- Diverse Learning Styles. The software accommodates a variety of learning styles; analyses are presented in tabular, graphic (two types), and written formats. This software is completely self-contained, with all functions and instructions on the disk.
- Extensive Database. The CD-ROM contains a database of the two most recent annual reports of more than 20 major companies from over a dozen different industries. These annual reports are complete and presented in full color. Some of the industries and companies in the database are:

Manufacturing	Browning Ferris Cooper Tire Emerson Electric
Health Care	Columbia Humana
Entertainment	Cineplex Odeon
Consumer Products	Rubbermaid Reebok
Computers	IBM Unisys
Airlines	UAL Delta Southwest
Retail	J.C. Penney Wal-Mart Toys "R" Us

- Case Studies. The CD-ROM also contains two case studies of simulated companies (Heartland Airways and Richland Home Centers). These case studies contain complete, well-articulated financial statements and notes, as well as related questions and assignments.

VISIT OUR INTERNET SITE!

New to this edition is the Needles Accounting Resource Center at:

http://www.hmco.com/college/needles/home.html

Look for the Internet icon in the assignment sections of the book: it tells you to visit our Internet resource center to help you with your homework! When you visit, you will also find links to many companies you have studied in the book, as well as other learning enhancements.

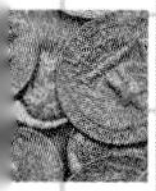

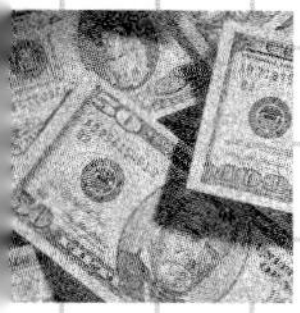

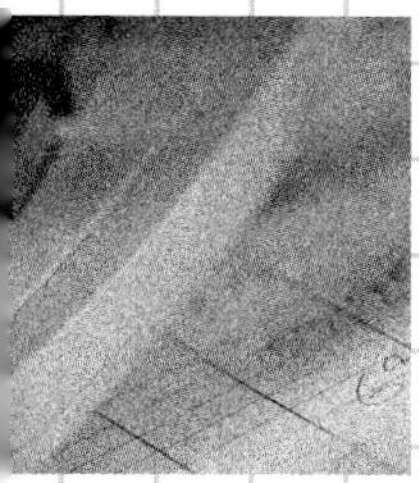

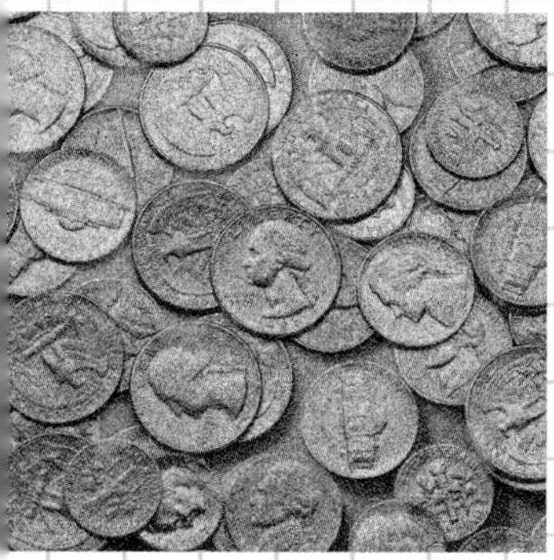

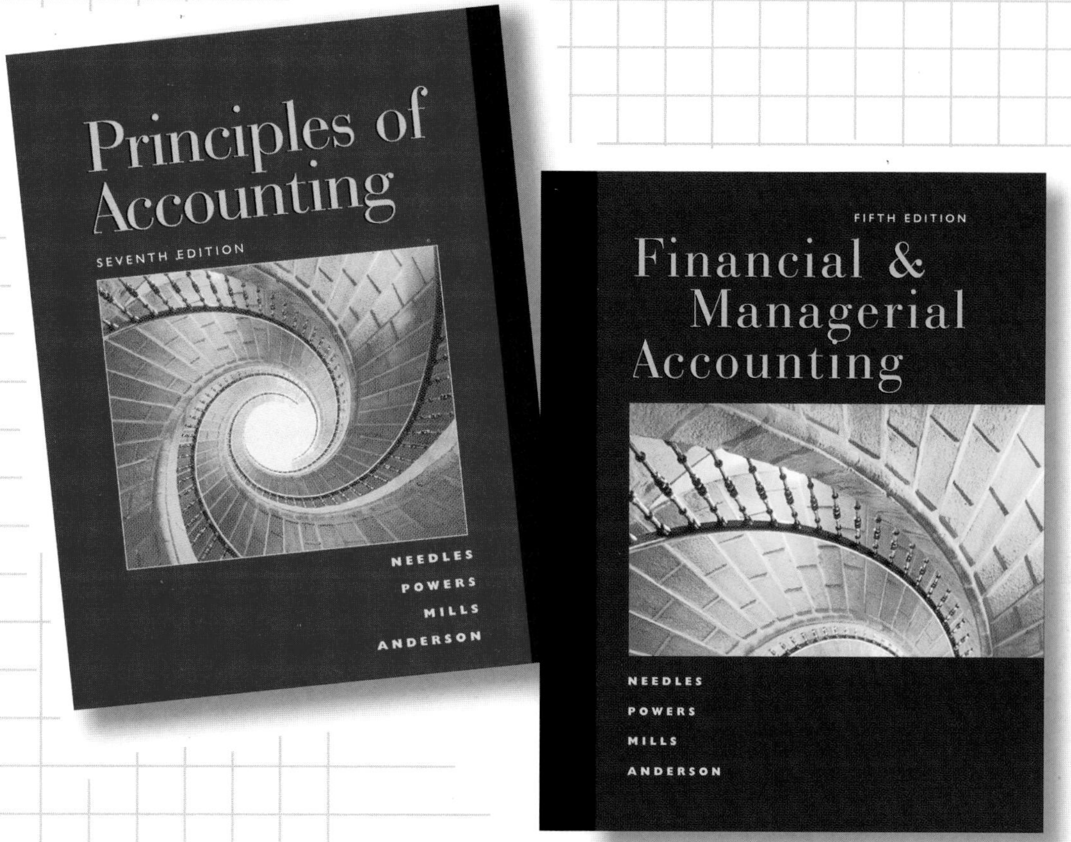
Principles of Accounting
SEVENTH EDITION
NEEDLES
POWERS
MILLS
ANDERSON
FIFTH EDITION
Financial & Managerial Accounting
NEEDLES
POWERS
MILLS
ANDERSON

With a great accounting program, interest accrues.

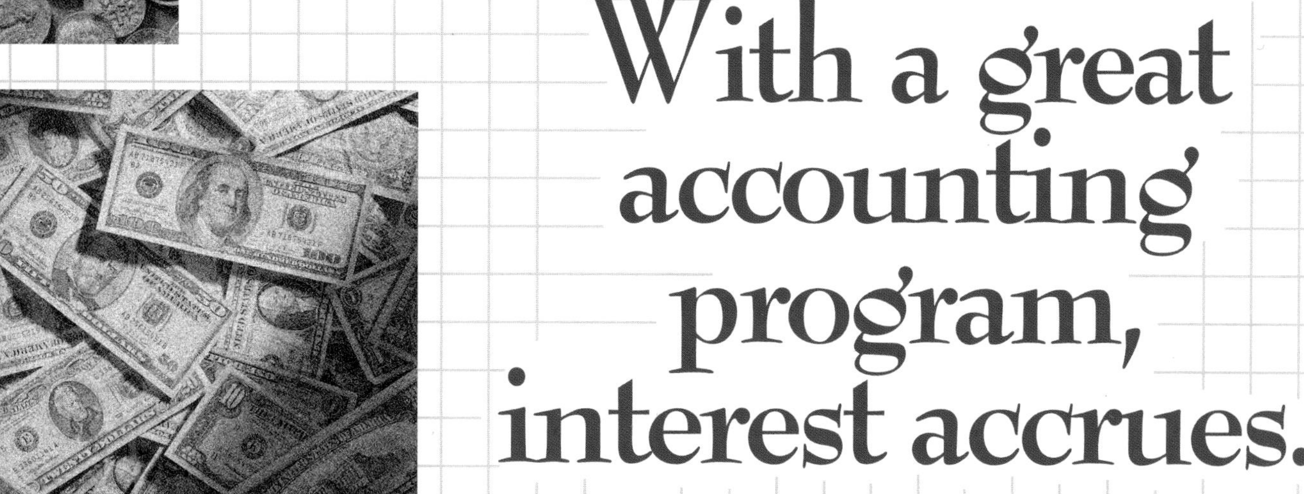

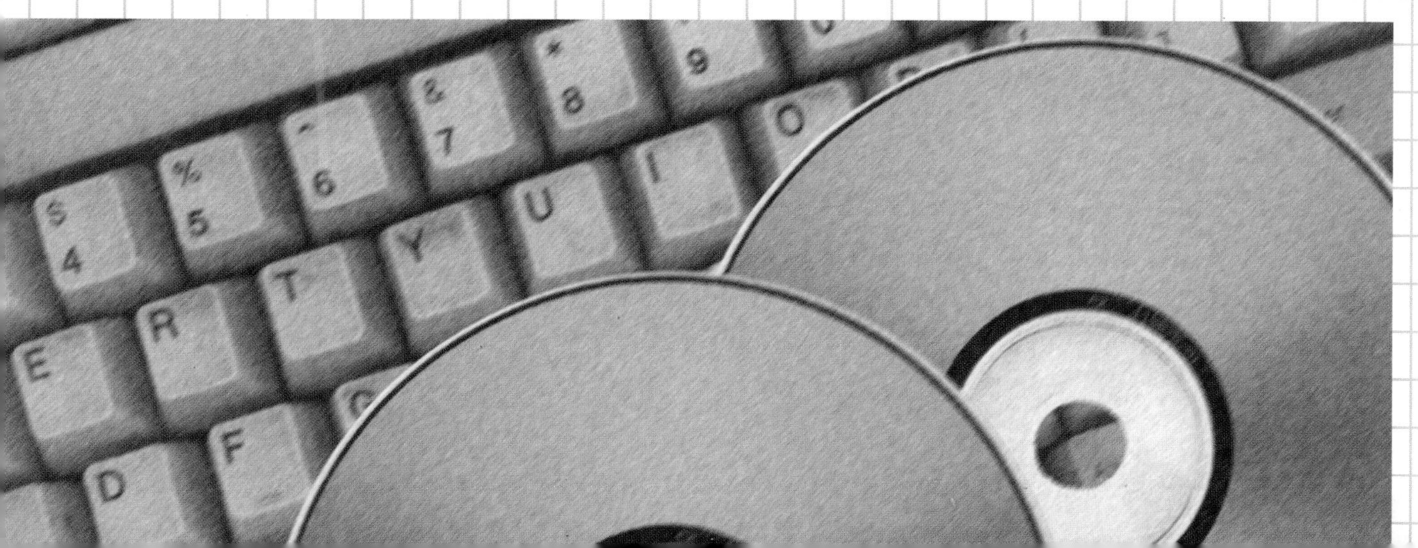

Count on experience

The authors of *Principles of Accounting* and *Financial & Managerial Accounting* have invested a great deal in teaching accounting—and it shows in the new editions, which integrate solid foundations with classroom flexibility. To help you master the changing requirements of accounting instruction and to meet requests for a stronger user orientation, the texts provide a conceptual framework with less emphasis on procedural details. The new editions offer more attention to management issues, a colorful new design, innovative instructional strategies, and expanded assignments on the skills most in demand in today's business world.

Belverd E. Needles, Jr.
DePaul University

An acclaimed expert in international accounting and accounting education, **Bel Needles** has earned numerous awards as an accounting educator. That pedagogical skill is reflected in the texts' focus on classroom applications as a bridge to the business world. For example, the class-tested **annual report project** teaches students how to interpret annual report information using the Fingraph® database, the Toys "R" Us report in the text, or any annual report.

Maximized real-world coverage also features financial data from such companies as Microsoft and US Airways; examples from Ford, Sears, Disney, American Airlines, General Mills, Oracle, and others; and **real-company video cases** (including Intel, Office Depot, Lotus, UPS and Enterprise Rent-A-Car) which underscore the role of accounting in management. Coming soon to the Accounting Resource Center Web Site, **Popular Press** will include current articles and exercises that support the texts' real-world approach.

Marian Powers
Northwestern University

New author **Marian Powers**, a professor in Northwestern University's Executive Program, provides **a fresh perspective**. Along with her extensive experience in executive education, focused on financial reporting and analysis, she has co-authored the best-selling *Financial Accounting* and its interactive multimedia financial analysis software.

To show students how the accounting cycle results in a published report, the texts' **financial reporting and analysis case** examines a hypothetical company in the context of real-world comparative data from such corporations as Oneida and Nike. The **Fingraph® Financial Analyst™ CD-ROM** demonstrates how managers use this financial information to analyze a company's performance, with financial and operating data drawn from an annual report database of 20 major companies.

Assignments using Fingraph®, as well as Excel and the Internet, give students new ways to apply their accounting knowledge. Another new technology resource, **Accounting On-line**, coming soon, will offer a complete program of web-based accounting instruction keyed directly to the texts' learning objectives.

Sherry K. Mills
New Mexico State University

Sherry Mills, an award-winning educator recognized for her innovation and excellence in teaching managerial accounting, now takes **an expanded role** in the author team. Her contributions support the extensive revision of managerial chapters and features throughout the texts.

The new editions offer **improved managerial coverage** across the full range of texts, along with more streamlined chapters, less procedural detail, and shorter problems for greater clarity. **Management decision cycle graphics** accompanying the learning objectives in each managerial chapter show how accounting information affects managers' business decisions. The texts devote more attention to **service organizations** in examples, end-of-chapter assignments, and other pedagogical materials.

Contemporary managerial topics such as activity-based costing, just-in-time management, total quality management, and target costing are integrated throughout the chapters. Learning objectives, decision points, and business bulletins also emphasize the connections between management accounting and both services and the management cycle.

in the classroom

A full range of options for introductory accounting

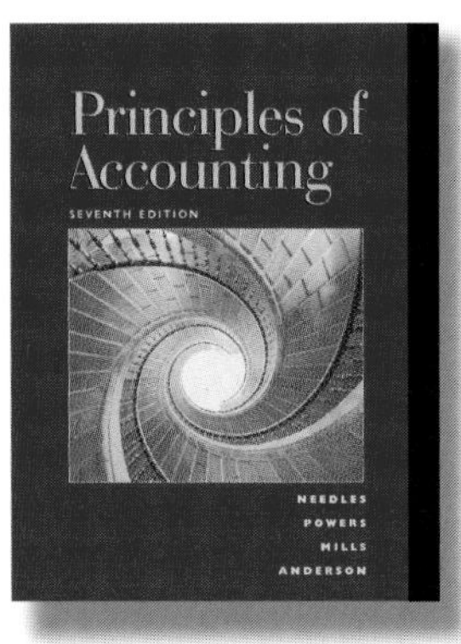

Principles of Accounting
Seventh Edition
Belverd E. Needles, Jr., DePaul University
Marian Powers, Northwestern University
Sherry K. Mills, New Mexico State University
Henry R. Anderson, University of Central Florida
Hardcover • 1280 pages • 27 chapters • ISBN: 0-395-92758-7

The leading text in the introductory accounting series, this book suits two-semester or three-quarter courses that stress financial accounting with some managerial accounting.

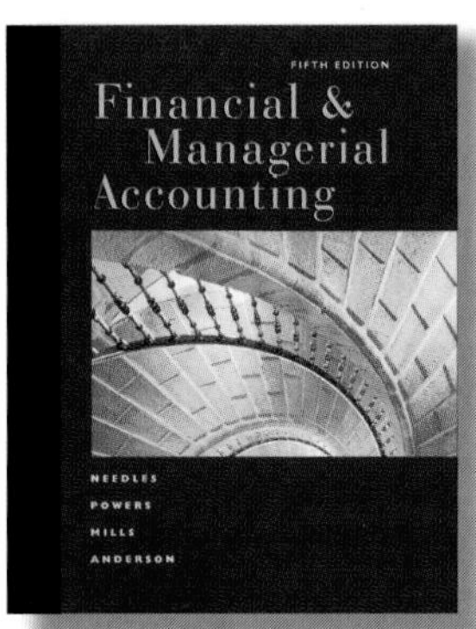

Financial & Managerial Accounting
Fifth Edition
Belverd E. Needles, Jr., DePaul University
Marian Powers, Northwestern University
Sherry K. Mills, New Mexico State University
Henry R. Anderson, University of Central Florida
Hardcover • 1264 pages • 28 chapters • ISBN: 0-395-92098-1

This complete volume, ideal for principles courses that include more managerial accounting, contains 14 chapters on financial accounting and 14 on managerial topics.

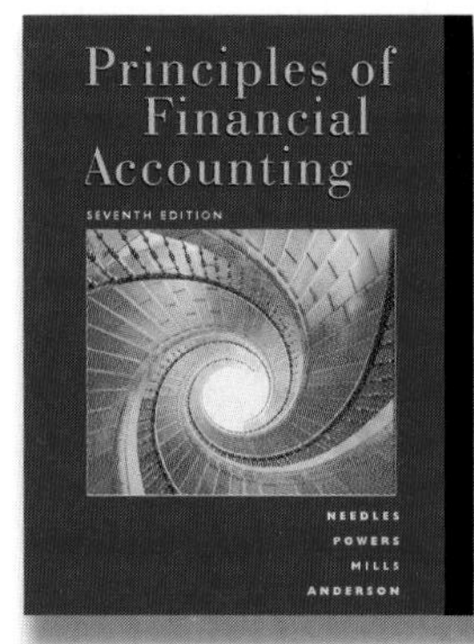

Principles of Financial Accounting
Seventh Edition
Belverd E. Needles, Jr., DePaul University
Marian Powers, Northwestern University
Sherry K. Mills, New Mexico State University
Henry R. Anderson, University of Central Florida
Paperback • 928 pages • 19 chapters • ISBN: 0-395-92629-7

For financial accounting courses that start with a sole proprietorship approach and principles courses that omit managerial topics, this text contains the 19 financial chapters of *Principles of Accounting*, 7/e.

with

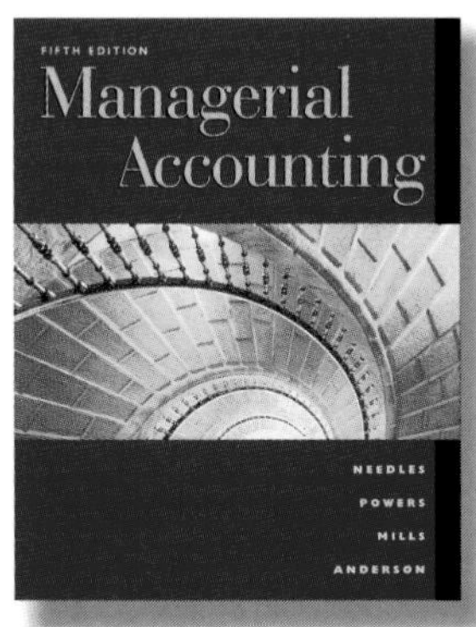

Managerial Accounting

Fifth Edition
Belverd E. Needles, Jr., DePaul University
Marian Powers, Northwestern University
Sherry K. Mills, New Mexico State University
Henry R. Anderson, University of Central Florida
Paperback • 1264 pages • 14 chapters • ISBN: 0-395-92099-X

Consisting of the 14 managerial chapters from *Financial & Managerial Accounting, 5/e*, this text is designed for the second semester of the financial/managerial accounting sequence.

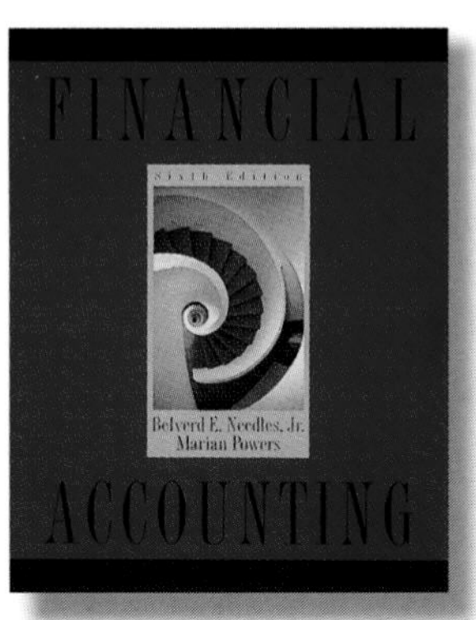

Financial Accounting

Sixth Edition
Belverd E. Needles, Jr., DePaul University
Marian Powers, Northwestern University
Hardcover • 864 pages • 16 chapters • ISBN: 0-395-85753-8

This best-selling financial accounting text serves the first term of two-term introductory accounting courses with a corporate approach.

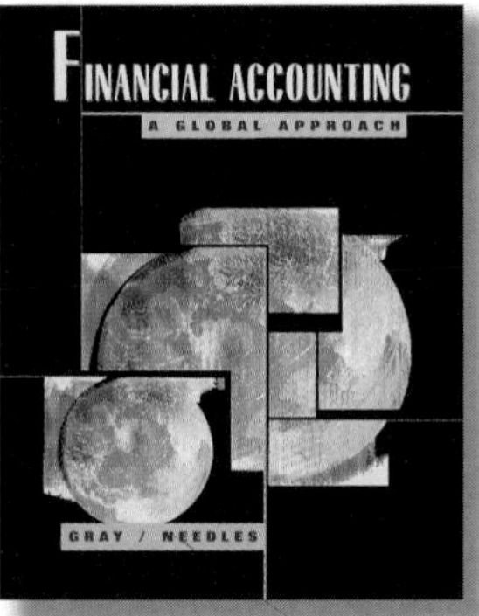

Financial Accounting: A Global Approach

Sidney J. Gray, Jr., University of New South Wales, Australia
Belverd E. Needles, DePaul University
Paperback • 608 pages • 14 chapters • ISBN: 0-395-83986-6

This adaptation of *Financial Accounting* offers a new global approach to introductory accounting. With international instead of U.S. standards, internationalized end-of-chapter assignments, and more international examples, this text is ideal for courses that emphasize international business.

more flexible choices

Supporting materials for ever

For Instructors

NEW! **Needles Accounting Resource Center Web Site**, organized by chapter, offers links to companies discussed in the text, links to current business articles related to chapter topics, Internet research activities, and the texts' Toys "R" Us cases, updated per the latest annual report.

NEW! **Exercises and Problems with Peachtree Accounting for Windows 5.0** and QuickBooks 6.0 Data CD-ROM and Booklet, packaged with Peachtree Accounting for Windows Release 5.0, extends exercises and problems from the texts for use with commercial general ledger packages.

NEW! **Peachtree for Instructor CD-ROM** contains all solutions and additional instructions for using and integrating Peachtree applications.

NEW! **Electronic Solutions** (Excel) makes it easy to manipulate, print, and post problems.

NEW! **PowerPoint Slides** based on lecture outlines follow the texts' learning objectives and provide a truly integrated classroom presentation tool.

NEW! **Excel Templates** cover all problems and alternate problems at the end of each chapter.

NEW! **Fingraph CD-ROM**, an interactive analytical tool, contains a database of real companies' financial reports, Fingraph® Financial Analyst™ software, assignment materials tied to the text, and the most recent Toys "R" Us annual report to update the texts' continuing case.

NEW! **Video Cases** consist of five vignettes of real companies—three on financial topics and two on managerial topics—that accompany cases and critical thinking assignments in the text.

Instructor's Annotated Edition includes marginal annotations on Critical Thinking Questions, Instructional Strategies, Points to Emphasize, Related Text Assignments, Discussion Questions, Teaching Notes, Enrichment Notes, Terminology Notes, Common Student Confusion, Clarification Notes, Parenthetical Notes, and Ethical Considerations.

Course Manual contains 11 teaching strategies, detailed notes on the learning improvement model, suggestions for course management, a chapter assignment learning objectives matrix, and chapter outlines.

Computerized Test Bank allows instructors to build tests automatically or choose, scramble, and edit questions to meet their needs. Special features include customized layouts and answer keys.

Solutions Transparencies are available for each end-of-chapter exercise, problem, alternate problem, and case.

Teaching Transparencies consist of art from the text, additional illustrations, and a chapter-by-chapter list of learning objectives.

Test Bank with Achievement Test Masters, the largest test bank available, contains over 4,000 exercises, problems, true/false questions, and multiple-choice questions, as well as short essay questions, alternatives for frequently asked problems, and achievement test masters for each chapter.

Instructor's Solutions Manual provides solutions to all text questions, exercises, problems, alternate problems, and cases, as well as a learning objectives chart and a difficulty and time chart.

General Mills, Inc. Annual Report Instructor's Solutions Manual aids instructors in using this financial analysis decision case based on a real company's annual report.

Micro-Tec Instructor's Solutions Manual supplements the computerized practice case covering a one-month accounting cycle for a sole proprietorship software wholesaler.

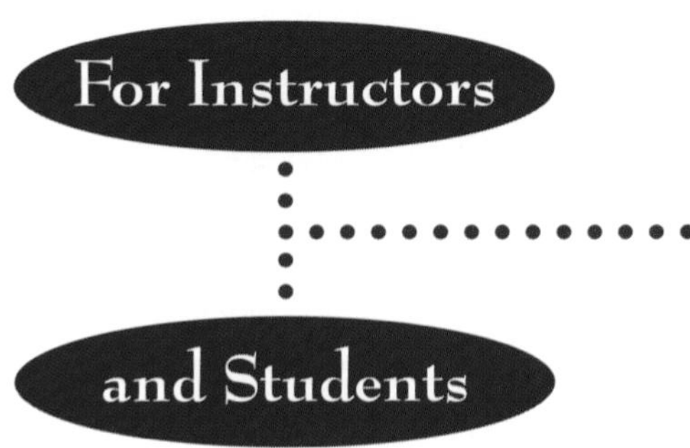

lassroom need

For Students

NEW! **Excel Templates** cover all problems and alternate problems at the end of each chapter.

NEW! **Fingraph CD-ROM**, an interactive analytical tool, contains a database of real financial reports from real companies (including Toys "R" Us, the continuing case in the text), Fingraph® Financial Analyst™ software, and text-related assignments.

NEW! **Annual Report CD** contains a database of 20 recent annual reports from over a dozen different industries to instruct students in reading and interpreting real-world financial information.

NEW! **Excel Spreadsheet Analysis: Cases for Managerial Reporting and Analysis** offer two learning approaches for one MRA in each chapter. To teach spreadsheeting skills, instructors can ask students to build their own spreadsheet using a blank template; to focus on analysis, they can start from a template equipped with all underlying links.

NEW! **Micro-Tec Disk**, an introductory case for manual or computer practice, covers a one-month accounting cycle for a sole proprietorship computer software wholesaler.

NEW! **Micro-Tec Workbook** supplements the computerized introductory practice case.

NEW! **Needles Accounting Resource Center Web Site**, organized by chapter, offers links to companies discussed in the text, links to current business articles related to chapter topics, Internet research activities, and the texts' Toys "R" Us cases, updated per the latest annual report.

Coming soon! **Accounting On-line**, a Web-based resource for both traditional students and distance learners, will be keyed directly to the texts' learning objectives. Along with lecture notes, PowerPoint slides, study guide material, quizzes, and sample tests, this resource will provide complete classroom management tools, customizable features, and discussion forums allowing collaborative group work.

Coming soon! **Popular Press ACE, A Cyber Evaluation,** a web-based self-testing system for students, builds quizzes by textbook chapter or topic with varying question formats such as multiple-choice, short-answer, true/false, and essay.

NEW! **Exercises and Problems with Peachtree Accounting for Windows 5.0** and Quickbooks 6.0 Data CD-ROM and Booklet, packaged with Peachtree Accounting for Windows Release 5.0, extends exercises and problems from the texts for use with commercial general ledger packages.

NEW! **Windows General Ledger** helps students to solve problems identified by icons in the text.

Accounting Transaction Tutor reinforces accounting concepts and procedures with exercises keyed to the texts' learning objectives, an on-line glossary, and diagnostic tests.

General Mills, Inc. Annual Report Financial Decision Case, 3/e, realistically introduces students to the final product of the financial accounting system from the viewpoint of financial statement users.

General Mills, Inc. Annual Report Student Workbook, packaged with the annual report, allows students to perform ratio analyses of profitability, liquidity, long term solvency, and market tests; conduct trend analyses; prepare common-size statements; and analyze statements of retained earnings and cash flow.

Study Guide provides a chapter-by-chapter review of major concepts and procedures presented in the text, organized by learning objective, as well as a summary of the texts' journal entries. It includes quizzes, exercises, and sections on "Testing Your Knowledge" and "Applying Your Knowledge."

Working Papers provide forms for each exercise, problem, and alternate problem in the text, including appropriate headings, beginning dates, and balances.

Houghton Mifflin Brief Accounting Dictionary helps students interpret definitions from college-level accounting textbooks. This 60-page reference, written by the same team as the prestigious *American Heritage Dictionary*, includes a pronunciation guide, easy-to-use grammar usage coding, and ample illustrations.

omplete teaching and learning tools

Profit from experience.

Principles of Accounting and *Financial & Managerial Accounting*

► To request an examination copy, call or fax the Faculty Services Center:
Tel: 800/733-1717 • Fax: 800/733-1810 or contact your Houghton Mifflin sales representative.

► For more information, consult the College Division home page: **www.hmco.com/college**

Editorial and International Offices
222 Berkeley Street
Boston, MA 02116

In Canada
Nelson Canada
1120 Birchmount Road
Scarborough, Ontario
CANADA M1K 5G4
Tel: 416/752-9100
Orders: 800/268-2222

In the United Kingdom, Europe, and the Middle East
Houghton Mifflin Co.
PO Box 269, Abingdon
Oxfordshire OX14 4YN, UK
Phone: 44 (0) 1235 833827
Fax: 44 (0) 1235 833829
E-mail: mifflin@compuserve.com

Principles of Accounting

INSTRUCTOR'S ANNOTATED EDITION

Seventh Edition

Belverd E. Needles, Jr. **Ph.D., C.P.A., C.M.A.**
DePaul University

Marian Powers **Ph.D.**
Northwestern University

Sherry K. Mills **Ph.D., C.P.A.**
New Mexico State University

Henry R. Anderson **Ph.D., C.P.A., C.M.A.**
Professor Emeritus, University of Central Florida

CONSULTING AUTHOR
James C. Caldwell **Ph.D., C.P.A.**
Andersen Consulting

CONTRIBUTING EDITOR
Susan V. Crosson **M.S. Accounting, C.P.A.**
Santa Fe Community College, Florida

Houghton Mifflin Company Boston New York

To Jennifer, Jeffrey, Annabelle, and Abigail
To Larry Mills, and to Zachary and Bill and Lois Snodgrass
To Sue Anderson, and to Deborah, Gregor, and Thomas Shewman, Howard and Nicole Anderson, Randy Anderson, and Hugh Anderson
To Bonnie Caldwell, Sharon Caldwell, Susan Painter, Ron Painter, Reagan Painter, Stephanie Trest, Glenn Trest, and Brendan Trest

SENIOR SPONSORING EDITOR: Anne Kelly
ASSOCIATE SPONSORING EDITOR: Margaret E. Monahan
SENIOR PROJECT EDITOR: Margaret M. Kearney
SENIOR PRODUCTION/DESIGN COORDINATOR: Sarah L. Ambrose
SENIOR MANUFACTURING COORDINATOR: Priscilla J. Abreu
MARKETING MANAGER: Juli Bliss

COVER DESIGN: Diana Coe
COVER IMAGE: Spiral Staircase–Spain by Joao Paulo—The Image Bank
PHOTO CREDITS: Page xlviii, © Index Stock/Phototake NYC; page 44, © Mark Wagner/Tony Stone Images; page 88, © H. Mark Weidman; page 130, © Charlotte Raymond/Science Source/Photo Researchers; page 170, © Koopman/MAK/Envision; page 216, © Paul S. Conrath/ Tony Stone Images; page 298, © 1998 Churchill & Klehr; page 304, Courtesy of International Business Machines Corporation. Unauthorized use is not permitted; page 340, © Jeffrey Coolidge/Image Bank; page 353, © Steven Needham/Envision; page 378, © Roberto Brosnan/Photonica; page 420, © Ira Wexler/Folio; page 436, © David O'Connor/Photonica; page 460, © Suzanne Smith/Gamma Liaison; page 506, © Jeff Hunter/The Image Bank; page 517, © Marc Loiseau/The Image Bank; page 540, © Shaun Egan/Tony Stone Images; page 544, © Index Stock; page 576, © Alan Becker/The Image Bank; page 618, © Comstock, Inc.; page 636, © Remo/Photonica; page 662, © Paul S. Howell/Gamma Liaison; page 708, © Bill Ellzey/Comstock, Inc.; page 721, © Don Carstens/Folio; page 764, © Thierry Dosogne/The Image Bank; page 768, © David Swanson/Gamma Liaison; page 810, © Philippe Sion/The Image Bank; page 819, © Steven Needham/Envision; page 850, © Mark Wagner/Tony Stone Images; page 890, © Peter Johansky/Envision; page 936, Ian Shaw/Tony Stone Images; page 980, © Gary Gladstone/Image Bank; page 1016, © C. Van Der Lende/Image Bank; page 1068, © David Gould/Image Bank; page 1110, © Grant Faint/The Image Bank; page 1146, © Zigy Kaluzny/Tony Stone Images.

Printed in the U.S.A.

Library of Congress Catalog Card No.: 98-72069

ISBN: 0-395-93530-X

123456789-VH-02 01 00 99 98

Contents in Brief

Contents

PART FOUR Measuring and Reporting Assets and Current Liabilities

About the Authors

Belverd E. Needles, Jr., Ph.D., C.P.A., C.M.A.

Belverd E. Needles, Jr. received his BBA and MBA degrees from Texas Tech University and his Ph.D. degree from the Unversity of Illinois. Dr. Needles teaches auditing and financial accounting at DePaul University, where he is the Arthur Andersen LLP Alumni Distinguished Professor and is an internationally known expert in international auditing and accounting education. He has published in leading journals in these fields and is the author or editor of more than twenty books and monographs.

Dr. Needles is active in many academic and professional organizations. He is president of the International Association for Accounting Education and Research and past president of the Federation of Schools of Accountancy. He has served as the elected U.S. representative to the European Accounting Association and chair of the International Accounting Section of the American Accounting Association. He has served as director of Continuing Education of the American Accounting Association. He serves on the Information Technology Executive Committee of the American Institute of CPAs. For the past five years he has served as the U.S. representative on the Education Committee of the International Federation of Accountants.

Dr. Needles has received the Distinguished Alumni Award from Texas Tech University, the Illinois CPA Society Outstanding Educator Award, the Joseph A. Silvoso Faculty Award of Merit from the Federation of Schools and Accountancy, the Ledger & Quill Award of Merit, and the Ledger & Quill Teaching Excellence Award. In 1992, he was named Educator of the Year by the national honorary society Beta Alpha Psi. In 1996, he received from the American Accounting Association the award of Outstanding International Accounting Educator.

Marian Powers, Ph.D.

Marian Powers earned her Ph.D. in accounting from the University of Illinois at Urbana. She has served on the accounting faculty of the Kellogg Graduate School of Management at Northwestern University, the University of Illinois at Chicago, and the Lake Forest Graduate School of Management. Since 1987, she has been a professor of accounting at the Allen Center for Executive Education at Northwestern University, specializing in teaching financial reporting and analysis to executives. She is co-author of several successful in-depth cases on financial analysis, and her research has been published in *The Accounting Review; The International Journal of Accounting; Issues in Accounting Education; The Journal of Accountancy; The Journal of Business, Finance, and Accounting;* and *Financial Management,* among others. Dr. Powers has received recognition and awards for her teaching.

Dr. Powers has been active in several professional organizations, including the Illinois CPA Society, the American Accounting Association, the European Accounting Association, the International Association of Accounting Education and Research, the American Society of Women Accountants, and the Education Foundation for Women in Accounting. She is currently serving as secretary of the Education Foundation for Women in Accounting. She is past president of the Chicago chapter and past national officer of the American Society of Women Accountants.

Henry R. Anderson, Ph.D., C.P.A., C.M.A.
Henry R. Anderson is KPMG Peat Marwick Professor Emeritus of Accounting at the University of Central Florida. He served as Director of UCF's School of Accounting for seven years; is the former Dean of the School of Business Administration & Economics at California State University, Fullerton; and was Assistant Director of the research staff of the Cost Accounting Standards Board, Washington, D.C. Dr. Anderson was National President of Beta Alpha Psi, 1981–82, and won the California CPA Society's 1981 Faculty Excellence Award and the 1987 Florida Excellence in Teaching Award from the College of Business at the University of Central Florida. He has been very active in the Institute of Management Accountants and has served on many committees of the American Accounting Association, the American Institute of Certified Public Accountants, and the Florida Institute of CPAs. Dr. Anderson is a graduate of Augustana College and the University of Missouri at Columbia.

Sherry K. Mills, Ph.D., C.P.A.
Sherry K. Mills is Associate Professor of Accounting at New Mexico State University, where she received the Outstanding Teaching Award in the College of Business Administration and Economics and the Burlington Northern Foundation Faculty Achievement Award at the university level in 1993. She also has been recognized for teaching innovations as a runner-up for the Boeing Award in 1993 and winner of the 1996 American Accounting Association's Innovation in Accounting Education Award. Dr. Mills has made presentations about accounting innovations at conferences held by the American Accounting Association, the Institute of Management Accountants, the International Association for Accounting Education, and the Accounting Education Change Commission. She currently is designing courses for the Manufacturing Engineering and Management curriculum, a joint project between the College of Business Administration and the College of Engineering at New Mexico State University. She received her Ph.D. from Texas Tech University.

Goals for PRINCIPLES OF ACCOUNTING, Seventh Edition

Our goal is for all students to become intelligent users of financial statements and to understand that financial information and related nonfinancial information, when interpreted and analyzed, will be useful to them in making critical business decisions throughout their careers.

Our goal is to provide the opportunity for the development in students of a wide skill set essential to success in business and management today.

Our goal, beginning with the Sixth Edition and continuing with the Seventh Edition, is to place more emphasis throughout the book on the use and analysis of accounting information by management and on the decisions that management makes regarding accounting information, including performance measurement.

Our goal is to make a significant improvement in the managerial accounting coverage.

Our goal is to reflect business practice as it is today in a context that is relevant and exciting to students.

Our goal is to provide exactly the right balance between conceptual understanding and technical application and analysis.

Our goal is to provide a complete supplemental learning system—including manual and technology applications for computer, CD-ROM, video tape, and Internet support—that directly facilitates student learning.

Our goal is to provide a complete support system for the instructor.

Preface

PRINCIPLES OF ACCOUNTING, Seventh Edition, is a first course in accounting for students with no previous training in accounting or business. This textbook is intended for use at the undergraduate level and is designed for both business and accounting majors. It is part of a well-integrated package for students and instructors that includes several manual and computer ancillaries. It has proven successful in traditional three-quarter or two-semester courses and has been used equally well in a three-semester sequence.

Decision Making and the Uses of Accounting Information

PRINCIPLES OF ACCOUNTING recognizes that a majority of the students in the first accounting course are business and management majors who will read, analyze, and interpret financial information throughout their careers. We believe the fundamental purpose of accounting is to provide information for decision making, and while not neglecting topics important for accounting majors,

> Our goal is for all students to become intelligent users of financial statements and to understand that financial information and related nonfinancial information, when interpreted and analyzed, will be useful to them in making critical business decisions throughout their careers.

Essential to PRINCIPLES OF ACCOUNTING is our conviction that the use of integrated learning objectives can significantly improve the teaching and learning of accounting. This system of learning by objectives enhances the role of the overall package, particularly the textbook, by achieving complete and thorough communication between instructor and student. Basic to this approach are the following objectives, which we have accomplished in this new revision:

- To write for business and management students as well as accounting majors
- To emphasize the role of accounting in decision making
- To make the content authoritative, practical, and contemporary
- To integrate the learning-by-objectives approach throughout the text, assignment material, and ancillaries
- To develop the most complete and flexible teaching-learning system available
- To adhere to a strict system of quality control

The success of the first six editions of PRINCIPLES OF ACCOUNTING has justified our confidence in this fundamental approach.

New Authors

The addition of two new authors, Dr. Marian Powers and Dr. Sherry K. Mills, over the past two editions strengthens the author team's expertise in the areas of (1) teaching business executives the latest tools of financial analysis and (2) the most current thinking on management's use of accounting information. With more than fifteen years of teaching experience at the undergraduate and graduate levels in both large and small classes, Marian Powers is an accomplished instructor who brings various instructional strategies to her financial accounting classes to develop critical thinking, group interaction, communication, and other broadening skills in students. In addition, she has taught thousands of executives how to read, interpret, and analyze corporate financial statements.

Sherry Mills, now contributing to PRINCIPLES OF ACCOUNTING for a second edition, has a reputation as an outstanding teacher and innovator in management accounting education. She has won the American Accounting Association's Innovation in Accounting Education Award and has taught contemporary management accounting topics in executive training. She brings a new approach to the managerial accounting chapters.

Essential Student Skills

The Seventh Edition of PRINCIPLES OF ACCOUNTING represents a major expansion of the decision-making approach and extends significantly the changes implemented in the Sixth Edition. The pedagogical system underlying PRINCIPLES OF ACCOUNTING is based on a model that encompasses a growing group of instructional strategies designed to develop and strengthen a broad skill set in students. This model, which includes learning objectives, the teaching-learning cycle, cognitive levels of learning, and output skills, is described in detail in the Course Manual that accompanies this text.

> Our goal is to provide the opportunity for the development in students of a wide skill set essential to success in business and management today.

Applying this model, the Seventh Edition achieves (1) a stronger decision-making approach with emphasis on performance measurement; (2) improved managerial accounting coverage, including integrated, contemporary discussions of state-of-the-art topics; (3) maximized real-world coverage; (4) reduction of procedural detail; and (5) reorganized and expanded assignment material to increase flexibility and to concentrate on developing students' critical thinking, group and team-building, communication, and financial statement analysis skills.

Stronger Decision-Making Approach with Emphasis on Performance Measurement

PRINCIPLES OF ACCOUNTING continues to emphasize the use of accounting information in decision making with a new focus on the importance this information plays in performance measurement.

> Our goal, beginning with the Sixth Edition and continuing with the Seventh Edition, is to place more emphasis throughout the book on the use and analysis of accounting information by management and on decisions that management makes regarding accounting information, including performance measurement.

Beginning with Chapter 1, we integrate the concept of using financial information in performance measurement and evaluation at appropriate points in the text. In Chapter 6, we introduce financial analysis ratios as evaluation tools and we then integrate them in subsequent financial chapters. These ratios are usually discussed in the "management issues" section at the beginning of the chapters, and we later bring all the ratios together in a comprehensive financial analysis of Sun Microsystems, Inc., in Chapter 18. In the managerial accounting chapters, we examine how the topics under consideration are used to enhance performance measurement.

Emphasis on Cash Flow Stemming from our goal of emphasizing performance measures is our decision to highlight cash flows as they relate to the liquidity objective of business. To this end, we introduce the statement of cash flows in Chapter 1 and we point out the difference between income measurement and cash flows in various chapters while reinforcing it through assignments. We examine the operating cycle, with its critical effect on cash flows, in Chapter 5 and we carry through with the integration of the receivables and inventory turnover ratios in Chapters 9 and 10. We illustrate management's need to carefully budget cash flows at the beginning of Chapter 9, *Short-Term Liquid Assets.* And, finally, we have extensively revised Chapter 17, *The Statement of Cash Flows.* This chapter begins with performance measures related to cash flows such as cash flow yield, cash flows to revenues and to assets, and free cash flows. While we now focus on the indirect method, which is used by 95 percent of all companies, we present the direct method as a supplemental objective, including sufficient assignment material for those who wish to cover this method fully. Cash budgeting is revisited again in Chapter 24, *The Budgeting Process.*

Visual Interest To show visually the relevance of accounting to business, attractive four-color photographs appear in every chapter. We employ additional contemporary graphics, often featuring visualizations of concepts, throughout. Most illustrations depicting concepts and relationships have been redrawn, and we have added many new illustrations to make the concepts easier to understand and the book more visually appealing.

Improved Managerial Coverage Including Integrated, Contemporary Discussions of State-of-the-Art Topics

This edition represents a major revision of the managerial accounting chapters, in terms of both structure and content.

> Our goal is to make a significant improvement in the managerial accounting coverage.

Reorganization of Material To improve flow and facilitate both the teaching and the learning processes, we have made the following major changes in the organization and presentation of chapter topics:

- We condensed the coverage of job order and process costing systems and combined these two Sixth Edition chapters (Chapters 22 and 23) into one Seventh Edition chapter (Chapter 22).
- To provide a smoother introduction to the budgeting process, we have moved cost-volume-profit analysis from Sixth Edition Chapter 24 to the beginning of Part Eight, *Information and Analysis for Planning and Controlling.*
- We now discuss responsibility accounting in the Seventh Edition chapter on budgeting (Chapter 24) rather than in the chapter on cost-volume-profit analysis, as we did in the Sixth Edition.

There are three major themes to the content revision of the managerial chapters.

Consistent Approach The managerial accounting chapters are now fully consistent with the focus in the financial accounting chapters on decision making, performance measurement, and the management issues associated with various topics. In Chapter 1, we define accounting as an information system that provides information for making the critical decisions needed to operate a business successfully. We carry this idea forward in the management accounting chapters by beginning each chapter with a learning objective linked to the management cycle. Also, we emphasize that costing systems can apply to both service businesses and manufacturing concerns. We use service companies as the focal point of all major examples and illustrations.

Contemporary Coverage We have mainstreamed contemporary topics such as activity-based costing, just-in time, total quality management, and target costing from the beginning of the introductory chapter and have integrated them at appropriate points throughout the chapters. This book presents state-of-the art techniques and shows how they are used to add value to a company's operations. Decision Points and Business Bulletins emphasize these techniques and other current trends—for example, the need to assign costs to such areas as research and development, legal activities, and human resources.

Systematic Improvement Every managerial chapter has been thoroughly revised in a systematic way with the assistance of an experienced developmental editor to achieve a concise, clear, understandable presentation. The result is shorter chapters, with simplified examples and greater congruence between chapters and substantially revised and improved assignment material.

Maximized Real-World Coverage

We have taken many steps to increase the real-world emphasis of the text.

> Our goal is to reflect business practice as it is today in a context that is relevant and exciting to students.

Periodically, we conduct interviews of businesspeople to ascertain current business practices. For example, material in Chapter 9, *Short-Term Liquid Assets,* and Chapter 12, *Current Liabilities,* is based on interviews with officials in the banking industry. In addition, we use information from annual reports of real companies and articles about them in business journals, such as *Business Week, Forbes,* and *The Wall Street Journal,* to enhance students' appreciation of the usefulness and relevance of accounting information. In total, more than 100 publicly held companies are offered in the text as illustrative examples. Our Internet web site provides direct links to most of the web pages for these companies.

Actual Financial Statements We have incorporated examples from the annual reports of or articles about real companies extensively in the text and assignment material. Chapter 6 presents the financial statements of Oneida, Inc., in graphical form using the Fingraph® Financial Analyst™ CD-ROM software that accompanies this book. A supplement to Chapter 6 contains a section entitled "How to Read an Annual Report," followed by the complete annual report of Toys "R" Us. The comprehensive financial analysis in Chapter 18 features the financial statements of Sun Microsystems, Inc. These are only a few examples of the scores of other well-known companies we use as examples throughout the text.

Decision Points Every chapter contains at least one Decision Point. Based on excerpts from real companies' annual reports or from articles in the business press, Decision Points present a situation requiring a decision by management or other users of accounting information and then demonstrate how the decision can be made using accounting information.

Business Bulletins We have added more Business Bulletins to each chapter of this edition. Business Bulletins are short items related to the chapter topics that show the relevance of accounting in four areas:

- Business Practice
- International Practice
- Technology in Practice
- Ethics in Practice

Real Companies in Assignments We have substantially increased the number of real companies appearing in the assignment materials.

International Accounting In recognition of the global economy in which all businesses operate today, we introduce international accounting examples in Chapter 1 and integrate them throughout the text. A small sampling of foreign companies mentioned in the text and assignments includes Takashimaya Co. (Japanese), Glaxco-Welcome (British), Philips Electronics, N.V. (Dutch), and Groupe Michelin (French).

Real-World Graphic Illustrations We offer, as a regular feature of the book, graphs or tables illustrating the relationship of actual business practices to chapter topics. Many of these illustrations are based on data from studies of 600 annual reports published in *Accounting Trends and Techniques.* Beginning with Chapter 6, most chapters display a graphic that shows selected ratios for selected industries based on Dun & Bradstreet data. Service industry examples include advertising and interstate trucking companies. Manufacturing industry examples include pharmaceutical and tableware companies.

Governmental and Not-for-Profit Organizations Acknowledging the importance of governmental and not-for-profit organizations in our society, we include discussions and examples of government and not-for-profit organizations at appropriate points.

Reduction of Procedural Detail

This edition furthers our efforts to reduce the procedural detail in the chapters and to decrease the amount of "pencil pushing" on the part of students completing the assignments.

> Our goal is to provide exactly the right balance between conceptual understanding and technical application and analysis.

Because our focus is on the application of concepts, we have substantially revised many chapters to reduce procedural detail. We have accomplished this goal by deleting unnecessary topics or by placing procedures that are not essential to conceptual understanding in supplemental objectives at the end of chapters. In the end-of-chapter assignments, we have scrutinized all exercises and problems with a view to reducing the number of journal entries and the amount of posting required, and we now employ T accounts more frequently as a form of analysis. Consistent with the emphasis on decision making and performance measurement, we have eliminated all journal entries from the managerial accounting chapters. The most significantly revised chapters in this regard are:

Chapter 1 Uses of Accounting Information and the Financial Statements

Chapter 5 Merchandising Operations

Chapter 6	Financial Reporting and Analysis
Chapter 11	Long-Term Assets
Chapter 14	Contributed Capital
Chapter 15	The Corporate Income Statement and the Statement of Stockholders' Equity
Chapter 16	Long-Term Liabilities
Chapter 17	The Statement of Cash Flows
Chapter 21	Operating Costs and Cost Allocation, Including Activity-Based Costing
Chapter 22	Product Costing: The Job Order and Process Costing Systems
Chapter 25	Cost Control Using Standard Costing and Variance Analysis
Chapter 26	Operating and Capital Expenditure Decision Analysis

Reorganized and Expanded Assignment Material

In answer to the demand for a more sophisticated skill set in students, coupled with greater pedagogical choice for faculty members, we have reorganized and expanded the end-of-chapter assignments and accompanying materials.

Our goal is to provide the most comprehensive and flexible set of assignments available involving real companies.

In recognition of the fact that our students need to be better prepared to communicate clearly, both in written and oral formats, we provide ample assignments to enhance student writing and interpersonal skills, including the writing of good business memorandums and working effectively in groups and teams.

NEW! **Video Cases** Five new 5-minute video vignettes, each accompanied by an in-text case, provide more real-world opportunities to reinforce key concepts and techniques. The cases work equally well as individual or group assignments, and all five include a written critical thinking component. Each video case serves as an introduction to the chapter in which it is found:

- *Intel Corporation* (Chapter 1) examines the business goals of liquidity and profitability and the business activities of financing, investing, and operating.
- *Office Depot, Inc.* (Chapter 5) discusses the merchandising company, the merchandising income statement, and the concept of the operating cycle.
- *Lotus Development Corporation* (Chapter 14) tells the history of Lotus from its beginning as a small start-up company through its growth to one of America's most successful companies and finally to its sale to IBM. The case emphasizes Lotus's equity financing needs along the way.
- *UPS* (Chapter 20) introduces management accounting, presents it in the context of the management cycle, and examines the concept of performance measures.
- *Enterprise Rent-A-Car* (Chapter 24) presents the budgeting process in the management cycle and describes the master budget process for a service company.

NEW! **The Annual Report Project** Because the use of real companies' annual reports is the most rapidly growing type of term project in the introductory accounting course, we provide with the Supplement to Chapter 6 a suggested annual report project that we have used in our own classes for several years. To allow for projects of varied comprehensiveness, we have developed four assignment options, including the use of the Fingraph® Financial Analyst™ CD-ROM software.

Building Your Knowledge Foundation This section consists of a variety of questions, exercises, and problems designed to develop basic knowledge, comprehension, and application of the concepts and techniques in the chapter.

Questions (Q) Fifteen to twenty-four review questions that cover the essential topics of the chapter.

Short Exercises (SE) Approximately ten very brief exercises suitable for classroom use.

Problems At least five extensive applications of chapter topics, often covering more than one learning objective, and often containing writing components. All problems may be worked on our Excel Templates software, and problems that may be solved on our General Ledger program are indicated by an icon.

Alternate Problems An alternative set of the most popular problems, which we have selected based on feedback from our study of users' syllabi.

Chapter Assignments: Critical Thinking, Communication, and Interpersonal Skills

This section consists of ten or more Skills Development (SD) cases and Financial and Managerial Reporting and Analysis (FRA and MRA) cases, usually based on real companies. All of these cases require critical thinking and communication skills in the form of writing. At least one assignment in each chapter requires students to practice good business communication skills by writing a memorandum reporting results and explaining recommendations. In addition, all cases are suitable for development of interpersonal skills through group activities: for selected cases that we have designated as especially appropriate for group activities, we provide specific instructions for applying a suggested group methodology.

Each Skills Development assignment has a specific purpose:

Conceptual Analysis Designed so a written solution is appropriate, but which may be used in other communication modes, these short cases address conceptual accounting issues and are based on real companies and situations.

Ethical Dilemma In recognition of the need for accounting and business students to be exposed in all their courses to ethical considerations, every chapter has a short case, often based on a real company, in which students must address an ethical dilemma directly related to the chapter content.

Research Activity These exercises enhance student learning and participation in the classroom by acquainting students with business periodicals, the use of annual reports and business references, and resources in the library and on the Internet. Some are designed to improve students' interviewing and observation skills through field activities at actual businesses. An icon in the margin indicates which activities can be researched on the Internet.

Decision-Making Practice In the role of decision maker, students are asked to extract relevant data from a case, make computations as necessary, and arrive at a decision. The decision maker may be a manager, an investor, an analyst, or a creditor.

Financial and Managerial Reporting and Analysis cases sharpen students' ability to comprehend and analyze financial and nonfinancial data:

Interpreting Financial and Management Reports These short cases abstracted from business articles and annual reports of well-known corporations and organizations such as Kmart, Sears, IBM, Chrysler, and UAL (United Airlines), as well as specially designed internal management scenarios, require students to extract relevant data, make computations, and interpret the results.

Formulating Management Reports Students strengthen analytical, critical thinking, and written communication skills with these assignments. They teach students how to examine, synthesize, and organize information with the object of preparing reports such as a memo to a company president identifying sources of waste, outlining performance measures to account for waste, and estimating the current costs associated with the waste.

International Company These exercises involve a company from another country that has had an accounting experience compatible with chapter content.

Toys "R" Us The reading and analysis of the actual Toys "R" Us annual report, contained in the Supplement to Chapter 6, forms the basis of these cases, which appear in the financial accounting chapters.

NEW! *Fingraph® Financial Analyst™* These cases in the financial accounting chapters are worked in conjunction with the Fingraph® Financial Analyst™ annual report database software. The annual reports of more than twenty well-known companies are included in the database, which students utilize to analyze financial statements.

NEW! *Excel Spreadsheet Analysis* New to the Seventh Edition, these assignments in the managerial accounting chapters require the use of a spreadsheet to conduct an analysis and include a written component for interpretation and decision making. Excel Spreadsheet Analysis: Cases for Management Reporting and Analysis, a software program containing all the cases, is available for student use.

Financial Analysis Cases Also accompanying the text are a series of comprehensive financial analysis cases that may be integrated throughout the course after Chapter 5 or may be used as capstone cases for the entire course. The first, *General Mills, Inc., Annual Report: A Decision Case in Financial Analysis,* uses the actual financial statements of General Mills Corporation. The other cases, *Heartland Airways, Inc.,* and *Richland Home Centers, Inc.,* present complete annual reports for an airline company and a home improvement retailing chain and guide students through a complete financial analysis. These cases may be assigned individually and also constitute excellent group assignments.

Readable, Accessible Text

Growing numbers of students who take the financial accounting course are from foreign countries, and English is a second language for them. To meet their needs fully, we as instructors must be aware of how the complexities and nuances of English, particularly business English, might hinder these students' understanding.

Each chapter of PRINCIPLES OF ACCOUNTING has been reviewed by business instructors who teach English As a Second Language (ESL) courses and English for Special Purposes courses, as well as by students taking these classes. With their assistance and advice, we have taken the following measures to ensure that the text is accessible.

- Word Choice: We replaced words and phrases that were unfamiliar to ESL students with ones they more readily recognize and understand. For instance, we substituted "raise" for "bolster," "require" for "call for," and "available" for "on hand."
- Length: Because short, direct sentences are more easily comprehended than sentences containing multiple clauses, we paid strict attention to the length and grammatical complexity of our sentences.
- Examples: Examples reinforce concepts discussed and help to make the abstract concrete. We have added simple, straightforward examples for further clarity.

THE INSTRUCTOR'S ANNOTATED EDITION

Marginal annotations constitute the major instructional advantage of the Instructor's Annotated Edition. We have developed a number of annotations, which appear adjacent to the appropriate text, with the aim of (1) aiding your use of the text and ancillaries; (2) enriching your lectures and class discussions by providing material that extends the text; and (3) offering strategies and tips for presenting material to your class. We also print icons in the margins, indicating which skills, such as communication or critical thinking, certain assignments are designed to build in students and when you can use some of the technological products provided in the ancillary package.

Help with Text and Ancillaries

Related Text Assignments In the student text, each learning objective is stated in the margin adjacent to relevant material. In the Instructor's Annotated Edition, each of those objectives is accompanied by an annotation citing related text assignments. These annotations indicate which end-of-chapter questions (Q), short exercises (SE), exercises (E), problems (P), skills development exercises (SD), financial reporting and analysis cases (FRA), and managerial reporting and analysis cases (MRA) apply to that learning objective.

Parenthetical Notes These notes generally present you with information about the book itself, such as where you might find more information on a particular subject.

Enrichment of Discussions and Lectures

Critical Thinking Questions These annotations accompany each Decision Point in the text. They pose at least one critical thinking question and they provide the answer.

Business-World Examples Short anecdotes drawn from real businesses help you extend the text's emphasis on real-world situations into the classroom.

Clarification Notes These notes further explain material in the text—for example, the difference between GAAP and the Internal Revenue Code—offering additional insight into the material.

Enrichment Notes Similar to Clarification Notes, these annotations offer interesting insights—such as historical perspectives—into certain topics and concepts. Although they aren't required learning, they will enhance students' appreciation of the material.

Ethical Considerations Recognizing the need for today's business students to be trained in ethics, we highlight certain areas that might engender ethical concern, thus providing a springboard for further classroom discussion.

Classroom Strategies and Tips

Instructional Strategy These in-text annotations are tied to end-of-chapter assignments. At least one Instructional Strategy annotation per chapter involves a group activity and is linked directly to a Skills Development exercise. Other Instructional Strategy annotations involve different types of learning activities and are keyed to exercises, problems, and cases.

Common Student Errors and Common Student Confusion These two annotations will alert you to topics and concepts that sometimes trouble or confuse students. An awareness of these areas is especially useful to inexperienced teachers, helping them clear up problems before they arise.

Discussion Questions Use these questions and their accompanying answers to stimulate classroom discussion and help you gauge your students' understanding of the material.

Points to Emphasize Particularly important topics and concepts that you may want to stress in your lectures and discussion are called out in these annotations.

Reinforcement Exercises These short, simples exercises offer you ideas on how to present particularly important or difficult material.

Teaching Notes From our own classroom experiences and those of other teachers, we have culled interesting strategies and fresh approaches to teaching certain topics.

Terminology Notes We identify alternate names, such as statement of financial position (for balance sheet), for some accounting terms.

Icons in the Instructor's Annotated Edition

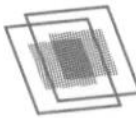

Teaching Transparencies icons designate figures that can be found in the Teaching Transparencies package.

Video icons accompany the video cases that introduce certain chapters in the text.

Communication icons identify assignments designed to help students develop their ability to communicate accounting information successfully.

Critical Thinking icons indicate assignments intended to strengthen students' critical thinking capabilities.

Group Activity icons are keyed to assignments that can be worked individually or in groups.

Memo icons appear alongside end-of-chapter exercises and cases that require students to communicate via business memorandums.

Ethics icons identify assignments that address ethical issues.

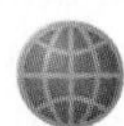

International icons indicate cases dealing with international companies and international accounting issues.

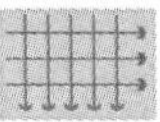

Spreadsheet icons designate problems that can be worked either manually or on the Excel Templates program that accompanies the text.

General Ledger icons designate problems that can be solved either manually or with the Windows General Ledger software that accompanies the text.

CD-ROM icons in the chapters themselves identify companies whose annual reports are provided on the Fingraph® Financial Analyst™ CD-ROM that accompanies the text. *CD-ROM* icons in the end-of-chapter assignments indicate cases that can be solved using the Fingraph software.

Internet icons identify assignments that can be worked using the Needles Accounting Resource Center web site.

Managerial Technology icons appear next to cases that can be solved with the help of the Excel Spreadsheet Analysis: Cases for Managerial Reporting and Analysis software that accompanies the text.

Supplementary Support Materials

Supplementary Learning Aids

Our goal is to provide a complete supplemental learning system—including manual and technology applications for computer, CD-ROM, videotape, and Internet support—that directly facilitates student learning.

Working Papers for Exercises and Problems

Study Guide

Accounting Transaction Tutor

General Ledger Software

NEW! **Exercises and Problems with Peachtree® Accounting for Windows Release 5.0 and QuickBooks® 6.0**

Excel Templates

NEW! **Excel Spreadsheet Analysis: Cases for Managerial Reporting and Analysis**

NEW! **Fingraph® Financial Analyst™ CD-ROM**

NEW! **Internet Web Site**

NEW! **Houghton Mifflin Brief Accounting Dictionary**

Financial Decision Cases and Practice Cases

Micro-Tec, Fifth Edition

Collegiate Ts

College Words and Sounds Store, Fourth Edition

General Mills, Inc., Annual Report, Third Edition

Heartland Airways, Inc., Third Edition

Richland Home Centers, Inc., Third Edition

Soft-Tec, Inc., Sixth Edition

Managerial Decision Cases

Aspen Food Products Company

McHenry Hotels, Inc., Second Edition

The Windham Company, Second Edition

Callson Industries, Inc.

Instructor's Support Materials

Our goal is to provide a complete support system for the instructor.

Instructor's Annotated Edition

Instructor's Solutions Manual

NEW! **Electronic Solutions**

Course Manual

Test Bank with Achievement Test Masters and Answers

Computerized Test Bank

Teaching Transparencies

Solutions Transparencies

NEW! **Powerpoint Classroom Presentation Software**

- **NEW!** **Video Cases**
- **NEW!** **Presentation Videos**
- **Master Teacher Videos**
- **Business Bulletin Videos**
- **NEW!** **Internet Web Site**
- **NEW!** **Instructor's Guide to Exercises and Problems with Peachtree® Accounting for Windows® Release 5.0 and Quickbooks® 6.0**

Acknowledgments

Preparing an accounting text is a long and demanding project that cannot really succeed without the help of one's colleagues. We are grateful to a large number of professors, other professional colleagues, and students for their many constructive comments on the text. Unfortunately, any attempt to list those who have helped means that some who have contributed would be slighted by omission. Some attempt, however, must be made to mention those who have been so helpful.

We wish to express our deep appreciation to our colleagues at DePaul University who have been extremely supportive and encouraging.

The thoughtful and meticulous work of Edward H. Julius (California Lutheran University) is reflected not only in the Study Guide but also in many other ways. We would also like to thank Paul J. Robertson (New Mexico State University) for his contribution to the Study Guide, Marion Taube (University of Pittsburgh) for her contribution to the Test Bank and the Working Papers, and Dick D. Wasson (Southwestern College) for his contribution to the Test Bank.

Also very important to the quality of this book is the supportive collaboration of our senior sponsoring editor, Anne Kelly. We further benefited from the ideas and guidance of our associate sponsoring editor, Peggy Monahan.

Others who have been supportive and have had an impact on this book throughout their reviews, suggestions, and class testing are:

Kym Anderson	
Gregory D. Barnes	Clarion University
Charles M. Betts	Delaware Technical & Community College
Michael C. Blue	Bloomsburg University
Cynthia Bolt-Lee	The Citadel
Gary R. Bower	Community College of Rhode Island
Lee Cannell	El Paso Community College
Lloyd Carroll	The Borough of Manhattan Community College
Naranjan Chipalkatti	Ohio Northern University
Stanley Chu	The Borough of Manhattan Community College
John D. Cunha	University of California—Berkeley
Mark W. Dawson	Duquesne University
Patricia A. Doherty	Boston University
Lizabeth England	American Language Academy
David Fetyko	Kent State University
Roxanne Gooch	Cameron University
Christine Uber Grosse	The American Graduate School of International Management
Dennis A. Gutting	Orange County Community College
Edward H. Julius	California Lutheran University
Howard A. Kanter	DePaul University

Kevin McClure	ESL Language Center
George McGowan	
Anita R. McKie	University of South Carolina—Aiken
Gail A. Mestas	
Michael F. Monahan	
Janette Moody	The Citadel
Jenine Moscove	
Glenn Owen	Alan Hancock College
Debra Parker-Fleming	Ohio Dominican College
Beth Brooks Patel	University of California—Berkeley
Yvonne Phangi-Hatami	The Borough of Manhattan Community College
LaVonda Ramey	Schoolcraft College
Roberta Rettner	American Ways
Donald Shannon	DePaul University
S. Murray Simons	Northeastern University
Ellen L. Sweatt	DeKalb College—Dunwoody
Marion Taube	University of Pittsburgh
Rita Taylor	University of Cincinnatti
Robert G. Unterman	Glendale Community College
Stan Weikert	College of the Canyons
Kay Westerfield	University of Oregon
Carol Yacht	
Glenn Allen Young	Tulsa Junior College
Marilyn J. Young	Tulsa Junior College

To the Student

How to Study Accounting Successfully

Whether you are majoring in accounting or in another business discipline, your introductory accounting course is one of the most important classes you will take, because it is fundamental to the business curriculum and to your success in the business world beyond college. The course has multiple purposes because its students have diverse interests, backgrounds, and purposes for taking it. What are your goals in studying accounting? Being clear about your goals can contribute to your success in this course.

Success in this class also depends on your desire to learn and your willingness to work hard. And it depends on your understanding of how the text complements the way your instructor teaches and the way you learn. A familiarity with how this text is structured will help you to study more efficiently, make better use of classroom time, and improve your performance on examinations and other assignments.

To be successful in the business world after you graduate, you will need a broad set of skills, which may be summarized as follows:

Technical/Analytical Skills A major objective of your accounting course is to give you a firm grasp of the essential business and accounting terminology and techniques that you will need to succeed in a business environment. With this foundation, you then can begin to develop the higher-level perception skills that will help you to acquire further knowledge on your own.

An even more crucial objective of this course is to help you develop analytical skills that will allow you to evaluate data. Well-developed analytical and decision-making skills are among the professional skills most highly valued by employers, and will serve you well throughout your academic and professional careers.

Communication Skills Another skill highly prized by employers is the ability to express oneself in a manner that is understood correctly by others. This can include writing skills, speaking skills, and presentation skills. Communication skills are developed through particular tasks and assignments and are improved through constructive criticism. Reading skills and listening skills support the direct communication skills.

Interpersonal Skills Effective interaction between two people requires a solid foundation of interpersonal skills. The success of such interaction depends on empathy, or the ability to identify with and understand the problems, concerns, and motives of others. Leadership, supervision, and interviewing skills also facilitate a professional's interaction with others.

Personal/Self Skills Personal/self skills form the foundation for growth in the use of all other skills. To succeed, a professional must take initiative, possess self-confidence, show independence, and be ethical in all areas of life. Personal/self skills can be enhanced significantly by the formal learning process and by peers and mentors who provide models upon which you can build. Accounting is just one course in your entire curriculum, but it can play an important role in your development of the above skills. Your instructor is interested in helping you gain both a knowledge of accounting and the more general skills you will need to succeed in the business world. The following sections describe how you can get the most out of this course.

The Teaching/Learning Cycle™

Both teaching and learning have natural, parallel, and mutually compatible cycles. This teaching/learning cycle, as shown in Figure 1, interacts with the basic structure of learning objectives in this text.

The Teaching Cycle The inner (tan) circle in Figure 1 shows the steps an instructor takes in teaching a chapter. Your teacher *assigns* material, *presents* the subject in lecture, *explains* by going over assignments and answering questions, *reviews* the subject prior to an exam, and *tests* your knowledge and understanding using examinations and other means of evaluation.

The Learning Cycle Moving outward, the next circle (green) in Figure 1 shows the steps you should take in studying a chapter. You should *preview* the material, *read* the chapter, *apply* your understanding by working the assignments, *review* the chapter, and *recall* and *demonstrate* your knowledge and understanding of the material on examinations and other assessments.

Integrated Learning Objectives Your textbook supports the teaching/learning cycle through the use of integrated learning objectives. Learning objectives are simply statements of what you should be able to do after you have completed a chapter. In Figure 1, the outside (blue) circle shows how learning objectives are integrated into your text and other study aids and how they interact with the teaching/learning cycle.

1. Learning objectives appear at the beginning of the chapter, as an aid to your teacher in making assignments and as a preview of the chapter for you.
2. Each learning objective is repeated in the text at the point where that subject is covered to assist your teacher in presenting the material and to help you organize your thoughts as you read the material.
3. Every exercise, problem, and case in the chapter assignments shows the applicable learning objective(s) so you can refer to the text if you need help.
4. A summary of the key points for each learning objective, a list of new concepts and terms referenced by learning objectives, and a review problem covering key learning objectives assist you in reviewing each chapter. Your Study Guide, also organized by learning objectives, provides for additional review.

Why Students Succeed Students succeed in their accounting course when they coordinate their personal learning cycle with their instructor's cycle. Students who do a good job of previewing their assignments, reading the chapters before the instructor is ready to present them, preparing homework assignments before they are discussed in class, and reviewing carefully will ultimately achieve their potential on exams. Those who get out of phase with their instructor, for whatever reason, will do poorly or fail. To ensure that your learning cycle is synchronized with your instructor's teaching cycle, check your study habits against these suggestions.

Figure 1
The Teaching/Learning Cycle™ with Integrated Learning Objectives

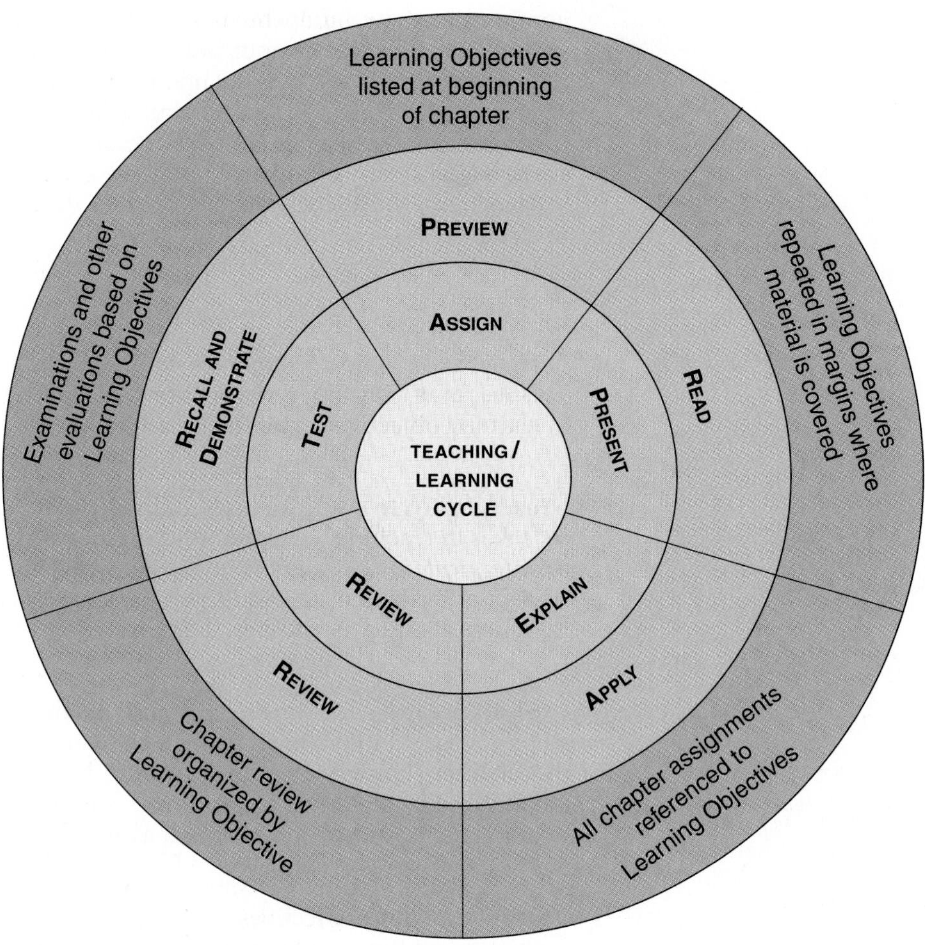

Previewing the Chapter

1. Read the learning objectives at the beginning of the chapter. These learning objectives specifically describe what you should be able to do after completing the chapter.
2. Study your syllabus. Know where you are in the course and where you are going. Know the rules of the course.
3. Realize that in an accounting course, each assignment builds on previous ones. If you do poorly in Chapter 1, you may have difficulty in Chapter 2 and be lost in Chapter 3.

Reading the Chapter

1. As you read each chapter, be aware of the learning objectives in the margins. They will tell you why the material is relevant.
2. Allow yourself plenty of time to read the text. Accounting is a technical subject. Accounting books are so full of information that almost every sentence is important.

3. Strive to understand why as well as how each procedure is done. Accounting is logical and requires reasoning. If you understand why something is done in accounting, there is little need to memorize.
4. Relate each new topic to its learning objective and be able to explain it in your own words.
5. Be aware of colors as you read. They are designed to help you understand the text. (See the chart on the back of your textbook.)
   Orange: All source documents and inputs are in orange.
   Aqua: All accounting forms, working papers, and accounting processes are shown in aqua.
   Purple: All financial statements, the output or final product of the accounting process, are shown in purple.
   Gray: In selected tables and illustrations, gray is used to heighten contrasts and aid understanding.
6. If there is something you do not understand, prepare specific questions for your instructor. Pinpoint the topic or concept that confuses you. Some students keep a notebook of points with which they have difficulty.

Applying the Chapter

1. In addition to understanding why each procedure is done, you must be able to do it yourself by working exercises, problems, and cases. Accounting is a "do-it-yourself" course.
2. Read assignments and instructions carefully. Each assignment has a specific purpose. The wording is precise, and a clear understanding of it will save time and improve your performance. Acquaint yourself with the end-of-chapter assignment materials in this text by reading the description of them in the Preface.
3. Try to work exercises, problems, and cases without referring to their discussions in the chapter. If you cannot work an assignment without looking in the chapter, you will not be able to work a similar problem on an exam. After you have tried on your own, refer to the chapter (based on the learning objective reference) and check your answer. Try to understand any mistakes you may have made.
4. Be neat and orderly. Sloppy calculations, messy papers, and general carelessness cause most errors on accounting assignments.
5. Allow plenty of time to work the chapter assignments. You will find that assignments seem harder and that you make more errors when you are feeling pressed for time.
6. Keep up with your class. Check your work against the solutions presented in class. Find your mistakes. Be sure you understand the correct solutions.
7. Note the part of each exercise, problem, or case that causes you difficulty so you can ask for help.
8. Attend class. Most instructors design classes to help you and to answer your questions. Absence from even one class can hurt your performance.

Reviewing the Chapter

1. Read the summary of learning objectives in the chapter review. Be sure you know the definitions of all the words in the review of concepts and terminology.
2. Review all assigned exercises, problems, and cases. Know them cold. Be sure you can work the assignments without the aid of the book.
3. Determine the learning objectives for which most of the problems were assigned. They refer to topics that your instructor is most likely to emphasize on an exam. Scan the text for such learning objectives and pay particular attention to the examples and illustrations.

4. Look for and scan other similar assignments that cover the same learning objectives. They may be helpful on an exam.
5. Review quizzes. Similar material will often appear on longer exams.
6. Attend any labs or visit any tutors your school provides, or see your instructor during office hours to get assistance. Be sure to have specific questions ready.

Taking Examinations

1. Arrive at class early so you can get the feel of the room and make a last-minute review of your notes.
2. Have plenty of sharp pencils and your calculator (if allowed) ready.
3. Review the exam quickly when it is handed out to get an overview of your task. Start with a part you know. It will give you confidence and save time.
4. Allocate your time to the various parts of the exam, and stick to your schedule. Every exam has time constraints. You need to move ahead and make sure you attempt all parts of the exam.
5. Read the questions carefully. Some may not be exactly like your homework assignments. They may approach the material from a slightly different angle to test your understanding and ability to reason, rather than your ability to memorize.
6. To avoid unnecessary errors, be neat, use good form, and show calculations.
7. Relax. If you have followed the above guidelines, your effort will be rewarded.

Preparing Other Assignments

1. Understand the assignment. Written assignments, term papers, computer projects, oral presentations, case studies, group activities, individual field trips, video critiques, and other activities are designed to enhance skills beyond your technical knowledge. It is essential to know exactly what your instructor expects. Know the purpose, audience, scope, and expected end product.
2. Allow plenty of time. "Murphy's Law" applies to such assignments: If anything can go wrong, it will.
3. Prepare an outline of each report, paper, or presentation. A project that is done well always has a logical structure.
4. Write a rough draft of each paper and report, and practice each presentation. Professionals always try out their ideas in advance and thoroughly rehearse their presentations. Good results are not accomplished by accident.
5. Make sure that each paper, report, or presentation is of professional quality. Instructors appreciate attention to detail and polish. A good rule of thumb is to ask yourself: Would I give this work to my boss?

Check Figures

Chapter 1
P 1. Total Assets: $21,640
P 2. Total Assets: $141,200
P 3. Total Assets: $21,120
P 4. Total Assets: $143,800
P 5. Total Assets: $48,750
P 6. Total Assets: $27,450
P 7. Total Assets: $115,000
P 8. Total Assets: $10,240

Chapter 2
P 1. No check figure
P 2. Trial Balance: $32,900
P 3. Trial Balance: $7,400
P 4. Trial Balance: $23,100
P 5. Trial Balance: $47,030
P 6. No check figure
P 7. Trial Balance: $21,080
P 8. Trial Balance: $61,420

Chapter 3
P 1. No check figure
P 2. No check figure
P 3. Adjusted Trial Balance: $212,334
P 4. Adjusted Trial Balance: $29,778
P 5. Adjusted Trial Balance: $1,284,418
P 6. No check figure
P 7. No check figure
P 8. Adjusted Trial Balance: $60,896

Chapter 4
P 1. Total Assets: $627,800
P 2. Total Assets: $113,616
P 3. October Adjusted Trial Balance: $10,288; Total Assets: $9,024; November Adjusted Trial Balance: $10,858; Total Assets: $9,204; Post-Closing Trial Balance: $9,344
P 4. Total Assets: $17,808
P 5. Total Assets: $247,148
P 6. Total Assets: $193,858
P 7. Total Assets: $56,808
P 8. Total Assets: $123,574

Chapter 5
P 1. 1. Net Income: $6,870
P 2. Net Income: $15,435
P 3. No check figure
P 4. 2. Net Income: $23,812; Total Assets: $66,336
P 5. 2. Net Income: $67,480; Total Assets: $244,530
P 6. No check figure
P 7. 1. Net Income: $47,882
P 8. Net Income: $5,261
P 9. No check figure

Chapter 6
P 1. No check figure
P 2. Net Loss: ($1,720)
P 3. Total Assets: $595,600
P 4. Current Ratio: 20x3, 2.3; 20x2, 3.5; Return on Assets: 20x3, 12.5%; 20x2, 11.0%
P 5. Net Income: $72,260; Total Assets: $1,083,800
P 6. No check figure
P 7. Net Income: $63,626
P 8. Current Ratio: 20x4, 2.0; 20x3, 2.6; Return on Assets: 20x4, 14.8%; 20x3, 13.2%

Chapter 7
P 1. May 31 Accounts Receivable debit balance: $870; May 31 Accounts Payable credit balance: $2,100
P 2. Cash total in cash receipts journal: $23,340; Cash total in cash payments journal: $17,012
P 3. Accounts Payable total: $22,418
P 4. Trial Balance: $91,616
P 5. Trial Balance: $52,630
P 6. June 30 Accounts Receivable debit balance: $3,020; June 30 Accounts Payable credit balance: $2,600
P 7. Cash total in cash receipts journal: $66,968; Cash total in cash payments journal: $28,644
P 8. Trial balance: $84,584

Chapter 8
P 1. No check figure
P 2. Adjusted book balance: $149,473.28
P 3. Adjusted book balance: $3,930
P 4. No check figure
P 5. Total Unpaid Vouchers: $6,216
P 6. No check figure
P 7. Adjusted book balance: $27,242.80
P 8. No check figure

Chapter 9
P 1. Short-Term Investments (at market): $903,875
P 2. No check figure
P 3. Amount of adjustment: $9,533
P 4. No check figure
P 5. Short-Term Investments (at market): $354,000
P 6. No check figure
P 7. Amount of Adjustment: $73,413.00
P 8. No check figure

Chapter 10
P 1. Cost of goods available for sale: $157,980
P 2. 1. Cost of goods sold: August, $4,578; September, $15,457
P 3. 1. Cost of goods sold: August, $4,560; September, $15,424
P 4. Estimated inventory shortage: At cost, $12,104; At retail, $17,800
P 5. Estimated loss of inventory in fire: $1,306,054
P 6. 1. Cost of goods available for sale: $10,560,000
P 7. 1. Cost of goods sold: April, $9,660; May, $22,119
P 8. 1. Cost of goods sold: April, $9,580; May, $21,991

Chapter 11:
P 1. Totals: Land: $723,900; Land Improvements: $142,000; Building: $1,383,600; Equipment: $210,800
P 2. 1. Depreciation, Year 3: a. $330,000; b. $264,000; c. $180,000
P 3. a. Gain on Sale of Road Grader: $3,600; b. Loss on Sale of Road Grader: $4,400; c. Gain on Exchange of Road Grader: $3,600; d. Loss on Exchange of Road Grader: $4,400; e. No gain recognized; f. Loss on Exchange of Road Grader: $4,400; g. Road Grader (new): $62,400; h. Road Grader (new): $70,400
P 4. Part A. c. Amortization Expense: $984,000; d. Loss on Exclusive License: $2,952,000; Part B. d. Leasehold Amortization Expense: $3,150; e. Leasehold Improvements Amortization Expense, $5,000
P 5. Total Depreciation Expense: 20x5: $26,560; 20x6: $37,520; 20x7: $31,456
P 6. Totals: Land: $426,212; Land Improvements: $166,560; Buildings: $833,940; Machinery: $1,262,640; Expense: $18,120
P 7. 1. Depreciation, Year 3: a. $54,250; b. $81,375; c. $53,407
P 8. Total Depreciation Expense: 20x5: $71,820; 20x6: $103,092; 20x7: $84,072

Chapter 12:
P 1. No check figure
P 2. No check figure
P 3. 1.b. Estimated Product Warranty Liability: $10,800
P 4. Payroll Taxes Expense: $31,938.70
P 5. 1. Net Pay, total: $8,176.32
P 6. No check figure
P 7. No check figure
P 8. 1.b. Estimated Product Warranty Liability: $10,080

Chapter 13:
P 1. 2f: Himes' share of income: $42,600
P 2. 3: Ruth's share of income: $32,160; Perry's share of loss: ($57,760)
P 3. d. Felicia, Capital: $48,000
P 4. Total cash distribution to the partners: $640,000
P 5. Cash distribution to Levenfeld: $254,800
P 6. 3: Norman's share of loss: ($76,000)
P 7. d. Ben's bonus: $12,000
P 8. Cash distribution to Li: $104,400

Chapter 14
P 1. 2. Total Stockholders' Equity: $345,400
P 2. 1: 20x5 Total dividends: Preferred, $210,000; Common, $190,000
P 3. No check figure
P 4. 2: Total Stockholders' Equity: $723,325
P 5. 2: Total Stockholders' Equity: $330,375
P 6. 2: Total Stockholders' Equity: $1,488,000
P 7. 1: 20x3 Total dividends: Preferred, $60,000; Common, $34,000
P 8. 2: Total Stockholders' Equity: $950,080

Chapter 15
P 1. 2. Difference in net income: $48,800
P 2. Income Before Extraordinary Items and Cumulative Effect of Accounting Change: $216,000
P 3. Income from Continuing Operations, December 31, 20x9: $551,250
P 4. Total Stockholders' Equity, Dec. 31, 20x7: $2,964,000
P 5. Retained Earnings: $250,000; Total Stockholders' Equity: $2,350,000
P 6. Total Stockholders' Equity: $2,802,800
P 7. Income Before Extraordinary Items and Cumulative Effect of Accounting Change: $410,000
P 8. Total Stockholders' Equity, Dec. 31, 20x3: $1,157,000
P 9. Retained Earnings: $397,000; Total Stockholders' Equity: $2,577,000

Chapter 16:
P 1. No check figure
P 2. No check figure
P 3. Bond Interest Expense: June 30, 20x1, $93,195; Sept. 30, 20x1, $193,800
P 4. No check figure
P 5. No check figure
P 6. No check figure
P 7. No check figure
P 8. Bond Interest Expense: June 30, 20x2, $289,332; Sept. 1, 20x2, $186,580

Chapter 17:
P 1. No check figure
P 2. 1. Net Cash Flows from: Operating Activities, $46,800; Investing Activities, ($14,400); Financing Activities, $102,000
P 3. 1. Net Cash Flows from: Operating Activities, ($106,000); Investing Activities, $34,000; Financing Activities, $44,000
P 4. 2. Same as P 3
P 5. Net Cash Flows from Operating Activities: $47,600
P 6. 1. Net Cash Flows from: Operating Activities, $548,000; Investing Activities: $6,000; Financing Activities, ($260,000)
P 7. No check figure
P 8. Net Cash Flows from: Operating Activities, $63,300; Investing Activities, ($12,900); Financing Activities, $7,000
P 9. 2. Same as P 8

Chapter 18:
P 1. No check figure
P 2. Increase: a, b, e, f, l, m
P 3. 1.c. Receivable turnover, 20x2: 14.1 times; 20x1: 14.4 times
P 4. 1.b. Quick ratio, Allison: 1.5 times; Marker: 1.2 times; 2.d. Return on equity, Allison: 8.8%; Marker, 4.9%
P 5. Increase: d, h, i
P 6. 1.a. Current ratio, 20x6: 1.9 times; 20x5: 1.0 times; 2.c. Return on assets, 20x6: 8.4%; 20x5: 6.6%
P 7. 1.b. Quick ratio, Emax: 0.4 times; Savlow: 1.0 times; 2.d. Return on equity, Emax: 11.8%; Savlow 8.8%

Chapter 19:
P 1. No check figure
P 2. No check figure
P 3. Investment in Sargent Company, Ending Balance: $320,000
P 4. Total Assets, Consolidated Balance Sheet: $4,488,000

P 5. Total Assets, Consolidated Balance Sheet: $1,280,000
P 6. No check figure
P 7. Investment in Albers Corporation, Ending Balance: $367,000

Chapter 20:
P 1. No check figure
P 2. Cutting/Lining, average hours per pair on Monday: .25 hours
P 3. No check figure
P 4. 2.a. Gross Margin: $181,200
2.d. Cost of Goods Manufactured: $253,500
P 5. 1.a. $4
1.e. $10
1.n. $10
P 6. Molding, Week 1, First Shift, hours per board: 3.50
P 7. No check figure
P 8. 2.a. Gross margin $191,800
2.d. Cost of Goods Manufactured: $312,100

Chapter 21:
P 1. 2. Total unit cost: $6.86
P 2. Cost of Goods Manufactured: $1,171,150
P 3. a. $2
f. $4
P 4. 2. Overhead applied to Job 2214: $29,717
P 5. 2. $69,280.40 Total costs assigned to Holstrum order, activity based costing approach
P 6. 1. Predetermined overhead rate for year 20x3: $5.014 per machine hour
P 7. 2. $41,805.60 Total costs assigned to Hines order, activity-based costing approach
P 8. 1.c. Rigger II: $10,665
BioScout: $13,940

Chapter 22:
P 1. 2. Cost of Units Sold $96,500
P 2. b. $66,500;
i. $57,800
P 3. 2. $35,168
P 4. 1.c. Cost of ending Work in Process Inventory: $18,900
P 5. 1.b. Total cost per equivalent unit: $1.20
P 6. b. $58,512
h. $65,448
P 7. 1. Total contract revenue, Job Order P-12: $30,238
P 8. 1.b. Total cost per equivalent unit: $2.12

Chapter 23:
P 1. 4. Cost per job: $81.56
P 2. 1. 7,500 billable hours
P 3. 3. $255
P 4. 2. 190,000 units
P 5. 1. 740 systems
P 6. 1.a. 3,500 units

Chapter 24:
P 1. 1. Total manufacturing costs budgeted for November: $578,500
P 2. 7. Income from Operations = $3,086
P 3. 1. Ending Cash Balance, August: $3,600
P 4. 1. Projected Net Income: $101,812
P 5. Ending Cash Balance, February: $919,400
P 6. 1. Net Income: $930,415
P 7. 1. Ending Cash Balance, February: ($1,450)
P 8. 1. Net Income: $52,404

Chapter 25:
P 1. 2. Total standard cost of front entrance, Year 20x0: $8,510
P 2. 1. Direct materials quantity variance—metal: $792 (U)
2. Direct labor efficiency variance—molding: $1,290 (U)
P 3. 2. Flexible budget formula = ($.35 × units produced) + $10,500
P 4. 1.a. Direct materials price variance, chemicals: $12,200 (F)
1.e. Controllable overhead variance: $3,100 (U)
P 5. c. $11.50
P 6. 1. Total standard direct materials cost per unit $169.62
P 7. 1. Direct materials price variance—liquid plastic: $386 (F)
2. Direct labor rate variance—Trimming/Packing: $56 (U)
P 8. 2. Direct materials quantity variance: $3,720 (U)
6. Manufacturing Overhead volume variance: $320 (F)

Chapter 26:
P 1. 1. Total relevant cost to make: $3,084,000
P 2. 1. Profit from special order: $7,725
P 3. 2. Total increase in profit from extended contract: $8,400
P 4. 1. Net income, Coupe Machine: $39,204; Net income, Metro Machine: $48,642
P 5. 1. Net present value: $16,573
P 6. 1. Total relevant cost to buy: $1,350,000
P 7. 1. Net income, Matthew Machine: $35,752.50; Net income, Kelley Machine: $41,475.00
P 8. 2. Net present value: ($27,730)

Chapter 27:
P 1. No check figure
P 2. 2. A-Bump, product unit cost: $150.00; unit selling price: $240.00
4. A-Bump, product unit cost: $178.11; unit selling price: $284.98
P 3. 2. Product unit cost, quarter ended 3/31/20x3: $10.49
P 4. 2. ABC total cost assigned to Life Spring order: $42,632
P 5. 1. East Division, total cost of nonconformance: $807,500
2. West Division, total cost of conformance as a percentage of sales: 8.35%
P 6. 2. ABC total cost assigned to Kujawa order: $71,415.40
P 7. 1. Currence Co., total cost of conformance: $533,600
2. Aspen Co., total cost of nonconformance as a percentage of sales: 6.45%
P 8. 1. Total materials cost: $199,300
2.b. Total cost per equivalent unit: $48.45

CHAPTER 1

Uses of Accounting Information and the Financial Statements

LEARNING OBJECTIVES

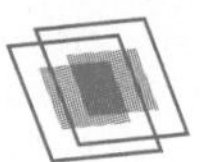

1. **Define *accounting,* identify business goals and activities, and describe the role of accounting in making informed decisions.**
2. **Identify the many users of accounting information in society.**
3. **Explain the importance of business transactions, money measure, and separate entity to accounting measurement.**
4. **Identify the three basic forms of business organization.**
5. **Define *financial position,* state the accounting equation, and show how they are affected by simple transactions.**
6. **Identify the four financial statements.**
7. **State the relationship of generally accepted accounting principles (GAAP) to financial statements and the independent CPA's report, and identify the organizations that influence GAAP.**
8. **Define *ethics* and describe the ethical responsibilities of accountants.**

DECISION POINT

MICROSOFT CORPORATION

Microsoft Corporation, the giant software company, is considered one of the world's most successful companies. Why is Microsoft considered successful? An ordinary person sees the quality of the company's enormously successful products like Microsoft Windows, Microsoft Word, and Microsoft Excel; an investment company and others with a financial stake in the company evaluate Microsoft and its management in financial terms. Many Microsoft employees have become millionaires by owning a part of the company through stock ownership. This success is reflected in the Financial Highlights from the company's 1997 annual report, shown here.[1]

Financial Highlights

(In millions, except earnings per share and return on net revenues)

	Year Ended June 30				
	1993	1994	1995	1996	**1997**
Net revenues	$3,753	$4,649	$5,937	$ 8,671	**$11,358**
Net income	953	1,146	1,453	2,195	**3,454**
Earnings per share	0.79	0.94	1.16	1.71	**2.63**
Return on net revenues	25.4%	24.7%	24.5%	25.3%	**30.4%**
Cash and short-term investments	$2,290	$3,614	$4,750	$ 6,940	**$ 8,966**
Total assets	3,805	5,363	7,210	10,093	**14,387**
Stockholders' equity	3,242	4,450	5,333	6,908	**10,777**

VIDEO CASE

INTEL CORPORATION

OBJECTIVES

- To examine the principal activities of a business enterprise: financing, investing and operating.
- To explore the principal performance goals of a business enterprise: liquidity and profitability.
- To relate these activities and goals to the financial statements.

BACKGROUND FOR THE CASE

You are probably familiar with the slogan "Intel Inside," from a marketing campaign for Intel Corporation, one of the most successful companies in the world. In 1971, Intel introduced the world's first microprocessor, which in turn made possible the personal computer (PC), which has changed the world. Today, Intel supplies the computing industry with chips, boards, systems, and software. Its principal products include:

- *Microprocessors.* Also called central processing units (CPUs), these are frequently described as the "brains" of a computer because they act as the central control for the processing of data in PCs. This category includes the famous Pentium® processor.
- *Networking and Communications Products.* These products enhance the capabilities and ease of use of PC systems by allowing users to talk to each other and to share information.
- *Semiconductor Products.* Semiconductors facilitate flash memory, making easily reprogrammable memory for computers, mobile phones, and many other products possible. Included in this category are embedded control chips that are programmed to regulate specific functions in products such as automobile engines, laser printers, disk drives, and home appliances.

Intel's customers include manufacturers of computers and computer systems, PC users, manufacturers of automobiles, and manufacturers of a wide range of industrial and telecommunications equipment.

For more information about Intel Corporation, visit the company's Web site through the Needles Accounting Resource Center at

http://www.hmco.com/college/needles/home.html

REQUIRED

View the video on Intel Corporation that accompanies this book. As you are watching the video, take notes related to the following:

1. All businesses engage in three basic activities—financing, investing, and operating—but how they engage in them differs from company to company. Describe in your own words the nature of each of these activities and give as many examples as you can of how Intel engages in each activity.
2. To be successful, all businesses must achieve two performance objectives—liquidity and profitability. Describe in your own words the nature of each of these goals and describe how each applies to Intel.
3. There are four financial statements that apply to business enterprises. Which statements are most closely associated with the goal of liquidity? Which statement is most closely associated with the goal of profitability? Which statement shows the financial position of the company?

These Financial Highlights contain a number of terms for common financial measures of all companies, large or small—measures by which a company's management is evaluated and by which others can evaluate a company in relation to other companies. It is easy to see the large increases at Microsoft over the years in such measures as net revenues, net income, total assets, and stockholders' equity, but what do these terms mean? What financial knowledge do Microsoft's managers need in order to measure progress toward their financial goals? What financial knowledge does anyone who is evaluating Microsoft in relation to other companies need in order to understand these measures?

Point to Emphasize: Management must have a good understanding of accounting to set financial goals and to make financial decisions. Management not only must understand how accounting information is compiled and processed, but also must realize that accounting information is imperfect and should be interpreted with caution.

Critical Thinking Question: Why would a business have more than one financial goal? **Answer:** Multiple financial goals signal that there is not just one measure of performance that is of interest to all users. For example, lenders' primary concern is cash flow, and owners are concerned with earnings and dividends.

Microsoft's managers must have a thorough knowledge of accounting to understand how the operations for which they are responsible contribute to the firm's overall financial health. People with a financial stake in the company, such as owners, investors, creditors, employees, attorneys, and government regulators, must also know accounting to evaluate the financial performance of a business. Anyone who aspires to any of these roles in a business requires a mastery of the terminology and concepts that underlie accounting, the way in which financial information is generated, and the way in which that information is interpreted and analyzed. The purpose of this course and this textbook is to assist you in acquiring that mastery.

Accounting as an Information System

OBJECTIVE 1

Define* accounting, *identify business goals and activities, and describe the role of accounting in making informed decisions

Related Text Assignments:
Q: 1, 2, 3, 4
E: 1
SD: 1, 4
FRA: 2, 4

Today's accountant focuses on the ultimate needs of decision makers who use accounting information, whether those decision makers are inside or outside the business. Accounting "is not an end in itself,"[2] but is *an information system that measures, processes, and communicates financial information about an identifiable economic entity.* An economic entity is a unit that exists independently—for example, a business, a hospital, or a governmental body. The central focus of this book is on business entities and business activities, although other economic units, such as hospitals and governmental units, will be mentioned at appropriate points in the text and assignment material.

Accounting provides a vital service by supplying the information decision makers need to make "reasoned choices among alternative uses of scarce resources in the

BUSINESS BULLETIN: BUSINESS PRACTICE

Accounting is a very old discipline. Forms of it have been essential to commerce for more than five thousand years. Accounting, in a version close to what we know today, gained widespread use in the 1400s, especially in Italy, where it was instrumental in the development of shipping, trade, construction, and other forms of commerce. This system of double-entry bookkeeping was documented by the famous Italian mathematician, scholar, and philosopher Fra Luca Pacioli. In 1494, Pacioli published his most important work, *Summa de Arithmetica, Geometrica, Proportioni et Proportionalita,* which contained a detailed description of accounting as practiced in that age. This book became the most widely read book on mathematics in Italy and firmly established Pacioli as the "Father of Accounting."

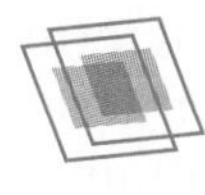

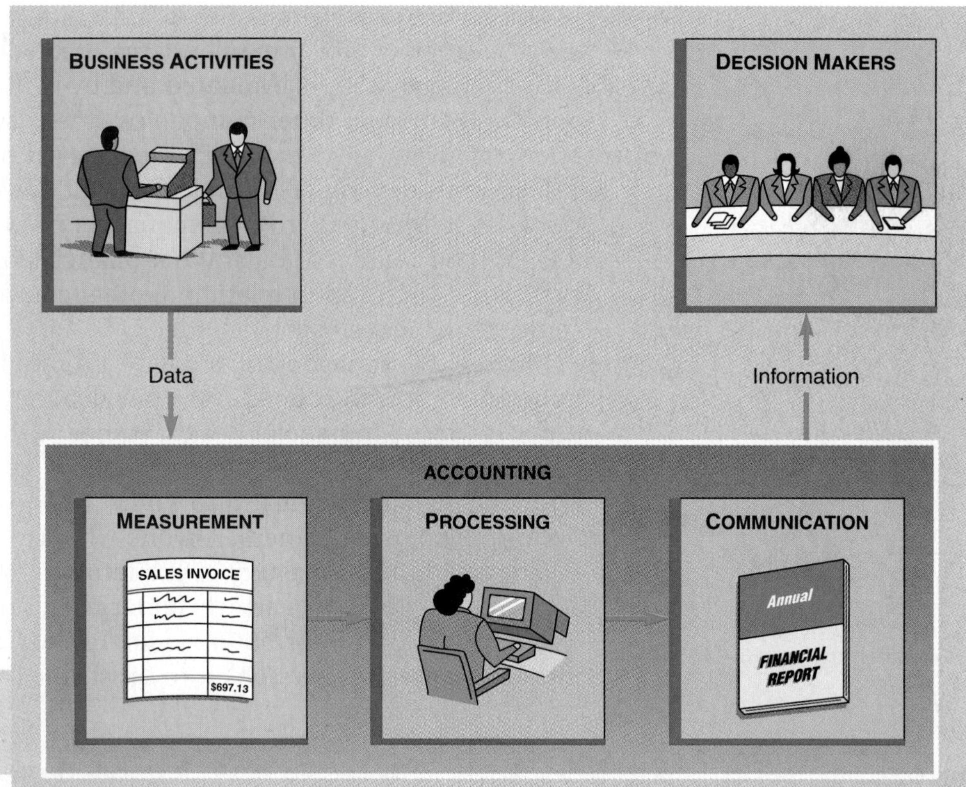

Figure 1
Accounting as an Information System

Point to Emphasize: It is the usefulness of the information generated by accounting that makes accounting a valuable discipline. That is, the primary purpose of accounting is to provide decision makers with financial information that can be used to make intelligent decisions.

conduct of business and economic activities."[3] As shown in Figure 1, accounting is a link between business activities and decision makers. First, accounting measures business activities by recording data about them for future use. Second, the data are stored until needed and then processed to become useful information. Third, the information is communicated, through reports, to decision makers. We might say that data about business activities are the inputs to the accounting system and that useful information for decision makers is the output.

Business Goals, Activities, and Performance Measures

A business is an economic unit that aims to sell goods and services to customers at prices that will provide an adequate return to its owners. For example, listed below are some companies and the principal goods or services they sell:

General Mills, Inc.	Food products
Reebok International Ltd.	Athletic footwear and clothing
Sony Corp.	Consumer electronics
Wendy's International Inc.	Food service
Hilton Hotels Corp.	Hotels and resorts service
Southwest Airlines Co.	Passenger airline service

Despite their differences, all these businesses have similar goals and engage in similar activities, as shown in Figure 2. Each must take in enough money from customers to pay all the costs of doing business, with enough left over as profit for the

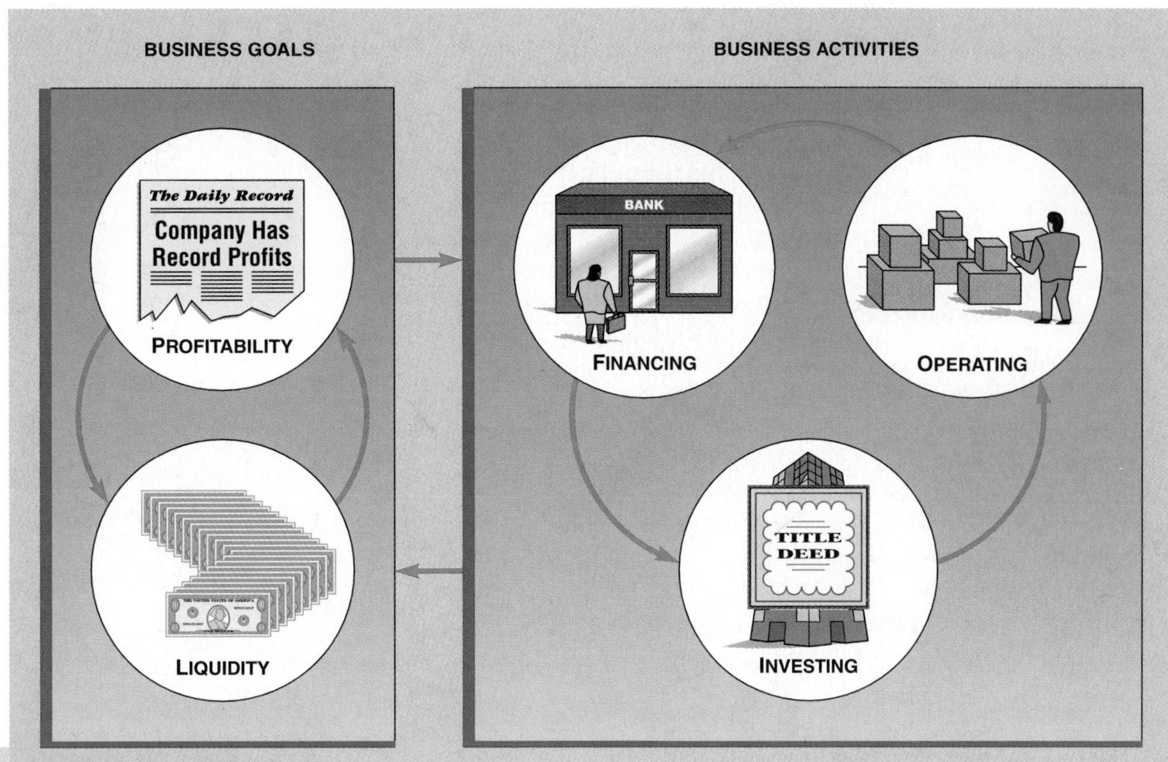

Figure 2
Business Goals and Activities

Discussion Question: What is the difference between profitability and liquidity? **Answer:** Profitability means earning enough income to attract and hold investment capital; liquidity means being able to pay debts when they fall due.

owners to want to stay in the business. This need to earn enough income to attract and hold investment capital is the goal of profitability. In addition, businesses must meet the goal of liquidity. Liquidity means having enough funds available to pay debts when they are due. For example, Toyota may meet the goal of profitability by selling many cars at a price that earns a profit, but if its customers do not pay for their cars quickly enough to enable Toyota to pay its suppliers and employees, the company may fail to meet the goal of liquidity. Both goals must be met if a company is to survive and be successful.

All businesses pursue their goals by engaging in similar activities. First, each business must engage in financing activities to obtain adequate funds, or capital, to begin and to continue operating. Financing activities include obtaining capital from owners and from creditors, such as banks and suppliers. They also include repaying creditors and paying a return to the owners. Second, each business must engage in investing activities to spend the capital it receives in ways that are productive and will help the business achieve its objectives. Investing activities include buying land, buildings, equipment, and other resources that are needed in the operation of the business, and selling these resources when they are no longer needed. Third, each business must engage in operating activities. In addition to the selling of goods and services to customers, operating activities include such actions as employing managers and workers, buying and producing goods and services, and paying taxes to the government.

An important function of accounting is to provide performance measures, which indicate whether or not managers are achieving the business goals and whether or not they are managing business activities well. For instance, earned income is a measure of profitability and cash flow is a measure of liquidity. Ratios of accounting

BUSINESS BULLETIN: BUSINESS PRACTICE

Microsoft Corporation projects its performance in meeting the major business objectives in its annual report:[4]

Liquidity: "Management believes existing cash and short-term investments together with funds generated from operations will be sufficient to meet the company's operating requirements in 1997."

Profitability: "This was a defining year (1996) for Microsoft, and our 21st consecutive year of growth in both revenues and profits. Windows 95 made a major contribution. Desktop application products' revenues were also very strong."

Microsoft's main business activities are shown at the right.

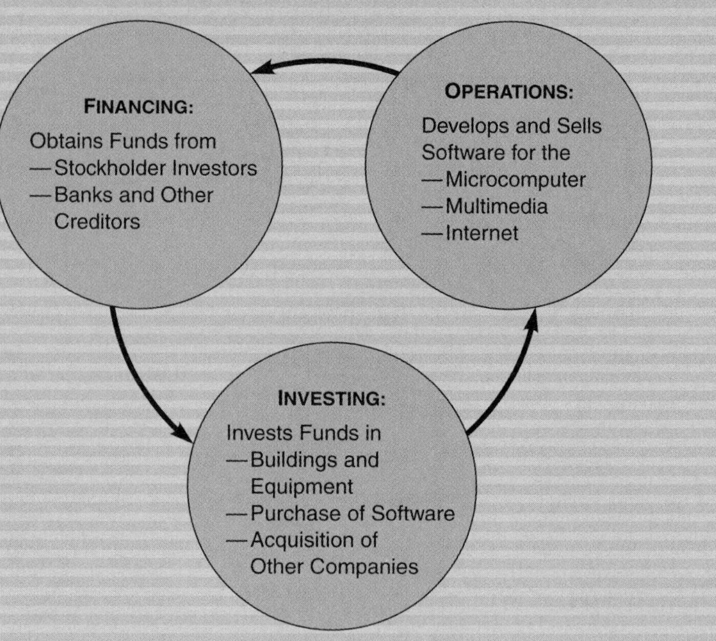

measures can also be used as performance measures. For instance, one performance measure for operating activities might be the ratio of expenses to the revenue of the business. A performance measure for financing activities might be the ratio of the money owed by the business to total resources controlled by the company. Since managers are usually evaluated on how well they achieve these and other performance measures, it is certainly in their best interest to know enough accounting so that they can understand how they are evaluated and how they can improve their performance.

Financial and Management Accounting

Accounting's role of assisting decision makers by measuring, processing, and communicating information is usually divided into the categories of management accounting and financial accounting. Although there is considerable overlap in the functions of management accounting and financial accounting, the two can be distinguished by who the principal users of the information will be. Management accounting provides internal decision makers who are charged with achieving the goals of profitability and liquidity with information about financing, investing, and operating activities. Managers and employees who conduct the activities of the business need information that tells them how they have done in the past and what they can expect in the future. For example, The Gap needs an operating report on each mall outlet that tells how much was sold at that outlet and what costs were incurred, and it needs a budget for each outlet that projects the sales and costs for the next year. Financial accounting generates reports and communicates them to external decision makers so that they can evaluate how well the business has achieved its goals. These reports to external users are called financial statements. The Gap, for instance, will send its financial statements to its owners (called *stockholders*), its banks and other creditors, and government regulators. Financial statements report directly on the goals of profitability and liquidity and are used extensively both inside and outside a business to evaluate the business's success. It is important for every person involved with a business to understand financial statements. They are a central feature of accounting and are the primary focus of this book.

Processing Accounting Information

Teaching Note: Students often have difficulty distinguishing between accounting and bookkeeping. Perhaps a Venn diagram showing bookkeeping as a small circle within a much larger circle identified as accounting can help make the distinction.

To avoid misunderstandings, it is important to distinguish accounting itself from the ways in which accounting information is processed by bookkeeping, the computer, and management information systems.

People often fail to understand the difference between accounting and bookkeeping. Bookkeeping is the process of recording financial transactions and keeping financial records. Mechanical and repetitive, bookkeeping is only a small—but important—part of accounting. Accounting, on the other hand, includes the design of an information system that meets the user's needs. The major goals of accounting are the analysis, interpretation, and use of information.

Point to Emphasize: Computerized accounting information is only as reliable and useful as the data input into the system. The accountant must have a thorough understanding of the concepts that underlie accounting to ensure the data's reliability and usefulness.

The computer is an electronic tool that is used to collect, organize, and communicate vast amounts of information with great speed. Accountants were among the earliest and most enthusiastic users of computers, and today they use microcomputers in all aspects of their work. It may appear that the computer is doing the accountant's job; in fact, it is only a tool that is instructed to do routine bookkeeping and to perform complex calculations.

With the widespread use of the computer today, a business's many information needs are organized into what is called a management information system (MIS). A management information system consists of the interconnected subsystems that provide the information needed to run an organization. The accounting information system is the most important subsystem because it plays the key role of managing the flow of economic data to all parts of an organization and to interested parties outside the organization.

Decision Makers: The Users of Accounting Information

OBJECTIVE 2

Identify the many users of accounting information in society

Related Text Assignments:
Q: 5, 6, 7, 8, 9
E: 1
SD: 1, 4

The people who use accounting information to make decisions fall into three categories: (1) those who manage a business; (2) those outside a business enterprise who have a direct financial interest in the business; and (3) those people, organizations, and agencies that have an indirect financial interest in the business, as shown in Figure 3. These categories apply to government and not-for-profit organizations as well as to profit-oriented ventures.

Management

Management, collectively, is the people who have overall responsibility for operating a business and for meeting its profitability and liquidity goals. In a small business, management may include the owners. In a large business, management more often consists of people who have been hired. Managers must decide what to do, how to do it, and whether the results match their original plans. Successful managers consistently make the right decisions based on timely and valid information. To make good decisions, managers need answers to such questions as: What was the company's net income during the past quarter? Is the rate of return to the owners adequate? Does the company have enough cash? Which products are most profitable?

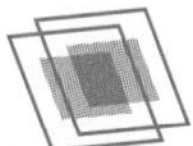

Teaching Note: An interesting way to present this learning objective is to ask your students to name the many users of financial information while you list them on the board or on an overhead transparency. Students should understand that the list in Figure 3 is not meant to be exhaustive.

Instructional Strategy: Assign SD 4 for homework. Change to require a half-page written answer. Discuss in class.

Figure 3
The Users of Accounting Information

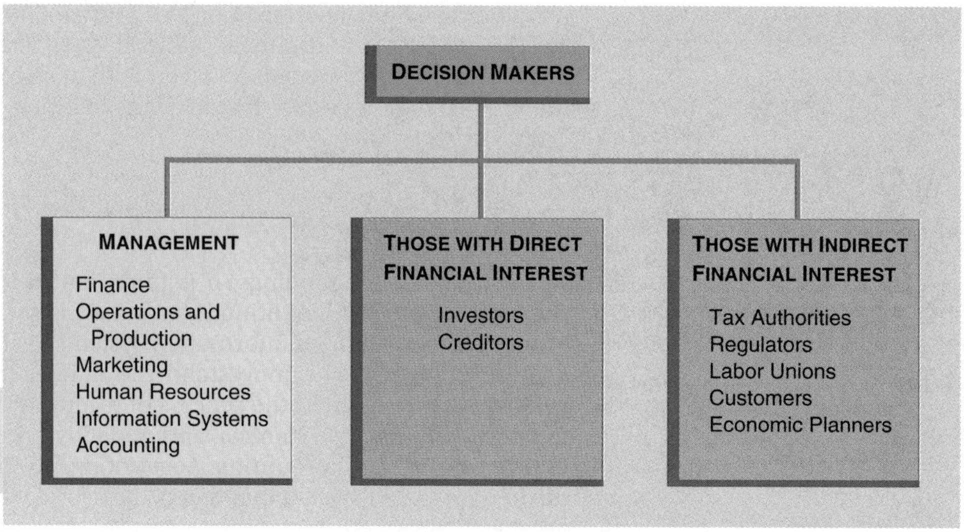

What is the cost of manufacturing each product? Because so many key decisions are based on accounting data, management is one of the most important users of accounting information.

Enrichment Note: Management is an *internal* user that requires its own set of accounting information.

In carrying out its decision-making process, management performs a set of functions essential to the operation of the business. Although larger organizations will have more elaborate operations, the same basic functions must be accomplished in all cases, and each requires accounting information for decision making. The basic management functions are:

Financing the business Financial management obtains financial resources so that the company can begin and continue operating.

Investing the resources of the business Asset management invests the financial resources of the business in productive assets that support the company's goals.

Producing goods and services Operations and production management develops and produces products and services.

Marketing goods and services Marketing management sells, advertises, and distributes goods and services.

Managing employees Human resource management encompasses the hiring, evaluation, and compensation of employees.

Providing information to decision makers Information systems management captures data about all aspects of the company's operations, organizes the data into usable information, and provides reports to internal managers and appropriate outside parties. Accounting plays a key role in this function.

Users with a Direct Financial Interest

Point to Emphasize: The primary external users of accounting information are investors and creditors.

Another group of decision makers who need accounting information are those with a direct financial interest in a business. They depend on accounting to measure and report information about how a business has performed. Most businesses periodically publish a set of general-purpose financial statements that report their success in meeting the goals of profitability and liquidity. These statements show what has happened in the past and are important indicators of what is going to happen in the future. Many people outside the company carefully study these financial reports. The two most important outside groups are investors and creditors.

BUSINESS BULLETIN: BUSINESS PRACTICE

John Connors, corporate controller of Microsoft, emphasizes that providing information to decision makers is an important accounting function, as follows:

> *The way I look at it, the controller's principal job is providing information that the business needs to make good decisions. . . . The real purpose is getting the information that managers need to do their jobs better, whether it is in sales and marketing, research and development, in the support groups, or operations.*[5]

Investors Those who invest or may invest in a business and acquire a part ownership are interested in its past success and its potential earnings. A thorough study of a company's financial statements helps potential investors judge the prospects for a profitable investment. After investing in a company, investors must continually review their commitment, again by examining the company's financial statements.

Creditors Most companies borrow money for both long- and short-term operating needs. Creditors, those who lend money or deliver goods and services before being paid, are interested mainly in whether a company will have the cash to pay interest charges and repay debt at the appropriate time. They study a company's liquidity and cash flow as well as its profitability. Banks, finance companies, mortgage companies, securities firms, insurance firms, suppliers, and other lenders must analyze a company's financial position before they make a loan.

Users with an Indirect Financial Interest

In recent years, society as a whole, through government and public groups, has become one of the biggest and most important users of accounting information. Users who need accounting information to make decisions on public issues include (1) tax authorities, (2) regulatory agencies, and (3) other groups.

Tax Authorities Government at every level is financed through the collection of taxes. Under federal, state, and local laws, companies and individuals pay many kinds of taxes, including federal, state, and city income taxes, social security and other payroll taxes, excise taxes, and sales taxes. Each tax requires special tax returns and often a complex set of records as well. Proper reporting is generally a matter of law and can be very complicated. The Internal Revenue Code, for instance, contains thousands of rules governing the preparation of the accounting information used in computing federal income taxes.

Regulatory Agencies Most companies must report to one or more regulatory agencies at the federal, state, and local levels. For example, all public corporations must report periodically to the Securities and Exchange Commission (SEC). This body, which was set up by Congress to protect the public, regulates the issuing, buying, and selling of stocks in the United States. Companies that are listed on a stock exchange also must meet the special reporting requirements of their exchange.

Other Groups Labor unions study the financial statements of corporations as part of preparing for contract negotiations. A company's income and costs often play an important role in these negotiations. Those who advise investors and creditors—financial analysts and advisers, brokers, underwriters, lawyers, economists, and the financial press—also have an indirect interest in the financial performance and prospects of a business. Consumers' groups, customers, and the general public have become more concerned about the financing and earnings of corporations as well as the effects that corporations have on inflation, the environment, social problems, and the quality of life. And economic planners, among them members of the President's Council of Economic Advisers and the Federal Reserve Board, use aggregated accounting information to establish economic policies and evaluate economic programs.

Government and Not-for-Profit Organizations

More than 30 percent of the U.S. economy is generated by government and not-for-profit organizations (hospitals, universities, professional organizations, and charities). The managers of these diverse entities need to understand and to use accounting information to perform the same functions as managers in businesses. They need to raise funds from investors, creditors, taxpayers, and donors, and to deploy scarce resources. They need to plan to pay for operations and repay creditors on a timely basis. Moreover, they have an obligation to report their financial performance to legislators, boards, and donors, as well as deal with tax authorities, regulators, and labor unions. Although most of the examples throughout this text focus on business enterprises, the same basic principles apply to government and not-for-profit organizations.

Accounting Measurement

OBJECTIVE 3

Explain the importance of business transactions, money measure, and separate entity to accounting measurement

Related Text Assignments:
Q: 10
SE: 1
E: 2, 3, 4
SD: 2

Terminology Note: *Measurement* means the analysis of transactions in terms of recognition, valuation, and classification. That is, it answers the question: How is this transaction best represented in the accounting records?

Accounting is an information system that measures, processes, and communicates financial information. In this section, you begin the study of the measurement aspects of accounting. Here you learn what accounting actually measures and study the effects of certain transactions on an organization's financial position.

To make an accounting measurement, the accountant must answer four basic questions:

1. What is measured?
2. When should the measurement be made?
3. What value should be placed on what is measured?
4. How should what is measured be classified?

All these questions deal with basic assumptions and generally accepted accounting principles, and their answers establish what accounting is and what it is not. Accountants in industry, professional associations, public accounting, government, and academic circles debate the answers to these questions constantly, and the answers change as new knowledge and practice require. But the basis of today's accounting practice rests on a number of widely accepted concepts and conventions, which are described in this book. We begin by focusing on question **1**: What is measured?

What Is Measured?

The world contains an unlimited number of things to measure and ways to measure them. For example, consider a machine that makes bottle caps. How many measurements of this machine could you make? You might start with size and then go on to location, weight, cost, or many other units of measurement. Some of these measurements are relevant to accounting; some are not. Every system must define what it measures, and accounting is no exception. Basically, financial accounting

Table 1. Partial Listing of Foreign Exchange Rates

Country	Price in $ U.S.	Country	Price in $ U.S.
Britain (pound)	1.69	Italy (lira)	0.0006
Canada (dollar)	0.71	Japan (yen)	0.008
France (franc)	0.173	Mexico (peso)	0.12
Germany (mark)	0.579	Philippines (peso)	0.03
Hong Kong (dollar)	0.13	Taiwan (dollar)	0.032

Source: Data from *The Wall Street Journal*, November 17, 1997.

uses money measures to gauge the impact of business transactions on separate business entities. The concepts of business transactions, money measure, and separate entity are discussed in the next sections.

Business Transactions as the Object of Measurement

Business transactions are economic events that affect the financial position of a business entity. Business entities can have hundreds or even thousands of transactions every day. These business transactions are the raw material of accounting reports.

Common Student Confusion: Students already have a feel for what a business transaction is, but they probably do not know the difference between an exchange transaction and a nonexchange transaction.

A transaction can be an exchange of value (a purchase, sale, payment, collection, or loan) between two or more independent parties. A transaction also can be an economic event that has the same effect as an exchange transaction but does not involve an exchange. Some examples of "nonexchange" transactions are losses from fire, flood, explosion, and theft; physical wear and tear on machinery and equipment; and the day-by-day accumulation of interest.

To be recorded, a transaction must relate directly to a business entity. For example, suppose a customer buys a shovel from Ace Hardware but has to buy a hoe from a competing store because Ace is out of hoes. The transaction in which the shovel was sold is entered in Ace's records. However, the purchase of the hoe from the competitor is not entered in Ace's records because even though it indirectly affects Ace economically, it does not involve a direct exchange of value between Ace and the customer.

Money Measure

All business transactions are recorded in terms of money. This concept is termed money measure. Of course, information of a nonfinancial nature may be recorded, but it is through the recording of monetary amounts that the diverse transactions and activities of a business are measured. Money is the only factor that is common to all business transactions, and thus it is the only practical unit of measure that can produce financial data that are alike and can be compared.

Point to Emphasize: The common unit of measurement in the United States for financial reporting purposes is the dollar.

The monetary unit a business uses depends on the country in which the business resides. For example, in the United States, the basic unit of money is the dollar. In Japan, it is the yen; in France, the franc; in Germany, the mark; and in the United Kingdom, the pound. If there are transactions between countries, exchange rates must be used to translate from one currency to another. An exchange rate is the value of one currency in terms of another. For example, a British person purchasing goods from a U.S. company and paying in U.S. dollars must exchange British pounds for U.S. dollars before making payment. In effect, the currencies are goods that can be bought and sold. Table 1 illustrates the exchange rates for several currencies in dollars. It shows the exchange rate for British pounds as $1.69 per pound on a particular date. Like the price of any good or service, these prices change frequently according to supply and demand for the currencies. For example, a few years earlier the exchange rate for British pounds was $1.20. Although our discussion in this book focuses on dollars, selected examples and certain assignments will be in foreign currencies.

The Concept of Separate Entity

Teaching Note: At this point, most students do not realize that there is a difference between separate *legal* entity and separate *economic* entity. Make the distinction, and emphasize that for accounting purposes a business is *always* separate and distinct from its owners, creditors, and customers.

For accounting purposes, a business is a separate entity, distinct not only from its creditors and customers but also from its owner or owners. It should have a completely separate set of records, and its financial records and reports should refer only to its own financial affairs.

For example, the Jones Florist Company should have a bank account that is separate from the account of Kay Jones, the owner. Kay Jones may own a home, a car, and other property, and she may have personal debts, but these are not the Jones Florist Company's resources or debts. Kay Jones also may own another business, say a stationery shop. If she does, she should have a completely separate set of records for each business.

Forms of Business Organization

OBJECTIVE 4

Identify the three basic forms of business organization

Related Text Assignments:
Q: 11
E: 3

There are three basic forms of business organization: sole proprietorships, partnerships, and corporations. Accountants recognize each form as an economic unit separate from its owners, although legally only the corporation is considered separate from its owners. Other legal differences among the three forms are summarized in Table 2 and discussed briefly in the following sections. In this book, we begin with accounting for the sole proprietorship because it is the simplest form of accounting. At critical points, however, we call attention to its essential differences from accounting for partnerships and corporations.

Table 2. Comparative Features of the Forms of Business Organization

	Sole Proprietorship	Partnership	Corporation
1. Legal status	Not a separate legal entity	Not a separate legal entity	Separate legal entity
2. Risk of ownership	Owner's personal resources at stake	Partners' personal resources at stake	Limited to investment in corporation
3. Duration or life	Limited by choice or death of owner	Limited by choice or death of any partner	Indefinite, possibly unlimited
4. Transferability of ownership	Sale by owner establishes new company	Changes in any partner's percentage of interest requires new partnership	Transferable by sale of stock
5. Accounting treatment	Separate economic unit	Separate economic unit	Separate economic unit

Point to Emphasize: In many ways, a sole proprietorship and a partnership are alike. A corporation, however, is very different from the other two forms of business organization.

Point to Emphasize: There are more sole proprietorships in the United States than either of the other two forms of businesses. However, they transact far less business in dollar terms than do corporations.

Sole Proprietorships

A sole proprietorship is a business owned by one person. This form of organization gives the individual a means of controlling the business apart from his or her personal interests. Legally, however, the proprietorship is the same economic unit as the individual. The individual receives all profits or losses and is liable for all obligations of the business. Proprietorships represent the largest number of businesses in the United States, but typically they are the smallest in size. The life of a sole proprietorship ends when the owner wants it to or when the owner dies or becomes incapacitated.

Point to Emphasize: A key disadvantage of the partnership is the unlimited liability of its owners. Unlimited liability can be avoided by organizing the business as a corporation.

Partnerships

A partnership is like a proprietorship in most ways except that it has more than one owner. A partnership is not a legal entity separate from the owners; it is an unincorporated association that brings together the talents and resources of two or more people. The partners share the profits and losses of the partnership according to an agreed-upon formula. Generally, any partner can bind the partnership to another party, and, if necessary, the personal resources of each partner can be called on to pay the obligations of the partnership. In some cases, one or more partners limit their liability, but at least one partner must have unlimited liability. A partnership must be dissolved when ownership changes—for example, when a partner leaves or dies. For the business to continue as a partnership, a new partnership must be formed.

Point to Emphasize: In a sole proprietorship or partnership, the owners generally manage the business. In a corporation, however, there is a separation between ownership and management. The owners (stockholders) elect a board of directors, which appoints managers to run the daily operations of the business.

Corporations

A corporation is a business unit that is legally separate from its owners (the stockholders). The owners, whose ownership is represented by shares of stock in the corporation, do not control the operations of the corporation directly. Instead, they elect a board of directors, which appoints managers to run the corporation for the benefit of the stockholders. In exchange for limited involvement in the corporation's actual operations, stockholders enjoy limited liability. That is, their risk of loss is limited to the amount they paid for their shares. If they want, stockholders can sell their shares to other people, without affecting corporate operations. Because of this limited liability, stockholders often are willing to invest in riskier, but potentially

BUSINESS BULLETIN: BUSINESS PRACTICE

Most people think of corporations as large national or global companies whose shares of stock are held by thousands of people and institutions. Indeed, corporations can be huge and have many stockholders. However, of the approximately 4 million corporations in the United States, only about 15,000 have stock that is publicly bought and sold. The vast majority of corporations are small businesses that are privately held by a few stockholders. In Illinois alone there are more than 250,000 corporations. For this reason, the study of corporations is just as relevant to small businesses as it is to large ones.

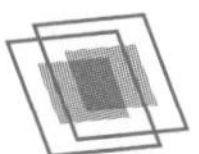

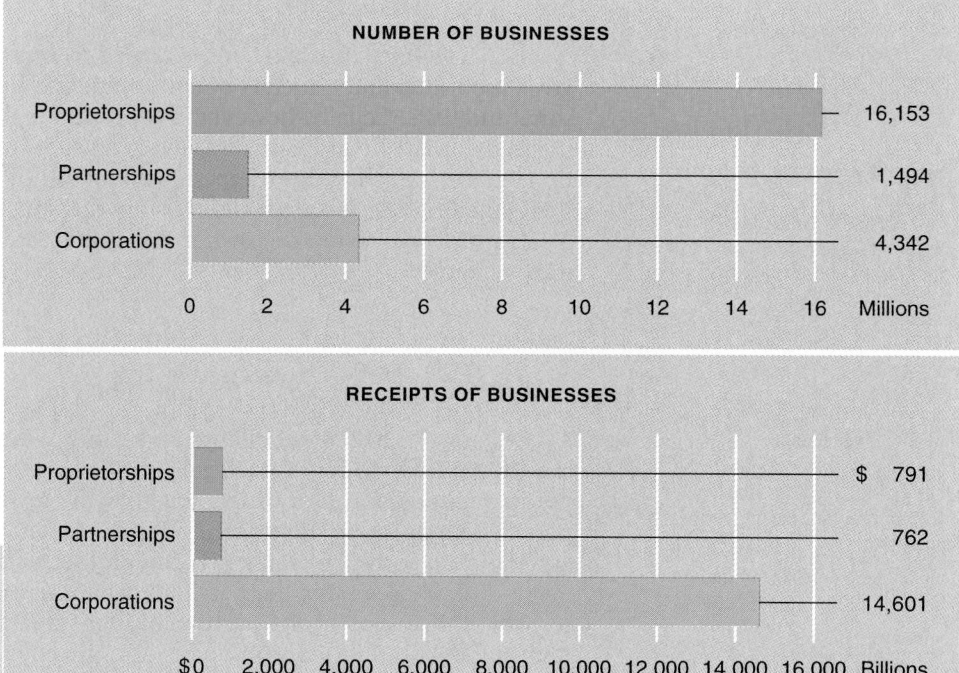

Figure 4
Number and Receipts of U.S. Proprietorships, Partnerships, and Corporations, 1995

Source: U.S. Treasury Department, Internal Revenue Service, *Statistics of Income Bulletin,* Spring 1997, pp. 200–203.

more profitable, activities. Also, because ownership can be transferred without dissolving the corporation, the life of the corporation is unlimited; it is not subject to the whims or health of a proprietor or partner.

Corporations have several important advantages over proprietorships and partnerships that make them very efficient in amassing capital for the formation and growth of very large companies. Even though corporations are fewer in number than proprietorships and partnerships, they contribute much more to the U.S. economy in monetary terms (see Figure 4). For example, in 1996 General Motors generated more revenue than all but thirty of the world's countries.

Financial Position and the Accounting Equation

OBJECTIVE 5

Define **financial position,** *state the accounting equation, and show how they are affected by simple transactions*

Related Text Assignments:
Q: 12, 13, 14, 15
SE: 2, 3, 4, 5, 6, 7, 8
E: 5, 6, 7, 8, 9, 10
P: 1, 2, 3, 5, 6, 8
SD: 5

Financial position refers to the economic resources that belong to a company and the claims against those resources at a point in time. Another term for claims is *equities.* Therefore, a company can be viewed as economic resources and equities:

Economic Resources = Equities

Every company has two types of equities, creditors' equities and owner's equity. Thus,

Economic Resources = Creditors' Equities + Owner's Equity

In accounting terminology, economic resources are called *assets* and creditors' equities are called *liabilities.* So the equation can be written like this:

Assets = Liabilities + Owner's Equity

This equation is known as the accounting equation. The two sides of the equation always must be equal, or "in balance."

Assets

Teaching Note: An effective way to introduce assets, liabilities, and owner's equity is to set up a skeleton balance sheet and ask your students to provide examples of each. Explain that assets are the resources of a business, the essence of which is expected future benefits.

Assets are economic resources owned by a business that are expected to benefit future operations. Certain kinds of assets—for example, cash and money owed to the company by customers (called *accounts receivable*)—are monetary items. Other assets—inventories (goods held for sale), land, buildings, and equipment—are nonmonetary physical things. Still other assets—the rights granted by patent, trademark, or copyright—are nonphysical.

Liabilities

Point to Emphasize: A liability is a debt or obligation that is satisfied with the payment of cash or the performance of a service.

Liabilities are present obligations of a business to pay cash, transfer assets, or provide services to other entities in the future. Among these obligations are debts of the business, amounts owed to suppliers for goods or services bought on credit (called *accounts payable*), borrowed money (for example, money owed on loans payable to banks), salaries and wages owed to employees, taxes owed to the government, and services to be performed.

As debts, liabilities are claims recognized by law. That is, the law gives creditors the right to force the sale of a company's assets if the company fails to pay its debts. Creditors have rights over owners and must be paid in full before the owners receive anything, even if payment of a debt uses up all the assets of a business.

Owner's Equity

Owner's equity represents the claims by the owner of a business to the assets of the business. It equals the residual interest, or *residual equity*, in the assets of an entity that remains after deducting the entity's liabilities. Theoretically, it is what would be left if all the liabilities were paid, and it is sometimes said to equal net assets. By rearranging the accounting equation, we can define owner's equity this way:

$$\text{Owner's Equity} = \text{Assets} - \text{Liabilities}$$

The four types of transactions that affect owner's equity are shown in Figure 5. Two of these transactions, owner's investments and owner's withdrawals, are assets that the owner either puts into the business or takes out of the business. For instance, if the owner of Shannon Realty, John Shannon, takes cash out of his personal bank account and deposits it in the business bank account, he has made an owner's investment. The assets (cash) of the business increase, and John Shannon's equity in those assets also increases. Conversely, if John Shannon takes cash out of

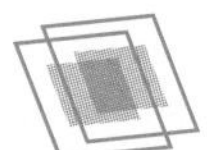

Teaching Note: A mnemonic for remembering which types of accounts affect owner's equity is *WIRE:* Withdrawals, Investments, Revenues, and Expenses.

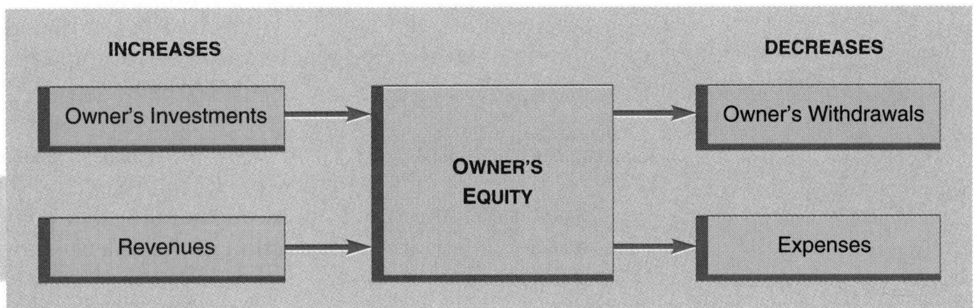

Figure 5
Four Types of Transactions That Affect Owner's Equity

the business bank account and deposits it in his personal bank account, he has made a withdrawal from the business. The assets of the business decrease, and John Shannon's equity in the business also decreases.

The other two types of transactions that affect owner's equity are revenues and expenses. Simply stated, revenues and expenses are the increases and decreases in owner's equity that result from operating a business. For example, the cash a customer pays (or agrees to pay in the future) to Shannon Realty in return for a service provided by the company is a revenue. The assets (cash or accounts receivable) of Shannon Realty increase, and the owner's equity in those assets also increases. On the other hand, the cash Shannon Realty pays out (or agrees to pay in the future) in the process of providing a service is an expense. Now the assets (cash) decrease or the liabilities (accounts payable) increase, and the owner's equity in the assets decreases.

Generally speaking, a company is successful if its revenues exceed its expenses. When revenues exceed expenses, the difference is called net income; when expenses exceed revenues, the difference is called net loss.

Some Illustrative Transactions

Let us now examine the effect of some of the most common business transactions on the accounting equation. Suppose that John Shannon opens a real estate agency called Shannon Realty on December 1. During December, his business engages in the transactions described in the following paragraphs. Exhibit 1 on page 20 summarizes these eleven illustrative transactions.

Owner's Investments John starts his business by depositing $50,000 in a bank account in the name of Shannon Realty. The transfer of cash from his personal account to the business account is an owner's investment. The first balance sheet of the new company would show the asset Cash and the owner's equity (John Shannon, Capital):

Point to Emphasize: The account name is "John Shannon, Capital," not "Owner's Equity" because capital accounts show the equity attributed to the specific owner.

Assets	=	**Owner's Equity (OE)**	
Cash		**John Shannon, Captial**	**Type of OE Transaction**
1. $50,000		$50,000	Owner's Investments

At this point, the company has no liabilities, and assets equal the owner's equity. The labels Cash and John Shannon, Capital are called accounts and are used by accountants to accumulate amounts that result from similar transactions. Transactions that affect owner's equity are identified by type so that similar types may later be grouped together on accounting reports.

Purchase of Assets with Cash John finds a good location and pays cash to purchase the lot for $10,000 and a small building on the lot for $25,000. This transaction does not change the total assets, liabilities, or owner's equity of Shannon Realty, but it does change the composition of the assets—it decreases Cash and increases Land and Building:

	Assets			=	Owners' Equity	
	Cash	Land	Building		John Shannon, Capital	Type of OE Transaction
bal.	$50,000				$50,000	
2.						
bal.	$15,000	$10,000	$25,000		$50,000	
	$50,000					

Point to Emphasize: The purchase of an asset does not affect owner's equity.

Purchase of Assets by Incurring a Liability Assets do not always have to be purchased with cash. They may also be purchased on credit, that is, on the basis of an agreement to pay for them later. Suppose Shannon Realty buys some office supplies for $500 on credit. This transaction increases the assets (Supplies) and increases the liabilities of Shannon Realty. This liability is designated by an account called Accounts Payable:

Point to Emphasize: Assets purchased on credit are recorded for the full amount at the time of the purchase.

	Assets				= Liabilities +	Owner's Equity	
	Cash	Supplies	Land	Building	Accounts Payable	John Shannon, Capital	Type of OE Transaction
bal.	$15,000		$10,000	$25,000		$50,000	
3.							
bal.	$15,000	$500	$10,000	$25,000	$500	$50,000	
	$50,500				$50,500		

Notice that this transaction increases both sides of the accounting equation to $50,500.

Payment of a Liability If Shannon Realty later pays $200 of the $500 owed for the supplies, both assets (Cash) and liabilities (Accounts Payable) decrease, but Supplies is unaffected:

Point to Emphasize: Payment of a liability does not affect owner's equity or the asset purchased on credit.

	Assets				= Liabilities +	Owner's Equity	
	Cash	Supplies	Land	Building	Accounts Payable	John Shannon, Capital	Type of OE Transaction
bal.	$15,000	$500	$10,000	$25,000	$500	$50,000	
4.							
bal.	$14,800	$500	$10,000	$25,000	$300	$50,000	
	$50,300				$50,300		

Notice that both sides of the accounting equation are still equal, although now at a total of $50,300.

Point to Emphasize: Revenues equal the price charged for the sale of goods or services.

Revenues Shannon Realty earns revenues in the form of commissions by selling houses for clients. Sometimes these commissions are paid to Shannon Realty immediately in the form of cash, and sometimes the client agrees to pay the commission later. In either case, the commission is recorded when it is earned and Shannon Realty has a right to a current or future receipt of cash. First, assume that Shannon Realty sells a house and receives a commission of $1,500 in cash. This transaction increases both assets (Cash) and owner's equity (John Shannon, Capital):

	Assets				= Liabilities +	Owner's Equity	
	Cash	Supplies	Land	Building	Accounts Payable	John Shannon, Capital	Type of OE Transaction
bal.	$14,800	$500	$10,000	$25,000	$300	$50,000	
5.	+1,500					+1,500	Commissions Earned
bal.	$16,300	$500	$10,000	$25,000	$300	$51,500	
	$51,800				$51,800		

Point to Emphasize: Revenues are recorded when they are earned, not necessarily when payments are received.

Now assume that Shannon Realty sells a house, in the process earning a commission of $2,000, and agrees to wait for payment of the commission. Because the commission has been earned now, a bill or invoice is sent to the client, and the transaction is recorded now. This revenue transaction increases both assets and owner's equity as before, but a new asset account, Accounts Receivable, shows that Shannon Realty is awaiting receipt of the commission:

	Assets					= Liabilities +	Owner's Equity	
	Cash	Accounts Receivable	Supplies	Land	Building	Accounts Payable	John Shannon, Capital	Type of OE Transaction
bal.	$16,300		$500	$10,000	$25,000	$300	$51,500	
6.		+$2,000					+2,000	Commissions Earned
bal.	$16,300	$2,000	$500	$10,000	$25,000	$300	$53,500	
	$53,800					$53,800		

As you progress in your study of accounting, you will be shown the use of separate accounts for revenues, like Commissions Earned.

Collection of Accounts Receivable Let us assume that a few days later Shannon Realty receives $1,000 from the client in transaction **6**. At that time, the asset Cash increases and the asset Accounts Receivable decreases:

	Assets					= Liabilities +	Owner's Equity	
	Cash	Accounts Receivable	Supplies	Land	Building	Accounts Payable	John Shannon, Capital	Type of OE Transaction
bal.	$16,300	$2,000	$500	$10,000	$25,000	$300	$53,500	
7.	+1,000	−1,000						
bal.	$17,300	$1,000	$500	$10,000	$25,000	$300	$53,500	
			$53,800				$53,800	

Notice that this transaction does not affect owner's equity because the commission revenue was already recorded in transaction **6**. Also notice that the balance of Accounts Receivable is $1,000, indicating that $1,000 is still to be collected.

Expenses Just as revenues are recorded when they are earned, expenses are recorded when they are incurred. Expenses can be paid in cash when they occur, or they can be paid later. If payment is going to be made later, a liability—for example, Accounts Payable or Wages Payable—increases. In both cases, owner's equity decreases. Assume that Shannon Realty pays $1,000 to rent some equipment for the office and $400 in wages to a part-time helper. These transactions reduce assets (Cash) and owner's equity (John Shannon, Capital):

	Assets					= Liabilities +	Owner's Equity	
	Cash	Accounts Receivable	Supplies	Land	Building	Accounts Payable	John Shannon, Capital	Type of OE Transaction
bal.	$17,300	$1,000	$500	$10,000	$25,000	$300	$53,500	
8.	−1,000						−1,000	Equipment Rental Expense
9.	−400						−400	Wages Expense
bal.	$15,900	$1,000	$500	$10,000	$25,000	$300	$52,100	
			$52,400				$52,400	

Now assume that Shannon Realty has not paid the $300 bill for utilities expense incurred for December. In this case, the effect on owner's equity is the same as when the expense is paid in cash, but instead of a reduction in assets, there is an increase in liabilities (Accounts Payable):

Exhibit 1. Summary of Effects of Illustrative Transactions on Financial Position

	Assets					= Liabilities +	Owner's Equity	
	Cash	Accounts Receiv-able	Supplies	Land	Building	Accounts Payable	John Shannon, Capital	Type of Owner's Equity Transaction
1.	$50,000						$50,000	Owner's Investment
2.	−35,000			+$10,000	+$25,000			
bal.	$15,000			$10,000	$25,000		$50,000	
3.			+$500			+$500		
bal.	$15,000		$500	$10,000	$25,000	$500	$50,000	
4.	−200					−200		
bal.	$14,800		$500	$10,000	$25,000	$300	$50,000	
5.	+1,500						+1,500	Commissions Earned
bal.	$16,300		$500	$10,000	$25,000	$300	$51,500	
6.		+$2,000					+2,000	Commissions Earned
bal.	$16,300	$2,000	$500	$10,000	$25,000	$300	$53,500	
7.	+1,000	−1,000						
bal.	$17,300	$1,000	$500	$10,000	$25,000	$300	$53,500	
8.	−1,000						−1,000	Equipment Rental Expense
9.	−400						−400	Wages Expense
bal.	$15,900	$1,000	$500	$10,000	$25,000	$300	$52,100	
10.						+300	−300	Utilities Expense
bal.	$15,900	$1,000	$500	$10,000	$25,000	$600	$51,800	
11.	−600						−600	Owner's Withdrawal
bal.	$15,300	$1,000	$500	$10,000	$25,000	$600	$51,200	
			$51,800			$51,800		

	Assets					= Liabilities +	Owner's Equity	
	Cash	Accounts Receiv-able	Supplies	Land	Building	Accounts Payable	John Shannon, Capital	Type of OE Transaction
bal.	$15,900	$1,000	$500	$10,000	$25,000	$300	$52,100	
10.						+300	−300	Utilities Expense
bal.	$15,900	$1,000	$500	$10,000	$25,000	$600	$51,800	
			$52,400				$52,400	

As you progress in your study of accounting, you will be shown the use of separate accounts for expenses, like Equipment Rental Expense, Wages Expense, and Utilities Expense.

Clarification Note: Owner's withdrawals do not qualify as expenses because they do not generate revenue.

Owner's Withdrawals John now withdraws $600 in cash from Shannon Realty and deposits it in his personal account. This transaction reduces assets (Cash) and owner's equity (John Shannon, Capital). Although, as can be seen below, withdrawals have the same effect on the accounting equation as expenses (see transactions **8** and **9**), it is important not to confuse them. Withdrawals are not expenses: Withdrawals are personal distributions of assets to the owner; expenses are incurred by the business in its operations.

	Assets					= Liabilities +	Owner's Equity	
	Cash	Accounts Receiv-able	Supplies	Land	Building	Accounts Payable	John Shannon, Capital	Type of OE Transaction
bal.	$15,900	$1,000	$500	$10,000	$25,000	$600	$51,800	
11.	−600						−600	Owner's Withdrawal
bal.	$15,300	$1,000	$500	$10,000	$25,000	$600	$51,200	
			$51,800				$51,800	

Communication Through Financial Statements

OBJECTIVE 6
Identify the four financial statements

Financial statements are the primary means of communicating important accounting information to users. It is helpful to think of these statements as models of the business enterprise because they show the business in financial terms. As is true of all models, however, financial statements are not perfect pictures of the real thing, but rather the accountant's best effort to represent what is real. Four major financial statements are used to communicate accounting information about a business: the income statement, the statement of owner's equity, the balance sheet, and the statement of cash flows.

Related Text Assignments:
Q: 16, 17, 18, 19, 20
SE: 9
E: 10, 11, 12, 13, 14
P: 4, 5, 7, 8
SD: 5
FRA: 1, 3, 4

Exhibit 2 illustrates the relationship among the four financial statements by showing how they would appear for Shannon Realty after the eleven sample transactions shown in Exhibit 1. It is assumed that the time period covered is the month of December, 20xx. Notice that each statement is headed in a similar way. Each heading identifies the company and the kind of statement. The income statement, the statement of owner's equity, and the statement of cash flows give the time period to which they apply; the balance sheet gives the specific date to which it applies. Much of this book deals with developing, using, and interpreting more complete versions of these basic statements.

Point to Emphasize: Businesses communicate financial information to decision makers in the form of four major financial statements.

The Income Statement

Terminology Note: The income statement is also called the *statement of earnings* and the *profit and loss statement.* Its purpose is to measure a company's performance over an accounting period.

The income statement summarizes the revenues earned and expenses incurred by a business over a period of time. Many people consider it the most important financial report because it shows whether or not a business achieved its profitability goal of earning an acceptable income. In Exhibit 2, Shannon Realty had revenues in the form of commissions earned of $3,500 ($2,000 of revenue earned on credit and $1,500 of cash). From this amount, total expenses of $1,700 were deducted (equipment rental expense of $1,000, wages expense of $400, and utilities expense of $300), to arrive at a net income of $1,800. To show that it applies to a period of time, the statement is dated "For the Month Ended December 31, 20xx."

The Statement of Owner's Equity

Terminology Note: The statement of owner's equity is also called the *capital statement.* It indicates changes in owner's capital over an accounting period.

The statement of owner's equity shows the change in the owner's capital over a period of time. In Exhibit 2, the beginning capital is zero because the company was started during this accounting period. During the month, John Shannon made an investment in the business of $50,000, and the company earned income (as shown on the income statement) of $1,800, for a total increase of $51,800. Deducted from this amount are the withdrawals for the month of $600, leaving an ending balance of $51,200 in the capital account.

The Balance Sheet

Terminology Note: The balance sheet is also called the *statement of financial position.* It represents two different views of a business: The left side shows the resources of the business; the right side shows who provided those resources (the creditors and the owner).

The purpose of a balance sheet is to show the financial position of a business on a certain date, usually the end of the month or year. For this reason, it often is called the *statement of financial position* and is dated as of a certain date. The balance sheet presents a view of the business as the holder of resources, or assets, that are equal to the claims against those assets. The claims consist of the company's liabilities and the owner's equity in the company. In Exhibit 2, Shannon Realty has several categories of assets, which total $51,800. These assets equal the total liabilities of $600 (Accounts Payable) plus the ending balance of owner's capital of $51,200. Notice that the owner's capital amount on the balance sheet comes from the ending balance on the statement of owner's equity.

The Statement of Cash Flows

Point to Emphasize: The purpose of the statement of cash flows is to explain the change in cash in terms of operating, investing, and financing activities over an accounting period. It provides valuable information that cannot be determined in an examination of the other three financial statements.

Whereas the income statement focuses on a company's profitability goal, the statement of cash flows is directed toward the company's liquidity goal. Cash flows are the inflows and outflows of cash into and out of a business. Net cash flows are the difference between the inflows and outflows. The statement of cash flows shows the cash produced by operating a business as well as important investing and financing transactions that take place during an accounting period. Exhibit 2 shows the statement of cash flows for Shannon Realty. Notice that the statement explains how the

Exhibit 2. Income Statement, Statement of Owner's Equity, Balance Sheet, and Statement of Cash Flows for Shannon Realty

Shannon Realty
Income Statement
For the Month Ended December 31, 20xx

Revenues		
Commissions Earned		$3,500
Expenses		
Equipment Rental Expense	$1,000	
Wages Expense	400	
Utilities Expense	300	
Total Expenses		1,700
Net Income		$1,800

Shannon Realty
Statement of Owner's Equity
For the Month Ended December 31, 20xx

John Shannon, Capital, December 1, 20xx		$ 0
Add Investments by John Shannon	$50,000	
Net Income for the Month	1,800	51,800
Subtotal		$51,800
Less Withdrawals by John Shannon		600
John Shannon, Capital, December 31, 20xx		$51,200

Shannon Realty
Statement of Cash Flows
For the Month Ended December 31, 20xx

Cash Flows from Operating Activities		
Net Income		$ 1,800
Noncash Expenses and Revenues Included in Income		
Increase in Accounts Receivable	($ 1,000)*	
Increase in Supplies	(500)	
Increase in Accounts Payable	600	(900)
Net Cash Flows from Operating Activities		$ 900
Cash Flows from Investing Activities		
Purchase of Land	($10,000)	
Purchase of Building	(25,000)	
Net Cash Flows from Investing Activities		(35,000)
Cash Flows from Financing Activities		
Investments by John Shannon	$50,000	
Withdrawals by John Shannon	(600)	
Net Cash Flows from Financing Activities		49,400
Net Increase (Decrease) in Cash		$15,300
Cash at Beginning of Month		0
Cash at End of Month		$15,300

*Parentheses indicate a negative impact or cash outflow.

Shannon Realty
Balance Sheet
December 31, 20xx

Assets		**Liabilities**	
Cash	$15,300	Accounts Payable	$ 600
Accounts Receivable	1,000		
Supplies	500	**Owner's Equity**	
Land	10,000	John Shannon, Capital	51,200
Building	25,000		
Total Assets	$51,800	Total Liabilities and Owner's Equity	$51,800

Point to Emphasize: Notice the sequence in which these financial statements must be prepared. Stress that the statement of owner's equity is a link between the income statement and the balance sheet and that the statement of cash flows is prepared last.

Instructional Strategy: Create a game with rewards. Divide the class into small groups and assign P 4 or P 7. The first group to complete the problem correctly wins. Prizes may include 1 or 2 extra points added to a quiz or test score, chocolate bars, novelty erasers, and such. If one of these problems was done for homework, use of the other one in this activity will reinforce learning. Another idea: Use FRA 1 for this activity.

Cash account changed during the period. Cash increased by $15,300. Operating activities produced net cash flows of $900, and financing activities produced net cash flows of $49,400. Investing activities used cash flows of $35,000.

Parenthetical Note: An entire chapter of this text is devoted to the statement of cash flows.

This statement is related directly to the other three statements. Notice that net income comes from the income statement and that investments by owners and withdrawals come from the statement of owner's equity. The other items in the statement represent changes in the balance sheet accounts: Accounts Receivable, Supplies, Accounts Payable, Land, and Building.

Generally Accepted Accounting Principles

OBJECTIVE 7

State the relationship of generally accepted accounting principles (GAAP) to financial statements and the independent CPA's report, and identify the organizations that influence GAAP.

Related Text Assignments:
Q: 21, 22, 23
E: 1, 15

Point to Emphasize: Explain that GAAP are constantly evolving, that they are not like laws of science. They are designed to measure the performance of businesses accurately. They can be abused to make a company look better on paper than it really is.

To ensure that financial statements will be understandable to their users, a set of practices, called generally accepted accounting principles (GAAP), has been developed to provide guidelines for financial accounting. Although the term has several meanings in the literature of accounting, perhaps this is the best definition: "Generally accepted accounting principles encompass the conventions, rules, and procedures necessary to define accepted accounting practice at a particular time."[6] In other words, GAAP arise from wide agreement on the theory and practice of accounting at a particular time. These "principles" are not like the unchangeable laws of nature found in chemistry or physics. They are developed by accountants and businesses to serve the needs of decision makers, and they can be altered as better methods evolve or as circumstances change.

In this book, we present accounting practice, or GAAP, as it is today. We also try to explain the reasons or theory on which the practice is based. Both theory and practice are important to the study of accounting. However, you should realize that accounting is a discipline that is always growing, changing, and improving. Just as years of research are necessary before a new surgical method or lifesaving drug can be introduced, it may take years for research and new discoveries in accounting to be commonly implemented. As a result, you may encounter practices that seem contradictory. In some cases, we point out new directions in accounting. Your instructor also may mention certain weaknesses in current theory or practice.

Financial Statements, GAAP, and the Independent CPA's Report

Point to Emphasize: The purpose of an audit is to lend credibility to a set of financial statements. The auditor does *not* attest to the absolute accuracy of the published information or to the value of the company as an investment. All he or she renders is an opinion, based on appropriate testing, about the fairness of the presentation of the financial information.

Because financial statements are representations by the management of a company and could be falsified for personal gain, all companies that sell ownership to the public and many companies that apply for sizable loans have their financial statements audited by an independent certified public accountant. Certified public accountants (CPAs) are licensed by all states for the same reason that lawyers and doctors are—to protect the public by ensuring the quality of professional service. One important attribute of CPAs is independence: They have no financial or other compromising ties with the companies they audit. This gives the public confidence in their work. The firms listed in Table 3 employ about 25 percent of all CPAs.

Ethical Consideration: To lend credibility to the work of the independent auditor, the profession has developed a set of guidelines that dictate appropriate professional behavior. Known as the AICPA Code of Professional Ethics, the current guidelines were adopted in 1988 and are based on earlier standards. Learning Objective 8 covers the topic of ethics in detail.

An independent CPA makes an audit, which is an examination of a company's financial statements and the accounting systems, controls, and records that produced them. The purpose of the audit is to ascertain that the financial statements have been prepared in accordance with generally accepted accounting principles. If the independent accountant is satisfied that this standard has been met, his or her report contains the following language:

> In our opinion, the financial statements . . . present fairly, in all material respects . . . in conformity with generally accepted accounting principles.

This wording emphasizes the fact that accounting and auditing are not exact sciences. Because the framework of GAAP provides room for interpretation and the application of GAAP necessitates the making of estimates, the auditor can render an

Enrichment Note: According to *Public Accounting Report,* the top-grossing U.S. accounting firm in 1996 was Andersen Worldwide, but the firm with the most partners was Ernst & Young.

Enrichment Note: The big six accounting firms may become the "big five." In 1998, Price Waterhouse and Coopers & Lybrand began discussing a possible merger.

Table 3. Large International Certified Public Accounting Firms

Firm	Home Office	Some Major Clients
Andersen Worldwide	Chicago	ITT, Texaco, United Airlines
Coopers & Lybrand	New York	AT&T, Ford
Deloitte & Touche	New York	General Motors, Procter & Gamble, Sears
Ernst & Young	New York	Coca-Cola, McDonald's, Mobil
KPMG Peat Marwick	New York	General Electric, Xerox
Price Waterhouse	New York	Du Pont, Exxon, IBM

opinion or judgment only that the financial statements *present fairly* or conform *in all material respects* to GAAP. The accountant's report does not preclude minor or immaterial errors in the financial statements. However, it does imply that on the whole, investors and creditors can rely on those statements. Historically, auditors have enjoyed a strong reputation for competence and independence. As a result, banks, investors, and creditors are willing to rely on an auditor's opinion when deciding to invest in a company or to make loans to a firm that has been audited. The independent audit is an important factor in the worldwide growth of financial markets.

Organizations That Influence Current Practice

Common Student Confusion: Regarding the organizations that influence GAAP, most students are familiar with the IRS and perhaps the SEC but have difficulty distinguishing among the others and learning their acronyms. The more you can "bring these organizations to life," the more understanding your students will have.

Point to Emphasize: The FASB is the primary source of GAAP.

Point to Emphasize: The AICPA is considered the primary organization of certified public accountants.

Enrichment Note: The SEC imposes its own very strict set of regulations on the companies it regulates, based in part on the standards set by the FASB.

Clarification Note: The GASB is responsible for issuing standards for state and local governments, whereas the FASB is responsible for issuing financial accounting standards for all other entities.

Enrichment Note: The primary purpose of the tax law is to generate revenue for the operation of the government, not to measure business income.

Many organizations directly or indirectly influence GAAP and so influence much of what is in this book. The Financial Accounting Standards Board (FASB) is the most important body for developing and issuing rules on accounting practice. This independent body issues Statements of Financial Accounting Standards. The American Institute of Certified Public Accountants (AICPA) is the professional association of certified public accountants and influences accounting practice through the activities of its senior technical committees. The Securities and Exchange Commission (SEC) is an agency of the federal government that has the legal power to set and enforce accounting practices for companies whose securities are offered for sale to the general public. As such, it has enormous influence on accounting practice. The Governmental Accounting Standards Board (GASB), which was established in 1984 under the same governing body as the Financial Accounting Standards Board, is responsible for issuing accounting standards for state and local governments.

With the growth of financial markets throughout the world, worldwide cooperation in the development of accounting principles has become a priority. The International Accounting Standards Committee (IASC) has approved more than thirty international standards, which have been translated into six languages.

U.S. tax laws that govern the assessment and collection of revenue for operating the federal government also influence accounting practice. Because a major source of the government's revenue is the income tax, these laws specify the rules for determining taxable income. These rules are interpreted and enforced by the Internal Revenue Service (IRS). In some cases, these rules conflict with good accounting practice, but they still are an important influence on that practice. Businesses use certain accounting practices simply because they are required by the tax laws. Sometimes companies follow an accounting practice specified in the tax laws to take advantage of rules that can help them financially. Cases where the tax laws affect accounting practice are noted throughout this book.

Professional Ethics and the Accounting Profession

OBJECTIVE 8

Define* ethics *and describe the ethical responsibilities of accountants

Related Text Assignments:
Q: 24
SD: 3

Instructional Strategy: Divide the class into small groups and assign each a different ethical dilemma from SD 3 to discuss. Each group will report the results of its discussion to the class and take questions from other students.

Enrichment Note: Professional accountants must avoid situations in which there is even the *appearance* of an impropriety.

Enrichment Note: When a professional accountant is in willful violation of the code of professional ethics, he or she runs the risk of criminal penalties.

Ethics is a code of conduct that applies to everyday life. It addresses the question of whether actions are right or wrong. Ethical actions are the product of individual decisions. You are faced with many ethical situations every day. Some may be potentially illegal—the temptation to take office supplies from your employer to use when you do homework, for example. Others are not illegal but are equally unethical—for example, deciding not to tell a fellow student who missed class that a test has been announced for the next class meeting. When an organization is said to act ethically or unethically, it means that individuals within the organization have made a decision to act ethically or unethically. When a company uses false advertising, cheats customers, pollutes the environment, treats employees poorly, or misleads investors by presenting false financial statements, members of management and other employees have made a conscious decision to act unethically. In the same way, ethical behavior within a company is a direct result of the actions and decisions of the company's employees.

Professional ethics is a code of conduct that applies to the practice of a profession. Like the ethical conduct of a company, the ethical actions of a profession are a collection of individual actions. As members of a profession, accountants have a responsibility, not only to their employers and clients but to society as a whole, to uphold the highest ethical standards. Historically, accountants have been held in high regard. For example, a survey of over one thousand prominent people in business, education, and government ranked the accounting profession second only to the clergy as having the highest ethical standards.[7] It is the responsibility of every person who becomes an accountant to uphold the high standards of the profession, regardless of the field of accounting the individual enters.

To ensure that its members understand the responsibilities of being professional accountants, the AICPA and each state have adopted codes of professional conduct that must be followed by certified public accountants. Fundamental to these codes is responsibility to the public, including clients, creditors, investors, and anyone else who relies on the work of the certified public accountant. In resolving conflicts among these groups, the accountant must act with integrity, even to the sacrifice of personal benefit. Integrity means that the accountant is honest and candid, and subordinates personal gain to service and the public trust. The accountant must also be objective. Objectivity means that he or she is impartial and intellectually honest. Furthermore, the accountant must be independent. Independence means avoiding all relationships that impair or even appear to impair the accountant's objectivity.

One way in which the auditor of a company maintains independence is by having no direct financial interest in the company and not being an employee of the

BUSINESS BULLETIN: ETHICS IN PRACTICE

One recent survey showed that 45 percent of the 1,000 largest U.S. companies have ethics programs or workshops. NYNEX, for example, has appointed an ethics officer, written a new code of conduct, put more than 1,500 managers through a formal training program, and provided its 94,000 employees with a whistle blowers' hotline. Companies with such comprehensive programs tend to receive significantly lower fines from federal judges if their employees are caught in illegal acts because the judges want to reward companies that are trying to be good corporate citizens.[8]

company. The accountant must exercise due care in all activities, carrying out professional responsibilities with competence and diligence. For example, an accountant must not accept a job for which he or she is not qualified, even at the risk of losing a client to another firm, and careless work is not acceptable. These broad principles are supported by more specific rules that public accountants must follow. (For instance, with certain exceptions, client information must be kept strictly confidential.) Accountants who violate the rules can be disciplined or even suspended from practice.

The Institute of Management Accountants (IMA), a professional organization, has adopted the Code of Professional Conduct for Management Accountants. This ethical code emphasizes that management accountants have a responsibility to be competent in their jobs, to keep information confidential except when authorized or legally required to disclose it, to maintain integrity and avoid conflicts of interest, and to communicate information objectively and without bias.[9]

Chapter Review

REVIEW OF LEARNING OBJECTIVES

1. **Define *accounting,* identify business goals and activities, and describe the role of accounting in making informed decisions.** Accounting is an information system that measures, processes, and communicates information, primarily financial in nature, about an identifiable entity for the purpose of making economic decisions. Management accounting focuses on the preparation of information primarily for internal use by management. Financial accounting is concerned with the development and use of accounting reports that are communicated to those external to the business organization as well as to management. Accounting is not an end in itself but a tool that provides the information that is necessary to make reasoned choices among alternative uses of scarce resources in the conduct of business and economic activities.
2. **Identify the many users of accounting information in society.** Accounting plays a significant role in society by providing information to managers of all institutions and to individuals with a direct financial interest in those institutions, including present or potential investors or creditors. Accounting information is also important to those with an indirect financial interest in the organization—for example, tax authorities, regulatory agencies, and economic planners.
3. **Explain the importance of business transactions, money measure, and separate entity to accounting measurement.** To make an accounting measurement, the accountant must determine what is measured, when the measurement should be made, what value should be placed on what is measured, and how what is measured should be classified. Generally accepted accounting principles define the objects of accounting measurement as business transactions, money measure, and separate entities. Relating these three concepts, financial accounting uses money measure to gauge the impact of business transactions on a separate business entity.
4. **Identify the three basic forms of business organization.** The three basic forms of business organization are sole proprietorships, partnerships, and corporations. Legally, sole proprietorships, which are formed by one individual, and partnerships, which are formed by more than one individual, are not separate from their owners. In accounting, however, they are treated as separate. Corporations, whose ownership is

represented by shares of stock, are separate entities for both legal and accounting purposes.

5. **Define *financial position,* state the accounting equation, and show how they are affected by simple transactions.** Financial position is the economic resources that belong to a company and the claims against those resources at a point in time. The accounting equation shows financial position in the equation form Assets = Liabilities + Owner's Equity. Business transactions affect financial position by decreasing or increasing assets, liabilities, or owner's equity in such a way that the accounting equation is always in balance.
6. **Identify the four financial statements.** Financial statements are the means by which accountants communicate the financial condition and activities of a business to those who have an interest in the business. The four basic financial statements are the income statement, the statement of owner's equity, the balance sheet, and the statement of cash flows.
7. **State the relationship of generally accepted accounting principles (GAAP) to financial statements and the independent CPA's report, and identify the organizations that influence GAAP.** Acceptable accounting practice consists of those conventions, rules, and procedures that make up generally accepted accounting principles at a particular time. GAAP are essential to the preparation and interpretation of financial statements and the independent CPA's report. Among the organizations that influence the formulation of GAAP are the Financial Accounting Standards Board, the American Institute of Certified Public Accountants, the Securities and Exchange Commission, and the Internal Revenue Service.
8. **Define *ethics* and describe the ethical responsibilities of accountants.** All accountants are required to follow a code of professional ethics, the foundation of which is responsibility to the public. Accountants must act with integrity, objectivity, and independence, and they must exercise due care in all their activities.

REVIEW OF CONCEPTS AND TERMINOLOGY

The following concepts and terms were introduced in this chapter:

LO 1 **Accounting:** An information system that measures, processes, and communicates financial information about an identifiable economic entity.

LO 5 **Accounting equation:** Assets = Liabilities + Owner's Equity.

LO 5 **Accounts:** The labels used by accountants to accumulate the amounts produced from similar transactions.

LO 7 **American Institute of Certified Public Accountants (AICPA):** The professional association of certified public accountants.

LO 5 **Assets:** Economic resources owned by a business that are expected to benefit future operations.

LO 7 **Audit:** An examination of a company's financial statements in order to render an independent professional opinion that they have been presented fairly, in all material respects, in conformity with generally accepted accounting principles.

LO 6 **Balance sheet:** The financial statement that shows the assets, liabilities, and owner's equity of a business at a point in time. Also called a *statement of financial position.*

LO 1 **Bookkeeping:** The process of recording financial transactions and keeping financial records.

LO 1 **Business:** An economic unit that aims to sell goods and services to customers at prices that will provide an adequate return to its owners.

LO 3 **Business transactions:** Economic events that affect the financial position of a business entity.

LO 6 **Cash flows:** The inflows and outflows of cash into and out of a business.

LO 7 **Certified public accountants (CPAs):** Public accountants who have met the stringent licensing requirements set by the individual states.

LO 1 **Computer:** An electronic tool for the rapid collection, organization, and communication of large amounts of information.

LO 4 **Corporation:** A business unit granted a state charter recognizing it as a separate legal entity having its own rights, privileges, and liabilities distinct from those of its owners.

LO 8 **Due care:** The act of carrying out professional responsibilities competently and diligently.

LO 8 **Ethics:** A code of conduct that addresses whether everyday actions are right or wrong.

LO 3 **Exchange rate:** The value of one currency in terms of another.

LO 5 **Expenses:** Decreases in owner's equity that result from operating a business.

LO 1 **Financial accounting:** The process of generating and communicating accounting information in the form of financial statements to those outside the organization.

LO 7 **Financial Accounting Standards Board (FASB):** The most important body for developing and issuing rules on accounting practice, called Statements of Financial Accounting Standards.

LO 5 **Financial position:** The economic resources that belong to a company and the claims (equities) against those resources at a point in time.

LO 1 **Financial statements:** The primary means of communicating important accounting information to users. They include the income statement, statement of owner's equity, balance sheet, and statement of cash flows.

LO 1 **Financing activities:** Activities undertaken by management to obtain adequate funds to begin and to continue operating a business.

LO 7 **Generally accepted accounting principles (GAAP):** The conventions, rules, and procedures that define accepted accounting practice at a particular time.

LO 7 **Governmental Accounting Standards Board (GASB):** The board responsible for issuing accounting standards for state and local governments.

LO 6 **Income statement:** The financial statement that summarizes the revenues earned and expenses incurred by a business over a period of time.

LO 8 **Independence:** The avoidance of all relationships that impair or appear to impair an accountant's objectivity.

LO 8 **Institute of Management Accountants (IMA):** A professional organization made up primarily of management accountants.

LO 8 **Integrity:** Honesty, candidness, and the subordination of personal gain to service and the public trust.

LO 7 **Internal Revenue Service (IRS):** The federal agency that interprets and enforces the tax laws governing the assessment and collection of revenue for operating the national government.

LO 7 **International Accounting Standards Committee (IASC):** The organization that encourages worldwide cooperation in the development of accounting principles; it has approved more than thirty international standards of accounting.

LO 1 **Investing activities:** Activities undertaken by management to spend capital in ways that are productive and will help a business achieve its objectives.

LO 5 **Liabilities:** Present obligations of a business to pay cash, transfer assets, or provide services to other entities in the future.

LO 1 **Liquidity:** Having enough funds available to pay debts when they are due.

LO 2 **Management:** Collectively, the people who have overall responsibility for operating a business and meeting its goals.

LO 1 **Management accounting:** The process of producing accounting information for the internal use of a company's management.

LO 1 **Management information system (MIS):** The interconnected subsystems that provide the information needed to run a business.

LO 3 **Money measure:** The recording of all business transactions in terms of money.

LO 5 **Net assets:** Assets minus liabilities; owner's equity.

LO 5 **Net income:** The difference between revenues and expenses when revenues exceed expenses.

LO 5 **Net loss:** The difference between expenses and revenues when expenses exceed revenues.

LO 8 **Objectivity:** Impartiality and intellectual honesty.

LO 1 **Operating activities:** Activities undertaken by management in the course of running the business.

LO 5 **Owner's equity:** The residual interest in the assets of a business entity that remains after deducting the entity's liabilities. Also called *residual equity.*

LO 5 **Owner's investments:** The assets that the owner puts into the business.

LO 5 **Owner's withdrawals:** The assets that the owner takes out of the business.

LO 4 **Partnership:** A business owned by two or more people.

LO 1 **Performance measures:** Indicators of achievement of business goals and management of business activities.

LO 8 **Professional ethics:** A code of conduct that applies to the practice of a profession.

LO 1 **Profitability:** The ability to earn enough income to attract and hold investment capital.

LO 5 **Revenues:** Increases in owner's equity that result from operating a business.

LO 2 **Securities and Exchange Commission (SEC):** An agency of the federal government set up by the U.S. Congress to protect the public by regulating the issuing, buying, and selling of stocks.

LO 3 **Separate entity:** A business that is treated as distinct from its creditors, customers, and owners.

LO 4 **Sole proprietorship:** A business owned by one person.

LO 6 **Statement of cash flows:** The financial statement that shows the inflows and outflows of cash from operating activities, investing activities, and financing activities over a period of time.

LO 6 **Statement of owner's equity:** The financial statement that shows the change in owner's capital over a period of time.

REVIEW PROBLEM

Effect of Transactions on the Accounting Equation

LO 5 Charlene Rudek finished law school in June and immediately set up her own law practice. During the first month of operation, she completed these transactions.

a. Began the practice by placing $2,000 in a bank account established for the business.
b. Purchased a law library for $900 cash.
c. Purchased office supplies for $400 on credit.
d. Accepted $500 in cash for completing a contract.
e. Billed clients $1,950 for services rendered during the month.
f. Paid $200 of the amount owed for office supplies.
g. Received $1,250 in cash from one client who had been billed previously for services rendered.
h. Paid rent expense for the month in the amount of $1,200.
i. Withdrew $400 from the practice for personal use.

REQUIRED

Show the effect of each of these transactions on the balance sheet equation by completing a table similar to Exhibit 1. Identify each owner's equity transaction.

ANSWER TO REVIEW PROBLEM

	Assets				= Liabilities +	Owner's Equity	
	Cash	Accounts Receiv-able	Office Supplies	Law Library	Accounts Payable	C. Rudek, Capital	Type of OE Transaction
a.	$2,000					$2,000	Owner's Investment
b.	−900			+$900			
bal.	$1,100			$900		$2,000	
c.			+$400		+$400		
bal.	$1,100		$400	$900	$400	$2,000	
d.	+500					+500	Legal Fees Earned
bal.	$1,600		$400	$900	$400	$2,500	
e.		+$1,950				+1,950	Legal Fees Earned
bal.	$1,600	$1,950	$400	$900	$400	$4,450	
f.	−200				−200		
bal.	$1,400	$1,950	$400	$900	$200	$4,450	
g.	+1,250	−1,250					
bal.	$2,650	$ 700	$400	$900	$200	$4,450	
h.	−1,200					−1,200	Rent Expense
bal.	$1,450	$ 700	$400	$900	$200	$3,250	
i.	−400					−400	Owner's Withdrawal
bal.	$1,050	$ 700	$400	$900	$200	$2,850	
		$3,050				$3,050	

Chapter Assignments

BUILDING YOUR KNOWLEDGE FOUNDATION

Questions

1. Why is accounting considered an information system?
2. What is the role of accounting in the decision-making process, and what broad business goals and activities does it help management to achieve and manage?
3. Distinguish between management accounting and financial accounting.
4. Distinguish among these terms: *accounting, bookkeeping,* and *management information systems.*
5. Which decision makers use accounting information?
6. A business is an economic unit whose goal is to sell goods and services to customers at prices that will provide an adequate return to the business owners. What functions must management perform to achieve that goal?
7. Why are investors and creditors interested in reviewing the financial statements of a company?
8. Among those who use accounting information are people and organizations with an indirect interest in the business entity. Briefly describe these people and organizations.
9. Why has society as a whole become one of the largest users of accounting information?

10. Use the terms *business transaction, money measure,* and *separate entity* in a single sentence that demonstrates their relevance to financial accounting.
11. How do sole proprietorships, partnerships, and corporations differ?
12. Define *assets, liabilities,* and *owner's equity.*
13. Arnold Smith's company has assets of $22,000 and liabilities of $10,000. What is the amount of the owner's equity?
14. What four elements affect owner's capital? How?
15. Give examples of the types of transactions that (a) increase assets and (b) increase liabilities.
16. What is the function of the statement of owner's equity?
17. Why is the balance sheet sometimes called the statement of financial position?
18. Contrast the purpose of the balance sheet with that of the income statement.
19. A statement for an accounting period that ends in June can be headed "June 30, 20xx" or "For the Year Ended June 30, 20xx." Which heading is appropriate for (a) a balance sheet and (b) an income statement?
20. How does the income statement differ from the statement of cash flows?
21. What are GAAP? Why are they important to the readers of financial statements?
22. What do auditors mean by the phrase "in all material respects" when they state that financial statements "present fairly, in all material respects . . . in conformity with generally accepted accounting principles"?
23. What organization has the most influence on GAAP?
24. Discuss the importance of professional ethics in the accounting profession.

Short Exercises

SE 1. LO 3 *Accounting Concepts*

Tell whether each of the following words or phrases relates most closely to (a) a business transaction, (b) a separate entity, or (c) a money measure.

1. Partnership
2. U.S. dollar
3. Payment of an expense
4. Corporation
5. Sale of an asset

SE 2. LO 5 *The Accounting Equation*

Determine the amount missing from each accounting equation below.

	Assets	=	Liabilities	+	Owner's Equity
1.	?		$25,000		$35,000
2.	$ 78,000		$42,000		?
3.	$146,000		?		$96,000

SE 3. LO 5 *The Accounting Equation*

Use the accounting equation to answer each question below.

1. The assets of Cruse Company are $480,000, and the liabilities are $360,000. What is the amount of the owner's equity?
2. The liabilities of Nabors Company equal one-fifth of the total assets. The owner's equity is $80,000. What is the amount of the liabilities?

SE 4. LO 5 *The Accounting Equation*

Use the accounting equation to answer each question below.

1. At the beginning of the year, Gilbert Company's assets were $180,000, and its owner's equity was $100,000. During the year, assets increased $60,000 and liabilities increased $10,000. What was owner's equity at the end of the year?
2. At the beginning of the year, Sailor Company had liabilities of $50,000 and owner's equity of $48,000. If assets increased by $20,000 and liabilities decreased by $15,000, what was owner's equity at the end of the year?

SE 5. LO 5 *The Accounting Equation and Net Income*

Use the following information and the accounting equation to determine the net income for the year for each alternative below.

	Assets	Liabilities
Beginning of the year	$ 70,000	$30,000
End of the year	100,000	50,000

1. No investments were made in the business and no withdrawals were made during the year.
2. Investments of $10,000 were made in the business, but no withdrawals were made during the year.
3. No investments were made in the business, but withdrawals of $2,000 were made during the year.

SE 6. LO 5 *The Accounting Equation and Net Income*

Murillo Company had assets of $140,000 and liabilities of $60,000 at the beginning of the year, and assets of $200,000 and liabilities of $70,000 at the end of the year. During the year, there was an investment of $20,000 in the business, and withdrawals of $24,000 were made. What amount of net income was earned during the year?

SE 7. LO 5 *Effect of Transactions on the Accounting Equation*

On a sheet of paper, list the numbers **1** through **6,** with columns labeled Assets, Liabilities, and Owner's Equity. In the columns, indicate whether each transaction below caused an increase (+), a decrease (−), or no change (NC) in assets, liabilities, and owner's equity.

1. Purchased equipment on credit.
2. Purchased equipment for cash.
3. Billed customers for services performed.
4. Received and immediately paid a utility bill.
5. Received payment from a previously billed customer.
6. The owner made an additional investment.

SE 8. LO 5 *Effect of Transactions on the Accounting Equation*

On a sheet of paper, list the numbers **1** through **6,** with columns labeled Assets, Liabilities, and Owner's Equity. In the columns, indicate whether each transaction below caused an increase (+), a decrease (−), or no change (NC) in assets, liabilities, and owner's equity.

1. Purchased supplies on credit.
2. Paid for previously purchased supplies.
3. Paid employee's weekly wages.
4. Cash withdrawal by owner.
5. Purchased a truck with cash.
6. Received a telephone bill to be paid next month.

SE 9. LO 6 *Preparation and Completion of a Balance Sheet*

Use the following accounts and balances to prepare a balance sheet for DeLay Company at June 30, 20x1, using Exhibit 2 as a model.

Accounts Receivable	$ 800
Wages Payable	250
Owner's Capital	13,750
Building	10,000
Cash	?

Exercises

E 1. LO 1 LO 2 LO 7 *The Nature of Accounting*

Match the terms on the left with the descriptions on the right.

____	1. Bookkeeping	a. Function of accounting
____	2. Creditors	b. Often confused with accounting
____	3. Measurement	c. User(s) of accounting information
____	4. Financial Accounting Standards Board (FASB)	d. Organization that influences current practice
____	5. Tax authorities	e. Tool that facilitates the practice of accounting
____	6. Computer	
____	7. Communication	
____	8. Securities and Exchange Commission (SEC)	
____	9. Investors	
____	10. Processing	
____	11. Management	
____	12. Management information system	

E 2. LO 3 *Business Transactions*

Theresa owns and operates a minimart. State which of the actions below are business transactions. Explain why any other actions are not regarded as transactions.

1. Theresa reduces the price of a gallon of milk in order to match the price offered by a competitor.
2. Theresa pays a high school student cash for cleaning up the driveway that is behind the market.
3. Theresa fills her son's car with gasoline in payment for restocking the vending machines and the snack food shelves.
4. Theresa pays interest to herself on a loan she made three years ago to the business.

E 3. LO 3 LO 4 *Accounting Concepts*

Financial accounting uses money measures to gauge the impact of business transactions on a separate business entity. Tell whether each of the following words or phrases relates most closely to (a) a business transaction, (b) a separate entity, or (c) a money measure.

1. Corporation
2. French franc
3. Sales of products
4. Receipt of cash
5. Sole proprietorship
6. U.S. dollar
7. Partnership
8. Owner's investments
9. Japanese yen
10. Purchase of supplies

E 4. LO 3 *Money Measure*

You have been asked to compare the sales and assets of four companies that make computer chips and determine which company is the largest in each category. You have gathered the following data, but they cannot be used for direct comparison because each company's sales and assets are in its own currency.

Company (Currency)	Sales	Assets
Inchip (U.S. dollar)	20,000,000	13,000,000
Wong (Taiwan dollar)	50,000,000	24,000,000
Mitzu (Japanese yen)	3,500,000,000	2,500,000,000
Works (German mark)	35,000,000	39,000,000

Assuming that the exchange rates in Table 1 are current and appropriate, convert all the figures to U.S. dollars and determine which company is the largest in sales and which is the largest in assets.

E 5. LO 5 *The Accounting Equation*

Use the accounting equation to answer each question that follows. Show any calculations you make.

1. The assets of Newport Company are $650,000, and the owner's equity is $360,000. What is the amount of the liabilities?
2. The liabilities and owner's equity of Fitzgerald Company are $95,000 and $32,000, respectively. What is the amount of the assets?
3. The liabilities of Emerald Company equal one-third of the total assets, and owner's equity is $120,000. What is the amount of the liabilities?
4. At the beginning of the year, Sherman's assets were $220,000 and its owner's equity was $100,000. During the year, assets increased $60,000 and liabilities decreased $10,000. What is the owner's equity at the end of the year?

E 6. LO 5 *Owner's Equity Transactions*

Identify the following transactions by marking each as an owner's investment (I), owner's withdrawal (W), revenue (R), expense (E), or not an owner's equity transaction (NOE).

a. Received cash for providing a service.
b. Took assets out of the business for personal expenses.
c. Received cash from a customer previously billed for a service.
d. Transferred assets to the business from a personal account.
e. Paid a service station for gasoline for a business vehicle.
f. Performed a service and received a promise of payment.
g. Paid cash to purchase equipment.
h. Paid cash to an employee for services performed.

E 7. LO 5 *Effect of Transactions on the Accounting Equation*

During the month of April, Andres Corporation had the following transactions:

a. Paid salaries for April, $5,400.
b. Purchased equipment on credit, $9,000.
c. Purchased supplies with cash, $300.
d. Additional investment by owner, $12,000.
e. Received payment for services performed, $1,800.
f. Made partial payment on equipment purchased in transaction **b,** $3,000.
g. Billed customers for services performed, $4,800.
h. Cash withdrawal by owner, $4,500.
i. Received payment from customers billed in transaction **g,** $900.
j. Received utility bill, $210.

On a sheet of paper, list the letters **a** through **j,** with columns labeled Assets, Liabilities, and Owner's Equity. In the columns, indicate whether each transaction caused an increase (+), a decrease (−), or no change (NC) in assets, liabilities, and owner's equity.

E 8. LO 5 *Examples of Transactions*

For each of the following categories, describe a transaction that would have the required effect on the elements of the accounting equation.

1. Increase one asset and decrease another asset.
2. Decrease an asset and decrease a liability.
3. Increase an asset and increase a liability.
4. Increase an asset and increase owner's equity.
5. Decrease an asset and decrease owner's equity.

E 9. LO 5 *Effect of Transactions on the Accounting Equation*

The total assets and liabilities at the beginning and end of the year for Pizarro Company are listed below.

	Assets	Liabilities
Beginning of the year	$110,000	$ 45,000
End of the year	200,000	120,000

Determine Pizarro Company's net income for the year under each of the alternatives that follow.

1. The owner made no investments in or withdrawals from the business during the year.
2. The owner made no investments in the business, but the owner withdrew $22,000 during the year.
3. The owner made an investment of $13,000, but made no withdrawals during the year.
4. The owner made an investment of $10,000 in the business and withdrew $22,000 during the year.

E 10. LO 5, LO 6 *Identification of Accounts*

1. Indicate whether each of the following accounts is an asset (A), a liability (L), or a part of owner's equity (OE).
   a. Cash
   b. Salaries Payable
   c. Accounts Receivable
   d. T. Booth, Capital
   e. Land
   f. Accounts Payable
   g. Supplies
2. Indicate whether each account would be shown on the income statement (IS), the statement of owner's equity (OE), or the balance sheet (BS).
   a. Repair Revenue
   b. Automobile
   c. Fuel Expense
   d. Cash
   e. Rent Expense
   f. Accounts Payable
   g. T. Booth, Withdrawals

E 11. LO 6 *Preparation of a Balance Sheet*

Listed in random order below are the balances for balance sheet items for the Glick Company as of June 30, 20xx.

Accounts Payable	$20,000	Accounts Receivable	$25,000
Building	45,000	Cash	10,000
R. Glick, Capital	85,000	Equipment	20,000
Supplies	5,000		

Sort the balances and prepare a balance sheet similar to the one in Exhibit 2.

E 12. Determine the amounts that correspond to the letters by completing the following independent sets of financial statements. (Assume no new investments by the owners.)

LO 6 *Completion of Financial Statements*

Income Statement	**Set A**	**Set B**	**Set C**
Revenues	$1,100	$ g	$240
Expenses	a	5,200	m
Net Income	$ b	$ h	$ 80
Statement of Owner's Equity			
Beginning Balance	$2,900	$15,400	$200
Net Income	c	1,600	n
Less Withdrawals	200	i	o
Ending Balance	$3,000	$ j	$ p
Balance Sheet			
Total Assets	$ d	$21,000	$ q
Liabilities	$1,600	$ 5,000	$ r
Owner's Equity	e	k	380
Total Liabilities and Owner's Equity	$ f	$ l	$580

E 13. Strickland Company engaged in the following activities during the year: Service Revenues, $52,800; Rent Expense, $4,800; Wages Expense, $33,080; Advertising Expense, $5,400; Utilities Expense, $3,600; and Bill Strickland, Withdrawals, $2,800. In addition, the year-end balances of selected accounts were as follows: Cash, $6,200; Accounts Receivable, $3,000; Supplies, $400; Land, $4,000; Accounts Payable, $1,800; and Bill Strickland, Capital, $8,680.

LO 6 *Preparation of Financial Statements*

Using good form, prepare the income statement, statement of owner's equity, and balance sheet for Strickland Company (assume the year ends on June 30, 20x2). (**Hint:** The amount given for Bill Strickland, Capital is the beginning balance.)

E 14. Diamond Company began the year 20x2 with cash of $86,000. In addition to earning a net income of $50,000 and making an owner's withdrawal of $30,000 for his personal use, Diamond borrowed $120,000 from the bank and purchased equipment for $180,000 with cash. Also, Accounts Receivable increased by $12,000 and Accounts Payable increased by $18,000.

LO 6 *Statement of Cash Flows*

Determine the amount of cash on hand at the end of the year (December 31) by preparing a statement of cash flows similar to the one in Exhibit 2.

E 15. Identify the accounting meaning of each of the following abbreviations: AICPA, SEC, GAAP, FASB, IRS, GASB, IASC, IMA, and CPA.

LO 7 *Accounting Abbreviations*

Problems

P 1. John Unger, after receiving his degree in computer science, started his own business, Regency Business Services Company. He completed the following transactions soon after starting the business:

LO 5 *Effect of Transactions on the Accounting Equation*

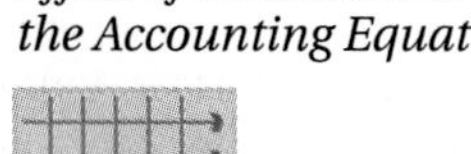

a. Deposited $18,000 in the bank to start the business and purchased a systems library with an additional investment of $1,840.
b. Paid current month's rent on an office, $720.
c. Purchased a minicomputer for cash, $14,000.
d. Purchased computer supplies on credit, $1,200.
e. Received revenue from a client, $1,600.
f. Billed a client on completion of a short project, $1,420.
g. Paid wages, $800.
h. Received a partial payment from the client billed in transaction **f,** $160.
i. Withdrew cash for personal expenses, $500.
j. Made a partial payment on the computer supplies purchased in transaction **d,** $400.

REQUIRED

1. Arrange the asset, liability, and owner's equity accounts in an equation similar to Exhibit 1, using the following account titles: Cash, Accounts Receivable, Supplies, Equipment, Systems Library, Accounts Payable, and John Unger, Capital.
2. Show by addition and subtraction, as in Exhibit 1, the effects of the transactions on the accounting equation. Show new balances after each transaction, and identify each owner's equity transaction by type.

P 2.
LO 5 *Effect of Transactions on the Accounting Equation*

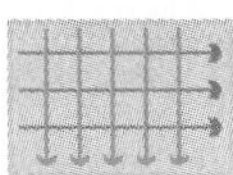

On October 1, Oscar Melendez started a new business, the Melendez Transport Company. During the month of October, the firm completed the following transactions:

a. Deposited $132,000 in a new bank account to establish Melendez Transport Company.
b. Purchased two trucks for cash, $86,000.
c. Purchased equipment on credit, $18,000.
d. Billed a customer for hauling goods, $2,400.
e. Received cash for hauling goods, $4,600.
f. Received cash payment from the customer billed in transaction **d,** $1,200.
g. Made a payment on the equipment purchased in transaction **c,** $10,000.
h. Paid wages in cash, $3,400.
i. Withdrew cash from the business for personal use, $2,400.

REQUIRED

1. Arrange the asset, liability, and owner's equity accounts in an equation similar to Exhibit 1, using the following account titles: Cash, Accounts Receivable, Trucks, Equipment, Accounts Payable, and Oscar Melendez, Capital.
2. Show by addition and subtraction, as in Exhibit 1, the effects of the transactions on the accounting equation. Show new balances after each transaction, and identify each owner's equity transaction by type.

P 3.
LO 5 *Effect of Transactions on the Accounting Equation*

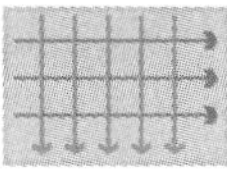

Dr. Barbara Getz, a psychologist, moved from her home town to set up an office in St. Louis. After one month, the business had the following assets: Cash, $5,600; Accounts Receivable, $1,360; Office Supplies, $600; and Office Equipment, $15,000. Owner's equity—the capital account—consisted of $17,360. The Accounts Payable were $5,200 for purchases of office equipment on credit. During a short period of time, the following transactions were completed:

a. Paid one month's rent, $700.
b. Billed patient for services rendered, $120.
c. Made payment on accounts owed, $600.
d. Paid for office supplies, $200.
e. Paid the secretary's salary, $600.
f. Received payment for services rendered from patients not previously billed, $1,600.
g. Made payment on accounts owed, $720.
h. Withdrew cash for living expenses, $1,000.
i. Paid telephone bill for current month, $140.
j. Received payment from patients previously billed, $580.
k. Purchased additional office equipment on credit, $600.

REQUIRED

1. Arrange the asset, liability, and owner's equity accounts in an equation similar to Exhibit 1, using the following account titles: Cash, Accounts Receivable, Office Supplies, Office Equipment, Accounts Payable, and Barbara Getz, Capital.
2. Enter the beginning balances for assets, liabilities, and owner's equity in your equation.
3. Show by addition and subtraction, as in Exhibit 1, the effects of the transactions on the accounting equation. Show new balances after each transaction, and identify each owner's equity transaction by type.

P 4.
LO 6 *Preparation of Financial Statements*

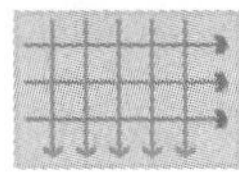

At the end of August 20xx, the Sheri Alexander, Capital account had a balance of $74,600. After operating during September, her Moon Valley Riding Club had the following account balances:

Cash	$17,400	Building	$60,000
Accounts Receivable	2,400	Horses	20,000
Supplies	2,000	Accounts Payable	35,600
Land	42,000		

In addition, the following transactions affected owner's equity:

Withdrawal by Sheri Alexander	$ 6,400	Salaries expense	$4,600
Investment by Sheri Alexander	32,000	Feed expense	2,000
Riding lesson revenue	12,400	Utilities expense	1,200
Locker rental revenue	3,400		

REQUIRED

Using Exhibit 2 as a model, prepare an income statement, a statement of owner's equity, and a balance sheet for Moon Valley Riding Club. (**Hint:** The final balance of Sheri Alexander, Capital is $108,200).

P 5.
LO 5
LO 6 *Effect of Transactions on the Accounting Equation and Preparation of Financial Statements*

On April 1, 20xx, AAFast Taxi Service began operation and engaged in the following transactions during April:

a. Investment by owner, Madeline Curry, $42,000.
b. Purchased taxi for cash, $19,000.
c. Purchased uniforms on credit, $400.
d. Received taxi fares in cash, $3,200.
e. Paid wages to part-time drivers, $500.
f. Purchased gasoline during month for cash, $800.
g. Purchased car washes during month on credit, $120.
h. Further investment by owner, $5,000.
i. Paid part of the amount owed for the uniforms purchased in transaction **c,** $200.
j. Billed major client for fares, $900.
k. Paid for automobile repairs, $250.
l. Withdrew cash from business for personal use, $1,000.

REQUIRED

1. Arrange the asset, liability, and owner's equity accounts in an equation similar to Exhibit 1, using these account titles: Cash, Accounts Receivable, Uniforms, Taxi, Accounts Payable, and Madeline Curry, Capital.
2. Show by addition and subtraction, as in Exhibit 1, the effects of the transactions on the accounting equation. Show new balances after each transaction, and identify each owner's equity transaction by type.
3. Using Exhibit 2 as a guide, prepare an income statement, a statement of owner's equity, and a balance sheet for AAFast Taxi Service.

Alternate Problems

P 6.
LO 5 *Effect of Transactions on the Accounting Equation*

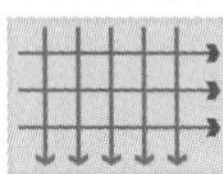

The Creative Frames Shop was started by Rosa Partridge in a small shopping center. In the first weeks of operation, she completed the following transactions:

a. Deposited $21,000 in an account in the name of the company to start the business.
b. Paid the current month's rent, $1,500.
c. Purchased store equipment on credit, $10,800.
d. Purchased framing supplies for cash, $5,100.
e. Received framing revenues, $2,400.
f. Billed customers for services, $2,100.
g. Paid utilities expense, $750.
h. Received payment from customers in transaction **f,** $600.
i. Made payment on store equipment purchased in transaction **c,** $5,400.
j. Withdrew cash for personal expenses, $1,200.

REQUIRED

1. Arrange the following asset, liability, and owner's equity accounts in an equation similar to Exhibit 1: Cash, Accounts Receivable, Framing Supplies, Store Equipment, Accounts Payable, and Rosa Partridge, Capital.
2. Show by addition and subtraction, as in Exhibit 1, the effects of the transactions on the accounting equation. Show new balances after each transaction, and identify each owner's equity transaction by type.

P 7.
LO 6 *Preparation of Financial Statements*

At the end of its first month of operation, March 20xx, Ellis Plumbing Company had the following account balances:

Cash	$58,600	Tools	$7,600
Accounts Receivable	10,800	Accounts Payable	8,600
Delivery Truck	38,000		

In addition, during the month of March, the following transactions affected owner's equity:

Investment by J. Ellis	$40,000	Repair revenue	$ 5,600
Withdrawal by J. Ellis	4,000	Salaries expense	16,600
Further investment by J. Ellis	60,000	Rent expense	1,400
Contract revenue	23,200	Fuel expense	400

REQUIRED

Using Exhibit 2 as a model, prepare an income statement, a statement of owner's equity, and a balance sheet for Ellis Plumbing Company. (**Hint**: The final balance of J. Ellis, Capital is $106,400.)

P 8.

LO 5 LO 6 *Effect of Transactions on the Accounting Equation and Preparation of Financial Statements*

Arrow Copying Service began operations and engaged in the following transactions during August 20xx:

a. Investment by owner, Myra Lomax, $10,000.
b. Paid current month's rent, $900.
c. Purchased copier for cash, $5,000.
d. Paid cash for paper and other copier supplies, $380.
e. Copying job payments received in cash, $1,780.
f. Copying job billed to major customer, $1,360.
g. Paid wages to part-time employees, $560.
h. Purchased additional copier supplies on credit, $280.
i. Received partial payment from customer in transaction **f,** $600.
j. Paid current month's utility bill, $180.
k. Made partial payment on supplies purchased in transaction **h,** $140.
l. Withdrew cash for personal use, $1,400.

REQUIRED

1. Arrange the asset, liability, and owner's equity accounts in an equation similar to Exhibit 1, using these account titles: Cash, Accounts Receivable, Supplies, Copier, Accounts Payable, and M. Lomax, Capital.
2. Show by addition and subtraction, as in Exhibit 1, the effects of the transactions on the accounting equation. Show new balances after each transaction, and identify each owner's equity transaction by type.
3. Using Exhibit 2 as a guide, prepare an income statement, a statement of owner's equity, and a balance sheet for Arrow Copying Service.

EXPANDING YOUR CRITICAL THINKING, COMMUNICATION, AND INTERPERSONAL SKILLS

Skills Development

CONCEPTUAL ANALYSIS

SD 1.

LO 1 LO 2 *Business Activities and Management Functions*

J.C. Penney Company, Inc., is America's largest department store company. According to its letter to stockholders, financial results didn't meet company expectations.

> J.C. Penney is implementing a number of strategic initiatives to ensure our competitiveness, to meet our growth objectives, and to provide a strong return on our stockholders' investment. These initiatives include: accelerated growth in our top 10 markets; expand our women's apparel and accessories business; speed merchandise to market; reduce our cost structure and enhance customer service.[10]

Communication
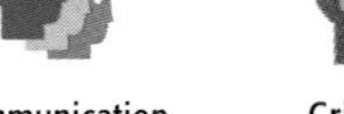

Critical Thinking

Group Activity

Memo

Ethics

International
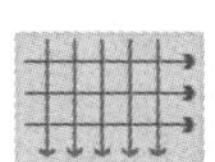
Spreadsheet

General Ledger

CD-ROM

Internet

To achieve its strategy, J.C. Penney must organize its management into functions that relate to the principal activities of a business. Discuss the three basic activities J.C. Penney will engage in to achieve its goals, and suggest some examples of each. What is the role of J.C. Penney's management, and what functions must its management perform to accomplish these activities?

SD 2. LO 3 *Concept of an Asset*

Southwest Airlines is one of the most successful airlines in the United States. Its annual report carries the following statement: "We are a company of People, not Planes. That is what distinguishes us from other airlines and other companies. At Southwest Airlines, People are our most important asset."[11] Are employees considered assets in the financial statements? Discuss in what sense Southwest Airlines considers its employees to be assets.

Ethical Dilemma

SD 3. LO 8 *Professional Ethics*

Discuss the ethical choices in the situations below. In each instance, determine the alternative courses of action, describe the ethical dilemma, and tell what you would do.

1. You are the payroll accountant for a small business. A friend asks you how much another employee is paid per hour.
2. As an accountant for the branch office of a wholesale supplier, you discover that several of the receipts the branch manager has submitted for reimbursement as selling expense actually stem from nights out with his spouse.
3. You are an accountant in the purchasing department of a construction company. When you arrive home from work on December 22, you find a large ham in a box marked "Happy Holidays—It's a pleasure to work with you." The gift is from a supplier who has bid on a contract your employer plans to award next week.
4. As an auditor with one year's experience at a local CPA firm, you are expected to complete a certain part of an audit in twenty hours. Because of your lack of experience, you know you cannot finish the job within that time. Rather than admit this, you are thinking about working late to finish the job and not telling anyone.
5. You are a tax accountant at a local CPA firm. You help your neighbor fill out her tax return, and she pays you $200 in cash. Because there is no record of this transaction, you are considering not reporting it on your tax return.
6. The accounting firm for which you work as a CPA has just won a new client, a firm in which you own 200 shares of stock that you received as an inheritance from your grandmother. Because it is only a small number of shares and you think the company will be very successful, you are considering not disclosing the investment.

Group Activity: Assign each case to a different group to resolve and report.

Research Activity

SD 4. LO 1 LO 2 *Need for Knowledge of Accounting*

Locate an article about a company from one of the following sources: the business section of your local paper or a nearby metropolitan daily, *The Wall Street Journal, Business Week, Forbes,* or the Needles Accounting Resource Center Web site at http://www.hmco.com/college/needles/home.html. List all the financial and accounting terms used in the article. Bring the article to class and be prepared to discuss how a knowledge of accounting would help a reader understand the content of the article.

Decision-Making Practice

SD 5. LO 5 LO 6 *Effect of Transactions on the Balance Sheet*

Instead of hunting for a summer job after finishing her junior year in college, Lucy Henderson organized a lawn service company in her neighborhood. To start her business on June 1, she deposited $1,350 in a new bank account in the name of her company. The $1,350 consisted of a $500 loan from her father and $850 of her own money.

Using the money in this checking account, Lucy rented lawn equipment, purchased supplies, and hired neighborhood high school students to mow and trim the lawns of neighbors who had agreed to pay her for the service. At the end of each month, she mailed bills to her customers.

On August 31, Lucy was ready to dissolve her business and go back to school for the fall quarter. Because she had been so busy, she had not kept any records other than her checkbook and a list of amounts owed to her by customers.

Her checkbook had a balance of $1,760, and the amount owed to her by customers totaled $435. She expected these customers to pay her during October. She planned to return unused supplies to Suburban Landscaping Company for a full credit of $25. When she brought back the rented lawn equipment, Suburban Landscaping also would return a deposit of $100 she had made in June. She owed Suburban Landscaping $260 for equipment rentals and supplies. In addition, she owed the students who had worked for her $50, and she still owed her father $350. Although Lucy feels she did quite well, she is not sure just how successful she was.

1. Prepare a balance sheet dated June 1 and one dated August 31 for Henderson Lawn Care Company.
2. Comment on the performance of Henderson Lawn Care Company by comparing the two balance sheets. Did the company have a profit or a loss? (Assume that Lucy used none of the company's assets for personal purposes.)
3. If Lucy wants to continue her business next summer, what kind of information from her recordkeeping system would help make it easier to tell whether or not she is earning a profit?

Financial Reporting and Analysis

Interpreting Financial Reports

FRA 1. LO 6 *Nature of Cash, Assets, and Net Income*

Merrill Lynch & Co., Inc., is a U.S.-based global financial services firm. Information for 1996 and 1995 adapted from the company's 1996 annual report is presented below.[12] (All numbers are in thousands.)

Merrill Lynch & Co., Inc.
Condensed Balance Sheets
December 27, 1996 and December 29, 1995
(in thousands)

	1996	1995
Assets		
Cash	$ 3,375,000	$ 3,091,000
Other Assets	209,641,000	173,766,000
Total Assets	$213,016,000	$176,857,000
Liabilities		
Total Liabilities	$205,797,000	$170,665,000
Owner's Equity		
Owner's Capital	$ 7,219,000	$ 6,192,000
Total Liabilities and Owner's Equity	$213,016,000	$176,857,000

Three students who were looking at Merrill Lynch's annual report were overheard to make the following comments:

Student A: What a great year Merrill Lynch had in 1996! The company earned net income of $36,159,000,000 because its total assets increased from $176,857,000,000 to $213,016,000,000.

Student B: But the change in total assets isn't the same as net income! The company had a net income of only $284,000,000 because cash increased from $3,091,000,000 to $3,375,000,000.

Student C: I see from the annual report that Merrill Lynch paid cash dividends (cash dividends are treated the same as owner's withdrawals) of $243,000,000 in 1996. Don't you have to take that into consideration when analyzing the company's performance?

REQUIRED

1. Comment on the interpretations of Students A and B, and then answer Student C's question.
2. Calculate Merrill Lynch's net income for 1996. (**Hint**: Reconstruct the statement of owner's equity.)

Group Activity: After discussing **1**, let groups compete to see which one can come up with the answer to **2** first.

INTERNATIONAL COMPANY

FRA 2.
LO 1 *The Goal of Profitability*

The Swedish company ***Volvo AB,*** the largest company in Scandinavia, had a difficult year in 1996. In the company's annual report, the president said in part, "The heavy losses incurred in our truck operations in the United States were a severe setback and earnings in Volvo Cars are still at an unsatisfactory level. . . . The efforts to strengthen Volvo's competitiveness and create sound profitability now have the highest priority."[13] Discuss the meaning of *profitability.* What other goal must a business achieve? Why is the goal of profitability important to Volvo's president? What is the accounting measure of profitability, and on which statement is it determined?

TOYS "R" US ANNUAL REPORT

FRA 3.
LO 6 *The Four Basic Financial Statements*

Refer to the Toys "R" Us annual report to answer the questions below. (Note that 1997 refers to the year ended February 1, 1997, and 1996 refers to the year ended February 3, 1996.) Keep in mind that every company, while following basic principles, adapts financial statements and terminology to its own special needs. Therefore, the complexity of the financial statements and the terminology in the Toys "R" Us statements will sometimes differ from those in the text.

1. What names does Toys "R" Us give its four basic financial statements? (Note that the use of the word "Consolidated" in the names of the financial statements simply means that these statements combine those of several companies owned by Toys "R" Us.)
2. Prove that the accounting equation works for Toys "R" Us on February 1, 1997, by finding the amounts for the following equation: Assets = Liabilities + Stockholders' Equity.
3. What were the total revenues of Toys "R" Us for the year ended February 1, 1997?
4. Was Toys "R" Us profitable in the year ended February 1, 1997? How much was net income in that year, and did it increase or decrease from the year ended February 3, 1996?
5. Did the company's cash and cash equivalents increase from February 3, 1996, to February 1, 1997? By how much? In what two places in the statements can this number be found or computed?

Group Activity: Assign above to in-class groups of three or four students. Set a time limit. The first group to answer all questions correctly wins.

FINGRAPH® FINANCIAL ANALYST™

FRA 4. Choose any company in the Fingraph® Financial Analyst™ CD-ROM software.

LO 1 *Financial Statements,*
LO 6 *Business Activities and Goals*

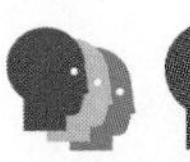

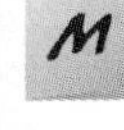

1. In the company's annual report, find a description of the business. What business is the company in? How would you describe its operating activities?
2. Find and identify the company's four basic financial statements. Which statement shows the resources of the business and the various claims to those resources? From the balance sheet, prove the balance sheet equation by showing that the company's assets equal its liabilities plus stockholders' equity. What is the company's largest category of assets? Which statement shows changes in all or part of the company's stockholders' equity during the year? Did the company pay any dividends in the last year?
3. Which statement is most closely associated with the company's profitability goal? How much net income did the company earn in the last year? Which statement is most closely associated with the company's liquidity goal? Did cash (and cash equivalents) increase in the last year? Which provided the most positive cash flows in the last year: operating, investing, or financing activities?
4. Prepare a one-page executive summary that highlights what you have learned from parts 1, 2, and 3. An executive summary is a short, easy-to-read report that emphasizes important information and conclusions by listing them by numbered paragraphs or bullet points.

ENDNOTES

1. Microsoft Corporation, *Annual Report,* 1997.
2. *Statement of Financial Accounting Concepts No. 1,* "Objectives of Financial Reporting by Business Enterprises" (Norwalk, Conn.: Financial Accounting Standards Board, 1978), par. 9.
3. Ibid.
4. Microsoft Corporation, *Annual Report,* 1996.
5. Kathy Williams and James Hart, "Microsoft: Tooling the Information Age," *Management Accounting,* May 1996, p. 42.
6. *Statement of the Accounting Principles Board No. 4,* "Basic Concepts and Accounting Principles Underlying Financial Statements of Business Enterprises" (New York: American Institute of Certified Public Accountants, 1970), par. 138.
7. Touche Ross & Co., "Ethics in American Business" (New York: Touche Ross & Co., 1988), p. 7.
8. *Business Week,* September 23, 1991, p. 65.
9. *Statement Number IC,* "Standards of Ethical Conduct for Management Accountants" (Montvale, N.J.: Institute of Management Accountants, 1983, revised 1997).
10. J.C. Penney Company, Inc., *Annual Report,* 1995.
11. Southwest Airlines Co., *Annual Report,* 1996.
12. Adapted from Merrill Lynch & Co., Inc., *Annual Report,* 1996.
13. Volvo AB, *Annual Report,* 1996.

CHAPTER 2

Measuring Business Transactions

LEARNING OBJECTIVES

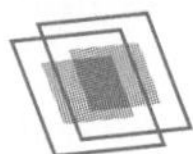

1. **Explain, in simple terms, the generally accepted ways of solving the measurement issues of recognition, valuation, and classification.**
2. **Describe the chart of accounts and recognize commonly used accounts.**
3. **Define *double-entry system* and state the rules for double entry.**
4. **Apply the steps for transaction analysis and processing to simple transactions.**
5. **Prepare a trial balance and describe its value and limitations.**
6. **Record transactions in the general journal.**
7. **Post transactions from the general journal to the ledger.**

DECISION POINT

CONTINENTAL AIRLINES, INC., and THE BOEING CO.

In June 1997, Continental Airlines, Inc., announced that it had ordered thirty-five Boeing jetliners, thirty 767 and five 777 aircraft.[1] The $4 billion order was part of an exclusive agreement that Boeing had negotiated with Continental. This exclusive twenty-year agreement to purchase only Boeing aircraft was the third such agreement with a major airline and positioned Boeing favorably against Airbus, its European competitor. How should this important order have been recorded, if at all, in the records of Continental and Boeing? When should the purchase and sale that results from this order be recorded in the companies' records?

The order obviously was an important event, one that had long-term consequences for both companies. But, as you will see in this chapter, it was not recorded in the accounting records of either company. At the time the order was placed, the aircraft were yet to be manufactured and would not begin to be delivered for several years. Even for "firm" orders, Boeing has cautioned that "an economic downturn could result in airline equipment requirements less than currently anticipated resulting in requests to negotiate the rescheduling or possible cancellation of firm orders."[2] The aircraft were not assets of Continental, and the company had not incurred a liability. No aircraft had been delivered or even built, so Continental was not obligated to pay at that point. And Boeing could not record any revenue until the aircraft were manufactured and delivered to Continental, and title to the aircraft shifted from Boeing to Continental. In prior years, Boeing experienced cancellation or extension of some previously firm orders because of adverse effects of the economy on the airline industry.

Point to Emphasize: Many students approach the topic of measurement (as well as accounting itself) as though it were fairly cut-and-dried. But they should realize that there are several ways to approach the recognition, valuation, and classification issues, only one of which, typically, follows GAAP. As shown in this Decision Point, the recognition issue is not always resolved easily.

Critical Thinking Question: How might other businesses use purchase orders?
Answer: Purchase orders are common in business. Examples include a supermarket ordering inventory or an appliance repair shop ordering parts and supplies.

To understand and use financial statements, it is important to know how to analyze events in order to determine the extent of their impact on those statements.

Measurement Issues

OBJECTIVE 1

Explain, in simple terms, the generally accepted ways of solving the measurement issues of recognition, valuation, and classification

Related Text Assignments:
Q: 1, 2, 3, 4, 5
SE: 1
E: 1, 2
P: 4, 7
SD: 1, 2, 3
FRA: 4

Terminology Note: *Recognize* here means to record a transaction or event.

Point to Emphasize: A purchase should not be recognized (recorded) before title is transferred because, until that point, the vendor has not fulfilled its contractual obligation and the buyer has no liability.

Business-World Example: Recognition is also a problem for franchisers, such as McDonald's, which cannot record initial franchise fees until they have performed the agreed-on services.

Business transactions are economic events that affect the financial position of a business entity. To measure a business transaction, the accountant must decide when the transaction occurred (the recognition issue), what value to place on the transaction (the valuation issue), and how the components of the transaction should be categorized (the classification issue).

These three issues—recognition, valuation, and classification—underlie almost every major decision in financial accounting today. They lie at the heart of accounting for pension plans, for mergers of giant companies, and for international transactions; and they allow the accountant to project and plan for the effects of inflation. In discussing the three basic issues, we follow generally accepted accounting principles and use an approach that promotes an understanding of the basic ideas of accounting. Keep in mind, however, that controversy does exist, and that some solutions to problems are not as cut-and-dried as they appear.

The Recognition Issue

The recognition issue refers to the difficulty of deciding when a business transaction should be recorded. Often the facts of a situation are known, but there is disagreement about *when* the event should be recorded. Suppose, for instance, that a company orders, receives, and pays for an office desk. Which of the following actions constitutes a recordable event?

1. An employee sends a purchase requisition to the purchasing department.
2. The purchasing department sends a purchase order to the supplier.
3. The supplier ships the desk.
4. The company receives the desk.
5. The company receives the bill from the supplier.
6. The company pays the bill.

The answer to this question is important because amounts in the financial statements are affected by the date on which a purchase is recorded. According to accounting tradition, the transaction is recorded when title to the desk passes from the supplier to the purchaser, creating an obligation to pay. Thus, depending on the

BUSINESS BULLETIN: BUSINESS PRACTICE

Many companies include in the "Summary of Significant Accounting Policies" section of their annual reports information on the recognition rules followed by the company. For instance, Sun Microsystems Inc., the large supplier of networked workstations, servers, and other computer software and hardware, describes its revenue recognition rules as follows:

> *Sun generally recognizes revenues from hardware and software sales at the time of shipment. Service revenues are recognized over the contractual period or as the services are provided.*[3]

details of the shipping agreement, the transaction is recognized (recorded) at the time of either action **3** or action **4.** This is the guideline that we generally use in this book. However, in many small businesses that have simple accounting systems, the transaction is not recorded until the bill is received (action **5**) or paid (action **6**) because these are the implied points of title transfer. The predetermined time at which a transaction should be recorded is the recognition point.

The recognition issue is not always solved easily. Consider the case of an advertising agency that is asked by a client to prepare a major advertising campaign. People may work on the campaign several hours a day for a number of weeks. Value is added to the plan as the employees develop it. Should this added value be recognized as the campaign is being produced or at the time it is completed? Normally, the increase in value is recorded at the time the plan is finished and the client is billed for it. However, if a plan is going to take a long period to develop, the agency and the client may agree that the client will be billed at key points during its development. A transaction is recorded at each billing.

Enrichment Note: The value of a transaction usually is based on a business document–a canceled check or an invoice. In general, appraisals or other subjective amounts are not recorded.

The Valuation Issue

Valuation is perhaps the most controversial issue in accounting. The valuation issue focuses on assigning a monetary value to a business transaction. Generally accepted accounting principles state that the appropriate value to assign to all business transactions—and therefore to all assets, liabilities, and components of owner's equity, including revenues and expenses, recorded by a business—is the original cost (often called *historical cost*).

Point to Emphasize: Assets, liabilities, and the components of owner's equity are not accounts, but account *classifications.* For example, Cash is a type of asset account, and Accounts Payable is a type of liability account.

Cost is defined here as the exchange price associated with a business transaction at the point of recognition. According to this guideline, the purpose of accounting is not to account for value in terms of worth, which can change after a transaction occurs, but to account for value in terms of cost at the time of the transaction. For example, the cost of an asset is recorded when the asset is acquired, and the value is held at that level until the asset is sold, expires, or is consumed. In this context, *value* means the cost at the time of the transaction. The practice of recording transactions at cost is referred to as the cost principle.

Suppose that a person offers a building for sale at $120,000. It may be valued for real estate taxes at $75,000, and it may be insured for $90,000. One prospective buyer may offer $100,000 for the building, and another may offer $105,000. At this point, several different, unverifiable opinions of value have been expressed. Finally, suppose the seller and a buyer settle on a price and complete the sale for $110,000. All of these figures are values of one kind or another, but only the last is sufficiently reliable to be used in the records. The market value of the building may vary over the years, but the building will remain on the new buyer's records at $110,000 until it

BUSINESS BULLETIN: BUSINESS PRACTICE

In many aspects of accounting, there are sometimes exceptions to the general rules. For instance, the cost principle is not followed in all parts of the financial statements. Investments, for example, are often accounted for at fair or market value because these investments are available for sale. The fair or market value is the best measure of the potential benefit to the company. Intel Corp., the large microprocessor company, states in its annual report:

> *All of the company's short- and long-term investments are classified as available-for-sale and are reported at fair value.*[4]

BUSINESS BULLETIN: ETHICS IN PRACTICE

Not only are the accounting solutions related to recognition, valuation, and classification important for good financial reporting, but they are also designed to help management fulfill its responsibilities to company owners and the public. At Bausch & Lomb, a maker of eye care products, the pursuit of results got out of hand. Under pressure to beat sales targets in 1993, contact lens managers shipped products that doctors never ordered and forced distributors to take up to two years of unwanted inventories. Also, the Hong Kong unit allegedly inflated revenues by faking sales of Ray-Ban sunglasses to customers. These actions helped the company meet targeted results. The CEO's bonus plan depended heavily on sales growth and earnings growth. By early 1994, Bausch & Lomb had achieved a market value of over $3.2 billion. But after disclosure that Bausch & Lomb had violated the recognition point, the company's market value declined more than 40 percent, to less than $1.8 billion.[5] Following proper accounting principles would have prevented management from falsely portraying the company. Appointing a new CEO and other management changes, as well as improved accounting procedures, are steps Bausch & Lomb took to regain some of its lost credibility.

is sold again. At that point, the accountant will record the new transaction at the new exchange price, and a profit or loss will be recognized.

The cost principle is used because the cost is verifiable. It results from the actions of independent buyers and sellers who come to an agreement on price. An exchange price is an objective price that can be verified by evidence created at the time of the transaction. It is this final price, verified by agreement of the two parties, at which the transaction is recorded.

The Classification Issue

The classification issue has to do with assigning all the transactions in which a business engages to appropriate categories, or accounts. For example, a company's ability to borrow money can be affected by the way in which its debts are categorized. Or a company's income can be affected by whether purchases of small items such as tools are considered repair expenses (a component of owner's equity) or equipment (assets). Proper classification depends not only on correctly analyzing the effect of each transaction on the business, but also on maintaining a system of accounts that reflects that effect. The rest of this chapter explains the classification of accounts and the analysis and recording of transactions.

Accounts and the Chart of Accounts

OBJECTIVE 2

Describe the chart of accounts and recognize commonly used accounts

In the measurement of business transactions, large amounts of data are gathered. These data require a method of storage. Businesspeople should be able to retrieve transaction data quickly and in usable form. In other words, there should be a filing system to sort out or classify all the transactions that occur in a business. This filing system consists of accounts. Recall that accounts are the basic storage units for accounting data and are used to accumulate amounts from similar transactions. An accounting system has a separate account for each asset, each liability, and each component of owner's equity, including revenues and expenses. Whether a company keeps records by hand or by computer, management must be able to refer to accounts so that it can study the company's financial history and plan for the future.

BUSINESS BULLETIN: BUSINESS PRACTICE

Today, most businesses, even the smallest, use computerized accounting systems. According to a study by Andersen Worldwide, the large accounting firm, 85 percent of small and midsize companies have computer systems. In small businesses, these systems are called *general ledger packages* and run on personal computers. The starting point for these systems is a chart of accounts that reflects the activities in which the business engages. Every company develops a chart of accounts for its own needs. Seldom do two companies have exactly the same chart of accounts. A small business may get by with a simple chart of accounts like that in Exhibit 1. A large, complicated business like Commonwealth Edison, the electric utility in Chicago, will have twelve or more digits in its account numbers and thousands of accounts in its chart of accounts.

Related Text Assignments:
Q: 6, 7, 8, 23
SE: 2
E: 3
FRA: 1

A very small company may need only a few dozen accounts; a multinational corporation may need thousands.

In a manual accounting system, each account is kept on a separate page or card. These pages or cards are placed together in a book or file called the general ledger. In the computerized systems that most companies have today, accounts are maintained on magnetic tapes or disks. However, as a matter of convenience, accountants still refer to the group of company accounts as the general ledger, or simply the *ledger.*

Point to Emphasize: A chart of accounts is a table of contents for the ledger. The accounts typically are listed in the same order as they appear in the ledger, and the numbering scheme should allow for some flexibility.

To help identify accounts in the ledger and to make them easy to find, the accountant often numbers them. A list of these numbers with the corresponding account names is called a chart of accounts. A very simple chart of accounts appears in Exhibit 1. Notice that the first digit refers to the major financial statement classifications. An account number that begins with the digit 1 represents an asset, an account number that begins with a 2 represents a liability, and so forth. The second and third digits refer to individual accounts. Notice the gaps in the sequence of numbers. These gaps allow the accountant to expand the number of accounts. The accounts in Exhibit 1 will be used in this chapter and in the next two chapters, through the sample case of the Joan Miller Advertising Agency.

Owner's Equity Accounts

In the chart of accounts in Exhibit 1, the revenue and expense accounts are separated from the other owner's equity accounts. The relationships of these accounts to each other and to the basic financial statements are shown in Figure 1. The distinctions among them are important for legal and financial reporting purposes.

First, for income tax reporting, financial reporting, and other purposes, the law requires that Capital and Withdrawals accounts be separated from revenues and expenses. The Capital account represents the owner's interest in the assets of the company. The Withdrawals account is used to record assets taken out of the business by the owner for personal use. These withdrawals are not described as salary or wages, although the owner may think of them as such, because there is no change in the ownership of the money withdrawn. In practice, the Withdrawals account often goes by other names, among them *Personal* and *Drawing*. Corporations do not use a Withdrawals account.

Second, management needs a detailed breakdown of revenues and expenses for budgeting and operating purposes. From these accounts, which are listed on the income statement, management can identify the sources of all revenues and the nature of all expenses. In this way, accounting gives management information about how it has achieved its primary goal of earning a net income.

Teaching Note: Explain that account names must be both concise and descriptive. Although some account names, such as Cash and Land, generally are fixed, others are not.

Teaching Note: Also explain that accounts are usually listed in the order in which they appear on the financial statements.

Common Student Confusion: Students frequently confuse the account Notes Receivable with the piece of paper called a *promissory note.* Also, they might not understand how notes receivable are assets for those who hold a note (it is a payment, not the note, that is a receivable). A visual demonstration should clear up any confusion.

Discussion Question: Why are prepaid expenses classified as an asset? **Answer:** Because they represent future benefits for which payment has already been made.

Common Student Confusion: At this point, many students do not know the difference between office supplies and office equipment. Explain that office supplies are consumed gradually, whereas office equipment remains intact.

Point to Emphasize: A liability is essentially a debt or obligation that is discharged with the disbursement of cash or with the performance of a service.

Exhibit 1. Chart of Accounts for a Small Business

Account Number	Account Name	Description
		Assets
111	Cash	Money and any medium of exchange, including coins, currency, checks, postal and express money orders, and money on deposit in a bank
112	Notes Receivable	Amounts due from others in the form of promissory notes (written promises to pay definite sums of money at fixed future dates)
113	Accounts Receivable	Amounts due from others from credit sales (sales on account)
114	Fees Receivable	Amounts arising from services performed but not yet billed to customers
115	Art Supplies	Prepaid expense; art supplies purchased and not used
116	Office Supplies	Prepaid expense; office supplies purchased and not used
117	Prepaid Rent	Prepaid expense; rent paid in advance and not used
118	Prepaid Insurance	Prepaid expense; insurance purchased and not expired; unexpired insurance
141	Land	Property owned for use in the business
142	Buildings	Structures owned for use in the business
143	Accumulated Depreciation, Buildings	Sum of the periodic allocation of the cost of buildings to expense
144	Art Equipment	Art equipment owned for use in the business
145	Accumulated Depreciation, Art Equipment	Sum of the periodic allocation of the cost of art equipment to expense
146	Office Equipment	Office equipment owned for use in the business
147	Accumulated Depreciation, Office Equipment	Sum of the periodic allocation of the cost of office equipment to expense
		Liabilities
211	Notes Payable	Amounts due to others in the form of promissory notes
212	Accounts Payable	Amounts due to others for purchases on credit

(continued)

Discussion Question: In what way are unearned revenues the opposite of prepaid expenses? **Answer:** With unearned revenues (a liability), cash is *received* in advance of performance. With prepaid expenses (an asset), cash is *paid* in advance of receiving a service.

Point to Emphasize: Although withdrawals are a component of owner's equity, they normally appear only in the statement of owner's equity, not in the owner's equity section of the balance sheet. In addition, they do not appear as an expense in the income statement.

Point to Emphasize: Although revenues and expenses are components of owner's equity, they appear in the income statement, not in the owner's equity section of the balance sheet. Figure 1 illustrates this point.

Exhibit 1. Chart of Accounts for a Small Business *(continued)*

Account Number	Account Name	Description
	Liabilities	
213	Unearned Art Fees	Unearned revenue; advance deposits for artwork to be provided in the future
214	Wages Payable	Amounts due to employees for wages earned and not paid
221	Mortgage Payable	Amounts due on loans that are backed by the company's property and buildings
	Owner's Equity	
311	Capital	Owner's investment in the company
312	Withdrawals	Assets withdrawn from the business by the owner for personal use
313	Income Summary	Temporary account used at the end of the accounting period to summarize revenues and expenses for the period
	Revenues	
411	Advertising Fees Earned	Revenues derived from performing advertising services
412	Art Fees Earned	Revenues derived from performing art services
	Expenses	
511	Wages Expense	Amounts earned by employees
512	Utilities Expense	Amounts for utilities, such as water, electricity, and gas, used
513	Telephone Expense	Amounts for telephone services used
514	Rent Expense	Amounts for rent on property and buildings used
515	Insurance Expense	Amounts for insurance used
516	Art Supplies Expense	Amounts for art supplies used
517	Office Supplies Expense	Amounts for office supplies used
518	Depreciation Expense, Buildings	Amount of buildings' cost allocated to expense
519	Depreciation Expense, Art Equipment	Amount of art equipment costs allocated to expense
520	Depreciation Expense, Office Equipment	Amount of office equipment costs allocated to expense
521	Interest Expense	Amount of interest on debts

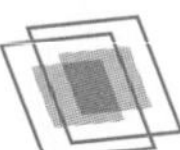

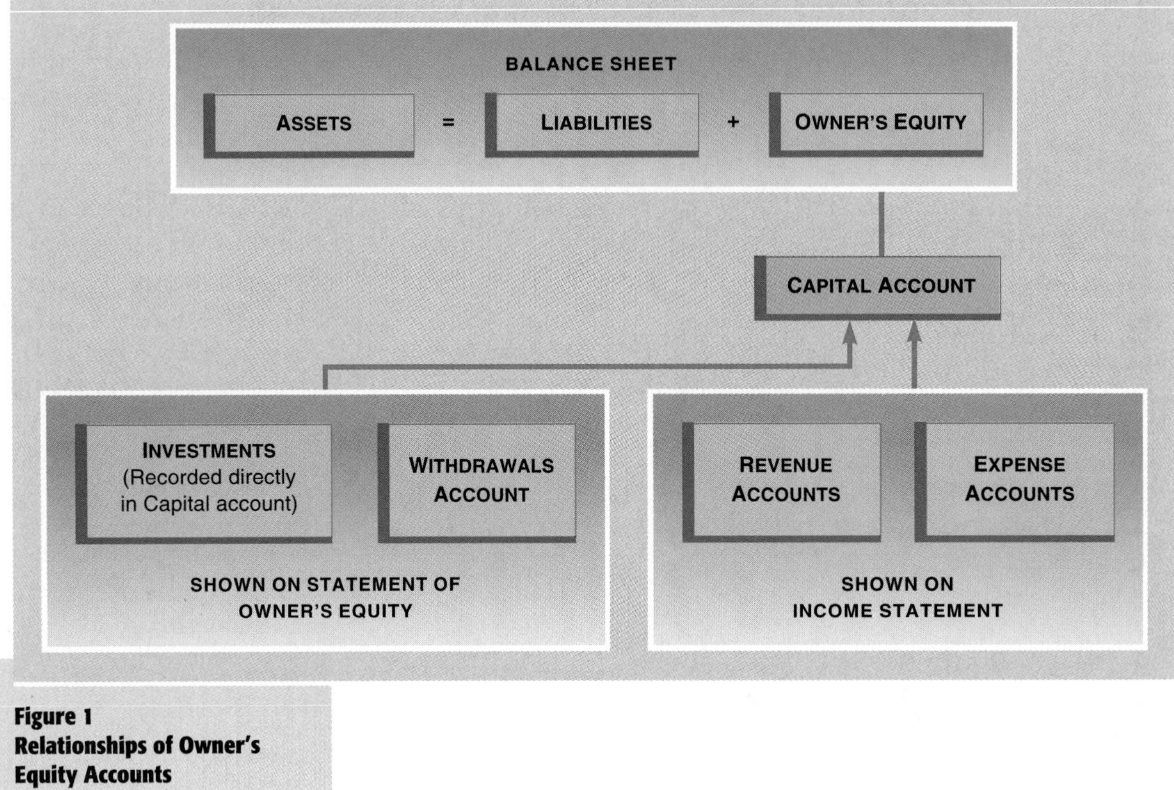

Figure 1
Relationships of Owner's Equity Accounts

Teaching Note: A mnemonic for the types of accounts that affect owner's equity is WIRE–Withdrawals, Investments, Revenues, and Expenses.

Account Titles

The names of accounts often confuse beginning accounting students because some of the words are new or have technical meanings. Also, the same asset, liability, or owner's equity account can have different names in different companies. (Actually, this is not so strange. People, too, often are called different names by their friends, families, and associates.) For example, Fixed Assets, Plant and Equipment, Capital Assets, and Long-Lived Assets are all names for long-term asset accounts. Even the most acceptable names change over time, and, out of habit, some companies use names that are out of date.

In general, an account title should describe what is recorded in the account. When you come across an account title that you do not recognize, you should examine the context of the name—whether it is classified as an asset, liability, or owner's equity component, including revenue or expense, on the financial statements—and look for the kind of transaction that gave rise to the account.

The Double-Entry System: The Basic Method of Accounting

OBJECTIVE 3

Define double-entry system *and state the rules for double entry*

Related Text Assignments:
Q: 9, 10, 11, 12, 13
FRA: 4

The double-entry system, the backbone of accounting, evolved during the Renaissance. As noted previously, the first systematic description of double-entry bookkeeping appeared in 1494, two years after Columbus discovered America, in a mathematics book written by Fra Luca Pacioli. Goethe, the famous German poet and dramatist, referred to double-entry bookkeeping as "one of the finest discoveries of the human intellect." And Werner Sombart, an eminent economist-sociologist, believed that "double-entry bookkeeping is born of the same spirit as the system of Galileo and Newton."

Point to Emphasize: Each transaction must include at least one debit and one credit, and the debit totals must equal the credit totals.

What is the significance of the double-entry system? The system is based on the *principle of duality,* which means that every economic event has two aspects—effort and reward, sacrifice and benefit, source and use—that offset or balance each other. In the double-entry system, each transaction must be recorded with at least one debit and one credit, so that the total dollar amount of debits and the total dollar amount of credits equal each other. Because of the way it is designed, the whole system is always in balance. All accounting systems, no matter how sophisticated, are based on the principle of duality.

The T Account

Point to Emphasize: A T account is simply an abbreviated version of a ledger account. T accounts are used by accountants, instructors, students, and textbooks to quickly analyze a set of transactions; ledger accounts are used in the accounting records.

Common Student Error: Many students have preconceived ideas about what *debit* and *credit* mean. They think that *debit* means "decrease" (or implies something bad) and that *credit* means "increase" (or implies something good). It is important that they realize that *debit* simply means "left side" and *credit* simply means "right side."

The T account is a good place to begin the study of the double-entry system. In its simplest form, an account has three parts: (1) a title, which describes the asset, the liability, or the owner's equity account; (2) a left side, which is called the debit side; and (3) a right side, which is called the credit side. This form of an account, called a T account because it resembles the letter *T,* is used to analyze transactions. It looks like this:

Title of Account

Debit (left) side	Credit (right) side

Any entry made on the left side of the account is a debit, or debit entry; and any entry made on the right side of the account is a credit, or credit entry. The terms *debit* (abbreviated Dr., from the Latin *debere*) and *credit* (abbreviated Cr., from the Latin *credere*) are simply the accountant's words for "left" and "right" (not for "increase" or "decrease"). We present a more formal version of the T account later in this chapter, where we examine the ledger account form.

The T Account Illustrated

In the chapter on uses of accounting information and the basic financial statements, Shannon Realty had several transactions that involved the receipt or payment of cash. These transactions can be summarized in the Cash account by recording receipts on the left (debit) side of the account and payments on the right (credit) side:

Point to Emphasize: Notice that the debits and credits do not act independently. That is, one is netted out against the other to produce the account balance.

Cash

(1)	50,000	(2)	35,000
(5)	1,500	(4)	200
(7)	1,000	(8)	1,000
		(9)	400
		(11)	600
	52,500		37,200
Bal.	15,300		

The cash receipts on the left total $52,500. (The total is written in small figures so that it cannot be confused with an actual debit entry.) The cash payments on the right total $37,200. These totals are simply working totals, or footings. Footings, which are calculated at the end of each month, are an easy way to determine cash on hand. The difference in dollars between the total debit footing and the total credit footing is called the balance, or *account balance.* If the balance is a debit, it is written on the left side. If it is a credit, it is written on the right side. Notice that Shannon Realty's Cash account has a debit balance of $15,300 ($52,500 − $37,200). This is the amount of cash the business has on hand at the end of the month.

Analyzing and Processing Transactions

The two rules of double-entry bookkeeping are that every transaction affects at least two accounts and that the total of the debits must equal the total of the credits. In other words, for every transaction, one or more accounts must be debited and one or more accounts must be credited, and the total dollar amount of the debits must equal the total dollar amount of the credits.

Look again at the accounting equation:

Assets = Liabilities + Owner's Equity

You can see that if a debit increases assets, then a credit must be used to increase liabilities or owner's equity because they are on opposite sides of the equal sign. Likewise, if a credit decreases assets, then a debit must be used to decrease liabilities or owner's equity. These rules can be shown as follows:

Teaching Note: Students often ask why the rules of debit and credit are what they are. Simply state that they are an *arbitrary* set of rules whose interrelationships make them work.

Assets		=	**Liabilities**		+	**Owner's Equity**	
Debit for increases (+)	Credit for decreases (−)		Debit for decreases (−)	Credit for increases (+)		Debit for decreases (−)	Credit for increases (+)

1. Increases in assets are debited to asset accounts. Decreases in assets are credited to asset accounts.
2. Increases in liabilities and owner's equity are credited to liability and owner's equity accounts. Decreases in liabilities and owner's equity are debited to liability and owner's equity accounts.

One of the more difficult points to understand is the application of double-entry rules to the owner's equity components. The key is to remember that withdrawals and expenses are deductions from owner's equity. Thus, transactions that *increase* withdrawals or expenses *decrease* owner's equity. Consider this expanded version of the accounting equation:

Reinforcement Exercise: To emphasize the importance of knowing the rules of debit and credit, have your students identify as a debit or a credit an increase in assets, a decrease in assets, an increase in liabilities, and so on.

Assets = Liabilities + Capital − Withdrawals + Revenues − Expenses

(Capital − Withdrawals + Revenues − Expenses = Owner's Equity)

This equation may be rearranged by shifting withdrawals and expenses to the left side, as follows:

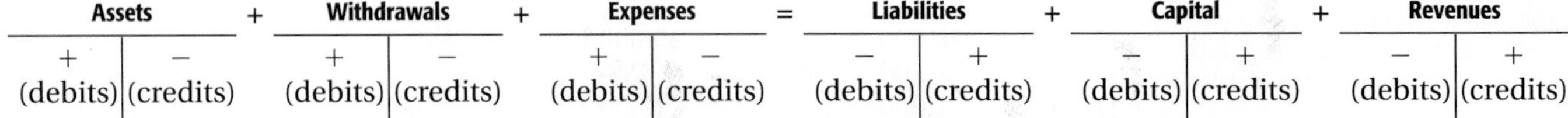

Assets		+	**Withdrawals**		+	**Expenses**		=	**Liabilities**		+	**Capital**		+	**Revenues**	
+ (debits)	− (credits)		+ (debits)	− (credits)		+ (debits)	− (credits)		− (debits)	+ (credits)		− (debits)	+ (credits)		− (debits)	+ (credits)

Note that the rules for double entry for all the accounts on the left of the equal sign are just the opposite of the rules for all the accounts on the right of the equal sign. Assets, withdrawals, and expenses are increased by debits and decreased by credits. Liabilities, capital, and revenues are increased by credits and decreased by debits.

With this basic information about double entry, it is possible to analyze and process transactions by following the five steps illustrated in Figure 2. To show how the steps are applied, assume that on June 1, Koenig Art Supplies borrows $100,000 from its bank on a promissory note. The transaction is analyzed and processed as follows:

Point to Emphasize: Identifying the accounts involved in a transaction takes practice. Often, account names are not used in the description of a transaction.

1. *Analyze the transaction to determine its effect on assets, liabilities, and owner's equity.* In this case, both an asset (Cash) and a liability (Notes Payable) increase. A

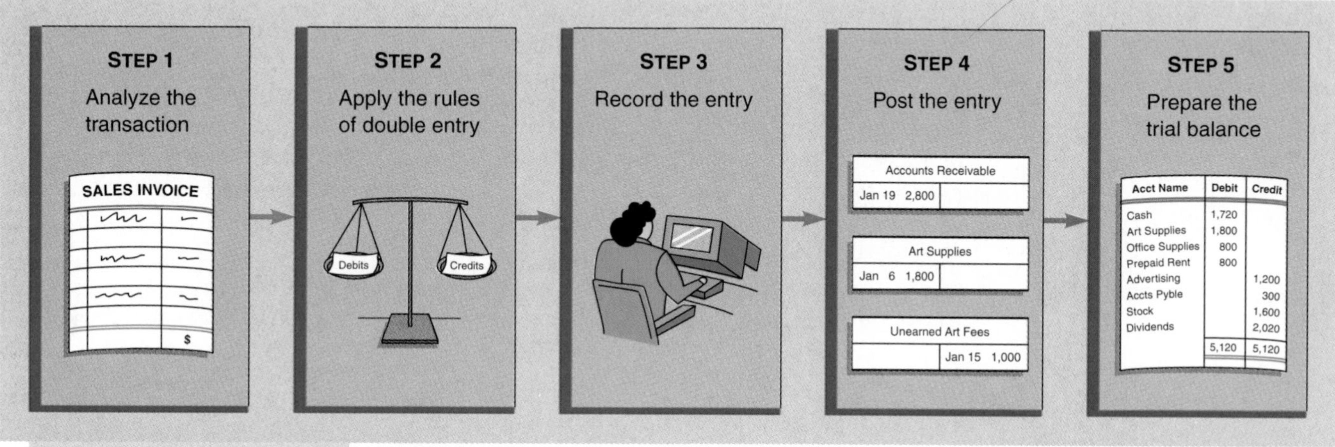

Figure 2
Analyzing and Processing Transactions

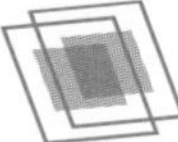

transaction is usually supported by some kind of source document—an invoice, a receipt, a check, or a contract. Here, a copy of the signed note would be the source document.

2. *Apply the rules of double entry.* Increases in assets are recorded by debits. Increases in liabilities are recorded by credits.
3. *Record the entry.* Transactions are recorded in chronological order in a journal. In one form of journal, which is explained in greater detail later on in this chapter, the date, the debit account, and the debit amount are recorded on one line, and the credit account and the credit amount are indented on the next line, as is shown below:

A = L + OE
\+ \+

		Dr.	**Cr.**
June 1	Cash	100,000	
	Notes Payable		100,000

This form is referred to as journal form and carries an explanation immediately following the entry. If more than one account is debited or credited, additional lines are used.

4. *Post the entry.* The entry is posted to the general ledger by transferring the date and amounts to the proper accounts. The T account is one form of ledger account.

Cash	
June 1 100,000	

Notes Payable	
	June 1 100,000

In formal records, step **3** is never omitted. However, for purposes of analysis, accountants often bypass step **3** and record entries directly in T accounts because doing so clearly and quickly shows the effects of transactions on the accounts. Some of the assignments in this chapter use the same approach to emphasize the analytical aspects of double entry.

5. *Prepare the trial balance to confirm the balance of the accounts.* Periodically, accountants prepare a trial balance to confirm that the accounts are still in balance after the recording and posting of transactions. Preparation of the trial balance is explained later in this chapter.

BUSINESS BULLETIN: TECHNOLOGY IN PRACTICE

In computerized accounting systems, it is essential that transactions be recorded properly because most of the subsequent processing is done automatically. Thus, the most important steps in the process are analyzing the transaction and applying the rules of double entry. The acronym GIGO describes what happens if transactions are incorrectly analyzed and recorded: **g**arbage **i**n, **g**arbage **o**ut.

Transaction Analysis Illustrated

OBJECTIVE 4

Apply the steps for transaction analysis and processing to simple transactions

In the next few pages, we examine the transactions for Joan Miller Advertising Agency during the month of January. In the discussion, we illustrate the principle of duality and show how transactions are recorded in the accounts.

January 1: Joan Miller invests $10,000 to start her own advertising agency.

A = L + OE
\+   +

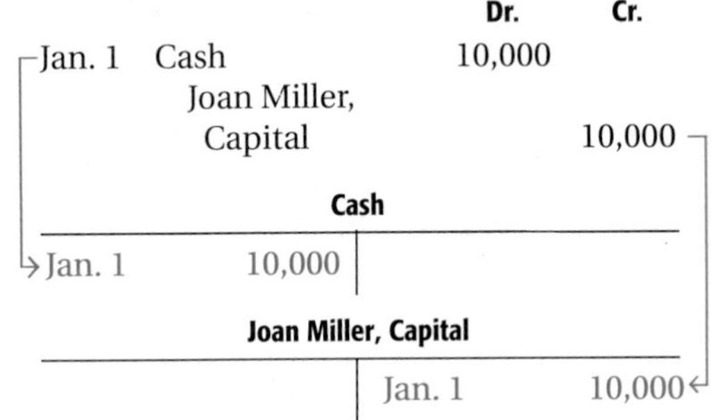

		Dr.	Cr.
Jan. 1	Cash	10,000	
	Joan Miller, Capital		10,000

Cash

Jan. 1	10,000		

Joan Miller, Capital

		Jan. 1	10,000

Transaction: Owner's investment.
Analysis: Assets increase. Owner's equity increases.
Rules: Increases in assets are recorded by debits. Increases in owner's equity are recorded by credits.
Entry: The increase in assets is recorded by a debit to Cash. The increase in owner's equity is recorded by a credit to Joan Miller, Capital.

Related Text Assignments:
Q: 14, 15, 16, 20
SE: 4, 5
E: 4, 5, 7, 12
P: 1, 2, 3, 4, 5, 6, 7, 8
SD: 2, 4, 5
FRA: 1, 2, 3, 4

Common Student Error: For this transaction, many students incorrectly credit "Owner's Equity" rather than Joan Miller, Capital. Remind them that owner's equity is an account *classification,* not an account title.

Analysis: If Joan Miller had invested assets other than cash in the business, the appropriate asset accounts would be debited.

Point to Emphasize: Notice the exchange of one asset for another asset.

January 2: Rents an office, paying two months' rent, $800, in advance.

A = L + OE
\+
−

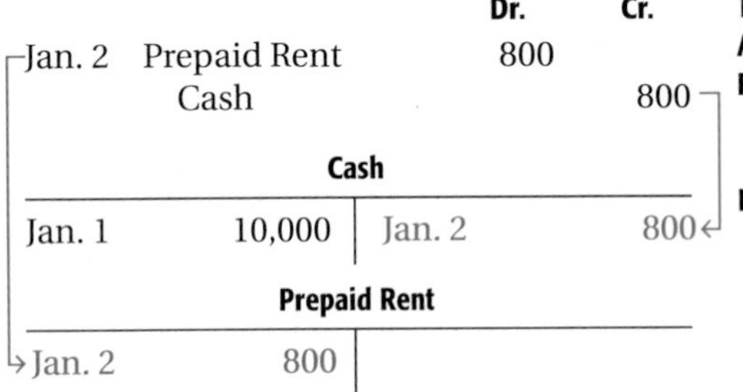

		Dr.	Cr.
Jan. 2	Prepaid Rent	800	
	Cash		800

Cash

Jan. 1	10,000	Jan. 2	800

Prepaid Rent

Jan. 2	800		

Transaction: Rent paid in advance.
Analysis: Assets increase. Assets decrease.
Rules: Increases in assets are recorded by debits. Decreases in assets are recorded by credits.
Entry: The increase in assets is recorded by a debit to Prepaid Rent. The decrease in assets is recorded by a credit to Cash.

Teaching Note: For this learning objective, it is extremely beneficial to discuss as many related end-of-chapter exercises and problems as time permits.

January 3: Orders art supplies, $1,800, and office supplies, $800.

Analysis: No entry is made because no transaction has occurred. According to the recognition issue, there is no liability until the supplies are shipped or received and there is an obligation to pay for them.

January 4: Purchases art equipment, $4,200, with cash.

A = L + OE
+
−

Common Student Error: Students often attach unnecessary verbs to account names. Point out that terms such as "Cash Paid" and "Art Equipment Purchased" are not acceptable account names.

		Dr.	Cr.
Jan. 4	Art Equipment	4,200	
	Cash		4,200

Cash

Jan. 1	10,000	Jan. 2	800
		4	4,200

Art Equipment

Jan. 4	4,200		

Transaction: Purchase of equipment.
Analysis: Assets increase. Assets decrease.
Rules: Increases in assets are recorded by debits. Decreases in assets are recorded by credits.
Entry: The increase in assets is recorded by a debit to Art Equipment. The decrease in assets is recorded by a credit to Cash.

January 5: Purchases office equipment, $3,000, from Morgan Equipment; pays $1,500 in cash and agrees to pay the rest next month.

A = L + OE
+ +
−

Point to Emphasize: Notice that the office equipment is recorded at the full $3,000, even though only half of it has been paid for.

		Dr.	Cr.
Jan. 5	Office Equipment	3,000	
	Cash		1,500
	Accounts Payable		1,500

Cash

Jan. 1	10,000	Jan. 2	800
		4	4,200
		5	1,500

Office Equipment

Jan. 5	3,000		

Accounts Payable

		Jan. 5	1,500

Transaction: Purchase of equipment and partial payment.
Analysis: Assets increase. Assets decrease. Liabilities increase.
Rules: Increases in assets are recorded by debits. Decreases in assets are recorded by credits. Increases in liabilities are recorded by credits.
Entry: The increase in assets is recorded by a debit to Office Equipment. The decrease in assets is recorded by a credit to Cash. The increase in liabilities is recorded by a credit to Accounts Payable.

January 6: Purchases art supplies, $1,800, and office supplies, $800, from Taylor Supply Company, on credit.

A = L + OE
+ +
+

Point to Emphasize: Notice that Accounts Payable is used when there is a delay between purchase and payment.

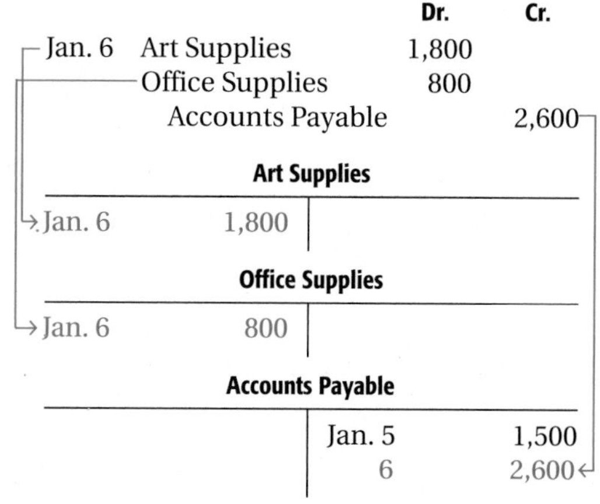

		Dr.	Cr.
Jan. 6	Art Supplies	1,800	
	Office Supplies	800	
	Accounts Payable		2,600

Art Supplies

Jan. 6	1,800		

Office Supplies

Jan. 6	800		

Accounts Payable

		Jan. 5	1,500
		6	2,600

Transaction: Purchase of supplies on credit.
Analysis: Assets increase. Liabilities increase.
Rules: Increases in assets are recorded by debits. Increases in liabilities are recorded by credits.
Entry: The increase in assets is recorded by debits to Art Supplies and Office Supplies. The increase in liabilities is recorded by a credit to Accounts Payable.

January 8: Pays for a one-year life insurance policy, $480, with coverage effective January 1.

A = L + OE
+
−

		Dr.	Cr.
Jan. 8	Prepaid Insurance	480	
	Cash		480

Cash

Jan. 1	10,000	Jan. 2	800
		4	4,200
		5	1,500
		8	480

Prepaid Insurance

Jan. 8	480		

Transaction: Insurance purchased in advance.
Analysis: Assets increase. Assets decrease.
Rules: Increases in assets are recorded by debits. Decreases in assets are recorded by credits.
Entry: The increase in assets is recorded by a debit to Prepaid Insurance. The decrease in assets is recorded by a credit to Cash.

January 9: Pays Taylor Supply Company $1,000 of the amount owed.

A = L + OE
− −

Point to Emphasize: Notice that Accounts Payable, not Art Supplies or Office Supplies, is debited. Also explain that a liability usually is credited before it can be debited.

		Dr.	Cr.
Jan. 9	Accounts Payable	1,000	
	Cash		1,000

Cash

Jan. 1	10,000	Jan. 2	800
		4	4,200
		5	1,500
		8	480
		9	1,000

Accounts Payable

Jan. 9	1,000	Jan. 5	1,500
		6	2,600

Transaction: Partial payment on a liability.
Analysis: Assets decrease. Liabilities decrease.
Rules: Decreases in liabilities are recorded by debits. Decreases in assets are recorded by credits.
Entry: The decrease in liabilities is recorded by a debit to Accounts Payable. The decrease in assets is recorded by a credit to Cash.

January 10: Performs a service for an automobile dealer by placing advertisements in the newspaper and collects a fee, $1,400.

A = L + OE
+ +

Common Student Error: Often, students credit the owner's Capital account and not the revenue account (such as Advertising Fees Earned). Although this is theoretically correct, they should know that, in practice, the owner's Capital account is not updated for revenues (or for expenses or withdrawals) until the end of the accounting period.

		Dr.	Cr.
Jan. 10	Cash	1,400	
	Advertising Fees Earned		1,400

Cash

Jan. 1	10,000	Jan. 2	800
10	1,400	4	4,200
		5	1,500
		8	480
		9	1,000

Advertising Fees Earned

		Jan. 10	1,400

Transaction: Revenue earned and cash collected.
Analysis: Assets increase. Owner's equity increases.
Rules: Increases in assets are recorded by debits. Increases in owner's equity are recorded by credits.
Entry: The increase in assets is recorded by a debit to Cash. The increase in owner's equity is recorded by a credit to Advertising Fees Earned.

January 12: Pays the secretary two weeks' wages, $600.

A = L + OE
−   −

		Dr.	Cr.
Jan. 12	Wages Expense	600	
	Cash		600

Cash

Jan. 1	10,000	Jan. 2	800
10	1,400	4	4,200
		5	1,500
		8	480
		9	1,000
		12	600

Wages Expense

Jan. 12	600		

Transaction: Payment of wages expense.
Analysis: Assets decrease. Owner's equity decreases.
Rules: Decreases in owner's equity are recorded by debits. Decreases in assets are recorded by credits.
Entry: The decrease in owner's equity is recorded by a debit to Wages Expense. The decrease in assets is recorded by a credit to Cash.

January 15: Accepts an advance fee, $1,000, for artwork to be done for another agency.

A = L + OE
+ +

Common Student Error: Here, many students credit Art Fees Earned, forgetting that a liability account is what must be credited.

		Dr.	Cr.
Jan. 15	Cash	1,000	
	Unearned Art Fees		1,000

Cash

Jan. 1	10,000	Jan. 2	800
10	1,400	4	4,200
15	1,000	5	1,500
		8	480
		9	1,000
		12	600

Unearned Art Fees

		Jan. 15	1,000

Transaction: Payment received for future services.
Analysis: Assets increase. Liabilities increase.
Rules: Increases in assets are recorded by debits. Increases in liabilities are recorded by credits.
Entry: The increase in assets is recorded by a debit to Cash. The increase in liabilities is recorded by a credit to Unearned Art Fees.

January 19: Performs a service by placing several major advertisements for Ward Department Stores. The fee, $2,800, is billed now but will be collected next month.

A = L + OE
+   +

Point to Emphasize: Notice that the revenue is recognized even though payment has not been received yet. Also, point out that Accounts Receivable is used when there is a delay between the sale of services or merchandise and payment.

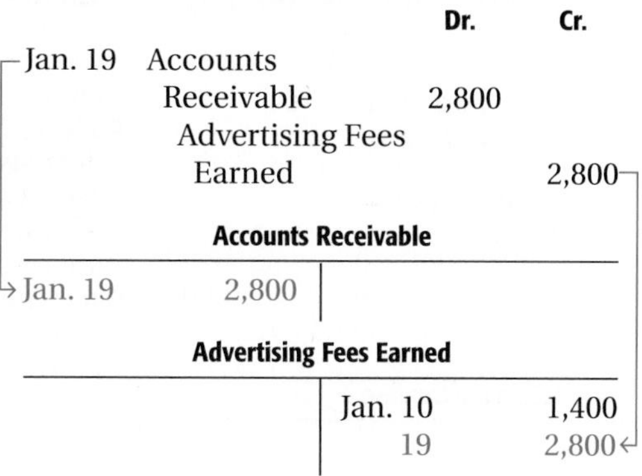

		Dr.	Cr.
Jan. 19	Accounts Receivable	2,800	
	Advertising Fees Earned		2,800

Accounts Receivable

Jan. 19	2,800		

Advertising Fees Earned

		Jan. 10	1,400
		19	2,800

Transaction: Revenue earned, to be received later.
Analysis: Assets increase. Owner's equity increases.
Rules: Increases in assets are recorded by debits. Increases in owner's equity are recorded by credits.
Entry: The increase in assets is recorded by a debit to Accounts Receivable. The increase in owner's equity is recorded by a credit to Advertising Fees Earned.

January 26: Pays the secretary two more weeks' wages, $600.

A = L + OE
− −

		Dr.	Cr.
Jan. 26	Wages Expense	600	
	Cash		600

Cash

Jan. 1	10,000	Jan. 2	800
10	1,400	4	4,200
15	1,000	5	1,500
		8	480
		9	1,000
		12	600
		26	600

Wages Expense

Jan. 12	600		
26	600		

Transaction: Payment of wages expense.
Analysis: Assets decrease. Owner's equity decreases.
Rules: Decreases in owner's equity are recorded by debits. Decreases in assets are recorded by credits.
Entry: The decrease in owner's equity is recorded by a debit to Wages Expense. The decrease in assets is recorded by a credit to Cash.

January 29: Receives and pays the utility bill, $100.

A = L + OE
− −

		Dr.	Cr.
Jan. 29	Utilities Expense	100	
	Cash		100

Cash

Jan. 1	10,000	Jan. 2	800
10	1,400	4	4,200
15	1,000	5	1,500
		8	480
		9	1,000
		12	600
		26	600
		29	100

Utilities Expense

Jan. 29	100		

Transaction: Payment of utilities expense.
Analysis: Assets decrease. Owner's equity decreases.
Rules: Decreases in owner's equity are recorded by debits. Decreases in assets are recorded by credits.
Entry: The decrease in owner's equity is recorded by a debit to Utilities Expense. The decrease in assets is recorded by a credit to Cash.

January 30: Receives (but does not pay) the telephone bill, $70.

A = L + OE
+ −

Discussion Question: Why are the expense and liability recognized at this point? After all, payment has not yet been made. **Answer:** An expense has been incurred because telephone services have been used. The obligation to pay exists.

		Dr.	Cr.
Jan. 30	Telephone Expense	70	
	Accounts Payable		70

Accounts Payable

Jan. 9	1,000	Jan. 5	1,500
		6	2,600
		30	70

Telephone Expense

Jan. 30	70		

Transaction: Expense incurred, to be paid later.
Analysis: Liabilities increase. Owner's equity decreases.
Rules: Decreases in owner's equity are recorded by debits. Increases in liabilities are recorded by credits.
Entry: The decrease in owner's equity is recorded by a debit to Telephone Expense. The increase in liabilities is recorded by a credit to Accounts Payable.

Discussion Question: Why are withdrawals not considered an expense?
Answer: Expenses are costs of operating a business, but withdrawals are assets that the owner takes out of the business.

A = L + OE
– –

January 31: Joan Miller withdraws $1,400 from the business for personal living expenses.

		Dr.	Cr.
Jan. 31	Joan Miller, Withdrawals	1,400	
	Cash		1,400

Cash

Jan. 1	10,000	Jan. 2	800
10	1,400	4	4,200
15	1,000	5	1,500
		8	480
		9	1,000
		12	600
		26	600
		29	100
		31	1,400

Joan Miller, Withdrawals

Jan. 31	1,400		

Transaction: Owner's withdrawal for personal use.
Analysis: Assets decrease. Owner's equity decreases.
Rules: Decreases in assets are recorded by credits. Decreases in owner's equity are recorded by debits.
Entry: The decrease in owner's equity is recorded by a debit to Joan Miller, Withdrawals. The decrease in assets is recorded by a credit to Cash.

Summary of Transactions

In Exhibit 2, the transactions for January are shown in their accounts and in relation to the accounting equation.

The Trial Balance

OBJECTIVE 5

Prepare a trial balance and describe its value and limitations

Related Text Assignments:
Q: 17, 18, 19, 24
SE: 3, 6, 7
E: 3, 6, 8, 9, 10, 11
P: 2, 3, 4, 5, 7, 8
SD: 5

Point to Emphasize: The trial balance is prepared at the end of the accounting period. It is an initial check that the ledger is in balance.

Instructional Strategy: Play a *Jeopardy*-type game using E 3 to reinforce account classifications and normal balance. All students participate by writing their own answers on a piece of paper, with headings as shown in the text. Consider performance-based rewards.

For every amount debited, an equal amount must be credited. This means that the total of debits and credits in the T accounts must be equal. To test this, the accountant periodically prepares a trial balance. Exhibit 3 shows a trial balance for Joan Miller Advertising Agency. It was prepared from the accounts in Exhibit 2.

The trial balance may be prepared at any time but is usually prepared on the last day of the month. Here are the steps in preparing a trial balance:

1. List each T account that has a balance, with debit balances in the left column and credit balances in the right column. Accounts are listed in the order in which they appear in the ledger.
2. Add each column.
3. Compare the totals of the columns.

In accounts in which increases are recorded by debits, the normal balance (the usual balance) is a debit balance; where increases are recorded by credits, the normal balance is a credit balance. Table 1 summarizes the normal account balances of the major account categories. According to the table, the T account Accounts Payable (a liability) typically has a credit balance and is copied into the trial balance as a credit balance.

Once in a while, a transaction leaves an account with a balance that is not "normal." For example, when a company overdraws its account at the bank, its Cash account (an asset) will show a credit balance instead of a debit balance. The "abnormal" balance should be copied into the trial balance columns as it stands, as a debit or a credit.

Exhibit 2. Summary of Sample Accounts and Transactions for Joan Miller Advertising Agency

Assets = Liabilities + Owner's Equity

Assets

Cash

Jan. 1	10,000	Jan. 2	800
10	1,400	4	4,200
15	1,000	5	1,500
		8	480
		9	1,000
		12	600
		26	600
		29	100
		31	1,400
	12,400		**10,680**
Bal.	**1,720**		

Accounts Receivable

Jan. 19	2,800		

Art Supplies

Jan. 6	1,800		

Office Supplies

Jan. 6	800		

Prepaid Rent

Jan. 2	800		

Prepaid Insurance

Jan. 8	480		

Art Equipment

Jan. 4	4,200		

Office Equipment

Jan. 5	3,000		

Liabilities

Accounts Payable

Jan. 9	1,000	Jan. 5	1,500
		6	2,600
		30	70
	1,000		**4,170**
		Bal.	**3,170**

Unearned Art Fees

		Jan. 15	1,000

Owner's Equity

Joan Miller, Capital

		Jan. 1	10,000

Joan Miller, Withdrawals

Jan. 31	1,400		

Advertising Fees Earned

		Jan. 10	1,400
		19	2,800
		Bal.	**4,200**

Wages Expense

Jan. 12	600		
26	600		
Bal.	**1,200**		

Utilities Expense

Jan. 29	100		

Telephone Expense

Jan. 30	70		

Teaching Note: Give your students several examples of errors made in the journal, ledger, and trial balance, and ask them to state whether or not each error produces an imbalance in the trial balance.

The trial balance proves whether or not the ledger is in balance. *In balance* means that the total of all debits recorded equals the total of all credits recorded. But the trial balance does not prove that the transactions were analyzed correctly or recorded in the proper accounts. For example, there is no way of determining from the trial balance that a debit should have been made in the Art Equipment account rather than the Office Equipment account. And the trial balance does not detect whether transactions have been omitted, because equal debits and credits will have been omitted. Also, if an error of the same amount is made in both a debit and a credit, it will not be discovered by the trial balance. The trial balance proves only that the debits and credits in the accounts are in balance.

Point to Emphasize: Notice that the accounts are listed in the same order as in the ledger. At this point, the Capital account does not reflect any revenues, expenses, or withdrawals for the period.

Exhibit 3. Trial Balance

Joan Miller Advertising Agency
Trial Balance
January 31, 20xx

Cash	$ 1,720	
Accounts Receivable	2,800	
Art Supplies	1,800	
Office Supplies	800	
Prepaid Rent	800	
Prepaid Insurance	480	
Art Equipment	4,200	
Office Equipment	3,000	
Accounts Payable		$ 3,170
Unearned Art Fees		1,000
Joan Miller, Capital		10,000
Joan Miller, Withdrawals	1,400	
Advertising Fees Earned		4,200
Wages Expense	1,200	
Utilities Expense	100	
Telephone Expense	70	
	$18,370	$18,370

If the debit and credit columns of the trial balance are not equal, look for one or more of the following errors: (1) a debit was entered in an account as a credit, or vice versa; (2) the balance of an account was computed incorrectly; (3) an error was made in carrying the account balance to the trial balance; or (4) the trial balance was summed incorrectly.

Other than simply incorrectly adding the columns, the two most common mistakes in preparing a trial balance are (1) recording an account with a debit balance as a credit, or vice versa, and (2) transposing two numbers when transferring an amount to the trial balance (for example, entering $23,459 as $23,549). The first of these mistakes causes the trial balance to be out of balance by an amount divisible

Teaching Note: A mnemonic for accounts with normal debit balances is AWE–Assets, Withdrawals, and Expenses.

Table 1. Normal Account Balances of Major Account Categories

	Increases Recorded by		Normal Balance	
Account Category	Debit	Credit	Debit	Credit
Assets	x		x	
Liabilities		x		x
Owner's Equity:				
Capital		x		x
Withdrawals	x		x	
Revenues		x		x
Expenses	x		x	

by 2. The second causes the trial balance to be out of balance by a number divisible by 9. Thus, if a trial balance is out of balance and the addition has been verified, determine the amount by which the trial balance is out of balance and divide it first by 2 and then by 9. If the amount is divisible by 2, look in the trial balance for an amount equal to the quotient. If you find the amount, it is probably in the wrong column. If the amount is divisible by 9, trace each amount to the ledger account balance, checking carefully for a transposition error. If neither of these techniques identifies the error, first recompute the balance of each account in the ledger, then, if the error still has not been found, retrace each posting from the journal to the ledger.

Some Notes on Presentation

A ruled line appears in financial reports before each subtotal or total to indicate that the amounts above are added or subtracted. It is common practice to use a double line under a final total to show that it has been checked, or verified.

Dollar signs ($) are required in all financial statements, including the balance sheet and income statement, and in the trial balance and other schedules. On these statements, a dollar sign should be placed before the first amount in each column and before the first amount in a column following a ruled line. Dollar signs in the same column are aligned. Dollar signs are not used in journals and ledgers.

Point to Emphasize: Placing a dash in the cents column is preferable to leaving it blank. (It's possible to infer from a blank cents column that the bookkeeper simply forgot to enter the figure for cents.)

On unruled paper, commas and decimal points are used in dollar amounts. On paper with ruled columns—like the paper in journals and ledgers—commas and decimal points are not needed. In this book, because most problems and illustrations are in whole dollar amounts, the cents column usually is omitted. When accountants deal with whole dollars, they often use a dash in the cents column to indicate whole dollars rather than take the time to write zeros.

Recording and Posting Transactions

OBJECTIVE 6

Record transactions in the general journal

Related Text Assignments:
Q: 20, 21, 23, 24
SE: 8
E: 12, 13
P: 3, 5, 8

Let us now take a look at the formal process of recording transactions in the general journal and posting them to the ledger.

The General Journal

Point to Emphasize: The journal is a chronological record of events. Only the general journal is discussed in this chapter.

Teaching Note: Refer students to Exhibit 4 as you describe the general journal.

As you have seen, transactions can be entered directly into the accounts. But this method makes identifying individual transactions or finding errors very difficult because the debit is recorded in one account and the credit in another. The solution is to record all transactions chronologically in a journal. The journal is sometimes called the *book of original entry* because it is where transactions first enter the accounting records. Later, the debit and credit portions of each transaction can be transferred to the appropriate accounts in the ledger.

A separate journal entry is used to record each transaction, and the process of recording transactions is called journalizing.

Most businesses have more than one kind of journal. The simplest and most flexible type, and the one we focus on in this chapter, is the general journal. Entries in the general journal include the following information about each transaction:

1. The date
2. The names of the accounts debited and the dollar amounts on the same lines in the debit column

Instructional Strategy: Have students work SD 2 in small groups. This exercise requires a journal entry and comprehension of Objective 1.

A = L + OE
\+ +
\+

A = L + OE
\+
−

Exhibit 4. The General Journal

General Journal					Page 1
Date		Description	Post. Ref.	Debit	Credit
20xx					
Jan.	6	Art Supplies		1,800	
		Office Supplies		800	
		Accounts Payable			2,600
		Purchase of art and office supplies on credit			
	8	Prepaid Insurance		480	
		Cash			480
		Paid one-year life insurance premium			

3. The names of the accounts credited and the dollar amounts on the same lines in the credit column
4. An explanation of the transaction
5. The account identification numbers, if appropriate

Exhibit 4 displays two of the earlier transactions for Joan Miller Advertising Agency. The procedure for recording transactions in the general journal follows:

Common Student Error: Check your students' journals for proper form. Frequent errors are forgetting to skip a space between entries, not indenting the credits, using the Post. Ref. column before posting is done, journalizing amounts that do not balance, entering a credit before a debit, and forgetting to enter the explanation.

Common Student Confusion: Invariably, a student asks if it matters *which* debit is listed first or *which* credit is listed before the others. The order does not matter, as long as all the debits in the entry are listed before any of the credits.

1. Record the date by writing the year in small figures on the first line at the top of the first column, the month on the next line of the first column, and the day in the second column opposite the month. For subsequent entries on the same page for the same month and year, the month and year can be omitted.
2. Write the exact names of the accounts debited and credited in the Description column. Write the names of the accounts debited next to the left margin of the second line, and indent the names of the accounts credited. The explanation is placed on the next line and further indented. The explanation should be brief but sufficient to explain and identify the transaction. A transaction can have more than one debit or credit entry; this is called a compound entry. In a compound entry, all debit accounts are listed before any credit accounts. (The January 6 transaction of Joan Miller Advertising Agency in Exhibit 4 is an example of a compound entry.)
3. Write the debit amounts in the appropriate column opposite the accounts to be debited, and write the credit amounts in the appropriate column opposite the accounts to be credited.
4. At the time the transactions are recorded, nothing is placed in the Post. Ref. (posting reference) column. (This column is sometimes called *LP* or *Folio.*) Later, if the company uses account numbers to identify accounts in the ledger, fill in the account numbers to provide a convenient cross-reference from the general journal to the ledger and to indicate that the entry has been posted to the ledger. If the accounts are not numbered, use a checkmark (√).
5. It is customary to skip a line after each journal entry.

OBJECTIVE 7

Post transactions from the general journal to the ledger

The General Ledger

The general journal is used to record the details of each transaction. The general ledger is used to update each account.

Teaching Note: Compare and contrast the structure of the general ledger (Exhibit 5) with that of the general journal (Exhibit 4). It is especially important at this point that students be able to compute account balances.

Exhibit 5. Accounts Payable in the General Ledger

General Ledger

Accounts Payable						Account No. 212	
						Balance	
Date		Item	Post. Ref.	Debit	Credit	Debit	Credit
20xx							
Jan.	5		J1		1,500		1,500
	6		J1		2,600		4,100
	9		J1	1,000			3,100
	30		J2		70		3,170

Related Text Assignments:
Q: 22, 23, 24
SE: 9
E: 13
P: 3, 5, 8

The Ledger Account Form

The T account is a simple, direct means of recording transactions. In practice, a somewhat more complicated form of the account is needed in order to record more information. The ledger account form, which contains four columns for dollar amounts, is illustrated in Exhibit 5.

The account title and number appear at the top of the account form. The date of the transaction appears in the first two columns as it does in the journal. The Item column is used only rarely to identify transactions, because explanations already appear in the journal. The Post. Ref. column is used to note the journal page where the original entry for the transaction can be found. The dollar amount of the entry is entered in the appropriate Debit or Credit column, and a new account balance is computed in the final two columns after each entry. The advantage of this form of account over the T account is that the current balance of the account is readily available.

Posting to the Ledger

Teaching Note: Explain that posting is much like sorting mail. It is a tedious, but necessary, procedure, conveniently accomplished by a computer.

After transactions have been entered in the journal, they must be transferred to the ledger. The process of transferring journal entry information from the journal to the ledger is called posting. Posting is usually done after several entries have been made—for example, at the end of each day or less frequently, depending on the number of transactions.

Through posting, each amount in the Debit column of the journal is transferred into the Debit column of the appropriate account in the ledger, and each amount in the Credit column of the journal is transferred into the Credit column of the appropriate account in the ledger (see Exhibit 6). The steps in the posting process are listed below:

1. In the ledger, locate the debit account named in the journal entry.
2. Enter the date of the transaction and, in the Post. Ref. column of the ledger, the journal page number from which the entry comes.
3. Enter in the Debit column of the ledger account the amount of the debit as it appears in the journal.
4. Calculate the account balance and enter it in the appropriate balance column.
5. Enter in the Post. Ref. column of the journal the account number to which the amount has been posted.
6. Repeat the same five steps for the credit side of the journal entry.

Instructional Strategy: To close class, let students summarize the flow of events through the accounting system by correctly ordering the items in Q 24.

Notice that step **5** is the last step in the posting process for each debit and credit. In addition to serving as an easy reference between the journal entry and the ledger account, this entry in the Post. Ref. column of the journal indicates that all steps for the item have been completed. This allows accountants who have been called away from their work to easily find where they were before the interruption.

Common Student Error: When students work their first posting assignment, they often misuse or forget to use the Post. Ref. columns. Emphasize the cross-referencing aspect of these columns.

A = L + OE
+ −

Exhibit 6. Posting from the General Journal to the Ledger

General Journal ② Page 2

Date		Description	Post. Ref.	Debit	Credit
20xx	②	①	⑤	③	
Jan.	30	Telephone Expense	513	70	
		Accounts Payable	212		70
		Received bill for telephone expense			

General Ledger

Accounts Payable — Account No. 212

Date		Item	Post. Ref.	Debit	Credit	Balance Debit	Balance Credit
20xx							
Jan.	5		J1		1,500		1,500
	6		J1		2,600		4,100
	9		J1	1,000			3,100
	30		J2		70		3,170

General Ledger

Telephone Expense — Account No. 513

Date		Item	Post. Ref.	Debit	Credit	Balance Debit	Balance Credit
20xx						④	
Jan.	30		J2	70		70	

Discussion Question: How would you know if a bookkeeper had posted only Telephone Expense and not Accounts Payable? **Answer:** The "513" would appear in the Post. Ref. column of the journal, but the "212" would not.

BUSINESS BULLETIN: TECHNOLOGY IN PRACTICE

In computerized accounting systems, posting is done automatically and the trial balance can be easily prepared as often as needed. Any accounts with abnormal balances are highlighted for investigation. Some general ledger software packages for small businesses list the trial balance amounts in a single column, with credit balances shown as minuses. In such cases, the trial balance is in balance if the total is zero.

Chapter Review

REVIEW OF LEARNING OBJECTIVES

1. **Explain, in simple terms, the generally accepted ways of solving the measurement issues of recognition, valuation, and classification.** To measure a business transaction, the accountant determines when the transaction occurred (the recognition issue), what value should be placed on the transaction (the valuation issue), and how the components of the transaction should be categorized (the classification issue). In general, recognition occurs when title passes, and a transaction is valued at the exchange price, the cost at the time the transaction is recognized. Classification refers to the categorizing of transactions according to a system of accounts.
2. **Describe the chart of accounts and recognize commonly used accounts.** An account is a device for storing data from transactions. There is one account for each asset, liability, and component of owner's equity, including revenues and expenses. The ledger is a book or file consisting of all of a company's accounts arranged according to a chart of accounts. Commonly used asset accounts are Cash, Notes Receivable, Accounts Receivable, Prepaid Expenses, Land, Buildings, and Equipment. Common liability accounts are Notes Payable, Accounts Payable, Wages Payable, and Mortgage Payable. Common owner's equity accounts are Capital, Withdrawals, and revenue and expense accounts.
3. **Define *double-entry system* and state the rules for double entry.** In the double-entry system, each transaction must be recorded with at least one debit and one credit so that the total dollar amount of the debits equals the total dollar amount of the credits. The rules for double entry are (1) increases in assets are debited to asset accounts; decreases in assets are credited to asset accounts; and (2) increases in liabilities and owner's equity are credited to those accounts; decreases in liabilities and owner's equity are debited to those accounts.
4. **Apply the steps for transaction analysis and processing to simple transactions.** The procedure for analyzing transactions is (1) analyze the effect of the transaction on assets, liabilities, and owner's equity; (2) apply the appropriate double-entry rule; (3) record the entry; (4) post the entry; and (5) prepare a trial balance.
5. **Prepare a trial balance and describe its value and limitations.** A trial balance is used to check that the debit and credit balances are equal. It is prepared by listing each account with its balance in the Debit or Credit column. Then the two columns are added and the totals are compared to test the balances. The major limitation of the trial balance is that even if debit and credit balances are equal, this does not guarantee that the transactions were analyzed correctly or recorded in the proper accounts.
6. **Record transactions in the general journal.** The general journal is a chronological record of all transactions. That record contains the date of each transaction, the names of the accounts and the dollar amounts debited and credited, an explanation of each entry, and the account numbers to which postings have been made.
7. **Post transactions from the general journal to the ledger.** After transactions have been entered in the general journal, they are posted to the ledger. Posting is done by transferring each amount in the Debit column of the general journal to the Debit column of the appropriate account in the ledger, and transferring each amount in the Credit column of the general journal to the Credit column of the appropriate account in the ledger. After each entry is posted, a new balance is entered in the appropriate Balance column.

REVIEW OF CONCEPTS AND TERMINOLOGY

The following concepts and terms were introduced in this chapter:

LO 3 **Balance:** The difference in dollars between the total debit footing and the total credit footing of an account. Also called *account balance.*

LO 2 **Chart of accounts:** A scheme that assigns a unique number to each account to facilitate finding the account in the ledger; also, the list of account numbers and titles.

LO 1 **Classification:** The process of assigning transactions to the appropriate accounts.

LO 6 **Compound entry:** An entry that has more than one debit or credit entry.

LO 1 **Cost:** The exchange price associated with a business transaction at the point of recognition.

LO 1 **Cost principle:** The practice of recording a transaction at cost.

LO 3 **Credit:** The right side of an account.

LO 3 **Debit:** The left side of an account.

LO 3 **Double-entry system:** The accounting system in which each transaction is recorded with at least one debit and one credit so that the total dollar amount of debits and the total dollar amount of credits equal each other.

LO 3 **Footings:** Working totals of columns of numbers. To *foot* means to total a column of numbers.

LO 6 **General journal:** The simplest and most flexible type of journal.

LO 2 **General ledger:** The book or file that contains all or groups of the company's accounts, arranged in the order of the chart of accounts. Also called *ledger.*

LO 6 **Journal:** A chronological record of all transactions; the place where transactions first enter the accounting records. Also called *book of original entry.*

LO 6 **Journal entry:** The notations in the journal that are used to record a single transaction.

LO 3 **Journal form:** A form of journal in which the date, the debit account, and the debit amount are recorded on one line and the credit account and credit amount on the next line.

LO 6 **Journalizing:** The process of recording transactions in a journal.

LO 7 **Ledger account form:** The form of account that has four dollar amount columns: one column for debit entries, one column for credit entries, and two columns (debit and credit) for showing the balance of the account.

LO 5 **Normal balance:** The usual balance of an account; also the side (debit or credit) that increases the account.

LO 7 **Posting:** The process of transferring journal entry information from the journal to the ledger.

LO 1 **Recognition:** The determination of when a business transaction should be recorded.

LO 1 **Recognition point:** The predetermined time at which a transaction should be recorded; usually, the point at which title passes to the buyer.

LO 3 **Source document:** An invoice, check, receipt, or other document that supports a transaction.

LO 3 **T account:** The simplest form of an account, used to analyze transactions.

LO 5 **Trial balance:** A comparison of the total of debit and credit balances in the ledger to check that they are equal.

LO 1 **Valuation:** The process of assigning a monetary value to a business transaction.

REVIEW PROBLEM

Transaction Analysis, General Journal, Ledger Accounts, and Trial Balance

LO 4 LO 5 LO 6 LO 7

After graduation from veterinary school, Laura Cox entered private practice. The transactions of the business through May 27 are as follows:

20xx

May 1 Laura Cox invested $2,000 in her business bank account.
3 Paid $300 for two months' rent in advance for an office.
9 Purchased medical supplies for $200 in cash.
12 Purchased $400 of equipment on credit, making a 25 percent down payment.
15 Delivered a calf for a fee of $35.
18 Made a partial payment of $50 on the equipment purchased May 12.
27 Paid a utility bill of $40.

REQUIRED

1. Record these entries in the general journal.
2. Post the entries from the journal to the following accounts in the ledger: Cash (111); Medical Supplies (115); Prepaid Rent (117); Equipment (144); Accounts Payable (212); Laura Cox, Capital (311); Veterinary Fees Earned (411); and Utilities Expense (512).
3. Prepare a trial balance as of May 31.

ANSWER TO REVIEW PROBLEM

1. Record the journal entries.

General Journal — **Page 1**

Date		Description	Post. Ref.	Debit	Credit
20xx					
May	1	Cash	111	2,000	
		Laura Cox, Capital	311		2,000
		Deposited $2,000 in the business bank account			
	3	Prepaid Rent	117	300	
		Cash	111		300
		Paid two months' rent in advance for an office			
	9	Medical Supplies	115	200	
		Cash	111		200
		Purchased medical supplies for cash			
	12	Equipment	144	400	
		Accounts Payable	212		300
		Cash	111		100
		Purchased equipment on credit, paying 25 percent down			
	15	Cash	111	35	
		Veterinary Fees Earned	411		35
		Collected fee for delivery of a calf			
	18	Accounts Payable	212	50	
		Cash	111		50
		Partial payment for equipment purchased May 12			
	27	Utilities Expense	512	40	
		Cash	111		40
		Paid utility bill			

2. Post the transactions to the ledger accounts.

General Ledger

Cash — **Account No. 111**

Date		Item	Post. Ref.	Debit	Credit	Balance Debit	Balance Credit
20xx							
May	1		J1	2,000		2,000	
	3		J1		300	1,700	
	9		J1		200	1,500	
	12		J1		100	1,400	
	15		J1	35		1,435	
	18		J1		50	1,385	
	27		J1		40	1,345	

Medical Supplies — **Account No. 115**

Date		Item	Post. Ref.	Debit	Credit	Balance Debit	Balance Credit
20xx							
May	9		J1	200		200	

Prepaid Rent — **Account No. 117**

Date		Item	Post. Ref.	Debit	Credit	Balance Debit	Balance Credit
20xx							
May	3		J1	300		300	

Equipment — **Account No. 144**

Date		Item	Post. Ref.	Debit	Credit	Balance Debit	Balance Credit
20xx							
May	12		J1	400		400	

Accounts Payable — **Account No. 212**

Date		Item	Post. Ref.	Debit	Credit	Balance Debit	Balance Credit
20xx							
May	12		J1		300		300
	18		J1	50			250

(continued)

Laura Cox, Capital — **Account No. 311**

Date		Item	Post. Ref.	Debit	Credit	Balance Debit	Balance Credit
20xx May	1		J1		2,000		2,000

Veterinary Fees Earned — **Account No. 411**

Date		Item	Post. Ref.	Debit	Credit	Balance Debit	Balance Credit
20xx May	15		J1		35		35

Utilities Expense — **Account No. 512**

Date		Item	Post. Ref.	Debit	Credit	Balance Debit	Balance Credit
20xx May	27		J1	40		40	

3. Complete the trial balance.

Laura Cox, Veterinarian
Trial Balance
May 31, 20xx

Cash	$1,345	
Medical Supplies	200	
Prepaid Rent	300	
Equipment	400	
Accounts Payable		$ 250
Laura Cox, Capital		2,000
Veterinary Fees Earned		35
Utilities Expense	40	
	$2,285	$2,285

Chapter Assignments

BUILDING YOUR KNOWLEDGE FOUNDATION

Questions

1. What three issues underlie most accounting measurement decisions?
2. Why is recognition an issue for accountants?
3. A customer asks the owner of a store to save an item for him and says that he will pick it up and pay for it next week. The owner agrees to hold it. Should this transaction be recorded as a sale? Explain your answer.
4. Why is it practical for accountants to rely on original cost for valuation purposes?
5. Under the cost principle, changes in value after a transaction is recorded are not usually recognized in the accounts. Comment on this possible limitation of using original cost in accounting measurements.
6. What is an account, and how is it related to the ledger?
7. Tell whether each of the following accounts is an asset account, a liability account, or an owner's equity account:
   a. Notes Receivable
   b. Land
   c. Withdrawals
   d. Bonds Payable
   e. Prepaid Rent
   f. Insurance Expense
   g. Service Revenue
8. In the owner's equity accounts, why do accountants maintain separate accounts for revenues and expenses rather than using the Capital account?
9. Why is the system of recording entries called the double-entry system? What is significant about this system?
10. "Double-entry accounting refers to entering a transaction in both the journal and the ledger." Comment on this statement.
11. "Debits are bad; credits are good." Comment on this statement.
12. What are the rules of double entry for (a) assets, (b) liabilities, and (c) owner's equity?
13. Why are the rules of double entry the same for liabilities and owner's equity?
14. What is the meaning of the statement "The Cash account has a debit balance of $500"?
15. Explain why debits, which decrease owner's equity, also increase expenses, which are a component of owner's equity.
16. What are the five steps in analyzing and processing a transaction?
17. What does a trial balance prove?
18. What is the normal balance of Accounts Payable? Under what conditions could Accounts Payable have a debit balance?
19. Can errors be present even though a trial balance balances? Explain your answer.
20. Is it a good idea to forgo the journal and enter a transaction directly into the ledger? Explain your answer.
21. In recording entries in a journal, which is written first, the debit or the credit? How is indentation used in the journal?
22. What is the relationship between the journal and the ledger?
23. Describe each of the following:
   a. Account
   b. Journal
   c. Ledger
   d. Book of original entry
   e. Post. Ref. column
   f. Journalizing
   g. Posting
   h. Footings
   i. Compound entry

24. List the following six items in sequence to illustrate the flow of events through the accounting system:
    a. Analysis of the transaction
    b. Debits and credits posted from the journal to the ledger
    c. Occurrence of the business transaction
    d. Preparation of the financial statements
    e. Entry made in the journal
    f. Preparation of the trial balance

Short Exercises

LO 1 *Recognition*

SE 1. Which of the following events would be recognized and entered in the accounting records of Hawthorne Company? Why?

Jan. 10 Hawthorne Company places an order for office supplies.
Feb. 15 Hawthorne Company receives the office supplies and a bill for them.
Mar. 1 Hawthorne Company pays for the office supplies.

LO 2 *Classification of Accounts*

SE 2. Tell whether each of the following accounts is an asset, a liability, a revenue, an expense, or none of these.

a. Accounts Payable
b. Supplies
c. Withdrawals
d. Fees Earned
e. Supplies Expense
f. Accounts Receivable
g. Unearned Revenue
h. Equipment

LO 5 *Normal Balances*

SE 3. Tell whether the normal balance of each account in **SE 2** is a debit or a credit.

LO 4 *Transaction Analysis*

SE 4. For each transaction below, tell which account is debited and which account is credited.

May 2 Joe Hurley started a computer programming business, Hurley's Programming Service, by investing $5,000.
5 Purchased a computer for $2,500 in cash.
7 Purchased supplies on credit for $300.
19 Received cash for programming services performed, $500.
22 Received cash for programming services to be performed, $600.
25 Paid the rent for May, $650.
31 Billed a customer for programming services performed, $250.

LO 4 *Recording Transactions in T Accounts*

SE 5. Set up T accounts and record each transaction in **SE 4.** Determine the balance of each account.

LO 5 *Preparing a Trial Balance*

SE 6. From the T accounts created in **SE 5,** prepare a trial balance dated May 31, 20x1.

LO 5 *Correcting Errors in a Trial Balance*

SE 7. The trial balance at the top of the next page is out of balance. Assuming that all balances are normal, place the accounts in proper order and correct the trial balance so that debits equal credits.

Sanders Boating Service
Trial Balance
January 31, 20x1

Cash	$2,000	
Accounts Payable	400	
Fuel Expense		$ 800
Unearned Service Revenue	250	
Accounts Receivable		1,300
Prepaid Rent		150
Sara Sanders, Capital		2,800
Service Revenue	1,750	
Wages Expense		300
Sara Sanders, Withdrawals		650
	$4,400	$6,000

SE 8. LO 6 *Recording Transactions in the General Journal*

Prepare a general journal form like the one in Exhibit 4 and label it Page 4. Record the following transactions in the journal.

Sept. 6 Billed a customer for services performed, $1,900.
16 Received partial payment from the customer billed on Sept. 6, $900.

SE 9. LO 7 *Posting to the Ledger Accounts*

Prepare ledger account forms like the ones in Exhibit 5 for the following accounts: Cash (111), Accounts Receivable (113), and Service Revenue (411). Post the transactions that are recorded in **SE 8** to the ledger accounts, at the same time making proper posting references.

Exercises

E 1. LO 1 *Recognition*

Which of the following events would be recognized and recorded in the accounting records of the Sabatini Company on the date indicated?

Feb. 17 Sabatini Company offers to purchase a tract of land for $280,000. There is a high likelihood that the offer will be accepted.
Mar. 7 Sabatini Company receives notice that its rent will be increased from $1,000 per month to $1,200 per month effective April 1.
Apr. 28 Sabatini Company receives its utility bill for the month of April. The bill is not due until May 10.
May 19 Sabatini Company places a firm order for new office equipment costing $42,000.
June 27 The office equipment ordered on May 19 arrives. Payment is not due until September 1.

E 2. LO 1 *Application of Recognition Point*

Infelice's Body Shop uses a large amount of supplies in its business. The following table summarizes selected transaction data for orders of supplies purchased:

Order	Date Shipped	Date Received	Amount
a	April 28	May 7	$300
b	May 8	13	750
c	10	16	400
d	15	21	600
e	25	June 1	750
f	June 3	9	500

Determine the total purchases of supplies for May alone under each of the following assumptions:

1. Infelice's Body Shop recognizes purchases when orders are shipped.
2. Infelice's Body Shop recognizes purchases when orders are received.

LO 2 LO 5 *Classification of Accounts*

E 3. Listed below are the ledger accounts of the Kedzie Service Company:

a. Cash
b. Accounts Receivable
c. Sandra Kedzie, Capital
d. Sandra Kedzie, Withdrawals
e. Service Revenue
f. Prepaid Rent
g. Accounts Payable
h. Investments in Stocks and Bonds
i. Bonds Payable
j. Land
k. Supplies Expense
l. Prepaid Insurance
m. Utilities Expense
n. Fees Earned
o. Unearned Revenue
p. Office Equipment
q. Rent Payable
r. Notes Receivable
s. Interest Expense
t. Notes Payable
u. Supplies
v. Interest Receivable

Complete the following table, indicating with two Xs for each account its classification and its normal balance (whether a debit or credit increases the account):

Type of Account

Item	Asset	Liability	Owner's Equity				Normal Balance (increases balance)	
			Owner's Capital	Owner's Withdrawals	Revenue	Expense	Debit	Credit
a.	x						x	

LO 4 *Transaction Analysis*

E 4. Analyze each of the following transactions, following the example below the list.

a. Benny James established Benny's Barber Shop by placing $2,400 in a bank account.
b. Paid two months' rent in advance, $840.
c. Purchased supplies on credit, $120.
d. Received cash for barbering services, $100.
e. Paid for supplies purchased in **c.**
f. Paid utility bill, $72.
g. Took cash out of the business for personal expenses, $100.

Example

a. The asset Cash was increased. Increases in assets are recorded by debits. Debit Cash, $2,400. A component of owner's equity, Benny James, Capital, was increased. Increases in owner's equity are recorded by credits. Credit Benny James, Capital, $2,400.

LO 4 *Recording Transactions in T Accounts*

E 5. Open the following T accounts: Cash; Repair Supplies; Repair Equipment; Accounts Payable; Michelle Donato, Capital; Michelle Donato, Withdrawals; Repair Fees Earned; Salaries Expense; and Rent Expense. Record the following transactions for the month of June directly in the T accounts; use the letters to identify the transactions in your T accounts. Determine the balance in each account.

a. Michelle Donato opened the Eastmoor Repair Service by investing $4,300 in cash and $1,600 in repair equipment.
b. Paid $400 for current month's rent.
c. Purchased repair supplies on credit, $500.
d. Purchased additional repair equipment for cash, $300.
e. Paid salary to a helper, $450.
f. Paid $200 of amount purchased on credit in **c.**
g. Withdrew $600 from business for living expenses.
h. Accepted cash for repairs completed, $1,860.

LO 5 *Trial Balance*

E 6. After recording the transactions in **E 5,** prepare a trial balance in proper sequence for Eastmoor Repair Service as of June 30, 20xx.

E 7. LO 4 *Analysis of Transactions*

Explain each transaction (**a** through **h**) entered in the following T accounts.

Cash

	Dr.		Cr.
a.	60,000	b.	15,000
g.	1,500	e.	3,000
h.	900	f.	4,500

Accounts Receivable

	Dr.		Cr.
c.	6,000	g.	1,500

Equipment

	Dr.		Cr.
b.	15,000	h.	900
d.	9,000		

Accounts Payable

	Dr.		Cr.
f.	4,500	d.	9,000

J. Seymour, Capital

	Dr.		Cr.
		a.	60,000

Service Revenue

	Dr.		Cr.
		c.	6,000

Wages Expense

	Dr.		Cr.
e.	3,000		

E 8. LO 5 *Preparing a Trial Balance*

The following accounts of the Barnes Service Company as of October 31, 20xx, are listed in alphabetical order. The amount of Accounts Payable is omitted.

Accounts Payable	?	Equipment	$24,000
Accounts Receivable	$ 6,000	Land	10,400
Alvin Barnes, Capital	62,900	Notes Payable	40,000
Building	68,000	Prepaid Insurance	2,200
Cash	18,000		

Prepare a trial balance with the proper heading (see Exhibit 3) and with the accounts listed in the chart of accounts sequence (see Exhibit 1). Compute the balance of Accounts Payable.

E 9. LO 5 *Effect of Errors on a Trial Balance*

Which of the following errors would cause a trial balance to have unequal totals? Explain your answers.

a. A payment to a creditor was recorded as a debit to Accounts Payable for $172 and a credit to Cash for $127.
b. A payment of $200 to a creditor for an account payable was debited to Accounts Receivable and credited to Cash.
c. A purchase of office supplies of $560 was recorded as a debit to Office Supplies for $56 and a credit to Cash for $56.
d. A purchase of equipment for $600 was recorded as a debit to Supplies for $600 and a credit to Cash for $600.

E 10. LO 5 *Correcting Errors in a Trial Balance*

This was the trial balance for Gilliam Services at the end of September:

Gilliam Services
Trial Balance
September 30, 20xx

Cash	$ 3,840	
Accounts Receivable	5,660	
Supplies	120	
Prepaid Insurance	180	
Equipment	8,400	
Accounts Payable		$ 4,540
R. Gilliam, Capital		11,560
R. Gilliam, Withdrawals		700
Revenues		5,920
Salaries Expense	2,600	
Rent Expense	600	
Advertising Expense	340	
Utilities Expense	26	
	$21,766	$22,720

The trial balance does not balance because of a number of errors. Gilliam's accountant compared the amounts in the trial balance with the ledger, recomputed the account balances, and compared the postings. He found the following errors:

a. The balance of Cash was understated by $400.
b. A cash payment of $420 was credited to Cash for $240.
c. A debit of $120 to Accounts Receivable was not posted.
d. Supplies purchased for $60 were posted as a credit to Supplies.
e. A debit of $180 to Prepaid Insurance was not posted.
f. The Accounts Payable account had debits of $5,320 and credits of $9,180.
g. The Notes Payable account, with a credit balance of $2,400, was not included in the trial balance.
h. The debit balance of R. Gilliam, Withdrawals was listed in the trial balance as a credit.
i. A $200 debit to R. Gilliam, Withdrawals was posted as a credit.
j. The actual balance of Utilities Expense, $260, was listed as $26 in the trial balance.

Prepare a correct trial balance.

LO 5 *Preparing a Trial Balance*

E 11. The Ferraro Construction Company builds foundations for buildings and parking lots. The following alphabetical list shows the account balances as of November 30, 20xx.

Accounts Payable	$ 11,700	Notes Payable	$60,000
Accounts Receivable	30,360	Office Trailer	6,600
Cash	?	Prepaid Insurance	13,800
Construction Supplies	5,700	Revenue Earned	52,200
Equipment	73,500	Supplies Expense	21,600
Fred Ferraro, Capital	120,000	Utilities Expense	1,260
Fred Ferraro, Withdrawals	23,400	Wages Expense	26,400

Prepare a trial balance for the company with the proper heading and with the accounts in balance sheet sequence. Determine the correct balance for the Cash account on November 30, 20xx.

LO 4
LO 6 *Analysis of Unfamiliar Transactions*

E 12. Managers and accountants often encounter transactions with which they are unfamiliar. Use your analytical skills to analyze and record in journal form the transactions below, which have not yet been discussed in the text.

a. Purchased merchandise inventory on account, $1,600.
b. Purchased marketable securities for cash, $4,800.
c. Returned part of merchandise inventory purchased in **a** for full credit, $500.
d. Sold merchandise inventory on account, $1,600 (record sale only).
e. Purchased land and a building for $600,000. Payment is $120,000 cash and a thirty-year mortgage for the remainder. The purchase price is allocated $200,000 to the land and $400,000 to the building.
f. Received an order for $24,000 in services to be provided. With the order was a deposit of $8,000.

LO 6
LO 7 *Recording Transactions in the General Journal and Posting to the Ledger Accounts*

E 13. Open a general journal form like the one in Exhibit 4, and label it Page 10. After opening the form, record the following transactions in the journal.

Dec. 14 Purchased an item of equipment for $6,000, paying $2,000 as a cash down payment.
28 Paid $3,000 of the amount owed on the equipment.

Prepare three ledger account forms like the one shown in Exhibit 5. Use the following account numbers: Cash, 111; Equipment, 144; and Accounts Payable, 212. Then post the two transactions from the general journal to the ledger accounts, being sure to make proper posting references.

Assume that the Cash account has a debit balance of $8,000 on the day prior to the first transaction.

Problems

LO 4 *Transaction Analysis*

P 1. The following accounts are applicable to Jackson Communications:

1. Cash
2. Accounts Receivable
3. Supplies
4. Prepaid Insurance
5. Equipment
6. Notes Payable
7. Accounts Payable
8. Capital
9. Withdrawals
10. Service Revenue
11. Rent Expense
12. Repair Expense

Jackson Communications completed the following transactions:

		Debit	Credit
a.	Paid for supplies purchased on credit last month.	7	1
b.	Billed customers for services performed.		
c.	Paid the current month's rent.		
d.	Purchased supplies on credit.		
e.	Received cash from customers for services performed but not yet billed.		
f.	Purchased equipment on account.		
g.	Received a bill for repairs.		
h.	Returned a portion of the equipment that was purchased in **f** for a credit.		
i.	Received payments from customers previously billed.		
j.	Paid the bill received in **g.**		
k.	Received an order for services to be performed.		
l.	Paid for repairs with cash.		
m.	Made a payment to reduce the principal of the note payable.		
n.	Withdrew cash for personal expenses.		

REQUIRED

Analyze each transaction and show the accounts affected by entering the corresponding numbers in the appropriate debit or credit column as shown in transaction **a.** Indicate no entry, if appropriate.

LO 4 *Transaction Analysis,*
LO 5 *T Accounts, and Trial Balance*

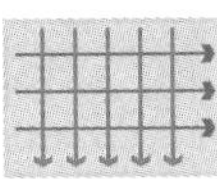

P 2. Donna Polonsky opened a secretarial school called Village Business School and engaged in the following transactions:

a. Contributed the following assets to the business:

Cash	$11,400
Word processors	8,600
Office equipment	7,200

b. Found a location for the business and paid the first month's rent, $520.
c. Paid for an advertisement announcing the opening of the school, $380.
d. Received applications from three students for a four-week secretarial program and two students for a ten-day keyboarding course. The students will be billed a total of $2,600.
e. Purchased supplies on credit, $660.
f. Billed the enrolled students, $2,600.
g. Paid an assistant one week's salary, $440.
h. Purchased a word processor, $960, and office equipment, $760, on credit.
i. Paid for the supplies purchased on credit in **e,** $660.
j. Repaired a broken word processor, paid cash, $80.
k. Billed new students who enrolled late in the course, $880.
l. Transferred cash to a personal checking account, $600.
m. Received partial payment from students previously billed, $2,160.
n. Paid a utility bill for the current month, $180.
o. Paid an assistant one week's salary, $440.
p. Received cash revenue from another new student, $500.

REQUIRED

1. Set up the following T accounts: Cash; Accounts Receivable; Supplies; Word Processors; Office Equipment; Accounts Payable; Donna Polonsky, Capital; Donna Polonsky, Withdrawals; Tuition Revenue; Salaries Expense; Utilities Expense; Rent Expense; Repair Expense; and Advertising Expense.
2. Record the transactions by entering debits and credits directly in the T accounts, using the transaction letter to identify each debit and credit.
3. Prepare a trial balance using today's date.

P 3.

LO 4 *Transaction Analysis,*
LO 5 *General Journal, Ledger*
LO 6 *Accounts, and Trial*
LO 7 *Balance*

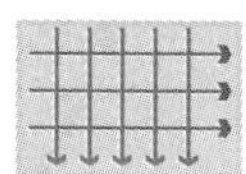

Kwan Lee began a rug cleaning business on October 1 and engaged in the following transactions during the month:

Oct. 1 Began business by transferring $6,000 from his personal bank account to the business bank account.
2 Ordered cleaning supplies, $500.
3 Purchased cleaning equipment for cash, $1,400.
4 Leased a van by making two months' lease payment in advance, $600.
7 Received the cleaning supplies ordered on October 2 and agreed to pay half the amount in ten days and the rest in thirty days.
9 Paid for repairs on the van with cash, $40.
12 Received cash for cleaning carpets, $480.
17 Paid half of the amount owed on supplies purchased on October 7, $250.
21 Billed customers for cleaning carpets, $670.
24 Paid for additional repairs on the van with cash, $40.
27 Received $300 from the customers billed on October 21.
31 Withdrew $350 from the business for personal use.

REQUIRED

1. Prepare journal entries to record the above transactions in the general journal (Pages 1 and 2). Use the accounts listed below.
2. Set up the following ledger accounts and post the journal entries: Cash (111); Accounts Receivable (113); Cleaning Supplies (115); Prepaid Lease (116); Cleaning Equipment (141); Accounts Payable (211); Kwan Lee, Capital (311); Kwan Lee, Withdrawals (312); Cleaning Revenues (411); Repair Expense (511).
3. Prepare a trial balance for Lee Carpet Cleaning Service as of October 31, 20xx.

P 4.

LO 1 *Transaction Analysis,*
LO 4 *Journal Form,*
LO 5 *T Accounts, and Trial Balance*

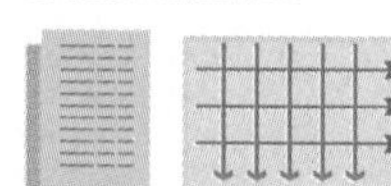

Jerry Green is a house painter. During the month of June, he completed the following transactions:

June 3 Began his business with equipment valued at $2,460 and placed $14,200 in a business checking account.
5 Purchased a used truck costing $3,800. Paid $1,000 in cash and signed a note for the balance.
7 Purchased supplies on account for $640.
8 Completed a painting job and billed the customer $960.
10 Received $300 in cash for painting two rooms.
11 Hired an assistant to work with him at $12 per hour.
12 Purchased supplies for $320 in cash.
13 Received a $960 check from the customer billed on June 8.
14 Paid $800 for an insurance policy for eighteen months' coverage.
16 Billed a customer $1,240 for a painting job.
18 Paid the assistant $300 for twenty-five hours' work.
19 Paid $80 for a tune-up for the truck.
20 Paid for the supplies purchased on June 7.
21 Purchased a new ladder (equipment) for $120 and supplies for $580, on account.
23 Received a telephone bill for $120, due next month.
24 Received $660 in cash from the customer billed on June 16.
25 Transferred $600 to a personal checking account.
26 Received $720 in cash for painting a five-room apartment.
28 Paid $400 on the note signed for the truck.
29 Paid the assistant $360 for thirty hours' work.

REQUIRED

1. Prepare journal entries to record these transactions in journal form. Use the accounts listed below.
2. Set up the following T accounts and post all the journal entries: Cash; Accounts Receivable; Supplies; Prepaid Insurance; Equipment; Truck; Notes Payable; Accounts Payable; Jerry Green, Capital; Jerry Green, Withdrawals; Painting Fees Earned; Wages Expense; Telephone Expense; and Truck Expense.
3. Prepare a trial balance for Green Painting Service as of June 30, 20xx.
4. Compare how recognition applies to the transactions of June 8 and 10 and how classification applies to the transactions of June 14 and 18.

P 5.

LO 4 *Transaction Analysis,*
LO 5 *General Journal, Ledger*
LO 6 *Accounts, and Trial*
LO 7 *Balance*

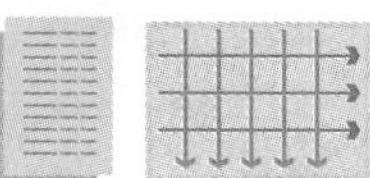

The Progressive Child Care Company provides babysitting and child-care programs. On August 31, 20xx, this was the company's trial balance:

Progressive Child Care Company
Trial Balance
August 31, 20xx

Cash (111)	$ 3,740	
Accounts Receivable (113)	3,400	
Equipment (141)	2,080	
Buses (143)	34,800	
Notes Payable (211)		$30,000
Accounts Payable (212)		3,280
Sharon Bromberg, Capital (311)		10,740
	$44,020	$44,020

During the month of September, the company completed the following transactions:

Sept. 3 Paid this month's rent, $540.
5 Received fees for this month's services, $1,300.
7 Purchased supplies on account, $170.
8 Reimbursed the bus driver for gas expenses, $80.
9 Ordered playground equipment, $2,000.
10 Paid part-time assistants for two weeks' services, $460.
12 Made a payment on account, $340.
13 Received payments from customers on account, $2,400.
15 Billed customers who had not yet paid for this month's services, $1,400.
16 Paid for the supplies purchased on September 7.
18 Purchased playground equipment for cash, $2,000.
19 Withdrew cash for personal expenses, $220.
20 Contributed equipment to the business, $580.
21 Paid this month's utility bill, $290.
24 Paid part-time assistants for two weeks' services, $460.
25 Received payment for one month's services from customers previously billed, $1,000.
26 Purchased gas and oil for the bus on account, $70.
29 Paid for a one-year insurance policy, $580.

REQUIRED

1. Enter these transactions in the general journal (Pages 17, 18, and 19).
2. Open accounts in the ledger for the accounts in the trial balance and the following accounts: Supplies (115); Prepaid Insurance (116); Sharon Bromberg, Withdrawals (312); Service Revenue (411); Rent Expense (511); Bus Expense (512); Wages Expense (513); and Utilities Expense (514).
3. Enter the August 31, 20xx, account balances from the trial balance.

4. Post the entries to the ledger accounts. Be sure to make the appropriate posting references in the journal and ledger as you post.
5. Prepare a trial balance as of September 30, 20xx.

Alternate Problems

LO 4 *Transaction Analysis*

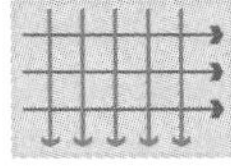

P 6. The following accounts are applicable to Omega Pool Service, a company that maintains swimming pools.

1. Cash	7. Capital
2. Accounts Receivable	8. Withdrawals
3. Supplies	9. Pool Services Revenue
4. Prepaid Insurance	10. Wages Expense
5. Equipment	11. Rent Expense
6. Accounts Payable	12. Utilities Expense

Omega Pool Service completed the following transactions.

		Debit	**Credit**
a.	Received cash from customers billed last month.	1	2
b.	Made a payment on accounts payable.	___	___
c.	Purchased a new one-year insurance policy in advance.	___	___
d.	Purchased supplies on credit.	___	___
e.	Billed a client for pool services.	___	___
f.	Made a rent payment for the current month.	___	___
g.	Received cash from customers for pool services.	___	___
h.	Paid wages for the staff.	___	___
i.	Ordered equipment.	___	___
j.	Paid the current month's utility bill.	___	___
k.	Received and paid for the equipment ordered in **i.**	___	___
l.	Returned for full credit some of the supplies purchased in **d** because they were defective.	___	___
m.	Paid for supplies purchased in **d,** less the return in **l.**	___	___
n.	Withdrew cash for personal expenses.	___	___

REQUIRED

Analyze each transaction and show the accounts affected by entering the corresponding numbers in the appropriate debit or credit columns as shown in transaction **a.** Indicate no entry, if appropriate.

LO 1 *Transaction Analysis,*
LO 4 *Journal Form,*
LO 5 *T Accounts, and Trial Balance*

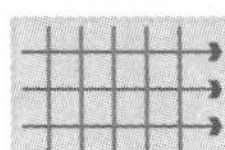

P 7. Bob Reeves won a concession to rent bicycles in the local park during the summer. In the month of May, Reeves completed the following transactions for his bicycle rental business:

May	3	Began business by placing $14,400 in a business checking account.
	6	Purchased supplies on account for $300.
	7	Purchased ten bicycles for $5,000, paying $2,400 down and agreeing to pay the rest in thirty days.
	9	Received $940 in cash for rentals during the first week of operation.
	10	Purchased a small shed to hold the bicycles and to use for other operations for $5,800 in cash.
	11	Paid $800 in cash for shipping and installation costs (considered an addition to the cost of the shed) to place the shed at the park entrance.
	14	Received $1,000 in cash for rentals during the second week of operation.
	15	Hired a part-time assistant to help out on weekends at $8 per hour.
	16	Paid a maintenance person $150 to clean the grounds.
	18	Paid the assistant $160 for a weekend's work.
	19	Paid $300 for the supplies purchased on May 6.
	20	Paid a $110 repair bill on bicycles.
	21	Received $1,100 in cash for rentals during the third week of operation.
	23	Paid the assistant $160 for a weekend's work.
	24	Billed a company $220 for bicycle rentals for an employees' outing.
	26	Paid the $200 fee for May to the Park District for the right to the bicycle concession.

28 Received $820 in cash for rentals during the week.
30 Paid the assistant $160 for a weekend's work.
31 Transferred $1,000 to a personal checking account.

REQUIRED

1. Prepare journal entries to record these transactions in journal form.
2. Set up the following T accounts and post all the journal entries: Cash; Accounts Receivable; Supplies; Shed; Bicycles; Accounts Payable; Bob Reeves, Capital; Bob Reeves, Withdrawals; Rental Revenue; Wages Expense; Maintenance Expense, Repair Expense; and Concession Fee Expense.
3. Prepare a trial balance for Reeves Rentals as of May 31, 20xx.
4. Compare how recognition applies to the transactions of May 24 and 28 and how classification applies to the transactions of May 11 and 16.

P 8. LO 4 LO 5 LO 6 LO 7 *Transaction Analysis, General Journal, Ledger Accounts, and Trial Balance*

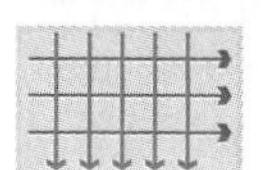

Boulevard Communications Company is a public relations firm. On April 30, 20xx, the company's trial balance looked like this:

Boulevard Communications Company
Trial Balance
April 30, 20xx

Cash (111)	$20,400	
Accounts Receivable (113)	11,000	
Supplies (115)	1,220	
Office Equipment (141)	8,400	
Accounts Payable (211)		$ 5,200
Ramesh Mehta, Capital (311)		35,820
	$41,020	$41,020

During the month of May, the company completed the following transactions:

May 3 Paid rent for May, $1,300.
5 Received cash from customers on account, $4,600.
6 Ordered supplies, $760.
8 Billed customers for services provided, $5,600.
10 Made a payment on accounts payable, $2,200.
13 Received the supplies ordered on May 6 and agreed to pay for them in thirty days, $760.
15 Paid salaries for the first half of May, $3,800.
16 Discovered some of the supplies were not as ordered and returned them for a full credit, $160.
18 Received cash from a customer for services provided, $9,600.
22 Paid the utility bill for May, $320.
23 Paid the telephone bill for May, $240.
27 Received a bill, to be paid in June, for advertisements placed in the local newspaper during the month of May to promote Boulevard Communications, $1,400.
28 Billed a customer for services provided, $5,400.
30 Paid salaries for the last half of May, $3,800.
31 Withdrew cash for personal use, $2,400.

REQUIRED

1. Enter these transactions in the general journal (Pages 22 and 23).
2. Open accounts in the ledger for the accounts in the trial balance and the following accounts: Ramesh Mehta, Withdrawals (312); Public Relations Fees (411); Salaries Expense (511); Rent Expense (512); Utilities Expense (513); Telephone Expense (514); and Advertising Expense (515).

3. Enter the April 30 account balances from the trial balance in the appropriate ledger account.
4. Post the entries to the ledger accounts. Be sure to make the appropriate posting references in the journal and ledger as you post.
5. Prepare a trial balance as of May 31, 20xx.

EXPANDING YOUR CRITICAL THINKING, COMMUNICATION, AND INTERPERSONAL SKILLS

Skills Development

CONCEPTUAL ANALYSIS

LO 1 *Valuation Issue*

SD 1. ***Nike, Inc.,*** manufactures and markets athletic shoes and related products. In one of the company's annual reports, under "Summary of Significant Accounting Policies," the following statement was made: "Property, plant, and equipment are recorded at cost."[6] Given that the property, plant, and equipment undoubtedly were purchased over several years and that the current value of those assets is likely to be very different from their original cost, tell what authoritative basis there is for carrying the assets at cost. Does accounting generally recognize changes in value subsequent to the purchase of property, plant, and equipment? Assume you are a Nike accountant. Write a memo to management explaining the rationale underlying Nike's approach.

LO 1 LO 4 *Recognition, Valuation, Classification Issues*

SD 2. ***Chambers Development,*** a landfill development company, announced a change in its accounting practices on March 17, 1992. The company said that the change would result in a restatement of 1991 earnings. News of the accounting change caused the stock price to drop from \$30½ to \$11⅛ in one day, and it continued to decline to a low of \$1⅞ by November 1994.

> At the core of the problem was how Chambers accounted for millions of dollars it was spending to develop landfills. The company's choice: charge the costs in the year in which they were incurred or over the life of the landfill. The first method would increase operating costs, thereby depressing current earnings. On the other hand, writing off the costs gradually—"capitalizing" them in accounting parlance—would boost current earnings.[7]

Chambers initially chose to capitalize these costs (record them as an asset) and expense them gradually over future years. The change to immediate expensing led to a reduction of prior years' earnings of \$362 million. The SEC required the restatement of Chambers's financial statements back to 1985, the year the company went public. The SEC determined that the amounts capitalized from 1989 through 1991 exceeded the reported pretax earnings. This means that instead of reporting profits each period, Chambers should have reported losses that it actually had.

The SEC discovered that management would set a target earnings level and back into the amount of costs to be capitalized to achieve the earnings target. The SEC investigation concluded "that the accounting practices that created millions of dollars in false profits were well outside the general bounds of generally accepted accounting practices. They were based on queered mathematics and an overzealous desire to please Wall Street, not an uncommon cause of corporate accounting scandals."[8]

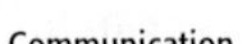
Communication

Critical Thinking

Group Activity

Memo

Ethics

International

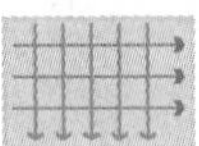
Spreadsheet

General Ledger

CD-ROM

Internet

REQUIRED

1. Prepare the journal entry that Chambers made to record landfill costs as an asset (prepaid landfill costs). Prepare the journal entry to reduce its prepaid landfill costs by $362 million.
2. Three issues that must be addressed when recording a transaction are recognition, valuation, and classification. Which of these issues were of most concern to the SEC in the Chambers case? Explain how each applies to the transactions in part **1.**

Group Activity: Students work in groups to complete part **1.** Discuss part **2** as a class.

Ethical Dilemma

SD 3. **LO 1** *Recognition Point and Ethical Considerations*

One of ***Penn Office Supplies Corporation***'s sales representatives, Jerry Hasbrow, is compensated on a commission basis and receives a substantial bonus for meeting his annual sales goal. The company's recognition point for sales is the day of shipment. On December 31, Jerry realizes that he needs sales of $2,000 to reach his sales goal and receive the bonus. He calls a purchaser for a local insurance company, whom he knows well, and asks him to buy $2,000 worth of copier paper today. The purchaser says, "But Jerry, that's more than a year's supply for us." Jerry says, "Buy it today. If you decide it's too much, you can return however much you want for full credit next month." The purchaser says, "Okay, ship it." The paper is shipped on December 31 and recorded as a sale. On January 15, the purchaser returns $1,750 worth of paper for full credit (okayed by Jerry) against the bill. Should the shipment on December 31 be recorded as a sale? Discuss the ethics of Jerry's action.

Group Activity: Divide the class into informal groups to discuss and report on the ethical issues of this case.

Research Activity

SD 4. **LO 4** *Transactions in a Business Article*

Locate an article on a company you recognize or on a company in a business that interests you in one of the following sources: a recent issue of a business journal (such as *Barron's, Fortune, The Wall Street Journal, Business Week,* or *Forbes*) or the Needles Accounting Resource Center Web site at http://www.hmco.com/college/needles/home.html. Read the article carefully, noting any references to transactions that the company engages in. These may be normal transactions (sales, purchases) or unusual transactions (a merger, the purchase of another company). Bring a copy of the article to class and be prepared to describe how you would analyze and record the transactions you have noted.

Decision-Making Practice

SD 5. **LO 4** **LO 5** *Transaction Analysis and Evaluation of a Trial Balance*

Ben Obi hired an attorney to help him start ***Obi Repairs Company.*** On June 1, Ben Obi invested $23,000 in cash in the business. When he paid the attorney's bill of $1,400, the attorney advised him to hire an accountant to keep his records. However, Ben was so busy that it was June 30 before he asked you to straighten out his records. Your first task is to develop a trial balance based on the June transactions.

After making the investment and paying the attorney, Ben borrowed $10,000 from the bank. He later paid $520, which included interest of $120, on this loan. He also purchased a pickup truck in the company's name, paying $5,000 down and financing $14,800. The first payment on the truck is due July 15. Ben then rented an office and paid three months' rent, $1,800, in advance. Credit purchases of office equipment for $1,400 and repair tools for $1,000 must be paid for by July 13.

In June, Obi Repairs completed repairs of $2,600, of which $800 were cash transactions. Of the credit transactions, $600 were collected during June, and $1,200 remained to be collected at the end of June. Wages of $800 were paid to employees. On June 30, the company received a $150 bill for June utilities and a $100 check from a customer for work to be completed in July.

1. Record the June transactions in journal form.
2. Set up T accounts, post the general journal entries to the T accounts, and determine the balance of each account.

3. Prepare a June 30 trial balance for Obi Repairs Company.
4. Ben Obi is unsure how to evaluate the trial balance. His Cash account balance is $24,980, which exceeds his original investment of $23,000 by $1,980. Did he make a profit of $1,980? Explain why the Cash account is not an indicator of business earnings. Cite specific examples to show why it is difficult to determine net income by looking solely at figures in the trial balance.

Financial Reporting and Analysis

INTERPRETING FINANCIAL REPORTS

FRA 1.
LO 2 LO 4 *Interpreting a Bank's Financial Statements*

First Chicago NBD Corp. is a large midwestern bank holding company. Selected accounts from the company's 1996 annual report are as follows (in millions):[9]

Cash and Due from Banks	$ 7,823	Investment Securities	$ 7,178
Loans to Customers	66,414	Deposits by Customers	63,669

REQUIRED

1. Indicate whether each of the accounts just listed is an asset, a liability, or a component of owner's equity on First Chicago NBD's balance sheet.
2. Assume that you are in a position to do business with First Chicago NBD. Prepare the entry on the bank's books in journal form to record each of the following transactions:
   a. You sell securities in the amount of $2,000 to the bank.
   b. You deposit the $2,000 received in step **a** in the bank.
   c. You borrow $5,000 from the bank.

INTERNATIONAL COMPANY

FRA 2.
LO 4 *Transaction Analysis*

Ajinomoto Company, a Japanese company with operations in twenty-two countries, is primarily engaged in the manufacture and sale of food products. Ajinomoto has approximately one-third of the global market for monosodium glutamate (Accent), a major seasoning product. The following selected aggregate cash transactions were reported in the statement of cash flows in Ajinomoto's 1996 annual report (amounts in millions of yen):[10]

Dividends paid	¥6,488	Proceeds from issuance of long-term debt	¥29,651
Purchase of investments	¥24,879	Repayment of long-term debt	¥22,577

REQUIRED

Prepare entries in journal form to record the above transactions.

Toys "R" Us Annual Report

FRA 3.
LO 4 *Transaction Analysis*

Refer to the balance sheet in the Toys "R" Us annual report. Prepare T accounts for the accounts Cash and Cash Equivalents, Accounts and Other Receivables, Prepaid Expenses and Other Current Assets, Accounts Payable, and Income Taxes Payable. Properly place the balance of the account at February 1, 1997, in the T accounts. Below are some typical transactions in which Toys "R" Us would engage. Analyze each transaction, enter it in the T accounts, and determine the balance of each account. Assume that all entries are in thousands.

a. Paid cash in advance for certain expenses, $20,000.
b. Received cash from customers billed previously, $35,000.
c. Paid cash for income taxes previously owed, $70,000.
d. Paid cash to suppliers for amounts owed, $120,000.

Fingraph® Financial Analyst™

FRA 4. Choose any company in the Fingraph® Financial Analyst™ CD-ROM software.

LO 1 LO 3 LO 4 *Transaction Identification*

1. From the company's annual report, determine the industry(ies) in which the company operates.
2. Find the summary of significant accounting policies that appears following the financial statements. In these policies, find examples of the application of recognition, valuation, and classification.
3. Identify six types of transactions that your company would commonly engage in. Are any of these transactions more common in the industry in which your company operates than in other industries? For each transaction, tell what account would typically be debited and what account would be credited.
4. Prepare a one-page executive summary that highlights what you have learned from parts **1, 2,** and **3.**

ENDNOTES

1. "Boeing Jets Worth $4 Billion Ordered," *Chicago Tribune,* June 11, 1997.
2. The Boeing Co., *Annual Report,* 1994.
3. Sun Microsystems Inc., *Annual Report,* 1997.
4. Intel Corp., *Annual Report,* 1997.
5. Mark Maremont, "Blind Ambition," *Business Week,* October 23, 1995.
6. Nike, Inc., *Annual Report,* 1996.
7. Boselovic, Len, "A Look at How the SEC Disposed of Chambers' Claims," *Pittsburgh Post-Gazette,* May 14, 1995.
8. Ibid.
9. First Chicago NBD Corp., *Annual Report,* 1996.
10. Ajinomoto Company, *Annual Report,* 1996.

CHAPTER 3

Measuring Business Income

LEARNING OBJECTIVES

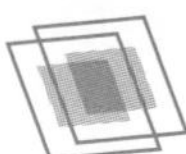

1. **Define *net income* and its two major components, *revenues* and *expenses*.**
2. **Explain the difficulties of income measurement caused by (a) the accounting period issue, (b) the continuity issue, and (c) the matching issue.**
3. **Define *accrual accounting* and explain two broad ways of accomplishing it.**
4. **State four principal situations that require adjusting entries.**
5. **Prepare typical adjusting entries.**
6. **Prepare financial statements from an adjusted trial balance.**

SUPPLEMENTAL OBJECTIVE

7. **Analyze cash flows from accrual-based information.**

DECISION POINT

GANNETT CO., INC.

Gannett Co., Inc., is the United States' largest newspaper publisher, with eighty-two dailies, including *USA Today*. The company also operates broadcasting stations and outdoor advertising businesses and provides other services. Gannett has 37,200 employees, and payroll is its largest expense.[1] During most of the year, payroll is recorded as an expense when it is paid. However, at the end of the year, employees may have earned compensation (wages or salaries) that will not be paid until the beginning of the next year. If these wages and salaries are not accounted for correctly, they will appear in the wrong year—the year in which they are paid instead of the year in which the company benefited from them. How does accounting solve this problem?

According to the concepts of accrual accounting and the matching rule, which you will learn in this chapter, the accountant must determine the amount of wages and salaries earned but not paid and record an adjusting entry for this amount as an expense of the current year and a liability to be paid the next year. In this way, expenses are correctly stated on the income statement and liabilities are correctly stated on the balance sheet. In the case of Gannett, the effect is significant. At the end of 1996, Gannett had a liability for compensation of $93,165,000. If an adjusting entry had not been made to record this liability and its related expense in 1996, income before taxes would have been overstated by $93,165,000. Given that income after deducting this expense in 1996 was $943,087,000, without the adjusting entry, readers of the financial statements would have been misled into thinking that Gannett's income was 9.9 percent greater than it actually was.

Critical Thinking Question: Why is it important for all companies to record identical business activities in the same manner? Consider the payroll example; then generalize. **Answer:** If all companies record a payroll adjusting entry in the same way, then users know that all payroll costs associated with revenues recorded are included in total expenses and resulting net income. In general, recording activities in a like manner increases the comparability of income among companies.

Profitability Measurement: The Role of Business Income

Point to Emphasize: An important purpose of accounting is to measure and report a business's profitability. The extent of the reported profit or loss communicates the company's success or failure.

Profitability is one of the two major goals of a business (the other being liquidity). For a business to succeed, or even to survive, it must earn a profit. The word profit, though, has many meanings. One is the increase in owner's equity that results from business operations. However, even this definition can be interpreted differently by economists, lawyers, businesspeople, and the public. Because the word *profit* has more than one meaning, accountants prefer to use the term *net income,* which can be precisely defined from an accounting point of view. Net income is reported on the income statement and is a performance measure used by management, owners, and others to monitor a business's progress in meeting the goal of profitability. Those who read income statements need to understand how the accountant defines net income and be aware of its strengths and weaknesses as a measure of company performance.

Net Income

OBJECTIVE 1

Define **net income** *and its two major components,* **revenues** *and* **expenses**

Related Text Assignments:
Q: 1, 2
SD: 5
FRA: 4

Net income is the net increase in owner's equity that results from the operations of a company and is accumulated in the owner's Capital account. Net income, in its simplest form, is measured by the difference between revenues and expenses when revenues exceed expenses:

$$\text{Net Income} = \text{Revenues} - \text{Expenses}$$

When expenses exceed revenues, a net loss occurs.

Common Student Confusion: At this point, students do not understand the difference between cash and revenue. Point out the difference in terms of both their placement in the financial statements and the intangible nature of revenue.

Revenues Revenues are increases in owner's equity resulting from selling goods, rendering services, or performing other business activities. In the simplest case, revenues equal the price of goods sold and services rendered over a specific period of time. When a business delivers a product or provides a service to a customer, it usually receives either cash or a promise to pay cash in the near future. The promise to pay is recorded in either Accounts Receivable or Notes Receivable. The revenue for a given period equals the total of cash and receivables from goods and services provided to customers during that period.

Point to Emphasize: The essence of revenue is that something has been *earned* through the sale of goods or services. That is why cash received through a loan does not constitute revenue.

Liabilities generally are not affected by revenues, and some transactions that increase cash and other assets do not produce revenues. For example a bank loan increases liabilities and cash but does not produce revenue. The collection of accounts receivable, which increases cash and decreases accounts receivable, does not produce revenue either. Remember that when a sale on credit takes place, the

BUSINESS BULLETIN: ETHICS IN PRACTICE

Accounting assumptions, such as periodicity, should not be applied in a way that will distort or obscure financial results. For instance, not until two years after Kurzweil Applied Intelligence sold its share of stock to the public for $10 per share was it revealed that the company had changed its fiscal year, thereby shifting losses of $1,000,000 to a previous year in order to show a profit in the year in which the shares were sold. This, together with other questionable accounting practices, gave a false picture of the company's prospects. After disclosure of these actions, the price of the company's stock dropped. Accounting practices are meant to inform the readers of financial results, not to deceive them.[2]

asset account Accounts Receivable increases; at the same time, an owner's equity revenue account increases. So counting the collection of the receivable as revenue later would be counting the same sale twice.

Not all increases in owner's equity arise from revenues. Owner investments increase owner's equity but are not revenue.

Point to Emphasize: The primary purpose of an expense is to generate revenue.

Expenses Expenses are decreases in owner's equity resulting from the costs of selling goods, rendering services, or performing other business activities. In other words, expenses are the costs of the goods and services used up in the course of earning revenues. Often called the *cost of doing business,* expenses include the cost of goods sold, the costs of activities necessary to carry on a business, and the costs of attracting and serving customers. Examples of expenses are salaries, rent, advertising, telephone service, and depreciation (allocation of cost) of a building or office equipment.

Business-World Example: Income measurement is difficult in many industries because of the uncertainties associated with their revenues and expenses. For example, in the period of the sale, cereal companies must recognize the expense associated with boxtops and coupons expected to be redeemed ultimately. And construction companies must estimate their revenues based upon a project's percentage of completion.

Just as not all cash receipts are revenues, not all cash payments are expenses. A cash payment to reduce a liability does not result in an expense. The liability, however, may have come from incurring a previous expense, such as advertising, that is to be paid later. There may also be two steps before an expenditure of cash becomes an expense. For example, prepaid expenses and plant assets (such as machinery and equipment) are recorded as assets when they are acquired. Later, as their usefulness expires in the operation of the business, their cost is allocated to expenses. In fact, expenses sometimes are called *expired costs.*

Not all decreases in owner's equity arise from expenses. Owner withdrawals decrease owner's equity, but they are not expenses.

The Accounting Period Issue

OBJECTIVE 2a

Explain the difficulties of income measurement caused by the accounting period issue

Related Text Assignments:
Q: 3, 4, 5
SE: 1
E: 1
SD: 1, 3
FRA: 1, 2

Point to Emphasize: Underscore the need for timely financial reports. The accounting periods must be of equal length so that one period can be compared to the next.

The accounting period issue involves the difficulty of assigning revenues and expenses to a short period of time, such as a month or a year. Not all transactions can be easily assigned to specific time periods. Purchases of buildings and equipment, for example, have effects that extend over many years. Accountants solve this problem by estimating the number of years the buildings or equipment will be in use and the cost that should be assigned to each year. In the process, they make an assumption about periodicity: that the net income for any period of time less than the life of the business, although tentative, is still a useful estimate of the net income for the period.

Generally, to make comparisons easier, the time periods are of equal length. Financial statements may be prepared for any time period. Accounting periods of less than one year—for example, a month or a quarter—are called *interim periods.* The twelve-month accounting period used by a company is called its fiscal year. Many companies use the calendar year, January 1 to December 31, for their fiscal year. Others find it convenient to choose a fiscal year that ends during a slack season rather than a peak season. In this case, the fiscal year corresponds to the company's yearly cycle of business activity. The time period should always be noted in the financial statements.

The Continuity Issue

OBJECTIVE 2b

Explain the difficulties of income measurement caused by the continuity issue

The process of measuring business income requires that certain expense and revenue transactions be allocated over several accounting periods. The number of accounting periods raises the continuity issue: How long will the business entity last? Many businesses last less than five years; in any given year, thousands of businesses go bankrupt. To prepare financial statements for an accounting period, the accountant must make an assumption about the ability of the business to survive.

BUSINESS BULLETIN: BUSINESS PRACTICE

The table on the right shows the diverse fiscal years used by some well-known companies. Many governmental and educational units use fiscal years that end June 30 or September 30.

Company	Last Month of Fiscal Year
American Greetings Corp.	February
Caesars World, Inc.	July
The Walt Disney Company	September
Eastman Kodak Company	December
Fleetwood Enterprises, Inc.	April
Lorimar	March
Mattel Inc.	December
MGM/UA Communications Co.	August
Polaroid Corp.	December

Business-World Example: The continuity assumption is set aside when an organization is formed for a limited venture, such as a World's Fair or an Olympics.

Specifically, unless there is evidence to the contrary, the accountant assumes that the business will continue to operate indefinitely, that the business is a going concern. Justification for all the techniques of income measurement rests on the assumption of continuity. For example, this assumption allows the cost of certain assets to be held on the balance sheet until a future year, when it will become an expense on the income statement.

Another example has to do with the value of assets on the balance sheet. The accountant records assets at cost and does not record subsequent changes in their value. But the value of assets to a going concern is much higher than the value of assets to a firm facing bankruptcy. In the latter case, the accountant may be asked to set aside the assumption of continuity and to prepare financial statements based on the assumption that the firm will go out of business and sell all of its assets at liquidation value—that is, for what they will bring in cash.

The Matching Issue

OBJECTIVE 2c

Explain the difficulties of income measurement caused by the matching issue

Revenues and expenses can be accounted for on a cash received and cash paid basis. This practice is known as the cash basis of accounting. Individuals and some businesses may use the cash basis of accounting for income tax purposes. Under this method, revenues are reported in the period in which cash is received, and expenses are reported in the period in which cash is paid. Taxable income, therefore, is calculated as the difference between cash receipts from revenues and cash payments for expenses.

Point to Emphasize: Although the cash basis often is used for tax purposes, it seldom produces an accurate measurement of a business's performance for financial reporting purposes.

Discussion Question: Suppose a company buys a building and expenses its cost in the year of the purchase. What financial reporting problem does this create, and what is the correct way to account for the building? **Answer:** Expensing the building immediately understates income (and total assets) in the year of the purchase and overstates income in the remaining years of the building's life. The cost of the building should be expensed over the years during which the building will benefit the business.

Although the cash basis of accounting works well for some small businesses and many individuals, it does not meet the needs of most businesses. As explained above, revenues can be earned in a period other than the one in which cash is received, and expenses can be incurred in a period other than the one in which cash is paid. To measure net income adequately, revenues and expenses must be assigned to the appropriate accounting period. The accountant solves this problem by applying the matching rule:

> Revenues must be assigned to the accounting period in which the goods are sold or the services performed, and expenses must be assigned to the accounting period in which they are used to produce revenue.

Direct cause-and-effect relationships seldom can be demonstrated for certain, but many costs appear to be related to particular revenues. The accountant recognizes these expenses and the related revenues in the same accounting period.

Discussion Question: Why must a company recognize warranty expense in the year of the sale rather than in the year of the repair or replacement? **Answer:** To measure a company's performance accurately, each expense must be matched with the related revenue. Otherwise, net income will be overstated and the liability will be understated.

Examples are the costs of goods sold and sales commissions. When there is no direct means of connecting expenses and revenues, the accountant tries to allocate costs in a systematic way among the accounting periods that benefit from the costs. For example, a building is converted from an asset to an expense by allocating its cost over the years during which the company benefits from its use.

Accrual Accounting

OBJECTIVE 3

***Define* accrual accounting and explain two broad ways of accomplishing it**

Related Text Assignments:
Q: 6, 7, 8
SE: 1
E: 1
SD: 1, 2, 3
FRA: 2

Common Student Error: Students have difficulty understanding the relationship between accrual accounting and the matching rule. Explain that accrual accounting is a set of *procedures* (such as journal entries) devised to follow the *guideline* known as the matching rule.

To apply the matching rule, accountants have developed accrual accounting. Accrual accounting "attempts to record the financial effects on an enterprise of transactions and other events and circumstances . . . in the periods in which those transactions, events, and circumstances occur rather than only in the periods in which cash is received or paid by the enterprise."[3] That is, accrual accounting consists of all the techniques developed by accountants to apply the matching rule. It is done in two general ways: (1) by recording revenues when earned and expenses when incurred and (2) by adjusting the accounts.

Recognizing Revenues When Earned and Expenses When Incurred

The first application of accrual accounting is the recognition of revenues when earned and expenses when incurred. For example, when Joan Miller Advertising Agency makes a sale on credit by placing advertisements for a client, revenue is recorded at the time of the sale by debiting Accounts Receivable and crediting Advertising Fees Earned. This is how the accountant recognizes the revenue from a credit sale before the cash is collected. Accounts Receivable serves as a holding account until payment is received. The process of determining when revenue is earned, and consequently when revenue should be recorded, is called revenue recognition.

When Joan Miller Advertising Agency receives its telephone bill, the expense is recognized both as having been incurred and as helping to produce revenue. The transaction is recorded by debiting Telephone Expense and crediting Accounts Payable. Until the bill is paid, Accounts Payable serves as a holding account. Notice that recognition of the expense does not depend on the payment of cash.

Adjusting the Accounts

Teaching Note: Students may ask why the accountant waits until the end of an accounting period to update certain revenues and expenses. Explain that even though the revenues and expenses theoretically have changed during the period, many as a result of time passing, there usually is no need to adjust them until the end of the period, when the financial statements are prepared. In fact, it would be impractical, even impossible, to adjust the accounts each time they are affected.

The second application of accrual accounting is adjusting the accounts. Adjustments are necessary because the accounting period, by definition, ends on a particular day. The balance sheet must list all assets and liabilities as of the end of that day, and the income statement must contain all revenues and expenses applicable to the period ending on that day. Although operating a business is a continuous process, there must be a cutoff point for the periodic reports. Some transactions invariably span the cutoff point; thus, some accounts need adjustment.

For example, some of the accounts in the end-of-the-period trial balance for Joan Miller Advertising Agency (Exhibit 1) do not show the correct balances for preparing the financial statements. The January 31 trial balance lists prepaid rent of $800. At $400 per month, this represents rent for the months of January and February. So on January 31, one-half of the $800, or $400, represents rent expense for January; the remaining $400 represents an asset that will be used in February. An adjustment is needed to reflect the $400 balance in the Prepaid Rent account on the balance sheet and the $400 rent expense on the income statement. As you will see on the following

Exhibit 1. Trial Balance for Joan Miller Advertising Agency

Joan Miller Advertising Agency Trial Balance January 31, 20xx		
Cash	$ 1,720	
Accounts Receivable	2,800	
Art Supplies	1,800	
Office Supplies	800	
Prepaid Rent	800	
Prepaid Insurance	480	
Art Equipment	4,200	
Office Equipment	3,000	
Accounts Payable		$ 3,170
Unearned Art Fees		1,000
Joan Miller, Capital		10,000
Joan Miller, Withdrawals	1,400	
Advertising Fees Earned		4,200
Wages Expense	1,200	
Utilities Expense	100	
Telephone Expense	70	
	$18,370	$18,370

pages, several other accounts in the Joan Miller Advertising Agency trial balance also do not reflect their correct balances. Like the Prepaid Rent account, they need to be adjusted.

The Adjustment Process

OBJECTIVE 4

State four principal situations that require adjusting entries

Related Text Assignments:
Q: 9, 10
E: 1
SD: 1, 2, 3, 4
FRA: 3, 4

Point to Emphasize: Each adjusting entry must include at least one balance sheet account and one income statement account. By definition, it cannot include a debit or a credit to Cash.

Accountants use adjusting entries to apply accrual accounting to transactions that span more than one accounting period. There are four situations in which adjusting entries are required, as illustrated in Figure 1. As shown, each situation affects one balance sheet account and one income statement account. Adjusting entries never involve the Cash account. The four types of adjusting entries may be stated as follows:

1. Costs have been recorded that must be allocated between two or more accounting periods. Examples are prepaid rent, prepaid insurance, supplies, and costs of a building. The adjusting entry in this case involves an asset account and an expense account.
2. Expenses have been incurred but not yet recorded. Examples are the wages that have been earned by employees in the current accounting period but after the last pay period. The adjusting entry involves an expense account and a liability account.
3. Revenues have been recorded that must be allocated between two or more accounting periods. An example is payments that have been collected for ser-

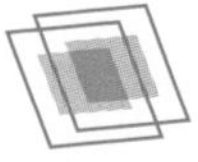

INCOME STATEMENT	BALANCE SHEET: Asset	BALANCE SHEET: Liability
Expense	1. Recorded costs are allocated between two or more accounting periods	2. Expenses are incurred but not yet recorded
Revenue	4. Revenues are earned but not yet recorded	3. Recorded unearned revenues are allocated between two or more accounting periods

Figure 1
The Four Types of Adjustments

Teaching Note: Before students can understand adjusting entries, they must fully comprehend the *nature* of each situation. A timeline can help explain the apportionment of interest and depreciation to accounting periods, and a calendar can help explain accrued wages.

Instructional Strategy: Divide the class into small groups and assign SD 3. Have each group write brief answers to all questions and hand them in. Discuss the ethical dilemma in class. If time allows, quickly tally students' written comments about whether management's recommendation is unethical.

vices yet to be rendered. The adjusting entry involves a liability account and a revenue account.

4. Revenues have been earned but not yet recorded. An example is fees earned but not yet collected or billed to customers. The adjusting entry involves an asset account and a revenue account.

Accountants often refer to adjusting entries as deferrals or accruals. A deferral is the postponement of the recognition of an expense already paid (Type 1 adjustment) or of a revenue received in advance (Type 3 adjustment). Recording of the receipt or payment of cash precedes the adjusting entry. An accrual is the recognition of a revenue (Type 4 adjustment) or expense (Type 2 adjustment) that has arisen but has not yet been recorded. No cash was received or paid prior to the adjusting entry; this will occur in a future accounting period.

Once again, we use Joan Miller Advertising Agency to illustrate the kinds of adjusting entries that most businesses make.

Type 1: Allocating Recorded Costs Between Two or More Accounting Periods (Deferred Expenses)

OBJECTIVE 5

Prepare typical adjusting entries

Related Text Assignments:
Q: 11, 12, 13, 14, 15, 16, 17, 18, 19
SE: 2, 3, 4, 5, 6
E: 2, 3, 4, 5, 6, 7, 8
P: 1, 2, 3, 4, 5, 6, 7, 8
SD: 5
FRA: 1

Point to Emphasize: The expired portion of a prepayment is converted to an expense; the unexpired portion remains an asset.

Organizations often make expenditures that benefit more than one period. These expenditures are usually debited to an asset account. At the end of the accounting period, the amount that has been used is transferred from the asset account to an expense account. Two of the more important kinds of adjustments are those for prepaid expenses and the depreciation of plant and equipment.

Prepaid Expenses Some expenses customarily are paid in advance. These expenditures are called prepaid expenses. Among them are rent, insurance, and supplies. At the end of an accounting period, a portion (or all) of these goods or services will have been used up or will have expired. An adjusting entry reducing the asset and increasing the expense, as shown in Figure 2, is always required. The amount of the adjustment equals the cost of the goods or services used up or expired. If adjusting entries for prepaid expenses are not made at the end of the period, both the balance sheet and the income statement will present incorrect information: The assets of the organization will be overstated, and the expenses of the organization will be understated. This means that owner's equity on the balance sheet and net income on the income statement will be overstated.

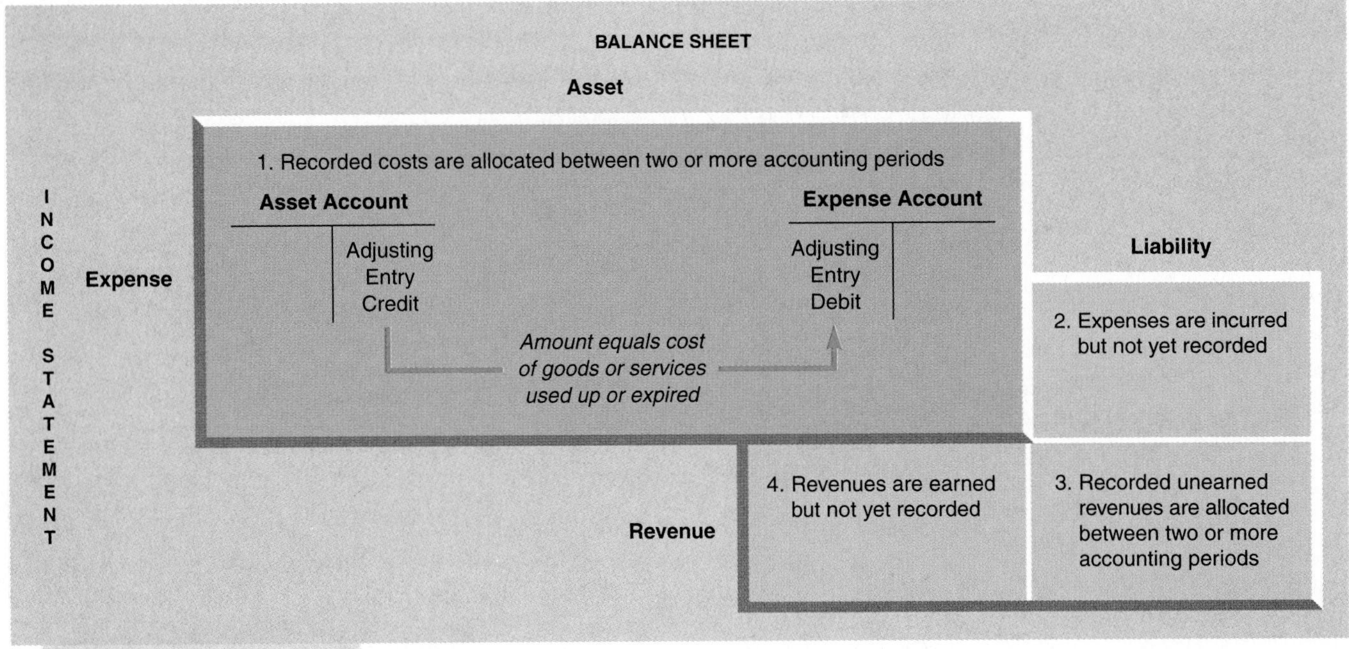

Figure 2
Adjustment for Prepaid (Deferred) Expenses

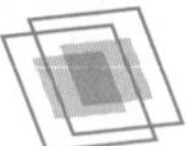

At the beginning of the month, Joan Miller Advertising Agency paid two months' rent in advance. This expenditure resulted in an asset consisting of the right to occupy the office for two months. As each day in the month passed, part of the asset's cost expired and became an expense. By January 31, one-half had expired and should be treated as an expense. This economic event is analyzed and recorded as follows:

Prepaid Rent (Adjustment a)

A = L + OE
–   –

		Dr.	Cr.
Jan. 31	Rent Expense	400	
	Prepaid Rent		400

Prepaid Rent

Jan. 2	800	Jan. 31	400

Rent Expense

Jan. 31	400

Transaction: Expiration of one month's rent.
Analysis: Assets decrease. Owner's equity decreases.
Rules: Decreases in owner's equity are recorded by debits. Decreases in assets are recorded by credits.
Entries: The decrease in owner's equity is recorded by a debit to Rent Expense. The decrease in assets is recorded by a credit to Prepaid Rent.

Reinforcement Exercise: XYZ Company pays $1,200 for six months' advance rent. Make the adjusting entry after one month's rent has expired. **Solution:**

Rent Expense	200	
Prepaid Rent		200

The Prepaid Rent account now has a balance of $400, which represents one month's rent paid in advance. The Rent Expense account reflects the $400 expense for the month of January.

Besides rent, Joan Miller Advertising Agency prepaid expenses for insurance, art supplies, and office supplies, all of which call for adjusting entries.

On January 8, the agency purchased a one-year life insurance policy, paying for it in advance. Like prepaid rent, prepaid insurance offers benefits (in this case, protection) that expire day by day. By the end of the month, one-twelfth of the protection had expired. The adjustment is analyzed and recorded as follows:

Prepaid Insurance (Adjustment b)

A = L + OE
−   −

Reinforcement Exercise: Before adjustment, the Prepaid Insurance account of XYZ Company had a balance of $7,200. As of the end of the period, $5,500 had not expired. Make the adjusting entry for expired insurance. **Solution:**

Insurance Expense	1,700	
Prepaid Insurance		1,700

		Dr.	Cr.
Jan. 31	Insurance Expense	40	
	Prepaid Insurance		40

Prepaid Insurance

Jan. 8	480	Jan. 31	40

Insurance Expense

Jan. 31	40		

Transaction: Expiration of one month's life insurance.
Analysis: Assets decrease. Owner's equity decreases.
Rules: Decreases in owner's equity are recorded by debits. Decreases in assets are recorded by credits.
Entries: The decrease in owner's equity is recorded by a debit to Insurance Expense. The decrease in assets is recorded by a credit to Prepaid Insurance.

Point to Emphasize: Notice that the cost of supplies consumed is inferred, not observed.

The Prepaid Insurance account now shows the correct balance, $440, and Insurance Expense reflects the expired cost, $40 for the month of January.

Early in the month, Joan Miller Advertising Agency purchased art supplies and office supplies. As Joan Miller prepared advertising designs for various clients, art supplies were consumed, and her secretary used office supplies. There is no need to account for these supplies every day because the financial statements are not prepared until the end of the month and the recordkeeping would involve too much work. Instead, Joan Miller makes a careful inventory of the art and office supplies at the end of the month. This inventory records the quantity and cost of those supplies that are still assets of the company—that are yet to be consumed.

Suppose the inventory shows that art supplies costing $1,300 and office supplies costing $600 are still on hand. This means that of the $1,800 of art supplies originally purchased, $500 worth were used up (became an expense) in January. Of the original $800 of office supplies, $200 worth were consumed.

Art Supplies and Office Supplies (Adjustments c and d)

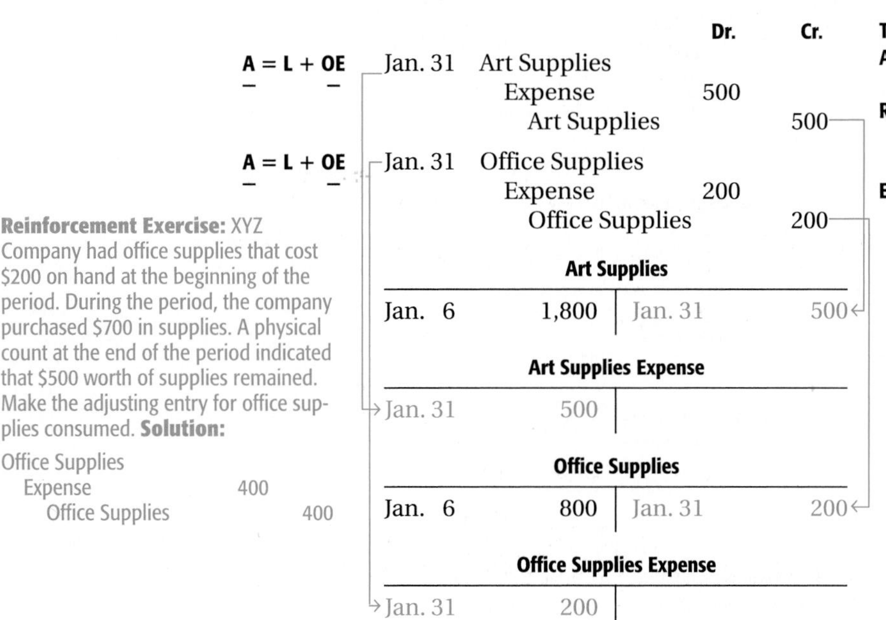

A = L + OE
−   −

A = L + OE
−   −

Reinforcement Exercise: XYZ Company had office supplies that cost $200 on hand at the beginning of the period. During the period, the company purchased $700 in supplies. A physical count at the end of the period indicated that $500 worth of supplies remained. Make the adjusting entry for office supplies consumed. **Solution:**

Office Supplies Expense	400	
Office Supplies		400

		Dr.	Cr.
Jan. 31	Art Supplies Expense	500	
	Art Supplies		500
Jan. 31	Office Supplies Expense	200	
	Office Supplies		200

Art Supplies

Jan. 6	1,800	Jan. 31	500

Art Supplies Expense

Jan. 31	500		

Office Supplies

Jan. 6	800	Jan. 31	200

Office Supplies Expense

Jan. 31	200		

Transaction: Consumption of supplies.
Analysis: Assets decrease. Owner's equity decreases.
Rules: Decreases in owner's equity are recorded by debits. Decreases in assets are recorded by credits.
Entries: The decreases in owner's equity are recorded by debits to Art Supplies Expense and Office Supplies Expense. The decreases in assets are recorded by credits to Art Supplies and Office Supplies.

The asset accounts Art Supplies and Office Supplies now reflect the correct balances, $1,300 and $600, respectively, of supplies that are yet to be consumed. In addition, the amount of art supplies used up during January is shown as $500 and the amount of office supplies used up is shown as $200.

Common Student Error: In accounting, depreciation refers only to the *allocation* of cost. Students, however, may continue to think about depreciation in the economic sense—that is, as the decline in value of an asset.

Point to Emphasize: The difficulty in fixing an asset's useful life is further evidence that the bottom-line figure is, at best, an estimate.

Depreciation of Plant and Equipment When an organization buys a long-term asset—a building, trucks, computers, store fixtures, or furniture—it is, in effect, prepaying for the usefulness of that asset for as long as it benefits the organization. Because a long-term asset is a deferral of an expense, the accountant must allocate the cost of the asset over its estimated useful life. The amount allocated to any one accounting period is called depreciation, or *depreciation expense.* Depreciation, like other expenses, is incurred during an accounting period to produce revenue.

It is often impossible to tell how long an asset will last or how much of the asset is used in any one period. For this reason, depreciation has to be estimated. Accountants have developed a number of methods for estimating depreciation and for dealing with the related complex problems. Here we look at the simplest case.

Suppose that Joan Miller Advertising Agency estimates that the art equipment for which it paid $4,200 and the office equipment for which it paid $3,000 will last five years (60 months) and will have zero value at the end of that time. The monthly depreciation of art equipment is $70 ($4,200 ÷ 60 months) and office equipment is $50 ($3,000 ÷ 60 months). These amounts represent the costs allocated to each month, and they are the amounts by which the asset accounts must be reduced and the expense accounts increased (reducing owner's equity).

Art Equipment and Office Equipment (Adjustments e and f)

A = L + OE
− −

		Dr.	Cr.
Jan. 31	Depreciation Expense, Art Equipment	70	
	Accumulated Depreciation, Art Equipment		70

A = L + OE
− −

		Dr.	Cr.
Jan. 31	Depreciation Expense, Office Equipment	50	
	Accumulated Depreciation, Office Equipment		50

Transaction: Recording depreciation expense.
Analysis: Assets decrease. Owner's equity decreases.
Rules: Decreases in owner's equity are recorded by debits. Decreases in assets are recorded by credits.
Entries: The owner's equity is decreased by debits to Depreciation Expense, Art Equipment and Depreciation Expense, Office Equipment. The assets are decreased by credits to Accumulated Depreciation, Art Equipment and Accumulated Depreciation, Office Equipment.

Reinforcement Exercise: XYZ Company purchased a company vehicle for $14,400. It is estimated that the vehicle will be used for six years and will be worthless after that time. Prepare the adjusting entry for depreciation after the company has used the vehicle for three months. **Solution:**

Depreciation Expense, Vehicle	600	
Accumulated Depreciation, Vehicle		600

Art Equipment

Jan. 4	4,200		

Accumulated Depreciation, Art Equipment

		Jan. 31	70

Office Equipment

Jan. 5	3,000		

Accumulated Depreciation, Office Equipment

		Jan. 31	50

Depreciation Expense, Art Equipment

Jan. 31	70		

Depreciation Expense, Office Equipment

Jan. 31	50		

BUSINESS BULLETIN: INTERNATIONAL PRACTICE

The privatization of businesses in Eastern Europe and the republics of the former Soviet Union has created a great need for Western accounting knowledge. Many managers from these countries are anxious to study accounting. Under the old governmental systems, the concept of net income as Westerners know it did not exist because the state owned everything and there was no such thing as income. The new businesses, because they are private, require accounting systems that recognize the importance of net income. In these new systems, it is necessary to make adjusting entries to record such things as depreciation and accrued expenses. Many Eastern European businesses have been suffering losses for years without knowing it and, as a result, are now in bad condition.

Teaching Note: To distinguish between depreciation expense and accumulated depreciation, first point out the difference in their placement in the financial statements. Then compare depreciation expense to a trip odometer in a car (which can be reset) and accumulated depreciation to an odometer (which cannot).

Accumulated Depreciation—A Contra Account Notice that in the previous analysis, the asset accounts are not credited directly. Instead, as shown in Figure 3, new accounts—Accumulated Depreciation, Art Equipment and Accumulated Depreciation, Office Equipment—are credited. These accumulated depreciation accounts are contra-asset accounts used to total the past depreciation expense on specific long-term assets. A contra account is a separate account that is paired with a related account—in this case an asset account. The balance of the contra account is shown on the financial statement as a deduction from the related account.

There are several types of contra accounts. In this case, the balance of Accumulated Depreciation, Art Equipment is shown on the balance sheet as a deduction from the associated account Art Equipment. Likewise, Accumulated Depreciation, Office Equipment is a deduction from Office Equipment. Exhibit 2

Figure 3
Adjustment for Depreciation

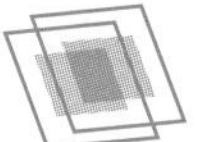

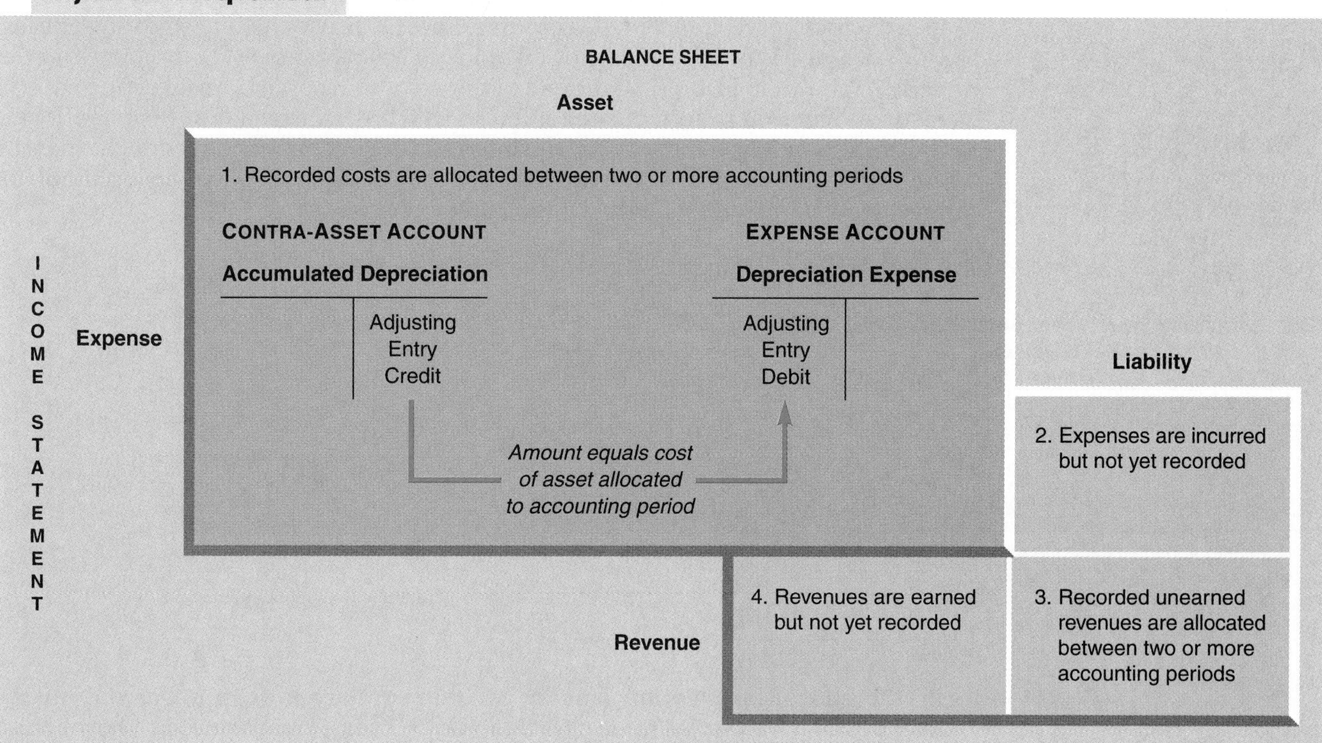

Exhibit 2. Plant and Equipment Section of the Balance Sheet

Joan Miller Advertising Agency
Partial Balance Sheet
January 31, 20xx

Plant and Equipment		
Art Equipment	$4,200	
Less Accumulated Depreciation	70	$4,130
Office Equipment	$3,000	
Less Accumulated Depreciation	50	2,950
Total Plant and Equipment		$7,080

shows the plant and equipment section of the balance sheet for Joan Miller Advertising Agency after these adjusting entries have been made.

A contra account is used for two very good reasons. First, it recognizes that depreciation is an estimate. Second, a contra account preserves the original cost of an asset: In combination with the asset account, it shows both how much of the asset has been allocated as an expense and the balance left to be depreciated. As the months pass, the amount of accumulated depreciation grows, and the net amount shown as an asset declines. In six months, Accumulated Depreciation, Art Equipment will show a balance of $420; when this amount is subtracted from Art Equipment, a net amount of $3,780 will remain. The net amount is called the carrying value, or *book value,* of the asset.

Type 2: Recognizing Unrecorded Expenses (Accrued Expenses)

At the end of an accounting period, there are usually expenses that have been incurred but not recorded in the accounts. These expenses require adjusting entries. One such case is interest on borrowed money. Each day, interest accumulates on the debt. As shown in Figure 4, at the end of the accounting period, an adjusting entry is made to record this accumulated interest, which is an expense of the period, and the corresponding liability to pay the interest. Other common unrecorded expenses are wages and salaries. As the expense and the corresponding liability accumulate, they are said to *accrue*—hence the term accrued expenses.

Accrued Wages Suppose the calendar for January looks like this:

Common Student Error: Some students may not understand why the adjustment in this example is for Monday through Wednesday, not for Thursday and Friday. Point out that Thursday and Friday are not covered in this accounting period.

Instructional Strategy: To reinforce the idea that every adjusting entry affects one balance sheet account and one income statement account, use FRA 3 or the Joan Miller Advertising Agency balance sheet in Exhibit 4. Ask students which balance sheet accounts are most likely to have had adjusting entries and what the corresponding income statement accounts would be.

January

Su	M	T	W	Th	F	Sa
	1	2	3	4	5	6
7	8	9	10	11	12	13
14	15	16	17	18	19	20
21	22	23	24	25	26	27
28	29	30	31			

By the end of business on January 31, the secretary at Joan Miller Advertising Agency will have worked three days (Monday, Tuesday, and Wednesday) beyond the last biweekly pay period, which ended on January 26. The employee has earned the

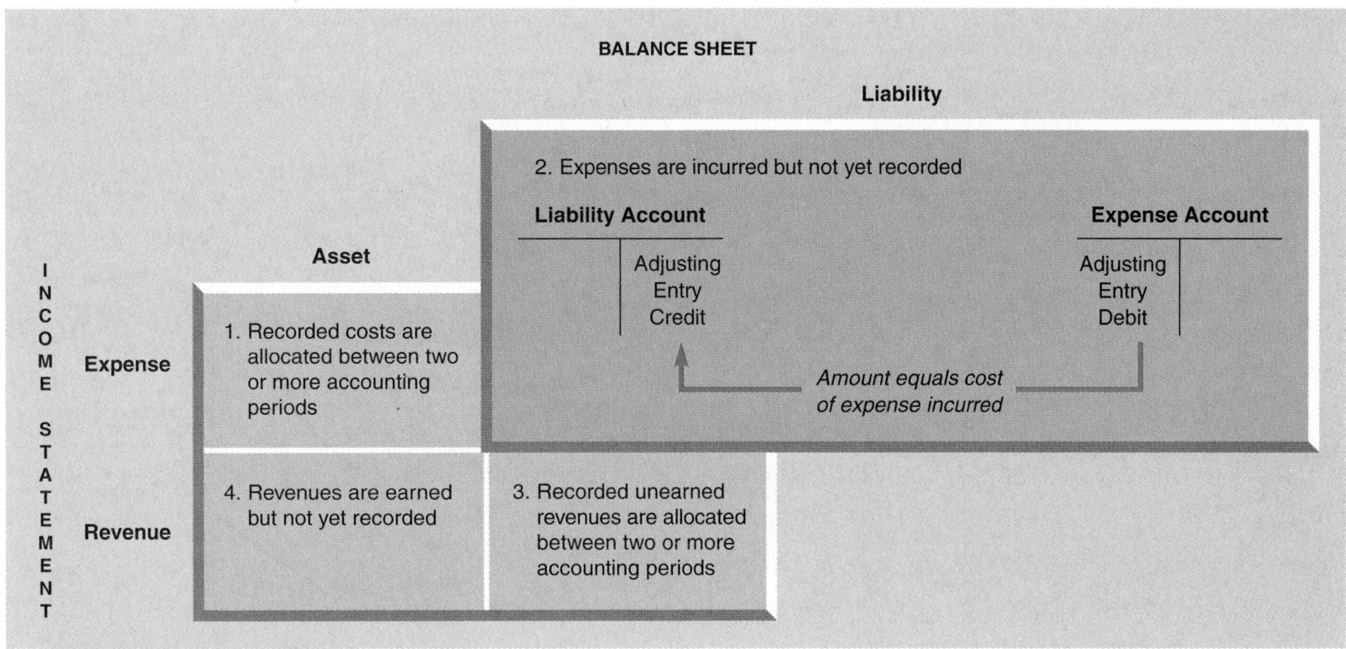

Figure 4
Adjustment for Unrecorded (Accrued) Expenses

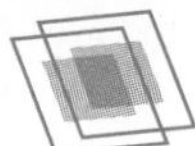

wages for these days, but she will not be paid until the regular payday in February. The wages for these three days are rightfully an expense for January, and the liabilities should reflect the fact that the company owes the secretary for those days. Because the secretary's wage rate is $600 every two weeks, or $60 per day ($600 ÷ 10 working days), the expense is $180 ($60 × 3 days).

Accrued Wages (Adjustment g)

A = L + OE
   + −

		Dr.	Cr.
Jan. 31	Wages Expense	180	
	Wages Payable		180

Wages Payable

		Jan. 31	180

Wages Expense

Jan. 12	600		
26	600		
31	180		

Transaction: Accrual of unrecorded expense.
Analysis: Liabilities increase. Owner's equity decreases.
Rules: Decreases in owner's equity are recorded by debits. Increases in liabilities are recorded by credits.
Entries: The decrease in owner's equity is recorded by a debit to Wages Expense. The increase in liabilities is recorded by a credit to Wages Payable.

Reinforcement Exercise: XYZ Company pays wages of $1,500 every Friday (for a five-day workweek). Assuming that the period ends on a Tuesday, prepare XYZ's adjusting entry. **Solution:**

Wages Expense	600	
Wages Payable		600

Point to Emphasize: Remember that an expense must be recorded in the period in which it is incurred, regardless of when payment is made.

The liability of $180 is now reflected correctly in the Wages Payable account. The actual expense incurred for wages during January, $1,380, is also correct.

Type 3: Allocating Recorded Unearned Revenues Between Two or More Accounting Periods (Deferred Revenues)

Point to Emphasize: Unearned Revenue is a liability because there is an obligation either to deliver goods or perform a service, or to return the payment. Once the goods have been delivered or the service performed, the liability is converted into revenue.

Just as expenses can be paid before they are used, revenues can be received before they are earned. When revenues are received in advance, the company has an obligation to deliver goods or perform services. Therefore, unearned revenues are shown in a liability account. For example, publishing companies usually receive payment in advance for magazine subscriptions. These receipts are recorded in a liability

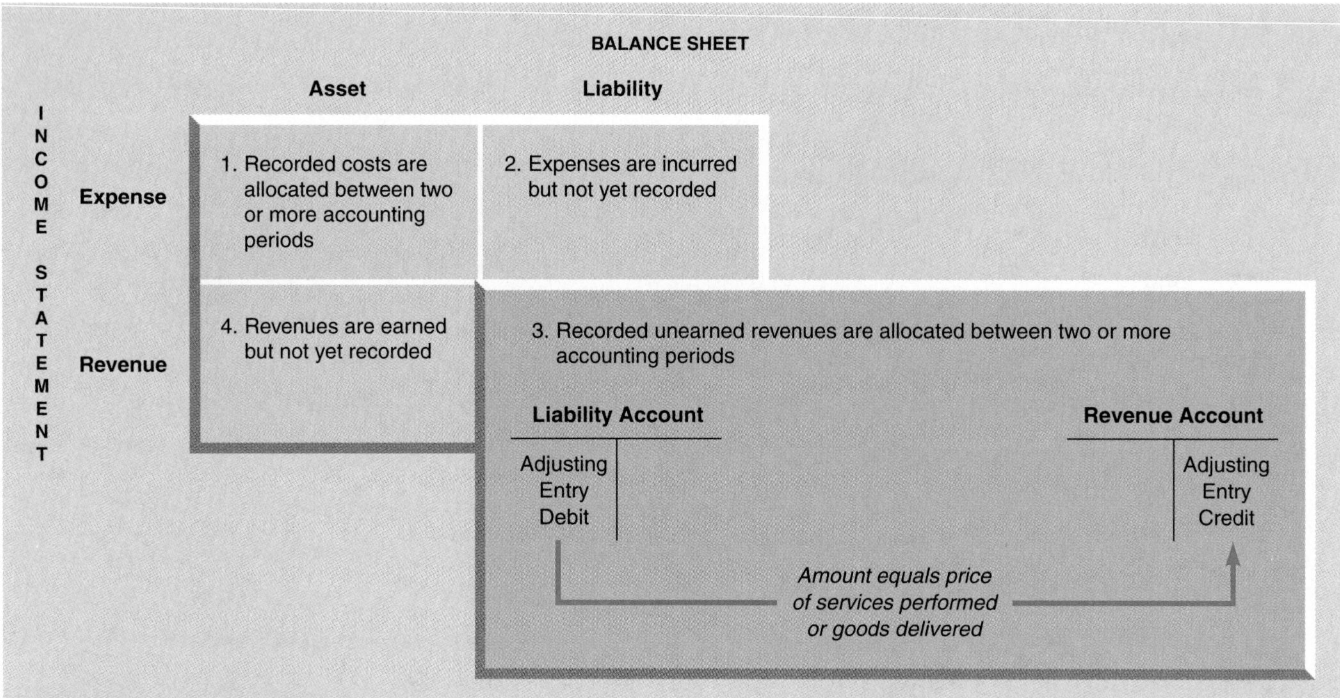

Figure 5
Adjustment for Unearned (Deferred) Revenues

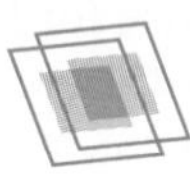

account. If the company fails to deliver the magazines, subscribers are entitled to their money back. As the company delivers each issue of the magazine, it earns a part of the advance payments. This earned portion must be transferred from the Unearned Subscriptions account to the Subscription Revenue account, as shown in Figure 5.

During the month of January, Joan Miller Advertising Agency received $1,000 as an advance payment for advertising designs to be prepared for another agency. Assume that by the end of the month, $400 of the design was completed and accepted by the other agency. Here is the transaction analysis:

Unearned Art Fees (Adjustment h)

A = L + OE
− +

		Dr.	Cr.
Jan. 31	Unearned Art Fees	400	
	Art Fees Earned		400

Unearned Art Fees

Jan. 31	400	Jan. 15	1,000

Art Fees Earned

		Jan. 31	400

Transaction: Performance of services paid for in advance.
Analysis: Liabilities decrease. Owner's equity increases.
Rules: Decreases in liabilities are recorded by debits. Increases in owner's equity are recorded by credits.
Entries: The decrease in liabilities is recorded by a debit to Unearned Art Fees. The increase in owner's equity is recorded by a credit to Art Fees Earned.

Reinforcement Exercise: XYZ Company received $500 in advance of performing a service. By the end of the period, one-fourth of the payment had been earned. Prepare the end-of-period adjustment.
Solution:

Unearned Revenues	125	
Revenue from Services		125

The liability account Unearned Art Fees now reflects the amount of work still to be performed, $600. The revenue account Art Fees Earned reflects the services performed and the revenue earned for them during January, $400.

Teaching Note: Distinguish between unearned revenues and accrued revenues by pointing out that with accrued revenues, cash is not received in advance or by the end of the period.

Type 4: Recognizing Unrecorded Revenues (Accrued Revenues)

Accrued revenues are revenues for which a service has been performed or goods delivered but for which no entry has been recorded. Any revenues earned but not

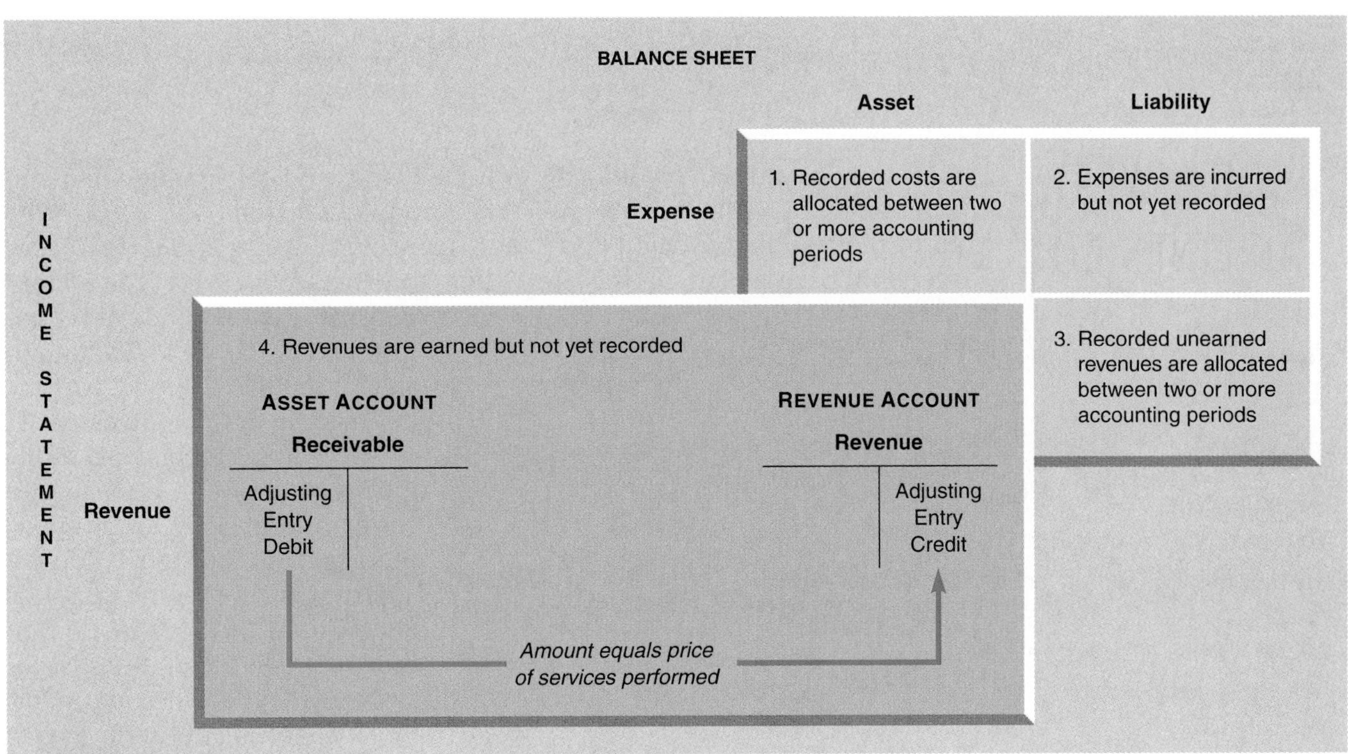

Figure 6
Adjustment for Unrecorded (Accrued) Revenues

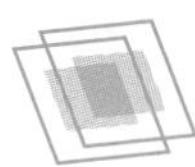

recorded during the accounting period call for an adjusting entry that debits an asset account and credits a revenue account, as shown in Figure 6. For example, the interest on a note receivable is earned day by day but may not be received until another accounting period. Interest Receivable should be debited and Interest Income should be credited for the interest accrued at the end of the current period.

Suppose that Joan Miller Advertising Agency has agreed to place a series of advertisements for Marsh Tire Company and that the first appears on January 31, the last day of the month. The fee of $200 for this advertisement, which has been earned but not recorded, should be recorded this way:

Accrued Advertising Fees (Adjustment i)

A = L + OE
\+   +

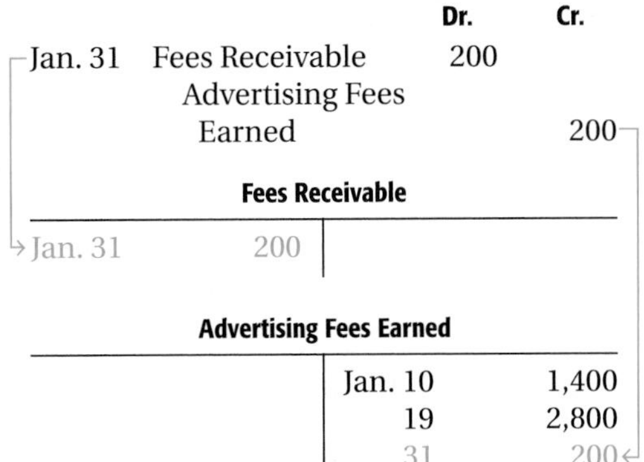

		Dr.	Cr.
Jan. 31	Fees Receivable	200	
	Advertising Fees Earned		200

Fees Receivable

Jan. 31	200		

Advertising Fees Earned

		Jan. 10	1,400
		19	2,800
		31	200

Transaction: Accrual of unrecorded revenue.
Analysis: Assets increase. Owner's equity increases.
Rules: Increases in assets are recorded by debits. Increases in owner's equity are recorded by credits.
Entries: The increase in assets is recorded by a debit to Fees Receivable. The increase in owner's equity is recorded by a credit to Advertising Fees Earned.

Reinforcement Exercise: By the end of the accounting period, a law firm has rendered $800 in legal services for which payment has not been received. Prepare the firm's end-of-period adjustment.
Solution:

Fees Receivable	800	
Legal Fees Earned		800

Now both the asset and the revenue accounts show the correct balance: The $200 in Fees Receivable is owed to the company, and the $4,400 in Advertising Fees Earned has been earned by the company during January. Marsh Tire Company will be billed for the series of advertisements when they are completed.

DECISION POINT

SOUTHWEST AIRLINES CO.

Adjustments can be very difficult to understand, and calculating them and entering them in the records takes time. You might be tempted to ask, "Why go to the trouble of making this adjustment? Why worry about it? Doesn't everything come out in the end when the transactions are completed? Because expenses and revenues in total are the same if you consider a multiyear period, isn't the net income in total unchanged?" In fact, adjustments are really quite important in evaluating a company. Consider, for example, the accrued liabilities (Type 2 adjustment) for Southwest Airlines Co. in 1996:[4] Why do you think the adjusting entries, especially accrued liabilities, are important in assessing the performance of the company?

Financial Highlights: Notes to Financial Statements

	Accrued Liabilities (in thousands)	
	1996	1995
Aircraft rentals	$121,384	$105,534
Employee profit sharing and savings plans	61,286	55,253
Vacation pay	44,763	38,777
Aircraft maintenance costs	25,942	31,463
Taxes, other than income	25,574	22,478
Interest	21,853	22,326
Other	79,945	73,588
	$380,747	$349,419

All adjusting entries are important because they help accountants compile information that is useful to management and other users. Adjusting entries are necessary in order to measure income and financial position in a relevant and useful way. Accrued liabilities are especially significant for Southwest Airlines. For example, the accrued liabilities of $380,747,000 represent 50 percent of the company's current liabilities, and they are almost double the company's net income. If these accruals had not been made in 1996, Southwest Airlines' net income would have been overstated by 184 percent!

Critical Thinking Question: If adjustments are not made, what type of operating performance measure would you have? **Answer:** Cash receipts from operations minus cash disbursements from operations yields net cash either from or used by operations. Remind students that adjusting entries never affect cash.

Adjusting entries also allow the comparison of financial statements from one accounting period to the next. Management, investors, and others can see whether the company is making progress in earning a profit or if the company has improved its financial position. If the adjustments for accrued liabilities are not recorded, not only will the income before income taxes for 1996 be overstated by $380,747,000, but the income before income taxes for 1997 will be understated by the same amount. This error will make 1997's earnings, whatever they may be, appear lower than they actually are. Also, even though one adjusting entry may seem insignificant, the cumulative effect of all adjusting entries can be great. The amount for the interest accrual, for example, is relatively small, but when all seven accruals are considered, the total effect is significant.

BUSINESS BULLETIN: TECHNOLOGY IN PRACT

In the accounting records, most accountants abbreviate the year by using the last t digits of the year, and most computer systems are programmed to handle dates the same way. For example, the year 1997 is written 97. But what happens after the year 2000? What will 04 represent? Is it 1904 or 2004? Most computer systems assume it is 1904. If a debt is due in 04, the computer can't figure out how long it is until it is due because 1997 minus 1904 gives a nonsense answer. Thus, the year 2000 is proving to be a major headache for computer users. A recent survey shows that 65 percent of the companies questioned are having to deal with this problem. For instance, *The Wall Street Journal* estimates that it will take 500 employees and cost $100 million to fix American Airlines, Inc.'s system. A major bank in Chicago expects to spend even more. There is even an Internet Web site for companies to share information about dealing with the problem.[5]

A Note About Journal Entries

Thus far we have presented a full analysis of each journal entry. The analyses showed you the thought process behind each entry. By now, you should be fully aware of the effects of transactions on the accounting equation and the rules of debit and credit. For this reason, in the rest of the book, journal entries are presented without full analysis.

Using the Adjusted Trial Balance to Prepare Financial Statements

OBJECTIVE 6

Prepare financial statements from an adjusted trial balance

Related Text Assignments:
Q: 20, 21
SE: 7, 8
E: 9
P: 4, 5

Point to Emphasize: The adjusted trial balance is a second check that the ledger is still in balance. Because it reflects updated information from the adjusting entries, it may be used to prepare the formal financial statements.

After adjusting entries have been recorded and posted, an adjusted trial balance is prepared by listing all accounts and their balances. If the adjusting entries have been posted to the accounts correctly, the adjusted trial balance should have equal debit and credit totals.

The adjusted trial balance for Joan Miller Advertising Agency is shown on the left side of Exhibit 3. Notice that some accounts, such as Cash and Accounts Receivable, have the same balances they have in the trial balance (see Exhibit 1) because no adjusting entries affected them. Some new accounts, such as Fees Receivable, depreciation accounts, and Wages Payable, appear in the adjusted trial balance, and other accounts, such as Art Supplies, Office Supplies, Prepaid Rent, and Prepaid Insurance, have balances different from those in the trial balance because adjusting entries did affect them.

From the adjusted trial balance, the financial statements can be easily prepared. The income statement is prepared from the revenue and expense accounts, as shown in Exhibit 3. Then, as shown in Exhibit 4, the statement of owner's equity and the balance sheet are prepared. Notice that the net income from the income statement is combined with withdrawals on the statement of owner's equity to give the net change in the Joan Miller, Capital account. The resulting balance of Joan Miller, Capital on January 31 is used on the balance sheet, as are the asset and liability accounts.

Exhibit 3. Relationship of Adjusted Trial Balance to Income Statement

Joan Miller Advertising Agency
Adjusted Trial Balance
January 31, 20xx

Cash	$ 1,720	
Accounts Receivable	2,800	
Fees Receivable	200	
Art Supplies	1,300	
Office Supplies	600	
Prepaid Rent	400	
Prepaid Insurance	440	
Art Equipment	4,200	
Accumulated Depreciation, Art Equipment		$ 70
Office Equipment	3,000	
Accumulated Depreciation, Office Equipment		50
Accounts Payable		3,170
Wages Payable		180
Unearned Art Fees		600
Joan Miller, Capital		10,000
Joan Miller, Withdrawals	1,400	
Advertising Fees Earned		4,400
Art Fees Earned		400
Wages Expense	1,380	
Utilities Expense	100	
Telephone Expense	70	
Rent Expense	400	
Insurance Expense	40	
Art Supplies Expense	500	
Office Supplies Expense	200	
Depreciation Expense, Art Equipment	70	
Depreciation Expense, Office Equipment	50	
	$18,870	$18,870

Joan Miller Advertising Agency
Income Statement
For the Month Ended January 31, 20xx

Revenues		
Advertising Fees Earned		$4,400
Art Fees Earned		400
Total Revenues		$4,800
Expenses		
Wages Expense	$1,380	
Utilities Expense	100	
Telephone Expense	70	
Rent Expense	400	
Insurance Expense	40	
Art Supplies Expense	500	
Office Supplies Expense	200	
Depreciation Expense, Art Equipment	70	
Depreciation Expense, Office Equipment	50	
Total Expenses		2,810
Net Income		$1,990

Discussion Question: Why is the income statement prepared before the statement of owner's equity, and that statement before the balance sheet? **Answer:** The net income figure is needed to prepare the statement of owner's equity, and the bottom-line figure of the statement of owner's equity is needed to prepare the balance sheet.

Exhibit 4. Relationship of Adjusted Trial Balance to Balance Sheet and Statement of Owner's Equity

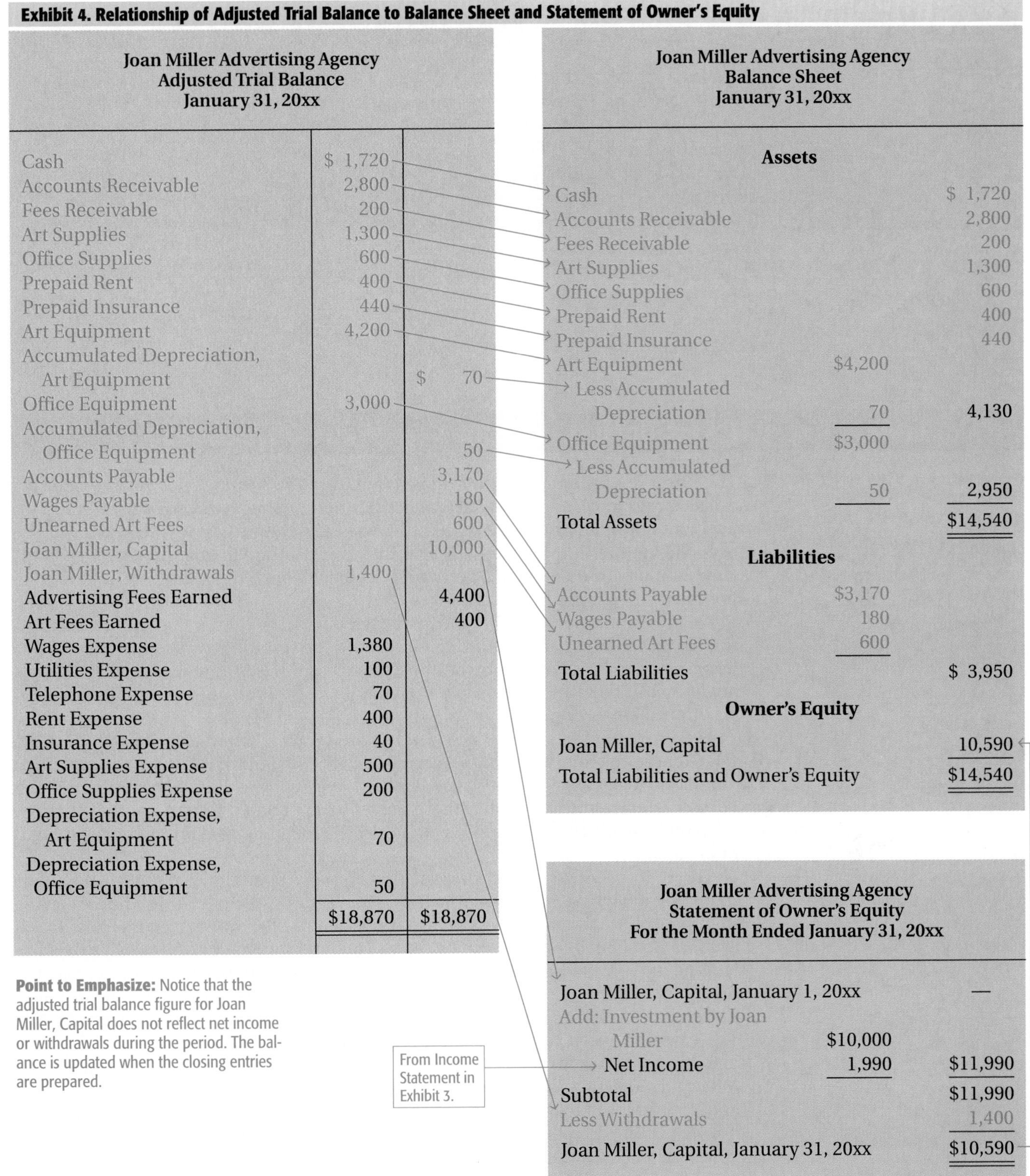

Joan Miller Advertising Agency
Adjusted Trial Balance
January 31, 20xx

Cash	$ 1,720	
Accounts Receivable	2,800	
Fees Receivable	200	
Art Supplies	1,300	
Office Supplies	600	
Prepaid Rent	400	
Prepaid Insurance	440	
Art Equipment	4,200	
Accumulated Depreciation, Art Equipment		$ 70
Office Equipment	3,000	
Accumulated Depreciation, Office Equipment		50
Accounts Payable		3,170
Wages Payable		180
Unearned Art Fees		600
Joan Miller, Capital		10,000
Joan Miller, Withdrawals	1,400	
Advertising Fees Earned		4,400
Art Fees Earned		400
Wages Expense	1,380	
Utilities Expense	100	
Telephone Expense	70	
Rent Expense	400	
Insurance Expense	40	
Art Supplies Expense	500	
Office Supplies Expense	200	
Depreciation Expense, Art Equipment	70	
Depreciation Expense, Office Equipment	50	
	$18,870	$18,870

Joan Miller Advertising Agency
Balance Sheet
January 31, 20xx

Assets		
Cash		$ 1,720
Accounts Receivable		2,800
Fees Receivable		200
Art Supplies		1,300
Office Supplies		600
Prepaid Rent		400
Prepaid Insurance		440
Art Equipment	$4,200	
Less Accumulated Depreciation	70	4,130
Office Equipment	$3,000	
Less Accumulated Depreciation	50	2,950
Total Assets		$14,540
Liabilities		
Accounts Payable	$3,170	
Wages Payable	180	
Unearned Art Fees	600	
Total Liabilities		$ 3,950
Owner's Equity		
Joan Miller, Capital		10,590
Total Liabilities and Owner's Equity		$14,540

Joan Miller Advertising Agency
Statement of Owner's Equity
For the Month Ended January 31, 20xx

Joan Miller, Capital, January 1, 20xx		—
Add: Investment by Joan Miller	$10,000	
Net Income	1,990	$11,990
Subtotal		$11,990
Less Withdrawals		1,400
Joan Miller, Capital, January 31, 20xx		$10,590

From Income Statement in Exhibit 3.

Point to Emphasize: Notice that the adjusted trial balance figure for Joan Miller, Capital does not reflect net income or withdrawals during the period. The balance is updated when the closing entries are prepared.

BUSINESS BULLETIN: TECHNOLOGY IN PRACTICE

In a computerized accounting system, adjusting entries may be entered just like any other transactions. However, since some adjusting entries, such as those for insurance expense and depreciation expense, may be similar for each accounting period, and others, such as those for accrued wages, may always involve the same accounts, the computer may be programmed to display the adjusting entries automatically so that all the accountant has to do is verify the amounts or enter the correct amounts. Then the adjusting entries are entered and posted and the adjusted trial balance is prepared with the touch of a button.

Cash Flows, Accrual Accounting, and Management Objectives

SUPPLEMENTAL OBJECTIVE 7

Analyze cash flows from accrual-based information

Related Text Assignments:
Q: 22
SE: 9, 10
E: 10, 11, 12
FRA: 4

The purpose of accrual accounting is to measure the earnings of a business during an accounting period. This measurement of net income is directly related to management's profitability goal. A company must earn a sufficient net income to survive over the long term. Management also has the short-range goal of achieving sufficient liquidity to meet its needs for cash to pay its ongoing obligations and to plan for borrowing money from the bank.

An important measure of liquidity is cash flow. Cash flow is the inflows and outflows of cash during an accounting period and the resulting availability of cash. It is important for managers to be able to use accrual-based financial information to analyze cash flows in order to plan payments to creditors and assess the need for short-term borrowing.

Every revenue or expense account on the income statement has one or more related accounts on the balance sheet. For instance, Supplies Expense is related to Supplies, Wages Expense to Wages Payable, and Art Fees Earned to Unearned Art Fees. As shown in this chapter, these accounts are related to one another through adjusting entries whose purpose is to apply the matching rule in the measurement of net income.

The cash flows generated or paid by company operations may also be determined by analyzing these relationships. For example, suppose that after receiving the financial statements in Exhibits 3 and 4, Joan Miller wants to know how much cash was expended for art supplies. On the income statement, Art Supplies Expense is $500, and on the balance sheet, Art Supplies is $1,300. Because January was the first month of operation for the company, there was no prior balance of art supplies, and so the amount of cash expended for art supplies during the month was $1,800. The cash flow used to purchase art supplies ($1,800) was much greater than the amount expensed in determining income ($500). In planning for February, Joan Miller Advertising Agency can anticipate that the cash needed may be less than the amount expensed because, given the large inventory of art supplies, it will probably not be necessary to buy art supplies for more than a month. Understanding these cash flow effects enables Joan Miller to better predict her business's need for cash during February.

The general rule for determining the cash flow received from any revenue or paid for any expense (except depreciation, which is a special case not covered here) is to determine the potential cash payments or cash receipts and deduct the amount not paid or received. The application of the general rule varies with the type of asset or liability account, which is shown as follows:

Type of Account	Potential Payment or Receipt	Not Paid or Received	Result
Prepaid Expense	Ending Balance + Expense for the Period	– Beginning Balance	= Cash Payments for Expenses
Unearned Revenue	Ending Balance + Revenue for the Period	– Beginning Balance	= Cash Receipts from Revenues
Accrued Expense	Beginning Balance + Expense for the Period	– Ending Balance	= Cash Payments for Expenses
Accrued Revenue	Beginning Balance + Revenue for the Period	– Ending Balance	= Cash Receipts from Revenues

Teaching Note: Balance sheet T accounts also work well to illustrate calculation of cash receipts and cash payments. Students have three pieces of information about the balance sheet account and must solve for one unknown. This approach reinforces the concept of normal balances. After the accrual number is entered, solve for the unknown cash effect.

For instance, assume that on May 31 a company had a balance of $480 in Prepaid Insurance and that on June 30 the balance was $670. If the insurance expense during June was $120, the amount of cash expended on insurance during June can be computed as follows:

Prepaid Insurance at June 30	$670
Insurance Expense during June	120
Potential cash payments for insurance	$790
Less Prepaid Insurance at May 31	480
Cash payments for insurance during June	$310

The beginning balance is deducted because it was paid in a prior accounting period. Note that the cash payments equal the expense plus the increase in the balance of the Prepaid Insurance account [$120 + ($670 − $480) = $310]. In this case, the cash paid was almost three times the amount of insurance expense. In future months, cash payments are likely to be less than the expense.

Chapter Review

REVIEW OF LEARNING OBJECTIVES

1. **Define *net income* and its two major components, *revenues* and *expenses*.** Net income is the net increase in owner's equity that results from the operations of a company. Net income equals revenues minus expenses, unless expenses exceed revenues, in which case a net loss results. Revenues equal the price of goods sold and services rendered during a specific period. Expenses are the costs of goods and services used up in the process of producing revenues.
2. **Explain the difficulties of income measurement caused by (a) the accounting period issue, (b) the continuity issue, and (c) the matching issue.** The accounting period issue recognizes that net income measurements for short periods of time are necessarily tentative. The continuity issue recognizes that even though businesses face an uncertain future, without evidence to the contrary, accountants must assume that a business will continue indefinitely. The matching issue has to do with the difficulty of assigning revenues and expenses to a period of time. It is addressed by applying the matching rule: Revenues must be assigned to the accounting period in which the goods are sold or the services performed, and expenses must be assigned to the accounting period in which they are used to produce revenue.
3. **Define *accrual accounting* and explain two broad ways of accomplishing it.** Accrual accounting consists of all the techniques developed by accountants to apply the matching rule. The two general ways of accomplishing accrual accounting are (1) by recognizing revenues when earned and expenses when incurred and (2) by adjusting the accounts.
4. **State four principal situations that require adjusting entries.** Adjusting entries are required (1) when recorded costs have to be allocated between two or more accounting periods, (2) when unrecorded expenses exist, (3) when recorded unearned revenues must be allocated between two or more accounting periods, and (4) when unrecorded revenues exist.

5. **Prepare typical adjusting entries.** The preparation of adjusting entries is summarized in the following table:

Type of Adjusting Entry	Type of Account		Balance Sheet Account Examples
	Debited	Credited	
1. Allocating recorded costs (previously paid, expired)	Expense	Asset (or contra-asset)	Prepaid Rent Prepaid Insurance Supplies Accumulated Depreciation, Buildings Accumulated Depreciation, Equipment
2. Accrued expenses (incurred, not paid)	Expense	Liability	Wages Payable Interest Payable
3. Allocating recorded unearned revenues (previously received, earned)	Liability	Revenue	Unearned Art Fees
4. Accrued revenues (earned, not received)	Asset	Revenue	Fees Receivable Interest Receivable

6. **Prepare financial statements from an adjusted trial balance.** An adjusted trial balance is prepared after adjusting entries have been posted to the accounts. Its purpose is to test whether the adjusting entries are posted correctly before the financial statements are prepared. The income statement is prepared from the revenue and expense accounts in the adjusted trial balance. The balance sheet is prepared from the asset and liability accounts in the adjusted trial balance and from the statement of owner's equity.

Supplemental Objective

7. **Analyze cash flows from accrual-based information.** Cash flow information bears on management's liquidity goal. The general rule for determining the cash flow effect of any revenue or expense (except depreciation, which is a special case not covered here) is to determine the potential cash payments or cash receipts and deduct the amount not paid or received.

REVIEW OF CONCEPTS AND TERMINOLOGY

The following concepts and terms were introduced in this chapter:

LO 2 **Accounting period issue:** The difficulty of assigning revenues and expenses to a short period of time.

LO 4 **Accrual:** The recognition of an expense or revenue that has arisen but has not yet been recorded.

LO 3 **Accrual accounting:** The attempt to record the financial effects of transactions and other events in the periods in which those transactions or events occur, rather than only in the periods in which cash is received or paid by the business. All the techniques developed by accountants to apply the matching rule.

LO 5 **Accrued expenses:** Expenses that have been incurred but are not recognized in the accounts; unrecorded expenses.

LO 5 **Accrued revenues:** Revenues for which a service has been performed or goods delivered but for which no entry has been made; unrecorded revenues.

LO 5 **Accumulated depreciation accounts:** Contra-asset accounts used to accumulate the depreciation expense of specific long-lived assets.

LO 6 **Adjusted trial balance:** A trial balance prepared after all adjusting entries have been recorded and posted to the accounts.

LO 4 **Adjusting entries:** Entries made to apply accrual accounting to transactions that span more than one accounting period.

LO 5 **Carrying value:** The unexpired portion of the cost of an asset. Also called *book value.*

LO 2 **Cash basis of accounting:** Accounting for revenues and expenses on a cash received and cash paid basis.

LO 2 **Continuity issue:** The difficulty associated with not knowing how long a business entity will survive.

LO 5 **Contra account:** An account whose balance is subtracted from an associated account in the financial statements.

LO 4 **Deferral:** The postponement of the recognition of an expense that already has been paid or of a revenue that already has been received.

LO 5 **Depreciation:** The portion of the cost of a tangible long-term asset allocated to any one accounting period. Also called *depreciation expense.*

LO 1 **Expenses:** Decreases in owner's equity resulting from the costs of goods and services used up in the course of earning revenues.

LO 2 **Fiscal year:** Any twelve-month accounting period used by an economic entity.

LO 2 **Going concern:** The assumption, unless there is evidence to the contrary, that a business entity will continue to operate indefinitely.

LO 2 **Matching rule:** Revenues must be assigned to the accounting period in which the goods are sold or the services performed, and expenses must be assigned to the accounting period in which they are used to produce revenue.

LO 1 **Net income:** The net increase in owner's equity that results from business operations and is accumulated in the owner's Capital account; revenues less expenses when revenues exceed expenses.

LO 1 **Net loss:** The net decrease in owner's equity that results from business operations when expenses exceed revenues. It is accumulated in the owner's Capital account.

LO 2 **Periodicity:** The recognition that net income for any period less than the life of the business, although tentative, is still a useful measure.

LO 5 **Prepaid expenses:** Expenses paid in advance that have not yet expired; an asset account.

LO 1 **Profit:** The increase in owner's equity that results from business operations.

LO 3 **Revenue recognition:** In accrual accounting, the process of determining when a sale takes place.

LO 1 **Revenues:** Increases in owner's equity resulting from selling goods, rendering services, or performing other business activities.

LO 5 **Unearned revenues:** Revenues received in advance for which the goods have not yet been delivered or the services performed; a liability account.

REVIEW PROBLEM

Determining Adjusting Entries, Posting to T Accounts, Preparing Adjusted Trial Balance, and Preparing Financial Statements

LO 5
LO 6 This was the unadjusted trial balance for Certified Answering Service on December 31, 20x2.

Certified Answering Service
Trial Balance
December 31, 20x2

Cash	$2,160	
Accounts Receivable	1,250	
Office Supplies	180	
Prepaid Insurance	240	
Office Equipment	3,400	
Accumulated Depreciation, Office Equipment		$ 600
Accounts Payable		700
Unearned Revenue		460
James Neal, Capital		4,870
James Neal, Withdrawals	400	
Answering Service Revenue		2,900
Wages Expense	1,500	
Rent Expense	400	
	$9,530	$9,530

The following information is also available:

a. Insurance that expired during December amounted to $40.
b. Office supplies on hand at the end of December totaled $75.
c. Depreciation for the month of December totaled $100.
d. Accrued wages at the end of December totaled $120.
e. Revenues earned for services performed in December but not yet billed on December 31 totaled $300.
f. Revenues earned in December for services performed that were paid in advance totaled $160.

REQUIRED

1. Prepare T accounts for the accounts in the trial balance and enter the balances.
2. Determine the required adjusting entries and record them directly to the T accounts. Open new T accounts as needed.
3. Prepare an adjusted trial balance.
4. Prepare an income statement, a statement of owner's equity, and a balance sheet for the month ended December 31, 20x2. The owner made no new investments during the month.

ANSWER TO REVIEW PROBLEM

1. T accounts set up and amounts from trial balance entered
2. Adjusting entries recorded

Cash

Bal.	2,160		

Accounts Receivable

Bal.	1,250		

Service Revenue Receivable

(e)	300		

Office Supplies

Bal.	180	(b)	105
Bal.	**75**		

Prepaid Insurance

Bal.	240	(a)	40
Bal.	**200**		

Office Equipment

Bal.	3,400		

Accumulated Depreciation, Office Equipment

		Bal.	600
		(c)	100
		Bal.	**700**

Accounts Payable

		Bal.	700

Unearned Revenue

(f)	160	Bal.	460
		Bal.	**300**

Wages Payable

		(d)	120

James Neal, Capital

		Bal.	4,870

James Neal, Withdrawals

Bal.	400		

Answering Service Revenue

		Bal.	2,900
		(e)	300
		(f)	160
		Bal.	**3,360**

Wages Expense

Bal.	1,500		
(d)	120		
Bal.	**1,620**		

Rent Expense

Bal.	400		

Insurance Expense

(a)	40		

Office Supplies Expense

(b)	105		

Depreciation Expense, Office Equipment

(c)	100		

3. Adjusted trial balance prepared

Certified Answering Service
Adjusted Trial Balance
December 31, 20x2

Cash	$ 2,160	
Accounts Receivable	1,250	
Service Revenue Receivable	300	
Office Supplies	75	
Prepaid Insurance	200	
Office Equipment	3,400	
Accumulated Depreciation, Office Equipment		$ 700
Accounts Payable		700
Unearned Revenue		300
Wages Payable		120
James Neal, Capital		4,870
James Neal, Withdrawals	400	
Answering Service Revenue		3,360
Wages Expense	1,620	
Rent Expense	400	
Insurance Expense	40	
Office Supplies Expense	105	
Depreciation Expense, Office Equipment	100	
	$10,050	$10,050

4. Financial statements prepared

Certified Answering Service
Income Statement
For the Month Ended December 31, 20x2

Revenues		
Answering Service Revenue		$3,360
Expenses		
Wages Expense	$1,620	
Rent Expense	400	
Insurance Expense	40	
Office Supplies Expense	105	
Depreciation Expense, Office Equipment	100	
Total Expenses		2,265
Net Income		$1,095

Certified Answering Service
Statement of Owner's Equity
For the Month Ended December 31, 20x2

James Neal, Capital, November 30, 20x2	$4,870
Net Income	1,095
Subtotal	$5,965
Less Withdrawals	400
James Neal, Capital, December 31, 20x2	$5,565

Certified Answering Service
Balance Sheet
December 31, 20x2

Assets		
Cash		$2,160
Accounts Receivable		1,250
Service Revenue Receivable		300
Office Supplies		75
Prepaid Insurance		200
Office Equipment	$3,400	
Less Accumulated Depreciation	700	2,700
Total Assets		$6,685
Liabilities		
Accounts Payable		$ 700
Unearned Revenue		300
Wages Payable		120
Total Liabilities		$1,120
Owner's Equity		
James Neal, Capital		5,565
Total Liabilities and Owner's Equity		$6,685

Chapter Assignments

BUILDING YOUR KNOWLEDGE FOUNDATION

Questions

1. Why does the accountant use the term *net income* instead of *profit?*
2. Define the terms *revenues* and *expenses.*
3. Why does the need for an accounting period cause problems?
4. What is the significance of the continuity assumption?
5. "The matching rule is the most significant concept in accounting." Do you agree with this statement? Explain your answer.
6. What is the difference between the cash basis and the accrual basis of accounting?
7. In what two ways is accrual accounting accomplished?
8. Why are adjusting entries necessary?
9. What are the four situations that require adjusting entries? Give an example of each.
10. "Some assets are expenses that have not expired." Explain this statement.
11. What do plant and equipment, office supplies, and prepaid insurance have in common?
12. What is the difference between accumulated depreciation and depreciation expense?
13. What is a contra account? Give an example.
14. Why are contra accounts used to record depreciation?
15. How does unearned revenue arise? Give an example.
16. Where does unearned revenue appear in the financial statements?
17. What accounting problem does a magazine publisher who sells three-year subscriptions have?
18. Under what circumstances does a company have accrued revenues? Give an example. What asset arises when the adjustment is made?
19. What is an accrued expense? Give two examples.
20. "Why worry about adjustments? Doesn't it all come out in the wash?" Discuss these questions.
21. Why is the income statement usually the first statement prepared from the adjusted trial balance?
22. To what management goals do the measurements of net income and cash flow relate?

Short Exercises

LO 2 LO 3 *Accrual Accounting Concepts*

SE 1. Match the concepts of accrual accounting on the right with the assumptions or actions on the left.

1. Assumes expenses can be assigned to the accounting period in which they are used to produce revenues
2. Assumes a business will last indefinitely
3. Assumes revenues are earned at a point in time
4. Assumes net income measured for a short period of time, such as one quarter, is a useful measure

a. periodicity
b. going concern
c. matching rule
d. revenue recognition

LO 5 *Adjustment for Prepaid Insurance*

SE 2. The Prepaid Insurance account began the year with a balance of $230. During the year, insurance in the amount of $570 was purchased. At the end of the year (December 31), the amount of insurance still unexpired was $350. Make the year-end entry in journal form to record the adjustment for insurance expense for the year.

SE 3. LO 5 *Adjustment for Supplies*

The Supplies account began the year with a balance of $190. During the year, supplies in the amount of $490 were purchased. At the end of the year (December 31), the inventory of supplies on hand was $220. Make the year-end entry in journal form to record the adjustment for supplies expense for the year.

SE 4. LO 5 *Adjustment for Depreciation*

The depreciation expense on office equipment for the month of March is $50. This is the third month that the office equipment, which cost $950, has been owned. Prepare the adjusting entry in journal form to record depreciation for March and show the balance sheet presentation for office equipment and related accounts after the adjustment.

SE 5. LO 5 *Adjustment for Accrued Wages*

Wages are paid each Saturday for a six-day workweek. Wages are currently running $690 per week. Make the adjusting entry required on June 30, assuming July 1 falls on a Tuesday.

SE 6. LO 5 *Adjustment for Unearned Revenue*

During the month of August, deposits in the amount of $550 were received for services to be performed. By the end of the month, services in the amount of $380 had been performed. Prepare the necessary adjustment for Service Revenue at the end of the month.

SE 7. LO 6 *Preparation of an Income Statement from an Adjusted Trial Balance*

The adjusted trial balance for Heller Company on December 31, 20x1, contains the following accounts and balances: Owner's Capital, $4,300; Withdrawals, $350; Service Revenue, $2,600; Rent Expense, $400; Wages Expense, $900; Utilities Expense, $200; Telephone Expense, $50; and Insurance Expense, $350. Prepare an income statement in proper form for the month of December.

SE 8. LO 6 *Preparation of a Statement of Owner's Equity*

Using the data in **SE 7,** prepare a statement of owner's equity for Heller Company.

SE 9. SO 7 *Determination of Cash Flows*

Wages Payable was $590 at the end of May and $920 at the end of June. Wages Expense for June was $2,300. How much cash was paid for wages during June?

SE 10. SO 7 *Determination of Cash Flows*

Unearned Revenue was $1,300 at the end of November and $900 at the end of December. Service Revenue was $5,100 for the month of December. How much cash was received for services provided during December?

Exercises

E 1. LO 2 LO 3 LO 4 *Applications of Accounting Concepts Related to Accrual Accounting*

The accountant for Demetra Company makes the assumptions or performs the activities listed below. Tell which of the following concepts of accrual accounting most directly relates to each assumption or action: (a) periodicity, (b) going concern, (c) matching rule, (d) revenue recognition, (e) deferral, and (f) accrual.

1. In estimating the life of a building, assumes that the business will last indefinitely.
2. Records a sale when the customer is billed.
3. Postpones the recognition of a one-year insurance policy as an expense by initially recording the expenditure as an asset.
4. Recognizes the usefulness of financial statements prepared on a monthly basis even though they are based on estimates.
5. Recognizes, by making an adjusting entry, wages expense that has been incurred but not yet recorded.
6. Prepares an income statement that shows the revenues earned and the expenses incurred during the accounting period.

E 2. LO 5 *Adjusting Entry for Unearned Revenue*

Lifestyle Company of Louisville, Kentucky, publishes a monthly magazine featuring local restaurant reviews and upcoming social, cultural, and sporting events. Subscribers pay for subscriptions either one year or two years in advance. Cash received from subscribers is credited to an account called Magazine Subscriptions Received in Advance.

On December 31, 20x3, the end of the company's fiscal year, the balance of this account was $1,000,000. Expiration of subscriptions is as follows:

During 20x3	$200,000
During 20x4	500,000
During 20x5	300,000

Prepare the adjusting entry in journal form for December 31, 20x3.

LO 5 *Adjusting Entries for Prepaid Insurance*

E 3. An examination of the Prepaid Insurance account shows a balance of $4,112 at the end of an accounting period, before adjustment. Prepare entries in journal form to record the insurance expense for the period under each of the following independent assumptions.

1. An examination of the insurance policies shows unexpired insurance that cost $1,974 at the end of the period.
2. An examination of the insurance policies shows that insurance that cost $694 has expired during the period.

LO 5 *Supplies Account: Missing Data*

E 4. Each column below represents a Supplies account:

	a	b	c	d
Supplies on hand, October 1	$396	$ 651	$294	$?
Supplies purchased during the month	78	?	261	2,892
Supplies consumed during the month	291	1,458	?	2,448
Supplies on hand, October 31	?	654	84	1,782

1. Determine the amounts indicated by the question marks in the columns.
2. Make the adjusting entry for Column **a,** assuming supplies purchased are debited to an asset account.

LO 5 *Adjusting Entry for Accrued Salaries*

E 5. Tru Vent has a five-day workweek and pays salaries of $70,000 each Friday.

1. Make the adjusting entry required on July 31, assuming that August 1 falls on a Wednesday.
2. Make the entry to pay the salaries on August 3.

LO 5 *Revenue and Expense Recognition*

E 6. Orlando Company produces computer software that is sold by Bond Systems Company. Orlando receives a royalty of 15 percent of sales. Royalties are paid by Bond Systems and received by Orlando semiannually on May 1 for sales made July through December of the previous year and on November 1 for sales made January through June of the current year. Royalty expense for Bond Systems and royalty income for Orlando in the amount of $12,000 were accrued on December 31, 20x2. Cash in the amounts of $12,000 and $20,000 was paid and received on May 1 and November 1, 20x3, respectively. Software sales during the July to December 20x3 period totaled $300,000.

1. Calculate the amount of royalty expense for Bond Systems and royalty income for Orlando during 20x3.
2. Record the appropriate adjusting entry made by each company on December 31, 20x3.

LO 5 *Adjusting Entries*

E 7. Prepare year-end adjusting entries for each of the following:

1. Office Supplies had a balance of $168 on January 1. Purchases debited to Office Supplies during the year amount to $830. A year-end inventory reveals supplies of $570 on hand.
2. Depreciation of office equipment is estimated to be $4,260 for the year.
3. Property taxes for six months, estimated at $1,750, have accrued but have not been recorded.
4. Unrecorded interest receivable on U.S. government bonds is $1,700.
5. Unearned Revenue has a balance of $1,800. Services for $600 received in advance have now been performed.
6. Services totaling $400 have been performed; the customer has not yet been billed.

LO 5 *Accounting for Revenue Received in Advance*

E 8. Antonia Soria, a lawyer, was paid $72,000 on April 1 to represent a client in certain real estate negotiations over the next twelve months.

1. Record the entries required in Soria's records on April 1 and at the end of the year, December 31.
2. How would this transaction be reflected in the income statement and balance sheet on December 31?

E 9. LO 6 *Preparation of Financial Statements*

Prepare the monthly income statement, statement of owner's equity, and balance sheet for Rogers Custodial Services from the data provided in this adjusted trial balance.

Rogers Custodial Services
Adjusted Trial Balance
August 31, 20xx

Cash	$ 4,590	
Accounts Receivable	2,592	
Prepaid Insurance	380	
Prepaid Rent	200	
Cleaning Supplies	152	
Cleaning Equipment	3,200	
Accumulated Depreciation, Cleaning Equipment		$ 320
Truck	7,200	
Accumulated Depreciation, Truck		720
Accounts Payable		420
Wages Payable		80
Unearned Janitorial Revenue		920
Chuck Rogers, Capital		15,034
Chuck Rogers, Withdrawals	2,000	
Janitorial Revenue		14,620
Wages Expense	5,680	
Rent Expense	1,200	
Gas, Oil, and Other Truck Expenses	580	
Insurance Expense	380	
Supplies Expense	2,920	
Depreciation Expense, Cleaning Equipment	320	
Depreciation Expense, Truck	720	
	$32,114	$32,114

E 10. SO 7 *Determination of Cash Flows*

After adjusting entries had been made, the 20x3 and 20x4 balance sheets of Hampton Company showed the following asset and liability amounts at the end of each year:

	20x3	**20x4**
Prepaid Insurance	$1,450	$1,200
Wages Payable	1,100	600
Unearned Fees	950	2,100

From the accounting records, the following amounts of cash disbursements and cash receipts for 20x4 were determined:

Cash disbursed to pay insurance premiums	$1,900
Cash disbursed to pay wages	9,750
Cash received for fees	4,450

Calculate the amount of insurance expense, wages expense, and fees earned that should be reported on the 20x4 income statement.

E 11. SO 7 *Determining Cash Flows*

Horowitz Newspaper Agency delivers morning, evening, and Sunday city newspapers to subscribers who live in the suburbs. Customers can pay a yearly subscription fee in advance (at a savings) or pay monthly after delivery of their newspapers. The following data are available for the Subscriptions Receivable and Unearned Subscriptions accounts at the beginning and end of October 20xx:

	October 1	October 31
Subscriptions Receivable	$ 7,600	$ 9,200
Unearned Subscriptions	22,800	19,600

The income statement shows subscriptions revenue for October of $44,800. Determine the amount of cash received from customers for subscriptions during October. Why is this calculation important to management?

SO 7 *Relationship of Expenses to Cash Paid*

E 12. The income statement for Jarvis Company included the following expenses for 20xx:

Rent Expense	$ 5,200
Interest Expense	7,800
Salaries Expense	83,000

Listed below are the related balance sheet account balances at year end for last year and this year:

	Last Year	This Year
Prepaid Rent	—	$ 900
Interest Payable	$1,200	—
Salaries Payable	5,000	9,600

1. Compute the cash paid for rent during the year.
2. Compute the cash paid for interest during the year.
3. Compute the cash paid for salaries during the year.

Problems

LO 5 *Determining Adjustments*

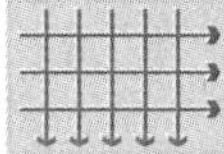

P 1. At the end of its fiscal year, the trial balance for Apollo Cleaners appears as follows:

Apollo Cleaners
Trial Balance
September 30, 20x2

Cash	$ 5,894	
Accounts Receivable	13,247	
Prepaid Insurance	1,700	
Cleaning Supplies	3,687	
Land	9,000	
Building	92,500	
Accumulated Depreciation, Building		$ 22,800
Accounts Payable		10,200
Unearned Dry Cleaning Revenue		800
Mortgage Payable		55,000
Marcos Apollo, Capital		28,280
Marcos Apollo, Withdrawals	5,000	
Dry Cleaning Revenue		60,167
Laundry Revenue		18,650
Wages Expense	50,665	
Cleaning Equipment Rent Expense	3,000	
Delivery Truck Expense	2,187	
Interest Expense	5,500	
Other Expenses	3,517	
	$195,897	$195,897

The following information is also available.

a. A study of insurance policies shows that $340 is unexpired at the end of the year.
b. An inventory of cleaning supplies shows $622 on hand.
c. Estimated depreciation on the building for the year is $6,400.
d. Accrued interest on the mortgage payable amounts to $500.
e. On September 1, the company signed a contract, effective immediately, with Stark County Hospital to dry clean, for a fixed monthly charge of $200, the uniforms used by doctors in surgery. The hospital paid for four months' service in advance.
f. Sales and delivery wages are paid on Saturday. The weekly payroll is $1,260. September 30 falls on a Thursday, and the company has a six-day pay week.

REQUIRED

All adjustments affect one balance sheet account and one income statement account. For each of the above situations, show the accounts affected, the amount of the adjustment (using a + or − to indicate an increase or decrease), and the balance of the account after the adjustment in the following format:

Balance Sheet Account	Amount of Adjustment (+ or −)	Balance after Adjustment	Income Statement Account	Amount of Adjustment (+ or −)	Balance after Adjustment

P 2. LO 5 *Preparing Adjusting Entries*

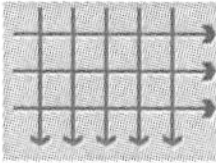

On June 30, the end of the current fiscal year, the following information was available to aid the Lincoln Company's accountants in making adjusting entries:

a. Among the liabilities of the company is a mortgage payable in the amount of $240,000. On June 30, the accrued interest on this mortgage amounted to $12,000.
b. On Friday, July 2, the company, which is on a five-day workweek and pays employees weekly, will pay its regular salaried employees $19,200.
c. On June 29, the company completed negotiations and signed a contract to provide services to a new client at an annual rate of $3,600.
d. The Supplies account showed a beginning balance of $1,615 and purchases during the year of $3,766. The end-of-year inventory revealed supplies on hand of $1,186.
e. The Prepaid Insurance account showed the following entries on June 30:

Beginning Balance	$1,530
January 1	2,900
May 1	3,366

The beginning balance represents the unexpired portion of a one-year policy purchased the previous year. The January 1 entry represents a new one-year policy, and the May 1 entry represents the additional coverage of a three-year policy.

f. The following table contains the cost and annual depreciation for buildings and equipment, all of which were purchased before the current year:

Account	Cost	Annual Depreciation
Buildings	$185,000	$ 7,300
Equipment	218,000	21,800

g. On June 1, the company completed negotiations with another client and accepted a payment of $21,000, representing one year's services paid in advance. The $21,000 was credited to Services Collected in Advance.
h. The company calculated that as of June 30 it had earned $3,500 on a $7,500 contract that would be completed and billed in August.

REQUIRED

Prepare adjusting entries for each item listed above.

P 3. This is the trial balance for the Executive Advisory Company on March 31, 20x3:

LO 5 *Determining Adjusting Entries, Posting to T Accounts, and Preparing an Adjusted Trial Balance*

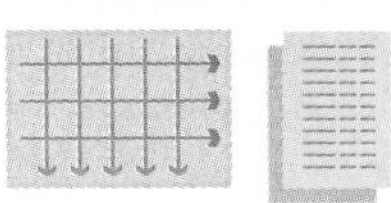

Executive Advisory Company
Trial Balance
March 31, 20x3

Cash	$ 25,572	
Accounts Receivable	49,680	
Office Supplies	1,982	
Prepaid Rent	2,800	
Office Equipment	13,400	
Accumulated Depreciation, Office Equipment		$ 3,200
Accounts Payable		3,640
Notes Payable		20,000
Unearned Fees		5,720
Barbara Podolski, Capital		58,774
Barbara Podolski, Withdrawals	30,000	
Fees Revenue		117,000
Salaries Expense	66,000	
Utilities Expense	3,500	
Rent Expense	15,400	
	$208,334	$208,334

The following information is also available:

a. Ending inventory of office supplies, $172.
b. Prepaid rent expired, $1,400.
c. Depreciation of office equipment for the period, $1,200.
d. Interest accrued on the note payable, $1,200.
e. Salaries accrued at the end of the period, $400.
f. Fees still unearned at the end of the period, $2,820.
g. Fees earned but not billed, $1,200.

REQUIRED

1. Open T accounts for the accounts in the trial balance plus the following: Fees Receivable; Interest Payable; Salaries Payable; Office Supplies Expense; Depreciation Expense, Office Equipment; and Interest Expense. Enter the balances.
2. Determine the adjusting entries and post them directly to the T accounts.
3. Prepare an adjusted trial balance.

P 4. Having graduated from college with a degree in accounting, Joyce Ozaki opened a small tax-preparation service. At the end of its second year of operation, Ozaki Tax Service had the trial balance shown at the top of the next page. The following information was also available:

LO 5
LO 6 *Determining Adjusting Entries and Tracing Their Effects to Financial Statements*

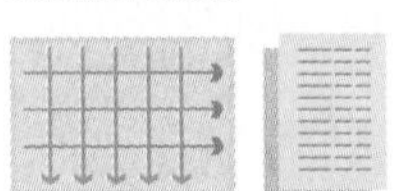

a. Office supplies on hand, December 31, 20x2, were $227.
b. Insurance still unexpired amounted to $120.
c. Estimated depreciation of office equipment was $410.
d. Estimated depreciation of the copier was $360.
e. The telephone expense for December was $19. This bill has been received but not recorded.
f. The services for all unearned tax fees had been performed by the end of the year.

Ozaki Tax Service Trial Balance December 31, 20x2		
Cash	$ 2,268	
Accounts Receivable	1,031	
Prepaid Insurance	240	
Office Supplies	782	
Office Equipment	4,100	
Accumulated Depreciation, Office Equipment		$ 410
Copier	3,000	
Accumulated Depreciation, Copier		360
Accounts Payable		635
Unearned Tax Fees		219
Joyce Ozaki, Capital		5,439
Joyce Ozaki, Withdrawals	6,000	
Fees Revenue		21,926
Office Salaries Expense	8,300	
Advertising Expense	650	
Rent Expense	2,400	
Telephone Expense	218	
	$28,989	$28,989

REQUIRED

1. Open T accounts for the accounts in the trial balance plus the following: Insurance Expense; Office Supplies Expense; Depreciation Expense, Office Equipment; and Depreciation Expense, Copier. Record the balances shown in the trial balance.
2. Determine the adjusting entries and post them directly to the T accounts.
3. Prepare an adjusted trial balance, an income statement, a statement of owner's equity, and a balance sheet.

P 5.
LO 5 LO 6 *Determining Adjusting Entries and Tracing Their Effects to Financial Statements*

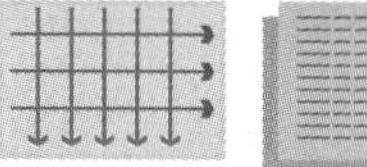

The Westland Limo Service was organized on January 1, 20x2, to provide limousine service between the airport and various suburban locations. It has just completed its second year of business. Its trial balance appears on the next page. John Cummings, the owner, made no investments during the year. The following information is also available:

a. To obtain space at the airport, Westland paid two years' rent in advance when it began business.
b. An examination of the firm's insurance policies reveals that $5,600 expired during the year.
c. To provide regular maintenance for the vehicles, a deposit of $24,000 was made with a local garage. An examination of maintenance invoices reveals that there are $21,888 in charges against the deposit.
d. An inventory of supplies shows $3,804 on hand.
e. All of the Westland Limo Service's limousines are depreciated at the rate of 12.5 percent a year. No limousines were purchased during the year.
f. A payment of $21,000 for one year's interest on notes payable is now due.
g. Unearned Passenger Service Revenue on December 31 includes $35,630 in tickets that were purchased by employers for use by their executives and that have not been redeemed. The rest have been redeemed.

Westland Limo Service
Trial Balance
December 31, 20x3

Cash (111)	$ 19,624	
Accounts Receivable (112)	28,454	
Prepaid Rent (117)	24,000	
Prepaid Insurance (118)	9,800	
Prepaid Maintenance (119)	24,000	
Supplies (141)	22,620	
Limousines (142)	400,000	
Accumulated Depreciation, Limousines (143)		$ 50,000
Notes Payable (211)		90,000
Unearned Passenger Service Revenue (212)		60,000
John Cummings, Capital (311)		156,422
John Cummings, Withdrawals (312)	40,000	
Passenger Service Revenue (411)		856,996
Gas and Oil Expense (511)	178,600	
Salaries Expense (512)	412,720	
Advertising Expense (513)	53,600	
	$1,213,418	$1,213,418

REQUIRED

1. Record the adjusting entries in the general journal (Page 14).
2. Open ledger accounts for the accounts in the trial balance plus the following: Interest Payable (213); Rent Expense (514); Insurance Expense (515); Supplies Expense (516); Depreciation Expense, Limousines (517); Maintenance Expense (518); and Interest Expense (519). Record the balances shown in the trial balance.
3. Post the adjusting entries from the general journal to the ledger accounts, showing the correct references.
4. Prepare an adjusted trial balance, an income statement, a statement of owner's equity, and a balance sheet.

Alternate Problems

LO 5 *Determining Adjustments*

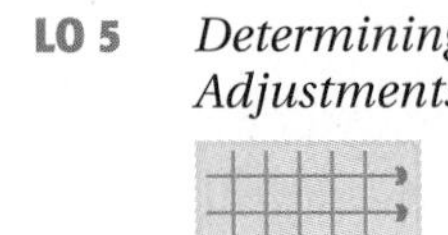

P 6. At the end of the first three months of operation, the trial balance of Citywide Answering Service appears as shown at the top of the next page. Ben Stuckey, the owner of Citywide, has hired an accountant to prepare financial statements to determine how well the company is doing after three months. Upon examining the accounting records, the accountant finds the following items of interest:

a. An inventory of office supplies reveals supplies on hand of $133.
b. The Prepaid Rent account includes the rent for the first three months plus a deposit for April's rent.
c. Depreciation on the equipment for the first three months is $208.
d. The balance of the Unearned Answering Service Revenue account represents a twelve-month service contract paid in advance on February 1.
e. On March 31, accrued wages total $80.

The balance of the Capital account represents investments by Ben Stuckey.

Citywide Answering Service
Trial Balance
March 31, 20x2

Cash	$ 3,482	
Accounts Receivable	4,236	
Office Supplies	903	
Prepaid Rent	800	
Equipment	4,700	
Accounts Payable		$ 2,673
Unearned Answering Service Revenue		888
Ben Stuckey, Capital		5,933
Ben Stuckey, Withdrawals	2,130	
Answering Service Revenue		9,002
Wages Expense	1,900	
Office Cleaning Expense	345	
	$18,496	$18,496

REQUIRED

All adjustments affect one balance sheet account and one income statement account. For each of the above situations, show the accounts affected, the amount of the adjustment (using a + or − to indicate an increase or decrease), and the balance of the account after the adjustment in the following format.

Balance Sheet Account	Amount of Adjustment (+ or −)	Balance after Adjustment	Income Statement Account	Amount of Adjustment (+ or −)	Balance after Adjustment

LO 5 *Preparing Adjusting Entries*

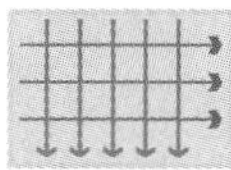

P 7. On May 31, the end of the current fiscal year, the following information was available to help Costa Company's accountants make adjusting entries:

a. The Supplies account showed a beginning balance of $4,348. Purchases during the year were $9,052. The end-of-year inventory revealed supplies on hand that cost $2,794.

b. The Prepaid Insurance account showed the following on May 31:

Beginning Balance	$ 7,160
February 1	8,400
April 1	14,544

The beginning balance represents the portion of a one-year policy that remained unexpired at the beginning of the current fiscal year. The February 1 entry represents a new one-year policy, and the April 1 entry represents additional coverage in the form of a three-year policy.

c. The following table contains the cost and annual depreciation for buildings and equipment, all of which were purchased before the current year:

Account	Cost	Annual Depreciation
Buildings	$572,000	$29,000
Equipment	748,000	70,800

d. On March 1, the company completed negotiations with a client and accepted payment of $33,600, which represented one year's services paid in advance. The $33,600 was credited to Unearned Service Revenue.

e. The company calculated that as of May 31, it had earned $8,000 on a $22,000 contract that would be completed and billed in September.

f. Among the liabilities of the company is a note payable in the amount of $600,000. On May 31, the accrued interest on this note amounted to $30,000.
g. On Saturday, June 2, the company, which is on a six-day workweek, will pay its regular salaried employees $24,600.
h. On May 29, the company completed negotiations and signed a contract to provide services to a new client at an annual rate of $35,000.

REQUIRED

Prepare adjusting entries for each item listed above.

P 8. Here is the trial balance for Crown Advisory Services on July 31:

LO 5 *Determining Adjusting Entries, Posting to T Accounts, and Preparing an Adjusted Trial Balance*

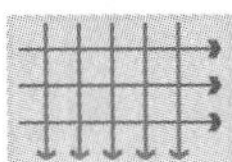

Crown Advisory Services
Trial Balance
July 31, 20xx

Cash	$ 8,250	
Accounts Receivable	4,125	
Office Supplies	1,331	
Prepaid Rent	660	
Office Equipment	4,620	
Accumulated Depreciation, Office Equipment		$ 770
Accounts Payable		2,970
Notes Payable		5,500
Unearned Fees		1,485
Molly Sklar, Capital		12,001
Molly Sklar, Withdrawals	11,000	
Fees Revenue		36,300
Salaries Expense	24,700	
Rent Expense	2,200	
Utilities Expense	2,140	
	$59,026	$59,026

The following information is also available:

a. Ending inventory of office supplies, $132.
b. Prepaid rent expired, $220.
c. Depreciation of office equipment for the period, $330.
d. Accrued interest expense at the end of the period, $275.
e. Accrued salaries at the end of the month, $165.
f. Fees still unearned at the end of the period, $583.
g. Fees earned but unrecorded, $1,100.

REQUIRED

1. Open T accounts for the accounts in the trial balance plus the following: Fees Receivable; Interest Payable; Salaries Payable; Office Supplies Expense; Depreciation Expense, Office Equipment; and Interest Expense. Enter the balances.
2. Determine the adjusting entries and post them directly to the T accounts.
3. Prepare an adjusted trial balance.

Skills Development

CONCEPTUAL ANALYSIS

LO 2 LO 3 LO 4 *Importance of Adjustments*

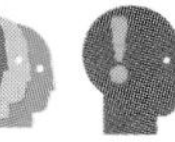

SD 1. ***Never Flake Company,*** which operated in the northeastern part of the United States, provided a rust-prevention coating for the underside of new automobiles. The company advertised widely and offered its services through new car dealers. When a dealer sold a new car, the salesperson attempted to sell the rust-prevention coating as an option. The protective coating was supposed to make cars last longer in the severe northeastern winters. A key selling point was Never Flake's warranty, which stated that it would repair any damage due to rust at no charge for as long as the buyer owned the car.

During the 1980s and most of the 1990s, Never Flake was very successful in generating enough cash to continue operations. But in 1998 the company suddenly declared bankruptcy. Company officials said that the firm had only $5.5 million in assets against liabilities of $32.9 million. Most of the liabilities represented potential claims under the company's lifetime warranty. It seemed that owners were keeping their cars longer in the 1990s than they had in the 1980s. Therefore, more damage was being attributed to rust. Discuss what accounting decisions could have helped Never Flake to survive under these circumstances.

Group Activity: Divide the class into groups to discuss this case. Then debrief as a class by asking a person from each group to comment.

LO 3 LO 4 *Application of Accrual Accounting*

SD 2. The ***Lyric Opera of Chicago*** is one of the largest and best-managed opera companies in the United States. Managing opera productions requires advance planning, including the development of scenery, costumes, and stage properties; the sale of tickets; and the collection of contributions. To measure how well the company is operating in any given year, accrual accounting must be applied to these and other transactions. At year end, April 30, 1997, Lyric Opera of Chicago's balance sheet showed Deferred Production Assets of $1,374,795 and Deferred Ticket Revenue of $16,604,605. Be prepared to discuss what accounting policies and adjusting entries are applicable to these accounts. Why are they important to Lyric Opera's management?

ETHICAL DILEMMA

LO 2 LO 3 LO 4 *Importance of Adjustments*

SD 3. ***Central Appliance Service Co.*** has achieved fast growth in the St. Louis area by selling service contracts on large appliances, such as washers, dryers, and refrigerators. For a fee, Central Appliance agrees to provide all parts and labor on an appliance after the regular warranty runs out. For example, by paying a fee of $200, a person who buys a dishwasher can add two years (years 2 and 3) to the regular one-year (year 1) warranty on the appliance. In 1999, the company sold service contracts in the amount of $1.8 million, all of which applied to future years. Management wanted all the sales recorded as revenues in 1999, contending that the amount of the contracts could be determined and the cash had been received. Discuss whether or not you agree with this logic. How would you record the cash receipts? What assumptions do you think should be made? Would you consider it unethical to follow management's recommendation? Who might be hurt or helped by this action?

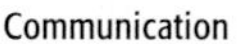

Communication | Critical Thinking | Group Activity | Memo | Ethics | International | Spreadsheet | General Ledger | CD-ROM | Internet

RESEARCH ACTIVITY

SD 4. LO 4 *The Importance of Accrued Expenses*

How important are accrued expenses? Randomly choose the annual reports of five companies from either your college's library or the Needles Accounting Resource Center Web site at http://www.hmco.com/college/needles/home.html. For each company, find the section of the balance sheet labeled "Current Liabilities" and identify the current liabilities that are accrued expenses (sometimes called accrued liabilities). More than one account may be involved. On a pad, write the information you find in four columns: name of company, total current liabilities, total accrued liabilities, and total accrued liabilities as a percentage of total current liabilities. Write a memorandum to your instructor listing the companies you chose, telling how you obtained their reports, reporting the data you have gathered in the form of a table, and stating a conclusion, with reasons, as to the importance of accrued expenses to the companies you studied. (**Hint:** Compute the average percentage of total accrued expenses for the five companies you chose.)

DECISION-MAKING PRACTICE

SD 5. LO 1 LO 5 *Adjusting Entries and Performance Evaluation*

Karen Jamison, the owner of a newsletter for managers of hotels and restaurants, has prepared condensed amounts from the financial statements for 20x3.

Revenues	$346,000
Expenses	282,000
Net Income	$ 64,000
Total Assets	$172,000
Liabilities	$ 48,000
Owner's Equity	124,000
Total Liabilities and Owner's Equity	$172,000

Given these figures, Jamison is planning to withdraw $50,000 for personal expenses. However, Jamison's accountant has found that the following items were overlooked:

a. Although the balance of the Printing Supplies account is $32,000, only $14,000 in supplies is on hand at the end of the year.
b. Depreciation of $20,000 on equipment has not been recorded.
c. Wages of $9,400 have been earned by employees but not recognized in the accounts.
d. A liability account called Unearned Subscriptions has a balance of $16,200, although it is determined that one-third of these subscriptions have been mailed to subscribers.

1. Prepare the necessary adjusting entries.
2. Recast the condensed financial statement figures after making the necessary adjustments.
3. Discuss the performance of Jamison's business after the adjustments have been made. (**Hint:** Compare net income to revenues and total assets before and after the adjustments.) Do you think that making the withdrawal is advisable?

Financial Reporting and Analysis

INTERPRETING FINANCIAL REPORTS

FRA 1. LO 2 LO 5 *Analysis of an Asset Account*

Walt Disney Company is engaged in the financing, production, and distribution of motion pictures and television programming. In Disney's 1996 annual report, the balance sheet contains an asset called Film and Television Costs. Film and Television Costs, which consists of the cost associated with producing films and television programs less the amount expensed, was $3,912,000,000 in 1996. The statement of cash flows reveals that the amount of film and television costs expensed (amortized) during 1996 was $2,966,000,000. The amount spent for new film productions was $3,678,000,000.[6]

REQUIRED

1. What are film and television costs and why would they be classified as an asset?
2. Prepare an entry to record the amount spent on new film and television production during 1996 (assume all expenditures are paid for in cash).

3. Prepare the adjusting entry that would be made to record the expense for film and television productions in 1996.
4. Can you suggest a method by which The Walt Disney Company might have determined the amount of the expense in **3** in accordance with the matching rule?

International Company

FRA 2.
LO 2 LO 3 *Account Identification and Accrual Accounting*

Takashimaya Company, Limited, is Japan's largest department store chain. An account on Takashimaya's balance sheet called Gift Certificates contains ¥45,370 million ($433 million).[7] Is this account an asset or a liability? What transaction gives rise to the account? How is this account an example of the application of accrual accounting? Explain the conceptual issues that must be resolved for an adjusting entry to be valid.

Toys "R" Us Annual Report

FRA 3.
LO 4 *Analysis of Balance Sheet and Adjusting Entries*

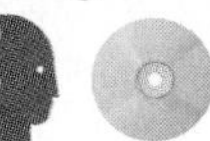

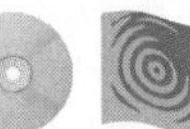

Refer to the balance sheet in the Toys "R" Us annual report. Examine the accounts listed in the current assets, property and equipment, and current liabilities sections. Which accounts are most likely to have had year-end adjusting entries? Tell the nature of the adjusting entries. For more information about the property and equipment section, refer to the notes to the consolidated financial statements.

Fingraph® Financial Analyst™

FRA 4.
LO 1 LO 4 SO 7 *Income Measurement and Adjustments*

Choose any company in the Fingraph® Financial Analyst™ CD-ROM software.

1. Does the company have a calendar year end or use some other fiscal year? Do you think the year end corresponds to the company's natural business year?
2. Find the company's balance sheet. From the asset accounts and liability accounts, find four examples of accounts that might have been related to an adjusting entry at the end of the year. For each example, tell whether the adjustment is a deferral or an accrual and suggest an income statement account that might be associated with it.
3. Find the summary of significant accounting policies, which appears following the financial statements. In these policies, find examples of the application of going concern and accrual accounting. Explain your choices of examples.
4. Prepare a one-page executive summary that highlights what you have learned from parts **1, 2,** and **3.**

ENDNOTES

1. Gannett Co., Inc., *Annual Report,* 1996.
2. "Where January Is the Cruelest Month," *Business Week,* June 4, 1994.
3. *Statement of Financial Accounting Concepts No. 1,* "Objectives of Financial Reporting by Business Enterprises" (Norwalk, Conn.: Financial Accounting Standards Board, 1978), par. 44.
4. Southwest Airlines Co., *Annual Report,* 1996.
5. Richard J. Koreto, "New Millennium Is Cause for Concern," *Journal of Accountancy,* October 1996.
6. The Walt Disney Company, *Annual Report,* 1996.
7. Takashimaya Company, Limited, *Annual Report,* 1996.

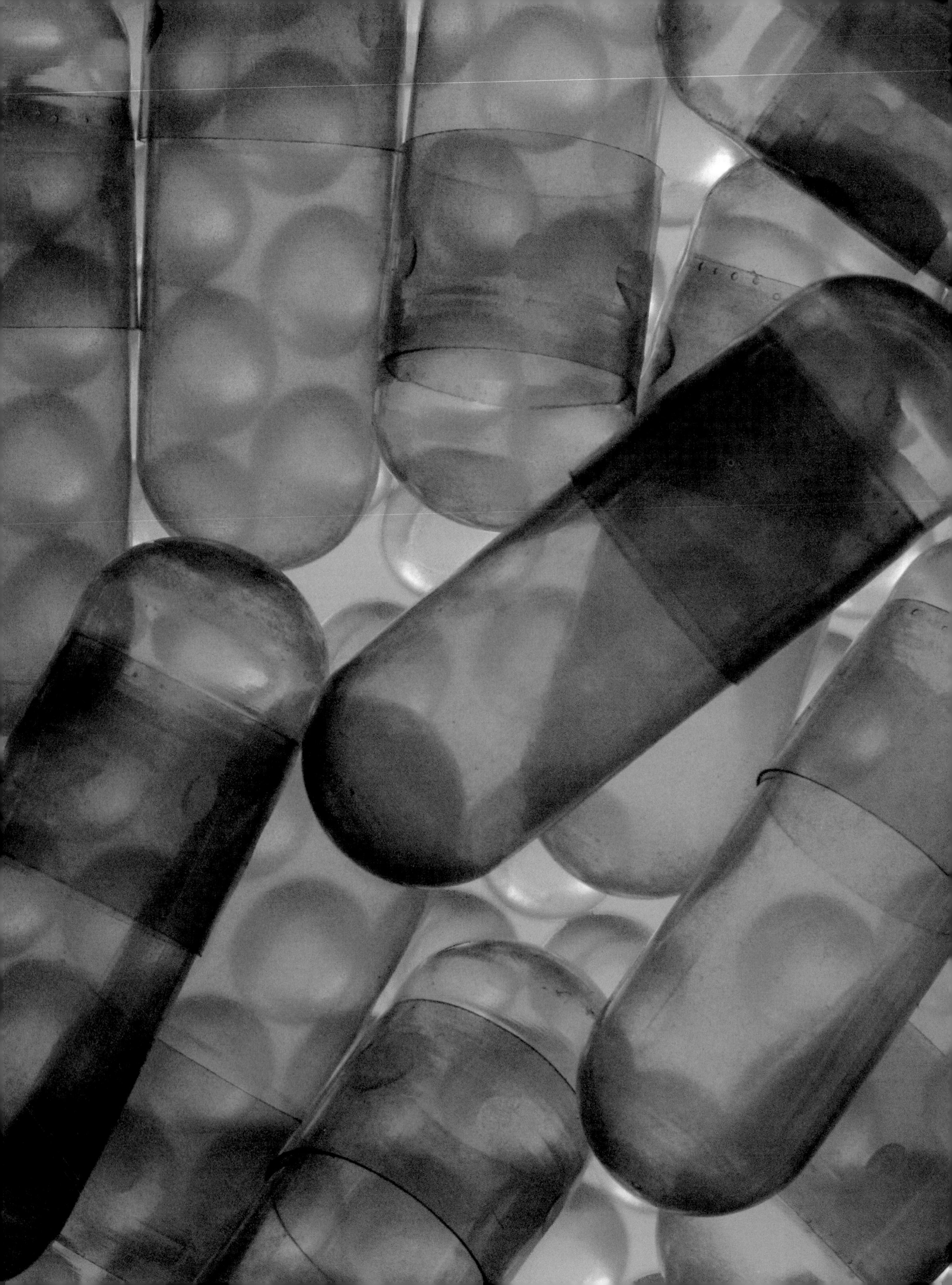

CHAPTER 4

Completing the Accounting Cycle

LEARNING OBJECTIVES

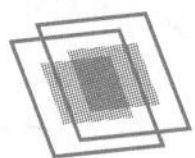

1. **State all the steps in the accounting cycle.**
2. **Explain the purposes of closing entries.**
3. **Prepare the required closing entries.**
4. **Prepare the post-closing trial balance.**
5. **Prepare reversing entries as appropriate.**
6. **Prepare a work sheet.**
7. **Use a work sheet for three different purposes.**

DECISION POINT

RHÔNE-POULENC RORER INC.

Critical Thinking Question: What economic conditions give interim financial statements greater importance for decision making? **Answer:** When prices or costs are changing rapidly, interim financial statements enable the business to respond quickly to ensure its profitability.

Rhône-Poulenc Rorer Inc., a French company, is one of the world's largest and most successful pharmaceutical companies, producing drugs that treat cancer and many other diseases. As a company whose shares are traded on the New York Stock Exchange, Rhône-Poulenc Rorer is required to prepare both annual and quarterly financial statements for its stockholders. Note the partial interim income statement from Rhône-Poulenc Rorer's "Mid-Year Progress Report" for 1996 that appears here.[1] This statement shows that Rhône-Poulenc Rorer increased its net sales and its net income by small amounts in the first half of 1996 when compared to the same period in 1995. Whether required by law or not, the preparation of *interim financial statements* every quarter, or even every month, is a good idea for all businesses because such reports give management an ongoing view of financial performance. What costs and time are involved in preparing interim financial statements?

Financial Highlights: Partial Interim Income Statement

(Unaudited—dollars and shares in millions except per share data)

	Six Months Ended June 30	
	1996	**1995**
Net sales	$2,618.5	$2,339.7
Cost of products sold	878.0	831.7
Selling, delivery, and administrative expenses	1,046.7	861.6
Research and development expenses	414.3	343.0
Operating income	279.5	303.4
Interest expense, net	84.5	23.0
Other (income) expense, net	(77.4)	10.3
Income before income taxes	272.4	270.1
Provision for income taxes	85.2	83.5
Net income	187.2	186.6

The preparation of interim financial statements throughout the year requires more effort than the preparation of a single set of financial statements for the entire year. Each time the financial statements are prepared,

Figure 1
Overview of the Accounting Cycle

Reinforcement Exercise: Have students list the sequence of steps in the accounting cycle and state the purpose of each step. (Figure 1 can be used as the basis for their answers.)

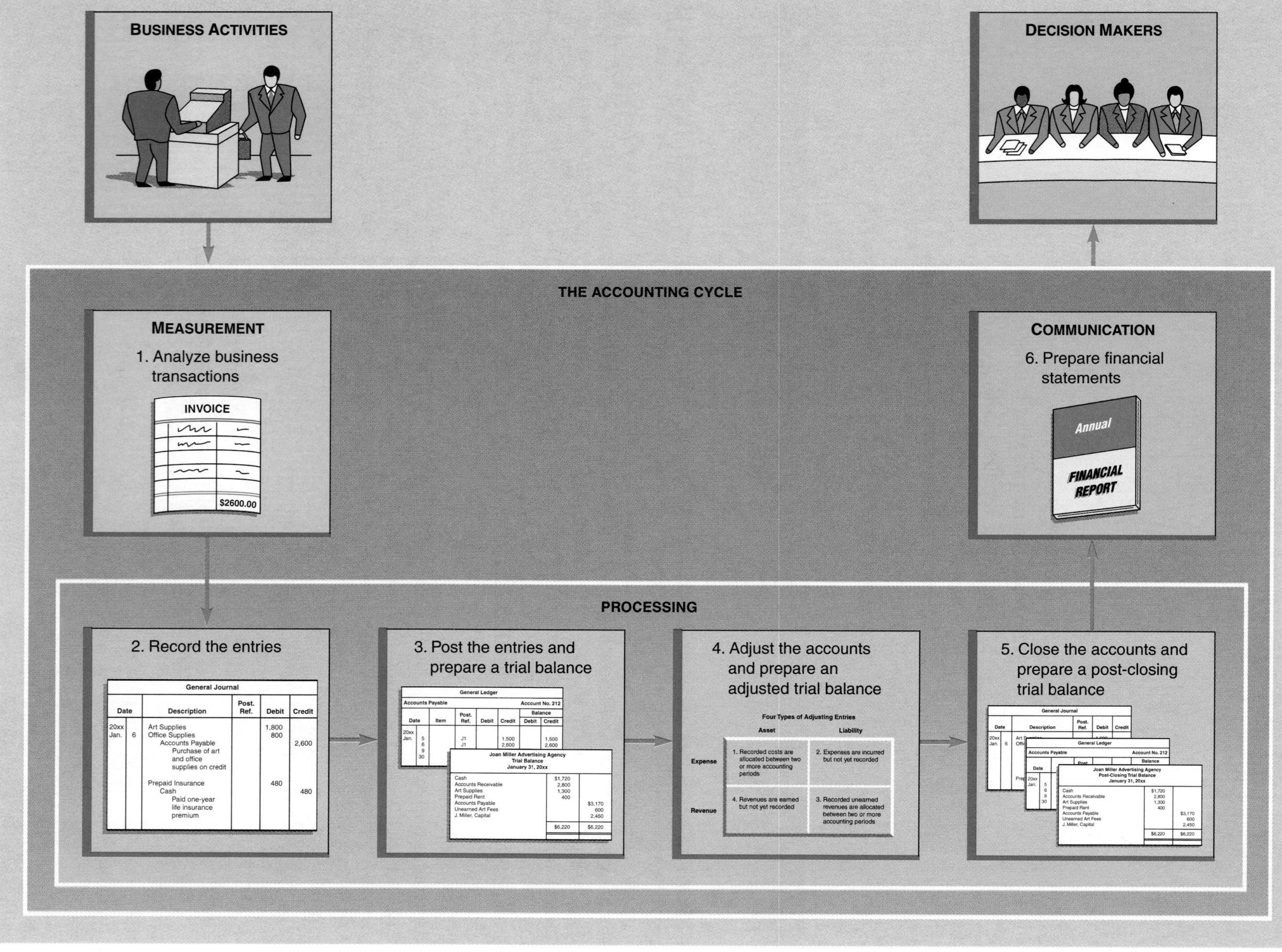

Clarification Note: The same set of accounting principles applies regardless of the accounting period chosen (month, quarter, or year). Preparing interim financial statements can be difficult and time-consuming because of the need to allocate certain costs and revenues to several different accounting periods.

adjusting entries must be determined, prepared, and recorded. Also, the ledger accounts must be prepared to begin the next accounting period. These procedures are time-consuming and costly. The advantages of preparing interim financial statements, even when they are not required, usually outweigh the costs, however, because such statements give management timely information for making decisions that will improve operations. This chapter explains the procedures used to prepare financial statements at the end of an accounting period, whether that period is a month, a quarter, or a year.

Overview of the Accounting Cycle

OBJECTIVE 1

State all the steps in the accounting cycle

Related Text Assignments:
Q: 1
SE: 1
P: 3
SD: 1, 3, 4, 5
FRA: 2, 3

Common Student Confusion: Even though most of the accounting cycle has been introduced by this point, students have difficulty both remembering the steps and understanding the rationale for their order. Remind them that steps 1 through 3 are carried out throughout the period, whereas steps 4 through 6 are carried out at the end of the period only.

The accounting cycle is a series of steps in the accounting system whose purpose is to measure business activities in the form of transactions and to transform these transactions into financial statements that will communicate useful information to decision makers. The steps in the accounting cycle, as illustrated in Figure 1, are as follows:

1. *Analyze* business transactions from source documents.
2. *Record* the entries in the journal.
3. *Post* the entries to the ledger and prepare a trial balance.
4. *Adjust* the accounts and prepare an adjusted trial balance.
5. *Close* the accounts and prepare a post-closing trial balance.
6. *Prepare* financial statements.

You are already familiar with steps 1–4 and 6. Step 5 is covered in this chapter. The order of these steps can vary to some extent depending on the system in place. For instance, the financial statements (step 6) may be completed before preparing the closing entries (step 5). In a computer system, step 6 usually must be done before step 5. The point is that all these steps must be accomplished to complete the accounting cycle. At key places in the accounting cycle, trial balances are prepared to ensure that the ledger remains in balance.

Closing Entries

OBJECTIVE 2

Explain the purposes of closing entries

Related Text Assignments:
Q: 2, 3, 4
SD: 4
FRA: 1

Teaching Note: Many students confuse adjusting and closing entries at this point. A quick review of the purpose of adjusting entries can help eliminate the confusion.

Balance sheet accounts are considered to be permanent accounts, or *real accounts,* because they carry their end-of-period balances into the next accounting period. On the other hand, revenue and expense accounts are temporary accounts, or *nominal accounts,* because they begin each accounting period with a zero balance, accumulate a balance during the period, and are then cleared by means of closing entries.

Closing entries are journal entries made at the end of an accounting period. They have two purposes. First, closing entries set the stage for the next accounting period by clearing revenue, expense, and withdrawal accounts of their balances. Remember that the income statement reports net income (or loss) for a single accounting period and shows revenues and expenses for that period only. For the income statement to present the activity of a single accounting period, the revenue and expense accounts must begin each new period with zero balances. The zero balances are obtained by using closing entries to clear the balances in the revenue and expense accounts at the end of each accounting period. The Withdrawals account is closed in a similar manner.

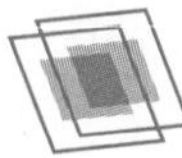

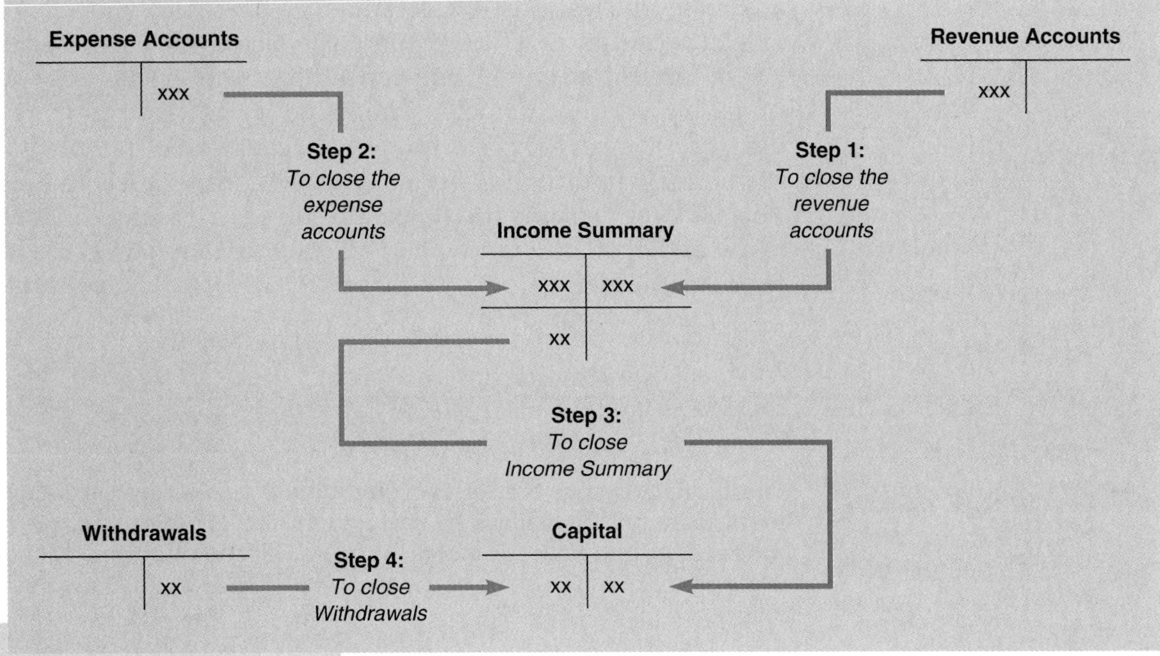

Figure 2
Overview of the Closing Process

Instructional Strategy: Divide the class into small groups and assign SD 3. Allow 8–10 minutes for group analysis, debrief the groups, and summarize the alternative strategies available to the assistant accountant.

Second, closing entries summarize a period's revenues and expenses. This is done by transferring the balances of revenues and expenses to the Income Summary account. This temporary account, which appears in the chart of accounts between the Withdrawals account and the first revenue account, provides a place to summarize all revenues and expenses. It is used only in the closing process and never appears in the financial statements.

The balance of the Income Summary account equals the net income or loss reported on the income statement. The net income or loss is then transferred to the Capital account. This is done because even though revenues and expenses are recorded in revenue and expense accounts, they actually represent increases and decreases in owner's equity. Closing entries transfer the net effect of increases (revenues) and decreases (expenses) to the owner's Capital account. An overview of the closing process is illustrated in Figure 2.

Required Closing Entries

OBJECTIVE 3

Prepare the required closing entries

Related Text Assignments:
Q: 5
SE: 2, 3, 4, 5, 6, 9
E: 1, 2, 8
P: 1, 2, 3, 4, 5, 6, 7, 8
SD: 4, 5
FRA: 1, 2

There are four important steps in closing the accounts:

1. Closing the credit balances from the income statement accounts to the Income Summary account
2. Closing the debit balances from the income statement accounts to the Income Summary account
3. Closing the Income Summary account balance to the Capital account
4. Closing the Withdrawals account balance to the Capital account

Each of these steps is accomplished by a closing entry. All the data needed to record the closing entries are found in the adjusted trial balance. The relationships of the four kinds of entries to the adjusted trial balance are shown in Exhibit 1.

Exhibit 1. Preparing Closing Entries from the Adjusted Trial Balance

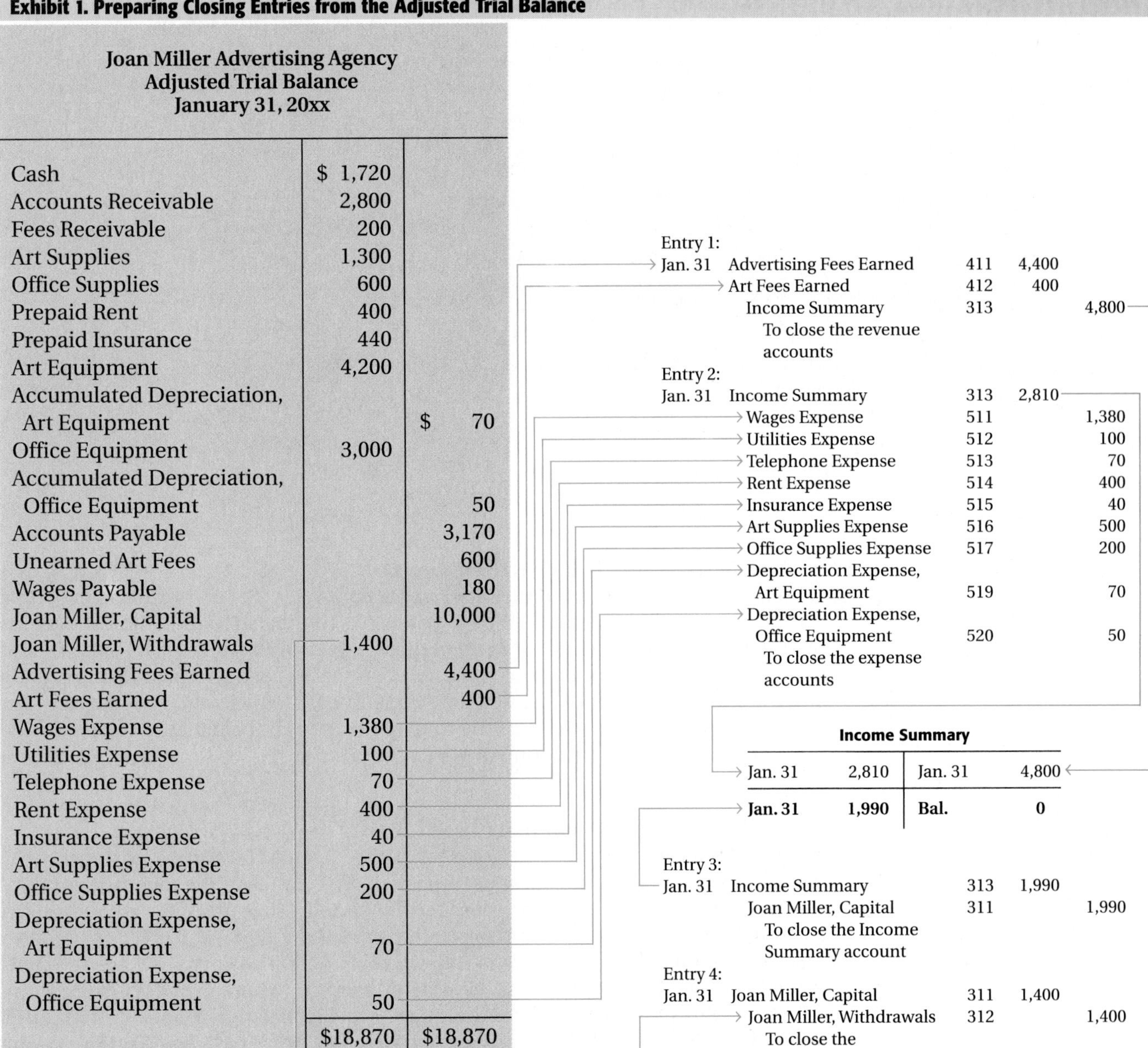

Joan Miller Advertising Agency
Adjusted Trial Balance
January 31, 20xx

Account	Debit	Credit
Cash	$ 1,720	
Accounts Receivable	2,800	
Fees Receivable	200	
Art Supplies	1,300	
Office Supplies	600	
Prepaid Rent	400	
Prepaid Insurance	440	
Art Equipment	4,200	
Accumulated Depreciation, Art Equipment		$ 70
Office Equipment	3,000	
Accumulated Depreciation, Office Equipment		50
Accounts Payable		3,170
Unearned Art Fees		600
Wages Payable		180
Joan Miller, Capital		10,000
Joan Miller, Withdrawals	1,400	
Advertising Fees Earned		4,400
Art Fees Earned		400
Wages Expense	1,380	
Utilities Expense	100	
Telephone Expense	70	
Rent Expense	400	
Insurance Expense	40	
Art Supplies Expense	500	
Office Supplies Expense	200	
Depreciation Expense, Art Equipment	70	
Depreciation Expense, Office Equipment	50	
	$18,870	$18,870

Entry	Date	Account	Ref.	Debit	Credit
Entry 1:	Jan. 31	Advertising Fees Earned	411	4,400	
		Art Fees Earned	412	400	
		Income Summary	313		4,800
		To close the revenue accounts			
Entry 2:	Jan. 31	Income Summary	313	2,810	
		Wages Expense	511		1,380
		Utilities Expense	512		100
		Telephone Expense	513		70
		Rent Expense	514		400
		Insurance Expense	515		40
		Art Supplies Expense	516		500
		Office Supplies Expense	517		200
		Depreciation Expense, Art Equipment	519		70
		Depreciation Expense, Office Equipment	520		50
		To close the expense accounts			

Income Summary

Jan. 31	2,810	Jan. 31	4,800
Jan. 31	**1,990**	**Bal.**	**0**

Entry	Date	Account	Ref.	Debit	Credit
Entry 3:	Jan. 31	Income Summary	313	1,990	
		Joan Miller, Capital	311		1,990
		To close the Income Summary account			
Entry 4:	Jan. 31	Joan Miller, Capital	311	1,400	
		Joan Miller, Withdrawals	312		1,400
		To close the Withdrawals account			

Enrichment Note: It is not absolutely necessary to use the Income Summary account when preparing closing entries. However, it does simplify the procedure. The Income Summary account is opened and closed with the preparation of closing entries.

Step 1: Closing the Credit Balances from Income Statement Accounts to the Income Summary Account On the credit side of the adjusted trial balance in Exhibit 1, two revenue accounts show balances: Advertising Fees Earned and Art Fees Earned. To close these two accounts, a journal entry must be made debiting each account in the amount of its balance and crediting the total to the Income Summary account. The effect of posting the entry is illustrated in Exhibit 2. Notice that the entry (1) sets the balances of the revenue accounts to zero and (2) transfers the total revenues to the credit side of the income Summary account.

Exhibit 2. Posting the Closing Entry of the Credit Balances from the Income Statement Accounts to the Income Summary Account

Advertising Fees Earned — Account No. 411

Date	Item	Post. Ref.	Debit	Credit	Balance Debit	Balance Credit
Jan. 10		J2		1,400		1,400
19		J2		2,800		4,200
31	Adj. (i)	J3		200		4,400
31	Closing	J4	4,400			—

Art Fees Earned — Account No. 412

Date	Item	Post. Ref.	Debit	Credit	Balance Debit	Balance Credit
Jan. 31	Adj. (h)	J3		400		400
31	Closing	J4	400			—

4,400
400
4,800

Income Summary — Account No. 313

Date	Item	Post. Ref.	Debit	Credit	Balance Debit	Balance Credit
Jan. 31	Closing	J4		4,800		4,800

Point to Emphasize: The Income Summary account now reflects the account balances that the revenue accounts contained before they were closed.

Step 2: Closing the Debit Balances from Income Statement Accounts to the Income Summary Account Several expense accounts show balances on the debit side of the adjusted trial balance in Exhibit 1. A compound entry is needed to credit each of these expense accounts for its balance and to debit the Income Summary account for the total. The effect of posting the closing entry is shown in Exhibit 3. Notice how the entry (1) reduces the expense account balances to zero and (2) transfers the total of the account balances to the debit side of the Income Summary account.

Point to Emphasize: In a net loss situation, debit the Capital account (to reduce it) and credit Income Summary (to close it).

Step 3: Closing the Income Summary Account to the Capital Account After the entries closing the revenue and expense accounts have been posted, the balance of the Income Summary account equals the net income or loss for the period. Since revenues are represented by the credit to Income Summary and expenses are represented by the debit to Income Summary, a net income is indicated by a credit balance (where revenues exceed expenses), and a net loss, by a debit balance (where expenses exceed revenues). At this point, the Income Summary account balance, whatever its nature, must be closed to the Capital account, as shown in Exhibit 1. The effect of posting

BUSINESS BULLETIN: BUSINESS PRACTICE

Performing routine accounting functions for other companies has become big business. The practice of managing a customer's information systems for a fixed fee is a form of *outsourcing.* By leaving the information systems operations to an outside company, management can devote its attention to income-earning activities. Electronic Data Systems, Inc., founded by H. Ross Perot in 1962 and the source of his fortune, is the largest company in this business (it was owned for several years by General Motors until 1997 and now is a separate company again). EDS had revenues exceeding $11 billion in 1997 and is very profitable.

Exhibit 3. Posting the Closing Entry of the Debit Balances from the Income Statement Accounts to the Income Summary Account

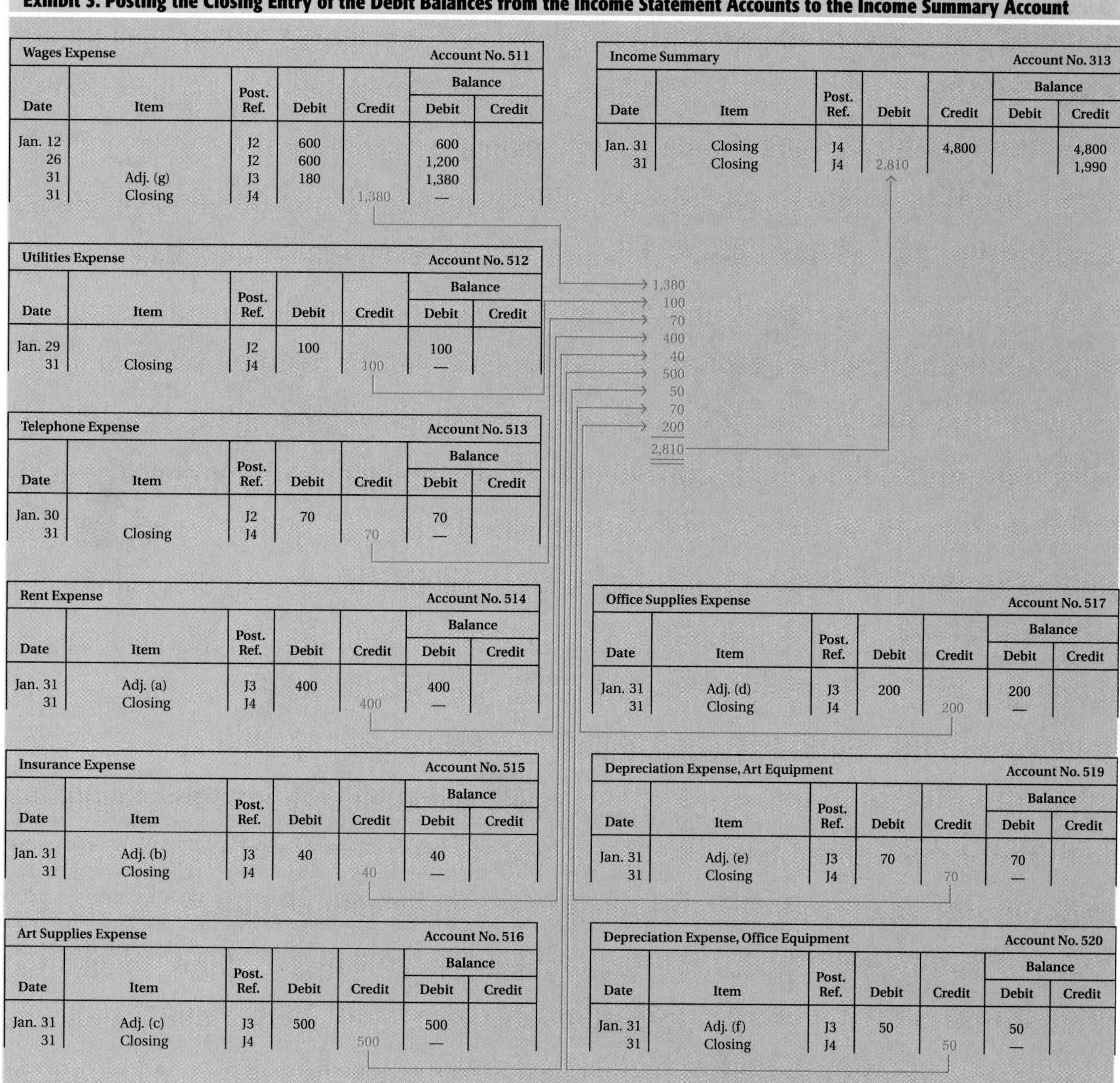

Wages Expense — Account No. 511

Date	Item	Post. Ref.	Debit	Credit	Balance Debit	Balance Credit
Jan. 12		J2	600		600	
26		J2	600		1,200	
31	Adj. (g)	J3	180		1,380	
31	Closing	J4		1,380	—	

Utilities Expense — Account No. 512

Date	Item	Post. Ref.	Debit	Credit	Balance Debit	Balance Credit
Jan. 29		J2	100		100	
31	Closing	J4		100	—	

Telephone Expense — Account No. 513

Date	Item	Post. Ref.	Debit	Credit	Balance Debit	Balance Credit
Jan. 30		J2	70		70	
31	Closing	J4		70	—	

Rent Expense — Account No. 514

Date	Item	Post. Ref.	Debit	Credit	Balance Debit	Balance Credit
Jan. 31	Adj. (a)	J3	400		400	
31	Closing	J4		400	—	

Insurance Expense — Account No. 515

Date	Item	Post. Ref.	Debit	Credit	Balance Debit	Balance Credit
Jan. 31	Adj. (b)	J3	40		40	
31	Closing	J4		40	—	

Art Supplies Expense — Account No. 516

Date	Item	Post. Ref.	Debit	Credit	Balance Debit	Balance Credit
Jan. 31	Adj. (c)	J3	500		500	
31	Closing	J4		500	—	

Income Summary — Account No. 313

Date	Item	Post. Ref.	Debit	Credit	Balance Debit	Balance Credit
Jan. 31	Closing	J4		4,800		4,800
31	Closing	J4	2,810			1,990

Office Supplies Expense — Account No. 517

Date	Item	Post. Ref.	Debit	Credit	Balance Debit	Balance Credit
Jan. 31	Adj. (d)	J3	200		200	
31	Closing	J4		200	—	

Depreciation Expense, Art Equipment — Account No. 519

Date	Item	Post. Ref.	Debit	Credit	Balance Debit	Balance Credit
Jan. 31	Adj. (e)	J3	70		70	
31	Closing	J4		70	—	

Depreciation Expense, Office Equipment — Account No. 520

Date	Item	Post. Ref.	Debit	Credit	Balance Debit	Balance Credit
Jan. 31	Adj. (f)	J3	50		50	
31	Closing	J4		50	—	

Discussion Question: The credit balance of the Income Summary account at this point ($1,990) represents what key measure? **Answer:** Net income.

Discussion Question: Could the Income Summary account contain a debit balance when the income statement accounts are closed to it? **Answer:** Yes, if a net loss had been incurred.

the closing entry when the company has a net income is shown in Exhibit 4. Notice the dual effect of (1) closing the Income Summary account and (2) transferring the balance, net income in this case, to Joan Miller's Capital account.

Step 4: Closing the Withdrawals Account to the Capital Account

The Withdrawals account shows the amount by which capital is reduced during the period by withdrawals of cash or other assets from the business for the owner's personal use. The debit balance of the Withdrawals account is closed to the Capital account, as shown in Exhibit 1. The

Exhibit 4. Posting the Closing Entry of the Income Summary Account to the Capital Account

Income Summary						Account No. 313
					Balance	
Date	Item	Post. Ref.	Debit	Credit	Debit	Credit
Jan. 31	Closing	J4		4,800		4,800
31	Closing	J4	2,810			1,990
31	Closing	J4	1,990			—

Joan Miller, Capital						Account No. 311
					Balance	
Date	Item	Post. Ref.	Debit	Credit	Debit	Credit
Jan. 1		J1		10,000		10,000
31	Closing	J4		1,990		11,990

Exhibit 5. Posting the Closing Entry of the Withdrawals Account to the Capital Account

Joan Miller, Withdrawals						Account No. 312
					Balance	
Date	Item	Post. Ref.	Debit	Credit	Debit	Credit
Jan. 31		J2	1,400		1,400	
31	Closing	J4		1,400	—	

Joan Miller, Capital						Account No. 311
					Balance	
Date	Item	Post. Ref.	Debit	Credit	Debit	Credit
Jan. 1		J1		10,000		10,000
31	Closing	J4		1,990		11,990
31	Closing	J4	1,400			10,590

Point to Emphasize: Notice that the Withdrawals account is closed to the Capital account, not to the Income Summary account.

effect of this closing entry, as shown in Exhibit 5, is to (1) close the Withdrawals account and (2) transfer the balance to the Capital account.

The Accounts After Closing

After all steps in the closing process have been completed and all closing entries have been posted to the accounts, the stage is set for the next accounting period. The ledger accounts of Joan Miller Advertising Agency, as they appear at this point, are shown in Exhibit 6. The revenue, expense, and Withdrawals accounts (temporary accounts) have zero balances. The Capital account has been increased to reflect the agency's net income and decreased for the owner's withdrawals. The balance sheet accounts (permanent accounts) show the correct balances, which are carried forward to the next period.

BUSINESS BULLETIN: TECHNOLOGY IN PRACTICE

When General Mills needed to speed up its year-end closing procedures, it selected a team from its Financial Reporting and Information Services Division to design an automated fiscal year-end accounting package. The team put together a system using software spreadsheets like Lotus 1-2-3 and Microsoft Excel to record and consolidate annual results. Not only did this accelerate the process, increase accuracy, reduce outside help and overtime, and provide flexibility, but its cost was very low because it used PCs and software that the company already owned. The whole process was reduced from nine weeks to just six workdays.[2]

Exhibit 6. The Accounts After Closing Entries Are Posted

Cash — Account No. 111

Date	Item	Post. Ref.	Debit	Credit	Balance Debit	Balance Credit
Jan. 1		J1	10,000		10,000	
2		J1		800	9,200	
4		J1		4,200	5,000	
5		J1		1,500	3,500	
8		J1		480	3,020	
9		J1		1,000	2,020	
10		J2	1,400		3,420	
12		J2		600	2,820	
15		J2	1,000		3,820	
26		J2		600	3,220	
29		J2		100	3,120	
31		J2		1,400	1,720	

Accounts Receivable — Account No. 113

Date	Item	Post. Ref.	Debit	Credit	Balance Debit	Balance Credit
Jan. 19		J2	2,800		2,800	

Fees Receivable — Account No. 114

Date	Item	Post. Ref.	Debit	Credit	Balance Debit	Balance Credit
Jan. 31	Adj. (i)	J3	200		200	

Art Supplies — Account No. 115

Date	Item	Post. Ref.	Debit	Credit	Balance Debit	Balance Credit
Jan. 6		J1	1,800		1,800	
31	Adj. (c)	J3		500	1,300	

Office Supplies — Account No. 116

Date	Item	Post. Ref.	Debit	Credit	Balance Debit	Balance Credit
Jan. 6		J1	800		800	
31	Adj. (d)	J3		200	600	

Prepaid Rent — Account No. 117

Date	Item	Post. Ref.	Debit	Credit	Balance Debit	Balance Credit
Jan. 2		J1	800		800	
31	Adj. (a)	J3		400	400	

Prepaid Insurance — Account No. 118

Date	Item	Post. Ref.	Debit	Credit	Balance Debit	Balance Credit
Jan. 8		J1	480		480	
31	Adj. (b)	J3		40	440	

Art Equipment — Account No. 144

Date	Item	Post. Ref.	Debit	Credit	Balance Debit	Balance Credit
Jan. 4		J1	4,200		4,200	

Accumulated Depreciation, Art Equipment — Account No. 145

Date	Item	Post. Ref.	Debit	Credit	Balance Debit	Balance Credit
Jan. 31	Adj. (e)	J3		70		70

Office Equipment — Account No. 146

Date	Item	Post. Ref.	Debit	Credit	Balance Debit	Balance Credit
Jan. 5		J1	3,000		3,000	

Accumulated Depreciation, Office Equipment — Account No. 147

Date	Item	Post. Ref.	Debit	Credit	Balance Debit	Balance Credit
Jan. 31	Adj. (f)	J3		50		50

Accounts Payable — Account No. 212

Date	Item	Post. Ref.	Debit	Credit	Balance Debit	Balance Credit
Jan. 5		J1		1,500		1,500
6		J1		2,600		4,100
9		J1	1,000			3,100
30		J2		70		3,170

Unearned Art Fees — Account No. 213

Date	Item	Post. Ref.	Debit	Credit	Balance Debit	Balance Credit
Jan. 15		J2		1,000		1,000
31	Adj. (h)	J3	400			600

Wages Payable — Account No. 214

Date	Item	Post. Ref.	Debit	Credit	Balance Debit	Balance Credit
Jan. 31	Adj. (g)	J3		180		180

(continued)

Teaching Note: A good way to review is to examine each ledger account and discuss where it fits (if at all) into the adjusting and closing procedures. The Cash account, for example, is never a part of adjusting or closing entries.

Exhibit 6. The Accounts After Closing Entries Are Posted *(continued)*

Joan Miller, Capital — Account No. 311

Date	Item	Post. Ref.	Debit	Credit	Balance Debit	Balance Credit
Jan. 1		J1		10,000		10,000
31	Closing	J4		1,990		11,990
31	Closing	J4	1,400			10,590

Joan Miller, Withdrawals — Account No. 312

Date	Item	Post. Ref.	Debit	Credit	Balance Debit	Balance Credit
Jan. 31		J2	1,400		1,400	
31	Closing	J4		1,400	—	

Income Summary — Account No. 313

Date	Item	Post. Ref.	Debit	Credit	Balance Debit	Balance Credit
Jan. 31	Closing	J4		4,800		4,800
31	Closing	J4	2,810			1,990
31	Closing	J4	1,990			—

Advertising Fees Earned — Account No. 411

Date	Item	Post. Ref.	Debit	Credit	Balance Debit	Balance Credit
Jan. 10		J2		1,400		1,400
19		J2		2,800		4,200
31	Adj. (i)	J3		200		4,400
31	Closing	J4	4,400			—

Art Fees Earned — Account No. 412

Date	Item	Post. Ref.	Debit	Credit	Balance Debit	Balance Credit
Jan. 31	Adj. (h)	J3		400		400
31	Closing	J4	400			—

Wages Expense — Account No. 511

Date	Item	Post. Ref.	Debit	Credit	Balance Debit	Balance Credit
Jan. 12		J2	600		600	
26		J2	600		1,200	
31	Adj. (g)	J3	180		1,380	
31	Closing	J4		1,380	—	

Utilities Expense — Account No. 512

Date	Item	Post. Ref.	Debit	Credit	Balance Debit	Balance Credit
Jan. 29		J2	100		100	
31	Closing	J4		100	—	

Telephone Expense — Account No. 513

Date	Item	Post. Ref.	Debit	Credit	Balance Debit	Balance Credit
Jan. 30		J2	70		70	
31	Closing	J4		70	—	

Rent Expense — Account No. 514

Date	Item	Post. Ref.	Debit	Credit	Balance Debit	Balance Credit
Jan. 31	Adj. (a)	J3	400		400	
31	Closing	J4		400	—	

Insurance Expense — Account No. 515

Date	Item	Post. Ref.	Debit	Credit	Balance Debit	Balance Credit
Jan. 31	Adj. (b)	J3	40		40	
31	Closing	J4		40	—	

Art Supplies Expense — Account No. 516

Date	Item	Post. Ref.	Debit	Credit	Balance Debit	Balance Credit
Jan. 31	Adj. (c)	J3	500		500	
31	Closing	J4		500	—	

Office Supplies Expense — Account No. 517

Date	Item	Post. Ref.	Debit	Credit	Balance Debit	Balance Credit
Jan. 31	Adj. (d)	J3	200		200	
31	Closing	J4		200	—	

Depreciation Expense, Art Equipment — Account No. 519

Date	Item	Post. Ref.	Debit	Credit	Balance Debit	Balance Credit
Jan. 31	Adj. (e)	J3	70		70	
31	Closing	J4		70	—	

Depreciation Expense, Office Equipment — Account No. 520

Date	Item	Post. Ref.	Debit	Credit	Balance Debit	Balance Credit
Jan. 31	Adj. (f)	J3	50		50	
31	Closing	J4		50	—	

Discussion Question: If Joan Miller, Capital is a permanent account, why is it a part of the closing procedure? **Answer:** Because Joan Miller, Capital is closed *into,* not closed *out.*

BUSINESS BULLETIN: INTERNATIONAL PRACTICE

For companies with extensive international operations, like Caterpillar Inc., Dow Chemical Co., Phillips Petroleum Company, Gillette Co., and Bristol-Myers Squibb Company, closing the records and preparing financial statements on a timely basis used to be a problem. It was common practice for foreign divisions of companies like these to end their fiscal year one month before the end of the fiscal year of their counterparts in the United States. This gave them the extra time they needed to perform closing procedures and mail the results back to U.S. headquarters to be used in preparation of the company's overall financial statements. This procedure is usually unnecessary today because high-speed computers and electronic communications enable companies to close records and prepare financial statements for both foreign and domestic operations in less than a week.

The Post-Closing Trial Balance

OBJECTIVE 4

Prepare the post-closing trial balance

Related Text Assignments:
Q: 6, 7
P: 3
SD: 4

Discussion Question: Which three types of accounts are absent from the post-closing trial balance? **Answer:** Revenue and expense accounts and the Withdrawals account.

Point to Emphasize: Notice that Joan Miller, Capital now reflects the correct month-end balance, $10,590.

Because it is possible to make errors in posting the closing entries to the ledger accounts, it is necessary to determine that all temporary accounts have zero balances and to double-check that total debits equal total credits by preparing a new trial balance. This final trial balance, called the post-closing trial balance, is shown in Exhibit 7 for Joan Miller Advertising Agency. Notice that only the balance sheet accounts show balances because the income statement accounts and the Withdrawals account have all been closed.

Exhibit 7. Post-Closing Trial Balance

Joan Miller Advertising Agency
Post-Closing Trial Balance
January 31, 20xx

Cash	$ 1,720	
Accounts Receivable	2,800	
Fees Receivable	200	
Art Supplies	1,300	
Office Supplies	600	
Prepaid Rent	400	
Prepaid Insurance	440	
Art Equipment	4,200	
Accumulated Depreciation, Art Equipment		$ 70
Office Equipment	3,000	
Accumulated Depreciation, Office Equipment		50
Accounts Payable		3,170
Unearned Art Fees		600
Wages Payable		180
Joan Miller, Capital		10,590
	$14,660	$14,660

Reversing Entries: The Optional First Step in the Next Accounting Period

LEARNING OBJECTIVE 5

Prepare reversing entries as appropriate

Related Text Assignments:
Q: 8, 9
SE: 7, 8
E: 3, 7
P: 4, 5, 8
SD: 2, 4

At the end of each accounting period, adjusting entries are made to bring revenues and expenses into conformity with the matching rule. A reversing entry is a general journal entry dated the first day of a new accounting period that is the exact reverse of an adjusting entry made at the end of the previous period. Reversing entries are optional. They simplify the bookkeeping process for transactions involving certain types of adjustments. Not all adjusting entries can be reversed. For the recording system used in this book, only adjustments for accruals (accrued revenues and accrued expenses) can be reversed. Deferrals cannot be reversed because such reversals would not simplify the bookkeeping process in future accounting periods.

To see how reversing entries can be helpful, consider the adjusting entry made in the records of Joan Miller Advertising Agency to accrue wages expense:

A = L + OE
    + −

Jan. 31	Wages Expense	180	
	Wages Payable		180
	To accrue unrecorded wages		

Point to Emphasize: Reversing entries are the opposite of adjusting entries and are dated the first day of the new period. They are never required.

When the secretary is paid on the next regular payday, the accountant would make this entry:

A = L + OE
− − −

Feb. 9	Wages Payable	180	
	Wages Expense	420	
	Cash		600
	Payment of two weeks' wages to secretary, $180 of which accrued in the previous period		

Discussion Question: What is the purpose of reversing entries? **Answer:** Reversing entries enable the bookkeeper to continue preparing routine journal entries early in the new period. (More complex entries are needed when reversing entries are not used.)

Point to Emphasize: Adjustments that eventually are followed by the receipt or payment of cash (that is, accruals) can be reversed. Adjustments that do not involve a cash follow-up (deferrals) cannot be reversed.

Notice that when the payment is made, if there is no reversing entry, the accountant must look in the records to find out how much of the $600 applies to the current accounting period and how much is applicable to the previous period. This may seem easy in our example, but think how difficult and time-consuming it would be if a company had hundreds of employees, especially if they were not all paid on the same schedule. A reversing entry helps solve the problem of applying revenues and expenses to the correct accounting period. It is exactly what its name implies: a reversal made by debiting the credits and crediting the debits of a previously made adjusting entry.

For example, notice the following sequence of entries and their effects on the ledger account Wages Expense:

1. Adjusting Entry
Jan. 31 Wages Expense 180
Wages Payable 180

2. Closing Entry
Jan. 31 Income Summary 1,380
Wages Expense 1,380

3. Reversing Entry
Feb. 1 Wages Payable 180
Wages Expense 180

4. Payment Entry
Feb. 9 Wages Expense 600
Cash 600

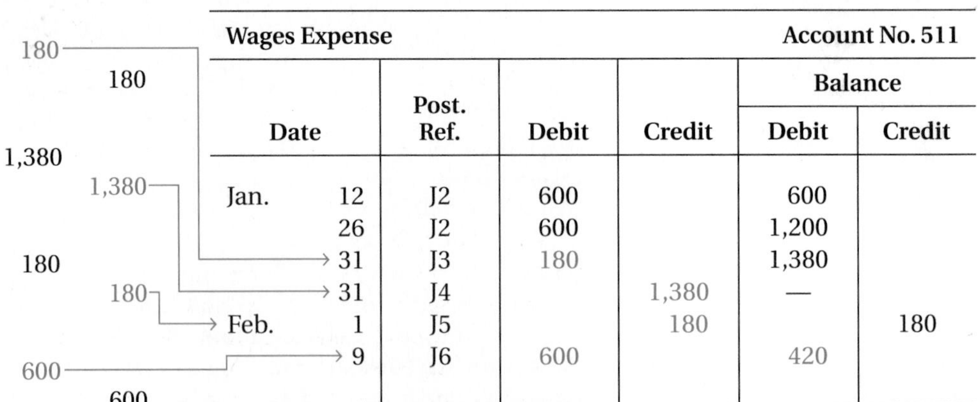

Wages Expense — **Account No. 511**

Date		Post. Ref.	Debit	Credit	Balance Debit	Balance Credit
Jan.	12	J2	600		600	
	26	J2	600		1,200	
	31	J3	180		1,380	
	31	J4		1,380	—	
Feb.	1	J5		180		180
	9	J6	600		420	

Entry 1 adjusted Wages Expense to accrue $180 in the January accounting period.

Entry 2 closed the $1,380 in Wages Expense for January to Income Summary, leaving a zero balance.

Point to Emphasize: Notice the abnormal credit balance as of February 1. This situation is "corrected" with the February 9 entry, an entry the bookkeeper can make easily.

Entry 3, the reversing entry, set up a credit balance of $180 on February 1 in Wages Expense, which is the expense recognized through the adjusting entry in January (and also reduced the liability account Wages Payable to a zero balance). The reversing entry always sets up an abnormal balance in the income statement account and produces a zero balance in the balance sheet account.

Entry 4 recorded the $600 payment of two weeks' wages as a debit to Wages Expense, automatically leaving a balance of $420, which represents the correct wages expense to date in February. The reversing entry simplified the process of making the payment entry on February 9.

Discussion Question: Is it "more accurate" to prepare reversing entries than not? **Answer:** No, because the same results are obtained whether or not reversing entries have been prepared.

Reversing entries apply to any accrued expenses or revenues. In the case of Joan Miller Advertising Agency, wages expense was the only accrued expense. However, the asset Fees Receivable was created as a result of the adjusting entry made to accrue fees earned but not yet billed. The adjusting entry for this accrued revenue would require the following reversing entry:

A = L + OE
− −

Feb. 1	Advertising Fees Earned	200	
	Fees Receivable		200
	To reverse the adjusting entry for accrued fees receivable		

Instructional Strategy: After reviewing the reversing entry for accrued revenue, check students' comprehension by dividing the class into pairs and assigning E 3. Use students' answers to summarize reversing entries for the entire class.

When the series of advertisements is finished, the company can credit all the proceeds to Advertising Fees Earned without regard to the amount accrued in the previous period. The credit will automatically be reduced to the amount earned during February by the $200 debit in the account.

As noted earlier, under the system of recording used in this book, reversing entries apply only to accruals. Reversing entries do not apply to deferrals, such as the entries that involve supplies, prepaid rent, prepaid insurance, depreciation, and unearned art fees.

The Work Sheet: An Accountant's Tool

LEARNING OBJECTIVE 6

Prepare a work sheet

Related Text Assignments:
Q: 10, 11, 12, 13, 14, 15, 16, 17
E: 4, 5
P: 4, 5, 8

As seen earlier, the flow of information that affects a business does not stop arbitrarily at the end of an accounting period. In preparing financial reports, accountants must collect relevant data to determine what should be included. For example, they need to examine insurance policies to see how much prepaid insurance has expired, examine plant and equipment records to determine depreciation, take an inventory of supplies on hand, and calculate the amount of accrued wages. These calculations, together with other computations, analyses, and preliminary drafts of statements, make up the accountants' working papers. Working papers are important for two reasons. First, they help accountants organize their work and thus avoid omitting important data or steps that affect the financial statements. Second, they provide evidence of past work so that accountants or auditors can retrace their steps and support the information in the financial statements.

A special kind of working paper is the work sheet. The work sheet is often used as a preliminary step in recording adjusting and closing entries and the preparation of financial statements. Using a work sheet lessens the possibility of leaving out an adjustment, helps the accountant check the arithmetical accuracy of the accounts, and facilitates the preparation of financial statements. The work sheet is never published and is rarely seen by management. It is a tool for the accountant.

Point to Emphasize: The work sheet is extremely useful when an accountant must prepare numerous adjustments. It is not a financial statement, it is not required, and it is not made public.

Because preparing a work sheet is a very mechanical process, many accountants use a microcomputer. In some cases, accountants use a spreadsheet program to prepare the work sheet. In other cases, they use general ledger software to prepare financial statements from the adjusted trial balance.

Preparing the Work Sheet

Point to Emphasize: For complicated end-of-period situations, the work sheet is ideal because incorrect information can be erased along the way. As a result, the correctly completed work sheet can be used to facilitate the preparation of formal adjusting and closing entries, which can be corrected only with additional formal entries.

So far, adjusting entries have been entered directly in the journal and posted to the ledger, and the financial statements have been prepared from the adjusted trial balance. The process has been relatively simple because Joan Miller Advertising Agency is a small company. For larger companies, which may require many adjusting entries, a work sheet is essential. To illustrate the preparation of the work sheet, we continue with the Joan Miller Advertising Agency example.

A common form of work sheet has one column for account names and/or numbers and ten more columns with the headings shown in Exhibit 8. Notice that the work sheet is identified by a heading that consists of (1) the name of the company, (2) the title "Work Sheet," and (3) the period of time covered (as on the income statement).

There are five steps in the preparation of a work sheet:

1. Enter and total the account balances in the Trial Balance columns.
2. Enter and total the adjustments in the Adjustments columns.
3. Enter and total the adjusted account balances in the Adjusted Trial Balance columns.
4. Extend the account balances from the Adjusted Trial Balance columns to the Income Statement columns or the Balance Sheet columns.
5. Total the Income Statement columns and the Balance Sheet columns. Enter the net income or net loss in both pairs of columns as a balancing figure, and recompute the column totals.

Point to Emphasize: The work sheet Trial Balance columns take the place of the "traditional" trial balance.

Common Student Confusion: Now that students are comfortable with the general ledger format, they are being asked to enter amounts into a new form, a working paper. Assure them that they will get used to the work sheet and that exactly the same rules of debit and credit apply.

1. **Enter and total the account balances in the Trial Balance columns.** The titles and balances of the accounts as of January 31 are copied directly from the ledger into the Trial Balance columns, as shown in Exhibit 8. When a work sheet is used, the accountant does not have to prepare a separate trial balance.
2. **Enter and total the adjustments in the Adjustments columns.** The required adjustments for Joan Miller Advertising Agency are entered in the Adjustments columns of the work sheet as shown in Exhibit 9. As each adjustment is entered, a letter is used to identify its debit and credit parts. The first adjustment, which is identified by the letter **a,** is to recognize rent expense, which results in a debit to Rent Expense and a credit to Prepaid Rent. In practice, this letter may be used to reference supporting computations or documentation underlying the adjusting entry, and it may simplify the recording of adjusting entries in the general journal.

   If an adjustment calls for an account that has not been used in the trial balance, the new account is added below the accounts listed in the trial balance. The trial balance includes only those accounts that have balances. For example, Rent Expense has been added in Exhibit 9. The only exception to this rule is the Accumulated Depreciation accounts, which have a zero balance only in the initial period of operation. Accumulated Depreciation accounts are listed immediately after their associated asset accounts.

   When all the adjustments have been made, the two Adjustments columns must be totaled. This step proves that the debits and credits of the adjustments are equal and generally reduces errors in the preparation of the work sheet.
3. **Enter and total the adjusted account balances in the Adjusted Trial Balance columns.** Exhibit 10 shows the adjusted trial balance. It is prepared by combining the amount of each account in the original Trial Balance columns with the corresponding amount in the Adjustments columns and entering each result in the Adjusted Trial Balance columns.

   Some examples from Exhibit 10 illustrate crossfooting, or adding and subtracting a group of numbers horizontally. The first line shows Cash with a debit balance of $1,720. Because there are no adjustments to the Cash account, $1,720 is

Common Student Confusion: Crossfooting is far more difficult than adding and subtracting vertically, especially when one must pay particular attention to debits versus credits. Assure students that it is normal to be uncomfortable with crossfooting at first, but that they will quickly become accustomed to it.

entered in the debit column of the Adjusted Trial Balance columns. The second line is Accounts Receivable, which shows a debit of $2,800 in the Trial Balance columns. Because there are no adjustments to Accounts Receivable, the $2,800 balance is carried over to the debit column of the Adjusted Trial Balance columns. The next line is Art Supplies, which shows a debit of $1,800 in the Trial Balance columns and a credit of $500 from adjustment **c** in the Adjustments columns. Subtracting $500 from $1,800 results in a $1,300 debit balance in the Adjusted Trial Balance columns. This process is followed for all the accounts, including those added below the trial balance totals. The Adjusted Trial Balance columns are then footed (totaled) to check the accuracy of the crossfooting.

4. **Extend the account balances from the Adjusted Trial Balance columns to the Income Statement columns or the Balance Sheet columns.** Every account in the adjusted trial balance is either a balance sheet account or an income statement account. Each account is extended to its proper place as a debit or credit in either the Income Statement columns or the Balance Sheet columns. The result of extending the accounts is shown in Exhibit 11. Revenue and expense accounts are copied to the Income Statement columns. Assets, liabilities, and the Capital and Withdrawals accounts are extended to the Balance Sheet columns. To avoid overlooking an account, extend the accounts line by line, beginning with the first line (which is Cash) and not omitting any subsequent lines. For instance, the Cash debit balance of $1,720 is extended to the debit column of the Balance Sheet columns, the Accounts Receivable debit balance of $2,800 is extended to the same debit column, and so forth. Each amount is carried across to only one column.

Discussion Question: Under what circumstances would the Income Statement and Balance Sheet columns balance when initially totaled? **Answer:** When net income equals exactly $0.

5. **Total the Income Statement columns and the Balance Sheet columns. Enter the net income or net loss in both pairs of columns as a balancing figure, and recompute the column totals.** This last step, as shown in Exhibit 12, is necessary to compute net income or net loss and to prove the arithmetical accuracy of the work sheet.

   Net income (or net loss) is equal to the difference between the total debits and credits of the Income Statement columns. It also equals the difference between the total debits and credits of the Balance Sheet columns.

Revenue (Income Statement credit column total)	$4,800
Expenses (Income Statement debit column total)	(2,810)
Net Income	$1,990

   In this case, revenues (credit column) exceed expenses (debit column). Consequently, the company has a net income of $1,990. The same difference is shown between the total debits and credits of the Balance Sheet columns.

   The $1,990 is entered in the debit side of the Income Statement columns to balance the columns, and it is entered in the credit side of the Balance Sheet columns to balance the columns. Remember that the excess of revenues over expenses (net income) increases owner's equity and that increases in owner's equity are recorded by credits.

   When a net loss occurs, the opposite rule applies. The excess of expenses over revenues—net loss—is placed in the credit side of the Income Statement columns as a balancing figure. It is then placed in the debit side of the Balance Sheet columns because a net loss decreases owner's equity, and decreases in owner's equity are recorded by debits.

   As a final check, the four columns are totaled again. If the Income Statement columns and the Balance Sheet columns do not balance, an account may have been extended or sorted to the wrong column, or an error may have been made in adding the columns. Of course, equal totals in the two pairs of columns are not absolute proof of accuracy. If an asset has been carried to the Income Statement

Point to Emphasize: Information from the work sheet simplifies the process of preparing formal adjusting entries.

Clarification Note: Theoretically, the formal adjusting entries can be prepared before the formal financial statements, or even before the work sheet itself is completed. However, they always precede the preparation of formal closing entries. It is in the preparation of formal adjusting entries that the value of identification letters becomes apparent.

Exhibit 13. Adjustments from Work Sheet Entered in the General Journal

General Journal — Page 3

Date		Description	Post. Ref.	Debit	Credit
20xx					
Jan.	31	Rent Expense	514	400	
		Prepaid Rent	117		400
		To recognize expiration of one month's rent			
	31	Insurance Expense	515	40	
		Prepaid Insurance	118		40
		To recognize expiration of one month's insurance			
	31	Art Supplies Expense	516	500	
		Art Supplies	115		500
		To recognize art supplies used during the month			
	31	Office Supplies Expense	517	200	
		Office Supplies	116		200
		To recognize office supplies used during the month			
	31	Depreciation Expense, Art Equipment	519	70	
		Accumulated Depreciation, Art Equipment	145		70
		To record depreciation of art equipment for a month			
	31	Depreciation Expense, Office Equipment	520	50	
		Accumulated Depreciation, Office Equipment	147		50
		To record depreciation of office equipment for a month			
	31	Wages Expense	511	180	
		Wages Payable	214		180
		To accrue unrecorded wages			
	31	Unearned Art Fees	213	400	
		Art Fees Earned	412		400
		To recognize performance of services paid for in advance			
	31	Fees Receivable	114	200	
		Advertising Fees Earned	411		200
		To accrue advertising fees earned but unrecorded			

debit column and a similar error involving revenues or liabilities has been made, the work sheet will still balance, but the net income figure will be wrong.

Using the Work Sheet

LEARNING OBJECTIVE 7

Use a work sheet for three different purposes

The completed work sheet assists the accountant in three principal tasks: (1) recording the adjusting entries, (2) recording the closing entries in the general journal to prepare the records for the beginning of the next period, and (3) preparing the financial statements.

Related Text Assignments:
Q: 18, 19
SE: 9
E: 6, 7, 8
P: 4, 5, 8
SD: 4

Recording the Adjusting Entries For Joan Miller Advertising Agency, the adjustments were determined while completing the work sheet because they are essential to the preparation of the financial statements. The adjusting entries may be recorded in the general journal at that point.

Recording the adjusting entries with appropriate explanations in the general journal, as shown in Exhibit 13, is an easy step. The information can be copied from the work sheet. Adjusting entries are then posted to the general ledger.

Recording the Closing Entries The four closing entries for Joan Miller Advertising Agency are entered in the journal and posted to the ledger as shown in Exhibits 1 through 5. All accounts that need to be closed, except for Withdrawals, may be found in the Income Statement columns of the work sheet.

Preparing the Financial Statements Once the work sheet has been completed, preparing the financial statements is simple because the account balances have been sorted into Income Statement and Balance Sheet columns. The income statement shown in Exhibit 14 was prepared from the account balances in the Income

Point to Emphasize: Demonstrate the ease with which the income statement can be prepared now that the work sheet has been completed.

Exhibit 14. Income Statement for Joan Miller Advertising Agency

Joan Miller Advertising Agency
Income Statement
For the Month Ended January 31, 20xx

Revenues		
Advertising Fees Earned		$4,400
Art Fees Earned		400
Total Revenues		$4,800
Expenses		
Wages Expense	$1,380	
Utilities Expense	100	
Telephone Expense	70	
Rent Expense	400	
Insurance Expense	40	
Art Supplies Expense	500	
Office Supplies Expense	200	
Depreciation Expense, Art Equipment	70	
Depreciation Expense, Office Equipment	50	
Total Expenses		2,810
Net Income		**$1,990**

Exhibit 15. Statement of Owner's Equity for Joan Miller Advertising Agency

Joan Miller Advertising Agency
Statement of Owner's Equity
For the Month Ended January 31, 20xx

Joan Miller, Capital, January 1, 20xx		—
Add: Investment by Joan Miller	$10,000	
Net Income	1,990	$11,990
Subtotal		$11,990
Less Withdrawals		1,400
Joan Miller, Capital, January 31, 20xx		$10,590

Discussion Question: At this point, what is the balance of Joan Miller, Capital on the books? **Answer:** $10,000. The Capital account does not reflect income (or loss) and withdrawals until the closing entries have been entered and posted.

Statement columns of Exhibit 12. The statement of owner's equity and the balance sheet for Joan Miller Advertising Agency are presented in Exhibits 15 and 16. The account balances for these statements are drawn from the Balance Sheet columns of the work sheet shown in Exhibit 12. Notice that the total assets and the total liabilities and owner's equity in the balance sheet are not the same as the totals of the

Exhibit 16. Balance Sheet for Joan Miller Advertising Agency

Joan Miller Advertising Agency
Balance Sheet
January 31, 20xx

Assets		
Cash		$ 1,720
Accounts Receivable		2,800
Fees Receivable		200
Art Supplies		1,300
Office Supplies		600
Prepaid Rent		400
Prepaid Insurance		440
Art Equipment	$4,200	
Less Accumulated Depreciation	70	4,130
Office Equipment	$3,000	
Less Accumulated Depreciation	50	2,950
Total Assets		$14,540
Liabilities		
Accounts Payable	$3,170	
Unearned Art Fees	600	
Wages Payable	180	
Total Liabilities		$ 3,950
Owner's Equity		
Joan Miller, Capital, January 31, 20xx		10,590
Total Liabilities and Owner's Equity		$14,540

BUSINESS BULLETIN: TECHNOLOGY IN PRACTICE

The work sheet is a good application for electronic spreadsheet software programs like Lotus 1-2-3 and Microsoft Excel. Constructing a work sheet using spreadsheet software takes time, but once it is done, the work sheet can be used over and over. The principal advantage of electronic preparation over manual preparation is that each time a number is entered or revised, the entire electronic work sheet is updated automatically, without the possibility of addition or extension mistakes. For example, if an error in an adjusting entry is corrected, the proper extensions to the other columns are made, all columns are re-added, and net income is recomputed. Of course, the software is purely mechanical. People are still responsible for inputting the correct numbers and equations initially.

Balance Sheet columns in the work sheet. The reason is that the Accumulated Depreciation and Withdrawals accounts have normal balances that appear in different columns from their associated accounts on the balance sheet. In addition, the owner's Capital account on the balance sheet is the amount determined on the statement of owner's equity. At this point, the financial statements have been prepared from the work sheet, not from the ledger accounts. For the ledger accounts to show the correct balances, the adjusting entries must be journalized and posted to the ledger.

Chapter Review

REVIEW OF LEARNING OBJECTIVES

1. **State all the steps in the accounting cycle.** The steps in the accounting cycle are (1) analyze business transactions from source documents, (2) record the entries in the journal, (3) post the entries to the ledger and prepare a trial balance, (4) adjust the accounts and prepare an adjusted trial balance, (5) close the accounts and prepare a post-closing trial balance, and (6) prepare the financial statements.
2. **Explain the purposes of closing entries.** Closing entries have two purposes. First, they clear the balances of all temporary accounts (revenue and expense accounts and owner's Withdrawals) so that they have zero balances at the beginning of the next accounting period. Second, they summarize a period's revenues and expenses in the Income Summary account so that the net income or loss for the period can be transferred as a total to owner's Capital.
3. **Prepare the required closing entries.** Closing entries are prepared by first transferring the revenue and expense account balances to the Income Summary account. Then the balance of the Income Summary account is transferred to the owner's Capital account. And, finally, the balance of the owner's Withdrawals account is transferred to the owner's Capital account.
4. **Prepare the post-closing trial balance.** As a final check on the balance of the ledger and to ensure that all temporary (nominal) accounts have been closed, a post-closing trial balance is prepared after the closing entries are posted to the ledger accounts.
5. **Prepare reversing entries as appropriate.** Reversing entries are optional entries dated the first day of the new accounting period to simplify routine bookkeeping procedures. They reverse certain adjusting entries made in the previous period. Under the system used in this text, they apply only to accruals.

6. **Prepare a work sheet.** There are five steps in the preparation of a work sheet: (1) Enter and total the account balances in the Trial Balance columns; (2) enter and total the adjustments in the Adjustments columns; (3) enter and total the adjusted account balances in the Adjusted Trial Balance columns; (4) extend the account balances from the Adjusted Trial Balance columns to the Income Statement or Balance Sheet columns; and (5) total the Income Statement and Balance Sheet columns, enter the net income or net loss in both pairs of columns as a balancing figure, and recompute the column totals.
7. **Use a work sheet for three different purposes.** A work sheet is useful in (1) recording the adjusting entries, (2) recording the closing entries, and (3) preparing the financial statements. The balance sheet and income statement can be prepared directly from the Balance Sheet and Income Statement columns of the completed work sheet. The statement of owner's equity is prepared using owner's Withdrawals, net income, additional investments, and the beginning balance of the owner's Capital account. Notice that the ending balance of owner's Capital does not appear on the work sheet. Adjusting entries can be recorded in the general journal directly from the Adjustments columns of the work sheet. Closing entries may be prepared from the Income Statement columns, except for owner's Withdrawals, which is found in the Balance Sheet columns.

REVIEW OF CONCEPTS AND TERMINOLOGY

The following concepts and terms were introduced in this chapter.

LO 1 **Accounting cycle:** The sequence of steps followed in the accounting system to measure business transactions and transform them into financial statements.

LO 2 **Closing entries:** Journal entries made at the end of an accounting period that set the stage for the next accounting period by clearing the temporary accounts of their balances, and that summarize a period's revenues and expenses.

LO 6 **Crossfooting:** Adding and subtracting numbers across a row.

LO 2 **Income Summary:** A temporary account used during the closing process that holds a summary of all revenues and expenses before the net income or loss is transferred to the owner's Capital account.

LO 2 **Permanent accounts:** Balance sheet accounts; accounts whose balances can extend past the end of an accounting period. Also called *real accounts.*

LO 4 **Post-closing trial balance:** A trial balance prepared at the end of the accounting period after all adjusting and closing entries have been posted; a final check on the balance of the ledger to ensure that all temporary accounts have zero balances and that total debits equal total credits.

LO 5 **Reversing entry:** A journal entry dated the first day of a new accounting period that is the exact opposite of an adjusting entry made on the last day of the prior accounting period.

LO 2 **Temporary accounts:** Accounts that show the accumulation of revenues and expenses over one accounting period; at the end of the accounting period, these account balances are transferred to owner's equity. Also called *nominal accounts.*

LO 6 **Working papers:** Documents used by accountants to organize their work and to support the information in the financial statements.

LO 6 **Work sheet:** A type of working paper used as a preliminary step in recording adjusting and closing entries and in the preparation of financial statements.

REVIEW PROBLEM

Preparation of Closing Entries

LO 3 At the end of the current fiscal year, the adjusted trial balance for Westwood Movers Company appeared as shown at the top of the next page.

REQUIRED

Prepare the necessary closing entries.

Westwood Movers Company
Adjusted Trial Balance
June 30, 20xx

Cash	$ 14,200	
Accounts Receivable	18,600	
Packing Supplies	10,400	
Prepaid Insurance	7,900	
Land	4,000	
Building	80,000	
Accumulated Depreciation, Building		$ 7,500
Trucks	106,000	
Accumulated Depreciation, Trucks		27,500
Accounts Payable		7,650
Unearned Storage Fees		5,400
Mortgage Payable		70,000
Art Burton, Capital		104,740
Art Burton, Withdrawals	18,000	
Moving Services Earned		159,000
Storage Fees Earned		26,400
Driver Wages Expense	94,000	
Fuel Expense	19,000	
Office Wages Expense	14,400	
Office Equipment Rental Expense	3,000	
Utilities Expense	4,450	
Insurance Expense	4,200	
Depreciation Expense, Building	4,000	
Depreciation Expense, Trucks	6,040	
	$408,190	$408,190

ANSWER TO REVIEW PROBLEM

June 30	Moving Services Earned	159,000	
	Storage Fees Earned	26,400	
	Income Summary		185,400
	To close the revenue accounts		
30	Income Summary	149,090	
	Driver Wages Expense		94,000
	Fuel Expense		19,000
	Office Wages Expense		14,400
	Office Equipment Rental Expense		3,000
	Utilities Expense		4,450
	Insurance Expense		4,200
	Depreciation Expense, Building		4,000
	Depreciation Expense, Trucks		6,040
	To close the expense accounts		
30	Income Summary	36,310	
	Art Burton, Capital		36,310
	To close the Income Summary account and transfer the balance to the Capital account		
30	Art Burton, Capital	18,000	
	Art Burton, Withdrawals		18,000
	To close the Withdrawals account		

Chapter Assignments

BUILDING YOUR KNOWLEDGE FOUNDATION

Questions

1. Resequence the following activities **a** through **f** to indicate the correct order of the accounting cycle.
   a. The transactions are entered in the journal.
   b. The financial statements are prepared.
   c. The transactions are analyzed from the source documents.
   d. The adjusting entries are prepared.
   e. The closing entries are prepared.
   f. The transactions are posted to the ledger.
2. What are the two purposes of closing entries?
3. What is the difference between adjusting entries and closing entries?
4. What is the purpose of the Income Summary account?
5. Which of the following accounts do not show a balance after the closing entries are prepared and posted?
   a. Insurance Expense
   b. Accounts Receivable
   c. Commission Revenue
   d. Prepaid Insurance
   e. Owner's Withdrawals
   f. Supplies
   g. Supplies Expense
   h. Owner's Capital
6. What is the significance of the post-closing trial balance?
7. Which of the following accounts would you expect to find on the post-closing trial balance?
   a. Insurance Expense
   b. Accounts Receivable
   c. Commission Revenue
   d. Prepaid Insurance
   e. Owner's Withdrawals
   f. Supplies
   g. Supplies Expense
   h. Owner's Capital
8. How do reversing entries simplify the bookkeeping process?
9. To what types of adjustments do reversing entries apply? To what types do they not apply?
10. Why are working papers important to accountants?
11. Why are work sheets never published and rarely seen by management?
12. Can the work sheet be used as a substitute for the financial statements? Explain your answer.
13. What is the normal balance (debit or credit) of the following accounts?
    a. Cash
    b. Accounts Payable
    c. Prepaid Rent
    d. Sam Jones, Capital
    e. Commission Revenue
    f. Sam Jones, Withdrawals
    g. Rent Expense
    h. Accumulated Depreciation, Office Equipment
    i. Office Equipment
14. Why should the Adjusted Trial Balance columns of the work sheet be totaled before the adjusted amounts are carried to the Income Statement and Balance Sheet columns?
15. What sequence should be followed in extending the amounts in the Adjusted Trial Balance columns to the Income Statement and Balance Sheet columns? Discuss your answer.
16. Do the Income Statement columns and the Balance Sheet columns of the work sheet balance after the amounts from the Adjusted Trial Balance columns are extended?
17. Do the totals of the Balance Sheet columns of the work sheet agree with the totals on the balance sheet? Explain your answer.

18. Should adjusting entries be posted to the ledger accounts before or after the closing entries? Explain your answer.
19. At the end of the accounting period, does the posting of adjusting entries to the ledger precede or follow the preparation of the work sheet?

Short Exercises

SE 1. LO 1 *Accounting Cycle*

Resequence the following activities to indicate the usual order of the accounting cycle.

a. Close the accounts.
b. Analyze the transactions.
c. Post the entries to the ledger.
d. Prepare the financial statements.
e. Adjust the accounts.
f. Record the transactions in the journal.
g. Prepare the post-closing trial balance.
h. Prepare the initial trial balance.
i. Prepare the adjusted trial balance.

SE 2. LO 3 *Closing Revenue Accounts*

Assuming credit balances at the end of the accounting period of $3,400 in Patient Services Revenues and $1,800 in Laboratory Fees Revenues, prepare the required closing entry. The accounting period ends December 31.

SE 3. LO 3 *Closing Expense Accounts*

Assuming debit balances at the end of the accounting period of $1,400 in Rent Expense, $1,100 in Wages Expense, and $500 in Other Expenses, prepare the required closing entry. The accounting period ends December 31.

SE 4. LO 3 *Closing the Income Summary Account*

Assuming that total revenues were $5,200 and total expenses were $3,000, prepare the journal entry to close the Income Summary account to the R. Richards, Capital account. The accounting period ends December 31.

SE 5. LO 3 *Closing the Withdrawals Account*

Assuming that withdrawals during the accounting period were $800, prepare the journal entry to close the R. Richards, Withdrawals account to the R. Richards, Capital account. The accounting period ends December 31.

SE 6. LO 3 *Posting Closing Entries*

Show the effects of the transactions in **SE 2** to **SE 5** by entering beginning balances in appropriate T accounts and recording the transactions. Assume that the R. Richards, Capital account has a beginning balance of $1,300.

SE 7. LO 5 *Preparation of Reversing Entries*

Below, indicated by letters, are the adjusting entries at the end of March. Prepare the required reversing entry.

Account Name	Debit	Credit
Prepaid Insurance		(a) 180
Accumulated Depreciation, Office Equipment		(b) 1,050
Salaries Expense	(c) 360	
Insurance Expense	(a) 180	
Depreciation Expense, Office Equipment	(b) 1,050	
Salaries Payable		(c) 360
	1,590	1,590

SE 8. LO 5 *Effects of Reversing Entries*

Assume that prior to the adjustments in **SE 7,** Salaries Expense had a debit balance of $1,800 and Salaries Payable had a zero balance. Prepare a T account for each of these accounts. Enter the beginning balance; post the adjustment for accrued salaries, the appropriate closing entry, and the reversing entry; and enter the transaction in the T accounts for a payment of $480 for salaries on April 3.

SE 9. Prepare the required closing entries for the year ended December 31, using the following items from the Income Statement columns of a work sheet and assuming that withdrawals by the owner, R. Carrera, were $6,000.

LO 3 LO 7 *Preparing Closing Entries from a Work Sheet*

Account Name	Income Statement	
	Debit	Credit
Repair Revenue		32,860
Wages Expense	12,260	
Rent Expense	1,800	
Supplies Expense	6,390	
Insurance Expense	1,370	
Depreciation Expense, Repair Equipment	2,020	
	23,840	32,860
Net Income	9,020	
	32,860	32,860

Exercises

E 1. The adjusted trial balance for the Nafzger Realty Corporation at the end of its fiscal year is shown below. Prepare the required closing entries.

LO 3 *Preparation of Closing Entries*

Nafzger Realty Corporation
Adjusted Trial Balance
December 31, 20xx

Cash	$ 7,275	
Accounts Receivable	2,325	
Prepaid Insurance	585	
Office Supplies	440	
Office Equipment	6,300	
Accumulated Depreciation, Office Equipment		$ 765
Automobile	6,750	
Accumulated Depreciation, Automobile		750
Accounts Payable		1,700
Unearned Management Fees		1,500
R. Nafzger, Capital		14,535
R. Nafzger, Withdrawals	7,000	
Sales Commissions Earned		31,700
Office Salaries Expense	13,500	
Advertising Expense	2,525	
Rent Expense	2,650	
Telephone Expense	1,600	
	$50,950	$50,950

LO 3 *Preparation of a Statement of Owner's Equity*

E 2. The Capital, Withdrawals, and Income Summary accounts for Wendell's Barber Shop are shown in T account form below. The closing entries have been recorded for the year ended December 31, 20x1.

Wendell Ross, Capital

12/31/x1	4,500	12/31/x0	13,000
		12/31/x1	9,500
		Bal.	**18,000**

Income Summary

12/31/x1	21,500	12/31/x1	31,000
12/31/x1	9,500		
Bal.	—		

Wendell Ross, Withdrawals

4/1/x1	1,500	12/31/x1	4,500
7/1/x1	1,500		
10/1/x1	1,500		
Bal.	—		

Prepare a statement of owner's equity for Wendell's Barber Shop.

LO 5 *Reversing Entries*

E 3. Selected June T accounts for Holmes Company are as follows:

Supplies

6/1 Bal.	860	6/30 Adjust.	1,280
Dec. purchases	940		
Bal.	**520**		

Supplies Expense

6/30 Adjust.	1,280	6/30 Closing	1,280
Bal.	—		

Wages Payable

		6/30 Adjust.	640
		Bal.	**640**

Wages Expense

June wages	3,940	6/30 Closing	4,580
6/30 Adjust.	640		
Bal.	—		

1. In which of these accounts would a reversing entry be helpful? Why?
2. Prepare the appropriate reversing entry.
3. Prepare the entry to record payments on July 3 for wages totaling $3,140. How much of this amount represents wages expense for July?

LO 6 *Preparation of a Trial Balance*

E 4. The following alphabetical list represents the accounts and balances for Natraj Realty on June 30, 20x3. All the accounts have normal balances.

Accounts Payable	$15,420	Natraj, Withdrawals	$27,000
Accounts Receivable	7,650	Office Equipment	15,510
Accumulated Depreciation,		Prepaid Insurance	1,680
Office Equipment	1,350	Rent Expense	7,200
Advertising Expense	1,800	Revenue from Commissions	57,900
Cash	7,635	Supplies	825
Natraj, Capital	30,630	Wages Expense	36,000

Prepare a trial balance by listing the accounts in the correct order, with the balances in the appropriate debit or credit column.

E 5. LO 6 *Completion of a Work Sheet*

The following is an alphabetically arranged list of accounts and balances, in highly simplified form. This information is for the month ended October 31, 20xx.

Trial Balance Accounts and Balances

Accounts Payable	$4	Rita Wilkins, Capital	$12
Accounts Receivable	7	Rita Wilkins, Withdrawals	6
Accumulated Depreciation, Office Equipment	1	Service Revenue	23
		Supplies	4
Cash	4	Unearned Revenues	3
Office Equipment	8	Utilities Expense	2
Prepaid Insurance	2	Wages Expense	10

1. Prepare a work sheet, entering the trial balance accounts in the order in which they would normally appear, and arranging the balances in the correct debit or credit column.
2. Complete the work sheet using the following information:
   a. Expired insurance, $1.
   b. Of the unearned revenue balance, $2 has been earned by the end of the month.
   c. Estimated depreciation on office equipment, $1.
   d. Accrued wages, $1.
   e. Unused supplies on hand, $1.

E 6. LO 7 *Derivation of Adjusting Entries and Preparation of Balance Sheet*

Below is a partial work sheet in which the Trial Balance and Income Statement columns have been completed. All amounts shown are in dollars.

	Trial Balance		Income Statement	
Account Name	**Debit**	**Credit**	**Debit**	**Credit**
Cash	14			
Accounts Receivable	24			
Supplies	22			
Prepaid Insurance	16			
Building	50			
Accumulated Depreciation, Building		16		
Accounts Payable		8		
Unearned Revenues		4		
T. L., Capital		64		
Revenues		88		92
Wages Expense	54		60	
	180	180		
Insurance Expense			8	
Supplies Expense			16	
Depreciation Expense, Building			4	
			88	92
Net Income			4	
			92	92

1. Show the adjustments that have been made in journal form.
2. Prepare a balance sheet.

E 7. LO 5 LO 7 *Preparation of Adjusting and Reversing Entries from Work Sheet Columns*

The items below are from the Adjustments columns of a work sheet that is dated June 30.

Account Name	Adjustments Debit	Adjustments Credit
Prepaid Insurance		(a) 240
Office Supplies		(b) 630
Accumulated Depreciation, Office Equipment		(c) 1,400
Accumulated Depreciation, Store Equipment		(d) 2,200
Office Salaries Expense	(e) 240	
Store Salaries Expense	(e) 480	
Insurance Expense	(a) 240	
Office Supplies Expense	(b) 630	
Depreciation Expense, Office Equipment	(c) 1,400	
Depreciation Expense, Store Equipment	(d) 2,200	
Salaries Payable		(e) 720
	5,190	5,190

1. Prepare the adjusting entries.
2. Where required, prepare appropriate reversing entries.

E 8. LO 3 LO 7 *Preparation of Closing Entries from the Work Sheet*

The items below are from the Income Statement columns of the work sheet of the DiPietro Repair Shop for the year ended December 31, 20xx.

Account Name	Income Statement Debit	Income Statement Credit
Repair Revenue		25,620
Wages Expense	8,110	
Rent Expense	1,200	
Supplies Expense	4,260	
Insurance Expense	915	
Depreciation Expense, Repair Equipment	1,345	
	15,830	25,620
Net Income	9,790	
	25,620	25,620

Prepare entries to close the revenue, expense, Income Summary, and Withdrawals accounts. Mr. DiPietro withdrew $5,000 during the year.

Problems

P 1. The adjusted trial balance for Deer Creek Tennis Club at the end of the company's fiscal year appears below.

LO 3 *Closing Entries Using T Accounts and Preparation of Financial Statements*

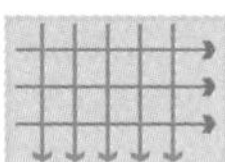

Deer Creek Tennis Club
Adjusted Trial Balance
June 30, 20x2

Cash	$ 26,200	
Prepaid Advertising	9,600	
Supplies	1,200	
Land	100,000	
Building	645,200	
Accumulated Depreciation, Building		$ 260,000
Equipment	156,000	
Accumulated Depreciation, Equipment		50,400
Accounts Payable		73,000
Wages Payable		29,000
Property Taxes Payable		22,500
Unearned Revenues, Locker Fees		3,000
Donna Webb, Capital		471,150
Donna Webb, Withdrawals	54,000	
Revenues from Court Fees		678,100
Revenues from Locker Fees		9,600
Wages Expense	351,000	
Maintenance Expense	51,600	
Advertising Expense	39,750	
Utilities Expense	64,800	
Supplies Expense	26,000	
Depreciation Expense, Building	30,000	
Depreciation Expense, Equipment	12,000	
Property Taxes Expense	22,500	
Miscellaneous Expense	6,900	
	$1,596,750	$1,596,750

REQUIRED

1. Prepare T accounts and enter the balance for Donna Webb, Capital; Donna Webb, Withdrawals; Income Summary; and all revenue and expense accounts.
2. Enter the four required closing entries in the T accounts, labeling the components a, b, c, and d as appropriate.
3. Prepare an income statement, a statement of owner's equity, and a balance sheet.

P 2. Lancaster Recreational Park, owned by Betty Schultz, rents campsites in a wooded park. The adjusted trial balance for Lancaster Recreational Park on June 30, 20x3, the end of the current fiscal year, is shown on the following page.

LO 3 *Closing Entries Using Journal Form and Preparation of Financial Statements*

REQUIRED

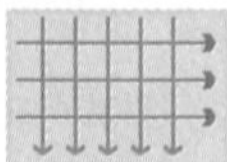

1. From the information given, prepare an income statement, a statement of owner's equity, and a balance sheet. Assume no additional investments by the owner.
2. Record the closing entries in journal form.
3. Assuming that Wages Payable represents wages accrued at the end of the accounting period, record the reversing entry required on July 1.

Lancaster Recreational Park
Adjusted Trial Balance
June 30, 20x3

Cash	$ 4,080	
Accounts Receivable	7,320	
Supplies	228	
Prepaid Insurance	1,188	
Land	30,000	
Building	91,800	
Accumulated Depreciation, Building		$ 21,000
Accounts Payable		3,450
Wages Payable		1,650
Betty Schultz, Capital		93,070
Betty Schultz, Withdrawals	36,000	
Campsite Rentals		88,200
Wages Expense	23,850	
Insurance Expense	3,784	
Utilities Expense	1,800	
Supplies Expense	1,320	
Depreciation Expense, Building	6,000	
	$207,370	$207,370

P 3. LO 1 LO 3 LO 4 *The Complete Accounting Cycle Without a Work Sheet: Two Months (second month optional)*

On October 1, 20xx, Jeff Romanoff opened Romanoff Appliance Service. During the month, he completed the following transactions for the company.

Oct.	1	Began business by depositing $5,000 in a bank account.
	1	Paid the rent for a store for one month, $425.
	1	Paid the premium on a one-year insurance policy, $480.
	2	Purchased repair equipment from Perry Company for $4,200. The terms were $600 down and $300 per month for one year. The first payment is due on November 1.
	5	Purchased repair supplies from Bridger Company on credit, $468.
	8	Paid cash for an advertisement in a local newspaper, $60.
	15	Received cash repair revenue for the first half of the month, $400.
	21	Paid Bridger Company on account, $225.
	31	Received cash repair revenue for the second half of October, $975.
	31	Owner withdrew cash for personal expenses, $300.

REQUIRED FOR OCTOBER

1. Prepare journal entries to record the October transactions.
2. Open the following accounts: Cash (111); Prepaid Insurance (117); Repair Supplies (119); Repair Equipment (144); Accumulated Depreciation, Repair Equipment (145); Accounts Payable (212); J. Romanoff, Capital (311); J. Romanoff, Withdrawals (312); Income Summary (313); Repair Revenue (411); Store Rent Expense (511); Advertising Expense (512); Insurance Expense (513); Repair Supplies Expense (514); and Depreciation Expense, Repair Equipment (515). Post the October journal entries to the ledger accounts.
3. Using the following information, record adjusting entries in the general journal and post to the ledger accounts.
   a. One month's insurance has expired.
   b. The remaining inventory of unused repair supplies is $169.
   c. The estimated depreciation on repair equipment is $70.

4. From the accounts in the ledger, prepare an adjusted trial balance. (Note: Normally a trial balance is prepared before adjustments, but this is omitted here to save time.)
5. From the adjusted trial balance, prepare an income statement, a statement of owner's equity, and a balance sheet for October.
6. Prepare and post closing entries.
7. Prepare a post-closing trial balance.

(*Optional*) During November, Jeff Romanoff completed the following transactions for Romanoff Appliance Service.

Nov.	1	Paid the monthly rent, $425.
	1	Made the monthly payment to Perry Company, $300.
	6	Purchased additional repair supplies on credit from Bridger Company, $863.
	15	Received cash repair revenue for the first half of the month, $914.
	20	Paid cash for an advertisement in the local newspaper, $60.
	23	Paid Bridger Company on account, $600.
	30	Received cash repair revenue for the last half of the month, $817.
	30	Withdrew cash for personal expenses, $300.

REQUIRED FOR NOVEMBER

8. Prepare and post journal entries to record the November transactions.
9. Using the following information, record adjusting entries in the general journal and post to the ledger accounts.
   a. One month's insurance has expired.
   b. The inventory of unused repair supplies is $413.
   c. The estimated depreciation on repair equipment is $70.
10. From the accounts in the ledger, prepare an adjusted trial balance.
11. From the adjusted trial balance, prepare the November income statement, statement of owner's equity, and balance sheet.
12. Prepare and post closing entries.
13. Prepare a post-closing trial balance.

P 4.

LO 3 *Preparation of a Work*
LO 5 *Sheet; Financial*
LO 6 *Statements; and*
LO 7 *Adjusting, Closing, and Reversing Entries*

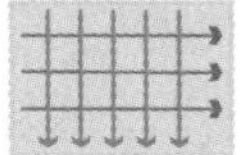

Jose Vargas opened his executive search service on July 1, 20x2. Some customers paid for his services after they were rendered, and others paid in advance for one year of service. After six months of operation, Vargas wanted to know how his business stood. The trial balance on December 31 appears below.

Vargas Executive Search Service
Trial Balance
December 31, 20x2

Cash	$ 1,713	
Prepaid Rent	1,800	
Office Supplies	413	
Office Equipment	15,750	
Accounts Payable		$ 3,173
Unearned Revenues		1,823
Jose Vargas, Capital		10,000
Jose Vargas, Withdrawals	5,200	
Search Revenue		20,140
Utilities Expense	1,260	
Wages Expense	9,000	
	$35,136	$35,136

REQUIRED

1. Enter the trial balance amounts in the Trial Balance columns of the work sheet. Remember that accumulated depreciation is listed with its asset account. Complete the work sheet using the following information:
   a. One year's rent had been paid in advance when Vargas began business.
   b. Inventory of unused office supplies, $75.
   c. One-half year's depreciation on office equipment, $900.
   d. Service rendered that had been paid for in advance, $863.
   e. Executive search services rendered during the month but not yet billed, $270.
   f. Wages earned by employees but not yet paid, $188.
2. From the work sheet, prepare an income statement, a statement of owner's equity, and a balance sheet.
3. From the work sheet, prepare adjusting and closing entries and, if required, reversing entries.
4. What is your evaluation of Vargas's first six months in business?

P 5.

LO 3 LO 5 LO 6 LO 7 *Preparation of a Work Sheet; Financial Statements; and Adjusting, Closing, and Reversing Entries*

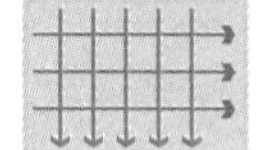

The following trial balance was taken from the ledger of Robinson Delivery Service on December 31, 20x2, the end of the company's fiscal year.

Robinson Delivery Service
Trial Balance
December 31, 20x2

Cash	$ 10,072	
Accounts Receivable	29,314	
Prepaid Insurance	5,340	
Delivery Supplies	14,700	
Office Supplies	2,460	
Land	15,000	
Building	196,000	
Accumulated Depreciation, Building		$ 53,400
Trucks	103,800	
Accumulated Depreciation, Trucks		30,900
Office Equipment	15,900	
Accumulated Depreciation, Office Equipment		10,800
Accounts Payable		9,396
Unearned Lockbox Fees		8,340
Mortgage Payable		72,000
Pearl Robinson, Capital		128,730
Pearl Robinson, Withdrawals	30,000	
Delivery Services Revenue		283,470
Lockbox Fees Earned		28,800
Truck Drivers' Wages Expense	120,600	
Office Salaries Expense	44,400	
Gas, Oil, and Truck Repairs Expense	31,050	
Interest Expense	7,200	
	$625,836	$625,836

REQUIRED

1. Enter the trial balance amounts in the Trial Balance columns of a work sheet and complete the work sheet using the following information:
   a. Expired insurance, $3,060.
   b. Inventory of unused delivery supplies, $1,430.

c. Inventory of unused office supplies, $186.
d. Estimated depreciation, building, $14,400.
e. Estimated depreciation, trucks, $15,450.
f. Estimated depreciation, office equipment, $2,700.
g. The company credits the lockbox fees of customers who pay in advance to the Unearned Lockbox Fees account. Of the amount credited to this account during the year, $5,630 had been earned by December 31.
h. Lockbox fees earned but unrecorded and uncollected at the end of the accounting period, $816.
i. Accrued but unpaid truck drivers' wages at the end of the year, $1,920.

2. Prepare an income statement, a statement of owner's equity, and a balance sheet. Assume no additional investments by Pearl Robinson.
3. Prepare adjusting, closing, and, if required, reversing entries from the work sheet.

Alternate Problems

LO 3 *Closing Entries Using T Accounts and Preparation of Financial Statements*

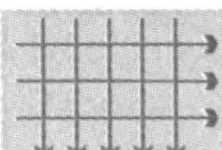

P 6. The adjusted trial balance for Whitehead Bowling Lanes at the end of the company's fiscal year appears below.

Whitehead Bowling Lanes
Adjusted Trial Balance
December 31, 20x3

Cash	$ 16,214	
Accounts Receivable	7,388	
Supplies	156	
Prepaid Insurance	300	
Land	5,000	
Building	100,000	
Accumulated Depreciation, Building		$ 27,200
Equipment	125,000	
Accumulated Depreciation, Equipment		33,000
Accounts Payable		30,044
Notes Payable		70,000
Unearned Revenues		300
Wages Payable		3,962
Property Taxes Payable		10,000
Ruth Accardo, Capital		60,813
Ruth Accardo, Withdrawals	24,000	
Revenues		618,263
Wages Expense	381,076	
Advertising Expense	30,200	
Maintenance Expense	84,100	
Supplies Expense	1,148	
Insurance Expense	1,500	
Depreciation Expense, Building	4,800	
Depreciation Expense, Equipment	11,000	
Utilities Expense	42,200	
Miscellaneous Expense	9,500	
Property Taxes Expense	10,000	
	$853,582	$853,582

REQUIRED

1. Prepare T accounts and enter the balance for Ruth Accardo, Capital; Ruth Accardo, Withdrawals; Income Summary; and all revenue and expense accounts.
2. Enter in the T accounts the four required closing entries, labeling the components a, b, c, and d as appropriate.
3. Prepare an income statement, a statement of owner's equity, and a balance sheet.

P 7. LO 3 *Closing Entries and Preparation of Financial Statements*

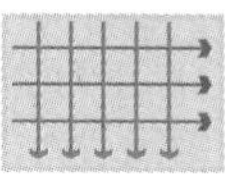

Hillcrest Campgrounds, owned by Cynthia Tobin, rents out campsites in a wooded park. The adjusted trial balance for Hillcrest Campgrounds on May 31, 20x2, the end of the current fiscal year, follows.

Hillcrest Campgrounds
Adjusted Trial Balance
May 31, 20x2

Cash	$ 2,040	
Accounts Receivable	3,660	
Supplies	114	
Prepaid Insurance	594	
Land	15,000	
Building	45,900	
Accumulated Depreciation, Building		$ 10,500
Accounts Payable		1,725
Wages Payable		825
Cynthia Tobin, Capital		46,535
Cynthia Tobin, Withdrawals	18,000	
Campsite Rentals		44,100
Wages Expense	11,925	
Insurance Expense	1,892	
Utilities Expense	900	
Supplies Expense	660	
Depreciation Expense, Building	3,000	
	$103,685	$103,685

REQUIRED

1. Record the closing entries in journal form.
2. From the information given, prepare an income statement, a statement of owner's equity, and a balance sheet. Assume no additional investments by the owner.

P 8. The following trial balance was taken from the ledger of Zolnay Package Delivery Company on August 31, 20x2, the end of the company's fiscal year.

LO 3 LO 5 LO 6 LO 7 *Preparation of a Work Sheet; Financial Statements; Adjusting, Closing, and Reversing Entries*

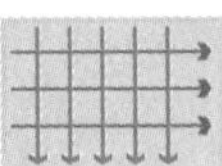

Zolnay Package Delivery Company
Trial Balance
August 31, 20x2

Cash	$ 5,036	
Accounts Receivable	14,657	
Prepaid Insurance	2,670	
Delivery Supplies	7,350	
Office Supplies	1,230	
Land	7,500	
Building	98,000	
Accumulated Depreciation, Building		$ 26,700
Trucks	51,900	
Accumulated Depreciation, Trucks		15,450
Office Equipment	7,950	
Accumulated Depreciation, Office Equipment		5,400
Accounts Payable		4,698
Unearned Lockbox Fees		4,170
Mortgage Payable		36,000
Ruth Zolnay, Capital		64,365
Ruth Zolnay, Withdrawals	15,000	
Delivery Services Revenue		141,735
Lockbox Fees Earned		14,400
Truck Drivers' Wages Expense	63,900	
Office Salaries Expense	22,200	
Gas, Oil, and Truck Repairs Expense	15,525	
	$312,918	$312,918

REQUIRED

1. Enter the trial balance amounts in the Trial Balance columns of a work sheet and complete the work sheet using the following information.
   a. Expired insurance, $1,530.
   b. Inventory of unused delivery supplies, $715.
   c. Inventory of unused office supplies, $93.
   d. Estimated depreciation, building, $7,200.
   e. Estimated depreciation, trucks, $7,725.
   f. Estimated depreciation, office equipment, $1,350.
   g. The company credits the lockbox fees of customers who pay in advance to the Unearned Lockbox Fees account. Of the amount credited to this account during the year, $2,815 had been earned by August 31.
   h. Lockbox fees earned but unrecorded and uncollected at the end of the accounting period, $408.
   i. Accrued but unpaid truck drivers' wages at the end of the year, $960.
2. Prepare an income statement, a statement of owner's equity, and a balance sheet. Assume no additional investments by Ruth Zolnay.
3. Prepare adjusting, closing, and, if required, reversing entries from the work sheet.

Skills Development

Conceptual Analysis

SD 1. LO 1 *Interim Financial Statements*

Ocean Oil Services Corporation provides services for drilling operations off the coast of Louisiana. The company has a significant amount of debt to River National Bank in Baton Rouge. The bank requires the company to provide it with financial statements every quarter. Explain what is involved in preparing financial statements every quarter.

SD 2. LO 5 *Accounting Efficiency*

Way Heaters Company, located just outside Milwaukee, Wisconsin, is a small, successful manufacturer of industrial heaters. The company's heaters are used, for instance, by candy manufacturers to heat chocolate. The company sells its heaters to some of its customers on credit with generous terms. The terms usually specify payment six months after purchase and an interest rate based on current bank rates. Because the interest on the loans accrues a little bit every day but is not paid until the due date of the note, it is necessary to make an adjusting entry at the end of each accounting period to debit Interest Receivable and credit Interest Income for the amount of the interest accrued but not paid to date. The company prepares financial statements every month. Keeping track of what has been accrued in the past is time-consuming because the notes carry different dates and interest rates. Discuss what the accountant can do to simplify the process of making the adjusting entry for accrued interest each month.

Ethical Dilemma

SD 3. LO 1 *Ethics and Time Pressure*

Jay Wheeler, the assistant accountant for ***WB Company,*** has made adjusting entries and is preparing the adjusted trial balance for the first six months of the year. Financial statements must be delivered to the bank by 5 o'clock to support a critical loan agreement. By noon, Jay cannot balance the adjusted trial balance. The figures are off by $1,320, so he increases the balance of the owner's Capital account by $1,320. He closes the accounts, prepares the statements, and sends them to the bank on time. Jay hopes that no one will notice the problem and believes that he can find the error and correct it by the end of next month. Are Jay's actions ethical? Why or why not? Did Jay have other alternatives?

Research Activity

SD 4. LO 1, LO 2, LO 3, LO 4, LO 5, LO 7 *Interview of a Local Businessperson*

Arrange to spend about an hour interviewing the owner, manager, or accountant of a local service or retail business. Your goal is to learn as much as you can about the accounting cycle of the person's business. Ask the interviewee to show you his or her accounting records and to tell you how such transactions as sales, purchases, payments, and payroll are handled. Examine the documents used to support the transactions. Look at any journals, ledgers, or work sheets. Does the business use a computer? Does it use its own accounting system, or does it use an outside or centralized service? Does it use the cash or the accrual basis of accounting? When does it prepare adjusting entries? When does it prepare closing entries? How often does it prepare financial statements? Does it prepare reversing entries? How do its procedures differ from those described in the text? When the interview is finished, organize and write up your findings and be prepared to present them to your class.

Communication

Critical Thinking

Group Activity

Memo

Ethics

International
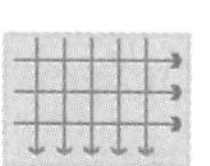
Spreadsheet

General Ledger

CD-ROM

Internet

Group Activity: Divide the class into groups and assign each group to a different type of business, such as shoe store, fast food, grocery, hardware, records, and others. Have the groups give presentations in class.

Decision-Making Practice

SD 5.
LO 1 *Conversion from Accrual*
LO 3 *to Cash Statement*

Adele's Secretarial Service is a simple business. Adele provides typing services for students at the local university. Her accountant prepared the income statement that appears below for the year ended June 30, 20x4.

Adele's Secretarial Service
Income Statement
For the Year Ended June 30, 20x4

Revenues		
Typing Services		$20,980
Expenses		
Rent Expense	$2,400	
Depreciation Expense, Office Equipment	2,200	
Supplies Expense	960	
Other Expenses	1,240	
Total Expenses		6,800
Net Income		$14,180

In reviewing this statement, Adele is puzzled. She knows she withdrew from the company $15,600 in cash for personal expenses, yet the cash balance in the company's bank account increased from $460 to $3,100 from last June 30 to this June 30. She wants to know how her net income could be less than the cash withdrawals she took out of the business if there is an increase in the cash balance.

Her accountant has completed the closing entries and shows her the balance sheets for June 30, 20x4, and June 30, 20x3. She explains that besides the change in the cash balance, accounts receivable from customers decreased by $1,480 and accounts payable increased by $380 (supplies are the only items Adele buys on credit). The only other asset or liability account that changed during the year was Accumulated Depreciation, Office Equipment, which increased by $2,200.

1. Verify the cash balance increase by preparing a statement that lists the receipts of cash and the expenditures of cash during the year.
2. Write a memorandum to Adele explaining why the accountant is answering her question by pointing out year-to-year changes in the balance sheet. Include in your memorandum an explanation of your treatment of depreciation expense, giving your reasons for the treatment.

Financial Reporting and Analysis

Interpreting Financial Reports

FRA 1.
LO 2 *Closing Entries*
LO 3

H&R Block, Inc., is the world's largest tax preparation service firm. In its 1997 annual report, the statement of earnings (in thousands) for the year ended April 30, 1997, appeared as shown on the next page.[3]

Revenues	
Service Revenues	$1,805,711
Royalties	110,519
Investment Income	20,730
Other Revenues	13,433
Total Revenues	$1,950,393
Expenses	
Employee Compensation and Benefits	$604,336
Occupancy and Equipment Expense	583,420
Marketing and Advertising Expense	239,255
Supplies, Freight, and Postage Expense	69,929
Other Operating Expenses	414,897
Total Expenses	$1,911,837
Earnings Before Income Taxes	$ 38,556
Income Taxes	14,613
Net Earnings	$ 23,943

The company reported distributing cash in the amount of $107,988,000 to the owners in 1997.

REQUIRED

1. Prepare, in journal form, the closing entries that would have been made by H&R Block on April 30, 1997. Treat income taxes as an expense, and treat cash distributions as withdrawals.
2. Based on the way you handled expenses and cash distributions in **1** and their ultimate effect on the owner's capital, what theoretical reason can you give for not including expenses and cash distributions in the same closing entry?

International Company

FRA 2. LO 1 LO 3 *Accounting Cycle and Closing Entries*

Nestlé S.A., maker of such well-known products as Nescafé, Lean Cuisine, and Perrier, is one of the largest and most internationally diverse companies in the world. Only 2 percent of its $47.8 billion in revenues comes from its home country of Switzerland, with the rest coming from sales in almost every other country of the world. Nestlé has over 220,000 employees in 70 countries[4] and is highly decentralized; that is, many of its divisions operate as separate companies in their countries. Managing the accounting operations of such a vast empire is a tremendous challenge. In what ways do you think the accounting cycle, including the closing process, would be the same for Nestlé as it is for Joan Miller Advertising Agency, and in what ways would it be different?

Toys "R" Us Annual Report

FRA 3. LO 1 *Fiscal Year, Closing Process, and Interim Reports*

Refer to the Notes to Consolidated Financial Statements in the Toys "R" Us annual report. When does Toys "R" Us end its fiscal year? What reasons can you give for the company's having chosen this date? From the standpoint of completing the accounting cycle, what advantages does this date have? Does Toys "R" Us prepare interim financial statements? What are the implications of interim financial statements for the accounting cycle?

Fingraph® Financial Analyst™

This activity is not applicable to the chapter.

ENDNOTES

1. Rhône-Poulenc Rorer Inc., *Mid-Year Progress Report,* 1996.
2. Earl E. Robertson and Dean Lockwood, "Tapping the Power of the PC at General Mills," *Management Accounting,* August 1994.
3. Adapted from H&R Block, Inc., *Annual Report,* 1997.
4. Nestlé S.A., *Annual Report,* 1996.

Comprehensive Problem: Joan Miller Advertising Agency

This problem continues with the Joan Miller Advertising Agency, the company used to illustrate the accounting cycle in the chapters on measuring business transactions, measuring business income, and completing the accounting cycle. It is necessary in some instances to refer to those chapters in completing this problem.

The January 31, 20xx, post-closing trial balance for the Joan Miller Advertising Agency is as follows:

Cash	$ 1,720	
Accounts Receivable	2,800	
Fees Receivable	200	
Art Supplies	1,300	
Office Supplies	600	
Prepaid Rent	400	
Prepaid Insurance	440	
Art Equipment	4,200	
Accumulated Depreciation, Art Equipment		$ 70
Office Equipment	3,000	
Accumulated Depreciation, Office Equipment		50
Accounts Payable		3,170
Unearned Art Fees		600
Wages Payable		180
Joan Miller, Capital		10,590
	$14,660	$14,660

During February, the agency engaged in the following transactions.

Feb. 1 Received an additional investment of cash from Joan Miller, $6,300.
2 Purchased additional office equipment with cash, $1,200.
5 Received art equipment transferred to the business from Joan Miller, $1,400.
6 Purchased additional office supplies with cash, $90.
7 Purchased additional art supplies on credit from Taylor Supply Company, $450.
8 Completed the series of advertisements for Marsh Tire Company that began on January 31 (see page 103) and billed Marsh Tire Company for the total services performed, including the accrued revenues (fees receivable) that had been recognized in an adjusting entry in January, $800.
9 Paid the secretary for two weeks' wages, $600.
12 Paid the amount due to Morgan Equipment for the office equipment purchased last month, $1,500.
13 Accepted an advance fee in cash for artwork to be done for another agency, $1,600.
14 Purchased a copier (office equipment) from Morgan Equipment for $2,100, paying $350 in cash and agreeing to pay the rest in equal payments over the next five months.
15 Performed advertising services and received a cash fee, $1,450.
16 Received payment on account from Ward Department Stores for services performed last month, $2,800.
19 Paid amount due for the telephone bill that was received and recorded at the end of January, $70.
20 Performed advertising services for Ward Department Stores and agreed to accept payment next month, $3,200.
21 Performed art services for a cash fee, $580.
22 Received and paid the utility bill for February, $110.
23 Paid the secretary for two weeks' wages, $600.
26 Paid the rent for March in advance, $400.
27 Received the telephone bill for February, which is to be paid next month, $80.
28 Paid out cash to Joan Miller as a withdrawal for personal living expenses, $1,400.

REQUIRED

1. Record in the general journal and post to the general ledger the reversing entries necessary on February 1 for Wages Payable and Fees Receivable (see Adjustment g on page 101 and Adjustment i on page 103). (Begin the general journal on Page 5.)
2. Record the transactions for February in the general journal.
3. Post the February transactions to the general ledger accounts.
4. Prepare a trial balance in the Trial Balance columns of a work sheet.
5. Prepare adjusting entries and complete the work sheet using the information below.
   a. One month's prepaid rent has expired, $400.
   b. One month's prepaid insurance has expired, $40.
   c. An inventory of art supplies reveals $600 still on hand on February 28.
   d. An inventory of office supplies reveals $410 still on hand on February 28.
   e. Depreciation on art equipment for February is calculated to be $100.
   f. Depreciation on office equipment for February is calculated to be $100.
   g. Art services performed for which payment has been received in advance total $1,300.
   h. Advertising services performed that will not be billed until March total $290.
   i. Three days' wages had accrued by the end of February.
6. From the work sheet prepare an income statement, a statement of owner's equity, and a balance sheet.
7. Record the adjusting entries in the general journal, and post them to the general ledger.
8. Record the closing entries in the general journal, and post them to the general ledger.
9. Prepare a post-closing trial balance.

This Comprehensive Problem covers all of the Learning Objectives in the chapters on measuring business transactions, measuring business income, and completing the accounting cycle.

03782

CHAPTER 5

Merchandising Operations

LEARNING OBJECTIVES

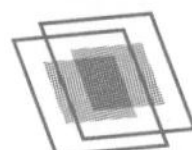

1. **Identify the management issues related to merchandising businesses.**
2. **Compare the income statements for service and merchandising concerns, and define the components of the merchandising income statement.**
3. **Distinguish between the periodic and the perpetual inventory systems, and explain the importance of taking a physical inventory.**
4. **Contrast and record transactions related to sales and purchases under the periodic and the perpetual inventory systems.**

SUPPLEMENTAL OBJECTIVES

5. **Prepare a work sheet and closing entries for a merchandising concern using the periodic inventory system.**
6. **Prepare a work sheet and closing entries for a merchandising concern using the perpetual inventory system.**
7. **Apply sales and purchases discounts to merchandising transactions.**

DECISION POINT

TARGET STORES

The management of a merchandising business has two key decisions to make: the price at which merchandise is sold and the level of service the company provides. For example, a department store can set the price of its merchandise at a relatively high level and provide a great deal of service. A discount store, on the other hand, may price its merchandise at a relatively low level and provide limited service. The following figures show that Target Stores, a division of Dayton-Hudson Corp., is successful.[1] What decisions did Target Stores' management make about pricing and service to achieve this success?

Target's chief executive officer says, "Target's ongoing financial success stems from our strategic differentiation. Target distinguishes itself from other discounters by providing its guests with quality, trend-right merchandise, superior service, a convenient shopping experience and competitive prices."[2] In other words, Target emphasizes high-quality, name-brand merchandise that might be sold at full price in specialty stores, but sells it at discount prices that are competitive with the prices of other discount stores that sell less well known merchandise. Target reduces operating expenses by operating very big stores that can be controlled by a minimum number of employees. By its efforts, Target was able to achieve record levels of profit margin "through strong sales momentum, improvement in gross margin rate and significant operating expense savings."[3]

Financial Highlights

(Millions of Dollars)

	1996	1995	1994
Revenues	**$17,853**	$15,807	$13,600
Operating profit	**$ 1,042**	$ 719	$ 732
Stores	**736**	670	611
Retail square feet*	**79,360**	71,108	64,446

*In thousands, reflects total square feet, less office, warehouse, and vacant space.

Critical Thinking Question: What types of costs can a merchandiser reduce to sell goods at a lower price while maintaining profitability? **Answer:** Labor costs, display costs, and retail store (rental) cost per square foot.

Business-World Example: In terms of sales dollars, the largest retailers in 1997 were Wal-Mart, Sears, and Kmart.

VIDEO CASE

OFFICE DEPOT, INC.

OBJECTIVES

- To become familiar with the nature of merchandising operations.
- To identify the management issues associated with a merchandising business.
- To show how gross margin and operating expenses affect the business goal of profitability.

BACKGROUND FOR THE CASE

All retailing companies are merchandising companies. Office Depot, Inc., is the world's largest office products retailer and one of the fastest-growing retailing companies in the world. Through its chain of office products superstores and delivery warehouses, the company serves the growing market of small and medium-size businesses, home offices, and individual consumers. A typical Office Depot store is 25,000 to 30,000 square feet in size and features over 6,000 name-brand products at prices that are generally 60 percent below manufacturers' suggested retail or catalog prices. Office Depot's merchandise assortment includes office supplies, business electronics, state-of-the-art computer hardware and software, office furniture, and a complete business service center. The company operates a national network of Customer Service Centers where customers can pick up purchases or have them delivered. The delivery business represents more than 30 percent of the company's total sales. Office Depot is expanding by opening megastores of approximately 50,000 square feet, free-standing furniture stores, and copying and publishing services outlets. The company is faced with intense competition from companies such as OfficeMax, Inc., and Staples, Inc.

For more information about Office Depot, Inc., visit the company's Web site through the Needles Accounting Resource Center Web site at

http://www.hmco.com/college/needles/home.html

REQUIRED

View the video on Office Depot, Inc., that accompanies this book. As you are watching the video, take notes related to the following questions:

1. All merchandising companies have inventories and need to control those inventories. In your own words, what is inventory and why is it important to implement controls over it? Identify the type of products that Office Depot typically has in inventory and some ways in which the company might control its inventory.
2. All merchandising companies have an operating cycle. Describe the operating cycle and explain how it applies to Office Depot.
3. All merchandising companies try to achieve the goal of profitability by producing a satisfactory gross margin and maintaining acceptable levels of operating expenses. What is gross margin, and how does it relate to operating expenses? Describe how Office Depot's operations affect gross margin and operating expenses in a way that enables the company to achieve superior profitability.

Management Issues in Merchandising Businesses

OBJECTIVE 1

Identify the management issues related to merchandising businesses

Related Text Assignments:
Q: 1, 2
SE: 1
E: 1, 2
P: 1, 7
SD: 1, 4
FRA: 2, 4, 5

Up to this point you have studied business and accounting issues related to the simplest type of business—the service business. Service businesses, such as advertising agencies and law firms, perform services for fees or commissions. Merchandising businesses, on the other hand, earn income by buying and selling products or merchandise. These companies, whether wholesale or retail, use the same basic accounting methods as do service companies, but the buying and selling of merchandise adds to the complexity of the process. As a foundation for discussing the accounting issues of merchandising businesses, we must first identify the management issues involved in running such a business.

Cash Flow Management

Merchandising businesses differ from service businesses in that they have goods on hand for sale to customers, called merchandise inventory, and they engage in a series of transactions called the operating cycle, as shown in Figure 1. The transactions in the operating cycle consist of (1) purchases of merchandise inventory for cash or on credit, (2) payment for purchases made on credit, (3) sales of merchandise inventory for cash or on credit, and (4) collection of cash from the sales. Purchases of merchandise are usually made on credit, so the merchandiser has a period of time before payment is due, but this period is generally less than the time it takes to sell the merchandise. Therefore, management will have to plan for cash flows from within the company or from borrowing to finance the inventory until it is sold and the resulting revenue is collected.

In the case of cash sales, sales of merchandise for cash, the cash is collected immediately. Sales on bank credit cards, such as VISA or MasterCard, are considered cash sales because funds from these sales are available to the merchandiser immediately. In the case of credit sales, sales of merchandise on credit, the company must wait a period of time before receiving the cash. Some very small retail stores may

Figure 1
The Operating Cycle of Merchandising Concerns

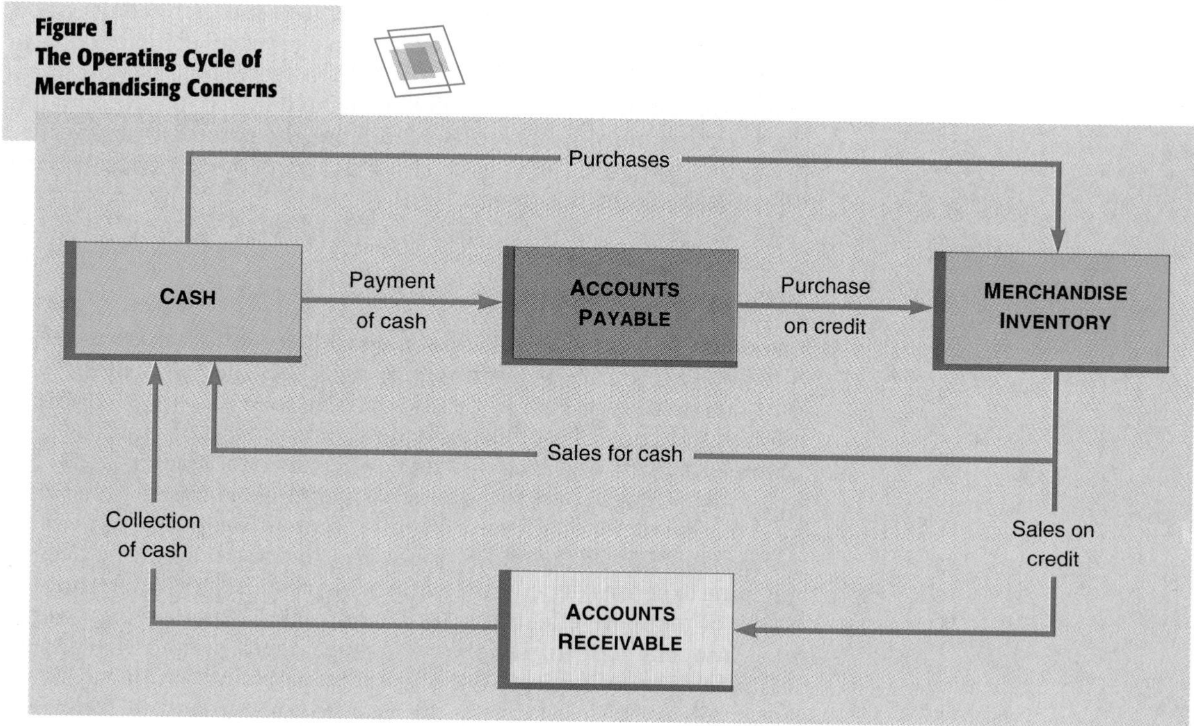

BUSINESS BULLETIN: BUSINESS PRACTICE

Warehouse clubs are big business, and Sam's Clubs, a division of Wal-Mart Stores, Inc., is one of the biggest. Individuals or small businesses join a warehouse club by paying a small annual membership fee and are then allowed to shop for groceries, drugs, office supplies, and many other products at discount prices. Clubs keep prices low by minimizing overhead costs and selling on a cash basis. Because warehouse clubs do not sell on credit, they traditionally have not sold to large companies, government agencies, or schools, which find it difficult to buy with cash. To expand into this market, a new division of Sam's Clubs, called Sam's Club Direct, sells directly to big organizations. The company says, "We're tapping into a giant source of new business. . . . This is a whole new ball game for the industry."[4] Selling on credit to large organizations affects the company's cash flow and may improve its profitability. It also affects the company's inventory systems and requires the company to establish new controls for sales and receipts on account.

have mostly cash sales and very few credit sales, whereas large wholesale concerns may have almost all credit sales. Most merchandising concerns, however, have a combination of cash and credit sales.

Regardless of the relationships of purchases, payments, cash and credit sales, and collections, the operators of a merchandising business must carefully manage cash flow, or liquidity. Such cash flow management involves planning the company's receipts and payments of cash. If a company is not able to pay its bills when they are due, it may be forced out of business. As mentioned above, merchandise that is purchased must often be paid for before it is sold and the cash from its sale collected. For example, if a retail business must pay for its purchases in thirty days, it must have cash available or arrange for borrowing if it cannot sell and collect for the merchandise in thirty days.

The operating cycle for a merchandising firm can be 120 days, or even longer. For example, Dillard Department Stores, Inc., a successful chain of department stores in the South and Southwest regions of the United States, has an operating cycle of about 220 days. Its inventory is on hand an average of 79 days, and it takes, on average, 141 days to collect its receivables. Since the company pays for its merchandise in an average of 65 days, a much shorter time, management must carefully plan its cash flow, including borrowing.

Profitability Management

In addition to managing cash flow, management must achieve a satisfactory level of profitability in terms of performance measures. It must sell its merchandise at a price that exceeds its cost by a sufficient margin to pay operating expenses and have enough left to provide sufficient income, or profitability. Profitability management is a complex activity that includes, first, achieving a satisfactory gross margin and, second, maintaining acceptable levels of operating expenses. Achieving a satisfactory gross margin depends on setting appropriate prices for merchandise and purchasing merchandise at favorable prices and terms. Maintaining acceptable levels of operating expenses depends on controlling expenses and operating efficiently.

One of the more effective ways of controlling expenses is to use operating budgets. An operating budget reflects management's operating plans and consists of detailed listings of projected selling and general and administrative expenses for a company. At key times during the year and at the end of the year, management

Exhibit 1. An Example of an Operating Budget

Fenwick Fashions Company Operating Budget For the Year Ended December 31, 20x2			
Operating Expenses	**Budget**	**Actual**	**Difference Under (Over) Budget**
Selling Expenses			
Sales Salaries Expense	$22,000	$22,500	($ 500)
Freight Out Expense	5,500	5,740	(240)
Advertising Expense	12,000	10,000	2,000
Insurance Expense, Selling	800	1,600	(800)
Store Supplies Expense	1,000	1,540	(540)
Total Selling Expenses	$41,300	$41,380	($ 80)
General and Administrative Expenses			
Office Salaries Expense	$23,000	$26,900	($3,900)
Insurance Expense, General	2,100	4,200	(2,100)
Office Supplies Expense	500	1,204	(704)
Depreciation Expense, Building	2,600	2,600	—
Depreciation Expense, Office Equipment	2,000	2,200	(200)
Total General and Administrative Expenses	$30,200	$37,104	($6,904)
Total Operating Expenses	$71,500	$78,484	($6,984)

( ) unfavorable difference

should compare the budget with actual expenses and make adjustments to operations as appropriate. An example operating budget for Fenwick Fashions Company is shown in Exhibit 1. Total selling expenses exceeded the budget by only $80, but four of the expense categories exceeded the budget by a total of $2,080. Management should investigate the possibility that underspending in advertising of $2,000 hid inefficiencies and waste in other areas. Also, sales may have been penalized by not spending the budgeted amount on advertising. Total general and administrative expenses exceed the budget by $6,904. Management should determine why large differences occurred for office salaries expense, insurance expense, and office supplies expense. The amount of insurance expense is usually set by the insurance company; thus an error in the initial budgeting of insurance expense may have caused the unfavorable result. The operating budget helps management focus on the specific areas that need attention.

Choice of Inventory System

Another issue the management of a merchandising business must address is the choice of inventory system. There are two basic systems of accounting for the many items in the merchandise inventory. Under the periodic inventory system, the inventory not yet sold, or on hand, is counted periodically, usually at the end of the accounting period. No detailed records of the actual inventory on hand are maintained during the accounting period. Under the perpetual inventory system, continuous records are kept of the quantity and, usually, the cost of individual items as they are bought and sold. The periodic inventory system is less costly to maintain than the perpetual inventory system, but it gives management less information about the current status of merchandise inventory. Given the number and diversity of items contained in the merchandise inventory of most businesses, the perpetual inventory system is usually more effective for providing information about quantities and ensuring optimal customer service. Management must choose the system or combination of systems that is best for achieving the company's goals.

Control of Merchandising Operations

The principal transactions of merchandising businesses, such as buying and selling, involve assets—cash, accounts receivable, and merchandise inventory—that are vulnerable to theft and embezzlement. One reason for this vulnerability is that cash and inventory are fairly easy to steal. Another is that these assets are usually involved in a large number of transactions, such as cash receipts, receipts on account, payments for purchases, and receipts and shipments of inventory, which can become difficult to monitor. If a merchandising company does not take steps to protect its assets, it can have high losses of cash and inventory. Management's responsibility is to establish an environment, accounting systems, and control procedures that will protect the company's assets. These systems and procedures are called the internal control structure.

Income Statement for a Merchandising Concern

OBJECTIVE 2

Compare the income statements for service and merchandising concerns, and define the components of the merchandising income statement

Related Text Assignments:
Q: 3, 4, 5, 6, 7
SE: 2, 3, 4
E: 3, 4, 5, 6
P: 1, 2, 7, 8
SD: 1, 4, 5
FRA: 1

Many service companies require only a simple income statement. For those companies, as shown in Figure 2, net income represents the difference between revenues and expenses. But merchandising companies, because they buy and sell merchandise inventory, require a more complex income statement. As shown in Figure 2, the income statement for a merchandiser consists of three major parts: (1) net sales, (2) cost of goods sold, and (3) operating expenses. There is also a subtotal for gross margin.

The main difference between a merchandiser's income statement and that of a service business is that the merchandiser must compute gross margin before operating expenses are deducted. In the following discussion, the income statement for Fenwick Fashions Company, presented in Exhibit 2, will serve as an example of a merchandising income statement.

Net Sales

The first major part of the merchandising income statement is net sales, or often simply *sales*. Net sales consist of the gross proceeds from sales of merchandise, or gross sales, less sales returns and allowances. Gross sales consist of total cash sales and total credit sales occurring during an accounting period. Even though the cash may not be collected until the following accounting period, revenue is recognized, under the revenue recognition rule, as being earned when title for merchandise passes from seller to buyer at the time of sale. Sales Returns and Allowances is a contra-revenue account used to accumulate cash refunds, credits on account, and

Point to Emphasize: A sale takes place when title to the goods transfers to the buyer.

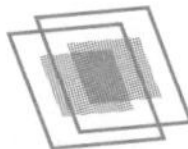

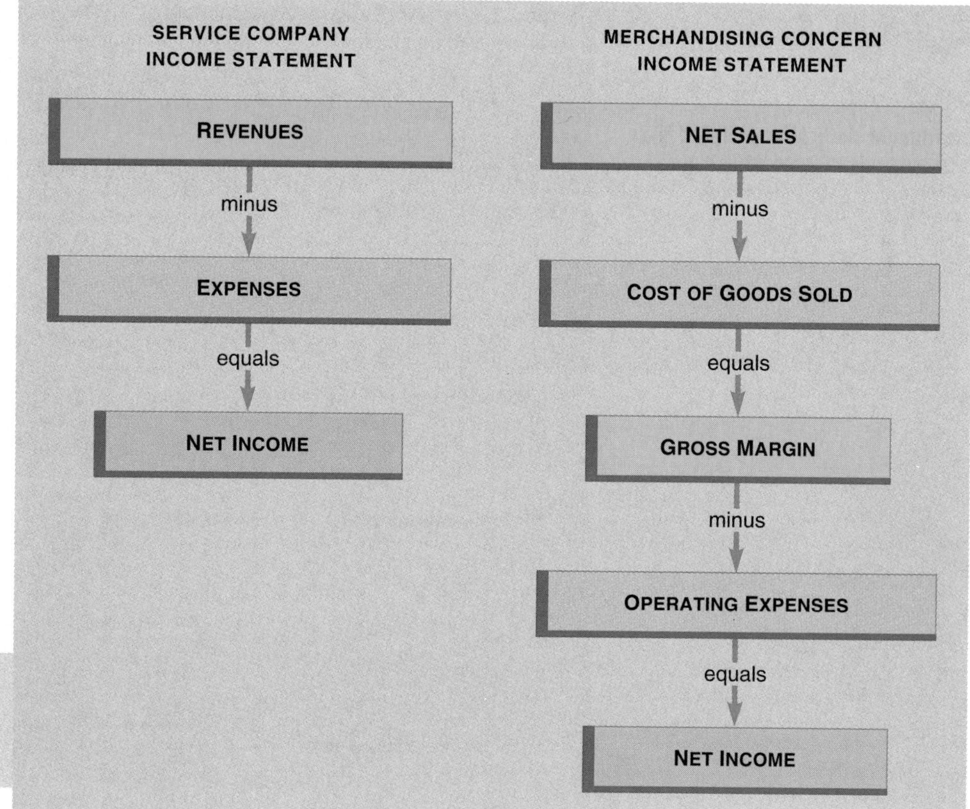

Figure 2
The Components of Income Statements for Service and Merchandising Companies

allowances off selling prices made to customers who have received defective or otherwise unsatisfactory products. If other discounts or allowances are given to customers (see supplemental objective 7, for instance), they also should be deducted from gross sales.

Management, investors, and others often use the amount of sales and trends suggested by sales as indicators of a firm's progress. Increasing sales suggest growth; decreasing sales indicate the possibility of decreased future earnings and other financial problems. To detect trends, comparisons are frequently made between the net sales of different accounting periods.

Cost of Goods Sold

Terminology Note: The cost of goods sold (also called the *cost of sales*) is an expense.

Enrichment Note: The matching rule precludes the cost of inventory from being expensed until the inventory has been sold.

The second part of the merchandising income statement is cost of goods sold, or often simply *cost of sales*, which is the amount a merchant paid for the merchandise sold during an accounting period. The method of computing cost of goods sold when using the periodic inventory method is sometimes confusing because it must take into account both merchandise inventory on hand at the beginning of the accounting period, called the beginning inventory, and merchandise inventory on hand at the end of the accounting period, called the ending inventory. The ending inventory appears on the balance sheet at the end of the accounting period and becomes the beginning inventory for the next accounting period.

The computation of cost of goods sold for Fenwick Fashions based on the income statement in Exhibit 2 is illustrated in Figure 3. The goods available for sale during the year is the sum of two factors, beginning inventory and the net cost of purchases

Exhibit 2. Merchandising Income Statement

Enrichment Note: Most published financial statements are condensed, eliminating much of the detail shown here.

Fenwick Fashions Company
Income Statement
For the Year Ended December 31, 20x2

Net Sales			
Gross Sales			$246,350
Less Sales Returns and Allowances			7,025
Net Sales			$239,325
Cost of Goods Sold			
Merchandise Inventory, December 31, 20x1		$ 52,800	
Purchases	$126,400		
Less Purchases Returns and Allowances	7,776		
Net Purchases	$118,624		
Freight In	8,236		
Net Cost of Purchases		126,860	
Goods Available for Sale		$179,660	
Less Merchandise Inventory, December 31, 20x2		48,300	
Cost of Goods Sold			131,360
Gross Margin			$107,965
Operating Expenses			
Selling Expenses			
Sales Salaries Expense	$ 22,500		
Freight Out Expense	5,740		
Advertising Expense	10,000		
Insurance Expense, Selling	1,600		
Store Supplies Expenses	1,540		
Total Selling Expenses		$ 41,380	
General and Administrative Expenses			
Office Salaries Expense	$ 26,900		
Insurance Expense, General	4,200		
Office Supplies Expense	1,204		
Depreciation Expense, Building	2,600		
Depreciation Expense, Office Equipment	2,200		
Total General and Administrative Expenses		37,104	
Total Operating Expenses			78,484
Net Income			$ 29,481

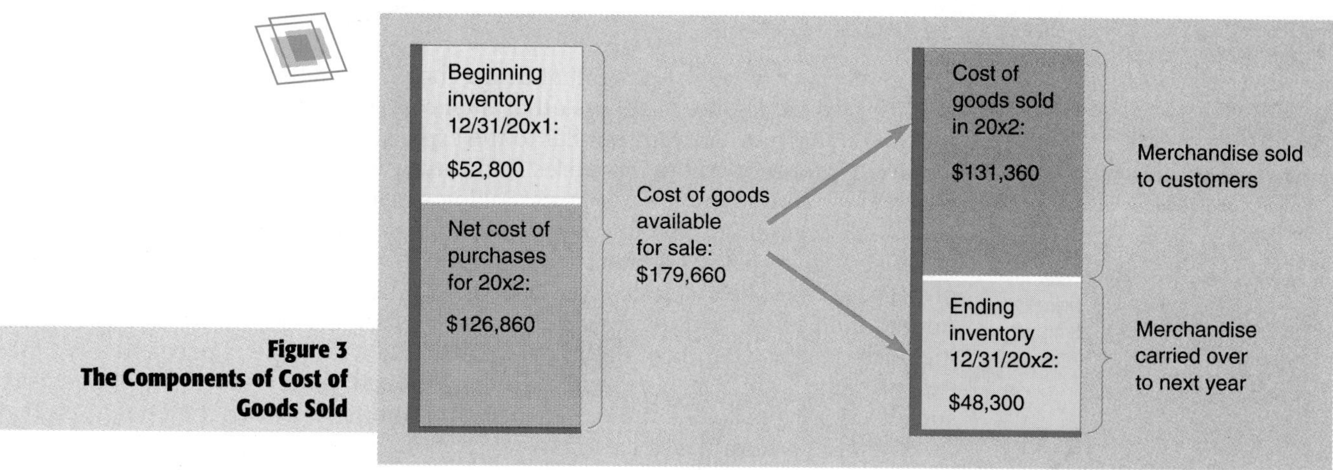

Figure 3
The Components of Cost of Goods Sold

during the year. In this case, the goods available for sale is $179,660 ($52,800 + $126,860).

Teaching Note: Once students understand the logic of the cost of goods sold calculation, this section of the income statement is clear to them; i.e., it is logical that beginning inventory plus inventory purchases equals the cost of goods *available* for sale. Similarly, by the end of the period, goods available for sale either are still on hand or have been sold during the period.

If a company sold all the goods available for sale during an accounting period, the cost of goods sold would equal the cost of goods available for sale. In most businesses, however, some merchandise will remain unsold and on hand at the end of the period. This merchandise, or ending inventory, must be deducted from the cost of goods available for sale to determine the cost of goods sold. In the case of Fenwick Fashions, the ending inventory on December 31, 20x2, is $48,300. Thus, the cost of goods sold is $131,360 ($179,660 − $48,300).

An important component of the cost of goods sold section is the net cost of purchases, which consists of net purchases plus any freight charges on the purchases. Net purchases equals total purchases less any deductions, such as purchases returns and allowances and any discounts allowed by suppliers for early payment (see supplemental objective 7). Because freight charges, or freight in, are a necessary cost to receive merchandise for sale, they are added to net purchases to arrive at the net cost of purchases. Freight in may also be called *transportation in.*

Gross Margin

Discussion Question: If a company sold all its goods to the public "at cost," would the company realize a profit of exactly $0? **Answer:** No. Its gross margin would equal $0, but the company would suffer a net loss equal to its operating expenses.

The difference between net sales and cost of goods sold on the merchandising income statement is gross margin, or *gross profit.* To be successful, merchants must sell goods for an amount greater than cost—that is, gross margin must be great enough to pay operating expenses and provide an adequate income. Management is interested in both the amount and the percentage of gross margin. The percentage of gross margin is computed by dividing the dollar amount of gross margin by net sales. In the case of Fenwick Fashions, the dollar amount of gross margin is $107,965 and the percentage of gross margin is 45.1 percent ($107,965 ÷ $239,325). This information is helpful in planning business operations. For instance, management may try to increase total sales dollars by reducing the selling price. This strategy reduces the percentage of gross margin, but it will work if the total items sold increase enough to raise the absolute amount of gross margin. This is the strategy followed by a discount warehouse store like Sam's Clubs. On the other hand, management may keep a high gross margin and attempt to increase sales and the amount of gross margin by increasing operating expenses such as advertising. This is the strategy followed by upscale specialty stores like Neiman Marcus. Other strategies to increase gross margin, such as improving purchasing methods to reduce cost of goods sold, can also be explored.

Parenthetical Note: When gross margin is insufficient to cover operating expenses, the company has suffered a net loss.

Point to Emphasize: The most common types of operating expenses are selling expenses and general and administrative expenses. They are deducted from gross margin on the income statement.

Instructional Strategy: To close this section and obtain student feedback, divide the class into pairs and assign E 7. Using the overhead or a flipchart, reveal the correct answers one by one and review as necessary. Consider giving 2 or 3 class participation points to teams with no mistakes and fewer points if mistakes are made.

Operating Expenses

The third major area of the merchandising income statement consists of operating expenses, which are the expenses other than cost of goods sold that are incurred in running a business. They are similar to the expenses of a service company. It is customary to group operating expenses into categories, such as selling expenses and general and administrative expenses. Selling expenses include the costs of storing goods and preparing them for sale, displaying, advertising, and otherwise promoting sales; making sales; and delivering goods to the buyer, if the seller bears the cost of delivery. The latter cost is often called freight out expense or *delivery expense.* Among the general and administrative expenses are general office expense, which includes expenses for accounting, personnel, credit and collections, and any other expenses that apply to overall operation. Although general occupancy expenses, such as rent expense, insurance expense, and utilities expense, are often classified as general and administrative expenses, they may also be allocated between the selling and the general and administrative categories. Careful planning and control of operating expenses can improve a company's profitability.

Net Income

Net income, the final figure or "bottom line" of the income statement, is what remains after operating expenses are deducted from gross margin. It is an important performance measure because it represents the amount of business earnings that accrue to the owners. It is the amount that is transferred to owner's equity from all the income-generating activities during the period. Both management and owners often use net income to measure whether a business has been operating successfully during the past accounting period.

Inventory Systems

OBJECTIVE 3

Distinguish between the periodic and the perpetual inventory systems, and explain the importance of taking a physical inventory

Related Text Assignments:
Q: 8, 9, 10, 11
SD: 2

As we have seen, merchandise inventory is a key factor in determining the cost of goods sold. Consequently, every merchandiser needs a useful and reliable system for determining both the quantity and the cost of the goods on hand. The two basic systems of accounting for the many items in the merchandise inventory are the periodic inventory system and the perpetual inventory system.

Periodic Inventory System

As discussed earlier, under the periodic inventory system the inventory on hand is counted periodically, usually at the end of the accounting period. No detailed records of the actual inventory on hand are maintained during the period. Cost of goods sold under the periodic inventory system is determined according to the format shown for Fenwick Fashions in Exhibit 2 and Figure 3. In the simplest case, the cost of inventory purchased is accumulated in a Purchases account. At the end of the accounting period, the cost of the physical inventory, based on an actual count, is deducted from the cost of goods available for sale to arrive at the cost of goods sold. Entries are made at the end of the accounting period to remove the beginning inventory (the last period's ending inventory) and to enter the ending inventory of the current period. As explained later in this chapter, these are the only entries made to the Merchandise Inventory account during the period. Consequently, the figure for inventory on hand is accurate only on the balance sheet date. As soon as any purchases or sales are made, the figure becomes a historical amount and remains so until the new ending inventory is entered at the end of the next accounting period.

BUSINESS BULLETIN: TECHNOLOGY IN PRACTICE

Many grocery stores, which traditionally used the periodic inventory system, now employ bar coding to update the physical inventory as items are sold. At the checkout counter, the cashier scans the electronic marking on each product, called a bar code or universal product code (UPC), into the cash register, which is linked to a computer. The price of the item appears on the cash register, and its sale is recorded by the computer. Bar coding has become common in all types of retail companies, and in manufacturing firms and hospitals as well. Some retail businesses now use the perpetual system for keeping track of the physical flow of inventory and the periodic system for preparing the financial statements.

Point to Emphasize: The valuation of ending inventory on the balance sheet is determined by multiplying the quantity of each inventory item by its unit cost.

Some retail and wholesale businesses use periodic inventory systems because they do not require much clerical work. If a business is fairly small, management can maintain control over inventory simply by observation or by use of an off-line system of cards or computer records. On the other hand, for larger businesses, the lack of detailed records may cause inefficiencies that lead either to lost sales or to high operating costs.

Perpetual Inventory System

Point to Emphasize: Under the perpetual inventory system, the Merchandise Inventory account and the Cost of Goods Sold account are updated with every sale.

Under the perpetual inventory system, records are kept of the quantity and, usually, the cost of individual items as they are bought or sold. The detailed data available under the perpetual inventory system enable management to respond to customers' inquiries about product availability, to order inventory more effectively and thus avoid running out of stock, and to control the financial costs associated with investments in the inventory. Under this system, the cost of each item is recorded in the Merchandise Inventory account when it is purchased. As merchandise is sold, its cost is transferred from the Merchandise Inventory account to the Cost of Goods Sold account. Thus, at all times the balance of the Merchandise Inventory account equals the cost of goods on hand, and the balance in Cost of Goods Sold equals the cost of merchandise sold to customers. The Purchases account is not used in a perpetual inventory system.

Enrichment Note: Although computerization has made the perpetual inventory system more popular in recent years, a physical count still should be made periodically to ensure that the actual number of goods on hand matches the quantity indicated by the computer records.

Traditionally, the periodic inventory system has been used by companies that sell items of low value in high volume because of the difficulty and expense of accounting for the purchase and sale of each item. Examples of such companies are drugstores, automobile parts stores, department stores, discount stores, and grain companies. In contrast, companies that sell items of high unit value, such as appliances or automobiles, tend to use the perpetual inventory system. This distinction between high and low unit value for inventory systems has blurred considerably in recent years because of the widespread use of computers. Although use of the periodic inventory system is still widespread, use of the perpetual inventory system has increased greatly.

Taking a Physical Inventory

Actually counting all merchandise on hand is called taking a physical inventory. This can be a difficult task because it is easy to leave items out or to count them twice. A physical inventory must be taken under both the periodic and the perpetual inventory systems.

Merchandise inventory includes all salable goods owned by a concern, regardless of where they are located—on shelves, in storerooms, in warehouses, or in trucks between warehouses and stores. It also includes goods in transit from suppliers if title to the goods has passed to the merchant. Ending inventory does not include merchandise that has been sold but has not yet been delivered to customers or goods that cannot be sold because they are damaged or obsolete. If the damaged or obsolete goods can be sold at a reduced price, however, they should be included in ending inventory at their reduced value.

The actual count is usually taken after the close of business on the last day of the fiscal year. To facilitate taking the physical inventory, many companies end their fiscal year in a slow season, when inventories are at relatively low levels. Retail department stores often end their fiscal year in January or February, for example. After hours, at night, or on the weekend, employees count all items and record the results on numbered inventory tickets or sheets, following procedures to make sure that no items are missed. Sometimes a store closes for all or part of a day for inventory taking. The use of bar coding to take inventory electronically has greatly facilitated the taking of a physical inventory in many companies.

Merchandising Transactions

OBJECTIVE 4

Contrast and record transactions related to sales and purchases under the periodic and the perpetual inventory systems

Related Text Assignments:
Q: 12, 13, 14, 15, 16, 17
SE: 5, 6, 7, 8
E: 7, 8, 9
P: 2, 3, 6, 8, 9
FRA: 3

Merchandising transactions can be divided into the two broad categories of sales transactions and purchases transactions. The ways in which these transactions are recorded differ somewhat under the periodic and the perpetual inventory systems. Before we discuss these transactions, some terms related to sales of merchandise need to be introduced.

Sales Terms

When goods are sold on credit, both parties should understand the amount and timing of payment as well as other terms of the purchase, such as who pays delivery or freight charges and what warranties or rights of return apply. Sellers quote prices in different ways. Many merchants quote the price at which they expect to sell their goods. Others, particularly manufacturers and wholesalers, provide a price list or catalogue and quote prices as a percentage (usually 30 percent or more) off the list or catalogue prices. These discounts are called trade discounts. For example, if an article was listed at $1,000 with a trade discount of 40 percent, or $400, the seller would record the sale at $600 and the buyer would record the purchase at $600. If the seller wishes to change the selling price, the trade discount can be raised or lowered. At times the trade discount may vary depending on the quantity purchased. The list price and related trade discount are used only to arrive at the agreed-on price; they do not appear in the accounting records.

Teaching Note: Students would benefit from looking at a comprehensive income statement for Fenwick Fashions Company before studying the individual sections. See Exhibit 2.

The terms of sale are usually printed on the sales invoice and thus constitute part of the sales agreement. Customary terms differ from industry to industry. In some industries, payment is expected in a short period of time, such as ten or thirty days. In these cases, the invoice is marked "n/10" or "n/30" (read as "net ten" or "net thirty"), meaning that the amount of the invoice is due either ten days or thirty days after the invoice date. If the invoice is due ten days after the end of the month, it is marked "n/10 eom."

Common Student Confusion: Students frequently confuse the terms *trade discount* and *sales discount.* A trade discount applies to the list or catalogue price. A sales discount applies to the sales price.

Enrichment Note: Early collection also has the advantage of reducing to zero the probability of a customer's defaulting.

In some industries it is customary to give discounts for early payments. These discounts, called sales discounts, are intended to increase the seller's liquidity by reducing the amount of money tied up in accounts receivable. An invoice that offers a sales discount might be labeled "2/10, n/30," which means that the buyer either can pay the invoice within ten days of the invoice date and take a 2 percent discount or can wait thirty days and then pay the full amount of the invoice. It is almost always advantageous for a buyer to take the discount because the saving of 2 percent over a period of 20 days (from the eleventh day to the thirtieth day) represents an effective annual rate of 36 percent (360 days ÷ 20 days × 2% = 36%). Most companies would be better off borrowing money to take the discount. The practice of giving sales discounts has been declining because it is costly to the seller and because, from the buyer's viewpoint, the amount of the discount is usually very small in relation to the price of the purchase. Accounting for sales discounts is covered in supplemental objective 7.

In some industries, it is customary for the seller to pay transportation costs and to charge a price that includes those costs. In other industries, it is customary for the purchaser to pay transportation charges on merchandise. Special terms designate whether the supplier or the purchaser pays the freight charges. FOB shipping point means that the supplier places the merchandise "free on board" at the point of origin, and the buyer bears the shipping costs. The title to the merchandise passes to the buyer at that point. For example, when the sales agreement for the purchase of a car says "FOB factory," the buyer must pay the freight from where the car was made to wherever he or she is located, and the buyer owns the car from the time it leaves the factory. On the other hand, FOB destination means that the supplier bears the transportation costs to the place where the merchandise is delivered. The supplier retains title until the merchandise reaches its destination and usually prepays the shipping costs, in which case the buyer makes no accounting entry for freight. The effects of these special shipping terms are summarized as follows:

Shipping Term	Where Title Passes	Who Pays the Cost of Transportation
FOB shipping point	At origin	Buyer
FOB destination	At destination	Seller

Transactions Related to Purchases of Merchandise

The primary difference in accounting between the perpetual and the periodic inventory systems is that under the perpetual inventory system, the Merchandise Inventory account is continuously adjusted because purchases, sales, and other inventory transactions are entered in the account as they occur. Purchases increase Merchandise Inventory, and purchases returns decrease it. As sales of goods occur, the cost of the goods is transferred from Merchandise Inventory to the Cost of Goods Sold account. Under the periodic inventory system, the Merchandise Inventory account stays at its beginning balance until the physical inventory is recorded at the end of the period. A Purchases account is used to accumulate the purchases of merchandise during the accounting period, and a Purchases Returns and Allowances account is used to accumulate returns and allowances of purchases. To illustrate these differences, purchase transactions made by Fenwick Fashions follow. Differences in the two systems are shown in blue.

Purchases of Merchandise on Credit

Oct. 3 Received merchandise purchased on credit from Neebok Company, invoice dated October 1, terms n/10, FOB shipping point, $4,890.

Periodic Inventory System

Oct. 3	Purchases	4,890	
	Accounts Payable		4,890
A = L + OE + −	Purchased merchandise from Neebok Company, terms n/10, FOB shipping point, invoice dated Oct. 1		

Perpetual Inventory System

Merchandise Inventory	4,890		
Accounts Payable		4,890	
Purchased merchandise from Neebok Company, terms n/10, FOB shipping point, invoice dated Oct. 1			A = L + OE + +

Under the periodic inventory system, Purchases is a temporary account. Its sole purpose is to accumulate the total cost of merchandise purchased for resale during an accounting period. (Purchases of other assets, such as equipment, are recorded in the appropriate asset account, not in the Purchases account.) The Purchases account does not indicate whether merchandise has been sold or is still on hand. Under the perpetual inventory system, the Purchases account is not necessary, because purchases are recorded directly in the Merchandise Inventory account.

Transportation Costs on Purchases

Oct. 4 Received bill from Transfer Freight Company for transportation costs on October 3 shipment, invoice dated October 1, terms n/10, $160.

Periodic Inventory System

Oct. 4	Freight In	160	
	Accounts Payable		160
	Transportation charges on Oct. 3 purchase, Transfer Freight Co., terms n/10, invoice dated Oct. 1		

A = L + OE
\+ −

Perpetual Inventory System

Freight In	160	
Accounts Payable		160
Transportation charges on Oct. 3 purchase, Transfer Freight Co., terms n/10, invoice dated Oct. 1		

A = L + OE
\+ −

Common Student Confusion: Students often confuse freight in and freight out expense. Explain that Freight In appears within the cost of goods sold section of the income statement and that Freight Out Expense appears as an operating expense.

Since most shipments contain many different items of merchandise, it is usually not practical to identify the specific cost of shipping each item. As a result, under both the periodic and the perpetual inventory systems, transportation costs on purchases are usually accumulated in a Freight In account.

In some cases, the seller pays the freight charges and bills them to the buyer as a separate item on the invoice. When this occurs, the entries are the same as in the October 3 example, except that an additional debit is made to Freight In for the amount of the freight charges and Accounts Payable is increased by a like amount.

Purchases Returns and Allowances

Oct. 6 Returned merchandise received from Neebok Company on October 3 for credit, $480.

Periodic Inventory System

Oct. 6	Accounts Payable	480	
	Purchases Returns and Allowances		480
	Merchandise from purchase of Oct. 3 returned to Neebok Company for full credit		

A = L + OE
− +

Perpetual Inventory System

Accounts Payable	480	
Merchandise Inventory		480
Merchandise from purchase of Oct. 3 returned to Neebok Company for full credit		

A = L + OE
− −

Point to Emphasize: Because the Purchases account is established with a debit, its contra accounts, Purchases Returns and Allowances and Purchases Discounts, are each established with a credit.

Enrichment Note: Accounts such as Purchases and Purchases Returns and Allowances are used only in conjunction with a periodic inventory system.

If a seller sends the wrong product or one that is otherwise unsatisfactory, the buyer may be allowed to return the item for a cash refund or credit on account, or the buyer may be given an allowance off the sales price. Under the periodic inventory system, the amount of the return or allowance is recorded in the Purchases Returns and Allowances account. This account is a contra-purchases account with a normal credit balance and is deducted from Purchases on the income statement. Under the perpetual inventory system, the returned merchandise is removed from the Merchandise Inventory account.

Payments on Account

Oct. 10 Paid in full the amount due to Neebok Company for the purchase of October 3, part of which was returned on October 6.

Periodic Inventory System				Perpetual Inventory System		
Oct. 10	Accounts Payable	4,410		Accounts Payable	4,410	
	Cash		4,410	Cash		4,410
A = L + OE − −	Made payment on account to Neebok Company $4,890 − $480 = $4,410			Made payment on account to Neebok Company $4,890 − $480 = $4,410		A = L + OE − −

Payments for merchandise purchased are the same under both systems.

Transactions Related to Sales of Merchandise

The primary difference in accounting for transactions related to sales under the perpetual and the periodic inventory systems pertains to the Cost of Goods Sold account. Under the perpetual inventory system, at the time of a sale, the cost of the merchandise is transferred from the Merchandise Inventory account to the Cost of Goods Sold account. In the case of a return, the cost of the merchandise is transferred from Cost of Goods Sold back to Merchandise Inventory. Under the periodic inventory system, the Cost of Goods Sold account is not used because the Merchandise Inventory account is not updated until the end of the accounting period. To illustrate these differences, transactions related to sales made by Fenwick Fashions follow. Differences in the two systems are indicated in blue.

Sales of Merchandise on Credit

Oct. 7 Sold merchandise on credit to Gonzales Distributors, terms n/30, FOB destination, $1,200; the cost of the merchandise was $720.

Periodic Inventory System				Perpetual Inventory System		
Oct. 7	Accounts Receivable	1,200		Accounts Receivable	1,200	
	Sales		1,200	Sales		1,200
A = L + OE + +	Sale of merchandise to Gonzales Distributors, terms n/30, FOB destination			Sale of merchandise to Gonzales Distributors, terms n/30, FOB destination		A = L + OE + +
				Cost of Goods Sold	720	
				Merchandise Inventory		720
				To transfer cost of merchandise inventory sold to Cost of Goods Sold account		A = L + OE − −

Point to Emphasize: Point out that there are more entries associated with a perpetual inventory system than with a periodic inventory system.

Sales of merchandise are handled in the same way under both inventory systems, except that under the perpetual inventory system, Cost of Goods Sold is updated by a transfer from Merchandise Inventory. In the case of cash sales, Cash rather than Accounts Receivable is debited for the amount of the sale.

Payment of Delivery Costs

Oct. 8 Paid transportation costs for the sale on October 7, $78.

Periodic Inventory System				Perpetual Inventory System		
Oct. 8	Freight Out Expense	78		Freight Out Expense	78	
	Cash		78	Cash		78
A = L + OE − −	Delivery costs on Oct. 7 sale			Delivery costs on Oct. 7 sale		A = L + OE − −

A seller will often absorb delivery or freight out costs in the belief that doing so will facilitate the sale of its products. These costs are accumulated in an account called

Delivery Expense or Freight Out Expense, which is shown as a selling expense on the income statement.

Returns of Merchandise Sold

Oct. 9 Merchandise sold on October 7 accepted back from Gonzales Distributors for full credit and returned to merchandise inventory, $300; the cost of the merchandise was $180.

Periodic Inventory System

Oct. 9	Sales Returns and Allowances	300	
	Accounts Receivable		300
A = L + OE − −	Return of merchandise from Gonzales Distributors		

Perpetual Inventory System

Sales Returns and Allowances	300	
Accounts Receivable		300
Return of merchandise from Gonzales Distributors		A = L + OE − −
Merchandise Inventory	180	
Cost of Goods Sold		180
To transfer cost of merchandise returned to the Merchandise Inventory account		A = L + OE + +

Point to Emphasize: Because the Sales account is established with a credit, its contra accounts, Sales Returns and Allowances and Sales Discounts, are each established with a debit.

Because returns and allowances to customers for wrong or unsatisfactory merchandise are often an indicator of customer dissatisfaction, such amounts are accumulated, under both methods, in a Sales Returns and Allowances account. This account is a contra-revenue account with a normal debit balance and is deducted from Sales on the income statement. Under the perpetual inventory system, the cost of the merchandise must also be transferred from the Cost of Goods Sold account back into the Merchandise Inventory account. If an allowance is made instead of accepting a return, or if the merchandise cannot be returned to inventory and resold, this transfer is not made.

Receipts on Account

Nov. 5 Received payment in full from Gonzales Distributors for sale of merchandise on Oct. 7, less the return on Oct. 9.

Periodic Inventory System

Nov. 5	Cash	900	
	Accounts Receivable		900
A = L + OE + −	Receipt on account from Gonzales Distributors $1,200 − $300 = $900		

Perpetual Inventory System

Cash	900	
Accounts Receivable		900
Receipt on account from Gonzales Distributors $1,200 − $300 = $900		A = L + OE + −

Receipts on account are recorded in the same way under both systems.

The Effect of the Perpetual Inventory System on the Income Statement

The merchandising income statement illustrated in Exhibit 2 uses the periodic inventory system. This may be determined by the presence of the computation of net cost of purchases and the figures for beginning and ending inventory. Under the perpetual inventory system, the Cost of Goods Sold account replaces these items. The gross margin for Fenwick Fashions would be presented as shown in Exhibit 3. In this example, Freight In is included in Cost of Goods Sold. Theoretically, freight in should be allocated between ending inventory and cost of goods sold, but most companies choose not to disclose freight in on the income statement because it is a relatively small amount.

Exhibit 3. Partial Income Statement Under the Perpetual Inventory System

Fenwick Fashions Company Partial Income Statement For the Year Ended December 31, 20x2	
Net Sales	
Gross Sales	$246,350
Less Sales Returns and Allowances	7,025
Net Sales	$239,325
Cost of Goods Sold*	131,360
Gross Margin	$107,965

*Freight In has been included in Cost of Goods Sold.

Inventory Losses

Enrichment Note: Inventory shortages could result from honest mistakes. That is, inventory could have been tagged with the wrong number.

Most companies experience losses of merchandise inventory from spoilage, shoplifting, and employee pilferage. When such losses occur, the periodic inventory system provides no means of tracking them because the costs are automatically included in the cost of goods sold. For example, assume that a company has lost $1,250 in stolen merchandise during an accounting period. When the physical inventory is taken, the missing items are no longer in stock, so they cannot be counted. Because the ending inventory does not contain these items, the amount subtracted from cost of goods available for sale is less than the amount would be if the goods were in stock. The cost of goods sold, then, is overstated by $1,250. In a sense, the cost of goods sold is inflated by the amount of merchandise that has been lost.

Clarification Note: An adjustment to the Merchandise Inventory account will be needed if the physical inventory reveals a difference between the actual inventory and the amount in the records.

The perpetual inventory system makes it easier to identify such losses. Because the Merchandise Inventory account is continuously updated for sales, purchases, and returns, the loss will show up as the difference between the inventory records and the physical inventory taken at the end of the accounting period. Once the amount of the loss has been identified, the ending inventory is updated by crediting the Merchandise Inventory account. The offsetting debit is usually listed as an increase in Cost of Goods Sold because the loss is considered a cost that reduces the company's gross margin.

BUSINESS BULLETIN: BUSINESS PRACTICE

In some industries a high percentage of sales returns is an accepted business practice. A book publisher like Simon & Schuster will produce and ship more copies of a best-seller than it expects to sell because, to gain the attention of potential buyers, copies must be distributed to a wide variety of outlets, such as bookstores, department stores, and discount stores. As a result, returns of unsold books may run as high as 30 to 50 percent of the books shipped. The same sales principles apply to magazines sold on newsstands, like *People,* and to popular recordings produced by companies like Motown Records. In all these businesses, management scrutinizes the Sales Returns and Allowances account for ways to reduce returns and increase profitability.

The Merchandising Work Sheet and Closing Entries

The work sheet for a merchandising company is basically the same as that for a service business, except that it includes the additional accounts that are needed to handle merchandising transactions. The treatment of these additional accounts differs depending on whether a company uses the periodic or the perpetual inventory system.

The Periodic Inventory System

SUPPLEMENTAL OBJECTIVE 5

Prepare a work sheet and closing entries for a merchandising concern using the periodic inventory system

Related Text Assignments:
Q: 18, 19, 20
SE: 9
E: 11
P: 4

The accounts for a merchandising company using the periodic inventory system generally include Sales, Sales Returns and Allowances, Sales Discounts, Purchases, Purchases Returns and Allowances, Purchases Discounts, Freight In, and Merchandise Inventory. Except for Merchandise Inventory, these accounts are treated in much the same way as revenue and expense accounts for a service company. On the work sheet, they are extended to the Income Statement columns. In the closing process, they are transferred to the Income Summary account.

The Merchandise Inventory account requires special treatment because, under the periodic inventory system, purchases of merchandise are accumulated in the Purchases account, and no entries are made to Merchandise Inventory during the accounting period. As a result, at the end of the period, the balance in Merchandise Inventory is the same as it was at the beginning of the period: the beginning inventory amount. To calculate net income, the closing entries must (1) remove the beginning inventory from the Merchandise Inventory account, (2) enter the ending inventory in the Merchandise Inventory account, and (3) transfer both inventory amounts to the Income Summary account. The following T accounts illustrate the flow of the inventory amounts at Fenwick Fashions.

Merchandise Inventory

Dec. 31, 20x1	Beginning Balance	52,800	Dec. 31, 20x2	52,800
Dec. 31, 20x2	Ending Balance	48,300		

Income Summary

Dec. 31, 20x2	52,800	Dec. 31, 20x2	48,300

Teaching Note: Remind your students that asset accounts are increased with debits and decreased with credits. Ending inventory must be established with a debit, and beginning inventory eliminated with a credit.

The beginning merchandise inventory was $52,800. This amount is removed from the Merchandise Inventory account by a credit, which leaves a zero balance, and transferred to the Income Summary account by a debit. The ending inventory was $48,300. This amount is entered in the Merchandise Inventory account by a debit and recorded in the Income Summary account by a credit. The results of the two closing entries mirror the calculation of cost of goods sold, in which beginning inventory is added to net cost of purchases and ending inventory is then subtracted. When beginning inventory is debited to the Income Summary account, it is, in effect, added to net purchases because the balance in the Purchases account is also debited to Income Summary through a closing entry. And when ending inventory is credited to Income Summary, it is, in effect, deducted from the sum of beginning inventory and net cost of purchases.

Keep these effects in mind while studying the work sheet for Fenwick Fashions Company shown in Exhibit 4. Each pair of columns in the work sheet and the closing entries are discussed in the following paragraphs.

Exhibit 4. Work Sheet for Fenwick Fashions Company: Periodic Inventory System

Fenwick Fashions Company
Work Sheet
For the Year Ended December 31, 20x2

Account Name	Trial Balance		Adjustments		Income Statement		Balance Sheet	
	Debit	Credit	Debit	Credit	Debit	Credit	Debit	Credit
Cash	29,410						29,410	
Accounts Receivable	42,400						42,400	
Merchandise Inventory	52,800				52,800	48,300	48,300	
Prepaid Insurance	17,400			(a) 5,800			11,600	
Store Supplies	2,600			(b) 1,540			1,060	
Office Supplies	1,840			(c) 1,204			636	
Land	4,500						4,500	
Building	20,260						20,260	
Accumulated Depreciation, Building		5,650		(d) 2,600				8,250
Office Equipment	8,600						8,600	
Accumulated Depreciation, Office Equipment		2,800		(e) 2,200				5,000
Accounts Payable		25,683						25,683
Gloria Fenwick, Capital		118,352						118,352
Gloria Fenwick, Withdrawals	20,000						20,000	
Sales		246,350				246,350		
Sales Returns and Allowances	7,025				7,025			
Purchases	126,400				126,400			
Purchases Returns and Allowances		7,776				7,776		
Freight In	8,236				8,236			
Sales Salaries Expense	22,500				22,500			
Freight Out Expense	5,740				5,740			
Advertising Expense	10,000				10,000			
Office Salaries Expense	26,900				26,900			
	406,611	406,611						
Insurance Expense, Selling			(a) 1,600		1,600			
Insurance Expense, General			(a) 4,200		4,200			
Store Supplies Expense			(b) 1,540		1,540			
Office Supplies Expense			(c) 1,204		1,204			
Depreciation Expense, Building			(d) 2,600		2,600			
Depreciation Expense, Office Equipment			(e) 2,200		2,200			
			13,344	13,344	272,945	302,426	186,766	157,285
Net Income					29,481			29,481
					302,426	302,426	186,766	186,766

Trial Balance Columns The first step in the preparation of the work sheet is to enter the balances from the ledger accounts into the Trial Balance columns. You are already familiar with this procedure.

Adjustments Columns The adjusting entries for Fenwick Fashions Company are entered in the Adjustments columns in the same way the adjusting entries were entered for service companies. Fenwick's adjusting entries involve insurance expired during the period (adjustment **a**), store and office supplies used during the period (adjustments **b** and **c**), and the depreciation of building and office equipment (adjustments **d** and **e**). No adjusting entry is made for merchandise inventory. After the adjusting entries are entered on the work sheet, the columns are totaled to prove that total debits equal total credits.

Omission of Adjusted Trial Balance Columns These two columns, which appeared in the work sheet for a service company, can be omitted. They are optional and are used when there are many adjusting entries to record. When only a few adjusting entries are required, as in the case of Fenwick Fashions Company, these columns are not necessary and may be omitted to save time.

Point to Emphasize No inventory-related entries are entered in the Adjustments columns of the work sheet.

Income Statement and Balance Sheet Columns After the Trial Balance columns have been totaled, the adjustments entered, and the equality of the columns proved, the balances are extended to the Income Statement and Balance Sheet columns. Again, begin with the Cash account at the top of the work sheet and move sequentially down the work sheet, one account at a time, entering each account balance in the correct Income Statement or Balance Sheet column.

Teaching Note: The mnemonic BEE reflects the treatment of inventory in the Income Statement and Balance Sheet columns: Beginning, Ending, and Ending amounts, starting with the debit side of the Income Statement columns.

Point to Emphasize: The Income Summary account does not appear on this work sheet.

As explained previously, the Merchandise Inventory row requires special treatment. The beginning inventory balance of $52,800 (which is already in the trial balance) is extended to the debit column of the Income Statement columns, as shown in Exhibit 4. This procedure has the effect of adding beginning inventory to net purchases because the Purchases account is also in the debit column of the Income Statement columns. The ending inventory balance of $48,300 (which is determined by the physical inventory and is not in the trial balance) is then inserted in the credit column of the Income Statement columns. This procedure has the effect of subtracting the ending inventory from goods available for sale in order to calculate the cost of goods sold. Finally, the ending merchandise inventory ($48,300) is inserted in the debit side of the Balance Sheet columns because it will appear on the balance sheet.

After all the items have been extended into the correct columns, the four columns are totaled. The net income or net loss is the difference between the debit and credit Income Statement columns. In this case, Fenwick Fashions Company has earned a net income of $29,481, which is extended to the credit side of the Balance Sheet columns. The four columns are then added to prove that total debits equal total credits.

Adjusting Entries The adjusting entries from the work sheet are now entered into the general journal and posted to the ledger, as they would be in a service company. There is no difference in this procedure between a service company and a merchandising company.

Closing Entries The closing entries for Fenwick Fashions Company appear in Exhibit 5. Notice that Merchandise Inventory is credited for the amount of the beginning inventory ($52,800) in the first entry and debited for the amount of the ending inventory ($48,300) in the second entry. Otherwise, these closing entries are very similar to those for a service company except that the merchandising accounts also must be closed to Income Summary. All income statement accounts with debit balances, including the merchandising accounts of Sales Returns and Allowances, Purchases, and Freight In, are credited in the first entry. The total of these accounts

Exhibit 5. Closing Entries for Fenwick Fashions Company: Periodic Inventory System

General Journal					Page 10
Date		Description	Post. Ref.	Debit	Credit
20x2		*Closing entries:*			
Dec.	31	Income Summary		272,945	
		Merchandise Inventory			52,800
		Sales Returns and Allowances			7,025
		Purchases			126,400
		Freight In			8,236
		Sales Salaries Expense			22,500
		Freight Out Expense			5,740
		Advertising Expense			10,000
		Office Salaries Expense			26,900
		Insurance Expense, Selling			1,600
		Insurance Expense, General			4,200
		Store Supplies Expense			1,540
		Office Supplies Expense			1,204
		Depreciation Expense, Building			2,600
		Depreciation Expense, Office Equipment			2,200
		To close the temporary expense and revenue accounts having debit balances and to remove the beginning inventory			
	31	Merchandise Inventory		48,300	
		Sales		246,350	
		Purchases Returns and Allowances		7,776	
		Income Summary			302,426
		To close the temporary expense and revenue accounts having credit balances and to establish the ending inventory			
	31	Income Summary		29,481	
		Gloria Fenwick, Capital			29,481
		To close the Income Summary account			
	31	Gloria Fenwick, Capital		20,000	
		Gloria Fenwick, Withdrawals			20,000
		To close the Withdrawals account			

($272,945) equals the total of the debit column in the Income Statement columns of the work sheet. All income statement accounts with credit balances—Sales and Purchases Returns and Allowances—are debited in the second entry. The total of these accounts ($302,426) equals the total of the Income Statement credit column in the work sheet. The third and fourth entries are used to close the Income Summary account and transfer net income to the Capital account, and to close the Withdrawals account to the Capital account.

Exhibit 6. Work Sheet for Fenwick Fashions Company: Perpetual Inventory System

Fenwick Fashions Company
Work Sheet
For the Year Ended December 31, 20x2

	Trial Balance		Adjustments		Income Statement		Balance Sheet	
Account Name	Debit	Credit	Debit	Credit	Debit	Credit	Debit	Credit
Cash	29,410						29,410	
Accounts Receivable	42,400						42,400	
Merchandise Inventory	48,300						48,300	
Prepaid Insurance	17,400			(a) 5,800			11,600	
Store Supplies	2,600			(b) 1,540			1,060	
Office Supplies	1,840			(c) 1,204			636	
Land	4,500						4,500	
Building	20,260						20,260	
Accumulated Depreciation, Building		5,650		(d) 2,600				8,250
Office Equipment	8,600						8,600	
Accumulated Depreciation, Office Equipment		2,800		(e) 2,200				5,000
Accounts Payable		25,683						25,683
Gloria Fenwick, Capital		118,352						118,352
Gloria Fenwick, Withdrawals	20,000						20,000	
Sales		246,350				246,350		
Sales Returns and Allowances	7,025				7,025			
Cost of Goods Sold	123,124				123,124			
Freight In	8,236				8,236			
Sales Salaries Expense	22,500				22,500			
Freight Out Expense	5,740				5,740			
Advertising Expense	10,000				10,000			
Office Salaries Expense	26,900				26,900			
	398,835	398,835						
Insurance Expense, Selling			(a) 1,600		1,600			
Insurance Expense, General			(a) 4,200		4,200			
Store Supplies Expense			(b) 1,540		1,540			
Office Supplies Expense			(c) 1,204		1,204			
Depreciation Expense, Building			(d) 2,600		2,600			
Depreciation Expense, Office Equipment			(e) 2,200		2,200			
			13,344	13,344	216,869	246,350	186,766	157,285
Net Income					29,481			29,481
					246,350	246,350	186,766	186,766

Point to Emphasize: The Income Summary account does not appear on this work sheet.

Exhibit 7. Closing Entries for Fenwick Fashions Company: Perpetual Inventory System

General Journal					Page 10
Date		Description	Post. Ref.	Debit	Credit
20x2		*Closing entries:*			
Dec.	31	Income Summary		216,869	
		Sales Returns and Allowances			7,025
		Cost of Goods Sold			123,124
		Freight In			8,236
		Sales Salaries Expense			22,500
		Freight Out Expense			5,740
		Advertising Expense			10,000
		Office Salaries Expense			26,900
		Insurance Expense, Selling			1,600
		Insurance Expense, General			4,200
		Store Supplies Expense			1,540
		Office Supplies Expense			1,204
		Depreciation Expense, Building			2,600
		Depreciation Expense, Office Equipment			2,200
		To close the temporary expense and revenue accounts having debit balances			
	31	Sales		246,350	
		Income Summary			246,350
		To close the temporary revenue account having a credit balance			
	31	Income Summary		29,481	
		Gloria Fenwick, Capital			29,481
		To close the Income Summary account			
	31	Gloria Fenwick, Capital		20,000	
		Gloria Fenwick, Withdrawals			20,000
		To close the Withdrawals account			

The Perpetual Inventory System

SUPPLEMENTAL OBJECTIVE 6

Prepare a work sheet and closing entries for a merchandising concern using the perpetual inventory system

Related Text Assignments:
Q: 19, 20
SE: 9
E: 12
P: 5

Under the perpetual inventory system, the Merchandise Inventory account is up to date at the end of the accounting period and therefore is not involved in the closing process. The reason for this is that, under the perpetual inventory system, purchases of merchandise are recorded directly in the Merchandise Inventory account and costs are transferred from the Merchandise Inventory account to the Cost of Goods Sold account as merchandise is sold. The work sheet for Fenwick Fashions Company, assuming the company uses the perpetual inventory system, is shown in Exhibit 6. Note that the ending merchandise inventory is $48,300 in both the Trial Balance and the Balance Sheet columns.

The closing entries for Fenwick Fashions Company, assuming that the perpetual inventory system is used, are shown in Exhibit 7. The Cost of Goods Sold account is closed to Income Summary along with the expense accounts because the Cost of Goods Sold account has a debit balance. No closing entries affect the Merchandise Inventory account.

Accounting for Discounts

Sales Discounts

SUPPLEMENTAL OBJECTIVE 7

Apply sales and purchases discounts to merchandising transactions

As mentioned earlier, some industries give sales discounts for early payment. Because it usually is not possible to know at the time of the sale whether the customer will pay in time to take advantage of them, sales discounts are recorded only at the time the customer pays. For example, assume that Fenwick Fashions Company sells merchandise to a customer on September 20 for $300, on terms of 2/10, n/60. This is the entry at the time of the sale:

A = L + OE
\+ +

Related Text Assignments:
Q: 21
SE: 10
E: 10, 13, 14
P: 6
SD: 3

Sept. 20	Accounts Receivable	300	
	Sales		300
	Sold merchandise on credit, terms 2/10, n/60		

The customer can take advantage of the sales discount any time on or before September 30, ten days after the date of the invoice. If the customer pays on September 29, the entry in Fenwick's records would look like this:

A = L + OE
\+ −
−

Sept. 29	Cash	294	
	Sales Discounts	6	
	Accounts Receivable		300
	Received payment for Sept. 20 sale; discount taken		

Point to Emphasize: Notice that Accounts Receivable must be credited for the full $300 even though only $294 has been received.

If the customer does not take advantage of the sales discount but waits until November 19 to pay for the merchandise, the entry would be as follows:

A = L + OE
\+
−

Nov. 19	Cash	300	
	Accounts Receivable		300
	Received payment for Sept. 20 sale; no discount taken		

Instructional Strategy: Divide the class into small groups and assign SD 3. Allow 8–10 minutes for group analysis, debrief the groups, and summarize.

At the end of the accounting period, the Sales Discounts account has accumulated all the sales discounts taken during the period. Because sales discounts reduce revenues from sales, Sales Discounts is a contra-revenue account with a normal debit balance that is deducted from gross sales in the income statement. Sales Discounts is treated the same as Sales Returns and Allowances on the work sheet and in the closing entries.

Purchases Discounts

Merchandise purchases are usually made on credit and sometimes involve purchases discounts for early payment. Purchases discounts are discounts taken for early payment for merchandise purchased for resale. They are to the buyer what sales discounts are to the seller. The amount of discounts taken is recorded in a separate account. Assume that Fenwick made a credit purchase of merchandise on November 12 for $1,500 with terms of 2/10, n/30 and returned $200 in merchandise on November 14. When payment is made, Fenwick's journal entry looks like this:

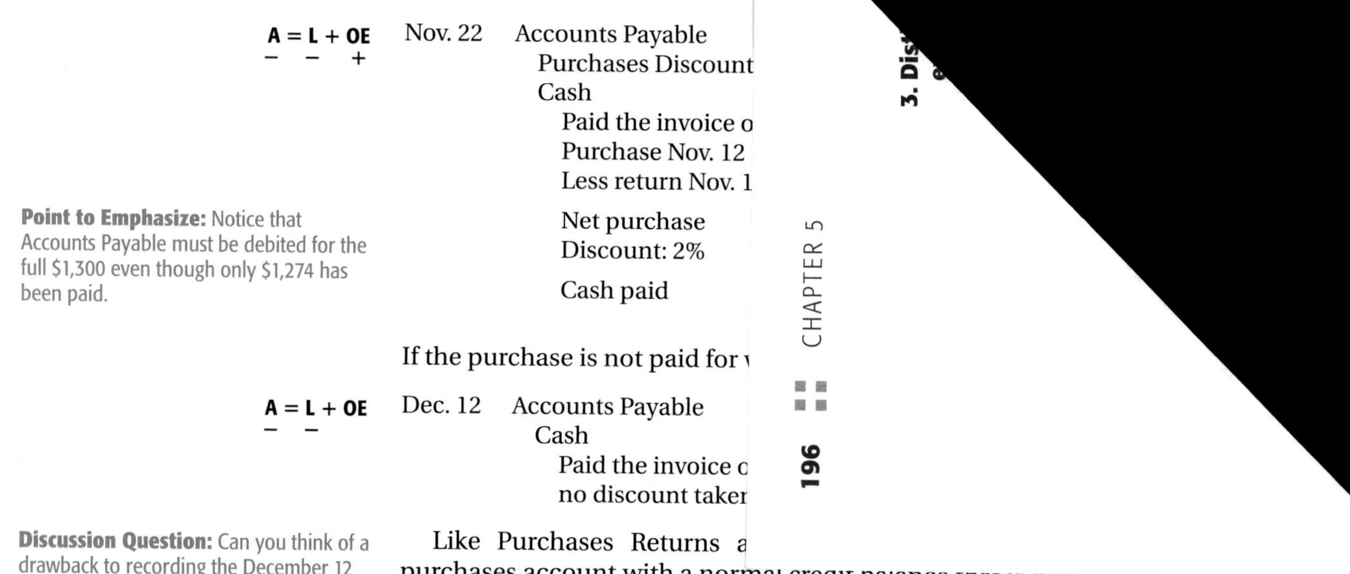

A = L + OE
− − +

Nov. 22 Accounts Payable
Purchases Discount
Cash
Paid the invoice o
Purchase Nov. 12
Less return Nov. 1
Net purchase
Discount: 2%
Cash paid

Point to Emphasize: Notice that Accounts Payable must be debited for the full $1,300 even though only $1,274 has been paid.

If the purchase is not paid for

A = L + OE
− −

Dec. 12 Accounts Payable
Cash
Paid the invoice c
no discount taker

Discussion Question: Can you think of a drawback to recording the December 12 payment in this way? **Answer:** No record was made of the discount that was lost.

Like Purchases Returns a purchases account with a normal credit balance that is deducted from Purchases on the income statement. If a company makes only a partial payment on an invoice, most creditors allow the company to take the discount applicable to the partial payment. The discount usually does not apply to freight, postage, taxes, or other charges that might appear on the invoice. Purchases Discounts is treated the same as Purchases Returns and Allowances on the work sheet and in the closing entries.

Chapter Review

REVIEW OF LEARNING OBJECTIVES

1. **Identify the management issues related to merchandising businesses.** Merchandising companies differ from service companies in that they earn income by buying and selling products or merchandise. The buying and selling of merchandise adds to the complexity of the business and raises four issues that management must address. First, the series of transactions that merchandising companies engage in (the operating cycle) requires careful cash flow management. Second, profitability management requires the company to price goods and control costs and expenses in ways that ensure the earning of an adequate income after operating expenses have been paid. Third, the company must choose whether to use the periodic or the perpetual inventory system. Fourth, management must establish an internal control structure that protects the assets of cash, merchandise inventory, and accounts receivable.
2. **Compare the income statements for service and merchandising concerns, and define the components of the merchandising income statement.** In the simplest case, the income statement for a service company consists only of revenues and expenses. The income statement for a merchandising company has three major parts: (1) net sales, (2) cost of goods sold, and (3) operating expenses. Gross margin is the difference between revenues from net sales and the cost of goods sold. Net income is the "bottom line" after operating expenses are deducted from the gross margin. Some important relationships associated with the computation of cost of goods sold are as follows:

$$\text{Gross Purchases} - \text{Purchases Returns and Allowances} + \text{Freight In} = \text{Net Cost of Purchases}$$

$$\text{Beginning Merchandise Inventory} + \text{Net Cost of Purchases} = \text{Goods Available for Sale}$$

$$\text{Goods Available for Sale} - \text{Ending Merchandise Inventory} = \text{Cost of Goods Sold}$$

inguish between the periodic and the perpetual inventory systems, and xplain the importance of taking a physical inventory. Merchandise inventory includes all salable goods owned, regardless of where they are located. Merchandise inventory can be determined by one of two systems. Under the *periodic inventory system,* the company usually waits until the end of an accounting period to take a physical inventory; it does not maintain detailed records of inventory on hand during the period. Under the *perpetual inventory system,* records are kept of the quantity and, usually, the cost of individual items of inventory throughout the year. The cost of goods sold is recorded as goods are transferred to customers, and the inventory balance is kept current throughout the year as items are bought and sold. Under both systems, a physical inventory, or physical count, is taken at the end of the accounting period—to determine cost of goods sold under the periodic inventory system and to detect inventory losses under the perpetual inventory system.

4. **Contrast and record transactions related to sales and purchases under the periodic and the perpetual inventory systems.** Sales terms define the amount and timing of payment, who pays delivery or freight charges, and what warranties or rights of return apply. Under the perpetual inventory system, the Merchandise Inventory account is continuously adjusted by entering purchases, sales, and other inventory transactions as they occur. Purchases increase the Merchandise Inventory account, and purchases returns decrease it. As goods are sold, their cost is transferred from the Merchandise Inventory account to the Cost of Goods Sold account. Under the periodic inventory system, in contrast, the Merchandise Inventory account stays at the beginning level until the physical inventory is recorded at the end of the period. A Purchases account is used to accumulate the purchases of merchandise during the accounting period, and a Purchases Returns and Allowances account is used to accumulate returns of and allowances on purchases. Under both systems, transportation costs on purchases are accumulated in the Freight In account, and transportation costs on sales are recorded as delivery expense or freight out expense.

Supplemental Objectives

5. **Prepare a work sheet and closing entries for a merchandising concern using the periodic inventory system.** Preparing a work sheet for a merchandising concern is much like preparing one for a service concern, except that there are additional accounts relating to merchandising transactions, such as Sales, Sales Returns and Allowances, Purchases, Purchases Returns and Allowances, and Freight In. These accounts must be extended to the appropriate Income Statement columns. Also, the beginning merchandise inventory from the trial balance is extended to the debit column of the Income Statement columns, and the ending balance of Merchandise Inventory is inserted in both the credit column of the Income Statement columns and the debit column of the Balance Sheet columns. The closing entries for a merchandising concern under the periodic inventory system are the same as those for a service business, with one exception. The exception is that the closing entries include a credit to Merchandise Inventory for the amount of the beginning inventory and a debit to Merchandise Inventory for the amount of the ending inventory.
6. **Prepare a work sheet and closing entries for a merchandising concern using the perpetual inventory system.** The work sheet under the perpetual inventory system is the same as the work sheet under the periodic inventory system, with two exceptions. First, since the Merchandise Inventory account is kept up to date, its ending balance is extended directly to the debit column of the Balance Sheet columns. There is no need to place it in the Income Statement columns. Second, the Cost of Goods Sold account replaces the Purchases and Purchases Returns and Allowances accounts and is extended to the debit column of the Income Statement columns. The closing entries for a merchandising concern under the perpetual inventory system are the same as those for a service business. There is no need to include the Merchandise Inventory account.
7. **Apply sales and purchases discounts to merchandising transactions.** Sales discounts are discounts for early payment. Terms of 2/10, n/30 mean that the buyer can

take a 2 percent discount if the invoice is paid within ten days of the invoice date. Otherwise, the buyer is obligated to pay the full amount in thirty days. Discounts on sales are recorded in the Sales Discounts account, and discounts on purchases are recorded in the Purchases Discounts account.

REVIEW OF CONCEPTS AND TERMINOLOGY

The following concepts and terms were introduced in this chapter:

LO 2 **Beginning inventory:** Merchandise on hand at the beginning of an accounting period.

LO 1 **Cash flow management:** The planning of a company's receipts and payments of cash.

LO 2 **Cost of goods sold:** The amount a merchant paid for the merchandise sold during an accounting period. Also called *cost of sales.*

LO 2 **Ending inventory:** Merchandise on hand at the end of an accounting period.

LO 4 **FOB destination:** A shipping term that means that the seller bears transportation costs to the place of delivery.

LO 4 **FOB shipping point:** A shipping term that means that the buyer bears transportation costs from the point of origin.

LO 2 **Freight in:** Transportation charges on merchandise purchased for resale. Also called *transportation in.*

LO 2 **Freight out expense:** Transportation charges on merchandise sold; an operating expense. Also called *delivery expense.*

LO 2 **Goods available for sale:** The sum of beginning inventory and the net cost of purchases during the period; the total goods available for sale to customers during an accounting period.

LO 2 **Gross margin:** The difference between net sales and cost of goods sold. Also called *gross profit.*

LO 2 **Gross sales:** Total sales for cash and on credit occurring during an accounting period.

LO 1 **Internal control structure:** A management-established environment, accounting systems, and control procedures designed to safeguard the assets of a business and provide reliable accounting records.

LO 1 **Merchandise inventory:** The goods on hand at any one time that are available for sale to customers.

LO 1 **Merchandising business:** A business that earns income by buying and selling products or merchandise.

LO 2 **Net cost of purchases:** Net purchases plus any freight charges on the purchases.

LO 2 **Net income:** For merchandising companies, what is left after deducting operating expenses from gross margin.

LO 2 **Net purchases:** Total purchases less any deductions, such as purchases returns and allowances and purchases discounts.

LO 2 **Net sales:** The gross proceeds from sales of merchandise less sales returns and allowances and any discounts. Also called *sales* on income statements.

LO 1 **Operating budget:** Management's operating plans as reflected by detailed listings of projected selling and general and administrative expenses.

LO 1 **Operating cycle:** A series of transactions that includes purchases of merchandise inventory for cash or on credit, payment for purchases made on credit, sales of merchandise inventory for cash or on credit, and collection of the cash from the sales.

LO 2 **Operating expenses:** The expenses other than cost of goods sold that are incurred in running a business.

LO 1 **Periodic inventory system:** A system for determining inventory on hand by a physical count at the end of an accounting period.

LO 1 **Perpetual inventory system:** A system for determining inventory by keeping continuous records of the quantity and, usually, the cost of individual items as they are bought and sold.

LO 3 **Physical inventory:** An actual count of all merchandise on hand at the end of an accounting period.

LO 1 **Profitability management:** The process of setting appropriate prices on merchandise, purchasing merchandise at favorable prices and terms, and maintaining acceptable levels of expenses.

LO 4 **Purchases:** A temporary account used under the periodic inventory system to accumulate the total cost of all merchandise purchased for resale during an accounting period.

SO 7 **Purchases discounts:** Discounts taken for prompt payment for merchandise purchased for resale; the Purchases Discounts account is a contra-purchases account.

LO 4 **Purchases Returns and Allowances:** A contra-purchases account used under the periodic inventory system to accumulate cash refunds, credits on account, and other allowances made by suppliers on merchandise originally purchased for resale.

LO 4 **Sales discount:** A discount given to a buyer for early payment for a sale made on credit; the Sales Discounts account is a contra-revenue account.

LO 2 **Sales Returns and Allowances:** A contra-revenue account used to accumulate cash refunds, credits on account, and other allowances made to customers who have received defective or otherwise unsatisfactory products.

LO 1 **Service business:** A business that earns income by performing a service for fees or commissions.

LO 4 **Trade discount:** A deduction (usually 30 percent or more) off a list or catalogue price.

REVIEW PROBLEM

Merchandising Transactions: Periodic and Perpetual Inventory Systems

LO 4 Dawkins Company engaged in the following transactions.

Oct. 1 Sold merchandise to Ernie Devlin on credit, terms n/30, FOB shipping point, $1,050 (cost, $630).

2 Purchased merchandise on credit from Ruland Company, terms n/30, FOB shipping point, $1,900.

2 Paid Custom Freight $145 for freight charges on merchandise received.

6 Purchased store supplies on credit from Arizin Supply House, terms n/30, $318.

9 Purchased merchandise on credit from LNP Company, terms n/30, FOB shipping point, $1,800, including $100 freight costs paid by LNP Company.

11 Accepted from Ernie Devlin a return of merchandise, which was returned to inventory, $150 (cost, $90).

14 Returned for credit $300 of merchandise received on October 2.

15 Returned for credit $100 of store supplies purchased on October 6.

16 Sold merchandise for cash, $500 (cost, $300).

22 Paid Ruland Company for purchase of October 2 less return of October 14.

23 Received full payment from Ernie Devlin for his October 1 purchase, less return on October 11.

REQUIRED

1. Prepare entries in journal form to record the transactions, assuming the periodic inventory system is used.
2. Prepare entries in journal form to record the transactions, assuming the perpetual inventory system is used.

ANSWER TO REVIEW PROBLEM

20xx	1. Periodic Inventory System			2. Perpetual Inventory System		
Oct. 1	Accounts Receivable	1,050		Accounts Receivable	1,050	
	Sales		1,050	Sales		1,050
	Sale on account to Ernie Devlin, terms n/30, FOB shipping point			Sale on account to Ernie Devlin, terms n/30, FOB shipping point		
				Cost of Goods Sold	630	
				Merchandise Inventory		630
				To transfer cost of merchandise sold to Cost of Goods Sold account		
2	Purchases	1,900		Merchandise Inventory	1,900	
	Accounts Payable		1,900	Accounts Payable		1,900
	Purchase on account from Ruland Company, terms n/30, FOB shipping point			Purchase on account from Ruland Company, terms n/30, FOB shipping point		
2	Freight In	145		Freight In	145	
	Cash		145	Cash		145
	Freight on previous purchase			Freight on previous purchase		
6	Store Supplies	318		Store Supplies	318	
	Accounts Payable		318	Accounts Payable		318
	Purchase of store supplies on account from Arizin Supply House, terms n/30			Purchase of store supplies on account from Arizin Supply House, terms n/30		
9	Purchases	1,700		Merchandise Inventory	1,700	
	Freight In	100		Freight In	100	
	Accounts Payable		1,800	Accounts Payable		1,800
	Purchase on account from LNP Company, terms n/30, FOB shipping point, freight paid by supplier			Purchase on account from LNP Company, terms n/30, FOB shipping point, freight paid by supplier		
11	Sales Returns and Allowances	150		Sales Returns and Allowances	150	
	Accounts Receivable		150	Accounts Receivable		150
	Return of merchandise from Ernie Devlin			Return of merchandise from Ernie Devlin		
				Merchandise Inventory	90	
				Cost of Goods Sold		90
				To transfer cost of merchandise returned to Merchandise Inventory		
14	Accounts Payable	300		Accounts Payable	300	
	Purchases Returns and Allowances		300	Merchandise Inventory		300
	Return of portion of merchandise purchased from Ruland Company			Return of portion of merchandise purchased from Ruland Company		
15	Accounts Payable	100		Accounts Payable	100	
	Store Supplies		100	Stores Supplies		100
	Return of store supplies (not merchandise) purchased on October 6 for credit			Return of store supplies (not merchandise) purchased on October 6 for credit		

	1. Periodic Inventory System *(continued)*			2. Perpetual Inventory System *(continued)*		
Oct. 16	Cash	500		Cash	500	
	Sales		500	Sales		500
	Sale of merchandise for cash			Sale of merchandise for cash		
				Cost of Goods Sold	300	
				Merchandise Inventory		300
				To transfer cost of merchandise sold to Cost of Goods Sold account		
22	Accounts Payable	1,600		Accounts Payable	1,600	
	Cash		1,600	Cash		1,600
	Payment on account to Ruland Company $1,900 − $300 = $1,600			Payment on account to Ruland Company $1,900 − $300 = $1,600		
23	Cash	900		Cash	900	
	Accounts Receivable		900	Accounts Receivable		900
	Receipt on account of Ernie Devlin $1,050 − $150 = $900			Receipt on account of Ernie Devlin $1,050 − $150 = $900		

Chapter Assignments

BUILDING YOUR KNOWLEDGE FOUNDATION

Questions

1. What four issues must be faced by managers of merchandising businesses?
2. What is the operating cycle of a merchandising business and why is it important?
3. What is the primary difference between the operations of a merchandising business and those of a service business, and how is it reflected on the income statement?
4. Is *freight in* an operating expense? Explain your answer.
5. Define *gross margin.* Why is it important?
6. During its first year in operation, D'Andrea Nursery had a cost of goods sold of $64,000 and a gross margin equal to 40 percent of sales. What was the dollar amount of the company's sales?
7. Could D'Andrea Nursery (in Question **6**) have a net loss for the year? Explain your answer.
8. What is the difference between the periodic inventory system and the perpetual inventory system?
9. Under the periodic inventory system, how must the amount of inventory at the end of the year be determined?
10. What are the principal differences in the handling of merchandise inventory in the accounting records under the periodic inventory system and the perpetual inventory system?
11. Discuss this statement: "The perpetual inventory system is the best system because management always needs to know how much inventory it has."
12. What is the difference between a trade discount and a sales discount?
13. The following prices and terms on 50 units of product were quoted by two companies.

	Price	Terms
Supplier A	$20 per unit	FOB shipping point
Supplier B	$21 per unit	FOB destination

Which supplier is quoting the better deal? Explain your answer.

14. What is the principal difference in accounting for the purchase and sale of merchandise under the perpetual inventory system and the periodic inventory system?
15. Lorres Hardware purchased the following items: (a) a delivery truck, (b) two dozen hammers, (c) supplies for its office workers, and (d) a broom for the janitor. Which items should be debited to the Purchases account under the periodic inventory system?
16. Under which inventory system is a Cost of Goods Sold account maintained? Why?
17. Why is it advisable to maintain a Sales Returns and Allowances account when the same result could be obtained by debiting each return or allowance to the Sales account?
18. Why is special treatment of the Merchandise Inventory account at the end of the accounting period of particular importance in the determination of net income under the periodic inventory system? What must be achieved in the account?
19. What are the principal differences between the work sheet for a merchandising company and that for a service company? Discuss in terms of the periodic and the perpetual inventory systems.
20. What are the principal differences between the closing entries for a merchandising company using the periodic inventory system and those for a company using the perpetual inventory system?
21. What is the normal balance of the Sales Discounts account? Is it an asset, a liability, an expense, or a contra-revenue account?

Short Exercises

LO 1 *Identification of Management Issues*

SE 1. Identify each of the following decisions as most directly related to (a) cash flow management, (b) profitability management, (c) choice of inventory system, or (d) control of merchandising operations.

1. Determination of how to protect cash from theft or embezzlement
2. Determination of the selling price of goods for sale
3. Determination of policies governing sales of merchandise on credit
4. Determination of whether to use the periodic or the perpetual inventory system

LO 2 *Merchandising Income Statement*

SE 2. Using the following data, prepare an income statement for Melchior Hardware for the month ended February 28.

Cost of Goods Sold	$30,000
General and Administrative Expenses	8,000
Net Sales	50,000
Selling Expenses	7,000

LO 2 *Cost of Goods Sold: Periodic Inventory System*

SE 3. Using the following data, prepare the cost of goods sold section of a merchandising income statement (periodic inventory system) for the month of July.

Freight In	$ 3,000
Merchandise Inventory, June 30, 20xx	25,000
Merchandise Inventory, July 31, 20xx	29,000
Purchases	97,000
Purchases Returns and Allowances	5,000

LO 2 *Cost of Goods Sold: Periodic Inventory System*

SE 4. Using the following data and assuming cost of goods sold is $230,000, prepare the cost of goods sold section of a merchandising income statement (periodic inventory system), including computation of the amount of purchases for the month of October.

Freight In	$12,000
Merchandise Inventory, Sept. 30, 20xx	33,000
Merchandise Inventory, Oct. 31, 20xx	44,000
Purchases	?
Purchases Returns and Allowances	9,000

SE 5. LO 4 *Purchases of Merchandise: Periodic Inventory System*

Record in journal form each of the following transactions, assuming the periodic inventory system is used.

Aug. 2 Purchased merchandise on credit from Campo Company, invoice dated August 1, terms n/10, FOB shipping point, $2,300.
3 Received bill from Nogel Shipping Company for transportation costs on August 2 shipment, invoice dated August 1, terms n/30, $210.
7 Returned damaged merchandise received from Campo Company on August 2 for credit, $360.
10 Paid in full the amount due to Campo Company for the purchase of August 2, part of which was returned on August 7.

SE 6. LO 4 *Purchases of Merchandise: Perpetual Inventory System*

Record in journal form the transactions in **SE 5** above, assuming the perpetual inventory system is used.

SE 7. LO 4 *Sales of Merchandise: Periodic Inventory System*

Record in journal form each of the following transactions, assuming the periodic inventory system is used.

Aug. 4 Sold merchandise on credit to Yehia Corporation, terms n/30, FOB destination, $1,200.
5 Paid transportation costs for sale of August 4, $110.
9 Merchandise sold on August 4 was accepted back from Yehia Corporation for full credit and returned to the merchandise inventory, $350.
Sept. 4 Received payment in full from Yehia Corporation for merchandise sold on August 4, less the return on August 9.

SE 8. LO 4 *Sales of Merchandise: Perpetual Inventory System*

Record in journal form the transactions in **SE 7** using the perpetual inventory system, assuming that the merchandise sold on August 4 cost $720 and the merchandise returned on August 9 cost $210.

SE 9. SO 5 SO 6 *Merchandise Inventory on the Work Sheet and in Closing Entries*

Pfenning Company had beginning merchandise inventory of $14,800 and ending merchandise inventory of $19,200. Where would these numbers appear on the work sheet and in the closing entries under (1) the periodic inventory system and (2) the perpetual inventory system?

SE 10. SO 7 *Sales and Purchases Discounts*

On April 15, the Bird Company sold merchandise to Nakabula Company for $1,500 on terms of 2/10, n/30. Record the entries in both Bird's and Nakabula's records for (1) the sale, (2) a return of merchandise on April 20 of $300, and (3) payment in full on April 25. Assume both companies use the periodic inventory system.

Exercises

E 1. LO 1 *Management Issues and Decisions*

The decisions and actions below were undertaken by the management of O'Leary Shoe Company. Indicate whether each action pertains primarily to (a) cash flow management, (b) profitability management, (c) choice of inventory system, or (d) control of merchandise operations.

1. Decided to mark each item of inventory with a magnetic tag that sets off an alarm if the tag is removed from the store before being deactivated.
2. Decided to reduce the credit terms offered to customers from thirty days to twenty days to speed up collection of accounts.
3. Decided that the benefits of keeping track of each item of inventory as it is bought and sold would exceed the costs of such a system and acted to implement the decision.
4. Decided to raise the price of each item of inventory to achieve a higher gross margin to offset an increase in rent expense.
5. Decided to purchase a new type of cash register that can be operated only by a person who knows a predetermined code.
6. Decided to switch to a new cleaning service that will provide the same service at a lower cost.

LO 1 *Operating Budget*

E 2. The operating budget and actual performance for the six months ended June 30, 20x1, for Tasheki Hardware Company appear as follows:

	Budget	Actual
Selling Expenses		
Sales Salaries Expense	$ 90,000	$102,030
Sales Supplies Expense	2,000	1,642
Rent Expense, Selling Space	18,000	18,000
Utilities Expense, Selling Space	12,000	11,256
Advertising Expense	15,000	21,986
Depreciation Expense, Selling Fixtures	6,500	6,778
Total Selling Expenses	$143,500	$161,692
General and Administrative Expenses		
Office Salaries Expense	$ 50,000	$47,912
Office Supplies Expense	1,000	782
Rent Expense, Office Space	4,000	4,000
Depreciation Expense, Office Equipment	3,000	3,251
Utilities Expense, Office Space	3,000	3,114
Postage Expense	500	626
Insurance Expense	2,000	2,700
Miscellaneous Expense	500	481
Total General and Administrative Expenses	$ 64,000	$ 62,866
Total Operating Expenses	$207,500	$224,558

1. Prepare an operating report that shows budget, actual, and difference.
2. Discuss the results, including identifying which differences most likely should be investigated by management.

LO 2 *Parts of the Income Statement: Missing Data*

E 3. Compute the dollar amount of each item indicated by a letter in the following table. Treat each horizontal row of numbers as a separate problem.

Sales	Beginning Inventory	Net Purchases	Ending Inventory	Cost of Goods Sold	Gross Margin	Operating Expenses	Net Income (Loss)
$250,000	$ **a**	$ 70,000	$ 20,000	$ **b**	$ 80,000	$ **c**	$24,000
d	24,000	**e**	36,000	216,000	120,000	80,000	40,000
460,000	44,000	334,000	**f**	**g**	100,000	**h**	(2,000)
780,000	80,000	**i**	120,000	**j**	**k**	240,000	80,000

LO 2 *Gross Margin from Sales Computation: Missing Data*

E 4. Determine the amount of gross purchases by preparing a partial income statement under the periodic inventory system and showing the calculation of gross margin from the following data: freight in, $13,000; cost of goods sold, $188,500; sales, $275,000; beginning inventory, $25,000; purchases returns and allowances, $4,000; ending inventory, $12,000.

LO 2 *Preparation of the Income Statement: Periodic Inventory System*

E 5. Using the selected year-end account balances as of December 31, 20x2, for the Mill Pond General Store that appear at the top of the next page, prepare a 20x2 income statement. The company uses the periodic inventory system. Beginning merchandise inventory was $26,000; ending merchandise inventory is $22,000.

Account Name	Debit	Credit
Sales		$297,000
Sales Returns and Allowances	$ 15,200	
Purchases	114,800	
Purchases Returns and Allowances		4,000
Freight In	5,600	
Selling Expenses	48,500	
General and Administrative Expenses	37,200	

E 6. LO 2 *Merchandising Income Statement: Missing Data, Multiple Years*

Determine the missing data for each letter in the following three income statements for Welch Wholesale Paper Company (in thousands).

	20x3	20x2	20x1
Gross Sales	$ **p**	$ **h**	$286
Sales Returns and Allowances	24	19	**a**
Net Sales	**q**	317	**b**
Merchandise Inventory, Beginning	**r**	**i**	38
Purchases	192	169	**c**
Purchases Returns and Allowances	31	**j**	17
Freight In	**s**	29	22
Net Cost of Purchases	189	**k**	**d**
Goods Available for Sale	222	212	182
Merchandise Inventory, Ending	39	**l**	42
Cost of Goods Sold	**t**	179	**e**
Gross Margin	142	**m**	126
Selling Expenses	**u**	78	**f**
General and Administrative Expenses	39	**n**	33
Total Operating Expenses	130	128	**g**
Net Income	**v**	**o**	27

E 7. LO 4 *Preparation of the Income Statement: Perpetual Inventory System*

Using the selected account balances at December 31, 20xx, for Nature's Adventure Store that follow, prepare an income statement for the year ended December 31, 20xx.

Account Name	Debit	Credit
Sales		$475,000
Sales Returns and Allowances	$ 23,500	
Cost of Goods Sold	280,000	
Freight In	13,500	
Selling Expenses	43,000	
General and Administrative Expenses	87,000	

The company uses the perpetual inventory system, and Freight In has not been included in Cost of Goods Sold.

LO 4 **E 8.** *Recording Purchases: Periodic and Perpetual Inventory Systems*

Give the entries to record each of the following transactions (1) under the periodic inventory system and (2) under the perpetual inventory system.

a. Purchased merchandise on credit, terms n/30, FOB shipping point, $7,500.
b. Paid freight on the shipment in transaction **a,** $405.
c. Purchased merchandise on credit, terms n/30, FOB destination, $4,200.
d. Purchased merchandise on credit, terms n/30, FOB shipping point, $7,800, which includes freight paid by the supplier of $600.
e. Returned part of the merchandise purchased in transaction **c,** $1,500.
f. Paid the amount owed on the purchase in transaction **a.**
g. Paid the amount owed on the purchase in transaction **d.**
h. Paid the amount owed on the purchase in transaction **c** less the return in **e.**

LO 4 **E 9.** *Recording Sales: Periodic and Perpetual Inventory Systems*

On June 15, the Pattis Company sold merchandise for $2,600 on terms of n/30 to Randle Company. On June 20, Randle Company returned some of the merchandise for a credit of $600, and on June 25, Randle paid the balance owed. Give Pattis's entries to record the sale, return, and receipt of payment (1) under the periodic inventory system and (2) under the perpetual inventory system. The cost of the merchandise sold on June 15 was $1,500, and the cost of the merchandise returned to inventory on June 20 was $350.

SO 7 **E 10.** *Purchases and Sales Involving Discounts*

The Ortiz Company purchased $9,200 of merchandise, terms 2/10, n/30, from the Goldbroch Company and paid for the merchandise within the discount period. Give the entries (1) by the Ortiz Company to record the purchase and payment and (2) by the Goldbroch Company to record the sale and receipt of payment. Both companies use the periodic inventory system.

SO 5 **E 11.** *Preparation of Closing Entries: Periodic Inventory System*

Selected account balances of the Mountain Grocery Store for the year ended December 31, 20xx, follow.

Account Name	Debit	Credit
Sales		$297,000
Sales Returns and Allowances	$ 11,000	
Sales Discounts	4,200	
Purchases	114,800	
Purchases Returns and Allowances		1,800
Purchases Discounts		2,200
Freight In	5,600	
Selling Expenses	48,500	
General and Administrative Expenses	37,200	

Beginning merchandise inventory was $26,000, and ending merchandise inventory is $22,000. Prepare closing entries, assuming that the owner of Mountain Grocery, Wilma Verplanck, withdrew $34,000 for personal expenses during the year.

SO 6 **E 12.** *Preparation of Closing Entries: Perpetual Inventory System*

Below are selected account balances of Fyles Company for the year ended December 31, 20xx.

Account Name	Debit	Credit
Sales		$297,000
Sales Returns and Allowances	$ 15,200	
Cost of Goods Sold	113,000	
Freight In	5,600	
Selling Expenses	48,500	
General and Administrative Expenses	37,200	

Prepare closing entries, assuming that the owner of Fyles Company, Angus Fyles, withdrew $40,000 for personal expenses during the year.

SO 7 *Sales Involving Discounts*

E 13. Give the entries to record the following transactions engaged in by Haq Company, which uses the periodic inventory system.

Mar. 1 Sold merchandise on credit to Duclos Company, terms 2/10, n/30, FOB shipping point, $500.
3 Accepted a return from Duclos Company for full credit, $200.
10 Received payment from Duclos Company for the sale, less the return and discount.
11 Sold merchandise on credit to Duclos Company, terms 2/10, n/30, FOB destination, $800.
31 Received payment for amount due from Duclos Company for the sale of March 11.

SO 7 *Purchases Involving Discounts*

E 14. Give the entries to record the following transactions engaged in by Fassad Company, which uses the periodic inventory system.

July 2 Purchased merchandise on credit from Brinsky Company, terms 2/10, n/30, FOB destination, invoice dated July 1, $800.
6 Returned merchandise to Brinsky Company for full credit, $100.
11 Paid Brinsky Company for purchase less return and discount.
14 Purchased merchandise on credit from Brinsky Company, terms 2/10, n/30, FOB destination, invoice dated July 12, $900.
31 Paid amount owed to Brinsky Company for purchase of July 14.

Problems

LO 1 LO 2 *Merchandising Income Statement: Periodic Inventory System*

P 1. Selected accounts from the adjusted trial balance for Reba's Retro Styles Shop for the end of the fiscal year, March 31, 20x4, are shown below. The merchandise inventory for Reba's Retro Styles Shop was $76,400 at the beginning of the year and $58,800 at the end of the year.

Reba's Retro Styles Shop
Partial Adjusted Trial Balance
March 31, 20x4

Sales		330,000
Sales Returns and Allowances	4,000	
Purchases	140,400	
Purchases Returns and Allowances		5,200
Freight In	4,600	
Store Salaries Expense	65,250	
Office Salaries Expense	25,750	
Advertising Expense	48,600	
Rent Expense	4,800	
Insurance Expense	2,400	
Utilities Expense	3,120	
Store Supplies Expense	5,760	
Office Supplies Expense	2,350	
Depreciation Expense, Store Equipment	2,100	
Depreciation Expense, Office Equipment	1,600	

REQUIRED

1. Using the information given, prepare an income statement for Reba's Retro Styles Shop. Store Salaries Expense; Advertising Expense; Store Supplies Expense; and

Depreciation Expense, Store Equipment are selling expenses. The other expenses are general and administrative expenses.

2. Based on your knowledge at this point in the course, how would you use the income statement for Reba's Retro Styles Shop to evaluate the company's profitability?

P 2. LO 2 LO 4 *Merchandising Income Statement: Perpetual Inventory System*

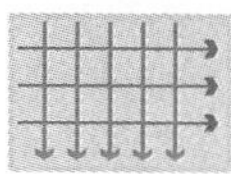

At the end of the fiscal year, August 31, 20x2, selected accounts from the adjusted trial balance for Ingram's Fashion Shop appeared as follows:

Ingram's Fashion Shop
Partial Adjusted Trial Balance
August 31, 20x2

Sales		162,000
Sales Returns and Allowances	2,000	
Cost of Goods Sold	61,400	
Freight In	2,300	
Store Salaries Expense	32,625	
Office Salaries Expense	12,875	
Advertising Expense	24,300	
Rent Expense	2,400	
Insurance Expense	1,200	
Utilities Expense	1,560	
Store Supplies Expense	2,880	
Office Supplies Expense	1,175	
Depreciation Expense, Store Equipment	1,050	
Depreciation Expense, Office Equipment	800	

REQUIRED

Using the information given, prepare an income statement for Ingram's Fashion Shop. Combine Freight In with Cost of Goods Sold. Store Salaries Expense; Advertising Expense; Store Supplies Expense; and Depreciation Expense, Store Equipment are selling expenses. The other expenses are general and administrative expenses.

P 3. LO 4 *Merchandising Transactions: Periodic and Perpetual Inventory Systems*

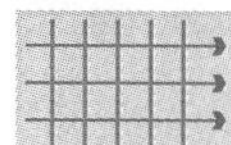

Yankee Company engaged in the following transactions in October.

Oct. 7 Sold merchandise on credit to Boris Lund, terms n/30, FOB shipping point, $3,000 (cost, $1,800).
8 Purchased merchandise on credit from Hilton Company, terms n/30, FOB shipping point, $6,000.
9 Paid Sherman Company for shipping charges on merchandise purchased on October 8, $254.
10 Purchased merchandise on credit from Main Company, terms n/30, FOB shipping point, $9,600, including $600 freight costs paid by Main.
13 Purchased office supplies on credit from Gaeta Company, terms n/15, $2,400.
14 Sold merchandise on credit to Sue Martin, terms n/30, FOB shipping point, $2,400 (cost, $1,440).
14 Returned damaged merchandise received from Hilton Company on October 8 for credit, $600.
17 Received check from Boris Lund for his purchase of October 7.
18 Returned a portion of the office supplies received on October 13 for credit because the wrong items were sent, $400.
19 Sold merchandise for cash, $1,800 (cost, $1,080).
20 Paid Main Company for purchase of October 10.
21 Paid Hilton Company the balance from transactions of October 8 and October 14.
24 Accepted from Sue Martin a return of merchandise, which was put back in inventory, $200 (cost, $120).

REQUIRED

1. Prepare entries in journal form to record the transactions, assuming the periodic inventory system is used.
2. Prepare entries in journal form to record the transactions, assuming the perpetual inventory system is used.

P 4. SO 5 *Work Sheet, Financial Statements, and Closing Entries for a Merchandising Company: Periodic Inventory System*

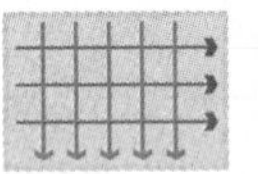

The following trial balance was taken from the ledger of Donnelly Bookstore at the end of its annual accounting period.

Donnelly Bookstore
Trial Balance
June 30, 20x2

Cash	$ 6,025	
Accounts Receivable	9,280	
Merchandise Inventory	29,450	
Store Supplies	1,911	
Prepaid Insurance	1,600	
Store Equipment	37,200	
Accumulated Depreciation, Store Equipment		$ 15,600
Accounts Payable		12,300
Ellen Donnelly, Capital		41,994
Ellen Donnelly, Withdrawals	12,000	
Sales		102,250
Sales Returns and Allowances	987	
Purchases	63,200	
Purchases Returns and Allowances		21,011
Freight In	2,261	
Sales Salaries Expense	21,350	
Rent Expense	3,600	
Other Selling Expenses	2,614	
Utilities Expense	1,677	
	$193,155	$193,155

REQUIRED

1. Assuming the company uses the periodic inventory system, enter the trial balance on a work sheet, and complete the work sheet using the following information: ending merchandise inventory, $33,227; ending store supplies inventory, $304; unexpired prepaid insurance, $200; estimated depreciation on store equipment, $4,300; sales salaries payable, $80; and accrued utilities expense, $150.
2. Prepare an income statement, a statement of owner's equity, and a balance sheet. Sales Salaries Expense; Other Selling Expenses; Store Supplies Expense; and Depreciation Expense, Store Equipment are all selling expenses.
3. From the work sheet, prepare the closing entries.

P 5. SO 6 *Work Sheet, Financial Statements, and Closing Entries for a Merchandising Company: Perpetual Inventory System*

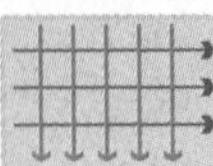

The year-end trial balance at the top of the next page was taken from the ledger of the Clay Party Costumes Company at the end of its annual accounting period on June 30, 20x2.

Clay Party Costumes Company Trial Balance June 30, 20x2		
Cash	$ 7,050	
Accounts Receivable	24,830	
Merchandise Inventory	88,900	
Store Supplies	3,800	
Prepaid Insurance	4,800	
Store Equipment	151,300	
Accumulated Depreciation, Store Equipment		$ 25,500
Accounts Payable		38,950
Jarrott Clay, Capital		161,350
Jarrott Clay, Withdrawals	24,000	
Sales		475,250
Sales Returns and Allowances	4,690	
Costs of Goods Sold	231,840	
Freight In	10,400	
Sales Salaries Expense	64,600	
Rent Expense	48,000	
Other Selling Expenses	32,910	
Utilities Expense	3,930	
	$701,050	$701,050

REQUIRED

1. Assuming the company uses the perpetual inventory system, enter the trial balance on a work sheet, and complete the work sheet using the following information: ending store supplies inventory, $550; expired insurance, $2,400; estimated depreciation on store equipment, $5,000; sales salaries payable, $650; and accrued utilities expense, $100.
2. Prepare an income statement, a statement of owner's equity, and a balance sheet. Sales Salaries Expense; Other Selling Expenses; Store Supplies Expense; and Depreciation Expense, Store Equipment are all selling expenses.
3. From the work sheet, prepare closing entries.

LO 4 SO 7 *Journalizing Merchandising Transactions, Including Discounts*

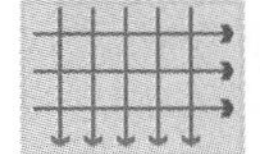

P 6. Below is a list of transactions for the Kimbassa Authentics Company for the month of January 20xx.

Jan. 2 Purchased merchandise on credit from Chang Company, terms 2/10, n/30, FOB destination, $7,400.
3 Sold merchandise on credit to B. St. Pierre, terms 1/10, n/30, FOB shipping point, $1,000.
5 Sold merchandise for cash, $700.
6 Purchased and received merchandise on credit from Oakland Company, terms 2/10, n/30, FOB shipping point, $4,200.
7 Received freight bill from North Port Express for shipment received on January 6, $570.
9 Sold merchandise on credit to R. Hayden, terms 1/10, n/30, FOB destination, $3,800.
10 Purchased merchandise from Chang Company, terms 2/10, n/30, FOB shipping point, $2,650, including freight costs of $150.
11 Received freight bill from North Port Express for sale to R. Hayden on January 9, $291.
12 Paid Chang Company for purchase of January 2.
13 Received payment in full for B. St. Pierre's purchase of January 3.

Jan. 14 Paid Oakland Company half the amount owed on the January 6 purchase. A discount is allowed on partial payment.
15 Returned faulty merchandise worth $300 to Chang Company for credit against purchase of January 10.
16 Purchased office supplies from GHI Co. for $478, terms n/10.
17 Received payment from R. Hayden for half of the purchase of January 9. A discount is allowed on partial payment.
18 Paid Chang Company in full for amount owed on purchase of January 10, less return on January 15.
19 Sold merchandise to M. Perez on credit, terms 2/10, n/30, FOB shipping point, $780.
20 Returned for credit several items of office supplies purchased on January 16, $128.
22 Issued a credit to M. Perez for returned merchandise, $180.
25 Paid for purchase of January 16, less return on January 20.
26 Paid freight company for freight charges for January 7 and 11.
27 Received payment of amount owed by M. Perez for purchase of January 19, less credit of January 22.
28 Paid Oakland Company for balance of January 6 purchase.
31 Sold merchandise for cash, $973.

REQUIRED

Prepare entries in journal form to record the transactions, assuming that the periodic inventory method is used.

Alternate Problems

P 7. **LO 1 LO 2** *Merchandising Income Statement: Periodic Inventory System*

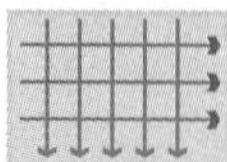

The data below come from the Abdul Lighting Shop's adjusted trial balance as of the fiscal year ended September 30, 20x5. The company's beginning inventory was $162,444; ending merchandise inventory is $153,328.

Abdul Lighting Shop
Partial Adjusted Trial Balance
September 30, 20x5

Sales		867,824
Sales Returns and Allowances	22,500	
Purchases	442,370	
Purchases Returns and Allowances		60,476
Freight In	20,156	
Store Salaries Expense	215,100	
Office Salaries Expense	53,000	
Advertising Expense	36,400	
Rent Expense	28,800	
Insurance Expense	5,600	
Utilities Expense	37,520	
Store Supplies Expense	928	
Office Supplies Expense	1,628	
Depreciation Expense, Store Equipment	3,600	
Depreciation Expense, Office Equipment	3,700	

REQUIRED

1. Prepare an income statement for the Abdul Lighting Shop. Store Salaries Expense; Advertising Expense; Store Supplies Expense; and Depreciation Expense, Store Equipment are selling expenses. The other expenses are general and administrative expenses.

2. Based on your knowledge at this point in the course, how would you use Abdul's income statement to evaluate the company's profitability?

P 8. LO 2 LO 4 *Merchandising Income Statement: Perpetual Inventory System*

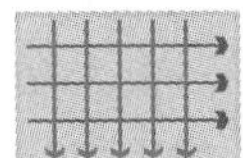

At the end of the fiscal year, June 30, 20x3, selected accounts from the adjusted trial balance for Tameka's Camera Store appeared as shown below.

Tameka's Camera Store
Partial Adjusted Trial Balance
June 30, 20x3

Sales		433,912
Sales Returns and Allowances	11,250	
Cost of Goods Sold	221,185	
Freight In	10,078	
Store Salaries Expense	107,550	
Office Salaries Expense	26,500	
Advertising Expense	18,200	
Rent Expense	14,400	
Insurance Expense	2,800	
Utilities Expense	8,760	
Store Supplies Expense	2,464	
Office Supplies Expense	1,814	
Depreciation Expense, Store Equipment	1,800	
Depreciation Expense, Office Equipment	1,850	

REQUIRED

Prepare an income statement for Tameka's Camera Store. Freight In should be combined with Cost of Goods Sold. Store Salaries Expense; Advertising Expense; Store Supplies Expense; and Depreciation Expense, Store Equipment are selling expenses. The other expenses are general and administrative expenses.

P 9. LO 4 *Merchandising Transactions: Periodic and Perpetual Inventory Systems*

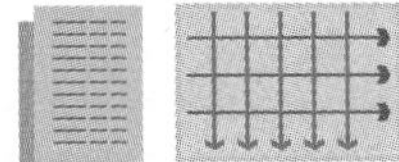

Fedor Company engaged in the following transactions in July.

July 1 Sold merchandise to Ji Ling on credit, terms n/30, FOB shipping point, $2,100 (cost, $1,260).
3 Purchased merchandise on credit from Roan Company, terms n/30, FOB shipping point, $3,800.
5 Paid Weston Freight for freight charges on merchandise received, $290.
6 Purchased store supplies on credit from Beans Supply Company, terms n/20, $636.
8 Purchased merchandise on credit from Lewisy Company, terms n/30, FOB shipping point, $3,600, which includes $200 freight costs paid by Lewisy Company.
12 Returned some of the merchandise received on July 3 for credit, $600.
15 Sold merchandise on credit to Iqbal Harris, terms n/30, FOB shipping point, $1,200 (cost, $720).
16 Returned some of the store supplies purchased on July 6 for credit, $200.
17 Sold merchandise for cash, $1,000 (cost, $600).
18 Accepted for full credit a return from Ji Ling and returned merchandise to inventory, $200 (cost, $120).
24 Paid Roan Company for purchase of July 3 less return of July 12.
25 Received full payment from Ji Ling for her July 1 purchase less the return on July 18.

REQUIRED

1. Prepare entries in journal form to record the transactions, assuming use of the periodic inventory system.
2. Prepare entries in journal form to record the transactions, assuming use of the perpetual inventory system.

Skills Development

Conceptual Analysis

SD 1.
LO 1 LO 2 *Merchandising Income Statement*

Village TV and ***TV Warehouse*** sell television sets and other video equipment in the Phoenix area. Village TV gives each customer individual attention, with employees explaining the features, advantages, and disadvantages of each video component. When a customer buys a television set or video system, Village provides free delivery, installs and adjusts the equipment, and teaches the family how to use it. TV Warehouse sells the same video components through showroom display. If a customer wants to buy a video component or a system, he or she fills out a form and takes it to the cashier for payment. After paying, the customer drives to the back of the warehouse to pick up the component, which he or she then takes home and installs. Village TV charges higher prices than TV Warehouse for the same components. Discuss how you would expect the income statements of Village TV and TV Warehouse to differ. Is it possible to tell which approach is more profitable?

Group Activity: Divide the class into informal groups. In addition to answering the above questions, ask each group to decide which store they would prefer to shop in and why. Allow 15 minutes and debrief immediately.

SD 2.
LO 3 *Periodic versus Perpetual Inventory Systems*

The Book Nook is a well-established chain of twenty bookstores in eastern Michigan. In recent years the company has grown rapidly, adding five new stores in regional malls. Management has relied on the manager of each store to place orders keyed to the market in his or her neighborhood, selected from a master list of available titles provided by the central office. Every six months, a physical inventory is taken, and financial statements are prepared using the periodic inventory system. At that time, books that have not sold well are placed on sale or, whenever possible, returned to the publisher. As a result of the company's fast growth, there are many new store managers, who management has found do not have the same ability to judge the market as do managers of the older, established stores. Thus, management is considering a recommendation to implement a perpetual inventory system and carefully monitor sales from the central office. Do you think The Book Nook should switch to the perpetual inventory system or stay with the periodic inventory system? Discuss the advantages and disadvantages of each system.

Ethical Dilemma

SD 3.
SO 7 *Ethics and Purchases Discounts*

The purchasing power of some customers is such that they can exert pressure on suppliers to go beyond the suppliers' customary allowances. For example, ***Wal-Mart*** represents more than 10 percent of annual sales for many suppliers, such as Fruit of the Loom, Rubbermaid, Sunbeam, and Coleman. *Forbes* magazine reports that while many of these suppliers allow a 2 percent discount if bills are paid within fifteen days, "Wal-Mart routinely pays its bills closer to 30 days and takes the 2 percent discount anyway on the gross amount of the invoice, not the net amount, which deducts for [trade] discounts and things like freight costs."[5] Identify three ways in which Wal-Mart's practice benefits Wal-Mart. Do you think this practice is unethical, or is it just good cash management on the part of Wal-Mart? Are the suppliers harmed by it?

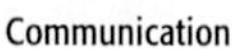
Communication

Critical Thinking

Group Activity

Memo

Ethics

International
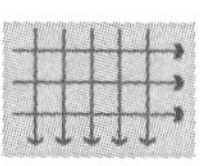
Spreadsheet

General Ledger

CD-ROM

Internet

Research Activity

LO 1 LO 2 *Merchandising Companies*

SD 4. Conduct an individual field trip by visiting any retail or wholesale business. It may be a business where you buy a product, a company where you work, or a family business. It is not necessary for you to talk to anyone at the business, but it may be helpful to do so. Determine why the business is a merchandising business. List the products or groups of products that the company sells. Does the company offer any services? How do services differ from merchandise? Make a list of the types of transactions the business engages in. Also identify and list all the operating expenses you can think of that would be relevant to this business. Organize your findings in the form of a memo to your instructor.

Decision-Making Practice

LO 2 *Analysis of Merchandising Income Statement*

SD 5. In 20x5 Les Solty opened a small retail store in a suburban mall. Called ***Solty Denim Company,*** the shop sold designer jeans. Les worked fourteen hours a day and controlled all aspects of the operation. All sales were for cash or bank credit card. The business was such a success that in 20x6 Les decided to open a second store in another mall. Because the new shop needed his attention, he hired a manager to work in the original store with two sales clerks. During 20x6 the new store was successful, but the operations of the original store did not match the first year's performance.

Concerned about this turn of events, Les compared the two years' results for the original store. The figures are as follows:

	20x6	20x5
Net Sales	$325,000	$350,000
Cost of Goods Sold	225,000	225,000
Gross Margin	$100,000	$125,000
Operating Expenses	75,000	50,000
Net Income	$ 25,000	$ 75,000

In addition, Les's analysis revealed that the cost and selling price of jeans were about the same in both years and that the level of operating expenses was roughly the same in both years, except for the new manager's $25,000 salary. Sales returns and allowances were insignificant amounts in both years.

Studying the situation further, Les discovered the following facts about the cost of goods sold:

	20x6	20x5
Gross purchases	$200,000	$271,000
Total purchases allowances	15,000	20,000
Freight in	19,000	27,000
Physical inventory, end of year	32,000	53,000

Still not satisfied, Les went through all the individual sales and purchase records for the year. Both sales and purchases were verified. However, the 20x6 ending inventory should have been $57,000, given the unit purchases and sales during the year. After puzzling over all this information, Les comes to you for accounting help.

1. Using Les's new information, recompute the cost of goods sold for 20x5 and 20x6, and account for the difference in net income between 20x5 and 20x6.
2. Suggest at least two reasons for the discrepancy in the 20x6 ending inventory. How might Les improve the management of the original store?

Financial Reporting and Analysis

INTERPRETING FINANCIAL REPORTS

FRA 1. LO 2 *Contrast of Operating Philosophies and Income Statements*

Wal-Mart Stores, Inc., and ***Kmart Corp.,*** two of the largest retailers in the United States, have different approaches to retailing. Their success has been different also. At one time, Kmart was larger than Wal-Mart. Today, Wal-Mart is almost three times as large. You can see the difference by analyzing their respective income statements and merchandise inventories. Selected information from their annual reports for the year ended January 31, 1997, is presented below. (All amounts are in millions.)

Wal-Mart: Net Sales, $104,859; Cost of Goods Sold, $83,663; Operating Expenses, $16,788; Ending Inventory, $15,897

Kmart: Net Sales, $31,437; Cost of Goods Sold, $24,390; Operating Expenses, $6,274; Ending Inventory, $6,354

REQUIRED

1. Prepare a schedule computing the gross margin and income from operations for both companies as dollar amounts and as percentages of net sales. Also, compute inventory as a percentage of the cost of goods sold.
2. From what you know about the different retailing approaches of these two companies, do the gross margins and incomes from operations you computed in **1** seem compatible with these approaches? What is it about the nature of Wal-Mart's operations that produces lower gross margin and lower operating expenses in percentages in comparison to Kmart? Which company's approach was more successful in the fiscal year ending January 31, 1997? Explain your answer.
3. Both companies have chosen a fiscal year that ends on January 31. Why do you suppose they made this choice? How realistic do you think the inventory figures are as indicators of inventory levels during the rest of the year?

FRA 2. LO 1 *Business Objectives and Income Statements*

Superior Products, Inc., is one of the nation's largest discount retailers, operating 216 stores in 30 states. In a letter to stockholders in the 1996 annual report (fiscal year ended January 31, 1997), the chairman and chief executive officer of the company stated, "Our operating plan for fiscal 1997 (year ended January 31, 1998) calls for moderate sales increases, continued improvement in gross margins, and a continuation of aggressive expense reduction programs." The following data are taken from the income statements presented in the 1997 annual report (in millions):

	Year Ended		
	January 30, 1998	**January 31, 1997**	**February 1, 1996**
Net Sales	$2,067	$2,142	$2,235
Cost of Goods Sold	1,500	1,593	1,685
Operating Expenses	466	486	502

REQUIRED

Did Superior Products, Inc., achieve the objective stated by its chairman? **Hint:** Prepare an income statement for each year and compute gross margin and operating expenses as percentages of net sales.

INTERNATIONAL COMPANY

FRA 3. LO 4 *Terminology for Merchandising Transactions in England*

Marks & Spencer is a large English retailer with department stores throughout England and in other European countries, especially France. The company also owns Brooks Brothers, the business clothing stores, in the United States. Merchandising terms in England differ from those in the United States. For instance, in England, the income statement is called the profit and loss account, sales is called turnover, merchandise inventory is called stocks, accounts receivable is called debtors, and accounts payable is called creditors. Of course, the amounts are stated in terms of pounds (£). In today's business world, it is important to understand and use terminology employed by professionals from other countries. Explain in your own words why the English may use the terms *profit and loss account, turnover, stocks, debtors,* and *creditors* in place of the American terms.

Toys "R" Us Annual Report

LO 1 *Operating Cycle*

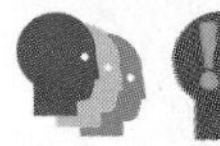
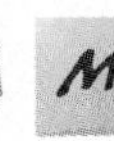

FRA 4. Refer to the Toys "R" Us annual report and to Figure 1 in this chapter. Write a memorandum to your instructor on the subject of the Toys "R" Us operating cycle. This memorandum should identify the most common transactions in the operating cycle as it applies to Toys "R" Us and should support the answer by referring to the importance of accounts receivable, accounts payable, and merchandise inventory in the Toys "R" Us financial statements. Complete the memorandum by explaining why this operating cycle is favorable to Toys "R" Us.

Fingraph® Financial Analyst™

LO 1 *Income Statement Analysis*

FRA 5. Choose any retail company from the Fingraph® Financial Analyst™ CD-ROM software and display the Income Statements Analysis: Income from Operations in tabular and graphical form for the company. Write an executive summary that analyzes the change in the company's income from operations from the first to the second year. In preparing your response, focus on the reasons the change occurred by answering the following questions: Did the company's income from operations improve or decline from the first to the second year? What was the relationship of the change to the change in net sales? Was the change in income from operations primarily due to a change in gross margin or a change in operating expenses? Suggest some possible reasons for the change in gross margin or operating expenses. Use percentages to support your answer.

ENDNOTES

1. Dayton-Hudson Corp., *Annual Report,* 1997.
2. Ibid.
3. Ibid.
4. John Schmeltzer, "Wal-Mart's Sam's Clubs Bend Rules for Big Firms," *The Wall Street Journal,* November 2, 1993.
5. Matthew Schifrin, "The Big Squeeze," *Forbes,* March 11, 1996.

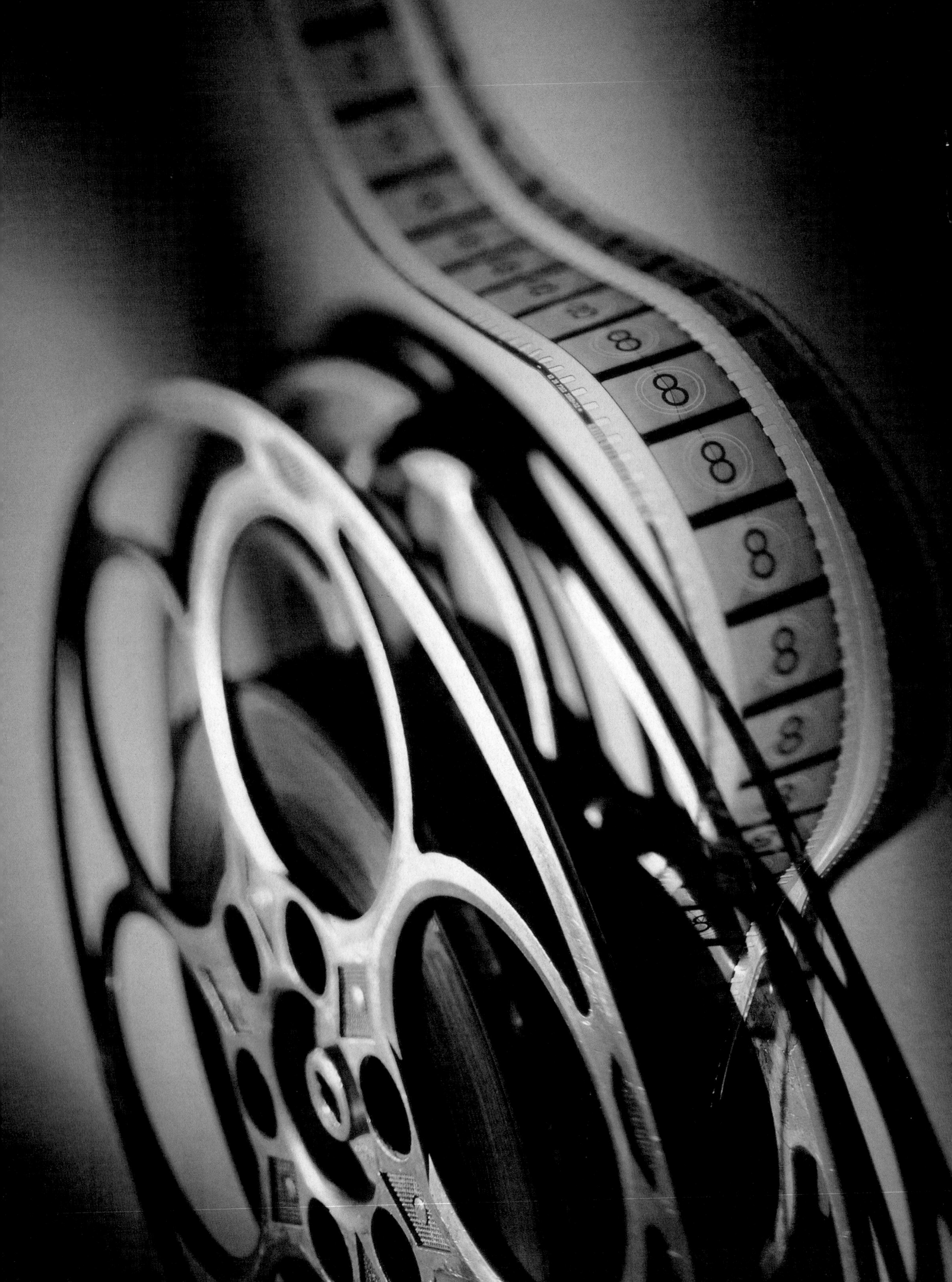

CHAPTER 6

cial Reporting nalysis

LEARNING OBJECTIVES

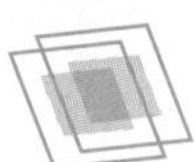

1. **State the objectives of financial reporting.**
2. **State the qualitative characteristics of accounting information and describe their interrelationships.**
3. **Define and describe the use of the conventions of *comparability* and *consistency, materiality, conservatism, full disclosure,* and *cost-benefit.***
4. **Explain management's responsibility for ethical financial reporting and define *fraudulent financial reporting.***
5. **Identify and describe the basic components of a classified balance sheet.**
6. **Prepare multistep and single-step classified income statements.**
7. **Evaluate liquidity and profitability using classified financial statements.**

DECISION POINT

THE WALT DISNEY COMPANY

The management of a corporation is judged by the company's financial performance. This financial performance is reported to stockholders and others outside the business in the company's published annual report, which includes the company's financial statements and other relevant information. Performance measures are usually based on the relationships of key data in the financial statements and are communicated by management to the reader. For large companies, this often means condensing a tremendous amount of information to a few numbers considered important by management. For example, what key measures does the management of The Walt Disney Company, a huge and highly successful entertainment company with Disney entertainment parks, ABC Broadcasting, ESPN, movies, and more, choose to focus on as its goals?

In its overview, Disney's management stated its performance in 1996 and illustrated it as follows:

> [T]he company's ongoing financial objective is to achieve 20% compound annual growth in earnings per share over any future five year period. Additionally, steady improvement in return on equity (ROE) remains a secondary, but important, financial objective.[1]

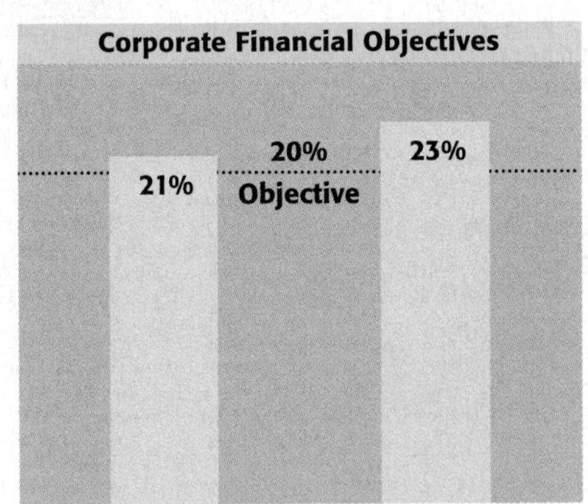

Compound Annual Earnings per Share Growth Rate 1991–1995 | Return on Average Shareholder's Equity 1995

Disney has chosen to highlight earnings growth and return on equity. The benchmark it has set is 20 percent growth and a

Critical Thinking Question: What financial statement information is most useful to investors? **Answer:** The most common response is net earnings. This response, however, is too narrow. Management compensation contracts focus not only on earnings but also on cash flows and asset utilization, which affect management behavior in achieving financial performance.

steady improvement in return on equity. Of course, investors and creditors will also want to do their own analysis of Disney. This will require a reading and interpretation of the financial statements and the calculation of other ratios. However, this analysis will be meaningless unless the reader understands financial statements and generally accepted accounting principles, on which the statements are based.

Also important to learning how to read and interpret financial statements is a comprehension of the categories and classifications used in balance sheets and income statements. Key financial ratios used in financial statement analysis are based on those categories. The chapter begins by describing the objectives, characteristics, and conventions that underlie the preparation of financial statements.

Objectives of Financial Information

OBJECTIVE 1

State the objectives of financial reporting

Related Text Assignments:
Q: 1
E: 2

Discussion Question: What is the difference between stocks and bonds? **Answer:** One difference is that stocks are a form of ownership interest, whereas bonds are a form of creditor interest.

The United States has a highly developed exchange economy. In this kind of economy, most goods and services are exchanged for money or claims to money instead of being used or bartered by their producers. Most business is carried on through corporations, including many extremely large firms that buy, sell, and obtain financing in U.S. and world markets.

By issuing stocks and bonds that are traded in financial markets, businesses can raise capital for production and marketing activities. Investors are interested mainly in returns from dividends and increases in the market price of their investments. Creditors want to know if the business can repay a loan plus interest in accordance with required terms. Thus investors and creditors both need to know if a company can generate adequate cash flows. Financial statements are important to both groups in making that judgment. They offer valuable information that helps investors and creditors judge a company's ability to pay dividends and repay debts with interest. In this way, the market puts scarce resources to work in the companies that can use them most efficiently.

The needs of users and the general business environment provide the basis for the Financial Accounting Standards Board's (FASB) three objectives of financial reporting.[2]

Point to Emphasize: Although people reading reports need some understanding of business, they do not need the skills required of a CPA.

1. **To furnish information useful in making investment and credit decisions** Financial reporting should offer information that can help present and potential investors and creditors make rational investment and credit decisions. The reports should be in a form that makes sense to those who have some understanding of business and are willing to study the information carefully.
2. **To provide information useful in assessing cash flow prospects** Financial reporting should supply information to help present and potential investors and creditors judge the amounts, timing, and risk of expected cash receipts from dividends or interest and the proceeds from the sale, redemption, or maturity of stocks or loans.
3. **To provide information about business resources, claims to those resources, and changes in them** Financial reporting should give information about the company's assets, liabilities, and owner's equity, and the effects of transactions on the company's assets, liabilities, and owner's equity.

Financial statements are the most important way of periodically presenting to parties outside the business the information that has been gathered and processed in the accounting system. For this reason, the financial statements—the balance sheet, the income statement, the statement of owner's equity, and the statement of cash flows—are the most important output of the accounting system. They are "general purpose" because they serve a wide audience. They are "external" because their users are outside the business. Because of a potential conflict of interest between managers, who must prepare the statements, and investors or creditors, who invest in or lend money to the business, the financial statements are often audited by outside accountants to increase confidence in their reliability.

Enrichment Note: The Securities and Exchange Commission (SEC) requires audited financial statements for publicly traded companies.

Qualitative Characteristics of Accounting Information

OBJECTIVE 2

State the qualitative characteristics of accounting information and describe their interrelationships

Related Text Assignments:
Q: 2
E: 2

Clarification Note: Financial statements are not perfect, but they should be free of material misstatements.

It is easy for students in their first accounting course to get the idea that accounting is 100 percent accurate. This idea is reinforced by the fact that all the problems in this and other introductory books can be solved. The numbers all add up; what is supposed to equal something else does. Accounting seems very much like mathematics in its precision. In this course, the basics of accounting are presented in a simple form to help you understand them. In practice, however, accounting information is neither simple nor precise, and it rarely satisfies all criteria. The FASB emphasizes this fact in the following statement:

> The information provided by financial reporting often results from approximate, rather than exact, measures. The measures commonly involve numerous estimates, classifications, summarizations, judgments and allocations. The outcome of economic activity in a dynamic economy is uncertain and results from combinations of many factors. Thus, despite the aura of precision that may seem to surround financial reporting in general and financial statements in particular, with few exceptions the measures are approximations, which may be based on rules and conventions, rather than exact amounts.[3]

The goal of accounting information—to provide the basic data that different users need to make informed decisions—is an ideal. The gap between the ideal and the actual provides much of the interest and controversy in accounting. To facilitate interpretation, the FASB has described the qualitative characteristics of accounting information, which are standards for judging that information. In addition, there are generally accepted conventions for recording and reporting that simplify interpretation. The relationships among these concepts are shown in Figure 1.

The most important qualitative characteristics are understandability and usefulness. Understandability depends on both the accountant and the decision maker. The accountant prepares the financial statements in accordance with accepted practices, generating important information that is believed to be understandable. But the decision maker must interpret the information and use it in making decisions. The decision maker must judge what information to use, how to use it, and what it means.

Reinforcement Exercise: Provide an example in which relevance would apply to a department of a company. For instance, a company prepares separate income schedules for each department. When management observes that a certain department (such as housewares) is not contributing on target to the company's profit, it uses that feedback to make other decisions. For example, management might take action to increase revenue in housewares or to abandon a housewares section and contribute that space and its resources to more profitable items.

For accounting information to meet the standard of usefulness, it must have two major qualitative characteristics: relevance and reliability. Relevance means that the information can make a difference in the outcome of a decision. In other words, another decision would be made if the relevant information were not available. To be relevant, information must provide feedback, help predict future conditions, and be timely. For example, the income statement provides information about how a company did over the past year (feedback), and it helps in planning for the next year (prediction). To be useful, however, the information must also be communicated soon enough after the end of the accounting period to enable the reader to make decisions (timeliness).

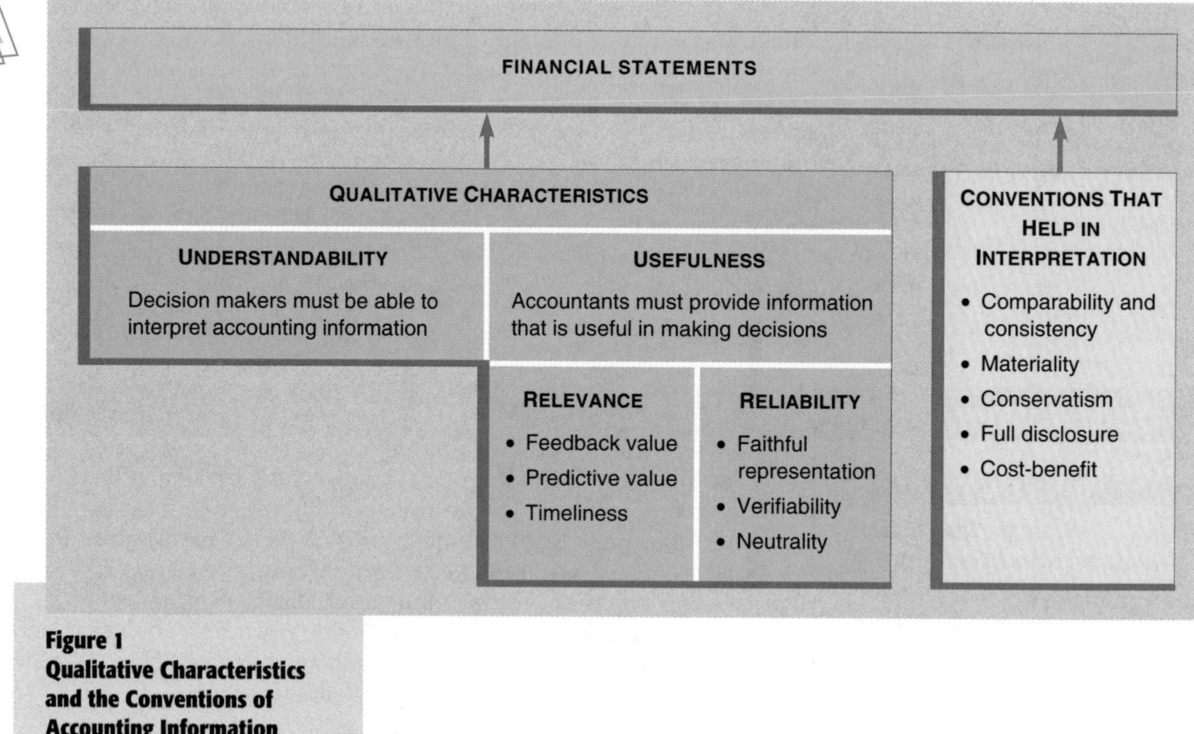

Figure 1
Qualitative Characteristics and the Conventions of Accounting Information

In addition to being relevant, accounting information must have reliability. In other words, the user must be able to depend on the information. It must represent what it is meant to represent. It must be credible and verifiable by independent parties using the same methods of measuring. It must also be neutral. Accounting should convey business activity as faithfully as possible without influencing anyone in a specific direction. For example, the balance sheet should represent the economic resources, obligations, and owner's equity of a business as faithfully as possible in accordance with generally accepted accounting principles, and the balance sheet should be verifiable by an auditor.

Conventions That Help in the Interpretation of Financial Information

OBJECTIVE 3

Define and describe the use of the conventions of comparability *and* consistency, materiality, conservatism, full disclosure, *and* cost-benefit

To a large extent, financial statements are based on estimates and arbitrary accounting rules of recognition and allocation. In this book, we point out a number of difficulties with financial statements. One is failing to recognize the changing value of the dollar caused by inflation. Another is treating intangibles, like research and development costs, as assets if they are purchased outside the company and as expenses if they are developed within the company. Such problems do not mean that financial statements are useless; the statements are essential. However, users must know how to interpret them.

To help in this interpretation, accountants depend on five conventions, or rules of thumb, in recording transactions and preparing financial statements: (1) comparability and consistency, (2) materiality, (3) conservatism, (4) full disclosure, and (5) cost-benefit.

Related Text Assignments:
Q: 3
SE: 1
E: 1, 2
P: 1, 6
SD: 1, 2

Comparability and Consistency

A characteristic that increases the usefulness of accounting information is comparability. Information about a company is more useful if it can be compared with similar facts about the same company over several time periods or about another company for the same time period. Comparability means that the information is presented in such a way that a decision maker can recognize similarities, differences, and trends over different time periods or between different companies.

Consistent use of accounting measures and procedures is important in achieving comparability. The consistency convention requires that an accounting procedure, once adopted by a company, remain in use from one period to the next unless users are informed of the change. Thus, without a note to the contrary, users of financial statements can assume that there has been no arbitrary change in the treatment of a particular transaction, account, or item that would affect the interpretation of the statements.

If management decides that a certain procedure is no longer appropriate and should be changed, generally accepted accounting principles require that the change and its dollar effect be described in the notes to the financial statements.

> The nature of and justification for a change in accounting principle and its effect on income should be disclosed in the financial statements of the period in which the change is made. The justification for the change should explain clearly why the newly adopted accounting principle is preferable.[4]

For example, in its 1992 annual report, Rubbermaid Incorporated stated that it changed its method of accounting for inventories in 1992 because management felt the new method improved the matching of resources and costs.

Materiality

Business-World Example: By definition, a $10 stapler is a long-term asset that, theoretically, should be capitalized and depreciated over its useful life. However, the convention of materiality allows the stapler to be expensed entirely in the year of purchase because its cost is small and writing it off in one year has no effect on anyone's decision making.

The term materiality refers to the relative importance of an item or event. If an item or event is material, it is probably relevant to the users of financial statements. In other words, an item is material if users would have done something differently if they had not known about the item. Accountants are often faced with decisions about small items or events that make little difference to users no matter how they are handled. For example, a large company may decide that expenditures for durable items of less than $500 should be charged as expenses rather than recorded as long-term assets and depreciated.

In general, an item is material if there is a reasonable expectation that knowing about it would influence the decisions of users of financial statements. The materiality of an item normally is determined by relating its dollar value to an element of the financial statements, such as net income or total assets. Some accountants feel that when an item is 5 percent or more of net income, it is material. However, materiality also depends on the nature of the item, not just its value. For example, in a multimillion-dollar company, a mistake in recording an item of $5,000 may not be important, but the discovery of a $5,000 bribe or theft can be very important. Also, many small errors can combine into a material amount. Accountants judge the materiality of many things, and the users of financial statements depend on their judgments being fair and accurate.

Point to Emphasize: Illegal acts involving small dollar amounts should still be investigated.

Common Student Error: Students sometimes think that the purpose of conservatism is to produce the lowest net income and lowest asset value. Stress that it is a guideline for choosing among GAAP alternatives and that it should be used with care.

Conservatism

Accountants try to base their decisions on logic and evidence that lead to the fairest report of what happened. In judging and estimating, however, accountants often are faced with uncertainties. In such cases, they look to the convention of conservatism.

This convention means that when accountants face major uncertainties about which accounting procedure to use, they generally choose the one that is least likely to overstate assets and income.

One of the most common applications of the conservatism convention is the use of the lower-of-cost-or-market method in accounting for inventories. Under this method, if the market value of an item is greater than its cost, the more conservative cost figure is used. If the market value falls below the cost, the more conservative market value is used. The latter situation often occurs in the computer industry.

Point to Emphasize: Stress that expensing a long-term asset in the period of purchase is not a GAAP alternative.

Conservatism can be a useful tool in doubtful cases, but its abuse leads to incorrect and misleading financial statements. Suppose that someone incorrectly applies the conservatism convention by expensing a long-term asset in the period of purchase. In this case, there is no uncertainty. Income and assets for the current period would be understated, and income in future periods would be overstated. For this reason, accountants depend on the conservatism convention only when there is uncertainty about which accounting procedure to use.

Full Disclosure

The convention of full disclosure requires that financial statements and their notes present all information that is relevant to the users' understanding of the company's financial condition. In other words, the statements should offer any explanation that is needed to keep them from being misleading. Explanatory notes are considered an integral part of the financial statements. For instance, as mentioned earlier, a change from one accounting procedure to another should be reported in the notes to the financial statements. In general, the form of the financial statements can affect their usefulness in making certain decisions. Also, certain items, such as the amount of depreciation expense on the income statement and the accumulated depreciation on the balance sheet, are essential to the readers of financial statements.

Enrichment Note: Any controversy arising after the balance sheet date must be disclosed in the statements. Suppose a firm purchased a piece of land for a future subdivision. Shortly after the end of its fiscal year, the firm is served papers to halt construction because the Environmental Protection Agency asserts that the land was once a toxic waste dump. This information, which obviously affects the users of the financial statements, must be disclosed in the statements for the just-ended fiscal year.

Other examples of disclosures required by the Financial Accounting Standards Board and other official bodies are the accounting procedures used in preparing the statements, important terms of the company's debt, commitments and contingencies, and important events taking place after the date of the statements. However, there is a point at which the statements become so cluttered that notes impede rather than help understanding. Beyond required disclosures, the application of the full-disclosure convention is based on the judgment of management and of the accountants who prepare the financial statements.

In recent years, the principle of full disclosure has also been influenced by users of accounting information. To protect investors and creditors, independent auditors, the stock exchanges, and the SEC have made more demands for disclosure by publicly owned companies. The SEC has been pushing especially hard for the enforcement of full disclosure. As a result, more and better information about corporations is available to the public today than ever before.

Business-World Example: Firms use the convention of cost-benefit for non-accounting decisions as well. Department stores could almost completely stop shoplifting if they were to hire five times as many clerks to watch customers. The benefit would be reduced shoplifting. The cost would be reduced sales (customers do not like being watched closely) and increased wages for clerks. Although shoplifting is a serious problem for department stores, clearly the benefit of reducing shoplifting in this way does not outweigh the cost.

Cost-Benefit

The cost-benefit convention underlies all the qualitative characteristics and conventions. It holds that the benefits to be gained from providing accounting information should be greater than the costs of providing it. Of course, minimum levels of relevance and reliability must be reached for accounting information to be useful. Beyond the minimum levels, however, it is up to the FASB and the SEC, which require the information, and the accountant, who provides the information, to judge the costs and benefits in each case. Most of the costs of providing information fall at first on the preparers; the benefits are reaped by both preparers and users.

Instructional Strategy: To check students' comprehension of accounting conventions, break the class into small groups to discuss SD 1. Randomly select groups to present their results. Each group could discuss a different convention as it applies to the case. Encourage class members to ask the presenters questions, and be prepared to ask questions yourself. Reward performance with class participation points.

Finally, both the costs and the benefits are passed on to society in the form of prices and social benefits from more efficient allocation of resources.

The costs and benefits of a particular requirement for accounting disclosure are both direct and indirect, immediate and deferred. For example, it is hard to judge the final costs and benefits of a far-reaching and costly regulation. The FASB, for instance, allows certain large companies to make a supplemental disclosure in their financial statements of the effects of changes on current costs. Most companies choose not to present such information because they believe the costs of producing and providing it exceed its benefits to the readers of their financial statements. Cost-benefit is a question faced by all regulators, including the FASB and the SEC. Even though there are no definitive ways of measuring costs and benefits, much of an accountant's work deals with these concepts.

Management's Responsibility for Ethical Reporting

OBJECTIVE 4

***Explain** management's responsibility for ethical financial reporting and **define** fraudulent financial reporting*

Related Text Assignments:
Q: 4
SD: 3, 4

The users of financial statements depend on the good faith of those who prepare the statements. Their dependence places a duty on a company's management and its accountants to act ethically in the reporting process. That duty is often expressed in the report of management's responsibilities that accompanies financial statements. For example, the report of the management of Quaker Oats Company, a company known for strong financial reporting and controls, states

> Management is responsible for the preparation and integrity of the Company's financial statements. The financial statements have been prepared in accordance with generally accepted accounting principles and necessarily include some amounts that are based on management's estimates and judgment.[5]

Quaker Oats's management also tells how it meets this responsibility:

> To fulfill its responsibility, management maintains a strong system of internal controls, supported by formal policies and procedures that are communicated throughout the Company. Management regularly evaluates its systems of internal control with an eye toward improvement. Management also maintains a staff of internal auditors who evaluate the adequacy of and investigate the adherence to these controls, policies, and procedures.[6]

The intentional preparation of misleading financial statements is called fraudulent financial reporting.[7] It can result from the distortion of records (the manipulation of inventory records), falsified transactions (fictitious sales or orders), or the misapplication of accounting principles (treating as an asset an item that should be expensed). There are many possible motives for fraudulent reporting—for instance, to obtain a higher price in the sale of a company, to meet the expectations of stockholders, or to obtain a loan. Other times, the incentive is personal gain, such as additional compensation, promotion, or avoidance of penalties for poor performance. The personal costs of such actions can be high—individuals who authorize or prepare fraudulent financial statements may face criminal penalties and financial loss. Others, including investors and lenders to the company, employees, and customers, suffer from fraudulent financial reporting as well.

Incentives for fraudulent financial reporting exist to some extent in every company. It is management's responsibility to insist on honest financial reporting, but it is also the company accountants' responsibility to maintain high ethical standards. Ethical reporting demands that accountants apply financial accounting concepts to present a fair view of the company's operations and financial position and to avoid misleading readers of the financial statements.

BUSINESS BULLETIN: ETHICS IN PRACTICE

There is a difference between management's choosing to follow accounting principles that are favorable to its actions and fraudulent financial reporting. For example, a company may choose to recognize revenue as soon as possible after a sale is made; however, when Oracle Corp., a software company, inflated its revenues and earnings by double-billing customers and failing to record product returns, it engaged in fraudulent financial reporting. The company agreed to settle charges brought by the Securities and Exchange Commission by paying a $100,000 fine. Management said the company's explosive growth in sales exceeded the ability of its internal control systems to detect errors.

Classified Balance Sheet

OBJECTIVE 5

Identify and describe the basic components of a classified balance sheet

Related Text Assignments:
Q: 5, 6, 7, 8, 9, 10, 11, 12, 13
SE: 2, 3
E: 3, 4
P: 3, 5
FRA: 4, 5

The balance sheets you have seen in the chapters thus far categorize accounts as assets, liabilities, and owner's equity. Because even a fairly small company can have hundreds of accounts, simply listing accounts in such broad categories is not particularly helpful to a statement user. Setting up subcategories within the major categories often makes financial statements much more useful. Investors and creditors study and evaluate the relationships among the subcategories. General-purpose external financial statements that are divided into useful subcategories are called classified financial statements.

The balance sheet presents the financial position of a company at a particular time. The subdivisions of the classified balance sheet shown in Exhibit 1 are typical of most companies in the United States. The subdivisions under owner's equity, of course, depend on the form of business.

Assets

Parenthetical Note: Examples of accounts that would be classified as "other assets" are long-term receivables and bond issue costs.

A company's assets are often divided into four categories: (1) current assets; (2) investments; (3) property, plant, and equipment; and (4) intangible assets. For simplicity, some companies group investments, intangible assets, and other miscellaneous assets into a category called "other assets." The categories are listed in the order of their presumed ease of conversion into cash. For example, current assets are usually more easily converted to cash than are property, plant, and equipment.

Current Assets Current assets are cash or other assets that are reasonably expected to be converted to cash, sold, or consumed within the next year or within the normal operating cycle of the business, whichever is longer. The normal operating cycle of a company is the average time needed to go from cash to cash. For example, cash is used to buy merchandise inventory, which is sold for cash or for a promise of cash if the sale is made on account. If a sale is made on account, the resulting receivable must be collected before the cycle is completed.

Point to Emphasize: Use one year as the current period unless the normal operating cycle happens to be longer.

The normal operating cycle for most companies is less than one year, but there are exceptions. Boeing Company, for example, can take more than one year to make commercial aircraft. The cost of those aircraft are considered current assets while they are being made because they will be sold in the current operating cycle. Another example is a company that sells on the installment basis. The payments for

Parenthetical Note: With some accounts–for example, Notes Receivable and Accounts Receivable–it is a toss-up which to list first.

Instructional Strategy: Play "Classification *Jeopardy*" using Exhibit 1 and E 3. Students could write their responses individually or play in 2 to 4 teams. Don't forget to have a Double *Jeopardy* question. Reward the winning team or individuals with bonus points on the next quiz or test.

Exhibit 1. Classified Balance Sheet for Shafer Auto Parts Company

Shafer Auto Parts Company
Balance Sheet
December 31, 20xx

Assets			
Current Assets			
Cash		$10,360	
Short-Term Investments		2,000	
Notes Receivable		8,000	
Accounts Receivable		35,300	
Merchandise Inventory		60,400	
Prepaid Insurance		6,600	
Store Supplies		1,060	
Office Supplies		636	
Total Current Assets			$124,356
Investments			
Land Held for Future Use			5,000
Property, Plant, and Equipment			
Land		$ 4,500	
Building	$20,650		
Less Accumulated Depreciation	8,640	12,010	
Delivery Equipment	$18,400		
Less Accumulated Depreciation	9,450	8,950	
Office Equipment	$ 8,600		
Less Accumulated Depreciation	5,000	3,600	
Total Property, Plant, and Equipment			29,060
Intangible Assets			
Trademark			500
Total Assets			$158,916
Liabilities			
Current Liabilities			
Notes Payable		$15,000	
Accounts Payable		23,883	
Salaries Payable		2,000	
Current Portion of Mortgage Payable		1,800	
Total Current Liabilities			$ 42,683
Long-Term Liabilities			
Mortgage Payable			17,800
Total Liabilities			$ 60,483
Owner's Equity			
Fred Shafer, Capital			98,433
Total Liabilities and Owner's Equity			$158,916

a television set or stove can be extended over twenty-four or thirty-six months, but such receivables are still considered current assets.

Cash is obviously a current asset. Temporary investments, notes and accounts receivable, and inventory are also current assets because they are expected to be converted to cash within the next year or during the normal operating cycle. On the balance sheet, they are listed in the order of their ease of conversion into cash.

Point to Emphasize: The firm does not consume prepaid expenses, but it does enjoy the benefit of the space rented, the insurance protection provided, and so forth.

Prepaid expenses, such as rent and insurance paid for in advance, and inventories of supplies bought for use rather than for sale should also be classified as current assets. Such assets are current in the sense that if they had not been bought earlier, a current outlay of cash would be needed to obtain them.[8]

Point to Emphasize: For an investment to be classified as current, management must intend to sell it within the next year or the current operating cycle, and it must be readily marketable.

In deciding whether an asset is current or noncurrent, the idea of "reasonable expectation" is important. For example, Short-Term Investments is an account used for temporary investments of idle cash or cash that is not immediately required for operating purposes. Management can reasonably expect to sell those securities as cash needs arise over the next year or operating cycle. Investments in securities that management does not expect to sell within the next year and that do not involve the temporary use of idle cash should be shown in the investments category of a classified balance sheet.

Investments The investments category includes assets, usually long term, that are not used in the normal operation of the business and that management does not plan to convert to cash within the next year. Items in that category are securities held for long-term investment, long-term notes receivable, land held for future use, plant or equipment not used in the business, and special funds established to pay off a debt or buy a building. Also included are large permanent investments in another company for the purpose of controlling that company.

Property, Plant, and Equipment The property, plant, and equipment category includes long-term assets used in the continuing operation of the business. They represent a place to operate (land and buildings) and equipment to produce, sell, deliver, and service the company's goods. Consequently, they may also be called *operating assets* or, sometimes, *fixed assets, tangible assets, long-lived assets,* or *plant assets.* Through depreciation, the costs of such assets (except land) are spread over the periods they benefit. Past depreciation is recorded in the Accumulated Depreciation accounts. The exact order in which property, plant, and equipment are listed on the balance sheet is not the same everywhere. In practice, accounts are often combined to make the financial statements less cluttered. For example:

Property, Plant, and Equipment

Land		$ 4,500
Buildings and Equipment	$47,650	
Less Accumulated Depreciation	23,090	24,560
Total Property, Plant, and Equipment		$29,060

Many companies simply show a single line with a total for property, plant, and equipment and provide the details in a note to the financial statements.

Property, plant, and equipment also includes natural resources owned by the company, such as forest lands, oil and gas properties, and coal mines. Assets that are not used in the regular course of business are listed in the investments category, as noted above.

Intangible Assets Intangible assets are long-term assets that have no physical substance but that have a value based on the rights or privileges that belong to their owner. Examples are patents, copyrights, goodwill, franchises, and trademarks. An intangible asset is recorded at cost, which is spread over the expected life of the right or privilege.

Other Assets Some companies use the category other assets to group all owned assets other than current assets and property, plant, and equipment. Other assets can include investments and intangible assets.

Liabilities

Liabilities are divided into the following two categories: current liabilities and long-term liabilities.

Current Liabilities The category current liabilities consists of obligations due to be paid or performed within one year or within the normal operating cycle of the business, whichever is longer. Current liabilities are typically paid from current assets or by incurring new short-term liabilities. They include notes payable, accounts payable, the current portion of long-term debt, salaries and wages payable, taxes payable, and customer advances (unearned revenues).

Discussion Question: How would a mortgage that is paid monthly for 120 months be classified? **Answer:** The portion due during the next year or the current operating cycle would be classified as a current liability; the portion due after the next year or the current operating cycle would be classified as a long-term liability.

Long-Term Liabilities The debts of a business that fall due more than one year in the future or beyond the normal operating cycle, or that are to be paid out of noncurrent assets, are long-term liabilities. Mortgages payable, long-term notes, bonds payable, employee pension obligations, and long-term lease liabilities generally fall in the category of long-term liabilities.

Owner's Equity

The terms *owner's equity, proprietorship, capital,* and *net worth* are used interchangeably to denote the owner's interest in a company. The first three terms are preferred to *net worth* because most assets are recorded at original cost rather than at current value. Consequently, the ownership section does not represent "worth." It really represents a claim against the assets of the company.

The accounting treatment of assets and liabilities is not usually affected by the form of business organization. However, the equity section of the balance sheet differs depending on whether the business is a sole proprietorship, a partnership, or a corporation.

Sole Proprietorship You already are familiar with the owner's equity section of a sole proprietorship, like the one shown in the balance sheet for Shafer Auto Parts Company in Exhibit 1:

Owner's Equity

Fred Shafer, Capital	$98,433

Partnership The equity section of the balance sheet for a partnership is called partners' equity and is much like that of the sole proprietorship. It might appear as follows:

Point to Emphasize: The only difference in equity between a sole proprietorship and a partnership is in the number of capital accounts.

Partners' Equity

A. J. Martin, Capital	$21,666	
R. C. Moore, Capital	35,724	
Total Partners' Equity		$57,390

Corporation Corporations are by law separate, legal entities that are owned by their stockholders. The equity section of a balance sheet for a corporation is called stockholders' equity and has two parts: contributed, or paid-in, capital and retained earnings. It might appear like this:

Stockholders' Equity

Contributed Capital		
Common Stock, $10 par value, 5,000 shares authorized, issued, and outstanding	$50,000	
Paid-in Capital in Excess of Par Value	10,000	
Total Contributed Capital		$60,000
Retained Earnings		37,500
Total Stockholders' Equity		$97,500

Remember that owner's equity accounts show the sources of and claims on assets. Of course, the claims are not on any particular asset but on the assets as a whole. It follows, then, that a corporation's contributed and earned capital accounts measure its stockholders' claims on assets and also indicate the sources of the assets. The contributed capital accounts reflect the amounts of assets invested by stockholders. Generally, contributed capital is shown on corporate balance sheets by two amounts: (1) the face, or par, value of issued stock and (2) the amounts paid in, or contributed, in excess of the par value per share. In the illustration above, stockholders invested amounts equal to par value of the outstanding stock (5,000 × $10) plus $10,000 more.

The Retained Earnings account is sometimes called *Earned Capital* because it represents the stockholders' claim to the assets earned from operations and reinvested in corporate operations. Distributions of assets to shareholders, called *dividends,* reduce the Retained Earnings account balance just as withdrawals of assets by the owner of a business lower the Capital account balance. Thus the Retained Earnings account balance, in its simplest form, represents the earnings of the corporation less dividends paid to stockholders over the life of the business.

Reading and Graphing Real Company Balance Sheets

Although financial statements usually follow the same general form as illustrated for Shafer Auto Parts Company, no two companies will have statements that are exactly alike. The balance sheet of Oneida Ltd., one of the oldest and largest makers of flatware, china, and other tableware, in Exhibit 2 is a good example. Note that two years of data are provided so that the change from one year to the next can be evaluated. Also note that the major classifications are similar but not identical to those for Shafer Auto Parts. For instance, there is a category called "Other Liabilities." Since this category appears after long-term debt, it represents longer-term liabilities, due more than one year from the balance sheet date. The word "Accrued" is used—"Accrued postretirement liability" and "Accrued pension liability"—and therefore, from our knowledge of accrued liabilities generally, we know that these liabilities are related to expenses that have been incurred and that were recorded through an adjusting entry; no cash has been paid as yet.

We may also observe that Oneida's stockholders' equity section is more complicated than the owner's equity section of Shafer Auto Parts. However, it is possible to look at the total stockholders' equity and know that this amount relates to the claims by the stockholders on the company.

When we look at columns of numbers, it is sometimes difficult to see the patterns. Graphical presentation of the statements is helpful in visualizing the changes that are taking place in a company's financial position. For example, Oneida's balance sheet from Exhibit 2 is presented graphically in Figure 2 using the Fingraph®

Exhibit 2. Balance Sheet for Oneida Ltd.

ONEIDA LTD., Consolidated Balance Sheet		
(In thousands)	**January 25, 1997**	January 27, 1996
ASSETS		
CURRENT ASSETS:		
Cash	**$ 3,183**	$ 2,847
Receivables	**50,246**	42,333
Inventories	**124,293**	126,043
Other current assets	**47,053**	40,707
Total current assets	**224,775**	211,930
PROPERTY, PLANT, AND EQUIPMENT:		
Land and buildings	**45,502**	42,625
Machinery and equipment	**149,927**	143,012
Total	**195,429**	185,637
Less accumulated depreciation	**116,283**	105,957
Property, plant, and equipment—net	**79,146**	79,680
OTHER ASSETS:		
Costs in excess of net assets acquired—net	**30,940**	
Deferred income taxes	**12,716**	12,341
Other	**2,651**	2,617
TOTAL	**$350,228**	$306,568
LIABILITIES AND STOCKHOLDERS' EQUITY		
CURRENT LIABILITIES:		
Short-term debt	**$ 15,593**	$ 24,067
Accounts payable	**14,176**	13,362
Accrued liabilities	**37,082**	29,646
Current installments of long-term debt	**29,703**	4,749
Total current liabilities	**96,554**	71,824
LONG-TERM DEBT	**68,126**	63,129
OTHER LIABILITIES:		
Accrued postretirement liability	**52,273**	50,932
Accrued pension liability	**5,666**	5,209
Other liabilities	**9,291**	9,174
Total	**67,230**	65,315
STOCKHOLDERS' EQUITY:		
Cumulative 6% preferred stock—$25 par value; authorized 95,660 shares, issued 88,640 and 88,989 shares, respectively; callable at $30 per share	**2,216**	2,225
Common stock—$1.00 par value; authorized 24,000,000 shares, issued 11,868,000 and 11,706,224 shares, respectively	**11,868**	11,706
Additional paid-in capital	**83,103**	81,150
Retained earnings	**39,893**	28,936
Equity adjustment from translation	**(8,468)**	(8,614)
Less cost of common stock held in treasury; 766,241 and 672,617 shares, respectively	**(10,156)**	(8,563)
Less unallocated ESOP shares of common stock of 8,531 and 34,347, respectively	**(138)**	(540)
Stockholders' equity	**118,318**	106,300
TOTAL	**$350,228**	$306,568

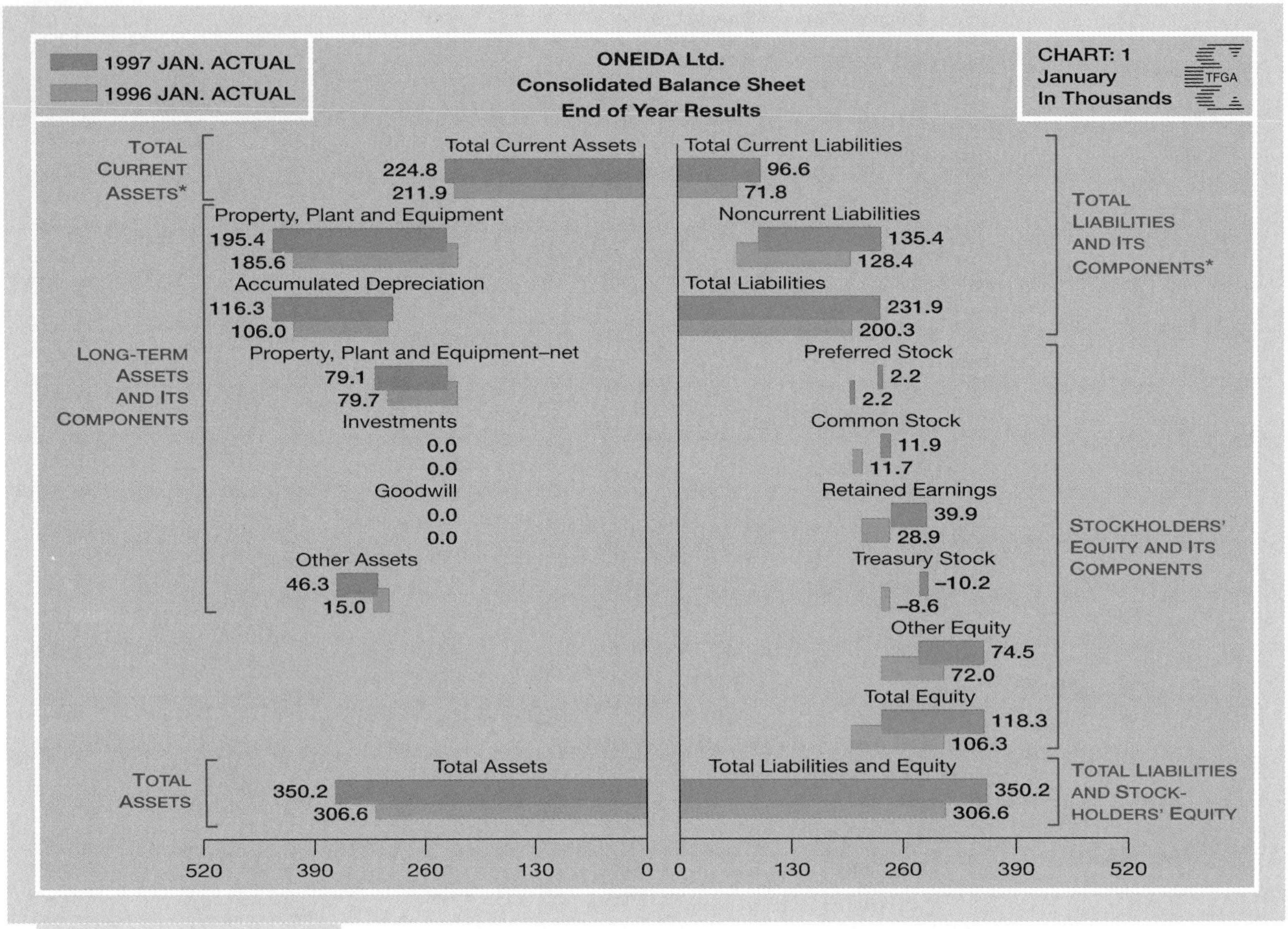

1997 JAN. ACTUAL
1996 JAN. ACTUAL

ONEIDA Ltd.
Consolidated Balance Sheet
End of Year Results

CHART: 1
January
In Thousands
TFGA

Group	Item	1997	1996
TOTAL CURRENT ASSETS*	Total Current Assets	224.8	211.9
LONG-TERM ASSETS AND ITS COMPONENTS	Property, Plant and Equipment	195.4	185.6
	Accumulated Depreciation	116.3	106.0
	Property, Plant and Equipment–net	79.1	79.7
	Investments	0.0	0.0
	Goodwill	0.0	0.0
	Other Assets	46.3	15.0
TOTAL ASSETS	Total Assets	350.2	306.6

Group	Item	1997	1996
TOTAL LIABILITIES AND ITS COMPONENTS*	Total Current Liabilities	96.6	71.8
	Noncurrent Liabilities	135.4	128.4
	Total Liabilities	231.9	200.3
STOCKHOLDERS' EQUITY AND ITS COMPONENTS	Preferred Stock	2.2	2.2
	Common Stock	11.9	11.7
	Retained Earnings	39.9	28.9
	Treasury Stock	−10.2	−8.6
	Other Equity	74.5	72.0
	Total Equity	118.3	106.3
TOTAL LIABILITIES AND STOCKHOLDERS' EQUITY	Total Liabilities and Equity	350.2	306.6

Axis: 520 390 260 130 0 0 130 260 390 520

Figure 2
Graphical Presentation of Oneida Ltd. Balance Sheets

*The components of total current assets and total current liabiliities are presented in another graph (not shown).

Financial Analyst™ CD-ROM software that accompanies this text. In the graph, total assets and its components are graphed on the left side, and total liabilities and its components, together with total stockholders' equity, are on the right side. The composition of the assets, liabilities, their relation to stockholders' equity, and the changes in them from 1996 to 1997 are clearly seen. These graphs show that overall

BUSINESS BULLETIN: BUSINESS PRACTICE

Accounting can be an issue even in the movies. Despite worldwide receipts of $300 million and additional millions in merchandise sales, Warner Bros. Inc. says the original *Batman* has not made a profit and may never do so. However, a lawsuit by two executive producers says that the studio's accounting is fraudulent and unconscionable. At issue is the measurement of "net profits," a percentage of which the producers are to receive. The problem is that the top actors like Jack Nicholson, the director, and others receive a share of every dollar that the movie generates and, as a result, have earned millions of dollars. Because of these shares, it is impossible for the movie ever to earn a "net profit." Thus, while others are paid handsomely, the two executive producers receive nothing. It pays to know something about accounting before signing your movie contract.

there were very few changes for Oneida from 1996 to 1997 in either totals or components. Also note that showing the balance sheet visually reduces the detailed clutter of the statement to the salient components for input to the graph. For instance, all other liabilities are combined and represented by a single component line.

Forms of the Income Statement

OBJECTIVE 6

Prepare multistep and single-step classified income statements

Related Text Assignments:
Q: 14, 15
SE: 4, 5, 6
E: 5, 6, 7
P: 2, 5, 7
FRA: 5

Teaching Note: The multistep income statement is a valuable analytical tool that is often overlooked. Analysts will frequently convert a single-step statement into a multistep one because the latter separates operating from nonoperating sources of net income. Investors want net income to result primarily from operations, not from one-time gains on sales of assets.

For internal management, a detailed income statement is helpful in analyzing the company's performance. But for external reporting purposes, the income statement is usually presented in condensed form. Condensed financial statements present only the major categories of the detailed financial statements. There are two common forms of the condensed income statement, the multistep form and the single-step form. The multistep form, illustrated in Exhibit 3, derives net income in the same step-by-step fashion as a detailed income statement would, except that only the totals of significant categories are given. Usually, some breakdown is shown for operating expenses, such as the totals for selling expenses and for general and administrative expenses. In the Shafer statement, gross margin less operating expenses is called income from operations and a new section, other revenues and expenses, has been added to include nonoperating revenues and expenses. The latter section includes revenues from investments (such as dividends and interest from stocks, bonds, and savings accounts) and interest earned on credit or notes extended to customers. It also includes interest expense and other expenses that result from borrowing money or from credit extended to the company. If the company has other revenues and expenses that are not related to normal business operations, they too are included in this part of the income statement. Thus an analyst who wants to compare two companies independent of their financing methods—that is, before considering other revenues and expenses—would focus on income from operations.

Exhibit 3. Condensed Multistep Income Statement for Shafer Auto Parts Company

Shafer Auto Parts Company
Income Statement
For the Year Ended December 31, 20xx

Net Sales		$289,656
Cost of Goods Sold		181,260
Gross Margin		$108,396
Operating Expenses		
Selling Expenses	$54,780	
General and Administrative Expenses	34,504	
Total Operating Expenses		89,284
Income from Operations		$ 19,112
Other Revenues and Expenses		
Interest Income	$ 1,400	
Less Interest Expense	2,631	
Excess of Other Expenses over Other Revenues		1,231
Net Income		$ 17,881

Exhibit 4. Condensed Single-Step Income Statement for Shafer Auto Parts Company

Shafer Auto Parts Company
Income Statement
For the Year Ended December 31, 20xx

Revenues		
Net Sales		$289,656
Interest Income		1,400
Total Revenues		$291,056
Costs and Expenses		
Cost of Goods Sold	$181,260	
Selling Expenses	54,780	
General and Administrative Expenses	34,504	
Interest Expense	2,631	
Total Costs and Expenses		273,175
Net Income		$ 17,881

Exhibit 5. Income Statement for Oneida Ltd.

ONEIDA LTD., Consolidated Statement of Operations for the years ended January 1997, 1996, and 1995

(In thousands)

	Year ended in January		
	1997	1996	1995
NET SALES	**$376,923**	$363,811	$335,831
COST OF SALES	**243,934**	236,560	222,639
GROSS MARGIN	**132,989**	127,251	113,192
OPERATING EXPENSES:			
Selling, advertising and distribution	**67,868**	66,693	64,873
General and administrative	**29,231**	27,350	24,408
Total	**97,099**	94,043	89,281
INCOME FROM OPERATIONS	**35,890**	33,208	23,911
OTHER EXPENSE	**832**	762	596
INTEREST EXPENSE	**6,503**	6,877	5,922
INCOME FROM CONTINUING OPERATIONS BEFORE INCOME TAXES	**28,555**	25,569	17,393
PROVISION FOR INCOME TAXES	**11,279**	10,144	7,306
INCOME FROM CONTINUING OPERATIONS	**17,276**	15,425	10,087
INCOME (LOSS) FROM DISCONTINUED OPERATIONS	**(304)**	2,663	3,406
NET INCOME	**$ 16,972**	$ 18,088	$ 13,493

The single-step form of income statement, illustrated in Exhibit 4, derives net income in a single step by putting the major categories of revenues in the first part of the statement and the major categories of costs and expenses in the second part. The multistep form and the single-step form each have advantages. The multistep form shows the components that are used in deriving net income; the single-step form has the advantage of simplicity. Approximately an equal number of large U.S. companies use each form in their public reports.

Net income from the income statement becomes an element of the statement of owner's equity.

Reading and Graphing Real Company Income Statements

As with the presentation of balance sheets, you will rarely find income statements that are exactly like the one for Shafer Auto Parts Company. You will encounter terms and structure that differ, such as those on the multistep income statement for Oneida Ltd. in Exhibit 5, where management provides three years of data for comparison purposes. Sometimes there may be components in the income statement that are not covered in this chapter. If this occurs, refer to the index at the end of the book to find the topic and read about it.

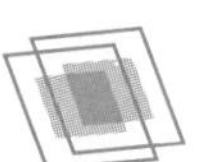

Using the Fingraph® Financial Analyst™ CD-ROM software that accompanies this text to graphically present Oneida's income from operations, as shown in Figure 3, helps to show the company's progress in meeting its profitability objectives. On the left side of the graph are the components of income from operations, beginning with total revenues at the top and ending with income from operations at the bottom. On

Figure 3
Graphical Presentation of Oneida Ltd. Income Statement

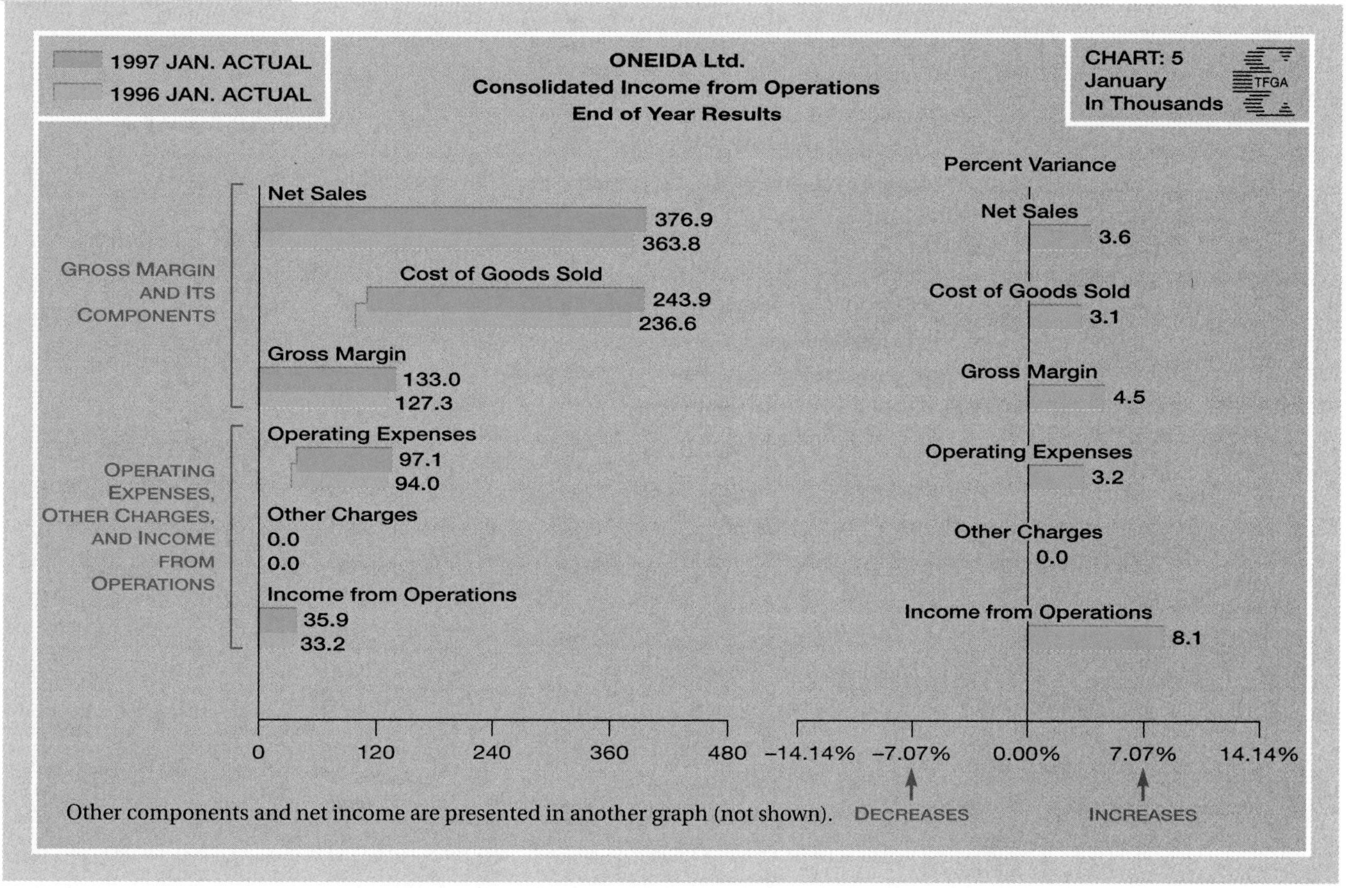

1997 JAN. ACTUAL
1996 JAN. ACTUAL
ONEIDA Ltd.
Consolidated Income from Operations
End of Year Results
CHART: 5
January
In Thousands
TFGA
GROSS MARGIN AND ITS COMPONENTS
Net Sales 376.9 363.8
Cost of Goods Sold 243.9 236.6
Gross Margin 133.0 127.3
OPERATING EXPENSES, OTHER CHARGES, AND INCOME FROM OPERATIONS
Operating Expenses 97.1 94.0
Other Charges 0.0 0.0
Income from Operations 35.9 33.2
0 120 240 360 480
Percent Variance
Net Sales 3.6
Cost of Goods Sold 3.1
Gross Margin 4.5
Operating Expenses 3.2
Other Charges 0.0
Income from Operations 8.1
−14.14% −7.07% 0.00% 7.07% 14.14%
DECREASES
INCREASES
Other components and net income are presented in another graph (not shown).

the right-hand side, the percentage changes in the components are graphed. Increases are shown on the right of the vertical column, and decreases are shown on the left. Income from operations increased by 8.1 percent, whereas gross margin increased by only 4.5 percent because operating expenses increased by only 3.2 percent.

A separate graphical presentation (not shown) is used to show the remainder of the income statement. The income statement shows annual increases in income from continuing operations. Net income, however, is variable. The reason for differences in profitability may be seen visually. The company discontinued (sold) an operation that was profitable in 1995 and 1996 but which had a loss in 1997.

When a company uses the single-step form, as Nike, Inc., the footwear company, does in Exhibit 6, most analysts will still calculate gross margin and income from operations and each component's percentages of revenues, as shown below for Nike, Inc.:

	1997	**Percent**	**1996**	**Percent**
Revenues	$9,186,539	100.0	$6,470,625	100.0
Cost of Sales	5,502,993	59.9	3,906,746	60.4
Gross Margin	$3,683,546	40.1	$2,563,879	39.6
Selling and Administrative	2,303,704	25.1	1,588,612	24.6
Income from Operations	$1,379,842	15.0	$ 975,267	15.0

From this analysis, it may be seen that Nike was able to maintain its profitability as measured by income from operations in percentage terms while increasing sales significantly. Gross margin improved slightly, but selling and administrative expenses increased as a percentage of revenues, offsetting the higher gross margin percentage. This type of analysis is often performed because a majority of public companies use some form of the single-step income statement.

Exhibit 6. Single-Step Income Statement for Nike, Inc.

NIKE, INC., CONSOLIDATED STATEMENTS OF INCOME

(In thousands, except per share data)

	Year Ended May 31		
	1997	1996	1995
Revenues	**$9,186,539**	$6,470,625	$4,760,834
Costs and expenses:			
Costs of sales	**5,502,993**	3,906,746	2,865,280
Selling and administrative	**2,303,704**	1,588,612	1,209,760
Interest expense	**52,343**	39,498	24,208
Other (income)/expense, net	**32,277**	36,679	11,722
	7,891,317	5,571,535	4,110,970
Income before income taxes	**1,295,222**	899,090	649,864
Income taxes	**499,400**	345,900	250,200
Net income	**$ 795,822**	$ 553,190	$ 399,664
Net income per common share	**$ 2.68**	$ 1.88	$ 1.36
Average number of common and common equivalent shares	**297,000**	293,608	294,012

The accompanying notes to consolidated financial statements are an integral part of this statement.

Source: Nike, Inc., *Annual Report,* 1997.

Using Classified Financial Statements

OBJECTIVE 7

Evaluate liquidity and profitability using classified financial statements

Related Text Assignments:
Q: 16, 17, 18, 19, 20
SE: 7, 8
E: 8, 9, 10
P: 4, 5, 8
SD: 5, 6
FRA: 1, 2, 3, 4, 5, 6

Discussion Question: How can a company be earning a profit but be forced out of business? **Answer:** A firm that sells on credit but does not collect its accounts receivable would not have enough cash to pay its obligations. (There are, of course, other valid answers to this question.)

Earlier in this chapter, you learned that financial reporting, according to the Financial Accounting Standards Board, seeks to provide information that is useful in making investment and credit decisions, in judging cash flow prospects, and in understanding business resources, claims to those resources, and changes in them. These objectives are related to two of the more important goals of management—maintaining adequate liquidity and achieving satisfactory profitability—because investors and creditors base their decisions largely on their assessment of a company's potential liquidity and profitability. The following analysis focuses on those two important goals.

In this section a series of charts shows average ratios for six industries based on data obtained from *Industry Norms and Key Business Ratios,* a publication of Dun and Bradstreet. There are two examples from service industries, advertising agencies and interstate trucking; two examples from merchandising industries, auto and home suppliers and grocery stores; and two examples from manufacturing, pharmaceuticals and tableware. Shafer Auto Parts Company, the example used in this chapter, falls into the auto and home supply industry.

Evaluating Liquidity

Liquidity means having enough money on hand to pay bills when they are due and to take care of unexpected needs for cash. Two measures of liquidity are working capital and the current ratio.

Working Capital The first measure, working capital, is the amount by which total current assets exceed total current liabilities. This is an important measure of liquidity because current liabilities are debts that must be paid or obligations that must be performed within one year and current assets are assets that will be realized in cash or used up within one year or one operating cycle, whichever is longer. By definition, current liabilities are paid out of current assets. So the excess of current assets over current liabilities is the net current assets on hand to continue business operations. It is the working capital that can be used to buy inventory, obtain credit, and finance expanded sales. Lack of working capital can lead to a company's failure.

Point to Emphasize: It is imperative that accounts be classified correctly before the ratios are computed. If accounts are not classified correctly, the ratios will not be correct.

For Shafer Auto Parts Company, working capital is computed as follows:

Current assets	$124,356
Less current liabilities	42,683
Working capital	$ 81,673

Current Ratio The second measure of liquidity, the current ratio, is closely related to working capital and is believed by many bankers and other creditors to be a good indicator of a company's ability to pay its bills and to repay outstanding loans. The current ratio is the ratio of current assets to current liabilities. For Shafer Auto Parts Company, it would be computed like this:

$$\text{Current Ratio} = \frac{\text{Current Assets}}{\text{Current Liabilities}} = \frac{\$124,356}{\$42,683} = 2.9$$

Thus Shafer has $2.90 of current assets for each $1.00 of current liabilities. Is that good or bad? The answer requires the comparison of this year's ratio with those of earlier years and with similar measures for successful companies in the same industry. The average current ratio varies widely from industry to industry, as shown in Figure 4. For interstate trucking companies, which have no merchandise inventory, the current ratio is 1.4. In contrast, auto and home supply companies, which carry large merchandise inventories, have an average current ratio of 2.1. Shafer Auto

Discussion Question: Why may a low current ratio be a sign of trouble? **Answer:** The business may have difficulty paying its obligations.

Business-World Example: Some successful companies, such as McDonald's, manage to have very low current ratios by carefully planning their cash flows.

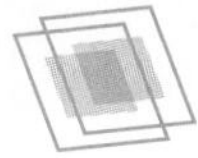

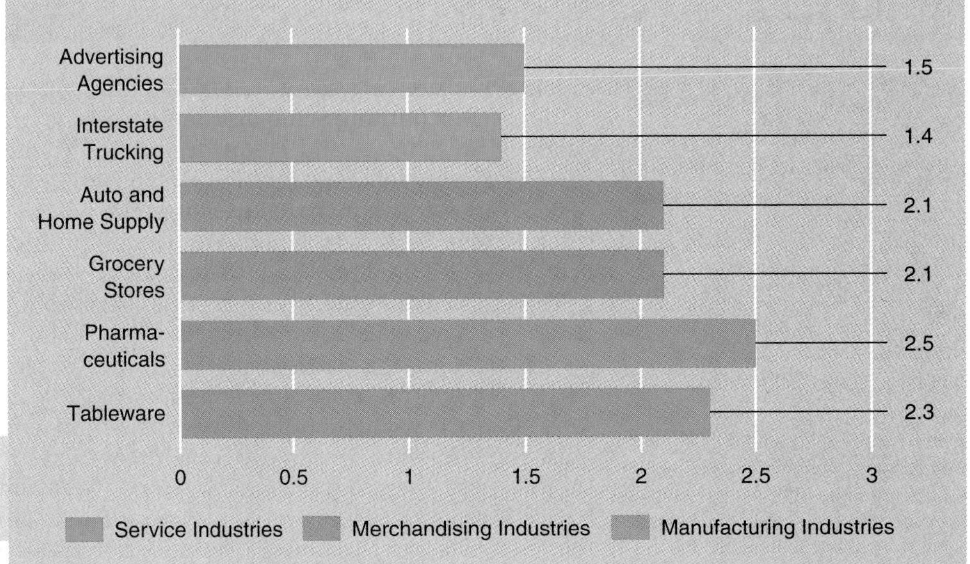

Figure 4
Average Current Ratio for Selected Industries

Source: Data from Dun and Bradstreet, *Industry Norms and Key Business Ratios,* 1996–97.

Discussion Question: Why is it inadvisable to have too high a current ratio? **Answer:** The firm could probably use the excess funds more effectively to increase its overall profit.

Parts Company, with a ratio of 2.9, exceeds the average for its industry. A very low current ratio, of course, can be unfavorable, but so can a very high one. The latter may indicate that a company is not using its assets effectively.

Evaluating Profitability

Just as important as paying bills on time is profitability—the ability to earn a satisfactory income. As a goal, profitability competes with liquidity for managerial attention because liquid assets, although important, are not the best profit-producing resources. Cash, for example, means purchasing power, but a satisfactory profit can be made only if purchasing power is used to buy profit-producing (and less liquid) assets, such as inventory and long-term assets.

Among the common measures of a company's ability to earn income are (1) profit margin, (2) asset turnover, (3) return on assets, (4) debt to equity, and (5) return on equity. To evaluate a company meaningfully, one must relate its profit performance to its past performance and prospects for the future as well as to the averages for other companies in the same industry.

Profit Margin

The profit margin shows the percentage of each sales dollar that results in net income. It is figured by dividing net income by net sales. It should not be confused with gross margin, which is not a ratio but rather the amount by which revenues exceed the cost of goods sold.

Shafer Auto Parts Company has a profit margin of 6.2 percent:

$$\text{Profit Margin} = \frac{\text{Net Income}}{\text{Net Sales}} = \frac{\$17{,}881}{\$289{,}656} = .062\ (6.2\%)$$

On each dollar of net sales, Shafer Auto Parts Company made 6.2 cents. A difference of 1 or 2 percent in a company's profit margin can mean the difference between a fair year and a very profitable one.

Asset Turnover

Asset turnover measures how efficiently assets are used to produce sales. Computed by dividing net sales by average total assets, it shows how many dollars of sales were generated by each dollar of assets. A company with a

Discussion Question: How could a company increase its asset turnover ratio? **Answer**: By managing assets better—by carrying minimum quantities of inventory and having efficient ordering procedures to avoid running out of merchandise.

Point to Emphasize: Average total assets equal assets at the beginning of the year plus assets at the end of the year, divided by 2.

higher asset turnover uses its assets more productively than one with a lower asset turnover. Average total assets is computed by adding total assets at the beginning of the year to total assets at the end of the year and dividing by 2.

Assuming that total assets for Shafer Auto Parts Company were \$148,620 at the beginning of the year, its asset turnover is computed as follows:

$$\text{Asset Turnover} = \frac{\text{Net Sales}}{\text{Average Total Assets}}$$

$$= \frac{\$289{,}656}{(\$158{,}916 + \$148{,}620) \div 2}$$

$$= \frac{\$289{,}656}{\$153{,}768} = 1.9 \text{ times}$$

Shafer Auto Parts Company produces \$1.90 in sales for each \$1.00 invested in average total assets. This ratio shows a meaningful relationship between an income statement figure and a balance sheet figure.

Return on Assets Both the profit margin and the asset turnover ratios have some limitations. The profit margin ratio does not take into consideration the assets necessary to produce income, and the asset turnover ratio does not take into account the amount of income produced. The return on assets ratio overcomes those deficiencies by relating net income to average total assets. It is computed like this:

$$\text{Return on Assets} = \frac{\text{Net Income}}{\text{Average Total Assets}}$$

$$= \frac{\$17{,}881}{(\$158{,}916 + \$148{,}620) \div 2}$$

$$= \frac{\$17{,}881}{\$153{,}768} = .116\ (11.6\%)$$

For each dollar invested, Shafer Auto Parts Company's assets generated 11.6 cents of net income. This ratio indicates the income-generating strength (profit margin) of the company's resources and how efficiently the company is using all its assets (asset turnover).

Return on assets, then, combines profit margin and asset turnover:

$$\frac{\text{Net Income}}{\text{Net Sales}} \times \frac{\text{Net Sales}}{\text{Average Total Assets}} = \frac{\text{Net Income}}{\text{Average Total Assets}}$$

$$\text{Profit Margin} \times \text{Asset Turnover} = \text{Return on Assets}$$

$$6.2\% \times 1.9 \text{ times} = 11.8\%^{*}$$

*The slight difference between 11.6 and 11.8 is due to rounding.

Thus a company's management can improve overall profitability by increasing the profit margin, the asset turnover, or both. Similarly, in evaluating a company's overall profitability, the financial statement user must consider the interaction of both ratios to produce return on assets.

Careful study of Figures 5, 6, and 7 shows the different ways in which the selected industries combine profit margin and asset turnover to produce return on assets. For instance, advertising agencies and tableware have a similar return on assets, but they achieve it in very different ways. Advertising agencies have a small profit margin, 3.2 percent, which when multiplied by a higher asset turnover, 4.0 times, gives a return on assets of 12.8 percent. Tableware, on the other hand, has a higher profit margin, 5.7 percent, and a lower asset turnover, 2.3 times, and produces a return on assets of 13.1 percent.

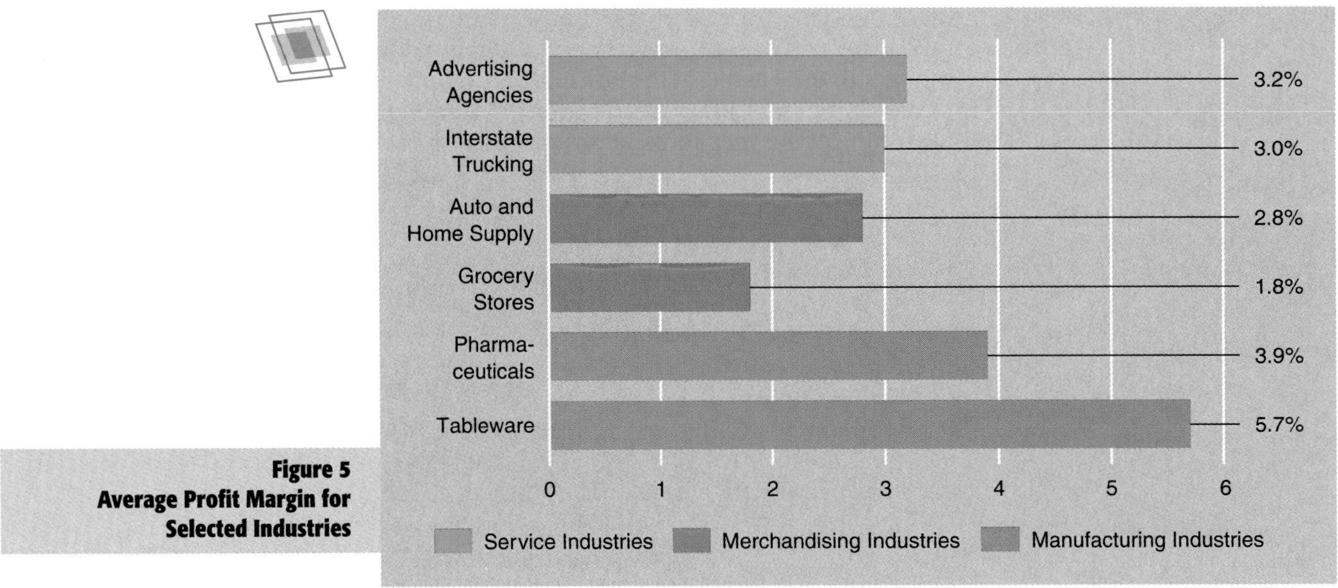

Figure 5
Average Profit Margin for Selected Industries

Source: Data from Dun and Bradstreet, *Industry Norms and Key Business Ratios,* 1996–97.

Shafer Auto Parts Company's profit margin of 6.2 percent is well above the auto and home supply industry average of 2.8 percent, but its turnover of 1.9 times lags behind the industry average of 2.8 times. Shafer is sacrificing asset turnover to achieve a high profit margin. It is clear that the strategy is working, because Shafer's return on assets of 11.6 percent exceeds the industry average of 7.8 percent.

Debt to Equity Another useful measure is the debt to equity ratio, which shows the proportion of the company financed by creditors in comparison to that financed by the owner. This ratio is computed by dividing total liabilities by owner's equity. Since the balance sheets of many companies do not show total liabilities, a short way of determining total liabilities is to deduct owner's equity from total

Point to Emphasize: A company with a low debt to equity ratio has a better chance of surviving in rough times. Debt requires additional expenses (interest) that must be paid.

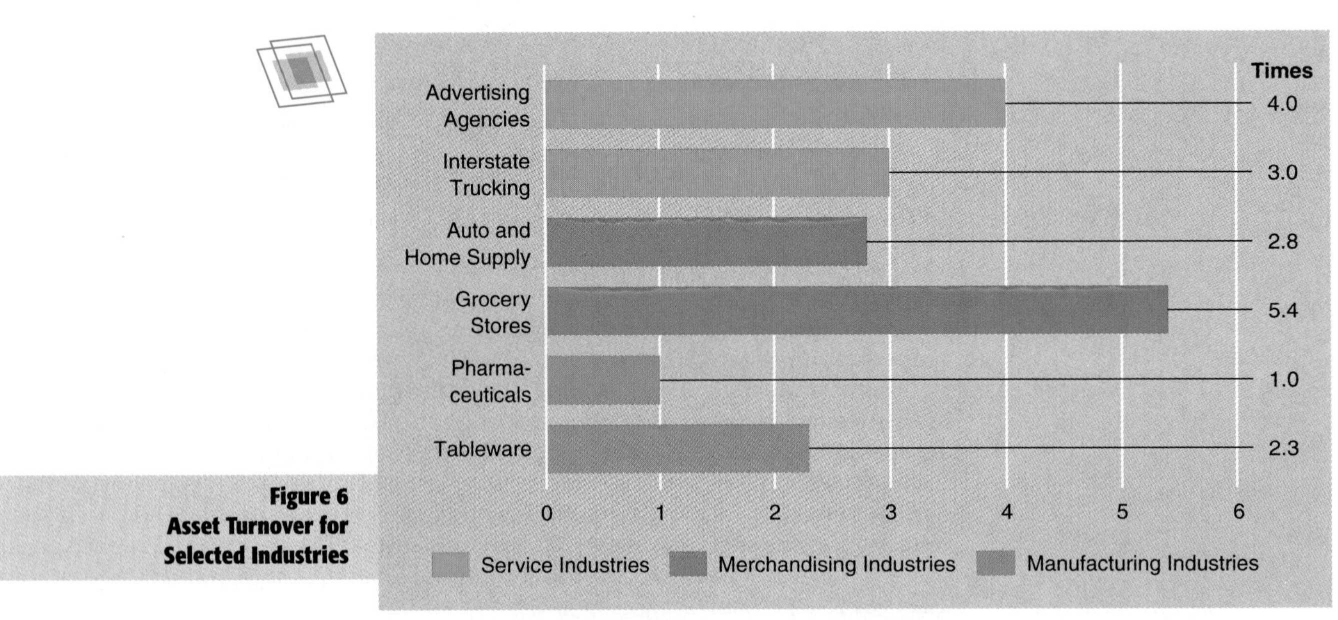

Figure 6
Asset Turnover for Selected Industries

Source: Data from Dun and Bradstreet, *Industry Norms and Key Business Ratios,* 1996–97.

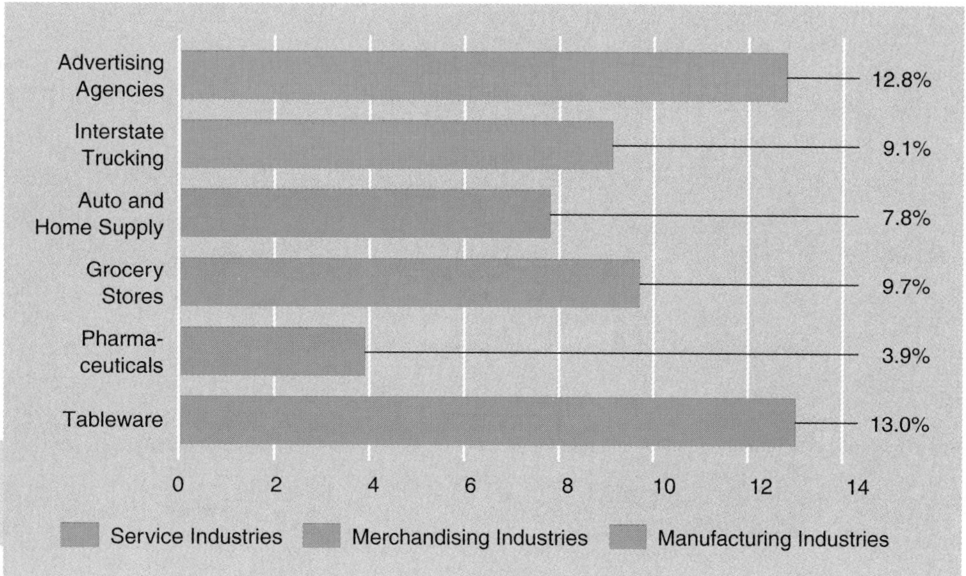

Figure 7
Return on Assets for Selected Industries

Source: Data from Dun and Bradstreet, *Industry Norms and Key Business Ratios,* 1996–97.

assets. A debt to equity ratio of 1.0 means that total liabilities equal owner's equity—that half of the company's assets are financed by creditors. A ratio of .5 would mean that one-third of the assets are financed by creditors. A company with a high debt to equity ratio is more vulnerable in poor economic times because it must continue to repay creditors. Owner's investments, on the other hand, do not have to be repaid, and withdrawals can be deferred if the company is suffering because of a poor economy.

The Shafer Auto Parts Company debt to equity ratio is computed as follows:

$$\text{Debt to Equity} = \frac{\text{Total Liabilities}}{\text{Owner's Equity}} = \frac{\$60{,}483}{\$98{,}433} = .614\ (61.4\%)$$

With a debt to equity ratio of 61.4 percent, which is less than 100 percent, Shafer Auto Parts Company receives less than half its financing from creditors and more than half from its owner, Fred Shafer.

The debt to equity ratio does not fit neatly into either the liquidity or the profitability category. It is clearly very important to liquidity analysis because it relates to debt and its repayment. However, the debt to equity ratio is also relevant to profitability for two reasons. First, creditors are interested in the proportion of the business that is debt financed because the more debt a company has, the more profit it must earn to protect the payment of interest to its creditors. Second, an owner is interested in the proportion of the business that is debt financed. The amount of interest that must be paid on the debt affects the amount of profit that is left to provide a return on the owner's investment. The debt to equity ratio also shows how much expansion is possible by borrowing additional long-term funds. Figure 8 shows that the debt to equity ratio in our selected industries varies from a low of 66.9 percent in the pharmaceutical industry to a high of 140.7 percent in interstate trucking.

Return on Equity Of course, Fred Shafer is interested in how much he has earned on his investment in the business. His return on equity is measured by the ratio of net income to average owner's equity. Taking the ending owner's equity from the balance sheet and assuming that beginning owner's equity is $100,553, Shafer's return on equity is computed as follows:

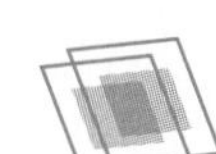

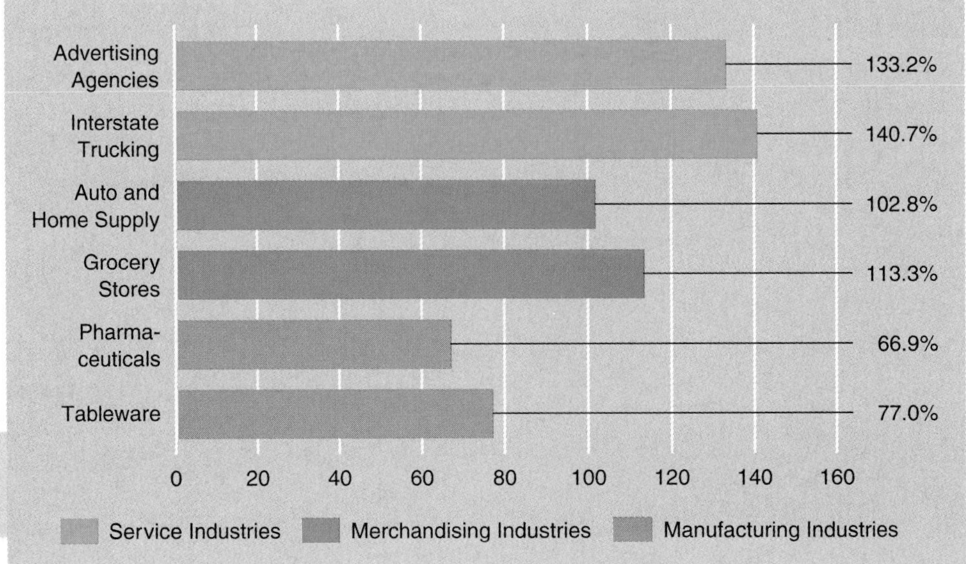

Figure 8
Average Debt to Equity for Selected Industries

Source: Data from Dun and Bradstreet, *Industry Norms and Key Business Ratios,* 1996–97.

$$\text{Return on Equity} = \frac{\text{Net Income}}{\text{Average Owner's Equity}}$$

$$= \frac{\$17{,}881}{(\$100{,}553 + \$98{,}433) \div 2}$$

$$= \frac{\$17{,}881}{\$99{,}493} = .180\ (18.0\%)$$

In 20xx, Shafer Auto Parts Company earned 18.0 cents for every dollar invested by the owner, Fred Shafer.

Whether or not this is an acceptable return depends on several factors, such as how much the company earned in prior years and how much other companies in the same industry earned. As measured by return on equity (Figure 9), advertising agencies are the most profitable of our sample industries, with a return on equity of 29.8 percent. Shafer Auto Parts Company's average return on equity of 18.0 percent exceeds the average of 15.9 percent for the auto and home supply industry.

Graphing Ratio Analysis Using the Fingraph® Financial Analyst™ CD-ROM software that accompanies this text to graphically present Oneida's profitability ratios involving net income, shown in Figure 10, helps to see visually the progress of

BUSINESS BULLETIN: BUSINESS PRACTICE

To what level of profitability should a company aspire? At one time, a company earning a 20 percent return on equity was considered among the elite. Walt Disney, Wal-Mart, Coca-Cola, and a few other companies were able to achieve this level of profitability. However, *The Wall Street Journal* reports that in the first quarter of 1995, for the first time, the average company of the Standard & Poor's 500 companies made a return on equity of 20.12 percent. It says that this performance is "akin to the average ball player hitting .350." [9] This means that stockholders' equity will double every four years. Why did this happen? First, a good business environment and cost cutting led to more profitable operations. Second, special charges and other accounting transactions reduced the amount of stockholders' equity for many companies.

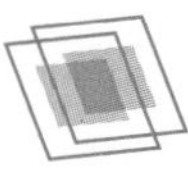

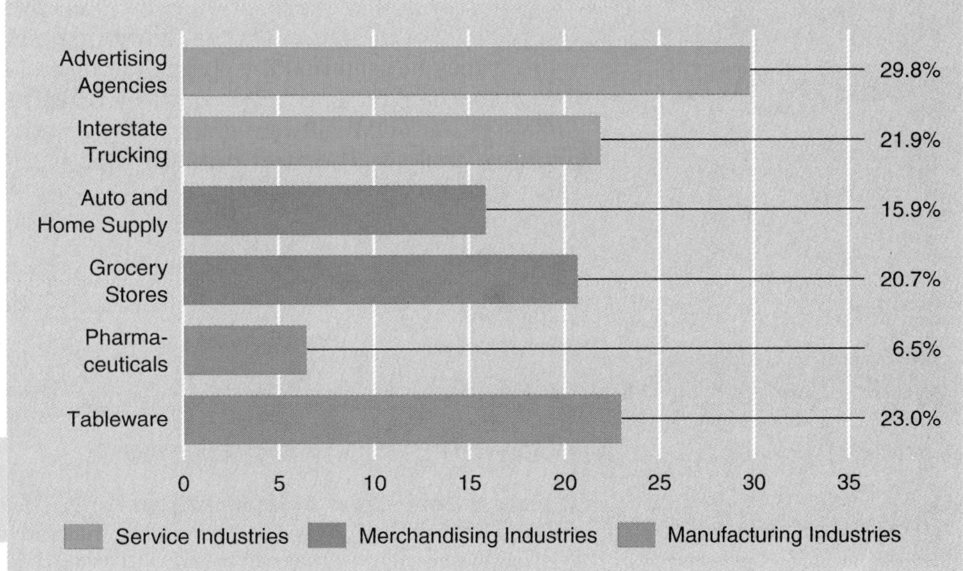

Figure 9
Average Return on Equity for Selected Industries

Source: Data from Dun and Bradstreet, *Industry Norms and Key Business Ratios,* 1996–97.

Figure 10
Graphical Presentation of Oneida Ltd. Profitability Ratios

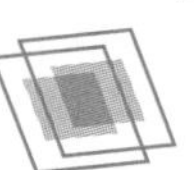

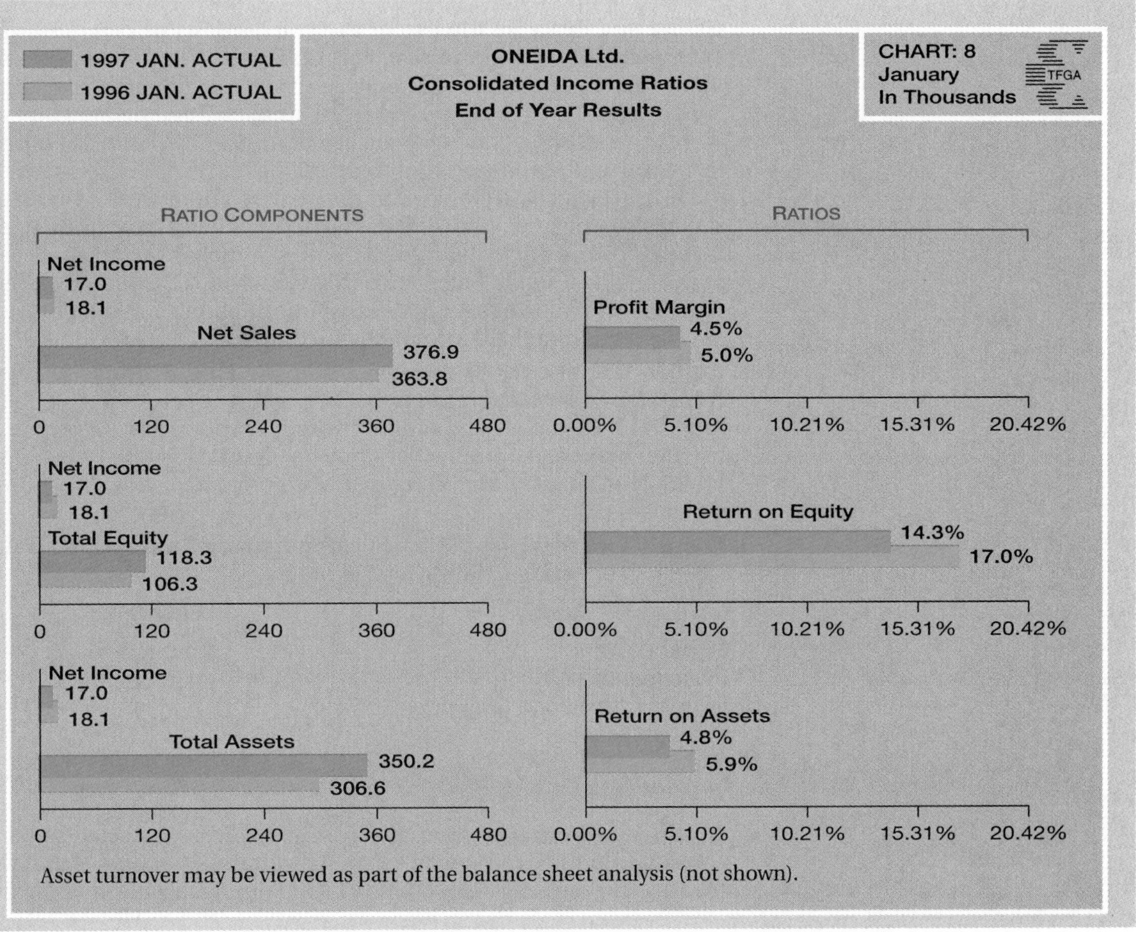

the company in meeting its profitability objectives. On the left of the figure are the components of the ratios. On the right of the figure are the ratios for the past two years. It may be seen that the changes in return on equity and return on assets are linked to changes in profit margin or asset turnover. The Fingraph® Financial Analyst™ CD-ROM software graphs all the ratios used in this book and provides narrative analysis. The asset turnover ratio is shown graphically with the balance sheet analysis.

Chapter Review

REVIEW OF LEARNING OBJECTIVES

1. **State the objectives of financial reporting.** The objectives of financial reporting are (1) to furnish the information needed to make investment and credit decisions; (2) to provide information that can be used to assess cash flow prospects; and (3) to provide information about business resources, claims to those resources, and changes in them.
2. **State the qualitative characteristics of accounting information and describe their interrelationships.** Understandability depends on the knowledge of the user and the ability of the accountant to provide useful information. Usefulness is a function of two primary characteristics: relevance and reliability. Information is relevant when it affects the outcome of a decision. Information that is relevant has feedback value and predictive value and is timely. To be reliable, information must represent what it is supposed to represent, must be verifiable, and must be neutral.
3. **Define and describe the use of the conventions of *comparability* and *consistency, materiality, conservatism, full disclosure,* and *cost-benefit.*** Because accountants' measurements are not exact, certain conventions have come to be applied in current practice to help users interpret financial statements. One of these conventions is consistency, which requires the use of the same accounting procedures from period to period and enhances the comparability of financial statements. The second is materiality, which has to do with the relative importance of an item. The third is conservatism, which entails using the procedure that is least likely to overstate assets and income. The fourth is full disclosure, which means including all relevant information in the financial statements. The fifth is cost-benefit, which suggests that above a minimum level of information, additional information should be provided only if the benefits derived from the information exceed the costs of providing it.
4. **Explain management's responsibility for ethical financial reporting and define *fraudulent financial reporting.*** Management is responsible for the preparation of financial statements in accordance with generally accepted accounting principles and for the internal controls that provide assurance that this objective is achieved. Fraudulent financial reporting is the intentional preparation of misleading financial statements.
5. **Identify and describe the basic components of a classified balance sheet.** A classified balance sheet is subdivided as follows:

Assets	Liabilities
Current Assets	Current Liabilities
Investments	Long-Term Liabilities
Property, Plant, and Equipment	**Owner's Equity**
Intangible Assets	(Content depends on the form of business)
(Other Assets)	

A current asset is an asset that can reasonably be expected to be realized in cash or consumed during the next year or the normal operating cycle, whichever is longer. Investments are long-term assets that are not usually used in the normal operation of a business. Property, plant, and equipment are long-term assets that are used in day-to-day operations. Intangible assets are long-term assets whose value stems from the rights or privileges they extend to the owner. A current liability is a liability that can reasonably be expected to be paid or performed during the next year or the normal operating cycle, whichever is longer. Long-term liabilities are debts that fall due more than one year in the future or beyond the normal operating cycle. The equity section for a corporation differs from that of a proprietorship in that it has subdivisions of contributed capital (the value of assets invested by stockholders) and retained earnings (stockholders' claim to assets earned from operations and reinvested in operations).

6. **Prepare multistep and single-step classified income statements.** Condensed income statements for external reporting can be in multistep or single-step form. The multistep form arrives at net income through a series of steps; the single-step form arrives at net income in a single step. There is usually a separate section in the multistep form for other revenues and expenses.
7. **Evaluate liquidity and profitability using classified financial statements.** One important use of classified financial statements is to evaluate a company's liquidity and profitability. Two simple measures of liquidity are working capital and the current ratio. Five simple measures of profitability are profit margin, asset turnover, return on assets, debt to equity, and return on equity.

REVIEW OF CONCEPTS AND TERMINOLOGY

The following concepts and terms were introduced in this chapter:

LO 7 **Asset turnover:** A measure of profitability that shows how efficiently assets are used to produce sales; net sales divided by average total assets.

LO 5 **Classified financial statements:** General-purpose external financial statements divided into useful subcategories.

LO 3 **Comparability:** The convention of presenting information in a way that enables decision makers to recognize similarities, differences, and trends over different time periods or between different companies.

LO 6 **Condensed financial statements:** Financial statements for external reporting that present only the major categories of information.

LO 3 **Conservatism:** The convention that requires that, when faced with equally acceptable alternatives, accountants must choose the one least likely to overstate assets and income.

LO 3 **Consistency:** The convention that requires that an accounting procedure, once adopted, not be changed from one period to another unless users are informed of the change.

LO 5 **Contributed capital:** The accounts that reflect the stockholders' investment in a corporation. Also called *paid-in capital.*

LO 3 **Conventions:** Rules of thumb or customary ways of recording transactions or preparing financial statements.

LO 3 **Cost-benefit:** The convention that holds that benefits gained from providing accounting information should be greater than the costs of providing that information.

LO 5 **Current assets:** Cash or other assets that are reasonably expected to be converted to cash, sold, or consumed within one year or within the normal operating cycle, whichever is longer.

LO 5 **Current liabilities:** Obligations due to be paid or performed within one year or within the normal operating cycle, whichever is longer.

LO 7 **Current ratio:** A measure of liquidity; current assets divided by current liabilities.

LO 7 **Debt to equity:** A ratio that measures the relationship of assets financed by creditors to those financed by owners; total liabilities divided by owner's equity.

LO 4 **Fraudulent financial reporting:** The intentional preparation of misleading financial statements.

LO 3 **Full disclosure:** The convention that requires that financial statements and their notes present all information relevant to the users' understanding of the company's financial condition.

LO 6 **Income from operations:** Gross margin less operating expenses.

LO 5 **Intangible assets:** Long-term assets that have no physical substance but that have a value based on rights or privileges that belong to their owner.

LO 5 **Investments:** Assets, usually long term, that are not used in the normal operation of a business and that management does not intend to convert to cash within the next year.

LO 7 **Liquidity:** Having enough money on hand to pay bills when they are due and to take care of unexpected needs for cash.

LO 5 **Long-term liabilities:** Debts that fall due more than one year in the future or beyond the normal operating cycle, or that are to be paid out of noncurrent assets.

LO 3 **Materiality:** The convention that refers to the relative importance of an item or event in a financial statement and its influence on the decisions of the users of financial statements.

LO 6 **Multistep form:** A form of condensed income statement that arrives at net income in the same steps as a detailed income statement but that presents only the totals of significant categories.

LO 5 **Other assets:** The balance sheet category that may include various types of assets other than current assets and property, plant, and equipment.

LO 6 **Other revenues and expenses:** The section of a multistep income statement that includes nonoperating revenues and expenses.

LO 7 **Profitability:** The ability of a business to earn a satisfactory income.

LO 7 **Profit margin:** A measure of profitability that shows the percentage of each sales dollar that results in net income; net income divided by net sales.

LO 5 **Property, plant, and equipment:** Tangible long-term assets used in the continuing operation of a business. Also called *operating assets, fixed assets, tangible assets, long-lived assets,* or *plant assets.*

LO 2 **Qualitative characteristics:** Standards for judging the information that accountants give to decision makers.

LO 2 **Relevance:** The qualitative characteristic of information bearing directly on the outcome of a decision.

LO 2 **Reliability:** The qualitative characteristic of information being representationally faithful, verifiable, and neutral.

LO 5 **Retained Earnings:** The account that reflects the stockholders' claim to the assets earned from operations and reinvested in corporate operations. Also called *Earned Capital.*

LO 7 **Return on assets:** A measure of profitability that shows how efficiently a company uses its assets to produce income; net income divided by average total assets.

LO 7 **Return on equity:** A measure of profitability that relates the amount earned by a business to the owner's investment in the business; net income divided by average owner's equity.

LO 6 **Single-step form:** A form of condensed income statement that arrives at net income in a single step.

LO 2 **Understandability:** The qualitative characteristic of communicating an intended meaning.

LO 2 **Usefulness:** The qualitative characteristic of information being relevant and reliable.

LO 7 **Working capital:** A measure of liquidity equal to the current assets on hand to continue business operations; total current assets minus total current liabilities.

REVIEW PROBLEM

Analyzing Liquidity and Profitability Using Ratios

LO 7 Flavin Shirt Company has faced increased competition from overseas shirtmakers in recent years. Key information for the last two years is as follows:

	20x2	20x1
Current Assets	$ 200,000	$ 170,000
Total Assets	880,000	710,000
Current Liabilities	90,000	50,000
Long-Term Liabilities	150,000	50,000
Owner's Equity	640,000	610,000
Sales	1,200,000	1,050,000
Net Income	60,000	80,000

Total assets and owner's equity at the beginning of 20x1 were $690,000 and $590,000, respectively.

REQUIRED

Use (1) liquidity analysis and (2) profitability analysis to document the declining financial position of Flavin Shirt Company.

ANSWER TO REVIEW PROBLEM

1. Liquidity analysis

	Current Assets	Current Liabilities	Working Capital	Current Ratio
20x1	$170,000	$50,000	$120,000	3.4
20x2	200,000	90,000	110,000	2.2
Decrease in working capital			($ 10,000)	
Decrease in current ratio				1.2

Both working capital and the current ratio declined because, although current assets increased by $30,000 ($200,000 − $170,000), current liabilities increased by a greater amount, $40,000 ($90,000 − $50,000), from 20x1 to 20x2.

2. Profitability analysis

	Net Income	Sales	Profit Margin	Average Total Assets	Asset Turnover	Return on Assets	Average Owner's Equity	Return on Equity
20x1	$80,000	$1,050,000	7.6%	$700,000[1]	1.50	11.4%	$600,000[3]	13.3%
20x2	60,000	1,200,000	5.0%	795,000[2]	1.51	7.5%	625,000[4]	9.6%
Increase (decrease)	($20,000)	$ 150,000	(2.6%)	$ 95,000	0.01	(3.9%)	$ 25,000	(3.7%)

[1]($690,000 + $710,000) ÷ 2
[2]($710,000 + $880,000) ÷ 2
[3]($590,000 + $610,000) ÷ 2
[4]($610,000 + $640,000) ÷ 2

Net income decreased by $20,000 despite an increase in sales of $150,000 and an increase in average total assets of $95,000. The results were decreases in profit margin from 7.6 percent to 5.0 percent and in return on assets from 11.4 percent to 7.5 percent. Asset turnover showed almost no change and so did not contribute to the decline in profitability. The decrease in return on equity from 13.3 percent to 9.6 percent was not as great as the decrease in return on assets because the growth in total assets was financed by debt instead of owner's equity, as shown by the following capital structure analysis.

	Total Liabilities	Owner's Equity	Debt to Equity Ratio
20x1	$100,000	$610,000	16.4%
20x2	240,000	640,000	37.5%
Increase	$140,000	$ 30,000	21.1%

Total liabilities increased by $140,000 while owner's equity increased by $30,000. As a result, the amount of the business financed by debt in relation to the amount of the business financed by owner's equity increased from 20x1 to 20x2.

Chapter Assignments

BUILDING YOUR KNOWLEDGE FOUNDATION

Questions

1. What are the three objectives of financial reporting?
2. What are the qualitative characteristics of accounting information, and what is their significance?
3. What are the accounting conventions? How does each help in the interpretation of financial information?
4. Who is responsible for preparing reliable financial statements, and what is a principal way of fulfilling the responsibility?
5. What is the purpose of classified financial statements?
6. What are four common categories of assets?
7. What criteria must an asset meet to be classified as current? Under what condition is an asset considered current even though it will not be realized as cash within a year? What are two examples of assets that fall into this category?
8. In what order should current assets be listed?
9. What is the difference between a short-term investment in the current assets section and a security in the investments section of the balance sheet?
10. What is an intangible asset? Give at least three examples.
11. Name the two major categories of liabilities.
12. What are the primary differences between the equity section of the balance sheet for a sole proprietorship or partnership and the corresponding section for a corporation?
13. Explain the difference between contributed capital and retained earnings.
14. Explain how the multistep form of income statement differs from the single-step form. What are the relative merits of each?
15. Why are other revenues and expenses separated from operating revenues and expenses in the multistep income statement?

16. Define *liquidity* and name two measures of liquidity.
17. How is the current ratio computed and why is it important?
18. Which is the more important goal—liquidity or profitability? Explain your answer.
19. Name five measures of profitability.
20. Evaluate the following statement: "Return on assets is a better measure of profitability than profit margin."

Short Exercises

SE 1. LO 3 *Accounting Conventions*

State which of the accounting conventions—comparability and consistency, materiality, conservatism, full disclosure, or cost-benefit—is being followed in each case below.

1. Management provides detailed information about the company's long-term debt in the notes to the financial statements.
2. A company does not account separately for discounts received for prompt payment of accounts payable because few such transactions occur and the total amount of the discounts is small.
3. Management eliminates a weekly report on property, plant, and equipment acquisitions and disposals because no one finds it useful.
4. A company follows the policy of recognizing a loss on inventory when the market value of an item falls below its cost but does nothing if the market value rises.
5. When several accounting methods are acceptable, management chooses a single method and follows that method from year to year.

SE 2. LO 5 *Classification of Accounts: Balance Sheet*

Tell whether each of the following accounts is a current asset; an investment; property, plant, and equipment; an intangible asset; a current liability; a long-term liability; owner's equity; or not on the balance sheet.

1. Delivery Trucks
2. Accounts Payable
3. Note Payable (due in ninety days)
4. Delivery Expense
5. Y. San, Capital
6. Prepaid Insurance
7. Trademark
8. Investment to Be Held Six Months
9. Interest Payable
10. Factory Not Used in Business

SE 3. LO 5 *Classified Balance Sheet*

Using the following accounts, prepare a classified balance sheet at May 31 year end: Accounts Payable, \$400; Accounts Receivable, \$550; Accumulated Depreciation, Equipment, \$350; Cash, \$100; Equipment, \$2,000; Franchise, \$100; Investments (long-term), \$250; Merchandise Inventory, \$300; Notes Payable (long-term), \$200; B. Pamp, Capital, ?; and Wages Payable, \$50.

SE 4. LO 6 *Classification of Accounts: Income Statement*

Tell whether each of the following accounts is part of net sales, cost of goods sold, operating expenses, other revenues and expenses, or not on the income statement.

1. Delivery Expense
2. Interest Expense
3. Unearned Revenue
4. Sales Returns and Allowances
5. Purchases
6. Depreciation Expense
7. Investment Income
8. Withdrawals

SE 5. LO 6 *Single-Step Income Statement*

Using the following accounts, prepare a single-step income statement at May 31 year end: Cost of Goods Sold, \$280; General Expenses, \$150; Interest Expense, \$70; Interest Income, \$30; Net Sales, \$800; and Selling Expenses, \$185.

SE 6. LO 6 *Multistep Income Statement*

Using the accounts presented in **SE 5,** prepare a multistep income statement.

SE 7. LO 7 *Liquidity Ratios*

Using the following information from a year-end balance sheet, compute working capital and the current ratio.

Accounts Payable	$ 7,000
Accounts Receivable	10,000
Cash	4,000
V. Smyth, Capital	20,000
Marketable Securities	2,000
Merchandise Inventory	12,000
Notes Payable in Three Years	13,000
Property, Plant, and Equipment	40,000

SE 8. LO 7 *Profitability Ratios*

Using the following information from a balance sheet and an income statement, compute the (1) profit margin, (2) asset turnover, (3) return on assets, (4) debt to equity, and (5) return on equity. (The previous year's total assets were $100,000 and owner's equity was $70,000.)

Total Assets	$120,000
Total Liabilities	30,000
Total Owner's Equity	90,000
Net Sales	130,000
Cost of Goods Sold	70,000
Operating Expenses	45,000

Exercises

E 1. LO 3 *Accounting Concepts and Conventions*

Each of the statements below violates a convention in accounting. State which of the following accounting conventions is violated: comparability and consistency, materiality, conservatism, full disclosure, or cost-benefit:

1. A series of reports that are time-consuming and expensive to prepare is presented to the board of directors each month even though the reports are never used.
2. A company changes its method of accounting for depreciation.
3. The company in **2** does not indicate in the financial statements that the method of depreciation was changed, nor does it specify the effect of the change on net income.
4. A new office building next to the factory is debited to the Factory account because it represents a fairly small dollar amount in relation to the factory.
5. The asset account for a pickup truck still used in the business is written down to what the truck could be sold for even though the carrying value under conventional depreciation methods is higher.

E 2. LO 1 LO 2 LO 3 *Financial Accounting Concepts*

The lettered items below represent a classification scheme for the concepts of financial accounting. Match each numbered term with the letter of the category in which it belongs.

a. Decision makers (users of accounting information)
b. Business activities or entities relevant to accounting measurement
c. Objectives of accounting information
d. Accounting measurement considerations
e. Accounting processing considerations
f. Qualitative characteristics
g. Accounting conventions
h. Financial statements

1. Conservatism
2. Verifiability
3. Statement of cash flows
4. Materiality
5. Reliability
6. Recognition
7. Cost-benefit
8. Understandability
9. Business transactions
10. Consistency

11. Full disclosure
12. Furnishing information that is useful to investors and creditors
13. Specific business entities
14. Classification
15. Management
16. Neutrality
17. Internal accounting control
18. Valuation
19. Investors
20. Timeliness
21. Relevance
22. Furnishing information that is useful in assessing cash flow prospects

E 3. LO 5 *Classification of Accounts: Balance Sheet*

The lettered items below represent a classification scheme for a balance sheet, and the numbered items are account titles. Match each account with the letter of the category in which it belongs.

a. Current assets
b. Investments
c. Property, plant, and equipment
d. Intangible assets
e. Current liabilities
f. Long-term liabilities
g. Owner's equity
h. Not on balance sheet

1. Patent
2. Building Held for Sale
3. Prepaid Rent
4. Wages Payable
5. Note Payable in Five Years
6. Building Used in Operations
7. Fund Held to Pay Off Long-Term Debt
8. Inventory
9. Prepaid Insurance
10. Depreciation Expense
11. Accounts Receivable
12. Interest Expense
13. Unearned Revenue
14. Short-Term Investments
15. Accumulated Depreciation
16. B. Dobecki, Capital

E 4. LO 5 *Classified Balance Sheet Preparation*

The following data pertain to a corporation: Cash, $31,200; Investment in Six-Month Government Securities, $16,400; Accounts Receivable, $38,000; Inventory, $40,000; Prepaid Rent, $1,200; Investment in Corporate Securities (long-term), $20,000; Land, $8,000; Building, $70,000; Accumulated Depreciation, Building, $14,000; Equipment, $152,000; Accumulated Depreciation, Equipment, $17,000; Copyright, $6,200; Accounts Payable, $51,000; Revenue Received in Advance, $2,800; Bonds Payable, $60,000; Common Stock, $10 par, 10,000 shares authorized, issued, and outstanding, $100,000; Paid-in Capital in Excess of Par Value, $50,000; and Retained Earnings, $88,200.

Prepare a classified balance sheet; omit the heading.

E 5. LO 6 *Classification of Accounts: Income Statement*

Using the classification scheme below for a multistep income statement, match each account with the letter of the category in which it belongs.

a. Net sales
b. Cost of goods sold
c. Selling expenses
d. General and administrative expenses
e. Other revenues and expenses
f. Not on income statement

1. Purchases
2. Sales Discounts
3. Merchandise Inventory (beginning)
4. Interest Income
5. Advertising Expense
6. Office Salaries Expense
7. Freight Out Expense
8. Prepaid Insurance
9. Utilities Expense
10. Sales Salaries Expense
11. Rent Expense
12. Purchases Returns and Allowances
13. Freight In
14. Depreciation Expense, Delivery Equipment
15. Taxes Payable
16. Interest Expense

LO 6 **E 6.** *Preparation of Income Statements*

The following data pertain to a sole proprietorship: Sales, $405,000; Cost of Goods Sold, $220,000; Selling Expenses, $90,000; General and Administrative Expenses, $60,000; Interest Expense, $4,000; and Interest Income, $3,000.

1. Prepare a condensed single-step income statement.
2. Prepare a condensed multistep income statement.

LO 6 **E 7.** *Condensed Multistep Income Statement*

A condensed single-step income statement appears below. Present this information in a condensed multistep income statement, and tell what insights can be obtained from the multistep form as opposed to the single-step form.

Serita Housewares Company
Income Statement
For the Year Ended June 30, 20xx

Revenues		
Net Sales	$1,197,132	
Interest Income	5,720	
Total Revenues		$1,202,852
Costs and Expenses		
Cost of Goods Sold	$ 777,080	
Selling Expenses	203,740	
General and Administrative Expenses	100,688	
Interest Expense	13,560	
Total Costs and Expenses		1,095,068
Net Income		$ 107,784

LO 7 **E 8.** *Liquidity Ratios*

The following accounts and balances are taken from the general ledger of Arago Company.

Accounts Payable	$ 49,800
Accounts Receivable	30,600
Cash	4,500
Current Portion of Long-Term Debt	30,000
Long-Term Investments	31,200
Marketable Securities	37,800
Merchandise Inventory	76,200
Notes Payable, 90 days	45,000
Notes Payable, 2 years	60,000
Notes Receivable, 90 days	78,000
Notes Receivable, 2 years	30,000
Prepaid Insurance	1,200
Property, Plant, and Equipment	180,000
F. Abruzzi, Capital	84,900
Salaries Payable	2,550
Supplies	1,050
Property Taxes Payable	3,750
Unearned Revenue	2,250

Compute the (1) working capital and (2) current ratio.

LO 7 **E 9.** *Profitability Ratios*

The following end-of-year amounts are taken from the financial statements of Simovich Company: Total Assets, $852,000; Total Liabilities, $344,000; Owner's Equity, $508,000; Net Sales, $1,564,000; Cost of Goods Sold, $972,000; Operating Expenses, $404,000; and

P 3. LO 5 *Classified Balance Sheet*

The following information was taken from the July 31, 20x3, post-closing trial balance of Inge Robotics Company.

Account Name	Debit	Credit
Cash	$ 31,000	
Short-Term Investments	33,000	
Notes Receivable	10,000	
Accounts Receivable	276,000	
Merchandise Inventory	145,000	
Prepaid Rent	1,600	
Prepaid Insurance	4,800	
Sales Supplies	1,280	
Office Supplies	440	
Deposit for Future Advertising	3,680	
Building, Not in Use	49,600	
Land	22,400	
Delivery Equipment	41,200	
Accumulated Depreciation, Delivery Equipment		$ 28,400
Franchise Fee	4,000	
Accounts Payable		114,600
Salaries Payable		5,200
Interest Payable		840
Long-Term Notes Payable		80,000
Ken Inge, Capital		394,960

REQUIRED

From the information provided, prepare a classified balance sheet.

P 4. LO 7 *Ratio Analysis: Liquidity and Profitability*

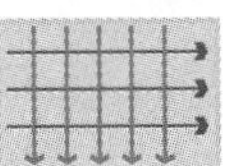

Cizer Products Company has been disappointed with its operating results for the past two years. As the accountant for the company, you have the following information available to you.

	20x3	20x2
Current Assets	$ 45,000	$ 35,000
Total Assets	145,000	110,000
Current Liabilities	20,000	10,000
Long-Term Liabilities	20,000	—
Owner's Equity	105,000	100,000
Net Sales	262,000	200,000
Net Income	16,000	11,000

Total assets and owner's equity at the beginning of 20x2 were $90,000 and $80,000, respectively.

REQUIRED

1. Compute the following measures of liquidity for 20x2 and 20x3: (a) working capital and (b) the current ratio. Comment on the differences between the years.
2. Compute the following measures of profitability for 20x2 and 20x3: (a) profit margin, (b) asset turnover, (c) return on assets, (d) debt to equity, and (e) return on equity. Comment on the change in performance from 20x2 to 20x3.

P 5. LO 5 LO 6 LO 7 *Classified Financial Statement Preparation and Evaluation*

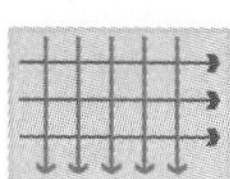

Enders Company sells outdoor sports equipment. At the December 31, 20x4, year end, the following financial information was available from the income statement: Administrative Expenses, $175,600; Cost of Goods Sold, $700,840; Interest Expense, $45,280; Interest Income, $5,600; Net Sales, $1,428,780; and Selling Expenses, $440,400.

The following information was available from the balance sheet (after closing entries were made): Accounts Payable, $65,200; Accounts Receivable, $209,600; Accumulated Depreciation, Delivery Equipment, $34,200; Accumulated Depreciation, Store Fixtures, $84,440; Cash, $56,800; Jon Enders, Capital, $718,600; Delivery Equipment, $177,000; Inventory, $273,080; Investment in Tsung Corporation (long term), $112,000; Investment in U.S. Government Securities (short term), $79,200; Long-Term Notes Payable, $200,000; Short-Term Notes Payable, $100,000; Prepaid Expenses, $11,520; and Store Fixtures, $283,240.

Total assets on December 31, 20x3, were $1,048,800, and withdrawals during 20x4 were $120,000.

REQUIRED

1. From the information above, prepare (a) an income statement in single-step form, (b) a statement of owner's equity, and (c) a classified balance sheet.
2. From the statements you have prepared, compute the following measures: (a) working capital and current ratio (for liquidity); and (b) profit margin, asset turnover, return on assets, debt to equity, and return on equity (for profitability).

Alternate Problems

P 6. LO 3 *Accounting Conventions*

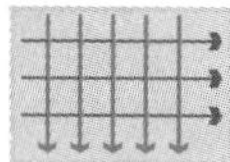

In each case below, accounting conventions *may* have been violated.

1. Schmidt Manufacturing Company uses the cost method for computing the balance sheet amount of inventory unless the market value of the inventory is less than the cost, in which case the market value is used. At the end of the current year, the market value is $221,000 and the cost is $240,000. Schmidt uses the $221,000 figure to compute current assets because management feels it is the more cautious approach.
2. Derhan Company has annual sales of $15,000,000. It follows a practice of charging any items that cost less than $300 to expenses in the year purchased. During the current year, it purchased several chairs for the executive conference rooms at $291 each, including freight. Although the chairs were expected to last for at least ten years, they were recorded as an expense in accordance with company policy.
3. Ho Company closed its books on July 31, 20x2, before preparing its annual report. On July 30, 20x2, a fire destroyed one of the company's two factories. Although the company had fire insurance and would not suffer a loss on the building, a significant decrease in sales in 20x3 was expected because of the fire. The fire damage was not reported in the 20x2 financial statements because the operations for that year were not affected by the fire.
4. Vasel Chemical Company spends a substantial portion of its profits on research and development. The company has been reporting its $7,500,000 expenditure for research and development as a lump sum, but management recently decided to begin classifying the expenditures by project even though its recordkeeping costs will increase.
5. During the current year, Igor Company changed from one generally accepted method of accounting for inventories to another generally accepted method.

REQUIRED

In each case, state the convention that is applicable and explain briefly whether or not (and why) the treatment is in accord with the convention and generally accepted accounting principles.

P 7. LO 6 *Forms of the Income Statement*

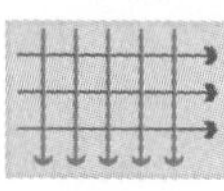

The income statement accounts from the June 30, 20x2, year-end adjusted trial balance of Nkosi Appliance Company appear at the top of the next page. Beginning merchandise inventory was $175,200 and ending merchandise inventory is $157,650. The company is a sole proprietorship.

Account Name	Debit	Credit
Sales		$541,230
Sales Returns and Allowances	$ 15,298	
Purchases	212,336	
Purchases Returns and Allowances		6,159
Freight In	11,221	
Sales Salaries Expense	102,030	
Sales Supplies Expense	1,642	
Rent Expense, Selling Space	18,000	
Utilities Expense, Selling Space	11,256	
Advertising Expense	21,986	
Depreciation Expense, Selling Fixtures	6,778	
Office Salaries Expense	47,912	
Office Supplies Expense	782	
Rent Expense, Office Space	4,000	
Depreciation Expense, Office Equipment	3,251	
Utilities Expense, Office Space	3,114	
Postage Expense	626	
Insurance Expense	2,700	
Miscellaneous Expense	481	
Interest Expense	3,600	
Interest Income		800

REQUIRED

From the information provided, prepare the following:

1. A detailed income statement.
2. A condensed income statement in multistep form.
3. A condensed income statement in single-step form.

P 8. **LO 7** *Ratio Analysis: Liquidity and Profitability*

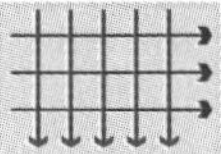

Below is a summary of data taken from the income statements and balance sheets for Ciller Plastics Company for the past two years.

	20x4	20x3
Current Assets	$ 366,000	$ 310,000
Total Assets	2,320,000	1,740,000
Current Liabilities	180,000	120,000
Long-Term Liabilities	800,000	580,000
Owner's Equity	1,340,000	1,040,000
Net Sales	4,600,000	3,480,000
Net Income	300,000	204,000

Total assets and owner's equity at the beginning of 20x3 were $1,360,000 and $840,000, respectively.

REQUIRED

1. Compute the following liquidity measures for 20x3 and 20x4: (a) working capital and (b) current ratio. Comment on the differences between the years.
2. Compute the following measures of profitability for 20x3 and 20x4: (a) profit margin, (b) asset turnover, (c) return on assets, (d) debt to equity, and (e) return on equity. Comment on the change in performance from 20x3 to 20x4.

Skills Development

CONCEPTUAL ANALYSIS

SD 1. LO 3 *Accounting Conventions*

Sulu Parking, which operates a seven-story parking building in downtown Chicago, has a calendar year end. It serves daily and hourly parkers, as well as monthly parkers who pay a fixed monthly rate in advance. The company traditionally has recorded all cash receipts as revenues when received. Most monthly parkers pay in full during the month prior to that in which they have the right to park. The company's auditors have said that beginning in 2000, the company should consider recording the cash receipts from monthly parking on an accrual basis, crediting Unearned Revenues. Total cash receipts for 2000 were $2,500,000, and the cash receipts received in 2000 and applicable to January 2001 were $125,000. Discuss the relevance of the accounting conventions of consistency, materiality, and full disclosure to the decision to record the monthly parking revenues on an accrual basis.

SD 2. LO 3 *Materiality*

Brown Electronics, Inc., operates a chain of consumer electronics stores in the Atlanta area. This year the company achieved annual sales of $50 million, on which it earned a net income of $2 million. At the beginning of the year, management implemented a new inventory system that enabled it to track all purchases and sales. At the end of the year, a physical inventory revealed that the actual inventory was $80,000 below what the new system indicated it should be. The inventory loss, which probably resulted from shoplifting, is reflected in a higher cost of goods sold. The problem concerns management but seems to be less important to the company's auditors. What is materiality? Why might the inventory loss concern management more than it does the auditors? Do you think the amount is material?

ETHICAL DILEMMA

SD 3. LO 4 *Ethics and Financial Reporting*

Dawes Software, located outside Boston, develops computer software and licenses it to financial institutions. The firm uses an aggressive accounting method that records revenues from the software it has developed on a percentage of completion basis. Consequently, revenue for partially completed projects is recognized based on the proportion of the project that is completed. If a project is 50 percent completed, then 50 percent of the contracted revenue is recognized. In 20x2, preliminary estimates for a $5 million project are that the project is 75 percent complete. Because the estimate of completion is a matter of judgment, management asks for a new report showing the project to be 90 percent complete. The change will enable senior managers to meet their financial goals for the year and thus receive substantial year-end bonuses. Do you think management's action is ethical? If you were the company controller and were asked to prepare the new report, would you do it? What action would you take?

Group Activity: Use in-class groups to debate the ethics of the action.

SD 4. LO 4 *Ethics and Financial Reporting*

Orion Microsystems, Inc., a Silicon Valley manufacturer of microchips for personal computers, has just completed its year-end physical inventory in advance of preparing financial statements. To celebrate, the entire accounting department goes out for a New Year's Eve party at a local establishment. As senior accountant, you join the fun. At the party, you fall into conversation with an employee of one of your main competitors. After a while, the employee reveals that the competitor plans to introduce a new product in sixty days that will make Orion's principal product obsolete.

Communication

Critical Thinking

Group Activity

Memo

Ethics

International

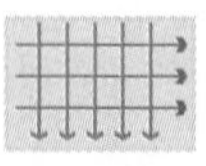
Spreadsheet

General Ledger

CD-ROM

Internet

On Monday morning, you go to the financial vice president with this information, stating that the inventory may have to be written down and net income reduced. To your surprise, the financial vice president says that you were right to come to her, but urges you to say nothing about the problem. She says, "It is probably a rumor, and even if it is true, there will be plenty of time to write down the inventory in sixty days." You wonder if this is the appropriate thing to do. You feel confident that your source knew what he was talking about. You know that the salaries of all top managers, including the financial vice president, are tied to net income. What is fraudulent financial reporting? Is this an example of fraudulent financial reporting? What action would you take?

Research Activity

SD 5. LO 7 *Annual Reports and Financial Analysis*

Obtain the annual report for a large, well-known company from either your college's library or the Needles Accounting Resource Center Web site at http://www.hmco.com/college/needles/home.html. In the annual report, identify the four basic financial statements and the notes to the financial statements. Perform a liquidity analysis, including the calculation of working capital and the current ratio. Perform a profitability analysis, calculating profit margin, asset turnover, return on assets, debt to equity, and return on equity. Be prepared to present your findings in class.

Decision-Making Practice

SD 6. LO 7 *Financial Analysis for Loan Decision*

Rosa Corona was recently promoted to loan officer at the ***First National Bank.*** She has authority to issue loans up to $50,000 without approval from a higher bank official. This week two small companies, Handy Harvey, Inc., and Sheila's Fashions, Inc., have each submitted a proposal for a six-month $50,000 loan. To prepare financial analyses of the two companies, Rosa has obtained the information summarized below.

Handy Harvey, Inc., is a local lumber and home improvement company. Because sales have increased so much during the past two years, Handy Harvey has had to raise additional working capital, especially as represented by receivables and inventory. The $50,000 loan is needed to assure the company of enough working capital for the next year. Handy Harvey began the year with total assets of $740,000 and stockholders' equity of $260,000, and during the past year the company had a net income of $40,000 on net sales of $760,000. The company's current unclassified balance sheet appears as follows:

Assets		Liabilities and Stockholders' Equity	
Cash	$ 30,000	Accounts Payable	$200,000
Accounts Receivable (net)	150,000	Notes Payable (short term)	100,000
Inventory	250,000	Notes Payable (long term)	200,000
Land	50,000	Common Stock	250,000
Buildings (net)	250,000	Retained Earnings	50,000
Equipment (net)	70,000		
Total Assets	$800,000	Total Liabilities and Stockholders' Equity	$800,000

Sheila's Fashions, Inc., has for three years been a successful clothing store for young professional women. The leased store is located in the downtown financial district. Sheila's loan proposal asks for $50,000 to pay for stocking a new line of women's suits during the coming season. At the beginning of the year, the company had total assets of $200,000 and total stockholders' equity of $114,000. Over the past year, the company earned a net income of $36,000 on net sales of $480,000. The firm's unclassified balance sheet at the current date appears as follows:

Assets		Liabilities and Stockholders' Equity	
Cash	$ 10,000	Accounts Payable	$ 80,000
Accounts Receivable (net)	50,000	Accrued Liabilities	10,000
Inventory	135,000	Common Stock	50,000
Prepaid Expenses	5,000	Retained Earnings	100,000
Equipment (net)	40,000		
Total Assets	$240,000	Total Liabilities and Stockholders' Equity	$240,000

1. Prepare a financial analysis of each company's liquidity before and after receiving the proposed loan. Also compute profitability ratios before and after, as appropriate. Write a brief summary of the effect of the proposed loan on each company's financial position.
2. Assume you are Rosa and you can make a loan to only one of these companies. Write a memorandum to the bank's vice president naming the company to which you would recommend loaning $50,000. Be sure to state what positive and negative factors could affect each company's ability to pay back the loan in the next year. Also indicate what other information of a financial or nonfinancial nature would be helpful in making a final decision.

Financial Reporting and Analysis

INTERPRETING FINANCIAL REPORTS

FRA 1. LO 7 *Profitability Analysis*

Two of the largest chains of grocery/drugstores in the United States are ***Albertson's Inc.*** and ***American Stores Co.*** (Jewel, Lucky, Acme, Osco, Sav-on, and others). In its fiscal year ended January 31, 1996, Albertson's had a net income of $465.0 million, and in its fiscal year ended December 31, 1995, American had net income of $316.8 million. It is difficult to judge which company is more profitable from those figures alone because they do not take into account the relative sales, sizes, and investments of the companies. Data (in millions) to complete a financial analysis of the two companies are presented below.[10]

	Albertson's	American Stores
Net Sales	$12,585.0	$18,308.9
Beginning Total Assets	3,621.7	7,031.6
Ending Total Assets	4,135.9	7,363.0
Beginning Total Liabilities	1,933.8	4,980.7
Ending Total Liabilities	2,183.4	5,008.5
Beginning Stockholders' Equity	1,687.9	2,050.9
Ending Stockholders' Equity	1,952.5	2,354.5

REQUIRED

1. Determine which company was more profitable by computing profit margin, asset turnover, return on assets, debt to equity, and return on equity for the two companies. Comment on the relative profitability of the two companies.
2. What do the ratios tell you about the factors that go into achieving an adequate return on assets in the grocery industry? For industry data, refer to Figures 5 through 9.
3. How would you characterize the use of debt financing in the grocery industry and the use of debt by the two companies?

Group Activity: Assign each ratio or company to a group and hold a class discussion.

FRA 2. LO 7 *Evaluation of Profitability*

Walt Half-Moon is the principal stockholder and president of ***Half-Moon Tapestries, Inc.***, which wholesales fine tapestries to retail stores. Because Half-Moon was not satisfied with the company earnings in 20x3, he raised prices in 20x4, increasing gross margin from sales from 30 percent in 20x3 to 35 percent in 20x4. Half-Moon is pleased that net income did go up from 20x3 to 20x4, as shown in the following comparative income statements.

	20x4	20x3
Revenues		
Net Sales	$611,300	$693,200
Costs and Expenses		
Cost of Goods Sold	$397,345	$485,240
Selling and Administrative Expenses	154,199	152,504
Total Costs and Expenses	$551,544	$637,744
Income Before Income Taxes	$ 59,756	$ 55,456
Income Taxes	15,000	14,000
Net Income	$ 44,756	$ 41,456

Total assets for Half-Moon Tapestries, Inc., at year end for 20x2, 20x3, and 20x4 were $623,390, $693,405, and $768,455, respectively. Has Half-Moon Tapestries' profitability really improved? (**Hint:** Compute profit margin and return on assets, and comment.)

What factors has Half-Moon overlooked in evaluating the profitability of the company? (**Hint:** Compute asset turnover and comment on the role it plays in profitability.)

FRA 3.
LO 7 *Financial Analysis with Industry Comparison*

REQUIRED

Exhibits 2 and 5 in this chapter contain the comparative balance sheet and income statement for Oneida Ltd. Assume you are the chief financial officer.

1. Compute liquidity ratios (working capital and current ratio) and profitability ratios (profit margin, asset turnover, return on assets, debt to equity, and return on equity) for 1996 and 1997 and show the industry ratios (except working capital) from Figures 4 to 9 in the chapter. Use income from continuing operations and end-of-year assets and stockholders' equity to compute the ratios.
2. Write a short memorandum to the board of directors in executive summary form summarizing changes in Oneida's liquidity and profitability performance from 1996 to 1997 compared with the industry averages.

International Company

FRA 4.
LO 5
LO 7 *Interpretation and Analysis of British Financial Statements*

Below is the classified balance sheet for the British company ***Glaxo Wellcome plc,*** a pharmaceutical firm with marketing and manufacturing operations in fifty-seven countries.[11]

Glaxo Wellcome plc and Subsidiaries
Consolidated Balance Sheets

	At 31.12.96 £m	At 31.12.95 £m
Fixed assets		
Tangible assets	3,853	4,165
Investments	93	96
	3,946	4,261
Current assets		
Stocks	804	811
Debtors	2,302	2,045
Asset for disposal	—	150
Investments	1,001	1,041
Cash at bank	261	233
	4,368	4,280
Creditors: amounts due within one year		
Loans and overdrafts	1,546	3,004
Other creditors	2,608	2,462
	4,154	5,466
Net current (liabilities)/assets	214	(1,186)
Total assets less current liabilities	4,160	3,075
Creditors: amounts due after one year		
Loans	1,607	1,343
Convertible bonds	92	123
Other creditors	147	71
	1,846	1,537
Provisions for liabilities and charges	1,047	1,317
Net assets	1,267	221
Capital and reserves		
Called up share capital	886	876
Share premium account	621	373
Goodwill reserve	(4,865)	(5,197)
Other reserves	4,583	4,039
Equity shareholders' funds	1,225	91
Equity minority interests	42	130
Capital employed	1,267	221

In the United Kingdom, the format used for classified financial statements is usually different from that used in the United States. To compare the financial statements of companies in different countries, it is important to develop the ability to interpret a variety of formats.

REQUIRED

1. For each line on Glaxo Wellcome plc's balance sheet, indicate the corresponding term that would be found on a U.S. balance sheet. (For this exercise, consider Provisions for Liabilities and Charges to be long-term liabilities.) What is the focus or rationale behind the format of the U.K. balance sheet?
2. Assuming that Glaxo Wellcome plc earned a net income of £1,997 million and £1,501 million in 1996 and 1995, respectively, compute the current ratio, debt to equity, return on assets, and return on equity for 1996 and 1995. (Use year-end amounts to compute ratios.)

Toys "R" Us Annual Report

FRA 5.
LO 5 LO 6 LO 7
Reading and Analyzing an Annual Report

Refer to the Toys "R" Us annual report to answer the following questions. (Note that 1997 refers to the year ended February 1, 1997, and 1996 refers to the year ended February 3, 1996.)

REQUIRED

1. Consolidated balance sheets: (a) Did the amount of working capital increase or decrease from 1996 to 1997? By how much? (b) Did the current ratio improve from 1996 to 1997? (c) Does the company have long-term investments or intangible assets? (d) Did the capital structure of Toys "R" Us change from 1996 to 1997? (e) What is the contributed capital for 1997? How does it compare with retained earnings?
2. Consolidated statements of earnings: (a) Did Toys "R" Us use a multistep or a single-step form of income statement? (b) Is it a comparative statement? (c) What is the trend of net earnings? (d) How significant are income taxes for Toys "R" Us? (e) Did the profit margin increase from 1996 to 1997? (f) Did asset turnover improve from 1996 to 1997? (g) Did the return on assets increase from 1996 to 1997? (h) Did the return on equity increase from 1996 to 1997? Total assets and total stockholders' equity for 1995 may be obtained from the financial highlights.
3. Multistep income statement: In Toys "R" Us's 1987 annual report, management stated that the company's "[operating] expense levels were among the best controlled in retailing [at] 18.8 percent. . . . We were able to operate with lower merchandise margins and still increase our earnings and return on sales." [12] Prepare a multistep income statement for Toys "R" Us down to income from operations for 1996 and 1997, excluding the other charges, and compute the ratios of gross margin, operating expenses, and income from operations to net sales. Comment on whether the company continued, as of 1997, to maintain the level of performance indicated by management in 1987. In 1987, gross margin was 31.2 percent and income from operations was 12.4 percent of net sales.

Fingraph® Financial Analyst™

FRA 6.
LO 7
Analysis of Oneida Ltd. or Toys "R" Us

Choose one or both of the following analyses:

1. *Alternate to FRA 3:* Analyze the Oneida Ltd. balance sheet and income statement using Fingraph® Financial Analyst™ CD-ROM software. To do this assignment you will need to enter the data from the Oneida financial statements shown in this chapter. Complete Part 1 of **FRA 3**. Prepare the memorandum required in Part 2 of **FRA 3** separately.
2. *Alternate to FRA 5:* Analyze the Toys "R" Us balance sheet and income statement using Fingraph® Financial Analyst™ CD-ROM software. The CD-ROM contains both the 1997 Toys "R" Us annual report that appears in this textbook and the 1998 annual report. Your instructor will specify which year to analyze. Complete requirements 1, 2, and 3 of **FRA 5**.

ENDNOTES

1. The Walt Disney Company, *Annual Report,* 1996.
2. "Objectives of Financial Reporting by Business Enterprises," *Statement of Financial Accounting Concepts No. 1* (Norwalk, Conn.: Financial Accounting Standards Board, 1978), pars. 32–54.
3. "Qualitative Characteristics of Accounting Information," *Statement of Financial Accounting Concepts No. 1* (Norwalk, Conn.: Financial Accounting Standards Board, 1980), par. 20.
4. Accounting Principles Board, "Accounting Changes," *Opinion No. 20* (New York: American Institute of Certified Public Accountants, 1971), par. 17.
5. Quaker Oats Company, *Annual Report,* 1997.
6. Ibid.
7. National Commission on Fraudulent Financial Reporting, *Report of the National Commission on Fraudulent Financial Reporting* (Washington, D.C., 1987), p. 2.
8. *Accounting Research and Terminology Bulletin,* final ed. (New York: American Institute of Certified Public Accountants, 1961), p. 20.
9. Roger Lowenstein, "The '20% Club' No Longer Is Exclusive," *The Wall Street Journal,* May 4, 1995.
10. Albertson's Inc. and American Stores Co., *Annual Reports,* January 31, 1996, and December 31, 1995, respectively.
11. Glaxo Wellcome plc, *Annual Report,* 1996.
12. Toys "R" Us, *Annual Report,* 1987.

How to Read an Annual Report

More than 4 million corporations are chartered in the United States. Most of these corporations are small, usually family-owned, businesses. They are called *private* or *closely held corporations* because their common stock is held by only a few people and is not available for sale to the public. Larger companies usually find it desirable to raise investment funds from many investors by issuing common stock to the public. These companies are called *public companies.* Although they are fewer in number than private companies, the total economic impact of public companies is much greater.

Public companies must register their common stock with the Securities and Exchange Commission (SEC), which regulates the issuance and subsequent trading of the stock of public companies. One important responsibility of the management of public companies under SEC rules is to report each year to the company's stockholders on the financial performance of the company. This report, called an *annual report,* contains the annual financial statements and other information about the company. Annual reports, which are a primary source of financial information about public companies, are distributed to all the company's stockholders and filed with the SEC. When filed with the SEC, the annual report is called the *S-1* because a Form S-1 is used to file the report. The general public may obtain a company's annual report by calling or writing the company. Many libraries have files of annual reports or have them available on electronic media such as *Compact Disclosure.* The annual reports of many companies can be accessed on the Internet by going to a company's home page on the World Wide Web. Also, many large companies file their S-1s electronically with the SEC. These annual reports and other filings may be accessed on the Internet at http://www.sec.gov/edgarhp.htm.

This supplement describes the major sections of the typical annual report and contains the complete annual report for one of the most successful retailers of this generation, *Toys "R" Us, In*c. In addition to stores that sell toys and other items for children, the company has opened a chain of stores that sell children's clothes, called Kids "R" Us. The Toys "R" Us annual report should be referred to in completing the case assignments related to the company in each chapter.

The Components of an Annual Report

In addition to the financial statements, the annual report contains the notes to the financial statements, a letter to the stockholders (or shareholders), a multiyear summary of financial highlights, a description of the business, management's discussion of operating results and financial condition, a report of management's responsibility, the auditors' report, and a list of directors and officers of the company.

Letter to the Stockholders

Traditionally, at the beginning of the annual report, there is a letter in which the top officers of a corporation tell stockholders about the performance of and prospects for the company. The president and the vice chairman of the board of Toys "R" Us wrote to the stockholders about the highlights of the past year, the outlook for the new year, expansion plans, corporate citizenship, and human resources. For example, they reported on future prospects as follows:

> While the 1996 holiday selling season fell short of our expectations—due primarily to a shortage of hot selling products like Tickle Me Elmo and Nintendo 64, as well as a limited selection of new video game software titles—we are pleased to report that even at this early stage in 1997, the demand for new products is very strong, and toy and video game manufacturers are geared up to meet that need. We fully expect that as a result of our traditional strength as *the* place to go for the best selection, in stock position and price, we will be able to meet the customers' expectations and generate increased sales and earnings for you, our stockholders.

Financial Highlights

The financial highlights section of the annual report presents key financial statistics for a ten-year period and is often accompanied by graphs. The Toys "R" Us annual report, for example, gives key figures for operations, financial position, and number of stores at year end and uses a graph to illustrate consolidated net sales for the last ten years. Other key figures are also shown graphically at appropriate points in the report. Note that the financial highlights section often includes nonfinancial data, such as number of stores.

In addition to financial highlights, an annual report will contain a detailed description of the products and divisions of the company. Some analysts tend to scoff at this section of the annual report because it often contains glossy photographs and other image-building material, but it should not be overlooked because it may provide useful information about past results and future plans.

Financial Statements

All companies present four basic financial statements. Toys "R" Us presents statements of earnings, balance sheets, statements of cash flows, and statements of stockholders' equity. Refer to the Toys "R" Us statements following this supplement during the discussion.

All of the Toys "R" Us financial statements are preceded by the word *consolidated.* A corporation issues *consolidated financial statements* when it consists of several companies and has combined their data for reporting purposes. For example, Toys "R" Us also operates Kids "R" Us and has combined that company's financial data with those of the Toys "R" Us stores.

Toys "R" Us also provides several years of data for each financial statement: two years for the balance sheet and three years for the others. Financial statements presented in this fashion are called *comparative financial statements.* Such statements are in accordance with generally accepted accounting principles and help readers to assess the company's performance over several years.

You may notice that the fiscal year for Toys "R" Us, instead of ending on the same date each year, ends on the Saturday nearest to the end of January. The reason is that Toys "R" Us is a retail company. It is common for retailers to end their fiscal years at a slow period after the busiest time of year.

In a note at the bottom of each page of the financial statements, the company reminds the reader that the accompanying notes are an integral part of the statements and must be consulted in interpreting the data.

Consolidated Statements of Earnings Toys "R" Us uses a modified single-step form of the income statement that includes all costs and expenses as a deduction from net sales to arrive at earnings before taxes on income. Income taxes are deducted in a separate step.

Net earnings is an alternative name for net income. The company also discloses the earnings per share, which is the net earnings divided by the weighted average number of shares of common stock held by stockholders during the year.

Consolidated Balance Sheets Toys "R" Us has a typical balance sheet for a merchandising company. In the assets and liabilities sections, the company separates out the current assets and the current liabilities. These are assets that will come available as cash or be used up in the next year and liabilities that will have to be paid or provided in the next year. These groupings help in understanding the company's liquidity.

Several items in the stockholders' equity section need further explanation. Common stock represents the number of shares outstanding at par value. Additional paid-in capital represents amounts invested by stockholders in excess of the par value of the common stock. Foreign currency translation adjustments occur because Toys "R" Us has foreign operations (see the chapter on international accounting and long-term investments). Treasury shares is a deduction from stockholders' equity that represents the cost of previously issued shares that have been bought back by the company.

Consolidated Statements of Cash Flows The preparation of the consolidated statement of cash flows is presented in the chapter on the statement of cash flows. Whereas the income statement reflects a company's profitability, the statement of cash flows reflects its liquidity. The statement provides information about a company's cash receipts, cash payments, and investing and financing activities during an accounting period.

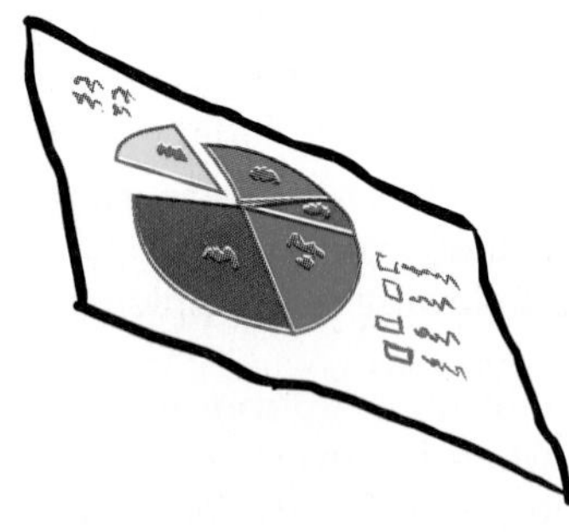

Refer to the consolidated statements of cash flows in the Toys "R" Us annual report. The first section shows cash flows from operating activities. It begins with the net earnings (income) from the consolidated statements of earnings and adjusts that figure to a figure that represents the net cash flows provided by operating activities. Among the adjustments are increases for depreciation and amortization, which are expenses that do not require the use of cash, and increases and decreases for the changes in the working capital accounts. In the year ended February 1, 1997, Toys "R" Us had net earnings of $427,400,000, and its net cash inflow from operating activities was $743,400,000. Added to net income are expenses that do not require a current outlay of cash, such as depreciation and amortization of $206,400,000. An increase of $14,300,000 in accounts and other receivables had a negative effect on

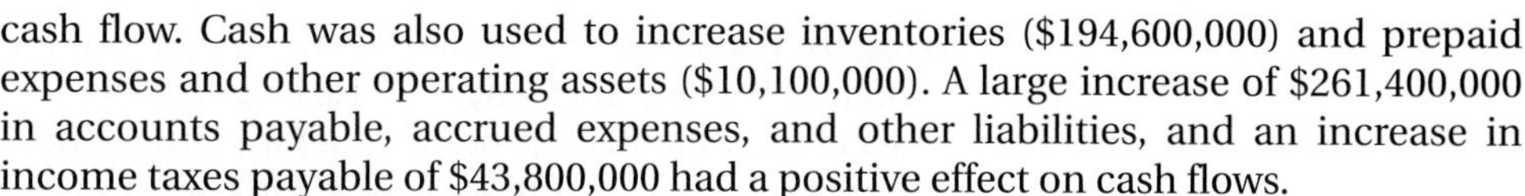

cash flow. Cash was also used to increase inventories ($194,600,000) and prepaid expenses and other operating assets ($10,100,000). A large increase of $261,400,000 in accounts payable, accrued expenses, and other liabilities, and an increase in income taxes payable of $43,800,000 had a positive effect on cash flows.

The second major section of the consolidated statements of cash flows is cash flows from investing activities. The main item in this category is capital expenditures, net, of $415,400,000. This shows that Toys "R" Us is a growing company.

The third major section of the consolidated statements of cash flows is cash flows from financing activities. You can see here that the sources of cash from financing activities are long-term borrowings of $325,400,000, and exercise of stock options of $28,500,000, which were helpful in paying for part of the capital expenditures in the investing activities section. Cash flows were used to reduce short-term borrowings and to make long-term debt repayments. In total, the company raised $211,100,000 from financing activities during the year.

At the bottom of the consolidated statements of cash flows, the net effect of the operating, investing, and financing activities on the cash balance may be seen. Toys "R" Us had an increase in cash and cash equivalents during the year of $558,200,000 and ended the year with $760,900,000 of cash and cash equivalents on hand.

The supplemental disclosures of cash flow information explain that Toys "R" Us intends the word *cash* to include not only cash but also highly liquid short-term investments called *cash equivalents.* This section also shows income tax and interest payments for the last three years.

Consolidated Statements of Stockholders' Equity Instead of a simple statement of retained earnings, Toys "R" Us presents a *statement of stockholders' equity.* This statement explains the changes in five components of stockholders' equity.

Notes to Consolidated Financial Statements

To meet the requirements of full disclosure, the company must add *notes to the financial statements* to help users interpret some of the more complex items. The notes are considered an integral part of the financial statements. In recent years, the need for explanation and further details has become so great that the notes often take more space than the statements themselves. The notes to the financial statements can be put into three broad groups: summary of significant accounting policies, explanatory notes, and supplementary information notes.

Summary of Significant Accounting Policies Generally accepted accounting principles require that the financial statements include a *summary of significant accounting policies.* In most cases, this summary is presented in the first note to the financial statements or as a separate section just before the notes. In this summary, the company tells which generally accepted accounting principles it has followed in preparing the statements. For example, in the Toys "R" Us report the company states the principles followed for property and equipment:

> Property and equipment are recorded at cost. Depreciation and amortization are provided using the straight-line method over the estimated useful lives of the assets or, where applicable, the terms of the respective leases, whichever is shorter.

Other important accounting policies listed by Toys "R" Us deal with fiscal year, principles of consolidation, merchandise inventories, preopening costs, capitalized interest, financial instruments, forward foreign exchange contracts, and the use of estimates.

Explanatory Notes Other notes explain some of the items in the financial statements. For example, Toys "R" Us showed the details of its Property and Equipment account, which is reproduced below. Other notes had to do with acquisition, other charges, seasonal financing and long-term debt, leases, stockholders' equity, taxes on income, the profit-sharing plan, stock options, foreign operations, and other matters.

	Useful Life (in years)	February 1, 1997	February 3, 1996
Land		**$ 821.2**	$ 802.4
Buildings	45–50	**1,834.3**	1,745.3
Furniture and equipment	5–20	**1,521.9**	1,351.9
Leaseholds and leasehold improvements	12½–50	**1,060.1**	959.0
Construction in progress		**37.1**	45.6
Leased property under capital leases		**30.6**	25.1
		5,305.2	4,929.3
Less accumulated depreciation and amortization		**1,257.8**	1,071.1
		$4,047.4	$3,858.2

Supplementary Information Notes In recent years, the FASB and the SEC have ruled that certain supplemental information must be presented with financial statements. Examples are the quarterly reports that most companies present to their stockholders and to the Securities and Exchange Commission. These quarterly reports, which are called *interim financial statements,* are in most cases reviewed but not audited by the company's independent CPA firm. In its annual report, Toys "R" Us presented unaudited quarterly financial data from its 1996 quarterly statements, which are shown in the following table (for the year ended February 1, 1997, dollars in millions, except per share amounts):

Year Ended February 1, 1997	First Quarter	Second Quarter	Third Quarter	Fourth Quarter
Net Sales	$1,645.5	$1,736.4	$1,883.0	$4,667.5
Cost of Sales	1,124.4	1,177.3	1,280.4	3,310.4
Other Charges	—	55.0	—	4.5
Net Earnings (Loss)	18.7	(7.5)	33.3	382.9
Earnings (Loss) per Share	$.07	$(.03)	$.12	$1.37

Interim data were presented for 1995 as well. Toys "R" Us also provides supplemental information on the market price of its common stock during the years. Other companies that engage in more than one line or type of business may present information for each business segment.

Report of Management's Responsibilities

A statement of management's responsibility for the financial statements and the internal control structure may accompany the financial statements. The management report of Toys "R" Us acknowledges management's responsibility for the integrity and objectivity of the financial information and for the system of internal controls. It mentions the company's internal audit program and its distribution of policies to employees. It also states that the company's financial statements have been audited.

Management's Discussion and Analysis

Management also presents a discussion and analysis of financial condition and results of operations. In this section, management explains the difference from one year to the next. For example, the management of Toys "R" Us describes the company's sales performance in the following way:

> The Company posted its 18th consecutive record sales year in 1996, reporting sales of $9.9 billion. Sales increased by 5.4% in 1996, 7.8% in 1995 and 10.1% in 1994. The sales growth is primarily attributable to the Company's continued store expansion and the increase in comparable U.S.A. toy store sales of 2% in 1996. The Company opened 102 new U.S.A. toy stores, 163 international toy stores, including franchise and joint venture stores, 22 children's clothing stores, 6 baby specialty stores and 2 superstores during the three year period. Comparable U.S.A. toy store sales decreased 2% in 1995 and increased 2% in 1994.

Its management of cash flows is described as follows:

> The seasonal nature of the business (approximately 47% of sales take place in the fourth quarter) typically causes cash to decline from the beginning of the year through October as inventory increases for the holiday selling season and funds are used for land purchases and construction of new stores, which usually open in the first ten months of the year. The Company has a $1 billion multi-currency unsecured committed revolving credit facility expiring in February 2000, from a syndicate of financial institutions. Cash requirements for operations, capital expenditures, lease commitments and the share repurchase program will be met primarily through operating activities, borrowings under the revolving credit facility, issuance of short-term commercial paper and other bank borrowings for foreign subsidiaries.

Report of Certified Public Accountants

The *independent auditors' report* deals with the credibility of the financial statements. This report by independent certified public accountants gives the accountants' opinion about how fairly these statements have been presented. Using financial statements prepared by managers without an independent audit would be like having a judge hear a case in which he or she was personally involved. Management, through its internal accounting system, is logically responsible for recordkeeping because it needs similar information for its own use in operating the business. The certified public accountants, acting independently, add the necessary credibility to management's figures for interested third parties. They report to the board of directors and the stockholders rather than to management.

In form and language, most auditors' reports are like the one shown in Figure 11. Usually such a report is short, but its language is very important. The report is divided into three parts.

1. The first paragraph identifies the financial statements subject to the auditors' report. This paragraph also identifies responsibilities. Company management is responsible for the financial statements, and the auditor is responsible for expressing an opinion on the financial statements based on the audit.

REPORT OF INDEPENDENT AUDITORS

To the Board of Directors and Stockholders
Toys"R"Us, Inc.

(1) We have audited the accompanying consolidated balance sheets of Toys"R"Us, Inc. and subsidiaries as of February 1, 1997 and February 3, 1996, and the related consolidated statements of earnings, stockholders' equity and cash flows for each of the three years in the period ended February 1, 1997. These financial statements are the responsibility of the Company's management. Our responsibility is to express an opinion on these financial statements based on our audits.

(2) We conducted our audits in accordance with generally accepted auditing standards. Those standards require that we plan and perform the audit to obtain reasonable assurance about whether the financial statements are free of material misstatement. An audit includes examining, on a test basis, evidence supporting the amounts and disclosures in the financial statements. An audit also includes assessing the accounting principles used and significant estimates made by management, as well as evaluating the overall financial statement presentation. We believe that our audits provide a reasonable basis for our opinion.

(3) In our opinion, the financial statements referred to above present fairly, in all material respects, the consolidated financial position of Toys"R"Us, Inc. and subsidiaries at February 1, 1997 and February 3, 1996, and the consolidated results of their operations and their cash flows for each of the three years in the period ended February 1, 1997, in conformity with generally accepted accounting principles.

Ernst & Young LLP

New York, New York
March 12, 1997

Figure 11
Auditors' Report for Toys "R" Us, Inc.

Source: Reprinted courtesy of Toys "R" Us, Inc. The notes to the financial statement, which are an integral part of the report, are not included.

2. The second paragraph, or *scope section,* states that the examination was made in accordance with generally accepted auditing standards. These standards call for an acceptable level of quality in ten areas established by the American Institute of Certified Public Accountants. This paragraph also contains a brief description of the objectives and nature of the audit.
3. The third paragraph, or *opinion section,* states the results of the auditors' examination. The use of the word *opinion* is very important because the auditor does not certify or guarantee that the statements are absolutely correct. To do so would go beyond the truth, since many items, such as depreciation, are based on estimates. Instead, the auditors simply give an opinion about whether, overall, the financial statements "present fairly," in all material respects, the financial position, results of operations, and cash flows. This means that the statements are prepared in accordance with generally accepted accounting principles. If, in the auditors' opinion, the statements do not meet accepted standards, the auditors must explain why and to what extent.

The Annual Report Project

Many instructors assign a term project that requires reading and analyzing a real annual report. The Annual Report Project described here is one that has proven successful in the authors' classes. It may be used with any company, including the Toys "R" Us Annual Report that is provided with this supplement.

The extent to which the financial analysis is required depends on the point in the course at which the Annual Report Project is assigned. Several options are provided in Instruction 3E, below.

Instructions:

1. Select an annual report of a company from those available on the Fingraph® Financial Analyst™ CD-ROM database that accompanies this text, or obtain one from the company, your library, or another source.

2. Library Research
   Identify the industry in which your company operates. Go to the library and find at least two articles in business periodicals that discuss the current situation in this industry or that present information about your company. Summarize the main points of these articles.

   Look up the company's stock price and dividend in the stock listing in *The Wall Street Journal.* On what stock exchange is the stock traded?

3. Your term project should consist of five or six double-spaced pages organized according to the following outline:

   A. Introduction
   Identify your company by writing a summary that includes the following elements:
   Name of the chief executive officer
   Home office
   Ending date of latest fiscal year
   Description of the principal products or services that the company provides
   Main geographic area of activity
   Name of the company's independent accountants (auditors). In your own words, what did the accountants say about the company's financial statements?
   The most recent price of the company's stock and its dividend per share. Be sure to provide the date for this information.

   B. Industry Situation and Company Plans
   Describe the industry and its outlook and summarize the company's future plans based on your library research and on reading the annual report. Be sure to read the letter to the stockholders and include relevant information about the company's plans from that discussion.

   C. Financial Statements
   Income Statement: Is the format most similar to a single-step or multistep format? Determine gross profit, income from operations, and net income for the last two years and comment on the increases or decreases in these amounts.

Balance Sheet: Show that Assets = Liabilities + Stockholders' Equity for the past two years.

Statement of Cash Flows: Are cash flows from operations more or less than net income for the past two years? Is the company expanding through investing activities? What is the company's most important source of financing? Overall, has cash increased or decreased over the past two years?

D. Accounting Policies

What are the significant accounting policies, if any, relating to revenue recognition, cash, short-term investments, merchandise inventories, property and equipment, and preopening costs?

What are the topics of the notes to the financial statements?

E. Financial Analysis

For the past two years, calculate and discuss the significance of the following ratios:

Option (a): Basic (After Chapter 6)

Liquidity Ratios
- Working capital
- Current ratio

Profitability Ratios
- Profit margin
- Asset turnover
- Return on assets
- Debt to equity
- Return on equity

Option (b): Basic with Enhanced Liquidity Analysis (After Chapter 10)

Liquidity Ratios
- Working capital
- Current ratio
- Receivable turnover
- Average days' sales uncollected
- Inventory turnover
- Average days' inventory on hand

Profitability Ratios
- Profit margin
- Asset turnover
- Return on assets
- Debt to equity
- Return on equity

Option (c): Comprehensive (After Chapter 18)

Liquidity Ratios
- Working capital
- Current ratio
- Receivable turnover
- Average days' sales uncollected
- Inventory turnover
- Average days' inventory on hand

Profitability Ratios
- Profit margin
- Asset turnover
- Return on assets
- Return on equity

Long-Term Solvency Ratios
- Debt to equity
- Interest coverage

Cash Flow Adequacy
- Cash flow yield
- Cash flows to sales
- Cash flows to assets
- Free cash flow

Market Strength Ratios
- Price/earnings per share
- Dividends yield

Option (d): Comprehensive using Fingraph® Financial Analyst™ software on the CD-ROM that accompanies this text.

A New **Generation**

1996

TOYS"R"US ANNUAL REPORT

YEAR ENDED FEBRUARY 1, 1997

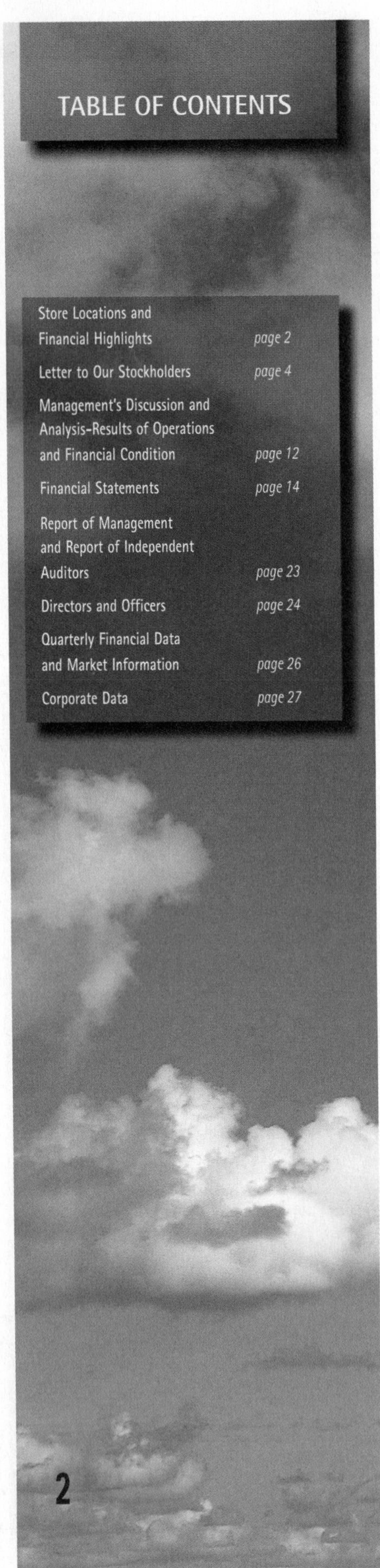

TABLE OF CONTENTS

STORE LOCATIONS

TOYS"R"US UNITED STATES - 682 LOCATIONS

Alabama - 7
Alaska - 1
Arizona - 11
Arkansas - 4
California - 84
Colorado - 11
Connecticut - 11
Delaware - 2
Florida - 44
Georgia - 18
Hawaii - 1
Idaho - 2
Illinois - 34
Indiana - 12
Iowa - 8
Kansas - 4
Kentucky - 8
Louisiana - 11
Maine - 2
Maryland - 19
Massachusetts - 19
Michigan - 25
Minnesota - 12
Mississippi - 5
Missouri - 12
Montana - 1
Nebraska - 3
Nevada - 4
New Hampshire - 5
New Jersey - 24*
New Mexico - 4
New York - 45
North Carolina - 16
North Dakota - 1
Ohio - 31
Oklahoma - 5
Oregon - 8
Pennsylvania - 31
Rhode Island - 1
South Carolina-8
South Dakota - 2
Tennessee - 14
Texas - 51
Utah - 5
Virginia - 22*
Vermont - 1
Washington - 14
West Virginia - 4
Wisconsin - 11
Puerto Rico - 4

* Includes a KidsWorld location.

TOYS"R"US INTERNATIONAL - 396 LOCATIONS

Australia - 22
Austria - 8
Belgium - 3
Canada - 61
Denmark - 9 (a)
France - 41
Germany - 58
Hong Kong - 4 (a)
Indonesia - 2 (a)
Israel - 3 (a)
Italy - 5 (a)
Japan - 51 (b)
Luxembourg - 1
Malaysia - 4 (a)
Netherlands - 9 (a)
Portugal - 3
Saudi Arabia - 1 (a)
Singapore - 4
South Africa - 6 (a)
Spain - 28
Sweden - 3 (a)
Switzerland - 4
Taiwan - 6 (a)
Turkey - 1 (a)
United Arab Emirates - 3 (a)
United Kingdom - 56

(a) Franchise or joint venture.
(b) 80 % owned.

KIDS"R"US UNITED STATES - 212 LOCATIONS

Alabama - 1
California - 24
Connecticut - 6
Delaware - 1
Florida - 10
Georgia - 4
Illinois - 20
Indiana - 7
Iowa - 1
Kansas - 1
Maine - 1
Maryland - 9
Massachusetts - 6
Michigan - 13
Minnesota - 2
Missouri - 5
Nebraska - 1
New Hampshire - 2
New Jersey - 18
New York - 22
North Carolina - 1
Ohio - 18
Pennsylvania - 14
Rhode Island - 1
Tennessee - 2
Texas - 9
Utah - 3
Virginia - 7
Wisconsin - 3

BABIES"R"US UNITED STATES - 82 LOCATIONS

Alabama - 2
Arizona - 1
California - 2
Colorado - 2
Florida - 10
Georgia - 7
Illinois - 4
Indiana - 2
Kansas - 1
Kentucky - 1
Louisiana - 1
Maryland - 3
Michigan - 1
Minnesota - 1
Missouri - 2
New Jersey - 3
New York - 1
North Carolina - 5
Ohio - 5
Oklahoma - 1
Pennsylvania - 2
South Carolina - 3
Tennessee - 4
Texas - 12
Virginia - 6

FINANCIAL HIGHLIGHTS

TOYS"R"US, INC. AND SUBSIDIARIES

(Dollars in millions except per share data)										Fiscal Year Ended
	Feb. 1, 1997*	Feb. 3, 1996*	Jan. 28, 1995	Jan. 29, 1994	Jan. 30, 1993	Feb. 1, 1992	Feb. 2, 1991	Jan. 28, 1990	Jan. 29, 1989	Jan. 31, 1988
OPERATIONS:										
Net Sales	**$ 9,932**	$ 9,427	$ 8,746	$ 7,946	$ 7,169	$ 6,124	$ 5,510	$ 4,788	$ 4,000	$ 3,137
Net Earnings	**427**	148	532	483	438	340	326	321	268	204
Earnings Per Share	**1.54**	.53	1.85	1.63	1.47	1.15	1.11	1.09	.91	.69
FINANCIAL POSITION AT YEAR END:										
Working Capital	**619**	326	484	633	797	328	177	238	255	225
Real Estate-Net	**2,411**	2,336	2,271	2,036	1,877	1,751	1,433	1,142	952	762
Total Assets	**8,023**	6,738	6,571	6,150	5,323	4,583	3,582	3,075	2,555	2,027
Long-Term Obligations	**909**	827	785	724	671	391	195	173	174	177
Stockholders' Equity	**4,191**	3,432	3,429	3,148	2,889	2,426	2,046	1,705	1,424	1,135
NUMBER OF STORES AT YEAR END:										
Toys"R"Us - United States	**680**	653	618	581	540	497	451	404	358	313
Toys"R"Us - International	**396**	337	293	234	167	126	97	74	52	37
Kids"R"Us - United States	**212**	213	204	217	211	189	164	137	112	74
Babies"R"Us - United States	**82**	-	-	-	-	-	-	-	-	-
KidsWorld - United States	**2**	-	-	-	-	-	-	-	-	-

*** After other charges as described in the Notes to the Consolidated Financial Statements.**

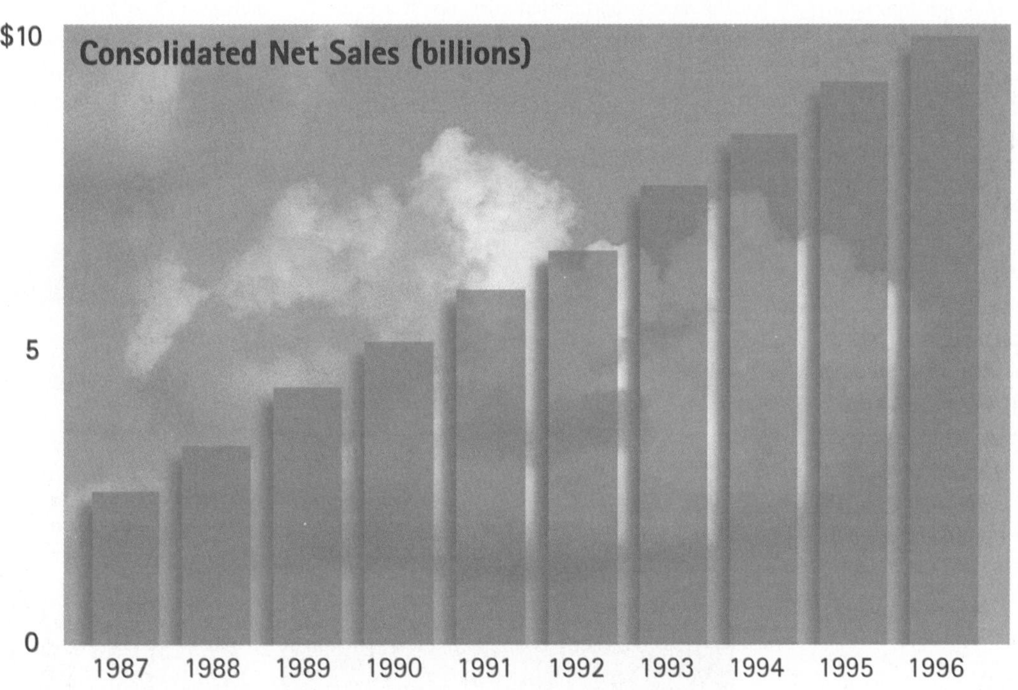

TO OUR STOCKHOLDERS

Introduction

In our annual report for the year ended February 3, 1980, our 85 toy stores in the United States reported net sales approaching $500 million. In our letter to our stockholders that year, we stated, "Much of this annual report is devoted to financial information. The true heart of our business, however, is our customer." During the next seventeen years, we grew our business to 1,372 stores in 27 countries, with sales approaching $10 billion. Delivering the best selection at great prices, we became the biggest toy store in town.

In 1997, just as in 1980, the heart of our business is the customer. In last year's annual report, we said that one of the major reasons we undertook our restructuring program was in response to our customers' feedback. In this letter, we will describe the many initiatives we have completed and are undertaking to improve our customers' shopping experience. By continuing to service the customer first and foremost, we will continue to grow profitably for you, our stockholders. We are confident that our ever-increasing emphasis on customer service will enhance our reputation as the finest retailer of children's products in the world.

1996 Financial Highlights

Our 1996 sales grew to $9.9 billion, a 5% percent increase over the $9.4 billion reported in the prior year. This is our 18th consecutive year of record sales since Toys"R"Us became a public company. In 1996, operating earnings more than doubled from the prior year and net earnings increased to $427.4 million versus $148.1 million in 1995. Earnings per share increased to $1.54 as compared to $.53 a year ago. Our results for both the 1996 and 1995 years were impacted by special charges. In 1996, a $37.8 million after tax charge was recorded for a judgement rendered against the Company related to a dispute involving a 1982 franchise agreement for toy store operations in the Middle East. In 1995, the Company underwent a strategic restructuring program and, as a result, incurred a $269.1 million after tax charge. Excluding the impact of these non-recurring charges, our 1996 net earnings increased 12% to $465.2 million from $417.2 million and earnings per share increased to $1.68 from $1.51 in the prior year.

1996 saw the successful implementation of our worldwide restructuring program. The most important initiative, our strategic inventory repositioning, has been completed. We have significantly streamlined our assortment and reduced the number of items we carry in our stores by more than 20%. This inventory repositioning program was initiated because the breadth of our assortment sometimes made our stores difficult to shop. Listening to our customers enabled us to enhance our selection advantage with larger facings and more dramatic presentations of desired items.

The other significant elements of our restructuring program, including store closings and the consolidation of certain distribution centers and administrative facilities, are substantially complete. Reducing our cost structure allows us to bring the right product to our stores more efficiently. Finally, the restructuring has had a positive financial impact. Our balance sheet is in excellent condition, as demonstrated by the significant decrease in debt, net of investments, and by our improved working capital and strong cash flow.

We are pleased to report that all of our divisions: Toys"R"Us - USA, International and Kids"R"Us, experienced comparable store sales increases and improved operating earnings for 1996.

Left: Michael Goldstein,
Vice Chairman and Chief Executive Officer
Right: Robert C. Nakasone,
President and Chief Operating Officer

While the 1996 holiday selling season fell short of our expectations – due primarily to a shortage of hot selling products like Tickle Me Elmo and Nintendo 64, as well as a limited selection of new video game software titles – we are pleased to report that even at this early stage in 1997, the demand for new products is very strong, and toy and video game manufacturers are geared up to meet that need. We fully expect that as a result of our traditional strength as the place to go for the best selection, in stock position and price, we will be able to meet the customers' expectations and generate increased sales and earnings for you, our stockholders.

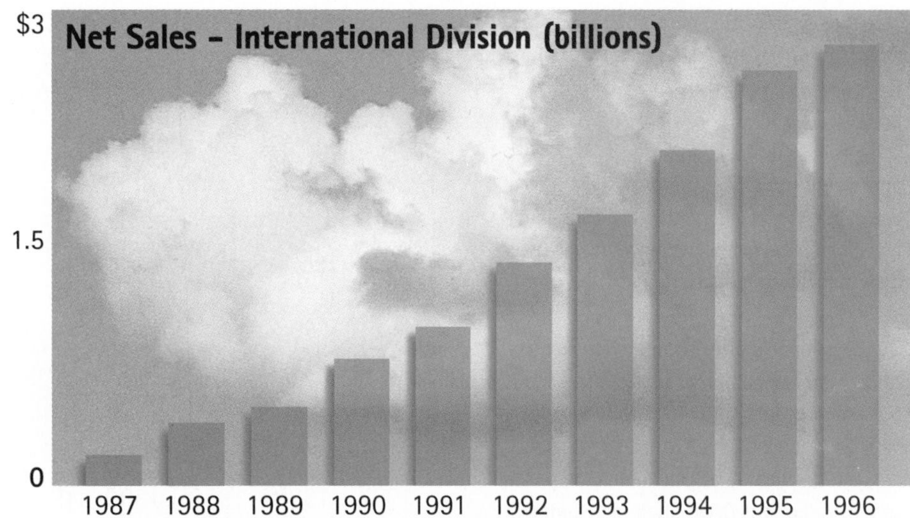

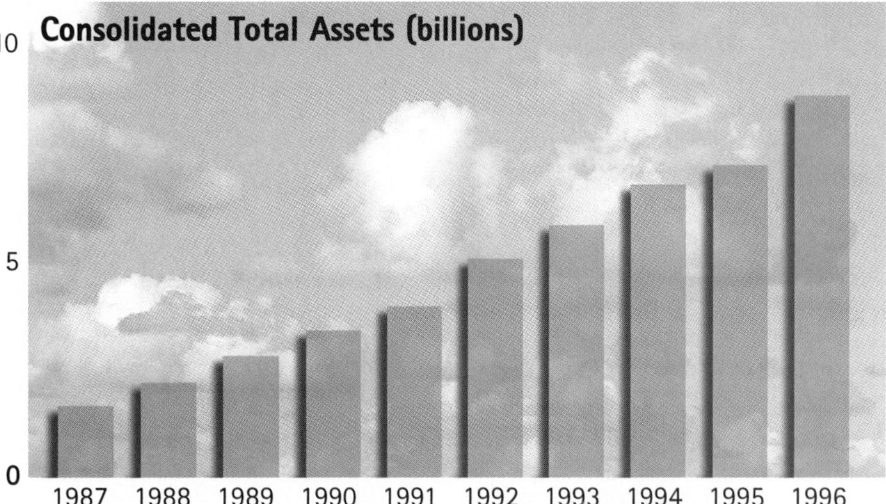

Our Customer Focus

Last year, we told you that we would unveil a revolutionary new toy store design in 1996 with the goal of creating a shopping experience like no other. We completed 13 of our "Concept 2000" stores in 1996 with outstanding results, both in terms of sales and customer satisfaction. The shopping environment we have created is completely different from the Toys"R"Us of yesterday. At the grand opening of our first "Concept 2000" store in Raritan, New Jersey, we overheard one of our customers say "people are going to shop for hours in this store." As a retailer, this is mighty praise indeed! In 1997, the "Concept 2000" format will be expanded as we will remodel 57 stores and all new toy stores in the United States will be built using this format.

In 1996, Toys"R"Us entered the superstore arena with the launch of Toys"R"Us KidsWorld, our 90,000 square foot prototype encompassing all of our formats – Toys"R"Us, Kids"R"Us and Babies"R"Us – under one roof. We know our customers are excited by this concept. Our two day grand opening in Elizabeth, New Jersey drew such enormous crowds that car traffic backed up the New Jersey Turnpike for miles. In our proud history, we have had many outstanding grand opening events, but the customer reaction to KidsWorld has been extraordinary. We are especially pleased with our licensed shops which provide our customers with food, fun, footwear and photographs. Our market research indicates the average customer stays in our KidsWorld store for well over an hour. Our goal of creating a new type of destination store for kids has been achieved.

Our customer focus has been extended to the existing base of our toy stores as well. In 1996, we rolled out 200 customer information centers, with more to follow. These provide a fixed single location in the center of the store where help can be received and questions can be answered. Due to the wide selection of merchandise we carry, as well as the shortage of hot product we have experienced, our customer information center is essential in improving our overall customer service. Through the use of our automated store inventory system, our customer information center enables us to communicate with our customer as never before.

And what better way to communicate with our customers than have them communicate with each other! While our Baby Registry has been available all year, we made registering even easier in 1996. We successfully tested in-store radio frequency technology and hand-held scanners and we'll use them to a greater extent in 1997. With this technology, our customers can now simply scan their desired selections for automatic registration into our computers. We complemented our Baby Registry this year by testing a Gift Registry where children can create a wish list for their families and friends, no matter where they live in the United States. This Gift Registry was tested in three of our markets this year and will be rolled out to the entire country beginning in 1997. Not only do our Registry programs make shopping easier, but they eliminate the time consuming process of returning or exchanging duplicate items and unwanted gifts.

Our revolving feature shop area continues to be a strong customer draw. While we are proud of our 1996 Toy Story, Barbie, Nerf and Hunchback of Notre Dame shops, we were thrilled by our customers' response to our Video Test Drive Shop last summer. We were able to provide first-hand playing experience on the new hardware platforms so that our customers could make educated decisions before making this significant purchase. We believe there is no retailer in the world as committed to the video game business as Toys"R"Us. In order to provide our customers with better in stock levels of high demand video game products, as well as computer software and VHS tapes, we will open our state-of the-art centralized "piece pick" operation in 1997. Centralized piece pick will allow us to distribute new titles across our chain faster than ever before. In addition, we can provide quicker inventory replenishment for these important categories.

Improving our in-stock levels at Toys"R"Us is an important element in our desire to improve our customer service. In 1996, one third of our chain installed a new sales floor replenishment tool which we call the Sales Improvement System. With the use of hand-held radio frequency technology, our associates can pinpoint the exact location of merchandise, not only on the sales floor, but also in our stockrooms. This will enable us to quickly identify out of stock or low stock positions and allow us to bring hot product to the sales floor quicker than ever.

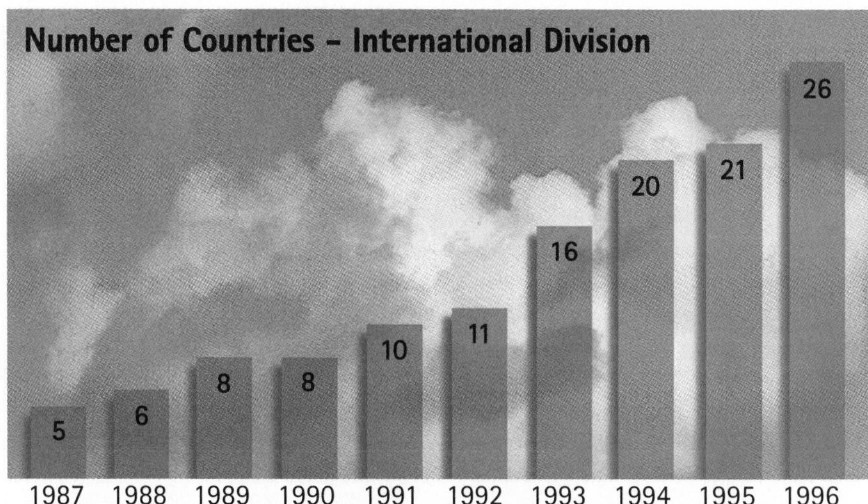

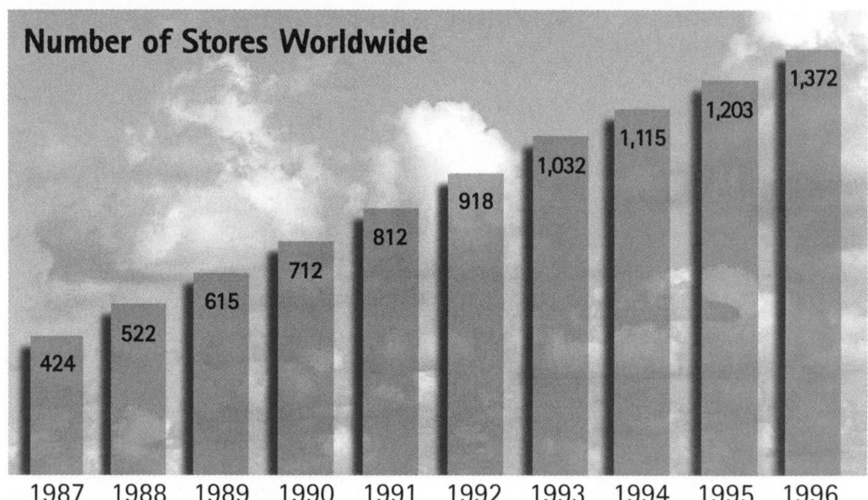

Babies"R"Us

In 1996, our newest division, Babies"R"Us, was born. We opened 6 Babies"R"Us stores, utilizing many elements from our "Concept 2000" store design and capitalizing on our Toys"R"Us and Kids"R"Us systems and infrastructure. Our merger with Baby Superstore on February 3, 1997 immediately makes Toys"R"Us a stronger player in the juvenile marketplace by adding 76 existing stores to the Babies"R"Us family. We have long admired the competitive spirit of the Baby Superstore associates and we recognize the value that they bring to Toys"R"Us in terms of their ability to provide outstanding customer service. Combining the successful Baby Superstore company with the financial resources, sophisticated distribution network and operational "know-how" of Toys"R"Us makes us the premier retailer of juvenile products in the United States.

Outlook

In 1996, we added 104 stores: 30 toy stores in the United States, 59 international toy stores, of which 27 were franchise stores, including our first franchise stores in Indonesia, Italy, Saudi Arabia, South Africa and Turkey, as well as 7 Kids"R"Us stores, 6 Babies"R"Us stores and 2 KidsWorld stores. In 1997, we intend to add approximately 105 stores: 25 USA toy stores in addition to the 57 Concept 2000 remodels, 40 international toy stores including 15 franchise stores, 5 Kids"R"Us stores and 20 Babies"R"Us stores in addition to converting the 76 Baby Superstore locations.

In terms of product, 1997 promises to be an exciting year for Toys"R"Us. The video game business remains strong and the introduction of Nintendo 64 into Europe should continue the excitement in another part of the world. In addition, the recent price reductions for Nintendo 64 and Sony Playstation should fuel the video game momentum not only in video hardware but software as well.

Licensed toy product related to movie releases has historically been successful for Toys"R"Us. Typically, a great movie license generates sales for us in many categories such as action figures, dolls, plush, party goods, and board and video games to name a few. This year there will be more children-oriented movies with related toy product than at any other point in our history. These movies include the Star Wars Trilogy and Little Mermaid re-releases, The Lost World: Jurassic Park, Batman and Robin, Hercules and Anastasia. We will be ready to supply our customers with exciting products related to all of these movies.

Corporate Citizenship

Toys"R"Us maintains a company-wide giving program focused on improving the health care needs of children by supporting many national and regional children's health care organizations.

The Counsel on Economic Priority recently awarded Toys"R"Us the Pioneer Award in Global Ethics. This award was the direct result of the implementation of our Code of Conduct for suppliers which outlines the Company's position against child labor and unsafe working conditions. In order for a vendor's product to be sold in any of our stores, they must comply with our Code of Conduct.

If you would like to receive more information on Toys"R"Us' corporate citizenship please write to Roger Gaston at the address noted on the back inside cover.

HUMAN RESOURCES

All of these initiatives are made possible by the excellent management team we have assembled here at Toys"R"Us. To prepare ourselves for 1997 and beyond, we have made the following important executive announcements:

ADDITIONS:

Roger C. Gaston
Senior Vice President - Human Resources

Mitchell Loukota
Vice President - Divisional Merchandise Manager
Toys "R" Us

Gregg Treadway
General Manager
Toys"R"Us

Antonio Urcelay
Managing Director - Toys"R"Us Iberia

David S. Walker
Vice President - Advertising
Kids"R"Us

PROMOTIONS:

Corporate & Toys"R"Us, USA

Robert J. Weinberg
Senior Vice President -
General Merchandise Manager

David Brewi
Vice President - Divisional Merchandise Manager

Thomas DeLuca
Vice President - Imports, Product Development and Safety Assurance

Truvillus Hall
General Manager

Charlene Mady
Vice President - Area Merchandise Planning

Gerald S. Parker
Vice President - Regional Operations

Timothy J. Slade
Vice President - Transportation and Traffic

William A. Stephenson
Vice President -
Merchandise Planning and Allocation

Kevin VanderGriend
General Manager

Robert S. Zarra
Vice President -
Internal Audit

Toys"R"Us, International

Larry D. Gardner
Vice President - Toys"R"Us Asia

Larry S. Johnson
Vice President - Franchise Markets

Michael C. Taylor
Vice President - Logistics

Kids"R"Us & Babies"R"Us

William Farrell
Vice President - Physical Distribution,
Kids"R"Us

Christopher M. Scherm
Vice President -
Divisional Merchandise Manager, Kids"R"Us

David E. Schoenbeck
Vice President - Operations, Babies"R"Us

We would like to thank Milton Gould and Harold Wit, who have served on our Board of Directors since we became a public company in 1978, for their guidance, counsel and contributions, in helping make Toys"R"Us the world's premier retailer of children's products. We extend to them our heartfelt thanks and best wishes for continued success, health and prosperity as they retire from our Board of Directors.

SUMMARY

We hope you are excited about all of the customer initiatives we will implement in 1997. We recognize our need for change and we are well on our way to implementing our strategic plan. We thank our associates throughout the world who are advancing our mission to grow our business and service our customer.

Yesterday, today and, most importantly, tomorrow our customers will remain the true heart of our business. Listening to our customers over the last two decades has made us strong. Listening harder to each and every one of our customers will make us even stronger.

We look forward to impressing our customers with outstanding service and impressing you, our stockholders, with outstanding results – And along the way, making children all over the world want to visit our stores again and again.

Sincerely,

Michael Goldstein
Vice Chairman and Chief Executive Officer

Robert C. Nakasone
President and Chief Operating Officer

March 24, 1997

Toys"R"Us is the world's premier retailer of children's products bringing toys, apparel, baby needs and much more to children (and their parents, too!)

Building Our Business with Customer Service

Today's highly competitive retail environment constantly challenges us to find more ways to distinguish the Toys"R"Us shopping experience. For the savvy, value-conscious consumer of the '90's, well-stocked shelves, great prices and sales promotions are expected from every retail store. There has to be "something more..." In response to this, we have been placing more and more emphasis on customer service. Throughout 1996, a number of opportunities enabled us to show our customers that we understand their needs, and that we are working towards providing the best service possible everyday... at every Toys"R"Us store.

Toys"R"Us Becomes a Public Company

1978

First Kid"R"Us Store Opens

1983

Toys"R"Us Goes International

1984

Concept 2000:

AND THE ADVENT OF CUSTOMER-FRIENDLY STORE DESIGN

In 1996, we unveiled thirteen stores with the innovative store format we call Concept 2000 – combining the ultimate in shopping convenience and aesthetics. Wider aisles, color-coded merchandise displays, attractive signage, specialty areas for video games and popular toys, animated icons and other visually stimulating features were introduced to entertain and motivate children and parents as they shop. Within our Concept 2000 and regular Toys"R"Us stores, we also enhanced service at our Customer Information Centers. Customers can now count on the assistance of trained employees who are able to access computer screens and identify product availability within our stores. In our Islands of Service program, we have sales assistants who are 'subject experts' in various categories to help customers answer product-specific questions and explain key product features.

We have successfully made our definition of Customer Service more expansive. Whether it is by giving our shoppers personalized attention and assistance, promoting key services that enhance the shopping experience, or simply by providing them with a pleasant environment in which to shop, we work to ensure customer satisfaction.

WHAT CUSTOMERS ARE SAYING ABOUT CONCEPT 2000:

"Walking into the new store, I was blown away by how much it has changed..."

"It was so much easier to find what I was looking for..."

"I was impressed by the merchandise displays and selection..."

"It was a pleasure to shop here because the store is so bright and colorful..."

"Wow!"

Toys"R"Us Opens First Store in Japan.

1991

Introduction of Baby Registry: A New Innovation in Customer Service

1993

Toys"R"Us Announces Worldwide Restructuring to Position Itself for a New Generation

1996

Toys"R"Us:

SPECIAL PROGRAMS AND NEW INITIATIVES

A welcome convenience for parents-to-be, the Toys"R"Us Baby Registry lets friends and family members find the right gifts for new parents with ease and confidence. After a simple registration process, parents-to-be can make their selection from any of the products in the store. With its focus on gift-giving for baby, this service shows our customers that we have thought of every shopping benefit!

Another new service coming soon is the Gift Registry. Kids simply sign up and create their own "wish list" with the toys they really want for birthdays, holidays and special occasions. Gift-givers will be able to choose the perfect gift every time! The Gift Registry will be rolled out to all stores beginning in 1997. We're exploring customer service opportunities on the Internet, too! Our new website (www.toysrus.com) provides fun for the kids , and gives parents direct access to store and product information instantly!

KidsWorld: TOTAL ONE-STOP SHOPPING

The two KidsWorld stores that opened in 1996 showcased the very best of one-stop shopping and customer service. Shoppers came for the full range of advantages from Toys"R"Us, Kids"R"Us and Babies"R"Us, plus other family-friendly "attractions" such as Kids Footlocker, Focus Pocus (a photo studio), Cartoon Cuts (a hair salon), Jeepers Junior (a restaurant), Fuzziwig's Candy Factory, plus arcade games and rides. Coming to KidsWorld means more than just a shopping trip. It's a real family event!

First Babies"R"Us Store Opens and Toys"R"Us Merges with Baby Superstore.

Toys"R"Us Redesigned for the 21st Century – "Concept 2000"

First KidsWorld Superstore Opens

1996

Babies"R"Us:

DELIVERING NEW OPPORTUNITIES FOR SUCCESS

There are great expectations for the newest arrival in the "R"Us family. In 1996, Babies"R"Us successfully opened six bright, spacious new stores (designed after the Concept 2000 model) that showcase total one-stop shopping and expert customer service. The recent merger with the Baby Superstore chain in February 1997 has quickly catapulted Babies"R"Us into the premier retailer of juvenile products in the country! Customers can expect advantages like an amazing product selection, everyday low prices, and the popular no-hassle returns policy. Other customer-friendly services include The Baby Registry that makes it easy for new parents to choose the gifts they want from friends and family, and the Special Orders desk where customers can order merchandise in specific styles or colors not currently available in the store. Our sales associates are expertly trained for customer interaction through classes, product seminars, videos and a regular product information newsletter. Expectant parents and gift-givers now have the ideal place to shop for everything for baby!

International:

HIGHLIGHTS FROM AROUND THE WORLD

Fifty-nine international Toys"R"Us stores opened in 1996, demonstrating our continuing growth as a global retailer. Franchise operations in Indonesia, Italy, Saudi Arabia, South Africa, and Turkey bring our current international presence to nearly 400 stores in 26 countries. Milestones for the year included the opening of our 50th store in Japan, and the celebration of our 10th year in Hong Kong. As the Toys"R"Us world gets bigger and better, new and exciting opportunities abound for strengthening relationships with all our customers!

MANAGEMENT'S DISCUSSION AND ANALYSIS - Results of Operations and Financial Condition

RESULTS OF OPERATIONS*

The Company posted its 18th consecutive record sales year in 1996, reporting sales of $9.9 billion. Sales increased by 5.4% in 1996, 7.8% in 1995 and 10.1% in 1994. The sales growth is primarily attributable to the Company's continued store expansion and the increase in comparable U.S.A. toy store sales of 2% in 1996. The Company opened 102 new U.S.A. toy stores, 163 international toy stores, including franchise and joint venture stores, 22 children's clothing stores, 6 baby specialty stores and 2 superstores during the three year period. Comparable U.S.A. toy store sales decreased 2% in 1995 and increased 2% in 1994.

Cost of sales as a percentage of sales decreased to 69.4% in 1996 from 69.9% in 1995 primarily due to an improved markup on basic toy products, partially offset by the strengthening of the lower margin video hardware business. Cost of sales as a percentage of sales increased in 1995 from 68.7% in 1994 primarily due to an intensively competitive retail environment, the Company's aggressive pricing strategy and an unfavorable shift in the merchandise mix.

Selling, advertising, general and administrative expenses as a percentage of sales were 20.3% in 1996, 20.1% in 1995 and 19.0% in 1994. The increases in 1996 and 1995 were primarily due to heavier advertising and promotional efforts, as well as the Company's increased emphasis on customer service.

The Company's 1996 results were impacted by a charge of $59.5 million ($37.8 million, net of tax benefits or $.14 cents per share) relating to an arbitration award rendered against the Company involving a dispute over a 1982 franchise agreement to operate stores in the Middle East. Although the arbitration award was recently confirmed in the District Courts, the Company has filed an appeal with the United States Court of Appeals for the Second Circuit.

The Company's 1995 results were impacted by charges of $396.6 million ($269.1 million, net of tax benefits or $.98 cents per share) to restructure its worldwide operations and to early adopt FAS No. 121, "Accounting for the Impairment of Long-Lived Assets and Long-Lived Assets to be Disposed Of." Elements of the restructuring plan are described below and in the notes to the consolidated financial statements and consisted of certain asset write offs and contractual obligations, primarily in the United States and Europe.

In 1996, the Company substantially completed its restructuring program action plan, including the closing of 3 Toys"R"Us and 7 Kids"R"Us stores in the United States, the consolidation of 3 distribution centers and various administrative facilities in the United States and Europe and, pending certain regulatory approvals, the franchising of 9 toy stores in the Netherlands. The Company also successfully completed the most important component of the restructuring program, its strategic inventory repositioning initiative designed to streamline the merchandise assortment in its toy stores and enhance its selection advantage. The Company has reduced the number of items carried in its toy stores by more than 20%.

At February 1, 1997, the Company had approximately $90 million of liabilities remaining for its restructuring program primarily relating to long-term lease obligations and other commitments. The Company believes these reserves are adequate to complete the restructuring program.

Interest expense decreased by 4.5% in 1996 as compared to 1995 primarily due to the Company's improved cash flow as a result of increased earnings, the benefits from its worldwide restructuring program and a $325.4 million medium term financing which replaced borrowings carrying higher interest rates. Interest expense increased in 1995 as compared to 1994 due to increased average borrowings and a change in the mix of borrowings and interest rates among countries.

The Company's effective tax rate was 36.5%, 44.2% and 37.0% in 1996, 1995 and 1994, respectively. The higher effective tax rate in 1995 was primarily due to the restructuring of its worldwide operations.

The Company believes that its risks attendant to foreign operations are minimal, as the countries in which it owns assets and operates stores are politically stable. The Company's foreign exchange risk management objectives are to stabilize cash flow from the effect of foreign currency fluctuations. The Company will, whenever practical, offset local investments in foreign currencies with borrowings denominated in the same currency. The Company also enters into forward foreign exchange contracts or purchases options to eliminate specific transaction currency risk.

*References to 1996, 1995, and 1994 are for the 52 weeks ended February 1, 1997, 53 weeks ended February 3, 1996 and the 52 weeks ended January 28, 1995.

International sales were unfavorably impacted by the translation of local currency results into U.S. dollars by approximately $150 million in 1996 and was favorably impacted by approximately $140 million and $90 million in 1995 and 1994, respectively. Neither the translation of local currency results into U.S. dollars nor inflation had a material effect on the Company's operating results for the last three years.

LIQUIDITY AND CAPITAL RESOURCES **

The Company's impressive financial position is evidenced by the liquidity of its assets and its strong cash flow.

The Company's newest division, Babies"R"Us opened its first 6 stores in 1996. The Company accelerated the growth of this division with the acquisition of Baby Superstore, Inc. on February 3, 1997 for 13 million treasury shares of the Company's common stock valued at approximately $376.0 million. This acquisition has been accounted for as a purchase at February 1, 1997, and the excess of purchase price over net assets acquired in the amount of $365.0 million has been recorded as goodwill and will be amortized over 40 years.

Baby Superstore, with 76 stores primarily in the southeast and midwest United States, was a leading retailer of baby and young children's products. The Company plans to operate these stores under its Babies"R"Us format, utilizing its Toys"R"Us and Kids"R"Us infrastructure to leverage its combined financial and operational strengths.

The Company's cash and cash equivalents have increased to $760.9 million at February 1, 1997 from $202.7 million at February 3, 1996. This increase is primarily attributable to the following factors: increased net earnings, due in part to the benefits of the Company's worldwide restructuring program, $67.5 million of cash received with the acquisition of Baby Superstore and an increase in net cash provided by financing activities of $112.1 million.

The Company's working capital improved to $618.9 million at February 1, 1997, from $326.1 million at February 3, 1996 due in part to the closing of a medium term $325.4 million financing in 1996, the proceeds of which reduced short term debt.

The long-term debt, net of current maturities, to equity percentage was 21.7% at February 1, 1997 as compared to 24.1% at February 3, 1996.

In 1997, the Company plans to open approximately 25 toy stores in the United States utilizing the new "Concept 2000" store design and also plans to remodel 57 toy stores in the United States to this format. The Company plans to open approximately 40 new international toy stores, including 15 franchise stores. Our newest division, Babies"R"Us, will open approximately 20 stores in the United States. Finally, there are plans to open approximately 5 Kids"R"Us children's clothing stores. The Company opened 89 toy stores in 1996, 80 in 1995 and 96 in 1994, and 7 Kids"R"Us children's clothing stores in 1996, 9 in 1995 and 6 in 1994. The Company also added its first 2 KidsWorld stores, one of which is a retrofit of an existing Toys"R"Us and Kids"R"Us location, and the first 6 Babies"R"Us stores in 1996. In addition to the stores closed in 1996 that were part of the Company's worldwide restructuring program, the Company closed 1 store in the United Kingdom in 1995 and 19 Kids"R"Us clothing stores in 1994 which did not meet its expectations. These closures did not have a significant impact on the Company's financial position.

For 1997, capital requirements for real estate, store and warehouse fixtures and equipment, leasehold improvements and other additions to property and equipment are estimated at $630 million (including real estate and related costs of $375 million). The Company's policy is to purchase its real estate where appropriate and it plans to continue this policy.

The Company has an existing $1 billion share repurchase program. As of February 1, 1997, the Company has repurchased 21.3 million shares of its common stock for $693.9 million under this program since it was announced in January of 1994.

The seasonal nature of the business (approximately 47% of sales take place in the fourth quarter) typically causes cash to decline from the beginning of the year through October as inventory increases for the holiday selling season and funds are used for land purchases and construction of new stores, which usually open in the first ten months of the year. The Company has a $1 billion multi-currency unsecured committed revolving credit facility expiring in February 2000, from a syndicate of financial institutions. Cash requirements for operations, capital expenditures, lease commitments and the share repurchase program will be met primarily through operating activities, borrowings under the revolving credit facility, issuance of short-term commercial paper and other bank borrowings for foreign subsidiaries.

**The Company's consolidated balance sheet at February 1, 1997 includes the effects of the acquisition of Baby Superstore, Inc.

CONSOLIDATED STATEMENTS OF EARNINGS

TOYS"R"US, INC. AND SUBSIDIARIES

(In millions except per share data)	February 1, 1997	February 3, 1996	January 28, 1995
			Year Ended
Net sales	**$ 9,932.4**	$ 9,426.9	$ 8,745.6
Costs and expenses:			
Cost of sales	**6,892.5**	6,592.3	6,008.0
Selling, advertising, general and administrative	**2,019.7**	1,894.8	1,664.2
Depreciation and amortization	**206.4**	191.7	161.4
Other charges	**59.5**	396.6	-
Interest expense	**98.6**	103.3	83.9
Interest and other income	**(17.4)**	(17.4)	(16.0)
	9,259.3	9,161.3	7,901.5
Earnings before taxes on income	**673.1**	265.6	844.1
Taxes on income	**245.7**	117.5	312.3
Net earnings	**$ 427.4**	$ 148.1	$ 531.8
Earnings per share	**$ 1.54**	$ .53	$ 1.85

See notes to consolidated financial statements.

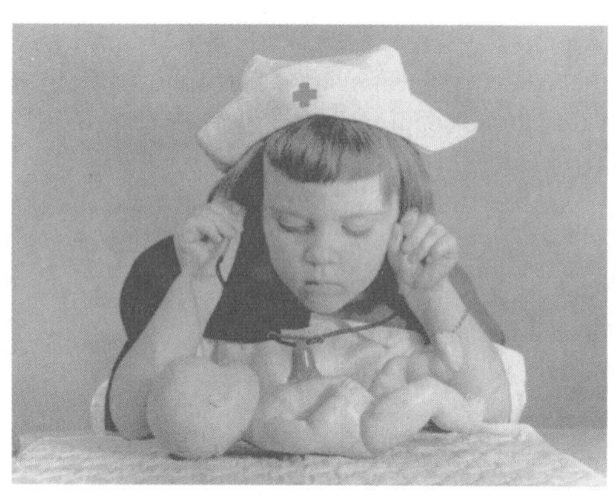

CONSOLIDATED BALANCE SHEETS

TOYS"R"US, INC. AND SUBSIDIARIES

(In millions)	February 1, 1997	February 3, 1996
ASSETS		
Current Assets:		
Cash and cash equivalents	$ 760.9	$ 202.7
Accounts and other receivables	142.1	128.9
Merchandise inventories	2,214.6	1,999.5
Prepaid expenses and other current assets	42.0	87.8
Total Current Assets	3,159.6	2,418.9
Property and Equipment:		
Real estate, net	2,410.6	2,336.0
Other, net	1,636.8	1,522.2
Total Property and Equipment	4,047.4	3,858.2
Goodwill	365.0	-
Other Assets	451.2	460.4
	$ 8,023.2	$ 6,737.5
LIABILITIES AND STOCKHOLDERS' EQUITY		
Current Liabilities:		
Short-term borrowings	$ 303.5	$ 332.8
Accounts payable	1,346.5	1,182.0
Accrued expenses and other current liabilities	720.0	438.1
Income taxes payable	170.7	139.9
Total Current Liabilities	2,540.7	2,092.8
Long-Term Debt	908.5	826.8
Deferred Income Taxes	222.5	228.7
Other Liabilities	160.9	156.9
Stockholders' Equity:		
Common stock	30.0	30.0
Additional paid-in capital	488.8	542.8
Retained earnings	4,120.1	3,692.7
Foreign currency translation adjustments	(60.6)	12.9
Treasury shares, at cost	(387.7)	(846.1)
Total Stockholders' Equity	4,190.6	3,432.3
	$ 8,023.2	$ 6,737.5

See notes to consolidated financial statements.

CONSOLIDATED STATEMENTS OF CASH FLOWS

TOYS"R"US, INC. AND SUBSIDIARIES

(In millions)			Year Ended
	February 1, 1997	February 3, 1996	January 28, 1995
CASH FLOWS FROM OPERATING ACTIVITIES			
Net earnings	**$ 427.4**	$ 148.1	$ 531.8
Adjustments to reconcile net earnings to net cash provided by operating activities:			
Other charges	**-**	396.6	-
Depreciation and amortization	**206.4**	191.7	161.4
Deferred income taxes	**23.4**	(66.7)	(14.5)
Changes in operating assets and liabilities:			
Accounts and other receivables	**(14.3)**	(10.8)	(17.4)
Merchandise inventories	**(194.6)**	(193.1)	(221.6)
Prepaid expenses and other operating assets	**(10.1)**	(15.7)	(31.7)
Accounts payable, accrued expenses and other liabilities	**261.4**	(150.5)	183.5
Income taxes payable	**43.8**	(49.3)	(2.0)
Net cash provided by operating activities	**743.4**	250.3	589.5
CASH FLOWS FROM INVESTING ACTIVITIES			
Cash received with the acquisition of Baby Superstore	**67.5**	-	-
Capital expenditures, net	**(415.4)**	(467.5)	(585.7)
Other assets	**(35.8)**	(67.4)	(44.6)
Net cash used in investing activities	**(383.7)**	(534.9)	(630.3)
CASH FLOWS FROM FINANCING ACTIVITIES			
Short-term borrowings, net	**(9.7)**	210.1	(117.2)
Long-term borrowings	**325.4**	82.2	34.6
Long-term debt repayments	**(133.1)**	(9.3)	(1.1)
Exercise of stock options	**28.5**	16.2	26.0
Share repurchase program	**-**	(200.2)	(469.7)
Sale of stock to Petrie Stores Corporation	**-**	-	161.6
Net cash provided by/(used in) financing activities	**211.1**	99.0	(365.8)
Effect of exchange rate changes on cash and cash equivalents	**(12.6)**	18.5	(15.5)
CASH AND CASH EQUIVALENTS			
Increase/(decrease) during year	**558.2**	(167.1)	(422.1)
Beginning of year	**202.7**	369.8	791.9
End of year	**$ 760.9**	$ 202.7	$ 369.8

SUPPLEMENTAL DISCLOSURES OF CASH FLOW INFORMATION

The Company considers its highly liquid investments purchased as part of its daily cash management activities to be cash equivalents. During 1996, 1995 and 1994, the Company made income tax payments of $177.2, $234.5 and $318.9 and interest payments (net of amounts capitalized) of $108.6, $118.4 and $123.6, respectively.

See notes to consolidated financial statements.

CONSOLIDATED STATEMENTS OF STOCKHOLDERS' EQUITY

TOYS"R"US, INC. AND SUBSIDIARIES

	Common Stock						
	Issued		In Treasury				
(In millions)	Shares	Amount	Shares	Amount	Additional paid-in capital	Retained earnings	Foreign currency translation adjustments
Balance, January 29, 1994	297.9	$ 29.8	(8.4)	$ (292.4)	$ 454.0	$ 3,012.8	$ (56.0)
Net earnings for the year	–	–	–	–	–	531.8	–
Share repurchase program	–	–	(13.1)	(469.7)	–	–	–
Exercise of stock options, net of tax benefit	0.1	–	1.1	41.9	(15.8)	–	–
Exchange with and sale of stock to Petrie Stores Corporation	–	–	2.2	78.5	83.1	–	–
Foreign currency translation adjustments	–	–	–	–	–	–	30.9
Balance, January 28, 1995	298.0	29.8	(18.2)	(641.7)	521.3	3,544.6	(25.1)
Net earnings for the year	–	–	–	–	–	148.1	–
Share repurchase program	–	–	(7.6)	(200.2)	–	–	–
Exercise of stock options, net of tax benefit	–	–	.9	34.2	(16.7)	–	–
Corporate inversion	2.4	0.2	(2.4)	(38.4)	38.2	–	–
Foreign currency translation adjustments	–	–	–	–	–	–	38.0
Balance, February 3, 1996	300.4	30.0	(27.3)	(846.1)	542.8	3,692.7	12.9
Net earnings for the year	–	–	–	–	–	427.4	–
Acquisition of Baby Superstore, Inc.	–	–	13.0	400.2	(24.2)	–	–
Exercise of stock options, net of tax benefit	–	–	1.7	58.2	(29.8)	–	–
Foreign currency translation adjustments	–	–	–	–	–	–	(73.5)
Balance, February 1, 1997	**300.4**	**$ 30.0**	**(12.6)**	**$ (387.7)**	**$ 488.8**	**$ 4,120.1**	**$(60.6)**

See notes to consolidated financial statements.

NOTES TO CONSOLIDATED FINANCIAL STATEMENTS

(Amounts in millions except per share data)

SUMMARY OF SIGNIFICANT ACCOUNTING POLICIES

Fiscal Year

The Company's fiscal year ends on the Saturday nearest to January 31. Reference to 1996, 1995 and 1994 are for the 52 weeks ended February 1, 1997, 53 weeks ended February 3, 1996 and the 52 weeks ended January 28, 1995, respectively.

Principles of Consolidation

The consolidated financial statements include the accounts of the Company and its subsidiaries. The consolidated balance sheet and statement of cash flows also reflect the acquisition of Baby Superstore, Inc. at February 1, 1997. All material intercompany balances and transactions have been eliminated. Assets and liabilities of foreign operations are translated at current rates of exchange at the balance sheet date while results of operations are translated at average rates in effect for the period. Translation gains or losses are shown as a separate component of stockholders' equity.

Merchandise Inventories

Merchandise inventories for the U.S.A. toy store operations, which represent over 60% of total inventories, are stated at the lower of LIFO (last-in, first-out) cost or market, as determined by the retail inventory method. If inventories had been valued at the lower of FIFO (first-in, first-out) cost or market, inventories would show no change at February 1, 1997 or February 3, 1996. All other merchandise inventories are stated at the lower of FIFO cost or market as determined by the retail inventory method.

Property and Equipment

Property and equipment are recorded at cost. Depreciation and amortization are provided using the straight-line method over the estimated useful lives of the assets or, where applicable, the terms of the respective leases, whichever is shorter.

The Company's policy to recognize impairment losses relating to long-lived assets is based on several factors including, but not limited to, management's plans for future operations, recent operating results and projected cash flows.

Preopening Costs

Preopening costs, which consist primarily of advertising, occupancy and payroll expenses, are amortized over expected sales to the end of the fiscal year in which the store opens.

Capitalized Interest

Interest on borrowed funds is capitalized during construction of property and is amortized by charges to earnings over the depreciable lives of the related assets. Interest of $3.3, $6.1 and $6.9 was capitalized during 1996, 1995 and 1994, respectively.

Financial Instruments

The carrying amounts reported in the balance sheets for cash and cash equivalents and short-term borrowings approximate their fair market values.

Forward Foreign Exchange Contracts

The Company enters into forward foreign exchange contracts to eliminate the risk associated with currency movement relating to its short-term intercompany loan program with foreign subsidiaries and inventory purchases denominated in foreign currency. Gains and losses, which offset the movement in the underlying transactions, are recognized as part of such transactions. Gross deferred unrealized gains and losses on the forward contracts were not material at either February 1, 1997 or February 3, 1996. The related receivable, payable and deferred gain or loss are included on a net basis in the balance sheet. The Company had approximately $205.0 of short term outstanding forward contracts at both February 1, 1997 and February 3, 1996 maturing in 1997 and 1996, respectively, which are entered into with counterparties that have high credit ratings and with which the Company has the contractual right to net forward currency settlements. In addition, the Company had a $325.4 currency swap obligation outstanding at February 1, 1997 related to its £200 note payable due 2001.

Use of Estimates

The preparation of financial statements in conformity with generally accepted accounting principles requires management to make estimates and assumptions that affect the amounts reported in the consolidated financial statements and accompanying notes. Actual results could differ from those estimates.

ACQUISITION

On February 3, 1997, the Company acquired all of the outstanding common shares of Baby Superstore, Inc. ("Baby Superstore") for 13 million shares of its treasury stock valued at approximately $376.0. Each Baby Superstore shareholder received .8121 of a share of Company stock for each Baby Superstore share, except for the Chairman and Chief Executive Officer of Baby Superstore who received .5150 of a share.

Baby Superstore, a leading retailer of baby and young children's products, opened its first store in 1971 and has operated as a public company since November, 1994. Baby Superstore operated 76 stores in 23 states, primarily in the southeast and midwest. Products sold by Baby Superstore were directed toward newborns and children up to three years old. The Company plans to operate substantially all the acquired stores.

This acquisition has been accounted for as a purchase at February 1, 1997. The excess of purchase price over net assets acquired of $365.0 has been recorded as goodwill and will be amortized on a straight-line basis over 40 years.

Consolidated pro forma income and earnings per share, as if the acquisition had taken place as of the beginning of 1995, would not have been materially different from the reported amounts for 1996 and 1995.

OTHER CHARGES

On July 12, 1996, an arbitrator rendered an award against the Company in connection with a dispute involving rights under a 1982 license agreement for toy store operations in the Middle East. Accordingly, the Company has recorded a provision of $59.5, ($37.8 after tax or $.14 cents per share) representing all costs in connection with this matter. The Company has filed an appeal with the United States Court of Appeals for the second circuit.

On February 1, 1996, the Company recorded charges of $396.6 ($269.1 after tax or $.98 cents per share) to restructure its worldwide operations (the "restructuring") and to early adopt Financial Accounting Standards Board ("FAS No. 121"), "Accounting for the Impairment of Long-Lived Assets and Long-Lived Assets to be Disposed Of." The restructuring charge included $184.0 related to strategic inventory repositioning, $84.4 related to the closing or franchising of 25 stores, $71.6 for the consolidation of three distribution centers and seven administrative facilities and $32.4 of other costs. Total restructuring and other charges were comprised of $208.8 relating to operations in the United States and $187.8 for international operations. The charge to early adopt FAS No.121 was $24.2, primarily related to a write down of certain store assets to fair value, based on discounted cash flows. At February 1, 1997, the Company had approximately $90 million of liabilities remaining for its restructuring program primarily relating to long-term lease obligations and other commitments. The Company believes these reserves are adequate to complete the restructuring program.

PROPERTY AND EQUIPMENT

	Useful Life (in years)	February 1, 1997	February 3, 1996
Land		$ 821.2	$ 802.4
Buildings	45-50	1,834.3	1,745.3
Furniture and equipment	5-20	1,521.9	1,351.9
Leaseholds and leasehold improvements	12 1\2-50	1,060.1	959.0
Construction in progress		37.1	45.6
Leased property under capital leases		30.6	25.1
		5,305.2	4,929.3
Less accumulated depreciation and amortization		1,257.8	1,071.1
		$ 4,047.4	$ 3,858.2

SEASONAL FINANCING AND LONG-TERM DEBT

	February 1, 1997	February 3, 1996
5.61% £200 note payable, due 2001(a)	$ 325.4	$ -
8 3\4% debentures, due 2021, net of expenses	198.2	198.1
Japanese yen loans payable at annual interest rates from 3.45% to 6.47%, due in varying amounts through 2012	150.2	178.3
4 7\8 % convertible subordinated notes payable, due October 2000(b)	115.0	-
8 1\4% sinking fund debentures, due 2017, net of discounts	88.4	88.3
Industrial revenue bonds, net of expenses (c)	70.0	74.2
7% British pound sterling loan payable, due quarterly through 2001(d)	67.1	77.3
Mortgage notes payable at annual interest rates from 6% to 11% (e)	12.2	19.2
Obligations under capital leases	17.1	12.8
11% British pound sterling Stepped Coupon Guaranteed Bonds	-	198.4
	1,043.6	846.6
Less current portion (f)	135.1	19.8
	$ 908.5	$ 826.8

(a) Supported by a £200 bank letter of credit. This note has been converted by an interest rate and currency swap to a floating rate, US dollar obligation at 3 month LIBOR less approximately 110 basis points.

(b) Obligation of Baby Superstore. Convertible into shares of the Company's common stock at the conversion price of $66.34. These notes are subject to an offer to purchase at par, plus accrued interest, which will close on April 16, 1997. Accordingly, these notes have been classified as current obligations.

(c) Bank letters of credit of $52.7, expiring in 1998, support certain of these industrial revenue bonds. The Company expects that the bank letters of credit will be renewed. The bonds have fixed or variable interest rates with an average rate of 3.4% at February 1, 1997.

(d) Collateralized by property with a carrying value of $159.5 at February 1, 1997.

(e) Collateralized by property and equipment with an aggregate carrying value of $18.2 at February 1, 1997.

(f) Included in accrued expenses and other current liabilities on the consolidated balance sheets.

The fair market value of the Company's long-term debt at February 1, 1997 was approximately $1,007.0. The fair market value was estimated using quoted market rates for publicly traded debt and estimated interest rates for non-public debt.

The Company has a $1 billion unsecured committed revolving credit facility expiring in February 2000. This multi-currency facility permits the Company to borrow at the lower of LIBOR plus a fixed spread or a rate set by competitive auction. The facility is available to support domestic commercial paper borrowings and to meet worldwide cash requirements.

Additionally, the Company also has lines of credit with various banks to meet the short-term financing needs of its foreign subsidiaries. The weighted average interest rate on short-term borrowings outstanding at February 1, 1997 and February 3, 1996 was 3.1% and 4.0%, respectively.

The annual maturities of long-term debt at February 1, 1997 are as follows:

1997	$ 135.1
1998	25.7
1999	26.4
2000	26.0
2001	334.0
2002 and subsequent	496.4
	$ 1,043.6

LEASES

The Company leases a portion of the real estate used in its operations. Most leases require the Company to pay real estate taxes and other expenses; some require additional amounts based on percentages of sales.

Minimum rental commitments under noncancelable operating leases having a term of more than one year as of February 1, 1997 are as follows:

	Gross minimum rentals	Sublease income	Net minimum rentals
1997	$ 331.8	$ 17.4	$ 314.4
1998	328.3	16.9	311.4
1999	326.3	15.6	310.7
2000	322.1	12.9	309.2
2001	317.5	11.8	305.7
2002 and subsequent	3,303.3	65.2	3,238.1
	$ 4,929.3	$ 139.8	$ 4,789.5

Total rental expense was as follows:

			Year ended
	February 1, 1997	February 3, 1996	January 28, 1995
Minimum rentals	**$ 295.3**	$ 284.3	$ 226.4
Additional amounts computed as percentages of sales	**5.5**	5.6	6.3
	300.8	289.9	232.7
Less sublease income	**18.8**	17.0	10.3
	$ 282.0	$ 272.9	$ 222.4

STOCKHOLDERS' EQUITY

The common shares of the Company, par value $.10 per share, were as follows:

	February 1, 1997	February 3, 1996
Authorized shares	**650.0**	650.0
Issued shares	**300.4**	300.4
Treasury shares	**12.6**	27.3
Issued and outstanding shares	**287.8**	273.1

Earnings per share is computed by dividing net earnings by the weighted average number of common shares outstanding after reduction for treasury shares and assuming exercise of dilutive stock options computed by the treasury stock method using the average market price during the year. Weighted average number of common and common equivalent shares used in computing earnings per share were 277.5, 276.9 and 287.4 at February 1, 1997, February 3, 1996 and January 28, 1995, respectively.

Effective January 1, 1996, the Company formed a new parent company (the "Surviving Company") thus making the former parent company (the "Predecessor Company") a wholly-owned subsidiary of the Surviving Company. As a result of this corporate inversion, each share of common stock of the Predecessor Company was converted into one share of common stock of the Surviving Company.

In April 1994, the Company entered into an agreement with Petrie Stores Corporation ("Petrie"), the then holder of 14% of the Company's outstanding Common Stock. The Company consummated its transaction with Petrie on January 24, 1995, wherein 42.1 shares of the Company's common stock were issued from its treasury in exchange for 39.9 shares of the Company's common stock and $165.0 in cash.

TAXES ON INCOME

The provisions for income taxes consist of the following:

			Year ended
	February 1, 1997	February 3, 1996	January 28, 1995
Current:			
Federal	**$ 135.9**	$ 137.1	$ 251.6
Foreign	**56.8**	26.7	29.2
State	**29.6**	20.4	46.0
	222.3	184.2	326.8
Deferred:			
Federal	**58.6**	(21.8)	8.9
Foreign	**(39.2)**	(41.6)	(24.7)
State	**4.0**	(3.3)	1.3
	23.4	(66.7)	(14.5)
Total tax provision	**$ 245.7**	$ 117.5	$ 312.3

The tax effects of temporary differences and carryforwards that give rise to significant portions of deferred tax assets and liabilities consist of the following:

			Year ended
	February 1, 1997	February 3, 1996	January 28, 1995
Deferred tax assets:			
Net operating loss carryforwards	**$154.8**	$108.9	$ 94.0
Restructuring	**53.1**	122.1	0.0
Other	**31.5**	21.4	35.9
Gross deferred tax assets	**239.4**	252.4	129.9
Valuation allowance	**(36.8)**	(29.5)	(17.9)
	$202.6	$222.9	$112.0
Deferred tax liabilities:			
Property, plant and equipment	**249.3**	245.0	217.0
LIFO inventory	**63.7**	64.3	49.9
Other tax	**3.8**	4.4	4.0
Gross deferred liability	**$316.8**	$313.7	$270.9
Net deferred tax liability	**$114.2**	$ 90.8	$158.9

A reconciliation of the federal statutory tax rate with the effective tax rate follows:

			Year ended
	February 1, 1997	February 3, 1996	January 28, 1995
Statutory tax rate	**35.0%**	35.0%	35.0%
State income taxes, net of federal income tax benefit	**3.7**	3.4	3.7
Foreign	**(2.3)**	(1.3)	(0.4)
Restructuring and other charges	**-**	7.2	-
Other, net	**0.1**	(0.1)	(1.3)
Effective tax rate	**36.5%**	44.2%	37.0%

Deferred income taxes are not provided on unremitted earnings of foreign subsidiaries that are intended to be indefinitely invested. Unremitted earnings were approximately $361.0 at February 1, 1997, exclusive of amounts that if remitted would result in little or no tax under current U.S. tax laws. Net income taxes of approximately $114.0 would be due if these earnings were to be remitted.

PROFIT SHARING PLAN

The Company has a profit sharing plan with a 401(k) salary deferral feature for eligible domestic employees. The terms of the plan call for annual contributions by the Company as determined by the Board of Directors, subject to certain limitations. The profit sharing plan may be terminated at the Company's discretion. Provisions of $30.8, $32.3 and $31.4 have been charged to earnings in 1996, 1995, and 1994, respectively.

STOCK OPTIONS

The Company has Stock Option Plans (the "Plans") which provide for the granting of options to purchase the Company's common stock to substantially all employees and non-employee directors of the Company. The Plans provide for the issuance of non-qualified options, incentive stock options, performance share options, performance units, stock appreciation rights, restricted shares and unrestricted shares. The Plans provide for a variety of vesting dates with the majority of the options vesting approximately five years from the date of grant. The options granted to non-employee directors are exercisable 20% each year on a cumulative basis commencing one year from the date of grant.

In addition to the aforementioned plans, 3.4 stock options were granted to certain senior executives during the period from 1988 to 1996 pursuant to stockholder approved individual plans. Of this total, 2.9 options vest 20% each year on a cumulative basis commencing one year from the date of grant with the balance of the options vesting five years from the date of grant. The exercise price per share of all options granted has been the average of the high and low market price of the Company's common stock on the date of grant. Most options must be exercised within ten years from the date of grant.

At February 1, 1997, an aggregate of 36.2 shares of authorized common stock were reserved for all of the Plans noted above, of which 13.0 were available for future grants. All outstanding options expire at dates ranging from May 1997 to January 2007.

Stock option transactions are summarized as follows:

	Shares Under Option		
	Incentive	Non-Qualified	Weighted-Average Exercise Price
Outstanding February 3, 1996	.2	20.2	$ 24.08
Granted *	.4	6.3	34.59
Exercised	(.2)	(2.1)	17.67
Canceled	-	(1.6)	25.20
Outstanding February 1, 1997	**.4**	**22.8**	**$25.82**
Options exercisable at February 1, 1997	-	**9.2**	**$24.15**

*Includes options assumed with the acquisition of Baby Superstore.

The Company utilizes a restoration feature to encourage the early exercise of options and retention of shares, thereby promoting increased employee share ownership. This feature provides for the grant of new options when previously owned shares of Company stock are used to exercise existing options. Restoration option grants are non-dilutive as they do not increase the combined number of shares of Company stock and options held by an employee prior to exercise. The new options are granted at a price equal to the fair market value on the date of the new grant, become exercisable six months from the date of grant and generally expire on the same date as the original options that were exercised.

The Company has adopted the disclosure only provisions of Statement of Financial Accounting Standards (FAS) No. 123, "Accounting for Stock-Based Compensation", issued in October 1995. In accordance with the provisions of FAS No. 123, the Company applies APB Opinion 25 and related interpretations in accounting for its stock option plans and, accordingly, does not recognize compensation cost. If the Company had elected to recognize compensation cost based on the fair value of the options granted at grant date as prescribed by FAS No. 123, net income and earnings per share would have been reduced to the pro forma amounts indicated in the table below:

	1996	1995
Net income-as reported	**$ 427.4**	$ 148.1
Net income-pro forma	**411.3**	139.5
Earning per share-as reported	**1.54**	.53
Earnings per share-pro forma	**1.48**	.50

The weighted-average fair value at date of grant for options granted in 1996 and 1995 were $24.58 and $31.49, respectively. The fair value of each option grant is estimated on the date of grant using the Black-Scholes option pricing model. As there were a number of options granted throughout the 1995 and 1996 years, a range of assumptions are provided below:

Expected stock price volatility	.241 - .328
Risk-free interest rate	5.0% - 7.1%
Weighted average expected life of options	6 years

The effects of applying FAS 123 and the results obtained through the use of the Black-Scholes option pricing model are not necessarily indicative of future values.

FOREIGN OPERATIONS

Certain information relating to the Company's foreign operations is set forth below. Corporate assets include all cash and cash equivalents and other related assets.

		Year ended	
	February 1, 1997	February 3, 1996	January 28, 1995
Sales			
Domestic	**$ 7,151.2**	$ 6,791.5	$ 6,644.8
Foreign	**2,781.2**	2,635.4	2,100.8
Total	**$ 9,932.4**	$ 9,426.9	$ 8,745.6
Operating Profit			
Domestic	**$ 692.2**	$ 432.8 [b]	$ 778.7
Foreign	**131.3**	(74.2)[c]	140.8
General corporate expenses	**(69.2)**[a]	(7.1)	(7.5)
Interest expense, net	**(81.2)**	(85.9)	(67.9)
Earnings before taxes on income	**$ 673.1**	$ 265.6	$ 844.1
Identifiable Assets			
Domestic	**$ 4,877.9**	$ 4,013.2	$ 3,950.5
Foreign	**2,345.6**	2,483.0	2,216.1
Corporate	**799.7**	241.3	404.6
Total	**$ 8,023.2**	$ 6,737.5	$ 6,571.2

(a) After an arbitration award charge of $59.5.
(b) After restructuring and other charges of $208.8.
(c) After restructuring and other charges of $187.8.

OTHER MATTERS

On May 22, 1996, the Staff of the Federal Trade Commission (the "FTC") filed an administrative complaint against the Company alleging that the Company is in violation of Section 5 of the Federal Trade Commission Act for its practices relating to warehouse clubs. The complaint alleges that the Company reached understandings with various suppliers that such suppliers not sell to the clubs the same items that they sell to the Company. The complaint also alleges that the Company "facilitated understandings" among the manufacturers that such manufacturers not sell to clubs. The complaint seeks an order that the Company cease and desist from this practice. Hearings on this complaint commenced on March 5, 1997.

Since the filing of the FTC complaint, several class action suits have been filed against the Company, alleging that the Company has violated certain state competition laws as a consequence of the behavior alleged in the FTC complaint. These class action suits seek damages in unspecified amounts and other relief under state law.

The Company believes that both its policy and its conduct in connection with the foregoing are within the law and plans to contest these actions vigorously. The Company also believes that these actions will not have a material adverse effect on its financial condition or results of operations.

REPORT OF MANAGEMENT

Responsibility for the integrity and objectivity of the financial information presented in this Annual Report rests with the management of Toys"R"Us. The accompanying financial statements have been prepared from accounting records which management believes fairly and accurately reflect the operations and financial position of the Company. Management has established a system of internal controls to provide reasonable assurance that assets are maintained and accounted for, in accordance with its policies and that transactions are recorded accurately on the Company's books and records.

The Company's comprehensive internal audit program provides for constant evaluation of the adequacy of the adherence to management's established policies and procedures. The Company has distributed to key employees its policies for conducting business affairs in a lawful and ethical manner.

The Audit Committee of the Board of Directors, which is comprised solely of outside directors, provides oversight to the financial reporting process through periodic meetings with our independent auditors, internal auditors and management.

The financial statements of the Company have been audited by Ernst & Young LLP, independent auditors, in accordance with generally accepted auditing standards, including a review of financial reporting matters and internal controls to the extent necessary to express an opinion on the consolidated financial statements.

Michael Goldstein
Vice Chairman and
Chief Executive Officer

Louis Lipschitz
Executive Vice President
and Chief Financial Officer

REPORT OF INDEPENDENT AUDITORS

The Board of Directors and Stockholders
Toys"R"Us, Inc.

We have audited the accompanying consolidated balance sheets of Toys"R"Us, Inc. and subsidiaries as of February 1, 1997 and February 3, 1996, and the related consolidated statements of earnings, stockholders' equity and cash flows for each of the three years in the period ended February 1, 1997. These financial statements are the responsibility of the Company's management. Our responsibility is to express an opinion on these financial statements based on our audits.

We conducted our audits in accordance with generally accepted auditing standards. Those standards require that we plan and perform the audit to obtain reasonable assurance about whether the financial statements are free of material misstatement. An audit includes examining, on a test basis, evidence supporting the amounts and disclosures in the financial statements. An audit also includes assessing the accounting principles used and significant estimates made by management, as well as evaluating the overall financial statement presentation. We believe that our audits provide a reasonable basis for our opinion.

In our opinion, the financial statements referred to above present fairly, in all material respects, the consolidated financial position of Toys"R"Us, Inc. and subsidiaries at February 1, 1997 and February 3, 1996, and the consolidated results of their operations and their cash flows for each of the three years in the period ended February 1, 1997, in conformity with generally accepted accounting principles.

Ernst & Young LLP

New York, New York
March 12, 1997

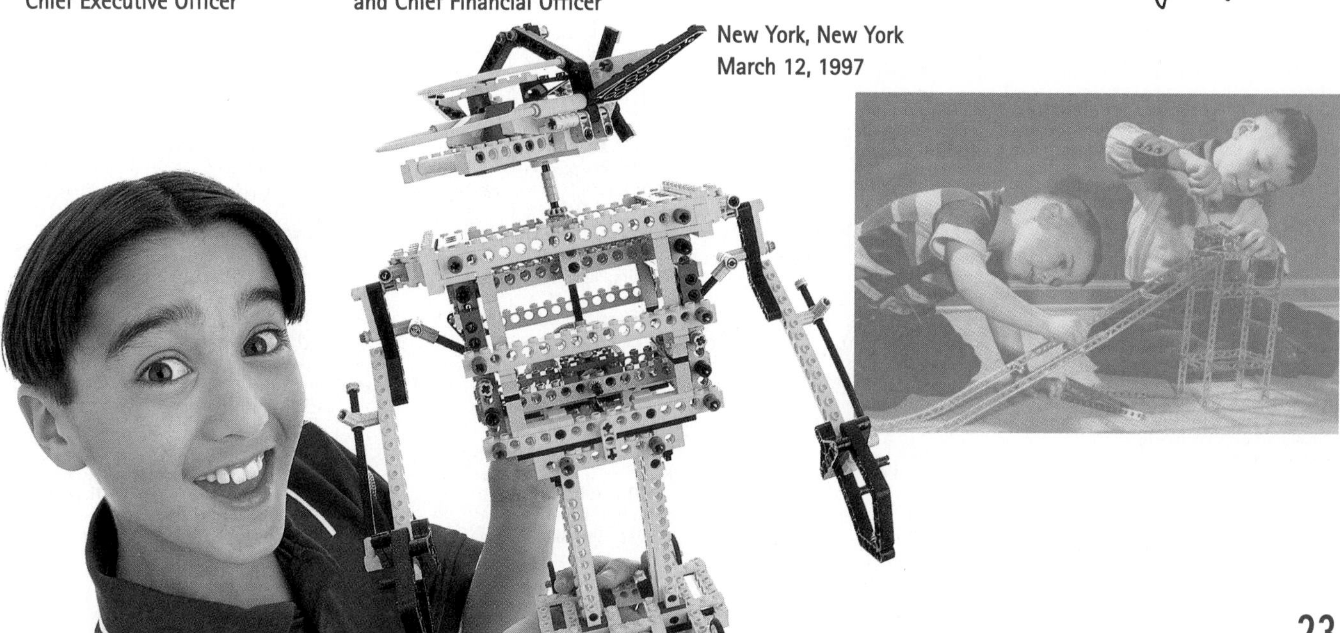

DIRECTORS AND OFFICERS

DIRECTORS

Charles Lazarus
Chairman of the Board of the Company

Robert A. Bernhard
Real Estate Developer

RoAnn Costin
President, Reservoir Capital Management, Inc.

Michael Goldstein
Vice Chairman and Chief Executive Officer of the Company

Milton S. Gould
Attorney-at-law; Of Counsel to LeBoeuf, Lamb, Greene & MacRae

Shirley Strum Kenny
President, State University of New York at Stony Brook

Norman S. Matthews
Former President, Federated Department Stores, Inc; Consultant

Howard W. Moore
Former Executive Vice President - General Merchandise Manager of the Company; Consultant

Robert C. Nakasone
President and Chief Operating Officer of the Company

Harold M. Wit
Managing Director, Allen & Company Incorporated, Investment Bankers

OFFICERS - CORPORATE AND ADMINISTRATIVE

Michael Goldstein
Vice Chairman and Chief Executive Officer

Robert C. Nakasone
President and Chief Operating Officer

Louis Lipschitz
Executive Vice President and Chief Financial Officer

Roger C. Gaston
Senior Vice President - Human Resources

Michael P. Miller
Senior Vice President - Real Estate

Thomas J. Reinebach
Senior Vice President and Chief Information Officer

Gayle C. Aertker
Vice President - Real Estate

Michael J. Corrigan
Vice President - Compensation and Benefits

Eileen C. Gabriel
Vice President - Information Systems

Jon W. Kimmins
Vice President - Treasurer

Joseph J. Lombardi
Vice President - Controller

Matthew J. Lombardi
Vice President - Information Technology

Michael L. Tumolo
Vice President - Counsel

Peter W. Weiss
Vice President - Taxes

Robert S. Zarra
Vice President - Internal Audit

Andre Weiss
Secretary - Partner-Schulte Roth & Zabel, LLP

TOYS"R"US UNITED STATES - OFFICERS AND GENERAL MANAGERS

Michael J. Madden
President - Store Operations

Robert J. Weinberg
Senior Vice President - General Merchandise Manager

Van H. Butler
Senior Vice President - Divisional Merchandise Manager

Ernest V. Speranza
Senior Vice President - Advertising/Marketing

David Brewi
Vice President - Divisional Merchandise Manager

Kristopher M. Brown
Vice President - Distribution and Traffic

Richard N. Cudrin
Vice President - Human Resources and Corporate Employee Relations

John F. Cummo
Vice President - Creative Services

Thomas DeLuca
Vice President - Imports, Product Development and Safety Assurance

Harvey J. Finkel
Vice President - Regional Operations

Martin E. Fogelman
Vice President - Divisional Merchandise Manager

Michael A. Gerety
Vice President - Store Planning

Debra M. Kachurak
Vice President - Operations Development

Mitchell Loukota
Vice President - Divisional Merchandise Manager

Charlene Mady
Vice President - Area Merchandise Planning

Gerald S. Parker
Vice President - Regional Operations

Lee Richardson
Vice President - Advertising

Timothy J. Slade
Vice President - Transportation and Traffic

John P. Sullivan
Vice President - Divisional Merchandise Manager

William A. Stephenson
Vice President - Merchandise Planning and Allocation

Dennis J. Williams
Vice President- Regional Operations and General Manager New York/Northern New Jersey

GENERAL MANAGERS

Robert F. Price
Vice President-
Southern California/
Arizona/Nevada/Hawaii

Thomas A. Drugan
Illinois/Wisconsin/Minnesota

Cathy Filion
Michigan/N.W. Ohio

Mark H. Haag
Pacific Northwest/Alaska

Truvillus Hall
Northern California/Utah

Michael K. Heffner
Alabama/Georgia/South
Carolina/Tennessee

Daniel D. Hlavaty
Central Ohio/Indiana/Kentucky

Richard A. Moyer
S.Texas/Louisiana/Mississippi

John J. Prawlocki
Florida/Puerto Rico

Edward F. Siegler
Maryland/Virginia/North Carolina

Carl P. Spaulding
New England

Gregg Treadway
Colorado/Kansas/Missouri/
Iowa/Nebraska

Kevin VanderGriend
N.E. Ohio/W. Pennsylvania/
N. New York

TOYS"R"US INTERNATIONAL - OFFICERS AND COUNTRY MANAGEMENT

Gregory R. Staley
President

Lawrence H. Meyer
Vice President -
Chief Financial Officer

Joan W. Donovan
Vice President -
General Merchandise Manager

Joseph Giamelli
Vice President -
Information Systems

Jeff Handler
Vice President -
International Advertising

Larry S. Johnson
Vice President -
Franchise Markets

Adam F. Szopinski
Vice President -
Operations

Michael C. Taylor
Vice President -
Logistics

Pierre Buuron
President -
Toys"R"Us Central Europe

Jacques LeFoll
President -
Toys"R"Us France/Belgium

David Rurka
Managing Director -
Toys"R"Us United Kingdom

John Schryver
Managing Director -
Toys"R"Us Australia

Manabu Tazaki
President -
Toys"R"Us Japan

Antonio Urcelay
Managing Director -
Toys"R"Us Iberia

Keith Van Beek
President-
Toys"R"Us Canada

Larry D. Gardner
Vice President -
Toys"R"Us Asia

Scott Chen
General Manager -
Toys"R"Us Taiwan

Joe Tang
General Manager -
Toys"R"Us Hong Kong

Michael Yeo
General Manager -
Toys"R"Us Singapore

KIDS"R"US/BABIES"R"US - OFFICERS*

Richard L. Markee
President -
Kids"R"Us and Babies"R"Us

Gwen Manto
Senior Vice President -
General Merchandise Manager

James G. Parros
Senior Vice President -
Stores and
Distribution Center Operations

Jonathan M. Friedman
Vice President -
Chief Financial Officer -
Kids"R"Us and Babies"R"Us

James L. Easton
Vice President -
Divisional Merchandise Manager

William Farrell
Vice President -
Physical Distribution

Jerel G. Hollens
Vice President -
Merchandise Planning and
Management Information Systems

*Kids"R"Us Officer, unless otherwise indicated.

Debra G. Hyman
Vice President -
Divisional Merchandise Manager

Elizabeth S. Jordan
Vice President -
Human Resources

John C. Morrow
Vice President -
Management Information Systems

Christopher M. Scherm
Vice President -
Divisional Merchandise Manager

David E. Schoenbeck
Vice President -
Operations - Babies "R" Us

David S. Walker
Vice President-
Advertising

UARTERLY FINANCIAL DATA AND MARKET INFORMATION

QUARTERLY FINANCIAL DATA

(In millions except per share data)

The following table sets forth certain unaudited quarterly financial information.

Year Ended	First Quarter	Second Quarter	Third Quarter	Fourth Quarter*
February 1, 1997				
Net Sales	$ 1,645.5	$ 1,736.4	$ 1,883.0	$ 4,667.5
Cost of Sales	1,124.4	1,177.3	1,280.4	3,310.4
Other Charges	-	55.0	-	4.5
Net Earnings (Loss)	18.7	(7.5)	33.3	382.9
Earnings (Loss) per Share	$ .07	$ (.03)	$ .12	$ 1.37
February 3, 1996				
Net Sales	$ 1,493.0	$ 1,614.2	$ 1,714.5	$ 4,605.2
Cost of Sales	1,017.3	1,104.5	1,168.5	3,302.0
Other Charges	-	-	-	396.6
Net Earnings	18.4	15.8	20.9	93.0
Earnings per Share	$ .07	$ .06	$ .08	$ .34

*For the 13 weeks ended February 1, 1997 and the 14 weeks ended February 3, 1996

MARKET INFORMATION

The Company's common stock is listed on the New York Stock Exchange. The following table reflects the high and low prices (rounded to the nearest one-eighth) based on New York Stock Exchange trading since January 28, 1995.

The Company has not paid any cash dividends, however, the Board of Directors of the Company reviews this policy annually.

The Company had approximately 32,300 Stockholders of Record on March 11,1997.

		High	Low
1995	1st Quarter	30 7\8	23 3\4
	2nd Quarter	29 1\2	24 1\4
	3rd Quarter	28 3\4	21 5\8
	4th Quarter	24 3\8	20 1\2
1996	1st Quarter	29 7\8	21 7\8
	2nd Quarter	30 7\8	23 3\4
	3rd Quarter	34 1\16	25 7\8
	4th Quarter	37 5\8	24 3\8

CORPORATE DATA

Annual Meeting

The Annual Meeting of the Stockholders of Toys"R"Us will be held at the Somerset Hills Hotel, 200 Liberty Corner Road, at exit 33 off I-78, Warren, NJ 07059 on Wednesday, June 4, 1997 10:00 A.M.

The office of the Company is located at

461 From Road
Paramus, New Jersey 07652
Telephone: 201-262-7800

General Counsel

Schulte Roth & Zabel, LLP
900 Third Avenue
New York, New York 10022

Independent Auditors

Ernst & Young, LLP
787 Seventh Avenue
New York, New York 10019

Stockholder Information

The Company will supply to any owner of Common Stock, upon written request to Mr. Louis Lipschitz of the Company at the above address and without charge, a copy of the Annual Report on Form 10-K for the year ended February 1, 1997, which has been filed with the Securities and Exchange Commission.

Stockholder information including quarterly earnings and other corporate news releases, can be obtained by calling 800-785-TOYS. Significant news releases are anticipated to be available as follows:

Call After...	For the following...
May 19, 1997	1st Quarter Results
Aug. 18, 1997	2nd Quarter Results
Nov. 17, 1997	3rd Quarter Results
Jan. 8, 1998	Christmas Sales Results
Mar. 11, 1998	1997 Results

Common Stock Listed

New York Stock Exchange,
Symbol: TOY

Registrar and Transfer Agent

American Stock Transfer and Trust Company
40 Wall Street, New York, New York 10005
Telephone: 718-921-8200

Visit us on the Internet at www.toysrus.com

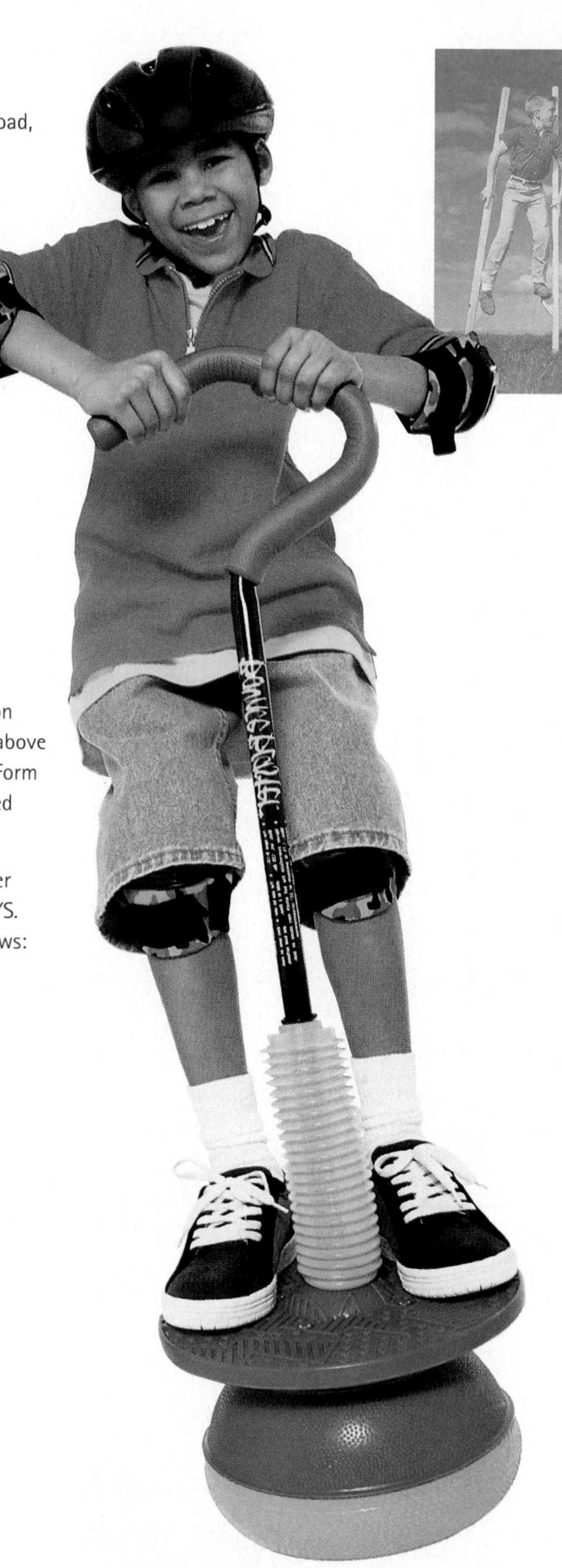

CHAPTER 7

Accounting Information Systems

LEARNING OBJECTIVES

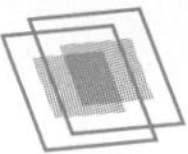

1. **Identify the principles of accounting systems design.**
2. **Describe how general ledger software and spreadsheet software are used in accounting.**
3. **Identify the basic elements of computer systems, and describe microcomputer accounting systems.**
4. **Explain how accountants use the Internet.**
5. **Explain the objectives and uses of special-purpose journals.**
6. **Explain the purposes and relationships of controlling accounts and subsidiary ledgers.**
7. **Construct and use a sales journal, purchases journal, cash receipts journal, cash payments journal, and other special-purpose journals as needed.**

DECISION POINT

FINE ARTS GALLERY AND FRAMING

Fine Arts Gallery and Framing, located in the South Fork Mall, was established two years ago to provide framing services. At that time, Gary Hoben, the owner, set up a computerized accounting system using Peachtree Complete Accounting™ for Windows.® His business is a sole proprietorship service business that uses Peachtree Complete's general journal and general ledger features. Because all sales were for cash or by credit card and because Hoben made a practice of paying all bills by the end of the month, the gallery had few receivables or payables. Over the past year, however, Hoben has added an inventory of color prints and posters, which carry a high profit margin. In addition, the new suppliers offer generous terms for payment. As a result, Hoben has allowed customers who buy framed prints or posters to pay over a period of three months. With the increased number and complexity of transactions involving inventory, accounts receivable, and accounts payable, Hoben's general journal/general ledger accounting system is now outdated. What kind of accounting system could Hoben use to handle the increased number and complexity of the store's transactions?

After analyzing the transactions in which his business engages, Hoben divided these transactions into five categories: credit sales, credit purchases, cash receipts, cash payments, and miscellaneous. Because more than 95 percent of the store's transactions fall into the first four categories, he decided to use Peachtree Complete's accounts payable and accounts receivable system. The accounts payable and accounts receivable system includes a

Critical Thinking Question: Will the use of a computerized accounting system for recording business transactions add more steps to the accounting cycle? Why or why not? **Answer:** No additional steps are added to the accounting cycle. However, the posting of transactions to the ledger and the preparation of a trial balance will be accomplished automatically, saving much time.

Point to Emphasize: The five kinds of transactions—credit sales, credit purchases, cash receipts, cash payments, and miscellaneous—are common in the typical business. In a manual system, a separate journal should be used for each type of transaction, with a general journal used for all other transactions. In a computer system, a separate function is chosen for each type.

separate or special-purpose journal for each of the categories that he defined. Hoben will use the general journal for his adjusting entries and some miscellaneous transactions. Because Hoben has been using Peachtree Complete's general journal/general ledger features for two years, he is eager to learn how to use the software's special journals and subsidiary ledgers. This chapter identifies the principles to consider when designing or buying a computerized accounting system and describes the basic features of computer hardware and software.

Principles of Accounting Systems Design

OBJECTIVE 1

Identify the principles of accounting systems design

Related Text Assignments:
Q: 1, 2
SE: 1
SD: 1, 2
FRA: 1, 2

Clarification Note: To work effectively with a computerized accounting system, students must understand how a manual accounting system works. A computerized system functions exactly like a manual system, except that it processes information at lightning speed.

Accounting systems summarize financial data about a business and organize the data into useful forms. Accountants communicate the results to management. The means by which an accounting system accomplishes these objectives is called data processing. Management uses the resulting information to make a variety of business decisions. As businesses have grown larger and more complex, the role of accounting systems has also grown. Today, the need for a total information system with accounting as its base is more pressing. For this reason, accountants must understand all phases of their company's operations as well as the latest development in systems design and technology.

Most businesses use computerized accounting systems that can be set up, monitored, and operated by accountants. However, their primary role is to provide timely accounting information to decision makers. Computer use does not eliminate the need to understand the accounting process. In fact, it is impossible to use accounting software without a basic knowledge of accounting. The opposite is also true: an accountant must have a basic knowledge of computer systems.

Analysis of computer system choices begins with the four general principles of accounting systems design: (1) cost-benefit principle, (2) control principle, (3) compatibility principle, and (4) flexibility principle.

Cost-Benefit Principle

Point to Emphasize: The cost of making a wrong decision is an intangible cost that can easily be overlooked in designing an accounting system. It is the systems analyst's job to strike the optimal balance between expected benefits and costs.

The most important systems principle, the cost-benefit principle, holds that the benefits derived from an accounting system and the information it generates must be equal to or greater than the system's cost. In addition to certain routine tasks—preparing payroll and tax reports and financial statements, and maintaining internal control—management may want or need other information. The benefits from that information must be weighed against both the tangible and the intangible costs of gathering it. Among the tangible costs are those for personnel, forms, and equipment. One of the intangible costs is the cost of wrong decisions stemming from the lack of good information. For instance, wrong decisions can lead to loss of sales, production stoppages, or inventory losses. Some companies have spent thousands of dollars on computer systems that do not offer enough benefits. On the other hand, some managers have failed to realize the important benefits that could be gained from investing in more advanced systems. It is the job of the accountant and the systems designer or analyst to weigh the costs and benefits.

Control Principle

Point to Emphasize: An accounting system should help protect the company's assets and provide reliable data.

The control principle requires that an accounting system provide all the features of internal control needed to protect the firm's assets and ensure that data are reliable. For example, before expenditures are made, they should be approved by a responsible member of management.

Compatibility Principle

Point to Emphasize: A systems analyst must carefully consider a business's activities and objectives, as well as the behavioral characteristics of its employees.

The compatibility principle holds that the design of an accounting system must be in harmony with the organizational and human factors of the business. The organizational factors have to do with the nature of a company's business and the formal roles its units play in meeting business objectives. For example, a company can organize its marketing efforts by region or by product. If a company is organized by region, its accounting system should report revenues and expenses by region. If a company is organized by product, its system should report revenues and expenses first by product and then by region.

The human factors of business have to do with the people within the organization and their abilities, behaviors, and personalities. The interest, support, and competence of a company's employees are very important to the success or failure of system design. In changing systems or installing new ones, the accountant must deal with the people who are presently carrying out or supervising existing procedures. Such people must understand, accept, and, in many cases, be trained in the new procedures.

Flexibility Principle

The flexibility principle holds that an accounting system must be flexible enough to allow the volume of transactions to grow and organizational changes to be made. Businesses do not stay the same. They grow, offer new products, add new branch offices, sell existing divisions, or make other changes that require adjustments in the accounting system. A carefully designed system allows a business to grow and change without making major alterations in the accounting system. For example, the chart of accounts should be designed to allow the addition of new asset, liability, owner's equity, revenue, and expense accounts.

Computer Software for Accounting

OBJECTIVE 2

Describe how general ledger software and spreadsheet software are used in accounting

Related Text Assignments:
Q: 3, 4

Accountants use a variety of software programs to assist them in performing their jobs. Two of the most important types of these are general ledger software and spreadsheet software.

General Ledger Software

General ledger software is the term commonly used to identify the group of integrated software programs that an accountant uses to perform major functions such as sales and accounts receivable, purchases and accounts payable, and payroll.

Today, most general ledger software is written using the Windows® operating system. Windows® has a graphical user interface (GUI). A graphical user interface employs symbols called icons to represent common operations. Examples of icons include a file folder, eraser, hourglass, and magnifying glass. When programs use Windows® as their graphical user interface, the program is termed "Windows®-compatible." The keyboard can be used in the traditional way, or a *mouse* or *trackball* may be used. The visual format and the ability to use a mouse or trackball make Windows®-compatible software easy to use.

Figure 1 shows how Peachtree Complete Accounting™ for Windows® uses a combination of text and icons. It is an example of what a graphical user interface looks like on your computer.

One of the benefits of Windows®-compatible software is the use of standardized terms and operations within software programs. Once you know how to use Peachtree Complete, you can use other Windows®-compatible applications, as they are similar.

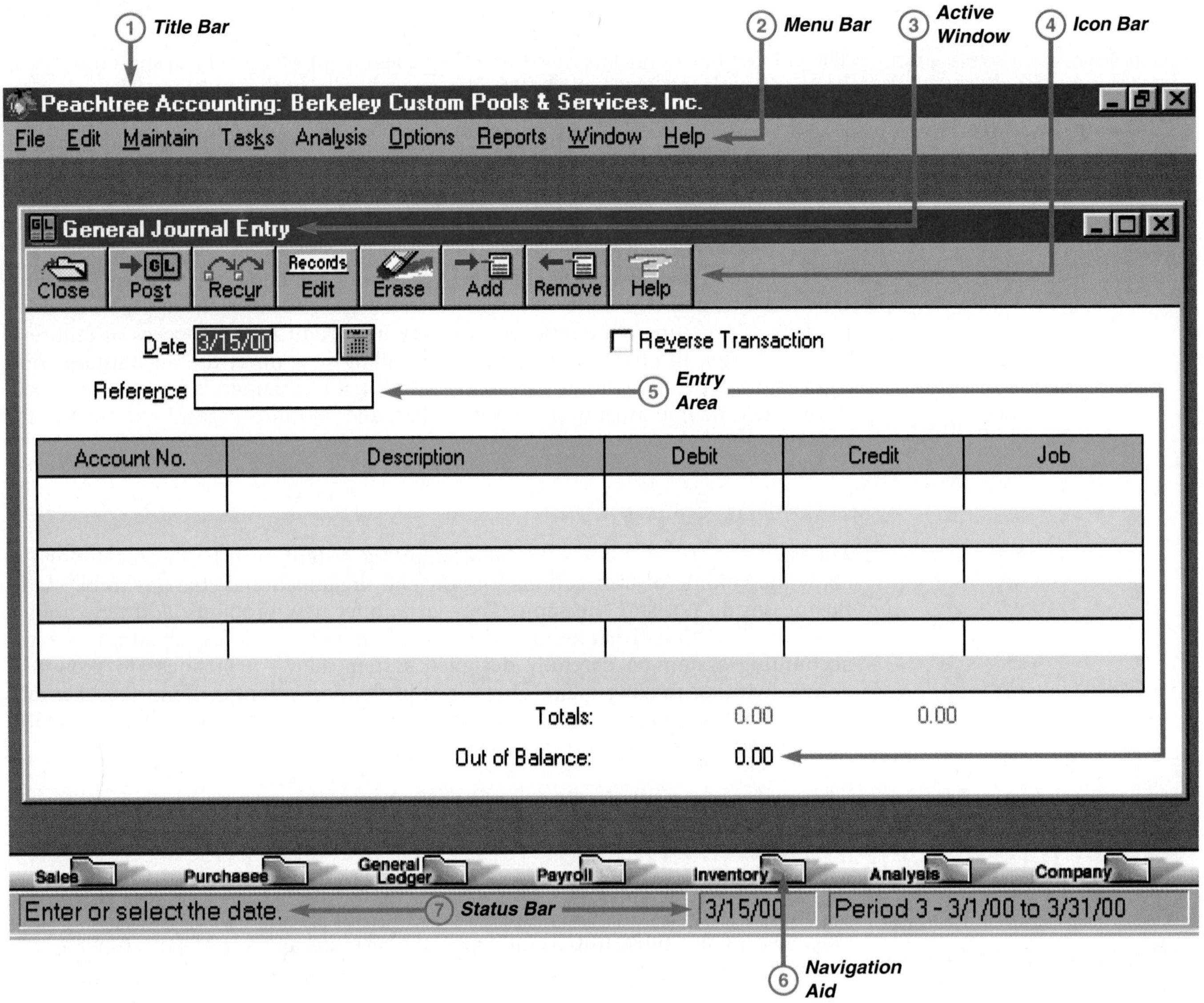

(1) ***Title Bar:*** The title bar is the bar at the top of your screen. When you enter the program, the name of the company is displayed on the title bar with Peachtree Accounting.

(2) ***Menu Bar:*** When you click on one of the menu bar headings, a submenu of options is pulled down or opened. These options are selected with a mouse or by holding down the <Alt> key and pressing the letter that is underlined in the desired menu bar option.

(3) ***Active Window:*** The "General Journal Entry" window has been chosen here in order to record an entry. This bar shows what window is open or "active."

(4) ***Icon Bar:*** The icon bar shows visual images that pertain to the window. Some icons are common to all windows, whereas other icons are specific to a particular window. You click on an icon to perform that function.

(5) ***Entry Area:*** This part of the screen is where information is entered for the journal entry.

(6) ***Navigation Aid:*** The navigation aid offers a graphical supplement to the menu bar. The major functions of the program are represented as icons or pictures that show you how tasks flow through the system.

(7) ***Status Bar:*** The gray bar (screen colors may vary) at the bottom of the window shows "help" information about the window, the current date, and the current accounting period.

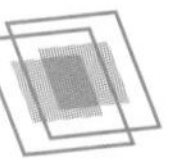

Figure 1
Graphical User Interface

Source: From Peachtree Complete Accounting for Windows. Reprinted by permission.

Three software programs available for this book are (1) General Ledger Software, (2) Peachtree Complete Accounting™ for Windows®, and (3) Quickbooks®. General Ledger Software is used to supplement end-of-chapter problems. It is designed for educational use and cannot be purchased commercially. Peachtree Complete and Quickbooks® can be purchased through retail stores. They can also be used with selected end-of-chapter problems.

BUSINESS BULLETIN: TECHNOLOGY IN PRACTICE

According to a recent survey of certified public accountants in public practice, industry, education, and government, more time was spent using spreadsheet software than any other kind of software. The other types of software used, in order of use, were word processing, tax accounting, general ledger, and database.[1]

Spreadsheet Software

Accountants use spreadsheet software in addition to general ledger software. General ledger software is effective for transactions that require double-entry accounting. Spreadsheets are used to analyze data. A spreadsheet is a grid made up of columns and rows into which are placed data or formulas used for financial planning, cost estimating, and other accounting tasks. Windows® Excel and Lotus 1-2-3 are popular commercial spreadsheet programs used for financial analysis and other spreadsheet applications.

Computerized Accounting Systems

OBJECTIVE 3

Identify the basic elements of computer systems, and describe microcomputer accounting systems

Related Text Assignments:
Q: 5, 6, 7
SE: 2, 3
SD: 1

Most businesses use computerized accounting systems. The parts of such systems may be put together in many different ways, and companies use their computers for many different purposes. A company's overall goal is to meet all its computing needs at the lowest possible cost. The computer system is the nerve center of the company. Large, multinational companies have vast computer resources, and use very powerful computers that are linked together to provide communication and data transfer around the world. However, even in these large companies and in most small companies, the PC or microcomputer system has become a critical element in the processing of information. This will be more critical as the Internet develops and companies begin using the Internet to communicate and transact business directly with vendors, suppliers, and clients.

Elements of a Computer System

Point to Emphasize: *Hardware* is another term for "computer equipment." Examples of hardware are disk drives, printers, terminals, and keyboards.

Hardware Hardware is the equipment needed to operate a computer system. Figure 2 shows the hardware in a typical PC or microcomputer system. The computer system includes components that are used to input data, such as the keyboard; the central processing unit (CPU) or network server for processing and storing data; and the printer or plotter for output. PCs process data using general ledger software and spreadsheet software. The day's transactions can be entered through the keyboard, observed on the monitor, then saved on the hard drive or floppy disk drive. Printed reports can be generated from the general ledger or spreadsheet program.

Point to Emphasize: *Software* is another term for "computer programs." Currently available software packages can accomplish a variety of accounting tasks.

Software A program is a set of instructions and steps that bring about the desired results in a computer system. Programs are known collectively as software. As mentioned earlier in the chapter, accounting tasks are performed by commercially available software programs such as Peachtree Complete Accounting™ for Windows®, Quickbooks®, Lotus 1-2-3, and Excel.

Figure 2
Microcomputer System

Source: Courtesy of IBM.

Often businesses link their computers together in a network environment. Networks can be configured as local area networks (LANs) or wide area networks (WANs). In a LAN, two or more computers in one location are networked. Computers that are networked in a classroom are an example of a LAN. Computers in different cities or around the world that are networked form a WAN. A large corporation's networked computers in different locations around the world are an example of a WAN.

Personnel The key personnel involved with a computer system are the systems analyst, the programmer, and the computer operator. The systems analyst designs the system on the basis of the organization's information needs, the programmer writes instructions for the computer, and the computer operator uses the computer to complete job-related tasks. In large organizations, the accountant works closely with the systems analyst to make sure that the accounting system is designed in accordance with the specific needs of the users of financial information. In smaller organizations, the company's owners or management often works with the certified public accounting firm to purchase and install commercial software that meets the company's needs.

BUSINESS BULLETIN: TECHNOLOGY IN PRACTICE

Not all companies have computers, but a recent survey of small and midsize companies by Arthur Andersen, LLP, the large accounting firm, showed that the percentage of non-computer companies stands at only 15 percent. One in two of the companies surveyed had personal computers for office employees, and half of them were on networks. More than half planned new technology or major upgrades in the next year. Internet usage among these companies was increasing. About one in four used the Internet for research and communication or had its own Web page. About one in twenty bought or sold goods over the Internet.[2]

BUSINESS BULLETIN: TECHNOLOGY IN PRACTICE

Many businesses achieve the computing power of mainframes, or large computers, by linking many microcomputers in a network. In a daisy chain network, the microcomputers are linked in a type of circle, or daisy chain. With this network, a person may have to go through several other microcomputers to reach a file or communicate with a person at another computer. In a home base, or star, network, all microcomputers are linked to a central switching point, or home base. A separate microcomputer called a server contains all the common data files, such as the accounting records, and is also linked to the home base. All users can access accounting records and other data files by going through the home base. This type of network is faster and more efficient than the daisy chain network.

Microcomputer Accounting Systems

Reinforcement Exercise: A good way to test your students' understanding of a typical accounting system is to ask them to match the source documents shown in Figure 3 with the related processing function.

Most small businesses purchase commercial accounting software that is already programmed to perform accounting functions. Most of these programs are organized so that each module performs a major task of the accounting system. A typical configuration of general ledger software is shown in Figure 3. Note that there is a software module, or feature, for each major accounting function—sales/accounts receivable, purchases/accounts payable, cash receipts, cash disbursements, payroll, and general journal. When these features interact with one another, the software is called an *integrated program.*

Figure 3
Microcomputer Accounting System Using General Ledger Software

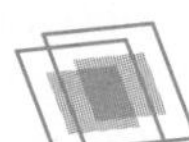

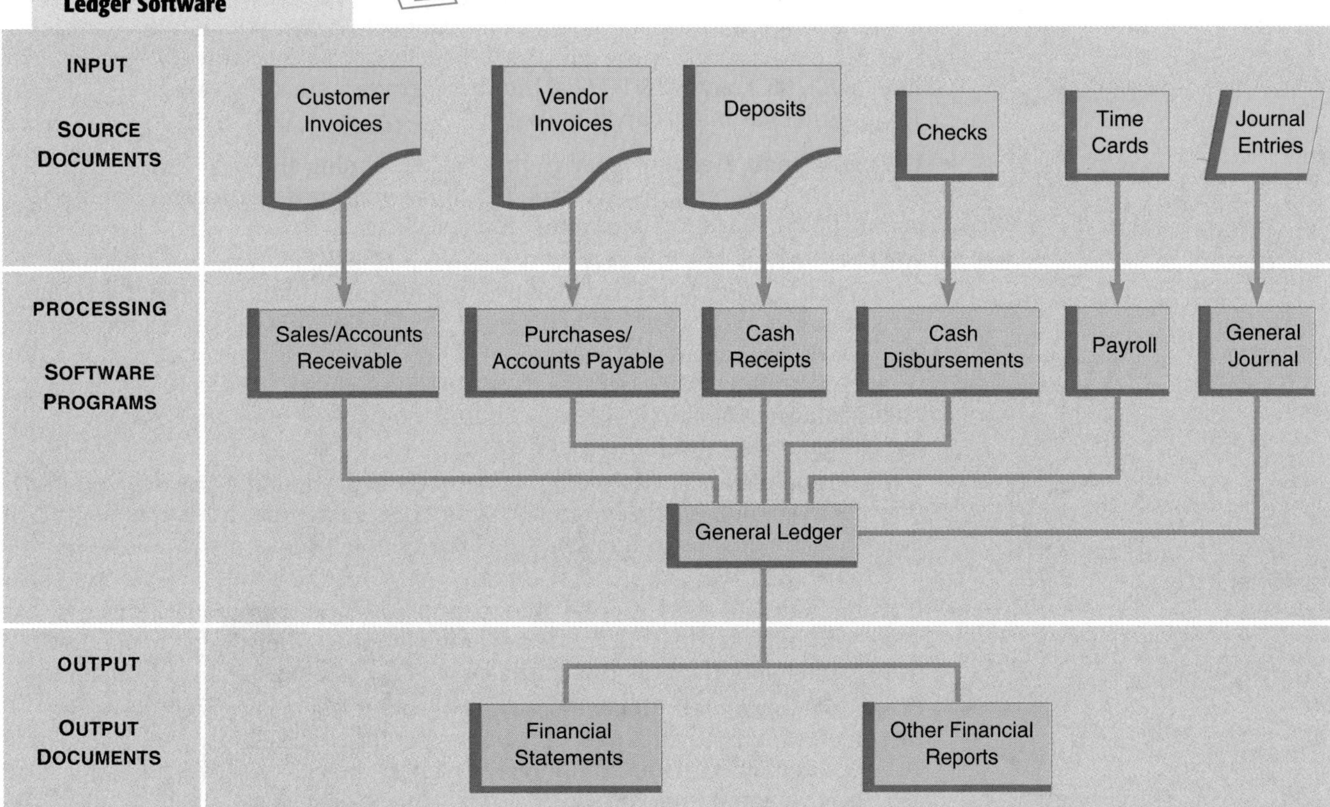

Point to Emphasize: At least one source document should support each business transaction entered in the records. The accounting system should provide easy reference to the source documents to facilitate subsequent examination (by an auditor, for example). Checks should be filed by check number after they have been returned by the bank, for instance.

Each transaction entered into the accounting system should be supported by source documents, or written evidence. Source documents verify that a transaction occurred and provide the details of the transaction. For example, a customer's invoice should support each sale on account, and a vendor's invoice should support each purchase. Even though the transactions are recorded by the computer in a file (on floppy disks or hard disks), the documents should be kept so that they can be examined at a later date if a question arises about the accuracy of the accounting records.

After transactions are processed, a procedure is followed to post them to and update the ledgers and to prepare the trial balance. Finally, the financial statements and other accounting reports are printed.

Peachtree Complete Accounting™ for Windows'® general ledger program allows either batch posting or real-time posting. In a batch posting system, source documents are recorded in the appropriate journal and saved. Posting is done at the end of the day, week, or month. In a real-time posting system, documents are posted as they are recorded in the journal. The basic goal of general ledger software is to computerize existing accounting tasks to make them less time-consuming and more accurate and dependable. However, it is important to understand, in principle, just what the computer is accomplishing. Knowledge of the underlying accounting process helps ensure that the accounting records are accurate, helps protect the assets of the business, and aids in the analysis of financial statements.

Accountants and the Internet

OBJECTIVE 4

Explain how accountants use the Internet

Related Text Assignments:
Q: 8
SD: 4
FRA: 1

The Internet is the world's largest computer network. The Internet allows any computer on the network to communicate with any other computer on the network. Internet usage is the fastest-growing part of the computer revolution. To access the Internet, a computer needs a modem that connects it to a phone line. A subscription to an Internet service provider (ISP) is usually necessary. Some ISPs are America Online (AOL), MCI, and AT&T. Local Internet providers are also available.

The Internet has many capabilities:

- **Electronic mail** Electronic mail (E-mail) is the sending and receiving of communications over a computer network. *Electronic mailing lists* are subscriptions to organizations that share a common interest.
- **World Wide Web** The World Wide Web is a repository that provides access to enormous amounts of information over the Internet. It can be compared to the biggest library in the world. When people type in a World Wide Web address, they may not only get access to the material at that location, but be in a position to do what is commonly called "surfing the Web." The software used to navigate the Web is known as a *browser.* The most popular browsers today are Netscape Navigator and Microsoft Internet Explorer.
- **Information retrieval** Information retrieval is the downloading of files from the Internet to an individual's computer. Companies sometimes offer upgrades of their software this way. Sometimes the information is free and sometimes there is a charge.
- **Bulletin boards** Bulletin boards allow people who have common interests to share information with one another over the Internet. Many hardware and software companies offer bulletin boards for technical support and troubleshooting.
- **Electronic commerce** Businesses and consumers increasingly are using the Internet for such activities as selling books, buying stocks, and paying bills. These practices and others using computers to conduct business transactions are called electronic commerce and provide new challenges for accountants in terms of keeping records of transactions and maintaining good internal controls.

BUSINESS BULLETIN: TECHNOLOGY IN PRACTICE

Accountants use the Internet for E-mail and for information retrieval. To find your way around the Internet, you use your browser and a *search engine.* Search engines are organized by subject, similar to the yellow pages or a library's catalog, and allow the user to find sources of information. Some popular search engines are Excite, Lycos, and Yahoo! There are many other features of the Internet that are also of interest to accountants. Newspapers and magazines such as *The New York Times, The Washington Post, Money,* and *Forbes* have Web sites. Many government agencies, such as the IRS, maintain Web sites. There is an *Electronic Accountant Newswire* available at Faulkner & Gray's Web site, http://www.faulknergray.com. Articles of interest to accountants are updated daily at this Web site. The public accounting firm Arthur Andersen has a Web subscription service called KnowledgeSpace™. Arthur Andersen says KnowledgeSpace™ will "sift, sort and interpret current news and relevant Arthur Andersen resources to help subscribers improve their business performance."

Manual Data Processing: Journals and Procedures

OBJECTIVE 5

Explain the objectives and uses of special-purpose journals

Related Text Assignments:
Q: 9
SE: 4
E: 1, 2
SD: 1, 5

The method of accounting described in prior chapters, and presented in Figure 4, is a form of manual data processing. It has been a useful way to present basic accounting theory and practice in small businesses. Data are fed into the system manually by entering each transaction from a source document into the general journal (which parallels the input device in a computer system). Then each debit and credit is posted to the correct ledger account (parallel to the processor and memory device). A work sheet (output device) is used as a tool to prepare the financial statements (output devices) that are distributed to users. This system, although useful for explaining the basic concepts of accounting, is actually used in only the smallest of companies.

Companies involved in more transactions, perhaps hundreds or thousands every week or every day, must have a more efficient and economical way of recording transactions in the journal and posting entries to the ledger. The easiest approach is to group typical transactions into common categories and use an input device called a special-purpose journal for each category. The objectives of special-purpose

Figure 4
Steps and Devices in a Manual Accounting System

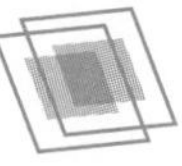

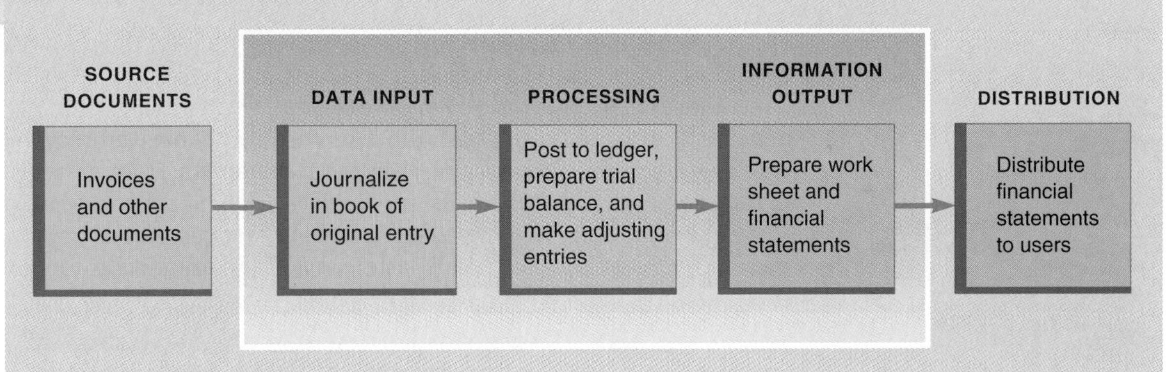

Instructional Strategy: Ask students to test their understanding of special-purpose journals by completing E 1 in class. Review the answers. Then check performance by asking how many missed 0–1, 2–3, 4–5, etc. Recommend SE 4 for those who want additional practice.

journals are efficiency, economy, and control. Although manual special-purpose journals are used by companies that have not yet computerized their systems, the concepts underlying special-purpose journals also underlie the software programs that drive computerized accounting systems.

Most business transactions—90 to 95 percent—fall into one of the following four categories. Each kind of transaction can be recorded in a special-purpose journal.

Point to Emphasize: Although a transaction could fall outside the four categories listed to the right, a transaction cannot fall into more than one category.

Transaction	Special-Purpose Journal	Posting Abbreviation
Sale of merchandise on credit	Sales journal	S
Purchase on credit	Purchases journal	P
Receipt of cash	Cash receipts journal	CR
Disbursement of cash	Cash payments journal	CP

Notice that these special-purpose journals correspond to the accounting functions shown in the microcomputer system in Figure 3, except for payroll.

Common Student Confusion: Students know that all transactions can be entered into the general journal, but they do not realize that special-purpose journals save considerable amounts of time and effort. Furthermore, students sometimes mistakenly enter all transactions initially into the general journal and then transcribe them into special-purpose journals. Students also enter detail in the special-purpose journal and then enter detail instead of totals in the ledgers.

The general journal is used to record transactions that do not fall into any of the special categories. For example, purchase returns, sales returns, and adjusting and closing entries are recorded in the general journal. (When transactions are posted from the general journal to the ledger accounts, the posting abbreviation is **J**.)

Using special-purpose journals greatly reduces the work involved in entering and posting transactions. For example, instead of posting every debit and credit for each transaction, in most cases only column totals—the sum of many transactions—are posted. In addition, labor can be divided, with each journal assigned to a different employee. This division of labor is important in establishing good internal control.

Controlling Accounts and Subsidiary Ledgers

OBJECTIVE 6

Explain the purposes and relationships of controlling accounts and subsidiary ledgers

Related Text Assignments:
Q: 10, 13
SE: 6, 8, 9, 10
E: 2, 5, 6, 7, 8
P: 1, 3, 4, 5, 6, 8
SD: 3, 5

Controlling accounts and subsidiary ledgers contain important details about the figures in special-purpose journals and other books of original entry. A controlling account, also called a *control account*, is an account in the general ledger that maintains the total balance of all related accounts in a subsidiary ledger. A subsidiary ledger is a ledger separate from the general ledger that contains a group of related accounts; the total of the balances in the subsidiary ledger accounts equals or ties in with the balance in the corresponding controlling account. For example, up to this point a single Accounts Receivable account has been used. But the balance in the single Accounts Receivable account does not tell how much each customer bought and paid for and how much each customer owes. Consequently, in practice, all companies that sell on credit keep an individual accounts receivable record for each customer. If a company has 6,000 credit customers, it has 6,000 accounts receivable.

BUSINESS BULLETIN: BUSINESS PRACTICE

Accounting information systems are obviously important for financial reporting, but they are increasingly becoming a means of providing good customer service as well. For instance, Walgreens, the world's largest prescription pharmacy company, has established direct communications with the insurance companies, employers, and government agencies that pay the bills of Walgreens' customers. From an accounting perspective, such links enhance Walgreens' profitability by eliminating rejected prescriptions, facilitating billing, and speeding collections. From the customers' point of view, instant communication with payers means faster service and immediate confirmation of payments—no forms, no paperwork, and no-hassle service.[3]

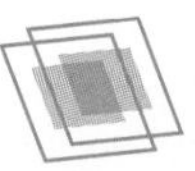

Figure 5
Relationship of Subsidiary Accounts to the Controlling Account

Including all those accounts with the other assets, liabilities, and owner's equity accounts would make the ledger very bulky. Therefore, companies take the individual customers' accounts out of the general ledger and place them in a separate, subsidiary ledger. In the accounts receivable subsidiary ledger, customers' accounts are filed either alphabetically or numerically (if account numbers are used).

When individual customers' accounts are put in an accounts receivable subsidiary ledger, the total balance is maintained in one Accounts Receivable account in the general ledger. The Accounts Receivable account in the general ledger is the controlling account in that its balance should equal the total of the individual account balances in the subsidiary ledger, as shown in Figure 5. Entries that involve accounts receivable, such as credit sales, must be posted to the individual customers' accounts every day. Postings to the controlling account in the general ledger are made at least once a month. When the amounts in the subsidiary ledger and the controlling account do not match, the accountant knows there is an error that must be found and corrected.

Discussion Question: What other general ledger accounts would be good candidates for controlling accounts? **Answer:** Any account, such as Notes Payable or Buildings, that requires a detailed listing of individual balances.

Most companies use an accounts payable subsidiary ledger as well. It is possible to use a subsidiary ledger for almost any account in the general ledger, such as Notes Receivable, Short-Term Investments, and Equipment, when management wants specific information on individual items.

Sales Journal

OBJECTIVE 7

Construct and use a sales journal, purchases journal, cash receipts journal, cash payments journal, and other special-purpose journals as needed

Related Text Assignments:
Q: 11, 12, 13
SE: 5, 6, 7, 8, 9, 10
E: 2, 3, 4, 5, 6, 7, 8
P: 1, 2, 3, 4, 5, 6, 7, 8
SD: 5

The sales journal is designed to contain all credit sales, and only credit sales. Cash sales are recorded in the cash receipts journal. Exhibit 1 illustrates a page from a typical sales journal. It shows the recording of six sales transactions involving five customers.

Notice how the sales journal saves time:

1. Only one line is needed to record each transaction. Each entry consists of a debit to a customer in Accounts Receivable and a corresponding credit to Sales.
2. The account names do not have to be written out because each entry automatically is debited to Accounts Receivable and credited to Sales.
3. No explanations are necessary because the function of the special-purpose journal is to record just one type of transaction. Only credit sales are recorded in the sales journal. Sales for cash are recorded in the cash receipts journal.

Instructional Strategy: To underscore the advantages and form of well-designed special-purpose journals, divide the class into small groups and ask each to complete a different required item in SD 5. If the class is large, several groups may work on the same item. State whether reference to the chapter is allowed. Reward groups with correct or best answers with one less required homework exercise or problem (preferable) from this chapter.

Point to Emphasize: The checkmarks indicate daily postings to the subsidiary accounts, which normally are listed in alphabetical or numerical order. Also, the column totals are posted to the appropriate general ledger accounts at the end of the month.

Exhibit 1. Sales Journal and Related Ledger Accounts

Sales Journal — Page 1

Date		Account Debited	Invoice Number	Terms	Post. Ref.	Amount (Debit/Credit Accounts Receivable/Sales)
July	1	Peter Clark	721	2/10, n/30	√	750
	5	Georgetta Jones	722	2/10, n/30	√	500
	8	Eugene Cumberland	723	2/10, n/30	√	335
	12	Maxwell Gertz	724	2/10, n/30	√	1,165
	18	Peter Clark	725	1/10, n/30	√	1,225
	25	Michael Powers	726	2/10, n/30	√	975
						4,950
						(114/411)

Post total at **end of month.**

Accounts Receivable — 114

Date		Post. Ref.	Debit	Credit	Balance Debit	Balance Credit
July	31	S1	4,950		4,950	

Sales — 411

Date		Post. Ref.	Debit	Credit	Balance Debit	Balance Credit
July	31	S1		4,950		4,950

4. Only one amount—the total credit sales for the month—has to be posted to the general ledger accounts. It is posted twice: once as a debit to Accounts Receivable and once as a credit to Sales. You can see the time this saves in Exhibit 1, with just six transactions. Imagine the time saved when there are hundreds of sales transactions.

Teaching Note: Working with special-purpose journals and subsidiary ledgers is a mechanical, not a mathematical, task. Accordingly, expect your students to be confused at first about where, when, and how transactions should be entered and posted. With practice, they will grasp the basic concepts.

Teaching Note: If terms of sale, including discounts, have not been previously covered, it is recommended that they be treated at this point.

Common Student Error: Students often forget to use the Post. Ref. columns of the ledger accounts, or they forget to reference the appropriate journal.

Parenthetical Note: The account number on the left is the account that was debited. The account number on the right is the account that was credited.

Summary of the Sales Journal Procedure Exhibit 2 shows the relationships between the sales journal, the accounts receivable subsidiary ledger, and the general ledger accounts. It also illustrates the procedure for using a sales journal, the steps of which are outlined in the list that follows.

1. Enter each sales invoice in the sales journal on a single line. Record the date, the customer's name, the invoice number, and the amount. No column is needed for the terms if the terms on all sales are the same.
2. At the end of each day, post each individual sale to the customer's account in the accounts receivable ledger. As each sale is posted, place a checkmark (or customer account number, if used) in the Post. Ref. (posting reference) column of the sales journal to indicate that it has been posted. In the Post. Ref. column of each customer's account, place an **S** and the sales journal page number (**S1** means Sales Journal—Page 1) to indicate the source of the entry.
3. At the end of the month, sum the Amount column in the sales journal to determine the total credit sales and post the total to the general ledger accounts (debit Accounts Receivable and credit Sales). Place the numbers of the accounts debited and credited beneath the total in the sales journal to indicate that this step has

Point to Emphasize: Accounts in the subsidiary ledger are maintained in alphabetical order. If account numbers are used to identify customers, the accounts would be listed in account number order.

Parenthetical Note: The daily posting to the individual accounts keeps the subsidiary ledger accounts up-to-date. The general ledger accounts, however, are normally recorded and reconciled with the subsidiary ledger once a month.

Discussion Question: Why are subsidiary accounts posted daily? **Answer:** (1) For control, to prevent customers from exceeding their credit limits. (2) To have up-to-date balances for customers wishing to pay their accounts.

Exhibit 2. Relationship of Sales Journal, General Ledger, and Accounts Receivable Subsidiary Ledger and the Posting Procedure

Sales Journal — Page 1

Date		Account Debited	Invoice Number	Terms	Post. Ref.	Amount (Debit/Credit Accounts Receivable/ Sales)
July	1	Peter Clark	721	2/10, n/30	√	750
	5	Georgetta Jones	722	2/10, n/30	√	500
	8	Eugene Cumberland	723	2/10, n/30	√	335
	12	Maxwell Gertz	724	2/10, n/30	√	1,165
	18	Peter Clark	725	1/10, n/30	√	1,225
	25	Michael Powers	726	2/10, n/30	√	975
						4,950
						(114/411)

Post individual amounts **daily** to subsidiary ledger accounts.

Post total at **end of month** to general ledger accounts.

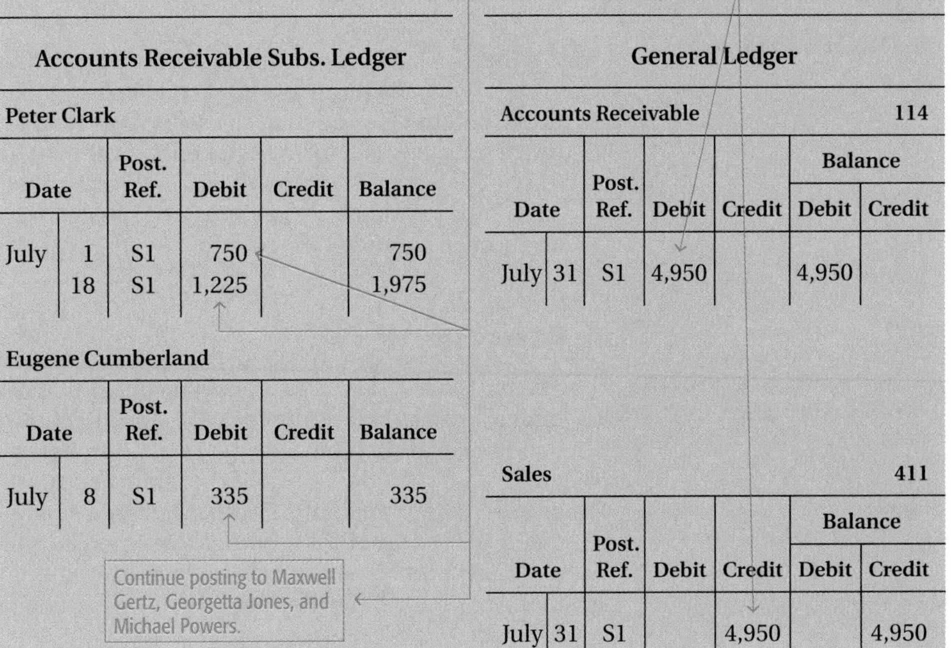

Accounts Receivable Subs. Ledger

Peter Clark

Date		Post. Ref.	Debit	Credit	Balance
July	1	S1	750		750
	18	S1	1,225		1,975

Eugene Cumberland

Date		Post. Ref.	Debit	Credit	Balance
July	8	S1	335		335

Continue posting to Maxwell Gertz, Georgetta Jones, and Michael Powers.

General Ledger

Accounts Receivable — 114

Date		Post. Ref.	Debit	Credit	Balance Debit	Balance Credit
July	31	S1	4,950		4,950	

Sales — 411

Date		Post. Ref.	Debit	Credit	Balance Debit	Balance Credit
July	31	S1		4,950		4,950

Point to Emphasize: In theory, the sum of the account balances from the subsidiary accounts must equal the balance in the related general ledger controlling account. In practice, however, the equality is verified only at the end of the month, when the general ledger is posted.

been completed. In the general ledger, indicate the source of the entry in the Post. Ref. column of each account.

4. Verify the accuracy of the posting by adding the account balances of the accounts receivable ledger and matching the total with the Accounts Receivable controlling account balance in the general ledger. You can do this by listing the accounts in a schedule of accounts receivable. As shown in Exhibit 3, the accounts are listed in the order in which they are maintained. This step is performed after collections on account in the cash receipts journal have been posted.

Discussion Question: In a schedule of accounts payable, what should the total accounts payable equal? **Answer:** It should equal the total in the Accounts Payable controlling account in the general ledger.

Exhibit 3. Schedule of Accounts Receivable

Mitchell's Used Car Sales Schedule of Accounts Receivable July 31, 20xx	
Peter Clark	$1,975
Eugene Cumberland	335
Maxwell Gertz	1,165
Georgetta Jones	500
Michael Powers	975
Total Accounts Receivable	$4,950

Point to Emphasize: Only the general ledger accounts are listed in the trial balance and financial statements.

The single controlling Accounts Receivable account in the general ledger summarizes all the individual accounts in the subsidiary ledger. Because the individual accounts are recorded daily and the controlling account is posted monthly, the total of the individual accounts in the accounts receivable ledger equals the controlling account only after the monthly posting. The monthly trial balance is prepared using only the general ledger accounts.

Sales Taxes Many retailers are required to collect a sales tax from their customers and periodically remit the total collected to the city or state. In such cases, an additional column is needed in the sales journal to record the credit to Sales Tax Payable on credit sales. The form of the entry is shown in Exhibit 4. The procedure for posting to the ledger is exactly the same as described above, except that the total of the Sales Tax Payable column must be posted as a credit to the Sales Tax Payable account at the end of the month.

Purchases Journal

Common Student Error: It is easy to forget that a cash purchase is entered into the cash payments journal, not into the purchases journal.

Point to Emphasize: Columns can be added to a special-purpose journal for accounts that are commonly used.

The purchases journal is used to record purchases on credit. It can take the form of either a single-column journal or a multicolumn journal. In a single-column journal, shown in Exhibit 5, only credit purchases of merchandise for resale to customers are recorded. This kind of transaction is recorded with a debit to Purchases and a credit to Accounts Payable. When a single-column purchases journal is used, credit purchases of things other than merchandise are recorded in the general journal. Cash purchases are never recorded in the purchases journal; they are recorded in the cash payments journal, which we explain later.

Exhibit 4. Section of a Sales Journal with a Column for Sales Tax

Sales Journal — Page 7

Date		Account Debited	Invoice Number	Terms	Post. Ref.	Debit	Credits	
						Accounts Receivable	Sales Tax Payable	Sales
Sept.	1	Ralph P. Hake	727	2/10, n/30	√	206	6	200

Teaching Note: Explain that the single-column purchases journal works exactly the same way as a sales journal, except that different ledger accounts are used.

Point to Emphasize: Accounts in the subsidiary ledger are generally maintained in alphabetical order. If account numbers are used to identify suppliers, the accounts would be listed in account number order.

Exhibit 5. Relationship of Single-Column Purchases Journal to the General Ledger and the Accounts Payable Subsidiary Ledger

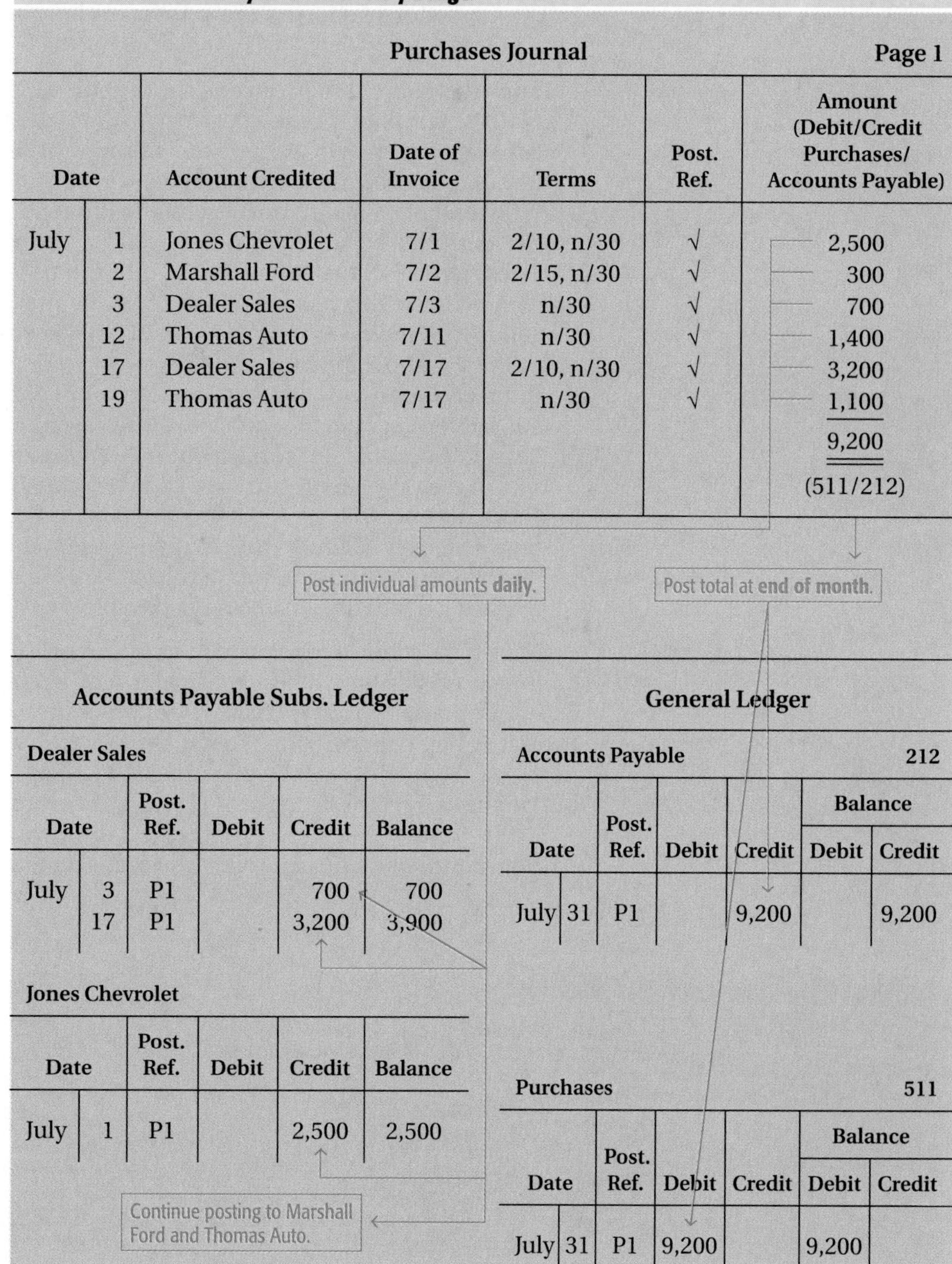

Purchases Journal — Page 1

Date		Account Credited	Date of Invoice	Terms	Post. Ref.	Amount (Debit/Credit Purchases/ Accounts Payable)
July	1	Jones Chevrolet	7/1	2/10, n/30	√	2,500
	2	Marshall Ford	7/2	2/15, n/30	√	300
	3	Dealer Sales	7/3	n/30	√	700
	12	Thomas Auto	7/11	n/30	√	1,400
	17	Dealer Sales	7/17	2/10, n/30	√	3,200
	19	Thomas Auto	7/17	n/30	√	1,100
						9,200
						(511/212)

Accounts Payable Subs. Ledger

Dealer Sales

Date		Post. Ref.	Debit	Credit	Balance
July	3	P1		700	700
	17	P1		3,200	3,900

Jones Chevrolet

Date		Post. Ref.	Debit	Credit	Balance
July	1	P1		2,500	2,500

General Ledger

Accounts Payable — 212

Date		Post. Ref.	Debit	Credit	Balance Debit	Balance Credit
July	31	P1		9,200		9,200

Purchases — 511

Date		Post. Ref.	Debit	Credit	Balance Debit	Balance Credit
July	31	P1	9,200		9,200	

Like Accounts Receivable, the Accounts Payable account in the general ledger is commonly used as a controlling account. The company keeps a separate account for each supplier in an accounts payable subsidiary ledger in order to know how much it owes each supplier. The process described above for using the accounts receivable subsidiary ledger and the general ledger controlling account also applies to the accounts payable subsidiary ledger and the general ledger controlling account. Thus, the total of the separate accounts in the accounts payable subsidiary ledger should equal the balance of the Accounts Payable controlling account in the general ledger. Here, too, the monthly total of the credit purchases posted to the individual accounts each day must equal the total credit purchases posted to the controlling account each month.

The procedure for using the purchases journal is much like that for using the sales journal.

1. Enter each purchase invoice in the purchases journal on a single line. Record the date, the supplier's name, the invoice date, the terms (if given), and the amount. It is not necessary to record the shipping terms in the Terms column because they do not affect the payment date.
2. At the end of each day, post each individual purchase to the supplier's account in the accounts payable subsidiary ledger. As each purchase is posted, place a checkmark in the Post. Ref. column of the purchases journal to show that it has been posted. Also place a **P** and the page number in the purchases journal (**P1** stands for Purchases Journal—Page 1) in the Post. Ref. column of each supplier's account to show the source of the entry.
3. At the end of the month, sum the Amount column and post the total to the general ledger accounts (a debit to Purchases and a credit to Accounts Payable). Place the numbers of the accounts debited and accounts credited beneath the total in the purchases journal to show that this step has been carried out.
4. Check the accuracy of the posting by adding the balances of the accounts payable ledger accounts and matching the total with the balance of the Accounts Payable controlling account in the general ledger. This step can be carried out by preparing a schedule of accounts payable.

Point to Emphasize: The multicolumn purchases journal can accommodate the purchase of *anything* on credit. Each column total (except the total of Other Accounts) must be posted at the end of the month.

The single-column purchases journal can be expanded to record credit purchases of things other than merchandise by adding separate debit columns for other accounts that are used often. For example, the multicolumn purchases journal in Exhibit 6 has columns for Freight In, Store Supplies, Office Supplies, and Other Accounts. Here, the total credits to Accounts Payable ($9,637) equal the total debits to Purchases, Freight In, Store Supplies, Office Supplies, and Other Accounts ($9,200 + $50 + $145 + $42 + $200). Again, the individual transactions in the Accounts Payable column are posted regularly to the accounts payable subsidiary ledger, and

Exhibit 6. A Multicolumn Purchases Journal

Purchases Journal **Page 1**

						Credit	Debits						
											Other Accounts		
Date		Account Credited	Date of Invoice	Terms	Post. Ref.	Accounts Payable	Purchases	Freight In	Store Supplies	Office Supplies	Account	Post. Ref.	Amount
July	1	Jones Chevrolet	7/1	2/10, n/30	√	2,500	2,500						
	2	Marshall Ford	7/2	2/15, n/30	√	300	300						
	2	Shelby Car Delivery	7/2	n/30	√	50		50					
	3	Dealer Sales	7/3	n/30	√	700	700						
	12	Thomas Auto	7/11	n/30	√	1,400	1,400						
	17	Dealer Sales	7/17	2/10, n/30	√	3,200	3,200						
	19	Thomas Auto	7/17	n/30	√	1,100	1,100						
	25	Osborne Supply	7/21	n/10	√	187			145	42			
	28	Auto Supply	7/28	n/10	√	200					Parts	120	200
						9,637	9,200	50	145	42			200
						(212)	(511)	(514)	(132)	(133)			(√)

BUSINESS BULLETIN: TECHNOLOGY IN PRACTICE

In manual accounting systems, subsidiary ledgers are often maintained in alphabetical order because that is a convenient way for people to organize information. With computers, however, numbers are much faster and easier to process than letters. For this reason, numbers are essential for all types of computer data processing. There are customer numbers, order numbers, social security numbers, product numbers, credit card numbers, and many more. When numbers are used, every account can be given a unique identification number. Then the potential confusion of having more than one Janet Smith or Juan Sanchez as customers can be avoided because each customer is assigned a different number.

the totals of each named account column in the journal are posted monthly to the correct general ledger accounts. Entries in the Other Accounts column are posted individually to the named accounts, and the column total is not posted.

Cash Receipts Journal

All transactions involving receipts of cash are recorded in the cash receipts journal. Examples of such transactions are cash from cash sales, cash from credit customers in payment of their accounts, and cash from other sources. The cash receipts journal must have several columns because, although all cash receipts require a debit to Cash, they require a variety of credit entries. Note the use of an Other Accounts column, the use of account numbers in the Post. Ref. column, and the daily posting of the credits to other accounts.

The cash receipts journal shown in Exhibit 7 has three debit columns and three credit columns. The three debit columns are as follows:

1. *Cash* Each entry must have an amount in this column because each transaction must be a receipt of cash.
2. *Sales Discounts* This company allows a 2 percent discount for prompt payment. Therefore, it is useful to have a column for sales discounts. Notice that in the transactions of July 8 and 28, the total of debits to Cash and Sales Discounts equals the credit to Accounts Receivable.
3. *Other Accounts* The Other Accounts column (sometimes called *Sundry Accounts*) is used for transactions that involve both a debit to Cash and a debit to some other account besides Sales Discounts.

These are the credit columns:

1. *Accounts Receivable* This column is used to record collections on account from customers. The customer's name is written in the Account Debited/Credited column so that the payment can be entered in the corresponding account in the accounts receivable subsidiary ledger. Postings to the individual accounts receivable accounts are usually done daily so that each customer's account balance is up-to-date.
2. *Sales* This column is used to record all cash sales during the month. Retail firms that use cash registers would make an entry at the end of each day for the total sales from each cash register for that day. The debit, of course, is in the Cash debit column.
3. *Other Accounts* This column is used for the credit portion of any entry that is neither a cash collection from accounts receivable nor a cash sale. The name of the account to be credited is indicated in the Account Debited/Credited column. For

Exhibit 7. Relationship of the Cash Receipts Journal to the General Ledger and the Accounts Receivable Subsidiary Ledger

Cash Receipts Journal — Page 1

Date		Account Debited/Credited	Post. Ref.	Debits: Cash	Debits: Sales Discounts	Debits: Other Accounts	Credits: Accounts Receivable	Credits: Sales	Credits: Other Accounts
July	1	Henry Mitchell, Capital	311	20,000					20,000
	5	Sales		1,200				1,200	
	8	Georgetta Jones	√	490	10		500		
	13	Sales		1,400				1,400	
	16	Peter Clark	√	750			750		
	19	Sales		1,000				1,000	
	20	Store Supplies	132	500					500
	24	Notes Payable	213	5,000					5,000
	26	Sales		1,600				1,600	
	28	Peter Clark	√	588	12		600		
				32,528	22		1,850	5,200	25,500
				(111)	(412)		(114)	(411)	(√)

Post individual amounts in Accounts Receivable ledger columns **daily.**

Post totals at **end of month.**

Total not posted.

Post individual amounts in Other Accounts column **daily.**

General Ledger

Cash — 111

Date		Post. Ref.	Debit	Credit	Balance Debit	Balance Credit
July	31	CR1	32,528		32,528	

Accounts Receivable — 114

Date		Post. Ref.	Debit	Credit	Balance Debit	Balance Credit
July	31	S1	4,950		4,950	
	31	CR1		1,850	3,100	

Store Supplies — 132

Date		Post. Ref.	Debit	Credit	Balance Debit	Balance Credit
Bal.					500	
July	20	CR1		500	—	

Accounts Receivable Subsidiary Ledger

Peter Clark

Date		Post. Ref.	Debit	Credit	Balance
July	1	S1	750		750
	16	CR1		750	—
	18	S1	1,225		1,225
	28	CR1		600	625

Georgetta Jones

Date		Post. Ref.	Debit	Credit	Balance
July	5	S1	500		500
	8	CR1		500	—

Continue posting to Notes Payable and Henry Mitchell, Capital.

Continue posting to Sales and Sales Discounts.

example, the transactions of July 1, 20, and 24 involve credits to accounts other than Accounts Receivable or Sales. These individual postings should be done daily (or weekly if there are just a few of them). If a company finds that it is consistently crediting a certain account in the Other Accounts column, it can add another credit column to the cash receipts journal for that particular account.

Point to Emphasize: The cash receipts journal can accommodate *all* receipts of cash. Daily postings are made, not only to the subsidiary accounts, but also to the "other accounts." The Other Accounts column totals, therefore, are not posted at the end of the month. Only at the end of the month are the control account balances meaningful or correct.

The procedure for posting the cash receipts journal, which is shown in Exhibit 7, is as follows:

1. Post the Accounts Receivable column daily to each individual account in the accounts receivable subsidiary ledger. The amount credited to the customer's account is the same as that credited to Accounts Receivable. A checkmark in the Post. Ref. column of the cash receipts journal indicates that the amount has been posted, and a **CR** plus the cash receipts journal page number (**CR1** means Cash Receipts Journal—Page 1) in the Post. Ref. column of each ledger account indicates the source of the entry.
2. Post the debits/credits in the Other Accounts columns daily, or at convenient short intervals during the month, to the general ledger accounts. As the individual items are posted, write the account number in the Post. Ref. column of the cash receipts journal to indicate that the posting has been done, and write **CR** and the page number of the cash receipts journal in the Post. Ref. column of each ledger account to indicate the source of the entry.
3. At the end of the month, total the columns in the cash receipts journal. The sum of the Debits column totals must equal the sum of the Credits column totals. This step is called *crossfooting.*

Debits Column Totals		**Credits Column Totals**	
Cash	$32,528	Accounts Receivable	$ 1,850
Sales Discounts	22	Sales	5,200
Other Accounts	0	Other Accounts	25,500
Total Debits	$32,550	Total Credits	$32,550

4. Post the Debits column totals as follows:
   a. Post the total of the Cash column as a debit to the Cash account.
   b. Post the total of the Sales Discounts column as a debit to the Sales Discounts account.
5. Post the Credits column totals as follows:
   a. Post the total of the Accounts Receivable column as a credit to the Accounts Receivable controlling account.
   b. Post the total of the Sales column as a credit to the Sales account.
6. Write the account numbers below each column in the cash receipts journal as the totals are posted to indicate that this step has been completed. A **CR** and the page number of the cash receipts journal are written in the Post. Ref. column of each account to indicate the source of the entry.
7. Notice that the total of the Other Accounts column is not posted to a general ledger account, because each entry is posted separately when the transaction occurs. The individual accounts are posted in step **2**. Place a checkmark (√) at the bottom of each Other Accounts column to show that postings in that column have been made and that the total is not posted.

Cash Payments Journal

Point to Emphasize: The cash payments journal can accommodate *all* cash payments. It functions like the cash receipts journal, although it uses some different general ledger accounts.

All transactions involving payments of cash are recorded in the cash payments journal (also called the *cash disbursements journal*). The cash payments journal shown in Exhibit 8 has three credit columns and two debit columns. The credit columns for the cash payments journal are as follows:

Exhibit 8. Relationship of the Cash Payments Journal to the General Ledger and the Accounts Payable Subsidiary Ledger

Cash Payments Journal — Page 1

Date		Ck. No.	Payee	Account Credited/Debited	Post. Ref.	Credits: Cash	Credits: Purchases Discounts	Credits: Other Accounts	Debits: Accounts Payable	Debits: Other Accounts
July	2	101	Sondra Tidmore	Purchases	511	400				400
	6	102	Daily Journal	Advertising Expense	612	200				200
	8	103	Siviglia Agency	Rent Expense	631	250				250
	11	104	Jones Chevrolet		√	2,450	50		2,500	
	16	105	Charles Kuntz	Salary Expense	611	600				600
	17	106	Marshall Ford		√	294	6		300	
	24	107	Grabow & Company	Prepaid Insurance	119	480				480
	27	108	Dealer Sales		√	3,136	64		3,200	
	30	109	A&B Equipment Company	Office Equipment	144	900				400
				Service Equipment	146					500
	31	110	Burns Real Estate	Notes Payable	213	5,000		10,000		
				Land	141					15,000
						13,710	120	10,000	6,000	17,830
						(111)	(512)	(√)	(212)	(√)

Post individual amounts in Other Accounts column **daily.**

Post individual amounts in Accounts Payable column **daily.**

Post totals at **end of month.**

Totals not posted.

General Ledger

Cash — 111

Date		Post. Ref.	Debit	Credit	Balance: Debit	Balance: Credit
July	31	CR1	32,528		32,528	
	31	CP1		13,710	18,818	

Prepaid Insurance — 119

Date		Post. Ref.	Debit	Credit	Balance: Debit	Balance: Credit
July	24	CP1	480		480	

Continue posting to Land, Office Equipment, Service Equipment, Notes Payable, Purchases, Salary Expense, Advertising Expense, and Rent Expense.

Continue posting to Purchases Discounts and Accounts Payable.

Accounts Payable Subsidiary Ledger

Dealer Sales

Date		Post. Ref.	Debit	Credit	Balance
July	3	P1		700	700
	17	P1		3,200	3,900
	27	CP1	3,200		700

Jones Chevrolet

Date		Post. Ref.	Debit	Credit	Balance
July	1	P1		2,500	2,500
	11	CP1	2,500		—

Marshall Ford

Date		Post. Ref.	Debit	Credit	Balance
July	2	P1		300	300
	17	CP1	300		—

1. *Cash* Each entry must have an amount in this column because each transaction must involve a payment of cash.
2. *Purchases Discounts* When purchases discounts are taken, they are recorded in this column.
3. *Other Accounts* This column is used to record credits to accounts other than Cash or Purchases Discounts. Notice that the July 31 transaction shows a purchase of land for $15,000, with a check for $5,000 and a note payable for $10,000.

The debit columns are as follows:

1. *Accounts Payable* This column is used to record payments to suppliers that have extended credit to the company. Each supplier's name is written in the Payee column so that the payment can be entered in his or her account in the accounts payable subsidiary ledger.
2. *Other Accounts* Cash can be expended for many reasons. Thus, an Other Accounts or Sundry Accounts column is needed in the cash payments journal. The title of the account to be debited is written in the Account Credited/Debited column, and the amount is entered in the Other Accounts debit column. If a company finds that a particular account appears often in the Other Accounts column, it can add another debit column to the cash payments journal.

The procedure for posting the cash payments journal, shown in Exhibit 8, is as follows:

1. Post the Accounts Payable column daily to the individual accounts in the accounts payable subsidiary ledger. Place a checkmark in the Post. Ref. column of the cash payments journal to indicate that the posting has been made.
2. Post the debits/credits in the Other Accounts debit/credit columns to the general ledger daily or at convenient short intervals during the month. As the individual items are posted, write the account number in the Post. Ref. column of the cash payments journal to indicate that the posting has been completed and **CP** plus the cash payments journal page number (**CP1** means Cash Payments Journal—Page 1) in the Post. Ref. column of each ledger account.
3. At the end of the month, the columns are footed and crossfooted. That is, the sum of the Credits column totals must equal the sum of the Debits column totals, as follows:

Credits Column Totals		**Debits Column Totals**	
Cash	$13,710	Accounts Payable	$ 6,000
Purchases Discounts	120	Other Accounts	17,830
Other Accounts	10,000	Total Debits	$23,830
Total Credits	$23,830		

4. Post the column totals for Cash, Purchases Discounts, and Accounts Payable at the end of the month to their respective accounts in the general ledger. Write the account number below each column in the cash payments journal as the total is posted to indicate that this step has been completed and **CP** plus the cash payments journal page number in the Post. Ref. column of each ledger account. Place a checkmark under the total of each Other Accounts column in the cash payments journal to indicate that the postings in the column have been made and that the total is not posted.

General Journal

Transactions that do not involve sales, purchases, cash receipts, or cash payments should be recorded in the general journal. Usually, there are only a few such transactions. The two examples that appear in Exhibit 9 require entries that do not fit in a

Point to Emphasize: The general journal is used only to record transactions that cannot be accommodated by the special-purpose journals. Whenever a controlling account is recorded, it must be "double posted" to the general ledger and the subsidiary accounts. All general journal entries are posted daily; column totals are neither obtained nor posted.

Exhibit 9. Transactions Recorded in the General Journal

General Journal — Page 1

Date		Description	Post. Ref.	Debit	Credit
July	25	Accounts Payable, Thomas Auto	212/√	700	
		Purchases Returns and Allowances	513		700
		Returned used car for credit; invoice date 7/11			
	26	Sales Returns and Allowances	413	35	
		Accounts Receivable, Maxwell Gertz	114/√		35
		Allowance for faulty tire			

special-purpose journal. They are a return of merchandise and an allowance from a supplier for credit. Adjusting and closing entries are also recorded in the general journal.

Notice that the entries in Exhibit 9 include a debit or a credit to a controlling account (Accounts Payable or Accounts Receivable). The name of the customer or supplier is also given. When this kind of debit or credit is made to a controlling account in the general journal, the entry must be posted twice: once to the controlling account and once to the individual account in the subsidiary ledger. This procedure keeps the subsidiary ledger equal to the controlling account as far as entries from the general journal are concerned. Notice that the July 26 transaction is posted by a debit to Sales Returns and Allowances in the general ledger (shown by the account number 413), by a credit to the Accounts Receivable controlling account in the general ledger (account number 114), and by a credit to the Maxwell Gertz account in the accounts receivable subsidiary ledger (checkmark).

The Flexibility of Special-Purpose Journals

Special-purpose journals reduce and simplify the work of accounting and allow for the division of labor. Such journals should be designed to fit the business in which they are used. As noted earlier, if certain accounts show up often in the Other

BUSINESS BULLETIN: ETHICS IN PRACTICE

Confidentiality is an important issue in the design and use of accounting information systems. For example, computer operators and other employees who have access to accounting records may know customers' credit histories as well as what they have purchased, how much they owe the company, and how punctually they pay their bills. And in many cases, customers may include friends, neighbors, and acquaintances. The payroll records also contain such sensitive information as salary levels. To avoid problems, it is good practice for businesses to restrict access to sensitive records to only those employees whose work depends on them and to make it clear that strict confidentiality must be maintained. The Institute of Management Accountants states that information should not be communicated to anyone inside or outside the company who is not authorized to receive it, except when disclosure is required by law.

Accounts column of a journal, it is a good idea to add a column for them when a new page of a special-purpose journal is prepared. Also, if certain transactions appear repeatedly in the general journal, it is a good idea to set up a new special-purpose journal.

Chapter Review

REVIEW OF LEARNING OBJECTIVES

1. **Identify the principles of accounting systems design.** The developers of an accounting system must keep in mind the four principles of systems design: the cost-benefit principle, the control principle, the compatibility principle, and the flexibility principle.
2. **Describe how general ledger software and spreadsheet software are used in accounting.** General ledger software is a group of integrated software programs that perform major accounting functions such as general ledger, purchases and accounts payable, sales and accounts receivable, payroll, and others in an integrated fashion. Some software uses icons in a graphical user interface to easily guide the accountant through the tasks. Spreadsheet software is also used widely by accountants for analysis.
3. **Identify the basic elements of computer systems, and describe microcomputer accounting systems.** Computerized accounting systems, regardless of their size, consist of the hardware or equipment, the programs or software, and the personnel to run the system. Most small companies use microcomputer accounting systems that use general ledger software to perform the major accounting functions.
4. **Explain how accountants use the Internet.** Accountants are increasingly using the Internet for electronic mail, for obtaining information or help on many issues via the World Wide Web and information retrieval, and for exchanging information on bulletin boards. Businesses are using the Internet for electronic commerce, which provides new challenges to the accountant.
5. **Explain the objectives and uses of special-purpose journals.** The typical manual data processing system uses several special-purpose journals, each designed to record one kind of transaction. Recording only one kind of transaction in each journal reduces and simplifies the accounting task and allows for the division of labor. The division of labor is important for internal control.
6. **Explain the purposes and relationships of controlling accounts and subsidiary ledgers.** Subsidiary ledgers contain individual accounts of a specific kind, such as customers' accounts (accounts receivable) or suppliers' accounts (accounts payable). The individual account records are kept separately in a subsidiary ledger to avoid making the general ledger too bulky. The total of the balances of the subsidiary ledger accounts should equal the balance of the controlling account in the general ledger because the individual items are posted daily to the subsidiary ledger accounts and the column totals are posted to the general ledger account monthly from the special-purpose journal.
7. **Construct and use a sales journal, purchases journal, cash receipts journal, cash payments journal, and other special-purpose journals as needed.** A special-purpose journal is constructed by devoting a single column to a particular account (for example, debits to Cash in the cash receipts journal and credits to Cash in the cash payments journal). Other columns in the journal depend on the kinds of transactions in which the company normally engages. Special-purpose journals also have columns for transaction dates, explanations or subsidiary account names, and posting references.

REVIEW OF CONCEPTS AND TERMINOLOGY

The following concepts and terms were introduced in this chapter.

LO 1 **Accounting systems:** The process that gathers data and puts them into useful form for communication of the results to management.

LO 4 **Bulletin boards:** A method for individuals with common interests to share information on the Internet.

LO 7 **Cash payments journal:** A multicolumn special-purpose journal used to record payments of cash. Also called *cash disbursements journal.*

LO 7 **Cash receipts journal:** A multicolumn special-purpose journal used to record transactions involving the receipt of cash.

LO 1 **Compatibility principle:** The principle that holds that the design of an accounting system must be in harmony with the organizational and human factors of the business.

LO 3 **Computer operator:** A person who uses a computer to complete job-related tasks.

LO 6 **Controlling account:** An account in the general ledger that summarizes the total balance of a group of related accounts in a subsidiary ledger. Also called *control account.*

LO 1 **Control principle:** The principle that holds that an accounting system must provide all the features of internal control needed to protect the firm's assets and ensure that data are reliable.

LO 1 **Cost-benefit principle:** The principle that holds that the benefits derived from an accounting system and the information it generates must be equal to or greater than its cost.

LO 1 **Data processing:** The means by which an accounting system gathers data, organizes them into useful forms, and issues the resulting information to users.

LO 4 **Electronic commerce:** The conducting of business transactions on computer networks, including the Internet.

LO 4 **Electronic mail (E-mail):** The sending and receiving of communications on the Internet.

LO 1 **Flexibility principle:** The principle that holds that an accounting system must be flexible enough to allow the volume of transactions to grow and organizational changes to be made.

LO 2 **General ledger software:** A group of integrated software programs that an accountant uses to direct the computer to carry out the major accounting functions.

LO 2 **Graphical user interface (GUI):** The employment of symbols, called icons, to represent common operations, making software easier to use.

LO 3 **Hardware:** The equipment needed to operate a computer system.

LO 2 **Icon:** A symbol representing a common operation that appears on the screen as part of a graphical user interface.

LO 4 **Information retrieval:** The downloading of free files from the Internet to a computer.

LO 4 **Internet:** The world's largest computer network; it allows communication among computers of individuals and organizations around the world.

LO 3 **Local area network (LAN):** A network of two or more computers in one location.

LO 5 **Manual data processing:** A system of accounting in which each transaction is entered manually from a source document into the general journal (input device) and each debit and credit is posted manually to the correct ledger account (processor and memory device) for the eventual preparation of financial statements (output devices).

LO 3 **Network:** The linking of two or more microcomputers to enable them to communicate with one another.

LO 3 **Program:** A set of instructions and steps that bring about a desired result in a computer system.

LO 3 **Programmer:** A person who writes instructions for a computer.

LO 7 **Purchases journal:** A single-column or multicolumn special-purpose journal used to record all purchases on credit.

LO 7 **Sales journal:** A type of special-purpose journal used to record credit sales.

LO 3 **Software:** The programs in a computer system.

LO 3 **Source documents:** The written evidence that supports each accounting transaction for each major accounting function.

LO 5 **Special-purpose journal:** An input device in an accounting system that is used to record a single type of transaction.

LO 2 **Spreadsheet:** A computerized grid of columns and rows into which are placed data or formulas used for financial planning, cost estimating, and other accounting tasks.

LO 6 **Subsidiary ledger:** A ledger separate from the general ledger that contains a group of related accounts; the total of the balances in the subsidiary ledger accounts must equal the balance of the related controlling account in the general ledger.

LO 3 **Systems analyst:** The person who designs a computer system on the basis of an organization's information needs.

LO 3 **Wide area network (WAN):** A network of two or more computers in widely separated locations.

LO 4 **World Wide Web:** The repository of vast amounts of information on the Internet.

REVIEW PROBLEM

Purchases Journal

LO 1
LO 5
LO 7 Caraban Company is a retail seller of hiking and camping gear. The company is installing a manual accounting system, and the accountant is trying to decide whether to use a single-column or a multicolumn purchases journal. Here is a list of several transactions related to purchases in the month of January.

Jan. 5 Received a shipment of merchandise from Simons Corporation, terms 2/10, n/30, FOB shipping point, invoice dated January 4, $2,875.

10 Received a bill from Allied Freight for the freight charges on the January 5 shipment, terms n/30, invoice dated January 4, $416.

15 Returned some of the merchandise received from Simons Corporation because it was not what was ordered, $315.

20 Purchased store supplies of $56 and office supplies of $117 from Mason Company, terms n/30, invoice dated January 20.

25 Received a shipment from Thomas Manufacturing, $1,882, which included supplier-paid freight charges of $175, terms n/30, FOB shipping point, invoice dated January 23.

REQUIRED

1. Record the transactions using a single-column purchases journal and a general journal, and show the posting reference for each journal entry. Use the following accounts: Store Supplies (116), Office Supplies (117), Accounts Payable (211), Purchases (611), Purchases Returns and Allowances (612), and Freight In (613).
2. Record the transactions using a multicolumn purchases journal and a general journal, total the purchases journal, and show the posting reference for each entry.
3. Using the principles of systems design, compare the single-column and multicolumn systems in terms of the number of journal entries and postings.

ANSWER TO REVIEW PROBLEM

1. Record the transactions in a single-column purchases journal and the general journal. Show the posting references.

Purchases Journal — **Page 1**

Date		Account Credited	Date of Invoice	Terms	Post. Ref.	Amount
Jan.	5	Simons Corporation	1/4	2/10, n/30	√	2,875

General Journal **Page 1**

Date		Description	Post. Ref.	Debit	Credit
Jan.	10	Freight In	613	416	
		Accounts Payable, Allied Freight	211/√		416
		Freight charges on Simons Corporation shipment, terms n/30, invoice dated January 4			
	15	Accounts Payable, Simons Corporation	211/√	315	
		Purchases Returns and Allowances	612		315
		Returned merchandise not ordered			
	20	Store Supplies	116	56	
		Office Supplies	117	117	
		Accounts Payable, Mason Company	211/√		173
		Purchased supplies, terms n/30, invoice dated January 20			
	25	Purchases	611	1,707	
		Freight In	613	175	
		Accounts Payable, Thomas Manufacturing	211/√		1,882
		Purchased merchandise, terms n/30; supplier paid shipping, invoice dated January 23			

2. Record the transactions in a multicolumn purchases journal and the general journal. Total the purchases journal and show posting references.

Purchases Journal **Page 1**

Date		Account Credited	Date of Invoice	Terms	Post. Ref.	Credit	Debits			
						Accounts Payable	Purchases	Freight In	Store Supplies	Office Supplies
Jan.	5	Simons Corporation	1/4	2/10, n/30	√	2,875	2,875			
	10	Allied Freight	1/4	n/30	√	416		416		
	20	Mason Company	1/20	n/30	√	173			56	117
	25	Thomas Manufacturing	1/23	n/30	√	1,882	1,707	175		
						5,346	4,582	591	56	117
						(211)	(611)	(613)	(116)	(117)

Each of these amounts is posted **daily** to the appropriate account in the subsidiary ledger.

Each of these totals is posted **monthly** to the applicable general ledger account.

General Journal					Page 1
Date		Description	Post. Ref.	Debit	Credit
Jan.	15	Accounts Payable, Simons Corporation	211/√	315	
		Purchases Returns and Allowances	612		315
		Returned merchandise not ordered			

This amount is posted both to the controlling account and to the subsidiary account.

This amount is posted to the general ledger account.

3. The single-column purchases journal requires four general journal entries plus one purchases journal entry, or twenty separate lines, including explanations. In addition, fifteen postings to the general ledger and the accounts payable subsidiary ledger are necessary. (Also, the total of the purchases journal must be posted twice at the end of the month: once as a debit to Accounts Payable and once as a credit to Purchases). The multicolumn purchases journal calls for just one general journal entry and four purchases journal entries. Only eight lines need to be written, and only seven postings must be made. (In addition, the column totals in the purchases journal must be posted at the end of the month).

   In applying the cost-benefit principle, the benefits of the multicolumn purchases journal in terms of journalizing and posting time saved are clear from this analysis. In addition, there are fewer chances for error when using the multicolumn purchases journal. So the control principle is better achieved under the second system. It is not possible to decide which system better meets the compatibility principle because we do not know the relative proportion of transaction types. For instance, if the number of transactions like the one for January 5 exceeds all the others by ten to one, the first system may be more compatible with the needs of the company. On the other hand, if there are many transactions like those for January 10, 20, and 25, the second system may be more compatible. Finally, in terms of the flexibility principle, the multicolumn purchases journal is obviously more flexible because it can handle more kinds of transactions and can be expanded to include columns for other accounts if necessary.

Chapter Assignments

BUILDING YOUR KNOWLEDGE FOUNDATION

Questions

1. What is the relationship of accounting systems to data processing?
2. Describe the four principles of accounting systems design.
3. What are two common types of software used by accountants, and how do they differ in terms of their use?
4. Why is a graphical user interface important to the successful use of general ledger software?
5. Describe the three basic elements of a computer system.
6. Data are the raw material of a computer system. Trace the flow of data through the different parts of a microcomputer accounting system.

7. How does a microcomputer accounting system using general ledger software relate to the major accounting functions?
8. In what ways can the Internet assist an individual in performing a job?
9. How do special-purpose journals save time in entering and posting transactions?
10. What is the purpose of the Accounts Receivable controlling account? What is its relationship to the accounts receivable subsidiary ledger?
11. Long Transit had 1,700 sales on credit during the current month.
    a. If the firm uses a two-column general journal to record sales, how many times will the word *Sales* be written?
    b. How many postings to the Sales account will have to be made?
    c. If the firm uses a sales journal, how many times will the word *Sales* be written?
    d. How many postings to the Sales account will have to be made?
12. Why are the cash receipts journal and cash payments journal crossfooted? When is this step performed?
13. A company has the following accounts with balances: 18 asset accounts, including the Accounts Receivable account but not the individual customers' accounts; 200 customer accounts; 8 liability accounts, including the Accounts Payable account but not the individual creditors' accounts; 100 creditor accounts; and 35 owner's equity accounts, including income statement accounts—a total of 361 accounts. How many accounts in total would appear in the general ledger?

Short Exercises

SE 1. **LO 1** *Principles of Accounting Information System Design*

Indicate whether each of the following statements concerning a newly installed accounting information system is most closely related to the (a) cost-benefit principle, (b) control principle, (c) compatibility principle, or (d) flexibility principle.

1. Procedures are put in place to make sure that the data entered into the system are reliable.
2. The system allows for growth in the number and types of transactions entered into by the company.
3. The system was installed after careful consideration of the additional costs in relation to the improved decision making that will result.
4. The system takes into account the various operations of the business and the capabilities of the people who will interact with the system.

SE 2. **LO 3** *Elements of a Computer System*

Indicate whether each of these elements in a newly installed accounting information system is most properly identified as (a) hardware, (b) software, or (c) personnel.

1. The computer program that instructs the computer to record and post transactions
2. The programmer who writes instructions for the computer
3. The devices that process and store data

SE 3. **LO 3** *Microcomputer Accounting System*

Assuming that a company uses a general ledger package for a microcomputer accounting system, indicate whether each source document listed below would provide input to (a) sales/accounts receivable, (b) purchases/accounts payable, (c) cash receipts, (d) cash disbursements, (e) payroll, or (f) the general journal.

1. Deposit slips
2. Time cards
3. Vendor invoices
4. Checks issued
5. Customer invoices
6. Documents for other journal entries

SE 4. **LO 5** *Transactions and Special-Purpose Journals*

Indicate whether each transaction listed below should be recorded in the (a) sales journal, (b) multicolumn purchases journal, (c) cash receipts journal, (d) cash payments journal, or (e) general journal.

1. Receipt on account
2. Purchase return on account
3. Sale on account
4. Purchase on account
5. Sale for cash
6. Payment on account

SE 5. **LO 7** *Sales Journal Transactions*

Using Exhibit 2 as a model, show how each of the following transactions should be entered in a sales journal. All terms are 2/10, n/30. If a transaction should not appear in the sales journal, tell where it should be recorded.

Oct. 1	Sold merchandise to S. Ruiz on credit, invoice no. 301, $350.
8	Sold merchandise to J. Sizemore for cash, $150.
15	Sold merchandise to F. Thomas on credit, invoice no. 302, $200.

Total and rule the journal.

SE 6. LO 6 LO 7 *Sales Journal Postings and Subsidiary Ledger*

Assuming the transactions in **SE 5** are the only sales transactions for the month of October, describe all the postings that would be made from the sales journal to the general ledger and the accounts receivable subsidiary ledger.

SE 7. LO 7 *Multicolumn Purchases Journal*

Using Exhibit 6 as a model, show how each of the following transactions should be entered in a multicolumn purchases journal. If a transaction should not appear in this journal, tell where it should be recorded.

Oct. 2	Purchased merchandise on credit from Carlson Electronics, invoice dated October 1, terms 2/10, n/30, $500.
4	Purchased merchandise on credit from Boyer Electrics, invoice dated October 2, terms 2/10, n/30, $650, including freight charges of $50.
6	Purchased supplies on credit from Ace Supplies, invoice dated October 5, terms n/30, $180, to be allocated one-third to store and two-thirds to office.
8	Purchased postage stamps at the post office for cash (check no. 101), $58.
9	Purchased equipment on credit from Jones Furniture Co., invoice dated October 9, terms n/EOM, $1,000.

Total and rule the journal.

SE 8. LO 6 LO 7 *Purchases Journal Postings and Subsidiary Ledger*

Assuming the transactions in **SE 7** are the only purchases transactions for the month of October, describe all the postings that would be made from the purchases journal to the general ledger and the accounts payable subsidiary ledger.

SE 9. LO 6 LO 7 *Cash Receipts Journal*

Using Exhibit 7 as a model, show how each of the following transactions should be entered in the cash receipts journal. If a transaction should not appear in this journal, tell where it should be recorded.

Oct. 8	Sold merchandise for cash to J. Sizemore, $150.
9	Received payment on account from S. Ruiz, $350 less 2 percent discount.
17	F. Thomas returned purchase of October 15 for full credit, $200.

Describe the postings that are required for each transaction.

SE 10. LO 6 LO 7 *Cash Payments Journal*

Using Exhibit 8 as a model, show how each of the following transactions should be entered in the cash payments journal. If a transaction should not appear in this journal, tell where it should be recorded.

Oct. 8	Issued check no. 101 to the U.S. Postal Service for postage, $58.
12	Issued check no. 102 to Carlson Electronics, $500 less 2 percent discount.

Describe the postings that are required for each transaction.

Exercises

E 1. LO 5 *Matching Transactions to Special-Purpose Journals*

A company uses a single-column sales journal, a single-column purchases journal, a cash receipts journal, a cash payments journal, and a general journal. In which journal would each of the following transactions be recorded?

1. Sold merchandise on credit
2. Sold merchandise for cash
3. Gave a customer credit for merchandise purchased on credit and returned
4. Paid a creditor
5. Paid office salaries
6. Received a customer's payment for merchandise previously purchased on credit
7. Recorded adjusting and closing entries
8. Purchased merchandise on credit
9. Purchased sales department supplies on credit
10. Purchased office equipment for cash
11. Returned merchandise purchased on credit
12. Paid income taxes

E 2. LO 5 LO 6 LO 7 *Characteristics of Special-Purpose Journals*

Padilla Corporation uses a single-column sales journal, a single-column purchases journal, a cash receipts journal, a cash payments journal, and a general journal.

1. In which of the journals listed above would you expect to find the fewest transactions recorded?
2. At the end of the accounting period, to which account or accounts should the total of the sales journal be posted as a debit and/or credit?
3. At the end of the accounting period, to which account or accounts should the total of the purchases journal be posted as a debit and/or credit?
4. What two subsidiary ledgers would probably be associated with the journals listed above? From which journals would postings normally be made to each of the two subsidiary ledgers?
5. In which of the journals are adjusting and closing entries made?

E 3. LO 7 *Identifying the Content of a Special-Purpose Journal*

Shown below is a page from a special-purpose journal.

				Debits		Credits		
Date		Account Credited	Post. Ref.	Cash	Sales Discount	Accounts Receivable	Sales	Other Accounts
		Balance Forward		79,598	1,574	20,408	8,564	52,200
May	25	Mae Johnson	√	980	20	1,000		
	26	Notes Receivable	115	2,240				2,000
		Interest Income	715					240
	27	Cash Sale		1,920			1,920	
	31	Virgil Thomas	√	400		400		
				85,138	1,594	21,808	10,484	54,440
				(111)	(412)	(114)	(411)	(√)

1. What kind of journal is this?
2. Explain each transaction.
3. Explain the following: (a) the numbers under the double rule, (b) the checkmarks entered in the Post. Ref. column, (c) the numbers 115 and 715 in the Post. Ref. column, and (d) the checkmark below the Other Accounts credit column.

E 4. LO 7 *Multicolumn Purchases Journal*

Gordon Company uses a multicolumn purchases journal similar to the one shown in Exhibit 6.

During the month of July, Gordon made the following purchases:

July 1 Purchased merchandise from Lujack Company on account for $5,400, invoice dated July 1, terms 2/10, n/30.

3 Received freight bill dated July 1 from Olinsky Freight for merchandise purchased July 1, $350, terms n/30.

18 Purchased supplies from Hobbs Company for $240; allocated half to the store and half to the office; invoice dated July 16, terms n/30.

23 Purchased merchandise from Pascale Company on account for $1,974; total included freight in of $174; invoice dated July 20, terms n/30, FOB shipping point.

27 Purchased office supplies from Hobbs Company for $96, invoice dated July 27, terms n/30.

31 Purchased a one-year insurance policy from Rathbun Associates, $480, invoice dated July 31, terms n/30.

1. Set up a multicolumn purchases journal similar to the one in Exhibit 6.
2. Enter the transactions listed above in the purchases journal. Then foot and crossfoot the columns.

E 5. LO 6 LO 7 *Finding Errors in Special-Purpose Journals*

A company records purchases in a single-column purchases journal and records purchases returns in its general journal. During the past month, an accounting clerk made each of the errors described below. Explain how each error might be discovered.

1. Correctly recorded a $191 purchase in the purchases journal but posted it to the creditor's account as a $119 purchase.
2. Made an error in totaling the Amount column of the purchases journal.
3. Posted a purchases return from the general journal to the Purchases Returns and Allowances account and the Accounts Payable account but did not post it to the creditor's account.
4. Made an error in determining the balance of a creditor's account.
5. Posted a purchases return to the Accounts Payable account but did not post it to the Purchases Returns and Allowances account.

E 6. LO 6 LO 7 *Posting from a Sales Journal*

Prokop Corporation began business on June 1. The company maintains a sales journal. The sales journal at the end of the month is shown below.

Sales Journal **Page 1**

Date		Account Debited	Invoice Number	Post. Ref.	Amount
June	3	Fran Smiley	1001		516
	8	Steve Pearl	1002		951
	12	Byung Koh	1003		642
	18	Fran Smiley	1004		291
	27	Maria Campos	1005		1,299
					3,699

1. Open general ledger accounts for Accounts Receivable (112) and Sales (411) and an accounts receivable subsidiary ledger with an account for each customer. Make the appropriate postings from the sales journal, inserting the posting references in the sales journal and in the ledger accounts as you work.
2. Prove the accounts receivable subsidiary ledger by preparing a schedule of accounts receivable.

E 7. LO 6 LO 7 *Identification of Transactions*

Hernandez Company uses a manual accounting system with a sales journal, purchases journal, cash receipts journal, cash payments journal, and general journal similar to those illustrated in the text. On October 31, the Sales account in the general ledger looked like this:

Sales **Account No. 411**

Date		Item	Post. Ref.	Debit	Credit	Balance Debit	Balance Credit
Oct.	31		S11		74,842		74,842
	31		CR7		42,414		117,256
	31		J17	117,256			—

On October 31, the J. Maroe account in the accounts receivable subsidiary ledger looked like this:

J. Maroe — **Account No. 10012**

Date		Item	Post. Ref.	Debit	Credit	Balance
Oct.	8		S10	4,216		4,216
	12		J14		564	3,652
	18		CR6		1,000	2,652

1. Write an explanation of each entry in the Sales account; include the journal from which the entry was posted.
2. Write an explanation of each entry in the J. Maroe account in the accounts receivable subsidiary ledger; include the journal from which the entry was posted.

LO 6 LO 7 *Identification of Transactions*

E 8. Aloez Company uses a sales journal, single-column purchases journal, cash receipts journal, cash payments journal, and general journal similar to those shown in the text. On April 30, the A. O'Malley account in the accounts receivable subsidiary ledger appeared as shown below.

A. O'Malley

Date		Item	Post. Ref.	Debit	Credit	Balance
Mar.	31		S4	2,448		2,448
Apr.	7		J7		192	2,256
	12		CR5		600	1,656
	17		S6	684		2,340

On April 30, the Li Company account in the accounts payable subsidiary ledger appeared as follows:

Li Company

Date		Item	Post. Ref.	Debit	Credit	Balance
Apr.	18		P7		6,078	6,078
	20		J9	636		5,442
	25		CP8	5,442		—

1. Write an explanation of each entry that affected the A. O'Malley account receivable, including the journal from which the entry was posted.
2. Write an explanation of each entry that affected the Li Company account payable, including the journal from which the entry was posted.

Problems

P 1. LO 6 LO 7 *Special-Purpose Journals and Subsidiary Ledgers*

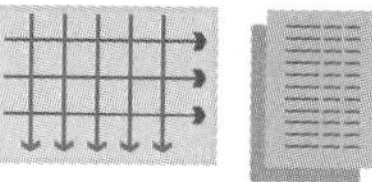

Manner Company is a small retail business that uses a manual accounting system similar to the one described in this chapter. At the end of April 20xx, the firm's accounts receivable and accounts payable subsidiary ledgers showed the following balances:

Accounts Receivable		**Accounts Payable**	
A. Barlett	$430	Baylor Company	$1,300
L. Lozowich	330	Gentrol Company	890
Total Accounts Receivable	$760	Total Accounts Payable	$2,190

During May, the company engaged in the following transactions:

May 2 Sold merchandise on credit to R. Wood, a new customer, $570, terms 2/10, n/30, invoice no. 1001.
4 Received payment in full from L. Lozowich, no discount allowed.
5 Paid Baylor Company the full amount owed less a 2 percent discount, check no. 201.
8 Accepted a return of merchandise for credit from R. Wood, $170.
9 Paid Gentrol Company the full amount owed, no discount allowed, check no. 202.
12 Received payment from R. Wood for amount due less discount.
15 Received partial payment from A. Barlett, no discount allowed, $230.
22 Purchased merchandise from Baylor Company, $1,200, terms 2/10, n/30, FOB destination, invoice dated May 22.
23 Sold merchandise on credit to L. Lozowich, $670, terms 2/10, n/30, invoice no. 1002.
26 Purchased merchandise from Gentrol Company, $1,500, terms 2/10, n/30, FOB destination, invoice dated May 23.
31 Returned merchandise to Gentrol Company for full credit, $600.

REQUIRED

1. Prepare a single-column sales journal, a single-column purchases journal, a cash receipts journal, a cash payments journal, and a general journal similar to the ones illustrated in the chapter. Use Page 1 for all references.
2. Open the following general ledger accounts: Accounts Receivable (112) and Accounts Payable (211).
3. Open the following accounts receivable subsidiary ledger accounts: A. Barlett, L. Lozowich, and R. Wood.
4. Open the following accounts payable subsidiary ledger accounts: Baylor Company and Gentrol Company.
5. Enter the transactions in the journals and post to the appropriate subsidiary ledger and general ledger accounts.
6. Foot and crossfoot the journals, and make the end-of-month postings applicable to Accounts Receivable and Accounts Payable.
7. Prove the control balances of Accounts Receivable and Accounts Payable by preparing schedules of accounts receivable and accounts payable.

P 2. LO 7 *Cash Receipts and Cash Payments Journals*

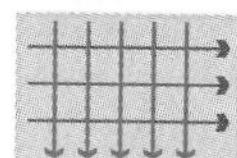

Stigman Company is a small retail business that uses a manual data processing system similar to the one described in the chapter. Among its special-purpose journals are multicolumn cash receipts and cash payments journals. These were the cash transactions for Stigman Company during the month of November:

Nov. 1 Paid November rent to R. Carsello, $1,000, with check no. 782.
3 Paid Cronos Wholesale on account, $2,300 less a 2 percent discount, check no. 783.
4 Received payment on account of $1,000, within the discount period, from J. Wilkes.
5 Cash sales, $2,632.
8 Paid Murray Freight on account, $598, with check no. 784.
9 The owner, Jerry Stigman, invested an additional $10,000 in cash and a truck valued at $14,000 in the business.
11 Paid Escobar Supply on account, $284, with check no. 785.

Nov. 14 Cash sales, $2,834.
15 Paid Murray Freight $310 for the freight on a shipment of merchandise received today, with check no. 786.
16 Paid Ludlow Company on account, $1,568 net a 2 percent discount, with check no. 787.
17 Received payment on account from P. Sibley, $120.
18 Cash sales, $1,974.
19 Received payment on a note receivable, $1,800 plus $36 interest.
20 Purchased office supplies from Escobar Supply, $108, with check no. 788.
21 Paid a note payable in full to Kenilworth Bank, $4,100 including $100 interest, with check no. 789.
24 Cash sales, $2,964.
25 Paid $500 less a 2 percent discount to Cronos Wholesale, with check no. 790.
26 Paid Linda Bisby, a sales clerk, $1,100 for her monthly salary, with check no. 791.
27 Purchased equipment from Buffalo Corporation for $16,000, paying $4,000 with check no. 792 and signing a note payable for the difference.
30 Jerry Stigman withdrew $1,200 from the business, using check no. 793.

REQUIRED

1. Enter these transactions in the cash receipts and cash payments journals.
2. Foot and crossfoot the journals.

P 3. LO 6 LO 7 *Purchases and General Journals*

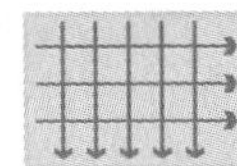

Mejias Lawn Supply Company uses a multicolumn purchases journal and general journal similar to those illustrated in the text. The company also maintains an accounts payable subsidiary ledger. The items below represent the company's credit transactions for the month of July.

July 2 Purchased merchandise from Noonan Fertilizer Company, $2,640.
3 Purchased office supplies of $166 and store supplies of $208 from Pagone Supply, Inc.
5 Purchased cleaning equipment from Whitlock Company, $1,856.
7 Purchased display equipment from Pagone Supply, Inc., $4,700.
10 Purchased lawn mowers from Toledo Lawn Equipment Company, for resale, $8,400 (which included transportation charges of $350).
14 Purchased merchandise from Noonan Fertilizer Company, $3,444.
18 Purchased a lawn mower from Toledo Lawn Equipment Company to be used in the business, $950 (which included transportation charges of $70).
23 Purchased store supplies from Pagone Supply, Inc., $54.
27 Returned a defective lawn mower purchased on July 10 for full credit, $750.

REQUIRED

1. Enter these transactions in a multicolumn purchases journal and the general journal. Assume that all terms are n/30 and that invoice dates are the same as the transaction dates.
2. Foot and crossfoot the purchases journal.
3. Open the following general ledger accounts: Store Supplies (116), Office Supplies (117), Lawn Equipment (142), Display Equipment (144), Cleaning Equipment (146), Accounts Payable (211), Purchases (611), Purchases Returns and Allowances (612), and Freight In (613). Open accounts payable subsidiary ledger accounts as needed. Post from the journals to the ledger accounts.

P 4. LO 6 LO 7 *Comprehensive Use of Special-Purpose Journals*

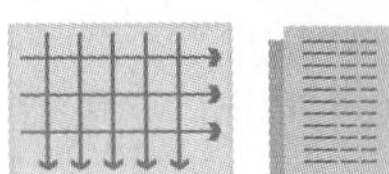

Bromberg Book Store opened its doors for business on May 1. During May, the following transactions took place:

May 1 Linda Bromberg started the business by depositing $42,000 in the new company's bank account.
3 Issued check no. C001 to Lomax Rentals for one month's rent, $1,000.
4 Received a shipment of books from Osgood Books, Inc., $15,680, invoice dated May 3, terms 5/10, n/60, FOB shipping point.
5 Received a bill for freight from Linden Shippers for previous day's shipment, $790, terms n/30.
6 Received a shipment from Forrest Books, $11,300, invoice dated May 6, terms 2/10, n/30, FOB shipping point.
7 Issued check no. C002 to Pappas Freight for transportation charges on previous day's shipment, $574.

May 8 Issued check no. C003 to Yoo Equipment Company for store equipment, $10,400.
9 Sold books to Horizon Center, $1,564, terms 5/10, n/30, invoice no. 1001.
10 Returned books to Osgood Books, Inc., for credit, $760.
11 Issued check no. C004 to WCAM for radio commercials, $470.
12 Issued check no. C005 to Osgood Books, Inc., for balance of amount owed less discount.
13 Cash sales for the first two weeks, $4,018. (To shorten this problem, cash sales are recorded at intervals instead of daily, as they would be in actual practice.)
14 Issued check no. C006 to Forrest Books, $6,000 less discount.
15 Signed a 90-day, 10 percent note for a bank loan and received the $20,000 in cash.
15 Sold books to Yosh Kawano, $260, terms n/30, invoice no. 1002.
16 Issued a credit memorandum to Horizon Center for returned books, $124.
17 Received payment in full from Horizon Center for balance owed less discount.
18 Sold books to Ruth Mayhew, $194, terms n/30, invoice no. 1003.
19 Received a shipment from Patton Publishing Company, $4,604, invoice dated May 18, terms 5/10, n/60.
20 Returned additional books purchased on May 4 to Osgood Books, Inc., for credit at gross price, $1,436.
21 Sold books to Horizon Center, $1,634, terms 5/10, n/30, invoice no. 1004.
23 Received a shipment from Osgood Books, Inc., $2,374, invoice dated May 19, terms 5/10, n/60, FOB shipping point.
24 Issued check no. C007 to Linden Shippers for balance owed on account plus shipping charges of $194 on previous day's shipment.
27 Cash sales for the second two weeks, $7,488.
29 Issued check no. C008 to Payroll Account for sales salaries for first four weeks of the month, $1,400.
31 Cash sales for the last four days of the month, $554.

REQUIRED

1. Prepare a sales journal, a multicolumn purchases journal, a cash receipts journal, a cash payments journal, and a general journal. Use Page 1 for all journal references.
2. Open the following general ledger accounts: Cash (111), Accounts Receivable (112), Store Equipment (141), Accounts Payable (211), Notes Payable (212), Linda Bromberg, Capital (311), Sales (411), Sales Discounts (412), Sales Returns and Allowances (413), Purchases (511), Purchases Discounts (512), Purchases Returns and Allowances (513), Freight In (514), Sales Salaries Expense (611), Advertising Expense (612), and Rent Expense (613).
3. Open the following accounts receivable subsidiary ledger accounts: Horizon Center, Yosh Kawano, and Ruth Mayhew.
4. Open the following accounts payable subsidiary ledger accounts: Forrest Books; Linden Shippers; Osgood Books, Inc.; and Patton Publishing Company.
5. Enter the transactions in the journals and post as appropriate.
6. Foot and crossfoot the journals, and make the end-of-month postings.
7. Prepare a trial balance of the general ledger, and prove the control balances of Accounts Receivable and Accounts Payable by preparing schedules of accounts receivable and accounts payable.

P 5.
LO 6 LO 7 *Comprehensive Use of Special-Purpose Journals*

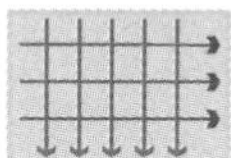

Midland Office Supply Company completed the following transactions in April 20xx:

Apr. 1 Issued check no. 2101 to Charles Realty for April rent, $2,200.
3 Received merchandise from Posten Company, $6,700, invoice dated April 3, terms 2/10, n/30, FOB shipping point.
4 Received freight bill from Mendes Transit for previous shipment, $552, terms n/10.
6 Sold merchandise to M. Donlin, $1,600, terms 2/10, n/30, invoice no. 3219.
7 Received a bill from WRZR for radio commercials, $634, terms n/25th of this month.
8 Received a credit memorandum from Posten Company for merchandise returned, $500.
9 Issued check no. 2102 to Kaporis Insurance for a two-year fire and casualty policy, $974.
10 Sold merchandise to T. Major, $1,680, terms 2/10, n/30, invoice no. 3220.

Apr. 11 Received merchandise from Posten Company, $3,700, invoice dated April 9, terms 2/10, n/30, FOB shipping point.
12 Received a freight bill from Mendes Transit for previous shipment, $412, terms n/10.
12 Issued a credit memorandum to T. Major for merchandise returned, $80.
13 Issued check no. 2103 to Posten Company for balance owed for the April 3 purchase less discount.
14 Issued check no. 2104 to Mendes Transit for balance owed.
15 Received payment in full less discount from M. Donlin.
15 Cash sales for the first half of the month, $20,850. (To shorten this problem, cash sales are recorded only twice a month instead of daily, as they would be in actual practice.)
17 Issued check no. 2105 to Van Buren Gas Company for monthly heating bill, $238.
18 Issued check no. 2106 to Posten Company for $2,000 less discount, in partial payment of amount owed.
19 Received payment from T. Major for half the amount owed less a 2 percent discount.
20 Sold merchandise to L. Ostrander, $700, terms 2/10, n/30, invoice no. 3221.
21 Received a credit memorandum from WRZR because two scheduled commercials were not played, $124.
22 Sold merchandise to T. Major, $318, terms 2/10, n/30, invoice no. 3222.
23 Issued check no. 2107 to Metropolitan Power Company for monthly utilities, $566.
24 Sold merchandise to M. Donlin, $992, terms 2/10, n/30, invoice no. 3223.
25 Received payment in full less discount from L. Ostrander.
25 Issued check no. 2108 to WRZR for balance of account.
27 Received merchandise from Rosati Company $5,400, invoice dated April 23, terms 2/10, n/30, FOB shipping point.
28 Issued check no. 2109 to Howell Freight for transportation on previous shipment, $638.
29 Issued check no. 2110 to Posten Company for balance of amount owed.
29 Issued check no. 2111, payable to Payroll Account, for monthly salaries, $8,400.
30 Cash sales for the last half of the month, $20,426.

REQUIRED

1. Prepare a sales journal, a multicolumn purchases journal, a cash receipts journal, a cash payments journal, and a general journal similar to the ones illustrated in this chapter. Use Page 1 for all journal references.
2. Open the following general ledger accounts: Cash (111), Accounts Receivable (112), Prepaid Insurance (113), Accounts Payable (211), Sales (411), Sales Discounts (412), Sales Returns and Allowances (413), Purchases (511), Purchases Discounts (512), Purchases Returns and Allowances (513), Freight In (514), Salaries Expense (521), Advertising Expense (522), Rent Expense (531), and Utilities Expense (532).
3. Open the following accounts receivable subsidiary ledger accounts: M. Donlin, T. Major, and L. Ostrander.
4. Open the following accounts payable subsidiary ledger accounts: Mendes Transit, Posten Company, Rosati Company, and WRZR.
5. Enter the transactions in the journals and post as appropriate.
6. Foot and crossfoot the journals, and make the end-of-month postings.
7. Prepare a trial balance of the general ledger, and prove the control balances of Accounts Receivable and Accounts Payable by preparing schedules of accounts receivable and accounts payable.

Alternate Problems

P 6. LO 6 LO 7 *Special-Purpose Journals and Subsidiary Ledgers*

Sachs Company, a small retail business, uses a manual accounting system similar to the one illustrated in this chapter. At the end of May 20xx, the accounts in the accounts receivable and accounts payable subsidiary ledgers showed the following balances:

Accounts Receivable		**Accounts Payable**	
T. Bakof	$ 870	Cellcor Inc.	$2,900
R. Banz	650	Visidyne Company	460
Total Accounts Receivable	$1,520	Total Accounts Payable	$3,360

During June, the company engaged in the following transactions:

June 2 Sold merchandise on credit to R. Banz, $920, terms 2/10, n/30, invoice no. 4001.
4 Received payment in full from R. Banz for the amount due at the beginning of June less a 2 percent discount.
5 Paid Cellcor Inc. the full amount owed less a 2 percent discount, check no. 501.
8 Accepted a return of merchandise from R. Banz, $220.
9 Paid Visidyne Company the full amount owed, no discount allowed, check no. 502.
12 Received payment from R. Banz for the amount due less the discount.
15 Received partial payment from T. Bakof, no discount allowed, $300.
22 Purchased merchandise from Visidyne Company, $1,700, terms 2/10, n/30, FOB destination, invoice dated June 21.
23 Sold merchandise on credit to F. Younger, $2,450, terms 2/10, n/30, invoice no. 4002.
26 Purchased merchandise from Cellcor Inc., $1,500, terms 2/10, n/30, FOB destination, invoice dated June 24.
30 Returned merchandise to Visidyne Company for full credit, $600.

REQUIRED

1. Prepare a sales journal, a single-column purchases journal, a cash receipts journal, a cash payments journal, and a general journal similar to the ones illustrated in the chapter. Use Page 1 for all references.
2. Open the following general ledger accounts: Accounts Receivable (112) and Accounts Payable (211).
3. Open the following accounts receivable subsidiary ledger accounts: T. Bakof, R. Banz, and F. Younger.
4. Open the following accounts payable subsidiary ledger accounts: Cellcor Inc. and Visidyne Company.
5. Enter the transactions in the journals and post to the appropriate subsidiary ledger and general ledger accounts.
6. Foot and crossfoot the journals, and make the end-of-month postings applicable to Accounts Receivable and Accounts Payable.
7. Prove the control balances of Accounts Receivable and Accounts Payable by preparing schedules of accounts receivable and accounts payable.

P 7.
LO 7 *Cash Receipts and Cash Payments Journals*

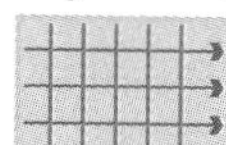

The items below detail all cash transactions by Baylor Company for the month of July. The company uses multicolumn cash receipts and cash payments journals similar to those illustrated in the chapter.

July 1 The owner, Eugene Baylor, invested $50,000 cash and $24,000 in equipment in the business.
2 Paid rent to Leonard Agency, $600, with check no. 75.
3 Cash sales, $2,200.
6 Purchased store equipment for $5,000 from Gilmore Company, with check no. 76.
7 Purchased merchandise for cash, $6,500, from Pascual Company, with check no. 77.
8 Paid Audretti Company invoice, $1,800, less 2 percent discount, with check no. 78 (assume that a payable has already been recorded).
9 Paid advertising bill, $350, to WOSU, with check no. 79.
10 Cash sales, $3,910.
12 Received $800 on account from B. Erring.
13 Purchased used truck for cash, $3,520, from Pettit Company, with check no. 80.
19 Received $4,180 from Monroe Company, in settlement of a $4,000 note plus interest.
20 Received $1,078 ($1,100 less $22 cash discount) from Young Lee.
21 Paid Baylor $2,000 from business for personal use by issuing check no. 81.
23 Paid Dautley Company invoice, $2,500, less 2 percent discount, with check no. 82.
26 Paid Haywood Company for freight on merchandise received, $60, with check no. 83.
27 Cash sales, $4,800.
28 Paid C. Murphy for monthly salary, $1,400, with check no. 84.

July 31 Purchased land from N. Archibald for $20,000, paying $5,000 with check no. 85 and signing a note payable for $15,000.

REQUIRED

1. Enter the preceding transactions in the cash receipts and cash payments journals.
2. Foot and crossfoot the journals.

P 8.

LO 6
LO 7

Comprehensive Use of Special-Purpose Journals

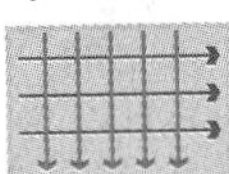

The following transactions were completed by Majid's Men's Wear during the month of May, its first month of operation:

May 1 Farouk Majid deposited $40,000 in the new company's bank account.
2 Issued check no. 101 to O'Neal Realty for one month's rent, $2,400.
3 Received merchandise from Worth Company, $14,000, invoice dated May 2, terms 2/10, n/60, FOB shipping point.
4 Received freight bill on merchandise purchased from Chappell Company, $1,928, terms n/20.
5 Issued check no. 102 to Kwan Company for store equipment, $14,800.
6 Borrowed $16,000 from the bank on a 90-day, 9 percent note.
7 Cash sales for the first week, $3,964. (To shorten this problem, cash sales are recorded weekly instead of daily, as they would be in actual practice.)
8 Sold merchandise to Newfield School, $1,800, terms 2/10, n/30, invoice no. 1001.
9 Sold merchandise to Scott Kravitz, $600, terms n/20, invoice no. 1002.
10 Purchased advertising in the *News-Chronicle*, $300, terms n/15.
11 Issued check no. 103 for purchase of May 3 less discount.
12 Issued a credit memorandum for merchandise returned by Scott Kravitz, $60.
15 Cash sales for the second week, $6,984.
16 Received merchandise from Worth Company, $3,800, invoice dated May 15, terms 2/10, n/60, FOB shipping point.
17 Received freight bill on merchandise purchased from Chappell Company, $524, terms n/20.
18 Received merchandise from Merullo Company, $2,800, invoice dated May 16, terms 1/10, n/60, FOB destination.
18 Received payment in full less discount from Newfield School.
20 Received a credit memorandum from Worth Company of $200 for merchandise returned.
21 Cash sales for the third week, $5,824.
23 Issued check no. 104 for the total amount owed Chappell Company.
24 Sold merchandise to Newfield School, $1,368, terms 2/10, n/30, invoice no. 1003.
25 Issued check no. 105 in payment of the amount owed Worth Company less discount.
26 Sold merchandise to Judy Ming, $744, terms n/20, invoice no. 1004.
27 Issued check no. 106 for the amount owed the *News-Chronicle*.
28 Cash sales for the fourth week, $3,948.
31 Issued check no. 107 to Payroll Account for sales salaries for the month of May, $7,200.

REQUIRED

1. Prepare a sales journal, a multicolumn purchases journal, a cash receipts journal, a cash payments journal, and a general journal. Use Page 1 for all journal references.
2. Open the following general ledger accounts: Cash (111), Accounts Receivable (112), Store Equipment (141), Accounts Payable (211), Notes Payable (212), Farouk Majid, Capital (311), Sales (411), Sales Discounts (412), Sales Returns and Allowances (413), Purchases (511), Purchases Discounts (512), Purchases Returns and Allowances (513), Freight In (514), Sales Salaries Expense (611), Advertising Expense (612), and Rent Expense (613).
3. Open the following accounts receivable subsidiary ledger accounts: Scott Kravitz, Judy Ming, and Newfield School.
4. Open the following accounts payable subsidiary ledger accounts: Chappell Company, Merullo Company, the *News-Chronicle*, and Worth Company.
5. Enter the transactions in the journals and post as appropriate.
6. Foot and crossfoot the journals, and make the end-of-month postings.
7. Prepare a trial balance of the general ledger and prove the control balances of Accounts Receivable and Accounts Payable by preparing schedules of accounts receivable and accounts payable.

Skills Development

CONCEPTUAL ANALYSIS

LO 1 LO 3 LO 5 *Accounting System Evaluation*

SD 1. ***Lessing Interiors*** is an interior design company that was started three years ago by Loretta Lessing. For the first two years of the company's life, Lessing helped clients plan the decorating of their luxury apartments in Manhattan. Lessing did not sell any furnishings herself but was paid an hourly fee plus a percentage of the total purchases made by her clients. Although the business was successful, it was very simple. And it required just a simple manual accounting system consisting of a general journal and a general ledger. During the past year, Lessing expanded. She opened a second-floor studio and began displaying and selling selected furnishings. She hired her first employees and began buying and selling on credit. As the number of her company's daily transactions multiplied, Lessing began to find the manual accounting system very burdensome. It was taking far too much time to record and post all the transactions. The company does not have a computer at present, but Lessing is thinking about buying one. She has come to you for help. Evaluate Lessing's current accounting system in terms of the principles of systems design (excluding the control principle) and make a recommendation about the types of accounting systems Lessing should consider installing. Write a memorandum to Lessing providing your analysis and recommendation.

LO 1 *Switching to a Computerized Accounting System*

SD 2. ***Kroch's & Brentano's*** operates full-service bookstores throughout the Chicago area. The firm is well known for excellent service and large inventories of books in a wide number of fields, such as art, history, business, technology, travel, and fiction. The company is willing to order any book in print.

The following paragraphs are from an article describing a change in the firm's data processing system.

> In a Wabash Avenue office brimming with hip-high piles of books, William Rickman agonizes over computerizing Kroch's & Brentano's 200,000-title inventory.
>
> The new technology, he frets, could make customers think Kroch's and its employees have become cold and distant. But Mr. Rickman, the 42-year-old president of Kroch's, doesn't know which books are selling or where—basic information most retailers cherish. Amazingly, the 20-store chain still uses manual inventory and sales systems.
>
> "We know we need the information, so we're doing it, but we want to make every effort to stay friendly and personal," he says.[4]

Do you think Mr. Rickman's fears are justified? What advantages related to merchandise inventory and sales will stem from implementing the new computer system? How can the possible disadvantages of the new system be overcome?

ETHICAL DILEMMA

LO 6 *Confidentiality of Accounting Records*

SD 3. Frank Santino is the accounting manager at the Ford and Toyota dealership in Petersburg, Texas, a town with a population of 50,000. At a barbecue, José Martinez, a close friend, mentions that he is planning to sell some land to Louis Johnson for $20,000 and will allow Johnson to pay him over a five-year period. Santino, who happened to have been reviewing the delinquent accounts at the dealership earlier in the day, knows that Johnson has a poor payment history and that his car may have to be repossessed. Martinez asks Santino what he thinks about the sale. What ethical issue is involved here? If you were Santino, would you warn Martinez about Johnson's credit record?

Communication

Critical Thinking

Group Activity

Memo

Ethics

International
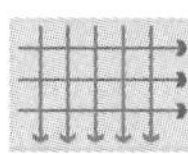
Spreadsheet

General Ledger

CD-ROM

Internet

RESEARCH ACTIVITY

LO 4 *Using the Internet*

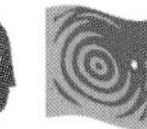

SD 4. Assume you have been asked by your boss, the owner of a small dress shop, to investigate general ledger software for her business. Both Peachtree Software and Intuit Software, the publisher of Quickbooks,® have Web pages. Access these Web sites through the Needles Accounting Resource Center Web site at http://www.hmco.com/college/needles/home/html. Study the information you find, and write a summary of the information and its usefulness. Can you assess the differences in the software approaches of the two companies and their applicability to a small dress shop?

DECISION-MAKING PRACTICE

LO 5 LO 6 LO 7 *Design of Special-Purpose Journals*

SD 5. ***RW Finer Foods Company,*** owned by Robert Washington, is a neighborhood grocery store that accepts cash or checks in payment for food. Known for its informality, the store has been very successful and has grown with the community. Along with that growth, however, has come an increase in the number of bad checks customers have written for purchases. Washington is concerned about the difficulty of accounting for these returned checks, so he has asked you to look into the problem.

In addition to a purchases journal and a cash payments journal, the company has a combination single-column sales and cash receipts journal. The combination journal has worked in the past because all sales are for cash (including checks), and almost all cash receipts represent sales transactions. Thus, the single column represents a debit to Cash and a credit to Sales.

The bad checks are recorded individually in the general journal by debiting Accounts Receivable and crediting Cash for the amount of the check and Returned Check Revenue for the amount of $10, which represents reimbursement of the service charge by the bank. When a customer pays off a bad check, another entry is made in the general journal debiting Cash and crediting Accounts Receivable. Washington keeps the returned checks in an envelope. When a customer comes in to pay one off, Washington gives the check back. No other records of the returned checks are maintained.

In studying the problem, you discover that the company is averaging ten returned checks per day, totaling $1,000. As part of the solution, you recommend that Washington issue check-cashing cards to customers whose credit is approved in advance. The card must be presented when a customer offers a check in payment for groceries. You recommend further that a special-purpose journal be established for the returned checks and returned check revenue, that a subsidiary ledger be maintained, and that the combination sales/cash receipts journal be expanded.

1. Draw and label the columns for the new returned checks journal and the expanded sales/cash receipts journal.
2. Assume that there are 300 returned checks and 280 collections per month and that the records are closed each month. How many written lines can be saved each month by recording returned checks and subsequent collections in the special journals? How many postings can be saved each month? (Ignore the effect of the subsidiary ledger.)
3. Describe the nature and use of the subsidiary ledger. What advantages do you see in having a subsidiary ledger?
4. Assuming that it takes approximately two and a half minutes to make each entry and related postings under the old system of recording bad checks and one minute to make each entry and related postings under the new system, what are the monthly savings if the cost is $20 an hour? What further, and possibly more significant, savings may be realized by using the new system?

Group Activity: After presenting parts **1** and **3** in class, divide the class into teams to work on parts **2** and **4.** Compare and discuss results.

Financial Reporting and Analysis

Interpreting Financial Reports

FRA 1.
LO 1 *Electronic Commerce on*
LO 4 *the Internet*

Amazon.com, which describes itself as the "Earth's Biggest Bookstore," is the leading Internet book seller. It might be described as a "virtual" bookstore because it carries only a relatively few books in its Seattle warehouse, far fewer than the average superstore, like Borders or Barnes & Noble. Buyers choose from a selection of 2.5 million books on the Internet and give credit card information to place an order. Amazon.com verifies the information and electronically sends the order to a wholesaler that packages and sends the order, usually within one day. Ninety-five percent of the books Amazon.com sells are delivered by these wholesalers, which charge a wholesale markup for handling and shipping. The cost of having to rely on wholesalers for distribution is one reason that Amazon.com has not yet reached profitability in spite of its success. As a result, the company is planning to expand its own distribution capability, which it believes it can do at a lower cost.[5]

1. Define electronic commerce and describe generally how conducting business on the Internet differs from conducting business in a retail store.
2. Describe how you believe the four principles of systems design apply to Amazon.com's sale and distribution of books as compared to a more traditional bookstore.
3. What changes in the application of these principles will occur if Amazon.com begins to do more of its own distribution?

Toys "R" Us Annual Report

FRA 2.
LO 1 *Principles of Accounting Systems Design*

In the Operational Highlights portion of the To the Stockholders section in the Toys "R" Us annual report supplement, management states that its goals are to streamline and reduce the number of items carried in inventory by more than 20 percent and to reduce the cost structure by bringing the right products to the stores more efficiently. To do this, the company uses satellite technology in North America that instantaneously links stores with headquarters' computer databases to make ordering, inventory control, and customer transaction authorization more cost-efficient. Explain how this computer technology and centralized databases comply with the principles of cost-benefit, control, compatibility, and flexibility.

International Company

This category is not applicable to this chapter.

Fingraph® Financial Analyst™

This category is not applicable to this chapter.

ENDNOTES

1. Douglas Prawitt, Marshall Romney, and Stanley Zarowin, "The Software CPAs Use," *Journal of Accountancy,* November 1997.
2. "Small Businesses Lining Up for New Technology," *Journal of Accountancy,* October 1996.
3. Walgreen, *Annual Report,* 1993.
4. Lisa Collins, "Top-Seller Kroch's Seeks a New Plot," *Crain's Chicago Business,* October 22, 1990.
5. Anthony Bianco, "Virtual Bookstores to Get Real," *Business Week,* October 27, 1997.

CHAPTER 8

Internal Control

LEARNING OBJECTIVES

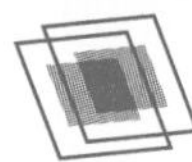

1. **Define *internal control* and identify the three elements of the internal control structure, including seven examples of control procedures.**
2. **Describe the inherent limitations of internal control.**
3. **Apply internal control procedures to common merchandising transactions.**
4. **Demonstrate the control of cash by preparing a bank reconciliation.**

SUPPLEMENTAL OBJECTIVES

5. **Demonstrate the use of a simple imprest system.**
6. **Define *voucher system* and describe the components of a voucher system.**
7. **Describe and carry out the five steps in operating a voucher system.**

DECISION POINT

DELL COMPUTER CORPORATION

Dell Computer Corporation is one of the fastest-growing businesses in the history of merchandising. The company sells computers by mail order and is known for providing good, fast service. But the fast growth causes problems for the company. In its early years, management acknowledged "[The company's] internal controls are having difficulty keeping up with its zooming growth. . . . The problems have made it difficult for the company to track its inventory and to accurately project supply and demand for the components that go into its personal computers. . . . The systems and the processes in the company didn't grow as fast as the business."[1] Why were these problems serious for Dell Computer, and what action should management have taken?

Problems with controls and systems are serious for all companies, including Dell, because they lead to loss of inventory, lost sales, and disgruntled customers. The mail-order computer business is very competitive, and Dell Computer could easily have lost its business and gone bankrupt if it had not addressed its growth-related problems. Management needed to institute new internal controls over purchases and inventory so that it could track all components and ship to customers soon after they placed their orders. As you will see in the next section, this goal can be achieved through a good internal control structure: a good control environment with an accounting and computer system that has specific procedures designed to manage and safeguard the inventory. Dell Computer Corporation was successful in remedying its problems and continues to be the leading mail-order computer company in the world.

Critical Thinking Question: Who loses if controls over assets are weak? **Answer:** Everyone. Owners earn less profit; managers and employees lose if losses affect their compensation or job security; customers lose because prices will rise to cover losses.

Internal Control Structure: Basic Elements and Procedures

A merchandising company can have high losses of cash and inventory if it does not take steps to protect its assets. The best way to do this is to set up and maintain a good internal control structure.

Internal Control Defined

OBJECTIVE 1

Define **internal control** *and identify the three elements of the internal control structure, including seven examples of control procedures*

Related Text Assignments:
Q: 1, 2, 3
SE: 1, 2, 3
E: 1, 2, 3, 4, 5
P: 4, 6
SD: 1, 3, 4
FRA: 1, 2, 3

Discussion Question: A good system of internal control accomplishes what four broad objectives? **Answer:** It safeguards the company assets, produces reliable accounting records, promotes operating efficiency, and encourages adherence to management's policies.

Internal control has traditionally been defined as all the policies and procedures management uses to protect the firm's assets and to ensure the accuracy and reliability of the accounting records. It also includes procedures that promote operating efficiency and encourage adherence to management's policies. In other words, management wants not only to safeguard assets and have reliable records, but also to maintain an efficient operation and ensure employees' compliance with its policies and procedures. To accomplish this, management establishes an internal control structure that consists of three elements: the control environment, the accounting system, and control procedures.[2]

The control environment is created by the overall attitude, awareness, and actions of management. It includes management's philosophy and operating style, organizational structure, methods of assigning authority and responsibility, and personnel policies and practices. Personnel should be qualified to handle responsibilities, which means that employees must be trained and informed. For example, the manager of a retail store should train employees to follow prescribed procedures for handling cash sales, credit card sales, and returns and refunds. It is clear that an accounting system, no matter how well designed, is only as good as the people who run it.

The control environment also includes regular reviews for compliance with procedures. For example, large companies often have a staff of internal auditors who review the company's system of internal control to see that it is working properly and that procedures are being followed. In smaller businesses, owners and managers should conduct these reviews.

As mentioned earlier, the accounting system consists of the methods and records established by management to identify, assemble, analyze, classify, record, and report a company's transactions, and to ensure that the goals of internal control are being met.

Finally, management uses control procedures to safeguard the company's assets and to ensure the reliability of the accounting records. These include:

Teaching Note: A good way to present the seven control procedures is to ask your students to explain how and why each procedure meets the goals of internal control. For example, the separation of duties is necessary so that the theft or error of one employee will most likely be discovered by another.

1. **Authorization** All transactions and activities should be properly authorized by management. In a retail store, for example, some transactions, such as normal cash sales, are authorized routinely; others, such as issuing a refund, may require a manager's approval.

2. **Recording transactions** To facilitate preparation of financial statements and to establish accountability for assets, all transactions should be recorded. In a retail store, for example, the cash register records sales, refunds, and other transactions internally on a paper tape or computer disk so that the cashier can be held responsible for the cash received and the merchandise removed during his or her shift.

3. **Documents and records** The design and use of adequate documents help ensure the proper recording of transactions. For example, to ensure that all transactions are recorded, invoices and other documents should be prenumbered and all numbers should be accounted for.

4. **Limited access** Access to assets should be permitted only with management's authorization. For example, retail stores should use cash registers, and only the cashier responsible for the cash in a register should have access to it. Other employees should not be able to open the cash drawer if the cashier is not present. Likewise, warehouses and storerooms should be accessible only to authorized personnel. Access to accounting records, including company computers, should also be controlled.

5. **Periodic independent verification** The records should be checked against the assets by someone other than the persons responsible for those records and assets. For example, at the end of each shift or day, the owner or store manager should count the cash in the cash drawer and compare that amount to the amounts recorded on the tape or computer disk in the cash register. Other examples of independent verification are the monthly bank reconciliation and periodic counts of physical inventory.

6. **Separation of duties** The organizational plan should separate functional responsibilities. Within a department, no one person should be in charge of authorizing transactions, operating the department, handling assets, and keeping records of assets. For example, in a stereo store, each employee should oversee only a single part of a transaction. A sales employee takes the order and writes out an invoice. Another employee receives the customer's cash or credit card payment and issues a receipt. Once the customer has a paid receipt, and only then, a third employee obtains the item from the warehouse and gives it to the customer. A person in the accounting department subsequently records the sales from the tape in the cash register, comparing them with the sales invoices and updating the inventory in the records. The separation of duties means that a mistake, careless or not, cannot be made without being seen by at least one other person.

Point to Emphasize: Actually, no control procedure can guarantee the prevention of theft. However, the more procedures there are in place, the less the likelihood of a theft occurring.

7. **Sound personnel procedures** Sound practices should be followed in managing the people who carry out the functions of each department. Among those practices are supervision, rotation of key people among different jobs, insistence that employees take vacations, and bonding of personnel who handle cash or inventories. Bonding is the process of carefully checking an employee's background and insuring the company against theft by that person. Bonding does not guarantee against theft, but it does prevent or reduce economic loss if theft occurs. Prudent personnel procedures help ensure that employees know their jobs, are honest, and will find it difficult to carry out and conceal embezzlement over a period of time.

Limitations of Internal Control

OBJECTIVE 2

Describe the inherent limitations of internal control

Related Text Assignments:
Q: 4
SE: 4
SD: 1, 4

No system of internal control is without its weaknesses. As long as control procedures are performed by people, the internal control system is vulnerable to human error. Errors may arise from misunderstandings, mistakes in judgment, carelessness, distraction, or fatigue. Separation of duties can be defeated through collusion by employees who secretly agree to deceive the company. Also, established procedures may be ineffective against employees' errors or dishonesty, or controls that may have initially been effective may later become ineffective because conditions have changed.[3] In certain cases, the costs of establishing and maintaining elaborate systems of internal control may exceed the benefits. In a small business, for example, active involvement by the owner can be a practical substitute for separation of some duties.

Internal Control over Merchandising Transactions

OBJECTIVE 3

Apply internal control procedures to common merchandising transactions

Related Text Assignments:
Q: 5, 6, 7, 8, 16
SE: 3, 5
P: 4, 6
SD: 1, 3, 4
FRA: 1, 3

Sound internal control procedures are needed in all aspects of a business, but particularly when assets are involved. Assets are especially vulnerable when they enter or leave a business. When sales are made, for example, cash or other assets enter the business, and goods or services leave the business. Procedures must be set up to prevent theft during those transactions.

Likewise, purchases of assets and payments of liabilities must be controlled. The majority of those transactions can be safeguarded by adequate purchasing and payroll systems. In addition, assets on hand, such as cash, investments, inventory, plant, and equipment, must be protected.

In this section, you will see how internal control procedures are applied to such merchandising transactions as cash sales, receipts, purchases, and cash payments. Similar procedures are applicable to service and manufacturing businesses.

Internal Control and Management Goals

Point to Emphasize: Maintaining internal control is especially complex and difficult for a merchandiser. Management must not only establish controls for cash sales receipts, purchases, and cash payments, but also go to great lengths to manage and protect its inventory.

When a system of internal control is applied effectively to merchandising transactions, it can achieve important management goals. For example, two key goals for the success of a merchandising business are

1. To prevent losses of cash or inventory owing to theft or fraud
2. To provide accurate records of merchandising transactions and account balances

Three broader goals for management are

1. To keep enough inventory on hand to sell to customers without overstocking
2. To keep enough cash on hand to pay for purchases in time to receive discounts
3. To keep credit losses as low as possible by making credit sales only to customers who are likely to pay on time

One control used in meeting broad management goals is the cash budget, which projects future cash receipts and disbursements. By maintaining adequate cash balances, a company is able to take advantage of discounts on purchases, prepare to borrow money when necessary, and avoid the damaging effects of being unable to pay bills when they are due. And by investing excess cash, the company can earn interest until the cash is needed.

Point to Emphasize: The separation of duties *can* be defeated through the collusion of two or more people.

A more specific accounting control is the separation of duties that involve the handling of cash. Such separation makes theft without detection extremely unlikely, unless two or more employees conspire. The separation of duties is easier in large businesses than in small ones, where one person may have to carry out several duties. The effectiveness of internal control over cash varies, depending on the size and the nature of the company. Most companies, however, should use the following procedures.

Teaching Note: Ask your students to explain how each control procedure listed acts to protect a business's cash. For example, payment by check not only provides evidence of payment, but also designates the payee as the only person who can convert the check into cash.

1. Separate the functions of authorization, recordkeeping, and custodianship of cash.
2. Limit the number of people who have access to cash.
3. Designate specific people who are responsible for handling cash.
4. Use banking facilities as much as possible, and keep the amount of cash on hand to a minimum.
5. Bond all employees who have access to cash.
6. Physically protect cash on hand by using cash registers, cashiers' cages, and safes.
7. Have a person who does not handle or record cash make unannounced audits of the cash on hand.

8. Record all cash receipts promptly.
9. Deposit all cash receipts promptly.
10. Make payments by check rather than by currency.
11. Have a person who does not authorize, handle, or record cash transactions reconcile the Cash account.

Notice that each of the foregoing procedures helps to safeguard cash by making it more difficult for any one individual who has access to cash to steal or misuse it undetected.

Control of Cash Sales Receipts

Cash payments for sales of goods and services can be received by mail or over the counter in the form of checks or currency. Whatever the source of the payments, cash should be recorded immediately upon receipt. This is usually done by making an entry in a cash receipts journal. Such a journal establishes a written record of cash receipts that should prevent errors and make theft more difficult.

Control of Cash Received Through the Mail Cash receipts that arrive by mail are vulnerable to theft by the employees who handle them. Payment by mail is increasing because of the expansion of mail-order sales. Therefore, to control mailed receipts, customers should be urged to pay by check instead of with currency.

Cash that comes in through the mail should be handled by two or more employees. The employee who opens the mail should make a list in triplicate of the money received. The list should contain each payer's name, the purpose for which the money was sent, and the amount. One copy goes with the cash to the cashier, who deposits the money. The second copy goes to the accounting department for recording. The third copy is kept by the person who opens the mail. Errors can be easily caught because the amount deposited by the cashier must agree with the amount received and the amount recorded in the cash receipts journal.

Control of Cash Received over the Counter Two common tools for controlling cash sales receipts are cash registers and prenumbered sales tickets. The amount of a cash sale should be rung up on a cash register at the time of the sale. The cash register should be placed so that the customer can see the amount recorded. Each cash register should have a locked-in tape on which it prints the day's transactions. At the

BUSINESS BULLETIN: TECHNOLOGY IN PRACTICE

One of the more difficult challenges facing computer programmers is to build good internal controls into computerized accounting programs. Such computer programs must include controls that prevent unintentional errors as well as unauthorized access and tampering. The programs prevent errors through reasonableness checks that, for example, may allow no transactions over a specified amount, mathematical checks that verify the arithmetic of transactions, and sequence checks that require documents and transactions to be in proper order. They typically use passwords and questions about randomly selected personal data to prevent unauthorized access to computer records. With unauthorized Internet access easily available to many systems, data encryption and firewalls are important. Data encryption is a way of coding data so that if it is stolen, it is useless to the thief. A firewall is a strong electronic barrier to access from outside a computer system.

end of the day, the cashier counts the cash in the cash register and turns it in to the cashier's office. Another employee takes the tape out of the cash register and records the cash receipts for the day in the cash receipts journal. The amount of cash turned in and the amount recorded on the tape should agree; if not, any differences must be accounted for. Large retail chains commonly monitor cash receipts by having each cash register tied directly into a computer that records each transaction as it occurs. Whether the elements are performed manually or by computer, separating responsibility for cash receipts, cash deposits, and recordkeeping is necessary to ensure good internal control.

Point to Emphasize: Notice that the cashier should not be allowed to remove the cash register tape or to record the day's cash receipts.

In some stores, internal control is further strengthened by the use of prenumbered sales tickets and a central cash register or cashier's office, where all sales are rung up and collected by a person who does not participate in the sale. The salesperson completes a prenumbered sales ticket at the time of sale, giving one copy to the customer and keeping a copy. At the end of the day, all sales tickets must be accounted for, and the sales total computed from the sales tickets should equal the total sales recorded on the cash register.

Control of Purchases and Cash Disbursements

Cash disbursements are particularly vulnerable to fraud and embezzlement. In one recent case, the treasurer of one of the nation's largest jewelry retailers was charged with having stolen over $500,000 by systematically overpaying federal income taxes and keeping the refund checks as they came back to the company.

To avoid such theft, cash should be paid only after the receipt of specific authorization supported by documents that establish the validity and amount of the claim. In addition, maximum possible use should be made of the principle of separation of duties in the purchase of goods and services and the payment for them. The degree of separation of duties varies, depending on the size of the business. Figure 1 shows how separation of duties can be maximized in large companies. In the figure, five internal units (the requesting department, the purchasing department, the accounting department, the receiving department, and the treasurer) and two external contacts (the supplier and the banking system) all play a role in the internal control plan. Notice that business documents are also crucial components of the plan.

Reinforcement Exercise: A good way to review the material in Figure 2 is to construct a quiz that asks students to match each business document with the preparer, recipient, and procedure. Students with little business experience often find this topic difficult to understand.

As shown in Figure 2, every action is documented and verified by at least one other person. For instance, the requesting department cannot work out a kickback scheme to make illegal payments to the supplier because the receiving department independently records receipts and the accounting department verifies prices. The receiving department cannot steal goods because the receiving report must equal the invoice. For the same reason, the supplier cannot bill for more goods than it ships. The accounting department's work is verified by the treasurer, and the treasurer ultimately is checked by the accounting department.

Using the forms shown with Figure 2, follow the typical sequence of documents used in this internal control plan for the purchase of twenty boxes of fax paper rolls. To begin, the credit office (requesting department) of Martin Maintenance Company fills out a formal request for a purchase, or purchase requisition for twenty boxes of fax paper rolls (Item 1). The department head approves it and forwards it to the purchasing department. The people in the purchasing department prepare a purchase order as shown in Item 2. The purchase order is addressed to the vendor (seller) and contains a description of the items ordered; the expected price, terms, and shipping date; and other shipping instructions. Martin Maintenance Company does not pay any bill that is not accompanied by a purchase order number.

Common Student Confusion: Students often think that a purchase requisition is the same as a purchase order. Emphasize that a purchase requisition is sent to the purchasing department and that a purchase order is sent to the vendor.

Point to Emphasize: *Invoice* is the business term for "bill." Notice that every business document must have a number, for purposes of reference.

After receiving the purchase order, the vendor, Henderson Supply Company, ships the goods and sends an invoice or bill (Item 3) to Martin Maintenance Company. The invoice gives the quantity and description of the goods delivered and

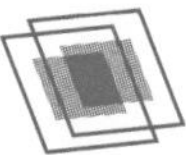

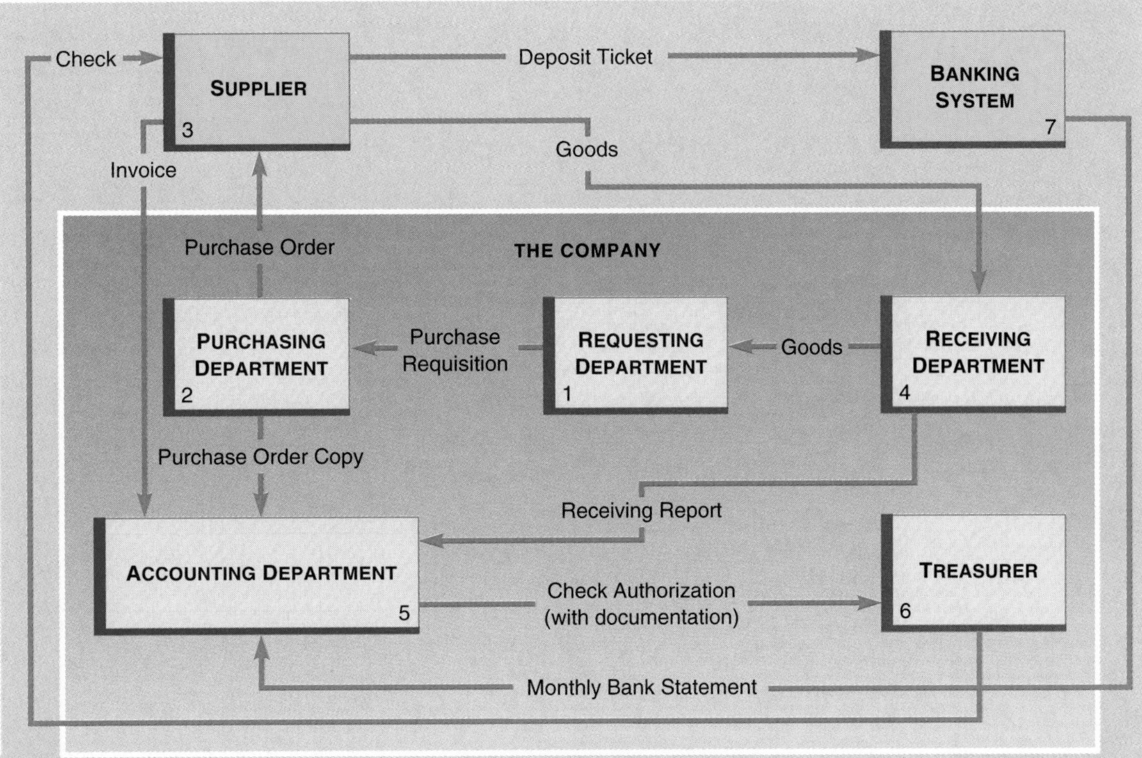

Figure 1
Internal Control for Purchasing and Paying for Goods and Services

the terms of payment. If goods cannot all be shipped immediately, the estimated date for shipment of the remainder is indicated.

When the goods reach the receiving department of Martin Maintenance Company, an employee writes the description, quantity, and condition of the goods on a form called a receiving report (Item 4). The receiving department does not receive a copy of the purchase order or invoice, so its employees do not know what should be received. Thus, they are not tempted to steal any excess goods that may be delivered.

The receiving report is sent to the accounting department, where it is compared with the purchase order and the invoice. If all is correct, the accounting department completes a check authorization and attaches it to the three supporting documents. The check authorization form shown in Item 5 has a space for each item to be checked off as it is examined. Notice that the accounting department has all the documentary evidence for the transaction but does not have access to the assets purchased. Nor does it write the check for payment. This means that the people performing the accounting function cannot gain by falsifying documents in an effort to conceal fraud.

Finally, the treasurer examines all the documents and issues an order to the bank for payment, called a check (Item 6), for the amount of the invoice less any appropriate discount. In some systems, the accounting department fills out the check so that all the treasurer has to do is inspect and sign it. The check is then sent to the supplier, with a remittance advice that shows what the check is for. A supplier who is not paid the proper amount will complain, of course, thus providing a form of

Figure 2
Internal Control Plan for Purchases and Cash Disbursements

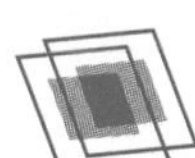

(1) **PURCHASE REQUISITION** No. 7077
Martin Maintenance Company

From: Credit Office Date: September 6, 20xx
To: Purchasing Department Suggested Vendor: Henderson Supply Company
Please purchase the following items:

Quantity	Number	Description
20 boxes	X 144	FAX paper rolls

Reason for Request
Six months' supply for office
Approved J.P.

To be filled in by Purchasing Department
Date ordered 9/8/20xx P.O. No. J 102

(2) **PURCHASE ORDER** No. J 102
Martin Maintenance Company
8428 Rocky Island Avenue
Chicago, Illinois 60643

To: Henderson Supply Company
2525 25th Street
Mesa, Illinois 61611

Date: September 8, 20xx
FOB: Destination
Ship by: September 12, 20xx
Terms: 2/10, n/30

Ship to: Martin Maintenance Company
Above Address

Please ship the following:

Quantity	✓	Number	Description	Price	Per	Amount
20 boxes		X 144	FAX paper rolls	12.00	box	$240.00

Purchase order number must appear on all shipments and invoices.
Ordered by Marsha Owen

(3) **INVOICE** No. 0468
Henderson Supply Company
2525 25th Street
Mesa, Illinois 61611

Date: September 12, 20xx
Your Order No.: J 102

Sold to:
Martin Maintenance Company
8428 Rocky Island Avenue
Chicago, Illinois 60643

Ship to: Same

Sales Representative: Joe Jacobs

Quantity		Description	Price	Per	Amount
Ordered	Shipped				
20	20	X 144 FAX paper rolls	12.00	box	$240.00

FOB Destination | Terms: 2/10, n/30 | Date Shipped: 9/12/20xx Via: Self

(4) **RECEIVING REPORT** No. JR065
Martin Maintenance Company
8428 Rocky Island Avenue
Chicago, Illinois 60643

Date: September 12, 20xx

Quantity	Number	Description	Condition
20 boxes	X 144	FAX paper rolls	O.K.

Received by B.M.

(5) **CHECK AUTHORIZATION**

	NO.	CHECK
Purchase Order	J 102	✓
Receiving Report	JR 065	✓
INVOICE	0468	✓
Price		✓
Calculations		✓
Terms		✓

Approved for Payment J Joseph

(6)
Martin Maintenance Company
8428 Rocky Island Avenue
Chicago, Illinois 60643

NO. 2570
61-153/313

9/21 20xx

PAY TO THE ORDER OF Henderson Supply Company $ 235.20

Two hundred thirty-five and 20/100 ---------- Dollars

THE LAKE PARK NATIONAL BANK
Chicago, Illinois

Martin Maintenance Company
by Arthur Martin

⑆03130153⑆ ⑈8030 647 4⑈

Remittance Advice

Date	P.O. No.	DESCRIPTION	AMOUNT
9/21/20xx	J 102	20 X 144 FAX paper rolls Supplier Inv. No. 0468 Less 2% discount Net Martin Maintenance Company	 $240.00 4.80 $235.20

Business Document	Prepared by	Sent to	Verification and Related Procedures
(1) Purchase requisition	Requesting department	Purchasing department	Purchasing verifies authorization.
(2) Purchase order	Purchasing department	Supplier	Supplier sends goods or services in accordance with purchase order.
(3) Invoice	Supplier	Accounting department	Accounting receives invoice from supplier.
(4) Receiving report	Receiving department	Accounting department	Accounting compares invoice, purchase order, and receiving report. Accounting verifies prices.
(5) Check authorization	Accounting department	Treasurer	Accounting attaches check authorization to invoice, purchase order, and receiving report.
(6) Check	Treasurer	Supplier	Treasurer verifies all documents before preparing check.
(7) Bank statement	Buyer's bank	Accounting department	Accounting compares amount and payee's name on returned check with check authorization.

(7)

Statement of Account with
THE LAKE PARK NATIONAL BANK
Chicago, Illinois

Martin Maintenance Company
8428 Rocky Island Avenue
Chicago, Illinois 60643

Checking Acct No
8030-647-4
Period covered
Sept.30-Oct.31,20xx

Previous Balance	Checks/Debits—No.	Deposits/Credits—No.	S.C.	Current Balance
$2,645.78	$4,319.33 --16	$5,157.12 --7	$12.50	$3,471.07

CHECKS/DEBITS			DEPOSITS/CREDITS		DAILY BALANCES	
Posting Date	Check No.	Amount	Posting Date	Amount	Date	Amount
					09/30	2,645.78
10/01	2564	100.00	10/01	586.00	10/01	2,881.78
10/01	2565	250.00	10/05	1,500.00	10/04	2,825.60
10/04	2567	56.18	10/06	300.00	10/05	3,900.46
10/05	2566	425.14	10/16	1,845.50	10/06	4,183.34
10/06	2568	17.12	10/21	600.00	10/12	2,242.34
10/12	2569	1,705.80	10/24	300.00CM	10/16	3,687.84
10/12	2570	235.20	10/31	25.62IN	10/17	3,589.09
10/16	2571	400.00			10/21	4,189.09
10/17	2572	29.75			10/24	3,745.59
10/17	2573	69.00			10/25	3,586.09
10/24	2574	738.50			10/28	3,457.95
10/24		5.00DM			10/31	3,471.07
10/25	2575	7.50				
10/25	2577	152.00				
10/28		118.14NSF				
10/28		10.00DM				
10/31		12.50SC				

Explanation of Symbols:

CM – Credit Memo
DM – Debit Memo
NSF – Non-Sufficient Funds

SC – Service Charge
EC – Error Correction
OD – Overdraft
IN – Interest on Average Balance

The last amount in this column is your balance.

Please examine; if no errors are reported within ten (10) days, the account will be considered to be correct.

BUSINESS BULLETIN: ETHICS IN PRACTICE

What happens to all the paper—records and documents of all sorts—generated by a company's accounting system? Some of it, of course, must be saved for tax and legal purposes, but much of it is discarded after a time. Because accounting records and documents contain much information that companies want to keep confidential, management is reluctant to simply throw the paper in the trash. As a result, a nationwide industry of information-destruction firms has grown up and produces annual revenues of more than $250 million. Companies such as DocuShred, Inc., of Pennsylvania specialize in picking up paper and shredding it in a confidential way. Some shredding machines can make confetti of up to ten tons of paper per hour at seven to fifteen cents per pound. This is cheaper, faster, and more secret than the companies could do it themselves. Data destruction companies recycle about 95 percent of the shredded paper.[4]

outside control over the payment. Using a deposit ticket, the supplier deposits the check in the bank, which returns the canceled check with Martin Maintenance Company's next bank statement (Item 7). If the treasurer has made the check out for the wrong amount (or altered a pre-filled-in check), the problem will show up in the bank reconciliation.

There are many variations of the system just described. This example is offered as a simple system that provides adequate internal control.

Preparing a Bank Reconciliation

OBJECTIVE 4

Demonstrate the control of cash by preparing a bank reconciliation

Related Text Assignments:
Q: 9, 10
SE: 6, 7
E: 6, 7, 8
P: 1, 2, 7
SD: 2

Rarely will the balance of a company's Cash account exactly equal the cash balance shown on the bank statement. Certain transactions shown in the company's records may not have been recorded by the bank, and certain bank transactions may not appear in the company's records. Therefore, a necessary step in internal control is to prove both the balance shown on the bank statement and the balance of Cash in the accounting records. A bank reconciliation is the process of accounting for the differences between the balance appearing on the bank statement and the balance of Cash according to the company's records. This process involves making additions to and subtractions from both balances to arrive at the adjusted cash balance.

The most common examples of transactions shown in the company's records but not entered in the bank's records are the following:

1. **Outstanding checks** These are checks that have been issued and recorded by the company but that do not yet appear on the bank statement.
2. **Deposits in transit** These are deposits that were mailed or taken to the bank but that were not received in time to be recorded on the bank statement.

Transactions that may appear on the bank statement but that have not been recorded by the company include the following:

1. **Service charges (SC)** Banks often charge a fee, or service charge, for the use of a checking account. Many banks base the service charge on a number of factors, such as the average balance of the account during the month or the number of checks drawn.

Enrichment Note: Periodically, banks detect individuals who are *kiting*. Kiting is the illegal issuing of checks when there is not enough money to cover them. Before one kited check clears the bank, a kited check from another account is deposited to cover it, making an endless circle.

Instructional Strategy: Students often assume that bank reconciliations do not present ethical dilemmas. Assign SD 3 to small groups for in-class discussion. Each group should appoint one member to take careful notes so that he or she can report results to the class. Challenge students to suggest at least five ways for Jean McGuire to respond. From a show of hands determine which alternative is favored and discuss why.

2. **NSF (non-sufficient funds) checks** An NSF check is a check deposited by the company that is not paid when the company's bank presents it to the maker's bank. The bank charges the company's account and returns the check so that the company can try to collect the amount due. If the bank has deducted the NSF check from the bank statement but the company has not deducted it from its book balance, an adjustment must be made in the bank reconciliation. The depositor usually reclassifies the NSF check from Cash to Accounts Receivable because the company must now collect from the person or company that wrote the check.
3. **Interest income** It is very common for banks to pay interest on a company's average balance. These accounts are sometimes money market accounts, but they can take other forms. Such interest is reported on the bank statement.
4. **Miscellaneous charges and credits** Banks also charge for other services, such as collection and payment of promissory notes, stopping payment on checks, and printing checks. The bank notifies the depositor of each deduction by including a debit memorandum with the monthly statement. A bank will sometimes serve as an agent in collecting on promissory notes for the depositor. In such a case, a credit memorandum will be included.

An error by either the bank or the depositor will, of course, require immediate correction.

Illustration of a Bank Reconciliation

Point to Emphasize: The ending bank statement balance does not represent the amount that should appear on the balance sheet for cash. There are events and items, such as deposits in transit and outstanding checks, that the bank is unaware of at the cutoff date. This is why a bank reconciliation must be prepared.

Assume that the October bank statement for Martin Maintenance Company indicates a balance on October 31 of $3,471.07 and that, in its records, Martin Maintenance Company has a cash balance on October 31 of $2,405.91. The bank statement is shown in Figure 2. The purpose of a bank reconciliation is to identify the items that make up the difference between these amounts and to determine the correct cash balance. The bank reconciliation for Martin Maintenance Company is given in Exhibit 1. The numbered items in the exhibit refer to the following:

1. A deposit in the amount of $276.00 was mailed to the bank on October 31 and has not been recorded by the bank.
2. Five checks issued in October or prior months have not yet been paid by the bank, as follows:

Check No.	Date	Amount
2551	Sept. 14	$150.00
2576	Oct. 24	40.68
2578	Oct. 31	500.00
2579	Oct. 31	370.00
2580	Oct. 31	130.50

3. The deposit for cash sales of October 6 was incorrectly recorded in Martin Maintenance Company's records as $330.00. The bank correctly recorded the deposit as $300.00.
4. Among the returned checks was a credit memorandum showing that the bank had collected a promissory note from A. Jacobs in the amount of $280.00, plus $20.00 in interest on the note. A debit memorandum was also enclosed for the $5.00 collection fee. No entry had been made on Martin Maintenance Company's records.
5. Also returned with the bank statement was an NSF check for $118.14. This check had been received from a customer named Arthur Clubb. The NSF check from Clubb was not reflected in the company's accounting records. A debit memorandum was included for the $10 returned check fee.

Clarification Note: A credit memorandum means that an amount was *added* to the bank balance; a debit memorandum means that an amount was *deducted.*

Exhibit 1. Bank Reconciliation

Martin Maintenance Company Bank Reconciliation October 31, 20xx		
Balance per bank, October 31		$3,471.07
① Add deposit of October 31 in transit		276.00
		$3,747.07
② Less outstanding checks:		
No. 2551	$150.00	
No. 2576	40.68	
No. 2578	500.00	
No. 2579	370.00	
No. 2580	130.50	1,191.18
Adjusted bank balance, October 31		**$2,555.89**
Balance per books, October 31		$2,405.91
Add:		
④ Notes receivable collected by bank	$280.00	
④ Interest income on note	20.00	
⑦ Interest income	25.62	325.62
		$2,731.53
Less:		
③ Overstatement of deposit of October 6	$ 30.00	
④ Collection fee	5.00	
⑤ NSF check of Arthur Clubb	118.14	
⑤ Returned check fee	10.00	
⑥ Service charge	12.50	175.64
Adjusted book balance, October 31		**$2,555.89**

Note: The circled numbers refer to the items listed in the text on the previous page and below.

Parenthetical Note: Even though the September 14 check was deducted on the September 30 reconciliation, it must be deducted again in each subsequent month in which it remains outstanding.

Clarification Note: It is possible to place an item in the wrong section of a bank reconciliation and still have it balance. The *correct* adjusted bank balance must be obtained.

Discussion Question: Some companies stipulate that checks they issue must be cashed within a certain period of time, such as sixty days, or the bank is instructed not to accept them. In a bank reconciliation, how should a company handle a check that was not deposited by the payee by the end of the stipulated time period? **Answer:** Add the amount to the balance per books.

6. The regular monthly service charge of $12.50 is shown on the statement. This charge had not yet been recorded by Martin Maintenance Company.
7. Interest earned by the company on the average balance was reported as $25.62.

Reinforcement Exercise: On May 31, a company's balance per bank is $750. Deposits in transit total $900, outstanding checks total $400, and the bank balance includes a $300 note receivable collected by the bank. What should the May 31 adjusted bank balance be? **Answer:** $1,250.

Note in Exhibit 1 that, starting from their separate balances, both the bank and book amounts are adjusted to the amount of $2,555.89. This adjusted balance is the amount of cash owned by the company on October 31 and thus is the amount that should appear on its October 31 balance sheet.

Recording Transactions After Reconciliation

Parenthetical Note: Notice that only those transactions the company was not aware of before receiving the bank statement are recorded.

The adjusted balance of cash differs from both the bank statement and Martin Maintenance Company's records. The bank balance will automatically become correct when outstanding checks are presented for payment and the deposit in transit is received and recorded by the bank. Entries must be made, however, for the transactions necessary to correct the book balance. All the items reported by the bank but not yet recorded by the company must be recorded in the general journal by means of the following entries:

Point to Emphasize: Every entry involves either a debit or a credit to Cash.

A = L + OE (+ − / +)	Oct. 31	Cash	300.00	
		Notes Receivable		280.00
		Interest Income		20.00
		Note receivable of $280.00 and interest of $20.00 collected by bank from A. Jacobs		
A = L + OE (+ / +)	Oct. 31	Cash	25.62	
		Interest Income		25.62
		Interest on average bank account balance		
A = L + OE (− / −)	31	Sales	30.00	
		Cash		30.00
		Correction of error in recording a $300.00 deposit as $330.00		
A = L + OE (+ −)	31	Accounts Receivable	128.14	
		Cash		128.14
		NSF check of Arthur Clubb returned by bank ($118.14 + $10.00)		
A = L + OE (− / −)	31	Bank Service Charges Expense	17.50	
		Cash		17.50
		Bank service charge ($12.50) and collection fee ($5.00) for October		

Instructional Strategy: To assess comprehension of check-writing procedures, ask students to complete SE 3 in class. After reviewing an answer, ask how many students responded correctly. When comprehension is low, ask student(s) with correct responses to explain further. Be prepared to assist as needed.

It is acceptable to record these entries in one or two compound entries to save time and space.

DECISION POINT

CAMPBELL SOUP CO.

Campbell Soup Co. was drowning in paperwork. The company had forty locations that processed accounts payable and weekly payrolls, which meant that eighty Cash accounts had to be maintained and the daily transactions of each tracked manually. Each month, checks were written to settle more than 1,300 transactions among divisions of the company, and any differences in cash records and cash on hand in thirty bank accounts had to be explained. What could Campbell Soup do to become more efficient and provide better information to management?

The company developed a system that concentrates its cash management activities in two personal computer networks that perform cash management, reporting, and information management. The system is integrated, and the flow of information is automatic. Cash and general ledger transactions are automatically generated, and a system was developed so that balances among divisions could be netted and checks would not have to be written to settle accounts. Because banking fees and balances are now closely monitored, the fees paid to banks dropped

Critical Thinking Question: How could a small business use information from bank statements and technology to reduce its cash management costs?

from $5 million per year to less than $1 million. And because duplication of effort has been reduced, the staff has been cut in half, which has led to savings of more than $400,000 per year.[5]

Answer: Using computer software to reconcile the cash balance with the bank statement will save time monthly. A detailed listing by category of all bank charges for previous periods may highlight areas where costs are controllable and could be reduced. Even small com-panies can save money by evaluating how they conduct business.

Petty Cash Procedures

SUPPLEMENTAL OBJECTIVE 5

Demonstrate the use of a simple imprest system

Related Text Assignments:
Q: 11, 12, 13, 14, 15, 16
SE: 8
E: 9, 10
P: 3, 8

It is not always practical to make every disbursement by check. For example, it is sometimes necessary to make small payments of cash for such things as postage stamps, incoming postage, shipping charges due, or minor purchases of pens, paper, and the like.

For situations in which it is inconvenient to pay by check, most companies set up a petty cash fund. One of the best methods of maintaining control over the fund is to use an imprest system. Under this system, a petty cash fund is established for a fixed amount. Each cash payment from the fund is documented by a voucher. Then the fund is periodically reimbursed, based on the vouchers, for the exact amount necessary to restore the original cash balance.

Establishing the Petty Cash Fund

Some companies have a regular cashier or other employee who administers the petty cash fund. To establish the fund, the company issues a check for an amount that is intended to cover two to four weeks of small expenditures. The check is cashed, and the money is placed in the petty cash box, drawer, or envelope.

The only entry required when the fund is established is to record the check.

A = L + OE
+
−

Oct. 14	Petty Cash	100.00	
	Cash		100.00
	To establish the petty cash fund		

Making Disbursements from the Petty Cash Fund

The custodian of the petty cash fund should prepare a petty cash voucher, or written authorization, for each expenditure, as shown in Figure 3. On each petty cash voucher, the custodian enters the date, amount, and purpose of the expenditure. The voucher is signed by the person who receives the payment.

The custodian should be informed that unannounced audits of the fund will be made occasionally. The cash in the fund plus the sum of the petty cash vouchers should at all times equal the amount shown in the Petty Cash account.

Point to Emphasize: Even though withdrawals from petty cash are generally small, the cumulative total over time can represent a substantial amount. Accordingly, an effective system of internal control must be established for the management of the fund.

Reimbursing the Petty Cash Fund

At specified intervals, when the fund becomes low, and at the end of an accounting period, the petty cash fund is replenished by a check issued to the custodian for the exact amount of the expenditures. From time to time, there may be minor discrepancies in the amount of cash left in the fund at the time of reimbursement. In those cases, the amount of the discrepancy is recorded in a Cash Short or Over account, as a debit if short or as a credit if over.

Assume that after two weeks the petty cash fund established earlier has a cash balance of $14.27 and petty cash vouchers as follows: postage, $25.00; supplies, $30.55; and freight in, $30.00. The entry to replenish, or replace, the fund would be:

Point to Emphasize: When the petty cash fund is replenished, the Petty Cash account is neither debited nor credited. But if the size of the fund is changed, there should be an entry to Petty Cash.

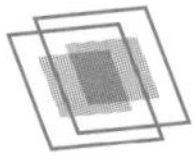

PETTY CASH VOUCHER

No. X 744

Date Oct. 23, 20xx

For Postage due

Charge to Postage Expense

Amount $2.86

W.S. — Approved by

Tom L. — Received by

Figure 3
Petty Cash Voucher

A = L + OE
+ −
− −
−

Oct. 28	Postage Expense	25.00	
	Supplies	30.55	
	Freight In	30.00	
	Cash Short or Over	.18	
	Cash		85.73
	To replenish the petty cash fund		

Notice that the Petty Cash account was not affected by the entry to replenish the fund. The Petty Cash account is debited only when the fund is established. Expense or asset accounts are debited each time the fund is replenished, including in this case $.18 to Cash Short or Over for a small cash shortage. In most cases, no further entries to the Petty Cash account are needed unless the firm wants to change the fixed amount of the fund.

The petty cash fund should be replenished at the end of an accounting period to bring it up to its fixed amount and ensure that changes in the other accounts involved are reflected in the current period's financial statements. If, through an oversight, the petty cash fund is not replenished at the end of the period, expenditures for the period still must appear on the income statement. They are shown through an adjusting entry debiting the expense accounts and crediting Petty Cash. The result is a reduction in the petty cash fund and the Petty Cash account by the amount of the adjusting entry. On the financial statements, the balance of the Petty Cash account is usually combined with other cash accounts.

Voucher Systems

SUPPLEMENTAL OBJECTIVE 6

Define* voucher system *and describe the components of a voucher system

Related Text Assignments:
Q: 17, 18, 19
SE: 9

Point to Emphasize: The purpose of a voucher system is to control expenditures through mandatory documentation and written authorization.

A voucher system is any system that gives documentary proof of and written authorization for business transactions. In this section, we present a voucher system designed to keep the tightest possible control over a company's expenditures. It consists of records and procedures for systematically gathering, recording, and paying expenditures. The system provides strong internal control by separating duties and responsibilities in the following functions:

1. Authorization of expenditures
2. Receipt of goods and services
3. Validation of liability by examination of invoices from suppliers for correctness of prices, extensions (quantity times price), shipping costs, and credit terms
4. Payment of expenditure by check, taking discounts when possible

Under a voucher system, every liability must be recorded as soon as it is incurred. A written authorization, called a voucher, is prepared for each expenditure when it becomes an obligation to pay, and checks are written only for approved vouchers. No one person has the authority both to incur expenses and to issue checks. In large companies, the duties of authorizing expenditures, verifying receipt of goods and services, checking invoices, recording liabilities, and issuing checks are divided among different people. So, for both accounting and management control, every expenditure must be carefully and routinely reviewed and verified before payment. For each transaction, the written approval leaves a trail of documentary evidence, or what is called an audit trail.

Although there is more than one way to set up a voucher system, most systems use (1) vouchers, (2) voucher checks, (3) a voucher register, and (4) a check register.

Vouchers

Point to Emphasize: A voucher serves the same purpose as a check authorization form.

Any business can use vouchers to control expenditures. A voucher is a written authorization for each expenditure and serves as the basis of an accounting entry. To facilitate tracking, all vouchers are sequentially numbered, and a separate voucher is attached to each bill as it comes in. In the cash disbursement system introduced earlier in this chapter, a voucher would replace the check authorization form. On the face of a typical voucher (Figure 4) are important information about the expenditure and the authorizing signatures required for payment. On the reverse side of the voucher is information about the accounts and amounts to be debited and credited. The voucher identifies the transaction by both voucher number and check number and is recorded in both the voucher register and the check register, as described in the following sections.

Voucher Checks

Point to Emphasize: Payment is made with a voucher check.

Although regular checks can be used effectively with a voucher system, many businesses use a form of voucher check, which tells the payee the reason why the check was issued. The information is written either on the check itself or on a detachable stub.

Voucher Register

Point to Emphasize: All approved vouchers are recorded in the voucher register.

The voucher register is the book of original entry in which vouchers are recorded after they have been approved. The voucher register takes the place of the purchases journal in companies that use special-purpose journals. There is one important difference between the two journals: All expenditures—expenses, payroll, plant, and equipment, as well as purchases of merchandise—are recorded in a voucher register; only purchases of merchandise on credit are recorded in a single-column purchases journal.

A voucher register appears in Exhibit 2. Notice that a column called Vouchers Payable replaces the Accounts Payable column. As you can see, the first entry in the voucher register records the receipt of a utility bill. It is recorded as a debit to Utilities Expense and a credit to Vouchers Payable (not Accounts Payable). On July 6, this utility bill was paid with check number 203.

Check Register

Point to Emphasize: A check register serves the same purpose as a cash payments journal.

In a voucher system, the check register, as shown in Exhibit 3, is the journal in which checks are listed as they are written. Consequently, it replaces the cash payments journal. Carefully study the connection between the voucher register and the check register. The incurrence of a liability is recorded in the voucher register; its payment is recorded in the check register.

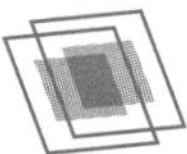

Parenthetical Note: A voucher not only provides for the necessary signatures but also includes information and document numbers that are important in creating an audit trail.

Thomas Appliance Company

Payee Belmont Products — Voucher No. 704
Address Gary, Indiana — Date Due 7/13
Date Paid 7/13
Terms 2/10, n/30 — Check No. 205

Date	Invoice No.	Description	Amount
7/3	XL1066	10 cases Model 70X14	1,200--

Approved M. N. Controller — Approved A. Thomas Treasurer

BACK OF VOUCHER

Account Debited	Acct. No.	Amount
Purchases	511	1,200.00
Freight In	512	
Rent Expense	631	
Salary Expense	611	
Utilities Expense	635	
Total		$1,200.00

Voucher No. 704
Payee Belmont Products
Address Gary, Indiana

Invoice Amount 1,200.00
Less Discount 24.00
Net 1,176.00
Date Due 7/13
Date Paid 7/13
Check No. 205

Figure 4
Front and Back of a Typical Voucher Form

Operation of a Voucher System

SUPPLEMENTAL OBJECTIVE 7

Describe and carry out the five steps in operating a voucher system

Related Text Assignments:
Q: 20, 21
SE: 10
P: 5

There are five steps in the operation of a voucher system:

1. Preparing the voucher
2. Recording the voucher
3. Paying the voucher
4. Posting the voucher and check registers
5. Summarizing unpaid vouchers

1. **Preparing the voucher** A voucher is prepared for each expenditure. All documents—purchase orders, invoices, and receiving reports—should be attached to the voucher when it is submitted for approval.

   Many companies pay their employees out of a separate payroll account. In such cases, a voucher is prepared to cover the total payroll. The check for the voucher is then deposited in the payroll account, and individual payroll checks are drawn on that account.

Exhibit 2. Voucher Register

Voucher Register

Date		Voucher No.	Payee	Payment Date	Payment Check No.	Credit Vouchers Payable	Debits Purchases	Debits Freight In	Debits Store Supplies
20xx									
July	1	701	Common Utility	7/6	203	75			
	2	702	Ade Realty	7/2	201	400			
	2	703	Buy Rite Supplies	7/6	202	25			
	3	704	Belmont Products	7/13	205	1,200	1,200		
	6	705	M&M Freight			60		60	
	7	706	J. Jay, Petty Cash	7/7	204	50			
	8	707	Belmont Products	7/18	208	600	600		
	11	708	M&M Freight			30		30	
	11	709	Mack Truck			5,600			
	12	710	Livingstone Wholesale	7/22	209	785	750	35	
	14	711	Payroll	7/14	206	2,200			
	17	712	First National Bank	7/17	207	4,250			
	20	713	Livingstone Wholesale			525	500	25	
	21	714	Belmont Products			400	400		
	24	715	M&M Freight			18		18	
	30	716	Payroll	7/30	210	2,200			
	31	717	J. Jay, Petty Cash	7/31	211	47		17	
	31	718	Maintenance Company			175			
	31	719	Store Supply Company			350			350
						18,990	3,450	185	350
						(211)	(511)	(512)	(116)

Point to Emphasize: The voucher register contains a Vouchers Payable column that functions exactly like the Accounts Payable column in a purchases journal.

2. **Recording the voucher** All approved vouchers should be recorded in the voucher register, as shown in Exhibit 2. For example, the entry for Voucher 704 corresponds to the information that is presented in Figure 4. Vouchers that do not have appropriate approvals or supporting documents should be investigated immediately.

Teaching Note: The mechanics of a voucher system are best understood by working a comprehensive problem. P 5 gives students an opportunity to practice these five steps.

3. **Paying the voucher** After a voucher has been recorded, it is placed in an unpaid voucher file. Many companies file their vouchers by due date and by vendor within due date, so that checks can be written at the appropriate times. Such a practice ensures that all discounts for prompt payment can be taken. After payment, vouchers are filed by voucher number.

   A few days before a voucher is due, a check for the correct amount, accompanied by the voucher and supporting documents, is presented to the individual

Exhibit 2. Voucher Register *(continued)*

Page 1

Debits								
Office Supplies	Sales Salaries Expense	Office Salaries Expense	Maintenance Expense, Selling	Maintenance Expense, Office	Utilities Expense	Other Accounts Name	Other Accounts No.	Other Accounts Amount
					75			
						Rent Expense	631	400
25								
						Petty Cash	121	50
						Trucks	148	5,600
	1,400	800						
						Notes Payable	212	4,000
						Interest Expense	645	250
	1,400	800						
20						Misc. Exp.	649	10
			100	75				
45	2,800	1,600	100	75	75			10,310
(117)	(611)	(612)	(621)	(622)	(635)			(✓)

Enrichment Note: The Other Accounts column enables the voucher register to accommodate any type of expenditure. The total of the Other Accounts column is not posted because it represents several different accounts, each of which is posted the day the transaction is entered into the voucher register.

authorized to sign checks. The payment is entered in the check register, as shown in Exhibit 3. For example, Belmont Products is paid with check no. 205. Both the date of payment and the check number are then entered in the voucher register on the same line as the corresponding voucher. This information is helpful in the preparation of a schedule of unpaid vouchers (see step **5**). If the net method of recording purchases is used instead of the gross method, a Discounts Lost debit column replaces the Purchases Discounts credit column.

Extra steps are required when there has been a purchase return or allowance that applies to a voucher. For example, suppose that part of a shipment of merchandise is defective and is returned to the supplier for credit. At the time the merchandise is returned or the allowance is given, an entry should be made in the general journal debiting Vouchers Payable and crediting Purchases Returns

Exhibit 3. Check Register

Check Register					Debit	Credits	
Date		Check No.	Payee	Voucher No.	Vouchers Payable	Purchases Discounts	Cash
20xx							
July	2	201	Ade Realty	702	400		400
	6	202	Buy Rite Supplies	703	25		25
	6	203	Common Utility	701	75		75
	7	204	J. Jay, Petty Cash	706	50		50
	13	205	Belmont Products	704	1,200	24	1,176
	14	206	Payroll	711	2,200		2,200
	17	207	First National Bank	712	4,250		4,250
	18	208	Belmont Products	707	600	12	588
	22	209	Livingstone Wholesale	710	785	15	770
	30	210	Payroll	716	2,200		2,200
	31	211	J. Jay, Petty Cash	717	47		47
					11,832	51	11,781
					(211)	(513)	(111)

Clarification Note: The check register in Exhibit 3 assumes the use of the gross method to handle discounts.

and Allowances, and a notation should be made on the voucher in the voucher file. At the time of payment, only the *net amount* of the voucher—the original amount less the return or allowance and any applicable discount—should be paid and recorded in the check register. Rather than noting the change on the voucher, some companies cancel the original voucher and prepare a new one for the amount to be paid.

4. **Posting the voucher and check registers** Posting the voucher and check registers is very similar to posting the purchases journal and cash payments journal. The only difference is that the Vouchers Payable account is substituted for the Accounts Payable account.
5. **Summarizing unpaid vouchers** Because the sum of the vouchers in the unpaid vouchers file should always equal the credit balance of the Vouchers Payable account, a subsidiary ledger is unnecessary. At the end of each accounting period, the unpaid voucher file should be totaled to prove the balance of the Vouchers Payable account. Exhibit 4 shows a schedule of unpaid vouchers, which is a list of all the unpaid vouchers according to the voucher register in Exhibit 2. The voucher register and the check register (Exhibit 3) are reconciled by simple subtraction.

Vouchers Payable credit from the voucher register	$18,990
Less Vouchers Payable debit from the check register	11,832
Vouchers Payable credit balance from the schedule of unpaid vouchers	$ 7,158

Sometimes the account title Vouchers Payable appears on a company's balance sheet. The preferred practice, however, is to use the more widely known and accepted term Accounts Payable, even when a voucher system is in place.

Exhibit 4. Schedule of Unpaid Vouchers

Thomas Appliance Company
Schedule of Unpaid Vouchers
July 31, 20xx

Payee	Voucher Number	Amount
M&M Freight	705	$ 60
M&M Freight	708	30
Mack Truck	709	5,600
Livingstone Wholesale	713	525
Belmont Products	714	400
M&M Freight	715	18
Maintenance Company	718	175
Store Supply Company	719	350
Total Unpaid Vouchers		$7,158

Point to Emphasize: The schedule total of $7,158 would appear as a liability on the July 31 balance sheet, usually labeled Accounts Payable.

Chapter Review

REVIEW OF LEARNING OBJECTIVES

1. **Define *internal control* and identify the three elements of the internal control structure, including seven examples of control procedures.** Internal controls are the policies and procedures management uses to protect the organization's assets and to ensure the accuracy and reliability of accounting records. They also work to maintain efficient operations and compliance with management's policies. The internal control structure consists of three elements: the control environment, the accounting system, and control procedures. Examples of control procedures are proper authorization of transactions; recording transactions to facilitate preparation of financial statements and to establish accountability for assets; use of well-designed documents and records; limited access to assets; periodic independent comparison of records and assets; separation of duties into the functions of authorization, operations, custody of assets, and recordkeeping; and use of sound personnel policies.
2. **Describe the inherent limitations of internal control.** A system of internal control relies on the people who implement it. Thus, the effectiveness of internal control is limited by the people involved. Human error, collusion, the interference of management, and the failure to recognize changed conditions all can contribute to a system's failure.
3. **Apply internal control procedures to common merchandising transactions.** Certain procedures strengthen internal control over sales, cash receipts, purchases, and cash disbursements. First, the functions of authorization, recordkeeping, and custody should be kept separate. Second, the accounting system should provide for physical protection of assets (especially cash and merchandise inventory), use of banking services, prompt recording and deposit of cash receipts, and payment by check. Third, the people who have access to cash and merchandise inventory should be specifically designated and their number limited. Fourth, employees who have access to cash or merchandise inventory should be bonded. Fifth, the Cash account should be reconciled each month, and unannounced audits of cash on hand should be made by an individual who does not authorize, handle, or record cash transactions.

4. **Demonstrate the control of cash by preparing a bank reconciliation.** The term *bank reconciliation* means accounting for the difference between the balance that appears on the bank statement and the balance in the company's Cash account. It involves adjusting both balances to arrive at the adjusted cash balance. The bank balance is adjusted for outstanding checks and deposits in transit. The depositor's book balance is adjusted for service charges, NSF checks, interest earned, and miscellaneous debits and credits.

Supplemental Objectives

5. **Demonstrate the use of a simple imprest system.** An imprest system is a method of controlling small cash expenditures by setting up a fund at a fixed amount and periodically reimbursing the fund by the amount necessary to restore the original balance. A petty cash fund, one example of an imprest system, is established by a debit to Petty Cash and a credit to Cash. It is replenished by debits to various expense or asset accounts and a credit to Cash. Each expenditure should be supported by a petty cash voucher.
6. **Define *voucher system* and describe the components of a voucher system.** A voucher system is any system that gives documentary proof of and written authorization for business transactions. It consists of authorizations (vouchers), voucher checks, a special journal to record the vouchers (voucher register), and a special journal to record the voucher checks (check register).
7. **Describe and carry out the five steps in operating a voucher system.** The five steps in operating a voucher system are (1) preparing the voucher, (2) recording the voucher, (3) paying the voucher, (4) posting the voucher and check registers, and (5) summarizing unpaid vouchers.

REVIEW OF CONCEPTS AND TERMINOLOGY

The following concepts and terms were introduced in this chapter:

SO 6 **Audit trail:** The documentary evidence of written approval created by key people as they routinely review and verify an expenditure before payment is made.

LO 4 **Bank reconciliation:** A procedure to account for the difference between the cash balance that appears on the bank statement and the balance of the Cash account in the depositor's records.

LO 1 **Bonding:** The process of carefully checking an employee's background and insuring the company against theft by that person.

LO 3 **Check:** A written order to a bank to pay the amount specified from funds on deposit.

LO 3 **Check authorization:** A form prepared by the accounting department after it has compared the receiving report for goods received with the purchase order and the invoice.

SO 6 **Check register:** In a voucher system, the journal in which voucher checks are listed as they are written.

LO 1 **Control environment:** The overall attitude, awareness, and actions of the owners and management of a business, as reflected in philosophy and operating style, organizational structure, methods of assigning authority and responsibility, and personnel policies and practices.

LO 1 **Control procedures:** Procedures and policies established by management to ensure that the objectives of internal control are met.

SO 5 **Imprest system:** A system for controlling small cash disbursements by establishing a fund at a fixed amount and periodically reimbursing the fund by the amount necessary to restore the original cash balance.

LO 1 **Internal control:** All the policies and procedures a company uses to safeguard its assets, check the accuracy and reliability of its accounting data, promote operational efficiency, and encourage adherence to its policies.

LO 1 **Internal control structure:** A structure established to safeguard the assets of a business and provide reliable accounting records; consists of the control environment, the accounting system, and control procedures.

LO 3 **Invoice:** A form sent to the purchaser by the vendor that describes the quantity and price of the goods or services delivered and the terms of payment.

SO 5 **Petty cash fund:** A fund for making small payments of cash when it is inconvenient to pay by check.

SO 5 **Petty cash voucher:** A form signed by a person who receives a cash payment from a petty cash fund; lists the date, amount, and purpose of the expenditure.

LO 3 **Purchase order:** A form prepared by a company's purchasing department and sent to a vendor, it describes the items ordered; their expected price, terms, and shipping date; and other shipping instructions.

LO 3 **Purchase requisition:** A formal written request for a purchase, prepared by the requesting department in an organization and sent to the purchasing department.

LO 3 **Receiving report:** A form prepared by the receiving department of a company; describes the quantity and condition of goods received.

SO 6 **Voucher:** A written authorization prepared for each business expenditure when it becomes a liability or obligation to pay.

SO 6 **Voucher check:** A form of check, used in a voucher system, that describes the reason for issuing the check.

SO 6 **Voucher register:** The book of original entry in which vouchers are recorded after they have been approved.

SO 6 **Voucher system:** Any system that gives documentary proof of and written authorization for business transactions.

REVIEW PROBLEM

Bank Reconciliation

LO 4 The information that follows comes from the records of the Maynard Company. The credit memorandum on April 15 is for the collection of a note, and includes $100 in interest. Checks numbered 1714 for $210 and 1715 for $70 were outstanding on March 31.

From the Cash Receipts Journal — Page 14

Date		Debit Cash
Apr.	1	560
	10	1,440
	17	780
	30	2,900
		5,680

From the Cash Payments Journal — Page 18

Date		Check Number	Credit Cash
Apr.	4	1716	580
	6	1717	800
	17	1718	1,050
	25	1719	110
			2,540

From the General Ledger

Cash — Account No. 111

Date		Item	Post. Ref.	Debit	Credit	Balance Debit	Balance Credit
Mar.	31	Balance				4,200	
Apr.	30		CR14	5,680		9,880	
	30		CP18		2,540	7,340	

From the Company's Bank Statement

Checks and Other Debits			Deposits		Balance	
Date	Check Number	Amount				
					4/1	4,480
4/5	1714	210	4/2	560	4/2	5,040
4/5	1716	580	4/11	1,440	4/5	4,250
4/12	1717	800	4/15	1,500CM	4/11	5,690
4/28		20SC	4/17	780	4/12	4,890
			4/28	10IN	4/15	6,390
					4/17	7,170
					4/28	7,160

CM–Credit Memo SC–Service Charge IN–Interest

REQUIRED

1. Prepare a bank reconciliation as of April 30, 20xx.
2. Prepare the necessary journal entries.

ANSWER TO REVIEW PROBLEM

1. Prepare a bank reconciliation.

Maynard Company
Bank Reconciliation
April 30, 20xx

Balance per bank, April 30, 20xx		$ 7,160
Add deposit of April 30, in transit		2,900
		$10,060
Less outstanding checks:		
No. 1715	$ 70	
No. 1718	1,050	
No. 1719	110	1,230
Adjusted bank balance, April 30, 20xx		$ 8,830
Balance per books, April 30, 20xx		$ 7,340
Add: Note collected by bank, including $100 of interest income	$1,500	
Interest income	10	1,510
		$ 8,850
Less service charge		20
Adjusted book balance, April 30, 20xx		$ 8,830

2. Prepare the journal entries.

Apr. 30	Cash	1,500	
	Notes Receivable		1,400
	Interest Income		100
	Collection of note by bank		
30	Cash	10	
	Interest Income		10
	Interest on bank account		
30	Bank Service Charges Expense	20	
	Cash		20
	Bank service charge for April		

Chapter Assignments

BUILDING YOUR KNOWLEDGE FOUNDATION

Questions

1. Most people think of internal control as a means of making fraud harder to commit and easier to detect. What are some other important purposes of internal control?
2. What are the three elements of the internal control structure?
3. What are some examples of control procedures?
4. Why is the separation of duties necessary to ensure sound internal control? What does this principle assume about the relationships of employees in a company and the possibility of two or more of them stealing from the company?
5. In a small business, it is sometimes impossible to separate duties completely. What are three other practices that a small business can follow to achieve the objectives of internal control over cash?
6. At Thrifty Variety Store, each sales clerk counts the cash in his or her cash drawer at the end of the day and then removes the cash register tape and prepares a daily cash form, noting any discrepancies. The information is checked by an employee in the cashier's office, who counts the cash, compares the total with the form, and then gives the cash to the cashier. What is the weakness in this system of internal control?
7. How does a movie theater control cash receipts?
8. For each of the following business documents, tell what department or person prepares it and what department or person receives it: purchase requisition, purchase order, invoice, receiving report, check authorization, check, deposit ticket, and bank statement.
9. Why is a bank reconciliation prepared?
10. Assume that each of the following items appeared on a bank reconciliation. Which item would be (1) an addition to the balance on the bank statement, (2) a deduction from the balance on the bank statement, (3) an addition to the balance on the books, or (4) a deduction from the balance on the books? Write the correct number next to each item.

    a. Outstanding checks
    b. Deposits in transit
    c. Bank service charge
    d. NSF check returned with statement
    e. Note collected by bank

    Which of the above items requires a journal entry?
11. What is the purpose of a petty cash fund? From the standpoint of internal control, what is the significance of the level at which the fund is established?

12. What account or accounts are debited when a petty cash fund is established? What account or accounts are debited when a petty cash fund is replenished?
13. What does a credit balance in the Cash Short or Over account indicate?
14. At the end of the day, the combined count of cash for all cash registers in a store reveals a cash shortage of $17.20. In what account would this cash shortage be recorded? Would the account be debited or credited?
15. Should a petty cash fund be replenished as of the last day of the accounting period? Explain your answer.
16. Explain how each of the following can contribute to internal control over cash: (a) a bank reconciliation; (b) a petty cash fund; (c) a cash register with printed receipts; (d) printed, prenumbered cash sales receipts; (e) regular vacations for the cashier; (f) two signatures on checks; and (g) prenumbered checks.
17. What is the greatest advantage of a voucher system?
18. Before a voucher for the purchase of merchandise is approved for payment, three documents should be compared to verify the amount of the liability. What are the three documents?
19. A company that presently uses a general journal, a sales journal, a purchases journal, a cash receipts journal, and a cash payments journal decides to adopt the voucher system. Which of the five journals would be changed or replaced? What would replace them?
20. What is the correct order for filing (a) unpaid vouchers and (b) paid vouchers?
21. When the voucher system is used, is there an Accounts Payable controlling account and an accounts payable subsidiary ledger? Be prepared to explain your answer.

Short Exercises

LO 1 *Purposes of Internal Control*

SE 1. Sara Morgan owns a gourmet coffee shop. Identify four ways in which good internal controls can help her operate her business.

LO 1 *Elements of Internal Control*

SE 2. Fell Company is a men's clothing store. Indicate whether each of the following elements of internal control is part of the (a) control environment, (b) accounting system, or (c) control procedures.

1. An organization plan calls for separation of duties in the handling of cash sales.
2. Charles Fell emphasizes to employees the importance of following specific procedures in the handling of cash.
3. All cash transactions are recorded automatically in the company's computer when the sales are rung up on the cash register.

LO 1
LO 3 *Internal Control Procedures*

SE 3. Match each of the following control procedures to the appropriate check-writing policy for a small business listed below.

a. Authorization
b. Recording transactions
c. Documents and records
d. Limited access
e. Periodic independent verification
f. Separation of duties
g. Sound personnel policies

1. The person who writes the checks to pay bills is different from the persons who authorize the payments and who keep the records of the payments.
2. The checks are kept in a locked drawer. The only person who has the key is the person who writes the checks.
3. The person who writes the checks is bonded.
4. Once each month the owner compares and reconciles the amount of money shown in the accounting records with the amount in the bank account.
5. Each check is approved by the owner of the business before it is mailed.
6. A check stub recording pertinent information is completed for each check.
7. Every day, all checks are recorded in the accounting records, using the information on the check stubs.

SE 4. LO 2 *Limitations of Internal Control*

Internal control is subject to several inherent limitations. Indicate whether each of the following situations is an example of (a) human error, (b) collusion, (c) changed conditions, or (d) cost-benefit considerations.

1. Effective separation of duties in a restaurant is impractical because the business is too small.
2. The cashier and the manager of a retail shoe store work together to circumvent the internal controls for the purpose of embezzling funds.
3. The cashier in a pizza shop does not understand the procedures for operating the cash register and thus fails to ring up all sales and to count the cash at the end of the day.
4. At a law firm, computer supplies were mistakenly delivered to the reception area instead of the receiving area because the supplier began using a different means of shipment. As a result, the receipt of the supplies was not recorded.

SE 5. LO 3 *Internal Control Documents for Purchases and Payments*

Indicate the letter of where each of the following documents would be prepared and the letter of where it would be sent.

a. Requesting department
b. Purchasing department
c. Receiving department
d. Accounting department
e. Treasurer
f. Supplier

1. Purchase requisition
2. Receiving report
3. Invoice
4. Check authorization
5. Check

SE 6. LO 4 *Elements of a Bank Reconciliation*

When a bank reconciliation is performed, is each of the following items (a) an addition to the balance per bank, (b) a deduction from the balance per bank, (c) an addition to the balance per books, or (d) a deduction from the balance per books?

1. Service charges (by the bank)
2. Deposits in transit
3. Interest income (shown on bank statement)
4. Outstanding checks

SE 7. LO 4 *Bank Reconciliation*

Prepare a bank reconciliation from the following information.

a. Balance per bank statement as of June 30, $2,586.58
b. Balance per books as of June 30, $1,308.87
c. Deposits in transit, $348.00
d. Outstanding checks, $1,611.11
e. Interest on average balance, $14.60

SE 8. SO 5 *Petty Cash Fund*

A petty cash fund was established at $100. At the end of May, the fund has a cash balance of $36 and petty cash vouchers for postage, $29, and office supplies, $34. Prepare the entry on May 31 to replenish the fund.

SE 9. SO 6 *Components of a Voucher System*

Identify which of the following statements describes the purpose of a (a) voucher, (b) voucher check, (c) voucher register, and (d) check register.

1. Provides a record of the payment of vouchers
2. Serves as a means of payment and notes the reason for the issuance of the payment
3. Provides a written authorization for each expenditure
4. Provides a record of all authorized expenditures

SE 10. SO 7 *Operation of a Voucher System*

Arrange the following actions in the order in which they would take place in the operation of a voucher system.

1. A voucher check is written for each recorded voucher on the due date and is recorded in the check register.
2. A voucher is prepared authorizing each expenditure.

3. A list of unpaid vouchers is prepared to prove the balance of the Vouchers Payable account.
4. Each authorized voucher is recorded in the voucher register.
5. Column totals in the voucher register and the check register and individual items in the Other Accounts column of the voucher register are posted to the appropriate accounts.

Exercises

LO 1 *Use of Accounting Records in Internal Control*

E 1. Careful scrutiny of accounting records and financial statements can lead to the discovery of fraud or embezzlement. Each of the following situations may indicate a possible breakdown in internal control. Indicate the nature of the possible fraud or embezzlement in each situation.

1. Wages expense for a branch office was 30 percent higher in 20x2 than in 20x1, even though the office was authorized to employ only the same four employees and raises were only 5 percent in 20x2.
2. Sales returns and allowances increased from 5 percent to 20 percent of sales in the first two months of 20x2, after record sales in 20x1 resulted in large bonuses being paid to the sales staff.
3. Gross margin decreased from 40 percent of net sales in 20x1 to 30 percent in 20x2, even though there was no change in pricing. Ending inventory was 50 percent less at the end of 20x2 than it was at the beginning of the year. There is no immediate explanation for the decrease in inventory.
4. A review of daily records of cash register receipts shows that one cashier consistently accepts more discount coupons for purchases than do the other cashiers.

LO 1 *Control Procedures*

E 2. Gary Hedly, who operates a small grocery store, has established the following policies with regard to the check-out cashiers.

1. Each cashier has his or her own cash drawer, to which no one else has access.
2. Each cashier may accept checks for purchases under $50 with proper identification. Checks over $50 must be approved by Hedly before they are accepted.
3. Every sale must be rung up on the cash register and a receipt given to the customer. Each sale is recorded on a tape inside the cash register.
4. At the end of each day Hedly counts the cash in the drawer and compares it to the amount on the tape inside the cash register.

Identify by letter which of the following conditions for internal control applies to each of the above policies.

a. Transactions are executed in accordance with management's general or specific authorization.
b. Transactions are recorded as necessary to permit preparation of financial statements and maintain accountability for assets.
c. Access to assets is permitted only as allowed by management.
d. At reasonable intervals, the records of assets are compared with the existing assets.

LO 1 *Internal Control Procedures*

E 3. Hazel's Video Store maintains the following policies with regard to purchases of new videotapes at each of its branch stores.

1. Employees are required to take vacations, and duties of employees are rotated periodically.
2. Once each month a person from the home office visits each branch to examine the receiving records and to compare the inventory of tapes with the accounting records.
3. Purchases of new tapes must be authorized by purchase order in the home office and paid for by the treasurer in the home office. Receiving reports are prepared in each branch and sent to the home office.
4. All new personnel receive one hour of training in how to receive and catalogue new tapes.
5. The company maintains a perpetual inventory system that keeps track of all tapes purchased, sold, and on hand.

Indicate by letter which of the following control procedures apply to each of the above policies (some may have several answers).

a. Authorization
b. Recording transactions
c. Documents and records
d. Limited access
e. Periodic independent verification
f. Separation of duties
g. Sound personnel policies

LO 1 *Internal Control Evaluation*

E 4. Developing a convenient means of providing sales representatives with cash for their incidental expenses, such as entertaining a client at lunch, is a problem many companies face. Under one company's plan, the sales representatives receive advances in cash from the petty cash fund. Each advance is supported by an authorization from the sales manager. The representative returns the receipt for the expenditure and any unused cash, which is replaced in the petty cash fund. The cashier of the petty cash fund is responsible for seeing that the receipt and the cash returned equal the advance. When the petty cash fund is reimbursed, the amount of the representative's expenditure is debited to Direct Sales Expense.

What is the weak point in this system? What fundamental principle of internal control is being ignored? What improvement in the procedure can you suggest?

LO 1 *Internal Control Evaluation*

E 5. An accountant is responsible for the following procedures: (1) receiving all cash; (2) maintaining the general ledger; (3) maintaining the accounts receivable subsidiary ledger that includes the individual records of each customer; (4) maintaining the journals for recording sales, purchases, and cash receipts; and (5) preparing monthly statements to be sent to customers. As a service to customers and employees, the company allows the accountant to cash checks of up to $50 with money from the cash receipts. When deposits are made, the checks are included in place of the cash receipts.

What weakness in internal control exists in this system?

LO 4 *Bank Reconciliation*

E 6. Prepare a bank reconciliation from the following information.

a. Balance per bank statement as of October 31, $8,454.54
b. Balance per books as of October 31, $6,138.04
c. Deposits in transit, $1,134.42
d. Outstanding checks, $3,455.92
e. Bank service charge, $5.00

LO 4 *Bank Reconciliation: Missing Data*

E 7. Compute the correct amounts to replace each letter in the following table.

Balance per bank statement	$ **a**	$26,700	$945	$5,970
Deposits in transit	1,800	**b**	150	375
Outstanding checks	4,500	3,000	**c**	225
Balance per books	10,350	28,200	675	**d**

LO 4 *Collection of a Note by a Bank*

E 8. Edmunds Corporation received a notice with its bank statement that the bank had collected a note for $4,000 plus $20 interest from B. Regalado and credited Edmunds Corporation's account for the total less a collection charge of $30.

Explain the effect that these items have on the bank reconciliation. Prepare a journal entry to record the information on the books of Edmunds Corporation.

SO 5 *Petty Cash Entries*

E 9. The petty cash fund of Lemke Company appeared as follows on July 31, 20xx (the end of the accounting period):

Cash on hand		$122.46
Petty cash vouchers		
Freight in	$45.72	
Postage	42.38	
Flowers for a sick employee	37.00	
Office supplies	52.44	177.54
Total		$300.00

Because there is cash on hand, is there a need to replenish the petty cash fund on July 31? Explain your answer. Prepare, in journal form, an entry to replenish the fund.

E 10. SO 5 *Petty Cash Transactions*

A small company maintains a petty cash fund for minor expenditures. In September and October, the following transactions took place:

a. The fund was established in the amount of $100.00 on September 1 from the proceeds of check no. 2707.
b. On September 30, the petty cash fund had cash of $15.46 and the following receipts on hand: postage, $40.00; supplies, $24.94; delivery service, $12.40; and rubber stamp, $7.20. Check no. 2778 was drawn to replenish the fund.
c. On October 31, the petty cash fund had cash of $22.06 and these receipts on hand: postage, $34.20; supplies, $32.84; and delivery service, $6.40. The petty cash custodian could not account for the shortage. Check no. 2847 was drawn to replenish the fund.

Prepare journal entries necessary to record each transaction.

Problems

P 1. LO 4 *Bank Reconciliation*

The following information is available for Hernandez Company as of November 30, 20xx.

a. Cash on the books as of November 30 amounted to $113,675.28. Cash on the bank statement for the same date was $141,717.08.
b. A deposit of $14,249.84, representing cash receipts of November 30, did not appear on the bank statement.
c. Outstanding checks totaled $7,293.64.
d. A check for $2,420.00 returned with the statement was recorded in the cash payments journal as $2,024.00. The check was for advertising.
e. The bank service charge for November amounted to $26.00.
f. The bank collected $36,400.00 for Hernandez Company on a note. The face value of the note was $36,000.00.
g. An NSF check for $1,140.00 from a customer, Emma Matthews, was returned with the statement.
h. The bank mistakenly deducted a check for $800.00 drawn by Mota Corporation.
i. The bank reported a credit of $960.00 for interest on the average balance.

REQUIRED

1. Prepare a bank reconciliation for Hernandez Company as of November 30, 20xx.
2. Prepare the journal entries necessary from the reconciliation.
3. State the amount of cash that should appear on the balance sheet as of November 30.

P 2. LO 4 *Bank Reconciliation*

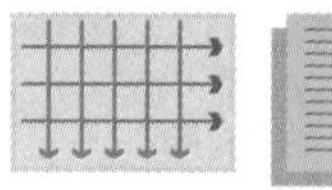
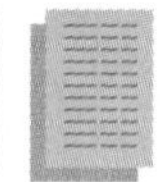

The information presented below and on the top of the next page comes from the records of the Kowalski Company.

From the Cash Receipts Journal		Page 9
Date		**Debit Cash**
Apr.	1	914
	8	1,012
	15	3,240
	22	2,646
	30	1,942
		9,754

From the Cash Payments Journal			Page 12
Date		**Check Number**	**Credit Cash**
Apr.	1	531	14
	3	532	283
	4	533	416
	5	534	27
		535 (voided)	
	6	536	5
	11	537	5,746
	12	538	709
	21	539	1,246
	22	540	76
			8,522

From the General Ledger

Cash — **Account No. 111**

Date		Item	Post. Ref.	Debit	Credit	Balance Debit	Balance Credit
Mar.	31	Balance				2,465	
Apr.	30		CR9	9,754		12,219	
	30		CP12		8,522	3,697	

TURNBULL NATIONAL BANK — **Statement of Kowalski Company, Jarvis and Oak Streets**

Checks/Debits Posting Date	Check No.	Amount	Deposits/Credits Posting Date	Amount	Daily Balances Date	Amount
					4/01	3,785.00
4/03	500	100.00	4/03	914.00	4/03	4,099.00
4/03	505	500.00	4/09	1,012.00	4/05	3,625.00
4/05	530	460.00	4/16	3,240.00	4/07	3,209.00
4/05	531	14.00	4/23	2,646.00	4/09	4,194.00
4/07	533	416.00	4/27	408.00CM	4/13	4,174.00
4/09	534	27.00	4/30	42.00IN	4/15	3,267.00
4/13	536	5.00			4/16	6,507.00
4/13		15.00NSF			4/23	9,153.00
4/15	538	907.00			4/25	3,407.00
4/25	537	5,746.00			4/27	3,739.00
4/27	540	76.00			4/30	3,777.00
4/30		4.00SC				

Code: CM–Credit Memo, DM–Debit Memo, IN–Interest, SC–Service Charge, NSF–Nonsufficient Funds

The NSF check was received from customer P. Kemp for merchandise. The credit memorandum represents a $400 note, plus interest, collected by the bank. Check number 535 was prepared improperly and has been voided. Check number 538 for a purchase of merchandise was recorded incorrectly in the cash payments journal as $709 instead of $907. On April 1, the following checks were outstanding: no. 500 for $100, no. 505 for $500, no. 529 for $260, and no. 530 for $460.

REQUIRED

1. Prepare a bank reconciliation as of April 30, 20xx.
2. Prepare the journal entries necessary to adjust the accounts.
3. What amount should appear on the balance sheet for Cash as of April 30?

P 3. SO 5 *Petty Cash Transactions*

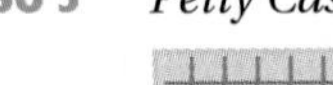
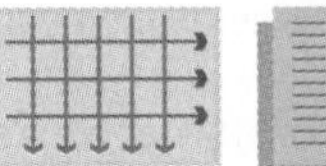

A small company maintains a petty cash fund for minor expenditures. The following transactions occurred in June and July.

a. The fund was established in the amount of $300.00 on June 1 from the proceeds of check no. 1515.
b. On June 30, the petty cash fund had cash of $46.38 and the following receipts on hand: postage, $120.00; supplies, $74.82; delivery service, $37.20; and rubber stamp, $21.60. Check no. 1527 was drawn to replenish the fund.

c. On July 31, the petty cash fund had cash of $66.18 and the following receipts on hand: postage, $102.60; supplies, $98.52; and delivery service, $19.20. The petty cash custodian could not account for the shortage. Check no. 1621 was written to replenish the fund.

REQUIRED

Prepare the journal entries necessary to record each transaction.

LO 1 LO 3 *Internal Control Procedures*

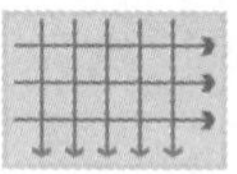

P 4. Eynon Sports Shop is a small neighborhood sporting goods store. The shop's owner, Sara Eynon, has set up a system of internal control over sales to prevent theft and to ensure the accuracy of the accounting records.

When a customer buys a product, the cashier writes up a sales invoice that describes the purchase, including the total price. All sales invoices are prenumbered sequentially.

If the sale is by credit card, the cashier runs the credit card through a scanner that verifies the customer's credit. The scanner prints out a receipt and a slip for the customer to sign. The signed slip is put in the cash register, and the customer is given the receipt and a copy of the sales invoice.

If the sale is by cash or check, the cashier rings it up on the cash register and gives change, if appropriate. Checks must be written for the exact amount of the purchase and must be accompanied by identification. The sale is recorded on a tape inside the cash register that cannot be accessed by the cashier. The cash register may be locked with a key. The cashier is the only person other than Eynon who has a key. The cash register must be locked when the cashier is not present. Refunds are made only with Eynon's approval, are recorded on prenumbered credit memorandum forms, and are rung up on the cash register.

At the end of each day, Eynon counts the cash and checks in the cash register and compares the total with the amount recorded on the tape inside the register. Eynon totals all the signed credit card slips and ensures that the total equals the amount recorded by the scanner. Eynon also makes sure that all sales invoices and credit memoranda are accounted for. Eynon prepares a bank deposit ticket for the cash, checks, and signed credit card slips, less $40 in change to be put in the cash register the next day, and removes the record of the day's credit card sales from the scanner. All the records are placed in an envelope that is sealed and sent to the company's accountant for verification and recording in the company records. On the way home, Eynon places the bank deposit in the night deposit box.

The company hires experienced cashiers who are bonded. The owner spends the first half-day with new cashiers, showing them the procedures and overlooking their work.

REQUIRED

Give an example of how each of the following control procedures is applied to internal control over sales and cash at Eynon Sports Shop: authorization, recording transactions, documents and records, limited access, periodic independent verification, separation of duties, and sound personnel procedures. Do not address controls over inventory.

SO 7 *Voucher System Transactions*

P 5. During the month of July, Treehouse Toy Shop had the following transactions.

July 1 Prepared voucher no. 205, payable to the petty cash cashier, to establish a petty cash fund, $500.
2 Issued check no. 330 for voucher no. 205.
3 Prepared voucher no. 206, payable to Khalit Distributing, for a shipment of merchandise, $1,600, invoice dated July 3, terms 2/10, n/60, FOB shipping point. Khalit prepaid freight of $120 and added it to the invoice, for a total of $1,720.
5 Prepared voucher no. 207, payable to Meehan Realty, for July rent, $2,400.
5 Issued check no. 331 for voucher no. 207.
6 Prepared voucher no. 208, payable to Shriver Distributors, for merchandise, $2,000, invoice dated July 6, terms 2/10, n/60, FOB shipping point.
7 Prepared voucher no. 209, payable to Garland Express, for freight in on July 6 shipment, $128, terms n/10.
8 Prepared voucher no. 210, payable to Crawford Hardware, for office equipment, $800, terms n/30.
10 Received credit memorandum from Shriver Distributors for damaged merchandise returned, $200.

July 11 Prepared voucher no. 211, payable to Shriver Distributors, for merchandise, $2,600, invoice dated July 10, terms 2/10, n/60, FOB shipping point.
12 Prepared voucher no. 212, payable to Garland Express, for freight in on July 11, $188, terms n/10.
13 Issued check no. 332 for voucher no. 206.
14 Prepared voucher no. 213, payable to the company's owner, Hilary Loeb, for her personal expenses, $2,000.
16 Issued check no. 333 for voucher no. 213.
16 Issued check no. 334 for voucher no. 208. There was a return on July 10.
17 Issued check no. 335 for voucher no. 209.
18 Prepared vouchers no. 214, 215, 216, and 217, for $1,200 each, payable to Kovler Furniture, for office furniture having an invoice price of $4,800, terms one-fourth down and one-fourth each month for three months.
19 Issued check no. 336 for voucher no. 214.
19 Issued check no. 337 for voucher no. 211.
20 Issued check no. 338 for voucher no. 212.
21 Prepared voucher no. 218, payable to Majumdar Supply, $540 ($380 to be charged to Store Supplies and $160 to Office Supplies), terms n/10.
22 Prepared voucher no. 219, payable to Belmonte Videocassettes, for merchandise, $660, invoice dated July 20, terms 2/10, n/30, FOB shipping point. Freight paid by shipper and included in invoice total, $60.
23 Prepared voucher no. 220, payable to Southfield National Bank, in payment of an $8,000 note plus $200 interest.
23 Issued check no. 339 for voucher no. 220.
25 Prepared voucher no. 221, payable to Howe Insurance Company, for a one-year policy, $960.
26 Issued check no. 340 for voucher no. 221.
27 Prepared voucher no. 222, payable to Shriver Distributors, for merchandise, $1,200, invoice dated July 26, terms 2/10, n/60, FOB shipping point.
28 Prepared voucher no. 223, payable to Garland Express, for freight in on shipment of July 27, $76.
29 Prepared voucher no. 224, payable to the Payroll Account, for monthly salaries, $15,800 (to be divided as follows: Sales Salaries Expense, $8,800, and Office Salaries Expense, $7,000).
29 Issued check no. 341 for voucher no. 224.
30 Issued check no. 342 for voucher no. 219.
31 Prepared voucher no. 225 to reimburse the petty cash fund. A count of the fund revealed cash on hand of $100 and the following receipts: postage, $88; office supplies, $68; collect telegram, $12; flowers for sick employee, $60; and delivery service, $108. The total of cash on hand and receipts was $64 less than the book balance of petty cash.
31 Issued check no. 343 for voucher no. 225.

REQUIRED

1. Record the transactions in a voucher register (Page 18), a check register (Page 12), and a general journal (Page 10). Record purchases at gross amounts. Total the voucher and check registers.
2. Prepare a Vouchers Payable account (211) and post those portions of the journal and register entries that affect this account. Assume the Vouchers Payable account had a zero balance on June 30.
3. Prove the balance of Vouchers Payable by preparing a schedule of unpaid vouchers.

Alternate Problems

LO 1 *Internal Control*
LO 3 *Procedures*

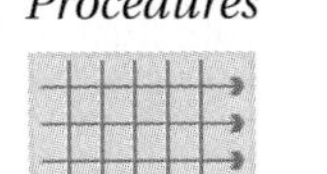

P 6. Langley Printers makes printers for personal computers and maintains a factory outlet showroom through which it sells its products to the public. The company's management has set up a system of internal controls over the inventory of printers to prevent theft and to ensure the accuracy of the accounting records.

All printers in inventory at the factory outlet are kept in a secured warehouse behind the showroom, except for the sample printers on display. Only authorized personnel may enter the warehouse. When a customer buys a printer, a sales invoice is written in triplicate by the cashier and is marked "paid." The sales invoices are sequentially numbered, and all must be accounted for. The cashier sends the pink copy of the completed invoice to the warehouse, gives the blue copy to the customer, and keeps the green copy. The customer drives around to the warehouse entrance. The warehouse attendant takes the blue copy of the invoice from the customer and gives the customer the printer and the pink copy of the invoice.

The company maintains a perpetual inventory system for the printers at the outlet. The warehouse attendant at the outlet signs an inventory transfer sheet for each printer received. An accountant at the factory is assigned responsibility for maintaining the inventory records based on copies of the inventory transfer sheets and the sales invoices. The records are updated daily and may be accessed by computer but not modified by the sales personnel and the warehouse attendant. The accountant also sees that all prenumbered inventory transfer sheets are accounted for and compares copies of them with the ones signed by the warehouse attendant. Once every three months the company's internal auditor takes a physical count of the printer inventory and compares the results with the perpetual inventory records.

All new employees are required to read a sales and inventory manual and receive a two-hour training session about the internal controls. They must demonstrate that they can perform the functions required of them.

REQUIRED

Give an example of how each of the following internal control procedures is applied to the printer inventory at Langley Printers' outlet showroom: authorization, recording transactions, documents and records, limited access, periodic independent verification, separation of duties, and sound personnel procedures. Do not address controls over cash.

P 7. **LO 4** *Bank Reconciliation*

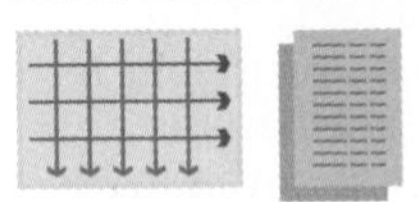

This information is available for Jorge Mendoza Company as of October 31, 20xx.

a. Cash on the books as of October 31 amounted to $21,327.08. Cash on the bank statement for the same date was $26,175.73.
b. A deposit of $2,610.47, representing cash receipts of October 31, did not appear on the bank statement.
c. Outstanding checks totaled $1,968.40.
d. A check for $960.00 returned with the statement was recorded incorrectly in the check register as $690.00. The check was made for a cash purchase of merchandise.
e. Bank service charges for October amounted to $12.50.
f. The bank collected for Jorge Mendoza Company $6,120.00 on a note. The face value of the note was $6,000.00.
g. An NSF check for $91.78 from a client, Beth Franco, came back with the statement.
h. The bank mistakenly charged to the company account a check for $425.00 drawn by another company.
i. The bank reported that it had credited the account for $170.00 in interest on the average balance for October.

REQUIRED

1. Prepare a bank reconciliation for Jorge Mendoza Company as of October 31, 20xx.
2. Prepare the journal entries necessary to adjust the accounts.
3. State the amount of cash that should appear on the balance sheet as of October 31.

P 8. **SO 5** *Petty Cash Transactions*

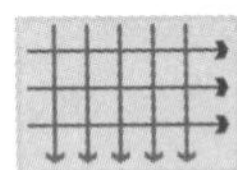

The Broadway Theater Company established a petty cash fund in its snack bar so that payment can be made for small deliveries on receipt. The following transactions occurred in July and August.

July 1 The fund was established in the amount of $400.00 from the proceeds of a check drawn for that purpose.

July 31 The petty cash fund has cash of $31.42 and the following receipts on hand: for merchandise received, $204.30; freight in, $65.74; laundry service, $84.00; and miscellaneous expense, $14.54. A check was drawn to replenish the fund.

Aug. 31 The petty cash fund has cash of $55.00 and the following receipts on hand: merchandise, $196.84; freight in, $76.30; laundry service, $84.00; and miscellaneous expense, $7.86. The petty cash custodian cannot account for the excess cash in the fund. A check is drawn to replenish the fund.

REQUIRED

In journal form, prepare the entries necessary to record each of these transactions.

Skills Development

Conceptual Analysis

SD 1.

LO 1 **LO 2** **LO 3** *System for Control of Supplies*

Industrial Services Company provides maintenance services to factories in the West Bend, Wisconsin, area. The company, which buys large amounts of cleaning supplies, has consistently been over budget in its expenditures for those items. In the past, supplies were left open in the warehouse so that the on-site supervisors could take them as needed. Periodically, a clerk in the accounting department ordered additional supplies from a long-time supplier. The only records maintained were records of purchases. Once a year, an inventory of supplies was made for the preparation of the financial statements.

To solve the budgetary problem, management recently implemented a new system for controlling and purchasing supplies. Under the new system, the cleaning supplies were placed in a secured storeroom overseen by a supplies clerk. Supplies are requisitioned by the supervisors of specific jobs. Each job receives a predetermined amount of supplies based on a study of the needs of that job. In the storeroom, the supplies clerk notes the levels of supplies and completes a purchase requisition when supplies are needed. The purchase requisition goes to the purchasing clerk, a new position, who is solely responsible for authorizing purchases and who prepares the purchase orders for suppliers. The prices of several suppliers are constantly monitored to ensure that the lowest price is obtained. When supplies are received from a vendor, the supplies clerk checks them in and prepares a receiving report, which is sent to accounting, where each payment to a supplier is documented by the purchase requisition, the purchase order, and the receiving report. The accounting department also maintains a record of supplies inventory, supplies requisitioned by supervisors, and supplies received. Once each month, a physical inventory of cleaning supplies in the storeroom is made by the warehouse manager and compared against the supplies inventory records maintained by the accounting department.

Demonstrate how the new system applies or does not apply to each of the seven control procedures described in this chapter. Is each new control procedure an improvement over the old system?

Ethical Dilemma

SD 2.

LO 4 *Inflating the Cash Account and the Bank Reconciliation*

Jean McGuire is the accountant for ***Slate Company.*** Among her responsibilities are the payment of bills and the preparation of the monthly bank reconciliation. On December 31, year end, McGuire's boss, Lydia Grunwald, instructed her to write checks for all the outstanding bills so that their amounts could be deducted for income tax purposes. Since payment of all the outstanding bills would have overdrawn the company's checking account by $78,000, McGuire had to hold the checks until sufficient funds were received. On January 2, when a check for $100,000 was received from a customer in payment of an account receivable, Grunwald, who did not want to report the negative balance of cash on the previous year's balance sheet, instructed McGuire to record the receipt as of December 31 and to show the check as a deposit in transit on the bank reconciliation. The checks written by McGuire on December 31 were mailed on January 3 and listed as outstanding checks on the bank reconciliation. Which of McGuire's and Grunwald's actions, if any, are unethical? Who may be harmed by their actions? What alternative actions could McGuire take?

 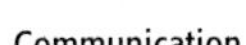
Communication

Critical Thinking

Group Activity

Memo

Ethics

International

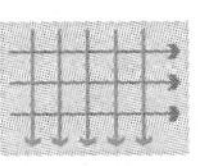
Spreadsheet

General Ledger

CD-ROM

Internet

Research Activity

LO 1
LO 3
Internal Controls

SD 3. Identify a retail business in your local shopping area or a local shopping mall, such as a bookstore, a clothing shop, a gift shop, a grocery, a hardware store, or a car dealership. Speak to someone who is knowledgeable about the store's internal controls. Find out the answers to the following questions and be prepared to discuss your findings in class.

1. How does the company protect against inventory theft and loss?
2. What control procedures, including authorization, recording transactions, documents and records, limited access, periodic independent verification, separation of duties, and sound personnel policies, does the company use?
3. Can you see these control procedures in use?

Group Activity: Assign teams to carry out the above assignment.

Decision-Making Practice

LO 1
LO 2
LO 3
Identifying Internal Control Weaknesses

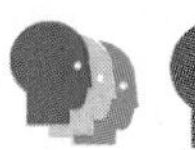

SD 4. ***Fleet's*** is a retail store with several departments. Its internal control procedures for cash sales and purchases are described in the following paragraphs.

Cash sales. Every cash sale is rung up on the department cash register by the sales clerk assigned to that department. The cash register produces a sales slip that is given to the customer with the merchandise. A carbon copy of the sales ticket is made on a continuous tape locked inside the machine. At the end of each day, a "total" key is pressed, and the machine prints the total sales for the day on the continuous tape. Then, the sales clerk unlocks the machine, reads the total sales figure, makes the entry in the accounting records for the day's cash sales, counts the cash in the drawer, places the basic $100 change fund back in the drawer, and gives the cash received to the cashier. The sales clerk then files the cash register tape and is ready for the next day's business.

Purchases. All goods are ordered by the purchasing agent upon the requests of the various department heads. When the goods are received, the receiving clerk prepares a receiving report in triplicate. One copy is sent to the purchasing agent, one copy is forwarded to the department head, and one copy is kept by the receiving clerk. Invoices are forwarded immediately to the accounting department to ensure payment before the discount period elapses. After payment, the invoice is forwarded to the purchasing agent for comparison with the purchase order and the receiving report and is then returned to the accounting office for filing.

For each of the above situations, identify at least one significant internal control weakness. What would you suggest to improve the system?

Financial Reporting and Analysis

Interpreting Financial Reports

LO 1
LO 3
Lapse of Internal Control

FRA 1. ***J. Walter Thompson Co. (JWT),*** is one of the world's largest advertising agencies, with more than $1 billion in billings per year. One of its smaller units is a television syndication unit that acquires rights to distribute television programming and sells those rights to local television stations, receiving in exchange advertising time that it sells to the agency's clients. Cash rarely changes hands between the unit and the television station, but the unit is supposed to recognize revenue when the television programs are exchanged for advertising time that later will be used by clients.

The Wall Street Journal reported on February 17, 1982, that the company "had discovered 'fictitious' accounting entries that inflated revenue at the television program syndication unit."[6] The article went on to say that "the syndication unit booked revenue of $29.3 million over a five-year period, but that $24.5 million of that amount was fictitious" and that "the accounting irregularities didn't involve an outlay of cash . . . and its [JWT's] advertising clients weren't improperly billed. . . . The fictitious sales were recorded in such a manner as to prevent the issuance of billings to advertising clients. The sole effect of these transactions was to overstate the degree to which the unit was achieving its revenue and profit objectives."

The chief financial officer of JWT indicated that "the discrepancies began to surface . . . when the company reorganized so that all accounting functions reported to the chief financial officer's central office. Previously, he said, 'we had been decentralized in accounting,' with the unit keeping its own books."

1. Suggest an entry to recognize revenue from the exchange of the right to televise a show for advertising time and an entry to bill a client for using the advertising time. Explain how the fraud was accomplished.
2. What would motivate the head of the syndication unit to perpetrate this fraud if no cash or other assets were stolen?
3. What principles of internal control were violated? How did correction of the weaknesses in internal control allow the fraud to be discovered?

INTERNATIONAL COMPANY

FRA 2.
LO 1 *Internal Control and Accounting Education in a Developing Country*

Zambia, a country in southern Africa, has 8.5 million inhabitants. It has an elected government and is moving toward capital markets through privatization of government-owned business. For example, the government-owned beer company was recently sold to private interests for $13 million. One national priority calls for the training of competent professional accountants, and the ***Zambian Centre for Accountancy Studies*** has been established with the assistance of the World Bank. There are only about 250 native-born certified accountants in all of Zambia. A state with a comparable population in the United States would have more than 20,000 certified public accountants. One reason for placing a priority on the training of accountants is the importance of good internal controls to the development of a country like Zambia. What are the purposes of internal control, and what are some ways in which such controls would aid the development of a country like Zambia? What are some other reasons for making accounting education a high national priority?

TOYS "R" US ANNUAL REPORT

FRA 3.
LO 1
LO 3 *Internal Control Considerations*

Refer to the annual report for Toys "R" Us in the supplement to Chapter 6. How many stores did Toys "R" Us operate in the United States and abroad in the most recent year? The typical store contains a showroom where customers wheel grocery carts down aisles to select toys and other products for purchase, a warehouse where larger items may be picked up after purchase, a bank of cash registers, and a service desk where returns and other unusual transactions can be authorized. Identify the main activities or transactions for which Toys "R" Us management would need to establish internal controls in each new store. Discuss the objectives of internal controls in each case.

FINGRAPH® FINANCIAL ANALYST™

This activity is not appropriate for this chapter.

ENDNOTES

1. Kyle Pope, "Dell Refocuses on Groundwork to Cope with Rocketing Sales," *The Wall Street Journal,* June 18, 1993.
2. *Professional Standards,* Vol. 1 (New York: American Institute of Certified Public Accountants, June 1, 1989), Sec. AU 319.06–11.
3. Ibid., Sec. AU 320.35.
4. Lynnette Khalfani, "Information-Destruction Finds Lucrative Business in Going to Waste," *The Wall Street Journal,* December 6, 1996.
5. James D. Moss, "Campbell Soup's Cutting Edge Cash Management," *Financial Executive,* September/October 1992.
6. Paul Blustein, "JWT Sees Pretax Write-Off of $18 Million; Fictitious Accounting Entries at Unit Cited," *The Wall Street Journal,* February 17, 1982, p. 16.

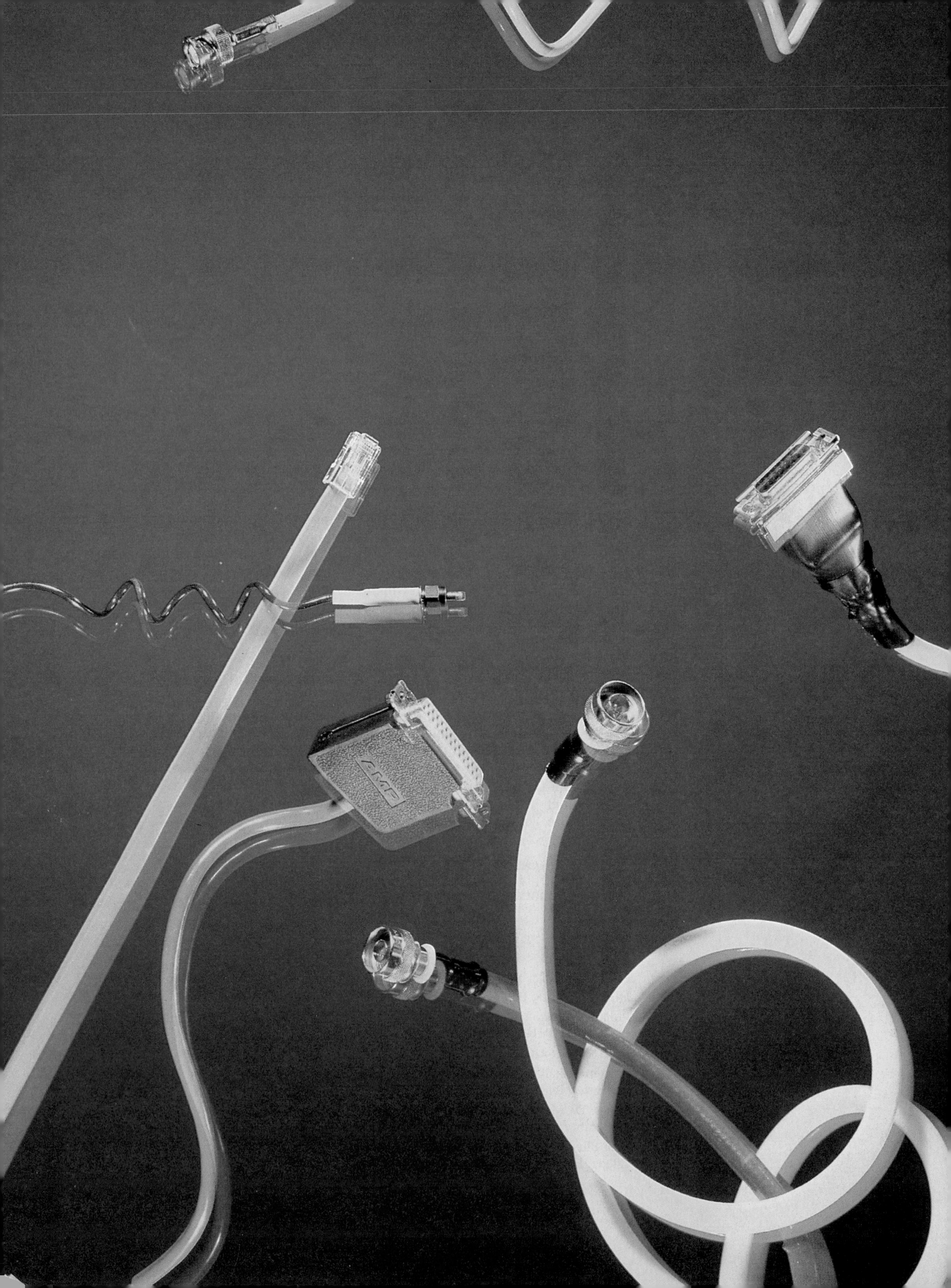
AMP

Short-Term Liquid Assets

LEARNING OBJECTIVES

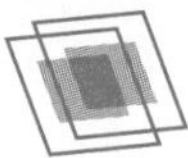

1. **Identify and explain the management issues related to short-term liquid assets.**
2. **Explain *cash, cash equivalents,* and the importance of electronic funds transfer.**
3. **Account for short-term investments.**
4. **Define *accounts receivable* and apply the allowance method of accounting for uncollectible accounts, using both the percentage of net sales method and the accounts receivable aging method.**
5. **Define and describe a *promissory note,* and make calculations and journal entries involving promissory notes.**

DECISION POINT

PIONEER ELECTRONIC CORPORATION

A company must use its assets to maximize income earned while maintaining liquidity. Pioneer Electronic Corporation, a leading provider of electronics for home, commerce, and industry, manages about $1.6 billion in short-term liquid assets. Short-term liquid assets are financial assets that arise from cash transactions, the investment of cash, and the extension of credit. What is the composition of these assets? Why are they important to Pioneer's management?

Pioneer's short-term liquid assets (in millions), as reported on the balance sheet in this Japanese company's 1996 annual report, are shown here.[1] These assets make up almost one-third of Pioneer's total assets, and they are very important to the company's strategy for meeting its goals. Effective asset management techniques ensure that these assets remain liquid and usable for the company's operations.

Financial Highlights

	Yen	Dollars
Cash and Cash Equivalents	¥ 86,513	$ 816.2
Short-Term Investments	3,488	32.9
Accounts Receivable, Net of Allowances of ¥3,504 ($33.0)	74,443	702.3
Notes Receivable, Net	7,511	70.9
Total Short-Term Liquid Assets	¥171,955	$1,622.3

A commonly used ratio for measuring the adequacy of short-term liquid assets is the quick ratio. The quick ratio is the ratio of short-term liquid assets to current liabilities. Since Pioneer's current liabilities are (in

Critical Thinking Question: For what types of businesses would you expect short-term liquid assets to be a large percentage of total assets? **Answer:** Financial institutions, credit card companies, and service businesses. For other examples, see Figure 3.

millions) ¥161,418 ($1,522.8), its quick ratio is 1.07, which is computed as follows:

$$\text{Quick Ratio} = \frac{\text{Short-Term Liquid Assets}}{\text{Current Liabilities}} = \frac{\$1,622,300,000}{\$1,522,800,000} = 1.07$$

A quick ratio of about 1.0 is a common benchmark, but it is more important to look at industry characteristics and at the trends for a particular company to see if the ratio is improving or not. A lower ratio may mean that a company is a very good manager of its short-term liquid assets. Pioneer has maintained a quick ratio of about 1.0 over several years. Through good cash management, the company has not tied up excess funds in quick assets relative to current liabilities. This chapter emphasizes management of, and accounting for, short-term liquid assets to achieve liquidity.

Management Issues Related to Short-Term Liquid Assets

OBJECTIVE 1

Identify and explain the management issues related to short-term liquid assets

Related Text Assignments:
Q: 1, 2
SE: 1, 2
E: 1, 2
P: 2, 6
SD: 1, 2, 3, 5, 6
FRA: 1, 3, 4, 5

The management of short-term liquid assets is critical to the goal of providing adequate liquidity. In dealing with short-term liquid assets, management must address three key issues: managing cash needs during seasonal cycles, setting credit policies, and financing receivables.

Managing Cash Needs During Seasonal Cycles

Most companies experience seasonal cycles of business activity during the year. These cycles involve some periods when sales are weak and other periods when sales are strong. There are also periods when expenditures are greater and periods when expenditures are smaller. In some companies, such as toy companies, college publishers, amusement parks, construction companies, and sports equipment companies, the cycles are dramatic, but all companies experience them to some degree.

Seasonal cycles require careful planning of cash inflows, cash outflows, borrowing, and investing. For example, Figure 1 might represent the seasonal cycles for a home improvement company like The Home Depot. As you can see, cash receipts

BUSINESS BULLETIN: BUSINESS PRACTICE

Big buyers often have significant power over small suppliers, and their cash management decisions can cause severe cash flow problems for the little companies that depend on them. For instance, in an effort to control costs and optimize cash flow, Ameritech Corporation told 70,000 suppliers that it would begin paying its bills in forty-five days instead of thirty days. Other large companies routinely take ninety days or more to pay. Small suppliers are so anxious to get the big companies' business that they fail to realize the implications of the deals they make until it is too late. When Earthly Elements, Inc., accepted a $10,000 order for dried floral gifts from a national home shopping network, management was ecstatic because the deal increased sales by 25 percent. But in four months, the resulting cash crunch forced the company to close down. When the shopping network finally paid for the big order six months later, it was too late to revive Earthly Elements.[2]

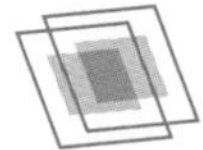

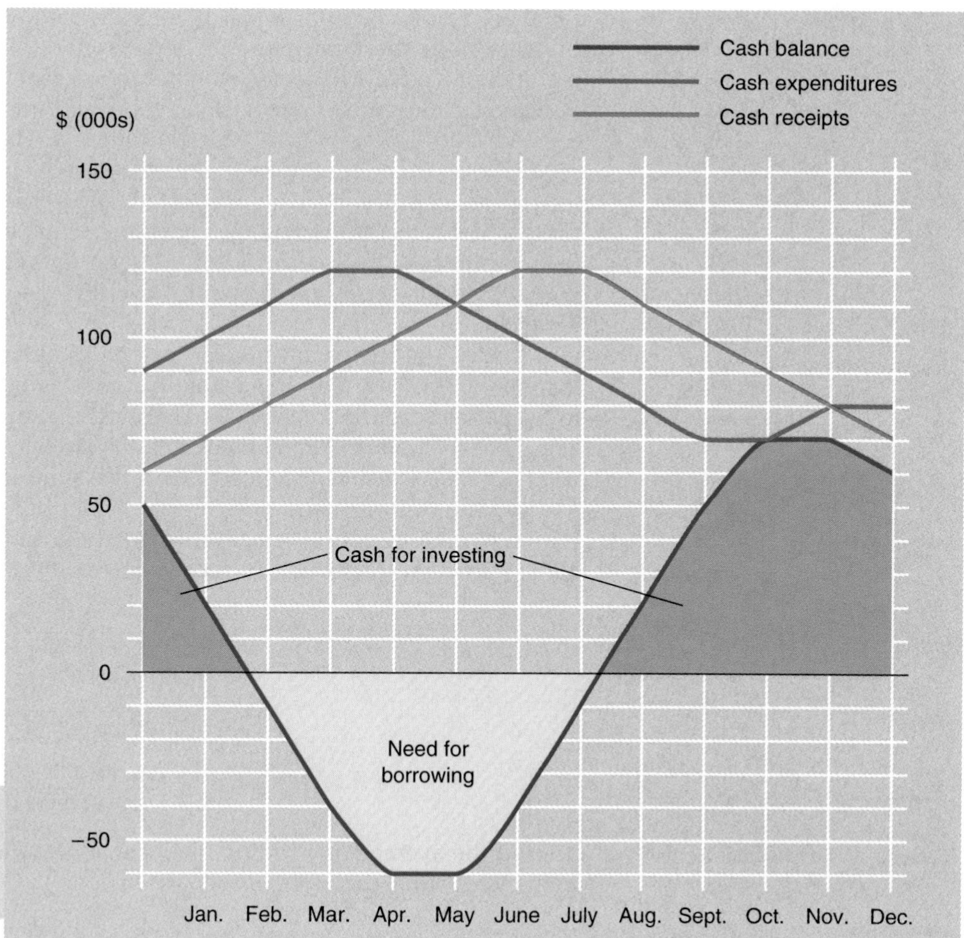

Figure 1
Seasonal Cycles and Cash Requirements for a Home Improvement Company

from sales are highest in the late spring, summer, and fall because that is when most people make home improvements. Sales are relatively low in the winter months. On the other hand, cash expenditures are highest in late winter and spring as the company builds up inventory for spring and summer selling. During the late summer, fall, and winter, the company has excess cash on hand that it needs to invest in a way that will earn a return, and yet permit access as needed. During the late spring and early summer, the company needs to plan for short-term borrowing to tide it over until cash receipts pick up later in the year. The discussion in this chapter of accounting for cash, cash equivalents, and short-term investments is directly related to managing for the seasonal cycles of a business.

Setting Credit Policies

Enrichment Note: Here is a chance to apply the economic concept of profit maximization. Profit is maximized when marginal revenue equals marginal cost. Thus, credit policy should equate the additional gross profit from credit sales with the cost of credit sales (i.e., bad debts).

Companies that sell on credit do so in order to be competitive and to increase sales. In setting credit terms, management must keep in mind both the terms the company's competitors are offering and the needs of its customers. Obviously, companies that sell on credit want customers who will pay the debts they incur. To increase the likelihood of selling only to customers who will pay on time, most companies develop control procedures and maintain a credit department. The credit department's responsibilities include the examination of each person or company that applies for credit and the approval or rejection of a credit sale to that customer. Typically, the credit department will ask for information about the customer's financial resources and debts. It may also check personal references and credit bureaus for further information. Then, based on the information it has gathered, the credit department will decide whether to extend credit to the customer.

Two common measures of the effect of a company's credit policies are receivable turnover and average days' sales uncollected. The receivable turnover reflects the relative size of a company's accounts receivable and the success of its credit and collection policies. It may also be affected by external factors, such as seasonal conditions and interest rates. It shows how many times, on average, the receivables were turned into cash during the accounting period. The average days' sales uncollected is a related measure that shows, on average, how long it takes to collect accounts receivable.

Turnover ratios usually consist of one balance sheet account and one income statement account. The receivable turnover is computed by dividing net sales by average net accounts receivable. Theoretically, the numerator should be net credit sales, but the amount of net credit sales is rarely made available in public reports, so total net sales is used. American Greetings is the second largest producer of greeting cards in the United States. The company's net sales in 1996 were $2,003,038,000, and its net trade accounts receivable in 1995 and 1996 were $324,329,000 and $353,671,000, respectively.[3] Its receivable turnover is computed as follows:

$$\text{Receivable Turnover} = \frac{\text{Net Sales}}{\text{Average Net Accounts Receivable}}$$

$$= \frac{\$2{,}003{,}038{,}000}{(\$324{,}329{,}000 + \$353{,}671{,}000) \div 2}$$

$$= \frac{\$2{,}003{,}038{,}000}{\$339{,}000{,}000} = 5.9 \text{ times}$$

Business-World Example: For many businesses with seasonal sales activity, such as Nordstrom's, Dillards, Marshall Fields, and Macy's, the fourth quarter produces more than 25 percent of annual sales. For such businesses, receivables are highest at the balance sheet date, resulting in an artificially low receivable turnover and high average days' sales uncollected.

Discussion Question: If a company's sales are made on 2/10, n/30 terms, what would you expect the average days' sales uncollected to be? **Answer:** The intent of credit discounts is to encourage early payment, but since not all customers will take advantage of these terms, an age of receivables of 15–25 days might be anticipated.

To find the average days' sales uncollected, the number of days in a year is divided by the receivable turnover, as follows:

$$\text{Average Days' Sales Uncollected} = \frac{365 \text{ days}}{\text{Receivable Turnover}} = \frac{365 \text{ days}}{5.9} = 61.9 \text{ days}$$

American Greetings turns its receivables 5.9 times a year, for an average of every 61.9 days. While this turnover period is longer than those of many companies, it is not unusual for greeting card companies because their credit terms allow retail outlets to receive and sell cards for various holidays, such as Easter, Thanksgiving, and Christmas, before paying for them. This example demonstrates the need to interpret ratios in light of the specific industry's practice. As may be seen from Figure 2, the receivable turnover ratio varies substantially from industry to industry. Grocery stores, for example, have a high turnover because that type of business has few receivables; the turnover in interstate trucking is 11.5 times because the typical credit term in that industry is thirty days. Pharmaceuticals' turnover is lower because that industry tends to have longer credit terms.

Financing Receivables

Financial flexibility is important to most companies. Companies that have significant amounts of assets tied up in accounts receivable may be unwilling or unable to wait until the receivables are collected to receive the cash they represent. Many companies have set up finance companies to help their customers finance the purchase of their products. For example, Ford Motor Co. has Ford Motor Credit Co. (FMCC), General Motors Corp. has General Motors Acceptance Corp. (GMAC), and Sears, Roebuck and Co. has Sears Roebuck Acceptance Corp. (SRAC). Some companies borrow funds by pledging their accounts receivable as collateral. If a company does not pay back its loan, the creditor can take the collateral, in this case the accounts receivable, and convert it to cash to satisfy the loan.

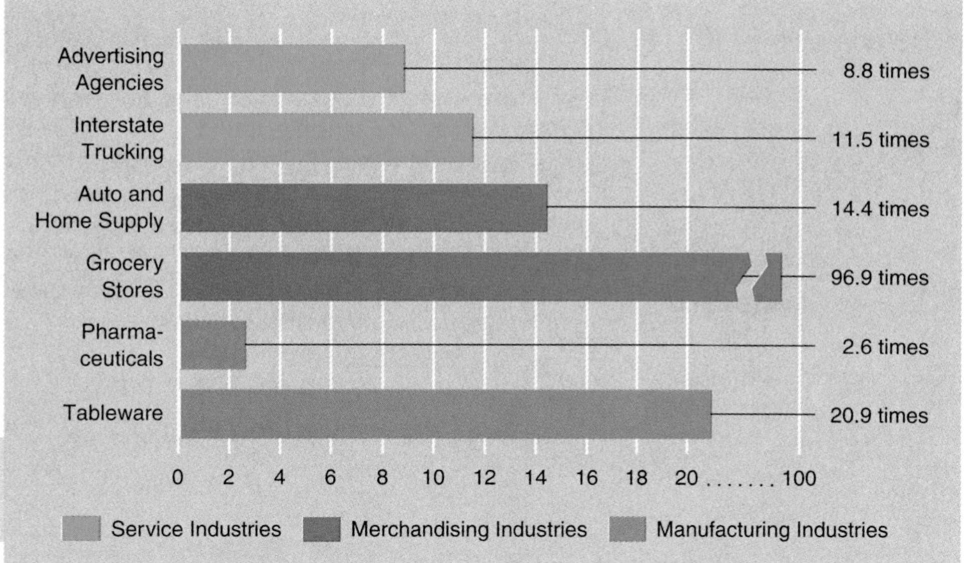

Figure 2
Receivable Turnover for Selected Industries

Source: Data from Dun and Bradstreet, *Industry Norms and Key Business Ratios,* 1996–1997.

Companies can also raise funds by selling or transferring accounts receivable to another entity, called a factor. The sale or transfer of accounts receivable, called factoring, can be done with or without recourse. *Without recourse* means that the factor that buys the accounts receivable bears any losses from uncollectible accounts. A company's acceptance of credit cards like VISA, MasterCard, or American Express is an example of factoring without recourse because the credit card issuers accept the risk of nonpayment.

With recourse means that the seller of the receivables is liable to the purchaser if the receivable is not collected. The factor, of course, charges a fee for its service. The fee for sales with recourse is usually about 1 percent of the accounts receivable. The fee is higher for sales without recourse because the factor's risk is greater. In accounting terminology, the seller of the receivables with recourse is said to be contingently liable. A contingent liability is a potential liability that can develop into a real liability if a possible subsequent event occurs. In this case, the subsequent event would be nonpayment of the receivable by the customer.

Teaching Note: The receivable turnover and average days' sales uncollected will appear better for a company that factors receivables than for a company that does not factor.

Circuit City Stores, Inc., is one of the nation's largest electronics and appliance retailers. To sell its products, the company offers its customers generous terms through its own credit card. The company is growing rapidly and needs the cash from these credit card receivables sooner than the customers have agreed to pay. To generate cash immediately from these receivables, the company sells them. After generating $551.1 million from selling receivables in 1997, the cumulative total amount of receivables sold but not yet collected was $2.59 billion, as follows:[4]

Financial Highlights

(Amounts in thousands)	1997
Securitized receivables	$2,594,651
Interest retained by company	(293,586)
Net receivables sold	$2,301,065
Net receivables sold with recourse	1,317,565
Net receivables sold without recourse	$ 983,500

BUSINESS BULLETIN: BUSINESS PRACTICE

How much cash is too much? Cyclical industries, such as the auto, paper, chemical, and airline industries, are sensitive to the ups and downs of the economy. To prepare for the downs, smart companies build up cash reserves during good times. Such prudence, however, can turn these companies into targets for corporate raiders. For example, in preparing for the next downturn, Chrysler built up a $7.3 billion cash reserve in 1995. Management said such a reserve was necessary if the company was to survive, but investor Kirk Kerkorian bid to take over the company because he said the company should not keep so much cash but should give it back to the shareholders in the form of dividends or by buying its stock back from shareholders. Kerkorian's strategy was to take over the company and use the company's own cash to pay for it.[5] Chrysler successfully fought off this takeover attempt, but the danger is still there.

Securitized receivables are those receivables sold both with and without recourse. The interest retained by the company is in effect a provision or allowance for customers who do not pay. The finance charges paid by customers on the accounts go to the buyers of the receivables to cover interest costs, uncollectible accounts, and servicing fees. The net receivables sold with recourse represents a contingent liability for the company. If the receivables are paid as expected, Circuit City will have no further liability.

Teaching Note: An example will help here. If Company A holds a note from company B of $10,000 that will pay $600 in interest, a bank may be willing to buy it for $9,600. The bank will receive $10,600 at maturity while earning $1,000 in interest.

Another method of financing receivables is through the discounting, or selling, of promissory notes held as notes receivable. Selling notes receivable is called discounting because the bank deducts the interest from the maturity value of the note to determine the proceeds. The holder of the note (usually the payee) endorses the note and delivers it to the bank. The bank expects to collect the maturity value of the note (principal plus interest) on the maturity date but also has recourse against the endorser or seller of the note. If the maker fails to pay, the endorser is liable to the bank for payment. The endorser has a contingent liability in the amount of the discounted notes that must be disclosed in the notes to the financial statements.

Cash and Cash Equivalents

OBJECTIVE 2

Explain **cash, cash equivalents,** *and the importance of electronic funds transfer*

Related Text Assignments:
Q: 3, 4
SE: 3
E: 3
SD: 1
FRA: 4

Enrichment Note: Most reporting practices are set by the FASB. This is an example of an SEC requirement for disclosure of information.

The annual report of Pioneer Electric Corp. refers to *cash and cash equivalents.* Of the two terms, *cash* is the easier to understand. It is the most liquid of all assets and the most readily available to pay debts. On the balance sheet, cash normally consists of coins and currency on hand, checks and money orders from customers, and deposits in bank checking accounts. Cash may also include a compensating balance, an amount that is not entirely free to be spent. A compensating balance is a minimum amount that a bank requires a company to keep in its bank account as part of a credit-granting arrangement. Such an arrangement restricts cash and may reduce a company's liquidity. Therefore, the SEC requires companies to disclose the amount of any compensating balances in a note to the financial statements.

The term *cash equivalents* is a little harder to understand. At times a company may find that it has more cash on hand than it needs to pay current obligations. Excess cash should not remain idle, especially during periods of high interest rates. Thus, management may periodically invest idle funds in time deposits or certificates of deposit at banks and other financial institutions, in government securities

BUSINESS BULLETIN: ETHICS IN PRACTICE

To combat the laundering of money by drug dealers, U.S. law requires banks to report cash transactions in excess of $10,000. Not to be deterred, money launderers began to sidestep the regulation by electronically transferring funds from overseas to banks, money exchanges, and brokerage firms. In response, the Treasury Department set up rules that require those institutions to keep records about the sources and recipients of all electronic transfers. Given the widespread use of electronic transfers in today's business world, it is questionable how much effect this action will have in the ongoing battle against drugs. Looking for drug money by combing the millions of transfers that occur every day is "like looking for a needle in a haystack."[6]

such as U.S. Treasury notes, or in other securities. Such actions are rightfully called investments. However, if the investments have a term of ninety days or less when they are purchased, they are called cash equivalents because the funds revert to cash so quickly that they are regarded as cash on the balance sheet. For example, Bell Atlantic follows this practice. Its policy is stated as follows: "The Company considers all highly liquid investments with a maturity of 90 days or less when purchased to be cash equivalents. Cash equivalents are stated at cost, which approximates market value."[7] A survey of the practices of 600 large U.S. corporations found that 63 of them, or 11 percent, used the term *cash* as the balance sheet caption and 478, or 80 percent, used the phrase *cash and cash equivalents* or *cash and equivalents*. Thirty-five companies, or 6 percent, combined cash with marketable securities.[8] The average amount of cash held can also vary by industry.

Most companies need to keep some currency and coins on hand. Currency and coins are needed for cash registers and for paying expenses that are impractical to pay by check. A company may need to advance cash to sales representatives for travel expenses, to divisions to cover their payrolls, and to individual employees to cash their paychecks.

One way to control a cash fund or cash advances is through the use of an imprest system. A common form of imprest system is a petty cash fund, which is established at a fixed amount. Each cash payment from the fund is documented by a receipt. Then the fund is periodically reimbursed, based on the documented expenditures, by the exact amount necessary to restore its original cash balance. The person responsible for the petty cash fund must always be able to account for its contents by having cash and receipts whose total equals the originally fixed amount.

Banking and Electronic Funds Transfer

Enrichment Note: Periodically, banks detect individuals who are *kiting*. Kiting is the illegal issuing of checks when there is not enough money to cover them. Before one kited check clears the bank, a kited check from another account is deposited to cover it, making an endless circle.

Banks greatly help businesses to control both cash receipts and cash disbursements. Banks serve as safe depositories for cash, negotiable instruments, and other valuable business documents, such as stocks and bonds. The checking accounts that banks provide improve control by minimizing the amount of currency a company needs to keep on hand and by supplying permanent records of all cash payments. Banks can also serve as agents in a variety of transactions, such as the collection and payment of certain kinds of debts and the exchange of foreign currencies.

Many companies commonly conduct transactions through a means of electronic communication called electronic funds transfer (EFT). Instead of writing checks to pay for purchases or to repay loans, the company arranges to have cash transferred electronically from its bank to another company's bank. Wal-Mart, for example, operates the largest electronic funds network in the retail industry and makes

BUSINESS BULLETIN: INTERNATIONAL PRACTICE

Electronic funds transfer has been an important facilitator of international business. Caterpillar Inc., for example, is a company that sells earth-moving equipment throughout the world. To ensure payment and reduce the funds tied up in receivables, Caterpillar uses electronic funds transfer. On prearranged terms, funds are electronically transferred from the customers' accounts to Caterpillar's account at the time orders are shipped. Worldwide, trillions of dollars in business transactions are electronically transferred every day.

75 percent of its payments to suppliers by this method. The actual cash, of course, is not transferred. For the banks, an electronic transfer is simply a bookkeeping entry.

In serving customers, banks may also offer automated teller machines (ATMs) for making deposits, withdrawing cash, transferring funds among accounts, and paying bills. Large consumer banks like Citibank, First Chicago, and Bank of America will process hundreds of thousands of ATM transactions each week. Many banks also give customers the option of paying bills over the telephone and with *debit cards.* When a customer makes a retail purchase using a debit card, the amount of the purchase is deducted directly from the buyer's bank account. The bank usually documents debit card transactions for the retailer, but the retailer must develop new internal controls to ensure that the transactions are recorded properly and that unauthorized transfers are not permitted. It is expected that within a few years 25 percent of all retail activity will be handled electronically.

Short-Term Investments

OBJECTIVE 3

Account for short-term investments

Related Text Assignments:
Q: 5, 6
SE: 4, 5
E: 4, 5
P: 1, 5
SD: 1, 6, 7

When investments have a maturity of more than ninety days but are intended to be held only until cash is needed for current operations, they are called short-term investments or marketable securities. Bell Atlantic states its policy on short-term investments as follows: "Short-term investments consist of investments that mature in 91 days to 12 months from the date of purchase."[9]

Investments that are intended to be held for more than one year are called long-term investments. Long-term investments are reported in an investments section of the balance sheet, not in the current assets section. Although long-term investments may be just as marketable as short-term assets, management intends to hold them for an indefinite period of time.

Securities that may be held as short-term or long-term investments fall into three categories, as specified by the Financial Accounting Standards Board: held-to-maturity securities, trading securities, and available-for-sale securities.[10] Trading securities are classified as short-term investments. Held-to-maturity securities and available-for-sale securities, depending on their length to maturity or management's intent to hold them, may be classified as either short-term or long-term investments. The three categories of securities when held as short-term investments are discussed here.

Held-to-Maturity Securities

Point to Emphasize: Any broker costs or taxes paid to acquire securities are part of the cost of the securities.

Held-to-maturity securities are debt securities that management intends to hold to their maturity date and whose cash value is not needed until that date. Such securities are recorded at cost and valued on the balance sheet at cost adjusted for the effects of interest. For example, suppose that on December 1, 20x1, Lowes Company pays $97,000 for U.S. Treasury bills, which are short-term debt of the federal government. The bills will mature in 120 days at $100,000. The following entry would be made by Lowes:

A = L + OE
+
−

20x1			
Dec. 1	Short-Term Investments	97,000	
	Cash		97,000
	Purchase of U.S. Treasury bills that mature in 120 days		

At Lowes' year end on December 31, the entry to accrue the interest income earned to date would be as follows:

A = L + OE
+ +

20x1			
Dec. 31	Short-Term Investments	750	
	Interest Income		750
	Accrual of interest on U.S. Treasury bills $3,000 × 30/120 = $750		

On December 31, the U.S. Treasury bills would be shown on the balance sheet as a short-term investment at their amortized cost of $97,750 ($97,000 + $750). When Lowes receives the maturity value on March 31, 20x2, the entry is as follows:

A = L + OE
+ +
−

20x2			
Mar. 31	Cash	100,000	
	Short-Term Investments		97,750
	Interest Income		2,250
	Receipt of cash at maturity of U.S. Treasury bills and recognition of related income		

Trading Securities

Discussion Question: What is the difference between investments in debt securities and investments in equity securities? **Answer:** Debt securities are to be redeemed at a specified time and pay a return in the form of interest. Equity securities are an ownership interest in an entity and are subject to market fluctuations. Return takes the form of dividends and increases in the price of the securities.

Trading securities are debt and equity securities bought and held principally for the purpose of being sold in the near term. Such securities are frequently bought and sold to generate profits on short-term changes in their prices. Trading securities are classified as current assets on the balance sheet and valued at fair value, which is usually the same as market value—for example, when securities are traded on a stock exchange or in the over-the-counter market.

An increase or decrease in the total trading portfolio (the group of securities held for trading purposes) is included in net income in the accounting period in which the increase or decrease occurs. For example, assume that Franklin Company purchases 10,000 shares of Mobil Corporation for $700,000 ($70 per share) and 5,000 shares of Texaco Inc. for $300,000 ($60 per share) on October 25, 20x1. The purchase is made for trading purposes; that is, management intends to realize a gain by holding the shares for only a short period. The entry to record the investment at cost follows:

A = L + OE
+
−

20x1			
Oct. 25	Short-Term Investments	1,000,000	
	Cash		1,000,000
	Investment in stocks for trading ($700,000 + $300,000 = $1,000,000)		

Assume that at year end Mobil's stock price has decreased to $60 per share and Texaco's has risen to $64 per share. The trading portfolio may now be valued at $920,000:

Security	Cost	Market Value
Mobil (10,000 shares)	$ 700,000	$600,000
Texaco (5,000 shares)	300,000	320,000
Totals	$1,000,000	$920,000

Since the current fair value of the portfolio is $80,000 less than the original cost of $1,000,000, an adjusting entry is needed, as follows:

A = L + OE
− −

20x1			
Dec. 31	Unrealized Loss on Investments	80,000	
	Allowance to Adjust Short-Term Investments to Market		80,000
	Recognition of unrealized loss on trading portfolio		

The unrealized loss will appear on the income statement as a reduction in income. (The loss is unrealized because the securities have not been sold.) The Allowance to Adjust Short-Term Investments to Market account appears on the balance sheet as a contra-asset, as follows:

Short-Term Investments (at cost)	$1,000,000
Less Allowance to Adjust Short-Term Investments to Market	80,000
Short-Term Investments (at market)	$ 920,000

or more simply,

Point to Emphasize: The Allowance to Adjust Short-Term Investments to Market account is never changed when securities are sold. It changes only with an adjusting entry at year end.

Short-Term Investments (at market value, cost is $1,000,000)	$ 920,000

If Franklin sells its 5,000 shares of Texaco for $70 per share on March 2, 20x2, a realized gain on trading securities is recorded as follows:

A = L + OE
\+ +
−

20x2			
Mar. 2	Cash	350,000	
	Short-Term Investments		300,000
	Realized Gain on Investments		50,000
	Sale of 5,000 shares of Texaco for $70 per share; cost was $60 per share		

The realized gain will appear on the income statement. Note that the realized gain is unaffected by the adjustment for the unrealized loss at the end of 20x1. The two transactions are treated independently. If the stock had been sold for less than cost, a realized loss on investments would have been recorded. Realized losses also appear on the income statement.

Let's assume that during 20x2 Franklin buys 2,000 shares of Exxon Corporation at $64 per share and has no transactions involving Mobil. Also assume that by December 31, 20x2, the price of Mobil's stock has risen to $75 per share, or $5 per share more than the original cost, and that Exxon's stock price has fallen to $58, or $6 less than the original cost. The trading portfolio now can be analyzed as follows:

Security	Cost	Market Value
Mobil (10,000 shares)	$700,000	$750,000
Exxon (2,000 shares)	128,000	116,000
Totals	$828,000	$866,000

Point to Emphasize: The entry to Allowance to Adjust Short-Term Investments to Market is equal to the change in the market value. Compute the new allowance and then compute the amount needed to change the account. The unrealized loss or gain is the other half of the entry.

The market value of the portfolio now exceeds the cost by $38,000 ($866,000 − $828,000). This amount represents the targeted ending balance for the Allowance to Adjust Short-Term Investments to Market account. Recall that at the end of 20x1, that account had a credit balance of $80,000, meaning that the market value of the trading portfolio was less than the cost. The account has no entries during 20x2 and thus retains its balance until adjusting entries are made at the end of the year. The adjustment for 20x2 must be $118,000—enough to result in a debit balance of $38,000 in the allowance account.

A = L + OE
\+ \+

20x2			
Dec. 31	Allowance to Adjust Short-Term Investments to Market	118,000	
	Unrealized Gain on Investments		118,000
	Recognition of unrealized gain on trading portfolio ($80,000 + $38,000 = $118,000)		

The 20x2 ending balance of the allowance account may be determined as follows:

Allowance to Adjust Short-Term Investments to Market

Dec. 31, 20x2 adj.	118,000	Dec. 31, 20x1 bal.	80,000
Dec. 31, 20x2 bal.	**38,000**		

The balance sheet presentation of short-term investment is as follows:

Short-Term Investments (at cost)	$828,000
Allowance to Adjust Short-Term Investments to Market	38,000
Short-Term Investments (at market)	$866,000

Instructional Strategy: To check students' comprehension of accounting for trading securities, assign SE 5. Students can work in self-selected teams of two or three. Groups that answer correctly may be rewarded with a bonus of two quiz points. State ground rules, such as whether notes or text may be used, before the activity begins.

or, more simply,

Short-Term Investments (at market value, cost is $828,000)	$866,000

If the company also holds held-to-maturity securities, they are included in short-term investments at cost adjusted for the effects of interest.

Available-for-Sale Securities

Available-for-sale securities are debt and equity securities that do not meet the criteria for either held-to-maturity or trading securities. They are accounted for in exactly the same way as trading securities, except that the unrealized gain or loss is not reported on the income statement, but is reported as a special item in the stockholders' equity section of the balance sheet.

Instructional Strategy: To underscore all the costs underlying credit sales and the matching principle, assign SD 2 to small groups in class. Debrief by listing responses on the chalkboard. Ask for student volunteers to summarize the key points. The case is a good lead-in to a discussion of how companies estimate uncollectible credit sales.

Dividend and Interest Income

Dividend and interest income for all three categories of investments is shown in the Other Income and Expenses section of the income statement.

Accounts Receivable

OBJECTIVE 4

Define **accounts receivable** ***and apply the allowance method of accounting for uncollectible accounts, using both the percentage of net sales method and the accounts receivable aging method***

Related Text Assignments:
Q: 7, 8, 9, 10, 11, 12, 13, 14, 15, 16, 17
SE: 6, 7, 8
E: 6, 7, 8, 9, 10, 11
P: 2, 3, 6, 7
SD: 2, 4, 5
FRA: 1, 2, 4

The other major types of short-term liquid assets are accounts receivable and notes receivable. Both result from credit sales to customers. Retail companies such as Sears, Roebuck and Co. have made credit available to nearly every responsible person in the United States. Every field of retail trade has expanded by allowing customers to make payments a month or more after the date of sale. What is not so apparent is that credit has expanded even more in the wholesale and manufacturing industries than at the retail level. The levels of accounts receivable in several industries are shown in Figure 3.

Accounts receivable are short-term liquid assets that arise from sales on credit to customers by wholesalers or retailers. This type of credit is often called **trade credit**. Terms on trade credit usually range from five to sixty days, depending on industry practice. For some companies that sell to consumers, **installment accounts receivable** constitute a significant portion of accounts receivable. Installment accounts receivable arise from the sale of goods on terms that allow the buyer to make a series of time payments. Department stores, appliance stores, furniture stores, used car companies, and other retail businesses often offer installment credit. Retailers such as J.C. Penney Company, Inc., and Sears, Roebuck and Co. have millions of dollars in installment accounts receivable. Although the payment period may be twenty-four months or more, installment accounts receivable are classified as current assets if such credit policies are customary in the industry.

On the balance sheet, the title Accounts Receivable is used for amounts arising from sales made to customers in the ordinary course of business. If loans or sales that do not fall into this category are made to employees, officers of the corporation, or owners, they should be shown separately with an asset title such as Receivables from Employees.

Normally, individual customer accounts receivable have debit balances, but sometimes customers overpay their accounts by mistake or in anticipation of future purchases. When individual customer accounts show credit balances, the total of the credits should be shown on the balance sheet as a current liability because the amounts must be refunded if future sales are not made to those customers.

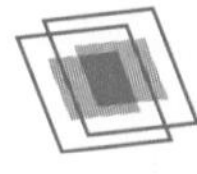

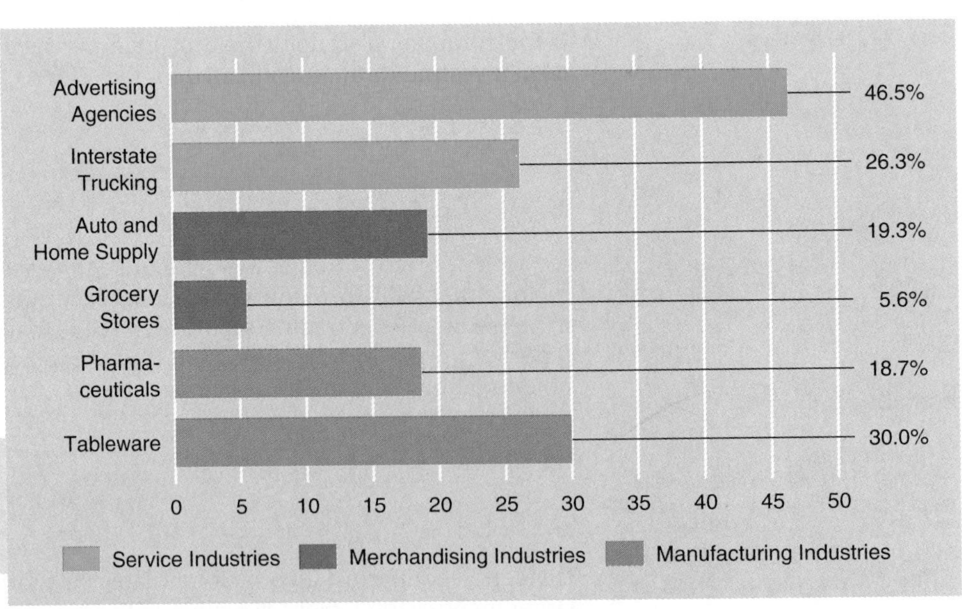

Figure 3
Accounts Receivable as a Percentage of Total Assets for Selected Industries

Source: Data from Dun and Bradstreet, *Industry Norms and Key Business Ratios*, 1996–1997.

Uncollectible Accounts and the Direct Charge-off Method

A company will always have some customers who cannot or will not pay their debts. The accounts owed by such customers are called uncollectible accounts, or *bad debts,* and are a loss or an expense of selling on credit. Why does a company sell on credit if it expects that some of its accounts will not be paid? The answer is that the company expects to sell much more than it would if it did not sell on credit, thereby increasing its earnings.

Some companies recognize the loss from an uncollectible account receivable at the time it is determined to be uncollectible by reducing Accounts Receivable directly and increasing Uncollectible Accounts Expense. Many small companies use this method because it is required in computing taxable income under federal tax regulations. However, companies that follow generally accepted accounting principles do not use the direct charge-off method in their financial statements because it makes no attempt to match revenues and expenses. They prefer the allowance method, which is explained in the next section.

Uncollectible Accounts and the Allowance Method

Under the allowance method of accounting for uncollectible accounts, bad debt losses are matched against the sales they help to produce. As mentioned earlier, when management extends credit to increase sales, it knows that it will incur some losses from uncollectible accounts. Those losses are expenses that occur at the time sales on credit are made and should be matched to the revenues they help to generate. Of course, at the time the sales are made, management cannot identify which customers will not pay their debts, nor can it predict the exact amount of money that will be lost. Therefore, to observe the matching rule, losses from uncollectible accounts must be estimated, and the estimate becomes an expense in the fiscal year in which the sales are made.

Common Student Error: Students frequently record uncollectible accounts expense in the year of the loss rather than in the year of the sale. Emphasize the need to follow the matching rule.

For example, let us assume that Cottage Sales Company made most of its sales on credit during its first year of operation, 20x2. At the end of the year, accounts receivable amounted to $100,000. On December 31, 20x2, management reviewed the collectible status of the accounts receivable. Approximately $6,000 of the $100,000 of accounts receivable were estimated to be uncollectible. Therefore, the uncollectible accounts expense for the first year of operation was estimated to be $6,000. The following adjusting entry would be made on December 31 of that year:

A = L + OE
−   −

20x2			
Dec. 31	Uncollectible Accounts Expense	6,000	
	Allowance for Uncollectible Accounts		6,000
	To record the estimated uncollectible accounts expense for the year		

Teaching Note: Students might understand the nature of the allowance account better if you use a T account for all transactions illustrated.

Uncollectible Accounts Expense appears on the income statement as an operating expense. Allowance for Uncollectible Accounts appears on the balance sheet as a contra account that is deducted from Accounts Receivable.[11] It reduces the accounts receivable to the amount expected to be realized, or collected in cash, as follows:

Current Assets		
Cash		$ 10,000
Short-Term Investments		15,000
Accounts Receivable	$100,000	
Less Allowance for Uncollectible Accounts	6,000	94,000
Inventory		56,000
Total Current Assets		$175,000

Accounts receivable may also be shown on the balance sheet as follows:

Accounts Receivable (net of allowance for uncollectible accounts of $6,000)	$94,000

Or they may be shown at "net," with the amount of the allowance for uncollectible accounts identified in a note to the financial statements. The estimated uncollectible amount cannot be identified with any particular customer; therefore, it is credited to a separate contra-asset account—Allowance for Uncollectible Accounts.

The allowance account will often have other titles, such as *Allowance for Doubtful Accounts* or *Allowance for Bad Debts.* Once in a while, the older phrase *Reserve for Bad Debts* will be seen, but in modern practice it should not be used. *Bad Debts Expense* is another title often used for Uncollectible Accounts Expense.

Estimating Uncollectible Accounts Expense

Ethical Consideration: Estimating bad debts is subjective and often an area of conflict. The IMA offers an ethics video that includes a vignette about the conflict between management and accountants over bad debt estimation.

Point to Emphasize: The accountant looks at the local economic conditions as well as national conditions in setting the estimated uncollectible accounts expense.

Discussion Question: What is the balance in Uncollectible Accounts Expense on the unadjusted trial balance? **Answer:** Zero. Uncollectible Accounts Expense is debited in the adjusting process (after the trial balance has been prepared).

As noted, it is necessary to estimate the expense to cover the expected losses for the year. Of course, estimates can vary widely. If management takes an optimistic view and projects a small loss from uncollectible accounts, the resulting net accounts receivable will be larger than if management takes a pessimistic view. The net income will also be larger under the optimistic view because the estimated expense will be smaller. The company's accountant makes an estimate based on past experience and current economic conditions. For example, losses from uncollectible accounts are normally expected to be greater in a recession than during a period of economic growth. The final decision, made by management, on the amount of the expense will depend on objective information, such as the accountant's analyses, and on certain qualitative factors, such as how investors, bankers, creditors, and others may view the performance of the company. Regardless of the qualitative considerations, the estimated losses from uncollectible accounts should be realistic.

The accountant may choose from two common methods for estimating uncollectible accounts expense for an accounting period: the percentage of net sales method and the accounts receivable aging method.

Point to Emphasize: The percentage of net sales method can be described as the income statement method to emphasize that the percentage of the net sales calculated is the amount expensed. That is, any previous balance in the allowance account is irrelevant in preparing the adjustment.

Percentage of Net Sales Method The percentage of net sales method asks, How much of this year's net sales will not be collected? The answer determines the amount of uncollectible accounts expense for the year. For example, the following balances represent the ending figures for Hassel Company for the year 20x9:

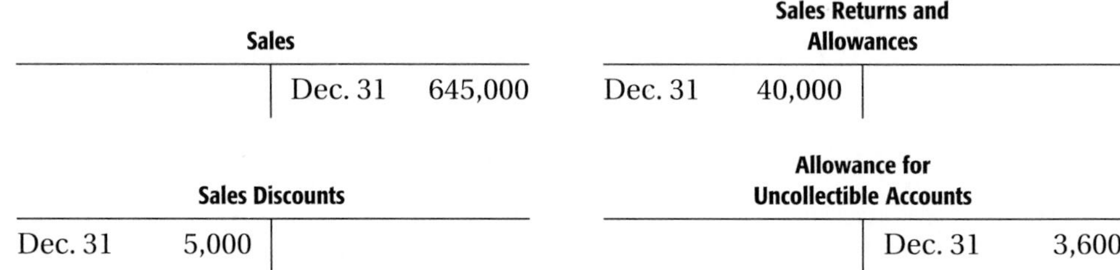

Sales

		Dec. 31	645,000

Sales Returns and Allowances

Dec. 31	40,000		

Sales Discounts

Dec. 31	5,000		

Allowance for Uncollectible Accounts

		Dec. 31	3,600

Below are the actual losses from uncollectible accounts for the past three years:

Year	Net Sales	Losses from Uncollectible Accounts	Percentage
20x6	$ 520,000	$10,200	1.96
20x7	595,000	13,900	2.34
20x8	585,000	9,900	1.69
Total	$1,700,000	$34,000	2.00

BUSINESS BULLETIN: INTERNATIONAL PRACTICE

Companies in emerging economies do not always follow the accounting practices accepted in the United States. The Shanghai Stock Exchange is one of the fastest-growing stock markets in the world. Few Chinese companies acknowledge that uncollected receivables are not worth full value even though many receivables have been outstanding for a year or more. It is common practice in the United States to write off receivables more than six months old. Now that Chinese companies like Shanghai Steel Tube and Shanghai Industrial Sewing Machine are making their shares of stock available to outsiders, they must estimate uncollectible accounts in accordance with international accounting standards. Recognition of this expense could easily wipe out annual earnings.[12]

In many businesses, net sales is understood to approximate net credit sales. If there are substantial cash sales, then net credit sales should be used. Management believes that uncollectible accounts will continue to average about 2 percent of net sales. The uncollectible accounts expense for the year 20x9 is therefore estimated to be

$$.02 \times (\$645{,}000 - \$40{,}000 - \$5{,}000) = .02 \times \$600{,}000 = \$12{,}000$$

The entry to record this estimate is

A = L + OE
−   −

20x9			
Dec. 31	Uncollectible Accounts Expense	12,000	
	Allowance for Uncollectible Accounts		12,000
	To record uncollectible accounts expense at 2 percent of $600,000 net sales		

After the above entry is posted, Allowance for Uncollectible Accounts will have a balance of $15,600.

Allowance for Uncollectible Accounts

	Dec. 31	3,600
	Dec. 31 adjustment	12,000
	Dec. 31 balance	**15,600**

Parenthetical Note: The percentage of net sales method, unlike the accounts receivable aging method, matches revenues with expenses.

The balance consists of the $12,000 estimated uncollectible accounts receivable from 20x9 sales and the $3,600 estimated uncollectible accounts receivable from previous years.

Enrichment Note: The aging method is often superior to the percentage of net sales method during changing economic times. For example, during a recession, more bad debts occur. The aging method automatically reflects the economic change as accounts receivable age because customers are unable to pay. A company using the percentage of net sales method must anticipate the change and modify the percentage it uses.

Accounts Receivable Aging Method The accounts receivable aging method asks the question, How much of the year-end balance of accounts receivable will not be collected? Under this method, the year-end balance of Allowance for Uncollectible Accounts is determined directly by an analysis of accounts receivable. The difference between the amount determined to be uncollectible and the actual balance of Allowance for Uncollectible Accounts is the expense for the year. In theory, this method should produce the same result as the percentage of net sales method, but in practice it rarely does.

The aging of accounts receivable is the process of listing each customer's receivable account according to the due date of the account. If the customer's account is past due, there is a possibility that the account will not be paid. And the further past

Exhibit 1. Analysis of Accounts Receivable by Age

Myer Company
Analysis of Accounts Receivable by Age
December 31, 20xx

Customer	Total	Not Yet Due	1–30 Days Past Due	31–60 Days Past Due	61–90 Days Past Due	Over 90 Days Past Due
A. Arnold	$ 150		$ 150			
M. Benoit	400			$ 400		
J. Connolly	1,000	$ 900	100			
R. Deering	250				$ 250	
Others	42,600	21,000	14,000	3,800	2,200	$1,600
Totals	$44,400	$21,900	$14,250	$4,200	$2,450	$1,600
Estimated percentage uncollectible		1.0	2.0	10.0	30.0	50.0
Allowance for Uncollectible Accounts	$ 2,459	$ 219	$ 285	$ 420	$ 735	$ 800

due an account is, the greater that possibility. The aging of accounts receivable helps management evaluate its credit and collection policies and alerts it to possible problems. The aging of accounts receivable for Myer Company is shown in Exhibit 1. Each account receivable is classified as being not yet due or as 1–30 days, 31–60 days, 61–90 days, or over 90 days past due. The estimated percentage uncollectible in each category is multiplied by the amount in each category to determine the estimated, or target, balance of Allowance for Uncollectible Accounts. In total, it is estimated that $2,459 of the $44,400 accounts receivable will not be collected.

Discussion Question: What is the balance before adjustment in Allowance for Uncollectible Accounts in the trial balance: debit, credit, or zero? **Answer:** There is no way to determine this, except in the first year of operations. The balance depends, in part, upon how quickly the entity writes off uncollectible accounts.

Once the target balance for Allowance for Uncollectible Accounts has been found, it is necessary to determine how much the adjustment is. The amount of the adjustment depends on the current balance of the allowance account. Let us assume two cases for the December 31 balance of Myer Company's Allowance for Uncollectible Accounts: (1) a credit balance of $800 and (2) a debit balance of $800.

In the first case, an adjustment of $1,659 is needed to bring the balance of the allowance account to $2,459, calculated as follows:

Discussion Question: What would cause a debit balance in the Allowance for Uncollectible Accounts account? **Answer:** The write-offs in an accounting period exceed the amount of the allowance.

Targeted Balance for Allowance for Uncollectible Accounts	$2,459
Less Current Credit Balance of Allowance for Uncollectible Accounts	800
Uncollectible Accounts Expense	$1,659

The uncollectible accounts expense is recorded as follows:

A = L + OE
− −

20xx			
Dec. 31	Uncollectible Accounts Expense	1,659	
	Allowance for Uncollectible Accounts		1,659
	To bring the allowance for uncollectible accounts to the level of estimated losses		

The resulting balance of Allowance for Uncollectible Accounts is $2,459, as follows:

Allowance for Uncollectible Accounts

		Dec. 31	800
		Dec. 31 adjustment	1,659
		Dec. 31 balance	**2,459**

In the second case, since Allowance for Uncollectible Accounts has a debit balance of $800, the estimated uncollectible accounts expense for the year will have to be $3,259 to reach the targeted balance of $2,459. This calculation is as follows:

Targeted Balance for Allowance for Uncollectible Accounts	$2,459
Plus Current Debit Balance of Allowance for Uncollectible Accounts	800
Uncollectible Accounts Expense	$3,259

The uncollectible accounts expense is recorded as follows:

20xx			
Dec. 31	Uncollectible Accounts Expense	3,259	
	Allowance for Uncollectible Accounts		3,259
	To bring the allowance for uncollectible accounts to the level of estimated losses		

A = L + OE
− −

Point to Emphasize: Describing the aging method as the balance sheet method emphasizes that the computation is based on ending accounts receivable, rather than on net sales for the period.

After this entry, Allowance for Uncollectible Accounts has a credit balance of $2,459, as shown below:

Allowance for Uncollectible Accounts

Dec. 31	800	Dec. 31 adjustment	3,259
		Dec. 31 balance	**2,459**

Comparison of the Two Methods Both the percentage of net sales method and the accounts receivable aging method estimate the uncollectible accounts expense in accordance with the matching rule, but as shown in Figure 4, they do so in different ways. The percentage of net sales method is an income statement approach. It assumes that a certain proportion of sales will not be collected, and this proportion is the *amount of Uncollectible Accounts Expense* for the accounting period. The accounts receivable aging method is a balance sheet approach. It assumes that a certain proportion of accounts receivable outstanding will not be collected. This proportion is the *targeted balance of the Allowance for Uncollectible Accounts account.* The expense for the accounting period is the difference between the targeted balance and the current balance of the allowance account.

Why Accounts Written Off Will Differ from Estimates Regardless of the method used to estimate uncollectible accounts, the total of accounts receivable written off in any given year will rarely equal the estimated uncollectible amount. The allowance account will show a credit balance when the total of accounts written off is less than the estimated uncollectible amount. The allowance account will show a debit balance when the total of accounts written off is greater than the estimated uncollectible amount.

Teaching Note: Bankruptcy as the point for writing off an account makes great sense to students. However, ask them what other events would justify writing off an account.

Writing Off an Uncollectible Account

When it becomes clear that a specific account receivable will not be collected, the amount should be written off to Allowance for Uncollectible Accounts. Remember that the uncollectible amount was already accounted for as an expense when the

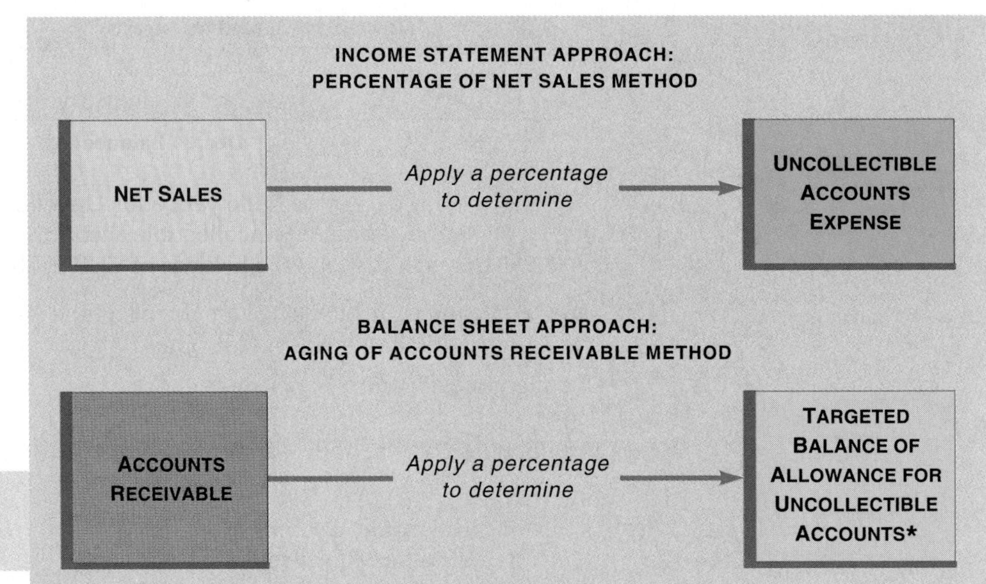

Figure 4
Two Methods of Estimating Uncollectible Accounts

*Add current debit balance or subtract current credit balance to determine uncollectible accounts expense.

allowance was established. For example, assume that on January 15, R. Deering, who owes Myer Company $250, is declared bankrupt by a federal court. The entry to *write off* this account is as follows:

A = L + OE
+
−

Jan. 15	Allowance for Uncollectible Accounts	250	
	Accounts Receivable		250
	To write off receivable from R. Deering as uncollectible; Deering declared bankrupt on January 15		

Common Student Error: When writing off an individual account, students frequently debit Uncollectible Accounts Expense rather than Allowance for Uncollectible Accounts.

Although the write-off removes the uncollectible amount from Accounts Receivable, it does not affect the estimated net realizable value of accounts receivable. The write-off simply reduces R. Deering's account to zero and reduces Allowance for Uncollectible Accounts by a similar amount, as the following table shows:

	Balances Before Write-off	Balances After Write-off
Accounts Receivable	$44,400	$44,150
Less Allowance for Uncollectible Accounts	2,459	2,209
Estimated Net Realizable Value of Accounts Receivable	$41,941	$41,941

Recovery of Accounts Receivable Written Off Occasionally, a customer whose account has been written off as uncollectible will later be able to pay some or all of the amount owed. When this happens, two journal entries must be made: one to reverse the earlier write-off (which is now incorrect), and another to show the collection of the account. For example, assume that on September 1, R. Deering, after his bankruptcy on January 15, notified the company that he would be able to pay

BUSINESS BULLETIN: TECHNOLOGY IN PRACTICE

Accountants generally believe that the accounts receivable aging method is the best way to estimate uncollectible accounts because it takes into consideration current circumstances, such as payment rates and economic conditions. However, since it is time-consuming to do an aging of accounts manually, the percentage of net sales method was commonly used in the past for preparing interim financial statements, such as monthly and quarterly reports. Now that most companies' accounts receivable are computerized, the aging of accounts receivable can be done much more quickly and easily. Indeed, many companies track the collection and aging of accounts receivable on a weekly or even a daily basis. As a result, the percentage of net sales method is used less often.

$100 of his account and sent a check for $50. The entries to record this transaction follow.

A = L + OE				
+ −	Sept. 1	Accounts Receivable	100	
		Allowance for Uncollectible Accounts		100
		To reinstate the portion of the account of R. Deering now considered collectible; originally written off January 15		

A = L + OE				
+ −	1	Cash	50	
		Accounts Receivable		50
		Collection from R. Deering		

Discussion Question: What would have been the entry to record the collection if there had been no write-off? **Answer:** Only the second entry on September 1 would have been journalized.

The collectible portion of R. Deering's account must be restored to his account and credited to Allowance for Uncollectible Accounts for two reasons. First, it turned out to be wrong to write off the full $250 on January 15 because only $150 was actually uncollectible. Second, the accounts receivable subsidiary account for R. Deering should reflect his ability to pay a portion of the money he owed despite his declaration of bankruptcy. Documentation of this action will give a clear picture of R. Deering's credit record for future credit action.

Notes Receivable

OBJECTIVE 5

Define and describe a promissory note, *and make* calculations and journal *entries involving promissory notes*

Related Text Assignments:
Q: 18, 19
SE: 9
E: 12, 13, 14, 15
P: 4, 8

A promissory note is an unconditional promise to pay a definite sum of money on demand or at a future date. The entity who signs the note and thereby promises to pay is called the *maker* of the note. The entity to whom payment is to be made is called the *payee*. The promissory note in Figure 5 is dated May 20, 20x1, and is an unconditional promise by the maker, Samuel Mason, to pay a definite sum, or principal ($1,000), to the payee, Cook County Bank & Trust Company, at the future date of August 18, 20x1. The promissory note bears an interest rate of 8 percent. The payee regards all promissory notes it holds that are due in less than one year as notes receivable in the current assets section of the balance sheet. The maker regards them as notes payable in the current liabilities section of the balance sheet.

This portion of the chapter is concerned primarily with notes received from customers. The nature of a business generally determines how frequently promissory notes are received from customers. Firms selling durable goods of high value, such

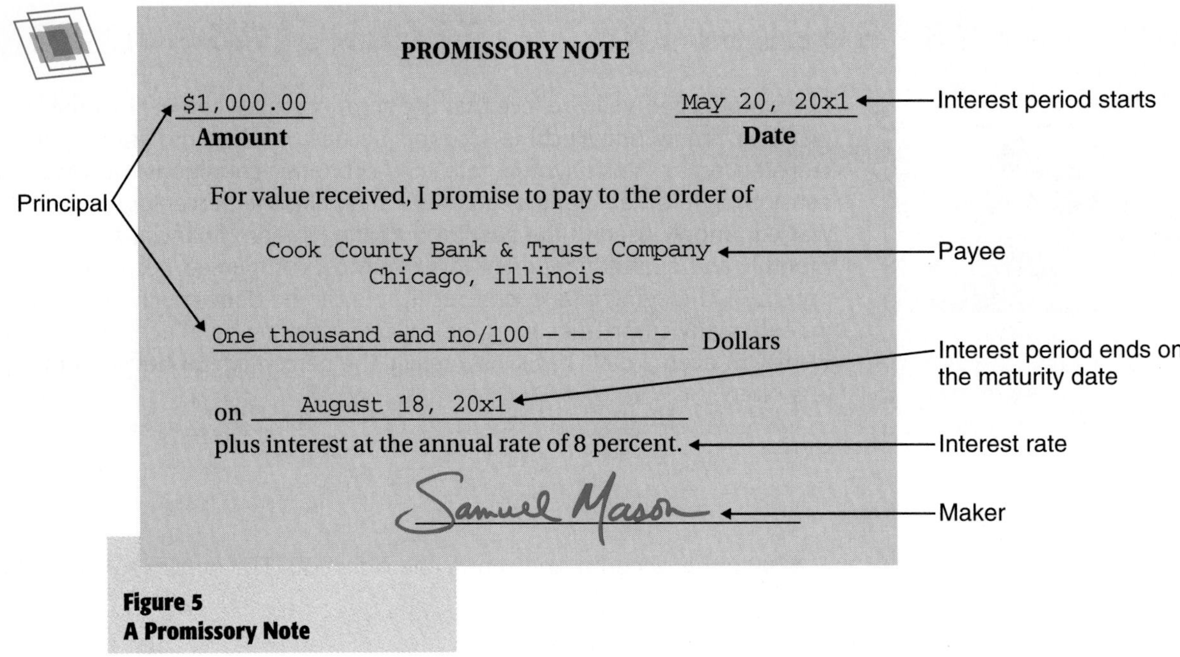
PROMISSORY NOTE

$1,000.00
Amount

May 20, 20x1
Date

For value received, I promise to pay to the order of

Cook County Bank & Trust Company
Chicago, Illinois

One thousand and no/100 - - - - - Dollars

on August 18, 20x1

plus interest at the annual rate of 8 percent.

Samuel Mason

Figure 5
A Promissory Note

as farm machinery and automobiles, will often accept promissory notes. Among the advantages of promissory notes are that they produce interest income and represent a stronger legal claim against a debtor than do accounts receivable. In addition, selling or discounting promissory notes to banks is a common financing method. Almost all companies will occasionally receive a note, and many companies obtain notes receivable in settlement of past-due accounts.

Computations for Promissory Notes

In accounting for promissory notes, several terms are important to remember. These terms are (1) maturity date, (2) duration of note, (3) interest and interest rate, and (4) maturity value.

Maturity Date The maturity date is the date on which the note must be paid. This date must either be stated on the promissory note or be determinable from the facts stated on the note. Among the most common statements of maturity date are the following:

1. A specific date, such as "November 14, 20xx"
2. A specific number of months after the date of the note, for example, "3 months after date"
3. A specific number of days after the date of the note, for example, "60 days after date"

Teaching Note: Another way to compute the duration of notes is to begin with the interest period, as follows:

90	Interest period
−11	days remaining in May (31 − 20)
79	
−30	days in June
49	
−31	days in July
18	due date in August

The maturity date is obvious when a specific date is stated. And when the maturity date is a number of months from the date of the note, one simply uses the same day in the appropriate future month. For example, a note that is dated January 20 and that is due in two months would be due on March 20.

When the maturity date is a specific number of days from the date of the note, however, the exact maturity date must be determined. In computing the maturity date, it is important to exclude the date of the note. For example, a note dated May 20 and due in 90 days would be due on August 18, computed as follows:

Days remaining in May (31 − 20)	11
Days in June	30
Days in July	31
Days in August	18
Total days	90

Duration of Note The duration of note is the length of time in days between a promissory note's issue date and its maturity date. Knowing the duration of the note is important because interest is calculated for the exact number of days. Identifying the duration is easy when the maturity date is stated as a specific number of days from the date of the note because the two numbers are the same. However, if the maturity date is stated as a specific date, the exact number of days must be determined. Assume that a note issued on May 10 matures on August 10. The duration of the note is 92 days, determined as follows:

Days remaining in May (31 − 10)	21
Days in June	30
Days in July	31
Days in August	10
Total days	92

Interest and Interest Rate The interest is the cost of borrowing money or the return for lending money, depending on whether one is the borrower or the lender. The amount of interest is based on three factors: the principal (the amount of money borrowed or lent), the rate of interest, and the loan's length of time. The formula used in computing interest is as follows:

$$\text{Principal} \times \text{Rate of Interest} \times \text{Time} = \text{Interest}$$

Interest rates are usually stated on an annual basis. For example, the interest on a \$1,000, one-year, 8 percent note would be \$80 ($\$1{,}000 \times 8/100 \times 1 = \$80$). If the term, or time period, of the note were three months instead of a year, the interest charge would be \$20 ($\$1{,}000 \times 8/100 \times 3/12 = \$20$).

When the term of a note is expressed in days, the exact number of days must be used in computing the interest. To keep the computation simple, let us compute interest on the basis of 360 days per year. Therefore, if the term of the above note were 45 days, the interest would be \$10, computed as follows: $\$1{,}000 \times 8/100 \times 45/360 = \$10$.

BUSINESS BULLETIN: BUSINESS PRACTICE

Practice as to the computation of interest varies. Most banks use a 365-day year for all loans, but some use a 360-day year for commercial loans. The brokerage firm of May Financial Corporation of Dallas, Texas, states in its customer loan agreement, "Interest is calculated on a 360-day basis." In Europe, use of a 360-day year is common. Financial institutions that use the 360-day basis earn slightly more interest than those that use the 365-day basis. In this book, we use a 360-day year to keep the computations simple.

Maturity Value The maturity value is the total proceeds of a note at the maturity date. The maturity value is the face value of the note plus interest. The maturity value of a 90-day, 8 percent, $1,000 note is computed as follows:

$$\begin{aligned}\text{Maturity Value} &= \text{Principal} + \text{Interest}\\ &= \$1{,}000 + (\$1{,}000 \times 8/100 \times 90/360)\\ &= \$1{,}000 + \$20\\ &= \$1{,}020\end{aligned}$$

There are also so-called non-interest-bearing notes. The maturity value is the face value, or principal amount. In this case, the principal includes an implied interest cost.

Illustrative Accounting Entries

Parenthetical Note: The entry to record receipt of a note does not include interest because interest has not yet been earned.

The accounting entries for promissory notes receivable fall into four groups: (1) recording receipt of a note, (2) recording collection on a note, (3) recording a dishonored note, and (4) recording adjusting entries.

Recording Receipt of a Note Assume that on June 1 a 12 percent, thirty-day note is received from a customer, J. Halsted, in settlement of an existing account receivable of $4,000. The entry for this transaction is as follows:

A = L + OE
+
−

June 1	Notes Receivable	4,000	
	Accounts Receivable		4,000
	Received 12 percent, 30-day note in payment of account of J. Halsted		

Recording Collection on a Note When the note plus interest is collected thirty days later, the entry is as follows:

A = L + OE
+ +
−

July 1	Cash	4,040	
	Notes Receivable		4,000
	Interest Income		40
	Collected 12 percent, 30-day note from J. Halsted		

Clarification Note: Dishonored notes are, in effect, not written off. The amounts are merely transferred to accounts receivable, which can be written off later.

Recording a Dishonored Note When the maker of a note does not pay the note at maturity, the note is said to be dishonored. The holder, or payee, of a dishonored note should make an entry to transfer the total amount due from Notes Receivable to an account receivable from the debtor. If J. Halsted dishonors her note on July 1, the following entry would be made.

A = L + OE
+ +
−

July 1	Accounts Receivable	4,040	
	Notes Receivable		4,000
	Interest Income		40
	12 percent, 30-day note dishonored by J. Halsted		

Enrichment Note: The interest rate on the account receivable is usually not the same as the rate on the note. It is usually higher than the rate on the note.

The interest earned is recorded because, although J. Halsted did not pay the note, she is still obligated to pay both the principal and the interest.

Two things are accomplished by transferring a dishonored note receivable into an Accounts Receivable account. First, this leaves the Notes Receivable account with only notes that have not matured and are presumably negotiable and collectible. Second, it establishes a record in the borrower's accounts receivable account that he or she has dishonored a note receivable. Such information may be helpful in deciding whether to extend future credit to the customer.

Recording Adjusting Entries A promissory note received in one period may not be due until a following accounting period. Because the interest on a note accrues by a small amount each day of the note's duration, it is necessary, according to the matching rule, to apportion the interest earned to the periods in which it belongs. For example, assume that on August 31 a sixty-day, 8 percent, $2,000 note was received and that the company prepares financial statements monthly. The following adjusting entry is necessary on September 30 to show how the interest earned for September has accrued.

A = L + OE
\+ +

Sept. 30	Interest Receivable	13.33	
	Interest Income		13.33
	To accrue 30 days' interest earned on a note receivable $2,000 × 8/100 × 30/360 = $13.33		

Reinforcement Exercise: What adjusting entry would the maker of the note have made on September 30? **Answer:** Debit Interest Expense, 13.33; credit Interest Payable, 13.33.

The account Interest Receivable is a current asset on the balance sheet. When payment of the note plus interest is received on October 30, the following entry is made.[13]

A = L + OE
\+ +
−

Oct. 30	Cash	2,026.67	
	Notes Receivable		2,000.00
	Interest Receivable		13.33
	Interest Income		13.34
	Receipt of note receivable plus interest		

Reinforcement Exercise: What journal entry would the maker of the note have made on October 30? **Answer:** Debit Notes Payable for 2,000.00, Interest Payable for 13.33, and Interest Expense for 13.34; credit Cash for 2,026.67.

As seen from these transactions, both September and October receive the benefit of one-half the interest earned.

Chapter Review

REVIEW OF LEARNING OBJECTIVES

1. **Identify and explain the management issues related to short-term liquid assets.** In managing short-term liquid assets, management must (1) consider the effects of seasonal cycles on the need for short-term investing and borrowing as the business's balance of cash fluctuates, (2) establish credit policies that balance the need for sales with the ability to collect, and (3) assess the need for additional cash flows through the financing of receivables.
2. **Explain *cash, cash equivalents,* and the importance of electronic funds transfer.** Cash consists of coins and currency on hand, checks and money orders received from customers, and deposits in bank accounts. Cash equivalents are investments that have a term of less than ninety days. Conducting transactions through electronic communication or electronic funds transfer is important because of its efficiency: Much of the paperwork associated with traditional recordkeeping is eliminated.
3. **Account for short-term investments.** Short-term investments may be classified as held-to-maturity securities, trading securities, and available-for-sale securities. Held-to-maturity securities are debt securities that management intends to hold to the maturity date; they are valued on the balance sheet at cost adjusted for the effects of interest. Trading securities are debt and equity securities bought and held principally for the purpose of being sold in the near term; they are valued at fair value or at market value. Unrealized gains or losses on trading securities appear on the income statement. Available-for-sale securities are debt and equity securities that do not meet the criteria for either held-to-maturity or trading securities. They are accounted for in the same way as trading securities, except that an unrealized gain or loss is reported as a special item in the stockholders' equity section of the balance sheet.

4. **Define *accounts receivable* and apply the allowance method of accounting for uncollectible accounts, using both the percentage of net sales method and the accounts receivable aging method.** Accounts receivable are amounts still to be collected from credit sales to customers. Because credit is offered to increase sales, uncollectible accounts associated with credit sales should be charged as expenses in the period in which the sales are made. However, because of the time lag between the sales and the time the accounts are judged uncollectible, the accountant must estimate the amount of bad debts in any given period.

   Uncollectible accounts expense is estimated by either the percentage of net sales method or the accounts receivable aging method. When the first method is used, bad debts are judged to be a certain percentage of sales during the period. When the second method is used, certain percentages are applied to groups of accounts receivable that have been arranged by due dates.

   Allowance for Uncollectible Accounts is a contra-asset account to Accounts Receivable. The estimate of uncollectible accounts is debited to Uncollectible Accounts Expense and credited to the allowance account. When an individual account is determined to be uncollectible, it is removed from Accounts Receivable by debiting the allowance account and crediting Accounts Receivable. If the written-off account should later be collected, the earlier entry should be reversed and the collection recorded in the normal way.

5. **Define and describe a *promissory note,* and make calculations and journal entries involving promissory notes.** A promissory note is an unconditional promise to pay a definite sum of money on demand or at a future date. Companies selling durable goods of high value, such as farm machinery and automobiles, often accept promissory notes, which can be sold to banks as a financing method.

   In accounting for promissory notes, it is important to know how to calculate the maturity date, duration of note, interest and interest rate, and maturity value. The accounting entries for promissory notes receivable fall into four groups: recording receipt of a note, recording collection on a note, recording a dishonored note, and recording adjusting entries.

REVIEW OF CONCEPTS AND TERMINOLOGY

The following concepts and terms were introduced in this chapter.

LO 4 **Accounts receivable:** Short-term liquid assets that arise from sales on credit at the wholesale or retail level.

LO 4 **Accounts receivable aging method:** A method of estimating uncollectible accounts based on the assumption that a predictable proportion of each dollar of accounts receivable outstanding will not be collected.

LO 4 **Aging of accounts receivable:** The process of listing each customer's receivable account according to the due date of the account.

LO 4 **Allowance for Uncollectible Accounts:** A contra-asset account that reduces accounts receivable to the amount that is expected to be collected in cash; also called *allowance for bad debts.*

LO 4 **Allowance method:** A method of accounting for uncollectible accounts by expensing estimated uncollectible accounts in the period in which the related sales take place.

LO 3 **Available-for-sale securities:** Debt and equity securities that do not meet the criteria for either held-to-maturity or trading securities.

LO 1 **Average days' sales uncollected:** A ratio that shows on average how long it takes to collect accounts receivable; 365 days divided by receivable turnover.

LO 2 **Cash:** Coins and currency on hand, checks and money orders from customers, and deposits in bank checking accounts.

LO 2 **Cash equivalents:** Short-term investments that will revert to cash in less than ninety days from when they are purchased.

LO 2 **Compensating balance:** A minimum amount that a bank requires a company to keep in its account as part of a credit-granting arrangement.

LO 1 **Contingent liability:** A potential liability that can develop into a real liability if a possible subsequent event occurs.

LO 4 **Direct charge-off method:** A method of accounting for uncollectible accounts by directly debiting an expense account when bad debts are discovered instead of using the allowance method; this method violates the matching rule but is required for federal income tax computations.

LO 1 **Discounting:** A method of selling notes receivable in which the bank deducts the interest from the maturity value of the note to determine the proceeds.

LO 5 **Dishonored note:** A promissory note that the maker cannot or will not pay at the maturity date.

LO 5 **Duration of note:** The length of time in days between a promissory note's issue date and its maturity date.

LO 2 **Electronic funds transfer (EFT):** The transfer of funds from one bank to another through electronic communication.

LO 1 **Factor:** An entity that buys accounts receivable.

LO 1 **Factoring:** The selling or transferring of accounts receivable.

LO 3 **Held-to-maturity securities:** Debt securities that management intends to hold to their maturity or payment date and whose cash value is not needed until that date.

LO 2 **Imprest system:** A system for controlling small cash disbursements by establishing a fund at a fixed amount and periodically reimbursing the fund by the amount necessary to restore its original cash balance.

LO 4 **Installment accounts receivable:** Accounts receivable that are payable in a series of time payments.

LO 5 **Interest:** The cost of borrowing money or the return for lending money, depending on whether one is the borrower or the lender.

LO 3 **Marketable securities:** Short-term investments intended to be held until needed to pay current obligations. Also called *short-term investments.*

LO 5 **Maturity date:** The date on which a promissory note must be paid.

LO 5 **Maturity value:** The total proceeds of a promissory note, including principal and interest, at the maturity date.

LO 5 **Notes payable:** Collective term for promissory notes owed by the entity (maker) who promises payment to other entities.

LO 5 **Notes receivable:** Collective term for promissory notes held by the entity to whom payment is promised (payee).

LO 4 **Percentage of net sales method:** A method of estimating uncollectible accounts based on the assumption that a predictable proportion of each dollar of sales will not be collected.

LO 5 **Promissory note:** An unconditional promise to pay a definite sum of money on demand or at a future date.

LO 1 **Quick ratio:** A ratio for measuring the adequacy of short-term liquid assets; short-term liquid assets divided by current liabilities.

LO 1 **Receivable turnover:** A ratio for measuring the average number of times receivables were turned into cash during an accounting period; net sales divided by average net accounts receivable.

LO 3 **Short-term investments:** Temporary investments of excess cash, intended to be held until needed to pay current obligations. Also called *marketable securities.*

LO 1 **Short-term liquid assets:** Financial assets that arise from cash transactions, the investment of cash, and the extension of credit.

LO 4 **Trade credit:** Credit granted to customers by wholesalers or retailers.

LO 3 **Trading securities:** Debt and equity securities bought and held principally for the purpose of being sold in the near term.

LO 4 **Uncollectible accounts:** Accounts receivable owed by customers who cannot or will not pay. Also called *bad debts.*

REVIEW PROBLEM

Estimating Uncollectible Accounts, Receivables Analysis, and Notes Receivable Transactions

LO 1
LO 4
LO 5

The Farm Implement Company sells merchandise on credit and also accepts notes for payment. During the year ended June 30, the company had net sales of $1,200,000, and at the end of the year it had Accounts Receivable of $400,000 and a debit balance in Allowance for Uncollectible Accounts of $2,100. In the past, approximately 1.5 percent of net sales have proved uncollectible. Also, an aging analysis of accounts receivable reveals that $17,000 in accounts receivable appears to be uncollectible.

The Farm Implement Company sold a tractor to R. C. Sims. Payment was received in the form of a $15,000, 9 percent, 90-day note dated March 16. On June 14, Sims dishonored the note. On June 29, the company received payment in full from Sims plus additional interest from the date of the dishonored note.

REQUIRED

1. Compute Uncollectible Accounts Expense and determine the ending balance of Allowance for Uncollectible Accounts and Accounts Receivable, Net under (a) the percentage of net sales method and (b) the accounts receivable aging method.
2. Compute the receivable turnover and average days' sales uncollected using the data from the accounts receivable aging method in **1** and assuming that the prior year's net accounts receivable were $353,000.
3. Prepare entries in journal form relating to the note received from R. C. Sims.

ANSWER TO REVIEW PROBLEM

1. Uncollectible Accounts Expense computed and balances determined.
   a. Percentage of net sales method:

   Uncollectible Accounts Expense = 1.5 percent × $1,200,000
   = $18,000

   Allowance for Uncollectible Accounts = $18,000 − $2,100
   = $15,900

   Accounts Receivable, Net = $400,000 − $15,900
   = $384,100

   b. Accounts receivable aging method:

   Uncollectible Accounts Expense = $2,100 + $17,000
   = $19,100

   Allowance for Uncollectible Accounts = $17,000

   Accounts Receivable, Net = $400,000 − $17,000
   = $383,000

2. Receivable turnover and average days' sales uncollected computed.

$$\text{Receivable Turnover} = \frac{\$1{,}200{,}000}{(\$353{,}000 + \$383{,}000)/2} = 3.3 \text{ times}$$

$$\text{Average Days' Sales Uncollected} = \frac{365 \text{ days}}{3.3} = 110.6 \text{ days}$$

3. Journal entries related to the note prepared.

Mar. 16	Notes Receivable	15,000.00	
	Sales		15,000.00
	Tractor sold to R. C. Sims; terms of note: 9 percent, 90 days		

June 14	Accounts Receivable	15,337.50	
	Notes Receivable		15,000.00
	Interest Income		337.50
	The note was dishonored by R. C. Sims Maturity value: $15,000 + ($15,000 × 9/100 × 90/360) = $15,337.50		
29	Cash	15,395.02	
	Accounts Receivable		15,337.50
	Interest Income		57.52
	Received payment in full from R. C. Sims $15,337.50 + ($15,337.50 × 9/100 × 15/360) $15,337.50 + $57.52 = $15,395.02		

Chapter Assignments

BUILDING YOUR KNOWLEDGE FOUNDATION

Questions

1. Why does a business need short-term liquid assets? What three issues does management face in managing short-term liquid assets?
2. What is a factor, and what do the terms *factoring with recourse* and *factoring without recourse* mean?
3. What items are included in the Cash account? What is a compensating balance?
4. How do cash equivalents differ from cash? From short-term investments?
5. What are the three kinds of securities held as short-term investments, and how are they valued at the balance sheet date?
6. What are unrealized gains and losses on trading securities? On what statement are they reported?
7. Which of the following lettered items should be in Accounts Receivable? If an item does not belong in Accounts Receivable, tell where on the balance sheet it does belong: (a) installment accounts receivable from regular customers, due monthly for three years; (b) debit balances in customers' accounts; (c) receivables from employees; (d) credit balances in customers' accounts; (e) receivables from officers of the company.
8. Why does a company sell on credit if it expects that some of the accounts will not be paid? What role does a credit department play in selling on credit?
9. What accounting rule is violated by the direct charge-off method of recognizing uncollectible accounts? Why?
10. According to generally accepted accounting principles, at what point in the cycle of selling and collecting does a loss on an uncollectible account occur?
11. Are the following terms different in any way: allowance for bad debts, allowance for doubtful accounts, allowance for uncollectible accounts?
12. What is the effect on net income of management's taking an optimistic versus a pessimistic view of estimated uncollectible accounts?
13. In what ways is Allowance for Uncollectible Accounts similar to Accumulated Depreciation? In what ways is it different?
14. What is the reasoning behind the percentage of net sales method and the accounts receivable aging method of estimating uncollectible accounts?
15. What procedure for estimating uncollectible accounts also gives management a view of the status of collections and the overall quality of accounts receivable?

16. After adjusting and closing the accounts at the end of the year, suppose that Accounts Receivable is $176,000 and Allowance for Uncollectible Accounts is $14,500. (a) What is the collectible value of Accounts Receivable? (b) If the $450 account of a bankrupt customer is written off in the first month of the new year, what will be the resulting collectible value of Accounts Receivable?
17. Why should an account that has been written off as uncollectible be reinstated if the amount owed is subsequently collected?
18. What is a promissory note? Who is the maker? Who is the payee?
19. What are the maturity dates of the following notes: (a) a 3-month note dated August 16, (b) a 90-day note dated August 16, and (c) a 60-day note dated March 25?

Short Exercises

LO 1 *Management Issues*

SE 1. Indicate whether each of the actions below is related to (a) managing cash needs during seasonal cycles, (b) setting credit policies, or (c) financing receivables.

1. Selling accounts receivable to a factor
2. Borrowing funds for short-term needs during slow periods
3. Conducting thorough checks of new customers' ability to pay
4. Investing cash that is not currently needed for operations

LO 1 *Short-Term Liquidity Ratios*

SE 2. Slater Company has cash of $20,000, short-term investments of $25,000, net accounts receivable of $45,000, inventory of $44,000, accounts payable of $60,000, and net sales of $360,000. Last year's net accounts receivable were $35,000. Compute the following ratios: quick ratio, receivable turnover, and average days' sales uncollected. Assume there are no current liabilities other than accounts payable.

LO 2 *Cash and Cash Equivalents*

SE 3. Compute the amount of cash and cash equivalents on Quay Company's balance sheet if, on the balance sheet date, it has coins and currency on hand of $500, deposits in checking accounts of $3,000, U.S. Treasury bills due in 80 days of $30,000, and U.S. Treasury bonds due in 200 days of $50,000.

LO 3 *Held-to-Maturity Securities*

SE 4. On May 31, Renata Company invested $49,000 in U.S. Treasury bills. The bills mature in 120 days at $50,000. Prepare entries to record the purchase on May 31; the adjustment to accrue interest on June 30, which is the end of the fiscal year; and the receipt of cash at the maturity date of September 28.

LO 3 *Trading Securities*

SE 5. Monika Corporation began investing in trading securities this year. At the end of 20x1, the following trading portfolio existed:

Security	Cost	Market Value
Sara Lee (10,000 shares)	$220,000	$330,000
Skyline (5,000 shares)	100,000	75,000
Totals	$320,000	$405,000

Prepare the necessary year-end adjusting entry on December 31 and the entry for the sale of all the Skyline shares on the following March 23 for $95,000.

LO 4 *Percentage of Net Sales Method*

SE 6. At the end of October, Mafa Company management estimates the uncollectible accounts expense to be 1 percent of net sales of $2,770,000. Give the entry to record the uncollectible accounts expense, assuming that the Allowance for Uncollectible Accounts has a debit balance of $14,000.

LO 4 *Accounts Receivable Aging Method*

SE 7. An aging analysis on June 30 of the accounts receivable of Texbar Corporation indicates uncollectible accounts of $43,000. Give the entry to record uncollectible accounts expense under each of the following independent assumptions: (a) Allowance for Uncollectible Accounts has a credit balance of $9,000 before adjustment, and (b) Allowance for Uncollectible Accounts has a debit balance of $7,000 before adjustment.

SE 8. LO 4 *Write-off of Accounts Receivable*

Key Company, which uses the allowance method, has an account receivable from Sandy Burgess of $4,400 that it deems to be uncollectible. Prepare the entries on May 31 to write off the account and on August 13 to record an unexpected receipt of $1,000 from Burgess. The company does not expect to collect more from Burgess.

SE 9. LO 5 *Notes Receivable Entries*

On August 25, Rostin Company received a 90-day, 9 percent note in settlement of an account receivable in the amount of $10,000. Record the receipt of the note, the accrual of interest at fiscal year end on September 30, and collection of the note on the due date.

Exercises

E 1. LO 1 *Management Issues*

Indicate whether each of the following actions is primarily related to (a) managing cash needs during seasonal cycles, (b) setting credit policies, or (c) financing receivables.

1. Buying a U.S. Treasury bill with cash that is not needed for a few months
2. Comparing receivable turnovers for two years
3. Setting policy on which customers may buy on credit
4. Selling notes receivable to a financing company
5. Borrowing funds for short-term needs during the period of the year when sales are low
6. Changing the terms for credit sales in an effort to reduce the average days' sales uncollected
7. Using a factor to provide operating funds
8. Establishing a department whose responsibility is to approve customers' credit

E 2. LO 1 *Short-Term Liquidity Ratios*

Using the following information selected from the financial statements of Holden Company, compute the quick ratio, the receivable turnover, and the average days' sales uncollected.

Current Assets	
Cash	$ 70,000
Short-Term Investments	170,000
Notes Receivable	240,000
Accounts Receivable, Net	200,000
Inventory	500,000
Prepaid Assets	50,000
Total Current Assets	$1,230,000
Current Liabilities	
Notes Payable	$ 300,000
Accounts Payable	150,000
Accrued Liabilities	20,000
Total Current Liabilities	$ 470,000
Net Sales	$1,600,000
Last Period's Accounts Receivable, Net	$ 180,000

E 3. LO 2 *Cash and Cash Equivalents*

At year end, Oppenheim Company had coins and currency in cash registers of $2,800, money orders from customers of $5,000, deposits in checking accounts of $32,000, U.S. Treasury bills due in eighty days of $90,000, certificates of deposits at the bank that mature in six months of $100,000, and U.S. Treasury bonds due in one year of $50,000. Calculate the amount of cash and cash equivalents that will be shown on the company's year-end balance sheet.

E 4. LO 3 *Held-to-Maturity Securities*

Arango Company experiences heavy sales in the summer and early fall, after which time it has excess cash to invest until the next spring. On November 1, 20x1, the company invested $194,000 in U.S. Treasury bills. The bills mature in 180 days at $200,000. Prepare entries to record the purchase on November 1; the adjustment to accrue interest on December 31, which is the end of the fiscal year; and the receipt of cash at the maturity date of April 30.

E 5. LO 3 *Trading Securities*

Ephrem Corporation began investing in trading securities and engaged in the following transactions.

Jan. 6 Purchased 7,000 shares of Quaker Oats stock, $30 per share.
Feb. 15 Purchased 9,000 shares of EG&G, $22 per share.

At June 30 year end, Quaker Oats was trading at $40 per share and EG&G was trading at $18 per share. Record the entries for the purchases. Then record the necessary year-end adjusting entry. (Include a schedule of the trading portfolio cost and market in the explanation.) Also record the entry for the sale of all the EG&G shares on August 20 for $16 per share. Is the last entry affected by the June 30 adjustment?

E 6. LO 4 *Percentage of Net Sales Method*

At the end of the year, Browne Enterprises estimates the uncollectible accounts expense to be .7 percent of net sales of $30,300,000. The current credit balance of Allowance for Uncollectible Accounts is $51,600. Prepare the entry in journal form to record the uncollectible accounts expense. What is the balance of Allowance for Uncollectible Accounts after this adjustment?

E 7. LO 4 *Accounts Receivable Aging Method*

Accounts Receivable of Ashly Company shows a debit balance of $52,000 at the end of the year. An aging analysis of the individual accounts indicates estimated uncollectible accounts to be $3,350.

Prepare the entry in journal form to record the uncollectible accounts expense under each of the following independent assumptions: (a) Allowance for Uncollectible Accounts has a credit balance of $400 before adjustment, and (b) Allowance for Uncollectible Accounts has a debit balance of $400 before adjustment. What is the balance of Allowance for Uncollectible Accounts after this adjustment?

E 8. LO 4 *Aging Method and Net Sales Method Contrasted*

At the beginning of 20xx, the balances for Accounts Receivable and Allowance for Uncollectible Accounts were $430,000 and $31,400, respectively. During the current year, credit sales were $3,200,000 and collections on account were $2,950,000. In addition, $35,000 in uncollectible accounts were written off.

Using T accounts, determine the year-end balances of Accounts Receivable and Allowance for Uncollectible Accounts. Then make the year-end adjusting entry to record the uncollectible accounts expense, and show the year-end balance sheet presentation of Accounts Receivable and Allowance for Uncollectible Accounts under each of the following conditions:

a. Management estimates the percentage of uncollectible credit sales to be 1.2 percent of total credit sales.
b. Based on an aging of accounts receivable, management estimates the end-of-year uncollectible accounts receivable to be $38,700.

Post the results of each entry to the T account for Allowance for Uncollectible Accounts.

E 9. LO 4 *Aging Method and Net Sales Method Contrasted*

During 20x1, Central Supply Company had net sales of $2,850,000. Most of the sales were on credit. At the end of 20x1, the balance of Accounts Receivable was $350,000 and Allowance for Uncollectible Accounts had a debit balance of $12,000. Management has two methods of estimating uncollectible accounts expense: (a) The percentage of uncollectible sales is 1.5 percent, and (b) based on an aging of accounts receivable, the end-of-year uncollectible accounts total $35,000. Make the end-of-year adjusting entry to record the uncollectible accounts expense under each method, and tell what the balance of Allowance for Uncollectible Accounts will be after each adjustment. Why are the results different, and which method is likely to be more reliable?

E 10. LO 4 *Entries for Uncollectible Accounts Expense*

The Poulakidas Parts Company sells merchandise on credit. During the fiscal year ended July 31, the company had net sales of $4,600,000. At the end of the year, it had Accounts Receivable of $1,200,000 and a debit balance in Allowance for Uncollectible Accounts of $6,800. In the past, approximately 1.4 percent of net sales have proved uncollectible. Also, an aging analysis of accounts receivable reveals that $60,000 of the receivables appear to be uncollectible. Prepare entries in journal form to record uncollectible accounts expense using: (a) the percentage of net sales method and (b) the accounts receivable aging method.

What is the resulting balance of Allowance for Uncollectible Accounts under each method? How would your answers under each method change if Allowance for

Uncollectible Accounts had a credit balance of $6,800 instead of a debit balance? Why do the methods result in different balances?

LO 4 *Accounts Receivable Transactions*

E 11. Assuming that the allowance method is being used, prepare entries in journal form to record the following transactions:

July 12, 20x4	Sold merchandise to Jean Snowden for $1,800, terms n/10.
Oct. 18, 20x4	Received $600 from Jean Snowden on account.
May 8, 20x5	Wrote off as uncollectible the balance of the Jean Snowden account when she declared bankruptcy.
June 22, 20x5	Unexpectedly received a check for $200 from Jean Snowden.

LO 5 *Interest Computations*

E 12. Determine the interest on the following notes.

a. $22,800 at 10 percent for 90 days
b. $16,000 at 12 percent for 60 days
c. $18,000 at 9 percent for 30 days
d. $30,000 at 15 percent for 120 days
e. $10,800 at 6 percent for 60 days

LO 5 *Notes Receivable Transactions*

E 13. Prepare entries in journal form to record the following transactions.

Jan. 16	Sold merchandise to Vacca Corporation on account for $36,000, terms n/30.
Feb. 15	Accepted a $36,000, 10 percent, 90-day note from Vacca Corporation in lieu of payment of account.
May 16	Vacca Corporation dishonored the note.
June 15	Received payment in full from Vacca Corporation, including interest at 10 percent from the date the note was dishonored.

LO 5 *Adjusting Entries: Interest Income*

E 14. Prepare entries in journal form (assuming reversing entries were not made) to record the following:

Dec. 1	Received a 90-day, 12 percent note for $10,000 from a customer for a sale of merchandise.
31	Made end-of-year adjustment for interest income.
Mar. 1	Received payment in full for note and interest.

LO 5 *Notes Receivable Transactions*

E 15. Prepare entries in journal form to record these transactions.

Jan. 5	Accepted a $4,800, 60-day, 10 percent note dated this day in granting a time extension on the past-due account of P. Hamnes.
Mar. 6	P. Hamnes paid the maturity value of his $4,800 note.
9	Accepted a $3,000, 60-day, 12 percent note dated this day in granting a time extension on the past-due account of V. Andrews.
May 8	When asked for payment, V. Andrews dishonored his note.
June 7	V. Andrews paid in full the maturity value of the note plus interest at 12 percent for the period since May 8.

Problems

LO 3 *Held-to-Maturity and Trading Securities*

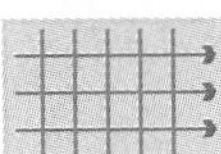

P 1. During certain periods, Chou Company invests its excess cash until it is needed. During 20x1 and 20x2, the company engaged in the following transactions.

20x1	
Jan. 16	Invested $146,000 in 120-day U.S. Treasury bills that had a maturity value of $150,000.
Apr. 15	Purchased 10,000 shares of Goodrich Paper common stock at $40 per share and 5,000 shares of Keuron Power Company common stock at $30 per share as trading securities.
May 16	Received maturity value of U.S. Treasury bills in cash.
June 2	Received dividends of $2.00 per share from Goodrich Paper and $1.50 per share from Keuron Power.
30	Made year-end adjusting entry for trading securities. Market price of Goodrich Paper shares is $32 per share and of Keuron Power shares is $35 per share.
Nov. 14	Sold all the shares of Goodrich Paper for $42 per share.

20x2
Feb. 15 Purchased 9,000 shares of Beacon Communications for $50 per share.
Apr. 1 Invested $195,500 in 120-day U.S. Treasury bills that had a maturity value of $200,000.
June 1 Received dividends of $2.20 per share from Keuron Power.
30 Made year-end adjusting entry for held-to-maturity securities.
30 Made year-end adjusting entry for trading securities. Market price of Keuron Power shares is $33 per share and of Beacon Communications shares is $60 per share.

REQUIRED

1. Prepare entries in journal form to record the preceding transactions, assuming that Chou Company's fiscal year ends on June 30.
2. Show the balance sheet presentation of short-term investments on June 30, 20x2.

P 2. LO 1 LO 4 *Methods of Estimating Uncollectible Accounts and Receivables Analysis*

On December 31 of last year, the balance sheet of Kakalatris Company had Accounts Receivable of $298,000 and a credit balance in Allowance for Uncollectible Accounts of $20,300. During the current year, the company's records included the following selected activities: (a) sales on account, $1,195,000; (b) sales returns and allowances, $73,000; (c) collections from customers, $1,150,000; (d) accounts written off as worthless, $16,000. In the past, the company had found that 1.6 percent of net sales would not be collected.

REQUIRED

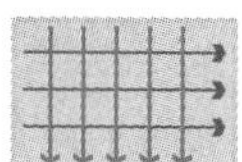

1. Prepare T accounts for Accounts Receivable and Allowance for Uncollectible Accounts. Enter the beginning balances, and show the effects on these accounts of the items listed above, summarizing the year's activity. Determine the ending balance of each account.
2. Compute Uncollectible Accounts Expense and determine the ending balance of Allowance for Uncollectible Accounts under (a) the percentage of net sales method and (b) the accounts receivable aging method, assuming an aging of the accounts receivable shows that $20,000 may be uncollectible.
3. Compute the receivable turnover and average days' sales uncollected, using the data from the accounts receivable aging method in **2**.
4. How do you explain the fact that the two methods in **2** result in different amounts for Uncollectible Accounts Expense? What rationale underlies each method?

P 3. LO 4 *Accounts Receivable Aging Method*

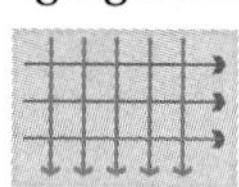

Girard Company uses the accounts receivable aging method to estimate uncollectible accounts. The Accounts Receivable account had a debit balance of $88,430 and Allowance for Uncollectible Accounts had a credit balance of $7,200 at the beginning of the year. During the year, the company had sales on account of $473,000, sales returns and allowances of $4,200, worthless accounts written off of $7,900, and collections from customers of $450,730. At the end of the year (December 31), a junior accountant for the company was preparing an aging analysis of accounts receivable. At the top of page 6 of the report, the following totals appeared:

Customer Account	Total	Not Yet Due	1–30 Days Past Due	31–60 Days Past Due	61–90 Days Past Due	Over 90 Days Past Due
Balance Forward	$89,640	$49,030	$24,110	$9,210	$3,990	$3,300

The following accounts remained to be classified to finish the analysis.

Account	Amount	Due Date
K. Foust	$ 930	Jan. 14 (next year)
K. Groth	620	Dec. 24
R. Mejias	1,955	Sept. 28
C. Polk	2,100	Aug. 16
M. Spears	375	Dec. 14
J. Yong	2,685	Jan. 23 (next year)
A. Zorr	295	Nov. 5
	$8,960	

From past experience, the company has found that the following rates are realistic to estimate uncollectible accounts.

Time	Percentage Considered Uncollectible
Not yet due	2
1–30 days past due	4
31–60 days past due	20
61–90 days past due	30
Over 90 days past due	50

REQUIRED

1. Complete the aging analysis of accounts receivable.
2. Determine the end-of-year balances (before adjustments) of Accounts Receivable and Allowance for Uncollectible Accounts.
3. Prepare an analysis computing the estimated uncollectible accounts.
4. Prepare the entry in journal form to record the estimated uncollectible accounts expense for the year (round the adjustment to the nearest whole dollar).

P 4. **LO 5** *Notes Receivable Transactions*

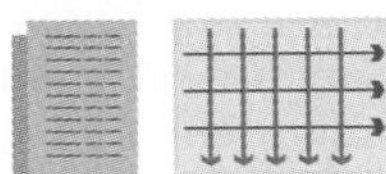

Minarcik Manufacturing Company sells truck beds. The company engaged in the following transactions involving promissory notes.

Jan. 10 Sold beds to Glynn Company for $30,000, terms n/10.
20 Accepted a 90-day, 12 percent promissory note in settlement of the account from Glynn.
Apr. 20 Received payment from Glynn Company for the note and interest.
May 5 Sold beds to Nanni Company for $20,000, terms n/10.
15 Received $4,000 cash and a 60-day, 13 percent note for $16,000 in settlement of the Nanni account.
July 14 When asked to pay, Nanni dishonored the note.
Aug. 2 Wrote off the Nanni account as uncollectible after receiving news that the company declared bankruptcy.
5 Received a 90-day, 11 percent note for $15,000 from Sayeed Company in settlement of an account receivable.
Nov. 3 When asked to pay, Sayeed dishonored the note.
9 Received payment in full from Sayeed, including 15 percent interest for the 6 days since the note was dishonored.

REQUIRED

Prepare entries in journal form to record the preceding transactions.

Alternate Problems

P 5. **LO 3** *Held-to-Maturity and Trading Securities*

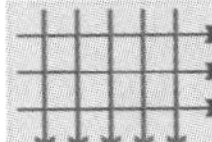

Wan Distributors follows a policy of investing excess cash until it is needed. During 20x1 and 20x2, the company engaged in the following transactions.

20x1
Feb. 1 Invested $97,000 in 120-day U.S. Treasury bills that had a maturity value of $100,000.
Mar. 30 Purchased 20,000 shares of Dataflex Company common stock at $16 per share and 12,000 shares of Gates Aviation, Inc., common stock at $10 per share as trading securities.
June 1 Received maturity value of U.S. Treasury bills in cash.
10 Received dividends of $.50 per share from Dataflex Company and $.25 per share from Gates Aviation, Inc.
30 Made year-end adjusting entry for trading securities. Market price of Dataflex Company shares is $13 per share and of Gates Aviation, Inc., shares is $12 per share.
Dec. 3 Sold all the shares of Dataflex Company for $12 per share.

20x2
Mar. 17 Purchased 15,000 shares of Biotech, Inc., for $9 per share.
May 31 Invested $116,000 in 120-day U.S. Treasury bills that had a maturity value of $120,000.

June 10 Received dividends of $.30 per share from Gates Aviation, Inc.
30 Made year-end adjusting entry for held-to-maturity securities.
30 Made year-end adjusting entry for trading securities. Market price of Gates Aviation, Inc., shares is $6 per share and of Biotech, Inc., shares is $11 per share.

REQUIRED

1. Prepare entries in journal form to record these transactions, assuming that Wan Distributors' fiscal year ends on June 30.
2. Show the balance sheet presentation of short-term investments on June 30, 20x2.

P 6.

LO 1 **LO 4** *Methods of Estimating Uncollectible Accounts and Receivables Analysis*

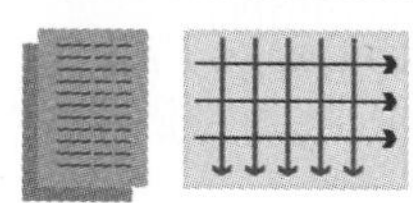

Hernandez Company had an Accounts Receivable balance of $320,000 and a credit balance in Allowance for Uncollectible Accounts of $16,700 at January 1, 20xx. During the year, the company recorded the following transactions.

a. Sales on account, $1,052,000
b. Sales returns and allowances by credit customers, $53,400
c. Collections from customers, $993,000
d. Worthless accounts written off, $19,800

The company's past history indicates that 2.5 percent of net credit sales will not be collected.

REQUIRED

1. Prepare T accounts for Accounts Receivable and Allowance for Uncollectible Accounts. Enter the beginning balances, and show the effects on these accounts of the items listed above, summarizing the year's activity. Determine the ending balance of each account.
2. Compute Uncollectible Accounts Expense and determine the ending balance of Allowance for Uncollectible Accounts under (a) the percentage of net sales method and (b) the accounts receivable aging method, assuming an aging of the accounts receivable shows that $24,000 may be uncollectible.
3. Compute the receivable turnover and average days' sales uncollected, using the data from the accounts receivable aging method in **2.**
4. How do you explain the fact that the two methods in **2** result in different amounts for Uncollectible Accounts Expense? What rationale underlies each method?

P 7.

LO 4 *Accounts Receivable Aging Method*

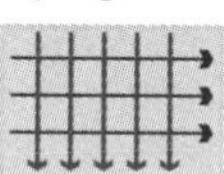

The Forsell Fashions Store uses the accounts receivable aging method to estimate uncollectible accounts. The balance of the Accounts Receivable account was a debit of $446,341 and the balance of Allowance for Uncollectible Accounts was a credit of $43,000 at February 1, 20x1. During the year, the store had sales on account of $3,724,000, sales returns and allowances of $63,000, worthless accounts written off of $44,300, and collections from customers of $3,214,000. As part of the end-of-year (January 31, 20x2) procedures, an aging analysis of accounts receivable is prepared. The totals of the analysis, which is partially complete, follow.

Customer Account	Total	Not Yet Due	1–30 Days Past Due	31–60 Days Past Due	61–90 Days Past Due	Over 90 Days Past Due
Balance Forward	$793,791	$438,933	$149,614	$106,400	$57,442	$41,402

The following accounts remain to be classified to finish the analysis.

Account	Amount	Due Date
J. Curtis	$10,977	January 15
T. Dawson	9,314	February 15 (next fiscal year)
M. Guokas	8,664	December 20
F. Javier	780	October 1
B. Loo	14,810	January 4
S. Qadri	6,316	November 15
A. Rosenthal	4,389	March 1 (next fiscal year)
	$55,250	

From past experience, the company has found that the following rates are realistic to estimate uncollectible accounts.

Time	Percentage Considered Uncollectible
Not yet due	2
1–30 days past due	5
31–60 days past due	15
61–90 days past due	25
Over 90 days past due	50

REQUIRED

1. Complete the aging analysis of accounts receivable.
2. Determine the end-of-year balances (before adjustments) of Accounts Receivable and Allowance for Uncollectible Accounts.
3. Prepare an analysis computing the estimated uncollectible accounts.
4. Prepare the entry in journal form to record the estimated uncollectible accounts expense for the year (round the adjustment to the nearest whole dollar).

LO 5 *Notes Receivable Transactions*

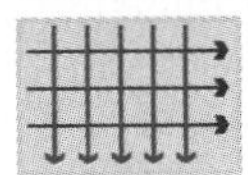

P 8. Zhon Importing Company engaged in the following transactions involving promissory notes.

Jan. 14 Sold merchandise to Whittaker Company for $18,500, terms n/30.
Feb. 13 Received $4,200 in cash from Whittaker Company and received a 90-day, 8 percent promissory note for the balance of the account.
May 14 Received payment in full from Whittaker Company.
15 Received a 60-day, 12 percent note from Ralph Sarkis Company in payment of a past-due account, $6,000.
July 14 When asked to pay, Ralph Sarkis Company dishonored the note.
20 Received a check from Ralph Sarkis Company for payment of the maturity value of the note and interest at 12 percent for the six days beyond maturity.
25 Sold merchandise to James Flowers Company for $18,000, with payment of $3,000 cash down and the remainder on account.
31 Received a $15,000, 45-day, 10 percent promissory note from James Flowers Company for the outstanding account receivable.
Sept. 14 When asked to pay, James Flowers Company dishonored the note.
25 Wrote off the James Flowers Company account as uncollectible following news that the company had declared bankruptcy.

REQUIRED

Prepare entries in journal form to record the preceding transactions.

Skills Development

Conceptual Analysis

SD 1. LO 1 LO 2 LO 3 *Management of Cash*

Academia Publishing Company publishes college textbooks in the sciences and humanities. More than 50 percent of the company's sales occur in July, August, and December. Its cash balances are largest in August, September, and January. During the rest of the year, its cash receipts are low. The corporate treasurer keeps the cash in a bank checking account earning little or no interest and pays bills from this account as they come due. To survive, the company has borrowed money during some slow sales months. The loans were repaid in the months when cash receipts were largest. A management consultant has suggested that the company institute a new cash management plan under which cash would be invested in marketable securities as it is received and securities would be sold when the funds are needed. In this way, the company will earn income on the cash and may realize a gain through an increase in the value of the securities, thus reducing the need for borrowing. The president of the company has asked you to assess the plan. Write a memorandum to the president that lays out the accounting implications of this cash management plan for cash and cash equivalents and for the three types of marketable securities. Include an assessment of the plan and any disadvantages to it.

SD 2. LO 1 LO 4 *Role of Credit Sales*

Mitsubishi Corp.,[14] a broadly diversified Japanese corporation, instituted a credit plan called Three Diamonds for customers who buy its major electronic products, such as large-screen televisions and videotape recorders, from specified retail dealers. Under the plan, approved customers who make purchases in July 1996 do not have to make any payments until September 1997 and pay no interest for the intervening months. Mitsubishi pays the dealer the full amount less a small fee, sends the customer a Mitsubishi credit card, and collects from the customer at the specified time. What was Mitsubishi's motivation for establishing such generous credit terms? What costs are involved? What are the accounting implications?

SD 3. LO 1 *Receivables Financing*

Siegel Appliances, Inc., is a small manufacturer of washing machines and dryers located in central Michigan. Siegel sells most of its appliances to large, established discount retail companies that market the appliances under their own names. Siegel sells the appliances on trade credit terms of n/60. If a customer wants a longer term, however, Siegel will accept a note with a term of up to nine months. At present, the company is having cash flow troubles and needs $5 million immediately. Its cash balance is $200,000, its accounts receivable balance is $2.3 million, and its notes receivable balance is $3.7 million. How might Siegel's management use its accounts receivable and notes receivable to raise the cash it needs? What are the company's prospects for raising the needed cash?

Group Activity: Assign to in-class groups and debrief.

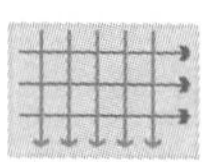

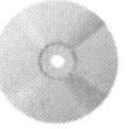

Communication | Critical Thinking | Group Activity | Memo | Ethics | International | Spreadsheet | General Ledger | CD-ROM | Internet

SD 4.
LO 4 *Estimation of Percentage of Uncollectible Accounts Receivable*

All companies that sell on credit face the risk of bad debt losses. For example, in 1995, ***L.A. Gear Inc.,*** a well-known maker of athletic footwear, had an allowance for uncollectible accounts of $7.6 million on gross accounts receivable of $54.2 million. Its 1995 sales were $296.6 million.[15] The percentage of uncollectible accounts receivable for 1995 was 14 percent of gross accounts receivable. What factors would determine the percentage uncollectible used by L.A. Gear Inc.? If actual collections of 1995 year-end receivables were less than $46.6 million ($54.2 − $7.6), how would the financial statements for 1995 and 1996 be affected?

ETHICAL DILEMMA

SD 5.
LO 1 *Ethics, Uncollectible*
LO 4 *Accounts, and Short-Term Objectives*

Fitzsimmons Designs, a successful retail furniture company, is located in an affluent suburb where a major insurance company has just announced a restructuring that will lay off 4,000 employees. Fitzsimmons sells quality furniture, usually on credit. Accounts Receivable represents one of the major assets of the company and, although the company's annual uncollectible accounts losses are not out of line, they represent a sizable amount. The company depends on bank loans for its financing. Sales and net income have declined in the past year, and some customers are falling behind in paying their accounts. George Fitzsimmons, owner of the business, knows that the bank's loan officer likes to see a steady performance. Therefore, he has instructed the controller to underestimate the uncollectible accounts this year to show a small growth in earnings. Fitzsimmons believes the short-term action is justified because future successful years will average out the losses, and since the company has a history of success, the adjustments are meaningless accounting measures anyway. Are Fitzsimmons's actions ethical? Would any parties be harmed by his actions? How important is it to try to be accurate in estimating losses from uncollectible accounts?

Group Activity: Assign to in-class groups and debate the ethical issues.

RESEARCH ACTIVITY

SD 6.
LO 1 *Stock and Treasury*
LO 3 *Investments*

Find a recent issue of *The Wall Street Journal* in your school library. Turn to the third, or C, section, entitled "Money & Investing." From the index at the top of the page, locate the listing of New York Stock Exchange (NYSE) stocks and turn to that page. From the listing of stocks, find five companies you have heard of, such as IBM, Deere, McDonald's, or Ford. Or, through the Needles Accounting Resource Center Web site at http://www.hmco.com/college/needles/home.html, access the home page of a broker such as Charles E. Schwab, Dean Witter, or A. G. Edwards. Locate the market listings and select five companies. Then, copy down the range of each company's stock price for the last year and the current closing price. Also, copy down the dividend, if any, per share. How much did the market values of the common stocks you picked vary in the last year? Do these data demonstrate the need to value short-term investments of this type at market? How does accounting for short-term investments in these common stocks differ from accounting for short-term investments in U.S. Treasury bills? How are dividends received on investments in these common stocks accounted for? Be prepared to hand in your notes and to discuss the results of your investigation in class.

DECISION-MAKING PRACTICE

SD 7.
LO 3 *Accounting for Short-Term Investments*

Norman Christmas Tree Company's business—the growing and selling of Christmas trees—is seasonal. By January 1, after its heavy selling season, the company has cash on hand that will not be needed for several months. The company has minimal expenses from January to October and heavy expenses during the harvest and shipping months of November and December. The company's management follows the practice of investing the idle cash in marketable securities, which can be sold as the funds are needed for operations. The company's fiscal year ends on June 30. On January 10 of the current year, the company has cash of $472,300 on hand. It keeps $20,000 on hand for operating expenses and invests the rest as follows:

$100,000 3-month Treasury bills	$ 97,800
1,000 shares of Ford Motor Co. ($30 per share)	30,000
2,500 shares of McDonald's ($50 per share)	125,000
2,100 shares of IBM ($95 per share)	199,500
Total short-term investments	$452,300

During the next few months, the company receives two quarterly cash dividends from each company (assume February 10 and May 10): $1 per share from Ford, $.125 per share from McDonald's, and $1.10 per share from IBM. The Treasury bills are redeemed at face value on April 10. On June 1 management sells 500 shares of McDonald's at $55 per share. On June 30 the market values of the investments are:

Ford Motor Co.	$41 per share
McDonald's	$46 per share
IBM	$90 per share

Another quarterly dividend is received from each company (assume August 10). All the remaining shares are sold on November 1 at the following prices:

Ford Motor Co.	$35 per share
McDonald's	$44 per share
IBM	$110 per share

REQUIRED

1. Record the investment transactions that occurred on January 10, February 10, April 10, May 10, and June 1. The Treasury bills are accounted for as held-to-maturity securities, and the stocks are trading securities. Prepare the required adjusting entry on June 30, and record the investment transactions on August 10 and November 1.
2. Explain how the short-term investments would be shown on the balance sheet on June 30.
3. After November 1, what is the balance of Allowance to Adjust Short-Term Investments to Market, and what will happen to this account next June?
4. What is your assessment of Norman Christmas Tree Company's strategy with regard to idle cash?

Financial Reporting and Analysis

INTERPRETING FINANCIAL REPORTS

FRA 1.

LO 1 LO 4 *Unbilled Accounts Receivable, Estimate of Uncollectibles, and Financial Ratios*

Systems & Computer Technology Corporation (SCT Corp) derives revenue primarily from OnSite services contracts, software sales and services, and maintenance and enhancements. The following is excerpted from the consolidated statements of operations for SCT Corporation:

	Year Ended September 30,	
Revenues	**1996**	1995
OnSite services	**$ 84,183,000**	$ 66,904,000
Software sales	**46,821,000**	40,376,000
Maintenance and enhancements	**42,013,000**	35,145,000
Software services	**41,552,000**	31,631,000
Interest and other revenue	**689,000**	2,092,000
	$215,258,000	$176,148,000

Fees from OnSite services are typically based on multiyear contracts ranging from five to ten years and provide a recurring revenue stream throughout the term of the contract.

For a typical OnSite services contract, services are performed and expenses are incurred by the company at a greater rate during the first several years than in the later years of the contract. Billings usually remain constant over the term of the contract. Revenue is recorded as work is performed; therefore, revenues usually exceed billings in the early years of the contract. The resulting excess is reflected on the company's balance sheet as unbilled accounts receivable as shown:

	September 30,	
	1996	1995
Current Assets		
Cash and short-term investments	**$12,303,000**	$15,312,000
Receivables, including $55,146,000 and $49,602,000 of earned revenues in excess of billings, net of allowance for doubtful accounts of $1,590,000 and $1,003,000	**77,161,000**	70,270,000
Prepaid expenses and other receivables	**10,208,000**	9,994,000
Total Current Assets	**$99,672,000**	$95,576,000

Of these unbilled receivables at September 30, 1996, 99 percent will be billed within the normal twelve-month business cycle, although unbilled receivables will continue to build. Total assets were $163.3 million and $151 million in 1996 and 1995, respectively.[16]

REQUIRED

1. Compute the ratio of receivables to total assets, the ratio of unbilled receivables to total receivables, and the ratio of unbilled receivables to OnSite revenues for both 1996 and 1995. Discuss how SCT's revenue recognition policy affects net income and cash flows.
2. Compute the percentage of gross receivables that the allowance for doubtful accounts represents. What does the change in the allowance imply?
3. Compute the 1996 receivable turnover. Exclude interest and other revenue from the computation. Discuss the impact of unbilled receivables on this ratio.

FRA 2. LO 4 *Accounting for Accounts Receivable*

Certified Co. is a major consumer goods company that sells over three thousand products in 135 countries. The company's annual report to the Securities and Exchange Commission presented the following data (in thousands) pertaining to net sales and accounts related to accounts receivable for 1997, 1998, and 1999:

	1999	1998	1997
Net Sales	$4,910,000	$4,865,000	$4,888,000
Accounts Receivable	523,000	524,000	504,000
Allowance for Uncollectible Accounts	18,600	21,200	24,500
Uncollectible Accounts Expense	15,000	16,700	15,800
Uncollectible Accounts Written Off	19,300	20,100	17,700
Recoveries of Accounts Previously Written Off	1,700	100	1,000

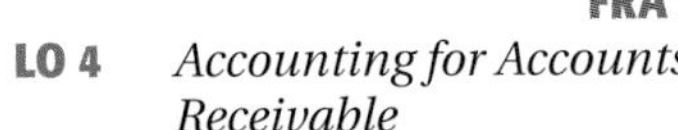

REQUIRED

1. Compute the ratios of Uncollectible Accounts Expense to Net Sales and to Accounts Receivable and of Allowance for Uncollectible Accounts to Accounts Receivable for 1997, 1998, and 1999.
2. Compute the receivable turnover and average days' sales uncollected for each year, assuming 1996 net accounts receivable are $465,000,000.
3. What is your interpretation of the ratios? What appears to be management's attitude with respect to the collectibility of accounts receivable over the three-year period?

INTERNATIONAL COMPANY

FRA 3. LO 1 *Interpretation of Ratios*

Philips Electronics, N.V., and ***Heineken, N.V.,*** are two of the most famous Dutch companies. Philips is a large, diversified electronics, music, and media company, and Heineken makes a popular beer. Philips is about six times bigger than Heineken, with 1995 revenues of 119 billion guilders versus 16 billion guilders. Ratios can help in comparing and understanding the companies. For example, the receivable turnovers for the companies for two past years are as follows:

	1995	1994
Philips	5.2 times	5.1 times
Heineken	8.0 times	8.3 times

What do the ratios tell you about the credit policies of the two companies? How long does it take each on average to collect a receivable? What do the ratios tell about the companies' relative needs for capital to finance receivables? Can you tell which company has a better credit policy? Explain your answers.

Toys "R" Us Annual Report

FRA 4.
LO 1 *Analysis of Short-Term*
LO 2 *Liquid Assets*
LO 4

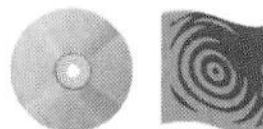

Refer to the Toys "R" Us annual report to answer the following questions.

1. How much cash and cash equivalents did Toys "R" Us have in 1997? Do you suppose most of that amount is cash in the bank or cash equivalents?
2. Toys "R" Us does not disclose an allowance for uncollectible accounts. How do you explain the lack of disclosure?
3. Compute the quick ratios for 1996 and 1997 and comment on them.
4. Compute receivable turnover and average days' sales uncollected for 1996 and 1997 and comment on Toys "R" Us credit policies. Accounts Receivable in 1995 were $115,900,000.

Fingraph® Financial Analyst™

FRA 5.
LO 1 *Analysis of Short-Term Liquid Assets*

Choose any two companies from the same industry in the Fingraph® Financial Analyst™ CD-ROM software. The industry chosen should be one in which accounts receivable is likely to be an important current asset. Suggested industries from which to choose are manufacturing, consumer products, consumer food and beverage, and computers.

1. Find and read in the annual reports for the companies you have selected any reference to cash and cash equivalents, short-term or marketable securities, and accounts receivable in the summary of significant accounting policies or notes to the financial statements.
2. Display and print for the companies you have selected (a) the Current Assets and Current Liabilities Analysis page and (b) the Liquidity and Asset Utilization Analysis page in tabular and graphical form. Prepare a table that compares the quick ratio, receivable turnover, and average days' receivable for both companies for two years.
3. Find and read the liquidity analysis section of management's discussion and analysis in each annual report.
4. Write a one-page executive summary that highlights the accounting policies for short-term liquid assets and compares the short-term liquidity position of the two companies. Include your assessment of the companies' relative liquidity and make reference to management's assessment. Include the Fingraph® pages and your table as an attachment to your report.

ENDNOTES

1. Pioneer Electronic Corporation, *Annual Report,* 1996.
2. Michael Selz, "Big Customers' Late Bills Choke Small Suppliers," *The Wall Street Journal,* June 22, 1994.
3. American Greetings Corp., *Annual Report,* 1996.
4. Adapted from Circuit City Stores, Inc., *Annual Report,* 1997.
5. Dave Kansas and Randall Smith, "How Much Cash a Firm Should Keep Is at Issue in Wake of Chrysler Bid," *The Wall Street Journal,* April 20, 1995.
6. Jeffrey Taylor, "Rules on Electronic Transfers of Money Are Being Tightened by U.S. Treasury," *The Wall Street Journal,* September 26, 1994.

7. Bell Atlantic Corporation, *Annual Report,* 1996.
8. *Accounting Trends & Techniques* (New York: American Institute of CPAs, 1997), p. 142.
9. Bell Atlantic Corporation, *Annual Report,* 1996.
10. *Statement of Financial Accounting Standards No. 115,* "Accounting for Certain Investments in Debt and Equity Securities" (Norwalk, Conn.: Financial Accounting Standards Board, 1993).
11. The purpose of Allowance for Uncollectible Accounts is to reduce the gross accounts receivable to the amount estimated to be collectible (net realizable value). The purpose of another contra account, Accumulated Depreciation, is *not* to reduce the gross plant and equipment accounts to realizable value. Rather, its purpose is to show how much of the cost of the plant and equipment has been allocated as an expense to previous accounting periods.
12. Craig S. Smith, "Chinese Companies Writing Off Old Debt," *The Wall Street Journal,* December 28, 1995.
13. Some firms may follow the practice of reversing the September 30 adjusting entry. Here we assume that a reversing entry is not made.
14. Information based on promotional brochures received from Mitsubishi Electric Corp.
15. L.A. Gear Inc., *Annual Report,* 1995.
16. Systems and Computer Technology Corporation, *Annual Report,* 1996.

RIGHT TRACK™
by THE JUNCTION
S
65% POLYESTER
COTTON

Inventories

LEARNING OBJECTIVES

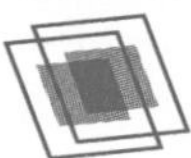

1. **Identify and explain the management issues associated with accounting for inventories.**
2. **Define *inventory cost* and relate it to goods flow and cost flow.**
3. **Calculate the pricing of inventory, using the cost basis under the periodic inventory system, according to the (a) specific identification method; (b) average-cost method; (c) first-in, first-out (FIFO) method; and (d) last-in, first-out (LIFO) method.**
4. **Apply the perpetual inventory system to the pricing of inventories at cost.**
5. **State the effects of inventory methods and misstatements of inventory on income determination and income taxes.**
6. **Apply the lower-of-cost-or-market (LCM) rule to inventory valuation.**

SUPPLEMENTAL OBJECTIVE

7. **Estimate the cost of ending inventory using the (a) retail inventory method and (b) gross profit method.**

DECISION POINT

J.C. PENNEY COMPANY, INC.

The management of inventory for profit is one of management's most complex and challenging tasks. In terms of dollars, the inventory of goods held for sale is one of the largest assets of a merchandising business. As a major retailer, with department stores in all fifty states and Puerto Rico, J.C. Penney Company, Inc., devotes almost 26 percent, or $5.7 billion, of its $22.1 billion in assets to inventories.[1] What challenges does J.C. Penney's management face in managing its inventory?

Not only must J.C. Penney's management purchase fashions and other merchandise that customers will want to buy, but it must also have the merchandise available in the right locations at the times when customers want to buy it. It also must try to minimize the cost of inventory while maintaining quality. To these ends, J.C. Penney maintains purchasing offices throughout the world, including Hong Kong, Taipei, Osaka, Seoul, Bangkok, Singapore, Bombay, and Florence. Quality assurance experts operate out of twenty-two domestic and fourteen international offices. Further, the amount of money tied up in inventory must be controlled because of the high cost of borrowing funds and storing inventory. Important accounting decisions include what assumptions to make about the flow of inventory costs, what prices to put on inventory, what inventory systems to use, and how to protect inventory against loss. Proper management of inventory helped J.C. Penney earn net income of $565 million in 1996, but small variations in any inventory decision can mean the difference between a net profit and a net loss.

Critical Thinking Question: How does competition influence inventory management issues? **Answer:** Profit making in a competitive environment requires management to control costs. For example, many businesses have reduced the level of excess inventory carried and place orders so that goods are received "just in time." This approach reduces financing and storage costs and requires suppliers to meet orders quickly.

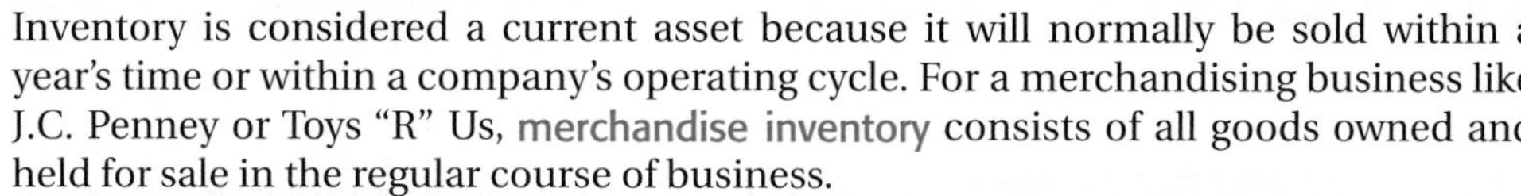

Management Issues Associated with Accounting for Inventories

OBJECTIVE 1

Identify and explain the management issues associated with accounting for inventories

Related Text Assignments:
Q: 1, 2, 3
SE: 1, 2
E: 1, 2
P: 1, 6
SD: 1, 4
FRA: 1, 3, 4, 5

Inventory is considered a current asset because it will normally be sold within a year's time or within a company's operating cycle. For a merchandising business like J.C. Penney or Toys "R" Us, merchandise inventory consists of all goods owned and held for sale in the regular course of business.

Inventories are also important for manufacturing companies. Because manufacturers are engaged in the actual making of products, they have three kinds of inventory: raw materials to be used in the production of goods, partially completed products (often called *work in process*), and finished goods ready for sale. For example, in its 1996 annual report, the National Semiconductor Corporation disclosed the following inventories (in millions):

Financial Highlights

	1996	1995
Inventories		
Raw materials	$ 39.1	$ 33.9
Work in process	208.5	165.9
Finished goods	78.1	63.2
Total inventories	$325.7	$263.0

Common Student Confusion: Even though merchandise inventory is one of a business's largest assets (in terms of dollars), students have difficulty envisioning it as a major asset since it often comprises thousands of items. A $2 million building is easier to visualize than $2 million in inventory.

In manufacturing operations, the costs of the work in process and the finished goods inventories include not only the cost of the raw materials that go into the product, but also the cost of the labor used to convert the raw materials to finished goods and the overhead costs that support the production process. Included in this latter category are such costs as indirect materials (for example, paint, glue, and nails), indirect labor (such as the salaries of supervisors), factory rent, depreciation of plant assets, utilities costs, and insurance costs. The methods for maintaining and pricing inventory explained in this chapter are applicable to manufactured goods, but since the details of accounting for manufacturing companies are usually covered as a managerial accounting topic, this chapter focuses on accounting for merchandising firms.

Applying the Matching Rule to Inventories

Point to Emphasize: Remind students that merchandise inventory appears on both the income statement and the balance sheet.

The American Institute of Certified Public Accountants states, "A major objective of accounting for inventories is the proper determination of income through the process of matching appropriate costs against revenues."[2] Note that the objective is the proper determination of income through the matching of costs and revenues, not the determination of the most realistic inventory value. These two objectives are sometimes incompatible, in which case the objective of income determination takes precedence.

The reason inventory accounting is so important to income measurement is linked to the way income is measured on the merchandising income statement. Recall that gross margin is computed as the difference between net sales and cost of goods sold and that cost of goods sold is dependent on the cost assigned to inventory or goods not sold. Because of those relationships, the higher the cost of ending inventory, the lower the cost of goods sold and the higher the resulting gross margin. Conversely, the lower the value assigned to ending inventory, the higher the cost of goods sold and the lower the gross margin. Because the amount of gross margin has a direct effect on the amount of net income, the amount assigned to ending inventory directly affects the amount of net income. *In effect, the value assigned to the ending inventory determines what portion of the cost of goods available for sale is assigned to cost of goods sold and what portion is assigned to the balance sheet as inventory to be carried over into the next accounting period.*

Assessing the Impact of Inventory Decisions

Figure 1 summarizes the management choices with regard to inventory systems and methods. The decisions usually result in different amounts of reported net income and, as a result, affect both the external evaluation of the company by investors and creditors and such internal evaluations as performance reviews, bonuses, and executive compensation. Because income is affected, the valuation of inventory may also have a considerable effect on the amount of income taxes paid. Federal income tax authorities have, therefore, been interested in the effects of various inventory valuation methods and have specific regulations about the acceptability of different methods. As a result, management is sometimes faced with the problem of balancing the goal of proper income determination with that of minimizing income taxes. Another consideration is that since the choice of inventory valuation method affects the amount of income taxes paid, it also affects a company's cash flows.

Evaluating the Level of Inventory

Discussion Question: What are some of the costs associated with carrying inventory? **Answer:** Insurance, property tax, and storage costs. There is also the possibility of additional spoilage and employee theft.

The level of inventory has important economic consequences for a company. Ideally, management wants to have a great variety and quantity on hand so that customers have a large choice and do not have to wait. Such an inventory policy is not

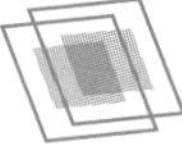

Enrichment Note: Management considers the behavior of inventory prices over time when selecting inventory costing methods.

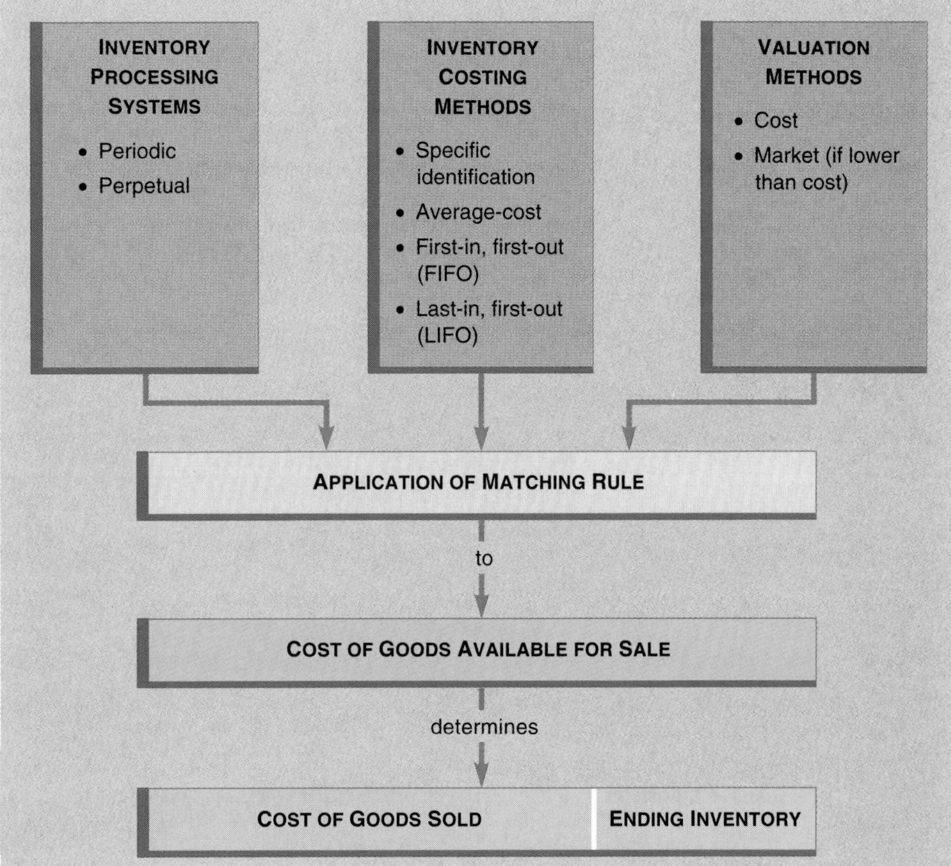

Figure 1
Management Choices in Accounting for Inventories

Instructional Strategy: Instead of lecturing on evaluating the level of inventory, assign SD 1 to small groups. Debrief the case by capturing results on the chalkboard or other media. Ask for a student volunteer to summarize the main points and close the exercise.

costless, however. The cost of handling and storage and the interest cost of the funds necessary to maintain high inventory levels are usually substantial. On the other hand, the maintenance of low inventory levels may result in lost sales and disgruntled customers. Common measures used in the evaluation of inventory levels are inventory turnover and its related measure, average days' inventory on hand. Inventory turnover is a measure similar to receivable turnover. It indicates the number of times a company's average inventory is sold during an accounting period. Inventory turnover is computed by dividing cost of goods sold by average inventory. For example, J.C. Penney's cost of goods sold was \$16.043 billion in 1996, and its merchandise inventory was \$5.722 billion at the end of 1996 and \$3.935 billion at the end of 1995. Its inventory turnover is computed as follows:

$$\text{Inventory Turnover} = \frac{\text{Cost of Goods Sold}}{\text{Average Inventory}}$$

$$= \frac{\$16{,}043{,}000{,}000}{(\$5{,}722{,}000{,}000 + \$3{,}935{,}000{,}000)/2}$$

$$= \frac{\$16{,}043{,}000{,}000}{\$4{,}828{,}500{,}000} = 3.3 \text{ times}$$

The average days' inventory on hand indicates the average number of days required to sell the inventory on hand. It is found by dividing the number of days in a year by the inventory turnover, as follows:

$$\text{Average Days' Inventory on Hand} = \frac{\text{Number of Days in a Year}}{\text{Inventory Turnover}}$$

$$= \frac{365 \text{ days}}{3.3 \text{ times}} = 110.6 \text{ days}$$

J.C. Penney turned its inventory over 3.3 times in 1996, or on average every 110.6 days. These figures are reasonable because J.C. Penney is in a business where fashions change every season, or about every 100 days. Management would want to sell all of each season's inventory within 90 days, even while making purchases for the next season. There are natural levels of inventory in every industry, as shown for selected merchandising and manufacturing industries in Figures 2 and 3. However, companies that are able to maintain their inventories at lower levels and still satisfy customer needs are the most successful.

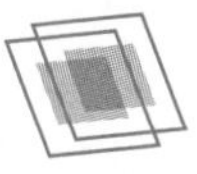

Enrichment Note: Inventory turnover will be systematically higher if year-end inventory levels are low. For example, Toys "R" Us inventory levels on January 31 are at their lowest point of the year.

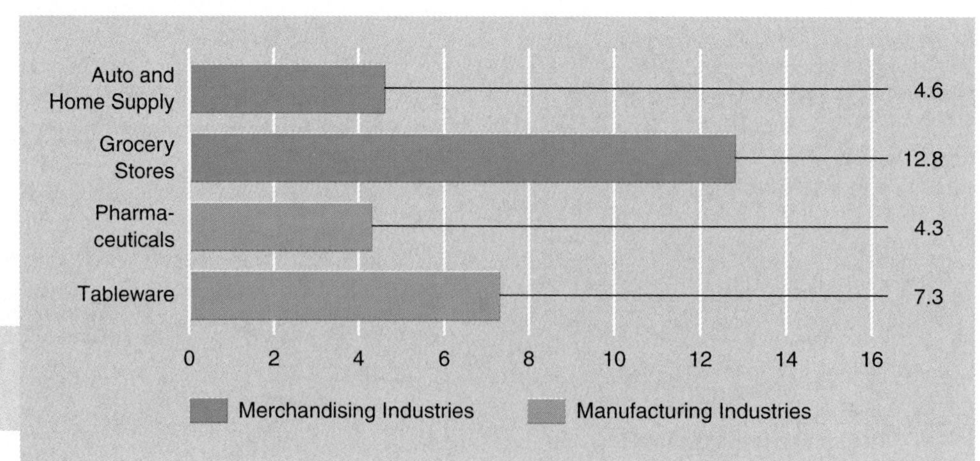

Figure 2
Inventory Turnover for Selected Industries

Source: Data from Dun & Bradstreet, *Industry Norms and Key Business Ratios,* 1996–97.

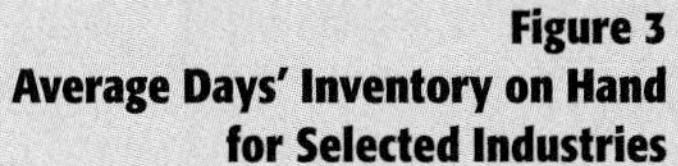

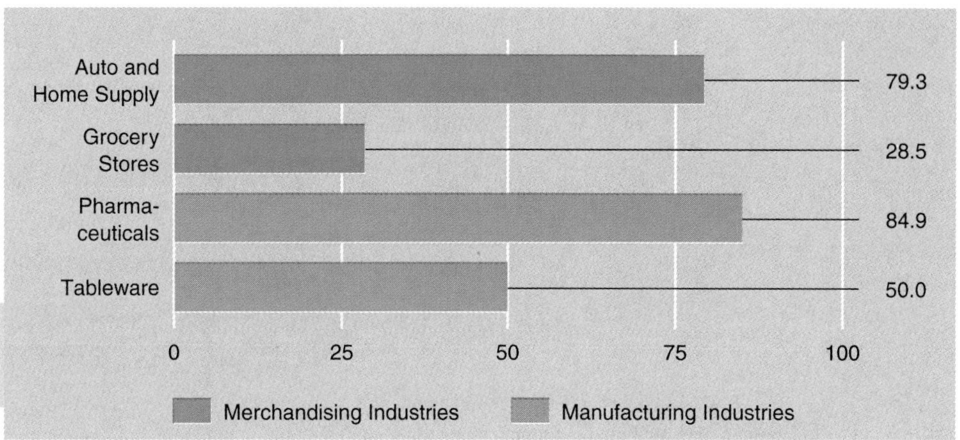

Figure 3
Average Days' Inventory on Hand for Selected Industries

Source: Data from Dun & Bradstreet, *Industry Norms and Key Business Ratios,* 1996–97.

Merchandising and manufacturing companies are attempting to reduce their levels of inventory by changing to a just-in-time operating environment. In such an environment, rather than stockpiling inventories for later use, companies work closely with suppliers to coordinate and schedule shipments so that goods arrive just at the time they are needed. Less money is tied up in inventories, and the costs associated with carrying inventories are reduced. For example, Pacific Bell was able to close six warehouses by implementing just-in-time inventory management.

Pricing Inventory Under the Periodic Inventory System

OBJECTIVE 2

Define inventory cost *and relate it to* goods flow *and* cost flow

Related Text Assignments:
Q: 4, 5, 6
SD: 5
FRA: 1

According to the AICPA, "The primary basis of accounting for inventories is cost, which has been defined generally as the price paid or consideration given to acquire an asset."[3] This definition of inventory cost has generally been interpreted to include the following costs: (1) invoice price less purchases discounts; (2) freight or transportation in, including insurance in transit; and (3) applicable taxes and tariffs. There are other costs—for ordering, receiving, and storing—that should in principle also be included in inventory cost. In practice, however, it is so difficult to allocate such costs to specific inventory items that they are usually considered expenses of the accounting period instead of inventory costs.

BUSINESS BULLETIN: BUSINESS PRACTICE

Managing the level of inventories is critical to a company's success. In 1995, Apple Computer, Inc.'s, earnings fell 48 percent in the fourth quarter because management grossly underestimated the market demand for the company's popular Macintosh computer based on the PowerPC processor. Apple's decision severely hurt the company's market share. Management responded by gearing up for what it saw as continuing strong demand.[4] By early 1996, only six months later, when inventories had been built up, demand had fallen off. Apple incurred a $740 million loss, the largest in its history. More than half the loss went to writing down the value of inventory it now could not sell.[5] After this fiasco, Apple's chief executive was replaced and the company's stature diminished rapidly.

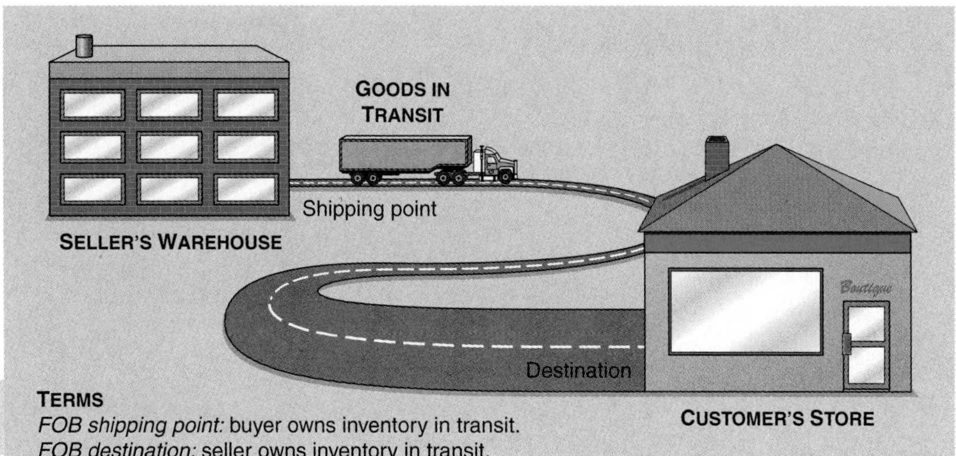

Figure 4
Merchandise in Transit

Business-World Example: When a customer orders merchandise from a catalogue company, he or she pays not only the price listed in the catalogue, but also such charges as shipping and insurance. Consequently, the cost is greater than the catalogue price.

Common Student Error: It would be helpful to review the terms *FOB shipping point* and *FOB destination,* as students often confuse the two.

Discussion Question: Who is responsible for taking and pricing the inventory? **Answer:** Company management is responsible for taking and pricing the inventory. Auditors observe that the inventory is properly taken and priced.

Merchandise in Transit

Because merchandise inventory includes all items owned by a company and held for sale, the status of any merchandise in transit, whether it is being sold or being purchased by the inventorying company, must be examined to determine if the merchandise should be included in the inventory count. As Figure 4 illustrates, neither the customer nor the buyer has physical possession of the merchandise. Ownership of these goods in transit is determined by the terms of the shipping agreement, which indicate whether title has passed. Outgoing goods shipped FOB (free on board) destination would be included in merchandise inventory, whereas those shipped FOB shipping point would not. Conversely, incoming goods shipped FOB shipping point would be included in merchandise inventory, but those shipped FOB destination would not.

Merchandise on Hand Not Included in Inventory

Point to Emphasize: Stress that the consignor will count as inventory all merchandise placed (consigned) at other locations.

At the time a physical inventory is taken, there may be merchandise on hand to which the company does not hold title. One category of such goods is merchandise that has been sold and is awaiting delivery to the buyer. Since the sale has been completed, title to the goods has passed to the buyer, and the merchandise should not be included in inventory. A second category is goods held on consignment. A consignment is merchandise placed by its owner (known as the *consignor*) on the premises of another company (the *consignee*) with the understanding that payment is expected only when the merchandise is sold and that unsold items may be returned to the consignor. Title to consigned goods remains with the consignor until the consignee sells the goods. Consigned goods should not be included in the physical inventory of the consignee because they still belong to the consignor.

Methods of Pricing Inventory at Cost

Enrichment Note: Businesses usually try to have the actual flow of inventory proceed in a FIFO manner. This means that the oldest merchandise would be sold first, leaving the freshest merchandise in inventory.

The prices of most kinds of merchandise vary during the year. Identical lots of merchandise may have been purchased at different prices. Also, when identical items are bought and sold, it is often impossible to tell which have been sold and which are still in inventory. For this reason, it is necessary to make an assumption about the order in which items have been sold. Because the assumed order of sale may or may not be the same as the actual order of sale, the assumption is really about the *flow of costs* rather than the *flow of physical inventory.*

The term goods flow refers to the actual physical movement of goods in the operations of a company, and the term cost flow refers to the association of costs with their *assumed* flow in the operations of a company. The assumed cost flow may or may not be the same as the actual goods flow. The possibility of a difference between cost flow and goods flow may seem strange at first, but it arises because several choices of assumed cost flow are available under generally accepted accounting principles. In fact, it is sometimes preferable to use an assumed cost flow that bears no relationship to goods flow because it gives a better estimate of income, which is the main goal of inventory valuation.

Accountants usually price inventory by using one of the following generally accepted methods, each based on a different assumption of cost flow: (1) specific identification method; (2) average-cost method; (3) first-in, first-out (FIFO) method; and (4) last-in, first-out (LIFO) method. The choice of method depends on the nature of the business, the financial effects of the methods, and the costs of implementing the methods.

To illustrate the four methods under the periodic inventory system, the following data for the month of June will be used.

Inventory Data—June 30

June 1	Inventory	50 units @ $1.00	$ 50
6	Purchase	50 units @ $1.10	55
13	Purchase	150 units @ $1.20	180
20	Purchase	100 units @ $1.30	130
25	Purchase	150 units @ $1.40	210
Goods Available for Sale		500 units	$625
Sales		280 units	
On hand June 30		220 units	

Notice that there is a total of 500 units available for sale at a total cost of $625. Stated simply, the problem of inventory pricing is to divide the $625 between the 280 units sold and the 220 units on hand. Recall that under the periodic inventory system, the inventory is not updated after each purchase and sale. Thus it is not necessary to know when the individual sales take place.

OBJECTIVE 3a

Calculate the pricing of inventory, using the cost basis under the periodic inventory system, according to the specific identification method

Related Text Assignments:
Q: 7, 8, 9
SE: 3, 4, 5, 6
E: 3, 4, 5, 7, 9
P: 1, 2, 6, 7

Specific Identification Method If the units in the ending inventory can be identified as coming from specific purchases, the specific identification method may be used to price the inventory by identifying the cost of each item in ending inventory. For instance, assume that the June 30 inventory consisted of 50 units from the June 1 inventory, 100 units from the purchase of June 13, and 70 units from the purchase of June 25. The cost assigned to the inventory under the specific identification method would be $268, determined as follows:

Periodic Inventory System—Specific Identification Method

50 units @ $1.00	$ 50	Cost of Goods Available for Sale	$625
100 units @ $1.20	120		
70 units @ $1.40	98	→ Less June 30 Inventory	268
220 units at a cost of	$268	Cost of Goods Sold	$357

The specific identification method might be used in the purchase and sale of high-priced articles, such as automobiles, heavy equipment, and works of art. Although this method may appear logical, it is not used by many companies

Discussion Question: Even if it were possible to track each individual inventory item, why would a company not do so? **Answer:** It would be excessively expensive to track which items were left in inventory. The cost would clearly exceed the benefit.

because it has two definite disadvantages. First, in many cases, it is difficult and impractical to keep track of the purchase and sale of individual items. Second, when a company deals in items that are identical but were purchased at different costs, deciding which items are sold becomes arbitrary; thus the company can raise or lower income by choosing to sell the lower- or higher-cost items.

OBJECTIVE 3b

Calculate the pricing of inventory, using the cost basis under the periodic inventory system, according to the average-cost method

Average-Cost Method Under the average-cost method, inventory is priced at the average cost of the goods available for sale during the period. Average cost is computed by dividing the total cost of goods available for sale by the total units available for sale. This gives an average unit cost that is applied to the units in ending inventory. In our illustration, the ending inventory would be $275, or $1.25 per unit, determined as follows:

Periodic Inventory System—Average-Cost Method

Cost of Goods Available for Sale ÷ Units Available for Sale = Average Unit Cost

$625 ÷ 500 units = $1.25

Ending Inventory: 220 units @ $1.25 =	$275
Cost of Goods Available for Sale	$625
Less June 30 Inventory	275
Cost of Goods Sold	$350

Business-World Example: The physical flow of goods sometimes may seem to dictate a particular method, such as in a milk producer's operations in which the perishable nature of the product requires a *physical flow* of FIFO. However, the milk producer's management can choose an inventory method based on an assumed *cost flow* that differs from FIFO such as average cost or LIFO.

The average-cost method tends to level out the effects of cost increases and decreases because the cost for the ending inventory calculated under this method is influenced by all the prices paid during the year and by the beginning inventory price. Some, however, criticize the average-cost method because they believe that recent costs are more relevant for income measurement and decision making.

OBJECTIVE 3c

Calculate the pricing of inventory, using the cost basis under the periodic inventory system, according to the first-in, first-out (FIFO) method

First-In, First-Out (FIFO) Method The first-in, first-out (FIFO) method is based on the assumption that the costs of the first items acquired should be assigned to the first items sold. The costs of the goods on hand at the end of a period are assumed to be from the most recent purchases, and the costs assigned to goods that have been sold are assumed to be from the earliest purchases. The FIFO method of determining inventory cost may be adopted by any business, regardless of the actual physical flow of goods, because the assumption is made regarding the flow of costs and not the flow of goods.

In our illustration, the June 30 inventory would be $301 when the FIFO method is used. It is computed as follows:

Periodic Inventory System—First-In, First-Out Method

150 units @ $1.40 from purchase of June 25	$210
70 units @ $1.30 from purchase of June 20	91
220 units at a cost of	$301
Cost of Goods Available for Sale	$625
Less June 30 Inventory	301
Cost of Goods Sold	$324

Enrichment Note: When you make a FIFO cost flow assumption, you use it even if you can prove that one of the first-purchased items is still in inventory. Let's say that for the first week of January, perfume was packaged in blue boxes, and then the company changed to red packaging. When you price inventory using the FIFO method, you assume the blue boxes (the older merchandise) were sold, even if you have some of them left in inventory.

The effect of the FIFO method is to value the ending inventory at the most recent costs and include earlier costs in cost of goods sold. During periods of consistently rising prices, the FIFO method yields the highest possible amount of net income, since cost of goods sold will show costs closer to the price level at the time the goods were purchased. Another reason for this result is that businesses tend to increase selling prices as costs rise, even when inventories were purchased before the price rise. The reverse effect occurs in periods of price decreases. Consequently, a major criticism of FIFO is that it magnifies the effects of the business cycle on income.

Last-In, First-Out (LIFO) Method The last-in, first-out (LIFO) method of costing inventories is based on the assumption that the costs of the last items purchased should be assigned to the first items sold and that the cost of ending inventory reflects the cost of the merchandise purchased earliest.

OBJECTIVE 3d

Calculate the pricing of inventory, using the cost basis under the periodic inventory system, according to the last-in, first-out (LIFO) method

Under this method, the June 30 inventory would be $249, computed as follows:

Periodic Inventory System—Last-In, First-Out Method

50 units @ $1.00 from June 1 inventory	$ 50
50 units @ $1.10 from purchase of June 6	55
120 units @ $1.20 from purchase of June 13	144
220 units at a cost of	$249
Cost of Goods Available for Sale	$625
Less June 30 Inventory	249
Cost of Goods Sold	$376

Business-World Example: An example of physical flow under LIFO would be a gravel pile. As gravel on top is sold, more is purchased and added on top. The gravel on the bottom may never be sold. Despite this LIFO physical flow, any acceptable cost flow assumption may be made.

Common Student Confusion: Students often reverse FIFO and LIFO. Remind them that under FIFO we assume that the first goods purchased are the first ones sold. Thus, we assume that we still have the ones purchased most recently.

Discussion Question: If your company uses LIFO and the inventory shown on your balance sheet is excessively low by replacement standards, how would you disclose this to the readers of your financial statements? **Answer:** By note.

The effect of LIFO is to value inventory at the earliest prices and to include in cost of goods sold the cost of the most recently purchased goods. This assumption, of course, does not agree with the actual physical movement of goods in most businesses.

There is, however, a strong logical argument to support LIFO, based on the fact that a certain size inventory is necessary in a going concern. When inventory is sold, it must be replaced with more goods. The supporters of LIFO reason that the fairest determination of income occurs if the current costs of merchandise are matched against current sales prices, regardless of which physical units of merchandise are sold. When prices are moving either upward or downward, the cost of goods sold will, under LIFO, show costs closer to the price level at the time the goods were sold. As a result, the LIFO method tends to show a smaller net income during inflationary times and a larger net income during deflationary times than other methods of inventory valuation. The peaks and valleys of the business cycle tend to be smoothed out. In inventory valuation, the flow of costs, and hence income determination, is more important than the physical movement of goods and balance sheet valuation.

BUSINESS BULLETIN: **BUSINESS PRACTICE**

A new type of retail business called the "category killer" seems to ignore the tenets of good inventory management. These retailers, such as The Home Depot, Inc., in home improvements, Barnes & Noble Inc. in bookstores, Wal-Mart Stores, Inc., in groceries and dry goods, Toys "R" Us, Inc., in toys, and Blockbuster Entertainment Corp. in videos, maintain huge inventories at such low prices that smaller competitors find it hard to compete. Although these companies have a large amount of money tied up in inventories, they maintain very sophisticated just-in-time operating environments that require suppliers to meet demanding standards for delivery of products and reduction of inventory costs. Some suppliers are required to stock the shelves and keep track of inventory levels. By minimizing handling and overhead costs and buying at favorably low prices, the category killers achieve great success.

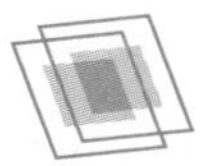

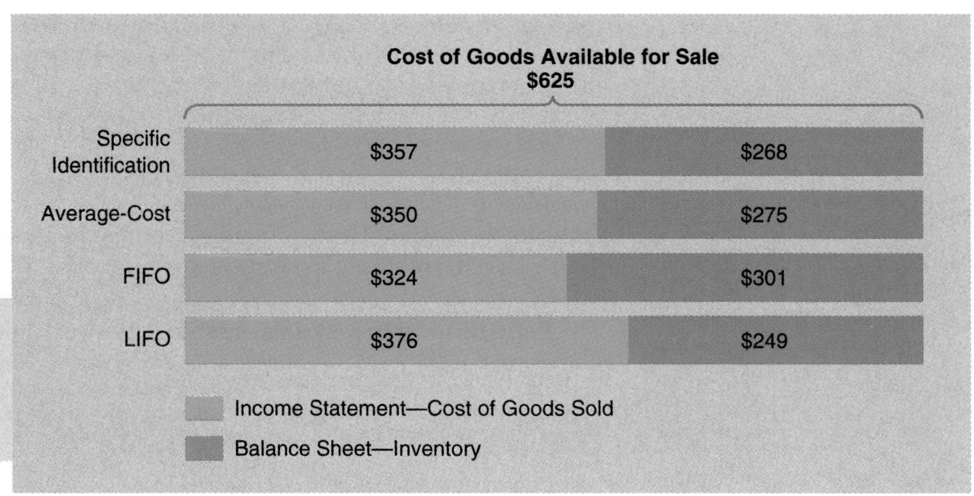

Figure 5
Summary of Cost Flow Assumptions' Impact on Income Statement and Balance Sheet Using Periodic Inventory System

An argument may also be made against the LIFO method. Because the inventory valuation on the balance sheet reflects earlier prices, it often gives an unrealistic picture of the current value of the inventory. Such balance sheet measures as working capital and current ratio may be distorted and must be interpreted carefully.

Figure 5 summarizes the impact of the four inventory cost allocation methods on the cost of goods sold as reported on the income statement and on inventory as reported on the balance sheet when a company uses the periodic inventory system. In periods of rising prices, the FIFO method yields the highest inventory valuation, the lowest cost of goods sold, and hence a higher net income. The LIFO method yields the lowest inventory valuation, the highest cost of goods sold, and thus a lower net income.

Pricing Inventory Under the Perpetual Inventory System

OBJECTIVE 4

Apply the perpetual inventory system to the pricing of inventories at cost

Related Text Assignments:
Q: 10
SE: 7, 8, 9
E: 6, 7
P: 3, 8
SD: 5

The pricing of inventories under the perpetual inventory system differs from pricing under the periodic inventory system. The difference occurs because under the perpetual inventory system, a continuous record of quantities and costs of merchandise is maintained as purchases and sales are made. Under the periodic inventory system, only the ending inventory is counted and priced. Cost of goods sold is determined by deducting the cost of the ending inventory from the cost of goods available for sale. Under the perpetual inventory system, cost of goods sold is accumulated as sales are made and costs are transferred from the Inventory account to Cost of Goods Sold. The cost of the ending inventory is the balance of the Inventory account. To illustrate pricing methods under the perpetual inventory system, the same data will be used as before, but specific sales dates and amounts will be added, as follows:

Inventory Data—June 30

June	1	Inventory	50 units @ $1.00
	6	Purchase	50 units @ $1.10
	10	Sale	70 units
	13	Purchase	150 units @ $1.20
	20	Purchase	100 units @ $1.30
	25	Purchase	150 units @ $1.40
	30	Sale	210 units
	30	Inventory	220 units

Pricing the inventory and cost of goods sold using the specific identification method is the same under the perpetual system as it was under the periodic system because cost of goods sold and ending inventory are based on the cost of the identified items sold and on hand. The perpetual system facilitates the use of the specific identification method because detailed records of purchases and sales are maintained.

Enrichment Note: An automated perpetual system still has considerable costs. These include the cost of automating the system, the cost of maintaining the system, and the cost of taking a physical inventory to check against the perpetual records.

Pricing the inventory and cost of goods sold using the average-cost method differs when the perpetual system is used. Under the periodic system, the average cost is computed for all goods available for sale during the month. Under the perpetual system, a moving average is computed after each purchase or series of purchases preceding the next sale, as follows:

Perpetual Inventory System—Average-Cost Method

June 1	Inventory	50 units @ $1.00	$ 50.00
6	Purchase	50 units @ $1.10	55.00
6	Balance	100 units @ $1.05	$105.00
10	Sale	70 units @ $1.05	(73.50)
10	Balance	30 units @ $1.05	$ 31.50
13	Purchase	150 units @ $1.20	180.00
20	Purchase	100 units @ $1.30	130.00
25	Purchase	150 units @ $1.40	210.00
25	Balance	430 units @ $1.28*	$551.50
30	Sale	210 units @ $1.28	(268.80)
30	Inventory	220 units @ $1.29*	$282.70
Cost of Goods Sold		$73.50 + $268.80	$342.30

*Rounded

The sum of the costs applied to sales becomes the cost of goods sold, $342.30. The ending inventory is the balance, or $282.70.

When pricing the inventory using the FIFO and LIFO methods, it is necessary to keep track of the components of inventory at each step of the way because as sales are made, the costs must be assigned in the proper order. To apply the FIFO method, the approach is as follows:

Perpetual Inventory System—FIFO Method

June 1	Inventory	50 units @ $1.00		$ 50.00
6	Purchase	50 units @ $1.10		55.00
10	Sale	50 units @ $1.00	($ 50.00)	
		20 units @ $1.10	(22.00)	(72.00)
10	Balance	30 units @ $1.10		$ 33.00
13	Purchase	150 units @ $1.20		180.00
20	Purchase	100 units @ $1.30		130.00
25	Purchase	150 units @ $1.40		210.00
30	Sale	30 units @ $1.10	($ 33.00)	
		150 units @ $1.20	(180.00)	
		30 units @ $1.30	(39.00)	(252.00)
30	Inventory	70 units @ $1.30	$ 91.00	
		150 units @ $1.40	210.00	$301.00
Cost of Goods Sold		$72.00 + $252.00		$324.00

Note that the ending inventory of $301 and the cost of goods sold of $324 are the same as the figures computed earlier under the periodic inventory system. This will always occur because the ending inventory under both systems will always consist of the last items purchased—in this case, the entire purchase of June 25 and 70 units from the purchase of June 20.

To apply the LIFO method, the approach is as follows:

Perpetual Inventory System—LIFO Method

June 1	Inventory	50 units @ $1.00		$ 50.00
6	Purchase	50 units @ $1.10		55.00
10	Sale	50 units @ $1.10	($ 55.00)	
		20 units @ $1.00	(20.00)	(75.00)
10	Balance	30 units @ $1.00		$ 30.00
13	Purchase	150 units @ $1.20		180.00
20	Purchase	100 units @ $1.30		130.00
25	Purchase	150 units @ $1.40		210.00
30	Sale	150 units @ $1.40	($210.00)	
		60 units @ $1.30	(78.00)	(288.00)
30	Inventory	30 units @ $1.00	$ 30.00	
		150 units @ $1.20	180.00	
		40 units @ $1.30	52.00	$262.00
Cost of Goods Sold		$75.00 + $288.00		$363.00

Notice that the ending inventory of $262 includes 30 units from the beginning inventory, all the units from the purchase of June 13, and 40 units from the purchase of June 20.

A comparison of the three cost flow assumptions or methods using a perpetual inventory system is shown in Figure 6. The relative relationship of the methods is the same as their relationship under the periodic inventory system, but some amounts have changed. For example, LIFO has the lowest inventory valuation regardless of the inventory system used, but the amount is $262 using the perpetual system versus $249 using the periodic system.

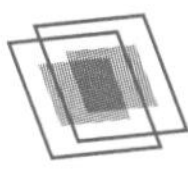

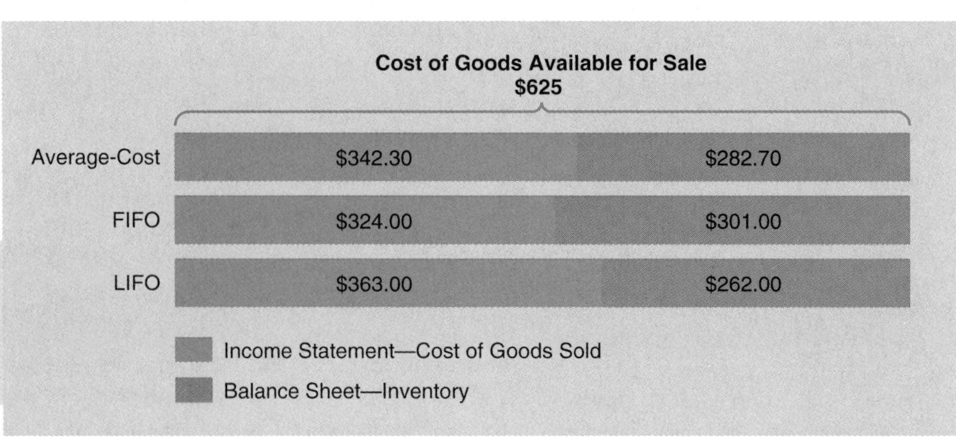

Figure 6
Summary of Cost Flow Assumptions' Impact on Income Statement and Balance Sheet Using Perpetual Inventory System

BUSINESS BULLETIN: TECHNOLOGY IN PRACTICE

Using the LIFO method under the perpetual inventory system is a very tedious process, especially if done manually. However, the development of faster and less expensive computer systems over the past ten years has made it easier for many companies to switch to LIFO and still use the perpetual inventory system. The availability of better technology may partially account for the increasing use of LIFO in the United States and may enable more companies to enjoy LIFO's economic benefits.

Comparison and Impact of Inventory Decisions and Misstatements

OBJECTIVE 5

State the effects of inventory methods and misstatements of inventory on income determination and income taxes

Related Text Assignments:
Q: 11, 12, 13, 14
SE: 10
E: 8, 9, 10
SD: 2, 3, 4, 6
FRA: 1, 2, 3, 4

The specific identification, average-cost, FIFO, and LIFO methods of pricing inventory under both the periodic and the perpetual inventory systems have now been illustrated. The effects of the four methods on net income are shown in Exhibit 1, using the same data as before and assuming June sales of $500. Because the specific identification method is based on actual cost, it is the same under both systems.

Keeping in mind that June was a period of rising prices, we can see that LIFO, which charges the most recent, and, in this case, the highest, prices to cost of goods sold, resulted in the lowest gross margin under both systems. Conversely, FIFO, which charges the earliest, and, in this case, the lowest, prices to cost of goods sold, produced the highest gross margin. The gross margin under the average-cost method is somewhere between those under LIFO and FIFO. Thus, it is clear that the average-cost method has a less pronounced effect. Note that ending inventory and gross margin under FIFO are always the same under both inventory systems.

Exhibit 1. Effects of Inventory Systems and Methods Computed

		Periodic Inventory System			Perpetual Inventory System†		
	Specific Identification Method	Average-Cost Method	First-In, First-Out Method	Last-In, First-Out Method	Average-Cost Method	First-In, First-Out Method	Last-In, First-Out Method
Sales	$500	$500	$500	$500	$500	$500	$500
Cost of Goods Sold							
Beginning Inventory	$ 50	$ 50	$ 50	$ 50			
Purchases	575	575	575	575			
Cost of Goods Available for Sale	$625	$625	$625	$625			
Less Ending Inventory	268	275	301	249	$283*	$301	$262
Cost of Goods Sold	$357	$350	$324	$376	$342*	$324	$363
Gross Margin	$143	$150	$176	$124	$158	$176	$137

*Rounded.
†Ending inventory under the perpetual inventory system is provided for comparison only. It is not used in the computation of cost of goods sold.

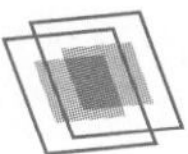

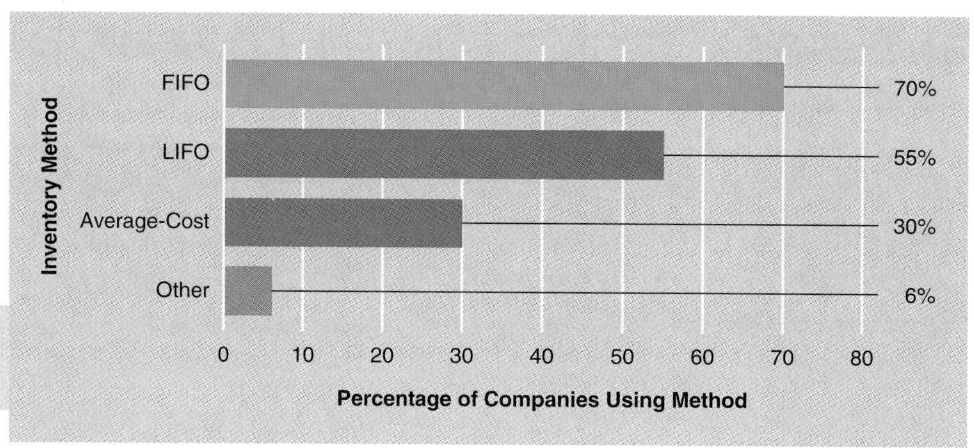

Figure 7
Inventory Costing Methods Used by 600 Large Companies

Total percentage exceeds 100 because some companies used different methods for different types of inventory.

Source: Reprinted with permission from *Accounting Trends and Techniques,* Copyright © 1997 by the American Institute of Certified Public Accountants, Inc.

Instructional Strategy: Use a *Jeopardy* team format to test student comprehension. Call out items from E 1 and E 9. Each correct answer wins one point. You might identify tougher questions as double *Jeopardy* items worth double points. The team with the highest score could earn bonus quiz points or be honored as reigning team champions.

During a period of declining prices, the reverse would occur. The LIFO method would produce a higher gross margin than the FIFO method. It is apparent that the method of inventory valuation has the greatest importance during prolonged periods of price changes in one direction, either up or down.

Because the specific identification method depends on the particular items sold, no generalization can be made about the effect of changing prices.

Effects on the Financial Statements

Discussion Question: What makes the assumption of inventory cost flows necessary? **Answer:** Changes in merchandise prices.

Each of the four methods of inventory pricing is acceptable for use in published financial statements. The FIFO, LIFO, and average-cost methods are widely used, as can be seen in Figure 7, which shows the inventory costing methods used by six hundred large companies. Each has its advantages and disadvantages, and none can be considered best or perfect. The factors that should be considered in choosing an inventory method are the trend of prices and the effects of each method on financial statements, income taxes, and management decisions.

A basic problem in determining the best inventory measure for a particular company stems from the fact that inventory affects both the balance sheet and the income statement. As we have seen, the LIFO method is best suited for the income statement because it matches revenues and cost of goods sold. But it is not the best measure of the current balance sheet value of inventory, particularly during a prolonged period of price increases or decreases. The FIFO method, on the other hand, is best suited to the balance sheet because the ending inventory is closest to current values and thus gives a more realistic view of the current financial assets of a business. Readers of financial statements must be alert to inventory methods and be able to assess their effects.

Effects on Income Taxes

The Internal Revenue Service has developed several rules for valuing inventories for federal income tax purposes. A company has a wide choice of methods, including specific identification, average-cost, FIFO, and LIFO, as well as lower-of-cost-or-

BUSINESS BULLETIN: BUSINESS PRACTICE

Does the accounting method a company uses affect management's operating decisions? It certainly does when taxes are involved! Recent research shows that among firms that use the LIFO inventory method, those with high tax rates are more likely to buy extra inventory at year end than those with low tax rates.[6] This behavior is predictable because LIFO deducts the most recent purchases, which are likely to have higher costs than earlier purchases, in determining taxable income. This action will result in lower income taxes.

market. But once a method has been chosen, it must be used consistently from one year to the next. The IRS must approve any change in the inventory valuation method for income tax purposes.[7] This requirement agrees with the rule of consistency in accounting, since changes in inventory method may cause income to fluctuate too much and would make income statements hard to interpret from year to year. A company may change its inventory method if there is a good reason for doing so. The nature and effect of the change must be shown on the company's financial statements.

Point to Emphasize: Stress that in periods of rising prices LIFO results in lower net income and thus lower taxes.

Many accountants believe that the use of the FIFO and average-cost methods in periods of rising prices causes businesses to report more than their true profit, resulting in the payment of excess income taxes. The profit is overstated because cost of goods sold is understated, relative to current prices. The company must buy replacement inventory at higher prices, but additional funds are also needed to pay income taxes. During the rapid inflation of 1979 to 1982, billions of dollars reported as profits and paid in income taxes were believed to be the result of poor matching of current costs and revenues under the FIFO and average-cost methods. Consequently, many companies, encouraged by the belief that prices will continue to rise, have since switched to the LIFO inventory method.

If a company uses the LIFO method in reporting income for tax purposes, the IRS requires that the same method be used in the accounting records. Also, the IRS will not allow the use of the lower-of-cost-or-market rule if LIFO is used to determine inventory cost. In such a case, only the LIFO cost can be used. This rule, however, does not preclude a company from using lower-of-LIFO-cost-or-market for financial reporting purposes (discussed later in this chapter).

Over a period of rising prices, a business that uses the LIFO method may find that for balance sheet purposes, its inventory is valued at a cost figure far below what it currently pays for the same items. Management must monitor this situation carefully, because if it should let the inventory quantity at year end fall below the beginning-of-the-year level, the company will find itself paying higher income taxes. Higher income before taxes results because the company expensed historical costs of inventory, which are below current costs. When this occurs, it is called a LIFO liquidation because sales have reduced inventories below the levels established in prior years.

A LIFO liquidation may be prevented by making enough purchases prior to year end to restore the desired inventory level. Sometimes a LIFO liquidation cannot be avoided because products are discontinued or supplies are interrupted, as in the case of a strike. In a recent year, forty of six hundred large companies reported a LIFO liquidation in which net income was increased because of the matching of older historical cost with present sales dollars.[8]

DECISION POINT

AMOCO CORPORATION

A company's inventory methods affect not only its reported profitability, but also its reported liquidity. In the case of a large company like Amoco Corporation, the effects can be complex and material. Like many companies, Amoco uses three of the methods in this chapter to cost its various types of inventory, which in 1996 totaled more than $1,069 million. In its statement of accounting policies, management explains its inventory methods: "Cost is determined under the last-in, first-out (LIFO) method for the majority of inventories of crude oil, petroleum products, and chemical products. The costs of remaining inventories are determined under the first-in, first-out (FIFO) or average cost methods." In a subsequent note on inventories, more detail is given:

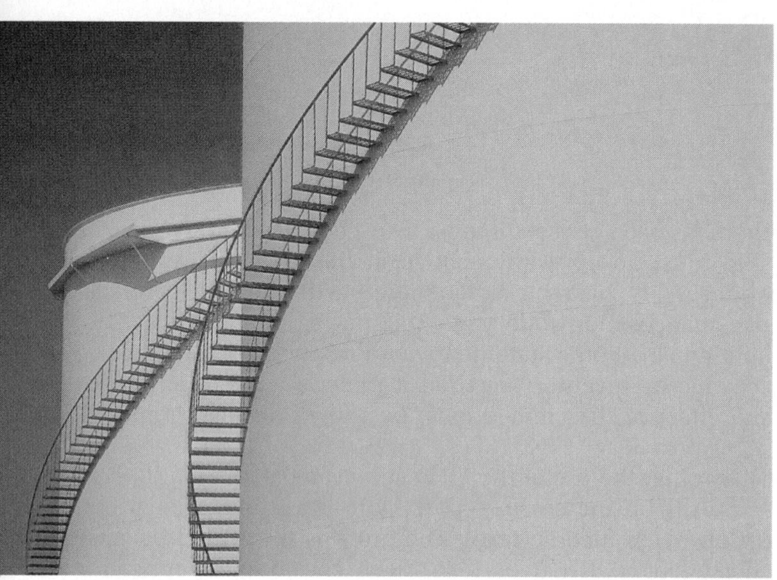

> Inventories carried under the LIFO method represented approximately 48 percent of total year-end inventory carrying values in 1996 and 53 percent in 1995.
>
> It is estimated that inventories would have been approximately $1,400 million higher than reported on December 31, 1996 and 1995, if the quantities valued on the LIFO basis were instead valued on the FIFO basis.[9]

Why was it important for Amoco to include such detail?

Critical Thinking Question: What is the amount by which current assets and working capital would increase for Amoco in 1996? **Answer:** $1,400 million.

The information in the note allows the reader to determine what Amoco's inventory value would be if the inventory were valued at current prices under FIFO rather than at older prices under LIFO. This allows more realistic computations of the company's liquidity ratios. Since the inventory would have been $1,400 million higher under FIFO than under LIFO, the more realistic inventory value is more than twice the reported amount of $1,069 million. The company's short-term liquidity position as measured by the current ratio is better than the reported figures would seem to indicate. However, the company's inventory turnover ratio and average days' inventory on hand will be adversely affected if the more realistic figures are used.

Enrichment Note: Physically counting, measuring, or weighing inventory is a tedious process. After inventory is counted, it must be priced and extended. Great care must be used to avoid errors.

Teaching Note: Mention that a percentage of the inventory will be recounted (verified). The same applies to pricing and extending the inventory. This internal control ensures the accuracy and reliability of the accounting data.

Effects of Misstatements in Inventory Measurement

The basic problem of separating goods available for sale into two components—goods sold and goods not sold—is that of assigning a cost to the goods not sold, the ending inventory. The portion of the goods available for sale not assigned to the ending inventory is used to determine the cost of goods sold.

Because the figures for ending inventory and cost of goods sold are related, a misstatement in the inventory figure at the end of the period will cause an equal misstatement in gross margin and income before income taxes in the income statement. The amount of assets and owner's equity on the balance sheet will also be misstated by the same amount. The consequences of overstatement and understatement of inventory are illustrated in the three simplified examples that follow. In each case, beginning inventory, net purchases, and cost of goods available for sale have been stated correctly. In the first example, ending inventory has been stated correctly. In the second example, ending inventory is overstated by $6,000; in the third example, ending inventory is understated by $6,000.

Example 1. Ending Inventory Correctly Stated at $10,000

Cost of Goods Sold for the Year		Income Statement for the Year	
Beginning Inventory	$12,000	Net Sales	$100,000
Net Cost of Purchases	58,000	→ Cost of Goods Sold	60,000
Cost of Goods Available for Sale	$70,000	Gross Margin	$ 40,000
Ending Inventory	10,000	Operating Expenses	32,000
Cost of Goods Sold	$60,000	Income Before Income Taxes	$ 8,000

Example 2. Ending Inventory Overstated by $6,000

Cost of Goods Sold for the Year		Income Statement for the Year	
Beginning Inventory	$12,000	Net Sales	$100,000
Net Cost of Purchases	58,000	→ Cost of Goods Sold	54,000
Cost of Goods Available for Sale	$70,000	Gross Margin	$ 46,000
Ending Inventory	16,000	Operating Expenses	32,000
Cost of Goods Sold	$54,000	Income Before Income Taxes	$ 14,000

Example 3. Ending Inventory Understated by $6,000

Cost of Goods Sold for the Year		Income Statement for the Year	
Beginning Inventory	$12,000	Net Sales	$100,000
Net Cost of Purchases	58,000	→ Cost of Goods Sold	66,000
Cost of Goods Available for Sale	$70,000	Gross Margin	$ 34,000
Ending Inventory	4,000	Operating Expenses	32,000
Cost of Goods Sold	$66,000	Income Before Income Taxes	$ 2,000

Discussion Question: When a company chooses the end of its fiscal year, what is one of the major considerations? **Answer:** To end the year when inventory is low, so that there will be less inventory to count, verify, and extend. Many department stores end their fiscal period on January 31.

In all three examples, the total cost of goods available for sale was $70,000. The difference in income before income taxes resulted from how this $70,000 was divided between ending inventory and cost of goods sold.

Because the ending inventory in one period becomes the beginning inventory in the following period, it is important to recognize that a misstatement in inventory valuation affects not only the current period but also the following period. Over a two-year period, the errors in income before income taxes will offset, or counterbalance, each other. In Example **2** above, for instance, the overstatement of ending inventory in 20x1 caused a $6,000 overstatement of beginning inventory in the following year, resulting in an understatement of income by $6,000 in the second year. This offsetting effect is illustrated in Table 1.

Point to Emphasize: Inventory errors will correct (counterbalance) themselves over a two-year period.

Table 1. Ending Inventory Overstated by $6,000

	With Inventory Correctly Stated	With Inventory at Dec. 31, 20x1, Overstated: Reported Net Income Will Be	With Inventory at Dec. 31, 20x1, Overstated: Reported Income Before Income Taxes Will Be Overstated (Understated)
Net Income for 20x1	$ 8,000	$14,000	$6,000
Net Income for 20x2	15,000	9,000	(6,000)
Total Net Income for Two Years	$23,000	$23,000	—

Because the total income before income taxes for the two years is the same, it may appear that one need not worry about inventory misstatements. However, the misstatements violate the matching rule. In addition, management, creditors, and investors make many decisions on an annual basis and depend on the accountant's determination of net income. The accountant has an obligation to make the net income figure for each year as useful as possible.

The effects of misstatements in inventory on income before income taxes are as follows:

Year 1	Year 2
Ending inventory overstated	**Beginning inventory overstated**
Cost of goods sold understated	Cost of goods sold overstated
Income before income taxes overstated	Income before income taxes understated
Ending inventory understated	**Beginning inventory understated**
Cost of goods sold overstated	Cost of goods sold understated
Income before income taxes understated	Income before income taxes overstated

A misstatement in inventory results in a misstatement in income before income taxes of the same amount. Thus the measurement of inventory is important.

BUSINESS BULLETIN: ETHICS IN PRACTICE

Income may be easily manipulated through accounting for inventory. For example, it is easy to misstate the amount of inventory or to overstate or understate inventory by including end-of-the-year purchase and sale transactions in the wrong fiscal year. In one case, *The Wall Street Journal* reported that Leslie Fay Company restated its earnings for three past years to reverse $81 million of pretax earnings. The situation was a "carefully concealed case of fraud" involving many members of the financial accounting staff. "Inventory was overstated, while the cost of making garments was understated in order to enhance profit figures." Such actions are obviously unethical and, in this case, led the company to bankruptcy and ruined the careers of most of its senior officers.[10]

Valuing Inventory at the Lower of Cost or Market (LCM)

OBJECTIVE 6

Apply the lower-of-cost-or-market (LCM) rule to inventory valuation

Related Text Assignments:
Q: 15, 16
SE: 11
E: 11
SD: 3
FRA: 4

Business-World Example: Certain types of businesses are more likely to use the lower-of-cost-or-market rule than others. For example, high-technology items such as computers and videodisk players tend to decrease in price over time.

Discussion Question: Which accounting convention supports the lower-of-cost-or-market rule? **Answer:** Conservatism.

Clarification Note: Cost must first be determined by the specific identification, FIFO, LIFO, or average-cost method before it can be compared with market cost.

Although cost is usually the most appropriate basis for valuation of inventory, there are times when inventory may properly be shown in the financial statements at less than its cost. If by reason of physical deterioration, obsolescence, or decline in price level the market value of inventory falls below its cost, a loss has occurred. This loss may be recognized by writing the inventory down to market or current replacement cost of inventory. For a merchandising company, market is the amount that the company would pay at the present time for the same goods, purchased from the usual suppliers and in the usual quantities. The lower-of-cost-or-market (LCM) rule requires that when the replacement cost of inventory falls below historical cost, the inventory is written down to the lower value and a loss is recorded. This rule is an example of the application of the convention of conservatism because the loss is recognized before an actual transaction takes place. Under historical cost accounting, the inventory remains at cost until it is sold. It may help in applying the LCM rule to think of it as the "lower-of-cost-or-replacement-cost" rule.[11] Approximately 90 percent of six hundred large companies report applying the LCM rule to their inventories.[12]

There are two basic methods of valuing inventories at the lower of cost or market accepted both by GAAP and for federal income tax purposes: (1) the item-by-item method and (2) the major category method. For example, a stereo shop could determine lower of cost or market for each kind of speaker, receiver, and turntable (item by item) or for all speakers, all receivers, and all turntables (major categories).

Item-by-Item Method

When the item-by-item method is used, cost and market values are compared for each item in inventory. Each individual item is then valued at its lower price (see Table 2).

Table 2. Lower of Cost or Market with Item-by-Item Method

		Per Unit		
	Quantity	Cost	Market	Lower of Cost or Market
Category I				
Item a	200	$1.50	$1.70	$ 300
Item b	100	2.00	1.80	180
Item c	100	2.50	2.60	250
Category II				
Item d	300	5.00	4.50	1,350
Item e	200	4.00	4.10	800
Inventory at the lower of cost or market				$2,880

Major Category Method

Under the major category method, the total cost and total market values for each category of items are compared. Each category is then valued at its lower amount (see Table 3).

Table 3. Lower of Cost or Market with Major Category Method

	Quantity	Per Unit Cost	Per Unit Market	Total Cost	Total Market	Lower of Cost or Market
Category I						
Item a	200	$1.50	$1.70	$ 300	$ 340	
Item b	100	2.00	1.80	200	180	
Item c	100	2.50	2.60	250	260	
Totals				$ 750	$ 780	$ 750
Category II						
Item d	300	5.00	4.50	$1,500	$1,350	
Item e	200	4.00	4.10	800	820	
Totals				$2,300	$2,170	2,170
Inventory at the lower of cost or market						$2,920

Valuing Inventory by Estimation

It is sometimes necessary or desirable to estimate the value of ending inventory. The methods most commonly used for this purpose are the retail method and the gross profit method.

Retail Method of Inventory Estimation

SUPPLEMENTAL OBJECTIVE 7a

Estimate the cost of ending inventory using the retail inventory method

Related Text Assignments:
Q: 17, 18, 19
E: 12, 13
P: 4, 5
FRA: 4

Point to Emphasize: Stress that when estimating inventory by the retail method, the inventory need not be counted.

The retail method as its name implies, is used in retail merchandising businesses to estimate the cost of ending inventory by using the ratio of cost to retail price. There are two principal reasons for its use. First, management usually requires that financial statements be prepared at least once a month. As taking a physical inventory is time-consuming and expensive, the retail method is used instead to estimate the value of inventory on hand. Second, because items in a retail store normally have a price tag or a universal product code, it is a common practice to take the physical inventory at retail from these price tags and codes and reduce the total value to cost through use of the retail method. The term *at retail* means the amount of the inventory at the marked selling prices of the inventory items.

When the retail method is used to estimate ending inventory, the records must show the beginning inventory at cost and at retail. The records must also show the amount of goods purchased during the period both at cost and at retail. The net sales at retail is, of course, the balance of the Sales account less returns and allowances. A simple example of the retail method is shown in Table 4.

Goods available for sale is determined both at cost and at retail by listing beginning inventory and net purchases for the period at cost and at their expected selling price, adding freight to the cost column, and totaling. The ratio of these two amounts (cost to retail price) provides an estimate of the cost of each dollar of retail sales value. The estimated ending inventory at retail is then determined by deducting sales for the period from the retail price of the goods that were available for sale during the period. The inventory at retail is then converted to cost on the basis of the ratio of cost to retail.

The cost of ending inventory may also be estimated by applying the ratio of cost to retail price to the total retail value of the physical count of the ending inventory.

Discussion Question: Why is Freight In not placed under the Retail column when using the retail method of inventory valuation? **Answer:** Businesses automatically price their goods high enough to cover freight charges.

Table 4. Retail Method of Inventory Valuation

	Cost	Retail
Beginning Inventory	$ 40,000	$ 55,000
Net Purchases for the Period (excluding Freight In)	107,000	145,000
Freight In	3,000	
Merchandise Available for Sale	$150,000	$200,000
Ratio of Cost to Retail Price: $\frac{\$150,000}{\$200,000} = 75\%$		
Net Sales During the Period		160,000
Estimated Ending Inventory at Retail		$ 40,000
Ratio of Cost to Retail	75%	
Estimated Cost of Ending Inventory	$ 30,000	

Applying the retail method in practice is often more difficult than this simple example because of such complications as changes in retail price during the year, different markups on different types of merchandise, and varying volumes of sales for different types of merchandise.

Gross Profit Method of Inventory Estimation

SUPPLEMENTAL OBJECTIVE 7b

Estimate the cost of ending inventory using the gross profit method

The gross profit method assumes that the ratio of gross margin for a business remains relatively stable from year to year. The gross profit method is used in place of the retail method when records of the retail prices of beginning inventory and purchases are not kept. It is considered acceptable for estimating the cost of inventory for interim reports, but it is not acceptable for valuing inventory in the annual financial statements. It is also useful in estimating the amount of inventory lost or destroyed by theft, fire, or other hazards. Insurance companies often use this method to verify loss claims.

The gross profit method is simple to use. First, figure the cost of goods available for sale in the usual way (add purchases to beginning inventory). Second, estimate the cost of goods sold by deducting the estimated gross margin from sales. Finally, deduct the estimated cost of goods sold from the goods available for sale to arrive at the estimated cost of ending inventory. This method is shown in Table 5.

Terminology Note: The gross profit method is also known as the *gross margin method.*

Point to Emphasize: Stress that it is highly desirable to maintain financial records off site. If records were destroyed, it would be difficult, if not impossible, to reconstruct the data necessary for the insurance claim.

Table 5. Gross Profit Method of Inventory Valuation

1. Beginning Inventory at Cost		$ 50,000
Purchases at Cost (including Freight In)		290,000
Cost of Goods Available for Sale		$340,000
2. Less Estimated Cost of Goods Sold		
Sales at Selling Price	$400,000	
Less Estimated Gross Margin of 30%	120,000	
Estimated Cost of Goods Sold		280,000
3. Estimated Cost of Ending Inventory		$ 60,000

Chapter Review

REVIEW OF LEARNING OBJECTIVES

1. **Identify and explain the management issues associated with accounting for inventories.** Included in inventory are goods owned, whether produced or purchased, that are held for sale in the normal course of business. Manufacturing companies also include raw materials and work in process. Among the issues management must face in accounting for inventories are allocating the cost of inventories in accordance with the matching rule, assessing the impact of inventory decisions, and evaluating the levels of inventory. The objective of accounting for inventories is the proper determination of income through the matching of costs and revenues, not the determination of the most realistic inventory value. Because the valuation of inventory has a direct effect on a company's net income, the choice of inventory systems and methods affects not only the amount of income taxes and cash flows but also the external and internal evaluation of the company. The level of inventory as measured by the inventory turnover and its related measure, average days' inventory on hand, is important to managing the amount of investment needed by a company.
2. **Define *inventory cost* and relate it to goods flow and cost flow.** The cost of inventory includes (1) invoice price less purchases discounts; (2) freight or transportation in, including insurance in transit; and (3) applicable taxes and tariffs. Goods flow relates to the actual physical flow of merchandise, whereas cost flow refers to the assumed flow of costs in the operations of the business.
3. **Calculate the pricing of inventory, using the cost basis under the periodic inventory system, according to the (a) specific identification method; (b) average-cost method; (c) first-in, first-out (FIFO) method; and (d) last-in, first-out (LIFO) method.** The value assigned to ending inventory is the result of two measurements: quantity and price. Quantity is determined by taking a physical inventory. The pricing of inventory is usually based on the assumed cost flow of the goods as they are bought and sold. One of four assumptions is usually made regarding cost flow. These assumptions are represented by four inventory methods. Inventory pricing can be determined by the specific identification method, which associates the actual cost with each item of inventory, but this method is rarely used. The average-cost method assumes that the cost of inventory is the average cost of goods available for sale during the period. The first-in, first-out (FIFO) method assumes that the costs of the first items acquired should be assigned to the first items sold. The last-in, first-out (LIFO) method assumes that the costs of the last items acquired should be assigned to the first items sold. The inventory method chosen may or may not be equivalent to the actual physical flow of goods.
4. **Apply the perpetual inventory system to the pricing of inventories at cost.** The pricing of inventories under the perpetual inventory system differs from pricing under the periodic system because under the perpetual system a continuous record of quantities and costs of merchandise is maintained as purchases and sales are made. Cost of goods sold is accumulated as sales are made and costs are transferred from the Inventory account to Cost of Goods Sold. The cost of the ending inventory is the balance of the Inventory account. Under the perpetual inventory system, the specific identification method and the FIFO method will produce the same results as under the periodic method. The results will differ for the average-cost method because a moving average is calculated prior to each sale rather than at the end of the accounting period, and for the LIFO method because the cost components of inventory change constantly as goods are bought and sold.
5. **State the effects of inventory methods and misstatements of inventory on income determination and income taxes.** During periods of rising prices, the LIFO method will show the lowest net income; FIFO, the highest; and average cost, in between. The opposite effects occur in periods of falling prices. No generalization can be made regarding the specific identification method. The Internal Revenue Service requires that if LIFO is used for tax purposes, it must also be used for financial statement purposes, and that the lower-of-cost-or-market rule cannot be applied to the

LIFO method. If the value of ending inventory is understated or overstated, a corresponding error—dollar for dollar—will be made in income before income taxes. Furthermore, because the ending inventory of one period is the beginning inventory of the next, the misstatement affects two accounting periods, although the effects are opposite.

6. **Apply the lower-of-cost-or-market (LCM) rule to inventory valuation.** The lower-of-cost-or-market rule can be applied to the above methods of determining inventory at cost. This rule states that if the replacement cost (market) of the inventory is lower than the inventory cost, the lower figure should be used. Valuation can be determined on an item-by-item or major category basis.

Supplemental Objective

7. **Estimate the cost of ending inventory using the (a) retail inventory method and (b) gross profit method.** Two methods of estimating the value of inventory are the retail inventory method and the gross profit method. Under the retail inventory method, inventory is determined at retail prices and is then reduced to estimated cost by applying a ratio of cost to retail price. Under the gross profit method, cost of goods sold is estimated by reducing sales by estimated gross margin. The estimated cost of goods sold is then deducted from the cost of goods available for sale to estimate the inventory.

REVIEW OF CONCEPTS AND TERMINOLOGY

The following concepts and terms were introduced in this chapter.

LO 3 **Average-cost method:** An inventory costing method in which inventory is priced at the average cost of the goods available for sale during the period.

LO 1 **Average days' inventory on hand:** The average number of days required to sell the inventory on hand; number of days in a year divided by inventory turnover.

LO 2 **Consignment:** Merchandise placed by its owner (the *consignor*) on the premises of another company (the *consignee*) with the understanding that payment is expected only when the merchandise is sold and that unsold items may be returned to the consignor.

LO 2 **Cost flow:** The association of costs with their assumed flow in the operations of a company.

LO 3 **First-in, first-out (FIFO) method:** An inventory costing method based on the assumption that the costs of the first items acquired should be assigned to the first items sold.

LO 2 **Goods flow:** The actual physical movement of goods in the operations of a company.

SO 7 **Gross profit method:** A method of inventory estimation based on the assumption that the ratio of gross margin for a business remains relatively stable from year to year.

LO 2 **Inventory cost:** The price paid or consideration given to acquire an asset; includes invoice price less purchases discounts, freight or transportation in, and applicable taxes and tariffs.

LO 1 **Inventory turnover:** A ratio indicating the number of times a company's average inventory is sold during an accounting period; cost of goods sold divided by average inventory.

LO 6 **Item-by-item method:** A lower-of-cost-or-market method of valuing inventory in which cost and market values are compared for each item in inventory, with each item then valued at its lower price.

LO 1 **Just-in-time operating environment:** An inventory management system in which companies seek to reduce their levels of inventory by working closely with suppliers to coordinate and schedule deliveries so that goods arrive just at the time they are needed.

LO 3 **Last-in, first-out (LIFO) method:** An inventory costing method based on the assumption that the costs of the last items purchased should be assigned to the first items sold.

LO 5 **LIFO liquidation:** The reduction of inventory below previous levels so that income is increased by the amount by which current prices exceed the historical cost of the inventory under LIFO.

LO 6 **Lower-of-cost-or-market (LCM) rule:** A method of valuing inventory at an amount below cost if the replacement (market) value is less than cost.

LO 6 **Major category method:** A lower-of-cost-or-market method of valuing inventory in which the total cost and total market values for each category of items are compared, with each category then valued at its lower amount.

LO 6 **Market:** Current replacement cost of inventory.

LO 1 **Merchandise inventory:** All goods owned and held for sale in the regular course of business.

SO 7 **Retail method:** A method of inventory estimation, used in retail merchandising businesses, under which inventory at retail value is reduced by the ratio of cost to retail price.

LO 3 **Specific identification method:** An inventory costing method in which the price of inventory is computed by identifying the cost of each item in ending inventory as coming from a specific purchase.

REVIEW PROBLEM

Periodic and Perpetual Inventory Systems

LO 3
LO 4 The table below summarizes the beginning inventory, purchases, and sales of Psi Company's single product during January.

Date		Beginning Inventory and Purchases			
		Units	Cost	Total	Sales Units
Jan. 1	Inventory	1,400	$19	$26,600	
4	Sale				300
8	Purchase	600	20	12,000	
10	Sale				1,300
12	Purchase	900	21	18,900	
15	Sale				150
18	Purchase	500	22	11,000	
24	Purchase	800	23	18,400	
31	Sale				1,350
Totals		4,200		$86,900	3,100

REQUIRED

1. Assuming that the company uses the periodic inventory system, compute the cost that should be assigned to ending inventory and to cost of goods sold using (a) the average-cost method, (b) the FIFO method, and (c) the LIFO method.
2. Assuming that the company uses the perpetual inventory system, compute the cost that should be assigned to ending inventory and to cost of goods sold using (a) the average-cost method, (b) the FIFO method, and (c) the LIFO method.

ANSWER TO REVIEW PROBLEM

	Units	Amount
Beginning Inventory	1,400	$26,600
Purchases	2,800	60,300
Available for Sale	4,200	$86,900
Sales	3,100	
Ending Inventory	1,100	

1. Periodic inventory system

   a. Average-cost method

Cost of goods available for sale	$86,900
Ending inventory consists of 1,100 units at $20.69*	22,759
Cost of goods sold	$64,141

*$86,900 ÷ 4,200 = $20.69†

†Rounded.

   b. FIFO method

Cost of goods available for sale		$86,900
Ending inventory consists of		
January 24 purchase (800 × $23)	$18,400	
January 18 purchase (300 × $22)	6,600	25,000
Cost of goods sold		$61,900

   c. LIFO method

Cost of goods available for sale	$86,900
Ending inventory consists of Beginning inventory (1,100 × $19)	20,900
Cost of goods sold	$66,000

2. Perpetual inventory system

   a. Average-cost method

Date		Units	Cost*	Amount*
Jan. 1	Inventory	1,400	$19.00	$26,600
4	Sale	(300)	19.00	(5,700)
4	Balance	1,100	19.00	$20,900
8	Purchase	600	20.00	12,000
8	Balance	1,700	19.35	$32,900
10	Sale	(1,300)	19.35	(25,155)
10	Balance	400	19.36	$ 7,745
12	Purchase	900	21.00	18,900
12	Balance	1,300	20.50	$26,645
15	Sale	(150)	20.50	(3,075)
15	Balance	1,150	20.50	$23,570
18	Purchase	500	22.00	11,000
24	Purchase	800	23.00	18,400
24	Balance	2,450	21.62	$52,970
31	Sale	(1,350)	21.62	(29,187)
31	Inventory	1,100	21.62	$23,783

Cost of Goods Sold: $5,700 + $25,155 + $3,075 + $29,187 = $63,117

*Rounded.

b. FIFO method

Date		Units	Cost	Amount
Jan. 1	Inventory	1,400	$19	$26,600
4	Sale	(300)	19	(5,700)
4	Balance	1,100	19	$20,900
8	Purchase	600	20	12,000
8	Balance	1,100	19	
		600	20	$32,900
10	Sale	(1,100)	19	
		(200)	20	(24,900)
10	Balance	400	20	$ 8,000
12	Purchase	900	21	18,900
12	Balance	400	20	
		900	21	$26,900
15	Sale	(150)	20	(3,000)
15	Balance	250	20	
		900	21	$23,900
18	Purchase	500	22	11,000
24	Purchase	800	23	18,400
24	Balance	250	20	
		900	21	
		500	22	
		800	23	$53,300
31	Sale	(250)	20	
		(900)	21	
		(200)	22	(28,300)
31	Inventory	300	22	
		800	23	$25,000

Cost of Goods Sold: $5,700 + $24,900 + $3,000 + $28,300 = $61,900

c. LIFO method

Date		Units	Cost	Amount
Jan. 1	Inventory	1,400	$19	$26,600
4	Sale	(300)	19	(5,700)
4	Balance	1,100	19	$20,900
8	Purchase	600	20	12,000
8	Balance	1,100	19	
		600	20	$32,900
10	Sale	(600)	20	
		(700)	19	(25,300)
10	Balance	400	19	$ 7,600
12	Purchase	900	21	18,900
12	Balance	400	19	
		900	21	$26,500
15	Sale	(150)	21	(3,150)
15	Balance	400	19	
		750	21	$23,350
18	Purchase	500	22	11,000
24	Purchase	800	23	18,400
24	Balance	400	19	
		750	21	
		500	22	
		800	23	$52,750
31	Sale	(800)	23	
		(500)	22	
		(50)	21	(30,450)
31	Inventory	400	19	
		700	21	$22,300

Cost of Goods Sold: $5,700 + $25,300 + $3,150 + $30,450 = $64,600

Chapter Assignments

BUILDING YOUR KNOWLEDGE FOUNDATION

Questions

1. What is merchandise inventory, and what is the primary objective of inventory measurement?
2. How does inventory for a manufacturing company differ from that for a merchandising company?
3. Why is the level of inventory important, and what are two common measures of inventory level?
4. What items should be included in the cost of inventory?
5. Fargo Sales Company is very busy at the end of its fiscal year on June 30. There is an order for 130 units of product in the warehouse. Although the shipping department tries, it cannot ship the product by June 30, and title has not yet passed. Should the 130 units be included in the year-end count of inventory? Why or why not?
6. What is the difference between goods flow and cost flow?
7. Do the FIFO and LIFO inventory methods result in different quantities of ending inventory?
8. Under which method of cost flow are (a) the earliest costs assigned to inventory, (b) the latest costs assigned to inventory, and (c) the average costs assigned to inventory?
9. What are the relative advantages and disadvantages of FIFO and LIFO from management's point of view?
10. Why do you think it is more expensive to maintain a perpetual inventory system?
11. In periods of steadily rising prices, which inventory method—average cost, FIFO, or LIFO—will give the (a) highest ending inventory cost, (b) lowest ending inventory cost, (c) highest net income, and (d) lowest net income?
12. May a company change its inventory cost method from year to year? Explain.
13. What is the relationship between income tax rules and inventory valuation methods?
14. If the merchandise inventory is mistakenly overstated at the end of 20x0, what is the effect on the (a) 20x0 net income, (b) 20x0 year-end balance sheet value, (c) 20x1 net income, and (d) 20x1 year-end balance sheet value?
15. In the phrase *lower of cost or market,* what is meant by the word *market?*
16. What methods can be used to determine the lower of cost or market?
17. Does using the retail inventory method mean that inventories are measured at retail value on the balance sheet? Explain.
18. For what reasons might management use the gross profit method of estimating inventory?
19. Which of the following inventory systems or methods do not require the taking of a physical inventory: (a) perpetual, (b) periodic, (c) retail, and (d) gross profit?

Short Exercises

LO 1 *Management Issues*

SE 1. Indicate whether each item listed below is associated with (a) allocating the cost of inventories in accordance with the matching rule, (b) assessing the impact of inventory decisions, or (c) evaluating the level of inventory.

1. Calculating the average number of days' inventory on hand
2. Ordering a supply of inventory to satisfy customer needs
3. Calculating the income tax effect of an inventory method
4. Deciding the cost to place on ending inventory

LO 1 *Inventory Turnover and Average Days' Inventory on Hand*

SE 2. During 20x1, Certeen Clothiers had beginning inventory of $240,000, ending inventory of $280,000, and cost of goods sold of $1,100,000. Compute the inventory turnover and average days' inventory on hand.

LO 3 **SE 3.** *Specific Identification Method*

Assume the following data with regard to inventory for Alexis Company:

Aug. 1	Inventory	80 units @ $10 per unit	$ 800
8	Purchase	100 units @ $11 per unit	1,100
22	Purchase	70 units @ $12 per unit	840
Goods Available for Sale		250 units	$2,740
Aug. 15	Sale	90 units	
28	Sale	50 units	
Inventory, August 31		110 units	

Assuming that the inventory consists of 60 units from the August 8 purchase and 50 units from the purchase of August 22, calculate the cost of ending inventory and cost of goods sold.

LO 3 **SE 4.** *Average-Cost Method—Periodic Inventory System*

Using the data in **SE 3,** calculate the cost of ending inventory and cost of goods sold according to the average-cost method under the periodic inventory system.

LO 3 **SE 5.** *FIFO Method—Periodic Inventory System*

Using the data in **SE 3,** calculate the cost of ending inventory and cost of goods sold according to the FIFO method under the periodic inventory system.

LO 3 **SE 6.** *LIFO Method—Periodic Inventory System*

Using the data in **SE 3,** calculate the cost of ending inventory and cost of goods sold according to the LIFO method under the periodic inventory system.

LO 4 **SE 7.** *Average-Cost Method—Perpetual Inventory System*

Using the data in **SE 3,** calculate the cost of ending inventory and cost of goods sold according to the average-cost method under the perpetual inventory system.

LO 4 **SE 8.** *FIFO Method—Perpetual Inventory System*

Using the data in **SE 3,** calculate the cost of ending inventory and cost of goods sold according to the FIFO method under the perpetual inventory system.

LO 4 **SE 9.** *LIFO Method—Perpetual Inventory System*

Using the data in **SE 3,** calculate the cost of ending inventory and cost of goods sold according to the LIFO method under the perpetual inventory system.

LO 5 **SE 10.** *Effects of Methods and Changing Prices*

Following the pattern of Exhibit 1, prepare a table with seven columns that shows the ending inventory and cost of goods sold for each of the results from your calculations in **SE 3** through **SE 9.** Comment on the results, including the effects of the different prices at which the merchandise was purchased. Which method(s) would result in the lowest income taxes?

LO 6 **SE 11.** *Lower of Cost or Market*

The following schedule is based on a physical inventory and replacement costs for one product line of men's shirts.

Item	Quantity	Cost per Unit	Market per Unit
Short sleeve	280	$24	$20
Long sleeve	190	28	29
Extra-long sleeve	80	34	35

Determine the value of this category of inventory at the lower of cost or market using (1) the item-by-item method and (2) the major category method.

Exercises

E 1. Indicate whether each item listed below is associated with (a) allocating the cost of inventories in accordance with the matching rule, (b) assessing the impact of inventory decisions, or (c) evaluating the level of inventory.

LO 1 *Management Issues Related to Inventory*

1. Computing inventory turnover
2. Application of the just-in-time operating environment
3. Determining the effects of inventory decisions on cash flows
4. Apportioning the cost of goods available for sale to ending inventory and cost of goods sold
5. Determining the effects of inventory methods on income taxes
6. Determining the assumption about the flow of costs into and out of the company

E 2. SaveMore Discount Stores is assessing its levels of inventory for 20x2 and 20x3 and has gathered the following data:

LO 1 *Inventory Ratios*

	20x3	20x2	20x1
Ending inventory	$128,000	$108,000	$92,000
Cost of goods sold	640,000	600,000	

Compute the inventory turnover and average days' inventory on hand for 20x2 and 20x3 and comment on the results.

E 3. Helen's Farm Store had the following purchases and sales of fertilizer during the year:

LO 3 *Periodic Inventory System and Inventory Costing Methods*

Jan. 1	Beginning Inventory	250 cases @ $23	$ 5,750
Feb. 25	Purchased	100 cases @ $26	2,600
June 15	Purchased	400 cases @ $28	11,200
Aug. 15	Purchased	100 cases @ $26	2,600
Oct. 15	Purchased	300 cases @ $28	8,400
Dec. 15	Purchased	200 cases @ $30	6,000
Total Goods Available for Sale		1,350	$36,550
Total Sales		1,000 cases	
Dec. 31	Ending Inventory	350 cases	

Assume that all of the June 15 purchase and 200 cases each from the January 1 beginning inventory, the October 15 purchase, and the December 15 purchase were sold.

Determine the costs that should be assigned to ending inventory and cost of goods sold under each of the following assumptions: (1) costs are assigned by the specific identification method; (2) costs are assigned by the average-cost method; (3) costs are assigned by the FIFO method; (4) costs are assigned by the LIFO method. What conclusions can be drawn about the effect of each method on the income statement and the balance sheet of Helen's Farm Store? Round your answers to the nearest whole number and assume the periodic inventory system.

E 4. During its first year of operation, Jefferson Company purchased 5,600 units of a product at $21 per unit. During the second year, it purchased 6,000 units of the same product at $24 per unit. During the third year, it purchased 5,000 units at $30 per unit. Jefferson Company managed to have an ending inventory each year of 1,000 units. The company uses the periodic inventory system.

LO 3 *Periodic Inventory System and Inventory Costing Methods*

Prepare cost of goods sold statements that compare the value of ending inventory and the cost of goods sold for each of the three years using (1) the FIFO method and (2) the LIFO method. From the resulting data, what conclusions can you draw about the relationships between changes in unit price and changes in the value of ending inventory?

E 5. LO 3 *Periodic Inventory System and Inventory Costing Methods*

In chronological order, the inventory, purchases, and sales of a single product for a recent month are as follows:

		Units	Amount per Unit
June 1	Beginning Inventory	300	$30
4	Purchase	800	33
8	Sale	400	60
12	Purchase	1,000	36
16	Sale	700	60
20	Sale	500	66
24	Purchase	1,200	39
28	Sale	600	66
29	Sale	400	66

Using the periodic inventory system, compute the cost of ending inventory, cost of goods sold, and gross margin. Use the average-cost, FIFO, and LIFO inventory costing methods. Explain the differences in gross margin produced by the three methods. Round unit costs to cents and totals to dollars.

E 6. LO 4 *Perpetual Inventory System and Inventory Costing Methods*

Using the data provided in **E 5** and assuming the perpetual inventory system, compute the cost of ending inventory, cost of goods sold, and gross margin. Use the average-cost, FIFO, and LIFO inventory costing methods. Explain the reasons for the differences in gross margin produced by the three methods. Round unit costs to cents and totals to dollars.

E 7. LO 3 LO 4 *Inventory Costing Methods: Periodic and Perpetual Systems*

During July 20x1, Bilden, Inc., sold 250 units of its product Dervex for $4,000. The following units were available:

	Units	Cost
Beginning Inventory	100	$ 2
Purchase 1	40	4
Purchase 2	60	6
Purchase 3	70	8
Purchase 4	80	10
Purchase 5	90	12

A sale of 100 units was made after purchase 1, and a sale of 150 units was made after purchase 4. Of the units sold, 100 came from beginning inventory and 150 from purchases 3 and 4.

Determine cost of goods available for sale and ending inventory in units. Then determine the costs that should be assigned to cost of goods sold and ending inventory under each of the following assumptions: (1) Costs are assigned under the periodic inventory system using (a) the specific identification method, (b) the average-cost method, (c) the FIFO method, and (d) the LIFO method. (2) Costs are assigned under the perpetual inventory system using (a) the average-cost method, (b) the FIFO method, and (c) the LIFO method. For each alternative, show the gross margin. Round unit costs to cents and totals to dollars.

E 8. LO 5 *Effects of Inventory Methods on Cash Flows*

Ross Products, Inc., sold 120,000 cases of glue at $40 per case during 20x1. Its beginning inventory consisted of 20,000 cases at a cost of $24 per case. During 20x1, it purchased 60,000 cases at $28 per case and later 50,000 cases at $30 per case. Operating expenses were $1,100,000, and the applicable income tax rate was 30 percent.

Using the periodic inventory system, compute net income using the FIFO method and the LIFO method for costing inventory. Which alternative produces the larger cash flow? The company is considering a purchase of 10,000 cases at $30 per case just before the year end. What effect on net income and on cash flow will this proposed purchase have under each method? (**Hint:** What are the income tax consequences?)

E 9. LO 3 LO 5 *Inventory Costing Method Characteristics*

The lettered items in the list below represent inventory costing methods. Write the letter of the method that each of the following statements *best* describes.

a. Specific identification
b. Average-cost
c. First-in, first-out (FIFO)
d. Last-in, first-out (LIFO)

1. Matches recent costs with recent revenues
2. Assumes that each item of inventory is identifiable
3. Results in the most realistic balance sheet valuation
4. Results in the lowest net income in periods of deflation
5. Results in the lowest net income in periods of inflation
6. Matches the oldest costs with recent revenues
7. Results in the highest net income in periods of inflation
8. Results in the highest net income in periods of deflation
9. Tends to level out the effects of inflation
10. Is unpredictable as to the effects of inflation

E 10. LO 5 *Effects of Inventory Errors*

Condensed income statements for Charron Company for two years are shown below.

	20x4	20x3
Sales	$126,000	$105,000
Cost of Goods Sold	75,000	54,000
Gross Margin	$ 51,000	$ 51,000
Operating Expenses	30,000	30,000
Income Before Income Taxes	$ 21,000	$ 21,000

After the end of 20x4, the company discovered that an error had resulted in a $9,000 understatement of the 20x3 ending inventory.

Compute the corrected income before income taxes for 20x3 and 20x4. What effect will the error have on income before income taxes and owner's equity for 20x5?

E 11. LO 6 *Lower-of-Cost-or-Market Rule*

Mercurio Company values its inventory, shown below, at the lower of cost or market. Compute Mercurio's inventory value using (1) the item-by-item method and (2) the major category method.

		Per Unit	
	Quantity	Cost	Market
Category I			
Item aa	200	$ 2.00	$ 1.80
Item bb	240	4.00	4.40
Item cc	400	8.00	7.50
Category II			
Item dd	300	12.00	13.00
Item ee	400	18.00	18.20

E 12. SO 7 *Retail Inventory Method*

Roseanne's Dress Shop had net retail sales of $500,000 during the current year. The following additional information was obtained from the accounting records:

	At Cost	At Retail
Beginning Inventory	$ 80,000	$120,000
Net Purchases (excluding Freight In)	280,000	440,000
Freight In	20,800	

1. Using the retail method, estimate the company's ending inventory at cost.
2. Assume that a physical inventory taken at year end revealed an inventory on hand of $36,000 at retail value. What is the estimated amount of inventory shrinkage (loss due to theft, damage, and so forth) at cost using the retail method?

E 13. SO 7 *Gross Profit Method*

Dale Nolan was at home watching television when he received a call from the fire department. His business was a total loss from fire. The insurance company asked him to prove his inventory loss. For the year, until the date of the fire, Dale's company had sales of $450,000 and purchases of $280,000. Freight in amounted to $13,700, and the beginning inventory was $45,000. It was Dale's custom to price goods to achieve a gross margin of 40 percent.

Compute Dale's estimated inventory loss.

Problems

LO 1 LO 3 *Periodic Inventory System and Inventory Costing Methods*

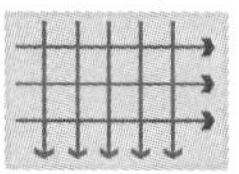

P 1. The Precision Door Company sold 2,200 doors during 20x2 at $160 per door. Its beginning inventory on January 1 was 130 doors at $56. Purchases made during the year were as follows:

February	225 doors @ $62
April	350 doors @ $65
June	700 doors @ $70
August	300 doors @ $66
October	400 doors @ $68
November	250 doors @ $72

The company's selling and administrative expenses for the year were $101,000, and the company uses the periodic inventory system.

REQUIRED

1. Prepare a schedule to compute the cost of goods available for sale.
2. Compute income before income taxes under each of the following inventory cost flow assumptions: (a) the average-cost method; (b) the FIFO method; and (c) the LIFO method.
3. Compute inventory turnover and average days' inventory on hand under each of the inventory cost flow assumptions in **2.** What conclusion can be made from this comparison?

LO 3 *Periodic Inventory System and Inventory Methods*

P 2. The inventory, purchases, and sales of Product BRS for August and September follow. The company closes its books at the end of each month and uses a periodic inventory system.

Aug.	1	Inventory	60 units @ $49
	7	Sale	20 units
	10	Purchase	100 units @ $52
	19	Sale	70 units
	31	Inventory	70 units
Sept.	4	Purchase	120 units @ $53
	11	Sale	110 units
	15	Purchase	50 units @ $54
	23	Sale	80 units
	25	Purchase	100 units @ $55
	27	Sale	100 units
	30	Inventory	50 units

REQUIRED

1. Compute the cost of the ending inventory on August 31 and September 30 using the average-cost method. In addition, determine cost of goods sold for August and September. Round unit costs to cents and totals to dollars.
2. Compute the cost of the ending inventory on August 31 and September 30 using the FIFO method. In addition, determine cost of goods sold for August and September.
3. Compute the cost of the ending inventory on August 31 and September 30 using the LIFO method. In addition, determine cost of goods sold for August and September.

LO 4 *Perpetual Inventory System and Inventory Methods*

P 3. Use the data provided in **P 2,** but assume that the company uses the perpetual inventory system. (**Hint:** In preparing the solutions required on the following page, it is helpful to determine the balance of inventory after each transaction, as shown in the Review Problem for this chapter.)

REQUIRED

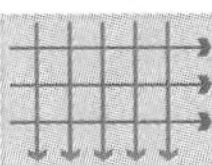

1. Determine the cost of ending inventory and cost of goods sold for August and September using the average-cost method. Round unit costs to cents and totals to dollars.
2. Determine the cost of ending inventory and cost of goods sold for August and September using the FIFO method.
3. Determine the cost of ending inventory and cost of goods sold for August and September using the LIFO method.

P 4. SO 7 *Retail Inventory Method*

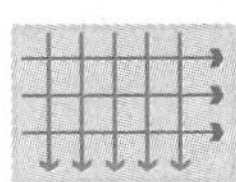

Maywood Company operates a large discount store and uses the retail inventory method to estimate the cost of ending inventory. Management suspects that in recent weeks there have been unusually heavy losses from shoplifting or employee pilferage. To estimate the amount of the loss, the company has taken a physical inventory and will compare the results with the estimated cost of inventory. Data from the accounting records of Maywood Company are as follows:

	At Cost	At Retail
March 1 Beginning Inventory	$102,976	$148,600
Purchases	143,466	217,000
Purchases Returns and Allowances	(4,086)	(6,400)
Freight In	1,900	
Sales		218,366
Sales Returns and Allowances		(1,866)
March 31 Physical Inventory		124,900

REQUIRED

1. Using the retail method, prepare a schedule to estimate the dollar amount of the store's year-end inventory at cost.
2. Use the store's cost to retail ratio to reduce the retail value of the physical inventory to cost.
3. Calculate the estimated amount of inventory shortage at cost and at retail.

P 5. SO 7 *Gross Profit Method*

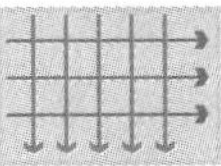

Jauss and Sons is a large retail furniture company that operates in two adjacent warehouses. One warehouse is a showroom, and the other is used to store merchandise. On the night of May 9, a fire broke out in the storage warehouse and destroyed the merchandise. Fortunately, the fire did not reach the showroom, so all the merchandise on display was saved.

Although the company maintained a perpetual inventory system, its records were rather haphazard, and the last reliable physical inventory had been taken on December 31. In addition, there was no control of the flow of the goods between the showroom and the warehouse. Thus, it was impossible to tell what goods should have been in either place. As a result, the insurance company required an independent estimate of the amount of loss. The insurance company examiners were satisfied when they were provided with the following information:

Merchandise Inventory on December 31	$1,454,800
Purchases, January 1 to May 9	2,412,200
Purchases Returns, January 1 to May 9	(10,706)
Freight In, January 1 to May 9	53,100
Sales, January 1 to May 9	3,959,050
Sales Returns, January 1 to May 9	(29,800)
Merchandise inventory in showroom on May 9	402,960
Average gross profit margin	44%

REQUIRED

Prepare a schedule that estimates the amount of the inventory lost in the fire.

Alternate Problems

P 6. LO 1, LO 3 *Periodic Inventory System and Inventory Costing Methods*

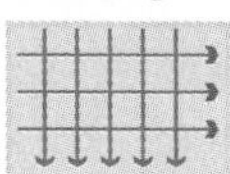

Premo Company merchandises a single product called Compak. The following data represent beginning inventory and purchases of Compak during the past year: January 1 inventory, 68,000 units at $11.00; February purchases, 80,000 units at $12.00; March purchases, 160,000 units at $12.40; May purchases, 120,000 units at $12.60; July purchases, 200,000 units at $12.80; September purchases, 160,000 units at $12.60; and November purchases, 60,000 units at $13.00. Sales of Compak totaled 786,000 units at $20 per unit. Selling and administrative expenses totaled $5,102,000 for the year, and Premo Company uses a periodic inventory system.

REQUIRED

1. Prepare a schedule to compute the cost of goods available for sale.
2. Compute income before income taxes under each of the following inventory cost flow assumptions: (a) the average-cost method; (b) the FIFO method; and (c) the LIFO method.
3. Compute inventory turnover and average days' inventory on hand under each of the inventory cost flow assumptions in **2.** What conclusion can be made from this comparison?

P 7. LO 3 *Periodic Inventory System and Inventory Methods*

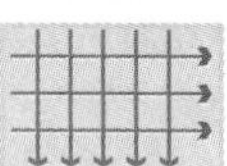

The inventory of Product D and data on purchases and sales for a two-month period follow. The company closes its books at the end of each month. It uses a periodic inventory system.

Apr.	1	Inventory	50 units @ $102
	5	Sale	30 units
	10	Purchase	100 units @ $110
	17	Sale	60 units
	30	Inventory	60 units
May	2	Purchase	100 units @ $108
	8	Sale	110 units
	14	Purchase	50 units @ $112
	18	Sale	40 units
	22	Purchase	60 units @ $117
	26	Sale	30 units
	30	Sale	20 units
	31	Inventory	70 units

REQUIRED

1. Compute the cost of ending inventory of Product D on April 30 and May 31 using the average-cost method. In addition, determine cost of goods sold for April and May. Round unit costs to cents and totals to dollars.
2. Compute the cost of the ending inventory on April 30 and May 31 using the FIFO method. In addition, determine cost of goods sold for April and May.
3. Compute the cost of the ending inventory on April 30 and May 31 using the LIFO method. In addition, determine cost of goods sold for April and May.

P 8. LO 4 *Perpetual Inventory System and Inventory Methods*

Use the data provided in **P 7,** but assume that the company uses the perpetual inventory system. (**Hint:** In preparing the solutions required below, it is helpful to determine the balance of inventory after each transaction, as shown in the Review Problem for this chapter.)

REQUIRED

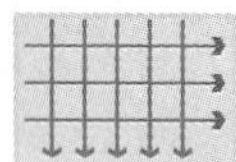

1. Determine the cost of ending inventory and cost of goods sold for April and May using the average-cost method. Round unit costs to cents and totals to dollars.
2. Determine the cost of ending inventory and cost of goods sold for April and May using the FIFO method.
3. Determine the cost of ending inventory and cost of goods sold for April and May using the LIFO method.

Skills Development

CONCEPTUAL ANALYSIS

SD 1. LO 1 *Evaluation of Inventory Levels*

The Gap, Inc., is one of the most important retailers of casual clothing for all members of the family. *Business Week* reports, "The Gap, Inc., is hell-bent on becoming to apparel what McDonald's is to food." With more than 1,100 stores already open, the company plans to open about 150 new stores per year for the next half decade. How does the company stay ahead of the competition? "One way is through frequent replenishment of mix-and-match inventory. That enables the company to clear out unpopular items fast—which prompts shoppers to check in on the new selections more often. . . . The Gap replaces inventory 7.5 times a year. That compares with 3.5 times at other specialty apparel stores."[13] One way in which The Gap controls inventory is by applying a just-in-time operating environment. How many days of inventory does The Gap have on hand on average compared to the competition? Discuss why those comparisons are important to The Gap. (Think of as many business and financial reasons as you can.) What is a just-in-time operating environment? Why is it important to achieving a favorable inventory turnover?

SD 2. LO 5 *LIFO Inventory Method*

Ninety-three percent of paper companies use the LIFO inventory method for the costing of inventories, whereas only 10 percent of computer equipment companies use LIFO.[14] Describe the LIFO inventory method. What effects does it have on reported income and income taxes during periods of price changes? Discuss why the paper industry would use LIFO, but most of the computer industry would not.

SD 3. LO 5, LO 6 *Lower of Cost or Market and Conservatism*

Mobil Corporation adopted the LIFO inventory method for its U.S. operations in 1957, when crude oil prices were only about $3 per barrel, but it did not adopt LIFO for its international operations until 1982, when crude oil prices were more than $30 per barrel. In 1994, the company adopted the lower-of-LIFO-cost-or-market method and, as a result, took a $250 million charge to earnings when crude oil prices dropped precipitously to less than $20 per barrel.[15] Explain why in this situation the lower-of-LIFO-cost-or-market method would result in the $250 million charge. Explain whether Mobil's domestic or international inventories would be more closely valued to market after the charge. Define the accounting convention of conservatism and tell how it explains the inconsistency between valuation of domestic and international inventories.

ETHICAL DILEMMA

SD 4. LO 1, LO 5 *Inventories, Income Determination, and Ethics*

Flare, Inc., which has a December 31 year end, designs and sells fashions for young professional women. Sandra Mason, president of the company, feared that the forecasted 2000 profitability goals would not be reached. She was pleased when Flare received a large order on December 30 from The Executive Woman, a retail chain of upscale stores for businesswomen. Mason immediately directed the controller to record the sale, which represented 13 percent of Flare's annual sales, but directed the inventory control department not to separate the goods for shipment until after January 1. Separated goods are not included in inventory because they have been sold. On December 31, the company's auditors arrived to observe the year-end taking of the physical inventory under the periodic inventory system. What will be the effect of Mason's action on Flare's 2000 profitability? What will be the effect on 2001 profitability? Was Mason's action ethical?

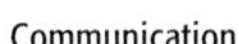
Communication

Critical Thinking

Group Activity

Memo

Ethics

International

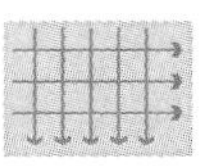
Spreadsheet

General Ledger

CD-ROM

Internet

RESEARCH ACTIVITY

LO 2 LO 4 *Retail Business Inventories*

SD 5. Make an appointment to visit a local retail business—a grocery, clothing, book, music, or appliance store, for example—and interview the manager for thirty minutes about the company's inventory accounting system. The store may be a branch of a larger company. Find out answers to the following questions, summarize your findings in a paper to be handed in, and be prepared to discuss your results in class.

What is the physical flow of merchandise into the store, and what documents are used in connection with this flow?

What documents are prepared when merchandise is sold?

Does the store keep perpetual inventory records? If so, does it keep the records in units only, or does it keep track of cost as well? If not, what system does the store use?

How often does the company take a physical inventory?

How are financial statements generated for the store?

What method does the company use to cost its inventory for financial statements?

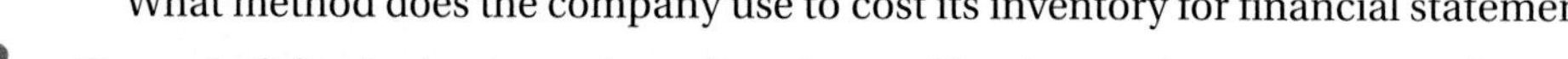

Group Activity: Assign teams to various types of businesses in your community.

DECISION-MAKING PRACTICE

LO 5 *Inventory Methods, Income Taxes, and Cash Flows*

SD 6. The ***Osaka Trading Company*** began business in 20x1 for the purpose of importing and marketing an electronic component used widely in digital appliances. It is now December 20, 20x1, and management is considering its options. Among its considerations is which inventory method to choose. It has decided to choose either the FIFO or the LIFO method. Under the periodic inventory system, the effects on net income of using the two methods are as follows:

	FIFO Method	LIFO Method
Sales: 500,000 units × $12	$6,000,000	$6,000,000
Cost of Goods Sold		
Purchases		
200,000 × $4	$ 800,000	$ 800,000
400,000 × $6	2,400,000	2,400,000
Total Purchases	$3,200,000	$3,200,000
Less Ending Inventory		
FIFO: 100,000 × $6	(600,000)	
LIFO: 100,000 × $4		(400,000)
Cost of Goods Sold	$2,600,000	$2,800,000
Gross Margin	$3,400,000	$3,200,000
Operating Expenses	2,400,000	2,400,000
Income Before Income Taxes	$1,000,000	$ 800,000
Income Taxes	300,000	240,000
Net Income	$ 700,000	$ 560,000

Also, management has an option to purchase an additional 100,000 units of inventory before year end at a price of $8 per unit, the price that is expected to prevail during 20x2. The income tax rate applicable to the company in 20x1 is 30 percent.

Business conditions are expected to be favorable in 20x2, as they were in 20x1. Management has asked you for advice. Analyze the effects of making the additional purchase. Then prepare a memorandum to Osaka management in which you compare cash outcomes under the four alternatives and advise management which inventory method to choose and whether to order the additional inventory. Be prepared to discuss your recommendations.

Financial Reporting and Analysis

INTERPRETING FINANCIAL REPORTS

LO 1 LO 2 LO 5 **FRA 1.** *LIFO, FIFO, and Income Taxes*

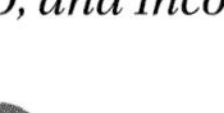

Hershey Foods Corp. is famous for its chocolate and confectionary products. A portion of the company's income statements for 1996 and 1995 follows (in thousands):[16]

	1996	1995
Net Sales	$3,989,308	$3,690,667
Cost of Goods Sold	2,302,089	2,126,274
Gross Margin	$1,687,219	$1,564,393
Selling, General, and Administrative Expenses	1,159,439	1,053,909
Income from Operations	$ 527,780	$ 510,484
Interest Expense, Net	48,043	44,833
Income Before Income Taxes	$ 479,737	$ 465,651
Provision for Income Taxes	206,551	184,034
Net Income	$ 273,186	$ 281,617

In a note on supplemental balance sheet information, Hershey indicated that most of its inventories are maintained using the last-in, first-out (LIFO) method. The company also reported that inventories (in thousands) using the LIFO method were $474,978 in 1996 and $397,570 in 1995. In addition, it reported that if valued using the first-in, first-out (FIFO) method, inventories (in thousands) would have been $552,589 in 1996 and $466,678 in 1995. In other words, inventory (in thousands) valued under FIFO would have been higher than the values under LIFO by $77,611 in 1996 and $69,108 in 1995.

REQUIRED

1. Prepare a schedule comparing net income for 1996 under the LIFO method with what it would have been under FIFO. Use a corporate income tax rate of 43.1 percent (Hershey's average tax rate in 1996).
2. Why do you suppose Hershey's management chooses to use the LIFO inventory method? On what economic conditions, if any, do those reasons depend? Given your calculations in **1,** do you believe the economic conditions relevant to Hershey were advantageous for using LIFO in 1996? Explain your answer.
3. Compute inventory turnover and average days' inventory on hand under each of the cost flow assumptions in **1.** What conclusion can be made from this comparison?

LO 5 **FRA 2.** *Misstatement of Inventory*

The Wall Street Journal reported that ***Crazy Eddie Inc.,*** a discount consumer electronics chain, seemed to be missing $45 million in merchandise inventory. "It was a shock," Elias Zinn, the new president and chief executive officer, was quoted as saying.[17]

The article went on to say that Mr. Zinn headed a management team that had taken control of Crazy Eddie after a new board of directors was elected at a shareholders' meeting. A count turned up only $75 million in inventory, compared with $126.7 million reported by the old management. Net sales could account for only $6.7 million of the difference. Mr. Zinn said he didn't know whether bookkeeping errors or an actual physical loss created the shortfall, although at least one store manager felt it was a bookkeeping error, because security is strong. "It would be hard for someone to steal anything," he said.

REQUIRED

1. What has been the effect of the misstatement of inventory on Crazy Eddie's reported earnings in prior accounting periods?
2. Is this a situation you would expect in a company that is experiencing financial difficulty? Explain.

International Company

FRA 3. LO 1 LO 5 *Inventory Levels and Methods*

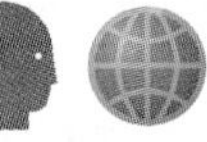

Two large Japanese diversified electronics companies are ***Pioneer Electronic Corporation*** and ***Yamaha Motor Co., Ltd.*** Both companies use the average-cost method and the lower-of-cost-or-market rule to account for inventories. The following data are for their 1996 fiscal years (in millions of yen).[18]

	Pioneer	Yamaha
Beginning Inventory	¥ 91,109	¥105,060
Ending Inventory	103,011	122,179
Cost of Goods Sold	365,108	556,883

Compare the inventory efficiency of Pioneer and Yamaha by computing the inventory turnover and average days' inventory on hand for both companies in 1996. Comment on the results. Most companies in the United States use the LIFO inventory method. How would inventory method affect your evaluation if you were to compare Pioneer and Yamaha to a U.S. company? What could you do to make the results comparable?

Toys "R" Us Annual Report

FRA 4. LO 1 LO 5 LO 6 SO 7 *Retail Inventory Method and Inventory Ratios*

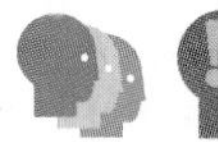

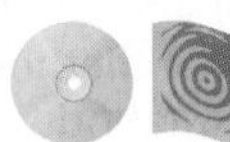

Refer to the note related to inventories in the Toys "R" Us Annual report to answer the following questions: What inventory method(s) does Toys "R" Us use? Why do you think that if LIFO inventories had been valued at FIFO, there would be no difference? Do you think many of the company's inventories are valued at market? Even though few companies use the retail inventory method, why do you think Toys "R" Us uses this method? Compute and compare the inventory turnover and average days' inventory on hand for Toys "R" Us for 1996 and 1997. Beginning 1996 inventory was $1,806,400,000.

Fingraph® Financial Analyst™

FRA 5. LO 1 *Analysis of Inventories and Operating Cycle*

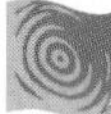

Select any two companies from the same industry on the Fingraph® Financial Analyst™ CD-ROM software. Choose an industry, such as manufacturing, consumer products, consumer food and beverage, or computers, in which inventory is likely to be an important current asset.

1. In the annual reports for the companies you have selected, read any reference to inventories in the summary of significant accounting policies or notes to the financial statements. What inventory method does the company use? What are the changes in and relative importance of raw materials, work in process, and finished goods inventories?
2. Display and print in tabular and graphical form the Liquidity and Asset Utilization Analysis page. Prepare a table that compares the inventory turnover and average days' inventory on hand for both companies for two years. Also include in your table the operating cycle by combining average days' inventory on hand with average days' sales uncollected.
3. Find and read references to inventories in the liquidity analysis section of management's discussion and analysis in each annual report.
4. Write a one-page executive summary that highlights the accounting policies for inventories, the relative importance and changes in raw materials, work in process, and finished goods, and compares the inventory utilization of the two companies, including reference to management's assessment. Comment specifically on the financing implications of the companies' relative operating cycles. Include the Fingraph® page and your table as an attachment to your report.

ENDNOTES

1. J.C. Penney Company, Inc., *Annual Report,* 1996.
2. American Institute of Certified Public Accountants, *Accounting Research Bulletin No. 43* (New York: AICPA, 1953), ch. 4.
3. American Institute of Certified Public Accountants, *Accounting Research Bulletin No. 43* (New York: AICPA, 1953), ch. 4.

4. Jim Carlton, "Apple's Net Fell 48% in 4th Quarter as Computer Shortages Hurt Results," *The Wall Street Journal,* October 19, 1995.
5. Jim Carlton, "Apple Posts Record $740 Million Loss, More than Doubles Planned Layoffs," *The Wall Street Journal,* April 18, 1996.
6. Micah Frankel and Robert Trezevant, "The Year-End LIFO Inventory Purchasing Decision: An Empirical Test," *The Accounting Review,* April 1994.
7. A single exception to this rule is that taxpayers must notify the IRS of a change to LIFO from another method, but they do not need to have advance IRS approval.
8. American Institute of Certified Public Accountants, *Accounting Trends & Techniques* (New York: AICPA, 1997).
9. Amoco Corporation, *Annual Report,* 1996.
10. Teri Agins, "Report Is Said to Show Pervasive Fraud at Leslie" and "Leslie Fay Co.'s Profits Restated for Past 3 Years," *The Wall Street Journal,* September 27 and 30, 1993.
11. In some cases, *market value* is determined by the *realizable value* of the inventory—the amount for which the goods can be sold—rather than by the amount for which the goods can be replaced. The circumstances in which realizable value determines market value are encountered in practice only occasionally, and the valuation procedures are technical enough to be addressed in a more advanced accounting course.
12. American Institute of Certified Public Accountants, *Accounting Trends & Techniques* (New York: AICPA, 1997).
13. "Everybody's Falling into The Gap," *Business Week,* September 23, 1991, p. 36.
14. American Institute of Certified Public Accountants, *Accounting Trends & Techniques* (New York: AICPA, 1997), p. 166.
15. Allanna Sullivan, "Accounting Change at Mobil Makes First-Quarter Profit a $145 Million Loss," *The Wall Street Journal,* August 1, 1994.
16. Adapted from Hershey Foods Corp., *Annual Report,* 1996.
17. Based on Ann Hagedorn, "Crazy Eddie Says About $45 Million of Goods Missing," *The Wall Street Journal,* November 20, 1987, p. 47.
18. Pioneer Electronics Corporation, *Annual Report,* 1996; and Yamaha Motor Co. Ltd., *Annual Report,* 1996.

Long-Term Assets

LEARNING OBJECTIVES

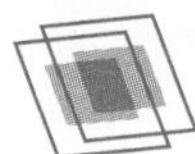

1. **Identify the types of long-term assets and explain the management issues related to accounting for them.**
2. **Distinguish between capital and revenue expenditures, and account for the cost of property, plant, and equipment.**
3. **Define *depreciation,* state the factors that affect its computation, and show how to record it.**
4. **Compute periodic depreciation under the (a) straight-line method, (b) production method, and (c) declining-balance method.**
5. **Account for the disposal of depreciable assets not involving exchanges.**
6. **Account for the disposal of depreciable assets involving exchanges.**
7. **Identify the issues related to accounting for natural resources and compute depletion.**
8. **Apply the matching rule to intangible assets, including research and development costs and goodwill.**

SUPPLEMENTAL OBJECTIVE

9. **Apply depreciation methods to problems of partial years, revised rates, groups of similar items, special types of capital expenditures, and cost recovery.**

DECISION POINT

H. J. HEINZ COMPANY

The effects of management's decisions regarding long-term assets are most apparent in the areas of reported total assets and net income. How does one learn about the significance of those items to a company? An idea of the extent of a company's long-term assets and their importance can be gained from the financial statements. For example, this list of assets (in thousands of dollars) is taken from the 1996 annual report of H. J. Heinz Company, one of the world's largest food companies. Of the company's almost $8.6 billion in total assets, about 30 percent consists of property, plant, and equipment, and another 28 percent is goodwill and other intangibles. On the income statement, depreciation and amortization expenses associated with those assets are $344 million, or

Financial Highlights		
(In thousands)	**1996**	**1995**
Property, Plant, and Equipment:		
Land	$ 62,243	$ 60,955
Buildings and leasehold improvements	824,308	804,762
Equipment, furniture, and other	3,333,493	3,138,937
	4,220,044	4,004,654
Less accumulated depreciation	1,603,216	1,470,278
Total property, plant, and equipment, net	$2,616,828	$2,534,376
Other Noncurrent Assets:		
Investments, advances, and other assets	$ 573,645	$ 543,032
Goodwill (net of amortization: 1996–$211,693 and 1995–$163,793)	1,737,478	1,682,933
Other intangibles (net of amortization: 1996–$141,886 and 1995–$117,430)	649,048	663,825
Total other noncurrent assets	$2,960,171	$2,889,790

Critical Thinking Question: Heinz has invested $4.2 billion in gross property, plant, and equipment and has expensed, as of 1996, slightly more than $1.6 billion. What does the $2.6 billion in total property, plant, and equipment, net represent?
Answer: It is the undepreciated acquisition cost of these assets. It will be allocated as depreciation expense to future accounting periods. It does not represent the value of the assets.

about 52 percent of net income, and on the statement of cash flows, more than $334 million was spent on new long-term assets.[1] This chapter deals with long-term assets: property, plant, and equipment and intangible assets.

Management Issues Related to Accounting for Long-Term Assets

OBJECTIVE 1

Identify the types of long-term assets and explain the management issues related to accounting for them

Related Text Assignments:
Q: 1, 2, 3, 4, 5, 6, 7
SE: 1
E: 1, 2
SD: 1, 7
FRA: 3, 4

Clarification Note: For an asset to be classified as property, plant, and equipment, it must be "put in use." This means that it is available for its intended purpose. An emergency generator is "put in use" when it is available for emergencies, even if it is never used.

Point to Emphasize: A computer used in the office would be considered plant and equipment, whereas an identical computer held for sale to customers would be considered inventory.

Long-term assets are assets that (1) have a useful life of more than one year, (2) are acquired for use in the operation of a business, and (3) are not intended for resale to customers. For many years, it was common to refer to long-term assets as *fixed assets,* but use of this term is declining because the word *fixed* implies that they last forever. The relative importance of long-term assets to various industries is shown in Figure 1. Long-term assets range from 22.6 percent of total assets in advertising agencies to 55.8 percent in interstate trucking.

Although there is no strict minimum useful life an asset must have to be classified as long term, the most common criterion is that the asset must be capable of repeated use for a period of at least a year. Included in this category is equipment used only in peak or emergency periods, such as generators.

Assets that are not used in the normal course of business should not be included in this category. Thus, land held for speculative reasons or buildings no longer used in ordinary business operations should not be included in the property, plant, and equipment category. Instead, they should be classified as long-term investments.

Finally, if an item is held for resale to customers, it should be classified as inventory—not plant and equipment—no matter how durable it is. For example, a printing press that is held for sale by a printing press manufacturer would be considered inventory, whereas the same printing press would be considered plant and equipment for a printing company that buys it for use in operations.

Long-term assets differ from current assets in that they support the operating cycle instead of being a part of it. They are also expected to benefit the business for a

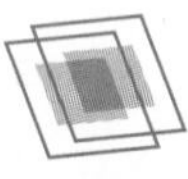

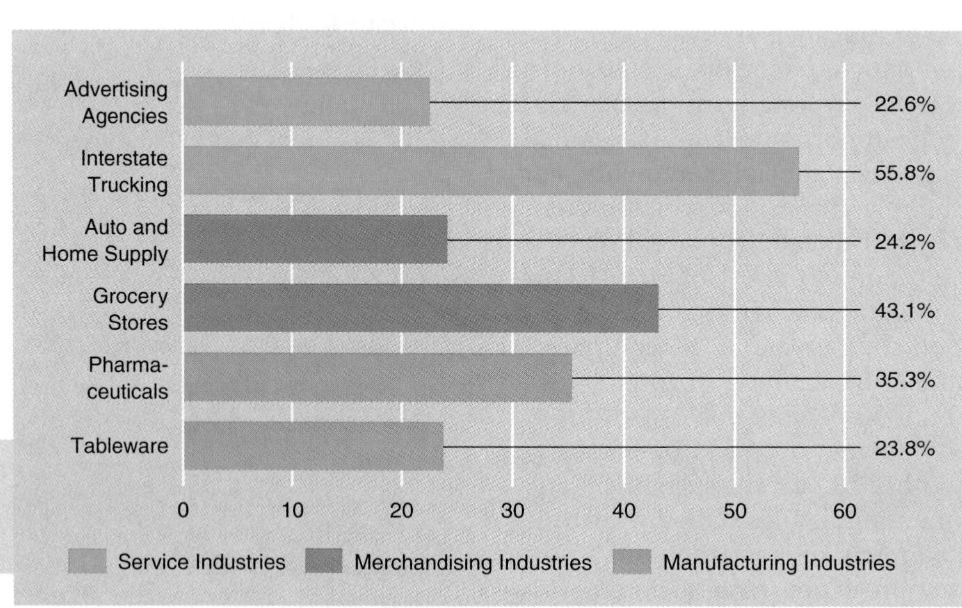

Figure 1
Long-Term Assets as a Percentage of Total Assets for Selected Industries

Source: Data from Dun & Bradstreet, *Industry Norms and Key Business Ratios,* 1996–97.

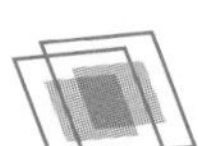

Point to Emphasize: For an asset to be classified as intangible, it must lack physical substance, be long term, and (normally) represent a legal right or advantage.

BALANCE SHEET Long-Term Assets	INCOME STATEMENT Expenses
Tangible Assets: long-term assets that have physical substance Land Plant, Buildings, Equipment (plant assets)	Land is not expensed because it has an unlimited life. **Depreciation:** periodic allocation of the cost of a tangible long-lived asset (other than land and natural resources) over its estimated useful life
Natural Resources: long-term assets purchased for the economic value that can be taken from the land and used up, as with ore, lumber, oil, and gas or other resources contained in the land Mines Timberland Oil and Gas Fields	**Depletion:** exhaustion of a natural resource through mining, cutting, pumping, or other extraction, and the way in which the cost is allocated
Intangible Assets: long-term assets that have no physical substance but have a value based on rights or advantages accruing to the owner Patents, Copyrights, Trademarks Franchises, Organizational Costs Leaseholds, Leasehold Improvements Goodwill	**Amortization:** periodic allocation of the cost of an intangible asset to the periods it benefits

Figure 2
Classification of Long-Term Assets and Corresponding Expenses

longer period than do current assets. Current assets are expected to be used up or converted to cash within one year or during the operating cycle, whichever is longer. Long-term assets are expected to last beyond that period. Long-term assets and their related expenses are summarized in Figure 2.

Point to Emphasize: The purchase of a long-term asset is in reality a prepayment for some form of future benefit.

Generally, long-lived assets are reported at carrying value, as presented in Figure 3. Carrying value is the unexpired part of the cost of an asset, not its market value; it is also called *book value.* If a long-lived asset loses some or all of its revenue-generating potential prior to the end of its useful life, the asset may be deemed impaired and its carrying value reduced. Asset impairment occurs when the sum of the expected cash flows from the asset is less than the carrying value of the asset.[2] Reducing carrying value to fair value, as measured by the present value of future cash flows, is an application of conservatism. All long-term assets are subject to an asset impairment evaluation. A reduction in carrying value as a result of impairment is recorded as a loss.

Facing deregulation and competition for the first time, six of the seven Baby Bell regional telephone companies, including Pacific Telesis, Bell South, and NYNEX, took writedowns in the billions of dollars. In the past, the cost of old equipment could be passed on to consumers through regulated rate increases, but with competition, rates are decreasing, not increasing. As a result, the future cash flows cannot

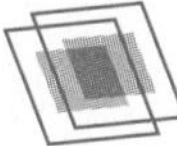

Plant Assets	Natural Resources	Intangible Assets
Less Accumulated Depreciation	Less Accumulated Depletion	Less Accumulated Amortization
Carrying Value	Carrying Value	Carrying Value

Figure 3
Carrying Value of Long-Term Assets on Balance Sheet

justify the recorded asset carrying values of aging copper telephone lines, switching gear, and other equipment. Estimated useful lives for these assets have been reduced by 50 percent or more. The writedowns have caused the companies to report operating losses.[3]

Deciding to Acquire Long-Term Assets

The decision to acquire a long-term asset involves a complex process. Methods of evaluating data to make rational decisions in this area are grouped under a topic called capital budgeting, which is usually covered as a managerial accounting topic. However, an awareness of the general nature of the problem is helpful in understanding the accounting issues related to long-term assets. To illustrate the acquisition decision, let us assume that Irena Markova, M.D., is considering the purchase of a $5,000 computer for her office. She estimates that if she purchases the computer, she can reduce the hours of a part-time employee sufficiently to save net cash flows of $2,000 per year for four years and that the computer will be worth $1,000 at the end of that period. These data are summarized as follows:

	20x1	20x2	20x3	20x4
Acquisition cost	($5,000)			
Net annual savings in cash flows	$2,000	$2,000	$2,000	$2,000
Disposal price				1,000
Net cash flows	($3,000)	$2,000	$2,000	$3,000

To place the cash flows on a comparable basis, it is helpful to use present value tables such as Tables 3 and 4 in the appendix on future value and present value tables. Assuming that the appropriate interest rate is 10 percent compounded annually, the purchase may be evaluated as follows:

		Present Value
Acquisition cost	Present value factor = 1.000 1.000 × $5,000	($5,000)
Net annual savings in cash flows	Present value factor = 3.170 (Table 4: 4 periods, 10%) 3.170 × $2,000	6,340
Disposal price	Present value factor = .683 (Table 3: 4 periods, 10%) .683 × $1,000	683
Net present value		$2,023

As long as the net present value is positive, Dr. Markova will earn at least 10 percent on the investment. In this case, the return is greater than 10 percent because the net present value is a positive $2,023. Based on this analysis, Dr. Markova makes the decision to purchase. However, there are other important considerations that have to be taken into account, such as the costs of training and maintenance, and the possibility that, because of unforeseen circumstances, the savings may not be as great as expected. In Dr. Markova's case, the decision to purchase is likely to be a good one because the net present value is both positive and large relative to the investment.

Information about a company's acquisitions of long-term assets may be found under investing activities in the statement of cash flows. For example, in referring to this section of its annual report, the management of ARCO Chemical Company, a manufacturer of chemicals used in consumer and industrial products, makes the following statement:

> Investment activities in 1995 included expenditures for plant and equipment of $195 million, which was comparable to the $184 million spent in 1994.[4]

Financing Long-Term Assets

In addition to deciding whether or not to acquire a long-term asset, management must decide how to finance the asset if it is acquired. Some companies are profitable enough to pay for long-term assets out of cash flows from operations, but when financing is needed, some form of long-term arrangement related to the life of the asset is usually most appropriate. For example, an automobile loan generally spans four or five years, whereas a mortgage loan on a house may span thirty years. For a major long-term acquisition, a company may issue capital stock, long-term notes, or bonds. A good place to study a company's long-term financing is in the financing activities section of the statement of cash flows. For instance, in discussing this section, ARCO Chemical Company's management states that "future cash requirements for capital expenditures, dividends and debt repayments, will be met by cash generated from operating activities and additional borrowing."[5] Another option a company may have is to lease long-term assets instead of buying them.

Applying the Matching Rule to Long-Term Assets

Accounting for long-term assets requires the proper application of the matching rule through the resolution of two important issues. The first is how much of the total cost to allocate to expense in the current accounting period. The second is how much to retain on the balance sheet as an asset to benefit future periods. To resolve these issues, four important questions about the acquisition, use, and disposal of each long-term asset, as illustrated in Figure 4, must be answered.

1. How is the cost of the long-term asset determined?
2. How should the expired portion of the cost of the long-term asset be allocated against revenues over time?
3. How should subsequent expenditures, such as repairs and additions, be treated?
4. How should disposal of the long-term asset be recorded?

Because of the long life of long-term assets and the complexity of the transactions involving them, management has many choices and estimates to make. For example, acquisition cost may be complicated by group purchases, trade-ins, or construction costs. In addition, to allocate the cost of the asset to future periods effectively, management must estimate how long the asset will last and what it will be worth at the end of its use. In making such estimates, it is helpful to think of a

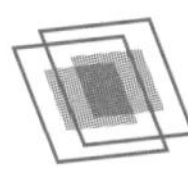

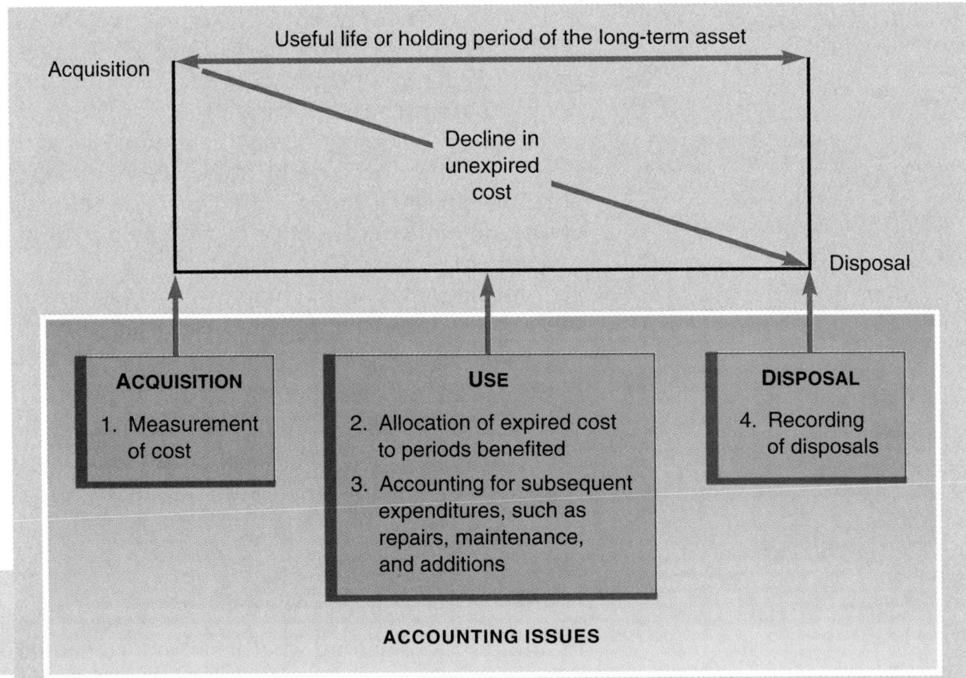

Figure 4
Issues of Accounting for Long-Term Assets

Clarification Note: Useful life is measured by the number of units a business expects to receive from an asset. It should not be confused with physical life, which is often much longer. If the management of a new business is having difficulty determining an asset's estimated useful life, it may obtain help from trade magazines. Nearly every industry has at least one.

long-term asset as a bundle of services to be used in the operation of the business over a period of years. A delivery truck may provide 100,000 miles of service over its life. A piece of equipment may have the potential to produce 500,000 parts. A building may provide shelter for 50 years. As each of those assets is purchased, the company is paying in advance for 100,000 miles, the capacity to produce 500,000 parts, or 50 years of service. In essence, each asset is a type of long-term prepaid expense. The accounting problem is to spread the cost of the services over the useful life of the asset. As the services benefit the company over the years, the cost becomes an expense rather than an asset.

Acquisition Cost of Property, Plant, and Equipment

OBJECTIVE 2

Distinguish between capital and revenue expenditures, and account for the cost of property, plant, and equipment

Related Text Assignments:
Q: 8, 9, 10
SE: 2, 3
E: 3, 4, 5, 14
P: 1, 6
SD: 4, 5
FRA: 3

The term expenditure refers to a payment or an obligation to make future payment for an asset, such as a truck, or a service, such as a repair. Expenditures may be classified as capital expenditures or revenue expenditures. A capital expenditure is an expenditure for the purchase or expansion of a long-term asset. Capital expenditures are recorded in the asset accounts because they benefit several future accounting periods. A revenue expenditure is an expenditure related to the repair, maintenance, and operation of a long-term asset. Revenue expenditures are recorded in the expense accounts because their benefits are realized in the current period.

Careful distinction between capital and revenue expenditures is important to the proper application of the matching rule. For example, if the purchase of an automobile is mistakenly recorded as a revenue expenditure, the total cost of the automobile is recorded as an expense on the income statement. As a result, current net income is reported at a lower amount (understated), and in future periods net income will be reported at a higher amount. If, on the other hand, a revenue expenditure, such as the painting of a building, were charged to an asset account,

Discussion Question: Dyeing a carpet may make it look almost new. Why then isn't that a capital expenditure? **Answer:** Although the carpet looks better, its fibers are not stronger, and it probably will not last significantly longer than it would have before the color was changed.

Discussion Question: The cost of mailing lists raises issues similar to those of software. Why would a company want to treat the cost of mailing lists as an asset? **Answer:** If mailing lists are treated as an asset, expenses will be lower in the first year, and thus net income will be higher.

Discussion Question: What theoretical reason might be given for recording the cost of mailing lists as an asset? **Answer:** The mailing lists will be used over and over and will benefit future accounting periods.

the expense of the current period would be understated. Current net income would be overstated by the same amount, and the net income of future periods would be understated.

Determining when a payment is an expense and when it is an asset is a matter of judgment, in the exercise of which management takes a leading role. For example, inconsistencies have existed in accounting for the costs of computer programs that run the systems for businesses. Some companies immediately write off the expense, whereas others treat it as a long-term intangible asset and amortize it year after year. As companies spend over $50 billion a year on this type of software, this is an important variable in the profitability of many companies. DST Systems Inc., a data processing company in Kansas City, spends $45 million per year on software for internal use, some of which it writes off when the software is developed by its own staff but capitalizes and amortizes over five years when it is bought off-the-shelf. The AICPA is issuing new rules to try to bring more standardization to these accounting issues, but considerable latitude will still exist, such as in determining how long the economic life of the software will be.[6]

General Approach to Acquisition Costs

The acquisition cost of property, plant, and equipment includes all expenditures reasonable and necessary to get the asset in place and ready for use. For example, the cost of installing and testing a machine is a legitimate cost of the machine. However, if the machine is damaged during installation, the cost of repairs is an operating expense and not an acquisition cost.

Point to Emphasize: Expenditures necessary to prepare an asset for its intended use are debited to the asset account.

Cost is easiest to determine when a purchase is made for cash. In that case, the cost of the asset is equal to the cash paid for the asset plus expenditures for freight, insurance while in transit, installation, and other necessary related costs. If a debt is incurred in the purchase of the asset, the interest charges are not a cost of the asset but a cost of borrowing the money to buy the asset. They are therefore an operating expense. An exception to this principle is that interest costs incurred during the construction of an asset are properly included as a cost of the asset.[7]

Expenditures such as freight, insurance while in transit, and installation are included in the cost of the asset because they are necessary if the asset is to function. Following the matching rule, they are allocated to the useful life of the asset rather than charged as expenses in the current period.

For practical purposes, many companies establish policies defining when an expenditure should be recorded as an expense or as an asset. For example, small expenditures for items that would normally be treated as assets may be treated as expenses because the amounts involved are not material in relation to net income. Thus, a wastebasket, which might last for years, would be recorded as a supplies expense rather than as a depreciable asset.

Some of the problems of determining the cost of a long-lived asset are demonstrated in the illustrations for land, land improvements, buildings, equipment, and group purchases presented in the next few sections.

Land

Point to Emphasize: Many costs may be incurred to prepare land for its intended use and condition. All such costs are debited to Land.

There are often expenditures in addition to the purchase price of land that should be debited to the Land account. Some examples are commissions to real estate agents; lawyers' fees; accrued taxes paid by the purchaser; costs of preparing the land to build on, such as draining, tearing down old buildings, clearing, and grading; and assessments for local improvements, such as streets and sewage systems. The cost of landscaping is usually debited to the Land account because such improvements are relatively permanent. Land is not subject to depreciation because it does not have a limited useful life.

Let us assume that a company buys land for a new retail operation. It pays a net purchase price of $170,000, pays brokerage fees of $6,000 and legal fees of $2,000,

Enrichment Note: While the costs of tearing down existing buildings can be minor, they can also be major. For example, companies spend millions of dollars imploding buildings to remove them and build new ones.

pays $10,000 to have an old building on the site torn down, receives $4,000 salvage from the old building, and pays $1,000 to have the site graded. The cost of the land will be $185,000.

Net purchase price		$170,000
Brokerage fees		6,000
Legal fees		2,000
Tearing down old building	$10,000	
Less salvage	4,000	6,000
Grading		1,000
Total cost		$185,000

Land Improvements Improvements to real estate, such as driveways, parking lots, and fences, have a limited life and are thus subject to depreciation. They should be recorded in an account called Land Improvements rather than in the Land account.

Buildings When an existing building is purchased, its cost includes the purchase price plus all repairs and other expenditures required to put it in usable condition. Buildings are subject to depreciation because they have a limited useful life. When a business constructs its own building, the cost includes all reasonable and necessary expenditures, such as those for materials, labor, part of the overhead and other indirect costs, architects' fees, insurance during construction, interest on construction loans during the period of construction, lawyers' fees, and building permits. If outside contractors are used in the construction, the net contract price plus other expenditures necessary to put the building in usable condition are included.

Enrichment Note: The electrical wiring and plumbing of a dental chair are included in the cost of the asset since they are a necessary cost of preparing the asset for use.

Equipment The cost of equipment includes all expenditures connected with purchasing the equipment and preparing it for use. Those expenditures include the invoice price less cash discounts; freight or transportation, including insurance; excise taxes and tariffs; buying expenses; installation costs; and test runs to ready the equipment for operation. Equipment is subject to depreciation.

Instructional Strategy: Form small groups and assign SD 4. Ask half the groups to prepare the role of the CFO and the other half, the role of the controller. In class, have representatives of each viewpoint role-play the situation. Follow up with questions and answers.

Group Purchases Sometimes land and other assets are purchased for a lump sum. Because land is a nondepreciable asset that has an unlimited life, it must have a separate ledger account, and the lump-sum purchase price must be apportioned between the land and the other assets. For example, assume that a building and the land on which it is situated are purchased for a lump-sum payment of $85,000. The apportionment can be made by determining the price of each if purchased separately and applying the appropriate percentages to the lump-sum price. Assume that appraisals yield estimates of $10,000 for the land and $90,000 for the building, if purchased separately. In that case, 10 percent of the lump-sum price, or $8,500, would be allocated to the land and 90 percent, or $76,500, would be allocated to the building, as follows:

	Appraisal	Percentage	Apportionment
Land	$ 10,000	10 ($10,000 ÷ $100,000)	$ 8,500 ($85,000 × 10%)
Building	90,000	90 ($90,000 ÷ $100,000)	76,500 ($85,000 × 90%)
Totals	$100,000	100	$85,000

BUSINESS BULLETIN: ETHICS IN PRACTICE

Determining the acquisition price of a long-term asset is not always as clear-cut as some might imagine, especially in the case of constructed assets. Management has considerable leeway, but if choices are questioned, the results can sometimes be costly. *The Wall Street Journal* reported that Chambers Development Co., a waste-disposal company, wrote off nearly $50 million when it decided to stop deferring costs related to the development of landfills. Previously, Chambers had been including certain indirect costs, such as executives' salaries and travel, legal, and public relations fees, as capital expenditures to be written off over the life of the landfill. *The Wall Street Journal* reported that Chambers portrayed the accounting change as the outcome of a theoretical debate about good accounting practice, but SEC investigators concluded that the accounting practices created fictitious profit beyond generally accepted accounting practices. Further write-offs may follow because of the large amount of interest the company is capitalizing as a cost of the landfill. On news of the accounting change, the company's stock price dropped 63 percent in one day.[8] After straightening out its accounting, Chambers was acquired by USA Waste for $424 million.

Accounting for Depreciation

OBJECTIVE 3

Define **depreciation,** *state the factors that affect its computation, and show how to record it*

Related Text Assignments:
Q: 11, 12, 13, 14
E: 6
P: 2, 7
SD: 1, 2
FRA: 1, 3

Depreciation accounting is described by the AICPA as follows:

> The cost of a productive facility is one of the costs of the services it renders during its useful economic life. Generally accepted accounting principles require that this cost be spread over the expected useful life of the facility in such a way as to allocate it as equitably as possible to the periods during which services are obtained from the use of the facility. This procedure is known as depreciation accounting, a system of accounting which aims to distribute the cost or other basic value of tangible capital assets, less salvage (if any), over the estimated useful life of the unit . . . in a systematic and rational manner. It is a process of allocation, not of valuation.[9]

This description contains several important points. First, all tangible assets except land have a limited useful life. Because of this limited useful life, the costs of these assets must be distributed as expenses over the years they benefit. Physical deterioration and obsolescence are the major causes of the limited useful life of a depreciable asset. The physical deterioration of tangible assets results from use and from exposure to the elements, such as wind and sun. Periodic repairs and a sound maintenance policy may keep buildings and equipment in good operating order and extract the maximum useful life from them, but every machine or building at some point must be discarded. The need for depreciation is not eliminated by repairs. Obsolescence is the process of becoming out of date. Because of fast-changing technology and fast-changing demands, machinery and even buildings often become obsolete before they wear out. Accountants do not distinguish between physical deterioration and obsolescence because they are interested in the length of an asset's useful life regardless of what limits that useful life.

Parenthetical Note: An older computer may be functioning as well as it did on the day of purchase, but it has become obsolete because much faster, more efficient computers are now available.

Second, the term *depreciation,* as used in accounting, does not refer to an asset's physical deterioration or decrease in market value over time. Depreciation means the allocation of the cost of a plant asset to the periods that benefit from the services of that asset. The term is used to describe the gradual conversion of the cost of the asset into an expense.

Point to Emphasize: Depreciation is the allocation of the historical cost of an asset, and any similarity between undepreciated cost and current market value is pure coincidence.

Third, depreciation is not a process of valuation. Accounting records are kept in accordance with the cost principle; they are not indicators of changing price levels. It is possible that, because of an advantageous purchase and specific market conditions, the market value of a building may rise. Nevertheless, depreciation must continue to be recorded because it is the result of an allocation, not a valuation, process. Eventually the building will wear out or become obsolete regardless of interim fluctuations in market value.

Factors That Affect the Computation of Depreciation

Four factors affect the computation of depreciation: (1) cost, (2) residual value, (3) depreciable cost, and (4) estimated useful life.

Cost As explained earlier in the chapter, cost is the net purchase price plus all reasonable and necessary expenditures to get the asset in place and ready for use.

Point to Emphasize: Residual value is the portion of an asset's acquisition cost expected to be recovered at the asset's disposal date.

Residual Value The residual value of an asset is its estimated net scrap, salvage, or trade-in value as of the estimated date of disposal. Other terms often used to describe residual value are *salvage value* and *disposal value.*

Point to Emphasize: It is depreciable cost, not historical cost, that is allocated over the useful life of a plant asset.

Depreciable Cost The depreciable cost of an asset is its cost less its residual value. For example, a truck that costs $12,000 and has a residual value of $3,000 would have a depreciable cost of $9,000. Depreciable cost must be allocated over the useful life of the asset.

Estimated Useful Life Estimated useful life is the total number of service units expected from a long-term asset. Service units may be measured in terms of years the asset is expected to be used, units expected to be produced, miles expected to be driven, or similar measures. In computing the estimated useful life of an asset, an accountant should consider all relevant information, including (1) past experience with similar assets, (2) the asset's present condition, (3) the company's repair and maintenance policy, (4) current technological and industry trends, and (5) local conditions such as weather.

BUSINESS BULLETIN: BUSINESS PRACTICE

Most airlines depreciate airplanes over an estimated useful life of ten to twenty years. But how long will a properly maintained airplane really last? In July 1968 Western Airlines paid $3.3 million for a new Boeing 737. Today, more than 78,000 flights later, this aircraft is still flying for a no-frills airline named Vanguard Airlines. During the course of its life, the owners of this aircraft have included Piedmont, Delta, US Airways, and other airlines. Virtually every part of the plane has been replaced over the years. Boeing believes the plane could theoretically make double the number of flights before it is retired.

The useful lives of many types of assets can be extended indefinitely if the assets are correctly maintained, but proper accounting in accordance with the matching rule would require depreciation over a "reasonable" useful life. Each airline that owned the plane would have accounted for the plane in this way.

Depreciation is recorded at the end of the accounting period by an adjusting entry that takes the following form:

A = L + OE			
− −	Depreciation Expense, Asset Name	XXX	
	Accumulated Depreciation, Asset Name		XXX
	To record depreciation for the period		

Methods of Computing Depreciation

Many methods are used to allocate the cost of plant assets to accounting periods through depreciation. Each is proper for certain circumstances. The most common methods are (1) the straight-line method, (2) the production method, and (3) an accelerated method known as the declining-balance method.

OBJECTIVE 4a

Compute periodic depreciation under the straight-line method

Related Text Assignments:
Q: 15, 16
SE: 4, 5, 6
E: 5, 6, 7
P: 2, 5, 7, 8
SD: 2
FRA: 1, 3, 4

Straight-Line Method When the straight-line method is used to calculate depreciation, the depreciable cost of the asset is spread evenly over the estimated useful life of the asset. The straight-line method is based on the assumption that depreciation depends only on the passage of time. The depreciation expense for each period is computed by dividing the depreciable cost (cost of the depreciating asset less its estimated residual value) by the number of accounting periods in the asset's estimated useful life. The rate of depreciation is the same in each year. Suppose, for example, that a delivery truck costs $10,000 and has an estimated residual value of $1,000 at the end of its estimated useful life of five years. The annual depreciation would be $1,800 under the straight-line method, calculated as follows:

$$\frac{\text{Cost} - \text{Residual Value}}{\text{Estimated Useful Life}} = \frac{\$10{,}000 - \$1{,}000}{5} = \$1{,}800$$

The depreciation for the five years would be as follows:

Clarification Note: The straight-line depreciation method should be used when approximately equal asset benefit is obtained each year.

Point to Emphasize: Residual value and useful life are, at best, educated guesses.

Instructional Strategy: In lieu of lecture and illustration, assign P 2 to small groups to prepare either in class or outside class. A member of each group will present part of P 2 and answer questions from the class. Encourage students to use good presentation skills. Review these, as necessary. Presenters may be randomly selected, so all should come prepared.

Depreciation Schedule, Straight-Line Method

	Cost	Yearly Depreciation	Accumulated Depreciation	Carrying Value
Date of purchase	$10,000	—	—	$10,000
End of first year	10,000	$1,800	$1,800	8,200
End of second year	10,000	1,800	3,600	6,400
End of third year	10,000	1,800	5,400	4,600
End of fourth year	10,000	1,800	7,200	2,800
End of fifth year	10,000	1,800	9,000	1,000

There are three important points to note from the depreciation schedule for the straight-line depreciation method. First, the depreciation is the same each year. Second, the accumulated depreciation increases uniformly. Third, the carrying value decreases uniformly until it reaches the estimated residual value.

OBJECTIVE 4b

Compute periodic depreciation under the production method

Production Method The production method of depreciation is based on the assumption that depreciation is solely the result of use and that the passage of time plays no role in the depreciation process. If we assume that the delivery truck from the previous example has an estimated useful life of 90,000 miles, the depreciation cost per mile would be determined as follows:

$$\frac{\text{Cost} - \text{Residual Value}}{\text{Estimated Units of Useful Life}} = \frac{\$10{,}000 - \$1{,}000}{90{,}000 \text{ miles}} = \$.10 \text{ per mile}$$

If we assume that the use of the truck was 20,000 miles for the first year, 30,000 miles for the second, 10,000 miles for the third, 20,000 miles for the fourth, and

10,000 miles for the fifth, the depreciation schedule for the delivery truck would appear as shown below.

Parenthetical Note: The production method is appropriate when a company has widely fluctuating rates of production. For example, carpet mills often close during the first two weeks in July. Charging a full month's depreciation would not achieve the goal of matching cost with revenue. Conversely, the same mills may run double shifts in September. At that time, twice the usual amount of depreciation should be charged.

Depreciation Schedule, Production Method

	Cost	Miles	Yearly Depreciation	Accumulated Depreciation	Carrying Value
Date of purchase	$10,000	—	—	—	$10,000
End of first year	10,000	20,000	$2,000	$2,000	8,000
End of second year	10,000	30,000	3,000	5,000	5,000
End of third year	10,000	10,000	1,000	6,000	4,000
End of fourth year	10,000	20,000	2,000	8,000	2,000
End of fifth year	10,000	10,000	1,000	9,000	1,000

There is a direct relation between the amount of depreciation each year and the units of output or use. Also, the accumulated depreciation increases each year in direct relation to units of output or use. Finally, the carrying value decreases each year in direct relation to units of output or use until it reaches the estimated residual value.

Under the production method, the unit of output or use employed to measure the estimated useful life of each asset should be appropriate for that asset. For example, the number of items produced may be an appropriate measure for one machine, but the number of hours of use may be a better measure for another. The production method should be used only when the output of an asset over its useful life can be estimated with reasonable accuracy.

OBJECTIVE 4c

Compute periodic depreciation under the declining-balance method

Parenthetical Note: Accelerated depreciation is appropriate for assets that provide the greatest benefits in their early years. Under such a method, depreciation charges will be high in years when revenue generation from the asset is high.

Point to Emphasize: The double-declining-balance method is the only method presented in which the residual value is not deducted before beginning the depreciation calculation.

Point to Emphasize: Under the double-declining-balance method, depreciation in the last year rarely equals the exact amount needed to reduce carrying value to residual value. Emphasize that depreciation in the last year is limited to the amount necessary to reduce carrying value to residual value.

Declining-Balance Method

An accelerated method of depreciation results in relatively large amounts of depreciation in the early years of an asset's life and smaller amounts in later years. Such a method, which is based on the passage of time, assumes that many kinds of plant assets are most efficient when new, and so provide more and better service in the early years of their useful life. It is consistent with the matching rule to allocate more depreciation to earlier years than to later years if the benefits or services received in the earlier years are greater.

An accelerated method also recognizes that changing technologies make some equipment lose service value rapidly. Thus, it is realistic to allocate more to depreciation in earlier years than in later years. New inventions and products result in obsolescence of equipment bought earlier, making it necessary to replace equipment sooner than if technology changed more slowly. Another argument in favor of an accelerated method is that repair expense is likely to be greater in later years than in earlier years. Thus, the total of repair and depreciation expense remains fairly constant over a period of years. This result naturally assumes that the services received from the asset are roughly equal from year to year.

The declining-balance method is the most common accelerated method of depreciation. Under this method, depreciation is computed by applying a fixed rate to the carrying value (the declining balance) of a tangible long-lived asset, resulting in higher depreciation charges during the early years of the asset's life. Though any fixed rate can be used, the most common rate is a percentage equal to twice the straight-line percentage. When twice the straight-line rate is used, the method is usually called the double-declining-balance method.

In our earlier example, the delivery truck had an estimated useful life of five years. Consequently, under the straight-line method, the depreciation rate for each year was 20 percent (100 percent ÷ 5 years).

Under the double-declining-balance method, the fixed rate is 40 percent (2 × 20 percent). This fixed rate is applied to the *remaining carrying value* at the end of each year. Estimated residual value is not taken into account in figuring depreciation except in a year when calculated depreciation exceeds the amount necessary to bring the carrying value down to the estimated residual value. The depreciation schedule for this method is as follows:

Depreciation Schedule, Double-Declining-Balance Method

	Cost	Yearly Depreciation		Accumulated Depreciation	Carrying Value
Date of purchase	$10,000		—	—	$10,000
End of first year	10,000	(40% × $10,000)	$4,000	$4,000	6,000
End of second year	10,000	(40% × $6,000)	2,400	6,400	3,600
End of third year	10,000	(40% × $3,600)	1,440	7,840	2,160
End of fourth year	10,000	(40% × $2,160)	864	8,704	1,296
End of fifth year	10,000		296*	9,000	1,000

*Depreciation limited to amount necessary to reduce carrying value to residual value: $296 = $1,296 (previous carrying value) − $1,000 (residual value).

Parenthetical Note: An asset remains on the books as long as it is in use. Even if the asset is fully depreciated, the company should not remove it from the books until it is taken out of service.

Note that the fixed rate is always applied to the carrying value at the end of the previous year. The depreciation is greatest in the first year and declines each year after that. Finally, the depreciation in the last year is limited to the amount necessary to reduce carrying value to residual value.

Comparing the Three Methods A visual comparison may provide a better understanding of the three depreciation methods described above. Figure 5 compares yearly depreciation and carrying value under the three methods. In the left-hand graph, which shows yearly depreciation, straight-line depreciation is uniform at $1,800 per year over the five-year period. However, the double-declining-balance method begins at an amount greater than straight-line ($4,000) and decreases each year to amounts that are less than straight-line (ultimately, $296). The production method does not generate a regular pattern because of the random fluctuation of the depreciation from year to year. The three yearly depreciation patterns are reflected in the graph of carrying value. In that graph, each method starts in the same place (cost of $10,000) and ends at the same place (residual value of $1,000). It is the patterns during the useful life of the asset that differ for each method. For instance, the carrying value under the straight-line method is always greater than that under the double-declining-balance method, except at the beginning and end of useful life.

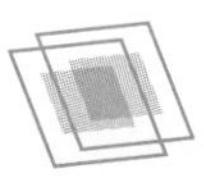

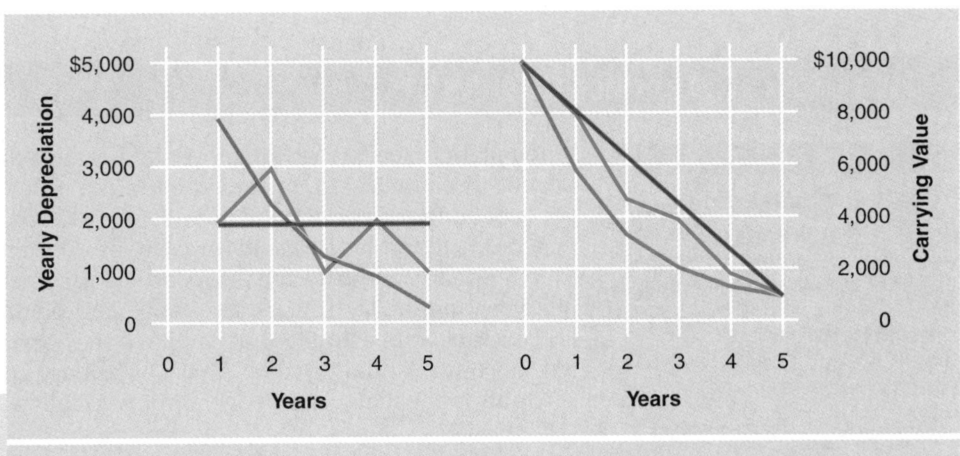

Figure 5
Graphical Comparison of Three Methods of Determining Depreciation

BUSINESS BULLETIN: BUSINESS PRACTICE

Most companies choose the straight-line method of depreciation for financial reporting purposes, as shown in Figure 6. Only about 15 percent use some type of accelerated method and 7 percent use the production method. These figures tend to be misleading about the importance of accelerated depreciation methods, however, especially when it comes to income taxes. Federal income tax laws allow either the straight-line method or an accelerated method, and for tax purposes, according to *Accounting Trends and Techniques,* about 75 percent of the six hundred large companies studied preferred an accelerated method. Companies use different methods of depreciation for good reason. The straight-line method can be advantageous for financial reporting because it can produce the highest net income, and an accelerated method can be beneficial for tax purposes because it can result in lower income taxes.

Clarification Note: Point out the conflicting objectives here. For financial reporting purposes, the objective is to accurately measure performance. For tax purposes, the objective is to minimize tax liability.

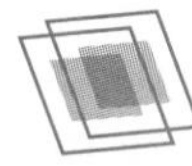

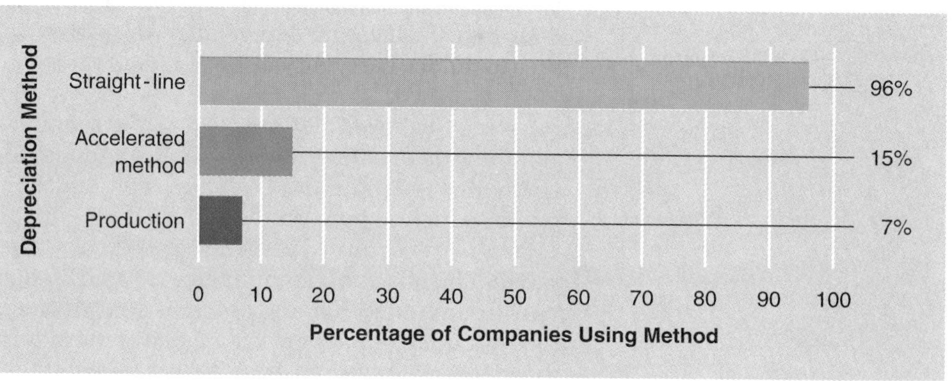

Figure 6
Depreciation Methods Used by 600 Large Companies

Total percentage exceeds 100 because some companies used different methods for different types of depreciable assets.

Source: Reprinted with permission from *Accounting Trends & Techniques,* Copyright © 1997 by American Institute of Certified Public Accountants, Inc.

Disposal of Depreciable Assets

OBJECTIVE 5

Account for the disposal of depreciable assets not involving exchanges

Related Text Assignments:
Q: 17, 18
SE: 7
E: 8, 9
P: 3
SD: 6

When plant assets are no longer useful because they are worn out or obsolete, they may be discarded, sold, or traded in on the purchase of new plant and equipment. For accounting purposes, a plant asset may be disposed of in three different ways: It may be (1) discarded, (2) sold for cash, or (3) exchanged for another asset. To illustrate how each of these cases is recorded, assume that MGC Company purchased a machine on January 1, 20x0, for $6,500 and planned to depreciate it on a straight-line basis over an estimated useful life of ten years. The residual value at the end of ten years was estimated to be $500. On January 1, 20x7, the balances of the relevant accounts in the plant asset ledger appear as follows:

Machinery			Accumulated Depreciation, Machinery	
6,500				4,200

Enrichment Note: Plant assets may also be disposed of by involuntary conversion (e.g., fire, theft, mud slide, flood) or condemnation by a governmental authority. For financial reporting purposes, involuntary conversions are treated in the same way as if the assets were discarded or sold.

On September 30, 20x7, management disposes of the asset. The next few sections illustrate the accounting treatment to record depreciation for the partial year and the disposal under several assumptions.

Depreciation for Partial Year

Teaching Note: Explain that when an asset is disposed of, a company must do two things. First, it must bring the depreciation up to date. Second, it must remove all evidence of ownership of the asset, including the contra account Accumulated Depreciation.

When a plant asset is discarded or disposed of in some other way, it is first necessary to record depreciation expense for the partial year up to the date of disposal. This step is required because the asset was used until that date and, under the matching rule, the accounting period should receive the proper allocation of depreciation expense.

In this illustration, MGC Company disposes of the machinery on September 30. The entry to record the depreciation for the first nine months of 20x7 (nine-twelfths of a year) is as follows:

A = L + OE
− −

Sept. 30	Depreciation Expense, Machinery	450	
	Accumulated Depreciation, Machinery		450
	To record depreciation up to date of disposal		

$$\frac{\$6{,}500 - \$500}{10} \times \frac{9}{12} = \$450$$

The relevant accounts in the plant asset ledger appear as follows after the entry is posted:

Machinery		Accumulated Depreciation, Machinery	
6,500			4,650

Discarded Plant Assets

Point to Emphasize: A fully depreciated asset is kept on the books as long as it is still being used in the business. When a physical count of plant assets is made and reconciled with the general ledger control account and the subsidiary ledger, all assets must be accounted for.

A plant asset rarely lasts exactly as long as its estimated life. If it lasts longer than its estimated life, it is not depreciated past the point at which its carrying value equals its residual value. The purpose of depreciation is to spread the depreciable cost of an asset over the estimated life of the asset. Thus, the total accumulated depreciation should never exceed the total depreciable cost. If an asset remains in use beyond the end of its estimated life, its cost and accumulated depreciation remain in the ledger accounts. Proper records will thus be available for maintaining control over plant assets. If the residual value is zero, the carrying value of a fully depreciated asset is zero until the asset is disposed of. If such an asset is discarded, no gain or loss results.

In the illustration, however, the discarded equipment has a carrying value of $1,850 at the time of its disposal. The carrying value is computed from the ledger accounts above as machinery of $6,500 less accumulated depreciation of $4,650. A loss equal to the carrying value should be recorded when the machine is discarded.

A = L + OE
+ −
−

Sept. 30	Accumulated Depreciation, Machinery	4,650	
	Loss on Disposal of Machinery	1,850	
	Machinery		6,500
	Discarded machine no longer used in the business		

Gains and losses on disposals of plant assets are classified as other revenues and expenses on the income statement.

Plant Assets Sold for Cash

The entry to record a plant asset sold for cash is similar to the one just illustrated except that the receipt of cash should also be recorded. The following entries show how to record the sale of a machine under three assumptions about the selling price. In the first case, the $1,850 cash received is exactly equal to the $1,850 carrying value of the machine; therefore, no gain or loss results.

A = L + OE
+
+
−

Sept. 30	Cash	1,850	
	Accumulated Depreciation, Machinery	4,650	
	Machinery		6,500
	Sale of machine for carrying value; no gain or loss		

In the second case, the $1,000 cash received is less than the carrying value of $1,850, so a loss of $850 is recorded.

A = L + OE
+ −
+
−

Sept. 30	Cash	1,000	
	Accumulated Depreciation, Machinery	4,650	
	Loss on Sale of Machinery	850	
	Machinery		6,500
	Sale of machine at less than carrying value; loss of $850 ($1,850 − $1,000) recorded		

In the third case, the $2,000 cash received exceeds the carrying value of $1,850, so a gain of $150 is recorded.

A = L + OE
+ +
−
+

Sept. 30	Cash	2,000	
	Accumulated Depreciation, Machinery	4,650	
	Gain on Sale of Machinery		150
	Machinery		6,500
	Sale of machine at more than the carrying value; gain of $150 ($2,000 − $1,850) recorded		

Exchanges of Plant Assets

OBJECTIVE 6

Account for the disposal of depreciable assets involving exchanges

Related Text Assignments:
Q: 19, 20
SE: 8
E: 8, 9
P: 3
SD: 6

Teaching Note: It is important for students to understand the difference between similar and dissimilar assets. For assets to be similar, they must be used for similar purposes. A typewriter, for example, is similar to a word processor. Dissimilar assets, such as a pickup truck and a cement mixer, are not used for similar purposes.

Businesses also dispose of plant assets by trading them in on the purchase of other plant assets. Exchanges may involve similar assets, such as an old machine traded in on a newer model, or dissimilar assets, such as a machine traded in on a truck. In either case, the purchase price is reduced by the amount of the trade-in allowance.

The basic accounting for exchanges of plant assets is similar to accounting for sales of plant assets for cash. If the trade-in allowance received is greater than the carrying value of the asset surrendered, there has been a gain. If the allowance is less, there has been a loss. There are special rules for recognizing these gains and losses, depending on the nature of the assets exchanged.

Exchange	Losses Recognized	Gains Recognized
For financial accounting purposes		
Of dissimilar assets	Yes	Yes
Of similar assets	Yes	No
For income tax purposes		
Of dissimilar assets	Yes	Yes
Of similar assets	No	No

Both gains and losses are recognized when a company exchanges dissimilar assets. Assets are dissimilar when they perform different functions or do not meet specific

Discussion Question: Are gains on similar assets completely unrecognized? **Answer:** No. Since the basis of the new asset is reduced by the unrecognized gain, there will be less depreciation expense over the life of the new asset.

monetary and type of business criteria for being considered similar assets. For financial accounting purposes, most exchanges are considered to be exchanges of dissimilar assets. In rare cases, when exchanges meet the specific criteria for them to be considered exchanges of similar assets, the gains are not recognized. In these cases, you could think of the trade-in as an extension of the life and usefulness of the original machine. Instead of recognizing a gain at the time of the exchange, the company records the new machine at the sum of the carrying value of the older machine plus any cash paid.[10]

Parenthetical Note: Recognizing losses but not gains on similar assets follows the convention of conservatism.

For income tax purposes, similar assets are defined as those performing the same function. Neither gains nor losses on exchanges of these assets are recognized in computing a company's income tax liability. Thus, in practice, accountants face cases where both gains and losses are recognized (exchanges of dissimilar assets), cases where losses are recognized and gains are not recognized (exchanges of similar assets), and cases where neither gains nor losses are recognized (exchanges of similar assets for income tax purposes). Since all these options are used in practice, they are all illustrated in the following paragraphs.

Loss Recognized on the Exchange A loss is recognized for financial accounting purposes on all exchanges in which a material loss occurs. To illustrate the recognition of a loss, let us assume that the firm in our example exchanges the machine for a newer, more modern machine on the following terms:

Discussion Question: What is the relationship, if any, between carrying value and trade-in value? **Answer:** There is none. Carrying value is original cost minus accumulated depreciation to date, whereas trade-in value is fair market value on the date of the exchange.

List price of new machine	$12,000
Trade-in allowance for old machine	(1,000)
Cash payment required	$11,000

In this case the trade-in allowance ($1,000) is less than the carrying value ($1,850) of the old machine. The loss on the exchange is $850 ($1,850 − $1,000). The following journal entry records this transaction under the assumption that the loss is to be recognized.

A = L + OE
\+ −
\+
−
−

Sept. 30	Machinery (new)	12,000	
	Accumulated Depreciation, Machinery	4,650	
	Loss on Exchange of Machinery	850	
	Machinery (old)		6,500
	Cash		11,000
	Exchange of machines		

Loss Not Recognized on the Exchange In the previous example, in which a loss was recognized, the new asset was recorded at the purchase price of $12,000 and a loss of $850 was recorded. If the transaction involves similar assets and is to be recorded for income tax purposes, the loss should not be recognized. In this case, the cost basis of the new asset will reflect the effect of the unrecorded loss. The cost basis is computed by adding the cash payment to the carrying value of the old asset:

Point to Emphasize: For income tax purposes, gains and losses on the exchange of similar assets are not recognized.

Carrying value of old machine	$ 1,850
Cash paid	11,000
Cost basis of new machine	$12,850

Note that no loss is recognized in the entry to record this transaction.

A = L + OE
\+
\+
−
−

Sept. 30	Machinery (new)	12,850	
	Accumulated Depreciation, Machinery	4,650	
	Machinery (old)		6,500
	Cash		11,000
	Exchange of machines		

Note that the new machinery is reported at the purchase price of $12,000 plus the unrecognized loss of $850. The nonrecognition of the loss on the exchange is, in effect, a postponement of the loss. Since depreciation of the new machine will be computed based on a cost of $12,850 instead of $12,000, the "unrecognized" loss results in more depreciation each year on the new machine than if the loss had been recognized.

Gain Recognized on the Exchange Gains on exchanges are recognized for accounting purposes when dissimilar assets are involved. To illustrate the recognition of a gain, we continue with our example, assuming the following terms and assuming the machines being exchanged serve different functions:

List price of new machine	$12,000
Trade-in allowance for old machine	(3,000)
Cash payment required	$ 9,000

Here the trade-in allowance ($3,000) exceeds the carrying value ($1,850) of the old machine by $1,150. Thus, there is a gain on the exchange, assuming that the price of the new machine has not been inflated to allow for an excessive trade-in value. In other words, a gain exists if the trade-in allowance represents the fair market value of the old machine. Assuming that this condition is true, the entry to record the transaction is as follows:

A = L + OE				
+	Sept. 30	Machinery (new)	12,000	
+ +		Accumulated Depreciation, Machinery	4,650	
−		Gain on Exchange of Machinery		1,150
−		Machinery (old)		6,500
		Cash		9,000
		Exchange of machines		

Gain Not Recognized on the Exchange When assets meeting the criteria for similar assets are exchanged, gains are not recognized for accounting or income tax purposes. The cost basis of the new machine must reflect the effect of the unrecorded gain. This cost basis is computed by adding the cash payment to the carrying value of the old asset.

Carrying value of old machine	$ 1,850
Cash paid	9,000
Cost basis of new machine	$10,850

The entry to record the transaction is as follows:

A = L + OE				
+	Sept. 30	Machinery (new)	10,850	
+		Accumulated Depreciation, Machinery	4,650	
−		Machinery (old)		6,500
−		Cash		9,000
		Exchange of machines		

As with the nonrecognition of losses, the nonrecognition of the gain on an exchange is, in effect, a postponement of the gain. In this illustration, when the new machine is eventually discarded or sold, its cost basis will be $10,850 instead of its original price of $12,000. Since depreciation will be computed on the cost basis of $10,850, the "unrecognized" gain is reflected in lower depreciation each year on the new machine than if the gain had been recognized.

Accounting for Natural Resources

OBJECTIVE 7

Identify the issues related to accounting for natural resources and compute depletion

Related Text Assignments:
Q: 21, 22
SE: 9
E: 10
FRA: 4

Clarification Note: Students often erroneously classify natural resources as intangible assets. Natural resources are correctly classified as components of property, plant, and equipment.

Enrichment Note: When determining the total units available for depletion, management uses only the total units that are economically feasible to extract. This follows the cost-benefit principle. That is, when the cost of extracting a mineral is greater than the expected profit from the sale of the mineral, the company stops extracting it.

Natural resources are shown on the balance sheet as long-term assets with such descriptive titles as Timberlands, Oil and Gas Reserves, and Mineral Deposits. The distinguishing characteristic of these assets is that they are converted into inventory by cutting, pumping, or mining. In terms of two of our examples, an oil field is a reservoir of unpumped oil, and a coal mine is a deposit of unmined coal. When the timber is cut, the oil is pumped, or the coal is mined, it becomes an inventory of the product to be sold. Natural resources are recorded at acquisition cost, which may also include some costs of development. As the resource is converted through the process of cutting, pumping, or mining, the asset account must be proportionally reduced. The carrying value of oil reserves on the balance sheet, for example, is reduced by a small amount for each barrel of oil pumped. As a result, the original cost of the oil reserves is gradually reduced, and depletion is recognized in the amount of the decrease.

Depletion

The term *depletion* is used to describe not only the exhaustion of a natural resource but also the proportional allocation of the cost of a natural resource to the units extracted. The costs are allocated in a way that is much like the production method used to calculate depreciation. When a natural resource is purchased or developed, there must be an estimate of the total units that will be available, such as barrels of oil, tons of coal, or board-feet of lumber. The depletion cost per unit is determined by dividing the cost of the natural resource (less residual value, if any) by the estimated number of units available. The amount of the depletion cost for each accounting period is then computed by multiplying the depletion cost per unit by the number of units pumped, mined, or cut and sold. For example, for a mine having an estimated 1,500,000 tons of coal, a cost of $1,800,000, and an estimated residual value of $300,000, the depletion charge per ton of coal is $1. Thus, if 115,000 tons of coal are mined and sold during the first year, the depletion charge for the year is $115,000. This charge is recorded as follows:

A = L + OE
− −

Dec. 31	Depletion Expense, Coal Deposits	115,000	
	Accumulated Depletion, Coal Deposits		115,000
	To record depletion of coal mine: $1 per ton for 115,000 tons mined and sold		

On the balance sheet, the mine would be presented as follows:

Coal Deposits	$1,800,000	
Less Accumulated Depletion	115,000	$1,685,000

Discussion Question: Why would an extracted natural resource be recorded as inventory until it is sold? **Answer:** The matching rule dictates that the extracted resource be treated as an asset until it is sold. At that point, the asset cost is converted into an expense.

Sometimes a natural resource that is extracted in one year is not sold until a later year. It is important to note that it would then be recorded as a depletion *expense* in the year it is *sold*. The part not sold is considered inventory.

Depreciation of Closely Related Plant Assets

Discussion Question: Why would a company abandon equipment that is still in good working condition? **Answer:** One reason is that it might cost the company more to dismantle the equipment and move it to another site than to abandon it.

Natural resources often require special on-site buildings and equipment, such as conveyors, roads, tracks, and drilling and pumping devices that are necessary to extract the resource. If the useful life of those assets is longer than the estimated time it will take to deplete the resource, a special problem arises. Because such long-term assets are often abandoned and have no useful purpose once all the resources have been extracted, they should be depreciated on the same basis as the

Discussion Question: Using the production method to depreciate long-term assets located at excavation sites is justified by which accounting convention? **Answer:** The matching rule.

depletion is computed. For example, if machinery with a useful life of ten years is installed on an oil field that is expected to be depleted in eight years, the machinery should be depreciated over the eight-year period, using the production method. That way, each year's depreciation will be proportional to the year's depletion. If one-sixth of the oil field's total reserves is pumped in one year, then the depreciation should be one-sixth of the machinery's cost minus the residual value. If the useful life of a long-term asset is less than the expected life of the depleting asset, the shorter life should be used to compute depreciation. In such cases, or when an asset will not be abandoned when the reserves are fully depleted, other depreciation methods, such as straight-line or declining-balance, are appropriate.

Development and Exploration Costs in the Oil and Gas Industry

The costs of exploration and development of oil and gas resources can be accounted for under either of two methods. Under successful efforts accounting, successful exploration—for example, the cost of a producing oil well—is a cost of the resource. This cost should be recorded as an asset and depleted over the estimated life of the resource. An unsuccessful exploration—such as the cost of a dry well—is written off immediately as a loss. Because of these immediate write-offs, successful efforts accounting is considered the more conservative method and is used by most large oil companies.

Exploration-minded independent oil companies, on the other hand, argue that the cost of dry wells is part of the overall cost of the systematic development of an oil field and thus a part of the cost of producing wells. Under this full-costing method, all costs, including the cost of dry wells, are recorded as assets and depleted over the estimated life of the producing resources. This method tends to improve earnings performance in the early years for companies using it. Either method is permitted by the Financial Accounting Standards Board.[11]

Accounting for Intangible Assets

OBJECTIVE 8

Apply the matching rule to intangible assets, including research and development costs and goodwill

Related Text Assignments:
Q: 23, 24, 25, 26, 27, 28, 29
SE: 10
E: 11
P: 4
SD: 3, 5
FRA: 2, 4

Point to Emphasize: Generally, intangible assets, including goodwill, are recorded only when purchased. An exception is the cost of internally developed computer software after a working prototype has been developed.

The purchase of an intangible asset is a special kind of capital expenditure. An intangible asset is long term, but it has no physical substance. Its value comes from the long-term rights or advantages it offers to its owner. The most common examples—patents, copyrights, leaseholds, leasehold improvements, trademarks and brand names, franchises, licenses, and goodwill—are described in Table 1. Some current assets, such as accounts receivable and certain prepaid expenses, have no physical substance, but they are not classified as intangible assets because they are short term. Intangible assets are both long term and nonphysical.

Intangible assets are accounted for at acquisition cost—that is, the amount that was paid for them. Some intangible assets, such as goodwill and trademarks, may be acquired at little or no cost. Even though they may have great value and be needed for profitable operations, they should not appear on the balance sheet unless they have been purchased from another party at a price established in the marketplace.

The accounting issues connected with intangible assets are the same as those connected with other long-lived assets. The Accounting Principles Board, in its *Opinion No. 17,* lists them as follows:

1. Determining an initial carrying amount
2. Accounting for that amount after acquisition under normal business conditions—that is, through periodic write-off or amortization—in a manner similar to depreciation.
3. Accounting for that amount if the value declines substantially and permanently.[12]

Table 1. Accounting for Intangible Assets

Type	Description	Accounting Treatment
Patent	An exclusive right granted by the federal government for a period of seventeen years to make a particular product or use a specific process.	The cost of successfully defending a patent in a patent infringement suit is added to the acquisition cost of the patent. Amortize over the useful life, which may be less than the legal life of seventeen years.
Copyright	An exclusive right granted by the federal government to the possessor to publish and sell literary, musical, or other artistic materials for a period of the author's life plus fifty years; includes computer programs.	Record at acquisition cost and amortize over the useful life, which is often much shorter than the legal life, but not to exceed forty years. For example, the cost of paperback rights to a popular novel would typically be amortized over a useful life of two to four years.
Leasehold	A right to occupy land or buildings under a long-term rental contract. For example, Company A, which owns but does not want to use a prime retail location, sells Company B the right to use it for ten years in return for one or more rental payments. Company B has purchased a leasehold.	Debit Leasehold for the amount of the rental payment, and amortize it over the remaining life of the lease. Payments to the lessor during the life of the lease should be debited to Lease Expense.
Leasehold improvements	Improvements to leased property that become the property of the lessor (the person who owns the property) at the end of the lease.	Debit Leasehold Improvements for the cost of improvements, and amortize the cost of the improvements over the remaining life of the lease.
Trademark, brand name	A registered symbol or name that can be used only by its owner to identify a product or service.	Debit Trademark or Brand Name for the acquisition cost, and amortize it over a reasonable life, not to exceed forty years.
Franchise, license	A right to an exclusive territory or market, or to exclusive use of a formula, technique, process, or design.	Debit Franchise or License for the acquisition cost, and amortize it over a reasonable life, not to exceed forty years.
Goodwill	The excess of the cost of a group of assets (usually a business) over the fair market value of the net assets if purchased individually.	Debit Goodwill for the acquisition cost, and amortize it over a reasonable life, not to exceed forty years.[13]

Terminology Note: Useful life refers to how long an intangible asset will be contributing income to a firm.

Besides these three problems, an intangible asset has no physical substance and, in some cases, may be impossible to identify. For these reasons, its value and its useful life may be quite hard to estimate.

The Accounting Principles Board has decided that a company should record as assets the costs of intangible assets acquired from others. However, the company should record as expenses the costs of developing intangible assets. Also, intangible assets that have a determinable useful life, such as patents, copyrights, and leaseholds, should be written off through periodic amortization over that useful life in much the same way that plant assets are depreciated. Even though some intangible

BUSINESS BULLETIN: BUSINESS PRACTICE

One of the most valuable intangible assets some companies have is a list of subscribers. For example, the Newark Morning Ledger Co., a newspaper chain, purchased a chain of Michigan newspapers whose list of 460,000 subscribers was valued at $68 million. In a 1993 decision, the U.S. Supreme Court upheld the company's right to amortize the value of the subscribers list because the company showed that the list had a limited useful life. The Internal Revenue Service had argued that the list had an indefinite life and therefore could not provide tax deductions through amortization. This ruling will benefit other types of businesses that purchase everything from bank deposits to pharmacy prescription files.[14]

Point to Emphasize: Intangible assets should never be amortized over more than forty years.

assets, such as goodwill and trademarks, have no measurable limit on their lives, they should still be amortized over a reasonable length of time (not to exceed forty years).

To illustrate these procedures, assume that Soda Bottling Company purchases a patent on a unique bottle cap for $18,000. The entry to record the patent would include $18,000 in the asset account Patents. Note that if Soda Bottling Company had developed the bottle cap internally instead of purchasing it from others, the costs of developing the cap, such as salaries of researchers, supplies used in testing, and costs of equipment, would have been expensed as incurred.

Assume now that Soda's management determines that, although the patent for the bottle cap will last for seventeen years, the product using the cap will be sold only for the next six years. The entry to record the annual amortization expense would be for $3,000 ($18,000 ÷ 6 years). Note that the Patents account is reduced directly by the amount of the amortization expense. This is in contrast to the treatment of other long-term asset accounts, for which depreciation or depletion is accumulated in separate contra accounts.

If the patent becomes worthless before it is fully amortized, the remaining carrying value is written off as a loss by removing it from the Patents account.

Research and Development Costs

Most successful companies carry out activities, possibly within a separate department, involving research and development. Among these activities are development of new products, testing of existing and proposed products, and pure research. In the past, some companies would record as assets those costs of research and development that could be directly traced to the development of specific patents, formulas, or other rights. Other costs, such as those for testing and pure research, were treated as expenses of the accounting period and deducted from income.

The Financial Accounting Standards Board has stated that all research and development costs should be treated as revenue expenditures and charged to expense in the period when incurred.[15] The board argues that it is too hard to trace specific costs to specific profitable developments. Also, the costs of research and development are continuous and necessary for the success of a business and so should be treated as current expenses. To support this conclusion, the board cites studies showing that 30 to 90 percent of all new products fail and that three-fourths of new-product expenses go to unsuccessful products. Thus, their costs do not represent future benefits.

Computer Software Costs

Point to Emphasize: Completely developed software should be protected by copyright.

Many companies develop computer programs or software to be sold or leased to individuals and companies. The costs incurred in creating a computer software product are considered research and development costs until the product has been proved to be technologically feasible. As a result, costs incurred before that point in the process should be charged to expense as incurred. A product is deemed to be technologically feasible when a detailed working program has been designed. After the working program has been developed, all software production costs are recorded as assets and amortized over the estimated economic life of the product using the straight-line method. If at any time the company cannot expect to realize from a software product the amount of its unamortized costs on the balance sheet, the asset should be written down to the amount expected to be realized.[16] Under new rules developed by the AICPA, software programs developed for internal use by a company may be capitalized and amortized over their estimated economic life.

Goodwill

Discussion Question: Why would a company spend thousands of dollars on goodwill? **Answer:** The company is paying for anticipated superior earnings and probably feels it will more than recoup the goodwill purchased.

The term *goodwill* is widely used by businesspeople, lawyers, and the public to mean different things. In most cases goodwill is taken to mean the good reputation of a company. From an accounting standpoint, goodwill exists when a purchaser pays more for a business than the fair market value of the net assets if purchased separately. Because the purchaser has paid more than the fair market value of the physical assets, there must be intangible assets. If the company being purchased does not have patents, copyrights, trademarks, or other identifiable intangible assets of value, the excess payment is assumed to be for goodwill. Goodwill exists because most businesses are worth more as going concerns than as collections of assets. Goodwill reflects all the factors that allow a company to earn a higher-than-market rate of return on its assets, including customer satisfaction, good management, manufacturing efficiency, the advantages of holding a monopoly, good locations, and good employee relations. The payment above and beyond the fair market value of the tangible assets and other specific intangible assets is properly recorded in the Goodwill account.

In *Opinion No. 17,* the Accounting Principles Board states that the benefits arising from purchased goodwill will in time disappear. It is hard for a company to keep having above-average earnings unless new factors of goodwill replace the old ones. For this reason, goodwill should be amortized or written off by systematic charges

BUSINESS BULLETIN: BUSINESS PRACTICE

Research and development expenditures can be substantial for many companies. For example, General Motors and IBM spent $8.0 billion and $4.7 billion, respectively, on research and development in 1996. Those amounts are about 5 percent of the companies' revenues. Research and development can be even costlier in high-tech fields like biotechnology, where Amgen, Inc., and Biogen spent 24 percent and 48 percent, respectively, of revenues.[17] Corporate spending on research and development is heaviest in the pharmaceutical and electronics industries, with an outlay of more than $118 billion in 1996.[18] Which of these costs are capitalized and amortized and which must be expensed immediately are obviously important questions for both the management and the stockholders of these companies.

to income over a reasonable number of future time periods. The total time period should in no case be more than forty years.[19]

Point to Emphasize: Goodwill equals purchase price minus adjusted net asset value.

Goodwill, as stated, should not be recorded unless it is paid for in connection with the purchase of a whole business. The amount to be recorded as goodwill can be determined by writing the identifiable net assets up to their fair market values at the time of purchase and subtracting the total from the purchase price. For example, assume that the owners of Company A agree to sell the company for \$11,400,000. If the net assets (total assets − total liabilities) are fairly valued at \$10,000,000, then the amount of the goodwill is \$1,400,000 (\$11,400,000 − \$10,000,000). If the fair market value of the net assets is later determined to be more or less than \$10,000,000, an entry is made in the accounting records to adjust the assets to the fair market value. The goodwill would then represent the difference between the adjusted net assets and the purchase price of \$11,400,000.

Special Problems of Depreciating Plant Assets

SUPPLEMENTAL OBJECTIVE 9

Apply depreciation methods to problems of partial years, revised rates, groups of similar items, special types of capital expenditures, and cost recovery

The illustrations used so far in this chapter have been simplified to explain the concepts and methods of depreciation. In actual business practice, there is often a need to (1) calculate depreciation for partial years, (2) revise depreciation rates based on new estimates of useful life or residual value, (3) group like items when calculating depreciation, (4) account for special types of capital expenditures, and (5) use the accelerated cost recovery method for tax purposes. The next sections discuss these five cases.

Related Text Assignments:
Q: 30, 31, 32, 33, 34, 35
E: 12, 13, 14, 15
P: 5, 8
FRA: 1

Depreciation for Partial Years

So far, the illustrations of depreciation methods have assumed that plant assets were purchased at the beginning or end of an accounting period. In most cases, however, businesses buy assets when they are needed and sell or discard them when they are no longer useful or needed. The time of year is normally not a factor in the decision. Consequently, it is often necessary to calculate depreciation for partial years.

For example, assume that a piece of equipment is purchased for \$3,600 and that it has an estimated useful life of six years and an estimated residual value of \$600. Assume also that it is purchased on September 5 and that the yearly accounting period ends on December 31. Depreciation must be recorded for four months, September through December, or four-twelfths of the year. This factor is applied to the calculated depreciation for the entire year. The four months' depreciation under the straight-line method is calculated as follows:

$$\frac{\$3,600 - \$600}{6 \text{ years}} \times 4/12 = \$167$$

For the other depreciation methods, most companies will compute the first year's depreciation and then multiply by the partial year factor. For example, if the company used the double-declining-balance method on the preceding equipment, the depreciation on the asset would be computed as follows:

$$\$3,600 \times 1/3 \times 4/12 = \$400$$

Typically, the depreciation calculation is rounded off to the nearest whole month because a partial month's depreciation is rarely material and the calculation is easier. In this case, depreciation was recorded from the beginning of September even though the purchase was made on September 5.

For all methods, the remainder (eight-twelfths) of the first year's depreciation is recorded in the next annual accounting period together with four-twelfths of the second year's depreciation.

Revision of Depreciation Rates

Enrichment Note: A poor estimate can occur when a defective piece of equipment is purchased.

Point to Emphasize: A change in an accounting estimate is not considered the correction of an error, but rather a revision based on new information.

Because a depreciation rate is based on an estimate of an asset's useful life, the periodic depreciation charge is seldom precise. Sometimes it is very inadequate or excessive. This situation may result from an underestimate or overestimate of the asset's useful life or from a wrong estimate of the residual value. What action should be taken when it is found, after several years of use, that a piece of equipment will last less time—or longer—than originally thought? Sometimes it is necessary to revise the estimate of useful life so that the periodic depreciation expense increases or decreases. Then, to reflect the revised situation, the remaining depreciable cost of the asset is spread over the remaining years of useful life.

With this technique, the annual depreciation expense is increased or decreased to reduce the asset's carrying value to its residual value at the end of its remaining useful life. To illustrate, assume that a delivery truck was purchased for $7,000 and has a residual value of $1,000. At the time of the purchase, the truck was expected to last six years, and it was depreciated on the straight-line basis. However, after two years of intensive use, it is determined that the truck will last only two more years, but that its estimated residual value at the end of the two years will still be $1,000. In other words, at the end of the second year, the truck's estimated useful life is reduced from six years to four years. At that time, the asset account and its related accumulated depreciation account would appear as follows:

Point to Emphasize: Allocate the remaining depreciable cost over the estimated remaining life.

Delivery Truck

Cost	7,000	

Accumulated Depreciation, Delivery Truck

	Depreciation, year 1	1,000
	Depreciation, year 2	1,000

The remaining depreciable cost is computed as follows:

Cost	minus	Depreciation Already Taken	minus	Residual Value		
$7,000	−	$2,000	−	$1,000	=	$4,000

The new annual periodic depreciation charge is computed by dividing the remaining depreciable cost of $4,000 by the remaining useful life of two years. Therefore, the new periodic depreciation charge is $2,000. The annual adjusting entry for depreciation for the next two years would be as follows:

A = L + OE
− −

Dec. 31	Depreciation Expense, Delivery Truck	2,000	
	Accumulated Depreciation, Delivery Truck		2,000
	To record depreciation expense for the year		

This method of revising depreciation is used widely in industry. It is also supported by the Accounting Principles Board of the AICPA in Accounting Principles Board *Opinion No. 9* and *Opinion No. 20*.

Group Depreciation

To say that the estimated useful life of an asset, such as a piece of equipment, is six years means that the average piece of equipment of that type is expected to last six years. In reality, some pieces may last only two or three years, and others may last eight or nine years, or longer. For this reason, and for reasons of convenience, large companies will group similar items, such as trucks, power lines, office equipment, or transformers, to calculate depreciation. This method is called group depreciation. Group depreciation is widely used in all fields of industry and business. A survey of large businesses indicated that 65 percent used group depreciation for all or part of their plant assets.[20]

Special Types of Capital Expenditures

Point to Emphasize: Other examples of betterments would include replacing stairs with an escalator in a department store and paving a gravel parking lot.

In addition to the acquisition of plant assets, natural resources, and intangible assets, capital expenditures also include additions and betterments. An addition is an enlargement to the physical layout of a plant asset. As an example, if a new wing is added to a building, the benefits from the expenditure will be received over several years, and the amount paid for it should be debited to the asset account. A betterment is an improvement that does not add to the physical layout of a plant asset. Installation of an air-conditioning system is an example of a betterment that will offer benefits over a period of years; therefore, its cost should be charged to an asset account.

Among the more usual kinds of revenue expenditures for plant equipment are the repairs, maintenance, lubrication, cleaning, and inspection necessary to keep an asset in good working condition. Repairs fall into two categories: ordinary repairs and extraordinary repairs. Ordinary repairs are expenditures that are necessary to maintain an asset in good operating condition. Trucks must have periodic tune-ups, their tires and batteries must be regularly replaced, and other routine repairs must be made. Offices and halls must be painted regularly, and broken tiles or woodwork must be replaced. Such repairs are a current expense.

Point to Emphasize: More examples of extraordinary repairs would be putting a new motor in a cement mixer and replacing the roof on a building, thereby extending its life.

Extraordinary repairs are repairs of a more significant nature—they affect the estimated residual value or estimated useful life of an asset. For example, a boiler for heating a building may be given a complete overhaul, at a cost of several thousand dollars, that will extend its useful life by five years. Typically, extraordinary repairs are recorded by debiting the Accumulated Depreciation account, under the assumption that some of the depreciation previously recorded has now been eliminated. The effect of this reduction in the Accumulated Depreciation account is to increase the carrying value of the asset by the cost of the extraordinary repair. Consequently, the new carrying value of the asset should be depreciated over the new estimated useful life.

Let us assume that a machine that cost $10,000 had no estimated residual value and an original estimated useful life of ten years. After eight years, the accumulated depreciation under the straight-line method was $8,000, and the carrying value was $2,000 ($10,000 − $8,000). At that point, the machine was given a major overhaul costing $1,500. This expenditure extended the machine's useful life three years beyond the original ten years. The entry for the extraordinary repair would be as follows:

A = L + OE
+
−

Jan. 4	Accumulated Depreciation, Machinery	1,500	
	Cash		1,500
	Extraordinary repair to machinery		

The annual periodic depreciation for each of the five years remaining in the machine's useful life would be calculated as follows:

Carrying value before extraordinary repairs	$2,000
Extraordinary repairs	1,500
Total	$3,500

$$\text{Annual periodic depreciation} = \frac{\$3{,}500}{5\text{ years}} = \$700$$

If the machine remains in use for the five years expected after the major overhaul, the total of the five annual depreciation charges of $700 will exactly equal the new carrying value, including the cost of the extraordinary repair.

Cost Recovery for Federal Income Tax Purposes

In 1986, Congress passed the Tax Reform Act of 1986, arguably the most sweeping revision of federal tax laws since the original enactment of the Internal Revenue Code in 1913. First, a company may elect to expense the first $17,500 of equipment expenditures rather than recording them as an asset. Second, a new method for writing off expenditures recorded as assets, the Modified Accelerated Cost Recovery System (MACRS), may be elected. MACRS discards the concepts of estimated useful life and residual value. Instead, it requires that a cost recovery allowance be computed (1) on the unadjusted cost of property being recovered, and (2) over a period of years prescribed by the law for all property of similar types. The accelerated method prescribed under MACRS for most property other than real estate is 200 percent declining balance with a half-year convention (only one half-year's depreciation is allowed in the year of purchase, and one half-year's depreciation is taken in the last year). In addition, the period over which the cost may be recovered is specified. Recovery of the cost of property placed in service after December 31, 1986, is calculated as prescribed in the 1986 law.

Congress hoped that MACRS would encourage businesses to invest in new plant and equipment by allowing them to write off such assets rapidly. MACRS accelerates the write-off of these investments in two ways. First, the prescribed recovery periods are often shorter than the estimated useful lives used for calculating depreciation for the financial statements. Second, the accelerated method allowed under the new law enables businesses to recover most of the cost of their investments early in the depreciation process.

Clarification Note: MACRS depreciation is used for tax purposes only. It cannot be used for financial reporting.

Tax methods of depreciation are not usually acceptable for financial reporting under generally accepted accounting principles because the recovery periods are shorter than the depreciable assets' estimated useful lives.

Chapter Review

REVIEW OF LEARNING OBJECTIVES

1. **Identify the types of long-term assets and explain the management issues related to accounting for them.** Long-term assets are assets that are used in the operation of a business, are not intended for resale, and have a useful life of more than one year. Long-term assets are either tangible or intangible. In the former category are land, plant assets, and natural resources. In the latter are trademarks, patents, franchises, goodwill, and other rights. The accounting issues associated with long-term assets relate to the decision to acquire the assets, the means of financing the assets, and the methods of accounting for the assets.
2. **Distinguish between capital and revenue expenditures, and account for the cost of property, plant, and equipment.** It is important to distinguish between capital expenditures, which are recorded as assets, and revenue expenditures, which are recorded as expenses. The error of classifying one as the other will have an important effect on net income. The acquisition cost of property, plant, and equipment includes all expenditures that are reasonable and necessary to get such an asset in place and

ready for use. Among these expenditures are purchase price, installation cost, freight charges, and insurance during transit.

3. **Define *depreciation*, state the factors that affect its computation, and show how to record it.** Depreciation is the periodic allocation of the cost of a plant asset over its estimated useful life. It is recorded by debiting Depreciation Expense and crediting a related contra-asset account called Accumulated Depreciation. Factors that affect the computation of depreciation are cost, residual value, depreciable cost, and estimated useful life.
4. **Compute periodic depreciation under the (a) straight-line method, (b) production method, and (c) declining-balance method.** Depreciation is commonly computed by the straight-line method, the production method, or an accelerated method. The straight-line method is related directly to the passage of time, whereas the production method is related directly to use. An accelerated method, which results in relatively large amounts of depreciation in earlier years and reduced amounts in later years, is based on the assumption that plant assets provide greater economic benefit in their earlier years than in later years. The most common accelerated method is the declining-balance method.
5. **Account for the disposal of depreciable assets not involving exchanges.** Long-term depreciable assets may be disposed of by being discarded, sold, or exchanged. When long-term assets are disposed of, it is necessary to record the depreciation up to the date of disposal and to remove the carrying value from the accounts by removing the cost from the asset account and the depreciation to date from the accumulated depreciation account. If a long-term asset is sold at a price that differs from its carrying value, there is a gain or loss that should be recorded and reported on the income statement.
6. **Account for the disposal of depreciable assets involving exchanges.** In recording exchanges of similar plant assets, a gain or loss may arise. According to the Accounting Principles Board, losses, but not gains, should be recognized at the time of the exchange. When a gain is not recognized, the new asset is recorded at the carrying value of the old asset plus any cash paid. For income tax purposes, neither gains nor losses are recognized in the exchange of similar assets. When dissimilar assets are exchanged, gains and losses are recognized under both accounting and income tax rules.
7. **Identify the issues related to accounting for natural resources and compute depletion.** Natural resources are wasting assets that are converted to inventory by cutting, pumping, mining, or other forms of extraction. Natural resources are recorded at cost as long-term assets. They are allocated as expenses through depletion charges as the resources are sold. The depletion charge is based on the ratio of the resource extracted to the total estimated resource. A major issue related to this subject is accounting for oil and gas reserves.
8. **Apply the matching rule to intangible assets, including research and development costs and goodwill.** The purchase of an intangible asset should be treated as a capital expenditure and recorded at acquisition cost, which in turn should be amortized over the useful life of the asset. The FASB requires that research and development costs be treated as revenue expenditures and charged as expenses in the periods of expenditure. Software costs are treated as research and development costs and expensed until a feasible working program is developed, after which time the costs may be capitalized and amortized over a reasonable estimated life. Goodwill is the excess of the amount paid for the purchase of a business over the fair market value of the net assets and is usually related to the superior earning potential of the business. It should be recorded only if paid for in connection with the purchase of a business, and it should be amortized over a period not to exceed forty years.

Supplemental Objective

9. **Apply depreciation methods to problems of partial years, revised rates, groups of similar items, special types of capital expenditures, and cost recovery.** In actual business practice, many factors affect depreciation calculations. It may be necessary to calculate depreciation for partial years because assets are bought and sold

throughout the year, or to revise depreciation rates because of changed conditions. Because it is often difficult to estimate the useful life of a single item, and because it is more convenient, many large businesses group similar items for purposes of depreciation. Companies must also consider certain special capital expenditures when calculating depreciation. For example, expenditures for additions and betterments are capital expenditures. Extraordinary repairs, which increase the residual value or extend the life of an asset, are also treated as capital expenditures, but ordinary repairs are revenue expenditures. For income tax purposes, rapid write-offs of depreciable assets are allowed through the Modified Accelerated Cost Recovery System. Such rapid write-offs are not usually acceptable for financial accounting because the shortened recovery periods violate the matching rule.

REVIEW OF CONCEPTS AND TERMINOLOGY

The following concepts and terms were introduced in this chapter.

LO 4 **Accelerated method:** A method of depreciation that allocates relatively large amounts of the depreciable cost of an asset to earlier years and reduced amounts to later years.

SO 9 **Addition:** An enlargement to the physical layout of a plant asset.

LO 1 **Amortization:** The periodic allocation of the cost of an intangible asset to the periods it benefits.

LO 1 **Asset impairment:** Loss of revenue-generating potential of a long-lived asset prior to the end of its useful life. The loss is computed as the difference between the asset's carrying value and its fair value, as measured by the present value of the expected cash flows.

SO 9 **Betterment:** An improvement that does not add to the physical layout of a plant asset.

LO 8 **Brand name:** A registered name that can be used only by its owner to identify a product or service.

LO 2 **Capital expenditure:** An expenditure for the purchase or expansion of a long-term asset, recorded in an asset account.

LO 1 **Carrying value:** The unexpired part of the cost of an asset, not its market value; also called *book value.*

LO 8 **Copyright:** An exclusive right granted by the federal government to the possessor to publish and sell literary, musical, or other artistic materials for a period of the author's life plus fifty years; includes computer programs.

LO 4 **Declining-balance method:** An accelerated method of depreciation in which depreciation is computed by applying a fixed rate to the carrying value (the declining balance) of a tangible long-lived asset.

LO 1 **Depletion:** The exhaustion of a natural resource through mining, cutting, pumping, or other extraction, and the way in which the cost is allocated.

LO 3 **Depreciable cost:** The cost of an asset less its residual value.

LO 1 **Depreciation:** The periodic allocation of the cost of a tangible long-lived asset (other than land and natural resources) over its estimated useful life.

LO 4 **Double-declining-balance method:** An accelerated method of depreciation in which a fixed rate equal to twice the straight-line percentage is applied to the carrying value (the declining balance) of a tangible long-lived asset.

LO 3 **Estimated useful life:** The total number of service units expected from a long-term asset.

LO 2 **Expenditure:** A payment or an obligation to make future payment for an asset or a service.

SO 9 **Extraordinary repairs:** Repairs that affect the estimated residual value or estimated useful life of an asset.

LO 8 **Franchise:** The right or license to an exclusive territory or market.

LO 7 **Full-costing:** A method of accounting for the costs of exploration and development of oil and gas resources in which all costs are recorded as assets and depleted over the estimated life of the producing resources.

LO 8 **Goodwill:** The excess of the cost of a group of assets (usually a business) over the fair market value of the net assets if purchased individually.

SO 9 **Group depreciation:** The grouping of similar items to calculate depreciation.

LO 1 **Intangible assets:** Long-term assets that have no physical substance but have a value based on rights or advantages accruing to the owner.

LO 8 **Leasehold:** A right to occupy land or buildings under a long-term rental contract.

LO 8 **Leasehold improvements:** Improvements to leased property that become the property of the lessor at the end of the lease.

LO 8 **License:** An exclusive right to a formula, technique, process, or design.

LO 1 **Long-term assets:** Assets that (1) have a useful life of more than one year, (2) are acquired for use in the operation of a business, and (3) are not intended for resale to customers; less commonly called *fixed assets.*

SO 9 **Modified Accelerated Cost Recovery System (MACRS):** A mandatory system of depreciation for income tax purposes, enacted by Congress in 1986, that requires a cost recovery allowance to be computed (1) on the unadjusted cost of property being recovered, and (2) over a period of years prescribed by the law for all property of similar types.

LO 1 **Natural resources:** Long-term assets purchased for the economic value that can be taken from the land and used up rather than for the value associated with the land's location.

LO 3 **Obsolescence:** The process of becoming out of date; a contributor, with physical deterioration, to the limited useful life of tangible assets.

SO 9 **Ordinary repairs:** Expenditures, usually of a recurring nature, that are necessary to maintain an asset in good operating condition.

LO 8 **Patent:** An exclusive right granted by the federal government for a period of seventeen years to make a particular product or use a specific process.

LO 3 **Physical deterioration:** Limitations on the useful life of a depreciable asset resulting from use and from exposure to the elements.

LO 4 **Production method:** A method of depreciation that assumes that depreciation is solely the result of use and that the passage of time plays no role in the depreciation process; it allocates depreciation based on the units of output or use during each period of an asset's useful life.

LO 3 **Residual value:** The estimated net scrap, salvage, or trade-in value of a tangible asset at the estimated date of disposal; also called *salvage value* or *disposal value.*

LO 2 **Revenue expenditure:** An expenditure for repairs, maintenance, or other services needed to maintain or operate a plant asset, recorded by a debit to an expense account.

LO 4 **Straight-line method:** A method of depreciation that assumes that depreciation depends only on the passage of time and that allocates an equal amount of depreciation to each accounting period in an asset's useful life.

LO 7 **Successful efforts accounting:** A method of accounting for oil and gas resources in which successful exploration is recorded as an asset and depleted over the estimated life of the resource and all unsuccessful efforts are immediately written off as losses.

LO 1 **Tangible assets:** Long-term assets that have physical substance.

LO 8 **Trademark:** A registered symbol or brand name that can be used only by its owner to identify a product or service.

REVIEW PROBLEM

Comparison of Depreciation Methods

Norton Construction Company purchased a cement mixer on January 1, 20x1, for $14,500. The mixer was expected to have a useful life of five years and a residual value of $1,000. The company engineers estimated that the mixer would have a useful life of 7,500 hours. It was used 1,500 hours in 20x1, 2,625 hours in 20x2, 2,250 hours in 20x3, 750 hours in 20x4, and 375 hours in 20x5. The company's year end is December 31.

REQUIRED

1. Compute the depreciation expense and carrying value for 20x1 to 20x5, using the following three methods: (a) straight-line, (b) production, and (c) double-declining-balance.
2. Prepare the adjusting entry to record the depreciation for 20x1 calculated in **1 (a).**

3. Show the balance sheet presentation for the cement mixer after the entry in **2** on December 31, 20x1.
4. What conclusions can you draw from the patterns of yearly depreciation?

ANSWER TO REVIEW PROBLEM

1. Depreciation computed:

Depreciation Method	Year	Computation	Depreciation	Carrying Value
a. Straight-line	20x1	\$13,500 × 1/5	\$2,700	\$11,800
	20x2	13,500 × 1/5	2,700	9,100
	20x3	13,500 × 1/5	2,700	6,400
	20x4	13,500 × 1/5	2,700	3,700
	20x5	13,500 × 1/5	2,700	1,000
b. Production	20x1	$\$13,500 \times \frac{1,500}{7,500}$	\$2,700	\$11,800
	20x2	$13,500 \times \frac{2,625}{7,500}$	4,725	7,075
	20x3	$13,500 \times \frac{2,250}{7,500}$	4,050	3,025
	20x4	$13,500 \times \frac{750}{7,500}$	1,350	1,675
	20x5	$13,500 \times \frac{375}{7,500}$	675	1,000
c. Double-declining-balance	20x1	\$14,500 × .4	\$5,800	\$ 8,700
	20x2	8,700 × .4	3,480	5,220
	20x3	5,220 × .4	2,088	3,132
	20x4	3,132 × .4	1,253*	1,879
	20x5		879*†	1,000

*Rounded.
†Remaining depreciation to reduce carrying value to residual value (\$1,879 − \$1,000 = \$879).

2. Adjusting entry prepared—straight-line method:

20x1			
Dec. 31	Depreciation Expense, Cement Mixer	2,700	
	Accumulated Depreciation, Cement Mixer		2,700
	To record depreciation expense, straight-line method		

3. Balance sheet presentation for 20x1 shown:

Property, Plant, and Equipment	
Cement Mixer	\$14,500
Less Accumulated Depreciation	2,700
	\$11,800

4. Conclusions drawn from depreciation patterns: The pattern of depreciation for the straight-line method differs significantly from that for the double-declining-balance method. In the earlier years, the amount of depreciation under the double-declining-balance method is significantly greater than the amount under the straight-line method. In the later years, the opposite is true. The carrying value under the straight-line method is greater than that under the double-declining-balance method at the end of all years except the fifth year. Depreciation under the production method differs from that under the other methods in that it follows no regular pattern. It varies with the amount of use. Consequently, depreciation is greatest in 20x2 and 20x3, which are the years of greatest use. Use declined significantly in the last two years.

Chapter Assignments

BUILDING YOUR KNOWLEDGE FOUNDATION

Questions

1. What are the characteristics of long-term assets?
2. Which of the following items would be classified as plant assets on the balance sheet? (a) A truck held for sale by a truck dealer, (b) an office building that was once the company headquarters but is now to be sold, (c) a typewriter used by a secretary of the company, (d) a machine that is used in manufacturing operations but is now fully depreciated, (e) pollution-control equipment that does not reduce the cost or improve the efficiency of a factory, (f) a parking lot for company employees.
3. Why is land different from other long-term assets?
4. What do accountants mean by the term *depreciation,* and what is its relationship to depletion and amortization?
5. What is asset impairment, and how does it affect the valuation of long-term assets?
6. How do cash flows relate to the decision to acquire a long-term asset, and how does the useful life of an asset relate to the means of financing it?
7. Why is it useful to think of a plant asset as a bundle of services?
8. What is the distinction between revenue expenditures and capital expenditures, why is it important, and what in general is included in the cost of a long-term asset?
9. Which of the following expenditures stemming from the purchase of a computer system would be charged to the asset account? (a) The purchase price of the equipment, (b) interest on the debt incurred to purchase the equipment, (c) freight charges, (d) installation charges, (e) the cost of special communications outlets at the computer site, (f) the cost of repairing a door that was damaged during installation, (g) the cost of adjustments to the system during the first month of operation.
10. Hale's Grocery obtained bids on the construction of a receiving dock at the back of its store. The lowest bid was $22,000. The company decided to build the dock itself, however, and was able to do so for $20,000, which it borrowed. The activity was recorded as a debit to Buildings for $22,000 and credits to Notes Payable for $20,000 and Gain on Construction for $2,000. Do you agree with the entry?
11. A firm buys technical equipment that is expected to last twelve years. Why might the equipment have to be depreciated over a shorter period of time?
12. A company purchased a building five years ago. The market value of the building is now greater than it was when the building was purchased. Explain why the company should continue depreciating the building.
13. Evaluate the following statement: "A parking lot should not be depreciated because adequate repairs will make it last forever."
14. Is the purpose of depreciation to determine the value of equipment? Explain your answer.
15. Contrast the assumptions underlying the straight-line depreciation method with the assumptions underlying the production depreciation method.
16. What is the principal argument supporting an accelerated depreciation method?
17. If a plant asset is sold during the year, why should depreciation be computed for the partial year prior to the date of the sale?
18. If a plant asset is discarded before the end of its useful life, how is the amount of loss measured?
19. When similar assets are exchanged, at what amount is the new asset recorded for federal income tax purposes?
20. When an exchange of similar assets occurs in which there is an unrecorded loss, is the taxpayer ever able to deduct or receive federal income tax credit for the loss?
21. Old Stake Mining Company computes the depletion rate of ore to be $2 per ton. During 20xx the company mined 400,000 tons of ore and sold 370,000 tons. What is the total depletion expense for the year?

22. Under what circumstances can a mining company depreciate its plant assets over a period of time that is less than their useful lives?
23. Because accounts receivable have no physical substance, can they be classified as intangible assets?
24. Under what circumstances can a company have intangible assets that do not appear on the balance sheet?
25. When the Accounting Principles Board indicates that accounting for intangible assets involves the same issues as accounting for tangible assets, what issues is it referring to?
26. How does the Financial Accounting Standards Board recommend that research and development costs be treated?
27. After spending three years developing a new software program for designing office buildings, Archi Draw Company recently completed the detailed working program. How does accounting for the costs of software development differ before and after the completion of a successful working program?
28. How is accounting for software development costs similar to and different from accounting for research and development costs?
29. Under what conditions should goodwill be recorded? Should it remain in the records permanently once it is recorded?
30. What basic procedure should be followed in revising a depreciation rate?
31. On what basis can depreciation be taken on a group of assets rather than on individual items?
32. What will be the effect on future years' income of charging an addition to a building to repair expense?
33. In what ways do an addition, a betterment, and an extraordinary repair differ?
34. How does an extraordinary repair differ from an ordinary repair? What is the accounting treatment for each?
35. What is the difference between depreciation for accounting purposes and the Modified Accelerated Cost Recovery System for income tax purposes?

Short Exercises

LO 1 *Management Issues*

SE 1. Indicate whether each of the following actions is primarily related to (a) acquisition of long-term assets, (b) financing of long-term assets, or (c) choosing methods and estimates related to long-term assets.

1. Deciding between common stock and long-term notes for the raising of funds
2. Relating the acquisition cost of a long-term asset to cash flows generated by the asset
3. Determining how long an asset will benefit the company
4. Deciding to use cash flows from operations to purchase long-term assets
5. Determining how much an asset will sell for when it is no longer useful to the company

LO 2 *Determining Cost of Long-Term Assets*

SE 2. Denecker Auto purchased a neighboring lot for a new building and parking lot. Indicate whether each of the following expenditures is properly charged to (a) Land, (b) Land Improvements, or (c) Buildings.

1. Paving costs
2. Architects' fee for building design
3. Cost of clearing the property
4. Cost of the property
5. Building construction costs
6. Lights around the property
7. Building permit
8. Interest on the construction loan

LO 2 *Group Purchase*

SE 3. Altshuler Company purchased property with a warehouse and parking lot for $750,000. An appraiser valued the components of the property if purchased separately as follows:

Land	$200,000
Land improvements	100,000
Building	500,000
Total	$800,000

Determine the cost to be assigned to each component.

SE 4. LO 4 *Straight-Line Method*

Vermont Sun Fitness Center purchased a new step machine for $5,500. The apparatus is expected to last four years and have a residual value of $500. What will be the depreciation expense for each year under the straight-line method?

SE 5. LO 4 *Production Method*

Assuming that the step machine in **SE 4** has an estimated useful life of 8,000 hours and was used for 2,400 hours in year 1, for 2,000 hours in year 2, for 2,200 hours in year 3, and for 1,400 hours in year 4, how much would depreciation expense be in each year?

SE 6. LO 4 *Double-Declining-Balance Method*

Assuming that the step machine in **SE 4** is depreciated using the declining-balance method at double the straight-line rate, how much would depreciation expense be in each year?

SE 7. LO 5 *Disposal of Plant Assets: No Trade-In*

New England Printing had a piece of equipment that cost $8,100 and on which $4,500 of accumulated depreciation had been recorded. The equipment was disposed of on January 4, the first day of business of the current year. Prepare the entries in journal form to record the disposal under each of the following assumptions:

1. It was discarded as having no value.
2. It was sold for $1,500 cash.
3. It was sold for $4,000 cash.

SE 8. LO 6 *Disposal of Plant Assets: Trade-In*

Prepare the entries in journal form to record the disposal referred to in **SE 7** under each of the following assumptions:

1. The equipment was traded in on dissimilar equipment that had a list price of $12,000. A $3,800 trade-in was allowed, and the balance was paid in cash. Gains and losses are to be recognized.
2. The equipment was traded in on dissimilar equipment that had a list price of $12,000. A $1,750 trade-in was allowed, and the balance was paid in cash. Gains and losses are to be recognized.
3. Same as **2,** except that the items are similar and gains and losses are not to be recognized.

SE 9. LO 7 *Natural Resources*

Lincoln Hills Company purchased land containing an estimated 4,000,000 tons of ore for $8,000,000. The land will be worth $1,200,000 without the ore after eight years of active mining. Although the equipment needed for the mining will have a useful life of twenty years, it is not expected to be usable and will have no value after the mining on this site is complete. Compute the depletion charge per ton and the amount of depletion expense for the first year of operation, assuming that 600,000 tons of ore were mined and sold. Also, compute the first-year depreciation on the mining equipment using the straight-line method, assuming a cost of $9,600,000 with no residual value.

SE 10. LO 8 *Intangible Assets: Computer Software*

Alpha-Links created a new software application for PCs. Its costs during research and development were $500,000, and its costs after the working program was developed were $350,000. Although its copyright may be amortized over forty years, management believes that the product will be viable for only five years. How should the costs be accounted for? At what value will the software appear on the balance sheet after one year?

Exercises

E 1. LO 1 *Management Issues*

Indicate whether each of the following actions is primarily related to (a) acquisition of long-term assets, (b) financing of long-term assets, or (c) choosing methods and estimates related to long-term assets.

1. Deciding to use the production method of depreciation
2. Allocating costs on a group purchase
3. Determining the total units a machine will produce
4. Deciding to borrow funds to purchase equipment
5. Estimating the savings a new machine will produce and comparing the amount to cost
6. Deciding whether to rent or buy a piece of equipment

LO 1 *Purchase Decision— Present Value Analysis*

E 2. Management is considering the purchase of a new machine for a cost of $12,000. It is estimated that the machine will generate positive net cash flows of $3,000 per year for five years and will have a disposal price at the end of that time of $1,000. Assuming an interest rate of 9 percent, determine if management should purchase the machine. Use Tables 3 and 4 in the appendix on future value and present value tables to determine the net present value of the new machine.

LO 2 *Determining Cost of Long-Term Assets*

E 3. Decatur Manufacturing purchased land next to its factory to be used as a parking lot. Expenditures incurred by the company were as follows: purchase price, $150,000; broker's fees, $12,000; title search and other fees, $1,100; demolition of a shack on the property, $4,000; general grading of property, $2,100; paving parking lots, $20,000; lighting for parking lots, $16,000; and signs for parking lots, $3,200. Determine the amounts that should be debited to the Land account and the Land Improvements account.

LO 2 *Group Purchase*

E 4. Linda Rollo purchased a car wash for $480,000. If purchased separately, the land would have cost $120,000, the building $270,000, and the equipment $210,000. Determine the amount that should be recorded in the new business's records for land, building, and equipment.

LO 2 LO 4 *Cost of Long-Term Asset and Depreciation*

E 5. Myron Walker purchased a used tractor for $35,000. Before the tractor could be used, it required new tires, which cost $2,200, and an overhaul, which cost $2,800. Its first tank of fuel cost $150. The tractor is expected to last six years and have a residual value of $4,000. Determine the cost and depreciable cost of the tractor and calculate the first year's depreciation under the straight-line method.

LO 3 LO 4 *Depreciation Methods*

E 6. Findlay Oil Company purchased a drilling truck for $90,000. The company expected the truck to last five years or 200,000 miles, with an estimated residual value of $15,000 at the end of that time. During 20x5, the truck was driven 48,000 miles. The company's year end is December 31. Compute the depreciation for 20x5 under each of the following methods, assuming that the truck was purchased on January 13, 20x4: (1) straight-line, (2) production, and (3) double-declining-balance. Using the amount computed in **3,** prepare the entry in journal form to record depreciation expense for the second year and show how the Drilling Truck account would appear on the balance sheet.

LO 4 *Declining-Balance Method*

E 7. Schwab Burglar Alarm Systems Company purchased a word processor for $2,240. It has an estimated useful life of four years and an estimated residual value of $240. Compute the depreciation charge for each of the four years using the double-declining-balance method.

LO 5 LO 6 *Disposal of Plant Assets*

E 8. A piece of equipment that cost $32,400 and on which $18,000 of accumulated depreciation had been recorded was disposed of on January 2, the first day of business of the current year. Prepare entries in journal form to record the disposal under each of the following assumptions:

1. It was discarded as having no value.
2. It was sold for $6,000 cash.
3. It was sold for $18,000 cash.
4. It was traded in on dissimilar equipment having a list price of $48,000. A $16,200 trade-in was allowed, and the balance was paid in cash. Gains and losses are to be recognized.
5. It was traded in on dissimilar equipment having a list price of $48,000. A $7,500 trade-in was allowed, and the balance was paid in cash. Gains and losses are to be recognized.
6. Same as **5,** except that the items are similar and gains and losses are not to be recognized.

LO 5 LO 6 *Disposal of Plant Assets*

E 9. A microcomputer was purchased by Juniper Company on January 1, 20x1, at a cost of $5,000. It is expected to have a useful life of five years and a residual value of $500. Assuming that the computer is disposed of on July 1, 20x4, record the partial year's depreciation for 20x4 using the straight-line method, and record the disposal under each of the following assumptions:

1. The microcomputer is discarded.
2. The microcomputer is sold for $800.

3. The microcomputer is sold for $2,200.
4. The microcomputer is exchanged for a new microcomputer with a list price of $9,000. A $1,200 trade-in is allowed on the cash purchase. The accounting approach to gains and losses is followed.
5. Same as **4,** except a $2,400 trade-in is allowed.
6. Same as **4,** except the income tax approach is followed.
7. Same as **5,** except the income tax approach is followed.
8. Same as **4,** except the microcomputer is exchanged for dissimilar office equipment.
9. Same as **5,** except the microcomputer is exchanged for dissimilar office equipment.

E 10. LO 7 *Natural Resource Depletion and Depreciation of Related Plant Assets*

Putney Mining Company purchased land containing an estimated 10 million tons of ore for a cost of $8,800,000. The land without the ore is estimated to be worth $1,600,000. The company expects that all the usable ore can be mined in ten years. Buildings costing $800,000 with an estimated useful life of thirty years were erected on the site. Equipment costing $960,000 with an estimated useful life of ten years was installed. Because of the remote location, neither the buildings nor the equipment has an estimated residual value. During its first year of operation, the company mined and sold 800,000 tons of ore.

1. Compute the depletion charge per ton.
2. Compute the depletion expense that Putney Mining should record for the year.
3. Determine the depreciation expense for the year for the buildings, making it proportional to the depletion.
4. Determine the depreciation expense for the year for the equipment under two alternatives: (a) making the expense proportional to the depletion and (b) using the straight-line method.

E 11. LO 8 *Amortization of Copyrights and Trademarks*

1. Fortunato Publishing Company purchased the copyright to a basic computer textbook for $20,000. The usual life of a textbook is about four years. However, the copyright will remain in effect for another fifty years. Calculate the annual amortization of the copyright.
2. Guzman Company purchased a trademark from a well-known supermarket for $160,000. The management of the company argued that because the trademark's value would last forever and might even increase, no amortization should be charged. Calculate the minimum amount of annual amortization that should be charged, according to guidelines of the appropriate Accounting Principles Board opinion.

E 12. SO 9 *Depreciation Methods: Partial Years*

Using the data given for Findlay Oil Company in **E 6,** compute the depreciation for calendar year 20x4 under each of the following methods, assuming that the truck was purchased on July 1, 20x4, and was driven 20,000 miles during 20x4: (1) straight-line, (2) production, and (3) double-declining-balance.

E 13. SO 9 *Revision of Depreciation Rates*

Broadleigh Hospital purchased a special x-ray machine for its operating room. The machine, which cost $311,560, was expected to last ten years, with an estimated residual value of $31,560. After two years of operation (and depreciation charges using the straight-line method), it became evident that the x-ray machine would last a total of only seven years. The estimated residual value, however, would remain the same. Given this information, determine the new depreciation charge for the third year on the basis of the revised estimated useful life.

E 14. LO 2, SO 9 *Special Types of Capital Expenditures*

Tell whether each of the following transactions related to an office building is a revenue expenditure (RE) or a capital expenditure (CE). In addition, indicate whether each transaction is an ordinary repair (OR), an extraordinary repair (ER), an addition (A), a betterment (B), or none of these (N).

1. The hallways and ceilings in the building are repainted at a cost of $8,300.
2. The hallways, which have tile floors, are carpeted at a cost of $28,000.
3. A new wing is added to the building at a cost of $175,000.
4. Furniture is purchased for the entrance to the building at a cost of $16,500.
5. The air-conditioning system is overhauled at a cost of $28,500. The overhaul extends the useful life of the air-conditioning system by ten years.
6. A cleaning firm is paid $200 per week to clean the newly installed carpets.

E 15. SO 9 *Extraordinary Repairs*

Regalado Manufacturing has an incinerator that originally cost $187,200 and now has accumulated depreciation of $132,800. The incinerator has completed its fifteenth year of service in an estimated useful life of twenty years. At the beginning of the sixteenth year, the company spent $42,800 repairing and modernizing the incinerator to comply with pollution-control standards. Therefore, the incinerator is now expected to last ten more years instead of five more years. It will not, however, have more capacity than it did in the past or a residual value at the end of its useful life.

1. Prepare the entry to record the cost of the repair.
2. Compute the carrying value of the incinerator after the entry.
3. Prepare the entry to record straight-line depreciation for the current year.

Problems

P 1. LO 2 *Determining Cost of Assets*

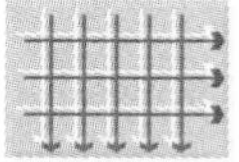

Muraskas Computers constructed a new training center in 20x2. You have been hired to manage the training center. A review of the accounting records lists the following expenditures debited to an asset account titled "Training Center."

Attorney's fee, land acquisition	$ 34,900
Cost of land	598,000
Architect's fee, building design	102,000
Building	1,020,000
Parking lot and sidewalk	135,600
Electrical wiring, building	164,000
Landscaping	55,000
Cost of surveying land	9,200
Training equipment, tables, and chairs	136,400
Installation of training equipment	68,000
Cost of grading the land	14,000
Cost of changes in building to soundproof rooms	59,200
Total account balance	$2,396,300

During the center's construction, someone from Muraskas Computers worked full time on the project. He spent two months on the purchase and preparation of the site, six months on the construction, one month on land improvements, and one month on equipment installation and training room furniture purchase and setup. His salary of $64,000 during this ten-month period was charged to Administrative Expense. The training center was placed in operation on November 1.

REQUIRED

Prepare a schedule with the following four column (Account) headings: Land, Land Improvements, Building, and Equipment. Place each of the expenditures above in the appropriate column. Total the columns.

P 2. LO 3 LO 4 *Comparison of Depreciation Methods*

Larson Manufacturing Company purchased a robot at a cost of $1,440,000 at the beginning of year 1. The robot has an estimated useful life of four years and an estimated residual value of $120,000. The robot, which should last 20,000 hours, was operated 6,000 hours in year 1; 8,000 hours in year 2; 4,000 hours in year 3; and 2,000 hours in year 4.

REQUIRED

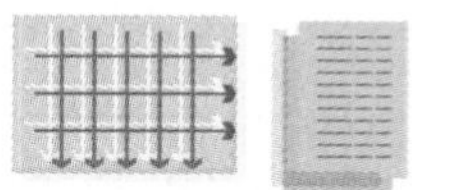

1. Compute the annual depreciation and carrying value for the robot for each year assuming the following depreciation methods: (a) straight-line, (b) production, and (c) double-declining-balance.
2. Prepare the adjusting entry that would be made each year to record the depreciation calculated under the straight-line method.
3. Show the balance sheet presentation for the robot after the adjusting entry in year 2 using the straight-line method.
4. What conclusions can you draw from the patterns of yearly depreciation and carrying value in **1**?

P 3. LO 5 LO 6 *Recording Disposals*

Pavlic Construction Company purchased a road grader for $58,000. The road grader is expected to have a useful life of five years and a residual value of $4,000 at the end of that time.

REQUIRED

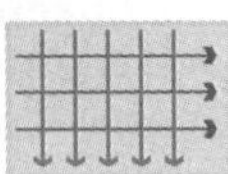

Prepare entries in journal form to record the disposal of the road grader at the end of the second year, assuming that the straight-line method is used and making the following additional assumptions:

a. The road grader is sold for $40,000 cash.
b. It is sold for $32,000 cash.
c. It is traded in on a dissimilar piece of machinery costing $66,000. A trade-in allowance of $40,000 is given, the balance is paid in cash, and gains or losses are recognized.
d. It is traded in on a dissimilar piece of machinery costing $66,000. A trade-in allowance of $32,000 is given, the balance is paid in cash, and gains or losses are recognized.
e. Same as **c,** except that it is traded for a similar road grader and Pavlic Construction Company follows accounting rules for the recognition of gains or losses.
f. Same as **d,** except that it is traded for a similar road grader and Pavlic Construction Company follows accounting rules for the recognition of gains or losses.
g. Same as **c,** except that it is traded for a similar road grader and gains or losses are not recognized for income tax purposes.
h. Same as **d,** except that it is traded for a similar road grader and gains or losses are not recognized for income tax purposes.

P 4. **LO 8** *Amortization of Exclusive License, Leasehold, and Leasehold Improvements*

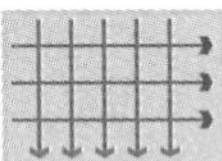

Part A: On January 1, Miracle Games purchased the exclusive license to make dolls based on the characters in a new hit television series called "Space Kids." The exclusive license cost $4,200,000, and there was no termination date on the rights. Immediately after signing the contract, the company sued a rival firm that claimed it had already received the exclusive license to the series characters. Miracle Games successfully defended its rights at a cost of $720,000. During the first year and the next, Miracle Games marketed toys based on the series. Because a successful television series lasts about five years, the company felt it could market the toys for three more years. However, before the third year of the series could get under way, a controversy arose between the two stars of the series and the producer. As a result, the stars refused to do the third year and the show was canceled, rendering exclusive rights worthless.

REQUIRED

Prepare entries in journal form to record the following: (a) purchase of the exclusive license; (b) successful defense of the license; (c) amortization expense, if any, for the first year; and (d) write-off of the license as worthless.

Part B: Evelyn Miripol purchased a six-year sublease on a building from the estate of the former tenant. It was a good location for her business, and the annual rent of $7,200, which had been established ten years before, was low. The cost of the sublease was $18,900. To use the building, Miripol had to make certain alterations. First she moved some panels at a cost of $3,400 and installed others for $12,200. Then she added carpet, lighting fixtures, and a sign at costs of $5,800, $6,200, and $2,400, respectively. All items except the carpet would last for at least twelve years. The expected life of the carpet was six years. None of the improvements would have a residual value at the end of those times.

REQUIRED

Prepare entries in journal form to record the following: (a) the payment for the sublease; (b) the payments for the alterations, panels, carpet, lighting fixtures, and sign; (c) the lease payment for the first year; (d) the amortization expense, if any, associated with the sublease; and (e) the amortization expense, if any, associated with the alterations, panels, carpet, lighting fixtures, and sign.

P 5. **LO 4** **SO 9** *Depreciation Methods and Partial Years*

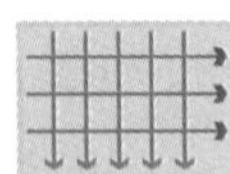

Isabel Lim purchased a laundry company. In addition to the washing machines, Lim installed a tanning machine and a refreshment center. Because each type of asset performs a different function, she has decided to use different depreciation methods. Data on each type of asset are summarized in the table below. The tanning machine was operated 2,100 hours in 20x5, 3,000 hours in 20x6, and 2,400 hours in 20x7.

Asset	Date Purchased	Cost	Installation Cost	Residual Value	Estimated Life	Depreciation Method
Washing machines	3/5/x5	$30,000	$4,000	$5,200	4 years	Straight-line
Tanning machine	4/1/x5	68,000	6,000	2,000	7,500 hours	Production
Refreshment center	10/1/x5	6,800	1,200	1,200	10 years	Double-declining-balance

REQUIRED

Assume the fiscal year ends December 31. Compute the depreciation expense for each item and the total depreciation expense for 20x5, 20x6, and 20x7. Round your answers to the nearest dollar and present them in a table with the headings shown below.

Asset	Computations	20x5	Depreciation 20x6	20x7

Alternate Problems

LO 2 *Determining Cost of Assets*

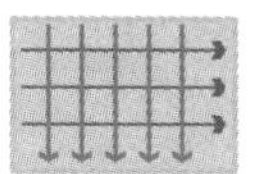

P 6. Flair Company began operation on January 1 of the current year. At the end of the year, the company's auditor discovered that all expenditures involving long-term assets had been debited to an account called Fixed Assets. An analysis of the account, which had a year-end balance of $2,644,972, disclosed that it contained the items presented below.

Cost of land	$ 316,600
Surveying costs	4,100
Transfer of title and other fees required by the county	920
Broker's fees for land	21,144
Attorney's fees associated with land acquisition	7,048
Cost of removing unusable timber from land	50,400
Cost of grading land	4,200
Cost of digging building foundation	34,600
Architect's fee for building and land improvements (80 percent building)	64,800
Cost of building construction	710,000
Cost of sidewalks	11,400
Cost of parking lots	54,400
Cost of lighting for grounds	80,300
Cost of landscaping	11,800
Cost of machinery	989,000
Shipping cost on machinery	55,300
Cost of installing machinery	176,200
Cost of testing machinery	22,100
Cost of changes in building to comply with safety regulations pertaining to machinery	12,540
Cost of repairing building that was damaged in the installation of machinery	8,900
Cost of medical bill for injury received by employee while installing machinery	2,400
Cost of water damage to building during heavy rains prior to opening the plant for operation	6,820
Account balance	$2,644,972

The timber that was cleared from the land was sold to a firewood dealer for $5,000. This amount was credited to Miscellaneous Income. During the construction period, two supervisors devoted their full time to the construction project. They earn annual salaries of $48,000 and $42,000, respectively. They spent two months on the purchase and preparation of the land, six months on the construction of the building (approximately one-sixth of which was devoted to improvements on the grounds), and one month on machinery installation. The plant began operation on October 1, and the supervisors returned to their regular duties. Their salaries were debited to Factory Salaries Expense.

REQUIRED

Prepare a schedule with the following column headings: Land, Land Improvements, Buildings, Machinery, and Expense. List the items and place each in the proper account. Negative amounts should be shown in parentheses. Total the columns.

LO 3 LO 4 *Comparison of Depreciation Methods*

P 7. Farentino Construction Company purchased a new crane for $360,500 at the beginning of year 1. The crane has an estimated residual value of $35,000 and an estimated useful life of six years. The crane is expected to last 10,000 hours. It was used 1,800 hours in year 1; 2,000 in year 2; 2,500 in year 3; 1,500 in year 4; 1,200 in year 5; and 1,000 in year 6.

REQUIRED

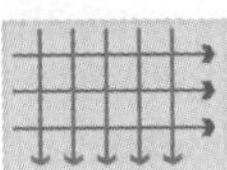

1. Compute the annual depreciation and carrying value for the new crane for each of the six years (round to nearest dollar where necessary) under each of the following methods: (a) straight-line, (b) production, and (c) double-declining-balance.
2. Prepare the adjusting entry that would be made each year to record the depreciation calculated under the straight-line method.
3. Show the balance sheet presentation for the crane after the adjusting entry in year 2 using the straight-line method.
4. What conclusions can you draw from the patterns of yearly depreciation and carrying value in **1**?

P 8. LO 4, SO 9 *Depreciation Methods and Partial Years*

Gottlieb Company operates three types of equipment. Because of the equipment's varied functions, company accounting policy requires the application of three different depreciation methods. Data on this equipment are summarized in the table below. Equipment 3 was used 2,000 hours in 20x5; 4,200 hours in 20x6; and 3,200 hours in 20x7.

Equipment	Date Purchased	Cost	Installation Cost	Estimated Residual Value	Estimated Life	Depreciation Method
1	1/12/x5	$171,000	$ 9,000	$18,000	10 years	Double-declining-balance
2	7/9/x5	191,100	15,900	21,000	10 years	Straight-line
3	10/2/x5	290,700	8,100	33,600	20,000 hours	Production

REQUIRED

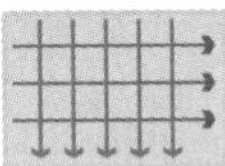

Assuming that the fiscal year ends December 31, compute the depreciation expense on each type of equipment and the total depreciation expense for 20x5, 20x6, and 20x7 by filling in a table with the headings shown below.

Equipment No.	Computations	Depreciation 20x5	Depreciation 20x6	Depreciation 20x7

EXPANDING YOUR CRITICAL THINKING, COMMUNICATION, AND INTERPERSONAL SKILLS

Skills Development

CONCEPTUAL ANALYSIS

SD 1. LO 1, LO 3 *Nature of Depreciation and Amortization and Estimated Useful Lives*

In its 1987 annual report, ***General Motors Corp.*** states,

> In the third quarter of 1987, the Corporation revised the estimated service lives of its plants and equipment and special tools retroactive to January 1, 1987. These revisions, which were based on 1987 studies of actual useful lives and periods of use, recognized current estimates of service lives of the assets and had the effect of reducing 1987 depreciation and amortization charges by $1,236.6 million or $2.53 per share of $1⅔ par value common stock.[21]

In 1987, General Motors' income before income taxes was $2,005.4 million. Discuss the purpose of depreciation and amortization. What is the estimated service life, and on what basis did General Motors change the estimates of the service lives of plants and equipment and special tools? What was the effect of this change on the corporation's income before income taxes? Is it likely that the company is in better condition economically as a result of the change? Does the company have more cash at the end of the year as a result? (Ignore income tax effects.)

Communication

Critical Thinking

Group Activity

Memo

Ethics

International
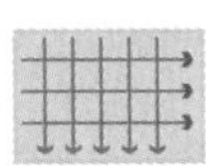
Spreadsheet
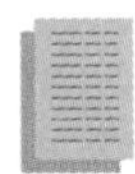
General Ledger

CD-ROM

Internet

SD 2.

LO 3 **LO 4** *Change of Depreciation Method*

Ford Motor Co., one of the nation's largest manufacturers of automobiles, changed from an accelerated depreciation method for financial reporting purposes to the straight-line method for assets acquired after January 1, 1993. As noted in Ford's 1995 annual report:

> Property and Equipment placed in service after December 31, 1992 are depreciated using the straight-line method of depreciation over the estimated useful life of the asset.[22]

What reasons can you give for Ford's choosing to switch to a straight-line method of depreciation? Discuss which of the two depreciation methods is the more conservative.

SD 3.

LO 8 *Trademarks*

The ***Quaker Oats Company's*** advertising campaign, "Gatorade is thirst aid for that deep down body thirst," infringed on a trademark held by ***Sands Taylor & Wood*** of Norwich Vermont, according to a 1990 ruling by a federal judge.[23] Sands Taylor & Wood had acquired the trademark "thirst aid" in a 1973 acquisition but was not using it at the time of the 1990 ruling. The judge determined that Gatorade had produced $247.3 million in income over the previous six years and reasoned that the advertising campaign was responsible for 10 percent of the product's sales. As a result, he awarded Sands Taylor & Wood $24.7 million plus legal fees and interest from 1984. He also prohibited Quaker Oats from further use of the phrase "thirst aid" in any advertising campaign for Gatorade, its largest-selling product.

What is a trademark, and why is it considered an intangible asset? Why does a trademark have value? For whom does a trademark have value? Be prepared to discuss how your answers apply to the case of Quaker Oats Company's use of "thirst aid."

Ethical Dilemma

SD 4.

LO 2 *Ethics and Allocation of Acquisition Costs*

Signal Company has purchased land and a warehouse for $18,000,000. The warehouse is expected to last twenty years and to have a salvage value equal to 10 percent of its cost. The chief financial officer (CFO) and the controller are discussing the allocation of the purchase price. The CFO believes that the largest amount possible should be assigned to the land because this action will improve reported net income in the future. Depreciation expense will be lower because land is not depreciated. He suggests allocating one-third, or $6,000,000, of the cost to the land. This results in depreciation expense each year of $540,000 [($12,000,000 − $1,200,000) ÷ 20 years]. The controller disagrees, arguing that the smallest amount possible, say one-fifth of the purchase price, should be allocated to the land, thereby saving income taxes, since the depreciation, which is tax deductible, will be greater. Under this plan, annual depreciation would be $648,000 [($14,400,000 − $1,440,000) ÷ 20 years]. The annual tax savings at a 30 percent tax rate is $32,400 [($648,000 − $540,000) × .30]. How will this decision affect the company's cash flows? Ethically speaking, how should the purchase cost be allocated? Who will be affected by the decision?

Group Activity: Have each group develop the position of one of the two roles for presentation and debate.

SD 5.

LO 2 **LO 8** *Ethics of Aggressive Accounting Policies*

Is it ethical to choose aggressive accounting practices to advance a company's business? ***America Online*** (AOL), the largest on-line service and Internet service provider in the United States, was one of the hottest stocks on Wall Street and one of the most aggressive in its choice of accounting principles. From its initial stock offering in 1992, its stock price was up over 2,000 percent by early 1996. Accounting is very important to AOL because earnings enable it to sell shares of stock and raise more cash to fund its phenomenal growth. AOL's strategy called for building the largest customer base in the industry. Consequently, it spent many millions of dollars each year marketing its services to new customers. Such costs are usually recognized as operating expenses in the year in which they are incurred. However, AOL treated these costs as long-term assets, called "deferred subscriber acquisition costs," and expensed them over several years, because the company said the average customer was going to stay with the company for three years or more. The company also recorded research and development costs as "product development costs" and amortized them over five years. Both of these practices are justifiable theoretically, but they are not common practice. If the standard or more conservative practice had been followed, the company would have had a net loss in every year it has been in business.[24] This result would have greatly limited AOL's ability to raise money and grow as it has. Explain in your own words management's rationale for adopting the accounting policies that it did. What could go wrong with management's plan? How would you evaluate the ethics of AOL's actions? Who benefits from the actions? Who is harmed by the actions? Have you seen any developments about AOL in the news?

RESEARCH ACTIVITY

SD 6. LO 5 LO 6 *SEC and Form 10-K*

Public corporations are required not only to communicate with their stockholders by means of an annual report, but also to submit an annual report to the Securities and Exchange Commission (SEC). The annual report to the SEC is called a 10-K and contains information in addition to that provided to stockholders. Most college and university libraries provide access to at least a selected number of 10-Ks. These 10-Ks may be on microfiche or on file with the companies' annual reports to stockholders. Find the 10-K for a single company in your school's library, or, through the Needles Accounting Resource Center Web site at http://www.hmco.com/college/needles/home.html, access the SEC's EDGAR files to locate a 10-K report. In that 10-K, Schedule 5 will contain information about the company's dispositions and acquisitions of property, plant, and equipment at carrying value. Schedule 6 will show the increases and decreases in the accumulated depreciation accounts. In the statement of cash flows, under investing activities, the cash proceeds from dispositions of property, plant, and equipment will be shown. Using the information from the statement of cash flows and the two related schedules, determine whether the company had a gain or loss from dispositions of property, plant, and equipment during the year. Be prepared to discuss your results in class.

DECISION-MAKING PRACTICE

SD 7. LO 1 *Purchase Decision and Time Value of Money Application*

Morningside Machine Works has successfully obtained a subcontract to manufacture parts for a new military aircraft. The parts are to be delivered over the next five years, and Morningside will be paid as the parts are delivered. To make the parts, new equipment will have to be purchased. Two types of equipment are available. Type A is conventional equipment that can be put into service immediately, and Type B requires one year to be put into service but is more efficient. Type A requires an immediate cash investment of $1,000,000 and will produce enough parts to provide net cash receipts of $340,000 each year for the five years. Type B may be purchased by signing a two-year non-interest-bearing note for $1,346,000. It is projected that Type B will produce net cash receipts of zero in year 1, $500,000 in year 2, $600,000 in year 3, $600,000 in year 4, and $200,000 in year 5. Neither type of equipment can be used on other contracts or will have any useful life remaining at the end of the contract. Morningside currently pays an interest rate of 16 percent to borrow money.

REQUIRED

1. What is the present value of the investment required for each type of equipment? (Use Table 3 in the appendix on future value and present value tables.)
2. Compute the net present value of each type of equipment based on your answer in 1 and the present value of the net cash receipts projected to be received. (Use Tables 3 and 4 in the appendix on future value and present value tables.)
3. Write a memorandum to the board of directors that recommends the option that appears to be best for Morningside based on your analysis (include **1** and **2** as attachments) and that explains why.

Financial Reporting and Analysis

INTERPRETING FINANCIAL REPORTS

FRA 1. LO 3 LO 4 SO 9 *Effects of Change in Accounting Method*

Depreciation expense is a significant expense for companies in which plant assets are a high proportion of assets. The amount of depreciation expense in a given year is affected by estimates of useful life and choice of depreciation method. In 1998, ***Century Steelworks Company,*** a major integrated steel producer, changed the estimated useful lives for its major production assets. It also changed the method of depreciation for other steel-making assets from straight-line to the production method.

The company's 1998 annual report states, "A recent study conducted by management shows that actual years-in-service figures for our major production equipment and machinery are, in most cases, higher than the estimated useful lives assigned to these assets. We have recast the depreciable lives of such assets so that equipment previously assigned a useful life of 8 to 26 years now has an extended depreciable life of 10 to 32 years." The report goes on to explain that the new production method of depreciation "recognizes that depreciation of production equipment and machinery correlates directly to both physical wear and tear and the passage of time. The production method of depreciation, which we have now initiated, more closely allocates the cost of these assets to the periods in which products are manufactured."

The report summarized the effects of both actions on the year 1998 as follows:

Incremental Increase in Net Income	**In Millions**	**Per Share**
Lengthened lives	$11.0	$ .80
Production method		
Current year	7.3	.53
Prior years	2.8	.20
Total increase	$21.1	$1.53

During 1998, Century Steelworks reported a net loss of $83,156,500 ($6.03 per share). Depreciation expense for 1998 was $87,707,200.

In explaining the changes, the controller of Century Steelworks was quoted in an article in *Business Journal* as follows: "There is no reason for Century Steelworks to continue to depreciate our assets more conservatively than our competitors do." But the article quotes an industry analyst who argues that by slowing its method of depreciation, Century Steelworks could be viewed as reporting lower-quality earnings.

REQUIRED

1. Explain the accounting treatment when there is a change in the estimated lives of depreciable assets. What circumstances must exist for the production method to produce the effect it did in relation to the straight-line method? What would Century Steelworks' net income or loss have been if the changes had not been made? What may have motivated management to make the changes?
2. What does the controller of Century Steelworks mean when he says that Century had been depreciating "more conservatively than our competitors do"? Why might the changes at Century Steelworks indicate, as the analyst asserts, "lower-quality earnings"? What risks might Century face as a result of its decision to use the production method of depreciation?

International Company

FRA 2.

LO 8 *Accounting for Trademarks and Goodwill: U.S. and British Rules*

When the British company ***Grand Metropolitan*** (Grand Met) purchased ***Pillsbury*** in 1989, it adopted British accounting policies with regard to intangibles. Many analysts feel this gives British companies advantages over U.S. companies, especially in buyout situations.[25] There are two major differences in accounting for intangibles between U.S. accounting standards and British accounting standards. First, under the U.S. rules, as discussed in this chapter, intangible assets such as trademarks are recorded at their acquisition cost, which is often nominal, and the cost is amortized over a reasonable life. Under British accounting standards, on the other hand, firms are able to record the value of trademarks for the purpose of increasing the total assets on their balance sheets. Further, they do not have to amortize the value if management can show that the value can be preserved through extensive brand support. Grand Met, therefore, elected to record such famous Pillsbury trademarks as the Pillsbury Doughboy, Green Giant vegetables, Häagen Dazs ice cream, and Van de Kamp fish at an estimated value and not to amortize them. Second, when one company purchases another company for more than the market value of the assets if purchased individually, under U.S. rules the excess is recorded as the asset Goodwill, which must be amortized over a period not to exceed forty years. Under British accounting rules, any goodwill resulting from a purchase lowers stockholders' equity directly, rather than being recorded as an asset and lowering net income through amortization over a number of years. Analysts say that these two rules made Pillsbury more valuable to Grand Met than to Pillsbury stockholders and thus led to Pillsbury's being bought by the British firm. Write a one- or two-page paper that addresses the following questions: What is the rationale behind the argument that the

British company has an advantage due to the differences between U.S. and British accounting principles? Do you agree with U.S. or British accounting rules regarding intangibles and goodwill? Defend your answers.

Toys "R" Us Annual Report

FRA 3.

LO 1 LO 2 LO 3 LO 4 *Long-Term Assets*

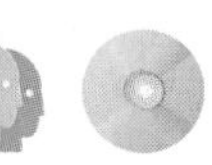

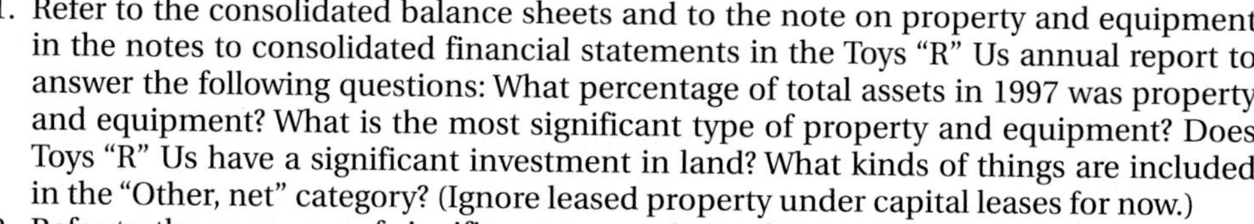

1. Refer to the consolidated balance sheets and to the note on property and equipment in the notes to consolidated financial statements in the Toys "R" Us annual report to answer the following questions: What percentage of total assets in 1997 was property and equipment? What is the most significant type of property and equipment? Does Toys "R" Us have a significant investment in land? What kinds of things are included in the "Other, net" category? (Ignore leased property under capital leases for now.)
2. Refer to the summary of significant accounting policies and to the note on property and equipment in the Toys "R" Us annual report. What method of depreciation does Toys "R" Us use? How is interest on construction of long-term assets accounted for? How long does management estimate its buildings to last as compared to furniture and equipment? What does this say about Toys "R" Us's need to remodel its stores?
3. Refer to the statement of cash flows in the Toys "R" Us annual report. How much did Toys "R" Us spend on property and equipment (capital expenditures, net) during 1997? Is this an increase or a decrease from prior years?
4. Refer to the other charges note to the financial statements. Among other charges in 1996, Toys "R" Us had a charge of $24,200,000 for asset impairment. What is an asset impairment? What long-lived assets were reduced to fair value? How does this affect the assets and earnings of the firm?

Fingraph® Financial Analyst™

FRA 4.

LO 1 LO 4 LO 7 LO 8 *Long-Term Assets*

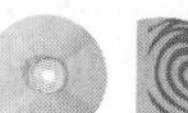

Choose any two companies from the same industry in the Fingraph® Financial Analyst™ CD-ROM software. The industry chosen should be one in which long-term assets are likely to be important. Choose an industry such as airlines, manufacturing, consumer products, consumer food and beverage, or computers.

1. In the annual reports for the companies you have selected, read the long-term asset section of the balance sheet and any reference to any long-term assets in the summary of significant accounting policies or notes to the financial statements. What are the most important long-term assets for each company? What depreciation methods do the companies use? Are there any long-term assets that appear to be characteristic of the industry? What intangible assets do the companies have, and how important are they?
2. Display and print in tabular and graphical form the Balance Sheet Analysis page. Prepare a table that compares the gross and net property, plant, and equipment.
3. Locate the statements of cash flows in the two companies' annual reports. Prepare another table that compares depreciation (and amortization) expense from the operating activities section with the net purchases of property, plant, and equipment (net capital expenditures) from the investing activities section for two years. Does depreciation (and amortization) expense exceed replacement of long-term assets? Are the companies expanding or reducing their property, plant, and equipment?
4. Find and read references to long-term assets and capital expenditures in management's discussion and analysis in each annual report.
5. Write a one-page executive summary that highlights the most important long-term assets and the accounting policies for long-term assets, and compares the investing activities of the two companies, including reference to management's assessment. Include the Fingraph® page and your tables as attachments to your report.

ENDNOTES

1. H. J. Heinz Company, *Annual Report*, 1996.
2. "Accounting for the Impairment of Long-Lived Assets and for Long-Lived Assets to Be Disposed of," *Statement of Financial Accounting Standards No. 121* (Norwalk, Conn.: Financial Accounting Standards Board, 1995).

3. Leslie Canley, "Pacific Telesis Plans a Charge of $3.3 Billion," *The Wall Street Journal,* September 8, 1995.
4. ARCO Chemical Company, *Annual Report,* 1995.
5. Ibid.
6. Elizabeth MacDonald, "CPA Groups' Plan Would Standardize the Accounting for Software Expenses," *The Wall Street Journal,* December 19, 1996.
7. "Capitalization of Interest Cost," *Statement of Financial Accounting Standards No. 34* (Norwalk, Conn.: Financial Accounting Standards Board, 1979), par. 9–11.
8. Len Boselovic, "A Look at How the SEC Disposed of Chambers' Claims," *Pittsburgh Post-Gazette,* May 14, 1995.
9. *Financial Accounting Standards: Original Pronouncements as of July 1, 1977* (Norwalk, Conn.: Financial Accounting Standards Board, 1977), ARB No. 43, Ch. 9, Sec. C, par. 5.
10. Accounting Principles Board, *Opinion No. 29,* "Accounting for Nonmonetary Transactions" (New York: American Institute of Certified Public Accountants, 1973) and Emerging Issues Task Force, *EITF Issue Summary 86-29,* "Nonmonetary Transactions: Magnitude of Boot and the Exceptions to the Use of Fair Value" (Norwalk, Conn.: Financial Accounting Standards Board, 1986). The specific criteria for similar assets are the subject of more advanced courses.
11. *Statement of Financial Accounting Standards No. 25,* "Suspension of Certain Accounting Requirements for Oil and Gas Producing Companies" (Norwalk, Conn.: Financial Accounting Standards Board, 1979).
12. Adapted from Accounting Principles Board, *Opinion No. 17,* "Intangible Assets" (New York: American Institute of Certified Public Accountants, 1970), par. 2.
13. The FASB is considering shortening the amortization period for goodwill.
14. "What's in a Name?" *Time,* May 3, 1993.
15. *Statement of Financial Accounting Standards No. 2,* "Accounting for Research and Development Costs" (Norwalk, Conn.: Financial Accounting Standards Board, 1974), par. 12.
16. *Statement of Financial Accounting Standards No. 86,* "Accounting for the Costs of Computer Software to be Sold, Leased, or Otherwise Marketed" (Norwalk, Conn.: Financial Accounting Standards Board, 1985).
17. Moody's OTC and Industrials Guides, 1997.
18. Louis Uchitelle, "Companies Reported Spending More on Research," *The New York Times,* November 7, 1997.
19. Accounting Principles Board, *Opinion No. 17,* par. 29.
20. Edward P. McTague, "Accounting for Trade-Ins of Operational Assets," *National Public Accountant* (January 1986), p. 39.
21. General Motors Corp., *Annual Report,* 1987.
22. Ford Motor Co., *Annual Report,* 1995.
23. James P. Miller, "Quaker Oats Loses Trademark Battle Over Gatorade Ad," *The Wall Street Journal,* December 19, 1990.
24. "Stock Gives Case the Funds He Needs to Buy New Technology," *Business Week,* April 15, 1996.
25. Joanne Lipman, "British Value Brand Names—Literally," *The Wall Street Journal,* February 9, 1989, p. B4; and "Brand Name Policy Boosts Assets," *Accountancy,* October 1988, pp. 38–39.

CHAPTER 12

Current Liabilities

LEARNING OBJECTIVES

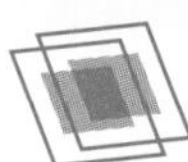

1. **Identify the management issues related to recognition, valuation, classification, and disclosure of current liabilities.**
2. **Identify, compute, and record definitely determinable and estimated current liabilities.**
3. **Define *contingent liability.***

SUPPLEMENTAL OBJECTIVE

4. **Compute and record the liabilities associated with payroll accounting.**

DECISION POINT

US AIRWAYS, INC.

Liabilities are one of the three major parts of the balance sheet. They are legal obligations for the future payment of assets or the future performance of services that result from past transactions. For example, the current and long-term liabilities of US Airways, Inc., which has total assets of more than \$6.9 billion, are shown here:[1] Current Maturities of Long-Term Debt, Accounts Payable, and Accrued Expenses for the most part will require an outlay of cash in the next year. Traffic Balances Payable will require payments to other airlines, but those may be partially offset by amounts owed from other airlines. Unused Tickets are tickets already paid for by passengers and represent services that must be performed. Long-Term Debt will require cash outlays in future years. Altogether these liabilities represent almost 75 percent of total assets. How does the decision of US Airways' management to incur so much debt relate to the goals of the business?

Terminology Note: US Airways uses "Accrued Expenses" to group liability accounts such as Salaries Payable and Interest Payable.

Enrichment Note: Unused tickets are often a significant liability for airlines. Like all service providers, airlines earn revenue by providing a service. The receipt of cash is usually incidental to revenue recognition.

Critical Thinking Question: What accounting concept underlies the recognition of the current liabilities called accrued expenses? **Answer:** The matching rule.

Liabilities are important because they are closely related to the goals of profitability and liquidity. Liabilities are sources of cash for operating and financing activities when they are incurred, but they are also obligations that use cash when they are paid as required. Achieving the appropriate level of liabilities is critical to business success. A company that has too few liabilities may not be earning up to its potential. A company that has too many liabilities, however, may be incurring excessive risks. This chapter focuses on the management and accounting issues

Financial Highlights
(in thousands)

	1996	1995
Current Liabilities	**\$ 84,259**	\$ 80,721
Current Maturities of Long-Term Debt	**438,951**	325,330
Accounts Payable	**715,576**	607,170
Traffic Balances Payable and Unused Tickets	**510,752**	495,489
Accrued Expenses	**1,099,181**	975,986
Total Current Liabilities	**2,848,719**	2,484,696
Long-Term Debt, Net of Current Maturities	**2,615,780**	2,717,085

involving current liabilities, including payroll liabilities and contingent liabilities.

Management Issues Related to Accounting for Current Liabilities

OBJECTIVE 1

Identify the management issues related to recognition, valuation, classification, and disclosure of current liabilities

Related Text Assignments:
Q: 1, 2, 3, 4, 5
SE: 1
E: 1
SD: 5
FRA: 1, 2, 3, 4

The primary reason for incurring current liabilities is to meet needs for cash during the operating cycle. The operating cycle is the process of converting cash to purchases, to sales, to accounts receivable, and back to cash. Most current liabilities arise in support of this cycle, as when accounts payable arise from purchases of inventory, accrued expenses arise from operating costs, and unearned revenues arise from customers' advance payments. Short-term debt is used to raise cash during periods of inventory buildup or while waiting for collection of receivables. Cash is used to pay current maturities of long-term debt and to pay off liabilities arising from operations.

Failure to manage the cash flows related to current liabilities can have serious consequences for a business. For instance, if suppliers are not paid on time, they may withhold shipments that are vital to a company's operations. Continued failure to pay current liabilities can lead to bankruptcy. To evaluate a company's ability to pay its current liabilities, three measures of liquidity—working capital, the current ratio, and the quick ratio—are often used. Current liabilities are a key component of each of these measures. They typically equal from 25 to 50 percent of total assets, as may be seen in Figure 1.

US Airways' short-term liquidity as measured by working capital is negative for both 1996 and 1995:

	Current Assets	−	Current Liabilities	=	Working Capital
1996	$2,310,194	−	$2,848,719	=	($538,525)
1995	$1,583,082	−	$2,484,696	=	($901,614)

This measure highlights the need for US Airways' management to focus on the management of short-term liquidity. It is common for airlines to have negative working capital because unearned ticket revenue is a current liability, but the cash from these ticket sales is quickly consumed in operations. On the assumption that only a small portion of unearned ticket revenues will be repaid to customers, unearned ticket revenue might be excluded from current liabilities for analysis purposes. The healthiest airlines have positive working capital when unearned ticket revenue is excluded. However, working capital for US Airways remains negative even after excluding unearned ticket revenues, highlighting serious liquidity issues.

The proper identification and management of current liabilities requires an understanding of how they are recognized, valued, classified, and disclosed.

Recognition of Liabilities

Timing is important in the recognition of liabilities. Failure to record a liability in an accounting period very often goes along with failure to record an expense. The two errors lead to an understatement of expense and an overstatement of income.

A liability is recorded when an obligation occurs. This rule is harder to apply than it might appear. When a transaction obligates a company to make future payments, a liability arises and is recognized, as when goods are bought on credit. However, current liabilities often are not represented by direct transactions. One of the key reasons for making adjusting entries at the end of an accounting period is to recognize unrecorded liabilities. Among these accrued liabilities are salaries payable and

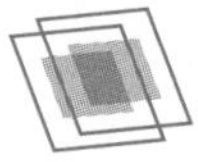

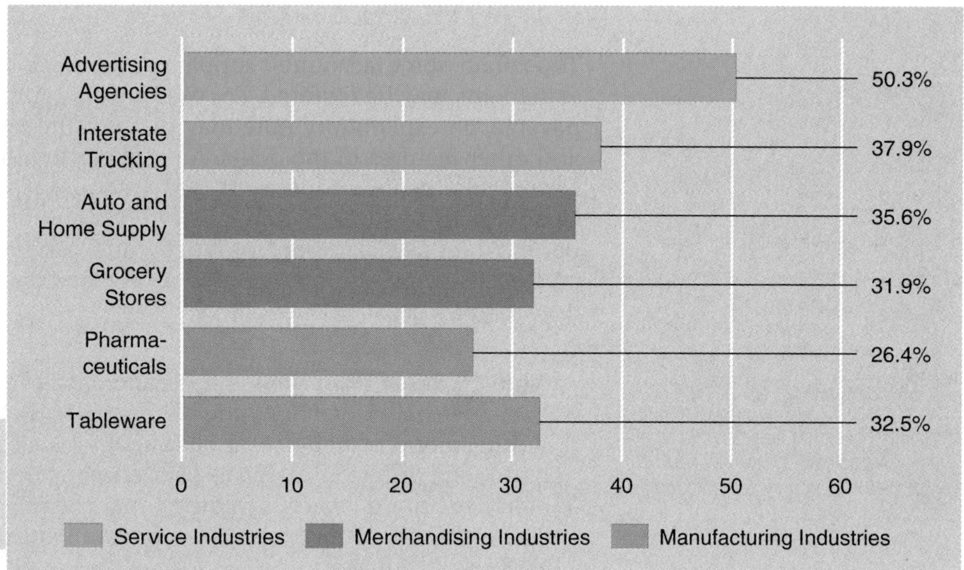

Figure 1
Current Liabilities as a Percentage of Total Assets for Selected Industries

Source: Data from Dun & Bradstreet, *Industry Norms and Key Business Ratios,* 1996–97.

Discussion Question: General Motors signs a new labor contract with the United Auto Workers calling for a raise of $1 per hour for all employees. What liability should GM record for the new contract? **Answer:** None. There is no liability for GM until the work is performed.

interest payable. Other liabilities that can only be estimated, such as taxes payable, must also be recognized through adjusting entries.

On the other hand, companies often enter into agreements for future transactions. For instance, a company may agree to pay an executive $50,000 a year for a period of three years, or a public utility may agree to buy an unspecified quantity of coal at a certain price over the next five years. Such contracts, though they are definite commitments, are not considered liabilities because they are for future—not past—transactions. As there is no current obligation, no liability is recognized.

Valuation of Liabilities

On the balance sheet, a liability is generally valued at the amount of money needed to pay the debt or at the fair market value of goods or services to be delivered. For most liabilities the amount is definitely known, but for some it must be estimated. For example, an automobile dealer who sells a car with a one-year warranty must provide parts and service during the year. The obligation is definite because the sale of the car has occurred, but the amount of the obligation can only be estimated. Such estimates are usually based on past experience and anticipated changes in the business environment. Additional disclosures of the fair value of liabilities may be required in the notes to the financial statements, as explained on the next page.

Classification of Liabilities

The classification of liabilities directly matches the classification of assets. Current liabilities are debts and obligations expected to be satisfied within one year or within the normal operating cycle, whichever is longer. Such liabilities are normally paid out of current assets or with cash generated from operations. Long-term liabilities, which are liabilities due beyond one year or beyond the normal operating cycle, have a different purpose. They are used to finance long-term assets, such as aircraft in the case of US Airways. The distinction between current and long-term liabilities is important because it affects the evaluation of a company's liquidity.

Disclosure of Liabilities

To explain some accounts, supplemental disclosure in the notes to the financial statements may be required. For example, if a company has a large amount of notes payable, an explanatory note may disclose the balances, maturities, interest rates, and other features of the debts. Any special credit arrangements, such as issues of commercial paper and lines of credit, should also be disclosed. For example, The Goodyear Tire & Rubber Company, which manufactures and sells tires, vehicle components, industrial rubber products, and rubber-related chemicals, disclosed its credit arrangements in the notes to the financial statements. Excerpts from that note follow.

Enrichment Note: Financial liabilities, such as loans, notes, and other borrowings, are considered financial instruments. The market value of financial instruments is reported in the notes to the financial statements.

Note 7A. Short Term Debt and Financing Arrangements

At December 31, 1996, the Company had short term uncommitted credit arrangements totaling $1.33 billion, of which $.90 billion were unused. These arrangements are available to the Company or certain of its international subsidiaries through various international banks at quoted market interest rates. There are no commitment fees or compensating balances associated with these arrangements.

The company had outstanding short term debt amounting to 428.1 million at December 31, 1996. Domestic short term debt represented $210.0 million of this total with a weighted average interest rate of 6.46% at December 31, 1996. . . . The remaining $218.1 million was international subsidiary short-term debt with a weighted average interest rate of 6.62% at December 31, 1996.[2]

This type of disclosure is helpful in assessing whether a company has additional borrowing power.

Common Categories of Current Liabilities

Current liabilities fall into two major groups: (1) definitely determinable liabilities and (2) estimated liabilities.

Definitely Determinable Liabilities

OBJECTIVE 2

Identify, compute, and record definitely determinable and estimated current liabilities

Related Text Assignments:
Q: 6, 7, 8, 9, 10, 11, 12, 13, 14, 15, 16
SE: 2, 3, 4, 5, 6, 7, 8
E: 2, 3, 4, 5, 6, 7, 8
P: 1, 2, 3, 6, 7, 8
SD: 1, 2, 3, 4, 5
FRA: 1, 2, 4

Current liabilities that are set by contract or by statute and can be measured exactly are called definitely determinable liabilities. The related accounting problems are to determine the existence and amount of each such liability and to see that it is recorded properly. Definitely determinable liabilities include accounts payable, bank loans and commercial paper, notes payable, accrued liabilities, dividends payable, sales and excise taxes payable, current portions of long-term debt, payroll liabilities, and unearned or deferred revenues.

Accounts Payable Accounts payable, sometimes called trade accounts payable, are short-term obligations to suppliers for goods and services. The amount in the Accounts Payable account is generally supported by an accounts payable subsidiary ledger, which contains an individual account for each person or company to whom money is owed.

Bank Loans and Commercial Paper Management will often establish a line of credit from a bank; this arrangement allows the company to borrow funds when

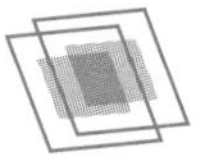

CASE 1: INTEREST STATED SEPARATELY

Chicago, Illinois August 31, 20xx

Sixty days after date I promise to pay First Federal Bank the sum of $5,000 with interest at the rate of 12% per annum.

Sandra Caron
Caron Corporation

CASE 2: INTEREST IN FACE AMOUNT

Chicago, Illinois August 31, 20xx

Sixty days after date I promise to pay First Federal Bank the sum of $5,000.

Sandra Caron
Caron Corporation

Figure 2
Two Promissory Notes: One with Interest Stated Separately; One with Interest in Face Amount

Point to Emphasize: On the balance sheet, the order of presentation for current liabilities is not as strict as for current assets. Generally, Accounts Payable appears first, and the rest follow.

they are needed to finance current operations. For example, Lowe's Companies, Inc., a large home improvement center and consumer durables company, reported in its 1996 annual report that "the company entered into a $300 million revolving credit facility with a syndicate of 13 banks. The facility expires on April 10, 2000 and is used to support the company's commercial paper program and for short term borrowing. . . . At January 31, 1997 there were no borrowings outstanding under this revolving credit facility."[3] A promissory note for the full amount of the line of credit is signed when the credit is granted, but the company has great flexibility in using the available funds. The company can increase its borrowing up to the limit when it needs cash and reduce the amount borrowed when it generates enough cash of its own. Both the amount borrowed and the interest rate charged by the bank may change daily. The bank may require the company to meet certain financial goals (such as maintaining specific profit margins, current ratios, or debt to equity ratios) to retain the line of credit.

Companies with excellent credit ratings may borrow short-term funds by issuing commercial paper, unsecured loans that are sold to the public, usually through professionally managed investment firms. The portion of a line of credit currently borrowed and the amount of commercial paper issued are usually combined with notes payable in the current liabilities section of the balance sheet. Details are disclosed in a note to the financial statements.

Clarification Note: Only the used portion of the line of credit is recognized as a liability in the financial statements.

Notes Payable Short-term notes payable, which also arise out of the ordinary course of business, are obligations represented by promissory notes. These notes may be used to secure bank loans, to pay suppliers for goods and services, and to secure credit from other sources.

The interest may be stated separately on the face of the note (Case 1 in Figure 2), or it may be deducted in advance by discounting it from the face value of the note (Case 2 in Figure 2). The entries to record the note in each case are shown on the next page.

Point to Emphasize: The effective interest rate on the loan in Case 2 is 12.24% ($100/$4,900 × 360/60).

	Case 1—Interest Stated Separately		
Aug. 31	Cash	5,000	
	Notes Payable		5,000
	Issued 60-day, 12% promissory note with interest stated separately		

Case 1: A = L + OE; + +

Case 2: A = L + OE; + − +

	Case 2—Interest in Face Amount		
Aug. 31	Cash	4,900	
	Discount on Notes Payable	100	
	Notes Payable		5,000
	Issued 60-day promissory note with $100 interest included in face amount		

Note that in Case 1 the money received equaled the face value of the note, whereas in Case 2 the money received ($4,900) was less than the face value ($5,000) of the note. The amount of the discount equals the amount of the interest for sixty days. Although the dollar amount of interest on each of these notes is the same, the effective interest rate is slightly higher in Case 2 because the amount received is slightly less ($4,900 in Case 2 versus $5,000 in Case 1). Discount on Notes Payable is a contra account to Notes Payable and is deducted from Notes Payable on the balance sheet.

On October 30, when the note is paid, each alternative is recorded as follows:

	Case 1—Interest Stated Separately		
Oct. 30	Notes Payable	5,000	
	Interest Expense	100	
	Cash		5,100
	Payment of note with interest stated separately		
	$\$5,000 \times \frac{60}{360} \times .12 = \$100$		

Case 1: A = L + OE; − − −

Case 2: A = L + OE; − −

A = L + OE; + −

	Case 2—Interest in Face Amount		
Oct. 30	Notes Payable	5,000	
	Cash		5,000
	Payment of note with interest included in face amount		
30	Interest Expense	100	
	Discount on Notes Payable		100
	Interest expense on note payable		

Accrued Liabilities A key reason for making adjusting entries at the end of an accounting period is to recognize and record liabilities that are not already in the accounting records. This practice applies to any type of liability. As you will see, accrued liabilities can include estimated liabilities.

Here the focus is on interest payable, a definitely determinable liability. Interest accrues daily on interest-bearing notes. At the end of the accounting period, an adjusting entry should be made in accordance with the matching rule to record the interest obligation up to that point in time. Let us again use the example of the two notes presented earlier in this chapter. If we assume that the accounting period ends on September 30, or thirty days after the issuance of the sixty-day notes, the adjusting entries for each case would be as follows:

	Case 1—Interest Stated Separately		
Sept. 30	Interest Expense	50	
	Interest Payable		50
	To record interest expense for 30 days on note with interest stated separately		
	$\$5,000 \times \frac{30}{360} \times .12 = \$50$		

Case 1: A = L + OE; + −

Case 2: A = L + OE; + −

	Case 2—Interest in Face Amount		
Sept. 30	Interest Expense	50	
	Discount on Notes Payable		50
	To record interest expense for 30 days on note with interest included in face amount		
	$\$100 \times \frac{30}{60} = \$50$		

Point to Emphasize: Both of the above entries have exactly the same impact on the financial statements.

In Case 2, Discount on Notes Payable will now have a debit balance of $50, which will become interest expense during the next thirty days.

Dividends Payable Cash dividends are a distribution of earnings by a corporation. The payment of dividends is solely the decision of the corporation's board of directors. A liability does not exist until the board declares the dividends. There is usually a short time between the date of declaration and the date of payment of dividends. During that short time, the dividends declared are considered current liabilities of the corporation.

Common Student Error: Students often try to compute sales tax on the basis of total cash collections rather than sales. Emphasize the difference between cash receipts and sales.

Sales and Excise Taxes Payable Most states and many cities levy a sales tax on retail transactions. There is a federal excise tax on some products, such as automobile tires. A merchant who sells goods subject to these taxes must collect the taxes and forward them periodically to the appropriate government agency. The amount of tax collected represents a current liability until it is remitted to the government. For example, assume that a merchant makes a $100 sale that is subject to a 5 percent sales tax and a 10 percent excise tax. Assuming that the sale takes place on June 1, the entry to record the sale is as follows:

A = L + OE
\+ + +
  \+

June 1	Cash	115	
	Sales		100
	Sales Tax Payable		5
	Excise Tax Payable		10
	Sale of merchandise and collection of sales and excise taxes		

Reinforcement Exercise: XYZ Company collects $171 from customers, which includes a 6% sales tax and an 8% excise tax. How much were sales? **Answer:** $150; $171 = sales + 6% sales tax + 8% excise tax = $171 ÷ 1.14 = $150.

The sale is properly recorded at $100, and the taxes collected are recorded as liabilities to be remitted at the proper times to the appropriate government agencies.

Enrichment Note: Liabilities such as bank loans, notes payable, and current portions of long-term debt are considered financial instruments.

Current Portions of Long-Term Debt If a portion of long-term debt is due within the next year and is to be paid from current assets, then that current portion is properly classified as a current liability. For example, suppose that a $500,000 debt is to be paid in installments of $100,000 per year for the next five years. The $100,000 installment due in the current year should be classified as a current liability. The remaining $400,000 should be classified as a long-term liability. Note that no journal entry is necessary. The total debt of $500,000 is simply reclassified when the financial statements are prepared, as follows:

Current Liabilities	
Current Portion of Long-Term Debt	$100,000
Long-Term Liabilities	
Long-Term Debt	400,000

Payroll Liabilities For most organizations, the cost of labor and related payroll taxes is a major expense. In some industries, such as banking and airlines, payroll costs represent more than half of all operating costs. Payroll accounting is important because complex laws and significant liabilities are involved. The employer is liable to employees for wages and salaries and to various agencies for amounts withheld from wages and salaries and for related taxes. The term **wages** refers to payment for the services of employees at an hourly rate. The term **salaries** refers to the compensation of employees who are paid at a monthly or yearly rate.

Because payroll accounting applies only to the employees of an organization, it is therefore important to distinguish between employees and independent contractors. Employees are paid a wage or salary by the organization and are under its direct supervision and control. Independent contractors are not employees of the organization, so they are not accounted for under the payroll system. They offer services to the organization for a fee, but they are not under its direct control or supervision. Some examples of independent contractors are certified public accountants, advertising agencies, and lawyers.

Instructional Strategy: Assign discussion of SD 3 to small groups in class. Ask one person from each group to present one alternative (not necessarily the group's choice as the best solution) and explain why that alternative would be ethical or unethical.

Figure 3 provides an illustration of payroll liabilities and their relationship to employee earnings and employer taxes and other costs. Two important observations may be made. First, the amount payable to employees is less than the amount of earnings. This occurs because employers are required by law or are requested by employees to withhold certain amounts from wages and send them directly to government agencies or other organizations. Second, the total employer liabilities exceed employee earnings because the employer must pay additional taxes and make other contributions, such as for pensions and medical care, that increase the cost. The most common withholdings, taxes, and other payroll costs are described below.

Point to Emphasize: In most of the end-of-chapter problems, students will not be required to compute income tax withholdings–those amounts will be given. They might be asked, however, to compute social security and Medicare withholdings and unemployment taxes.

Enrichment Note: For many organizations, a large portion of the cost of labor is not reflected in employees' regular paychecks. Vacation pay, sick pay, personal days, health insurance, life insurance, and pensions are some of the additional costs that may be negotiated between employers and employees.

Common Student Confusion: Students often have difficulty understanding the difference between employee-related and employer-related payroll liabilities.

Point to Emphasize: Remember that FICA, FUTA, and state unemployment insurance payroll taxes are borne by the employer, and thus are an additional expense to the business.

Federal Income Taxes Federal income taxes are collected on a "pay as you go" basis. Employers are required to withhold appropriate taxes from employees' paychecks and pay them to the Internal Revenue Service.

State and Local Income Taxes Most states and some local governments have income taxes. In most cases, the procedures for withholding are similar to those for federal income taxes.

Social Security (FICA) Tax The social security program (the Federal Insurance Contribution Act) offers retirement and disability benefits and survivor's benefits. About 90 percent of the people working in the United States fall under the provisions of this program. The 1998 social security tax rate of 6.20 percent was paid by *both* employee and employer on the first $68,400 earned by an employee during the calendar year. Both the rate and the base to which it applies are subject to change in future years.

Medicare Tax A major extension of the social security program is Medicare, which provides hospitalization and medical insurance for persons over age 65. In 1998, the Medicare tax rate was 1.45 percent of gross income, with no limit, paid by *both* employee and employer.

Medical Insurance Many organizations provide medical benefits to employees. Often, the employee contributes a portion of the cost through withholdings from income and the employer pays the rest, usually a greater amount, to the insurance company. Some proposals for national health-care reform, if they become law, could change substantially the way medical insurance is funded and provided in this country.

Pension Contributions Many organizations also provide pension benefits to employees. In a manner similar to that for medical insurance, a portion of the pension contribution is withheld from the employee's income and the rest is paid by the organization to the pension fund.

Federal Unemployment Insurance (FUTA) Tax This tax, referred to as FUTA after the Federal Unemployment Tax Act, is intended to pay for programs to help unemployed workers. It is paid *only* by employers and recently was 6.2 percent of the first $9,000 earned by each employee. Against this federal tax, however, the employer is allowed a credit for unemployment taxes paid to the state. The maximum credit is 5.4 percent of the first $9,000 earned by each employee. Most states set their rate at this maximum. Thus, the FUTA tax most often paid is .8 percent (6.2 percent − 5.4 percent) of the taxable wages.

State Unemployment Insurance Tax All state unemployment programs provide for unemployment compensation to be paid to eligible unemployed workers. This compensation is paid out of the fund provided by the 5.4 percent of the first $7,000 (varies in some states) earned by each employee. In some states, employers with favorable employment records may be entitled to pay less than 5.4 percent.

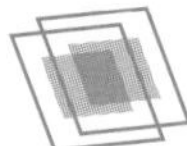

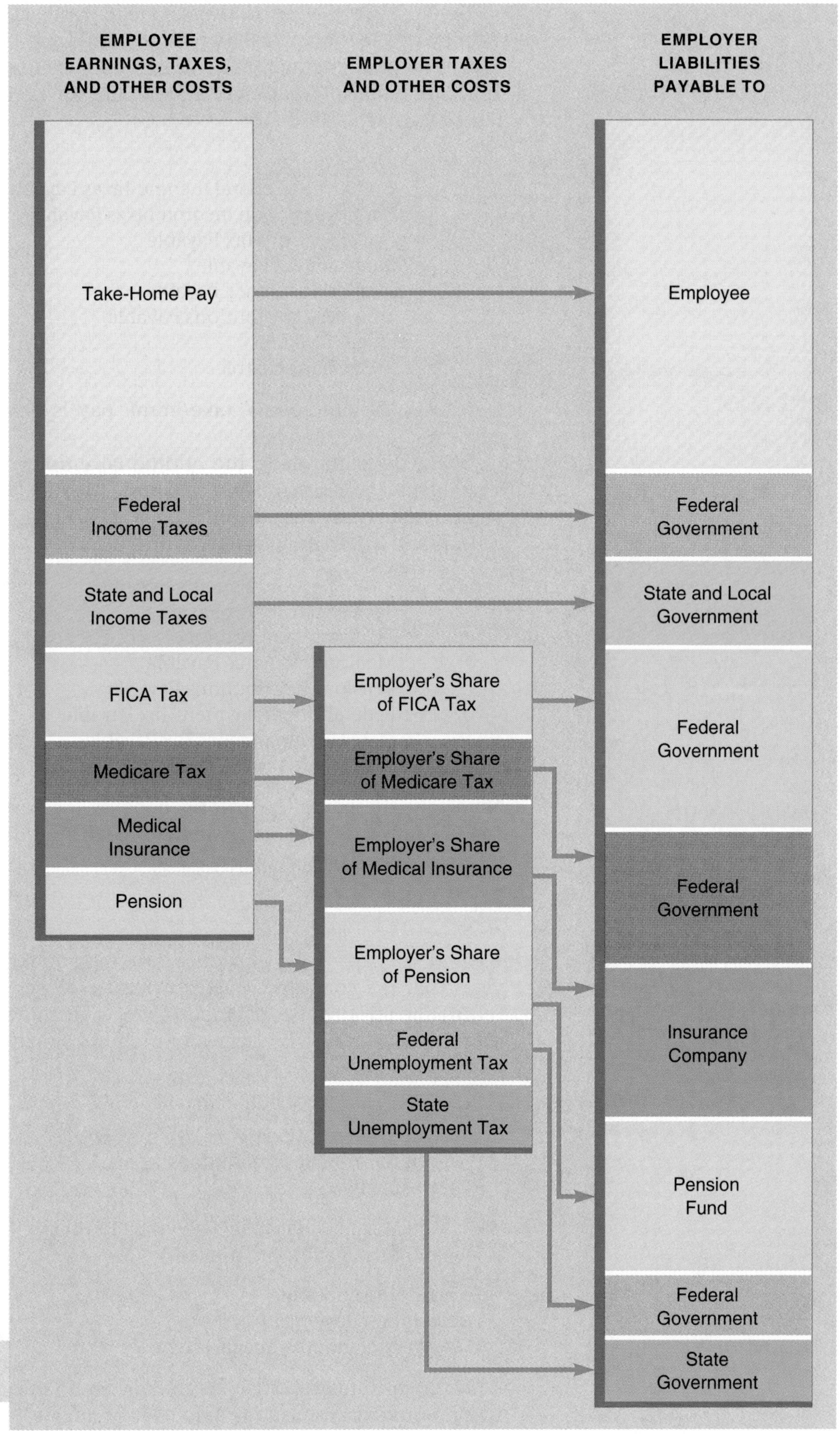

Figure 3
Illustration of Payroll Liabilities

To illustrate the recording of the payroll, assume that on February 15 total employee wages are $32,500, with withholdings of $5,400 for federal income taxes, $1,200 for state income taxes, $2,015 for social security tax, $471 for Medicare tax, $900 for medical insurance, and $1,300 for pension contributions. The entry to record this payroll follows.

A = L + OE	Date	Account	Debit	Credit
+ −	Feb. 15	Wages Expense	32,500	
+		Employees' Federal Income Taxes Payable		5,400
+		Employees' State Income Taxes Payable		1,200
+		Social Security Tax Payable		2,015
+		Medicare Tax Payable		471
+		Medical Insurance Payable		900
+		Pension Contributions Payable		1,300
+		Wages Payable		21,214
		To record payroll		

Note that the employees' take-home pay is only $21,214, although $32,500 was earned.

Using the same data, the additional employer taxes and other benefits costs would be recorded as follows, assuming that the payroll taxes correspond to the discussion above and that the employer pays 80 percent of the medical insurance premiums and half of the pension contributions.

A = L + OE	Date	Account	Debit	Credit
+ −	Feb. 15	Payroll Taxes and Benefits Expense	9,401	
+		Social Security Tax Payable		2,015
+		Medicare Tax Payable		471
+		Medical Insurance Payable		3,600
+		Pension Contributions Payable		1,300
+		Federal Unemployment Tax Payable		260
+		State Unemployment Tax Payable		1,755
		To record payroll taxes and other costs		

Note that the payroll taxes and benefits increase the total cost of the payroll to $41,901 ($9,401 + $32,500), which exceeds by almost 29 percent the amount earned by employees. This is a typical situation.

Business-World Example: See the Decision Point about US Airways at the beginning of this chapter for an example of an unearned revenue account with a substantial balance.

Unearned Revenues Unearned revenues represent obligations for goods or services that the company must provide or deliver in a future accounting period in return for an advance payment from a customer. For example, a publisher of a monthly magazine who receives annual subscriptions totaling $240 would make the following entry.

A = L + OE	Account	Debit	Credit
+ +	Cash	240	
	Unearned Subscriptions		240
	Receipt of annual subscriptions in advance		

The publisher now has a liability of $240 that will be reduced gradually as monthly issues of the magazine are mailed.

A = L + OE	Account	Debit	Credit
− +	Unearned Subscriptions	20	
	Subscription Revenues		20
	Delivery of monthly magazine issues		

Many businesses, such as repair companies, construction companies, and special-order firms, ask for a deposit or advance from a customer before they will begin work. Such advances are also current liabilities until the goods or services are delivered.

BUSINESS BULLETIN: TECHNOLOGY IN PRACTICE

The processing of payroll is an ideal application for computers because it is a very routine and complex procedure that must be done with absolute accuracy: Employees want to be paid exactly what they are owed, and failure to pay the taxes and other costs as required can result in severe penalties and high interest charges. Consequently, many companies purchase carefully designed and tested computer software for use in preparing the payroll. Other companies do not process their own payroll but rely on outside businesses that specialize in providing such services. Many of these service suppliers, such as Automatic Data Processing, Inc., are successful and fast growing.

DECISION POINT

AMERICAN AIRLINES, INC.

In the early 1980s American Airlines, Inc., developed a frequent-flyer program that gave free trips and other awards to customers based on the number of miles they flew on the airline. Since then, the number of similar programs offered by other airlines has mushroomed, and it is estimated that 38

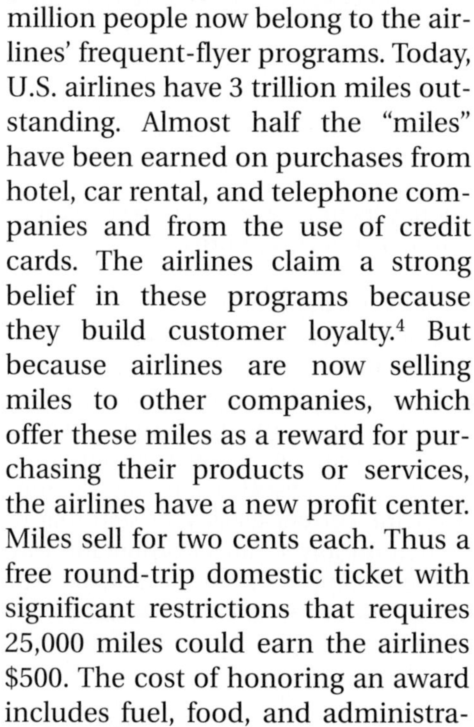

million people now belong to the airlines' frequent-flyer programs. Today, U.S. airlines have 3 trillion miles outstanding. Almost half the "miles" have been earned on purchases from hotel, car rental, and telephone companies and from the use of credit cards. The airlines claim a strong belief in these programs because they build customer loyalty.[4] But because airlines are now selling miles to other companies, which offer these miles as a reward for purchasing their products or services, the airlines have a new profit center. Miles sell for two cents each. Thus a free round-trip domestic ticket with significant restrictions that requires 25,000 miles could earn the airlines $500. The cost of honoring an award includes fuel, food, and administration. American estimates that a $500 ticket costs just $92.50 to honor. United figures that its liability is just $42.39 per award. However, the fact that United's cost estimate is less than half American's suggests a wide range to these cost estimates. If these figures are good estimates of the true costs, then the airlines have a profit on miles sold. Of course, the airlines must

Critical Thinking Question: Would any part of estimated frequent-flyer liability be classified as noncurrent? **Answer:** Most frequent-flyer programs assign an expiration date to earned miles. While some allocation method based on expiration and past redemption rates could be used, the current classification is most common since miles can be redeemed any time prior to expiration.

also provide free ticket awards on miles that result from air travel and do not bring in additional revenue. However, the airlines say that the cost is not significant because on average only about two-thirds of domestic airline seats are filled, leaving plenty of room for free travelers. According to this theory, if a free traveler occupies a seat that would otherwise have been empty, the incremental cost is minimal.

Today, 7 to 8 percent of all passengers are traveling on free tickets. Estimated liabilities such as those associated with frequent-flyer plans are becoming an important consideration when evaluating an airline's financial position.

Estimated Liabilities

Point to Emphasize: Estimated liabilities are recorded and presented on the financial statements in the same way as definitely determinable liabilities. The only difference is that estimated liabilities involve some uncertainty in their computation.

Estimated liabilities are definite debts or obligations of which the exact dollar amount cannot be known until a later date. Since there is no doubt about the existence of the legal obligation, the primary accounting problem is to estimate and record the amount of the liability. Examples of estimated liabilities are income taxes, property taxes, product warranties, and vacation pay.

Income Taxes The income of a corporation is taxed by the federal government, most state governments, and some cities and towns. The amount of income taxes liability depends on the results of operations. Often the results are not known until after the end of the year. However, because income taxes are an expense in the year in which income is earned, an adjusting entry is necessary to record the estimated tax liability. The entry is as follows:

A = L + OE
\+ −

Dec. 31	Income Taxes Expense	53,000	
	Estimated Income Taxes Payable		53,000
	To record estimated federal income taxes		

Sole proprietorships and partnerships do *not* pay income taxes. Their owners must report their share of the firm's income on their individual tax returns.

Property Tax Payable Property taxes are levied on real property, such as land and buildings, and on personal property, such as inventory and equipment. Property taxes are a main source of revenue for local governments. They are usually assessed annually against the property involved. Because the fiscal years of local governments and their assessment dates rarely correspond to a firm's fiscal year, it is necessary to estimate the amount of property tax that applies to each month of the year. Assume, for instance, that a local government has a fiscal year of July 1 to June 30, that its assessment date is November 1 for the current fiscal year, and that its payment date is December 15. Assume also that on July 1, Janis Corporation estimates that its property tax assessment for the coming year will be $24,000. The adjusting entry to be made on July 31, which would be repeated on August 31, September 30, and October 31, would be as follows:

Enrichment Note: The process of accruing property tax each month could be applied to income taxes if a company desires monthly financial statements.

A = L + OE
\+ −

July 31	Property Tax Expense	2,000	
	Estimated Property Tax Payable		2,000
	To record estimated property tax expense for the month $24,000 ÷ 12 months = $2,000		

On November 1, the firm receives a property tax bill for $24,720. The estimate that was made in July was too low. The charge should have been $2,060 per month. Because the difference between the actual assessment and the estimate is small, the company decides to absorb in November the amount undercharged in the previous four months. Therefore, the property tax expense for November is $2,300 [$2,060 + 4($60)] and is recorded as follows:

A = L + OE
 + −

Nov. 30	Property Tax Expense	2,300	
	Estimated Property Tax Payable		2,300
	To record estimated property tax		

The Estimated Property Tax Payable account now has a balance of $10,300. The entry to record payment on December 15 would be as follows:

A = L + OE
± −

Dec. 15	Estimated Property Tax Payable	10,300	
	Prepaid Property Tax	14,420	
	Cash		24,720
	Payment of property tax		

Discussion Question: Where does the account Prepaid Property Tax appear in the financial statements? **Answer:** In the current asset section.

Beginning December 31 and each month afterward until June 30, property tax expense is recorded by a debit to Property Tax Expense and a credit to Prepaid Property Tax in the amount of $2,060. The total of these seven entries will reduce the Prepaid Property Tax account to zero on June 30.

Product Warranty Liability When a firm places a warranty or guarantee on its product at the time of sale, a liability exists for the length of the warranty. The cost of the warranty is properly debited to an expense account in the period of sale because it is a feature of the product or service sold and thus is included in the price paid by the customer for the product. On the basis of experience, it should be possible to estimate the amount the warranty will cost in the future. Some products or services will require little warranty service; others may require much. Thus, there will be an average cost per product or service.

Discussion Question: Recording product warranty expense in the year of the sale follows which accounting rule? **Answer:** The matching rule.

Instructional Strategy: Assign E 6 to small groups in class. The exercise works well as a substitute for a lecture on warranties or can be used to check students' comprehension and application skills.

For example, assume that a muffler company guarantees that it will replace free of charge any muffler it sells that fails during the time the buyer owns the car. The company charges a small service fee for replacing the muffler. This guarantee is an important selling feature for the firm's mufflers. In the past, 6 percent of the mufflers sold have been returned for replacement under the guarantee. The average cost of a muffler is $25. Assume that during July, 350 mufflers were sold. The accrued liability would be recorded as an adjustment at the end of July as follows:

A = L + OE
 + −

July 31	Product Warranty Expense	525	
	Estimated Product Warranty Liability		525
	To record estimated product warranty expense:		
	Number of units sold	350	
	Rate of replacement under warranty	× .06	
	Estimated units to be replaced	21	
	Estimated cost per unit	×$ 25	
	Estimated liability for product warranty	$525	

Point to Emphasize: The date of the December 5 entry is not important. It would be the same if it happened during January or July. Note that the debit is to the liability account and not to the warranty expense account.

When a muffler is returned for replacement under the warranty, the cost of the muffler is charged against the Estimated Product Warranty Liability account. For example, assume that on December 5 a customer returns with a defective muffler and pays a $10 service fee to have the muffler replaced. Assume that this particular muffler cost $20. The entry is as follows:

A = L + OE
± − +

Dec. 5	Cash	10	
	Estimated Product Warranty Liability	20	
	Service Revenue		10
	Merchandise Inventory		20
	Replacement of muffler under warranty		

BUSINESS BULLETIN: BUSINESS PRACTICE

Estimated liabilities are presenting greater challenges to accountants as many companies attempt to mimic the success of frequent-flyer programs. For example, if you frequently stay at Holiday Inns, you can earn a three-day tour of castles in the Bavarian Alps, a Magnavox computer, or a Canon Camcorder. Rent cars from Avis or Thrifty and earn points to stay at Sheraton Hotels. Rent cars from Dollar or General and earn a $1,000 U.S. savings bond. If you have a MasterCard issued by General Motors, for every dollar you spend, you receive a nickel credit toward a new car, up to $500 per year. Buy from vendors like MCI, Club Med, Hertz, General Electric Capital, Eddie Bauer, and Spiegel and earn credits toward a retirement account. In each company, accountants must estimate how and when consumers will redeem their points as well as the costs of providing the premiums.[5]

Vacation Pay Liability In most companies, employees earn the right to paid vacation days or weeks as they work during the year. For example, an employee may earn two weeks of paid vacation for each fifty weeks of work. Therefore, the person is paid fifty-two weeks' salary for fifty weeks' work. Theoretically, the cost of the two weeks' vacation should be allocated as an expense over the whole year so that month-to-month costs will not be distorted. The vacation pay represents 4 percent (two weeks' vacation divided by fifty weeks) of a worker's pay. Every week worked earns the employee a small fraction (4 percent) for vacation pay.

Vacation pay liability can amount to a substantial amount of money. For example, in its annual report Delta Airlines reported at its 1997 year end a vacation pay liability of $463 million.[6]

Reinforcement Exercise: Durling Corp. offers four weeks of paid vacation per year to all employees. Because of this, no employees leave. What is the vacation pay expense for the month of April if the combined salary expense is $18,000? **Answer:** $1,500 (4/48 × $18,000).

Suppose that a company with a vacation policy of two weeks of paid vacation for each fifty weeks of work has a payroll of $21,000, of which $1,000 was paid to employees on vacation for the week ended April 20. Because of turnover and rules regarding term of employment, not every employee in the company will collect vacation pay, and so it is assumed that 75 percent of employees will ultimately collect vacation pay. The computation of vacation pay expense based on the payroll of employees not on vacation ($21,000 − $1,000) is as follows: $20,000 × 4 percent × 75 percent = $600. The entry to record vacation pay expense for the week ended April 20 is as follows:

A = L + OE
　　+ −

Apr. 20	Vacation Pay Expense	600	
	Estimated Liability for Vacation Pay		600
	Estimated vacation pay expense		

At the time employees receive their vacation pay, an entry is made debiting Estimated Liability for Vacation Pay and crediting Cash or Wages Payable. For example, the entry to record the $1,000 paid to employees on vacation during August is as follows:

A = L + OE
− −

Aug. 31	Estimated Liability for Vacation Pay	1,000	
	Cash (or Wages Payable)		1,000
	Wages of employees on vacation		

The treatment of vacation pay presented in this example may also be applied to other payroll costs, such as bonus plans and contributions to pension plans.

Contingent Liabilities

OBJECTIVE 3

Define contingent liability

Related Text Assignments:
Q: 17, 18
SE: 2
SD: 4
FRA: 2, 4

Point to Emphasize: Contingencies are recorded when they are probable and an amount can be reasonably estimated.

A contingent liability is not an existing liability. Rather, it is a potential liability because it depends on a future event arising out of a past transaction. For instance, a construction company that built a bridge may have been sued by the state for using poor materials. The past transaction is the building of the bridge under contract. The future event is the outcome of the lawsuit, which is not yet known.

Two conditions have been established by the FASB for determining when a contingency should be entered in the accounting records: (1) the liability must be probable and (2) it must be reasonably estimated.[7] Estimated liabilities such as the estimated income taxes liability, warranty liability, and vacation pay liability that were described earlier meet those conditions. Therefore, they are accrued in the accounting records. Potential liabilities that do not meet both conditions (probable and reasonably estimated) are reported in the notes to the financial statements. Losses from such potential liabilities are recorded when the conditions set by the FASB are met. The following example of contingent liabilities comes from the notes in an annual report of Humana, Inc., one of the largest health services organizations.

Discussion Question: As an investor, would you find Humana's disclosure sufficient to reach a decision? **Answer:** There is no right answer to this question, but many investors would be interested in additional details, such as the amount of loss and the likelihood of such losses.

> Management continually evaluates contingencies based upon the best available evidence. In addition, allowances for loss are provided currently for disputed items that have continuing significance, such as certain third-party reimbursements and deductions that continue to be claimed in current cost reports and tax returns.
>
> Management believes that allowances for loss have been provided to the extent necessary and that its assessment of contingencies is reasonable. To the extent that resolution of contingencies results in amounts that vary from management's estimates, earnings will be charged or credited.
>
> Hospitals' principal contingencies are described below:
>
> **Revenues**—Certain third-party payments are subject to examination by agencies administering the programs. Management is contesting certain issues raised in audits of prior year cost reports.
>
> **Professional Liability Risks**—Hospitals has provided for loss for professional liability risks based upon actuarially determined estimates. Actual settlements and expenses incident thereto may differ from the provisions for loss.
>
> **Interest Rate Agreements**—Hospitals has entered into agreements which reduce the impact of changes in interest rates on its floating rate long-term debt. In the event of nonperformance by other parties to these agreements,

BUSINESS BULLETIN: BUSINESS PRACTICE

Many companies promote their products by issuing coupons that offer "cents off" or other enticements for purchasers. Since four out of five shoppers use coupons, companies are forced by competition to distribute them. The total value of unredeemed coupons, each of which represents a potential liability for the issuing company, is truly staggering. NCH Promotional Services, a company owned by Dun & Bradstreet, estimates that almost 300 billion coupons were issued in 1995. Of course, the liability depends on how many of the coupons will actually be redeemed. NCH estimates that number at approximately 6 billion, or about 2 percent. That is not a large percentage, but the value of the redeemed coupons is estimated to be more than $4 billion.[8]

Hospitals may incur a loss that is based on the difference between market rates and the contract rates.

Income Taxes—Management is contesting adjustments proposed by the Internal Revenue Service for prior years.

Litigation—Various suits and claims arising in the ordinary course of business are pending against Hospitals.[9]

Contingent liabilities may also arise from failure to follow government regulations, from discounted notes receivable, and from guarantees of the debt of other companies.

Payroll Accounting Illustrated

SUPPLEMENTAL OBJECTIVE 4

Compute and record the liabilities associated with payroll accounting

Related Text Assignments:
Q: 19, 20, 21
SE: 9, 10
E: 9, 10, 11
P: 4, 5
SD: 5

Earlier in this chapter, the liabilities associated with payroll accounting were identified and discussed. This section will focus on the calculations, records, and control requirements of payroll accounting. To demonstrate the concepts, the illustrations are shown in manual format, but, in actual practice, most businesses (including small businesses) use a computer to process payroll.

Computation of an Employee's Take-Home Pay

Besides setting minimum wage levels, the federal Fair Labor Standards Act (also called the Wages and Hours Law) regulates overtime pay. Employers who take part in interstate commerce must pay overtime to employees who work beyond forty hours a week or more than eight hours a day. This pay must be at least one and one-half times the regular rate. Work on Saturdays, Sundays, or holidays may also call for overtime or some sort of premium pay under separate wage agreements. Overtime pay under union or other employment contracts may exceed these minimums.

Discussion Question: What would change if Mr. Jones had worked six hours on Wednesday and eleven hours on Thursday? **Answer:** His pay would go up by $8 because of the two extra hours of overtime.

For example, suppose that the employment contract of Robert Jones calls for a regular wage of $8 an hour, one and one-half times the regular rate for work over eight hours in any weekday, and twice the regular rate for work on Saturdays, Sundays, or holidays. He works the following days and hours during the week of January 18, 20xx.

Day	Total Hours Worked	Regular Time	Overtime
Monday	10	8	2
Tuesday	8	8	0
Wednesday	8	8	0
Thursday	9	8	1
Friday	10	8	2
Saturday	2	0	2
	47	40	7

Jones's wages would be calculated as follows:

Regular time	40 hours × $8	$320
Overtime, weekdays	5 hours × $8 × 1.5	60
Overtime, weekend	2 hours × $8 × 2	32
Total wages		$412

Once Jones's wages are known, his take-home pay can be calculated. Since his total earnings for the week of January 18 are $412.00, his social security tax is 6.2

WEEKLY PAYROLL PERIOD—EMPLOYEE MARRIED												
		And the number of withholding allowances claimed is—										
And the wages are—		0	1	2	3	4	5	6	7	8	9	10 or more
At least	*But less than*	The amount of income tax to be withheld will be—										
$300	$310	$37	$31	$26	$20	$14	$ 9	$ 3	$ 0	$ 0	$0	$0
310	320	38	33	27	22	16	10	5	0	0	0	0
320	330	40	34	29	23	17	12	6	1	0	0	0
330	340	41	36	30	25	19	13	8	2	0	0	0
340	350	43	37	32	26	20	15	9	4	0	0	0
350	360	44	39	33	28	22	16	11	5	0	0	0
360	370	46	40	35	29	23	18	12	7	1	0	0
370	380	47	42	36	31	25	19	14	8	2	0	0
380	390	49	43	38	32	26	21	15	10	4	0	0
390	400	50	45	39	34	28	22	17	11	5	0	0
400	410	52	46	41	35	29	24	18	13	7	1	0
410	420	53	48	42	37	31	25	20	14	8	3	0
420	430	55	49	44	38	32	27	21	16	10	4	0

Figure 4
Sample Withholding Table

percent, or $25.54 (he has not earned over $68,400), and his Medicare tax is 1.45 percent, or $5.97. The amount to be withheld for federal income taxes depends in part on Jones's earnings and in part on the number of his exemptions. All employees are required by law to indicate exemptions by filing a Form W-4 (Employee's Withholding Exemption Certificate). Every employee is entitled to one exemption for himself or herself and one for each dependent. Based on the information in the Form W-4, the amount of withholding is determined by referring to a withholding table provided by the Internal Revenue Service. For example, the withholding table in Figure 4 shows that for Jones, a married employee who has a total of four exemptions and is paid weekly, the withholding on total wages of $412 is $31. Actual withholding tables change periodically to reflect changes in tax rates and laws. Assume also that Jones's union dues are $2.00, his medical insurance premiums are $7.60, his life insurance premium is $6.00, he places $15.00 per week in savings bonds, and he contributes $1.00 per week to United Charities. His net (take-home) pay is computed as follows:

Point to Emphasize: The expense to the company is the gross earnings, not the net take-home pay.

Total earnings		$412.00
Deductions		
Federal income taxes withheld	$31.00	
Social security tax	25.54	
Medicare tax	5.97	
Union dues	2.00	
Medical insurance	7.60	
Life insurance	6.00	
Savings bonds	15.00	
United Charities contribution	1.00	
Total deductions		94.11
Net (take-home) pay		$317.89

Exhibit 1. Payroll Register

Payroll Register **Pay Period: Week ended January 18**

		Earnings			Deductions								Payment		Distribution	
Employee	Total Hours	Regular	Overtime	Gross	Federal Income Taxes	Social Security Tax	Medicare Tax	Union Dues	Medical Insurance	Life Insurance	Savings Bonds	Other: A—United Charities	Net Earnings	Check No.	Sales Wages Expense	Office Wages Expense
Linda Duval	40	160.00		160.00	11.00	9.92	2.32		5.80				130.96	923		160.00
John Franks	44	160.00	24.00	184.00	14.00	11.41	2.67	2.00	7.60			A 10.00	136.32	924	184.00	
Samuel Goetz	40	400.00		400.00	53.00	24.80	5.80		10.40	14.00		A 3.00	289.00	925	400.00	
Robert Jones	47	320.00	92.00	412.00	31.00	25.54	5.97	2.00	7.60	6.00	15.00	A 1.00	317.89	926	412.00	
Billie Matthews	40	160.00		160.00	14.00	9.92	2.32		5.80				127.96	927		160.00
Rosaire O'Brien	42	200.00	20.00	220.00	22.00	13.64	3.19	2.00	5.80				173.37	928	220.00	
James Van Dyke	40	200.00		200.00	20.00	12.40	2.90		5.80				158.90	929		200.00
		1,600.00	136.00	1,736.00	165.00	107.63	25.17	6.00	48.80	20.00	15.00	14.00	1,334.40		1,216.00	520.00

Payroll Register

The payroll register, which is prepared each pay period, is a detailed listing of the firm's total payroll. A payroll register is presented in Exhibit 1. Note that the name, hours, earnings, deductions, and net pay of each employee are listed. Compare the entry for Robert Jones in the payroll register with the January 18 entry in the employee earnings record of Robert Jones presented in Exhibit 2. Except for the first column, which lists the employee names, and the last two columns, which show the wage or salary as either sales or office expense, the columns are the same. The columns help employers record the payroll in the accounting records and meet legal reporting requirements. The last two columns in Exhibit 1 are needed to divide the expenses in the accounting records into selling and administrative categories.

Exhibit 2. Employee Earnings Record

Employee Earnings Record

Employee's Name Robert Jones Social Security Number 444-66-9999
Address 777 20th Street Sex Male Employee No. 705
Marshall, Michigan 52603 Single ____ Married X Weekly Pay Rate ____
Date of Birth September 20, 1962 Exemptions (W-4) 4 Hourly Rate $8
Position Sales Assistant Date of Employment July 15, 1988 Date Employment Ended ____

20xx		Earnings			Deductions								Payment		
Period Ended	Total Hours	Regular	Overtime	Gross	Federal Income Taxes	Social Security Tax	Medicare Tax	Union Dues	Medical Insurance	Life Insurance	Savings Bonds	Other: A—United Charities	Net Earnings	Check No.	Cumula-tive Gross Earnings
Jan 4	40	320.00	0	320.00	17.00	19.84	4.64	2.00	7.60	6.00	15.00	A 1.00	246.92	717	320.00
11	44	320.00	48.00	368.00	23.00	22.82	5.34	2.00	7.60	6.00	15.00	A 1.00	285.24	822	688.00
18	47	320.00	92.00	412.00	31.00	25.54	5.97	2.00	7.60	6.00	15.00	A 1.00	317.89	926	1,100.00

BUSINESS BULLETIN: ETHICS IN PRACTICE

Payroll fraud is a common form of financial wrongdoing because there are strong motivations for both the employee and the employer to cheat. Some employees want to be paid cash "under the table" to avoid income, social security, and Medicare taxes. Some employers may wish to avoid paying their share of social security and Medicare taxes as well as other payroll taxes and employee benefits. Therefore, the Internal Revenue Service cracks down on cheaters. It investigates, for example, the relationships between restaurants' revenues and the tip income that employees report on their tax returns. Severe penalties, including prison terms, can result from false reporting. Good accounting records and controls over payroll help ensure compliance with the law.

Recording the Payroll

Discussion Question: How would the credits in the January 18 entry be presented on the financial statements? **Answer:** They are all current liabilities. Since most of them are small, they probably would be aggregated into "Other Payables" or a similar category.

The journal entry for recording the payroll is based on the column totals from the payroll register. The journal entry to record the January 18 payroll follows. Note that each account debited or credited is a total from the payroll register. If the payroll register is considered a special-purpose journal, the column totals can be posted directly to the ledger accounts, with the correct account numbers shown at the bottom of each column.

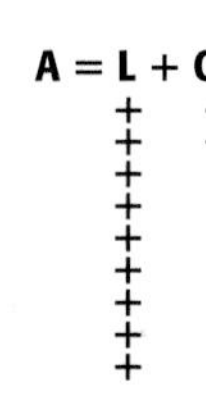

Date	Account	Debit	Credit
Jan. 18	Sales Wages Expense	1,216.00	
	Office Wages Expense	520.00	
	Employees' Federal Income Taxes Payable		165.00
	Social Security Tax Payable		107.63
	Medicare Tax Payable		25.17
	Union Dues Payable		6.00
	Medical Insurance Premiums Payable		48.80
	Life Insurance Premiums Payable		20.00
	Savings Bonds Payable		15.00
	United Charities Payable		14.00
	Wages Payable		1,334.40
	To record payroll		

Employee Earnings Record

Point to Emphasize: Payroll is one of the easiest elements of a business to computerize.

Each employer must keep a record of earnings and withholdings for each employee. Most companies today use computers to maintain such records, but some small companies may still use manual records. The manual form of employee earnings record for Robert Jones is shown in Exhibit 2. This form is designed to help the employer meet legal reporting requirements. Each deduction must be shown to have been paid to the proper agency, and the employee must receive a report of the deductions made each year.

Most of the columns in Exhibit 2 are self-explanatory. Note, however, the column on the far right for cumulative gross earnings (total earnings to date). This record helps the employer comply with the rule of applying social security and unemployment taxes only up to the maximum wage levels. At the end of the year, the employer reports to the employee on Form W-2, the Wage and Tax Statement, the total earnings and tax deductions for the year, which the employee uses to complete his or her individual tax return. The employer sends a copy of the W-2 to the Internal Revenue Service. Thus, the IRS can check whether the employee has reported all income earned from that employer.

Recording Payroll Taxes

According to Exhibit 1, the gross payroll for the week ended January 18 was $1,736.00. Because it was the first month of the year, all employees had accumulated less than the $68,400 and $9,000 maximum taxable salaries. Therefore, the total social security tax was $107.63 and the total Medicare tax was $25.17 (equal to the tax on employees), the total FUTA tax was $13.89 (.008 × $1,736.00), and the total state unemployment tax was $93.74 (.054 × $1,736.00). The entry to record this expense and related liability is as follows:

A = L + OE				
+ −	Jan. 18	Payroll Taxes Expense	240.43	
+		Social Security Tax Payable		107.63
+		Medicare Tax Payable		25.17
+		Federal Unemployment Tax Payable		13.89
+		State Unemployment Tax Payable		93.74
		To record payroll taxes		

Discussion Question: Where would the credits appear in the financial statements if the statements were prepared as of the date of the entry? **Answer:** They are all current liabilities. Since they are small, they would probably be aggregated into "Other Payables" or a similar category.

Teaching Note: Internal control affects the bookkeeping system used to pay taxes and payroll. However, any system must debit the liabilities established and credit Cash. If you approach the entry from a financial statement perspective (debit current liabilities and credit Cash), you can then discuss the internal control issues relating to the bookkeeping particulars.

Payment of Payroll and Payroll Taxes

After the weekly payroll is recorded, as illustrated earlier, a liability of $1,334.40 exists for wages payable. How this liability will be paid depends on the system used by the company. Many companies use a special payroll account against which payroll checks are drawn. Under this system, a check for total net earnings for this payroll ($1,334.40) must be drawn on the regular checking account and deposited in the special payroll account before the payroll checks are issued to the employees. If a voucher system is combined with a special payroll account, a voucher for the total wages payable is prepared and recorded in the voucher register as a debit to Payroll Bank Account and a credit to Vouchers Payable.

The combined social security and Medicare taxes (both employees' and employer's shares) and the federal income taxes must be paid at least quarterly. More frequent payments are required when the total liability exceeds $500. The federal unemployment insurance tax is paid yearly if the amount is less than $100. If the liability for FUTA tax exceeds $100 at the end of any quarter, a payment is necessary. Payment dates vary among the states. Other payroll deductions must be paid in accordance with the particular contracts or agreements involved.

Chapter Review

REVIEW OF LEARNING OBJECTIVES

1. **Identify the management issues related to recognition, valuation, classification, and disclosure of current liabilities.** Liabilities represent present legal obligations for future payment of assets or future performance of services. They result from past transactions and should be recognized when there is a transaction that obligates the company to make future payments. Liabilities are valued at the amount of money necessary to satisfy the obligation or the fair value of goods or services that must be delivered. Liabilities are classified as current or long term. Supplemental disclosure is required when the nature or details of the obligations would help in understanding the liability.

2. **Identify, compute, and record definitely determinable and estimated current liabilities.** Two principal categories of current liabilities are definitely determinable liabilities and estimated liabilities. Although definitely determinable liabilities, such as accounts payable, notes payable, dividends payable, accrued liabilities, and the current portion of long-term debt, can be measured exactly, the accountant must still be careful not to overlook existing liabilities in these categories. Estimated liabilities, such as liabilities for income taxes, property taxes, and product warranties, definitely exist, but the amounts must be estimated and recorded properly.
3. **Define *contingent liability*.** A contingent liability is a potential liability arising from a past transaction and dependent on a future event. Examples are lawsuits, income tax disputes, discounted notes receivable, guarantees of debt, and failure to follow government regulations.

Supplemental Objective

4. **Compute and record the liabilities associated with payroll accounting.** Computations for payroll liabilities must be made for the compensation to each employee, for withholdings from each employee's total pay, and for the employer's portion of payroll taxes. The salary and deductions for each employee are recorded each pay period in the payroll register. From the payroll register, the details of each employee's earnings are transferred to the employee's earnings record. The column totals of the payroll register are used to prepare an entry that records the payroll and accompanying liabilities. The employer's share of social security and Medicare taxes and the federal and state unemployment taxes as well as any liabilities for other fringe benefits must then be recorded.

REVIEW OF CONCEPTS AND TERMINOLOGY

The following concepts and terms were introduced in this chapter.

LO 2 **Commercial paper:** A means of borrowing short-term funds by using unsecured loans that are sold directly to the public, usually through professionally managed investment firms.

LO 3 **Contingent liability:** A potential liability that depends on a future event arising out of a past transaction.

LO 1 **Current liabilities:** Debts and obligations expected to be satisfied within one year or within the normal operating cycle, whichever is longer.

LO 2 **Definitely determinable liabilities:** Current liabilities that are set by contract or by statute and can be measured exactly.

SO 4 **Employee earnings record:** A record of earnings and withholdings for an individual employee.

LO 2 **Estimated liabilities:** Definite debts or obligations of which the exact amounts cannot be known until a later date.

LO 1 **Liabilities:** Legal obligations for the future payment of assets or the future performance of services that result from past transactions.

LO 2 **Line of credit:** A preapproved arrangement with a commercial bank that allows a company to borrow funds as needed.

LO 1 **Long-term liabilities:** Debts or obligations due beyond one year or beyond the normal operating cycle.

SO 4 **Payroll register:** A detailed listing of a firm's total payroll that is prepared each pay period.

LO 2 **Salaries:** Compensation to employees who are paid at a monthly or yearly rate.

LO 2 **Unearned revenues:** Revenues received in advance for which the goods will not be delivered or the services performed during the current accounting period.

LO 2 **Wages:** Payment for services of employees at an hourly rate.

REVIEW PROBLEM

Notes Payable Transactions and End-of-Period Entries

LO 2 McLaughlin, Inc., whose fiscal year ends June 30, 20xx, completed the following transactions involving notes payable.

May 11	Purchased a small crane by issuing a 60-day, 12 percent note for $54,000. The face of the note does not include interest.
16	Obtained a $40,000 bank loan to finance a temporary increase in receivables by signing a 90-day, 10 percent note. The face value includes interest.
June 30	Made the end-of-year adjusting entry to accrue interest expense.
30	Made the end-of-year adjusting entry to recognize interest expired on the note.
30	Made the end-of-year closing entry pertaining to interest expense.
July 10	Paid the note plus interest on the crane purchase.
Aug. 14	Paid off the note to the bank.

REQUIRED

Prepare entries in journal form for the above transactions.

ANSWER TO REVIEW PROBLEM

Prepare general journal entries.

Date	Account	Debit	Credit
20xx			
May 11	Equipment	54,000	
	Notes Payable		54,000
	Purchase of crane with 60-day, 12% note		
16	Cash	39,000	
	Discount on Notes Payable	1,000	
	Notes Payable		40,000
	Loan from bank obtained by signing 90-day, 10% note; discount $40,000 × .10 × 90/360 = $1,000		
June 30	Interest Expense	900	
	Interest Payable		900
	To accrue interest expense $54,000 × .12 × 50/360 = $900		
30	Interest Expense	500	
	Discount on Notes Payable		500
	To recognize interest on note $1,000 × 45/90 = $500		
30	Income Summary	1,400	
	Interest Expense		1,400
	To close interest expense		
July 10	Notes Payable	54,000	
	Interest Payable	900	
	Interest Expense	180	
	Cash		55,080
	Payment of note on equipment $54,000 × .12 × 60/360 = $1,080		
Aug. 14	Notes Payable	40,000	
	Cash		40,000
	Payment of bank loan		
14	Interest Expense	500	
	Discount on Notes Payable		500
	Interest expense on matured note $1,000 − $500 = $500		

Chapter Assignments

BUILDING YOUR KNOWLEDGE FOUNDATION

Questions

1. What are liabilities?
2. Why is the timing of liability recognition important in accounting?
3. At the end of the accounting period, Janson Company had a legal obligation to accept delivery of and pay for a truckload of hospital supplies the following week. Is this legal obligation a liability?
4. Ned Johnson, a star college basketball player, received a contract from the Midwest Blazers to play professional basketball. The contract calls for a salary of $300,000 a year for four years, dependent on his making the team in each of those years. Should this contract be considered a liability and recorded on the books of the basketball team?
5. What is the rule for classifying a liability as current?
6. What are a line of credit and commercial paper? Where do they appear on the balance sheet?
7. A bank is offering Diane Wedge two alternatives for borrowing $2,000. The first alternative is a $2,000, 12 percent, 30-day note. The second alternative is a $2,000, 30-day note discounted at 12 percent. (a) What entries are required by Diane Wedge to record the two loans? (b) What entries are needed by Diane to record the payment of the two loans? (c) Which alternative favors Diane, and why?
8. Where should the Discount on Notes Payable account appear on the balance sheet?
9. When can a portion of long-term debt be classified as a current liability?
10. What are three types of employer-related payroll liabilities?
11. How does an employee differ from an independent contractor?
12. Who pays social security and Medicare taxes?
13. Why are unearned revenues classified as liabilities?
14. What is definite about an estimated liability?
15. Why are income taxes payable considered to be estimated liabilities?
16. When does a company incur a liability for a product warranty?
17. What is a contingent liability, and how does it differ from an estimated liability?
18. What are some examples of contingent liabilities? For what reason is each a contingent liability?
19. What role does the W-4 form play in determining the withholding for estimated federal income taxes?
20. How can the payroll register be used as a special-purpose journal?
21. Why is an employee earnings record necessary, and how does it relate to the W-2 form?

Short Exercises

LO 1 *Issues in Accounting for Liabilities*

SE 1. Indicate whether each of the following actions relates to (a) recognition of liabilities, (b) valuation of liabilities, (c) classification of liabilities, or (d) disclosure of liabilities.

1. Determining that a liability will be paid in less than one year
2. Estimating the amount of a liability
3. Providing information about when liabilities are due and the interest rate that they carry
4. Determining when a liability arises

SE 2. LO 2 LO 3 *Types of Liabilities*

Indicate whether each of the following is (a) a definitely determinable liability, (b) an estimated liability, or (c) a contingent liability.

1. Dividends Payable
2. Pending litigation
3. Income Taxes Payable
4. Current portion of long-term debt
5. Vacation Pay Liability
6. Guaranteed loans of another company

SE 3. LO 2 *Interest Expense: Interest Not Included in Face Value of Note*

On the last day of August, Gross Company borrowed $60,000 on a bank note for 60 days at 10 percent interest. Assume that interest is stated separately. Prepare the following entries in journal form: (1) August 31, recording of note; and (2) October 30, payment of note plus interest.

SE 4. LO 2 *Interest Expense: Interest Included in Face Value of Note*

Assume the same facts as in **SE 3,** except that interest of $1,000 is included in the face amount of the note and the note is discounted at the bank on August 31. Prepare the following entries in journal form: (1) August 31, recording of note; and (2) October 30, payment of note and recording of interest expense.

SE 5. LO 2 *Payroll Withholdings, Taxes, and Other Costs*

Tell whether each of the following payroll withholdings, taxes, and other costs is generally a withholding only from the employee's wages (W), both a withholding from the employee's wages and a tax or cost to the employer (WE), or a tax or cost only to the employer (E).

1. Employee's federal income taxes
2. State unemployment insurance tax
3. Social security (FICA) tax
4. Medicare tax
5. Medical insurance
6. Federal unemployment insurance (FUTA) tax
7. Pension contributions
8. Employee's state and local income taxes

SE 6. LO 2 *Payroll Entries*

The following payroll totals for the month of April were taken from the payroll register of Coover Corporation: salaries, $223,000.00; federal income taxes withheld, $31,440.00; social security tax withheld, $13,826.00; Medicare tax withheld, $3,233.50; medical insurance deductions, $6,580.00; and salaries subject to unemployment taxes, $156,600.00. Prepare entries in journal form to record (1) accrual of the monthly payroll and (2) accrual of employer's payroll expense, assuming social security and Medicare taxes equal to the amounts for employees, a federal unemployment insurance tax of .8 percent, a state unemployment tax of 5.4 percent, and medical insurance premiums for which the employer pays 80 percent of the cost.

SE 7. LO 2 *Product Warranty Liability*

Rainbow Corp. manufactures and sells travel clocks. Each clock costs $25 to produce and sells for $50. In addition, each clock carries a warranty that provides for free replacement if it fails for any reason during the two years following the sale. In the past, 5 percent of the clocks sold have had to be replaced under the warranty. During October, Rainbow sold 52,000 clocks, and 2,800 clocks were replaced under the warranty. Prepare entries in journal form to record the estimated liability for product warranties during the month and the clocks replaced under warranty during the month.

SE 8. LO 2 *Vacation Pay Liability*

The employees of Chan Services receive two weeks of paid vacation each year. Seventy percent of the employees qualify for vacation. Assuming the September payroll is $150,000, including $12,000 paid to employees on vacation, how much is the vacation pay expense for September? What is the ending balance of the Estimated Liability for Vacation Pay account, assuming a beginning balance of $16,000?

SE 9. SO 4 *Payroll Taxes*

Kristof Company and its employees are subject to a 6.2 percent social security tax on wages up to $68,400 and a 1.45 percent Medicare tax with no limit. The company is subject to a 5.4 percent state unemployment tax and a .8 percent federal unemployment tax up to $9,000 per employee. The company has two employees: A. Burns, who has cumulative earnings of $77,000 and earned $7,000 in the month of December, and C. Dunn, who has cumulative earnings of $5,000 and earned $1,000 during December. Compute the total payroll taxes for the employees and the employer for December.

SE 10. SO 4 *Payroll Earnings, Withholdings, and Taxes*

Last week, Manuel Kardo worked 44 hours. He is paid $10 per hour and receives one and one-half times his regular rate for hours worked over 40. Kardo has withholdings of $45 for federal income taxes, $10 for state income taxes, $23 for health insurance, 6.2 percent for social security tax, and 1.45 percent for Medicare tax. Compute Kardo's take-home pay. Also compute the total cost of Kardo to his employer, assuming that Kardo's cumulative wages are over the limit for unemployment taxes and that the company makes a health-care contribution of $75.

Exercises

E 1. LO 1 *Issues in Accounting for Liabilities*

Indicate whether each of the following actions relates to (a) recognition of liabilities, (b) valuation of liabilities, (c) classification of liabilities, or (d) disclosure of liabilities.

1. Setting a liability at the fair market value of goods to be delivered
2. Relating the payment date of a liability to the length of the operating cycle
3. Recording a liability in accordance with the matching rule
4. Providing information about financial instruments on the balance sheet
5. Estimating the amount of "cents off" coupons that will be redeemed
6. Categorizing a liability as long-term debt

E 2. LO 2 *Interest Expense: Interest Not Included in Face Value of Note*

On the last day of October, Ostrand Company borrows $30,000 on a bank note for 60 days at 12 percent interest. Assume that interest is not included in the face amount. Prepare the following entries in journal form: (1) October 31, recording of note; (2) November 30, accrual of interest expense; and (3) December 30, payment of note plus interest.

E 3. LO 2 *Interest Expense: Interest Included in Face Value of Note*

Assume the same facts as in **E 2,** except that interest is included in the face amount of the note and the note is discounted at the bank on October 31. Prepare the following entries in journal form: (1) October 31, recording of note; (2) November 30, recognition of interest accrued on note; and (3) December 30, payment of note and recording of interest expense.

E 4. LO 2 *Sales and Excise Taxes*

Alert Dial Service billed its customers a total of $980,400 for the month of August, including 9 percent federal excise tax and 5 percent sales tax.

1. Determine the proper amount of service revenue to report for the month.
2. Prepare an entry in journal form to record the revenue and related liabilities for the month.

E 5. LO 2 *Payroll Entries*

At the end of October, the payroll register for Lathrop Bandmill Corporation contained the following totals: wages, $185,500; social security tax withheld, $11,501; federal income taxes withheld, $47,442; state income taxes withheld, $7,818; Medicare tax withheld, $2,689.75; medical insurance deductions, $6,435; and wages subject to unemployment taxes, $28,620.

Prepare entries in journal form to record (1) accrual of the monthly payroll and (2) accrual of employer payroll expenses, assuming social security and Medicare taxes equal to the amount for employees, a federal unemployment insurance tax of .8 percent, a state unemployment tax of 5.4 percent, and medical insurance premiums for which the employer pays 80 percent of the cost.

E 6. LO 2 *Product Warranty Liability*

Keystone Company manufactures and sells electronic games. Each game costs $25 to produce and sells for $45. In addition, each game carries a warranty that provides for free replacement if it fails for any reason during the two years following the sale. In the past, 7 percent of the games sold had to be replaced under the warranty. During July, Keystone sold 26,000 games and 2,800 games were replaced under the warranty.

1. Prepare an entry in journal form to record the estimated liability for product warranties during the month.
2. Prepare an entry in journal form to record the games replaced under warranty during the month.

E 7. LO 2 *Vacation Pay Liability*

Crosstown Corporation currently allows each employee who has worked at the company for one year three weeks' paid vacation. Based on studies of employee turnover and previous experience, management estimates that 65 percent of the employees will qualify for vacation pay this year.

1. Assume that Crosstown's July payroll is $600,000, of which $40,000 is paid to employees on vacation. Figure the estimated employee vacation benefit for the month.
2. Prepare an entry in journal form to record the employee benefit for July.
3. Prepare an entry in journal form to record the pay to employees on vacation.

E 8. LO 2 *Estimated Liability*

Great Plains Airways has initiated a frequent-flyer program in which enrolled passengers accumulate miles of travel that may be redeemed for rewards such as free trips or upgrades from coach to first class. Great Plains estimates that approximately 2 percent of its passengers are traveling for free as a result of this program. During 20x1, Great Plains Airways had total revenues of $16,000,000,000.

In January 20x2, passengers representing tickets of $300,000 flew free. Prepare the December 20x1 year-end adjusting entry to record the estimated liability for this program and the January 20x2 entry for the free tickets used. Can you suggest how these transactions would be recorded if the estimate of the free tickets were to be considered a deferred revenue (revenue received in advance) rather than an estimated liability? How is each treatment an application of the matching rule?

E 9. SO 4 *Social Security, Medicare, and Unemployment Taxes*

Muzzy Company is subject to a 5.4 percent state unemployment insurance tax and a .8 percent federal unemployment insurance tax after credits. Currently, both federal and state unemployment taxes apply to the first $9,000 earned by each employee. Social security and Medicare taxes in effect at this time are 6.20 and 1.45 percent, respectively. The social security tax is levied for both employee and employer on the first $68,400 earned by each employee during the year. During the current year, the cumulative earnings for each employee of the company are as follows:

Employee	Cumulative Earnings	Employee	Cumulative Earnings
Botala, J.	$28,620	Gosliga, M.	$16,760
Cohn, A.	5,260	Harrington, P.	6,420
Dwyer, G.	32,820	Lebeau, C.	51,650
Esposito, R.	30,130	Miklos, D.	32,100
Furchgott, B.	70,000	Offray, V.	36,645
Gonzalez, N.	5,120	Tung, S.	5,176

1. Prepare and complete a schedule with the following columns: Employee Name, Cumulative Earnings, Earnings Subject to Social Security Tax, Earnings Subject to Medicare Tax, and Earnings Subject to Unemployment Taxes. Total the columns.
2. Compute the social security and Medicare taxes and the federal and state unemployment taxes for Muzzy Company for the year.

E 10. SO 4 *Net Pay Calculation and Payroll Entries*

Linda Lightfoot is an employee whose overtime pay is regulated by the Fair Labor Standards Act. Her hourly rate is $8, and during the week ended July 11, she worked 42 hours. Linda claims two exemptions on her W-4 form. So far this year she has earned $8,650. Each week $12 is deducted from her paycheck for medical insurance.

1. Compute the following items related to the pay for Linda Lightfoot for the week of July 11: (a) total pay, (b) federal income taxes withholding (use Figure 4), (c) social security and Medicare taxes (assume rates of 6.2 percent and 1.45 percent, respectively), and (d) net pay.
2. Prepare an entry in journal form to record the wages expense and related liabilities for Linda Lightfoot for the week ended July 11.

E 11. SO 4 *Payroll Transactions*

Jian-Jin Ye earns a salary of $70,000 per year. Social security and Medicare taxes are 6.2 percent on salary up to $68,400 and 1.45 percent on total salary. Federal unemployment insurance taxes are 6.2 percent of the first $9,000; however, a credit is allowed equal to the state unemployment insurance taxes of 5.4 percent on the $9,000. During the year, $15,000 was withheld for federal income taxes, $3,000 for state income taxes, and $1,500 for medical insurance.

1. Prepare an entry in journal form summarizing the payment of $70,000 to Ye during the year.
2. Prepare an entry in journal form summarizing the employer payroll taxes and other costs on Ye's salary for the year. Assume the company pays 80 percent of the total premiums for medical insurance.
3. Determine the total cost paid by Jian-Jin Ye's employer to employ Ye for the year.

Problems

P 1. **LO 2** *Notes Payable Transactions and End-of-Period Entries*

Landover Corporation, whose fiscal year ends June 30, completed the following transactions involving notes payable:

May 11	Signed a 90-day, 12 percent, $66,000 note payable to Village Bank for a working capital loan. The face value included interest. Proceeds received were $64,020.
21	Obtained a 60-day extension on an $18,000 trade account payable owed to a supplier by signing a 60-day, $18,000 note. Interest is in addition to the face value, at the rate of 14 percent.
June 30	Made end-of-year adjusting entry to accrue interest expense.
30	Made end-of-year adjusting entry to recognize prepaid interest expense.
July 20	Paid off the note plus interest due the supplier.
Aug. 9	Paid amount due to the bank on the 90-day note.

REQUIRED

Prepare entries in journal form for the notes payable transactions.

P 2. **LO 2** *Property Tax and Vacation Pay Liabilities*

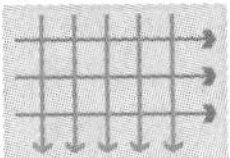

Kubek Corporation prepares monthly financial statements and ends its fiscal year on June 30, the same as the local government. In July 20x1, your first month as accountant for the company, you find that the company has not previously accrued estimated liabilities. In the past, the company, which has a large property tax bill, has charged the property tax to the month in which the bill is paid. The tax bill for the year ended June 30, 20x1, was $72,000, and it is estimated that the tax will increase by 8 percent for the year ending June 30, 20x2. The tax bill is usually received on September 1, to be paid November 1.

You also discover that employees who have worked for the company for one year are allowed to take two weeks' paid vacation each year. The cost of the vacations has been charged to expense in the month of payment. Approximately 80 percent of the employees qualify for this benefit. You suggest to management that the proper accounting treatment of these expenses is to spread their cost over the entire year. Management agrees and asks you to make the necessary adjustments.

REQUIRED

1. Figure the proper monthly charge to property tax expense and prepare entries in journal form for the following:

July 31	Accrual of property tax expense
Aug. 31	Accrual of property tax expense
Sept. 30	Accrual of property tax expense (assume the actual bill is $81,720)
Oct. 31	Accrual of property tax expense
Nov. 1	Payment of property tax
30	Recording of monthly property tax expense

2. Assume that the total payroll for July is $1,136,000. This amount includes $42,600 paid to employees on paid vacations.
   a. Compute the vacation pay expense for July.
   b. Prepare an entry in journal form on July 31 to record the accrual of vacation pay expense for July.
   c. Prepare an entry in journal form, dated July 31, to record the wages of employees on vacation in July (ignore payroll deductions and taxes).

P 3. **LO 2** *Product Warranty Liability*

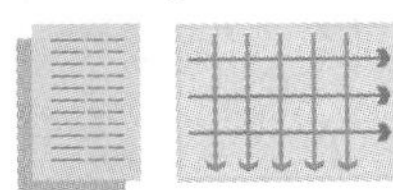

Marrero Company is engaged in the retail sale of washing machines. Each machine has a twenty-four-month warranty on parts. If a repair under warranty is required, a charge for the labor is made. Management has found that 20 percent of the machines sold require some work before the warranty expires. Furthermore, the average cost of replacement parts has been $120 per repair. At the beginning of June, the account for the estimated liability for product warranties had a credit balance of $28,600. During June, 112 machines were returned under the warranty. The cost of the parts used in repairing the machines was $17,530, and $18,884 was collected as service revenue for the labor involved. During the month, Marrero Company sold 450 new machines.

REQUIRED

1. Prepare entries in journal form to record each of the following: (a) the warranty work completed during the month, including related revenue; (b) the estimated liability for product warranties for machines sold during the month.
2. Compute the balance of the Estimated Product Warranty Liability account at the end of the month.

SO 4 *Payroll Entries*

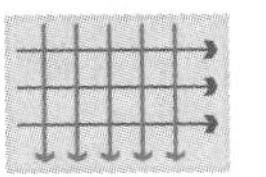

P 4. The following payroll totals for the month of April were taken from the payroll register of Coover Corporation: sales salaries, $116,400; office salaries, $57,000; general salaries, $49,600; social security tax withheld, $13,826; Medicare tax withheld, $3,233.50; income taxes withheld, $31,440; medical insurance premiums, $6,580; life insurance premiums, $3,760; salaries subject to unemployment taxes, $156,600. Fifty percent of medical and life insurance premiums are paid by the employer.

REQUIRED

Prepare entries in journal form to record the following: (1) accrual of the monthly payroll, (2) payment of the net payroll, (3) accrual of employer's payroll taxes and expenses (assuming social security and Medicare taxes equal to the amounts for employees, a federal unemployment insurance tax of .8 percent, and a state unemployment tax of 5.4 percent), and (4) payment of all liabilities related to the payroll (assuming that all are paid at the same time).

SO 4 *Payroll Register and Related Entries*

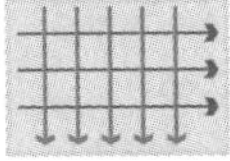

P 5. Huizenga Dairy Company has seven employees. Employees paid hourly receive a set rate for regular hours plus one and one-half times their hourly rate for overtime hours. They are paid every two weeks. The salaried employees are paid monthly on the last biweekly payday of each month. The employees and company are subject to social security tax of 6.2 percent up to a maximum of $68,400 for each employee and to Medicare tax of 1.45 percent. The unemployment insurance tax rates are 5.4 percent for the state and .8 percent for the federal government. The unemployment insurance tax applies to the first $9,000 earned by each employee and is levied only on the employer.

The company maintains a supplemental benefits plan that includes medical insurance, life insurance, and additional retirement funds for employees. Under the plan, each employee contributes 4 percent of her or his gross income as a payroll withholding, and the company matches the amount. Data for the November 30 payroll, the last payday of November, follow.

Employee	Hours: Regular	Hours: Overtime	Pay Rate	Cumulative Gross Pay Excluding Current Pay Period	Federal Income Taxes to Be Withheld
Epstein, D.	80	5	$ 8.00	$ 4,867.00	$ 71.00
Hladik, W.	80	4	6.50	3,954.00	76.00
Melchior, P.*	Salary	—	5,000.00	55,000.00	985.00
Nuovo, V.	80	—	5.00	8,250.00	32.00
Rasmussen, L.*	Salary	—	2,000.00	20,000.00	294.00
Tang, M.	80	20	10.00	12,000.00	103.00
Von Bruns, B.*	Salary	—	1,500.00	15,000.00	210.00

*Denotes administrative personnel; the rest are sales. P. Melchior's cumulative gross pay includes a $5,000 bonus paid early in the year.

REQUIRED

1. Prepare a payroll register for the pay period ended November 30. The payroll register should have the following columns:

Employee	Deductions	Net Pay
Total Hours	Federal Income Taxes	Distribution
Earnings	Social Security Tax	Sales Wages Expense
Regular	Medicare Tax	Administrative Salaries Expense
Overtime	Supplemental Benefits Plan	
Gross		
Cumulative		

2. Prepare an entry in journal form to record the payroll and related liabilities for deductions for the period ended November 30.
3. Prepare entries in journal form to record the employer's payroll taxes and contribution to the supplemental benefits plan.
4. Prepare the November 30 entries (a) to transfer sufficient cash from the company's regular checking account to a special payroll disbursement account and (b) to pay the employees.

Alternate Problems

LO 2 *Notes Payable Transactions and End-of-Period Entries*

P 6. Prentiss Paper Company, whose fiscal year ends December 31, completed the following transactions involving notes payable.

20x1
Nov. 25 Purchased a new loading cart by issuing a 60-day, 10 percent note for $21,600.
Dec. 16 Borrowed $25,000 from the bank to finance inventory by signing a 90-day note. The face value of the note includes interest of $750. Proceeds received were $24,250.
31 Made the end-of-year adjusting entry to accrue interest expense.
31 Made the end-of-year adjusting entry to recognize the interest expired on the note.

20x2
Jan. 24 Paid off the loading cart note.
Mar. 16 Paid off the inventory note to the bank.

REQUIRED

Prepare entries in journal form for these transactions.

LO 2 *Payroll Entries*

P 7. At the end of October, the payroll register for Lindos Corporation contained the following totals: sales salaries, $176,220; office salaries, $80,880; administrative salaries, $113,900; federal income taxes withheld, $94,884; state income taxes withheld, $15,636; social security tax withheld, $23,002; Medicare tax withheld, $5,379.50; medical insurance premiums, $12,870; life insurance premiums, $11,712; union dues deductions, $1,368; and salaries subject to unemployment taxes, $57,240. Fifty percent of medical and life insurance premiums are paid by the employer.

REQUIRED

Prepare entries in journal form to record the (1) accrual of the monthly payroll, (2) payment of the net payroll, (3) accrual of employer's payroll taxes and expenses (assuming social security and Medicare taxes equal to the amount for employees, a federal unemployment insurance tax of .8 percent, and a state unemployment tax of 5.4 percent), and (4) payment of all liabilities related to the payroll (assuming that all are paid at the same time).

LO 2 *Product Warranty Liability*

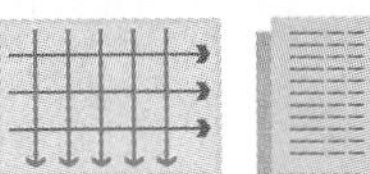

P 8. The Citation Company manufactures and sells food processors. The company guarantees the processors for five years. If a processor fails, it is replaced free, but the customer is charged a service fee for handling. In the past, management has found that only 3 percent of the processors sold required replacement under the warranty. The average food processor costs the company $120. At the beginning of September, the account for estimated liability for product warranties had a credit balance of $104,000. During September, 250 processors were returned under the warranty. Service fees of $4,930 were collected for handling. During the month, the company sold 2,800 food processors.

REQUIRED

1. Prepare entries in journal form to record (a) the cost of food processors replaced under warranty and (b) the estimated liability for product warranties for processors sold during the month.
2. Compute the balance of the Estimated Product Warranty Liability account at the end of the month.

Skills Development

Conceptual Analysis

SD 1.
LO 2 *Identification of Current Liabilities*

Several businesses and organizations and a current liability from the balance sheet of each are listed below. Discuss the nature of each current liability (definitely determinable or estimated), how each arose, and how the obligation is likely to be fulfilled.

Institute of Management Accountants: Deferred Revenues—Membership Dues

The Foxboro Company: Advances on Sales Contracts

UNC Incorporated: Current Portion of Long-Term Debt

Hurco Companies, Inc.: Accrued Warranty Expense

Affiliated Publications, Inc.: Deferred Subscription Revenues

Geo. A Hormel & Company: Accrued Advertising

SD 2.
LO 2 *Frequent-Flyer Plan*

America South Airways instituted a frequent-flyer program under which passengers accumulate points based on the number of miles they fly on the airline. One point is awarded for each mile flown, with a minimum of 750 miles given for any flight. Because of competition in 1997, the company began a triple mileage bonus plan under which passengers received triple the normal mileage points. In the past, about 1.5 percent of passenger miles were flown by passengers who had converted points to free flights. With the triple mileage program, it is expected that a 2.5 percent rate will be more appropriate for future years. During 1997 the company had passenger revenues of $966.3 million and passenger transportation operating expenses of $802.8 million before depreciation and amortization. Operating income was $86.1 million. The AICPA is considering requiring airline companies to recognize frequent-flyer plans in their accounting records. What is the appropriate rate to use to estimate free miles? What would be the effect of the estimated liability for free travel by frequent flyers on 1997 net income? Describe several ways to estimate the amount of this liability. Be prepared to discuss the arguments for and against recognizing this liability.

Ethical Dilemma

SD 3.
LO 2 *Known Legal Violations*

Tower Restaurant is a large seafood restaurant in the suburbs of Chicago. Joe Murray, an accounting student at a nearby college, recently secured a full-time accounting job at the restaurant. Joe felt fortunate to have a good job that accommodated his class schedule because the local economy was very bad. After a few weeks on the job, Joe realized that his boss, the owner of the business, was paying the kitchen workers in cash and was not withholding federal and state income taxes or social security and Medicare taxes. Joe understands that federal and state laws require these taxes to be withheld and paid to the appropriate agency in a timely manner. Joe also realizes that if he raises this issue, he may lose his job. What alternatives are available to Joe? What action would you take if you were in Joe's position? Why did you make this choice?

Group Activity: Use in class groups. Debrief by asking each group for an alternative. Then debate the ethics of each alternative.

Communication

Critical Thinking

Group Activity

Memo

Ethics

International

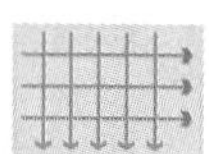
Spreadsheet

General Ledger

CD-ROM

Internet

RESEARCH ACTIVITY

SD 4. LO 2 LO 3 *Basic Research Skills*

Indexes for business periodicals, in which you can look up topics of interest, are available in your school library. Three of the most important of these indexes are the *Business Periodicals Index, The Wall Street Journal Index,* and the *Accountants' Index.* Using one or more of these indexes, locate and photocopy two articles related to bank financing, commercial paper, product warranties, airline frequent-flyer plans, or contingent liabilities. Keep in mind that you may have to look under related topics to find an article. For example, to find articles about contingent liabilities, you might look under litigation, debt guarantees, environmental losses, or other topics. For each of the two articles, write a short summary of the situation and tell how it relates to accounting for the topic as described in the text. Be prepared to discuss your results in class.

DECISION-MAKING PRACTICE

SD 5. LO 1 LO 2 SO 4 *Identification of Current Liabilities*

Jerry Highland opened a small television repair shop, ***Highland Television Repair,*** on January 2, 20xx. He also sold a small line of television sets. Highland's wife was the sole salesperson for the television sets, and Highland was the only person doing repairs. (Highland had worked for another television repair store for twenty years, where he was the supervisor of six repairpersons.) The new business was such a success that he hired two assistants on March 1, 20xx. In October, Highland realized that he had failed to file any tax reports for his business since its inception and therefore probably owed a considerable amount of taxes. Since Highland has limited experience in running a business, he has brought all his business records to you for help. The records include a checkbook, canceled checks, deposit slips, invoices from his suppliers, a notice of annual property taxes of $4,620 due to the city on November 1, 20xx, and a promissory note to his father-in-law for $5,000. He wants you to determine what his business owes the government and other parties.

You analyze all his records and determine the following:

Unpaid supplies invoices	$ 3,160
Sales (excluding sales tax)	88,540
Workers' salaries	20,400
Repair revenues	120,600

You learn that the company has deducted $952 from the two employees' salaries for federal income taxes owed to the government. The current social security tax is 6.2 percent on maximum earnings of $68,400 for each employee, and the current Medicare tax is 1.45 percent (no maximum earnings). The FUTA tax is 5.4 percent to the state and .8 percent to the federal government on the first $9,000 earned by each employee, and each employee earned more than $9,000. Highland has not filed a sales tax report to the state (5 percent of sales).

1. Given these limited facts, determine Highland Television Repair's current liabilities as of October 31, 20xx.
2. What additional information would you want from Highland to satisfy yourself that all current liabilities have been identified?

Financial Reporting and Analysis

INTERPRETING FINANCIAL REPORTS

FRA 1. LO 1 LO 2 *Analysis of Current Liabilities for a Bankrupt Company*

Trans World Airlines, Inc., is a major airline that has experienced financial difficulties since 1988. In TWA's 1989 annual report, management referred to the company's deteriorating liquidity as follows:[10]

> TWA's net working capital deficit was $55.5 million at December 31, 1989, representing a reduction of $82.6 million from net working capital of $27.1 million at December 31, 1988. Working capital deficits are not unusual in the airline industry because of the large advance ticket sales current liability account.

In 1991, the company declared bankruptcy. By 1993, the company had reorganized and came out of bankruptcy. The company's current liabilities and current assets at December 31 for 1989 and 1994 were as follows (in thousands):

	1994	1989
Current liabilities:		
Current maturities of long-term debt	$1,102,146	$ 127,301
Current obligations under capital leases	47,593	93,194
Advance ticket sales	172,044	276,549
Accounts payable, principally trade	117,461	387,256
Accounts payable to affiliated companies	3,092	8,828
Securities sold, not yet purchased	—	82,302
Accrued expenses:		
Employee compensation and vacations earned	109,715	148,175
Contributions to retirement and pension trusts	33,393	14,711
Interest on debt and capital leases	68,717	86,761
Taxes	16,968	33,388
Other accrued expenses	175,868	122,295
Total	$1,846,997	$1,380,760
Current assets:		
Cash and cash equivalents	$121,306	$ 454,415
Marketable securities	—	10,355
Receivables, less allowance for doubtful accounts, $13,432 in 1989 and $14,832 in 1994	240,804	435,061
Receivables from affiliated companies	—	15,506
Due from brokers	—	70,636
Spare parts, materials, and supplies, less allowance for obsolescence, $38,423 in 1989 and $20,928 in 1994	156,662	227,098
Prepaid expenses and other	48,768	112,232
Total	$567,540	$1,325,303

REQUIRED

1. Identify any current liabilities that did not require a current outlay of cash and identify any current estimated liabilities for 1989 and 1994. Why was management not worried about the cash flow consequences of advance ticket sales?
2. For 1989 and 1994, which current assets would not generate cash inflow, and which would most likely be available to pay for the remaining current liabilities? Compare the amount of these current assets with the amount of current liabilities other than those identified in **1** as not requiring a cash outlay.
3. In light of the calculations in **2,** comment on TWA's liquidity for 1989 and 1994 and its ability to operate successfully after bankruptcy. Identify several alternative sources of additional cash.

International Company

FRA 2.

LO 1 *Classification and*
LO 2 *Disclosure of Current*
LO 3 *Liabilities and*
Contingent Liabilities

The German company ***Man Nutzfahrzeuge Aktiengesellschaft*** is one of the largest truck companies in the world. Accounting in Germany differs in some respects from that in the United States. A good example of the difference is the placement and classification of liabilities. On the balance sheet, Man places liabilities below a detailed stockholders' equity section. Man does not distinguish between current and long-term liabilities; however, a note to the financial statements does disclose the amount of the liabilities due within one year. Those liabilities are primarily what we call *definitely determinable liabilities,* such as loans and accounts and notes payable. Estimated liabilities do not seem to appear in this category. In contrast, there is an asset category called *current assets,* which is similar to that found in the United States. In another note to the financial statements, the company lists what it calls *contingent liabilities,* which have not been recorded and do not appear on the balance sheet. These include liabilities for hire and leasing contracts, guarantees of loans of other companies, and warranties on trucks.[11] What do you think of the idea of combining all liabilities, whether short-term or long-term, as a single item on the balance sheet? Do you think any of the contingent liabilities should be recorded and shown on the balance sheet?

Toys "R" Us Annual Report

FRA 3.

LO 1 *Short-Term Liabilities and Seasonality*

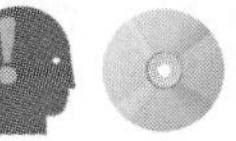
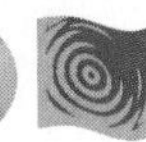

Refer to the balance sheet and the liquidity and capital resources section of Management's Discussion—Results of Operations and Financial Condition in the Toys "R" Us annual report to answer the following questions. What percentage of total assets are current liabilities for Toys "R" Us, and how does this percentage compare to that in other industries, as represented by Figure 1? Toys "R" Us is a seasonal business. Would you expect short-term borrowings and accounts payable to be unusually high or unusually low at the balance sheet date of February 1, 1997? How does management use short-term financing to meet its needs for cash during the year?

Fingraph® Financial Analyst™

FRA 4.

LO 1
LO 2
LO 3
Current Liability and Working Capital Analysis

Choose any two companies from the same industry in the Fingraph® Financial Analyst™ CD-ROM software. The industry chosen should be one in which current liabilities are likely to be important. Choose an industry such as airlines, manufacturing, consumer products, consumer food and beverage, or computers.

1. In the annual reports for the companies you have selected, read the current liability section of the balance sheet and any reference to any current liabilities in the summary of significant accounting policies or notes to the financial statements. What are the most important current liabilities for each company? Are there any current liabilities that appear to be characteristic of the industry? Which current liabilities are definitely determinable and which appear to be accrued liabilities?
2. Display and print in tabular and graphical form the Current Assets and Current Liabilities Analysis page. Prepare a table that compares the current ratio and working capital for both companies for two years.
3. Find and read references to current liabilities in the liquidity analysis section of management's discussion and analysis in each annual report.
4. Write a one-page executive summary that highlights the most important types of current liabilities for this industry and compares the current ratio and working capital trends of the two companies, including reference to management's assessment. Include the Fingraph® page and your table as an attachment to your report.

ENDNOTES

1. US Airways, Inc., *Annual Report,* 1996.
2. The Goodyear Tire & Rubber Company, *Annual Report,* 1996.
3. Lowe's Companies, Inc., *Annual Report,* 1996.
4. Scott McCartney, "Free Airline Miles Become a Potent Tool for Selling Everything," *The Wall Street Journal,* April 16, 1996.
5. Brigid McMenamin, "The Great Giveaway," *Forbes,* January 18, 1993.
6. Delta Airlines, *Annual Report,* 1997.
7. *Statement of Financial Accounting Standards No. 5,* "Accounting for Contingencies" (Norwalk, Conn.: Financial Accounting Standards Board, 1975).
8. Raju Narisetti, "P&G Ad Chief Plots Demise of the Coupon," *The Wall Street Journal,* April 17, 1996.
9. Adapted from Humana, Inc., *Annual Report,* 1992.
10. Trans World Airlines, Inc., *Annual Report,* 1989 and 1994.
11. Man Nutzfahrzeuge Aktiengesellschaft, *Annual Report,* 1997.

8
5
2

CHAPTER 13

Partnerships

LEARNING OBJECTIVES

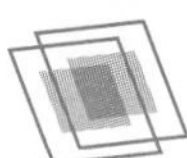

1. **Identify the principal characteristics, advantages, and disadvantages of the partnership form of business.**
2. **Record partners' investments of cash and other assets when a partnership is formed.**
3. **Compute and record the income or losses that partners share, based on stated ratios, capital balance ratios, and partners' salaries and interest.**
4. **Record a person's admission to a partnership.**
5. **Record a person's withdrawal from a partnership.**
6. **Compute the distribution of assets to partners when they liquidate their partnership.**

DECISION POINT

Many people think of partnerships as relatively small business organizations, and usually they are right. However, some partnerships, among them law firms, investment companies, real estate companies, and accounting firms, are very large. An example is Ernst & Young International, an integrated professional services firm with 660 locations in 130 countries. The firm provides accounting and auditing services, tax services, and management consulting services. With 80,000 employees, it is one of the largest partnerships in the world. In 1997, the firm had revenues of $8.1 billion, $4.4 billion of which came from the United States. How does a partnership this large organize to accomplish its objectives?[1]

Ernst & Young International is organized as a limited liability partnership. In a normal partnership, the personal financial resources of all partners are subject to risk of loss if the partnership suffers a loss it cannot bear. Accounting firms are at risk of suffering large losses as a result of lawsuits from investors who lose money investing in a company audited by the accounting firm. Because Ernst & Young is organized as a limited liability partnership, partners are liable to the extent of their partnership interest in the firm but do not subject their other personal assets to risk.

Every partnership has a unique partnership agreement. It is unlikely that any other partnership has an agreement exactly the same as Ernst & Young's. Ernst & Young has announced a merger with KPMG Peat Marwick, another large international accounting firm. For the merger to go through, the partners of both firms will have to agree to the new partnership agreement. This chapter examines many of the considerations that go into drafting such an agreement.

ERNST & YOUNG INTERNATIONAL

Critical Thinking Question: How does a partnership located only in the United States differ from one with offices around the world? **Answer:** While technology permits worldwide communication, accommodations, such as the translation of monetary amounts from international operations into U.S. dollars, would be required to summarize total partnership performance.

Business-World Example: Because of mergers, the former "Big Eight" has been reduced to the "Big Six." They are Arthur Andersen & Co., Coopers & Lybrand, Deloitte & Touche, Ernst & Young, KPMG Peat Marwick, and Price Waterhouse. Proposed mergers, if consummated, will reduce the "Big Six" to the "Big Four."

Partnership Characteristics

OBJECTIVE 1

Identify the principal characteristics, advantages, and disadvantages of the partnership form of business

Related Text Assignments:
Q: 1, 2, 3, 4, 5
SE: 1
SD: 1, 3, 4
FRA: 1, 2

Point to Emphasize: Partnerships and sole proprietorships are not legal entities; corporations are. All three, however, are considered accounting entities.

The Uniform Partnership Act, which has been adopted by most states, defines a partnership as "an association of two or more persons to carry on as co-owners of a business for profit." Partnerships are treated as separate entities in accounting. They differ in many ways from the other forms of business. The next few paragraphs describe some of the important characteristics of a partnership.

Voluntary Association

A partnership is a voluntary association of individuals rather than a legal entity in itself. Therefore, a partner is responsible under the law for his or her partners' business actions within the scope of the partnership. A partner also has unlimited liability for the debts of the partnership. Because of these potential liabilities, an individual must be allowed to choose the people who join the partnership. A person should select as partners individuals who share his or her business objectives.

Partnership Agreement

A partnership is easy to form. Two or more competent people simply agree to be partners in a common business purpose. Their agreement is known as a partnership agreement. The partnership agreement does not have to be in writing; however, good business practice calls for a written document that clearly states the details of the arrangement. The contract should specify the name, location, and purpose of the business; the partners and their respective duties; the investments of each partner; the methods for distributing income and losses; and the procedures for the admission and withdrawal of partners, the withdrawal of assets allowed each partner, and the liquidation (termination) of the business.

Limited Life

Enrichment Note: Many types of organizations have been created by law. They include S corporations and limited partnerships. Each provides legal (especially tax) advantages and disadvantages.

Because a partnership is formed by a contract between partners, it has a limited life: Anything that ends the contract dissolves the partnership. A partnership is dissolved when (1) a new partner is admitted, (2) a partner withdraws, (3) a partner goes bankrupt, (4) a partner is incapacitated (to the point where he or she cannot perform as obligated), (5) a partner retires, (6) a partner dies, or (7) the partnership ends according to the partnership agreement (for example, when a large project is completed). However, if the partners want the partnership to continue legally, the partnership agreement can be written to cover each of these situations. For example, the partnership agreement can state that if a partner dies, the remaining partner or partners must purchase the deceased partner's capital at book value from the heirs.

Mutual Agency

Each partner is an agent of the partnership within the scope of the business. Because of this mutual agency, any partner can bind the partnership to a business agreement as long as he or she acts within the scope of the company's normal operations. For example, a partner in a used-car business can bind the partnership through the purchase or sale of used cars. But this partner cannot bind the partnership to a contract to buy men's clothing or any other goods that are not related to the used-car business. Because of mutual agency, it is very important for an individual to choose business partners who have integrity and who share his or her business objectives.

BUSINESS BULLETIN: INTERNATIONAL PRACTICE

American businesses are expanding into emerging markets throughout the world. Many of these markets, such as Hungary, Poland, the Czech Republic, India, and China, are in the process of privatizing public entities. This means that operations such as steel mills, cement factories, and utilities that were previously run by the government are being converted into private enterprises. Many countries require that local investors own a substantial proportion of the newly formed businesses. One way of accomplishing this is to form joint ventures, which match a country's need for outside capital and operational know-how with investors' interest in business expansion and profitability. Joint ventures often take the form of partnerships among two or more corporations and other investors. For example, Caterpillar, the large U.S. heavy equipment producer, has formed a joint venture with Amo Zil, a Russian car producer, to produce fuel-injection systems for diesel motors. Under the joint venture, called Novodiesel, Caterpillar receives 51 percent ownership in return for its capital investment, and the local company retains 49 percent ownership.[2] Any income or losses from operations will be divided among the participants according to a predetermined agreement.

Unlimited Liability

Point to Emphasize: Unlimited liability means that potential responsibility for debts is not limited by one's investment, as it is in a corporation. Each person is personally liable for all debts of the partnership, including those arising from contingent liabilities such as lawsuits. Liability can be avoided only by filing for personal bankruptcy.

All partners have unlimited liability for their company's debt, which means that each partner is personally liable for all the debts of the partnership. If a partnership is in poor financial condition and cannot pay its debts, the creditors must first satisfy their claims from the assets of the partnership. If the assets are not enough to pay all debts, the creditors can seek payment from the personal assets of each partner. If one partner's personal assets are used up before the debts are paid, the creditors can claim additional assets from the remaining partners who are able to pay. Each partner, then, could be required by law to pay all the debts of the partnership.

Co-ownership of Partnership Property

When individuals invest property in a partnership, they give up the right to their separate use of the property. The property becomes an asset of the partnership and is owned jointly by all the partners.

Participation in Partnership Income

Each partner has the right to share in the company's income and the responsibility to share in its losses. The partnership agreement should state the method of distributing income and losses to each partner. If the agreement describes how income should be shared but does not mention losses, losses are distributed in the same way as income. If the partners fail to describe the method of income and loss distribution in the partnership agreement, the law states that income and losses must be shared equally.

Point to Emphasize: There is no federal income tax on partnerships. However, an informational return must be filed, and partners are taxed at their personal rates. There may be state or local business taxes assessed on a partnership, however. One example of this is the Michigan Single Business Tax.

Advantages and Disadvantages of Partnerships

Partnerships have both advantages and disadvantages. One advantage is that a partnership is easy to form, change, and dissolve. Also, a partnership facilitates the pooling of capital resources and individual talents; it has no corporate tax burden (because a partnership is not a legal entity for tax purposes, it does not have to pay a federal income tax, as do corporations, but must file an informational return); and it gives the partners a certain amount of freedom and flexibility.

On the other hand, there are the following disadvantages: the life of a partnership is limited; one partner can bind the partnership to a contract (mutual agency); the partners have unlimited personal liability; and it is more difficult for a partnership to raise large amounts of capital and to transfer ownership interests than it is for a corporation.

Critical Thinking Question: What makes limited partnerships attractive to investors? **Answer:** Limited risk and price per unit of ownership. If price per unit is low enough, demand for ownership units may increase.

DECISION POINT

ALLIANCE CAPITAL MANAGEMENT LIMITED PARTNERSHIP

An exception to the unlimited liability rule is the limited partnership. A limited partnership differs from a regular partnership in that limited partners do not have unlimited liability. Their possible losses are normally restricted to the amount of their investment. In exchange for limited liability, the limited partners give up control of the business to a general partner, someone who manages day-to-day operations and usually has unlimited liability. During the 1980s, limited partnerships were widely used to obtain financing for many projects, such as locating and drilling oil and gas wells, manufacturing airplanes, and developing real estate (including shopping centers, office buildings, and apartment complexes). Alliance Capital Management Corporation, an investment adviser, decided to raise additional capital by allowing the public to buy partnership shares in the company. It formed a limited partnership, with itself as the general partner[3]. Did Alliance make a good decision by choosing the limited partnership form of organization to meet its objective?

Although the limited partnership form of business reduces investors' possible losses, many investors lost their investments in the 1980s when tax laws changed and prices collapsed. However, investment company limited partnerships, including Alliance Capital Management Limited Partnership, were notable exceptions. In 1988, Alliance sold 7,475,000 units (a *unit* is a share of ownership in a partnership) to the public at $10 per unit. Alliance Capital Management Limited Partnership is now one of the largest investment advisers, offering investment management services to corporate clients and individual investors. The partnership now manages more than $70 billion in assets. The company's units sell on the New York Stock Exchange and can be purchased by any investor. In late 1997, the units were trading at about $39 each. In addition to seeing an increase in the value of their units, the limited partners received cash distributions of $2.96 per share, an annual return of about 8.4 percent.

Clarification Note: Limited partnerships, like corporations, confine the limited partner's loss to the amount of his or her investment. A partner's loss in an ordinary partnership is limited only by personal bankruptcy laws.

Enrichment Note: Several legal formats bridge the gap between general partnership and corporation; a limited partnership is just one of them. Each type of organization can have both legal and tax advantages.

Accounting for Partners' Equity

OBJECTIVE 2

Record partners' investments of cash and other assets when a partnership is formed

Related Text Assignments:
Q: 6
SE: 2
E: 1
P: 1, 5
SD: 3

Although accounting for a partnership is very similar to accounting for a sole proprietorship, there are differences. One is that the owner's equity in a partnership is called partners' equity. In accounting for partners' equity, it is necessary to maintain separate Capital and Withdrawals accounts for each partner and to divide the income and losses of the company among the partners. The differences in the Capital accounts of a sole proprietorship and a partnership are shown below.

SOLE PROPRIETORSHIP		PARTNERSHIP			
Blake, Capital		**Desmond, Capital**		**Frank, Capital**	
	50,000		30,000		40,000
Blake, Withdrawals		**Desmond, Withdrawals**		**Frank, Withdrawals**	
12,000		5,000		6,000	

In the partners' equity section of the balance sheet, the balance of each partner's Capital account is listed separately.

Liabilities and Partners' Equity

Total Liabilities		$28,000
Partners' Equity		
Desmond, Capital	$25,000	
Frank, Capital	34,000	
Total Partners' Equity		59,000
Total Liabilities and Partners' Equity		$87,000

Each partner invests cash or other assets or a combination of the two in the partnership according to the partnership agreement. Noncash assets should be valued at their fair market value on the date they are transferred to the partnership. The assets invested by a partner are debited to the proper account, and the total amount is credited to the partner's Capital account.

To show how partners' investments are recorded, let's assume that Jerry Adcock and Rose Villa have agreed to combine their capital and equipment in a partnership

BUSINESS BULLETIN: BUSINESS PRACTICE

Some highly visible businesses are organized as partnerships. For instance, the restaurant chain Planet Hollywood is a partnership. The chain, which operates flamboyant movie-theme restaurants, opened the first Planet Hollywood in New York in 1991 and followed with eleven others from Maui to Minneapolis. Two dozen more are planned from Tel Aviv to Paris. A majority of the company is owned by Chief Executive Officer Robert Earl, a veteran restaurant manager, and Keith Barish, whose films include *Sophie's Choice.* Other partners include such celebrities as Sylvester Stallone, Arnold Schwarzenegger, Bruce Willis, and Demi Moore. Because the success of the stars' investments is tied to the success of the partnership, they are motivated to make personal appearances on behalf of the restaurants. Mr. Stallone says, "I am very involved in this, more than my financial advisors would like."[4]

to operate a jewelry store. According to their partnership agreement, Adcock will invest $28,000 in cash and $37,000 worth of furniture and displays, and Villa will invest $40,000 in cash and $30,000 worth of equipment. Related to the equipment is a note payable for $10,000, which the partnership assumes. The journal entries to record the partners' initial investments are as follows:

	20x1			
A = L + OE + + +	July 1	Cash	28,000	
		Furniture and Displays	37,000	
		Jerry Adcock, Capital		65,000
		Initial investment of Jerry Adcock in Adcock and Villa		
A = L + OE + + + +	1	Cash	40,000	
		Equipment	30,000	
		Note Payable		10,000
		Rose Villa, Capital		60,000
		Initial investment of Rose Villa in Adcock and Villa		

Teaching Note: When accounts receivable are among the assets invested, they are recorded at the gross amounts. An allowance for uncollectible accounts is also recorded. The net result is the realizable value of the accounts receivable.

Point to Emphasize: Old book values from previous entities are irrelevant to the new entity.

Point to Emphasize: Villa's noncash contribution is equal to the fair market value of the equipment less the amount owed on the equipment.

The values assigned to the assets would be included in the partnership agreement. These values can differ from those carried on the partners' personal books. For example, the equipment that Rose Villa contributed had a value of only $22,000 on her books, but its market value had increased considerably after she purchased it. The book value of Villa's equipment is not important. The fair market value of the equipment at the time of transfer *is* important, however, because that value represents the amount of money Villa has invested in the partnership. Later investments are recorded the same way.

Distribution of Partnership Income and Losses

OBJECTIVE 3

Compute and record the income or losses that partners share, based on stated ratios, capital balance ratios, and partners' salaries and interest

Related Text Assignments:
Q: 7, 8, 9
SE: 3, 4, 5
E: 2, 3, 4
P: 1, 2, 5, 6
SD: 2
FRA: 1

Point to Emphasize: The division of income is one area in which a partnership differs from a corporation. In corporations each common share receives an equal dividend. Partners can use any method they agree on to divide partnership income.

Income and losses can be distributed according to whatever method the partners specify in the partnership agreement. To avoid later disputes, the agreement should be specific and clear. If a partnership agreement does not mention the distribution of income and losses, the law requires that they be shared equally by all partners. Also, if a partnership agreement mentions only the distribution of income, the law requires that losses be distributed in the same ratio as income.

The income of a partnership normally has three components: (1) return to the partners for the use of their capital (called *interest on partners' capital*), (2) compensation for direct services the partners have rendered (partners' salaries), and (3) other income for any special characteristics or risks individual partners may bring to the partnership. The breakdown of total income into its three components helps clarify how much each partner has contributed to the firm.

If all partners contribute equal capital, have similar talents, and spend the same amount of time in the business, then an equal distribution of income and losses would be fair. However, if one partner works full time in the firm and another devotes only a fourth of his or her time, then the distribution of income or losses should reflect the difference. (This concept would apply to any situation in which the partners contribute unequally to the business.)

Several ways for partners to share income are (1) by stated ratios, (2) by capital balance ratios, and (3) by salaries to the partners and interest on partners' capital, with the remaining income shared according to stated ratios. *Salaries* and *interest* here are not the same as *salaries expense* and *interest expense* in the ordinary sense

Point to Emphasize: The computations of each partner's share of net income are relevant to the closing entries in which the Income Summary account is closed to the partners' Capital accounts.

of the terms. They do not affect the amount of reported net income. Instead, they refer to ways of determining each partner's share of net income or loss on the basis of time spent and money invested in the partnership.

Stated Ratios

One method of distributing income and losses is to give each partner a stated ratio of the total income or loss. If each partner is making an equal contribution to the firm, each can assume the same share of income and losses. It is important to understand that an equal contribution to the firm does not necessarily mean an equal capital investment in the firm. One partner may devote more time and talent to the firm, whereas the second partner may make a larger capital investment. And, if the partners contribute unequally to the firm, unequal stated ratios—60 percent and 40 percent, perhaps—can be appropriate.

Common Student Confusion: Students often change the entry to close out Income Summary when the method of distributing partnership income changes. Regardless of how partnership income is divided, the accounts used in the entry to close out Income Summary never change. When there are losses to a partner or the partnership, the debits and credits switch, but the accounts are always the same.

Let's assume that Adcock and Villa had a net income last year of $30,000. Their partnership agreement states that the percentages of income and losses distributed to Jerry Adcock and Rose Villa should be 60 percent and 40 percent, respectively. The computation of each partner's share of the income and the journal entry to show the distribution are as follows:

Adcock ($30,000 × .60)	$18,000
Villa ($30,000 × .40)	12,000
Net Income	$30,000

A = L + OE	Date	Account	Debit	Credit
	20x2			
−	June 30	Income Summary	30,000	
+		Jerry Adcock, Capital		18,000
+		Rose Villa, Capital		12,000
		Distribution of income for the year to the partners' Capital accounts		

Capital Balance Ratios

If invested capital produces the most income for the partnership, then income and losses may be distributed according to capital balances. The ratio used to distribute income and losses here may be based on each partner's capital balance at the beginning of the year or on the average capital balance of each partner during the year. The partnership agreement must describe the method to be used.

Ratios Based on Beginning Capital Balances To show how the first method works, let's look at the beginning capital balances of the partners in Adcock and Villa. At the start of the fiscal year, July 1, 20x1, Jerry Adcock, Capital showed a $65,000 balance, and Rose Villa, Capital showed a $60,000 balance. (Actually, these balances reflect the partners' initial investment; the partnership was formed on July 1, 20x1.) The total partners' equity in the firm, then, was $125,000 ($65,000 + $60,000). Each partner's capital balance at the beginning of the year divided by the total partners' equity at the beginning of the year is that partner's beginning capital balance ratio.

	Beginning Capital Balance	Beginning Capital Balance Ratio
Jerry Adcock	$ 65,000	65,000 ÷ 125,000 = .52 = 52%
Rose Villa	60,000	60,000 ÷ 125,000 = .48 = 48%
	$125,000	

The income that each partner should receive when distribution is based on beginning capital balance ratios is determined by multiplying the total income by each partner's capital ratio. If we assume that income for the year was $140,000, Jerry Adcock's share of that income was $72,800, and Rose Villa's share was $67,200.

Jerry Adcock	$140,000 × .52 =	$ 72,800
Rose Villa	140,000 × .48 =	67,200
		$140,000

Ratios Based on Average Capital Balances If Adcock and Villa use beginning capital balance ratios to determine the distribution of income, they do not consider any investments or withdrawals made during the year. But investments and withdrawals usually change the partners' capital ratios. If the partners believe that their capital balances are going to change dramatically during the year, they can choose average capital balance ratios as a fairer means of distributing income and losses.

The following T accounts show the activity over the year in Adcock and Villa's partners' Capital and Withdrawals accounts.

Jerry Adcock, Capital

	7/1/x1	65,000

Jerry Adcock, Withdrawals

1/1/x2	10,000	

Rose Villa, Capital

	7/1/x1	60,000
	2/1/x2	8,000

Rose Villa, Withdrawals

11/1/x1	10,000	

Jerry Adcock withdrew $10,000 on January 1, 20x2, and Rose Villa withdrew $10,000 on November 1, 20x1, and invested an additional $8,000 of equipment on February 1, 20x2. Again, the income for the year's operation (July 1, 20x1, to June 30, 20x2) was $140,000. The calculations for the average capital balances and the distribution of income are as follows:

Average Capital Balances

Partner	Date	Capital Balance ×	Months Unchanged	=	Total		Average Capital Balance
Adcock	July–December	$65,000 ×	6	=	$390,000		
	January–June	55,000 ×	6	=	330,000		
			12		$720,000	÷ 12 =	$ 60,000
Villa	July–October	$60,000 ×	4	=	$240,000		
	November–January	50,000 ×	3	=	150,000		
	February–June	58,000 ×	5	=	290,000		
			12		$680,000	÷ 12 =	56,667
					Total average capital		$116,667

Average Capital Balance Ratios

$$\text{Adcock} = \frac{\text{Adcock's Average Capital Balance}}{\text{Total Average Capital}} = \frac{\$\ 60{,}000}{\$116{,}667} = .514 = 51.4\%$$

$$\text{Villa} = \frac{\text{Villa's Average Capital Balance}}{\text{Total Average Capital}} = \frac{\$\ 56{,}667}{\$116{,}667} = .486 = 48.6\%$$

Distribution of Income

Partner	Income	×	Ratio	=	Share of Income
Adcock	$140,000	×	.514	=	$ 71,960
Villa	$140,000	×	.486	=	68,040
				Total income	$140,000

Instructional Strategy: To check students' ability to apply LO 3, divide the class into small groups and ask each group to complete two items from P 1, part 2 (such as 2a and 2f). Vary the assignments, but try to assign each item to at least two groups. Allow time for completion. Then have a representative of each group present the answer to one item, using the chalkboard, overheads, or flip charts. If the presenter has difficulty, a member of the backup group may help.

Notice that to determine the distribution of income (or loss), you have to determine (1) the average capital balances, (2) the average capital balance ratios, and (3) each partner's share of income or loss. To compute each partner's average capital balance, you have to examine the changes that have taken place during the year in each partner's capital balance, changes that are the product of further investments and withdrawals. The partner's beginning capital is multiplied by the number of months the balance remains unchanged. After the balance changes, the new balance is multiplied by the number of months it remains unchanged. The process continues until the end of the year. The totals of these computations are added and then divided by 12 to determine the average capital balances. Once the average capital balances are determined, the method of figuring capital balance ratios for sharing income and losses is the same as that used for beginning capital balances.

Salaries, Interest, and Stated Ratios

Point to Emphasize: Partnership income or loss cannot be divided solely on the basis of salaries or interest. An additional component, such as stated ratios, is needed.

Teaching Note: Students often enter salaries and interest as expenses. Remind them that using salaries and interest to divide income or loss among partners has no effect on the income statement. Partners' salaries and interest are used only to allow the equitable division of the partnership's net income.

Reinforcement Exercise: What is the entry for Adcock and Villa on June 30 if net income is $14,000? **Answer:** $7,500 for Adcock and $6,500 for Villa. The salaries ($15,000 total) are distributed first, which leaves a $1,000 negative balance to be distributed equally.

Partners generally do not contribute equally to a firm. To make up for unequal contributions, a partnership agreement can allow for partners' salaries, interest on partners' capital balances, or a combination of both in the distribution of income. Again, salaries and interest of this kind are not deducted as expenses before the partnership income is determined. They represent a method of arriving at an equitable distribution of income or loss.

To illustrate an allowance for partners' salaries, we assume that Adcock and Villa have agreed that they will receive salaries—$8,000 for Adcock and $7,000 for Villa—and that any remaining income will be divided equally between them. Each salary is charged to the appropriate partner's Withdrawals account when paid. If we assume the same $140,000 income for the first year, the calculations for Adcock and Villa are as shown below.

	Income of Partner		Income Distributed
	Adcock	Villa	
Total Income for Distribution			$140,000
Distribution of Salaries			
Adcock	$ 8,000		
Villa		$ 7,000	(15,000)
Remaining Income After Salaries			$125,000
Equal Distribution of Remaining Income			
Adcock ($125,000 × .50)	62,500		
Villa ($125,000 × .50)		62,500	(125,000)
Remaining Income			—
Income of Partners	$70,500	$69,500	$140,000

Salaries allow for differences in the services that partners provide the business. However, they do not take into account differences in invested capital. To allow for capital differences, each partner can receive a stated interest on his or her invested capital in addition to salary. Suppose that Jerry Adcock and Rose Villa agree to pay annual salaries of $8,000 for Adcock and $7,000 for Villa, to receive 10 percent interest on their beginning capital balances, and to share any remaining income equally. If we assume income of $140,000, the calculations for Adcock and Villa are as follows:

	Income of Partner		
	Adcock	**Villa**	**Income Distributed**
Total Income for Distribution			$140,000
Distribution of Salaries			
Adcock	$ 8,000		
Villa		$ 7,000	(15,000)
Remaining Income After Salaries			$125,000
Distribution of Interest			
Adcock ($65,000 × .10)	6,500		
Villa ($60,000 × .10)		6,000	(12,500)
Remaining Income After Salaries and Interest			$112,500
Equal Distribution of Remaining Income			
Adcock ($112,500 × .50)	56,250		
Villa ($112,500 × .50)		56,250	(112,500)
Remaining Income			—
Income of Partners	$70,750	$69,250	$140,000

Clarification Note: If there is a negative balance after salaries or salaries and interest have been distributed, the terms *Remaining Income After Salaries* and *Remaining Income After Salaries and Interest* become *Negative Balance After Salaries* and *Negative Balance After Salaries and Interest.* The computation proceeds in exactly the same way, regardless of whether the balance is positive or negative.

Enrichment Note: When negotiating a partnership agreement, be sure to look at (and negotiate on) the impact of both profits (net income) and losses.

If the partnership agreement allows for the distribution of salaries or interest or both, the amounts must be allocated to the partners even if profits are not enough to cover the salaries and interest. In fact, even if the company has a loss, these allocations must still be made. The negative balance or loss after the allocation of salaries and interest must be distributed according to the stated ratio in the partnership agreement, or equally if the agreement does not mention a ratio.

For example, let's assume that Adcock and Villa agreed to the following conditions for the distribution of income and losses:

	Salaries	Interest	Beginning Capital Balance
Adcock	$70,000	10 percent of beginning	$65,000
Villa	60,000	capital balances	60,000

The income for the first year of operation was $140,000. At the top of the next page is the computation for the distribution of the income and loss.

On the income statement for the partnership, the distribution of income or losses is shown below the net income figure. Exhibit 1 shows how this is done.

	Income of Partner		Income Distributed
	Adcock	Villa	
Total Income for Distribution			$140,000
Distribution of Salaries			
Adcock	$70,000		
Villa		$60,000	(130,000)
Remaining Income After Salaries			$ 10,000
Distribution of Interest			
Adcock ($65,000 × .10)	6,500		
Villa ($60,000 × .10)		6,000	(12,500)
Negative Balance After Salaries and Interest			($ 2,500)
Equal Distribution of Negative Balance*			
Adcock ($2,500 × .50)	(1,250)		
Villa ($2,500 × .50)		(1,250)	2,500
Remaining Income			—
Income of Partners	$75,250	$64,750	$140,000

*Notice that the negative balance is distributed equally because the agreement does not indicate how income and losses should be distributed after salaries and interest are paid.

Exhibit 1. Partial Income Statement for Adcock and Villa

Adcock and Villa
Partial Income Statement
For the Year Ended June 30, 20x2

Net Income		$140,000
Distribution to the Partners		
Adcock		
Salary Distribution	$70,000	
Interest on Beginning Capital Balance	6,500	
Total	$76,500	
One-Half of Remaining Negative Amount	(1,250)	
Share of Net Income		$ 75,250
Villa		
Salary Distribution	$60,000	
Interest on Beginning Capital Balance	6,000	
Total	$66,000	
One-Half of Remaining Negative Amount	(1,250)	
Share of Net Income		$ 64,750
Net Income Distributed		$140,000

Dissolution of a Partnership

OBJECTIVE 4

Record a person's admission to a partnership

Related Text Assignments:
Q: 10, 11
SE: 6, 7, 8
E: 5
P: 3, 5, 7
SD: 5

Dissolution of a partnership occurs whenever there is a change in the original association of partners. When a partnership is dissolved, the partners lose their authority to continue the business as a going concern. This does not necessarily mean that the business operation is ended or interrupted, but it does mean—from a legal and an accounting standpoint—that the separate entity ceases to exist. The remaining partners can act for the partnership in finishing the affairs of the business or form a new partnership that will be a new accounting entity. The dissolution of a partnership takes place through the admission of a new partner, the withdrawal of a partner, or the death of a partner.

Business-World Example: Dissolution of a partnership is a legal issue. Consider Ernst & Young, which admits over one hundred partners each year. The entity continues to operate despite the legal changes it must make.

Point to Emphasize: Admission of a new partner never has an impact on net income. Regardless of the price a new partner pays, there are never any income statement accounts in the entry to admit a new partner.

Admission of a New Partner

The admission of a new partner dissolves the old partnership because a new association has been formed. Dissolving the old partnership and creating a new one require the consent of all the old partners and the ratification of a new partnership agreement. When a new partner is admitted, a new partnership agreement should be in place.

An individual can be admitted into a partnership in one of two ways: (1) by purchasing an interest in the partnership from one or more of the original partners or (2) by investing assets in the partnership.

Purchasing an Interest from a Partner When an individual is admitted to a firm by purchasing an interest from an old partner, each partner must agree to the change. The transaction is a personal one between the old and new partners, but the interest purchased must be transferred from the Capital account of the selling partner to the Capital account of the new partner.

Suppose that Jerry Adcock decides to sell his interest, assumed to be $70,000, in Adcock and Villa to Richard Davis for $100,000 on August 31, 20x3, and that Rose Villa agrees to the sale. The entry to record the sale on the partnership books looks like this:

A = L + OE
−
+

20x3			
Aug. 31	Jerry Adcock, Capital	70,000	
	Richard Davis, Capital		70,000
	Transfer of Jerry Adcock's equity to Richard Davis		

Point to Emphasize: When a partner sells his or her interest directly to a new partner, the partner, not the partnership, realizes the gain or loss. In this case, Adcock has a gain of $30,000, but the assets, liabilities, and total equity of the partnership do not change.

Notice that the entry records the book value of the equity, not the amount Davis pays. The amount Davis pays is a personal matter between him and Adcock. Because the amount paid does not affect the assets or liabilities of the firm, it is not entered in the records.

Here's another example of a purchase: Assume that Richard Davis purchases half of Jerry Adcock's $70,000 interest in the partnership and half of Rose Villa's interest, assumed to be $80,000, by paying a total of $100,000 to the two partners on August 31, 20x3. The entry to record this transaction on the partnership books would be as follows:

A = L + OE	20x3			
−	Aug. 31	Jerry Adcock, Capital	35,000	
−		Rose Villa, Capital	40,000	
+		Richard Davis, Capital		75,000
		Transfer of half of Jerry Adcock's and Rose Villa's equity to Richard Davis		

Investing Assets in a Partnership When a new partner is admitted through an investment in the partnership, both the assets and the partners' equity in the firm increase. The increase occurs because the assets the new partner invests become partnership assets, and as partnership assets increase, partners' equity increases as well. For example, assume that Jerry Adcock and Rose Villa have agreed to allow Richard Davis to invest $75,000 in return for a one-third interest in their partnership. The Capital accounts of Jerry Adcock and Rose Villa are assumed to be $70,000 and $80,000, respectively. Davis's $75,000 investment equals a one-third interest in the firm after the investment is added to the previously existing capital of the partnership.

Clarification Note: If the account did not reflect the current value of the assets, the asset accounts (and Capital accounts) would need to be adjusted before admitting the new partner.

Jerry Adcock, Capital	$ 70,000
Rose Villa, Capital	80,000
Davis's investment	75,000
Total capital after Davis's investment	$225,000
One-third interest = $225,000 ÷ 3 =	$ 75,000

The journal entry to record Davis's investment is as follows:

A = L + OE	20x3			
+ +	Aug. 31	Cash	75,000	
		Richard Davis, Capital		75,000
		Admission of Richard Davis to a one-third interest in the company		

Bonus to the Old Partners Sometimes a partnership may be so profitable or otherwise advantageous that a new investor is willing to pay more than the actual dollar interest he or she receives in the partnership. For instance, suppose an individual pays $100,000 for an $80,000 interest in a partnership. The $20,000 excess of the payment over the interest purchased is a bonus to the original partners. The bonus must be distributed to the original partners according to the partnership agreement. When the agreement does not cover the distribution of bonuses, a bonus should be distributed to the original partners in accordance with the method for distributing income and losses.

Point to Emphasize: The original partners receive a bonus because the entity is worth more as a going concern than the fair value of the net assets would otherwise indicate. That is, the new partner is paying for unrecorded partnership value.

Assume that Adcock and Villa has operated for several years and that the partners' capital balances and the stated ratios for distribution of income and loss are as follows:

Partners	Capital Balances	Stated Ratios
Adcock	$160,000	55%
Villa	140,000	45%
	$300,000	100%

Richard Davis wants to join the firm. He offers to invest $100,000 on December 1 in return for a one-fifth interest in the business and income. The original partners agree to the offer. The computation of the bonus to the original partners follows:

Partners' equity in the original partnership		$300,000
Cash investment by Richard Davis		100,000
Partners' equity in the new partnership		$400,000
Partners' equity assigned to Richard Davis ($400,000 × ⅕)		$ 80,000
Bonus to the original partners		
Investment by Richard Davis	$100,000	
Less equity assigned to Richard Davis	80,000	$ 20,000
Distribution of bonus to original partners		
Jerry Adcock ($20,000 × .55)	$ 11,000	
Rose Villa ($20,000 × .45)	9,000	$ 20,000

Reinforcement Exercise: What would the entry be if Davis pays $700,000 for a 40 percent ownership in the partnership?
Answer:

Cash	700,000	
Jerry Adcock, Capital		165,000
Rose Villa, Capital		135,000
Richard Davis, Capital		400,000

The journal entry that records Davis's admission to the partnership is shown below.

A = L + OE
\+   + + +

20x3			
Dec. 1	Cash	100,000	
	Jerry Adcock, Capital		11,000
	Rose Villa, Capital		9,000
	Richard Davis, Capital		80,000
	Investment by Richard Davis for a one-fifth interest in the firm, and the bonus paid to the original partners		

Bonus to the New Partner There are several reasons for a partnership to want a new partner. A firm in financial trouble might need additional cash. Or the original partners, wanting to expand the firm's markets, might need more capital than they themselves can provide. Also, the partners might know a person who would bring a unique talent to the firm. Under such conditions, a new partner could be admitted to the partnership with the understanding that part of the original partners' capital will be transferred (credited) to the new partner's Capital account as a bonus.

Enrichment Note: Human capital plays a large part in the profitability of entities traditionally organized as partnerships (for example, accounting firms, legal firms, and medical practices). When a new partner is admitted, this human capital is recognized in the Capital account of the new partner who receives a bonus.

For example, suppose that Jerry Adcock and Rose Villa have invited Richard Davis to join the firm. Davis is going to invest $60,000 on December 1 for a one-fourth interest in the company. The stated ratios for distribution of income or loss for Adcock and Villa are 55 percent and 45 percent, respectively. If Davis is to receive a one-fourth interest in the firm, the interest of the original partners represents a three-fourths interest in the business. The computation of Davis's bonus is as follows:

Total equity in partnership		
Jerry Adcock, Capital		$160,000
Rose Villa, Capital		140,000
Investment by Richard Davis		60,000
Partners' equity in the new partnership		$360,000
Partners' equity assigned to Richard Davis ($360,000 × ¼)		$ 90,000
Bonus to new partner		
Equity assigned to Richard Davis	$90,000	
Less cash investment by Richard Davis	60,000	$ 30,000
Distribution of bonus from original partners		
Jerry Adcock ($30,000 × .55)	$16,500	
Rose Villa ($30,000 × .45)	13,500	$ 30,000

The journal entry to record the admission of Davis to the partnership is shown below.

A = L + OE	20x3			
+ −	Dec. 1	Cash	60,000	
−		Jerry Adcock, Capital	16,500	
+		Rose Villa, Capital	13,500	
		Richard Davis, Capital		90,000
		To record the investment by Richard Davis of cash and a bonus from Adcock and Villa		

Withdrawal of a Partner

OBJECTIVE 5

Record a person's withdrawal from a partnership

Related Text Assignments:
SE: 6, 9
E: 6
P: 3, 7
SD: 3

Point to Emphasize: There is no impact on the income statement of a partnership when a partner withdraws. The only change is on the balance sheet.

Since a partnership is a voluntary association, a partner usually has the right to withdraw at any time. However, to avoid disputes when a partner does decide to withdraw or retire, a partnership agreement should describe the procedures to be followed. The agreement should specify (1) whether or not an audit will be performed, (2) how the assets will be reappraised, (3) how a bonus will be determined, and (4) by what method the withdrawing partner will be paid.

There are several ways in which an individual can withdraw from a partnership. A partner can (1) sell his or her interest to another partner with the consent of the remaining partners, (2) sell his or her interest to an outsider with the consent of the remaining partners, (3) withdraw assets equal to his or her capital balance, (4) withdraw assets that are less than his or her capital balance (in which case the remaining partners receive a bonus), or (5) withdraw assets that are greater than his or her capital balance (in which case the withdrawing partner receives a bonus). These alternatives are illustrated in Figure 1.

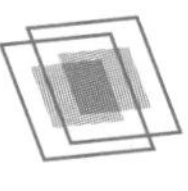

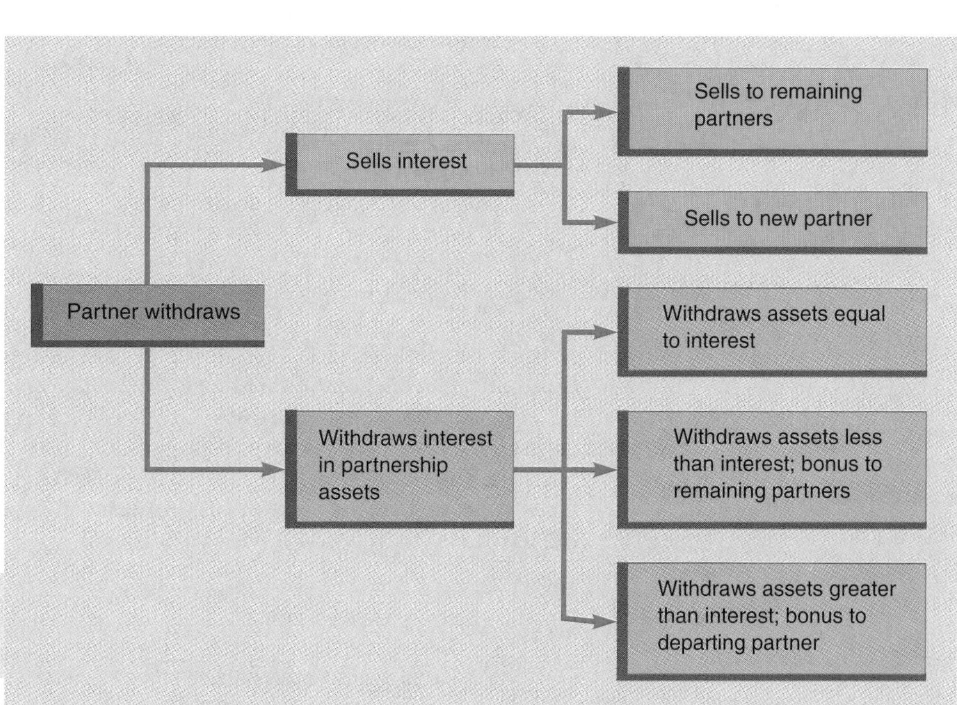

Figure 1
Alternative Ways for a Partner to Withdraw

BUSINESS BULLETIN: BUSINESS PRACTICE

The withdrawal of partners can cause a financial strain on a partnership. For instance, in 1994 Goldman, Sachs & Co., the last major Wall Street investment company still organized as a partnership, was scrambling to raise more than $250 million to compensate for the withdrawal of twenty-three partners. The retirements caused a decrease in equity capital of about $400 million, which represented almost 10 percent of the firm's capital. Goldman was looking for private investors to make up for the losses.[5] The majority of Wall Street investment companies, such as Merrill Lynch & Co., Inc., and Salomon Brothers Inc., are organized as corporations. An advantage of this form of organization is that managers who want to leave their jobs can sell their stock to other investors without affecting the firms' capital.

Withdrawal by Selling Interest When a partner sells his or her interest to another partner or to an outsider with the consent of the other partners, the transaction is personal; it does not change the partnership assets or the partners' equity. For example, let's assume that the capital balances of Adcock, Villa, and Davis are $140,000, $100,000, and $60,000, respectively, for a total of $300,000.

Point to Emphasize: Selling a partnership interest does not affect the assets and liabilities of the partnership. Therefore, total equity remains unchanged. The only effect of a partner's selling his or her interest to the existing partners or to a new partner is the change of names in the partners' equity section of the balance sheet.

Villa wants to withdraw from the partnership and is reviewing two offers for her interest. The offers are (1) to sell her interest to Davis for $110,000 or (2) to sell her interest to Judy Jones for $120,000. The remaining partners have agreed to either potential transaction. Because Davis and Jones would pay for Villa's interest from their personal assets, the partnership accounting records would show only the transfer of Villa's interest to Davis or Jones. The entries to record these possible transfers are as follows:

A = L + OE			
	1. If Villa's interest is purchased by Davis:		
− +	Rose Villa, Capital	100,000	
	Richard Davis, Capital		100,000
	Sale of Villa's partnership interest to Davis		

A = L + OE			
	2. If Villa's interest is purchased by Jones:		
− +	Rose Villa, Capital	100,000	
	Judy Jones, Capital		100,000
	Sale of Villa's partnership interest to Jones		

Withdrawal by Removing Assets A partnership agreement can allow a withdrawing partner to remove assets from the firm equal to his or her capital balance. Assume that Richard Davis decides to withdraw from Adcock, Villa, Davis & Company. Davis's capital balance is $60,000. The partnership agreement states that he can withdraw cash from the firm equal to his capital balance. If there is not enough cash, he must accept a promissory note from the new partnership for the balance. The remaining partners ask that Davis take only $50,000 in cash because of a cash shortage at the time of his withdrawal; he agrees to this request. The following journal entry records Davis's withdrawal:

A = L + OE				
− + −	20x3 Jan. 21	Richard Davis, Capital	60,000	
		Cash		50,000
		Notes Payable, Richard Davis		10,000
		Withdrawal of Richard Davis from the partnership		

When a withdrawing partner removes assets that represent less than his or her capital balance, the equity he or she leaves in the business is divided among the remaining partners according to their stated ratios. This distribution is considered a bonus to the remaining partners. When a withdrawing partner takes out assets greater than his or her capital balance, the excess is treated as a bonus to the withdrawing partner. The remaining partners absorb the bonus according to their stated ratios. Alternative arrangements can be spelled out in the partnership agreement.

Point to Emphasize: Even if a bonus was involved, Davis's Capital account would be debited for $60,000 to eliminate it.

Death of a Partner

When a partner dies, the partnership is dissolved because the original association has changed. The partnership agreement should state the actions to be taken. Normally, the books are closed and financial statements are prepared. Those actions are necessary to determine the capital balance of each partner on the date of the death. The agreement may also indicate whether an audit should be conducted, assets appraised, and a bonus recorded, as well as the procedures for settling with the heirs. The remaining partners may purchase the deceased's equity, sell it to outsiders, or deliver specified business assets to the estate. If the firm intends to continue, a new partnership must be formed.

Instructional Strategy: Divide the class into small groups and ask the groups to prepare one- to two-minute presentations of their solutions to SD 3. If effective presentation skills have been taught, have the class evaluate each presenter's skills. Award bonus class-participation points to presenters who are rated very good or excellent by the class.

Liquidation of a Partnership

OBJECTIVE 6

Compute the distribution of assets to partners when they liquidate their partnership

Related Text Assignments:
Q: 12, 13
SE: 10
E: 7, 8
P: 4, 5, 8

The liquidation of a partnership is the process of ending the business, of selling enough assets to pay the partnership's liabilities, and distributing any remaining assets among the partners. Liquidation is a special form of dissolution. When a partnership is liquidated, the business will not continue.

The partnership agreement should indicate the procedures to be followed in the case of liquidation. Usually, the books are adjusted and closed, with the income or loss distributed to the partners. As the assets of the business are sold, any gain or loss should be distributed to the partners according to the stated ratios. As cash becomes available, it must be applied first to outside creditors, then to partners' loans, and finally to the partners' capital balances.

BUSINESS BULLETIN: BUSINESS PRACTICE

Partners in professional accounting firms are often held in high esteem and envied for the high incomes that some of them make. Partners in large accounting firms can make over $200,000 per year, with top partners drawing over $700,000. However, consideration of those incomes should take into account the risks that partners take and the fact that the incomes of partners in small accounting firms are often much lower. Partners are not compensated in the same way as managers in corporations. Partners' income is not guaranteed, but rather is based on the performance of the partnership. Also, each partner is required to make a substantial investment of capital in the partnership. This capital remains at risk for as long as the partner chooses to stay in the partnership. For instance, in one notable instance, when many savings and loan institutions were failing, the partners in a major accounting firm lost their total investments as well as their income when their firm was subjected to lawsuits and other losses. The firm was eventually liquidated.

Teaching Note: Be sure to emphasize the liquidation procedure step by step. To liquidate a partnership, the partners first must sell the assets and pay the liabilities (or distribute them to the partners). Second, any gains or losses from the sales of assets must be allocated to the partners. Third, when only cash remains, it is paid to the partners. Fourth, when a partner has a negative capital balance, he or she is obligated to pay the deficiency. Otherwise, the remaining partners must absorb the deficiency.

The process of liquidation can have a variety of financial outcomes. We look at two: (1) assets sold for a gain and (2) assets sold for a loss. For both alternatives, we make the assumptions that the books have been closed for Adcock, Villa, Davis & Company and that the following balance sheet exists before liquidation.

Adcock, Villa, Davis & Company
Balance Sheet
February 2, 20x4

Assets		**Liabilities**	
Cash	$ 60,000	Accounts Payable	$120,000
Accounts Receivable	40,000	**Partners' Equity**	
Merchandise Inventory	100,000		
Plant Assets (net)	200,000	Adcock, Capital	85,000
Total Assets	$400,000	Villa, Capital	95,000
		Davis, Capital	100,000
		Total Liabilities and Partners' Equity	$400,000

The stated ratios of Adcock, Villa, and Davis are 3:3:4, or 30, 30, and 40 percent, respectively.

Gain on Sale of Assets

Suppose that the following transactions took place in the liquidation of Adcock, Villa, Davis & Company.

1. The accounts receivable were collected for $35,000.
2. The inventory was sold for $110,000.
3. The plant assets were sold for $200,000.
4. The accounts payable of $120,000 were paid.
5. The gain of $5,000 from the realization of the assets was distributed according to the partners' stated ratios.
6. The partners received cash equivalent to the balances of their Capital accounts.

These transactions are summarized in the statement of liquidation in Exhibit 2. The journal entries with their assumed transaction dates are as follows:

Terminology Note: Notice the proper use of the term *realization* in the February 13 and 14 entries. *Realization* means "conversion into cash."

					Explanation on Statement of Liquidation
20x4					
A = L + OE: + − ; −	Feb. 13	Cash	35,000		1
		Gain or Loss from Realization	5,000		
		Accounts Receivable		40,000	
		Collection of accounts receivable			
A = L + OE: + − ; +	14	Cash	110,000		2
		Merchandise Inventory		100,000	
		Gain or Loss from Realization		10,000	
		Sale of inventory			

Exhibit 2. Statement of Liquidation Showing Gain on Sale of Assets

Adcock, Villa, Davis & Company
Statement of Liquidation
February 2–20, 20x4

Explanation	Cash	Other Assets	Accounts Payable	Adcock, Capital (30%)	Villa, Capital (30%)	Davis, Capital (40%)	Gain (or Loss) from Realization
Balance 2/2/x4	$ 60,000	$340,000	$120,000	$85,000	$95,000	$100,000	
1. Collection of Accounts Receivable	35,000	(40,000)					($ 5,000)
	$ 95,000	$300,000	$120,000	$85,000	$95,000	$100,000	($ 5,000)
2. Sale of Inventory	110,000	(100,000)					10,000
	$205,000	$200,000	$120,000	$85,000	$95,000	$100,000	$ 5,000
3. Sale of Plant Assets	200,000	(200,000)					
	$405,000	—	$120,000	$85,000	$95,000	$100,000	$ 5,000
4. Payment of Liabilities	(120,000)		(120,000)				
	$285,000		—	$85,000	$95,000	$100,000	$ 5,000
5. Distribution of Gain (or Loss) from Realization				1,500	1,500	2,000	(5,000)
	$285,000			$86,500	$96,500	$102,000	—
6. Distribution to Partners	(285,000)			(86,500)	(96,500)	(102,000)	
	—			—	—	—	

	Date	Account	Debit	Credit	Explanation on Statement of Liquidation
	20x4				
A = L + OE + −	Feb. 16	Cash Plant Assets Sale of plant assets	200,000	 200,000	3
A = L + OE − −	16	Accounts Payable Cash Payment of accounts payable	120,000	 120,000	4
A = L + OE − + + +	20	Gain or Loss from Realization Jerry Adcock, Capital Rose Villa, Capital Richard Davis, Capital Distribution of the gain on assets ($10,000 gain minus $5,000 loss) to the partners	5,000	 1,500 1,500 2,000	5

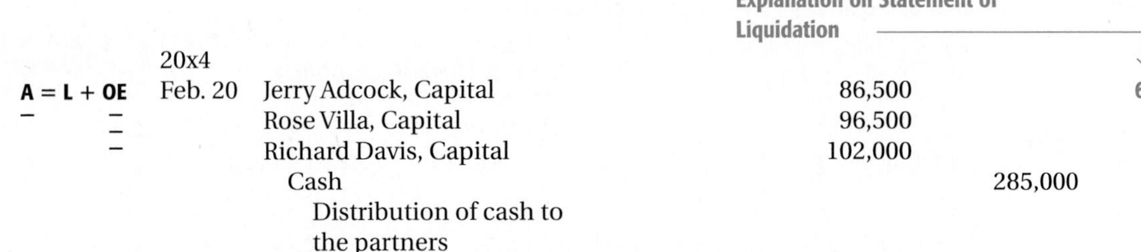

A = L + OE					Explanation on Statement of Liquidation
	20x4				
− −	Feb. 20	Jerry Adcock, Capital	86,500		6
−		Rose Villa, Capital	96,500		
−		Richard Davis, Capital	102,000		
		Cash		285,000	
		Distribution of cash to the partners			

Notice that the cash distributed to the partners is the balance in their respective Capital accounts. Cash is not distributed according to the partners' stated ratios.

Loss on Sale of Assets

We discuss two cases involving losses on the sale of a company's assets. In the first, the losses are small enough to be absorbed by the partners' capital balances. In the second, one partner's share of the losses is too large for his capital balance to absorb.

Point to Emphasize: The case here is almost the same as the previous one because losses are allocated on the same basis as gains. The only difference is that entry 3 in this case and entry 5 in the first case switch the debits and credits.

When a firm's assets are sold at a loss, the partners share the loss on liquidation according to their stated ratios. For example, assume that during the liquidation of Adcock, Villa, Davis & Company, the total cash received from the collection of accounts receivable and the sale of inventory and plant assets was $140,000. The statement of liquidation appears in Exhibit 3, and the journal entries for the liquidation are as follows:

Point to Emphasize: This example uses a compound entry for what was included in entries 1, 2, and 3 in the first example. If students have difficulty with the concept, here is an opportunity to break the entry down into its three component parts.

A = L + OE					Explanation on Statement of Liquidation
	20x4				
+ −	Feb. 15	Cash	140,000		1
−		Gain or Loss from Realization	200,000		
−		Accounts Receivable		40,000	
−		Merchandise Inventory		100,000	
		Plant Assets		200,000	
		Collection of accounts receivable and the sale of inventory and plant assets			
A = L + OE					
− −	16	Accounts Payable	120,000		2
		Cash		120,000	
		Payment of accounts payable			
A = L + OE					
−	20	Jerry Adcock, Capital	60,000		3
−		Rose Villa, Capital	60,000		
−		Richard Davis, Capital	80,000		
+		Gain or Loss from Realization		200,000	
		Distribution of the loss on assets to the partners			
A = L + OE					
− −	20	Jerry Adcock, Capital	25,000		4
−		Rose Villa, Capital	35,000		
−		Richard Davis, Capital	20,000		
		Cash		80,000	
		Distribution of cash to the partners			

Exhibit 3. Statement of Liquidation Showing Loss on Sale of Assets

Adcock, Villa, Davis & Company
Statement of Liquidation
February 2–20, 20x4

Explanation	Cash	Other Assets	Accounts Payable	Adcock, Capital (30%)	Villa, Capital (30%)	Davis, Capital (40%)	Gain (or Loss) from Realization
Balance 2/2/x4	$ 60,000	$340,000	$120,000	$85,000	$95,000	$100,000	
1. Collection of Accounts Receivable and Sale of Inventory and Plant Assets	140,000	(340,000)					($200,000)
	$200,000	—	$120,000	$85,000	$95,000	$100,000	($200,000)
2. Payment of Liabilities	(120,000)		(120,000)				
	$ 80,000		—	$85,000	$95,000	$100,000	($200,000)
3. Distribution of Gain (or Loss) from Realization				(60,000)	(60,000)	(80,000)	200,000
	$ 80,000			$25,000	$35,000	$ 20,000	—
4. Distribution to Partners	(80,000)			(25,000)	(35,000)	(20,000)	
	—			—	—	—	

In some liquidations, a partner's share of the loss is greater than his or her capital balance. In such a situation, because partners are subject to unlimited liability, the partner must make up the deficit in his or her Capital account from personal assets. For example, suppose that after the sale of assets and the payment of liabilities, the remaining assets and partners' equity of Adcock, Villa, Davis & Company look like this:

Assets		
Cash		$ 30,000
Partners' Equity		
Adcock, Capital	$25,000	
Villa, Capital	20,000	
Davis, Capital	(15,000)	$ 30,000

Richard Davis must pay $15,000 into the partnership from personal funds to cover his deficit. If he pays cash to the partnership, the following entry would record the cash contribution.

A = L + OE
+ +

20x4			
Feb. 20	Cash	15,000	
	Richard Davis, Capital		15,000
	Additional investment of Richard Davis to cover the negative balance in his Capital account		

Discussion Question: What is the balance in Richard Davis, Capital after the February 20 entry? **Answer:** Zero.

After Davis pays $15,000, there is enough cash to pay Adcock and Villa their capital balances and, thus, to complete the liquidation. The transaction is recorded like this:

A = L + OE
− −

20x4			
Feb. 20	Jerry Adcock, Capital	25,000	
	Rose Villa, Capital	20,000	
	Cash		45,000
	Distribution of cash to the partners		

Discussion Question: Under what condition might Adcock and Villa allow Davis not to pay? **Answer:** Legally, Adcock and Villa can force Davis into personal bankruptcy and see what could be recovered in court. They might not choose this course of action because the legal costs could outweigh the potential recovery.

If a partner does not have the cash to cover his or her obligations to the partnership, the remaining partners share the loss according to their established stated ratios. Remember that all partners have unlimited liability. As a result, if Richard Davis cannot pay the $15,000 deficit in his Capital account, Adcock and Villa must share the deficit according to their stated ratios. Each has a 30 percent stated ratio, so each must pay 50 percent of the losses that Davis cannot pay. The new stated ratios are computed this way:

	Old Ratios	**New Ratios**
Adcock	30%	30 ÷ 60 = .50 = 50%
Villa	30%	30 ÷ 60 = .50 = 50%
	60%	100%

And the journal entries to record the transactions are as follows:

A = L + OE
−
−
+

20x4			
Feb. 20	Jerry Adcock, Capital	7,500	
	Rose Villa, Capital	7,500	
	Richard Davis, Capital		15,000
	Transfer of Davis's deficit to Adcock and Villa		

A = L + OE
− −
−

20	Jerry Adcock, Capital	17,500	
	Rose Villa, Capital	12,500	
	Cash		30,000
	Distribution of cash to the partners		

Davis's inability to meet his obligations at the time of liquidation does not relieve him of his liabilities to Adcock and Villa. If he is able to pay his liabilities at some time in the future, Adcock and Villa can collect the amount of Davis's deficit that they absorbed.

Chapter Review

REVIEW OF LEARNING OBJECTIVES

1. **Identify the principal characteristics, advantages, and disadvantages of the partnership form of business.** A partnership has several major characteristics that distinguish it from the other forms of business. It is a voluntary association of two or more people who combine their talents and resources to carry on a business. Their joint effort should be supported by a partnership agreement that spells out the venture's operating procedures. A partnership is dissolved by a partner's admission, withdrawal, or death, and therefore has a limited life. Each partner acts as an agent of the partnership within the scope of normal operations and is personally liable for the partnership's debts. Property invested in the partnership becomes an asset of the partnership, owned jointly by all the partners. And, finally, each partner has the right to share in the company's income and the responsibility to share in its losses.

   The advantages of a partnership are the ease of its formation and dissolution, the opportunity to pool several individuals' talents and resources, the lack of corporate tax burden, and the freedom of action each partner enjoys. The disadvantages are the limited life of a partnership, mutual agency, the unlimited personal liability of the partners, and the difficulty of raising large amounts of capital and transferring partners' interest.
2. **Record partners' investments of cash and other assets when a partnership is formed.** A partnership is formed when the partners contribute cash, other assets, or a combination of both to the business. The details are stated in the partnership agreement. Initial investments are recorded with a debit to Cash or another asset account and a credit to the investing partner's Capital account. The recorded amount of the other assets should be their fair market value on the date of transfer to the partnership. In addition, a partnership can assume an investing partner's liabilities. When this occurs, the partner's Capital account is credited with the difference between the assets invested and the liabilities assumed.
3. **Compute and record the income or losses that partners share, based on stated ratios, capital balance ratios, and partners' salaries and interest.** The partners must share income and losses in accordance with the partnership agreement. If the agreement says nothing about the distribution of income and losses, the partners share them equally. Common methods used for distributing income and losses include stated ratios, capital balance ratios, and salaries and interest on capital investments. Each method tries to measure the individual partner's contribution to the operations of the business. Stated ratios usually are based on the partners' relative contributions to the partnership. When capital balance ratios are used, income or losses are divided strictly on the basis of each partner's capital balance. The use of salaries and interest on capital investment takes into account both efforts (salary) and capital investment (interest) in dividing income or losses among the partners.
4. **Record a person's admission to a partnership.** An individual is admitted to a partnership by purchasing a partner's interest or by contributing additional assets. When an interest is purchased, the withdrawing partner's capital is transferred to the new partner. When the new partner contributes assets to the partnership, it may be necessary to recognize a bonus shared or borne by the original partners or by the new partner.
5. **Record a person's withdrawal from a partnership.** A person can withdraw from a partnership by selling his or her interest in the business to the remaining partners or a new partner, or by withdrawing company assets. When assets are withdrawn, the amount can be equal to, less than, or greater than the partner's capital interest. When assets that have a value less than or greater than the partner's interest are withdrawn, a bonus is recognized and distributed among the remaining partners or to the departing partner.
6. **Compute the distribution of assets to partners when they liquidate their partnership.** The liquidation of a partnership entails selling the assets necessary to pay the company's liabilities and then distributing any remaining assets to the partners.

Any gain or loss on the sale of the assets is shared by the partners according to their stated ratios. When a partner has a deficit balance in a Capital account, that partner must contribute personal assets equal to the deficit. When a partner does not have personal assets to cover a capital deficit, the deficit must be absorbed by the solvent partners according to their stated ratios.

REVIEW OF CONCEPTS AND TERMINOLOGY

The following concepts and terms were introduced in this chapter:

LO 4 **Bonus:** An amount that accrues to the original partners when a new partner pays more to the partnership than the interest received or that accrues to the new partner when the amount paid to the partnership is less than the interest received.

LO 4 **Dissolution:** The loss of authority to continue a partnership as a separate entity due to a change in the original association of partners.

LO 1 **Limited life:** A characteristic of a partnership; the fact that any event that breaches the partnership agreement—including the admission, withdrawal, or death of a partner—terminates the partnership.

LO 1 **Limited partnership:** A form of partnership in which limited partners' liabilities are limited to their investment and general partners with unlimited liability operate the business.

LO 6 **Liquidation:** A special form of dissolution in which a business ends by selling assets, paying liabilities, and distributing any remaining assets to the partners.

LO 1 **Mutual agency:** A characteristic of a partnership; the authority of each partner to act as an agent of the partnership within the scope of the business's normal operations.

LO 2 **Partners' equity:** The owner's equity in a partnership.

LO 1 **Partnership:** An association of two or more people to carry on as co-owners of a business for profit.

LO 1 **Partnership agreement:** The contractual relationship between partners that identifies the details of their partnership.

LO 1 **Unlimited liability:** A characteristic of a partnership; the fact that each partner has personal liability for all the debts of the partnership.

REVIEW PROBLEM

Distribution of Income and Admission of a Partner

LO3
LO4
Jack Holder and Dan Williams reached an agreement in 20x7 to pool their resources and form a partnership to manufacture and sell university T-shirts. In forming the partnership, Holder and Williams contributed $100,000 and $150,000, respectively. They drafted a partnership agreement stating that Holder was to receive an annual salary of $6,000 and Williams was to receive 3 percent interest annually on his original investment of $150,000 in the business. Income and losses after salary and interest were to be shared by Holder and Williams in a 2:3 ratio.

REQUIRED

1. Compute the income or loss that Holder and Williams share, and prepare the required entries in journal form, assuming the partnership made $27,000 income in 20x7 and suffered a $2,000 loss in 20x8 (before salary and interest).
2. Assume that Jean Ratcliffe offers Holder and Williams $60,000 for a 15 percent interest in the partnership on January 1, 20x9. Holder and Williams agree to Ratcliffe's offer because they need her resources to expand the business. The capital balances of Holder and Williams are $113,600 and $161,400, respectively, on January 1, 20x9. Record the admission of Ratcliffe to the partnership, assuming that her investment represents a 15 percent interest in the total partners' capital and that a bonus will be distributed to Holder and Williams in the ratio of 2:3.

ANSWER TO REVIEW PROBLEM

1. Compute the income or loss distribution to the partners.

	Income of Partner		Income
	Holder	Williams	Distributed
20x7			
Total Income for Distribution			$27,000
Distribution of Salary			
Holder	$ 6,000		(6,000)
Remaining Income After Salary			$21,000
Distribution of Interest			
Williams ($150,000 × .03)		$ 4,500	(4,500)
Remaining Income After Salary and Interest			$16,500
Distribution of Remaining Income			
Holder ($16,500 × ⅖)	6,600		
Williams ($16,500 × ⅗)		9,900	(16,500)
Remaining Income			—
Income of Partners	$12,600	$14,400	$27,000
20x8			
Total Loss for Distribution			($ 2,000)
Distribution of Salary			
Holder	$ 6,000		(6,000)
Negative Balance After Salary			($ 8,000)
Distribution of Interest			
Williams ($150,000 × .03)		$ 4,500	(4,500)
Negative Balance After Salary and Interest			($12,500)
Distribution of Negative Balance			
Holder ($12,500 × ⅖)	(5,000)		
Williams ($12,500 × ⅗)		(7,500)	12,500
Remaining Loss			—
Income and Loss of Partners	$ 1,000	($ 3,000)	($ 2,000)

Entry in Journal Form—20x7

Income Summary	27,000	
Jack Holder, Capital		12,600
Dan Williams, Capital		14,400
Distribution of income for the year to the partners' Capital accounts		

Entry in Journal Form—20x8

Dan Williams, Capital	3,000	
Income Summary		2,000
Jack Holder, Capital		1,000
Distribution of the loss for the year to the partners' Capital accounts		

2. Record the admission of a new partner.

Capital Balance and Bonus Computation

Ratcliffe, Capital = (Original Partners' Capital + New Partner's Investment) × 15%
= ($113,600 + $161,400 + $60,000) × .15 = $50,250
Bonus = New Partner's Investment − Ratcliffe, Capital
= $60,000 − $50,250
= $9,750

Distribution of Bonus

Holder = $9,750 × ⅖ =	$3,900
Williams = $9,750 × ⅗ =	5,850
Total bonus	$9,750

Entry in Journal Form

20x9			
Jan. 1	Cash	60,000	
	Jack Holder, Capital		3,900
	Dan Williams, Capital		5,850
	Jean Ratcliffe, Capital		50,250
	Sale of a 15 percent interest in the partnership to Jean Ratcliffe and the bonus paid to the original partners		

Chapter Assignments

BUILDING YOUR KNOWLEDGE FOUNDATION

Questions

1. Briefly define *partnership* and list several important characteristics of the partnership form of business.
2. Leon and Jon are partners in a drilling operation. Leon purchased a drilling rig to be used in the partnership's operations. Is Leon's purchase binding on Jon even though Jon was not involved in it? Explain your answer.
3. What is the meaning of unlimited liability when applied to a partnership? Describe a form of partnership that limits investors' liability.
4. The partnership agreement for Anne and Jin-Li does not disclose how they will share income and losses. How would the income and losses be shared in this partnership?
5. What are several key advantages of a partnership? What are some disadvantages?
6. Charles contributes $10,000 in cash and a building with a book value of $40,000 and fair market value of $50,000 to the Charles and Dean partnership. What is the balance of Charles's Capital account in the partnership?
7. Oscar Perez and Leah Torn are forming a partnership. What are some factors they should consider in deciding how income is to be divided?
8. Sue and Ari share income and losses in their partnership in a 3:2 ratio. The firm's net income for the current year is $80,000. How would the distribution of income be recorded in the journal?
9. Kathy and Roger share income in their partnership in a 2:4 ratio. Kathy and Roger receive salaries of $6,000 and $10,000, respectively. How would they share a net income of $22,000 before salaries?
10. Carol purchases Mary's interest in the Mary and Leo partnership for $62,000. Mary has a $57,000 capital interest in the partnership. How would this transaction be recorded in the partnership books?

11. Dan and Augie each own a $50,000 interest in a partnership. They agree to admit Bea as a partner by selling her a one-third interest for $80,000. How large a bonus will be distributed to Dan and Augie?
12. Describe how the dissolution of a partnership differs from the liquidation of a partnership.
13. In the liquidation of a partnership, José's Capital account showed a $5,000 debit balance after all the creditors had been paid. What obligation does José have to the partnership?

Short Exercises

LO 1 *Partnership Characteristics*

SE 1. Indicate whether each statement below is a reflection of (a) voluntary association, (b) a partnership agreement, (c) limited life, (d) mutual agency, or (e) unlimited liability.

1. A partner may be required to pay the debts of the partnership out of personal assets.
2. A partnership must be dissolved when a partner is admitted, withdraws, retires, or dies.
3. Any partner can bind the partnership to a business agreement.
4. A partner does not have to remain a partner if he or she does not want to.
5. Details of the arrangements among partners are specified in a written contract.

LO 2 *Partnership Formation*

SE 2. Bob contributes cash of $12,000 and Kim contributes office equipment that cost $10,000 but is valued at $8,000 to the formation of a new partnership. Prepare the entry in journal form to form the partnership.

LO 3 *Distribution of Partnership Income*

SE 3. During the first year, the Bob and Kim partnership (see **SE 2**) earned an income of $5,000. Assume the partners agreed to share income and losses in the ratio of the beginning balances of their capital accounts. How much income should be transferred to each Capital account?

LO 3 *Distribution of Partnership Income*

SE 4. During the first year, the Bob and Kim partnership (see **SE 2**) earned an income of $5,000. Assume the partners agreed to share income and losses by figuring interest on the beginning capital balances at 10 percent and dividing the remainder equally. How much income should be transferred to each Capital account?

LO 3 *Distribution of Partnership Income*

SE 5. During the first year, the Bob and Kim partnership (see **SE 2**) earned an income of $5,000. Assume the partners agreed to share income and losses by figuring interest on the beginning capital balances at 10 percent, allowing a salary of $6,000 to Bob, and dividing the remainder equally. How much income (or loss) should be transferred to each Capital account?

LO 4
LO 5 *Withdrawal of a Partner and Admission of a Partner*

SE 6. After a year of operating as partners, the Capital accounts of Bob and Kim are $15,000 and $10,000, respectively. Kim withdraws from the partnership by selling her interest in the business to Sonia for $8,000. What will be the Capital account balances of the partners in the new Bob and Sonia partnership? Prepare the journal entry to record the transfer of ownership on the partnership books.

LO 4 *Admission of a New Partner*

SE 7. After a year of operating as partners, the Capital accounts of Bob and Kim are $15,000 and $10,000, respectively. Sonia buys a one-sixth interest in the partnership by investing cash of $11,000. What will be the Capital account balances of the partners in the new Bob, Kim, and Sonia partnership, assuming a bonus to the old partners, who share income and losses equally? Prepare the entry in journal form to record the transfer of ownership on the partnership books.

LO 4 *Admission of a New Partner*

SE 8. After a year of operating as partners, the Capital accounts of Bob and Kim are $15,000 and $10,000, respectively. Sonia buys a one-fourth interest in the partnership by investing cash of $5,000. What will be the Capital account balances of the partners in the new Bob, Kim, and Sonia partnership, assuming that the new partner receives a bonus and that Bob and Kim share income and losses equally? Prepare the entry in journal form to record the transfer of ownership on the partnership books.

SE 9. LO 5 *Withdrawal of a Partner*

After several years of operating as partners, the Capital accounts of Bob, Kim, and Sonia are $25,000, $16,000, and $9,000, respectively. Sonia decides to leave the partnership and is allowed to withdraw $9,000 in cash. Prepare the entry in journal form to record the withdrawal on the partnership books.

SE 10. LO 6 *Liquidation of a Partnership*

After a year of operating as partners, the Capital accounts of Bob and Kim are $15,000 and $10,000, respectively. The firm has cash of $12,000 and office equipment of $13,000. The partners decide to liquidate the partnership. The office equipment is sold for only $4,000. Assuming the partners share income and losses in the ratio of one-third to Bob and two-thirds to Kim, how much cash will be distributed to each partner in liquidation?

Exercises

E 1. LO 2 *Partnership Formation*

Martin Brill and Ruben Olivo are watch repairmen who want to form a partnership and open a jewelry store. They have an attorney prepare their partnership agreement, which indicates that assets invested in the partnership will be recorded at their fair market value and that liabilities will be assumed at book value. The assets contributed by each partner and the liabilities assumed by the partnership are as follows:

Assets	**Martin Brill**	**Ruben Olivo**	**Total**
Cash	$40,000	$30,000	$70,000
Accounts Receivable	52,000	20,000	72,000
Allowance for Uncollectible Accounts	4,000	3,000	7,000
Supplies	1,000	500	1,500
Equipment	20,000	10,000	30,000
Liabilities			
Accounts Payable	$32,000	$ 9,000	$41,000

Prepare the entry in journal form necessary to record the original investments of Brill and Olivo in the partnership.

E 2. LO 3 *Distribution of Income*

Walker Parks and Lonnie Tucker agreed to form a partnership. Parks contributed $200,000 in cash, and Tucker contributed assets with a fair market value of $400,000. The partnership, in its initial year, reported net income of $120,000. Calculate the distribution of the first year's income to the partners under each of the following conditions:

1. Parks and Tucker failed to include stated ratios in the partnership agreement.
2. Parks and Tucker agreed to share income and losses in a 3:2 ratio.
3. Parks and Tucker agreed to share income and losses in the ratio of their original investments.
4. Parks and Tucker agreed to share income and losses by allowing 10 percent interest on original investments and sharing any remainder equally.

E 3. LO 3 *Distribution of Income or Losses: Salary and Interest*

Assume that the partnership agreement of Parks and Tucker in **E 2** states that Parks and Tucker are to receive salaries of $20,000 and $24,000, respectively; that Parks is to receive 6 percent interest on his capital balance at the beginning of the year; and that the remainder of income and losses are to be shared equally. Calculate the distribution of the income or losses under the following conditions:

1. Income totaled $120,000 before deductions for salaries and interest.
2. Income totaled $48,000 before deductions for salaries and interest.
3. There was a loss of $2,000.
4. There was a loss of $40,000.

E 4. LO 3 *Distribution of Income: Average Capital Balance*

Fran and Laura operate a furniture rental business. Their capital balances on January 1, 20x7, were $160,000 and $240,000, respectively. Fran withdrew cash of $32,000 from the business on April 1, 20x7. Laura withdrew $60,000 cash on October 1, 20x7. Fran and Laura distribute partnership income based on their average capital balances each year. Income for 20x7 was $160,000. Compute the income to be distributed to Fran and Laura using their average capital balances in 20x7.

E 5. LO 4 *Admission of a New Partner: Recording a Bonus*

Jorge, Ramon, and Hubert have equity in a partnership of $40,000, $40,000, and $60,000, respectively, and they share income and losses in a ratio of 1:1:3. The partners have agreed to admit Jesse to the partnership. Prepare entries in journal form to record the admission of Jesse to the partnership under the following conditions:

1. Jesse invests $60,000 for a 20 percent interest in the partnership, and a bonus is recorded for the original partners.
2. Jesse invests $60,000 for a 40 percent interest in the partnership, and a bonus is recorded for Jesse.

E 6. LO 5 *Withdrawal of a Partner*

Ronald, Ted, and Steve are partners. They share income and losses in the ratio of 3:2:1. Steve's Capital account has a $120,000 balance. Ronald and Ted have agreed to let Steve take $160,000 of the company's cash when he retires from the business. What entry in journal form must be made on the partnership's books when Steve retires, assuming that a bonus to Steve is recognized and absorbed by the remaining partners?

E 7. LO 6 *Partnership Liquidation*

Assume the following assets, liabilities, and partners' equity in the Nguyen and Carlson partnership on December 31, 20xx:

Assets	=	**Liabilities**	+	**Nguyen, Capital**	+	**Carlson, Capital**
$160,000	=	$10,000	+	$90,000	+	$60,000

The partnership has no cash. When the partners agree to liquidate the business, the assets are sold for $120,000 and the liabilities are paid. Nguyen and Carlson share income and losses in a ratio of 3:1.

1. Prepare a statement of liquidation.
2. Prepare entries in journal form for the sale of assets, payment of liabilities, distribution of loss from realization, and final distribution of cash to Nguyen and Carlson.

E 8. LO 6 *Partnership Liquidation*

Harriet, Chris, and Sue are partners in a tanning salon. The assets, liabilities, and capital balances as of July 1, 20x7, are as follows:

Assets	$480,000
Liabilities	160,000
Harriet, Capital	140,000
Chris, Capital	40,000
Sue, Capital	140,000

Because competition is strong, business is declining, and the partnership has no cash, the partners have decided to sell the business. Harriet, Chris, and Sue share income and losses in a ratio of 3:1:1, respectively. The assets were sold for $260,000, and the liabilities were paid. Chris has no other assets and will not be able to cover any deficits in her Capital account. How will the ending cash balance be distributed to the partners?

Problems

P 1. LO 2 LO 3 *Partnership Formation and Distribution of Income*

In January 20x1, Tom Himes and Jeff Palmer agreed to produce and sell chocolate candies. Tom contributed $240,000 in cash to the business. Jeff contributed the building and equipment, valued at $220,000 and $140,000, respectively. The partnership had an income of $84,000 during 20x1 but was less successful during 20x2, when income was only $40,000.

REQUIRED

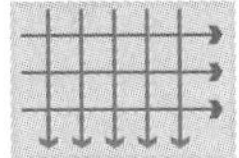

1. Prepare the entry in journal form to record the investment of both partners in the partnership.
2. Determine the share of income for each partner in 20x1 and 20x2 under each of the following conditions: (a) The partners agreed to share income equally. (b) The partners failed to agree on an income-sharing arrangement. (c) The partners agreed to share income according to the ratio of their original investments. (d) The partners agreed to share income by allowing interest of 10 percent on their original investments and dividing the remainder equally. (e) The partners agreed to share income by allowing salaries of $40,000 for Himes and $28,000 for Palmer, and dividing the remainder equally. (f) The partners agreed to share income by paying salaries of $40,000 to Himes and $28,000 to Palmer, allowing interest of 9 percent on their original investments, and dividing the remainder equally.

P 2. LO 3 *Distribution of Income: Salary and Interest*

Ruth and Perry are partners in a tennis shop. They have agreed that Ruth will operate the store and receive a salary of $104,000 per year. Perry will receive 10 percent interest on his average capital balance during the year of $500,000. The remaining income or losses are to be shared by Ruth and Perry in a 2:3 ratio.

REQUIRED

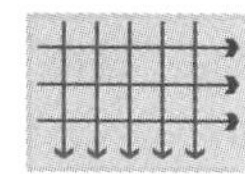

Determine each partner's share of income and losses under each of the following conditions. In each case, the income or loss is stated before the distribution of salary and interest.

1. Income was $168,000.
2. Income was $88,000.
3. The loss was $25,600.

P 3. LO 4 LO 5 *Admission and Withdrawal of a Partner*

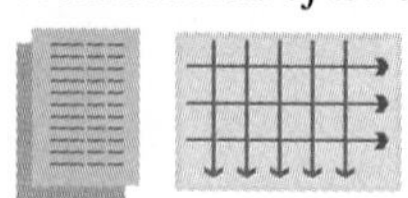

Pat, Connie, and Janice are partners in Manitow Woodwork Company. Their capital balances as of July 31, 20x4, are as follows:

Pat, Capital		Connie, Capital		Janice, Capital	
	45,000		15,000		30,000

Each partner has agreed to admit Felicia to the partnership.

REQUIRED

Prepare entries in journal form to record Felicia's admission to or Pat's withdrawal from the partnership under each of the following independent conditions: (a) Felicia pays Pat $12,500 for 20 percent of Pat's interest in the partnership. (b) Felicia invests $20,000 cash in the partnership and receives an interest equal to her investment. (c) Felicia invests $30,000 cash in the partnership for a 20 percent interest in the business. A bonus is to be recorded for the original partners on the basis of their capital balances on July 31, 20x4. (d) Felicia invests $30,000 cash in the partnership for a 40 percent interest in the business. The original partners give Felicia a bonus according to the ratio of their capital balances on July 31, 20x4. (e) Pat withdraws from the partnership, taking $52,500. The excess of assets over the partnership interest is distributed according to the balances of the Capital accounts. (f) Pat withdraws by selling her interest directly to Felicia for $60,000.

P 4. LO 6 *Partnership Liquidation*

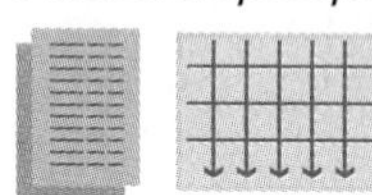

Conroy, Esposito, and Wetzel are partners in a retail lighting store. They share income and losses in the ratio of 2:2:1, respectively. The partners have agreed to liquidate the partnership. Here is the partnership balance sheet before the liquidation:

Conroy, Esposito, and Wetzel Partnership
Balance Sheet
August 31, 20x7

Assets		Liabilities	
Cash	$ 280,000	Accounts Payable	$ 360,000
Other Assets	880,000	**Partners' Equity**	
Total Assets	$1,160,000		
		Conroy, Capital	400,000
		Esposito, Capital	240,000
		Wetzel, Capital	160,000
		Total Liabilities and Partners' Equity	$1,160,000

The other assets were sold on September 1, 20x7, for $720,000. Accounts payable were paid on September 4, 20x7. The remaining cash was distributed to the partners on September 11, 20x7.

REQUIRED

1. Prepare a statement of liquidation.
2. Prepare the following entries in journal form: (a) the sale of the other assets, (b) payment of the accounts payable, (c) the distribution of the partners' gain or loss on liquidation, and (d) the distribution to the partners of the remaining cash.

P 5. LO 2, LO 3, LO 4, LO 6 *Comprehensive Partnership Transactions*

The following events pertain to a partnership formed by Ray Facchini and Bob Locasio to operate a floor-cleaning company:

20x1

Feb. 14 The partnership was formed. Facchini transferred to the partnership $80,000 cash, land worth $80,000, a building worth $480,000, and a mortgage on the building of $240,000. Locasio transferred to the partnership $40,000 cash and equipment worth $160,000.

Dec. 31 During 20x1, the partnership earned income of just $84,000. The partnership agreement specifies that income and losses are to be divided by paying salaries of $40,000 to Facchini and $60,000 to Locasio, allowing 8 percent interest on beginning capital investments, and dividing any remainder equally.

20x2

Jan. 1 To improve the prospects for the company, the partners decided to take in a new partner, Gary Levenfeld, who had experience in the floor-cleaning business. Levenfeld invested $156,000 for a 25 percent interest in the business. A bonus was transferred in equal amounts from the original partners' Capital accounts to Levenfeld's Capital account.

Dec. 31 During 20x2, the company earned income of $87,200. The new partnership agreement specified that income and losses would be divided by paying salaries of $60,000 to Locasio and $80,000 to Levenfeld (no salary to Facchini), allowing 8 percent interest on beginning capital balances after Levenfeld's admission, and dividing the remainder equally.

20x3

Jan. 1 Because it appeared that the business could not support the three partners, the partners decided to liquidate the partnership. The asset and liability accounts of the partnership were as follows: Cash, $407,200; Accounts Receivable, $68,000; Land, $80,000; Building (net), $448,000; Equipment (net), $236,000; Accounts Payable, $88,000; and Mortgage Payable, $224,000. The equipment was sold for $200,000. The accounts payable were paid. The loss was distributed equally to the partners' Capital accounts. A statement of liquidation was prepared, and the remaining assets and liabilities were distributed. Facchini agreed to accept cash plus the land and building at book value and the mortgage payable as payment for his share. Locasio accepted cash and the accounts receivable for his share. Levenfeld was paid in cash.

REQUIRED

Prepare entries in journal form to record all of the facts above. Support your computations with schedules, and prepare a statement of liquidation in connection with the January 1, 20x3, entries.

Alternate Problems

P 6. LO 3 *Distribution of Income: Salaries and Interest*

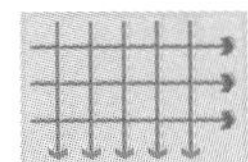

Norman, Philip, and Daniel are partners in the South Central Company. The partnership agreement states that Norman is to receive 8 percent interest on his capital balance at the beginning of the year, Philip is to receive a salary of $100,000 a year, and Daniel will be paid interest of 6 percent on his average capital balance during the year. Norman, Philip, and Daniel will share any income or loss after salary and interest in a 5:3:2 ratio. Norman's capital balance at the beginning of the year was $600,000, and Daniel's average capital balance for the year was $720,000.

REQUIRED

Determine each partner's share of income and losses under each of the following conditions. In each case, the income or loss is stated before the distribution of salary and interest.

1. Income was $545,200.
2. Income was $155,600.
3. The loss was $56,800.

P 7. LO 4 LO 5 *Admission and Withdrawal of a Partner*

Max, Luisa, and Vida are partners in the Image Gallery. The balances in the Capital accounts of Max, Luisa, and Vida as of November 30, 20xx, are $50,000, $60,000, and $90,000, respectively. The partners share income and losses in a ratio of 2:3:5.

REQUIRED

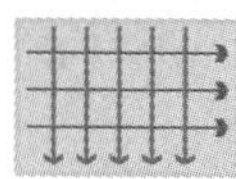

Prepare journal entries for each of the following independent conditions: (a) Ben pays Vida $100,000 for four-fifths of Vida's interest. (b) Ben is to be admitted to the partnership with a one-third interest for a $100,000 cash investment. (c) Ben is to be admitted to the partnership with a one-third interest for a $160,000 cash investment. A bonus, based on the partners' ratio for income and losses, is to be distributed to the original partners when Ben is admitted. (d) Ben is to be admitted to the partnership with a one-third interest for an $82,000 cash investment. A bonus is to be given to Ben on admission. (e) Max withdraws from the partnership, taking $66,000 in cash. (f) Max withdraws from the partnership by selling his interest directly to Ben for $70,000.

P 8. LO 6 *Partnership Liquidation*

The balance sheet of the Tulip Partnership as of July 31, 20xx, follows.

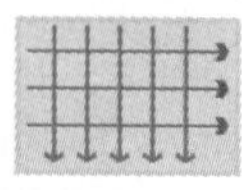

Tulip Partnership
Balance Sheet
July 31, 20xx

Assets		**Liabilities**	
Cash	$ 6,000	Accounts Payable	$480,000
Accounts Receivable	120,000	**Partners' Equity**	
Inventory	264,000		
Equipment (net)	462,000	Tuni, Capital	72,000
Total Assets	$852,000	Li, Capital	180,000
		Ippo, Capital	120,000
		Total Liabilities and Partners' Equity	$852,000

Tuni, Li, and Ippo share income and losses in the ratio of 5:3:2. Because of a mutual disagreement, the partners have decided to liquidate the business.

Assume that Tuni cannot contribute any additional personal assets to the company during liquidation and that the following transactions occurred during liquidation: (a) Accounts receivable were sold for 60 percent of their book value. (b) Inventory was sold for $276,000. (c) Equipment was sold for $300,000. (d) Accounts payable were paid in full. (e) Gain or loss from realization was distributed to the partners' Capital accounts. (f) Tuni's deficit was transferred to the remaining partners in their new income and loss ratio. (g) The remaining cash was distributed to Li and Ippo.

REQUIRED

1. Prepare a statement of liquidation.
2. Prepare entries in journal form to liquidate the partnership and distribute any remaining cash.

Skills Development

CONCEPTUAL ANALYSIS

SD 1.
LO 1 *Partnership Agreement*

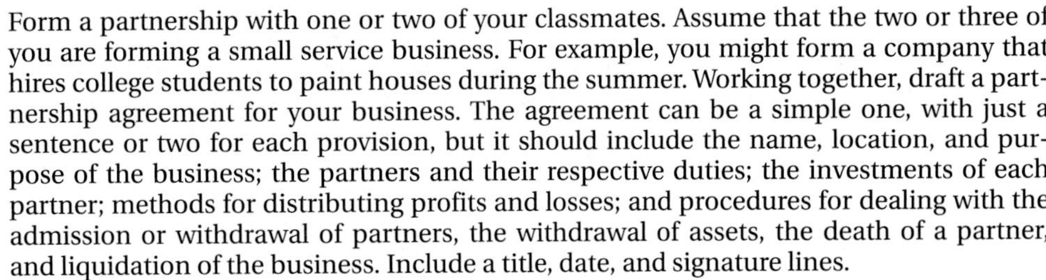

Form a partnership with one or two of your classmates. Assume that the two or three of you are forming a small service business. For example, you might form a company that hires college students to paint houses during the summer. Working together, draft a partnership agreement for your business. The agreement can be a simple one, with just a sentence or two for each provision, but it should include the name, location, and purpose of the business; the partners and their respective duties; the investments of each partner; methods for distributing profits and losses; and procedures for dealing with the admission or withdrawal of partners, the withdrawal of assets, the death of a partner, and liquidation of the business. Include a title, date, and signature lines.

Group Activity: Assign groups to prepare partnership agreements.

SD 2.
LO 3 *Distribution of Partnership Income and Losses*

List, Donohue, and Han, who are forming a partnership to operate an antiques gallery, are discussing how income and losses should be distributed. Among the facts they are considering are the following:

a. List will contribute cash for operations of $100,000, Donohue will contribute a collection of antiques valued at $300,000, and Han will not contribute any assets.
b. List and Han will handle day-to-day business operations. Han will work full time, and List will devote about half-time to the partnership. Donohue will not devote time to day-to-day operations. A full-time clerk in a retail store would make about $20,000 in a year, and a full-time manager would receive about $30,000.
c. The current interest rate on long-term bonds is 8 percent.

You have just been hired as the partnership's accountant. Write a memorandum describing an equitable plan for distributing income and losses. State your reasons why this plan is equitable. According to your plan, which partner will gain the most if the partnership is very profitable, and which will lose the most if the partnership has large losses?

ETHICAL DILEMMA

SD 3.
LO 1
LO 2
LO 5 *Death of Partner*

South Shore Realty was started twenty years ago when J. B. Taylor, C. L. Sklar, and L. A. Hodges established a partnership to sell real estate near Galveston, Texas. The partnership has been extremely successful. In 20xx, Taylor, the senior partner, who in recent years had not been very active in the partnership, died. Unfortunately, the partnership agreement is vague about how the partnership interest of a partner who dies should be valued. It simply states that "the estate of a deceased partner shall receive compensation for his or her interest in the partnership in a reasonable time after death." The attorney for Taylor's family believes that the estate should receive one-third of the assets of the partnership based on the fair market value of the net assets (total assets less total liabilities). The total assets of the partnership are $10 million in the accounting records, but the assets are worth at least $20 million. Because the firm's total liabilities are $4 million, the attorney is asking for $5.3 million (one third of $16 million). Sklar and Hodges do not agree, but all parties want to avoid a protracted, expensive lawsuit. They have decided to put the question to an arbitrator, who will make a determination of the settlement.

Here are some other facts that may or may not be relevant. The current balances in the partners' Capital accounts are $1.5 million for Taylor, $2.5 million for Sklar, and $2.0

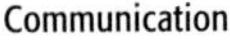
Communication

Critical Thinking

Group Activity

Memo

Ethics

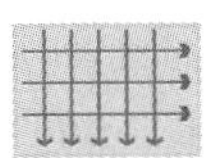
International

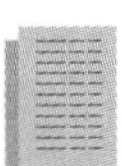
Spreadsheet

General Ledger

CD-ROM

Internet

million for Hodges. Net income in 20xx is to be distributed to the Capital accounts in the ratio of 1:4:3. Before Taylor's semiretirement, the distribution ratio was 3:3:2. Assume you or your group is the arbitrator and develop what you would consider a fair distribution of assets to Taylor's estate. Defend your solution.

RESEARCH ACTIVITY

SD 4.
LO 1 *Basic Research Skills*

The limited partnership is a form of business that was particularly important to the U.S. economy in the 1980s. To find the latest developments or to study the practical applications of a particular subject, such as limited partnerships, it is helpful to use periodical indexes in the library to find articles relating to that subject. Three periodical indexes relevant to accounting and business are *The Accountant's Index,* the *Business Periodicals Index,* and *The Wall Street Journal Index.* Use one or more of those periodical indexes in your school library to find three articles about limited partnerships. Sometimes the articles are not listed under the topic Limited Partnerships; instead, they appear under the uses of limited partnerships. Some examples are real estate, investments, research and development, and cattle or livestock. Write a short summary of each article, relating the content of the article to the content of this chapter or explaining why the limited partnership form of business was important in the situation described in the article.

DECISION-MAKING PRACTICE

SD 5.
LO 4 *Potential Partnership Purchase*

The ***A-One Fitness Center,*** owned by John Kiel and Sunjat Patel, has been very successful since its inception five years ago. John and Sunjat work ten to eleven hours a day at the business. They have decided to expand by opening up another fitness center in the north part of town. John has approached you about becoming a partner in the business. He and Sunjat are interested in you because of your experience in operating a small gym. Also, they need additional funds to expand their business. Projected income after the expansion but before partners' salaries for the next five years is as follows:

20x1	20x2	20x3	20x4	20x5
$100,000	$120,000	$130,000	$140,000	$150,000

Currently, John and Sunjat each draw a $25,000 salary and share remaining profits equally. They are willing to give you an equal share of the business for $142,000. You will receive a $25,000 salary and one-third of the remaining profits. You would work the same hours as John and Sunjat. Your salary for the next five years where you currently work is expected to be as follows:

20x1	20x2	20x3	20x4	20x5
$34,000	$38,000	$42,000	$45,000	$50,000

Here is financial information for the A-One Fitness Center:

Current Assets	$ 45,000	Long-Term Liabilities	100,000
Plant and Equipment, net	365,000	John Kiel, Capital	140,000
Current Liabilities	50,000	Sunjat Patel, Capital	120,000

1. Compute your capital balance if you decide to join John and Sunjat in the fitness center partnership.
2. Analyze your expected income for the next five years.
3. Should you invest in the A-One Fitness Center?
4. Assume that you do not consider John and Sunjat's offer of partnership to be a good one. Develop a counteroffer that you would be willing to accept (be realistic).

Financial Reporting and Analysis

INTERPRETING FINANCIAL REPORTS

FRA 1.
LO 1
LO 3 *Effects of Lawsuit on Partnership*

The ***Springfield Clinic*** is owned and operated by ten local doctors as a partnership. Recently, a paralyzed patient sued the clinic for malpractice, for a total of $20 million. The clinic carries malpractice liability insurance in the amount of $10 million. There is no provision for the possible loss from this type of lawsuit in the partnership's financial statements. The condensed balance sheet for 20xx follows.

Springfield Clinic
Condensed Balance Sheet
December 31, 20xx

Assets		
Current Assets	$246,000	
Property, Plant, and Equipment (net)	750,000	
Total Assets		$996,000
Liabilities and Partners' Equity		
Current Liabilities	$180,000	
Long-Term Debt	675,000	
Total Liabilities		$855,000
Partners' Equity		141,000
Total Liabilities and Partners' Equity		$996,000

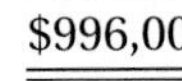

1. How should information about the lawsuit be disclosed in the December 31, 20xx, financial statements of the partnership?
2. Assume that the clinic and its insurance company settle out of court by agreeing to pay a total of $10.1 million, of which $100,000 must be paid by the partnership. What effect will the payment have on the clinic's December 31, 20xx, financial statements? Discuss the effect of the settlement on the Springfield Clinic doctors' personal financial situations.

INTERNATIONAL COMPANY

LO 1 *International Joint Ventures*

FRA 2. ***Wal-Mart,*** the large discounter, formed a joint venture with ***Dillard Department Stores,*** a company that owns 231 department stores mainly in the southern part of the United States, and ***Grupe Cifra,*** a Mexican company, to open department stores in Mexico. Dillard owns 50 percent of the joint venture, and Wal-Mart and Cifra split the other 50 percent. Dillard operates the stores; Wal-Mart assists in logistics, recruitment, and technology; and Cifra provides access to the markets.[6] What advantages does a joint venture have over a single company in entering a new market in another country? What are the potential disadvantages?

TOYS "R" US ANNUAL REPORT

The partnership chapter is not applicable to Toys "R" Us.

FINGRAPH® FINANCIAL ANALYSIS™

The partnership chapter is not applicable to this case.

ENDNOTES

1. Ernst & Young International, *Annual Report,* 1997.
2. "What's New in Your Industry," *Business Eastern Europe,* December 20, 1993.
3. Information excerpted from the 1990 and 1997 annual reports of Alliance Capital Management Limited Partnership.
4. David J. Jefferson, "At Planet Hollywood, the Star of the Show Isn't Stallone, It's Earl," *The Wall Street Journal,* June 21, 1994.
5. Anita Raghavan, "Goldman Scrambles to Find $250 Million in Equity Capital from Private Investors," *The Wall Street Journal,* September 15, 1994.
6. "Wal-Mart Joins Dillard in Mexico Store Venture," *Chicago Tribune,* October 15, 1994.

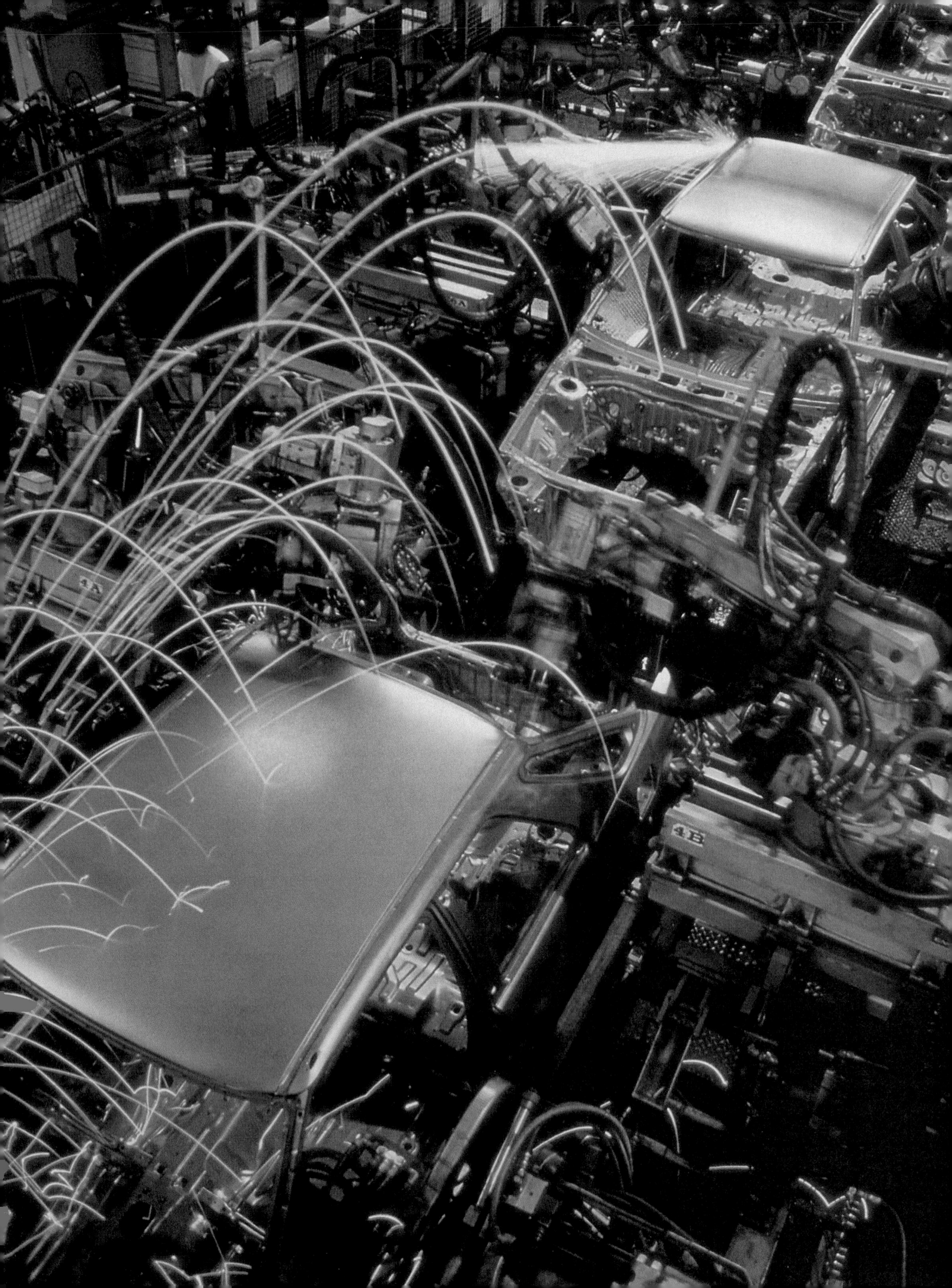
4A
4B

Contributed Capital

LEARNING OBJECTIVES

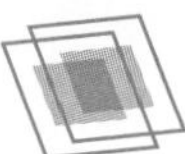

1. **Identify and explain the management issues related to contributed capital.**
2. **Define organization costs and state their effects on financial reporting.**
3. **Identify the components of stockholders' equity.**
4. **Account for cash dividends.**
5. **Identify the characteristics of preferred stock, including the effect on distribution of dividends.**
6. **Account for the issuance of stock for cash and other assets.**
7. **Account for treasury stock.**
8. **Account for the exercise of stock options.**

DECISION POINT

GENERAL MOTORS CORPORATION

One way corporations raise new capital is by issuing stock. In each of the past five years, General Motors Corporation, a major automotive manufacturer, has issued common stock, including almost $2 billion in the past three years, as shown in the Financial Highlights from the statement of cash flows.[1]

What are some reasons General Motors' management chooses to satisfy some of its needs for new capital by issuing common stock? What are some disadvantages of this approach?

Financial Highlights

(In millions of dollars)

	1996	1995	1994
Proceeds from issuing common stock	$480	$453	$1,017

There are advantages to financing with common stock. First, financing with common stock is less risky than financing with bonds, because dividends on common stock are not paid unless the board of directors decides to pay them. In contrast, if the interest on bonds is not paid, a company can be forced into bankruptcy. Second, when a company does not pay a cash dividend, the cash generated by profitable operations can be invested in the company's operations. Third, and most important for General Motors, a company may need the proceeds of a common stock issue to improve the balance between liabilities and stockholders' equity. The company lost more than $23.5 billion in 1992, drastically reducing its stockholders' equity. However, by issuing common stock over the next several years, the company improved its debt to equity ratio and its credit rating.

On the other hand, issuing common stock has certain disadvantages. Unlike the interest on bonds, dividends paid on stock are not tax deductible.

Critical Thinking Question: On the balance sheet, is contributed capital reported at current market value or at the market value on the date of issue? **Answer:** Market value at the date of issue. Contributed capital does not fluctuate with market value changes.

VIDEO CASE

LOTUS DEVELOPMENT CORPORATION

OBJECTIVES

- To become familiar with the advantages of a corporation, especially in equity financing.
- To identify the ways investors obtain return on investment in a corporation.
- To show how stock buybacks affect return on equity as a measure of profitability.

BACKGROUND FOR THE CASE

The story of software giant Lotus Development Corporation is a prototype of the recent history of high-technology companies. When Lotus was founded in the early 1980s, its landmark spreadsheet program Lotus 1-2-3 was an overnight sensation at corporations because of its ability to make rapid calculations based on mathematical relationships in large databases. Lotus 1-2-3 went far beyond the rudimentary spreadsheets that preceded it by incorporating a database module and graphics capability. In October 1983, investors stampeded for the company's initial public offering of 2.6 million shares at $18 per share for a total of $55 million. For several years the company had no real competition. By 1992, more than 11 million units of Lotus 1-2-3 had been sold, but the company was unable to solidify its position by developing any new blockbuster products. Microsoft gained on Lotus and eventually passed it with its spreadsheet program Excel. Finally, Lotus developed a hit "groupware" product called Lotus Notes, which boosts productivity by enabling co-workers to share information and work together electronically on complex tasks. The large audit firm Coopers & Lybrand, for example, networks more than 2,000 auditors all over the world and the knowledge of experts in various parts of the firm via Lotus Notes. Many other big companies such as Ford, Unilever, and Citicorp are also using Lotus Notes successfully. The success of Notes attracted the notice of IBM, which had failed to develop its own groupware product. In 1995, IBM made a hostile takeover bid for Lotus and bought out the company. In fewer than fifteen years, Lotus had gone from an intriguing startup to a mature company with sales of more than $1 billion and, finally, to a takeover candidate for a giant competitor.

For more information about Lotus, which is now a division of IBM, visit the company's or IBM's web site through the Needles Accounting Resource Center at:
http://www.hmco.com/college/needles/home.html

REQUIRED

View the video on Lotus Development Corporation that accompanies this book. As you are watching the video, take notes related to the following questions:

1. All corporations must raise equity capital in the form of common stock. In your own words, what is common stock? What is the relationship of par value to market value of the common stock? What is an initial public offering (IPO)? Why was this IPO important in Lotus's early history?
2. Investors in corporations desire to receive an adequate return on their investment. What are the ways investors can receive a return? In what way did Lotus's shareholders receive a return?
3. From 1991 to 1993, the Lotus board of directors authorized the repurchase of 7,700,000 shares of the company's approximately 44,000,000 shares. (1) What impact will the repurchase of these shares have on the investors' return? (2) What role did the takeover by IBM play in achieving an adequate return to Lotus shareholders?
4. Return on equity is a common measure of management's ability to meet the company's profitability goal. What role do common stock buybacks (purchases of treasury stock) play in the company's increasing return on equity?

Furthermore, when it issues more stock, the corporation dilutes its ownership. This means that the current stockholders must yield some control to the new stockholders. It is important for accountants to understand the nature and characteristics of corporations as well as the process of accounting for a stock issue and other types of stock transactions.

Management Issues Related to Contributed Capital

OBJECTIVE 1

Identify and explain the management issues related to contributed capital

Related Text Assignments:
Q: 1, 2, 3, 4, 5, 8
SE: 1, 2
E: 1
P: 2, 7
SD: 1, 4, 5, 6
FRA: 1, 4, 5

A corporation is defined as "a body of persons granted a charter legally recognizing them as a separate entity having its own rights, privileges, and liabilities distinct from those of its members."[2] In other words, a corporation is a legal entity separate and distinct from its owners.

The management of contributed capital is a critical component in the financing of a corporation. Important issues faced by management in the area of contributed capital are forming a corporation, managing under the corporate form of business, using equity financing, determining dividend policies, and evaluating performance using return on equity.

Forming a Corporation

To form a corporation, most states require individuals, called incorporators, to sign an application and file it with the proper state official. This application contains the articles of incorporation. If approved by the state, these articles become, in effect, a contract, called the company charter, between the state and the incorporators. The company is then authorized to do business.

The authority to manage the corporation is delegated by the stockholders to the board of directors and by the board of directors to the corporate officers (see Figure 1). That is, the stockholders elect the board of directors, which sets company policies and chooses the corporate officers, who in turn carry out the corporate policies by managing the business.

Stockholders A unit of ownership in a corporation is called a share of stock. The articles of incorporation state the maximum number of shares of stock that the corporation will be allowed, or authorized, to issue. The number of shares held by stockholders is the outstanding capital stock; this may be less than the number authorized in the articles of incorporation. To invest in a corporation, a stockholder transfers cash or other resources to the corporation. In return, the stockholder receives shares of stock representing a proportionate share of ownership in the corporation. Afterward, the stockholder may transfer the shares at will. Corporations may have more than one kind of capital stock, but here we will refer only to common stock.

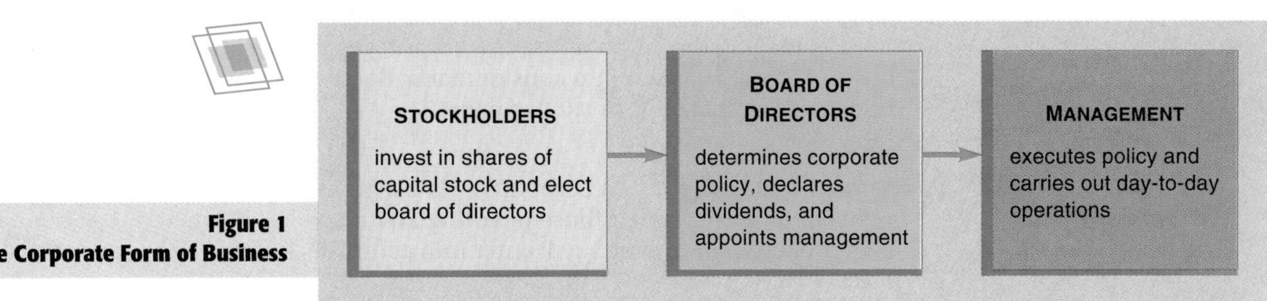

Figure 1
The Corporate Form of Business

Board of Directors As noted, the stockholders elect the board of directors, which in turn decides on the major business policies of the corporation. Among the specific duties of the board are authorizing contracts, setting executive salaries, and arranging major loans with banks. The declaration of dividends is also an important function of the board of directors. Only the board has the authority to declare dividends. Dividends are distributions of resources, generally in the form of cash, to the stockholders. Paying dividends is one way of rewarding stockholders for their investment when the corporation has been successful in earning a profit. (The other way is through a rise in the market value of the stock.) Although there is usually a delay of two or three weeks between the time the board declares a dividend and the date of the actual payment, we shall assume that declaration and payment are made on the same day.

The board of directors will vary in composition from company to company, but in most cases it will contain several officers of the corporation and several outsiders. Today, the formation of an audit committee with several outside directors is encouraged to make sure that the board will be objective in evaluating management's performance. One function of the audit committee is to engage the company's independent auditors and review their work. Another is to make sure that proper systems exist to safeguard the company's resources and ensure that reliable accounting records are kept.

Management The board of directors appoints managers to carry out the corporation's policies and run day-to-day operations. The management consists of the operating officers, who are generally the president, vice presidents, controller, treasurer, and secretary. Besides being responsible for running the business, management has the duty of reporting the financial results of its administration to the board of directors and the stockholders. Though management must, at a minimum, make a comprehensive annual report, it may and generally does report more often. The annual reports of large public corporations are available to the public. Excerpts from many of them will be used throughout this book.

Managing Under the Corporate Form of Business

Although there are fewer corporations than sole proprietorships and partnerships in the United States, the corporate form of business dominates the economy in total dollars of assets and output of goods and services. Corporations are well suited to today's trends toward large organizations, international trade, and professional management. Figure 2 illustrates the corporation's ability to raise large amounts of capital by showing the amount and sources of new funds raised by corporations over the last six years for which data are available. There were dramatic increases in the amount of funds raised after 1990. In 1994, the amount of new corporate capital in that year was $954 billion, of which $801 billion, or 84 percent, came from new bond issues; $115 billion, or 12.1 percent, came from new common stock issues; and $37 billion, or 3.9 percent, came from preferred stock issues.

In managing the corporation, the advantages and disadvantages of this form of business must be taken into consideration. Some of the advantages of the corporation are described on the next two pages.

Separate Legal Entity A corporation is a separate legal entity that has most of the rights of a person except those of voting and marrying. As such, it can buy, sell, or own property; sue and be sued; enter into contracts; hire and fire employees; and be taxed.

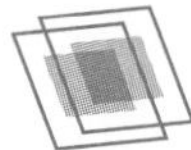

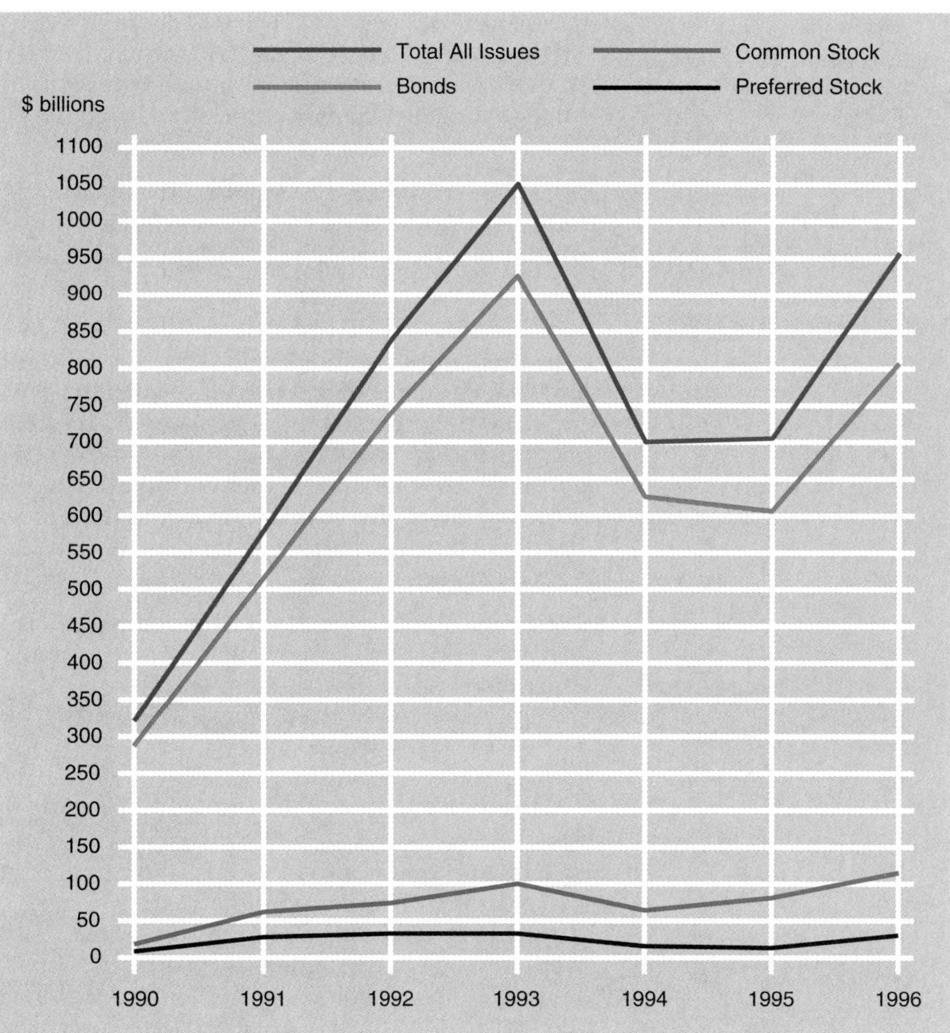

Figure 2
Sources of Capital Raised by Corporations in the United States

Source: Data from *Securities Industry Yearbook 1997–1998* (New York: Securities Industry Association, 1997), p. 985.

Common Student Error: After reading about limited liability, students often think that it's possible to incorporate, borrow much of the needed capital, and walk away from the business if it doesn't work. Emphasize that lenders qualify a corporation for a loan as they would a person. If a corporation does not have a credit history or a good credit rating, a loan will not be granted in its name only. Others, such as the corporation's officers, will be required to co-sign the note and will therefore be personally liable.

Point to Emphasize: Creditors generally do not have to pursue partners' assets on a prorated basis. They can try to recover their losses from any partner.

Limited Liability Because a corporation is a separate legal entity, it is responsible for its own actions and liabilities. This means that a corporation's creditors can satisfy their claims only against the assets of the corporation, not against the personal property of the corporation's owners. Because the owners are not responsible for the corporation's debts, their liability is limited to the amount of their investment. The personal property of sole proprietors and partners, however, generally is available to creditors.

Ease of Capital Generation It is fairly easy for a corporation to raise capital because shares of ownership in the business are available to a great number of potential investors for a small amount of money. As a result, a single corporation can be owned by many people.

Ease of Transfer of Ownership A share of stock, a unit of ownership in a corporation, is transferable. A stockholder can normally buy and sell shares of stock without affecting the activities of the corporation or needing the approval of other owners.

Point to Emphasize: Make sure students understand that *ease of capital generation* means the ability to expand a business or to venture into other markets more readily.

Enrichment Note: It is easy to transfer ownership if the stock is traded on a major stock exchange. If the stock is issued by a closely held corporation, securing a buyer can take a long time.

Lack of Mutual Agency There is no mutual agency in the corporate form of business. If a stockholder, acting as an owner, tries to enter into a contract for the corporation, the corporation is not bound by the contract. But in a partnership, because of mutual agency, all the partners can be bound by one partner's actions.

Continuous Existence Another advantage of the corporation's existence as a separate legal entity is that an owner's death, incapacity, or withdrawal does not affect the life of the corporation. The life of a corporation is set by its charter and regulated by state laws.

Centralized Authority and Responsibility The board of directors represents the stockholders and delegates the responsibility and authority for the day-to-day operation of the corporation to a single person, usually the president. Operating power is not divided among the many owners of the business. The president may delegate authority over certain segments of the business to others, but he or she is held accountable to the board of directors. If the board is dissatisfied with the performance of the president, it can replace him or her.

Professional Management Large corporations are owned by many people, the vast majority of whom are unequipped to make timely decisions about business operations. So, in most cases, management and ownership are separate. This allows a corporation to hire the best talent available to manage the business.

The disadvantages of the corporation include the following:

Discussion Question: What are some government agencies that regulate businesses? Answer: The Securities and Exchange Commission (SEC), the Occupational Safety and Health Administration (OSHA), the Federal Trade Commission (FTC), the Environmental Protection Agency (EPA), the Nuclear Regulatory Commission (NRC), the Equal Employment Opportunity Commission (EEOC), the Interstate Commerce Commission (ICC), the National Transportation Safety Board (NTSB), the Federal Aviation Administration (FAA), and the Federal Communications Commission (FCC).

Government Regulation Corporations must meet the requirements of state laws. As "creatures of the state," corporations are subject to greater control and regulation by the state than are other forms of business. Corporations must file many reports with the state in which they are chartered. Also, corporations that are publicly held must file reports with the Securities and Exchange Commission and with the stock exchanges. Meeting those requirements is very costly.

Taxation A major disadvantage of the corporate form of business is double taxation. Because a corporation is a separate legal entity, its earnings are subject to federal and state income taxes, which may be as much as 35 percent of corporate earnings. If any of the corporation's after-tax earnings are then paid out as dividends, the earnings are taxed again as income to the stockholders. In contrast, the earnings of sole proprietorships and partnerships are taxed only once, as personal income to the owners.

Limited Liability Above, we cited limited liability as an advantage of incorporation, but it also can be a disadvantage. Limited liability restricts the ability of a small corporation to borrow money. Because creditors can lay claim only to the assets of the corporation, they limit their loans to the level secured by those assets or ask stockholders to guarantee the loans personally.

Separation of Ownership and Control Just as limited liability can be a drawback, so can the separation of ownership and control. Sometimes management makes decisions that are not good for the corporation as a whole. Poor communication can also make it hard for stockholders to exercise control over the corporation or even to recognize that management's decisions are harmful.

BUSINESS BULLETIN: BUSINESS PRACTICE

To help with the initial issue of capital stock, called an initial public offering (IPO), a corporation often uses an underwriter—an intermediary between the corporation and the investing public. For a fee—usually less than 1 percent of the selling price—the underwriter guarantees the sale of the stock. The corporation records the amount of the net proceeds of the offering—what the public paid less the underwriter's fee, legal and printing expenses, and any other direct costs of the offering—in its capital stock and additional paid-in capital accounts. In 1997, General Motors spun off its Hertz car rental division as a separate company in one of the largest recent IPOs.

Point to Emphasize: In effect, the underwriter buys the stock from the corporation at a set price. The stock price in the secondary markets can be above or below the commitment to the corporation. Thus, the underwriter can gain or lose on the transaction and is exposed to a certain amount of risk.

Discussion Question: Ask your students to list some of the U.S. stock exchanges. **Answer:** The New York Stock Exchange, the American Stock Exchange, NASDAQ, the Boston Stock Exchange, the Philadelphia Stock Exchange, the Midwest Stock Exchange, and the Pacific Stock Exchange.

Point to Emphasize: Securing a large number of authorized shares of stock with the original articles of incorporation is wise for two reasons. First, additional shares can be offered at a later date without delay; second, additional time and money do not have to be spent amending the charter to increase the number of authorized shares.

Point to Emphasize: Par value is usually a small amount, $1 up to $10. The amount is arbitrary and has primarily legal significance.

Using Equity Financing

A share of stock is a unit of ownership in a corporation. A stock certificate is issued to the owner. It shows the number of shares of the corporation's stock owned by the stockholder. Stockholders can transfer their ownership at will. When they do, they must sign their stock certificate and send it to the corporation's secretary. In large corporations that are listed on the organized stock exchanges, stockholders' records are hard to maintain. Such companies can have millions of shares of stock, thousands of which change ownership every day. Therefore, they often appoint independent registrars and transfer agents (usually banks and trust companies) to help perform the secretary's duties. The outside agents are responsible for transferring the corporation's stock, maintaining stockholders' records, preparing a list of stockholders for stockholders' meetings, and paying dividends.

When a corporation applies for a charter, the articles of incorporation specify the maximum number of shares of stock the corporation is allowed to issue. This number represents authorized stock. Most corporations are authorized to issue more shares of stock than are necessary at the time of organization, which allows for future stock issues to raise additional capital. For example, if a corporation plans to expand in the future, it will be able to sell the unissued shares of stock that were authorized in its charter. If a corporation immediately issues all of its authorized stock, it cannot issue more stock unless it applies to the state for a change in charter.

The charter also shows the par value of the stock that has been authorized. Par value is an arbitrary amount assigned to each share of stock. It must be recorded in the capital stock accounts and constitutes the legal capital of a corporation. Legal capital equals the number of shares issued times the par value; it is the minimum amount that can be reported as contributed capital. Par value usually bears little if any relationship to the market value or book value of the shares. When a corporation is formed, a memorandum entry can be made in the general journal giving the number and description of authorized shares.

Determining Dividend Policies

The board of directors has sole authority to declare dividends, but the dividend policies are influenced by senior managers, who usually serve as members of the board. Receiving dividends from a corporation is one of the two ways stockholders can earn a return on their investment in the company. The other way is to sell their shares of stock for more than they paid for them. Investors evaluate the amount of dividends received with the ratio dividends yield. Dividends yield measures the current return to an investor in the form of dividends and is computed by dividing the

BUSINESS BULLETIN: INTERNATIONAL PRACTICE

Daimler-Benz AG, the huge German automaker famous for Mercedes-Benz cars, became the first German company to be listed on the New York Stock Exchange in 1993. This was a significant step because German accounting standards are very different from U.S. standards. Both Daimler-Benz and the Securities and Exchange Commission had to compromise for the listing to occur. Now small German companies are seeking to make initial public offerings (IPOs) in the United States because in Germany, where large banks handle much of the financing, "there is no place for *small-cap* companies."[3] Over a period of time when there were 271 IPOs in the United States, there were only 85 IPOs in Germany.

dividends per share by the market price per share. For instance, the dividends yield (shown in Figure 3) for Abbott Laboratories, a large, successful pharmaceutical company, is computed as follows:

Enrichment Note: Due to the rise in prices of stocks during the 1990s, the average dividends yield has declined and the average P/E ratio has increased.

$$\text{Dividends Yield} = \frac{\text{Dividends per Share}}{\text{Market Price per Share}} = \frac{\$1.08}{\$64.3125} = 1.7\%$$

Since the yield on corporate bonds exceeds 8 percent, the shareholders of Abbott Labs must expect some of their return to come from increases in the price of the shares. A measure of investors' confidence in a company's future is the price/earnings (P/E) ratio, which is calculated by dividing the market price per share by the earnings per share. The price/earnings ratio will vary as market price per share fluctuates daily and the amount of earnings per share changes. From Figure 3, the price/earnings ratio for Abbott Labs is 25 times, which was computed by using its most recent annual earnings per share, as follows:

$$\text{Price/Earnings (P/E) Ratio} = \frac{\text{Market Price per Share}}{\text{Earnings per Share}} = \frac{\$64.3125}{\$2.57} = 25 \text{ times}$$

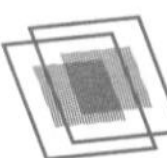

Figure 3
Stock Quotations on the New York Stock Exchange

NYSE COMPOSITE TRANSACTIONS

52 Weeks Hi	52 Weeks Lo	Stock	Sym	Div	Yld %	PE	Vol 100's	Hi	Lo	Close	Net Chg
20	13 1/4	AJL PepsTR	AJP	1.44	8.9	...	504	16 1/8	15 7/8	16 1/8	+ 1/8
24 3/4	20 1/4	♣AMLI Resdntl	AML	1.72	7.3	19	351	23 5/8	23 1/16	23 5/8	+ 1/4
56 11/16	32 7/8	♣AMP	AMP	1.04	2.0	44	4417	53 3/4	51 5/8	53	+ 1/8
118 1/2	78 1/4	AMR	AMR		...	9	4407	114	111 5/16	111 5/16	−1 3/4
50 3/4	40 7/8	♣ARCO Chm	RCM	2.80	6.0	19	698	47 1/2	46 3/4	47	+ 1/4
41	28 5/16	ASA	ASA	1.20	3.8	...	1274	31 7/8	31 3/8	31 3/4	+ 1/8
46 1/8	30 3/4	AT&T	T	1.32	3.1	14	61576	44 3/16	43 1/16	43 3/16	− 3/8
35 1/8	28 1/4	AXA-UAP ADR	AXA	.65p	...	...	363	34 5/16	33 15/16	34 1/4	+ 1/2
s 40 3/4	10 1/2	AamesFnl	AAM	.13	.8	11	5558	16 5/8	16	16 5/16	+ 1/16
n▲26 3/16	24 1/2	AbbeyNtl		2.19	8.4	...	44	26 1/4	26 3/16	26 3/16	+ 1/8
68 15/16	48 3/4	AbbotLab	ABT	1.08	1.7	25	13615	65 7/16	68 1/8	64 5/16	−3/16
27 5/16	12 1/2	Abercrombie A	ANF		...	...	391	26 7/8	26 7/16	26 3/4	+ 3/8
21	12 5/8	Abitibi g	ABY	.40	...	...	271	17	16 3/4	16 15/16	+ 1/16
28	17 3/4	♣Acceptins	AIF		...	13	87	26 7/8	26 3/8	26 3/4	+ 7/16

Source: The Wall Street Journal, October 6, 1997. Reprinted by permission of *The Wall Street Journal.*

Since the market price is 25 times earnings, investors are paying what for most companies would be a high price in relation to earnings, expecting this drug company to continue its success. Caution must be taken in interpreting high P/E ratios because unusually low earnings can produce a high result.

Companies usually pay dividends to stockholders only when they have experienced profitable operations. For example, Apple Computer, Inc., paid a dividend beginning in 1987 but suspended its dividend payments in 1996 to conserve cash after large operating losses in 1995. Factors other than earnings affect the decision to pay dividends. First, the expected volatility of earnings is a factor. If a company has years of good earnings followed by years of poor earnings, the board may want to keep dividends low so as not to give a false impression of sustained high earnings. For instance, for years General Motors Corporation followed the practice of having a fairly stable dividend yield and paying a bonus dividend in especially good years. Second, the level of dividends affects cash flows. Some companies may not have the cash to pay higher dividends because operations are not generating cash at the level of earnings or because the companies are investing the cash in future operations. For instance, Abbott Labs pays a dividend of only $1.08 per share in spite of earning $2.57 per share because management feels the cash generated by the earnings is better spent for other purposes, such as researching and developing new drugs that will generate revenue in the future. It is partly due to Abbott's investment in new products that stockholders are willing to pay a high price for Abbott Laboratories stock.

Evaluating Performance Using Return on Equity

The ratio return on equity is the most important ratio associated with the stockholders' equity section because it is a common measure of management's performance. For instance, when *Business Week* and *Forbes* rate companies on their success, return on equity is the major basis of this evaluation. Also, the compensation of top executives is often tied to return on equity benchmarks. This ratio is computed for Abbott Labs from information in the company's 1996 annual report, as follows:

Point to Emphasize: A company can improve its return on equity by increasing net income or by reducing average stockholders' equity.

$$\text{Return on Equity} = \frac{\text{Net Income}}{\text{Average Stockholders' Equity}}$$

$$= \frac{\$1{,}882{,}033{,}000}{(\$4{,}820{,}182{,}000 + \$4{,}396{,}847{,}000) \div 2}$$

$$= 40.8\%$$

Abbott Labs' healthy return on equity of 40.8 percent depends, of course, on the amount of net income the company earns, but it also depends on the level of stockholders' equity. This level can be affected by management decisions. First, it depends on the amount of stock a company sells to the public. Management can keep the stockholders' equity at a minimum by financing the business with cash flows from operations and with debt instead of with stock. However, the use of debt to finance the business increases a company's risk because the interest and principal of the debt must be paid in a timely manner. In the case of common stock, dividends may be suspended if there is a cash shortage. With a debt to equity ratio of over 1.0, Abbott Labs is taking advantage of the leverage provided by debt. Second, management can reduce the number of shares in the hands of the public by buying back its shares on the open market. The cost of these shares, which are called treasury stock, has the effect of reducing the amount of stockholders' equity and thereby increasing the return on equity. Many companies follow this practice instead of paying or increasing dividends because it puts money into the hands of stockholders in the form of market price appreciation without creating a commitment to higher dividends in the future. For example, during the last three years, Abbott

BUSINESS BULLETIN: BUSINESS PRACTICE

In recent years, there has been a surge in stock buybacks for the purpose of increasing return on equity and stock prices. Records were set in 1995 and 1996. Coca-Cola, IBM, Philip Morris, and McDonald's are recent examples of companies with consistently large buyback policies.[4] From 1984 to 1996, Coca-Cola repurchased 1 billion shares, which improved its earnings per share results and return on equity. Since January 1995, IBM has bought back more than $13.2 billion of its stock and recently announced another $3.5 billion share repurchase program.[5]

These buybacks helped boost stock prices, yet some companies, like Champion International, Owens-Corning, Gillette, Monsanto, and Eaton, are resisting pressures to buy back shares. These companies believe that if, instead of buying back shares, they invest that cash in their existing operations, returns for stockholders will be even better. Eaton's management says a share buyback program would provide only half of the company's goal of earning a 20 percent return on equity.[6]

Laboratories purchased more than 59 million shares of its common stock at a cost of $2.2 billion.[7] Abbott Labs' stock repurchases improved the company's return on equity.

Organization Costs

OBJECTIVE 2

Define organization costs and state their effects on financial reporting

Related Text Assignments:
Q: 6, 7, 15
SE: 3
P: 1, 4, 5, 6, 8

Point to Emphasize: Organization costs are classified as intangible or other assets, and usually are amortized over five years.

The costs of forming a corporation are called organization costs. Such costs, which are incurred before the corporation begins operations, include state incorporation fees and attorneys' fees for drawing up the articles of incorporation. They also include the cost of printing stock certificates, accountants' fees for services rendered in registering the firm's initial stock, and other expenditures necessary for forming the corporation. These costs are recorded as a debit to Organization Costs and a credit to Cash, or possibly to contributed capital if services are exchanged for stock.

Theoretically, organization costs benefit the entire life of the corporation. For that reason, a case can be made for recording them as intangible assets and amortizing them over the years of the life of the corporation. However, the life of a corporation normally is not known, so accountants amortize organization costs over the early years of a corporation's life. Because federal income tax regulations allow organization costs to be amortized over five years or more, most companies amortize these costs over a five-year (sixty-month) period.[8] The amortization is recorded with a debit to Amortization Expense and a credit to Organization Costs. Organization costs normally appear as other assets or as intangible assets on the balance sheet.

Components of Stockholders' Equity

OBJECTIVE 3

Identify the components of stockholders' equity

In a corporation's balance sheet, the owners' claims to the business are called stockholders' equity and are presented on the balance sheet as shown on the next page. Notice that the equity section of the corporate balance sheet is divided into two parts: (1) contributed capital and (2) retained earnings. Contributed capital represents the investments made by the stockholders in the corporation. Retained earnings are the earnings of the corporation since its inception, less any losses, dividends, or transfers to contributed capital. Retained earnings are not a pool of funds

Stockholders' Equity		
Contributed Capital		
Preferred Stock, $50 par value, 1,000 shares authorized, issued, and outstanding		$ 50,000
Common Stock, $5 par value, 30,000 shares authorized, 20,000 shares issued and outstanding	$100,000	
Paid-in Capital in Excess of Par Value, Common	50,000	150,000
Total Contributed Capital		$200,000
Retained Earnings		60,000
Total Stockholders' Equity		$260,000

Related Text Assignments:
Q: 15
SE: 4
E: 2, 3, 4
P: 1, 4, 5, 6, 8
SD: 1, 5, 6
FRA: 1, 3, 4, 5

Teaching Note: Explain to students how the account title Retained Earnings describes its function completely: These are the earnings of a corporation that have not been paid out in dividends, that have been retained in the business. Also point out the intangible nature of retained earnings.

Discussion Question: How is it possible for a corporation to have more shares issued than it has outstanding? **Answer:** When it has repurchased some shares, which are called *treasury stock*.

Instructional Strategy: SD 6 works well as an in-class role-play. In preparation, form small groups. Assign one financing alternative to each group and ask groups to meet between classes to analyze their alternative's impact and consider its pros and cons. In class, select representatives of the various groups to act as management, presenting and defending their group's alternative to the board (the rest of the class). Then have the board vote on the best alternative. Discuss the results, and, if desired, award bonus quiz points to the role players.

to be distributed to the stockholders; they represent, instead, earnings reinvested in the corporation.

In keeping with the convention of full disclosure, the contributed-capital part of the stockholders' equity section of the balance sheet gives a great deal of information about the corporation's stock: the kinds of stock; their par value; and the number of shares authorized, issued, and outstanding.

Common Stock

A corporation can issue two basic types of stock: common stock and preferred stock. If only one kind of stock is issued by the corporation, it is called common stock. Common stock is the company's residual equity. This means that all other creditors' and preferred stockholders' claims to the company's assets rank ahead of those of the common stockholders in case of liquidation. Because common stock is generally the only stock that carries voting rights, it represents the means of controlling the corporation.

The issued stock of a corporation is the shares sold or otherwise transferred to stockholders. For example, a corporation can be authorized to issue 500,000 shares of stock but may choose to issue only 300,000 shares when the company is organized. The holders of those 300,000 shares own 100 percent of the corporation. The remaining 200,000 shares of stock are unissued shares. No rights or privileges are associated with them until they are issued.

Outstanding stock is stock that has been issued and is still in circulation. A share of stock is not outstanding if the issuing corporation has repurchased it or if a stockholder has given it back to the company that issued it. So, a company can have more shares issued than are currently outstanding. Issued shares that are bought back and held by the corporation are called treasury stock, which we discuss in detail later in this chapter. The relationship of authorized, issued, unissued, outstanding, and treasury shares is illustrated in Figure 4.

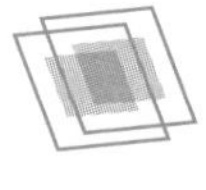

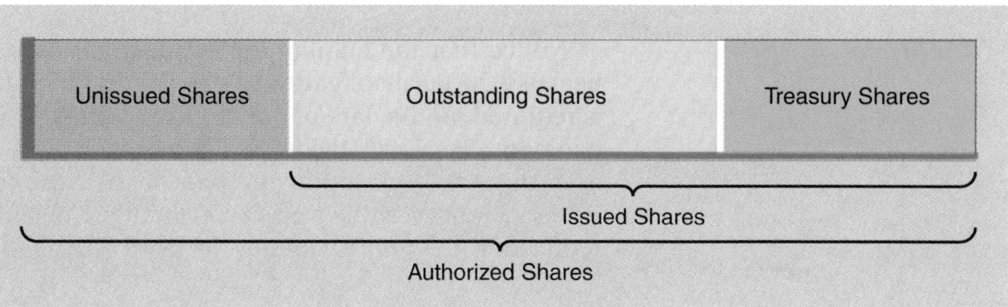

Figure 4
Relationship of Authorized, Unissued, Issued, Outstanding, and Treasury Shares

Dividends

OBJECTIVE 4

Account for cash dividends

Related Text Assignments:
Q: 9, 10
SE: 5
E: 5, 6
P: 1, 4, 5, 6, 8
SD: 5
FRA: 3

Discussion Question: What are some reasons that the board of directors of a corporation with sufficient cash and retained earnings might vote *against* declaring a dividend? **Answer:** If the cash is needed for significant expansion; if the board of directors wants to liquidate debt and improve the overall financial position of the company; if there are major uncertainties threatening the corporation (such as a pending lawsuit or a possible work force strike); and if the economy is poor and the board of directors decides it would be prudent to keep resources for difficult times.

Discussion Question: On which financial statement does the account Cash Dividends Declared appear? **Answer:** It appears on either the statement of retained earnings or the statement of stockholders' equity.

Dividends can be paid quarterly, semiannually, annually, or at other times decided on by the board. Most states do not allow the board to declare a dividend that exceeds retained earnings. When a dividend that exceeds retained earnings is declared, the corporation is, in essence, returning to the stockholders part of their contributed capital. It is called a liquidating dividend and is usually paid when a company is going out of business or reducing its operations. Having sufficient retained earnings in itself does not justify the distribution of a dividend. If cash or other readily distributable assets are not available for distribution, the company might have to borrow money to pay a dividend—an action most boards of directors want to avoid.

There are three important dates associated with dividends. In order of occurrence, they are (1) the date of declaration, (2) the date of record, and (3) the date of payment. The date of declaration is the date on which the board of directors formally declares that a dividend is going to be paid. The date of record is the date on which ownership of the stock of a company, and therefore of the right to receive a dividend, is determined. Individuals who own the stock on the date of record will receive the dividend. Between that date and the date of payment, the stock is said to be ex-dividend. If one person sells the shares of stock to another, the right to the cash dividend remains with the first person; it does not transfer with the shares to the second person. The date of payment is the date on which the dividend is paid to the stockholders of record.

To illustrate the accounting for cash dividends, we assume that the board of directors has decided that sufficient cash is available to pay a $56,000 cash dividend to the common stockholders. The process has two steps. First, the board declares the dividend as of a certain date. Second, the dividend is paid. Assume that the dividend is declared on February 21, 20xx, for stockholders of record on March 1, 20xx, to be paid on March 11, 20xx. Here are the entries to record the declaration and payment of the cash dividend.

Date of Declaration

A = L + OE
    + −

Feb. 21	Cash Dividends Declared	56,000	
	Cash Dividends Payable		56,000
	Declaration of a cash dividend to common stockholders		

Date of Record

Mar. 1 No entry is required. This date is used simply to determine the owners of the stock who will receive the dividends. After this date (starting March 2), the shares are ex-dividend.

Date of Payment

A = L + OE
− −

Mar. 11	Cash Dividends Payable	56,000	
	Cash		56,000
	Payment of cash dividends declared February 21		

Teaching Note: Explain that Cash Dividends Declared is to a corporation what Withdrawals is to a sole proprietorship.

Notice that the liability for the dividend is recorded on the date of declaration because the legal obligation to pay the dividend is established on that date. No entry is required on the date of record. The liability is liquidated, or settled, on the date of payment. The Cash Dividends Declared account is a temporary stockholders' equity account that is closed at the end of the accounting period by debiting Retained Earnings and crediting Cash Dividends Declared. Retained Earnings are thereby reduced by the total dividends declared during the period.

Some companies do not pay dividends. A company may not have any earnings. Or the cash generated by operations may need to be kept in the company for business purposes, perhaps expansion of the plant. Investors in growth companies expect a return on their investment in the form of an increase in the market value of their stock.

Preferred Stock

OBJECTIVE 5

Identify the characteristics of preferred stock, including the effect on distribution of dividends

Related Text Assignments:
Q: 10, 11, 12
SE: 6
E: 3, 7, 8
P: 2, 4, 5, 7, 8
SD: 2, 5

The second kind of stock a company can issue is called preferred stock. Both common stock and preferred stock are sold to raise money. But investors in preferred stock have different investment goals from investors in common stock. In fact, a corporation may offer several different classes of preferred stock, each with distinctive characteristics to attract different investors. Preferred stock has preference over common stock in one or more areas. Most preferred stock has one or more of the following characteristics: preference as to dividends, preference as to assets of the business in liquidation, convertibility, and a callable option.

Preference as to Dividends Preferred stocks ordinarily have a preference over common stock in the receipt of dividends; that is, the holders of preferred shares must receive a certain amount of dividends before the holders of common shares can receive dividends. The amount that preferred stockholders must be paid before common stockholders can be paid is usually stated in dollars per share or as a percentage of the face value of the preferred shares. For example, a corporation can issue a preferred stock and pay an annual dividend of $4 per share, or it might issue a preferred stock at $50 par value and pay a yearly dividend of 8 percent of par value, also $4 per share.

Discussion Question: All other things being equal, which would have a higher market value, cumulative or noncumulative preferred stock? **Answer:** Cumulative preferred stock, because unpaid dividends carry over to subsequent years.

Preferred stockholders have no guarantee of ever receiving dividends: The company must have earnings and the board of directors must declare dividends on preferred shares before any liability arises. The consequences of not declaring a dividend to preferred stockholders in the current year vary according to the exact terms under which the shares were issued. In the case of noncumulative preferred stock, if the board of directors fails to declare a dividend to preferred stockholders in a given year, the company is under no obligation to make up the missed dividend in future years. In the case of cumulative preferred stock, however, the fixed dividend amount per share accumulates from year to year, and the whole amount must be paid before any common dividends can be paid. Dividends not paid in the year they are due are called dividends in arrears.

Assume that a corporation has been authorized to issue 10,000 shares of $100 par value, 5 percent cumulative preferred stock, and that the shares have been issued and are outstanding. If no dividends were paid in 20x1, at the end of the year there would be preferred dividends of $50,000 (10,000 shares × $100 × .05 = $50,000) in arrears. If dividends are paid in 20x2, the preferred stockholders' dividends in arrears plus the 20x2 preferred dividends must be paid before any dividends on common stock can be paid.

Discussion Question: Why is it necessary to disclose dividends in arrears? After all, they do not represent a legitimate liability. **Answer:** To alert potential investors in common stock that those dividends must be paid before common shareholders receive any dividends.

Dividends in arrears are not recognized as liabilities because no liability exists until the board declares a dividend. A corporation cannot be sure it is going to make a profit. So, of course, it cannot promise dividends to stockholders. However, if a company has dividends in arrears, the amount should be reported either in the body of the financial statements or in a note. The following note appeared in a steel company's annual report.

> On January 1, 20xx, the company was in arrears by $37,851,000 ($1.25 per share) on dividends to its preferred stockholders. The company must pay all dividends in arrears to preferred stockholders before paying any dividends to common stockholders.

Suppose that on January 1, 20x1, a corporation issued 10,000 shares of $10 par, 6 percent cumulative preferred stock and 50,000 shares of common stock. The first year's operations resulted in income of only $4,000. The corporation's board of directors declared a $3,000 cash dividend to the preferred stockholders. The dividend picture at the end of 20x1 was as follows:

20x1 dividends due preferred stockholders ($100,000 × .06)	$6,000
Less 20x1 dividends declared to preferred stockholders	3,000
20x1 preferred stock dividends in arrears	$3,000

Now, suppose that in 20x2 the company earned income of $30,000 and wanted to pay dividends to both the preferred and the common stockholders. Because the preferred stock is cumulative, the corporation must pay the $3,000 in arrears on the preferred stock, plus the current year's dividends on its preferred stock, before it can distribute a dividend to the common stockholders. For example, assume that the corporation's board of directors declared a $12,000 dividend to be distributed to preferred and common stockholders. The dividend would be distributed as follows:

20x2 declaration of dividends	$12,000
Less 20x1 preferred stock dividends in arrears	3,000
Available for 20x2 dividends	$ 9,000
Less 20x2 dividends due preferred stockholders ($100,000 × .06)	6,000
Remainder available to common stockholders	$3,000

And this is the journal entry when the dividend is declared:

A = L + OE				
+ −	Dec. 31	Cash Dividends Declared	12,000	
		Cash Dividends Payable		12,000
		Declaration of a $9,000 cash dividend to preferred stockholders and a $3,000 cash dividend to common stockholders		

Preference as to Assets Many preferred stocks have preference in terms of the assets of the corporation in the case of liquidation. If the corporation's existence is terminated, the preferred stockholders have a right to receive the par value of their stock or a larger stated liquidation value per share before the common stockholders receive any share of the company's assets. This preference can also include any dividends in arrears owed to the preferred stockholders.

Point to Emphasize: Many companies that liquidate do not have enough assets to pay creditors. Consequently, there is nothing left for shareholders, common or preferred. Most companies that liquidate do so because business has been bad.

Convertible Preferred Stock A corporation can make its preferred stock more attractive to investors by adding convertibility. People who hold convertible preferred stock can exchange their shares of preferred stock for shares of the company's common stock at a ratio stated in the preferred stock contract. Convertibility appeals to investors for two reasons. First, like all preferred stockholders, owners of convertible stock are more likely to receive regular dividends than are common stockholders. Second, if the market value of a company's common stock rises, the conversion feature allows the preferred stockholders to share in the increase. The rise in value would come either through increases in the value of the preferred stock or through conversion to common stock.

Enrichment Note: When a preferred shareholder converts to common stock, he or she gains voting rights but loses the dividend and liquidation preference. Conversion back to preferred stock is not an option.

For example, suppose that a company issues 1,000 shares of 8 percent, $100 par value convertible preferred stock for $100 per share. Each share of stock can be converted into five shares of the company's common stock at any time. The market value of the common stock is now $15 per share. In the past, an owner of the com-

BUSINESS BULLETIN: BUSINESS PRACTICE

Preferred stock represents a flexible means of achieving goals that cannot be achieved with common stock. For example, in 1997, Microsoft Corporation issued almost $1 billion in preferred stock even though the company probably did not need the cash.[9] Since Microsoft does not pay and has no plans to pay a dividend on its common stock, this preferred stock satisfies the desire of investors who want to own Microsoft stock but who want to buy stocks that pay a dividend. The preferred stock pays a fixed dividend and is convertible into common stock or convertible notes, or the company guarantees it can be redeemed at face value for cash in three years. In return for this flexibility and low risk, the possible gain of converting the preferred stock into common stock is limited to 25 to 30 percent. A Microsoft vice president says, "If you own the preferred, you get a dividend yield and downside protection, but the upside is capped."[10]

mon stock could expect dividends of about $1 per share per year. The owner of one share of preferred stock, on the other hand, now holds an investment that is approaching a value of $100 on the market and is more likely to receive dividends than is the owner of common stock.

Assume that in the next several years, the corporation's earnings increase, and the dividends paid to common stockholders also increase, to $3 per share. In addition, assume that the market value of a share of common stock rises from $15 to $30. Preferred stockholders can convert each of their preferred shares into five common shares and increase their dividends from $8 on each preferred share to the equivalent of $15 ($3 on each of five common shares). Furthermore, the market value of each share of preferred stock will be close to the $150 value of the five shares of common stock because each share can be converted into five shares of common stock.

Callable Preferred Stock Most preferred stock is callable preferred stock. That is, it can be redeemed or retired at the option of the issuing corporation at a price stated in the preferred stock contract. A stockholder must surrender nonconvertible preferred stock to the corporation when asked to do so. If the preferred stock is convertible, the stockholder can either surrender the stock to the corporation or convert it into common stock when the corporation calls the stock. The *call price,* or redemption price, is usually higher than the par value of the stock. For example, a $100 par value preferred stock might be callable at $103 per share. When preferred stock is called and surrendered, the stockholder is entitled to (1) the par value of the stock, (2) the call premium, (3) any dividends in arrears, and (4) a portion of the current period's dividend, prorated by the proportion of the year to the call date.

A corporation may call its preferred stock for several reasons. First, the company may want to force conversion of the preferred stock to common stock because the cash dividend paid on the equivalent common stock is lower than the dividend paid on the preferred shares. Second, it may be possible to replace the outstanding preferred stock on the current market with a preferred stock at a lower dividend rate or with long-term debt, which can have a lower after-tax cost. Third, the company may simply be profitable enough to retire the preferred stock.

Retained Earnings

Retained earnings, the other component of stockholders' equity, represent stockholders' claims to the assets of the company resulting from profitable operations.

Accounting for Stock Issuance

OBJECTIVE 6

Account for the issuance of stock for cash and other assets

Related Text Assignments:
Q: 13
SE: 7, 8
E: 4, 9, 10
P: 1, 4, 5, 6, 8
SD: 5
FRA: 1

Point to Emphasize: Legal capital is the minimum amount that can be reported as contributed capital. For the protection of creditors, dividends cannot be declared that would reduce capital below the amount of legal capital.

Point to Emphasize: When stock is issued with no par and no stated value, all proceeds represent legal capital and are recorded as capital stock. Because stock may be issued at different prices, the legal capital per share varies.

A share of capital stock may be either par or no-par. The value of par stock is stated in the corporate charter and must be printed on each share of stock. Par value can be $.10, $1, $5, $100, or any other amount established by the organizers of the corporation. The par values of common stocks tend to be lower than those of preferred stocks.

Par value is the amount per share that is entered into the corporation's capital stock accounts and that makes up the legal capital of the corporation. A corporation cannot declare a dividend that would cause stockholders' equity to fall below the legal capital of the firm. Therefore, the par value is a minimum cushion of capital that protects creditors. Any amount in excess of par value received from the issuance of stock is recorded in the Paid-in Capital in Excess of Par Value account and represents a portion of the company's contributed capital.

No-par stock is capital stock that does not have a par value. There are several reasons for issuing stock without a par value. One is that some investors confuse par value with the market value of stock instead of recognizing it as an arbitrary figure. Another reason is that most states do not allow an original stock issue below par value and thereby limit a corporation's flexibility in obtaining capital.

No-par stock can be issued with or without a stated value. The board of directors of a corporation issuing no-par stock may be required by state law to place a stated value on each share of stock or may choose to do so as a matter of convenience. The stated value can be any value set by the board, although some states specify a minimum amount. The stated value can be set before or after the shares are issued if the state law is not specific.

If a company issues no-par stock without a stated value, all proceeds are recorded in the Capital Stock account. That amount becomes the corporation's legal capital unless a different amount is specified by state law. Because additional shares of the stock can be issued at different prices, the per-share credit to the Capital Stock account will not be uniform. This is a key way in which no-par stock without a stated value differs from par value stock or no-par stock with a stated value.

When no-par stock with a stated value is issued, the shares are recorded in the Capital Stock account at the stated value. Any amount that is received in excess of the stated value is recorded in the Paid-in Capital in Excess of Stated Value account. The amount in excess of the stated value is part of the corporation's contributed capital. However, the stated value is normally considered to be the legal capital of the corporation.

Par Value Stock

When par value stock is issued, the appropriate capital stock account (usually Common Stock or Preferred Stock) is credited for the par value regardless of whether the proceeds are more or less than the par value. For example, assume that Bradley Corporation is authorized to issue 20,000 shares of $10 par value common stock and actually issues 10,000 shares at $10 per share on January 1, 20xx. The entry to record the stock issue at par value would be as follows:

A = L + OE
\+ \+

Jan. 1	Cash	100,000	
	Common Stock		100,000
	Issued 10,000 shares of $10 par value common stock for $10 per share		

Cash is debited for $100,000 (10,000 shares × $10), and Common Stock is credited for an equal amount because the stock was sold for par value.

When stock is issued for a price greater than par, the proceeds in excess of par are credited to a capital account called Paid-in Capital in Excess of Par Value, Common. For example, assume that the 10,000 shares of Bradley common stock sold for $12 per share on January 1, 20xx. The entry to record the issuance of the stock at the price in excess of par value would be as follows:

A = L + OE
\+ +

Jan. 1	Cash	120,000	
	Common Stock		100,000
	Paid-in Capital in Excess of Par Value, Common		20,000
	Issued 10,000 shares of $10 par value common stock for $12 per share		

Cash is debited for the proceeds of $120,000 (10,000 shares × $12), and Common Stock is credited for the total par value of $100,000 (10,000 shares × $10). Paid-in Capital in Excess of Par Value, Common is credited for the differences of $20,000 (10,000 shares × $2). The amount in excess of par value is part of the corporation's contributed capital and will be included in the stockholders' equity section of the balance sheet. The stockholders' equity section for Bradley Corporation immediately following the stock issue would appear as follows:

Point to Emphasize: Common Stock and Paid-in Capital in Excess of Par Value are separated for legal purposes. Their effect on the company's balance sheet is the same.

Contributed Capital	
Common Stock, $10 par value, 20,000 shares authorized, 10,000 shares issued and outstanding	$100,000
Paid-in Capital in Excess of Par Value, Common	20,000
Total Contributed Capital	$120,000
Retained Earnings	—
Total Stockholders' Equity	$120,000

If a corporation issues stock for less than par, an account called Discount on Capital Stock is debited for the difference. The issuance of stock at a discount rarely occurs because it is illegal in many states.

No-Par Stock

As mentioned earlier, stock can be issued without a par value. However, most states require that all or part of the proceeds from the issuance of no-par stock be designated as legal capital, which cannot be withdrawn except in liquidation. The purpose of this requirement is to protect the corporation's assets for creditors. Assume that Bradley Corporation's capital stock is no-par common and that 10,000 shares are issued on January 1, 20xx at $15 per share. The $150,000 (10,000 shares × $15) in proceeds would be recorded as shown in the following entry.

A = L + OE
\+ +

Jan. 1	Cash	150,000	
	Common Stock		150,000
	Issued 10,000 shares of no-par common stock for $15 per share		

Because the stock does not have a stated or par value, all proceeds of the issue are credited to Common Stock and are part of the company's legal capital.

Most states allow the board of directors to put a stated value on no-par stock, and that value represents the corporation's legal capital. Assume that Bradley's board puts a $10 stated value on its no-par stock. The entry to record the issue of 10,000 shares of no-par common stock with a $10 stated value for $15 per share would appear as shown on the following page:

A = L + OE			
+ +	Jan. 1	Cash	150,000	
		Common Stock		100,000
		Paid-in Capital in Excess of Stated Value, Common		50,000
		Issued 10,000 shares of no-par common stock with $10 stated value for $15 per share		

Notice that the legal capital credited to Common Stock is the stated value decided by the board of directors. Notice also that the account Paid-in Capital in Excess of Stated Value, Common is credited for $50,000. The $50,000 is the difference between the proceeds ($150,000) and the total stated value ($100,000). Paid-in Capital in Excess of Stated Value is presented on the balance sheet in the same way as Paid-in Capital in Excess of Par Value.

Issuance of Stock for Noncash Assets

Point to Emphasize: Even though the board of directors has the right to determine the fair market value of property that is exchanged for stock, it cannot establish the amount arbitrarily. It must do so in a prudent fashion, using all the information at its disposal.

Stock can be issued for assets or services other than cash. The problem is to determine the dollar amount that should be recorded for the exchange. The generally preferred rule is to record the transaction at the fair market value of what the corporation is giving up—in this case, the stock. If the fair market value of the stock cannot be determined, the fair market value of the assets or services received can be used. Transactions of this kind usually involve the use of stock to pay for land or buildings or for the services of attorneys and others who helped organize the company.

When there is an exchange of stock for noncash assets, the board of directors has the right to determine the fair market value of the property. Suppose that when Bradley Corporation was formed on January 1, 20xx, its attorney agreed to accept 100 shares of its $10 par value common stock for services rendered. At the time the stock was issued, its market value could not be determined. However, for similar services the attorney would have billed the company $1,500. The entry to record the noncash transaction is as follows:

A = L + OE				
+ + +	Jan. 1	Organization Costs	1,500	
		Common Stock		1,000
		Paid-in Capital in Excess of Par Value, Common		500
		Issued 100 shares of $10 par value common stock for attorney's services		

Reinforcement Exercise: Have students record the transaction if the stock had been traded for land with an appraised value of $15,000. **Answer:** The entry would be the same because the rule is to record the exchange at the fair market value of what the company is giving up, if that can be determined. In this case, it was easily determined.

Now suppose that two years later Bradley Corporation exchanged 1,000 shares of its $10 par value common stock for a piece of land. At the time of the exchange, the stock was selling on the market for $16 per share. The entry to record the exchange would be as follows:

A = L + OE				
+ + +	Jan. 1	Land	16,000	
		Common Stock		10,000
		Paid-in Capital in Excess of Par Value, Common		6,000
		Issued 1,000 shares of $10 par value common stock with a market value of $16 per share for a piece of land		

BUSINESS BULLETIN: BUSINESS PRACTICE

Recent years have proved to be hot times for initial public offerings (IPOs); such offerings of a company's stock to the public for the first time reached unprecedented levels as small companies took advantage of all-time record highs in the stock market. For example, when Gateway 2000, a North Sioux City, South Dakota, mail-order computer marketer, offered 10.9 million shares at $15 per share, the price rose to above $20 per share on the first day of trading.[11] The stock of another company, Boston Chicken, a mid-western fast-food company, more than doubled in price on the first day, climbing from $20 to over $48 per share. Some analysts noted that the good fortune of Gateway and Boston Chicken would continue only as long as the companies maintained fast sales growth. Disappointing sales could cause the stocks to plunge.[12] By 1997, Gateway 2000 stock had risen to $60 per share, whereas the price of Boston Chicken shares had dropped to $34.

Treasury Stock

OBJECTIVE 7

Account for treasury stock

Related Text Assignments:
Q: 14, 15
SE: 9, 10
E: 2, 6, 11, 12
P: 3, 4, 5, 8
SD: 3
FRA: 2, 4, 5

Treasury stock is capital stock, either common or preferred, that has been issued and later reacquired by the issuing company and has not subsequently been resold or retired. The company normally gets the stock back by purchasing the shares on the market.

It is common for companies to buy and hold their own stock. In a recent year, 385, or 64 percent, of six hundred large companies held treasury stock.[13] A company may purchase its own stock for several reasons:

1. It may want stock to distribute to employees through stock option plans.
2. It may be trying to maintain a favorable market for its stock.
3. It may want to increase its earnings per share.
4. It may want to have additional shares of stock available for such activities as purchasing other companies.
5. It may want to prevent a hostile takeover.

Discussion Question: Is treasury stock the same as unissued stock? **Answer:** No. Treasury stock represents shares that have been issued but are no longer outstanding. Unissued shares, on the other hand, have never been in circulation.

Enrichment Note: In 1995 and 1996, American companies bought back more shares than they sold to the public.

A treasury stock purchase reduces the assets and stockholders' equity of the company. It is not considered a purchase of assets, as the purchase of shares in another company would be. Treasury stock is capital stock that has been issued but is no longer outstanding. Treasury shares can be held for an indefinite period of time, reissued, or retired. Like unissued stock, treasury stock has no rights until it is reissued. Treasury stock does not have voting rights, rights to cash dividends and stock dividends, or rights to share in assets during liquidation of the company, and it is not considered to be outstanding in the calculation of book value. However, there is one major difference between unissued shares and treasury shares: A share of stock that originally was issued at par value or greater and fully paid for, and that then was reacquired as treasury stock, can be reissued at less than par value without negative consequences.

Purchase of Treasury Stock When treasury stock is purchased, it is normally recorded at cost. The transaction reduces both the assets and the stockholders' equity of the firm. For example, assume that on September 15 the Caprock Corporation purchases 1,000 shares of its common stock on the market at a price of $50 per share. The purchase would be recorded as shown on the next page:

A = L + OE
− −

Sept. 15	Treasury Stock, Common	50,000	
	Cash		50,000
	Acquired 1,000 shares of the company's common stock for $50 per share		

The treasury shares are recorded at cost. The par value, stated value, or original issue price of the stock is ignored.

Discussion Question: What effect does the purchase of treasury stock have on return on equity? **Answer:** Since treasury stock reduces equity, the return on equity will increase.

The stockholders' equity section of Caprock's balance sheet shows the cost of the treasury stock as a deduction from the total of contributed capital and retained earnings.

Contributed Capital	
Common Stock, $5 par value, 100,000 shares authorized, 30,000 shares issued, 29,000 shares outstanding	$ 150,000
Paid-in Capital in Excess of Par Value, Common	30,000
Total Contributed Capital	$ 180,000
Retained Earnings	900,000
Total Contributed Capital and Retained Earnings	$1,080,000
Less Treasury Stock, Common (1,000 shares at cost)	50,000
Total Stockholders' Equity	$1,030,000

Notice that the number of shares issued, and therefore the legal capital, has not changed, although the number of outstanding shares has decreased as a result of the transaction.

Instructional Strategy: Assign E 11 or E 12 to pairs of students. Randomly select pairs to present each journal entry and discuss its effect on total equity. Students' presentations may substitute for the instructor's lecture.

Sale of Treasury Stock Treasury shares can be sold at cost, above cost, or below cost. For example, assume that on November 15 the 1,000 treasury shares of the Caprock Corporation are sold for $50 per share. The following entry records the transaction:

A = L + OE
\+ +

Nov. 15	Cash	50,000	
	Treasury Stock, Common		50,000
	Reissued 1,000 shares of treasury stock for $50 per share		

Point to Emphasize: Gains and losses on the reissue of treasury stock are never recognized as such. Instead, the accounts Retained Earnings and Paid-in Capital, Treasury Stock are used.

When treasury shares are sold for an amount greater than their cost, the excess of the sales price over cost should be credited to Paid-in Capital, Treasury Stock. No gain should be recorded. For example, suppose that on November 15 the 1,000 treasury shares of the Caprock Corporation are sold for $60 per share. The entry for the reissue would be as follows:

A = L + OE
\+ +
\+

Nov. 15	Cash	60,000	
	Treasury Stock, Common		50,000
	Paid-in Capital, Treasury Stock		10,000
	Sale of 1,000 shares of treasury stock for $60 per share; cost was $50 per share		

Point to Emphasize: Treasury Stock, Common is eliminated (credited) based on the original $50 per share cost.

If treasury shares are sold below their cost, the difference is deducted from Paid-in Capital, Treasury Stock. When this account does not exist or its balance is insufficient to cover the excess of cost over the reissue price, Retained Earnings absorbs the excess. No loss is recorded. For example, suppose that on September 15, the Caprock Corporation bought 1,000 shares of its common stock on the market at a price of $50 per share. The company sold 400 shares of its stock on October 15 for

$60 per share and the remaining 600 shares on December 15 for $42 per share. The entries for these transactions follow:

A = L + OE				
− −	Sept. 15	Treasury Stock, Common	50,000	
		Cash		50,000
		Purchase of 1,000 shares of treasury stock at $50 per share		

A = L + OE				
+ + +	Oct. 15	Cash	24,000	
		Treasury Stock, Common		20,000
		Paid-in Capital, Treasury Stock		4,000
		Sale of 400 shares of treasury stock for $60 per share; cost was $50 per share		

A = L + OE				
+ − − +	Dec. 15	Cash	25,200	
		Paid-in Capital, Treasury Stock	4,000	
		Retained Earnings	800	
		Treasury Stock, Common		30,000
		Sale of 600 shares of treasury stock for $42 per share; cost was $50 per share		

Clarification Note: Retained Earnings is debited only when the Paid-in Capital, Treasury Stock account has been depleted. In this case, the credit balance of $4,000 is exhausted completely before Retained Earnings absorbs the excess.

In the entry for the December 15 transaction, Retained Earnings is debited for $800 because the 600 shares were sold for $4,800 less than cost. That amount is $800 greater than the $4,000 of paid-in capital generated by the sale of the 400 shares of treasury stock on October 15.

Retirement of Treasury Stock If a company determines that it will not reissue stock it has purchased, with the approval of its stockholders it can retire the stock. When shares of stock are retired, all items related to those shares are removed from the related capital accounts. When treasury stock whose acquisition price is less than the original contributed capital is retired, the difference is recognized in Paid-in Capital, Retirement of Stock. However, when the acquisition price is more than was received when the stock was first issued, the difference is a reduction in stockholders' equity and is debited to Retained Earnings. For instance, suppose that instead of selling the 1,000 shares of treasury stock it purchased for $50,000,

BUSINESS BULLETIN: INTERNATIONAL PRACTICE

In the United States, it is accepted practice that a company does not report profits from trading in its own stock on the income statement, but this is not the case in other countries. Only if foreign companies raise money in the United States or are listed on a major U.S. stock exchange must they comply with U.S. accounting rules. Because more and more Americans are investing in emerging markets, investors need to realize that U.S. accounting and disclosure rules may not apply. For example, in Mexico a company can record a gain from reselling its own treasury stock. *Forbes* reported that Cemex, a huge Mexican cement company, customarily reports nonoperating items with little explanation. Only by searching in the notes does one discover that one-third of Cemex's $495 million in 1991 pretax profits came from gains on treasury stock transactions.[14]

A = L + OE
−
−
+

Caprock decides to retire the shares on November 15. Assuming that the $5 par value common stock was originally issued at $6 per share, this entry records the retirement:

Nov. 15	Common Stock	5,000	
	Paid-in Capital in Excess of Par Value, Common	1,000	
	Retained Earnings	44,000	
	Treasury Stock, Common		50,000
	Retirement of 1,000 shares that cost $50 per share and were issued originally at $6 per share		

Clarification Note: Common Stock and Paid-in Capital in Excess of Par Value, Common are eliminated based on the original $6 issue price. The remaining $44 per share is absorbed by Retained Earnings.

Exercising Stock Options

OBJECTIVE 8

Account for the exercise of stock options

Related Text Assignments:
Q: 16
SE: 11
E: 13
P: 5
SD: 5
FRA: 4, 5

More than 85 percent of public companies encourage the ownership of their common stock through a stock option plan, which is an agreement to issue stock to employees according to specified terms.[15] Under some plans, the option to purchase stock applies to all employees equally, and the stock is purchased at a price close to its market value at the time of purchase. In such situations, the stock issue is recorded in the same way as a stock issue to an outsider. If, for example, we assume that on March 30 the employees of a company purchased 2,000 shares of $10 par value common stock at the current market value of $25 per share, the entry would be as follows:

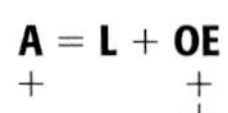

Mar. 30	Cash	50,000	
	Common Stock		20,000
	Paid-in Capital in Excess of Par Value, Common		30,000
	Issued 2,000 shares of $10 par value common stock under employee stock option plan		

In other cases, the stock option plan gives employees the right to purchase stock in the future at a fixed price. This type of plan, which is usually offered only to management personnel, both compensates and motivates management because the market value of a company's stock is tied to the company's performance. As the market value of the stock goes up, the difference between the option price and the market price grows, which increases management's compensation. On the date stock options are granted, the fair value of the options must be estimated and the amount in excess of the exercise price must be either recorded as compensation expense over the grant period or reported in the notes to the financial statements.[16] If a company chooses to record compensation expense, additional paid-in capital will increase as a result. Most companies are expected to choose to report the excess of fair value over exercise price in the notes to the financial statements. The notes must include the impact on net income and earnings per share of not recording compensation expense.

If note disclosure is the preferred method of reporting compensation costs, then when an option eventually is exercised and the stock is issued, the entry is similar to the one above. For example, assume that on July 1, 20x1, a company grants its key management personnel the option to purchase 50,000 shares of $10 par value common stock at its then-current market value of $15 per share. Suppose that one of the firm's vice presidents exercises the option to purchase 2,000 shares on March 30, 20x2, when the market price is $25 per share. The following entry would record the issue:

BUSINESS BULLETIN: BUSINESS PRACTICE

Stock options are also used by companies to attract and keep top managers. When Eastman Kodak Company hired George Fisher away from Motorola, the company gave him options to purchase approximately 750,000 shares of Kodak stock. Compensation consultants put a value of between $13 million and $17 million on the package and said that such compensation was appropriate for an executive hired to turn a company around, as Fisher was charged to do at Kodak. Fisher was given options to purchase 742,000 shares at $57.97 per share and 7,910 shares at $63.19 per share. The average price per share at the time the options were granted was $63.19. Thus, if Fisher could increase the price of the shares by improving the company's profitability, he would stand to gain. When Fisher left Motorola, he gave up unexercised options worth $6.4 million.[17] By 1997 Eastman Kodak was so successful that the stock price was $90, and Fisher received more stock options extending through the year 2000.[18]

A = L + OE
\+   +
       +

20x2			
Mar. 30	Cash	30,000	
	Common Stock		20,000
	Paid-in Capital in Excess of Par Value, Common		10,000
	Issued 2,000 shares of $10 par value common stock under the employee stock option plan		

Point to Emphasize: A corporation records compensation expense only if the market price exceeds the option price on the grant date. The actual gain realized by the vice president here is not recognized in the corporate records.

Although the vice president has a gain of $20,000 (the $50,000 market value less the $30,000 option price), no compensation expense is recorded. Estimation of the fair value of options at the grant date is the subject of future courses. Information pertaining to employee stock option plans should be discussed in the notes to the financial statements.[19]

Chapter Review

REVIEW OF LEARNING OBJECTIVES

1. **Identify and explain the management issues related to contributed capital.** The management of contributed capital is a critical component in the financing of a corporation, which is a legal entity separate and distinct from its owners. The issues faced by management in the area of contributed capital are forming a corporation, managing under the corporate form of business, using equity financing, determining dividend policies, and evaluating performance using return on equity.
2. **Define organization costs and state their effects on financial reporting.** The costs of organizing a corporation are recorded on the balance sheet as intangible assets at cost. The costs are usually amortized as expenses over five years.
3. **Identify the components of stockholders' equity.** Stockholders' equity consists of contributed capital and retained earnings. Contributed capital includes two basic types of stock: common stock and preferred stock. When only one type of security is issued, it is common stock. Common stockholders have voting rights; they also share in the earnings of the corporation.

Retained earnings, the other component of stockholders' equity, represents the claim of stockholders to the assets of the company resulting from profitable operations. These are earnings that have been invested in the corporation.

4. **Account for cash dividends.** The liability for payment of cash dividends arises on the date of declaration by the board of directors. The declaration is recorded with a debit to Cash Dividends Declared and a credit to Cash Dividends Payable. The date of record, on which no entry is required, establishes the stockholders who will receive the cash dividend on the date of payment. Payment is recorded with a debit to Cash Dividends Payable and a credit to Cash.
5. **Identify the characteristics of preferred stock, including the effect on distribution of dividends.** Preferred stock, like common stock, is sold to raise capital. But the investors in preferred stock have different objectives. To attract such investors, corporations usually give them a preference—in terms of receiving dividends and assets—over common stockholders. The dividend on preferred stock is generally figured first; then the remainder goes to common stock. If the preferred stock is cumulative and in arrears, the amount in arrears must be allocated to preferred stockholders before any allocation is made to common stockholders. In addition, certain preferred stock is convertible. Preferred stock is often callable at the option of the corporation.
6. **Account for the issuance of stock for cash and other assets.** A corporation's stock is normally issued for cash and other assets. The majority of states require that stock be issued at a minimum value called legal capital. Legal capital is represented by the par or stated value of the stock.

   When stock is issued for cash at par or stated value, Cash is debited and Common Stock or Preferred Stock is credited. When stock is sold at an amount greater than par or stated value, the excess is recorded in Paid-in Capital in Excess of Par or Stated Value.

   Sometimes stock is issued for noncash assets. Then, the accountant must decide how to value the stock. The general rule is to record the stock at its market value. If this value cannot be determined, the fair market value of the asset received is used to record the transaction.
7. **Account for treasury stock.** Treasury stock is stock that a company has issued and later reacquired but not resold or retired. A company may acquire its own stock to create stock option plans, maintain a favorable market for the stock, increase earnings per share, or purchase other companies. Treasury stock is similar to unissued stock in that it does not have rights until it is reissued. However, treasury stock can be resold at less than par value without penalty. The accounting treatment for treasury stock is as shown below.

Treasury Stock Transaction	Accounting Treatment
Purchase of treasury stock	Debit Treasury Stock and credit Cash for the cost of the shares.
Sale of treasury stock at the same price as the cost of the shares	Debit Cash and credit Treasury Stock for the cost of the shares.
Sale of treasury stock at an amount greater than the cost of the shares	Debit Cash for the reissue price of the shares, and credit Treasury Stock for the cost of the shares and Paid-in Capital, Treasury Stock for the excess.
Sale of treasury stock at an amount less than the cost of the shares	Debit Cash for the reissue price; debit Paid-in Capital, Treasury Stock for the difference between the reissue price and the cost of the shares; and credit Treasury Stock for the cost of the shares. If Paid-in Capital, Treasury Stock does not exist or its balance is not large enough to cover the difference, Retained Earnings should absorb the difference.

8. **Account for the exercise of stock options.** Companywide stock option plans are used to encourage employees to own a part of the company. Other plans are offered only to management personnel, both to compensate and to motivate them. Usually, the issue of stock to employees under stock option plans is recorded like the issue of stock to any outsider.

REVIEW OF CONCEPTS AND TERMINOLOGY

The following concepts and terms were introduced in this chapter.

LO 1 **Articles of incorporation:** An official document filed with and approved by a state that authorizes the incorporators to do business as a corporation.

LO 1 **Audit committee:** A subgroup of the board of directors of a corporation that is charged with ensuring that the board will be objective in reviewing management's performance; it engages the company's independent auditors and reviews their work.

LO 1 **Authorized stock:** The maximum number of shares a corporation can issue without changing its charter with the state.

LO 5 **Callable preferred stock:** Preferred stock that can be redeemed or retired at a stated price at the option of the corporation.

LO 3 **Common stock:** Shares of stock that carry voting rights but that rank below preferred stock in terms of dividends and the distribution of assets.

LO 5 **Convertible preferred stock:** Preferred stock that can be exchanged for common stock at the option of the holder.

LO 1 **Corporation:** A separate legal entity having its own rights, privileges, and liabilities distinct from those of its owners.

LO 5 **Cumulative preferred stock:** Preferred stock on which unpaid dividends accumulate over time and must be satisfied in any given year before a dividend can be paid to common stockholders.

LO 4 **Date of declaration:** The date on which the board of directors declares a dividend.

LO 4 **Date of payment:** The date on which payment of a dividend is made.

LO 4 **Date of record:** The date on which ownership of stock for the purpose of receiving a dividend is determined.

LO 1 **Dividend:** The distribution of a corporation's assets (usually cash) to its stockholders.

LO 5 **Dividends in arrears:** Dividends on cumulative preferred stock that remain unpaid in the year they were due.

LO 1 **Dividends yield:** Current return to stockholders in the form of dividends; dividends per share divided by market price per share.

LO 1 **Double taxation:** The act of taxing corporate earnings twice—once as the net income of the corporation and once as the dividends distributed to stockholders.

LO 4 **Ex-dividend:** A description of capital stock between the date of record and the date of payment, when the right to a dividend already declared on the stock remains with the person who sells the stock and does not transfer to the person who buys it.

LO 1 **Initial public offering (IPO):** Common stock issue of a company that is selling its stock to the public for the first time.

LO 3 **Issued stock:** The shares of stock sold or otherwise transferred to stockholders.

LO 1 **Legal capital:** The number of shares of stock issued times the par value; the minimum amount that can be reported as contributed capital.

LO 4 **Liquidating dividend:** A dividend that exceeds retained earnings; usually paid when a corporation goes out of business or reduces its operations.

LO 5 **Noncumulative preferred stock:** Preferred stock that does not oblige the issuer to make up a missed dividend in a subsequent year before paying dividends to common stockholders.

LO 6 **No-par stock:** Capital stock that does not have a par value.

LO 2 **Organization costs:** The costs of forming a corporation.

LO 3 **Outstanding stock:** Stock that has been issued and is still in circulation.

LO 1 **Par value:** An arbitrary amount assigned to each share of stock; used to determine the legal capital of a corporation.

LO 5 **Preferred stock:** Stock that has preference over common stock, usually in terms of dividends and the distribution of assets.

LO 1 **Price/earnings (P/E) ratio:** A measure of confidence in a company's future; market price per share divided by earnings per share.

LO 3 **Residual equity:** The common stock of a corporation.

LO 1 **Return on equity:** A measure of management performance; net income divided by average stockholders' equity.

LO 1 **Share of stock:** A unit of ownership in a corporation.

LO 6 **Stated value:** A value assigned by the board of directors of a corporation to no-par stock.

LO 1 **Stock certificate:** A document issued to a stockholder indicating the number of shares of stock the stockholder owns.

LO 8 **Stock option plan:** An agreement to issue stock to employees according to specified terms.

LO 7 **Treasury stock:** Capital stock, either common or preferred, that has been issued and reacquired by the issuing company but has not been resold or retired.

LO 1 **Underwriter:** An intermediary between the corporation and the investing public who facilitates an issue of stock or other securities for a fee.

REVIEW PROBLEM

Stock Journal Entries and Stockholders' Equity

LO 1 LO 2 LO 3 LO 4 LO 5 LO 6 LO 7

The Beta Corporation was organized in 20x1 in the state of Arizona. Its charter authorized the corporation to issue 1,000,000 shares of $1 par value common stock and an additional 25,000 shares of 4 percent, $20 par value cumulative convertible preferred stock. Here are the transactions that related to the company's stock during 20x1.

Feb. 1	Issued 100,000 shares of common stock for $125,000.
15	Issued 3,000 shares of common stock for accounting and legal services. The services were billed to the company at $3,600.
Mar. 15	Issued 120,000 shares of common stock to Edward Jackson in exchange for a building and land that had appraised values of $100,000 and $25,000, respectively.
Apr. 2	Purchased 20,000 shares of common stock for the treasury at $1.25 per share from an individual who changed his mind about investing in the company.
July 1	Issued 25,000 shares of preferred stock for $500,000.
Sept. 30	Sold 10,000 of the shares in the treasury for $1.50 per share.
Dec. 31	The board declared dividends of $24,910 payable on January 15 to stockholders of record on January 8. Dividends included preferred stock cash dividends for one-half year.

For the period ended December 31, 20x1, the company reported net income of $40,000 and earnings per common share of $.15. At December 31, the market price per common share was $1.60.

REQUIRED

1. Record these transactions in journal form. Following the December 31 entry to record dividends, show dividends payable for each class of stock.
2. Prepare the stockholders' equity section of the Beta Corporation balance sheet as of December 31, 20x1. (**Hint**: Use net income and dividends to calculate retained earnings.)
3. Calculate dividends yield on common stock, price/earnings ratio of common stock, and return on equity.

ANSWER TO REVIEW PROBLEM

1. Prepare the journal entries.

20x1				
Feb.	1	Cash	125,000	
		Common Stock		100,000
		Paid-in Capital in Excess of Par Value, Common		25,000
		Issue of 100,000 shares of $1 par value common stock for $1.25 per share		
	15	Organization Costs	3,600	
		Common Stock		3,000
		Paid-in Capital in Excess of Par Value, Common		600
		Issue of 3,000 shares of $1 par value common stock for billed accounting and legal services of $3,600		
Mar.	15	Building	100,000	
		Land	25,000	
		Common Stock		120,000
		Paid-in Capital in Excess of Par Value, Common		5,000
		Issue of 120,000 shares of $1 par value common stock for a building and land appraised at $100,000 and $25,000, respectively		
April.	2	Treasury Stock, Common	25,000	
		Cash		25,000
		Purchase of 20,000 shares of common stock for the treasury at $1.25 per share		
July	1	Cash	500,000	
		Preferred Stock		500,000
		Issue of 25,000 shares of $20 par value preferred stock for $20 per share		
Sept.	30	Cash	15,000	
		Treasury Stock, Common		12,500
		Paid-in Capital, Treasury Stock		2,500
		Sale of 10,000 shares of treasury stock at $1.50 per share; original cost was $1.25 per share		
Dec.	31	Cash Dividends Declared	24,910	
		Cash Dividends Payable		24,910
		Declaration of a $24,910 cash dividend to preferred and common stockholders		

Total dividend	$24,910
Less preferred stock cash dividend $500,000 × .04 × 6/12	10,000
Common stock cash dividend	$14,910

2. Prepare the stockholders' equity section of the balance sheet.

Beta Corporation
Balance Sheet
December 31, 20x1

Stockholders' Equity

Contributed Capital		
Preferred Stock, 4% cumulative convertible, $20 par value, 25,000 shares authorized, issued, and outstanding		$500,000
Common Stock, $1 par value, 1,000,000 shares authorized, 223,000 shares issued, and 213,000 shares outstanding	$223,000	
Paid-in Capital in Excess of Par Value, Common	30,600	
Paid-in Capital, Treasury Stock	2,500	256,100
Total Contributed Capital		$756,100
Retained Earnings		15,090*
Total Contributed Capital and Retained Earnings		$771,190
Less Treasury Stock, Common (10,000 shares, at cost)		12,500
Total Stockholders' Equity		$758,690

*Retained Earnings = $40,000 − $24,910 = $15,090.

3. Calculate dividends yield on common stock, price/earnings ratio of common stock, and return on equity.

Dividends per Share = $14,910 Common Stock Dividend ÷ 213,000 Common Shares Outstanding = $.07

$$\text{Dividends Yield} = \frac{\text{Dividends per Share}}{\text{Market Price per Share}} = \frac{\$.07}{\$1.60} = 4.4\%$$

$$\text{Price/Earnings (P/E) Ratio} = \frac{\text{Market Price per Share}}{\text{Earnings per Share}} = \frac{\$1.60}{\$.15} = 10.7 \text{ times}$$

The opening balance of stockholders' equity on February 1, 20x1 was $125,000.

$$\text{Return on Equity} = \frac{\text{Net Income}}{\text{Average Stockholders' Equity}}$$

$$= \frac{\$40{,}000}{(\$758{,}690 + \$125{,}000) \div 2}$$

$$= 9.1\%$$

Chapter Assignments

BUILDING YOUR KNOWLEDGE FOUNDATION

Questions

1. What are the issues related to contributed capital facing management?
2. Identify and explain several advantages of the corporate form of business.
3. Identify and explain several disadvantages of the corporate form of business.
4. What is dividends yield, and what do investors learn from it?
5. What is the price/earnings (P/E) ratio, and what does it measure?
6. What are the organization costs of a corporation?
7. What is the proper accounting treatment of organization costs?
8. What is the legal capital of a corporation, and what is its significance?
9. Describe the significance of the following dates as they relate to dividends: (a) date of declaration, (b) date of record, and (c) date of payment.
10. Explain the accounting treatment of cash dividends.
11. What are dividends in arrears, and how should they be disclosed in the financial statements?
12. Define the terms *cumulative, convertible,* and *callable* as they apply to preferred stock.
13. How is the value of stock determined when stock is issued for noncash assets?
14. Define *treasury stock* and explain why a company would purchase its own stock.
15. What is the proper classification of the following accounts on the balance sheet? Indicate whether stockholders' equity accounts are contributed capital, retained earnings, or contra stockholders' equity. (a) Organization Costs; (b) Common Stock; (c) Treasury Stock; (d) Paid-in Capital, Treasury Stock; (e) Paid-in Capital in Excess of Par Value, Common; (f) Paid-in Capital in Excess of Stated Value, Common; and (g) Retained Earnings.
16. What is a stock option plan and why does a company have one?

Short Exercises

LO 1 *Management Issues*

SE 1. Indicate whether each of the actions below is related to (a) forming a corporation, (b) managing under the corporate form of business, (c) using equity financing, (d) determining dividend policies, or (e) evaluating performance using return on equity.

1. Considering whether to make a distribution to stockholders
2. Controlling day-to-day operations not necessarily by the owners
3. Determining whether to issue preferred or common stock
4. Compensating management based on the company's meeting or exceeding the targeted return on equity
5. Issuing shares (not to exceed the maximum of authorized shares)
6. Transferring shares from one owner to another without the approval of other owners
7. Deciding who will be the officers and board of directors

LO 1 *Advantages and Disadvantages of a Corporation*

SE 2. Identify whether each of the following characteristics is an advantage or a disadvantage of the corporate form of business.

1. Ease of transfer of ownership
2. Taxation
3. Separate legal entity
4. Lack of mutual agency
5. Government regulation
6. Continuous existence

SE 3. **LO 2** *Effect of Organization Costs*

At the beginning of 20x1, Matson Company incurred two organization costs: (1) attorney's fees with a market value of $5,000, paid with 3,000 shares of $1 par value common stock, and (2) incorporation fees paid to the state of $3,000. Calculate total organization costs. Assuming that the company elects to write off organization costs over five years, what will be the effect of these costs on the balance sheet and income statement after one year?

SE 4. **LO 3** *Stockholders' Equity*

Prepare the stockholders' equity section of Lincoln Corporation's balance sheet from the following accounts and balances on December 31, 20xx.

Account	Balance	
	Debit	Credit
Common Stock, $10 par value, 60,000 shares authorized, 40,000 shares issued, and 39,000 shares outstanding		$400,000
Paid-in Capital in Excess of Par Value, Common		200,000
Retained Earnings		30,000
Treasury Stock, Common (1,000 shares, at cost)	$15,000	

SE 5. **LO 4** *Cash Dividends*

Blancone Corporation has authorized 100,000 shares of $1 par value common stock, of which 80,000 are issued and 70,000 are outstanding. On May 15, the board of directors declared a cash dividend of $.10 per share payable on June 15 to stockholders of record on June 1. Prepare the entries, as necessary, for each of the three dates.

SE 6. **LO 5** *Preferred Stock Dividends with Dividends in Arrears*

The Vergennes Corporation has 1,000 shares of its $100, 8 percent cumulative preferred stock outstanding and 20,000 shares of its $1 par value common stock outstanding. In its first three years of operation, the board of directors of Vergennes Corporation paid cash dividends as follows: 20x1, none; 20x2, $20,000; and 20x3, $40,000.

Determine the total cash dividends and dividends per share paid to the preferred and common stockholders during each of the three years.

SE 7. **LO 6** *Issuance of Stock*

Ferrisburg Company is authorized to issue 100,000 shares of common stock. The company sold 5,000 shares at $12 per share. Prepare journal entries to record the sale of stock for cash under each of the following independent alternatives: (1) The stock has a par value of $5, and (2) the stock has no par value but a stated value of $1 per share.

SE 8. **LO 6** *Issuance of Stock for Noncash Assets*

Borneo Corporation issued 8,000 shares of its $1 par value common stock in exchange for some land. The land had a fair market value of $50,000.

Prepare the journal entries necessary to record the issuance of the stock for the land under each of the following independent conditions: (1) The stock was selling for $7 per share on the day of the transaction, and (2) management attempted to place a value on the common stock but could not do so.

SE 9. **LO 7** *Treasury Stock Transactions*

Prepare the journal entries necessary to record the following stock transactions of the Lemner Company during 20xx.

Oct. 1 Purchased 1,000 shares of its own $2 par value common stock for $20, the current market price.
17 Sold 250 shares of treasury stock purchased on Oct. 5 for $25 per share.
21 Sold 400 shares of treasury stock purchased on Oct. 5 for $18 per share.

SE 10. **LO 7** *Retirement of Treasury Stock*

On October 28, 20xx, the Lemner Company (**SE 9**) retired the remaining 350 shares of treasury stock. The shares were originally issued at $5 per share. Prepare the necessary journal entry.

SE 11. LO 8 *Exercise of Stock Options* On June 6, Winston Leno exercised his option to purchase 10,000 shares of Plunkett Company $1 par value common stock at an option price of $4. The market price per share was $4 on the grant date and $18 on the exercise date. Record the transaction on Plunkett's books.

Exercises

E 1. LO 1 *Dividends Yield and Price/Earnings Ratio* In 20x1, Kessler Corporation earned $2.20 per share and paid a dividend of $1.00 per share. At year end, the price of its stock was $33 per share. Calculate the dividends yield and the price/earnings ratio.

E 2. LO 3 LO 7 *Stockholders' Equity* The accounts and balances below were taken from the records of Jamil Corporation on December 31, 20xx.

Account	Balance Debit	Balance Credit
Preferred Stock, $100 par value, 9% cumulative, 20,000 shares authorized, 12,000 shares issued and outstanding		$1,200,000
Common Stock, $12 par value, 90,000 shares authorized, 60,000 shares issued and outstanding		720,000
Paid-in Capital in Excess of Par Value, Common		388,000
Retained Earnings		46,000
Treasury Stock	$60,000	

Prepare a stockholders' equity section for Jamil Corporation's balance sheet.

E 3. LO 3 LO 5 *Characteristics of Common and Preferred Stock* Indicate whether each characteristic listed below is more closely associated with common stock (C) or preferred stock (P).

1. Often receives dividends at a set rate
2. Is considered the residual equity of a company
3. Can be callable
4. Can be convertible
5. More likely to have dividends that vary in amount from year to year
6. Can be entitled to receive dividends not paid in past years
7. Likely to have full voting rights
8. Receives assets first in liquidation
9. Generally receives dividends before other classes of stock

E 4. LO 3 LO 6 *Stock Journal Entries and Stockholders' Equity* The Winkler Hospital Supply Corporation was organized in 20xx. The company was authorized to issue 100,000 shares of no-par common stock with a stated value of $5 per share, and 20,000 shares of $100 par value, 6 percent noncumulative preferred stock. On March 1 the company issued 60,000 shares of its common stock for $15 per share and 8,000 shares of its preferred stock for $100 per share.

1. Prepare the journal entries to record the issuance of the stock.
2. Prepare the company's stockholders' equity section of the balance sheet immediately after the common and preferred stock was issued.

E 5. LO 4 *Cash Dividends* Downey Corporation has secured authorization from the state for 200,000 shares of $10 par value common stock. There are 160,000 shares issued and 140,000 shares outstanding. On June 5, the board of directors declared a $.50 per share cash dividend to be paid on June 25 to stockholders of record on June 15. Prepare the journal entries necessary to record these events.

E 6. LO 4 LO 7 *Cash Dividends*

Gayle Corporation has 500,000 authorized shares of $1 par value common stock, of which 400,000 are issued, including 40,000 shares of treasury stock. On October 15, the board of directors declared a cash dividend of $.25 per share payable on November 15 to stockholders of record on November 1. Prepare the entries, as necessary, for each of the three dates.

E 7. LO 5 *Cash Dividends with Dividends in Arrears*

The Matsuta Corporation has 10,000 shares of its $100 par value, 7 percent cumulative preferred stock outstanding, and 50,000 shares of its $1 par value common stock outstanding. In its first four years of operation, the board of directors of Matsuta Corporation paid cash dividends as follows: 20x1, none; 20x2, $120,000; 20x3, $140,000; 20x4, $140,000.

Determine the dividends per share and total cash dividends paid to the preferred and common stockholders during each of the four years.

E 8. LO 5 *Preferred and Common Cash Dividends*

The Levinson Corporation pays dividends at the end of each year. The dividends paid for 20x1, 20x2, and 20x3 were $80,000, $60,000, and $180,000, respectively.

Calculate the total amount of dividends paid each year to the common and preferred stockholders if each of the following capital structures is assumed: (1) 20,000 shares of $100 par, 6 percent noncumulative preferred stock and 60,000 shares of $10 par common stock. (2) 10,000 shares of $100 par, 7 percent cumulative preferred stock and 60,000 shares of $10 par common stock. There were no dividends in arrears at the beginning of 20x1.

E 9. LO 6 *Issuance of Stock*

Foth Company is authorized to issue 200,000 shares of common stock. On August 1, the company issued 10,000 shares at $25 per share. Prepare journal entries to record the issuance of stock for cash under each of the following independent alternatives:

1. The stock has a par value of $25.
2. The stock has a par value of $10.
3. The stock has no par value.
4. The stock has a stated value of $1 per share.

E 10. LO 6 *Issuance of Stock for Noncash Assets*

On July 1, 20xx, Elk Grove, a new corporation, issued 20,000 shares of its common stock for a corporate headquarters building. The building has a fair market value of $600,000 and a book value of $400,000. Because the corporation is new, it is not possible to establish a market value for the common stock.

Record the issuance of stock for the building, assuming the following conditions: (1) The par value of the stock is $10 per share; (2) the stock is no-par stock; and (3) the stock has a stated value of $4 per share.

E 11. LO 7 *Treasury Stock Transactions*

Prepare the journal entries necessary to record the following stock transactions of the Vishniac Company during 20xx.

May 5 Purchased 400 shares of its own $2 par value common stock for $20 per share, the current market price.
17 Sold 150 shares of treasury stock purchased on May 5 for $22 per share.
21 Sold 100 shares of treasury stock purchased on May 5 for $20 per share.
28 Sold the remaining 150 shares of treasury stock purchased on May 5 for $19.00 per share.

E 12. LO 7 *Treasury Stock Transactions Including Retirement*

Prepare the journal entries necessary to record the following stock transactions of Armstrong Corporation, which represent all treasury stock transactions entered into by the company.

June 1 Purchased 2,000 shares of its own $30 par value common stock for $70 per share, the current market price.
10 Sold 500 shares of treasury stock purchased on June 1 for $80 per share.
20 Sold 700 shares of treasury stock purchased on June 1 for $58 per share.
30 Retired the remaining shares purchased on June 1. The original issue price was $42 per share.

E 13. LO 8 *Grant and Exercise of Stock Options*

On January 1, 20x8, Jennifer Ling received an option to purchase 10,000 shares of $1 par value common stock at the January 1, 20x8, market price of $13 per share. The fair market value of the options on the date of grant was $16 per share, and the options expire on December 31, 20x8. Record the entry to recognize compensation expense for 20x8 and describe the alternative method of reporting in the notes to the financial statements. Jennifer Ling exercised her options on November 30, 20x8. Record the issuance of stock.

Problems

P 1. LO 2, LO 3, LO 4, LO 6 *Organization Costs, Stock and Dividend Journal Entries, and Stockholders' Equity*

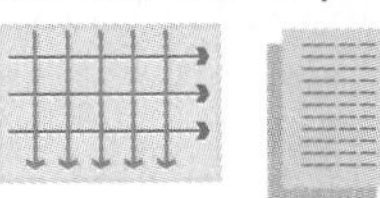

On March 1, 20xx, Blanco Corporation began operations with a charter from the state that authorized 100,000 shares of $4 par value common stock. Over the next quarter, the firm engaged in the following transactions:

Mar. 1	Issued 30,000 shares of common stock, $200,000.
2	Paid fees associated with obtaining the charter and organizing the corporation, $24,000.
Apr. 10	Issued 13,000 shares of common stock, $130,000.
May 31	The board of directors declared a $.20 per share cash dividend to be paid on June 15 to shareholders of record on June 10.

REQUIRED

1. Record the transactions indicated above in journal form.
2. Prepare the stockholders' equity section of Blanco Corporation's balance sheet on May 31, 20xx. Net income earned during the first quarter, $24,000.
3. Assuming that the payment for organization costs on March 2 was going to be amortized over five years, what adjusting entry was made on May 31 to record three months' amortization?
4. How does the adjusting entry in **3** affect the firm's balance sheet, including the resulting amount of organization costs?

P 2. LO 1, LO 5 *Preferred and Common Stock Dividends and Dividends Yield*

The Laqueur Corporation had both common stock and preferred stock outstanding from 20x4 through 20x6. Information about each stock for the three years is as follows:

Type	Par Value	Shares Outstanding	Other
Preferred	$100	20,000	7% cumulative
Common	10	600,000	

The company paid $70,000, $400,000, and $550,000 in dividends for 20x4 through 20x6, respectively. The market price per common share was $15.00 and $17.00 per share at year-end 20x5 and 20x6, respectively.

REQUIRED

1. Determine the dividend per share and total dividends paid to the common and preferred stockholders each year.
2. Repeat the computations performed in **1**, with the assumption that the preferred stock was noncumulative.
3. Calculate the 20x5 and 20x6 dividends yield for common stock using dividends per share computed in **2.**

P 3. LO 7 *Treasury Stock Transactions*

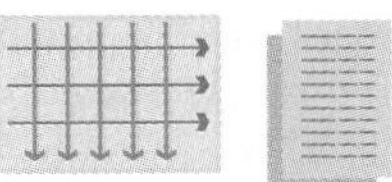

The Meier Company was involved in the following treasury stock transactions during 20xx.

a. Purchased 52,000 shares of its $2 par value common stock on the market for $40 per share.
b. Sold 16,000 shares of the treasury stock for $42 per share.
c. Sold 12,000 shares of the treasury stock for $38 per share.
d. Sold 20,000 shares of the treasury stock for $34 per share.

e. Purchased an additional 8,000 shares for $36 per share.
f. Retired all the remaining shares of treasury stock. All shares originally were issued at $16 per share.

REQUIRED

Record these transactions in journal form.

P 4. LO 2 LO 3 LO 4 LO 5 LO 6 LO 7 *Comprehensive Stockholders' Equity Transactions*

Harrington Plastics Corporation was chartered in the state of Massachusetts. The company was authorized to issue 10,000 shares of $100 par value, 6 percent preferred stock and 100,000 shares of no-par common stock. The common stock has a $1 stated value. The stock-related transactions for the quarter ended May 31, 20xx, were as follows:

Mar. 3	Issued 10,000 shares of common stock for $60,000 worth of services rendered in organizing and chartering the corporation.
15	Issued 16,000 shares of common stock for land, which had an asking price of $100,000. The common stock had a market value of $6 per share.
22	Issued 5,000 shares of preferred stock for $500,000.
May 4	Issued 10,000 shares of common stock for $60,000.
10	Purchased 2,500 shares of common stock for the treasury for $6,500.
15	Declared a quarterly cash dividend on the outstanding preferred stock and $.05 per share on common stock outstanding, payable on May 30 to stockholders of record on May 25.
25	Date of record for cash dividends.
30	Paid cash dividends.

REQUIRED

1. Record transactions for the quarter ended May 31, 20xx, in journal form.
2. Prepare the stockholders' equity section of the company's balance sheet as of May 31, 20xx. Net income for the quarter was $23,000.

P 5. LO 2 LO 3 LO 4 LO 5 LO 6 LO 7 LO 8 *Comprehensive Stockholders' Equity Transactions and T Accounts*

In January 20xx, the Schell Corporation was organized and authorized to issue 2,000,000 shares of no-par common stock and 50,000 shares of 5 percent, $50 par value, noncumulative preferred stock. The stock-related transactions for the first year's operations follow.

Jan. 19	Sold 15,000 shares of the common stock for $31,500. State law requires a minimum of $1 stated value per share.
21	Issued 5,000 shares of common stock to attorneys and accountants for services valued at $11,000 and provided during the organization of the corporation.
Feb. 7	Issued 30,000 shares of common stock for a building that had an appraised value of $78,000.
Mar. 22	Purchased 10,000 shares of common stock for the treasury at $3 per share.
July 15	Issued 5,000 shares of common stock to employees under a stock option plan that allows any employee to buy shares at the current market price, which today is $3 per share.
Aug. 1	Sold 2,500 shares of treasury stock for $4 per share.
Sept. 1	Declared a cash dividend of $.15 per common share to be paid on September 25 to stockholders of record on September 15.
15	Cash dividends date of record.
25	Paid cash dividends to stockholders of record on September 15.
Oct. 30	Issued 4,000 shares of common stock for a piece of land. The stock was selling for $3 per share, and the land had a fair market value of $12,000.
Dec. 15	Issued 2,200 shares of preferred stock for $50 per share.

REQUIRED

1. Record the above transactions in T accounts. Prepare T accounts for Cash; Land; Building; Organization Costs; Cash Dividends Payable; Preferred Stock; Common Stock; Paid-in Capital in Excess of Stated Value, Common; Paid-in Capital, Treasury Stock; Retained Earnings; Treasury Stock, Common; and Cash Dividends Declared.
2. Prepare the stockholders' equity section of Schell Corporation's balance sheet as of December 31, 20xx. Net income earned during the year was $100,000.

Alternate Problems

P 6. LO 2, LO 3, LO 4, LO 6 *Organization Costs, Stock and Dividend Journal Entries, and Stockholders' Equity*

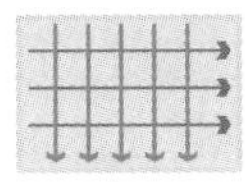

Lasser Corporation began operations on September 1, 20xx. The corporation's charter authorized 300,000 shares of $8 par value common stock. Lasser Corporation engaged in the following transactions during its first quarter:

Sept.	1	Issued 50,000 shares of common stock, $500,000.
	1	Paid an attorney $32,000 to help organize the corporation and obtain the corporate charter from the state.
Oct.	2	Issued 80,000 shares of common stock, $960,000.
Nov.	30	The board of directors declared a cash dividend of $.40 per share to be paid on December 15 to stockholders of record on December 10.

REQUIRED

1. Prepare journal entries to record the first-quarter transactions.
2. Prepare the stockholders' equity section of Lasser Corporation's November 30, 20xx balance sheet. Net income for the quarter was $80,000.
3. Assuming that the payment to the attorney on September 1 was going to be amortized over five years, what adjusting entry was made on November 30?
4. How does the adjusting entry in **3** affect the balance sheet, including the resulting amount of organization costs?

P 7. LO 1, LO 5 *Preferred and Common Stock Dividends and Dividends Yield*

The Theoharis Corporation had the following stock outstanding from 20x1 through 20x4.

Preferred stock: $50 par value, 8 percent cumulative, 10,000 shares authorized, issued, and outstanding

Common stock: $5 par value, 200,000 shares authorized, issued, and outstanding.

The company paid $30,000, $30,000, $94,000, and $130,000 in dividends during 20x1, 20x2, 20x3, and 20x4, respectively. The market price per common share was $7.25 and $8.00 per share at year end 20x3 and 20x4, respectively.

REQUIRED

1. Determine the dividend per share and the total dividends paid to common stockholders and preferred stockholders in 20x1, 20x2, 20x3, and 20x4.
2. Perform the same computations, with the assumption that the preferred stock was noncumulative.
3. Calculate the 20x3 and 20x4 dividends yield for common stock, using the dividends per share computed in **2.**

P 8. LO 2, LO 3, LO 4, LO 5, LO 6, LO 7 *Comprehensive Stockholders' Equity Transactions*

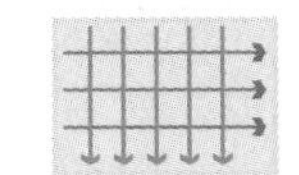

Wojcik, Inc., was organized and authorized to issue 10,000 shares of $100 par value, 9 percent preferred stock and 100,000 shares of no-par, $10 stated value common stock on July 1, 20xx. Stock-related transactions for Wojcik were as follows:

July	1	Issued 20,000 shares of common stock at $22 per share.
	1	Issued 1,000 shares of common stock at $22 per share for services rendered in connection with the organization of the company.
	2	Issued 4,000 shares of preferred stock at par value for cash.
	10	Issued 5,000 shares of common stock for land on which the asking price was $120,000. Market value of the stock was $24. Management wishes to record the land at full market value of the stock.
Aug.	2	Purchased 3,000 shares of common stock for the treasury at $26 per share.
	10	Declared a cash dividend for one month on the outstanding preferred stock and $.04 per share on common stock outstanding, payable on August 22 to stockholders of record on August 12.
	12	Date of record for cash dividends.
	22	Paid cash dividends.

REQUIRED

1. Record the transactions in journal form.
2. Prepare the stockholders' equity section of the balance sheet as it would appear on August 31, 20xx. Net income for July and August was $50,000.

Skills Development

CONCEPTUAL ANALYSIS

SD 1. LO 1 LO 3 *Reasons for Issuing Common Stock*

For decades ***Allstate Corporation,*** one of the largest automobile, home, and life insurance companies in the United States, was a division of ***Sears, Roebuck and Co.*** In June 1993, the company had an initial public offering that raised $2.5 billion, as the public bought 19.9 percent of Allstate common shares for $27 per share. Sears retained 80.1 percent of the shares. The company had paid an estimated $2.5 billion in claims as a result of Hurricane Andrew in Florida the previous year, but it expected to return to profitable operations in 1993 and 1994. Allstate's chief executive officer was quoted as saying, "Going public really focused us."[20] What advantages are there to Sears and Allstate in raising money by issuing common stock rather than bonds? Why would the chief executive officer say that going public "really focused us"?

SD 2. LO 5 *Reasons for Issuing Preferred Stock*

Preferred stock is a hybrid security that has some of the characteristics of stock and some of the characteristics of bonds. Historically, preferred stock has not been a popular means of financing. In the last few years, however, it has become more attractive to companies and individual investors alike, and investors are buying large amounts because of high yields. Large preferred stock issues have been made by banks such as ***Chase Manhattan, Citicorp, Republic New York,*** and ***Wells Fargo,*** as well as other companies. The dividend yields on these stocks are over 9 percent, higher than the interest rates on comparable bonds.[21] Especially popular are preferred equity redemption convertible stocks, or PERCs, which are automatically convertible into common stock after three years if the company does not redeem or call them first and retire them. What reasons can you give for the popularity of preferred stock, and of PERCs in particular, when the tax-deductible interest on bonds is less costly? Discuss both the company's and the investor's standpoints.

SD 3. LO 7 *Purposes of Treasury Stock*

Many companies in recent years have bought back their common stock. For example, because ***Time Warner*** viewed its stock as substantially undervalued, it announced plans to buy back 4 percent of its outstanding shares in an effort to raise its market price. ***Kodak*** plans to contribute half of its $1 billion buyback program to its pension plan. Other companies are awash in cash because interest rates have declined, they have laid off employees to cut costs, and their need to make investments has decreased. ***IBM,*** with large cash holdings, has spent almost $3 billion this year buying back its stock and has said it will spend as much as $2.5 billion more. IBM chose to buy back shares in lieu of raising its dividend. What are the reasons that companies buy back their own shares? What is the effect of common stock share buybacks on earnings per share, return on equity, return on assets, debt to equity, and the current ratio?

ETHICAL DILEMMA

SD 4. LO 1 *Ethics of Incorporating an Accounting Firm*

Traditionally, accounting firms have organized as partnerships or as professional corporations, a form of corporation that in many ways resembles a partnership. In recent years, some accounting firms have had large judgments imposed upon them as a result of lawsuits by investors who lost money when they invested in companies the firms have audited that went bankrupt. Because of the increased risk of large losses from malprac-

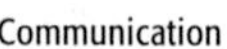
Communication

Critical Thinking

Group Activity

Memo

Ethics

International

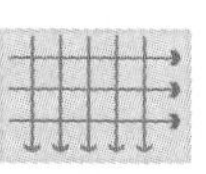
Spreadsheet

General Ledger

CD-ROM

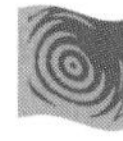
Internet

tice suits, accounting firms are allowed to incorporate as long as they maintain a minimum level of partners' capital and carry malpractice insurance. Some accounting practitioners feel that incorporating would be a violation of their responsibility to the public. What features of the corporate form of business would be most advantageous to the partners of an accounting firm? Do you think it is a violation of the public trust for an accounting firm to incorporate?

Research Activity

SD 5. LO 1 LO 3 LO 4 LO 5 LO 6 LO 8 *Reading Corporate Annual Reports*

Select the annual reports of three corporations, using one or more of the following sources: your library, the Fingraph® Financial Analyst™ CD-ROM software that accompanies this text, or the Needles Accounting Resource Center Web site at http://www.hmco.com/college/needles/home.html. You can choose them from the same industry or at random, at the direction of your instructor. (**Note:** You may be asked to use these companies again in the Research Activities in later chapters.) Prepare a table with a column for each corporation. Then answer the following questions for each corporation: Does the corporation have preferred stock? If so, what are the par value and the indicated dividend, and is the preferred stock cumulative or convertible? Is the common stock par value or no-par? What is the par value or stated value? What cash dividends, if any, were paid in the past year? What is the dividends yield? From the notes to the financial statements, determine whether the company has an employee stock option plan. What are some of its provisions? What is the return on equity? Be prepared to discuss the characteristics of the stocks and dividends for your selected companies in class.

Decision-Making Practice

SD 6. LO 1 LO 3 *Analysis of Alternative Financing Methods*

Companies offering services to the computer technology industry are growing quickly. Participating in this growth, ***Northeast Servotech Corporation*** has expanded rapidly in recent years. Because of its profitability, the company has been able to grow without obtaining external financing. This fact is reflected in its current balance sheet, which contains no long-term debt. The liability and stockholders' equity sections of the balance sheet on March 31, 20xx, follow.

Northeast Servotech Corporation
Balance Sheet
March 31, 20xx

Liabilities		
Current Liabilities		$ 500,000
Stockholders' Equity		
Common Stock, $10 par value, 500,000 shares authorized, 100,000 shares issued and outstanding	$1,000,000	
Paid-in Capital in Excess of Par Value, Common	1,800,000	
Retained Earnings	1,700,000	
Total Stockholders' Equity		4,500,000
Total Liabilities and Stockholders' Equity		$5,000,000

The company now has the opportunity to double its size by purchasing the operations of a rival company for $4,000,000. If the purchase goes through, Northeast Servotech will become the top company in its specialized industry in the northeastern part of the country. The problem for management is how to finance the purchase. After much study and discussion with bankers and underwriters, management has prepared three financing alternatives to present to the board of directors, which must authorize the purchase and the financing.

Alternative A: The company could issue $4,000,000 of long-term debt. Given the company's financial rating and the current market rates, management believes the company will have to pay an interest rate of 17 percent on the debt.

Alternative B: The company could issue 40,000 shares of 12 percent, $100 par value preferred stock.

Alternative C: The company could issue 100,000 additional shares of $10 par value common stock at $40 per share.

Management explains to the board that the interest on the long-term debt is tax-deductible and that the applicable income tax rate is 40 percent. The board members know that a dividend of $.80 per share of common stock was paid last year, up from $.60 and $.40 per share in the two years before that. The board has had a policy of regular increases in dividends of $.20 per share. The board feels that each of the three financing alternatives is feasible and now wants to study the financial effects of each alternative.

1. Prepare a schedule to show how the liabilities and stockholders' equity sections of Northeast Servotech's balance sheet would look under each alternative, and compute the debt to equity ratio (total liabilities ÷ total stockholders' equity) for each.
2. Compute and compare the cash needed to pay the interest or dividends for each kind of new financing net of income taxes in the first year.
3. How might the cash needed to pay for the financing change in future years under each alternative?
4. Prepare a memorandum to the board of directors that evaluates the alternatives in order of preference based on cash flow effects, giving arguments for and against each one.

Group Activity: Assign the alternatives to different groups to analyze and present to the class as the "board of directors."

Financial Reporting and Analysis

INTERPRETING FINANCIAL REPORTS

LO 1 LO 3 LO 6 *Effect of Stock Issue*

FRA 1. ***Netscape Communications Corporation*** is a leading provider of software, applications, and tools that link people and information over networks, the Internet, and the World Wide Web. Netscape went public with an IPO in June 1995 and issued shares at a price of $14 per share. On November 14, 1996, Netscape announced a common stock issue in an ad in *The Wall Street Journal:*

6,440,000 Shares
NETSCAPE
Common Stock
Price $53¾ a share

If Netscape sold all these shares at the offering price of $53.75, the net proceeds before issue costs would be $346.15 million.

A portion of the stockholders' equity section of the balance sheet adapted from Netscape's 1995 annual report is shown below.

	1995	1994
	(in thousands)	
Common Stock, $.0001 par value, 200,000,000 shares authorized, 12,003,594 shares in 1994 and 81,063,158 shares in 1995 issued and outstanding	$ 8	$ 1
Additional Paid-in Capital	196,749	18,215
Accumulated Deficit	(16,314)	(12,873)

1. Assume the net proceeds from the sale of 6,440,000 shares at $53.75 were $342.6 million after issue costs. Record the stock issuance on Netscape's accounting records in journal form.
2. Prepare the portion of the stockholders' equity section of the balance sheet shown above after the issue of the common stock, based on the information given. Round all answers to the nearest thousand.
3. Based on your answer in **2,** did Netscape have to increase its authorized shares to undertake this stock issue?
4. What amount per share did Netscape receive and how much did Netscape's underwriters receive to help in issuing the stock if investors paid $53.75 per share? What do the underwriters do to earn their fee?

LO 7 **FRA 2.** *Purpose of Treasury Stock and Its Retirement*

The board of directors of ***Wm. Wrigley Jr. Company,*** the chewing gum company, has adopted a policy of retiring shares of common stock held in the corporate treasury "to the extent not required for issuance under the MIP [Management Incentive Plan or stock option plan]." The company began 1995 with a balance of 192,000 common shares in the treasury at a cost of $9,034,000. During the year the company purchased 261,000 shares of its own common stock for $11,811,000, reissued 54,000 shares for $2,293,000 that cost $2,449,000, and retired 180,000 shares that cost $8,218,000 and had originally been issued at $24,000.[22] What is the ending balance, in number of shares and dollar amount, of Treasury Stock on December 31, 1995? What reasons does management have to purchase shares of the company's stock? Why do you think the board of directors wants to retire treasury shares? Did management follow the board's stated policy with regard to treasury shares?

International Company

LO 3
LO 4 **FRA 3.** *Stockholders' Equity and Dividends*

Roche Group is a giant Swiss pharmaceutical company. Its stockholders' equity below shows how little importance common stock, called share capital, typically plays in the financing of Swiss companies.[23]

	1996	1995
Shareholders' Equity (in millions of Swiss Francs)		
Share Capital	160	160
Retained Earnings	20,620	17,394
Total Shareholders' Equity	20,780	17,554

When Swiss companies need financing, they often rely on debt financing from large Swiss banks and from other debt markets. With only 160 million Swiss francs in share capital, Roche has had few stock issues in its history. This amount compares to over 18 billion Swiss francs in liabilities. Also, Roche has been enormously profitable, having built up retained earnings of more than 20 billion Swiss francs over the years. The company also pays a good dividend that totaled 863 million Swiss francs in 1996. Record in journal form the declaration and issue of dividends in 1996. Assuming that dividends and net income were the only factors that affected retained earnings during 1996, how much did Roche earn in 1996 in U.S. dollars (use an exchange rate of 1.4 Swiss francs to the dollar)?

Toys "R" Us Annual Report

LO 1
LO 3
LO 7
LO 8 **FRA 4.** *Stockholders' Equity*

Refer to the Toys "R" Us annual report to answer the following questions.

1. What type of capital stock does Toys "R" Us have? What is the par value? How many shares are authorized, issued, and outstanding at the end of 1997?
2. What is the dividends yield for Toys "R" Us and its relationship to the investors' total return? Does the company rely mostly on stock or on earnings for its stockholders' equity?

3. From the statement of stockholders' equity how has management's policy with regard to treasury stock changed over the past three years? What favorable effects did the stock buybacks in the first two years have and how were the treasury shares used in the third year?
4. Does the company have a stock option plan? To whom do the stock options apply? Do employees have significant stock options? Given the market price of the stock shown in the report, do these options represent significant value to the employees?
5. Calculate and discuss the price/earnings ratio and return on equity for 1996 and 1997. The average share price for the fourth quarter was $22.50 and $31.00 for 1996 and 1997, respectively.

FINGRAPH® FINANCIAL ANALYST™

FRA 5.

LO 1 LO 3 LO 7 LO 8 *Stockholders' Equity Analysis*

Select any two companies from the same industry in the Fingraph® Financial Analyst™ CD-ROM software.

1. In the annual reports for the companies you have selected, identify the stockholders' equity section of the balance sheet and reference to any stockholders' equity accounts in the summary of significant accounting policies or notes to the financial statements. Do the companies have more than one kind of capital stock? What are the characteristics of each type of capital stock? Do the companies have treasury stock? Do the companies have an employee stock option plan?
2. Find the earnings per share and dividends per share in the annual reports for both companies. Also, find in the financial section of your local paper the current market prices of the companies' common stock. Prepare a table that summarizes this information and also shows the price/earnings ratio and the dividends yield.
3. Locate the statements of cash flows in the two companies' annual reports. Has the company issued capital stock or repurchased its stock in the last three years?
4. Find and read references to capital stock in management's discussion and analysis in each annual report.
5. Write a one-page executive summary that highlights the types of capital stock for these companies, significance of treasury stock, employee stock option plan, and compares the price/earnings ratio and the dividends yield trends of the two companies, including reference to management's assessment. Include your table as an attachment to your report.

ENDNOTES

1. General Motors Corporation, *Annual Report,* 1996.
2. Copyright© 1996 by Houghton Mifflin Company. Adapted and reprinted by permission from *The American Heritage Dictionary of the English Language,* Third Edition.
3. John H. Christy, "The Americanization of Matthias Zahn," *Forbes,* March 13, 1995.
4. "The Buyback Monster," *Forbes,* November 17, 1997.
5. "IBM Plans $3.5 Billion Buyback," *International Herald Tribune,* April 30, 1997.
6. Fred R. Bleakley, "Management Problem: Reinvest High Profits or Please Institutions?" *The Wall Street Journal,* October 16, 1995.
7. Abbott Laboratories, *Annual Report,* 1996.
8. The FASB allows organization costs to be amortized over a period of up to forty years.
9. Microsoft Corporation, Inc., *Annual Report,* 1997.
10. G. Christian Hill, "Microsoft Plans Preferred Issue of $750 Million," *The Wall Street Journal,* December 3, 1996.
11. Kyle Pope and Warren Getler, "Gateway 2000's New Shares Jump 28% Amid Keen Interest in Computer Issues," *The Wall Street Journal,* December 9, 1993.
12. William Power, "Boston Chicken Soars by 143% on Its IPO Day," *The Wall Street Journal,* November 10, 1993.
13. American Institute of Certified Public Accountants, *Accounting Trends & Techniques* (New York: AICPA, 1996), p. 271.

14. Roula Khalaf, "Free-Style Accounting," *Forbes,* March 1, 1993.
15. American Institute of Certified Public Accountants, *Accounting Trends & Techniques* (New York: AICPA, 1996).
16. *Statement of Accounting Standards No. 123,* "Accounting for Stock-Based Compensation" (Norwalk, Conn.: Financial Accounting Standards Board, 1995).
17. Wendy Bounds, "Kodak Gives Fisher Options to Purchase 750,000 of Its Shares," *The Wall Street Journal,* December 20, 1993.
18. Emily Nelson, "Eastman Kodak CEO Fisher Extends Employment Contract Through 2000," *The Wall Street Journal,* February 27, 1997.
19. Stock options are discussed here in the context of employee compensation. They can also be important features of complex corporate capitalization arrangements.
20. Hillary Durgin, "A New Hand Dealt to 1990s Allstate," *Crain's Chicago Business,* December 20, 1993.
21. Tom Herman, "Preferreds' Rich Yields Blind Some Investors to Risks," *The Wall Street Journal,* March 24, 1992.
22. Wm. Wrigley Jr. Company, *Annual Report,* 1995.
23. Roche Group, *Annual Report,* 1996.

The Corporate Income Statement and the Statement of Stockholders' Equity

LEARNING OBJECTIVES

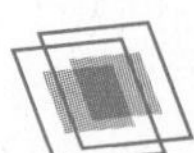

1. **Identify the issues related to evaluating the quality of a company's earnings.**
2. **Prepare a corporate income statement.**
3. **Show the relationships among income taxes expense, deferred income taxes, and net of taxes.**
4. **Describe the disclosure on the income statement of discontinued operations, extraordinary items, and accounting changes.**
5. **Compute earnings per share.**
6. **Prepare a statement of stockholders' equity.**
7. **Account for stock dividends and stock splits.**
8. **Calculate book value per share.**

DECISION POINT

General Electric Company (GE) is one of the most successful companies of all time. For many years, GE has prided itself on its consistent growth in earnings—a feat not accomplished by many other companies. As good as General Electric is, however, interpreting its results is not always easy. For instance, consider General Electric's performance for the five-year period 1992 through 1996, as measured by earnings per share.[1] Earnings from continuing operations have indeed increased from year to year, but net earnings have shown more variation. Someone who does not understand the structure and use of corporate income statements may be confused by the apparent contradiction of these numbers. What is the explanation?

Financial Highlights

(Per share)	**1996**	1995	1994	1993	1992
Earnings from continuing operations	$4.40	$3.90	$3.46	$2.45	$2.41
Net earnings	4.40	3.90	2.77	2.52	2.75

Earnings per share is the "bottom line" that many investors look at to judge the success or failure of a company, but looking just at the bottom line may be misleading because the corporate income statement can include a number of infrequent increases or decreases, more or less at the discretion

Critical Thinking Question: Why is it important to know which items included in earnings are recurring and which are one-time items? **Answer:** Earnings from continuing operations before nonrecurring items give a good signal about future results. In assessing the company's future earnings potential, nonrecurring items are excluded because they are not expected to continue.

of management, that result in variations like those shown for General Electric. *The Wall Street Journal* reports that while General Electric is an excellent company, part of its success in achieving consistent increases in earnings is "earnings management, the orchestrated timing of gains and losses to smooth out bumps and, especially, avoid a decline. . . . To smooth out fluctuations, GE frequently offsets one-time gains from big asset sales with restructuring charges; that keeps earnings from rising so high that they can't be topped the following year."[2] Knowledge of issues involving quality of earnings and the components of corporate income statements is essential to understanding and analyzing the operations of companies like General Electric.

Performance Measurement: Quality of Earnings Issues

OBJECTIVE 1

Identify the issues related to evaluating the quality of a company's earnings

Related Text Assignments:
Q: 1, 2, 3
SE: 1
E: 1
P: 1
SD: 1, 4
FRA: 1, 6

Current and expected earnings are an important factor to consider in evaluating a company's performance and analyzing its prospects. In fact, a survey of two thousand members of the Association for Investment Management and Research indicated that the two most important economic indicators in evaluating common stocks were expected changes in earnings per share and expected return on equity.[3] Net income is a key component of both measures. Because of the importance of net income, or the "bottom line," in measures of a company's prospects, there is significant interest in evaluating the quality of the net income figure, or the quality of earnings. The quality of a company's earnings refers to the substance of earnings and their sustainability into future accounting periods and may be affected by (1) the accounting methods and estimates the company's management chooses and (2) the nature of nonoperating items in the income statement.

Choice of Accounting Methods and Estimates

Point to Emphasize: Two companies in the same industry could have comparable earnings quantity but not comparable earnings quality. In order to assess the quality of reported earnings, one must know the methods and estimates used to compute income. GAAP allows several choices of methods and estimates, all yielding different results.

Choices of accounting methods and estimates affect a firm's operating income. To assure proper matching of revenues and expenses, accounting requires cost allocations and estimates of data that will not be known with certainty until some future date. For example, accountants estimate the useful life of assets when they are acquired. However, technological obsolescence could shorten the expected useful life, or excellent maintenance and repairs could lengthen it. The actual useful life will not be known with certainty until some future date. The choice of estimate affects both current and future operating income.

Because there is considerable latitude in the choice of estimates, management and other financial statement users must be aware of the impact of accounting estimates on reported operating income. Estimates include percentage of uncollectible accounts receivable, sales returns, useful life, residual or salvage value, total units of production, total recoverable units of natural resource, amortization period, expected warranty claims, and expected environmental cleanup costs.

These estimates are not all equally important to every firm. The relative importance of each estimate depends on the industry in which the firm operates. For example, the estimate of uncollectible receivables for a credit card firm, such as American Express, or a financial services firm, such as Bank of America, can have a material impact on earnings, but the choice of useful life may be less important because depreciable assets represent only a small percentage of total assets. Toys "R" Us has very few receivables, but it has substantial investment in depreciable assets; thus choice of useful life and residual value are much more important than uncollectible accounts receivable.

Business-World Example: The problems in the savings and loan industry are a good example of the importance of estimating uncollectible accounts, which have an impact on both earnings and assets.

Ethical Consideration: Ask your students what ethical considerations exist when making accounting estimates.

The choice of methods also affects a firm's operating income. Generally accepted accounting methods include uncollectible receivable methods (net sales or aging of accounts receivable), inventory methods [last-in, first-out (LIFO), first-in, first-out (FIFO), or average-cost], depreciation methods (accelerated, production, or straight-line), and revenue recognition methods. These methods are designed to match revenues and expenses. Costs are allocated based on a determination of the benefits to the current period (expenses) versus the benefits to future periods (assets). The expenses are estimates, and the period or periods benefited cannot be demonstrated conclusively. The estimates are also subjective, because in practice it is hard to justify one method of estimation over another.

For these reasons, management, the accountant, and the financial statement user need to understand the possible effects of different accounting procedures on net income and financial position. Some methods and estimates are more conservative than others because they tend to produce a lower net income in the current period. For example, suppose that two companies have similar operations, but one uses FIFO for inventory costing and straight-line (SL) for computing depreciation, whereas the other uses LIFO for inventory costing and double-declining-balance (DDB) for computing depreciation. The income statements of the two companies might appear as follows:

	FIFO and SL	**LIFO and DDB**
Net Sales	$500,000	$500,000
Goods Available for Sale	$300,000	$300,000
Less Ending Inventory	60,000	50,000
Cost of Goods Sold	$240,000	$250,000
Gross Margin	$260,000	$250,000
Less: Depreciation Expense	$ 40,000	$ 80,000
Other Expenses	170,000	170,000
Total Operating Expenses	$210,000	$250,000
Operating Income	$ 50,000	$ 0

The operating income for the firm using LIFO and DDB is lower because, in periods of rising prices, the LIFO inventory costing method produces a higher cost of goods sold, and, in the early years of an asset's useful life, accelerated depreciation yields a

BUSINESS BULLETIN: **BUSINESS PRACTICE**

Quality of earnings is an important issue for investors. For example, analysts for Twentieth Century Mutual Funds, a major investment company, make adjustments to a company's reported financial performance to create a more accurate picture of the company's ongoing operations. Assume a paper company reports earnings of $1.30 per share, which makes year-to-year comparisons unusually strong. Upon further investigation, however, it is found that the per share number includes a one-time gain on the sale of assets of $.25 per share. Twentieth Century would list the company in its database as earning only $1.05 per share. "These kinds of adjustments help assure long-term decisions aren't based on one-time events."[4]

higher depreciation expense. The result is lower operating income. However, future operating income is expected to be higher.

Discussion Questions: 1. Who is responsible for the content of financial statements? 2. Which group's performance is being reported on in financial statements? **Answer:** 1. Management is responsible for the content of financial statements. 2. Financial statements report on the performance of management. *Note:* Students should be aware that when a group is responsible for reporting on its own activity, usually the best or most favorable position will be reported. Ethical considerations may also be mentioned here.

The $50,000 difference in operating income stems only from the differences in accounting methods. Differences in the estimated lives and residual values of the plant assets could lead to an even greater variation. In practice, of course, differences in net income occur for many reasons, but the user must be aware of the discrepancies that can occur as a result of the accounting methods chosen by management. In general, an accounting method or estimate that results in lower current earnings is considered to produce a better quality of operating income.

The existence of such alternatives could cause problems in the interpretation of financial statements were it not for the conventions of full disclosure and consistency. Full disclosure requires that management explain the significant accounting policies used in preparing the financial statements in a note to the statements. Consistency requires that the same accounting procedures be followed from year to year. If a change in procedure is made, the nature of the change and its monetary effect must be explained in a note.

Nature of Nonoperating Items

The corporate income statement consists of several components, as shown in Exhibit 1. The top of the statement presents income from current ongoing operations, called income from continuing operations. The lower part of the statement can contain such nonoperating items as discontinued operations, extraordinary gains and losses, and effects of accounting changes. Those items may drastically affect the bottom line, or net income, of the company. In fact, in Exhibit 1, earnings per common share associated with continuing operations were $2.81, but net income per share was $3.35, or 19.2 percent higher.

For practical reasons, the calculations of trends and ratios are based on the assumption that net income and other components are comparable from year to

BUSINESS BULLETIN: ETHICS IN PRACTICE

External users of financial statements depend on management's honesty and openness in disclosing factual information about a company. In the vast majority of cases, management's reports are reliable, but on occasion, employees (called *whistle-blowers*) may publicly disclose wrongdoing on the part of their company. For instance, employees have accused various divisions of Teledyne, Inc., a large defense contractor, of financial misdeeds. The charges include keeping two sets of records, overbilling the government, and making illegal payments to Egyptian officials. Although whistle-blowers are protected by law, their actions often harm their careers. A former Teledyne employee, for example, who complained about poor equipment, improper training, and shipments of untested components claims to have been banished to a dingy corner of the plant.[5] Such allegations had a negative effect on the market's view of Teledyne and must be considered when analyzing the company. As it turned out, these allegations were only the tip of the iceberg. Over the years Teledyne pleaded guilty to several cases of fraud and settled other cases. Years later, *The Wall Street Journal* reported that after "lackluster results and years of bruising criminal and civil allegations that it cheated . . . the government" the company was merged into another company and went out of existence as a separate company.[6]

Exhibit 1. A Corporate Income Statement

Junction Corporation Income Statement For the Year Ended December 31, 20xx		
Revenues		$925,000
Less Costs and Expenses		500,000
Income from Continuing Operations Before Taxes		$425,000
Income Taxes Expense		144,500
Income from Continuing Operations		$280,500
Discontinued Operations		
Income from Operations of Discontinued Segment (net of taxes, $35,000)	$90,000	
Loss on Disposal of Segment (net of taxes, $42,000)	(73,000)	17,000
Income Before Extraordinary Items and Cumulative Effect of Accounting Change		$297,500
Extraordinary Gain (net of taxes, $17,000)		43,000
Subtotal		$340,500
Cumulative Effect of a Change in Accounting Principle (net of taxes, $5,000)		(6,000)
Net Income		$334,500
Earnings per Common Share:		
Income from Continuing Operations		$ 2.81
Discontinued Operations (net of taxes)		.17
Income Before Extraordinary Items and Cumulative Effect of Accounting Change		$ 2.98
Extraordinary Gain (net of taxes)		.43
Cumulative Effect of Accounting Change (net of taxes)		(.06)
Net Income		$ 3.35

Point to Emphasize: Discontinued operations, extraordinary gains and losses, and the cumulative effect of a change in accounting principle must appear as separate items below income from continuing operations. They are all shown net of taxes.

Business-World Example: Discontinued operations, extraordinary items, and cumulative effects of a change in accounting principle are more likely to occur in large, public corporations. A knowledge of these items is important when analyzing the financial results of such companies. These items do not occur as frequently in small, private business corporations.

Point to Emphasize: Income from continuing operations is different from net income; it is a better indicator of future performance than net income.

year and from company to company. However, in making interpretations, the astute analyst will always look beyond the ratios to the quality of the components. For example, in a recent year, AT&T wrote off $7 billion for retiree health benefits and another $1.3 billion to cover future disability and severance payments. Despite those huge losses, the company's stock price was higher because income from operations before those charges was up for the year.[7] Although such write-offs reduce a company's net worth, they usually do not affect current cash flows or operations and in most cases are ignored by analysts assessing current performance.

Point to Emphasize: These examples also stress that a single year's information is not adequate without a trend for use as a reference.

In some cases, a company may boost income by including one-time gains. For example, Dayton-Hudson, a retail merchandising company that owns department stores such as Marshall Field's and Mervyn's, used a gain from an accounting adjustment to bolster an otherwise lackluster earnings report. For the full year, net income decreased 2 percent, but without the gain, net income would have decreased 30 percent. Weak earnings were camouflaged by a one-time $107 million gain after taxes from an accounting change.[8] The quality of Dayton-Hudson's earnings is in fact lower than it might appear on the surface. Unless analysts go beyond the "bottom line" in analyzing and interpreting financial reports, they can come to the wrong conclusions.

Instructional Strategy: Quality of earnings issues, in many cases, call attention to ethical considerations. To explore those issues, ask students to complete SD 4 as a one-page written assignment to be graded and discussed in class. Use a straw poll to assess students' agreement with the viewpoints expressed.

The Corporate Income Statement

OBJECTIVE 2

Prepare a corporate income statement

Related Text Assignments:
SE: 2
E: 2, 3
P: 2, 3, 7
SD: 2, 5
FRA: 5, 6

Parenthetical Note: Both single-step and multistep income statements are commonly used in corporate annual reports. Whichever format is used, the income statement must be all-inclusive.

Accounting organizations have not specified the format of the income statement because they have considered flexibility more important than a standard format. Either the single-step or the multistep form can be used. However, the accounting profession has taken the position that income for a period should be all-inclusive, comprehensive income, which is different from net income.[9] Comprehensive income is the change in a company's equity during a period from sources other than owners and includes net income, change in unrealized investment gains and losses, and other items affecting equity. Beginning in 1998, companies must report comprehensive income and its components as a separate financial statement, or as part of another financial statement. Net income or loss for a period includes all revenues, expenses, gains, and losses over the period, except for prior period adjustments. As a result, several items must be added to the income statement, among them discontinued operations, extraordinary items, and accounting changes. In addition, earnings per share figures must be disclosed. Exhibit 1 illustrates a corporate income statement and the required disclosures. The following sections discuss the components of the corporate income statement, beginning with income taxes expense.

Income Taxes Expense

OBJECTIVE 3

Show the relationships among income taxes expense, deferred income taxes, and net of taxes

Related Text Assignments:
Q: 4, 5
SE: 3
E: 3, 4, 5
P: 2, 3, 7
SD: 5
FRA: 3

Corporations determine their taxable income (the amount on which taxes are paid) by subtracting allowable business deductions from includable gross income. The federal tax laws determine which business expenses may be deducted and which cannot be deducted from taxable gross income.[10]

The tax rates that apply to a corporation's taxable income are shown in Table 1. A corporation with taxable income of $70,000 would have a federal income tax liability of $12,500: $7,500 (the tax on the first $50,000 of taxable income) plus $5,000 (25 percent of the $20,000 earned in excess of $50,000).

Income taxes expense is the expense recognized in the accounting records on an accrual basis that applies to income from continuing operations. This expense may or may not equal the amount of taxes actually paid by the corporation and recorded as income taxes payable in the current period. The amount payable is determined from taxable income, which is measured according to the rules and regulations of the income tax code.

Enrichment Note: The federal income tax is progressive. That is, the rate increases as taxable income increases.

Table 1. Tax Rate Schedule for Corporations, 1998*

Taxable Income		Tax Liability	
Over	But Not Over		Of the Amount Over
—	$ 50,000	0 + 15%	—
$ 50,000	75,000	$ 7,500 + 25%	$ 50,000
75,000	100,000	13,750 + 34%	75,000
100,000	335,000	22,250 + 39%	100,000
335,000	10,000,000	113,900 + 34%	335,000
10,000,000	15,000,000	3,400,000 + 35%	10,000,000
15,000,000	18,333,333	5,150,000 + 38%	15,000,000
18,333,333	—	6,416,667 + 35%	18,333,333

*Tax rates are subject to change by Congress.

Common Student Confusion: Most people think it is illegal to keep accounting records on a different basis from income tax records. They don't realize that it is normal because the Internal Revenue Code and GAAP often do not agree. To work with two conflicting sets of guidelines, the accountant must keep two sets of records.

For the sake of convenience, most small businesses keep their accounting records on the same basis as their tax records, so that the income taxes expense on the income statement equals the income taxes liability to be paid to the Internal Revenue Service (IRS). This practice is acceptable when there is no material difference between the income on an accounting basis and the income on an income tax basis. However, the purpose of accounting is to determine net income in accordance with generally accepted accounting principles, not to determine taxable income and tax liability.

Management has an incentive to use methods that minimize the firm's tax liability, but accountants, who are bound by accrual accounting and the materiality concept, cannot let tax procedures dictate their method of preparing financial statements if the result would be misleading. As a consequence, there can be a material difference between accounting and taxable incomes, especially in larger businesses. This discrepancy can result from differences in the timing of the recognition of revenues and expenses under the two accounting methods. Some possible variations are shown below.

	Accounting Method	**Tax Method**
Expense recognition	Accrual or deferral	At time of expenditure
Accounts receivable	Allowance	Direct charge-off
Inventories	Average cost	FIFO
Depreciation	Straight-line	Modified Accelerated Cost Recovery System

Deferred Income Taxes

Point to Emphasize: The discrepancy between GAAP-based tax expense and Internal Revenue Code-based tax liability produces the need for the Deferred Income Taxes account.

Accounting for the difference between income taxes expense based on accounting income and the actual income taxes payable based on taxable income is accomplished by a technique called income tax allocation. The amount by which income taxes expense differs from income taxes payable is reconciled in an account called Deferred Income Taxes. For example, Junction Corporation shows income taxes expense of $144,500 on its income statement but has actual income taxes payable to the IRS of $92,000. The entry to record the estimated income taxes expense applicable to income from continuing operations using the income tax allocation procedure would appear as follows:

A = L + OE
    + −

Dec. 31	Income Taxes Expense	144,500	
	Income Taxes Payable		92,000
	Deferred Income Taxes		52,500
	To record estimated current and deferred income taxes		

In other years, it is possible for Income Taxes Payable to exceed Income Taxes Expense, in which case the same entry is made except that Deferred Income Taxes is debited.

The Financial Accounting Standards Board has issued specific rules for recording, measuring, and classifying deferred income taxes.[11] Deferred income taxes are recognized for the estimated future tax effects resulting from temporary differences in the valuation of assets, liabilities, equity, revenues, expenses, gains, and losses for tax and financial reporting purposes. Temporary differences include revenues and expenses or gains and losses that are included in taxable income before or after they are included in financial income. In other words, the recognition point for revenues, expenses, gains, and losses is not the same for tax and financial reporting. For example, advance payments for goods and services, such as magazine subscriptions, are not recognized in financial income until the product is shipped, but for tax purposes they are usually recognized as revenue when cash is received. The result is that taxes paid exceed tax expense, which creates a deferred income tax asset (or prepaid taxes).

Clarification Note: Deferred Income Taxes is classified as a liability when it has a credit balance and as an asset when it has a debit balance. It is further classified as either current or long-term depending on when it is expected to reverse.

Classification of deferred income taxes as current or noncurrent depends on the classification of the related asset or liability that created the temporary difference. For example, the deferred income tax asset mentioned above would be classified as current if unearned subscription revenue is classified as a current liability. On the other hand, the temporary difference arising from depreciation is related to a long-term depreciable asset. Therefore, the resulting deferred income tax would be classified as long-term. However, if a temporary difference isn't related to an asset or liability, then it is classified as current or noncurrent based on its expected date of reversal. Temporary differences and the classification of deferred income taxes that results are covered in depth in more advanced courses.

Each year, the balance of the Deferred Income Taxes account is evaluated to determine whether it still accurately represents the expected asset or liability in light of legislated changes in income tax laws and regulations. If changes have occurred, an adjusting entry to bring the account balance into line with current laws is required. For example, a decrease in corporate income tax rates, like the one that occurred in 1987, means that a company with deferred income tax liabilities will pay less in taxes in future years than the amount indicated by the credit balance of its Deferred Income Taxes account. As a result, the company would debit Deferred Income Taxes to reduce the liability and credit Gain from Reduction in Income Tax Rates. This credit increases the reported income on the income statement. If the tax rate increases in future years, a loss would be recorded and the deferred income tax liability would be increased.

In any given year, the amount a company pays in income taxes is determined by subtracting (or adding, as the case may be) the deferred income taxes for that year, as reported in the notes to the financial statements, from (or to) income taxes expense, which is reported in the financial statements. In subsequent years, the amount of deferred income taxes can vary based on changes in tax laws and rates.

Some understanding of the importance of deferred income taxes to financial reporting can be gained from studying a survey of the financial statements of six hundred large companies. About 68 percent reported deferred income taxes with a credit balance in the long-term liability section of the balance sheet.[12]

Net of Taxes

Teaching Note: To present a conceptual overview of intraperiod tax allocation, draw a box and label it total income taxes expense. Then, divide the box into five sections and label them continuing operations, discontinued operations, extraordinary items, cumulative effect, and prior period adjustments. Finally, explain that if the income tax is not divided among the appropriate sections of the income statement or statement of retained earnings, the figures in those statements will be distorted. The idea is to let the tax follow the item.

The phrase net of taxes, as used in Exhibit 1, means that the effect of applicable taxes (usually income taxes) has been considered in determining the overall effect of an item on the financial statements. The phrase is used on the corporate income statement when a company has items that must be disclosed in a separate section. Each such item should be reported net of the applicable income taxes to avoid distorting the income taxes expense associated with ongoing operations and the resulting net operating income.

For example, assume that a corporation with operating income before taxes of $120,000 has a total tax expense of $66,000 and that the total income includes a gain of $100,000 on which a tax of $30,000 is due. Also assume that the gain is not part of normal operations and must be disclosed separately on the income statement as an extraordinary item (explained later). This is how the tax expense would be reported on the income statement.

Operating Income Before Taxes	$120,000
Income Taxes Expense	36,000
Income Before Extraordinary Item	$ 84,000
Extraordinary Gain (net of taxes, $30,000)	70,000
Net Income	$154,000

If all the tax expense were deducted from operating income before taxes, both the income before extraordinary item and the extraordinary gain would be distorted.

A company follows the same procedure in the case of an extraordinary loss. For example, assume the same facts as before except that the total tax expense is only $6,000 because of a $100,000 extraordinary loss. The result is a $30,000 tax saving, as shown below.

Operating Income Before Taxes	$120,000
Income Taxes Expense	36,000
Income Before Extraordinary Item	$ 84,000
Extraordinary Loss (net of taxes, $30,000)	(70,000)
Net Income	$ 14,000

In Exhibit 1, the total of the income tax items is $149,500. That amount is allocated among five statement components, as follows:

Income taxes expense on income from continuing operations	$144,500
Income tax on income from a discontinued segment	35,000
Income tax saving on the loss on the disposal of the segment	(42,000)
Income tax on the extraordinary gain	17,000
Income tax saving on the cumulative effect of a change in accounting principle	(5,000)
Total income taxes expense	$149,500

Discontinued Operations

OBJECTIVE 4

Describe the disclosure on the income statement of discontinued operations, extraordinary items, and accounting changes

Related Text Assignments:
Q: 6, 7, 8
E: 3
P: 2, 3, 7
SD: 1, 2, 5
FRA: 5, 6

Enrichment Note: A segment is a separate line of business or class of customer; it must be distinguishable physically and operationally for financial reporting purposes. Discontinuing *part* of a segment does not qualify for separate disclosure in this section.

Point to Emphasize: To qualify as extraordinary, an event must be unusual (not in the ordinary course of business) and must not be expected to occur again in the foreseeable future. Occasionally, judgment must be exercised when it is not clear whether an event meets these two criteria.

Large companies in the United States usually have many segments. A segment may be a separate major line of business or serve a separate class of customer. For example, a company that makes heavy drilling equipment may also have another line of business, such as the manufacture of mobile homes. A large company may discontinue or otherwise dispose of certain segments of its business that do not fit its future plans or are not profitable. Discontinued operations are segments of a business that are no longer part of its ongoing operations. Generally accepted accounting principles require that gains and losses from discontinued operations be reported separately in the income statement. Such separation makes it easier to evaluate the ongoing activities of the business.

In Exhibit 1, the disclosure of discontinued operations has two parts. One part shows that after the date of the decision to discontinue, the income from operations of the segment that has been disposed of was $90,000 (net of $35,000 taxes). The other part shows that the loss from the disposal of the segment was $73,000 (net of $42,000 tax saving). Computation of the gains or losses is covered in more advanced accounting courses. The disclosure has been described, however, to give a complete view of the corporate income statement.

Extraordinary Items

The Accounting Principles Board, in its *Opinion No. 30,* defines extraordinary items as "events or transactions that are distinguished by their unusual nature *and* by the infrequency of their occurrence."[13] Unusual and infrequent occurrences are explained in the opinion as follows:

> Unusual Nature—the underlying event or transaction should possess a high degree of abnormality and be of a type clearly unrelated to, or only incidentally related to, the ordinary and typical activities of the entity, taking into account the environment in which the entity operates.

Infrequency of Occurrence—the underlying event or transaction should be of a type that would not reasonably be expected to recur in the foreseeable future, taking into account the environment in which the entity operates.[14]

If an item is both unusual and infrequent (and material in amount), it should be reported separately from continuing operations on the income statement. The disclosure allows readers to identify gains or losses in income that would not be expected to happen again soon. Items usually treated as extraordinary include (1) an uninsured loss from flood, earthquake, fire, or theft; (2) a gain or loss resulting from the passage of a new law; (3) the expropriation (taking) of property by a foreign government; and (4) a gain or loss from the early retirement of debt. Gains or losses from extraordinary items should be reported on the income statement after discontinued operations. And they should be shown net of applicable taxes. In a recent year, fifty-six (9 percent) of six hundred large companies reported extraordinary items on their income statements.[15] In Exhibit 1, the extraordinary gain was $43,000 after applicable taxes of $17,000.

Accounting Changes

Enrichment Note: A change in accounting method (principle) violates the convention of consistency. Such a change is allowed, however, when it can be demonstrated that the new method will produce more useful financial statements. The effect of the change is disclosed just above net income on the income statement.

Consistency, which is one of the basic conventions of accounting, means that companies must apply the same accounting principles from year to year. However, a company is allowed to make accounting changes if current procedures are incorrect or inappropriate. For example, a change from the FIFO to the LIFO inventory method can be made if there is adequate justification for the change. Adequate justification usually means that if the change occurs, the financial statements will better show the financial activities of the company. A company's desire to lower the amount of income taxes it pays is not considered adequate justification for an accounting change. If justification does exist and an accounting change is made, generally accepted accounting principles require the disclosure of the change in the financial statements.

Ethical Consideration: Some accounting changes can produce a significant increase in net income without an accompanying improvement in performance. The user of financial statements should be aware that some businesses implement an accounting change solely for the increase in net income that results.

The cumulative effect of an accounting change is the effect that the new accounting principle would have had on net income in prior periods if it had been applied instead of the old principle. This effect is shown on the income statement immediately after extraordinary items.[16] For example, assume that in the five years prior to 20xx, the Junction Corporation had used the straight-line method to depreciate its machinery. This year, the company retroactively changed to the double-declining-balance method of depreciation. The controller computed the cumulative effect of the change in depreciation charges (net of taxes) as $6,000, as shown below.

Cumulative, 5-year double-declining-balance depreciation	$29,000
Less cumulative, 5-year straight-line depreciation	18,000
Before tax effect	11,000
Income tax savings	5,000
Cumulative effect of accounting change	$ 6,000

Instructional Strategy: Ask small groups to complete SD 2 in class. Randomly select 2 or 3 groups to present their position and supporting arguments. Summarize by emphasizing the key points presented and adding any omitted points.

Relevant information about the accounting change is shown in the notes to the financial statements. The change results in $11,000 of depreciation expense for prior years being deducted in the current year, in addition to the current year's depreciation costs included in the $500,000 costs and expenses section of the income statement. This expense must be shown in the current year's income statement as a reduction in income (see Exhibit 1). In 1995, seventy-seven, or 13 percent, of six hundred large companies reported changes in accounting procedures.[17] Further study of accounting changes is left to more advanced accounting courses.

Earnings per Share

OBJECTIVE 5

Compute earnings per share

Related Text Assignments:
Q: 9, 10, 11
SE: 4
E: 3, 6
P: 2, 3, 7
SD: 4
FRA: 6

Enrichment Note: Earnings per share is a measure of a corporation's profitability. It is one of the most closely watched financial statement ratios in the business world. Its disclosure, within or below the income statement, is required.

Readers of financial statements use earnings per share information to judge a company's performance and to compare it with the performance of other companies. Because such information is so important, the Accounting Principles Board concluded that earnings per share of common stock should be presented on the face of the income statement.[18] As shown in Exhibit 1, the information is usually disclosed just below the net income.

An earnings per share amount is always shown for (1) income from continuing operations, (2) income before extraordinary items and the cumulative effect of accounting changes, (3) the cumulative effect of accounting changes, and (4) net income. If the statement shows a gain or loss from discontinued operations or a gain or loss on extraordinary items, earnings per share amounts can also be presented for them. The per share data below from Fleetwood Enterprises, Inc.'s income statement show why it is a good idea to study the components of earnings per share.[19]

Financial Highlights

	Years ended April 30		
	1996	1995	1994
Net income per common and equivalent share:			
Continuing operations	$1.50	$1.63	$1.30
Discontinued operations	.21	.19	.16
Cumulative effect of accounting change	—	—	(.03)
Total	$1.71	$1.82	$1.43

Note that net income (loss) was influenced by special items in all three years reported. In 1994, special items actually increased income from continuing operations of $.13 per share to a net profit of $1.43 per share; in 1995, special items increased net income per share by more than 11 percent. In 1996 the company had special items that increased earnings per share of $.21 per share; thus 100 percent of reported net income per share is attributable to continuing operations.

Basic earnings per share is net income applicable to common stock divided by the weighted-average number of common shares outstanding. To compute this figure, one must determine if during the year the number of common shares outstanding changed, and if the company paid preferred stock dividends.

When a company has only common stock and has the same number of shares outstanding throughout the year, the earnings per share computation is simple. From Exhibit 1, we know that Junction Corporation reported net income of $334,500. Assume that the company had 100,000 shares of common stock outstanding for the entire year. The earnings per share of common stock is computed as follows:

$$\text{Earnings per Share} = \frac{\$334{,}500}{100{,}000 \text{ shares}}$$
$$= \$3.35 \text{ per share}$$

Point to Emphasize: The earnings per share calculation is based on the weighted-average number of shares outstanding during the year, much like the calculation of interest on a bank account.

If the number of shares outstanding changes during the year, it is necessary to figure the weighted-average number of shares outstanding for the year. Suppose that

Junction Corporation had the following amounts of common shares outstanding during various periods of the year: January–March, 100,000 shares; April–September, 120,000 shares; and October–December, 130,000 shares. The weighted-average number of common shares outstanding and basic earnings per share would be found this way:

100,000 shares × ¼ year	25,000
120,000 shares × ½ year	60,000
130,000 shares × ¼ year	32,500
Weighted-average shares outstanding	$117,500

$$\text{Basic Earnings per Share} = \frac{\text{Net Income}}{\text{Weighted-Average Common Shares Outstanding}}$$

$$= \frac{\$334{,}500}{117{,}500 \text{ shares}}$$

$$= \$2.85 \text{ per share}$$

If a company has nonconvertible preferred stock outstanding, the dividend for that stock must be subtracted from net income before earnings per share for common stock are computed. Suppose that Junction Corporation has preferred stock on which the annual dividend is $23,500. Earnings per share on common stock would be $2.65 [($334,500 − $23,500) ÷ 117,500 shares].

Companies with a capital structure in which there are no bonds, stocks, or stock options that could be converted into common stock are said to have a simple capital structure. The earnings per share for these companies is computed as shown on the previous page. Some companies, however, have a complex capital structure, which includes exercisable stock options or convertible stocks and bonds. Those convertible securities have the potential of diluting the earnings per share of common stock. *Potential dilution* means that a stockholder's proportionate share of ownership in a company could be reduced through the conversion of stocks or bonds or the exercise of stock options, which would increase the total shares outstanding.

For example, suppose that a person owns 10,000 shares of a company, which equals 2 percent of the outstanding shares of 500,000. Now, suppose that holders of convertible bonds convert the bonds into 100,000 shares of stock. The person's 10,000 shares would then equal only 1.67 percent (10,000 ÷ 600,000) of the outstanding shares. In addition, the added shares outstanding would lower earnings per share and would most likely lower market price per share.

BUSINESS BULLETIN: **BUSINESS PRACTICE**

Sometimes a change in accounting principle is mandated by the Financial Accounting Standards Board. For many companies, such a change has a dramatic effect on reported earnings. However, accounting changes made at management's discretion usually have a positive or income-increasing effect. For example, in 1996 Bell Atlantic Corporation, a diversified telecommunications company, reported a one-time voluntary change in accounting principles associated with publishing its directories. The amount of the cumulative effect of change in accounting principle increased net income by $142.1 million or 8.2%, from $1,739.4 million to $1,881.5 million. If the company had not made the change in 1996, its net income would have fallen 6.4%, from $1,858.3 million to $1,739.4 million. Instead, the company reported a small increase in its net income.[20]

Point to Emphasize: A company with potentially dilutive securities (such as convertible preferred stock or bonds) has a complex capital structure and must present two earnings per share figures—basic and diluted. The latter figure is the more conservative of the two.

Because stock options and convertible preferred stocks or bonds have the potential to dilute earnings per share, they are referred to as potentially dilutive securities. When a company has a complex capital structure, it must report two earnings per share figures: basic earnings per share and diluted earnings per share.[21] Diluted earnings per share are calculated by adding all potentially dilutive securities to the denominator of the basic earnings per share calculation. This figure shows stockholders the maximum potential effect of dilution of their ownership position in the company.

For fiscal years ending prior to December 15, 1997, a corporation with a complex capital structure may have reported primary earnings per share and fully diluted earnings per share. Primary earnings per share considered only some potentially dilutive securities in its calculation, whereas diluted earnings per share included all potentially dilutive securities.

The computation of diluted earnings per share is a complex process and is reserved for more advanced courses.

The Statement of Stockholders' Equity

OBJECTIVE 6

Prepare a statement of stockholders' equity

Related Text Assignments:
Q: 12, 13
SE: 5, 6, 7
E: 7, 8
P: 4, 5, 6, 8, 9
SD: 5, 6
FRA: 2, 4, 5, 6

Enrichment Note: The majority of annual reports contain a statement of stockholders' equity because it discloses far more than a statement of retained earnings.

The statement of stockholders' equity, also called the *statement of changes in stockholders' equity,* summarizes the changes in the components of the stockholders' equity section of the balance sheet. More and more companies are using this statement in place of the statement of retained earnings because it reveals much more about the year's stockholders' equity transactions. In the statement of stockholders' equity in Exhibit 2, for example, the first line shows the beginning balance of each account in the stockholders' equity section. Each subsequent line discloses the effects of transactions on those accounts. It is possible to determine from the statement that during 20x1 Tri-State Corporation issued 5,000 shares of common stock for $250,000, had a conversion of $100,000 of preferred stock into common stock, declared and issued a 10 percent stock dividend on common stock, had a net purchase of treasury shares of $24,000, earned net income of $270,000, and paid cash dividends on both preferred and common stock. The ending balances of the accounts are presented at the bottom of the statement. Those accounts and balances make up the stockholders' equity section of Tri-State's balance sheet on December 31, 20x1, as shown in Exhibit 3.

Retained Earnings

Notice that in Exhibit 2 the Retained Earnings column has the same components as the statement of retained earnings. The retained earnings of a company are the part of stockholders' equity that represents stockholders' claims to assets arising from the earnings of the business. Retained earnings equal a company's profits since the date of its inception, less any losses, dividends to stockholders, or transfers to contributed capital.

Common Student Error: Students often confuse retained earnings with cash. Point out that retained earnings are intangible and represent a general ownership claim on the assets of the corporation.

It is important to remember that retained earnings are not the assets themselves. The existence of retained earnings means that assets generated by profitable operations have been kept in the company to help it grow or to meet other business needs. A credit balance in Retained Earnings is *not* directly associated with a specific amount of cash or designated assets. Rather, such a balance means that assets as a whole have been increased.

Point to Emphasize: In accounting, a deficit is a negative (debit) balance in Retained Earnings. It is not the same thing as a net loss, which reflects the performance in just one accounting period.

Retained Earnings can carry a debit balance. Generally, this happens when a company's dividends and subsequent losses are greater than its accumulated profits from operations. In such a case, the firm is said to have a deficit (debit balance) in

Exhibit 2. A Statement of Stockholders' Equity

Tri-State Corporation
Statement of Stockholders' Equity
For the Year Ended December 31, 20x1

	Preferred Stock $100 Par Value 8% Convertible	Common Stock $10 Par Value	Paid-in Capital in Excess of Par Value, Common	Retained Earnings	Treasury Stock	Total
Balance, December 31, 20x0	$400,000	$300,000	$300,000	$600,000	—	$1,600,000
Issuance of 5,000 Shares of Common Stock		50,000	200,000			250,000
Conversion of 1,000 Shares of Preferred Stock into 3,000 Shares of Common Stock	(100,000)	30,000	70,000			—
10 Percent Stock Dividend on Common Stock, 3,800 Shares		38,000	152,000	(190,000)		—
Purchase of 500 Shares of Treasury Stock					($24,000)	(24,000)
Net Income				270,000		270,000
Cash Dividends						
Preferred Stock				(24,000)		(24,000)
Common Stock				(47,600)		(47,600)
Balance, December 31, 20x1	$300,000	$418,000	$722,000	$608,400	($24,000)	$2,024,400

Instructional Strategy: To check comprehension of balance sheet effects, ask students to write responses to SE 6. After five minutes, have students switch papers and correct each other's answers. Ask for volunteers to explain each answer.

Point to Emphasize: The statement of stockholders' equity is a labeled calculation of the change in each stockholders' equity account over the period.

Common Student Confusion: Students have difficulty understanding that a restriction on retained earnings (also called an *appropriation* or *reserve*) is not the same as setting aside cash. To restrict retained earnings is to communicate to the users of financial statements that the retained earnings available for dividends have been reduced.

Retained Earnings. A deficit is shown in the stockholders' equity section of the balance sheet as a deduction from contributed capital.

A corporation may be required or may want to restrict all or a portion of its retained earnings. A restriction on retained earnings means that dividends can be declared only to the extent of the *unrestricted* retained earnings. The following are several reasons a company might restrict retained earnings.

1. *A contractual agreement.* For example, bond indentures may place a limitation on the dividends the company can pay.
2. *State law.* Many states do not allow a corporation to distribute dividends or purchase treasury stock if doing so reduces equity below a minimum level because this would impair the legal capital of the company.
3. *Voluntary action by the board of directors.* Often a board decides to retain assets in the business for future needs. For example, the company may be planning to build a new plant and may want to show that dividends will be limited to save enough money for the building. A company might also restrict retained earnings to show a possible future loss of assets resulting from a lawsuit.

A restriction on retained earnings does not change the total retained earnings or stockholders' equity of the company. It simply divides retained earnings into two parts: restricted and unrestricted. The unrestricted amount represents earnings kept in the business that the company can use for dividends and other purposes. Also, the restriction of retained earnings does not restrict cash or other assets in any way.

Exhibit 3. Stockholders' Equity Section of a Balance Sheet

Tri-State Corporation
Stockholders' Equity
December 31, 20x1

Contributed Capital		
Preferred Stock, $100 par value, 8% convertible, 10,000 shares authorized, 3,000 shares issued and outstanding		$300,000
Common Stock, $10 par value, 100,000 shares authorized, 41,800 shares issued, 41,300 shares outstanding	$418,000	
Paid-in Capital in Excess of Par Value, Common	722,000	1,140,000
Total Contributed Capital		$1,440,000
Retained Earnings		608,400
Total Contributed Capital and Retained Earnings		$2,048,400
Less Treasury Stock, Common (500 shares, at cost)		24,000
Total Stockholders' Equity		$2,024,400

Point to Emphasize: The ending balances on the statement of stockholders' equity are transferred to the stockholders' equity section of the balance sheet.

It simply explains to the readers of the financial statements that a certain amount of assets generated by earnings will remain in the business for the purpose stated. It is still management's job to make sure that there is enough cash or assets on hand to fulfill the purpose. Also, the removal of a restriction does not necessarily mean that the board of directors is then able to declare a dividend.

The most common way to disclose restricted retained earnings is by reference to a note to the financial statements. For example:

Teaching Note: To help your students understand that a restriction simply reduces unrestricted retained earnings—that it does not change total retained earnings—draw a box and label it unrestricted retained earnings. Divide the box into two parts, labeling one part unrestricted and the other part restricted.

Retained Earnings (Note 15) $900,000

Note 15:
Because of plans to expand the capacity of the clothing division, the board of directors has restricted retained earnings available for dividends by $300,000.

BUSINESS BULLETIN: INTERNATIONAL PRACTICE

Restrictions on retained earnings, called *reserves,* are much more common in some foreign countries than in the United States. In Sweden, for instance, reserves are used to respond to fluctuations in the economy. The Swedish tax code allows companies to set up contingency reserves for the purpose of maintaining financial stability. Appropriations to those reserves reduce taxable income and income taxes. The reserves become taxable when they are reversed, but they are available to absorb losses should they occur. For example, although Skandia Group, a large Swedish insurance company, incurred a net loss of SK348 million in 1995, the unrestricted retained earnings increased from SK311 million to SK583 million because the company reduced its restricted reserves. Skandia Group paid its customary cash dividend and still had SK7.0 billion in restricted reserves.[22]

Stock Dividends

OBJECTIVE 7

Account for stock dividends and stock splits

Related Text Assignments:
Q: 14, 15
SE: 6, 8, 9
E: 9, 10, 11
P: 4, 5, 6, 8, 9
SD: 3, 5, 6
FRA: 6

A stock dividend is a proportional distribution of shares of a corporation's stock to its shareholders. A stock dividend does not change the firm's assets and liabilities because there is no distribution of assets, as there is when a cash dividend is distributed. A board of directors may declare a stock dividend for several reasons:

1. It may want to give stockholders some evidence of the company's success without paying a cash dividend, which would affect working capital.
2. It may seek to reduce the stock's market price by increasing the number of shares outstanding, although this goal is more often met by a stock split.
3. It may want to make a nontaxable distribution to stockholders. Stock dividends that meet certain conditions are not considered income, so they are not taxed.
4. It may wish to increase the company's permanent capital by transferring an amount from retained earnings to contributed capital.

The total stockholders' equity is not affected by a stock dividend. The effect of a stock dividend is to transfer a dollar amount from retained earnings to the contributed capital section on the date of declaration. The amount transferred is the fair market value (usually, the market price) of the additional shares to be issued. The laws of most states specify the minimum value of each share transferred under a stock dividend, which is normally the minimum legal capital (par or stated value). However, generally accepted accounting principles state that market value reflects the economic effect of small stock distributions (less than 20 to 25 percent of a company's outstanding common stock) better than par or stated value does. For this reason, market price should be used to account for small stock dividends.[23]

To illustrate the accounting for a stock dividend, let us assume that Caprock Corporation has the following stockholders' equity structure.

Contributed Capital	
Common Stock, $5 par value, 100,000 shares authorized, 30,000 shares issued and outstanding	$ 150,000
Paid-in Capital in Excess of Par Value, Common	30,000
Total Contributed Capital	$ 180,000
Retained Earnings	900,000
Total Stockholders' Equity	$1,080,000

Suppose that the board of directors declares a 10 percent stock dividend on February 24, distributable on March 31 to stockholders of record on March 15, and that the market price of the stock on February 24 is $20 per share. The entries to record the declaration and distribution of the stock dividend are shown below.

Date of Declaration

A = L + OE
−
+

Feb. 24	Stock Dividends Declared	60,000	
	Common Stock Distributable		15,000
	Paid-in Capital in Excess of Par Value, Common		45,000
	Declared a 10% stock dividend on common stock, distributable on March 31 to stockholders of record on March 15: 30,000 shares × .10 = 3,000 shares 3,000 shares × $20/share = $60,000 3,000 shares × $5/share = $15,000		

Point to Emphasize: For a small stock dividend, the portion of retained earnings transferred is determined by multiplying the number of shares to be distributed by the stock's market price on the date of declaration.

Date of Record

Mar. 15 No entry required.

Date of Distribution

A = L + OE
−
+

Mar. 31	Common Stock Distributable	15,000	
	Common Stock		15,000
	Distribution of a stock dividend of 3,000 shares		

Point to Emphasize: The declaration of a stock dividend results in a reshuffling of stockholders' equity. That is, a portion of retained earnings is converted (by closing the Stock Dividends Declared account) into contributed capital. Total stockholders' equity is not affected. Retained earnings are transferred at the time of the recording (date of declaration) and not at the closing of the Stock Dividends Declared account.

Point to Emphasize: Common Stock Distributable is a contributed capital (stockholders' equity) account, not a liability. When the shares are issued, this account is converted into Common Stock.

The effect of this stock dividend is to permanently transfer the market value of the stock, $60,000, from retained earnings to contributed capital and to increase the number of shares outstanding by 3,000. The Stock Dividends Declared account is used to record the total amount of the stock dividend. Retained Earnings is reduced by the amount of the stock dividend when the Stock Dividends Declared account is closed to Retained Earnings at the end of the accounting period. Common Stock Distributable is credited for the par value of the stock to be distributed (3,000 × $5 = $15,000).

In addition, when the market value is greater than the par value of the stock, Paid-in Capital in Excess of Par Value, Common must be credited for the amount by which the market value exceeds the par value. In this case, the total market value of the stock dividend ($60,000) exceeds the total par value ($15,000) by $45,000. No entry is required on the date of record. On the distribution date, the common stock is issued by debiting Common Stock Distributable and crediting Common Stock for the par value of the stock ($15,000).

Common Stock Distributable is not a liability account because there is no obligation to distribute cash or other assets. The obligation is to distribute additional shares of capital stock. If financial statements are prepared between the date of declaration and the date of distribution, Common Stock Distributable should be reported as part of contributed capital.

Contributed Capital	
Common Stock, $5 par value, 100,000 shares authorized, 30,000 shares issued and outstanding	$ 150,000
Common Stock Distributable, 3,000 shares	15,000
Paid-in Capital in Excess of Par Value, Common	75,000
Total Contributed Capital	$ 240,000
Retained Earnings	840,000
Total Stockholders' Equity	$1,080,000

Three points can be made from this example. First, the total stockholders' equity is the same before and after the stock dividend. Second, the assets of the corporation are not reduced as in the case of a cash dividend. Third, the proportionate ownership in the corporation of any individual stockholder is the same before and after the stock dividend. To illustrate these points, assume that a stockholder owns 1,000 shares before the stock dividend. After the 10 percent stock dividend is distributed, this stockholder would own 1,100 shares, as illustrated below.

Reinforcement Exercise: A corporation with 6,000 shares of $100 par value common stock outstanding declares a 15 percent stock dividend on a day when the stock's market price is $120 per share. Make the journal entry on the declaration date.

Answer:

Stock Dividends Declared	108,000	
Common Stock Distributable		90,000
Paid-in Capital in Excess of Par Value, Common		18,000

Stockholders' Equity	**Before Dividend**	**After Dividend**
Common Stock	$ 150,000	$ 165,000
Paid-in Capital in Excess of Par Value, Common	30,000	75,000
Total Contributed Capital	$ 180,000	$ 240,000
Retained Earnings	900,000	840,000
Total Stockholders' Equity	$1,080,000	$1,080,000
Shares Outstanding	30,000	33,000
Stockholders' Equity per Share	$ 36.00	$ 32.73

Point to Emphasize:
$36.00 × 1,000 = $36,000
$32.73 × 1,100 = $36,003 (rounded)

Stockholder's Investment

Shares owned	1,000	1,100
Shares outstanding	30,000	33,000
Percentage of ownership	3⅓%	3⅓%
Proportionate investment ($1,080,000 × .03⅓)	$36,000	$36,000

Both before and after the stock dividend, the stockholders' equity totals $1,080,000 and the stockholder owns 3⅓ percent of the company. The proportionate investment (stockholders' equity times percentage ownership) stays at $36,000.

Point to Emphasize: When a large (greater than 20 to 25 percent) stock dividend is declared, the transfer from retained earnings is based on the stock's par or stated value, not on its market value.

All stock dividends have an effect on the market price of a company's stock. But some stock dividends are so large that they have a material effect. For example, a 50 percent stock dividend would cause the market price of the stock to drop about 33 percent because the increase is now one-third of shares outstanding. The AICPA has decided that large stock dividends, those greater than 20 to 25 percent, should be accounted for by transferring the par or stated value of the stock on the date of declaration from retained earnings to contributed capital.[24]

DECISION POINT

CHRYSLER CORPORATION

In May 1996, Chrysler Corporation's board of directors raised the company's dividend for the fifth time in two years and the stockholders voted a 2-for-1 stock split. These moves were viewed very positively by the stock market, which pushed Chrysler's shares above $67 per share. Just a year earlier the stock price had been $43 and the dividend was less than half the new level.[25] How does a stock split differ from a stock dividend and a cash dividend? Why would the board of directors and the stockholders take these actions? Why did the market and the stockholders respond so positively to these actions?

These are important questions for internal management and external investors in the company. A 2-for-1 stock split gives stockholders one additional share of common stock for each share they own. Stock dividends also give stockholders additional shares based on the value of their holdings, but they have a different effect on the stockholders' equity section of the balance sheet. A cash dividend is a distribution of cash based on the number of shares owned. Chrysler's recent prosperity is the probable reason for the action, as the market usually views stock splits as symbols of success. By doubling the number of shares outstanding, the Chrysler stock split will reduce the market value per share; this will make the stock more readily tradable and more easily available to the ordinary investor. The market value per share will be about half of $67 per share, and each stockholder will own twice as many shares. Transactions

Critical Thinking Question: What are the effects of stock splits, stock dividends, and cash dividends on earnings per share? **Answer:** Earnings per share are reduced by stock splits and stock dividends because the number of shares has increased. Cash dividends have no effect on earnings per share.

involving stock dividends and stock splits affect the financial structure of a company and are important strategic actions that both managers and investors should understand.

Stock Splits

A stock split occurs when a corporation increases the number of issued shares of stock and reduces the par or stated value proportionally. A company may plan a stock split when it wants to lower the stock's market value per share and increase the demand for the stock at this lower price. This action may be necessary if the market value per share has become so high that it hinders the trading of the stock. An example of this strategy is shown in the Decision Point on Chrysler Corporation.

To illustrate a stock split, suppose that Caprock Corporation has 30,000 shares of $5.00 par value stock outstanding. The market value is $70.00 per share. The corporation plans a 2-for-1 split. This split will lower the par value to $2.50 and increase the number of shares outstanding to 60,000. A stockholder who previously owned 400 shares of the $5.00 par stock would own 800 shares of the $2.50 par stock after the split. When a stock split occurs, the market value tends to fall in proportion to the increase in outstanding shares of stock. For example, a 2-for-1 stock split would cause the price of the stock to drop by approximately 50 percent, to about $35.00. It would also halve earnings per share and cash dividends per share (if the board does not increase the dividend). The lower price and the increase in shares tend to promote the buying and selling of shares.

Business-World Example: Stock splits greater than 2 for 1 are unusual. Splits such as 3 for 2 or 4 for 3 are far more common. On occasion, companies whose stock sells for a very low price will perform a reverse stock split, which reduces the number of shares and increases the market price.

A stock split does not increase the number of shares authorized. Nor does it change the balances in the stockholders' equity section of the balance sheet. It simply changes the par value and the number of shares issued, both shares outstanding and shares held as treasury stock. Therefore, an entry is not necessary. However, it is appropriate to document the change by making a memorandum entry in the general journal.

July 15 The 30,000 shares of $5 par value common stock that are issued and outstanding were split 2 for 1, resulting in 60,000 shares of $2.50 par value common stock issued and outstanding.

The change for the Caprock Corporation is as follows:

Before Stock Split (from page 634)

Contributed Capital	
Common Stock, $5 par value, 100,000 shares authorized, 30,000 shares issued and outstanding	$ 150,000
Paid-in Capital in Excess of Par Value, Common	30,000
Total Contributed Capital	$ 180,000
Retained Earnings	900,000
Total Stockholders' Equity	$1,080,000

After Stock Split

Contributed Capital	
Common Stock, $2.50 par value, 100,000 shares authorized, 60,000 shares issued and outstanding	$ 150,000
Paid-in Capital in Excess of Par Value, Common	30,000
Total Contributed Capital	$ 180,000
Retained Earnings	900,000
Total Stockholders' Equity	$1,080,000

Point to Emphasize: A stock split affects only the common stock calculation. In this case, there are twice as many shares after the split, but par value is now half of what it was.

Point to Emphasize: As long as the newly outstanding shares do not exceed the previously authorized shares, permission from the state is not needed for a stock split.

Although the amount of stockholders' equity per share would be half as much, each stockholder's proportionate interest in the company would remain the same.

If the number of split shares will exceed the number of authorized shares, the board of directors must secure state and stockholders' approval before it can issue additional shares.

Book Value

OBJECTIVE 8

Calculate book value per share

Related Text Assignments:
Q: 16
SE: 10
E: 12
P: 6
SD: 5, 6
FRA: 1, 5, 6

Discussion Question: What is the significance of book value per share of stock? **Answer:** Book value per share represents the equity of one share of stock in the net assets (assets minus liabilities) of a corporation. It can apply to both common and preferred stock.

The word *value* is associated with shares of stock in several ways. Par value or stated value is set when the stock is authorized and establishes the legal capital of a company. Neither par value nor stated value has any relationship to a stock's book value or market value. The book value of a company's stock represents the total assets of the company less its liabilities. It is simply the stockholders' equity of the company or, to look at it another way, the company's net assets. The book value per share, therefore, represents the equity of the owner of one share of stock in the net assets of the corporation. That value, of course, does not necessarily equal the amount the shareholder would receive if the company were sold or liquidated. It differs in most cases because assets are usually recorded at historical cost, not at the current value at which they could be sold.

To determine the book value per share when a company has only common stock outstanding, divide the total stockholders' equity by the total common shares outstanding. In computing the shares outstanding, common stock distributable is included. Treasury stock (shares previously issued and now held by the company), however, is not included. For example, suppose that Caprock Corporation has total stockholders' equity of $1,030,000 and 29,000 shares outstanding after recording the purchase of treasury shares. The book value per share of Caprock's common stock is $35.52 ($1,030,000 ÷ 29,000 shares).

If a company has both preferred and common stock, the determination of book value per share is not so simple. The general rule is that the call value (or par value, if a call value is not specified) of the preferred stock plus any dividends in arrears is subtracted from total stockholders' equity to determine the equity pertaining to common stock. As an illustration, refer to the stockholders' equity section of Tri-State Corporation's balance sheet in Exhibit 3. Assuming that there are no dividends in arrears and that the preferred stock is callable at $105, the equity pertaining to common stock is calculated as follows:

Total stockholders' equity	$2,024,400
Less equity allocated to preferred shareholders (3,000 shares × $105)	315,000
Equity pertaining to common shareholders	$1,709,400

BUSINESS BULLETIN: BUSINESS PRACTICE

Although book value per share often bears little relationship to market value per share, some investors use the relationship between the two as a rough indicator of the relative value of the stock. For example, in early 1991, the stock of Chrysler Corporation had a book value per share of $31 and a market value per share of $14. By 1996, at the time of the stock split discussed in the previous decision point, the book value had climbed to about $40 per share but the market value per share had risen much more, to $67 per share. Other factors being equal, investors were more optimistic about Chrysler's prospects in 1996 than they were in 1991.

Point to Emphasize: To determine the equity applicable to common shareholders, subtract the total call value of preferred stock plus any dividends in arrears (if the preferred stock is cumulative) from total stockholders' equity. To determine the book value per share, simply divide the equity applicable to each type of stock by the number of shares.

There are 41,300 shares of common stock outstanding (41,800 shares issued less 500 shares of treasury stock). The book values per share are computed as follows:

Preferred Stock: $315,000 ÷ 3,000 shares = $105 per share
Common Stock: $1,709,400 ÷ 41,300 shares = $41.39 per share

If we assume the same facts except that the preferred stock is 8 percent cumulative and that one year of dividends is in arrears, the stockholders' equity would be allocated as follows:

Total stockholders' equity		$2,024,400
Less: Call value of outstanding preferred shares	$315,000	
Dividends in arrears ($300,000 × .08)	24,000	
Equity allocated to preferred shareholders		339,000
Equity pertaining to common shareholders		$1,685,400

The book values per share are then as follows:

Preferred Stock: $339,000 ÷ 3,000 shares = $113 per share
Common Stock: $1,685,400 ÷ 41,300 shares = $40.81 per share

Undeclared preferred dividends fall into arrears on the last day of the fiscal year (the date when the financial statements are prepared). Also, dividends in arrears do not apply to unissued preferred stock.

Chapter Review

REVIEW OF LEARNING OBJECTIVES

1. **Identify the issues related to evaluating the quality of a company's earnings.** Current and prospective net income is an important component in many ratios used to evaluate a company. The user should recognize that the quality of reported net income can be influenced by certain choices made by management. First, management exercises judgment in choosing the accounting methods and estimates that are used in computing net income. Second, discontinued operations, extraordinary gains or losses, and changes in accounting methods may affect net income positively or negatively.
2. **Prepare a corporate income statement.** The corporate income statement shows comprehensive income—all revenues, expenses, gains, and losses for the accounting period, except for prior period adjustments. The top part of the corporate income statement includes all revenues, costs and expenses, and income taxes that pertain to continuing operations. The bottom part of the statement contains any or all of the following: discontinued operations, extraordinary items, and accounting changes. Earnings per share data should be shown at the bottom of the statement, below net income.
3. **Show the relationships among income taxes expense, deferred income taxes, and net of taxes.** Income taxes expense is the taxes applicable to income from operations on an accrual basis. Income tax allocation is necessary when differences between accrual-based accounting income and taxable income cause a material difference between income taxes expense as shown on the income statement and actual income tax liability. The difference between income taxes expense and income taxes payable is debited or credited to an account called Deferred Income Taxes. *Net of taxes* is a phrase used to indicate that the effect of taxes has been considered when showing an item on the income statement.
4. **Describe the disclosure on the income statement of discontinued operations, extraordinary items, and accounting changes.** Because of their unusual nature, a gain or loss on discontinued operations and on extraordinary items, and the cumulative effect of accounting changes must be disclosed on the income statement sepa-

rately from continuing operations and net of income taxes. Relevant information about any accounting change is shown in the notes to the financial statements.

5. **Compute earnings per share.** Stockholders and other readers of financial statements use earnings per share data to evaluate a company's performance and to compare it with the performance of other companies. Therefore, earnings per share data are presented on the face of the income statement. The amounts are computed by dividing the income applicable to common stock by the number of common shares outstanding for the year. If the number of shares outstanding has varied during the year, then the weighted-average number of shares outstanding should be used in the computation. When the company has a complex capital structure, both basic and diluted earnings per share must be disclosed on the face of the income statement.
6. **Prepare a statement of stockholders' equity.** A statement of stockholders' equity shows changes over the period in each component of the stockholders' equity section of the balance sheet. This statement reveals much more about the transactions that adjust stockholders' equity than does the statement of retained earnings.
7. **Account for stock dividends and stock splits.** A stock dividend is a proportional distribution of shares of a corporation's stock to the company's stockholders. Here is a summary of the key dates and accounting treatment of stock dividends.

Key Date	Stock Dividend
Date of declaration	Debit Stock Dividends Declared for the market value of the stock to be distributed (if it is a small stock dividend), and credit Common Stock Distributable for the stock's par value and Paid-in Capital in Excess of Par Value, Common for the excess of the market value over the stock's par value.
Date of record	No entry.
Date of distribution	Debit Common Stock Distributable and credit Common Stock for the par value of the stock that has been distributed.

A stock split is usually undertaken to reduce the market value of a company's stock and improve the demand for the stock. Because there is normally a decrease in the par value of the stock in proportion to the number of additional shares issued, a stock split has no effect on the dollar amounts in the stockholders' equity accounts. The split should be recorded in the general journal by a memorandum entry only.

8. **Calculate book value per share.** Book value per share is the stockholders' equity per share. It is calculated by dividing stockholders' equity by the number of common shares outstanding plus shares distributable. When a company has both preferred and common stock, the call or par value of the preferred stock plus any dividends in arrears is deducted from total stockholders' equity before dividing by the common shares outstanding.

REVIEW OF CONCEPTS AND TERMINOLOGY

The following concepts and terms were introduced in this chapter.

LO 5 **Basic earnings per share:** The net income applicable to common stock divided by the weighted-average number of common shares outstanding.

LO 8 **Book value:** The total assets of a company less its liabilities; stockholders' equity.

LO 8 **Book value per share:** The equity of the owner of one share of stock in the net assets of the corporation.

LO 5 **Complex capital structure:** A capital structure that includes convertible preferred stocks or bonds, or stock options that can be converted into common stock.

LO 2 **Comprehensive income:** The change in a company's equity during a period from sources other than owners; it includes net income, change in unrealized investment gains and losses, and other items affecting equity.

LO 4 **Cumulative effect of an accounting change:** The effect that a different accounting principle would have had on the net income of prior periods if it had been used instead of the old principle.

LO 3 **Deferred Income Taxes:** The account used to record the difference between the Income Taxes Expense and Income Taxes Payable accounts.

LO 6 **Deficit:** A debit balance in the Retained Earnings account.

LO 5 **Diluted earnings per share:** The net income applicable to common stock divided by the sum of the weighted-average number of common shares outstanding plus potentially dilutive securities.

LO 4 **Discontinued operations:** Segments of a business that are no longer part of its ongoing operations.

LO 4 **Extraordinary items:** Events or transactions that are both unusual in nature and infrequent in occurrence.

LO 3 **Income tax allocation:** An accounting method used to accrue income taxes expense on the basis of accounting income whenever there are differences between accounting and taxable income.

LO 3 **Net of taxes:** Taking into account the effect of applicable taxes (usually income taxes) on an item to determine the overall effect of the item on the income statement.

LO 5 **Potentially dilutive securities:** Stock options and convertible preferred stocks or bonds, which have the potential to dilute earnings per share.

LO 1 **Quality of earnings:** The substance of earnings and their sustainability into future accounting periods.

LO 6 **Restriction on retained earnings:** The required or voluntary identification of a portion of retained earnings that cannot be used to declare dividends.

LO 6 **Retained earnings:** Stockholders' claims to assets arising from the earnings of the business; the accumulated earnings of a corporation from its inception, minus any losses, dividends, or transfers to contributed capital.

LO 4 **Segments:** Distinct parts of business operations, such as lines of business or classes of customer.

LO 5 **Simple capital structure:** A capital structure in which there are no stocks, bonds, or stock options that can be converted into common stock.

LO 6 **Statement of stockholders' equity:** A financial statement that summarizes changes in the components of the stockholders' equity section of the balance sheet; also called *statement of changes in stockholders' equity.*

LO 7 **Stock dividend:** A proportional distribution of shares of a corporation's stock to its stockholders.

LO 7 **Stock split:** An increase in the number of outstanding shares of stock accompanied by a proportionate reduction in the par or stated value.

REVIEW PROBLEM

Comprehensive Stockholders' Equity Transactions

LO 6 LO 7 LO 8 The stockholders' equity of the Szatkowski Company on June 30, 20x1, is shown below.

Contributed Capital	
Common Stock, no par value, $6 stated value, 1,000,000 shares authorized, 250,000 shares issued and outstanding	$1,500,000
Paid-in Capital in Excess of Stated Value, Common	820,000
Total Contributed Capital	$2,320,000
Retained Earnings	970,000
Total Stockholders' Equity	$3,290,000

Stockholders' equity transactions for the next fiscal year were as follows:

a. The board of directors declared a 2-for-1 stock split.
b. The board of directors obtained authorization to issue 50,000 shares of $100 par value, 6 percent noncumulative preferred stock, callable at $104.
c. Issued 12,000 shares of common stock for a building appraised at $96,000.
d. Purchased 8,000 shares of the company's common stock for $64,000.
e. Issued 20,000 shares of preferred stock for $100 per share.

f. Sold 5,000 shares of treasury stock for $35,000.
g. Declared cash dividends of $6 per share on preferred stock and $.20 per share on common stock.
h. Date of record.
i. Paid the preferred and common stock cash dividends.
j. Declared a 10 percent stock dividend on common stock. The market value was $10 per share. The stock dividend is distributable after the end of the fiscal year.
k. Closed Net Income for the year, $340,000.
l. Closed the Cash Dividends Declared and Stock Dividends Declared accounts to Retained Earnings.

Because of a loan agreement, the company is not allowed to reduce retained earnings below $100,000. The board of directors determined that this restriction should be disclosed in the notes to the financial statements.

1. Record the preceding transactions in journal form.
2. Prepare the stockholders' equity section of the company's balance sheet on June 30, 20x2, including appropriate disclosure of the restriction on retained earnings.
3. Compute the book values per share of common stock on June 30, 20x1 and 20x2, and of preferred stock on June 30, 20x2, using end-of-year shares outstanding.

ANSWER TO REVIEW PROBLEM

1. Prepare the journal entries.

	Debit	Credit
a. Memorandum entry: 2-for-1 stock split, common, resulting in 500,000 shares issued and outstanding of no par value common stock with a stated value of $3		
b. No entry required.		
c. Building	96,000	
Common Stock		36,000
Paid-in Capital in Excess of Stated Value, Common		60,000
Issued 12,000 shares of common stock for a building appraised at $96,000		
d. Treasury Stock, Common	64,000	
Cash		64,000
Purchased 8,000 shares of common stock for the treasury for $8 per share		
e. Cash	2,000,000	
Preferred Stock		2,000,000
Issued 20,000 shares of $100 par value preferred stock at $100 per share		
f. Cash	35,000	
Retained Earnings	5,000	
Treasury Stock, Common		40,000
Sold 5,000 shares of treasury stock for $35,000, originally purchased for $8 per share		
g. Cash Dividends Declared	221,800	
Cash Dividends Payable		221,800
Declaration of cash dividends of $6 per share on 20,000 shares of preferred stock and $.20 per share on 509,000 shares of common stock:		

20,000 × $6	=	$120,000
509,000 × $.20	=	101,800
		$221,800

h. No entry required.		
i. Cash Dividends Payable	221,800	
Cash		221,800
Paid cash dividends to preferred and common stockholders		
j. Stock Dividends Declared	509,000	
Common Stock Distributable		152,700
Paid-in Capital in Excess of Stated Value, Common		356,300
Declaration of a 50,900-share stock dividend (509,000 × .10) on \$3 stated value common stock at a market value of \$509,000 (50,900 × \$10)		
k. Income Summary	340,000	
Retained Earnings		340,000
To close the Income Summary account to Retained Earnings		
l. Retained Earnings	730,800	
Cash Dividends Declared		221,800
Stock Dividends Declared		509,000
To close the Cash Dividends Declared and Stock Dividends Declared accounts to Retained Earnings		

2. Prepare the stockholders' equity section of the balance sheet.

Szatkowski Company
Stockholders' Equity
June 30, 20x2

Contributed Capital		
Preferred Stock, \$100 par value, 6% noncumulative, 50,000 shares authorized, 20,000 shares issued and outstanding		\$2,000,000
Common Stock, no par value, \$3 stated value, 1,000,000 shares authorized, 512,000 shares issued, 509,000 shares outstanding	\$1,536,000	
Common Stock Distributable, 50,900 shares	152,700	
Paid-in Capital in Excess of Stated Value, Common	1,236,300	2,925,000
Total Contributed Capital		\$4,925,000
Retained Earnings (Note x)		574,200
Total Contributed Capital and Retained Earnings		\$5,499,200
Less Treasury Stock, Common (3,000 shares, at cost)		24,000
Total Stockholders' Equity		\$5,475,200

Note x: The board of directors has restricted retained earnings available for dividends by the amount of \$100,000 as required under a loan agreement.

3. Compute the book values.

June 30, 20x1
Common Stock: $3,290,000 ÷ 250,000 shares = $13.16 per share
June 30, 20x2
Preferred Stock: Call price of $104 per share equals book value per share
Common Stock:
($5,475,200 − $2,080,000) ÷ (509,000 shares + 50,900 shares) =
$3,395,200 ÷ 559,900 shares = $6.06 per share

Chapter Assignments

BUILDING YOUR KNOWLEDGE FOUNDATION

Questions

1. What is quality of earnings, and what are two ways in which quality of earnings can be affected?
2. Why would the reader of financial statements be interested in management's choice of accounting methods and estimates? Give an example.
3. In the first quarter of 1994, AT&T, the giant telecommunications company, reported a net loss because it reduced its income by $1.3 billion, or $.96 per share, as a result of changing its method of accounting for disability and severance payments. Without this charge, the company would have earned $1.15 billion, or $.85 per share. Where on the corporate income statement do you find the effects of changes in accounting principles? As an analyst, how would you treat this accounting change?
4. "Accounting income should be geared to the concept of taxable income because the public understands that concept." Comment on this statement, and tell why income tax allocation is necessary.
5. Nabisco had about $1.3 billion of deferred income taxes in 1996, equal to about 11 percent of total liabilities. This percentage has risen or remained steady for many years. Given management's desire to put off the payment of taxes as long as possible, the long-term growth of the economy and inflation, and the definition of a liability (probable future sacrifice of economic benefits arising from present obligations), make an argument for not accounting for deferred income taxes.
6. Why should a gain or loss on discontinued operations be disclosed separately on the income statement?
7. Explain the two major criteria for extraordinary items. How should extraordinary items be disclosed in the financial statements?
8. When an accounting change occurs, what disclosures must be made in the financial statements?
9. How are earnings per share disclosed in the financial statements?
10. When does a company have a simple capital structure? A complex capital structure?
11. What is the difference between basic and diluted earnings per share?
12. What is the difference between the statement of stockholders' equity and the stockholders' equity section of the balance sheet?
13. When does a company have a deficit in retained earnings?
14. Explain how the accounting treatment of stock dividends differs from that of cash dividends.
15. What is the difference between a stock dividend and a stock split? What is the effect of each on the capital structure of the corporation?
16. Would you expect a corporation's book value per share to equal its market value per share? Why or why not?

Short Exercises

SE 1. LO 1 *Quality of Earnings*

Each of the following items is a quality of earnings issue. Indicate whether the item is (a) an accounting method, (b) an accounting estimate, or (c) a nonoperating item. For any item for which the answer is (a) or (b), indicate which alternative is usually the more conservative choice.

1. LIFO versus FIFO
2. Extraordinary loss
3. Ten-year useful life versus fifteen-year useful life
4. Effect of change in accounting principle
5. Straight-line versus accelerated method
6. Discontinued operations
7. Immediate write-off versus amortization
8. Increase in percentage of uncollectible accounts versus a decrease

SE 2. LO 2 *Corporate Income Statement*

Assume that the Griswold Company's chief financial officer gave you the following information: Net Sales, $720,000; Cost of Goods Sold, $350,000; Loss from Discontinued Operations (net of income tax benefit of $70,000), $200,000; Loss on Disposal of Discontinued Operations (net of income tax benefit of $16,000), $50,000; Operating Expenses, $130,000; Income Taxes Expense on Continuing Operations, $100,000. From this information, prepare the company's income statement for the year ended June 30, 20xx. (Ignore earnings per share information.)

SE 3. LO 3 *Use of Corporate Income Tax Rate Schedule*

Using the corporate tax rate schedule in Table 1, compute the income tax liability for taxable income of (1) $400,000 and (2) $20,000,000.

SE 4. LO 5 *Earnings per Share*

During 20x1, the Jimmo Corporation reported a net income of $669,200. On January 1, Jimmo had 360,000 shares of common stock outstanding. The company issued an additional 240,000 shares of common stock on August 1. In 20x1, the company had a simple capital structure. During 20x2, there were no transactions involving common stock, and the company reported net income of $870,000. Determine the weighted-average number of common shares outstanding for 20x1 and 20x2. Also, compute earnings per share for 20x1 and 20x2.

SE 5. LO 6 *Statement of Stockholders' Equity*

Refer to the statement of stockholders' equity for Tri-State Corporation in Exhibit 2 to answer the following questions: (1) At what price per share were the 5,000 shares of common stock sold? (2) What was the conversion price per share of the common stock? (3) At what price was the common stock selling on the date of the stock dividend? (4) At what price per share was the treasury stock purchased?

SE 6. LO 6 LO 7 *Effects of Stockholders' Equity Actions*

Tell whether each of the following actions will increase, decrease, or have no effect on total assets, total liabilities, and total stockholders' equity.

1. Declaration of a stock dividend
2. Declaration of a cash dividend
3. Stock split
4. Restriction of retained earnings
5. Purchase of treasury stock

SE 7. LO 6 *Restriction of Retained Earnings*

Swift Company has a lawsuit filed against it. The board took action to restrict retained earnings in the amount of $2,500,000 on May 31, 20x1, pending the outcome of the suit. On May 31, the company had retained earnings of $3,725,000. Show how the restriction on retained earnings would be disclosed as a note to the financial statements.

SE 8. LO 7 *Stock Dividends*

On February 15, Green Mountain Corporation's board of directors declared a 2 percent stock dividend applicable to the outstanding shares of its $10 par value common stock, of which 200,000 shares are authorized, 130,000 are issued, and 20,000 are held in the treasury. The stock dividend was distributable on March 15 to stockholders of record on March 1. On February 15, the market value of the common stock was $15 per share. On March 30, the board of directors declared a $.50 per share cash dividend. No other stock transactions have occurred. Record the necessary transactions on February 15, March 1, March 15, and March 30.

SE 9. LO 7 *Stock Split*

On August 10, the board of directors of Symula International declared a 3-for-1 stock split of its $9 par value common stock, of which 800,000 shares were authorized and 250,000 were issued and outstanding. The market value on that date was $60 per share. On the same date, the balance of Paid-in Capital in Excess of Par Value, Common was $6,000,000, and the balance of Retained Earnings was $6,500,000. Prepare the stockholders' equity section of the company's balance sheet after the stock split. What journal entry, if any, is needed to record the stock split?

SE 10. LO 8 *Book Value for Preferred and Common Stock*

Given the stockholders' equity section of the Talmage Corporation's balance sheet shown below, what is the book value per share for both the preferred and the common stock?

Contributed Capital		
Preferred Stock, $100 par value, 8 percent cumulative, 10,000 shares authorized, 500 shares issued and outstanding*		$ 50,000
Common Stock, $10 par value, 100,000 shares authorized, 40,000 shares issued and outstanding	$400,000	
Paid-in Capital in Excess of Par Value, Common	516,000	916,000
Total Contributed Capital		$ 966,000
Retained Earnings		275,000
Total Stockholders' Equity		$1,241,000

*The preferred stock is callable at $104 per share, and one year's dividends are in arrears.

Exercises

E 1. LO 1 *Effect of Alternative Accounting Methods*

At the end of its first year of operations, a company calculated its ending merchandise inventory according to three different accounting methods, as follows: FIFO, $95,000; average-cost, $90,000; LIFO, $86,000. If the average-cost method is used by the company, net income for the year would be $34,000.

1. Determine net income if the FIFO method is used.
2. Determine net income if the LIFO method is used.
3. Which method is more conservative?
4. Will the consistency convention be violated if the company chooses to use the LIFO method?
5. Does the full-disclosure convention require disclosure of the inventory method selected by management in the financial statements?

E 2. LO 2 *Corporate Income Statement*

Assume that the Shortall Furniture Company's chief financial officer gave you the following information: Net Sales, $1,900,000; Cost of Goods Sold, $1,050,000; Extraordinary Gain (net of income taxes of $3,500), $12,500; Loss from Discontinued Operations (net of income tax benefit of $30,000), $50,000; Loss on Disposal of Discontinued Operations (net of income tax benefit of $13,000), $35,000; Selling Expenses, $50,000; Administrative Expenses, $40,000; Income Taxes Expense on Continuing Operations, $300,000.

From this information, prepare the company's income statement for the year ended June 30, 20xx. (Ignore earnings per share information.)

E 3. LO 2 LO 3 LO 4 LO 5 *Corporate Income Statement*

The following items are components in the income statement of Cohen Corporation for the year ended December 31, 20x1:

Sales	$500,000
Cost of Goods Sold	(275,000)
Operating Expenses	(112,500)
Total Income Taxes Expense for Period	(82,350)
Income from Operations of a Discontinued Segment	80,000
Gain on Disposal of Segment	70,000
Extraordinary Gain on Retirement of Bonds	36,000
Cumulative Effect of a Change in Accounting Principle	(24,000)
Net Income	$192,150
Earnings per Share	$.96

Recast the 20x1 income statement in proper multistep form, including allocating income taxes to appropriate items (assume a 30 percent income tax rate) and showing earnings per share figures (200,000 shares outstanding).

E 4. LO 3 *Use of Corporate Income Tax Rate Schedule*

Using the corporate tax rate schedule in Table 1, compute the income tax liability for the following situations:

Situation	Taxable Income
A	$ 70,000
B	85,000
C	320,000

E 5. LO 3 *Income Tax Allocation*

The Delcampo Corporation reported the following accounting income before income taxes, income taxes expense, and net income for 20x2 and 20x3:

	20x2	20x3
Income before income taxes	$280,000	$280,000
Income taxes expense	88,300	88,300
Net income	$191,700	$191,700

Also, on the balance sheet, deferred income taxes liability increased by $38,400 in 20x2 and decreased by $18,800 in 20x3.

1. How much did Delcampo Corporation actually pay in income taxes for 20x2 and 20x3?
2. Prepare entries in journal form to record income taxes expense for 20x2 and 20x3.

E 6. LO 5 *Earnings per Share*

During 20x1, the Heath Corporation reported a net income of $1,529,500. On January 1, Heath had 700,000 shares of common stock outstanding. The company issued an additional 420,000 shares of common stock on October 1. In 20x1, the company had a simple capital structure. During 20x2, there were no transactions involving common stock, and the company reported net income of $2,016,000.

1. Determine the weighted-average number of common shares outstanding each year.
2. Compute earnings per share for each year.

E 7. LO 6 *Restriction of Retained Earnings*

The board of directors of the Suplicki Company has approved plans to acquire another company during the coming year. The acquisition should cost approximately $550,000. The board took action to restrict retained earnings of the company in the amount of $550,000 on July 17, 20x1. On July 31, the company had retained earnings of $975,000. Show how the restriction on retained earnings can be disclosed as a note to the financial statements.

E 8. LO 6 *Statement of Stockholders' Equity*

The stockholders' equity section of Kolb Corporation's balance sheet on December 31, 20x2 appears as follows:

Contributed Capital	
Common Stock, $2 par value, 500,000 shares authorized, 400,000 shares issued and outstanding	$ 800,000
Paid-in Capital in Excess of Par Value, Common	1,200,000
Total Contributed Capital	$2,000,000
Retained Earnings	4,200,000
Total Stockholders' Equity	$6,200,000

Prepare a statement of stockholders' equity for the year ended December 31, 20x3, assuming the following transactions occurred in sequence during 20x3:

a. Issued 10,000 shares of $100 par value, 9 percent cumulative preferred stock at par after obtaining authorization from the state.
b. Issued 40,000 shares of common stock in connection with the conversion of bonds having a carrying value of $600,000.
c. Declared and issued a 2 percent common stock dividend. The market value on the date of declaration was $14 per share.
d. Purchased 10,000 shares of common stock for the treasury at a cost of $16 per share.

e. Earned net income of $460,000.
f. Declared and paid the full year's dividend on preferred stock and a dividend of $.40 per share on common stock outstanding at the end of the year.

E 9. LO 7 *Journal Entries: Stock Dividends*

The Geyer Company has 30,000 shares of its $1 par value common stock outstanding. Record the following transactions as they relate to the company's common stock:

July 17 Declared a 10 percent stock dividend on common stock to be distributed on August 10 to stockholders of record on July 31. Market value of the stock was $5 per share on this date.
31 Record date.
Aug. 10 Distributed the stock dividend declared on July 17.
Sept. 1 Declared a $.50 per share cash dividend on common stock to be paid on September 16 to stockholders of record on September 10.

E 10. LO 7 *Stock Split*

The Colson Company currently has 500,000 shares of $1 par value common stock authorized with 200,000 shares outstanding. The board of directors declared a 2-for-1 split on May 15, when the market value of the common stock was $2.50 per share. The Retained Earnings balance on May 15 was $700,000. Paid-in Capital in Excess of Par Value, Common on this date was $20,000.

Prepare the stockholders' equity section of the company's balance sheet before and after the stock split. What journal entry, if any, would be necessary to record the stock split?

E 11. LO 7 *Stock Split*

On Janury 15, the board of directors of Fuquat International declared a 3-for-1 stock split of its $12 par value common stock, of which 800,000 shares were authorized and 200,000 were issued and outstanding. The market value on that date was $45 per share. On the same date, the balance of Paid-in Capital in Excess of Par Value, Common was $4,000,000, and the balance of Retained Earnings was $8,000,000.

Prepare the stockholders' equity section of the company's balance sheet before and after the stock split. What journal entry, if any, is needed to record the stock split?

E 12. LO 8 *Book Value for Preferred and Common Stock*

The stockholders' equity section of the Colombus Corporation's balance sheet is shown below.

Contributed Capital		
Preferred Stock, $100 per share, 6 percent cumulative, 10,000 shares authorized, 200 shares issued and outstanding*		$ 20,000
Common Stock, $5 par value, 100,000 shares authorized, 10,000 shares issued, 9,000 shares outstanding	$50,000	
Paid-in Capital in Excess of Par Value, Common	28,000	78,000
Total Contributed Capital		$ 98,000
Retained Earnings		95,000
Total Contributed Capital and Retained Earnings		$193,000
Less Treasury Stock, Common (1,000 shares at cost)		15,000
Total Stockholders' Equity		$178,000

*The preferred stock is callable at $105 per share, and one year's dividends are in arrears.

Determine the book value per share for both the preferred and the common stock.

Problems

LO 1 *Effect of Alternative Accounting Methods*

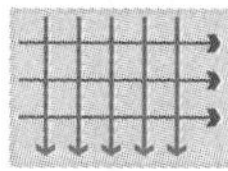

P 1. Nam Company began operations this year. At the beginning of 20xx, the company purchased plant assets of $450,000, with an estimated useful life of ten years and no salvage value. During the year, the company had net sales of $650,000, salaries expense of $100,000, and other expenses of $40,000, excluding depreciation. In addition, Nam Company purchased inventory as follows:

January 15	400 units at $200	$ 80,000
March 20	200 units at $204	40,800
June 15	800 units at $208	166,400
September 18	600 units at $206	123,600
December 9	300 units at $210	63,000
Total	2,300 units	$473,800

At the end of the year, a physical inventory disclosed 500 units still on hand. The managers of Nam Company know they have a choice of accounting methods, but are unsure how those methods will affect net income. They have heard of the FIFO and LIFO inventory methods and the straight-line and double-declining-balance depreciation methods.

REQUIRED

1. Prepare two income statements for Nam Company, one using the FIFO and straight-line methods, the other using the LIFO and double-declining-balance methods.
2. Prepare a schedule accounting for the difference in the two net income figures obtained in **1.**
3. What effect does the choice of accounting method have on Nam's inventory turnover? What conclusions can you draw?
4. How does the choice of accounting methods affect Nam's return on assets? Assume the company's only assets are cash of $40,000, inventory, and plant assets. Use year-end balances to compute the ratios. Is your evaluation of Nam's profitability affected by the choice of accounting methods?

LO 2
LO 3
LO 4
LO 5 *Corporate Income Statement*

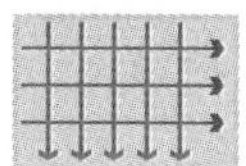

P 2. Income statement information for the Shah Corporation during 20x1 is as follows:

a. Administrative expenses, $220,000.
b. Cost of goods sold, $880,000.
c. Cumulative effect of a change in inventory methods that decreased income (net of taxes, $56,000), $120,000.
d. Extraordinary loss from a storm (net of taxes, $20,000), $40,000.
e. Income taxes expense, continuing operations, $84,000.
f. Net sales, $1,780,000.
g. Selling expenses, $380,000.

REQUIRED

Prepare Shah Corporation's income statement for 20x1, including earnings per share, information assuming a weighted average of 200,000 shares of common stock outstanding for 20x1.

LO 2
LO 3
LO 4
LO 5 *Corporate Income Statement and Evaluation of Business Operations*

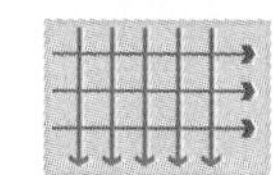

P 3. During 20x9 Lutton Corporation engaged in a number of complex transactions to restructure the business—selling off a division, retiring bonds, and changing accounting methods. The company has always issued a simple single-step income statement, and the accountant has accordingly prepared the December 31 year-end income statements for 20x8 and 20x9, shown at the top of the next page.

The president of the company, Karen Lutton, is pleased to see that both net income and earnings per share increased by 22 percent from 20x8 to 20x9 and intends to announce to the stockholders that the restructuring is a success.

REQUIRED

1. Recast the 20x9 and 20x8 income statements in proper multistep form, including allocating income taxes to appropriate items (assume a 30 percent income tax rate) and showing earnings per share figures (200,000 shares outstanding).
2. What is your assessment of the restructuring plan and business operations in 20x9?

Lutton Corporation
Income Statements
For the Years Ended December 31, 20x9 and 20x8

	20x9	20x8
Net Sales	$3,500,000	$4,200,000
Cost of Goods Sold	(1,925,000)	(2,100,000)
Operating Expenses	(787,500)	(525,000)
Income Taxes Expense	(576,450)	(472,500)
Income from Operations of a Discontinued Segment	560,000	
Gain on Disposal of Discontinued Segment	490,000	
Extraordinary Gain on Retirement of Bonds	252,000	
Cumulative Effect of a Change in Accounting Principle	(168,000)	
Net Income	$1,345,050	$1,102,500
Earnings per share	$ 6.73	$ 5.51

P 4. LO 6 LO 7 *Stock Dividend and Stock Split Transactions and Stockholders' Equity*

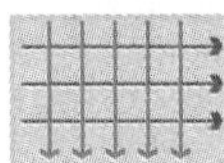

The stockholders' equity section of the balance sheet of Borkowski Corporation as of December 31, 20x6, was as follows:

Contributed Capital	
Common Stock, $4 par value, 500,000 shares authorized, 200,000 shares issued and outstanding	$ 800,000
Paid-in Capital in Excess of Par Value, Common	1,000,000
Total Contributed Capital	$1,800,000
Retained Earnings	1,200,000
Total Stockholders' Equity	$3,000,000

The following transactions occurred in 20x7 for Borkowski Corporation:

Feb. 28 The board of directors declared a 10 percent stock dividend to stockholders of record on March 25 to be distributed on April 5. The market value on this date is $16.
Mar. 25 Date of record for stock dividend.
Apr. 5 Issued stock dividend.
Aug. 3 Declared a 2-for-1 stock split.
Nov. 20 Purchased 18,000 shares of the company's common stock at $8 per share for the treasury.
Dec. 31 Declared a 5 percent stock dividend to stockholders of record on January 25 to be distributed on February 5. The market value per share was $9.

REQUIRED

1. Record the transactions for Borkowski Corporation in T accounts.
2. Prepare the stockholders' equity section of the company's balance sheet as of December 31, 20x7. Assume net income for 20x7 is $108,000.

P 5. LO 6 LO 7 *Dividends and Stock Split Transactions, and Stockholders' Equity*

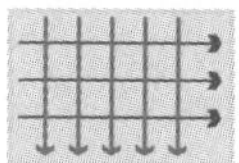

The stockholders' equity section of the Kurland Blind and Awning Company's balance sheet as of December 31, 20x6, was as follows:

Contributed Capital	
Common Stock, $2 par value, 3,000,000 shares authorized, 500,000 shares issued and outstanding	$1,000,000
Paid-in Capital in Excess of Par Value, Common	400,000
Total Contributed Capital	$1,400,000
Retained Earnings	1,080,000
Total Stockholders' Equity	$2,480,000

The company was involved in the following stockholders' equity transactions during 20x7:

Mar. 5	Declared a $.40 per share cash dividend to be paid on April 6 to stockholders of record on March 20.
20	Date of record.
Apr. 6	Paid the cash dividend.
June 17	Declared a 10 percent stock dividend to be distributed August 17 to stockholders of record on August 5. The market value of the stock was $14 per share.
Aug. 5	Date of record.
17	Distributed the stock dividend.
Oct. 2	Split its stock 3 for 1.
Dec. 27	Declared a cash dividend of $.20 payable January 27, 20x8, to stockholders of record on January 14, 20x8.

On December 9, the board of directors restricted retained earnings for a pending lawsuit in the amount of $200,000. The restriction should be shown on the firm's financial statements.

REQUIRED

1. Record the 20x7 transactions in journal form.
2. Prepare the stockholders' equity section of the company's balance sheet as of December 31, 20x7, with an appropriate disclosure of the restriction on retained earnings. Assume net income for the year is $400,000.

P 6. LO 6 LO 7 LO 8 *Comprehensive Stockholders' Equity Transactions*

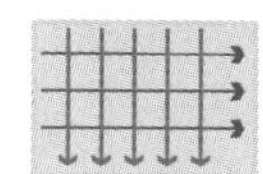

On December 31, 20x1, the stockholders' equity section of the Pucinski Company's balance sheet appeared as follows:

Contributed Capital	
Common Stock, $8 par value, 200,000 shares authorized, 60,000 shares issued and outstanding	$ 480,000
Paid-in Capital in Excess of Par Value, Common	1,280,000
Total Contributed Capital	$1,760,000
Retained Earnings	824,000
Total Stockholders' Equity	$2,584,000

Selected transactions involving stockholders' equity in 20x2 are as follows: On January 4, the board of directors obtained authorization for 20,000 shares of $40 par value noncumulative preferred stock that carried an indicated dividend rate of $4 per share and was callable at $42 per share. On January 14, the company sold 12,000 shares of the preferred stock at $40 per share and issued another 2,000 in exchange for a building valued at $80,000. On March 8, the board of directors declared a 2-for-1 stock split on the common stock. On April 20, after the stock split, the company purchased 3,000 shares of common stock for the treasury at an average price of $12 per share; 1,000 of these shares subsequently were sold on May 4 at an average price of $16 per share. On July 15, the board of directors declared a cash dividend of $4 per share on the preferred stock and $.40 per share on the common stock. The date of record was July 25. The dividends were paid on August 15. The board of directors declared a 15 percent stock dividend on November 28, when the common stock was selling for $20. The record date for the stock dividend was December 15, and the dividend was to be distributed on January 5. The board of directors noted that note disclosure must be made of a bank loan agreement that requires minimum retained earnings. No cash dividends can be declared or paid if retained earnings fall below $100,000.

REQUIRED

1. Record the above transactions in journal form.
2. Prepare the stockholders' equity section of the company's balance sheet as of December 31, 20x2, including an appropriate disclosure of the restrictions on retained earnings. Net loss for 20x2 was $218,000. (**Hint:** Use T accounts to keep track of transactions.)
3. Compute the book value per share for preferred and common stock (including common stock distributable) on December 31, 20x1 and 20x2, using end-of-year shares outstanding.

Alternate Problems

LO 2 LO 3 LO 4 LO 5 *Corporate Income Statement*

P 7. Information concerning operations of the Benedict Shoe Corporation during 20xx is as follows:

a. Administrative expenses, $180,000.
b. Cost of goods sold, $840,000.
c. Cumulative effect of an accounting change in depreciation methods that increased income (net of taxes, $40,000), $84,000.
d. Extraordinary loss from an earthquake (net of taxes, $72,000), $120,000.
e. Sales (net), $1,800,000.
f. Selling expenses, $160,000.
g. Income taxes expense applicable to continuing operations, $210,000.

REQUIRED

Prepare the corporation's income statement for the year ended December 31, 20xx, including earnings per share information. Assume a weighted average of 100,000 common shares outstanding during the year.

LO 6 LO 7 *Stock Dividend and Stock Split Transactions and Stockholders' Equity*

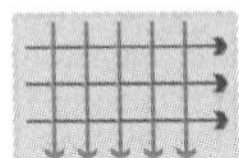

P 8. The stockholders' equity section of Bargiel Linen Mills, Inc., as of December 31, 20x2, was as follows:

Contributed Capital	
Common Stock, $6 par value, 500,000 shares authorized, 80,000 shares issued and outstanding	$ 480,000
Paid-in Capital in Excess of Par Value, Common	150,000
Total Contributed Capital	$ 630,000
Retained Earnings	480,000
Total Stockholders' Equity	$1,110,000

A review of the stockholders' equity records of Bargiel Linen Mills, Inc., disclosed the following transactions during 20x3.

Mar. 25	The board of directors declared a 5 percent stock dividend to stockholders of record on April 20 to be distributed on May 1. The market value of the common stock was $11 per share.
Apr. 20	Date of record for the stock dividend.
May 1	Issued the stock dividend.
Sept. 10	Declared a 3-for-1 stock split.
Dec. 15	Declared a 10 percent stock dividend to stockholders of record on January 15 to be distributed on February 15. The market price on this date is $3.50 per share.

REQUIRED

1. Record the transactions for Bargiel Linen Mills, Inc., in T accounts.
2. Prepare the stockholders' equity section of the company's balance sheet as of December 31, 20x3. Assume net income for 20x3 is $47,000.

P 9. The balance sheet of the Yao Clothing Company disclosed the following stockholders' equity as of September 30, 20x1:

LO 6 **LO 7** *Dividends and Stock Split Transactions and Stockholders' Equity*

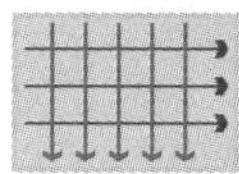

Contributed Capital	
Common Stock, $4 par value, 1,000,000 shares authorized, 300,000 shares issued and outstanding	$1,200,000
Paid-in Capital in Excess of Par Value, Common	740,000
Total Contributed Capital	$1,940,000
Retained Earnings	700,000
Total Stockholders' Equity	$2,640,000

The following stockholders' equity transactions were completed during the next fiscal year in the order presented:

20x1	
Dec. 17	Declared a 10 percent stock dividend to be distributed January 20 to stockholders of record on January 1. The market value per share on the date of declaration was $8.
20x2	
Jan. 1	Date of record.
20	Distributed the stock dividend.
Apr. 14	Declared a $.50 per share cash dividend. The cash dividend is payable May 15 to stockholders of record on May 1.
May 1	Date of record.
15	Paid the cash dividend.
June 17	Split its stock 2 for 1.
Sept. 15	Declared a cash dividend of $.30 per share payable October 10 to stockholders of record October 1.

On September 14, the board of directors restricted retained earnings for plant expansion in the amount of $300,000. The restriction should be shown in the financial statements.

REQUIRED

1. Record the above transactions in journal form.
2. Prepare the stockholders' equity section of the company's balance sheet as of September 30, 20x2, with an appropriate disclosure of the restriction of retained earnings. Assume net income for the year is $300,000.

Skills Development

Conceptual Analysis

LO 1 **LO 4** *Classic Quality of Earnings*

SD 1. On Tuesday, January 19, 1988, ***International Business Machines Corp. (IBM),*** the world's largest computer manufacturer, reported greatly increased earnings for the fourth quarter of 1987. Despite this reported gain in earnings, the price of IBM's stock on the New York Stock Exchange declined by $6 per share to $111.75. In sympathy with this move, most other technology stocks also declined.[26]

IBM's fourth-quarter net earnings rose from $1.39 billion, or $2.28 a share, to $2.08 billion, or $3.47 a share, an increase of 49.6 percent and 52.2 percent over the year-earlier period. Management declared that these results demonstrated the effectiveness of IBM's efforts to become more competitive and that, despite the economic uncertainties of 1988, the company was planning for growth.

The apparent cause of the stock price decline was that the huge increase in income could be traced to nonrecurring gains. Investment analysts pointed out that IBM's high earnings stemmed primarily from factors such as a lower tax rate. Despite most analysts' expectations of a tax rate between 40 and 42 percent, IBM's rate was a low 36.4 percent, down from the previous year's 45.3 percent.

In addition, analysts were disappointed in IBM's revenue growth. Revenues within the United States were down, and much of the growth in revenues came through favorable currency translations, increases that might not be repeated. In fact, some estimates of the fourth-quarter earnings attributed $.50 per share to currency translations and another $.25 to tax-rate changes.

Other factors contributing to the rise in earnings were one-time transactions, such as the sale of Intel Corporation stock and bond redemptions, along with a corporate stock buyback program that reduced the amount of stock outstanding in the fourth quarter by 7.4 million shares.

The analysts were concerned about the quality of IBM's earnings. Identify four quality of earnings issues reported in the case and the analysts' concern about each. In percentage terms, what is the impact of the currency changes on fourth-quarter earnings? Comment on management's assessment of IBM's performance. Do you agree with management? (Optional question: What has IBM's subsequent performance been?) Be prepared to discuss your answers to the questions in class.

LO 2 **LO 4** *Interpretation of Corporate Income Statement*

SD 2. ***General Motors*** is a major automotive manufacturing company with supporting financing and insurance operations. The independent auditors' report indicates that the company has changed some of its accounting principles as follows:[27]

> As discussed in Note 1 to the financial statements, effective January 1, 1995, the Corporation changed its method of accounting for sales to daily rental car companies (EITF No. 95). Also as discussed in Note 1 and 4 to the financial statements, respectively, effective January 1, 1994, the Corporation changed its method of accounting for postemployment benefits (SFAS No. 112) and certain investments in debt and equity securities (SFAS No. 115).

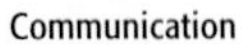
Communication

Critical Thinking

Group Activity

Memo

Ethics

International
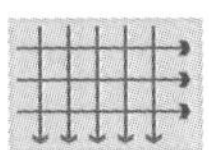
Spreadsheet

General Ledger

CD-ROM

Internet

The latter change had no impact on the income statement. Further, the notes reveal that on June 7, 1996, General Motors split off its Electronic Data Systems operations, which were reported as discontinued operations. Because the discontinued operation was split off and not sold, there was no gain or loss on the transaction. The accounting changes and discontinued operations disclosed in the company's income statement were as follows:

	1996	1995	1994
Income from continuing operations	$4,589	$5,404	$4,296
Income (loss) from discontinued operations (Note 2)	(5)	105	349
Cumulative effect of accounting changes (Note 1)	—	(52)	(751)
Net Income	$4,584	$5,457	$3,894
Earnings per share (Note 20)			
$1-2/3 par value from continuing operations	$6.07	$7.14	$5.74
Income (loss) from discontinued operations (Note 2)	(0.01)	0.14	0.46
Cumulative effect of accounting changes (Note 1)	—	(0.07)	(1.05)
Net earnings attributable to $1-2/3 par value	$ 6.06	$ 7.21	$ 5.15

1. Identify the amounts in the partial income statement for each item mentioned in the independent auditors' report.
2. Define discontinued operations. Why are discontinued operations shown separately on the income statement?
3. Define the cumulative effect of changes in accounting principles. Were the changes here instigated by management, or were they mandated by outside authorities? If mandated, by whom?
4. Why are several figures given for earnings per common share? Which earnings (loss) per common share figure would you say is most relevant to future operations? Why is it the most relevant?

ETHICAL DILEMMA

SD 3. LO 7 *Ethics and Stock Dividends*

For twenty years ***Bass Products Corporation,*** a public corporation, has followed the practice of paying a cash dividend every quarter and has promoted itself to investors as a stable, reliable company. Recent competition from Asian companies has negatively affected its earnings and cash flows. As a result, Sandra Bass, president of the company, is proposing that the board of directors declare a stock dividend of 5 percent this year instead of a cash dividend. She says, "This will maintain our consecutive dividend record and will not require any cash outflow." What is the difference between a cash dividend and a stock dividend? Why does a corporation usually distribute either kind of dividend, and how does each affect the financial statements? Is the action proposed by Bass ethical?

SD 4. LO 1 LO 5 *Effect of Alternative Accounting Methods on Executive Compensation*

At the beginning of 20x1, Ted Lazzerini retired as president and principal stockholder in ***Tedtronics Corporation,*** a successful producer of personal computer equipment. As an incentive to the new management, Lazzerini supported the board of directors' new executive compensation plan, which provides cash bonuses to key executives for years in which the company's earnings per share equal or exceed the current dividends per share of $2.00, plus a $.20 per share increase in dividends for each future year. Thus, for management to receive the bonuses, the company must earn per-share income of $2.00 the first year, $2.20 the second, $2.40 the third, and so forth. Since Lazzerini owns 500,000 of the 1,000,000 common shares outstanding, the dividend income will provide for his retirement years. He is also protected against inflation by the regular increase in dividends. Earnings and dividends per share for the first three years of operation under the new management follow.

	20x3	20x2	20x1
Earnings per share	$2.50	$2.50	$2.50
Dividends per share	2.40	2.20	2.00

During this time, management earned bonuses totaling more than $1 million under the compensation plan. Lazzerini, who had taken no active part on the board of directors, began to worry about the unchanging level of earnings and decided to study the company's annual report more carefully. The notes to the annual report revealed the following information:

a. Management changed from the LIFO inventory method to the FIFO method in 20x1. The effect of the change was to decrease cost of goods sold by $200,000 in 20x1, $300,000 in 20x2, and $400,000 in 20x3.
b. Management changed from the double-declining-balance accelerated depreciation method to the straight-line method in 20x2. The effect of this change was to decrease depreciation by $400,000 in 20x2 and by $500,000 in 20x3.
c. In 20x3, management increased the estimated useful life of intangible assets from five to ten years. The effect of this change was to decrease amortization expense by $100,000 in 20x3.

1. Compute earnings per share for each year according to the accounting methods in use at the beginning of 20x1. (Use common shares outstanding.)
2. Is the action of the executives ethical? Have the executives earned their bonuses? What serious effect has the compensation package apparently had on the net assets of Tedtronics Corporation? How could Lazzerini have protected himself from what has happened?

Research Activity

SD 5.
LO 2 LO 3 LO 4 LO 6 LO 7 LO 8 *Corporate Income Statement, Statement of Stockholders' Equity, and Book Value*

Select the annual reports of three corporations, using one or more of the following sources: your library, the Fingraph® Financial Analyst™ CD-ROM software that accompanies this text, or the Needles Accounting Resource Center Web site at http://www.hmco.com/college/needles/home.html. You may choose companies from the same industry or at random, at the direction of your instructor. (If you completed the related research activity in the chapter on contributed capital, use the same three companies.) Prepare a table with a column for each corporation. Then, for any year covered by the balance sheet, the statement of stockholders' equity, and the income statement, answer the following questions: Does the company own treasury stock? Was any treasury stock bought or retired? Did the company declare a stock dividend or a stock split? What other transactions appear in the statement of stockholders' equity? Has the company deferred any income taxes? Were there any discontinued operations, extraordinary items, or accounting changes? Compute the book value per common share for the company. In *The Wall Street Journal* or the financial section of another daily newspaper, find the current market price of each company's common stock and compare it to the book value you computed. Should there be any relationship between the two values? Be prepared to discuss your answers to these questions in class.

Decision-Making Practice

SD 6.
LO 6 LO 7 LO 8 *Analyzing Effects of Stockholders' Equity Transactions*

***Metzger Steel Corporation** (MSC)* is a small specialty steel manufacturer located in northern Alabama that has been owned by the Metzger family for several generations. Arnold Metzger is a major shareholder in MSC by virtue of his having inherited 200,000 shares of common stock in the company. Arnold has not shown much interest in the business because of his enthusiasm for archaeology, which takes him to far parts of the world. However, when he received the minutes of the last board of directors meeting, he questioned a number of transactions involving stockholders' equity. He asks you, as a person with a knowledge of accounting, to help him interpret the effect of these transactions on his interest in MSC.

You begin by examining the stockholders' equity section of MSC's December 31, 20x1, balance sheet.

Metzger Steel Corporation
Stockholders' Equity
December 31, 20x1

Contributed Capital	
Common Stock, $10 par value, 5,000,000 shares authorized, 1,000,000 shares issued and outstanding	$10,000,000
Paid-in Capital in Excess of Par Value, Common	25,000,000
Total Contributed Capital	$35,000,000
Retained Earnings	20,000,000
Total Stockholders' Equity	$55,000,000

Then you read the relevant parts of the minutes of the December 15, 20x2, meeting of the firm's board of directors:

Item A: The president reported the following transactions involving the company's stock during the last quarter.

October 15. Sold 500,000 shares of authorized common stock through the investment banking firm of T.R. Kendall at a net price of $50 per share.

November 1. Purchased 100,000 shares for the corporate treasury from Lucy Metzger at a price of $55 per share.

Item B: The board declared a 2-for-1 stock split (accomplished by halving the par value and doubling each stockholder's shares), followed by a 10 percent stock dividend. The board then declared a cash dividend of $2 per share on the resulting shares. Cash dividends are declared on outstanding shares and shares distributable. All these transactions are applicable to stockholders of record on December 20 and are payable on January 10. The market value of MSC stock on the board meeting date after the stock split was estimated to be $30.

Item C: The chief financial officer stated that he expected the company to report net income for the year of $4,000,000.

1. Prepare a stockholders' equity section of MSC's balance sheet as of December 31, 20x2, that reflects the transactions above. (**Hint:** Use T accounts to analyze the transactions. Also, use a T account in order to keep track of the shares of common stock outstanding.)
2. Write a memorandum to Arnold Metzger that shows the book value per share and Metzger's percentage of ownership at the beginning and end of the year. Explain the difference and state whether Metzger's position has improved during the year. Tell why or why not and state how Metzger may be able to maintain his percentage of ownership.

Financial Reporting and Analysis

INTERPRETING FINANCIAL REPORTS

FRA 1.
LO 1 *Quality of Earnings,*
LO 8 *Book Value, Stock Price*

In a recent article, ***International Business Machines Corp. (IBM)*** came under heavy criticism for repeated write-offs and restructuring charges that have lowered earnings. For example, in July 1993 IBM took a pretax $8.9 billion write-off for personnel retrenchment. The company also took a pretax $1.84 billion charge in the third quarter of 1995 for goodwill in its acquisition of Lotus Development Corporation. In December 1995, IBM announced that it expected to take a pretax $800 million fourth-quarter charge to reflect new closings and cutbacks that were to take place over the next year. After IBM's announcement, the stock price fell from $93.75 to $89.38 as of December 20, 1995. One analyst observed that "IBM's book value today is lower than it was twelve years ago. This means that excluding dividends, the cumulative earnings of the past 12 years have been wiped out."[28]

REQUIRED

1. How do write-offs and restructuring charges relate to the quality of earnings?
2. While analysts often exclude nonrecurring items such as write-offs from their analyses, what reasons would you give for including them in an analysis of IBM? What does a lower stock price mean?
3. Explain how IBM's book value could be lower than it was twelve years ago.

LO 6 *Interpretation of Statement of Stockholders' Equity*

FRA 2. The consolidated statement of stockholders' equity for ***Jackson Electronics, Inc.,*** a manufacturer of a broad line of electrical components, appears as presented below.

Jackson Electronics, Inc.
Consolidated Statement of Stockholders' Equity
(in thousands)

	Preferred Stock	Common Stock	Paid-in Capital in Excess of Par Value, Common	Retained Earnings	Treasury Stock, Common	Total
Balance at September 30, 20x1	$2,756	$3,902	$14,149	$119,312	($ 942)	$139,177
Year Ended September 30, 20x2						
Net income	—	—	—	18,753	—	18,753
Redemption and retirement of Preferred Stock (27,560 shares)	(2,756)	—	—	—	—	(2,756)
Stock options exercised (89,000 shares)	—	89	847	—	—	936
Purchases of Common Stock for treasury (501,412 shares)	—	—	—	—	(12,552)	(12,552)
Issuance of Common Stock (148,000 shares) in exchange for convertible subordinated debentures	—	148	3,635	—	—	3,783
Issuance of Common Stock (715,000 shares) for cash	—	715	24,535	—	—	25,250
Issuance of 500,000 shares of Common Stock in exchange for investment in Electrix Company shares	—	500	17,263	—	—	17,763
Cash dividends—Common Stock ($.80 per share)	—	—	—	(3,086)	—	(3,086)
Balance at September 30, 20x2	$ —	$5,354	$60,429	$134,979	($13,494)	$187,268

REQUIRED

Jackson Electronics, Inc.'s, statement of stockholders' equity has eight summary transactions. Show that you understand this statement by preparing an entry in journal form with an explanation for each. In each case, if applicable, determine the average price per common share. Sometimes you will also have to make assumptions about an offsetting part of the entry. For example, assume that debentures (long-term bonds) are recorded at face value and that employees pay cash for stock purchased under Jackson Electronics, Inc.'s, employee incentive plans.

Group Activity: Assign each transaction to a different group to develop the entry and present the explanation to the class.

FRA 3.
LO 3 *Analysis of Income Taxes from Annual Report*

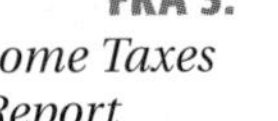
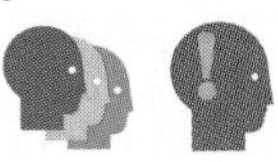

In its 1996 annual report, ***Sara Lee Corporation,*** an international food and packaged products company based in Chicago, provided the following data about its current and deferred income tax provisions (in millions):[29]

	1996	
	Current	**Deferred**
Federal	$166	$25
Foreign	237	10
State	28	(4)
	$431	$31

REQUIRED

1. What was the 1996 income taxes expense? Record in journal form the overall income tax liability for 1996, using income tax allocation procedures.
2. In the long-term liability section of the balance sheet, Sara Lee shows deferred income taxes of $333 million in 1996 versus $273 million in 1995. This shows an increase in the amount of deferred income taxes. How do such deferred income taxes arise? What would cause deferred income taxes to increase? Give an example of this process. Given the definition of a liability, do you see a potential problem with the company's classifying deferred income taxes as a liability?

International Company

FRA 4.
LO 6 *Restriction of Retained Earnings*

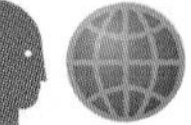

In some countries, including Japan, the availability of retained earnings for the payment of dividends is restricted. The following disclosure appeared in the annual report of ***Yamaha Motor Company, Ltd.,*** the Japanese motorcycle manufacturer.[30]

> The Commercial Code of Japan provides that an amount not less than 10 percent of the total of cash dividends and bonuses to directors and corporate auditors paid be appropriated as a legal reserve until such reserve equals 25 percent of stated capital. The legal reserve may be used to reduce a deficit or may be transferred to stated capital, but is not available as dividends.

Stated capital is equivalent to common stock. For Yamaha, this legal reserve amounted to ¥3 billion, or $30.8 million. How does this practice differ from that in the United States? Why do you think it is government policy in Japan? Do you think it is a good idea?

Toys "R" Us Annual Report

FRA 5.
LO 2 *Corporate Income*
LO 4 *Statement, Statement of*
LO 6 *Stockholders' Equity, and*
LO 8 *Book Value per Share*

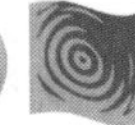

Refer to the Toys "R" Us annual report to answer the following questions.

1. Does Toys "R" Us have discontinued operations, extraordinary items, or cumulative changes in accounting principles? Would you say the income statement for Toys "R" Us is relatively simple or relatively complex?
2. What transactions most commonly affect the stockholders' equity section of the balance sheet of Toys "R" Us? Examine the statement of stockholders' equity.
3. Compute the book value of Toys "R" Us stock in 1997 and 1996 and compare it to the market price. What interpretation do you place on these relationships?

Fingraph® Financial Analyst™

FRA 6.
LO 1 *Stockholders' Equity*
LO 2 *Analysis*
LO 4
LO 5
LO 6
LO 7
LO 8

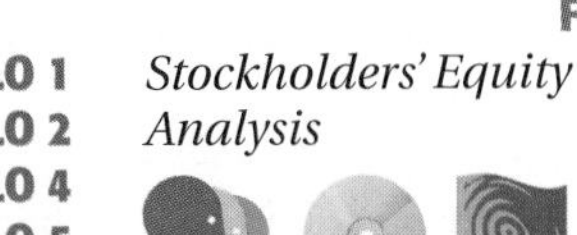

Choose any two companies from the same industry in the Fingraph® Financial Analyst™ CD-ROM software.

1. In the annual reports for the companies you have selected, identify the corporate income statement and its summary of significant accounting policies, usually the first note to the financial statements. Did the companies report any discontinued operations, extraordinary items, or accounting changes? What percentage impact did these items have on earnings per share? Summarize the methods and estimates each company uses in a table. If the company changed its accounting methods, was the change

the result of a new accounting standard or a voluntary choice by management? Evaluate the quality of earnings for each company.

2. Did the companies report a statement of stockholders' equity or summarize the changes in stockholders' equity in the notes only? Did the companies declare any stock dividends or stock splits? Calculate book value per common share.
3. Find in the financial section of your local paper the current market prices of the companies' common stock. Discuss the difference between market price per share and book value per share.
4. Find and read references to earnings per share in management's discussion and analysis in each annual report.
5. Write a one-page executive summary that highlights the quality of earnings for these companies, the relationship of book value and market value, and the existence or absence of stock splits or dividends, including reference to management's assessment. Include your table as an attachment to your report.

ENDNOTES

1. General Electric Company, *Annual Report,* 1996.
2. "How General Electric Damps Fluctuations in Its Annual Earnings," *The Wall Street Journal,* November 3, 1994.
3. Cited in *The Week in Review* (Deloitte Haskins & Sells), February 28, 1985.
4. "Up to the Minute, Down to the Wire," *Twentieth Century Mutual Funds Newsletter,* 1996.
5. "At Teledyne, A Chorus of Whistle-blowers," *Business Week,* December 14, 1992.
6. Erle Norton and Andy Posztor, "Ludlum Agrees to a Merger with Teledyne," *The Wall Street Journal,* April 2, 1996.
7. "Accounting Rule Change Will Erase AT&T Earnings," *Chicago Tribune,* January 15, 1994.
8. "Accounting Gain Helps Dayton Hudson Results," *Chicago Tribune,* March 11, 1994.
9. *Statement of Financial Accounting Standards No. 130,* "Reporting Comprehensive Income" (Norwalk, Conn.: Financial Accounting Standards Board, 1997).
10. Rules for calculating and reporting taxable income in specialized industries such as banking, insurance, mutual funds, and cooperatives are highly technical and may vary significantly from those discussed in this chapter.
11. *Statement of Financial Accounting Standards No. 109,* "Accounting for Income Taxes" (Norwalk, Conn.: Financial Accounting Standards Board, 1992).
12. American Institute of Certified Public Accountants, *Accounting Trends & Techniques* (New York: American Institute of Certified Public Accountants, 1996), p. 245.
13. Accounting Principles Board, *Opinion No. 30,* "Reporting the Results of Operations" (New York: American Institute of Certified Public Accountants, 1973), par. 20.
14. Ibid.
15. American Institute of Certified Public Accountants, *Accounting Trends & Techniques* (New York: American Institute of Certified Public Accountants, 1996), p. 390.
16. Accounting Principles Board, *Opinion No. 20,* "Accounting Changes" (New York: American Institute of Certified Public Accountants, 1971), par. 20.
17. American Institute of Certified Public Accountants, *Accounting Trends & Techniques* (New York: American Institute of Certified Public Accountants, 1996), p. 547.
18. Accounting Principles Board, *Opinion No. 15,* "Earnings per Share" (New York: American Institute of Certified Public Accountants, 1969), par. 12.
19. Fleetwood Enterprises, Inc., *Annual Report,* 1996.
20. Bell Atlantic Corporation, *Annual Report,* 1996.
21. *Statement of Financial Accounting Standards No. 128,* "Earnings per Share and the Disclosure of Information About Capital Structure" (Norwalk, Conn.: Financial Accounting Standards Board, 1997).
22. Skandia Group, *Annual Report,* 1996.
23. *Accounting Research Bulletin No. 43* (New York: American Institute of Certified Public Accountants, 1953), chap. 7, sec. B, par. 10.

24. Ibid., par. 13.
25. Angelo B. Henderson, "Chrysler Declares 2-for-1 Stock Split and Increases Its Dividend by 17%," *The Wall Street Journal,* May 17, 1996.
26. "Technology Firms Post Strong Earnings But Stock Prices Decline Sharply," *The Wall Street Journal,* January 21, 1988; Donald R. Seace, "Industrials Plunge 57.2 Points—Technology Stocks' Woes Cited," *The Wall Street Journal,* January 21, 1988.
27. Adapted from General Motors, *Annual Report,* 1996.
28. Fred R. Bleakley, "Spate of Writeoffs Mostly Please Investors, but Analysts Warn Profit May Be Distorted," *The Wall Street Journal,* December 21, 1995.
29. Sara Lee Corporation, *Annual Report,* 1996.
30. Yamaha Motor Company, Ltd., *Annual Report,* 1996.

CHAPTER 16

Long-Term Liabilities

LEARNING OBJECTIVES

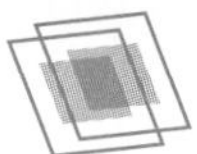

1. **Identify the management issues related to issuing long-term debt.**
2. **Identify and contrast the major characteristics of bonds.**
3. **Record the issuance of bonds at face value and at a discount or premium.**
4. **Use present values to determine the value of bonds.**
5. **Use the straight-line and effective interest methods to amortize (a) bond discounts and (b) bond premiums.**
6. **Account for bonds issued between interest dates and make year-end adjustments.**
7. **Account for the retirement of bonds and the conversion of bonds into stock.**
8. **Explain the basic features of mortgages payable, installment notes payable, long-term leases, and pensions and other postretirement benefits as long-term liabilities.**

DECISION POINT

AT&T CORPORATION

Long-term liabilities, or long-term debt, are obligations of a business that are due to be paid after one year or beyond the operating cycle, whichever is longer. Decisions related to the issuance of long-term debt are among the most important that management has to make because, next to the success or failure of a company's operations, how the company finances its operations is the most important factor in the company's long-term viability. AT&T Corporation is a company that has a large amount of long-term debt, as shown by the following figures for 1996 in the Financial Highlights.[1] Total long-term liabilities are almost twice stockholders' equity, and the debt to equity ratio is 1.7 ($35,257 ÷ $20,295). What factors might have influenced AT&T's management to incur such a large amount of debt?

Financial Highlights	
(In millions)	
Liabilities	
Total current liabilities	$16,318
Long-term debt	$ 7,883
Long-term benefit-related liabilities	3,037
Deferred income taxes	4,827
Other long-term liabilities and deferred credits	3,192
Total long-term liabilities	$18,939
Total liabilities	$35,257
Stockholders' equity	20,295
Total liabilities and stockholders' equity	$55,552

In the past, AT&T was the nation's long-distance telephone company. The investments in power lines, transformers, computers, and other types of property, plant, and equipment required for this business are enormous. These are mostly long-term assets, and the most sensible way to finance them is through long-term financing. When the business was protected from competition, management could reasonably predict sufficient earnings and cash flow to meet the debt and interest

Critical Thinking Question: Why are pension obligations recorded as an expense and liability now, since they will not be paid for many years? **Answer:** Under accrual accounting, the benefits to the company accrue while the employee is working.

obligations. Also, over the years, AT&T has been very generous to employees in promising benefits that will be paid after the employees retire. Now that AT&T is facing open competition for its markets, the company must reassess not only the kind of business it is but also the amount and kinds of debt it carries. The amount and type of debt a company incurs will depend on many factors, including the nature of the business, its competitive environment, the state of the financial markets, and the predictability of its earnings.

Management Issues Related to Issuing Long-Term Debt

OBJECTIVE 1

Identify the management issues related to issuing long-term debt

Related Text Assignments:
Q: 1
SE: 1
E: 1
SD: 6
FRA: 4, 5, 6

Profitable operations and short-term credit are seldom sufficient for a growing business that must invest in long-term assets and in research and development and other activities that will produce income in future years. For such assets and activities, the company requires funds that will be available for longer periods of time. Two key sources of long-term funds are the issuance of capital stock and the issuance of long-term debt in the form of bonds, notes, mortgages, and leases. The management issues related to issuing long-term debt are (1) whether or not to have long-term debt, (2) how much long-term debt to have, and (3) what types of long-term debt to have.

The Decision to Issue Long-Term Debt

A key decision faced by management is whether to rely solely on stockholders' equity—capital stock issued and retained earnings—for long-term funds for the business or to rely partially on long-term debt for those funds.

Since long-term debts represent financial commitments that must be paid at maturity and interest or other payments that must be paid periodically, common stock would seem to have two advantages over long-term debt: It does not have to be paid back, and dividends on common stock are usually paid only if the company earns sufficient income. Long-term debt does, however, have some advantages over common stock:

1. **Stockholder control.** Since bondholders and other creditors do not have voting rights, common stockholders do not relinquish any control of the company.
2. **Tax effects.** The interest on debt is tax deductible, whereas dividends on common stock are not. For example, if a corporation pays $100,000 in interest and the income tax rate is 30 percent, the net cost to the corporation is $70,000 because it will save $30,000 on its income taxes. To pay $100,000 in dividends, the company would have to earn $142,857 before taxes ($100,000 ÷ .70).
3. **Financial leverage.** If a corporation is able to earn more on its assets than it pays in interest on debt, all of the excess will increase its earnings for stockholders. This concept is called financial leverage or *trading on the equity.* For example, if a company is able to earn 12 percent, or $120,000, on a $1,000,000 investment financed by long-term 10 percent notes, it will earn $20,000 before taxes ($120,000 − $100,000). Financial leverage makes heavily debt-financed investments in office buildings and shopping centers attractive to investors: They hope to earn a return that exceeds the cost of the interest on the underlying debt. The debt to equity ratio is considered an overall measure of the financial leverage of a company.

Despite these advantages, using debt financing is not always in a company's best interest. First, since cash is required to make periodic interest payments and to pay

Point to Emphasize: Although carrying a lot of debt is risky, there *are* some advantages to issuing bonds instead of stock. First, bond interest expense is tax-deductible for the issuing corporation, whereas dividends paid on stock are not. Second, issuing bonds is a way to raise capital without diluting ownership of the corporation. The challenge is to determine the optimal balance between stocks and bonds so that the advantages of each can be enjoyed.

back the principal amount of the debt at the maturity date, a company whose plans for earnings do not pan out, whose operations are subject to ups and downs, or whose cash flow is weak can be in danger. If the company fails to meet its obligations, it can be forced into bankruptcy by creditors. In other words, a company may become overcommitted. Consider, for example, the heavily debt-financed airline industry in recent years. Companies such as TWA and Continental Airlines became bankrupt because they could not make payments on their long-term debt and other liabilities. Second, financial leverage can work against a company if the earnings from its investments do not exceed its interest payments. This happened during the savings and loan crisis when long-term debt was used to finance the construction of office buildings that subsequently could not be leased for enough money to cover interest payments.

How Much Debt

Although some companies carry amounts of total debt that exceed 100 percent of their stockholders' equity, many companies carry less, as can be seen from Figure 1, which shows the average debt to equity for selected industries. The range is from about 67 percent to 142 percent of equity. Clearly the use of debt financing varies widely across industries. Firms that own a high percentage of long-term assets would be looking to long-term financing as an option. We saw previously that AT&T has a very high debt to equity ratio of 250 percent. Financial leverage makes it advantageous to have long-term debt so long as the company earns a satisfactory income and is able to make interest payments and repay the debt at maturity. Since failure to make timely interest payments could possibly force a company into bankruptcy, it is important for companies to assess the risk of default or nonpayment of interest or principal.

A common measure of how much risk a company is undertaking with its debt is the interest coverage ratio. It measures the degree of protection a company has from default on interest payments. This measure can help to assess the safety of AT&T in light of its huge amount of debt. This ratio for AT&T, which in 1996 had income

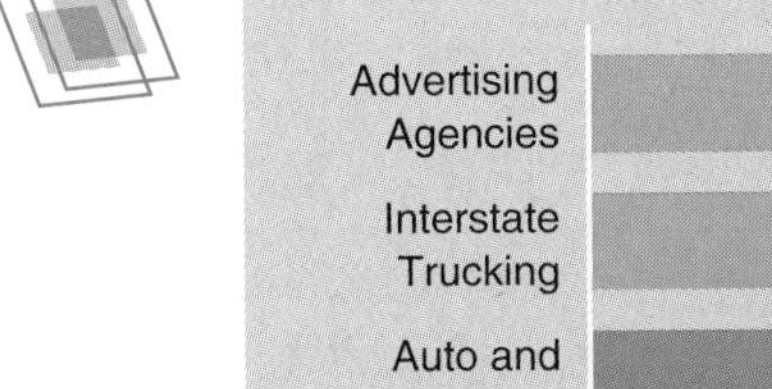

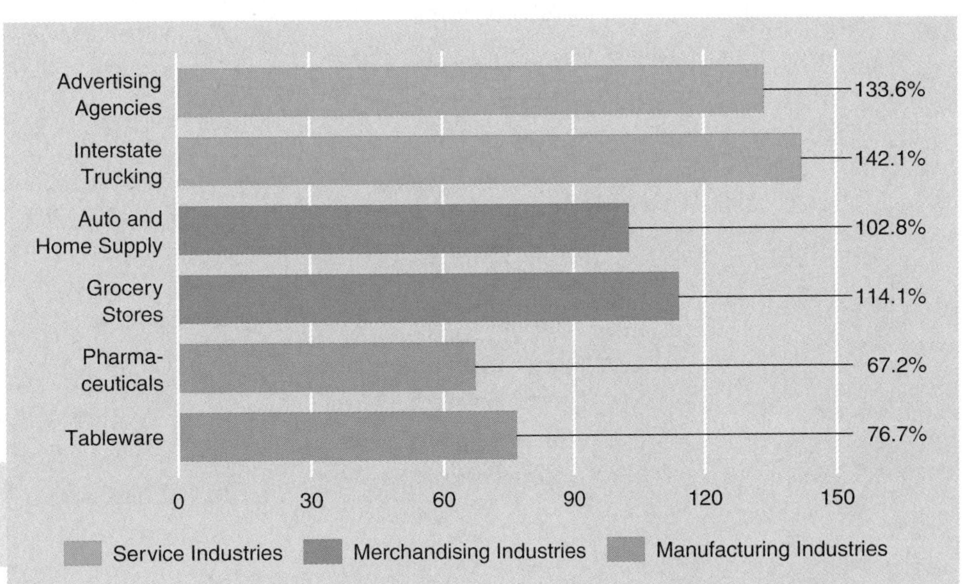

Figure 1
Average Debt to Equity for Selected Industries

Source: Data from Dun & Bradstreet, *Industry Norms and Key Business Ratios,* 1996–97.

before taxes of $8,866 million and interest expense of $334 million, is computed as follows:

$$\text{Interest Coverage Ratio} = \frac{\text{Income Before Taxes} + \text{Interest Expense}}{\text{Interest Expense}}$$

$$= \frac{\$8,866,000,000 + \$334,000,000}{334,000,000}$$

$$= 27.5 \text{ times}$$

This ratio shows that the interest expense for AT&T is covered 27.5 times. The coverage ratio is high for AT&T, which in previous years had much lower coverage ratios. The trend shows the effects of the dramatic changes that are occurring in AT&T's industry and the results of the company's restructuring of its financing strategies.

What Types of Long-Term Debt

The most common type of long-term debt is long-term bonds (most of which are also called debentures). These can have many different characteristics, including the time until repayment, the amount of interest, whether or not the company can elect to repay early, and whether the bonds can be converted into other securities like common stock. However, there are many other types of long-term debt. Some examples are long-term notes, mortgages, and long-term leases. AT&T, for example, has a mixture of long-term obligations, as shown by the following excerpt from its 1996 annual report (in millions):

Financial Highlights: Long-Term Obligations

(This table shows the outstanding long-term debt obligations at December 31)

Interest Rates (b)	Maturities	1996
Debentures		
4⅜% to 4¾%	1998–1999	**$ 500**
5⅛% to 6%	2000–2001	**500**
8⅛% to 8⅝%	1997–2031	**1,996**
Notes		
4¼% to 7¾%	1997–2025	**4,341**
7⅘% to 8 19/20%	1997–2025	**786**
9% to 13%	1997–2020	**60**
Variable rate	1997–2054	**115**
		8,298
Other		**112**
Less: Unamortized discount—net		**64**
Total long-term obligations		**8,346**
Less: Amounts maturing within one year		**463**
Net long-term obligations		**$7,883**

It is important that managers know the characteristics of the various types of long-term liabilities so that they can structure a company's long-term financing to the best advantage of the company.

BUSINESS BULLETIN: BUSINESS PRACTICE

Missing interest payments on debt is serious business for companies. On March 3, 1995, Trans World Airlines, Inc. (TWA) reached the end of a thirty-day grace period on the payment of $255 million of interest on its long-term notes. Standard & Poor's lowered the company's debt rating to D, its lowest category. If TWA had not paid by the end of the day, any group representing at least 25 percent of its noteholders could have forced the company into bankruptcy by invoking an acceleration notice that would make all the loans due immediately.[2] This action would have been unfortunate because the company was recovering after many years of losses. The company was able to meet the interest payment and continue its recovery, but it incurred another disastrous shock when one of its Paris-bound planes exploded after taking off from New York in June 1996.

The Nature of Bonds

OBJECTIVE 2

Identify and contrast the major characteristics of bonds

Related Text Assignments:
Q: 2, 3
SD: 4, 6
FRA: 6

Enrichment Note: An investor who purchases debt securities, such as bonds or notes, is a creditor of the organization, not an owner. Debt securities normally carry a maturity date and require the organization to make periodic interest payments.

Common Student Confusion: Students often confuse the terms *indenture* and *debenture* because they sound alike. Point out that an indenture is a bond contract, whereas a debenture is an unsecured bond.

Parenthetical Note: Bonds are quoted as a percentage of face value; stock is quoted as a dollar amount.

A bond is a security, usually long term, representing money borrowed from the investing public by a corporation or some other entity. (Bonds are also issued by the U.S. government, state and local governments, and foreign companies and countries to raise money.) A bond must be repaid at a specified time and requires periodic payments of interest.[3] Interest is usually paid semiannually (twice a year). Bonds must not be confused with stocks. Because stocks are shares of ownership, stockholders are owners. Bondholders are creditors. Bonds are promises to repay the amount borrowed, called the *principal,* and interest at a specified rate on specified future dates.

A bondholder receives a bond certificate as evidence of the organization's debt. In most cases, the face value (denomination) of the bond is $1,000 or some multiple of $1,000. A bond issue is the total number of bonds issued at one time. For example, a $1,000,000 bond issue could consist of a thousand $1,000 bonds. Because a bond issue can be bought and held by many investors, the organization usually enters into a supplementary agreement called a bond indenture. The bond indenture defines the rights, privileges, and limitations of the bondholders. It generally describes such things as the maturity date of the bonds, interest payment dates, interest rate, and other characteristics of the bonds. Repayment plans and restrictions also may be covered.

The prices of bonds are stated in terms of a percentage of face value. A bond issue quoted at 103½ means that a $1,000 bond costs $1,035 ($1,000 × 1.035). When a bond sells at exactly 100, it is said to sell at face or par value. When it sells above 100, it is said to sell at a premium; below 100, at a discount. A $1,000 bond quoted at 87.62 would be selling at a discount and would cost the buyer $876.20.

A bond indenture can be written to fit the financing needs of an individual organization. As a result, the bonds being issued in today's financial markets have many different features. Several of the more important ones are described in the following paragraphs.

Secured or Unsecured Bonds

Bonds can be either secured or unsecured. If issued on the general credit of the organization, they are unsecured bonds (also called *debenture bonds*). Secured bonds give the bondholders a pledge of certain assets as a guarantee of repayment.

BUSINESS BULLETIN: INTERNATIONAL PRACTICE

When U.S. companies need cash, one ready source is a bond issue, but this source of funds is not available in many other countries. For instance surprising as it may seem, Japan, the world's second largest economy and financial system, has only a fledgling corporate bond market. Whereas regular corporate bonds account for 31 percent of U.S. corporate debt, only 57, or 2 percent, of the 2,500 publicly listed companies in Japan have any domestic bonds outstanding. Japanese companies have traditionally relied on loans from big Japanese banks when they need cash. This has caused problems for Japanese companies in the 1990s because Japanese banks have not had the funds to lend them as a result of the collapse of the real estate industry in Japan.[4] Similar problems have occurred more recently in other Asian countries.

Parenthetical Note: A debenture of a solid company actually might be a less risky investment than a secured bond of an unstable company.

The security identified by a secured bond can be any specific asset of the organization or a general category of asset, such as property, plant, or equipment.

Term or Serial Bonds

Point to Emphasize: An advantage of issuing serial bonds is that the organization retires the bonds over a period of years, rather than all at once.

When all the bonds of an issue mature at the same time, they are called term bonds. For instance, an organization may issue $1,000,000 worth of bonds, all due twenty years from the date of issue. If the bonds in an issue mature on several different dates, the bonds are serial bonds. An example of serial bonds would be a $1,000,000 issue that calls for retiring $200,000 of the principal every five years. This arrangement means that after the first $200,000 payment is made, $800,000 of the bonds would remain outstanding for the next five years. In other words, $1,000,000 is outstanding for the first five years, $800,000 for the second five years, and so on. An organization may issue serial bonds to ease the task of retiring its debt.

Registered or Coupon Bonds

Most bonds issued today are registered bonds. The names and addresses of the owners of such bonds must be recorded with the issuing organization. The organization keeps a register of the owners and pays interest by check to the bondholders of record on the interest payment date. Coupon bonds generally are not registered with the organization; instead, they bear interest coupons stating the amount of interest due and the payment date. The bondholder removes the coupons from the bonds on the interest payment dates and presents them at a bank for collection.

Accounting for Bonds Payable

OBJECTIVE 3

Record the issuance of bonds at face value and at a discount or premium

When the board of directors of a corporation decides to issue bonds, it customarily presents the proposal to the stockholders. If the stockholders agree to the issue, the company prints the certificates and draws up an appropriate legal document. The bonds are then authorized for issuance. It is not necessary to make a journal entry for the authorization, but most companies prepare a memorandum in the Bonds Payable account describing the issue. This note lists the number and value of bonds authorized, the interest rate, the interest payment dates, and the life of the bonds.

Related Text Assignments:
Q: 4, 5
SE: 2, 3, 5, 7
E: 2, 3, 4, 5, 10, 12
P: 1, 2, 3, 5, 6, 7, 8
SD: 1, 5
FRA: 1

Once the bonds are issued, the corporation must pay interest to the bondholders over the life of the bonds (in most cases, semiannually) and the principal of the bonds at maturity.

Balance Sheet Disclosure of Bonds

Point to Emphasize: Bonds payable are presented on the balance sheet as either a current or a long-term liability, depending on the maturity date and method of retiring the bonds.

Bonds payable and unamortized discounts or premiums (which we explain later) are typically shown on a company's balance sheet as long-term liabilities. However, if the maturity date of the bond issue is one year or less and the bonds will be retired using current assets, Bonds Payable should be listed as a current liability. If the issue is to be paid with segregated assets or replaced by another bond issue, the bonds should still be shown as a long-term liability.

Important provisions of the bond indenture are reported in the notes to the financial statements, as illustrated by the earlier excerpt from the AT&T annual report. Often reported with them is a list of all bond issues, the kinds of bonds, interest rates, any securities connected with the bonds, interest payment dates, maturity dates, and effective interest rates.

Bonds Issued at Face Value

Instructional Strategy: Assign SD 5 for in-class discussion. Its tie-in to financial markets and the business press is excellent, and it reinforces the user's perspective on financial accounting information.

Suppose that the Vason Corporation has authorized the issuance of $100,000 of 9 percent, five-year bonds on January 1, 20x0. According to the bond indenture, interest is to be paid on January 1 and July 1 of each year. Assume that the bonds are sold on January 1, 20x0, for their face value. The entry to record the issuance is as follows:

A = L + OE
\+ \+

20x0			
Jan. 1	Cash	100,000	
	Bonds Payable		100,000
	Sold $100,000 of 9%, 5-year bonds at face value		

As stated above, interest is paid on January 1 and July 1 of each year. Therefore, the corporation would owe the bondholders $4,500 interest on July 1, 20x0:

Common Student Error: When calculating semiannual interest, students often use the annual rate (9 percent in this case) by mistake, rather than half the annual rate.

$$\begin{aligned} \text{Interest} &= \text{Principal} \times \text{Rate} \times \text{Time} \\ &= \$100{,}000 \times .09 \times \frac{6}{12}\text{ year} \\ &= \$4{,}500 \end{aligned}$$

The interest paid to the bondholders on each semiannual interest payment date (January 1 or July 1) would be recorded as follows:

A* = L + OE
− −
*assumes cash paid

Bond Interest Expense	4,500	
Cash (or Interest Payable)		4,500
Paid (or accrued) semiannual interest to bondholders of 9%, 5-year bonds		

Face Interest Rate and Market Interest Rate

Discussion Question: Under what circumstance does a bond sell at face value? **Answer:** When the face interest rate of the bond is identical to the market interest rate for similar bonds on the date of issue.

When issuing bonds, most organizations try to set the face interest rate as close as possible to the market interest rate. The face interest rate is the rate of interest paid to bondholders based on the face value, or principal, of the bonds. The rate and amount are fixed over the life of the bond. An organization must decide in advance what the face interest rate will be to allow time to file with regulatory bodies, publicize the issue, and print the certificates.

The market interest rate is the rate of interest paid in the market on bonds of similar risk. It is also referred to as the *effective interest rate.* The market interest rate

BUSINESS BULLETIN: BUSINESS PRACTICE

The price for many bonds may be found daily in business publications like *The Wall Street Journal.* For instance, shown to the right are the quotations for a number of AT&T Corporation bonds.[5] The first quoted bond is an AT&T bond with a face interest rate of 4¾ percent that is due in 1998. The current yield is 4.8 percent based on the closing price of 99 17/32. Ten $1,000 bonds were traded (volume), and the last sale was up by 1/32 point from the previous day.

New York Exchange Bonds

Corporation Bonds (Volume) $22,427,000

Bonds	Cur Yld	Vol	Close	Net Chg
ATT 4¾98	4.8	10	99 17/32	+ 1/32
ATT 4⅜99	4.4	75	98½	...
ATT 6s00	6.0	210	100⅛	+ ½
ATT 5⅛01	5.2	125	98⅛	+ ¼
ATT 7⅛02	6.8	70	104¼	+ ½
ATT 6¾04	6.5	92	103⅞	+ 1⅛
ATT 7s05	6.8	5	103½	+ ¼
ATT 8.2s05	7.8	5	104⅞	− ¾
ATT 7½06	6.9	70	108⅛	+ ⅝
ATT 8⅛22	7.5	58	107⅞	+ ⅜
ATT 8⅛24	7.5	27	107¾	+ ⅝
ATT 8.35s25	7.6	20	110	...
ATT 8⅝31	7.8	5	110½	− ¼

Point to Emphasize: When bonds with an interest rate different from the market rate are issued, they sell at a discount or premium. The discount or premium acts as an equalizing factor.

fluctuates daily. Because an organization has no control over the market interest rate, there is often a difference between the market interest rate and the face interest rate on the issue date. The result is that the issue price of the bonds does not always equal their face value. If the market interest rate is higher than the face interest rate, the issue price will be less than the face value and the bonds are said to be issued at a discount. The discount equals the excess of the face value over the issue price. On the other hand, if the market interest rate is lower than the face interest rate, the issue price will be more than the face value and the bonds are said to be issued at a premium. The premium equals the excess of the issue price over the face value.

Bonds Issued at a Discount

Point to Emphasize: The carrying amount is always the face value of the bonds plus the unamortized premium or less the unamortized discount. The carrying amount always approaches the face value.

Suppose that the Vason Corporation issues $100,000 of 9 percent, five-year bonds at 96.149 on January 1, 20x0, when the market interest rate is 10 percent. In this case, the bonds are being issued at a discount because the market interest rate exceeds the face interest rate. The following entry records the issuance of the bonds at a discount.

A = L + OE
\+ ±

20x0				
Jan. 1	Cash		96,149	
	Unamortized Bond Discount		3,851	
	Bonds Payable			100,000
	Sold $100,000 of 9%, 5-year bonds at 96.149			
	Face amount of bonds	$100,000		
	Less purchase price of bonds ($100,000 × .96149)	96,149		
	Unamortized bond discount	$ 3,851		

In the entry, Cash is debited for the amount received ($96,149), Bonds Payable is credited for the face amount ($100,000) of the bond liability, and the difference ($3,851) is debited to Unamortized Bond Discount. If a balance sheet is prepared right after the bonds are issued at a discount, the liability for bonds payable is reported as follows:

Point to Emphasize: The unamortized bond discount is subtracted from Bonds Payable on the balance sheet. The carrying value will be below the face value until the maturity date.

Long-Term Liabilities		
9% Bonds Payable, due 1/1/x5	$100,000	
Less Unamortized Bond Discount	3,851	$96,149

Unamortized Bond Discount is a contra-liability account: Its balance is deducted from the face amount of the bonds to arrive at the carrying value, or present value, of the bonds. The bond discount is described as unamortized because it will be amortized (written off) over the life of the bonds.

Bonds Issued at a Premium

When bonds have a face interest rate above the market rate for similar investments, they are issued at a price above the face value, or at a premium. For example, assume that the Vason Corporation issues $100,000 of 9 percent, five-year bonds for $104,100 on January 1, 20x0, when the market interest rate is 8 percent. This means that investors will purchase the bonds at 104.1 percent of their face value. The issuance would be recorded as follows:

A = L + OE
\+ \+

20x0			
Jan. 1	Cash	104,100	
	Unamortized Bond Premium		4,100
	Bonds Payable		100,000
	Sold $100,000 of 9%, 5-year bonds at 104.1 ($100,000 × 1.041)		

Right after this entry is made, bonds payable would be presented on the balance sheet as follows:

Point to Emphasize: The unamortized bond premium is *added* to Bonds Payable on the balance sheet. The carrying value will be above the face value until the maturity date.

Long-Term Liabilities		
9% Bonds Payable, due 1/1/x5	$100,000	
Unamortized Bond Premium	4,100	$104,100

The carrying value of the bonds payable is $104,100, which equals the face value of the bonds plus the unamortized bond premium. The cash received from the bond issue is also $104,100. This means that the purchasers were willing to pay a premium of $4,100 to buy these bonds because their face interest rate was higher than the market interest rate.

Bond Issue Costs

Point to Emphasize: A separate Bond Issue Costs account is usually established and amortized over the life of the issue.

Most bonds are sold through underwriters, who receive a fee for taking care of the details of marketing the issue or for taking a chance on receiving the selling price. Such costs are connected with the issuance of bonds. Because bond issue costs benefit the whole life of a bond issue, it makes sense to spread the costs over that period. It is generally accepted practice to establish a separate account for bond issue costs and to amortize them over the life of the bonds. However, issue costs decrease the amount of money a company receives from a bond issue. They have the effect, then, of raising the discount or lowering the premium on the issue. As a result, bond issue costs can be spread over the life of the bonds through the amortization of a discount or premium. Because this method simplifies recordkeeping, we assume in

BUSINESS BULLETIN: BUSINESS PRACTICE

In 1993, interest rates on long-term debt were at historically low levels, which induced some companies to attempt to lock in those low costs for long periods. One of the most aggressive companies in that regard was The Walt Disney Company, which issued $150 million of 100-year bonds at a yield of only 7.5 percent. It was the first time since 1954 that 100-year bonds had been issued. Some analysts wondered if even Mickey Mouse could survive 100 years. Investors who purchase these bonds are taking a financial risk because if interest rates rise, which they are likely to do, then the market value of the bonds will decrease. Since then, other companies, including The Coca-Cola Company and Columbia HCA Healthcare, have followed suit with 100-year bonds.[6]

the text and problems of this book that all bond issue costs increase the discounts or decrease the premiums of bond issues.

Using Present Value to Value a Bond

OBJECTIVE 4

Use present values to determine the value of bonds

Related Text Assignments:
SE: 4
E: 6, 7, 8, 13
FRA: 1

Teaching Note: Explain that the amount buyers are willing to pay for an investment is normally based on what they expect to receive in return, taken at present value. In the case of a bond, the theoretical value equals the present value of the periodic interest payments plus the present value of the maturity value. The discount rate is set at the market rate (what investors are looking for), not at the face rate.

Present value is relevant to the study of bonds because the value of a bond is based on the present value of two components of cash flow: (1) a series of fixed interest payments and (2) a single payment at maturity.[7] The amount of interest a bond pays is fixed over its life. However, the market interest rate varies from day to day. Thus, the amount investors are willing to pay for a bond changes as well.

Assume, for example, that a particular bond has a face value of $10,000 and pays fixed interest of $450 every six months (a 9 percent annual rate). The bond is due in five years. If the market interest rate today is 14 percent, what is the present value of the bond?

To determine the present value of the bond, we use Table 4 in the appendix on future value and present value tables to calculate the present value of the periodic interest payments of $450, and we use Table 3 in the same appendix to calculate the present value of the single payment of $10,000 at maturity. Since interest payments are made every six months, the compounding period is half a year. Because of this, it is necessary to convert the annual rate to a semiannual rate of 7 percent (14 percent divided by two six-month periods per year) and to use ten periods (five years multiplied by two six-month periods per year). Using this information, we compute the present value of the bond.

Present value of 10 periodic payments at 7% (from Table 4 in the appendix on future value and present value tables): $450 × 7.024	$3,160.80
Present value of a single payment at the end of 10 periods at 7% (from Table 3 in the appendix on future value and present value tables): $10,000 × .508	5,080.00
Present value of $10,000 bond	$8,240.80

The market interest rate has increased so much since the bond was issued (from 9 percent to 14 percent) that the value of the bond is only $8,240.80 today. That amount is all investors would be willing to pay at this time for a bond that provides income of $450 every six months and a return of the $10,000 principal in five years.

If the market interest rate falls below the face interest rate, say to 8 percent (4 percent semiannually), the present value of the bond will be greater than the face value of $10,000.

Point to Emphasize: It is customary to amortize a premium or discount on interest payment dates and at the end of the accounting period.

Present value of 10 periodic payments at 4% (from Table 4 in the appendix on future value and present value tables): \$450 × 8.111	\$ 3,649.95
Present value of a single payment at the end of 10 periods at 4% (from Table 3 in the appendix on future value and present value tables): \$10,000 × .676	6,760.00
Present value of \$10,000 bond	\$10,409.95

Amortizing a Bond Discount

OBJECTIVE 5a

Use the straight-line and effective interest methods to amortize bond discounts

Related Text Assignments:
Q: 6, 7
SE: 2, 3, 7
E: 2, 3, 4, 5, 9, 12
P: 1, 2, 3, 4, 5, 6, 7, 8
SD: 2

In the example on page 670, Vason Corporation issued \$100,000 of five-year bonds at a discount because the market interest rate of 10 percent exceeded the face interest rate of 9 percent. The bonds were sold for \$96,149, resulting in an unamortized bond discount of \$3,851. Because this discount affects interest expense in each year of the bond issue, the bond discount should be amortized (reduced gradually) over the life of the issue. This means that the unamortized bond discount will decrease gradually over time, and that the carrying value of the bond issue (face value less unamortized discount) will increase gradually. By the maturity date of the bond, the carrying value of the issue will equal its face value, and the unamortized bond discount will be zero.

Calculation of Total Interest Cost

Discussion Question: Why is a bond discount considered a component of total interest cost? **Answer:** Because a bond discount represents the amount in excess of the issue price that must be paid by the corporation at the time of maturity.

When bonds are issued at a discount, the effective interest rate paid by the company is greater than the face interest rate on the bonds. The reason is that the interest cost to the company is the stated interest payments *plus* the amount of the bond discount. That is, although the company does not receive the full face value of the bonds on issue, it still must pay back the full face value at maturity. The difference between the issue price and the face value must be added to the total interest payments to arrive at the actual interest expense. The full cost to the corporation of issuing the bonds at a discount is as follows:

Cash to be paid to bondholders	
Face value at maturity	\$100,000
Interest payments (\$100,000 × .09 × 5 years)	45,000
Total cash paid to bondholders	\$145,000
Less cash received from bondholders	96,149
Total interest cost	\$ 48,851

Or, alternatively:

Interest payments (\$100,000 × .09 × 5 years)	\$ 45,000
Bond discount	3,851
Total interest cost	\$ 48,851

The total interest cost of \$48,851 is made up of \$45,000 in interest payments and the \$3,851 bond discount, so the bond discount increases the interest paid on the bonds from the stated interest rate to the effective interest rate. The *effective interest rate* is the real interest cost of the bond over its life.

For each year's interest expense to reflect the effective interest rate, the discount must be allocated over the remaining life of the bonds as an increase in the interest expense each period. The process of allocation is called *amortization of the bond discount.* Thus, interest expense for each period will exceed the actual payment of interest by the amount of the bond discount amortized over the period.

Point to Emphasize: The discount on a zero coupon bond represents the interest that will be paid (in its entirety) on the maturity date.

Some companies and governmental units issue bonds that do not require periodic interest payments. These bonds, called zero coupon bonds, are simply a promise to pay a fixed amount at the maturity date. They are issued at a large discount because the only interest earned by the buyer or paid by the issuer is the discount. For example, a five-year, $100,000 zero coupon bond issued at a time when the market rate is 14 percent, compounded semiannually, would sell for only $50,800. That amount is the present value of a single payment of $100,000 at the end of five years. The discount of $49,200 ($100,000 − $50,800) is the total interest cost; it is amortized over the life of the bond.

Methods of Amortizing a Bond Discount

There are two ways of amortizing bond discounts or premiums: the straight-line method and the effective interest method.

Straight-Line Method The straight-line method is the easier of the two, with equal amortization of the discount for each interest period. Suppose that the interest payment dates for the Vason Corporation bond issue are January 1 and July 1. The amount of the bond discount amortized and the interest cost for each semiannual period are calculated in four steps.

1. $$\text{Total Interest Payments} = \text{Interest Payments per Year} \times \text{Life of Bonds} = 2 \times 5 = 10$$

2. $$\text{Amortization of Bond Discount per Interest Period} = \frac{\text{Bond Discount}}{\text{Total Interest Payments}} = \frac{\$3{,}851}{10} = \$385^*$$

*Rounded.

3. $$\text{Cash Interest Payment} = \text{Face Value} \times \text{Face Interest Rate} \times \text{Time} = \$100{,}000 \times .09 \times 6/12 = \$4{,}500$$

4. $$\text{Interest Cost per Interest Period} = \text{Interest Payment} + \text{Amortization of Bond Discount} = \$4{,}500 + \$385 = \$4{,}885$$

On July 1, 20x0, the first semiannual interest date, the entry would be as follows:

A* = L + OE
− −
*assumes cash paid

20x0			
July 1	Bond Interest Expense	4,885	
	Unamortized Bond Discount		385
	Cash (or Interest Payable)		4,500
	Paid (or accrued) semiannual interest to bondholders and amortized the discount on 9%, 5-year bonds		

Notice that the bond interest expense is $4,885, but the amount paid to the bondholders is the $4,500 face interest payment. The difference of $385 is the credit to Unamortized Bond Discount. This lowers the debit balance of the Unamortized

Enrichment Note: Although the straight-line method of amortization is easier to apply than the effective interest method, it is theoretically inferior because it does not apply a uniform rate of interest (as does the effective interest method). It can be used, however, if the amount does not differ materially from the effective interest amount. (The amounts are material if they affect a decision or the evaluation of the company.)

Bond Discount account and raises the carrying value of the bonds payable by $385 each interest period. Assuming that no changes occur in the bond issue, this entry will be made every six months for the life of the bonds. When the bond issue matures, there will be no balance in the Unamortized Bond Discount account, and the carrying value of the bonds will be $100,000—exactly equal to the amount due the bondholders.

The straight-line method has long been used, but it has a certain weakness. Because the carrying value goes up each period and the bond interest expense stays the same, the rate of interest falls over time. Conversely, when the straight-line method is used to amortize a premium, the rate of interest rises over time. Therefore, the Accounting Principles Board has ruled that the straight-line method can be used only when it does not lead to a material difference from the effective interest method.[8]

Teaching Note: Students may be overwhelmed when they first encounter a bond amortization schedule. It might be helpful to begin by explaining how a mortgage program works and how the principal and interest portions of the payment change each month. Then, draw an analogy between the principal balance and a bond's carrying value (Column F). Amortization of a bond premium works exactly like a mortgage program: amortization of a discount works in the opposite way (the principal actually is *increasing* each period).

Effective Interest Method To compute the interest and amortization of a bond discount for each interest period under the effective interest method, a constant interest rate is applied to the carrying value of the bonds at the beginning of the interest period. This constant rate equals the market rate, or effective rate, at the time the bonds are issued. The amount to be amortized each period is the difference between the interest computed by using the effective rate and the actual interest paid to bondholders.

As an example, we use the same facts presented earlier—a $100,000 bond issue at 9 percent, with a five-year maturity and interest to be paid twice a year. The market, or effective, interest rate at the time the bonds were issued was 10 percent. The bonds were sold for $96,149, a discount of $3,851. The interest and amortization of the bond discount are shown in Table 1.

Table 1. Interest and Amortization of a Bond Discount: Effective Interest Method

	A	B	C	D	E	F
Semiannual Interest Period	Carrying Value at Beginning of Period	Semiannual Interest Expense at 10% to Be Recorded* (5% × A)	Semiannual Interest to Be Paid to Bondholders (4½% × $100,000)	Amortization of Bond Discount (B − C)	Unamortized Bond Discount at End of Period (E − D)	Carrying Value at End of Period (A + D)
0					$3,851	$ 96,149
1	$96,149	$4,807	$4,500	$307	3,544	96,456
2	96,456	4,823	4,500	323	3,221	96,779
3	96,779	4,839	4,500	339	2,882	97,118
4	97,118	4,856	4,500	356	2,526	97,474
5	97,474	4,874	4,500	374	2,152	97,848
6	97,848	4,892	4,500	392	1,760	98,240
7	98,240	4,912	4,500	412	1,348	98,652
8	98,652	4,933	4,500	433	915	99,085
9	99,085	4,954	4,500	454	461	99,539
10	99,539	4,961†	4,500	461	—	100,000

*Rounded to the nearest dollar.
†Last period's interest expense equals $4,961 ($4,500 + $461); it does not equal $4,977 ($99,539 × .05) because of the cumulative effect of rounding.

The amounts in the table (using period 1) were computed as follows:

Column A: The carrying value of the bonds is their face value less the unamortized bond discount ($100,000 − $3,851 = $96,149).

Column B: The interest expense to be recorded is the effective interest. It is found by multiplying the carrying value of the bonds by the effective interest rate for one-half year ($96,149 × .10 × 6/12 = $4,807).

Column C: The interest paid in the period is a constant amount computed by multiplying the face value of the bonds by their face interest rate by the interest time period ($100,000 × .09 × 6/12 = $4,500).

Column D: The discount amortized is the difference between the effective interest expense to be recorded and the interest to be paid on the interest payment date ($4,807 − $4,500 = $307).

Column E: The unamortized bond discount is the balance of the bond discount at the beginning of the period less the current period amortization of the discount ($3,851 − $307 = $3,544). The unamortized discount decreases each interest payment period because it is amortized as a portion of interest expense.

Column F: The carrying value of the bonds at the end of the period is the carrying value at the beginning of the period plus the amortization during the period ($96,149 + $307 = $96,456). Notice that the sum of the carrying value and the unamortized discount (Column F + Column E) always equals the face value of the bonds ($96,456 + $3,544 = $100,000).

Point to Emphasize: The bond interest expense recorded exceeds the amount of interest paid because of the amortization of the bond discount. The matching rule dictates that the discount be amortized over the life of the bond.

The entry to record the interest expense is exactly like the one used when the straight-line method is applied. However, the amounts debited and credited to the various accounts are different. Using the effective interest method, the entry for July 1, 20x0, would be as follows:

A* = L + OE
− + −
***assumes cash paid**

20x0			
July 1	Bond Interest Expense	4,807	
	Unamortized Bond Discount		307
	Cash (or Interest Payable)		4,500
	Paid (or accrued) semiannual interest to bondholders and amortized the discount on 9%, 5-year bonds		

Notice that it is not necessary to prepare an interest and amortization table to determine the amortization of a discount for any one interest payment period. It is necessary only to multiply the carrying value by the effective interest rate and subtract the interest payment from the result. For example, the amount of discount to be amortized in the seventh interest payment period is $412, calculated as follows: ($98,240 × .05) − $4,500.

Visual Summary of the Effective Interest Method The effect on carrying value and interest expense of the amortization of a bond discount using the effective interest method can be seen in Figure 2 (which is based on the data from Table 1). Notice that initially the carrying value (the issue price) is less than the face value, but that it gradually increases toward the face value over the life of the bond issue. Notice also that interest expense exceeds interest payments by the amount of the bond discount amortized. Interest expense increases gradually over the life of the bond because it is based on the gradually increasing carrying value (multiplied by the market interest rate).

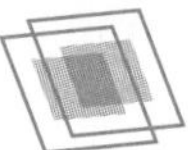

Point to Emphasize: The bond interest expense *increases* each period because the carrying value of the bonds (the principal on which the interest is calculated) increases each period.

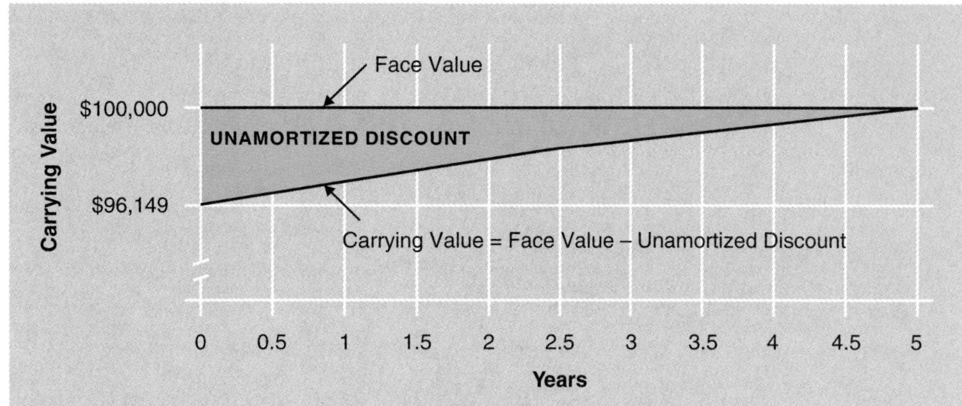

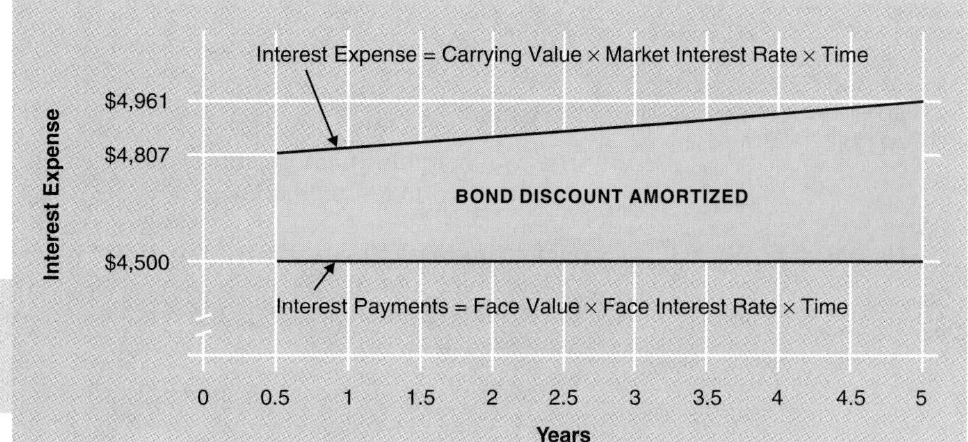

Figure 2
Carrying Value and Interest Expense—Bonds Issued at a Discount

Amortizing a Bond Premium

OBJECTIVE 5b

Use the straight-line and effective interest methods to amortize bond premiums

In our example on page 671, Vason Corporation issued $100,000 of five-year bonds at a premium because the market interest rate of 8 percent was less than the face interest rate of 9 percent. The bonds were sold for $104,100, which resulted in an unamortized premium of $4,100. Like a discount, a premium must be amortized over the life of the bonds so that it can be matched to its effects on interest expense during that period. In the following sections, the total interest cost is calculated and the bond premium is amortized using the straight-line and the effective interest methods.

Calculation of Total Interest Cost

Because the bondholders paid more than face value for the bonds, the premium of $4,100 ($104,100 − $100,000) represents an amount that the bondholders will not receive at maturity. The premium is in effect a reduction, in advance, of the total interest paid on the bonds over the life of the bond issue.

The total interest cost over the issue's life can be computed as follows:

Cash to be paid to bondholders	
Face value at maturity	$100,000
Interest payments ($100,000 × .09 × 5 years)	45,000
Total cash paid to bondholders	$145,000
Less cash received from bondholders	104,100
Total interest cost	$ 40,900

Or, alternatively:

Interest payments ($100,000 × .09 × 5 years)	$ 45,000
Less bond premium	4,100
Total interest cost	$ 40,900

Discussion Question: Why is a bond premium deducted from interest payments in calculating total interest cost? **Answer:** Because a bond premium represents a bonus paid for a bond that the corporation never has to return to the bondholders. In effect, it counters the higher-than-market interest the corporation is paying on the bond.

Notice that the total interest payments of $45,000 exceed the total interest cost of $40,900 by $4,100, the amount of the bond premium.

Methods of Amortizing a Bond Premium

The two methods of amortizing a bond premium are the straight-line method and the effective interest method.

Straight-Line Method Under the straight-line method, the bond premium is spread evenly over the life of the bond issue. As with bond discounts, the amount of the bond premium amortized and the interest cost for each semiannual period are computed in four steps.

1. Total Interest Payments = Interest Payments per Year × Life of Bonds
   = 2 × 5 = 10
2. $$\text{Amortization of Bond Premium per Interest Period} = \frac{\text{Bond Premium}}{\text{Total Interest Payments}} = \frac{\$4{,}100}{10} = \$410$$

Point to Emphasize: The bond interest expense recorded is less than the amount of the interest paid because of the amortization of the bond premium. The matching rule dictates that the premium be amortized over the life of the bond.

3. Cash Interest Payment = Face Value × Face Interest Rate × Time
   = $100,000 × .09 × $\frac{6}{12}$ = $4,500
4. Interest Cost per Interest Period = Interest Payment − Amortization of Bond Premium
   = $4,500 − $410 = $4,090

On July 1, 20x0, the first semiannual interest date, the entry would be:

A* = L + OE
 −   −   −
*assumes cash paid

20x0			
July 1	Bond Interest Expense	4,090	
	Unamortized Bond Premium	410	
	Cash (or Interest Payable)		4,500
	Paid (or accrued) semiannual interest to bondholders and amortized the premium on 9%, 5-year bonds		

Notice that the bond interest expense is $4,090, but the amount received by the bondholders is the $4,500 face interest payment. The difference of $410 is the debit to Unamortized Bond Premium. This lowers the credit balance of the Unamortized

Point to Emphasize: Whether a bond is originally sold at a discount or a premium, on the maturity date its carrying value will equal its face value.

Bond Premium account and the carrying value of the bonds payable by $410 each interest period. Assuming that the bond issue remains unchanged, the same entry will be made on every semiannual interest date over the life of the bond issue. When the bond issue matures, there will be no balance in the Unamortized Bond Premium account, and the carrying value of the bonds payable will be $100,000, exactly equal to the amount due the bondholders.

As noted earlier in this chapter, the straight-line method should be used only when it does not lead to a material difference from the effective interest method.

Effective Interest Method Under the straight-line method, the effective interest rate changes constantly, even though the interest expense is fixed, because the effective interest rate is determined by comparing the fixed interest expense with a carrying value that changes as a result of amortizing the discount or premium. To apply a fixed interest rate over the life of the bonds based on the actual market rate at the time of the bond issue requires the use of the effective interest method. Under this method, the interest expense decreases slightly each period (see Table 2, Column B) because the amount of the bond premium amortized increases slightly (Column D). This occurs because a fixed rate is applied each period to the gradually decreasing carrying value (Column A).

The first interest payment is recorded as follows:

A* = L + OE
– – –
*assumes cash paid

20x0			
July 1	Bond Interest Expense	4,164	
	Unamortized Bond Premium	336	
	Cash (or Interest Payable)		4,500
	Paid (or accrued) semiannual interest to bondholders and amortized the premium on 9%, 5-year bonds		

Teaching Note: To test understanding, ask students why the amounts in each column increase, decrease, or remain the same. For example, the amounts in Column B decrease because the carrying value (the principal on which interest is calculated) decreases each period.

Table 2. Interest and Amortization of a Bond Premium: Effective Interest Method

	A	B	C	D	E	F
Semiannual Interest Period	Carrying Value at Beginning of Period	Semiannual Interest Expense at 8% to Be Recorded* (4% × A)	Semiannual Interest to Be Paid to Bondholders (4½% × $100,000)	Amortization of Bond Premium (C − B)	Unamortized Bond Premium at End of Period (E − D)	Carrying Value at End of Period (A − D)
0					$4,100	$104,100
1	$104,100	$4,164	$4,500	$336	3,764	103,764
2	103,764	4,151	4,500	349	3,415	103,415
3	103,415	4,137	4,500	363	3,052	103,052
4	103,052	4,122	4,500	378	2,674	102,674
5	102,674	4,107	4,500	393	2,281	102,281
6	102,281	4,091	4,500	409	1,872	101,872
7	101,872	4,075	4,500	425	1,447	101,447
8	101,447	4,058	4,500	442	1,005	101,005
9	101,005	4,040	4,500	460	545	100,545
10	100,545	3,955†	4,500	545	—	100,000

*Rounded to the nearest dollar.
†Last period's interest expense equals $3,955 ($4,500 − $545); it does not equal $4,022 ($100,545 × .04) because of the cumulative effect of rounding.

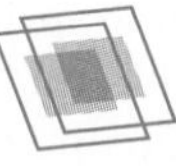

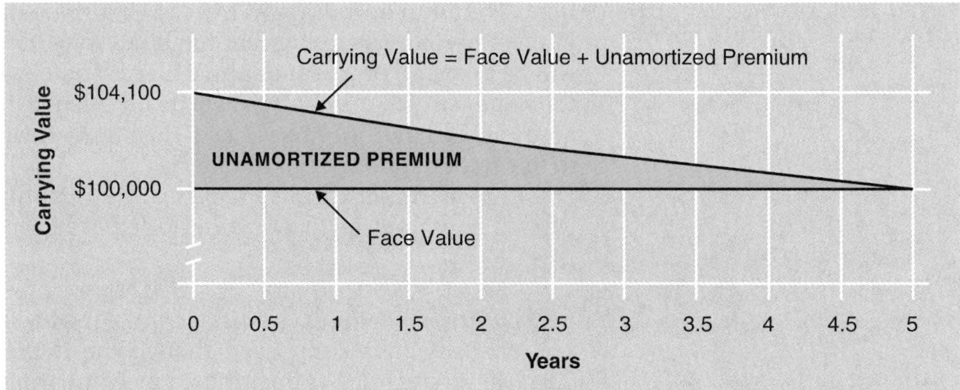

Point to Emphasize: Over the life of a bond, the premium or discount amortized increases each period.

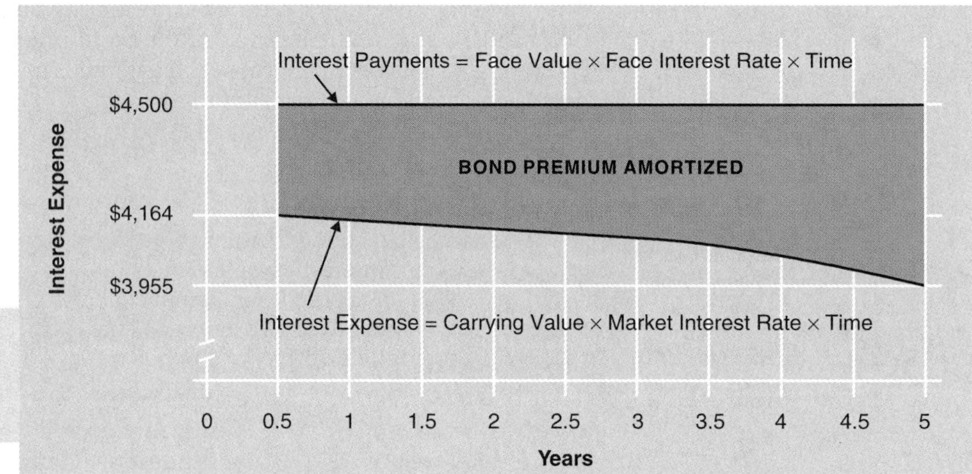

Figure 3
Carrying Value and Interest Expense—Bonds Issued at a Premium

Notice that the unamortized bond premium (Column E) decreases gradually to zero as the carrying value decreases to the face value (Column F). To find the amount of premium amortized in any one interest payment period, subtract the effective interest expense (the carrying value times the effective interest rate, Column B) from the interest payment (Column C). In semiannual interest period 5, for example, the amortization of premium is $393, calculated as follows: $4,500 − ($102,674 × .04).

Visual Summary of the Effective Interest Method The effect of the amortization of a bond premium using the effective interest method on carrying value and interest expense can be seen in Figure 3 (based on data from Table 2). Notice that initially the carrying value (issue price) is greater than the face value, but that it gradually decreases toward the face value over the life of the bond issue. Notice also that interest payments exceed interest expense by the amount of the premium amortized, and that interest expense decreases gradually over the life of the bond because it is based on the gradually decreasing carrying value (multiplied by the market interest rate).

BUSINESS BULLETIN: TECHNOLOGY IN PRACTICE

Interest and amortization tables like those in Tables 1 and 2 are ideal applications for computer spreadsheet software such as Lotus 1-2-3 and Microsoft Excel. Once the tables have been constructed with the proper formula in each cell, only five variables must be entered to produce the entire table. The five variables are the face value of the bonds, the selling price, the life of the bonds, the face interest rate, and the effective interest rate.

Other Bonds Payable Issues

OBJECTIVE 6

Account for bonds issued between interest dates and make year-end adjustments

Related Text Assignments:
Q: 8
SE: 3, 5, 6, 7
E: 4, 5, 9, 10, 11, 12
P: 1, 2, 3, 5, 6, 7, 8

Teaching Note: Students will better understand the concept if you duplicate Figure 4 and explain the timeline shown. Point out that this procedure eliminates difficulties that would otherwise be encountered by the issuing corporation.

Several other issues arise in accounting for bonds payable. Among them are the sale of bonds between interest payment dates, the year-end accrual of bond interest expense, the retirement of bonds, and the conversion of bonds into common stock.

Sale of Bonds Between Interest Dates

Bonds may be issued on an interest payment date, as in the previous examples, but they are often issued between interest payment dates. The generally accepted method of handling bonds issued in this manner is to collect from investors the interest that would have accrued for the partial period preceding the issue date. Then, when the first interest period is completed, the corporation pays investors the interest for the entire period. Thus, the interest collected when bonds are sold is returned to investors on the next interest payment date.

There are two reasons for following this procedure. The first is a practical one. If a company issued bonds on several different days and did not collect the accrued interest, records would have to be maintained for each bondholder and date of purchase. In such a case, the interest due each bondholder would have to be computed on the basis of a different time period. Clearly, large bookkeeping costs would be incurred under this kind of system. On the other hand, if accrued interest is collected when the bonds are sold, on the interest payment date the corporation can pay the interest due for the entire period, eliminating the extra computations and costs.

The second reason for collecting accrued interest in advance is that when that amount is netted against the full interest paid on the interest payment date, the resulting interest expense represents the amount for the time the money was borrowed. For example, assume that the Vason Corporation sold $100,000 of 9 percent, five-year bonds for face value on May 1, 20x0, rather than on January 1, 20x0, the issue date. The entry to record the sale of the bonds is as follows:

A = L + OE
\+ \+ \+

20x0			
May 1	Cash	103,000	
	Bond Interest Expense		3,000
	Bonds Payable		100,000
	Sold 9%, 5-year bonds at face value plus 4 months' accrued interest $100,000 × .09 × 4/12 = $3,000		

Teaching Note: Point out that this is one of the few times an expense account is credited (other than when it is closed). Then, refer to the ledger account, which demonstrates that the net effect is the recording of two months' interest (May and June).

As shown, Cash is debited for the amount received, $103,000 (the face value of $100,000 plus four months' accrued interest of $3,000). Bond Interest Expense is credited for the $3,000 of accrued interest, and Bonds Payable is credited for the face value of $100,000.

When the first semiannual interest payment date arrives, the following entry is made:

A* = L + OE
− −
*assumes cash paid

20x0			
July 1	Bond Interest Expense	4,500	
	Cash (or Interest Payable)		4,500
	Paid (or accrued) semiannual interest $100,000 × .09 × 6/12 = $4,500		

Notice that the entire half-year interest is both debited to Bond Interest Expense and credited to Cash because the corporation pays bond interest only once every six months, in full six-month amounts. This process is illustrated in Figure 4. The actual interest expense for the two months that the bonds were outstanding is $1,500. This amount is the net balance of the $4,500 debit to Bond Interest Expense on July 1 less the $3,000 credit to Bond Interest Expense on May 1. You can see these steps clearly in the T account for Bond Interest Expense below.

Bond Interest Expense

Bal.	0	May 1	3,000
July 1	4,500		
Bal.	1,500		

Year-End Accrual for Bond Interest Expense

Bond interest payment dates rarely correspond with a company's fiscal year. Therefore, an adjustment must be made at the end of the accounting period to accrue the interest expense on the bonds from the last payment date to the end of the fiscal year. Further, if there is any discount or premium on the bonds, it must also be amortized for the fractional period.

Remember that in an earlier example, Vason Corporation issued $100,000 in bonds on January 1, 20x0, at 104.1 (see page 671). Suppose the company's fiscal year ends on September 30, 20x0. In the period since the interest payment and amortization of the premium on July 1, three months' worth of interest has accrued, and the following adjusting entry under the effective interest method must be made.

A = L + OE
+ −
−

20x0			
Sept. 30	Bond Interest Expense	2,075.50	
	Unamortized Bond Premium	174.50	
	Interest Payable		2,250.00
	To record accrual of interest on 9% bonds payable for 3 months and amortization of one-half of the premium for the second interest payment period		

Clarification Note: The matching rule dictates that both the accrued interest and the amortization of a premium or discount be recorded at year end. Refer to Table 2 for premium-amortization figures.

This entry covers one-half of the second interest period. Unamortized Bond Premium is debited for $174.50, which is one-half of $349, the amortization of the premium for the second period from Table 2. Interest Payable is credited for $2,250, three months' interest on the face value of the bonds ($100,000 × .09 × 3/12). The net debit figure of $2,075.50 ($2,250 − $174.50) is the bond interest expense for the three-month period.

When the January 1, 20x1, payment date arrives, the entry to pay the bondholders and amortize the premium is as follows:

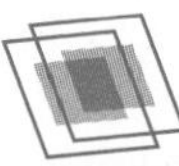

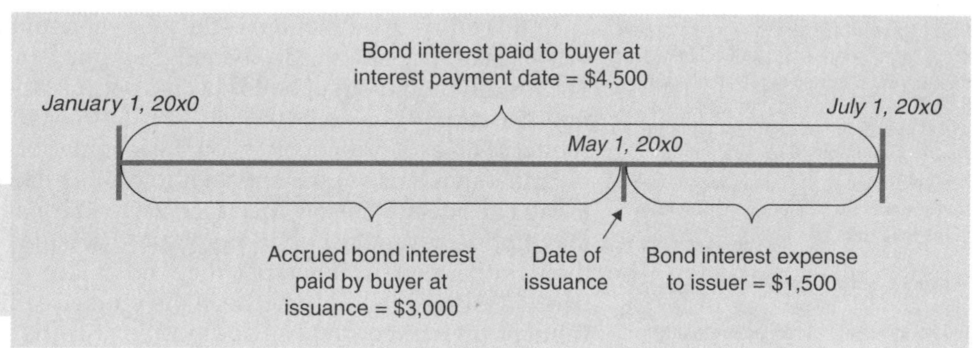

Figure 4
Effect on Bond Interest Expense When Bonds Are Issued Between Interest Dates

A = L + OE
− − −
+

20x1			
Jan. 1	Bond Interest Expense	2,075.50	
	Interest Payable	2,250.00	
	Unamortized Bond Premium	174.50	
	Cash		4,500.00
	Paid semiannual interest including interest previously accrued, and amortized the premium for the period since the end of the fiscal year		

As shown here, one-half ($2,250) of the amount paid ($4,500) was accrued on September 30. Unamortized Bond Premium is debited for $174.50, the remaining amount to be amortized for the period ($349.00 − $174.50). The resulting bond interest expense is the amount that applies to the three-month period from October 1 to December 31.

Bond discounts are recorded at year end in the same way as bond premiums. The difference is that the amortization of a bond discount increases interest expense instead of decreasing it, as a premium does.

Retirement of Bonds

OBJECTIVE 7

Account for the retirement of bonds and the conversion of bonds into stock

Related Text Assignments:
Q: 9, 10
SE: 8, 9
E: 13, 14, 15
P: 4, 5
FRA: 2

Most bond issues give the company a chance to buy back and retire the bonds at a specified call price, usually above face value, before maturity. Such bonds are known as callable bonds, and give the company flexibility in financing its operations. For example, if bond interest rates drop, the company can call its bonds and reissue debt at a lower interest rate. A company might also call its bonds if it has earned enough to pay off the debt, the reason for having the debt no longer exists, or it wants to restructure its debt to equity ratio. The bond indenture states the time period and the prices at which the bonds can be redeemed. The retirement of a bond issue before its maturity date is called early extinguishment of debt.

Let's assume that Vason Corporation can call or retire the $100,000 of bonds issued at a premium (page 671) at 105, and that it decides to do so on July 1, 20x3. (To simplify the example, the retirement is made on an interest payment date.) Because the bonds were issued on January 1, 20x0, the retirement takes place on the seventh interest payment date. Assume that the entry for the required interest payment and the amortization of the premium has been made. The entry to retire the bonds is as follows:

A = L + OE
− − −
−

20x3			
July 1	Bonds Payable	100,000	
	Unamortized Bond Premium	1,447	
	Loss on Retirement of Bonds	3,553	
	Cash		105,000
	Retired 9% bonds at 105		

Point to Emphasize: When interest rates drop, corporations frequently refinance their bonds at the lower rate, much like homeowners who refinance their mortgage loans when interest rates go down. Even though a call premium is usually paid to extinguish the bonds, the interest saved makes the refinancing cost-effective in the long run.

Teaching Note: Explain that the goal is to eliminate from the books any reference to the bonds being retired. Any resulting gain or loss is treated as extraordinary.

In this entry, the cash paid is the face value times the call price ($100,000 × 1.05 = $105,000). The unamortized bond premium can be found in Column E of Table 2. The loss on retirement of bonds occurs because the call price of the bonds is greater than the carrying value ($105,000 − $101,447 = $3,553). The loss, if material, is presented as an extraordinary item on the income statement.

Sometimes a rise in the market interest rate can cause the market value of bonds to fall considerably below their face value. If it has the cash to do so, the company may find it advantageous to purchase the bonds on the open market and retire them, rather than wait and pay them off at face value. An extraordinary gain is recognized for the difference between the purchase price of the bonds and the carrying value of the retired bonds. For example, assume that because of a rise in interest rates, Vason Corporation is able to purchase the $100,000 bond issue on the open market at 85, making it unnecessary to call the bonds at the higher price of 105. Then, the entry would be as follows:

A = L + OE
− − +
   −

20x3			
July 1	Bonds Payable	100,000	
	Unamortized Bond Premium	1,447	
	Cash		85,000
	Gain on Retirement of Bonds		16,447
	Purchased and retired 9% bonds at 85		

DECISION POINT

MACRONIX INTERNATIONAL

Macronix International Co., Ltd., an electronics company from Taiwan, issued $200,000,000 of 1% convertible bonds due in 2007 at face value. The bonds could be converted into shares of the company's common stock that traded in the United States at the equivalent rate of $1.543 per share. In other words, a holder of a $1,000 bond could convert it into 648 shares ($1,000 ÷ $1.543) of common stock.[9] The day before, the company's stock had traded on the NASDAQ exchange at the equivalent of $1.40. What advantages and disadvantages did Macronix's management weigh in deciding to issue convertible bonds rather than another security, such as nonconvertible bonds or common stock?

Several factors are favorable to the issuance of convertible bonds. First, the interest rate of 1 percent is much less than the company would have had to offer if the bonds were not convertible. An investor is willing to give up some current interest for the prospect that the value of the stock will increase, and therefore the value of the bonds will also increase. For example, if the common stock rises from $1.40 to more than $1.543 per share, the market value of the bond will begin to rise based on changes in the price of the common stock, not on

Critical Thinking Question: Which parties (creditors, owners, or management) benefit the most from the issuance of callable, convertible debentures?
Answer: Management probably benefits most because the callable and convertible features provide Macronix with financial flexibility as interest rates and stock prices vary.

changes in interest rates. If the common stock were to rise to $3, the market value of a $1,000 bond would rise to $1,944 (648 shares × $3). A second advantage is that Macronix did not have to give up any current control of the company. Unlike stockholders, bondholders do not have voting rights. A third benefit is tax savings. Interest paid on bonds is fully deductible for income tax purposes, whereas cash dividends on common stock are not. Fourth, the company's income will be affected favorably if the company earns a return that exceeds the interest cost of the debentures. For example, if the company uses the funds for a purpose that earns 10 percent, the return will be ten times the interest cost of 1 percent. Finally, the convertible feature offers financial flexibility. If the price of the stock rises above $1.543, management can avoid repaying the bonds by calling them for redemption, thereby forcing the bondholders to convert their bonds into common stock. The bondholders will agree to convert because the common stock they will receive will be worth more than they would receive if the bonds were redeemed.

One major disadvantage of debentures is that interest must be paid semiannually. Inability to make an interest payment could force the company into bankruptcy. Common stock dividends are declared and paid only when the board of directors decides to do so. Another disadvantage is that when the bonds are converted, they become new outstanding common stock and no longer have the features of bonds. Macronix's management obviously felt that the advantages of its choice outweighed the disadvantages.

Conversion of Bonds into Common Stock

Bonds that can be exchanged for other securities of the corporation (in most cases, common stock) are called convertible bonds. Convertibility enables an investor to make more money if the market price of the common stock rises, because the value of the bonds then rises. However, if the common stock price does not rise, the investor still holds the bonds and receives both the periodic interest payments and the principal at the maturity date.

When a bondholder wishes to convert bonds into common stock, the common stock is recorded at the carrying value of the bonds. The bond liability and the associated unamortized discount or premium are written off the books. For this reason, no gain or loss on the transaction is recorded. For example, suppose that Vason Corporation's bonds are not called on July 1, 20x3. Instead, the corporation's bondholders decide to convert all the bonds to $8 par value common stock under a convertible provision of 40 shares of common stock for each $1,000 bond. The entry would be as follows:

A = L + OE
    − +

20x3			
July 1	Bonds Payable	100,000	
	Unamortized Bond Premium	1,447	
	Common Stock		32,000
	Paid-in Capital in Excess of Par Value, Common		69,447
	Converted 9% bonds payable into $8 par value common stock at a rate of 40 shares for each $1,000 bond		

Point to Emphasize: The credits to the contributed capital accounts are based on the carrying value of the bonds converted. As a result, no gain or loss is recognized. If only a portion of the bonds had been converted, proportionate shares of the balances in Bonds Payable and Unamortized Bond Premium would be eliminated.

The unamortized bond premium is found in Column E of Table 2. At a rate of 40 shares for each $1,000 bond, 4,000 shares will be issued, with a total par value of

$32,000 (4,000 × $8). The Common Stock account is credited for the amount of the par value of the stock issued. In addition, Paid-in Capital in Excess of Par Value, Common is credited for the difference between the carrying value of the bonds and the par value of the stock issued ($101,447 − $32,000 = $69,447). No gain or loss is recorded.

Other Long-Term Liabilities

OBJECTIVE 8

Explain the basic features of mortgages payable, installment notes payable, long-term leases, and pensions and other postretirement benefits as long-term liabilities

Related Text Assignments:
Q: 11, 12, 13, 14, 15, 16
SE: 10
E: 16, 17, 18, 19
SD: 3, 6
FRA: 3, 5, 6

A company may have other long-term liabilities besides bonds. The most common are mortgages payable, installment notes payable, long-term leases, and pensions and other postretirement benefits.

Mortgages Payable

A mortgage is a long-term debt secured by real property. It is usually paid in equal monthly installments. Each monthly payment includes interest on the debt and a reduction in the debt. Table 3 shows the first three monthly payments on a $50,000, 12 percent mortgage. The mortgage was obtained on June 1, and the monthly payments are $800. According to the table, the entry to record the July 1 payment would be as follows:

A = L + OE
− −

July 1	Mortgage Payable	300	
	Mortgage Interest Expense	500	
	Cash		800
	Made monthly mortgage payment		

Teaching Note: Draw three rectangles of equal size to represent the monthly fixed mortgage payment. Divide each rectangle into two parts, principal and interest, and reduce the interest section with each successive rectangle. Point out that interest is always calculated first, and that principal reduction equals whatever remains of the mortgage payment.

Notice from the entry and from Table 3 that the July 1 payment represents interest expense of $500 ($50,000 × .12 × $\frac{1}{12}$) and a reduction in the debt of $300 ($800 − $500). Therefore, the unpaid balance is reduced to $49,700 by the July payment. August's interest expense is slightly less than July's because of the decrease in the debt.

Installment Notes Payable

Point to Emphasize: Although both mortgages payable and installment notes payable involve a series of payments, mortgages are used to finance real estate, whereas installment notes are used to finance other types of assets.

A long-term note can be paid at its maturity date by making a lump-sum payment that includes the amount borrowed plus the interest. Often, however, the terms of a note will call for a series of periodic payments. Such a note is called an installment note payable because each payment includes the interest to date plus a repayment of part of the amount that was borrowed. For example, let's assume that on December 31, 20x1, $100,000 is borrowed on a 15 percent installment note, to be paid annually over five years. The entry to record the note is as follows:

A = L + OE
\+ +

20x1			
Dec. 31	Cash	100,000	
	Notes Payable		100,000
	Borrowed $100,000 at 15% on a 5-year installment note		

Payments of Accrued Interest Plus Equal Amounts of Principal Installment notes most often call for payments consisting of accrued interest plus equal amounts of principal repayment. The amount of each installment decreases because the amount of principal on which the accrued interest is owed decreases by the amount of the previous principal payment. Banks use installment notes to finance equipment purchases by businesses; such notes are also common for other kinds of pur-

Point to Emphasize: This schedule is the same as the schedule in Table 2 (amortization of a bond premium).

Table 3. Monthly Payment Schedule on a $50,000, 12 Percent Mortgage

	A	B	C	D	E
Payment Date	Unpaid Balance at Beginning of Period	Monthly Payment	Interest for 1 Month at 1% on Unpaid Balance* (1% × A)	Reduction in Debt (B − C)	Unpaid Balance at End of Period (A − D)
June 1					$50,000
July 1	$50,000	$800	$500	$300	49,700
Aug. 1	49,700	800	497	303	49,397
Sept. 1	49,397	800	494	306	49,091

*Rounded to the nearest dollar.

chases when payment is spread over several years. They can be set up on a revolving basis whereby the borrower can borrow additional funds as the installments are paid. Moreover, the interest rate charged on installment notes may be adjusted periodically as market interest rates change.

Point to Emphasize: The only way to set up equal principal payments each period is to vary the total payment made. That is, the total payment equals the uniform principal payment plus a decreasing interest payment.

On our sample installment note for $100,000, the principal declines by an equal amount each year for five years, or by $20,000 per year ($100,000 ÷ 5 years). The interest is calculated on the balance of the note that remains each year. Because the balance of the note declines each year, the amount of interest also declines. For example, the entries for the first two payments of the installment note follow:

A = L + OE
− − −

20x2			
Dec. 31	Notes Payable	20,000	
	Interest Expense	15,000	
	Cash		35,000
	Made first installment payment on note $100,000 × .15 = $15,000		

A = L + OE
− − −

20x3			
Dec. 31	Notes Payable	20,000	
	Interest Expense	12,000	
	Cash		32,000
	Made second installment payment on note $80,000 × .15 = $12,000		

Notice that the amount of the payment decreases from $35,000 to $32,000 because the amount of interest accrued on the note has decreased from $15,000 to $12,000. The difference of $3,000 is the interest on the $20,000 that was repaid in 20x2. Each subsequent payment decreases by $3,000, as the note itself decreases by $20,000 each year until it is fully paid. This example assumes that the repayment of principal and the interest rate remain the same from year to year.

Payments of Accrued Interest Plus Increasing Amounts of Principal Less commonly, the terms of an installment note, like those used for leasing equipment, may call for equal periodic (monthly or yearly) payments of accrued interest plus increasing amounts of principal. Under this method, the interest is deducted from the equal payments to determine the amount by which the principal will be reduced each year.

This procedure, presented in Table 4, is very similar to that for mortgages, shown in Table 3. Each equal payment of $29,833 is allocated between interest and principal reduction. Each year the interest is calculated on the remaining principal. As the

Table 4. Payment Schedule on a $100,000, 15 Percent Installment Note

	A	B	C	D	E
Payment Date	Unpaid Principal at Beginning of Period	Equal Annual Payment	Interest for 1 Year at 15% on Unpaid Principal* (15% × A)	Reduction in Principal (B − C)	Unpaid Principal at End of Period (A − D)
					$100,000
20x2	$100,000	$29,833	$15,000	$14,833	85,167
20x3	85,167	29,833	12,775	17,058	68,109
20x4	68,109	29,833	10,216	19,617	48,492
20x5	48,492	29,833	7,274	22,559	25,933
20x6	25,933	29,833	3,900†	25,933	—

*Rounded to the nearest dollar.

†The last year's interest equals $3,900 ($29,833 − $25,933); it does not exactly equal $3,890 ($25,933 × .15) because of the cumulative effect of rounding.

Point to Emphasize: This situation, unlike the previous one, is exactly the same as a typical mortgage payment plan.

principal decreases, the annual interest also decreases, and because the payment remains the same, the amount by which the principal decreases becomes larger each year. The entries for the first two years, with data taken from Table 4, follow:

A = L + OE
− − −

20x2			
Dec. 31	Notes Payable	14,833	
	Interest Expense	15,000	
	Cash		29,833
	Made first installment payment on note		

A = L + OE
− − −

20x3			
Dec. 31	Notes Payable	17,058	
	Interest Expense	12,775	
	Cash		29,833
	Made second installment payment on note		

Similar entries will be made for the next three years.

How is the equal annual payment calculated? Because the $100,000 borrowed is the present value of the five equal annual payments at 15 percent interest, present value tables can be used to calculate the annual payments. Using Table 4 from the appendix on future value and present value tables, the calculation is made as shown below:

Periodic Payment × Factor (Table 4 in the appendix on future value and present value tables: 15%, 5 periods) = Present Value

Periodic Payment × 3.352 = $100,000

Periodic Payment = $100,000 ÷ 3.352 = $29,833

Table 4 shows that five equal annual payments of $29,833 at 15 percent will reduce the principal balance to zero (except for the discrepancy due to rounding).

Long-Term Leases

There are several ways for a company to obtain new operating assets. One way is to borrow money and buy the asset. Another is to rent the equipment on a short-term

Instructional Strategy: Assign SD 6 in class to small groups. Restate the expected response so that students stay focused. Collect the memos. One way to debrief is to ask two students to enact a role-play, with one as the CFO and the other as a staff member. A second approach to debriefing is to solicit one issue from each group until the list is complete. Grade memos as class participation or written assignment. Award bonus points for role playing.

lease. A third way is to obtain the equipment on a long-term lease. The first two methods do not create accounting problems. In the first case, the asset and liability are recorded at the amount paid, and the asset is subject to periodic depreciation. In the second case, the lease is short term in relation to the asset's useful life, and the risks of ownership remain with the lessor. This type of agreement is called an operating lease. It is proper accounting to treat operating lease payments as an expense and to debit the amount of each monthly payment to Rent Expense.

The third alternative, a long-term lease, is one of the fastest-growing ways of financing operating equipment in the United States today. It has several advantages. For instance, a long-term lease requires no immediate cash payment, the rental payment is deducted in full for tax purposes, and it costs less than a short-term lease. Acquiring the use of plant assets under long-term leases does cause several accounting challenges, however. Often, such leases cannot be canceled. Also, their duration may be about the same as the useful life of the asset. Finally, they may provide for the lessee to buy the asset at a nominal price at the end of the lease. The lease is much like an installment purchase because the risks of ownership are transferred to the lessee. Both the lessee's available assets and its legal obligations (liabilities) increase because the lessee must make a number of payments over the life of the asset.

Terminology Note: From the lessee's point of view, a lease is treated as either an operating lease or a capital lease. An operating lease is a true lease and is treated as such. A capital lease, however, is in substance an installment purchase, and the leased asset and related liability must be recognized at their present value.

Point to Emphasize: Under a capital lease, depreciation must be recorded by the lessee, using any allowable method. Depreciation is *not* recorded under an operating lease, however, because the leased asset is not recognized on the lessee's books.

The Financial Accounting Standards Board has described this kind of long-term lease as a capital lease. The term reflects the provisions of such a lease, which make the transaction more like a purchase or sale on installment. The FASB has ruled that in the case of a capital lease, the lessee must record an asset and a long-term liability equal to the present value of the total lease payments during the lease term. In doing so, the lessee must use the present value at the beginning of the lease.[10] Much like a mortgage payment, each lease payment consists partly of interest expense and partly of repayment of debt. Further, depreciation expense is figured on the asset and entered on the records of the lessee.

Suppose, for example, that Isaacs Company enters into a long-term lease for a machine used in its manufacturing operations. The lease terms call for an annual payment of $4,000 for six years, which approximates the useful life of the machine (see Table 5). At the end of the lease period, the title to the machine passes to Isaacs.

Table 5. Payment Schedule on a 16 Percent Capital Lease

	A	B	C	D
Year	Lease Payment	Interest (16%) on Unpaid Obligation* (D × 16%)	Reduction of Lease Obligation (A − B)	Balance of Lease Obligation (D − C)
Beginning				$14,740
1	$ 4,000	$2,358	$ 1,642	13,098
2	4,000	2,096	1,904	11,194
3	4,000	1,791	2,209	8,985
4	4,000	1,438	2,562	6,423
5	4,000	1,028	2,972	3,451
6	4,000	549†	3,451	—
	$24,000	$9,260	$14,740	

*Computations are rounded to the nearest dollar.
†The last year's interest equals $549 ($4,000 − $3,451); it does not exactly equal $552 ($3,451 × .16) because of the cumulative effect of rounding.

This lease is clearly a capital lease and should be recorded as an asset and a liability according to FASB *Statement No. 13.*

A lease is a periodic payment for the right to use an asset or assets. Present value techniques can be used to place a value on the asset and on the corresponding liability associated with a capital lease. If Isaac's interest cost is 16 percent, the present value of the lease payments can be computed as follows:

Periodic Payment × Factor (Table 4 in the appendix on future value and present value tables: 16%, 6 periods) = Present Value

$4,000 × 3.685 = $14,740

The entry to record the lease contract is as follows:

A = L + OE
\+ +

Equipment Under Capital Lease	14,740	
Obligations Under Capital Lease		14,740
To record capital lease on machinery		

Equipment Under Capital Lease is classified as a long-term asset; Obligations Under Capital Lease is classified as a long-term liability. Each year, Isaacs must record depreciation on the leased asset. Using straight-line depreciation, a six-year life, and no salvage value, the following entry would record the depreciation:

A = L + OE
− −

Depreciation Expense, Equipment Under Capital Lease	2,457	
Accumulated Depreciation, Equipment Under Capital Lease		2,457
To record depreciation expense on capital lease		

The interest expense for each year is computed by multiplying the interest rate (16 percent) by the amount of the remaining lease obligation. Table 5 shows these calculations. Using the data in the table, the first lease payment would be recorded as follows:

A = L + OE
− − −

Interest Expense (Column B)	2,358	
Obligations Under Capital Lease (Column C)	1,642	
Cash		4,000
Made payment on capital lease		

Pensions

Most employees who work for medium- and large-sized companies are covered by some sort of pension plan. A pension plan is a contract between a company and its employees in which the company agrees to pay benefits to the employees after they retire. Most companies contribute the full cost of the pension, but sometimes the employees also pay part of their salary or wages toward their pension. The contributions from both parties are typically paid into a pension fund, from which benefits are paid to retirees. In most cases, pension benefits consist of monthly payments to retired employees and other payments on disability or death.

Teaching Note: Students often have difficulty understanding the difference between a defined contribution plan and a defined benefit plan. An example or two of actual pension situations, such as your own, would make the distinction clear.

There are two kinds of pension plans. Under a *defined contribution plan,* the employer is required to contribute an annual amount specified by an agreement between the company and its employees or a resolution of the board of directors. Retirement payments depend on the amount of pension payments the accumulated contributions can support. Under a *defined benefit plan,* the employer's annual contribution is the amount required to fund pension liabilities arising from employment in the current year, but the exact amount will not be determined until the retirement and death of the current employees. Under a defined benefit plan, the amount of future benefits is fixed, but the annual contributions vary depending on

BUSINESS BULLETIN: ETHICS IN PRACTICE

Accounting sometimes has a profound impact on our lives. When the FASB adopted SFAS No. 106, which requires companies to account for postretirement medical benefits on an accrual basis in accordance with the matching rule rather than on a cash basis in a distant year when the benefits are paid, companies had to face up to the cost of promising such benefits. Because the management of many companies, including Unisys Corporation, McDonnell Douglas Corporation, and Navistar International Corporation, had not realized the magnitude of the promises they had made, they were compelled to reduce health care benefits to retirees. As a result, many retirees are finding that they have lost benefits they had counted on receiving. According to one study, almost two-thirds of U.S. companies will have scaled back or eliminated benefits.[11] By making companies aware of the real cost of health care, accounting has played a significant role in making health care reform a key political issue. Some people think the FASB should have left well enough alone and not required companies to report these costs. What do you think?

assumptions about how much the pension fund will earn. Under a defined contribution plan, each year's contribution is fixed, but the benefits vary depending on how much the pension fund earns.

Accounting for annual pension expense under a defined contribution plan is simple. After the required contribution is determined, Pension Expense is debited and a liability (or Cash) is credited.

Point to Emphasize: Accounting for a defined benefit plan is far more complex than accounting for a defined contribution plan. Fortunately, accountants can rely on the calculations of professional actuaries, whose expertise includes the mathematics of pension plans.

Accounting for annual expense under a defined benefit plan is one of the most complex topics in accounting; thus, the intricacies are reserved for advanced courses. In concept, however, the procedure is simple. First, the amount of pension expense is determined. Then, if the amount of cash contributed to the fund is less than the pension expense, a liability results, which is reported on the balance sheet. If the amount of cash paid to the pension plan exceeds the pension expense, a prepaid expense arises and appears on the asset side of the balance sheet. For example, the 1996 annual report for Philip Morris Companies, Inc. included among assets on the balance sheet a prepaid pension of $814 million.

In accordance with the FASB's *Statement No. 87,* all companies should use the same actuarial method to compute pension expense.[12] However, because of the need to estimate many factors, such as the average remaining service life of active employees, the expected long-run return on pension plan assets, and expected future salary increases, the computation of pension expense is not simple. In addition, actuarial terminology further complicates pension accounting. In nontechnical terms, the pension expense for the year includes not only the cost of the benefits earned by people working during the year but interest costs on the total pension obligation (which are calculated on the present value of future benefits to be paid) and other adjustments. Those costs are reduced by the expected return on the pension fund assets.

Since 1989, all employers whose pension plans do not have sufficient assets to cover the present value of their pension benefit obligations (on a termination basis) must record the amount of the shortfall as a liability on their balance sheets. The investor no longer has to read the notes to the financial statements to learn whether or not the pension plan is fully funded. However, if a pension plan does have sufficient assets to cover its obligations, then no balance sheet reporting is required or permitted.

Other Postretirement Benefits

Point to Emphasize: Other postretirement benefits should be expensed when earned by the employee, not when received after retirement. This practice conforms to the matching rule.

In addition to pensions, many companies provide health care and other benefits to employees after retirement. In the past, these other postretirement benefits were accounted for on a cash basis; that is, they were expensed when the benefits were paid, after an employee had retired. The FASB has concluded, however, that those benefits are earned by the employee, and that, in accordance with the matching rule, they should be estimated and accrued during the period of time the employee is working.[13]

The estimates must take into account assumptions about retirement age, mortality, and, most significantly, future trends in health care benefits. Like pension benefits, such future benefits should be discounted to the current period. In a field test conducted by the Financial Executives Research Foundation, it was determined that the change to accrual accounting increased postretirement benefits by two to seven times the amount recognized on a cash basis.

Chapter Review

REVIEW OF LEARNING OBJECTIVES

1. **Identify the management issues related to issuing long-term debt.** Long-term debt is used to finance long-term assets and business activities that have long-term earnings potential, such as property, plant, and equipment and research and development. In issuing long-term debt, management must decide (1) whether or not to have long-term debt, (2) how much long-term debt to have, and (3) what types of long-term debt to have. Among the advantages of long-term debt financing are that (1) common stockholders do not relinquish any control, (2) interest on debt is tax deductible, and (3) financial leverage may increase earnings. Disadvantages of long-term financing are that (1) interest and principal must be repaid on schedule, and (2) financial leverage can work against a company if a project is not successful.
2. **Identify and contrast the major characteristics of bonds.** A bond is a security that represents money borrowed from the investing public. When a corporation issues bonds, it enters into a contract, called a bond indenture, with the bondholders. The bond indenture identifies the major conditions of the bonds. A corporation can issue several types of bonds, each having different characteristics. For example, a bond issue may or may not require security (secured versus unsecured bonds). It may be payable at a single time (term bonds) or at several times (serial bonds). And the holder may receive interest automatically (registered bonds) or may have to return coupons to receive interest payable (coupon bonds).
3. **Record the issuance of bonds at face value and at a discount or premium.** When bonds are issued, the bondholders pay an amount equal to, less than, or greater than the bonds' face value. Bondholders pay face value for bonds when the interest rate on the bonds approximates the market rate for similar investments. The issuing corporation records the bond issue at face value as a long-term liability in the Bonds Payable account.

   Bonds are issued at an amount less than face value when their face interest rate is lower than the market rate for similar investments. The difference between the face value and the issue price is called a discount and is debited to Unamortized Bond Discount.

   When the face interest rate on bonds is greater than the market interest rate on similar investments, investors are willing to pay more than face value for the bonds. The difference between the issue price and the face value is called a premium and is credited to Unamortized Bond Premium.

4. **Use present values to determine the value of bonds.** The value of a bond is determined by summing the present values of (a) the series of fixed interest payments of the bond issue and (b) the single payment of the face value at maturity. Tables 3 and 4 in the appendix on future value and present value tables should be used in making these computations.
5. **Use the straight-line and effective interest methods to amortize (a) bond discounts and (b) bond premiums.** When bonds are sold at a discount or a premium, the interest rate is adjusted from the face rate to an effective rate that is close to the market rate when the bonds were issued. Therefore, bond discounts or premiums have the effect of increasing or decreasing the interest expense on the bonds over their life. Under these conditions, it is necessary to amortize the discount or premium over the life of the bonds by using either the straight-line method or the effective interest method.

   The straight-line method allocates a fixed portion of the bond discount or premium each interest period to adjust the interest payment to interest expense. The effective interest method, which is used when the effects of amortization are material, results in a constant rate of interest on the carrying value of the bonds. To find interest and the amortization of discounts or premiums, the effective interest rate is applied to the carrying value of the bonds (face value minus the discount or plus the premium) at the beginning of the interest period. The amount of the discount or premium to be amortized is the difference between the interest figured by using the effective rate and that obtained by using the face rate. The results of using the effective interest method on bonds issued at a discount or a premium are summarized below and compared with issuance at face value.

	Bonds Issued at		
	Face Value	**Discount**	**Premium**
Trend in carrying value over bond term	Constant	Increasing	Decreasing
Trend in interest expense over bond term	Constant	Increasing	Decreasing
Interest expense versus interest payments	Interest expense = interest payments	Interest expense > interest payments	Interest expense < interest payments
Classification of bond discount or premium	Not applicable	Contra-liability (deducted from Bonds Payable)	Liability (added to Bonds Payable)

6. **Account for bonds issued between interest dates and make year-end adjustments.** When bonds are sold on dates between the interest payment dates, the issuing corporation collects from investors the interest that has accrued since the last interest payment date. When the next interest payment date arrives, the corporation pays the bondholders interest for the entire interest period.

   When the end of a corporation's fiscal year does not fall on an interest payment date, the corporation must accrue bond interest expense from the last interest payment date to the end of the company's fiscal year. This accrual results in the inclusion of the interest expense in the year incurred.

7. **Account for the retirement of bonds and the conversion of bonds into stock.** Callable bonds can be retired before maturity at the option of the issuing corporation. The call price is usually an amount greater than the face value of the bonds, so the corporation usually recognizes a loss on the retirement of bonds. An extraordinary gain can be recognized on the early extinguishment of debt when a company purchases its bonds on the open market at a price below carrying value. This happens when a rise in the market interest rate causes the market value of the bonds to fall.

   Convertible bonds allow the bondholder to convert bonds to stock in the issuing corporation. In this case, the common stock issued is recorded at the carrying value of the bonds being converted. No gain or loss is recognized.

8. **Explain the basic features of mortgages payable, installment notes payable, long-term leases, and pensions and other postretirement benefits as long-term liabilities.** A mortgage is a long-term debt secured by real property. It usually is paid in equal monthly installments. Each payment is partly interest expense and partly debt repayment. Installment notes payable are long-term notes that are paid in a series of payments. Part of each payment is interest, and part is repayment of principal. If a long-term lease is a capital lease, the risks of ownership lie with the lessee. Like a mortgage payment, each lease payment is partly interest and partly a reduction of debt. For a capital lease, both an asset and a long-term liability should be recorded. The liability should be equal to the present value at the beginning of the lease of the total lease payments over the lease term. The recorded asset is subject to depreciation. Pension expense must be recorded in the current period. Other postretirement benefits should be estimated and accrued while the employee is still working.

REVIEW OF CONCEPTS AND TERMINOLOGY

The following concepts and terms were introduced in this chapter.

LO 2 **Bond:** A security, usually long term, representing money borrowed from the investing public by a corporation or some other entity.

LO 2 **Bond certificate:** Evidence of an organization's debt to a bondholder.

LO 2 **Bond indenture:** A supplementary agreement to a bond issue that defines the rights, privileges, and limitations of bondholders.

LO 2 **Bond Issue:** The total value of bonds issued at one time.

LO 7 **Callable bonds:** Bonds that an organization can buy back and retire at a call price before maturity.

LO 7 **Call price:** A specified price, usually above face value, at which a corporation may, at its option, buy back and retire bonds before maturity.

LO 8 **Capital lease:** A long-term lease in which the risk of ownership lies with the lessee and whose terms resemble a purchase or sale on installment.

LO 7 **Convertible bonds:** Bonds that can be exchanged for other securities of the corporation, usually its common stock.

LO 2 **Coupon bonds:** Bonds that are usually not registered with the issuing organization but instead bear interest coupons stating the amount of interest due and the payment date.

LO 3 **Discount:** The amount by which the face value of a bond exceeds the issue price; occurs when the market interest rate is higher than the face interest rate.

LO 7 **Early extinguishment of debt:** The retirement of a bond issue before its maturity date.

LO 5 **Effective interest method:** A method of amortizing bond discounts or premiums that applies a constant interest rate, the market rate at the time the bonds were issued, to the carrying value of the bonds at the beginning of each interest period.

LO 3 **Face interest rate:** The rate of interest paid to bondholders based on the face value of the bonds.

LO 1 **Financial leverage:** The ability to increase earnings for stockholders by earning more on assets than is paid in interest on debt incurred to finance the assets; also called *trading on the equity.*

LO 8 **Installment note payable:** A long-term note paid off in a series of payments, of which part is interest and part is repayment of principal.

LO 1 **Interest coverage ratio:** A measure of the degree of protection a company has from default on interest payments; income before taxes and interest expense divided by interest expense.

LO 3 **Market interest rate:** The rate of interest paid in the market on bonds of similar risk; also called *effective interest rate.*

LO 8 **Mortgage:** A long-term debt secured by real property; usually paid in equal monthly installments, of which part is interest and part is repayment of principal.

LO 8 **Operating lease:** A short-term or cancelable lease in which the risks of ownership lie with the lessor, and whose payments are recorded as a rent expense.

LO 8 **Other postretirement benefits:** Health care and other nonpension benefits paid to a worker after retirement but earned while the employee is still working.

LO 8 **Pension fund:** A fund established through contributions from an employer (and, sometimes, employees) from which payments are made to employees after retirement or on disability or death.

LO 8 **Pension plan:** A contract between a company and its employees under which the company agrees to pay benefits to the employees after they retire.

LO 3 **Premium:** The amount by which the issue price of a bond exceeds its face value; occurs when the market interest rate is lower than the face interest rate.

LO 2 **Registered bonds:** Bonds for which the names and addresses of bondholders are recorded with the issuing organization.

LO 2 **Secured bonds:** Bonds that give the bondholders a pledge of certain assets as a guarantee of repayment.

LO 2 **Serial bonds:** A bond issue with several different maturity dates.

LO 5 **Straight-line method:** A method of amortizing bond discounts or premiums that allocates a discount or premium equally over each interest period of the life of a bond.

LO 2 **Term bonds:** Bonds of a bond issue that all mature at the same time.

LO 2 **Unsecured bonds:** Bonds issued on the general credit of an organization; also called *debenture bonds.*

LO 5 **Zero coupon bonds:** Bonds that do not pay periodic interest but that promise to pay a fixed amount on the maturity date.

REVIEW PROBLEM

Interest and Amortization of a Bond Discount, Bond Retirement, and Bond Conversion

LO 3
LO 5
LO 7

When the Merrill Manufacturing Company was expanding its metal window division, it did not have enough capital to finance the expansion. So, management sought and received approval from the board of directors to issue bonds. The company planned to issue $5,000,000 of 8 percent, five-year bonds in 20x1. Interest would be paid on June 30 and December 31 of each year. The bonds would be callable at 104, and each $1,000 bond would be convertible into 30 shares of $10 par value common stock.

On January 1, 20x1, the bonds were sold at 96 because the market rate of interest for similar investments was 9 percent. The company decided to amortize the bond discount by using the effective interest method. On July 1, 20x3, management called and retired half the bonds, and investors converted the other half into common stock.

REQUIRED

1. Prepare an interest and amortization schedule for the first five interest payment dates.
2. Prepare the journal entries to record the sale of the bonds, the first two interest payments, the bond retirement, and the bond conversion.

ANSWER TO REVIEW PROBLEM

1. Prepare a schedule for the first five interest periods.

Interest and Amortization of Bond Discount

Semiannual Interest Payment Date	Carrying Value at Beginning of Period	Semiannual Interest Expense* (9% × ½)	Semiannual Interest Paid per Period (8% × ½)	Amortization of Discount	Unamortized Bond Discount at End of Period	Carrying Value at End of Period
Jan. 1, 20x1					$200,000	$4,800,000
June 30, 20x1	$4,800,000	$216,000	$200,000	$16,000	184,000	4,816,000
Dec. 31, 20x1	4,816,000	216,720	200,000	16,720	167,280	4,832,720
June 30, 20x2	4,832,720	217,472	200,000	17,472	149,808	4,850,192
Dec. 31, 20x2	4,850,192	218,259	200,000	18,259	131,549	4,868,451
June 30, 20x3	4,868,451	219,080	200,000	19,080	112,469	4,887,531

*Rounded to the nearest dollar.

2. Prepare the journal entries.

Date		Account	Debit	Credit
20x1				
Jan.	1	Cash	4,800,000	
		Unamortized Bond Discount	200,000	
		Bonds Payable		5,000,000
		Sold $5,000,000 of 8%, 5-year bonds at 96		
June	30	Bond Interest Expense	216,000	
		Unamortized Bond Discount		16,000
		Cash		200,000
		Paid semiannual interest and amortized the discount on 8%, 5-year bonds		
Dec.	31	Bond Interest Expense	216,720	
		Unamortized Bond Discount		16,720
		Cash		200,000
		Paid semiannual interest and amortized the discount on 8%, 5-year bonds		
20x3				
July	1	Bonds Payable	2,500,000	
		Loss on Retirement of Bonds	156,235	
		Unamortized Bond Discount		56,235
		Cash		2,600,000
		Called $2,500,000 of 8% bonds and retired them at 104 $112,469 × ½ = $56,235*		
	1	Bonds Payable	2,500,000	
		Unamortized Bond Discount		56,234
		Common Stock		750,000
		Paid-in Capital in Excess of Par Value, Common		1,693,766
		Converted $2,500,000 of 8% bonds into common stock: 2,500 × 30 shares = 75,000 shares 75,000 shares × $10 = $750,000 $112,469 − $56,235 = $56,234 $2,500,000 − ($56,234 + $750,000) = $1,693,766		

*Rounded.

Chapter Assignments

BUILDING YOUR KNOWLEDGE FOUNDATION

Questions

1. What are the advantages and disadvantages of issuing long-term debt?
2. What are a bond certificate, a bond issue, and a bond indenture? What information is found in a bond indenture?
3. What are the essential differences between (a) secured and debenture bonds, (b) term and serial bonds, and (c) registered and coupon bonds?
4. Napier Corporation sold $500,000 of 5 percent $1,000 bonds on the interest payment date. What would the proceeds from the sale be if the bonds were issued at 95, at 100, and at 102?
5. If you were about to buy bonds on which the face interest rate was less than the market interest rate, would you expect to pay more or less than par value for the bonds?
6. Why does the amortization of a bond discount increase interest expense to an amount greater than interest paid? Why does the amortization of a premium have the opposite effect?
7. When the effective interest method of amortizing a bond discount or premium is used, why does the amount of interest expense change from period to period?
8. When bonds are issued between interest dates, why is it necessary for the issuer to collect an amount equal to accrued interest from the buyer?
9. Why would a company want to exercise the call provision of a bond when it can wait to pay off the debt?
10. What are the advantages of convertible bonds to the company issuing them and to the investor?
11. What are the two components of a uniform monthly mortgage payment?
12. What are the two methods of repaying an installment note?
13. Under what conditions is a long-term lease called a capital lease? Why should an accountant record both an asset and a liability in connection with this type of lease? What items should appear on the income statement as the result of a capital lease?
14. What is a pension plan? What is a pension fund?
15. What is the difference between a defined contribution plan and a defined benefit plan? In general, how is expense determined under each plan? What assumptions must be made to account for the expenses of such a plan?
16. What are other postretirement benefits, and how does the matching rule apply?

Short Exercises

SE 1. LO 1 *Bond Versus Common Stock Financing*

Indicate whether each of the following is an advantage or a disadvantage of using long-term bond financing rather than issuing common stock.

1. Interest paid on bonds is tax deductible.
2. Sometimes projects are not as successful as planned.
3. Financial leverage can have a negative effect when investments do not earn as much as the interest payments on the related debt.
4. Bondholders do not have voting rights in a corporation.
5. Positive financial leverage may be achieved.

SE 2. LO 3 LO 5 *Journal Entries for Interest Using the Straight-Line Method*

On April 1, 20x1, Taylor Corporation issued $4,000,000 in 8.5 percent, five-year bonds at 98. The semiannual interest payment dates are April 1 and October 1. Prepare journal entries for the issue of the bonds by Taylor on April 1, 20x1, and the first two interest payments on October 1, 20x1, and April 1, 20x2. Use the straight-line method and ignore year-end accruals.

SE 3. LO 3 LO 5 LO 6 *Journal Entries for Interest Using the Effective Interest Method*

On March 1, 20xx, River Front Freight Company sold $100,000 of its 9.5 percent, twenty-year bonds at 106. The semiannual interest payment dates are March 1 and September 1. The effective interest rate is approximately 8.9 percent. The company's fiscal year ends August 31. Prepare journal entries to record the sale of the bonds on March 1, the accrual of interest and amortization of premium on August 31, and the first interest payment on September 1. Use the effective interest method to amortize the premium.

SE 4. LO 4 *Valuing Bonds Using Present Value*

Mine-Mart, Inc., is considering the sale of two bond issues. Choice A is a $400,000 bond issue that pays semiannual interest of $32,000 and is due in twenty years. Choice B is a $400,000 bond issue that pays semiannual interest of $30,000 and is due in fifteen years. Assume that the market rate of interest for each bond is 12 percent. Calculate the amount that Mine-Mart, Inc., will receive if both bond issues occur. (Calculate the present value of each bond issue and sum.)

SE 5. LO 3 LO 6 *Journal Entries for Bond Issues*

Macrofilm Company is authorized to issue $900,000 in bonds on June 1. The bonds carry a face interest rate of 8 percent, with interest to be paid on June 1 and December 1. Prepare journal entries for the issue of the bonds under the independent assumptions that (a) the bonds are issued on September 1 at 100 and (b) the bonds are issued on June 1 at 103.

SE 6. LO 6 *Sale of Bonds Between Interest Dates*

Tripp Corporation sold $200,000 of 9 percent, ten-year bonds for face value on September 1, 20xx. The issue date of the bonds was May 1, 20xx. The company's fiscal year ends on December 31, and this is its only bond issue. Record the sale of the bonds on September 1 and the first semiannual interest payment on November 1, 20xx. What is the bond interest expense for the year ending December 31, 20xx?

SE 7. LO 3 LO 5 LO 6 *Year-End Accrual of Bond Interest*

On October 1, 20x1, Alexus Corporation issued $500,000 of 9 percent bonds at 96. The bonds are dated October 1 and pay interest semiannually. The market rate of interest is 10 percent, and the company's year end is December 31. Prepare the entries to record the issuance of the bonds, the accrual of the interest on December 31, 20x1, and the payment of the first semiannual interest on April 1, 20x2. Assume that the company does not use reversing entries and uses the effective interest method to amortize the bond discount.

SE 8. LO 7 *Journal Entry for Bond Retirement*

The Falstaf Corporation has outstanding $800,000 of 8 percent bonds callable at 104. On December 1, immediately after the payment of the semiannual interest and the amortization of the bond discount were recorded, the unamortized bond discount equaled $21,000. On that date, $480,000 of the bonds were called and retired. Prepare the entry to record the retirement of the bonds on December 1.

SE 9. LO 7 *Journal Entry for Bond Conversion*

The Degas Corporation has $1,000,000 of 6 percent bonds outstanding. There is $20,000 of unamortized discount remaining on the bonds after the March 1, 20x2, semiannual interest payment. The bonds are convertible at the rate of 20 shares of $10 par value common stock for each $1,000 bond. On March 1, 20x2, bondholders presented $600,000 of the bonds for conversion. Prepare the journal entry to record the conversion of the bonds.

SE 10. LO 8 *Mortgage Payable*

Sternberg Corporation purchased a building by signing a $300,000 long-term mortgage with monthly payments of $2,400. The mortgage carries an interest rate of 8 percent. Prepare a monthly payment schedule showing the monthly payment, the interest for the month, the reduction in debt, and the unpaid balance for the first three months. (Round to the nearest dollar.)

Exercises

E 1. LO 1 *Interest Coverage Ratio*

Compute the interest coverage ratios for 20x1 and 20x2 from the partial income statements of Evergreen Company:

	20x2	20x1
Income from operations	$23,890	$18,460
Interest expense	5,800	3,300
Income before income taxes	$18,090	$15,160
Income taxes	5,400	4,500
Net income	$12,690	$10,660

E 2. LO 3, LO 5 *Journal Entries for Interest Using the Straight-Line Method*

Berkshire Corporation issued $4,000,000 in 10.5 percent, ten-year bonds on February 1, 20x1, at 104. The semiannual interest payment dates are February 1 and August 1.

Prepare journal entries for the issue of bonds by Berkshire on February 1, 20x1, and the first two interest payments on August 1, 20x1, and February 1, 20x2. Use the straight-line method and ignore year-end accruals.

E 3. LO 3, LO 5 *Journal Entries for Interest Using the Straight-Line Method*

McAllister Corporation issued $8,000,000 in 8.5 percent, five-year bonds on March 1, 20x1, at 96. The semiannual interest payment dates are March 1 and September 1.

Prepare journal entries for the issue of the bonds by McAllister on March 1, 20x1, and the first two interest payments on September 1, 20x1, and March 1, 20x2. Use the straight-line method and ignore year-end accruals.

E 4. LO 3, LO 5, LO 6 *Journal Entries for Interest Using the Effective Interest Method*

The Mayfair Drapery Company sold $500,000 of 9.5 percent, twenty-year bonds on April 1, 20xx, at 106. The semiannual interest payment dates are April 1 and October 1. The effective interest rate is approximately 8.9 percent. The company's fiscal year ends September 30.

Prepare journal entries to record the sale of the bonds on April 1, the accrual of interest and amortization of premium on September 30, and the first interest payment on October 1. Use the effective interest method to amortize the premium.

E 5. LO 3, LO 5, LO 6 *Journal Entries for Interest Using the Effective Interest Method*

On March 1, 20x1, the Sperlazzo Corporation issued $1,200,000 of 10 percent, five-year bonds. The semiannual interest payment dates are March 1 and September 1. Because the market rate for similar investments was 11 percent, the bonds had to be issued at a discount. The discount on the issuance of the bonds was $48,670. The company's fiscal year ends February 28.

Prepare journal entries to record the bond issue on March 1, 20x1; the payment of interest and the amortization of the discount on September 1, 20x1; the accrual of interest and the amortization of the discount on February 28, 20x2; and the payment of interest on March 1, 20x2. Use the effective interest method. (Round answers to the nearest dollar.)

E 6. LO 4 *Valuing Bonds Using Present Value*

Sessions, Inc., is considering the sale of two bond issues. Choice A is an $800,000 bond issue that pays semiannual interest of $64,000 and is due in twenty years. Choice B is an $800,000 bond issue that pays semiannual interest of $60,000 and is due in fifteen years. Assume that the market interest rate for each bond is 12 percent.

Calculate the amount that Sessions, Inc., will receive if both bond issues are made. (**Hint:** Calculate the present value of each bond issue and sum.)

E 7. LO 4 *Valuing Bonds Using Present Value*

Use the present value tables in the appendix on future value and present value tables to calculate the issue price of a $1,200,000 bond issue in each of the following independent cases, assuming that interest is paid semiannually.

a. A ten-year, 8 percent bond issue; the market interest rate is 10 percent.
b. A ten-year, 8 percent bond issue; the market interest rate is 6 percent.
c. A ten-year, 10 percent bond issue; the market interest rate is 8 percent.
d. A twenty-year, 10 percent bond issue; the market interest rate is 12 percent.
e. A twenty-year, 10 percent bond issue; the market interest rate is 6 percent.

E 8. LO 4 *Zero Coupon Bonds*

The state of Vermont needs to raise $100,000,000 for highway repairs. Officials are considering issuing zero coupon bonds, which do not require periodic interest payments. The current market interest rate for the bonds is 10 percent. What face value of bonds must be issued to raise the needed funds, assuming the bonds will be due in thirty years and compounded annually? How would your answer change if the bonds were due in fifty years? How would both answers change if the market interest rate were 8 percent instead of 10 percent?

E 9. LO 5, LO 6 *Journal Entries for Interest Payments Using the Effective Interest Method*

The long-term debt section of the Fleming Corporation's balance sheet at the end of its fiscal year, December 31, 20x1, was as follows:

Long-Term Liabilities		
Bonds Payable—8%, interest payable 1/1 and 7/1, due 12/31/03	$1,000,000	
Less Unamortized Bond Discount	80,000	$920,000

Prepare the journal entries relevant to the interest payments on July 1, 20x2, December 31, 20x2, and January 1, 20x3. Assume an effective interest rate of 10 percent.

E 10. LO 3 LO 6 *Journal Entries for Bond Issue*

Computer Alternatives, Inc., is authorized to issue $1,800,000 in bonds on June 1. The bonds carry a face interest rate of 9 percent, which is to be paid on June 1 and December 1.

Prepare journal entries for the issue of the bonds by Computer Alternatives, Inc., under the assumptions that (a) the bonds are issued on September 1 at 100 and (b) the bonds are issued on June 1 at 105.

E 11. LO 6 *Sale of Bonds Between Interest Dates*

Marina Corporation sold $400,000 of 12 percent, ten-year bonds at face value on September 1, 20xx. The issue date of the bonds was May 1, 20xx.

1. Record the sale of the bonds on September 1 and the first semiannual interest payment on November 1, 20xx.
2. The company's fiscal year ends on December 31 and this is its only bond issue. What is the bond interest expense for the year ending December 31, 20xx?

E 12. LO 3 LO 5 LO 6 *Year-End Accrual of Bond Interest*

Swoboda Corporation issued $1,000,000 of 9 percent bonds on October 1, 20x1, at 96. The bonds are dated October 1 and pay interest semiannually. The market interest rate is 10 percent, and the company's fiscal year ends on December 31.

Prepare the entries to record the issuance of the bonds, the accrual of the interest on December 31, 20x1, and the first semiannual interest payment on April 1, 20x2. Assume the company does not use reversing entries and uses the effective interest method to amortize the bond discount.

E 13. LO 4 LO 7 *Time Value of Money and Early Extinguishment of Debt*

Feldman, Inc., has a $1,400,000, 8 percent bond issue that was issued a number of years ago at face value. There are now ten years left on the bond issue, and the market interest rate is 16 percent. Interest is paid semiannually.

1. Using present value tables, figure the current market value of the bond issue.
2. Record the retirement of the bonds, assuming the company purchases the bonds on the open market at the calculated value.

E 14. LO 7 *Journal Entry for Bond Retirement*

The Okado Corporation has outstanding $1,600,000 of 8 percent bonds callable at 104. On September 1, immediately after recording the payment of the semiannual interest and the amortization of the discount, the unamortized bond discount equaled $42,000. On that date, $960,000 of the bonds were called and retired.

Prepare the entry to record the retirement of the bonds on September 1.

E 15. LO 7 *Journal Entry for Bond Conversion*

The Gallery Corporation has $400,000 of 6 percent bonds outstanding. There is $20,000 of unamortized discount remaining on these bonds after the July 1, 20x8, semiannual interest payment. The bonds are convertible at the rate of 40 shares of $5 par value common stock for each $1,000 bond. On July 1, 20x8, bondholders presented $300,000 of the bonds for conversion.

Prepare the journal entry to record the conversion of the bonds.

E 16. LO 8 *Mortgage Payable*

Antilles Corporation purchased a building by signing a $150,000 long-term mortgage with monthly payments of $2,000. The mortgage carries an interest rate of 12 percent.

1. Prepare a monthly payment schedule showing the monthly payment, the interest for the month, the reduction in debt, and the unpaid balance for the first three months. (Round to the nearest dollar.)
2. Prepare journal entries to record the purchase and the first two monthly payments.

E 17. LO 8 *Recording Lease Obligations*

Ramos Corporation has leased a piece of equipment that has a useful life of twelve years. The terms of the lease are $43,000 per year for twelve years. Ramos currently is able to borrow money at a long-term interest rate of 15 percent. (Round answers to the nearest dollar.)

1. Calculate the present value of the lease.
2. Prepare the journal entry to record the lease agreement.
3. Prepare the entry to record depreciation of the equipment for the first year using the straight-line method.
4. Prepare the entries to record the lease payments for the first two years.

E 18. LO 8 *Installment Notes Payable: Unequal Payments*

Assume that on December 31, 20x1, $40,000 is borrowed on a 12 percent installment note, to be paid annually over four years. Prepare the entry to record the note and the first two annual payments, assuming that the principal is paid in equal annual installments and the interest on the unpaid balance accrues annually. How would your answer change if the interest rate rose to 13 percent in 20x3?

E 19. LO 8 *Installment Notes Payable: Equal Payments*

Assume that on December 31, 20x1, $40,000 is borrowed on a 12 percent installment note, to be paid in equal annual payments over four years. Calculate to the nearest dollar the amount of each equal payment, using Table 4 from the appendix on future value and present value tables. Prepare a payment schedule table similar to Table 4 in the text, and record the first two annual payments.

Problems

P 1. LO 3, LO 5, LO 6 *Bond Transactions—Straight-Line Method*

Weiskopf Corporation has $8,000,000 of 9.5 percent, twenty-five-year bonds dated March 1, with interest payable on March 1 and September 1. The company's fiscal year ends on November 30, and it uses the straight-line method to amortize bond premiums or discounts.

REQUIRED

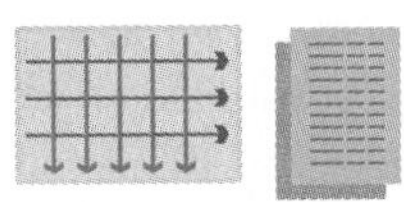

1. Assume the bonds are issued at 103.5 on March 1. Prepare journal entries for March 1, September 1, and November 30.
2. Assume the bonds are issued at 96.5 on March 1. Prepare journal entries for March 1, September 1, and November 30.
3. Assume the bonds are issued on June 1 at face value plus accrued interest. Prepare journal entries for June 1, September 1, and November 30.

P 2. LO 3, LO 5, LO 6 *Bond Transactions—Effective Interest Method*

Pandit Corporation has $20,000,000 of 10.5 percent, twenty-year bonds dated June 1, with interest payment dates of May 31 and November 30. The company's fiscal year ends December 31. It uses the effective interest method to amortize bond premiums or discounts. (Round amounts to the nearest dollar.)

REQUIRED

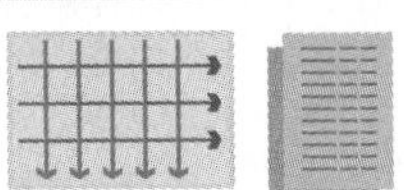

1. Assume the bonds are issued at 103 on June 1 to yield an effective interest rate of 10.1 percent. Prepare journal entries for June 1, November 30, and December 31.
2. Assume the bonds are issued at 97 on June 1 to yield an effective interest rate of 10.9 percent. Prepare journal entries for June 1, November 30, and December 31.
3. Assume the bonds are issued at face value plus accrued interest on August 1. Prepare journal entries for August 1, November 30, and December 31.

P 3. LO 3, LO 5, LO 6 *Bonds Issued at a Discount and a Premium*

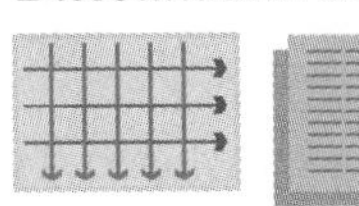
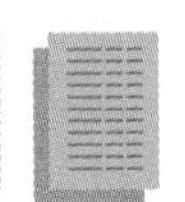

Bannchi Corporation issued bonds twice during 20x1. The transactions were as follows:

20x1

- Jan. 1 Issued $2,000,000 of 9.2 percent, ten-year bonds dated January 1, 20x1, with interest payable on June 30 and December 31. The bonds were sold at 98.1, resulting in an effective interest rate of 9.5 percent.
- Apr. 1 Issued $4,000,000 of 9.8 percent, ten-year bonds dated April 1, 20x1, with interest payable on March 31 and September 30. The bonds were sold at 102, resulting in an effective interest rate of 9.5 percent.
- June 30 Paid semiannual interest on the January 1 issue and amortized the discount, using the effective interest method.
- Sept. 30 Paid semiannual interest on the April 1 issue and amortized the premium, using the effective interest method.
- Dec. 31 Paid semiannual interest on the January 1 issue and amortized the discount, using the effective interest method.
- 31 Made an end-of-year adjusting entry to accrue interest on the April 1 issue and to amortize half the premium applicable to the second interest period.

20x2

- Mar. 31 Paid semiannual interest on the April 1 issue and amortized the premium applicable to the second half of the second interest period.

REQUIRED

Prepare journal entries to record the bond transactions. (Round amounts to the nearest dollar.)

P 4. LO 5 LO 7 *Bond Interest and Amortization Table and Bond Retirements*

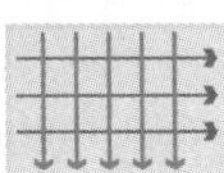

In 20x1, Tagore Corporation was authorized to issue $3,000,000 of unsecured bonds, due March 31, 20x6. The bonds carried a face interest rate of 11.6 percent, payable semiannually on March 31 and September 30, and were callable at 104 any time after March 31, 20x4. All the bonds were issued on April 1, 20x1, at 102.261, a price that yielded an effective interest rate of 11 percent.

On April 1, 20x4, Tagore Corporation called one-half of the outstanding bonds and retired them.

REQUIRED

1. Prepare a table similar to Table 2 to show the interest and amortization of the bond premium for ten interest payment periods, using the effective interest method. (Round results to the nearest dollar.)
2. Calculate the amount of loss on early retirement of one-half of the bonds on April 1, 20x4.

P 5. LO 3 LO 5 LO 6 LO 7 *Comprehensive Bond Transactions*

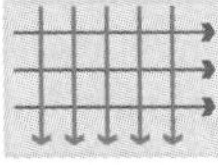

Over a period of three years, DaSilva Corporation, a company whose fiscal year ends on December 31, engaged in the following transactions involving two bond issues.

20x1

July 1	Issued $20,000,000 of 12 percent convertible bonds at 96. The bonds are convertible into $20 par value common stock at the rate of 20 shares of stock for each $1,000 bond. Interest is payable on June 30 and December 31, and the market rate of interest is 13 percent.
Dec. 31	Made the semiannual interest payment and amortized the bond discount.

20x2

June 1	Issued $40,000,000 of 9 percent bonds at face value plus accrued interest. Interest is payable on February 28 and August 31. The bonds, dated March 1, 20x2, are callable at 105, and the market rate of interest is 9 percent.
30	Made the semiannual interest payment on the 12 percent bonds and amortized the bond discount.
Aug. 31	Made the semiannual interest payment on the 9 percent bonds.
Dec. 31	Made the semiannual interest payment and amortized the discount on the 12 percent bonds, and accrued interest on the 9 percent bonds.

20x3

Feb. 28	Made the semiannual interest payment on the 9 percent bonds.
June 30	Made the semiannual interest payment and amortized the bond discount on the 12 percent bonds.
July 1	Accepted all the 12 percent bonds for conversion into common stock.
31	Called and retired all of the 9 percent bonds, including accrued interest.

REQUIRED

Prepare journal entries to record the bond transactions, making all necessary accruals and using the effective interest method. (Round all calculations to the nearest dollar.)

Alternate Problems

P 6. LO 3 LO 5 LO 6 *Bond Transactions—Straight-Line Method*

Marconi Corporation has $10,000,000 of 10.5 percent, twenty-year bonds dated June 1, with interest payment dates of May 31 and November 30. The company's fiscal year ends on December 31. It uses the straight-line method to amortize bond premiums or discounts.

REQUIRED

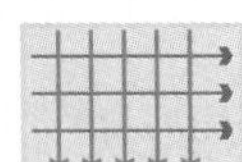

1. Assume the bonds are issued at 103 on June 1. Prepare journal entries for June 1, November 30, and December 31.
2. Assume the bonds are issued at 97 on June 1. Prepare journal entries for June 1, November 30, and December 31.
3. Assume the bonds are issued at face value plus accrued interest on August 1. Prepare journal entries for August 1, November 30, and December 31.

P 7. LO 3 LO 5 LO 6 *Bond Transactions—Effective Interest Method*

Aparicio Corporation has $8,000,000 of 9.5 percent, twenty-five-year bonds dated March 1, with interest payable on March 1 and September 1. The company's fiscal year ends on November 30. It uses the effective interest method to amortize bond premiums or discounts. (Round amounts to the nearest dollar.)

REQUIRED

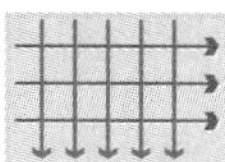

1. Assume the bonds are issued at 102.5 on March 1 to yield an effective interest rate of 9.2 percent. Prepare journal entries for March 1, September 1, and November 30.
2. Assume the bonds are issued at 97.5 on March 1 to yield an effective interest rate of 9.8 percent. Prepare journal entries for March 1, September 1, and November 30.
3. Assume the bonds are issued on June 1 at face value plus accrued interest. Prepare journal entries for June 1, September 1, and November 30.

P 8. LO 3, LO 5, LO 6 *Bonds Issued at a Discount and a Premium*

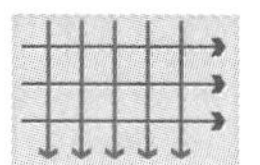

Maldonado Corporation issued bonds twice during 20x2. A summary of the transactions involving the bonds follows.

20x2

Jan. 1 Issued $6,000,000 of 9.9 percent, ten-year bonds dated January 1, 20x2, with interest payable on December 31 and June 30. The bonds were sold at 102.6, resulting in an effective interest rate of 9.4 percent.

Mar. 1 Issued $4,000,000 of 9.2 percent, ten-year bonds dated March 1, 20x2, with interest payable March 1 and September 1. The bonds were sold at 98.2, resulting in an effective interest rate of 9.5 percent.

June 30 Paid semiannual interest on the January 1 issue and amortized the premium, using the effective interest method.

Sept. 1 Paid semiannual interest on the March 1 issue and amortized the discount, using the effective interest method.

Dec. 31 Paid semiannual interest on the January 1 issue and amortized the premium, using the effective interest method.

31 Made an end-of-year adjusting entry to accrue interest on the March 1 issue and to amortize two-thirds of the discount applicable to the second interest period.

20x3

Mar. 1 Paid semiannual interest on the March 1 issue and amortized the remainder of the discount applicable to the second interest period.

REQUIRED

Prepare journal entries to record the bond transactions. (Round amounts to the nearest dollar.)

EXPANDING YOUR CRITICAL THINKING, COMMUNICATION, AND INTERPERSONAL SKILLS

Skills Development

Conceptual Analysis

SD 1. LO 3 *Bond Interest Rates and Market Prices*

RJR Nabisco issued high-interest debt as part of a buyout of the company in the 1980s. The following statement relates to a refinancing plan designed to help the company deal with this debt.

> The refinancing plan's chief objective is to purge away most of the reset bonds of 2007 and 2009. These bonds have proved to be an immense headache for RJR. . . . That's because the bonds' interest rate must be reset [changed] so that they [the bonds] trade at full face value. The bonds had sunk to a deep discount earlier this year, raising the prospect that RJR might have to accept a painfully high reset rate of 20% or more to meet its reset obligations.[14]

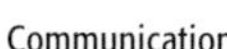

Communication

Critical Thinking

Group Activity

Memo

Ethics

International

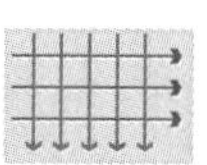

Spreadsheet

General Ledger

CD-ROM

Internet

What is a "deep discount," and what causes bonds to sell at a deep discount? Who loses when they do? What does "the bonds' interest rate must be reset so that they trade at full face value" mean? Why would this provision in the covenant be "an immense headache" to RJR Nabisco?

SD 2.

LO 5 *Nature of Zero Coupon Notes*

The Wall Street Journal reported, "Financially ailing ***Trans World Airlines*** has renegotiated its agreement to sell its 40 landing and takeoff slots and three gates at O'Hare International Airport to ***American Airlines***." Instead of receiving a lump-sum cash payment in the amount of $162.5 million, TWA elected to receive a zero coupon note from American that would be paid off in monthly installments over a twenty-year period. Since the 240 monthly payments total $500 million, TWA placed a value of $500 million on the note and indicated that the bankruptcy court would not have accepted the lower lump-sum cash payment. How does this zero coupon note differ from the zero coupon bonds described earlier in this chapter? Explain the difference between the $162.5 million cash payment and the $500 million. Is TWA right in placing a $500 million price on the sale?[15]

SD 3.

LO 8 *Lease Financing*

Federal Express Corporation, known for overnight delivery and distribution of high-priority goods and documents throughout the world, has an extensive fleet of aircraft and vehicles. In its 1996 annual report, the company stated that it "utilizes certain aircraft, land, facilities, and equipment under capital and operating leases which expire at various dates through 2024. In addition, supplemental aircraft are leased under agreements which generally provide for cancellation upon 30 days' notice." The annual report further stated that the minimum commitments for capital leases and noncancelable operating leases for 1997 were $15,561,000 and $724,161,000, respectively.[16] What is the difference between a capital lease and an operating lease? How do the accounting procedures for the two types of leases differ? How do you interpret management's reasoning in placing some aircraft under capital leases and others under operating leases? Why do you think the management of FedEx leases most of its aircraft instead of buying them?

Ethical Dilemma

SD 4.

LO 2 *Bond Indenture and Ethical Reporting*

Celltech Corporation, a biotech company, has a $24,000,000 bond issue outstanding that has several restrictive provisions in its bond indenture. Among them are requirements that current assets exceed current liabilities by a ratio of 2 to 1 and that income before income taxes exceed the annual interest on the bonds by a ratio of 3 to 1. If those requirements are not met, the bondholders can force the company into bankruptcy. The company is still awaiting Food and Drug Administration (FDA) approval of its new product CMZ-12, a cancer treatment drug. Management had been counting on sales of CMZ-12 in 2000 to meet the provisions of the bond indenture. As the end of the fiscal year approaches, the company does not have sufficient current assets or income before taxes to meet the requirements. Roger Landon, the chief financial officer, proposes, "Since we can assume that FDA approval will occur in early 2001, I suggest we book sales and receivables from our major customers now in anticipation of next year's sales. This action will increase our current assets and our income before taxes. It is essential that we do this to save the company. Look at all the people who will be hurt if we don't do it." Is Landon's proposal acceptable accounting? Is it ethical? Who could be harmed by it? What steps might management take?

Research Activity

SD 5.

LO 3 *Reading the Bond Markets*

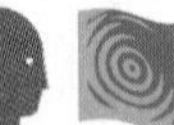

Obtain a copy of a recent issue of *The Wall Street Journal* from your school or local library. Or, if you have access to an Internet service, visit *The Wall Street Journal's* home page. In the newspaper, find Section C, "Money & Investing," and turn to the page where the New York Exchange Bonds are listed. Notice, first, the Dow Jones Bond Averages of twenty bonds, ten utilities, and ten industrials. Are the averages above or below 100? Is this a premium or a discount? Is the market interest rate above or below the face rate of the average bond? Now, identify three bonds from those listed. Choose one that sells at a discount, one that sells at a premium, and one that sells for approximately 100. For each bond, write the name of the company, the face interest rate, the year the bond is due, the current yield, and the current closing market price. (Some bonds have the letters *cv* in the Yield column. This means the bonds are convertible into common stock and the yield may not be meaningful.) For each bond, explain the relationships between the face interest rate, the current yield, and the closing price. What other factors affect the current yield of a bond? Be prepared to discuss your findings.

Decision-Making Practice

SD 6.
LO 1 *Issuance of Long-Term*
LO 2 *Bonds Versus Leasing*
LO 8

The ***Weiss Chemical Corporation*** plans to build or lease a new plant that will produce liquid fertilizer for the agricultural market. The plant is expected to cost $800,000,000 and will be located in the southwestern United States. The company's chief financial officer, Sharon Weiss, has spent the last several weeks studying different means of financing the plant. From her talks with bankers and other financiers, she has decided that there are two basic choices: The plant can be financed through the issuance of a long-term bond or through a long-term lease. Details for the two options are given below.

a. Issue $800,000,000 of twenty-five-year, 16 percent bonds secured by the new plant. Interest on the bonds would be payable semiannually.
b. Sign a twenty-five-year lease for an existing plant calling for lease payments of $65,400,000 on a semiannual basis.

Weiss wants to know what the effect of each choice will be on the company's financial statements. She estimates that the useful life of the plant is twenty-five years, at which time it is expected to have an estimated residual value of $80,000,000.

Weiss plans a meeting to discuss the alternatives. Prepare a short memorandum to her identifying the issues that should be considered in making this decision. (**Note:** You are not asked to discuss the factors or to recommend an action.)

Financial Reporting and Analysis

Interpreting Financial Reports

FRA 1.
LO 3 *Contrasting Types of*
LO 4 *Bonds and Present Value*

A bond or note with no periodic interest payments sounds like a car with no motor. But some large companies are issuing such bonds. For example, in 1981, ***J.C. Penney Company, Inc.,*** advertised in the business press and sold $200,000,000 of zero coupon bonds due in 1989. The price, however, was not $200,000,000 but only 33.247 percent of $200,000,000. In other words, the investor paid about $332,470 initially and in eight years collected $1,000,000. The advantage to J.C. Penney was that it did not have to pay a cent of interest for eight years. It did, of course, have to produce the full face value of the notes at the maturity date. For the investor, a return would be guaranteed regardless of the market interest rate over the eight years, as long as J.C. Penney was able to pay off the notes at the maturity date. The J.C. Penney zero coupon bonds can be contrasted with the financing transactions that occurred at about the same time at two other companies of similar quality: ***Transamerica Corporation*** and ***Greyhound Corporation.*** Transamerica sold $200,000,000 (face value) of thirty-year bonds with 6.5 percent annual interest at a price of $480.67 per $1,000 bond. Greyhound issued $75,000,000 of ten-year notes carrying an interest rate of 14.25 percent at 100.

REQUIRED

1. Using Tables 3 and 4 in the appendix on future value and present value tables, compute the effective interest rates for the three debt issues. Which issue would have been the most attractive to investors?
2. Federal tax laws require the payment of income taxes on amortized interest income from low-coupon bonds and notes as well as on interest that is actually paid. In light of this, would your answer to **1** change? What factors other than the effective interest rate and income taxes would you consider important in deciding which of these bonds was the best investment?

FRA 2.
LO 7 *Characteristics, Advantages, and Disadvantages of Convertible Debt*

Delta Air Lines has $800 million in 3.23 percent convertible subordinated notes due June 15, 2003.[17] In fiscal years 1995 and 1994, there was $179 million and $202 million of unamortized discount, respectively, on these notes. Similar nonconvertible notes issued by Delta carry an interest rate of 9.875 percent and have no discount. Accounting for notes is similar to that for bonds.

REQUIRED

How much interest was paid on these notes in fiscal 1995? How much was interest expense in 1995? What is the approximate effective interest rate? What reasons can you suggest for Delta's management's choosing notes that are convertible into common stock rather than simply issuing nonconvertible notes or issuing common stock directly? Are there any disadvantages to this approach? In 1996, all of the 3.23% convertible subordinated notes were converted into $3 par value common stock at a time when the discount was $178 million. What was the impact of this action on Delta's balance sheet? Does it have a favorable or unfavorable impact on Delta's debt to equity ratio?

FRA 3.
LO 8 *Lease Financing*

UAL Corporation, owner of United Airlines, stated in its 1996 annual report that it had leased some of its planes for terms of four to twenty-six years. Some leases carried the right of first refusal to purchase the aircraft at fair market value at the end of the lease term, and others set the price at fair market value or a percentage of cost.[18]

On United's December 31, 1996, balance sheet, the following accounts appeared (in millions):

Owned—Flight Equipment	$8,393
Capital Leases—Flight Equipment	1,775
Current Obligations Under Capital Leases	132
Long-Term Obligations Under Capital Leases	1,325

Expected payments in 1997 were $943 million for operating leases and $206 million for capital leases.

REQUIRED

1. How would you characterize the differences between the aircraft leases described in the first paragraph as operating leases and those described as capital leases? Explain your answer.
2. Explain in general the difference in accounting for (a) operating and capital leases and (b) Owned—Flight Equipment and Capital Leases—Flight Equipment.

International Company

FRA 4.
LO 1 *Analysis of Interest Coverage*

Japanese companies have historically relied more on debt financing and are more highly leveraged than U.S. companies. For instance, ***NEC Corporation*** and ***Sanyo Electric Co.,*** two large Japanese electronics companies, had debt to equity ratios of about 4.0 and 3.5, respectively, in 1997. From the selected data from the companies' annual reports below (in millions of yen), compute the interest coverage ratios for the two companies for the two years and comment on the riskiness of the companies and on the trends presented.

	NEC		Sanyo	
	1997	**1996**	**1997**	**1996**
Interest Expense	60,463	69,793	31,765	9,821
Income Before Income Taxes	121,222	151,318	41,486	3,485

Group Activity: Assign the two companies to different groups to calculate the ratios and discuss the results. Debrief by discussing the advantages and disadvantages of a debt-laden capital structure.

Toys "R" Us Annual Report

FRA 5.
LO 1 *Business Practice, Long-*
LO 8 *Term Debt, and Leases*

Refer to the Financial Statements and the Notes to Consolidated Financial Statements in the Toys "R" Us annual report and answer the following questions.

1. Is it the practice of Toys "R" Us to own or lease most of its property and equipment?
2. What proportion of total assets is financed with long-term debt? Calculate Toys "R" Us's interest coverage ratios for 1996 and 1997 and comment on the trend.
3. In what countries has Toys "R" Us incurred long-term debt? Which maturity date is farthest in the future?
4. Does Toys "R" Us lease property predominantly under capital leases or under operating leases? How much was rental expense for operating leases in 1997?

FINGRAPH® FINANCIAL ANALYST™

FRA 6. Select any two companies from the same industry on the Fingraph® Financial Analyst™ CD-ROM software.

LO 1 *Long-Term Liability*
LO 2 *Analysis*
LO 8

1. In the annual reports for the companies you have selected, identify the long-term liabilities from the balance sheet and any reference to any long-term liabilities in the summary of significant accounting policies or notes to the financial statements. There is likely to be a separate note for each type of long-term liability. What are the most important current liabilities for each company? What are the most important long-term liabilities for each company?
2. Display and print in tabular and graphical form the Balance Sheet Analysis page. Prepare a table that compares the debt to equity and interest coverage ratios for both companies for two years.
3. Locate the statements of cash flows in the two companies' annual reports. Have the companies been increasing or decreasing their long-term debt? If increasing, what were each company's most important sources of long-term financing over the past two years? If decreasing, which liabilities are being decreased?
4. Find and read references to long-term liabilities in management's discussion and analysis in each annual report.
5. Write a one-page executive summary that highlights the most important types of long-term liabilities for these companies, identifies accounting policies for specific long-term liabilities, and compares the debt to equity and interest coverage trends of the two companies, including reference to management's assessment. Include the Fingraph® page and your table as an attachment to your report.

ENDNOTES

1. AT&T Corporation, *Annual Report,* 1996.
2. Susan Carey, "TWA Today Faces a Key Deadline on Senior Notes," *The Wall Street Journal,* March 3, 1995.
3. At the time this chapter was written, the market interest rates on corporate bonds were volatile. Therefore, the examples and problems in this chapter use a variety of interest rates to demonstrate the concepts.
4. Quentin Hardy, "Japanese Companies Need to Raise Cash, But First a Bond Market Must Be Built," *The Wall Street Journal,* October 20, 1992.
5. Quotations from *The Wall Street Journal,* January 27, 1998. Reprinted by permission of Wall Street Journal, © 1998 Dow Jones & Company, Inc. All Rights Reserved Worldwide.
6. Fred Vogelstein, "The 100 Year Bond Is Coming Back, But Is It Good?" *The Wall Street Journal,* November 22, 1995.
7. A knowledge of present value concepts, as presented in the appendix on time value of money, is necessary to an understanding of this section.
8. Accounting Principles Board, *Opinion No. 21,* "Interest on Receivables and Payables" (New York: American Institute of Certified Public Accountants, 1971), par. 15.
9. Macronix International Co., Ltd. display advertisement in *The Wall Street Journal,* February 25, 1997. International companies are traded in the United States in units of ten shares called ADRs.
10. *Statement of Financial Accounting Standards No. 13,* "Accounting for Leases" (Norwalk, Conn.: Financial Accounting Standards Board, 1976), par. 10.
11. Larry Light, Kelly Holland, and Kevin Kelly, "Honest Balance Sheets, Broken Promises," *Business Week,* November 23, 1992.
12. *Statement of Financial Accounting Standards No. 87,* "Employers' Accounting for Pensions" (Norwalk, Conn.: Financial Accounting Standards Board, 1985).
13. *Statement of Financial Accounting Standards No. 106,* "Employers' Accounting for Postretirement Benefits Other Than Pensions" (Norwalk, Conn.: Financial Accounting Standards Board, 1990).
14. George Anders, "RJR Nabisco Moves to Retire Most Troublesome Junk Bonds," *The Asian Wall Street Journal,* July 17, 1990.
15. Stanley Ziemba, "TWA, American Revise O'Hare Gate Agreement," *The Wall Street Journal,* May 13, 1992.
16. FedEx Corporation, *Annual Report,* 1996.
17. Delta Airlines, *Annual Report,* 1995 and 1996.
18. UAL Corporation, *Annual Report,* 1996.

CHAPTER 17

The Statement of Cash Flows

LEARNING OBJECTIVES

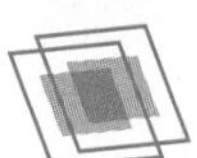

1. **Describe the statement of cash flows, and define *cash* and *cash equivalents.***
2. **State the principal purposes and uses of the statement of cash flows.**
3. **Identify the principal components of the classifications of cash flows, and state the significance of noncash investing and financing transactions.**
4. **Analyze the statement of cash flows.**
5. **Use the indirect method to determine cash flows from operating activities.**
6. **Determine cash flows from (a) investing activities and (b) financing activities.**
7. **Use the indirect method to prepare a statement of cash flows.**

SUPPLEMENTAL OBJECTIVES

8. **Prepare a work sheet for the statement of cash flows.**
9. **Use the direct method to determine cash flows from operating activities and prepare a statement of cash flows.**

DECISION POINT

MARRIOTT INTERNATIONAL, INC.

Marriott International, Inc., is a world leader in lodging and contract services. The balance sheet, income statement, and statement of stockholders' equity presented in the company's annual report give an excellent picture of management's philosophy and performance.

Those three financial statements are essential to the evaluation of a company, but they do not tell the entire story. Some information that they do not contain is presented in a fourth statement, the statement of cash flows, as shown in the Financial Highlights on the next page.[1] This statement shows how much cash was generated by the company's operations during the past three years and how much was used in or came from investing and financing activities. Marriott feels that maintaining adequate cash flows is important to the future of the company. In fact, Marriott's emphasis on cash flows is reflected in its executive compensation plan for its chief executive officer and senior executive officers. A review of the plan indicates that a measure of cash flows, at the firm or business group level, is the financial measure given the highest weight in determining compensation. Why would Marriott emphasize cash flows to such an extent?

Strong cash flows are essential to management's key goal of liquidity. If cash flows exceed the amount needed for operations and expansion, the

Critical Thinking Question: How does Marriott's shift from earnings to cash flows as a means of evaluating managers benefit the company's profitability? **Answer:** The shift motivates managers to improve cash flows from operations. If underlying that improvement is better collection of receivables and lower levels of inventory, then earnings will benefit from lower asset financing costs.

Point to Emphasize: It is common practice to combine the change in cash for the period with the beginning cash to produce the ending cash balance.

Financial Highlights: Consolidated Statement of Cash Flows

Marriott International, Inc. and Subsidiaries

Fiscal years ended January 3, 1996, December 29, 1995, and December 30, 1994	**1996**	1995	1994
		(in millions)	
Operating Activities			
Net income	**$306**	$247	$200
Adjustments to reconcile to cash from operations:			
Depreciation and amortization	**156**	129	117
Income taxes	**65**	42	23
Timeshare activity, net	**(95)**	(192)	(44)
Other	**62**	57	70
Working capital changes:			
Accounts receivable	**(52)**	(36)	(38)
Inventories	**14**	(7)	–
Other current assets	**3**	(10)	(4)
Accounts payable and accruals	**143**	139	73
Cash from operations	**602**	369	397
Investing Activities			
Capital expenditures	**(326)**	(153)	(115)
Acquisitions	**(331)**	(254)	–
Dispositions of property and equipment	**65**	42	–
Loans to Host Marriott Corporation	**(16)**	(210)	(48)
Loan repayments from Host Marriott Corporation	**141**	250	30
Other	**(82)**	(232)	(49)
Cash used in investing activities	**(549)**	(557)	(182)
Financing Activities			
Issuances of long-term debt	**–**	556	255
Repayments of long-term debt	**(137)**	(341)	(309)
Issuance of convertible subordinated debt	**288**	–	–
Issuances of common stock	**43**	40	29
Dividends paid	**(40)**	(35)	(35)
Purchases of treasury stock	**(158)**	(17)	(189)
Cash provided by (used in) financing activities	**(4)**	203	(249)
Increase/(Decrease) in Cash and Equivalents	**49**	15	(34)
Cash and Equivalents, beginning of year	**219**	204	238
Cash and Equivalents, end of year	**$268**	$219	$204

Instructional Strategy: Using information in P 1 and P 7, create a *Jeopardy* game. State a transaction and have students provide the cash flow classification. Use each item again, asking, "What is the effect on cash?" Spread difficult transactions as evenly as possible. Award prizes, which could include class participation points of varying levels, to top teams.

company will not have to borrow additional funds. The excess cash flows will be available to reduce the company's debt and improve its financial position by lowering its debt to equity ratio. Another reason for the emphasis on cash flows may be the belief that strong cash flows from operations create shareholder value or increase the market value of the company's stock.

Point to Emphasize: The statement of cash flows helps financial statement users answer many questions that cannot be answered readily by referring to the other three financial statements. It fills the gaps by disclosing a business's inflows and outflows of cash, categorized by activity, during the period.

The statement of cash flows demonstrates management's commitments for the company in ways that are not readily apparent in the other financial statements. For example, the statement of cash flows can show whether management's focus is on the short term or the long term. This statement is required by the FASB[2] and satisfies the FASB's long-held position that a primary objective of financial statements is to provide investors and creditors with information about a company's cash flows.[3]

Overview of the Statement of Cash Flows

OBJECTIVE 1

Describe the statement of cash flows, and define **cash** *and* **cash equivalents**

Related Text Assignments:
Q: 1, 2
E: 1
P: 1, 7

Discussion Question: Why are money market accounts, commercial paper (short-term notes), and U.S. Treasury bills considered cash equivalents? **Answer:** Because they are highly liquid, temporary (ninety days or less) holding places for cash that is not currently needed to operate the business. They can be converted quickly into cash if needed.

The statement of cash flows shows how a company's operating, investing, and financing activities have affected cash during an accounting period. It explains the net increase (or decrease) in cash during the accounting period. For purposes of preparing this statement, cash is defined to include both cash and cash equivalents. Cash equivalents are defined by the FASB as short-term, highly liquid investments, including money market accounts, commercial paper, and U.S. Treasury bills. A company maintains cash equivalents to earn interest on cash that would otherwise remain unused temporarily. Suppose, for example, that a company has $1,000,000 that it will not need for thirty days. To earn a return on this amount, the company may place the cash in an account that earns interest (such as a money market account); it may loan the cash to another corporation by purchasing that corporation's short-term note (commercial paper); or it may purchase a short-term obligation of the U.S. government (a Treasury bill). In this context, short-term refers to original maturities of ninety days or less. Since cash and cash equivalents are considered the same, transfers between the Cash account and cash equivalents are not treated as cash receipts or cash payments. In effect, cash equivalents are combined with the Cash account on the statement of cash flows.

Cash equivalents should not be confused with short-term investments or marketable securities, which are not combined with the Cash account on the statement of cash flows. Purchases of marketable securities are treated as cash outflows and sales of marketable securities as cash inflows on the statement of cash flows. In this chapter, cash will be assumed to include cash and cash equivalents.

Purposes of the Statement of Cash Flows

OBJECTIVE 2

State the principal purposes and uses of the statement of cash flows

Related Text Assignments:
Q: 3, 4

The primary purpose of the statement of cash flows is to provide information about a company's cash receipts and cash payments during an accounting period. A secondary purpose of the statement is to provide information about a company's operating, investing, and financing activities during the accounting period. Some information about those activities may be inferred by examining other financial statements, but it is on the statement of cash flows that all the transactions affecting cash are summarized.

Point to Emphasize: Management uses the statement of cash flows to make various investing and financing decisions. Investors and creditors, on the other hand, use the statement primarily to assess cash flow prospects, as outlined in *Statement of Financial Accounting Concepts No. 1* of the FASB.

Internal and External Uses of the Statement of Cash Flows

The statement of cash flows is useful internally to management and externally to investors and creditors. Management uses the statement to assess liquidity, to determine dividend policy, and to evaluate the effects of major policy decisions involving investments and financing. In other words, management may use the statement to determine if short-term financing is needed to pay current liabilities, to decide whether to raise or lower dividends, and to plan for investing and financing needs.

Investors and creditors will find the statement useful in assessing the company's ability to manage cash flows, to generate positive future cash flows, to pay its liabilities, to pay dividends and interest, and to anticipate its need for additional financing. Also, they may use the statement to explain the differences between net income on the income statement and the net cash flows generated from operations. In addition, the statement shows both the cash and the noncash effects of investing and financing activities during the accounting period.

Classification of Cash Flows

OBJECTIVE 3

Identify the principal components of the classifications of cash flows, and state the significance of noncash investing and financing transactions

Related Text Assignments:
Q: 5, 6
SE: 1
E: 1
P: 1, 7
SD: 2, 3
FRA: 2, 4

Teaching Note: Refer your students to a completed statement of cash flows, like the ones shown in Exhibits 4 and 7, so that they can become aware of their goal. Then help them distinguish among the three types of activities. Operating activities arise from the day-to-day sale of goods and services, investing activities involve long-term assets and investments, and financing activities deal with stockholders' equity accounts and debt (borrowing).

Discussion Question: If noncash investing and financing transactions do not produce cash flows, why must they be disclosed? **Answer:** Because they involve activities that might be considered important to the reader. Also, many noncash transactions involve a simultaneous inflow and outflow of cash and will require cash flows in the future.

The statement of cash flows classifies cash receipts and cash payments into the categories of operating, investing, and financing activities. The components of these activities are illustrated in Figure 1 and summarized below.

1. Operating activities include the cash effects of transactions and other events that enter into the determination of net income. Included in this category as cash inflows are cash receipts from customers for goods and services, interest and dividends received on loans and investments, and sales of trading securities. Included as cash outflows are cash payments for wages, goods and services, expenses, interest, taxes, and purchases of trading securities. In effect, the income statement is changed from an accrual to a cash basis.
2. Investing activities include the acquiring and selling of long-term assets, the acquiring and selling of marketable securities other than trading securities or cash equivalents, and the making and collecting of loans. Cash inflows include the cash received from selling long-term assets and marketable securities and from collecting loans. Cash outflows include the cash expended for purchases of long-term assets and marketable securities and the cash loaned to borrowers.
3. Financing activities include obtaining resources from or returning resources to owners and providing them with a return on their investment, and obtaining resources from creditors and repaying the amounts borrowed or otherwise settling the obligations. Cash inflows include the proceeds from issues of stocks and from short-term and long-term borrowing. Cash outflows include the repayments of loans (excluding interest) and payments to owners, including cash dividends. Treasury stock transactions are also considered financing activities. Repayments of accounts payable or accrued liabilities are not considered repayments of loans under financing activities, but are classified as cash outflows under operating activities.

A company will occasionally engage in significant noncash investing and financing transactions involving only long-term assets, long-term liabilities, or stockholders' equity, such as the exchange of a long-term asset for a long-term liability or the settlement of a debt by issuing capital stock. For instance, a company might take out a long-term mortgage for the purchase of land and a building. Or it might convert long-term bonds into common stock. Such transactions represent significant investing and financing activities, but they would not be reflected on the statement of cash flows because they do not involve either cash inflows or cash outflows. However, since one purpose of the statement of cash flows is to show investing and financing activities, and since such transactions will affect future cash flows, the FASB has determined that they should be disclosed in a separate schedule as part of the statement of cash flows. In this way, the reader of the statement will see the company's investing and financing activities more clearly.

Format of the Statement of Cash Flows

The statement of cash flows, as shown in the Financial Highlights for Marriott International on page 710, is divided into three sections. The first section, cash flows

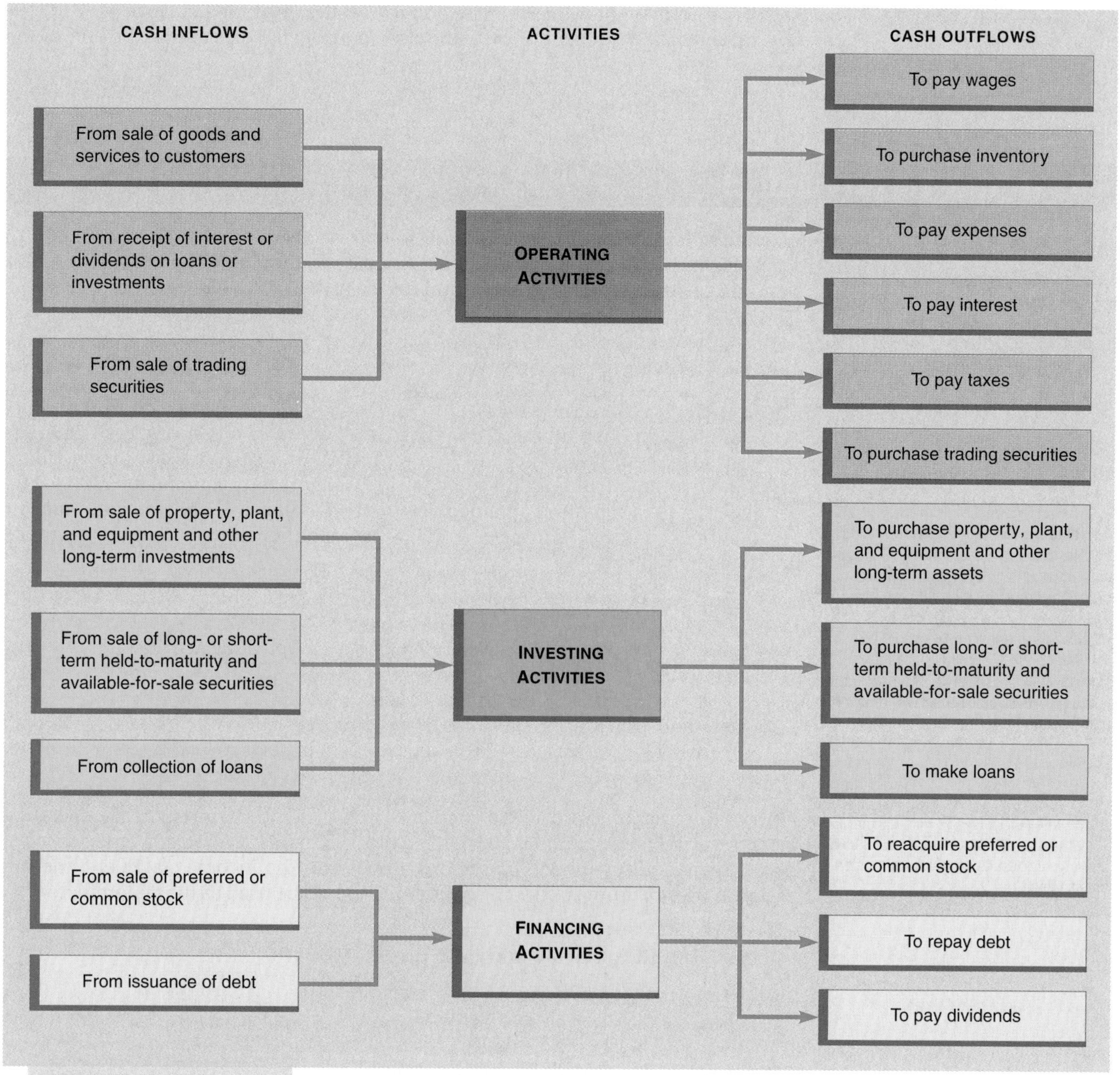

CASH INFLOWS	ACTIVITIES	CASH OUTFLOWS
From sale of goods and services to customers From receipt of interest or dividends on loans or investments From sale of trading securities	OPERATING ACTIVITIES	To pay wages To purchase inventory To pay expenses To pay interest To pay taxes To purchase trading securities
From sale of property, plant, and equipment and other long-term investments From sale of long- or short-term held-to-maturity and available-for-sale securities From collection of loans	INVESTING ACTIVITIES	To purchase property, plant, and equipment and other long-term assets To purchase long- or short-term held-to-maturity and available-for-sale securities To make loans
From sale of preferred or common stock From issuance of debt	FINANCING ACTIVITIES	To reacquire preferred or common stock To repay debt To pay dividends

Figure 1
Classification of Cash Inflows and Cash Outflows

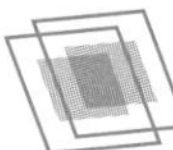

from operating activities, is presented using the indirect method. This is the most common method and is explained in learning objective 5 of this chapter. The other two sections of the statement of cash flows are the cash flows from investing activities and the cash flows from financing activities. The individual cash inflows and outflows from investing and financing activities are shown separately in their respective categories. Normally, cash outflows for the purchase of plant assets are shown separately from cash inflows from the disposal of plant assets. However, some companies follow the practice of combining these two lines to show the net amount of outflow, because the inflows are not usually material.

A reconciliation of the beginning and ending balances of cash is shown near the bottom of the statement. It shows that Marriott International had a net increase in cash of $49 million in 1996, which together with the beginning balance of $219 million results in $268 million of cash and cash equivalents on hand at the end of the year.

Analyzing the Statement of Cash Flows

OBJECTIVE 4

Analyze the statement of cash flows

Related Text Assignments:
Q: 7, 8
SE: 2, 3
E: 2
P: 2, 3, 4, 6, 8, 9
SD: 3, 4
FRA: 1, 2, 3, 4

Enrichment Note: The cash flow yield enables users to assess whether sufficient cash flows underlie earnings. Serious questions would be raised if cash flow yield was less than 1.0. For example, receivables and inventories could be growing too fast, perhaps signaling a slowdown in sales growth or a problem managing receivables collection or inventory levels.

Point to Emphasize: The change in cash shown in the comparative balance sheets provides a check figure for the statement of cash flows.

Like the other financial statements, the statement of cash flows can be analyzed to reveal significant relationships. Two areas analysts examine when studying a company are cash-generating efficiency and free cash flow.

Cash-Generating Efficiency

Cash-generating efficiency is the ability of a company to generate cash from its current or continuing operations. Three ratios are helpful in measuring cash-generating efficiency: cash flow yield, cash flows to sales, and cash flows to assets. These ratios are computed and discussed below for Marriott International for 1996.[4] Data for the computations are obtained from the Financial Highlights for Marriott International on page 710 and below; all dollar amounts used to compute the ratios are stated in millions.

Cash flow yield is the ratio of net cash flows from operating activities to net income, as follows:

$$\text{Cash Flow Yield} = \frac{\text{Net Cash Flows from Operating Activities}}{\text{Net Income}} = \frac{\$602}{\$306} = 2.0 \text{ times}$$

Marriott International provides a good cash flow yield of 2.0 times; that is, operating activities are generating about 100 percent more cash flow than net income. If special items, such as discontinued operations, appear on the income statement and are material, income from continuing operations should be used as the denominator.

Financial Highlights for Marriott International

(In millions of dollars)

	1996	1995	1994
Net Sales	$10,172	$8,961	$8,415
Total Assets	5,075	4,018	3,207

Cash flows to sales is the ratio of net cash flows from operating activities to sales.

$$\text{Cash Flows to Sales} = \frac{\text{Net Cash Flows from Operating Activities}}{\text{Net Sales}} = \frac{\$602}{\$10,172} = 5.9\%$$

Marriott generates cash flows to sales of 5.9 percent. The company generated a positive but relatively small percentage of net cash from sales.

BUSINESS BULLETIN: BUSINESS PRACTICE

New accounting standards issued by the FASB can have a significant impact on financial reporting. Melville Corporation, a shoe manufacturer and retailer, reported a loss of $657.1 million in 1995 as a result of asset impairment charges of $982.4 million due to adoption of SFAS No. 121. These one-time charges reflect a decline in the value of long-term assets and meant a loss of $657.1 million instead of a $325.3 million net income.[5]

Readers of the financial statements need to understand the cash flow consequences of these one-time charges because they are often referred to as paper items that do not affect cash flows. Melville Corporation had positive cash flows from operations of $345.5 million in 1995, because the writedown of long-term assets was not a cash outflow in that year. However, in the year of the purchase, a cash outflow occurred in anticipation of future cash inflows. Now that it has been determined that the assets will not generate the expected cash inflows, the assets' decline in value is appropriately deducted in determining net income because future cash flows will be negatively affected. One purpose of financial reporting is to provide information about future cash flows. The net loss reported by Melville Corporation reflects reduced future cash flows.

Cash flows to assets is the ratio of net cash flows from operating activities to average total assets, as follows:

$$\begin{aligned}\text{Cash Flows to Assets} &= \frac{\text{Net Cash Flows from Operating Activities}}{\text{Average Total Assets}}\\ &= \frac{\$602}{(\$5{,}075 + \$4{,}018)/2}\\ &= 13.2\%\end{aligned}$$

The cash flows to assets is much higher than cash flows to sales because Marriott has an excellent asset turnover ratio (sales ÷ average total assets) of about 2.2 times. Cash flows to sales and cash flows to assets are closely related to the profitability measures profit margin and return on assets. They exceed those measures by the amount of the cash flow yield ratio because cash flow yield is the ratio of net cash flows from operating activities to net income.

Instructional Strategy: Ask students to compute the cash flow measures called for in FRA 1 as homework. Then, in class, form small groups and have them complete the required analysis. Remind students that in evaluating any measure, it's important to look in detail at all components. Discuss the groups' results, and, on the chalkboard, list all causes of the decline in cash flow performance.

Although Marriott's cash flow yield and cash flows to assets are relatively good, its efficiency at generating cash flows from operating activities, as measured by cash flows to sales, could be improved.

Free Cash Flow

It would seem logical for the analysis to move along to investing and financing activities. For example, in 1996 there is a net cash outflow of $549 million in the investing activities section, which could indicate that the company is expanding. However, that figure mixes capital expenditures for plant assets, which reflect management's expansion of operations, with the acquisition of another hotel chain and loans to and repayments from Host Marriott Corporation. Also, cash flows from financing activities were a negative $4 million, but that figure combines financing activities associated with long-term debt and stocks with dividends paid to stockholders. While something can be learned by looking at those broad categories, many analysts find it more informative to go beyond them and focus on a computation called free cash flow.

Free cash flow is the amount of cash that remains after deducting the funds the company must commit to continue operating at its planned level. The commitments must cover current or continuing operations, interest, income taxes, dividends, and net capital expenditures. Cash requirements for current or continuing operations, interest, and income taxes must be paid or the company's creditors and the government can take legal action. Although the payment of dividends is not strictly required, dividends normally represent a commitment to stockholders. If these payments are reduced or eliminated, stockholders will be unhappy and the price of the company's stock will fall. Net capital expenditures represent management's plans for the future.

If free cash flow is positive, it means that the company has met all of its planned cash commitments and has cash available to reduce debt or expand. A negative free cash flow means that the company will have to sell investments, borrow money, or issue stock in the short term to continue at its planned levels. If free cash flow remains negative for several years, a company may not be able to raise cash by selling investments or issuing stock or bonds.

Since cash commitments for current or continuing operations, interest, and income taxes are incorporated in cash flows from current operations, free cash flow for Marriott is computed as follows (in millions):

Enrichment Note: Dividends should be a distribution of the operating success of the firm. If a company has negative net cash flows from operating activities or an amount of net cash flows inadequate to cover payment of dividends, it will have to borrow money, issue stock, or sell assets to pay a dividend.

$$\begin{aligned}\text{Free Cash Flow} &= \text{Net Cash Flows from Operating Activities} - \text{Dividends} \\ &\quad - \text{Purchases of Plant Assets} + \text{Sales of Plant Assets} \\ &= \$602 - \$40 - \$326 + \$65 \\ &= \$301\end{aligned}$$

Purchases and sales of plant assets appear in the investing activities section of the statement of cash flows. Marriott reports both capital expenditures and dispositions of property and equipment. Dividends are found in the financing activities section. Marriott has positive free cash flow of $301 million and can use this cash to partially fund its business acquisitions. Looking at the financing activities section, it may be seen that the company repaid long-term debt of $137 million while issuing new debt of $288 million. Marriott also issued common stock in the amount of $43 million and purchased treasury stock for $158 million. The result is that financing activities, with net cash used of only $4 million, had little overall effect.

Cash flows can vary from year to year, so it is best to look at trends in cash flow measures over several years when analyzing a company's cash flows. For example, Marriott International's 1995 cash flow yield was only 1.5 times ($369 million ÷ $247 million). This is because, although net income rose about 24 percent in 1996, cash

BUSINESS BULLETIN: BUSINESS PRACTICE

Because the statement of cash flows has been around for only a decade, no generally accepted analyses have yet been developed. For example, the term *free cash flow* is commonly used in the business press, but there is no agreement on its definition. An article in *Forbes* defines free cash flow as "cash available after paying out capital expenditures and dividends, *but before taxes and interest*"[6] [emphasis added]. In *The Wall Street Journal,* free cash flow was defined as "operating income less maintenance-level capital expenditures."[7] The definition with which we are most in agreement is the one used in *Business Week,* which is net cash flows from operating activities less net capital expenditures and dividends. This "measures truly discretionary funds—company money that an owner could pocket without harming the business."[8]

flows from operations increased 63 percent. Management sums up in the annual report:

> **Cash from Operations**
> The company's operations generate substantial amounts of cash with only limited reinvestment requirements.[9]

In fact, all the cash flow measures improved from 1995 to 1996 as a result of this increase in cash flows from operations.

The Indirect Method of Preparing the Statement of Cash Flows

OBJECTIVE 5

Use the indirect method to determine cash flows from operating activities

Related Text Assignments:
Q: 9, 10, 11
SE: 4, 5
E: 3, 4, 5
SD: 1

To demonstrate the preparation of the statement of cash flows, we will work through an example step by step. The data for this example are presented in Exhibits 1 and 2. Those two exhibits present Ryan Corporation's balance sheets for December 31, 20x1 and 20x0, and its 20x1 income statement. Since the changes in the balance sheet accounts will be used for analysis, those changes are shown in Exhibit 1. Whether the change in each account is an increase or a decrease is also shown. In addition, Exhibit 2 contains data about transactions that affected noncurrent accounts. Those transactions would be identified by the company's accountants from the records.

There are four steps in preparing the statement of cash flows:

1. Determine cash flows from operating activities.
2. Determine cash flows from investing activities.
3. Determine cash flows from financing activities.
4. Use the information obtained in the first three steps to compile the statement of cash flows.

Determining Cash Flows from Operating Activities

Common Student Confusion: Because so much of financial accounting focuses on accrual accounting, students may have difficulty converting to a cash accounting basis. Explain that net income doesn't necessarily represent the cash generated from operating activities because it is based primarily on revenue earned (not received) and expenses incurred (not paid).

Point to Emphasize: The direct and indirect methods relate only to the operating activities section of the statement of cash flows. They are both acceptable for financial reporting purposes.

Point to Emphasize: The direct and indirect methods will always produce the same net figure. The direct method, however, is more easily understood by the average reader because it results in a more straightforward presentation of operating cash flows than does the indirect method.

The first step in preparing the statement of cash flows is to determine cash flows from operating activities. The income statement indicates a business's success or failure in earning an income from its operating activities, but it does not reflect the inflow and outflow of cash from those activities. The reason is that the income statement is prepared on an accrual basis. Revenues are recorded even though the cash for them may not have been received, and expenses are recorded even though the cash for them may not have been expended. As a result, to arrive at cash flows from operations, the figures on the income statement must be converted from an accrual basis to a cash basis.

There are two methods of converting the income statement from an accrual basis to a cash basis: the direct method and the indirect method. Under the direct method, each item in the income statement is adjusted from the accrual basis to the cash basis. The result is a statement that begins with cash receipts from sales and interest and deducts cash payments for purchases, operating expenses, interest payments, and income taxes to arrive at net cash flows from operating activities. The indirect method on the other hand, does not require the individual adjustment of each item in the income statement, but lists only those adjustments necessary to convert net income to cash flows from operations. Because the indirect method is more common, it will be used to illustrate the conversion of the income statement to a cash basis in the sections that follow. The direct method is presented in a supplemental objective at the end of the chapter.

Exhibit 1. Comparative Balance Sheets with Changes in Accounts Indicated for Ryan Corporation

Ryan Corporation
Comparative Balance Sheets
December 31, 20x1 and 20x0

	20x1	20x0	Change	Increase or Decrease
Assets				
Current Assets				
Cash	$ 46,000	$ 15,000	$ 31,000	Increase
Accounts Receivable (net)	47,000	55,000	(8,000)	Decrease
Inventory	144,000	110,000	34,000	Increase
Prepaid Expenses	1,000	5,000	(4,000)	Decrease
Total Current Assets	$238,000	$185,000	$ 53,000	
Investments Available for Sale	$115,000	$127,000	($ 12,000)	Decrease
Plant Assets				
Plant Assets	$715,000	$505,000	$210,000	Increase
Accumulated Depreciation	(103,000)	(68,000)	(35,000)	Increase
Total Plant Assets	$612,000	$437,000	$175,000	
Total Assets	$965,000	$749,000	$216,000	
Liabilities				
Current Liabilities				
Accounts Payable	$ 50,000	$ 43,000	$ 7,000	Increase
Accrued Liabilities	12,000	9,000	3,000	Increase
Income Taxes Payable	3,000	5,000	(2,000)	Decrease
Total Current Liabilities	$ 65,000	$ 57,000	$ 8,000	
Long-Term Liabilities				
Bonds Payable	295,000	245,000	50,000	Increase
Total Liabilities	$360,000	$302,000	$ 58,000	
Stockholders' Equity				
Common Stock, $5 par value	$276,000	$200,000	$ 76,000	Increase
Paid-in Capital in Excess of Par Value, Common	189,000	115,000	74,000	Increase
Retained Earnings	140,000	132,000	8,000	Increase
Total Stockholders' Equity	$605,000	$447,000	$158,000	
Total Liabilities and Stockholders' Equity	$965,000	$749,000	$216,000	

Point to Emphasize: The indirect method begins with net income and adjusts up or down to produce net cash flows from operating activities.

The indirect method, as illustrated in Figure 2, focuses on items from the income statement that must be adjusted to reconcile net income to net cash flows from operating activities. The items that require attention are those that affect net income but not net cash flows from operating activities, such as depreciation and amortization, gains and losses, and changes in the balances of current asset and current liability accounts. The reconciliation of Ryan Corporation's net income to net cash flows from operating activities is shown in Exhibit 3. Each adjustment is discussed in the following sections.

Exhibit 2. Income Statement and Other Information on Noncurrent Accounts for Ryan Corporation

Ryan Corporation
Income Statement
For the Year Ended December 31, 20x1

Net Sales		$698,000
Cost of Goods Sold		520,000
Gross Margin		$178,000
Operating Expenses (including Depreciation Expense of $37,000)		147,000
Operating Income		$ 31,000
Other Income (Expenses)		
Interest Expense	($23,000)	
Interest Income	6,000	
Gain on Sale of Investments	12,000	
Loss on Sale of Plant Assets	(3,000)	(8,000)
Income Before Income Taxes		$ 23,000
Income Taxes		7,000
Net Income		$ 16,000

Other transactions affecting noncurrent accounts during 20x1:

1. Purchased investments in the amount of $78,000.
2. Sold investments for $102,000 that cost $90,000.
3. Purchased plant assets in the amount of $120,000.
4. Sold plant assets that cost $10,000 with accumulated depreciation of $2,000 for $5,000.
5. Issued $100,000 of bonds at face value in a noncash exchange for plant assets.
6. Repaid $50,000 of bonds at face value at maturity.
7. Issued 15,200 shares of $5 par value common stock for $150,000.
8. Paid cash dividends in the amount of $8,000.

Common Student Error: Students often have the mistaken notion that items such as depreciation expense represent cash inflows since they are added back to net income under the indirect method. These items, however, represent no cash flow and are added back to cancel the deductions taken when arriving at accrual-based net income.

Depreciation Cash payments for plant assets, intangibles, and natural resources occur when the assets are purchased and are reflected as investing activities on the statement of cash flows at that time. When depreciation expense, amortization expense, and depletion expense appear on the income statement, they simply indicate allocations of the costs of the original purchases to the current accounting period; they do not affect net cash flows in the current period. The amount of such

Figure 2
Indirect Method of Determining Net Cash Flows from Operating Activities

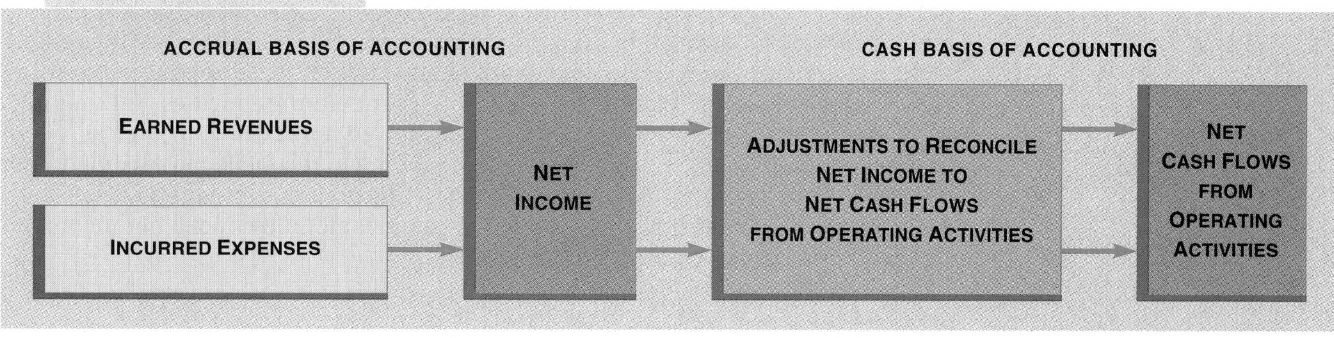

Exhibit 3. Schedule of Cash Flows from Operating Activities: Indirect Method

Ryan Corporation Schedule of Cash Flows from Operating Activities For the Year Ended December 31, 20x1		
Cash Flows from Operating Activities		
Net Income		$16,000
Adjustments to Reconcile Net Income to Net Cash Flows from Operating Activities		
Depreciation	$37,000	
Gain on Sale of Investments	(12,000)	
Loss on Sale of Plant Assets	3,000	
Changes in Current Assets and Current Liabilities		
Decrease in Accounts Receivable	8,000	
Increase in Inventory	(34,000)	
Decrease in Prepaid Expenses	4,000	
Increase in Accounts Payable	7,000	
Increase in Accrued Liabilities	3,000	
Decrease in Income Taxes Payable	(2,000)	14,000
Net Cash Flows from Operating Activities		$30,000

Point to Emphasize: Operating expenses on the income statement include depreciation expense, which does not require a cash outlay.

expenses can usually be found by referring to the income statement or a note to the financial statements.

For Ryan Corporation, the income statement reveals depreciation expense of $37,000, which would have been recorded as follows:

A = L + OE
− −

Depreciation Expense	37,000	
Accumulated Depreciation		37,000
To record annual depreciation on plant assets		

Parenthetical Note: It is possible to earn a profit yet realize a negative cash flow from operating activities. Similarly, it is possible to suffer a net loss yet realize a positive cash flow from operating activities.

The recording of depreciation involved no outlay of cash. Thus, as cash flow was not affected, an adjustment for depreciation is needed to increase net income by the amount of depreciation recorded.

Clarification Note: Gains and losses by themselves do not represent cash flows; they are merely bookkeeping adjustments. For example, when a long-term asset is sold, it is the *proceeds* (cash received), not the gain or loss, that constitute cash flow.

Gains and Losses Gains and losses that appear on the income statement also do not affect cash flows from operating activities and need to be removed from this section of the statement of cash flows. The cash receipts generated from the disposal of the assets that resulted in the gains or losses are shown in the investing section of the statement of cash flows. Therefore, gains and losses are removed from net income to reconcile net income to cash flows from operating activities. For example, on the income statement, Ryan Corporation showed a $12,000 gain on the sale of investments, and this is subtracted from net income to reconcile net income to net cash flows from operating activities. Also, Ryan Corporation showed a $3,000 loss on the sale of plant assets, and this is added to net income to reconcile net income to net cash flows from operating activities.

DECISION POINT

SURVEY OF LARGE COMPANIES

The direct method and the indirect method of determining cash flows from operating activities produce the same results. Although it will accept either method, the FASB recommends that the direct method be used. If the direct method of reporting net cash flows from operating activities is used, reconciliation of net income to net cash flows from operating activities must be provided in a separate schedule (the indirect method). Despite the FASB's recommendation, a survey of large companies showed that an overwhelming majority, 98 percent, chose to use the indirect method. Of six hundred companies, only eleven chose the direct approach.[10] Why did so many choose the indirect approach?

The reasons for choosing the indirect method may vary, but chief financial officers tend to prefer it because it is easier and less expensive to prepare. Moreover, because the FASB requires the reconciliation of net income (accrual) to cash flow (operations) as a supplemental schedule, the indirect method has to be implemented anyway.

A knowledge of the direct method helps managers and the readers of financial statements perceive the underlying causes for the differences between reported net income and cash flows from operations. The indirect method is a practical way of presenting the differences. Both methods have advantages.

Critical Thinking Question: Which method of determining cash flows from operations requires a greater understanding of accounting for the average user of financial statements? Why? **Answer:** The indirect method, because its focus on the differences and plus or minus effects of the reconciling accounts may be difficult for an inexperienced user to interpret.

Changes in Current Assets Decreases in current assets other than cash have positive effects on cash flows, and increases in current assets have negative effects on cash flows. For example, refer to the balance sheets and income statement for Ryan Corporation in Exhibits 1 and 2. Note that net sales in 20x1 were $698,000 and that Accounts Receivable decreased by $8,000. Thus, cash received from sales was $706,000, calculated as follows:

Clarification Note: A decrease in a current asset frees up invested cash, thereby increasing cash flow. An increase in a current asset consumes cash, thereby decreasing cash flow.

$$\$706,000 = \$698,000 + \$8,000$$

Collections were $8,000 more than sales recorded for the year. This relationship may be illustrated as follows:

Point to Emphasize: The difference between accrual sales and cash receipts from customers is the change in accounts receivable.

Accounts Receivable

	Debit		Credit	
	Beg. Bal.	55,000	706,000 →	Cash Receipts from Customers
Sales to Customers →		698,000		
	End. Bal.	**47,000**		

Thus, to reconcile net income to net cash flows from operating activities, the $8,000 decrease in Accounts Receivable is added to net income.

Inventory may be analyzed in the same way. For example, Exhibit 1 shows that Inventory increased by $34,000 from 20x0 to 20x1. This means that Ryan Corporation expended $34,000 more in cash for purchases than was included in cost of goods sold on the income statement. As a result of this expenditure, net income is higher than the net cash flows from operating activities, so $34,000 must be deducted from net income.

Using the same logic, the decrease of $4,000 in Prepaid Expenses is added to net income to reconcile net income to net cash flows from operations.

Clarification Note: An increase in a current liability represents a postponement of a cash payment, which frees up cash and increases cash flow in the current period. A decrease in current liabilities consumes cash, thereby decreasing cash flow.

Changes in Current Liabilities Changes in current liabilities have the opposite effects on cash flows from those of changes in current assets. Increases in current liabilities are added to net income, and decreases in current liabilities are deducted from net income to reconcile net income to net cash flows from operating activities. For example, note from Exhibit 1 that Ryan Corporation had a $7,000 increase in Accounts Payable from 20x0 to 20x1. This means that Ryan Corporation paid $7,000 less to creditors than what appears as purchases on the income statement. This relationship may be visualized as follows:

Accounts Payable

Cash Payments to Suppliers ←	Debit	Credit	
	547,000	Beg. Bal. 43,000	
		554,000*	← Purchases
		End. Bal. 50,000	

*Purchases = Cost of Goods Sold ($520,000) + Increase in Inventory ($34,000).

As a result, $7,000 is added to net income to reconcile net income to net cash flows from operating activities.

Using this same logic, the increase of $3,000 in Accrued Liabilities is added to net income and the decrease of $2,000 in Income Taxes Payable is deducted from net income to reconcile net income to net cash flows from operating activities.

Schedule of Cash Flows from Operating Activities In summary, Exhibit 3 shows that by using the indirect method, net income of $16,000 has been adjusted by reconciling items totaling $14,000 to arrive at net cash flows from operating activities of $30,000. This means that although net income was $16,000, Ryan Corporation actually had net cash flows available from operating activities of $30,000 to use for purchasing assets, reducing debts, or paying dividends.

Summary of Adjustments The effects of items on the income statement that do not affect cash flows may be summarized as follows:

	Add to or Deduct from Net Income
Depreciation Expense	Add
Amortization Expense	Add
Depletion Expense	Add
Losses	Add
Gains	Deduct

The adjustments for increases and decreases in current assets and current liabilities may be summarized as follows.

Teaching Note: Under the indirect method, net income must be adjusted for the effect of certain current assets and current liabilities. A simple mnemonic device is "Add CLI-CAD." That is, you add to net income Current Liability Increases and Current Asset Decreases.

	Add to Net Income	Deduct from Net Income
Current Assets		
Accounts Receivable (net)	Decrease	Increase
Inventory	Decrease	Increase
Prepaid Expenses	Decrease	Increase
Current Liabilities		
Accounts Payable	Increase	Decrease
Accrued Liabilities	Increase	Decrease
Income Taxes Payable	Increase	Decrease

Determining Cash Flows from Investing Activities

OBJECTIVE 6a

Determine cash flows from investing activities

Related Text Assignments:
Q: 12, 13
SE: 6, 7
E: 6, 7, 8

Point to Emphasize: Investing activities involve long-term assets and short- or long-term investments. Both inflows and outflows of cash are contained in this section of the statement of cash flows.

The second step in preparing the statement of cash flows is to determine cash flows from investing activities. Each account involving cash receipts and cash payments from investing activities is examined individually. The objective is to explain the change in each account balance from one year to the next.

Investing activities center on the long-term assets shown on the balance sheet, but they also include transactions affecting short-term investments from the current assets section of the balance sheet and investment gains and losses from the income statement. The balance sheets in Exhibit 1 show that Ryan Corporation has long-term assets of investments and plant assets, but no short-term investments. The income statement in Exhibit 2 shows that Ryan has investment-related items in the form of a gain on the sale of investments and a loss on the sale of plant assets. The schedule at the bottom of Exhibit 2 lists the following five items pertaining to investing activities in 20x1:

1. Purchased investments in the amount of $78,000.
2. Sold investments for $102,000 that cost $90,000.
3. Purchased plant assets in the amount of $120,000.
4. Sold plant assets that cost $10,000 with accumulated depreciation of $2,000 for $5,000.
5. Issued $100,000 of bonds at face value in a noncash exchange for plant assets.

The following paragraphs analyze the accounts related to investing activities to determine their effects on Ryan Corporation's cash flows.

Investments The objective here is to explain the corporation's $12,000 decrease in investments, all of which are classified as available-for-sale securities. This is accomplished by analyzing the increases and decreases in the Investments account to determine the effects on the Cash account. Purchases increase investments, and sales decrease investments. Item **1** in Ryan's list of investing activities shows purchases of $78,000 during 20x1. The transaction is recorded as follows:

A = L + OE
\+
−

Investments	78,000	
Cash		78,000
Purchase of investments		

The entry shows that the effect of this transaction is a $78,000 decrease in cash flows.

Point to Emphasize: The $102,000 price obtained, not the $12,000 gain, constitutes the cash flow here.

Item **2** in the list shows a sale of investments for $102,000 that cost $90,000, which results in a gain of $12,000. This transaction was recorded as follows:

A = L + OE
\+ +
−

Cash	102,000	
Investments		90,000
Gain on Sale of Investments		12,000
Sale of investments for a gain		

The effect of this transaction is a $102,000 increase in cash flows. Note that the gain on sale of investments is included in the $102,000. This is the reason it was excluded earlier in computing cash flows from operations. If it had been included in that section, it would have been counted twice.

The $12,000 decrease in the Investments account during 20x1 has now been explained, as seen in the following T account.

Investments

Beg. Bal.	127,000	Sales	90,000
Purchases	78,000		
End. Bal.	**115,000**		

The cash flow effects from these transactions are shown in the Cash Flows from Investing Activities section on the statement of cash flows as follows:

Point to Emphasize: Both the inflow and the outflow of cash are reported; they are not netted together.

Purchase of Investments	($ 78,000)
Sale of Investments	102,000

Notice that purchases and sales are listed separately as cash outflows and cash inflows to give readers of the statement a complete view of investing activity. Some companies prefer to combine them into a single net amount.

If Ryan Corporation had short-term investments or marketable securities, the analysis of cash flows would be the same.

Plant Assets In the case of plant assets, it is necessary to explain the changes in both the asset account and the related accumulated depreciation account. According to Exhibit 1, Plant Assets increased by $210,000 and Accumulated Depreciation increased by $35,000. Purchases increase plant assets, and sales decrease plant assets. Accumulated depreciation is increased by the amount of depreciation expense and decreased by the removal of the accumulated depreciation associated with plant assets that are sold. Three items listed in Exhibit 2 affect plant assets. Item **3** in the list on the previous page indicates that Ryan Corporation purchased plant assets totaling $120,000 during 20x1, as shown by this entry:

A = L + OE
+
−

Plant Assets	120,000	
Cash		120,000
Purchase of plant assets		

This transaction results in a cash outflow of $120,000.

Item **4** states that Ryan Corporation took plant assets that had cost $10,000 and had accumulated depreciation of $2,000, and sold them for $5,000, which resulted in a loss of $3,000. The entry to record this transaction is as follows:

A = L + OE
+ −
+
−

Cash	5,000	
Accumulated Depreciation	2,000	
Loss on Sale of Plant Assets	3,000	
Plant Assets		10,000
Sale of plant assets at a loss		

Point to Emphasize: Even though a loss was suffered on the sale, a positive cash flow of $5,000 was realized and will be reported in the investing activities section of the statement. When the indirect approach is used, the loss must be eliminated with an "add-back" to net income.

Note that in this transaction the positive cash flow is equal to the amount of cash received, or $5,000. The loss on the sale of plant assets is included here and excluded from the operating activities section by adjusting net income for the amount of the loss. The amount of a loss or gain on the sale of an asset is determined by the amount of cash received and does not represent a cash outflow or inflow.

The disclosure of these two transactions in the investing activities section of the statement of cash flows is as follows:

Purchase of Plant Assets	($120,000)
Sale of Plant Assets	5,000

As with investments, cash outflows and cash inflows are not combined here, but are sometimes combined into a single net amount.

Item **5** on the list of Ryan's investing activities is a noncash exchange that affects two long-term accounts, Plant Assets and Bonds Payable. It was recorded as follows:

A = L + OE			
+ +	Plant Assets	100,000	
	Bonds Payable		100,000
	Issued bonds at face value for plant assets		

Teaching Note: To help students understand the dual nature of this transaction, have them imagine that $100,000 in bonds is issued for cash, which is immediately used to purchase $100,000 in plant assets.

Although this transaction does not involve an inflow or outflow of cash, it is a significant transaction involving both an investing activity (the purchase of plant assets) and a financing activity (the issue of bonds payable). Because one purpose of the statement of cash flows is to show important investing and financing activities, the transaction is listed in a separate schedule, either at the bottom of the statement of cash flows or accompanying the statement, as follows:

Schedule of Noncash Investing and Financing Transactions

Issue of Bonds Payable for Plant Assets	$100,000

Through our analysis of the preceding transactions and the depreciation expense for plant assets of $37,000, all the changes in the plant assets accounts have now been accounted for, as shown in the following T accounts:

Plant Assets

Beg. Bal.	505,000	Sale	10,000
Cash Purchase	120,000		
Noncash Purchase	100,000		
End. Bal.	**715,000**		

Accumulated Depreciation

Sale	2,000	Beg. Bal.	68,000
		Dep. Exp.	37,000
		End. Bal.	**103,000**

If the balance sheet had included specific plant asset accounts, such as Buildings and Equipment and their related accumulated depreciation accounts, or other long-term asset accounts, such as intangibles or natural resources, the analysis would have been the same.

Determining Cash Flows from Financing Activities

OBJECTIVE 6b

Determine cash flows from financing activities

Point to Emphasize: Financing activities involve stockholders' equity accounts and short- and long-term borrowings. Because dividends paid involve retained earnings, they are appropriately included in this category.

The third step in preparing the statement of cash flows is to determine cash flows from financing activities. The procedure is similar to the analysis of investing activities, including treatment of related gains or losses. The only difference is that the accounts to be analyzed are the short-term borrowings, long-term liabilities, and stockholders' equity accounts. Cash dividends from the statement of stockholders' equity must also be considered. Since Ryan Corporation does not have short-term borrowings, only long-term liabilities and stockholders' equity accounts are considered here. The following items from Exhibit 2 pertain to Ryan Corporation's financing activities in 20x1:

5. Issued $100,000 of bonds at face value in a noncash exchange for plant assets.
6. Repaid $50,000 of bonds at face value at maturity.
7. Issued 15,200 shares of $5 par value common stock for $150,000.
8. Paid cash dividends in the amount of $8,000.

Bonds Payable Exhibit 1 shows that Bonds Payable increased by $50,000 in 20x1. This account is affected by items **5** and **6.** Item **5** was analyzed in connection with plant assets. It is reported on the schedule of noncash investing and financing transactions (see Exhibit 4 on page 728), but it must be remembered here in preparing the T account for Bonds Payable. Item **6** results in a cash outflow, which can be seen in the following transaction.

A = L + OE			
− −	Bonds Payable	50,000	
	Cash		50,000
	Repayment of bonds at face value at maturity		

This cash outflow is shown in the financing activities section of the statement of cash flows as follows:

Repayment of Bonds	($50,000)

From these transactions, the change in the Bonds Payable account can be explained as follows:

Bonds Payable

Repayment	50,000	Beg. Bal.	245,000
		Noncash Issue	100,000
		End. Bal.	**295,000**

If Ryan Corporation had notes payable, either short-term or long-term, the analysis would be the same.

Common Stock As with plant assets, related stockholders' equity accounts should be analyzed together. For example, Paid-in Capital in Excess of Par Value, Common should be examined with Common Stock. In 20x1 Ryan Corporation's Common Stock account increased by $76,000 and Paid-in Capital in Excess of Par Value, Common increased by $74,000. Those increases are explained by item **7,** which states that Ryan Corporation issued 15,200 shares of stock for $150,000. The entry to record the cash inflow was as follows:

A = L + OE			
+ + +	Cash	150,000	
	Common Stock		76,000
	Paid-in Capital in Excess of Par Value, Common		74,000
	Issued 15,200 shares of $5 par value common stock		

The cash inflow is shown in the financing activities section of the statement of cash flows as follows:

Issue of Common Stock $150,000

Parenthetical Note: The purchase of treasury stock would also qualify as a financing activity, but would appear as a cash outflow.

The analysis of this transaction is all that is needed to explain the changes in the two accounts during 20x1, as follows:

Common Stock

	Beg. Bal.	200,000
	Issue	76,000
	End. Bal.	**276,000**

Paid-in Capital in Excess of Par Value, Common

	Beg. Bal.	115,000
	Issue	74,000
	End. Bal.	**189,000**

Retained Earnings At this point in the analysis, several items that affect retained earnings have already been dealt with. For instance, in the case of Ryan Corporation, net income was used as part of the analysis of cash flows from operating activities. The only other item affecting the retained earnings of Ryan

Corporation is the payment of $8,000 in cash dividends (item **8** on the list on page 725), as reflected by the following transaction.

A = L + OE
− −

Retained Earnings	8,000	
Cash		8,000
Cash dividends for 20x1		

Ryan Corporation would have declared the dividend before paying it and therefore would have debited the Cash Dividends Declared account instead of Retained Earnings, but after paying the dividend and closing the Cash Dividends Declared account to Retained Earnings, the effect is as shown. Cash dividends are displayed in the financing activities section of the statement of cash flows:

Point to Emphasize: It is dividends paid, not dividends declared, that appear in the statement of cash flows.

Dividends Paid	($8,000)

The following T account shows the change in the Retained Earnings account.

Retained Earnings

Dividends	8,000	Beg. Bal.	132,000
		Net Income	16,000
		End. Bal.	**140,000**

Compiling the Statement of Cash Flows

OBJECTIVE 7

Use the indirect method to prepare a statement of cash flows

Related Text Assignments:
SE: 8
E: 9, 10
P: 2, 3, 4, 8, 9
SD: 4

At this point in the analysis, all income statement items have been analyzed, all balance sheet changes have been explained, and all additional information has been taken into account. The resulting information may now be assembled into a statement of cash flows for Ryan Corporation, as presented in Exhibit 4. The Schedule of Noncash Investing and Financing Transactions is presented at the bottom of the statement.

Preparing the Work Sheet

SUPPLEMENTAL OBJECTIVE 8

Prepare a work sheet for the statement of cash flows

Related Text Assignments:
Q: 14, 15
E: 10
P: 4, 9

Previous sections illustrated the preparation of the statement of cash flows for Ryan Corporation, a relatively simple company. To assist in preparing the statement of cash flows for more complex companies, accountants have developed a work sheet approach. The work sheet approach employs a special format that allows for the systematic analysis of all the changes in the balance sheet accounts to arrive at the statement of cash flows. In this section, the work sheet approach is demonstrated using the statement of cash flows for Ryan Corporation. The work sheet approach uses the indirect method of determining cash flows from operating activities because of its basis in changes in the balance sheet accounts.

Procedures in Preparing the Work Sheet

Point to Emphasize: A statement of cash flows work sheet is especially helpful in complex business situations. The work sheet takes the indirect approach.

The work sheet for Ryan Corporation is presented in Exhibit 5. The work sheet has four columns, labeled as follows:

Column A: Description

Column B: Account balances for the end of the prior year (20x0)

Column C: Analysis of transactions for the current year

Column D: Account balances for the end of the current year (20x1)

Teaching Note: Have your students analyze a completed statement of cash flows, such as the one here, and list the five or six activities that had the greatest effect (positive or negative) on cash flows. Then have them summarize, in a short paragraph, management's generation and application of cash during the period.

Enrichment Note: Published financial statements include three years of cash flow information, not just the single year shown in Exhibit 4.

Exhibit 4. Statement of Cash Flows: Indirect Method

Ryan Corporation
Statement of Cash Flows
For the Year Ended December 31, 20x1

Cash Flows from Operating Activities		
Net Income		$ 16,000
Adjustments to Reconcile Net Income to Net Cash Flows from Operating Activities		
Depreciation	$ 37,000	
Gain on Sale of Investments	(12,000)	
Loss on Sale of Plant Assets	3,000	
Changes in Current Assets and Current Liabilities		
Decrease in Accounts Receivable	8,000	
Increase in Inventory	(34,000)	
Decrease in Prepaid Expenses	4,000	
Increase in Accounts Payable	7,000	
Increase in Accrued Liabilities	3,000	
Decrease in Income Taxes Payable	(2,000)	14,000
Net Cash Flows from Operating Activities		$ 30,000
Cash Flows from Investing Activities		
Purchase of Investments	($ 78,000)	
Sale of Investments	102,000	
Purchase of Plant Assets	(120,000)	
Sale of Plant Assets	5,000	
Net Cash Flows from Investing Activities		(91,000)
Cash Flows from Financing Activities		
Repayment of Bonds	($ 50,000)	
Issue of Common Stock	150,000	
Dividends Paid	(8,000)	
Net Cash Flows from Financing Activities		92,000
Net Increase (Decrease) in Cash		$ 31,000
Cash at Beginning of Year		15,000
Cash at End of Year		$ 46,000
Schedule of Noncash Investing and Financing Transactions		
Issue of Bonds Payable for Plant Assets		$100,000

Five steps are followed in preparing the work sheet. As you read each one, refer to Exhibit 5.

1. Enter the account names from the balance sheets (Exhibit 1) in column A. Note that all accounts with debit balances are listed first, followed by all accounts with credit balances.
2. Enter the account balances for 20x0 in column B and the account balances for 20x1 in column D. In each column, total the debits and the credits. The total debits should equal the total credits in each column. (This is a check of whether all accounts were correctly transferred from the balance sheets.)

Exhibit 5. Work Sheet for the Statement of Cash Flows

Ryan Corporation
Work Sheet for Statement of Cash Flows
For the Year Ended December 31, 20x1

(A) Description	(B) Account Balances 12/31/x0	(C) Analysis of Transactions: Debit	Analysis of Transactions: Credit	(D) Account Balances 12/31/x1
Debits				
Cash	15,000	(x) **31,000**		46,000
Accounts Receivable (net)	55,000		(b) 8,000	47,000
Inventory	110,000	(c) 34,000		144,000
Prepaid Expenses	5,000		(d) 4,000	1,000
Investments Available for Sale	127,000	(h) 78,000	(i) 90,000	115,000
Plant Assets	505,000	(j) 120,000	(k) 10,000	715,000
		(l) 100,000		
Total Debits	817,000			1,068,000
Credits				
Accumulated Depreciation	68,000	(k) 2,000	(m) 37,000	103,000
Accounts Payable	43,000		(e) 7,000	50,000
Accrued Liabilities	9,000		(f) 3,000	12,000
Income Taxes Payable	5,000	(g) 2,000		3,000
Bonds Payable	245,000	(n) 50,000	(l) 100,000	295,000
Common Stock	200,000		(o) 76,000	276,000
Paid-in Capital	115,000		(o) 74,000	189,000
Retained Earnings	132,000	(p) 8,000	(a) 16,000	140,000
Total Credits	817,000	425,000	425,000	1,068,000
Cash Flows from Operating Activities				
Net Income		(a) 16,000		
Decrease in Accounts Receivable		(b) 8,000		
Increase in Inventory			(c) 34,000	
Decrease in Prepaid Expenses		(d) 4,000		
Increase in Accounts Payable		(e) 7,000		
Increase in Accrued Liabilities		(f) 3,000		
Decrease in Income Taxes Payable			(g) 2,000	
Gain on Sale of Investments			(i) 12,000	
Loss on Sale of Plant Assets		(k) 3,000		
Depreciation Expense		(m) 37,000		
Cash Flows from Investing Activities				
Purchase of Investments			(h) 78,000	
Sale of Investments		(i) 102,000		
Purchase of Plant Assets			(j) 120,000	
Sale of Plant Assets		(k) 5,000		
Cash Flows from Financing Activities				
Repayment of Bonds			(n) 50,000	
Issue of Common Stock		(o) 150,000		
Dividends Paid			(p) 8,000	
		335,000	304,000	
Net Increase in Cash			(x) **31,000**	
		335,000	335,000	

See related **Parenthetical Note** on the next page.

3. Below the data entered in step **2,** insert the headings Cash Flows from Operating Activities, Cash Flows from Investing Activities, and Cash Flows from Financing Activities, leaving several lines of space between each one. As you do the analysis in step **4,** write the results in the appropriate categories.
4. Analyze the changes in each balance sheet account, using information from both the income statement (see Exhibit 2) and other transactions affecting noncurrent accounts during 20x1. (The procedures for this analysis are presented in the next section.) Enter the results in the debit and credit columns. Identify each item with a letter. On the first line, identify the change in cash with an (x). In a complex situation, these letters will refer to a list of explanations on another working paper.
5. When all the changes in the balance sheet accounts have been explained, add the debit and credit columns in both the top and the bottom portions of column C. The debit and credit columns in the top portion should equal each other. They should *not* be equal in the bottom portion. If no errors have been made, the difference between columns in the bottom portion should equal the increase or decrease in the Cash account, identified with an (x) on the first line of the work sheet. Add this difference to the lesser of the two columns, and identify it as either an increase or a decrease in cash. Label the change with an (x) and compare it with the change in Cash on the first line of the work sheet, also labeled (x). The amounts should be equal, as they are in Exhibit 5, where the net increase in cash is $31,000. Also, the new totals from the debit and credit columns should be equal.

Parenthetical Note: The work sheet would handle a net decrease in cash in the opposite way—as a credit at the top of the work sheet and as a debit to balance at the bottom.

When the work sheet is complete, the statement of cash flows may be prepared using the information in the lower half of the work sheet.

Analyzing the Changes in Balance Sheet Accounts

The most important step in preparing the work sheet is the analysis of the changes in the balance sheet accounts (step **4**). Although a number of transactions and reclassifications must be analyzed and recorded, the overall procedure is systematic and not overly complicated. It is as follows:

1. Record net income.
2. Account for changes in current assets and current liabilities.
3. Use the information about other transactions to account for changes in noncurrent accounts.
4. Reclassify any other income and expense items not already dealt with.

Parenthetical Note for Exhibit 5: For every change in a balance sheet account (except Cash), a corresponding activity is identified. Transaction (l) would appear as a noncash investing and financing transaction in the statement of cash flows. Also, note the way that Cash is handled: primarily as a balancing figure.

In the following explanations, the identification letters refer to the corresponding transactions and reclassifications in the work sheet.

a. *Net Income* Net income results in an increase in Retained Earnings. Under the indirect method, it is the starting point for determining cash flows from operating activities. Under this method, additions and deductions are made to net income to arrive at cash flows from operating activities. Work sheet entry **a** is as follows:

Point to Emphasize: Retained Earnings is analyzed on the work sheet through net income and dividends paid.

(a) Cash Flows from Operating Activities: Net Income	16,000	
Retained Earnings		16,000

b–g. *Changes in Current Assets and Current Liabilities* Entries **b** to **g** record the effects on cash flows of the changes in current assets and current liabilities. In each case, there is a debit or credit to the current asset or current liability to account for the change from year to year and a corresponding debit or credit in the operating activities section of the work sheet. For example, work sheet entry **b** records the decrease in Accounts Receivable as a credit (decrease) to Accounts Receivable and as a debit in the operating activities section because the decrease has a positive effect on cash flows, as follows:

(b) Cash Flows from Operating Activities:		
Decrease in Accounts Receivable	8,000	
Accounts Receivable		8,000

Work sheet entries **c–g** reflect the effects on cash flows from operating activities of the changes in the other current assets and current liabilities. As you study these entries, note how the effects of each entry on cash flows are automatically determined by debits or credits reflecting changes in the balance sheet accounts.

(c) Inventory	34,000	
Cash Flows from Operating Activities:		
Increase in Inventory		34,000
(d) Cash Flows from Operating Activities:		
Decrease in Prepaid Expenses	4,000	
Prepaid Expenses		4,000
(e) Cash Flows from Operating Activities:		
Increase in Accounts Payable	7,000	
Accounts Payable		7,000
(f) Cash Flows from Operating Activities:		
Increase in Accrued Liabilities	3,000	
Accrued Liabilities		3,000
(g) Income Taxes Payable	2,000	
Cash Flows from Operating Activities:		
Decrease in Income Taxes Payable		2,000

h–i. *Investments* Among the other transactions affecting noncurrent accounts during 20x1 (see Exhibit 2), two pertain to investments. One is the purchase for $78,000, and the other is the sale at $102,000. The purchase is recorded on the work sheet as a cash flow in the investing activities section, as follows:

(h) Investments	78,000	
Cash Flows from Investing Activities:		
Purchase of Investments		78,000

Note that instead of a credit to Cash, a credit entry with the appropriate designation is made in the appropriate section in the lower half of the work sheet. The sale transaction is more complicated because it involves a gain that appears on the income statement and is included in net income. The work sheet entry shows this gain as follows:

(i) Cash Flows from Investing Activities:		
Sale of Investments	102,000	
Investments		90,000
Cash Flows from Operating Activities:		
Gain on Sale of Investments		12,000

Clarification Note: Even though the gain on sale in (i) and the loss on sale in (k) are identified with the operating activities section, they do not represent cash flows.

This entry records the cash inflow in the investing activities section, accounts for the remaining difference in the Investments account, and removes the gain on sale of investments from net income.

j–m. *Plant Assets and Accumulated Depreciation* The four transactions that affect plant assets and the related accumulated depreciation are the purchase of plant assets, the sale of plant assets at a loss, the noncash exchange of bonds for plant assets, and the depreciation expense for the year. Because these transactions may appear complicated, it is important to work through them systematically when preparing the work sheet. First, the purchase of plant assets for $120,000 is entered (entry **j**) in the same way the purchase of investments was entered in entry **h:**

(j) Plant Assets	120,000	
Cash Flows from Investing Activities:		
Purchase of Plant Assets		120,000

Second, the sale of plant assets is similar to the sale of investments, except that a loss is involved, as follows:

(k) Cash Flows from Investing Activities:		
Sale of Plant Assets	5,000	
Cash Flows from Operating Activities:		
Loss on Sale of Plant Assets	3,000	
Accumulated Depreciation	2,000	
Plant Assets		10,000

The cash inflow from this transaction is $5,000. The rest of the entry is necessary in order to add the loss back into net income in the operating activities section of the statement of cash flows (since it was deducted to arrive at net income and no cash outflow resulted) and to record the effects on plant assets and accumulated depreciation.

The third transaction (entry **l**) is the noncash issue of bonds for the purchase of plant assets, as follows:

(l) Plant Assets	100,000	
Bonds Payable		100,000

Point to Emphasize: A noncash investing and financing transaction, such as the one here, is entered on the work sheet as a debit and credit to balance sheet accounts. No cash flow activity is identified.

Note that this transaction does not affect Cash. Still, it needs to be recorded because the objective is to account for all changes in the balance sheet accounts. It is listed at the end of the statement of cash flows (Exhibit 4) in the schedule of noncash investing and financing transactions.

At this point, the increase of $210,000 ($715,000 − $505,000) in plant assets has been explained by the two purchases less the sale ($120,000 + $100,000 − $10,000 = $210,000), but the change in Accumulated Depreciation has not been completely explained. The depreciation expense for the year needs to be entered, as follows:

(m) Cash Flows from Operating Activities:		
Depreciation Expense	37,000	
Accumulated Depreciation		37,000

Point to Emphasize: It is depreciation expense, not accumulated depreciation, that appears in the statement of cash flows and is identified here with the operating activities section.

The debit is to the operating activities section of the work sheet because, as explained earlier in the chapter, no current cash outflow is required for depreciation expense. The effect of this debit is to add the amount for depreciation expense back into net income. The $35,000 increase in Accumulated Depreciation has now been explained by the sale transaction and the depreciation expense (−$2,000 + $37,000 = $35,000).

n. *Bonds Payable* Part of the change in Bonds Payable was explained in entry **l** when a noncash transaction, a $100,000 issue of bonds in exchange for plant assets, was entered. All that remains to be entered is the repayment, as follows:

(n) Bonds Payable	50,000	
Cash Flows from Financing Activities:		
Repayment of Bonds		50,000

o. *Common Stock and Paid-in Capital in Excess of Par Value, Common* One transaction affects both these accounts. It is an issue of 15,200 shares of $5 par value common stock for a total of $150,000. The work sheet entry follows.

(o) Cash Flows from Financing Activities:		
Issue of Common Stock	150,000	
Common Stock		76,000
Paid-in Capital in Excess of Par Value, Common		74,000

p. *Retained Earnings* Part of the change in Retained Earnings was recognized when net income was entered (entry **a**). The only remaining effect to be recognized is the $8,000 in cash dividends paid during the year, as follows:

(p) Retained Earnings	8,000	
Cash Flows from Financing Activities:		
Dividends Paid		8,000

Parenthetical Note: Cash is identified with the letter x because its entry on the work sheet is different in nature from all the others. That is, the change in cash equals the net effect on cash of entries **a** through **p.** It therefore acts as a balancing figure.

x. *Cash* The final step is to total the debit and credit columns in the top and bottom portions of the work sheet and then to enter the net change in cash at the bottom of the work sheet. The columns in the upper half equal $425,000. In the lower half, the debit column totals $335,000 and the credit column totals $304,000. The credit difference of $31,000 (entry **x**) equals the debit change in cash on the first line of the work sheet.

The Direct Method of Preparing the Statement of Cash Flows

SUPPLEMENTAL OBJECTIVE 9

Use the direct method to determine cash flows from operating activities and prepare a statement of cash flows

Related Text Assignments:
Q: 16
SE: 9, 10
E: 11, 12
P: 5, 6

To this point in the chapter, the indirect method of preparing the statement of cash flows has been used. In this section, the direct method is presented. First, the use of the direct method to determine net cash flows from operating activities is covered. Then the statement of cash flows under the direct method is illustrated.

Determining Cash Flows from Operating Activities

The principal difference between the indirect and the direct methods appears in the cash flows from operating activities section of the statement of cash flows. As you have seen, the indirect method starts with net income from the income statement and converts it to net cash flows from operating activities by adding or subtracting items that do not affect net cash flows. The direct method takes a different approach. It converts each item on the income statement to its cash equivalent, as illustrated in Figure 3. For instance, sales are converted to cash receipts from sales, and purchases are converted to cash payments for purchases. Exhibit 6 shows the schedule of cash flows from operating activities under the direct method for Ryan Corporation. The conversion of the components of Ryan Corporation's income statement to those figures is explained in the following paragraphs.

Figure 3
Direct Method of Determining Net Cash Flows from Operating Activities

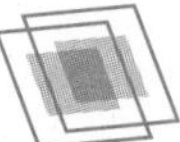

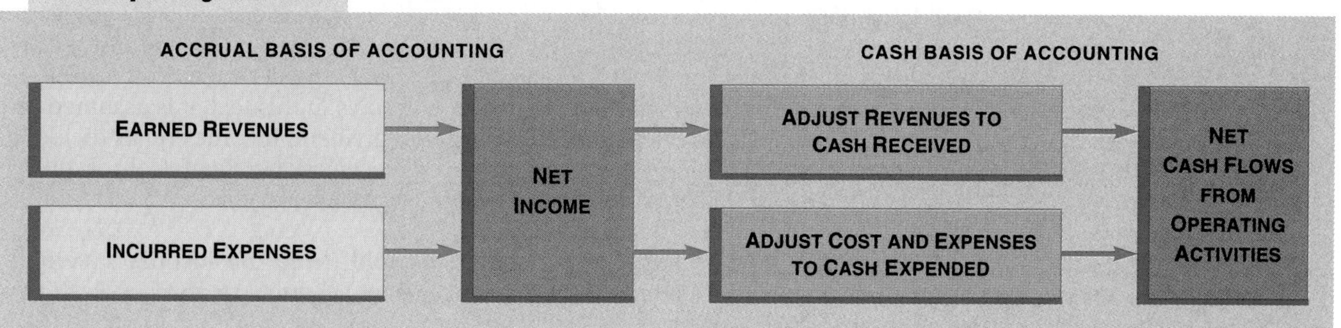

Exhibit 6. Schedule of Cash Flows from Operating Activities: Direct Method

Ryan Corporation Schedule of Cash Flows from Operating Activities For the Year Ended December 31, 20x1		
Cash Flows from Operating Activities		
Cash Receipts from		
Sales	$706,000	
Interest Received	6,000	$712,000
Cash Payments for		
Purchases	$547,000	
Operating Expenses	103,000	
Interest	23,000	
Income Taxes	9,000	682,000
Net Cash Flows from Operating Activities		$ 30,000

Cash Receipts from Sales Sales result in a positive cash flow for a company. Cash sales are direct cash inflows. Credit sales are not, because they are originally recorded as accounts receivable. When they are collected, they become cash inflows. You cannot, however, assume that credit sales are automatically inflows of cash, because the collections of accounts receivable in any one accounting period are not likely to equal credit sales. Receivables may be uncollectible, sales from a prior period may be collected in the current period, or sales from the current period may be collected in the next period. For example, if accounts receivable increase from one accounting period to the next, cash receipts from sales will not be as great as sales. On the other hand, if accounts receivable decrease from one accounting period to the next, cash receipts from sales will exceed sales.

The relationships among sales, changes in accounts receivable, and cash receipts from sales are reflected in the following formula:

Parenthetical Note: A decrease in accounts receivable during the period occurs when more has been collected than realized in accrual-based sales. The decrease, therefore, must be added to (or an increase subtracted from) sales to produce cash receipts from sales.

$$\text{Cash Receipts from Sales} = \text{Sales} \begin{cases} + \text{ Decrease in Accounts Receivable} \\ \text{or} \\ - \text{ Increase in Accounts Receivable} \end{cases}$$

Refer to the balance sheets and income statement for Ryan Corporation in Exhibits 1 and 2. Note that sales were $698,000 in 20x1 and that accounts receivable decreased by $8,000. Thus, cash received from sales is $706,000:

$$\$706,000 = \$698,000 + \$8,000$$

Collections were $8,000 more than sales recorded for the year.

Cash Receipts from Interest and Dividends Although interest and dividends received are most closely associated with investment activity and are often called investment income, the FASB has decided to classify the cash received from these items as operating activities. To simplify the examples in this text, it is assumed that interest income equals interest received and that dividend income equals dividends received. Thus, based on Exhibit 2, interest received by Ryan Corporation is assumed to equal $6,000, which is the amount of interest income.

Cash Payments for Purchases Cost of goods sold (from the income statement) must be adjusted for changes in two balance sheet accounts to arrive at cash payments for purchases. First, cost of goods sold must be adjusted for changes in inventory to arrive at net purchases. Then, net purchases must be adjusted for the change in accounts payable to arrive at cash payments for purchases. If inventory has increased from one accounting period to another, net purchases will be greater than cost of goods sold because net purchases during the period have exceeded the dollar amount of the items sold during the period. If inventory has decreased, net purchases will be less than cost of goods sold. Conversely, if accounts payable have increased, cash payments for purchases will be less than net purchases; if accounts payable have decreased, cash payments for purchases will be greater than net purchases.

These relationships may be stated in equation form as follows:

Parenthetical Note: A decrease in accounts payable during the period occurs when more has been paid for goods than has been purchased. The decrease, therefore, must be added to (or an increase subtracted from) cost of goods sold, along with an adjustment for the change in inventory, to produce cash payments for purchases.

$$\text{Cash Payments for Purchases} = \text{Cost of Goods Sold} \left\{ \begin{array}{l} + \text{ Increase in Inventory} \\ \text{or} \\ - \text{ Decrease in Inventory} \end{array} \right. \left\{ \begin{array}{l} + \text{ Decrease in Accounts Payable} \\ \text{or} \\ - \text{ Increase in Accounts Payable} \end{array} \right.$$

From Exhibits 1 and 2, cost of goods sold is $520,000, inventory increased by $34,000, and accounts payable increased by $7,000. Thus, cash payments for purchases is $547,000, as the following calculation shows:

$$\$547{,}000 = \$520{,}000 + 34{,}000 - \$7{,}000$$

In this example, Ryan Corporation purchased $34,000 more inventory than it sold and paid out $7,000 less in cash than it made in purchases. The net result is that cash payments for purchases exceeded cost of goods sold by $27,000 ($547,000 – $520,000).

Cash Payments for Operating Expenses Just as cost of goods sold does not represent the amount of cash paid for purchases during an accounting period, operating expenses do not match the amount of cash paid to employees, suppliers, and others for goods and services. Three adjustments must be made to operating expenses to arrive at the cash outflows. The first adjustment is for changes in prepaid expenses, such as prepaid insurance or prepaid rent. If prepaid assets increase during the accounting period, more cash will have been paid out than appears on the income statement as expenses. If prepaid assets decrease, the expenses shown on the income statement will exceed the cash spent.

The second adjustment is for changes in liabilities resulting from accrued expenses, such as wages payable and payroll taxes payable. If accrued liabilities increase during the accounting period, operating expenses on the income statement will exceed the cash spent. And if accrued liabilities decrease, operating expenses will fall short of cash spent.

Discussion Question: Why must depreciation, amortization, and depletion be subtracted from operating expenses when computing cash payments for operating expenses? **Answer:** The three expenses are legitimate accrual-based expenses, but they do not represent cash disbursements; they are merely *paper* allocations of cost. They must be eliminated in converting from an accrual to a cash basis.

The third adjustment is made because certain expenses do not require a current outlay of cash; those expenses must be subtracted from operating expenses to arrive at cash payments for operating expenses. The most common expenses in this category are depreciation expense, amortization expense, and depletion expense. For example, Ryan Corporation recorded 20x1 depreciation expense of $37,000. No cash payment was made in this transaction. Therefore, to the extent that operating expenses include depreciation and similar items, an adjustment is needed to reduce operating expenses to the amount of cash expended.

The three adjustments to operating expenses are summarized in the equations that follow.

$$\text{Cash Payments for Operating Expenses} = \text{Operating Expenses} \left\{ \begin{array}{l} + \text{ Increase in Prepaid Expenses} \\ \text{or} \\ - \text{ Decrease in Prepaid Expenses} \end{array} \right. \left\{ \begin{array}{l} + \text{ Decrease in Accrued Liabilities} \\ \text{or} \\ - \text{ Increase in Accrued Liabilities} \end{array} \right. \left\{ \begin{array}{l} - \text{ Depreciation and Other Noncash Expenses} \end{array} \right.$$

According to Exhibits 1 and 2, Ryan's operating expenses (including depreciation of $37,000) were $147,000, prepaid expenses decreased by $4,000, and accrued liabilities increased by $3,000. As a result, Ryan Corporation's cash payments for operating expenses are $103,000, computed as follows:

$$\$103{,}000 = \$147{,}000 - \$4{,}000 - \$3{,}000 - \$37{,}000$$

If there are prepaid expenses and accrued liabilities that are *not* related to specific operating expenses, they are not included in these computations. One example is income taxes payable, which is the accrued liability related to income taxes expense. The cash payment for income taxes will be discussed shortly.

Cash Payments for Interest The FASB classifies cash payments for interest as operating activities, although some authorities argue that they should be considered financing activities because of their association with loans incurred to finance the business. The FASB feels that interest expense is a cost of operating a business, and this is the position followed in this text. Also, for the sake of simplicity, all examples in this text assume that interest payments are equal to interest expense on the income statement. Thus, based on Exhibit 2, Ryan Corporation's interest payments are assumed to be $23,000 in 20x1.

Cash Payments for Income Taxes The amount of income taxes expense that appears on the income statement rarely equals the amount of income taxes actually paid during the year. To determine cash payments for income taxes, income taxes (from the income statement) is adjusted by the change in Income Taxes Payable. If Income Taxes Payable increased during the accounting period, cash payments for taxes will be less than the expense shown on the income statement. If Income Taxes Payable decreased, cash payments for taxes will exceed income taxes on the income statement. In other words, the following equation is applicable:

Parenthetical Note: A decrease in Income Taxes Payable during the year occurs when more has been paid than recorded as accrual-based Income Taxes Expense. The decrease therefore must be added to (or an increase subtracted from) Income Taxes Expense to obtain cash payments for income taxes.

$$\text{Cash Payments for Income Taxes} = \text{Income Taxes} \begin{cases} + \text{ Decrease in Income Taxes Payable} \\ \text{or} \\ - \text{ Increase in Income Taxes Payable} \end{cases}$$

In 20x1, Ryan Corporation showed income taxes of $7,000 on its income statement and a decrease of $2,000 in Income Taxes Payable on its balance sheets (see Exhibits 1 and 2). As a result, cash payments for income taxes during 20x1 were $9,000, calculated as follows:

$$\$9{,}000 = \$7{,}000 + \$2{,}000$$

Compiling the Statement of Cash Flows

The Ryan Corporation's statement of cash flows under the direct method is presented in Exhibit 7. The only differences between that statement of cash flows and the one based on the indirect method shown in Exhibit 4 occur in the first and last sections. The middle sections, which present cash flows from investing activities and financing activities, net increases or decreases in cash, and the schedule of noncash investing and financing activities, are the same under both methods.

The first section of the statement in Exhibit 7 shows the net cash flows from operating activities on a direct basis, as presented in Exhibit 6. The last section is the same as the cash flows from operating activities section of the statement of cash flows under the indirect method (see Exhibit 4). The FASB believes that when the direct method is used, a schedule must be provided that reconciles net income to net cash flows from operating activities. Thus, the statement of cash flows under the direct method includes a section that accommodates the main difference between it and the indirect method.

Exhibit 7. Statement of Cash Flows: Direct Method

Ryan Corporation
Statement of Cash Flows
For the Year Ended December 31, 20x1

Cash Flows from Operating Activities		
Cash Receipts from		
Sales	$706,000	
Interest Received	6,000	$712,000
Cash Payments for		
Purchases	$547,000	
Operating Expenses	103,000	
Interest	23,000	
Income Taxes	9,000	682,000
Net Cash Flows from Operating Activities		$ 30,000
Cash Flows from Investing Activities		
Purchase of Investments	($ 78,000)	
Sale of Investments	102,000	
Purchase of Plant Assets	(120,000)	
Sale of Plant Assets	5,000	
Net Cash Flows from Investing Activities		(91,000)
Cash Flows from Financing Activities		
Repayment of Bonds	($ 50,000)	
Issue of Common Stock	150,000	
Dividends Paid	(8,000)	
Net Cash Flows from Financing Activities		92,000
Net Increase (Decrease) in Cash		$ 31,000
Cash at Beginning of Year		15,000
Cash at End of Year		$ 46,000

Schedule of Noncash Investing and Financing Transactions

Issue of Bonds Payable for Plant Assets		$100,000

Reconciliation of Net Income to Net Cash Flows from Operating Activities

Net Income		$ 16,000
Adjustments to Reconcile Net Income to Net Cash Flows from Operating Activities		
Depreciation	$ 37,000	
Gain on Sale of Investments	(12,000)	
Loss on Sale of Plant Assets	3,000	
Changes in Current Assets and Current Liabilities		
Decrease in Accounts Receivable	8,000	
Increase in Inventory	(34,000)	
Decrease in Prepaid Expenses	4,000	
Increase in Accounts Payable	7,000	
Increase in Accrued Liabilities	3,000	
Decrease in Income Taxes Payable	(2,000)	14,000
Net Cash Flows from Operating Activities		$ 30,000

Point to Emphasize: When the direct method is used, a supplemental reconciliation of net income to net cash flows from operating activities must also be presented.

Chapter Review

REVIEW OF LEARNING OBJECTIVES

1. **Describe the statement of cash flows, and define *cash and cash equivalents*.** The statement of cash flows explains the changes in cash and cash equivalents from one accounting period to the next by showing cash inflows and cash outflows from the operating, investing, and financing activities of a company for an accounting period. For purposes of preparing the statement of cash flows, *cash* is defined to include cash and cash equivalents. *Cash equivalents* are short-term (ninety days or less), highly liquid investments, including money market accounts, commercial paper, and U.S. Treasury bills.

2. **State the principal purposes and uses of the statement of cash flows.** The primary purpose of the statement of cash flows is to provide information about a company's cash receipts and cash payments during an accounting period. Its secondary purpose is to provide information about a company's operating, investing, and financing activities. The statement is useful to management as well as to investors and creditors in assessing the liquidity of a business, including its ability to generate future cash flows and to pay debts and dividends.

3. **Identify the principal components of the classifications of cash flows, and state the significance of noncash investing and financing transactions.** Cash flows may be classified as stemming from (1) operating activities, which include the cash effects of transactions and other events that enter into the determination of net income; (2) investing activities, which include the acquiring and selling of long- and short-term marketable securities and property, plant, and equipment, and the making and collecting of loans, excluding interest; or (3) financing activities, which include the obtaining and returning or repaying of resources, excluding interest, to owners and creditors. Noncash investing and financing transactions are also important because they are exchanges of assets and/or liabilities that are of interest to investors and creditors when evaluating the financing and investing activities of a business.

4. **Analyze the statement of cash flows.** In analyzing a company's statement of cash flows, analysts tend to focus on cash-generating efficiency and free cash flow. Cash-generating efficiency is a company's ability to generate cash from its current or continuing operations. Three ratios used in measuring cash-generating efficiency are cash flow yield, cash flows to sales, and cash flows to assets. Free cash flow is the cash that remains after deducting funds a company must commit to continue operating at its planned level. Such commitments must cover current or continuing operations, interest, income taxes, dividends, and net capital expenditures.

5. **Use the indirect method to determine cash flows from operating activities.** Under the indirect method, net income is adjusted for all noncash effects and for items that need to be converted from an accrual to a cash basis to arrive at a cash flow basis, as follows:

Cash Flows from Operating Activities		
Net Income		XXX
Adjustments to Reconcile Net Income to Net Cash Flows from Operating Activities		
(List of individual items)	XXX	XXX
Net Cash Flows from Operating Activities		XXX

6. **Determine cash flows from (a) investing activities and (b) financing activities.** Cash flows from investing activities are determined by identifying the cash flow effects of the transactions that affect each account relevant to investing activities. Such accounts include all long-term assets and short-term marketable securities. The same procedure is followed for financing activities, except that the accounts involved are short-term borrowings, long-term liabilities, and stockholders' equity. The effects of

gains and losses reported on the income statement must also be considered. After the changes in the balance sheet accounts from one accounting period to the next have been explained, all the cash flow effects should have been identified.

7. **Use the indirect method to prepare a statement of cash flows.** The statement of cash flows lists cash flows from operating activities, investing activities, and financing activities, in that order. The sections on investing and financing activities are prepared by examining individual accounts involving cash receipts and cash payments from investing and financing activities to explain year-to-year changes in the account balances. Significant noncash transactions are included in a schedule of noncash investing and financing transactions that accompanies the statement of cash flows.

Supplemental Objectives

8. **Prepare a work sheet for the statement of cash flows.** A work sheet is useful in preparing the statement of cash flows for complex companies. The basic procedures are to analyze the changes in the balance sheet accounts for their effects on cash flows (in the top portion of the work sheet) and to classify those effects according to the format of the statement of cash flows (in the lower portion of the work sheet). When all changes in the balance sheet accounts have been explained and entered on the work sheet, the change in the Cash account will also be explained, and all necessary information will be available to prepare the statement of cash flows. The work sheet approach lends itself to the indirect method of preparing the statement of cash flows.

9. **Use the direct method to determine cash flows from operating activities and prepare a statement of cash flows.** The principal difference between a statement of cash flows prepared under the direct method and one prepared under the indirect method appears in the cash flows from operating activities section. Instead of beginning with net income and making additions and subtractions, as is done with the indirect method, the direct method converts each item on the income statement to its cash equivalent by adjusting for changes in the related current asset or current liability accounts and for other items such as depreciation. The rest of the statement of cash flows is the same under the direct method, except that a schedule that reconciles net income to net cash flows from operating activities must be included.

REVIEW OF CONCEPTS AND TERMINOLOGY

The following concepts and terms were introduced in this chapter.

LO 1 **Cash:** For purposes of the statement of cash flows, both cash and cash equivalents.

LO 1 **Cash equivalents:** Short-term (ninety days or less), highly liquid investments, including money market accounts, commercial paper, and U.S. Treasury bills.

LO 4 **Cash flows to assets:** The ratio of net cash flows from operating activities to average total assets.

LO 4 **Cash flows to sales:** The ratio of net cash flows from operating activities to sales.

LO 4 **Cash flow yield:** The ratio of net cash flows from operating activities to net income.

LO 4 **Cash-generating efficiency:** The ability of a company to generate cash from its current or continuing operations.

LO 5 **Direct method:** The procedure for converting the income statement from an accrual basis to a cash basis by separately adjusting each item in the income statement.

LO 3 **Financing activities:** Business activities that involve obtaining resources from or returning resources to owners and providing them with a return on their investment, and obtaining resources from creditors and repaying any amounts borrowed or otherwise settling the obligations.

LO 4 **Free cash flow:** The amount of cash that remains after deducting the funds a company must commit to continue operating at its planned level; net cash flows from operating activities minus dividends minus net capital expenditures.

LO 5 **Indirect method:** The procedure for converting the income statement from an accrual basis to a cash basis by adjusting net income for items that do not affect cash flows, including depreciation, amortization, depletion, gains, losses, and changes in current assets and current liabilities.

LO 3 **Investing activities:** Business activities that involve the acquiring and selling of long-term assets, the acquiring and selling of marketable securities other than trading securities or cash equivalents, and the making and collecting of loans.

LO 3 **Noncash investing and financing transactions:** Significant investing and financing transactions that do not involve an actual cash inflow or outflow but involve only long-term assets, long-term liabilities, or stockholders' equity, such as the exchange of a long-term asset for a long-term liability or the settlement of a debt by issuing capital stock.

LO 3 **Operating activities:** Business activities that involve the cash effects of transactions and other events that enter into the determination of net income.

LO 1 **Statement of cash flows:** A primary financial statement that shows how a company's operating, investing, and financing activities have affected cash during an accounting period.

REVIEW PROBLEM

The Statement of Cash Flows

LO 4 The 20x2 income statement for Northwest Corporation is presented below and the com-
LO 5 parative balance sheets for the years 20x2 and 20x1 are shown on the next page.
LO 6
LO 7
SO 9

Northwest Corporation
Income Statement
For the Year Ended December 31, 20x2

Net Sales		$1,650,000
Cost of Goods Sold		920,000
Gross Margin		$ 730,000
Operating Expenses (including Depreciation Expense of $12,000 on Buildings and $23,100 on Equipment, and Amortization Expense of $4,800)		470,000
Operating Income		$ 260,000
Other Income (Expenses)		
Interest Expense	($55,000)	
Dividend Income	3,400	
Gain on Sale of Investments	12,500	
Loss on Disposal of Equipment	(2,300)	(41,400)
Income Before Income Taxes		$ 218,600
Income Taxes		52,200
Net Income		$ 166,400

Northwest Corporation
Comparative Balance Sheets
December 31, 20x2 and 20x1

	20x2	20x1	Change	Increase or Decrease
	Assets			
Cash	$ 115,850	$ 121,850	($ 6,000)	Decrease
Accounts Receivable (net)	296,000	314,500	(18,500)	Decrease
Inventory	322,000	301,000	21,000	Increase
Prepaid Expenses	7,800	5,800	2,000	Increase
Long-Term Investments	36,000	86,000	(50,000)	Decrease
Land	150,000	125,000	25,000	Increase
Buildings	462,000	462,000	—	—
Accumulated Depreciation, Buildings	(91,000)	(79,000)	(12,000)	Increase
Equipment	159,730	167,230	(7,500)	Decrease
Accumulated Depreciation, Equipment	(43,400)	(45,600)	2,200	Decrease
Intangible Assets	19,200	24,000	(4,800)	Decrease
Total Assets	$1,434,180	$1,482,780	($ 48,600)	
	Liabilities and Stockholders' Equity			
Accounts Payable	$ 133,750	$ 233,750	($100,000)	Decrease
Notes Payable (current)	75,700	145,700	(70,000)	Decrease
Accrued Liabilities	5,000	—	5,000	Increase
Income Taxes Payable	20,000	—	20,000	Increase
Bonds Payable	210,000	310,000	(100,000)	Decrease
Mortgage Payable	330,000	350,000	(20,000)	Decrease
Common Stock, $10 par value	360,000	300,000	60,000	Increase
Paid-in Capital in Excess of Par Value	90,000	50,000	40,000	Increase
Retained Earnings	209,730	93,330	116,400	Increase
Total Liabilities and Stockholders' Equity	$1,434,180	$1,482,780	($ 48,600)	

The following additional information was taken from the company's records:

a. Long-term investments (available-for-sale securities) that cost $70,000 were sold at a gain of $12,500; additional long-term investments were made in the amount of $20,000.
b. Five acres of land were purchased for $25,000 to build a parking lot.
c. Equipment that cost $37,500 with accumulated depreciation of $25,300 was sold at a loss of $2,300; new equipment costing $30,000 was purchased.
d. Notes payable in the amount of $100,000 were repaid; an additional $30,000 was borrowed by signing notes payable.
e. Bonds payable in the amount of $100,000 were converted into 6,000 shares of common stock.
f. The Mortgage Payable account was reduced by $20,000 during the year.
g. Cash dividends declared and paid were $50,000.

REQUIRED

1. Prepare a schedule of cash flows from operating activities using the (a) indirect method and (b) direct method.
2. Prepare a statement of cash flows using the indirect method.
3. Compute cash flow yield, cash flows to sales, cash flows to assets, and free cash flow for 20x2.

ANSWER TO REVIEW PROBLEM

1. (a) Prepare a schedule of cash flows from operating activities using the indirect method.

Northwest Corporation
Schedule of Cash Flows from Operating Activities
For the Year Ended December 31, 20x2

Cash Flows from Operating Activities		
Net Income		$166,400
Adjustments to Reconcile Net Income to		
Net Cash Flows from Operating Activities		
Depreciation Expense, Buildings	$ 12,000	
Depreciation Expense, Equipment	23,100	
Amortization Expense, Intangible Assets	4,800	
Gain on Sale of Investments	(12,500)	
Loss on Disposal of Equipment	2,300	
Changes in Current Assets		
and Current Liabilities		
Decrease in Accounts Receivable	18,500	
Increase in Inventory	(21,000)	
Increase in Prepaid Expenses	(2,000)	
Decrease in Accounts Payable	(100,000)	
Increase in Accrued Liabilities	5,000	
Increase in Income Taxes Payable	20,000	(49,800)
Net Cash Flows from Operating Activities		$116,600

1. (b) Prepare a schedule of cash flows from operating activities using the direct method.

Northwest Corporation
Schedule of Cash Flows from Operating Activities
For the Year Ended December 31, 20x2

Cash Flows from Operating Activities		
Cash Receipts from		
Sales	$1,668,500[1]	
Dividends Received	3,400	$1,671,900
Cash Payments for		
Purchases	$1,041,000[2]	
Operating Expenses	427,100[3]	
Interest	55,000	
Income Taxes	32,200[4]	1,555,300
Net Cash Flows from Operating Activities		$ 116,600

1. $1,650,000 + $18,500 = $1,668,500
2. $920,000 + $100,000 + $21,000 = $1,041,000
3. $470,000 + $2,000 − $5,000 − ($12,000 + $23,100 + $4,800) = $427,100
4. $52,200 − $20,000 = $32,200

2. Prepare a statement of cash flows using the indirect method.

Northwest Corporation
Statement of Cash Flows
For the Year Ended December 31, 20x2

Cash Flows from Operating Activities		
Net Income		$166,400
Adjustments to Reconcile Net Income to Net Cash Flows from Operating Activities		
Depreciation Expense, Buildings	$ 12,000	
Depreciation Expense, Equipment	23,100	
Amortization Expense, Intangible Assets	4,800	
Gain on Sale of Investments	(12,500)	
Loss on Disposal of Equipment	2,300	
Changes in Current Assets and Current Liabilities		
Decrease in Accounts Receivable	18,500	
Increase in Inventory	(21,000)	
Increase in Prepaid Expenses	(2,000)	
Decrease in Accounts Payable	(100,000)	
Increase in Accrued Liabilities	5,000	
Increase in Income Taxes Payable	20,000	(49,800)
Net Cash Flows from Operating Activities		$116,600
Cash Flows from Investing Activities		
Sale of Long-Term Investments	$ 82,500[1]	
Purchase of Long-Term Investments	(20,000)	
Purchase of Land	(25,000)	
Sale of Equipment	9,900[2]	
Purchase of Equipment	(30,000)	
Net Cash Flows from Investing Activities		17,400
Cash Flows from Financing Activities		
Repayment of Notes Payable	($100,000)	
Issuance of Notes Payable	30,000	
Reduction in Mortgage	(20,000)	
Dividends Paid	(50,000)	
Net Cash Flows from Financing Activities		(140,000)
Net Increase (Decrease) in Cash		($ 6,000)
Cash at Beginning of Year		121,850
Cash at End of Year		$115,850

Schedule of Noncash Investing and Financing Transactions

Conversion of Bonds Payable into Common Stock	$100,000

1. $70,000 + $12,500 (gain) = $82,500
2. $37,500 − $25,300 = $12,200 (book value) − $2,300 (loss) = $9,900

3. Compute cash flow yield, cash flows to sales, cash flows to assets, and free cash flow for 20x2.

$$\text{Cash Flow Yield} = \frac{\$116{,}600}{\$166{,}400} = .7 \text{ times}$$

$$\text{Cash Flows to Sales} = \frac{\$116{,}600}{\$1{,}650{,}000} = 7.1\%$$

$$\text{Cash Flows to Assets} = \frac{\$116{,}600}{(\$1{,}434{,}180 + \$1{,}482{,}780)/2} = 8.0\%$$

$$\text{Free Cash Flow} = \$116{,}600 - \$50{,}000 - \$25{,}000 - \$30{,}000 + \$9{,}900 = \$21{,}500$$

Chapter Assignments

BUILDING YOUR KNOWLEDGE FOUNDATION

Questions

1. In the statement of cash flows, what is the term *cash* understood to include?
2. To earn a return on cash on hand during 20x3, Sallas Corporation transferred $45,000 from its checking account to a money market account, purchased a $25,000 Treasury bill, and invested $35,000 in common stocks. How will each of these transactions affect the statement of cash flows?
3. What are the purposes of the statement of cash flows?
4. Why is the statement of cash flows needed when most of the information in it is available from a company's comparative balance sheets and income statement?
5. What are the three classifications of cash flows? Give some examples of each.
6. Why is it important to disclose certain noncash transactions? How should they be disclosed?
7. Define *cash-generating efficiency* and identify three ratios that measure cash-generating efficiency.
8. Define *free cash flow* and identify its components. What does it mean to have a positive or a negative free cash flow?
9. What are the essential differences between the direct method and the indirect method of determining cash flows from operations?
10. In determining net cash flows from operating activities (assuming the indirect method is used), what are the effects on cash generated of the following items: (a) an increase in accounts receivable, (b) a decrease in inventory, (c) an increase in accounts payable, (d) a decrease in wages payable, (e) depreciation expense, and (f) amortization of patents?
11. Cell-Borne Corporation had a net loss of $12,000 in 20x1 but had positive cash flows from operations of $9,000. What conditions may have caused this situation?
12. What is the proper treatment on the statement of cash flows of a transaction in which a building that cost $50,000 with accumulated depreciation of $32,000 is sold at a loss of $5,000?
13. What is the proper treatment on the statement of cash flows of (a) a transaction in which buildings and land are purchased by the issuance of a mortgage for $234,000 and (b) a conversion of $50,000 in bonds payable into 2,500 shares of $6 par value common stock?
14. Why is the work sheet approach considered to be more compatible with the indirect method than with the direct method of determining cash flows from operations?
15. Assuming in each of the following independent cases that only one transaction occurred, what transactions would be likely to cause (a) a decrease in investments

and (b) an increase in common stock? How would each case be treated on the work sheet for the statement of cash flows?

16. Glen Corporation has the following other income and expense items: interest expense, $12,000; interest income, $3,000; dividend income, $5,000; and loss on the retirement of bonds, $6,000. How does each of these items appear on or affect the statement of cash flows, assuming the direct method is used?

Short Exercises

SE 1. LO 3 *Classification of Cash Flow Transactions*

Tosca Corporation engaged in the transactions below. Identify each as (a) an operating activity, (b) an investing activity, (c) a financing activity, (d) a noncash transaction, or (e) none of the above.

1. Sold land for a gain.
2. Declared and paid a cash dividend.
3. Paid interest.
4. Issued common stock for plant assets.
5. Issued preferred stock.
6. Borrowed cash on a bank loan.

SE 2. LO 4 *Cash-Generating Efficiency Ratios and Free Cash Flow*

In 20x2, Wu Corporation had year-end assets of $550,000, net sales of $790,000, net income of $90,000, net cash flows from operating activities of $180,000, purchases of plant assets of $120,000, sales of plant assets of $20,000, and paid dividends of $40,000. In 20x1, year-end assets were $500,000. Calculate the cash-generating efficiency ratios of cash flow yield, cash flows to sales, and cash flows to assets. Also calculate free cash flow.

SE 3. LO 4 *Cash Flow Efficiency and Free Cash Flow*

Examine the cash flow measures in **3** of the review problem on page 744. Discuss the meaning of these ratios.

SE 4. LO 5 *Computing Cash Flows from Operating Activities: Indirect Method*

Specialty Products Corporation had a net income of $33,000 during 20x1. During the year the company had depreciation expense of $14,000. Accounts receivable increased by $11,000, and accounts payable increased by $5,000. Those were the company's only current assets and current liabilities. Use the indirect method to determine cash flows from operating activities.

SE 5. LO 5 *Computing Cash Flows from Operating Activities: Indirect Method*

During 20x1, Ayzarian Corporation had a net income of $72,000. Included on the income statement was depreciation expense of $8,000 and amortization expense of $900. During the year, accounts receivable decreased by $4,100, inventories increased by $2,700, prepaid expenses decreased by $500, accounts payable decreased by $7,000, and accrued liabilities decreased by $850. Use the indirect method to determine cash flows from operating activities.

SE 6. LO 6 *Cash Flows from Investing Activities and Noncash Transactions*

During 20x1, Rhode Island Company purchased land for $750,000. It paid $250,000 in cash and signed a $500,000 mortgage for the rest. The company also sold a building that had originally cost $180,000, on which it had $140,000 of accumulated depreciation, for $190,000 cash and a gain of $150,000. Prepare the cash flows from investing activities and schedule of noncash investing and financing transactions sections of the statement of cash flows.

SE 7. LO 6 *Cash Flows from Financing Activities*

During 20x1, South Carolina Company issued $1,000,000 in long-term bonds at 96, repaid $150,000 of bonds at face value, paid interest of $80,000, and paid dividends of $50,000. Prepare the cash flows from the financing activities section of the statement of cash flows.

SE 8. LO 7 *Identifying Components of the Statement of Cash Flows*

Assuming the indirect method is used to prepare the statement of cash flows, tell whether each item below would appear (a) in cash flows from operating activities, (b) in cash flows from investing activities, (c) in cash flows from financing activities, (d) in the schedule of noncash investing and financing transactions, or (e) not on the statement of cash flows at all.

1. Dividends paid
2. Cash receipts from sales
3. Decrease in accounts receivable
4. Sale of plant assets
5. Gain on sale of investment
6. Issue of stock for plant assets
7. Issue of common stock
8. Net income

SE 9. SO 9 *Cash Receipts from Sales and Cash Payments for Purchases: Direct Method*

During 20x2, Nebraska Wheat Company, a marketer of whole-grain products, had sales of $426,500. The ending balance of Accounts Receivable was $127,400 in 20x1 and $96,200 in 20x2. Also, during 20x2, Nebraska Wheat Company had cost of goods sold of $294,200. The ending balance of inventory was $36,400 in 20x1 and $44,800 in 20x2. The ending balance of Accounts Payable was $28,100 in 20x1 and $25,900 in 20x2. Using the direct method, calculate cash receipts from sales and cash payments for purchases in 20x2.

SE 10. SO 9 *Cash Payments for Operating Expenses and Income Taxes: Direct Method*

During 20x2, Nebraska Wheat Company had operating expenses of $79,000 and income taxes expense of $12,500. Depreciation expense of $20,000 for 20x2 was included in operating expenses. The ending balance of Prepaid Expenses was $3,600 in 20x1 and $2,300 in 20x2. The ending balance of Accrued Liabilities (excluding Income Taxes Payable) was $3,000 in 20x1 and $2,000 in 20x2. The ending balance of Income Taxes Payable was $4,100 in 20x1 and $3,500 in 20x2. Calculate cash payments for operating expenses and income taxes in 20x2 using the direct method.

Exercises

E 1. LO 1 LO 3 *Classification of Cash Flow Transactions*

Horizon Corporation engaged in the following transactions. Identify each as (a) an operating activity, (b) an investing activity, (c) a financing activity, (d) a noncash transaction, or (e) not on statement of cash flow.

1. Declared and paid a cash dividend.
2. Purchased a long-term investment.
3. Received cash from customers.
4. Paid interest.
5. Sold equipment at a loss.
6. Issued long-term bonds for plant assets.
7. Received dividends on securities held.
8. Issued common stock.
9. Declared and issued a stock dividend.
10. Repaid notes payable.
11. Paid employees their wages.
12. Purchased a 60-day Treasury bill.
13. Purchased land.

E 2. LO 4 *Cash-Generating Efficiency Ratios and Free Cash Flow*

In 20x5, Black Wolf Corporation had year-end assets of $4,800,000, net sales of $6,600,000, net income of $560,000, net cash flows from operating activities of $780,000, dividends of $240,000, and net capital expenditures of $820,000. In 20x4, year-end assets were $4,200,000. Calculate the cash-generating efficiency ratios of cash flow yield, cash flows to sales, and cash flows to assets. Also calculate free cash flow.

E 3. LO 5 *Cash Flows from Operating Activities: Indirect Method*

The condensed single-step income statement of Union Chemical Company, a distributor of farm fertilizers and herbicides, appears as follows:

Sales		$6,500,000
Less: Cost of Goods Sold	$3,800,000	
Operating Expenses (including depreciation of $410,000)	1,900,000	
Income Taxes	200,000	5,900,000
Net Income		$ 600,000

Selected accounts from the company's balance sheets for 20x2 and 20x1 are as follows:

	20x2	20x1
Accounts Receivable	$1,200,000	$850,000
Inventory	420,000	510,000
Prepaid Expenses	130,000	90,000
Accounts Payable	480,000	360,000
Accrued Liabilities	30,000	50,000
Income Taxes Payable	70,000	60,000

Present in good form a schedule of cash flows from operating activities using the indirect method.

LO 5 **E 4.** *Computing Cash Flows from Operating Activities: Indirect Method*

During 20x1, Mayfair Corporation had a net income of $41,000. Included on the income statement was depreciation expense of $2,300 and amortization expense of $300. During the year, accounts receivable increased by $3,400, inventories decreased by $1,900, prepaid expenses decreased by $200, accounts payable increased by $5,000, and accrued liabilities decreased by $450. Determine cash flows from operating activities using the indirect method.

LO 5 **E 5.** *Preparing a Schedule of Cash Flows from Operating Activities: Indirect Method*

For the year ended June 30, 20xx, net income for Dedam Corporation was $7,400. The following is additional information: (a) Depreciation expense was $2,000; (b) accounts receivable increased by $4,400 during the year; (c) inventories increased by $7,000, and accounts payable increased by $14,000 during the year; (d) prepaid rent decreased by $1,400, and salaries payable increased by $1,000; and (e) income taxes payable decreased by $600 during the year. Use the indirect method to prepare a schedule of cash flows from operating activities.

LO 6 **E 6.** *Computing Cash Flows from Investing Activities: Investments*

Krieger Company's T account for long-term available-for-sale investments at the end of 20x3 is as follows:

Investments

Beg. Bal.	38,500	Sales	39,000
Purchases	58,000		
End. Bal.	**57,500**		

In addition, Krieger's income statement shows a loss on the sale of investments of $6,500. Compute the amounts to be shown as cash flows from investing activities and show how they are to appear on the statement of cash flows.

LO 6 **E 7.** *Computing Cash Flows from Investing Activities: Plant Assets*

The T accounts for plant assets and accumulated depreciation for Krieger Company at the end of 20x3 are as follows:

Plant Assets

Beg. Bal.	65,000	Disposals	23,000
Purchases	33,600		
End. Bal.	**75,600**		

Accumulated Depreciation

Disposals	14,700	Beg. Bal.	34,500
		Depreciation	10,200
		End. Bal.	**30,000**

In addition, Krieger Company's income statement shows a gain on sale of plant assets of $4,400. Compute the amounts to be shown as cash flows from investing activities and show how they are to appear on the statement of cash flows.

LO 6 **E 8.** *Determining Cash Flows from Investing and Financing Activities*

All transactions involving Notes Payable and related accounts engaged in by Krieger Company during 20x3 are as follows:

Cash	18,000	
Notes Payable		18,000
Bank loan		
Patent	30,000	
Notes Payable		30,000
Purchase of patent by issuing note payable		
Notes Payable	5,000	
Interest Expense	500	
Cash		5,500
Repayment of note payable at maturity		

Determine the amounts of the transactions affecting financing activities and show how they are to appear in the statement of cash flows for 20x3.

E 9. LO 7 *Preparing the Statement of Cash Flows: Indirect Method*

Bradbury Corporation's 20x2 income statement and its comparative balance sheets for June 30, 20x2 and 20x1, follow.

Bradbury Corporation
Income Statement
For the Year Ended June 30, 20x2

Sales	$468,000
Cost of Goods Sold	312,000
Gross Margin	$156,000
Operating Expenses	90,000
Operating Income	$ 66,000
Interest Expense	5,600
Income Before Income Taxes	$ 60,400
Income Taxes	24,600
Net Income	$ 35,800

Bradbury Corporation
Comparative Balance Sheets
June 30, 20x2 and 20x1

	20x2	20x1
Assets		
Cash	$139,800	$ 25,000
Accounts Receivable (net)	42,000	52,000
Inventory	86,800	96,800
Prepaid Expenses	6,400	5,200
Furniture	110,000	120,000
Accumulated Depreciation, Furniture	(18,000)	(10,000)
Total Assets	$367,000	$289,000
Liabilities and Stockholders' Equity		
Accounts Payable	$ 26,000	$ 28,000
Income Taxes Payable	2,400	3,600
Notes Payable (long-term)	74,000	70,000
Common Stock, $10 par value	230,000	180,000
Retained Earnings	34,600	7,400
Total Liabilities and Stockholders' Equity	$367,000	$289,000

Additional information: (a) Issued $44,000 note payable for purchase of furniture; (b) sold furniture that cost $54,000 with accumulated depreciation of $30,600 at carrying value; (c) recorded depreciation on the furniture during the year, $38,600; (d) repaid a note in the amount of $40,000; (e) issued $50,000 of common stock at par value; and (f) declared and paid dividends of $8,600. Without using a work sheet, prepare a statement of cash flows for 20x2 using the indirect method.

E 10. LO 7 SO 8 *Preparing a Work Sheet for the Statement of Cash Flows: Indirect Method*

Using the information in **E 9,** prepare a work sheet for the statement of cash flows for Bradbury Corporation for 20x2. From the work sheet, prepare a statement of cash flows using the indirect method.

E 11. SO 9 *Computing Cash Flows from Operating Activities: Direct Method*

Europa Corporation engaged in the following transactions in 20x2. Using the direct method, compute the various cash flows from operating activities as required.

a. During 20x2, Europa Corporation had cash sales of $41,300 and sales on credit of $123,000. During the same year, accounts receivable decreased by $18,000. Determine the cash receipts from sales during 20x2.
b. During 20x2, Europa Corporation's cost of goods sold was $119,000. During the same year, merchandise inventory increased by $12,500 and accounts payable decreased by $4,300. Determine the cash payments for purchases during 20x2.
c. During 20x2, Europa Corporation had operating expenses of $45,000, including depreciation of $15,600. Also during 20x2, related prepaid expenses decreased by $3,100 and relevant accrued liabilities increased by $1,200. Determine the cash payments for operating expenses to suppliers of goods and services during 20x2.
d. Europa Corporation's income taxes expense for 20x2 was $4,300. Income taxes payable decreased by $230 that year. Determine the cash payments for income taxes during 20x2.

E 12. SO 9 *Preparing a Schedule of Cash Flows from Operating Activities: Direct Method*

The income statement for the Karsko Corporation follows.

Karsko Corporation
Income Statement
For the Year Ended June 30, 20xx

Sales		$122,000
Cost of Goods Sold		60,000
Gross Margin		$ 62,000
Operating Expenses		
Salaries Expense	$32,000	
Rent Expense	16,800	
Depreciation Expense	2,000	50,800
Income Before Income Taxes		$ 11,200
Income Taxes		2,400
Net Income		$ 8,800

Additional information: (a) Accounts receivable increased by $4,400 during the year; (b) inventories increased by $7,000, and accounts payable increased by $14,000 during the year; (c) prepaid rent decreased by $1,400, while salaries payable increased by $1,000; and (d) income taxes payable decreased by $600 during the year. Using the direct method, prepare a schedule of cash flows from operating activities as illustrated in Exhibit 6.

Problems

LO 1 LO 3 *Classification of Transactions*

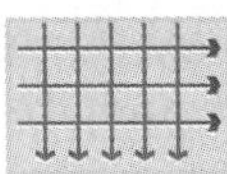

P 1. Analyze each transaction below and place *X*'s in the appropriate columns to indicate its classification and its effect on cash flows using the indirect method.

	Cash Flow Classification				Effect on Cash		
Transaction	Operating Activity	Investing Activity	Financing Activity	Noncash Transaction	Increase	Decrease	No Effect
1. Earned a net income.							
2. Declared and paid cash dividend.							
3. Issued stock for cash.							
4. Retired long-term debt by issuing stock.							
5. Paid accounts payable.							
6. Purchased inventory with cash.							
7. Purchased a one-year insurance policy with cash.							
8. Purchased a long-term investment with cash.							
9. Sold trading securities at a gain.							
10. Sold a machine at a loss.							
11. Retired fully depreciated equipment.							
12. Paid interest on debt.							
13. Purchased available-for-sale securities (long-term).							
14. Received dividend income.							
15. Received cash on account.							
16. Converted bonds to common stock.							
17. Purchased ninety-day Treasury bill.							

LO 4 LO 7 *The Statement of Cash Flows: Indirect Method*

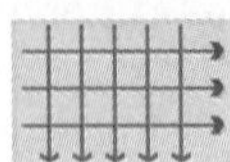

P 2. The comparative balance sheets for Mateo Fabrics, Inc., for December 31, 20x3 and 20x2, appear on the next page. Additional information about Mateo Fabrics's operations during 20x3: (a) Net income, $56,000; (b) building and equipment depreciation expense amounts, $30,000 and $6,000, respectively; (c) equipment that cost $27,000 with accumulated depreciation of $25,000 sold at a gain of $10,600; (d) equipment purchases, $25,000; (e) patent amortization, $6,000; purchase of patent, $2,000; (f) funds borrowed by issuing notes payable, $50,000; notes payable repaid, $30,000; (g) land and building purchased for $324,000 by signing a mortgage for the total cost; (h) 3,000 shares of $20 par value common stock issued for a total of $100,000; and (i) cash dividend, $18,000.

Mateo Fabrics, Inc.
Comparative Balance Sheets
December 31, 20x3 and 20x2

	20x3	20x2
Assets		
Cash	$189,120	$ 54,720
Accounts Receivable (net)	204,860	150,860
Inventory	225,780	275,780
Prepaid Expenses	—	40,000
Land	50,000	—
Building	274,000	—
Accumulated Depreciation, Building	(30,000)	—
Equipment	66,000	68,000
Accumulated Depreciation, Equipment	(29,000)	(48,000)
Patents	8,000	12,000
Total Assets	$958,760	$553,360
Liabilities and Stockholders' Equity		
Accounts Payable	$ 21,500	$ 73,500
Notes Payable	20,000	—
Accrued Liabilities (current)	—	24,600
Mortgage Payable	324,000	—
Common Stock, $20 par value	360,000	300,000
Paid-in Capital in Excess of Par Value	114,400	74,400
Retained Earnings	118,860	80,860
Total Liabilities and Stockholders' Equity	$958,760	$553,360

REQUIRED

1. Using the indirect method, prepare a statement of cash flows for Mateo Fabrics, Inc. (Do not use a work sheet.)
2. Why did Mateo Fabrics have an increase in cash of $134,400 when it recorded net income of $56,000? Discuss and interpret.
3. Compute and assess cash flow yield and free cash flow for 20x3.

P 3. LO 4 LO 7 *Statement of Cash Flows: Indirect Method*

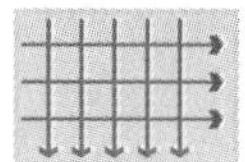

The comparative balance sheets for Bausch Ceramics, Inc., for December 31, 20x3 and 20x2, appear on the next page. The following is additional information about Bausch Ceramics' operations during 20x3: (a) Net income was $96,000; (b) building and equipment depreciation expense amounts were $80,000 and $60,000, respectively; (c) intangible assets were amortized in the amount of $20,000; (d) investments in the amount of $116,000 were purchased; (e) investments were sold for $150,000, on which a gain of $34,000 was recorded; (f) the company issued $240,000 in long-term bonds at face value; (g) a small warehouse building with the accompanying land was purchased through the issue of a $320,000 mortgage; (h) the company paid $40,000 to reduce mortgage payable during 20x3; (i) the company borrowed funds in the amount of $60,000 by issuing notes payable and repaid notes payable in the amount of $180,000; and (j) cash dividends in the amount of $36,000 were declared and paid.

REQUIRED

1. Using the indirect method, prepare a statement of cash flows for Bausch Ceramics. (Do not use a work sheet.)
2. Why did Bausch Ceramics experience a decrease in cash in a year in which it had a net income of $96,000? Discuss and interpret.
3. Compute and assess cash flow yield and free cash flow for 20x3.

Bausch Ceramics, Inc.
Comparative Balance Sheets
December 31, 20x3 and 20x2

	20x3	20x2
Assets		
Cash	$ 277,600	$ 305,600
Accounts Receivable (net)	738,800	758,800
Inventory	960,000	800,000
Prepaid Expenses	14,800	26,800
Long-Term Investments	440,000	440,000
Land	361,200	321,200
Building	1,200,000	920,000
Accumulated Depreciation, Building	(240,000)	(160,000)
Equipment	480,000	480,000
Accumulated Depreciation, Equipment	(116,000)	(56,000)
Intangible Assets	20,000	40,000
Total Assets	$4,136,400	$3,876,400
Liabilities and Stockholders' Equity		
Accounts Payable	$ 470,800	$ 660,800
Notes Payable (current)	40,000	160,000
Accrued Liabilities	10,800	20,800
Mortgage Payable	1,080,000	800,000
Bonds Payable	1,000,000	760,000
Common Stock	1,200,000	1,200,000
Paid-in Capital in Excess of Par Value	80,000	80,000
Retained Earnings	254,800	194,800
Total Liabilities and Stockholders' Equity	$4,136,400	$3,876,400

P 4. LO 4 LO 7 SO 8 *The Work Sheet and the Statement of Cash Flows: Indirect Method*

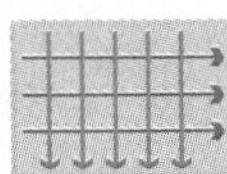

Use the information for Bausch Ceramics, Inc., given in **P 3** to complete the following requirements.

REQUIRED

1. Prepare a work sheet for the statement of cash flows for Bausch Ceramics, Inc.
2. Answer requirements **1, 2,** and **3** in **P 3** if that problem was not assigned.

P 5. SO 9 *Cash Flows from Operating Activities: Direct Method*

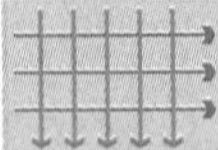

The income statement for Broadwell Clothing Store is at the top of the next page. The following is additional information: (a) Other sales and administrative expenses include depreciation expense of $104,000 and amortization expense of $36,000; (b) accrued liabilities for salaries were $24,000 less than the previous year, and prepaid expenses were $40,000 more than the previous year; and (c) during the year accounts receivable (net) increased by $288,000, accounts payable increased by $228,000, and income taxes payable decreased by $14,400.

Broadwell Clothing Store
Income Statement
For the Year Ended June 30, 20xx

Net Sales		$4,900,000
Cost of Goods Sold		
Beginning Inventory	$1,240,000	
Net Cost of Purchases	3,040,000	
Goods Available for Sale	$4,280,000	
Ending Inventory	1,400,000	
Cost of Goods Sold		2,880,000
Gross Margin		$2,020,000
Operating Expenses		
Sales and Administrative Salaries Expense	$1,112,000	
Other Sales and Administrative Expenses	624,000	
Total Operating Expenses		1,736,000
Income Before Income Taxes		$ 284,000
Income Taxes		78,000
Net Income		$ 206,000

REQUIRED

Using the direct method, prepare a schedule of cash flows from operating activities as illustrated in Exhibit 6.

LO 4 SO 9 **P 6.** *Statement of Cash Flows: Direct Method*

Gutierrez Corporation's 20x2 income statement and its comparative balance sheets as of June 30, 20x2 and 20x1 appear as follows:

Gutierrez Corporation
Income Statement
For the Year Ended June 30, 20x2

Sales		$2,081,800
Cost of Goods Sold		1,312,600
Gross Margin		$ 769,200
Operating Expenses (including Depreciation Expense of $120,000)		378,400
Income from Operations		$ 390,800
Other Income (Expenses)		
Loss on Disposal of Equipment	($ 8,000)	
Interest Expense	(75,200)	(83,200)
Income Before Income Taxes		$ 307,600
Income Taxes		68,400
Net Income		$ 239,200

Gutierrez Corporation
Comparative Balance Sheets
June 30, 20x2 and 20x1

	20x2	20x1
Assets		
Cash	$ 334,000	$ 40,000
Accounts Receivable (net)	200,000	240,000
Inventory	360,000	440,000
Prepaid Expenses	1,200	2,000
Property, Plant, and Equipment	1,256,000	1,104,000
Accumulated Depreciation, Property, Plant, and Equipment	(366,000)	(280,000)
Total Assets	$1,785,200	$1,546,000
Liabilities and Stockholders' Equity		
Accounts Payable	$ 128,000	$ 84,000
Notes Payable (due in 90 days)	60,000	160,000
Income Taxes Payable	52,000	36,000
Mortgage Payable	720,000	560,000
Common Stock, $5 par value	400,000	400,000
Retained Earnings	425,200	306,000
Total Liabilities and Stockholders' Equity	$1,785,200	$1,546,000

The following is additional information about 20x2: (a) equipment that cost $48,000 with accumulated depreciation of $34,000 was sold at a loss of $8,000; (b) land and building were purchased in the amount of $200,000 through an increase of $200,000 in the mortgage payable; (c) a $40,000 payment was made on the mortgage; (d) the notes were repaid, but the company borrowed an additional $60,000 through the issuance of a new note payable; and (e) a $120,000 cash dividend was declared and paid.

REQUIRED

1. Use the direct method to prepare a statement of cash flows. Include a supporting schedule of noncash investing and financing transactions. Do not use a work sheet, and do not include a reconciliation of net income to net cash flows from operating activities.
2. What are the primary reasons for Gutierrez Corporation's large increase in cash from 20x1 to 20x2?
3. Compute and assess cash flow yield and free cash flow for 20x2.

Alternate Problems

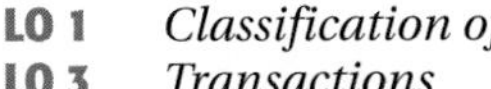

LO 1 LO 3 *Classification of Transactions*

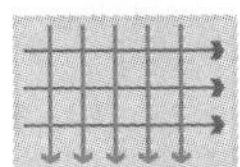

P 7. Analyze each transaction below and place *X*'s in the appropriate columns to indicate its classification and its effect on cash flows using the indirect method.

Transaction	Cash Flow Classification				Effect on Cash		
	Operating Activity	Investing Activity	Financing Activity	Noncash Transaction	Increase	Decrease	No Effect
1. Incurred a net loss.							
2. Declared and issued a stock dividend.							
3. Paid a cash dividend.							
4. Collected accounts receivable.							
5. Purchased inventory with cash.							
6. Retired long-term debt with cash.							
7. Sold available-for-sale securities at a loss.							
8. Issued stock for equipment.							
9. Purchased a one-year insurance policy with cash.							
10. Purchased treasury stock with cash.							
11. Retired a fully depreciated truck (no gain or loss).							
12. Paid interest on note.							
13. Received cash dividend on investment.							
14. Sold treasury stock.							
15. Paid income taxes.							
16. Transferred cash to money market account.							
17. Purchased land and building with a mortgage.							

LO 4
LO 7

P 8. *The Statement of Cash Flows: Indirect Method*

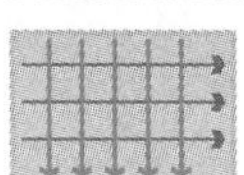

Meridian Corporation's comparative balance sheets as of December 31, 20x2 and 20x1, and its income statement for the year ended December 31, 20x2, follow.

Meridian Corporation
Comparative Balance Sheets
December 31, 20x2 and 20x1

	20x2	20x1
Assets		
Cash	$ 82,400	$ 25,000
Accounts Receivable (net)	82,600	100,000
Inventory	175,000	225,000
Prepaid Rent	1,000	1,500
Furniture and Fixtures	74,000	72,000
Accumulated Depreciation, Furniture and Fixtures	(21,000)	(12,000)
Total Assets	$394,000	$411,500
Liabilities and Stockholders' Equity		
Accounts Payable	$ 71,700	$100,200
Income Taxes Payable	700	2,200
Notes Payable (long-term)	20,000	10,000
Bonds Payable	50,000	100,000
Common Stock, $10 par value	120,000	100,000
Paid-in Capital in Excess of Par Value	90,720	60,720
Retained Earnings	40,880	38,380
Total Liabilities and Stockholders' Equity	$394,000	$411,500

Meridian Corporation
Income Statement
For the Year Ended December 31, 20x2

Net Sales		$804,500
Cost of Goods Sold		563,900
Gross Margin		$240,600
Operating Expenses (including Depreciation Expense of $23,400)		224,700
Income from Operations		$ 15,900
Other Income (Expenses)		
Gain on Disposal of Furniture and Fixtures	$ 3,500	
Interest Expense	(11,600)	(8,100)
Income Before Income Taxes		$ 7,800
Income Taxes		2,300
Net Income		$ 5,500

The following is additional information about 20x2: (a) Furniture and fixtures that cost $17,800 with accumulated depreciation of $14,400 were sold at a gain of $3,500; (b) furniture and fixtures were purchased in the amount of $19,800; (c) a $10,000 note payable was paid and $20,000 was borrowed on a new note; (d) bonds payable in the amount of $50,000 were converted into 2,000 shares of common stock; and (e) $3,000 in cash dividends were declared and paid.

REQUIRED

1. Using the indirect method, prepare a statement of cash flows. Include a supporting schedule of noncash investing and financing transactions. (Do not use a work sheet.)
2. What are the primary reasons for Meridian Corporation's large increase in cash from 20x1 to 20x2, despite its low net income?
3. Compute and assess cash flow yield and free cash flow for 20x2.

P 9. LO 4, LO 7, SO 8 *The Work Sheet and the Statement of Cash Flows: Indirect Method*

Use the information for Meridian Corporation given in **P 8** to answer the following requirements.

REQUIRED

1. Prepare a work sheet to gather information for the preparation of the statement of cash flows.
2. Answer requirements **1, 2,** and **3** if that problem was not assigned.

EXPANDING YOUR CRITICAL THINKING, COMMUNICATION, AND INTERPERSONAL SKILLS

Skills Development

CONCEPTUAL ANALYSIS

SD 1. LO 5 *Direct Versus Indirect Method*

AST Research, Inc., a computer company, uses the direct method of presenting cash flows from operating activities in its statement of cash flows. As noted in the text, 98 percent of large companies use the indirect method.[11] Explain the difference between the direct and indirect methods of presenting cash flows from operating activities. Then choose either the direct or the indirect method and tell why it is the best way of presenting cash flows from operations. Be prepared to discuss your opinion in class.

ETHICAL DILEMMA

SD 2. LO 3 *Ethics and Cash Flow Classifications*

Chemical Waste Treatment, Inc., is a fast-growing company that disposes of chemical wastes. The company has an $800,000 line of credit at its bank. One section in the loan agreement says that the ratio of cash flows from operations to interest expense must exceed 3.0. If this ratio falls below 3.0, the company must reduce the balance outstanding on its line of credit to one-half the total line if the funds borrowed against the line of credit exceed that amount. After the end of the fiscal year, the controller informs the president: "We will not meet the ratio requirements on our line of credit in 20x2 because interest expense was $1.2 million and cash flows from operations were $3.2 million. Also, we have borrowed 100 percent of our line of credit. We do not have the cash to reduce the credit line by $400,000." The president says, "This is a serious situation. To pay our ongoing bills, we need our bank to increase our line of credit, not decrease it. What can

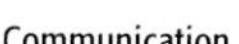
Communication

Critical Thinking

Group Activity

Memo

Ethics

International
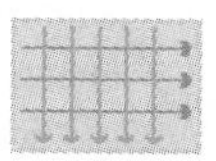
Spreadsheet

General Ledger

CD-ROM

Internet

we do?" "Do you recall the $500,000 two-year note payable for equipment?" replied the controller. "It is now classified as 'Proceeds from Notes Payable' in cash flows provided from financing activities in the statement of cash flows. If we move it to cash flows from operations and call it 'Increase in Payables,' it would increase cash flows from operations to $3.7 million and put us over the limit." "Well, do it," ordered the president. "It surely doesn't make any difference where it is on the statement. It is an increase in both places. It would be much worse for our company in the long term if we failed to meet this ratio requirement." What is your opinion of the president's reasoning? Is the president's order ethical? Who benefits and who is harmed if the controller follows the president's order? What are management's alternatives? What would you do?

RESEARCH ACTIVITY

SD 3. LO 3 LO 4 *Basic Research Skills*

   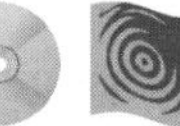

Select the annual reports of three corporations, using one or more of the following sources: your library, the Fingraph® Financial Analyst™ CD-ROM software that accompanies this text, or the Needles Accounting Resource Center Web site at http://www.hmco.com/college/needles/home.html. You may choose them from the same industry or at random, at the direction of your instructor. (If you did a related exercise in a previous chapter, use the same three companies.) Prepare a table with a column for each corporation. Then, for any year covered by the statement of cash flows, answer the following questions: Does the company use the direct or the indirect approach? Is net income more or less than net cash flows from operating activities? What are the major causes of differences between net income and net cash flows from operating activities? Compute cash flow efficiency ratios and free cash flow. Does the dividend appear secure? Did the company make significant capital expenditures during the year? How were the expenditures financed? Do you notice anything unusual about the investing and financing activities of your companies? Do the investing and financing activities provide any insights into management's plan for each company? If so, what are they? Be prepared to discuss your findings in class.

DECISION-MAKING PRACTICE

SD 4. LO 4 LO 7 *Analysis of Cash Flow Difficulty*

May Hashimi, president of ***Hashimi Print Gallery, Inc.***, is examining the following income statement, which has just been handed to her by her accountant, Lou Klein, CPA.

Hashimi Print Gallery, Inc.
Income Statement
For the Year Ended December 31, 20x2

Net Sales	$884,000
Cost of Goods Sold	508,000
Gross Margin	$376,000
Operating Expenses (including Depreciation Expense of $20,000)	204,000
Operating Income	$172,000
Interest Expense	24,000
Income Before Income Taxes	$148,000
Income Taxes	28,000
Net Income	$120,000

After looking at the statement, Hashimi said to Klein, "Lou, the statement seems to be well done, but what I need to know is why I don't have enough cash to pay my bills this month. You show that I earned $120,000 in 20x2, but I have only $24,000 in the bank. I know I bought a building on a mortgage and paid a cash dividend of $48,000, but what else is going on?" Klein replied, "To answer your question, we have to look at comparative balance sheets and prepare another type of statement. Take a look at these balance sheets." The statements handed to Hashimi follow.

Hashimi Print Gallery, Inc.
Comparative Balance Sheets
December 31, 20x2 and 20x1

	20x2	20x1
Assets		
Cash	$ 24,000	$ 40,000
Accounts Receivable (net)	178,000	146,000
Inventory	240,000	180,000
Prepaid Expenses	10,000	14,000
Building	400,000	—
Accumulated Depreciation	(20,000)	—
Total Assets	$832,000	$380,000
Liabilities and Stockholders' Equity		
Accounts Payable	$ 74,000	$ 96,000
Income Taxes Payable	6,000	4,000
Mortgage Payable	400,000	—
Common Stock	200,000	200,000
Retained Earnings	152,000	80,000
Total Liabilities and Stockholders' Equity	$832,000	$380,000

1. To what statement is Klein referring? From the information given, prepare the additional statement using the indirect method.
2. Hashimi Print Gallery, Inc., has a cash problem despite profitable operations. Why?

Financial Reporting and Analysis

INTERPRETING FINANCIAL REPORTS

FRA 1.

LO 4 *Cash-Generating Efficiency and Free Cash Flow*

The statement of cash flows for ***Tandy Corporation,*** the owner of Radio Shack and other retail store chains, appears on the next page. For the two years shown, compute the cash-generating efficiency ratios of cash flow yield, cash flows to sales, and cash flows to assets. Also compute free cash flow for the two years. Assume that you report to an investment analyst who has asked you to analyze Tandy's statement of cash flows for 1995 and 1996. Prepare a memorandum to the investment analyst that assesses Tandy's cash-generating efficiency and evaluates its available free cash flow in light of its financing activities. Are there any special operating circumstances that should be taken into consideration? Refer to your computations and to Tandy's Statement of Cash Flows as attachments. The following data come from Tandy's annual report (in thousands):[12]

	1996	1995	1994
Net Sales	$6,285.5	$5,839.1	$4,943.7
Total Assets	2,583.4	2,722.1	3,243.8

Tandy Corporation
Statement of Cash Flows
For the Years Ended December 31, 1996 and 1995

(In millions)	1996	1995
Cash flows from operating activities:		
Net income (loss)	**$ (91.6)**	$211.9
Adjustments to reconcile net income (loss) to net cash provided by operating activities:		
Impairment of long-lived assets	**112.8**	—
Provision for restructuring cost and other charges	**253.5**	1.1
Gain on sale of extended service contracts	—	—
Gain on sale of credit card portfolios	—	—
Depreciation and amortization	**108.6**	92.0
Deferred income taxes and other items	**(127.8)**	20.1
Provision for credit losses and bad debts	**2.8**	15.7
Changes in operating assets and liabilities:		
Sale of credit card portfolios	—	342.8
Receivables	**8.0**	167.4
Inventories	**(0.1)**	(23.3)
Other current assets	**3.2**	3.2
Accounts payable, accrued expenses and income taxes	**38.1**	(157.9)
Net cash provided by operating activities	**307.5**	673.0
Investing activities:		
Additions to property, plant and equipment	**(174.8)**	(226.5)
Proceeds from sale of property, plant and equipment	**2.8**	42.0
Proceeds from sale of divested operations	—	—
Payment on AST note	**60.0**	6.7
Other investing activities	**(0.9)**	(2.5)
Net cash (used) provided by investing activities	**(112.9)**	(180.3)
Financing activities:		
Purchases of treasury stock	**(232.9)**	(502.2)
Sales of treasury stock to employee stock purchase program	**39.4**	44.6
Proceeds from exercise of stock options	**7.4**	18.2
Dividends paid, net of taxes	**(52.5)**	(63.0)
Changes in short-term borrowings, net	**40.9**	(1.8)
Additions to long-term borrowings	**8.0**	10.3
Repayments of long-term borrowings	**(26.9)**	(60.9)
Net cash used by financing activities	**(216.6)**	(554.8)
Decrease in cash and cash equivalents	**(22.0)**	(62.1)
Cash and cash equivalents, at the beginning of the year	**143.5**	205.6
Cash and cash equivalents, at the end of the year	**$121.5**	$143.5

INTERNATIONAL COMPANY

LO 3 LO 4 *Format and Interpretation of Statement of Cash Flows*

FRA 2. The format of the statement of cash flows can differ from country to country. One of the more interesting presentations, as shown below, is that of ***Guinness PLC,*** a large British liquor company that distributes Johnny Walker Scotch and many other products.[13] (The word *group* means the same as *consolidated* in the United States.) What differences can you identify between this British statement of cash flows and the one used in the United States? In what ways do you find the Guinness format more useful than the format used in the United States? Assume that net cash flows from operating activities are computed similarly in both countries, except for the items shown.

Guinness PLC
Group Cash Flow Statement
For the Years Ended 31 December 1996 and 1995

	1996 £m	1995 £m
Cash flow from operating activities	**1,020**	**989**
Interest received	25	33
Interest paid	(178)	(153)
Dividends paid to minority shareholders in subsidiary undertakings	(34)	(22)
Returns on investments and servicing of finance	**(187)**	**(142)**
United Kingdom corporation tax paid	(194)	(127)
Overseas tax paid	(61)	(81)
Taxation	**(255)**	**(208)**
Purchase of tangible fixed assets:		
Spirits	(58)	(56)
Brewing	(134)	(123)
Sale of tangible fixed assets	22	24
Capital expenditure and financial investment	**(170)**	**(155)**
Free cash flow before dividends	**408**	**484**
Purchase of subsidiary undertakings	(38)	(15)
Purchase of long term investments	(4)	(16)
Disposals	5	90
Acquisitions and disposals	**(37)**	**59**
Equity dividends paid	(294)	(285)
Cash inflow before use of liquid resources and financing	**77**	**258**
Decrease/(increase) in liquid resources	390	(231)
Financing:		
Issue of ordinary share capital (employee share schemes)	23	26
Repurchase of shares	(466)	—
Increase/(decrease) in debt	32	(40)
Increase in cash in the period	**56**	**13**

Toys "R" Us Annual Report

LO 4

FRA 3. *Analysis of the Statement of Cash Flows*

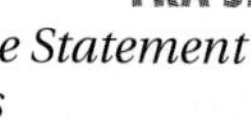

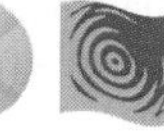

Refer to the statement of cash flows in the Toys "R" Us annual report to answer the following questions:

1. Does Toys "R" Us use the direct or the indirect method of reporting cash flows from operating activities? Other than net earnings, what are the most important factors affecting cash flows from operating activities? Explain the trend of each.
2. Based on the cash flows from investing activities, would you say that Toys "R" Us is a contracting or an expanding company?
3. Calculate the cash flow yield, cash flows to sales, cash flows to assets, and free cash flow for the last three years for Toys "R" Us. How would you evaluate the company's cash-generating efficiency? Does Toys "R" Us need external financing? If so, where has it come from?

Fingraph® Financial Analyst™

LO 3
LO 4

FRA 4. *Cash Flow Analysis*

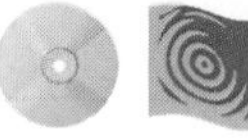

Choose any two companies from the same industry in the Fingraph® Financial Analyst™ CD-ROM software.

1. In the annual reports for the companies you have selected, identify the statement of cash flows. Do the companies use the direct or indirect form of the statement?
2. Display and print in tabular and graphical form the Statement of Cash Flows: Operating Activities Analysis page. Prepare a table that compares the cash flow yield, cash flows to sales, and cash flows to assets for both companies for two years. Are the ratios moving in the same or opposite directions? Study the operating activities sections of the statements to determine the main causes of differences between the net income and cash flows from operations. How do the companies compare?
3. Display and print in tabular and graphical form the Statement of Cash Flows: Investing and Financing Activities Analysis page. Prepare a table that compares the free cash flow for both companies for two years. How do the companies compare? Are the companies growing or contracting? Study the investing and financing activities sections of the statements to determine the main causes of differences between the companies.
4. Find and read references to cash flows in the liquidity analysis section of management's discussion and analysis in each annual report.
5. Write a one-page executive summary that reports your findings from parts **1–4,** including your assessment of the companies' comparative liquidity. Include the Fingraph® pages and your tables as attachments to your report.

ENDNOTES

1. Marriott International, Inc., *Annual Report,* 1996.
2. *Statement of Financial Accounting Standards No. 95,* "Statement of Cash Flows" (Norwalk, Conn.: Financial Accounting Standards Board, 1987).
3. *Statement of Financial Accounting Concepts No. 1,* "Objectives of Financial Reporting for Business Enterprises" (Norwalk, Conn.: Financial Accounting Standards Board, 1978), par. 37–39.
4. Marriott International, Inc., *Annual Report,* 1996.
5. Melville Corporation, *Annual Report,* 1995.
6. Gary Slutsker, "Look at the Birdie and Say: 'Cash Flow,'" *Forbes,* October 25, 1993.
7. Jonathan Clements, "Yacktman Fund Is Bloodied but Unbowed," *The Wall Street Journal,* November 8, 1993.
8. Jeffrey Laderman, "Earnings, Schmearnings—Look at the Cash," *Business Week,* July 24, 1989.
9. Marriott International, Inc., *Annual Report,* 1996.
10. American Institute of Certified Public Accountants, *Accounting Trends & Techniques* (New York: AICPA, 1997), p. 461.
11. American Institute of Certified Public Accountants, *Accounting Trends & Techniques* (New York: AICPA, 1997), p. 461.
12. Tandy Corporation, *Annual Report,* 1996.
13. Adapted from Guinness PLC, *Annual Report,* 1996.

Feb 21
May 21
Aug 21
Nov 21
Aug 22
Nov 22
Feb 23
Aug 23
Nov 24
Feb 25
Aug 25
Feb 26
114:05
112:24
103:29
108:18
102:19
91:30
107:20
109:15
114:07
112:26
103:31
108:20
102:21
92:00
−28 6.93
−29 6.93
−28 6.93
−27 6.93
May
Aug
Nov
260
250
248

CHAPTER 18

Financial Statement Analysis

LEARNING OBJECTIVES

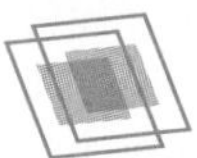

1. **Describe and discuss the objectives of financial statement analysis.**
2. **Describe and discuss the standards for financial statement analysis.**
3. **State the sources of information for financial statement analysis.**
4. **Apply horizontal analysis, trend analysis, and vertical analysis to financial statements.**
5. **Apply ratio analysis to financial statements in a comprehensive evaluation of a company's financial situation.**

DECISION POINT

MOODY'S INVESTORS SERVICE, INC.

Moody's Investors Service, Inc., rates the bonds and other indebtedness of companies on the basis of safety—that is, the likelihood of repayment. Investors rely on this service when making investments in bonds and other long-term company debt. *The Wall Street Journal* reported on February 26, 1997, that Moody's had downgraded $1.1 billion in Apple Computer, Inc.'s, long-term debt. This downgrade was one of a series that have occurred in the last few years because of Apple's declining sales and net losses. Moody's lowered the rating on Apple's senior unsecured debt to B3 from B1 and its subordinated debt to Caa from B3. Bonds with a B rating or lower are considered speculative. On what basis would Moody's decide to upgrade or lower the bond rating of a company? According to *The Wall Street Journal* "Moody's said it expected Apple's market share to continue to decline against PC's using Microsoft Corp.'s Windows operating system. That will result in deteriorating operating performance and erosion of support from independent software makers."[1]

This case demonstrates several features of the evaluation of a company's financial prospects. First, the analysis is rooted in the financial statements (for example, sales, profits, and cash flows). Second, it is directed toward the future (for example, expected erosion in Apple's market share). Third, the operating environment must be taken into consideration (for example, strong competition). Fourth, judgment is involved (for example, after its first debt rating downgrade, Moody's determined that subsequent downgrades of Apple's long-term debt were needed).

Critical Thinking Question: When determining bond ratings, why would short-term performance be included in the evaluation? **Answer:** If business cycles create varying earnings and cash flow patterns, risk increases. Higher risk requires higher returns to creditors. For example, in a weak year, interest payments or current principal repayments might be difficult or impossible to make because cash flows are inadequate.

Point to Emphasize: Because a reevaluation by Moody's can have such a serious impact on a company, many relationships and interrelationships must be calculated and evaluated before a decision is rendered.

Enrichment Note: A bond-rating reevaluation is often triggered by poor earnings performance.

Objectives of Financial Statement Analysis

OBJECTIVE 1

Describe and discuss the objectives of financial statement analysis

Related Text Assignments:
Q: 1, 2
SE: 1
E: 1

Financial statement analysis comprises all the techniques employed by users of financial statements to show important relationships in the financial statements. Users of financial statements fall into two broad categories: internal and external. Management is the main internal user. However, because the people who run a company have inside information on operations, other techniques are available to them. The main focus here is on the external users of financial statements and the analytical techniques they employ.

Creditors make loans in the form of trade accounts, notes, or bonds. They expect them to be repaid according to specified terms and receive interest on the notes and bonds payable. Investors buy capital stock, from which they hope to receive dividends and an increase in value. Both groups face risks. The creditor faces the risk that the debtor will fail to pay back the loan. The investor faces the risks that dividends will be reduced or not paid and that the market price of the stock will drop. For both groups, the goal is to achieve a return that makes up for the risk. In general, the greater the risk taken, the greater the return required as compensation.

Any one loan or any one investment can turn out badly. As a result, most creditors and investors put their funds into a portfolio or a group of loans or investments. The portfolio allows them to average both the returns and the risks. Nevertheless, individual decisions about the loans and stock in the portfolio must still be made. It is in making those individual decisions that financial statement analysis is most useful. Creditors and investors use financial statement analysis in two general ways: (1) to judge past performance and current position and (2) to judge future potential and the risk connected with that potential.

Assessment of Past Performance and Current Position

Point to Emphasize: Past performance is a measure of certainty, whereas trends and projections are surrounded with varying degrees of risk and uncertainty.

Past performance is often a good indicator of future performance. Therefore, an investor or creditor looks at the trend of past sales, expenses, net income, cash flow, and return on investment not only as a means for judging management's past performance but also as a possible indicator of future performance. In addition, an analysis of current position will tell, for example, what assets the business owns and what liabilities must be paid. It will also tell what the cash position is, how much debt the company has in relation to equity, and what levels of inventories and receivables exist. Knowing a company's past performance and current position is often important in achieving the second general objective of financial analysis.

Assessment of Future Potential and Related Risk

Information about the past and present is useful only to the extent that it bears on decisions about the future. An investor judges the potential earning ability of a company because that ability will affect the market price of the company's stock and the amount of dividends the company will pay. A creditor judges the potential debt-paying ability of the company.

Teaching Note: It is wise to review some basic considerations associated with projections, such as not projecting results for activities that fall outside the range of the predicting data and determining whether the environment has changed since the predicting data were generated.

The riskiness of an investment or loan depends on how easy it is to predict future profitability or liquidity. If an investor can predict with confidence that a company's earnings per share will be between \$2.50 and \$2.60 in the next year, the investment is less risky than if the earnings per share are expected to fall between \$2.00 and \$3.00. For example, the potential associated with an investment in an established and stable electric utility, or a loan to it, is relatively easy to predict on the basis of the company's past performance and current position. The potential associated with a small microcomputer manufacturer, on the other hand, may be much harder to predict. For this reason, the investment in or loan to the electric utility carries less risk than the investment in or loan to the small microcomputer company.

Often, in return for taking a greater risk, an investor in the microcomputer company will demand a higher expected return (increase in market price plus dividends) than will an investor in the utility company. Also, a creditor of the microcomputer company will demand a higher interest rate and possibly more assurance of repayment (a secured loan, for instance) than a creditor of the utility company. The higher interest rate reimburses the creditor for assuming a higher risk.

Standards for Financial Statement Analysis

OBJECTIVE 2

Describe and discuss the standards for financial statement analysis

When analyzing financial statements, decision makers must judge whether the relationships they have found are favorable or unfavorable. Three commonly used standards of comparison are (1) rule-of-thumb measures, (2) past performance of the company, and (3) industry norms.

Related Text Assignments:
Q: 3, 4
SE: 1
E: 1
SD: 1

Common Student Error: Students tend to accept rules of thumb as rigid values. Explain that rules of thumb evolve and change as the environment changes. Not long ago, a higher current ratio than today's was considered satisfactory.

Rule-of-Thumb Measures

Many financial analysts, investors, and lenders employ ideal, or rule-of-thumb, measures for key financial ratios. For example, it has long been thought that a current ratio (current assets divided by current liabilities) of 2:1 is acceptable. The credit-rating firm of Dun & Bradstreet, in its *Industry Norms and Key Business Ratios,* offers such rules of thumb as the following:

> Current debt to tangible net worth. Ordinarily, a business begins to pile up trouble when this relationship exceeds 80%.
>
> Inventory to net working capital. Ordinarily, this relationship should not exceed 80%.

Although such measures may suggest areas that need further investigation, there is no proof that the specified levels are the best for any company. A company with a current ratio higher than 2:1 may have a poor credit policy (resulting in accounts receivable being too large), too much inventory, or poor cash management. Another company may have a ratio that is lower than 2:1 as a result of excellent management in all three of those areas. Thus, rule-of-thumb measures must be used with great care.

Past Performance of the Company

An improvement over rule-of-thumb measures is the comparison of financial measures or ratios of the same company over a period of time. This standard will give the analyst at least some basis for judging whether the measure or ratio is getting better or worse. It may also be helpful in showing possible future trends. However, since trends reverse at times, such projections must be made with care. Another problem with trend analysis is that the past may not be a useful measure of adequacy. In other words, past performance may not be enough to meet present needs. For example, even if return on total investment improved from 3 percent one year to 4 percent the next, the 4 percent return may in fact not be adequate.

DECISION POINT

PEPSICO, INC.

Most people think of PepsiCo, Inc., as a maker of soft drinks. In fact, the company is also involved in snack foods (Frito-Lay) and restaurants (Pizza Hut, Taco Bell, and KFC). The overall success of PepsiCo as reflected in its financial statements is affected by the relative amounts of investment and earnings in each of its very different businesses. How should a financial analyst assess the impact of each of these three segments on the company's overall financial performance?

In accordance with FASB *Statement No. 131,* PepsiCo reports key information about its three segments in a note to the financial statements in its annual report (see Exhibit 1). The analyst can learn a lot about the company from this information. For example, net sales and operating profit for each segment are shown for the past three years. Note that for the combined segments, net sales have grown each year, but operating profit has declined. On January 23, 1997, PepsiCo, in an effort to focus on its more profitable segments, announced plans to spin off its restaurant segment, and before year-end 1997, PepsiCo had spun off its restaurants as Tricom Corporation. From the operating profit data in Exhibit 1, the restaurant segment was less profitable than beverages and snack foods. In 1996, beverages experienced lower operating profits because of problems with international operations. Identifiable assets, capital spending, and depreciation and amortization expense of each segment are also indicated in the note. Segment information allows the analyst to see the profitability of each business and to identify where management is investing most for the future. The information about net sales, segment operating profits, and identifiable assets by geographic area is also useful. It is interesting to note, for instance, that although PepsiCo's net sales in Europe are increasing, its operating profits in this region are declining.

Critical Thinking Question: Are domestic or international operations more profitable for PepsiCo? What factors contribute to this trend? **Answer:** Domestic sales are more profitable, as measured by operating profit divided by net sales (1996 margins are domestic, 13.0%, and international, .9%). Factors that contribute to this profitability trend include: (1) U.S. operations have greater economies of scale; (2) the cost of operating in foreign markets is generally greater; (3) international sales prices could be set lower to gain market share; and (4) tariffs charged by foreign countries decrease earnings.

Industry Norms

One way of making up for the limitations of using past performance as a standard is to use industry norms. Such norms will tell how the company being analyzed compares with the average of other companies in the same industry. For example, suppose that other companies in an industry have an average rate of return on total investment of 8 percent. In such a case, 3 and 4 percent returns are probably not adequate. Industry norms can also be used to judge trends. Suppose that a company's profit margin dropped from 12 to 10 percent because of a downward turn in the economy. A finding that other companies in the same industry had experienced an average drop in profit margin from 12 to 4 percent would indicate that the first company being analyzed did relatively well. Sometimes, instead of industry averages, data for the industry leader or a specific competitor are used for analysis.

Exhibit 1. Segment Information for PepsiCo, Inc.

INDUSTRY SEGMENTS

	1996	1995	1994
NET SALES			
Beverages	**$10,524**	$10,382	$ 9,566
Snack Foods	**9,680**	8,545	8,264
Restaurants	**11,441**	11,328	10,521
	$31,645	$30,255	$28,351
OPERATING PROFIT (b)			
Beverages	**$ 890**	$ 1,309	$ 1,217
Snack Foods	**1,608**	1,432	1,377
Restaurants	**511**	430	730
Combined Segments	**3,009**	3,171	3,324
Equity (Loss) Income	**(266)**	(3)	38
Unallocated Expenses, net	**(197)**	(181)	(161)
Operating Profit	**$ 2,546**	$ 2,987	$ 3,201
Depreciation Expense			
Beverages	**$ 440**	$ 445	$ 385
Snack Foods	**346**	304	297
Restaurants	**546**	579	539
Corporate	**7**	7	7
	$ 1,339	$ 1,335	$ 1,228
Amortization of Intangible Assets			
Beverages	**$ 164**	$ 166	$ 165
Snack Foods	**41**	41	42
Restaurants	**96**	109	105
	$ 301	$ 316	$ 312

	1996	1995	1994
Capital Spending (a)			
Beverages	**$ 650**	$ 566	$ 677
Snack Foods	**973**	769	532
Restaurants	**665**	750	1,072
Corporate	**9**	34	7
	$ 2,297	$ 2,119	$ 2,288
United States	**$ 1,613**	$ 1,496	$ 1,492
International	**684**	623	796
	$ 2,297	$ 2,119	$ 2,288
Acquisitions and Investments in Unconsolidated Affiliates (c)			
Beverages	**$ 75**	$ 323	$ 195
Snack Foods	**–**	82	12
Restaurants	**1**	70	148
	$ 76	$ 475	$ 355
United States	**$ 16**	$ 73	$ 88
International	**60**	402	267
	$ 76	$ 475	$ 355
Identifiable Assets			
Beverages	**$ 9,816**	$10,032	$ 9,566
Snack Foods	**6,279**	5,451	5,044
Restaurants	**6,435**	6,759	7,203
Investments in Unconsolidated Affiliates	**1,375**	1,635	1,295
Corporate	**607**	1,555	1,684
	$24,512	$25,432	$24,792

GEOGRAPHIC AREAS (d)

	Net Sales			**Segment Operating Profit (Loss)**			**Identifiable Assets**		
	1996	1995	1994	**1996**(e)	1995(e)	1994	**1996**	1995	1994
Europe	**$ 2,865**	$ 2,783	$ 2,177	**$ (90)**	$ (65)	$ 17	**$ 3,159**	$ 3,127	$ 3,062
Canada	**1,340**	1,299	1,244	**134**	86	82	**1,354**	1,344	1,342
Mexico	**1,334**	1,228	2,023	**116**	80	261	**661**	637	995
Other	**3,658**	3,437	2,782	**(73)**	342	258	**2,628**	2,629	2,196
Total International	**9,197**	8,747	8,226	**87**	443	618	**7,802**	7,737	7,595
United States	**22,448**	21,508	20,125	**2,922**	2,728	2,706	**14,728**	14,505	14,218
Combined Segments	**$31,645**	$30,255	$28,351	**$3,009**	$3,171	$3,324	**22,530**	22,242	21,813
Investments in Unconsolidated Affiliates							**1,375**	1,635	1,295
Corporate							**607**	1,555	1,684
							$24,512	$25,432	$24,792

(a) Included immaterial, noncash amounts related to capital leases, largely in the restaurants segment.

(b) See Items Affecting Comparability on page 43.

(c) Included immaterial noncash amounts related to treasury stock and debt issued.

(d) The results of centralized concentrate manufacturing operations in Puerto Rico and Ireland have been allocated based upon sales to the respective geographic areas.

(e) The unusual impairment, disposal and other charges reduced combined segment operating profit by $822 (United States - $246, Europe - $69, Mexico - $4, Other - $503) in 1996 and $503 (United States - $302, Europe - $119, Mexico - $21, Canada - $30, Other - $31) in 1995 (see Items Affecting Comparability on page 43).

Source: PepsiCo, Inc., *Annual Report*, 1996, p. 44.

There are three limitations to using industry norms as standards. First, two companies that seem to be in the same industry may not be strictly comparable. Consider two companies said to be in the oil industry. The main business of one may be purchasing oil products and marketing them through service stations. The other, an international company, may discover, produce, refine, and market its own oil products. The operations of these two companies cannot be compared because they are different.

Second, most large companies today operate in more than one industry. Some of these diversified companies or *conglomerates,* operate in many unrelated industries. The individual segments of a diversified company generally have different rates of profitability and different degrees of risk. In analyzing the consolidated financial statements of such companies, it is often impossible to use industry norms as standards. There are simply no other companies that are similar enough. A requirement by the Financial Accounting Standards Board, presented in *Statement No. 131,* provides a partial solution to this problem. It states that diversified companies must report segment profit or loss, certain revenue and expense items, and segment assets for each of their operating segments. Depending on how the company is organized for resource allocation in assessing performance, segment information may be reported for operations in different industries or in different geographical areas, or for major customers.[2]

Teaching Note: Students often understand business segments if they are described according to the "Sack of Money Theory." Each segment represents an investment that is evaluated and reviewed frequently by the home office or parent company and that can remain an active investment or be replaced by a more attractive one.

The third limitation of industry norms is that companies in the same industry with similar operations may use different acceptable accounting procedures. That is, different methods may be used to value inventories, or different methods may be used to depreciate similar assets. Even so, if little information about a company's prior performance is available, industry norms probably offer the best available standards for judging current performance—as long as they are used with care.

Sources of Information

OBJECTIVE 3

State the sources of information for financial statement analysis

Related Text Assignments:
Q: 5
SE: 2
E: 1
SD: 2, 3, 4

Point to Emphasize: Since published financial statements represent a major source of information for financial analysis, it is important for students to understand the content of the accounts that make up those statements.

The external analyst is often limited to using publicly available information about a company. The major sources of information about publicly held corporations are reports published by the company, SEC reports, business periodicals, and credit and investment advisory services.

Reports Published by the Company

The annual report of a publicly held corporation is an important source of financial information. The main parts of an annual report are (1) management's analysis of the past year's operations, (2) the financial statements, (3) the notes to the statements, including the principal accounting procedures used by the company, (4) the auditors' report, and (5) a summary of operations for a five- or ten-year period. Most publicly held companies also publish interim financial statements each quarter. Those reports present limited information in the form of condensed financial statements, which need not be subjected to a full audit by the independent auditor. The interim statements are watched closely by the financial community for early signs of important changes in a company's earnings trend.

SEC Reports

Publicly held corporations must file annual reports, quarterly reports, and current reports with the Securities and Exchange Commission (SEC). All such reports are available to the public at a small charge. The SEC calls for a standard form for the annual report (Form 10-K) that contains more information than the published annual report. For that reason, Form 10-K is a valuable source of information. It is available free of charge to stockholders of the company. The quarterly report (Form 10-Q) presents important facts about interim financial performance. The current report (Form 8-K) must be filed within a few days of the date of certain significant events, such as the sale or purchase of a division of the company or a change in auditors. This report is often the first indicator of important changes that may affect the company's financial performance in the future. Many company reports that are filed with the Securities and Exchange Commission are now available on the Internet at http://www.sec.gov/edgarhp.htm.

Business Periodicals and Credit and Investment Advisory Services

Financial analysts must keep up with current events in the financial world. Probably the best source of financial news is *The Wall Street Journal,* which is published every business day and is the most complete financial newspaper in the United States. Some helpful magazines, published every week or every two weeks, are *Forbes, Barron's, Fortune,* and the *Commercial and Financial Chronicle.*

For further details about the financial history of companies, the publications of such services as Moody's Investors Service, Inc., and Standard & Poor's are useful. Data on industry norms, average ratios and relationships, and credit ratings are available from such agencies as The Dun & Bradstreet Corp. In its *Industry Norms and Key Business Ratios,* Dun & Bradstreet offers an annual analysis giving fourteen ratios for each of 125 industry groups, classified as retailing, wholesaling, manufacturing, and construction. *Annual Statement Studies,* published by Robert Morris Associates, presents many facts and ratios for 223 different industries. A number of private services are also available for a yearly fee.

An example of specialized financial reporting that is readily available to the public is Moody's *Handbook of Dividend Achievers,* which profiles companies that have increased their dividends consistently over the past ten years. A sample listing from that publication—for PepsiCo, Inc.—is shown in Exhibit 2. A wealth of information about the company is summarized on one page: the market action of its stock; summaries of its business operations, recent developments, and prospects; earnings and dividend data; annual financial data for the past six or seven years; and other information. From the data contained in those summaries, it is possible to do many of the trend analyses and calculate the ratios explained in this chapter.

BUSINESS BULLETIN: TECHNOLOGY IN PRACTICE

Performance reports and other financial information, stock quotes, reference data, and news about companies and markets are available instantaneously to individuals on the Internet through such services as Prodigy, CompuServe, and America Online. The Internet is an international web of computer-driven communications systems that links tens of millions of homes and businesses through telephone, cable, and computer networks. Combined with the services of brokers like Charles Schwab & Co., Inc., that allow customers to use their own computers to buy and sell stock and other securities, individuals have access to resources equivalent to those used by many professional analysts.

Exhibit 2. Sample Listing from Moody's *Handbook of Dividend Achievers*

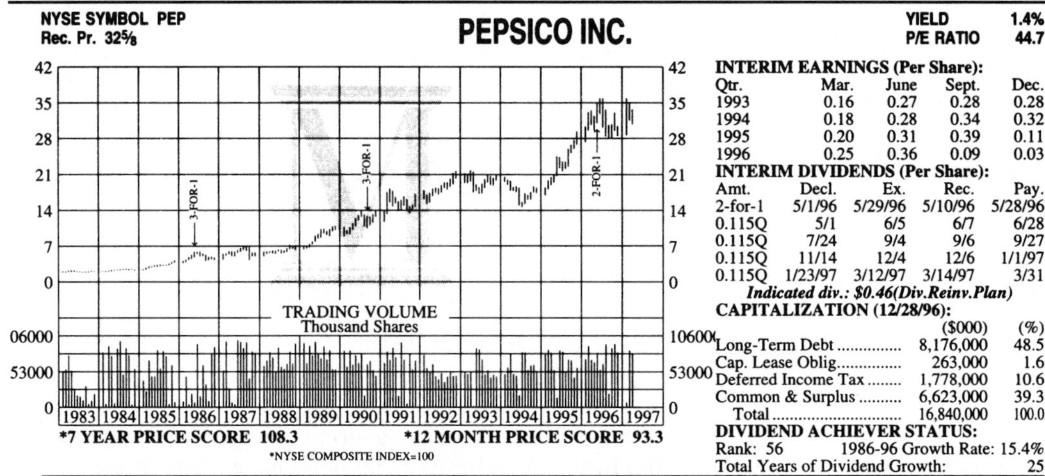

NYSE SYMBOL PEP
Rec. Pr. $32\frac{5}{8}$

PEPSICO INC.

YIELD	1.4%
P/E RATIO	44.7

INTERIM EARNINGS (Per Share):

Qtr.	Mar.	June	Sept.	Dec.
1993	0.16	0.27	0.28	0.28
1994	0.18	0.28	0.34	0.32
1995	0.20	0.31	0.39	0.11
1996	0.25	0.36	0.09	0.03

INTERIM DIVIDENDS (Per Share):

Amt.	Decl.	Ex.	Rec.	Pay.
2-for-1	5/1/96	5/29/96	5/10/96	5/28/96
0.115Q	5/1	6/5	6/7	6/28
0.115Q	7/24	9/4	9/6	9/27
0.115Q	11/14	12/4	12/6	1/1/97
0.115Q	1/23/97	3/12/97	3/14/97	3/31

Indicated div.: $0.46(Div.Reinv.Plan)

CAPITALIZATION (12/28/96):

	($000)	(%)
Long-Term Debt	8,176,000	48.5
Cap. Lease Oblig.	263,000	1.6
Deferred Income Tax	1,778,000	10.6
Common & Surplus	6,623,000	39.3
Total	16,840,000	100.0

DIVIDEND ACHIEVER STATUS:
Rank: 56 1986-96 Growth Rate: 15.4%
Total Years of Dividend Growth: 25

RECENT DEVELOPMENTS: For the year ended 12/28/96, net income was $1.15 billion compared with $1.61 billion a year earlier. The 1996 and 1995 results include nonrecurring charges of $716.0 million and $384.0 million, respectively. Sales rose 4.6% to $31.65 billion. Operating results were dampened by lower results at Pizza Hut and Taco Bell and dramatic losses from PEP's international beverage businesses. Results from North American beverages, global snacks, international restaurants and KFC were improved.

PROSPECTS: On 1/23/97, PEP announced that it plans to spin off its restaurant businesses to shareholders of the Company by the end of 1997. The spin-off will include the operations of Pizza Hut, Taco Bell and KFC, consisting of approximately 29,000 restauruants and more that $20.00 billion in annual retail sales as of 12/28/96. The spin-off will allow the Company to sharpen its focus on its core businesses, which will consist of its snack foods and beverage operations. Also, PEP is examining the sale of its Pepsico Food Systems unit.

BUSINESS

PEPSICO, INC. operates on a worldwide basis within three distinct business segments: soft drinks, snackfoods and restaurants. The soft drinks segment, which accounted for 33% of sales in 1996 (21% of operating profit), manufactures concentrates, and markets Pepsi-Cola, Diet Pepsi, Mountain Dew, Slice and allied brands worldwide, and 7-up internationally. This segment also operates soft drink bottling businesses principally in the United States. Snack Foods, 31% (60%), manufactures and markets snack chips through Frito-Lay Inc. Well-known brands include: Doritos, Ruffles and Lays. The Restaurant segment, 36% (19%), consists of Pizza Hut, Taco Bell and KFC.

ANNUAL EARNINGS AND DIVIDENDS PER SHARE

	12/28/96	12/30/95	12/31/94	12/25/93	12/26/92	12/28/91	12/29/90
Earnings Per Share	**0.72**	**1.00**	**1.11**	**0.98**	**0.81**	**0.68**	**0.69**
Dividends Per Share	**0.43**	**0.38**	**0.34**	**0.29**	**0.25**	**0.22**	**0.184**
Dividend Payout %	**59.7**	**38.0**	**30.6**	**29.6**	**30.9**	**32.4**	**26.7**

ANNUAL FINANCIAL DATA

RECORD OF EARNINGS (IN MILLIONS):							
Total Revenues	31,645.0	30,421.0	28,472.4	25,020.7	21,970.0	19,607.9	17,802.7
Costs and Expenses	28,798.0	27,118.0	24,959.0	21,810.5	19,332.9	17,276.3	15,558.0
Depreciation & Amort	1,719.0	1,740.0	1,576.5	1,444.2	1,214.9	1,034.5	884.0
Operating Profit	2,546.0	2,987.0	3,201.2	2,906.5	2,371.2	2,122.9	2,055.6
Inc Fr Cont Opers Bef Income Taxes	2,047.0	2,432.0	2,664.4	2,422.5	1,898.8	1,670.3	1,667.4
Income Taxes	898.0	826.0	880.4	834.6	597.1	590.1	576.8
Net Income	1,149.0	1,606.0	[1] 1,784.0	1,587.9	[2] 1,301.7	1,080.2	[3] 1,090.6
Aver. Shs. Outstg. (000)	1,606,000	1,608,000	1,607,200	1,620,200	1,613,400	1,605,000	1,597,400

[1] Before acctg. change dr$32,000,000. [2] Before acctg. change dr$927,400,000. [3] Before disc. op. dr$13,700,000.

BALANCE SHEET (IN MILLIONS):							
Cash and Cash Equivalents	786.0	1,498.0	1,488.1	1,856.2	2,058.4	2,036.0	1,815.7
Receivables, Net	2,516.0	2,407.0	2,050.9	1,883.4	1,588.5	1,481.7	1,414.7
Inventories	1,038.0	1,051.0	970.0	924.7	768.8	661.5	585.8
Gross Property	17,840.0	16,751.0	16,130.1	14,250.0	12,095.2	10,501.7	8,977.7
Accumulated Depreciation	7,649.0	6,881.0	6,247.3	5,394.4	4,653.2	3,907.0	3,266.8
Long-Term Debt	8,176.0	8,215.0	8,542.3	7,442.6	7,964.8	7,806.2	5,600.1
Capital Lease Obligations	263.0	294.0	298.2	...	...	...	...
Net Stockholders' Equity	6,623.0	7,313.0	6,856.1	6,338.7	5,355.7	5,545.4	4,904.2
Total Assets	24,512.0	25,432.0	24,792.0	23,705.8	20,951.2	18,775.1	17,143.4
Total Current Assets	5,139.0	5,546.0	5,072.2	5,164.1	4,842.3	4,566.1	4,081.4
Total Current Liabilities	5,139.0	5,230.0	5,270.4	6,574.9	4,324.4	3,722.1	4,770.5
Net Working Capital	...	316.0	d198.2	d1,410.8	517.9	844.0	d689.1
Year End Shs Outstg (000)	1,545,000	1,576,000	1,579,800	1,597,600	1,597,600	1,578,200	1,576,780
STATISTICAL RECORD:							
Operating Profit Margin %	8.0	9.8	11.2	11.6	10.8	10.8	11.5
Return on Equity %	17.3	22.0	26.0	25.1	24.3	19.5	22.2
Return on Assets %	4.7	6.3	7.2	6.7	6.2	5.8	6.4
Average Yield %	1.4	1.6	2.0	1.5	1.4	1.5	1.6
P/E Ratio	49.8-37.8	29.4-17.0	18.6-13.2	22.3-17.6	26.9-18.8	26.8-17.3	20.3-13.0
Price Range	$35\frac{7}{8}$-$27\frac{1}{4}$	$29\frac{3}{8}$-17	$20\frac{5}{8}$-$14\frac{5}{8}$	$21\frac{7}{8}$-$17\frac{1}{4}$	$21\frac{3}{4}$-$15\frac{1}{4}$	$18\frac{1}{4}$-$11\frac{3}{4}$	14-9

Statistics are as originally reported.

OFFICERS:
R.A. Enrico, Chmn. & C.E.O.
K.M. von der Heyden, Vice Chm. & C.F.O.
E.V. Lahey, Jr., Sr. V.P., Gen. Coun. & Sec.

INCORPORATED: NC, Dec., 1986

PRINCIPAL OFFICE: 700 Anderson Hill Rd., Purchase, NY 10577-1444

TELEPHONE NUMBER: (914) 253-2000
FAX: (914) 253-2070
NO. OF EMPLOYEES: 486,000
ANNUAL MEETING: In May
SHAREHOLDERS: 207,000
INSTITUTIONAL HOLDINGS:
No. of Institutions: 1,452
Shares Held: 844,281,498

REGISTRAR(S): Bank of Boston, Boston, MA

TRANSFER AGENT(S): Bank of Boston, Boston, MA

Source: From Moody's *Handbook of Dividend Achievers.* Copyright © 1997. Reprinted by permission of Moody's Investors Services.

Tools and Techniques of Financial Analysis

OBJECTIVE 4

Apply horizontal analysis, trend analysis, and vertical analysis to financial statements

Related Text Assignments:
Q: 6, 7, 8
SE: 3, 4, 5
E: 2, 3, 4
P: 1
SD: 5
FRA: 1

Teaching Note: Horizontal analysis can be likened to comparing oneself at the present time to oneself over an extended period of time.

Point to Emphasize: Traditional horizontal analysis presents trends in terms of nominal dollars. Advanced analysis might adjust data over several time periods to remove any inflation effect or price-level changes.

Few numbers are very significant when looked at individually. It is their relationship to other numbers or their change from one period to another that is important. The tools of financial analysis are intended to show relationships and changes. Among the more widely used tools are horizontal analysis, trend analysis, vertical analysis, and ratio analysis. To illustrate these tools, a comprehensive financial analysis of Sun Microsystems, Inc., is performed. Sun Microsystems was formed in 1982 and has emerged as a global leader in network computing. The company developed many of the core networking technologies that today are the basis of the Internet and corporate intranets, including the widely adopted Java technology.

Horizontal Analysis

Generally accepted accounting principles require the presentation of comparative financial statements that give financial information for the current year and the previous year. A common starting point for studying such statements is horizontal analysis, which begins with the computation of changes from the previous year to the current year in both dollar amounts and percentages. The percentage change must be computed to relate the size of the change to the size of the dollar amounts involved. A change of $1 million in sales is not as impressive as a change of $1 million in net income, because sales is a larger amount than net income.

Exhibits 3 and 4 present the comparative balance sheets and income statements, respectively, for Sun Microsystems, Inc., with the dollar and percentage changes shown. The percentage change is computed as follows:

$$\text{Percentage Change} = 100 \times \left(\frac{\text{Amount of Change}}{\text{Base Year Amount}}\right)$$

The base year in any set of data is always the first year being studied. For example, from 1996 to 1997, Sun Microsystems' total current assets increased by $695 million, from approximately $3,034 million to $3,728 million, or by 22.9 percent. This is computed as follows:

$$\text{Percentage Change} = 100 \times \left(\frac{\$695 \text{ million}}{\$3{,}034 \text{ million}}\right) = 22.9\%$$

An examination of the components of current assets in the comparative balance sheet shows many changes from 1996 to 1997. For example, there were the large increases in deferred tax assets and accounts receivables of 61.5 percent and 38.1 percent, respectively. Also, cash and cash equivalents increased 24.8 percent, and other current assets increased 12.8 percent. However, it is important to consider the changes in dollars as well as in percentages. Consider again the changes in deferred tax assets and accounts receivable. In dollar terms, the increase in accounts receivable, $460 million, is more than four times the increase in deferred tax assets, $109 million. The increase in accounts receivable is in fact the primary reason for the increase in current assets. Overall, this and other increases far outweighed the decreases in short-term investments and inventories from 1996 to 1997. Further, net property, plant, and equipment increased 49.8 percent, or $266 million. With such a large increase in total assets, one expects to see growth in liabilities and equity. The comparative balance sheets show substantial growth in both these areas.

From the income statements in Exhibit 4, the most important result is that net revenues increased by $1,504 million, or 21.2 percent, while total costs and expenses increased by only $1,152 million, or 17.9 percent. Cost of sales and research and development increased 10.2 percent and 26.5 percent, respectively. The result of these favorable relationships is that operating income increased by $352 million, or 52.1 percent, and net income increased by $286 million, or 60.0 percent.

Reinforcement Exercise: To demonstrate the effect of the law of large numbers, show the percentage impact of a change of a given dollar amount on two ratios that have the same answer but differ greatly in data size. **Example:** Net Income as a percentage of Sales.
A: NI ($200,000) divided by Sales ($1,000,000) = 20% NI to Sales.
B: NI ($20,000) divided by Sales ($100,000) = 20% NI to Sales.
Assume a $10,000 reduction in Net Income. A then becomes NI ($190,000) divided by Sales ($1,000,000) = 19% NI to Sales, or a 5% decrease. B now becomes NI ($10,000) divided by Sales ($100,000) = 10%, or a 50% decrease for the same dollar amount.

Exhibit 3. Comparative Balance Sheets with Horizontal Analysis

Sun Microsystems, Inc.
Consolidated Balance Sheets
June 30, 1997 and 1996

(In thousands)	1997	1996	Increase (Decrease) Amount	Increase (Decrease) Percentage
Assets				
Current Assets				
Cash and Cash Equivalents	$ 660,170	$ 528,854	$131,316	24.8
Short-Term Investments	452,590	460,743	(8,153)	(1.8)
Accounts Receivable, Net of Allowances of $196,091 in 1997 and $100,730 in 1996	1,666,523	1,206,612	459,911	38.1
Inventories	437,978	460,914	(22,936)	(5.0)
Deferred Tax Assets	286,720	177,554	109,166	61.5
Other Current Assets	224,469	199,059	25,410	12.8
Total Current Assets	$3,728,450	$3,033,736	$694,714	22.9
Property, Plant and Equipment	$1,658,341	$1,282,384	$375,957	29.3
Accumulated Depreciation and Amortization	(858,448)	(748,535)	109,913	14.7
Net Property, Plant and Equipment	$ 799,893	$ 533,849	$266,044	49.8
Other Assets, Net	168,931	233,324	(64,393)	(27.6)
Total Assets	$4,697,274	$3,800,909	$896,365	23.6
Liabilities and Stockholders' Equity				
Current Liabilities				
Short-Term Borrowings	$ 100,930	$ 49,161	$ 51,769	105.3
Accounts Payable	468,912	325,067	143,845	44.3
Accrued Payroll-Related Liabilities	337,412	282,778	54,634	19.3
Accrued Liabilities and Other	625,600	518,772	106,828	20.6
Deferred Service Revenues	197,616	140,157	57,459	41.0
Income Taxes Payable	118,568	134,934	(16,366)	(12.1)
Current Portion of Long-Term Debt	—	38,400	(38,400)	(100.0)
Total Current Liabilities	$1,849,038	$1,489,269	$359,769	24.2
Long-Term Debt and Other Obligations	106,299	60,154	46,145	76.7
Total Stockholders' Equity	2,741,937	2,251,486	490,451	21.8
Total Liabilities and Stockholders' Equity	$4,697,274	$3,800,909	$896,365	23.6

Source: Sun Microsystems, Inc., *Annual Report*, 1997.

Enrichment Note: Trend analysis is usually done for a five-year period to reflect the general five-year economic cycle that affects the U.S. economy. Cycles of other lengths exist and are tracked by the National Bureau of Economic Research. Trend analysis needs to use the appropriate cycle time to cover the complete cycle's impact on the business being studied.

Trend Analysis

A variation of horizontal analysis is trend analysis, in which percentage changes are calculated for several successive years instead of for two years. Trend analysis, with its long-run view, is important because it may point to basic changes in the nature of a business. In addition to comparative financial statements, most companies present a summary of operations and data about other key indicators for five or more years. Domestic and international net revenues from Sun Microsystems' summary of operations together with a trend analysis are presented in Exhibit 5.

Exhibit 4. Comparative Income Statements with Horizontal Analysis

Sun Microsystems, Inc.
Consolidated Income Statements
For the Years Ended June 30, 1997 and 1996

			Increase (Decrease)	
(In thousands, except per share amounts)	1997	1996	Amount	Percentage
Net Revenues	$8,598,346	$7,094,751	$1,503,595	21.2
Costs and Expenses				
Cost of Sales	$4,320,460	$3,921,228	$ 399,232	10.2
Research and Development	825,968	653,044	172,924	26.5
Selling, General and Administrative	2,402,442	1,787,567	614,875	34.4
Nonrecurring Charges	22,958	57,900	(34,942)	(60.3)
Total Costs and Expenses	$7,571,828	$6,419,739	$1,152,089	17.9
Operating Income	$1,026,518	$ 675,012	$ 351,506	52.1
Gain on Sale of Equity Investment	62,245	—	62,245	NA
Interest Income	39,899	42,976	(3,077)	(7.2)
Interest Expense	(7,455)	(9,114)	1,659	18.2
Income Before Income Taxes	$1,121,207	$ 708,874	$ 412,333	58.2
Provision for Income Taxes	358,787	232,486	126,301	54.3
Net Income	$ 762,420	$ 476,388	$ 286,032	60.0
Net Income per Common and Common-Equivalent Share	$ 1.96	$ 1.21	$ .75	62.0
Common and Common-Equivalent Shares Used in the Calculation of Net Income per Share	388,967	393,380	(4,413)	(1.1)

Source: Sun Microsystems, Inc., *Annual Report*, 1997.

Exhibit 5. Trend Analysis

Sun Microsystems, Inc.
Net Revenues and Operating Income
Trend Analysis

	1997	1996	1995	1994	1993
Dollar Values (in millions)					
Net Revenues	$8,598	$7,095	$5,902	$4,690	$4,309
Operating Income	1,027	675	500	277	241
Trend Analysis (in percentages)					
Net Revenues	199.5	164.7	137.0	108.8	100.0
Operating Income	426.1	280.1	207.5	114.9	100.0

Source: Sun Microsystems, Inc., *Annual Report*, 1997.

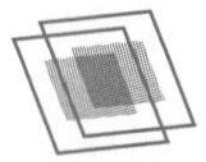

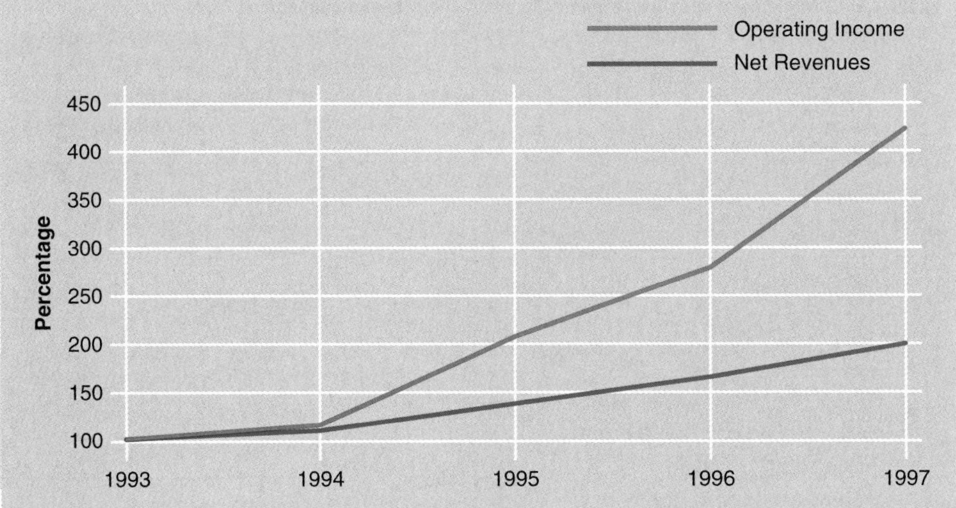

Figure 1
Trend Analysis Presented Graphically for Sun Microsystems, Inc.

Trend analysis uses an index number to show changes in related items over a period of time. For index numbers, the base year is equal to 100 percent. Other years are measured in relation to that amount. For example, the 1997 index for net revenues was figured as follows (dollar amounts in millions):

$$\text{Index} = 100 \times \left(\frac{\text{Index Year Amount}}{\text{Base Year Amount}}\right) = 100 \times \left(\frac{\$8{,}598}{\$4{,}309}\right) = 199.5$$

A study of the trend analysis in Exhibit 5 clearly shows that operating income has grown faster than net revenues at Sun Microsystems. However, both net revenues and operating income have shown increases every year. These trends may be seen visually in Figure 1.

Vertical Analysis

In vertical analysis, percentages are used to show the relationship of the different parts to a total in a single statement. The accountant sets a total figure in the statement equal to 100 percent and computes each component's percentage of that total. (The figure would be total assets or total liabilities and stockholders' equity on the balance sheet, and net revenues or net sales on the income statement.) The resulting statement of percentages is called a common-size statement. Common-size balance sheets and income statements for Sun Microsystems are shown in pie-chart form in Figures 2 and 3, and in financial statement form in Exhibits 6 and 7.

Vertical analysis is useful for comparing the importance of specific components in the operation of a business. Also, comparative common-size statements can be used to identify important changes in the components from one year to the next. For Sun Microsystems, the composition of assets in Exhibit 6, illustrated in Figure 2, shifted from other assets toward net property, plant, and equipment, whereas liabilities showed a small shift to long-term liabilities from stockholders' equity. The main conclusion that can be drawn from this analysis of Sun Microsystems is that current assets and current liabilities make up a large portion of the company and that the company's financial structure has little long-term debt.

Common Student Error: Because percentages look identical in their presentation, students must be warned to discern what base amount is used when a percentage describes an item. For example, inventory may be 50 percent of *total current assets* but only 10 percent of *total assets.*

The common-size income statements in Exhibit 7, illustrated in Figure 3, show that Sun Microsystems improved its cost of sales from 1996 to 1997 by 5.1 percent of revenues (55.3 – 50.2). This improvement resulted in increased gross margin, operating income, and net income as a percentage of net revenues. Selling, general, and

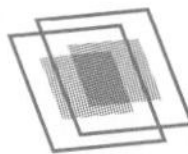

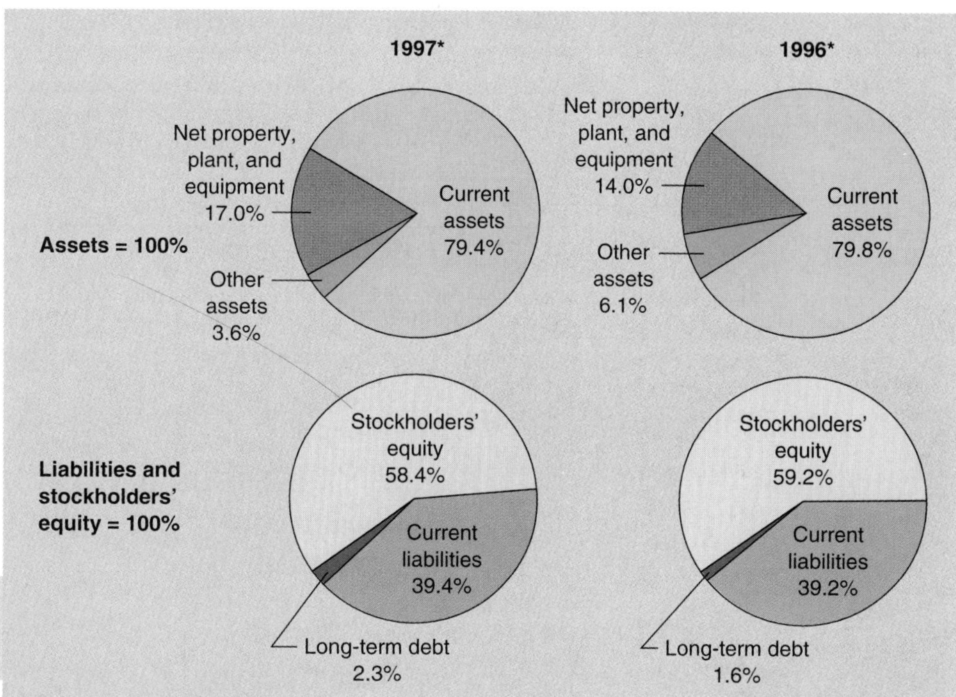

Figure 2
Common-Size Balance Sheets Presented Graphically

* Rounding causes some additions not to total precisely.

administrative expenses increased 2.7 percent of net revenues, which is the primary reason why total costs and expenses decreased only 2.4 percent of net revenues. Also, the company continued to invest over 9 percent of its net revenues in research and development.

Parenthetical Note: Common-size statements can be used in some situations to compare characteristics of firms reporting in different currencies.

Common-size statements are often used to make comparisons between companies. They allow an analyst to compare the operating and financing characteristics of two companies of different size in the same industry. For example, the analyst might want to compare Sun Microsystems with other companies in terms of

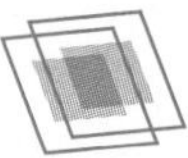

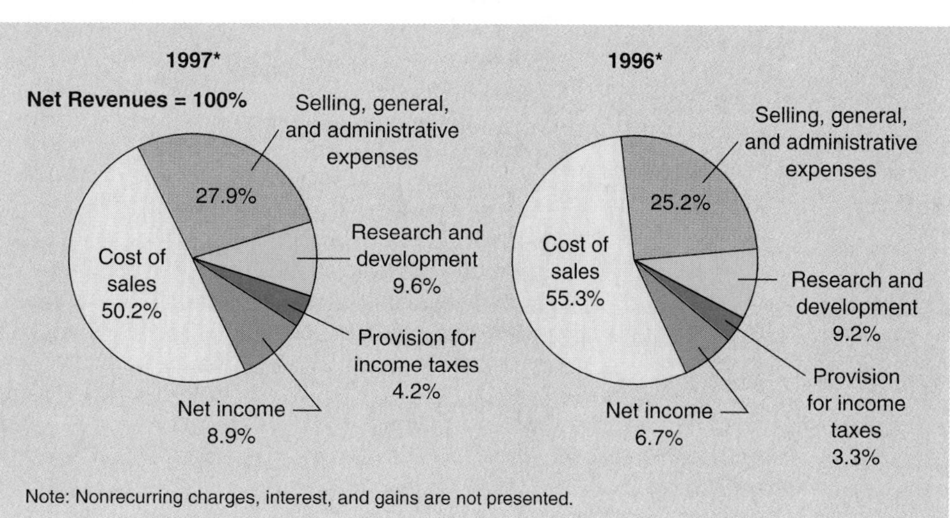

Figure 3
Common-Size Income Statements Presented Graphically

* Rounding causes some additions not to total precisely.

Exhibit 6. Common-Size Balance Sheets

Sun Microsystems, Inc.
Common-Size Balance Sheets
June 30, 1997 and 1996

	1997*	1996*
Assets		
Current Assets	79.4%	79.8%
Net Property, Plant, and Equipment	17.0	14.0
Other Assets, Net	3.6	6.1
Total Assets	100.0%	100.0%
Liabilities and Stockholders' Equity		
Current Liabilities	39.4%	39.2%
Long-Term Debt and Other Obligations	2.3	1.6
Total Liabilities	41.6%	40.8%
Total Stockholders' Equity	58.4	59.2
Total Liabilities and Stockholders' Equity	100.0%	100.0%

*Amounts do not precisely total 100 percent in all cases due to rounding.
Source: Sun Microsystems, Inc., *Annual Report*, 1997.

Exhibit 7. Common-Size Income Statements

Sun Microsystems, Inc.
Common-Size Income Statements
For the Years Ended June 30, 1997 and 1996

	1997*	1996*
Net Revenues	100.0%	100.0%
Costs and Expenses		
Cost of Sales	50.2%	55.3%
Research and Development	9.6	9.2
Selling, General and Administrative	27.9	25.2
Nonrecurring Charges	.3	.8
Total Costs and Expenses	88.1%	90.5%
Operating Income	11.9%	9.5%
Gain on Sale of Equity Investment	.8	—
Interest, Net	.4	.5
Income Before Income Taxes	13.1%	10.0%
Provision for Income Taxes	4.2	3.3
Net Income	8.9%	6.7%

*Rounding causes some additions and subtractions not to total precisely.
Source: Sun Microsystems, Inc., *Annual Report*, 1997.

percentage of total assets financed by debt or in terms of selling, general, and administrative expenses as a percentage of net revenues. Common-size statements would show those and other relationships.

Ratio Analysis

Ratio analysis is an important way to state meaningful relationships between the components of the financial statements. To be most meaningful, the interpretation of ratios must include a study of the underlying data. Ratios are guides or shortcuts that are useful in evaluating a company's financial position and operations and making comparisons with results in previous years or with other companies. The primary purpose of ratios is to point out areas needing further investigation. They should be used in connection with a general understanding of the company and its environment. Ratios may be expressed in several ways. For example, a ratio of net income of $100,000 to sales of $1,000,000 may be stated as (1) net income is 1/10 or 10 percent of sales; (2) the ratio of sales to net income is 10 to 1 (10:1), or sales are 10 times net income; or (3) for every dollar of sales, the company has an average net income of 10 cents.

Comprehensive Illustration of Ratio Analysis

OBJECTIVE 5

Apply ratio analysis to financial statements in a comprehensive evaluation of a company's financial situation

The management's discussion and analysis section of Sun Microsystems' annual report states, "The company's financial condition strengthened as of fiscal 1997 year end when compared with fiscal 1996."[3] To verify this statement, a comprehensive ratio analysis is used to compare Sun Microsystems' performance for the years 1996 and 1997 with regard to the following objectives: (1) liquidity, (2) profitability, (3) long-term solvency, (4) cash flow adequacy, and (5) market strength. Most data for the analyses come from the financial statements presented in Exhibits 3 and 4. Other data are presented as needed.

Related Text Assignments:
Q: 9, 10, 11, 12, 13, 14, 15, 16
SE: 6, 7, 8, 9, 10
E: 5, 6, 7, 8, 9, 10
P: 2, 3, 4, 5, 6, 7
SD: 1, 5
FRA: 2, 3, 4

Point to Emphasize: When comparing company ratios to published ratios, be aware that publishers often redefine the contents of the ratios. While the general content is similar, variations occur. Be sure to evaluate exactly what information a published source says it uses to calculate its ratios.

Teaching Note: To reinforce the different presentations of ratios, avoid the use of only one format in class discussion. Present one format and ask a student to express the relationship in a different format.

Enrichment Note: Other classifications of ratios may be presented. Some of these include productivity ratios and efficiency ratios.

Evaluating Liquidity

Liquidity is a company's ability to pay bills when they are due and to meet unexpected needs for cash. All the ratios that relate to liquidity involve working capital or some part of it, because it is out of working capital that debts are paid. The objective of liquidity is also closely related to the cash flow ratios.

The liquidity ratios from 1996 to 1997 for Sun Microsystems are presented in Exhibit 8. The current ratio and the quick ratio are measures of short-term debt-paying ability. The principal difference between the two is that the numerator of the current ratio includes inventories and prepaid expenses. Inventories take longer to convert to cash than do the current assets included in the numerator of the quick ratio. Both ratios remained constant from 1996 to 1997. The current ratio was 2.0 times, and the quick ratio was 1.5 times. The primary reason for the consistent results is that current assets and current liabilities grew at similar rates.

Analysis of two major components of current assets, receivables and inventory, shows contrasting trends. The major change in this category of ratios is in the receivable turnover. The relative size of the accounts receivable and the effectiveness of credit policies are measured by the receivable turnover, which fell from 6.3 times in 1996 to 6.0 times in 1997. The related ratio of average days' sales uncollected increased by almost three days, from 57.9 days in 1996 to 60.8 days in 1997. The inventory turnover, which measures the relative size of inventories, also worsened. Inventory turnover declined from 10.0 times in 1996 to 9.6 times in 1997. This

Exhibit 8. Liquidity Ratios of Sun Microsystems, Inc.

(Dollar amounts in thousands)	1997	1996
Current ratio: Measure of short-term debt-paying ability		
Current Assets / Current Liabilities	$3,728,450 / $1,849,038 = 2.0 times	$3,033,736 / $1,489,269 = 2.0 times
Quick ratio: Measure of short-term debt-paying ability		
(Cash + Marketable Securities + Receivables) / Current Liabilities	($660,170 + $452,590 + $1,666,523) / $1,849,038	($528,854 + $460,743 + $1,206,612) / $1,489,269
	= $2,779,283 / $1,849,038 = 1.5 times	= $2,196,209 / $1,489,269 = 1.5 times
Receivable turnover: Measure of relative size of accounts receivable balance and effectiveness of credit policies		
Net Sales / Average Accounts Receivable*	$8,598,346 / (($1,666,523 + $1,206,612)/2)	$7,094,751 / (($1,206,612 + $1,046,374)/2)
	= $8,598,346 / $1,436,568 = 6.0 times	= $7,094,751 / $1,126,493 = 6.3 times
Average days' sales uncollected: Measure of average time taken to collect receivables		
Days in Year / Receivable Turnover	365 days / 6.0 times = 60.8 days	365 days / 6.3 times = 57.9 days
Inventory turnover: Measure of relative size of inventory		
Cost of Goods Sold / Average Inventory*	$4,320,460 / (($437,978 + $460,914)/2)	$3,921,228 / (($460,914 + $325,172)/2)
	= $4,320,460 / $449,446 = 9.6 times	= $3,921,228 / $393,043 = 10.0 times
Average days' inventory on hand: Measure of average days taken to sell inventory		
Days in Year / Inventory Turnover	365 days / 9.6 times = 38.0 days	365 days / 10.0 times = 36.5 days

*1995 figures are derived from the statement of cash flows in Sun Microsystems' annual report.
Source: Sun Microsystems, Inc., *Annual Report*, 1997.

Teaching Note: Review the concept of balance sheet classification according to liquidity.

Point to Emphasize: Profit often is expressed in many different ways in accounting literature. Examples are net income before income taxes, net income after income taxes, and net operating income. If students are aware of the content of net income data in profitability ratios, they will draw appropriate conclusions about the results of ratio computation.

results in an unfavorable increase in average days' inventory on hand from 36.5 days in 1996 to 38.0 days in 1997. When taken together, this means that Sun Microsystems, operating cycle, or the time it takes to sell products and collect for them, increased from 94.4 days in 1996 (57.9 days + 36.5 days) to 98.8 days in 1997 (60.8 days + 38.0 days). This increase represents a small decline in liquidity. Overall, Sun Microsystems' liquidity remains strong.

Evaluating Profitability

The objective of profitability relates to a company's ability to earn a satisfactory income so that investors and stockholders will continue to provide capital to the company. A company's profitability is also closely linked to its liquidity because

Exhibit 9. Profitability Ratios of Sun Microsystems, Inc.

(Dollar amounts in thousands)	1997	1996
Profit margin: Measure of net income produced by each dollar of sales		
Net Income* / Net Sales	$\frac{\$762,420}{\$8,598,346} = 8.9\%$	$\frac{\$476,388}{\$7,094,751} = 6.7\%$
Asset turnover: Measure of how efficiently assets are used to produce sales		
Net Sales / Average Total Assets†	$\frac{\$8,598,346}{(\$4,697,274 + \$3,800,909)/2}$	$\frac{\$7,094,751}{(\$3,800,909 + \$3,545,000)/2}$
	$= \frac{\$8,598,346}{\$4,249,092} = 2.0$ times	$= \frac{\$7,094,751}{\$3,672,955} = 1.9$ times
Return on assets: Measure of overall earning power or profitability		
Net Income / Average Total Assets†	$\frac{\$762,420}{\$4,249,092} = 17.9\%$	$\frac{\$476,388}{\$3,672,955} = 13.0\%$
Return on equity: Measure of the profitability of stockholders' investments		
Net Income / Average Stockholders' Equity†	$\frac{\$762,420}{(\$2,741,937 + \$2,251,486)/2}$	$\frac{\$476,388}{(\$2,251,486 + \$2,122,595)/2}$
	$= \frac{\$762,420}{\$2,496,712} = 30.5\%$	$= \frac{\$476,388}{\$2,187,041} = 21.8\%$

*In comparing companies in an industry, some analysts use income before income taxes as the numerator to eliminate the effect of differing tax rates among firms.

†1995 figures are from the eleven-year financial history or the statements of stockholders' equity in Sun Microsystems' annual report.

Source: Sun Microsystems, Inc., *Annual Report*, 1997.

earnings ultimately produce cash flow. For this reason, evaluating profitability is important to both investors and creditors. The profitability ratios of Sun Microsystems, Inc., are shown in Exhibit 9.

Enrichment Note: In both asset turnover and return on assets, the analysis is improved if only productive assets are used in the calculations. For example, unfinished new plant construction or investments in obsolete or nonoperating plants could be removed from the asset base to give a better picture of the productivity of assets.

All measures of Sun Microsystems' profitability improved from 1996 to 1997, primarily because of the large increase in net income. The reasons for the increase were discussed in the sections on horizontal and vertical analysis. Profit margin, which measures the net income produced by each dollar of sales, increased from 6.7 to 8.9 percent, and asset turnover, which measures how efficiently assets are used to produce sales, increased from 1.9 to 2.0 times. The result is an improvement in the overall earning power of the company, or return on assets, from 13.0 to 17.9 percent. These relationships may be illustrated as follows:

	Profit Margin		**Asset Turnover**		**Return on Assets**
	Net Income / Net Sales	×	Net Sales / Average Total Assets	=	Net Income / Average Total Assets
1997	8.9%	×	2.0	=	17.8%
1996	6.7%	×	1.9	=	12.7%

Instructional Strategy: Divide the class into small groups and ask them to discuss SD 1. After about ten minutes, debrief the case. This exercise highlights the links between profit margin, return on equity, and market value. To summarize, review profit margin × asset turnover = return on assets. The difference between return on assets and return on equity is a function of leverage.

The slight difference in the two sets of return on assets figures results from the rounding of the ratios used in the above computation. Finally, the profitability of stockholders' investments, or return on equity, became more favorable, increasing from 21.8 percent to 30.5 percent.

Exhibit 10. Long-Term Solvency Ratios of Sun Microsystems, Inc.

(Dollar amounts in thousands)	1997	1996
Debt to equity ratio: Measure of capital structure and leverage		
Total Liabilities / Stockholders' Equity	$1,955,337 / $2,741,937 = .7 times	$1,549,423 / $2,251,486 = .7 times
Interest coverage ratio: Measure of creditors' protection from default on interest payments		
(Income Before Income Taxes + Interest Expense) / Interest Expense	($1,121,207 + $7,455) / $7,455 = 151.4 times	($708,874 + $9,114) / $9,114 = 78.8 times

Source: Sun Microsystems, Inc., *Annual Report*, 1997.

Evaluating Long-Term Solvency

Discussion Question: What is the difference between liquidity and solvency? **Answer:** Liquidity is a firm's ability to meet its current obligations, whereas solvency is a firm's ability to meet its maturing obligations as they become due, without losing the ability to continue operations.

Long-term solvency has to do with a company's ability to survive for many years. The aim of long-term solvency analysis is to detect early signs that a company is on the road to bankruptcy. Studies have indicated that accounting ratios can show as much as five years in advance that a company may fail.[4] Declining profitability and liquidity ratios are key indicators of possible business failure. Two other ratios that analysts often consider when assessing long-term solvency are debt to equity and interest coverage. Long-term solvency ratios are shown in Exhibit 10.

Increasing amounts of debt in a company's capital structure mean that the company is becoming more heavily leveraged. This condition negatively affects long-term solvency because it represents increasing legal obligations to pay interest periodically and the principal at maturity. Failure to make those payments can result in bankruptcy. The debt to equity ratio measures capital structure and leverage by showing the amount of a company's assets provided by creditors in relation to the amount provided by stockholders. Sun Microsystems' debt to equity ratio was only .7 times in both 1996 and 1997. It is noteworthy to recall from Exhibit 3 that the company has primarily short-term debt and little long-term debt and that the company has ample current assets as reflected by the current ratio and the quick ratio. All of these are positive factors for the company's long-term solvency. As to the future, "The Company believes the level of financial resources is a significant competitive factor in its industry, and it may choose at any time to raise additional capital through debt or equity financing to strengthen its financial position, facilitate growth, and provide the Company with additional flexibility to take advantage of business opportunities that may arise."[5]

If debt is risky, why have any? The answer is that the level of debt is a matter of balance. Despite its riskiness, debt is a flexible means of financing certain business operations. Sun Microsystems is using debt to finance what management plans to be a temporary increase in inventory. The interest paid on that debt is deductible for income tax purposes, whereas dividends on stock are not. Because debt usually carries a fixed interest charge, the cost of financing can be limited and leverage can be used to advantage. If the company is able to earn a return on assets greater than the cost of interest, it makes an overall profit.[6] However, the company runs the risk of not earning a return on assets equal to the cost of financing those assets, thereby incurring a loss.

Business-World Example: Because of innovative financing plans and other means of acquiring assets, a beneficial modern-day ratio is the fixed charges ratio. This ratio includes interest, lease payments, and all other fixed obligations that must be met through earnings.

The interest coverage ratio measures the degree of protection creditors have from a default on interest payments. Because of its small amount of long-term debt, Sun

Exhibit 11. Cash Flow Adequacy Ratios of Sun Microsystems, Inc.

(Dollar amounts in thousands)	1997	1996
Cash flow yield: Measure of a company's ability to generate operating cash flows in relation to net income		
Net Cash Flows from Operating Activities* / Net Income	$\frac{\$1,105,088}{\$762,420}$ = 1.4 times	$\frac{\$688,314}{\$476,388}$ = 1.4 times
Cash flows to sales: Measure of the ability of sales to generate operating cash flows		
Net Cash Flows from Operating Activities* / Net Sales	$\frac{\$1,105,088}{\$8,598,346}$ = 12.9%	$\frac{\$688,314}{\$7,094,751}$ = 9.7%
Cash flows to assets: Measure of the ability of assets to generate operating cash flows		
Net Cash Flows from Operating Activities* / Average Total Assets†	$\frac{\$1,105,088}{(\$4,697,274 + \$3,800,909)/2}$ = $\frac{\$1,105,088}{\$4,249,092}$ = 26.0%	$\frac{\$688,314}{(\$3,800,909 + \$3,545,000)/2}$ = $\frac{\$688,314}{\$3,672,955}$ = 18.7%
Free cash flow: Measure of cash generated or cash deficiency after providing for commitments		
Net Cash Flows from Operating Activities* − Dividends − Net Capital Expenditures*	$1,105,088 − $0 − $554,018 = $551,070	$688,314 − $0 − $295,638 = $392,676

*These figures are from the statements of cash flows in Sun Microsystems' annual report.
†The 1995 figure is from the eleven-year financial history in Sun Microsystems' annual report.
Source: Sun Microsystems, Inc., *Annual Report,* 1997.

Microsystems has large interest coverage ratios of 78.8 times in 1996 and 151.4 times in 1997. Interest coverage is not a problem for the company.

Evaluating Cash Flow Adequacy

Because cash flows are needed to pay debts when they are due, cash flow measures are closely related to the objectives of liquidity and long-term solvency. Sun Microsystems' cash flow adequacy ratios are presented in Exhibit 11. By most measures, the company's ability to generate positive operating cash flows showed improvement from 1996 to 1997. Key to those increases is the fact that net cash flows from operating activities had a large increase, from $688 million in 1996 to $1,105 million in 1997, while net income, net sales, and average total assets increased by lesser percentages. Cash flow yield, or the relationship of cash flows from operating activities to net income, remained unchanged at 1.4 times. Cash flows to sales, or the ability of sales to generate operating cash flows, increased from 9.7 percent to 12.9 percent. Cash flows to assets, or the ability of assets to generate operating cash flows, increased from 18.7 percent to 26.0 percent.

Free cash flow, the cash generated after providing for commitments, also increased and remains very positive primarily because capital expenditures were increased by a smaller amount than the increase in net cash flows from operating activities and because the company pays no dividends. Management's comment with regard to cash flows in the future is, "The Company believes that the liquidity provided by existing cash and short-term investment balances and the borrowing

Exhibit 12. Market Strength Ratios of Sun Microsystems, Inc.

	1997	1996
Price/earnings ratio: Measure of investor confidence in a company		
$\frac{\text{Market Price per Share*}}{\text{Earnings per Share}}$	$\frac{\$37.2190}{\$1.96}$ = 19.0 times	$\frac{\$29.4375}{\$1.21}$ = 24.3 times
Dividends yield: Measure of the current return to an investor in a stock		
$\frac{\text{Dividends per Share}}{\text{Market Price per Share}}$	Sun Microsystems does not pay a dividend.	

*Market price is from Sun Microsystems' annual report.
Source: Sun Microsystems, Inc., *Annual Report*, 1997.

arrangements . . . may have to be supplemented with additional resources to provide sufficient capital to meet the Company's capital requirements through fiscal 1998."[7]

Evaluating Market Strength

Teaching Note: To stimulate student questions and discussion, present market strength ratios for several well-known companies directly from a financial publication, such as *The Wall Street Journal.*

The market price of a company's stock is of interest to the analyst because it represents what investors as a whole think of the company at a point in time. Market price is the price at which the stock is bought and sold. It provides information about how investors view the potential return and risk connected with owning the company's stock. Market price by itself is not very informative for this purpose, however. Companies differ in number of outstanding shares and amount of underlying earnings and dividends. Thus, market price must be related to earnings by considering the price/earnings ratio and the dividends yield. Those ratios for Sun Microsystems appear in Exhibit 12 and have been computed using the market price for Sun Microsystems' stock at the end of 1996 and 1997.

The price/earnings (P/E) ratio, which measures investor confidence in a company, is the ratio of the market price per share to earnings per share. The P/E ratio is useful in comparing the relative values placed on the earnings of different companies and in comparing the value placed on a company's shares in relation to the overall market. With a lower P/E ratio, the investor obtains more underlying earnings per dollar invested. However, Sun Microsystems' P/E ratio decreased from 24.3 times in 1996 to 19.0 times in 1997. In effect, investors probably do not believe that the more than 60 percent increase in earnings per share is sustainable in future years. It does not signal a lack of confidence by investors in Sun Microsystems. It is an indication that investors think the company will continue to increase earnings in future years. The dividends yield measures a stock's current return to an investor in the form of dividends. Because Sun Microsystems pays no dividend, it may be concluded that investors expect their return from owning the company's stock to come from increases in its market value.

Common Student Error: Students often confuse dividends and earnings per share in this calculation. Clarify by emphasizing the cash flow nature of dividends and the wealth increase concept of earnings.

Summary of the Financial Analysis of Sun Microsystems, Inc.

This ratio analysis clearly shows that Sun Microsystems' financial condition is strong, as measured by its liquidity, long-term solvency, and cash flow adequacy ratios. The company's profitability is excellent and increased from 1996 to 1997, as measured by its profitability ratios. This performance has been rewarded by a higher market price per share.

Chapter Review

REVIEW OF LEARNING OBJECTIVES

1. **Describe and discuss the objectives of financial statement analysis.** Creditors and investors, as well as managers, use financial statement analysis to judge the past performance and current position of a company, and also to judge its future potential and the risk associated with it. Creditors use the information gained from their analysis to make reliable loans that will be repaid with interest. Investors use the information to make investments that will provide a return that is worth the risk.
2. **Describe and discuss the standards for financial statement analysis.** Three commonly used standards for financial statement analysis are rule-of-thumb measures, the company's past performance, and industry norms. Rule-of-thumb measures are weak because of the lack of evidence that they can be widely applied. The past performance of a company can offer a guideline for measuring improvement but is not helpful in judging performance relative to other companies. Although the use of industry norms overcomes this last problem, its disadvantage is that firms are not always comparable, even in the same industry.
3. **State the sources of information for financial statement analysis.** The main sources of information about publicly held corporations are company-published reports, such as annual reports and interim financial statements; SEC reports; business periodicals; and credit and investment advisory services.
4. **Apply horizontal analysis, trend analysis, and vertical analysis to financial statements.** Horizontal analysis involves the computation of changes in both dollar amounts and percentages from year to year. Trend analysis is an extension of horizontal analysis in that percentage changes are calculated for several years. The changes are usually computed by setting a base year equal to 100 and calculating the results for subsequent years as percentages of that base year. Vertical analysis uses percentages to show the relationship of the component parts to a total in a single statement. The resulting financial statements, which are expressed entirely in percentages, are called common-size statements.
5. **Apply ratio analysis to financial statements in a comprehensive evaluation of a company's financial situation.** A comprehensive ratio analysis includes the evaluation of a company's liquidity, profitability, long-term solvency, cash flow adequacy, and market strength. The ratios for measuring these characteristics are found in Exhibits 8 to 12.

REVIEW OF CONCEPTS AND TERMINOLOGY

The following concepts and terms were introduced in this chapter.

LO 5 **Asset turnover:** Net sales divided by average total assets. Used to measure how efficiently assets are used to produce sales.

LO 5 **Average days' inventory on hand:** Days in the year divided by inventory turnover. Shows the average number of days taken to sell inventory.

LO 5 **Average days' sales uncollected:** Days in the year divided by receivable turnover. Shows the speed at which receivables are turned over—literally, the number of days, on average, that a company must wait to receive payment for credit sales.

LO 4 **Base year:** In financial analysis, the first year to be considered in any set of data.

LO 5 **Cash flows to assets:** Net cash flows from operating activities divided by average total assets. Used to measure the ability of assets to generate operating cash flows.

LO 5 **Cash flows to sales:** Net cash flows from operating activities divided by net sales. Used to measure the ability of sales to generate operating cash flows.

LO 5 **Cash flow yield:** Net cash flows from operating activities divided by net income. Used to measure the ability of a company to generate operating cash flows in relation to net income.

LO 4 **Common-size statement:** A financial statement in which the components of a total figure are stated in terms of percentages of that total.

LO 5 **Current ratio:** Current assets divided by current liabilities. Used as an indicator of a company's liquidity and short-term debt-paying ability.

LO 5 **Debt to equity ratio:** Total liabilities divided by stockholders' equity. Used to measure the relationship of debt financing to equity financing, or the extent to which a company is leveraged.

LO 2 **Diversified companies:** Companies that operate in more than one industry; also called *conglomerates*.

LO 5 **Dividends yield:** Dividends per share divided by market price per share. Used as a measure of the current return to an investor in a stock.

LO 1 **Financial statement analysis:** All the techniques used to show important relationships among amounts in financial statements.

LO 5 **Free cash flow:** Net cash flows from operating activities minus dividends minus net capital expenditures. Used to measure cash generated after providing for commitments.

LO 4 **Horizontal analysis:** A technique for analyzing financial statements that involves the computation of changes in both dollar amounts and percentages from the previous to the current year.

LO 4 **Index number:** In trend analysis, a number from which changes in related items over a period of time are measured. Calculated by setting the base year equal to 100 percent.

LO 5 **Interest coverage ratio:** Income before income taxes plus interest expense divided by interest expense. Used as a measure of the degree of protection creditors have from a default on interest payments.

LO 3 **Interim financial statements:** Financial statements issued for a period of less than one year, usually a quarter or a month.

LO 5 **Inventory turnover:** The cost of goods sold divided by average inventory. Used to measure the relative size of inventory.

LO 5 **Operating cycle:** The time it takes to sell products and collect for them; average days' inventory on hand plus average days' sales uncollected.

LO 1 **Portfolio:** A group of loans or investments designed to average the returns and risks of a creditor or investor.

LO 5 **Price/earnings (P/E) ratio:** Market price per share divided by earnings per share. Used as a measure of investor confidence in a company and as a means of comparison among stocks.

LO 5 **Profit margin:** Net income divided by net sales. Used to measure the percentage of each revenue dollar that contributes to net income.

LO 5 **Quick ratio:** The more liquid current assets—cash, marketable securities or short-term investments, and receivables—divided by current liabilities. Used as a measure of short-term debt-paying ability.

LO 4 **Ratio analysis:** A technique of financial analysis in which meaningful relationships are shown between the components of the financial statements.

LO 5 **Receivable turnover:** Net sales divided by average accounts receivable. Used as a measure of the relative size of a company's accounts receivable and the success of its credit and collection policies; shows how many times, on average, receivables were turned into cash during the period.

LO 5 **Return on assets:** Net income divided by average total assets. Used to measure the amount earned on each dollar of assets invested. A measure of overall earning power, or profitability.

LO 5 **Return on equity:** Net income divided by average stockholders' equity. Used to measure how much income was earned on each dollar invested by stockholders.

LO 4 **Trend analysis:** A type of horizontal analysis in which percentage changes are calculated for several successive years instead of for two years.

LO 4 **Vertical analysis:** A technique for analyzing financial statements that uses percentages to show the relationships of the different parts to the total in a single statement.

REVIEW PROBLEM

Comparative Analysis of Two Companies

LO 5 Maggie Washington is considering an investment in one of two fast-food restaurant chains because she believes the trend toward eating out more often will continue. Her choices have been narrowed to Quik Burger and Big Steak, whose balance sheets and income statements appear below.

Balance Sheets
December 31, 20xx
(in thousands)

	Quik Burger	Big Steak
Assets		
Cash	$ 2,000	$ 4,500
Accounts Receivable (net)	2,000	6,500
Inventory	2,000	5,000
Property, Plant, and Equipment (net)	20,000	35,000
Other Assets	4,000	5,000
Total Assets	$30,000	$56,000
Liabilities and Stockholders' Equity		
Accounts Payable	$ 2,500	$ 3,000
Notes Payable	1,500	4,000
Bonds Payable	10,000	30,000
Common Stock, $1 par value	1,000	3,000
Paid-in Capital in Excess of Par Value, Common	9,000	9,000
Retained Earnings	6,000	7,000
Total Liabilities and Stockholders' Equity	$30,000	$56,000

Income Statements
For the Year Ended December 31, 20xx
(in thousands, except per share amounts)

	Quik Burger	Big Steak
Net Sales	$53,000	$86,000
Costs and Expenses		
Cost of Goods Sold	$37,000	$61,000
Selling Expenses	7,000	10,000
Administrative Expenses	4,000	5,000
Total Costs and Expenses	$48,000	$76,000
Income from Operations	$ 5,000	$10,000
Interest Expense	1,400	3,200
Income Before Income Taxes	$ 3,600	$ 6,800
Income Taxes	1,800	3,400
Net Income	$ 1,800	$ 3,400
Earnings per Share	$ 1.80	$ 1.13

The statements of cash flows show that net cash flows from operations were $2,200,000 for Quik Burger and $3,000,000 for Big Steak. Net capital expenditures were $2,100,000 for Quik Burger and $1,800,000 for Big Steak. Dividends of $500,000 were paid by Quik Burger and $600,000 by Big Steak. The market prices of the stocks of Quik Burger and Big Steak were $30 and $20, respectively. Financial information pertaining to prior years is not readily available to Maggie Washington. Assume that all notes payable are current liabilities and that all bonds payable are long-term liabilities.

REQUIRED

Conduct a comprehensive ratio analysis of Quik Burger and Big Steak and compare the results. The analysis should be performed using the following steps (use end-of-year balances for averages and round all ratios and percentages to one decimal place):

1. Prepare an analysis of liquidity.
2. Prepare an analysis of profitability.
3. Prepare an analysis of long-term solvency.
4. Prepare an analysis of cash flow adequacy.
5. Prepare an analysis of market strength.
6. Compare the two companies by inserting the ratio calculations from the preceding five steps in a table with the following column headings: Ratio Name, Quik Burger, Big Steak, and Company with More Favorable Ratio. Indicate in the last column the company that apparently had the more favorable ratio in each case. (Consider differences of .1 or less to be neutral.)
7. In what ways would having access to prior years' information aid this analysis?

ANSWER TO REVIEW PROBLEM

Ratio Name	Quik Burger	Big Steak
1. **Liquidity analysis**		
a. Current ratio	$\frac{\$2{,}000 + \$2{,}000 + \$2{,}000}{\$2{,}500 + \$1{,}500} = \frac{\$6{,}000}{\$4{,}000} = 1.5$ times	$\frac{\$4{,}500 + \$6{,}500 + \$5{,}000}{\$3{,}000 + \$4{,}000} = \frac{\$16{,}000}{\$7{,}000} = 2.3$ times
b. Quick ratio	$\frac{\$2{,}000 + \$2{,}000}{\$2{,}500 + \$1{,}500} = \frac{\$4{,}000}{\$4{,}000} = 1.0$ times	$\frac{\$4{,}500 + \$6{,}500}{\$3{,}000 + \$4{,}000} = \frac{\$11{,}000}{\$7{,}000} = 1.6$ times
c. Receivable turnover	$\frac{\$53{,}000}{\$2{,}000} = 26.5$ times	$\frac{\$86{,}000}{\$6{,}500} = 13.2$ times
d. Average days' sales uncollected	$\frac{365}{26.5} = 13.8$ days	$\frac{365}{13.2} = 27.7$ days
e. Inventory turnover	$\frac{\$37{,}000}{\$2{,}000} = 18.5$ times	$\frac{\$61{,}000}{\$5{,}000} = 12.2$ times
f. Average days' inventory on hand	$\frac{365}{18.5} = 19.7$ days	$\frac{365}{12.2} = 29.9$ days

Ratio Name	Quik Burger	Big Steak
2. Profitability analysis		
a. Profit margin	$\frac{\$1,800}{\$53,000} = 3.4\%$	$\frac{\$3,400}{\$86,000} = 4.0\%$
b. Asset turnover	$\frac{\$53,000}{\$30,000} = 1.8$ times	$\frac{\$86,000}{\$56,000} = 1.5$ times
c. Return on assets	$\frac{\$1,800}{\$30,000} = 6.0\%$	$\frac{\$3,400}{\$56,000} = 6.1\%$
d. Return on equity	$\frac{\$1,800}{\$1,000 + \$9,000 + \$6,000} = \frac{\$1,800}{\$16,000} = 11.3\%$	$\frac{\$3,400}{\$3,000 + \$9,000 + \$7,000} = \frac{\$3,400}{\$19,000} = 17.9\%$
3. Long-term solvency analysis		
a. Debt to equity ratio	$\frac{\$2,500 + \$1,500 + \$10,000}{\$1,000 + \$9,000 + \$6,000} = \frac{\$14,000}{\$16,000} = .9$ times	$\frac{\$3,000 + \$4,000 + \$30,000}{\$3,000 + \$9,000 + \$7,000} = \frac{\$37,000}{\$19,000} = 1.9$ times
b. Interest coverage ratio	$\frac{\$3,600 + \$1,400}{\$1,400} = \frac{\$5,000}{\$1,400} = 3.6$ times	$\frac{\$6,800 + \$3,200}{\$3,200} = \frac{\$10,000}{\$3,200} = 3.1$ times
4. Cash flow adequacy analysis		
a. Cash flow yield	$\frac{\$2,200}{\$1,800} = 1.2$ times	$\frac{\$3,000}{\$3,400} = .9$ times
b. Cash flows to sales	$\frac{\$2,200}{\$53,000} = 4.2\%$	$\frac{\$3,000}{\$86,000} = 3.5\%$
c. Cash flows to assets	$\frac{\$2,200}{\$30,000} = 7.3\%$	$\frac{\$3,000}{\$56,000} = 5.4\%$
d. Free cash flow	$2,200 − $500 − $2,100 = (400)	$3,000 − $600 − $1,800 = $600
5. Market strength analysis		
a. Price/earnings ratio	$\frac{\$30}{\$1.80} = 16.7$ times	$\frac{\$20}{\$1.13} = 17.7$ times
b. Dividends yield	$\frac{\$500,000/1,000,000}{\$30} = 1.7\%$	$\frac{\$600,000/3,000,000}{\$20} = 1.0\%$

6. **Comparative analysis**

Ratio Name	Quik Burger	Big Steak	Company with More Favorable Ratio*
1. Liquidity analysis			
a. Current ratio	1.5 times	2.3 times	Big Steak
b. Quick ratio	1.0 times	1.6 times	Big Steak
c. Receivable turnover	26.5 times	13.2 times	Quik Burger
d. Average days' sales uncollected	13.8 days	27.7 days	Quik Burger
e. Inventory turnover	18.5 times	12.2 times	Quik Burger
f. Average days' inventory on hand	19.7 days	29.9 days	Quik Burger
2. Profitability analysis			
a. Profit margin	3.4%	4.0%	Big Steak
b. Asset turnover	1.8 times	1.5 times	Quik Burger
c. Return on assets	6.0%	6.1%	Neutral
d. Return on equity	11.3%	17.9%	Big Steak
3. Long-term solvency analysis			
a. Debt to equity ratio	.9 times	1.9 times	Quik Burger
b. Interest coverage ratio	3.6 times	3.1 times	Quik Burger
4. Cash flow adequacy analysis			
a. Cash flow yield	1.2 times	.9 times	Quik Burger
b. Cash flows to sales	4.2%	3.5%	Quik Burger
c. Cash flows to assets	7.3%	5.4%	Quik Burger
d. Free cash flow	($400)	$600	Big Steak
5. Market strength analysis			
a. Price/earnings ratio	16.7 times	17.7 times	Big Steak
b. Dividends yield	1.7%	1.0%	Quik Burger

*This analysis indicates the company with the apparently more favorable ratio. Class discussion may focus on conditions under which different conclusions may be drawn.

7. **Usefulness of prior years' information**
Prior years' information would be helpful in two ways. First, turnover, return, and cash flows to assets ratios could be based on average amounts. Second, a trend analysis could be performed for each company.

Chapter Assignments

BUILDING YOUR KNOWLEDGE FOUNDATION

Questions

1. What are the differences and similarities in the objectives of investors and creditors in using financial statement analysis?
2. What role does risk play in making loans and investments?
3. What standards of comparison are commonly used to evaluate financial statements, and what are their relative merits?
4. Why would a financial analyst compare the ratios of Steelco, a steel company, with the ratios of other companies in the steel industry? What factors might invalidate such a comparison?

5. Where may an investor look for information about a publicly held company in which he or she is thinking of investing?
6. Why would an investor want to see both horizontal and trend analyses of a company's financial statements?
7. What does the following sentence mean: "Based on 1980 equaling 100, net income increased from 240 in 1996 to 260 in 1997"?
8. What is the difference between horizontal and vertical analysis?
9. What is the purpose of ratio analysis?
10. Under what circumstances would a current ratio of 3:1 be good? Under what circumstances would it be bad?
11. In a period of high interest rates, why are receivable turnover and inventory turnover especially important?
12. The following statements were made on page 35 of the November 6, 1978, issue of *Fortune* magazine: "Supermarket executives are beginning to look back with some nostalgia on the days when the standard profit margin was 1 percent of sales. Last year the industry overall margin came to a thin 0.72 percent." How could a supermarket earn a satisfactory return on assets with such a small profit margin?
13. Company A and Company B both have net incomes of $1,000,000. Is it possible to say that these companies are equally successful? Why or why not?
14. Circo Company has a return on assets of 12 percent and a debt to equity ratio of .5. Would you expect return on equity to be more or less than 12 percent?
15. What amount is common to all cash flow adequacy ratios? To what other groups of ratios are the cash flow adequacy ratios most closely related?
16. The market price of Company J's stock is the same as that of Company Q's. How might you determine whether investors are equally confident about the future of these companies?

Short Exercises

LO 1
LO 2
SE 1. *Objectives and Standards of Financial Statement Analysis*

Indicate whether each of the following items is (a) an objective or (b) a standard of comparison of financial statement analysis.

1. Industry norms
2. Assessment of the company's past performance
3. The company's past performance
4. Assessment of future potential and related risk
5. Rule-of-thumb measures

LO 3
SE 2. *Sources of Information*

For each piece of information listed below, indicate whether the *best* source would be (a) reports published by the company, (b) SEC reports, (c) business periodicals, or (d) credit and investment advisory services.

1. Current market value of a company's stock
2. Management's analysis of the past year's operations
3. Objective assessment of a company's financial performance
4. Most complete body of financial disclosures
5. Current events affecting the company

LO 4
SE 3. *Trend Analysis*

Using 2000 as the base year, prepare a trend analysis for the following data, and tell whether the results suggest a favorable or unfavorable trend. (Round your answers to one decimal place.)

	20x2	20x1	20x0
Net sales	$158,000	$136,000	$112,000
Accounts receivable (net)	43,000	32,000	21,000

LO 4 *Horizontal Analysis*

SE 4. Compute the amount and percentage changes for the income statements that appear below, and comment on the changes from 20x0 to 20x1. (Round the percentage changes to one decimal place.)

SiteWorks, Inc.
Comparative Income Statements
For the Years Ended December 31, 20x1 and 20x0

	20x1	20x0
Net Sales	$180,000	$145,000
Cost of Goods Sold	112,000	88,000
Gross Margin	$ 68,000	$ 57,000
Operating Expenses	40,000	30,000
Operating Income	$ 28,000	$ 27,000
Interest Expense	7,000	5,000
Income Before Income Taxes	$ 21,000	$ 22,000
Income Taxes	7,000	8,000
Net Income	$ 14,000	$ 14,000
Earnings per Share	$ 1.40	$ 1.40

LO 4 *Vertical Analysis*

SE 5. Express the comparative balance sheets that follow as common-size statements, and comment on the changes from 20x0 to 20x1. (Round computations to one decimal place.)

SiteWorks, Inc.
Comparative Balance Sheets
December 31, 20x1 and 20x0

	20x1	20x0
Assets		
Current Assets	$ 24,000	$ 20,000
Property, Plant, and Equipment (net)	130,000	100,000
Total Assets	$154,000	$120,000
Liabilities and Stockholders' Equity		
Current Liabilities	$ 18,000	$ 22,000
Long-Term Liabilities	90,000	60,000
Stockholders' Equity	46,000	38,000
Total Liabilities and Stockholders' Equity	$154,000	$120,000

LO 5 *Liquidity Analysis*

SE 6. Using the information for SiteWorks, Inc., in **SE 4** and **SE 5,** compute the current ratio, quick ratio, receivable turnover, average days' sales uncollected, inventory turnover, and average days' inventory on hand for 20x0 and 20x1. Inventories were $4,000 in 19x9 $5,000 in 20x0, and $7,000 in 20x1. Accounts Receivable were $6,000 in 19x9, $8,000 in

20x0, and $10,000 in 20x1. There were no marketable securities or prepaid assets. Comment on the results. (Round computations to one decimal place.)

SE 7. LO 5 *Profitability Analysis*

Using the information for SiteWorks, Inc., in **SE 4** and **SE 5,** compute the profit margin, asset turnover, return on assets, and return on equity for 20x0 and 20x1. In 19x9, total assets were $100,000 and total stockholders' equity was $30,000. Comment on the results. (Round computations to one decimal place.)

SE 8. LO 5 *Long-Term Solvency Analysis*

Using the information for SiteWorks, Inc., in **SE 4** and **SE 5,** compute the debt to equity and interest coverage ratios for 20x0 and 20x1. Comment on the results. (Round computations to one decimal place.)

SE 9. LO 5 *Cash Flow Adequacy Analysis*

Using the information for SiteWorks, Inc., in **SE 4, SE 5,** and **SE 7,** compute the cash flow yield, cash flows to sales, cash flows to assets, and free cash flow for 20x0 and 20x1. Net cash flows from operating activities were $21,000 in 20x0 and $16,000 in 20x1. Net capital expenditures were $30,000 in 20x0 and $40,000 in 20x1. Cash dividends were $6,000 in both years. Comment on the results. (Round computations to one decimal place.)

SE 10. LO 5 *Market Strength Analysis*

Using the information for SiteWorks, Inc., in **SE 4, SE 5,** and **SE 9,** compute the price/earnings and dividends yield ratios for 20x0 and 20x1. The company had 10,000 shares of common stock outstanding in both years. The price of SiteWorks' common stock was $30 in 20x0 and $20 in 20x1. Comment on the results. (Round computations to one decimal place.)

Exercises

E 1. LO 1 LO 2 LO 3 *Objectives, Standards, and Sources of Information for Financial Statement Analysis*

Identify each of the following as (a) an objective of financial statement analysis, (b) a standard for financial statement analysis, or (c) a source of information for financial statement analysis:

1. Average ratios of other companies in the same industry
2. Assessment of the future potential of an investment
3. Interim financial statements
4. Past ratios of the company
5. SEC Form 10-K
6. Assessment of risk
7. A company's annual report

E 2. LO 4 *Horizontal Analysis*

Compute the amount and percentage changes for the following balance sheets, and comment on the changes from 20x1 to 20x2. (Round the percentage changes to one decimal place.)

Lindquist Company
Comparative Balance Sheets
December 31, 20x2 and 20x1

	20x2	20x1
Assets		
Current Assets	$ 37,200	$ 25,600
Property, Plant, and Equipment (net)	218,928	194,400
Total Assets	$256,128	$220,000
Liabilities and Stockholders' Equity		
Current Liabilities	$ 22,400	$ 6,400
Long-Term Liabilities	70,000	80,000
Stockholders' Equity	163,728	133,600
Total Liabilities and Stockholders' Equity	$256,128	$220,000

LO 4 *Trend Analysis*

E 3. Using 20x1 as the base year, prepare a trend analysis of the following data, and tell whether the situation shown by the trends is favorable or unfavorable. (Round your answers to one decimal place.)

	20x5	20x4	20x3	20x2	20x1
Net sales	$25,520	$23,980	$24,200	$22,880	$22,000
Cost of goods sold	17,220	15,400	15,540	14,700	14,000
General and administrative expenses	5,280	5,184	5,088	4,896	4,800
Operating income	3,020	3,396	3,572	3,284	3,200

LO 4 *Vertical Analysis*

E 4. Express the comparative income statements that follow as common-size statements, and comment on the changes from 20x1 to 20x2. (Round computations to one decimal place.)

Lindquist Company
Comparative Income Statements
For the Years Ended December 31, 20x2 and 20x1

	20x2	20x1
Net Sales	$424,000	$368,000
Cost of Goods Sold	254,400	239,200
Gross Margin	$169,600	$128,800
Selling Expenses	$106,000	$ 73,600
General Expenses	50,880	36,800
Total Operating Expenses	$156,880	$110,400
Net Operating Income	$ 12,720	$ 18,400

LO 5 *Liquidity Analysis*

E 5. Partial comparative balance sheet and income statement information for Lum Company follows.

	20x2	20x1
Cash	$ 6,800	$ 5,200
Marketable Securities	3,600	8,600
Accounts Receivable (net)	22,400	17,800
Inventory	27,200	24,800
Total Current Assets	$ 60,000	$ 56,400
Current Liabilities	$ 20,000	$ 14,100
Net Sales	$161,280	$110,360
Cost of Goods Sold	$108,800	101,680
Gross Margin	$ 52,480	$ 8,680

The year-end balances for Accounts Receivable and Inventory were $16,200 and $25,600, respectively, in 20x0. Compute the current ratio, quick ratio, receivable turnover, average days' sales uncollected, inventory turnover, and average days' inventory on hand for each year. (Round computations to one decimal place.) Comment on the change in the company's liquidity position from 20x1 to 20x2.

LO 5 *Turnover Analysis*

E 6. Alberto's Men's Shop has been in business for four years. Because the company has recently had a cash flow problem, management wonders whether there is a problem with receivables or inventories. Here are selected figures from the company's financial statements (in thousands):

	20x4	20x3	20x2	20x1
Net sales	$288	$224	$192	$160
Cost of goods sold	180	144	120	96
Accounts receivable (net)	48	40	32	24
Merchandise inventory	56	44	32	20

Compute receivable turnover and inventory turnover for each of the four years, and comment on the results relative to the cash flow problem that Alberto's Men's Shop has been experiencing. Round computations to one decimal place.

LO 5 *Profitability Analysis*

E 7. At year end, Canzoneri Company had total assets of $640,000 in 20x0, $680,000 in 20x1, and $760,000 in 20x2. Its debt to equity ratio was .67 in all three years. In 20x1, the company had net income of $77,112 on revenues of $1,224,000. In 20x2, the company had net income of $98,952 on revenues of $1,596,000. Compute the profit margin, asset turnover, return on assets, and return on equity for 20x1 and 20x2. Comment on the apparent cause of the increase or decrease in profitability. (Round the percentages and other ratios to one decimal place.)

LO 5 *Long-Term Solvency and Market Strength Ratios*

E 8. An investor is considering investing in the long-term bonds and common stock of Companies X and Y. Both companies operate in the same industry. In addition, both companies pay a dividend per share of $4, and a yield of 10 percent on their long-term bonds. Other data for the two companies follow:

	Company X	Company Y
Total assets	$2,400,000	$1,080,000
Total liabilities	1,080,000	594,000
Income before income taxes	288,000	129,600
Interest expense	97,200	53,460
Earnings per share	3.20	5.00
Market price of common stock	40	47.50

Compute the debt to equity, interest coverage, price/earnings (P/E), and dividends yield ratios, and comment on the results. (Round computations to one decimal place.)

LO 5 *Cash Flow Adequacy Analysis*

E 9. Using the data below, taken from the financial statements of Liarano, Inc., compute the cash flow yield, cash flows to sales, cash flows to assets, and free cash flow. (Round computations to one decimal place.)

Net sales	$6,400,000
Net income	704,000
Net cash flows from operating activities	912,000
Total assets, beginning of year	5,780,000
Total assets, end of year	6,240,000
Cash dividends	240,000
Net capital expenditures	596,000

LO 5 *Preparation of Statements from Ratios and Incomplete Data*

E 10. On the next page are the income statement and balance sheet of Pandit Corporation, with most of the amounts missing. Pandit's only interest expense is on long-term debt. Its debt to equity ratio is .5, its current ratio 3:1, its quick ratio 2:1, the receivable turnover 4.5, and its inventory turnover 4.0. The return on assets is 10 percent. All ratios are based on the current year's information. Complete the financial statements using the information presented. Show supporting computations.

Pandit Corporation
Income Statement
For the Year Ended December 31, 20x1
(in thousands of dollars)

Net Sales		$18,000
Cost of Goods Sold		(a)
Gross Margin		$ (b)
Operating Expenses		
Selling Expenses	$ (c)	
Administrative Expenses	234	
Total Operating Expenses		(d)
Income from Operations		(e)
Interest Expense		162
Income Before Income Taxes		(f)
Income Taxes		620
Net Income		$ (g)

Pandit Corporation
Balance Sheet
December 31, 20x1
(in thousands of dollars)

Assets		
Cash	$ (h)	
Accounts Receivable (net)	(i)	
Inventories	(j)	
Total Current Assets		$ (k)
Property, Plant, and Equipment (net)		5,400
Total Assets		$ (l)
Liabilities and Stockholders' Equity		
Current Liabilities	$ (m)	
Bonds Payable, 9% interest	(n)	
Total Liabilities		$ (o)
Common Stock, $20 par value	$3,000	
Paid-in Capital in Excess of Par Value, Common	2,600	
Retained Earnings	4,000	
Total Stockholders' Equity		9,600
Total Liabilities and Stockholders' Equity		$ (p)

Problems

LO 4 **P 1.** *Horizontal and Vertical Analysis*

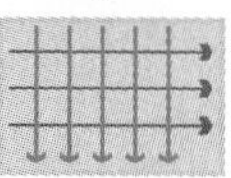

The condensed comparative income statements and balance sheets of Mariano Corporation follow. All figures are given in thousands of dollars.

Mariano Corporation
Comparative Income Statements
For the Years Ended December 31, 20x2 and 20x1

	20x2	20x1
Net Sales	$3,276,800	$3,146,400
Cost of Goods Sold	2,088,800	2,008,400
Gross Margin	$1,188,000	$1,138,000
Operating Expenses		
Selling Expenses	$ 476,800	$ 518,000
Administrative Expenses	447,200	423,200
Total Operating Expenses	$ 924,000	$ 941,200
Income from Operations	$ 264,000	$ 196,800
Interest Expense	65,600	39,200
Income Before Income Taxes	$ 198,400	$ 157,600
Income Taxes	62,400	56,800
Net Income	$ 136,000	$ 100,800
Earnings per Share	$ 3.40	$ 2.52

Mariano Corporation
Comparative Balance Sheets
December 31, 20x2 and 20x1

	20x2	20x1
Assets		
Cash	$ 81,200	$ 40,800
Accounts Receivable (net)	235,600	229,200
Inventory	574,800	594,800
Property, Plant, and Equipment (net)	750,000	720,000
Total Assets	$1,641,600	$1,584,800
Liabilities and Stockholders' Equity		
Accounts Payable	$ 267,600	$ 477,200
Notes Payable (short-term)	200,000	400,000
Bonds Payable	400,000	—
Common Stock, $10 par value	400,000	400,000
Retained Earnings	374,000	307,600
Total Liabilities and Stockholders' Equity	$1,641,600	$1,584,800

REQUIRED

Perform the following analyses. Round all ratios and percentages to one decimal place.

1. Prepare schedules showing the amount and percentage changes from 20x1 to 20x2 for Mariano's comparative income statements and balance sheets.
2. Prepare common-size income statements and balance sheets for 20x1 and 20x2.
3. Comment on the results in **1** and **2** by identifying favorable and unfavorable changes in the components and composition of the statements.

P 2. LO 5 *Analyzing the Effects of Transactions on Ratios*

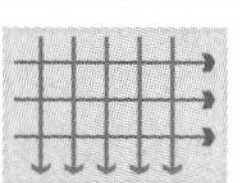

Rader Corporation engaged in the transactions listed in the first column of the following table. Opposite each transaction is a ratio and space to indicate the effect of each transaction on the ratio.

Transaction	Ratio	Effect: Increase	Effect: Decrease	Effect: None
a. Sold merchandise on account.	Current ratio			
b. Sold merchandise on account.	Inventory turnover			
c. Collected on accounts receivable.	Quick ratio			
d. Wrote off an uncollectible account.	Receivable turnover			
e. Paid on accounts payable.	Current ratio			
f. Declared cash dividend.	Return on equity			
g. Incurred advertising expense.	Profit margin			
h. Issued stock dividend.	Debt to equity ratio			
i. Issued bond payable.	Asset turnover			
j. Accrued interest expense.	Current ratio			
k. Paid previously declared cash dividend.	Dividends yield			
l. Purchased treasury stock.	Return on assets			
m. Recorded depreciation expense.	Cash flow yield			

REQUIRED

Place an *X* in the appropriate column to show whether the transaction increased, decreased, or had no effect on the indicated ratio.

P 3. LO 5 *Ratio Analysis*

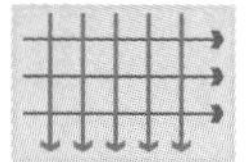

Additional data for Mariano Corporation in 20x2 and 20x1 follow. This information should be used in conjunction with the data in **P 1.**

	20x2	20x1
Net cash flows from operating activities	($196,000,000)	$144,000,000
Net capital expenditures	$ 40,000,000	$ 65,000,000
Dividends paid	$ 44,000,000	$ 34,400,000
Number of common shares	40,000,000	40,000,000
Market price per share	$18	$30

Selected balances at the end of 20x0 were Accounts Receivable (net), $206,800; Inventory, $547,200; Total Assets, $1,465,600; and Stockholders' Equity, $641,200. All of Mariano's notes payable were current liabilities; all of the bonds payable were long-term liabilities.

REQUIRED

Perform the following analyses. Round all answers to one decimal place, and consider changes of .1 or less to be neutral. After making the calculations, indicate whether each ratio improved or deteriorated from 20x1 to 20x2 by writing *F* for favorable or *U* for unfavorable.

1. Prepare a liquidity analysis by calculating for each year the (a) current ratio, (b) quick ratio, (c) receivable turnover, (d) average days' sales uncollected, (e) inventory turnover, and (f) average days' inventory on hand.
2. Prepare a profitability analysis by calculating for each year the (a) profit margin, (b) asset turnover, (c) return on assets, and (d) return on equity.
3. Prepare a long-term solvency analysis by calculating for each year the (a) debt to equity ratio and (b) interest coverage ratio.
4. Prepare a cash flow adequacy analysis by calculating for each year the (a) cash flow yield, (b) cash flows to sales, (c) cash flows to assets, and (d) free cash flows.
5. Prepare a market strength analysis by calculating for each year the (a) price/earnings ratio, and (b) dividends yield.

LO 5 *Comprehensive Ratio Analysis of Two Companies*

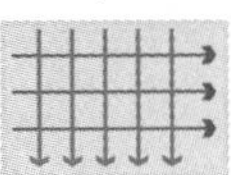

P 4. Willis Rowe is considering an investment in the common stock of a chain of retail department stores. He has narrowed his choice to two retail companies, Allison Corporation and Marker Corporation, whose income statements and balance sheets are shown below and on the next page. During the year, Allison Corporation paid a total of $50,000 in dividends. The market price per share of its stock is currently $30. In comparison, Marker Corporation paid a total of $114,000 in dividends, and the current market price of its stock is $38 per share. Allison Corporation had net cash flows from operations of $271,500 and net capital expenditures of $625,000. Marker Corporation had net cash flows from operations of $492,500 and net capital expenditures of $1,050,000. Information for prior years is not readily available. Assume that all notes payable are current liabilities and all bonds payable are long-term liabilities.

	Allison Corporation	Marker Corporation
Assets		
Cash	$ 80,000	$ 192,400
Marketable Securities	203,400	84,600
Accounts Receivable (net)	552,800	985,400
Inventories	629,800	1,253,400
Prepaid Expenses	54,400	114,000
Property, Plant, and Equipment (net)	2,913,600	6,552,000
Intangibles and Other Assets	553,200	144,800
Total Assets	$4,987,200	$9,326,600
Liabilities and Stockholders' Equity		
Accounts Payable	$ 344,000	$ 572,600
Notes Payable	150,000	400,000
Income Taxes Payable	50,200	73,400
Bonds Payable	2,000,000	2,000,000
Common Stock, $10 par value	1,000,000	600,000
Paid-in Capital in Excess of Par Value, Common	609,800	3,568,600
Retained Earnings	833,200	2,112,000
Total Liabilities and Stockholders' Equity	$4,987,200	$9,326,600

	Allison Corporation	Marker Corporation
Net Sales	$12,560,000	$25,210,000
Costs and Expenses		
Cost of Goods Sold	$ 6,142,000	$14,834,000
Selling Expenses	4,822,600	7,108,200
Administrative Expenses	986,000	2,434,000
Total Costs and Expenses	$11,950,600	$24,376,200
Income from Operations	$ 609,400	$ 833,800
Interest Expense	194,000	228,000
Income Before Income Taxes	$ 415,400	$ 605,800
Income Taxes	200,000	300,000
Net Income	$ 215,400	$ 305,800
Earnings per Share	$ 2.15	$ 5.10

REQUIRED

Conduct a comprehensive ratio analysis for each company, using the available information. Compare the results. Round percentages and ratios to one decimal place, and consider changes of .1 or less to be indeterminate. This analysis should be done in the following steps:

1. Prepare an analysis of liquidity by calculating for each company the (a) current ratio, (b) quick ratio, (c) receivable turnover, (d) average days' sales uncollected, (e) inventory turnover, and (f) average days' inventory on hand.
2. Prepare an analysis of profitability by calculating for each company the (a) profit margin, (b) asset turnover, (c) return on assets, and (d) return on equity.
3. Prepare an analysis of long-term solvency by calculating for each company the (a) debt to equity ratio and (b) interest coverage ratio.
4. Prepare an analysis of cash flow adequacy by calculating for each company the (a) cash flow yield, (b) cash flows to sales, (c) cash flows to assets, and (d) free cash flow.
5. Prepare an analysis of market strength by calculating for each company the (a) price/earnings ratio and (b) dividends yield.
6. Compare the two companies by inserting the ratio calculations from **1** through **5** in a table with the following column headings: Ratio Name, Allison Corporation, Marker Corporation, and Company with More Favorable Ratio. Indicate in the right-hand column which company had the more favorable ratio in each case.
7. How could the analysis be improved if information from prior years were available?

Alternate Problems

P 5. LO 5 *Analyzing the Effects of Transactions on Ratios*

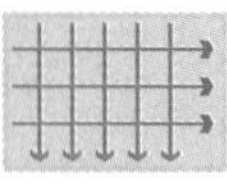

Estevez Corporation engaged in the transactions listed in the first column of the table on the next page. Opposite each transaction is a ratio and space to mark the effect of each transaction on the ratio.

Transaction	Ratio	Effect: Increase	Decrease	None
a. Issued common stock for cash.	Asset turnover			
b. Declared cash dividend.	Current ratio			
c. Sold treasury stock.	Return on equity			
d. Borrowed cash by issuing note payable.	Debt to equity ratio			
e. Paid salaries expense.	Inventory turnover			
f. Purchased merchandise for cash.	Current ratio			
g. Sold equipment for cash.	Receivable turnover			
h. Sold merchandise on account.	Quick ratio			
i. Paid current portion of long-term debt.	Return on assets			
j. Gave sales discount.	Profit margin			
k. Purchased marketable securities for cash.	Quick ratio			
l. Declared 5% stock dividend.	Current ratio			
m. Purchased a building.	Free cash flow			

REQUIRED

Place an *X* in the appropriate column to show whether the transaction increased, decreased, or had no effect on the indicated ratio.

LO 5 *Ratio Analysis*

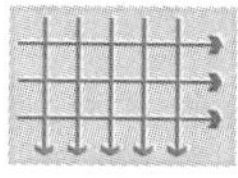

P 6. The condensed comparative income statements and balance sheets of Schumacker Corporation appear below and on the next page. All figures are given in thousands of dollars, except earnings per share.

Schumacker Corporation
Comparative Income Statements
For the Years Ended December 31, 20x6 and 20x5

	20x6	20x5
Net Sales	$1,638,400	$1,573,200
Costs and Expenses		
Cost of Goods Sold	$1,044,400	$1,004,200
Selling Expenses	238,400	259,000
Administrative Expenses	223,600	211,600
Total Costs and Expenses	$1,506,400	$1,474,800
Income from Operations	$ 132,000	$ 98,400
Interest Expense	32,800	19,600
Income Before Income Taxes	$ 99,200	$ 78,800
Income Taxes	31,200	28,400
Net Income	$ 68,000	$ 50,400
Earnings per Share	$ 1.70	$ 1.26

Schumacker Corporation
Comparative Balance Sheets
December 31, 20x6 and 20x5

	20x6	20x5
Assets		
Cash	$ 40,600	$ 20,400
Accounts Receivable (net)	117,800	114,600
Inventory	287,400	297,400
Property, Plant, and Equipment (net)	375,000	360,000
Total Assets	$820,800	$792,400
Liabilities and Stockholders' Equity		
Accounts Payable	$133,800	$238,600
Notes Payable	100,000	200,000
Bonds Payable	200,000	—
Common Stock, $5 par value	200,000	200,000
Retained Earnings	187,000	153,800
Total Liabilities and Stockholders' Equity	$820,800	$792,400

Additional data for Schumacker Corporation in 20x6 and 20x5 follow.

	20x6	20x5
Net cash flows from operating activities	$106,500,000	$86,250,000
Net capital expenditures	$22,500,000	$16,000,000
Dividends paid	$22,000,000	$17,200,000
Number of common shares	40,000,000	40,000,000
Market price per share	$9	$15

Selected balances (in thousands) at the end of 20x4 were Accounts Receivable (net), $103,400; Inventory, $273,600; Total Assets, $732,800; and Stockholders' Equity, $320,600. All of Schumacker's notes payable were current liabilities; all of the bonds payable were long-term liabilities.

REQUIRED

Perform the following analyses. Round percentages and ratios to one decimal place, and consider changes of .1 or less to be neutral. After making the calculations, indicate whether each ratio had a favorable (F) or unfavorable (U) change from 20x5 to 20x6.

1. Conduct a liquidity analysis by calculating for each year the (a) current ratio, (b) quick ratio, (c) receivable turnover, (d) average days' sales uncollected, (e) inventory turnover, and (f) average days' inventory on hand.
2. Conduct a profitability analysis by calculating for each year the (a) profit margin, (b) asset turnover, (c) return on assets, and (d) return on equity.
3. Conduct a long-term solvency analysis by calculating for each year the (a) debt to equity ratio and (b) interest coverage ratio.
4. Conduct a cash flow adequacy analysis by calculating for each year the (a) cash flow yield, (b) cash flows to sales, (c) cash flows to assets, and (d) free cash flow.
5. Conduct a market strength analysis by calculating for each year the (a) price/earnings ratio and (b) dividends yield.

P 7. **LO 5** *Comprehensive Ratio Analysis of Two Companies*

José Trevás has decided to invest some of his savings in common stock. He feels that the chemical industry has good growth prospects and has narrowed his choice to two companies in that industry. As a final step in making the choice, he has decided to perform a comprehensive ratio analysis of the two companies, Emax and Savlow. Income statement and balance sheet data for the two companies appear below.

	Emax	**Savlow**
Net Sales	$9,486,200	$27,287,300
Costs and Expenses		
Cost of Goods Sold	$5,812,200	$18,372,400
Selling Expenses	1,194,000	1,955,700
Administrative Expenses	1,217,400	4,126,000
Total Costs and Expenses	$8,223,600	$24,454,100
Income from Operations	$1,262,600	$ 2,833,200
Interest Expense	270,000	1,360,000
Income Before Income Taxes	$ 992,600	$ 1,473,200
Income Taxes	450,000	600,000
Net Income	$ 542,600	$ 873,200
Earnings per Share	$ 1.55	$ .87

	Emax	**Savlow**
Assets		
Cash	$ 126,100	$ 514,300
Marketable Securities (at cost)	117,500	1,200,000
Accounts Receivable (net)	456,700	2,600,000
Inventories	1,880,000	4,956,000
Prepaid Expenses	72,600	156,600
Property, Plant, and Equipment (net)	5,342,200	19,356,000
Intangibles and Other Assets	217,000	580,000
Total Assets	$8,212,100	$29,362,900
Liabilities and Stockholders' Equity		
Accounts Payable	$ 517,400	$ 2,342,000
Notes Payable	1,000,000	2,000,000
Income Taxes Payable	85,200	117,900
Bonds Payable	2,000,000	15,000,000
Common Stock, $1 par value	350,000	1,000,000
Paid-in Capital in Excess of Par Value, Common	1,747,300	5,433,300
Retained Earnings	2,512,200	3,469,700
Total Liabilities and Stockholders' Equity	$8,212,100	$29,362,900

During the year, Emax paid a total of $140,000 in dividends, and its current market price per share is $20. Savlow paid a total of $600,000 in dividends during the year, and its current market price per share is $9. Emax had net cash flows from operations of $771,500 and net capital expenditures of $450,000. Savlow had net cash flows from operations of $843,000 and net capital expenditures of $1,550,000. Information pertaining to prior years is not readily available. Assume that all notes payable are current liabilities and that all bonds payable are long-term liabilities.

REQUIRED

Conduct a comprehensive ratio analysis of Emax and of Savlow, using the current end-of-year data. Compare the results. Round all ratios and percentages to one decimal place. This analysis should be done in the following steps:

1. Prepare an analysis of liquidity by calculating for each company the (a) current ratio, (b) quick ratio, (c) receivable turnover, (d) average days' sales uncollected, (e) inventory turnover, and (f) average days' inventory on hand.
2. Prepare an analysis of profitability by calculating for each company the (a) profit margin, (b) asset turnover, (c) return on assets, and (d) return on equity.
3. Prepare an analysis of long-term solvency by calculating for each company the (a) debt to equity ratio and (b) interest coverage ratio.
4. Prepare an analysis of cash flow adequacy by calculating for each company the (a) cash flow yield, (b) cash flows to sales, (c) cash flows to assets, and (d) free cash flow.
5. Prepare an analysis of market strength by calculating for each company the (a) price/earnings ratio and (b) dividends yield.
6. Compare the two companies by inserting the ratio calculations from **1** through **5** in a table with the following column headings: Ratio Name, Emax, Savlow, and Company with More Favorable Ratio. Indicate in the right-hand column of the table which company had the more favorable ratio in each case.
7. How could the analysis be improved if information from prior years were available?

EXPANDING YOUR CRITICAL THINKING, COMMUNICATION, AND INTERPERSONAL SKILLS

Skills Development

CONCEPTUAL ANALYSIS

SD 1. LO 2 LO 5 *Standards for Financial Analysis*

Helene Curtis, a well-known, publicly owned corporation, became a take-over candidate and sold out in the 1990s after years of poor profit performance. "By almost any standard, Chicago-based Helene Curtis rates as one of America's worst-managed personal care companies. In recent years its return on equity has hovered between 10% and 13%, well below the industry average of 18% to 19%. Net profit margins of 2% to 3% are half that of competitors. . . . As a result, while leading names like Revlon and Avon are trading at three and four times book value, Curtis trades at less than two-thirds book value."[8] Considering that many companies in other industries are happy with a return on equity of 10 percent to 13 percent, why is this analysis so critical of Curtis's performance? Assuming that Curtis could double its profit margin, what other information would be

Communication

Critical Thinking

Group Activity

Memo

Ethics

International
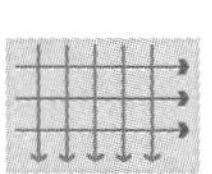
Spreadsheet

General Ledger

CD-ROM

Internet

necessary to project the resulting return on stockholders' investment? Why are Revlon's and Avon's stocks trading for more than Curtis's? Be prepared to discuss your answers to these questions in class.

SD 2.
LO 3 *Use of Investors Service*

Refer to Exhibits 1 and 2, which contain the segment information for ***PepsiCo, Inc.,*** and its listing in Moody's *Handbook of Dividend Achievers*. Assume that an investor has asked you to assess PepsiCo's recent history and prospects. Write a memorandum to the investor that addresses the following points:

1. PepsiCo's business segments and their relative importance. (In what three business segments does PepsiCo, Inc., operate, and what is the relative size of each in terms of their sales and operating income? Which business segment appears to be the most profitable?)
2. PepsiCo's earnings history. (What generally has been the relationship between PepsiCo's return on assets and its return on equity over the years 1990 to 1996? What does this tell you about the way the company is financed? What figures back up your conclusion?)
3. The trend of PepsiCo's stock price and price/earnings ratio for the seven years shown.
4. PepsiCo's prospects, including developments that are likely to affect the future of the company.

Ethical Dilemma

SD 3.
LO 3 *Management of Earnings*

In 1993, *The Wall Street Journal* reported that ***H. J. Heinz Co.,*** the famous maker of catsup and many other food products, earned a quarterly income of $.75 per share, which included a gain on sale of assets of $.24 per share. Income from continuing operations was only $.51 per share, or 16 percent below the previous year's figure. The paper was critical of Heinz's use of a one-time gain to increase earnings: "In recent years, H. J. Heinz Co. has been spicing up its earnings with special items. The latest quarter is no exception." An analyst was quoted as saying that Heinz had not admitted the slump in its business but had "started including nonrecurring items in the results they were showing. That created an artificially high base of earnings that they can no longer match."[9] Do you think it is unethical for a company's management to increase earnings periodically through the use of one-time transactions, such as sales of assets, on which it has a profit? What potential long-term negative effects might this practice have for Heinz?

Research Activity

SD 4.
LO 3 *Use of Investors Services*

Find *Moody's Investors Service* or *Standard & Poor's Industry Guide* using one or more of the following sources: your library, the Fingraph® Financial Analyst™ CD-ROM that accompanies this text, or the Needles Accounting Resource Center Web site at http://www.hmco.com/college/needles/home.html. Locate the reports on three corporations. You may choose the corporations at random or choose them from the same industry, if directed to do so by your instructor. (If you did a related exercise in a previous chapter, use the same three companies.) Write a summary of what you learned about each company's financial performance and its prospects for the future, and be prepared to discuss your findings in class.

Decision-Making Practice

SD 5.
LO 4 *Effect of One-Time Item*
LO 5 *on Loan Decision*

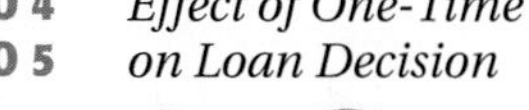

Apple a Day, Inc., and ***Unforgettable Edibles, Inc.,*** both operate food catering businesses in the metropolitan area. Their customers include *Fortune* 500 companies, regional firms, and individuals. The two firms reported similar profit margins for the current year, and both determine bonuses for managers based on reaching a target profit margin and return on equity. Each firm has submitted a loan request to you as a loan officer for City National Bank.

	Apple a Day	Unforgettable Edibles
Net Sales	$625,348	$717,900
Cost of Goods Sold	225,125	287,080
Gross Margin	$400,223	$430,820
Operating Expenses	281,300	371,565
Operating Income	$118,923	$ 59,255
Gain on Sale of Real Estate		81,923
Interest Expense	(9,333)	(15,338)
Income Before Income Taxes	$109,590	$125,840
Income Taxes	25,990	29,525
Net Income	$ 83,600	$ 96,315
Average Stockholders' Equity	$312,700	$390,560

REQUIRED

1. Perform a vertical analysis and prepare a common-size income statement for each firm. Compute profit margin and return on equity.
2. Discuss these results, the bonus plan for management, and loan considerations. Make a recommendation as to which company is a better risk for receiving the loan.

Financial Reporting and Analysis

Interpreting Financial Reports

FRA 1. LO 4 *Trend Analysis*

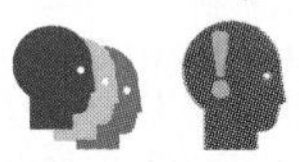

H. J. Heinz Company is a global company engaged in several lines of business, including food service, infant foods, condiments, pet foods, tuna, and weight control food products. Below is a five-year summary of operations and other related data for Heinz.

Five-Year Summary of Operations and Other Related Data
H.J. Heinz Company and Subsidiaries

	1996	1995	1994	1993	1992
	(Dollars in thousands, except per share data)				
Summary of Operations					
Sales	**$9,112,265**	$8,086,794	$7,046,738	$7,103,374	$6,581,867
Cost of products sold	**5,775,357**	5,119,597	4,381,745	4,530,563	4,102,816
Interest expense	**277,411**	210,585	149,243	146,491	134,948
Provision for income taxes	**364,342**	346,982	319,442	185,838	346,050
Income before cumulative effect of accounting change	**659,319**	591,025	602,944	529,943	638,295
Cumulative effect of FAS No. 106 adoption	**—**	—	—	(133,630)	—
Net income	**659,319**	591,025	602,944	396,313	638,295
Other Related Data					
Dividends paid:					
Common	**381,871**	345,358	325,887	297,009	270,512
Preferred	**56**	64	71	78	86
Total assets	**8,623,691**	8,247,188	6,381,146	6,821,321	5,931,901
Total debt	**3,363,828**	3,401,076	2,166,703	2,613,736	1,902,483
Shareholders' equity	**2,706,757**	2,472,869	2,338,551	2,320,996	2,367,398

REQUIRED

Prepare a trend analysis for Heinz and discuss. Identify important trends and tell whether the trends are favorable or unfavorable. Discuss significant relationships among the trends.

INTERNATIONAL COMPANY

LO 5 **FRA 2.** *Analyzing Non-U.S. Financial Statements*

When dealing with non-U.S. companies, the analyst is often faced with financial statements that do not follow the same format as the statements of U.S. companies. The 1996 balance sheet and the profit and loss account (income statement) for ***Granada Group,***[10] a leading British hotel, restaurant, and media company, present such a situation. The statements are below and on the next page.

Show that you can read these British financial statements by computing as many of the following ratios as you can: (a) current ratio, (b) receivable turnover, (c) inventory turnover, (d) profit margin, (e) asset turnover, (f) return on assets, (g) return on equity,

Granada Group
Balance Sheet

At 28 September 1996	**£m**	**1996 £m**
Fixed assets:		
Tangible assets		4,834.5
Investments		462.0
		5,296.5
Current assets:		
Stocks	190.9	
Debtors: amounts falling due within one year	664.4	
Debtors: amounts falling due after more than one year	267.5	
Cash, short term deposits and liquid investments	428.1	
	1,550.9	
Creditors: amounts falling due within one year:		
Borrowings	382.0	
Other creditors	1,685.0	
	2,067.0	
Net current (liabilities)/assets		(516.1)
Total assets less current liabilities		4,780.4
Creditors: amounts falling due after more than one year:		
Borrowings	3,561.5	
Other creditors	70.9	
		3,632.4
Provisions for liabilities and charges		55.8
Net assets		1,092.2
Capital and reserves:		
Called up share capital		231.0
Share premium account		82.5
Revaluation reserve		163.3
Merger reserve		(134.2)
Profit and loss account		645.2
Shareholders' funds		987.8
Minority interests		104.4
		1,092.2

Granada Group Profit and Loss Account	
For the 52 weeks ended 28 September 1996	**1996 £ m**
Turnover:	3,816.9
Depreciation on tangible assets	184.6
Staff costs	928.6
Net other operating costs	2,104.0
	3,217.2
Operating profit:	599.7
Profit on disposal of businesses	1.6
Profit before interest and taxation	601.3
Net interest	196.5
Profit on ordinary activities before taxation	404.8
Tax on profit on ordinary activities	108.3
Profit on ordinary activities after taxation	296.5
Minority interests	2.1
Profit for the financial period	294.4
Dividends on shares	121.6
Amount transferred to reserves	172.8
Earnings per share (basic)	37.0p
Earnings per share (fully diluted)	35.6p

and (h) debt to equity. Use year-end figures to compute ratios that normally require averages. Indicate what data are missing for any ratio you are not able to compute. What terms or accounts did you have trouble interpreting? How do you evaluate the usefulness of the formats of the British financial statements compared to the formats of U.S. financial statements?

Group Activity: Assign groups to prepare an analysis of Granada. Allow one week for this project to be completed.

Toys "R" Us Annual Report

FRA 3.
LO 5 *Comprehensive Ratio Analysis*

   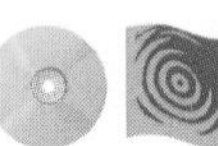

Refer to the Toys "R" Us annual report, and conduct a comprehensive ratio analysis that compares data from 1997 and 1996. If you have been computing ratios for Toys "R" Us in previous chapters, you may prepare a table that summarizes the ratios for 1997 and 1996 and show calculations only for the ratios not previously calculated. If this is the first time you are doing a ratio analysis for Toys "R" Us, show all your computations. In either case, after each group of ratios, comment on the performance of Toys "R" Us. Round your calculations to one decimal place. Prepare and comment on the following categories of ratios:

Liquidity analysis: Current ratio, quick ratio, receivable turnover, average days' sales uncollected, inventory turnover, and average days' inventory on hand

Profitability analysis: Profit margin, asset turnover, return on assets, and return on equity (Comment on the effect of the restructuring in 1996 on the company's profitability.)

Long-term solvency analysis: Debt to equity ratio and interest coverage ratio

Cash flow adequacy analysis: Cash flow yield, cash flows to sales, cash flows to assets, and free cash flow

Market strength analysis: Price/earnings ratio and dividends yield

FINGRAPH® FINANCIAL ANALYST™

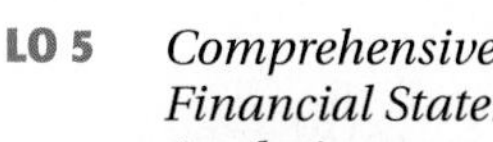

LO 5 *Comprehensive Financial Statement Analysis*

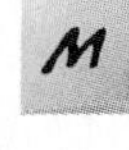

FRA 4. Choose any company in the Fingraph® Financial Analyst™ CD-ROM software database.

1. Display and print for the company you have selected the following pages:
   a. Balance Sheet Analysis
   b. Current Assets and Current Liabilities Analysis
   c. Liquidity and Asset Utilization Analysis
   d. Income from Operations Analysis
   e. Statement of Cash Flows: Operating Activities Analysis
   f. Statement of Cash Flows: Investing and Financing Activities Analysis
   g. Market Strength Analysis
2. Prepare an executive summary that describes the financial condition and performance of your company for the past two years. Attach the pages you printed above in support of your analysis.

ENDNOTES

1. "Credit Ratings," *The Wall Street Journal*, February 26, 1997.
2. *Statement of Financial Accounting Standards No. 131*, "Segment Disclosures" (Norwalk, Conn.: Financial Accounting Standards Board, 1997).
3. Sun Microsystems, Inc., *Annual Report*, 1997.
4. William H. Beaver, "Alternative Accounting Measures as Indicators of Failure," *Accounting Review*, January 1968; and Edward Altman, "Financial Ratios, Discriminant Analysis and the Prediction of Corporate Bankruptcy," *Journal of Finance*, September 1968.
5. Sun Microsystems, Inc., "Management's Discussion and Analysis," *Annual Report*, 1997.
6. In addition, there are advantages to being a debtor in periods of inflation because the debt, which is fixed in dollar amount, may be repaid with cheaper dollars.
7. Sun Microsystems, Inc., "Management's Discussion and Analysis," *Annual Report*, 1997.
8. *Forbes*, November 13, 1978, p. 154.
9. "Heinz's 25% Jump in 2nd-Period Profit Masks Weakness," *The Wall Street Journal*, December 8, 1993.
10. Granada Group, *Annual Report*, 1996.

CHAPTER 19

International Accounting and Long-Term Investments

LEARNING OBJECTIVES

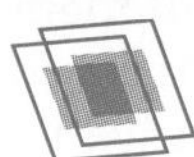

1. **Define *exchange rate* and record transactions that are affected by changes in foreign exchange rates.**
2. **Describe the restatement of a foreign subsidiary's financial statements in U.S. dollars.**
3. **Describe the progress toward international accounting standards.**
4. **Identify the classifications of long-term investments in bonds and stocks.**
5. **Apply the cost adjusted to market method and the equity method as appropriate in accounting for long-term investments.**
6. **Explain when to prepare consolidated financial statements, and describe the uses of such statements.**
7. **Prepare the consolidated balance sheet at acquisition date for a purchase at (a) book value and (b) other than book value.**
8. **Prepare a consolidated income statement.**

DECISION POINT

SANDOZ LTD. and GERBER PRODUCTS CO. (Part 1)

Sandoz Ltd., a $10.3 billion Swiss pharmaceutical and chemicals company, stunned the investment community in 1994 with an agreement to buy Gerber Products Co., the leading U.S. baby foods company, for $3.7 billion. Although Gerber had been rumored to be a buyout candidate, the price of $53 a share, or almost $20 more than the then-current price on the New York Stock Exchange, was more than had been expected. However, according to *Business Week*, working in Sandoz's favor is the fact that "the Swiss franc's strength against the dollar makes this the perfect time to buy in the U.S."[1] Why does a strong franc, and by implication a weak dollar, play a role in Sandoz's purchase of Gerber?

When U.S. firms deal with other U.S. firms, or when Swiss firms deal with other Swiss firms, the relative values of the two countries' currencies do not play a role. Because the parties come from the same country, they are dealing in the same currency. However, when a U.S. firm and a Swiss firm engage in transactions, the relative values of their two currencies assume an important role. For example, if the U.S. dollar is "weak" in relation to the Swiss franc, Swiss francs will "purchase" more dollars. Such is the case with Gerber and Sandoz. The dollar purchase price of Gerber's assets may not look especially attractive to another U.S. company. But when the price is

Critical Thinking Question: What are the future implications of fluctuating currencies for Sandoz as the new owner of Gerber Products Co.? **Answer:** Any future transactions or transfers of funds from Gerber to its Swiss parent, or vice versa, will be exposed to exchange rate fluctuations. For example, if Gerber pays a cash dividend to Sandoz when the U.S. dollar is strong relative to the Swiss franc, Sandoz will receive fewer francs for each dollar of dividend.

Point to Emphasize: When both parties to a transaction deal in the same currency, no foreign currency problem exists. When the parties deal in different currencies, however, the fluctuating exchange rates create a need for special accounting procedures.

seen in terms of Swiss francs, as Sandoz sees it, it is a bargain. When the U.S. dollar is low in relation to other currencies, foreign companies are motivated to purchase U.S. assets and companies.

International Accounting

OBJECTIVE 1

Define** exchange rate **and record transactions that are affected by changes in foreign exchange rates

Related Text Assignments:
Q: 1, 2
SE: 1, 2
E: 1, 2
P: 1
SD: 1, 2, 4
FRA: 3

Point to Emphasize: Foreign investment in U.S. companies is widespread, as is U.S. investment in foreign companies.

Enrichment Note: Students are often eager to learn more about foreign currencies. A handout listing a number of countries and their currencies provides students with a useful reference for this chapter.

As businesses grow, they naturally look for new sources of supply and new markets in other countries. Today, it is common for businesses, called multinational or transnational corporations, to operate in more than one country, and many of them operate throughout the world. Table 1 shows the extent of the foreign business of five of the largest U.S. corporations. IBM, for example, has operations in eighty countries and receives over 60 percent of its sales from outside the United States. Other industrial countries, such as Switzerland, France, Germany, Great Britain, the Netherlands, and Japan, have also given rise to numerous worldwide corporations. For example, 98 percent of the sales of Nestlé, the large Swiss food company, are made outside Switzerland. Examples of companies that receive more than half of their sales from outside their home countries are Michelin, the French tire maker; Mercedes-Benz, the German automobile company; Unilever, the British/Netherlands consumer products company; and Sony, the Japanese electronics company. More than five hundred companies are listed on at least one stock exchange outside their home country.

In addition, sophisticated investors no longer restrict their investment activities to domestic securities markets. Many Americans invest in foreign securities markets, and non-Americans invest heavily in the stock market in the United States. Figure 1 shows that from 1980 to 1996, the total value of securities traded on the world's stock markets has increased over eighteenfold, with the U.S. share of the pie declining from 55 to 52 percent. Emerging markets in the rest of the world have increased from 16 percent to 29 percent.

Foreign business transactions have two major effects on accounting. First, most sales or purchases of goods and services in other countries involve different currencies. Thus, one currency needs to be translated into another, using exchange rates.[2] An exchange rate is the value of one currency in terms of another. For example, an English person purchasing goods from a U.S. company and paying in U.S. dollars must exchange British pounds for U.S. dollars before making payment. In effect, currencies are goods that can be bought and sold. Table 2 lists the exchange rates of several currencies in terms of dollars. It shows the exchange rate for the British

Table 1. Extent of Foreign Revenues for Selected U.S. Companies

Company	Foreign Revenues (millions)	Total Revenues (millions)	Foreign Revenues (percentage)
Exxon	$89,608	$116,728	76.8
General Motors	51,000	164,069	31.1
Mobil	48,533	72,267	67.2
Ford Motor	48,104	146,991	32.7
IBM	46,552	75,947	61.3

Source: "The 100 Largest U.S. Multinationals," *Forbes,* July 28, 1997. Reprinted by permission of *Forbes* Magazine © Forbes, Inc., 1997.

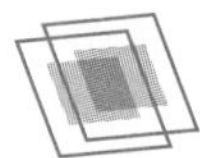

Discussion Question: Conducting international business causes what two accounting problems for U.S. companies? **Answer:** First, foreign companies often do not follow U.S. accounting standards, creating comparability problems. Second, the use of different currencies creates a translation problem.

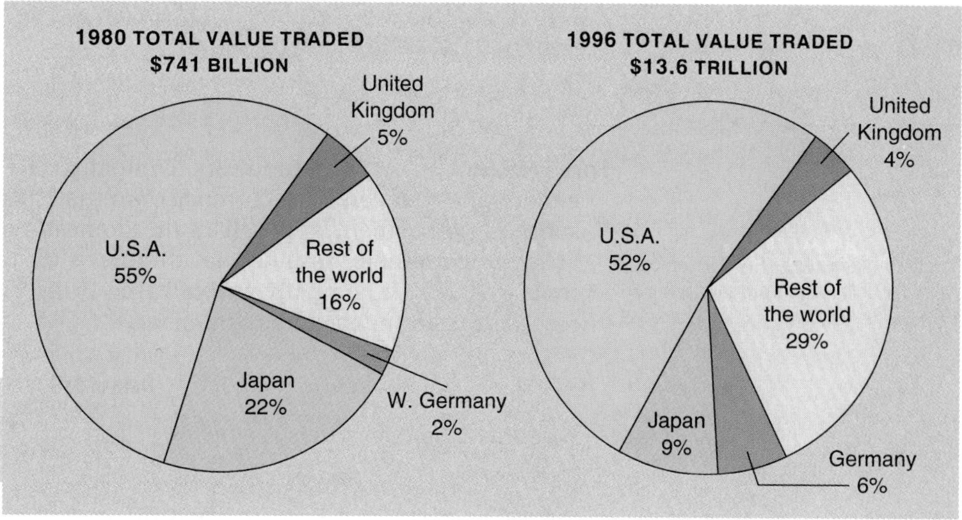

Figure 1
Value of Securities Traded on the World's Stock Markets

Source: International Finance Corporation, *Emerging Stock Markets Factbook,* © 1997.

pound as $1.69 per pound on a particular date. Like the price of any good or service, these prices change on a daily basis according to supply and demand for the currencies. Accounting for these price changes in recording foreign transactions and preparing financial statements for foreign subsidiaries is the subject of the next two sections.

The second major effect of international business on accounting is that financial standards differ from country to country, which makes comparisons among companies from different countries more difficult. Some of the obstacles to achieving comparability and some of the progress in solving the problem are discussed later in this chapter.

Accounting for Transactions in Foreign Currencies

Among the first activities of an expanding company in the international market are the buying and selling of goods and services. For example, a U.S. maker of precision tools may expand by selling its product to foreign customers. Or it might lower its product cost by buying a less expensive part from a source in another country. In previous chapters, all transactions were recorded in dollars, and it was assumed that the dollar is a uniform measure in the same way that the inch and the centimeter are. But in the international marketplace, a transaction may take place in Japanese

Common Student Error: Students often find published tables such as this one confusing, and frequently apply the exchange rates backward. Emphasize that on this date (November 17, 1997), $1.69 would be needed to acquire one British pound.

Table 2. Partial Listing of Foreign Exchange Rates

Country	Price in $ U.S.	Country	Price in $ U.S.
Britain (pound)	1.69	Italy (lira)	.0006
Canada (dollar)	.71	Japan (yen)	.0080
France (franc)	.173	Mexico (peso)	.12
Germany (mark)	.579	Philippines (peso)	.030
Hong Kong (dollar)	.13	Taiwan (dollar)	.032

Source: Data from *The Wall Street Journal,* November 17, 1997.

yen, British pounds, or some other currency. The values of these currencies in relation to the dollar rise and fall daily.

Foreign Sales When a domestic company sells merchandise abroad, it may bill either in its own country's currency or in the foreign currency. If the billing and the subsequent payment are both in the domestic currency, no accounting problem arises. For example, assume that the precision toolmaker sells $160,000 worth of tools to a British company and bills the British company in dollars. The entry to record the sale and payment is familiar:

Point to Emphasize: The U.S. company must use dollars to record sales and purchases in its records.

Date of Sale

A = L + OE			
+ +	Accounts Receivable, British company	160,000	
	Sales		160,000

Date of Payment

A = L + OE			
+	Cash	160,000	
−	Accounts Receivable, British company		160,000

However, if the U.S. company bills the British company in British pounds and accepts payment in pounds, the U.S. company may incur an exchange gain or loss. A gain or loss will occur if the exchange rate between dollars and pounds changes between the date of sale and the date of payment. Since gains and losses tend to offset one another, a single account is used during the year to accumulate the activity. The net exchange gain or loss is reported on the income statement. For example, assume that the sale of $160,000 above was billed as £100,000, reflecting an exchange rate of 1.60 (that is, $1.60 per pound) on the sale date. Now assume that by the date of payment, the exchange rate has fallen to 1.50. The entries to record the transactions follow:

Point to Emphasize: Exchange gains and losses occur when there is a timing difference between sale and payment. The larger the time span, the more likely it is that a difference will occur.

Date of Sale

A = L + OE			
+ +	Accounts Receivable, British company	160,000	
	Sales		160,000
	£100,000 × $1.60 = $160,000		

Date of Payment

A = L + OE			
+ −	Cash	150,000	
−	Exchange Gain or Loss	10,000	
	Accounts Receivable, British company		160,000
	£100,000 × $1.50 = $150,000		

The U.S. company has incurred an exchange loss of $10,000 because it agreed to accept a fixed number of British pounds in payment, and the value of each pound dropped before the payment was made. Had the value of the pound in relation to the dollar increased, the U.S. company would have made an exchange gain.

Foreign Purchases Purchases are the opposite of sales. The same logic applies to them, except that the relationship of exchange gains and losses to changes in exchange rates is reversed. For example, assume that the maker of precision tools purchases $15,000 of a certain part from a Japanese supplier. If the purchase and subsequent payment are made in U.S. dollars, no accounting problem arises.

Date of Purchase

A = L + OE + −	Purchases	15,000	
	Accounts Payable, Japanese company		15,000

Date of Payment

A = L + OE − −	Accounts Payable, Japanese company	15,000	
	Cash		15,000

However, the Japanese company may bill the U.S. company in yen and be paid in yen. If so, the U.S. company will incur an exchange gain or loss if the exchange rate changes between the date of purchase and the date of payment. For example, assume that the transaction is for 2,500,000 yen and the exchange rates on the dates of purchase and payment are \$.0090 and \$.0085 per yen, respectively. The entries follow.

Date of Purchase

A = L + OE + −	Purchases	22,500	
	Accounts Payable, Japanese company		22,500
	¥2,500,000 × \$.0090 = \$22,500		

Date of Payment

A = L + OE − − +	Accounts Payable, Japanese company	22,500	
	Exchange Gain or Loss		1,250
	Cash		21,250
	¥2,500,000 × \$.0085 = \$21,250		

In this case the U.S. company received an exchange gain of \$1,250 because it agreed to pay a fixed ¥2,500,000, and between the dates of purchase and payment the exchange value of the yen decreased in relation to the dollar.

Point to Emphasize: Unrealized gains and losses may reverse themselves quickly, so reporting such gains and losses in quarterly statements may produce unnecessary concern. Differences between years may be important, but differences between quarters of the current reporting year may not be critical.

Realized Versus Unrealized Exchange Gain or Loss The preceding illustration dealt with completed transactions (in the sense that payment was completed). In each case, the exchange gain or loss was recognized on the date of payment. If financial statements are prepared between the sale or purchase and the subsequent receipt or payment, and exchange rates have changed, there will be unrealized gains or losses. The Financial Accounting Standards Board, in its *Statement No. 52,* requires that exchange gains and losses "shall be included in determining net income for the period in which the exchange rate changes."[3] The requirement includes interim (quarterly) statements and applies whether or not a transaction is complete.

This ruling has caused much debate. Critics charge that it gives too much weight to fleeting changes in exchange rates, causing random changes in earnings that hide long-run trends. Others believe that the use of current exchange rates to value receivables and payables as of the balance sheet date is a major step toward economic reality (current values). To illustrate, we will use the preceding case, in which a U.S. company buys parts from a Japanese supplier. We will assume that the transaction has not been completed by the balance sheet date, when the exchange rate is \$.0080 per yen:

	Date	Exchange Rate (\$ per Yen)
Date of purchase	Dec. 1	.0090
Balance sheet date	Dec. 31	.0080
Date of payment	Feb. 1	.0085

The accounting effects of the unrealized gain are as follows:

	Dec. 1	Dec. 31	Feb. 1
Purchase recorded in U.S. dollars (billed as ¥2,500,000)	$22,500	$22,500	$22,500
Dollars to be paid to equal ¥2,500,000 (¥2,500,000 × exchange rate)	22,500	20,000	21,250
Unrealized gain (or loss)	—	$ 2,500	
Realized gain (or loss)			$ 1,250

A = L + OE
+ −

Dec. 1	Purchases	22,500	
	Accounts Payable, Japanese company		22,500

A = L + OE
− +

Dec. 31	Accounts Payable, Japanese company	2,500	
	Exchange Gain or Loss		2,500

A = L + OE
− − −

Feb. 1	Accounts Payable, Japanese company	20,000	
	Exchange Gain or Loss	1,250	
	Cash		21,250

Discussion Question: Why was an exchange gain recorded on December 31? **Answer:** Between the purchase date and the balance sheet date, the dollar got stronger relative to the yen. Therefore, fewer dollars would be needed to acquire the yen necessary to settle the debt. The dollar savings is recognized on the books as an unrealized gain.

In this case, the original sale was billed in yen by the Japanese company. Following the rules of *Statement No. 52*, an exchange gain of $2,500 is recorded on December 31, and an exchange loss of $1,250 is recorded on February 1. Even though these large fluctuations do not affect the net exchange gain of $1,250 for the whole transaction, the effect on each year's income statements may be important.

Restatement of Foreign Subsidiary Financial Statements

OBJECTIVE 2

Describe the restatement of a foreign subsidiary's financial statements in U.S. dollars

Related Text Assignments:
Q: 3
FRA: 3

Growing companies often expand by setting up or buying foreign subsidiaries. If a foreign subsidiary is more than 50 percent owned and the parent company exercises control, then the foreign subsidiary should be included in the consolidated financial statements (see the discussion of parent and subsidiary companies later in this chapter). The consolidation procedure is the same as that for domestic subsidiaries, except that the statements of the foreign subsidiary must be restated in the reporting currency before consolidation takes place. The reporting currency is the currency in which the consolidated financial statements are presented. Clearly, it makes no sense to combine the assets of a Mexican subsidiary stated in pesos with the assets of the U.S. parent company stated in dollars. Most U.S. companies present their financial statements in U.S. dollars, so the following discussion assumes that the U.S. dollar is the reporting currency used.[4]

Parenthetical Note: The restatement process is typically covered in an advanced accounting course. It consists of multiplying the foreign currency figure for each account by the appropriate exchange rate.

Restatement is the stating of one currency in terms of another. The method of restatement depends on the foreign subsidiary's functional currency. The functional currency is the currency of the place where the subsidiary carries on most of its business. Generally, it is the currency in which a company earns and spends its cash. The functional currency to be used depends on the kind of foreign operation in which the subsidiary takes part. There are two broad types of foreign operation. Type I includes those that are fairly self-contained and integrated within a certain country or economy. Type II includes those that are mainly a direct and integral part or extension of the parent company's operations. As a general rule, Type I subsidiaries use the currency of the country in which they are located, and Type II subsidiaries use the currency of the parent company. If the parent company is a U.S. company, the functional currency of a Type I subsidiary will be the currency of the country in which the subsidiary carries on its business, and the functional currency of a Type II subsidiary will be the U.S. dollar. *Statement No. 52* makes an exception when a Type I subsidiary operates in a country in which there is hyperinflation (as a

Teaching Note: A brief introduction to the Eurodollar and the new European Currency Unit might be appropriate at this point.

rule of thumb, more than 100 percent cumulative inflation over three years), such as Brazil or Argentina. In such a case, the subsidiary is treated as a Type II subsidiary, with the functional currency being the U.S. dollar.

The Search for Comparability of International Accounting Standards

OBJECTIVE 3

Describe the progress toward international accounting standards

Related Text Assignments:
Q: 4, 5
SD: 3
FRA: 2

Teaching Note: Students are usually not familiar with the accounting systems of other countries. Short discussions of the effects that methods such as replacement cost have on the balance sheet and income statement help students realize the extent of this problem.

International investors need to compare the financial position and results of operations of companies from different countries. At present, however, few standards of accounting are recognized worldwide.[5] For example, the LIFO method of valuing inventory is the most popular in the United States, but it is not acceptable in most European countries. As another example, historical cost is strictly followed in Germany, replacement cost is used by some companies in the Netherlands, and a mixed system, allowing lower of cost or market in some cases, is used in the United States and England. Even the formats of financial statements differ from country to country. In England and France, for example, the order in which the balance sheets are presented is almost the reverse of that in the United States. In those countries, property, plant, and equipment is the first listing in the assets section.

A number of major problems stand in the way of setting international standards.[6] One is that accountants and users of accounting information have not been able to agree on the goals of financial statements. Some other problems are differences in the way the accounting profession has developed in various countries, differences in the laws regulating companies, and differences in government and other requirements. Further difficulties are created by differences among countries in the basic economic factors affecting financial reporting, inconsistencies in practices recommended by the accounting profession in different countries, and the influence of tax laws on financial reporting.

Some efforts have been made to achieve greater international understanding and uniformity of accounting practice. The Accountants International Study Group, formed in 1966 and consisting of the AICPA and similar bodies in Canada, England and Wales, Ireland, and Scotland, has issued reports that survey and compare accounting practices in the member countries. Probably the best hopes for finding areas of agreement among all the different countries are the International Accounting Standards Committee (IASC) and the International Federation of Accountants (IFAC). The IASC was formed in 1973 as a result of an agreement by accountancy bodies in Australia, Canada, France, Germany, Japan, Mexico, the Netherlands, the United Kingdom and Ireland, and the United States. More than one hundred professional accountancy bodies from over seventy countries now support the IASC.

The role of the IASC is to contribute to the development and adoption of accounting principles that are relevant, balanced, and comparable throughout the world by formulating and publicizing accounting standards and encouraging their observance in the presentation of financial statements.[7] The standards issued by the IASC are generally followed by large multinational companies that are clients of international accounting firms. The IASC has been especially helpful to companies in developing economies that do not have the financial history or resources to develop accounting standards. The IASC is currently engaged in a major project to improve financial reporting worldwide by introducing a set of international accounting standards that will be acceptable to the world's securities regulators, such as the SEC in the United States. If successful, the effort should make it easier for companies to raise equity capital and list their stocks in other countries.

Teaching Note: A brief discussion of the problem of international reciprocity of accounting credentials provides additional insight into the problems of bringing consistency to accounting procedures.

The IFAC, which was formed in 1977 and also includes most of the world's accountancy organizations, fully supports the work of the IASC and recognizes the IASC as the sole body having responsibility and authority to issue pronouncements

BUSINESS BULLETIN: INTERNATIONAL PRACTICE

Many foreign companies that do business in the United States have started showing in the notes to the financial statements the major differences between income in their own country and income calculated under U.S. GAAP. For instance, the following table is adapted from the annual report of Grand Metropolitan, the large British branded products company (Pillsbury, Burger King, Häagen Dazs, etc.):[8]

Financial Highlights

(in millions of pounds)	**1996**	1995
Operating Income in accordance with UK GAAP	**345**	592
US GAAP adjustments:		
Brands	**(97)**	(85)
Goodwill and other intangibles	**(58)**	(100)
Property and investment transactions	**3**	209
Restructuring and integration costs	**(89)**	(16)
Pensions and other benefits	**(8)**	(5)
Other items	**11**	(6)
Deferred taxation	**83**	35
Approximate operating income in accordance with US GAAP	**190**	624

Accounting for intangibles, such as brand names, trademarks, and goodwill, presents major differences between British and U.S. GAAP. For example, brand names that are carried as assets must be written off over time as amortization costs in the United States but not in the United Kingdom. Purchased goodwill may be written off against stockholders' equity in the United Kingdom but must be capitalized and amortized in the United States. Also, timing of the recognition of property transactions and one-time charges such as restructurings can cause significant differences. The United Kingdom does not normally require deferred taxation accounting, as is required in the United States. These disclosures are very helpful in calculating profitability ratios for Grand Metropolitan and comparing them with those of U.S. companies.

on international accounting standards. The IFAC's objective is to develop international guidelines for auditing, ethics, education, and management accounting. Every five years an International Congress is held to judge the progress toward achieving these objectives.

In Europe, attempts are also being made to harmonize accounting standards. The European Community has issued a directive (4th) requiring certain minimum and uniform reporting and disclosure standards for financial statements. Other directives deal with uniform rules for preparing consolidated financial statements (7th) and qualifications of auditors (8th). In recent years, the European Community has paid considerable attention to the comparability of financial reporting as the organization moves toward the goal of a single European market.

The road to international harmony is a difficult one. However, there is reason for optimism because an increasing number of countries are recognizing the appropriateness of international accounting standards in international trade and commerce.

DECISION POINT

SANDOZ LTD. and GERBER PRODUCTS CO. (Part 2)

Corporations often find it desirable to invest in the securities of other corporations with the intent of holding those securities for an indefinite period. There are many reasons for making such long-term investments. One reason, of course, is simple: the prospect of earning a return on investment. Another might be to establish a more formal business relationship with a company with which the investing company has ties. As noted in the first Decision Point in this chapter, in 1994, Sandoz, a Swiss pharmaceutical and chemicals company with some food lines, purchased Gerber Products Co., a U.S. baby foods company, at a price that seemed high in relation to the market. What reasons might these companies have had for entering into this agreement even though their products are different?

Although analysts believe that management will find it difficult to meld the two companies, each company gains something it feels it needs in order to remain competitive in the global marketplace. Sandoz has almost no presence in North America, and its chairman, Marc Moret, says, "Gerber's excellent image and exceptional market strength in North America give a strong base in child nutrition on which we will expand internationally." Although it is the leader in baby foods in North America and Latin America, Gerber has been very weak in Europe and has lacked the financial strength to improve its situation. Sandoz will provide Gerber with the global marketing and distribution network it sorely needs. "The most important ingredient in our future is extending the Gerber franchise in the international arena," said Gerber Chairman Alfred A. Piergalini.[9]

Critical Thinking Question: Could Sandoz Ltd. have accomplished its objectives with less than 100 percent ownership of Gerber Products? **Answer:** Yes, Sandoz needed to purchase only enough shares to gain control (greater than 50 percent of all shares outstanding). However, by purchasing 100 percent ownership, Sandoz has no Gerber Products shareholders to which it must directly report.

Long-Term Investments

OBJECTIVE 4

Identify the classifications of long-term investments in bonds and stocks

Related Text Assignments:
Q: 6, 7
E: 4
SD: 5
FRA: 4

One corporation may invest in another corporation by purchasing bonds or stocks. These investments may be either short term or long term. In this section, we are concerned with long-term investments.

Long-Term Investments in Bonds

Like all investments, investments in bonds are recorded at cost, which is the price of the bonds plus the broker's commission. When bonds are purchased between interest payment dates, the purchaser must also pay an amount equal to the interest that has accrued on the bonds since the last interest payment date. Then, on the next

BUSINESS BULLETIN: ETHICS IN PRACTICE

In the United States, insider trading, or making use of inside information for personal gain, is unethical and usually illegal. The officers and employees of a public company are not allowed to buy or sell shares of stock in their own company in advance of the release of significant information; only after the information is released to the stockholders and the general public can insiders make such trades. The Securities and Exchange Commission (SEC) vigorously prosecutes any individual, whether employed by the company in question or not, who buys or sells shares of a publicly held company based on information that is not yet available to the public. This is not always true in other countries. Until recently insider trading was not illegal in Germany, but with the goal of expanding its securities markets, Germany recently reformed its securities laws. It established the Federal Authority for Securities Trading (FAST), in part to oversee insider trading activities. However, only 7 FAST staff members handle these investigations compared with approximately 84 SEC staff members. In a notable case in Germany, over 100 employees, managers, and board members of SAP A.G. are being investigated for insider trading.[10] Other countries continue to permit insider trading.

Instructional Strategy: Assign SD 3, based on this Business Bulletin, to small groups in class. Expect a variety of responses to questions 3 and 4. Class discussion of the groups' results could include a show of hands for or against the U.S. practice.

interest payment date, the purchaser receives an interest payment for the whole period. The payment for accrued interest should be recorded as a debit to Interest Income, which will be offset by a credit to Interest Income when the semiannual interest is received.

Subsequent accounting for a corporation's long-term bond investments depends on the classification of the bonds. If the company may at some point decide to sell the bonds, they are classified as available-for-sale securities. If the company plans to hold the bonds until they are paid off on their maturity date, they are considered held-to-maturity securities. Except in industries like insurance and banking, it is unusual for companies to buy the bonds of other companies with the express purpose of holding them until they mature, which can be in ten to thirty years. Therefore, most firms classify long-term bond investments as available-for-sale securities. Such bonds are subsequently accounted for at fair value, much like equity or stock investments are. Fair value is usually the market value. When bonds are intended to be held to maturity, which is rare, they are accounted for not at fair value but at cost, adjusted for the amortization of their discount or premium. The procedure is similar to accounting for long-term bond liabilities, except that separate accounts for discounts and premiums are not used.

Long-Term Investments in Stock

All long-term investments in stocks are recorded at cost, in accordance with generally accepted accounting principles. The treatment of the investment in the accounting records after the initial purchase depends on the extent to which the investing company can exercise significant influence or control over the operating and financial policies of the other company.

The Accounting Principles Board defined the important terms *significant influence* and *control* in its *Opinion No. 18.* Significant influence is the ability to affect the operating and financial policies of the company whose shares are owned, even though the investor holds 50 percent or less of the voting stock. Ability to influence a company may be shown by representation on the board of directors, participation in policy making, material transactions between the companies, exchange of managerial personnel, and technological dependency. For the sake of uniformity, the

BUSINESS BULLETIN: TECHNOLOGY IN PRACTICE

The global transmission of financial and other information is a rapidly growing business. Global revenues from network services, which include data network management and data interchanges among suppliers and banks, are growing rapidly. Because of the substantial investments needed to tap this market, large companies are forming alliances by making long-term investments in other companies. For example, Ameritech Corporation, a Chicago-based telephone company, invested $472 million for a 30 percent share in General Electric Information Services Company, a company that creates and markets data-transmission products and services to businesses. In this way, Ameritech was able to get a toehold in the market without having to develop it from scratch.[11]

APB decided that unless there is proof to the contrary, an investment of 20 percent or more of the voting stock should be presumed to confer significant influence. An investment of less than 20 percent of the voting stock would not confer significant influence.[12]

Control is defined as the ability of the investing company to decide the operating and financial policies of the other company. Control is said to exist when the investing company owns more than 50 percent of the voting stock of the company in which it has invested.

Point to Emphasize: Influence and control are related specifically to equity holdings, not debt holdings.

Thus, in the absence of information to the contrary, a noninfluential and noncontrolling investment would be less than 20 percent ownership. An influential but noncontrolling investment would be 20 to 50 percent ownership. And a controlling investment would be more than 50 percent ownership. The accounting treatment differs for each kind of investment.

OBJECTIVE 5

Apply the cost adjusted to market method and the equity method as appropriate in accounting for long-term investments

Related Text Assignments:
Q: 8, 11
SE: 3, 4, 5, 6
E: 3, 4, 5, 6
P: 2, 3, 6, 7
SD: 5
FRA: 4

Discussion Question: Why is a decrease in long-term investments not recorded as a loss in the current period? **Answer:** Because the loss is not realized. The only true loss occurs when a financial transaction confirms it. The contra-equity account discloses the temporary decline.

Noninfluential and Noncontrolling Investment Available-for-sale securities are debt or equity securities that are not classified as trading or held-to-maturity securities. When equity securities are involved, the further criterion is that they be noninfluential and noncontrolling investments of less than 20 percent of the voting stock. The Financial Accounting Standards Board requires a cost adjusted to market method for accounting for available-for-sale securities. Under this method, available-for-sale securities must be recorded initially at cost and thereafter adjusted periodically through the use of an allowance account to reflect changes in the market value.[13]

Available-for-sale securities are classified as long term if management intends to hold them for more than one year. When accounting for long-term available-for sale securities, the unrealized gain or loss resulting from the adjustment is not reported on the income statement, but is reported as a special item in the stockholders' equity section of the balance sheet and in comprehensive income disclosure.

At the end of each accounting period, the total cost and the total market value of these long-term stock investments must be determined. If the total market value is less than the total cost, the difference must be credited to a contra-asset account called Allowance to Adjust Long-Term Investments to Market. Because of the long-term nature of the investment, the debit part of the entry, which represents a decrease in value below cost, is treated as a temporary decrease and does not appear as a loss on the income statement. It is shown in a contra-stockholders' equity account called Unrealized Loss on Long-Term Investments. Thus, both of these accounts are balance sheet accounts. If the market value exceeds the cost, the allowance account is added to Long-Term Investments and the unrealized gain appears as an addition to stockholders' equity.[14]

When long-term investments in stock are sold, the difference between the sale price and what the stock cost is recorded and reported as a realized gain or loss on the income statement. Dividend income from such investments is recorded by a debit to Cash and a credit to Dividend Income.

For example, assume the following facts about the long-term stock investments of Coleman Corporation:

Point to Emphasize: On April 1, 20x1, a *change in policy* requires the sale. This points out that intent is often the only difference between long-term investments and short-term investments.

June 1, 20x0	Paid cash for the following long-term investments: 10,000 shares of Durbin Corporation common stock (representing 2 percent of outstanding stock) at $25 per share; 5,000 shares of Kotes Corporation common stock (representing 3 percent of outstanding stock) at $15 per share.
Dec. 31, 20x0	Quoted market prices at year end: Durbin common stock, $21; Kotes common stock, $17.
Apr. 1, 20x1	Change in policy required sale of 2,000 shares of Durbin Corporation common stock at $23.
July 1, 20x1	Received cash dividend from Kotes Corporation equal to $.20 per share.
Dec. 31, 20x1	Quoted market prices at year end: Durbin common stock, $24; Kotes common stock, $13.

Entries to record these transactions follow.

Investment

A = L + OE
+ −

20x0			
June 1	Long-Term Investments	325,000	
	Cash		325,000
	Investments in Durbin common stock (10,000 shares × $25 = $250,000) and Kotes common stock (5,000 shares × $15 = $75,000)		

Year-End Adjustment

A = L + OE
− −

20x0			
Dec. 31	Unrealized Loss on Long-Term Investments	30,000	
	Allowance to Adjust Long-Term Investments to Market		30,000
	To record reduction of long-term investment to market		

Company	Shares	Market Price	Total Market	Total Cost
Durbin	10,000	$21	$210,000	$250,000
Kotes	5,000	17	85,000	75,000
			$295,000	$325,000

Point to Emphasize: *Total* cost and *total* market or fair value are used to determine the adjustment.

Total Cost − Total Market Value = $325,000 − $295,000 = $30,000

Sale

A = L + OE
+ − −

20x1			
Apr. 1	Cash	46,000	
	Loss on Sale of Investments	4,000	
	Long-Term Investments		50,000
	Sale of 2,000 shares of Durbin common stock 2,000 × $23 = $46,000 2,000 × $25 = 50,000 Loss $ 4,000		

Dividend Received

			Debit	Credit
A = L + OE	20x1			
+ +	July 1	Cash	1,000	
		Dividend Income		1,000
		Receipt of cash dividend from Kotes stock 5,000 × \$.20 = \$1,000		

Year-End Adjustment

			Debit	Credit
A = L + OE	20x1			
+ +	Dec. 31	Allowance to Adjust Long-Term Investments to Market	12,000	
		Unrealized Loss on Long-Term Investments		12,000
		To record the adjustment in long-term investment so it is reported at market		

Clarification Note: The \$12,000 here represents a loss recovery from the previous period.

Instructional Strategy: To reinforce year-end adjustments, assign SE 3 and then SE 4. Encourage students to work together. Tell students there will be a short quiz afterwards. After debriefing, and before the quiz, practice one more time with "what-if" questions. For example: assume the same facts as in SE 4, except that market value is \$590,000. What is the December 31 entry? Immediately follow up with a two- or three-question quiz.

The adjustment equals the previous balance (\$30,000 from the December 31, 20x0 entry) minus the new balance (\$18,000), or \$12,000. The new balance of \$18,000 is the difference at the present time between the total market value and the total cost of all investments. It is figured as follows:

Company	Shares	Market Price	Total Market	Total Cost
Durbin	8,000	\$24	\$192,000	\$200,000
Kotes	5,000	13	65,000	75,000
			\$257,000	\$275,000

Total Cost − Total Market Value = \$275,000 − \$257,000 = \$18,000

The Allowance to Adjust Long-Term Investments to Market and the Unrealized Loss on Long-Term Investments are reciprocal contra accounts, each with the same dollar balance, as can be shown by the effects of these transactions on the T accounts:

CONTRA-ASSET ACCOUNT — Allowance to Adjust Long-Term Investments to Market

	Debit		Credit
20x1	12,000	20x0	30,000
		Bal. 20x1	18,000

CONTRA-STOCKHOLDERS' EQUITY ACCOUNT — Unrealized Loss on Long-Term Investments

	Debit		Credit
20x0	30,000	20x1	12,000
Bal. 20x1	18,000		

The Allowance account reduces long-term investments by the amount by which the cost of the investments exceeds market; the Unrealized Loss account reduces stockholders' equity by a similar amount. The opposite effects will exist if market value exceeds cost, resulting in an unrealized gain.

Influential but Noncontrolling Investment As we have seen, ownership of 20 percent or more of a company's voting stock is considered sufficient to influence the operations of that corporation. When this is the case, the investment in the stock of the influenced company should be accounted for using the equity method. The equity method presumes that an investment of 20 percent or more is more than a passive investment, and that therefore the investing company should share proportionately in the success or failure of the investee company. The three main features of this method are as follows:

Point to Emphasize: The income or loss on an investment stems from the reported income or loss of the influenced company.

1. The investor records the original purchase of the stock at cost.
2. The investor records its share of the investee's periodic net income as an increase

in the Investment account, with a corresponding credit to an income account. In like manner, the investor records its share of the investee's periodic loss as a decrease in the Investment account, with a corresponding debit to a loss account.

3. When the investor receives a cash dividend, the asset account Cash is increased and the Investment account is decreased.

To illustrate the equity method of accounting, we will assume the following facts about an investment by Vassor Corporation. On January 1 of the current year, Vassor Corporation acquired 40 percent of the voting common stock of Block Corporation for $180,000. With this share of ownership, Vassor Corporation can exert significant influence over the operations of Block Corporation. During the year, Block Corporation reported net income of $80,000 and paid cash dividends of $20,000. The entries to record these transactions by Vassor Corporation are as follows:

Investment

A = L + OE			
+ −	Investment in Block Corporation	180,000	
	Cash		180,000
	Investment in Block Corporation common stock		

Recognition of Income

A = L + OE			
+ +	Investment in Block Corporation	32,000	
	Income, Block Corporation Investment		32,000
	Recognition of 40% of income reported by Block Corporation		
	40% × $80,000 = $32,000		

Receipt of Cash Dividend

A = L + OE			
+ −	Cash	8,000	
	Investment in Block Corporation		8,000
	Cash dividend from Block Corporation		
	40% × $20,000 = $8,000		

Discussion Question: Under the equity method, why are dividends received credited to the Investment account? **Answer:** The dividends represent a return of or decrease in the investment in Block Corporation.

The balance of the Investment in Block Corporation account after these transactions is $204,000, as shown here:

Investment in Block Corporation

Investment	180,000	Dividend received	8,000
Share of income	32,000		
Balance	204,000		

Controlling Investment In some cases, an investor who owns less than 50 percent of the voting stock of a company may exercise such powerful influence that for all practical purposes the investor controls the policies of the other company. Nevertheless, ownership of more than 50 percent of the voting stock is required for accounting recognition of control. When a controlling interest is owned, a parent-subsidiary relationship is said to exist. The investing company is known as the parent company, the other company as the subsidiary. Because the two corporations are separate legal entities, each prepares separate financial statements. However, owing to their special relationship, they are viewed for public financial reporting

BUSINESS BULLETIN: BUSINESS PRACTICE

The purchase of one company by another is an extremely significant transaction not only for the companies involved but for the economy as a whole. Corporate buyouts increased 37 percent in 1996 to a record $492.9 billion. The four largest buyouts were as follows:[15]

Buyer	Seller	Dollar Value (billions)
Bell Atlantic	NYNEX	$19.5
SBC Communications	Pacific Telesis	16.7
Boeing	McDonnell Douglas	13.3

These consolidations represent a trend toward larger and more concentrated business. They also represent significant accounting challenges. This buyout activity has continued through 1997 and into 1998.

purposes as a single economic entity. For this reason, they must combine their financial statements into a single set of statements called consolidated financial statements.

Common Student Error: Students often fail to recognize that parents and subsidiaries are separate legal entities even though they combine their financial reports at year end.

Accounting for consolidated financial statements is very complex. It is usually the subject of an advanced accounting course. However, most large public corporations have subsidiaries and must prepare consolidated financial statements. It is therefore important to have some understanding of accounting for consolidations.

The proper accounting treatments for long-term investments in stock are summarized in Table 3.

Table 3. Accounting Treatments of Long-Term Investments in Stock

Level of Ownership	Percentage of Ownership	Accounting Treatment
Noninfluential and noncontrolling	Less than 20%	Cost initially; investment adjusted subsequent to purchase for changes in market value.
Influential but noncontrolling	Between 20% and 50%	Equity method; investment valued subsequently at cost plus investor's share of income (or minus investor's share of loss) minus dividends received.
Controlling	More than 50%	Financial statements consolidated.

Consolidated Financial Statements

OBJECTIVE 6

Explain when to prepare consolidated financial statements, and describe the uses of such statements

Related Text Assignments:
Q: 9, 10, 12
SE: 6
E: 6
FRA: 1

Most major corporations find it convenient for economic, legal, tax, or other reasons to operate in parent-subsidiary relationships. When we speak of a large company such as Ford, IBM, or Texas Instruments, we generally think of the parent company, not of its many subsidiaries. When considering investment in one of these firms, however, the investor wants a clear financial picture of the total economic entity. The main purpose of consolidated financial statements is to give such a view of the parent and subsidiary firms by treating them as if they were one company. On a consolidated balance sheet, the Inventory account includes the inventory held by the parent and all its subsidiaries. Similarly, on the consolidated income statement, the Sales account is the total revenue from sales by the parent and all its subsidiaries. This overview helps management and stockholders of the parent company judge the company's progress in meeting its goals. Long-term creditors of the parent also find consolidated statements useful because of their interest in the long-range financial health of the company.

Discussion Question: Where would you find information about individual subsidiaries? **Answer:** The annual report will usually have information about lines of business or major segments but not the full financial statements of each subsidiary. If the subsidiary is not wholly owned, it will have its own filings with the SEC.

In the past, it was acceptable not to consolidate the statements of certain subsidiaries, even though the parent owned a controlling interest, when the business of the subsidiary was not homogeneous with that of the parent. For instance, a retail company or an automobile manufacturer might have had a wholly-owned finance subsidiary that was not consolidated. However, such practices were criticized because they tended to remove certain assets (accounts and notes receivable) and certain liabilities (borrowing by the finance subsidiary) from the consolidated financial statements. For example, in 1986, General Motors's financing subsidiary, GMAC, with assets of $90 billion and liabilities of $84 billion, was carried as a long-term investment of $6 billion on GM's balance sheet. It was also argued by those who favored consolidation that financing arrangements such as these are an integral part of the overall business. The Financial Accounting Standards Board ruled that, effective in 1988, all subsidiaries in which the parent owns a controlling interest (more than 50 percent) must be consolidated with the parent for financial reporting purposes.[16] As a result, with few exceptions, the financial statements of all majority-owned subsidiaries must now be consolidated with the parent company's financial statements for external reporting purposes. Some companies, such as General Electric Corporation, present separate statements for their finance subsidiaries in their annual report in addition to the consolidated statements.

Methods of Accounting for Business Combinations

Point to Emphasize: Business combinations are recorded by using either the purchase method or the pooling of interests method, depending upon whether certain criteria have been met. The discussions that follow focus on the purchase method.

Interests in subsidiary companies may be acquired by paying cash; issuing long-term bonds, other debt, or common or preferred stock; or working out some combination of these forms of payment, such as exchanging shares of the parent's own unissued capital stock for the outstanding shares of the subsidiary's capital stock. For parent-subsidiary relationships that arise when cash is paid or debt or preferred stock is issued, it is mandatory to use the purchase method, which is explained below. For simplicity, our illustrations assume payment in cash. In the special case of establishing a parent-subsidiary relationship through an exchange of common stock, the pooling of interests method may be appropriate. This latter method is the subject of more advanced courses.

Consolidated Balance Sheet

In preparing consolidated financial statements under the purchase method, similar accounts from the separate statements of the parent and the subsidiaries are combined. Some accounts result from transactions between the parent and the subsidiary. Examples are debt owed by one of the entities to the other and sales and purchases between the two entities. When considering the group of companies as a single business, it is not appropriate to include these accounts in the group financial statements; the purchases and sales are only transfers between different parts of the business, and the payables and receivables do not represent amounts due to or receivable from outside parties. For this reason, it is important that certain eliminations be made. These eliminations avoid the duplication of accounts and reflect the financial position and operations from the standpoint of a single entity. Eliminations appear only on the work sheets used in preparing consolidated financial statements. They are never shown in the accounting records of either the parent or the subsidiary. There are no consolidated journals or ledgers.

Point to Emphasize: The parent and the subsidiary each maintain individual accounting records as separate entities. Work sheet eliminations remove only duplications that occur in consolidation and the effects of intercompany transactions.

Another good example of accounts that result from transactions between the two entities is the Investment in Subsidiary account in the parent's balance sheet and the stockholders' equity section of the subsidiary. When the balance sheets of the two companies are combined, these accounts must be eliminated to avoid duplicating these items in the consolidated financial statements.

To illustrate the preparation of a consolidated balance sheet under the purchase method, we will use the following balance sheets for Parent and Subsidiary companies:

Accounts	Parent Company	Subsidiary Company
Cash	$100,000	$25,000
Other Assets	760,000	60,000
Total Assets	$860,000	$85,000
Liabilities	$ 60,000	$10,000
Common Stock, $10 par value	600,000	55,000
Retained Earnings	200,000	20,000
Total Liabilities and Stockholders' Equity	$860,000	$85,000

100 Percent Purchase at Book Value Suppose that Parent Company purchases 100 percent of the stock of Subsidiary Company for an amount exactly equal to Subsidiary's book value. The book value of Subsidiary Company is $75,000 ($85,000 − $10,000). Parent Company would record the purchase as shown below:

A = L + OE
+
−

Investment in Subsidiary Company	75,000	
Cash		75,000
Purchase of 100 percent of Subsidiary Company at book value		

OBJECTIVE 7a

Prepare the consolidated balance sheet at acquisition date for a purchase at book value

It is helpful to use a work sheet like the one shown in Exhibit 1 in preparing consolidated financial statements. Note that the balance of Parent Company's Cash account is now $25,000 and that Investment in Subsidiary Company is shown as an asset in Parent Company's balance sheet, reflecting the purchase of the subsidiary. To prepare a consolidated balance sheet, it is necessary to eliminate the investment in the subsidiary. This procedure is shown by elimination entry **1** in Exhibit 1. This elimination entry does two things. First, it eliminates the double counting that would take place when the net assets of the two companies are combined. Second, it eliminates the stockholders' equity section of Subsidiary Company.

The theory underlying consolidated financial statements is that parent and subsidiary are a single entity. The stockholders' equity section of the consolidated

Exhibit 1. Work Sheet for Preparation of Consolidated Balance Sheet

Parent and Subsidiary Companies
Work Sheet for Consolidated Balance Sheet
As of Acquisition Date

Accounts	Balance Sheet, Parent Company	Balance Sheet, Subsidiary Company	Eliminations		Consolidated Balance Sheet
			Debit	Credit	
Cash	25,000	25,000			50,000
Investment in Subsidiary Company	75,000			(1) 75,000	
Other Assets	760,000	60,000			820,000
Total Assets	860,000	85,000			870,000
Liabilities	60,000	10,000			70,000
Common Stock, $10 par value	600,000	55,000	(1) 55,000		600,000
Retained Earnings	200,000	20,000	(1) 20,000		200,000
Total Liabilities and Stockholders' Equity	860,000	85,000	75,000	75,000	870,000

(1) Elimination of intercompany investment.

Related Text Assignments:
Q: 13, 14, 15, 16
SE: 7, 8, 9, 10
E: 7, 8, 9, 10
P: 4, 5
FRA: 1

balance sheet is the same as that of Parent Company. So after eliminating the Investment in Subsidiary Company account and the stockholders' equity of the subsidiary, we can take the information from the right-hand column in Exhibit 1 and present it in the following form:

Parent and Subsidiary Companies
Consolidated Balance Sheet
As of Acquisition Date

Cash	$ 50,000	Liabilities	$ 70,000
Other Assets	820,000	Common Stock	600,000
		Retained Earnings	200,000
Total Assets	$870,000	Total Liabilities and Stockholders' Equity	$870,000

Discussion Question: If the parent purchased the entire subsidiary, why is investment in Subsidiary Company only $75,000 and not the total asset value of $85,000? **Answer:** The parent can purchase only the equity of the subsidiary stockholders, which equals assets minus liabilities.

Less than 100 Percent Purchase at Book Value A parent company does not have to purchase 100 percent of a subsidiary to control it. If it purchases more than 50 percent of the voting stock of the subsidiary company, it will have legal control. In the consolidated financial statements, therefore, the total assets and liabilities of the subsidiary are combined with the assets and liabilities of the parent. However, it is still necessary to account for the interests of those stockholders of the subsidiary company who own less than 50 percent of the voting stock. These are the minority

Exhibit 2. Work Sheet Showing Elimination of Less than 100 Percent Ownership

Parent and Subsidiary Companies
Work Sheet for Consolidated Balance Sheet
As of Acquisition Date

Accounts	Balance Sheet, Parent Company	Balance Sheet, Subsidiary Company	Eliminations		Consolidated Balance Sheet
			Debit	Credit	
Cash	32,500	25,000			57,500
Investment in Subsidiary Company	67,500			(1) 67,500	
Other Assets	760,000	60,000			820,000
Total Assets	860,000	85,000			877,500
Liabilities	60,000	10,000			70,000
Common Stock, $10 par value	600,000	55,000	(1) 55,000		600,000
Retained Earnings	200,000	20,000	(1) 20,000		200,000
Minority Interest				(1) 7,500	7,500
Total Liabilities and Stockholders' Equity	860,000	85,000	75,000	75,000	877,500

(1) Elimination of intercompany investment. Minority interest equals 10 percent of subsidiary's stockholders' equity.

Common Student Error: Students often believe that minority stockholders have no influence or rights in the subsidiary. While they may or may not have significant influence, they do have the full rights accorded to any stockholder in the subsidiary company.

Point to Emphasize: When the elimination entry is made, all of the subsidiary's stockholders' equity is eliminated. The percentage not owned by the parent company is assigned to minority interest.

stockholders, and their minority interest must appear on the consolidated balance sheet as an amount equal to their percentage of ownership times the net assets of the subsidiary.

Suppose that the same Parent Company buys, for $67,500, only 90 percent of Subsidiary Company's voting stock. In this case, the portion of the company purchased has a book value of $67,500 (90% × $75,000). The work sheet used for preparing the consolidated balance sheet appears in Exhibit 2. The elimination is made in the same way as in the case above, except that the minority interest must be accounted for. All of the Investment in Subsidiary Company ($67,500) is eliminated against all of Subsidiary Company's stockholders' equity ($75,000). The difference ($7,500, or 10% × $75,000) is set as minority interest.

There are two ways to classify minority interest on the consolidated balance sheet. One is to place it between long-term liabilities and stockholders' equity. The other is to consider the stockholders' equity section as consisting of (1) minority interest and (2) Parent Company's stockholders' equity, as shown here:

Minority Interest	$ 7,500
Common Stock	600,000
Retained Earnings	200,000
Total Stockholders' Equity	$807,500

Purchase at More or Less than Book Value The purchase price of a business depends on many factors, such as the current market price, the relative strength of the buyer's and seller's bargaining positions, and the prospects for future earnings. Thus, it is only by chance that the purchase price of a subsidiary will equal the book

OBJECTIVE 7b

Prepare the consolidated balance sheet at acquisition date for a purchase at other than book value

Point to Emphasize: In current accounting practice, the book (recorded) value of a company probably will not reflect the true value of the net assets of the business. Examples might be a parcel of land, a well-maintained building, or a trademark reported at cost, adjusted for amortization, that is worth much more than the reported amount.

Point to Emphasize: Regardless of the circumstances, the Investment in Subsidiary Company account must be eliminated completely and should not appear on the consolidated balance sheet.

Discussion Question: When is it appropriate to record goodwill in financial records? **Answer:** When the purchase price of a business exceeds the fair market value of the net assets purchased.

Point to Emphasize: In these examples, neither company has goodwill on its balance sheet, but goodwill is "created" when consolidated statements are prepared.

value of the subsidiary's equity. Usually, it will not. For example, a parent company may pay more than the book value of a subsidiary to purchase a controlling interest if the assets of the subsidiary are understated. In that case, the recorded historical cost less depreciation of the subsidiary's assets may not reflect current market values. The parent may also pay more than book value if the subsidiary has something that the parent wants, such as an important technical process, a new and different product, or a new market. On the other hand, the parent may pay less than book value for its share of the subsidiary's stock if the subsidiary's assets are not worth their depreciated cost. Or the subsidiary may have suffered heavy losses, causing its stock to sell at rather low prices.

The Accounting Principles Board has provided the following guidelines for consolidating a purchased subsidiary and its parent when the parent pays more than book value for its investment in the subsidiary:

> First, all identifiable assets acquired . . . and liabilities assumed in a business combination . . . should be assigned a portion of the cost of the acquired company, normally equal to their fair values at date of acquisition.
>
> Second, the excess of the cost of the acquired company over the sum of the amounts assigned to identifiable assets acquired less liabilities assumed should be recorded as goodwill.[17]

To illustrate the application of these principles, we will assume that Parent Company purchases 100 percent of Subsidiary Company's voting stock for $92,500, or $17,500 more than book value. Parent Company considers $10,000 of the $17,500 to be due to the increased value of Subsidiary's other assets and $7,500 of the $17,500 to be due to the overall strength that Subsidiary Company would add to Parent Company's organization. The work sheet used for preparing the consolidated balance sheet appears in Exhibit 3. All of the Investment in Subsidiary Company ($92,500) has been eliminated against all of Subsidiary Company's stockholders' equity ($75,000). The excess of cost over book value ($17,500) has been debited in the amounts of $10,000 to Other Assets and $7,500 to a new account called Goodwill, or *Goodwill from Consolidation.*

The amount of goodwill is determined as follows:

Cost of investment in subsidiary	$92,500
Book value of subsidiary	75,000
Excess of cost over book value	$17,500
Portion of excess attributable to undervalued long-term assets of subsidiary	10,000
Portion of excess attributable to goodwill	$ 7,500

On the consolidated balance sheet, Goodwill appears as an asset representing the portion of the excess of the cost of the investment over book value that cannot be allocated to any specific asset. Other Assets appears on the consolidated balance sheet at the combined total of $830,000 ($760,000 + $60,000 + $10,000).

When the parent pays less than book value for its investment in the subsidiary, Accounting Principles Board *Opinion No. 16,* paragraph 87, requires that the excess of book value over cost of the investment be used to lower the carrying value of the subsidiary's long-term assets. The reasoning behind this is that market values of long-lived assets (other than marketable securities) are among the least reliable of estimates, since a ready market does not usually exist for such assets. In other words, the APB advises against using negative goodwill, except in very special cases.

Intercompany Receivables and Payables If either the parent or the subsidiary company owes money to the other, there will be a receivable on the creditor com-

Exhibit 3. Work Sheet Showing Elimination When Purchase Cost Is Greater than Book Value

Parent and Subsidiary Companies
Work Sheet for Consolidated Balance Sheet
As of Acquisition Date

Accounts	Balance Sheet, Parent Company	Balance Sheet, Subsidiary Company	Eliminations		Consolidated Balance Sheet
			Debit	Credit	
Cash	7,500	25,000			32,500
Investment in Subsidiary Company	92,500			(1) 92,500	
Other Assets	760,000	60,000	(1) 10,000		830,000
Goodwill			(1) 7,500		7,500
Total Assets	860,000	85,000			870,000
Liabilities	60,000	10,000			70,000
Common Stock, $10 par value	600,000	55,000	(1) 55,000		600,000
Retained Earnings	200,000	20,000	(1) 20,000		200,000
Total Liabilities and Stockholders' Equity	860,000	85,000	92,500	92,500	870,000

(1) Elimination of intercompany investment. Excess of cost over book value ($92,500 − $75,000 = $17,500) is allocated to Other Assets ($10,000) and to Goodwill ($7,500).

pany's individual balance sheet and a payable on the debtor company's individual balance sheet. When a consolidated balance sheet is prepared, both the receivable and the payable should be eliminated because, from the viewpoint of the consolidated entity, neither the asset nor the liability exists. In other words, it does not make sense for a company to owe money to itself. The eliminating entry would be made on the work sheet by debiting the payable and crediting the receivable for the amount of the intercompany loan.

The Consolidated Income Statement

OBJECTIVE 8

Prepare a consolidated income statement

Related Text Assignments:
Q: 12, 17
SE: 10
E: 11

The consolidated income statement for a consolidated entity is prepared by combining the revenues and expenses of the parent and subsidiary companies. The procedure is the same as that for preparing a consolidated balance sheet. That is, intercompany transactions are eliminated to prevent double counting of revenues and expenses. Several intercompany transactions affect the consolidated income statement. They are: (1) sales and purchases of goods and services between parent and subsidiary (purchases for the buying company and sales for the selling company); (2) income and expenses related to loans, receivables, or bond indebtedness between parent and subsidiary; and (3) other income and expenses from intercompany transactions.

To illustrate the eliminating entries, we will assume the following transactions between a parent and its wholly owned subsidiary. Parent Company made sales of $120,000 in goods to Subsidiary Company, which in turn sold all the goods to others. Subsidiary Company paid Parent Company $2,000 interest on a loan from the parent.

Exhibit 4. Work Sheet Showing Eliminations for Preparing a Consolidated Income Statement

Parent and Subsidiary Companies
Work Sheet for Consolidated Income Statement
For the Year Ended December 31, 20xx

Accounts	Income Statement, Parent Company	Income Statement, Subsidiary Company	Eliminations		Consolidated Income Statement
			Debit	Credit	
Sales	430,000	200,000	(1) 120,000		510,000
Other Revenues	60,000	10,000	(2) 2,000		68,000
Total Revenues	490,000	210,000			578,000
Cost of Goods Sold	210,000	150,000		(1) 120,000	240,000
Other Expenses	140,000	50,000		(2) 2,000	188,000
Total Cost and Expenses	350,000	200,000			428,000
Net Income	140,000	10,000	122,000	122,000	150,000

(1) Elimination of intercompany sales and purchases.
(2) Elimination of intercompany interest income and interest expense.

Teaching Note: Describe the parent and subsidiary as one consolidated entity for reporting purposes. Then explain that items such as intercompany loans must be eliminated because an entity cannot owe itself money.

The work sheet in Exhibit 4 shows how to prepare a consolidated income statement. The purpose of the eliminating entries is to treat the two companies as a single entity. Thus, it is important to include in Sales only those sales made to outsiders and to include in Cost of Goods Sold only those purchases made from outsiders. This goal is met with the first eliminating entry, which eliminates the $120,000 of intercompany sales and purchases by a debit of that amount to Sales and a credit of that amount to Cost of Goods Sold. As a result, only sales to outsiders ($510,000) and purchases from outsiders ($240,000) are included in the Consolidated Income

BUSINESS BULLETIN: INTERNATIONAL PRACTICE

Changes in international accounting standards can motivate business strategies involving billions of dollars. For instance, in 1994, European companies rushed to buy up U.S. companies. Roche Holding Ltd., the Swiss pharmaceutical giant, paid $5.3 billion in cash for Syntex Corp. and, as discussed in the Decision Points in this chapter, Sandoz Ltd., another Swiss pharmaceutical giant, paid $3.7 billion for Gerber Products Co. What prompted their hurry? Under 1994 international accounting standards, when Swiss and other European companies made acquisitions, they could write off the goodwill in the year they made the deal. Since most of the purchase prices represented goodwill—the difference between the value of the assets purchased and the price paid—the current year benefited from substantially lower taxes and future years' earnings would not be burdened with write-offs. However, beginning January 1, 1995, European companies had to write off goodwill over twenty years, which delayed the tax write-offs and caused future earnings to be lower. As a result, the acquired companies were worth more to the European companies if their purchases were completed in 1994.[18]

Point to Emphasize: Intercompany sales or purchases are not true revenues or expenses; they are only paper transactions to provide for an exchange between affiliates. True revenues and expenses occur only when transactions are with parties *external* to the firm.

Statement column. The intercompany interest income and expense are eliminated by a debit to Other Revenues and a credit to Other Expenses.

Other Consolidated Financial Statements

Public corporations also prepare consolidated statements of retained earnings and consolidated statements of cash flows. For examples of these statements, see the financial statements in the Toys "R" Us, Inc., annual report.

Chapter Review

REVIEW OF LEARNING OBJECTIVES

1. **Define *exchange rate* and record transactions that are affected by changes in foreign exchange rates.** An *exchange rate* is the value of one currency stated in terms of another. A domestic company may make sales or purchases abroad in either its own country's currency or a foreign currency. If a transaction (sale or purchase) and its resolution (receipt or payment) are made in the domestic currency, no accounting problem arises. However, if the transaction and its resolution are made in a foreign currency and the exchange rate changes between the time of the transaction and its resolution, an exchange gain or loss will occur and should be recorded.
2. **Describe the restatement of a foreign subsidiary's financial statements in U.S. dollars.** Foreign financial statements are converted to U.S. dollars by multiplying the appropriate exchange rates by the amounts in the foreign financial statements. In general, the rates that apply depend on whether the subsidiary is separate and self-contained (Type I) or an integral part of the parent company (Type II).
3. **Describe the progress toward international accounting standards.** There has been some progress toward establishing international accounting standards, especially through the efforts of the International Accounting Standards Committee and the International Federation of Accountants. However, there still are serious inconsistencies in financial reporting among countries. These inconsistencies make the comparison of financial statements from different countries difficult.
4. **Identify the classifications of long-term investments in bonds and stocks.** Long-term investments in bonds fall into two categories. First, bond investments classified as available-for-sale are recorded at cost and subsequently accounted for at fair value. Second, bond investments classified as held-to-maturity are accounted for at the amortized cost.

   Long-term stock investments fall into three categories. First are noninfluential and noncontrolling investments, which represent less than 20 percent ownership. Second are influential but noncontrolling investments, which represent 20 percent to 50 percent ownership. Third are controlling interest investments, which represent more than 50 percent ownership.
5. **Apply the cost adjusted to market method and the equity method as appropriate in accounting for long-term investments.** The cost adjusted to market method is used to account for noninfluential and noncontrolling investments in stock. Under this method, investments are initially recorded at cost and then adjusted to market value based on overall portfolio valuations. The equity method is used to account for influential but noncontrolling investments. Under this method, the investment is initially recorded at cost and then adjusted for the investor's share of the investee's net income or loss and subsequent dividends.
6. **Explain when to prepare consolidated financial statements, and describe the uses of such statements.** The FASB requires that consolidated financial statements be prepared when an investing company has legal and effective control over another company. Control exists when the parent company owns more than 50 percent of the voting stock of the subsidiary company. Consolidated financial statements are useful

to investors and others because they treat the parent company and its subsidiaries realistically, as an integrated economic unit.

7. **Prepare the consolidated balance sheet at acquisition date for a purchase at (a) book value and (b) other than book value.** At the date of acquisition, a work sheet entry is made to eliminate the investment from the parent company's financial statements and the stockholders' equity section of the subsidiary's financial statements. The assets and liabilities of the two companies are combined. If the parent owns less than 100 percent of the subsidiary, minority interest equal to the percentage of the subsidiary owned by minority stockholders multiplied by the stockholders' equity in the subsidiary will appear on the consolidated balance sheet. If the cost of the parent's investment in the subsidiary is greater than the subsidiary's book value, on the balance sheet, an amount equal to the excess of cost over book value will be allocated to undervalued subsidiary assets and to goodwill. If the cost of the parent's investment in the subsidiary is less than book value, the excess of book value over cost should be used to reduce the book value of the long-term assets (other than long-term marketable securities) of the subsidiary.
8. **Prepare a consolidated income statement.** When consolidated income statements are prepared, intercompany sales, purchases, interest income, interest expense, and other income and expenses from intercompany transactions must be eliminated to avoid double counting of these items.

REVIEW OF CONCEPTS AND TERMINOLOGY

The following concepts and terms were introduced in this chapter.

LO 4 **Available-for-sale securities:** Investments held by a company that it may at some point decide to sell.

LO 5 **Consolidated financial statements:** Financial statements that reflect the combined operations of a parent company and its subsidiaries.

LO 4 **Control:** The ability of an investing company to decide the operating and financial policies of another company through ownership of more than 50 percent of that other company's voting stock.

LO 5 **Cost adjusted to market method:** A method of accounting for available-for-sale securities at cost adjusted for changes in the market value of the securities.

LO 6 **Eliminations:** Entries made on consolidation work sheets to eliminate transactions between parent and subsidiary companies.

LO 5 **Equity method:** The method of accounting for long-term investments in which the investor records its share of the investee's periodic net income or loss as an increase or decrease in the Investment account and dividends as a decrease in the Investment account. Used when the investing company exercises significant influence over the other company.

LO 1 **Exchange gain or loss:** A gain or loss due to exchange rate fluctuation that is reported on the income statement.

LO 1 **Exchange rate:** The value of one currency in terms of another.

LO 2 **Functional currency:** The currency of the place where a subsidiary carries on most of its business.

LO 7 **Goodwill (*goodwill from consolidation*):** The amount paid for a subsidiary that exceeds the fair value of the subsidiary's assets less its liabilities.

LO 4 **Held-to-maturity securities:** Investments in debt securities that a company expects to hold until their maturity date.

LO 4 **Insider trading:** The practice of buying or selling shares of a publicly held company based on information that has not yet been made available to the public.

LO 7 **Minority interest:** The amount recorded on a consolidated balance sheet that represents the holdings of stockholders who own less than 50 percent of the voting stock of a subsidiary.

LO 1 **Multinational (transnational) corporations:** Companies that operate in more than one country.

LO 5 **Parent company:** An investing company that owns a controlling interest in another company.

LO 6 **Purchase method:** A method of accounting for parent-subsidiary relationships in which similar accounts from separate statements are combined. Used when the investing company owns more than 50 percent of a subsidiary.

LO 2 **Reporting currency:** The currency in which consolidated financial statements are presented.

LO 2 **Restatement:** The stating of one currency in terms of another.

LO 4 **Significant influence:** The ability of an investing company to affect the operating and financial policies of another company, even though the investor holds 50 percent or less of the voting stock.

LO 5 **Subsidiary:** An investee company in which a controlling interest is owned by another company.

REVIEW PROBLEM

Consolidated Balance Sheet: Less than 100 Percent Ownership

LO 7 In a cash transaction, Taylor Company purchased 90 percent of the outstanding stock of Schumacher Company for $763,200 on June 30, 20xx. Directly after the acquisition, separate balance sheets of the companies appeared as follows:

	Taylor Company	Schumacher Company
Assets		
Cash	$ 400,000	$ 48,000
Accounts Receivable	650,000	240,000
Inventory	1,000,000	520,000
Investment in Schumacher Company	763,200	—
Plant and Equipment (net)	1,500,000	880,000
Other Assets	50,000	160,000
Total Assets	$4,363,200	$1,848,000
Liabilities and Stockholders' Equity		
Accounts Payable	$ 800,000	$ 400,000
Long-Term Debt	1,000,000	600,000
Common Stock, $5 par value	2,000,000	800,000
Retained Earnings	563,200	48,000
Total Liabilities and Stockholders' Equity	$4,363,200	$1,848,000

Additional information: (a) Schumacher Company's other assets represent a long-term investment in Taylor Company's long-term debt. The debt was purchased for an amount equal to Taylor's carrying value of the debt. (b) Taylor Company owes Schumacher Company $100,000 for services rendered.

REQUIRED

Prepare a work sheet for preparing a consolidated balance sheet as of the acquisition date.

ANSWER TO REVIEW PROBLEM

Taylor and Schumacher Companies
Work Sheet for Consolidated Balance Sheet
June 30, 20xx

Accounts	Balance Sheet, Taylor Company	Balance Sheet, Schumacher Company	Eliminations		Consolidated Balance Sheet
			Debit	Credit	
Cash	400,000	48,000			448,000
Accounts Receivable	650,000	240,000		(3) 100,000	790,000
Inventory	1,000,000	520,000			1,520,000
Investment in Schumacher Company	763,200			(1) 763,200	
Plant and Equipment (net)	1,500,000	880,000			2,380,000
Other Assets	50,000	160,000		(2) 160,000	50,000
Total Assets	4,363,200	1,848,000			5,188,000
Accounts Payable	800,000	400,000	(3) 100,000		1,100,000
Long-Term Debt	1,000,000	600,000	(2) 160,000		1,440,000
Common Stock, $5 par value	2,000,000	800,000	(1) 800,000		2,000,000
Retained Earnings	563,200	48,000	(1) 48,000		563,200
Minority Interest				(1) 84,800	84,800
Total Liabilities and Stockholders' Equity	4,363,200	1,848,000	1,108,000	1,108,000	5,188,000

(1) Elimination of intercompany investment. Minority interest equals 10 percent of Schumacher Company's stockholders' equity [10% × ($800,000 + $48,000) = $84,800].
(2) Elimination of intercompany long-term debt.
(3) Elimination of intercompany receivables and payables.

Chapter Assignments

BUILDING YOUR KNOWLEDGE FOUNDATION

Questions

1. What does it mean to say that the exchange rate for the French franc in terms of the U.S. dollar is .15? If a bottle of French perfume costs 200 francs, how much will it cost in dollars?
2. If an American firm does business with a German firm and all their transactions take place in German marks, which firm may incur exchange gains or losses, and why?
3. What is the difference between a functional currency and a reporting currency?

4. If you as an investor were trying to evaluate the relative performance of General Motors, Volkswagen, and Toyota Motors from their published financial statements, what problems might you encounter (other than a language problem)?
5. What are some of the obstacles to uniform international accounting standards, and what efforts are being made to overcome them?
6. Why are the concepts of significant influence and control important in accounting for long-term investments?
7. For each of the following categories of long-term investments, briefly describe the applicable percentage of ownership and accounting treatment: (a) noninfluential and noncontrolling investment, (b) influential but noncontrolling investment, and (c) controlling investment.
8. What is meant by a parent-subsidiary relationship?
9. Would the stockholders of American Home Products Corporation be more interested in the consolidated financial statements of the overall company than in the statements of its many subsidiaries? Explain.
10. The 1987 annual report for Merchant Corporation included the following statement in its Summary of Principal Accounting Policies: "*Principles applied in consolidation.*—Majority-owned subsidiaries are consolidated, except for leasing and finance companies and those subsidiaries not considered to be material." How did this practice change in 1988, and why?
11. Also in Merchant's annual report, in the Summary of Principal Accounting Policies, was the following statement: "*Investments.*—Investments in companies in which Merchant has significant influence in management are on the equity basis." What is the equity basis of accounting for investments, and why did Merchant use it in this case?
12. Why should intercompany receivables, payables, sales, and purchases be eliminated in the preparation of consolidated financial statements?
13. The following item appears on Merchant's consolidated balance sheet: "Minority Interest—$50,000." Explain how this item arose and where you would expect to find it on the consolidated balance sheet.
14. Why may the price paid to acquire a controlling interest in a subsidiary company exceed the subsidiary's book value?
15. The following item also appears on Merchant's consolidated balance sheet: "Goodwill from Consolidation—$70,000." Explain how this item arose and where you would expect to find it on the consolidated balance sheet.
16. Subsidiary Corporation has a book value of $100,000, of which Parent Corporation purchases 100 percent for $115,000. None of the excess of cost over book value is attributed to tangible assets. What is the amount of goodwill from consolidation?
17. Subsidiary Corporation, a wholly-owned subsidiary, has total sales of $500,000, $100,000 of which were made to Parent Corporation. Parent Corporation has total sales of $1,000,000, including sales of all items purchased from Subsidiary Corporation. What is the amount of sales on the consolidated income statement?

Short Exercises

SE 1. LO 1 *Recording Sales: Fluctuating Exchange Rate*

Prepare an entry to record a sale by a U.S. company on account on September 12 in the amount of DM 420,000 to a German company. Also, record the subsequent collection in full in marks on October 12. On September 12 the exchange rate was $.70 per mark, and on October 12 it was $.60 per mark.

SE 2. LO 1 *Recording Purchases: Fluctuating Exchange Rate*

Prepare an entry to record a purchase by a U.S. company on account on September 12 in the amount of DM 420,000 from a German company. Also, record the subsequent payment in full in marks on October 12. On September 12 the exchange rate was $.70 per mark, and on October 12 it was $.60 per mark.

SE 3.
LO 5 *Cost Adjusted to Market Method*

At December 31, 20x1, the market value of The Cedar Deck Company's portfolio of long-term available-for-sale securities was $320,000. The cost of these securities was $285,000. Prepare the entry to adjust the portfolio to market at year end, assuming that the company did not have any long-term investments prior to 20x1.

SE 4.
LO 5 *Cost Adjusted to Market Method*

Refer to your answer to **SE 3** and assume that at December 31, 20x2, the cost of The Cedar Deck Company's portfolio of long-term available-for-sale securities was $640,000 and that its market value was $600,000. Prepare the entry to record the 20x2 year-end adjustment.

SE 5.
LO 5 *Equity Method*

Sturchio Company owns 30 percent of Raymond Company. In 20x1, Raymond Company earned $120,000 and paid $80,000 in dividends. Prepare journal entries for Sturchio Company's records on December 31 to reflect this information. Assume that the dividends are received on December 31.

SE 6.
LO 5 LO 6 *Methods of Accounting for Long-Term Investments*

For each of the investments listed below, tell which of the following methods should be used for external financial reporting: (a) cost adjusted to market method, (b) equity method, (c) consolidation of parent and subsidiary financial statements.

1. 49 percent investment in Motir Corporation
2. 51 percent investment in Saris Corporation
3. 5 percent investment in Ransor Corporation

SE 7.
LO 7 *Purchase of 100 Percent at Book Value*

Maple House Corporation buys 100 percent ownership of Winter Sweets Corporation for $50,000. At the time of the purchase, Winter Sweets' stockholders' equity consists of $10,000 in common stock and $40,000 in retained earnings, and Maple House's stockholders' equity consists of $100,000 in common stock and $200,000 in retained earnings. After the purchase, what would be the amount, if any, of the following accounts on the consolidated balance sheet: Goodwill, Minority Interest, Common Stock, and Retained Earnings?

SE 8.
LO 7 *Purchase of Less than 100 Percent at Book Value*

Assume the same facts as in **SE 7** except that the purchase was 80 percent of Winter Sweets Corporation for $40,000. After the purchase, what would be the amount, if any, of the following accounts on the consolidated balance sheet: Goodwill, Minority Interest, Common Stock, and Retained Earnings?

SE 9.
LO 7 *Purchase of 100 Percent at More than Book Value*

Assume the same facts as in **SE 7** except that the purchase of 100 percent of Winter Sweets Corporation was for $60,000. After the purchase, what would be the amount, if any, of the following accounts on the consolidated balance sheet: Goodwill, Minority Interest, Common Stock, and Retained Earnings? Assume that the fair value of Winter Sweets' net assets equals their book value.

SE 10.
LO 7 LO 8 *Intercompany Transactions*

T Company owns 100 percent of C Company. Some of the separate accounts from the balance sheets and income statements for T Company and C Company appear below:

	T Company	C Company
Accounts Receivable	$ 230,000	$150,000
Accounts Payable	180,000	90,000
Sales	1,200,000	890,000
Cost of Goods Sold	710,000	540,000

What would be the combined amount of each of the above accounts on the consolidated financial statements assuming the following additional information: (a) C Company sold to T Company merchandise at cost in the amount of $270,000; (b) all of the merchandise sold by C Company to T Company had been resold by T Company to customers, but it still owes C Company $60,000 for the merchandise.

Exercises

E 1. LO 1 *Recording International Transactions: Fluctuating Exchange*

New York Corporation purchased a special-purpose machine from Stuttgart Corporation on credit for DM 50,000. At the date of purchase, the exchange rate was $.55 per mark. On the date of the payment, which was made in marks, the value of the mark had increased to $.60.

Prepare journal entries to record the purchase and payment in New York Corporation's accounting records.

E 2. LO 1 *Recording International Transactions*

U.S. Corporation made a sale on account to U.K. Company on November 15 in the amount of £300,000. Payment was to be made in British pounds on February 15. U.S. Corporation's fiscal year is the same as the calendar year. The British pound was worth $1.70 on November 15, $1.58 on December 31, and $1.78 on February 15.

Prepare journal entries to record the sale, year-end adjustment, and collection on U.S. Corporation's books.

E 3. LO 5 *Long-Term Investments*

Heard Corporation has the following portfolio of long-term available-for-sale securities at year end:

Company	Percentage of Voting Stock Held	Cost	Year-End Market Value
N Corporation	4	$160,000	$190,000
O Corporation	12	750,000	550,000
P Corporation	5	60,000	110,000
Total		$970,000	$850,000

The Unrealized Loss on Long-Term Investments account and the Allowance to Adjust Long-Term Investments to Market account each currently have a balance of $80,000 from the last accounting period. Prepare the year-end adjustment to reflect the above information.

E 4. LO 4, LO 5 *Long-Term Investments: Cost Adjusted to Market and Equity Methods*

On January 1, Mueller Corporation purchased, as long-term investments, 8 percent of the voting stock of Schott Corporation for $500,000 and 45 percent of the voting stock of Choy Corporation for $2 million. During the year, Schott Corporation had earnings of $200,000 and paid dividends of $80,000. Choy Corporation had earnings of $600,000 and paid dividends of $400,000. The market value of neither investment changed during the year. Which of these investments should be accounted for using the cost adjusted to market method? Which using the equity method? At what amount should each investment be carried on the balance sheet at year end? Give a reason for each choice.

E 5. LO 5 *Long-Term Investments: Equity Method*

On January 1, 20xx, Romano Corporation acquired 40 percent of the voting stock of Burke Corporation, an amount sufficient to exercise significant influence over Burke Corporation's activities, for $2,400,000 in cash. On December 31, Romano determined that Burke paid dividends of $400,000 but incurred a net loss of $200,000 for 20xx. Prepare journal entries in Romano Corporation's records to reflect this information.

E 6. LO 5, LO 6 *Methods of Accounting for Long-Term Investments*

Diversified Corporation has the following long-term investments:

1. 60 percent of the common stock of Calcor Corporation
2. 13 percent of the common stock of Virginia, Inc.
3. 50 percent of the nonvoting preferred stock of Camrad Corporation
4. 100 percent of the common stock of its financing subsidiary, DCF, Inc.
5. 35 percent of the common stock of the French company Maison de Boutaine
6. 70 percent of the common stock of the Canadian company Alberta Mining Company

For each of these investments, tell which of the following methods should be used for external financial reporting, and why.

a. Cost adjusted to market method
b. Equity method
c. Consolidation of parent and subsidiary financial statements

E 7. LO 7 *Elimination Entry for a Purchase at Book Value*

The Lardner Manufacturing Company purchased 100 percent of the common stock of the Gwynn Manufacturing Company for $300,000. Gwynn's stockholders' equity included common stock of $200,000 and retained earnings of $100,000. Prepare the eliminating entry in journal form that would appear on the work sheet for consolidating the balance sheets of these two entities as of the acquisition date.

E 8. LO 7 *Elimination Entry and Minority Interest*

The stockholders' equity section of the Brandt Corporation's balance sheet appeared as follows on December 31:

Common Stock, $10 par value, 40,000 shares authorized and issued	$400,000
Retained Earnings	48,000
Total Stockholders' Equity	$448,000

Assume that Wegner Manufacturing Company owns 80 percent of the voting stock of Brandt Corporation and paid $11.20 for each share. In journal form, prepare the entry (including minority interest) to eliminate Wegner's investment and Brandt's stockholders' equity that would appear on the work sheet used in preparing the consolidated balance sheet for the two firms.

E 9. LO 7 *Consolidated Balance Sheet with Goodwill*

On September 1, Y Company purchased 100 percent of the voting stock of Z Company for $960,000 in cash. The separate condensed balance sheets immediately after the purchase follow:

	Y Company	Z Company
Other Assets	$2,206,000	$1,089,000
Investment in Z Company	960,000	—
Total Assets	$3,166,000	$1,089,000
Liabilities	$ 871,000	$ 189,000
Common Stock, $1 par value	1,000,000	300,000
Retained Earnings	1,295,000	600,000
Total Liabilities and Stockholders' Equity	$3,166,000	$1,089,000

Prepare a work sheet for preparing the consolidated balance sheet immediately after Y Company acquired control of Z Company. Assume that any excess cost of the investment in the subsidiary over book value is attributable to goodwill from consolidation.

E 10. LO 7 *Analyzing the Effects of Elimination Entries*

Some of the separate accounts from the balance sheets for A Company and B Company, just after A Company purchased 85 percent of B Company's voting stock for $1,530,000 in cash, follow:

	A Company	B Company
Accounts Receivable	$2,600,000	$ 800,000
Interest Receivable, Bonds of B Company	14,400	—
Investment in B Company	1,530,000	—
Investment in B Company Bonds	360,000	—
Accounts Payable	1,060,000	380,000
Interest Payable, Bonds	64,000	40,000
Bonds Payable	1,600,000	1,000,000
Common Stock	2,000,000	1,200,000
Retained Earnings	1,120,000	600,000

Accounts Receivable and Accounts Payable included the following: B Company owed A Company $100,000 for services rendered, and A Company owed B Company $132,000 for purchases of merchandise. A bought B Company's bonds for an amount equal to B's carrying value of the bonds. Determine the amount, including minority interest, that would appear on the consolidated balance sheet for each of the accounts listed.

E 11. LO 8 *Preparation of Consolidated Income Statement*

Polonia Company has owned 100 percent of Cardwell Company since 20x0. The income statements of these two companies for the year ended December 31, 20x1, follow.

	Polonia Company	Cardwell Company
Net Sales	$3,000,000	$1,200,000
Cost of Goods Sold	1,500,000	800,000
Gross Margin	$1,500,000	$ 400,000
Less: Selling Expenses	$ 500,000	$ 100,000
General and Administrative Expenses	600,000	200,000
Total Operating Expenses	$1,100,000	$ 300,000
Income from Operations	$ 400,000	$ 100,000
Other Income	120,000	—
Net Income	$ 520,000	$ 100,000

Additional information: (a) Cardwell Company purchased $560,000 of inventory from Polonia Company, which had been sold to Cardwell Company customers by the end of the year. (b) Cardwell Company leased its building from Polonia Company for $120,000 per year.

Prepare a consolidated income statement work sheet for the two companies for the year ended December 31, 20x1. Ignore income taxes.

Problems

LO 1 *International Transactions*

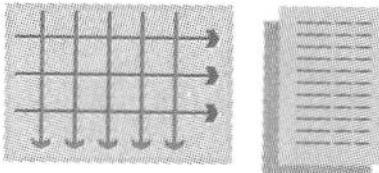

P 1. Mountain States Company, whose year end is June 30, engaged in the following international transactions (exchange rates in parentheses):

May 15 Purchased goods from a Japanese firm for $110,000; terms n/10 in U.S. dollars (yen = $.0080).
17 Sold goods to a German company for $165,000; terms n/30 in marks (mark = $.55).
21 Purchased goods from a Mexican company for $120,000; terms n/30 in pesos (peso = $.0004).
25 Paid for the goods purchased on May 15 (yen = $.0085).
31 Sold goods to an Italian firm for $200,000; terms n/60 in lire (lira = $.0005).
June 5 Sold goods to a British firm for $56,000; terms n/10 in U.S. dollars (pound = $1.30).
7 Purchased goods from a Japanese firm for $221,000; terms n/30 in yen (yen = $.0085).
15 Received payment for the sale made on June 5 (pound = $1.80).
16 Received payment for the sale made on May 17 (mark = $.60).
17 Purchased goods from a French firm for $66,000; terms n/30 in U.S. dollars (franc = $.16).
20 Paid for the goods purchased on May 21 (peso = $.0003).
22 Sold goods to a British firm for $108,000; terms n/30 in pounds (pound = $1.80).
30 Made year-end adjusting entries for incomplete foreign exchange transactions (franc = $.17; peso = $.0003; mark = $.60; lira = $.0003; pound = $1.70; yen = $.0090).
July 7 Paid for the goods purchased on June 7 (yen = $.0085).
19 Paid for the goods purchased on June 17 (franc = $.15).
22 Received payment for the goods sold on June 22 (pound = $1.60).
30 Received payment for the goods sold on May 31 (lira = $.0004).

REQUIRED Prepare entries in journal form for these transactions.

P 2. **LO 5** *Long-Term Investment Transactions*

Mazurek Corporation made the following transactions in its Long-Term Investments account over a two-year period:

20x0

Apr.	1	Purchased with cash 20,000 shares of Cheevers Company stock for $152 per share.
June	1	Purchased with cash 15,000 shares of Abbado Corporation stock for $72 per share.
Sept.	1	Received a $1 per share dividend from Cheevers Company.
Nov.	1	Purchased with cash 25,000 shares of Frankel Corporation stock for $110 per share.
Dec.	31	Market values per share of shares held in the Long-Term Investments account were as follows: Cheevers Company, $140; Abbado Corporation, $32; and Frankel Corporation, $122.

20x1

Feb.	1	Because of unfavorable prospects for Abbado Corporation, Abbado stock was sold for cash at $40 per share.
May	1	Purchased with cash 10,000 shares of Schulian Corporation for $224 per share.
Sept.	1	Received $2 per share dividend from Cheevers Company.
Dec.	31	Market values per share of shares held in the Long-Term Investments account were as follows: Cheevers Company, $160; Frankel Corporation, $140; and Schulian Corporation, $200.

REQUIRED

Prepare entries to record these transactions in the Mazurek Corporation records. Assume that all investments represent less than 20 percent of the voting stock of the company whose stock was acquired.

P 3. **LO 5** *Long-Term Investments: Equity Method*

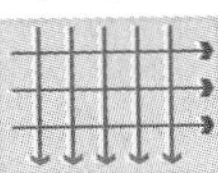

The Yu Company owns 40 percent of the voting stock of the Sargent Company. The Investment account for this company on the Yu Company's balance sheet had a balance of $300,000 on January 1, 20xx. During 20xx, the Sargent Company reported the following quarterly earnings and dividends paid:

Quarter	Earnings	Dividends Paid
1	$ 40,000	$20,000
2	30,000	20,000
3	80,000	20,000
4	(20,000)	20,000
	$130,000	$80,000

The Yu Company exercises a significant influence over the operations of the Sargent Company and therefore uses the equity method to account for its investment.

REQUIRED

1. Prepare the entries in journal form that the Yu Company must make each quarter in accounting for its investment in the Sargent Company.
2. Prepare a T account for the investment in common stock of the Sargent Company. Enter the beginning balance, relevant portions of the entries made in **1**, and the ending balance.

P 4. **LO 7** *Consolidated Balance Sheet: Less than 100 Percent Ownership*

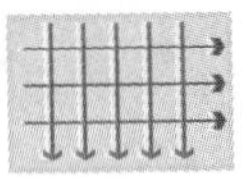

In a cash transaction, Kamper Company purchased 70 percent of the outstanding stock of Woolf Company for $593,600 cash on June 30, 20xx. Immediately after the acquisition, the separate balance sheets of the companies appeared as follows on the next page.

Additional information: (a) Woolf Company's other assets represent a long-term investment in Kamper Company's long-term debt. The debt was purchased for an amount equal to Kamper's carrying value of the debt. (b) Kamper Company owes Woolf Company $80,000 for services rendered.

REQUIRED

Prepare a work sheet for preparing a consolidated balance sheet as of the acquisition date.

	Kamper Company	Woolf Company
Assets		
Cash	$ 320,000	$ 48,000
Accounts Receivable	520,000	240,000
Inventory	800,000	520,000
Investment in Woolf Company	593,600	—
Property, Plant, and Equipment (net)	1,200,000	880,000
Other Assets	40,000	160,000
Total Assets	$3,473,600	$1,848,000
Liabilities and Stockholders' Equity		
Accounts Payable	$ 640,000	$ 400,000
Long-Term Debt	800,000	600,000
Common Stock, $10 par value	1,600,000	800,000
Retained Earnings	433,600	48,000
Total Liabilities and Stockholders' Equity	$3,473,600	$1,848,000

LO 7 *Consolidated Balance Sheet: Cost Exceeding Book Value*

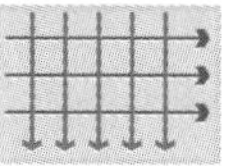

P 5. The balance sheets of Magreb and Nicario Companies as of December 31, 20xx are as follows.

	Magreb Company	Nicario Company
Assets		
Cash	$ 120,000	$ 80,000
Accounts Receivable	200,000	60,000
Investment in Nicario Company	700,000	—
Property, Plant, and Equipment	200,000	360,000
Total Assets	$1,220,000	$500,000
Liabilities and Stockholders' Equity		
Accounts Payable	$ 220,000	$ 60,000
Common Stock, $20 par value	800,000	400,000
Retained Earnings	200,000	40,000
Total Liabilities and Stockholders' Equity	$1,220,000	$500,000

REQUIRED

Prepare a consolidated balance sheet work sheet for the Magreb and Nicario Companies. Assume that the Magreb Company purchased 100 percent of Nicario's common stock for $700,000 immediately prior to December 31, 20xx. Also assume that $160,000 of the excess of cost over book value is attributable to the increased value of Nicario Company's property, plant, and equipment. The rest of the excess is considered by the Magreb Company to be goodwill.

Alternate Problems

P 6. LO 5 *Long-Term Investments Transactions*

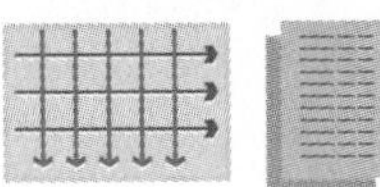

On January 2, 20x0, the Healey Company made several long-term investments in the voting stock of various companies. It purchased 10,000 shares of Zweig at $4.00 a share, 15,000 shares of Kamb at $6.00 a share, and 6,000 shares of Rodriguez at $9.00 a share. Each investment represents less than 20 percent of the voting stock of the company. The remaining securities transactions of Healey during 20x0 were as follows:

May 5 Purchased with cash 6,000 shares of Drennan stock for $6.00 per share. This investment represents less than 20 percent of the Drennan voting stock.
July 16 Sold the 10,000 shares of Zweig stock for $3.60 per share.
Sept. 30 Purchased with cash 5,000 additional shares of Kamb for $6.40 per share. This investment still represents less than 20 percent of the voting stock.
Dec. 31 The market values per share of the stock in the Long-Term Investments account were as follows: Kamb, $6.50; Rodriguez, $8.00; and Drennan, $4.00.

Healey's transactions in securities during 20x1 were as follows:

Feb. 1 Received a cash dividend from Kamb of $.20 per share.
July 15 Sold the 6,000 Rodriguez shares for $8.00 per share.
Aug. 1 Received a cash dividend from Kamb of $.20 per share.
Sept. 10 Purchased 3,000 shares of Parmet for $14.00 per share. This investment represents less than 20 percent of the voting stock of the company.
Dec. 31 The market values per share of the stock in the Long-Term Investments account were as follows: Kamb, $6.50; Drennan, $5.00; and Parmet, $13.00.

REQUIRED

Prepare the journal entries to record all of Healey Company's transactions in long-term investments during 20x0 and 20x1.

P 7. LO 5 *Long-Term Investments: Equity Method*

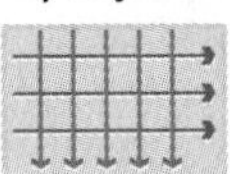

Mathis Corporation owns 35 percent of the voting stock of Albers Corporation. The Investment account on the books of Mathis Corporation as of January 1, 20xx, was $360,000. During 20xx, Albers Corporation reported the following quarterly earnings and dividends:

Quarter	Earnings	Dividends Paid
1	$ 80,000	$ 50,000
2	120,000	50,000
3	60,000	50,000
4	(40,000)	50,000
	$220,000	$200,000

Because of the percentage of voting shares Mathis owns, it can exercise significant influence over the operations of Albers Corporation. Therefore, Mathis Corporation must account for the investment using the equity method.

REQUIRED

1. Prepare the entries in journal form that Mathis Corporation must make each quarter to record its share of earnings and dividends.
2. Prepare a T account for Mathis Corporation's investment in Albers, and enter the beginning balance, the relevant entries from **1**, and the ending balance.

EXPANDING YOUR CRITICAL THINKING, COMMUNICATION, AND INTERPERSONAL SKILLS

Skills Development

CONCEPTUAL ANALYSIS

SD 1. **LO 1** *Effect of Change in Exchange Rate*

Compagnie Générale des Etablissements Michelin, the famous French maker of Michelin tires, became the world's largest tiremaker when it purchased the U.S. tiremaker Uniroyal Goodrich Tire Company in 1990. *The Wall Street Journal* reported that excluding Uniroyal Goodrich sales, sales revenue in fiscal 1990 decreased 4.4 percent to 52.74 billion francs. The decrease was due mainly to the weak dollar in 1990. Michelin executives said, the article reported, that about 25 percent of Michelin's sales, not counting those of Uniroyal Goodrich, were exports to the United States. Without the dollar's drop, revenue expressed in francs would have increased instead of decreased.[19] Explain why a weak dollar would lead to a decrease in Michelin's sales. Why are sales of Uniroyal Goodrich excluded from this discussion?

SD 2. **LO 1** *Effects of Changes in Exchange Rates*

Japan Air Lines, one of the world's top-ranking airlines, has an extensive global network of passenger and cargo services. The company engages in sales and purchase transactions throughout the world. At the end of the year, it will have receivables and payables in many currencies that must be translated into yen for preparation of its consolidated financial statements. The company's 1997 annual report notes that these receivables and payables are translated at the applicable year-end rates. What will be the financial effects (exchange gain or loss) under each of the following independent assumptions about changes in the exchange rates since the transactions that gave rise to the receivables or payables occurred? (1) Receivables exceed payables, and on average the yen has risen relative to other currencies. (2) Receivables exceed payables, and on average the yen has fallen relative to other currencies. (3) Payables exceed receivables, and on average the yen has risen relative to other currencies. (4) Payables exceed receivables, and on average the yen has fallen relative to other currencies. Suggest some ways in which Japan Air Lines can minimize the effects of the fluctuations in exchange rates as they relate to receivables and payables.

ETHICAL DILEMMA

SD 3. **LO 3** *Insider Trading*

Refer to the Business Bulletin: Ethics in Practice on page 820 in the chapter to answer the following questions:

1. What is meant by the phrase "insider trading"?
2. Why do you think insider trading is unethical and illegal in the United States and now in Germany?
3. Why do you think insider trading is an allowable practice in some other countries?
4. Do you think the prohibition of insider trading in the United States is the correct approach? Why or why not?

Group Activity: Divide the class into groups to discuss the above questions. Also, ask the groups to consider why what is considered ethical differs from country to country. Debrief in class.

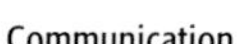
Communication

Critical Thinking

Group Activity

Memo

Ethics

International

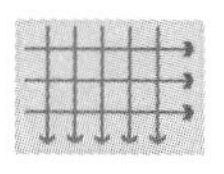
Spreadsheet

General Ledger

CD-ROM

Internet

Research Activity

SD 4. **LO 1** *Reading and Analyzing Foreign Currency Markets*

Go to the section of the library where recent issues of *The Wall Street Journal* are located. From the index on the front page of Section C, "Money & Investing," find the page number of world markets. In the "Currency Trading" portion of that page, find a table entitled "Exchange Rates." This table shows the exchange rates of the currencies of about fifty countries with the U.S. dollar. Choose the currency of any country in which you are interested. Write down the value of that currency in U.S. dollar equivalents for one day in the first week of each month for the past six months, as reported in *The Wall Street Journal*. Prepare a chart that shows the variation in exchange rate for this currency over this time period. Assuming that you run a company that exports goods to the country you chose, would you find the change in exchange rate over the past six months favorable or unfavorable? Assuming that you run a company that imports goods from the country you chose, would you find the change in exchange rate over the past six months favorable or unfavorable? Explain your answers and tell what business practices you would follow to offset any adverse effects of exchange rate fluctuations. Be prepared to discuss your results in class.

Decision-Making Practice

SD 5. **LO 4** **LO 5** *Accounting for Investments*

Gulf Coast Corporation is a successful oil and gas exploration business in the southwestern part of the United States. At the beginning of 20xx, the company made investments in three companies that perform services in the oil and gas industry. The details of each of these investments are presented in the next three paragraphs.

Gulf Coast purchased 100,000 shares of Marsh Service Corporation at a cost of $16 per share. Marsh has 1.5 million shares outstanding, and during 20xx paid dividends of $.80 per share on earnings of $1.60 per share. At the end of the year, Marsh's shares were selling for $24 per share.

Gulf Coast also purchased 2 million shares of Crescent Drilling Company at $8 per share. Crescent has 10 million shares outstanding. In 20xx, Crescent paid a dividend of $.40 per share on earnings of $.80 per share. During the current year the president of Gulf Coast was appointed to the board of directors of Crescent. At the end of the year, Crescent's stock was selling for $12 per share.

In another action, Gulf Coast purchased 1 million of Logan Oil Field Supplies Company's 5 million outstanding shares at $12 per share. The president of Gulf Coast sought membership on the board of directors of Logan but was rebuffed by Logan's board when shareholders representing a majority of Logan's outstanding stock stated that they did not want to be associated with Gulf Coast. Logan paid a dividend of $.80 per share and reported a net income of only $.40 per share for the year. By the end of the year, the price of its stock had dropped to $4 per share.

REQUIRED

1. What principal factors must you consider in order to determine how to account for Gulf Coast's investments? Should they be shown on the balance sheet as short-term or long-term investments? What factors affect this decision?
2. For each of the three investments, make entries in journal form for each of the following: (a) initial investment, (b) receipt of cash dividend, and (c) recognition of income (if appropriate).
3. What adjusting entry (if any) is required at the end of the year?
4. Assuming that Gulf Coast's investment in Logan is sold after the first of the year for $6 per share, what journal entry would be made? Assuming no other transactions and that the market value of the remaining investment in Marsh held by Gulf Coast exceeds cost by $2,400,000 at the end of the second year, what adjusting entry (if any) would be required?

Financial Reporting and Analysis

INTERPRETING FINANCIAL REPORTS

FRA 1.
LO 6 LO 7 *Effects of Consolidating Finance Subsidiaries*

Metropolitan Stores Corporation is one of the largest owners of discount appliance stores in the United States. It owns Highway Superstores, among several other discount chains. The company has a wholly owned finance subsidiary to finance its accounts receivable. Condensed 1997 balance sheets for Metropolitan Stores and its finance subsidiary (in millions) are shown below.[20] The fiscal year ends January 31.

	Metropolitan Stores Corporation	Finance Subsidiary
Assets		
Current Assets (except Accounts Receivable)	$ 866	$ 1
Accounts Receivable (net)	293	869
Property, Equipment, and Other Assets	933	—
Investment in Finance Subsidiary	143	—
Total Assets	$2,235	$870
Liabilities and Stockholders' Equity		
Current Liabilities	$ 717	$ 10
Long-Term Liabilities	859	717
Stockholders' Equity	659	143
Total Liabilities and Stockholders' Equity	$2,235	$870

Total sales to customers were $4 billion. The Financial Accounting Standards Board's *Statement No. 94* requires all majority-owned subsidiaries to be consolidated in the parent company's financial statements. Metropolitan's management believes that it is misleading to consolidate the finance subsidiary because it distorts the real operations of the company. You are asked to assess the effects of the statement on Metropolitan Stores' financial position.

REQUIRED

1. Prepare a consolidated balance sheet for Metropolitan Stores and its finance subsidiary.
2. Demonstrate the effects of FASB *Statement No. 94* by computing the following ratios for Metropolitan Stores before and after the consolidation in **1:** receivable turnover, average days' sales uncollected, and debt to equity (use year-end balances).
3. What are some of the other ratios that will be affected by the implementation of FASB *Statement No. 94?* Does consolidation assist investors and creditors in assessing the risk of investing in Metropolitan Stores' securities or loaning the company money? Relate your answer to your calculations in **2.** What do you think of management's position?

INTERNATIONAL COMPANY

FRA 2.
LO 3 *Differences Between U.S. and U.K. Accounting Principles*

Cable and Wireless, plc, is a major global communications company that provides business networks and mobile communications in Europe, the Caribbean, and Asia. This United Kingdom company publishes its financial statements in accordance with generally accepted accounting principles (GAAP) in the United Kingdom but includes in its annual report a very interesting summary of the differences that would result if selected financial data were presented in accordance with GAAP in the United States, as follows on the next page (in millions).[21]

	Per U.K. GAAP		Per U.S. GAAP	
Effect of Differences	**1996 £m**	**1995 £m**	**1996 £m**	**1995 £m**
Net income (as below)	607	252	546	208
Stockholders' equity	3,259	3,339	3,815	3,367

	1996 £m	1995 £m
Net income as reported under U.K. GAAP	607	252
U.S. GAAP adjustments:		
Amortisation of goodwill	(20)	(17)
Goodwill written off in respect of sale of subsidiary undertakings	3	21
Capitalisation of interest	2	1
Deferred tax—full provision	(31)	(86)
—tax effect of other U.S. GAAP reconciling items	7	(4)
Pension costs	(7)	13
Restructuring costs	(21)	22
Other	3	(4)
Minority interests	3	10
Net income under U.S. GAAP	546	208

Assume that an investment analyst has asked you to evaluate Cable and Wireless's profitability. Prepare a memorandum that shows the calculation of return on equity for 1995 and 1996 under U.K. GAAP and U.S. GAAP, using year-end amounts. Indicate which country's GAAP shows better results. Explain the role of goodwill and intangibles in this difference. (**Hint:** Recall that purchased goodwill is shown as an asset and is amortized on the income statement in the United States, whereas it is deducted from stockholders' equity and does not appear on the income statement in the United Kingdom.) Identify two other important differences in accounting principles between U.K. GAAP and U.S. GAAP. Also, comment on whether accounting principles appear to be more conservative under U.K. GAAP or U.S. GAAP.

TOYS "R" US ANNUAL REPORT

FRA 3.
LO 1 LO 2 *Effects of Foreign Exchange*

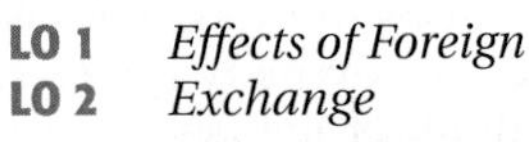

Refer to the Toys "R" Us annual report to answer the following questions. In Management's Discussion, management states that "International sales were unfavorably impacted by the translation of local currency results into U.S. dollars by approximately $150 million in 1996." In a note to the financial statements, management indicates that the company has borrowed money in Japanese yen. Would a strong or a weak dollar have a favorable effect on international sales? Does the same conclusion hold for the money borrowed in Japanese yen?

FINGRAPH® FINANCIAL ANALYST™

FRA 4.
LO 4 LO 5 *Long-Term Investments Analysis*

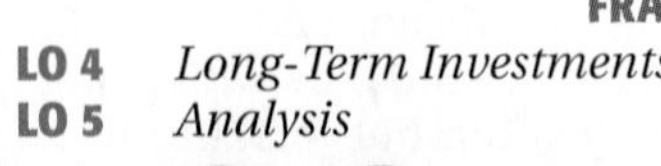

Select any two companies from the same industry on the Fingraph® Financial Analyst™ CD-ROM software.

1. In the annual reports for the companies you have selected, identify the balance sheet accounts and notes to the financial statements associated with long-term investments. What type of long-term investments does each company have? Are the investments valued at cost or market? What is the difference between cost and market value? Did the companies report unrealized gains and losses on their investments?

Summarize in a table the types of investments, how they are valued, and the amount of cost and market value and unrealized gains and losses.

2. Identify the income statements for the companies you selected. Did the companies report any interest or dividend income? If so, what are these amounts? An examination of the notes may be necessary.
3. Write a one-page executive summary that highlights the types of long-term investments and their valuation, and the impact on net income in the current year, including reference to management's assessment. Include your table as an attachment to your report.

ENDNOTES

1. "Strained Peas, Strained Profits," *Business Week,* June 6, 1994.
2. At the time this chapter was written, exchange rates were fluctuating rapidly. Thus, the examples, exercises, and problems in this book use exchange rates in the general range for the countries involved.
3. *Statement of Financial Accounting Standards No. 52,* "Foreign Currency Translation" (Norwalk, Conn.: Financial Accounting Standards Board, 1981), par. 15.
4. This section is based on the requirements of *Statement of Financial Accounting Standards No. 52,* "Foreign Currency Translation" (Norwalk, Conn.: Financial Accounting Standards Board, 1981).
5. *Financial Reporting: An International Survey* (New York: Price Waterhouse, May 1995).
6. *International Accounting and Auditing Trends* (Princeton, N.J.: CIFAP Publications, 5th ed., 1996).
7. "International Accounting Standards Committee Objectives and Procedures," *Professional Standards* (New York: American Institute of Certified Public Accountants, 1988), Volume B, Section 9000, par. 24–27.
8. Grand Metropolitan, *Annual Report,* 1996.
9. Richard Gibson, "Gerber Missed the Boat in Quest to Go Global, So It Turned to Sandoz," *The Wall Street Journal,* May 24, 1994.
10. Greg Steinmetz and Cacilie Rohwedder, "SAP Insider Probe Points to Reforms Needed in Germany," *The Wall Street Journal,* May 8, 1997.
11. John J. Keller, "Ameritech, GE Plan $472 Million Data Venture," *The Wall Street Journal,* December 21, 1993.
12. The Financial Accounting Standards Board points out in its *Interpretation No. 35* (May 1981) that although the presumption of significant influence applies when 20 percent or more of the voting stock is held, the rule is not a rigid one. All relevant facts and circumstances should be examined in each case to find out whether or not significant influence exists. For example, the FASB notes five circumstances that may remove the element of significant influence: (1) The company files a lawsuit against the investor or complains to a government agency; (2) the investor tries and fails to become a director; (3) the investor agrees not to increase its holdings; (4) the company is operated by a small group that ignores the investor's wishes; (5) the investor tries and fails to obtain additional information from the company that is not available to other stockholders.
13. *Statement of Financial Accounting Standards No. 115,* "Accounting for Certain Investments in Debt and Equity Securities" (Norwalk, Conn.: Financial Accounting Standards Board, 1993).
14. If the decrease in value is deemed permanent, a different procedure is followed to record the decline in market value of the long-term investment. A loss account that appears on the income statement is debited instead of the Unrealized Loss account.
15. John Schmettzer, "Mergers Blast into New Orbit," *Chicago Tribune,* January 1, 1997 © Copyrighted Chicago Tribune Company. All rights reserved. Used with permission.
16. *Statement of Financial Accounting Standards No. 94,* "Consolidation of All Majority-Owned Subsidiaries" (Norwalk, Conn.: Financial Accounting Standards Board, 1987).
17. Accounting Principles Board, *Opinion No. 16,* "Business Combinations" (New York: Accounting Principles Board, 1970), par. 87.
18. John Templeman, "The Swiss Are Coming! The Swiss Are Coming!" *Business Week,* June 6, 1994.
19. E. S. Browning, "Michelin Sees Heavy Net Loss for the Year," *The Wall Street Journal,* October 19, 1990.
20. Metropolitan Stores Corporation, *Annual Report,* 1997.
21. Cable and Wireless, plc, *Annual Report,* 1996.

Introduction to Management Accounting

LEARNING OBJECTIVES

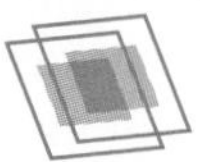

1. **Define *management accounting* and distinguish between management accounting and financial accounting.**
2. **Explain the management cycle and its connection to management accounting.**
3. **Identify the new management philosophies for continuous improvement and discuss the role of management accounting in implementing these philosophies.**
4. **Define *performance measures,* recognize the uses of these measures in the management cycle, and prepare an analysis of nonfinancial data.**
5. **Identify the important questions a manager must consider before requesting or preparing a management report.**
6. **Compare accounting for inventories and cost of goods sold in merchandising and manufacturing organizations.**
7. **Identify various approaches managers use to classify costs and show how the purpose of a manager's cost analysis can change the classification of a single cost item.**
8. **Identify the standards of ethical conduct for management accountants.**

DECISION POINT

GENERAL MOTORS

Prosperous organizations identify key success factors, such as satisfying customer needs, developing excellent manufacturing processes, leading the market with innovative products, and developing technological advances. General Motors Corp. (GM) has all of these key success factors in mind as it leads the market with the introduction of EV1, the first electric vehicle to be mass-produced in the United States.[1] This vehicle is an alternative to fossil-fueled cars and uses rechargeable batteries. Lightweight aluminum frames (chassis), magnesium seat frames, and special exterior panels made of a lightweight composite material are some examples of the technological advances in materials used in the EV1. Less weight yields better battery efficiency, a feature customers want.

Workers put aluminum car parts together with an adhesive and then bake the frame in an oven, rather than welding the parts. Suppliers deliver premade parts to the factory floor, thus reducing the number of workers and machines used in production. After the tires are mounted, a worker drives the car to other stations, thus eliminating the conveyors traditionally used

Critical Thinking Question: Which of the items mentioned in the Decision Point are direct materials? indirect materials? direct labor? indirect labor? other manufacturing overhead? **Answer:** Direct materials: chassis, seat frames, exterior panels, premade parts, tires, windshields; indirect materials: adhesive; direct labor: workers who glue and bake the frame; indirect labor: driver to other stations; other manufacturing overhead: depreciation of robot and portable "stations." The costs of these items are part of the product cost of the EV1.

VIDEO CASE

UPS

OBJECTIVES

- To define management accounting.
- To describe the management cycle and its connection to management accounting
- To recognize performance measures.

BACKGROUND FOR THE CASE

UPS, one of the largest package distribution companies in the world, transports more than three billion parcels and documents annually. UPS supports its commitment to serving the needs of customers throughout the world with more than 500 airplanes, 147,000 vehicles, and 2,400 facilities in over 200 countries. Like many other companies, UPS relies on management accounting information to plan, execute, review, and report its business activities. Management accounting helps managers at UPS make better decisions about embracing new technology, managing environmental issues, and improving fuel efficiency.

For more information about UPS, visit the company's web site through the Needles Accounting Resource Center at

http://www.hmco.com/college/needles/home.html

REQUIRED

View the video on UPS that accompanies this book. As you are watching the video, take notes related to the following questions:

1. In your words, how would you define management accounting?
2. Describe the management cycle and explain how management accounting information helps managers at UPS move through each stage of the management cycle.
3. Define the term "performance measures" and give examples of some performance measures used by UPS.

to transport heavier cars. A robot installs windshields that contain an invisible electronic film to defrost the glass, and portable "stations" allow assembly to be expanded from 2,000 cars per year to 10,000 or more. The $34,000 cars are leased for $480 to $680 per month.

All of these changes demonstrate GM's desire to reestablish its reputation as a technology leader. The company has invested more than $1.5 billion in the EV1 electric car project and has earned 30 patents from developing the EV1. Now General Motors needs objective, quantifiable performance measures for the key success factors mentioned above. What is management accounting's role in the design and production of a vehicle like the EV1? What performance measures would you suggest for developing excellent manufacturing processes and satisfying customer needs related to the EV1?

Management accounting has provided and will continue to provide General Motors with relevant, useful information for making decisions about the selling and leasing prices for the car and the cost of new materials, new production processes, outsourcing premade parts assemblies through suppliers, and leasing cars. Management accounting uses tools such as budgets and performance measures to help GM managers develop, manufacture, sell, and distribute the EV1 using limited resources. Budgets influence daily operating goals for the workers and provide benchmarks for evaluating the workers' performance. Performance measures for the production process at GM include the time to complete one cycle of the production process, number of setups, and time to rework errors in the production process. Number of customer complaints, number of service change notices, and number of customer referrals are potential performance measures of customer satisfaction. As GM continues to improve the EV1 by introducing new materials, such as a nickel-metal hybrid battery to increase by more than 180 miles the miles driven before recharge, management accounting will provide quantifiable information to support GM's achievement of its strategic key success factors.

What Is Management Accounting?

OBJECTIVE 1

Define management accounting *and distinguish between management accounting and financial accounting*

Related Text Assignments:
Q: 1, 2, 3, 4, 5
SE: 1
E: 1
MRA: 1

Management accounting consists of accounting techniques and procedures for gathering and reporting financial, production, and distribution data to meet management's information needs. The management accountant is expected to provide timely, accurate information—including budgets, standard costs, variance analyses, support for day-to-day operating decisions, and analyses of capital expenditures. The Institute of Management Accountants defines **management accounting** as

> the process of identification, measurement, accumulation, analysis, preparation, interpretation, and communication of financial [as well as nonfinancial] information used by management to plan, evaluate, and control within the organization and to assure appropriate use and accountability for its resources.[2]

The information that management accountants gather and analyze is used to support the actions of management. All business managers need accurate and timely information to support pricing, planning, operating, and many other types of decisions. Managers of manufacturing, merchandising, government, and service

Table 1. Comparison of Management and Financial Accounting

Areas of Comparison	Management Accounting	Financial Accounting
Report format	Flexible format, driven by user's needs	Based on generally accepted accounting principles
Purpose of reports	Provide information for planning, control, performance measurement, and decision making	Report on past performance
Primary users	Employees, managers, suppliers	Owners, lenders, customers, government agencies
Units of measure	Historical or future dollar; physical measure in time or number of objects	Historical dollar
Nature of information	Future-oriented; objective for decision making; more subjective for planning; rely on estimates	Historical, objective
Frequency of reports	Prepared as needed; may or may not be on a regular basis	Prepared on a regular basis (minimum of once a year)

Common Student Error: Students often think that management accounting is a subordinate activity to financial accounting. Management accounting is a process that includes financial accounting, tax accounting, information analysis, and other accounting activities.

Point to Emphasize: Financial accounting requires consistency and comparability to ensure the usefulness of information to those outside the firm. Management accounting can use innovative analyses and presentation techniques to enhance information's usefulness to management within the firm.

organizations all depend on management accounting information. Multidivisional corporations need large amounts of information and more complex accounting and reporting systems than do small businesses. But small- and medium-sized businesses make use of certain types of financial and operating information as well. The types of data needed to ensure efficient operating conditions do not depend entirely on an organization's size.

Management accounting information helps organizations make better decisions. Such decisions make all organizations become more cost-effective and help manufacturing, retail, and service organizations become more profitable. Financial accounting takes the results of management decisions about the actual operating, investing, and financing activities and prepares reports for external parties (investors, creditors, and governmental agencies).

Both management accounting and financial accounting (1) provide an information system crucial to reporting and analysis, (2) provide reports used by individuals to analyze and make decisions, and (3) develop relevant, objective product cost information for valuing inventories included on the balance sheet.

Table 1 compares management accounting to financial accounting. Management of accounting data is essential for management planning, control, performance measurement, and decision making. Employees and managers need accounting information to handle daily operations efficiently and effectively to achieve the organization's goals. Management reports are very flexible. Either historical or future information may be reported without any formal guidelines or restrictions. The information may communicate dollar amounts or physical measures of time or objects, such as number of hours worked or number of inspections. The information may be relevant and objective for decision-making purposes or may be more subjective for estimating future activities. Management accounting reports can be prepared monthly, quarterly, or annually. Management may also request reports daily or for special purposes.

Common Student Error: Students often have difficulty relating to accounting techniques that do not rely on the double-entry format.

Teaching Note: Emphasize again that many accounting activities take place in cycles of different duration, and that some activities—special analyses, for example—are done occasionally or just once.

In contrast, financial accounting communicates economic information to external parties. In profit-generating organizations, such as manufacturing, retail, and service organizations, owners and creditors contribute money to assist managers in investing in resources and generating profits from operating activities. Government agencies, such as the Internal Revenue Service and the Securities and Exchange Commission, also require reports. Managers must distribute financial reports to those parties to show the organization's actual performance. The reports are historical and measured in dollars. Generally accepted accounting principles require that specific standards and procedures be followed in the preparation of these reports. Financial reports include objective information that is prepared and distributed regularly, usually on an annual basis.

Connecting Management Accounting to the Management Cycle

OBJECTIVE 2

Explain the management cycle and its connection to management accounting

Related Text Assignments:
Q: 6, 7, 8
SE: 2
E: 2

Teaching Note: Ask a student to apply the management cycle to a personal activity, such as taking a vacation, applying for a job, obtaining a college degree, or raising funds for a campus organization.

To better understand the relationship between management and management accounting, let's take a look at the management cycle and the connections between it and management accounting.

The Management Cycle

Management is expected to use resources wisely, operate profitably, pay debts, and abide by laws and regulations. These expectations motivate managers to establish the objectives, goals, and strategic plans of the organization and to guide and control operating, investing, and financing activities to reach those goals. The management process differs from organization to organization, but traditionally management operates in four stages: (1) planning, (2) executing, (3) reviewing, and (4) reporting. Figure 1 illustrates these stages as an overall management cycle. Each stage of the cycle is discussed below.

Planning Management needs to plan the future operating, investing, and financing activities of the organization. Appropriate objectives and goals must be established and organizational policies enacted. Strategic planning represents the formulation of long-term strategies and related goals, objectives, and organizational policies. Management strives to complement the organization's strategic plans with annual operating plans. The development of strategic and operating plans requires managers to make decisions concerning various alternatives. These plans often include expectations about the performance of individuals, working teams, products, or services.

Executing Planning alone does not guarantee satisfactory operating results. Management must implement the strategic and operating plans by executing activities, or tasks, in a way that maximizes the use of available resources. Smooth operations require one or more of the following: (1) hiring and training of personnel, (2) properly matching human and technical resources to the work that must be done, (3) purchasing or leasing facilities, (4) maintaining an inventory of products for sale,

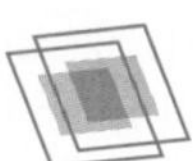

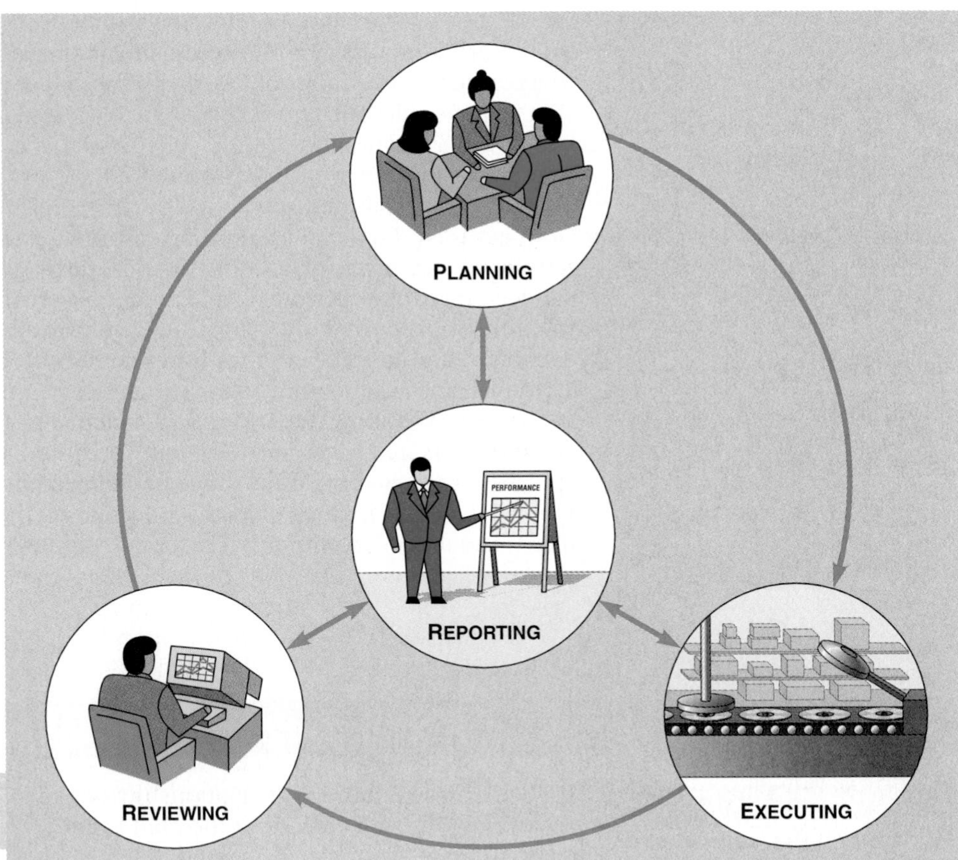

Figure 1
The Management Cycle

and (5) identifying operating activities, or tasks, that minimize waste and improve the quality of the products or services.

Management executes the plan by overseeing the daily operations of the organization. In small organizations, managers often have much direct contact with their employees. They supervise their employees and interact with them to help them learn or complete a task or to improve their performance. In larger, more complex organizations, there may be less direct contact between managers and employees. Instead of directly watching employees, management monitors performance by measuring the actual time taken to complete an activity (for example, number of inspection hours) or the frequency of an activity (such as number of inspections).

Reviewing In many organizations, financial rewards are given to those managers who follow the plan and manage their resources well. Thus, control of operations becomes very important to managers. Often managers compare actual performance to the expected performance established at the planning stage. Any significant differences are then identified for further analysis. Problems that arise may be corrected, or the original plans may be revised as a result of changes in the organization's operating environment. Ideally, the adjustments made in the review stage will improve the performance of future activities.

Point to Emphasize: Revenue and expenses accumulated in accounting systems for financial reporting purposes are also used in management accounting to support budgeting of next year's business activities.

Reporting Because managers have an obligation to use resources wisely, management is responsible for reporting the results of operations to external parties. Periodic summaries of past performance are sent to stockholders, creditors, and other people and groups who are interested in the organization's operations. Also, internal reports about plans and reviews of past performance provide useful information for management decision making.

Management Accounting Connections to the Management Cycle

Management accounting serves the multiple information needs of managers by (1) developing plans and analyzing alternatives; (2) communicating plans to key personnel; (3) evaluating performance; (4) reporting the results of activities; and (5) accumulating, maintaining, and processing an organization's financial and nonfinancial information. These management accounting activities complement the management cycle.

For example, let's suppose that Abbie Awani is about to open her own retail business, Sweet Treasures Candy Store. She plans to purchase candy and other confections from various candy manufacturers and to sell them after some repackaging. What types of information does Abbie need before she opens the doors of her new store? Her first need is for a business plan so that she can apply for a start-up loan from a local bank. This plan includes a full description of the business as well as a complete budget for the first two years of operations. The budget includes a forecasted income statement, a forecasted statement of cash flows, and a forecasted balance sheet at the end of the second year.

Since Abbie does not have a financial background, she will consult a local accounting firm to help her with this project. But she can provide relevant input into the business plan. She needs to decide (1) the types of candy she wants to sell; (2) the volume of sales she anticipates; (3) the selling price for each product; (4) the monthly costs of leasing or purchasing facilities, employing personnel, and maintaining the facilities; and (5) the number of display counters, storage units, and cash registers that she will need.

Teaching Note: This is an opportunity to stress to students the role of accounting in starting and operating a business.

Once she obtains the loan and opens the business, Abbie's information needs continue. She must now measure how well her business is doing. She also needs budgeted information as her guide to evaluate the store's performance. Spending on advertising campaigns, pricing for special sales, and hiring temporary versus full-time personnel are decisions that are also linked to her business plan. Actual revenues and expenses must be compared to the planned amounts and any differences explained. Reasons for such differences may lead Abbie to change parts of her original business plan.

Abbie may also want to measure and evaluate the past performance of employees. This information will help her to develop new strategies or goals. For example, keeping a record of the number of complaints about poor customer service can help her improve quality by finding better ways to train personnel or change the service-delivery process.

Thus Sweet Treasures Candy Store needs management accounting information about the purchase of display counters and office equipment; the selection, training, and rewarding of employees; and the marketing, production, and distribution of its products. Abbie can use this information to plan operations, organize resources, execute business activities, and review the performance of her employees and her business.

Teaching Note: Look through recent periodicals for examples of organizations that have made important decisions about a plant, a product, or a marketing strategy. Use these examples to demonstrate the relevance of management accounting to current business issues.

This example illustrates the connection between management accounting and the management cycle. Management accounting can provide a constant source of relevant information. Compare Abbie's activities and informational needs with the management cycle shown in Figure 1. She started with a business plan, organized her thoughts, planned actions, executed those actions, and reviewed the results. Accounting information helped her to develop her business plan, communicate that plan to the banker and employees, evaluate the performance of employees, and report the results of operations for a period of time. As you can see, accounting plays a critical role in managing the operations of an organization.

Meeting the Demands of Global Competition

During the 1970s and 1980s, the United States lost its dominance in the world marketplace. Countries such as Japan, Germany, Great Britain, and Korea successfully entered many product markets with high-quality, low-cost goods. Customers around the world were pleased with the quality of the new products and purchased them in large numbers. Most affected by the emergence of foreign competition were the automobile, television and VCR equipment, appliance, steel, and audio equipment industries. These industries represented a significant portion of the United States' manufacturing sector, and hundreds of companies were affected. American management had to develop the means to cope with this world-class competition.

New Management Philosophies and Management Accounting

OBJECTIVE 3

Identify the new management philosophies for continuous improvement and discuss the role of management accounting in implementing these philosophies

Related Text Assignments:
Q: 9, 10, 11, 12
SE: 3
E: 3
SD: 1

Three significant new management philosophies evolved in the United States to deal with expanding global competition: just-in-time operating techniques, total quality management, and activity-based management. In addition, flexible manufacturing systems have been developed to assist in improving quality and reducing manufacturing time.

The just-in-time (JIT) operating environment is an organizational environment in which personnel are hired and raw materials and facilities are purchased and used only as needed; emphasis is on the elimination of waste. Workers are trained to be multiskilled, and production processes are consolidated to allow workers to operate several different machines or processes. Raw materials and parts are scheduled to be delivered when they are needed in the production process, so materials inventories are reduced significantly. Products are produced continuously, so work in process inventories are very small. Goods are usually produced only when an order is received and are shipped when completed, so inventories of finished goods are reduced. Adopting the JIT operating environment results in reduced production time, reduced investment in raw materials inventory, reduced materials waste, higher-quality goods, and reduced production costs. Funds that are no longer invested in high inventory levels can be redirected according to the goals of the strategic plan. The accounting system responds to the new environment by tracking the costs of the product differently. JIT processes help management accountants assign more accurate costs to the product and identify costs of waste and inefficient manufacturing activities.

Total quality management (TQM), is an environment in which all functions work together to build quality into the organization's product or service. TQM has many of the same characteristics as the JIT operating philosophy. Workers function as team members and are empowered to make operating decisions that improve both the product or service and the work environment. TQM focuses on improved product quality by identifying and reducing or eliminating the waste of resources caused by poor product or service quality. Emphasis is placed on using resources efficiently and effectively to prevent poor quality and on examining current operations to spot possible causes of poor quality. Improved quality of both the work environment and the product or service is the goal of TQM. Like JIT, TQM results in reduced waste of materials, higher-quality goods, and lower production costs in a manufacturing environment and time savings and higher-quality services in service organizations.

To determine the impact of poor quality on profits, management uses accounting information about the magnitude and classification of the costs of quality. The costs of quality include both the costs of achieving quality (such as training costs and inspection costs) and the costs of poor quality (such as rework costs and costs of handling customer complaints). Managers use cost of quality information to (1) connect strategic goals of the organization with daily operating activities, (2) stimulate improvement by involving everyone, (3) identify opportunities for reducing customer dissatisfaction, (4) identify major opportunities for cost reduction, and (5) determine the costs of quality relative to net income.

Activity-based management (ABM) is an approach to managing an organization that identifies all major operating activities, determines what resources are consumed by each activity, identifies what causes resource usage of each activity, and categorizes the activities as either adding value to a product or service or being nonvalue-adding. ABM includes a management accounting practice called activity-based costing. Activity-based costing (ABC) is a system that identifies all of an organization's major operating activities (both production and nonproduction), traces costs to those activities, and then determines which products or services use the resources and services supplied by those activities. Activities that add value to a product or service, as perceived by the customer, are known as value-adding activities. Such activities are enhanced to improve product or service quality and customer satisfaction. All other activities are called nonvalue-adding activities. Nonvalue-adding activities that are needed because they support the organization are focal points for cost reduction. Nonvalue-adding activities that do not support the organization are eliminated. ABM results in reduced costs, reduced waste of resources, increased efficiency, and increased customer satisfaction.

Activity-based costing is most often used to improve the assignment of overhead costs to products or services. More accurate costs allow managers to make better product or service pricing decisions and decisions about expanding or contracting certain market segments.

The Goal: Continuous Improvement

One of the most valuable lessons to be gained from the emergence of stiff global competition is that management cannot afford to become complacent. While the United States rested on its laurels as the world's most productive nation, countries around the globe were perfecting their productive capabilities. Because our industry had been lulled into self-satisfaction, other countries equaled and surpassed our levels of quality and productivity. What followed was a period of catch-up by American companies. The concept of continuous improvement evolved during this period. Organizations that adhere to continuous improvement are never satisfied with what is; they constantly seek a better method, product, service, process, or resource. Their goal is perfection in everything they do.

Parenthetical Note: New management philosophies continue to evolve from the goal of continuous improvement. A few for further study are the theory of constraints (see *The Goal* by Goldratt and Cox), open book management (*The Great Game of Business* by Jack Stack), balanced scorecard (*The Balanced Scorecard* by Kaplan), and systems thinking (numerous books and articles).

JIT, TQM, and ABM all have perfection by means of continuous improvement as their goal. Figure 2 shows how each approach tries to accomplish its goal. In the just-in-time operating environment, management wages a relentless war on waste:

BUSINESS BULLETIN: BUSINESS PRACTICE

The Internal Revenue Service (IRS) wants to continually improve the quality of its services and reduce the costs of collecting tax revenues from individuals who fail to submit tax returns or who file tax returns but do not pay their taxes. The Field Collection function is responsible for this service. The IRS measures the performance of IRS Field Collection offices and revenue officers based on (1) total dollars collected, (2) number of delinquent taxpayer accounts closed (in total and in subtotals of taxpayers who paid in full, agreed to pay in installments, etc.), and (3) number of delinquent taxpayer investigations. The IRS believes these measures will guide its employees to increase revenue collection, reduce costs of collection, increase job satisfaction, and improve the productivity of the Field Collection function within the organization.[3]

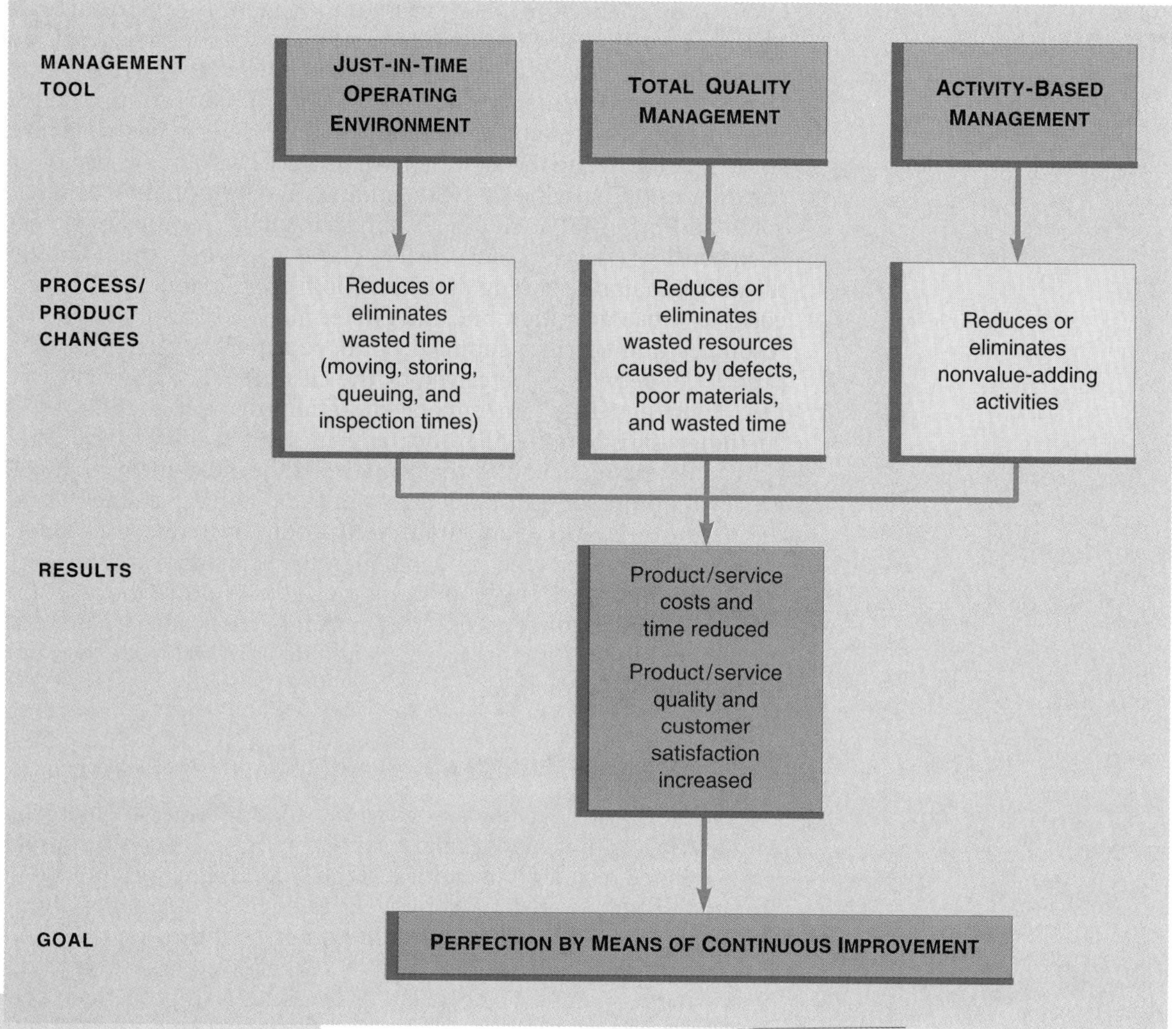

Figure 2
The Continuous Improvement Environment

wasted time, wasted space, and wasted use of materials. All employees are encouraged to continuously look for ways to improve processes and save time. Total quality management focuses on improving the quality of the product or service and the work environment. It pursues continuous improvement by reducing the number of defective products and the amount of wasted time to complete a task or provide a service. Activity-based management focuses on the ongoing reduction or elimination of nonvalue-adding activities as its way of seeking continuous improvement.

Each of these management tools can be used as an individual system, or parts of them can be combined to create a new operating environment. Some aspects of them can be employed in service industries, such as banking, as well as in manufacturing. By continuously trying to improve and fine-tune operations, these new management tools contribute to the same basic results for any organization: Product or service costs and delivery time are reduced, and the quality of the product or service and customer satisfaction are increased. If American organizations continuously improve upon all these results, the United States will catch up with and then surpass its competition.

Performance Measures and the Analysis of Nonfinancial Data

OBJECTIVE 4

Define* performance measures, *recognize the uses of these measures in the management cycle, and prepare an analysis of nonfinancial data

Related Text Assignments:
Q: 13, 14, 15, 16
SE: 4
E: 4
P: 1, 2, 6
SD: 1, 4
MRA: 3, 4

Teaching Strategy: In class, ask students to work in teams to identify other examples of financial and nonfinancial performance measures. Emphasize that the measure should tie to a specific object.

Instructional Strategy: Divide the class into groups and ask them to discuss SD 1. Each group will report its results to the class. Emphasize that the activities they discussed are used to continuously improve the skills and knowledge required to be an expert. Suggest that continuous improvement applies to every activity we perform—as individuals or as members of an organization.

Discussion Question: What measures could be used to express poor quality?
Answers: Dollar measures (cost of rework, cost of spoilage) and nondollar measures (number of rejected units, rework labor hours, or percentage of good units to total production).

Performance measures are quantitative tools that provide an indication of an organization's performance in relation to a specific process, activity, or task or to an expected outcome. Performance measures may be financial or nonfinancial. Financial performance measures include return on investment, net income as a percentage of sales, and the costs of poor quality as a percentage of sales. All of these examples use monetary information to measure the performance of a profit-generating organization or its segments, such as divisions, departments, product lines, sales territories, or operating activities.

Nonfinancial performance measures can include the number of times an object (product, service, activity, or person) occurs or the time taken to perform a task. Examples include number of customer complaints, number of orders shipped the same day, hours of inspection, and time to fill an order. Such performance measures are useful in reducing or eliminating waste and inefficiencies in operating activities.

Management uses performance measures in all stages of the management cycle. In the planning stage, management establishes performance measures to motivate future performance that supports the goals and objectives of the strategic plan. For example, many organizations want employees to increase quality, reduce costs, increase customer satisfaction, and increase efficiency and timeliness. As you will recall from earlier in the chapter, Abbie Awani selected the number of customer complaints as a performance measure to monitor service quality.

During the executing stage, performance measures guide and motivate the performance of employees and assist in assigning costs to products, departments, or operating activities. Abbie will record the number of customer complaints during the year. She can group the information by type of complaint or the employee involved in the service.

In the reviewing stage, management uses performance measures to improve future performance by analyzing significant differences between actual and planned performance. By comparing the actual and planned number of customer complaints, Abbie can identify problem areas and consider solutions.

In the reporting stage, performance measurement information is useful in communicating performance evaluations and developing new budgets. If Abbie needed a formal report, she could have her accountant prepare a performance evaluation analysis based on this information.

To measure increased quality, the management of a manufacturing organization needs information about and trend analysis of the number of items that require rework, the amount of scrapped materials and products, the total time devoted to inspection, and the time spent on product development, design, and testing. Improvements in production and delivery can be measured by trends in throughput time (the total production time per unit per product type), total delivery time by customer and geographic location, raw materials spoilage and scrap rates, production bottlenecks (slowdowns), and completed production. Customer satisfaction can be measured by trends in the number of product warranty claims and the number of products returned (analyzed by product line and by customer), retention of customers, product reorders by customers, and time spent on product repairs and adjustments in the field.

These analyses of nonfinancial data also measure how well management has been able to reduce operating costs. Reducing or eliminating the need to rework defective units or the incurrence of scrap also reduces the cost of a product. If throughput time is reduced, the costs connected with the time saved—such as storage costs, inspection labor time costs, and product moving costs—are also reduced. Improved product quality reduces or eliminates warranty claims and service work, thus reducing product costs.

Exhibit 1. Analysis of Nonfinancial Data–Bank

Kings Beach National Bank
Summary of Number of Customers Served
For the Quarter Ended December 31, 20xx

Part A

	Number of Customers Served			
Window	**October**	**November**	**December**	**Quarter Totals**
1	5,428	5,186	5,162	15,776
2	5,280	4,820	4,960	15,060
3	4,593	4,494	4,580	13,667
Totals	15,301	14,500	14,702	44,503

Part B

	Number of Customers Served per Hour			
Window	**October**	**November**	**December**	**Quarter Averages**
1	31.93	30.51	30.36	30.93
2	31.06	28.35	29.18	29.53
3	27.02	26.44	26.94	26.80
Totals	90.01	85.30	86.48	87.26
Average per hour per window	30.00	28.43	28.83	29.09

Part C: Graphic Comparison of the Number of Customers Served per Hour

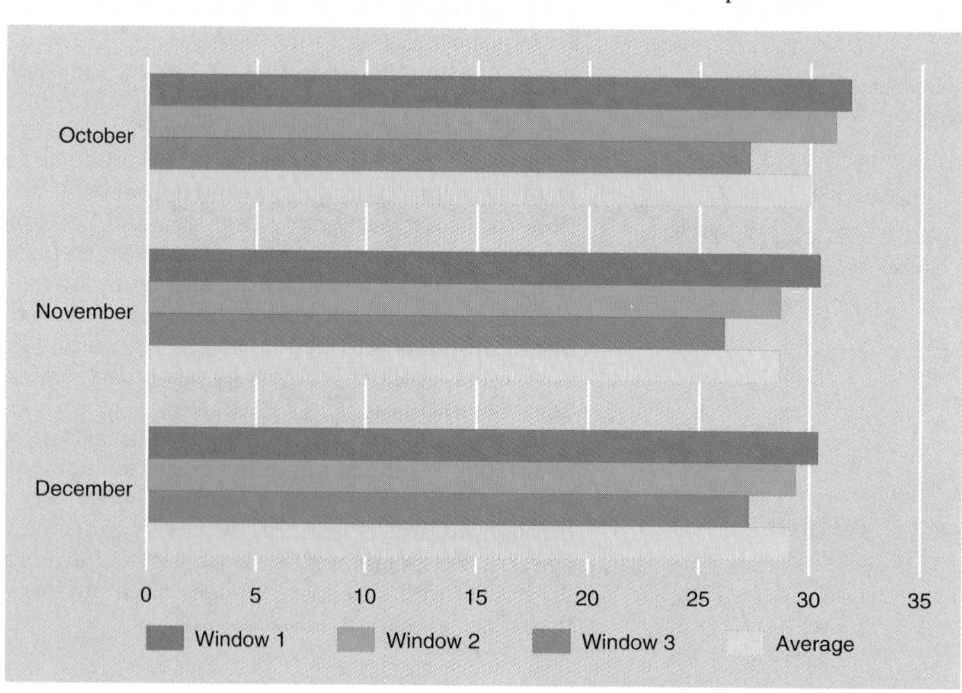

Teaching Note: Explain how using nonfinancial measures in an international business environment often eliminates the problems associated with different currencies and different accounting standards.

Notice that all of these performance measures are nonfinancial and are critical in today's operating environment. In addition, all are part of the decision-supporting data management needs and are expected to be supplied by the management accounting information system.

Accountants are often confronted with problems that require such nonfinancial measures as machine hours, labor hours, units of output, number of employees, and number of requests for a particular service. The following example illustrates a situation in which a manager requires nonfinancial data to make an informed decision in a service organization.

Lynda Babb supervises tellers at Kings Beach National Bank. The bank has three drive-up windows, each with a full-time teller. Historically, each teller served an average of thirty customers per hour. However, on November 1, 20xx, management implemented a new check-scanning procedure that has cut back the number of customers served per hour.

Data on the number of customers served for the three-month period ended December 31, 20xx, are shown in Part A of Exhibit 1. Each teller works an average of 170 hours per month. Window 1 is always the busiest; Windows 2 and 3 receive progressively less business. The October figure of thirty customers per hour is derived from the averages for all three windows.

Ms. Babb is preparing a report for management on the effects of the new procedure. Part B of Exhibit 1 shows her analysis of the number of customers served over the three months by each teller window. She computed the number of customers served per hour by dividing the number of customers served by the monthly average hours worked per teller (170). By averaging the customer service rates for the three tellers, she got 28.43 for November and 28.83 for December. As you can see, the service rate has decreased. But December's average is higher than November's, which means the tellers, as a whole, are becoming more accustomed to the new procedure. Part C of Exhibit 1 is a graphic comparison of the number of customers served per hour.

How to Prepare a Management Accounting Report or Analysis

OBJECTIVE 5

Identify the important questions a manager must consider before requesting or preparing a management report

Related Text Assignments:
Q: 17
SE: 5
E: 5
P: 3, 7
SD: 3
MRA: 2, 3

Point to Emphasize: Stress the concepts of generating useful information and reducing information overload.

As a manager, you may have to recommend the purchase of a particular machine, request money to develop a new form of packaging, or present a marketing plan for your organization's most popular product or service. Regardless of the assignment, you will have to prepare some type of report. Often the report will require relevant accounting information to support your position.

The keys to successful report preparation are the four *W*'s: Why? Who? What? and When? Keep the following points in mind as you prepare your report.

- **Why?** Know the purpose of the report. Focus on it as you write.
- **Who?** Identify the audience for your report. Communicate at a level that matches your audience's understanding of the issue and their familiarity with accounting information. A detailed, informal report may be appropriate for your manager, but a more concise summary may be necessary for other audiences, such as the president or board of directors of your organization.
- **What?** What information is needed? *Select the relevant information.* Know the sources of this information. You may draw information from specific documents or from interviews with knowledgeable managers and employees.

  What method of presentation is best? *Develop the most effective method of presentation.* The information should be relevant and easy to read and understand. You may need to include visual presentations, such as bar charts or graphs to present accounting information.

- **When?** Know the due date for the report. Strive to prepare an accurate report on a timely basis. Remember that you may have to balance accuracy and timeliness. Some accuracy may be lost if the report is urgent.

You have an opportunity to develop your skills in reporting accounting information. At the end of each management accounting chapter, you will find Managerial Reporting and Analysis problems that ask you to formulate reports that include accounting information.

Merchandising Versus Manufacturing Organizations

OBJECTIVE 6

Compare accounting for inventories and cost of goods sold in merchandising and manufacturing organizations

Related Text Assignments:
Q: 18
SE: 6
E: 6
P: 4, 5, 8

Discussion Question: Is a fast-food restaurant a merchandising establishment or a manufacturing operation? **Answer:** Students may decide that it is a merchandising operation, manufacturer, or both. Use this example to stress that manufacturing operations are also in the business of selling a product.

Teaching Note: Demonstrate to students that the work in process inventory is the source of goods for the finished goods inventory in a manufacturing organization, just as purchases are the source of goods for the merchandise inventory in a merchandising organization.

Merchandising organizations and manufacturing organizations prepare income statements and balance sheets for owners, creditors, and other outside parties. Both types of organizations maintain levels of inventory and calculate gross margin using sales and cost of goods sold information. However, merchandising organizations are less complex than manufacturing organizations.

Merchandising organizations

- purchase products that are ready for resale,
- maintain only one inventory account on the balance sheet, and
- include the cost of purchases in the calculation of cost of goods sold.

Manufacturing organizations

- design and manufacture products for sale,
- reflect three inventory accounts on the balance sheet, and
- determine the cost of goods manufactured to include in the calculation of cost of goods sold.

Merchandising organizations, such as Wal-Mart, Toys "R" Us, and Home Depot, purchase products that are ready for resale. These organizations maintain one inventory account, called Merchandise Inventory, that reflects the costs of products held for resale. To calculate the cost of goods sold for a merchandising organization, the following equation is used:

$$\text{Cost of Goods Sold} = \begin{array}{c}\text{Beginning}\\\text{Merchandise}\\\text{Inventory}\end{array} + \begin{array}{c}\textbf{Net Cost of}\\\textbf{Purchases}\end{array} - \begin{array}{c}\text{Ending}\\\text{Merchandise}\\\text{Inventory}\end{array}$$

For example, Sweet Treasures Candy Store had a balance of \$3,000 in the Merchandise Inventory account on January 1, 20xx. During the year, the company purchased candy products totaling \$23,000 (adjusted for purchase discounts, purchases returns and allowances, and freight-in). At December 31, 20xx, the Merchandise Inventory balance was \$4,500. The cost of goods sold is thus \$21,500.

$$\text{Cost of Goods Sold} = \$3,000 + \$23,000 - \$4,500 = \$21,500$$

Manufacturing organizations, such as Motorola, Sony, and IBM, use materials, labor, and manufacturing overhead to manufacture products for sale. Materials are purchased and used in the production process. The Materials Inventory account shows the balance of the cost of unused materials. During the production process, the costs of manufacturing the product are accumulated in the Work in Process Inventory account. The balance of the Work in Process Inventory account represents the costs of unfinished product. Once the product is complete and ready for sale, the cost of the goods manufactured is reflected in the Finished Goods Inventory account. The balance in the Finished Goods Inventory account is the cost of unsold completed product. When the product is sold, the manufacturing organization calculates the cost of goods sold using the following equation:

$$\text{Cost of Goods Sold} = \begin{matrix}\text{Beginning}\\ \text{Finished Goods}\\ \text{Inventory}\end{matrix} + \begin{matrix}\textbf{Cost of}\\ \textbf{Goods}\\ \textbf{Manufactured}\end{matrix} - \begin{matrix}\text{Ending}\\ \text{Finished Goods}\\ \text{Inventory}\end{matrix}$$

For example, Hatcher Candy Company, a supplier to Sweet Treasures Candy Store, had a balance of $52,000 in the Finished Goods Inventory account on January 1, 20xx. During the year, Hatcher manufactured candy products totaling $144,000. At December 31, 20xx, the Finished Goods Inventory balance was $78,000. The cost of goods sold is $118,000.

$$\text{Cost of Goods Sold} = \$52{,}000 + \$144{,}000 - \$78{,}000 = \$118{,}000$$

Both of these organizations use the following income statement format:

$$\text{Sales} - \text{Cost of Goods Sold} = \text{Gross Margin} - \text{Operating Expenses} = \text{Net Income}$$

Figure 3 compares the inventories and cost of goods sold sections for merchandising and manufacturing organizations. By combining the beginning Merchandise Inventory balance with the net cost of purchases for Sweet Treasures Candy Store, we calculate a "pie" called *cost of goods available for sale.* By counting and valuing unsold merchandise in the Merchandise Inventory account, we slice from the pie the ending Merchandise Inventory balance for the balance sheet, leaving the cost of goods sold for the income statement. Similarly, if we combine the beginning Finished Goods Inventory balance with the cost of goods manufactured for Hatcher Candy Company, we calculate a "pie" called *cost of goods available for sale.* By counting and valuing the unsold products in Finished Goods Inventory, we can slice from the pie the ending Finished Goods Inventory balance for the balance sheet, leaving the cost of goods sold for the income statement.

Cost Classifications and Their Uses

OBJECTIVE 7

Identify various approaches managers use to classify costs and show how the purpose of a manager's cost analysis can change the classification of a single cost item

Related Text Assignments:
Q: 19, 20, 21, 22
SE: 7
E: 7

Cost management is a necessary element of long-term success for an organization. Because managers are accountable to a variety of external parties, they must be aware of costs. Managers will focus on ways to operate efficiently, provide quality products or services, and satisfy customer needs. An understanding of cost classification will help managers select and use relevant information for planning, executing, reviewing, and reporting purposes.

A single cost can be classified and used in several different ways, depending on the purpose of the analysis. For example, managers may want to (1) trace costs to cost objects (cost traceability), (2) calculate the number of units that must be sold to obtain a certain level of profit (cost behavior), (3) identify costs of activities that do and do not add value to a product or service (value-adding versus nonvalue-adding costs), or (4) prepare an income statement for the owner (financial reporting).

Cost Traceability

Managers rely on management accountants to trace costs to cost objects, such as products or services, sales territories, departments, or operating activities. By tracing costs as directly as possible to cost objects, managers can thus develop a fairly

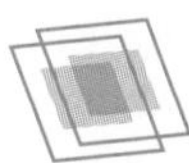

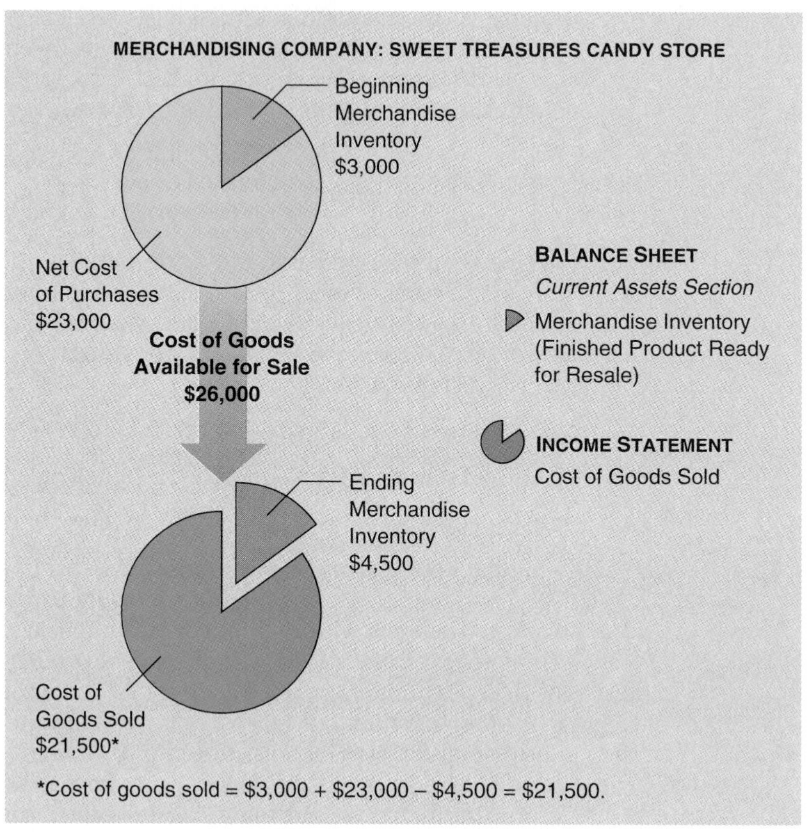

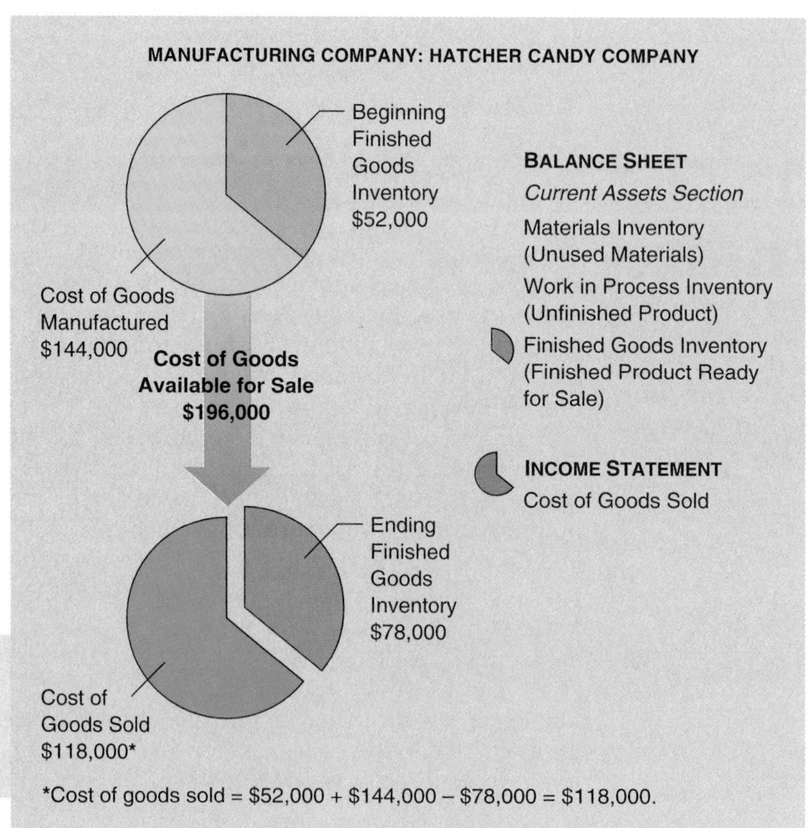

Figure 3
Comparison of the Inventories and Cost of Goods Sold Sections for Merchandising and Manufacturing Organizations

accurate measurement of costs. Managers use these direct and indirect measures of costs to support pricing decisions or decisions to reallocate resources to other cost objects.

Direct costs are costs that can be conveniently or economically traced to a cost object. For example, the wages of production line workers can be conveniently traced to the product, because the time worked and the related hourly wages can be easily found by looking at time cards and payroll records. Similarly, the costs of an engine can be easily traced to an automobile's cost.

In some cases, however, even though a material becomes part of a finished product, the expense of actually tracing its cost is too great. Some examples include nails in furniture, bolts in automobiles, and rivets in airplanes. These costs are considered indirect costs of the product. Indirect costs are costs that cannot be conveniently or economically traced to a cost object. Even though indirect costs may be difficult to trace, they must be included in the cost of a product. Therefore, management accountants use a formula to assign indirect costs to products. For example, insurance costs for the factory cannot be conveniently traced to individual products, but, for the sake of accuracy, they must be included in each product's cost. Management accountants solve the problem by assigning a portion of the factory insurance costs to each product manufactured.

Costs are classified as direct or indirect depending on the manager's needs. Regardless of the type of organization—service, retail, or manufacturing—classifying costs is important. The following examples illustrate a cost object and its related direct and indirect costs for three kinds of organizations.

- In a service organization, such as an accounting firm, costs can be traced to a specific service, such as tax return preparation. Direct costs for tax return preparation services include the costs of tax return forms, computer usage, and labor to prepare the return. Indirect costs include the costs of office rental, utilities, secretarial labor, telephone expenses, and depreciation of office furniture.
- In a retail organization, such as a department store, costs can be traced to a department. For example, the direct costs of the shoe department include the costs of shoes and the wages of employees working in that department. Indirect costs include the costs of utilities, insurance, property taxes, storage, and handling.
- In a manufacturing organization, costs can be traced to the product. Direct costs of the product include the costs of direct materials and direct labor. Indirect costs include the costs of utilities, depreciation of equipment, insurance, property taxes, inspection, maintenance of machinery, storage, handling, and cleaning.

Cost Behavior

Instructional Strategy: Divide the class into small groups. Ask groups to identify three fixed and three variable costs found in all fast-food restaurants and discuss why it is important for managers to identify those costs. Groups may present their findings to the class and take questions from other students.

Managers are also interested in the way costs respond to changes in volume or activity. By analyzing these patterns of behavior, managers gain information about the impact of changes in selling prices or operating costs on the net income of the organization. Costs can be separated into variable costs or fixed costs. A variable cost is a cost that changes in direct proportion to a change in productive output (or any other measure of volume). A fixed cost is a cost that remains constant within a defined range of activity or time period.

Viewing costs as variable or fixed is important to managers of any type of organization. The following examples illustrate variable and fixed costs for service, retail, and manufacturing organizations:

- A landscaping service has variable costs that include the cost of landscaping materials and direct labor to plant the materials for each landscaping project. Fixed costs include the costs of depreciation on trucks and equipment, nursery rent, insurance, and property taxes.

- A retail used-car dealership has variable costs that include the cost of the used cars sold and sales commissions. Fixed costs include the costs of building and lot rental, depreciation on office equipment, and salaries of the receptionist and accountant.
- A lawn mower manufacturer has variable costs that include the costs of direct materials, direct labor, indirect materials (bolts, nails, lubricants), and indirect labor (inspection and maintenance labor). Fixed costs include the costs of supervisory salaries and depreciation on buildings.

Value-Adding Versus Nonvalue-Adding Costs

In the spirit of continuous improvement, managers examine operating activities and processes in their organization. Their goal is to reduce or eliminate activities that do not add value to the products or services. The organization identifies the characteristics of the product or service that customers value and would be willing to pay for. This information influences the design of future products or the delivery of future services. The organization's management also identifies the operating activities that provide the value. Activities that do not add value are reduced or eliminated. A value-adding cost is the cost of an operating activity that increases the market value of a product or service. A nonvalue-adding cost is the cost of an operating activity that adds cost to a product or service but does not increase its market value. The depreciation of a machine that shapes a part assembled into the final product is a value-adding cost; depreciation of a sales department automobile is a nonvalue-adding cost. Costs incurred to improve the quality of a product are value-adding costs if the customer is willing to pay more for the higher-quality product; if not, they are nonvalue-adding costs because they do not increase the product's market value. The costs of administrative activities such as accounting and personnel are nonvalue-adding costs; they are necessary for the operation of the business, but they do not add value to the product.

Costs for Financial Reporting

Teaching Note: The concepts of product costs and period costs can also be explained using the matching rule: Product costs must be charged to the period in which the product generates revenue, and period costs are charged against the revenue of the current period.

Managers must prepare financial statements for external parties using a required format based on generally accepted accounting principles. Income statements prepared for owners, creditors, and other outside parties must reflect expenditures separated into product costs and period costs. Classifying expenditures into product (cost of goods sold) and period (selling and administrative) costs is called the *absorption approach* to income statement preparation.

BUSINESS BULLETIN: ETHICS IN PRACTICE

United Parcel Service (UPS) has taken a proactive role in its commitment to efficient and responsible management of resources. UPS recycles computer paper, letter envelopes, and delivery notices, and it also records delivery information electronically, which saves an estimated 30,000 trees annually. UPS also helps customers protect the environment by (1) devising the best packaging methods to prevent product damage and minimize waste and (2) developing national package-retrieval services to collect a customer's packaging. For example, Ethan Allen, Inc., a furniture maker and retailer, uses UPS's services to retrieve foam-sheet shipping material, which makes money for Ethan Allen in addition to reducing its disposal costs.[4]

Table 2. Cost Classification and Cost Analyses

	Purpose of Cost Classification			
Cost Examples	Traceability to Product	Cost Behavior	Value	Financial Reporting
Sugar for candy	Direct	Variable	Value-adding	Product
Depreciation on mixing machine	Indirect	Fixed	Value-adding	Product
Sales commission	—*	Variable	Value-adding**	Period
Accountant's salary	—*	Fixed	Nonvalue-adding	Period

*Sales commission and accountant's salary are not product costs. Therefore, these costs are not directly or indirectly traceable in traditional business operations.
**Sales commission can be value-adding because customers' perceptions of the salesperson and the selling experience can strongly affect their perceptions of the product's or service's market value.

Point to Emphasize: Product costs remain assets until they are expensed and transferred from the Finished Goods Inventory account to Cost of Goods Sold.

Business-World Example: To demonstrate that the length of time costs remain in inventory is not a consideration in determining product costs, ask the class to identify the product costs and period costs of a local fast-food operation. Such operations maintain a direct materials inventory, have a rapid turnover in work in process inventory, and have virtually no finished goods inventory at any given time.

Product costs or inventoriable costs, include the three elements of manufacturing cost: direct materials, direct labor, and manufacturing overhead. The product costs for units sold in the accounting period are included in the cost of goods sold section of the income statement. The product costs of unsold units are shown in the Finished Goods Inventory balance on the balance sheet. Prime costs are the primary costs of production, which are the sum of direct materials costs and direct labor costs, while conversion costs are the costs of converting raw materials into finished product, which include direct labor and manufacturing overhead costs.

Period costs, or noninventoriable costs, are the costs of resources consumed during the current period. For example, selling and administrative expenses are period costs because those activities were performed to generate the revenues of the current period.

A single cost item can be classified in different ways depending on the purpose of the cost analysis. Table 2 provides examples.

Standards of Ethical Conduct for Practitioners of Management Accounting and Financial Management

OBJECTIVE 8

Identify the standards of ethical conduct for management accountants

Related Text Assignments:
Q: 23, 24
SE: 8
E: 8
SD: 2

Managers are responsible to external parties (for example, owners, creditors, governmental agencies, and the local community) for the proper use of organizational resources and the financial reporting of their actions. Conflicts may arise that require managers to balance the interests of all external parties. For example, the community wants a safe living environment, while owners seek to maximize profits. If management decides to purchase an expensive device to extract pollutants from the production process, it will protect the community, but profits will decline. The benefit will be greater for the community than for the owners. On the other hand, management could achieve higher profits for the owners by purchasing a less expensive, less effective pollution device that may harm the community. Such potential conflicts between external parties can create ethical dilemmas for management and for accountants.

Management accountants and financial managers have a responsibility to help management balance the needs of the various external parties. Thus the accounting profession must operate with the highest standards of performance. To provide

Exhibit 2. Standards of Ethical Conduct for Practitioners of Management Accounting and Financial Management

Practitioners of management accounting and financial management have an obligation to the public, their profession, the organization they serve, and themselves, to maintain the highest standards of ethical conduct. In recognition of this obligation, the Institute of Management Accountants has promulgated the following standards of ethical conduct for practitioners of management accounting and financial management. Adherence to these standards, both domestically and internationally, is integral to achieving the Objectives of Management Accounting. Practitioners of management accounting and financial management shall not commit acts contrary to these standards nor shall they condone the commission of such acts by others within their organizations.

Competence. Practitioners of management accounting and financial management have a responsibility to:

- Maintain an appropriate level of professional competence by ongoing development of their knowledge and skills.
- Perform their professional duties in accordance with relevant laws, regulations, and technical standards.
- Prepare complete and clear reports and recommendations after appropriate analysis of relevant and reliable information.

Confidentiality. Practitioners of management accounting and financial management have a responsibility to:

- Refrain from disclosing confidential information acquired in the course of their work except when authorized, unless legally obligated to do so.
- Inform subordinates as appropriate regarding the confidentiality of information acquired in the course of their work and monitor their activities to assure the maintenance of that confidentiality.
- Refrain from using or appearing to use confidential information acquired in the course of their work for unethical or illegal advantage either personally or through third parties.

Integrity. Practitioners of management accounting and financial management have a responsibility to:

- Avoid actual or apparent conflicts of interest and advise all appropriate parties of any potential conflict.
- Refrain from engaging in any activity that would prejudice their ability to carry out their duties ethically.
- Refuse any gift, favor, or hosptiality that would influence or would appear to influence their actions.
- Refrain from either actively or passively subverting the attainment of the organization's legitimate and ethical objectives.
- Recognize and communicate professional limitations or other constraints that would preclude responsible judgment or successful performance of an activity.

(continued)

Discussion Question: Does the competence standard apply to areas other than technical competence? **Answer:** A management accountant or financial manager needs management skills, quantitative methods, and an understanding of economics and finance to perform quality work. These are also covered by the competence standard.

Ethical Consideration: Ask students to identify situations in which confidentiality is required.

guidance, the Institute of Management Accountants has formally adopted standards of ethical conduct for practitioners of management accounting and financial management. Those standards emphasize that management accountants have responsibilities in the areas of competence, confidentiality, integrity, and objectivity. The full statement is presented in Exhibit 2.

Chapter Review

REVIEW OF LEARNING OBJECTIVES

1. **Define *management accounting* and distinguish between management accounting and financial accounting.** Management accounting is the process of identifying, measuring, accumulating, analyzing, preparing, interpreting, and communicating information used by management to plan, evaluate, and control an organization within and to ensure that its resources are used and accounted for appropriately. Management accounting reports provide information for planning, control,

Exhibit 2. Standards of Ethical Conduct for Practitioners of Management Accounting and Financial Management (*continued*)

- Communicate unfavorable as well as favorable information and professional judgments or opinions.
- Refrain from engaging in or supporting any activity that would discredit the profession.

Objectivity. Practitioners of management accounting and financial management have a responsibility to:

- Communicate information fairly and objectively.
- Disclose fully all relevant information that could reasonably be expected to influence an intended user's understanding of the reports, comments, and recommendations presented.

Resolution of Ethical Conflict. In applying the standards of ethical conduct, practitioners of management accounting and financial management may encounter problems in identifying unethical behavior or in resolving an ethical conflict. When faced with significant ethical issues, practitioners of management accounting and financial management should follow the established policies of the organization bearing on the resolution of such conflict. If these policies do not resolve the ethical conflict, such practitioner should consider the following courses of action:

- Discuss such problems with the immediate superior except when it appears that the superior is involved, in which case the problem should be presented initially to the next higher managerial level. If a satisfactory resolution cannot be achieved when the problem is initially presented, submit the issues to the next higher managerial level.

  If the immediate superior is the chief executive officer, or equivalent, the acceptable reviewing authority may be a group such as the audit committee, executive committee, board of directors, board of trustees, or owners. Contact with levels above the immediate superior should be initiated only with the superior's knowledge, assuming the superior is not involved. Except where legally prescribed, communication of such problems to authorities or individuals not employed or engaged by the organization is not considered appropriate.
- Clarify relevant ethical issues by confidential discussion with an objective advisor (e.g., IMA Ethics Counselling Service) to obtain a better understanding of possible courses of action.
- Consult your own attorney as to legal obligations and rights concerning the ethical conflict.
- If the ethical conflict still exists after exhausting all levels of internal review, there may be no other recourse on significant matters than to resign from the organization and to submit an informative memorandum to an appropriate representative of the organization. After resignation, depending on the nature of the ethical conflict, it may also be appropriate to notify other parties.

Source: From *Standards of Ethical Conduct for Practitioners of Management Accounting and Financial Management.*" Institute of Management Accountants, July 1997. Reprinted by permission.

Ethical Consideration: Ask students to identify the dollar-value limits on gifts, lunches, or favors that would not violate the integrity standard. Then ask them, "What is your price?" or "What amount would influence your behavior?" This often stimulates lively discussion.

Point to Emphasize: It is crucial for business students to recognize situations that give rise to ethical conflicts and to be prepared to address these issues.

performance measurement, and decision making to employees, managers, and suppliers when they need such information. Management accounting reports follow a flexible format and present subjective, future-oriented information expressed in dollar amounts or physical measures. In contrast, financial accounting reports provide information about the past performance of an organization to owners, lenders, customers, and government agencies on a regular basis. Financial accounting reports follow strict guidelines defined by generally accepted accounting principles and present objective information shown in historical dollars.

2. **Explain the management cycle and its connection to management accounting.** Traditionally, management operates in four stages: planning, executing, reviewing, and reporting. Strategic and operating plans prepare managers for the execution of activities that put those plans into action. A review of the actual performance in relation to planned performance helps in the evaluation of management's success in guiding and motivating personnel. Reports reflect the results of planning, executing, and reviewing operations and may be prepared externally for stockholders, creditors, or other external parties or internally for management and employees.
3. **Identify the new management philosophies for continuous improvement and discuss the role of management accounting in implementing these philosophies.** The new approaches to management include the just-in-time (JIT) operating environment, total quality management (TQM), and activity-based management

(ABM). All of these approaches are designed to achieve continuous improvement by increasing product or service quality, reducing resource waste, and reducing cost. Management accounting helps managers design better information systems that are sensitive to changes in production processes in a JIT operating environment, requests for information about quality costs (TQM), and assignment of overhead costs to products or services (ABC).

4. **Define *performance measures,* recognize the uses of these measures in the management cycle, and prepare an analysis of nonfinancial data.** Performance measures are quantitative tools that provide an indication of an organization's performance in relation to a specific goal or expected outcome. Performance measures are used in the management cycle to plan future performance, to guide and motivate current performance and assign costs during the executing stage, and to improve future performance through the analysis of significant differences between actual and planned performance. Management accountants have always been responsible for analyzing nonfinancial data. Today's globally competitive environment has created additional demand for nonfinancial analyses centered on increasing the quality of an organization's products or services, reducing production and delivery time, and satisfying customers. Among the performance measures used in these analyses are units of output, time measures, and scrap incurrence rates.
5. **Identify the important questions a manager must consider before requesting or preparing a management report.** Report preparation depends on the four *W*'s: Why? What? Who? and When? The why question is answered by stating the purpose of the report. Once that has been stated, the report maker must determine what information the report should contain to satisfy that purpose. The who question can take several forms: For whom is the report being prepared? To whom should the report be distributed? Who will read it? Finally, there is the question of when. When is the report due?
6. **Compare accounting for inventories and cost of goods sold in merchandising and manufacturing organizations.** A merchandising organization purchases a product that is ready for resale when it is received. Only one account, Merchandise Inventory, is used to record and account for items in inventory. The cost of goods sold is simply the difference between the cost of goods available for sale and the ending merchandise inventory. A manufacturing organization, because it creates a product, maintains three inventory accounts: Materials Inventory, Work in Process Inventory, and Finished Goods Inventory. Manufacturing costs flow through all three inventory accounts. During the accounting period, the cost of completed products is transferred to the Finished Goods Inventory account; the cost of units that have been sold is transferred to the Cost of Goods Sold account.
7. **Identify various approaches managers use to classify costs and show how the purpose of a manager's cost analysis can change the classification of a single cost item.** A single cost item can be classified and used by managers to (1) trace costs to cost objects (direct versus indirect costs), (2) calculate the number of units that must be sold to obtain a certain level of profit (variable versus fixed costs), (3) identify costs of activities that do and do not add value to a product or service (value-adding versus nonvalue-adding costs), or (4) prepare an income statement for outside parties (product versus period costs).
8. **Identify the standards of ethical conduct for management accountants.** Standards of ethical conduct govern management accountants' competence, confidentiality, integrity, and objectivity. These standards help management accountants recognize and avoid situations and activities that compromise their honesty, loyalty, and ability to supply management with accurate and relevant information.

REVIEW OF CONCEPTS AND TERMINOLOGY

The following concepts and terms were introduced in this chapter:

LO 3 **Activity-based costing (ABC):** A system that identifies all of an organization's major operating activities (both production and nonproduction), traces costs to those activities, and then determines which products or services use the resources and services supplied by those activities.

LO 3 **Activity-based management (ABM):** An approach to managing an organization that identifies all major operating activities, determines what resources are consumed by each activity, identifies what causes resource usage of each activity, and categorizes the activities as either adding value to a product or service or being nonvalue-adding; emphasis is on the reduction or elimination of nonvalue-adding activities.

LO 3 **Continuous improvement:** The management concept that one should never be satisfied with what is; one should always seek a better method, product, service, process, or resource.

LO 7 **Conversion costs:** The costs of converting raw materials into finished product, which are the sum of direct labor costs and manufacturing overhead costs.

LO 7 **Direct cost:** Any cost that can be conveniently or economically traced to a specific cost object; a manufacturing cost that is easily traced to a specific product.

LO 7 **Fixed cost:** A cost that remains constant within a defined range of activity or time period.

LO 7 **Indirect cost:** Any cost that cannot be conveniently or economically traced to a specific cost object.

LO 7 **Inventoriable cost:** See *product cost.*

LO 3 **Just-in-time (JIT) operating environment:** An organizational environment in which personnel are hired and raw materials and facilities are purchased and used only as needed; emphasis is on the elimination of waste.

LO 1 **Management accounting:** The process of identification, measurement, accumulation, analysis, preparation, interpretation, and communication of financial and nonfinancial information used by management to plan, evaluate, and control the organization within and to assure appropriate use and accountability for its resources.

LO 7 **Noninventoriable cost:** See *period costs.*

LO 3 **Nonvalue-adding activity:** A production- or service-related activity that adds cost to a product or service, but, from a customer's perspective, does not increase its value.

LO 7 **Nonvalue-adding cost:** The cost of an operating activity that adds cost to a product or service but does not increase its market value.

LO 4 **Performance measures:** Quantitative tools that provide an indication of an organization's performance in relation to a specific goal or expected outcome.

LO 7 **Period costs:** The costs of resources consumed during the current period; they cannot be inventoried.

LO 7 **Prime costs:** The primary costs of production, which are the sum of the direct materials costs and the direct labor costs.

LO 7 **Product cost:** Inventoriable costs that include the three elements of manufacturing cost: direct materials, direct labor, and manufacturing overhead.

LO 3 **Total quality management (TQM):** An environment in which all functions work together to build quality into the organization's product or service.

LO 3 **Value-adding activity:** A production- or service-related activity that adds cost to a product or service, but, from a customer's perspective, also increases its value.

LO 7 **Value-adding cost:** The cost of an operating activity that increases the market value of a product or service.

LO 7 **Variable cost:** A cost that changes in direct proportion to a change in productive output (or any other measure of volume).

REVIEW PROBLEM

Analysis of Nonfinancial Data

LO 4 Youngdale Painting, Inc., is a house-painting company located in Phoenix. The company employs painters specializing in interior walls or exterior trim. Recently Mr. Youngdale assigned two interior painters and three exterior trim painters to two school projects. He prepared a projection of work hours for the Yakima High School and Jerome Elementary School projects for the month of June, as shown at the top of the next page.

Projected Hours to Be Worked

	Week 1	Week 2	Week 3	Week 4	Totals
Interior	80	80	80	80	320
Exterior	120	120	120	120	480

On July 2, Mr. Youngdale assembled the actual hour data shown below:

Actual Hours Worked

	Week 1	Week 2	Week 3	Week 4	Totals
Interior	96	108	116	116	436
Exterior	104	108	116	108	436

Mr. Youngdale is concerned about the excess hours worked during June.

REQUIRED

1. For each group of painters (interior and exterior), prepare an analysis that shows the projected hours, the actual hours worked, and the number of hours over or under the projected hours for each week and in total.
2. Using the same information, prepare one line graph for the interior painters and another line graph for the exterior painters. Place the weeks on the *X* axis and the number of hours on the *Y* axis.
3. Using the information from 1 and 2, identify which group of painters worked more hours than planned and offer several reasons for the additional hours.

ANSWER TO REVIEW PROBLEM

1. **Interior Painters**

Week	Projected Hours to Be Worked	Actual Hours Worked	Hours Worked Under or (Over) Projected
1	80	96	(16)
2	80	108	(28)
3	80	116	(36)
4	80	116	(36)
Total	320	436	(116)

Exterior Painters

Week	Projected Hours to Be Worked	Actual Hours Worked	Hours Worked Under or (Over) Projected
1	120	104	16
2	120	108	12
3	120	116	4
4	120	108	12
Total	480	436	44

2.

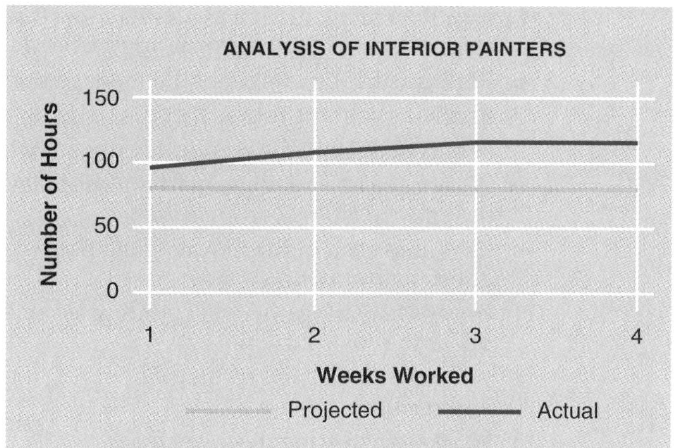

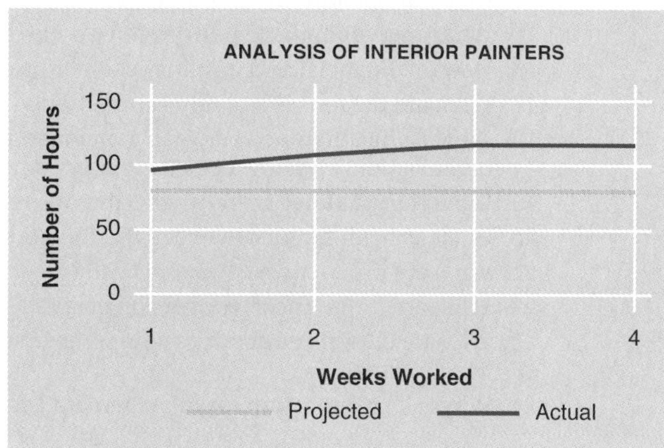

3. The interior painters took more time to complete the jobs than was anticipated by Mr. Youngdale. Possible reasons for the additional hours include:
   a. The quality of the paint or painting materials may have been poor, which would require the walls to be repainted.
   b. One of the painters may have been inexperienced or recently hired. If that person lacked training, he or she may have worked more slowly than anticipated, or the other painter may have had to take extra time to train him or her.
   c. The customer may have requested a different color or finish after the painting had started. As a result, the painters had to repaint some areas.
   d. Mr. Youngdale underestimated the amount of time required for interior painting.

Chapter Assignments

BUILDING YOUR KNOWLEDGE FOUNDATION

Questions

1. What is management accounting?
2. What effect does the size of an organization have on the amount or type of financial information needed by management?
3. How is management accounting similar to financial accounting?
4. How do management accounting and financial accounting differ in terms of report format, reasons for report preparation, and the parties to whom management is accountable?

5. How do management accounting reports and financial accounting reports differ in terms of units of measure, nature of information, and timing of preparation?
6. What are the four stages of the management cycle?
7. Briefly explain the four stages of the management cycle.
8. How is management accounting linked to the management cycle?
9. What three new management philosophies or approaches have developed in response to global competition?
10. How does each of the new management philosophies affect an organization's operating environment?
11. How have management accounting systems adapted to changes in an organization's operating environment?
12. What are the desired results of adopting any one of the three new management approaches?
13. What are performance measures?
14. Give examples of financial performance measures.
15. What are nonfinancial performance measures? Give examples.
16. How are financial and nonfinancial performance measures used?
17. What are the four *W*'s of report preparation? Explain the importance of each.
18. What is the difference between a merchandising organization and a manufacturing organization, and how does it affect accounting for inventories?
19. What is the difference between a direct cost and an indirect cost?
20. What is the difference between a value-adding cost and a nonvalue-adding cost?
21. What are product costs? period costs?
22. What are prime costs? conversion costs?
23. Why are ethical standards of competence so important to the work of management accountants?
24. Why is it so important for management accountants to maintain their integrity?

Short Exercises

SE 1. LO 1 *Management Accounting Versus Financial Accounting*

Management accounting differs from financial accounting in a number of ways. Tell whether each of the following characteristics relates to management accounting (MA) or financial accounting (FA).

1. Focuses on various segments of the business entity
2. Demands objectivity
3. Relies on the criterion of usefulness rather than formal guidelines or restrictions for gathering information
4. Measures units in historical dollars
5. Reports information on a regular basis
6. Uses only monetary measures for reports
7. Adheres to generally accepted accounting principles
8. Prepares reports whenever needed

SE 2. LO 2 *The Management Cycle*

Indicate whether each of the following management activities is part of the planning stage (P), the executing stage (E), the reviewing stage (REV), or the reporting stage (REP) of the management cycle.

1. Complete a balance sheet and income statement at the end of the year
2. Train a store clerk to complete a cash sale
3. Meet with department store managers to develop performance measures for sales personnel
4. Rent a local warehouse to store excess inventory of clothing
5. Evaluate the performance of the shoe department by examining the significant differences between the department's actual and planned expenses for the month
6. Prepare an annual budget of anticipated sales for each department and the entire store

SE 3. LO 3 *JIT and Continuous Improvement*

The just-in-time operating environment focuses on reducing or eliminating the waste of resources. Resources include physical assets such as machinery and buildings, labor time, and materials and parts used in the production process. Choose one of these resources and tell how it could be wasted. How can an organization prevent the waste of that resource? How can the concept of continuous improvement be implemented to reduce the waste of that resource?

SE 4. LO 4 *Analysis of Nonfinancial Data*

Spectrum Technologies has been having a problem with the computerized welding operation in its dialogic extractor product line. The extractors are used to sift through and separate various types of metal shavings into piles of individual metals for recycling and scrap sales. The time for each welding operation has been increasing at an erratic rate. Management has asked that the time intervals be analyzed to see if the cause of the problem can be determined. The number of parts welded per shift during the previous week is reported below. What can you deduce from the information that may help management solve the welding operation problem?

	Machine Number	Monday	Tuesday	Wednesday	Thursday	Friday
First shift:						
Kovacs	1	642	636	625	617	602
Abington	2	732	736	735	729	738
Geisler	3	745	726	717	694	686
Second shift:						
Deragon	1	426	416	410	404	398
Berwager	2	654	656	661	664	670
Grass	3	526	524	510	504	502

SE 5. LO 5 *Managerial Report Preparation*

Melissa Mertz, president of Mertz Industries, asked controller Rick Caputo to prepare a report on the use of electricity by each of the organization's five divisions. Increases in electricity costs ranged from 20 to 35 percent in the divisions over the past year. What questions should Rick ask before he begins his analysis?

SE 6. LO 6 *Merchandising Versus Manufacturing*

Based on the following information, decide whether the Vikram Company is a merchandising organization or a manufacturing organization. List reasons for your answer.

Beginning Work in Process Inventory	$3,800
Materials Used	2,350
Overhead Costs	4,250
Direct Labor Costs	1,500
Cost of Goods Sold	9,340
Ending Materials Inventory	2,430
Beginning Finished Goods Inventory	4,800
Ending Finished Goods Inventory	7,250

SE 7. LO 7 *Cost Classification*

Indicate whether each of the following is a product (PR) or a period (PER) cost and a variable (V) or a fixed (F) cost. Also indicate whether each adds value (VA) or does not add value (NVA) to the product.

1. Production supervisor's salary
2. Sales commission
3. Wages of a production line worker

SE 8. LO 8 *Ethical Conduct*

Gary Louskip, a management accountant for Pegstone Cosmetics Company, has lunch every day with his good friend Joe Blaik, a management accountant for Shepherd Cosmetics, Inc., a competitor of Pegstone. Last week, Gary couldn't decide how to treat some information in a report he was preparing, so he discussed the information with Joe. Is Gary adhering to the ethical standards of management accountants? Defend your answer.

Exercises

E 1. LO 1 *Definitions of Management Accounting*

There are many definitions and descriptions of management accounting. The Institute of Management Accountants, in *Statement No. 1A* in its series *Statements on Management Accounting,* defined management accounting as

> the process of identification, measurement, accumulation, analysis, preparation, interpretation, and communication of financial information used by management

to plan, evaluate, and control within the organization and to assure appropriate use and accountability for its resources. Management accounting also comprises the preparation of financial reports for nonmanagement groups such as shareholders, creditors, regulatory agencies, and tax authorities.[5]

In *The Modern Accountant's Handbook,* management (managerial) accounting is described as follows:

> Managerial accounting, although generally anchored to the financial accounting framework, involves a broader information-processing system. It deals in many units of measure and produces a variety of reports designed for specific purposes. Its scope encompasses the past, the present, and the future. Its purposes include short- and long-range planning, cost determination, control of activities, assessment of objectives and program performance, and provision of basic information for decision making.[6]

1. Compare these two statements about management accounting.
2. Explain this statement: "It is impossible to distinguish the point at which financial accounting ends and management accounting begins."

LO 2 *The Management Cycle*

E 2. Indicate whether each of the following management activities is part of the planning stage (P), the executing stage (E), the reviewing stage (REV), or the reporting stage (REP) of the management cycle in a local hospital.

1. Lease five Ford ambulances for the current year
2. Compare the actual number of patient days in the hospital to the planned number of patient days for the year
3. Develop a strategic plan for a new pediatric wing of the hospital
4. Prepare a report showing the past performance of the emergency room
5. Develop standards or expectations about the performance of the hospital admittance area for the next year
6. Prepare and distribute the hospital's balance sheet and income statement to the board of directors
7. Maintain an inventory of bed linens and bath towels for hospital patients
8. Formulate a corporate policy for the treatment and final disposition of hazardous waste materials in the hospital
9. Prepare a report of the types and amounts of hazardous waste materials removed from the hospital in the last three months
10. Monitor the time taken to deliver food trays to patients staying in the hospital

LO 3 *New Management Philosophies*

E 3. Recently, you were dining with three chief financial officers who were attending a seminar on new management tools and approaches to improving operations. During dinner, they shared information about their organizations' current operating environments. Excerpts from the dinner conversation are presented below. Tell whether each excerpt describes activity-based management (ABM), just-in-time operations (JIT), or total quality management (TQM).

CFO 1: We believe that quality can be achieved through carefully designed production processes. Therefore, we have an environment in which the time to move, store, queue, and inspect materials and products is greatly reduced. We have reduced inventories by purchasing and using materials only as needed.

CFO 2: Your approach is good. However, we are more concerned with our total operating environment, so we have a strategy that asks all employees to contribute to the achievement of quality, both for our products and for our production processes. We focus on eliminating poor product quality by targeting and reducing waste and inefficiencies in our current operating methods.

CFO 3: Our organization has adopted a strategy for quality products that incorporates many of your approaches. We also want to manage our resources effectively, but we do so by monitoring operating activities. All activities are analyzed, and the ones that do not add value to products are reduced or eliminated.

LO 4 *Nonfinancial Data Analysis*

E 4. Greenacres Landscapes, Inc., specializes in lawn installations requiring California bluegrass sod. The sod comes in 1-yard squares. The organization uses the guideline of 500 square yards per person per hour to evaluate the performance of its sod layers.

During the first week of March, the following actual data were collected.

Employee	Hours Worked	Square Yards of Sod Planted
P. Thompson	38	18,240
L. May	45	22,500
B. Pratt	40	19,800
E. Yu	42	17,640
R. Hardin	44	22,880
B. Harty	45	21,500

Evaluate the performance of the six employees.

LO 5 *Report Preparation*

E 5. Jim Herndon is the sales manager for All-Occasions Greeting Cards, Inc. At the beginning of the year, the organization introduced a new line of humorous birthday cards into the U.S. market. Now management is holding a strategic planning meeting to plan next year's operating activities. One item on the agenda is to review the success of the new birthday card line and the need to change the selling price or stimulate sales volume in the five sales territories. For the October 31 meeting, Jim was asked to prepare a report addressing these issues. His report was to include profits generated in each sales territory for the birthday card line only.

On October 31 Jim arrived late at the meeting and immediately distributed his report to the members of the strategic planning team. The report consisted of comments made by seven of Jim's leading sales representatives. The comments were broad in scope and touched only lightly on the success of the new card line. Jim was pleased that he had met the deadline to distribute the report, but the other team members were disappointed in the information he had provided.

Using the four *W*'s for report presentation, comment on Jim's effectiveness in preparing a report for the strategic planning team.

LO 6 *Merchandising Versus Manufacturing*

E 6. Indicate whether the accounting information from each of the following accounts refers to the operations of a merchandising organization (MER), a manufacturing organization (MANF), or both merchandising and manufacturing organizations (BOTH).

1. Finished Goods Inventory
2. Merchandise Inventory
3. Cost of Goods Sold
4. Net Cost of Purchases
5. Materials Inventory
6. Cost of Goods Manufactured
7. Gross Margin
8. Net Income
9. Operating Expenses

LO 7 *Cost Classifications*

E 7. Tell whether each of the following costs for a bicycle manufacturer is a product cost or a period cost, a direct cost or an indirect cost of the bicycle, and a variable cost or a fixed cost.

	Cost Classification		
	Product or Period	**Direct or Indirect**	**Variable or Fixed**
Example: Bicycle tire	Product	Direct	Variable
1. Depreciation on office computer			
2. Labor to assemble bicycle			
3. Labor to inspect bicycle			
4. President's salary			
5. Lubricant for wheels			

LO 8 *Professional Ethics*

E 8. Ron Kowalski went to work for Billings Industries five years ago. He was recently promoted to cost accounting manager and now has a new boss, Ted Young, the corporate controller. Last week, Ron and Ted went to a two-day professional development program on accounting changes in the new manufacturing environment. During the first hour of the first day's program, Ted disappeared and Ron didn't see him again until the cocktail hour. The same thing happened on the second day. During the trip home, Ron asked Ted if he enjoyed the conference. He replied:

> Ron, the golf course was excellent. You play golf. Why don't you join me during the next conference? I haven't sat in on one of those sessions in ten years. This is my

R&R time. Those sessions are for the new people. My experience is enough to keep me current. Plus, I have excellent people to help me as we adjust our accounting system to the changes being implemented on the production floor.

Does Ron have an ethical dilemma? If so, what is it? What are his options? How would you solve his problem? Be prepared to defend your answer.

Problems

LO 4 **P 1.** *Using Nonfinancial Data*

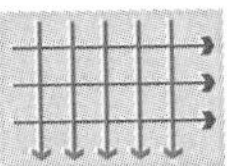

Clearlake Candy Company recently developed its strategic plan based on the philosophy of total quality management. Clearlake wants to sell candies with the highest quality in color, texture, shape, and taste. To meet quality standards, management chose many quality performance measures, including the number of rejected candy canes. Working with Janeece Hammond, the process supervisor, management decided that no more than 50 candy canes should be rejected daily throughout the year.

Using the data gathered about the actual number of rejected candy canes in Week 1 of 20xx, Janeece Hammond prepared the following summary and graph.

Week 1, 20xx	Maximum Number of Rejected Allowed Candy Canes	Actual Number of Rejected Candy Canes	Variance Under (Over) Allowed Maximum
Monday	50	60	(10)
Tuesday	50	63	(13)
Wednesday	50	58	(8)
Thursday	50	59	(9)
Friday	50	62	(12)
Total for the Week	250	302	(52)
Daily Average	50	60.4	

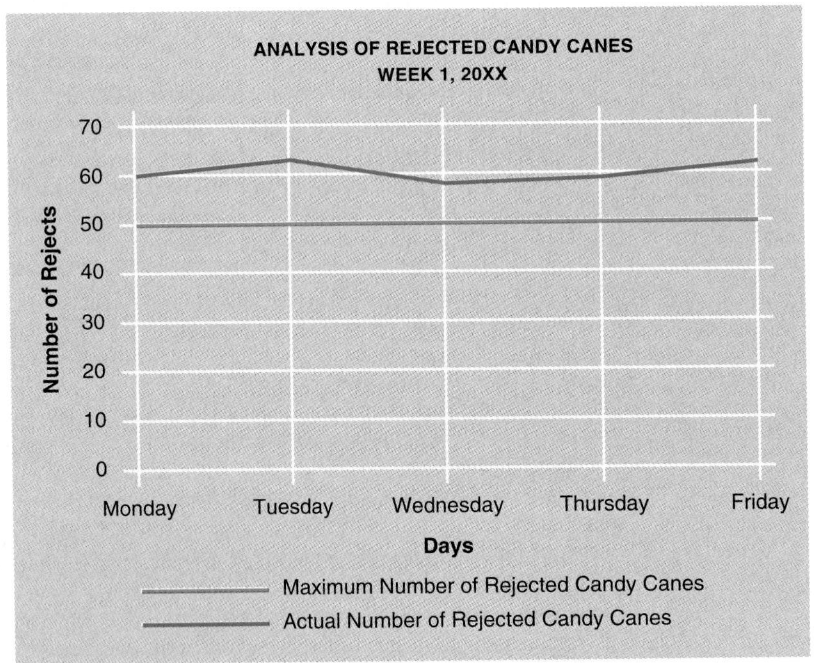

Because the variance was 20.8 percent (52 ÷ 250), Janeece decided to analyze the data further. She found that the rejected candy canes either contained too little sugar (ingredients), were not circular in shape (shaping), or were undercooked (cooking time). The number of rejects in each category follows at the top of the next page.

Week 1, 20xx	Reasons for Rejects
Ingredients	40
Shaping	195
Cooking Time	67
Total	302

Janeece worked with the cooks the following week to review the recipe, including ingredients, quantities, and cooking instructions. She trained the cooks to measure quantities more precisely, to shape the candy more carefully, and to time the cooking process more accurately. Then, in Week 3 of 20xx, she gathered the following information on the actual number of rejected candy canes and reasons for the rejects.

Week 3, 20xx	Actual Number of Rejects
Monday	20
Tuesday	21
Wednesday	22
Thursday	19
Friday	18
Total	100

Week 3, 20xx	Reasons for Rejects
Ingredients	7
Shaping	63
Cooking Time	30
Total	100

REQUIRED

1. Analyze the activity in Week 3 of 20xx by preparing a table showing each day's maximum number of rejected candy canes allowed (50 candy canes), actual number of rejected candy canes, and variance under (over) the maximum number allowed each day. In addition, prepare a graph comparing the maximum and actual numbers of rejected candy canes each day for Week 3.
2. Analyze the change in reasons for rejects between Weeks 1 and 3 by preparing a table showing the frequency of each reason for rejecting a candy cane for each week. In addition, prepare a graph comparing the reasons for each week.
3. Based on the information, how successful was Janeece in increasing the quality of the candy canes made at Clearlake? What recommendations, if any, would you make about monitoring the candy production process in the future?

P 2.

LO 4 *Nonfinancial Data Analysis: Manufacturing*

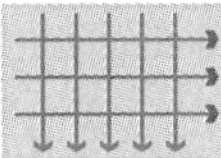

Ekin Enterprises makes shoes for every major sport. The Awesome Shoe, one of the organization's leading products, is lightweight, long wearing, and inexpensive. Production of the Awesome Shoe involves five different departments: (1) the Cutting/Lining Department, where cloth tops are cut and lined; (2) the Molding Department, where the shoe's rubber base is formed; (3) the Bonding Department, where the cloth top is bonded to the rubber base; (4) the Soling Department, where the sole is attached to the rubber base; and (5) the Finishing Department, where the shoe is trimmed, stitched, and laced.

Recently, manufacturing costs have increased for the Awesome Shoe. Controller Avery Berger has been investigating the production process to determine the problems. Everything points to the labor hours required to make the shoe. Actual labor hours worked in a recent week are as follows.

	Actual Hours Worked					
Operation	Monday	Tuesday	Wednesday	Thursday	Friday	Total
Cutting/Lining	300	310	305	300	246	1,461
Molding	144	186	183	200	246	959
Bonding	456	434	488	450	492	2,320
Soling	408	434	366	400	492	2,100
Finishing	600	620	549	625	615	3,009

The company has estimated the following labor hours for each department to complete a pair of Awesome Shoes: Cutting/Lining, .2 hour; Molding, .1 hour; Bonding, .4 hour; Soling, .3 hour; and Finishing, .5 hour. During the week under review, the number of Awesome Shoes produced was 1,200 pairs on Monday; 1,240 pairs on Tuesday; 1,220 pairs on Wednesday; 1,250 pairs on Thursday; and 1,230 pairs on Friday.

REQUIRED

1. Prepare an analysis to determine the average actual labor hours worked per day per pair of Awesome Shoes for each operation in the production process. (*Note:* Hours worked per pair of shoes = actual hours worked each day ÷ number of pairs of shoes produced each day.)
2. Prepare a graph showing the percentage of actual labor hours worked over/(under) the target level for the week.
3. By comparing the average actual labor hours worked from **1** with the expected labor hours per pair of shoes per department, prepare an analysis showing the differences in each operation for each day. Identify reasons for the differences.

P 3. LO 5 *Approach to Report Preparation*

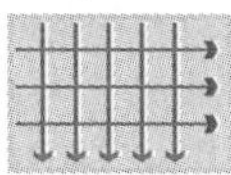

Lancer Industries, Inc., is deciding whether to expand its Jeans by Lorraine line of women's clothing. Sales in units of this product were 22,500, 28,900, and 36,200 in 20xx, 20x1, and 20x2, respectively. The product has been very profitable, averaging 35 percent profit (above cost) over the three-year period. Lancer has ten sales representatives covering seven states in the Northeast. Present production capacity is about 40,000 pairs of jeans per year. There is adequate plant space for additional equipment, and the labor needed can be easily hired and trained.

The organization's management is made up of four vice presidents: the vice president of marketing, the vice president of production, the vice president of finance, and the vice president of management information systems. Each vice president is directly responsible to the president, Lorraine Lancer.

REQUIRED

1. What types of information will Ms. Lancer need before she can decide whether to expand the Jeans by Lorraine product line?
2. Assume that one of the reports needed to support Ms. Lancer's decision is an analysis of sales over the past three years. This analysis should be broken down by sales representative. How would each of the four *W*'s pertain to this report?
3. Design a format for the report in **2.**

P 4. LO 6 *Manufacturing Company Balance Sheet*

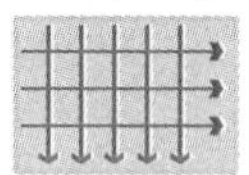

The analysis below shows the balance sheet accounts at Hooley Manufacturing Company after closing entries were made.

Ledger Accounts	Debit	Credit
Cash	$ 26,000	
Accounts Receivable	30,000	
Materials Inventory, 12/31/xx	42,000	
Work in Process Inventory, 12/31/xx	27,400	
Finished Goods Inventory, 12/31/xx	52,700	
Production Supplies and Tools	8,600	
Land	200,000	
Factory Building	400,000	
Accumulated Depreciation, Building		$ 110,000
Factory Equipment	250,000	
Accumulated Depreciation, Equipment		72,000
Sales Warehouse	148,000	
Accumulated Depreciation, Warehouse		35,000
Patents	27,300	
Accounts Payable		101,800
Mortgage Payable		400,000
Common Stock		260,000
Retained Earnings, 12/31/xx		233,200
	$1,212,000	$1,212,000

REQUIRED

1. Manufacturing organizations use assets that are not needed in merchandising organizations.
   a. List the titles of the asset accounts that are specifically related to manufacturing organizations.
   b. List the titles of the asset, liability, and equity accounts that you could expect to see on the balance sheets of both manufacturing and merchandising organizations.
2. Assuming that the following information reflects the results of operations for 20xx, calculate the (a) gross margin, (b) cost of goods sold, (c) cost of goods available for sale, and (d) cost of goods manufactured.

Net Income	$133,200
Operating Expenses	48,000
Sales	450,000
Finished Goods Inventory, 1/1/xx	68,000

P 5. LO 6 *Inventories, Cost of Goods Sold, and Net Income*

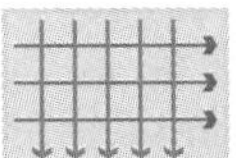

The analyses below contain incomplete data for (1) a merchandizing organization and (2) a manufacturing organization.

REQUIRED

1. Fill in the missing data for the merchandising organization.

	First Quarter	Second Quarter	Third Quarter	Fourth Quarter
Sales	$9	$ **e**	$15	$ **k**
Gross Margin	**a**	4	5	**l**
Ending Merchandise Inventory	5	**f**	5	**m**
Beginning Merchandise Inventory	4	**g**	**h**	5
Net Cost of Purchases	**b**	7	9	**n**
Net Income	3	2	**i**	2
Operating Expenses	**c**	2	2	4
Cost of Goods Sold	5	6	**j**	11
Cost of Goods Available for Sale	**d**	12	15	15

2. Fill in the missing data for the manufacturing organization.

	First Quarter	Second Quarter	Third Quarter	Fourth Quarter
Ending Finished Goods Inventory	$**a**	$ 3	$ **h**	$ 6
Cost of Goods Sold	6	3	5	**l**
Net Income	1	3	1	**m**
Cost of Goods Available for Sale	8	**d**	10	13
Cost of Goods Manufactured	5	**e**	**i**	8
Gross Margin	4	**f**	**j**	7
Operating Expenses	3	**g**	5	6
Beginning Finished Goods Inventory	**b**	2	3	**n**
Sales	**c**	10	**k**	14

Alternate Problems

P 6. LO 4 *Nonfinancial Data Analysis: Manufacturing*

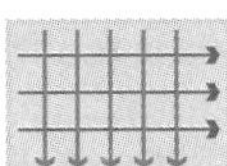

Seaflyer Surfboards, Inc., manufactures state-of-the-art surfboards and related equipment. Stacy Hopper is manager of the West Indies branch. The production process involves the following departments and tasks: (1) the Molding Department, where the board's base is molded; (2) the Sanding Department, where the base is sanded after being taken out of the mold; (3) the Fiber-Ap Department, where a fiberglass coating is applied; and (4) the Finishing Department, where a finishing coat of fiberglass is applied and the board is inspected. After the molding process, all functions are performed by hand.

Ms. Hopper is concerned about the hours being worked by her employees. The West Indies branch utilizes a two-shift labor force. The actual hours worked for the past four weeks are summarized on the next page.

	Actual Hours Worked–First Shift				
Department	**Week 1**	**Week 2**	**Week 3**	**Week 4**	**Totals**
Molding	420	432	476	494	1,822
Sanding	60	81	70	91	302
Fiber-Ap	504	540	588	572	2,204
Finishing	768	891	952	832	3,443

	Actual Hours Worked–Second Shift				
Department	**Week 1**	**Week 2**	**Week 3**	**Week 4**	**Totals**
Molding	360	357	437	462	1,616
Sanding	60	84	69	99	312
Fiber-Ap	440	462	529	506	1,937
Finishing	670	714	782	726	2,892

Expected labor hours per product for each operation are: Molding, 3.4 hours; Sanding, .5 hour; Fiber-Ap, 4.0 hours; and Finishing, 6.5 hours. Actual units completed were as follows:

Week	**First Shift**	**Second Shift**
1	120	100
2	135	105
3	140	115
4	130	110

REQUIRED

1. Prepare an analysis of each week to determine the average actual labor hours worked per board for each phase of the production process and for each shift.
2. Using the information from **1** and the expected labor hours per board for each department, prepare an analysis showing the differences in each phase of each shift. Identify reasons for the differences.

P 7. **LO 5** *Approach to Report Preparation*

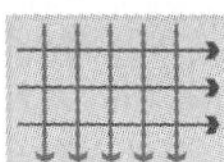

Amy Green recently purchased Yardcare, Inc., a wholesale distributor of lawn- and garden-care equipment and supplies. The organization, headquartered in Baltimore, Maryland, has four distribution centers: Boston, Massachusetts; Rye, New York; Reston, Virginia; and Lawrenceville, New Jersey. The distribution centers service fourteen eastern states. Company profits were $225,400, $337,980, and $467,200 for 20xx, 20x1, and 20x2, respectively.

Shortly after purchasing the organization, Ms. Green appointed people to fill the following positions: vice president, marketing; vice president, distribution; corporate controller; and vice president, research and development. Ms. Green has called a meeting of her management group. She wishes to create a deluxe retail lawn and garden center that would include a large, fully landscaped plant and tree nursery. The purposes of the retail center would be (1) to test equipment and supplies before selecting them for sales and distribution and (2) to showcase the effects of using the company's products. The retail center must also make a profit on sales.

REQUIRED

1. What types of information will Ms. Green need before deciding whether to create the retail lawn and garden center?
2. One of the reports Ms. Green needs to support her decision is an analysis of all possible plants and trees that could be planted and their ability to grow in the possible locations for the new retail center. The report would be prepared by the vice president of research and development. How would each of the four *W*'s pertain to this report?
3. Design a format for the report in **2.**

P 8. **LO 6** *Manufacturing Organization Balance Sheet*

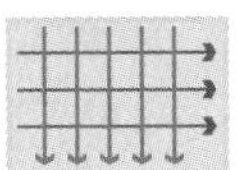

The analysis below shows the balance sheet accounts at Greencrest Manufacturing Company after closing entries were made.

Ledger Accounts	Debit	Credit
Cash	$ 34,000	
Accounts Receivable	27,000	
Materials Inventory, 12/31/xx	31,000	
Work in Process Inventory, 12/31/xx	47,900	
Finished Goods Inventory, 12/31/xx	54,800	
Production Supplies	5,700	
Small Tools	9,330	
Land	160,000	
Factory Building	575,000	
Accumulated Depreciation, Building		$ 199,000
Factory Equipment	310,000	
Accumulated Depreciation, Factory Equipment		137,000
Patents	33,500	
Accounts Payable		26,900
Insurance Premiums Payable		6,700
Income Taxes Payable		41,500
Mortgage Payable		343,000
Common Stock		200,000
Retained Earnings, 12/31/xx		334,130
	$1,288,230	$1,288,230

REQUIRED

1. Manufacturing organizations use assets that are not needed by merchandising organizations.
   a. List the titles of the asset accounts that are specifically related to manufacturing organizations.
   b. List the titles of the asset, liability, and equity accounts that you could expect to see on the balance sheets of both manufacturing and merchandising organizations.
2. Assuming that the following information reflects the results of operations for 20xx, calculate the (a) gross margin, (b) cost of goods sold, (c) cost of goods available for sale, and (d) cost of goods manufactured.

Net Income	$138,130
Operating Expenses	53,670
Sales	500,000
Finished Goods Inventory, 1/1/xx	50,900

Skills Development

Conceptual Analysis

SD 1. LO 3, LO 4 *Continuous Improvement*

Achieving high quality requires high standards of performance. And to maintain high standards of quality, individuals and organizations must continuously improve their performance. To illustrate this, select your favorite sport or hobby.

1. Answer the following questions:
   a. What standards would you establish to assess your actual performance?
   b. What process would you design to achieve high quality in your performance?
   c. When do you know you have achieved high quality in your performance?
   d. Once you know you perform well, how easy would it be for you to maintain that level of expertise?
   e. What can you do to continuously improve your performance?
2. If you owned a business, which of the questions in **1** would be important to answer?
3. Answer the questions in **1,** assuming you own a business.

Ethical Dilemma

SD 2. LO 8 *Professional Ethics*

Grace Albems is controller for the ***Atlanta Corporation.*** Grace has been with the company for seventeen years and is being considered for the job of chief financial officer (CFO). Her boss, the current CFO, will be Atlanta Corporation's new president. Grace has just discussed the year-end closing with her boss, who made the following statement during the conversation:

> Grace, why are you so inflexible? I'm only asking you to postpone the write-off of the $2,500,000 obsolete inventory for ten days so that it won't appear on this year's financial statements. Ten days! Do it. Your promotion is coming up, you know. Make sure you keep all the possible outcomes in mind as you complete your year-end work. Oh, and keep this conversation confidential—just between you and me. OK?

Identify the ethical issue or issues involved and state the appropriate solution to the problem. Be prepared to defend your answer.

Research Activity

SD 3. LO 5 *Management Reports*

The registrar's office is responsible for maintaining a record of each student's grades and credits for use by students, instructors, and administrators.

1. Assume that you are a manager in the registrar's office and that you recently joined a team of managers to review the grade-reporting process. State how you would prepare a grade report for students and a grade report for instructors by answering the following questions.
   a. Who will read the grade report?
   b. Why must the registrar's office prepare the grade report?
   c. What information should the grade report contain?
   d. When is the grade report due?

Communication

Critical Thinking

Group Activity

Memo

Ethics

International

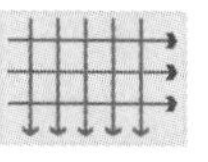
Spreadsheet

Managerial Technology

Internet

2. Why do differences exist between the information in a grade report for students and the information in a grade report for instructors?
3. Visit the registrar's office of your school in person, or access it through your school's home page. Obtain a copy of your grade report and a copy of the forms the registrar's office uses to report grades to instructors at your school. Compare the information on the actual grade report forms to the information you listed in **1** above. Explain any differences.
4. What can the registrar's office do to make sure that grade reports present all necessary information in a manner that communicates effectively to users?

Decision-Making Practice

LO 4 *Nonfinancial Data Analysis*

SD 4. As a subcontractor in the jet aircraft industry, ***Air Gears Manufacturing Company*** specializes in the production of housings for landing gears on jet airplanes. Production begins on Machine 1, which bends pieces of metal into cylinder-shaped housings and trims off the rough edges. Machine 2 welds the seam of the cylinder and pushes the entire piece into a large die to mold the housing into its final shape.

Joe Mee, the production supervisor, believes that too much scrap (wasted metal) is created in the current process. To help him, James Kincaid began preparing an analysis by comparing the amounts of actual scrap generated with the amounts of expected scrap for production in the last four weeks. His incomplete report follows.

Air Gears Manufacturing Company
Comparison of Actual Scrap and Expected Scrap
Four-Week Period

	Scrap in Pounds		Difference	
	Actual	**Expected**	**Pounds**	**Percentage**
Machine 1				
Week 1	36,720	36,720		
Week 2	54,288	36,288		
Week 3	71,856	35,856		
Week 4	82,440	35,640		
Machine 2				
Week 1	43,200	18,180		
Week 2	39,600	18,054		
Week 3	7,200	18,162		
Week 4	18,000	18,108		

Because of a death in his family, James is unable to complete the analysis. Joe asks you to complete the following tasks and submit a recommendation to him.

1. Present the information in two ways.
   a. Prepare a table that shows the difference between the actual and the expected scrap in pounds per machine per week. Calculate the difference in pounds and as a percentage (divide the difference in pounds by the expected pounds of scrap for each week). If the actual poundage of scrap is less than the expected poundage, record the difference as a negative. (This means there is less scrap than expected.)
   b. Prepare a line graph for each machine showing the weeks on the *X* axis and the pounds of scrap on the *Y* axis.
2. Examine the differences for the four weeks for each machine and determine which machine operation is creating excessive scrap.
3. What could cause these problems?
4. What could Joe do to identify the specific cause of such problems sooner?
5. Write a memo summarizing your findings in **1** through **4** above.

Managerial Reporting and Analysis

Interpreting Management Reports

MRA 1.

LO 1 *Management Information Needs*

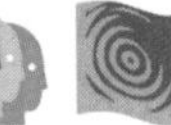

Obtain a copy of a recent annual report for a publicly held organization in which you have a particular interest. (Copies of annual reports are available at your campus library, a local public library, on the Internet, or by direct request to an organization.) Assume that you have just been appointed to a middle-management position in a division of the organization you have chosen. You are interested in obtaining information that will help you better manage the activities of your division and have decided to thoroughly review the contents of the annual report in an attempt to learn as much as possible. You particularly want to know about:

1. Size of inventory maintained
2. Ability to earn income
3. Reliance on debt financing
4. Types, volume, and prices of products or services sold
5. Type of production process used
6. Management's long-range strategies
7. Success (profitability) of the division's various product lines
8. Efficiency of operations
9. Operating details of your division

REQUIRED

1. Write a brief description of the organization and its products, services, or activities.
2. From a review of the financial statements and the accompanying disclosure notes, prepare a written summary of the information you found that pertained to items **1** through **9** above.
3. Is any of the information you seek in other sections of the annual report? If so, which information, and where is it found?
4. The annual report also includes other types of information you may find helpful in your new position. In outline form, summarize the additional information you think will help you.

Formulating Management Reports

MRA 2.

LO 5 *Management Information Needs*

In **MRA 1**, you examined your new employer's annual report and noted some useful information. You still wish to find out if your new division's products are competitive, but cannot find the necessary information in the annual report.

REQUIRED

1. What kinds of information do you want to know about your competition?
2. Why is this information relevant? (Link your response to a particular decision about your organization's products or services. For example, you might seek information to help you determine a new selling price.)
3. From what sources could you obtain the information you need?
4. When would you want to obtain this information?
5. Create a report that will communicate your findings to your superior.

International Company

MRA 3.

LO 4
LO 5 *Management Information Needs*

McDonald's is the leading competitor in the fast-food restaurant business. More than 40 percent of McDonald's restaurants are located outside the United States. One component of McDonald's marketing strategy is to increase sales by expanding its foreign markets. The company uses financial and nonfinancial as well as quantitative and qualitative information in making decisions about new restaurant locations in foreign markets. For example, the following types of information would be important to such a decision: the cost of a new building (financial quantitative information), the estimated number of hamburgers to be sold in the first year (nonfinancial quantitative information), and site desirability (qualitative information).

REQUIRED

You are a member of a management team that must decide whether or not to open a new restaurant in England. Identify at least two examples each of the (a) financial quantitative, (b) nonfinancial quantitative, and (c) qualitative information you will need before you can make a decision.

Group Activity: Divide the class into groups and ask them to discuss this MRA. Then debrief the entire class by asking one person from each group to summarize his or her group's discussion.

Excel Spreadsheet Analysis

MRA 4.
LO 4 *Nonfinancial Data*

Refer to assignment P 6 in this chapter. Ms. Hopper needs to analyze the work performed by each shift in each department during Weeks 1 through 4.

REQUIRED

1. For each department, calculate the average labor hours worked per board for each shift during Weeks 1 through 4. (*Note:* Hours worked per board = hours worked each week ÷ boards produced each week.)
2. Using the ChartWizard and the information from **1** for each department, prepare a line graph that compares the hours per board worked by the first and second shifts and the estimate for that department during Weeks 1 through 4. Below is the suggested format to use for the information table necessary to complete the line graph for the Molding Department.

Molding Department

	Week 1	Week 2	Week 3	Week 4
First shift	3.5	3.2	3.4	3.8
Second shift	3.6	3.4	3.8	4.2
Estimated	3.4	3.4	3.4	3.4

3. Examine the four graphs that you prepared in **2.** Which shift is more efficient in all four departments? List some reasons for the differences between the shifts.

ENDNOTES

1. *Source:* "Electric Car Drives Factory Innovation," *The Wall Street Journal,* February 27, 1997, p. B1.
2. Institute of Management Accountants, *Statement No. 1A* (New York, 1982). Since this definition was prepared, the importance of nonfinancial information has increased significantly. The words in brackets were added by the authors.
3. *Source:* Based on John B. MacArthur, "Cost Management at the IRS," *Management Accounting,* Institute of Management Accountants, November 1996, pp. 42–48.
4. *Source:* www.ups.com/about/inits.html
5. National Association of Accountants, "Definition of Management Accounting," from *Statements on Management Accounting,* Statement Number 1A, March 19, 1981. Copyright © 1987 by McGraw-Hill, Inc. Reprinted by permission.
6. James Don Edwards and Homer A. Black, *The Modern Accountant's Handbook* (Homewood, IL: Dow Jones-Irwin, 1976), p. 830.

CHAPTER 21

Operating Costs and Cost Allocation, Including Activity-Based Costing

LEARNING OBJECTIVES

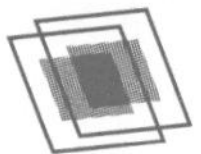

1. **State how managers use operating cost information and product costs in the management cycle.**
2. **Define and give examples of the three elements of product cost and compute a product's unit cost for a manufacturing organization.**
3. **Describe the flow of product-related activities, documents, and costs through the Materials Inventory, Work in Process Inventory, and Finished Goods Inventory accounts.**
4. **Prepare a statement of cost of goods manufactured and an income statement for a manufacturing organization.**
5. **Define *cost allocation* and explain the process of manufacturing overhead allocation using cost objects, cost pools, and cost drivers.**
6. **Calculate product unit cost using the traditional allocation of manufacturing overhead costs.**
7. **Define and explain *activity-based costing.***
8. **Calculate product unit cost using activity-based costing to assign manufacturing overhead costs.**
9. **Apply costing concepts to a service organization.**

DECISION POINT

SUPER BAKERY

Super Bakery supplies unique, reasonably priced, quality donuts and other baked goods to schools, hospitals, and others in the institutional baked goods market. With a staff of nine full-time employees, Super Bakery's sales reached $8.5 million in 1994. Super Bakery is a "virtual" corporation because it performs only a few strategic functions. Other functions typically performed by employees are outsourced to external companies specializing in each function. Super Bakery focuses on customer-related activities, such as taking a customer order, pricing the order, scheduling production, selecting and packing the ordered items, and billing and collecting customer accounts. A network of independent brokers sell the baked goods, and contractors produce, store, and ship them.[1]

Although Super Bakery outsources functions to outside brokers, manufacturers, and trucking companies, it must still control the quality and the

Critical Thinking Question: Accurate cost estimates provide more accurate profit estimates. Why can assigning an accurate cost to a customer order be difficult at Super Bakery? **Answer:** Each customer order usually consumes a different amount of resources. For example: (1) freight costs vary depending on shipping distance and order size; (2) manufacturing costs are higher at manufacturing plants in California than in Indiana; (3) some customers place more frequent orders than others.

cost of those services to minimize the risk of losing business. Brokers must effectively sell and promote the products to customers. Quality standards must be met for the products and the production processes. Trucking companies must deliver undamaged products on time. Super Bakery also faces the challenge of pricing sales orders accurately, because the cost of serving a customer can vary depending on the size and location of the customer's organization. How can management accounting help Super Bakery?

Super Bakery uses a performance reporting and activity-based costing system. This system is a component of an organization's management accounting information system. The activity-based costing (ABC) system accumulates cost information and assigns costs to a cost object, such as products or services, and reports performance after measuring the actual performance and comparing it to the organization's plan. ABC helps determine more accurate product costs for pricing and profitability decisions and requires nonfinancial measures that are also useful for measuring and evaluating performance. To manage costs and profitability at Super Bakery, the primary focus is on the cost of a sales order, which includes the cost of the baked goods ordered and the costs of freight, storage, selling, discounts, and order-taking service associated with the order. If such cost information is estimated in advance, it will help managers make better pricing and profitability decisions about each sales order.

ABC systems include nonfinancial performance measures (called *cost drivers*) useful for both assigning costs and measuring performance. To assign indirect costs to a cost object (customer, order, common carrier), cost drivers, such as number of customer complaints, number of days from order receipt to delivery, and number of orders damaged in shipment, are selected. Cost drivers, when properly matched, can also be used to measure and evaluate employee, broker, or contractor performance. In many companies that use ABC, management will choose cost drivers that not only minimize waste or inefficiency but also persuade individuals to perform well.

Operating Costs and the Management Cycle

OBJECTIVE 1

State how managers use operating cost information and product costs in the management cycle

Related Text Assignments:
Q: 1, 2
SE: 1
E: 1

Teaching Note: To help students see the complete management cycle for each type of organization, move through the cycle for manufacturing, retail, and service organizations separately, adding your own illustrations.

One of the primary goals of a company is to be profitable. Because owners expect to earn profits, managers have a responsibility to use resources wisely and generate revenues that will exceed the costs of the organization's operating, investing, and financing activities. In this chapter, we will focus on operating costs related to production activities in a manufacturing organization and to service activities in a service organization. First, let's look at operating costs and the management cycle for manufacturing, retail, and service companies.

In the management cycle, managers use operating cost information to plan, execute, review, and report the results of operating activities. Figure 1 provides an overview of operating costs and the management cycle. In the planning stage, managers of manufacturing organizations, such as John Deere, Motorola, or General Motors, use the estimated product cost portion of operating cost information to develop production, direct materials, direct labor, and manufacturing overhead budgets and to determine selling prices or sales levels required to cover all costs. In retail organizations, such as Sears, PepBoys, or Macy's, managers work with estimates of the cost of merchandise purchases to develop budgets for purchases and net income and to determine selling prices or sales levels required to cover all costs. In service organizations, like Citibank, Columbia Healthcare, or Andersen

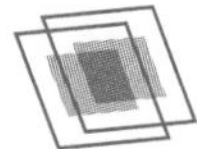

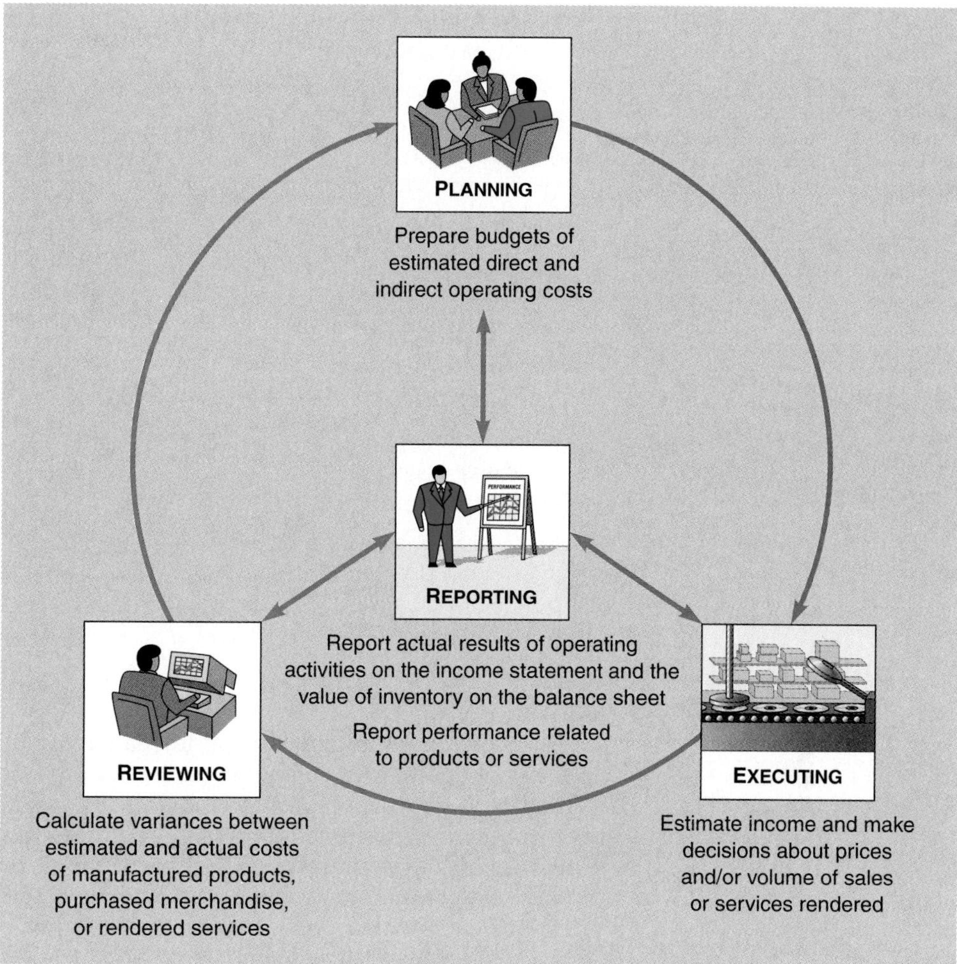

Figure 1
Operating Costs and the Management Cycle

Consulting, managers utilize the estimated costs of rendering services to develop budgets, estimate fees, and plan human resource needs.

In the executing stage, managers of manufacturing organizations use estimated product unit costs to estimate the gross margin or operating income on products sold or to make decisions about dropping a product line, outsourcing the manufacture of a part or subassembly to another manufacturer, bidding on a special order, or negotiating a selling price. In retail organizations, managers work with the estimated cost of merchandise purchases to estimate gross margin, operating income, or value of merchandise sold or to make decisions about reducing selling prices for clearance sales, offering lower selling prices for bulk sales orders, or dropping a product line. In service organizations, managers find the estimated cost of services helpful in estimating profitability or making decisions about bidding on future service assignments or projects, lowering the fee to charge a customer, dropping a service provided, or negotiating a fee.

In the reviewing stage, managers want to know about significant differences between estimated costs and actual costs. The identification of variances between estimated and actual product costs (for manufacturing organizations), estimated and actual costs of merchandise purchased (for retail organizations), and estimated and actual costs of services rendered (for service organizations) helps managers to determine the causes of cost overruns and enables them to adjust future actions to reduce potential problems.

In the reporting stage, managers expect to see financial statements that include the actual costs associated with operating activities in the executing stage of the

Clarification Note: Operating cost information is also needed for the management of selling, promoting, shipping, accounting, and general business activities.

Table 1. Examples of Types and Uses of Operating Cost Information for Different Types of Organizations

	Type of Organization		
	Manufacturing	**Retail**	**Service**
Operating cost information needed by management	Cost to manufacture the product	Cost to purchase the product	Cost to provide the service
Uses of cost information:			
To measure historical or future profits	Yes	Yes	Yes
To decide the selling price for regular or special sales or services provided	Yes	Yes	Yes
To value finished goods or merchandise inventories	Yes	Yes	Not applicable

management cycle and also performance evaluation reports that summarize the variance analyses calculated in the reviewing stage. This is true for manufacturing, retail, and service organizations.

Table 1 lists examples of the types and uses of operating cost information for different types of organizations. In this textbook, we will follow the traditional practices of organizations in costing products and services. For a manufacturing organization, the product costs include the costs of direct materials, direct labor, and manufacturing overhead. For a retail organization, the costs of a purchased product include adjustments for freight-in costs, purchase returns and allowances, and purchase discounts. And for a service organization, the costs to provide a service include the costs of labor and related overhead. Ultimately, a company is profitable only when revenues from sales or services rendered exceed the *full* cost of the products or services. The full cost includes the cost to manufacture or purchase a product or to render a service plus the costs of marketing, distributing, installing, repairing, and replacing a product or the costs of marketing and supporting the delivery of services.

Elements of Product Costs

OBJECTIVE 2

Define and give examples of the three elements of product cost and compute a product's unit cost for a manufacturing organization

Product costs include all costs related to the manufacturing process. The three elements of product cost are (1) direct materials costs, (2) direct labor costs, and (3) manufacturing overhead costs, which are indirect manufacturing costs.

Direct Materials Costs

All manufactured products are made from basic direct materials. Direct materials costs are the costs of materials that can be conveniently and economically traced to specific units of product. Some examples of direct materials are iron ore for steel, sheet steel for automobiles, and sugar for candy.

BUSINESS BULLETIN: TECHNOLOGY IN PRACTICE

Technology and new manufacturing processes of the 1990s have produced entirely new patterns of product costs. The three elements of product cost are still direct materials, direct labor, and manufacturing overhead. However, the percentage that each element contributes to the total cost of a product has changed. During the 1950s, 1960s, and 1970s, direct labor was the dominant cost element, making up over 40 percent of total product cost. Direct materials contributed 35 percent and manufacturing overhead around 25 percent of total cost. Seventy-five percent of total product cost was a direct cost, traceable to the product. Improved production technology caused a dramatic shift in the three product cost elements. People were replaced by machines, and direct labor was reduced significantly. Today, only 50 percent of the cost of a product is directly traceable to the product; the other 50 percent is manufacturing overhead, an indirect cost.

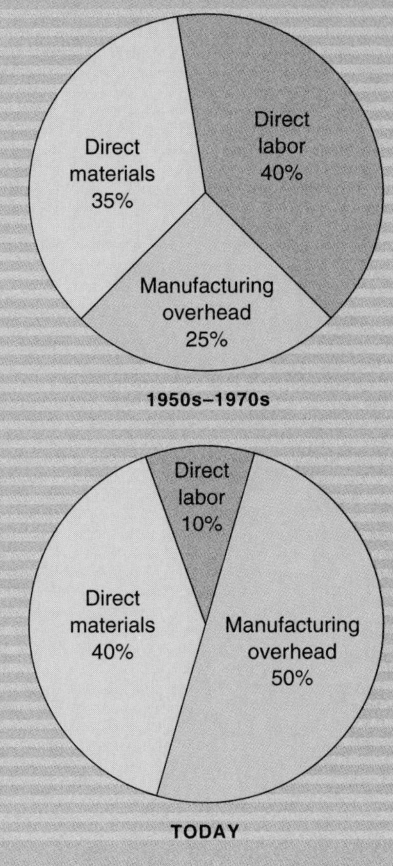

Related Text Assignments:
Q: 3, 4, 5, 6, 7, 8
SE: 2, 3
E: 2
P: 1
SD: 3

Discussion Question: Under what conditions would materials such as paint or small parts be accounted for as direct materials? **Answer:** When their relative costs are high and have a material effect on product cost.

Discussion Question: Is the paint on a toy (or other object) a direct or an indirect material? **Answer:** The paint is physically a direct material because it is attached to the product. However, because it is inexpensive, it is often accounted for as an indirect cost.

Point to Emphasize: Direct materials and direct labor are costs that can be conveniently and economically traced to the product. This is an application of cost-benefit analysis.

Direct Labor Costs

The manufacturing process includes all activities required to make a product, including maintenance, handling, inspecting, moving, and storing. Direct labor costs are the costs of labor to complete activities involved in the production process that can be conveniently and economically traced to specific units of product. The wages of machine operators and other workers involved in actually shaping the product are direct labor costs.

Manufacturing Overhead Costs

The third element of product cost includes all manufacturing costs that cannot be classified as direct materials or direct labor costs. Manufacturing overhead costs are production-related costs that cannot be practically or conveniently traced directly to an end product. This assortment of costs is also called *factory overhead, factory burden,* or *indirect manufacturing costs.* Two common components of manufacturing overhead costs are indirect materials costs and indirect labor costs. Indirect materials costs are the costs of materials that cannot be conveniently or economically traced to a unit of product. Labor costs for production-related activities that cannot be conveniently or economically traced to a unit of product are indirect labor costs. Examples of the major components of manufacturing overhead costs are as follows:

Indirect materials costs: costs of nails, rivets, lubricants, and small tools

Indirect labor costs: costs of labor for maintenance, inspection, engineering design, supervision, materials handling, and machine handling

Other indirect manufacturing costs: costs of building maintenance, machinery and tool maintenance, property taxes, property insurance, pension costs, depreciation on plant and equipment, rent expense, and utilities expense

As indirect costs, manufacturing overhead costs are allocated to a product's cost using traditional or activity-based costing methods, which will be explained later in this chapter.

To illustrate product costs and the manufacturing process, we will learn how Angelo Sanchez, owner of Angelo's Rolling Suitcases, Inc., operates part of his business. In 1990, Angelo Sanchez began building rolling suitcases, versions of the flight crew bag used for years by airline pilots and flight attendants. Angelo's rolling suitcases are designed to roll along easily and steadily, holding belongings for a three-day trip and providing a luggage rack with a strap to hold a briefcase and computer. The suitcases are made of ballistic nylon fabric wrapped around a rigid frame with a retractable pull handle at one end and wheels at the other end. Stair skids protect the fabric from abrasion, and carrying handles on the side and top of the bag improve handling. The direct materials costs for the rolling suitcase include the costs of the frame, ballistic nylon fabric, retractable pull handle, and wheels. Indirect materials costs include the costs of zippers, interior mesh storage pockets, garment straps, carrying handles, stair skids, and wheel lubricants. Direct labor costs include the costs of labor used to build the rolling suitcase. Indirect labor costs include the costs of labor associated with moving the materials to the production area and inspecting the rolling suitcase during its construction. In addition to the indirect materials and indirect labor costs, manufacturing overhead costs include depreciation on the building and equipment used to make the rolling suitcases and the utilities, insurance, property taxes, and insurance expenses related to the manufacturing plant.

Computing the Unit Cost of a Product for a Manufacturing Company

Point to Emphasize: Many management decisions require estimates of future costs. Managers often use actual cost as a basis for estimating future cost.

The product unit cost, or manufacturing cost of a single unit of product, is computed by dividing the total cost of direct materials, direct labor, and manufacturing overhead for the units produced by the total number of units produced.

$$\text{Product Unit Cost} = \frac{\text{Total Direct Materials} + \text{Direct Labor} + \text{Manufacturing Overhead for Units Produced}}{\text{Total Units Produced}}$$

Unit cost information helps managers price products and calculate gross margin and net income. Managers or accountants can calculate the product unit cost using actual costing, normal costing, or standard costing methods. Table 2 summarizes the use of actual or estimated costs for the three cost-measurement methods.

The actual costing method uses the *actual* costs of direct materials, direct labor, and manufacturing overhead to calculate the actual product unit cost at the end of the accounting period, when actual costs are known. The actual product unit cost is assigned to the finished goods inventory on the balance sheet and to the cost of goods sold on the income statement. For example, assume that Angelo's Rolling Suitcases, Inc., produced 30 rolling suitcases on December 28, 20xx, for a corporate customer in Salt Lake City. Jamie Estrada, the company's accountant, calculated

Table 2. Summary of the Use of Actual or Estimated Costs in Three Cost-Measurement Methods

Clarification Note: Estimated costs are also called *projected, standard, predetermined,* or *budgeted costs.*

Product Cost Elements	Actual Costing	Normal Costing	Standard Costing
Direct materials	Actual costs	Actual costs	Estimated costs
Direct labor	Actual costs	Actual costs	Estimated costs
Manufacturing overhead	Actual costs	Estimated costs	Estimated costs

that the actual costs for the Salt Lake City order were direct materials, $540; direct labor, $420; and manufacturing overhead, $240. The actual product unit cost for the order was $40.

Direct materials ($540 ÷ 30 rolling suitcases)	$18
Direct labor ($420 ÷ 30 rolling suitcases)	14
Manufacturing overhead ($240 ÷ 30 rolling suitcases)	8
Product cost per rolling suitcase ($1,200 ÷ 30 rolling suitcases)	$40

In this case, the product unit cost was computed when the job ended and all cost information was known. What if a company needs this information during the year, when the actual direct materials costs and direct labor costs are known but the actual manufacturing overhead costs are uncertain? Here, the product unit cost will include an estimate of the manufacturing overhead applied to the product.

The normal costing method combines the *actual* direct materials and direct labor costs with the *estimated* manufacturing overhead costs to determine a normal product unit cost. This method is simple and allows a smoother, more even assignment of manufacturing overhead costs to production during the year. It also contributes to better pricing decisions and profitability estimates. However, any difference between the estimated and the actual costs must be identified and removed so that the financial statements show only the actual product costs at the end of the year.

Assume that normal costing was used to price the Salt Lake City order, and that manufacturing overhead was applied to the product's cost using an estimated, or predetermined, overhead rate of 60 percent of direct labor costs. Based on that method, the costs for the order included the actual direct materials cost of $540.00, the actual direct labor cost of $420.00, and the *applied* manufacturing overhead cost of $252.00 ($420.00 × .6). The normalized product unit cost was $40.40.

Direct materials ($540.00 ÷ 30 rolling suitcases)	$18.00
Direct labor ($420.00 ÷ 30 rolling suitcases)	14.00
Manufacturing overhead ($252.00 ÷ 30 rolling suitcases)	8.40
Product cost per rolling suitcase ($1,212 ÷ 30 rolling suitcases)	$40.40

In this case, the product unit cost was computed using actual and estimated cost information. Later in this chapter, we will discuss various methods of assigning manufacturing overhead costs to finished products.

What if managers need product costing information before the accounting period begins, so that they can control operating activities? Or, what if an organization is pricing a proposed product for a customer? In such situations, product unit costs must be estimated, and the standard costing method can be helpful. This method allows actual costs to be compared to budgeted, or estimated, costs to identify significant variances that require management attention. The *estimated* (or standard) direct materials, direct labor, and manufacturing overhead costs determine the standard product unit cost, which is useful as a benchmark for pricing decisions during the year and for controlling product costs.

Assume Angelo's must place a bid to manufacture 20 rolling suitcases for a new Italian customer. Using standard cost information, Jamie has *estimated* the following cost information: $20 per unit for direct materials, $15 per unit for direct labor, and $9 for manufacturing overhead (assuming a standard, or predetermined, overhead rate of 60 percent of direct labor cost). The standard cost per unit would be $44.

Direct materials	$20
Direct labor	15
Manufacturing overhead ($15 × .6)	9
Product cost per rolling suitcase	$44

The $44 product unit cost is useful for estimating the gross margin for the job and deciding the price to bid for the Italian company's business. Standard costing is discussed in more detail in another chapter.

Manufacturing Inventory Accounts

OBJECTIVE 3

Describe the flow of product-related activities, documents, and costs through the Materials Inventory, Work in Process Inventory, and Finished Goods Inventory accounts

Related Text Assignments:
Q: 9, 10
SE: 4, 5
E: 3, 4
SD: 3

Teaching Note: Turn the classroom into a factory. Starting at the door, walk through the factory, explaining the flow of activities and the three inventory accounts. Use construction blocks or a simple product to demonstrate.

Manufacturing organizations use a number of production and production-related activities to transform materials into finished products. Materials are brought into the organization through purchasing, receiving, inspecting, moving, and storing activities. Production activities convert the materials into a finished product using labor, equipment, and other resources. Moving and storing activities transfer the completed product to the finished goods storage area. The accounting system tracks these activities as product costs flowing through the Direct Materials Inventory, Work in Process Inventory, and Finished Goods Inventory accounts. The Direct Materials Inventory account shows the balance of unused direct materials, the Work in Process Inventory account records the manufacturing costs incurred and assigned to partially completed units of product, and the Finished Goods Inventory account holds the costs assigned to all completed products that have not been sold.

Selling and administrative activities are also important in a manufacturing organization. Marketing, packaging, and shipping activities play a role in making the product available to buyers, and customer billing, collection of accounts receivable, and payment of suppliers help keep the company in sound financial shape. Such selling and administrative costs are accumulated as period costs for the purposes of financial reporting.

Document Flows and Cost Flows Through the Inventory Accounts

In many companies, accountants accumulate and report manufacturing costs based on source documents that support production and production-related activities. Looking at how the source documents for the three elements of manufacturing cost relate to the flow of costs through the three inventory accounts for a manufacturing organization provides insight into when an activity must be recorded in the accounting records. Figure 2 (on pages 900-901) summarizes the relationships among the production-related activities, the documents for each of the three cost elements, and the inventory account(s) that are affected by the activities. An organization may use paper documents or computer-transmitted information to communicate with suppliers, customers, or internal departments.

To illustrate the document flow and changes in inventory balances for production activities, we will continue with our example of Angelo's Rolling Suitcases, Inc.

Purchasing Direct Materials When Angelo receives or expects to receive a *sales order* from a customer, the purchasing process starts with a *purchase request* for specific quantities of direct materials needed but not currently available in the materials storeroom. A qualified manager approves the request. Based on the information in the purchase request, the Purchasing Department sends *purchase orders* to its suppliers. When the direct materials arrive, an employee on the receiving dock counts and examines them and prepares a *receiving report*. Later, an accounting clerk matches the information on the receiving report with the descriptions and quantities listed on the purchase order. A material handler moves the newly arrived materials from the receiving area to the materials storeroom. Soon, Angelo receives a *vendor's invoice* requesting payment for the purchased direct materials. The cost of those materials increases the balance of Angelo's Direct Materials Inventory account.

Teaching Note: Some companies use sophisticated computer programs to match receipts to purchase orders.

Materials Requisition and Conversion When the rolling suitcases are scheduled for production, the storeroom clerk receives a *materials request form*. The materials request form is essential for controlling direct materials. Besides providing the supervisor's approval signature, it describes the types and quantities of materials the storeroom clerk must pick and send to the production area, and it authorizes the release of those materials into production. If the materials request form has been approved by the appropriate manager, the storeroom clerk has the material handler move the materials to the production floor. The cost of the direct materials increases the balance of the Work in Process Inventory account and decreases the balance of the Direct Materials Inventory account.

The production employees assemble the rolling suitcases using frames, fabric, pull handles, wheels, and indirect materials. Each production employee prepares a *time card* to track the amount of time worked each day. The costs of the direct labor and manufacturing overhead used to manufacture the rolling suitcases increase the balance of the Work in Process Inventory account.

Product Completion and Sale Employees place completed rolling suitcases in individual boxes, then move and store the boxes in the finished goods storeroom until the scheduled shipment date. The balance of the Finished Goods Inventory account increases and the balance of the Work in Process Inventory account decreases for the cost of the completed rolling suitcases.

When suitcases are sold, a clerk prepares a *sales invoice* while another clerk fills the order by removing the rolling suitcases from the storeroom, packaging them, and shipping them to the customer. A *shipping document* shows the quantity and description of the products shipped. The cost of the rolling suitcases sold increases the Cost of Goods Sold account and decreases the balance of the Finished Goods Inventory account.

The Manufacturing Cost Flow

Manufacturing cost flow is the flow of manufacturing costs (direct materials, direct labor, and manufacturing overhead) from their incurrence through the Direct Materials Inventory, Work in Process Inventory, and Finished Goods Inventory accounts into the Cost of Goods Sold account. A defined, structured manufacturing cost flow is the foundation for product costing, inventory valuation, and financial reporting. The manufacturing cost flow as it relates to the accounts in the general ledger and the production activity at Angelo's Rolling Suitcases, Inc., for the year ended December 31, 20xx, are summarized in Figure 3 on page 902. In this

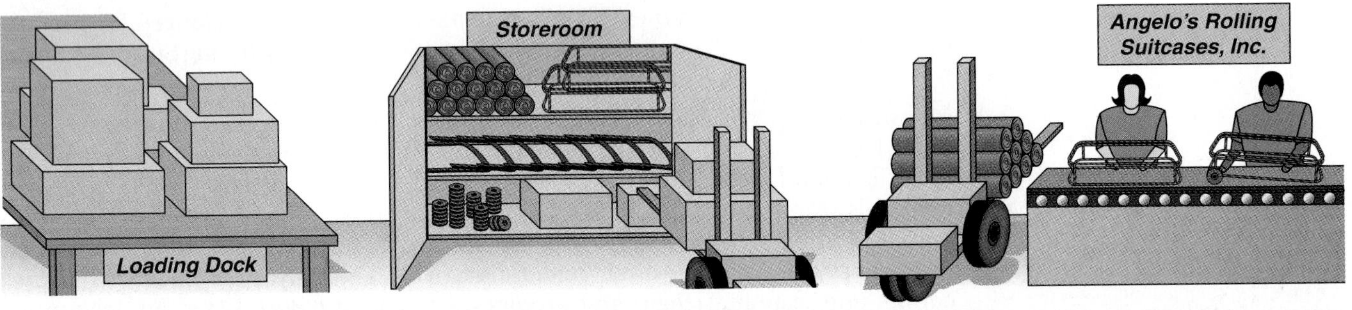

	ACTIVITY	Purchase, receive, inspect, move, and store direct materials in direct materials storeroom	Move direct materials to production area
	DOCUMENT	Purchase request Purchase order Receiving report Vendor's invoice	Materials request
INVENTORY ACCOUNT AFFECTED/ CHANGE IN BALANCE	**DIRECT MATERIALS INVENTORY**	Increases for cost of direct materials purchased	Decreases for cost of direct materials used in the production process
	WORK IN PROCESS INVENTORY		Increases for cost of direct materials used in the production process
	FINISHED GOODS INVENTORY		

Figure 2
Activities, Documents, and Cost Flows Through the Inventory Accounts of a Manufacturing Organization

illustration, we will assume that the accountant has adjusted the inventory account balances to reflect only actual costs. Using the actual cost information, the accountant can prepare financial statements for the company.

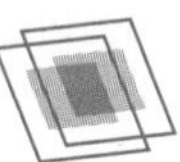

The Direct Materials Inventory account shows the balance of unused direct materials. The costs of direct materials purchased increase the Direct Materials Inventory account balance, while the costs of direct materials requested and used by the Production Department decrease the balance. The following formula shows the activity in this account for Angelo's Rolling Suitcases, Inc., for the year ended December 31, 20xx:

Direct Materials Inventory, Ending Balance	=	Direct Materials Inventory, Beginning Balance	+	Cost of Direct Materials Purchased	−	Cost of Direct Materials Used
$5,000	=	$10,000	+	$20,000	−	$25,000

The Work in Process Inventory account records the balance of partially completed units of product. As direct materials and direct labor are used, their costs are added to the Work in Process Inventory account. The cost of manufacturing overhead for the current period is also added. The total costs of direct materials, direct labor, and manufacturing overhead incurred and charged to production during an accounting period are called total manufacturing costs. Total manufacturing costs increase the balance of the Work in Process Inventory account.

As goods are finished, they are moved to the finished goods storage area. The cost of all units completed and moved to the finished goods storage is the cost of goods manufactured. The cost of goods manufactured for the period decreases the balance

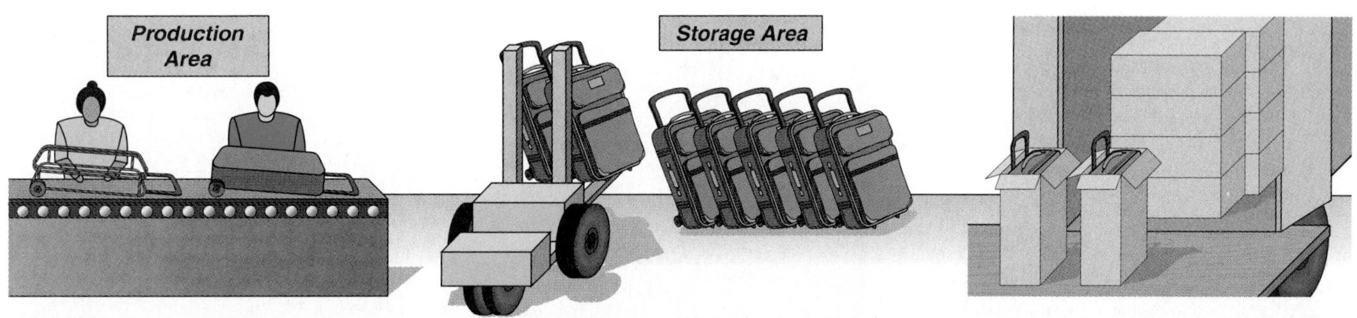

Convert direct materials into finished product using direct labor and manufacturing overhead Package some types of products	Move completed units of product of finished goods to storage area	Sell units of product to customer; pack and ship product
Time card Job card Vendors' invoices for manufacturing overhead items	Job card	Sales invoice Shipping document
Increases for costs of direct labor and manufacturing overhead	Decreases for cost of completed units of product	
	Increases for cost of completed units of product	Decreases for cost of completed units of product

Point to Emphasize: When costs are transferred from one inventory account to another in a manufacturing company, they remain assets. They are inventoriable product costs and are not expensed until the finished goods are sold.

Teaching Note: It is often helpful to show that Materials Inventory and Work in Process Inventory support the production process, while Finished Goods Inventory supports the sales and distribution functions.

of the Work in Process Inventory account. The following formulas show the activity in the Work in Process Inventory account for Angelo's Rolling Suitcases, Inc., for the year ended December 31, 20xx:

Total Manufacturing Costs	=	Cost of Direct Materials Used	+	Direct Labor Costs	+	Manufacturing Overhead Costs
\$43,000	=	\$25,000	+	\$12,000	+	\$6,000

Work in Process Inventory, Ending Balance	=	Work in Process Inventory, Beginning Balance	+	Total Manufacturing Costs	−	Cost of Goods Manufactured
\$15,000	=	\$2,000	+	\$43,000	−	\$30,000

The Finished Goods Inventory account holds the balance of costs assigned to all completed products that have not been sold by a manufacturing company. The cost of goods manufactured increases the balance, while the cost of goods sold decreases the balance. The following formula shows the activity in the Finished Goods Inventory account for Angelo's Rolling Suitcases, Inc., for the year ended December 31, 20xx:

Point to Emphasize: When a sale occurs, Accounts Receivable and Sales are increased by the *revenue* amount. Cost of Goods Sold is increased and Finished Goods Inventory decreased by the *cost* amount, or inventory carrying value.

Finished Goods Inventory, Ending Balance	=	Finished Goods Inventory, Beginning Balance	+	Cost of Goods Manufactured	−	Cost of Goods Sold
\$12,000	=	\$6,000	+	\$30,000	−	\$24,000

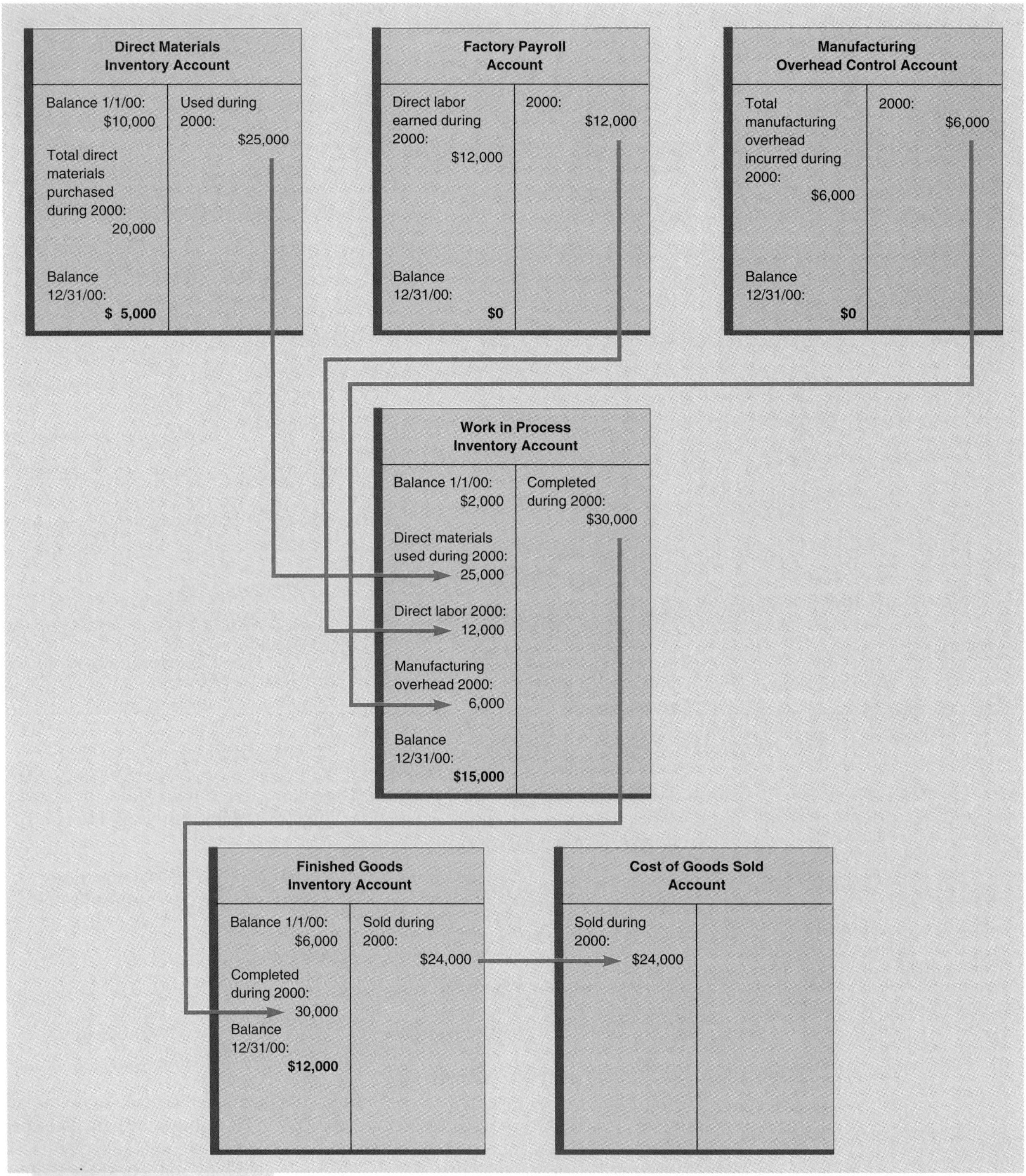

Direct Materials Inventory Account	
Balance 1/1/00: $10,000	Used during 2000: $25,000
Total direct materials purchased during 2000: 20,000	
Balance 12/31/00: **$ 5,000**	

Factory Payroll Account	
Direct labor earned during 2000: $12,000	2000: $12,000
Balance 12/31/00: **$0**	

Manufacturing Overhead Control Account	
Total manufacturing overhead incurred during 2000: $6,000	2000: $6,000
Balance 12/31/00: **$0**	

Work in Process Inventory Account	
Balance 1/1/00: $2,000	Completed during 2000: $30,000
Direct materials used during 2000: 25,000	
Direct labor 2000: 12,000	
Manufacturing overhead 2000: 6,000	
Balance 12/31/00: **$15,000**	

Finished Goods Inventory Account	
Balance 1/1/00: $6,000	Sold during 2000: $24,000
Completed during 2000: 30,000	
Balance 12/31/00: **$12,000**	

Cost of Goods Sold Account	
Sold during 2000: $24,000	

Figure 3
Manufacturing Cost Flow: An Example

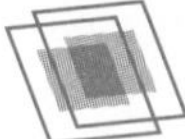

Manufacturing and Reporting

OBJECTIVE 4

Prepare a statement of cost of goods manufactured and an income statement for a manufacturing organization

Related Text Assignments:
Q: 11, 12, 13
SE: 6
E: 5
P: 2, 3
MRA: 1, 3

The financial statements of manufacturing organizations differ very little from those of merchandising organizations. Account titles on the balance sheet of manufacturers are similar to those used by merchandisers. The primary difference between the balance sheets is the use of three inventory accounts by manufacturing organizations versus only one by merchandising organizations. Even the income statements for a merchandiser and a manufacturer are similar. However, manufacturers use the heading Cost of Goods Manufactured in place of the Purchases account. Also, the Merchandise Inventory account is replaced by the Finished Goods Inventory account.

The key to preparing an income statement for a manufacturing organization is to determine the cost of goods manufactured. This dollar amount is calculated on the statement of cost of goods manufactured. This special statement is based on an analysis of the Work in Process Inventory account.

Statement of Cost of Goods Manufactured

The flow of manufacturing costs, shown in Figure 3, provides the basis for accounting for manufacturing costs. In this process, all manufacturing costs incurred are considered product costs. They are used to compute ending inventory balances and the cost of goods sold. At the end of the period, the flow of all manufacturing costs incurred during the period is summarized in the statement of cost of goods manufactured. This statement gives the dollar amount of costs for products completed and moved to finished goods inventory during the period. The cost of goods manufactured should be the same as the amount transferred from the Work in Process Inventory account to the Finished Goods Inventory account during the period.

The statement of cost of goods manufactured for Angelo's Rolling Suitcases, Inc., is shown in Exhibit 1. The statement is complex, so we piece it together in three steps. The first step is to compute the cost of direct materials used. To do so, we add the beginning balance in the Direct Materials Inventory account to the direct materials purchased ($10,000 + $20,000). The subtotal represents the cost of direct materials available for use during the period ($30,000). Then, we subtract the ending balance of Direct Materials Inventory from the cost of direct materials available for use. The difference is the cost of direct materials used during the period ($30,000 − $5,000 = $25,000).

Calculating total manufacturing costs for the period is the second step. As shown in Figure 3, the costs of direct materials used and direct labor are added to total manufacturing overhead costs incurred during the period.

Computation of Total Manufacturing Costs

Cost of Direct Materials Used	$25,000
Add Direct Labor Costs	12,000
Add Total Manufacturing Overhead Costs	6,000
Total Manufacturing Costs	$43,000

The third step shown in Exhibit 1 is to determine the total cost of goods manufactured for the period. The beginning Work in Process Inventory balance is added to total manufacturing costs for the period to arrive at the total cost of work in process during the period. From this amount, the ending Work in Process Inventory balance is subtracted to get the cost of goods manufactured ($45,000 − $15,000 = $30,000).

The term *total manufacturing costs* should not be confused with the cost of goods manufactured. To understand the difference between these two dollar

Exhibit 1. Statement of Cost of Goods Manufactured and Income Statement for a Manufacturing Organization

Angelo's Rolling Suitcases, Inc.
Statement of Cost of Goods Manufactured
For the Year Ended December 31, 20xx

Step One	Direct Materials Used		
	Direct Materials Inventory, January 1, 20xx	$10,000	
	Direct Materials Purchased	20,000	
	Cost of Direct Materials Available for Use	$30,000	
	Less Direct Materials Inventory, December 31, 20xx	5,000	
	Cost of Direct Materials Used		$25,000
Step Two	Direct Labor		12,000
	Manufacturing Overhead		6,000
	Total Manufacturing Costs		$43,000
Step Three	Add Work in Process Inventory, January 1, 20xx		2,000
	Total Cost of Work in Process During the Year		$45,000
	Less Work in Process Inventory, December 31, 20xx		15,000
	Cost of Goods Manufactured		$30,000

Angelo's Rolling Suitcases, Inc.
Income Statement
For the Year Ended December 31, 20xx

Sales		$50,000
Cost of Goods Sold		
Finished Goods Inventory, January 1, 20xx	$ 6,000	
Cost of Goods Manufactured	30,000	
Total Cost of Finished Goods Available for Sale	$36,000	
Less Finished Goods Inventory, December 31, 20xx	12,000	
Cost of Goods Sold		24,000
Gross Margin		$26,000
Selling and Administrative Expenses		16,000
Net Income		$10,000

amounts, look again at the preceding computations. Total manufacturing costs of $43,000 incurred during the period are added to the beginning balance in Work in Process Inventory. Costs of $2,000 in the beginning balance are, by definition, costs from an earlier period. The costs of two accounting periods are now being mixed to arrive at the total cost of work in process during the period ($43,000 + $2,000 = $45,000). The costs of products still in process ($15,000) are then subtracted from the total cost of work in process during the year. The remainder, $30,000, is the cost of goods manufactured (completed) during the current year. It is assumed that the items in beginning inventory were completed first. The costs attached to the ending balance of Work in Process Inventory are part of the current period's total manufacturing costs. However, they will not become part of the cost of goods manufactured until the next period, when the products are completed.

Common Student Error: It is important that students do not confuse the cost of goods manufactured with the cost of goods sold.

Teaching Note: An alternative to the cost of goods manufactured calculation uses the cost flow concept. Current manufacturing costs (direct materials, direct labor, and manufacturing overhead) become the cost of goods manufactured if the Work in Process Inventory balance remains unchanged in the accounting period. Similarly, the cost of goods manufactured becomes the cost of goods sold if the Finished Goods Inventory remains unchanged in the period.

Cost of Goods Sold and the Income Statement

Exhibit 1 demonstrates the relationship between the income statement and the statement of cost of goods manufactured. The total amount of the cost of goods manufactured during the period is carried over to the income statement. There, it is used to compute the cost of goods sold. The beginning balance of Finished Goods Inventory is added to the cost of goods manufactured to get the total cost of finished goods available for sale during the period ($6,000 + $30,000 = $36,000). The cost of goods sold is then computed by subtracting the ending balance in Finished Goods Inventory (the cost of goods completed but not sold) from the total cost of finished goods available for sale ($36,000 − $12,000 = $24,000). The cost of goods sold is considered an expense in the period in which the related products are sold.

Cost Allocation

OBJECTIVE 5

Define *cost allocation* and explain the process of manufacturing overhead allocation using cost objects, cost pools, and cost drivers

Related Text Assignments:
Q: 14, 15, 16, 17
SE: 7, 8, 9
E: 6, 7, 8
P: 4, 6, 8
SD: 1
MRA: 4

Teaching Note: Allocation, by its very nature, is a relatively arbitrary process. It is important to stress that a rational allocation scheme is best. Rational allocation approaches help avoid behavioral problems for management.

Managers need accurate and timely product costs to estimate profits and inventory values and to make pricing decisions during the year. The product cost elements of direct materials and direct labor can be easily traced to a product, but manufacturing overhead costs are indirect costs that must be collected and allocated in some manner. Cost allocation is the process of assigning collected indirect costs to specific cost objects using an allocation base that represents a major function of the business. A cost object is the destination of an assigned or allocated cost. For purposes of product costing, cost allocation is the assignment of manufacturing overhead costs to the product (cost object) during the accounting period.

To understand cost allocation, you also need to understand the terms *cost pool* and *cost driver.* For purposes of product costing, a cost pool is a collection of overhead costs related to a cost object (a production-related activity). A cost driver is an activity that causes the cost pool to increase in amount as the cost driver increases in volume. Cost allocation requires (1) the pooling of manufacturing overhead costs that are affected by a common activity and (2) the selection of a cost driver whose activity level causes a change in the cost pool.

The Manufacturing Overhead Allocation Process

The process of allocating manufacturing overhead costs is part of the management cycle presented in Figure 1. In the planning stage, manufacturing overhead costs are estimated and a rate is calculated. In the executing stage, manufacturing overhead costs are assigned to products during the production process and manufacturing overhead costs are incurred and recorded. In the reviewing stage, the difference between the actual and applied manufacturing overhead costs is calculated and analyzed. The difference is then reported in the reporting stage. In addition, the actual manufacturing overhead costs are reported in the cost of goods sold on the income statement and the ending Work in Process and Finished Goods Inventory balances on the balance sheet.

The process of manufacturing overhead allocation includes four steps. Figure 4 shows the relationship of the four steps over a time period that includes the planning process and the actual manufacturing process for one year. Figure 4 also describes each step and its timing, procedure, and journal entry, if needed. In Step 1, the planning step, the management accountant calculates a predetermined overhead rate in traditional settings or an activity pool rate in activity-based costing settings. If a rate is calculated before an accounting period begins, managers can better estimate the product costs by assigning manufacturing overhead costs more smoothly over units of production during the year. For example, using a single, plantwide overhead rate requires grouping all of the estimated manufacturing overhead costs into one cost pool with direct labor hours or machine hours as the cost driver. No journal entry is required because no business activity has occurred.

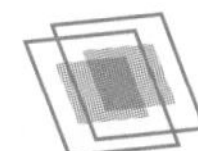

Figure 4
The Manufacturing Overhead Allocation Process

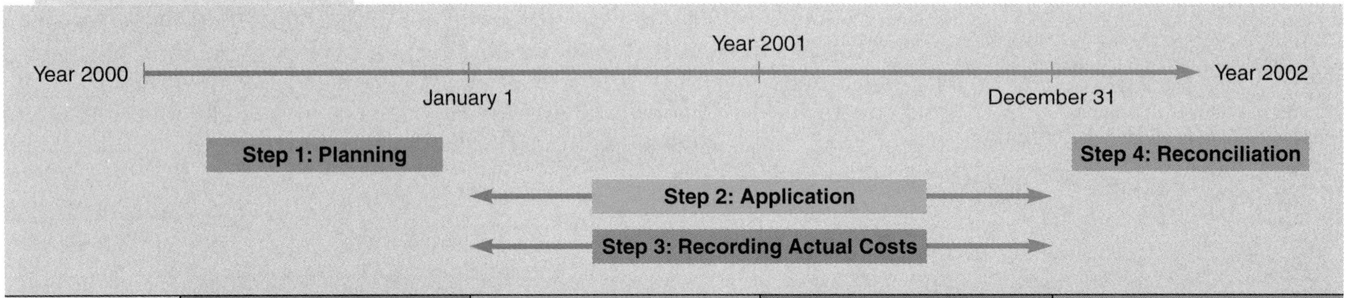

Year 2000 — January 1 — Year 2001 — December 31 — Year 2002

Step 1: Planning (before January 1)
Step 2: Application (January 1 to December 31)
Step 3: Recording Actual Costs (January 1 to December 31)
Step 4: Reconciliation (after December 31)

	Step 1: Planning	Step 2: Application	Step 3: Recording Actual Costs	Step 4: Reconciliation
Description	Calculate a predetermined manufacturing overhead rate	Apply manufacturing overhead costs to production	Record actual manufacturing overhead costs	Calculate the difference between applied and actual manufacturing overhead costs
When	Before accounting period	During accounting period as units are produced	During accounting period as costs are incurred	At the end of the accounting period
Procedure	Divide the cost pool of total estimated overhead costs by the total estimated cost driver level	Multiply the predetermined overhead rate for each cost pool by the actual cost driver level	Record actual manufacturing overhead costs when incurred	Calculate and record the difference between the actual and applied manufacturing overhead costs
Journal entry?	No	Yes Increase Work in Process Inventory account Decrease Manufacturing Overhead Control account	Yes Increase Manufacturing Overhead Control account Decrease asset accounts Increase contra assets or liability accounts	Yes If applied > actual, then Increase Manufacturing Overhead Control account Decrease Cost of Goods Sold account If applied < actual, then Increase Cost of Goods Sold account Decrease Manufacturing Overhead Control account

In Step 2, the management accountant applies the estimated manufacturing overhead costs to the product's costs as units are manufactured. The actual cost driver level (for example, the actual number of direct labor hours used to complete the product) is multiplied by the predetermined manufacturing overhead rate or activity pool rate for that cost driver. The purpose of this calculation is to assign a fairly consistent manufacturing overhead cost to each unit produced during the accounting period. The accountant records the allocation, or application, of overhead to the product by increasing the Work in Process Inventory account and reducing the Manufacturing Overhead Control account.

During the accounting period the management accountant records the actual manufacturing overhead costs when incurred (Step 3). These costs will be part of the actual product cost and include the costs of indirect materials, indirect labor, depreciation, property taxes, and other accrued production costs. Recording the actual manufacturing overhead costs requires an increase in the Manufacturing Overhead Control account and a decrease in asset accounts or an increase in contra asset or liability accounts.

Instructional Strategy: Divide the class into small groups and assign SD 1. Groups may present their results to the class and take questions from other students. Emphasize that knowing product costs can help in designing a quality product despite cost constraints.

At the end of the accounting period, during Step 4, the reconciliation step, management accountants calculate the difference between the allocated, or applied, manufacturing overhead costs and the actual manufacturing overhead costs. If the manufacturing overhead costs applied to production during the accounting period are greater than (over) the actual manufacturing overhead costs, the difference in the amounts represents overapplied overhead costs. The accountant increases the Manufacturing Overhead Control account and decreases the Cost of Goods Sold account by this difference, assuming the difference is not material. If the difference is material, adjustments are made to the Work in Process Inventory, Finished Goods Inventory, and Cost of Goods Sold accounts. If the manufacturing overhead costs applied to production during the accounting period are less than (under) the actual manufacturing overhead costs, the difference in the amounts is underapplied overhead costs. The accountant increases the Cost of Goods Sold account and decreases the Manufacturing Overhead Control account by this difference, assuming the difference is not material. The adjustment for overapplied or underapplied overhead costs, whether it is immaterial or material, is necessary to reflect the actual manufacturing overhead costs on the income statement.

The Importance of Good Estimates

A predetermined manufacturing overhead rate has two primary uses. First, it enables managers to make more timely decisions about pricing products and controlling costs. The product cost calculated at the end of the period when all of the product costs are known is more accurate. However, when the overhead portion of product cost is estimated in advance, managers can compare actual and estimated costs throughout the year and more quickly correct the problems that caused the under- or overallocation of overhead costs. Second, an advance estimate allows the management accountant to allocate manufacturing overhead costs more equitably to each unit produced.

Actual manufacturing overhead costs fluctuate from month to month due to the timing of the costs and the variability of the amounts. For example, some manufacturing overhead costs (such as supervisors' salaries and depreciation on equipment) may be expensed monthly. Others (like payroll taxes) may be paid quarterly, and still others (like property taxes and insurance) may be paid annually. In addition, hourly indirect labor costs (such as machine maintenance and material handling) fluctuate with changes in production levels.

The successful allocation of manufacturing overhead costs depends on two factors. One is a careful estimate of the total manufacturing overhead costs. The other is a good forecast of the activity used as the cost driver.

Estimating total manufacturing overhead costs is critical. If the estimate is wrong, the manufacturing overhead rate will be wrong. This will cause an overstatement or understatement of the product unit cost. If overstated product unit cost information is relied upon, the organization may fail to bid on profitable projects because the costs appear to be too high. If understated product unit cost information is used, the organization may accept business that is not as profitable as expected. So, to provide managers with reliable product unit costs, the management accountant must be careful to include all manufacturing overhead items and to forecast the costs of those items accurately.

The budgeting process normally includes estimated manufacturing overhead costs. Managers who use production-related resources will provide cost estimates for direct and indirect production-related activities. For example, the managers for material handling and inspecting at Angelo's Rolling Suitcases, Inc., can estimate the costs related to their departments' activities. The accountant then includes their cost estimates in developing total manufacturing overhead costs. In addition, the managers need to carefully estimate the cost driver level. An understated cost driver level will cause an overstatement of the predetermined manufacturing overhead rate (the cost is spread over a lesser level), and an overstated cost driver level will cause an understatement of the predetermined manufacturing overhead rate (the cost is spread over a greater level).

In the remaining learning objectives of this chapter, we will present two approaches to manufacturing overhead allocation. We will use the first two steps of the four-step overhead allocation process to demonstrate these approaches.

Manufacturing Overhead Allocation Using the Traditional Approach

OBJECTIVE 6

Calculate product unit cost using the traditional allocation of manufacturing overhead costs

Related Text Assignments:
SE: 8, 9
E: 6, 7, 8, 9
P: 4, 6, 8
SD: 1
MRA: 4

Common Student Error: Students often think that because a cost is not traced directly to a product, it is not a product cost. Stress that all manufacturing costs, both direct and indirect, are product costs.

Many organizations continue to use one predetermined overhead rate to apply manufacturing overhead to a product cost. This approach is especially useful if companies manufacture only one product or a few very similar products requiring the same production processes and production-related activities, such as setup, inspection, and material handling. The total manufacturing overhead costs represent one cost pool, and a traditional activity base, such as direct labor hours, direct labor costs, machine hours, or units of production, becomes the cost driver.

Figure 5 illustrates the application of one cost pool of manufacturing overhead costs to two product lines. As we continue with our example of Angelo's Rolling Suitcases, Inc., let's assume that Angelo's will be selling two product lines in 20x1, a regular model and a deluxe model. The deluxe model has additional pockets, a wider handle that locks in a closed position, and a larger main storage area. Suppose that Jamie chooses direct labor hours as the cost driver. For the next year, Jamie estimates that manufacturing overhead costs will amount to \$200,000 and that total direct labor hours worked will be 40,000 hours.

The first step using the traditional approach is to compute the predetermined overhead rate, as shown in Step 1 of Table 3:

$$\text{Predetermined Overhead Rate} = \frac{\$200{,}000}{\text{40,000 Direct Labor Hours}} = \$5 \text{ per Direct Labor Hour}$$

The second step is to apply manufacturing overhead to the products (see Table 3). During the year, 25,000 direct labor hours were used to produce 10,000 regular rolling suitcases and 15,000 direct labor hours were used to produce 5,000 deluxe rolling suitcases. When Jamie used the predetermined overhead rate, the portion of the manufacturing overhead cost applied to the regular rolling suitcases totaled \$125,000 (\$5 × 25,000 DLH), or \$12.50 per unit (\$125,000 ÷ 10,000 units); and the

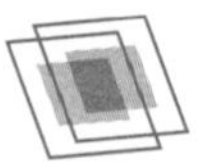

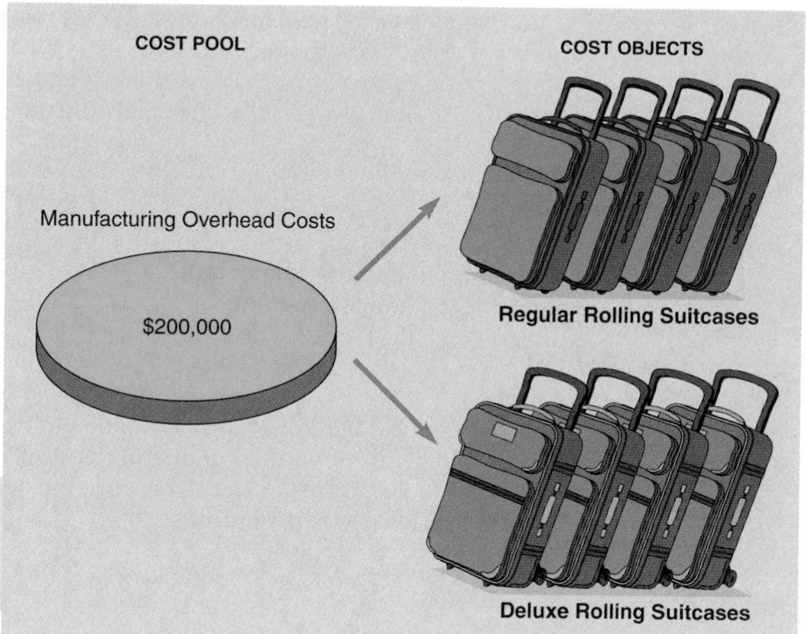

Figure 5
Using the Traditional Approach to Allocate Manufacturing Overhead Costs to Production

Table 3. Assignment of Manufacturing Overhead Costs and Calculation of Product Unit Cost: Traditional Approach

Step 1. Calculate the predetermined overhead rate.

Cost Pool Description	Estimated Cost Pool Amount	Cost Driver	Cost Driver Level	Predetermined Overhead Rate
Manufacturing overhead	$200,000	Direct labor hours (DLH)	40,000 DLH	$5 per DLH

Step 2. Apply manufacturing overhead costs to production.

	Regular		Deluxe	
	Cost Driver Level	Cost Applied	Cost Driver Level	Cost Applied
Overhead costs applied:				
Manufacturing overhead: $5 per DLH	× 25,000 DLH	$125,000	× 15,000 DLH	$75,000
Number of units		÷ 10,000		÷ 5,000
Manufacturing overhead cost per unit		$ 12.50		$ 15.00

Product Unit Cost

	Regular Rolling Suitcase	Deluxe Rolling Suitcase
Product costs per unit:		
Direct materials	$40.00	$ 42.00
Direct labor	37.50	45.00
Manufacturing overhead	12.50	15.00
Product unit cost	$90.00	$102.00

portion applied to the deluxe rolling suitcases totaled $75,000 ($5 × 15,000 DLH), or $15.00 per unit ($75,000 ÷ 5,000 units).

Jamie also wanted to calculate the normalized product unit cost during the accounting period. She gathered the following data for the two product lines:

	Regular Rolling Suitcase	Deluxe Rolling Suitcase
Actual direct materials cost per unit	$40.00	$42.00
Actual direct labor cost per unit	37.50	45.00
Prime cost per unit	$77.50	$87.00

At the bottom of Table 3 is Jamie's calculation of the product unit cost for each product line. The deluxe model's product unit cost of $102.00 is higher than the regular model's product unit cost of $90.00 because the deluxe model required more expensive materials and more labor time.

Activity-Based Costing

OBJECTIVE 7

Define and explain **activity-based costing**

Related Text Assignments:
Q: 18, 19
P: 8
SD: 1
MRA: 4

Point to Emphasize: Underscore that indirect costs are allocated to cost objects using an appropriate allocation scheme.

Suppose you and three of your friends are planning to take a skiing trip during the winter break. You call a local travel agency to obtain an estimated cost for a three-day winter skiing package. The package includes skiing, food, lodging, and entertainment. The travel agent quotes a flat fee of $400 per person, or a total of $1,600. But you and your friends prefer not to pay a flat fee. Instead, you would prefer to plan your own trip and identify the cost of each activity (skiing, eating, sleeping, entertainment).

How would you assign the $1,600 total cost of the trip to four people? The easiest way would be to follow the travel agent's approach and require each person to pay a flat fee of $400, which is one-fourth of the total cost. But what if one person does not plan to ski? Should that person pay for a portion of the skiing costs? What if another person eats much more than the other three people? Should he or she pay the same amount for food as everyone else? What if two people plan to stay only two days? Should they pay the full price?

The issue is how to assign costs fairly if each individual is involved in different activities. The people who ski should bear the skiing costs. The individual who eats more than the others should pay a larger portion of the food costs, and the ones who leave one day early should not be charged for the activities on the final day. Each individual, then, is accountable to the others for making a fair payment relative to his or her level of involvement in each activity.

The fair assignment of costs also applies to cost management. From the 1950s through the 1970s, traditional overhead allocation methods used cost drivers such as direct labor hours, direct labor costs, or machine hours to allocate a plantwide overhead cost pool to products. However, since the mid-1980s, organizations in the United States have been faced with increasing competition from foreign companies. Foreign competitors sold products of equal or better quality at lower prices than those of U.S. organizations. One weakness was that many U.S. organizations used a product costing system that did not accurately assign manufacturing overhead costs to the product lines and then used these inaccurate product unit costs when making pricing decisions. Inaccurate manufacturing overhead costs led to inaccurate product unit costs and poor pricing decisions. As a result, many organizations lost market share because they set their selling prices too high in very competitive markets. Other organizations lost profits because they set their selling prices too low in markets with little or no competition. In response, U.S. organizations began to

BUSINESS BULLETIN: BUSINESS PRACTICE

A common challenge for companies implementing activity-based costing (ABC) is to limit the number of cost drivers used for overhead cost assignment. The management accountants at Dayton Technologies, an extruded-plastics business unit of Alcoa, have developed an ABC model that includes eleven cost pools using eleven different cost drivers. The initial design included forty cost drivers but was reduced to eleven for the following reasons:

- constraints of data availability and collectibility,
- difficulty in managing a large number of drivers in the model, and
- practical relevance of the cost driver to the users of the ABC information.

The model reports an ABC contribution margin for the company's products and customers. The ABC contribution margin equals the total sales minus variable costs minus other directly traceable costs identified by the ABC system. The calculation of the ABC contribution margin includes approximately 80 percent of the total costs. Dayton Technologies uses the ABC contribution margin to improve decisions about keeping or dropping product lines and negotiating future business with customers.[2]

(1) continuously improve their product/service quality, (2) critically evaluate their operating processes, and (3) overhaul their product costing systems to more accurately identify the costs of their products or services. In the search for more accurate product costing, many organizations embraced activity-based costing (ABC). Since its introduction as a viable cost assignment technique, organizations in the United States and throughout the world have adopted ABC.

Activity-based costing (ABC) is an approach to cost assignment that calculates a more accurate product cost by categorizing all indirect costs by activity, tracing the indirect costs to those activities, and assigning activity costs to products using a cost driver that is related to the cause of the cost. A company that uses ABC to assign manufacturing overhead costs to products identifies production-related activities and the events and circumstances that cause, or drive, those activities, such as number of inspections, number of moves, or maintenance hours. As a result, many smaller cost pools are created from the single manufacturing overhead cost pool that was traditionally used. This means that the management accountant will apply manufacturing overhead costs to a product by calculating a predetermined overhead rate, or cost pool rate, for each cost pool and then using that rate and a cost driver amount to determine the portion of manufacturing overhead costs to apply. The management accountant must work with managers to select an appropriate number of cost pools for manufacturing overhead. Since each cost pool requires a cost driver, the benefit of grouping manufacturing overhead costs into several smaller pools to obtain more accurate product costs is offset by the additional costs of measuring many different cost drivers. A system must be designed to capture the actual cost driver amounts.

ABC will improve the accuracy of product costs for organizations that sell many different types of products (product diversity) or use varying, significant amounts of different production-related activities to complete the products (process complexity). To remain competitive in our current global marketplace, many organizations are selling a wider range of products or services (product or service diversity). For example, twenty years ago, Taco Bell carried only six food items. Today the menu at Taco Bell offers more than twenty-five food items. This diversity of product lines requires more careful cost allocation, especially when it comes to making decisions about pricing products, outsourcing processes to other organizations, or choosing to keep or drop a food item from the menu.

For other organizations, some products are more complicated to manufacture, store, move, package, or ship than others (process complexity). For example, an auto parts distributor receives, stores, picks, moves, consolidates, packs, and ships auto parts to auto dealers. The major operating costs of the distributor are overhead costs, which it allocates based on the cost to purchase a part for resale. Under this system, more expensive parts, such as car radios, receive a greater allocation of overhead costs than do less expensive parts, such as windshields. However, compared to a car radio, a glass windshield, because it is delicate, costs the distributor more to move, store, pack, and ship. If ABC were used, the cost of the windshield would increase to reflect a fairer allocation of the distributor's overhead costs. Thus, ABC, by fairly allocating overhead costs, would provide managers with better information for making decisions, such as pricing car radios, windshields and other auto parts; choosing to discontinue selling windshields; or reducing the amount of storage space.

Manufacturing Overhead Allocation Using ABC

OBJECTIVE 8

Calculate product unit cost using activity-based costing to assign manufacturing overhead costs

Related Text Assignments:
SE: 10
E: 9
P: 5, 7, 8
MRA: 4

Figure 6 illustrates the use of ABC to allocate manufacturing overhead costs to two product lines. Earlier in the chapter, Jamie Estrada, accountant for Angelo's Rolling Suitcases, Inc., calculated product unit cost by computing one manufacturing overhead rate for one cost pool and applying that rate to the direct labor hours used to manufacture the regular and deluxe rolling suitcase models. As we continue with our example, we find that Angelo is concerned about the product cost for each model. Angelo believes that the difference in cost between the regular and deluxe models should be more than $12. He has asked Jamie to review her estimate. Jamie found no error when she rechecked the calculation of direct materials costs and direct labor costs. However, she believes manufacturing overhead cost allocation could be misleading, so she wants to use activity-based costing to obtain a more accurate product cost.

Jamie analyzed the production-related activities and decided that the estimated $200,000 in manufacturing overhead cost could be grouped into four cost pools. The first cost pool, setup, includes estimated total costs of $70,000 for indirect labor and indirect materials used in preparing machines and workers for each batch of production. The second cost pool, which covers inspection, includes $60,000 for salaries and other costs of indirect materials, indirect labor, and depreciation on testing equipment. Packaging, the third cost pool, includes estimated total costs of $50,000 for indirect materials, indirect labor, and equipment depreciation for each order. The last cost pool, building, includes estimated total overhead costs of $20,000 for building depreciation, maintenance, janitorial wages, property taxes, insurance, security, and all other costs not related to the first three cost pools.

After identifying the four cost pools, Jamie selected a cost driver and estimated the cost driver level for each cost pool. The following schedule shows those amounts by product line and in total.

	Estimated Cost Driver Level		
Cost Driver	Regular	Deluxe	Total
Number of setups	300	400	700
Number of inspections	150	350	500
Packaging hours	600	1,400	2,000
Machine hours	4,000	6,000	10,000

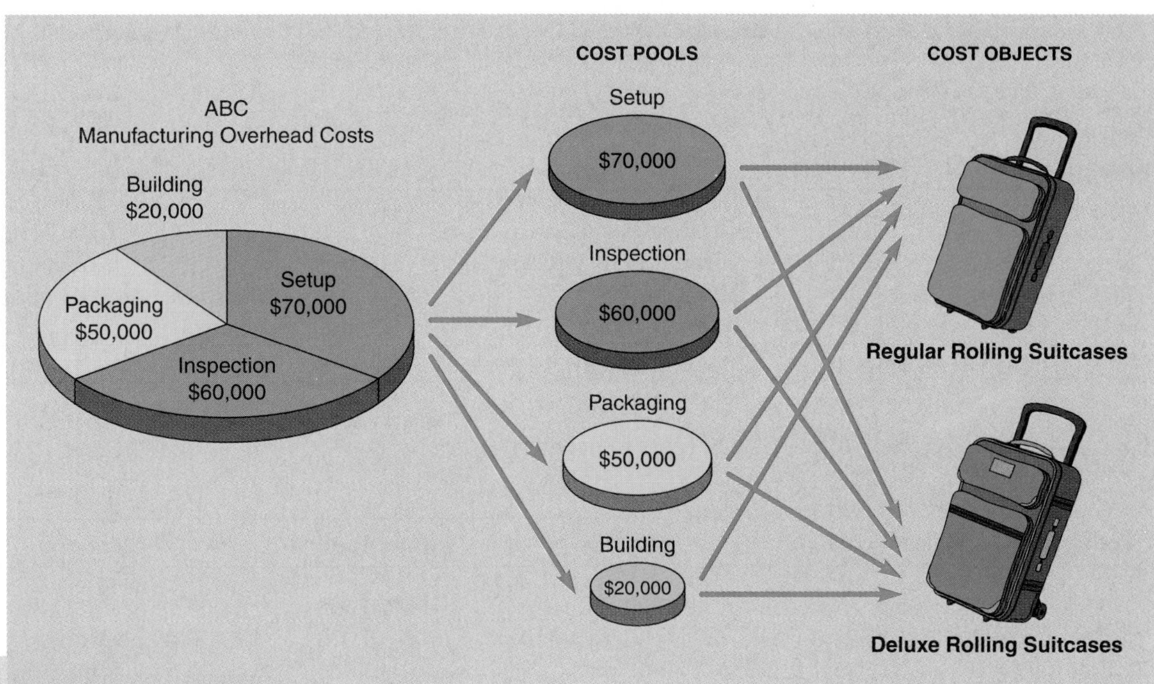

Figure 6
Using ABC to Allocate Manufacturing Overhead Costs to Production

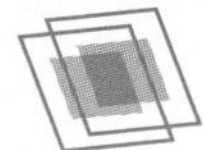

After identifying cost pools, estimated cost pool amounts, cost drivers, and estimated cost driver levels, Jamie performed the first step of the overhead allocation process by calculating the cost pool rate for each cost pool. The cost pool rate is the estimated cost pool amount divided by the estimated cost driver level. Step 1 of Table 4 shows the cost pool rates to be $100 per setup, $120 per inspection, $25 per packaging hour, and $2 per machine hour.

In the second step, Jamie applied manufacturing overhead to the two product lines using the cost driver levels for each cost driver shown in the schedule above. Step 2 of Table 4 shows those calculations. For example, during the year, Jamie applied $30,000 in setup costs ($100 × 300 setups) to the regular model and $40,000 ($100 × 400 setups) to the deluxe model. After applying the overhead costs from the four cost pools to the product lines, Jamie estimated that total manufacturing overhead costs of $71,000, or $7.10 per suitcase ($71,000 ÷ 10,000 units), applied to the regular model and $129,000, or $25.80 per suitcase ($129,000 ÷ 5,000 units), applied to the deluxe model.

Jamie also wanted to calculate the normalized product unit cost for the accounting period. At the bottom of Table 4 is Jamie's calculation of the product unit cost for each product line. The product unit cost is $112.80 for the deluxe model and $84.60 for the regular model.

Jamie presented the following information to Angelo:

	Regular Rolling Suitcase	Deluxe Rolling Suitcase
Product unit cost: One manufacturing overhead cost pool	$90.00	$102.00
Product unit cost: ABC with four cost pools	84.60	112.80
Difference: decrease (increase)	$5.40	($10.80)

Table 4. Assignment of Manufacturing Overhead Costs and Calculation of Product Unit Cost: ABC Approach

Step 1. Calculate the overhead cost pool rates.

Cost Pool Description	Estimated Cost Pool Amount	Cost Driver	Cost Driver Level	Cost Pool Rates
Setup	$ 70,000	Number of setups	700 setups	$100 per setup
Inspection	60,000	Number of inspections	500 inspections	$120 per inspection
Packaging	50,000	Packaging hours	2,000 packaging hours	$ 25 per packaging hour
Building	20,000	Machine hours	10,000 machine hours	$ 2 per machine hour
	$200,000			

Step 2. Apply manufacturing overhead costs to production.

		Regular		Deluxe	
Cost Pool	Cost Pool Rate	Cost Driver Level	Cost Applied	Cost Driver Level	Cost Applied
Setup	$100 per setup	× 300 setups	$30,000	× 400 setups	$ 40,000
Inspection	$120 per inspection	× 150 inspections	18,000	× 350 inspections	42,000
Packaging	$ 25 per packaging hour	× 600 packaging hours	15,000	× 1,400 packaging hours	35,000
Building	$ 2 per machine hour	× 4,000 machine hours	8,000	× 6,000 machine hours	12,000
Total			$71,000		$129,000
Number of units			÷ 10,000		÷ 5,000
Manufacturing overhead cost per unit			$7.10		$25.80

Product Unit Cost

	Regular Rolling Suitcase	Deluxe Rolling Suitcase
Product costs per unit:		
Direct materials	$40.00	$ 42.00
Direct labor	37.50	45.00
Manufacturing overhead	7.10	25.80
Product unit cost	$84.60	$112.80

Because ABC fairly assigned more costs to the product line that used more resources, it provided a more accurate product unit cost estimate. The increased information about the production requirements for the deluxe model that went into the ABC product unit cost calculation also provided valuable insights. Angelo found that the deluxe model costs more because the product requires (1) more setups and machine hours due to changes in the handle and number of pockets, (2) more inspections to test the new handle, and (3) more hours to complete special packaging requirements that allow retailers to display the rolling suitcase in a "carry-on" package at stores in airport terminals. The product unit cost of the deluxe model is higher for two reasons. First, the product requires more production and production-related activities to be completed and ready for sale. Second, the deluxe model's manufacturing overhead cost per unit is greater, in part, because the estimated

BUSINESS BULLETIN: TECHNOLOGY IN PRACTICE

Walker, a financial software organization, uses computer mainframes, client/server systems, Internet browsers on desktops, and network computing to help multimillion-dollar organizations manage vast amounts of transactions that are accessed frequently by suppliers, employees, and customers. Organizations in the utility industry as well as the packaged goods, transportation, banking, insurance, and telecommunications fields need to translate accounting data into business information for decision making. For example, Ryder uses a general ledger software package designed by Walker to analyze the profitability of each of its trucks and routes. Walker also helps some organizations use electronic data interchange (EDI) and Internet technology to assist their customers in making payments on their accounts and to allow their suppliers to check the payment status of their invoices.[3]

overhead was spread over fewer units than for the regular model. Based on the results of this analysis, Angelo may want to reconsider some of his short-term decisions regarding the manufacture and sale of these two product lines.

Cost Allocation in Service Organizations

OBJECTIVE 9

Apply costing concepts to a service organization

Related Text Assignments:
Q: 20, 21
SE: 11
E: 10
SD: 2, 4
MRA: 2

Instructional Strategy: Divide the class into small groups and assign MRA 2, part 1. Ask students to apply the uses of cost information about maintenance activities to the management cycle (see Figure 1). Groups may present their results to the class and answer questions from other students. Emphasize that cost information for any operating, investing, or financing activity helps managers, at any point in the management cycle.

Many organizations provide services to other organizations or to the general public. Services are labor-intensive processes supported by indirect labor and overhead costs. Managers of service organizations need to classify costs in different ways depending upon the purpose of the analysis. For example, the owner of a tax-preparation service would like to trace costs to the preparation of particular types of returns, such as personal tax returns, payroll tax reports, and estate tax returns. This allows her to see how profitable each type of service is. The manager of a nursery may classify the costs of a landscaping service into variable and fixed components to calculate the minimum number of landscaping projects needed to make a targeted profit. And the direct labor costs for tax-preparation or landscaping work will be a value-added cost to those respective services.

Processing loans, representing people in courts of law, selling insurance policies, and computing people's income taxes are typical services performed by professionals. Because no products are manufactured in the course of providing such services, service organizations have no direct materials costs. Nonetheless, specific costs arise that must be included when computing the cost of providing a service.

The most important cost in a service organization would be the professional labor involved, and the usual standard is applicable; that is, the direct labor cost must be traceable to the service rendered. In addition to the labor cost, any type of organization, whether manufacturing, retail, service, or not-for-profit—incurs overhead costs. In a service organization, the overhead costs associated with and incurred for the purpose of offering a service are classified as service overhead (like manufacturing overhead) and, along with professional labor costs, are considered service costs (like product costs) rather than period costs.

For example, assume that the Loan Department at the Seminole Bank of Commerce wants to determine the total costs incurred in processing a typical loan application. Its policy for the past five years has been to charge a $150 fee for processing a home-loan application. Barbara Hasegawa, the chief loan officer, thinks the fee is far too low. Considering the way operating costs have soared in the past five years, she proposes that the fee be doubled. You have been asked to compute the cost of processing a typical home-loan application.

The following information concerning the processing of loan applications has been given to you.

Direct professional labor:	
Loan processors' monthly salaries:	
4 people at $3,000 each	$12,000
Indirect monthly Loan Department overhead costs:	
Chief loan officer's salary	$ 4,500
Telephone	750
Depreciation	5,750
Legal advice	2,460
Customer relations	640
Credit check function	1,980
Internal audit function	2,400
Utilities	1,690
Clerical personnel	3,880
Miscellaneous	1,050
Total overhead costs	$25,100

In addition, you discover that all appraisals and title searches are performed by people outside the bank; their fees are treated as separate loan costs. One hundred home-loan applications are usually processed each month.

The Loan Department performs several other functions in addition to processing home-loan applications. Roughly one-half of the department is involved in loan collection. After determining how many of the processed loans were not home loans, you conclude that only 25 percent of the overhead costs of the Loan Department were applicable to the processing of home-loan applications. The cost of processing one home-loan application can be computed as follows:

Direct professional labor cost:	
$12,000 ÷ 100	$120.00
Service overhead cost:	
$25,100 × 25% ÷ 100	62.75
Total processing cost per loan	$182.75

Finally, you conclude that the chief loan officer was correct; the present fee does not cover the current costs of processing a typical home-loan application. However, doubling the loan fee seems inappropriate. To allow for a profit margin, the loan fee could be raised to $225 or $250.

Chapter Review

REVIEW OF LEARNING OBJECTIVES

1. **State how managers use operating cost information and product costs in the management cycle.** Managers use operating cost information and product costs as they plan, execute, review, and report during the management cycle. Managers in manufacturing, retail, or service organizations use operating cost and product cost information to measure historical or future profits, decide the selling price for regular or special sales or services provided, and to value finished goods or merchandise inventories.

2. **Define and give examples of the three elements of product cost and compute a product's unit cost for a manufacturing organization.** Direct materials are materials that become part of the finished product and that can be conveniently and economically traced to specific product units. The sheet metal used to manufacture cars is an example of a direct material. Direct labor costs include all labor costs for specific work that can be conveniently and economically traced to specific product units. A machine operator's wages are a direct labor cost. All other production-related costs—for utilities, depreciation on equipment, and operating supplies, for example—are classified and accounted for as manufacturing overhead costs. These costs cannot be conveniently or economically traced to end products, so they are assigned to products by a cost allocation method.

   The unit cost of a product is made up of the costs of direct materials, direct labor, and manufacturing overhead. These three cost elements are accumulated for a batch of products as they are produced. When the batch has been completed, the number of units produced is divided into the total costs incurred to determine the product unit cost. The product unit cost will include estimated costs if normal or standard costing methods are used.

3. **Describe the flow of product-related activities, documents, and costs through the Materials Inventory, Work in Process Inventory, and Finished Goods Inventory accounts.** The flow of costs through the inventory accounts begins when costs are incurred for direct materials, direct labor, and manufacturing overhead. Materials costs flow first into the Materials Inventory account, which is used to record the costs of materials when they are received and again when they are issued for use in a production process. All manufacturing-related costs—direct materials, direct labor, and manufacturing overhead—are recorded in the Work in Process Inventory account as the production process begins. When products are completed, their costs are transferred from the Work in Process Inventory account to the Finished Goods Inventory account. Costs remain in the Finished Goods Inventory account until the products are sold, at which time they are transferred to the Cost of Goods Sold account.

4. **Prepare a statement of cost of goods manufactured and an income statement for a manufacturing organization.** The cost of goods manufactured is a key component of the income statement for a manufacturing organization. Determining the cost of goods manufactured involves three steps: (1) computing the cost of materials used, (2) computing total manufacturing costs for the period, and (3) computing the cost of goods manufactured. This last figure, taken from the statement of cost of goods manufactured, is used in the income statement to compute the cost of goods sold.

5. **Define *cost allocation* and explain the process of manufacturing overhead allocation using cost objects, cost pools, and cost drivers.** Cost allocation is the process of assigning pooled indirect costs to specific cost objects using an allocation base that represents a major function of the business. The allocation of manufacturing overhead requires the pooling of manufacturing overhead costs that are affected by a common activity and the selection of a cost driver whose activity level causes a change in the cost pool. A cost pool is a pool of overhead costs related to a cost object (the destination of an assigned or allocated cost). A cost driver is an activity that causes the cost pool to increase in amount as the cost driver increases.

   The four steps of the manufacturing overhead allocation process are planning, application, recording actual costs, and reconciliation. In the planning step, the predetermined overhead rate is calculated. In the application step, manufacturing overhead costs are applied to the product costs during production. In the recording actual costs step, the actual manufacturing overhead costs are recorded in the accounting records when the costs are incurred. In the reconciliation step, the difference between the actual and applied manufacturing overhead costs is calculated and the Cost of Goods Sold account is corrected for an immaterial amount of over- or underapplied manufacturing overhead costs to the products. If the difference is material, adjustments are made to the Work in Process Inventory, Finished Goods Inventory, and Cost of Goods Sold accounts.

6. **Calculate product unit cost using the traditional allocation of manufacturing overhead costs.** The normal costing method applies manufacturing overhead costs to a product's cost by estimating a predetermined manufacturing overhead rate and multiplying that rate by the actual cost driver level. The total applied manufacturing

overhead cost is added to the actual costs of direct materials and direct labor in order to determine the total product cost. The product unit cost is the total product cost divided by the total units produced.

7. **Define and explain *activity-based costing.*** Activity-based costing (ABC) is an approach to cost assignment that calculates a more accurate product cost by (1) categorizing all indirect costs by activity and (2) tracing costs to those activities, and (3) assigning activity costs to products using a cost driver that is related to the cause of the cost. For manufacturing organizations, activity-based costing improves the accuracy of the allocation of manufacturing overhead costs to products. ABC is particularly useful for companies with product diversity or variations in the amounts of production-related activities needed to manufacture different product lines.
8. **Calculate product unit cost using activity-based costing to assign manufacturing overhead costs.** When ABC is used, manufacturing overhead costs are grouped into smaller cost pools related to specific activities. Cost drivers are identified and cost driver levels are estimated for each cost pool. Each cost pool rate is calculated by dividing the estimated cost pool amount by the cost driver level. Manufacturing overhead, which is represented in the cost pools, is applied to the product's cost by multiplying the cost pool rate by the actual cost driver amount. The total applied manufacturing overhead cost is added to the cost of direct materials and direct labor to determine the total product cost. The product unit cost is the total product cost divided by the total units produced.
9. **Apply costing concepts to a service organization.** Most types of costs incurred by a manufacturer and called product costs are also incurred by a service organization. The only important difference is that a service organization does not deal with a physical product that can be assembled, stored, and valued. Services are rendered and cannot be held in inventory. Because no products are manufactured in the course of providing services, service organizations have no materials costs. To determine the cost of performing a particular service, professional labor and service-related overhead costs are included in the analysis.

REVIEW OF CONCEPTS AND TERMINOLOGY

The following concepts and terms were introduced in this chapter.

LO 7 **Activity-based costing:** A cost assignment approach that calculates a more accurate product cost by categorizing all indirect costs by activity, tracing the indirect costs to those activities, and assigning activity costs to products using a cost driver that is related to the cause of the cost.

LO 2 **Actual costing:** A method of cost measurement using the actual costs of direct materials, direct labor, and manufacturing overhead to calculate the product unit cost.

LO 5 **Cost allocation:** The process of assigning collected indirect costs to specific cost objects using an allocation base that represents a major function of the business.

LO 5 **Cost driver:** An activity that causes the cost pool to increase in amount as the cost driver increases in volume.

LO 5 **Cost object:** The destination of an assigned, or allocated, cost.

LO 3 **Cost of goods manufactured:** The total manufacturing costs attached to units of a product completed during an accounting period and moved to finished goods storage.

LO 5 **Cost pool:** A collection of overhead costs or other indirect costs related to a cost object.

LO 2 **Direct labor costs:** Costs of labor to complete activities involved in the production process that can be conveniently and economically traced to specific units of product.

LO 2 **Direct materials costs:** Costs of materials that can be conveniently and economically traced to specific units of product.

LO 3 **Direct Materials Inventory account:** An inventory account showing the balance of the cost of unused direct materials.

LO 3 **Finished Goods Inventory account:** An inventory account that holds the costs assigned to all completed products that have not been sold by a manufacturing company.

LO 2 **Indirect labor costs:** Labor costs for production-related activities that cannot be conveniently or economically traced to a unit of product.

LO 2 **Indirect materials costs:** The costs of minor materials and other production supplies that cannot be conveniently or economically traced to a unit of product.

LO 3 **Manufacturing cost flow:** The flow of manufacturing costs (direct materials, direct labor, and manufacturing overhead) from their incurrence through the Direct Materials Inventory, Work in Process Inventory, and Finished Goods Inventory accounts to the Cost of Goods Sold account.

LO 2 **Manufacturing overhead costs:** A varied collection of production-related costs that cannot be practically or conveniently traced to an end product. Also called *factory overhead, factory burden,* or *indirect manufacturing costs.*

LO 2 **Normal costing:** A method that combines the *actual* direct materials and direct labor costs with the *estimated* manufacturing overhead costs to determine a normal product unit cost.

LO 2 **Product unit cost:** The manufacturing cost of a single unit of product; total cost of direct materials, direct labor, and manufacturing overhead for the units produced divided by the total units produced.

LO 2 **Standard costing:** A method of cost measurement using the estimated costs of direct materials, direct labor, and manufacturing overhead to calculate the product unit cost for purposes of cost control.

LO 4 **Statement of cost of goods manufactured:** A formal statement summarizing the flow of all manufacturing costs incurred during an accounting period.

LO 3 **Total manufacturing costs:** The total costs of direct materials, direct labor, and manufacturing overhead incurred and charged to production during an accounting period.

LO 3 **Work in Process Inventory account:** An inventory account used to record all manufacturing costs incurred and assigned to partially completed units of product.

REVIEW PROBLEM

Cost of Goods Manufactured—Three Fundamental Steps

LO 2
LO 3
LO 4

In addition to the year-end balance sheet and income statement, the management of Nikita Company requires the controller to prepare a statement of cost of goods manufactured. During 20xx, $361,920 of direct materials were purchased. Operating cost data and inventory account balances for 20xx follow:

Account	Balance
Direct Labor (10,430 hours at $9.50 per hour)	$ 99,085
Plant Supervision	42,500
Indirect Labor (20,280 hours at $6.25 per hour)	126,750
Factory Insurance	8,100
Utilities, Factory	29,220
Depreciation, Factory Building	46,200
Depreciation, Factory Equipment	62,800
Manufacturing Supplies	9,460
Factory Repair and Maintenance	14,980
Selling and Administrative Expenses	76,480
Direct Materials Inventory, January 1, 20xx	26,490
Work in Process Inventory, January 1, 20xx	101,640
Finished Goods Inventory, January 1, 20xx	148,290
Direct Materials Inventory, December 31, 20xx	24,910
Work in Process Inventory, December 31, 20xx	100,400
Finished Goods Inventory, December 31, 20xx	141,100

REQUIRED

1. Compute the cost of materials used during the year.
2. Given the cost of materials used, compute the total manufacturing costs for the year.
3. Given the total manufacturing costs for the year, compute the cost of goods manufactured during the year.
4. Assuming 13,397 units were manufactured during the year, what was the actual product unit cost?

ANSWER TO REVIEW PROBLEM

1. Compute the cost of materials used.

Direct Materials Inventory, January 1, 20xx	$ 26,490
Add Direct Materials Purchased (net)	361,920
Cost of Direct Materials Available for Use	$388,410
Less Direct Materials Inventory, December 31, 20xx	24,910
Cost of Direct Materials Used	$363,500

2. Compute the total manufacturing costs.

Cost of Direct Materials Used		$363,500
Add Direct Labor Costs		99,085
Add Total Manufacturing Overhead Costs		
Plant Supervision	$ 42,500	
Indirect Labor	126,750	
Factory Insurance	8,100	
Utilities, Factory	29,220	
Depreciation, Factory Building	46,200	
Depreciation, Factory Equipment	62,800	
Manufacturing Supplies	9,460	
Factory Repair and Maintenance	14,980	
Total Manufacturing Overhead Costs		340,010
Total Manufacturing Costs		$802,595

3. Compute the cost of goods manufactured.

Total Manufacturing Costs	$802,595
Add Work in Process Inventory, January 1, 20xx	101,640
Total Cost of Work in Process During the Year	$904,235
Less Work in Process Inventory, December 31, 20xx	100,400
Cost of Goods Manufactured	$803,835

4. Compute the actual product unit cost.

$$\frac{\text{Cost of Goods Manufactured}}{\text{Number of Units Manufactured}} = \frac{\$803{,}835}{13{,}397} = \$60^*$$

*Rounded.

Chapter Assignments

BUILDING YOUR KNOWLEDGE FOUNDATION

Questions

1. How do managers use operating cost information?
2. Explain the full cost of a product or service.
3. What are the three kinds of manufacturing costs included in a product's cost?
4. Define *direct materials costs.*
5. How is a direct cost different from an indirect cost?
6. What characteristics identify a cost as part of manufacturing overhead?
7. How are direct labor costs different from indirect labor costs?
8. Explain the difference between actual costing and normal costing.

9. Identify and describe the three inventory accounts used by a manufacturing company.
10. What is meant by the term *manufacturing cost flow?*
11. Describe how to compute the cost of direct materials used.
12. Describe how total manufacturing costs differ from the cost of goods manufactured.
13. How is the cost of goods manufactured used in computing the cost of goods sold?
14. What is cost allocation?
15. Explain the relationship between cost objects, cost pools, and cost drivers. Give an example of each.
16. List the four steps of the manufacturing overhead allocation process. Briefly explain each step.
17. What are two primary uses of a predetermined manufacturing overhead rate?
18. What is activity-based costing?
19. When would a company find activity-based costing to be an appropriate approach to cost assignment?
20. "The concept of product costs is not applicable to service organizations." Is this statement correct? Defend your answer.
21. Why do service organizations need unit cost information?

Short Exercises

SE 1. LO 1 *Distinguishing the Costs of a Product*

Ray Christopher, owner of Candlelight, Inc., was given the following list of costs he incurs in his candle business. Examine the list and identify the costs that Ray should *not* include in the full cost of making and selling candles.

1. Salary of Mary, the office employee
2. Cost of delivering candles to Candles Plus, a buyer
3. Cost of wax
4. Sales commission on a sale to Candles Plus
5. Cost to custom-design Christmas candles

SE 2. LO 2 *Elements of Manufacturing Cost*

Flora Rose, the bookkeeper at Candlelight, Inc., must group the costs to manufacture candles. Tell whether each of the following items should be classified as direct materials (DM), direct labor (DL), manufacturing overhead (MO), or none of the three (N).

1. Depreciation of the cost of vats to hold melted wax
2. Cost of wax
3. Rent on the factory where candles are made
4. Cost of George's time to dip the wicks into the wax
5. Cost of coloring for candles
6. Cost of Ray's time to design candles for Halloween
7. Sam's commission to sell candles to Candles Plus

SE 3. LO 2 *Computing Product Unit Cost*

What is the product unit cost for Job 14, which consists of 300 units and has total manufacturing costs of direct materials, $4,500; direct labor, $7,500; and manufacturing overhead, $3,600?

SE 4. LO 3 *Manufacturing Cost Flow*

Given the following information, compute the ending balances of the Direct Materials Inventory, Work in Process Inventory, and Finished Goods Inventory accounts.

Direct Materials Inventory, beginning balance	$ 23,000
Work in Process Inventory, beginning balance	25,750
Finished Goods Inventory, beginning balance	38,000
Direct materials purchased	85,000
Direct materials placed into production	74,000
Direct labor costs	97,000
Manufacturing overhead costs	35,000
Cost of goods completed	123,000
Cost of goods sold	93,375

SE 5. LO 3 *Document Flows for a Manufacturing Organization*

Identify the document needed to support each of the following transactions.

1. Placing an order for direct materials with a supplier
2. Recording direct labor time at the beginning and end of each work shift
3. Receiving direct materials at the shipping dock
4. Recording the costs of a specific job requiring direct materials, direct labor, and overhead
5. Issuing direct materials into production
6. Billing the customer for a completed order
7. A request from the Production Scheduling Department for the purchase of direct materials

SE 6. LO 4 *Income Statement for a Manufacturing Organization*

Using the following information from C.L.I.N.T. Company, prepare an income statement for 20xx.

Net Sales	$900,000
Finished Goods Inventory, January 1, 20xx	45,000
Cost of Goods Manufactured	585,000
Finished Goods Inventory, December 31, 20xx	60,000
Operating Expenses	270,000
Interest Expense	5,000
Tax Rate	34%

SE 7. LO 5 *Calculation of Underapplied or Overapplied Overhead*

At year end, records show actual manufacturing overhead costs incurred were $25,870 and the amount of manufacturing overhead costs applied to production was $27,000. Identify the amount of under- or overapplied manufacturing overhead and indicate whether the Cost of Goods Sold account should be increased or decreased to adjust the balance to reflect actual manufacturing overhead costs.

SE 8. LO 5 LO 6 *Computation of Predetermined Overhead Rate*

Compute the predetermined overhead rate per service request for the Maintenance Department if estimated overhead costs are $18,290 and the number of estimated service requests is 3,100.

SE 9. LO 5 LO 6 *Application of Manufacturing Overhead to Production*

Calculate the amount of manufacturing overhead costs applied to production if the predetermined overhead rate is $4 per direct labor hour and 1,200 direct labor hours were worked.

SE 10. LO 8 *Activity-Based Costing and Cost Drivers*

Kloezeman Clothiers Company relies on the information from its activity-based costing system when setting prices for its products. Compute ABC rates from the following budgeted data for each of the activity centers.

	Budgeted Cost	Budgeted Cost Driver
Cutting/Stitching	$5,220,000	145,000 machine hours
Trimming/Packing	998,400	41,600 operator hours
Designing	1,187,500	62,500 designer hours

SE 11. LO 9 *Unit Costs in a Service Business*

Pickerson's Picking Services provides inexpensive, high-quality labor for farmers growing vegetable and fruit crops. In June, Pickerson paid laborers $4,000 to pick 500 acres of winter-grown onions. Pickerson incurred overhead costs of $2,400 for onion- and lettuce-picking services in June. This included the costs of transporting the laborers to the various fields; providing facilities, food, and beverages for the laborers; and scheduling, billing, and collecting from the farmers. Of this amount, 50 percent was related to picking onions. Compute the cost per acre to pick onions.

Exercises

E 1. LO 1 *Distinguishing the Costs of Products*

Identify each of the following as a cost of a manufactured product (M), a cost of a purchased product (P), or both (B).

1. Warehouse costs for merchandise
2. Cost of utilities used in the factory
3. Advertising costs

4. Building rent
5. Product design costs
6. Cost of direct materials
7. Delivery costs
8. Display cases for merchandise
9. Parts in assembly operations
10. Production supervisor's salary

E 2. LO 2 *Unit Cost Determination*

The Rose Winery is one of the finest and oldest wineries in the country. One of its most famous products is a red table wine called Olen Millot. The wine is made from Olen Millot grapes grown in Missouri's Ozark region. Recently, management has become concerned about the increasing cost of making Olen Millot and needs to find out if the current $10 per bottle selling price is adequate. The winery would like to make about a 25 percent profit on the sale of each bottle of wine. The following information is given to you for analysis.

Batch size	10,550 bottles
Costs	
Direct Materials	
Olen Millot grapes	$22,155
Chancellor grapes	9,495
Bottles	5,275
Direct Labor	
Pickers/loaders	2,110
Crusher	422
Processors	8,440
Bottler	1,688
Storage and racking	11,605
Manufacturing overhead	
Depreciation, equipment	2,743
Depreciation, building	5,275
Utilities	1,055
Indirect labor	6,330
Supervision	7,385
Supplies	3,165
Storage fixtures	2,532
Chemicals	4,220
Repairs	1,477
Miscellaneous	633
Total production costs	$96,005

1. Compute the unit cost per bottle for materials, labor, and manufacturing overhead.
2. What would you advise management regarding the price per bottle of Olen Millot wine? Defend your answer.

E 3. LO 3 *Documentation*

Magellan Company manufactures a complete line of music boxes. Seventy percent of its products are standard items and are produced in long production runs. The remaining 30 percent of the music boxes are special orders involving specific requests for tunes. The special order boxes cost from three to six times as much as the standard product because of the use of additional materials and labor.

Howard Smith, the controller, recently received a complaint memorandum from V. Whatley, the production supervisor, because of the new network of source documents added to the existing cost accounting system. The new documents include a purchase request, a purchase order, a receiving report, and a materials request. Mr. Whatley claims that the forms represent extra busy work and interrupt the normal flow of production.

Prepare a written memorandum from Howard Smith to Mr. Whatley that fully explains the purpose of each type of document.

E 4. LO 3 *Cost Flows and Inventory Accounts*

For each of the following activities, identify the inventory account (Direct Materials Inventory, Work in Process Inventory, Finished Goods Inventory), if any, that is affected. If an inventory account is affected, indicate whether the account balance will increase or decrease. *Example:* Moved completed units to finished goods inventory. *Answer:* Increase Finished Goods Inventory, Decrease Work in Process Inventory. If no inventory account is affected, use "None of these" as your answer.

1. Moved materials requested by production.
2. Sold units of product to customer.
3. Purchased and received direct materials for production.
4. Used direct labor and factory overhead in the production process.
5. Received payment from customer.
6. Purchased office supplies and paid cash.
7. Paid monthly office rent.

E 5. LO 4 *Statement of Cost of Goods Manufactured*

The following information about the manufacturing costs incurred by the Earth Company for the month ended August 31, 20xx, is available.

Purchases of direct materials during August totaled $139,000.

Direct labor was 3,400 hours at $8.75 per hour.

The following manufacturing overhead costs were incurred: utilities, $5,870; supervision, $16,600; indirect supplies, $6,750; depreciation, $6,200; insurance, $1,830; and miscellaneous, $1,100.

Inventory accounts on August 1 were as follows: Direct Materials Inventory, $48,600; Work in Process Inventory, $54,250; and Finished Goods Inventory, $38,500. Inventory accounts on August 31 were as follows: Direct Materials Inventory, $50,100; Work in Process Inventory, $48,400; and Finished Goods Inventory, $37,450.

From the information given, prepare a statement of cost of goods manufactured.

E 6. LO 5 LO 6 *Computation of Predetermined Overhead Rate*

The overhead costs used by Trinity Industries, Inc., to compute its predetermined overhead rate for 20x1 are listed below.

Indirect materials and supplies	$ 79,200
Repairs and maintenance	14,900
Outside service contracts	17,300
Indirect labor	79,100
Factory supervision	42,900
Depreciation, machinery	85,000
Factory insurance	8,200
Property taxes	6,500
Heat, light, and power	7,700
Miscellaneous manufacturing overhead	5,760
	$346,560

A total of 45,600 machine hours was used as the 20x1 allocation base. In 20x2, all overhead costs except depreciation, property taxes, and miscellaneous manufacturing overhead are expected to increase by 10 percent. Depreciation should increase by 12 percent, and a 20 percent increase in property taxes and miscellaneous manufacturing overhead is expected. Plant capacity in terms of machine hours used will increase by 4,400 hours in 20x2.

1. Compute the 20x1 predetermined overhead rate. (Carry your answer to three decimal places.)
2. Compute the predetermined overhead rate for 20x2. (Carry your answer to three decimal places.)

E 7. LO 5 LO 6 *Computation and Application of Overhead Rate*

Bullock Compumatics specializes in the analysis and reporting of complex inventory costing projects. Materials costs are minimal, consisting entirely of operating supplies (computer diskettes, inventory sheets, and other recording tools). Labor is the highest single expense item, totaling $693,000 for 75,000 hours of work in 20xx. Manufacturing overhead costs for 20xx were $916,000 and were applied to specific jobs on the basis of labor hours worked. In 20x1 the company anticipates a 25 percent increase in manufacturing overhead costs. Labor costs will increase by $130,000, and the number of hours worked is expected to increase 20 percent.

1. Determine the total amount of manufacturing overhead anticipated by the company in 20x1.
2. Compute the predetermined manufacturing overhead rate for 20x1. (Round your answer to the nearest penny.)
3. During April 20x1, 11,980 labor hours were worked. Calculate the manufacturing overhead amount assigned to April production.

E 8. LO 5 LO 6 *Disposition of Overapplied Overhead (Extension of E 7)*

At the end of 20x1, Bullock Compumatics had compiled a total of 89,920 labor hours worked. The actual manufacturing overhead incurred was $1,143,400.

1. Using the predetermined overhead rate computed in **E 7**, determine the total amount of manufacturing overhead applied to operations during 20x1.
2. Compute the amount of overapplied overhead for the year.
3. Will Cost of Goods Sold be increased or decreased to correct the overapplication of manufacturing overhead?

E 9. LO 6 LO 8 *Activities and Activity-Based Costing*

Yu Enterprises produces antennas for telecommunications equipment. One of the most important parts of the company's new just-in-time production process is quality control. Initially, a traditional cost accounting system was used to assign quality control costs to products. All costs of the Quality Control Department were included in the plant's overhead cost pool and allocated to products based on direct labor dollars. Recently, the firm implemented an activity-based costing system. The activities, cost drivers, and rates for the quality control function are summarized below, along with cost allocation information from the traditional system. Also shown is information related to one order of the Qian model antenna, Order HQ14. Compute the quality control cost that would be assigned to the Qian model order under both the traditional approach and the activity-based costing approach.

Traditional costing approach:
Quality control costs were assigned at a rate of 12 percent of direct labor dollars. Order HQ14 was charged with $9,350 of direct labor costs.

Activity-based costing approach:
Quality Control Function

Activities	Cost Drivers	Cost Pool Rates	Order HQ14 Activity Usage
Incoming materials inspection	Types of materials used	$17.50 per type of material	17 types of materials
In-process inspection	Number of products	$0.06 per product	2,400 products
Tool and gauge control	Number of processes per cell	$26.50 per process	11 processes
Product certification	Per order	$94.00 per order	1 order

E 10. LO 9 *Unit Costs in a Service Business*

Hector Franco provides custom farming services to owners of five-acre alfalfa fields. In July, he earned $2,400 by cutting, turning, and baling 3,000 bales of alfalfa. In the same month, he incurred the following costs: gas, $150; tractor maintenance, $115; and labor, $600. His annual tractor depreciation was $1,500. What was Franco's cost per bale? What was his revenue per bale? Should he increase the amount he charges the owners for his custom farming services?

Problems

P 1. LO 2 *Computation of Unit Cost*

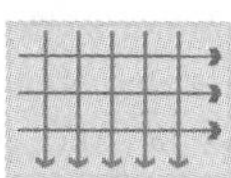

Banff Industries, Inc., manufactures video discs for several of the leading recording studios in the United States and Europe. Department 85 is responsible for the electronic circuitry within each disc. Department 82 applies the plastic-like surface to the discs and packages them for shipment. A recent order for 4,000 discs from the JAZ Company was produced during July. For this job, the departments incurred the costs (at the top of the next page) to complete and ship the goods in July.

	Department	
	85	82
Direct materials used	$14,720	$1,960
Direct labor	3,400	1,280
Manufacturing overhead	3,680	2,400

REQUIRED

1. Compute the unit cost for each of the two departments.
2. Compute the total unit cost for the JAZ Company order.
3. The selling price for this order was $7 per unit. Was the selling price adequate? List the assumptions and/or computations upon which you based your answer. What suggestions would you make to Banff Industries' management concerning the pricing of future orders?

P 2. LO 4 *Statement of Cost of Goods Manufactured*

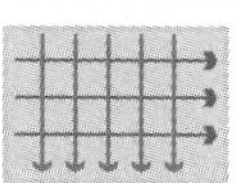

Unger Manufacturing Company produces a line of Viking ship replicas that is sold at Scandinavian gift shops throughout the world. Inventory account balances on May 1, 20xx were Direct Materials Inventory, $190,400; Work in Process Inventory, $96,250; and Finished Goods Inventory, $52,810. April 30, 20x1 inventory account balances were Direct Materials Inventory, $186,250; Work in Process Inventory, $87,900; and Finished Goods Inventory, $56,620.

During the 20xx–20x1 fiscal year, $474,630 of direct materials were purchased, and payroll records indicated that direct labor costs totaled $215,970. Overhead costs for the period included indirect materials and supplies, $77,640; indirect labor, $192,710; depreciation, building, $19,900; depreciation, equipment, $14,240; heating, $19,810; electricity, $8,770; repairs and maintenance, $12,110; liability and fire insurance, $2,980; property taxes, building, $3,830; design and rework, $23,770; and supervision, $92,290. Other costs for the period included selling costs, $41,720, and administrative salaries, $102,750.

REQUIRED

Prepare a statement of cost of goods manufactured for the fiscal year ended April 30, 20x1.

P 3. LO 4 *Statement of Cost of Goods Manufactured and Cost of Goods Sold*

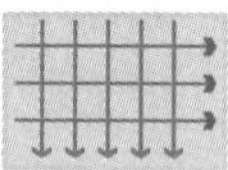

Placita Corp. makes irrigation sprinkler systems for farmers in semi-arid and desert climates. Rajesh Balaji, the new controller for the organization, can find only partial information for the past year, which is presented below.

	Clovis Division	Lamesa Division	Childress Division	Grady Division
Direct materials used	$3	$ 7	$ **g**	$ 8
Total manufacturing costs	6	**d**	**h**	14
Manufacturing overhead costs	1	3	2	**j**
Direct labor costs	**a**	6	4	4
Ending Work in Process Inventory	**b**	3	2	5
Cost of goods manufactured	7	20	12	**k**
Beginning Work in Process Inventory	2	**e**	3	**l**
Ending Finished Goods Inventory	2	6	**i**	9
Beginning Finished Goods Inventory	3	**f**	5	7
Cost of goods sold	**c**	18	13	9

REQUIRED

Using the information given, compute the unknown values. Show your computations.

P 4. LO 5 LO 6 *Application of Manufacturing Overhead*

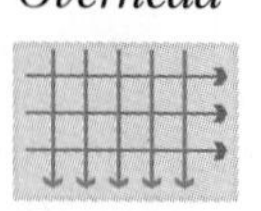

Classic Cosmetics Company applies manufacturing overhead costs on the basis of machine hours. The current predetermined overhead rate is computed by using data from the two prior years, in this case 20xx and 20x1, adjusted to reflect expectations for the current year, 20x2. The controller prepared the overhead rate analysis for 20x2 using the information at the top of the next page.

In 20x2, utilities are expected to increase by 40 percent over the previous year; indirect labor, employee benefits, and miscellaneous manufacturing overhead are expected to increase by 30 percent; insurance and depreciation are expected to increase by 20 percent; and supervision and janitorial services are expected to increase by 10 percent. Machine hours are expected to total 68,832.

	20xx	20x1
Machine hours	47,800	57,360
Manufacturing overhead costs:		
Indirect labor	$ 18,100	$ 23,530
Employee benefits	22,000	28,600
Manufacturing supervision	16,800	18,480
Utilities	10,350	14,490
Factory insurance	6,500	7,800
Janitorial services	11,000	12,100
Depreciation, factory and machinery	17,750	21,300
Miscellaneous manufacturing overhead	5,750	7,475
Total manufacturing overhead	$108,250	$133,775

REQUIRED

1. Compute the projected costs and the predetermined overhead rate for 20x2 using the information about expected cost increases. (Carry your answer to three decimal places.)
2. Assume that the company actually surpassed its sales and operating expectations in 20x2. Jobs completed during the year and the related machine hours used were as follows:

Job No.	Machine Hours
2214	12,300
2215	14,200
2216	9,800
2217	13,600
2218	11,300
2219	8,100

Total machine hours were 69,300. Determine the amount of manufacturing overhead to be applied to each job and to total production during 20x2. (Round answers to whole dollars.)

3. Assume that $165,845 of manufacturing overhead was incurred during the year. Was overhead underapplied or overapplied in 20x2? By how much? Should the Cost of Goods Sold account be increased or decreased to reflect actual manufacturing overhead costs?

P 5. LO 8 *Activities and Activity-Based Costing*

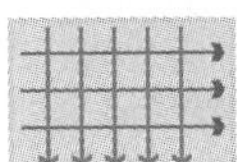

Berina Computer Company, which has been in operation for ten years, produces a line of minicomputers. Holstrum, Ltd., placed an order for eighty minicomputers and the order has just been completed. Berina recently shifted to an activity-based system of cost assignment. Sandra Alvarez, the controller, is interested in finding out the impact that the ABC system had on the Holstrum order. Raw materials, purchased parts, and production labor costs for the Holstrum order are as follows:

Cost of raw materials	$36,750.00	Production direct labor hours	220
Cost of purchased parts	21,300.00	Average direct labor pay rate	$15.25

Other operating costs are as follows:

Traditional costing data using a single, plantwide overhead rate:
Manufacturing overhead costs were assigned at a rate of 270 percent of direct labor dollars.

Activity-based costing data:

Activities	Cost Drivers	Cost Pool Rates	Activity Usage for Holstrum Order
Electrical engineering design	Engineering hours	$19.50 per engineering hour	32 engineering hours
Work cell setup	Number of setups	$29.40 per setup	11 setups
Parts production work cell	Machine hours	$26.30 per machine hour	134 machine hours
Product testing cell	Cell hours	$32.80 per cell hour	52 cell hours
Packaging work cell	Cell hours	$17.50 per cell hour	22 cell hours

Building occupancy-related overhead costs are allocated at a rate of $9.80 per parts production work cell machine hour.

REQUIRED

1. Using the traditional costing approach, compute the total cost of the Holstrum order.
2. Using the activity-based costing approach, compute the total cost of the Holstrum order.
3. What difference in the amount of cost assigned to the Holstrum order resulted from the shift to activity-based costing? Does the use of activity-based costing guarantee cost reduction for every product?

Alternate Problems

LO 5
LO 6
Application of Manufacturing Overhead

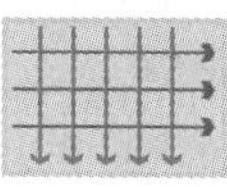

P 6. Chan Products, Inc., uses a predetermined manufacturing overhead rate in its production, assembly, and testing departments. One rate is used for the entire company and is based on machine hours. The current rate was determined by analyzing data from the previous two years and projecting figures for the current year, adjusted for expected changes. Mr. Yu is about to compute the rate to be used in 20x3 using the following data.

	20x1	20x2
Machine hours	38,000	41,800
Manufacturing overhead costs:		
Indirect materials	$ 44,500	$ 57,850
Indirect labor	21,200	25,440
Supervision	37,800	41,580
Utilities	9,400	11,280
Labor-related costs	8,200	9,020
Depreciation, factory	9,800	10,780
Depreciation, machinery	22,700	27,240
Property taxes	2,400	2,880
Insurance	1,600	1,920
Miscellaneous manufacturing overhead	4,400	4,840
Total manufacturing overhead	$162,000	$192,830

In 20x3, indirect materials are expected to increase by 30 percent over the previous year. Indirect labor, utilities, machinery depreciation, property taxes, and insurance are expected to increase by 20 percent. All other expenses are expected to increase by 10 percent. Machine hours are estimated to be 45,980 for 20x3.

REQUIRED

1. Compute the projected costs and the predetermined manufacturing overhead rate for year 20x3 using the information about expected cost increases. (Round your answer to three decimal places.)
2. During 20x3, Chan Products, Inc., produced the following jobs using the machine hours shown.

Job No.	Machine Hours	Job No.	Machine Hours
H–142	7,840	H–201	10,680
H–164	5,260	H–218	12,310
H–175	8,100	H–304	2,460

   Determine the amount of manufacturing overhead applied to each job in 20x3. What was the total manufacturing overhead applied during the year? (Round answers to the nearest dollar.)
3. Actual manufacturing overhead for 20x3 was $234,485. Was overhead underapplied or overapplied in 20x3? By how much? Should the Cost of Goods Sold account be increased or decreased to reflect actual overhead costs?

LO 8

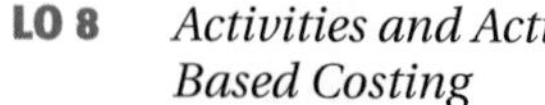

Activities and Activity-Based Costing

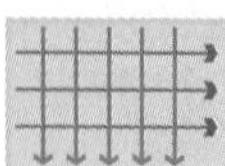

P 7. Maltz Products, Inc., produces a line of fax machines for wholesale distributors in the Pacific Northwest. Hines Company ordered 150 Model 14 fax machines and Maltz has just completed packaging the order. Before the Hines order is shipped, the controller has asked for a unit cost analysis comparing the amounts determined under the company's old traditional costing system with amounts computed under the new activity-based costing system. Raw materials, purchased parts, and production labor costs for the Hines order are as follows:

Cost of raw materials	$17,450.00	Production direct labor hours	140
Cost of purchased parts	$14,800.00	Average direct labor pay rate	$16.50

Other operating costs are as follows:

Traditional costing data using a single, plantwide overhead rate:
Manufacturing overhead costs were assigned at a rate of 240 percent of direct labor dollars.

Activity-based costing data:

Activities	Cost Drivers	Cost Pool Rates	Activity Usage for Hines Order
Engineering systems design	Engineering hours	$28.00 per engineering hour	18 engineering hours
Work cell setup	Number of setups	$42.00 per setup	8 setups
Parts production work cell	Machine hours	$37.50 per machine hour	84 machine hours
Product assembly cell	Cell hours	$44.00 per cell hour	36 cell hours
Packaging work cell	Cell hours	$28.50 per cell hour	28 cell hours

Building occupancy-related overhead costs are allocated at a rate of $10.40 per parts production work cell machine hour.

REQUIRED

1. Using the traditional costing approach with a single, plantwide overhead rate, compute the total cost of the Hines order.
2. Using the activity-based costing approach, compute the total cost of the Hines order.
3. What difference in the amount of cost assigned to the Hines order resulted from the shift to activity-based costing? Does the use of activity-based costing guarantee cost reduction for every product?

P 8. **LO 5 LO 6 LO 7 LO 8** *Application of Manufacturing Overhead: Traditional and Activity-Based Costing Approaches*

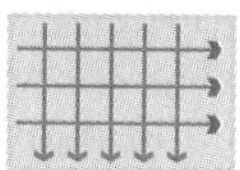

Shark Scout, Inc., manufactures underwater vehicles. Oil companies use the Rigger II to examine offshore oil rigs, and marine biology research foundations use the BioScout for research studies along coastlines. The company's San Diego factory is semiautomated and requires some direct labor. Blanca Gonzales, the controller, used normal costing to calculate the product unit cost for both product lines. Blanca calculated a traditional predetermined overhead rate of $13.75 per direct labor hour. A summary of the product unit cost and other relevant information under normal costing follow:

	Rigger II	BioScout
Product costs per unit:		
Direct materials	$ 10,000.00	$12,000.00
Direct labor	450.00	600.00
Manufacturing overhead	412.50*	550.00**
Product unit cost	$ 10,862.50	$13,150.00
Units of production	400	100
Estimated direct labor hours	12,000	4,000
Estimated manufacturing overhead costs	$220,000	

* Applied to Rigger II = $13.75 per direct labor hour × 30 direct labor hours per unit
** Applied to BioScout = $13.75 per direct labor hour × 40 direct labor hours per unit

Blanca believes that the product unit cost is too low for the BioScout line. After carefully watching the production process, she believes that the BioScout requires much more attention than the Rigger II, since suppliers perform many subassemblies for the Rigger II, and the intricate design of the BioScout requires more production-related activities to complete the production process. Blanca created four overhead activity pools, grouped the estimated manufacturing overhead costs into related cost pools, selected a cost driver for each pool, and estimated the cost driver for each product line, as shown in the following summary.

Overhead Activity Pool	Estimated Activity Cost Pool
Setup	$70,000
Inspection	20,000
Engineering	50,000
Assembly	80,000
Total	$220,000

Cost Driver	Rigger II Cost Driver Level	BioScout Cost Driver Level	Total Cost Driver Level
Number of setups	250	450	700
Number of inspections	150	350	500
Engineering hours	600	1,400	2,000
Machine hours	5,000	5,000	10,000

REQUIRED

1. Using the activity-based costing approach:
   a. Calculate the overhead cost pool rates for each cost pool.
   b. Compute the overhead costs applied to each product line by cost pool and in total.
   c. Calculate the product unit cost for each product line.
2. What differences in the costs assigned to the two product lines resulted from the shift to activity-based costing?

EXPANDING YOUR CRITICAL THINKING, COMMUNICATION, AND INTERPERSONAL SKILLS

Skills Development

CONCEPTUAL ANALYSIS

SD 1.

LO 5 LO 6 LO 7 *Computation of Predetermined Overhead Rates*

Both ***Brown Company*** and ***Santo Corporation*** use predetermined overhead rates for product costing, inventory valuation, and sales quotations. The two businesses are about the same size, and they compete in the corrugated box industry. Brown Company's management believes that because the predetermined overhead rate is an estimated measure, the controller's department should spend little effort in developing it. The company computes the rate once a year based on a trend analysis of the previous year's costs. No one monitors its accuracy during the year.

Santo Corporation takes a much more sophisticated approach. One person in the controller's office is responsible for developing predetermined overhead rates on a monthly basis. All cost estimates are checked carefully to make sure they are realistic. Accuracy checks are done routinely during each monthly closing analysis, and forecasts of changes in business activity are taken into account.

Assume you are a consultant who has been hired by the ***Corwin Corporation,*** an East Coast manufacturer of corrugated boxes. Lisa Nyman wants you to recommend the best approach for developing overhead rates. Based on your knowledge of the practices described above, write a memo to Lisa Nyman that will answer the following questions.

1. What are the advantages and disadvantages of each company's approach to developing predetermined overhead rates?
2. Which company has taken the more cost-effective approach to developing predetermined overhead rates? Defend your answer.
3. Is an accurate overhead rate most important for product costing, inventory valuation, or sales quotations? Why?
4. Would activity-based costing (ABC) be better than the two approaches discussed above? What conditions should exist before a company adopts ABC?

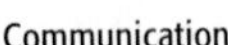
Communication

Critical Thinking

Group Activity

Memo

Ethics

International

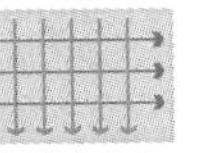
Spreadsheet

Managerial Technology

Internet

Ethical Dilemma

SD 2.
LO 9 *Preventing Pollution and the Costs of Waste Disposal*

Pleasanton Power Plant currently provides power to a metropolitan area of 4 million people. Tamika Simms, the controller for the plant, just returned from a conference about the Environmental Protection Agency's regulations concerning pollution prevention. She met with Jake Gates, the president of the company, to discuss the impact of the EPA's regulations on the plant.

"Jake, I'm really concerned. We haven't been monitoring the disposal of the radioactive material we send to the Digger Disposal Plant. If Digger is disposing of our waste material improperly, we could be sued," said Tamika. "We also haven't been recording the costs of the waste as part of our product cost. Ignoring that cost will have a negative impact on our decision about the next rate hike."

"Tamika, don't worry. I don't think we need to concern ourselves with the waste we send to Digger. We pay them to dispose of it. They take it off of our hands, and it's their responsibility to manage its disposal. As for the cost of waste disposal, I think we would have a hard time justifying a rate increase based on a requirement to record the full cost of waste as a cost of producing power. Let's just forget about waste and its disposal as a component of our power cost. We can get our rate increase without mentioning waste disposal," replied Jake.

What responsibility does Pleasanton Power Plant have to monitor the condition of the waste at the Digger Disposal Plant? Should Tamika take Jake's advice to ignore waste disposal costs in calculating the cost of power? Be prepared to discuss your response.

Research Activity

SD 3.
LO 2
LO 3 *Variable and Fixed Costs*

Make a trip to a local fast-food restaurant. Observe all aspects of the operation and take notes on the entire process. Describe the procedures used to take, process, and fill an order and get the food to the customer. Based on your observations, make a list of the costs incurred by the owner. Then identify at least three direct costs and three indirect costs of making sandwiches. Bring your notes to class and report your findings.

Group Activity: Divide the class into groups and ask them to discuss this SD. Then ask a person from each group to summarize his or her group's discussion.

Decision-Making Practice

SD 4.
LO 9 *Unit Costs for a Service Business*

Keaton Municipal Hospital relies heavily on cost data to keep its pricing structures in line with those of competitors. The hospital provides a wide range of services, including nursing care in intensive care units, intermediate care units, the neonatal (newborn) nursery, and nursing administration.

Ella Walton, the hospital's controller, is concerned about the profits being generated from the thirty-bed intensive care unit (ICU), so she is reviewing current billing procedures. The focus of Ella's analysis is Keaton's billing per patient day. The billing per patient day equals the cost of a patient day in the ICU plus a markup of an additional 40 percent of cost to cover other operating costs and to generate a profit.

ICU patient costs include the following:

Doctors' care	2 hours per day @ $360 per hour (actual)
Special nursing care	4 hours per day @ $85 per hour (actual)
Regular nursing care	24 hours per day @ $28 per hour (average)
Medications	$237 per day (average)
Medical supplies	$134 per day (average)
Room rental	$350 per day (average)
Food and services	$140 per day (average)

One other significant cost is equipment, which costs about $185,000 per room. Ella has determined that the cost per patient day for the equipment is $179.

Paul Sautter, the hospital director, has asked Ella to review the current billing procedure and compare it to another procedure using industry averages to determine the billing per patient day.

1. Compute the cost per patient per day.
2. Compute the billing per patient day using the hospital's existing markup rate. Round answers to whole dollars.

3. Many hospitals use separate markup rates for each cost when preparing billing statements. Industry averages revealed the following markup rates:

Equipment	30 percent	Medications	50
Doctors' care	50	Medical supplies	50
Special nursing care	40	Room rental	30
Regular nursing care	50	Food and services	25

Using these rates, recompute the billing per patient day in the ICU. Round answers to whole dollars.

4. Based on your findings in **2** and **3,** which billing procedure would you recommend to the hospital's director? Why? Be prepared to discuss your response.

Managerial Reporting and Analysis

INTERPRETING MANAGEMENT REPORTS

MRA 1.

LO 4 *Analyzing Financial Statements*

Rico Manufacturing Company makes sheet metal products for heating and air conditioning installations. For the past several years, the income of the company has been declining, and this past year, 20x1, was particularly poor. The company's statement of cost of goods manufactured and its income statement for 20xx and 20x1 are shown below and on the following page.

Rico Manufacturing Company
Statements of Cost of Goods Manufactured
For the Years Ended December 31, 20x1 and 20xx

	20x1		20xx	
Direct Materials Used				
Direct Materials Inventory, January 1	$ 91,240		$ 93,560	
Direct Materials Purchased (net)	987,640		959,940	
Cost of Direct Materials Available for Use	$1,078,880		$1,053,500	
Less Direct Materials Inventory, December 31	95,020		91,240	
Cost of Direct Materials Used		$ 983,860		$ 962,260
Direct Labor Costs		571,410		579,720
Manufacturing Overhead Costs				
Indirect Labor	$ 182,660		$ 171,980	
Power	34,990		32,550	
Insurance	22,430		18,530	
Supervision	125,330		120,050	
Depreciation	75,730		72,720	
Other Manufacturing Costs	41,740		36,280	
Total Manufacturing Overhead Costs		482,880		452,110
Total Manufacturing Costs		$2,038,150		$1,994,090
Add Work in Process Inventory, January 1		148,875		152,275
Total Cost of Work in Process During the Year		$2,187,025		$2,146,365
Less Work in Process Inventory, December 31		146,750		148,875
Cost of Goods Manufactured		$2,040,275		$1,997,490

Rico Manufacturing Company
Income Statements
For the Years Ended December 31, 20x1 and 20xx

	20x1		20xx	
Net Sales		$2,942,960		$3,096,220
Cost of Goods Sold				
Finished Goods Inventory, January 1	$ 142,640		$ 184,820	
Cost of Goods Manufactured	2,040,275		1,997,490	
Total Cost of Finished Goods Available for Sale	$2,182,915		$2,182,310	
Less Finished Goods Inventory, December 31	186,630		142,640	
Cost of Goods Sold		1,996,285		2,039,670
Gross Margin		$ 946,675		$1,056,550
Selling and Administrative Expenses				
Sales Salaries and Commission Expense	$ 394,840		$ 329,480	
Advertising Expense	116,110		194,290	
Other Selling Expenses	82,680		72,930	
Administrative Expenses	242,600		195,530	
Total Selling and Administrative Expenses		836,230		792,230
Income from Operations		$ 110,445		$ 264,320
Other Revenues and Expenses				
Interest Expense		54,160		56,815
Income Before Income Taxes		$ 56,285		$ 207,505
Less Income Taxes Expense		19,137		87,586
Net Income		$ 37,148		$ 119,919

You have been asked to comment on why the company's profitability has deteriorated.

REQUIRED

1. In preparing your comments on the decline in income, compute the following ratios for each year:
   a. Ratios of cost of direct materials used to total manufacturing costs, direct labor costs to total manufacturing costs, and total manufacturing overhead costs to total manufacturing costs. Round to one decimal place.
   b. Ratios of sales salaries and commission expense, advertising expense, other selling expenses, administrative expenses, and total selling and administrative expenses to net sales. Round to one decimal place.
   c. Ratios of gross margin to net sales, total selling and administrative expenses to net sales, and net income to net sales. Round to one decimal place.
2. From your evaluation of the ratios computed in **1**, state the probable causes of the decline in net income.
3. What other factors or ratios do you believe should be considered in determining the cause of the company's decreased income?

FORMULATING MANAGEMENT REPORTS

MRA 2.
LO 9 *Management Decision for a Supporting Service Function*

As the manager of grounds maintenance for ***INNET,*** a large insurance company in California, you are responsible for maintaining the grounds surrounding the three buildings, the six entrances to the property, and the recreational facilities, which include a golf course, a soccer field, jogging and bike paths, and tennis, basketball, and volleyball courts. Maintenance activities include gardening (watering, mowing, trimming, sweeping, and removing debris) and upkeep of land improvements (repairing concrete and gravel areas and replacing damaged or worn recreational equipment).

Early in January 20x2, you received a memo from the president requesting information about the cost of operating your department for the last twelve months. She has received a bid from Fantastic Landscapes, Inc., to perform the gardening activities you now perform. You are to prepare a cost report that will help the president in deciding whether to continue gardening activities within the company or to outsource the work to another company.

REQUIRED

1. Before preparing your report, answer the following questions.
   a. What kinds of information do you need about your department?
   b. Why is this information relevant?
   c. Where would you go to obtain this information (sources)?
   d. When would you want to obtain this information?
2. Prepare a draft of the cost report that would best communicate the costs of your department. Show only headings and line items. How would you change your report if the president asked you to reduce the costs of operating your department?
3. One of your department's costs is Maintenance Expense, Garden Equipment.
   a. Is it a direct or indirect cost for the Grounds Maintenance Department?
   b. Is it a product or a period cost?
   c. Is it a variable or a fixed cost?
   d. Does the activity add value to the provision of insurance services?
   e. Is it a budgeted or an actual cost in your report?

INTERNATIONAL COMPANY

MRA 3.
LO 4 *Management Information Needs*

The ***Muntok Pharmaceuticals Corporation*** manufactures the majority of its three pharmaceutical products in Indonesia. Inventory information for April 20x1 was as follows:

Account	April 30	April 1
Direct Materials Inventory	$228,100	$258,400
Work in Process Inventory	127,200	138,800
Finished Goods Inventory	114,100	111,700

Purchases of direct materials for April were $612,600, which included natural materials, basic organic compounds, catalysts, and suspension agents. Direct labor costs were $160,000, and actual manufacturing overhead costs were $303,500. Net sales for the company's three pharmaceutical products for April were $2,188,400. General and administrative expenses were $362,000. Income is taxed at a rate of 34 percent.

REQUIRED

1. Prepare a statement of cost of goods manufactured and an income statement for the month ended April 30.
2. Explain why the total manufacturing costs do not equal the cost of goods manufactured.
3. What additional information would you need to determine the profitability of each pharmaceutical product line?
4. Tell whether each of the following is a product cost or a period cost:
   a. Import duties for suspension agent materials
   b. Shipping expenses to deliver manufactured products to the United States
   c. Rent on manufacturing facilities in Jakarta
   d. Salary of the American production line manager working at the Indonesian manufacturing facilities
   e. Training costs for an Indonesian accountant

Excel Spreadsheet Analysis

MRA 4.

LO 5 **LO 6** **LO 7** **LO 8** *Application of Manufacturing Overhead: Traditional and Activity-Based Costing Approaches*

Refer to assignment **P 8** in this chapter. Assume that Blanca Gonzales, the controller of Shark Scout, Inc., has received some additional information from the production manager, James Koloc. Mr. Koloc reported that robotic equipment has been installed on the factory floor to increase productivity. Depreciation and other machine costs for the robots will increase total manufacturing overhead from $220,000 to $320,000 for the year, which will increase the assembly activity cost pool from $80,000 to $180,000. The cost driver level for the assembly cost pool will change from 5,000 machine hours to 2,000 machine hours for the Rigger II and from 5,000 machine hours to 8,000 machine hours for the BioScout. The cost driver levels and cost pool amounts for setup, inspection, and engineering activities will remain the same.

REQUIRED

1. Using the traditional approach:
   a. Calculate the predetermined overhead rate.
   b. Compute the amount of the total manufacturing overhead costs applied to each product line.
   c. Calculate the product unit cost for each product line.
2. Using the activity-based costing approach:
   a. Calculate the manufacturing overhead cost pool rates for each cost pool.
   b. Compute the manufacturing overhead costs applied to each product line by cost pool and in total.
   c. Calculate the product unit cost for each product line.
3. Complete the following table and discuss the differences in the costs assigned to the two product lines resulting from the additional information in this assignment.

Product unit cost	Rigger II	BioScout
Traditional		
Activity-based costing		
Difference: decrease (increase)		

ENDNOTES

1. Tim R.V. Davis and Bruce L. Darling, "ABC in a Virtual Corporation," *Management Accounting*, Institute of Management Accountants, October 1996, pp. 18–26.
2. Neal R. Pemberton, Logan Arumugam, and Nabil Hassan, "From Obstacles to Opportunities," *Management Accounting*, Institute of Management Accountants, March 1996, pp. 20–27.
3. Kathy Williams and James Hart, "Walker: Deploying a Mainframe Solution," *Management Accounting*, Institute of Management Accountants, June 1997, pp. 49–52.

Product Costing: The Job Order and Process Costing Systems

LEARNING OBJECTIVES

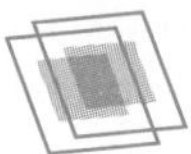

1. **Identify the types of product costing systems and state how managers use product costing information.**
2. **Explain the cost flow in a job order costing system.**
3. **Prepare a job order cost card and compute a job order's product unit cost.**
4. **Explain the product flow and the cost flow in a process costing system.**
5. **Prepare a process cost report: (a) use a schedule of equivalent production to compute equivalent units of production, (b) use a unit cost analysis schedule to compute product unit cost for a specific time period, and (c) complete a cost summary schedule that assigns costs to units completed and transferred out during the period, and compute the ending balance in the Work in Process Inventory account.**
6. **Compare the characteristics of the job order and process costing systems and explain the role of the Work in Process Inventory account(s) in the two product costing systems.**
7. **Evaluate operating performance using product costing information.**

DECISION POINT

KUNDE ESTATE WINERY

Kunde Estate Winery is located in California's Sonoma Valley. Kunde is considered an estate winery because it grows or controls the growth of at least 95 percent of the grapes it uses in its wines. The wine-making process differs for white and red wines, but both must be aged from eight to eighteen months in stainless steel tanks or oak barrels before being bottled and released for distribution.[1]

Determining the product unit cost of a bottle of wine creates special problems and requires the blending of the job order and process costing approaches into a hybrid system. The process of taking the picked grapes and turning them into a fermented solution requires a process costing approach. But once the wine maker begins to work with the fermented solutions, blending other types of grapes with varietals such as Cabernet Sauvignon or Chardonnay, the uniqueness of the resulting wines suggests

Critical Thinking Question: Why is it important to design product costing systems that reflect production processes? **Answer:** To help managers make better product costing and pricing decisions.

the need for a job order system. Tracing production and aging costs to specific lots of wine involves many allocations, but tracking the cost of blending and refining the wine requires a different kind of attention. What types of problems do wineries encounter in this critical costing area? How could Kunde Estate Winery overcome this problem?

Blending takes place during the aging process and usually begins about three months after the initial solution of crushed, destemmed grapes was produced. The wine maker experiments with different combinations of grapes at different stages in the eight- to eighteen-month aging process. Some white varietals can be easily developed, whereas some red varietals are very complex and take months to develop. The controller at Kunde Winery created a tracking system that records the activities of the wine maker. The time spent on each batch of each varietal wine is recorded. Then, all costs connected with the wine maker's activities are assigned to a batch or lot of wine based on the amount of time the wine maker took to produce it. The new approach is a version of activity-based costing applied to a hybrid product costing system.

Types of Product Costing Systems and Their Uses

OBJECTIVE 1

Identify the types of product costing systems and state how managers use product costing information

Related Text Assignments:
Q: 1, 2, 3, 4
SE: 1
E: 1, 2
SD: 1
MRA: 1, 2, 3

One important purpose of a management accounting system is to determine the cost of manufacturing an individual product or batch of products or of constructing a large product, such as a bridge or a jet airplane. Such management accounting systems differ widely from one company to another, but each system is designed to provide information that management believes is important. To determine the cost of producing or constructing something, two basic product costing systems have been developed, the job order costing system and the process costing system. A job order costing system is a product costing system used by both service and manufacturing organizations that make large, unique, or special-order products. Under such a system, the costs of direct materials, direct labor, and manufacturing overhead are traced to specific job orders or batches of products. Companies such as Flour Construction and Boeing Company would use a job order approach. A process costing system is a product costing system used by organizations that have a continuous production flow yielding large amounts of similar products or liquids. Under such a system, the costs of direct materials, direct labor, and manufacturing overhead are first traced to a process or work cell and then assigned to the products produced by that process or work cell. Pepsi Cola Co. and Porter Paint Company would use a process costing system.

These two product costing systems are each designed for a specific type of production activity. But few actual production processes fit either of the production environments described. As discussed in the Decision Point about Kunde Estate Winery, the production process dictates the type of product costing system a company needs. As the production process changes, so does the product costing system. The typical product costing system in actual use incorporates parts of both the job order and the process costing systems to create a hybrid system designed specifically for a particular production process. It would be impossible to study all actual systems because they number in the thousands. However, by learning the terms and procedures connected with the basic job order and process costing systems, managers can adapt to any operating environment and help design product costing systems that fit their specific information needs.

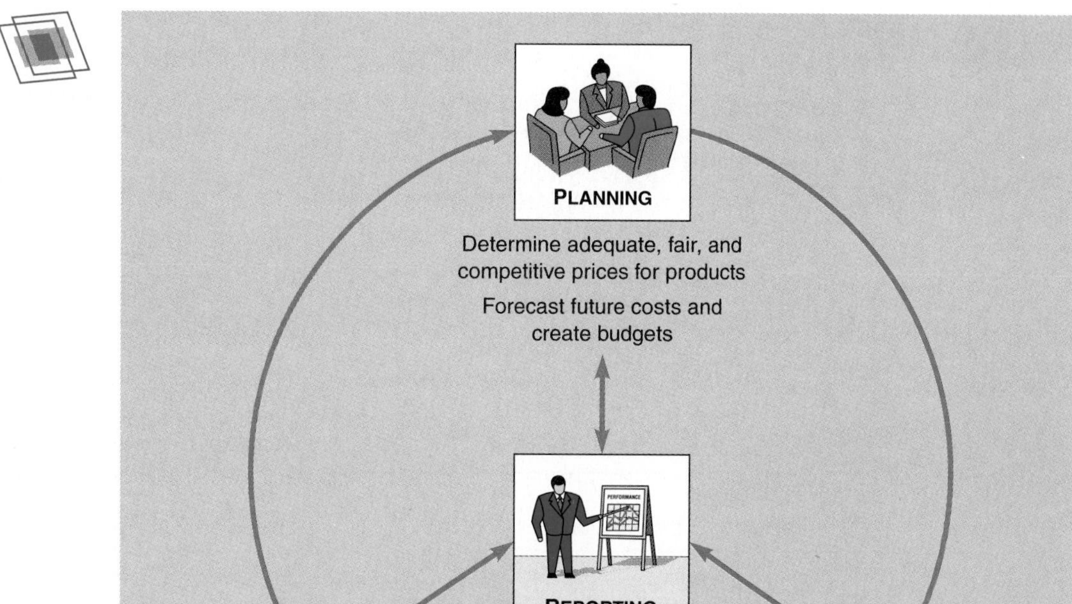

Figure 1
Product Costing and the Management Cycle

Product costing information is useful throughout the management cycle, as illustrated in Figure 1. During the planning stage, knowledge of unit costs helps managers determine adequate, fair, and competitive prices for products. In addition, managers use product cost information to forecast future costs and create budgets for the next operating period.

Managers often make decisions about the quality and cost of a product. For example, they may decide to improve the quality of a product or to lower a product's unit cost by using cheaper direct materials. Such decisions are implemented during the executing stage of the management cycle by making changes in design, purchasing, or production.

A decision to change a product's quality or cost can have far-reaching effects. For example, a decision to improve quality may cause product costs to rise, and a decision to cut product costs may cause quality to decline. Managers watch for such changes during the reviewing stage of the management cycle. The information gathered during the reviewing stage enables managers to control operations and costs. If operating costs have risen too high, a product unit cost can be broken down into its many components to analyze where costs can be cut. If product quality is suffering, the design, purchasing, and production processes can be studied to determine the source of the problem.

Finally, during the reporting stage of the management cycle, the management accountant prepares internal reports that show the period's actual product costs

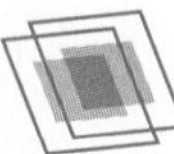

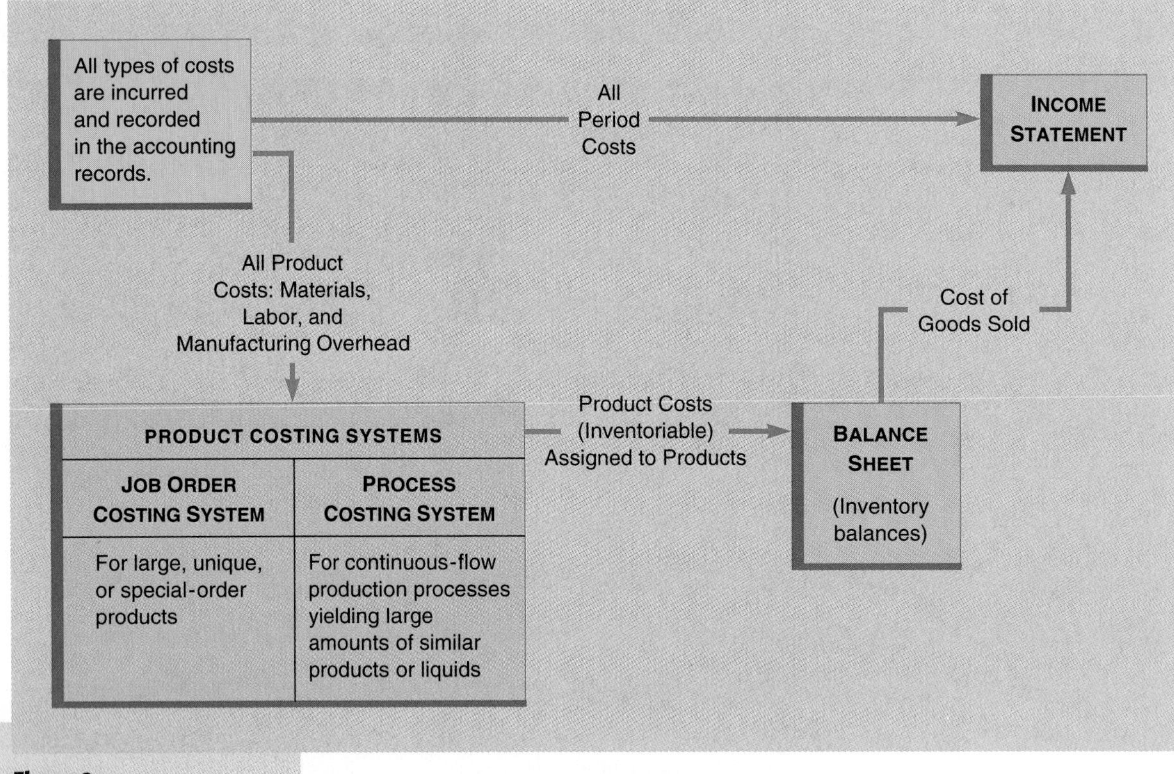

Figure 2
The Role of the Product Costing System

and compare them to budgeted costs. Managers use such reports to assess and adjust operations and plan for the future. Product unit costs are also used in financial reporting to determine inventory balances on the balance sheet and the cost of goods sold on the income statement.

The role of the product costing system is illustrated in Figure 2. First, costs of all types are incurred and recorded in various accounting records, including the general ledger. Period costs, once recorded, are used directly in developing the income statement. They are not used to develop product unit costs. All product costs—the costs of direct materials, direct labor, and manufacturing overhead—are routed through the product costing system, where they are assigned to the products produced. Product costing information is used to compute the ending balances of both the work in process and the finished goods inventories on the balance sheet. Product costs are also used to compute the cost of goods sold during the period, an important amount shown on the income statement.

Job Order Versus Process Costing

The job order costing system and the process costing system both have the same objective: to account for an organization's product costs and provide unit cost information for pricing, cost planning and control, inventory valuation, and income statement preparation. As illustrated in Figure 2, the product costing system provides end-of-period values for the Cost of Goods Sold account on the income statement and the Work in Process Inventory and Finished Goods Inventory accounts on the balance sheet.

Point to Emphasize: In a job order costing system, the specific job or batch of product, not a department or work center, is the focus of cost accumulation.

Job order costing begins when an organization receives a job order. A job order is a customer order for a specific number of specially designed, made-to-order products. To compute the product unit cost, the total manufacturing costs for each job are accumulated and divided by the number of good units produced. Users of job order costing systems include manufacturers of ships, airplanes, large machines, bridges, and buildings. An organization may also use job order costing when producing a set quantity of a product, such as 500 identical lawn mowers, to replenish inventory. The job order here would be the batch size produced.

Instructional Strategy: To reinforce the concept that product cost information is useful to managers, ask students to complete MRA 1. Divide the class into groups and have them compare answers. Then debrief the entire class by asking one person from each group to summarize his or her group's findings.

The continuous flow of a production process signals the need for a process costing system. Tracking individual costs to individual products is too difficult and too expensive and does not result in significantly different product costs. One gallon of green paint is identical to the next gallon. One brick looks just like the next brick. Each product is similar to the next and should cost the same amount to produce. A process costing system accumulates the costs of materials, labor, and manufacturing overhead for each process or work cell and assigns those costs equally to the products produced during a particular time period. Industries that produce paint, beverages, bricks, canned foods, milk, and paper are typical users of the process cost system. Companies that adopt the just-in-time operating philosophy also usually employ process costing procedures, because a continuous flow work cell or process is central to a JIT operation.

Product Costing in Service Organizations

Product costing is often associated with manufacturing organizations. However, some of the approaches to product costing discussed and illustrated in this chapter are also used by service organizations. For example, tracing labor and service overhead costs to specific jobs is useful for business consulting firms, accounting firms, automobile repair organizations, and home maintenance companies such as plumbers or electricians. Service organizations need to trace costs to the services they perform or design. Since a service is usually customer-specific, service organizations use job order costing. Because process costing is applied to operations that have a continuous flow or that produce large numbers of similar products, it is not adaptable to service organizations. A specific discussion of service costing is presented later in this chapter.

The Job Order Costing System

OBJECTIVE 2

Explain the cost flow in a job order costing system

Related Text Assignments:
Q: 5, 6, 7
SE: 2
E: 3
P: 1, 2, 6
SD: 4
MRA: 3

Remember that a job order costing system is designed to gather costs for a specific order or batch of products to help determine product unit costs. Price setting, production scheduling, and other management tasks related to job orders depend on information from the management accounting system. This is why it is necessary to maintain a system that gives timely, correct data about product costs. In this section, we see how the three main cost elements—direct materials, direct labor, and manufacturing overhead—are accounted for in a job order costing system. Notice that all inventory balances in a job order costing system are kept on a perpetual basis and that all production costs are included in the analysis.

Incurring Materials, Labor, and Manufacturing Overhead Costs

A basic part of a job order costing system is the set of procedures and accounts used when the company incurs materials, labor, and manufacturing overhead costs. In order to help control such costs, businesses use various documents to support each

Point to Emphasize: Product unit cost in a job order costing system is the total cost of the job or batch divided by the number of items in the job or batch. This is an average cost of the number of good units manufactured for that job or batch.

transaction. The effective use of procedures and documents generates timely, accurate information for managers and facilitates the smooth and continuous flow of information through the accounting records.

Materials Careful use of direct materials improves a company's overall efficiency and profitability by conserving productive resources and saving their related costs. At the same time, good records ensure accountability. So, controlling the physical materials used in production and keeping good records increase the opportunity to earn a profit.

To help record and control direct materials costs, accountants rely on a series of documents, including purchase requisitions, purchase orders, receiving reports, inventory records, and materials requisitions. Through these documents, direct materials are ordered, received, stored, and issued into production. Information from purchase requisitions enables the tracing of direct materials costs to specific jobs or batches of product and identifies the amount of indirect materials to be charged to manufacturing overhead.

Teaching Note: It is often helpful to describe the acquisition process and the purpose of the various documents related to this information cycle.

Labor Labor is one production resource that cannot be stored and used later, so it must be accounted for carefully. Time cards and job cards are used to record labor costs as they are incurred. Time cards keep track of the total time each employee works per day, and job cards track the amount of time each employee works on a particular job or other labor classification. Direct labor costs that can be traced directly to a job or batch of products are charged to the Work in Process Inventory Control account, and all indirect labor costs flow through the Manufacturing Overhead Control account.

Discussion Question: What is the purpose of maintaning both time cards and job cards? **Answer:** Time cards are used for payroll purposes, whereas job cards are used to distribute the costs of labor to various job orders worked on during the period.

Manufacturing Overhead All indirect manufacturing costs are classified as manufacturing overhead. Like direct materials and direct labor costs, manufacturing overhead costs require documents to support their recording and payment. As described above, materials requests support the use of indirect materials and supplies, and job cards track indirect labor; vendors' invoices support most of the other indirect costs. In a job order costing system, all manufacturing overhead costs are charged to the Manufacturing Overhead Control account, and separate subsidiary accounts are maintained to keep track of the individual kinds of overhead costs. Using a predetermined overhead rate, manufacturing overhead costs are assigned to individual jobs by decreasing the Manufacturing Overhead Control account and increasing the Work in Process Inventory Control account.

Cost Flow in a Job Order Costing System

Because a job order costing system emphasizes cost flow, it is important to understand how the various costs are incurred, recorded, and transferred within the system. This cost flow, along with the job order cost cards and the subsidiary ledgers for materials and finished goods inventories, form the core of the job order costing system. Understanding the cost flow enables you to fully understand how the system works.

The job order cost flow at Wasa Boat Company is diagrammed in Exhibit 1 on pages 944-945. Referring to Exhibit 1 will help you picture the flow of each cost in the following discussion.

Beginning Inventory Balances In Exhibit 1, the word *control* is found in all three inventory account titles, which means that each inventory account has a subsidiary ledger backing up its totals. The beginning balance of the Materials Inventory Control account is $123,000. It includes $83,000 of Material 5X, $37,000 of Material 14Q, and $3,000 of operating supplies. These amounts correspond to the beginning balances in the materials subsidiary ledger, shown in the lower part of Exhibit 1. The Work in Process Inventory Control account's beginning balance of $40,080 is related entirely to Job 16F, as shown on the subsidiary ledger's job order cost card. There is no beginning balance in Finished Goods Inventory Control, which means that all previously completed orders have been shipped.

Purchase of Direct Materials and Supplies During the period, the Wasa Boat Company bought direct materials and supplies totaling $99,400. Two transactions supported those purchases. Transaction **1** totaled $91,200 and involved the purchase of $57,200 of Material 5X and $34,000 of Material 14Q. Transaction **2** was the purchase of $8,200 of operating supplies.

Teaching Note: It is helpful to briefly explain the role of requisition forms and the controls they represent.

Requisition of Direct Materials and Supplies into Production Transaction **3** shows the requisition of materials and supplies into production. A total of $188,000 of direct materials costs are transferred from the Materials Inventory Control account to the Work in Process Inventory Control account. From the materials subsidiary ledger, you can see that the $188,000 is made up of $124,000 of Material 5X and $64,000 of Material 14Q. In addition, $9,600 of operating supplies were used. Since supplies are an indirect material, their cost was transferred to the Manufacturing Overhead Control account.

Ethical Consideration: Ask your students to describe the ethical considerations related to using requisitions or other control procedures within a business. For example, the quantity of materials requisitioned must be limited to those needed for a specific job.

Labor Costs for the Period The total cost of factory labor for the period was $240,000. As shown by Transaction **4,** this amount was entered in the Factory Payroll account. Factory Payroll is a clearing account, which means that it holds costs for only a short time, until they are distributed to the various production accounts. This distribution is shown in Transaction **5.** Of the total, $164,000 is for direct labor and is transferred directly to the Work in Process Inventory Control account. The remaining $76,000 is for indirect labor and is transferred to the Manufacturing Overhead Control account.

Point to Emphasize: Payroll liability distribution and payroll cost distribution are not the same.

Accounting for Other Manufacturing Overhead Costs Thus far, indirect materials and indirect labor have been the only costs charged to the Manufacturing Overhead Control account. Transaction **6** shows that other cash payments totaling $29,500 have been made during the period. Those cash payments were for electricity, $6,300; maintenance and repairs, $16,900; factory liability and fire insurance, $2,800; and property taxes, $3,500. The noncash expense of depreciation must also be accounted for in Manufacturing Overhead. Transaction **7** records the adjustment of $24,000 for the depreciation of plant, machinery, and equipment.

Point to Emphasize: Manufacturing Overhead Control is a cost pool of various manufacturing overhead accounts.

Applying Manufacturing Overhead Costs to Production For manufacturing overhead costs to be included in the production costs of the period, they must be applied using a predetermined overhead rate. The Wasa Boat Company's current overhead rate is 85 percent of direct labor dollars. In Transaction **8,** manufacturing overhead costs are applied to production by transferring $139,400 (85% of $164,000) from the Manufacturing Overhead Control account to the Work in Process Inventory Control account.

Point to Emphasize: Manufacturing overhead application is an assignment procedure using a predetermined overhead rate and an actual measured activity (machine hours, for example).

Tracing Costs to Specific Jobs At this point, all of the period's production costs have been transferred to the Work in Process Inventory Control account. Now it is necessary to relate the costs to specific jobs. This is done by tracing each cost in the Work in Process Inventory Control account to the job order cost cards in the subsidiary ledgers. (A job order cost card is a document on which all costs incurred in the production of a particular job order are recorded.) The Work in Process Inventory Control account at the top of Exhibit 1 shows that the total cost of direct materials used was $188,000. By looking at the job order cost cards at the bottom of

Exhibit 1. The Job Order Costing System—Wasa Boat Company

Materials Inventory Control

Beg. Bal.	123,000	Requisitions:	
(1) Purchases	91,200	Direct Materials	188,000 (3)
(2) Purchases	8,200	Supplies	9,600 (3)
End. Bal.	**24,800**		

Work in Process Inventory Control

Beg. Bal.	40,080	Completed	388,080 (9)
(3) Direct Materials Used	188,000		
(5) Direct Labor	164,000		
(8) Overhead	139,400		
End. Bal.	**143,400**		

Factory Payroll

(4) Wages Earned	240,000	Direct Labor	164,000 (5)
		Indirect Labor	76,000 (5)

Manufacturing Overhead Control

(3) Supplies Used	9,600	Applied	139,400 (8)
(5) Indirect Labor	76,000		
(6) Other	29,500		
(7) Adjustment	24,000		
	139,100		139,400
(11) To close	300		
	—		

SUBSIDIARY LEDGERS

MATERIALS LEDGER

Material 5X

Beg. Bal.	83,000	Used	124,000 (3)
(1) Purchases	57,200		
End. Bal.	**16,200**		

Material 14Q

Beg. Bal.	37,000	Used	64,000 (3)
(1) Purchases	34,000		
End. Bal.	**7,000**		

Operating Supplies Inventory

Beg. Bal.	3,000	Used	9,600 (3)
(2) Purchases	8,200		
End. Bal.	**1,600**		

JOB ORDER COST CARDS

Job 16F

Costs from the previous period	40,080
Direct Materials	103,800
Direct Labor	132,000
Manufacturing Overhead	112,200
Completed Cost	388,080

Job 23H

Direct Materials	84,200
Direct Labor	32,000
Manufacturing Overhead	27,200
Ending Balance	143,400

Exhibit 1, you can see that $103,800 of the total cost of direct materials was used for Job 16F and $84,200 was used for Job 23H. In the same way, the total direct labor costs of $164,000 can be traced to $132,000 for Job 16F and $32,000 for Job 23H. And the total manufacturing overhead cost of $139,400 can be traced to $112,200 for Job 16F and $27,200 for Job 23H.

At the end of the period, Job 16F has a total cost of $388,080 and Job 23H has a total cost of $143,400. At this point Job 16F has been completed, so its total cost is transferred to the Finished Goods Inventory Control account, as shown by

Finished Goods Inventory Control

Beg. Bal.	—	Sold	352,800 (10)
(9) Completed During Period	388,080		
End. Bal.	**35,280**		

Cost of Goods Sold

(10) Sold During Period	352,800	Adjustment	300 (11)
End. Bal.	**352,500**		

Reinforcement Exercises: Costs for Week 2 in the Cutting Department of ABC Company are: cutting machine operators' wages, $500; supervisor's salary, $300; supplies used, $100; materials cut, $400; and miscellaneous factory costs, $200. Which costs are assigned to Work in Process Inventory Control, and which are assigned to Manufacturing Overhead Control? **Answer:** Cutting machine operators' wages (direct labor) and materials cut (direct materials) are assigned to Work in Process Inventory Control. The supervisor's salary, supplies used, and miscellaneous factory costs are assigned to Manufacturing Overhead Control.

Teaching Note: Parts of entries 4 and 5 are not posted in Exhibit 1. Although they are necessary for an accurate accounting of payroll, they do not deal directly with product costs. Exhibit 1 focuses only on the flow of product costs through the accounts.

FINISHED GOODS LEDGER

Product 16F

Beg. Bal.	—	Sold	352,800 (10)
(9) Completed	388,080		
End. Bal.	**35,280**		

Product 23H

Beg. Bal.	—		

Transaction **9**. The ending balance in the Work in Process Inventory Control account is $143,400. That amount corresponds to the ending balance shown on the job order cost card for Job 23H because Job 23H is still in process at the end of the period.

Accounting for Completed Units The costs of completed units are placed in the Finished Goods Inventory Control account until the units are shipped to customers. At the Wasa Boat Company, units costing $388,080 (Job 16F) were completed and transferred to the Finished Goods Inventory Control account during the period.

Units from Job 16F with costs totaling $352,800 were then sold to customers, as shown by Transaction **10.** Their sale left an ending balance of $35,280 in the Finished Goods Inventory Control account. That balance corresponds to the ending balance for Product 16F in the finished goods subsidiary ledger.

Enrichment Note: The example shows the company used a perpetual inventory system. In a periodic inventory system, the cost of goods sold is calculated at the end of the period.

Accounting for Units Sold The costs of all units sold during the period are transferred from the Finished Goods Inventory Control account to the Cost of Goods Sold account. Transaction **10** shows this transfer of costs at the Wasa Boat Company.

Reinforcement Exercise: Bass Catcher's Lures reported actual manufacturing overhead of $100,000, a predetermined overhead application rate of $.50 per lure, and total lures manufactured of 205,500. Is manufacturing overhead underapplied or overapplied and by how much?
Answer: $2,750 overapplied [(205,500 × $.50) − $100,000].

Disposing of Underapplied or Overapplied Overhead For the final step, we return to the Manufacturing Overhead Control account. During the period, a total of $139,100 was charged to this account and $139,400 of manufacturing overhead was applied to production activities. As a result, manufacturing overhead was overapplied by $300. Rather than try to trace such a small amount to all of the units worked on during the period, the company prefers to close the overapplied balance to the Cost of Goods Sold account. Since production was overcharged by the amount of overapplied overhead, Transaction **11** closes out the balance in the Manufacturing Overhead Control account and reduces the total charges in the Cost of Goods Sold account by the $300.

The Job Order Cost Card

OBJECTIVE 3

Prepare a job order cost card and compute a job order's product unit cost

Related Text Assignments:
Q: 8, 9
SE: 3
E: 4, 5
P: 1, 2, 3, 6, 7
SD: 2,4

As shown in the discussion of Exhibit 1, job order cost cards play a key role in the job order costing system. Because all manufacturing costs are accumulated in the Work in Process Inventory Control account, a separate accounting procedure is needed to relate those costs to specific jobs. The solution is a subsidiary ledger made up of job order cost cards. Each job being worked on has a job order cost card. As costs are incurred, they are classified by job and recorded on the appropriate job order cost card.

A typical job order cost card is shown in Figure 3. Each card has space for direct materials, direct labor, and manufacturing overhead costs. It also includes the job order number, product specifications, the name of the customer, the date of the order, the projected completion date, and a cost summary. As each department incurs materials and labor costs, the individual job order cost cards are updated. Manufacturing overhead, as applied, is also posted to the job order cost cards. Job

BUSINESS BULLETIN: **BUSINESS PRACTICE**

Xerox Corporation had a problem with errors in its customer billing process. In fact, an analysis revealed that each billing error cost the company an average of $106. The cost per billing error was computed using the salaries of the people answering customer complaints about billing errors and the costs of related postage, computer time, and clerical support. A quality improvement team of Xerox employees created a series of Captain Zero cartoons illustrating typical billing bloopers. The result was a significant decrease in billing errors and a steady rise in customer satisfaction with the billing process. This simple change in business practice saved Xerox over $110,000 in the six-month period under review—and cost only about $7,000.[2]

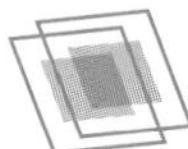

JOB ORDER COST CARD
Wasa Boat Company
New Port Richey, Florida

Job Order No. 16F

Product Specs: Model GB30-Mark I: 30 foot fiberglass sailing sloop with full galley

Customer: Hinds Yachts, Inc.

Date of Order: February 10, 20xx

Date of Completion: October 28, 20xx

Cost Summary:

Direct Materials	$120,200
Direct Labor	144,800
Manufacturing Overhead	123,080
Total	$388,080
Units Completed	11 (eleven)

Product Unit Cost $35,280

Direct Materials:

Dept. 1	$96,500
Dept. 2	23,700
Dept. 3	-0-
Total	$120,200

Direct Labor:

Dept. 1	$43,440
Dept. 2	60,960
Dept. 3	40,400
Total	$144,800

Applied Manufacturing Overhead:

Dept. 1	$36,924
Dept. 2	51,816
Dept. 3	34,340
Total	$123,080

Figure 3
Job Order Cost Card

Terminology Note: A job order cost card can take the form of an actual card in a card file, a reporting form on a clipboard, a computer file, or a record in a data base. Each form captures essentially the same information.

order cost cards for incomplete jobs make up the subsidiary ledger for the Work in Process Inventory Control account. To ensure correctness, the ending balance in the Work in Process Inventory Control account is compared with the total of the costs shown on the job order cost cards.

Computing Product Unit Costs

Product unit costs are fairly simple to calculate in a job order costing system. All costs of direct materials, direct labor, and manufacturing overhead are recorded on a job order cost card as a job progresses toward completion. When a job is finished, the costs on its job order cost card are totaled. The product unit cost is computed by dividing the total costs for the job by the number of good units produced.

The cost data for completed Job 16F are shown on the job order cost card in Figure 3. Eleven sailing sloops were produced at a total cost of $388,080. This worked out to a cost of $35,280 per sloop before adjustments. As shown in Exhibit 1, however, only ten of the sloops were actually shipped during the period. Because the amount of overapplied overhead was small, the entire $300 was used to reduce the cost of the ten sloops sold. The cost of one sloop still remains in the Finished Goods Inventory Control account at the unadjusted amount.

Job Order Costing in Service Organizations

Janesco Plumbing Company employs 30 people and serves the metropolitan Minneapolis area. The company earns roughly half of its revenue from plumbing installations in new homes and half from plumbing repairs and remodeling of existing homes. Job order cost cards are used to keep track of the costs incurred for each plumbing job. Job costs are categorized as direct materials, direct labor, or service overhead. Each job is based on a contract that requires the customer to pay for all costs incurred plus a predetermined amount of profit. Such contracts are called *cost-plus contracts,* and the "plus" provides a profit based on the amount of costs incurred.

The job order cost card for one of Janesco Plumbing's new home projects is shown in Figure 4. Costs have been categorized into three activities: plumbing system design, system installation, and job-site cleanup. Costs have been tracked to this job, the Clorisson Job, for the duration of the project, and now that the job has been finished, it is time to complete the job order cost card. The service overhead charge for plumbing system design is 30 percent of engineering labor cost, and the service overhead cost for system installation is 50 percent of direct labor cost. Total costs incurred for this job were $29,560. The cost-plus contract has a 25 percent profit guarantee, so $7,390 of profit margin is added to the total cost to arrive at the total contract revenue of $36,950, which is the amount billed to the customer. Janesco finds it useful to compare the cost of each activity to the total costs incurred. On the Clorisson job, 10.01 percent of the costs were design-related, 87.96 percent were installation-related, and 2.03 percent went for cleanup activities.

This example can be applied to almost any type of service organization, from auto repair shops to home pool companies to landscape businesses. Organizations such as banks and insurance companies also use job order costing to track the costs of the services they offer. It is important for them to know the service unit costs of such activities as processing loan applications or developing insurance policies.

The Process Costing System

OBJECTIVE 4

Explain the product flow and cost flow in a process costing system

Related Text Assignments:
Q: 10, 11
SE: 4
E: 6
SD: 3
MRA: 3

A process costing system is needed by businesses that manufacture liquid products or that continuously manufacture the same product over an extended time period. Products flow in a FIFO (first-in, first-out) manner. In such a process, it is difficult to determine when one batch ends and another begins.

Production Flows in a Process Costing System

In companies that use process costing, the steps in the production process can combine in hundreds of ways. Two basic production flows are illustrated in Figure 5. Example 1 shows a series of three processing steps or departments. The completed product from one department becomes the direct materials for the next department. Such a production flow can include from two to a dozen or more departments, or processes. The product unit cost is the sum of the cost elements in all departments.

Example 2 in Figure 5 shows a different kind of production flow. Again there are three departments, but the product does not flow through all departments in a simple 1-2-3 order. Instead, two separate products are developed, one in Department X and the other in Department Y. Both products then go to Department Z, where they are joined with a third direct material, Material AH. The unit cost transferred to the Finished Goods Inventory account when the products are completed includes cost elements from Departments X, Y, and Z.

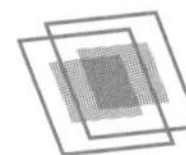

JOB ORDER COST CARD
Janesco Plumbing Company
Minneapolis, Minnesota

Customer: Clorisson
Contract Date: January 12, 20xx
Contract Type: Cost-Plus
Type of Service: New Home
Target Completion Date: October 15, 20xx
Job Status: Completed

Costs Charged to Job	**Previous Months**	**Current Month**	**Total Cost**
Plumbing System Design			
Supplies	$750	$0	$750
Engineering Labor	1,450	250	1,700
Service Overhead *(30% of Engineering Labor)*	435	75	510
Totals	$2,635	$325	$2,960
System Installation			
Materials and Supplies	$3,450	$2,150	$5,600
Direct Labor	7,200	6,400	13,600
Service Overhead *(50% of Direct Labor)*	3,600	3,200	6,800
Totals	$14,250	$11,750	$26,000
Job-Site Cleanup			
Janitorial Service Cost	$75	$525	$600
Totals	$16,960	$12,600	$29,560

Cost Summary to Date	**Total Cost**	**Percentage of Total Cost**
Plumbing System Design	$2,960	10.01%
System Installation	26,000	87.96%
Job-Site Cleanup	600	2.03%
Totals	$29,560	100.00%
Profit Margin (25%)	7,390	
Total Contract Revenue	$36,950	

Figure 4
Job Order Cost Card–Service Organization

Point to Emphasize: In process costing, costs are assigned to production processes; in job order costing, costs are assigned to jobs.

Cost Flows in a Process Costing System

Because of the nature of a process industry, products flow in a first-in, first-out (FIFO) pattern. In a FIFO production flow, the first item entering the process must be the first one completed. The production flows diagrammed in Figure 5 are based on a FIFO pattern.

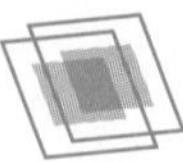

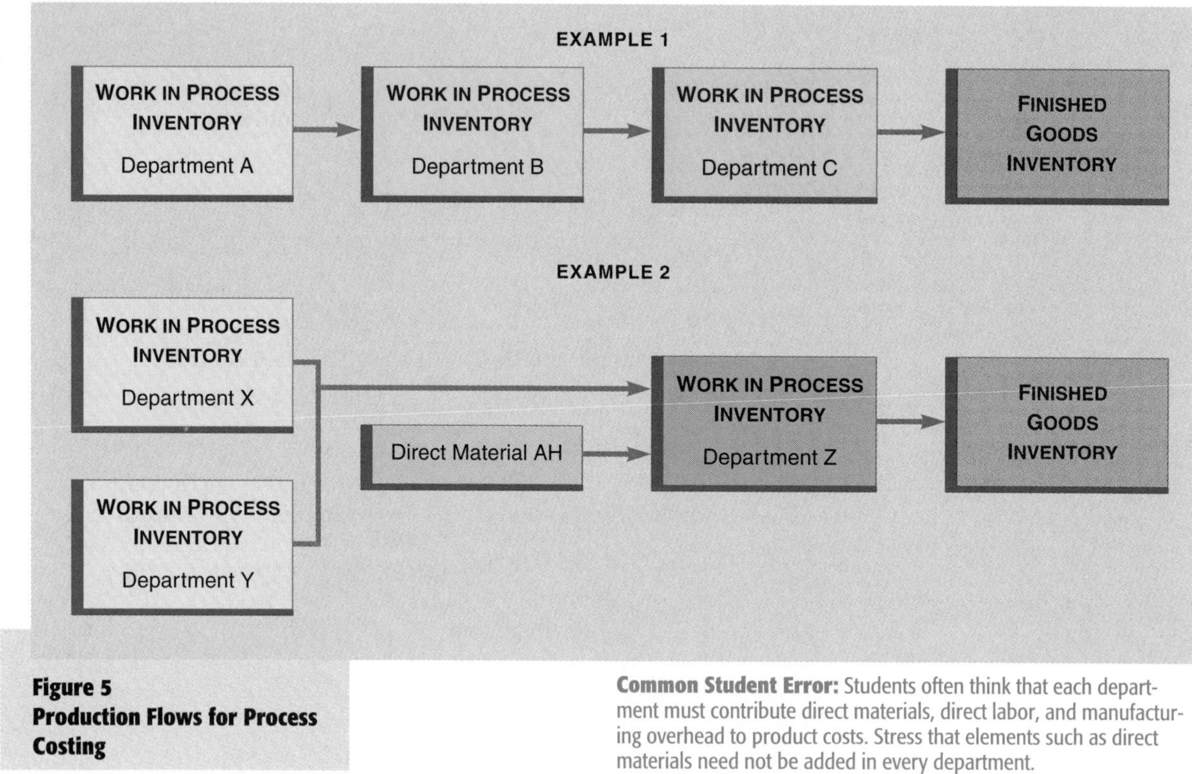

Figure 5
Production Flows for Process Costing

Common Student Error: Students often think that each department must contribute direct materials, direct labor, and manufacturing overhead to product costs. Stress that elements such as direct materials need not be added in every department.

Point to Emphasize: Total product cost is a flow-through concept in which each department's work adds cost to the product.

In process costing, costs are assigned to products using the FIFO costing approach. Under this approach, the cost flow follows the product flow. Just as the first products to be introduced into the production process are the first products to be completed, the costs assigned to the first products are the first costs to be transferred out of the production center or department.

OBJECTIVE 5a

Prepare a process cost report: Use a schedule of equivalent production to compute equivalent units of production

The Process Cost Report

A process cost report helps managers track and analyze costs in a process costing system. The process cost report consists of three schedules: the schedule of equivalent production, the unit cost analysis schedule, and the cost summary schedule.

Related Text Assignments:
Q: 12, 13, 14, 15, 16, 17
SE: 5, 6, 7, 8
E: 7, 8, 9, 10, 11
P: 4, 5, 8
MRA: 4

Teaching Note: Stress the need to focus on the work done in the current period only.

Teaching Note: Emphasize that work in the current period is applied to three distinct product groups: units in beginning Work in Process Inventory, which must be completed; goods started and completed during the period; and goods started but not completed by the end of the accounting period.

The Schedule of Equivalent Production A key feature of a process costing system is the computation of equivalent units of production for each department or process for each accounting period. This computation is needed before product unit costs can be computed. In process costing, an averaging approach is used. No attempt is made to associate costs with particular job orders. Instead, all manufacturing costs incurred in a department or process are divided by the units produced during the period. There are, however, several important questions to answer about the number of units produced. Exactly how many units were produced? Do we count only those units completed during the period? What about partly completed units in the beginning work in process inventory? Do we count them even if only part of the work needed to complete them was done during the period? And what about products in the ending work in process inventory? Is it proper to focus on only those units started and completed during the period?

The answers to all these questions relate to the concept of equivalent production. Equivalent production (also called *equivalent units*) is a measure of the number of equivalent whole units produced in a period of time. This measure restates partly

BUSINESS BULLETIN: BUSINESS PRACTICE

A study conducted by the Institute of Management Accountants found that 52 percent of 112 companies surveyed used process costing procedures. Of the companies that used process costing, 58 percent used the FIFO cost flow assumption, 21 percent used a variant of the FIFO approach, and 21 percent used an approach called average costing.[3]

Common Student Error: The percentage of completion for beginning Work in Process Inventory is for informational purposes only. Since equivalent production is a results-oriented concept, the amount of effort required to *complete* beginning Work in Process Inventory is the relevant percentage.

Point to Emphasize: The concept of good output is a central theme. Equivalent production is calculated as an output concept.

completed units in terms of equivalent whole units. The number of equivalent units produced is equal to the sum of (1) total units started and completed during the period and (2) an amount representing the work done on partially completed products in both the beginning and the ending work in process inventories. A percentage of completion factor is applied to partially completed units to calculate the number of equivalent whole units.

Figure 6 illustrates the computation of equivalent units. One computer was in process at the beginning of Week 2, three were started and completed during Week 2, and one was still in process at period end. Actually, one-half (.5) of Computer A and three-quarters (.75) of Computer E were completed during Week 2. The total equivalent units for the month are found by adding together the units started and completed (3.0) and the units partly completed (.5 and .75). Therefore, equivalent production for Week 2 is 4.25 units.

Figure 6
Computation of Equivalent Units

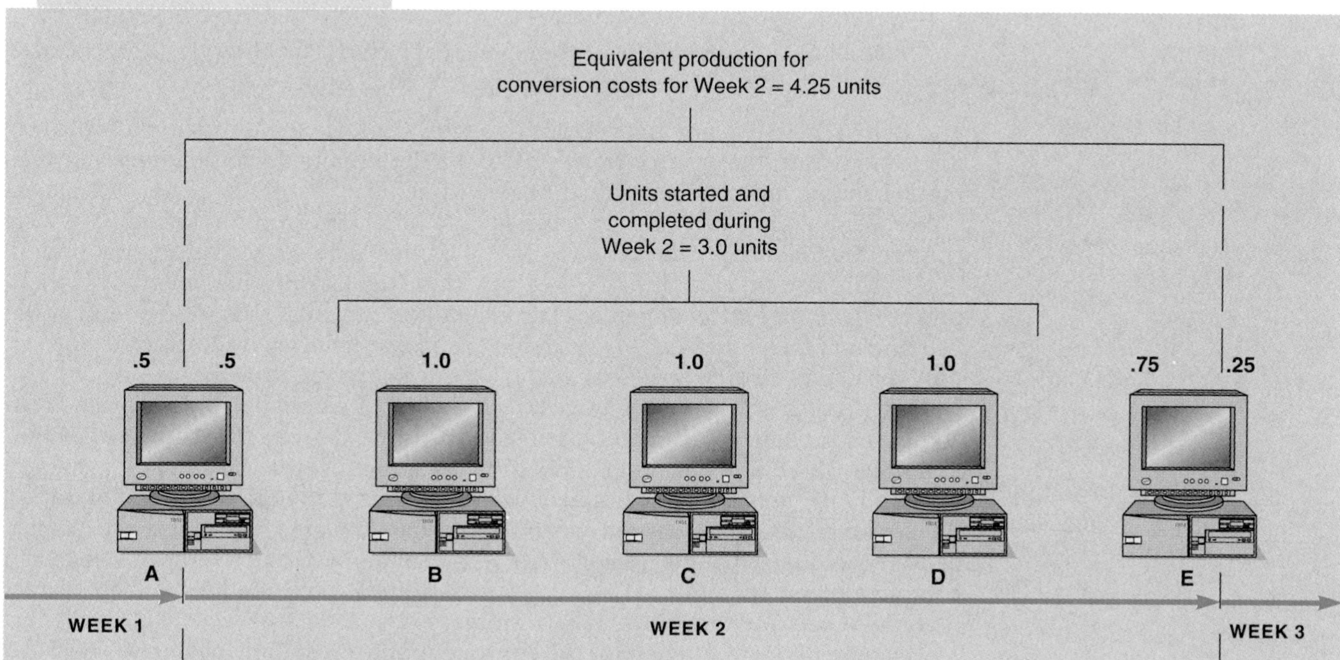

Conversion costs (the cost of direct labor and manufacturing overhead) are incurred uniformly as each computer moves through production. Equivalent production for Week 2 is 4.25 units for conversion costs. But materials costs are all added to production at the beginning of the process. Since four computers entered production in Week 2 (computers B, C, D, and E), equivalent production for the week is 4.0 units for materials costs.

The foregoing method is used to determine equivalent production for conversion costs, which are the combined total of direct labor and manufacturing overhead costs incurred by a production department. Because direct labor and manufacturing overhead are often incurred uniformly throughout the production process, it is convenient to combine them when determining unit cost.

Raw materials are usually added at the beginning of a process, however, so equivalent units for direct materials costs are computed in a different way. As shown in Figure 6, direct materials for Computer A were added in Week 1 and therefore do not influence equivalent units for direct materials in Week 2. However, direct materials for Computer E were *all* added to production in Week 2. So, 3.0 (units started and completed—Computers B, C, and D) is added to 1.0 (unit started but not completed—Computer E) to get the equivalent units for direct materials for Week 2, 4.0 units.

Common Student Error: Since many sample situations simplify the solution by stating that direct materials are added at the beginning of the process, students often think that direct materials are always placed in production then. Explain situations in which direct materials are added at different stages of production (e.g., for paint, packaging cans are added at the end).

Once you know the number of equivalent units produced, you can compute unit costs for direct materials and conversion costs for each department or work cell in the production process. The equations for computing the unit cost amounts are as follows (note the role of equivalent units):

$$\text{Unit Cost for Direct Materials} = \frac{\text{Total Direct Materials Costs}}{\text{Equivalent Units for Direct Materials Costs}}$$

$$\text{Unit Cost for Conversion Costs} = \frac{\text{Total Labor and Manufacturing Overhead Costs}}{\text{Equivalent Units for Conversion Costs}}$$

Computing Equivalent Production: No Beginning Work in Process Inventory We will now take a closer look at the computation of equivalent production. First we will assume that there are no units in beginning work in process inventory. In such a case, we need to consider only (1) units started and completed during the period and (2) units started but not completed. By definition, the number of units started but not completed equals the number of units in the ending work in process inventory. Equivalent production consists of two amounts:

Amount 1: Units started and completed = (number of units) × 100 percent

Amount 2: Equivalent units in ending work in process inventory = (number of units) × (average percentage of completion)

The *sum* of these two amounts equals the equivalent whole units completed during the period. Percentage of completion factors are obtained from engineering estimates or supervisors in the production departments.

For example, assume that at Karlsson Clothing, Inc., records for January 20xx contain the following information: (1) 47,500 units were started during the period; (2) 6,200 units were partially complete at period end; (3) units in the ending work in process inventory were 60 percent completed; (4) raw materials were added at the beginning of the process, and conversion costs were incurred uniformly throughout the process; (5) no units were lost or spoiled during the month.

The schedule of equivalent production, in which the period's equivalent units are computed for both direct materials costs and conversion costs, is shown in Exhibit 2. Because there were no units in beginning work in process inventory, dashes are entered in the appropriate columns. All 41,300 units started and completed during the period (47,500 units started − 6,200 units not completed) have received 100 percent of the direct materials, direct labor, and manufacturing overhead needed to complete them. Therefore, 41,300 equivalent units are recorded in both the Direct Materials Costs and the Conversion Costs columns.

The next step is to account for the equivalent units in ending inventory. The 6,200 units have received 100 percent of the direct materials, which were added to each product as it entered the production process. Therefore, 6,200 equivalent units are entered in the Direct Materials Costs column. However, conversion costs (direct

Exhibit 2. Equivalent Units: No Beginning Inventory

Karlsson Clothing, Inc.
Schedule of Equivalent Production
For the Month Ended January 31, 20xx

Units—Stage of Completion	Units to Be Accounted For	Equivalent Units: Direct Materials Costs	Equivalent Units: Conversion Costs
Beginning inventory—units started last period but completed in this period	—	—	—
Units started and completed in this period	41,300	41,300	41,300
Ending inventory—units started but not completed in this period	6,200		
(Direct materials costs—100% complete)		6,200	
(Conversion costs—60% complete)			3,720
Totals	47,500	47,500	45,020

labor and manufacturing overhead) are added uniformly as the products move through the process. The 6,200 units in ending inventory are only 60 percent complete. Equivalent whole units are determined by multiplying the number of units by the percentage completed:

6,200 units × 60% completion = 3,720 equivalent units

When the columns are totaled, we find that for January, there were 47,500 equivalent units for direct materials costs and 45,020 equivalent units for conversion costs.

Point to Emphasize: Units in beginning work in process inventory represent work accomplished in the previous accounting period that has already been assigned a certain portion of its total cost. These units must be completed in the current period, incurring additional costs.

Common Student Error: The number of units started and completed is not the same as the total number of units completed during the period. Total units completed includes two categories–units in beginning work in process inventory and units started and completed.

Computing Equivalent Production: With Beginning Work in Process Inventory In reality, it is rare to find a manufacturer that has no beginning work in process inventory. By definition, process costing techniques are used in industries where production flows continuously or where there are long runs of identical products. Because there is usually something in process at month end, there are always units in beginning work in process inventory in the following period. Thus, we turn our analysis to such a situation, expanding the previous example.

For February 20xx, the records for Karlsson Clothing, Inc., showed that (1) the 6,200 units in beginning work in process inventory (60 percent complete at the beginning of February) were finished during the month and (2) 57,500 units were started during the period, of which 5,000 units were partially complete (45 percent) at period end and constituted the ending work in process inventory.

In February, Karlsson Clothing, Inc., had units in both the beginning work in process inventory and the ending work in process inventory. To compute equivalent units, we must be careful to account for only the work done in February. The computation of equivalent units is illustrated in Exhibit 3. Units in beginning inventory were 60 percent complete for conversion costs before the period began, and 100

Exhibit 3. Equivalent Units: With Beginning Inventory

Karlsson Clothing, Inc.
Schedule of Equivalent Production
For the Month Ended February 28, 20xx

		Equivalent Units	
Units—Stage of Completion	Units to Be Accounted For	Direct Materials Costs	Conversion Costs
Beginning inventory—units started last period but completed in this period	6,200		
(Direct materials costs—100% complete)		—	
(Conversion costs—60% complete)			2,480
Units started and completed in this period	52,500	52,500	52,500
Ending inventory—units started but not completed in this period	5,000		
(Direct materials costs—100% complete)		5,000	
(Conversion costs—45% complete)			2,250
Totals	63,700	57,500	57,230

percent complete for direct materials costs. All direct materials were added during the preceding period. Therefore, for those units, no equivalent units of direct materials costs were applicable to February, and only 40 percent of the conversion costs were needed to complete the units. As shown in Exhibit 3, equivalent units of conversion costs are 2,480 (6,200 units × 40 percent, the remaining percentage of completion). Computations for units started and completed, and for ending inventory, are similar to those for January.

Note that our examples cover only two of the hundreds of possible process costing situations. Nonetheless, they establish the procedures necessary to solve all process costing problems using FIFO product and cost flows.

OBJECTIVE 5b

Prepare a process cost report: Use a unit cost analysis schedule to compute product unit cost for a specific time period

The Unit Cost Analysis Schedule Thus far we have focused on accounting for *units* of productive output. In the schedule of equivalent production, we computed units to be accounted for and equivalent units for direct materials costs and conversion costs. Once such unit information is determined, we can turn our attention to dollar information.

The unit cost analysis schedule is used to accumulate all costs charged to the Work in Process Inventory account of each department and production process and to compute the cost per equivalent unit for direct materials costs and conversion costs. As shown in Exhibit 4, a unit cost analysis schedule has two parts: the total cost analysis and the computation of equivalent unit costs.

Exhibit 4. Unit Cost Determination

Karlsson Clothing, Inc.
Unit Cost Analysis Schedule
For the Month Ended February 28, 20xx

Total Cost Analysis	Costs from Beginning Inventory		Costs from Current Period		Total Costs to Be Accounted For
Direct materials costs	$20,150		$189,750		$209,900
Conversion costs	21,390		320,488		341,878
Totals	$41,540		$510,238		$551,778
Computation of Equivalent Unit Costs	**Costs from Current Period**	÷	**Equivalent Units**	=	**Cost per Equivalent Unit**
Direct materials costs	$189,750		57,500		$3.30
Conversion costs	320,488		57,230		5.60
Totals	$510,238				$8.90

The following additional information is available for Karlsson Clothing, Inc., for February 20xx:

Costs from beginning inventory	
Direct materials costs	$ 20,150
Conversion costs	21,390
Costs for the current period	
Direct materials costs	189,750
Conversion costs	320,488

This information enables us to complete the unit cost analysis schedule. As shown in Exhibit 4, all costs for the period are accumulated in the part of the schedule labeled "Total Cost Analysis." Included are the direct materials costs and conversion costs from the beginning inventory and the direct materials costs and conversion costs incurred during the current period. These costs are summed in the Total Costs to Be Accounted For column. At Karlsson Clothing, Inc., total costs to be accounted for equal $551,778, which is the sum of $209,900 in direct materials costs and $341,878 in conversion costs.

Point to Emphasize: All costs must be accounted for. A department might lose units through scrap or waste, but all costs must be accounted for.

Teaching Note: Explain that in a process costing system, costs must be assigned to production units to transfer costs to the next process or department and eventually to finished goods inventory.

Common Student Error: Students often round product unit costs to even cents or dollars. Rounding may cause a significant difference in total costs, giving the impression that the costs have been miscalculated. Suggest that students carry product unit costs to three decimal places where appropriate.

In the Computation of Equivalent Unit Costs section of the unit cost analysis schedule, *only current period costs* are used. The direct materials costs and conversion costs for the period are divided by their respective units of equivalent production for the period to arrive at the cost per equivalent unit. The second part of Exhibit 4 shows that at Karlsson Clothing, Inc., the total $8.90 cost per equivalent unit consists of $3.30 per equivalent unit for direct materials costs ($189,750 ÷ 57,500 equivalent units) plus $5.60 per equivalent unit for conversion costs ($320,488 ÷ 57,230 equivalent units). Note that the equivalent units were taken from the schedule of equivalent production in Exhibit 3.

Costs attached to units in beginning inventory are *not* included in the computation of February equivalent unit costs. Under the FIFO cost flow assumption, separate costing analyses are used for each accounting period. Therefore, costs attached to beginning inventory are treated separately, in the cost summary schedule.

OBJECTIVE 5c

Prepare a process cost report: Complete a cost summary schedule that assigns costs to units completed and transferred out during the period, and compute the ending balance in the Work in Process Inventory account

Point to Emphasize: The cost summary schedule and its supporting calculations are developed for the purpose of assigning a value to *one* transaction—the transfer of goods from one department to another or to finished goods inventory. The ending balance in the Work in Process Inventory account represents the costs that remain after this transfer.

The Cost Summary Schedule The final phase of the process costing analysis is to prepare the cost summary schedule, shown in Exhibit 5. This schedule helps to determine the costs to be transferred to the Finished Goods Inventory account of a department or production process and the ending balance in the Work in Process Inventory account. The information in this schedule comes from the schedule of equivalent production and the unit cost analysis schedule.

Exhibit 5 shows that at Karlsson Clothing, Inc., the costs transferred to the Finished Goods Inventory account included $41,540 attached to the 6,200 units in beginning inventory, the costs of completing the units in beginning inventory, and the costs of producing the 52,500 units started and completed during February. Exhibit 3 shows that 2,480 equivalent units of conversion costs were required to complete the 6,200 units in the beginning work in process inventory. Because the equivalent unit conversion cost for February is $5.60, the cost to complete the units carried over from January was $13,888 (2,480 units × $5.60). The 52,500 units started and completed in February each cost $8.90 to produce. Their combined cost of $467,250 is added to the $55,428 required to produce the 6,200 units from beginning inventory to arrive at the total of $522,678 transferred to the Finished Goods Inventory account.

Exhibit 5. Ending Inventory Computation

Karlsson Clothing, Inc.
Cost Summary Schedule
For the Month Ended February 28, 20xx

	Cost of Goods Transferred to Finished Goods Inventory	Cost of Ending Work in Process Inventory
Beginning inventory*		
Costs from preceding period	$ 41,540	
Costs to complete this period		
Direct materials costs: none	—	
Conversion costs: 2,480 units × $5.60	13,888	
Subtotal	$ 55,428	
Units started and completed*		
52,500 units × $8.90	467,250	
Ending inventory*		
Direct materials costs: 5,000 units × $3.30		$16,500
Conversion costs: 2,250 units × $5.60		12,600
Totals	$522,678	$29,100

Computational check:	
Costs to Finished Goods Inventory	$522,678
Costs in ending Work in Process Inventory	29,100
Total costs to be accounted for (see unit cost analysis schedule)	$551,778

*Unit figures come from the schedule of equivalent production for February (Exhibit 3).

Point to Emphasize: Only current period costs are assigned in FIFO process costing. Prior period costs have already been assigned to beginning work in process inventory.

Point to Emphasize: The costs being transferred to the Finished Goods Inventory account are those costs previously assigned to beginning work in process inventory, the current period costs needed to complete the beginning work in process inventory, and the costs of units started and completed in the current accounting period.

All costs remaining in the Work in Process Inventory account after the costs of completed units have been transferred out represent the cost of the units in process at period end. As shown in the second column of Exhibit 5, at Karlsson Clothing, Inc., the ending Work in Process Inventory balance of $29,100 consists of $16,500 of direct materials costs (5,000 units × $3.30 per unit) and $12,600 of conversion costs (5,000 units × 45 percent × $5.60 per unit). Note that the unit figures come from the schedule of equivalent production (Exhibit 3).

To complete the cost summary schedule, a computational check is performed. The total cost of completed units transferred to the Finished Goods Inventory account is added to the costs of unfinished units in the Work in Process Inventory account to arrive at the total costs to be accounted for. This figure should equal the total costs to be accounted for as calculated in the unit cost analysis schedule. If the two totals are not equal, the difference may be due to rounding or a computational error. At Karlsson Clothing, Inc., the two figures are the same, so we know that all costs have been accounted for and that no calculation errors were made in the February cost analysis.

Comparison of Job Order Costing and Process Costing

OBJECTIVE 6

Compare the characteristics of the job order and process costing systems and explain the role of the Work in Process Inventory account(s) in the two product costing systems

Related Text Assignments:
Q: 18, 19
SE: 9
MRA: 3

Point to Emphasize: The product cost arrived at by both job order and process costing systems is an average cost. Process costing usually averages cost over a greater volume of product.

The job order costing and the process costing systems differ in key ways because they are designed to serve two different environments. The main characteristics of the job order costing and process costing systems may be summarized and compared as follows:

Job Order Costing System	Process Costing System
1. Collects manufacturing costs and assigns them to specific jobs or batches of product.	1. Collects manufacturing costs and groups them by department, work center, or work cell.
2. Measures costs for each completed job.	2. Measures costs in terms of units completed in specific time periods.
3. Uses one Work in Process Inventory Control account supported by a subsidiary ledger of job order cost cards.	3. Uses several Work in Process Inventory accounts, one for each department, work center, or work cell.

BUSINESS BULLETIN: INTERNATIONAL PRACTICE

The auto maker Daihatsu Motor Company, of Osaka, Japan, employs a system called Kaizen costing to help control product costs. Although not a product costing system in itself, Kaizen costing supports the continuous improvement environment adopted by Daihatsu management. Kaizen costing is a cost-reduction technique that aims at reducing actual costs below anticipated or budgeted costs. So instead of trying to meet budgeted goals, managers at Daihatsu try to meet or exceed budgeted output targets at below budgeted costs. Improvements in product design, production techniques, marketing, and distribution channels all help the company reduce product costs below budget. Kaizen costing is one way of introducing continuous improvement into the operating and product costing systems of a company.[4]

Cost Flows Through the Work in Process Inventory Accounts

Accounting for the costs of direct materials, direct labor, and manufacturing or service overhead is similar for job order costing and process costing. Under both systems, materials and supplies must be purchased and requisitioned into production, wages for direct labor must be paid to employees and charged to production accounts, and manufacturing overhead must be assigned to production using an appropriate allocation base. Therefore, the flow of costs into the Work in Process Inventory account is very similar in the two product costing systems.

The main difference between job order costing and process costing is the way in which costs are assigned to products. The Work in Process Inventory account plays a major role in cost assignment. Figure 7 illustrates the cost flow in the two systems. In a job order costing system, costs are charged to one Work in Process Inventory Control account and then traced to specific jobs or orders. The balance in the Work in Process Control account is supported by a subsidiary ledger containing all of the job order cost cards for the period. All product costs flow through the same Work in Process Inventory Control account. Because products and/or jobs differ in this type of environment, differing amounts of costs are assigned to each job.

In a process costing system, an averaging technique is used to develop product costs. A separate Work in Process Inventory account is maintained for each activity in the operating process. Unit costs are computed for each activity for a specific time period. Each Work in Process Inventory account is charged for only the production costs needed for its operation. A product's unit cost is the total of the unit costs computed for each activity within the production process. Because the products in a process costing environment are either identical or use the same production process, averaging can be used to assign costs to products.

Product Costing and ABC

In the traditional approach to product costing, two kinds of costs are accumulated in the Work in Process Inventory account—the costs that can be traced directly to the job or process (direct materials costs and direct labor costs) and the indirect production costs that are assigned using a predetermined overhead rate (overhead costs). This traditional approach was used in the Wasa Boat Company case and the Karlsson Clothing, Inc., example earlier in this chapter. Activity-based costing (ABC) may also be used to assign costs in a job order or process costing system. You will recall that in an activity-based costing system, all costs are first divided into two groups—those that are directly traceable to a product, process, or department (including directly traceable overhead costs such as electricity and operating supplies) and those that are not directly traceable to a cost objective. The nontraceable costs are then categorized by activity (such as setup costs, engineering costs, and materials purchasing costs) and a cost driver is identified for each activity. The cost driver is closely linked to the cause of the cost and becomes the basis for assigning costs to the job or process that used the activity's resources. For example, machine setup costs could be assigned to jobs or processes based on the number of setups required and used. Companywide costs that cannot be linked to an operating activity, such as plant insurance and building and grounds maintenance, are grouped together and assigned using a base such as square footage.

When ABC is used in a job order setting, the single overhead rate is replaced with a rate per cost driver for each activity. As a result, several computations are needed to transfer overhead costs to the Work in Process Inventory account instead of the single transfer used in the Wasa Boat Company example. Once the activity costs have been assigned to the Work in Process Inventory account, the remainder of the cost flow is the same as illustrated in the Wasa case.

When ABC is used in a process costing system, the only schedule affected is the unit cost analysis. No changes are necessary in either the schedule of equivalent

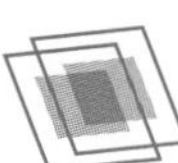

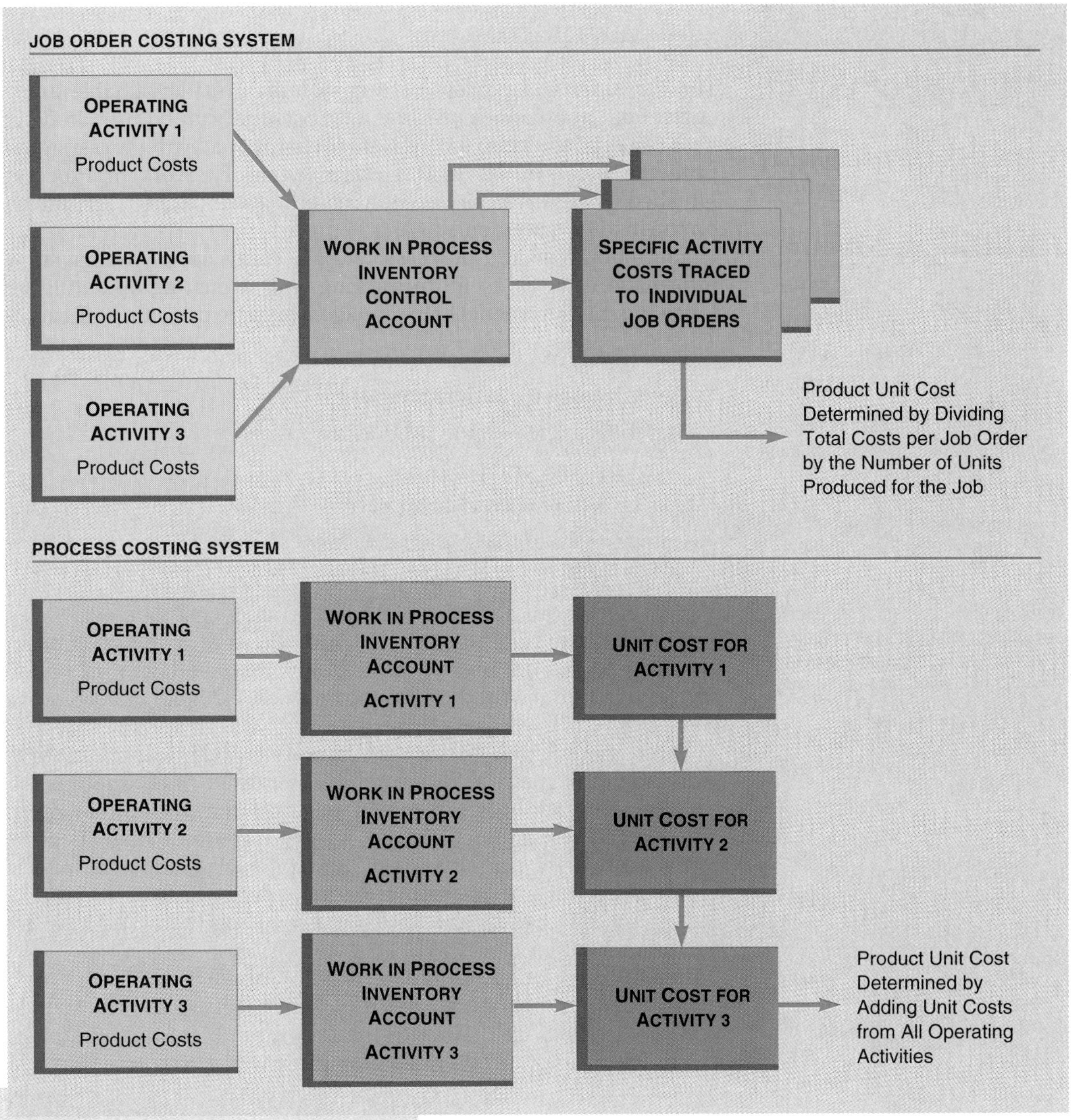

JOB ORDER COSTING SYSTEM

OPERATING ACTIVITY 1
Product Costs

OPERATING ACTIVITY 2
Product Costs

OPERATING ACTIVITY 3
Product Costs

WORK IN PROCESS INVENTORY CONTROL ACCOUNT

SPECIFIC ACTIVITY COSTS TRACED TO INDIVIDUAL JOB ORDERS

Product Unit Cost Determined by Dividing Total Costs per Job Order by the Number of Units Produced for the Job

PROCESS COSTING SYSTEM

OPERATING ACTIVITY 1
Product Costs

WORK IN PROCESS INVENTORY ACCOUNT
ACTIVITY 1

UNIT COST FOR ACTIVITY 1

OPERATING ACTIVITY 2
Product Costs

WORK IN PROCESS INVENTORY ACCOUNT
ACTIVITY 2

UNIT COST FOR ACTIVITY 2

OPERATING ACTIVITY 3
Product Costs

WORK IN PROCESS INVENTORY ACCOUNT
ACTIVITY 3

UNIT COST FOR ACTIVITY 3

Product Unit Cost Determined by Adding Unit Costs from All Operating Activities

Figure 7
Comparison of Cost Flows in Job Order and Process Costing Systems: The Role of the Work in Process Inventory Account(s)

production or the cost summary schedule. Under the traditional approach to process costing, the unit cost analysis schedule identifies two kinds of costs—direct materials costs and conversion costs. ABC allows more tracing of costs to the Work in Process Inventory accounts; as a result, the unit cost analysis schedule for an ABC process costing system includes three cost categories: (1) direct materials costs, (2) conversion costs that are directly traceable, and (3) conversion costs that must be assigned using an arbitrary allocation base. The two amounts for conversion costs are added together and divided by the equivalent units for conversion costs to determine the unit cost. The remainder of the process cost report is the same as illustrated earlier in the chapter.

Using Product Costing Information to Evaluate Performance

OBJECTIVE 7

Evaluate operating performance using product costing information

Related Text Assignments:
Q: 20
SE: 10
E: 12
MRA: 1, 2, 4

The job order and process costing systems provide valuable information to managers. Both approaches provide unit costs that can be used in determining a product's price. In addition, the information supplied by the two systems is used to compute the balances in the Materials Inventory, Work in Process Inventory, and Finished Goods Inventory accounts on the balance sheet and the cost of goods sold on the income statement.

Both job order and process costing systems supply managers with much other information that is useful in tracking and evaluating operating performance. The following measurements help managers analyze operating efficiency:

Cost trends of a product or product line

Units produced per time period

Materials usage per unit produced

Labor cost per unit produced

Special order needs of customers

Comparisons of the cost-effectiveness of changing to a more advanced production process

Teaching Note: Remind students that performance measures are quantitative tools that help managers assess the performance of a specific process or expected outcome.

Cost trends can be developed from product cost data over several time periods. Such trends can help managers identify areas of rising costs or areas where cost-effectiveness has improved. Tracking units produced per time period, a figure that is easily pulled from a product costing analysis, can help managers evaluate operating efficiency.

Direct materials and labor costs represent a significant portion of a product's cost and should be monitored constantly. Trends in direct materials usage and labor costs per unit produced can help managers determine optimal resource usage.

Anticipating customers' needs is very important to managers. Job order cost cards summarize the size, costs, and type of product a specific customer has ordered. By tracking such information, managers can see which customers are increasing their orders and which are reducing them and take action to improve customer relations.

Finally, decisions to purchase new, automated machinery and equipment are often based on the savings that the change is expected to produce. Managers can estimate product unit costs for the new equipment and compare them with cost trends for the existing equipment to decide whether to accept or reject a purchase.

Chapter Review

REVIEW OF LEARNING OBJECTIVES

1. **Identify the types of product costing systems and state how managers use product costing information.** Two basic product costing systems have been developed to determine the cost of producing or constructing something. A job order costing system is used by companies that make large, unique, or special-order products. Under such a system, the costs of direct materials, direct labor, and manufacturing overhead are traced to and assigned to specific job orders or batches of product. A

process costing system is used by companies that produce large amounts of similar products or liquids or that have a continuous production flow. Under such a system, the costs of direct materials, direct labor, and manufacturing overhead are first traced to processes or work cells and then assigned to the products produced by that process or work cell.

Managers use product costing information in many ways. First, product unit cost is an important element in determining an adequate, fair, and competitive selling price for a product. Second, product costing information often forms the basis for forecasting future costs. Controlling current operations and costs is also facilitated by product cost information. Finally, product unit costs are used to determine the inventory balances reported on the balance sheet and the cost of goods sold reported on the income statement, so they also assist in financial reporting.

2. **Explain the cost flow in a job order costing system.** A job order costing system uses a perpetual inventory approach. The costs of materials and supplies are first charged to the Materials Inventory Control account and to the respective materials accounts in the subsidiary ledger. Labor costs are first accumulated in the Factory Payroll account. The various manufacturing overhead costs are charged to the Manufacturing Overhead Control account. As products are manufactured, the costs of direct materials and direct labor are transferred to the Work in Process Inventory Control account. Manufacturing overhead costs are applied and charged to the Work in Process Inventory Control account using a predetermined overhead rate. Those charges are used to reduce the balance in the Manufacturing Overhead Control account. When products and jobs are completed, the costs assigned to them are transferred to the Finished Goods Inventory Control account. Then, when the products are sold and shipped, their costs are transferred to the Cost of Goods Sold account.

3. **Prepare a job order cost card and compute a job order's product unit cost.** All costs of direct materials, direct labor, and manufacturing overhead for a particular job are accumulated on a job order cost card. When the job has been completed, those costs are totaled. The total is then divided by the number of good units produced to find the product unit cost for that order. The product unit cost is entered on the job order cost card and used to value items in inventory.

4. **Explain the product flow and the cost flow in a process costing system.** Process costing is used to account for the production of liquids or for long, continuous production runs of identical products. Thus, products flow in a FIFO pattern (first in, first out). Once a product is started into production, it flows on to completion. In a process costing system, manufacturing costs are handled differently than in a job order costing system. Following a FIFO costing approach, unit costs are computed using only current period cost and unit data. Costs attached to units in the beginning work in process inventory are treated separately. The unit costs are assigned to completed units and to units in the ending work in process inventory.

5. **Prepare a process cost report: (a) use a schedule of equivalent production to compute equivalent units of production, (b) use a unit cost analysis schedule to compute product unit cost for a specific time period, and (c) complete a cost summary schedule that assigns costs to units completed and transferred out during the period, and compute the ending balance in the Work in Process Inventory account.** Equivalent units are computed using information about (1) units in the beginning work in process inventory and their percentage of completion, (2) units started and completed during the period, and (3) units in the ending work in process inventory and their percentage of completion. If materials were added at the beginning of the manufacturing process, no materials are added to the units in beginning inventory during the current period, so no units are included in the computation of equivalent units. All units started during the period receive the full amount of materials. Equivalent units for costs added uniformly throughout the process are computed by multiplying the percentage completed in the current period by the total units in the respective categories mentioned above.

   Unit costs are found by using a unit cost analysis schedule. Direct materials costs for units in beginning inventory and direct materials costs of the current period are added. The same procedure is followed for conversion costs. Total costs to be accounted for are found by adding the total direct materials costs and the conversion costs.

Following FIFO costing procedures, the unit cost for direct materials is found by dividing the direct materials costs for the current period by the equivalent unit amount for direct materials. The same procedure is followed for conversion costs. Then the unit costs for direct materials and conversion costs are added to yield the total unit cost for the period.

The first part of the cost summary schedule is used to compute the costs assigned to units completed and transferred out during the period. The cost of producing the units in the beginning inventory is determined by adding the costs transferred in from the preceding period and the conversion costs needed to complete the units during the current period. That amount is added to the total cost of producing all units started and completed during the period. The result is the total cost to be transferred to the Finished Goods Inventory account. The second part of the cost summary schedule assigns costs to units still in process at period end. Unit costs for direct materials and conversion costs are multiplied by their respective equivalent units. The total equals the balance in the Work in Process Inventory account at the end of the period.

6. **Compare the characteristics of the job order and process costing systems and explain the role of the Work in Process Inventory account(s) in the two product costing systems.** Both the job order and the process costing systems are basic, traditional approaches to management accounting. In a job order costing system, (1) manufacturing costs are assigned to specific jobs or batches of product, (2) costs are measured for each job, rather than for a set time period, and (3) one Work in Process Inventory Control account is used in the accounting system. In a process costing system, (1) manufacturing costs are grouped by department or work center, (2) costs are measured in terms of a weekly or monthly time period, and (3) several Work in Process Inventory accounts are used, one for each major part of the operating process.

   The primary difference between job order costing and process costing is the way in which costs are assigned to products. This difference can be seen in the role the Work in Process Inventory account plays in the assignment of costs. In a job order costing system, costs charged to the Work in Process Inventory Control account are traced to specific jobs or orders. The balance in the Work in Process Inventory Control account is supported by a subsidiary record containing all of the period's job order cost cards. In a process costing system, an averaging technique is used to develop product costs. Costs are accumulated in separate Work in Process Inventory accounts, one for each part of the process. Unit costs are computed for each part of the process for a specific time period and assigned to the products produced during that period.

7. **Evaluate operating performance using product costing information.** Both the job order and the process costing systems supply information that managers can use to track and evaluate the operating performance of an organization. The following measurements can help managers analyze operating efficiency: cost trends of a product or product line; units produced per time period; materials usage per unit produced; labor cost per unit produced; special order needs of customers; and cost effectiveness comparisons of shifting to a more advanced production process.

REVIEW OF CONCEPTS AND TERMINOLOGY

The following concepts and terms were introduced in this chapter:

LO 5 **Conversion costs:** The combined total of direct labor and manufacturing overhead costs incurred by a production department.

LO 5 **Cost summary schedule:** A process costing schedule that is used to determine the costs to be transferred to the Finished Goods Inventory account of a department or production process and the ending balance of the Work in Process Inventory account.

LO 5 **Equivalent production:** A measure of the number of equivalent whole units produced in a period of time. Also called *equivalent units.*

LO 4 **FIFO costing approach:** A process costing method in which cost flow follows product flow. Just as the first products to be introduced into the production process are the first products to be completed, the costs assigned to those first products are the first costs to be transferred out of the production center or department.

LO 1 **Job order:** A customer order for a specific number of specially designed, made-to-order products.

LO 2 **Job order cost card:** A document on which all costs incurred in the production of a particular job order are recorded; part of the subsidiary ledger for the Work in Process Inventory Control account.

LO 1 **Job order costing system:** A product costing system used by both service and manufacturing organizations that make large, unique, or special-order products; the costs of direct materials, direct labor, and manufacturing overhead are traced to specific job orders or batches of products.

LO 1 **Process costing system:** A product costing system used by organizations that have a continuous production flow yielding large amounts of similar products or liquids; the costs of direct materials, direct labor, and manufacturing overhead are first traced to a process or work cell and then assigned to the products produced by that process or work cell.

LO 5 **Process cost report:** A set of three schedules that help managers track and analyze costs in a process costing system; it consists of the schedule of equivalent production, the unit cost analysis schedule, and the cost summary schedule.

LO 5 **Schedule of equivalent production:** A process costing schedule in which a period's equivalent units are computed for both direct materials costs and conversion costs.

LO 5 **Unit cost analysis schedule:** A process costing statement used to accumulate all costs charged to the Work in Process Inventory account of each department or production process and to compute cost per equivalent unit for materials costs and conversion costs.

REVIEW PROBLEM

The Process Costing System

LO 5 Newell Company of Scottsdale, Arizona, produces a line of sunscreen products, all of which must go through the same blending process. At September 1, 20xx, the Blending Department had 1,400 units in process, 100 percent complete as to direct materials costs and 40 percent complete as to conversion costs. During September, 52,500 units were started into production. At the close of operations on September 30, 1,250 units remained in process, with 100 percent of direct materials costs and 20 percent of the conversion costs added. Cost information for September is summarized below:

Beginning work in process inventory	
Direct materials costs	$ 3,575
Conversion costs	1,054
Costs for September	
Direct materials costs	133,875
Conversion costs	99,446

Output of the Blending Department is transferred to the Bottling Department where, prior to bottling, special ingredients are added to the blended solution to form the different sunscreen products.

REQUIRED

1. Using the FIFO process costing approach, prepare the following schedules for the Blending Department for September 20xx: (a) schedule of equivalent production, (b) unit cost analysis schedule, and (c) cost summary schedule.
2. From the information in the cost summary schedule, prepare the computational check, identify the amount that should be transferred out of the Work in Process Inventory account, and state where those dollars should be transferred.

ANSWER TO REVIEW PROBLEM

1. Schedule of equivalent production, unit cost analysis schedule, and cost summary schedule

Newell Company
Blending Department
Process Cost Report
For the Month Ended September 30, 20xx

a. Schedule of equivalent production

Units—Stage of Completion	Units to Be Accounted For	Equivalent Units: Direct Materials Costs	Equivalent Units: Conversion Costs	
Beginning inventory—units started last period but completed this period	1,400			
(Direct materials costs—100% complete)		—		
(Conversion costs—40% complete)			840	(60% of 1,400)
Units started and completed in this period (52,500 – 1,250)	51,250	51,250	51,250	
Ending inventory—units started but not completed in this period	1,250			
(Direct materials costs—100% complete)		1,250		
(Conversion costs—20% complete)			250	(20% of 1,250)
Totals	53,900	52,500	52,340	

b. Unit cost analysis schedule

Total Cost Analysis	Costs from Beginning Inventory	Costs from Current Period	Total Costs to Be Accounted For
Direct materials costs	$3,575	$133,875	$137,450
Conversion costs	1,054	99,446	100,500
Totals	$4,629	$233,321	$237,950

Computation of Equivalent Unit Costs	Costs from Current Period	÷	Equivalent Units	=	Cost per Equivalent Unit
Direct materials costs	$133,875		52,500		$2.55
Conversion costs	99,446		52,340		1.90
Totals	$233,321				$4.45

c. Cost summary schedule

	Cost of Goods Transferred to Bottling Department	Cost of Ending Work in Process Inventory
Beginning inventory		
Beginning balance	$ 4,629	
Cost to complete		
840 units × $1.900 per unit	1,596	
Total beginning inventory	$ 6,225	
Units started and completed		
51,250 units × $4.450 per unit	228,063	
Ending inventory		
Direct materials costs		
1,250 units × $2.550 per unit		$3,188
Conversion costs		
250 units × $1.900 per unit		475
Totals	$234,288	$3,663

2. Computational check

Costs to Bottling Department	$234,288
Costs in ending Work in Process Inventory	3,663
Difference due to rounding	(1)
Total costs to be accounted for (see unit cost analysis schedule)	$237,950

Units costing $234,288 were completed during September and should be transferred to the Work in Process Inventory account of the Bottling Department.

Chapter Assignments

BUILDING YOUR KNOWLEDGE FOUNDATION

Questions

1. Identify four ways in which managers use product costing information.
2. Describe the importance of a product costing system to (a) the preparation of financial statements and (b) profitability.
3. Identify two ways in which product costing information is useful during the management cycle.
4. What is a job order costing system? What types of organizations use such a system?
5. How does materials usage influence a company's efficiency and profitability?
6. "Purchased labor services cannot be stored and used later." Discuss this statement.
7. What is the nature of the Manufacturing Overhead Control account?
8. What is the purpose of the job order cost card? Identify the types of information recorded on this document.

9. Explain the process of computing product unit cost in a job order costing system. How are the necessary data accumulated?
10. What is a process costing system? What types of companies are likely to employ a process costing system?
11. Explain the FIFO approach for assigning costs to products in a process costing system.
12. What three schedules comprise the process cost report?
13. Define the term *equivalent production* (or *equivalent units*).
14. Define the term *conversion costs*. Why are conversion costs used in process costing computations?
15. Why is it easier to compute equivalent units without units in beginning inventory than with units in beginning inventory?
16. What are the purposes of the unit cost analysis schedule?
17. What two important dollar amounts come from the cost summary schedule? How do they relate to the year-end financial statements?
18. What are the similarities and differences between a job order costing system and a process costing system? (Focus on the characteristics of each system.)
19. "In job order costing, one Work in Process Inventory account is used for all jobs. In process costing, several Work in Process Inventory accounts are used." Explain these statements.
20. What type of operating performance can be evaluated by (a) units produced per time period, (b) labor cost per unit produced, and (c) special-order needs of customers?

Short Exercises

SE 1. **LO 1** *Uses of Product Costing Information*

Hill's Kennel provides boarding for dogs and cats. Aruber Hill must make several decisions soon. Write *yes* or *no* to indicate whether knowing the cost to board one animal per day (the product unit cost) can help Aruber answer the following questions.

1. Is the boarding fee high enough to cover my costs?
2. How much profit will I make if I board an average of ten dogs per day for fifty weeks?
3. What costs can I reduce so that I can compete with the boarding fee charged by my competitor?

SE 2. **LO 2** *Documentation for a Job Order Costing System*

Identify the document needed to support each of the following transactions.

1. Placing an order for raw materials with a supplier
2. Recording direct labor time at the beginning and end of each work shift
3. Receiving raw materials at the shipping dock
4. Producing a job requiring direct materials, direct labor, and manufacturing overhead
5. Issuing direct materials into production
6. Using water and electricity in the production process
7. A request from the Production Scheduling Department for the purchase of raw materials

SE 3. LO 3 *Computation of Product Unit Cost*

Complete the following job order cost card for six custom-built computer systems.

Job Order No. 168		Gatekeeper 3000 Apache City, North Dakota	
Customer: Robert Arthur		Direct Materials:	
		Dept. 1	$ 3,540
Date of Order: April 4, 20xx		Dept. 2	2,820
		Total	$ ____
Date of Completion: June 18, 20xx		Direct Labor:	
		Dept. 1	$ 2,340
Cost Summary:		Dept. 2	1,620
Direct Materials	$ ____	Total	$ ____
Direct Labor	____	Applied Manufacturing Overhead:	
Manufacturing Overhead	____	Dept. 1	$ 2,880
Total	$ ____	Dept. 2	2,550
Units Completed	____	Total	$ ____
Product Unit Cost	$ ____		

SE 4. LO 4 *Product Flow Diagram*

Draw a diagram showing the flow of production for product A. Product A goes through Department 1, Department 2, Department 4, and Department 5. Direct materials are added in Departments 1 and 4, and direct labor and manufacturing overhead are added in every department.

SE 5. LO 5 *Equivalent Production: No Beginning Inventory*

Given the following information from Blue Blaze's records for July 20xx, compute the equivalent units of production.

Beginning inventory	—
Units started during the period	17,000
Units partially completed	2,500
Percentage of completion of ending work in process inventory	70%

Direct materials are added at the beginning of the process, and conversion costs are added uniformly throughout the process.

SE 6. LO 5 *Equivalent Production: Beginning Inventory*

Assume the same information as in **SE 5,** except that there were 3,000 units in beginning work in process inventory, 100 percent complete as to direct materials and 40 percent complete as to conversion costs. Compute the equivalent units of production for the month.

SE 7. LO 5 *Unit Cost Determination*

Using the information from **SE 5** and the following information, compute the total cost per equivalent unit.

Costs for the period	
Direct materials costs	$20,400
Conversion costs	32,500

SE 8. LO 5 *Cost Summary Schedule*

Using the information from **SE 5** and **SE 7,** prepare a cost summary schedule.

SE 9. LO 6 *Process Versus Job Order Costing*

Indicate whether each of the following is a characteristic of job order costing or of process costing.

1. Several Work in Process Inventory accounts are used, one for each department or part in the process.
2. Costs are grouped by department, work center, or work cell.
3. Costs are measured for each completed job.
4. Only one Work in Process Inventory account is used.
5. Costs are measured in terms of units completed in specific time periods.
6. Costs are assigned to specific jobs or batches of product.

SE 10. LO 7 *Measuring Performance with Product Cost Data*

The following are the weekly average direct materials costs per unit for two products from an operating department. What use could the department manager make of this information?

Week	Product A	Product B
1	$45.20	$23.90
2	46.10	23.80
3	48.30	23.80
4	49.60	23.60

Exercises

E 1. LO 1 *Product Versus Period Costs*

Pak's Printing Company specializes in wedding invitations. Pak needs information to budget next year's activities. Write *yes* or *no* to indicate whether each piece of information listed below is likely to be available in the company's product costing system.

1. Cost of paper and envelopes
2. Printing machine setup costs
3. Depreciation of printing machinery
4. Advertising costs
5. Repair costs for printing machinery
6. Costs to deliver stationery to customers
7. Cost of office supplies
8. Costs to design a wedding invitation
9. Cost of ink
10. Sales commissions

E 2. LO 1 *Costing Systems: Industry Linkage*

Which of the following products would typically be accounted for using a job order costing system? Which would be accounted for using a process costing system? (a) paint, (b) automobiles, (c) jet aircraft, (d) bricks, (e) large milling machines, (f) liquid detergent, (g) aluminum compressed-gas cylinders of standard size and capacity, (h) aluminum compressed-gas cylinders with a special fiberglass overwrap for a Mount Everest expedition, (i) standard nails produced from wire, (j) television sets, (k) printed wedding invitations, (l) a limited edition of lithographs, (m) flea collars for pets, (n) high-speed lathes with special-order thread drills, (o) breakfast cereal, and (p) an original evening gown.

E 3. LO 2 *Cost Flow in a Job Order Costing System*

The three manufacturing cost elements—direct materials, direct labor, and manufacturing overhead—flow through a job order costing system in a structured, orderly fashion. Specific general ledger accounts, subsidiary ledgers, and source documents are used to verify and record cost information. In both paragraph and diagram form, describe the cost flow in a job order costing system.

E 4. LO 3 *Computation of Unit Cost*

Clothes-Minded Corporation manufactures a full line of women's apparel. During February 20xx, the company worked on three special orders: A–5, A–7, and B–4. Cost and production data for each order follow.

	Job A-5	Job A-7	Job B-4
Direct materials			
Fabric Q	$20,840	$22,980	$27,660
Fabric Z	1,400	2,200	3,440
Fabric YB	5,260	6,920	10,900
Direct labor			
Garmentmaker	$ 9,900	$11,400	$17,200
Layout	5,450	6,425	8,210
Packaging	3,950	4,875	6,090
Manufacturing overhead			
120% of direct labor dollars	?	?	?
Number of units produced	700	775	1,482

1. Compute the total cost associated with each job. Show the subtotals for each cost category.
2. Compute the product unit cost for each job. (Round your computations to the nearest penny.)

LO 3 **E 5.** *Preparation of Job Order Cost Card and Computation of Product Unit Cost*

During the month of January, the Kramer Cabinet Company worked on six different orders for specialty kitchen cabinets. Job 62, manufactured for T.G. Products, Inc., was begun on January 18 and completed on January 28. Partial data from Job 62's job order cost card are summarized below.

	Costs	Machine Hours Used
Direct materials		
Cedar	$8,900	
Pine	6,320	
Hardware	3,930	
Assembly supplies	988	
Direct labor		
Sawing Department	$2,880	120
Shaping Department	2,200	220
Finishing Department	2,250	180
Assembly Department	2,890	50

A total of thirty-four cabinets was included in Job 62. The current predetermined manufacturing overhead rate is $21.60 per machine hour. From the information given, prepare a job order cost card similar to Figure 3. The cedar and pine are placed into production in the Sawing Department. The hardware and supplies are placed into production in the Assembly Department. (Round to whole dollars where appropriate.)

LO 4 **E 6.** *Product Flow in a Process Costing System*

Briter Paint Company uses a process costing system to analyze the costs incurred in making paint. Production of Superior Brand starts in the Blending Department, where materials SM and HA are added to a water base. The solution is heated to 70° Celsius and transferred to the Mixing Department, where it is mixed for one hour. Then the paint goes to the Settling/Canning Department, where it is cooled and put into 4-liter cans. Direct labor and manufacturing overhead charges are incurred uniformly throughout each part of the paint-making process.

In diagram form, show the product flow for Superior Brand paint.

LO 5 **E 7.** *Equivalent Units: No Beginning Inventories*

Salazar Stone Company produces slumpstone bricks. Though it has been in operation for only twelve months, the company already enjoys a good reputation. During its first year, direct materials for 600,000 bricks were put into production; 586,000 bricks were completed and transferred to finished goods inventory. The remaining bricks were still in process at year end, 60 percent complete. In the company's process costing system, all direct materials are added at the beginning of the process. Conversion costs are incurred uniformly throughout the production process.

From this information, prepare a schedule of equivalent production for the year ending December 31, 20xx.

E 8. LO 5 *Equivalent Units: Beginning Inventories*

Zwick Enterprises makes Dewberry Shampoo for professional hair stylists. On January 1, 20xx, 5,200 liters of shampoo were in process, 80 percent complete as to conversion costs and 100 percent complete as to direct materials costs. During the month, 212,500 liters of direct materials were put into production. Data for work in process inventory on January 31, 20xx were as follows: shampoo, 4,500 liters; stage of completion, 60 percent of conversion costs and 100 percent of direct materials content.

From this information, prepare a schedule of equivalent production for the month.

E 9. LO 5 *Unit Cost Determination*

Neff Kitchenwares, Inc., manufactures sets of heavy-duty cookware. Production has just been completed for July 20xx. At the beginning of July, the Work in Process Inventory account showed materials costs of $31,700 and conversion costs of $29,400. Cost of materials used in July was $275,373; conversion costs were $175,068. During the month, 15,190 sets were started and completed. A schedule of equivalent production for July has already been prepared. It shows a total of 16,450 equivalent sets as to materials costs and 16,210 equivalent sets as to conversion costs.

With this information, prepare a unit cost analysis schedule for July.

E 10. LO 5 *Cost Summary Schedule*

The Kristoff Bakery produces Kringle coffee bread. It uses a process costing system for internal recordkeeping. In August 20xx, beginning inventory was 450 units, 100 percent complete as to direct materials costs and 10 percent as to conversion costs, and had a value of $655. Units started and completed during the month totaled 14,200. Ending inventory was 410 units, 100 percent complete as to direct materials costs and 70 percent as to conversion costs. Unit costs per equivalent unit for August were direct materials costs, $1.40, and conversion costs, $.80.

Using the information given, compute the cost of goods transferred to the Finished Goods Inventory account, the cost remaining in the Work in Process Inventory account, and the total costs to be accounted for.

E 11. LO 5 *Work in Process Inventory Accounts in Process Costing Systems*

ATK, Inc., makes a chemical used as a food preservative during a manufacturing process involving Departments A and B. The company had the following total costs and unit costs for completed production last month, when 10,000 pounds of the chemical were manufactured.

	Total Cost	Unit Cost
Department A		
Direct materials	$10,000	$1.00
Direct labor	2,600	.26
Manufacturing overhead	1,300	.13
Totals, Dept. A	$13,900	$1.39
Department B		
Direct materials	$ 3,000	$ .30
Direct labor	700	.07
Manufacturing overhead	1,000	.10
Totals, Dept. B	$ 4,700	$ .47
Totals	$18,600	$1.86

1. How many Work in Process Inventory accounts would ATK use?
2. What dollar amount of the chemical's production cost was transferred from Department A to Department B last month?
3. What dollar amount was transferred from Department B to the Finished Goods Inventory account?
4. What dollar amount is useful in estimating a selling price for one pound of the chemical?

E 12. LO 7 *Measuring Performance with Nonfinancial Product Data*

During the month of December, Lazar Products Company conducted a study of the productivity of their three-machine metal-trimming center. The data were condensed into product units per hour so that managers could analyze the productivity of individual machine operators. The target output established for the year was 125 units per hour. From the data presented below, analyze the productivity of the three machine operators.

Week	Operator 1	Operator 2	Operator 3
1	119/hr.	129/hr.	124/hr.
2	120/hr.	127/hr.	124/hr.
3	122/hr.	125/hr.	123/hr.
4	124/hr.	122/hr.	124/hr.

Problems

P 1. LO 2 LO 3 *Job Order Cost Flow*

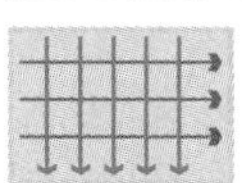

Toni Eatros is the chief financial officer for Chadwick Industries, a company that makes special-order printers for personal computers. Her records for February 20xx revealed the following information.

Beginning inventory balances	
Direct Materials Inventory Control	$27,550
Work in Process Inventory Control	22,900
Finished Goods Inventory Control	19,800
Direct materials purchased and received	
February 6	$ 7,300
February 12	8,110
February 24	5,890
Direct labor costs	
February 14	$13,950
February 28	13,230
Direct materials requisitioned into production	
February 4	$ 9,280
February 13	5,940
February 25	7,600

Job order cost cards for jobs in process on February 28 showed the following totals.

Job No.	Direct Materials	Direct Labor	Manufacturing Overhead
J–10	$3,220	$1,810	$2,534
J–14	3,880	2,110	2,954
J–30	2,980	1,640	2,296
J–16	4,690	2,370	3,318

The predetermined manufacturing overhead rate for the month was 140 percent of direct labor dollars. Sales for February totaled $154,400, which represented a 60 percent markup over the cost of production.

REQUIRED

1. Compute the cost of units completed during the month.
2. What was the total cost of units sold during February?
3. Using T accounts, reconstruct the transactions for February.
4. Determine the ending balances in the inventory accounts.
5. During the first week of March, Jobs J–10 and J–14 were completed. No additional direct materials costs were incurred, but Job J–10 needed $720 more direct labor, and Job J–14 required additional direct labor of $1,140. Job J–10 was 40 units; Job J–14, 55 units. Compute the product unit cost for each completed job.

P 2. **LO 2 LO 3** *Job Order Costing: Unknown Quantity Analysis*

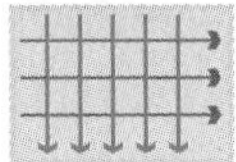

L-Tech Enterprises makes an assortment of computer support equipment. Byron Jones, the new controller for the organization, can find only partial information from the past two months, which is presented below.

Account/Transaction	May	June
Direct Materials Inventory Control, Beginning	$ 36,200	$ **e**
Work in Process Inventory Control, Beginning	56,500	**f**
Finished Goods Inventory Control, Beginning	44,200	**g**
Direct Materials Purchased	**a**	96,120
Direct Materials Requisitioned	82,320	**h**
Direct Labor Costs	**b**	72,250
Manufacturing Overhead Applied	53,200	**i**
Cost of Units Completed	**c**	221,400
Cost of Units Sold	209,050	**j**
Direct Materials Inventory Control, Ending	38,870	41,950
Work in Process Inventory Control, Ending	**d**	**k**
Finished Goods Inventory Control, Ending	47,900	51,180

The current year's predetermined overhead rate is 80 percent of direct labor dollars.

REQUIRED

Using the information given, compute the unknown values. Show your computations.

P 3. **LO 3** *The Job Order Cost Card—Service Company*

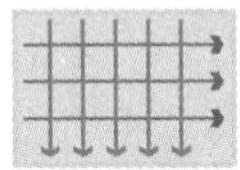

Galley & Associates is a CPA firm located in Rock Island, Illinois. The firm deals primarily in tax and audit work. For billing of major audit engagements, the firm uses cost-plus profit agreements and the profit factor used is 25 percent of total job cost. Costs are accumulated for three primary activities: Preliminary Analysis; Field Work; and Report Development. Current service overhead rates based on billable hours are: Preliminary Analysis, $12 per hour; Field Work, $20 per hour; and Report Development, $16 per hour. Supplies are treated as direct materials, traceable to each engagement. Audits for two clients, Bergholm, Inc. and Hill House Restaurants, are currently in process. During March 20xx costs related to these audits were as follows:

	Bergholm Inc.	Hill House Restaurants
Beginning balances		
Preliminary Analysis	$2,160	$2,150
Field Work	710	3,460
Report Development	0	420
Work during March		
Preliminary Analysis		
Supplies	$ 910	$ 200
Labor: hours	60	12
dollars	$1,200	$ 240
Field Work		
Supplies	$ 650	$ 890
Labor: hours	120	230
dollars	$4,800	$9,200
Report Development		
Supplies	$ 350	$ 390
Labor: hours	30	140
dollars	$ 900	$4,200

REQUIRED

1. Create the job order cost cards for the two audit engagements. Include a cost summary to date for the three primary activities and compute the cost of each activity as a percentage of the total cost.
2. The Hill House Restaurants audit was completed by the end of March. What will be the billing amount for this audit engagement?
3. What is Galley & Associates' March ending Audit-in-Process account balance?

P 4. LO 5 *Process Costing: No Beginning Inventories*

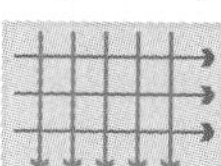

The Cee Gee Chewing Gum Company, which produces several flavors of bubble gum, began production of a new kumquat-flavored gum on June 1, 20xx. Two basic direct materials, gum base and kumquat-flavored sweetener, are blended at the beginning of the process. Direct labor and manufacturing overhead costs are incurred uniformly throughout the blending process. During June, 135,000 kilograms of gum base and 270,000 kilograms of kumquat additive were used at costs of $122,500 and $80,000, respectively. Direct labor charges were $299,200, and manufacturing overhead costs applied during June were $284,000. The ending work in process inventory was 21,600 kilograms. All direct materials have been added to those units, and 25 percent of the conversion costs have been assigned. Output from the Blending Department is transferred to the Packing Department.

REQUIRED

1. Prepare (a) a schedule of equivalent production, (b) a unit cost analysis schedule, and (c) a cost summary schedule for the Blending Department for June.
2. From the information in the cost summary schedule, prepare the computational check, identify the amount that should be transferred out of the Work in Process Inventory account, and state where those dollars should be transferred.

P 5. LO 5 *Process Costing: With Beginning Inventories*

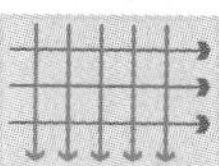

Waukesha Bottling Company manufactures and sells several different kinds of soft drinks. Direct materials (sugar syrup and artificial flavor) are added at the beginning of production in the Mixing Department. Direct labor and manufacturing overhead costs are applied to products throughout the process. During August 20xx, beginning inventory for the citrus flavor was 1,200 gallons, 80 percent complete. Ending inventory was 1,800 gallons, 50 percent complete. Production data showed 120,000 gallons started during August. A total of 119,400 gallons was completed and transferred to the Bottling Department. Beginning inventory costs were $610 for direct materials and $676 for conversion costs. Current period costs were $60,000 for direct materials and $83,538 for conversion costs.

REQUIRED

1. Prepare for the Mixing Department for August (a) a schedule of equivalent production, (b) a unit cost analysis schedule, and (c) a cost summary schedule.
2. From the information in the cost summary schedule, prepare the computational check, identify the amount that should be transferred out of the Work in Process Inventory account, and state where those dollars should be transferred.

Alternate Problems

P 6. LO 2 LO 3 *Job Order Costing: Unknown Quantity Analysis*

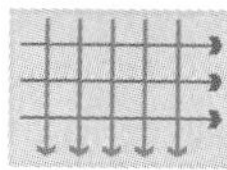

Partial operating data for the Perfect Picture Company are presented below. Management has decided the predetermined overhead rate for the current year is 120 percent of direct labor dollars.

Account/Transaction	June	July
Beginning Direct Materials Inventory Control	$ **a**	$ **e**
Beginning Work in Process Inventory Control	89,605	**f**
Beginning Finished Goods Inventory Control	79,764	67,660
Direct Materials Requisitioned	59,025	**g**
Direct Materials Purchased	57,100	60,216
Direct Labor Costs	48,760	54,540
Manufacturing Overhead Applied	**b**	**h**
Cost of Units Completed	**c**	231,861
Cost of Goods Sold	166,805	**i**
Ending Direct Materials Inventory Control	32,014	27,628
Ending Work in Process Inventory Control	**d**	**j**
Ending Finished Goods Inventory Control	67,660	30,515

REQUIRED

Using the data provided, compute the unknown values. Show all your computations.

P 7. LO 3 *The Job Order Cost Card: Service Company*

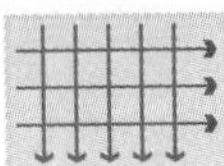

Southeast Engineering Co. specializes in designing automated characters and displays for theme parks. Cost-plus profit contracts are used, and the company's profit factor is 30 percent of total cost. A job order costing system is used to track the costs associated with the development of each project. Costs are accumulated for three primary activities: Bid and Proposal; Design; and Prototype Development. Current service overhead rates based on engineering hours are as follows: Bid and Proposal, $18 per hour; Design, $22 per hour; and Prototype Development, $20 per hour. Supplies are treated as direct materials, traceable to each job. Two projects, P–12 and P–19, were worked on during January 20xx. The costs for these projects are as follows.

	P–12	P–19
Beginning balances:		
Bid and Proposal	$1,420	$ 940
Design	2,910	0
Prototype Development	2,410	0
Work during January:		
Bid and Proposal		
Supplies	0	$2,300
Labor: hours	12	68
dollars	$ 192	$1,088
Design		
Supplies	$1,400	$ 290
Labor: hours	64	26
dollars	$1,280	$ 520
Prototype Development		
Special materials	$6,744	$2,400
Labor: hours	120	25
dollars	$2,880	$ 600

REQUIRED

1. Create the job order cost cards for the two projects. Include a cost summary to date for the three primary activities and compute the cost of each activity as a percentage of the total cost.
2. Project P–12 was completed on January 31. Customer A approved of the proto-type product and plans to produce 12 special characters using the design and specifications created by Project P–12. What dollar amount will Customer A use as the cost of design for each of its products? (Round to the nearest dollar.)
3. What is Southeast Engineering Co.'s January ending Contract in Process Inventory balance?

P 8. LO 5 *Process Costing: With Beginning Inventories*

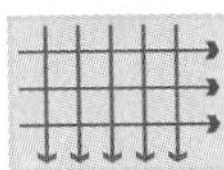

Lacho Liquid Extracts Company produces a line of fruit extracts for use in making homemade products such as wines, jams and jellies, pies, and meat sauces. Fruits are introduced into the production process in pounds; the product emerges in quarts (one pound of input equals one quart of output). On June 1, 20xx, 4,250 units were in process. All materials had been added and the units were 70 percent complete as to conversion costs. Direct materials costs of $5,070 and conversion costs of $2,910 were attached to the units in beginning work in process inventory. During June, 61,300 pounds of fruit were added: apples, 23,500 pounds costing $21,600; grapes, 22,600 pounds costing $29,920; and bananas, 15,200 pounds costing $22,040. Direct labor for the month totaled $24,630, and manufacturing overhead costs applied were $31,375. On June 30, 20xx, 3,400 units remained in process. All direct materials had been added, and 50 percent of conversion costs had been incurred.

REQUIRED

1. Prepare for June (a) a schedule of equivalent production, (b) a unit cost analysis schedule, and (c) a cost summary schedule.
2. From the information in the cost summary schedule, prepare the computational check, identify the amount that should be transferred out of the Work in Process Inventory account, and state where those dollars should be transferred.

Skills Development

Conceptual Analysis

SD 1. LO 1 *Changing the Accounting System*

International Commcable produces several types of communications cable for a worldwide market. Since the manufacturing process is continuous, a process costing system is used to develop product costs. Until recently, costs were accumulated monthly, and revised product costs were made available to management by the tenth of the following month. With the installation of a computer-integrated manufacturing system, cost information is now available as soon as each production run is finished. The production superintendent has asked the controller to change the accounting system so that product unit costs are available the day following production.

Prepare a memorandum to the corporate vice president justifying the proposed change in the accounting system. Identify reasons that the controller can use to support the production superintendent's request. What benefits would be obtained from the proposed modification? Be prepared to share your ideas with your classmates.

Ethical Dilemma

SD 2. LO 3 *Ethical Job Order Costs*

Kevin Rodgers, the production manager for ***Stitts Metal Products Company,*** entered the office of controller Ed Harris and asked, "Ed, what gives here? I was charged for 330 direct labor hours on Job AD22 and my records show that we only spent 290 hours on that job. That 40-hour difference caused the total cost of direct labor and manufacturing overhead for the job to increase by over $5,500. Are my records wrong or was there an error in the direct labor assigned to the job?" Ed responded, "Don't worry about it, Kevin. This job won't be used in your quarterly performance evaluation. Job AD22 was a federal government job, a cost-plus-fixed-fee contact, so the more costs we assign to it, the more profit we make. We decided to add a few hours to the job in case there is some follow-up work to do. You know how fussy the feds are with their close tolerances."

What should Kevin Rodgers do? Discuss Ed Harris's costing procedure.

Research Activity

SD 3. LO 4 *Process Costing Systems*

Locate an article about a company that you believe would use a process costing system. Conduct your search using the business section of your local newspaper, *The Wall Street Journal,* company annual reports, or the Needles Accounting Resource Center Web site at http://www.hmco.com/college/needles/home.html.

Prepare a short report that includes the company's name, its product(s), and a description of its production process. Bring this information to class to share with your classmates. Be sure to identify the article's title, author(s), and publication date.

Communication

Critical Thinking

Group Activity

Memo

Ethics

International

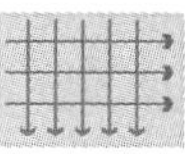
Spreadsheet

Managerial Technology

Internet

Decision-Making Practice

SD 4.

LO 2 **LO 3** *Analysis of Job Order Costing Systems*

Reed Manufacturing Company is a small family-owned business that makes specialty plastic products. Started three years ago, the company has grown quickly and now employs ten production people. Because of its size, the company uses a job order costing system that was designed around a periodic inventory system. Work sheets and special analyses are used to account for manufacturing costs and inventory valuations.

Two months ago, in May 20xx, the company's accountant quit. You have been called in to help management. The following information has been given to you.

Beginning inventory balances (1/1/20xx):	
Direct Materials	$50,500
Work in Process (Job K–2)	59,650
Finished Goods (Job K–1)	77,600
Direct materials requisitioned into production during 20xx:	
Job K–2	$33,850
Job K–4	54,300
Job K–6	82,400
Direct labor for the year:	
Job K–2	$25,300
Job K–4	33,480
Job K–6	45,600

The company purchased direct materials only once (in February), for $126,500. All jobs use the same direct materials. For the current year, the company has been using a manufacturing overhead application rate of 150 percent of direct labor dollars. So far, two jobs, K–2 and K–4, have been completed, and Jobs K–1 and K–2 have been shipped to customers. Job K–1 contained 3,200 units; Job K–2, 5,500 units; and Job K–4, 4,600 units.

1. Calculate the product unit costs for Jobs K–1, K–2, and K–4, and the costs so far for Job K–6.
2. From the information given, prepare a T account analysis and compute the current balances in the three inventory accounts and the Cost of Goods Sold account.
3. The president has asked you to analyze the current job order costing system. Do you think the system be changed? How? Why? Prepare an outline of your response to the president.

Group Activity: Ask students to complete **1** individually. Then have students work in groups to complete **2** and **3.** Select one person from each group to report the group's findings to the class.

Managerial Reporting and Analysis

INTERPRETING MANAGEMENT REPORTS

MRA 1.
LO 1 *Interpreting*
LO 7 *Nonfinancial Data*

Maynard Manufacturing supplies engine parts to ***Ralston Cycle Company,*** a major U.S. manufacturer of motorcycles. Maynard, like all parts suppliers for Ralston, has always added a healthy profit margin to its cost when calculating its selling price to Ralston. Recently, however, several new suppliers have offered to provide parts to Ralston for lower prices than Maynard has been charging.

Because Maynard wants to keep Ralston's business, a team of managers analyzed the company's production costs and decided to make minor changes in the company's production process. No new equipment was purchased, and no additional labor was required. Instead, the machines were rearranged and some of the work was reassigned.

To monitor the effectiveness of the changes, Maynard introduced four new performance measures to its information system: square feet of floor space used in production, inventory levels, lead time (total time required for a part to move through the production process), and productivity (number of parts manufactured per person per day). Maynard's goal was to reduce the quantities of the first three performance measures and to increase the quantity of the fourth.

A section of a recent management report, shown below, summarizes the quantities for each performance measure before and after the changes were made to the production process.

Measure	Before	After	Improvement
Floor space in square feet	198	97	51%
Inventory in dollars	$21,444	$10,772	50%
Lead time in minutes	17	11	35%
Productivity (parts/person/day)	515	1,152	124%

REQUIRED

1. Do you believe Maynard improved the quality of its production process and the quality of its engine parts? Explain your answer.
2. Do you believe Maynard was able to lower its selling price to Ralston? Explain your answer.
3. Was the design of the product costing system affected by the introduction of the new measures? Explain your answer.
4. Do you believe that the new measures caused a change in Maynard's cost per engine part? In what way?
5. What impact did the introduction of these new measures have on Maynard's income statement and balance sheet?

FORMULATING MANAGEMENT REPORTS

MRA 2.
LO 1 *Product Costing Systems*
LO 7 *and Nonfinancial Data*

Refer to the information in **MRA 1.** Bertha Riley, who is the president of ***Maynard Manufacturing,*** wants to improve the quality of the company's operations and products. She believes waste exists in the design and manufacture of standard engine parts. To begin the improvement process, she has asked you to (1) identify sources of waste, (2) develop performance measures to account for the waste, and (3) estimate the current costs associated with such waste. She has asked you to write a memo presenting your findings within two weeks so that she can begin strategic planning to revise the selling price for engine parts to Ralston.

You have identified two sources of costly waste. The Production Department is redoing work that was not done correctly the first time, and the Engineering Design Department is redesigning products that were not designed according to customer specifications the first time. Having improper designs has caused the company to buy parts that are not used in production. You have also obtained the following information from the product costing system:

Direct labor costs	$673,402
Engineering design costs	124,709
Indirect labor costs	67,200
Depreciation on production equipment	84,300
Supervisors' salaries	98,340
Direct materials costs	432,223
Indirect materials costs	44,332

REQUIRED

1. In preparation for writing your memo, answer the following questions.
   a. For whom are you preparing the memo? What is the appropriate length of the memo?
   b. Why are you preparing the memo?
   c. What information is needed for the memo? Where can you get such information? What performance measure would you suggest for each activity? Is the accounting information sufficient for your memo?
   d. When is the memo due? What can be done to provide accurate and timely information?
2. Prepare an outline of the sections you would want in your memo.

INTERNATIONAL COMPANY

MRA 3.
LO 1 LO 2 LO 4 LO 6 *Design of a Product Costing System*

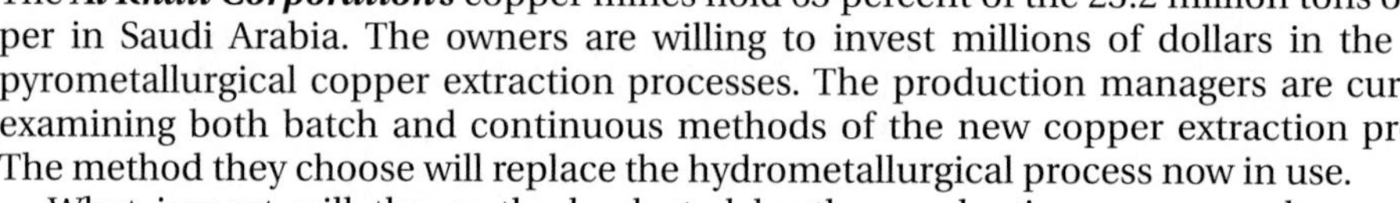

The ***Al Khali Corporation's*** copper mines hold 63 percent of the 23.2 million tons of copper in Saudi Arabia. The owners are willing to invest millions of dollars in the latest pyrometallurgical copper extraction processes. The production managers are currently examining both batch and continuous methods of the new copper extraction process. The method they choose will replace the hydrometallurgical process now in use.

What impact will the method selected by the production managers have on the design of the product costing system? What impact would changing from hydrometallurgical to pyrometallurgical processing have on the design of the product costing system if both processes use continuous methods of extraction?

EXCEL SPREADSHEET ANALYSIS

MRA 4.
LO 5 LO 7 *Process Costing: One Process—Two Time Periods*

Seader Corporation produces a line of home products in its Fargo, North Dakota, plant. The Shaping Department has been making two-gallon chili pots for the past three months. The production process has been automated so the product can now be produced in one operation rather than in the three operations that were needed before the new machinery was purchased. All direct materials are added at the beginning of the process, and conversion costs are incurred uniformly throughout the process. Operating data for May and June, 20xx, were as follows:

	May	June
Beginning Work in Process Inventory		
Units (May: 40% complete)	220	?
Direct materials costs	$ 400	$ 360
Conversion costs	$ 125	$ 134
Production during the month		
Units started	24,000	31,000
Direct materials costs	$35,000	$74,400
Conversion costs	$26,000	$29,695
Ending Work in Process Inventory		
Units (May: 70% complete; June: 60% complete)	200	320
Unit cost		
Direct materials costs	$ 1.800	$?
Conversion costs	.958	?
Product unit cost	$ 2.758	$?

REQUIRED

1. Using the appropriate template on your Computer-Aided Learning diskette, prepare a complete process costing report for June 20xx, including (a) a schedule of equivalent units, (b) a unit cost analysis schedule, and (c) a cost summary schedule. (Round unit costs to three decimal places; round all other dollar amounts to the nearest dollar.)
2. Check your cost summary results by verifying that the cost of units completed and transferred to the Finished Goods Inventory account plus the ending balance in the Work in Process Inventory account equal the total costs to be accounted for in the unit cost analysis schedule.
3. Analyze the product costing results of the Shaping Department for the current month versus those of the previous month. What is the most significant change? What are some possible causes of this change?

ENDNOTES

1. John Y. Lee and Brian G. Jacobs, "Kunde Estate Winery: A Case Study in Cost Accounting," *CMA Magazine,* The Society of Management Accountants (Canada), April 1993, pp. 15–19.
2. David M. Buehlmann and Donald Stover, "How Xerox Solves Quality Problems," *Management Accounting,* Institute of Management Accountants, September 1993, pp. 33–36.
3. Rex C. Hunter, Frank R. Urbancic, and Donald E. Edwards, "Process Costing: Is It Relevant?" *Management Accounting,* Institute of Management Accountants, December 1989, p. 53.
4. Yasuhiro Monden and John Lee, "How a Japanese Auto Maker Reduces Costs," *Management Accounting,* Institute of Management Accountants, August 1993, pp. 22–26.

CHAPTER 23

Cost-Volume-Profit Analysis and Variable Costing

LEARNING OBJECTIVES

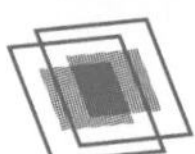

1. **Define *cost behavior* and explain how managers make use of this concept in the management cycle.**
2. **Identify specific types of variable and fixed cost behavior, and define and discuss the relationships of operating capacity and relevant range to cost behavior.**
3. **Define *mixed cost,* and use the high-low method to separate the variable and fixed components of a mixed cost.**
4. **Define *cost-volume-profit analysis* and discuss how managers use this analysis.**
5. **Compute a breakeven point in units of output and in sales dollars, and prepare a breakeven graph.**
6. **Define *contribution margin* and use the concept to determine a company's breakeven point for a single product and for multiple products.**
7. **Apply cost-volume-profit analysis to estimated levels of future sales and to changes in costs and selling prices.**
8. **Apply cost-volume-profit analysis to a service business.**

DECISION POINT

CUMMINS ENGINE COMPANY, INC.

Cummins Engine Company, Inc., is a manufacturing company whose main office is located in Columbus, Indiana.[1] Cummins facilities in the United States, Mexico, and China manufacture diesel engines and other parts for large trucks. The costs of manufacturing equipment used to produce engines (which include the B and C Series) are considered fixed because the equipment can be used over a long period of time.

But equipment does not last forever. Equipment deteriorates, and some pieces become outdated when new, more productive models are introduced. The depreciable costs of the equipment are assigned to engines using a modified units-of-production method. This method considers both the life of the equipment (maximum economic life) and its usage (total productive capacity).

Management must decide when to replace equipment as well as when to purchase additional equipment so that the business can change its manufacturing processes to produce a new series of engines that will meet the latest emissions requirements. How does the relationship of fixed costs to the company's production volume and its profit play a role in the decision process?

Critical Thinking Question: What factors affect the replacement of manufacturing equipment? **Answer:** Usage, obsolescence, and maintenance needs of the equipment; volume of business; and planned net income.

To generate income, the revenue generated from the sale of B and C Series engines must exceed the costs of using the equipment to produce the engines (depreciation expense) and other costs related to designing, manufacturing, selling, and shipping the engines. Management decides the best method of assigning equipment costs to the units produced. When making plans to purchase additional equipment, management must first estimate the projected volume of engine production, the costs involved, and the projected net income. With those projections in mind, management can decide how much new equipment it needs to meet the company's goal.

Cost Behavior Patterns

OBJECTIVE 1

Define **cost behavior** ***and explain how managers make use of this concept in the management cycle***

Related Text Assignments:
Q: 1, 2
SE: 1
SD: 1

Teaching Note: Cost behavior is closely linked to the concept of cost controllability. Generally, variable costs can be controlled more easily in the short run than can fixed costs.

The expectation that an organization's management will generate income for its owners and maintain liquidity for its creditors requires managers to find ways to make good decisions. One common way to make good decisions is to use cost behavior to analyze alternative courses of action. Cost behavior is the way costs respond to changes in volume or activity. Some costs vary with volume or operating activity; others remain fixed as volume changes. Between these two extremes are costs that exhibit characteristics of both. An understanding of cost behavior is most helpful as managers move through the planning, executing, and reporting stages of the management cycle, as shown in Figure 1.

In the planning stage, managers want to know how many units must be sold to cover all costs or to generate a targeted amount of income. Managers want to know how changes in planned operating, investing, or financing activities will affect income. As German sports shoe manufacturer Adidas completed the acquisition of Salomon SA, a French ski and sporting goods maker, its management began to estimate income from future operations. They used cost behavior to estimate how the addition of new lines of sporting equipment, such as Salomon skis and snowboards, Taylor Made golf clubs, and Mavic cycling equipment, would contribute to the organization's income.

Car manufacturers, such as Chrysler, also use cost behavior in the planning stage to decide how to change the output of trucks and cars to meet changing sales demand. If increased demand for trucks suggests the need to increase truck production and decrease car production, management can use cost behavior analysis to estimate the changes in income for those product lines. Since the truck segment is more profitable for Chrysler, the company's net income should increase if truck production is increased.

Managers use information about cost behavior in almost every decision they make. For example, the management at Cummins Engine must understand the changes in income that can be caused by a decision to buy new, more productive manufacturing equipment or to launch an advertising campaign to promote a new series of engines. Throughout the executing stage of the management cycle, management must understand cost behavior to determine the impact of its decisions on income.

Managers at Adidas, Chrysler, and Cummins Engine will also need to understand cost behavior during the reporting stage of the management cycle. Variable costing income statements, which are discussed later in this chapter, are commonly used to analyze the impact of changes in cost and sales on the profitability of product lines, sales territories, customers, departments, or other segments. Other reports based on cost behavior are used in decisions about eliminating a product line, accepting

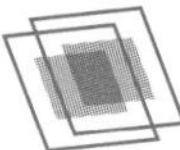

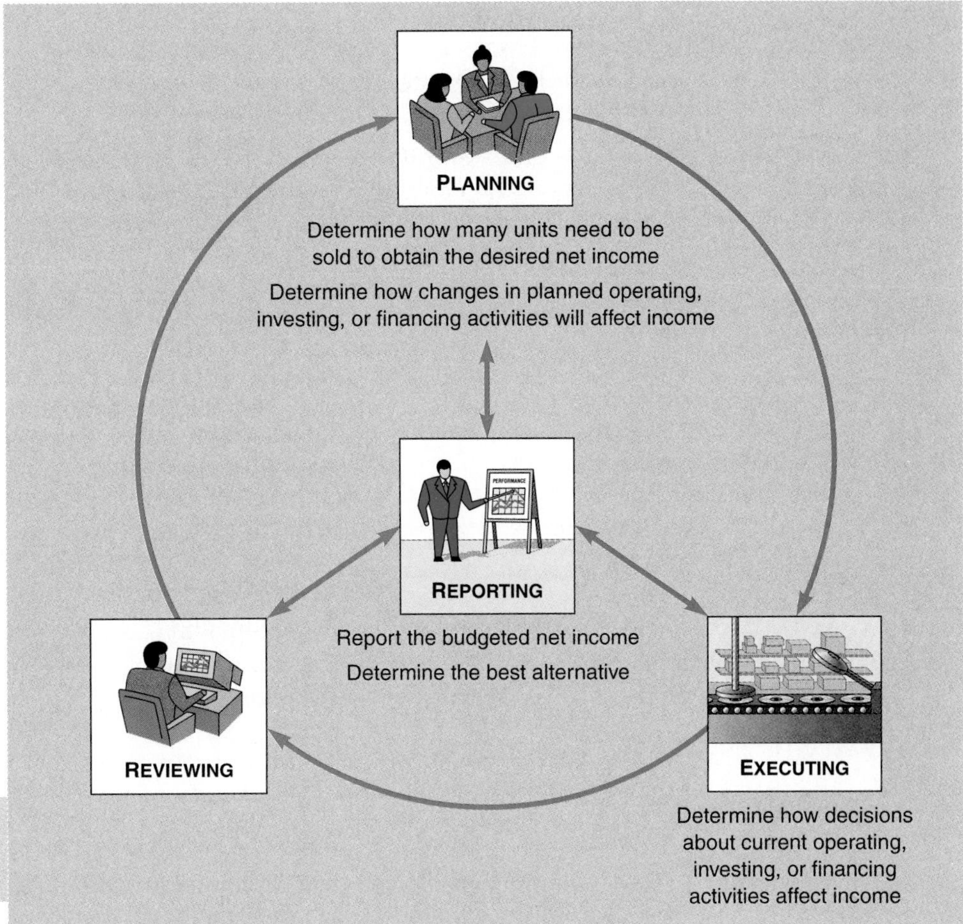

Figure 1
The Use of Cost Behavior in the Management Cycle

special orders, and contracting with other companies to provide services previously performed internally.

Our discussion in this chapter will focus primarily on cost behavior as it relates to production activity. But cost behavior can be observed in other activities. For example, increases in the number of shipments affect shipping costs; the number of units sold or total sales revenue affects the cost of sales commissions; and the number of customers billed or the number of hours to bill affects total billing costs. Costs behave in much the same way in service organizations as they do in manufacturing organizations. We look specifically at the costs of service organizations later in the chapter.

OBJECTIVE 2

Identify specific types of variable and fixed cost behavior, and define and discuss the relationships of operating capacity and relevant range to cost behavior

The Behavior of Variable Costs

Total costs that change in direct proportion to changes in productive output (or any other measure of volume) are called variable costs. To explore how variable costs work, consider tire costs for Land Rover, a maker of off-road vehicles. Each new vehicle has four tires, and each tire costs $48. The total cost of tires, then, is $192 for one car, $384 for two, $576 for three, $768 for four, $960 for five, $1,920 for ten, and $19,200 for one hundred. In the production of off-road vehicles, the total cost of tires is a variable cost. On a per unit basis, however, a variable cost remains constant. In this case, the cost of tires per vehicle is $192 whether the auto maker produces one car or one hundred cars. True, the cost of tires varies depending on the

Table 1. Examples of Variable, Fixed, and Mixed Costs

Costs	Manufacturing Company— Desk Manufacturer	Service Company— Bank	Merchandising Company— Department Store
Variable	Direct materials Direct labor (hourly) Indirect labor (hourly) Operating supplies Small tools	Computer equipment leasing (based on usage) Computer operators (hourly) Operating supplies Data storage disks	Merchandise to sell Sales commissions Shelf stockers (hourly)
Fixed	Depreciation, machinery and building Insurance premiums Labor (salaried) Supervisory salaries Property taxes	Depreciation, furniture and fixtures Insurance premiums Salaries: Programmers Systems designers Bank administrators Rent, buildings	Depreciation, building Insurance premiums Buyers (salaried) Supervisory salaries Property taxes (on equipment and building)
Mixed	Electrical power Telephone Heat	Electrical power Telephone Heat	Electrical power Telephone Heat

Related Text Assignments:
Q: 3, 4, 5, 6, 7, 8, 9
SE: 2
E: 1, 2
P: 1
SD: 1, 4

Terminology Note: By definition, there are no variable costs at the level of zero production, which is why variable costs are sometimes described as the direct costs of production, sales, and administration.

Point to Emphasize: Variable costs change in *direct proportion* to changes in activity. That is, they increase *in total* with an increase in volume and decrease *in total* with a decrease in volume, but they remain the same on a *per unit* basis.

Point to Emphasize: Variable costs are incurred in all functional areas, not just in manufacturing.

Enrichment Note: In the theory that underlies the just-in-time operating environment, theoretical capacity acts as a benchmark, a relatively constant reference point until a total capacity adjustment is made (such as adding more plant or equipment).

Terminology Note: Practical capacity is sometimes called *engineering capacity.*

number purchased, and discounts are available for purchases of large quantities. But once the purchase has been made, the cost per tire is established. Table 1 lists other examples of variable costs. All of those costs—whether incurred by a manufacturer, a service business, or a merchandiser—are variable based on either productive output or total sales.

Operating Capacity Because variable costs increase or decrease in direct proportion to volume or output, it is important to know an organization's operating capacity. Operating capacity is the upper limit of an organization's productive output capability, given its existing resources. It describes just what an organization can accomplish in a given time period. Operating capacity, or volume, can be expressed in several ways, including total labor hours, total machine hours, and total units of output. Any increase in volume or activity over operating capacity requires additional expenditures for building, machinery, personnel, and operations. In our discussion of cost behavior patterns, we assume that operating capacity is constant and that all activity occurs within the limits of current operating capacity. Cost behavior patterns can change when additional operating capacity is added.

There are three common measures, or types, of operating capacity: theoretical, or ideal, capacity; practical capacity; and normal capacity. Theoretical (ideal) capacity is the maximum productive output for a given period, assuming that all machinery and equipment are operating at optimum speed, without interruption. Theoretical capacity is useful in estimating maximum production levels, but an organization never operates at ideal capacity. In fact, the concept had little relationship to actual operations until the advent of the just-in-time operating environment. The concept that drives the just-in-time environment is the continuous improvement of operations, with the long-term goal of approaching ideal capacity.

Practical capacity is theoretical capacity reduced by normal and expected work stoppages. Production is interrupted by machine breakdowns and downtime for retooling, repairs and maintenance, and employees' work breaks. Such normal interruptions and the resulting reductions in output are considered when measuring practical capacity.

Most organizations do not operate at either theoretical or practical capacity. Both measures include excess capacity, extra machinery and equipment kept on standby. This extra equipment is used when regular equipment is being repaired. Also, during a slow season, a company may use only part of its equipment, or it may work just one or two shifts instead of around the clock. Because it is necessary to consider so many different circumstances, managers often use a measure called normal capacity, rather than practical capacity, when planning operations. Normal capacity is the average annual level of operating capacity needed to meet expected sales demand. The sales demand figure is adjusted for seasonal changes and business and economic cycles. Therefore, normal capacity is a realistic measure of what an organization is likely to produce, not what it can produce.

Business-World Example: A time period of five years is often used to calculate average activity for normal capacity. This common time frame corresponds to the five-year economic cycle in the U.S. economy. Certain industries use different time periods to correspond to specific cycles in their industries.

Each variable cost should be related to an appropriate measure of capacity, but, in many cases, more than one measure of capacity applies. Operating costs can be related to machine hours used or total units produced. Sales commissions, on the other hand, usually vary in direct proportion to total sales dollars.

There are two reasons for carefully selecting the basis for measuring the activity of variable costs. First, an appropriate activity base simplifies cost planning and control. Second, the management accountant must combine (aggregate) many variable costs with the same activity base so that the costs can be analyzed in a reasonable way. Such aggregation also provides information that allows management to predict future costs.

Terminology Note: An activity base is often called *denominator activity;* it is the activity for which relationships are established. The basic relationships should not change greatly if activity fluctuates around this level of denominator activity.

The general guide for selecting an activity base is to relate costs to their most logical or causal factor. For example, machinery setup costs should be considered variable in relation to the number of setup operations needed for a particular job or function. This approach allows machinery setup costs to be budgeted and controlled more effectively.

Linear Relationships and the Relevant Range The traditional definition of a variable cost assumes that there is a linear relationship between cost and volume, that costs go up or down as volume increases or decreases. You saw that relationship in our tire example earlier. Figure 2 shows another linear relationship. Here, each unit of output requires $2.50 of labor cost. Total labor costs grow in direct proportion to the increase in units of output: For two units, total labor costs are $5.00; for six units, the organization incurs $15.00 in labor costs.

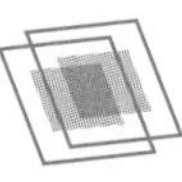

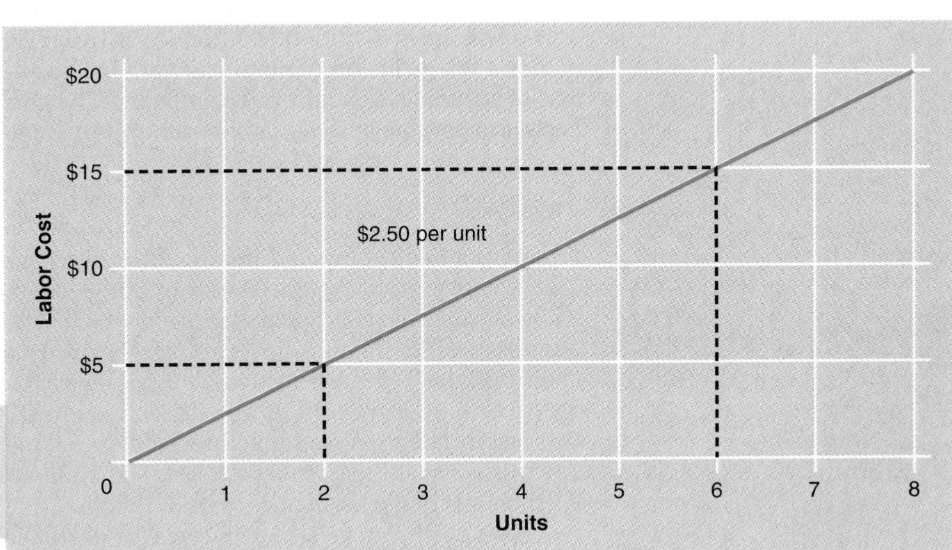

Figure 2
A Common Variable-Cost Behavior Pattern: A Linear Relationship

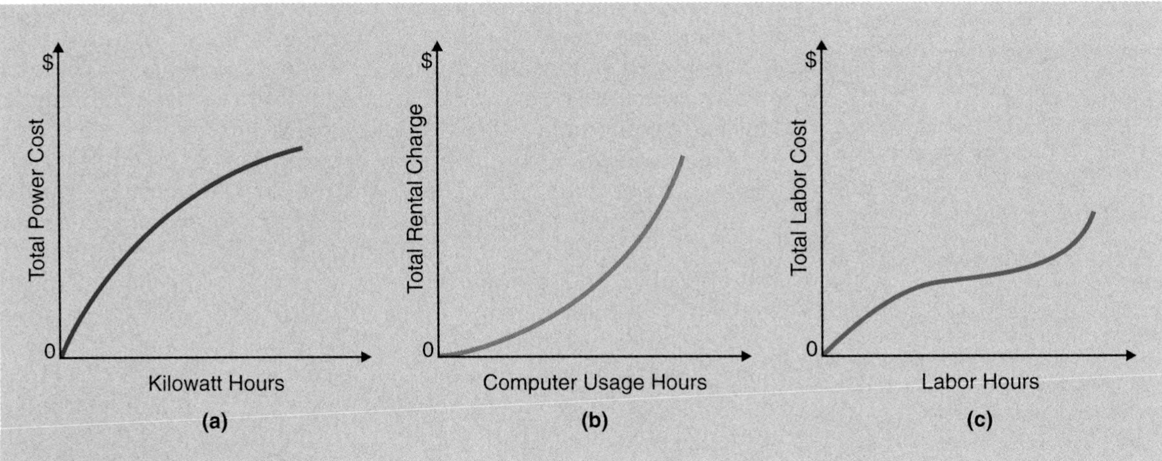

Figure 3
Other Variable-Cost Behavior Patterns: Nonlinear Relationships

Many costs, however, vary with operating activity in a nonlinear fashion. In Figure 3, graph (a) shows the behavior of power costs as usage increases and the unit cost of power consumption falls. Graph (b) shows the behavior of rental costs when each additional hour of computer usage costs more than the previous hour. And graph (c) shows how labor costs vary as efficiency increases and decreases. These three nonlinear cost patterns are variable in nature, but they differ from the straight-line variable-cost pattern shown in Figure 2.

Variable costs with linear relationships to a volume measure are easy to analyze and project for cost planning and control. Nonlinear variable costs are not easy to use. But all costs must be included in an analysis if the results are to be useful to management. To simplify cost analysis procedures and make variable costs easier to use, accountants have developed a method of converting nonlinear variable costs into linear variable costs. This method is called *linear approximation* and relies upon the concept of relevant range. Relevant range is the span of activity in which a company expects to operate. Within that range, many nonlinear costs can be estimated using the straight-line linear approximation approach illustrated in Figure 4. Those estimated costs can then be treated as part of the other variable costs.

Terminology Note: Relevant range is that range of activity in which costs are expected to behave as predicted.

A linear approximation of a nonlinear variable cost is not a precise measure, but it allows the inclusion of nonlinear variable costs in cost behavior analysis, and the loss of accuracy is usually not significant. The goal is to help management estimate costs and prepare budgets, and linear approximation helps accomplish that goal.

The Behavior of Fixed Costs

Fixed costs behave much differently from variable costs. Fixed costs are total costs that remain constant within a relevant range of volume or activity. Remember that a relevant range of activity is the range in which actual operations are likely to occur.

Terminology Note: Because fixed costs are expected to hold relatively steady over the entire relevant range of activity, they can be described as the costs of providing capacity.

Look back at Table 1 for examples of fixed costs. The desk manufacturer, the bank, and the department store all incur depreciation costs and fixed annual insurance premiums. In addition, all salaried personnel have fixed earnings for a particular period. The desk manufacturer and the department store own their buildings and must pay annual property taxes. The bank, on the other hand, pays an annual fixed rental charge for the use of its building.

As the examples in Table 1 suggest, a particular time period is identified when discussing fixed costs because, according to economic theory, all costs tend to be

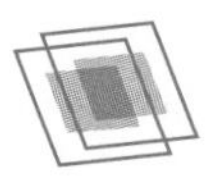

Clarification Note: Nonlinear costs can be roughly estimated by treating them as if they were linear (variable) costs within set limits of volume.

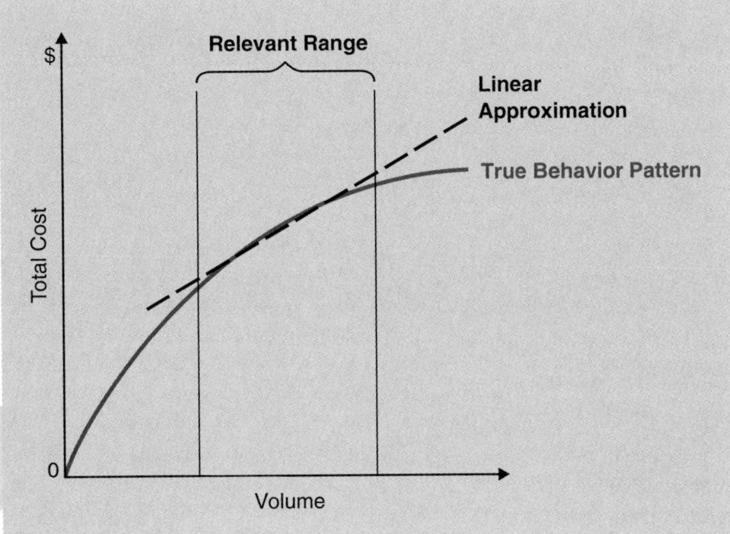

Figure 4
The Relevant Range and Linear Approximation

variable in the long run. A change in plant capacity, machinery, labor requirements, or other production factors causes fixed costs to increase or decrease. Thus, a cost is fixed only within a limited time period. For planning purposes, management usually considers a one-year time period: Fixed costs are expected to be constant within that period.

Of course, fixed costs change when activity exceeds the relevant range. For example, assume that a local manufacturing organization needs one supervisor for an eight-hour work shift. Production can range from zero to 500,000 units per month per shift; the relevant range, then, is from zero to 500,000 units. The supervisor's salary is $4,000 per month. The cost behavior analysis is as follows:

Units of Output per Month	Total Supervisory Salaries per Month
0–500,000	$4,000
Over 500,000	**$8,000**

If a maximum of 500,000 units can be produced per month per shift, any output above 500,000 units would require another work shift and another supervisor. Like all fixed costs, the new fixed cost remains constant in total within the new relevant range.

What about unit costs? Fixed costs per unit change as volume increases or decreases. *Unit fixed costs vary inversely with activity or volume.* On a per unit basis, fixed costs go down as volume goes up. That pattern holds true as long as the firm is operating within the relevant range of activity. Look at how supervisory costs per unit fall as the volume of activity increases within the relevant range.

Volume of Activity	Cost per Unit
100,000 units	$4,000 ÷ 100,000 = $.0400
300,000 units	$4,000 ÷ 300,000 = $.0133
500,000 units	$4,000 ÷ 500,000 = $.0080
600,000 units	**$8,000** ÷ 600,000 = $.0133

The per unit cost increases to $.0133 at the 600,000-unit level because that activity level is above the relevant range, which means another shift must be added and another supervisor must be hired.

Figure 5 shows this behavior pattern. The fixed supervisory costs for the first 500,000 units of production are $4,000. Those costs hold steady at $4,000 for any

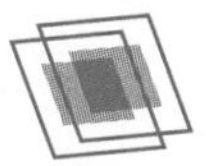

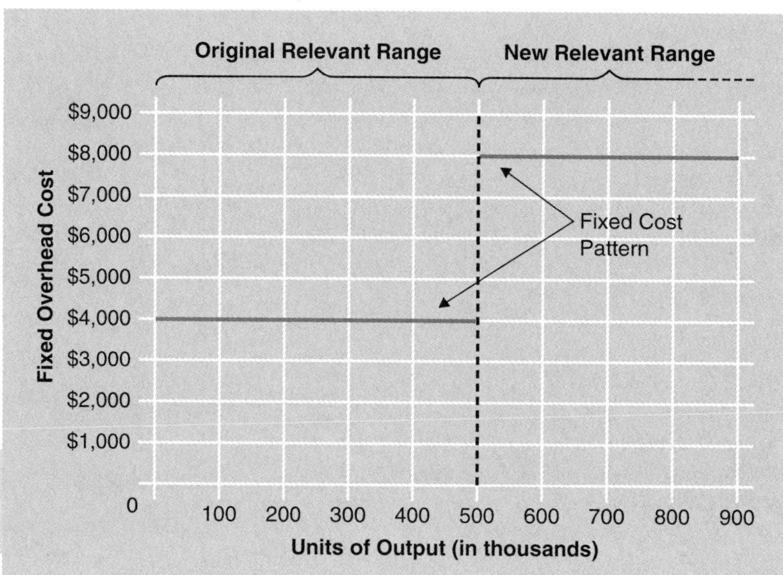

Figure 5
A Common Fixed-Cost Behavior Pattern

level of output within the relevant range. But if output goes above 500,000 units, another supervisor must be hired, pushing fixed supervisory costs to $8,000.

Mixed Costs

OBJECTIVE 3

Define mixed cost, *and use the high-low method to separate the variable and fixed components of a mixed cost*

Some costs cannot be classified as either variable or fixed. A mixed cost has both variable and fixed cost components. Part of the cost changes with volume or usage, and part of the cost is fixed over the period. Telephone cost is an example. Monthly telephone cost includes charges for long-distance calls plus a service charge and charges for extra telephones. The long-distance charges are variable because they depend on the amount of use; the service charge and the cost of the additional telephones are fixed costs.

Related Text Assignments:
Q: 10, 11, 12
SE: 2, 3
E: 3
P: 1
SD: 4

Examples of Mixed Costs Many costs have both variable and fixed components. Utilities costs often fall into this category. Like telephone costs, electricity and gas heat costs normally consist of a fixed base amount and additional charges related to usage. Figure 6 shows just two of the many behavior patterns of mixed costs. Graph (a) depicts the total telephone cost for an organization. The monthly bill begins with a fixed charge for the service and increases as long-distance calls are made. Graph (b)

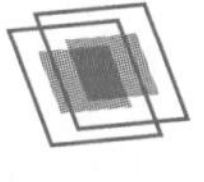

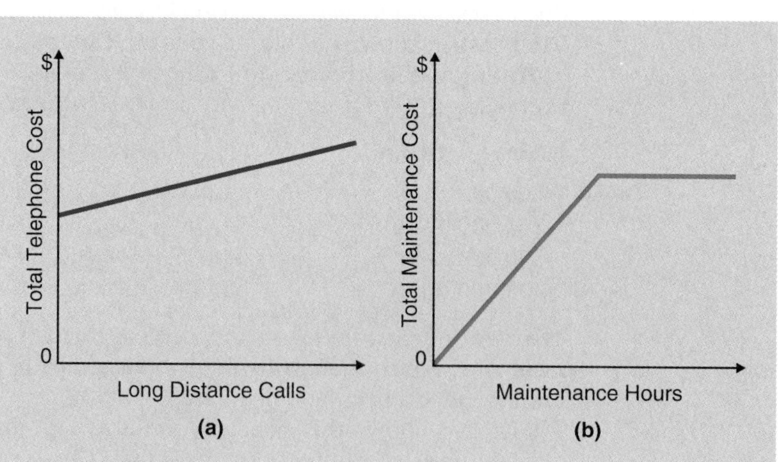

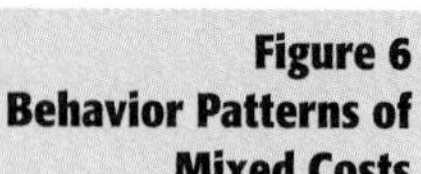

Figure 6
Behavior Patterns of Mixed Costs

Point to Emphasize: Many cost accounts in a business fall into the mixed-cost category.

Reinforcement Exercise: Ask your students to consider their personal expenses, and to classify each of the following as variable, fixed, or mixed:

Rent (fixed)
Water (mixed)
Electricity (mixed)
Gasoline (variable)
Postage (variable)

Point to Emphasize: A scatter diagram is a useful tool for cost analysis. A scatter diagram can be posted with original data and then updated as new information becomes available. As time passes, the diagram presents a visual display of cost behavior and any changes that have occurred. In addition, such a diagram is easy to create and maintain.

depicts a special contractual arrangement: The annual cost of equipment maintenance provided by an outside company increases for each maintenance hour worked, up to a maximum per period. After the maximum is reached, additional maintenance is done at no cost.

High-Low Method of Separating Costs For cost planning and control, mixed costs must be divided into their respective variable and fixed components. The separate components can then be grouped with other variable and fixed costs for analysis. When there is doubt about the behavior pattern of a particular cost, especially a mixed cost, it helps to plot past costs and related measures of volume in a scatter diagram. A scatter diagram is a chart of plotted points that helps determine if there is a linear relationship between a cost item and its related activity measure. It is a form of linear approximation. If the diagram suggests that a linear relationship exists, a cost line can be imposed on the data by either visual means or statistical analysis.

For example, last year, the Evelio Corporation's Winter Park Division incurred the following machine hours and electricity costs.

Month	Machine Hours	Electricity Costs
January	6,250	$ 24,000
February	6,300	24,200
March	6,350	24,350
April	6,400	24,600
May	6,300	24,400
June	6,200	24,300
July	6,100	23,900
August	6,050	23,600
September	6,150	23,950
October	6,250	24,100
November	6,350	24,400
December	6,450	24,700
Totals	75,150	$290,500

Figure 7 shows a scatter diagram of these data. The diagram suggests that there is a linear relationship between machine hours and the cost of electricity. To determine

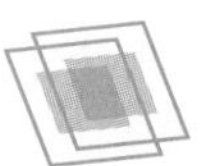

Point to Emphasize: A scatter diagram shows how closely volume and costs correlate. A tight, closely associated group of data is better for linear approximation than a random or circular pattern of data points.

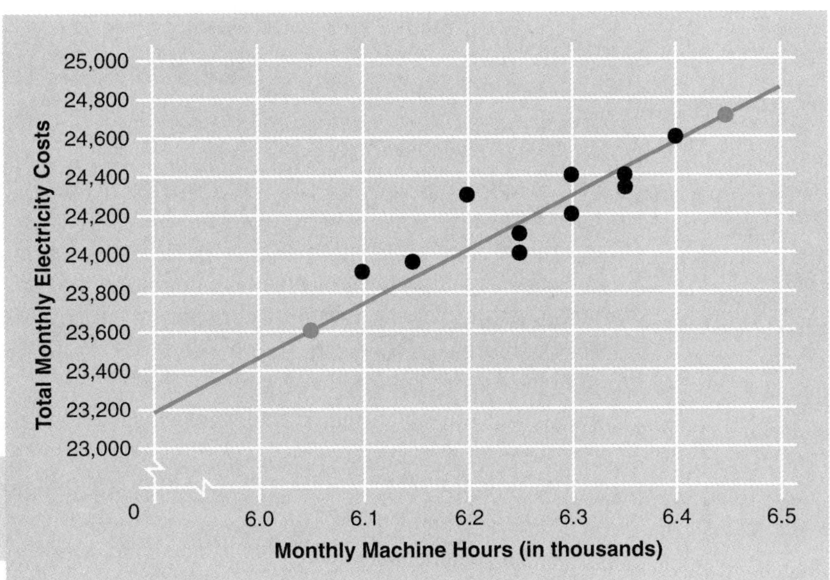

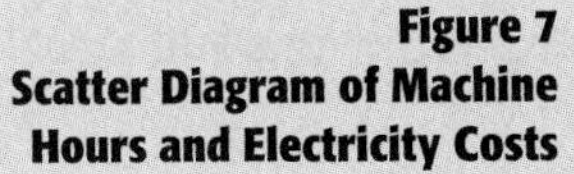
Figure 7
Scatter Diagram of Machine Hours and Electricity Costs

Enrichment Note: The high-low method is based on the premise that only two points are necessary to define a linear cost-volume relationship.

Point to Emphasize: The disadvantage of using the high-low method is that it is based on only two data observations. If one or both data points are not representative of the remaining data set, the estimate of variable and fixed costs may not be accurate. The advantage is that the method can be used when limited data are available.

Clarification Note: If the highest or lowest level of activity occurs more than once in the data set and each occurrence has a different cost value, the *average* of all the values for that level of activity should be used.

the variable and fixed components of this mixed cost, we apply the high-low method, a common, three-step approach to separating variable and fixed costs.

Step 1: Calculate the variable cost per activity base.
Select the periods of highest and lowest activity within the accounting period. In our example, the Winter Park Division experienced its highest machine-hour activity in December and its lowest machine-hour activity in August. Find the difference between the highest and lowest amounts for both the machine hours and their related electricity costs.

Volume	Month	Activity Level	Cost
Highest	December	6,450 machine hours	$24,700
Lowest	August	6,050 machine hours	23,600
Difference		400 machine hours	$ 1,100

To determine the variable cost per machine hour, divide the difference in cost by the difference in machine hours.

$$\text{Variable Cost per Machine Hour} = \$1{,}100 \div 400 \text{ Machine Hours}$$
$$= \$2.75 \text{ per Machine Hour}$$

Step 2: Calculate the total fixed costs.
Compute total fixed costs for a month by selecting the information from the month with either the highest or the lowest volume. Let's select the month with the highest volume.

$$\text{Total Fixed Costs} = \text{Total Costs} - \text{Total Variable Costs}$$
$$\text{Total Fixed Costs for December} = \$24{,}700.00 - (6{,}450 \times \$2.75) = \$6{,}962.50$$

You can check your answer by recalculating total fixed costs using the month with the lowest activity. Total fixed costs will be the same.

$$\text{Total Fixed Costs for August} = \$23{,}600.00 - (6{,}050 \times \$2.75) = \$6{,}962.50$$

BUSINESS BULLETIN: BUSINESS PRACTICE

Socially conscious investors are seeking more environmental information from companies. Companies must disclose in the notes to the financial statements any information about contingencies or liabilities from environmental contamination. Companies may also voluntarily include environmental information in their annual reports. Because environmental information affects investors' decisions, managers must consider the financial consequences of business decisions that affect the environment. Information that must be considered in profit planning and cost-volume-profit analysis includes:

- An estimate of the costs (or range of costs) necessary to meet environmental obligations
- An indication of when, if, and how those costs have been recorded in the accounting records
- The possible effects of those environmental obligations on the future financial well-being of the company[2]

Instructional Strategy: To check students' comprehension of the high-low method, assign E 3. Students can work in self-selected teams of two or three. Groups that answer correctly may be rewarded with a bonus of 2 quiz points. State ground rules, such as whether notes or text may be used, before activity begins.

Step 3: Calculate the formula to estimate the total costs within the relevant range.

Total Cost per Month = \$6,962.50 + \$2.75 per Machine Hour

Remember that the cost formula will work only within the relevant range. In this example, the formula would work for amounts between 6,050 machine hours and 6,450 machine hours. To estimate the electricity costs for machine hours outside the relevant range (in this case, below 6,050 machine hours or above 6,450 machine hours), a new cost formula must be calculated.

Cost-Volume-Profit Analysis

OBJECTIVE 4

Define **cost-volume-profit analysis** *and discuss how managers use this analysis*

Related Text Assignments:
Q: 13, 14
SE: 4
MRA: 1, 3

Suppose Ford Motor Co. wants to plan operations for the upcoming model year. How do managers know the correct amounts of materials and parts to purchase? Will additional workers need to be hired? Will there be enough space on existing assembly lines or must new facilities be constructed? What should the selling price of the cars be to meet the company's target net income for the year? These questions cannot be answered until the anticipated volume for the year is estimated. Once a target volume has been developed, the costs of production for the period and product pricing can be computed using cost-volume-profit analysis.

Cost-volume-profit (C-V-P) analysis is an examination of the cost behavior patterns that underlie the relationships among cost, volume of output, and profit, which we will refer to as net income. C-V-P analysis is a tool for both planning and control. The process involves a number of techniques and problem-solving procedures based on the cost behavior patterns in an organization. The techniques express relationships among revenue, sales mix, cost, volume, and net income. These relationships provide a general model of financial activity that management can use for short-range planning, evaluating performance, and analyzing alternatives.

For planning, managers can use C-V-P analysis to calculate net income when sales volume is known. Or, through C-V-P analysis, management can decide the level of sales needed to reach a target amount of net income. C-V-P analysis is also used extensively in budgeting.

The C-V-P relationship is expressed in a simple equation.

Sales Revenue = Variable Costs + Fixed Costs + Net Income

Or,

$$S = VC + FC + NI$$

Point to Emphasize: Because C-V-P analysis involves grouping costs by cost behavior, it helps managers identify relevant costs for decision-making. Often, variable costs are relevant to a decision while many fixed costs are not.

Instructional Strategy: Assign MRA 3. Divide the class into groups, and ask the students to discuss the MRA. Then debrief the entire class by asking one student from each group to summarize his or her group's findings for one or more of the requirements.

Cost-volume-profit analysis is a way of measuring how well the departments in an organization are doing. At the end of a period, sales volume and related actual costs are analyzed to find actual net income. A department's performance is measured by comparing actual costs with expected costs, costs that have been computed by applying C-V-P analysis to actual sales volume. The result is a performance report on which management can base the control of operations.

Basic C-V-P analysis can also be applied to measure the effects of alternative choices: changes in variable and fixed costs, expansion or contraction of sales volume, increases or decreases in selling prices, or other changes in operating methods or policies. Cost-volume-profit analysis is useful for making decisions about product pricing, product mix analysis (when an organization produces more than one product or offers more than one service), adding or deleting a product line, and accepting special orders. There are many applications of C-V-P analysis, and all are used by managers to plan and control operations effectively.

BUSINESS BULLETIN: INTERNATIONAL PRACTICE

How does C-V-P analysis in Japan, Germany, Great Britain, or Canada differ from the same analysis in the United States? The only difference is in the measures used. The procedures and formulas remain the same. Instead of expressing volume in pounds or gallons, these countries use metric measures such as grams and liters. Whereas our cost and profit amounts are expressed in dollars, Japan's amounts would be in yen, Germany's in German marks, Great Britain's in British pounds, and Canada's in Canadian dollars. Most management accounting procedures and analyses are appropriate for use by companies in any free economy. All that changes are the units of measurement.

Breakeven Analysis

OBJECTIVE 5

Compute a breakeven point in units of output and in sales dollars, and prepare a breakeven graph

Related Text Assignments:
Q: 15
SE: 5
E: 4, 5
P: 2, 5
SD: 2
MRA: 1

Common Student Error: When asked to identify the breakeven point, students often name the intersection of the total revenue and total cost lines in the breakeven graph. Explain that this point is just the product of a set of coordinates. The breakeven point must be described in terms of units or sales dollars.

Discussion Question: What is the purpose of identifying the breakeven point when the concept of zero profit is not a business organization's goal? **Answer:** The breakeven point represents the *minimum* level of sales. Any lower sales volume results in a loss.

Teaching Note: Display a breakeven graph. Then, ask students to describe the effect of several individual adjustments to the model, such as an increase in selling price, a decrease in variable cost per unit, or an increase in fixed costs. Ask them to describe the movement of the breakeven point along either the revenue line or the cost line as each adjustment is made. Demonstrate the effect with a straightedge.

Breakeven analysis uses the basic elements of cost-volume-profit relationships. The breakeven point is the point at which total revenues equal total costs. Breakeven, then, is the point at which an organization begins to earn net income. When a new venture or product line is being planned, the likelihood of success can be quickly measured by finding the project's breakeven point. If, for instance, breakeven is 50,000 units and the total market is only 25,000 units, the idea should be abandoned promptly.

Sales (S), variable costs (VC), and fixed costs (FC) are used to compute the breakeven point, which can be stated in terms of sales units or sales dollars. The general equation for finding the breakeven point is:

$$S = VC + FC$$

For example, Dakota Products, Inc., makes special wooden stands for portable compact disk players that include a protective storage compartment for the disks. Variable costs are \$50 per unit, and fixed costs average \$20,000 per year. Each wooden stand sells for \$90. Given this information, we can compute the breakeven point for this product in sales units (x equals sales units):

$$\begin{aligned} S &= VC + FC \\ \$90x &= \$50x + \$20{,}000 \\ \$40x &= \$20{,}000 \\ x &= 500 \text{ Units} \end{aligned}$$

and in sales dollars:

$$\$90 \times 500 \text{ Units} = \$45{,}000$$

We can also make a rough estimate of the breakeven point using a graph. This method is less exact, but it does yield meaningful data. Figure 8 shows a breakeven graph for Dakota Products, Inc. This graph has five parts.

1. A horizontal axis in volume or units of output
2. A vertical axis in dollars of revenue
3. A line running horizontally from the vertical axis at the level of fixed costs
4. A total cost line that begins at the point where the fixed cost line crosses the vertical axis and slopes upward to the right (The slope of the line depends on the variable cost per unit.)
5. A total revenue line that begins at the origin of the vertical and horizontal axes and slopes upward to the right (The slope depends on the selling price per unit.)

At the point where the total revenue line crosses the total cost line, revenues equal total costs. The breakeven point, stated in either units or dollars of sales, is

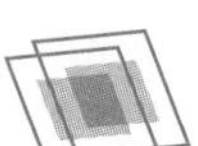

Point to Emphasize: Graphs can be very powerful management tools because they visually depict relationships between revenues and expenses that otherwise might not be evident.

Point to Emphasize: Sensitivity analysis is one of the important benefits of using C-V-P analysis. Different variables can be adjusted and the resulting impact on net income can be evaluated.

Business-World Example: The C-V-P model shown in Figure 8 is a static model. The modern business environment is dynamic–prices, advertising, and wages all fluctuate. These variables can be expressed in computer simulation languages to produce a dynamic model.

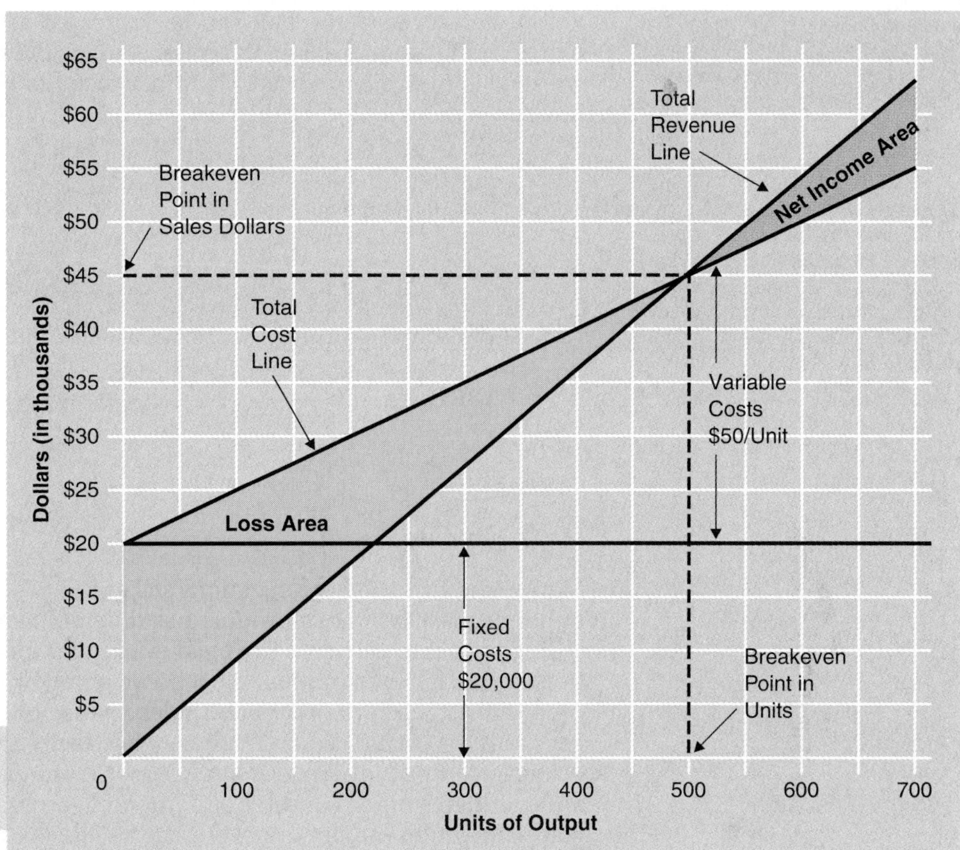

Figure 8
Graphic Breakeven Analysis: Dakota Products, Inc.

Discussion Question: Why does the total revenue line start at the origin (zero units, zero dollars) of the graph while the total cost line usually starts higher on the vertical axis? **Answer:** At zero sales, there is zero revenue; at zero sales and production, there is no variable cost, yet fixed costs still exist.

found by extending broken lines from this point to the axes. As Figure 8 shows, Dakota Products, Inc., will break even when 500 wooden stands have been made and sold for $45,000.

Contribution Margin

OBJECTIVE 6

Define **contribution margin** *and use the concept to determine a company's breakeven point for a single product and for multiple products*

Related Text Assignments:
Q: 16
SE: 6, 7
E: 5, 6, 7
P: 2, 4, 5
SD: 3
MRA: 1

A simpler method of determining the breakeven point uses contribution margin. Contribution margin is what remains after total variable costs are subtracted from sales. A product line's contribution margin represents its net contribution to paying off fixed costs and earning net income.

$$S - VC = CM$$

And net income is what remains after fixed costs are paid and subtracted from the contribution margin.

$$CM - FC = NI$$

The following example uses contribution margin to determine the profitability of Dakota Products, Inc.

Point to Emphasize: The maximum *total contribution* a unit of product can make is its selling price. After paying for itself (variable costs), a product provides a contribution margin to help pay total fixed costs and then earn net income.

		Units Produced and Sold		
Symbols		**250**	**500**	**750**
S	Sales revenue ($90 per unit)	$22,500	$45,000	$67,500
VC	Less variable costs ($50 per unit)	12,500	25,000	37,500
CM	Contribution margin ($40 per unit)	$10,000	$20,000	$30,000
FC	Less fixed costs	20,000	20,000	20,000
NI	Net income (net loss)	($10,000)	—	$10,000

Common Student Error: Explain that *contribution margin* equals sales minus variable costs, whereas *gross margin* equals sales minus the cost of goods sold.

Reinforcement Exercise: ABC Company sells its single product at $20 each. Variable costs per unit are $8, and the fixed cost for the period is $96,000. How many units must be sold to break even? **Answer:** Contribution margin = $20 − $8 = $12. Breakeven units = $96,000 ÷ $12 = 8,000 units.

The breakeven point (BE) can be expressed as the point at which contribution margin minus total fixed costs equals zero (or the point at which contribution margin equals total fixed costs). In terms of units of product, the equation for the breakeven point looks like this:

$$(\text{CM per Unit} \times \text{BE Units}) - \text{FC} = 0$$

The formula that also generates the breakeven point in units is

$$\text{BE Units} = \frac{\text{FC}}{\text{CM per Unit}}$$

To show how the formula works, we use the data for Dakota Products, Inc.

$$\text{BE Units} = \frac{\text{FC}}{\text{CM per Unit}} = \frac{\$20{,}000}{\$90 - \$50} = \frac{\$20{,}000}{\$40} = 500 \text{ Units}$$

Multiple Products

Many manufacturing organizations sell a variety of products to satisfy different customer needs. Often each product has different variable and fixed costs or different selling prices. To calculate the breakeven point for each product, the unit contribution margin for each product must be weighted by the sales mix. The sales mix is the proportion of each product's unit sales relative to the organization's total unit sales. Let's assume that Dakota Products, Inc., sells two types of wooden stands for portable compact disk players: the Floor Stand model, which is placed on the floor and has high storage capacity, and the Tabletop model, which is smaller and can be placed in entertainment units. If Dakota sells 500 units, of which 300 units are Floor Stands and 200 units are Tabletops, the sales mix would be 3:2. For every 3 Floor Stand models sold, 2 Tabletop models are sold. The sales mix can also be stated in percentages. Of the 500 units sold, 60 percent (300 ÷ 500) are Floor Stand sales and 40 percent (200 ÷ 500) are Tabletop sales (see Figure 9).

The breakeven point for multiple products can be completed in three steps. We will illustrate using Dakota Products, Inc.'s 60/40 percent sales mix, total fixed costs of $32,000, and the selling price, variable cost per unit, and contribution margin per unit for each product line presented in Step 1 below.

Step 1: Compute the weighted-average contribution margin.
Calculate the weighted-average contribution margin by multiplying the contribution margin for each product by its percentage of the sales mix.

	Sales		Variable Costs		Contribution Margin (CM)		Percentage of Sales Mix		Weighted-Average CM
Floor Stand	$90	−	$50	=	$40	×	.60	=	$24
Tabletop	$40	−	$20	=	$20	×	.40	=	$ 8
Weighted-average contribution margin									$32

Step 2: Calculate the weighted-average breakeven point.
Compute the weighted-average breakeven point by dividing total fixed costs by the weighted-average contribution margin.

Weighted-Average Breakeven Point = Total Fixed Costs ÷ Weighted-Average Contribution Margin

1,000 Units = $32,000 ÷ $32

Step 3: Calculate the breakeven point for each product.
Multiply the weighted-average breakeven point by each product's percentage of the sales mix.

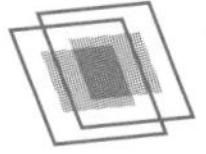

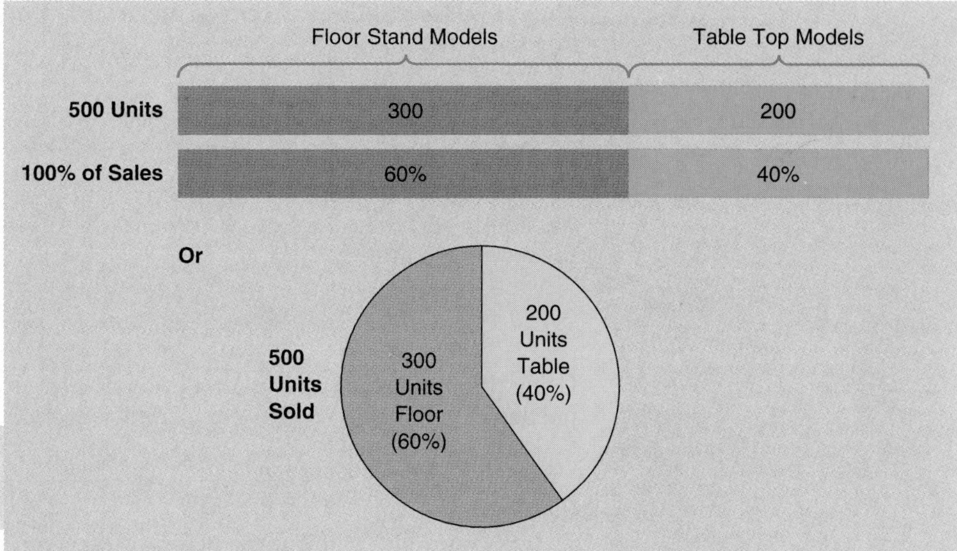

Figure 9
Sales Mix for Dakota Products, Inc.

		Weighted-Average Breakeven Point		**Sales Mix**		**Breakeven Point**
Floor Stand	=	1,000 units	×	.60	=	600 units
Tabletop	=	1,000 units	×	.40	=	400 units

To verify, determine the contribution margin of each product and subtract the total fixed costs.

Contribution margin	
Floor Stand = 600 × $40 =	$24,000
Tabletop = 400 × $20 =	8,000
Total contribution margin	$32,000
Less fixed costs	32,000
Net income	—

Planning Future Sales

OBJECTIVE 7

Apply cost-volume-profit analysis to estimated levels of future sales and to changes in costs and selling prices.

Related Text Assignments:
Q: 17, 18
SE: 8
E: 7, 8
P: 2, 3, 4, 6
SD: 3
MRA: 2, 4

Enrichment Note: The incremental approach also can be used in "what if" analysis. The firm's net income or loss is affected by the unit sales difference times the unit contribution margin.

The primary goal of a business venture is not to break even; it is to generate net income. C-V-P analysis adjusted for targeted net income can be used to estimate the profitability of a venture. In fact, the approach is excellent for "what if" analysis, in which the accountant selects several scenarios and computes the anticipated net income for each. For instance, what if sales increase by 17,000 units? What effect will the increase have on anticipated net income? What if sales increase by only 6,000 units? What if fixed costs are reduced by $14,500? What if the variable unit cost increases by $1.40? Each of these scenarios generates a different amount of net income or loss.

To illustrate how C-V-P analysis can be applied, assume that the president of Dakota Products, Inc., Les Tibbs, has set $4,000 in net income as the goal for the year. If all the data in our earlier example stay as they were, how many compact disk stands must Dakota Products, Inc., make and sell to reach the target net income? Again, *x* equals the number of units.

$$\begin{aligned} S &= VC + FC + NI \\ \$90x &= \$50x + \$20{,}000 + \$4{,}000 \\ \$40x &= \$24{,}000 \\ x &= 600 \text{ Units} \end{aligned}$$

The answer is 600 units. To check the accuracy of the answer, insert all known data into the equation.

$$S - VC - FC = NI$$
$$(600 \text{ Units} \times \$90) - (600 \times \$50) - \$20{,}000 = \$4{,}000$$
$$\$54{,}000 - \$30{,}000 - \$20{,}000 = \$4{,}000$$

The contribution margin approach can also be used for profit planning. To do so, we simply add the target net income to the numerator of the contribution margin breakeven equation:

$$\text{Target Sales Units} = \frac{FC + NI}{\text{CM per Unit}}$$

Using the data from the Dakota Products, Inc., example, the number of sales units needed to generate $4,000 in net income is computed this way:

$$\text{Target Sales Units} = \frac{FC + NI}{\text{CM per Unit}} = \frac{\$20{,}000 + \$4{,}000}{\$40} = \frac{\$24{,}000}{\$40} = 600 \text{ Units}$$

Let's continue to look at the planning activities of Dakota Products, Inc. The contribution income statement below focuses on cost behavior, not cost function. All variable costs related to production, selling, and administration are subtracted from sales to determine the total contribution margin. All fixed costs related to production, selling, and administration are subtracted from the total contribution margin to determine net income. This format is used internally by managers to help make decisions about the company's operations.

Dakota Products, Inc.
Contribution Income Statement
For the Year Ended December 31, 20xx

	Per Unit	Total for 600 Units
Sales revenue	$90	$54,000
Less variable costs	50	30,000
Contribution margin	$40	$24,000
Less fixed costs		20,000
Net income		$ 4,000

Mr. Tibbs wants the members of the planning team to consider three alternatives to the original plan shown in the contribution income statement. In the following sections, we examine each alternative and its impact on net income. In the summary, we will review our work and analyze the different breakeven points.

Alternative 1: Decrease Variable Costs, Increase Sales Volume The planning team worked with production, purchasing, and sales employees to determine the net income if the company purchased and used pine rather than oak to make the wooden compact disk stands. If pine is used, the direct materials cost per unit will decrease by $3. The company plans to stain the pine to meet the needs of a new customer group, which will increase the sales volume by 10 percent. What will be the estimated net income for this alternative? What will be the impact of this alternative on net income?

Teaching Note: Before working each alternative, ask students to determine the change in the breakeven point (an increase or decrease) due to each change in variables. See Exhibit 1 for new breakeven point calculations.

SOLUTION

	Per Unit	Total for 660 units
Sales revenue	$90	$59,400
Less variable costs	47	31,020
Contribution margin	$43	$28,380
Less fixed costs		20,000
Net income		$ 8,380
Increase in net income ($8,380 − $4,000)		$ 4,380

A different way to determine the impact of changes in selling price, cost, or sales volume on net income is to analyze only the information that changes between the original plan and the proposed alternative. In Alternative 1, variable costs will decrease by $3 (from $50 to $47), which will increase the contribution margin per unit by $3 (from $40 to $43) for the 600 wooden stands planned to be sold. This will increase the total contribution margin and net income by $1,800 ($3 × 600).

In addition, a sales increase of 60 units (.10 × 600) will increase the total contribution margin and net income by $2,580 ($43 × 60). The total increase in net income due to the decrease in variable costs and the increase in sales volume will be $4,380.

SOLUTION

Analysis of Changes Only

Increase in contribution margin from	
Planned sales [($43 − $40) × 600 units]	$1,800
Additional sales ($43 × 60 units)	2,580
Increase in net income	$4,380

Alternative 2: Increase Fixed Costs, Increase Sales Volume Rather than change the direct materials, the marketing department suggested that a $500 increase in advertising costs would increase sales volume by 5 percent. What will be the estimated net income for this alternative? What will be the impact of this alternative on net income?

SOLUTION

	Per Unit	Total for 630 units
Sales revenue	$90	$56,700
Less variable costs	50	31,500
Contribution margin	$40	$25,200
Less fixed costs		20,500
Net income		$ 4,700
Increase in net income ($4,700 − $4,000)		$ 700

Additional advertising costs will affect both sales volume and fixed costs. The sales volume will increase by 30 stands from 600 units to 630 units (600 × 1.05), which increases the total contribution margin and net income by $1,200 (from $24,000 to $25,200). Fixed costs will increase from $20,000 to $20,500, which decreases net income by $500. The increase in net income will be $700 ($1,200 − $500).

SOLUTION

Analysis of Changes Only

Increase in contribution margin from additional units sold [$40 × (600 × .05)]	$1,200
Less increase in fixed costs	500
Increase in net income	$700

Alternative 3: Increase Selling Price, Decrease Sales Volume Mr. Tibbs asked the planning team to evaluate the impact of a $10 increase in selling price on the company's net income. The planning team believes that their competitors are selling the same product at a lower price. By increasing the selling price, the team estimates that the sales volume will decrease by 15 percent. What will be the estimated net income for this alternative? What will be the impact of this alternative on net income?

SOLUTION

	Per Unit	Total for 510 Units
Sales revenue	$100	$51,000
Less variable costs	50	25,500
Contribution margin	$ 50	$25,500
Less fixed costs		20,000
Net income		$ 5,500
Increase in net income ($5,500 − $4,000)		$ 1,500

The $3,000 decrease in sales revenue is more than offset by the $4,500 decrease in variable costs, resulting in an increase in the contribution margin and net income of $1,500.

SOLUTION

Analysis of Changes Only

Increase in contribution margin from increasing selling price ($10 increase in selling price × 510 units sold)	$5,100
Decrease in contribution margin from decrease in sales volume ($40 contribution margin per unit × 90 sales units lost)	(3,600)
Increase in net income	$1,500

Comparative Summary In preparation for a meeting with Mr. Tibbs, the planning team at Dakota Products, Inc., compiled the summary presented in Exhibit 1. It compares the three alternatives to the original plan and shows how changes in variable and fixed costs, selling price, and sales volume will affect the breakeven point.

Note that the decrease in variable costs (direct materials) proposed in Alternative 1 increases the contribution margin per unit (from $40 to $43), which reduces the breakeven point. Since fewer sales dollars are required to cover variable costs, the breakeven point is reached sooner, at a sales volume of 465 units, which is lower than the breakeven point of 500 units in the original plan. In Alternative 2 the increase in fixed costs has no effect on the contribution margin per unit, but it does require the total contribution margin to cover more fixed costs before reaching the breakeven point. Thus, the breakeven point of 513 units is higher than the breakeven point of 500 units in the original plan. The increase in selling price in Alternative 3 increases the contribution margin per unit, which reduces the

Exhibit 1. Comparative Summary of Alternatives at Dakota Products, Inc.

	Original Plan Totals for 600 Units	Alternative 1 Decrease Direct Materials Cost for 660 Units	Alternative 2 Increase Advertising for 630 Units	Alternative 3 Increase Selling Price for 510 Units
Sales revenue	$54,000	$59,400	$56,700	$51,000
Less variable costs	30,000	31,020	31,500	25,500
Contribution margin	$24,000	$28,380	$25,200	$25,500
Less fixed costs	20,000	20,000	20,500	20,000
Net income	$ 4,000	$ 8,380	$ 4,700	$ 5,500
Breakeven point in whole units				
$20,000 FC ÷ $40 CM	500			
$20,000 FC ÷ $43 CM		465		
$20,500 FC ÷ $40 CM			513	
$20,000 FC ÷ $50 CM				400

breakeven point. Since more sales dollars are available to cover fixed costs, the breakeven point of 400 units is lower than the breakeven point for the original plan.

Which plan should Mr. Tibbs choose? If he selects the alternative with the highest net income shown in Exhibit 1, he would choose Alternative 1. However, if he focuses on the breakeven point, he may prefer to choose Alternative 3. Since the breakeven point for that alternative is 400 units, Dakota Products, Inc., can begin generating net income more quickly.

Remember that the breakeven point provides a "ballpark" estimate of the number of units that must be sold to cover the total costs. Additional qualitative information may help Mr. Tibbs make a better decision. Will customers perceive that the quality of the compact disk stands is lower if the company uses pine rather than oak as proposed in Alternative 1? Has the company chosen the best form of advertising to yield a 5 percent increase in sales volume for Alternative 2? Will the increase in selling price suggested in Proposal 3 create more than a 15 percent decline in unit sales? Management accountants provide the quantitative information for planning, but managers must also be sensitive to qualitative factors, such as product quality, reliability and quality of suppliers, and availability of human and technical resources.

Assumptions Underlying C-V-P Analysis

Cost-volume-profit analysis is useful only under certain conditions and only when certain assumptions hold true. These assumptions and conditions are as follows:

Point to Emphasize: A company's sales mix can be very dynamic. If the mix is constantly changing, the erroneous assumption of stability may undermine the C-V-P analysis.

1. The behavior of variable and fixed costs can be measured accurately.
2. Costs and revenues have a close linear approximation. For example, if costs rise, revenues rise proportionately.
3. Efficiency and productivity hold steady within the relevant range of activity.
4. Cost and price variables also hold steady during the period being planned.
5. The sales mix does not change during the period being planned.
6. Production and sales volume are roughly equal.

If one or more of these conditions and assumptions are absent, the C-V-P analysis may be misleading.

Applying Cost-Volume-Profit Analysis to a Service Business

OBJECTIVE 8

Apply cost-volume-profit analysis to a service business

Related Text Assignments:
Q: 19, 20
SE: 9
E: 8, 9
P: 1

Now we will see how C-V-P analysis can be applied to a service business by studying four decisions that were made by a mortgage company. Assume that Lynn Chumbley, the manager of the Appraisal Department at Portland Mortgage Company, wants to plan the home appraisal activities that are required for each mortgage loan application. The following information has been estimated for the next year.

Service fee revenue: $400 per appraisal

Variable costs: Direct professional labor, $160 per appraisal
County survey map fee, $99 per appraisal

Mixed costs: Monthly service overhead:

Volume	Month	Activity Level	Cost
Highest	March	106 appraisals	$20,346
Lowest	February	98 appraisals	20,018

Estimated average home appraisals per month next year: 100

Decision 1: Estimating Service Overhead Costs Lynn would like to estimate the total service overhead cost of appraisals for next year. Use the high-low method to calculate the cost formulas that will estimate service overhead costs for next year.

Step 1: Calculate the variable service overhead cost per appraisal.

Variable Service Overhead Cost per Appraisal = (Highest Cost − Lowest Cost) ÷ (Highest Volume − Lowest Volume)
= ($20,346 − $20,018) ÷ (106 − 98)
= $328 ÷ 8 Appraisals = $41

Step 2: Calculate the total fixed service overhead costs.

Total Fixed Service Overhead Costs = Total Service Overhead Costs − Total Variable Service Overhead Costs

Total Fixed Service Overhead Costs for March = $20,346 − ($41 × 106) = $16,000

Step 3: State the formula for total service overhead costs for one month.

Total Service Overhead Costs = Total Fixed Service Overhead Costs + (Variable Rate × Estimated Number of Appraisals)
= $16,000 + ($41 per Appraisal × Number of Appraisals)

Step 4: Calculate the total service overhead costs for one month, assuming that 100 appraisals will be made.

Total Overhead Service Costs = $16,000 + ($41 × 100) = $20,100

Decision 2: Determining the Breakeven Point Lynn would also like to know how many appraisals must be performed each month to cover the fixed and variable appraisal costs. Calculate the breakeven point.

$$\begin{aligned} \text{Let } x &= \text{Number of Appraisals per Month at Breakeven Point} \\ S &= VC + FC \\ \$400x &= \$300x + \$16{,}000 \\ \$100x &= \$16{,}000 \\ x &= 160 \text{ Appraisals per Month} \end{aligned}$$

The variable rate of $300 per appraisal includes the variable service overhead rate, the direct professional labor, and the county survey map fee ($41 + $160 + $99).

BUSINESS BULLETIN: TECHNOLOGY IN PRACTICE

Corporations engage in millions of transactions daily that must be recorded and reported. For example, in 1996 General Motors processed 17 million transactions, and VISA recorded millions of transactions for the 77.2 million cards in circulation, generating $60.6 billion in charges. Today, companies and their accountants need technology that will help them manage such large volumes of data. The many different departments, branches, or divisions within an organization contribute to the inflow and outflow of data. The spread of operations to multiple locations requires that organizations move away from centralized mainframe processing to flexible distributed database systems. A distributed database system allows a user to make a query from any site without knowing where the data are located. Data can be updated from several sites, and the changes are made simultaneously to all relevant databases. Operations are continuous, and each user sees a single system even though a multiple, distributed system exists.[3]

Decision 3: Determining the Effect of a Change in Operating Costs Lynn is worried because an average of only 100 appraisals can be performed each month and the estimated breakeven point is 160 appraisals per month. Due to strong competition in the community, the mortgage company cannot increase its fee. Lynn has been asked to reduce costs so that the mortgage company can profit from home appraisal activities. Lynn reviewed the appraisal activity and determined that improved scheduling of appraisals would reduce travel time. The current professional labor cost of $160 per appraisal covers the fee of one appraiser working four hours at $40 per hour. By scheduling the jobs based on location, Lynn can reduce the appraisers' travel time by 50 percent. As a result, the professional labor cost will decrease to $80 [(.50 × 4 hours) × $40 per hour] for one appraiser working two hours at $40 per hour. The new scheduling process will increase fixed costs by $200 per month. What would be the new breakeven point?

$$\begin{aligned}
\text{Let } x &= \text{Number of Appraisals per Month at Breakeven Point}\\
S &= VC + FC\\
\$400x &= \$220x + \$16{,}200\\
\$180x &= \$16{,}200\\
x &= 90 \text{ Appraisals per Month}
\end{aligned}$$

Variable costs become $220 ($300 − $80) per appraisal due to the reduced labor costs. This change increases the contribution margin by $80 per appraisal. Fixed costs increase from $16,000 to $16,200. The increase in the contribution margin is greater than the increase in the fixed costs, so the breakeven point decreases from 160 appraisals per month to 90 appraisals per month.

Decision 4: Estimating Net Income What would be the net income if the new scheduling process is implemented and 100 appraisals are performed each month?

$$\begin{aligned}
\text{Let NI} &= \text{Net Income When 100 Appraisals Are Performed}\\
NI &= S - VC - FC\\
NI &= \$400\,(100) - \$220\,(100) - \$16{,}200\\
NI &= \$40{,}000 - \$22{,}000 - \$16{,}200 = \$1{,}800
\end{aligned}$$

Chapter Review

REVIEW OF LEARNING OBJECTIVES

1. **Define *cost behavior* and explain how managers make use of this concept in the management cycle.** Cost behavior is the way costs respond to changes in volume or activity. Some costs vary in relation to volume or operating activity; other costs remain fixed as volume changes. Cost behavior depends on whether the focus is total costs or cost per unit. Variable costs vary in total as volume changes but are fixed per unit; fixed costs are fixed in total as volume changes but vary per unit. Managers use information about cost behavior in almost every decision they make. Whenever managers are asked to make a decision, they must always deal with cost ramifications, and they must understand and anticipate cost behavior patterns if they are to decide correctly.
2. **Identify specific types of variable and fixed cost behavior, and define and discuss the relationships of operating capacity and relevant range to cost behavior.** Total costs that change in direct proportion to changes in productive output (or any other volume measure) are called variable costs. Hourly wages, the cost of operating supplies, direct materials costs, and the cost of merchandise are all variable costs. Total fixed costs remain constant within a relevant range of volume or activity. They change only when activity exceeds the anticipated relevant range because, for example, new equipment or new buildings must be purchased, higher insurance premiums and property taxes must be paid, or additional supervisory personnel must be hired to accommodate the increased activity.
3. **Define *mixed cost*, and use the high-low method to separate the variable and fixed components of a mixed cost.** A mixed cost, such as the cost of electricity, has both variable and fixed cost components. The high-low method, which identifies a linear relationship between activity level and cost, is the easiest way to separate variable costs from fixed costs in a mixed cost.
4. **Define *cost-volume-profit analysis* and discuss how managers use this analysis.** Cost-volume-profit analysis is an examination of the cost behavior patterns that underlie the relationships among cost, volume of output, and net income. C-V-P analysis is a tool for both planning and control. The process involves a number of techniques and problem-solving procedures based on the cost behavior patterns in an organization. This form of analysis provides a general model of financial activity that management can use for short-range planning, evaluating performance, and analyzing alternatives.
5. **Compute a breakeven point in units of output and in sales dollars, and prepare a breakeven graph.** The breakeven point is the point at which total revenues equal total costs, the point at which net sales equal variable costs plus fixed costs. Once the number of units needed to break even is known, the number can be multiplied by the product's selling price to determine the breakeven point in sales dollars.

   A breakeven graph is made up of a horizontal axis (units) and a vertical axis (dollars). Three lines are plotted: The fixed cost line runs horizontally from the point on the vertical axis representing total fixed cost. The total cost line begins at the intersection of the fixed cost line and the vertical axis and runs upward to the right. The total revenue line runs from the intersection of the two axes upward to the right. The slope of the total cost line is determined by the variable cost per unit; the slope of the total revenue line is determined by the selling price per unit. The point at which the total cost and the total revenue lines cross determines the breakeven point in units or in dollars.
6. **Define *contribution margin* and use the concept to determine a company's breakeven point for a single product and for multiple products.** Contribution margin is the excess of revenues over all variable costs related to a particular sales volume. A product's contribution margin represents its net contribution to paying off fixed costs and earning net income. The breakeven point in units can be computed by dividing total fixed costs by the contribution margin per unit. A sales mix is used to calculate the breakeven point for each product when a company sells more than one product.

7. Apply cost-volume-profit analysis to estimated levels of future sales and to changes in costs and selling prices. The addition of targeted net income to the breakeven equation makes it possible to plan levels of operation that yield targeted net income. The formula in terms of contribution margin is

$$\text{Target Sales Units} = \frac{\text{FC} + \text{NI}}{\text{CM per Unit}}$$

8. Apply cost-volume-profit analysis to a service business. A service business can use cost-volume-profit analysis to separate mixed costs into their variable and fixed portions, calculate a breakeven point, and plan net income when changes in cost, volume, or price occur.

REVIEW OF CONCEPTS AND TERMINOLOGY

The following concepts and terms were introduced in this chapter.

LO 5 **Breakeven point:** The point at which total revenues equal total costs.

LO 6 **Contribution margin:** The remainder after total variable costs are subtracted from sales.

LO 1 **Cost behavior:** The way costs respond to changes in volume or activity.

LO 4 **Cost-volume-profit (C-V-P) analysis:** An examination of the cost behavior patterns that underlie the relationships among cost, volume of output, and net income.

LO 2 **Excess capacity:** Machinery and equipment kept on standby.

LO 2 **Fixed costs:** Total costs that remain constant within a relevant range of volume or activity.

LO 3 **High-low method:** A three-step approach to separating a mixed cost into its variable and fixed components.

LO 3 **Mixed costs:** Costs that have both variable and fixed components; part of the cost changes with volume or usage, and part of the cost is fixed over the period.

LO 2 **Normal capacity:** The average annual level of operating capacity needed to meet expected sales demand.

LO 2 **Operating capacity:** The upper limit of an organization's productive output capability, given its existing resources.

LO 2 **Practical capacity:** Theoretical capacity reduced by normal and expected work stoppages.

LO 2 **Relevant range:** The span of activity in which a company expects to operate.

LO 6 **Sales mix:** The proportion of each product's unit sales relative to the organization's total unit sales.

LO 3 **Scatter diagram:** A chart of plotted points that helps determine if there is a linear relationship between a cost item and its related activity measure.

LO 2 **Theoretical capacity:** The maximum productive output for a given period, assuming that all machinery and equipment are operating at optimum speed, without interruption. Also called *ideal capacity.*

LO 2 **Variable costs:** Total costs that change in direct proportion to changes in productive output or any other measure of volume.

REVIEW PROBLEM

Breakeven/Profit Planning Analysis

LO 5
LO 6
LO 7

Instrument City, Inc., is a major producer of pipe organs. Its Model D14 is a double-manual organ with a large potential market. On the next page is a summary of data from 20x1 operations for Model D14.

Variable costs per unit	
Direct materials	$ 2,300
Direct labor	800
Manufacturing overhead	600
Selling expense	500
Total fixed costs	
Manufacturing overhead	195,000
Advertising	55,000
Administrative expense	68,000
Selling price per unit	9,500

REQUIRED

1. Compute the 20x1 breakeven point in units.
2. Instrument City sold sixty-five D14 models in 20x1. How much net income did the firm realize?
3. Management is considering alternative courses of action for 20x2. (Use the figures from **2** and treat each alternative independently.)
   a. Calculate the number of units that must be sold to generate a net income of $95,400. Assume that costs and selling price remain constant.
   b. Calculate the net income if the company increases the number of units sold by 20 percent and cuts the selling price by $500 per unit.
   c. Determine the number of units that must be sold to break even if advertising is increased by $47,700.
   d. If variable costs are cut by 10 percent, find the number of units that must be sold to generate net income of $125,000.

ANSWER TO REVIEW PROBLEM

1. Compute the breakeven point in units for 20x1.

$$\text{Breakeven Units} = \frac{\text{FC}}{\text{CM per Unit}} = \frac{\$318{,}000}{\$9{,}500 - \$4{,}200} = \frac{\$318{,}000}{\$5{,}300} = 60 \text{ Units}$$

2. Calculate net income from sales of sixty-five units.

Units sold	65
Units required to break even	60
Units over breakeven	5

20x1 net income = $5,300 per unit × 5 = $26,500

Contribution margin equals sales minus all variable costs. Contribution margin per unit equals the amount of sales dollars remaining, after variable costs have been subtracted, to cover fixed costs and earn net income. If all fixed costs have been absorbed by the time breakeven is reached, the entire contribution margin of each unit sold in excess of breakeven represents net income.

3. a. Calculate the number of units that must be sold to generate net income of $95,400.

$$\text{Target Sales Units} = \frac{\text{FC} + \text{NI}}{\text{CM per Unit}}$$

$$= \frac{\$318{,}000 + \$95{,}400}{\$5{,}300} = \frac{\$413{,}400}{\$5{,}300} = 78 \text{ Units}$$

b. Calculate net income if unit sales increase 20 percent and unit selling price decreases by $500.

Sales revenue [78(65 × 1.20) units at $9,000 per unit]	$702,000
Less variable costs (78 units × $4,200)	327,600
Contribution margin	$374,400
Less fixed costs	318,000
Net income	$ 56,400

c. Determine the number of units needed to break even if advertising costs (fixed cost) increase by $47,700.

$$\text{BE Units} = \frac{\text{FC}}{\text{CM per Unit}}$$

$$= \frac{\$318{,}000 + \$47{,}700}{\$5{,}300} = \frac{\$365{,}700}{\$5{,}300} = 69 \text{ Units}$$

d. Calculate the number of units that must be sold to generate a net income of $125,000 if variable costs decrease by 10 percent.

$$\text{CM per Unit} = \$9{,}500 - (\$4{,}200 \times .9) = \$9{,}500 - \$3{,}780 = \$5{,}720$$

$$\text{Target Sales Units} = \frac{\text{FC} + \text{NI}}{\text{CM per Unit}}$$

$$= \frac{\$318{,}000 + \$125{,}000}{\$5{,}720} = \frac{\$443{,}000}{\$5{,}720} = 77.45 \text{ or } 78 \text{ Units}$$

Chapter Assignments

BUILDING YOUR KNOWLEDGE FOUNDATION

Questions

1. Define *cost behavior.*
2. Why is an understanding of cost behavior useful to managers?
3. What is the difference between theoretical capacity and practical capacity?
4. Why does a company never operate at theoretical capacity?
5. Define *excess capacity.*
6. What is normal capacity? Why is normal capacity considered more relevant and useful than either theoretical or practical capacity?
7. What does *relevant range of activity* mean?
8. What makes variable costs different from fixed costs?
9. "Fixed costs remain constant in total but decrease per unit as productive output increases." Explain this statement.
10. What is a mixed cost? Give an example.
11. What is a scatter diagram?
12. Describe the high-low method of separating mixed costs.
13. Define *cost-volume-profit analysis.*
14. Identify two uses of C-V-P analysis and explain their significance to management.
15. Define *breakeven point.* Why is information about the breakeven point important to managers?
16. Define *contribution margin* and describe its use in breakeven analysis.
17. State the equation that determines target sales units using the elements of fixed costs, target net income, and contribution margin per unit.
18. What conditions must be met for C-V-P computations to be accurate?
19. Give examples of ways in which C-V-P analysis can be used in a service organization.
20. Compare and contrast breakeven analysis for manufacturing organizations to breakeven analysis for service organizations.

Short Exercises

SE 1. LO 1 *Concept of Cost Behavior*

Patrick's Hat Makers is in the business of designing specialty hats. The material that goes into producing a derby costs $4.50 per unit, and Patrick's pays each of its two full-time hat makers $250 per week. If hat maker A makes 15 derbies in one week, what is the variable cost per derby, and what is this worker's fixed cost per derby? If hat maker B makes only 12 derbies in one week, what are this worker's variable and fixed costs per derby? (Round to two decimal places where necessary.)

SE 2. LO 2 LO 3 *Identification of Variable, Fixed, and Mixed Costs*

Identify the following as either fixed costs, variable costs, or mixed costs.

1. Direct materials
2. Telephone expense
3. Operating supplies
4. Personnel manager's salary
5. Factory building rent payment

SE 3. LO 3 *Mixed Costs: High-Low Method*

Using the high-low method and the following information, compute the monthly variable costs per telephone hour and fixed costs for Sadiko Corporation.

Month	Business Telephone Hours	Telephone Expenses
April	96	$4,350
May	93	4,230
June	105	4,710

SE 4. LO 4 *Cost-Volume-Profit Analysis*

Delacruz, Inc., wishes to make a net income of $20,000. The company has variable costs of $80 per unit and fixed costs of $12,000. How much must Delacruz charge per unit if 4,000 units are sold?

SE 5. LO 5 *Computing the Breakeven Point*

How many units must Marsik Company sell to break even if the selling price per unit is $8.50, variable costs are $4.30 per unit, and fixed costs are $3,780?

SE 6. LO 6 *Contribution Margin*

Using the contribution margin approach, find the breakeven point in units for Dubois Consumer Products if the selling price per unit is $11, the variable cost per unit is $6, and the fixed costs are $5,500.

SE 7. LO 6 *Cost-Volume-Profit Analysis for Multiple Products*

Using the contribution margin approach, find the breakeven point in units for Lacy Products' two products. Product A's selling price per unit is $10 and its variable cost per unit is $4. Product B's selling price per unit is $8 and its variable cost per unit is $5. Fixed costs are $15,000 and the sales mix of Product A to Product B is 2:1.

SE 8. LO 7 *Contribution Margin and Projected Profit*

If Sandoval Watches sells 300 watches at $48 per watch and has variable costs of $18 per watch and fixed costs of $4,000, what is the projected net income?

SE 9. LO 8 *Cost Behavior in a Service Business*

Eye Spy, a private investigation firm, has the following costs for December.

Direct labor: $190 per case
Service overhead, December

Salary for director of investigations	$ 4,800
Telephone	930
Depreciation	8,300
Legal advice	2,300
Supplies	590
Advertising	360
Utilities	1,560
Wages for clerical personnel	2,000
Total service overhead	$20,840

Service overhead for October: $21,150
Service overhead for November: $21,350

The number of cases investigated during October, November, and December was 93, 97, and 91, respectively.

Compute the variable and fixed cost components of service overhead. Then determine the variable and fixed costs per case for December. (Round to nearest dollar where necessary.)

Exercises

LO 2 **E 1.** *Identification of Variable and Fixed Costs*

Indicate whether each of the following costs of productive output is usually considered variable or fixed: (1) packing materials for stereo components, (2) real estate taxes, (3) gasoline for a delivery truck, (4) property insurance, (5) depreciation expense of buildings (straight-line method), (6) supplies, (7) indirect materials, (8) bottles used to package liquids, (9) license fees for company cars, (10) wiring used in radios, (11) machine helper's wages, (12) wood used in bookcases, (13) city operating license, (14) machine depreciation based on machine hours of usage, (15) machine operator's hourly wages, and (16) cost of required outside inspection of each unit produced.

LO 2 **E 2.** *Variable Cost Analysis*

Speedy Oil Change has been in business for six months. Each oil change requires an average of four quarts of oil. The cost of oil to Speedy Oil Change is $.50 per quart. The estimated number of cars that will be serviced in the next three months is 240, 288, and 360.

1. Compute the cost of oil for each of the three months and the total cost for all three months. Fill in the blanks in the following table.

Month	Cars to Be Serviced	Required Quarts/Car	Cost/Quart	Total Cost/Month
1	240	4	$.50	_____
2	288	4	.50	_____
3	360	4	.50	_____
Three-month total	888			_____

2. Complete the following sentences by choosing the words that best describe the cost behavior at Speedy Oil Change.

   Cost per unit (increased, decreased, remained constant).

   Total variable cost per month (increased, decreased) as the quantity of oil used (increased, decreased).

LO 3 **E 3.** *Mixed Costs: High-Low Method*

Elder Electronics Company manufactures major appliances. The company just had its most successful year because of increased interest in its refrigerators. While preparing the budget for next year, Arnelle Autrey, the company's controller, compiled the following data.

Month	Volume in Machine Hours	Electricity Costs
July	6,000	$60,000
August	5,000	53,000
September	4,500	49,500
October	4,000	46,000
November	3,500	42,500
December	3,000	39,000

Using the high-low method, determine (1) the variable electricity cost per machine hour, (2) the monthly fixed electricity cost, and (3) the total variable electricity costs and fixed electricity costs for the six-month period.

LO 5 **E 4.** *Graphical Analysis*

Identify the letter of the point, line segment, or area of the breakeven graph on the next page that correctly completes each of the following statements.

1. The maximum possible operating loss is
   a. *A.* c. *B.*
   b. *D.* d. *F.*
2. The breakeven point in sales dollars is
   a. *C.* c. *A.*
   b. *D.* d. *G.*

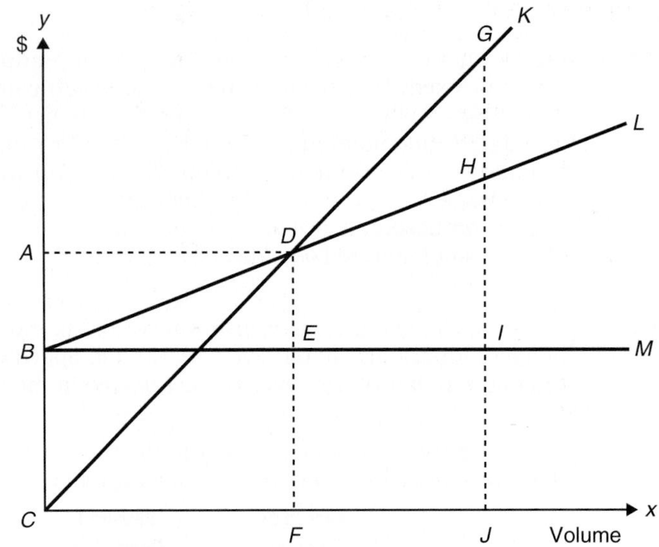

3. At volume *F*, total contribution margin is
   a. *C.* c. *E.*
   b. *D.* d. *G.*
4. Net income is represented by area
   a. *KDL.* c. *BDC.*
   b. *KCJ.* d. *GCJ.*
5. At volume *J*, total fixed costs are represented by
   a. *H.* c. *I.*
   b. *G.* d. *J.*
6. If volume increases from *F* to *J*, the change in total costs is
   a. *HI* minus *DE.* c. *BC* minus *DF.*
   b. *DF* minus *HJ.* d. *AB* minus *DE.*

E 5. LO 5 LO 6 *Breakeven Analysis*

Gleason Manufacturing Company produces head covers for golf clubs. The company expects to generate net income next year. It anticipates fixed manufacturing costs of $126,500 and fixed general and administrative expenses of $82,030 for the year. Variable manufacturing and selling costs per set of head covers will be $4.65 and $2.75, respectively. Each set will sell for $13.40.

1. Compute the breakeven point in sales units.
2. Compute the breakeven point in sales dollars.
3. If the selling price is increased to $14 per unit and fixed general and administrative expenses are cut by $33,465, what would the new breakeven point be in units?
4. Prepare a graph to illustrate the breakeven point found in **2.**

E 6. LO 6 *Calculate Breakeven Point for Multiple Products*

Marine Aquarium, Inc., manufactures and sells aquariums, water pumps, and air filters using a sales mix of 1:2:2. Using the contribution margin approach, find the breakeven point in units for each product. The company's fixed costs are $26,000. Other information is as follows:

	Selling Price per Unit	Variable Cost per Unit
Aquariums	$60	$25
Water pumps	20	12
Air filters	10	3

E 7. LO 6 LO 7 *Contribution Margin/Profit Planning*

ICT Systems, Ltd., makes undersea missiles for nuclear submarines. Management has just been offered a government contract that may generate a net income for the company. The contract purchase price is $130,000 per unit, but the number of units to be purchased has not yet been decided. The company's fixed costs are budgeted at $3,973,500, and the variable costs are $68,500 per unit.

1. Compute the number of units the company should agree to make at the stated contract price to earn a target net income of $1,500,000.
2. Using a lighter material, the variable unit cost can be reduced by $1,730, but total fixed overhead will increase by $27,500. How many units must be produced to make $1,500,000 in net income?
3. Using the figures in **2,** how many additional units must be produced to increase net income by $1,264,600?

LO 7
LO 8
Planning Future Sales

E 8. Short-term automobile rentals are the specialty of Frugal Auto Rentals, Inc. Average variable operating costs have been $12.50 per day per automobile. The company owns sixty cars. Fixed operating costs for the next year are expected to be $145,500. Average daily rental revenue per automobile is expected to be $34.50. Management would like to earn a net income of $47,000 during the year.

1. Calculate the total number of daily rentals the company must have during the year to earn the target net income.
2. On the basis of your answer to **1**, determine the number of days on the average that each automobile must be rented.
3. Find the total revenue for the year needed to earn net income of $47,000.
4. What would the total rental revenue be if fixed operating costs could be lowered by $5,180 and target net income increased to $70,000?

LO 8
Cost Behavior in a Service Business

E 9. Leo Zapata, CPA, provides tax services in Rio Bravo. To prepare standard short-form tax returns, he incurred the following costs for the previous three months.

Direct professional labor: $50 per tax return

Service overhead (included telephone, depreciation on equipment and building, tax forms, office supplies, wages of clerical personnel, and utilities): January, $18,500; February, $20,000; March, $17,000.

Number of tax returns prepared: January, 850; February, 1,000; March, 700.

1. Determine the variable and fixed cost components of the Service Overhead account.
2. What would be the estimated total cost per tax return if Leo's CPA firm prepares 825 standard short-form tax returns in April?

Problems

LO 2
LO 3
LO 8
Cost Behavior and Projection

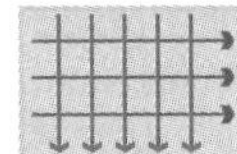

P 1. Bright Auto, Inc., which opened for business on March 1, 20x1, specializes in revitalizing automobile exteriors. *Detailing* is the term used to describe the process. The objective is to detail an automobile until it looks like it just rolled off the showroom floor. Area market research indicates that a full exterior detail should cost about $100. The company has just completed its first year of business and has asked its accountants to analyze the operating results. Management wants costs divided into variable, fixed, and mixed components and would like them projected for the coming year. Anticipated volume for next year is 1,100 jobs.

The process used to detail a car's exterior is as follows:

1. One $20-per-hour employee spends twenty minutes cleaning the car's exterior.
2. One can per car of Tars-Off, a cleaning compound, is used on the trouble spots.
3. A chemical compound called Buff Glow 7 is used to remove oxidants from the paint surface and restore the natural oils to the paint.
4. Poly Wax is applied by hand, allowed to sit for ten minutes, and then buffed off.
5. The final step is an inspection to see that all wax and debris have been removed.

On average, two hours are spent on each car, including the cleaning time and wait time for the wax. The following first-year operating information for Bright Auto is provided to the accountant.

Number of automobiles detailed	840
Labor per auto	2 hours at $20.00 per hour
Containers of Tars-Off consumed	840 at $3.50 per can
Pounds of Buff Glow 7 consumed	105 pounds at $32.00 per pound
Pounds of Poly Wax consumed	210 pounds at $8.00 per pound
Rent	$1,400.00 per month

During the year, utilities costs ranged from $800 for 40 jobs in March to $1,801 for 110 jobs in August.

REQUIRED

1. Classify the costs as variable, fixed, or mixed.
2. Using the high-low method, separate the mixed costs into their variable and fixed components. Use number of jobs as the basis.
3. Project the same costs for next year, assuming that the anticipated increase in activity will occur and that fixed costs will remain constant.
4. Compute the unit cost per job for next year.
5. Based on your answer to **4,** should the price remain at $100 per job?

P 2. LO 5, LO 6, LO 7 *Breakeven Analysis*

Billings & Brown, a law firm in downtown San Diego, is considering the development of a legal clinic for middle- and low-income clients. Paraprofessional help would be employed, and a billing rate of $18 per hour would be used. The paraprofessionals would be law students who would work for only $9 per hour. Other variable costs are anticipated to be $5.40 per hour, and annual fixed costs are expected to total $27,000.

REQUIRED

1. Compute the breakeven point in billable hours.
2. Compute the breakeven point in total billings.
3. Find the new breakeven point in total billings if fixed costs should go up by $2,340.
4. Using the original figures, compute the breakeven point in total billings if the billing rate is decreased by $1 per hour, variable costs are decreased by $.40 per hour, and fixed costs go down by $3,600.

P 3. LO 7 *Planning Future Sales*

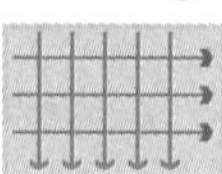

Lesko Financial Corporation is a subsidiary of Polansky Enterprises. Processing loan applications is the main task of the corporation. Last year, Polly Bar, the manager of the Loan Department, established a policy of charging a $250 fee for every loan application processed. Next year's variable costs have been projected as follows: loan consultant's wages, $15.50 per hour (a loan application takes five hours to process); supplies, $2.40 per application; and other variable costs, $5.60 per application. Annual fixed costs include depreciation of equipment, $8,500; building rental, $14,000; promotional costs, $12,500; and other fixed costs, $8,099.

REQUIRED

1. Using the contribution margin approach, compute the number of loan applications the company must process to (a) break even and (b) earn a net income of $14,476.
2. Continuing the same approach, compute the number of applications the company must process to earn a target net income of $20,000 if promotional costs increase by $5,662.
3. Assuming the original information and the processing of 500 applications, compute the loan application fee the company must charge if the target net income is $41,651.
4. Bar believes that 750 loan applications is the maximum number her staff can handle. How much more can be spent on promotional costs if the highest fee tolerable to the customer is $280, if variable costs cannot be reduced, and if the target net income for such an application loan is $50,000?

P 4. LO 6, LO 7 *Planning Future Sales*

Vitale Company has a maximum capacity of 200,000 units per year. Variable manufacturing costs are $12 per unit. Fixed manufacturing overhead is $600,000 per year. Variable selling and administrative costs are $5 per unit, and fixed selling and administrative costs are $300,000 per year. The current sales price is $23 per unit.

REQUIRED

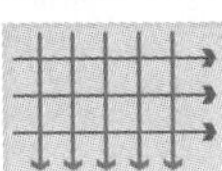

1. What is the breakeven point in (a) sales units and (b) sales dollars?
2. How many units must be sold to earn a target net income of $240,000 per year?
3. A strike at a major supplier has caused a material shortage, so the current year's production and sales are limited to 160,000 units. Top management is planning to reduce fixed costs to $841,000 to partially offset the effect on net income of the reduced sales. Variable cost per unit is the same as last year. The company already has sold 30,000 units at the regular selling price of $23 per unit.
   a. How much of the fixed costs was covered by the total contribution margin of the first 30,000 units sold?
   b. What contribution margin per unit will be needed on the remaining 130,000 units to cover the remaining fixed costs and to earn $210,000 in net income this year?

Alternate Problems

LO 5 *Breakeven Analysis*
LO 6

P 5. At the beginning of each year, the accounting department at Zia Lighting, Ltd., must find the point at which projected sales revenue will equal total budgeted variable and fixed costs. The company makes custom-made, low-voltage outdoor lighting systems. Each system sells for an average of $435. Variable costs per unit are $210. Total fixed costs for the year are estimated to be $166,500.

REQUIRED

1. Compute the breakeven point in sales units.
2. Compute the breakeven point in sales dollars.
3. Find the new breakeven point in sales units if the fixed costs should go up by $10,125.
4. Using the original figures, compute the breakeven point in sales units if the selling price decreases to $425 per unit, fixed costs go up by $15,200, and variable costs decrease by $15 per unit.

LO 7 *Planning Future Sales: Contribution Margin Approach*

P 6. Yoli Bingaman is president of the ASU Plastics Division of Land Industries. Management is considering a new product featuring a dashing medieval knight posed on a beautiful horse. Called Chargin' Knight, this product is expected to have global market appeal and become the mascot for many high school and university athletic teams. Expected variable unit costs are as follows: direct materials, $18.50; direct labor, $4.25; production supplies, $1.10; selling costs, $2.80; and other, $1.95. The following are annual fixed costs: depreciation, building and equipment, $36,000.00; advertising, $45,000.00; and other, $11,400.00. Land Industries plans to sell the product for $55.00.

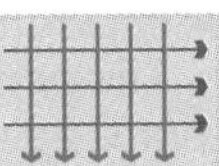

REQUIRED

1. Using the contribution margin approach, compute the number of products the company must sell to (a) break even and (b) earn a net income of $70,224.
2. Using the same data, compute the number of products that must be sold to earn a target net income of $139,520 if advertising costs rise by $40,000.
3. Assuming the original information and sales of 10,000 units, compute the new selling price the company must use to make a net income of $131,600.
4. According to the vice president of marketing, Pete Rice, the most optimistic annual sales estimate for the product would be 15,000 units, and the highest competitive selling price the company can charge is $52.00 per unit. How much more can be spent on fixed advertising costs if the selling price is $52.00, if the variable costs cannot be reduced, and if the target net income for 15,000 unit sales is $251,000?

Skills Development

CONCEPTUAL ANALYSIS

SD 1.
LO 1 *Concept of Cost Behavior*
LO 2

Pacific Coast Shrimp Company is a very small company. It owns an ice house and shrimp preparation building, a refrigerated van, and three shrimp boats. Steven Black inherited the company from his father three months ago. The company employs three boat crews of four people each and five processing workers. Willman and Yang, a local accounting firm, has kept the company's financial records for many years.

In her last analysis of operations, Su Yang stated that the company's fixed-cost base of $100,000 is satisfactory for this type and size of business. However, variable costs have averaged 70 percent of sales over the last two years, a percentage that is too high for the volume of business. For example, last year only 30 percent of the company's sales revenue of $300,000 contributed toward covering the fixed costs. As a result, the company reported a $10,000 operating loss.

Black wants to improve the company's net income, but he is confused by Yang's explanation of the fixed and variable costs. Prepare a response to Black from Yang in which you explain the concept of cost behavior as it relates to Pacific Coast's operations. Include ideas for improving the company's net income based on changes in fixed and variable costs.

ETHICAL DILEMMA

SD 2.
LO 5 *Breaking Even and Ethics*

Cindy Ginsberg is the supervisor of the new product division of ***Fricker Corp.,*** located in Jackson, Wyoming. Ginsberg's annual bonus is based on the success of new products and is computed on the amount of sales over and above each product's projected breakeven point. In reviewing the computations supporting her most recent bonus, she found that a large order for 7,500 units of product WR4, which had been refused by a customer and returned to the company, had been included in the calculations. She later found out that the company's accountant had labeled the return as an overhead expense and had charged the entire cost of the returned order to the plantwide manufacturing overhead account. The result was that product WR4 exceeded breakeven by more than 5,000 units and Cindy's bonus from that product amounted to over $800. What actions should Ginsberg take? Be prepared to discuss your response.

RESEARCH ACTIVITY

SD 3.
LO 6 *Projecting Revenues and*
LO 7 *Costs*

Select a company on the Internet or refer to the Needles Accounting Resource Center Web site at http://www.hmco.com/college/needles/home.html for links to selected companies. Study the Letter to the Stockholders in the most recent annual report for the company you have chosen. Many initiatives or actions discussed in this section were part of the company's strategic plan and were included in planning activities for the year. Identify at least three initiatives or actions that you believe were part of the company's planning activities for the year that affected sales or costs. Also identify one initiative or action that the company is planning for the coming year that you would expect to affect revenue or expenses for next year.

Group Activity: Divide the class into groups and ask them to discuss this SD. Then debrief the entire class by asking one person from each group to summarize his or her group's findings.

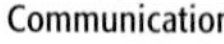
Communication

Critical Thinking

Group Activity

Memo

Ethics

International

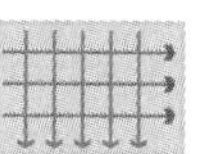
Spreadsheet

Managerial Technology

Internet

DECISION-MAKING PRACTICE

LO 2 LO 3 *Mixed Costs*

SD 4. Officials of the ***Minnetonka Golf and Tennis Club*** are putting together a budget for the year ending December 31, 20xx. A problem has caused the budget to be delayed by more than four weeks. Ray Lobo, the club treasurer, indicated that two expense items were creating the problem. The items were difficult to account for because they were called "mixed costs," and he did not know how to break them down into their variable and fixed components. An accountant friend and golfing partner told him to use the high-low method to divide the costs into their variable and fixed parts.

The two cost categories are Electricity Expense and Repairs and Maintenance Expense. Information pertaining to last year's spending patterns and the measurement activity connected with each cost are as shown below.

	Electricity Expense		Repairs and Maintenance	
Month	**Amount**	**Kilowatt Hours**	**Amount**	**Labor Hours**
January	$ 7,500	210,000	$ 7,578	220
February	8,255	240,200	7,852	230
March	8,165	236,600	7,304	210
April	8,960	268,400	7,030	200
May	7,520	210,800	7,852	230
June	7,025	191,000	8,126	240
July	6,970	188,800	8,400	250
August	6,990	189,600	8,674	260
September	7,055	192,200	8,948	270
October	7,135	195,400	8,674	260
November	8,560	252,400	8,126	240
December	8,415	246,600	7,852	230
Totals	$92,550	2,622,000	$96,416	2,840

1. Using the high-low method, compute the variable cost rates used last year for each expense. What was the monthly fixed cost for electricity and for repairs and maintenance?
2. Compute the total variable cost and total fixed cost for each expense category for last year.
3. Lobo believes that for the coming year the electricity rate will increase by $.005 and the repairs rate will rise by $1.20. Usage of all items and their fixed cost amounts will remain constant. Compute the projected total cost for each category. How will these increases in costs affect the club's profits and cash flow?

Managerial Reporting and Analysis

INTERPRETING MANAGEMENT REPORTS

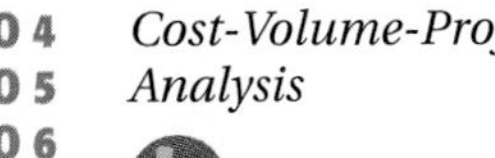

LO 4 LO 5 LO 6 *Cost-Volume-Profit Analysis*

MRA 1. ***Nambe-Casa, Ltd.,*** is an international importer-exporter of fine china. The company was formed in 1963 in Albuquerque, New Mexico. The company has distribution centers in the United States, Europe, and Australia. Although very successful in its early years, the company's profitability has steadily declined. As a member of a management team selected to gather information for the next strategic planning meeting, you are asked to review the most recent income statement for the company. The income statement is on the next page. Sales in 20x1 were 15,000 sets of fine china.

Nambe-Casa, Ltd. Contribution Income Statement For the Year Ended December 31, 20x1		
Sales		$13,500,000
Less Variable Costs		
Purchases	$6,000,000	
Distribution	2,115,000	
Sales Commissions	1,410,000	
Total Variable Costs		9,525,000
Contribution Margin		$ 3,975,000
Less Fixed Costs		
Distribution	$ 985,000	
Selling	1,184,000	
General and Administrative	871,875	
Total Fixed Costs		3,040,875
Net Income		$ 934,125

REQUIRED

1. For each set of fine china, calculate the (a) selling price, (b) variable purchases cost, (c) variable distribution cost, (d) variable sales commission; and (e) contribution margin.
2. Calculate the breakeven point in units and in sales dollars.
3. Historically, variable costs should be about 60 percent of sales. What was the ratio of variable costs to sales for 20x1? List three actions Nambe-Casa could take to correct the difference.
4. What would have been the impact on fixed costs if Nambe-Casa had sold only 14,000 sets of fine china?

Formulating Management Reports

MRA 2.
LO 7 *Cost-Volume-Profit Analysis*

Refer to the information in **MRA 1**. In January 20x2, Laura Casa, the president and chief executive officer of Nambe-Casa, Ltd., conducted a strategic planning meeting with her officers. Below is a summary of the information provided by two of the officers.

> Rita O'Toole, vice president of sales: A review of the competitors indicates that the selling price of a set of china should be lowered to $890. We plan to sell 15,000 sets of fine china again in 20x2. To encourage increased sales, we should raise sales commissions to 12 percent of the selling price.

> Maurice Moonitz, vice president of distribution: We have signed a contract with a new shipping line for foreign shipments. We will be able to reduce the fixed distribution costs by 10 percent and reduce variable distribution costs by 4 percent.

Laura needs your help. She is concerned that the changes may not improve net income sufficiently in 20x2. If net income does not increase by at least 10 percent, she will want to find other ways to reduce the company's costs. Since the new year has already started and changes need to be made quickly, she requests your report within five days.

REQUIRED

1. Prepare an estimated contribution income statement for 20x2. Your report should show the budgeted (estimated) net income based on the information provided above and in **MRA 1**. Will the changes improve net income sufficiently? Explain.
2. In preparation for writing your report, answer the following questions:
   a. Who needs the report?
   b. Why are you preparing the report?
   c. What were the sources of information for your report?
   d. When is the report due?

International Company

MRA 3.
LO 4 *C-V-P Analysis and Decision Making*

The ***Goslar Corporation*** cuts stones used in the construction and restoration of cathedrals throughout Europe. Granite, marble, and sandstone are cut into a variety of dimensions for walls, ceilings, and floors. The German-based company has operations in Italy and Switzerland. Otto Schrock, the controller, recently determined that the breakeven point was $325,000 in sales. In preparation for a quarterly planning meeting, Otto must provide information for the following six proposals, which will be discussed individually by the planning team.

a. Increase the selling price of marble slabs by 10 percent.
b. Change the sales mix to respond to the increased sales demand for marble slabs. As a result, the company would increase production of marble slabs and decrease the production and sales of sandstone, the least profitable product.
c. Increase fixed production costs by $40,000 annually for the depreciation of new stone-cutting equipment.
d. Increase the variable costs by 1 percent for increased export duties on foreign sales.
e. Decrease the sales volume of the sandstone slabs because of political upheavals in eastern Europe.
f. Decrease the number of days that a customer can wait before paying without being charged interest.

REQUIRED

1. For each proposal, determine if cost-volume-profit (C-V-P) analysis would provide useful financial information.
2. Indicate whether each proposal that lends itself to C-V-P analysis would show an increase, decrease, or no impact on net income. Consider each decision separately.

Excel Spreadsheet Analysis

MRA 4.
LO 7 *Planning Future Sales*

Refer to the information in **MRA 2**. In January 20x2, Laura Casa gathered information about a decrease in the selling price of a set of china to $890, an increase in sales commissions to 12 percent of the selling price, a decrease in fixed distribution costs of 10 percent, a decrease in variable distribution costs of 4 percent, and planned sales of 15,000 sets. Based on an analysis of this information she found that Nambe-Casa would not increase its 20x2 net income by at least 10 percent over the previous year's income.

Rita O'Toole reported that a new salesperson had just obtained a sales contract with an Australian distributor for 4,500 sets of china. The selling price, variable purchases cost per unit, 12 percent sales commission, and total fixed costs will be the same, but the variable distribution costs will be $160 per unit.

REQUIRED

Using Excel spreadsheet, complete the following:

1. Calculate the desired net income for 20x2.
2. Prepare a contribution margin income statement for 20x2 based on the information presented in **MRA 1** and the adjustments presented in **MRA 2**. Do you agree with Ms. Casa that Nambe-Casa's projected net income for 20x2 will be less than the net income for 20x1? Explain.
3. Calculate the total contribution margin from the Australian sales.
4. Prepare a revised contribution margin income statement for 20x2 by combining the information from **2** and **3** above.
5. Does Nambe-Casa need the Australian sales to satisfy the desired net income requirement for 20x2?

ENDNOTES

1. Linda Hall and Jane Lambert, "Cummins Engine Changes Its Depreciation," *Management Accounting*, Institute of Management Accountants, July 1996, pp. 30–36.
2. Jerry G. Kreuze, Gale E. Newell, and Stephen J. Newell, "What Companies Are Reporting," *Management Accounting*, Institute of Management Accountants, July 1996, p. 42.
3. Paul Hooper and John Page, "Relational Databases: An Accountant's Primer," *Management Accounting*, Institute of Management Accountants, October 1996, pp. 48–53.

CHAPTER 24

The Budgeting Process

LEARNING OBJECTIVES

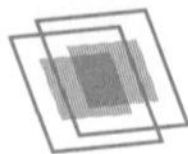

1. **Define *budgeting* and explain its role in the management cycle.**
2. **Explain the basic principles of budgeting.**
3. **Describe the master budget process for different types of organizations, and list the guidelines for preparing budgets.**
4. **Prepare a budgeted income statement and supporting operating budgets.**
5. **Prepare a cash budget.**
6. **Prepare a budgeted balance sheet.**
7. **Define *responsibility accounting* and discuss its relation to responsibility centers.**

DECISION POINT

THE HON COMPANY

The HON Company, the largest manufacturer of mid-priced office furniture in the United States and Canada, wants to improve productivity and customer service while developing new products and services. However, balancing incremental improvements with innovation is difficult. The HON Company, one of nine subsidiaries of HON Industries, operates as a profit center. The managers of HON Company are responsible for generating profits and managing resources in accordance with its parent company's strategic plan. The company feels tremendous pressure to compete in an industry that has a few major customers who want good quality, low prices, and on-time delivery. To manage costs and make full use of production capacity, managers at the HON Company use a process called continuous quarterly budgeting to implement their budgets. At the beginning of each quarter, teams work to create a four-quarter budget. Through this budgeting process, top management expects to motivate others to continuously improve productivity and reduce delivery time while planning the introduction of new products and variations of existing products.[1]

How does the quarterly budget process work? First, a team from sales and marketing develops a sales budget by product, geographic territory, and distribution channel. The president and senior staff review the sales budget to see that it meets the goals of the strategic plan. Second, the scheduling team prepares a production and shipping schedule to coordinate those activities at the different manufacturing plants. Third, managers responsible for one of the five functional areas (research and development; production; distribution; customer service; and selling, general, and administrative) prepare cost/expense budgets. Fourth, the company accounting group reviews the budgets and analyzes the contents to see that the budgets reflect the strategic plan. Fifth, the HON Company controller prepares a complete set of budgeted financial statements and additional information, including

Critical Thinking Question: How do you think management minimizes the time required to prepare continuous quarterly budgets? **Answer:** A computerized budgeting system allows managers to change only specific items as needed and to transfer information more quickly to higher-level managers.

VIDEO CASE

ENTERPRISE RENT-A-CAR

OBJECTIVES

- To become familiar with the budgeting process and budgets
- To understand the relationship between strategic plans and operating budgets
- To describe the role of budgeting in the management cycle

BACKGROUND FOR THE CASE

Enterprise Rent-A-Car does not have the high profile most of its competitors enjoy because it does not rent vehicles at airport locations; however, with over $3.5 billion in annual revenues (revenue growth of more than 25 percent per year for the last eleven years) and more than 3,300 locations, it is the largest car rental company in the United States and one of the top fifty privately owned companies. The forty-year old company focuses on the home-city market, which is divided into two segments. The first segment serves people who need replacement vehicles when their own cars are not available—for instance, when they are scheduled for lengthy repair work. The second segment serves people with discretionary needs for another or different type of car for a short period, such as for a weekend trip or vacations. Enterprise prides itself on providing excellent customer service, including free delivery and pickup of all rentals. The company accomplishes its goals by providing incentives to motivate employees, coupled with a decentralized organization that allows great latitude in decision making. Enterprise's managers prepare budgets to integrate, coordinate, and communicate the operating plans necessary to achieve these strategic objectives. The budgeting system must allow measurement of performance for each location and each employee. Good systems and budgeting also facilitate the company's objective of expanding into global markets in Canada, the United Kingdom, and Germany.

For more information about Enterprise Rent-A-Car, visit the company's Web site through the Needles Accounting Resource Center at

http://www.hmco.com/college/needles/home.html

REQUIRED

View the video on Enterprise Rent-A-Car that accompanies this book. As you are watching the video, take notes related to the following questions:

1. As part of the planning process, many large, successful companies prepare budgets. In your words, explain what a budget is and list all of the reasons you believe a company like Enterprise would prepare a set of budgets.
2. Companies that prepare strategic plans also prepare budgets. What is the relationship between Enterprise's strategic plans and its operating budgets?
3. What is the role of budgeting in the management cycle?

productivity measures, budgeted sales attributable to new product introductions, and major equipment expenditures.

The value of this approach for HON Company results from the preparation of the budgets on a quarterly basis. This continuous process informs employees about new products and procedures and permits improvements to occur more quickly. Continuous quarterly budgeting successfully connects strategic planning to operations by helping the workers see the corporate vision, target their actions to support the vision, and monitor the results of their actions. Continuous quarterly budgeting helps the managers and employees of the HON Company to continuously improve productivity and customer service while integrating innovation through the development of new products.

The Budgeting Process

OBJECTIVE 1

Define **budgeting** *and explain its role in the management cycle*

Related Text Assignments:
Q: 1, 2, 3, 4, 5, 6
SE: 1, 2, 3
E: 1, 2
SD: 1, 3

Point to Emphasize: A budget is a management tool. The quality of the tool, when used in the proper manner, influences the quality of the results achieved.

Point to Emphasize: The preparation stage is the planning part of the budgeting process. Budgeting also helps control operations.

Point to Emphasize: Cost control is not the same as cost reduction. The concept of control recognizes that costs must be incurred but should be incurred in the proper amounts to achieve an organization's desired goals.

Enrichment Note: Any budget, even a poorly prepared one, is probably better than no budget at all. As the budgeting process is refined, the benefits to the organization will increase.

Planning is an important ongoing process for organizations. A review of the current use of available resources for financing, investing, and operating activities is necessary to plan for the efficient use of future resources. **Budgeting** is the process of identifying, gathering, summarizing, and communicating financial and nonfinancial information about an organization's future activities. The budgeting process provides managers with the opportunity to carefully match the goals of the organization with the resources necessary to accomplish those goals.

Budgets are synonymous with managing an organization. The term *organization* is important because budgets are used in government and not-for-profit organizations (such as hospitals, universities, professional organizations, and charities) as well as in profit-oriented businesses. All types of organizations rely on plans to help them accomplish their objectives. All types of organizations have managers whose responsibilities are determined by top management or a board of directors; budgets are used to plan for and assess those areas of responsibility and to measure managers' performance. All organizations need cash to purchase resources to accomplish their goals. Whenever cash needs to be managed and accounted for, budgets are used. Budgets establish (1) minimum desired or target levels of cash receipts and (2) limits on the spending of cash for particular purposes. The primary difference between not-for-profit and profit-oriented organizations is that a profit-oriented organization sells a product or service for the purpose of making a profit. Profit-oriented organizations often call their budgeting function a profit-planning activity.

A **budget** is a plan of action that forecasts future transactions, activities, and events in financial or nonfinancial terms. Used as planning documents, budgets can communicate information, coordinate activities and resource usage, motivate employees, and evaluate performance. Budgets come in many forms. Some budgets present financial information based on the availability of resources. Those budgets should reflect a fair assignment of resources to various organizational activities over a future period. For example, a cash budget shows the planned use of cash resources for operating, investing, and financing activities. Other budgets show planned activities to meet certain requirements or standards established in the planning stage. For example, a production budget shows planned production in units. Exhibit 1 contains two simple budgets prepared for diverse purposes. These budgets are illustrations rather than official guidelines for budget preparation.

The budgeting process is as important in today's globally competitive operating environment as it is in more traditional settings. In fact, budgeting becomes even

Exhibit 1. Examples of Budgets

Example A

State University Knights
Alumni Club
Revenues and Expenditures Budget
Homecoming Activities—20x1

Budgeted Revenues		
Football Concession Sales	$32,500	
Homecoming Dance Tickets (1,200 at $20)	24,000	
Parking Fees	1,425	
Total Budgeted Revenues		$57,925
Budgeted Expenditures		
Dance Music Group	$ 7,500	
Hall Rental	2,000	
Refreshments	2,600	
Printing Costs	1,450	
Concession Purchases	12,200	
Clean-up Costs	4,720	
Miscellaneous	800	
Total Budgeted Expenditures		31,270
Excess of Revenues Over Expenditures*		$26,655

*To be contributed to State University's Scholarship Fund.

Example B

Scottsdale Resort
Room Occupancy Budget
For the Year Ended December 31, 20x2

	Projected Occupancy							
	Singles (50)		Doubles (80)		Mini Suites (10)		Luxury Suites (6)	
Month	Rooms	%	Rooms	%	Rooms	%	Rooms	%
January	20	40.0	30	37.5	2	20.0	1	16.7
February	24	48.0	36	45.0	3	30.0	1	16.7
March	28	56.0	42	52.5	4	40.0	2	33.3
April	32	64.0	50	62.5	5	50.0	2	33.3
May	44	88.0	60	75.0	6	60.0	2	33.3
June	46	92.0	74	92.5	7	70.0	3	50.0
July	50	100.0	78	97.5	9	90.0	4	66.7
August	50	100.0	80	100.0	10	100.0	5	83.3
September	48	96.0	78	97.5	10	100.0	6	100.0
October	34	68.0	60	75.0	8	80.0	5	83.3
November	30	60.0	46	57.5	2	20.0	3	50.0
December	34	68.0	50	62.5	4	40.0	4	66.7

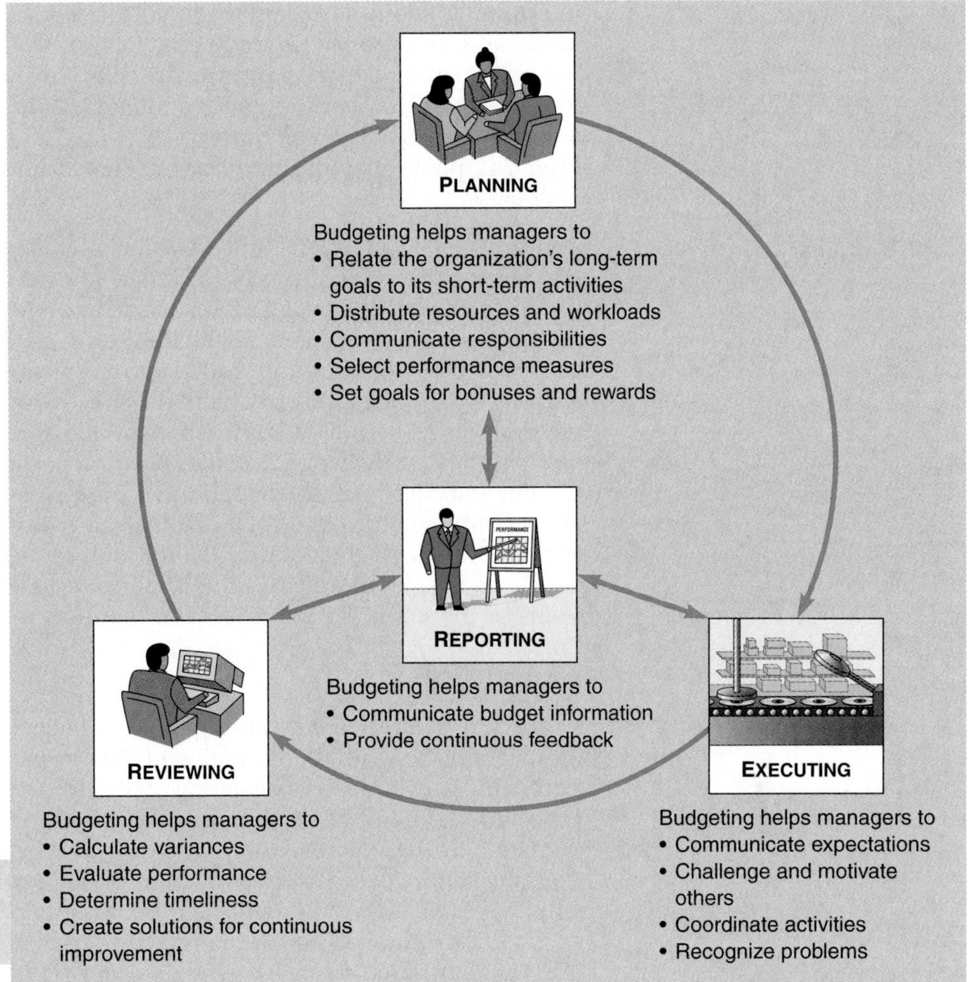

Figure 1
Budgeting and the Management Cycle

more important when just-in-time (JIT) or total quality management (TQM) concepts are applied and when computers and other electronic operating and data accumulation devices are used. In these new environments, actual operating data are made available quickly, and budgets are updated continuously to accommodate management's need for performance evaluation. The principles of budgeting do not change in the new operating environments, but the speed and timing with which they are applied does.

Budgeting and the Management Cycle

Managers in profit-oriented organizations work to generate profits and pay debts as they become due because investors and creditors expect them to do so. To achieve the goals of profitability and liquidity, managers of many organizations use the budgeting process throughout the management cycle to help plan, execute, review, and report the organization's financing, investing, and operating activities. Figure 1 illustrates the relationships between budgeting and the management cycle. Budgets originate in the planning stage, which is the stage that we emphasize in this chapter. It is important to develop relevant, timely budgets during the planning stage because managers will rely on the resulting budget information when making decisions during the executing and reviewing stages. Budget information is quantifiable information about an organization's future activities and the revenues or expenses associated with those activities. Reports formally communicate budget information. We will illustrate the relationship between budgeting and the management cycle in the context of Hi-Flyer Company, a manufacturer of flying disks used for recreation and tournament play. The owner, Skye King, believes that the future growth of Hi-Flyer Company depends on a good budgeting process.

Planning The planning process often includes the development of long-range and short-range plans to achieve important success factors, such as high-quality products, reasonable cost, and timely delivery. Mr. King believes that budgets help his organization's managers match long-term goals with short-term business activities by carefully distributing workloads and resources throughout the organization, such as to specific products, departments, sales territories, and activities. In the planning stage, budget teams use budget information to communicate responsibilities to individuals who are accountable for a particular segment of the organization. Careful selection and introduction of performance measures can challenge and influence the performance of individuals or teams to achieve goals and earn bonuses and rewards for their efforts. Senior management recently selected profits, number of units sold, and cycle time (the time to take, manufacture, and ship a sales order) as measures of performance for bonuses to individuals and teams at Hi-Flyer Company.

Executing During the executing stage, managers use budget information for communication, benchmarking, and problem recognition. The managers of Hi-Flyer Company use budget information daily, weekly, and monthly to communicate expectations about the performance of activities and the availability of resources for segments of the organization. For example, Abe Dillon, the production manager, uses the planned units of production as an operating target for the production employees. He has also established the number of reworks as a performance measure to motivate workers to manufacture quality products. In addition, Mr. King uses standard product costs, generated during the budget process, to submit bids for sales orders, estimate profits, and calculate the expected profitability of a product during the operating period.

Reviewing In the reviewing stage, managers calculate variances, evaluate performance, review the timeliness of activities performed, and create solutions for continuous improvement. As mentioned earlier, Hi-Flyer's managers use the performance measures developed during the planning stage as targets for actual performance during the executing stage. By comparing the budget and actual information, they can identify variances between planned and actual activity. They review the variances to identify waste and inefficiencies in production, sales, purchasing, packing, shipping, accounting, and other business activities. If problems are identified, they can work together to find solutions that will enable the organization to continuously improve its products and processes. Hi-Flyer's managers perform budget analyses on a regular basis because it helps chart the course of future operations and provides a means of evaluating past performance. If Hi-Flyer Company establishes realistic goals, then comparing the actual results with budgeted targets can help management assess how well the organization performed.

Point to Emphasize: Although we present the four stages of the management cycle linearly, organizations are dynamic and managers may move through one stage, such as the executing stage, more often than another stage, such as the planning stage. For example, as part of the reviewing stage, a manager may evaluate performance reports on a weekly basis. On the other hand, as part of the planning stage, a manager may prepare a capital expenditures budget for new equipment only once a year.

Reporting The reporting stage occurs throughout the year because managers need to continuously report on budget information and provide feedback about the organization's operating, investing, and financing activities. Budgets are reports showing plans for future actions. As such, they serve as a reference point for many other reports. For example, performance reports based on budget information sup-

BUSINESS BULLETIN: TECHNOLOGY IN PRACTICE

When an organization decides to market its products or services on the Internet's World Wide Web, it must create a Web site and build the site's costs into its budget. Developing a Web site includes making decisions about access to the Internet, content on the site (online brochures or product news), graphic design, and functionality. In addition to basic development costs, the organization will incur costs for faster connections, database applications that update information easily, and animations and three-dimensional logos. After the Web site has been developed, additional costs include monthly site maintenance fees, database development, and network integration. In addition, those who choose to use a custom domain server pay a yearly licensing fee to Internic, a government agency that oversees Internet activity.

port bonuses and promotions. Other budget-based reports support operating decisions. In this chapter, we will focus on how budgets are prepared during the planning stage. In the next chapter, we will discuss the use of budget information in the reviewing stage of the management cycle.

Basic Principles of Budgeting

OBJECTIVE 2

Explain the basic principles of budgeting

Related Text Assignments:
Q: 7, 8, 9, 10, 11
SE: 4
E: 3, 4
SD: 1, 2, 3, 4
MRA: 1, 2

Discussion Question: Describe some additional benefits of budgeting. **Answer:** (1) There will be improved communication between business segments, (2) managers will become better general business managers and acquire a better understanding of the business environment, and (3) managers will better understand the impact of their actions on other business operations.

Point to Emphasize: Because long-range plans are developed by top management, communication is necessary to inform lower levels of management of those goals.

Enrichment Note: Long-range plans are often expressed in more subjective terms, such as increasing market share, becoming the industry leader, or having the best quality in the market.

Budget preparation contributes to an organization's success in three ways. First, preparing a budget forces management to look ahead and plan both long- and short-range goals and events. Second, the entire management team must work together to make and carry out the plans. Third, by comparing the budget with actual results, it is possible to review performance at all levels of management.

Long-Range Goals Annual operating plans cannot be made unless the people preparing the budget know the direction that top management expects for the organization. Long-range goals, which are projections covering a five- to ten-year period, must be set by top management. Those goals should take into consideration economic and industry forecasts, employee-management relationships, and the structure and role of management in leading the organization. And they should include statements about the expected quality of products or services, growth rates, and desired market share.

Vague aims are not sufficient. The long-term goals should set specific targets and expected timetables and name the people responsible for achieving the goals. For example, assume that one of O'Toole Corporation's long-term goals is to control 15 percent of its product's market. At present the company holds only 4 percent of the market. The company's long-term goals may state that the vice president of marketing is to develop plans and strategies to ensure that the company controls 10 percent of the market in five years and increases its share to 15 percent by the end of ten years.

Once all goals have been developed, they should be compiled into a total long-range plan. This plan should include a spectrum of targets and goals and give direction to the company's efforts to achieve those goals. It should include future profit projections and spell out in general terms new products and services.

Short-Range Goals and Strategies The long-range goals must be carefully developed because they are used to prepare yearly operating plans and targets. The short-range plan involves every part of the enterprise and is much more detailed than the long-range goals.

Point to Emphasize: As plans are formulated for time periods closer to the current date, they become more specific and quantified. The annual budget is a very specific plan of action.

To arrive at the short-range plan, the long-range goals must be restated in terms of what should be accomplished during the next year. Decisions must be made about sales and profit targets by product or service, human resource needs and expected changes, and plans for introducing new products or services. The resulting short-range targets and goals form the basis for the organization's operating budget for the year.

Once management has set the short-range goals, the controller or budget director takes charge of preparing the budget. This person designs a complete set of budget-development plans and a timetable with deadlines for all levels and parts of the year's operating plan. Specific people must be named to carry out each part of the budget's development, and their responsibilities, targets, and deadlines must be clearly described.

The Master Budget

OBJECTIVE 3

Describe the master budget process for different types of organizations, and list the guidelines for preparing budgets

Related Text Assignments:
Q: 12, 13, 14, 15
SE:5
E: 5
SD: 1, 2, 4
MRA: 2, 4

Teaching Note: At this point, discuss spreadsheet applications in budgeting, as well as the linking of spreadsheets.

Suppose you want to start a new business, but you must obtain a bank loan to supply some of the cash you need to begin operations. Before the bank will agree to loan you money, you must demonstrate that you can repay the principal and interest with cash generated by profitable operations. To do so, you will prepare a set of budgeted, or pro forma, financial statements for the bank to review. Now assume that you receive the bank loan and that, over ten years, your company becomes quite successful. Every year you would continue to prepare a set of budgeted financial statements so that you could match long-term goals to short-term activities and plan for the resources necessary to operate, finance, and invest in your business.

A master budget is a set of budgets that consolidate an organization's financial information into budgeted financial statements for a future period of time. A master budget includes a set of operating budgets that support a budgeted income statement. In addition, a master budget presents a set of financial budgets that include a budgeted balance sheet, a cash budget, and a capital expenditures budget. Regardless of the type of organization, the master budget provides helpful information for planning, executing, reviewing, and reporting organizational activities. Figures 2, 3, and 4 display the preparation of a master budget for a manufacturing organization, a retail organization, and a service organization, respectively.

The master budget process has some similarities in all three types of organizations. All three types of organizations need a set of operating budgets to support the budgeted income statement. The budget information from the operating budgets and the capital expenditures budget affects the cash budget and the budgeted balance sheet. The cash budget also provides information for the budgeted balance sheet.

The main difference in the master budget process for the three types of organizations involves the preparation of operating budgets for the budgeted income statement. The operating budgets for a manufacturing organization like Intel or John Deere include budgets for sales, production, direct materials purchases, direct labor, manufacturing overhead, cost of goods manufactured, and selling and administrative expenses. The preparation of those budgets for a manufacturing organization will be explained under the next learning objective.

A retail organization like J.C. Penney or Home Depot must know what products to sell, the estimated quantities to be sold, and the selling price for each. This helps the organization plan the amount of resources needed to sell the merchandise. A retail organization must purchase merchandise for resale and incur expenses for employee payroll, utilities, taxes, insurance, rent, advertising, sales commissions, accounting, and other expenses. Managers may need to purchase long-term assets, such as buildings, equipment, and display cases to store, display, and sell merchan-

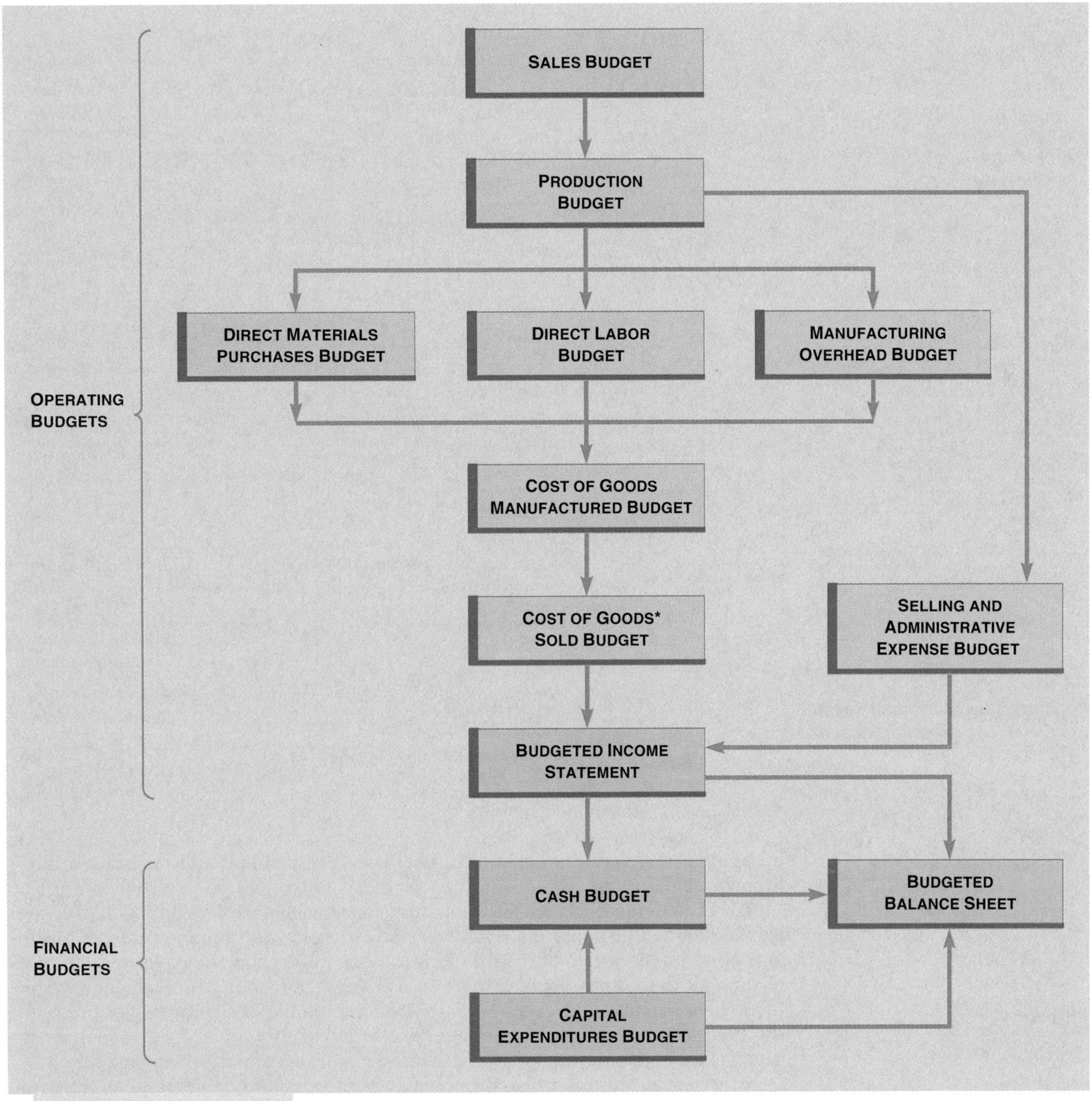

SALES BUDGET

PRODUCTION BUDGET

DIRECT MATERIALS PURCHASES BUDGET

DIRECT LABOR BUDGET

MANUFACTURING OVERHEAD BUDGET

OPERATING BUDGETS

COST OF GOODS MANUFACTURED BUDGET

COST OF GOODS* SOLD BUDGET

SELLING AND ADMINISTRATIVE EXPENSE BUDGET

BUDGETED INCOME STATEMENT

CASH BUDGET

BUDGETED BALANCE SHEET

FINANCIAL BUDGETS

CAPITAL EXPENDITURES BUDGET

Figure 2
Preparation of a Master Budget for a Manufacturing Organization

*Some organizations choose to include the cost of goods sold budget in the budgeted income statement.

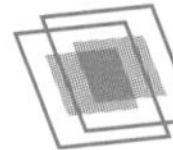

dise. To manage the use of these resources, retail managers and accountants prepare operating budgets to support a budgeted income statement. The operating budgets for a retail organization include a sales budget, a purchases budget, a cost of goods sold budget, and a selling and administrative expense budget. The sales budget is prepared first because it is used to estimate sales volume and revenues. Once managers know how many sales dollars to expect, and the quantity to be sold, they can develop other budgets that will enable them to manage the organization's resources to generate profits on those sales. The purchases budget determines the

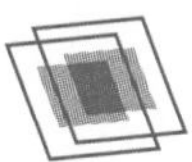

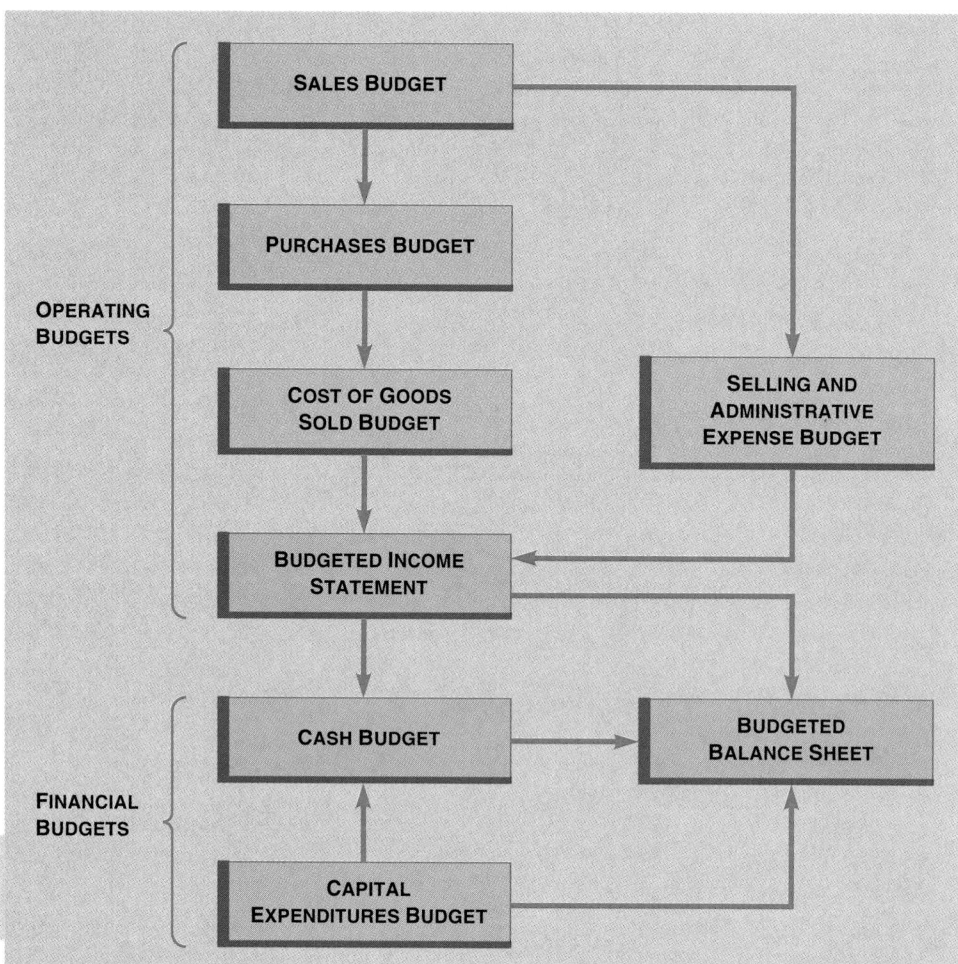

Figure 3 Preparation of a Master Budget for a Retail Organization

quantity of merchandise needed to meet the sales demand and maintain a minimum level of inventory.

Rather than manufacture and sell products, service organizations such as Union Pacific Railroad or Columbia Healthcare invest money in human resources to provide services. Managers of service organizations must know the types and amounts of services to perform. Managers must also know the labor hours needed to complete those services, the level of expertise of their employees, and the labor rates for the planned services. In addition, service organizations must incur expenses for utilities, taxes, insurance, rent, advertising, accounting, and other expenses.

A service organization also prepares a set of operating budgets to support the budgeted income statement. The operating budgets include budgets for service revenue, labor, services overhead, and selling and administrative expenses. The labor budget reflects the estimated labor hours and labor rates to provide the services. The managers use this information to estimate the amount of human and technical resources needed for the accounting period and to set prices for services.

Guidelines for Budget Preparation

Attention to the suggestions presented in Table 1 will help managers improve the quality of the budgets they prepare. Managers need to know why the budget is being prepared, who will read and use it, how the information will be presented, and where the information can be found. Meaningful, accurate information is gathered from

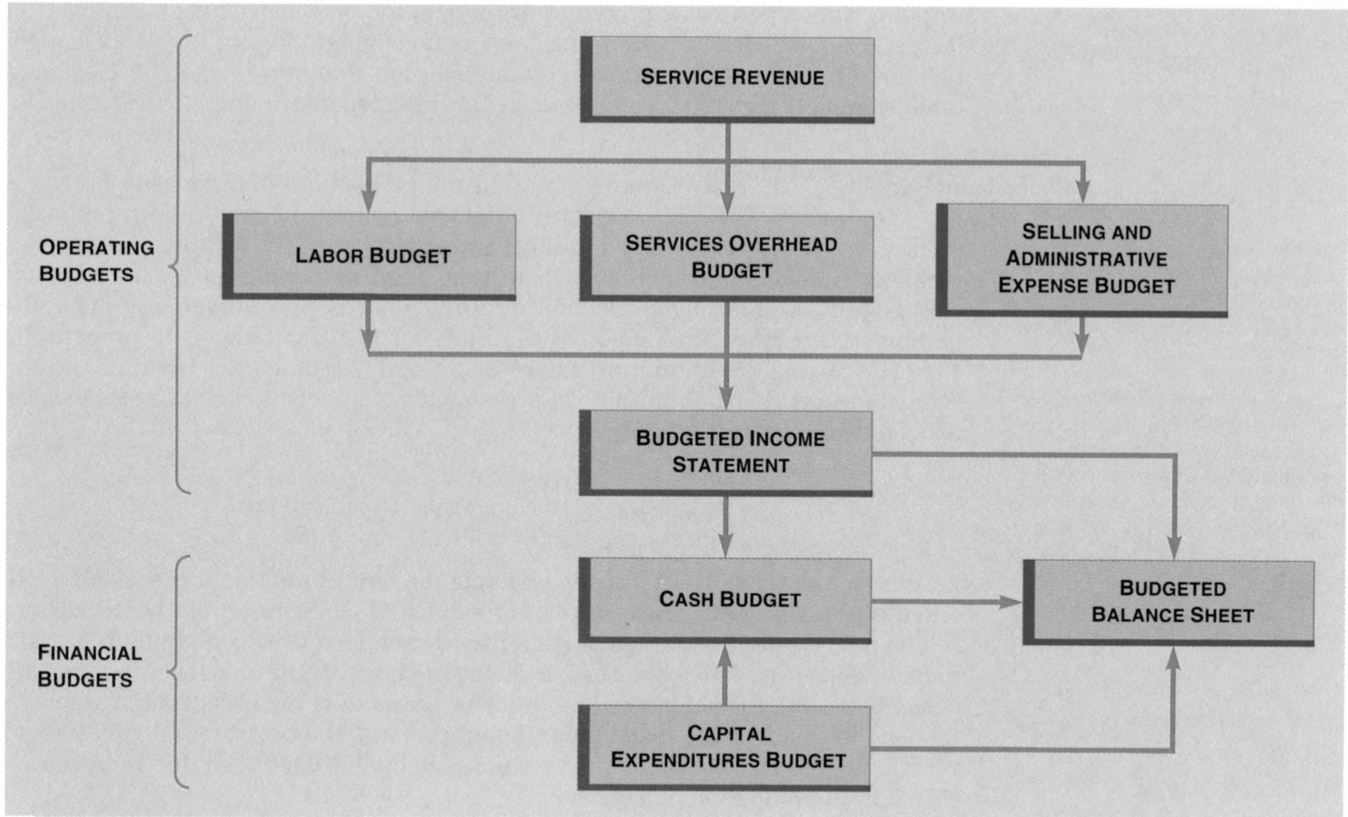

Figure 4
Preparation of a Master Budget for a Service Organization

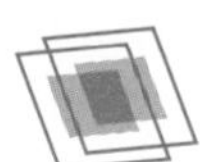

appropriate documents or interviews with the employees, suppliers, or managers who are responsible for the related areas. The title or heading includes the organization's name, the type of budget, and the accounting period under consideration. Several revisions may be required before the final version is ready to distribute.

The Operating Budgets

OBJECTIVE 4

Prepare a budgeted income statement and supporting operating budgets

Related Text Assignments:
Q: 16, 17, 18
SE: 6, 8
E: 6, 7, 8, 9, 10
P: 1, 2, 4, 6, 8
SD: 2, 4
MRA: 2, 4

Procedures for preparing a master budget vary from one organization to another. Since it is impossible to cover all procedures found in actual practice, the following discussion will illustrate one approach to preparing a budgeted income statement and supporting operating budgets for a manufacturing organization. Remember that by applying the tools of cost behavior and cost-volume-profit analysis and by

Table 1. Guidelines for Budget Preparation

- Know the purpose of the budget.
- Identify the user group and their information needs.
- Begin the budget with a clearly stated title or heading.
- Identify the format for the budget, and use appropriate formulas and calculations to derive the quantitative information.
- Label the budget's components, and list the unit and financial data in an orderly manner.
- Know the sources of budget information.
- Revise the budget until all planning decisions are included.

working with a particular product costing method, you can prepare any kind of budget. We have already stated that there is no standard format to use for budget preparation; the only universal requirements are that the budget be clear and understandable and that it communicate the intended information to the reader.

Point to Emphasize: The sales budget is the only budget subject to customer demand. Therefore, it must provide input data for all period budgets that depend on its numbers.

Discussion Question: What are some of the sources of information used to prepare the sales forecast and the sales budget? **Answer:** Sales force projections, top management projections, quantitative projections from historical data, information from trade associations, and leading economic indicators.

Sales Budget

The beginning point for the preparation of the master budget is the sales budget. The sales budget is a detailed plan, expressed in both units and dollars, that identifies expected product (or service) sales for a future period. Sales managers use this information to plan sales- and marketing-related activities as well as human, physical, and technical resource needs. Accountants use the information to determine estimated cash receipts for the cash budget. To prepare the sales budget, management must know the estimated selling price per unit and the estimated sales demand in units. The sales budget reflects the total budgeted sales using the following equation:

$$\text{Total Budgeted Sales} = \text{Estimated Selling Price per Unit} \times \text{Estimated Sales in Units}$$

Although the calculation is easy, selecting the best estimates for the selling price and the sales volume can be difficult. The estimated selling price may be the current selling price, or it may change in response to such factors as competition. An estimated selling price below the current selling price may be needed if competitors are currently selling the same product at lower prices or if the organization wants to increase its share of the market. On the other hand, the organization may plan to sell at a higher price because the product's quality has increased due to improved materials or production processes.

In addition, the estimated sales volume is very important because it will affect the level of operating activities and the amount of resources necessary to operate. Production, packing, shipping, accounting, purchasing, selling, and administrative activities require resources that will increase in varying degrees with increases in the estimated sales volume. A sales forecast can help to determine an estimated sales volume. A sales forecast is a projection of sales demand (the estimated sales in units) based on an analysis of external and internal factors. External factors influencing a sales forecast include:

1. The state of the local and the national economies
2. The state of the industry's economy
3. The nature of the competition, their sales volume, and selling price

Internal factors influencing a sales forecast include:

1. The number of units sold in prior periods
2. The organization's credit policies
3. The organization's collection policies
4. The organization's pricing policies
5. Any new products the organization plans to introduce into the market
6. The capacity of the organization's manufacturing facilities

Exhibit 2 illustrates the sales budget for Hi-Flyer Company. The sales budget states sales information for the Hi-Flyer products in both units and dollar revenue amounts for each quarter and for the entire year. The estimated selling price is $5 per unit in response to the highly competitive marketplace. The sales forecast shows highly seasonable sales activity that causes the estimated sales volume to fluctuate between 10,000 and 40,000 Hi-Flyers per quarter in 20x1. If Hi-Flyer Company sold more than one product, separate schedules or a comprehensive sales budget could be prepared to show the total budgeted sales by product.

Exhibit 2. Sales Budget

Hi-Flyer Company
Sales Budget
For the Year Ended December 31, 20x1

	Quarter				
	1	2	3	4	Year
Sales in Units	10,000	30,000	10,000	40,000	90,000
× Selling Price per Unit	$ 5	$ 5	$ 5	$ 5	$ 5
Total Sales	$50,000	$150,000	$50,000	$200,000	$450,000

Point to Emphasize: The production budget must provide for sufficient goods to meet current sales and must ensure that finished goods inventory levels are maintained according to company policy.

Production Budget The production budget is a detailed schedule that identifies the products or services that must be produced or provided to meet sales and inventory needs. Production managers use this information to plan for the technical and human resources needed to complete production-related activities. To prepare this budget, management must know the sales target in units (see the sales budget in Exhibit 2) and the desired level of ending finished goods inventory for each period. The desired level of ending finished goods inventory is often stated as a percentage of the next period's budgeted unit sales. For example, Hi-Flyer Company's desired level of ending finished goods inventory is 10 percent of the next quarter's unit sales of Hi-Flyers.

The following formula identifies the production needs for each accounting period.

Total Production Units	=	Budgeted Sales in Units	+	Desired Units of Ending Finished Goods Inventory	−	Desired Units of Beginning Finished Goods Inventory

BUSINESS BULLETIN: INTERNATIONAL PRACTICE

An organization selling in foreign markets must consider each market's special characteristics when developing a sales budget. The differences among regions and countries require the preparation of a separate sales budget for each market. Here are some examples of factors a company must consider when marketing abroad.[2]

Region/Country	Dominant and Distinctive Market Characteristic
Canada	North American Free Trade Agreement
Eastern Europe	Recent democratization and uncertain trade regulations
France	Price controls
Japan	Complex distribution system
Pacific Rim	New area with many developing countries offering a growing consumer base

Exhibit 3. Production Budget

Hi-Flyer Company
Production Budget
For the Year Ended December 31, 20x1

	Quarter 1	Quarter 2	Quarter 3	Quarter 4	Year
Sales in Units (Exhibit 2)	10,000	30,000	10,000	40,000	90,000
Add Desired Units of Ending Finished Goods Inventory	3,000	1,000	4,000	1,500	1,500
Desired Total Units	13,000	31,000	14,000	41,500	91,500
Less Desired Units of Beginning Finished Goods Inventory	1,000	3,000	1,000	4,000	1,000
Total Production Units	12,000	28,000	13,000	37,500	90,500

Note 1: Desired units of ending finished goods inventory = 10% of *next* quarter's budgeted sales.
Note 2: Desired units of beginning finished goods inventory = 10% of *current* quarter's budgeted sales.
Note 3: Assume that budgeted sales for the first quarter of 20x2 = 15,000 units.

Exhibit 3 illustrates the production budget for Hi-Flyer Company. Notice that each quarter's desired total units of ending finished goods inventory become the next quarter's desired total units of beginning finished goods inventory. If we assume that the budgeted units for the first quarter of 20x2 are 15,000 units, then the ending finished goods inventory for the fourth quarter of 20x1 will be 1,500 units (.10 × 15,000 units). This amount also represents the desired total units of ending finished goods inventory for 20x1. The 1,000 units in the beginning finished goods inventory for the first quarter are also the desired total units of beginning finished goods inventory for the year 20x1. A production budget for a service organization will show the required labor hours to generate the planned revenues for each period. Organizations that manufacture a variety of products or provide many different types of services may prepare either separate schedules for each product or service or one comprehensive production budget. This information helps managers to schedule production and service activities.

Point to Emphasize: The direct materials purchases budget must reflect both quantities of materials to be acquired and purchase prices. Those quantities and prices will be used again in the preparation of the cash budget.

Direct Materials Purchases Budget The direct materials purchases budget is a detailed schedule that identifies the purchases required for budgeted production and inventory needs and the costs associated with those needs. The purchasing function uses this information to plan purchases of direct materials, while the accountant uses the same information to estimate cash payments to suppliers. Thus, this budget reflects both the quantity and the cost of direct materials purchases.

To prepare this budget, management must know the production needs (see the production budget in Exhibit 3), the desired level of the direct materials inventory for each period, and the estimated per unit cost of direct materials. The desired level of ending direct materials inventory is usually stated as a percentage of the next period's production needs. In our example, Hi-Flyer Company's desired level of ending direct materials inventory is 20 percent of the next quarter's production needs.

The first step is to calculate the total production needs in ounces because the Hi-Flyer flying disk requires 10 ounces of plastic per disk. The total production needs in ounces for the quarter is the number of Hi-Flyer disks budgeted for production in the quarter multiplied by 10 ounces of plastic per disk. In the second step, the fol-

Exhibit 4. Direct Materials Purchases Budget

Hi-Flyer Company
Direct Materials Purchases Budget
For the Year Ended December 31, 20x1

	Quarter 1	Quarter 2	Quarter 3	Quarter 4	Year
Total Production Units (Exhibit 3)	12,000	28,000	13,000	37,500	90,500
× 10 Ounces per Unit	10	10	10	10	10
Total Production Needs in Ounces	120,000	280,000	130,000	375,000	905,000
Add Desired Ounces of Ending Direct Materials Inventory	56,000	26,000	75,000	30,000	30,000
	176,000	306,000	205,000	405,000	935,000
Less Desired Ounces of Beginning Direct Materials Inventory	24,000	56,000	26,000	75,000	24,000
Total Ounces of Direct Materials to Be Purchased	152,000	250,000	179,000	330,000	911,000
× Cost per Ounce	$ .05	$ .05	$ .05	$ .05	$ .05
Total Cost of Direct Materials Purchases	$ 7,600	$ 12,500	$ 8,950	$ 16,500	$ 45,550

Note 1: Desired ounces of ending direct materials inventory = 20% of *next* quarter's budgeted production needs in ounces.
Note 2: Desired ounces of beginning direct materials inventory = 20% of *current* quarter's budgeted production needs in ounces.
Note 3: Assume that budgeted production needs in ounces for the first quarter of 20x2 = 150,000 ounces.
Note 4: The desired direct materials inventory balance at January 1, 20x1 = 24,000 ounces × $.05 per ounce = $1,200 and at December 31, 20x1 = 30,000 ounces × $.05 per ounce = $1,500.

lowing formula creates the direct materials purchases in units for each accounting period in the budget.

Total Units of Direct Materials To Be Purchased	=	Total Production Needs in Units of Direct Materials	+	Desired Units of Ending Direct Materials Inventory	−	Desired Units of Beginning Direct Materials Inventory

The third step is to calculate the cost of the direct materials purchases by multiplying the total unit purchases of direct materials by the direct materials cost of $.05 per ounce (the cost that was estimated by the Purchasing Department). Exhibit 4 illustrates the direct materials purchases budget for Hi-Flyer Company. Notice that each quarter's desired units of ending direct materials inventory becomes the next quarter's desired units of beginning direct materials inventory. If we assume that the budgeted ounces for the first quarter of 20x2 are 150,000 ounces, then the ending direct materials inventory for the fourth quarter of 20x1 will be 30,000 ounces (.20 × 150,000 ounces). This amount also represents the desired units of ending direct materials inventory for the year 20x1. The 24,000 ounces of the first quarter's beginning direct materials inventory is also the desired units of beginning direct materials inventory for the year 20x1. In this example, Hi-Flyer Company uses only one direct material. Organizations that purchase a large variety of materials or parts for production may prepare either separate schedules for each material required or one comprehensive direct materials purchases budget.

Exhibit 5. Direct Labor Budget

Hi-Flyer Company
Direct Labor Budget
For the Year Ended December 31, 20x1

	Quarter				
	1	2	3	4	Year
Total Production Units (Exhibit 3)	12,000	28,000	13,000	37,500	90,500
× Direct Labor Hours per Unit	.1	.1	.1	.1	.1
Total Direct Labor Hours	1,200	2,800	1,300	3,750	9,050
× Direct Labor Cost per Hour	$ 6	$ 6	$ 6	$ 6	$ 6
Total Direct Labor Cost	$ 7,200	$16,800	$ 7,800	$22,500	$54,300

Direct Labor Budget The direct labor budget is a detailed schedule that identifies the direct labor needs for a future period and the labor costs associated with those needs. The Production Department uses direct labor hours to schedule the number of employees and the hours that each will work, while the accountant uses direct labor costs to estimate the cash payments to direct labor workers. The information in the direct labor budget also helps the Human Resources Department plan for hiring new employees, training current and new employees, or reducing the number of employees.

The first step in preparing a direct labor budget is to estimate the total direct labor hours by multiplying the estimated direct labor hours per unit by the anticipated units of production (see Exhibit 3). The second step is to calculate the total budgeted direct labor cost by multiplying the estimated total direct labor hours by the estimated direct labor cost per hour. The Human Resources Department provides an estimate of the hourly labor wages for these workers.

$$\text{Total Budgeted Direct Labor Cost} = \text{Estimated Total Direct Labor Hours} \times \text{Estimated Direct Labor Cost per Hour}$$

Exhibit 5 illustrates the direct labor budget for Hi-Flyer Company using these formulas to estimate the total budgeted direct labor cost. The Production Department needs an estimated .10 direct labor hours to complete one Hi-Flyer. The Human Resources Department estimates a direct labor cost of $6 per direct labor hour. In this example, Hi-Flyer Company needs only one production department. Organizations that require varying production processes and varying levels of expertise may prepare either separate schedules for each type of labor or one comprehensive direct labor budget.

Teaching Note: Variable manufacturing overhead estimates may be based on units produced or other consumption measures, such as direct labor hours, number of employees, or machine hours.

Manufacturing Overhead Budget The manufacturing overhead budget is a detailed schedule of anticipated manufacturing costs, other than direct materials and direct labor costs, that must be incurred to meet the production expectations of a future period. The manufacturing overhead budget has two purposes: (1) to integrate the overhead cost budgets developed by the managers of production and production-related service departments and (2) to group information for the calculation of manufacturing overhead rates for the forthcoming accounting period.

The presentation of manufacturing overhead budget information is flexible. Grouping information by activities is useful for organizations using activity-based

Exhibit 6. Manufacturing Overhead Budget

Hi-Flyer Company
Manufacturing Overhead Budget
For the Year Ended December 31, 20x1

	Quarter				
	1	2	3	4	Year
Variable Overhead Costs					
Indirect Materials	$ 2,160	$ 5,040	$ 2,340	$ 6,750	$ 16,290
Employee Benefits	2,880	6,720	3,120	9,000	21,720
Inspection	1,080	2,520	1,170	3,375	8,145
Maintenance and Repair	1,920	4,480	2,080	6,000	14,480
Utilities	3,600	8,400	3,900	11,250	27,150
Total Variable Overhead	$11,640	$27,160	$12,610	$36,375	$ 87,785
Fixed Overhead Costs					
Depreciation, Machinery	$ 2,810	$ 2,810	$ 2,810	$ 2,810	$ 11,240
Depreciation, Building	3,225	3,225	3,225	3,225	12,900
Supervision	9,000	9,000	9,000	9,000	36,000
Maintenance and Repair	2,150	2,150	2,150	2,150	8,600
Other Overhead Expenses	3,175	3,175	3,175	3,175	12,700
Total Fixed Overhead	$20,360	$20,360	$20,360	$20,360	$ 81,440
Total Manufacturing Overhead Costs	$32,000	$47,520	$32,970	$56,735	$169,225

costing. This approach helps the accountant to more easily determine the application rates for each cost pool. The Hi-Flyer Company prefers to group information into variable and fixed costs for cost-volume-profit analysis during the executing stage of the management cycle (see Exhibit 6). The manufacturing overhead rate for Hi-Flyer Company is the estimated total manufacturing costs divided by the estimated total direct labor hours. The predetermined manufacturing overhead rate for 20x1 is $18.70 per direct labor hour ($169,225 ÷ 9,050 direct labor hours), or $1.87 per unit ($18.70 per direct labor hour ÷ .10 direct labor hours per unit). The variable portion of the manufacturing overhead rate is $9.70 per direct labor hour, which includes indirect materials, $1.80; employee benefits, $2.40; inspection, $.90; maintenance and repair, $1.60; and utilities, $3.00.

Point to Emphasize: Remember that selling and administrative expenses are period costs, not product costs.

Selling and Administrative Expense Budget A selling and administrative expense budget is a detailed plan of operating expenses, other than those of the production function, needed to support the sales and overall operations of the organization for a future period. The accountant uses the estimated selling and administrative expense budget to estimate cash payments for products or services used in nonproduction-related activities. Exhibit 7 illustrates the selling and administrative expense budget for Hi-Flyer Company, which groups expenses into variable and fixed components for purposes of cost-volume-profit analysis and profit planning.

Cost of Goods Manufactured Budget The cost of goods manufactured budget is a detailed schedule that summarizes the costs of production for a future period. The sources of budget information for the total manufacturing costs are the budgets for direct materials, direct labor, and manufacturing overhead (Exhibits 4, 5, and 6).

Exhibit 7. Selling and Administrative Expense Budget

Hi-Flyer Company
Selling and Administrative Expense Budget
For the Year Ended December 31, 20x1

	Quarter				
	1	2	3	4	Year
Variable Selling and Administrative Expenses					
Delivery Expenses	$ 800	$ 2,400	$ 800	$ 3,200	$ 7,200
Sales Commissions	1,000	3,000	1,000	4,000	9,000
Accounting	700	2,100	700	2,800	6,300
Other Administrative Expenses	400	1,200	400	1,600	3,600
Total Variable Selling and Administrative Expenses	$ 2,900	$ 8,700	$ 2,900	$11,600	$ 26,100
Fixed Selling and Administrative Expenses					
Sales Salaries	$ 4,500	$ 4,500	$ 4,500	$ 4,500	$ 18,000
Executive Salaries	12,750	12,750	12,750	12,750	51,000
Depreciation, Office Equipment	925	925	925	925	3,700
Taxes and Insurance	1,700	1,700	1,700	1,700	6,800
Total Fixed Selling and Administrative Expenses	$19,875	$19,875	$19,875	$19,875	$ 79,500
Total Selling and Administrative Expenses	$22,775	$28,575	$22,775	$31,475	$105,600

Exhibit 8. Cost of Goods Manufactured Budget

Hi-Flyer Company
Cost of Goods Manufactured Budget
For the Year Ended December 31, 20x1

			Sources of Data
Direct Materials Used			
Direct Materials Inventory, January 1, 20x1	$ 1,200		Exhibit 4, Note 4
Purchases for 20x1	45,550		Exhibit 4
Cost of Direct Materials Available for Use	$46,750		
Less Direct Materials Inventory, December 31, 20x1	1,500		Exhibit 4, Note 4
Cost of Direct Materials Used		$ 45,250	
Direct Labor Costs		54,300	Exhibit 5
Manufacturing Overhead Costs		169,225	Exhibit 6
Total Manufacturing Costs		$268,775	
Work-in-Process Inventory, January 1, 20x1*		—	
Less Work-in-Process Inventory, December 31, 20x1*		—	
Cost of Goods Manufactured		$268,775	

*It is a company policy to have no units in process at the beginning or end of the year.

Most manufacturing organizations anticipate some work in process at the beginning or end of the future period, although we assume that the Hi-Flyer Company has a policy of no work in process on January 1 or December 31 of any year. Exhibit 8 summarizes the costs of production for Hi-Flyer Company. The budgeted, or standard, product unit cost for one Hi-Flyer is rounded to \$2.97 (\$268,775 ÷ 90,500 units).

Budgeted Income Statement

Teaching Note: Time spent explaining the interrelationships of each of the operating budgets and the projected financial statements will help eliminate some student questions later.

Once the operating budgets have been prepared, the budget director or the controller can prepare the budgeted income statement for the period. A budgeted income statement projects an organization's net income based on the estimated revenues and expenses for a future period. Information about projected sales and costs comes from several operating budgets. Hi-Flyer Company's budgeted income statement for 20x1 is shown in Exhibit 9. Note that the right side of the exhibit identifies the sources of key elements so you can trace the statement's development. At this point, you can review the overall preparation of the operating budgets by comparing the preparation flow in Figure 2 to the schedules in Exhibits 2 through 9. You will notice that the budgeted cost of goods sold was included in the budgeted income statement instead of being shown as a separate schedule.

Exhibit 9. Budgeted Income Statement

Hi-Flyer Company
Budgeted Income Statement
For the Year Ended December 31, 20x1

			Sources of Data
Sales		\$450,000	Exhibit 2
Cost of Goods Sold			
Finished Goods Inventory, January 1, 20x1*	\$ 2,970		
Cost of Goods Manufactured	268,775		Exhibit 8
Total Cost of Goods Available for Sale	\$271,745		
Less Finished Goods Inventory, December 31, 20x1*	4,455		
Cost of Goods Sold		267,290	
Gross Margin		\$182,710	
Less Selling and Administrative Expenses		105,600	Exhibit 7
Income from Operations		\$ 77,110	
Less Interest Expense (8% × \$70,000)		5,600	
Income Before Income Taxes		\$ 71,510	
Less Income Taxes Expense (30%)		21,453	
Net Income		\$ 50,057	

*Finished goods inventory balances assume that product unit costs were the same in 20x0 and 20x1.

January 1	December 31	
1,000 units	1,500 units	(Exhibit 3)
× \$2.97	× \$2.97	(Exhibit 8)
\$2,970	\$4,455	

Capital Expenditures Budget

A capital expenditures budget is a detailed plan outlining the amount and timing of anticipated capital expenditures for a future period. Buying equipment, building a new store outlet, purchasing and installing a materials handling system, or acquiring another business are examples of capital expenditure decisions that require a capital expenditures budget. Budgeting for capital expenditures decisions is discussed in another chapter. In our illustration, Hi-Flyer Company plans to purchase a new extrusion machine for $30,000. The company will pay $15,000 in the first quarter of 20x1, when the order is placed, and $15,000 in the second quarter of 20x1, when the equipment is received.

Cash Budgeting

OBJECTIVE 5

Prepare a cash budget

Related Text Assignments:
Q: 19
SE: 7, 9
E: 11
P: 3, 5, 7
MRA: 3

Point to Emphasize: The cash budget depends heavily on information from the operating budgets. Therefore, errors in those budgets could be compounded in the cash budget.

A cash budget is a projection of the cash receipts and cash payments for a future period. It summarizes the cash flow forecasts of planned transactions in all phases of a master budget. This information helps managers plan for short-term loans when the cash balance is low and for short-term investments when the cash balance is high. The elements of a cash budget can relate to operating, investing, or financing activities, as shown by the examples in Table 2.

The cash budget excludes some planned noncash transactions, such as depreciation expense, amortization expense, issuance and receipt of stock dividends, uncollectible accounts expense, and gains and losses on sales of assets. Some organizations also exclude deferred taxes and accrued interest.

Information about cash receipts comes from several sources, including the sales budget, cash collection records and trends, the budgeted income statement, the cash budgets from previous periods, and financial records of notes, stocks, and bonds. Information about cash payments comes from operating budgets, capital expenditures budgets, the previous year's financial statements, loan records, and the budgeted income statement. The accountant will convert credit sales to cash inflows and materials purchases to cash outflows and disclose those conversions on supporting schedules for the cash budget.

Table 2. Elements of a Cash Budget

Activities	Cash Receipts From	Cash Payments For
Operating	Cash sales Cash collections on credit sales	Purchases of direct materials Purchases of operating supplies Direct labor Manufacturing overhead expenses Selling expenses Administrative expenses
Investing	Sale of investments Sale of long-term assets Interest income from investments Cash dividends from investments	Purchase of investments Purchase of long-term assets
Financing	Loan proceeds Proceeds from sale of stock Proceeds from sale of bonds	Loan repayment Interest expense Cash dividends to stockholders

Exhibit 10. Schedule of Expected Cash Collections from Customers

Hi-Flyer Company
Schedule of Expected Cash Collections from Customers
For the Year Ended December 31, 20x1

	Quarter				
	1	2	3	4	Year
Accounts Receivable, Dec. 31, 20x0	$38,000	$ 10,000	—	—	$ 48,000
Cash Sales	10,000	30,000	$10,000	$ 40,000	90,000
Collections of Credit Sales					
First Quarter ($40,000)	24,000	12,000	4,000		40,000
Second Quarter ($120,000)		72,000	36,000	12,000	120,000
Third Quarter ($40,000)			24,000	12,000	36,000
Fourth Quarter ($160,000)				96,000	96,000
Total Cash to Be Collected from Customers	$72,000	$124,000	$74,000	$160,000	$430,000

Note 1: 20% of sales are cash sales, 80% are credit sales. Credit sales are collected as follows: 60% of all credit sales collected in quarter of sale, 30% collected in quarter following sale, 10% collected in second quarter following sale.
Note 2: The Accounts Receivable balance at December 31, 20x0, is $48,000, which is $8,000 from 20x0 third quarter sales [($100,000 × .80) × .10] and $40,000 from 20x0 fourth quarter sales [($125,000 × .80) × .40].
Note 3: The Accounts Receivable balance at December 31, 20x1, is $68,000, which is $4,000 from the third quarter's sales [($50,000 × .80) × .10] and $64,000 from the fourth quarter's sales [($200,000 × .80) × .40].

Teaching Note: Students will not understand how certain amounts in the cash budget are determined. Be sure to identify which figures are given and which ones must be obtained mathematically.

Preparing a Cash Budget In our illustration, the cash budget summarizes cash inflows and cash outflows for the four quarters of 20x1 and for the entire year. A useful format for the preparation of a cash budget is:

Estimated Ending Cash Balance	=	Total Estimated Cash Receipts	−	Total Estimated Cash Payments	+	Estimated Beginning Cash Balance

Many organizations also need to prepare supporting schedules for cash inflows or cash outflows that fluctuate over time. For example, the Hi-Flyer Company expects to receive cash from cash sales and credit sales in 20x1. The projected collection of that cash is shown in Exhibit 10, the schedule of expected cash collections from customers. Cash sales will represent 20 percent of the current quarter's sales, and the remaining 80 percent of sales will be credit sales. Experience has shown that 60 percent of all credit sales are collected in the quarter of sale, 30 percent are collected in the quarter following sale, and 10 percent are collected in the second quarter following sale.

Exhibit 10 shows that in the first quarter of 20x1, Hi-Flyer Company will collect $38,000 of the $48,000 balance of accounts receivable at December 31, 20x0. The company will collect the remaining portion of the $48,000 balance ($10,000) in the second quarter of 20x1. The estimated ending balance of Accounts Receivable at December 31, 20x1, is $68,000, which is $4,000 from the third quarter's credit sales [($50,000 × .80) × .10] plus $64,000 from the fourth quarter's sales [($200,000 × .80) × .40]. The expected cash collections from this exhibit flow to the total cash receipts section of the cash budget.

Our illustration continues with the preparation of a schedule of expected cash payments for direct materials. To simplify the illustration, Hi-Flyer Company will

Exhibit 11. Schedule of Expected Cash Payments for Direct Materials

Hi-Flyer Company
Schedule of Expected Cash Payments for Direct Materials
For the Year Ended December 31, 20x1

	Quarter				
	1	2	3	4	Year
Accounts Payable, Dec. 31, 20x0	$4,200	—	—	—	$ 4,200
First Quarter ($7,600)	3,800	$ 3,800			7,600
Second Quarter ($12,500)		6,250	$ 6,250		12,500
Third Quarter ($8,950)			4,475	$ 4,475	8,950
Fourth Quarter ($16,500)				8,250	8,250
Total Cash Payments for Direct Materials	$8,000	$10,050	$10,725	$12,725	$41,500

Note 1: 50% of the direct materials purchases are paid in the quarter of purchase and 50% are paid in the following quarter.
Note 2: The Accounts Payable balance at December 31, 20x0, is $4,200, or 50% of the 20x0 fourth-quarter direct materials purchases of $8,400.
Note 3: The Accounts Payable balance at December 31, 20x1 is $8,250, or 50% of the fourth-quarter direct materials purchases of $16,500.

pay 50 percent of the invoices it receives in the quarter of purchase and the remaining 50 percent in the following quarter. The estimated ending balance of Accounts Payable at December 31, 20x1, is $8,250 (50 percent of the fourth-quarter direct materials purchases of $16,500). Exhibit 11 shows the schedule for 20x1, which supports the first line of the cash payments section of the cash budget.

The cash budget in Exhibit 12 lists the cash receipts and cash payments, as well as the cash increase or decrease for the period. The cash increase or decrease plus the period's beginning cash balance equals the ending cash balance for the period. In the example in Exhibit 12, you can see that the beginning cash balance for the first quarter was $20,000. This amount also represents the beginning cash balance for the year 20x1. In addition, notice that each quarter's budgeted ending cash balance becomes the next quarter's beginning cash balance. To assist you in following the development of this budget, the sources for all information are listed on the right side of the exhibit.

Many organizations maintain a minimum cash balance to cover unusual expenditures. If the ending cash balance on the cash budget falls below the minimum required cash level, short-term borrowing may be necessary during the year to cover planned cash payments. If the ending cash balance is significantly larger than the organization needs, the excess cash may be invested in short-term securities to generate additional income.

Let's examine the 20x1 cash budget for the Hi-Flyer Company presented in Exhibit 12. If we assume that management wants a minimum of $10,000 cash available at the end of each quarter, the balance at the end of the first quarter indicates a problem. Hi-Flyer's management has several options in managing the low cash balance for the first quarter. The organization can borrow cash to cover the first quarter's cash needs, delay purchase of the equipment until the second quarter, or reduce some of the operating expenses. On the other hand, the balance at the end of the fourth quarter may be excessively high, thus leading management to invest a portion of the idle cash in short-term securities.

Exhibit 12. Cash Budget

Hi-Flyer Company
Cash Budget
For the Year Ended December 31, 20x1

	Quarter 1	Quarter 2	Quarter 3	Quarter 4	Year	Sources of Data
Cash Receipts						
Expected Cash Collections from Customers	$ 72,000	$124,000	$74,000	$160,000	$430,000	Exhibit 10
Total Cash Receipts	$ 72,000	$124,000	$74,000	$160,000	$430,000	
Cash Payments						
Direct Materials	$ 8,000	$ 10,050	$10,725	$ 12,725	$ 41,500	Exhibit 11
Direct Labor	7,200	16,800	7,800	22,500	54,300	Exhibit 5
Indirect Materials	2,160	5,040	2,340	6,750	16,290	Exhibit 6
Employee Benefits	2,880	6,720	3,120	9,000	21,720	Exhibit 6
Inspection	1,080	2,520	1,170	3,375	8,145	Exhibit 6
Maintenance and Repair	1,920	4,480	2,080	6,000	14,480	Exhibit 6
Utilities	3,600	8,400	3,900	11,250	27,150	Exhibit 6
Supervision	9,000	9,000	9,000	9,000	36,000	Exhibit 6
Maintenance and Repair	2,150	2,150	2,150	2,150	8,600	Exhibit 6
Other Overhead Expenses	3,175	3,175	3,175	3,175	12,700	Exhibit 6
Delivery Expenses	800	2,400	800	3,200	7,200	Exhibit 7
Sales Commissions	1,000	3,000	1,000	4,000	9,000	Exhibit 7
Accounting	700	2,100	700	2,800	6,300	Exhibit 7
Other Administrative Expenses	400	1,200	400	1,600	3,600	Exhibit 7
Sales Salaries	4,500	4,500	4,500	4,500	18,000	Exhibit 7
Executive Salaries	12,750	12,750	12,750	12,750	51,000	Exhibit 7
Taxes and Insurance	1,700	1,700	1,700	1,700	6,800	Exhibit 7
Capital Expenditures	15,000	15,000	—	—	30,000	Note 1
Interest Expense	1,400	1,400	1,400	1,400	5,600	Exhibit 9
Income Taxes	5,363	5,363	5,363	5,364	21,453	Exhibit 9
Total Cash Payments	$ 84,778	$117,748	$74,073	$123,239	$399,838	
Cash Increase (Decrease)	$(12,778)	$ 6,252	$ (73)	$ 36,761	$ 30,162	
Beginning Cash Balance	20,000	7,222	13,474	13,401	20,000	
Ending Cash Balance	$ 7,222	$ 13,474	$13,401	$ 50,162	$ 50,162	

Note: A new extrusion machine costing $30,000 will be paid in two quarterly installments of $15,000 each in the first and second quarter of 20x1.

Budgeted Balance Sheet

OBJECTIVE 6

Prepare a budgeted balance sheet

The final step in developing the master budget is to prepare a budgeted balance sheet. A budgeted balance sheet projects the financial position of an organization for a future period. As shown in Figure 2, all budgeted information is used in this process. The budgeted balance sheet at December 31, 20x1, for the Hi-Flyer

Related Text Assignments:
SE: 10
P: 4, 8

Terminology Note: Budgeted financial statements often are referred to as forecasted financial statements or pro forma statements.

Company is illustrated in Exhibit 13. To assist you in following the development of this statement, the sources of all information are listed on the right side of the exhibit and notes are included at the bottom.

Budget Implementation

When the master budget is completed, management must decide whether to accept the proposed master budget and the planned operating results it presents, or change the plans and revise the budget. Once the master budget has been accepted, it must be implemented.

Point to Emphasize: Proper communication cannot be overemphasized because good communication can eliminate many of the problems that typically arise in the budget process.

Budget implementation is the responsibility of the budget director. Two elements discussed earlier—communication and support—determine the success of this process. Proper communication of expectations and targets to all key people in the organization is essential. All involved employees must know what is expected of them and must receive directions on how to achieve their goals. Equally important, top management must support the budgeting process and encourage implementation of the budget. The process will succeed only if middle- and lower-level managers can see that top management is truly interested in the outcome and willing to reward people for meeting the budget goals.

Responsibility Accounting

OBJECTIVE 7

Define **responsibility accounting** *and discuss its relation to responsibility centers*

Related Text Assignments:
Q: 20, 21, 22, 23
SE: 11, 12
E: 12

Many organizations develop strategic plans that include the allocation of resources to areas of responsibility. For example, Chrysler Corp. allocates resources to its Eagle, Jeep, and Plymouth automotive divisions. The managers of those divisions will be responsible for revenue generation and cost management. In addition, those managers may also be given resources to invest in assets that will support the growth of the automotive division. Within each division, other managers are responsible for manufacturing subassemblies or assembling automobiles. The performance of all the managers is evaluated in terms of their ability to manage their areas of responsibility.

To assist in the strategic planning process, many organizations have established responsibility accounting systems. Responsibility accounting is an information system that (1) classifies financial data according to areas of responsibility in an organization and (2) reports each area's activities by including only the revenue and

BUSINESS BULLETIN: BUSINESS IN PRACTICE

Hexacomb Corporation and other companies use budgets in their "open-book management" system to motivate employees to achieve company goals. Hexacomb's "beat the budget" bonus system helps employees earn bonuses based on their plant's performance. Management consults with employees at each of the company's seven plants to develop an annual budget. Scorecards, which include an income statement, a balance sheet, and relevant nonfinancial measures, are distributed throughout the plants to track performance against budget. Managers and employees review the financial information each month and adjust operating activities, if necessary. If profits exceed the budgeted amount for the seven plants, half of the excess profits are placed into a bonus pool. Employees collect the bonus if their plant beats its budget.[3]

Exhibit 13. Budgeted Balance Sheet

Hi-Flyer Company Budgeted Balance Sheet For the Year Ended December 31, 20x1				Sources of Data
Assets				
Current Assets				
Cash		$ 50,162		Exhibit 12
Accounts Receivable		68,000		Exhibit 10
Direct Materials Inventory		1,500		Exhibit 8
Work in Process Inventory		—		Exhibit 8, Note
Finished Goods Inventory		4,455		Exhibit 9, Note
Total Current Assets			$124,117	
Property, Plant, and Equipment				
Land		$ 50,000		
Plant and Equipment	$200,000			Note 1
Less Accumulated Depreciation	45,000	155,000		Note 2
Total Property, Plant, and Equipment			205,000	
Total Assets			$329,117	
Liabilities				
Current Liabilities				
Accounts Payable			$ 8,250	Exhibit 11, Note 3
Total Current Liabilities			$ 8,250	
Long-Term Liabilities				
Notes Payable			70,000	Note 3
Total Liabilities			$ 78,250	
Stockholders' Equity				
Contributed Capital				
Common Stock		$150,000		Note 4
Retained Earnings		100,867		Note 5
Total Stockholders' Equity			250,867	
Total Liabilities and Stockholders' Equity			$329,117	

Note 1: The Plant and Equipment balance includes the $30,000 equipment purchase.

Note 2: The Accumulated Depreciation balance includes the 20x1 depreciation expense totaling $27,840 for Machinery, Building, and Equipment ($11,240, $12,900, and $3,700, respectively).

Note 3: Management plans no change in the Notes Payable balance.

Note 4: Management plans no change in the Common Stock balance.

Note 5: The Retained Earnings balance at December 31 equals the beginning Retained Earnings balance plus the 20x1 projected net income ($50,810 and $50,057, respectively).

Point to Emphasize: Responsibility accounting units may not coincide with functional reporting units. Functions such as production, sales, inventory management, and finance may be found in various combinations within a responsibility center. Alternatively, there may be several responsibility centers in a given functional area.

Instructional Strategy: Ask students to work in small groups to identify the responsibility centers within the business school or program at your college. Students should be able to recognize instructors, department heads, deans or directors, computer services representatives, counselors, and placement directors and must recognize their plans and their attainment. Use group responses to build class discussion.

cost categories that the assigned manager can control. A responsibility center is an organizational unit whose manager has been assigned the responsibility of managing a portion of the organization's resources. The activity of a responsibility center dictates the extent of the manager's responsibility. If a responsibility center involves only costs, it is called a cost center. On the other hand, if a manager is responsible for both revenues and costs, and for the resulting profits, the department is called a profit center. Finally, an investment center is a responsibility center whose manager is responsible for profit generation and can, in addition, make significant decisions about the assets the center uses. In the case of Chrysler Corp., the Eagle, Jeep, and Plymouth divisions may be investment centers or profit centers, whereas a single assembly plant may be a cost center.

Organizational Structure and Reporting

A responsibility accounting system establishes a communications network within the organization that is ideal for gathering information about operations in the planning, executing, and reviewing stages of the management cycle. The system is used to prepare budgets by areas of responsibility and to report the actual results of each responsibility center. The report for a responsibility center includes only those cost and revenue items the manager of that center can control. This approach ensures that managers will not be held responsible for items they cannot control.

By examining a corporate organization chart and a series of related managerial reports, you can see how a responsibility accounting system works. Figure 5 shows a typical management hierarchy, with the three vice presidents reporting to the corporate president. In the figure, the sales and finance areas are condensed to emphasize the manufacturing area. The production managers of Divisions A and B report to the vice president of manufacturing. In Division B, the managers of the Stamping Department, Painting Department, and Assembly Department report to the division's production manager.

In a responsibility accounting system, operating reports for each level of management are tailored to individual needs. Because a responsibility accounting system provides a report for every manager and because lower-level managers report

BUSINESS BULLETIN: ETHICS IN PRACTICE

Managers need to develop a strong ethical culture within their organizations so that they can minimize unethical or illegal activities. Unethical behavior in organizations hurts business. As employee productivity and loyalty decrease, employee turnover and absenteeism increase. As a result the organization may project a poor image to customers, suppliers, and the community. A loss of faith and confidence in the organization becomes expensive. Organizations can spend as much as $5,000 per employee on efforts to control unethical behavior. So, how can managers influence the ethical culture of their organizations? They can:

- Develop a code of ethics that communicates the organization's ethical values.
- Increase employee awareness through training programs.
- Provide a process to guide employees when they are facing an ethical dilemma.
- Develop a process to promote, watch, and positively influence the ethical behavior of the organization's employees.
- Demonstrate ethical behavior personally.[4]

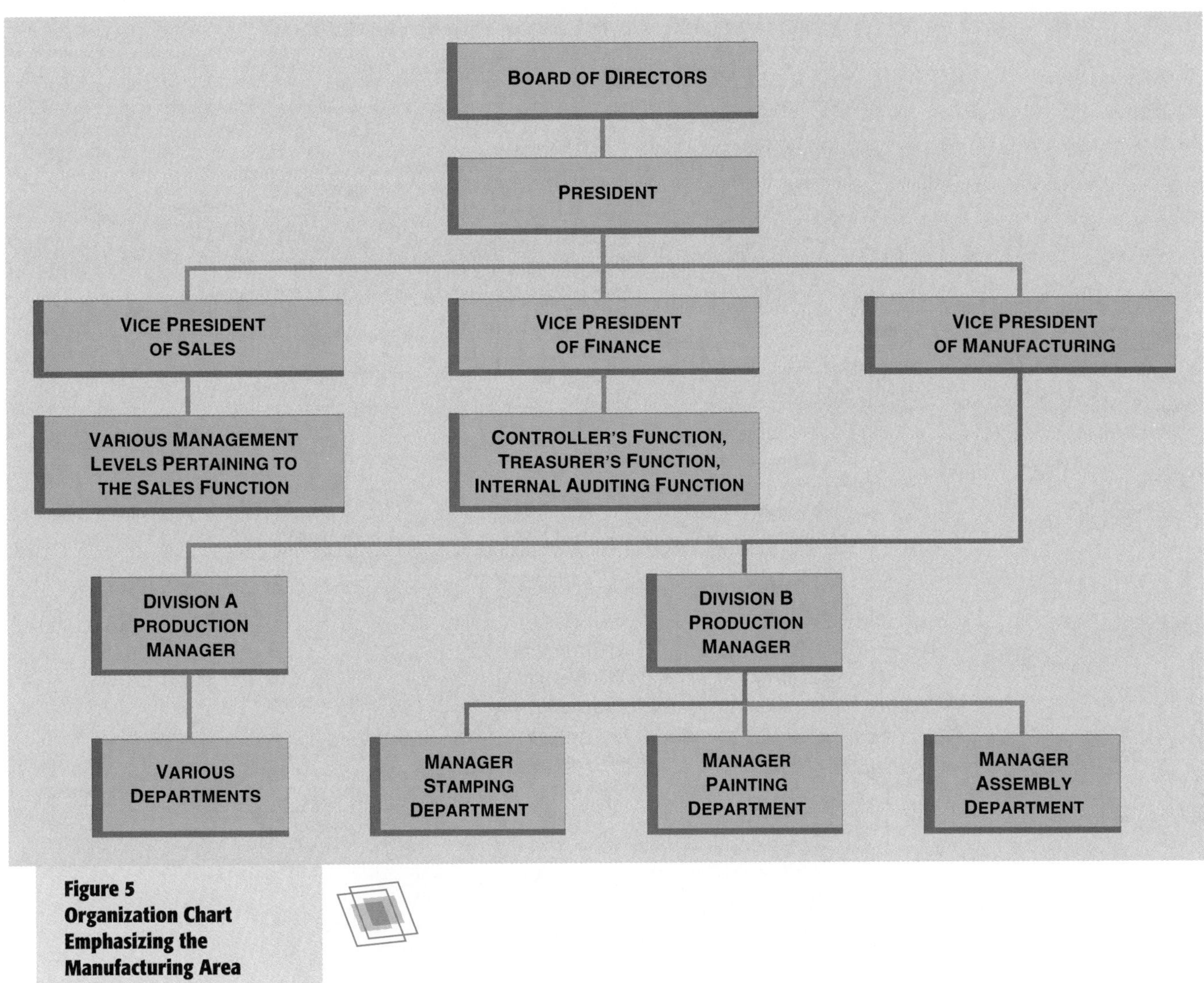

Figure 5
Organization Chart Emphasizing the Manufacturing Area

to higher-level managers, the same costs and revenues may appear in several reports. When lower-level operating data are included in higher-level reports, the data are summarized.

Based on the managerial hierarchy presented in Figure 5, Exhibit 14 illustrates how the responsibility reporting network is tied together. At the department level, the report lists cost items under the manager's control and compares expected (or budgeted) costs with actual costs. This comparison is a measure of operating performance. The manager who receives the report on the Stamping Department should be particularly concerned with direct materials costs and maintenance salaries, for they are significantly over budget. Also, the underutilization of small tools may signal problems with productivity in that department.

Point to Emphasize: Determination of the lowest level of responsibility is necessary because detail is lost as summary reports are prepared.

The production manager of Division B is responsible for the three operating departments plus controllable divisionwide costs. The production manager's report includes a summary of results from the Stamping Department as well as from the other areas of responsibility. At the division level, the report does not present detailed data for each department; only department totals appear. As shown in Exhibit 14, the data are even more condensed in the vice president's report. Only corporate and summarized divisional data about costs controllable by the vice president are included.

Exhibit 14. Reporting Within a Responsibility Accounting System

Manufacturing: Vice President — Monthly Report: November

Amount Budgeted	Controllable Cost	Actual Amount	Over (Under) Budget
	Central production		
$ 281,400	scheduling	$ 298,100	$16,700
179,600	Office expenses	192,800	13,200
19,800	Operating expenses	26,200	6,400
339,500	Division A	348,900	9,400
426,200	Division B	399,400	(26,800)
$1,246,500	Totals	$1,265,400	$18,900

Division B: Production Manager — Monthly Report: November

Amount Budgeted	Controllable Cost	Actual Amount	Over (Under) Budget
	Division expenses		
$101,800	Salaries	$ 96,600	($ 5,200)
39,600	Utilities	39,900	300
25,600	Insurance	21,650	(3,950)
	Departments		
46,600	Stamping	48,450	1,850
69,900	Painting	64,700	(5,200)
142,700	Assembly	128,100	(14,600)
$426,200	Totals	$399,400	($26,800)

Stamping Department: Manager — Monthly Report: November

Amount Budgeted	Controllable Cost	Actual Amount	Over (Under) Budget
$22,500	Direct materials	$23,900	$1,400
14,900	Factory labor	15,200	300
2,600	Small tools	1,400	(1,200)
5,100	Maintenance salaries	6,000	900
1,000	Supplies	1,200	200
500	Other costs	750	250
$46,600	Totals	$48,450	$1,850

Chapter Review

REVIEW OF LEARNING OBJECTIVES

1. **Define *budgeting* and explain its role in the management cycle.** Budgeting is the process of identifying, gathering, summarizing, and communicating financial and nonfinancial information about future activities in an organization. Budgeting helps managers (1) relate the organization's long-term goals to short-term activities and distribute resources during the planning stage; (2) communicate expectations, motivate others, and coordinate activities during the executing stage; (3) evaluate performance and solve problems during the reviewing stage; and (4) communicate budget information, report the organization's financing, investing, and operating activities, and provide continuous feedback during the reporting stage of the management cycle.

2. **Explain the basic principles of budgeting.** Budgeting principles relate to (1) long-range goals and (2) short-range goals and strategies. Every organization needs to set long-range goals and convert them into plans for product or service offerings. The long-range goals must be restated in terms of short-range goals and strategies, which provide plans for the annual product or service offerings and associated profit plans. The budget development plans and timetable must also be set up.

3. **Describe the master budget process for different types of organizations, and list the guidelines for preparing budgets.** A master budget is a set of budgets that consolidate an organization's financial information into budgeted financial statements for a future period of time. A master budget includes a budgeted income statement supported by a set of operating budgets, a budgeted balance sheet, and a cash budget. The operating budgets (1) for a manufacturing organization include budgets for sales, production, direct materials purchases, direct labor, manufacturing overhead, and selling and administrative expenses; (2) for a retail organization include budgets for sales, merchandise purchases, and selling and administrative expenses; and (3) for a service organization include budgets for service revenue, labor, services overhead, and selling and administrative expenses. Preliminary planning involves knowing the purpose of the budget, the user group and their information needs, the sources of budget information, and the budget components.

4. **Prepare a budgeted income statement and supporting operating budgets.** The initial step in preparing a budgeted income statement is to prepare a sales budget. After preparing the sales budget, managers or accountants at a manufacturing organization prepare a production budget followed by budgets for direct materials purchases, direct labor, manufacturing overhead, selling and administrative expenses, cost of goods manufactured, and cost of goods sold. The information from these operating budgets supports the information on the budgeted income statement.

5. **Prepare a cash budget.** A cash budget is a projection of the cash receipts and cash payments for a future period. A cash budget summarizes the cash flow results of planned transactions for a future period. A cash budget discloses the organization's projected ending cash balance and shows a manager when short-term borrowing or investing may be appropriate.

   The preparation of a cash budget begins with the projection of all expected sources of cash. Next, all expected cash payments are found by analyzing all other operating budgets and the capital expenditures budget within the master budget. The difference between these two totals is the cash increase or decrease anticipated for the period. This total, combined with the period's beginning cash balance, yields the ending cash balance.

6. **Prepare a budgeted balance sheet.** The final step in the master budget process is to prepare a budgeted balance sheet for the company. All budgeted data are used in this process.

7. **Define *responsibility accounting* and discuss its relation to responsibility centers.** Responsibility accounting is an information reporting system that (1) classifies financial data according to areas of responsibility in an organization and (2) reports each area's activities by including only revenue and cost categories that the assigned manager can control. A responsibility accounting system personalizes accounting

reports. It is composed of a series of reports, one for each person with responsibility for cost control. Within a responsibility accounting system, a responsibility center is an organizational unit for which reports are prepared.

REVIEW OF CONCEPTS AND TERMINOLOGY

The following concepts and terms were introduced in this chapter:

LO 1 **Budget:** A plan of action that forecasts future transactions, activities, and events in financial or nonfinancial terms.

LO 6 **Budgeted balance sheet:** A statement that projects the financial position of an organization for a future period.

LO 4 **Budgeted income statement:** A statement that projects an organization's net income based on estimated revenues and expenses for a future period.

LO 1 **Budget information:** Quantifiable information about an organization's future activities and the revenues or expenses associated with those activities.

LO 1 **Budgeting:** The process of identifying, gathering, summarizing, and communicating financial and nonfinancial information about an organization's future activities.

LO 4 **Capital expenditures budget:** A detailed plan outlining the amount and timing of anticipated capital expenditures for a future period.

LO 5 **Cash budget:** A projection of the cash receipts and cash payments for a future period.

LO 7 **Cost center:** A responsibility center, such as a department or division, whose manager is responsible only for the costs incurred by that center.

LO 4 **Cost of goods manufactured budget:** A detailed schedule that summarizes the costs of production for a future period.

LO 4 **Direct labor budget:** A detailed schedule that identifies the direct labor needs for a future period and the labor costs associated with those needs.

LO 4 **Direct materials purchases budget:** A detailed schedule that identifies the purchases required for budgeted production and inventory needs and the costs associated with those needs.

LO 7 **Investment center:** A responsibility center whose manager is responsible for profit generation and can make significant decisions about the assets the center uses.

LO 4 **Manufacturing overhead budget:** A detailed schedule of anticipated manufacturing costs, other than direct materials and direct labor costs, that must be incurred to meet the production expectations of a future period.

LO 3 **Master budget:** A set of budgets that consolidate an organization's financial information into budgeted financial statements for a future period of time.

LO 4 **Production budget:** A detailed schedule that identifies the products or services that must be produced or provided to meet budgeted sales and inventory needs.

LO 7 **Profit center:** A responsibility center whose manager is responsible for revenues and costs and the resulting profits.

LO 7 **Responsibility accounting:** An information reporting system that (1) classifies financial data according to areas of responsibility in an organization and (2) reports each area's activities by including only the revenue and cost categories that the assigned manager can control.

LO 7 **Responsibility center:** An organizational unit whose manager has been assigned the responsibility of managing a portion of the organization's resources. This includes, but is not limited to, cost centers, profit centers, and investment centers.

LO 4 **Sales budget:** A detailed plan, expressed in both units and dollars, that identifies expected product (or service) sales for a future period.

LO 4 **Sales forecast:** A projection of sales demand based on an analysis of external and internal factors.

LO 4 **Selling and administrative expense budget:** A detailed plan of operating expenses, other than those of the production function, needed to support the sales and overall operations of the organization for a future period.

REVIEW PROBLEM

Cash Budget Preparation

LO 5 Pearce Information Processing Company provides word processing services for its clients. Pearce uses state-of-the-art equipment and employs five data entry personnel, who each average 160 hours of work a month. The following table sets out information developed by the budget officer.

	Actual—20x0		Forecast—20x1		
	November	December	January	February	March
Client billings (sales)	$25,000	$35,000	$25,000	$20,000	$40,000
Selling and administrative expenses	12,000	13,000	12,000	11,000	12,500
Operating supplies purchased	2,500	3,500	2,500	2,500	4,000
Processing overhead	3,200	3,500	3,000	2,500	3,500

The company has a bank loan of $12,000 at a 12 percent annual interest rate. Interest is paid monthly, and $2,000 of the principal of the loan is due on February 28, 20x1. No capital expenditures are anticipated for the first quarter of the coming year. Income taxes of $4,550 for calendar year 20x0 are due and payable on March 15, 20x1. The company's five employees earn $8.50 an hour, and all payroll-related labor benefit costs are included in processing overhead. For the items included in the table, assume the following conditions.

Client billings	60% are cash sales collected during the month of sale 30% are collected in the first month following the sale 10% are collected in the second month following the sale
Operating supplies	Paid for in the month purchased
Selling and administrative expenses and processing overhead	Paid in the month following the cost's incurrence

The beginning cash balance on January 1, 20x1, is expected to be $13,840.

REQUIRED

Prepare a monthly cash budget for Pearce Information Processing Company for the three-month period ending March 31, 20x1.

ANSWER TO REVIEW PROBLEM

Here is the three-month cash budget for Pearce Information Processing Company.

Pearce Information Processing Company
Monthly Cash Budget
For the Three-Month Period Ended March 31, 20x1

	January	February	March	Totals
Cash Receipts				
Client billings	$28,000	$23,000	$32,500	$83,500
Cash Payments				
Operating supplies	$ 2,500	$ 2,500	$ 4,000	$ 9,000
Direct labor	6,800	6,800	6,800	20,400
Selling and administrative expenses	13,000	12,000	11,000	36,000
Processing overhead	3,500	3,000	2,500	9,000
Interest expense	120	120	100	340
Loan payment	—	2,000	—	2,000
Income tax payment	—	—	4,550	4,550
Total cash payments	$25,920	$26,420	$28,950	$81,290
Cash Increase (Decrease)	$ 2,080	($ 3,420)	$ 3,550	$ 2,210
Beginning Cash Balance	13,840	15,920	12,500	13,840
Ending Cash Balance	$15,920	$12,500	$16,050	$16,050

Details supporting the individual computations within the cash budget are as follows:

	January	February	March
November	$ 2,500	—	—
December	10,500	$ 3,500	—
January	15,000	7,500	$ 2,500
February	—	12,000	6,000
March	—	—	24,000
	$28,000	$23,000	$32,500
Operating supplies			
All paid in the month purchased	$ 2,500	$ 2,500	$ 4,000
Direct labor			
5 employees × 160 hours a month × $8.50 an hour	6,800	6,800	6,800
Selling and administrative expenses			
Paid in the month following incurrence	13,000	12,000	11,000
Processing overhead			
Paid in the month following incurrence	3,500	3,000	2,500
Interest expense			
January and February = 1% of $12,000	120	120	
March = 1% of $10,000			100
Loan payment	—	2,000	—
Income tax payment	—	—	4,550

The ending cash balances of $15,920, $12,500, and $16,050 for January, February, and March 20x1, respectively, appear to be comfortable but not too large for the company.

Chapter Assignments

BUILDING YOUR KNOWLEDGE FOUNDATION

Questions

1. Define *budgeting.*
2. What is a budget? What type of information can be included in a budget?
3. Give examples of ways that budgeting can help managers during the planning stage of the management cycle.
4. Give examples of ways that budgeting can help managers during the executing stage of the management cycle.
5. Give examples of ways that budgeting can help managers during the reviewing stage of the management cycle.
6. Give examples of ways that budgeting can help managers during the reporting stage of the management cycle.
7. List three ways in which budget preparation contributes to an organization's success.
8. Distinguish between long-range plans and yearly operating plans.
9. What factors should influence the development of long-range goals?
10. What is the purpose of the following budgeting principle? "Restate the long-range plans in terms of short-range plans for products or services and a detailed profit plan."
11. Explain how budgets are developed once management has set short-range goals.
12. What is a master budget? What is its purpose?
13. In what ways are master budgets similar for manufacturing, retail, and service organizations?
14. Explain the differences between the master budget for a retail organization and the master budget for a service organization.
15. List the guidelines for the preparation of a budget.
16. What is a sales forecast? What are some factors that influence the estimation of future unit sales?
17. What are the three steps in preparing a direct materials purchases budget?
18. What are the two steps in preparing a direct labor budget?
19. List four items not found on a cash budget.
20. Define *responsibility accounting.*
21. Describe a responsibility accounting system.
22. How does a company's organizational structure affect its responsibility accounting system?
23. Compare and contrast a cost or expense center, a profit center, and an investment center.

Short Exercises

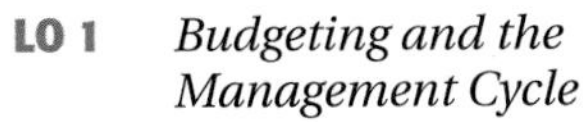

LO 1 *Budgeting and the Management Cycle*

SE 1. State whether each of the following management activities requiring the use of budget information is part of the planning stage (P), the executing stage (E), the reviewing stage (REV), or the reporting stage (REP) of the management cycle.

1. Coordinate the purchasing, production, selling, and shipping activities.
2. Select performance measures to monitor the timeliness of the shipping activities.
3. Calculate variances between the planned direct materials and the actual direct materials used in production last month.
4. Develop a budget to distribute the organization's resources to the various operating segments.
5. Prepare a report showing the performance of the production department for the last three months.

SE 2. LO 1 *Manager's Budget Uses*

Jim Gray is the manager of a shoe department in a local discount department store. His supervisor has indicated that Jim's goal is to increase the number of pairs of shoes sold by 20 percent. The department sold 8,000 pairs of shoes last year. Two shoe salespersons currently work for Jim. What type of budgets should Jim use to help achieve his sales goal? What kinds of information should these budgets provide?

SE 3. LO 1 *Budgetary Control*

Andrea Kral likes to analyze the results of her tree nursery operations by comparing the actual operating results with budgeted figures from the beginning of the year. If the business generates large profits, she often overlooks the differences between actual and budgeted data. But if profits are low, she spends many hours analyzing those differences. If you were Andrea, would you approach budgetary control in a similar manner? If not, what changes would you make to her approach?

SE 4. LO 2 *Budgeting Principles*

The basic principles of budgeting have just been discussed with the dashboard assembly team at the Rockford Automobile Company. The team is participating in the company's budgeting process for the first time. One team member asked the controller to explain how the long-range goals principles relate to the short-range goals and strategies principles. How should the controller respond?

SE 5. LO 3 *Master Budget Components*

The master budget is a compilation of many departmental or functional forecasts for the coming year or operating cycle. What is the most important forecast made in relation to the master budget? List the reasons for your answer. Which budgets must be prepared before you can develop a direct materials purchases budget?

SE 6. LO 4 *Operating Budget Preparation*

Lockwood Company expects to sell 50,000 units of its product in the coming year. Each unit sells for $45. Sales brochures and supplies are expected to cost $7,000 for the year. Three sales representatives cover the southeast region. Their individual base salary is $20,000, and they earn a sales commission of 5 percent of the selling price of the units they sell. The sales representatives supply their own transportation, and they are reimbursed for travel at a rate of $.40 per mile. Based on the current year's mileage, the sales representatives are expected to drive a total of 75,000 miles next year. From the information provided, calculate the budgeted selling expenses for the coming year.

SE 7. LO 5 *Operating Budget Preparation*

BK Insurance Co. specializes in term life insurance contracts. Cash collection experience shows that 20 percent of billed premiums are collected in the month prior to being due, 60 percent are paid in the month they are due, and 16 percent are paid in the month following their due date. Four percent of the billed premiums are paid late (in the second month following their due date) and include a 10 percent penalty payment. Total billing notices were: January, $58,000; February, $62,000; March, $66,000; April, $65,000; May, $60,000; and June, $62,000. How much cash does the company expect to collect in May?

SE 8. LO 4 *Budgeted Gross Margin*

Operating budgets for the Constantine Company revealed the following information: net sales, $450,000; beginning direct materials inventory, $23,000; materials purchased, $185,000; beginning work in process inventory, $64,700; beginning finished goods inventory, $21,600; direct labor costs, $34,000; manufacturing overhead applied, $67,000; ending work in process inventory, $61,200; ending direct materials inventory, $18,700; and ending finished goods inventory, $16,300. Compute the company's budgeted gross margin.

SE 9. LO 5 *Cash Budget*

The following direct materials purchase projections are for the Martinson Corp. Experience has shown that the company pays 60 percent of the purchases on account in the month of purchase and 40 percent in the month following the purchase. Prepare a schedule of expected cash payments for direct materials for the first quarter of 20x1.

	Purchases on Account	**Cash Purchases**
December 20x0	$40,000	$20,000
January 20x1	60,000	30,000
February 20x1	50,000	25,000
March 20x1	70,000	35,000

SE 10. LO 6 *Budgeted Balance Sheet*

Shadow Corporation's budgeted data showed total projected assets for the coming year of $4,650,000. Total liabilities were expected to be $1,900,000. Common stock and retained earnings make up the entire stockholders' equity section of the balance sheet.

Common stock remains at its beginning balance of $1,500,000. The projected net income for the year is $349,600. What was the balance of retained earnings at the beginning of the budget period?

LO 7 *Identification of Controllable Costs*

SE 11. Bill Faries is the manager of the Paper Cutting Department in Division A of Warren Paper Products. From the following list, identify the costs that are controllable by Bill.

1. Salaries of cutting machine workers
2. Cost of cutting machine parts
3. Cost of electricity for Division A
4. Lumber Department hauling costs
5. Vice president's salary

LO 7 *Cost Centers, Profit Centers, and Investment Centers*

SE 12. Identify the following as a cost center, a profit center, or an investment center.

1. In business unit A, the manager is responsible for generating cash inflows and incurring costs with the goal of making the most money for the company. The manager has no responsibility for assets.
2. Business unit B produces a component that is not sold to an external party.

Exercises

LO 1 *Budgeting and the Management Cycle*

E 1. Joe Mee manages a golf and tennis resort. Indicate whether each of the following management activities requiring the use of budget information is part of the planning stage (P), the executing stage (E), the reviewing stage (REV), or the reporting stage (REP) of the management cycle.

1. Joe develops a budget to distribute limited resources to the Pro Shop, facilities maintenance, golf and tennis operations, hotel operations, and restaurant operations.
2. Joe challenges the employees to increase the volume of customers eating in the restaurant by 10 percent as set forth in the restaurant's budget.
3. Joe selects the number of golf lessons given each month as a measure of performance for the golf course operations.
4. After three months of operations, the resort's accountant prepares a performance report for the restaurant.
5. Joe analyzes the restaurant's performance report and finds that sales volume is 25 percent lower than planned.
6. Joe meets with restaurant managers and employees to discuss operations and surveys resort guests for one month. Based on his findings, Joe expands the number of food items offered on the menu, increases advertising for the restaurant, and replaces the cook.
7. Rita Baines, the manager of golf operations, uses the budgeted number of golf lessons to motivate the golf pros to provide more lessons. However, Rita notices that the quality of the golf lessons does not improve.
8. At the end of the month, Rita calculates the variance between the actual number of golf lessons given and the budgeted number of golf lessons. She finds that fewer lessons were given than originally planned.
9. Rita prepares a variance report and gives it to the golf pros for review.
10. Rita selects the number of hours of golf instruction as a new performance measure for the remainder of the year.

LO 1 *Budget Objectives*

E 2. You recently attended a workshop on budgeting and overheard the following comments as you moved to the refreshment table.

1. "Budgets look the same regardless of the size of an organization and the role of the budget process in management."
2. "Budgets can include financial or nonfinancial data. In our organization, we plan the number of hours to be worked and the number of customer contacts we want our salespeople to make."
3. "All budgets are complicated. You have to be an expert to prepare one."
4. "Budgets do not need to be highly accurate or very meaningful. No one stays within a budget in our organization."

Do you agree or disagree with each comment? Explain.

E 3. LO 2 *Budgeting Principles*

The managers of Colorado Calendars, Inc., recently held a planning meeting to develop goals for the company. The company's success has been influenced by the managers' willingness to effectively follow budgeting principles. These principles include long-range goals and short-range goals and strategies. Identify the group of budgeting principles related to the following actions taken by the management team.

1. The management team considered economic and industry forecasts, employee-management relationships, and the structure and role of management in forecasting the next ten-year period.
2. Decisions were made about next year's sales and profit targets by calendar line and sales territory based on the forecast for the next ten years.

E 4. LO 2 *Budgeting Principles*

Assume that you work in the accounting department of a small wholesale warehousing business. Inspired by a seminar on budgeting that she recently attended, the president wants to develop a budgeting system and has asked you to direct it.

State the points that you should communicate to the president about the initial steps in the budgeting process. Concentrate on principles related to long-range goals and short-range goals and strategies.

E 5. LO 3 *Components of a Master Budget*

Identify the order in which the following budgets are prepared within the master budget process. Use the letters *a* through g, with the first budget to be prepared as *a*.

1. Production budget
2. Direct labor budget
3. Direct materials purchases budget
4. Sales budget
5. Budgeted balance sheet
6. Cash budget
7. Budgeted income statement

E 6. LO 4 *Sales Budget Preparation*

Quarterly and annual sales for 20x1 for the Crosson Manufacturing Company are shown below.

Crosson Manufacturing Company
Actual Sales Revenue
For the Year Ended December 31, 20x1

Product Class	January–March	April–June	July–September	October–December	Annual Totals	Estimated 20x2 Percent Increases by Product Class
Marine Products	$ 44,500	$ 45,500	$ 48,200	$ 47,900	$ 186,100	10%
Mountain Products	36,900	32,600	34,100	37,200	140,800	5%
River Products	29,800	29,700	29,100	27,500	116,100	30%
Hiking Products	38,800	37,600	36,900	39,700	153,000	15%
Running Products	47,700	48,200	49,400	49,900	195,200	25%
Biking Products	65,400	65,900	66,600	67,300	265,200	20%
Totals	$263,100	$259,500	$264,300	$269,500	$1,056,400	

Prepare the 20x2 sales budget for the company. Show both quarterly and annual totals for each product class.

E 7. LO 4 *Production Budget Preparation*

Ed Julius, the controller for the All-in-One Door Company, is preparing a production budget for 20xx. The company's policy is to maintain a finished goods inventory equal to one-half of the following month's sales. Complete the following production budget for the first quarter using the information provided. Budgeted sales for April are 7,000 doors.

	January	February	March
Desired sales in units	5,000	4,000	6,000
Desired ending finished goods inventory	2,000	?	?
Desired total units	7,000		
Less desired beginning finished goods inventory	2,500	?	?
Production needs	4,500	?	?

LO 4 *Direct Materials Purchases Budget*

E 8. The All-in-One Door Company manufactures garage door units. These units include hinges, door panels, and other hardware. Prepare a direct materials purchases budget for the first quarter of 20xx based on budgeted production of 16,000 garage door units. Ed Julius, the controller, has provided the following information.

Hinges	4 sets per door	$11.00 a set
Door panels	4 panels per door	$27.00 a panel
Other hardware	1 lock per door	$31.00 a lock
	1 handle per door	$22.50 a handle
	2 roller tracks per door	$16.00 for a set of 2 roller tracks
	8 rollers per door	$4.00 a roller

Assume no beginning or ending quantities of direct materials inventory.

LO 4 *Direct Labor Budget Preparation*

E 9. Whitmore Metals Company manufactures three products in a single plant with two departments: Cutting and Grinding. The company has estimated costs for products T, M, and B and is currently analyzing direct labor hour requirements for the budget year 20x1. The department data follow:

	Cutting	Grinding
Estimated Hours per Unit		
Product T	1.1	.5
Product M	.6	2.9
Product B	3.2	1.0
Hourly Labor Rate	$9	$7

Budgeted unit production in 20x1 is 21,000 of Product T, 36,000 of Product M, and 30,000 of Product B. Prepare a direct labor budget for 20x1 that shows the budgeted direct labor costs for each department and for the company as a whole.

LO 4 *Manufacturing Overhead Budget*

E 10. Denise Talley is chief financial officer of the London division of Talley Corporation, a multinational company operating with three divisions. As part of the budgeting process, Talley's staff is developing the manufacturing overhead budget for 20x1. The division estimates that 50,000 units will be manufactured during the year. The budgeted cost information follows:

	Variable Rate per Unit	Total Fixed Costs
Indirect Materials	$1.00	
Indirect Labor	4.00	
Supplies	.40	
Repairs and Maintenance	3.00	$ 40,000
Electricity	.10	20,000
Factory Supervision		180,000
Insurance		25,000
Property Taxes		35,000
Depreciation, Machinery		82,000
Depreciation, Building		72,000

From the data given, prepare the 20x1 manufacturing overhead budget for the division.

E 11. LO 5 *Cash Budget Preparation—Revenues*

Magrone Car Care, Inc., is an automobile maintenance and repair organization with outlets throughout the midwestern United States. Judy McCullough, the budget director for the home office, is beginning to assemble next quarter's cash budget. Sales are projected as follows:

	On Account	Cash
October 20x1	$452,000	$196,800
November 20x1	590,000	214,000
December 20x1	720,500	218,400

McCullough's past collection results for sales on account indicate the following pattern.

Month of sale	40%
1st month following sale	30%
2nd month following sale	28%
Uncollectible	2%

Sales on account during the months of August and September were $346,000 and $395,000, respectively.

What are the purposes of preparing a cash budget? Compute the amount of cash to be collected from customers during each month of the last quarter.

E 12. LO 7 *Identification of Controllable Costs*

Contro Corporation produces computer equipment. Production has a three-tier management structure, as follows:

Vice president, production
↖ Plant superintendent
↖ Production supervisors

Identify each cost item below as variable (V), fixed (F), or mixed (M). Then identify the manager responsible for that cost.

1. Repair and maintenance costs
2. Materials handling costs
3. Direct labor
4. Supervisors' salaries
5. Maintenance of plant grounds
6. Depreciation, equipment
7. Plant superintendent's salary
8. Materials usage costs
9. Storage, finished goods inventory
10. Property taxes, plant
11. Depreciation, plant

Problems

P 1. LO 4 *Budget Preparation*

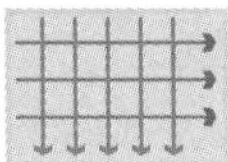

The main product of Cho Sun Enterprises, Inc., is a multipurpose hammer that carries a lifetime guarantee. The steps in the manufacturing process have been combined by using modern, automated equipment. A list of cost and production information for the Cho Sun hammer follows.

Direct materials
- Anodized steel: 2 kilograms per hammer at $1.60 per kilogram
- Leather strapping for the handle: .5 square meter per hammer at $4.40 per square meter
- (Packing materials are returned to the manufacturer and thus are not included as part of cost of goods sold.)

Direct labor
- Forging operation: $12.50 per labor hour; 6 minutes per hammer
- Leather-wrapping operation: $12.00 per direct labor hour; 12 minutes per hammer

Manufacturing overhead
- Forging operation: rate equals 70 percent of department's direct labor dollars
- Leather-wrapping operation: rate equals 50 percent of department's direct labor dollars

For the three months ending December 31, 20x1, Cho Sun's management expects to produce 54,000 hammers in October, 52,000 hammers in November, and 50,000 hammers in December.

Assume no beginning or ending balances of direct materials inventory or work in process inventory for the year.

REQUIRED

1. For the three-month period ending December 31, 20x1, prepare monthly production cost information for the manufacture of the Cho Sun hammer. Classify the costs as direct materials, direct labor, or manufacturing overhead and show the computation methods used.
2. Prepare a cost of goods manufactured budget for the hammer. Show monthly cost data and combined totals for the quarter for each cost category.

P 2. LO 4 *Comprehensive Budgeted Income Statement*

Bobby Blue began manufacturing operations for Blue's Bath Oils in 20x2. His biggest customer is a national retail store chain that sells hair and bath products. Mr. Blue would like an estimate of the company's income from operations for 20x2.

REQUIRED

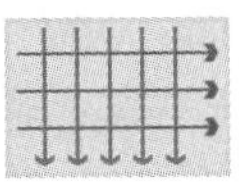

Calculate the company's income from operations by completing the following operating budgets and budgeted income statement for Blue's Bath Oils.

1. Sales Budget

Blue's Bath Oils
Sales Budget
For the Year Ended December 31, 20x2

	Quarter 1	Quarter 2	Quarter 3	Quarter 4	Year
Sales in Units	4,000	3,000	5,000	5,000	17,000
× Selling Price per Unit	$ 5	?	?	?	?
Total Sales	$20,000	?	?	?	?

2. Production Budget

Blue's Bath Oils
Production Budget
For the Year Ended December 31, 20x2

	Quarter 1	Quarter 2	Quarter 3	Quarter 4	Year
Sales in Units (Budget 1)	4,000	?	?	?	?
Add Desired Units of Ending Finished Goods Inventory	300	?	?	**600**	**600**
Desired Total Units	4,300				
Less Desired Units of Beginning Finished Goods Inventory	**400**	?	?	?	**400**
Total Production Units	3,900	?	?	?	?

Note 1: Desired units of ending finished goods inventory = 10% of *next* quarter's budgeted sales.
Note 2: Desired units of beginning finished goods inventory = 10% of *current* quarter's budgeted sales.

3. Direct Materials Purchases Budget

Blue's Bath Oils
Direct Materials Purchases Budget
For the Year Ended December 31, 20x2

	Quarter				
	1	2	3	4	Year
Total Production Units (Budget 2)	3,900	3,200	5,000	5,100	17,200
× 3 Ounces per Unit	3	?	?	?	?
Total Production Needs in Ounces	11,700	?	?	?	?
Add Desired Ounces of Ending Direct Materials Inventory	1,920	?	?	**3,600**	**3,600**
	13,620				
Less Desired Ounces of Beginning Direct Materials Inventory	**2,340**	?	?	?	**2,340**
Total Ounces of Direct Materials to be Purchased	11,280	?	?	?	
× Cost per Ounce	$ .10	?	?	?	?
Total Cost of Direct Materials Purchases	$ 1,128	?	?	?	?

Note 1: Desired ounces of ending direct materials inventory = 20% of *next* quarter's budgeted production needs in ounces.
Note 2: Desired ounces of beginning direct materials inventory = 20% of *current* quarter's budgeted production needs in ounces.
Note 3: Assume that budgeted production needs in ounces for the first quarter of 20x3 = 18,000 ounces.

4. Direct Labor Budget

Blue's Bath Oils
Direct Labor Budget
For the Year Ending December 31, 20x2

	Quarter				
	1	2	3	4	Year
Total Production Units (Budget 2)	3,900	?	?	?	?
× Direct Labor Hours per Unit	.1	?	?	?	?
Total Direct Labor Hours	390	?	?	?	?
× Direct Labor Cost per Hour	$ 7	?	?	?	?
Total Direct Labor Cost	$2,730	?	?	?	?

5. Manufacturing Overhead Budget

Blue's Bath Oils
Manufacturing Overhead Budget
For the Year Ended December 31, 20x2

	Quarter				
	1	2	3	4	Year
Variable Overhead Costs					
Indirect Materials ($.05)	$ 195	?	?	?	?
Employee Benefits ($.25)	975	?	?	?	?
Inspection ($.10)	390	?	?	?	?
Maintenance and Repair ($.15)	585	?	?	?	?
Utilities ($.05)	195	?	?	?	?
Total Variable Overhead	$2,340	?	?	?	?
Fixed Overhead Costs					
Depreciation, Machinery	$ 500	?	?	?	?
Depreciation, Building	700	?	?	?	?
Supervision	1,800	?	?	?	?
Maintenance and Repair	400	?	?	?	?
Other Overhead Expenses	600	?	?	?	?
Total Fixed Overhead	$4,000	?	?	?	?
Total Manufacturing Overhead Costs	$6,340	?	?	?	?

6. Selling and Administrative Expense Budget

Blue's Bath Oils
Selling and Administrative Expense Budget
For the Year Ended December 31, 20x2

	Quarter				
	1	2	3	4	Year
Variable Selling and Administrative Expenses					
Delivery Expenses ($.10)	$ 400	?	?	?	?
Sales Commissions ($.15)	600	?	?	?	?
Accounting ($.05)	200	?	?	?	?
Other Administrative Expenses ($.20)	800	?	?	?	?
Total Variable Selling and Administrative Expenses	$2,000	?	?	?	?
Fixed Selling and Administrative Expenses					
Sales Salaries	$5,000	?	?	?	?
Depreciation, Office Equipment	900	?	?	?	?
Taxes and Insurance	1,700	?	?	?	?
Total Fixed Selling and Administrative Expenses	$7,600	?	?	?	?
Total Selling and Administrative Expenses	$9,600	?	?	?	?

7. Cost of Goods Manufactured Budget

Blue's Bath Oils
Cost of Goods Manufactured Budget
For the Year Ended December 31, 20x2

Direct Materials Used			
Direct Materials Inventory, January 1, 20x2			
Purchases for 20x2	?		(Budget 3)
Cost of Materials Available for Use			
Less Direct Materials Inventory, December 31, 20x2	?		
Cost of Direct Materials Used			
Direct Labor Costs			(Budget 4)
Manufacturing Overhead Costs		?	(Budget 5)
Total Manufacturing Costs			
Work-in-Process Inventory, January 1, 20x2*			
Less Work-in-Process Inventory, December 31, 20x2*		?	
Cost of Goods Manufactured		?	

*It is a company policy to have no units in process at year end.

8. Budgeted Income Statement

Blue's Bath Oils
Budgeted Income Statement
For the Year Ended December 31, 20x2

Sales			
Cost of Goods Sold			
Finished Goods Inventory, January 1, 20x2			
Cost of Goods Manufactured	?		(Budget 7)
Cost of Goods Available for Sale			
Less Finished Goods Inventory, December 31, 20x2	?		
Cost of Goods Sold		?	
Gross Margin			
Less Selling and Administrative Expenses		?	(Budget 6)
Income from Operations		?	

LO 5 *Basic Cash Budget*

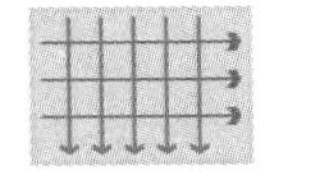

P 3. Produce Mart, Inc., is the creation of Leo Lynz. Lynz's dream was to develop the biggest produce store with the widest selection of fresh fruits and vegetables in the northern Illinois area. In three years, he accomplished his objective. Eighty percent of his business is conducted on credit with area retail enterprises, and 20 percent of the produce sold is to walk-in customers at his retail outlet on a cash only basis.

Collection experience has shown that 50 percent of all credit sales are collected during the month of sale, 30 percent are received in the month following the sale, and 20 percent are collected in the second month after the sale. Lynz has asked you to prepare a cash budget for the quarter ending September 30, 20x3.

Operating data for the period are as follows: Total sales in May were $132,000, and in June, $135,000. Anticipated sales include July, $139,000; August, $152,500; and September, $168,500. Purchases for the quarter are expected to be $87,400 in July; $97,850 in August; and $111,450 in September. All purchases are for cash.

Other projected costs for the quarter include salaries and wages of $36,740 in July, $38,400 in August, and $40,600 in September; and monthly costs of $2,080 for heat, light, and power; $750 for bank collection fees; $3,850 for rent; $2,240 for supplies; $3,410 for depreciation of equipment; $2,570 for equipment repairs; and $950 for miscellaneous expenses. The corporation's cash balance at June 30, 20x3, was $5,490.

REQUIRED

1. Prepare a cash budget by month for the quarter ending September 30, 20x3.
2. Should Produce Mart, Inc., anticipate taking out a loan during the quarter? How much should be borrowed? When? (**Note:** Management has a $3,000 minimum monthly cash balance policy.)

P 4. **LO 4, LO 6** *Budgeted Financial Statements*

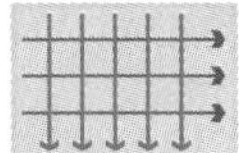

The Bank of the West has asked the president of Montoya Products, Inc., for a budgeted income statement and budgeted balance sheet for the quarter ending June 30, 20x1. These documents will be used to support the company's request for a loan. A quarterly master budget is routinely prepared by the company, so the president indicated that the requested documents would be forwarded to the bank.

To date (April 2), the following operating budgets have been developed. Sales: April, $220,400, May, $164,220, and June, $165,980; direct materials purchases for the period, $96,840; direct materials usage, $102,710; direct labor expenses, $71,460; manufacturing overhead, $79,940; selling and administrative expenses, $143,740; capital expenditures, $125,000 (to be spent on June 29); cost of goods manufactured, $252,880; and cost of goods sold, $251,700.

Balance sheet account balances at March 31, 20x1 were: Cash, $28,770; Accounts Receivable, $26,500; Direct Materials Inventory, $23,910; Work in Process Inventory, $31,620; Finished Goods Inventory, $36,220; Prepaid Expenses, $7,200; Plant, Furniture, and Fixtures, $498,600; Accumulated Depreciation, Plant, Furniture, and Fixtures, $141,162; Patents, $90,600; Accounts Payable, $39,600; Notes Payable, $105,500; Common Stock, $250,000; and Retained Earnings, $207,158.

Monthly cash balances for the quarter are projected to be: April 30, $20,490; May 31, $35,610; and June 30, $45,400. During the quarter, accounts receivable are supposed to increase by 30 percent, patents will go up by $6,500, prepaid expenses will remain constant, accounts payable will go down by 10 percent, and the company will make a $5,000 payment on the note payable ($4,100 is principal reduction). The federal income tax rate is 34 percent and the second quarter's tax is paid in July. Depreciation for the quarter will be $6,420, which was already included in the manufacturing overhead budget. No dividends were paid.

REQUIRED

1. Prepare a budgeted income statement for the quarter ending June 30, 20x1. Round answers to the nearest dollar.
2. Prepare a budgeted balance sheet as of June 30, 20x1.

P 5. **LO 5** *Cash Budget Preparation: Comprehensive*

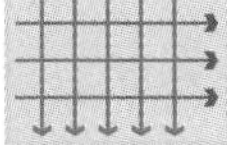

Black Hills Ski Resort, Inc., has been in business for twenty-two years. Although the skiing season is difficult to predict, the company operates under the assumption that all of its revenues will be generated during the first three months of the calendar year. Routine maintenance and repair work are done during the remaining nine-month period. The following projections for 20x2 were developed by Sandy Potts, the company budget director.

Cash Receipts

Lift tickets: January, 16,800 people @ $22; February, 17,400 people @ $23; and March, 17,800 people @ $24
Food sales: January, $62,000; February, $56,000; and March, $62,000
Skiing lessons: January, $158,000; February, $134,000; and March, $158,000
Equipment sales and rental: January, $592,000; February, $496,000; and March, $592,000
Liquor sales: January, $124,000; February, $92,000; and March, $104,000

Cash Payments

Salaries:
- Ski area:
  - Lift operators: 12 people @ $2,500 per month for January, February, and March (first quarter)
  - Instruction and equipment rental: 24 people @ $2,700 per month for first quarter
  - Maintenance: $35,000 per month for first quarter, and a total of $96,000 for the rest of the year
- Customer service: Shuttle bus drivers, 10 people @ $1,400 per month for first quarter
- Medical: 8 people @ $6,400 per month for first quarter
- Food service: 24 people @ $1,800 per month for first quarter

Purchases:
- Food: $30,000 per month for the first quarter
- Ski equipment: Purchases of $340,000 in both January and February plus a $700,000 purchase anticipated in December 20x2
- Liquor: $50,000 in each month of the first quarter
- Tickets and supplies: $50,000 in January, $40,000 in February, and $80,000 in December 20x2

Advertising: $40,000 in January, $30,000 in February, and a total of $90,000 from April through the end of the year

Fire and liability insurance: January and June premium payments of $8,000

Medical facility costs: $15,000 per month during first quarter

Utilities: $5,000 per month for the first quarter and $1,000 per month for the rest of the year

Lift maintenance: $25,000 per month for the first quarter and $10,000 per month for the rest of the year

Property taxes: $180,000 due in June

Federal income taxes: 20x1 taxes of $364,000 due in March

The beginning cash balance for 20x2 is anticipated to be $10,000.

REQUIRED

Prepare a cash budget for Black Hills Ski Resort, Inc., for 20x2, using the following column headings.

Item	January	February	March	April–December	Year

Alternate Problems

LO 4 *Budgeted Income Statement*

P 6. Catie Burns is the budget director for Overland Spectaculars, Inc., a multinational company based in Maryland. Overland Spectaculars, Inc., organizes and coordinates art shows and auctions throughout the world. Budgeted and actual costs and expenses for 20x4 are compared in the following schedule.

	20x4 Amounts	
Expense Item	**Budget**	**Actual**
Salaries expense, staging	$ 240,000	$ 256,400
Salaries expense, executive	190,000	223,600
Travel costs	320,000	326,010
Auctioneer services	270,000	224,910
Space rental costs	125,500	123,290
Printing costs	96,000	91,250
Advertising expense	84,500	91,640
Insurance, merchandise	42,400	38,650
Insurance, liability	32,000	33,550
Home office costs	104,600	109,940
Shipping costs	52,500	56,280
Miscellaneous	12,500	12,914
Total expenses	$1,570,000	$1,588,434
Net receipts	$3,100,000	$3,184,600

For 20x5, the following fixed costs have been budgeted: executive salaries, $220,000; advertising expense, $95,000; merchandise insurance, $40,000; and liability insurance, $34,000. Additional information follows.

a. Net receipts are expected to be $3,200,000 in 20x5.
b. Staging salaries will increase 20 percent over 20x4 actual figures.
c. Travel costs are expected to be 11 percent of net receipts.
d. Auctioneer services will be billed at 9.5 percent of net receipts.
e. Space rental costs will go up 20 percent from 20x4 budgeted amounts.
f. Printing costs are expected to be $95,000 in 20x5.
g. Home office costs are budgeted for $115,000 in 20x5.
h. Shipping costs are expected to rise 20 percent over 20x4 budgeted amounts.
i. Miscellaneous expenses for 20x5 will be budgeted at $14,000.

REQUIRED

1. Prepare the company's budgeted income statement for 20x5. Assume that only services are being sold and that there is no cost of sales. (Net receipts equal gross margin.) Use a 34 percent federal income tax rate.
2. Should the budget director be worried about the trend in the company's operations? Be specific.

LO 5 *Basic Cash Budget*

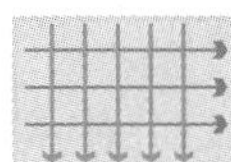

P 7. Lisa Santelli is president of Tri-State Nurseries, Inc. This corporation has four locations and has been in business for six years. Each retail outlet offers over 300 varieties of plants and trees. James Ash, the controller, has been asked to prepare a cash budget for the Southern Division for the first quarter of 20x2.

Projected data supporting the budget are summarized as follows. Collection history for the accounts receivable has shown that 30 percent of all credit sales are collected in the month of sale, 60 percent in the month following the sale, and 8 percent in the second month following the sale. Two percent of the credit sales are uncollectible. Purchases are all paid for in the month following the purchase. As of December 31, 20x1 the Southern Division had a cash balance of $4,800.

Sales (60 percent on credit)		**Purchases**	
November 20x1	$ 80,000	December 20x1	$43,400
December 20x1	100,000	January 20x2	62,350
January 20x2	60,000	February 20x2	49,720
February 20x2	80,000	March 20x2	52,400
March 20x2	70,000		

Salaries and wages are projected to be $12,600 in January; $16,600 in February; and $10,600 in March. Monthly costs are estimated to be: utilities, $2,110; collection fees, $850; rent, $2,650; equipment depreciation, $2,720; supplies, $1,240; small tools, $1,570; and miscellaneous, $950.

REQUIRED

1. Prepare a cash budget by month for the Southern Division for first quarter 20x2.
2. Should Tri-State Nurseries, Inc., anticipate taking out a loan for the Southern Division during the quarter? How much should be borrowed? When? (**Note:** Management maintains a $3,000 minimum cash balance at each location.)

LO 4 *Budgeted Financial*
LO 6 *Statements*

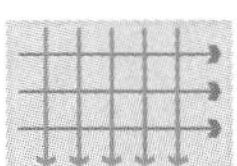

P 8. Voyager Video Company, Inc., produces and markets two popular video games, "Fifth Galaxy" and "Young Pathfinder." The company's closing balance sheet account balances for 20x0 are as follows: Cash, $18,735; Accounts Receivable, $19,900; Direct Materials Inventory, $18,510; Work in Process Inventory, $24,680; Finished Goods Inventory, $21,940; Prepaid Expenses, $3,420; Plant and Equipment, $262,800; Accumulated Depreciation, Plant and Equipment, $55,845; Other Assets, $9,480; Accounts Payable, $52,640; Mortgage Payable, $70,000; Common Stock, $90,000; and Retained Earnings, $110,980.

Operating budgets for the first quarter of 20x1 revealed the following: direct materials purchases, $58,100; direct materials usage, $62,400; direct labor expense, $42,880; manufacturing overhead, $51,910; selling expenses, $35,820; general and administrative expenses, $60,240; capital expenditures, $0; ending cash balances by month: January, $34,610; February, $60,190; March, $54,802; cost of goods manufactured, $163,990; and cost of goods sold, $165,440.

Sales per month are projected to be \$125,200 for January, \$105,100 for February, and \$112,600 for March. Accounts receivable will double during the quarter, and accounts payable will decrease by 20 percent. Mortgage payments for the quarter will total \$6,000, of which \$2,000 is interest expense. Prepaid expenses are expected to go up by \$20,000, and other assets are projected to increase 50 percent over the budget period. Depreciation for plant and equipment (already included in the manufacturing overhead budget) averages 5 percent of total Plant and Equipment per year. Federal income taxes (34 percent of profits) are payable in April. No dividends were paid.

REQUIRED

1. Prepare a budgeted income statement for the quarter ending March 31, 20x1.
2. Prepare a budgeted balance sheet as of March 31, 20x1.

Skills Development

CONCEPTUAL ANALYSIS

SD 1. *The Budgeting Process*
LO 1
LO 2
LO 3

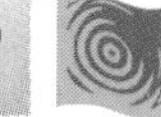

Many organizations believe the budgeting process is wasteful and ineffective. Managers and employees can spend too much time focusing on budgeting mechanics rather than on strategic issues. They can also forget to review nonvalue-adding activities that waste resources. Finally, they may select budget information and use budget formats that fail to communicate the short-term business activities needed to achieve long-term goals. Place yourself in the role of a budget director for a company. Prepare a memorandum to the company's owner justifying the need for budgeting. Also suggest ways to make the budgeting process, the budget information, and the budgets themselves efficient, effective, and meaningful. (**Note:** For help in completing this assignment, look for the article written by Jeffrey A. Schmidt, "Is It Time to Replace Traditional Budgeting?" *Journal of Accountancy,* October 1992, pp. 103–107, located on the Needles Accounting Resource Center Web site at http://www.hmco.com/college/needles/home.html.)

Group Activity: Ask students to complete the assignment individually. Then have students work in groups to prepare (1) an argument justifying the use of budgeting and (2) a list of ways to make the budgeting process, the budget information, and the budgets efficient, effective, and meaningful. Select one person from each group to report the group's findings to the class.

ETHICAL DILEMMA

SD 2. *Ethical Considerations in the Budgeting Process*
LO 2
LO 3
LO 4

Gus Kamp is manager of the Repairs and Maintenance (R&M) Department, a cost center at ***Phoenix Industries.*** Mr. Kamp is responsible for preparing the annual budget for his department. For 20x2, he turned in the following budgeted information to the company's budget director. The 20x2 figures are 20 percent above the 20x1 budget figures. Most managers in the company inflate their budget numbers by at least 10 percent because their bonuses depend upon how much below budget they operate.

Cost Category	Budget 20x1	Actual 20x1	Budget 20x2
Supplies	$ 20,000	$ 16,000	$ 24,000
Labor	80,000	82,000	96,000
Utilities	8,500	8,000	10,200
Tools	12,500	9,000	15,000
Hand-carried equipment	25,000	16,400	30,000
Cleaning materials	4,600	4,200	5,520
Miscellaneous	2,000	2,100	2,400
Totals	$152,600	$137,700	$183,120

The director has questioned some of the numbers. Mr. Kamp defended them by saying that he expects a significant increase in repairs and maintenance activity in 20x2.

What are the real reasons for the increased budgeted data? What are the ethical considerations of this situation?

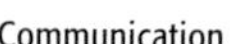
Communication

Critical Thinking

Group Activity

Memo

Ethics

International

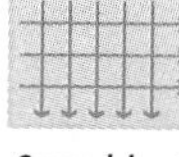
Spreadsheet

Managerial Technology

Internet

Research Activity

SD 3. *The Budgeting Process*
LO 1
LO 2

  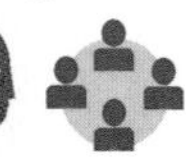

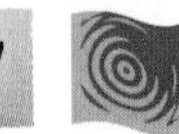

Managers of the HON Company and HON Industries use relevant operational information to prepare quarterly budgets for the next year. HON's Web site presents the actual results of some of the long-range and short-range plans that were originally included in company budgets. Prepare a short, typewritten report that includes a list of the historical or planned events, activities, or factors that would influence the information in the next period's budget for HON Industries. Conduct your research by reviewing the Decision Point in this chapter, the *Management Accounting* article on which the Decision Point is based, and/or the most recent Operations Review in the Investor Relations section of the HON Industries Web site (see the Needles Accounting Resource Center Web site at http://www.hmco.com/college/needles/home.html for access to these materials.)

Decision-Making Practice

SD 4. *Effective Budgeting Procedures*
LO 2
LO 3
LO 4

During the past ten years, ***Squizzero Enterprises*** has practiced participative budgeting all the way from the maintenance personnel to the president's staff. Gradually, however, the objectives of honesty and decisions made in the best interest of the company as a whole have given way to division-benefiting decisions. Ralph Banerjee, the corporate controller, has asked Maggie Neff, the budget director, to carefully analyze this year's divisional budgets before incorporating them into the company's master budget.

The Motor Division was the first of six divisions to submit its 20x5 budget request to the corporate office. Its summary income statement and notes appear on the next page.

1. Recast the Motor Division's budgeted income statement into the following format (round percentages to two places):

	Budget—12/31/x4		Budget—12/31/x5	
Account	**Amount**	**Percent of Sales**	**Amount**	**Percent of Sales**

2. Actual results for 20x4 revealed the following information about revenues and cost of goods sold.

	Amount	Percent of Sales
Net Sales		
Radios	$ 780,000	43.94%
Appliances	640,000	36.06%
Telephones	280,000	15.77%
Miscellaneous	75,000	4.23%
Net Sales	$1,775,000	100.00%
Less Cost of Goods Sold	763,425	43.01%
Gross Margin	$1,011,575	56.99%

On the basis of this information and your analysis in **1**, what should the budget director say to the managers of the Motor Division? Mention specific areas of the budget that need to be revised.

Squizzero Enterprises
Motor Division
Budgeted Income Statement
For the Years Ended December 31, 20x4 and 20x5

	Budget 12/31/x4	Budget 12/31/x5	Increase (Decrease)
Net Sales			
Radios	$ 850,000	$ 910,000	$ 60,000
Appliances	680,000	740,000	60,000
Telephones	270,000	305,000	35,000
Miscellaneous	84,400	90,000	5,600
Net Sales	$1,884,400	$2,045,000	$160,600
Less Cost of Goods Sold	750,960	717,500[1]	(33,460)
Gross Margin	$1,133,440	$1,327,500	$194,060
Operating Expenses			
Wages			
Warehouse	$ 94,500	$ 102,250	$ 7,750
Purchasing	77,800	84,000	6,200
Delivery/Shipping	69,400	74,780	5,380
Maintenance	42,650	45,670	3,020
Salaries			
Supervisory	60,000	92,250	32,250
Executive	130,000	164,000	34,000
Purchases, Supplies	17,400	20,500	3,100
Merchandise Moving Equipment			
Maintenance	72,400	82,000	9,600
Depreciation	62,000	74,750[2]	12,750
Building Rent	96,000	102,500	6,500
Sales Commissions	188,440	204,500	16,060
Insurance			
Fire	12,670	20,500	7,830
Liability	18,200	20,500	2,300
Utilities	14,100	15,375	1,275
Taxes			
Property	16,600	18,450	1,850
Payroll	26,520	41,000	14,480
Miscellaneous	4,610	10,250	5,640
Total Operating Expenses	$1,003,290	$1,173,275	$169,985
Income from Operations	$ 130,150	$ 154,225	$ 24,075

1. Less expensive merchandise will be purchased in 20x5 to boost profits.
2. Depreciation is increased because of a need to buy additional equipment to handle increased sales.

Managerial Reporting and Analysis

INTERPRETING MANAGEMENT REPORTS

MRA 1.
LO 2 *Interpreting Budget Formulation Policies*

Husin Corporation is a manufacturing company with annual sales of $25,000,000. The controller, Victor Subroto, appointed Yolanda Alvillar as budget director. She created the following budget formulation policy based on a calendar-year accounting period.

May 20x2	Meeting of corporate officers and budget director to discuss corporate plans for 20x3.
June 20x2	Meeting(s) of division managers, department heads, and budget director to communicate 20x3 corporate objectives. At this time, relevant background data are distributed to all managers and a time schedule is established for development of 20x3 budget data.
July 20x2	Managers and department heads continue to develop budget data. Complete 20x3 monthly sales forecasts by product line and receive final sales estimates from sales vice president.
Aug. 20x2	Complete 20x3 monthly production activity and anticipated inventory level plans. Division managers and department heads should communicate preliminary budget figures to budget director for coordination and distribution to other operating areas.
Sept. 20x2	Development of preliminary 20x3 master budget. Revised budget data from all functional areas to be received. Budget director will coordinate staff activities, integrating labor requirements, direct materials and supplies requirements, unit cost estimates, cash requirements, and profit estimates, and prepare preliminary 20x3 master budget.
Oct. 20x2	Meeting with corporate officers to discuss preliminary 20x3 master budget; any corrections, additions, or deletions to be communicated to budget director by corporate officers; all authorized changes to be incorporated into the 20x3 master budget.
Nov. 20x2	Submit final draft of 20x3 master budget to corporate officers for approval. Publish approved budget and distribute to all corporate officers, division managers, and department heads.

REQUIRED

1. Comment on the proposed budget formulation policy.
2. What changes in the policy would you recommend?

FORMULATING MANAGEMENT REPORTS

MRA 2.
LO 2 *Budgeted Financial*
LO 3 *Statement Preparation*
LO 4

Assume that you have just signed a partnership agreement with your cousin Eddie to open a bookstore near the college campus. You believe that you will be able to provide excellent services at prices lower than your local competition. In order to begin operations, Eddie and you have decided to apply for a small business loan from the Small Business Administration (SBA). Part of the application requires that you submit financial statements that will forecast the bookstore's first two years of operating activity and its financial position at the end of the second year. The application is due within six weeks. Because of your expertise in accounting and business, Eddie has asked you to develop the budgeted financial statements.

REQUIRED

1. List the budgeted financial statements and supporting schedules you believe you must prepare.
2. Who needs the budgeted financial statements?
3. Why are you preparing budgeted financial statements?
4. What information do you need to develop on the budgeted financial statements? How will you obtain the information?
5. When must you have the budgeted financial statements prepared?
6. In what ways can Eddie and you use the budgeted financial statements that you have prepared?

INTERNATIONAL COMPANY

MRA 3.
LO 5 *Goals and the Budgeting Process*

3M manufactures a variety of products ranging from office supplies to household sponges and laser imagers for CAT scanners to reflective materials for roads. Because of the company's aggressive research and development activities, many of these products have been redesigned to satisfy the needs of Asian customers. Business has been so successful that sales in the Asia-Pacific division of 3M have doubled in the past five years. Facilities are in Malaysia, South Korea, India, Thailand, and Taiwan.[5]

Based on 3M's strategic plan for next year, two goals for the Asia-Pacific division have been developed. These goals include a 25 percent growth in sales volume and construction of a $14 million manufacturing plant in Shanghai that will begin operations in the third quarter of the year.

REQUIRED

The manager for the Asia-Pacific division is preparing the cash budget for next year's operations. How would the budgeted cash receipts and cash payments on the cash budget be affected by these two goals?

EXCEL SPREADSHEET ANALYSIS

MRA 4.
LO 3
LO 4 *The Budgeting Process*

Refer to the Hi-Flyer Company's master budget presented in this chapter for the year ending December 31, 20x1. Skye King has decided to increase the budgeted sales in the first quarter by 5,000 units to reflect sales to a new customer in Canada. The expenses for this sale will include direct materials, direct labor, variable manufacturing overhead, and variable selling and administrative expenses. The delivery expense for the Canadian customer will be $.18 per unit rather than the regular $.08 per unit. The desired units of beginning finished goods inventory will remain at 1,000 units.

REQUIRED

Use the Excel spreadsheet of the exhibits found in the chapter and the changes stated above to complete the following:

1. Prepare a revised budgeted income statement and supporting operating budgets.
2. What was the change in income from operations? Would you recommend accepting the order? Why?

ENDNOTES

1. Ralph Drtina, Steve Hoeger, and John Schaub, "Continuous Budgeting at the HON Company," *Management Accounting,* Institute of Management Accountants, January 1996, pp. 20–24.
2. From, "Budgeting for an International Business," Paul V. Mannino and Ken Milani. *Management Accounting,* February, 1992, p. 39. Reprinted courtesy of the Institute of Management Accountants.
3. John Case, "Opening the Books," *Harvard Business Review,* March–April 1997, pp. 118–126.
4. Adapted from Larry Ponemon, "Building an Effective Business Ethics Process," *Management Accounting,* Institute of Management Accountants, June 1996, p. 16.
5. "3M: Business Booms in Asia," *Asian Business,* Vol. 29, No. 22, February 1993, pp. 9–10.

Cost Control Using Standard Costing and Variance Analysis

LEARNING OBJECTIVES

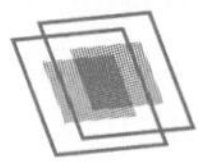

1. **Define *standard costs* and describe how managers use standard costs in the management cycle.**
2. **State the purposes for using standard costs.**
3. **Identify the six elements of, and compute, a standard unit cost.**
4. **Describe how to control costs through variance analysis.**
5. **Compute and analyze direct materials variances.**
6. **Compute and analyze direct labor variances.**
7. **Define and prepare a flexible budget.**
8. **Compute and analyze manufacturing overhead variances.**
9. **Explain how variances are used to evaluate managers' performance.**

DECISION POINT

THE RUBICON GROUP

The Rubicon Group, of Oak Brook, Illinois, is an employee-owned consulting company that specializes in identifying computer hardware, software, and process-support solutions to business problems. It designs and installs comprehensive distribution, financial, and manufacturing software systems. One of the company's specialties is cost control. As part of its service in this area, Rubicon provides clients with current and standard cost updates, a comprehensive cost worksheet package, a variance report tracking standard and actual costs, and a gross profit and price evaluation. For manufacturers, the cost control analysis looks at current and standard costs for machine setup, materials, labor, and variable and fixed manufacturing overhead. Rubicon's cost control system can track variances for making an individual part, specific routed parts, or all parts manufactured by a client company. The company's operating manual states that its cost control system "offers users both the tools and the flexibility to establish, analyze, and report the following financial management functions: standard cost generation, cost inquiries, and evaluation of cost changes."[1] How can these three functions aid management in controlling operating costs?

Creating a set of standard costs provides management with benchmarks to use in evaluating actual operating costs. They are targets for analyzing

Critical Thinking Question: Why should management be interested in knowing about materials cost changes? **Answer:** So that management can adjust prices of goods to reflect those changes.

actual spending trends. Cost inquiries are used to continuously monitor market price and operating cost changes. If these changes are permanent, the changes are used to update standard costs. The evaluation of changes in costs provides management with information about the causes of variances. Once the cause of a variance is known, management can make decisions to correct any related operating problem.

Standard Costs in Today's Business Environment

OBJECTIVE 1

Define* standard costs *and describe how managers use* standard costs *in the management cycle

Related Text Assignments:
Q: 1, 2
SE: 1
E: 1
SD: 3

Standard costing is a budgetary control technique. In a standard costing system, standard costs for direct materials, direct labor, and manufacturing overhead flow through the inventory accounts and eventually into the Cost of Goods Sold account. Instead of using actual costs for product costing purposes, standard costs are used. Standard costs are realistically predetermined costs that are developed from analyses of both past operating costs, quantities, and times and future costs and operating conditions.

Once standard costs have been developed, managers use them as tools for cost planning and control. Figure 1 shows how standard costs are used during the management cycle. During the planning stage, after projected sales and production targets for the upcoming year are established, standard costs can be used to estimate costs for direct materials, direct labor, and variable manufacturing overhead. The estimated costs serve as goals for product costing. They can also be used in product distribution and pricing. Standard costs not only aid in the development of budgets, but they also serve as yardsticks for evaluating capital expenditures. If the price a vendor charges differs from the anticipated standard price, the manager should question the difference.

During the executing stage, dollar, time, and quantity standards are applied to the work being done. The reviewing stage occurs at the end of the accounting period—whether it be a week, a month, or a quarter. At that time, the actual costs incurred are compared with standard costs, and the difference is computed. The difference between a standard cost and an actual cost is called a variance. Variances provide measures of performance that can be used to control costs. The amount of a variance provides one measure of the significance of the variance. But managers should look beyond the amount of a variance and try to determine its cause or causes. By analyzing the causes of variances, managers can identify inefficient functions within departments or work cells and take action to improve them. Variances from standard costs can also be used to evaluate an individual manager's performance.

During the reporting stage, standard costs are used to report on operations and managerial performance. When a variance report is tailored to a manager's specific responsibilities, it will provide much useful information about how well operations are proceeding and how well the manager is controlling them.

Standard costing has traditionally been used to measure and evaluate operating performance in manufacturing settings. Today, standard costing can be applied by managers in service organizations such as Barnett Bank and Liberty Mutual Insurance Company. The only difference between using standard costs in a manufacturing company and in a service organization is that there are no direct materials costs in a service environment. But labor and overhead costs are very much a part of providing services and must be planned and controlled. Therefore, managers in service organizations can also use standard costs and measure performance through variance analysis.

Instructional Strategy: Have students prepare SD 3 individually. In class, form small groups and ask group members to share the main points of their articles with each other. Then have the groups decide whether or not labor-intensive companies should calculate labor-based variances. Emphasize that managers should know when this form of variance analysis is appropriate.

In today's globally competitive manufacturing environment, managers use new approaches to performance evaluation. Instead of concentrating exclusively on production efficiency and cost control, they are also concerned with reducing processing time and improving quality, customer satisfaction, and the number of on-time

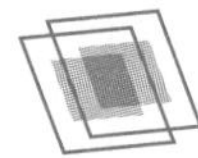

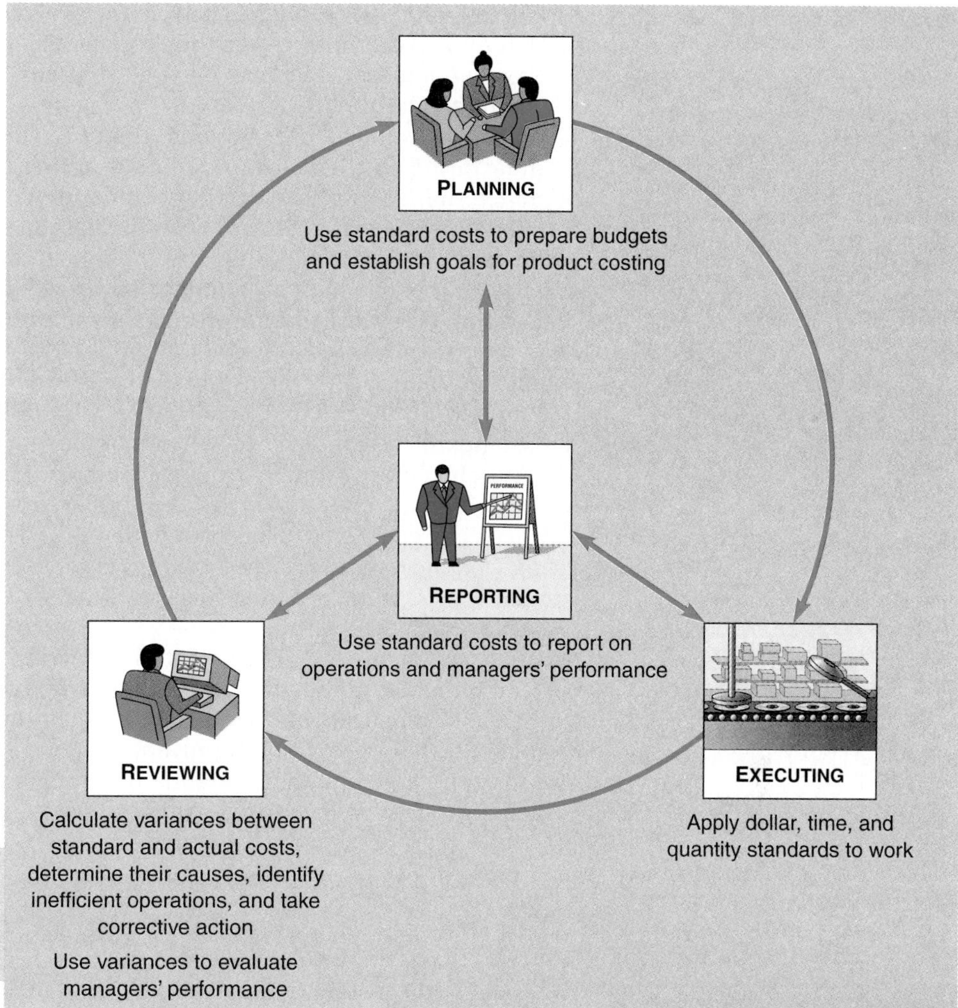

Figure 1
Standard Costing, Variance Analysis, and the Management Cycle

deliveries. This approach requires new measures of performance that track processing time, quality, customer responses, and delivery results. The importance of labor-related standard costs and variances has been reduced because direct labor costs have dropped significantly. However, standard costs and variance analysis are still very much in use for direct materials and manufacturing overhead.

The Nature and Purpose of Standard Costing

OBJECTIVE 2

State the purposes for using standard costs

Related Text Assignments:
Q: 3, 4
SE: 2
SD: 2, 3

Accountants do not build a full cost accounting system from standard costs alone. Standard costs are used with existing job order or process costing systems. When a company uses standard costs, all costs affecting the inventory accounts and the Cost of Goods Sold account are recorded using standard, or predetermined, costs rather than actual costs incurred. In this section, we examine the nature and purpose of standard costs—their components, their development, and their use in product costing. Later in the chapter we concentrate on their use in cost control and evaluating managers' performance.

Standard costs are predetermined costs for direct materials, direct labor, and manufacturing overhead. They are usually expressed as the cost per unit of finished product or process. Standard costs share two very important characteristics with predetermined overhead costs: both forecast the dollar amounts to be used in product costing, and both depend on projected costs for budgeted items. But that is where the similarity ends.

Teaching Note: At this point students may have difficulty understanding the difference between predetermined overhead rates and a standard overhead cost. Compare and contrast the two for greater clarity.

Standard costing focuses on *total* unit cost, which includes all three elements of manufacturing cost. The computation of standard costs is more detailed than that of predetermined overhead costs. Whereas predetermined overhead rates are usually based on past costs, standard costs are based on engineering estimates, forecasted demand, worker input, time and motion studies, and type and quality of direct materials. One drawback to standard costing is that it is expensive to use. Since a predetermined overhead rate provides some of the same data as a standard overhead rate, a company that cannot afford to add standard costing to its cost system should continue to use predetermined overhead rates.

Point to Emphasize: Standard costs are necessary for planning and control. Budgets are developed from standard costs, and performance is measured against standard costs.

Standard costing is a total cost concept. In a fully integrated standard costing system, standard costs replace all actual manufacturing costs. Accounts such as Direct Materials Inventory, Work in Process Inventory, Finished Goods Inventory, and Cost of Goods Sold are maintained and reported in terms of standard costs. All inventory balances are computed using standard unit costs. The management accountant keeps separate records of actual costs to compare what should have been spent (the standard costs) with the actual costs incurred.

Point to Emphasize: Updating time and dollar standards for valid reasons produces more meaningful standards. However, if the updates are too frequent, the standards may lose credibility and be perceived as moving targets by managers.

There are, then, several reasons for introducing standard costs into a cost accounting system. They are useful in preparing operating budgets. They make it easier to pinpoint production costs that must be controlled and to evaluate the performance of managers and workers. They help in setting realistic prices, and they simplify procedures for valuing inventories and product costing. Although expensive to set up and maintain, a standard costing system can save a company money by helping to reduce waste and inefficiency.

The Development of Standard Costs

OBJECTIVE 3

Identify the six elements of, and compute, a standard unit cost

Related Text Assignments:
Q: 5, 6, 7
SE: 3
E: 2, 3
P: 1, 6

A standard unit cost for a manufactured product has six parts: (1) the direct materials price standard, (2) the direct materials quantity standard, (3) the direct labor time standard, (4) the direct labor rate standard, (5) the standard variable manufacturing overhead rate, and (6) the standard fixed manufacturing overhead rate. To develop a standard unit cost, we must identify and analyze each of these elements. For service organizations, only the last four apply because those organizations do not use raw materials or parts in their operations.

Standard Direct Materials Cost The standard direct materials cost is found by multiplying the standard price for direct materials by the standard quantity for direct materials. If the standard price for a certain item is \$2.75 and a specific job calls for a standard quantity of 8 of the items, the standard direct materials cost for that job is \$22.00 (8 × \$2.75).

The direct materials price standard is a careful estimate of the cost of a specific direct material in the next accounting period. The purchasing agent is responsible for developing price standards for all direct materials. When estimating a direct materials price standard, the purchasing agent must take into account all possible price increases, changes in available quantities, and new sources of supply. The purchasing agent also makes the actual purchases.

Discussion Question: Why wouldn't a purchasing agent purchase the least costly materials available to stay within a direct materials price standard? **Answer:** The *quality* of the direct materials purchased must remain consistent so that excess spoilage and waste do not occur during the production process and cause unfavorable quantity variances.

The direct materials quantity standard is an estimate of the amount of direct materials to be used. It is influenced by product engineering specifications, the quality of direct materials, the age and productivity of machinery, and the quality and experience of the work force. Some scrap and waste may be unavoidable, so they are included in the estimate. Production managers or cost accountants usually establish and monitor direct materials quantity standards, although engineers, purchasing agents, and machine operators may contribute to the development of these standards.

Standard Direct Labor Cost The standard direct labor cost for a product, task, or job order is calculated by multiplying the standard hours of direct labor by the standard wage for direct labor. If a product takes 1.5 standard direct labor hours to produce and the standard direct labor rate is $8.40 per hour, then the product's standard direct labor cost is $12.60 ($8.40 × 1.5).

Teaching Note: In explaining direct labor time and rate standards, emphasize two points: First, both standards are based on an average of the different levels of skilled workers, and second, both are related to the production of one unit or batch.

The direct labor time standard is the expected time required for each department, machine, or process to complete the production of one unit or one batch of output. Current time and motion studies of workers and machines as well as past employee and machine performance are the basic input for the development of this standard. In many cases, standard time per unit is a small fraction of an hour. The direct labor time standard should be revised whenever a machine is replaced or the quality of the labor force changes. Meeting time standards is the responsibility of the department manager or supervisor.

Standard labor rates are fairly easy to develop because labor rates are either set by a labor contract or defined by the company. Direct labor rate standards are the hourly direct labor costs that are expected to prevail during the next accounting period for each function or job classification. Although rate ranges are established for each type of worker and rates vary within these ranges based on experience and length of service, an average standard rate is developed for each task. Even if the person actually making the product is paid more or less than the standard rate, the standard rate is used to calculate the standard direct labor cost.

Standard Manufacturing Overhead Cost The standard manufacturing overhead cost is the sum of the estimates for variable and fixed manufacturing overhead costs in the next accounting period. It is based on standard rates computed in much the same way as the predetermined manufacturing overhead rate discussed earlier. One important difference, however, is that the standard manufacturing overhead rate is made up of two parts, one for variable costs and one for fixed costs. The reason for computing the standard variable and fixed manufacturing overhead rates separately is that different application bases are generally required. The standard variable manufacturing overhead rate is total budgeted variable manufacturing overhead costs divided by an expression of capacity, such as the expected number of standard machine hours or direct labor hours. (Other bases may be used if machine hours or direct labor hours are not good predictors (or drivers) of variable manufacturing overhead costs.) Using standard machine hours as the basis, the formula is:

Teaching Note: Using an overhead cost as an example, help students review the differences between fixed and variable costs.

$$\text{Standard Variable Manufacturing Overhead Rate} = \frac{\text{Total Budgeted Variable Manufacturing Overhead Costs}}{\text{Expected Number of Standard Machine Hours}}$$

The standard fixed manufacturing overhead rate is total budgeted fixed manufacturing overhead costs divided by an expression of capacity, usually normal capacity in terms of standard hours or units. The denominator is expressed in the same terms (direct labor hours, machine hours, and so forth) used to compute the variable manufacturing overhead rate. The formula is:

$$\text{Standard Fixed Manufacturing Overhead Rate} = \frac{\text{Total Budgeted Fixed Manufacturing Overhead Costs}}{\text{Normal Capacity in Terms of Standard Machine Hours}}$$

Point to Emphasize: Normal capacity is the average annual level of operating capacity needed to meet expected sales demand; it is the level of activity at which a company expects to operate.

Using normal capacity as the application basis ensures that all fixed manufacturing overhead costs have been applied to units produced by the time normal capacity is reached.

Using Standards for Product Costing

Using standard costs eliminates the need to calculate unit costs from actual cost data every week or month or for each batch produced. Once standard costs are developed for direct materials, direct labor, and manufacturing overhead, a total standard unit cost can be computed at any time.

With standard cost elements, the following amounts are determined: (1) cost of purchased direct materials entered into Direct Materials Inventory, (2) cost of goods requisitioned out of Direct Materials Inventory and into Work in Process Inventory, (3) cost of direct labor charged to Work in Process Inventory, (4) cost of manufacturing overhead applied to Work in Process Inventory, (5) cost of goods completed and transferred to Finished Goods Inventory, and (6) cost of units sold and charged to Cost of Goods Sold. In other words, all transactions affecting the three inventory accounts and the Cost of Goods Sold account are expressed in terms of standard costs, no matter what the amount of actual costs incurred.

For example, Bokinski Industries, Inc., uses a standard costing system. Recently, the company updated the standards for its line of automatic pencils. New standards include the following: Direct materials price standards are \$9.20 per square foot for casing materials and \$2.25 for each movement mechanism. Direct materials quantity standards are .025 square foot of casing materials per pencil and one movement mechanism per pencil. Direct labor time standards are .01 hour per pencil for the Stamping Department and .05 hour per pencil for the Assembly Department. Direct labor rate standards are \$8.00 per hour for the Stamping Department and \$10.20 per hour for the Assembly Department. Standard manufacturing overhead rates are \$12.00 per direct labor hour for the standard variable manufacturing overhead rate and \$9.00 per direct labor hour for the standard fixed manufacturing overhead rate. The standard cost of making one automatic pencil would be computed as follows.

Point to Emphasize: Underscore that the \$4.33 standard cost represents the *desired* cost to produce one pencil.

Direct materials costs	
Casing (\$9.20 per sq. ft. × .025 sq. ft.)	\$ .23
One movement mechanism	2.25
Direct labor costs	
Stamping Department (.01 hour per pencil × \$8.00 per hour)	.08
Assembly Department (.05 hour per pencil × \$10.20 per hour)	.51
Manufacturing overhead	
Variable manufacturing overhead (.06 hour per pencil × \$12.00 per hour)	.72
Fixed manufacturing overhead (.06 hour per pencil × \$9.00 per hour)	.54
Total standard cost of one automatic pencil	\$4.33

Using Variance Analysis to Control Operations

OBJECTIVE 4

Describe how to control costs through variance analysis

Related Text Assignments:
Q: 8, 9, 10, 11
SE: 4
SD: 1, 2
MRA: 2

Although a standard costing system can be useful in both cost planning and cost control, it has traditionally been associated primarily with cost control and the evaluation of operating performance. Managers of manufacturing operations, as well as those responsible for selling and service functions, constantly compare the costs of what was expected to happen with the costs of what did happen. By examining the differences—or variances—between standard and actual costs, managers can learn much valuable information.

Variance analysis is the process of computing the differences between standard (or budgeted) costs and actual costs and identifying the causes of those differences.

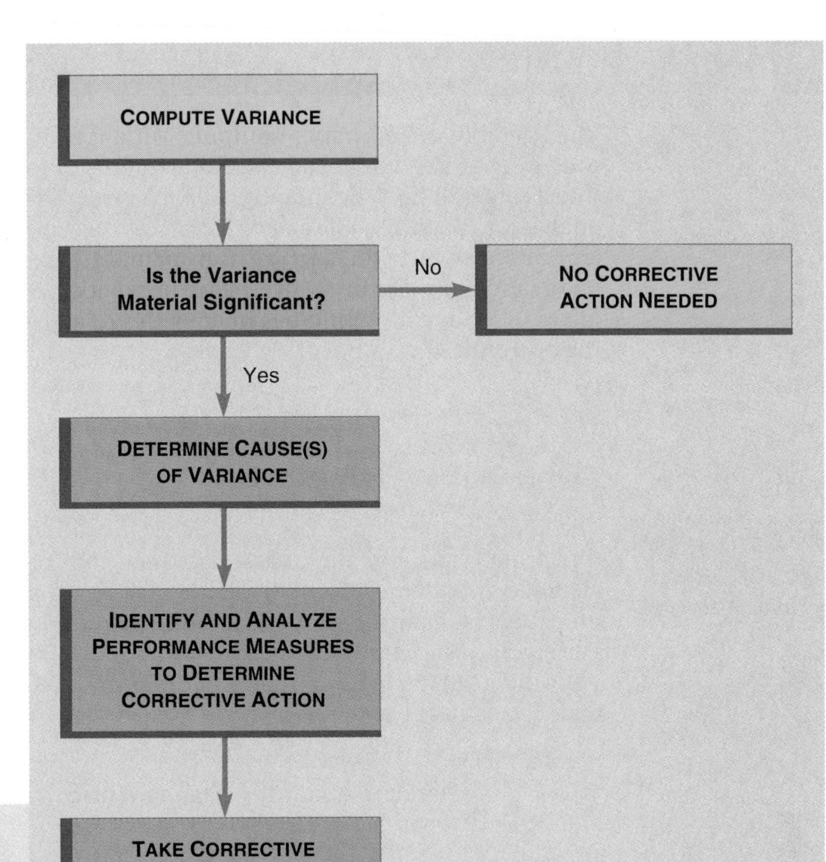

Figure 2
Using Variance Analysis to Control Costs

But just identifying the cause(s) of a variance does not necessarily solve the problem. Therefore we will also discuss some financial and nonfinancial performance measures that can be used to track the cause of a problem and suggest possible ways to correct it.

Point to Emphasize: Many companies use a percentage, such as plus or minus 3 percent of standard, to determine if the dollar amount of variance is material.

Several steps are needed to get to the root of a problem and to correct it. As shown in Figure 2, first you must compute the variance. If the variance is insignificant, actual operating results are close to anticipated operating conditions and no corrective action is needed. If the variance is significant, the management accountant analyzes it to identify its cause. Knowing the cause of a variance usually helps the accountant pinpoint the areas or activities that need to be monitored. The accountant then chooses the best performance measures to track those activities, analyzes the results, and determines the action needed to correct the problem. The final step is to take the required corrective action.

As we focus on the variances related to direct materials, direct labor, and manufacturing overhead, we will follow the process outlined in Figure 2. Computing the amount of the variance is important. But it is also important to remember that identifying the amount of a variance does nothing to prevent it from occurring again in the future. Managers need to know the cause of a variance. We will identify many examples of operating problems that might cause each of the variances to occur. Once the cause is known, specific performance measures can be identified and analyzed to help the manager determine the best solution to the problem so corrective action can be taken.

Computing and Analyzing Variances

Management accountants compute variances for whole cost categories, such as total direct materials costs, and for elements of that category, like the price of each direct material and the quantity of each direct material used. The more detailed an analysis is, the more effective it is in controlling costs. We will limit our analysis to six variances, two for each of the main cost elements of direct materials, direct labor, and manufacturing overhead. In practice, companies can use dozens of variances in many different types of activities to assist them in controlling and improving operating conditions.

Direct Materials Variances

OBJECTIVE 5

Compute and analyze direct materials variances

Related Text Assignments:
Q: 12, 13, 15
SE: 5
E: 4
P: 2, 4, 7, 8
MRA: 3

The total direct materials cost variance is the difference between the standard cost of direct materials and the actual cost incurred for those items. Let us assume, for example, that Ramos Company makes leather chairs. Each chair should use 4 yards of leather (standard quantity), and the standard price of leather is $6.00 per yard. During August, Ramos Company purchased 760 yards of leather costing $5.90 per yard and used the leather to produce 180 chairs. The total direct materials cost variance is calculated as follows:

Standard cost		
Standard quantity × standard price	=	
(180 chairs × 4 yards per chair) × $6.00 per yard	=	
720 yards × $6.00 per yard	=	$4,320
Less actual cost		
Actual quantity × actual price	=	
760 yards × $5.90 per yard	=	4,484
Total direct materials cost variance		$ 164 (U)

Here actual cost exceeds standard cost. The situation is unfavorable, as indicated by the *U* placed in parentheses after the dollar amount. An *F* designates a favorable situation.

To find the area or people responsible for the variance, the total direct materials cost variance must be broken down into two parts: the direct materials price variance and the direct materials quantity variance. The direct materials price variance is the difference between the standard price and the actual price, multiplied by the actual quantity purchased. For Ramos Company, the direct materials price variance is computed as follows:

Point to Emphasize: The direct materials price variance relates to the difference between the standard cost of purchased materials and the actual cost of purchased materials. This variance does not relate to the use of materials in the production process.

Common Student Error: Students often compute variances correctly, but fail to identify whether the variance is favorable or unfavorable. Stress the importance of identifying the type or direction of the variance for proper analysis of problems.

Standard price	$6.00
Less actual price	5.90
Difference	$ .10 (F)

Direct Materials Price Variance = (Standard Price − Actual Price) × Actual Quantity
= $ .10 (F) × 760 yards
= $76 (F)

Because the direct materials purchased cost less than the standard cost, the variance is favorable.

The direct materials quantity variance is the difference between the standard quantity and the actual quantity used, multiplied by the standard price.

BUSINESS BULLETIN: BUSINESS PRACTICE

The globally competitive business environment has caused managers in many companies to revise their costing systems, in particular their standard costing systems. In traditional systems, variance analysis focused on the efficient use of direct materials and direct labor. Defects and product rework were expected, and their anticipated amounts were incorporated into the standards. Excess production that built inventories was not penalized. Today, tracking product quality and avoiding inventory buildups are major concerns. Consequently, revised standard costing systems track product quality and rates of production as well as the efficient use of resources. Quality variances are computed to indicate the production costs wasted on defective units. One approach to calculating a quality variance is as follows:

(Total Units Produced − Good Units Produced) × Standard Cost per Unit

Overproduction is also frowned on in the new global operating environment. To help track overproduction, a production variance can be computed as follows:

(Good Units Produced − Scheduled Units) × Standard Cost per Unit

The two new variances can be incorporated into an existing standard costing system to monitor product defects and prevent overproduction. Direct materials price and quantity variances and direct labor rate and efficiency variances are still necessary to help measure the efficiency of resource usage.[2]

Standard quantity (180 × 4 yards per chair)	720 yards
Less actual quantity	760 yards
Difference	40 yards (U)

Direct Materials Quantity Variance = (Standard Quantity − Actual Quantity) × Standard Price
= 40 yards (U) × $6 per yard
= $240 (U)

Because more direct material was used than prescribed, the direct materials quantity variance is unfavorable.

If the calculations are correct, the sum of the direct materials price variance and the direct materials quantity variance should equal the total direct materials cost variance.

Direct materials price variance	$ 76 (F)
Direct materials quantity variance	240 (U)
Total direct materials cost variance	$164 (U)

Sometimes cost relationships are easier to interpret in diagram form. Figure 3 illustrates the analysis just described. Notice that direct materials are purchased at actual cost but entered into the Direct Materials Inventory account at standard price; therefore, the direct materials price variance of $76 (F) is known when costs are entered into Direct Materials Inventory. As shown in Figure 3, the standard quantity times the standard price is the amount entered into the Work in Process Inventory account.

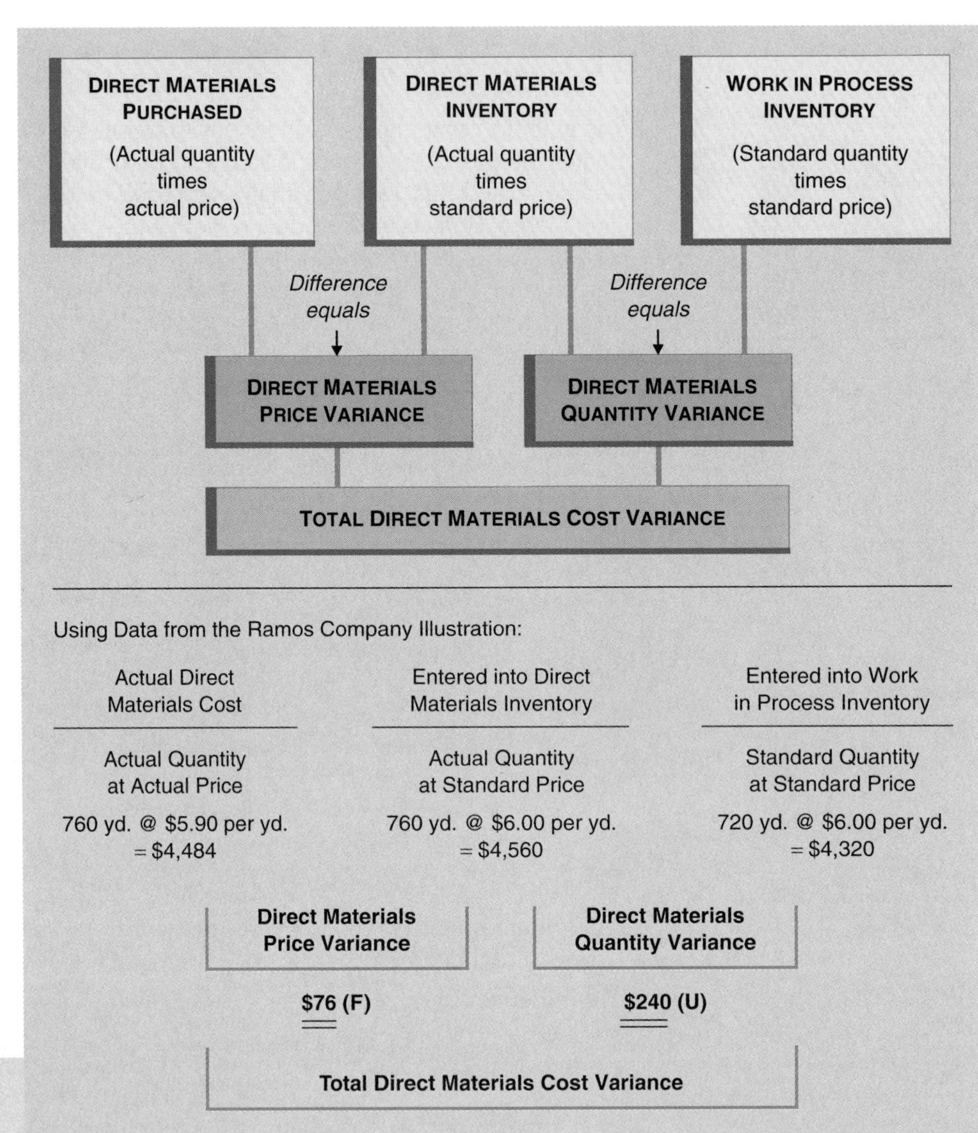

Figure 3
Direct Materials Variance Analysis

Taking Corrective Action—Ramos Company Managers of the Ramos Company were concerned because the direct materials price variances and quantity variances had been occurring in the production of leather chairs for some time and because, as in our analysis, the price variances were always favorable and the quantity variances were always unfavorable. The purchasing manager had contacted vendors about possible price changes, but no changes had occurred. By tracking the purchasing activity for three months, the management accountant discovered that a lower grade of leather had been purchased at a reduced price. No authorization had been given to the purchasing agent for such a substitution. After a careful analysis, the manager of engineering determined that the substitute leather was not appropriate and that the company should return to purchasing the originally specified leather. Further analysis revealed that the unfavorable quantity variance was also caused by using the substitute leather. By tracking the purchasing activity, the managers at Ramos Company were able to solve the variance problem in the direct materials costs of producing leather chairs.

Direct Labor Variances

OBJECTIVE 6

Compute and analyze direct labor variances

Related Text Assignments:
Q: 14
SE: 6
E: 5
P: 2, 4, 7, 8
SD: 4
MRA: 2, 3

Teaching Note: Note the similarities between direct labor cost variances and direct materials cost variances. If your students can do the analyses for one, they can do the analyses for the other. The computation of the direct labor rate variance is very similar to the computation of the direct materials price variance. Computations for the direct labor efficiency variance and the direct materials quantity variance are also similar.

The procedure for finding cost variances in direct labor parallels the procedure for finding variances in direct materials. The total direct labor cost variance is the difference between the standard direct labor cost for the good units produced and the actual direct labor costs incurred. (Good units are the total units produced less the units that are scrapped or need to be reworked.) At the Ramos Company, each chair requires 2.4 standard direct labor hours, and the standard direct labor rate is $8.50 per hour. During August, 450 direct labor hours were used to make 180 chairs at an average pay rate of $9.20 per hour. The total direct labor cost variance is computed below.

Standard cost	
Standard hours allowed × standard rate =	
(180 chairs × 2.4 hours per chair) × $8.50 per hour =	
432 hours × $8.50 per hour =	$3,672
Less actual cost	
Actual hours × actual rate = 450 hours × $9.20 =	4,140
Total direct labor cost variance	$ 468 (U)

Both the actual direct labor hours per chair and the actual direct labor rate varied from the standard. For effective performance evaluation, management must know how much of the total cost arose from differing direct labor rates and how much from varying direct labor hours. This information is found by computing the direct labor rate variance and the direct labor efficiency variance.

The direct labor rate variance is the difference between the standard direct labor rate and the actual direct labor rate, multiplied by the actual direct labor hours worked.

Standard rate	$8.50
Less actual rate	9.20
Difference	$ .70 (U)

Direct Labor Rate Variance = (Standard Rate − Actual Rate) × Actual Hours
= $ .70 (U) × 450 hours
= $315 (U)

The direct labor efficiency variance is the difference between standard direct labor hours allowed for the good units produced and the actual direct labor hours worked, multiplied by the standard direct labor rate.

Standard hours allowed (180 chairs × 2.4 hours per chair)	432 hours
Less actual hours worked	450 hours
Difference	18 hours (U)

Direct Labor Efficiency Variance = (Standard Hours Allowed − Actual Hours Worked) × Standard Rate
= 18 hours (U) × $8.50 per hour
= $153 (U)

The following check shows that the direct labor rate and efficiency variances have been computed correctly:

Direct labor rate variance	$315 (U)
Direct labor efficiency variance	153 (U)
Total direct labor cost variance	$468 (U)

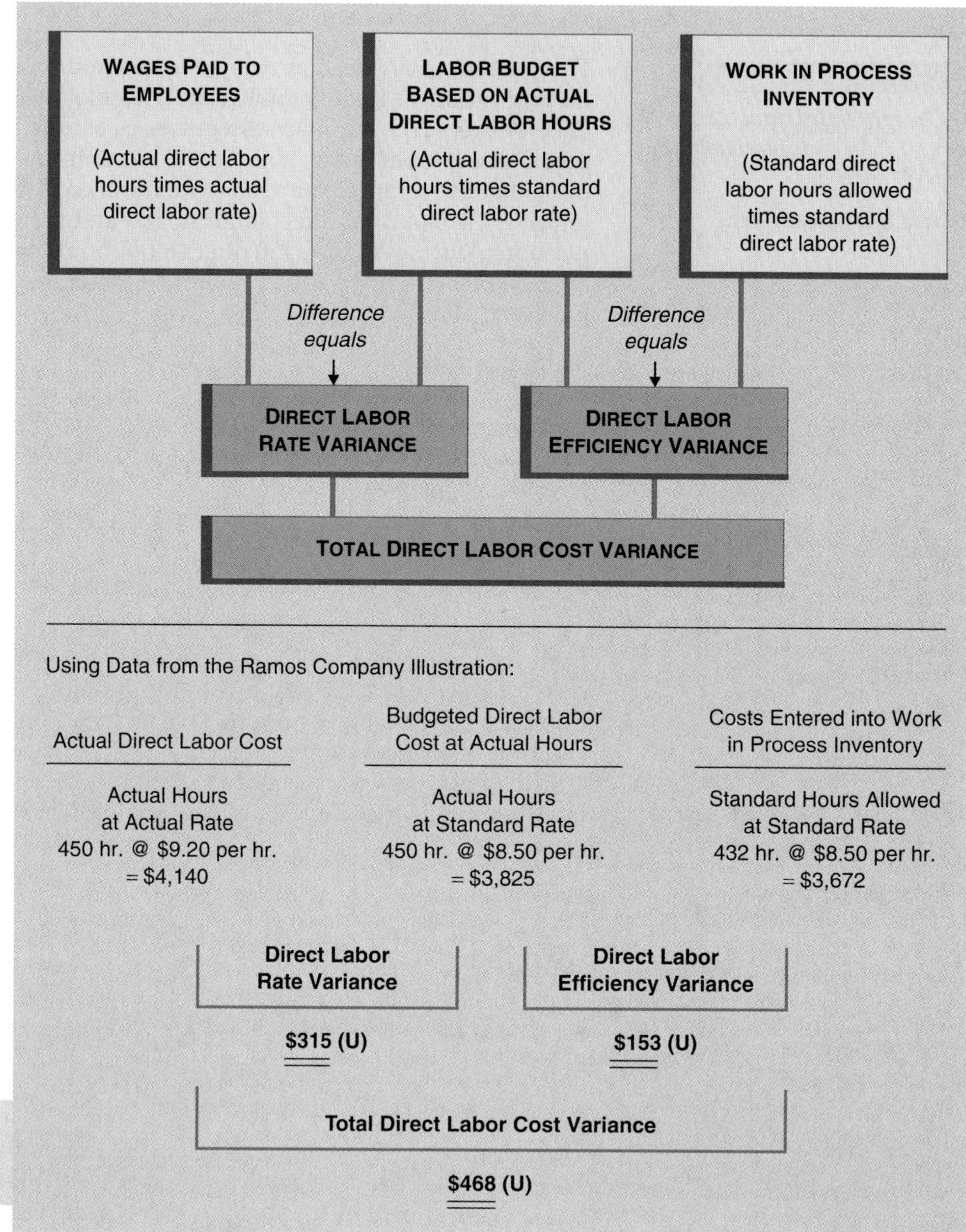

Figure 4
Direct Labor Variance Analysis

Figure 4 summarizes the direct labor variance analysis. Unlike direct materials variances, the direct labor rate and efficiency variances are usually computed and recorded at the same time, because direct labor is not stored in an inventory account before use. Data from Ramos Company in the lower portion of Figure 4 illustrate this approach to direct labor variance analysis.

Taking Corrective Action—Ramos Company Because both the direct labor rate variance and the direct labor efficiency variance were unfavorable, the management of the Ramos Company wanted to find out their causes. By analyzing employee time cards, it was discovered that a machine operator from another department had taken the place of a chair assembly worker who was ill. The machine operator made $9.20 per hour while the assembly worker earned the standard $8.50 per hour rate. When questioned about the unfavorable efficiency variance, the assembly supervisor identified two causes. First, the machine operator had to learn assembly skills on the job, so his assembly time was longer than the standard time per chair. Second, the materials handling people were partially to blame because they delivered parts late on five different occasions. Management decided to keep a close eye on the materials handling function by tracking delivery times and number of delays for the next three months. Once the new data are collected and analyzed, corrective action can be taken.

Manufacturing Overhead Variances

Controlling manufacturing overhead costs is more difficult than controlling direct materials and direct labor costs because the responsibility for manufacturing overhead costs is hard to assign. In addition, many types of both variable and fixed manufacturing overhead costs may contribute to variances from standard costs. Most fixed manufacturing overhead costs are not controlled by specific department managers, but if variable manufacturing overhead costs can be related to departments or activities, some control is possible.

OBJECTIVE 7

Define and prepare a flexible budget

Related Text Assignments:
Q: 16, 17
SE: 7
E: 6
P: 3
MRA: 1, 4

Using a Flexible Budget The type of budget a company uses strongly affects the accuracy of its manufacturing overhead variance analysis. The budgets discussed earlier were *static,* or fixed, budgets. They forecast revenues and expenses for one level of sales and production. The entire master budget is usually prepared for a single level of output, but many things can happen over a year's time that will cause actual output to differ from the estimated output. If a company produces more products than predicted, total production costs should also rise. In such a situation, comparing actual production costs with static budgeted amounts will automatically show large variances.

Exhibit 1 presents data for Bradford Industries, Inc. As you can see, actual costs exceed budgeted costs by $14,300, or 7.2 percent. Most managers would consider

Exhibit 1. Performance Analysis: Comparison of Actual and Budgeted Data

Bradford Industries, Inc.
Performance Report—Berwyn Division
For the Year Ended December 31, 20xx

Cost Category	Budget*	Actual†	Difference Under (Over) Budget
Direct materials	$ 42,000	$ 46,000	($ 4,000)
Direct labor	68,250	75,000	(6,750)
Manufacturing overhead			
Variable			
Indirect materials	10,500	11,500	(1,000)
Indirect labor	14,000	15,250	(1,250)
Utilities	7,000	7,600	(600)
Other	8,750	9,750	(1,000)
Fixed			
Supervisory salaries	19,000	18,500	500
Depreciation	15,000	15,000	—
Utilities	4,500	4,500	—
Other	10,900	11,100	(200)
Totals	$199,900	$214,200	($14,300)

*Budget based on expected productive output of 17,500 units.
†Actual cost of producing 19,100 units.

Exhibit 2. Flexible Budget: Total Performance

Bradford Industries, Inc.
Flexible Budget—Berwyn Division
For the Year Ended December 31, 20xx

Cost Category	Units Produced 15,000	17,500	20,000	Variable Cost per Unit*
Direct materials	$ 36,000	$ 42,000	$ 48,000	$2.40
Direct labor	58,500	68,250	78,000	3.90
Variable manufacturing overhead				
Indirect materials	9,000	10,500	12,000	.60
Indirect labor	12,000	14,000	16,000	.80
Utilities	6,000	7,000	8,000	.40
Other	7,500	8,750	10,000	.50
Total variable costs	$129,000	$150,500	$172,000	$8.60
Fixed manufacturing overhead				
Supervisory salaries	$ 19,000	$ 19,000	$ 19,000	
Depreciation	15,000	15,000	15,000	
Utilities	4,500	4,500	4,500	
Other	10,900	10,900	10,900	
Total fixed manufacturing overhead costs	$ 49,400	$ 49,400	$ 49,400	
Total costs	$178,400	$199,900	$221,400	

Flexible budget formula:
Total budgeted costs = (variable cost per unit × number of units produced) + budgeted fixed costs = ($8.60 × units produced) + $49,400

Note: Activity expressed in units was used as the basis for this analysis. When units are used, direct material and direct labor costs are included in the analysis. Flexible budgets are commonly restricted to overhead costs. In such cases, machine hours or direct labor hours are used in place of units produced.
*Computed by dividing the dollar amount in any column by the respective level of activity.

Point to Emphasize: Flexible budgets allow for the comparison and analysis of costs at a budgeted volume with actual costs at the same volume.

such an overrun to be significant. But was there really a cost overrun? The budgeted amounts are based on an expected output of 17,500 units, but actual output was 19,100 units. Thus, the static budget for 17,500 units is inadequate for judging performance. Before analyzing the performance of the Berwyn Division, we must change the budgeted data to reflect an output of 19,100 units.

This can be accomplished by using a flexible budget. A flexible budget is a summary of expected costs for a *range* of activity levels, geared to changes in the level of productive output. Unlike a static budget, a flexible budget provides forecasted data that can be adjusted automatically for changes in the level of output. The flexible budget (also called a *variable budget*) is primarily a cost control tool used in evaluating performance.

Exhibit 2 presents a flexible budget for Bradford Industries, Inc., with budgeted data for 15,000, 17,500, and 20,000 units of output. The total cost of a variable cost item is found by multiplying the number of units produced by the variable cost for one unit of that item. For example, in the Berwyn Division, direct materials will cost $36,000 if 15,000 units are produced (15,000 units × $2.40). The important part of

Exhibit 3. Performance Report Using Flexible Budget Data

Bradford Industries, Inc. Performance Report—Berwyn Division For the Year Ended December 31, 20xx			
Cost Category (Variable Unit Cost)	Budget Based on 19,100 Units Produced	Actual Costs of 19,100 Units	Difference Under (Over) Budget
Direct materials ($2.40)	$ 45,840	$ 46,000	($160)
Direct labor ($3.90)	74,490	75,000	(510)
Manufacturing overhead			
Variable			
Indirect materials ($.60)	11,460	11,500	(40)
Indirect labor ($.80)	15,280	15,250	30
Utilities ($.40)	7,640	7,600	40
Other ($.50)	9,550	9,750	(200)
Fixed			
Supervisory salaries	19,000	18,500	500
Depreciation	15,000	15,000	—
Utilities	4,500	4,500	—
Other	10,900	11,100	(200)
Totals	$213,660	$214,200	($540)

this illustration is the flexible budget formula shown at the bottom. The flexible budget formula is an equation that determines the correct budgeted cost for any level of productive activity. It consists of a per unit amount for variable costs and a total amount for fixed costs. In Exhibit 2, the $8.60 variable cost per unit is computed in the far right column, and the $49,400 is found in the fixed cost section of the analysis. Using this formula, you can draw up a budget for the Berwyn Division at any level of output.

Exhibit 3 shows a performance report prepared using the flexible budget data in Exhibit 2. Variable unit costs have been multiplied by 19,100 units to arrive at the total budgeted figures. Fixed overhead information has been carried over from the flexible budget developed in Exhibit 2. As the new performance report shows, costs exceeded budgeted amounts during the year by only $540, or less than three-tenths of one percent. In other words, when we use a flexible budget, we find that the performance of the Berwyn Division is almost on target.

At the Bradford Company, a flexible budget is used to analyze overall performance. At the Ramos Company, a flexible budget is used only to analyze manufacturing overhead costs. Exhibit 4 shows the Ramos Company's flexible budget for manufacturing overhead costs for the Chair Assembly Department. Whereas the Bradford Industries' flexible budget was based on units of output, the Ramos Company's budget uses direct labor hours as the expression of activity. Thus, in the Ramos budget, variable costs vary with the number of direct labor hours worked. Total fixed manufacturing overhead costs remain constant. The flexible budget formula in such cases is (variable costs per direct labor hour × number of direct labor hours) + budgeted fixed manufacturing overhead costs. As shown at the bottom of Exhibit 4, the specific flexible budget formula for the Ramos Company is ($5.75 × number of DLH) + $1,300.

Exhibit 4. Flexible Budget: Manufacturing Overhead Costs

Ramos Company
Flexible Budget—Manufacturing Overhead
Chair Assembly Department
For an Average One-Month Period

Cost Category	Direct Labor Hours (DLH) 300	400	500	Variable Cost per DLH
Budgeted variable manufacturing overhead				
Indirect materials	$ 450	$ 600	$ 750	$1.50
Indirect labor	600	800	1,000	2.00
Supplies	225	300	375	.75
Utilities	300	400	500	1.00
Other	150	200	250	.50
Total budgeted variable manufacturing overhead costs	$1,725	$2,300	$2,875	$5.75
Budgeted fixed manufacturing overhead				
Supervisory salaries	$ 600	$ 600	$ 600	
Depreciation	400	400	400	
Other	300	300	300	
Total budgeted fixed manufacturing overhead costs	$1,300	$1,300	$1,300	
Total budgeted manufacturing overhead costs	$3,025	$3,600	$4,175	

Flexible budget formula:
Total budgeted manufacturing overhead costs = (variable costs per direct labor hour × number of DLH) + budgeted fixed manufacturing overhead costs = ($5.75 × number of DLH) + $1,300

The flexible budget in Exhibit 4 shows overhead costs for 300, 400, and 500 direct labor hours. However, this month Ramos Company did not operate at exactly one of those activity levels. Instead, it operated at 432 direct labor hours. To find the total budgeted manufacturing overhead costs for the month, simply insert 432 direct labor hours in the flexible budget formula: ($5.75 × 432 DLH) + $1,300 = $3,784.

OBJECTIVE 8

Compute and analyze manufacturing overhead variances

Related Text Assignments:
Q: 18, 19
SE: 8
E: 7, 8, 9
P: 4, 5, 8
SD: 4
MRA: 2, 4

Analyzing Manufacturing Overhead Variances Analyses of manufacturing overhead variances differ in degree of detail. The basic approach is to compute the total manufacturing overhead variance, which is the difference between the actual manufacturing overhead costs incurred and the standard manufacturing overhead costs applied to production using the standard variable and fixed manufacturing overhead rates. The total manufacturing overhead variance is then divided into two parts: the controllable manufacturing overhead variance and the manufacturing overhead volume variance.

In our example, Ramos Company budgeted standard variable manufacturing overhead costs of $5.75 per direct labor hour plus $1,300 of fixed manufacturing overhead costs for the month of August (see the flexible budget formula). Normal capacity was set at 400 direct labor hours per month. The company incurred $4,100 of actual manufacturing overhead costs in August.

Before finding the manufacturing overhead variances, the total standard manufacturing overhead rate must be calculated. The total standard manufacturing over-

Teaching Strategy: Students usually have little trouble understanding direct materials and direct labor variances, but have more difficulty with manufacturing overhead variances. Be prepared to spend extra time on manufacturing overhead variance analysis.

head rate has two parts. One is the variable rate of $5.75 per direct labor hour. The other is the standard fixed manufacturing overhead rate, which is found by dividing budgeted fixed manufacturing overhead ($1,300) by normal capacity. The result is $3.25 per direct labor hour ($1,300 ÷ 400 hours). So, the total standard manufacturing overhead rate is $9.00 per direct labor hour ($5.75 + $3.25). The total budgeted fixed manufacturing overhead costs divided by normal capacity provides a rate that assigns fixed manufacturing overhead costs to products in a way that is consistent with expected output. The total manufacturing overhead variance is computed as follows:

Standard manufacturing overhead costs applied to good units produced	
$9.00 per direct labor hour × (180 chairs × 2.4 hr. per chair)	$3,888
Less actual manufacturing overhead costs incurred	4,100
Total manufacturing overhead variance	$ 212 (U)

Point to Emphasize: The controllable manufacturing overhead variance focuses on the amount of good units produced and examines the difference between actual manufacturing overhead costs incurred and standard costs allowed at the actual level of production attained.

This amount can be divided into two parts: the controllable manufacturing overhead variance and the manufacturing overhead volume variance. The controllable manufacturing overhead variance is the difference between the actual manufacturing overhead costs incurred and the manufacturing overhead costs budgeted for the level of production reached. Thus, the controllable manufacturing overhead variance for Ramos Company for August is as follows:

Budgeted manufacturing overhead (flexible budget) for 180 chairs:		
Variable manufacturing overhead cost for 432 direct labor hours (180 chairs × 2.4 hr. per chair) × $5.75 per direct labor hour	$2,484	
Budgeted fixed manufacturing overhead cost	1,300	
Total budgeted manufacturing overhead		$3,784
Less actual manufacturing overhead costs incurred		4,100
Controllable manufacturing overhead variance		$ 316 (U)

Point to Emphasize: The manufacturing overhead volume variance concentrates on fixed manufacturing overhead costs. This variance measures the effective use of productive capacity and related production facilities.

In this example, the controllable manufacturing overhead variance is unfavorable; the company spent more than had been budgeted.

The manufacturing overhead volume variance is the difference between the manufacturing overhead costs budgeted for the level of production achieved and the manufacturing overhead costs applied to production using the standard variable and fixed manufacturing overhead rates. Continuing with the Ramos Company example, we have the following:

Standard manufacturing overhead costs applied for 432 direct labor hours (180 chairs × 2.4 hr. per chair) × $9.00 per direct labor hour	$3,888
Less budgeted manufacturing overhead (see above)	3,784
Manufacturing overhead volume variance	$ 104 (F)

Checking the computations, we find that the two variances do equal the total manufacturing overhead variance.

Point to Emphasize: The total manufacturing overhead variance should be the sum of the controllable manufacturing overhead variance and the manufacturing overhead volume variance. Students can check their math with this final calculation.

Controllable manufacturing overhead variance	$316 (U)
Manufacturing overhead volume variance	104 (F)
Total manufacturing overhead variance	$212 (U)

Because the manufacturing overhead volume variance gauges the use of existing facilities and capacity, a volume variance will occur if more or less capacity than normal is used. In this example, 400 direct labor hours is considered normal use of facilities. Fixed manufacturing overhead costs are applied on the basis of standard hours allowed. So in the example, manufacturing overhead was applied on the basis of 432 hours, even though the fixed manufacturing overhead rate was computed using 400 hours (normal capacity). Thus, more fixed costs would be applied to products than were budgeted. Because the products can absorb no more than actual costs incurred, this level of production would tend to lower unit cost. Thus, when capacity exceeds the expected amount, the result is a favorable manufacturing overhead volume variance. When capacity does not meet the normal level, not all of the fixed manufacturing overhead costs will be applied to units produced. It is then necessary to add the amount of underapplied fixed manufacturing overhead to the cost of the good units produced, thereby increasing their unit cost. This condition is unfavorable.

Figure 5 summarizes the analysis of manufacturing overhead variance. As explained earlier, to determine the controllable manufacturing overhead variance, the management accountant subtracts the budgeted manufacturing overhead amount (using a flexible budget for the level of output achieved) from the actual manufacturing overhead costs incurred. A positive result means an unfavorable variance because actual costs were greater than budgeted costs. The controllable manufacturing overhead variance is favorable if the difference is negative. Subtracting total manufacturing overhead applied from budgeted manufacturing overhead at the level of output achieved yields the manufacturing overhead volume variance. Again, a positive result means an unfavorable variance; a negative result, a favorable variance. The data from the Ramos Company example are shown in the lower part of Figure 5. Carefully check the solution in the figure with that computed on the previous page.

Taking Corrective Action—Ramos Company The manager of Ramos Company's Chair Assembly Department found that the unfavorable controllable variance of \$316 was caused by higher than anticipated usage of indirect materials and the inefficient assembly skills of the borrowed machine operator. To obtain more specific information, the manager asked the management accountant to study the use of indirect materials over a period of three months.

The borrowed machine operator took 450 hours to do 432 standard hours of work, but the 432 standard hours were well above normal capacity of 400 direct labor hours. The overutilization of capacity resulted in a favorable volume variance of \$104. The cause was traced to high seasonal demand for the product that pressed the company to use almost all of its capacity. Management decided not to do anything about the volume variance because it fell within a range that had been anticipated.

Manufacturing Overhead Variance Analysis in an Activity-Based Costing System

When organizations such as Ingersoll Milling Machine Co. and Saturn Automobile Co. adopt an activity-based costing system, costs are traced to activities within departments rather than accumulated for whole departments, as in a traditional costing system. Thus, if Department A has three activities, costs are accumulated separately for each of the three activities rather than for the department as a whole. The approach to variance analysis then changes to focus on the activities, not the department. Direct materials costs and direct labor costs are traced directly to an activity, just as if each activity were a department. From that point on, variance analyses of direct materials and direct labor costs for an activity are the same as they were in our previous discussion based on departments.

Activity-based costing changes the analysis of overhead variance in one very significant way: Each activity has a different cost driver, so the basis of the variance analysis changes from one activity to another. We no longer analyze overhead using a single measure, such as direct labor hours or machine hours, as an expression of capacity.

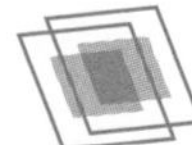

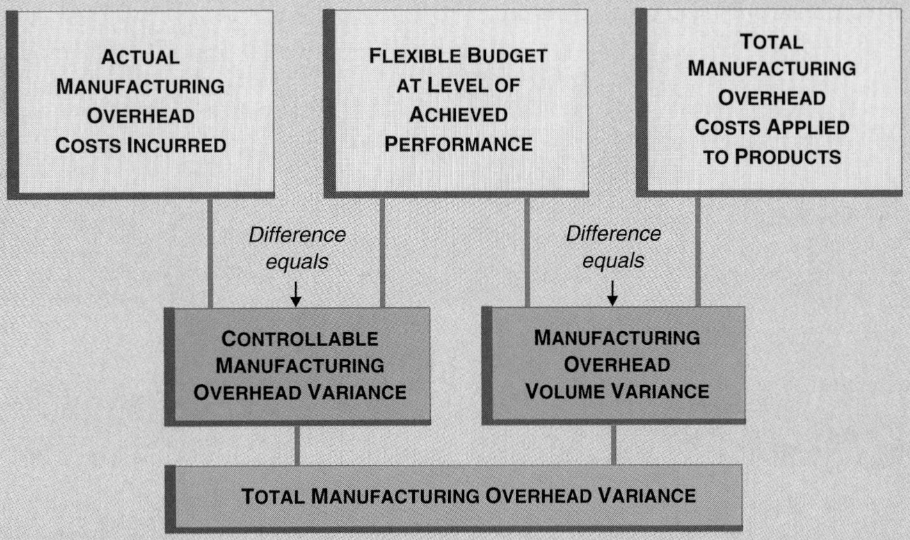

ACTUAL MANUFACTURING OVERHEAD COSTS INCURRED

FLEXIBLE BUDGET AT LEVEL OF ACHIEVED PERFORMANCE

TOTAL MANUFACTURING OVERHEAD COSTS APPLIED TO PRODUCTS

Difference equals ↓ CONTROLLABLE MANUFACTURING OVERHEAD VARIANCE

Difference equals ↓ MANUFACTURING OVERHEAD VOLUME VARIANCE

TOTAL MANUFACTURING OVERHEAD VARIANCE

Using Data from the Ramos Company Illustration:

Actual Manufacturing Overhead Costs Incurred	Flexible Budget at Level of Achieved Performance		Total Manufacturing Overhead Costs Applied to Products
(Given in example)	Variable rate times standard hours allowed*	$5.75 × 432 hours = $2,484	Variable: $5.75 × 432 hours = $2,484
	Plus budgeted fixed costs	1,300	Fixed: $3.25 × 432 hours = 1,404
$4,100		**$3,784**	**$3,888**

Controllable Manufacturing Overhead Variance $316 (U)

Manufacturing Overhead Volume Variance $104 (F)

Total Manufacturing Overhead Variance = $212 (U)

Figure 5
Manufacturing Overhead Variance Analysis

* Standard hours allowed (achieved performance level) is computed by multiplying good units produced times required standard direct labor time per unit. The computation is as follows:

180 chairs produced x 2.4 hours per chair = 432 standard hours allowed

Figure 6 illustrates how overhead variance analysis changes when an organization uses an activity-based system. We still want to compute a controllable overhead variance and an overhead volume variance, but we now must compute those variances for each activity. Assume, as shown in Figure 6, that an organization has three activities: Setup Activity, Work Cell Activity, and Repairs and Maintenance Activity. The overhead variance analysis for the Setup Activity shown in Figure 6 is structured in the same way as the analysis shown in Figure 5, and it is very similar to that used to analyze the overhead variances of a department. The primary difference is the cost driver used in the analysis. Here the cost driver is the number of setup hours.

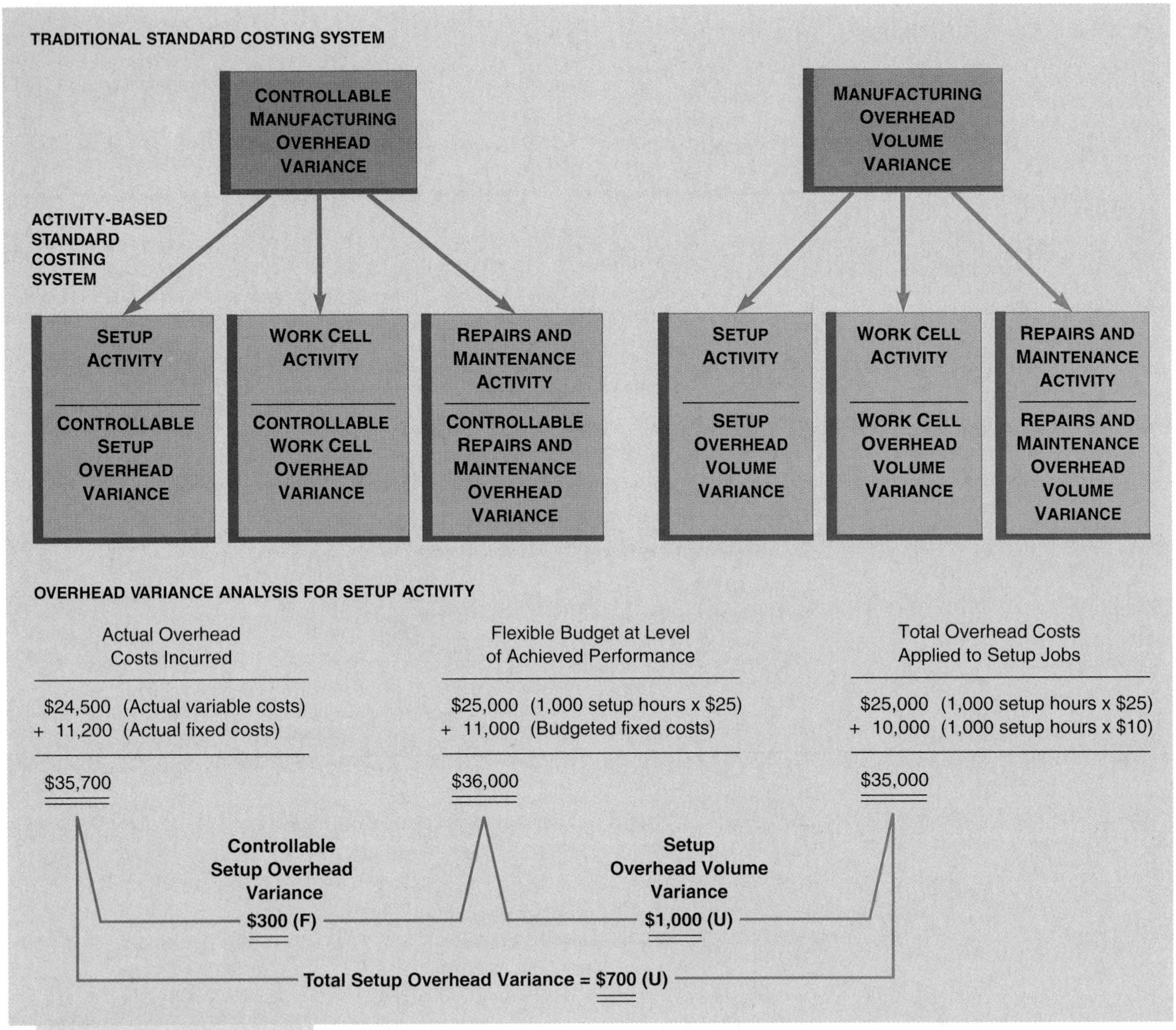

TRADITIONAL STANDARD COSTING SYSTEM

CONTROLLABLE MANUFACTURING OVERHEAD VARIANCE

MANUFACTURING OVERHEAD VOLUME VARIANCE

ACTIVITY-BASED STANDARD COSTING SYSTEM

Setup Activity	Work Cell Activity	Repairs and Maintenance Activity	Setup Activity	Work Cell Activity	Repairs and Maintenance Activity
Controllable Setup Overhead Variance	Controllable Work Cell Overhead Variance	Controllable Repairs and Maintenance Overhead Variance	Setup Overhead Volume Variance	Work Cell Overhead Volume Variance	Repairs and Maintenance Overhead Volume Variance

OVERHEAD VARIANCE ANALYSIS FOR SETUP ACTIVITY

Actual Overhead Costs Incurred	Flexible Budget at Level of Achieved Performance	Total Overhead Costs Applied to Setup Jobs
$24,500 (Actual variable costs)	$25,000 (1,000 setup hours x $25)	$25,000 (1,000 setup hours x $25)
+ 11,200 (Actual fixed costs)	+ 11,000 (Budgeted fixed costs)	+ 10,000 (1,000 setup hours x $10)
$35,700	$36,000	$35,000

Controllable Setup Overhead Variance $300 (F)

Setup Overhead Volume Variance $1,000 (U)

Total Setup Overhead Variance = $700 (U)

Figure 6
Manufacturing Overhead Variance Analysis: Traditional Versus Activity-Based Standard Costing Systems

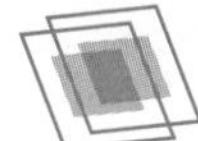

To analyze the controllable overhead variance and the overhead volume variance of the Setup Activity, you need to know the following information:

Actual variable overhead costs of the Setup Activity	$24,500
Actual fixed overhead costs of the Setup Activity	$11,200
Setup hours worked	1,000 hours
Total capacity of the Setup Activity in hours	1,100 hours
Budgeted fixed overhead costs	$11,000
Variable overhead rate for the Setup Activity	$25 per setup hour
Fixed overhead rate for the Setup Activity	$10 per setup hour

Instructional Strategy: Have students solve E 8 and E 9. Then ask them to compare their answers to see what changes had to be made when overhead variances were analyzed in an ABC system.

Using the same approach to overhead variance analysis discussed earlier, we determine that the controllable overhead variance for the Setup Activity is $300 (F), which is computed by subtracting $35,700 of actual overhead costs from the budgeted total of $36,000. It is favorable because the activity spent less than anticipated.

BUSINESS BULLETIN: TECHNOLOGY IN PRACTICE

"You can't manage what you can't measure." To control the operations of an organization, managers must continuously monitor operating conditions. Traditional accounting techniques provided some help to managers, but the preparation of operating reports often took several days, or even several weeks. By the time a manager got the necessary information, in many cases, the problems had recurred or even gotten worse.

Modern technology has led to the creation of Continuous Control Monitoring (CCM). CCM is a management accounting practice that provides managers with continuous, current measurements of operations. Computer analyses provide almost instantaneous variances from standards so that managers can quickly take corrective action.[3]

The overhead volume variance of $1,000 (U) occurred because the activity did not operate at full capacity. They failed to use 100 hours of setup labor, which resulted in $1,000 of underapplied fixed overhead (100 hours × $10 fixed overhead rate). A similar approach would be used to analyze overhead variances for the Work Cell Activity and the Repairs and Maintenance Activity. As mentioned earlier, a different cost driver would be used for each of those activities.

Using Variances in Performance Evaluation

OBJECTIVE 9

Explain how variances are used to evaluate managers' performance

Related Text Assignments:
Q: 20
SE: 9
E: 10
P: 4
MRA: 1, 2

Point to Emphasize: The computation of variances is only one step in the cost control process. True success depends on the effective communication of those variances to the appropriate managers and the identification and follow-up of the problem areas causing the variances.

Point to Emphasize: The accountant is responsible for computing the variances, but the manager is responsible for identifying the cause(s) and taking corrective action.

The effective evaluation of managers' performance depends on both human factors and company policies. Using variances from standard costs in a manager's performance report adds accuracy to the evaluation process.

The human factor is the key to meeting corporate goals. People do the planning, people perform the operating processes, and people evaluate and are evaluated. To ensure effectiveness and fairness when setting up a performance evaluation process, management should develop appropriate policies and get direct input from managers and employees. More specifically, a company's management should establish policies and procedures for (1) preparing operational plans, (2) assigning responsibility for performance, (3) communicating operational plans to key personnel, (4) evaluating each area of responsibility, (5) identifying the causes of significant variances, and (6) taking corrective action to eliminate problems.

Variance analysis tends to pinpoint efficient and inefficient operating areas better than do basic comparisons of actual and budgeted data. Breaking down cost differences into more detailed variances helps to identify the causes for the differences. The key to preparing a performance report based on standard costs and related variances is to follow company policy by (1) identifying the personnel responsible for each significant variance, (2) determining the causes for each variance, and (3) developing a reporting format suited to the task. Performance reports should be tailored to each manager's responsibilities. They should be clear and accurate and should explain in detail why the department or activity met or did not meet operating expectations. Managers should be held accountable for only those cost areas under their control.

Exhibit 5 shows a performance report for the manager of Ramos Company's Chair Assembly Department. The report summarizes all of the cost data and variances for direct materials, direct labor, and manufacturing overhead. In addition, it identifies the causes of all of the variances and the corrective actions taken. This

Exhibit 5. Managerial Performance Report Using Variance Analysis

Ramos Company
Managerial Performance Report
Chair Assembly Department
For the Month Ended August 31, 20xx

Productivity Summary

Normal capacity (direct labor hours, or DLH)	400 DLH
Capacity performance level achieved (standard hours allowed)	432 DLH
Good units produced	180 chairs

Cost and Variance Analysis

	Standard Cost	Actual Cost Incurred	Total Variance	Variance Breakdown: Amount	Variance Breakdown: Type
Direct materials	$ 4,320	$ 4,484	$164 (U)	$ 76 (F)	Direct materials price variance
				240 (U)	Direct materials quantity variance
Direct labor	3,672	4,140	468 (U)	315 (U)	Direct labor rate variance
				153 (U)	Direct labor efficiency variance
Manufacturing overhead	3,888	4,100	212 (U)	316 (U)	Controllable manufacturing overhead variance
				104 (F)	Manufacturing overhead volume variance
Totals	$11,880	$12,724	$844 (U)	$844 (U)	

Causes of Variances	Actions Taken
Direct materials price variance:	
Substitute direct material purchased at reduced price	Substitute direct material not appropriate—returned to original direct material
Direct materials quantity variance:	
Poor quality of substitute direct material	Substitute direct material not appropriate—returned to original direct material
Direct labor rate variance:	
Machine operator replaced assembly worker	Temporary replacement—assembly worker ill
Direct labor efficiency variance:	
Machine operator replaced assembly worker	Temporary replacement—assembly worker ill
Late delivery of parts to assembly floor	Material delivery times and number of delays being tracked
Controllable manufacturing overhead variance:	
Indirect materials usage too high—caused by replacement worker's lack of skill	Study of indirect materials usage being conducted
Manufacturing overhead volume variance:	
High number of product orders caused by seasonal demand	No action necessary

report enables the plant superintendent to review the manager's actions and evaluate his or her performance. A point to remember is that the mere occurrence of a variance does not indicate poor performance. However, if a variance consistently occurs, if no cause is identified, and if no corrective action is taken, the manager may be suspected of poor performance. The report in Exhibit 5 suggests that the manager of the Chair Assembly Department has the operation under control because the causes of the variances have been identified and corrective actions have been taken.

Chapter Review

REVIEW OF LEARNING OBJECTIVES

1. **Define *standard costs* and describe how managers use standard costs in the management cycle.** Standard costs are realistically predetermined costs that are developed from analyses of both past costs, quantities, and times and future costs and operating conditions. In a standard costing system, standard costs for direct materials, direct labor, and manufacturing overhead flow through the inventory accounts and eventually into the Cost of Goods Sold account. Instead of using actual costs for product costing purposes, standard costs are used.

   Once standard costs have been developed, managers use them as tools for planning and budgeting. Once the projected sales and production unit targets for the upcoming year are established, planned costs for direct materials, direct labor, and variable manufacturing overhead can be computed using standard costs. The resulting costs serve as targets or goals for product costing. They can also be used in product distribution and pricing. At the end of an accounting period, actual costs incurred are compared with standard costs and the differences are computed. These differences, called variances, provide measures of performance that can be used to control costs.
2. **State the purposes for using standard costs.** Standard costs are predetermined costs for direct materials, direct labor, and manufacturing overhead that are usually expressed as a cost per unit of finished product. Standard costs are useful for preparing operating budgets and evaluating performance. They help in identifying production costs that require control, in establishing realistic prices, and in simplifying procedures for valuing inventories and product costing.
3. **Identify the six elements of, and compute, a standard unit cost.** The six elements of a standard unit cost are (1) the direct materials price standard, (2) the direct materials quantity standard, (3) the direct labor time standard, (4) the direct labor rate standard, (5) the standard variable manufacturing overhead rate, and (6) the standard fixed manufacturing overhead rate. The direct materials price standard is found by carefully considering expected price increases, changes in available quantities, and possible new sources of supply. The direct materials quantity standard expresses the expected quantity to be used. It is affected by product engineering specifications, the quality of direct materials, the age and productivity of the machines, and the quality and experience of the work force. The direct labor time standard is based on current time and motion studies of workers and machines and by past employee and machine performance. Labor union contracts and company personnel policies influence direct labor rate standards. Standard variable and fixed manufacturing overhead rates are found by dividing total budgeted variable and fixed manufacturing overhead costs by an appropriate application base.

   A product's total standard unit cost is computed by adding the following costs: (1) direct materials cost (equals direct materials price standard times direct materials quantity standard), (2) direct labor cost (equals direct labor time standard times direct labor rate standard), and (3) manufacturing overhead cost (equals standard variable and standard fixed manufacturing overhead rate times standard direct labor hours allowed per unit).

4. **Describe how to control costs through variance analysis.** A standard costing system has traditionally been associated with cost control activities and the evaluation of operating performance. Managers of manufacturing operations, as well as those responsible for selling and service functions, constantly compare the costs of what was expected to happen with the costs of what did happen. By examining the differences—or variances—between standard and actual costs, managers can learn much valuable information. Variance analysis is a four-step approach. The first step is to compute the variance. If the variance is insignificant, actual operating results are close to or equal to anticipated operating conditions and no corrective action is needed. If the variance is significant, the management accountant analyzes it to identify its cause (step 2). Knowing the cause of a problem or variance usually helps the accountant pinpoint the areas or activities that need to be monitored. Step 3 involves identifying the performance measures that track those activities. The final step is to take the approaches needed to correct the problem.
5. **Compute and analyze direct materials variances.** An analysis of the direct materials price and quantity variances helps to explain causes of differences between standard and actual direct materials costs. The direct materials price variance is computed by finding the difference between the standard price and the actual price per unit and multiplying it by the actual quantity purchased. The direct materials quantity variance is the difference between the standard quantity that should have been used and the actual quantity used, multiplied by the standard price.
6. **Compute and analyze direct labor variances.** Causes for the difference between standard direct labor costs and actual direct labor costs are identified by analyzing the direct labor rate and direct labor efficiency variances. The direct labor rate variance is computed by determining the difference between the standard labor rate and the actual labor rate and multiplying it by the actual labor hours worked. The direct labor efficiency variance is equal to the difference between the standard hours allowed for the number of good units produced and the actual hours worked, multiplied by the standard direct labor rate for the operation being analyzed.
7. **Define and prepare a flexible budget.** A flexible budget is a summary of anticipated costs for a range of activity levels, geared to changes in productive output. Variable, fixed, and total costs are given for several levels of capacity or output. From those data the management accountant derives the flexible budget formula. This formula, which can be applied to any level of productive output, allows management to evaluate the performance of individuals, departments, or processes.
8. **Compute and analyze manufacturing overhead variances.** The total manufacturing overhead variance is equal to the amount of under- or overapplied manufacturing overhead costs for the period. An analysis of the controllable manufacturing overhead variance and the manufacturing overhead volume variance will help to explain why the amount of manufacturing overhead applied to units produced differed from the manufacturing overhead costs incurred. The controllable manufacturing overhead variance is the difference between the actual manufacturing overhead costs incurred and the manufacturing overhead costs budgeted for the level of production achieved (based on the flexible budget). The manufacturing overhead volume variance is the difference between the manufacturing overhead budgeted for the level of production achieved and the total manufacturing overhead costs applied to production using the standard variable and fixed manufacturing overhead rates. When an organization adopts an activity-based costing system, costs are traced to activities within departments rather than accumulated for whole departments. If a department has three activities, costs are accumulated separately for each of the three activities rather than for the department as a whole. Direct materials costs and direct labor costs are traced to an activity, just as if the activity were a department. From that point on, variance analyses for those two costs follow the same approach as variance analyses for a department. Activity-based costing changes the analysis of overhead costs in one very significant way: Each activity has a different cost driver, so the basis of the variance analysis changes from one activity to another.
9. **Explain how variances are used to evaluate managers' performance.** The effective evaluation of managers' performance depends on both human factors and company policies. Using variances from standard costs in a manager's performance report adds accuracy to the evaluation process. To ensure effectiveness and fairness when

setting up a performance evaluation process, management should develop appropriate policies and get direct input from managers and employees. More specifically, a company's management should establish policies and procedures for (1) preparing operational plans, (2) assigning responsibility for performance, (3) communicating operational plans to key personnel, (4) evaluating each area of responsibility, (5) identifying the causes of significant variances, and (6) taking corrective action to eliminate problems.

The key to preparing a performance report based on standard costs and related variances is to follow company policy by (1) identifying the personnel responsible for each variance, (2) determining the causes for each variance, and (3) developing a reporting format suited to the task. Performance reports should be tailored to each manager's responsibilities.

REVIEW OF CONCEPTS AND TERMINOLOGY

The following concepts and terms were introduced in this chapter.

LO 8 **Controllable manufacturing overhead variance:** The difference between actual manufacturing overhead costs incurred and the manufacturing overhead costs budgeted for the level of production reached.

LO 6 **Direct labor efficiency variance:** The difference between standard direct labor hours allowed for the good units produced and actual direct labor hours worked, multiplied by the standard direct labor rate.

LO 3 **Direct labor rate standards:** The hourly direct labor costs that are expected to prevail during the next accounting period for each function or job classification.

LO 6 **Direct labor rate variance:** The difference between the standard direct labor rate and the actual direct labor rate, multiplied by the actual direct labor hours worked.

LO 3 **Direct labor time standard:** The expected time required for each department, machine, or process to complete production of one unit or one batch of output.

LO 3 **Direct materials price standard:** A careful estimate of the cost of a specific direct material in the next accounting period.

LO 5 **Direct materials price variance:** The difference between the standard price and the actual price, multiplied by the actual quantity purchased.

LO 3 **Direct materials quantity standard:** An estimate of the amount of direct materials to be used, influenced by product engineering specifications, quality of direct materials, age and productivity of machinery, and quality and experience of the work force.

LO 5 **Direct materials quantity variance:** The difference between the standard quantity and the actual quantity used, multiplied by the standard price.

LO 7 **Flexible budget:** A summary of expected costs for a range of activity levels, geared to changes in the level of productive output; also called *variable budget.*

LO 7 **Flexible budget formula:** An equation that determines the correct budgeted cost for any level of productive output.

LO 8 **Manufacturing overhead volume variance:** The difference between the manufacturing overhead costs budgeted for the level of production achieved and the manufacturing overhead costs applied to production using the standard variable and fixed manufacturing overhead rates.

LO 1 **Standard costs:** Realistically predetermined costs that are developed from analyses of both past operating costs, quantities, and times and future costs and operating conditions.

LO 3 **Standard direct labor cost:** The standard hours of direct labor multiplied by the standard wage for direct labor.

LO 3 **Standard direct materials cost:** The standard price for direct materials multiplied by the standard quantity for direct materials.

LO 3 **Standard fixed manufacturing overhead rate:** Total budgeted fixed manufacturing overhead costs divided by an expression of capacity, usually normal capacity in terms of standard hours or units.

LO 3 **Standard manufacturing overhead cost:** The sum of the estimates for variable and fixed manufacturing overhead costs in the next accounting period.

LO 3 **Standard variable manufacturing overhead rate:** Total budgeted variable manufacturing overhead costs divided by an expression of capacity, such as the expected number of standard machine hours or standard direct labor hours.

LO 6 **Total direct labor cost variance:** The difference between standard direct labor cost for the good units produced and the actual direct labor costs incurred.

LO 5 **Total direct materials cost variance:** The difference between the standard cost for direct materials and the actual cost incurred for those items.

LO 8 **Total manufacturing overhead variance:** The difference between the actual manufacturing overhead costs incurred and the standard manufacturing overhead costs applied to production using the standard variable and fixed manufacturing overhead rates.

LO 1 **Variance:** The difference between a standard cost and an actual cost.

LO 4 **Variance analysis:** The process of computing the differences between standard (or budgeted) costs and actual costs and identifying the causes of those differences.

REVIEW PROBLEM
Variance Analysis

LO 3 LO 5 LO 6 LO 7 LO 8

Sosnow Manufacturing Company has a standard costing system and keeps all cost standards up to date. The company's main product is copper water pipe, which is made in a single department. The standard variable costs for one unit of finished pipe are:

Direct materials (3 sq meters @ $12.50 per sq. meter)	$37.50
Direct labor (1.2 hours @ $9.00 per hour)	10.80
Variable manufacturing overhead (1.2 hr. @ $5.00 per direct labor hour)	6.00
Standard variable cost per unit	$54.30

Normal capacity is 15,000 direct labor hours, and budgeted fixed manufacturing overhead costs for the year were $54,000. During the year, the company produced and sold 12,200 units. Related transactions and actual cost data for the year were as follows: Direct materials consisted of 37,500 square meters purchased and used; unit purchase cost was $12.40 per square meter. Direct labor consisted of 15,250 direct labor hours worked at an average labor rate of $9.20 per hour. Actual manufacturing overhead costs incurred for the period consisted of variable manufacturing overhead costs of $73,200 and fixed manufacturing overhead costs of $55,000.

REQUIRED

Using the data given, compute the following:

1. Standard hours allowed
2. Standard fixed manufacturing overhead rate
3. Direct materials price variance
4. Direct materials quantity variance
5. Direct labor rate variance
6. Direct labor efficiency variance
7. Controllable manufacturing overhead variance
8. Manufacturing overhead volume variance

ANSWER TO REVIEW PROBLEM

1. Standard Hours Allowed = Good Units Produced × Standard Direct Labor Hours per Unit

   = 12,200 units × 1.2 direct labor hours per unit = 14,640 hours

2. Standard Fixed Manufacturing Overhead Rate $= \dfrac{\text{Budgeted Fixed Manufacturing Overhead Cost}}{\text{Normal Capacity}}$

$= \dfrac{\$54{,}000}{15{,}000 \text{ direct labor hours}}$

$= \underline{\underline{\$3.60}}$ per direct labor hour

3. Direct materials price variance:

Price difference:	Standard price	$12.50 per sq. meter
	Less actual price paid	12.40 per sq. meter
	Difference	$ .10 (F)

Direct Materials Price Variance = (Standard Price − Actual Price) × Actual Quantity
= $.10 (F) × 37,500 sq. meters
= $3,750 (F)

4. Direct materials quantity variance:

Quantity difference:	Standard quantity (12,200 units × 3 sq. meters)	36,600 sq. meters
	Less actual quantity used	37,500 sq. meters
	Difference	900 (U)

Direct Materials Quantity Variance = (Standard Quantity − Actual Quantity) × Standard Price
= 900 sq. meters (U) × $12.50 per sq. meter
= $11,250 (U)

5. Direct labor rate variance:

Rate difference:	Standard labor rate	$9.00 per hour
	Less actual labor rate	9.20 per hour
	Difference	$ .20 (U)

Direct Labor Rate Variance = (Standard Rate − Actual Rate) × Actual Hours
= $.20 (U) × 15,250 hours
= $3,050 (U)

6. Direct labor efficiency variance:

Difference in hours:	Standard hours allowed	14,640 hours*
	Less actual hours worked	15,250 hours
	Difference	610 (U)

Direct Labor Efficiency Variance = (Standard Hours Allowed − Actual Hours Worked) × Standard Rate
= 610 hours (U) × $9.00 per hour
= $5,490 (U)

*12,200 units produced × 1.2 hours per unit = 14,640 hours.

7. Controllable manufacturing overhead variance

Budgeted manufacturing overhead for 14,640 hours		
Variable manufacturing overhead cost (14,640 labor hours × $5.00 per hour)	$73,200	
Budgeted fixed manufacturing overhead	54,000	
Total budgeted manufacturing overhead		$127,200
Less actual manufacturing overhead incurred		$128,200
Controllable manufacturing overhead variance		$ 1,000 (U)

8. Manufacturing overhead volume variance

Total budgeted manufacturing overhead (see computation in 7)		$127,200
Less manufacturing overhead applied		
Variable: 14,640 labor hours × $5.00 per hour	$73,200	
Fixed: 14,640 labor hours × $3.60 per hour	52,704	
Total manufacturing overhead applied		125,904
Manufacturing overhead volume variance		$ 1,296 (U)

Chapter Assignments

BUILDING YOUR KNOWLEDGE FOUNDATION

Questions

1. What are standard costs?
2. Can standard costing be used by a service organization? Explain your answer.
3. What do predetermined overhead costing and standard costing have in common? How are they different?
4. "Standard costing is a total cost concept in that standard unit costs are determined for direct materials, direct labor, and manufacturing overhead." Explain this statement.
5. Name the six elements used to compute a standard unit cost.
6. Identify three factors that could affect a direct materials price standard.
7. What general ledger accounts are affected by a standard costing system?
8. "Performance is evaluated by comparing what did happen with what should have happened." What is meant by this statement? Relate your comments to the budgetary control process.
9. What is a variance?
10. What is variance analysis?
11. How can variances help management control operations?
12. What is the formula for computing a direct materials price variance?
13. How would you interpret an unfavorable direct materials price variance?
14. Identify two possible causes of a direct labor rate variance and describe the measures used to track performance in those areas. Then do the same for a direct labor efficiency variance.
15. Can an unfavorable direct materials quantity variance be caused, at least in part, by a favorable direct materials price variance? Explain.
16. What is a flexible budget? What is its purpose?
17. What are the two parts of the flexible budget formula? How are they related to each other?
18. Distinguish between the controllable manufacturing overhead variance and the manufacturing overhead volume variance.
19. If standard hours allowed exceed normal hours, will the period's manufacturing overhead volume variance be favorable or unfavorable? Explain your answer.
20. What is the key to preparing a performance report based on standard costs and related variances?

Short Exercises

LO 1 *Uses of Standard Costs*

SE 1. Jensen Corporation is considering the installation of a standard costing system. Dan Barkus, the manager of the Missouri Division, attended the corporate meeting where Leah Eisen, the controller, discussed the proposal. Dan asked, "Leah, how will this new system benefit me? How will I use the new system?" Prepare Leah's response to Dan.

LO 2 *Purposes of Standard Costs*

SE 2. You are a consultant and a client asks you why companies augment their cost accounting systems with standard costs. Prepare your response, listing several purposes for introducing standard costs into a cost accounting system.

LO 3 *Standard Unit Cost Computation*

SE 3. Given the following information, compute the standard unit cost of Product JLT.

Direct materials quantity standard:	5 pounds per unit
Direct materials price standard:	$10.20 per pound
Direct labor time standard:	.4 hours per unit
Direct labor rate standard:	$10.75 per hour
Variable manufacturing overhead rate standard:	$7.00 per machine hour
Fixed manufacturing overhead rate standard:	$11.00 per machine hour
Machine hour standard:	2 hours per unit

LO 4 *Cost Variance Analysis*

SE 4. Des Jardins Metal Works produces lawn sculptures. The company follows a practice of analyzing only variances that differ by more than 5 percent from the standard cost. The controller computed the following direct labor efficiency variances for March.

	Direct Labor Efficiency Variance	**Standard Direct Labor Cost**
Product 4	$1,240 (U)	$26,200
Product 6	3,290 (F)	41,700
Product 7	2,030 (U)	34,300
Product 9	1,620 (F)	32,560
Product 12	2,810 (U)	59,740

Identify the variances that should be analyzed for cause. Round to two decimal places. Also identify possible causes of the variances.

LO 5 *Direct Materials Variances*

SE 5. Given the standard costs in **SE 3** and the following actual cost and usage data, compute the direct materials price and direct materials quantity variances.

Direct materials purchased and used	55,000 pounds
Price paid for direct materials	$10.00 per pound
Number of good units produced	11,000 units

LO 6 *Direct Labor Variances*

SE 6. Given the standard costs in **SE 3** and the following actual cost and usage data, compute the direct labor rate and direct labor efficiency variances.

Direct labor hours used	4,950 hours
Total cost of direct labor	$53,460
Number of good units produced	11,000 units

LO 7 *Flexible Budget Preparation*

SE 7. Prepare a flexible budget for 10,000, 12,000, and 14,000 units of output, given the following information.

Variable costs	
Direct materials	$8.00 per unit
Direct labor	$2.50 per unit
Variable manufacturing overhead	$6.00 per unit
Total budgeted fixed manufacturing overhead	$81,200

SE 8. LO 8 *Manufacturing Overhead Variances*

Ron-Mar Products uses a standard costing system. The following information about manufacturing overhead was generated during August:

Standard variable manufacturing overhead rate	$2 per machine hour
Standard fixed manufacturing overhead rate	$3 per machine hour
Actual variable manufacturing overhead costs	$443,200
Actual fixed manufacturing overhead costs	$698,800
Budgeted fixed manufacturing overhead costs	$700,000
Standard machine hours per unit	12
Good units produced	18,940
Actual machine hours	228,400

Compute the controllable manufacturing overhead variance and the manufacturing overhead volume variance.

SE 9. LO 9 *Evaluating Managerial Performance*

Derrick Shirley, the production manager at AWA Industries, received a report containing the following information from Gina Masamoto, the company controller.

	Actual	**Standard**	**Variance**
Direct Materials	$38,200	$36,600	$1,600 (U)
Direct Labor	19,450	19,000	450 (U)
Manufacturing overhead	62,890	60,000	2,890 (U)

Gina asked for a response. If you were Derrick, what would you do? What additional information does Derrick need to prepare his response?

Exercises

E 1. LO 1 *Uses of Standard Costs*

Deb Nicodemus has just assumed the duties of controller for Hinkley Market Research Company. She is concerned that the methods used for cost planning and control do not accurately track the operations of the business. She plans to suggest to the company's president, Jefferson Hinkley, that a standard costing system be created for budgeting and cost control. The new system could be incorporated into the existing accounting system. The anticipated cost of installing the new costing system and training managers is around $7,500. Prepare a memo from Deb to Jefferson Hinkley that defines a standard costing system and outlines its uses and benefits.

E 2. LO 3 *Development of Standard Costs*

McCain Corp. maintains a complete standard costing system and is in the process of updating its direct materials and direct labor standards for Product 20B. The following data have been accumulated.

Direct Materials

In the previous period, 20,500 units were produced and 32,800 square yards of direct materials were used to produce them.

Three suppliers of direct materials will be used in the coming period: Supplier A will provide 20 percent of the materials at a cost of $3.60 per square yard, Supplier B will be responsible for 50 percent at a cost of $3.80 per square yard, and Supplier C will ship 30 percent at a cost of $3.70 per square yard.

Direct Labor

During the previous period, 57,400 direct labor hours were worked, 34,850 hours on machine H and 22,550 hours on machine K.

Machine H operators earned $9.40 per hour and machine K operators earned $9.20 per hour last period. The new labor contract calls for a 10 percent increase in labor rates for the coming period.

From the information above, compute the direct materials quantity and price standards and the direct labor time and rate standards for each machine listed for the coming accounting period.

E 3. LO 3 *Standard Unit Cost Computation*

Tara Aerodynamics, Inc., makes electronically equipped weather-detecting balloons for university meteorology departments. Recent nationwide inflation has caused the company management to order that standard costs be recomputed. New direct materials price standards are $600.00 per set for electronic components and $13.50 per square meter for heavy-duty canvas. Direct materials quantity standards include one set of electronic components and 100 square meters of heavy-duty canvas per balloon. Direct labor time standards are 26 hours per balloon for the Electronics Department and 19 hours per balloon for the Assembly Department. Direct labor rate standards are $11.00 per hour for the Electronics Department and $10.00 per hour for the Assembly Department. Standard manufacturing overhead rates are $16.00 per direct labor hour for the standard variable manufacturing overhead rate and $12.00 per direct labor hour for the standard fixed manufacturing overhead rate.

Using the production standards provided, compute the standard unit cost of one weather balloon.

E 4. LO 5 *Direct Materials Price and Quantity Variances*

The Febor Elevator Company manufactures small hydroelectric elevators with a maximum capacity of ten passengers. One of the direct materials used by the Production Department is heavy-duty carpeting for the floor of the elevator. The direct materials quantity standard used for the month ended April 30, 20xx was 8 square yards per elevator. During April, the purchasing agent purchased this carpeting at $11 per square yard; the standard price for the period was $12. Ninety elevators were completed and sold during April; the Production Department used an average of 8.5 square yards of carpet per elevator.

Calculate Febor Elevator Company's direct materials price and quantity variances for carpet for April 20xx.

E 5. LO 6 *Direct Labor Rate and Efficiency Variances*

Goetz Foundry, Inc., manufactures castings used by other companies in the production of machinery. For the past two years, the largest selling product has been a casting for an eight-cylinder engine block. Standard direct labor hours per engine block are 1.8 hours. The labor contract requires that $14 per hour be paid to all direct labor employees. During June, 16,500 engine blocks were produced. Actual direct labor hours and costs for June were 29,900 hours and $433,550, respectively.

1. Compute the direct labor rate variance for eight-cylinder engine blocks during June.
2. Using the same data, compute the direct labor efficiency variance for eight-cylinder engine blocks during June. Check your answer, assuming that the total direct labor variance is $17,750 (U).

E 6. LO 7 *Flexible Budget Preparation*

Fixed manufacturing overhead costs for the Bernard Company for 20xx are expected to be as follows: depreciation, $72,000; supervisory salaries, $92,000; property taxes and insurance, $26,000; and other fixed manufacturing overhead, $14,500. Total fixed manufacturing overhead is thus expected to be $204,500. Variable costs per unit are expected to be as follows: direct materials, $16.50; direct labor, $8.50; operating supplies, $2.60; indirect labor, $4.10; and other variable manufacturing overhead costs, $3.20.

Prepare a flexible budget for the following levels of production: 18,000 units, 20,000 units, and 22,000 units. What is the flexible budget formula for 20xx?

E 7. LO 8 *Manufacturing Overhead Variances*

Theodore Company produces handmade clamming buckets that are sold to distributors along the Atlantic coast of North Carolina. The company incurred $12,400 of actual manufacturing overhead costs in May. Budgeted standard manufacturing overhead costs for May were $4 of variable manufacturing overhead costs per direct labor hour plus $1,500 in fixed manufacturing overhead costs. Normal capacity was set at 2,000 direct labor hours per month. In May, the company was able to produce 10,100 clamming buckets. The time standard is .2 direct labor hours per clamming bucket.

Compute the total manufacturing overhead variance, the controllable manufacturing overhead variance, and the manufacturing overhead volume variance for May.

E 8. LO 8 *Manufacturing Overhead Variances*

Ridgeway Industries uses a standard costing system that includes flexible budgeting for cost planning and control. The 20xx monthly flexible budget for manufacturing overhead costs is $200,000 of fixed costs plus $5.20 per machine hour. Monthly normal capacity of 100,000 machine hours is used to compute the standard fixed manufacturing overhead rate. During December 20xx, plant workers recorded 105,000 actual machine hours. The standard machine hours allowed for good production during December was only 98,500. Actual manufacturing overhead costs incurred during December totaled $441,000 of variable costs and $204,500 of fixed costs.

Compute (1) the under- or overapplied manufacturing overhead during December and (2) the controllable manufacturing overhead variance and the manufacturing overhead volume variance.

E 9. LO 8 *Overhead Variance Analysis in an ABC System*

Lewis Paper Company produces rolled paper products that are used by various book publishing and newspaper companies. The company adopted an activity-based costing system and now analyzes variances for over thirty activities within the Production Division. The Machine Setup Activity is used by seven different work cells and is involved in each product line's size or type of paper change. Information about the Machine Setup Activity for June follows.

Actual variable overhead costs of the activity	$95,900
Actual fixed overhead costs of the activity	$38,000
Setup hours worked	3,400 hours
Total capacity of the activity in hours	3,200 hours
Budgeted fixed overhead costs	$38,400
Variable overhead rate for the activity	$28 per setup hour
Fixed overhead rate for the activity	$12 per setup hour

Compute (1) the under- or overapplied overhead for the Machine Setup Activity during June and (2) the activity's controllable overhead variance and the overhead volume variance for the month.

E 10. LO 9 *Evaluating Managerial Performance*

Scott Loman is a project manager for Beam Construction Company. Recently the company's controller sent him a performance report for the Aims Apartment Complex project. Included in the report was an unfavorable direct labor efficiency variance of $1,900 for roof structure. What types of information does Scott need to analyze before he can respond to the unfavorable direct labor efficiency variance that is his responsibility?

Problems

P 1. LO 3 *Developing and Using Standard Costs*

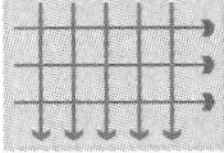

Prefabricated houses are the specialty of Kentish Homes, Inc., of Dallas, Texas. Although Kentish Homes produces many models, and customers can even special order a home, 60 percent of the company's business comes from the sale of the Citadel, a three-bedroom, 1,400-square-foot home with an impressive front entrance. The six basic direct materials used to manufacture the entrance with their standard costs for 20x1 are as follows: wood framing materials, $2,140; deluxe front door, $480; door hardware, $260; exterior siding, $710; electrical materials, $580; and interior finishing materials, $1,520.

Three types of direct labor are used to build this section: carpenter, 30 hours at $12 per hour; door specialist, 4 hours at $14 per hour; and electrician, 8 hours at $16 per hour. In 20x1, the company used a manufacturing overhead rate of 40 percent of total direct materials cost.

During 20x2, the cost of wood framing materials is expected to increase by 20 percent. The deluxe front door will need two suppliers: Supplier A will produce 40 percent of the company's needs at $490 per door; Supplier B, 60 percent at $500 per door. The cost of the door hardware will increase by 10 percent, and the cost of electrical materials will increase by 20 percent. Exterior siding cost should decrease by $16 per unit. The cost of interior finishing materials is expected to remain the same. The carpenter's wages will increase by $1 per hour, while the door specialist's wages should remain the same. The electrician's wages will increase by $.50 per hour. Finally, the manufacturing overhead rate will decrease to 25 percent of total direct materials cost. All other costs will remain the same.

REQUIRED

1. Compute the total standard cost of direct materials per front entrance for 20x1.
2. Using your answer to **1**, compute the total standard unit cost for the Citadel's entrance in 20x1.
3. Compute the new standard unit cost per front entrance for the year 20x2.

P 2. LO 5 LO 6 *Direct Materials and Direct Labor Variances*

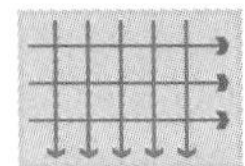

Neff Trophy Company produces a variety of athletic awards, most in the form of trophies or mounted replicas of athletes in action. Lisa Neff, the president of the company, is in the process of developing a standard costing system. The company produces six standard sizes. The deluxe trophy stands three feet tall above the base. Direct materials standards include one pound of metal supported by an 8-ounce wooden base. Standard prices for 20xx were $3.30 per pound of metal and $.45 per ounce of wood.

Direct labor is used in both the Molding and the Trimming/Finishing Departments. Direct labor standards for deluxe trophies specify .2 hours of direct labor in the Molding Department and .4 hours in the Trimming/Finishing Department. Standard direct labor rates for deluxe trophies are $10.75 per hour in the Molding Department and $12.00 per hour in the Trimming/Finishing Department.

During January 20xx, 16,400 deluxe trophies were made. Actual production data were as follows:

Direct Materials	
Metal	16,640 pounds @ $3.25 per pound
Wood	131,400 ounces @ $.48 per ounce
Direct Labor	
Molding	3,400 hours @ $10.60 per hour
Trimming/Finishing	6,540 hours @ $12.10 per hour

REQUIRED

1. Compute the direct materials price and quantity variances for metal and wood.
2. Compute the direct labor rate and efficiency variances for the Molding and the Trimming/Finishing Departments.

P 3. LO 7 *Flexible Budget and Performance Evaluation*

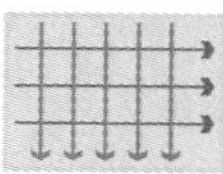

Marwick Home Products Company manufactures a complete line of kitchen glassware. The Cottonwood Division specializes in 12-ounce drinking glasses. Sheila Sapinski, the superintendent of the Cottonwood Division, has asked the controller to prepare a performance report for April 20xx. The following report was handed to her a few days later:

Cost Category	Budget*	Actual Costs Incurred During April	Variance
Direct materials (variable)	$ 5,000	$ 4,975	$ 25 (F)
Direct labor (variable)	6,000	5,850	150 (F)
Indirect labor (variable)	1,500	1,290	210 (F)
Supplies (variable)	1,000	960	40 (F)
Heat and power (variable)	1,500	1,325	175 (F)
Other variable costs	2,500	2,340	160 (F)
Heat and power (fixed)	3,500	3,500	—
Depreciation (fixed)	4,200	4,200	—
Insurance and taxes (fixed)	1,200	1,200	—
Other fixed costs	1,600	1,600	—
Totals	$28,000	$27,240	$760 (F)

*Based on normal capacity of 50,000 units.

Sapinski questioned the controller on the report, stating: "Profits have been decreasing in recent months but this report indicates that our production process is operating efficiently."

REQUIRED

1. Prepare a flexible budget for the Cottonwood Division using production levels of 45,000 units, 50,000 units, and 55,000 units.
2. What is the flexible budget formula?
3. Assume the Cottonwood Division produced 46,560 units in April and that all fixed costs remained constant. Prepare a revised performance report using actual capacity as a basis.
4. Which report is more meaningful for performance evaluation, the original one above or the revised one? Why?

P 4. LO 5 LO 6 LO 8 LO 9 *Direct Materials, Direct Labor, and Manufacturing Overhead Variances*

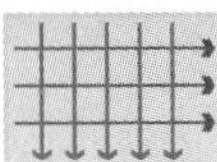

During 20x2, Gregor Laboratories, Inc., researched and perfected a cure for the common cold. Called Cold-Gone, the product consists of a series of five tablets and sells for $28.00 per package. Standard unit costs for this product were developed in late 20x2 for use in 20x3. Per package, the standard unit costs were: chemical ingredients, 6 ounces at $1.00 per ounce; packaging, $1.20; direct labor, .8 hour at $14.00 per hour; standard variable manufacturing overhead, $4.00 per direct labor hour; and standard fixed manufacturing overhead, $6.00 per direct labor hour.

In the first quarter of 20x3, the peak season for colds, demand for the new product rose beyond even the wildest expectations of management. During those three months, the company produced and sold over one-half million packages of Cold-Gone. During the first week in April, 50,000 packages were produced using materials for 50,200 packages costing $60,240. Chemical use was 305,000 ounces costing $292,800. Direct labor was 40,250 direct labor hours at a total cost of $579,600. Total variable manufacturing overhead was $161,100 and total fixed manufacturing overhead, $242,000. Budgeted fixed manufacturing overhead for the period was $240,000.

REQUIRED

1. Compute (a) all direct materials price variances, (b) all direct materials quantity variances, (c) the direct labor rate variance, (d) the direct labor efficiency variance, (e) the controllable manufacturing overhead variance, and (f) the manufacturing overhead volume variance.
2. Prepare a performance report based on your variance analysis and suggest possible causes for each significant variance.

P 5. LO 8 *Variance Review: Missing Information*

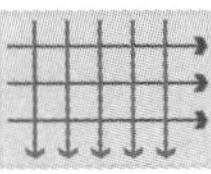

The identification of over- or underapplied manufacturing overhead is the reason for analyzing overhead variances. The controllable manufacturing overhead and manufacturing overhead volume variances are interrelated. Dion Corporation uses a standard costing system.

	Dion Corporation
Actual machine hours	8,550
Standard machine hours allowed	8,750
Normal capacity in machine hours	(e)
Total manufacturing overhead rate per machine hour	(c)
Standard variable manufacturing overhead rate	$ 2.50
Standard fixed manufacturing overhead rate	(d)
Actual variable and fixed manufacturing overhead	(f)
Total manufacturing overhead applied	(b)
Budgeted fixed manufacturing overhead	$76,500
Total manufacturing overhead variance	(a)
Controllable manufacturing overhead variance	$ 900 (F)
Manufacturing overhead volume variance	$ 2,250 (F)

REQUIRED

Fill in the unknown amounts by analyzing the data for the company. Capacities are expressed in machine hours. (**Hint:** Use the structure of Figure 5 in this chapter as a guide for your analysis.)

Alternate Problems

P 6. **LO 3** *Development of Standards: Direct Materials*

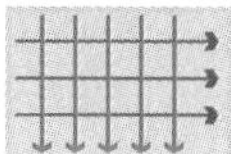

Clockworks, Ltd., assembles clock movements for grandfather clocks. Each movement has four components to assemble: the clock facing, the clock hands, the time movement, and the spring assembly. For the current year, 20x1, the company used the following standard costs: clock facing, $15.90; clock hands, $12.70; time movement, $66.10; and spring assembly, $52.50.

Prices and sources of materials are expected to change in 20x2. Sixty percent of the facings will be supplied by Company A at $19.50 each, and the remaining 40 percent will be purchased from Company B at $18.80 each. The hands are produced for Clockworks, Ltd., by Olesha Hardware, Inc., and will cost $16.40 per set in 20x2. Time movements will be purchased from three Swiss sources: Company Q, 30 percent of total need at $70.50 per movement; Company R, 20 percent at $69.50; and Company S, 50 percent at $71.90. Spring assemblies will be purchased from a French company and are expected to increase in cost by 20 percent.

REQUIRED

1. Determine the total standard direct materials cost per unit for 20x2.
2. If the company could guarantee the purchase of 2,500 sets of hands from Olesha Hardware, Inc., the unit cost would be reduced by 20 percent. Find the resulting standard direct materials unit cost.
3. Substandard spring assemblies can be purchased at $50.00, but 20 percent of them will be unusable and cannot be returned. Compute the standard direct materials unit cost if the company follows this procedure, assuming the original facts of the case for the remaining data. The cost of the defective materials will be spread over good units produced.

P 7. **LO 5** **LO 6** *Direct Materials and Direct Labor Variances*

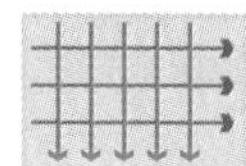

The Kawalski Packaging Company makes plastic baskets for food wholesalers. Each Type R basket is made of .8 grams of liquid plastic and .6 grams of an additive that includes color and hardening agents. The standard prices are $.15 per gram of liquid plastic and $.09 per gram of additive.

Two kinds of direct labor are required: molding and trimming/packing. The direct labor time and rate standards per 100-basket batch are as follows: molding, 1.0 hours per batch at an hourly rate of $12; trimming/packing, 1.2 hours per batch at $10 per hour.

During 20xx, the company produced 48,000 Type R baskets. Actual materials used were 38,600 grams of liquid plastic at a total cost of $5,404 and 28,950 grams of additive at a cost of $2,895. Actual direct labor included 480 hours for molding at a total cost of $5,664, and 560 hours for trimming/packing at $5,656.

REQUIRED

1. Compute the direct materials price and quantity variances for both the liquid plastic and the additive.
2. Compute the direct labor rate and efficiency variances for the molding and trimming/packing processes.

P 8. **LO 5** **LO 6** **LO 8** *Direct Materials, Direct Labor, and Manufacturing Overhead Variances*

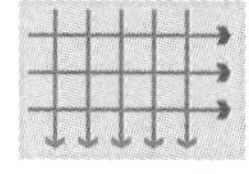

The Doormat Division of Robertson Rug Company produces a line of all-vinyl mats. Each doormat calls for .4 meters of vinyl material that costs $3.10 per meter. Standard direct labor hours and cost per doormat are .2 hour and $1.84 (.2 hour × $9.20 per hour), respectively. The division's current standard variable overhead rate is $1.50 per direct labor hour, and the standard fixed manufacturing overhead rate is $.80 per direct labor hour.

In August the division manufactured and sold 60,000 doormats. During the month, 25,200 meters of vinyl material were used at a total cost of $73,080. The total actual manufacturing overhead costs for August were $28,200, of which $18,200 were variable. The total number of direct labor hours worked was 10,800, and the factory payroll for direct labor for August was $95,040. Normal monthly capacity for the year has been set at 58,000 doormats. Budgeted fixed manufacturing overhead for the period was $9,280.

REQUIRED

Compute (1) the direct materials price variance, (2) the direct materials quantity variance, (3) the direct labor rate variance, (4) the direct labor efficiency variance, (5) the controllable manufacturing overhead variance, and (6) the manufacturing overhead volume variance.

Skills Development

CONCEPTUAL ANALYSIS

SD 1.

LO 4 *Cost Control Using Variance Analysis*

Holding down operating costs is an ongoing challenge for managers. The lower the costs incurred, the higher the profit. But two factors make a target profit difficult to achieve. First, dozens of possible operating inefficiencies may occur, ranging from human error to unexpected machine breakdowns. Each occurrence causes costs to escalate. On the other hand, if costs are so strictly controlled that cheaper resources are used, the quality of the product or service may suffer and total sales may decline. To control costs and still produce high-quality goods or services, managers must continually assess operating activities by analyzing both financial and nonfinancial data.

Write a short paper discussing how variance analysis helps managers to accomplish cost control objectives. Focus on both the financial and the nonfinancial data used in a standard costing system.

ETHICAL DILEMMA

SD 2.

LO 2 *An Ethical Question*
LO 4 *Involving Standard Costs*

Jason Bramwell is the manager of standard costing systems at ***Ragnar Industries, Inc.*** Standard costs are developed for all product-related direct materials, direct labor, and manufacturing overhead costs and are used for pricing products, for costing all inventories, and for performance evaluation of all purchasing and production line managers. The company updates standard costs whenever costs, prices, or rates change by 3 percent or more; in addition, all standard costs are reviewed and updated annually in December. This practice provided currently attainable standards that were appropriate for use in valuing year-end inventories on Ragnar Industries' financial statements.

On November 30, 20x2, Jason received a memo from the company's chief financial officer. The memo said that the company was considering the purchase of another company and that Jason and his staff were to concentrate their full effort on analyzing the proposed transaction and ignore adjusting the standards until February or March. In late November, prices on over twenty raw materials were reduced by 10 percent or more and a new labor contract reduced several categories of labor rates. Lower standard costs would result in lower inventories, higher cost of goods sold due to inventory write-downs, and lower net income for the year. Jason believed that the company was facing an operating loss and that the assignment to evaluate the proposed major purchase was designed primarily to keep his staff from revising and lowering the standards. Jason questioned the CFO about the assignment and reiterated the need for updating the standard costs, but he was again told to ignore the update procedure and concentrate on the company purchase. The proposed purchase never materialized, and Jason and his staff were removed from the assignment in early February.

Assess Jason's actions in this situation. Did he follow all ethical paths to solve the problem? What are the consequences of not adjusting the standard costs?

Communication

Critical Thinking

Group Activity

Memo

Ethics

International

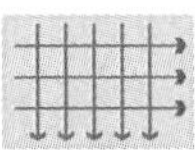
Spreadsheet

Managerial Technology

Internet

Research Activity

SD 3.

LO 1 **LO 2** *The Relevance of Standard Costing*

Standard costs and the variances for direct materials, direct labor, and manufacturing overhead generated by a standard costing system have been used to control costs and evaluate performance for many years. Standard costs are also used in the pricing of new products. In recent years, the standard costing approach has been called irrelevant to the measurement of operations. Locate an article written about this topic within the last five years in the periodical *Management Accounting*, published monthly by the Institute of Management Accountants or on the Needles Accounting Resource Center Web site at http://www.hmco.com/college/needles/home.html. Identify the issues addressed by the author(s). Is the article positive or negative toward standard costs? What role does the globally competitive environment play in the points being made by the author(s)? Prepare a formal two-page summary of the article. Also prepare an outline that you would use if called upon to report your findings to your classmates.

Group Activity: Have students work in groups to complete **SD 3**. Select one person from each group to report the group's findings to the class.

Decision-Making Practice

SD 4.

LO 6 **LO 8** *Annuity Life Insurance Company—Standard Costing in a Service Industry*

The ***Annuity Life Insurance Company*** (ALIC) markets several types of life insurance policies, but its permanent, twenty-year life annuity policy (P20A) is its most popular product. The P20A policy sells in $10,000 increments and features variable percentages of whole life insurance and single-payment annuity, depending on the potential policyholder's needs and age. An entire department is devoted to developing and marketing the P20A policy. ALIC has determined that both the policy developer and the policy salesperson contribute to the creation of each policy, so ALIC categorizes these people as direct labor for variance analysis, cost control, and performance evaluation. For unit costing, each $10,000 increment is considered 1 unit. Thus, a $90,000 policy is counted as 9 units.

Standard unit cost information for the period is as follows:

Direct labor	
Policy developer	
3 hours at $12.00 per hour	$ 36.00
Policy salesperson	
8.5 hours at $14.20 per hour	120.70
Operating overhead	
Variable operating overhead	
11.5 hours at $26.00 per hour	299.00
Fixed operating overhead	
11.5 hours at $18.00 per hour	207.00
Standard unit cost	$662.70

Actual costs incurred during January for the 265 units sold were as follows:

Direct labor	
Policy developers	
848 hours at $12.50 per hour	$10,600.00
Policy salespeople	
2,252.5 hours at $14.00 per hour	31,535.00
Operating overhead	
Variable operating overhead	78,440.00
Fixed operating overhead	53,400.00

Normal monthly capacity was 260 units, and the budgeted fixed operating overhead for the month was $53,820.

1. Compute the standard hours allowed in January for policy developers and policy salespeople.
2. What should have been the total standard costs for January? What were the total actual costs incurred for January? Compute the total cost variance for the period.
3. Compute the direct labor rate and efficiency variances for policy developers and policy salespeople.
4. Compute the operating overhead variances for January.
5. Identify possible causes for each variance and suggest possible solutions.

Managerial Reporting and Analysis

INTERPRETING MANAGEMENT REPORTS

MRA 1.
LO 7 *Flexible Budgets and*
LO 9 *Performance Evaluation*

Boris Realtors, Inc., specializes in home resales. Revenue is earned from selling fees. Commissions for salespersons, listing agents, and listing companies are the main costs for the company. Business has improved steadily over the last ten years. As usual, Bonnie Boris, the managing partner of Boris Realtors, Inc., received a report summarizing the performance for the most recent year.

Boris Realtors, Inc.
Performance Report
For the Year Ended December 31, 20xx

	Budget*	Actual**	Difference Under (Over) Budget
Total Selling Fees	$2,052,000	$2,242,200	($190,200)
Less Variable Costs			
Sales Commissions	$1,102,950	$1,205,183	($102,233)
Automobile	36,000	39,560	(3,560)
Advertising	93,600	103,450	(9,850)
Home Repairs	77,400	89,240	(11,840)
General Overhead	656,100	716,970	(60,870)
	$1,966,050	$2,154,403	($188,353)
Less Fixed Costs			
General Overhead	60,000	62,300	(2,300)
Total Costs	$2,026,050	$2,216,703	($190,653)
Net Income	$ 25,950	$ 25,497	$ 453

*Budgeted data based on 180 home resales.
**Actual selling fees and operating costs of 200 home resales.

REQUIRED

1. Analyze the performance report. What does it say about the performance of the company? Is the performance report reliable? Explain.
2. Calculate the budgeted selling fee and budgeted variable costs per home resale.
3. Prepare a performance report using a flexible budget based on the actual number of home resales.
4. Analyze the report you prepared in **3.** What does it say about the performance of the company? Is the performance report reliable? Explain.
5. What recommendations would you make to improve next year's performance?

FORMULATING MANAGEMENT REPORTS

MRA 2.
LO 4 LO 6 LO 8 LO 9 *Preparing Performance Reports*

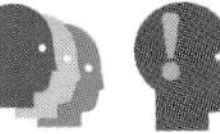

Troy Corrente, the president of ***Forest Valley Spa,*** is concerned about the spa's operating performance in March 20xx. He carefully budgeted his costs so that he could reduce the 20xx membership fees. Now he needs to monitor those costs to make sure that the spa's profits are at the level he expected.

He has asked you, as the controller for the spa, to prepare a performance report for the operating labor and overhead costs. He also wants you to analyze the report and suggest possible causes for any problems you find. He needs your work immediately so that any problems can be quickly solved.

The following information is available:

	Standard	Actual
Variable costs		
Operating labor	$10,880	$12,150
Utilities	2,880	3,360
Repairs and maintenance	5,760	7,140
Fixed costs		
Depreciation, equipment	2,600	2,680
Rent	3,280	3,280
Other	1,704	1,860
Totals	$27,104	$30,470

Normal operating hours call for eight operators to work 160 hours each per month. During March, nine operators worked an average of 150 hours each.

REQUIRED

1. Answer the following questions about preparing performance reports.
   a. Who needs the performance report?
   b. Why are you preparing the performance report?
   c. What information do you need to develop the performance report? How will you obtain that information?
   d. When must you have the performance report and analysis prepared?
2. With this limited information, compute the operating labor rate variance, the operating labor efficiency variance, and the operating controllable overhead variance.
3. Prepare a performance report for the month. Analyze the report and suggest possible causes for any problems that you find.

INTERNATIONAL COMPANY

MRA 3.
LO 5 LO 6 *Variance Analysis*

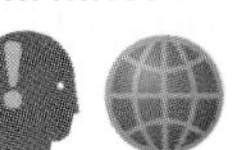

Ming Nu recently became the controller of a joint venture in Hong Kong. Ming created a standard costing system to help plan for and control the company's activities. After completing the first quarter of operations using standard costing, Ming met with the budget team, which included managers from purchasing, engineering, production, and personnel. He asked them to share any problems that occurred during the quarter. He planned to use the information to analyze the variances that his staff would calculate.

REQUIRED

For each of the following situations, identify the direct materials and/or direct labor variance(s) that could be affected and indicate the direction (favorable or unfavorable) of those variances.

a. The production department used highly skilled, higher-paid workers.
b. Machines were improperly adjusted.
c. Direct labor personnel worked more carefully to manufacture the product.
d. The product design engineer substituted a direct material that was less expensive and of lower quality.
e. The Purchasing Department bought higher-quality materials at a higher price.
f. A major supplier used a less-expensive mode of transportation to deliver the raw materials.
g. Work was halted for two hours because of a power disruption.

EXCEL SPREADSHEET ANALYSIS

MRA 4. LO 7 LO 8 *Flexible Budget Development and Manufacturing Overhead Variance Analysis*

Ella Mae Collins is the controller for ***FH Industries.*** She has asked you, her new assistant, to prepare an analysis from the following data related to projected and actual manufacturing overhead costs for October 20xx:

	Standard Variable Costs per Machine Hour (MH)	Actual Variable Costs Incurred in October
Indirect materials and supplies	$1.10	$ 2,380
Indirect machine setup labor	2.50	5,090
Materials handling	1.40	3,950
Maintenance and repair	1.50	2,980
Utilities	.80	1,490
Miscellaneous	.10	200
Totals	$7.40	$16,090

	Budgeted Fixed Manufacturing Overhead	Actual Fixed Manufacturing Overhead in October
Supervisory salaries	$ 3,630	$ 3,630
Machine depreciation	8,360	8,580
Other	1,210	1,220
Totals	$13,200	$13,430

During October, the number of good units produced was used to compute the 2,100 standard machine hours allowed. Your analysis of this data should include the steps outlined below.

REQUIRED

1. Prepare a monthly flexible budget for the company for operating activity at 2,000 machine hours, 2,200 machine hours, and 2,500 machine hours.
2. Formulate a flexible budget formula for the company.
3. The company's normal operating capacity is 2,200 machine hours per month. Compute the fixed manufacturing overhead rate at this level of activity. Then break the rate down into individual rates for each element of fixed manufacturing overhead.
4. Prepare a detailed comparative cost analysis for October. All variable and fixed manufacturing overhead costs should be included. Your report form should include the following five columns: (a) cost category, (b) cost per machine hour, (c) costs applied, (d) actual costs incurred, and (e) variance.
5. Develop a manufacturing overhead variance analysis for October that identifies the controllable manufacturing overhead variance and the manufacturing overhead volume variance.
6. Prepare an analysis of the variances. Are some of the fixed costs controllable by the manager? Defend your answer.

ENDNOTES

1. http://www.rubgrp.com/main.html. Other sources include brochures and practice manual pages received from The Rubicon Group and a personal telephone interview with Dennis Evans, of the Rubicon Group, January 30, 1998.
2. Carole Cheatham, "Updating Standard Cost Systems," *Journal of Accountancy,* The American Institute of Certified Public Accountants, December 1990, pp. 57–60.
3. http://www.euro.net/innovation/Management_Base_/Man_Guide_Rel_1.081/controlandmonitoring.html, July 14, 1997.

A
B
B
C
48
48

Operating and Capital Expenditure Decision Analyses

LEARNING OBJECTIVES

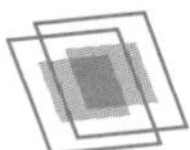

1. Describe the decision environment facing managers and state how managers use decision-support information in the management cycle.
2. Identify the steps in the management decision process and define *relevant decision information.*
3. Use incremental analysis to develop decision data.
4. Prepare evaluations of alternatives for (a) make-or-buy decisions, (b) special order decisions, (c) sales mix decisions, and (d) sell or process-further decisions.
5. Identify three techniques commonly used to analyze proposed capital expenditures, and explain the measures of projected costs and revenues used in those analyses.
6. Use (a) the accounting rate-of-return method, (b) the payback period method, and (c) the net present value method to analyze proposed capital expenditures.

DECISION POINT

FIREMAN'S FUND INSURANCE COMPANY

Fireman's Fund Insurance Company is one of the top twenty property and casualty insurance companies in the United States. Fifty major field offices serve the needs of the company's 6,000 independent insurance agents and brokers. Eighty percent of the company's business is commercial and the remainder is personal insurance. The company offers hundreds of different types of policies, which has made it difficult to track the profitability of individual product lines.

To set appropriate premium rates, knowledge of both policy costs and claims experience is necessary, so Fireman's Fund developed a system for tracking such costs. Specific activities of company personnel have been identified, and operating costs are accumulated and traced to the policies that utilize those services. Claims are also monitored by policy type and geographic location. How does such a cost-tracking system help managers make decisions about the company's numerous types of insurance policies?

Fireman's Fund's new accounting system allows the company to make decisions about the profitability of insurance policies by type as well as by geographic location. Once identified, unprofitable policy types and locations can be analyzed to determine whether they should be eliminated. If operating costs are too high, controls may be instituted to limit them.

Critical Thinking Question: How can the cost-tracking system reduce waste?
Answer: By identifying and monitoring specific activities, managers can identify wasteful, costly activities.

The ability to track and analyze patterns, such as claims by geographic region, helps managers decide whether to raise premiums or eliminate a policy type. By improving its ability to track costs, the company can determine the sources of its profits and manage its resources more effectively.[1]

Decision Information for Managers

OBJECTIVE 1

Describe the decision environment facing managers and state how managers use decision-support information in the management cycle

Related Text Assignments:
Q: 1
SE: 1
E: 1

Managers must make decisions every day. Some decisions have short-term effects on the organization, while others affect operations far into the future. No matter what type of decision managers face, they need relevant, accurate information on which to base their choice. Sometimes managers need financial information; at other times, they need nonfinancial data, such as projected product or service delivery time or anticipated demand for units. Decision information can come from existing data, such as standard product costs or current budgets, or from special decision analyses that must be researched and prepared. Because management accountants provide the information and perform the analyses managers need, they are important members of an organization's decision-making team.

The typical decisions managers make include (1) whether to buy parts from an outside vendor or to make them internally; (2) which special orders to accept; (3) which products, services, or divisions are unprofitable and whether they should be discontinued; (4) which products or services are the most profitable and whether their markets can be expanded; (5) whether a product should be sold as is or processed further; (6) which alternative for purchasing a machine is most advantageous; and (7) whether a process should be automated and what effects automation would have. The Decision Point about Fireman's Fund Insurance Company examined aspects of decision types 3 and 4 as they pertain to a service business.

Each type of decision involves uncertainties that can be resolved by obtaining appropriate information. The sources of information are endless and may be found both inside and outside the organization. Managers should always be aware of their environment and identify, remember, and even record relevant information whenever it surfaces. Internal sources include regular organization reports, personal observation of practices and processes, organization meetings, specific requests for information from other functions and departments, direct involvement in organization activities, and results and actions that are related to past decisions. External sources include professional meetings and conferences, training and professional development seminars, journals and business publications, and analyses of the competition.

Decision making usually involves selecting the best of two or more alternative courses of action. In many cases, one of those alternatives is to do nothing. Even doing nothing can alter financial measures. For example, sales will decrease if customers want new products but a manager chooses not to purchase a machine designed to expand the product line. Before selecting an alternative, a manager will gather as much information about all alternatives as time will permit. Some of that information will focus on details, such as productivity estimates of various machines, while other information will spell out the broader financial consequences of each alternative. The manager must analyze the information supporting each decision, identify the most likely alternatives, project the results of each alter-

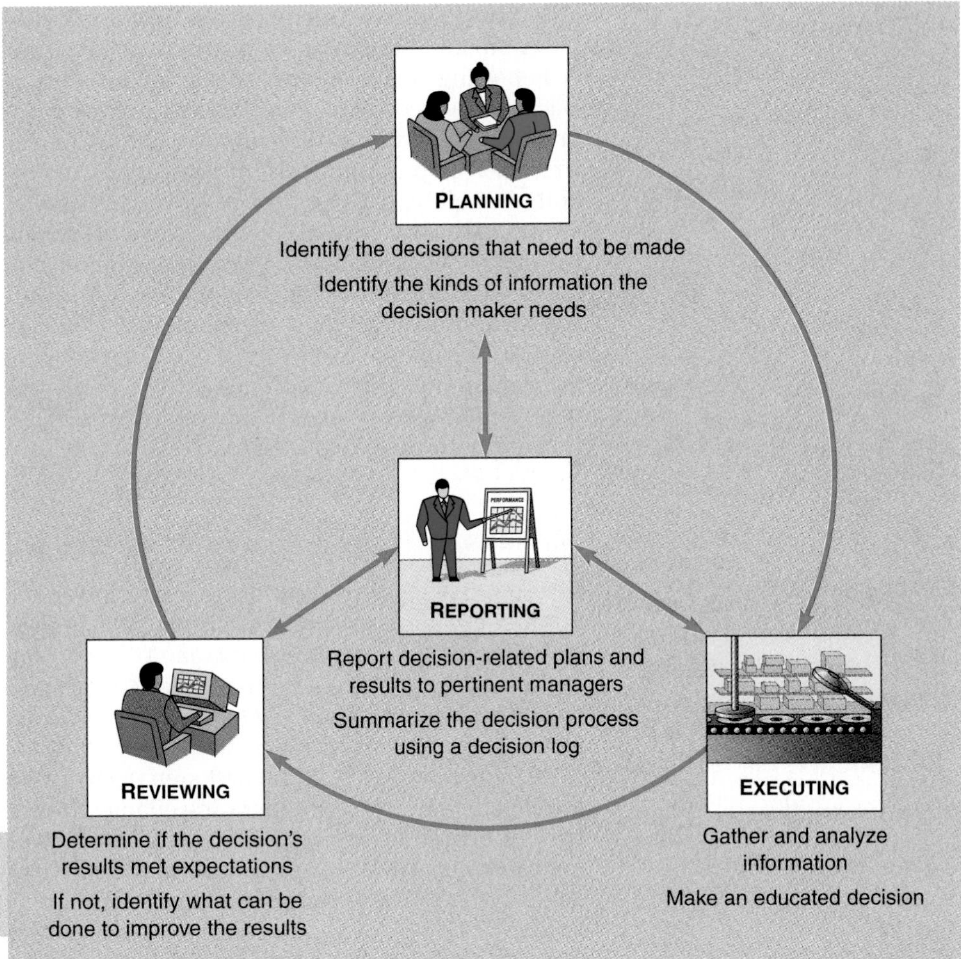

Figure 1
Decision-Support Information and the Management Cycle

native, and then make a decision. Mathematical formulas and computer programs are useful in organizing and analyzing decision support information, but the actual decision is made by the manager.

As illustrated in Figure 1, decision making is an integral part of the management cycle. In the planning stage, managers must identify the kinds of decisions that need to be made. For example, Jason Corporation is planning to expand one of its product lines. The decision facing management is whether to make the additional parts needed for the expansion or to purchase them from an outside vendor. Before the managers can begin the decision process, they need to know what kinds of information will support their decision. In this case, the managers need to know the costs of making the parts and the costs of buying them from an outside supplier.

In the executing stage of the management cycle, information is gathered and analyzed and a decision is made. At the Jason Corporation, when all the costs of making versus buying the needed parts have been assembled and analyzed, management can make an educated decision.

In the reviewing stage of the management cycle, each decision is evaluated to determine if the forecasted results were obtained. If the results are not as predicted, corrective action must be identified and taken. Suppose that the management of Jason Corporation decided to purchase the parts they need from an outside supplier. Once the purchasing process is underway, the managers will want to compare actual costs with the projected costs on which their decision was based. They will also want to know if the parts are being delivered on time and if they are meeting the company's standards for quality.

Reporting takes place continuously during the decision-making process. Decision-related plans and results should be promptly reported to the managers involved. In addition, for each decision, a log should be maintained that summarizes each step in the decision process. Such a log can provide useful information, both during the reviewing stage and when similar decisions are made in the future. At the Jason Corporation, the managers prepared and received many reports about the make-or-buy decision. During the planning stage, reports helped the managers analyze the costs of making versus buying the parts. During the executing stage, the managers issued a report explaining their decision and specifying how to implement it. During the reviewing stage, the managers received many reports analyzing the actual and forecasted costs of the parts, delivery data, and levels of quality. Periodically, the managers prepared reports that evaluated the success of the decision and recommended future actions.

The Management Decision Process

OBJECTIVE 2

***Identify the steps in the management decision process and define* relevant decision information**

Related Text Assignments:
Q: 2, 3
SE: 2, 3
E: 2, 3, 4, 8
SD: 1, 3

Instructional Strategy: To bring the concept of the management decision process to life, have students complete SD 1 individually. In class, form small groups, and ask group members to share the contents of the letters they wrote. Also ask the groups to discuss how the process would differ for purchasing a fleet of cars. A representative of each group can summarize his or her group's discussion for the entire class as the instructor highlights the similarities and differences of the groups' results.

Decision making is the process of analyzing and selecting a course of action from a number of alternatives. The decision-making process becomes complex when several alternatives must be evaluated. Although many decisions are unique and are not made according to strict rules, certain events occur frequently in the analysis of business problems. The five steps managers take in making decisions and following up on them is known as the management decision process.

As shown in Figure 2, the first step in the process is the discovery of an existing problem or a need for an operating change, such as the expansion or contraction of current operating capacity. In step 2, the management accountant works with the managers involved in the decision to identify all reasonable courses of action that will solve the problem or create the needed change. In step 3, the management accountant prepares a thorough analysis of each alternative course of action, identifying its total savings, possible additional costs, and other financial effects. Each alternative may require different cost information and involve different types of analyses. In some cases, past experience may provide useful information, but in other cases, the organization may have no previous experience or information.

In step 4, after studying the information gathered by the management accountant, the manager selects the best course of action. Note, however, that this is not the end of the decision-making process. In step 5, after the decision has been carried out, the management accountant studies its impact on the organization's operations. The resulting postdecision audit gives management feedback about the decision's results. If the solution is not completely satisfactory or if the problem still exists, a new course of action is needed and the decision process begins again. If the decision solved the problem or satisfied the operating need, then the decision process is complete.

Relevant Decision Information

Once managers determine that a project is worthy of consideration, they must obtain information about all the alternative courses of action. Management accounting supports decision making by presenting comparative analyses of alternative actions. For each alternative, it is necessary to determine the estimated costs, revenues, and resource requirements. The volume of data, however, should not be overwhelming. The management accountant must select the appropriate amount of relevant information about each alternative.

How does the management accountant decide which information is relevant and which is not? Relevant decision information is data about future costs, revenues, and

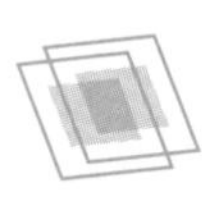

Point to Emphasize: The postdecision audit (step 5) is vital to the management decision process, but it is often overlooked once the decision is made (step 4). Overlooking the final step can undermine the entire decision-making process.

No need for further action (no problem)

1 Discover a problem or need for change

2 Identify the alternative courses of action

3 Analyze the effects of each alternative on business operations

4 Select the best alternative

5 Conduct a postdecision audit (feedback)

Figure 2
The Management Decision Process

resource usage that differ among the alternatives being evaluated. Facts that are the same for each alternative are not relevant. For example, assume that a company is considering the purchase of a computer-assisted machine to replace a labor-intensive operation. Four machines are being considered. If projected total sales are the same for each of the four alternatives, sales information should not appear in the comparative evaluation. Similarly, although the accountant may use past data to prepare cost estimates of alternatives, historical data are not relevant to projections of future operations and do not guide managers in choosing between alternatives.

Let's look at how the management decision cycle and relevant decision information relate to the decision process. Assume that the management of the Huertas Company has discovered that its manual accounts payable system is inefficient and needs to be replaced by an automated system (decision step **1**—discovery of a need). A task force has identified two companies that sell automated equipment that would satisfy the Huertas Company's needs (decision step **2**—identification of alternative courses of action). The following annual costs have been gathered for each alternative, including keeping the old manual system:

	Keep Manual System	**Automated System 1**	**Automated System 2**
Supervisory salaries	$40,000	$20,000	$20,000
Clerical wages	56,000	—	—
Computer lease cost	—	45,000	42,000
Electricity costs	12,000	18,000	17,500
Operating supplies	6,000	10,000	12,000
Controller's salary	60,000	60,000	60,000

The controller's staff prepared the comparative analysis shown in Exhibit 1 and presented it to management (decision step **3**—analysis of alternatives). Based on

Exhibit 1. Comparative Analysis—Huertas Company

Huertas Company
Comparative Analysis
Accounts Payable Systems

Relevant Costs	Alternative 1 Keep Manual System	Alternative 2 Lease Automated System 1	Alternative 3 Lease Automated System 2
Supervisory salaries	$ 40,000	$20,000	$20,000
Clerical wages	56,000	—	—
Computer lease cost	—	45,000	42,000
Electricity costs	12,000	18,000	17,500
Operating supplies	6,000	10,000	12,000
Total relevant costs	$114,000	$93,000	$91,500

Low-cost alternative

that analysis, management chose Automated System 2 because it will cost $1,500 less to operate than System 1 and because keeping the manual system would be the most costly choice of all (decision step **4**—selection of the best alternative). Note that the controller's salary was not included in the analysis in Exhibit 1 because it is the same for all alternatives and is, therefore, irrelevant. Once Automated System 2 is installed, the management accountant will study its costs to make sure the correct decision was made (decision step **5**—postdecision audit).

Incremental Analysis

OBJECTIVE 3

Use incremental analysis to develop decision data

Related Text Assignments:
Q: 4, 5
SE: 4
E: 4
MRA: 2, 3

Teaching Note: Incremental analysis is a technique used not only by businesses, but also by individuals to solve daily problems. You might reinforce this concept by asking your students to perform an incremental analysis to decide which of two vehicles, a Saturn coupe and a Lincoln Town Car, to purchase, given different operating costs and gas mileage.

Incremental analysis helps managers to compare alternative projects by focusing on differences in projected revenues and costs. The management accountant organizes relevant information to determine which alternative contributes the most to profits or incurs the lowest costs. Only data that differ for each alternative appear in the report. For example, assume that a management accountant is preparing a report to help the management of the Thomas Company decide which of two mill blade grinders, C or W, to buy. The accountant has collected the following estimated annual sales and operating costs for the two machines.

	Grinder C	Grinder W
Increase in revenue	$16,200	$19,800
Increase in annual operating costs		
Direct materials	4,800	4,800
Direct labor	2,200	4,100
Variable manufacturing overhead	2,100	3,050
Fixed manufacturing overhead (depreciation included)	5,000	5,000

An incremental analysis shows increases or decreases in revenues and costs that arise from each alternative. Since direct materials and fixed manufacturing overhead costs are the same for each alternative, they are not included in the analysis.

Point to Emphasize: Both revenues and costs come into play in an incremental analysis. In the Difference column, positive numbers indicate increases in revenues or savings, and negative numbers (numbers in parentheses) indicate costs.

Exhibit 2. Incremental Analysis–Thomas Company

Thomas Company
Incremental Analysis

	Grinder C	Grinder W	Difference in Favor of Grinder W
Increase in revenues	$16,200	$19,800	$3,600
Increase in operating costs			
Direct labor	$ 2,200	$ 4,100	($1,900)
Variable manufacturing overhead	2,100	3,050	(950)
Total increase in operating costs	$ 4,300	$ 7,150	($2,850)
Resulting change in income	$11,900	$12,650	$ 750

If you assume that the purchase prices and the useful lives of the two grinders are the same, the incremental analysis in Exhibit 2 shows that Grinder W generates $750 more in income than Grinder C. Thus, the decision based on this report is to purchase Grinder W.

Since incremental analysis focuses on the differences between alternatives, it identifies both the benefits and the drawbacks of each. An incremental analysis simplifies the evaluation for the decision maker and reduces the time needed to choose the best course of action.

Contribution Margin Reporting and Decisions

The contribution margin format of income reporting, as discussed in the chapter on cost-volume-profit analysis and variable costing, is used a great deal in decision analysis. It is most commonly used when an organization is deciding whether to eliminate a product line or operating segment, such as a division. It is also used to evaluate new product lines, optimize product sales mix, and make decisions based on the contributions of different sales territories. Many of these uses are explained in detail later in this chapter.

Special Decision Reports

Point to Emphasize: An incremental analysis should not be limited to quantifiable data. Subjective and qualitative data should always be incorporated into the decision when appropriate.

Income statements in the contribution margin format and incremental analyses work best when comparing quantitative information. In some cases, however, managers might be considering many alternatives, each of which is best in certain circumstances. One may generate more profits, while another diversifies the organization's product line. A third alternative may prevent a huge layoff, bolstering the organization's goodwill. Even though several equally good alternatives may be available, management must choose only one. In such cases, qualitative information must support or replace the quantitative analyses, and the management accountant must use imagination to prepare a special decision report that demonstrates which alternative is best under the circumstances.

For most special decision reports, there is no one correct, set structure. Experienced accountants prepare such reports to fit individual situations. In this course, you can solve most of the problems by following the examples in the text.

BUSINESS BULLETIN: ETHICS IN PRACTICE

When Roger B. Smith, the former chairman and CEO of General Motors, was interviewed on the subject of ethics, he had the following to say. ". . . the world is not neat and orderly, and arriving at an ethical decision can be difficult. It has been wisely observed that 'It is easy to do what is right; it is hard to know what is right.' . . . In the final analysis, each of us must exercise individual judgment and answer to our own conscience. As General Motors employees, we should never do anything we would be ashamed to explain to our family or afraid to see on the front page of the local newspaper.

"Ethical conduct in business goes beyond this, however. For example, one of the basic needs top management has is to receive reliable data and honest opinions from people throughout the organization. Management needs to hear bad news as well as good news. Too often, subordinates are reluctant to tell all of the details of a project or assignment that has failed or is in trouble. This very human trait occurs in all walks of life, whether personal, business, or government, and contributes to the making of bad decisions. In short, ethics is an essential element of success in business."[2]

But remember that in practice, management accountants must create report formats appropriate to existing circumstances. Such challenges contribute to the dynamic role of the management accountant.

Operating Decisions

Many business decisions can be made using income statements generated by variable costing and incremental analysis. In this section, we use those tools to select the best alternative when managers face (1) make-or-buy decisions, (2) special order decisions, (3) sales mix decisions, and (4) sell or process-further decisions.

Make-or-Buy Decisions

OBJECTIVE 4a

Prepare evaluations of alternatives for make-or-buy decisions

Related Text Assignments:
Q: 6, 7, 8, 9, 10
SE: 5, 6, 7
E: 5, 6, 7
P: 1, 2, 3, 6
SD: 2
MRA: 1

A common problem facing managers of manufacturing organizations is whether to make or to buy some or all of the parts used in product assembly. The goal of make-or-buy analysis is to help management select the more profitable choice by identifying the costs of each alternative and their effects on revenues and existing costs. The following factors are needed for this analysis.

To Make	To Buy
Need for additional machinery	Purchase price of item
Variable costs of making the item	Rent or net cash flow to be generated from vacated space in factory
Incremental fixed costs	Salvage value of unused machinery

The case of the Trenot Electronics Company illustrates a make-or-buy decision. For the past five years, the firm has purchased a small transistor casing from an outside supplier at a cost of $1.25 per casing. The supplier just informed Trenot Electronics that it is raising the price 20 percent, effective immediately. Trenot has idle machinery that could be adjusted to produce the casings. Trenot estimates the cost of direct materials at $84 per 100 casings, the amount of direct labor at three minutes of labor per casing at a rate of $8 per direct labor hour, and the cost of vari-

Common Student Error: When performing a make-or-buy analysis, students often incorporate irrelevant information, such as depreciation and other fixed costs. Emphasize that the production costs of manufacturing an item in-house are relevant only if they can be avoided by purchasing the necessary materials from an outside supplier.

Exhibit 3. Incremental Analysis: Make-or-Buy Decision

Trenot Electronics Company
Make-or-Buy Decision
Incremental Analysis

	Make	Buy	Difference in Favor of Make
Direct materials			
(20,000 ÷ 100 × $84)	$16,800	—	($16,800)
Direct labor			
(20,000 ÷ 20 × $8)	8,000	—	(8,000)
Variable manufacturing overhead			
(20,000 ÷ 20 × $4)	4,000	—	(4,000)
To purchase completed casings			
(20,000 × $1.50)	—	$30,000	30,000
Totals	$28,800	$30,000	$ 1,200

able manufacturing overhead at $4 per direct labor hour. Fixed manufacturing overhead includes $4,000 of depreciation per year and $6,000 of other fixed costs. Annual production and usage would be 20,000 casings. The space and machinery to produce the casing would be idle if the part were purchased. Should Trenot Electronics Company make or buy the casings?

Incremental analysis enables the accountant to organize the relevant data in a make-or-buy decision. Management can use the accountant's report to quickly analyze all relevant costs or revenues and to use that information to select the best alternative.

Exhibit 3 presents an incremental analysis of the two alternatives. All relevant costs are listed. Because the machinery has already been purchased and neither the machinery nor the required factory space has any other use, the depreciation costs and other fixed manufacturing overhead costs are the same for both alternatives, so they are not relevant to the decision. The cost of making the needed casings is $28,800. The cost of buying 20,000 casings will be $30,000 at the increased purchase price. The company would save $1,200 by making the casings, and it should do so.

Special Order Decisions

OBJECTIVE 4b

Prepare evaluations of alternatives for special order decisions

Management is often faced with special order decisions, that is, whether to accept or reject unexpected orders for products at prices below normal market prices. Special orders usually call for the manufacture of large numbers of similar products to be sold in bulk (packaged in large containers). Special order analysis is designed to help management decide whether to accept or reject a special order.

A number of factors must be taken into consideration when making a special order decision. Because management did not expect the order, it is not included in annual cost or sales estimates. And, since such an order is a one-time event, it should not be included in cost or revenue estimates for subsequent years. A company should consider a special order only if unused capacity exists. Moreover, before a firm accepts a special order, it must be sure that the products involved are sufficiently different from its regular product line to avoid violating federal price discrimination laws.

Goodman Sporting Goods, Inc., manufactures a complete line of sports equipment. Deck Enterprises operates a large chain of discount stores. Deck has approached Goodman with a special order for 30,000 special cross-stitched baseballs to be bulk packed in boxes containing 500 baseballs each. Deck is willing to pay $2.45 per baseball.

The Goodman Accounting Department knows that annual expected production is 400,000 baseballs, the current year's production is 410,000 baseballs, and the maximum production capacity is 450,000 baseballs. The following additional information is available:

Point to Emphasize: Even though the cost per baseball (based on production of 400,000) is $3.00, the relevant costs for making this decision are $2.00 (direct materials, direct labor, and variable overhead) plus the bulk packaging cost of $2,500. The fixed costs and usual packaging costs are irrelevant because they are not incremental with this special order.

Unit cost data	
Direct materials	$ .90
Direct labor	.60
Manufacturing overhead	
Variable	.50
Fixed ($100,000 ÷ 400,000)	.25
Packaging per unit	.30
Advertising ($60,000 ÷ 400,000)	.15
Other fixed selling and administrative costs ($120,000 ÷ 400,000)	.30
Total unit cost	$ 3.00
Unit selling price	$ 4.00
Total estimated bulk packaging costs (30,000 baseballs: 500 per box)	$2,500

Should Goodman Sporting Goods, Inc., accept Deck's offer?

A comparative analysis in the contribution margin format appears in Exhibit 4. The report shows net income for the Baseball Division's operations both with and without the Deck offer. The only costs affected by the order are for direct materials, direct labor, variable manufacturing overhead, and packaging. Packaging costs will increase, but only by the amount of the added bulk packaging. All other costs will remain the same. The net result of accepting the special order is an $11,000 increase in contribution margin (and net income). This amount is verified by the following computation.

$$\begin{aligned}\text{Net Gain} &= [(\text{Unit Selling Price} - \text{Unit Variable Mfg. Costs}) \times \text{Units}] - \text{Bulk Packaging Costs}\\ &= [(\$2.45 - \$2.00) \times 30{,}000] - \$2{,}500\\ &= \$13{,}500 - \$2{,}500\\ &= \$11{,}000\end{aligned}$$

Thus, the analysis reveals that the special order from Deck Enterprises should be accepted.

For special order analysis, both contribution margin analysis and incremental analysis can be used. In this case, because we wanted to see how the decision would affect net income, we used contribution margin analysis. Incremental analysis would have eliminated all fixed costs because they were the same for each alternative. Contribution margin analysis highlights the effect of changes in variable costs on contribution margin and net income.

The fixed costs of existing facilities would normally not change if a special order were accepted and are, therefore, usually irrelevant to the decision. If, on the other hand, additional fixed costs would be incurred, they would be relevant to the decision. Examples of relevant fixed costs include the purchase of additional machinery, an increase in supervisory help, or an increase in insurance premiums required by a specific order.

Point to Emphasize: The difference in net income equals the $11,000 computed earlier.

Exhibit 4. Contribution Margin Analysis: Special Order Decision

Goodman Sporting Goods, Inc.
Special Order Decision
Contribution Margin Analysis

	Without Deck Order (410,000 products)	With Deck Order (440,000 products)
Sales	$1,640,000	$1,713,500
Less variable costs		
Direct materials	$ 369,000	$ 396,000
Direct labor	246,000	264,000
Variable manufacturing overhead	205,000	220,000
Packaging costs	123,000	125,500
Total variable costs	$ 943,000	$1,005,500
Contribution margin	$ 697,000	$ 708,000
Less fixed costs		
Manufacturing overhead	$ 100,000	$ 100,000
Advertising	60,000	60,000
Selling and administrative	120,000	120,000
Total fixed costs	$ 280,000	$ 280,000
Net income	$ 417,000	$ 428,000

Sales Mix Decisions

OBJECTIVE 4c

Prepare evaluations of alternatives for sales mix decisions.

Point to Emphasize: When resources such as direct materials or direct labor are scarce, the objective is to maximize the contribution margin per unit of scarce resource.

Profit analysis and maximization are possible only when the profitability of all product lines is known. How does General Motors Corporation determine which of its automobile products is most profitable? GM may also wish to determine which product or products contribute the most to company profitability in relation to the amount of capital assets or other scarce resources needed to produce the item(s). To answer these questions, the accountant must measure the contribution margin of each product. The next step is to determine a set of ratios of contribution margin to the required limiting resource. Once this step is completed, management should request a marketing study to identify the upper limits of demand on the most profitable products. If product profitability can be computed and adequate market demand exists, management should shift production to the more profitable products, given the company's resources.

Many kinds of decisions can be related to the approach described here. Sales mix analysis determines the most profitable combination of sales when a company produces more than one product or offers more than one service. Closely related to sales mix analysis is the product line profitability study, which is designed to discover which products are losing money for the company. The same decision approach is used, but the goal is to eliminate any unprofitable product line(s). Another area of study is corporate segment analysis. The contribution margin approach is again used, this time with the goal of isolating production costs to identify any unprofitable segment(s). If corrective action is not possible, management should eliminate the noncontributing segment(s). Even though we will not give specific examples of a

Point to Emphasize: Although Product S yields the lowest contribution margin per unit, only one machine hour (the scarce resource) is required. In this unique situation, Product S is the best of the three alternative products to market; Product C is the worst.

Exhibit 5. Contribution Margin Analysis: Sales Mix Decision

Bradley Enterprises
Sales Mix Decision
Contribution Margin Analysis

	Product C	Product S	Product F
Unit sales price	$24.00	$18.00	$32.00
Variable costs			
Manufacturing	$12.50	$10.00	$18.75
Selling	6.50	5.00	6.25
Total variable costs	$19.00	$15.00	$25.00
Contribution margin per unit (A)	$ 5.00	$ 3.00	$ 7.00
Machine hours required per unit (B)	2	1	2.5
Contribution margin per machine hour (A ÷ B)	$ 2.50	$ 3.00	$ 2.80

product line profitability study or a corporate segment analysis, it is important to remember that they use the same technique as sales mix analysis.

Assume that the management of Bradley Enterprises is analyzing its sales mix. The company manufactures three products—C, S, and F—using the same production equipment. The total productive capacity is being used. Following are the product line statistics.

	Product C	Product S	Product F
Current production and sales (units)	20,000	30,000	18,000
Machine hours per product	2	1	2.5
Selling price per unit	$24.00	$18.00	$32.00
Unit variable manufacturing costs	$12.50	$10.00	$18.75
Unit variable selling costs	$6.50	$5.00	$6.25

Should the company try to sell more of one product and less of another?

Because total productive capacity is being used, the only way to expand the production of one product is to reduce the production of another. The sales mix analysis of Bradley Enterprises is shown in Exhibit 5. Though contribution reporting is used here, contribution margin per product is not the important figure for a decision about shifts in sales mix. In the analysis, Product F has the highest contribution margin per unit. However, all products use the same machinery and all machine hours are filled. So machine hours are the scarce resource.

The analysis in Exhibit 5 goes one step beyond the computation of contribution margin per unit. A sales mix decision such as this one should use two decision variables: contribution margin per unit and machine hours required per unit. For instance, Product C requires two machine hours to generate $5 of contribution margin. But Product S would generate $6 of contribution margin using the same two machine hours. For this reason, we have calculated contribution margin per machine hour. Based on this information, management can readily see that they should produce and sell as much of Product S as possible. Next, they should push Product F. If any productive capacity remains, they should manufacture product C.

Sell or Process-Further Decisions

OBJECTIVE 4d

Prepare evaluations of alternatives for sell or process-further decisions

Sometimes two or more products or services are created simultaneously from a common raw material or input. Such products, called joint products, cannot be identified as separate products during some or all of the production process. Only at a specific point, called the split-off point, do joint products become separate and identifiable. Petroleum manufacturing often results in joint products. For example, when Exxon Corporation refines crude oil, it is only after the split-off point that gasoline, motor oil, and kerosene become identifiable as separate products.

Some products may be sold at the split-off point and others may be processed further. Extra processing adds value to a product and increases its selling price, but it also adds costs. Thus, manufacturers must often decide which approach will be more profitable. Sell or process-further analysis helps managers determine whether to sell a joint product at the split-off point or process it further. This technique enables managers to analyze the incremental costs and revenues of the two possible courses of action to see whether the increase in total revenue will exceed the additional costs of processing. *Joint costs incurred before split-off do not affect the decision.* Those costs are irrelevant to the decision because they are incurred regardless of the point at which the products are sold. Only future costs that will differ between alternatives are relevant to the decision.

Maximizing profits is the objective of sell or process-further decisions. For example, assume that Hilbrich Gardening Supplies, Inc., produces various products to enhance plant growth. In one process, three products—Gro-Pow, Gro-Pow II, and Gro-Supreme—emerge from the joint initial phase. For each 20,000-pound batch of materials converted into products, $120,000 in joint production costs are incurred. At split-off, 50 percent of the output becomes Gro-Pow, 30 percent becomes Gro-Pow II, and 20 percent becomes Gro-Supreme. Each product must be processed beyond split-off, and the following additional variable costs are incurred.

Product	Pounds	Additional Processing Costs
Gro-Pow	10,000	$24,000
Gro-Pow II	6,000	38,000
Gro-Supreme	4,000	33,500
Totals	20,000	$95,500

Linda & Parks Landscapers has offered to purchase any or all joint products at split-off for the following prices per pound: Gro-Pow, $8; Gro-Pow II, $24; and Gro-Supreme, $40. To help decide whether to sell at split-off or process the products further, Hilbrich management requested an incremental analysis. This analysis is to compare increases in revenue and increases in processing costs for each alternative.

Exhibit 6 reveals the selling prices of the three products at split-off and if processed further. This exhibit also contains the incremental analysis. As illustrated, products Gro-Pow and Gro-Supreme should be processed further since each will cause a significant increase in overall company profit. If Gro-Pow II can be sold to Linda & Parks Landscapers, the company will avoid a $2,000 loss from further processing. Note that the $120,000 in joint processing costs are irrelevant to the decision since they will be incurred with either alternative.

Measuring incremental costs for additional processing beyond split-off can create problems. Additional costs of direct materials, direct labor, and variable manufacturing overhead are incremental since they are caused by additional processing. However, supervisors' salaries, property taxes, insurance, and other fixed costs incurred regardless of the production decision are not incremental costs. Incremental processing costs should include only production costs if a product is

Exhibit 6. Incremental Analysis: Sell or Process-Further Decision

Hilbrich Gardening Supplies, Inc.
Sell or Process-Further Decision
Incremental Analysis

Unit selling price data

Product	If Sold at Split-Off	If Sold After Processing Further
Gro-Pow	$ 8	$12
Gro-Pow II	24	30
Gro-Supreme	40	50

Incremental analysis per 20,000-pound batch

Product	(1) Pounds	(2) Total Revenue if Sold at Split-Off	(3) Total Revenue if Sold After Processing Further	(4) Incremental Revenue (3) − (2)	(5) Incremental Costs	(6) Effect on Overall Profit (4) − (5)
Gro-Pow	10,000	$ 80,000	$120,000	$40,000	$24,000	$16,000
Gro-Pow II	6,000	144,000	180,000	36,000	38,000	(2,000)
Gro-Supreme	4,000	160,000	200,000	40,000	33,500	6,500

processed beyond split-off. Fixed manufacturing overhead costs common to other production activity must be excluded from a sell or process-further incremental analysis.

Capital Expenditure Decisions

OBJECTIVE 5

Identify three techniques commonly used to analyze proposed capital expenditures, and explain the measures of projected costs and revenues used in those analyses

Related Text Assignments:
Q: 11, 12, 13
SE: 8
MRA: 3

Among the most significant decisions facing management are capital expenditure decisions which are decisions about when and how much to spend on capital facilities. A capital facility could include machinery, systems, or processes; building additions, renovations, or new structures; or entire new divisions or product lines. Thus, decisions about installing new equipment, replacing old equipment, expanding the production area by adding to a building, buying or building a new factory, or acquiring another company are all examples of capital expenditure decisions. Spending on capital assets is expensive. A new factory or production system may cost millions of dollars and require several years to implement. When making capital expenditure decisions, managers must be careful to select the alternative that contributes the most to profits.

Capital Budgeting: A Cooperative Venture

The process of making decisions about capital expenditures is called capital budgeting, or *capital expenditure decision analysis.* This analysis is an important tool for large corporations, such as MicroSoft, and for smaller companies, like Standard Locknut & Lockwasher, Inc., in Westfield, Indiana. Capital budgeting consists of

Discussion Question: What is capital budgeting? **Answer:** Capital budgeting is a decision process for the purchase of capital facilities such as buildings and equipment.

identifying the need for a capital facility, analyzing courses of action to meet the need, preparing reports for managers, choosing the best alternative, and rationing funds among competing needs. People in every part of the organization participate in capital budgeting. Financial analysts supply a target cost of capital or desired rate of return and an estimate of how much money can be spent annually on capital facilities. Marketing specialists predict sales trends and new product demands, which help in determining operations that need expansion or new equipment. Managers at all levels help identify facility needs and often prepare preliminary cost estimates of the desired capital expenditures. The same people implement the project selected and try to keep results within revenue and cost estimates.

The management accountant gathers and organizes the required information into a workable, readable form. Generally, he or she applies one or more decision evaluation methods to the information gathered for each alternative. The most common evaluation methods are: (1) the accounting rate-of-return method, (2) the payback period method, and (3) the net present value method. The accounting rate-of-return method is designed to measure the benefit of a potential capital expenditure project by dividing the project's average annual net income by the average cost of the investment. The rates of the projects competing for the same investment funds are compared, and the ones that earn the required minimum rate are approved for implementation. Under the payback period method, the decision to invest in a capital project is based on the minimum length of time it will take to earn back in cash the amount of the initial investment. Under the net present value method, all future cash flows for each proposed project are discounted to their present value, the amount of the initial investment is subtracted from the sum of those amounts, and the projects with the highest positive net present value—the amount that exceeds the initial investment—are selected for implementation. Before we can expand on the use of these methods to evaluate proposed capital expenditures, we must explore the cost and revenue measures relevant to the decision process.

Cost and Revenue Measures Used in Capital Budgeting

When evaluating a proposed capital expenditure, the management accountant must predict how the new asset will perform and how it will benefit the organization. Various measures of costs and revenues are used to estimate the benefits to be derived from such projects.

Point to Emphasize: Accrual-based net income is incorporated into the accounting rate-of-return calculation. Net cash flow, however, is the basis for the payback period and net present value methods.

Net Income and Cash Flow Each capital expenditure analysis must include a measure of the expected benefit from the investment project. For the accounting rate-of-return method, this measure is net income, calculated in the usual way. Increases in net income resulting from the capital expenditure must be determined for each alternative. All other methods of evaluating capital expenditure proposals use projected cash flows. Net cash inflow, the balance of increases in cash receipts over increases in cash payments resulting from a capital expenditure, is used in evaluating capital projects when either the payback period or the net present value method is employed. In some cases, equipment replacement decisions involve alternatives that do not increase current revenue. In such cases, cost savings measure the benefits resulting from the proposed capital investments. Either net cash flow or cost savings can be used as a basis for an evaluation, but one should not be confused with the other. If cash receipts are involved in the analysis, then net cash flow is used. If only cash outlays are involved, then cost savings are used. Each of the alternatives must be measured and evaluated consistently.

Equal Versus Unequal Cash Flows Projected cash flows may be the same for each year of an asset's life or they may vary from year to year. Unequal cash flows are common and must be analyzed for each year of an asset's life. Proposed projects with equal annual cash flows require less detailed analysis. A project with equal cash flows and one with unequal cash flows are both illustrated and explained later in this chapter.

Point to Emphasize: The book value of an asset targeted for replacement is irrelevant because it simply represents the undepreciated portion of a sunk cost. The proceeds upon sale, however, are relevant.

Book Value of Assets Book value is the undepreciated portion of the original cost of a long-term asset. When evaluating a decision to replace an asset, the book value of the old asset is irrelevant since it is a past, or historical, cost and will not be altered by the decision. Net proceeds from the asset's sale or disposal are relevant, however, because the proceeds affect cash flows and may differ for each alternative.

Clarification Note: Although depreciation is a noncash expense, it actually produces a cash inflow from its tax-deductibility and resulting tax savings.

Depreciation Expense Since depreciation is a noncash expense requiring no cash outlay during the period, it is irrelevant to decision analyses based on cash flow.

Disposal or Salvage Values Proceeds from the sale of an old asset are current cash inflows and are relevant to evaluating a proposed capital expenditure. Projected disposal or salvage values of replacement equipment are also relevant because they represent future cash inflows and usually differ among alternatives. Remember, salvage values will be received at the end of the asset's estimated life.

Time Value of Money Cash flows of equal dollar amounts separated by an interval of time have different current values, a phenomenon known as the time value of money. The values differ because of the effect of compound interest. This concept assumes that invested funds should provide a return and the amount of that return is compounded annually by an interest factor or rate.

Accounting Rate-of-Return Method

OBJECTIVE 6a

Use the accounting rate-of-return method to analyze proposed capital expenditures

Related Text Assignments:
Q: 14, 15, 16, 17
SE: 9
E: 9, 10, 11, 12
P: 4, 5, 7, 8
SD: 4
MRA: 3, 4

The accounting rate-of-return method is a crude but easy way to measure the estimated performance of a capital investment. With this method, expected performance is measured using two variables: (1) estimated annual net income from the project and (2) average investment cost. The basic equation is as follows:

$$\text{Accounting Rate of Return} = \frac{\text{Project's Average Annual Net Income}}{\text{Average Investment Cost}}$$

To compute average annual net income, use the cost and revenue data prepared for evaluating the project. Average investment in a proposed capital facility is figured as follows:

$$\text{Average Investment} = \left(\frac{\text{Total Investment} - \text{Salvage Value}}{2}\right) + \text{Salvage Value}$$

To see how this equation is used in evaluating a capital expenditure decision, assume the Gordon Company is interested in purchasing a new bottling machine. The company's management will consider only those projects that promise to yield more than a 16 percent return. Estimates for the proposal include revenue increases of $17,900 a year and operating cost increases of $11,696 a year (including depreciation and taxes). The cost of the machine is $51,000. Its salvage value is $3,000. To determine if the company should invest in the machine, compute the accounting rate of return as follows:

$$\begin{aligned}\text{Accounting Rate of Return} &= \frac{\$17{,}900 - \$11{,}696}{\left(\frac{\$51{,}000 - \$3{,}000}{2}\right) + \$3{,}000} \\ &= \frac{\$6{,}204}{\$27{,}000} \\ &= 22.98\%\end{aligned}$$

Point to Emphasize: The accounting rate-of-return method is appealing because it is easy to understand. It has flaws, however, such as the omission of the time value of money.

The projected rate of return is higher than the 16 percent minimum desired rate, so management should think seriously about making the investment.

The accounting rate-of-return method is widely used because it is easy to understand and apply. It does have several disadvantages, however. First, because net income is averaged over the life of the investment, it is not a reliable figure. Actual net income may vary considerably from the estimates. Second, the method is unreliable if estimated annual income differs from year to year. Finally, the time value of money is not considered in the computations. Thus, future and present dollars are treated as equal.

Cash Flow and the Payback Period Method

OBJECTIVE 6b

Use the payback period method to analyze proposed capital expenditures

Discussion Question: What does the payback period method measure? **Answer:** It measures the estimated length of time necessary to recover in cash the cost of an investment.

Instead of measuring the rate of return, many managers estimate the cash flow generated by a capital investment. Their goal is to determine the minimum time it will take to recover the initial investment. If two investment alternatives are being studied, management should choose the investment that pays back its initial cost in the shortest time. That period of time is known as the payback period, and the method of evaluation is called the payback period method. The payback period is computed as follows.

$$\text{Payback Period} = \frac{\text{Cost of Investment}}{\text{Annual Net Cash Inflow}}$$

To apply the payback period method to the proposed capital investment of the Gordon Company, determine the net cash flow. To do so, first find and eliminate the effects of all noncash revenue and expense items included in the analysis of net income. In this case, the only noncash expense or revenue is machine depreciation. To calculate this amount, you must know the asset's life and the depreciation method. Suppose the Gordon Company uses the straight-line method of depreciation, and the new bottling machine will have a ten-year estimated service life. Using this information and the facts given earlier, the payback period is computed as follows.

Teaching Note: Your students may wonder why the estimated salvage value is ignored in this calculation. Explain that the payback period logically must be the same, regardless of the expected salvage value. In addition, they may be confused by the \$4,800 deduction for depreciation. Explain that depreciation is merely being "backed out" because it is a noncash expense.

$$\text{Annual Depreciation} = \frac{\text{Cost} - \text{Salvage Value}}{10 \text{ (years)}}$$

$$= \frac{\$51{,}000 - \$3{,}000}{10}$$

$$= \$4{,}800 \text{ per year}$$

$$\text{Payback Period} = \frac{\text{Cost of Machine}}{\text{Cash Revenue} - \text{Cash Expenses}}$$

$$= \frac{\$51{,}000}{\$17{,}900 - (\$11{,}696 - \$4{,}800)}$$

$$= \frac{\$51{,}000}{\$11{,}004}$$

$$= 4.635 \text{ years}$$

If the company's desired payback period is five years or less, this proposal would be approved.

If a proposed capital expenditure has unequal annual net cash inflows, the payback period is determined by subtracting each annual amount (in chronological order) from the cost of the capital facility. When a zero balance is reached, the payback period is determined. This will often occur in the middle of a year. The portion of the final year is computed by dividing the amount needed to reach zero into the entire year's cash inflow. The Review Problem at the end of the chapter illustrates this process.

BUSINESS BULLETIN: BUSINESS PRACTICE

Activity-based costing (ABC) is often used in the preparation of an organization's annual operating budget. In such cases, data must be broken down by the various activities of the organization. The same approach can be taken to creating decision information for capital budgeting. Using ABC, the management accountant identifies the operating activities believed to be affected by the decision and forecasts cash flows for each of the activities. This approach provides a more detailed look at future cash flows and increases the accuracy of the forecasts supporting the decision.[3]

Like the accounting rate of return method, the payback period method is widely used because it is easy to compute and understand. However, the disadvantages of this approach far outweigh its advantages. First, the payback method does not measure profitability. Second, it ignores differences in the present values of cash flows from different periods; thus it does not adjust cash flows for the time value of money. Finally, the payback period method emphasizes the time it takes to recover the investment rather than the long-run return on the investment.

Net Present Value Method

OBJECTIVE 6c

Use the net present value method to analyze proposed capital expenditures

Point to Emphasize: The net present value method carefully considers the time value of money. That is, it discounts all cash inflows and outflows to their present values so a valid assessment can be made in terms of current dollars.

Managers expect a capital asset to yield returns for its entire useful life. Capital budgeting techniques that treat cash flows from varying periods as if they have the same value in current dollars do not properly value the returns from an investment. As mentioned earlier, this is a shortcoming of both the accounting rate-of-return method and the payback period method.

The net present value method, in contrast, evaluates a capital investment by discounting its future cash flows to their present values. The multipliers used to find the present values of future cash flows are given in the present value tables in the appendix on future value and present value tables. Which multipliers to use is determined by connecting the minimum desired rate of return and the life of the asset or the length of time for which the amount is being discounted. Each cash inflow and cash outflow to be realized over the life of the asset is discounted to the present. If the present value of all expected future net cash inflows is greater than the amount of the current investment, the expenditure meets the minimum desired rate of return, and the project should be carried out.

The method of calculating a project's net present value depends on whether the annual cash flows are equal or unequal. If all annual net cash flows (inflows less outflows) are equal, the discount factor comes from Table 4 in the appendix on future value and present value tables. That table gives multipliers for the present value of $1 received each period for a given number of periods. If annual cash flows are equal, one computation will cover all periods involved. If, however, expected cash inflows and outflows differ from year to year, each year's cash flow must be individually discounted to the present. Such discount factors are found in Table 3 of the same appendix. The multipliers in that table are used to find the present value of $1 to be received (or paid out) at the end of a given number of periods.

The following example shows the difference in the present value analysis of expenditures with equal and unequal cash flows. Suppose the Janus Metal Products Company is deciding which of two stamping machines to buy. The blue machine has equal expected annual net cash inflows and the black machine has unequal annual cash flows.

	Blue Machine	Black Machine
Purchase price: January 1, 20x1	$16,500	$16,500
Salvage value	—	—
Estimated useful life	5 years	5 years
Estimated net cash inflows		
20x1	$5,000	$6,000
20x2	$5,000	$5,500
20x3	$5,000	$5,000
20x4	$5,000	$4,500
20x5	$5,000	$4,000

Point to Emphasize: A minimum desired rate of return is built into the net present value calculation. A positive net present value means the minimum rate has been surpassed. A negative net present value means it has not.

The company's minimum desired rate of return is 16 percent. Which—if either—of the two alternatives should be chosen?

The evaluation process is shown in Exhibit 7. The analysis of the blue machine is easier to prepare because it generates equal annual cash flows. The present value of net cash inflows for the five-year period for the blue machine is found by first locating the appropriate multiplier in Table 4 of the appendix on future value and present value tables. By matching the row for five years with the column for 16 percent, the factor 3.274 is found. Multiplying that factor by the $5,000 annual cash inflow yields $16,370, the present value of the total cash inflows from the blue machine. Comparing that figure with the machine's $16,500 purchase price results in a negative net present value of $130.

Analysis of the black machine gives a different result. Multipliers for this part of the analysis are found by using the same 16 percent rate. But five multipliers must be used, one for each year of the asset's life. Table 3 in the appendix on future value and present value tables applies here since each annual amount must be discounted to the present. For the black machine, the $16,851.50 present value of net cash

Point to Emphasize: The black machine (positive net present value) is worth serious consideration, whereas the blue machine (negative net present value) is not.

Exhibit 7. Net Present Value Analysis: Equal Versus Unequal Cash Flows

Janus Metal Products Company
Capital Expenditure Analysis
Net Present Value Method

Blue Machine	
Present value of cash inflows: ($5,000 × 3.274)	$16,370.00
Less purchase price of machine	16,500.00
Negative net present value	($ 130.00)
Black Machine	
Present value of cash inflows	
20x1 ($6,000 × .862)	$ 5,172.00
20x2 ($5,500 × .743)	4,086.50
20x3 ($5,000 × .641)	3,205.00
20x4 ($4,500 × .552)	2,484.00
20x5 ($4,000 × .476)	1,904.00
Total	$16,851.50
Less: Purchase price of machine	16,500.00
Positive net present value	$ 351.50

inflows is more than the $16,500 purchase price of the machine. Thus, there is a positive net present value of $351.50.

A positive net present value means the return on the asset exceeds the 16 percent minimum desired rate of return. A negative figure means the rate of return is below the minimum cutoff point. In the Janus Metal Products case, the right decision would be to purchase the black machine.

Enrichment Note: If possible, all three capital expenditure evaluation methods should be employed, to see if they agree.

The incorporation of the time value of money in the evaluation of a proposed capital expenditure is the main advantage of the net present value method. This method also measures total cash flows from an investment over its estimated useful life, so total profitability can be brought into the analysis as well. The principal disadvantage of the net present value method is that its computations are more difficult than those of the payback period method and the accounting rate-of-return method. As a result, many managers prefer the two simpler methods.

Tax Considerations in Capital Expenditure Decisions

In profit-oriented organizations, income taxes alter the amount and timing of cash flows of projects under consideration. To accurately assess the benefits of a capital expenditure, the management accountant must include the effects of taxes in the decision analysis. However, because of the complexity of the corporate tax tables and their impact on cash flow projections, a detailed discussion of the effects of income taxes on capital expenditure decisions has been left for a more advanced course.

Chapter Review

REVIEW OF LEARNING OBJECTIVES

1. **Describe the decision environment facing managers and state how managers use decision-support information in the management cycle.** Decision making usually involves the selection of the best of two or more alternative courses of action. Managers must analyze the information supporting each alternative, identify the most likely alternatives, project the results of each alternative, and then make a decision. Managers obtain information from sources both internal and external to their organizations. Internal sources include regular company reports, personal observation of practices and processes, company meetings, specific requests for information from other functions and departments, direct involvement in company activities, and results and actions related to past decisions. External sources include professional meetings and conferences, training and professional development seminars, journals and business publications, and analyses of the competition.

   Before selecting an alternative, a manager will gather as much information about all alternatives as time will permit. Some of that information will focus on details, such as productivity estimates of various machines, while other information will spell out the broader financial consequences of each alternative. Mathematical formulas and computer programs are useful in organizing and analyzing decision-support information, but the actual decision is made by the manager.

   Decision making is an integral part of the management cycle. During the planning stage, managers must identify the kind of decision they need to make and the kinds of information they need to support their decision. During the executing stage, information is gathered and analyzed and a decision is made. During the reviewing stage, the decision is evaluated to determine if the forecasted results were obtained and if corrective action is necessary. Reporting occurs continuously throughout the decision-making process.
2. **Identify the steps in the management decision process and define relevant decision information.** The decision process begins with the identification of an exist-

ing problem or the need for an operating change. Then the management accountant works with the appropriate managers to identify all reasonable courses of action to solve the problem or create the needed change. Next, the management accountant prepares a thorough analysis to determine the effects of each alternative on operations. Based on that information, the decision maker chooses the best alternative. After the decision has been carried out, the accountant should conduct a postdecision audit to see if the decision was correct or if other needs have arisen. Relevant decision information is any data about future costs, revenues, or resource usage that differ among the alternative courses of action. Projected sales or estimated costs of direct materials and direct labor, if they differ for each decision alternative, are examples of relevant information.

3. **Use incremental analysis to develop decision data.** In incremental analysis, alternatives are compared by looking only at their differences. After identifying the potential increases or decreases in costs and revenues that result from each alternative, the accountant highlights the relevant data. They are the values that differ among the alternatives. Only those values are included in the incremental analysis.

4. **Prepare evaluations of alternatives for (a) make-or-buy decisions, (b) special order decisions, (c) sales mix decisions, and (d) sell or process-further decisions.** Make-or-buy analysis helps managers decide whether to make or buy a part used in product assembly by identifying the costs of each alternative and their effects on revenues and existing costs. An incremental analysis of the expected costs and revenues for each alternative identifies the best alternative. To analyze special orders, the accountant must determine if there is unused capacity and find the lowest acceptable selling price for a product. Generally, fixed costs are irrelevant to the decision since those costs are covered by regular operations. Contribution margin analysis shows whether the special order increases income. Sales mix analysis is used to find the most profitable combination of sales when a company uses a common scarce resource to make more than one product. (A similar approach may be used for decisions based on the profitability of sales territories, service lines, or corporate segments.) The analysis uses the contribution margin format but goes one step further by examining the contribution margin per unit of scarce resource. Sell or process-further analysis is based on comparisons of incremental costs and revenues of selling a joint product at the split-off point or processing it further. Joint processing costs are irrelevant to this decision because they are identical for both alternatives.

5. **Identify three techniques commonly used to analyze proposed capital expenditures, and explain the measures of projected costs and revenues used in those analyses.** The accounting rate-of-return method is designed to measure the benefit of a potential capital expenditure project by dividing the project's average annual net income by the average cost of the investment. Using the payback period method, the decision to invest in a capital project is based on the minimum length of time it will take to earn back in cash the amount of the initial investment. Using the net present value method, all future cash flows for each proposed project are discounted back to their present value, the amount of the investment is subtracted from those amounts, and the ones with the highest positive net present value—the amount that exceeds the initial investment—are selected for implementation.

   The accounting rate-of-return method requires measures of net income. Other methods of evaluating capital expenditures evaluate net cash inflow or cash savings. The accountant must estimate whether the cash flows in each period are equal or unequal. Book values and depreciation expense of assets awaiting replacement are irrelevant. The net proceeds from the sale of an old asset and the estimated salvage value of a new asset represent future cash flows and must be part of the estimated benefit of a project. Proceeds from the sale of old assets and depreciation expense on replacement equipment change future cash flows and are relevant to cash flow analyses.

6. **Use (a) the accounting rate-of-return method, (b) the payback period method, and (c) the net present value method to analyze proposed capital expenditures.** When managers use the accounting rate-of-return method to evaluate proposed capital expenditures, they select the alternative that yields the highest ratio of average annual net income to average cost of investment and that exceeds the minimum desired rate of return. The payback period method of evaluating a proposed capital

expenditure identifies the project that recoups the original amount of the investment in the shortest time period. The net present value method incorporates the time value of money. Present values of future net cash inflows are measured to see if they exceed the current cost of the capital expenditure being evaluated.

REVIEW OF CONCEPTS AND TERMINOLOGY

The following concepts and terms were introduced in this chapter:

LO 5 **Accounting rate-of-return method:** A capital investment evaluation method designed to measure the benefit of a potential capital project; calculated by dividing the project's average annual net income by the average cost of the investment.

LO 5 **Book value:** The undepreciated portion of the original cost of a long-term asset.

LO 5 **Capital budgeting:** The process of making decisions about capital expenditures. It includes identifying the need for a capital facility, analyzing different courses of action to meet that need, preparing the reports for management, choosing the best alternative, and rationing funds among competing capital projects; also called *capital expenditure decision analysis.*

LO 5 **Capital expenditure decision:** A management decision about when and how much to spend on capital facilities.

LO 3 **Incremental analysis:** A technique used in decision analysis that compares alternatives by focusing on the differences in their projected revenues and costs.

LO 4 **Joint products:** Two or more products or services that are created simultaneously from a common raw material or input and cannot be identified as separate products until the split-off point in the process.

LO 4 **Make-or-buy analysis:** A decision analysis that helps management choose whether to make or buy some or all parts used in product assembly by identifying the costs of each alternative and their effects on revenues and existing costs.

LO 2 **Management decision process:** The five steps managers take in making decisions and following up on them.

LO 5 **Net cash inflow:** The balance of increases in cash receipts over increases in cash payments resulting from a proposed capital expenditure.

LO 5 **Net present value method:** A capital investment evaluation method that discounts future cash flows to their present value; the present value of all the future cash flows is compared with the amount of the proposed expenditure to determine if the investment should be made.

LO 5 **Noncash expense:** An expense that did not require a cash outlay during the period under review.

LO 5 **Payback period method:** A capital investment evaluation method that bases the decision to invest in a capital project on the minimum length of time it will take to earn back in cash the amount of the initial investment.

LO 2 **Relevant decision information:** Data about future costs, revenues, and resource usage that differ among the alternatives being evaluated.

LO 4 **Sales mix analysis:** A decision analysis designed to determine the most profitable combination of sales when a company produces more than one product or offers more than one service.

LO 4 **Sell or process-further analysis:** A decision analysis designed to help management determine whether to sell a joint product at split-off or process it further to increase its market price and profits.

LO 4 **Special order analysis:** A decision analysis designed to help management determine whether to accept or reject unexpected special product orders at prices below normal market prices.

LO 4 **Split-off point:** A specific point in the production or development process at which two or more joint products or services become separate and identifiable.

LO 5 **Time value of money:** The concept that cash flows of equal dollar amounts separated by a time interval have different present values because of the effect of compound interest.

REVIEW PROBLEM

Capital Expenditure Decision Analysis

LO 5
LO 6
The Roland Construction Company specializes in developing large shopping centers. The company is considering the purchase of a new earth-moving machine and has gathered the following information:

Purchase price	$600,000
Salvage value	$100,000
Useful life	4 years
Depreciation method	Straight line
Desired payback period	3 years
Minimum rate of return	15%

The cash flow estimates are as follows:

Year	Cash Inflows	Cash Outflows	Net Cash Inflow
1	$ 500,000	$260,000	$240,000
2	450,000	240,000	210,000
3	400,000	220,000	180,000
4	350,000	200,000	150,000
Totals	$1,700,000	$920,000	$780,000

REQUIRED

1. Analyze the Roland Construction Company's investment in the new earth-moving machine. In your analysis use (a) the accounting rate-of-return method, (b) the payback period method, and (c) the net present value method.
2. Summarize your findings from **1** and recommend a course of action.

ANSWER TO REVIEW PROBLEM

1. The increase in net income is as follows:

Year	Net Cash Inflow	Depreciation	Projected Net Income
1	$240,000	$125,000	$115,000
2	210,000	125,000	85,000
3	180,000	125,000	55,000
4	150,000	125,000	25,000
Totals	$780,000	$500,000	$280,000

1a. Accounting rate-of-return method

$$\text{Accounting Rate of Return} = \frac{\text{Average Annual Net Income}}{\text{Average Investment Cost}}$$

$$= \frac{\$280{,}000 \div 4}{\left(\frac{\$600{,}000 - \$100{,}000}{2}\right) + \$100{,}000} = \frac{\$70{,}000}{\$350{,}000}$$

$$= 20\%$$

1b. Payback period method

Total cash investment		$600,000
Less cash-flow recovery		
Year 1	$240,000	
Year 2	210,000	
Year 3 ($\frac{5}{6}$ of $180,000)	150,000	(600,000)
Unrecovered investment		$ 0

Payback period: 2.833 (2$\frac{5}{6}$) years, or 2 years 10 months

1c. Net present value method (Multipliers are from Table 3 in the appendix on future value and present value tables.)

Year	Net Cash Flow	Present-Value Multiplier	Present Value
1	$240,000	.870	$208,800
2	210,000	.756	158,760
3	180,000	.658	118,440
4	150,000	.572	85,800
4	100,000 (salvage)	.572	57,200
Total present value			$629,000
Less cost of original investment			600,000
Positive net present value			$ 29,000

2. Roland Construction Company: Summary of Decision Analysis

	Decision Measures	
	Desired	**Predicted**
Accounting rate of return	15%	20%
Payback period	3 years	2.833 years
Net present value	—	$29,000

Based on the calculations in **1**, the proposed investment in the earth-moving machine meets all company criteria for such investments. Given these results, the company should invest in the machine.

Chapter Assignments

BUILDING YOUR KNOWLEDGE FOUNDATION

Questions

1. What are seven common types of business decisions?
2. Describe the five steps of the management decision cycle.
3. What is relevant decision information? What are the two important characteristics of such information?
4. What are the objectives of incremental analysis? What types of decision analyses depend on the incremental approach?
5. When must decision analysis go beyond the comparison of quantitative information? What is the solution?
6. What factors must be included in a make-or-buy decision?
7. What justifies excluding fixed manufacturing overhead costs from a special order analysis? When are fixed costs relevant to the special order decision?
8. In sales mix decisions, what criteria can be used to select products that will maximize net income?
9. Why are joint processing costs irrelevant to the decision to sell a product at split-off or process it further?
10. Is incremental analysis important to the sell or process-further decision? If so, why?
11. What is a capital expenditure? List some types of capital expenditures.
12. Define *capital budgeting.*
13. Distinguish between cost savings and net cash flow.
14. What is the importance of equal versus unequal cash flows in capital expenditure decisions? Are cash flows relevant to the accounting rate-of-return method of decision analysis? The payback period method? The net present value method?

15. What is a crude but easy method for evaluating capital expenditures? List the advantages and disadvantages of that method.
16. What is the formula for determining the payback period? Is this evaluation technique accurate? Defend your answer.
17. Discuss the statement, "To treat all future income flows alike ignores the time value of money."

Short Exercises

SE 1. LO 1 *Information Sources for Decision Support*

Identify each of the following as an internal or external source of information for decision making.

1. Company meetings
2. Professional meetings
3. Requests for specific information from other departments
4. Business publications or trade journals
5. Results and actions related to past management decisions

SE 2. LO 2 *Management Decision Cycle*

Number the actions below 1 through 5 to indicate the order in which they are performed.

a. Selection of the superior alternative
b. Discovery of a problem or need for change
c. Analysis of the effects of each alternative on business operations
d. Postdecision analysis
e. Identification of alternative courses of action

SE 3. LO 2 *Identifying Relevant Information*

Identify which of the following items are relevant to the decision analysis. Why are the other items irrelevant?

	Alternative 1	Alternative 2
1. Expected sales increase	$300,000	$325,000
2. Purchase price of machine	75,000	80,000
3. Cost of direct materials	40,000	40,000
4. Labor of machine operator	25,000	25,000
5. Machine maintenance costs	14,000	12,000

SE 4. LO 3 *Incremental Analysis*

Fonseca Corporation has assembled the following information related to the decision to purchase a new automated degreasing machine. Using incremental analysis and relevant information, compute the difference in favor of the Vogle machine.

	Harvey Machine	Vogle Machine
Increase in revenues	$43,200	$49,300
Increase in annual operating costs		
Direct materials	12,200	12,200
Direct labor	10,200	10,600
Variable manufacturing overhead	24,500	26,900
Fixed manufacturing overhead (including depreciation)	12,400	12,400

SE 5. LO 4 *Make-or-Buy Decision*

Zorich Company assembles products from a group of interconnecting parts. Some of the parts are produced by the company and some are purchased from outside vendors. Part 23X has been purchased in the past, but the supplier has just increased its price by 35 percent, to $10 per unit for the first 5,000 units and $9 per additional unit ordered each year. The company uses 7,500 units of Part 23X each year. Should the company continue to purchase the part or should it begin making the part?

Unit cost to make and sell the part	
Direct materials	$3.50
Direct labor	1.75
Variable manufacturing overhead	4.25
Variable selling costs for the assembled product	3.75

SE 6. LO 4 *Special Order Decision*

Bixler Company has received a special order for 1,000 units of Product YTZ at a selling price of $20 per unit. This order is over and above normal production, and budgeted production and sales targets have already been exceeded for the year. Capacity exists to satisfy the special order. No selling costs will be incurred in connection with this order. Unit costs to manufacture and sell Product YTZ are as follows: Direct materials, $7.60; direct labor, $3.75; variable manufacturing overhead, $9.25; fixed manufacturing costs, $4.85; variable selling costs, $2.75; and fixed general and administrative costs, $6.75. Should Bixler Company accept the order?

SE 7. LO 4 *Sell or Process-Further Decision*

Perez Industries produces three products from a single operation. Product A sells for $3 per unit, Product B sells for $6 per unit, and Product C sells for $9 per unit. When B is processed further, there are additional unit costs of $3, and its new selling price is $10 per unit. Each product is allocated $2 of joint costs from the initial production operation. Should Product B be processed further, or should it be sold at the end of the initial operation?

SE 8. LO 5 *Capital Budgeting Cost and Revenue Measures*

Matsuki Corp. is analyzing a proposal to purchase a computer-integrated boring mill. The machine will be able to produce an entire product line in a single operation. Projected annual net cash inflow from the machine is $180,000 and projected net income is $120,000. Why is projected net income lower than projected net cash inflow? Identify possible causes for the $60,000 difference.

SE 9. LO 6 *Capital Expenditure Decision*

Swift Communications, Inc., is considering the purchase of a new piece of computerized data transmission equipment. Estimated annual net cash inflow for the new equipment is $575,000. The equipment costs $2 million, has a five-year estimated useful life, and will have no salvage value at the end of the five years. The company requires a maximum payback period of four years and a minimum rate of return of 12 percent. Compute the payback period and the net present value of the equipment. Should the company buy it?

Exercises

E 1. LO 1 *Information Sources*

Tara Hollis, the owner of Cresent Cement Company, must decide whether to replace the current cement production process with a process using the newest technology. Indicate whether each of the following information sources is internal or external to the organization.

1. A presentation about the use of current technology for the manufacture of cement that Tara attended at the national conference
2. Tara's personal observation of the current production activities at the plant
3. A report about the output of the current production process prepared by Tara's vice president of operations
4. A summary of information from leading trade journals about the latest techniques used by competitors
5. A presentation by sales representatives of a company that manufactures machines that process cement

E 2. LO 2 *Steps in the Management Decision Cycle*

Troy Corrente owns Corrente's Department Store in Salt Lake City. The store's profits had declined, so Troy had to decide how to remedy the situation. Number the actions below 1 through 5 to indicate the order in which Troy would have performed them.

a. Troy decided to close the Cosmetics Department.
b. Troy realized that the store's declining profits may have been due to the poor sales performance of one or more departments.
c. Troy reviewed the profitability in each department and found that profits in the Women's Clothing Department had dropped. The sales clerks suggested that closing the Cosmetics Department had reduced the flow of traffic into their department.
d. Troy gathered monthly sales and expense information directly related to each department in the store. He noticed that the Cosmetics Department was operating at a loss.
e. Troy believed that he would have to decide whether to keep or drop an unprofitable department.

E 3. LO 2 *Relevant Costs and Revenues*

Silverton Enterprises manufactures household metal products, such as window frames, light fixtures, and doorknobs. In 20xx the company produced 10,000 special oblong doorknobs but sold only 2,000 of the doorknobs at $20.00 each. The remaining 8,000 units cannot be sold through Silverton's normal channels.

The costs of the unsold units were as follows:

Direct materials	$ 6.00
Direct labor	3.00
Variable manufacturing overhead	1.00
Fixed manufacturing overhead	4.00
Cost per knob	$14.00

The 8,000 oblong knobs can be sold to a scrap dealer in another state for $7.00 each. A license for doing business in this state will cost Silverton $400. Shipping expenses will average $.10 per knob.

1. Identify the relevant costs and revenues for the scrap sale alternative.
2. Assume the oblong knobs can be reprocessed to produce round knobs that normally have the same $14.00 unit cost components and sell for $16.00 each. Rework costs will be $9.00 per unit. Determine the alternative that will minimize the overall loss: (a) doing nothing, (b) reprocessing the knobs (assuming a market exists for the reworked knobs), or (c) selling them as scrap.

E 4. LO 2 LO 3 *Relevant Data and Incremental Analysis*

Carl Bezner, the business manager for Chesney Industries, must select a new computer and word processing package for his secretary. Rental of Model A, which is similar to the model now being used, is $3,200 per year. Model B is a deluxe computer that rents for $3,900 per year, but will require a new desk for the secretary. The annual desk rental charge is $750. The secretary's salary of $1,200 per month will not change. If Model B is rented, $280 in annual software training costs will be incurred. Model B has greater capacity and is expected to save $2,550 per year in part-time secretarial wages. Upkeep and operating costs will not differ between the two models.

1. Identify the relevant data in this problem.
2. Prepare an incremental analysis to aid the business manager in his decision.

E 5. LO 4 *Make-or-Buy Decision*

One component of a radio produced by Retoric Audio Systems, Inc., is currently being purchased for $210 per 100 parts. Management is studying the possibility of manufacturing that component. Annual production (usage) at Retoric is 70,000 units; fixed costs (all of which remain unchanged whether the part is made or purchased) are $38,500; and variable costs are $.90 per unit for direct materials, $.50 per unit for direct labor, and $.60 per unit for manufacturing overhead.

Using incremental analysis, decide whether Retoric Audio Systems, Inc., should manufacture the part or continue to purchase it from an outside vendor.

E 6. LO 4 *Special Order Decision*

Olga Antiquities, Ltd., produces antique-looking lampshades. Management has just received a special order for 1,000 shades and must decide whether to accept it. Shishkova Furniture Company, the purchaser, is offering to pay $22.00 per shade and shipping costs. The variable production costs per shade include $9.20 for direct materials, $4.00 for direct labor, and $3.80 for variable manufacturing overhead. The current year's production is 20,000 shades and maximum capacity is 25,000 shades. Fixed costs, including manufacturing overhead, advertising, and selling and administrative costs total $70,000. The normal selling price is $30.00 per shade. Shipping costs average $3.00 per shade.

Determine whether or not Olga Antiquities should accept the special order.

E 7. LO 4 *Scarce-Resource Usage*

Brunner, Inc., manufactures two products that require both machine processing and labor operations. Although there is unlimited demand for both products, Brunner could devote all its capacities to a single product. Unit prices, cost data, and processing requirements are:

	Product A	**Product M**
Unit selling price	$95	$250
Unit variable costs	$55	$120
Machine hours per unit	0.4	1.4
Labor hours per unit	2	6

In 20xx the company will be limited to 160,000 machine hours and 120,000 labor hours.

1. Compute the most profitable combination of products to be produced in 20xx.
2. Compute the contribution margin for the total product volume computed in **1.**

E 8. LO 2 *Analysis of Relevant Information*

Barnett & Co., a scrap-metal company, supplies area steel companies with recycled materials. The company collects scrap metal, sorts and cleans it, and compresses it into one-ton blocks for easy handling. Increased demand for recycled metals has caused Mr. Barnett to consider purchasing an additional metal-compressing machine. He has narrowed the choice to two models. The company's management accountant has gathered the following information about each model.

	Model 1	**Model 2**
Purchase price	$100,000	$120,000
Salvage value	12,000	20,000
Annual depreciation*	8,800	10,000
Resulting increases in annual sales	182,000	210,000
Annual operating costs		
Direct materials	70,000	80,000
Direct labor	40,000	40,000
Operating supplies	3,600	4,000
Indirect labor	24,000	36,000
Insurance and taxes	1,600	2,000
Plant rental	8,000	8,000
Electricity	1,000	1,120
Other overhead	5,000	5,680

*Computed using the straight-line method.

List the revenue and cost items relevant to the decision.

E 9. LO 6 *Capital Expenditure Decision: Accounting Rate-of-Return Method*

Heber Corporation manufactures metal hard hats for construction workers. Recently, management has tried to raise productivity to meet the growing demand from the real estate industry. The company is now thinking about a new stamping machine. Management has decided that only capital expenditures that yield a 14 percent return will be accepted. The management accountant projects that the new machine will cost $325,000, revenue will increase by $98,400 per year, the salvage value of the new machine will be $32,500, and operating cost increases (including depreciation) will be $74,600 per year.

Using the accounting rate-of-return method, decide whether the company should invest in the machine. (Show all computations to support your decision.)

E 10. LO 6 *Capital Expenditure Decision: Payback Period Method*

Super Sounds, Inc., a manufacturer of stereo speakers, is thinking about adding a new injection molding machine. The machine could produce speaker parts that the company now buys from outsiders. The machine has an estimated life of fourteen years and will cost $425,000. Gross cash revenue from the machine will be about $400,000 per year, and related cash expenses should total $310,050. The payback period as set by management should be five years or less.

Use the payback period method to determine whether the company should invest in the new machine. Show your computations to support your answer.

E 11. LO 6 *Using the Present Value Tables*

For each of the following situations, identify the correct multiplier to use from the tables in the appendix on future value and present value tables, and compute the appropriate present value.

1. Annual net cash inflow of $35,000 for five years, discounted at 16%
2. An amount of $25,000 to be received at the end of ten years, discounted at 12%
3. The amount of $28,000 to be received at the end of two years, and $15,000 to be received at the end of years 4, 5, and 6, discounted at 10%
4. Annual net cash inflow of $22,500 for twelve years, discounted at 14%
5. The following five years of cash inflows, discounted at 10%:

Year 1	$35,000
Year 2	20,000
Year 3	30,000
Year 4	40,000
Year 5	50,000

6. The amount of $70,000 to be received at the beginning of year 7, discounted at 14%

E 12.
LO 6 *Capital Expenditure Decision: Net Present Value Method*

Jefferson and Associates wants to buy an automatic extruding machine. The equipment would have a useful life of six years, cost $220,000, and increase annual net cash inflows by $57,500. Assume there is no salvage value at the end of six years. The company's minimum desired rate of return is 14 percent.

Using the net present value method, prepare an analysis to determine whether the company should purchase the machine.

Problems

P 1.
LO 4 *Make-or-Buy Decision*

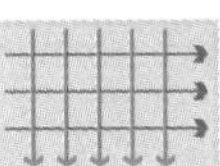

The Carothers Furniture Company is famous for its dining room furniture. One full department is engaged in the production of the Cottonwood line, an elegant but affordable dining room set. To date, the company has been manufacturing all pieces of the set, including the six chairs.

Management has just received word that a company in Durango, Colorado, is willing to produce the chairs for Carothers at a total purchase price of $3,000,000 for the annual demand. Company records show that the following costs have been incurred in the production of the chairs: wood materials, $22.50 per chair; cloth materials, $8.50 per chair; direct labor, 1.2 hours per chair at $12.00 per hour; variable manufacturing overhead, $5.00 per direct labor hour; fixed manufacturing overhead, depreciation, $135,000; and fixed manufacturing overhead, other, $109,400. Fixed manufacturing overhead would continue whether or not the chairs are produced. Assume that idle facilities cannot be used for any other purpose and that annual usage is 60,000 chairs.

REQUIRED

1. Prepare an incremental analysis to determine whether the chairs should be made by the company or purchased from the outside supplier in Durango.
2. Compute the variable unit cost to make one chair and to buy one chair.

P 2.
LO 4 *Special Order Decision*

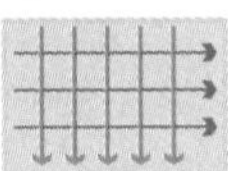

On March 26, Rio Fria Industries received a special order request for 150 ten-foot aluminum fishing boats. Operating on a fiscal year ending May 31, the division already has orders that will allow them to produce at budget levels for the period. However, extra capacity exists to produce the additional 150 boats.

The terms of the special order call for a selling price of $625 per boat, and the customer will pay all shipping costs. No sales personnel were involved in soliciting the order.

The ten-foot fishing boat has the following cost estimates: direct materials, aluminum, two $4' \times 8'$ sheets at $145 per sheet; direct labor, 14 hours at $14.50 per hour; variable manufacturing overhead, $5.75 per direct labor hour; fixed manufacturing overhead, $4.50 per direct labor hour; variable selling expenses, $46.50 per boat; and variable shipping expenses, $57.50 per boat.

REQUIRED

1. Prepare an analysis for management to use in deciding whether to accept or reject the special order. What decision should be made?
2. To make a $9,000 profit on the order, what would be the lowest possible price that the company could charge per boat?

P 3.
LO 4 *Sell or Process-Further Decision*

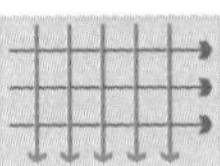

Meyers Marketing, Inc., has developed a promotional program for a large shopping center in Tampa, Florida. After investing $360,000 in developing the original promotion campaign, the firm is ready to present its client with an add-on contract offer that includes the original promotion areas of (1) TV advertising program, (2) series of brochures for mass mailing, and (3) special rotating BIG SALE schedule for 10 of the 28 tenants in the shopping center. On the next page are the revenue terms from the original contract with the shopping center and the offer for an add-on contract, which extends the original contract terms.

Meyers estimates that the following additional costs will be incurred by extending the contract.

	TV Program	**Brochures**	**BIG SALE Schedule**
Direct labor	$30,000	$ 9,000	$7,000
Variable overhead costs	22,000	14,000	6,000
Traceable fixed overhead costs	2,400	800	400

	Contract Terms	
	Original Contract Terms	Extended Contract Including Add-On Terms
TV advertising program	$520,000	$ 580,000
Brochures	210,000	230,000
Rotating BIG SALE schedule	170,000	190,000
Totals	$900,000	$1,000,000

REQUIRED

1. Compute the costs that will be incurred for each part of the add-on portion of the contract.
2. Should Meyers Marketing, Inc., offer the add-on contract or should it ask for a final settlement check based on the original contract only? Defend your answer.
3. If management of the shopping center indicated the terms of the add-on contract were negotiable, how should Meyers respond?

LO 6 *Accounting Rate-of-Return and Payback Period Methods*

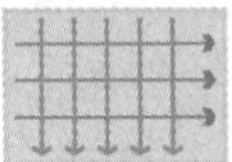

P 4. Blue Island Corporation wants to buy a new rubber-stamping machine. The machine will provide the company with a new product line: pressed rubber food trays for kitchens. Two machines are being considered; the data applicable to each machine follow.

	Coupe Machine	Metro Machine
Estimated annual increase in revenue	$450,000	$500,000
Purchase price	280,000	300,000
Salvage value	28,000	30,000
Traceable annual costs		
Direct materials	161,670	157,500
Direct labor	65,250	92,300
Factory supervision	26,000	26,000
Indirect labor	62,480	82,750
Electrical power	7,200	7,200
Other manufacturing overhead	42,800	33,550
Taxes	20,196	25,058
Estimated useful life in years	10	10

Depreciation is computed using the straight-line method net of salvage value. The company's minimum desired rate of return is 16 percent, and the maximum allowable payback period is 4.5 years.

REQUIRED

1. Compute how the company's net income will change under each alternative.
2. Compute the projected accounting rate of return for each machine.
3. Compute the payback period for each machine.
4. Based on the information in **2** and **3,** which machine should be purchased? Why?

LO 6 *Capital Expenditure Decision: Net Present Value Method*

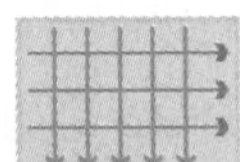

P 5. The Chateau is a famous restaurant in the French Quarter of New Orleans. "Bouillabaisse Kathryn" is the house specialty. Management is currently considering the purchase of a machine that would prepare all the ingredients, automatically mix them, and cook the dish to the restaurant's specifications. The machine will function for an estimated twelve years, and the purchase price, including installation, is $250,000. Estimated salvage value is $25,000. This labor-saving device is expected to increase cash flows by an average of $42,000 per year during its estimated useful life. For purposes of capital expenditure decisions, the restaurant uses a 12 percent minimum desired rate of return.

REQUIRED

1. Using the net present value method, determine if the company should purchase the machine. Support your answer.
2. If management had decided on a minimum desired rate of return of 14 percent, should the machine be purchased? Show all computations to support your answer.

Alternate Problems

P 6. LO 4 *Make-or-Buy Decision*

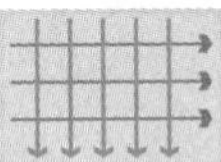

The Ralston Refrigerator Company purchases and installs defrost clocks in its products. The clocks cost $144 per case, and each case contains twelve clocks. The supplier recently gave advance notice that, effective in thirty days, the price will rise by 50 percent. The company has idle equipment that, with only a few minor changes, could be used to produce similar defrost clocks.

The following cost estimates have been prepared under the assumption that the company could make the product itself. Direct materials would cost $9.00 per clock. Direct labor would be ten minutes per clock at a labor rate of $12.00 per hour. Variable manufacturing overhead would be $6.50 per clock. Fixed manufacturing overhead, which would be incurred under either decision alternative, would be $32,420 a year for depreciation and $234,000 a year for other costs. Production and usage are estimated at 75,000 clocks a year. (Assume that idle equipment cannot be used for any other purpose.)

REQUIRED

1. Prepare an incremental analysis to determine whether the defrost clocks should be made within the company or purchased from the outside supplier at the higher price.
2. Compute the total unit cost to make one clock and to buy one clock after the price hike.

P 7. LO 6 *Accounting Rate-of-Return and Payback Period Methods*

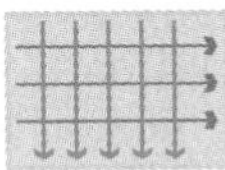

The Lambros Company is expanding its production facilities to include a new product line, a sporty automobile tire rim. If the company bought a new computerized machine, tire rims could be produced with little labor cost. The controller has identified two machines that could do the job. Following are the details about each machine.

	Matthew Machine	Kelley Machine
Estimated annual increase in revenue	$280,000.00	$280,000.00
Purchase price	490,000.00	510,000.00
Salvage value	49,000.00	51,000.00
Traceable annual costs		
Direct materials	75,000.00	60,000.00
Direct labor	21,700.00	36,900.00
Electrical power	4,900.00	4,900.00
Factory supervision	15,750.00	15,750.00
Factory supplies	25,150.00	24,700.00
Other manufacturing overhead	31,300.00	40,250.00
Taxes	15,322.50	17,775.00
Estimated useful life in years	8	12

The company uses the straight-line depreciation method. The minimum desired rate of return is 12 percent. The maximum payback period is six years.

REQUIRED

1. Compute the change in the company's net income arising from each alternative.
2. Compute the projected accounting rate of return for each machine.
3. Compute the payback period for each machine.
4. Based on the information generated in **2** and **3**, which machine should be purchased? Why?

P 8. LO 6 *Capital Expenditure Decision: Net Present Value Method*

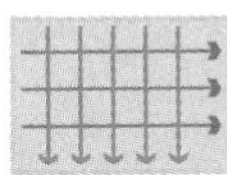

The management of Mega-Tuff Plastics has been looking at a proposal to purchase a new plastic injection-style molding machine. With the new machine, the company would not have to buy small plastic parts to use in production. The estimated useful life of the machine is fifteen years, and the purchase price, including all setup charges, is $400,000. Salvage value is estimated to be $40,000. The net addition to the company's cash inflow due to the savings from making the parts is estimated to be $66,000 a year. Mega-Tuff Plastic's management has decided on a minimum desired rate of return of 14 percent.

REQUIRED

1. Using the net present value method, determine if the company should purchase the machine. Support your answer.
2. If management had decided on a minimum desired rate of return of 16 percent, should the machine be purchased? Show all computations to support your answer.

Skills Development

Conceptual Analysis

SD 1. **LO 2** *Management Decision Cycle*

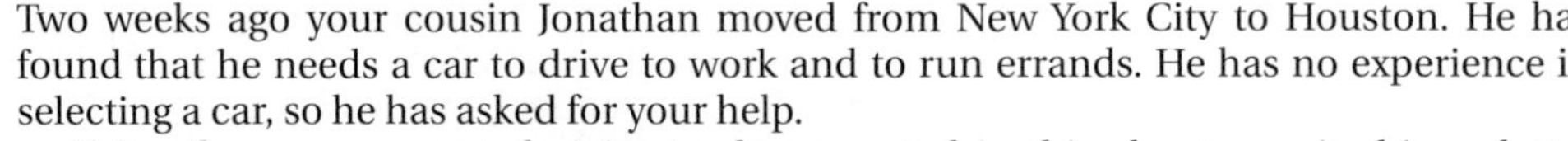

Two weeks ago your cousin Jonathan moved from New York City to Houston. He has found that he needs a car to drive to work and to run errands. He has no experience in selecting a car, so he has asked for your help.

Using the management decision cycle presented in this chapter, write him a letter explaining how he can approach making this decision.

How would your response change if the president of your company asked you to help make a decision about acquiring a fleet of cars for use by sales personnel?

Ethical Dilemma

SD 2. **LO 4** *Ethics of a Make-or-Buy Decision*

Karen Gore is the assistant controller for ***Railing Corp.,*** a leading producer of home appliances. Her friend, Ed Jason, is the supervisor of the Cookware Department. Jason has the authority to decide whether parts are purchased from outside vendors or manufactured in his department. Gore recently conducted an internal audit of the parts being manufactured in the Cookware Department, including a check of the prices currently charged by vendors for similar parts. She found over a dozen parts that could be purchased for less than they cost the company to produce. When she approached Jason about the situation, he replied that if those parts were purchased from outside vendors, two automated machines would be idled for several hours a week. Increased machine idle time would have a negative effect on his performance evaluation and could reduce his yearly bonus. He reminded Gore that he was in charge of the decision to make or purchase those parts and asked her not to pursue the matter any further.

What should Gore do in this situation? Discuss her options.

Research Activity

SD 3. **LO 2** *Identifying Relevant Decision Information*

Assume you want to take a two-week vacation. Select two destinations for your vacation and gather information about them from brochures, magazines, travel agents, and people you know. Then list the relevant quantitative and qualitative information in its order of importance to your decision. Analyze the information and select a destination. What factors were the most important to your decision? Why? What factors were the least important to your decision? Why? How would the process of identifying relevant decision information differ if you were asked by the president of your company to prepare a budget for the next training meeting, to be held at a location of your choice?

Decision-Making Practice

SD 4. **LO 6** *Using Net Present Value*

The ***McCall Hotel Syndicate*** owns four resort hotels in Europe. Because the Paris operation has been booming over the past five years, management has decided to build an addition. The proposed wing, which will increase the hotel's capacity by 20 percent, can be built at a cost of $30,000,000. The new structure will have a salvage value of $3,000,000 and will be depreciated on a straight-line basis over its twenty-year estimated useful life.

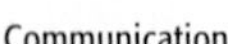
Communication

Critical Thinking

Group Activity

Memo

Ethics

International

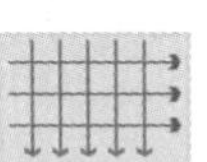
Spreadsheet

Managerial Technology

Internet

Erin McVan, the controller, has started an analysis of the net present value for the project. She has calculated the annual net cash inflow by subtracting the increase in cash operating expenses from the increase in cash inflows from room rentals.

Year	Annual Net Cash Inflow
1–7 (each year)	$3,809,700
8	4,007,700
9	4,535,700
10–20 (each year)	4,733,700

Capital investment projects must generate a 12 percent minimum rate of return to qualify for consideration.

Using net present value analysis, calculate the annual cash inflow, evaluate the proposal, and make a recommendation to management.

Group Activity: Have students work in groups to complete **SD 4.** Select one person from each group to report the group's findings to the class.

Managerial Reporting and Analysis

INTERPRETING MANAGEMENT REPORTS

MRA 1.
LO 4 *Special Order Decision*

Roscoe Can Opener Company is a subsidiary of ***Boedigheimer Appliances, Inc.*** The can opener Roscoe produces is in strong demand. Sales during the present year, 20x2, are expected to hit the 1,000,000 unit mark. Full plant capacity is 1,150,000 units, but the 1,000,000-unit mark was considered normal capacity for the current year. The following unit price and cost breakdown is applicable in 20x2:

	Per Unit
Sales price	$22.50
Less manufacturing costs	
Direct materials	$6.00
Direct labor	2.50
Overhead: Variable	3.50
Fixed	1.50
Total manufacturing costs	$13.50
Gross margin	$ 9.00
Less selling and administrative expenses	
Selling: Variable	$ 1.50
Fixed	1.00
Administrative, fixed	1.25
Packaging, variable*	.75
Total selling and administrative expenses	$ 4.50
Net income	$ 4.50

*Three types of packaging are available: deluxe, $.75/unit; plain, $.50/unit; and bulk pack, $.25/unit.

During November, the company received three special-order requests from large chain-store companies. Those orders are not part of the budgeted 1,000,000-unit sales for 20x2, but company officials think that sufficient capacity exists for one order to be accepted. Orders received and their terms are:

Order 1: 75,000 can openers @ $20.00 per unit, deluxe packaging

Order 2: 90,000 can openers @ $18.00 per unit, plain packaging

Order 3: 125,000 can openers @ $15.75 per unit, bulk packaging

Since the orders were placed directly with company officials, no variable selling costs will be incurred.

REQUIRED

1. Analyze the profitability of each of the three special orders.
2. Which special order should be accepted?

Formulating Management Reports

MRA 2.
LO 3 *Formulating an Income Statement Using the Contribution Margin Format*

Gloria Belasco recently purchased the ***Bella Vista Country Club*** in Tucson, Arizona. The club offers swimming, golfing, and tennis as well as dining services for its members. Belasco is unfamiliar with the actual operating activities of those areas. Because you are the controller for the country club's operations, Belasco has asked you to formulate a report that shows how each activity or service contributed to the profitability of the country club in the year ended December 31, 20x3. The information you provide will assist Belasco in deciding whether to keep or eliminate one or more areas.

REQUIRED

1. In preparation for writing your report, answer the following questions.
   a. What kinds of information do you need about each area?
   b. Why is the information relevant?
   c. Where would you find the information?
   d. When would you want to obtain the information?
2. Prepare a draft of your report, omitting the actual numbers. Show only the headings and line items.
3. Assume that Belasco wants to increase the membership of the country club and will invest a large sum of money to promote membership sales. How would you structure the report differently to address such a decision?

International Company

MRA 3.
LO 3 *Using Qualitative*
LO 5 *Information in Capital*
LO 6 *Expenditure Decisions*

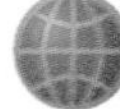

The board of directors of the ***Tanashi Corporation*** met to review a number of proposals involving the use of capital to improve the quality of company products. A proposal submitted by a production line manager requested the purchase of new computer-integrated machines to replace the older machines in one of the ten production departments at the Tokyo plant. Although the manager had presented quantitative information to support the purchase of the new machines, the board members asked the following important questions related to the proposal.

1. Why do we want to replace the old machines? Have they deteriorated? Are they obsolete?
2. Will the new machines require less cycle time?
3. Can we reduce inventory levels or save floor space by replacing the old machines?
4. How expensive is the software used with the new machines?
5. Will we be able to find highly skilled employees to maintain the new machines? Or can we find workers who are trainable? What would it cost to train those workers? Would the training disrupt the staff by causing relocations?
6. Would the implementation of the machines be delayed because of the time required to recruit new workers?
7. What impact would the new machines have on the other parts of the manufacturing systems? Would the company lose some of the flexibility in its manufacturing systems if it introduced the new machines?

The board members believe that the qualitative information needed to answer their questions could lead to the rejection of the project, even though it would have been accepted based on the quantitative information.

REQUIRED

1. Identify the questions that can be answered with quantitative information. Give examples of the quantitative information that could be used.
2. Identify the questions that can be answered with qualitative information. Explain why such information could negatively influence the capital expenditure decision even though the quantitative information suggests a positive outcome.

EXCEL SPREADSHEET ANALYSIS

LO 6 *Excel Analysis*

MRA 4. ***Harper Corporation*** is an international plumbing equipment and supply company located in Southern California. The manager of the Pipe Extruding Division is considering the purchase of a computerized copper pipe extruding machine that costs $120,000. The machine has a six-year life, and its expected salvage value after six years of use will be 10 percent of its original cost. Cash revenue generated by the new machine is projected to be $50,000 in year 1 and will increase by $10,000 each year for the next five years. Variable cash operating costs will be materials and parts, 25 percent of revenue; machine labor, 5 percent of revenue; and manufacturing overhead, 15 percent of revenue. Fixed manufacturing overhead consists entirely of machine depreciation computed on a straight-line basis. First-year sales and marketing cash outflows are expected to be $10,500 and will decrease by 10 percent each year over the life of the new machine. Anticipated cash administrative expenses will be $2,500 per year. The company uses a 15 percent minimum desired rate of return for all capital investment analyses.

REQUIRED

1. Prepare an Excel spreadsheet that will compute the net present value of the anticipated cash flows for the life of the proposed new extruding machine. Use the following format:

		Projected Cash Outflows							
Future Time Period	**Projected Cash Revenue**	**Materials and Parts**	**Machine Labor**	**Manufacturing Overhead**	**Sales and Marketing**	**Admin-istrative Expenses**	**Projected Net Cash Inflow**	**Present Value Multiplier**	**Present Value of Future Cash Inflows**

Should the company invest in the new machine?

2. After careful analysis, the controller has determined that the variable rate for materials and parts can be reduced to 22 percent of revenue. Will this reduction in cash flow change the company's decision to invest in the new machine? Explain.
3. The marketing manager has determined that the initial estimate of sales and marketing cash expenses was too high and has reduced the initial estimate by $1,000. The 10 percent annual reductions are still expected to occur. Together with the change in **2,** will this reduction affect the initial investment decision? Explain your answer.

ENDNOTES

1. Michael Crane and John Meyer, "Focusing on True Costs in a Service Organization," *Management Accounting,* Institute of Management Accountants, February 1993, pp. 41–45.
2. From Roger B. Smith, "Ethics in Business: An Essential Element of Success," *Management Accounting,* June 1990, p. 50. Reprinted by permission of the Institute of Management Accountants.
3. Steve Coburn, Hugh Grove, and Tom Cook, "How ABC Was Used in Capital Budgeting," *Management Accounting,* Institute of Management Accountants, May 1997, pp. 38–46.

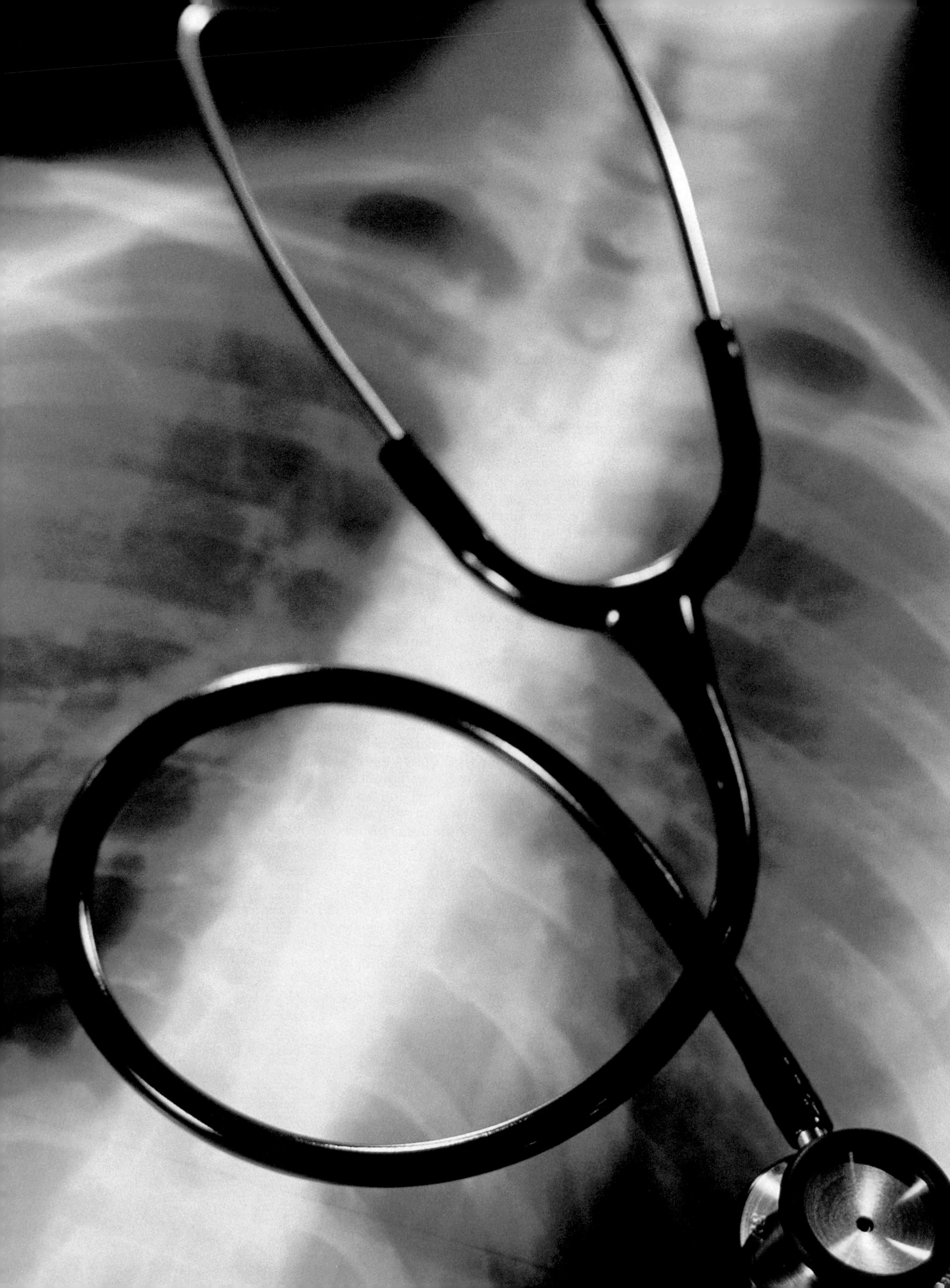

CHAPTER 27

Just-in-Time Operations and Measures of Quality

LEARNING OBJECTIVES

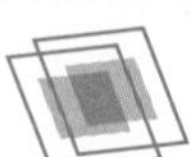

1. **Define and explain the *just-in-time operating philosophy* and identify the elements of a JIT operating environment.**
2. **Compare the traditional approach to production with just-in-time operations.**
3. **Relate JIT to activity-based costing, identify a product's or service's value chain, and distinguish between value-adding and nonvalue-adding activities.**
4. **Compute product costs for an organization that employs an ABC system in a JIT operating environment.**
5. **Define and explain *total quality management,* and identify and compute the costs of quality for products and services.**
6. **Use nonfinancial measures of quality to evaluate operating performance.**

DECISION POINT

GROUP HEALTH COOPERATIVE OF PUGET SOUND

Group Health Cooperative of Puget Sound is a health maintenance organization (HMO) headquartered in Seattle that serves over 480,000 people in the state of Washington. GHC's original cost management system was primarily designed to meet financial reporting needs and was used for several decades without being updated. GHC's management found, however, that to remain profitable in the highly competitive HMO industry, it needed significantly more information of varying kinds. In response, in 1989, the organization began the ongoing process of redesigning its cost management system. Using the principles of total quality management, the organization developed an extensive cost management database that captures as much data as possible about business operations.[1]

Since GHC is a service organization, the new cost management system focuses on the costs of delivering health care services. It enables management to identify the full cost of operating its delivery system, including both the direct costs of delivering health care to patients and the overhead costs of administering the program. The new cost management system allows management accountants to analyze costs by (1) treatment patterns, such as uses of specific services; (2) treatment differences, such as uses of inpatient versus outpatient hospital care; (3) patient diagnosis; (4) market segment, such as users of Medicare; and (5) service location. Why did competition pressure GHC to redesign its cost management system? How has the role of the cost management system changed for the managers of GHC?

For managers to perform their jobs effectively in today's highly competitive environment, they need more than just after-the-fact financial results. They need detailed, timely information, both financial and nonfinancial, about every aspect of their operation. For such information, they depend on the cost management system. When the cost management system is well constructed and uses the latest database technology, it becomes the focal point for all operating information. It is no longer a source of financial data only.

The Just-in-Time Operating Environment

OBJECTIVE 1

Define and explain the **just-in-time operating philosophy** *and identify the elements of a JIT operating environment*

Related Text Assignments:
Q: 1, 2, 3, 4, 5
SE: 1
E: 1, 2
P: 1
SD: 1
MRA: 2

Critical Thinking Question: What role must management play in successfully implementing a JIT operating environment? **Answer:** Management must anticipate the potential problems and make plans for dealing with employees' reactions to change. To gain employees' trust and respect, they must actively support and participate in implementing and monitoring JIT operations.

Point to Emphasize: JIT is an operating environment that must be adopted by everyone in a company before its total benefits can be realized.

Discussion Question: Ask your students if they have discussed any of these concepts in other courses, but under different names—for example, quality circles, pull-through production, or zero-defects programs.

Many organizations that formerly relied on traditional production processes are changing to new operating and managing approaches, particularly the just-in-time (JIT) operating environment. Organizations that adopt the JIT approach to production must redesign their manufacturing facilities and the events that trigger the production process. The just-in-time (JIT) operating philosophy requires that all resources, including materials, personnel, and facilities, be used only as needed. Its objectives are to improve productivity and eliminate waste. JIT is based on continuous production flow and requires that each part of the production process work in concert with the other parts. Direct labor workers are assigned expanded responsibilities, which helps to reduce waste in labor cost, space, and production time. JIT production methods require virtually no materials inventory because direct materials and parts are scheduled to arrive from suppliers as needed. JIT can also reduce work in process and finished goods inventories by as much as 90 percent, which significantly lowers the amount of working capital devoted to inventories.

The first step in achieving JIT operating efficiencies is to redesign the plant layout, moving machines and processes closer together to cut throughput time. The Japanese took the redesign one step further by automating the new processes. Automated JIT operations moved Japanese industry into world prominence. Japanese manufacturers were able to improve product quality while decreasing waste. The result was significant cost savings that were reflected in lower prices. The Japanese also increased the productivity of their factories as they approached total capacity. Their success has prompted manufacturers in other countries to change from traditional production methods to the new automated JIT environments. And the movement toward automated JIT operations will continue as more and more organizations enter world markets.

Organizations that want to adopt a JIT operating environment must reevaluate their current operations and implement new ways of producing goods or services. Underlying the new methods are several basic concepts.

Simple is better.

The quality of the product or service is critical.

The work environment must emphasize continuous improvement.

Maintaining inventories wastes resources and may hide poor work.

Any activity or function that does not add value to the product should be eliminated or reduced.

Goods should be produced only when needed.

Workers must be multiskilled and must participate in improving efficiency and product quality.

Elements of the JIT Operating Environment

Among the organizations that have adopted elements of JIT are Caterpillar Inc. and Harley-Davidson, Inc. To implement a JIT operating environment, an organization must be prepared to

1. Maintain minimum inventory levels.
2. Develop pull-through production planning and scheduling.
3. Purchase materials and produce products as needed, in smaller lot sizes.
4. Perform quick, inexpensive machine setups.
5. Create flexible manufacturing work cells.
6. Develop a multiskilled work force.
7. Maintain high levels of product quality.
8. Enforce a system of effective preventive maintenance.
9. Encourage continuous improvement of the work environment.[2]

This section describes each element and its impact on costs, product quality, and productivity.

Maintain Minimum Inventory Levels

Discussion Question: Why is inventory sometimes described as a nonproductive asset? **Answer:** Inventory is an idle asset; it is held to smooth a production or selling process. As such, resources are used for its maintenance that could be used in productive activities.

One objective of a JIT operating environment is to maintain minimum inventory levels. In contrast to the traditional environment, in which parts, materials, and supplies are purchased far in advance and stored until the Production Department needs them, in a JIT environment, raw materials and parts are purchased and received only when needed. The system lowers costs by reducing (1) the space needed for inventory storage, (2) the amount of materials handling, and (3) the amount of inventory obsolescence. There is less need for inventory control facilities, personnel, and recordkeeping. The amount of work in process inventory waiting to be processed and the amount of working capital tied up in all inventories decrease significantly.

Develop Pull-Through Production Planning and Scheduling

Point to Emphasize: Pull-through production represents a change in concept. Instead of producing goods in anticipation of customers' needs, customers' orders trigger the production process.

Pull-through production is a system in which a customer's order triggers the purchase of materials and the scheduling of production for the required products. In contrast, traditional manufacturing operations use the *push-through method,* whereby products are manufactured in long production runs and stored in anticipation of customers' orders.

Purchase Materials and Produce Products as Needed, in Smaller Lot Sizes

With pull-through production, the size of customers' orders determines the size of production runs, and the organization purchases materials and parts as needed. Low inventory levels are maintained, but machines have to be set up more frequently, resulting in more work stoppages.

Perform Quick, Inexpensive Machine Setups

In the past, managers felt that it was more cost-effective to produce large inventories because producing small batches increases the number of machine setups. The success of JIT over the last ten years has disproved this belief. By placing machines in more efficient locations and scheduling similar products on common machine groupings, setup time can be minimized. In addition, workers become more experienced and more efficient when they perform frequent setups.

Create Flexible Manufacturing Work Cells

Enrichment Note: Traditional environments emphasize *functional* departments that tend to combine similar activities.

In a traditional factory layout, all similar machines are grouped together, forming functional departments. Products are routed through each department in sequence, so that all necessary operations are completed in order. This process can take several days or weeks, depending on the size and complexity of the job.

By changing the factory layout, the JIT operating environment cuts the manufacturing time of a product from days to hours, or from weeks to days. In many cases, time can be reduced more than 80 percent by ensuring that all machines needed for sequential processing are placed together. The new cluster of machinery forms a flexible work cell, an autonomous production line that can perform all required operations efficiently and continuously. The flexible work cell handles products of similar shape or size, what is called a family of products. Product families require minimum setup changes as workers move from one job to the next. The more flexible the work cell, the greater the potential to minimize total production time.

Develop a Multiskilled Work Force

In the flexible work cells of a JIT environment, workers may be required to operate several types of machines simultaneously. Therefore, they must learn new operating skills. Many work cells are run by only one operator, who, for example, may have to set up and retool machines and even perform routine maintenance on them. In short, a JIT operating environment requires a multiskilled work force.

Multiskilled workers have been very effective in contributing to the high levels of productivity achieved by Japanese companies. In the United States, union contracts often restrict workers to a single skill. Thus, some organizations may encounter difficulties in training workers to run work cells.

Maintain High Levels of Product Quality

Point to Emphasize: That inspection is necessary is an admission that problems with quality do occur. Continuous inspection throughout production as opposed to inspection only at the end of the process creates awareness at the point where a problem occurs.

Point to Emphasize: Product quality is a corporate goal. Everyone must work toward high-quality finished goods to achieve that goal.

JIT operations result in high-quality products because high-quality raw materials are used and because inspections are routinely made throughout the production process. According to JIT philosophy, inspection as a separate step does not add value to the product, so the JIT environment incorporates inspection into ongoing operations. JIT machine operators inspect the products as they pass through the manufacturing process. An operator who detects a flaw determines its cause. The operator even may help the engineer or quality control person find a way to correct the problem. Once an operator finds a defect, he or she shuts down the work cell and fixes the problem to prevent the production of similarly flawed products. This integrated inspection procedure, combined with quality raw materials, produces high-quality finished goods.

Enforce a System of Effective Preventive Maintenance

Point to Emphasize: In the JIT environment, normal operating activities–setup, production, and maintenance–still take place. But the timing of those activities is altered to promote smoother operations and to minimize downtime.

When an organization rearranges its machinery into flexible manufacturing work cells, each machine becomes an integral part of its cell. If one machine breaks down, the entire cell stops functioning. Because the product cannot be easily routed to another machine while the malfunctioning machine is repaired, continuous JIT operations require an effective system of preventive maintenance. Preventing machine breakdowns is considered more important and more cost-effective than keeping machines running continuously. Machine operators are trained to perform minor repairs as they detect problems. Machines are serviced regularly—much like an automobile—to help guarantee continued operation. The machine operator conducts routine maintenance during periods of downtime between orders. (Remember that in a JIT setting, the work cell does not operate unless there is a customer order for the product. Machine operators take advantage of such downtime to perform maintenance.)

Encourage Continuous Improvement of the Work Environment

The JIT environment fosters loyalty among workers, who are likely to see themselves as part of a team because they are so deeply involved in the production process. Machine operators must have the skills to run several types of machines, be able to detect defective products, suggest measures to correct problems, and maintain the machinery within their work cell. In addition, each worker is encouraged to make suggestions for improving the production process. Japanese companies receive thousands of employee suggestions and implement a high percentage of them. And workers are rewarded for suggestions that improve the process. Such an environment supports workers' initiative and benefits the company.

Traditional Versus Just-in-Time Production

OBJECTIVE 2

Compare the traditional approach to production with just-in-time operations

Related Text Assignments:
Q: 6, 7
SE: 2
E: 2, 3
P: 1
SD: 3, 4
MRA: 2, 3

Teaching Note: Students who have not been exposed to a manufacturing environment often do not understand the concepts and terminology of production. A brief explanation of terms may encourage students to study these new concepts.

The most effective way to differentiate between traditional and JIT operating environments is to analyze and compare product flow and plant layout. The just-in-time approach attempts to eliminate all waste, including wasted materials and wasted time, so it focuses on minimizing the time it takes to make and ship a product or to develop and deliver a service. We will examine the differences in a manufacturing environment, but the JIT philosophy can be applied to any operation.

The Traditional Manufacturing Environment

The Stay-Tite Company uses a traditional manufacturing process to produce screws, bolts, shoe nails, and specialty fasteners. Figure 1 shows the plant layout, and Figure 2 shows the operations needed to produce a fastener.

The arrows and numbers in Figure 1 indicate the sequence of events in the manufacturing process. Raw materials arrive at the plant as coils of wire of various thicknesses. The wire is fed into a heading machine, which cuts the wire to length and forms the head. The headed blanks are then collected in large movable bins for temporary storage, until they are transported to the next department. If the headed blank needs a slot, it is moved to the Slotting Department. Then the products are again collected in movable bins. The next operation is threading the fastener, either by cutting away the excess metal or by rolling the headed blank between two dies to form the thread (similar to rolling a pencil between your hands).

At this point, although the product looks like a screw or bolt, it needs additional processing to become a finished product. This occurs in operations **5** through **9** in Figure 1. Some fasteners may need to be pointed, and all fasteners must be washed to remove excess oils and foreign materials. Inspection is necessary to determine if the product meets specifications. Some fasteners require heat treatment and plating, and some batches need special packaging.

Throughout the process, the products are stored and moved in large bins from one operation to the next. Finally, they are transported to the finished goods storage area to await sale and shipment.

Figure 1 also shows the location of several support services in the traditional plant. Notice that production support services—repair and maintenance, inventory

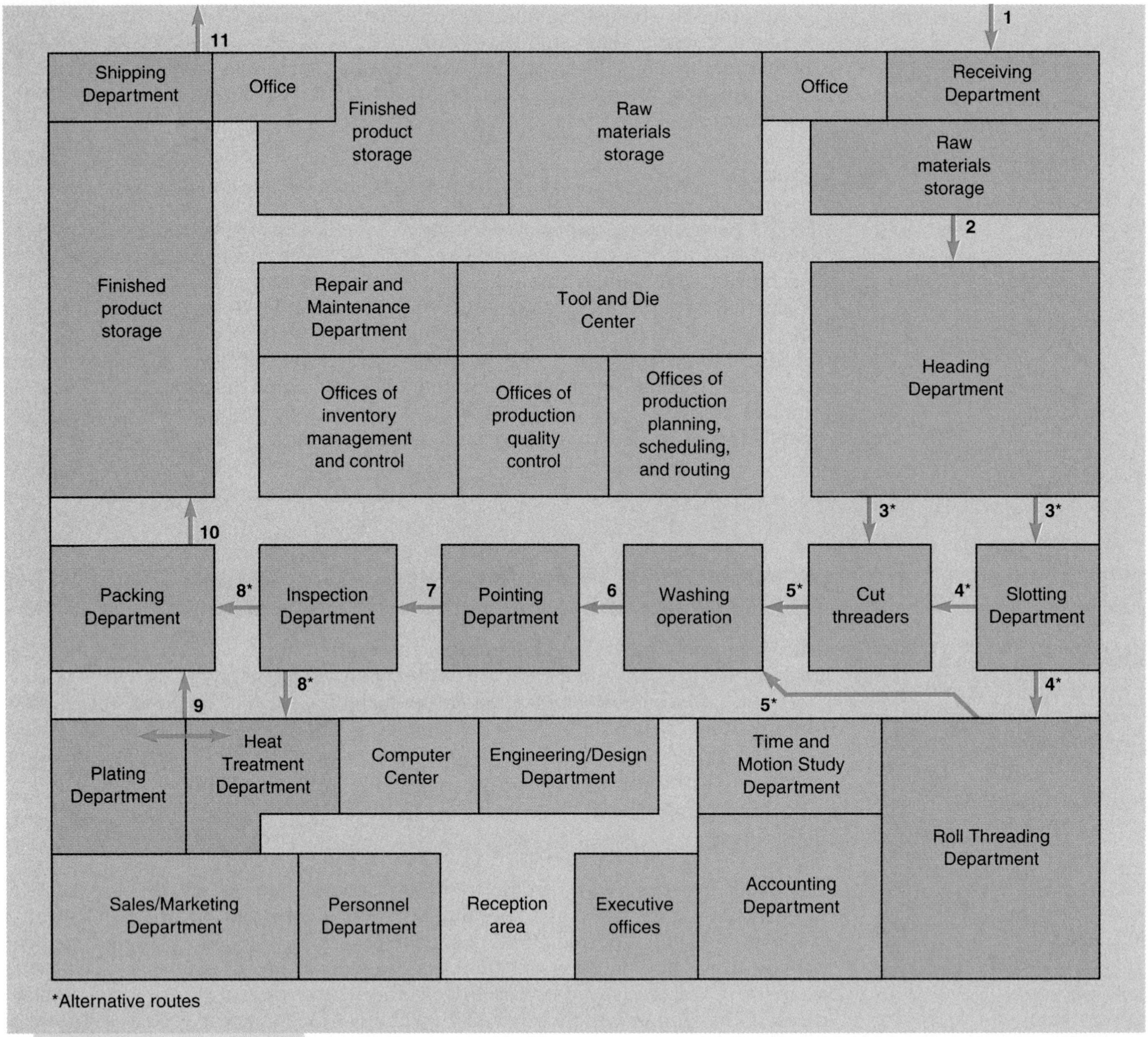

Figure 1
The Plant Layout of a Factory Using Traditional Manufacturing Operations

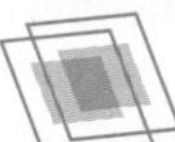

control, quality control, and scheduling and routing—are located in the middle of the factory. The lower part of Figure 1 shows other common support services. Accounting, time and motion study, engineering, computer services, sales, personnel, and executive activities all support the production, sale, or distribution of the company's products.

The JIT Manufacturing Environment

The layout of a JIT production environment is quite different from the traditional factory floor. As discussed earlier, equipment is arranged to form small, autonomous production lines, called work cells or islands. Each work cell has a complete set of machines that produces a product from start to finish. Machine operators run several different machines, help set up production runs, and identify and repair

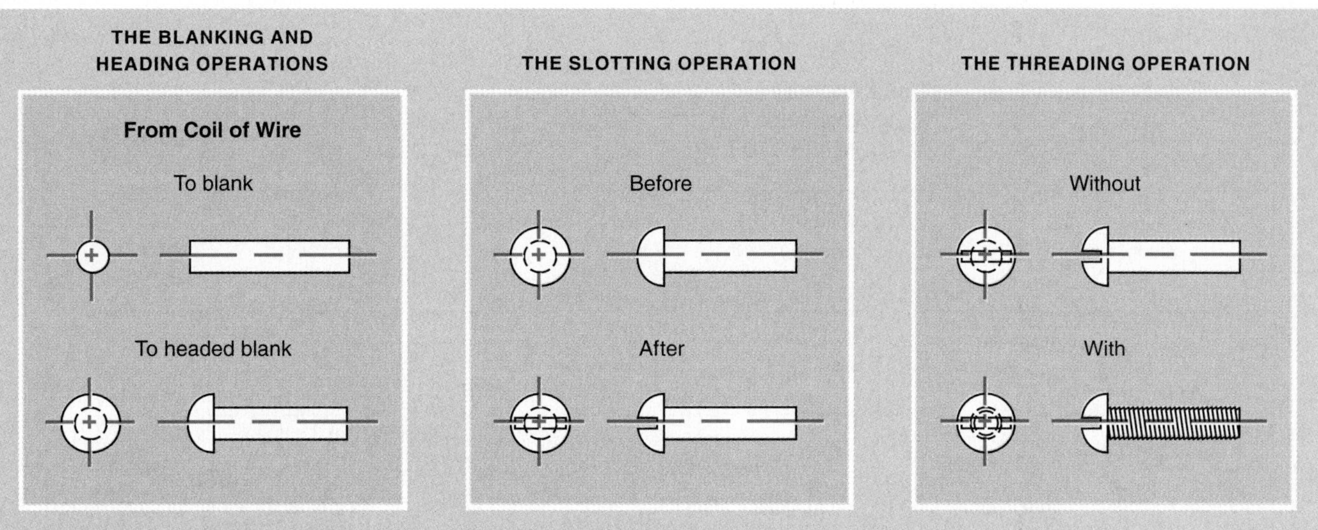

Figure 2
Steps in the Production of a Fastener

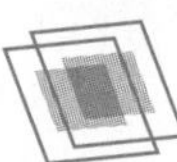

machinery that needs maintenance. Operators are also encouraged to spot areas of inefficiency.

Figure 3 shows how the factory layout of the Stay-Tite Company could be converted into a JIT operating environment. Instead of having large departments containing dozens of similar machines (like the Heading Department in Figure 1), the JIT environment has small operating cells that start and complete a product in minimal time, with minimal movement and storage. Each of the six headers begins a separate operating cell.

In Subplant A, existing machinery is relocated to form JIT work cells. Raw materials are received as they are needed and are unloaded in the materials storage area adjacent to the header scheduled to fill that order. Each of the six work cells includes heading, slotting, threading, and pointing machines, as necessary. Each cell is designed to work on different sizes and types of fasteners. Instead of work in process inventory sitting in travel bins as it moves from one department to the next, wire is fed into the header automatically. The headed blanks move on a conveyer belt to subsequent operations. If an order's specifications call for additional processing, such as heat treatment or plating, the computerized routing system moves the products to those locations. Packaging is the final phase; then, the goods are shipped to the customer. An order for fasteners is completed in a matter of hours, as compared to the days or weeks required when a batch is moved and queued for each departmental operation.

Subplant B in Figure 3 contains three flexible manufacturing systems. A flexible manufacturing system (FMS) is an integrated set of computerized machines and systems designed to complete a series of operations automatically. An FMS often completes a product from beginning to end without the product's being touched or moved by hand. Raw materials are fed in at one end of the FMS machine, and a finished product emerges at the other end.

Assume that FMS1 in Subplant B makes a special type of fastener called a sems screw. To manufacture a sems screw, a locking washer is placed on the screw blank before the threading operation. Once the threads have been rolled on, the washer becomes part of the finished product; it cannot be removed. This FMS cell produces all types and sizes of sems fasteners from start to finish. Each part of the cell represents a different operation—heading, slotting, lock washer fitting, threading, or pointing. All operations are computerized, and the manufacturing process is continuous. When the sems fasteners have been packaged, they are sent to the finished goods area to be shipped to the customer.

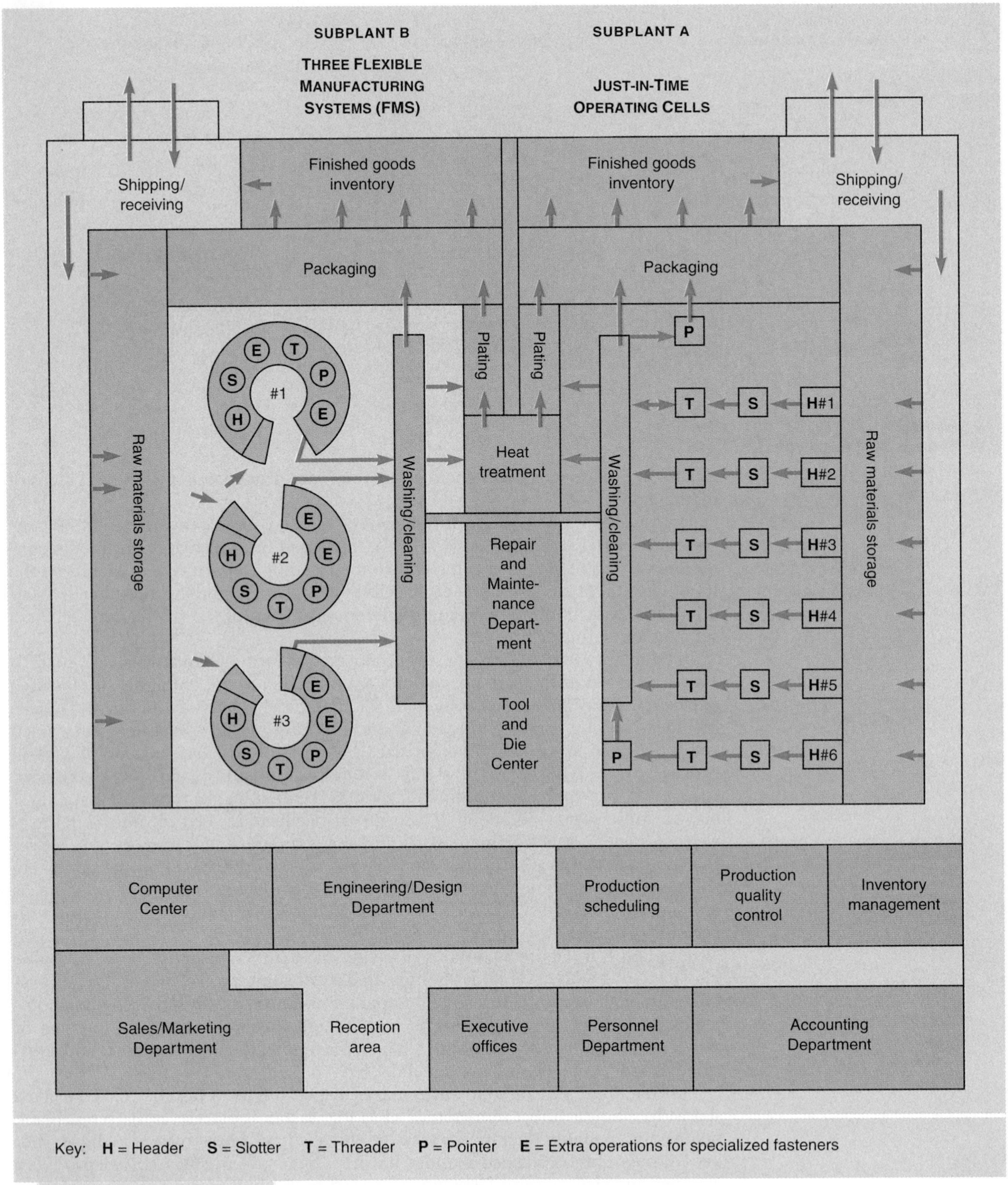

SUBPLANT B

THREE FLEXIBLE MANUFACTURING SYSTEMS (FMS)

SUBPLANT A

JUST-IN-TIME OPERATING CELLS

Shipping/receiving

Finished goods inventory

Finished goods inventory

Shipping/receiving

Packaging

Packaging

Raw materials storage

#1
E T S P H E

#2
E H E S P T

#3
E H E S P T

Washing/cleaning

Plating

Plating

Heat treatment

Repair and Maintenance Department

Tool and Die Center

Washing/cleaning

P

T S H#1

T S H#2

T S H#3

T S H#4

T S H#5

P T S H#6

Raw materials storage

Computer Center

Engineering/Design Department

Production scheduling

Production quality control

Inventory management

Sales/Marketing Department

Reception area

Executive offices

Personnel Department

Accounting Department

Key: H = Header S = Slotter T = Threader P = Pointer E = Extra operations for specialized fasteners

Figure 3
The Plant Layout of a Factory with a JIT Production Environment

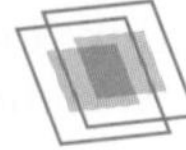

BUSINESS BULLETIN: BUSINESS PRACTICE

Self-directed work teams (SDWTs) are an important element of today's work environment. "A SDWT is a group of employees who have day-to-day responsibilities for managing themselves and a whole work process that delivers a service or a product."[3] Managing such a group of people requires a radical switch from traditional autocratic methods. A successful SDWT manager must play the following roles:

Leader—Holds an inspiring and motivating vision to which team members can make personal commitments.

Role model—"Walks the walk," demonstrating the desired behaviors.

Coach—Teaches and helps team members realize their potential, ensures accountability, and maintains authority.

Business analyzer—Brings the big picture perspective to the team, translates changes in business environment into opportunities for the team.

Advocate—Opens doors for the team, manages senior support, challenges status quo and artificial barriers that limit team performance.

Facilitator—Brings together resources, information, technologies and does whatever it takes to allow the team to be successful.

Customer advocate—Keeps close to the customers, understands their needs, and brings the customer perspective to the team.

Some aspects of the plant layout in Figure 3 are similar to the traditional arrangement in Figure 1. For example, supporting services, such as the Tool and Die Center and the Repair and Maintenance Department, remain close to the manufacturing operation. Heat-treating facilities are very expensive and heat-treated products are still batch-processed, so both subplant layouts share the same heat-treating furnaces.

The remaining parts of the factory in Figure 3 have been redesigned to satisfy the needs of the JIT production process. In particular, the support functions located in the lower part of the layout are similar, but the Computer Center and the Engineering/Design Department have been enlarged. Production scheduling, production quality control, and inventory management have been reduced and moved to the managerial office area because they need to be closer to the computer area than to the production process. In general, many support functions are too expensive to maintain and simply add cost to the product. In our example, the Time and Motion Study Department falls into that category. When a company switches to a JIT operating environment, several support functions are either reduced significantly or eliminated.

JIT, ABC, and the Value Chain

OBJECTIVE 3

Relate JIT to activity-based costing, identify a product's or service's value chain, and distinguish between value-adding and nonvalue-adding activities

In an earlier chapter, you were introduced to activity-based costing as a means of assigning overhead costs to products or services. But activity-based costing is more than an approach to cost assignment. To implement ABC, an organization must analyze its entire operation to identify all activities involved in getting its product or service to the customer. Identifying activities, tracing costs to those activities, and assigning the costs to products or services using cost drivers is only one aspect of an ABC system. Once an activity is identified, it can be analyzed, its value to the organization assessed, and then improved upon or eliminated. It is at this point that ABC

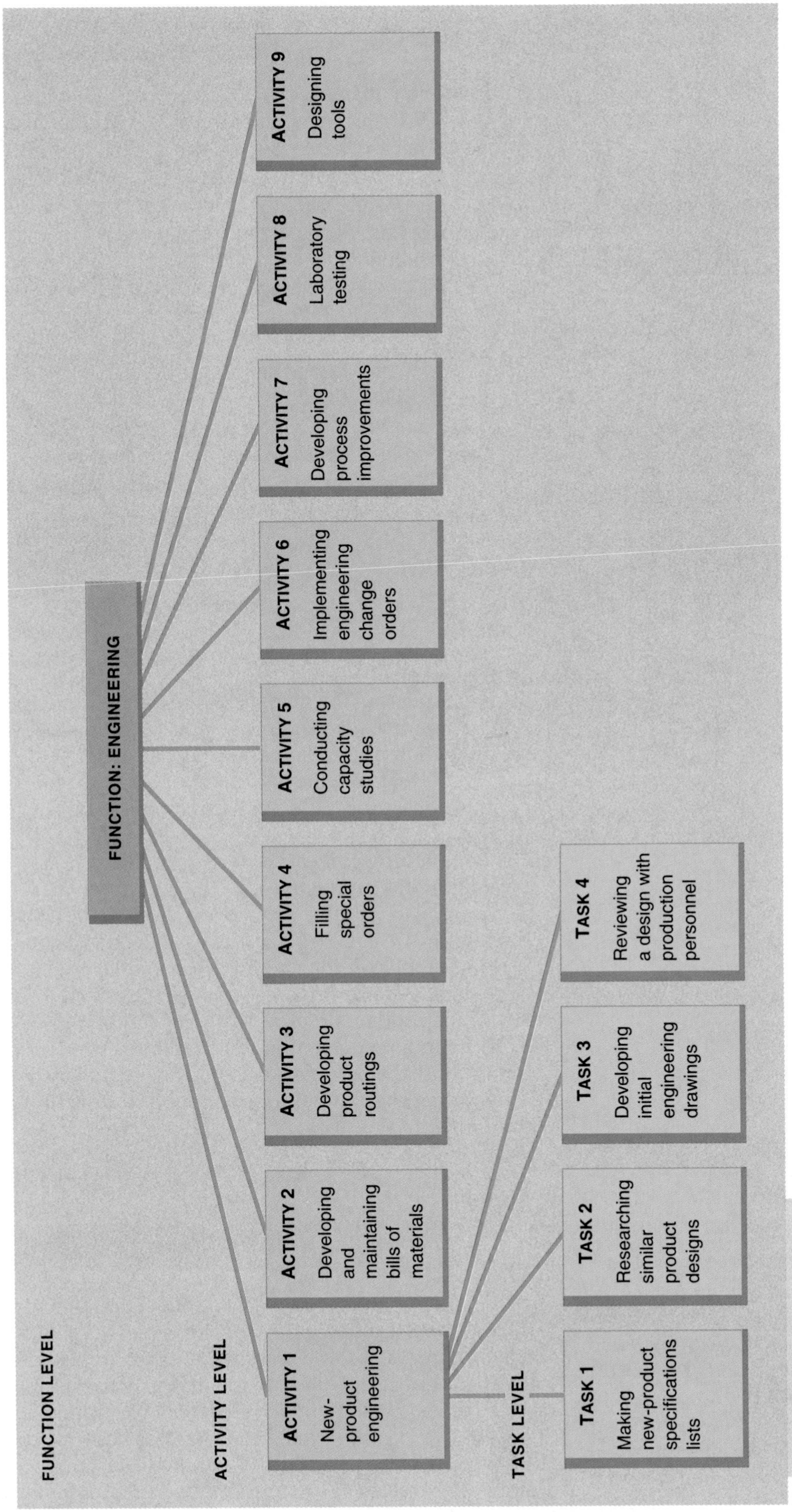

FUNCTION LEVEL

FUNCTION: ENGINEERING

ACTIVITY LEVEL

ACTIVITY 1 New-product engineering

ACTIVITY 2 Developing and maintaining bills of materials

ACTIVITY 3 Developing product routings

ACTIVITY 4 Filling special orders

ACTIVITY 5 Conducting capacity studies

ACTIVITY 6 Implementing engineering change orders

ACTIVITY 7 Developing process improvements

ACTIVITY 8 Laboratory testing

ACTIVITY 9 Designing tools

TASK LEVEL

TASK 1 Making new-product specifications lists

TASK 2 Researching similar product designs

TASK 3 Developing initial engineering drawings

TASK 4 Reviewing a design with production personnel

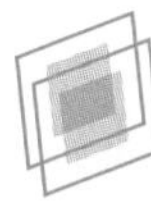

Figure 4
Elements Underlying a Cost Management System

Related Text Assignments:
Q: 8, 9
SE: 3
MRA: 2, 3, 4

becomes a valuable tool in the JIT environment. Activities become the key to minimizing throughput time, and they are identified and evaluated using an approach called process value analysis.

Process Value Analysis—Identifying the Activities

Identifying the activities in an operating process is an important but difficult task. How detailed should the identification process be? What exactly is an activity? Is every action taken in the organization considered an activity? Obviously, the activities identified should be detailed enough so that all essential areas are included, but trying to associate costs with too many areas is not cost-effective. A balanced approach, such as process value analysis, is best. Process value analysis (PVA) is the process of identifying all activities and relating them to events that create or drive the need for the activities and the resources consumed.

From a cost management viewpoint, a business is composed of functions, activities, and tasks. Figure 4 shows the relationships among functions, activities, and tasks. A function is a group of activities that have a common purpose or objective. The functions of a manufacturing organization include product design, engineering, production, distribution, marketing and sales, and customer service. An activity is an action that is needed to accomplish the purpose or objective of a function. As shown in Figure 4, the activities of an engineering department, or function, might include new-product engineering, developing and maintaining bills (lists) of materials used, developing product routings, filling special orders, conducting capacity studies, implementing engineering change orders, developing ways to improve the process, laboratory testing, and designing tools. Tasks are the work elements or operating steps needed to perform and complete an activity. The tasks of a new-product engineering activity might include making a list of specifications for a new product, researching similar product designs, developing an initial set of engineering drawings, and reviewing the design with production personnel. There can be hundreds of tasks for each activity, and many activities supporting each function.

Enrichment Note: Some activities or functions occur before production; their costs are sometimes called *upstream costs.* Other activities or functions occur after production; their costs are called *downstream costs.* In the new operating environment, both upstream and downstream costs are part of a product's total cost.

Activities can be identified as either value-adding or nonvalue-adding. Value-adding activities add value to a product or service as perceived by the customer. They involve resources and related costs that customers feel are necessary and important to satisfying their needs. Nonvalue-adding activities are production- or service-related activities that add cost to a product or service but do not increase its market value. All value-adding activities in a process form a value chain. The value chain of a product or service consists of all the activities in its development path that contribute to its value and marketability. Figure 5 illustrates the value chain of

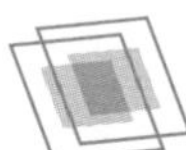

Figure 5
The Value Chain in an Automobile Production Facility

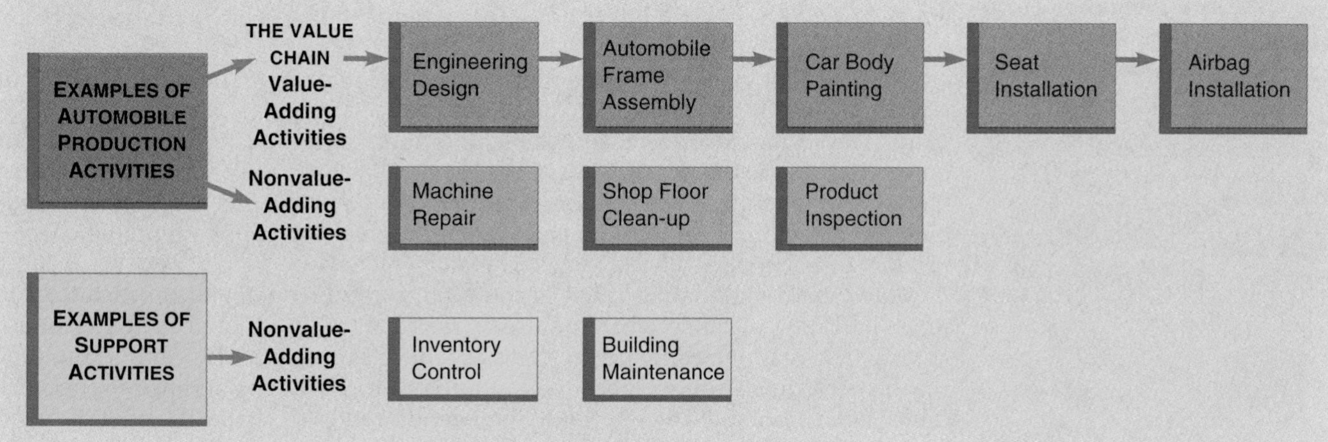

selected activities in the assembly of an automobile. Included are engineering design, automobile frame assembly, car body painting, seat installation, and airbag installation. Figure 5 also shows several types of nonvalue-adding activities, some of which are related directly to the production process and some of which are support activities. They include machine repair, shop floor clean-up, product inspection, inventory control, and building maintenance.

ABC assists managers in a JIT environment to reduce costs and product throughput time by matching costs to activities. To use activity-based costing, an organization must (1) identify all activities in its operating process, (2) develop methods to trace costs to those activities, and (3) identify the primary causes (cost drivers) of the costs for each activity. Process value analysis (PVA) enables management to identify those activities that add value to a product and those that simply add cost.[4] PVA enables managers to look critically at all phases of their operation. It helps them lower costs by reducing or eliminating nonvalue-adding activities. And it improves cost traceability, which can make product costing significantly more accurate and lower costs even more. In addition, managers can use value chain analysis to monitor the operating process to ensure continuous improvements in quality and throughput time. ABC forces managers to focus on their operation's activities, which in turn helps them to increase efficiency by performing those activities just in time.

Not all nonvalue-adding activities are wasteful and therefore automatically targeted for elimination. Every organization maintains support activities without which it could not operate. Although support activities are not included in the value chain, they foster smooth operations. For example, consider the data processing activity in a manufacturing company. It does not add value to the products, but because it is the center of the company's information system, it is a critical activity. Although its costs should be controlled, the activity itself should not be eliminated. A separate inspection activity, on the other hand, is typical of a traditional manufacturing environment and can be eliminated. In a JIT environment, inspection is incorporated into the duties of the work cell operator. Inspection is still performed, but not by people whose primary function is inspection. Machine workers now do the inspecting as they develop the products.

Accounting for Product Costs in a JIT/ABC Environment

OBJECTIVE 4

Compute product costs for an organization that employs an ABC system in a JIT operating environment

Related Text Assignments:
Q: 10, 11, 12, 13
SE: 4
E: 4, 5
P: 2, 3, 4, 6
SD: 2
MRA: 4

When a firm shifts from a traditional to a JIT manufacturing environment, the management accounting system must take a new approach to evaluating costs. If a company also chooses to adopt activity-based costing, additional changes must be made. These changes will affect how costs are determined and what measures are used to monitor performance.

JIT operations can be implemented without the purchase of new equipment, but most organizations add automated equipment when they shift to the new environment. The result is an increase in machine hours and a decrease in direct labor hours. The characteristics of labor also change. Direct labor workers no longer just help shape the product; they are responsible for many tasks that used to be considered indirect labor. Examples include machine setups, machine maintenance, and product inspection.

Many traditional management accounting procedures depend on measures of direct labor. For instance, accountants use measures of direct labor to find standard cost variances and to estimate the costs of potential projects. Most important, they rely on measures of direct labor to compute product unit costs. However, because direct labor hours and dollars are significantly reduced in the JIT environment, costs must be assigned differently. In the new setting, indirect costs may be assigned using machine hours as a basis. In addition, computerized processes and systems, such as activity-based costing, increase the accountant's ability to trace costs to the specific activities that generate them.

Classifying Costs

The JIT work cell and the goal of reducing or eliminating nonvalue-adding activities change the way costs are classified and assigned in a JIT operating environment. The traditional production process can be divided into five parts, or time frames:

Processing time	The actual amount of time spent working on a product
Inspection time	The time spent either looking for product flaws or reworking defective units
Moving time	The time spent moving a product from one operation or department to another
Queue time	The time a product spends waiting to be worked on once it arrives at the next operation or department
Storage time	The time a product spends in materials storage, work in process inventory, or finished goods inventory

Parenthetical Note: The concept of conversion costs is the same as it was in the discussion of process costing.

Clarification Note: While separate inspection costs are reduced, some additional time is added to production because the machine operator is now performing the inspection function. The objectives are to reduce *total* costs and to increase quality.

In product costing under JIT, costs associated with processing time are grouped as either materials costs or conversion costs. Conversion costs include the total of direct labor and manufacturing overhead costs incurred by a production department, JIT work cell, or other work center.

The costs traceable to the other four time frames are not necessary to the production process and are either reduced or eliminated through process and cost control measures. Inspection costs, for instance, are reduced significantly because the cell operator performs inspections. The costs associated with moving the work in process inventory from department to department are reduced because the factory layout is redesigned. Many of the costs of queue time are reduced or eliminated by using work cells. Storage costs are also reduced significantly or eliminated. When the JIT production process operates optimally, raw materials and parts arrive from vendors just in time to be used in the work cells, goods flow continuously through the work cells, and finished products are packaged and shipped immediately to customers. In this way, a large percentage of the old costs of inventory storage are eliminated. Indirect product costs that are not eliminated must still be treated as manufacturing overhead and charged to work cells as part of conversion costs.

Accounting for product costs under JIT is not a complicated procedure; it is summarized in Table 1. A product cost is classified as either a materials cost or a conversion cost. Product costs are traced to work cells. The process costing method is then used to determine product unit costs.

Cost Allocation

In a traditional manufacturing organization, direct labor hours or dollars are a common basis for allocating manufacturing overhead costs to products. Direct labor is the largest cost component of finished goods and is considered the primary cause of manufacturing overhead costs. Therefore, most manufacturing overhead costs are allocated to products based on direct labor hours or dollars.

In the new manufacturing environment, because flexible automated work cells decrease the reliance on direct labor, other measures must replace direct labor in the allocation of overhead costs to finished goods. Two changes in cost allocation are made: (1) the work order is replaced by other measures of production and (2) direct labor and manufacturing overhead costs are merged and accounted for as conversion costs.

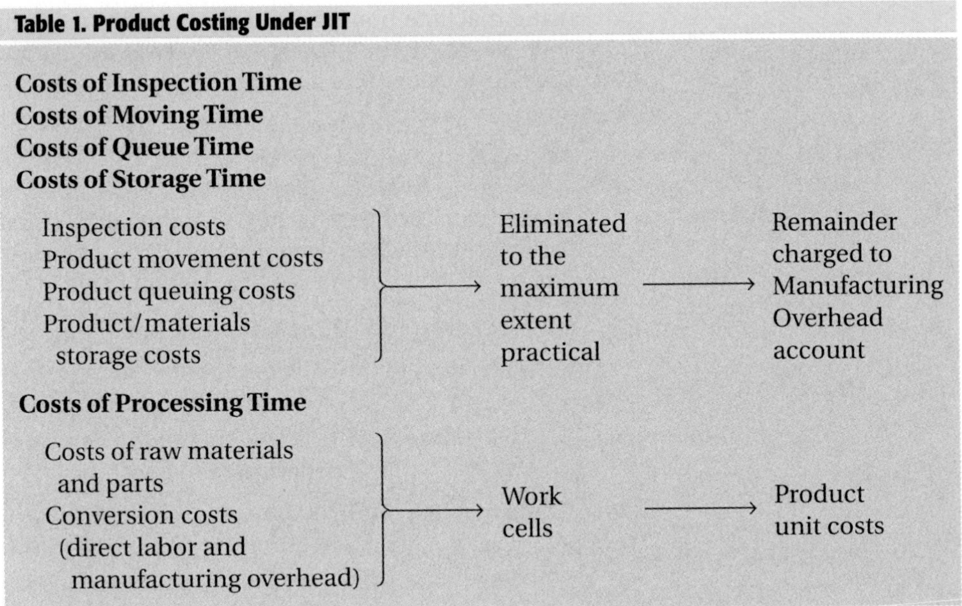
Table 1. Product Costing Under JIT

Costs of Inspection Time
Costs of Moving Time
Costs of Queue Time
Costs of Storage Time

Inspection costs Product movement costs Product queuing costs Product/materials storage costs	→ Eliminated to the maximum extent practical	→ Remainder charged to Manufacturing Overhead account

Costs of Processing Time

Costs of raw materials and parts Conversion costs (direct labor and manufacturing overhead)	→ Work cells	→ Product unit costs

The work order is a key document in a traditional manufacturing system. Direct labor time is accumulated as the order moves from one operation to the next. When the job is complete, the work order contains a record of all direct labor time required for the job. This information enables the accountant to determine the cost of direct labor and to apply manufacturing overhead costs. Work cells and continuous production eliminate the need for work orders. Daily production schedules are maintained, and costs are assigned to the work completed during the day. Detailed reporting, such as the completion of documents like the work order, is not a part of the simplified JIT process.

In the JIT operating environment, indirect costs have little correlation with direct labor hours. The key measure is *throughput time,* the time it takes to move a product through the entire production process. So machine hours become more important than labor hours. Measures of product movement are used to apply conversion costs to products via process costing. In addition, theoretical capacity is used to establish the application rates for conversion costs. (A primary objective of the JIT environment is to produce at theoretical capacity.)

Point to Emphasize: Theoretical capacity is used as the rate base because it is a goal of management in the new operating environment.

Sophisticated computer monitoring of the work cells allows many costs to be traced directly to the cells where products are manufactured. As Table 2 shows, several costs that used to be treated as indirect costs and applied to products using a labor base are treated as direct costs of a work cell. They are directly traceable to the JIT production cell. If standard costs are used, products are costed using predetermined rates for materials and conversion costs. Because each cell manufactures similar products to minimize setup time, materials and conversion costs should be nearly uniform per product per cell. The costs of materials handling, utilities, operating supplies, and supervision can be traced directly to work cells as they are incurred. Depreciation charges are based on units of output, not on time, so depreciation can also be charged directly to work cells based on the number of units produced. Building occupancy costs, property and casualty insurance premiums, and property taxes remain indirect costs and must be allocated to the production cells for inclusion in the conversion cost.

The result of all of these changes is an entirely new approach to product costing. Accounting for direct materials and direct labor remains much the same as in a traditional setting, but accounting for the manufacturing overhead costs changes dra-

Table 2. Changes Caused by JIT: Direct Versus Indirect Costs

Traditional Environment		JIT Environment
Direct	Materials and parts	Direct
Direct	Direct labor	Direct
Indirect	Repairs and maintenance	Direct to work cell
Indirect	Materials handling	Direct to work cell
Indirect	Operating supplies	Direct to work cell
Indirect	Utility costs	Direct to work cell
Indirect	Supervision	Direct to work cell
Indirect	Depreciation	Direct to work cell
Indirect	Supporting service functions	Mostly direct to work cell
Indirect	Building occupancy	Indirect
Indirect	Insurance and taxes	Indirect

matically. These differences can be seen in the case of Tomhank Co., which produces remote control door-opening devices. The company recently converted to a just-in-time operating environment and is also considering changing from a traditional product costing approach to activity-based costing. Michael Marchak, the controller, has been asked to compute the cost of order no. 1142 using both traditional costing and ABC so that the two methods can be compared and analyzed. A summary of the data pertaining to order no. 1142 follows.

Raw materials and labor costs	
Cost of raw materials	$1,650.00
Direct labor hours	30
Average direct labor pay rate	$14.50

Other operating costs include the following.

Traditional Costing Data

Manufacturing overhead costs were assigned at a rate of 350 percent of direct labor dollars.

Activity-Based Costing Data

Activities	Cost Drivers	Cost Assignment Rates	Activity Usage for Order No. 1142
Engineering design	Engineering hours	$25.00 per engineering hour	12 engineering hours
Work cell setup	Number of setups	$28.00 per setup	3 setups
Production work cell	Machine hours	$17.50 per machine hour	24 machine hours
Final tuning	Number of processes	$34.00 per process	3 processes
Packaging/shipping work cell	Cell hours	$38.25 per cell hour	2 cell hours

Building occupancy-related overhead costs are allocated at a rate of $6.50 per production work cell machine hour in the ABC approach.

Michael found that the total costs assigned to order no. 1142 under the two methods would be as follows on the next page.

	Traditional Costing Approach	Activity-Based Costing Approach
Raw materials cost	$1,650.00	$1,650.00
Direct labor cost ($14.50 × 30 hours)	435.00	435.00
Manufacturing overhead cost (traditional costing approach)($14.50 per hour × 30 hours × 350%)	1,522.50	
Cost of activities		
Engineering design		
$25.00 per engineering hour × 12 engineering hours		300.00
Work cell setup		
$28.00 per setup × 3 setups		84.00
Production work cell		
$17.50 per machine hour × 24 machine hours		420.00
Final tuning		
$34.00 per process × 3 processes		102.00
Packaging/shipping work cell		
$38.25 per cell hour × 2 cell hours		76.50
Building occupancy-related overhead		
$6.50 × 24 machine hours		156.00
Total costs assigned to order no. 1142	$3,607.50	$3,223.50

The change to activity-based costing reduced the amount of costs assigned to this order by $384.00, from $3,607.50 to $3,223.50.

Accounting for Product and Service Quality

OBJECTIVE 5

Define and explain total quality management, *and identify and compute the costs of quality for products and services*

Related Text Assignments:
Q: 14, 15
SE: 5
E: 6
P: 5, 7
SD: 3
MRA: 1

Point to Emphasize: Quality is not a technical issue; it is a cultural issue. Quality can be achieved only when all personnel are dedicated to its basic principles.

In the past, U.S. manufacturers often sacrificed or ignored quality in an attempt to lower prices to meet world competition. At the same time, Japan and other countries increased the quality of their goods while lowering prices. To survive in global markets, companies such as AT&T and General Motors Corp. must produce quality products or services at competitive prices. Quality, however, is not something that an organization can simply add at some point in the production process or assume will happen automatically. Inspections can detect bad products, but they do not ensure quality. Managers need reliable measures of quality to meet the goal of producing high-quality, reasonably priced products or services. They need to create a total quality management environment. Total quality management (TQM) is an organizational environment in which all functions work together to build quality into the organization's products or services. The first stage of a TQM environment identifies and manages the costs of quality. The second stage analyzes performance using nonfinancial measures and requires that all operating processes and products be improved continuously.

Cost-Based Measures of Quality[5]

To the average person, quality means that one product or service is better than another—possibly because of design, durability, or some other attribute. In a business setting, however, quality is an operating environment in which a company's product or service meets a customer's specifications the first time it is produced or delivered. The costs of quality are the costs specifically associated with the achieve-

BUSINESS BULLETIN: INTERNATIONAL PRACTICE

Although the value of human resources is never shown on a balance sheet, it is an organization's most important asset. Because intellectual capital is intangible, it is very difficult to measure, so accountants have shied away from quantifying and reporting its value. But that is changing. The Swedish firm Skandia AFS (Assurance and Financial Services) is one of many organizations around the world that are beginning to measure and report the value of their human capital. Skandia created a top management position entitled Director of Intellectual Capital and now publishes a supplement to its annual report presenting measures of this valuable asset. Among the new measures are annual comparisons of (1) information technology investments as a percentage of total expenses, (2) information technology employees as a percentage of all employees, (3) innovative business development expenses as a percentage of total expenses, and (4) the amount of production from newly launched projects. Also tracked is the amount of gross insurance premiums per employee, a bottom-line measure of the impact of human resource utilization and refined business practices on the amount of new business.[6]

ment or nonachievement of product or service quality. Total costs of quality include (1) costs of good quality incurred to ensure the successful development of a product or service and (2) costs of poor quality incurred to transform a faulty product or service into one that is acceptable to the customer.

The costs of quality make up a significant portion of a product's or service's total cost. In his book *Thriving on Chaos,* Tom Peters states that the costs of poor quality consume 25 percent of all labor and assets in manufacturing organizations; in service organizations, they can run as high as 40 percent of labor and asset costs.[7] Therefore, controlling the costs of quality strongly affects profitability. Today's managers should be able to identify the activities associated with improving quality and should be aware of the cost of resources used to achieve high quality.

Teaching Note: The costs of quality can usually be measured directly. However, some subjective costs are also associated with poor quality, such as the loss of goodwill and the potential loss of future sales. Discuss accounting for such costs with your students.

The costs of quality have two components: the costs of conformance, which are the costs incurred to produce a quality product or service, and the costs of nonconformance, which are the costs incurred to correct the defects in a product or service. Costs of conformance are made up of prevention costs and appraisal costs. Prevention costs are the costs associated with the prevention of defects and failures in products and services. Appraisal costs are the costs of activities that measure, evaluate, or audit products, processes, or services to ensure conformance to quality standards and performance requirements. The costs of nonconformance include internal failure costs and external failure costs. Internal failure costs are the costs incurred when defects are discovered before a product or service is delivered to a customer. Costs incurred after the delivery of defective goods or services are called external failure costs. Examples of each cost category are shown in Table 3. Notice that there is a trade-off between the two major categories: If a company spends money on the costs of conformance, the costs of nonconformance should be reduced. However, if little attention is paid to the costs of conformance, then the costs of nonconformance may escalate.

The management accountant is responsible for supplying the information used by managers to control the costs of quality. The overall objective is to avoid costs of nonconformance because internal and external failures affect customers' satisfaction. High initial costs of conformance are justified when they minimize total costs of quality over the life cycle of the product or service. The cost-based measures of quality listed at the bottom of Table 3 are used and explained in the illustrative problem that follows in a few pages.

Table 3. Costs and Measures of Quality

Costs of Conformance to Customer Standards

Prevention costs

Quality training of employees	Design and development of quality equipment
Design review	Quality improvement projects
Quality planning activities	On-line statistical process control
Quality engineering	
Preventive maintenance	

Appraisal costs

Sample preparation	Vendor audits and sample testing
All inspection activities	Maintenance of test equipment
Setup for testing	Quality audits
Product simulation and development	Maintenance of equipment used for quality enhancement

Costs of Nonconformance to Customer Standards

Internal failure costs

Scrap and rework	Failure analysis
Reinspection of rework	Inventory control and scheduling costs
Quality-related downtime	Downgrading because of defects
Losses caused by vendor scrap	

External failure costs

Loss of goodwill and future orders	Returned goods
Warranty claims and adjustments	Investigation of defects
Customer complaint processing	Product recalls
Customer service	Product liability suits

Measures of Quality

Total costs of quality as a percentage of net sales
Ratio of conformance costs to total costs of quality
Ratio of nonconformance costs to total costs of quality
Nonconformance costs as a percentage of net sales

Nonfinancial Measures of Quality

OBJECTIVE 6

Use nonfinancial measures of quality to evaluate operating performance

Related Text Assignments:
Q: 16, 17, 18
SE: 6
E: 7
P: 5, 7
MRA: 1

By measuring the costs of quality, an organization learns how much it has spent in its efforts to improve product or service quality. But critics say that tracking historical data to account for quality performance does little to help production and engineering people enhance quality. What managers need is a measurement and evaluation system that signals poor quality early enough in the process that they can correct problems before a defective product reaches the customer. Implementing a policy of continuous improvement satisfies this need and is the second stage of total quality management.

Nonfinancial measures of operating performance, identified and reported in a timely manner to engineering and production managers, are used to augment traditional cost-based measures in JIT/TQM operations. Although cost control is still an important consideration, a commitment to ongoing product improvement encourages activities that enhance product quality, from design to delivery. As explained

Instructional Strategy: To help the students see the richness and variety of quality reports, divide the class into small groups and assign MRA 1. Ask the groups to present their results, and list key points on the board or screen for class discussion.

Point to Emphasize: The cost of quality is a long-term rather than a short-term measurement. Because of the objective of continuous improvement, the entire product life cycle must be considered.

Enrichment Note: One of the reasons for Japanese success is their increased emphasis on the engineering function, as opposed to the U.S. emphasis on the production function.

Point to Emphasize: Because of the reliance on vendors in JIT, the purchasing company often provides suppliers with technical, managerial, or problem-solving help that the vendors might not be able to afford otherwise.

earlier, those activities, or cost drivers, cause costs. By controlling the nonfinancial performance measures of production activities, managers ultimately maximize the financial return from operations.

Measures of Product Design Quality Problems with quality are often caused by poor design. Most automated production operations use computer-aided design (CAD), a computer-based engineering system with a built-in program to detect product design flaws. Such computer programs automatically identify faultily designed parts or manufacturing processes so that engineers can correct them before actual production begins. The management accountant is not directly involved in this process but should be aware of the existence and use of product design control measures.

Measures of High-Quality Raw Materials One of the most significant changes for an organization that is converting to a JIT/TQM operating environment occurs in the organization's relationship with suppliers of raw materials and parts. Instead of dealing with dozens of suppliers, looking for the lowest costs, JIT companies analyze their vendors to determine which are most reliable, deal in high-quality goods, have a record of timely deliveries, and charge competitive prices. Once such vendors are identified, they become an integral part of the production team. A JIT organization works closely with its vendors to ensure a continuing supply of high-quality raw materials and parts. Vendors may even contribute to product design to ensure that the correct materials and parts are used. The management accountant should conduct the necessary analyses to identify and monitor reliable vendors, so that high-quality, well-priced materials are available when they are needed.

Terminology Note: A control system that utilizes in-process controls is often called a *feed-forward control system.* It monitors inputs to a process, anticipates problems, and makes necessary corrections before unusable output is produced.

Measures of In-Process and Delivery Controls Automated machinery linked to a flexible manufacturing system can easily be programmed with in-process product control mechanisms. Product quality problems are detected by computer-programmed control techniques, and corrective action is taken when a problem is detected. No longer is it necessary to wait for a specified inspection point to detect a product flaw. In-process controls form a continuous inspection system that highlights trouble spots, significantly reduces scrap, cuts overall product rework machine time, and eliminates the nonvalue-adding product costs of traditional inspection activities. Although management accountants are not expected to develop and program FMS in-process quality controls, they should understand the control points and maintain records of the rates of defective parts produced. Because product delivery is part of overall quality, the accountant should also maintain records to track the performance of the firm's delivery systems.

Point to Emphasize: Notice the emphasis on customer satisfaction. This emphasis drives the quality and value chain network.

Measures of Customer Acceptance The sale and shipment of a product no longer marks the end of performance measurement. Customer follow-up helps evaluate total customer satisfaction. Accounting measures used to determine the degree of customer acceptance include (1) the percentage of shipments returned by customers, (2) the number and types of customer complaints, (3) the percentage of shipments accepted by customers, and (4) an analysis of the number and causes of warranty claims. Several companies have developed their own customer satisfaction indexes from these measures so they can compare different product lines over different time periods.

Table 4 contains a summary of the nonfinancial measures of quality used by management accountants as discussed above. This is only a sample of the many nonfinancial measures used to monitor quality. These measures help a company move toward its goal of continuously seeking to produce higher-quality products and to improve production processes.

Table 4. Nonfinancial Measures of Quality Used by Management Accountants

Measures of High-Quality Raw Materials	
Vendor quality analysis	An analysis of the quality of materials and parts received; prepared for each vendor used
Vendor delivery analysis	An analysis of timely vendor deliveries; prepared for each vendor used
Measures of In-Process and Delivery Controls	
Production quality level	Defective parts per million; usually tracked by product line
Percentage of on-time deliveries	Percentage of total shipments received by the promised date
Measures of Customer Acceptance	
Returned-order percentage	Number of shipments returned by customers as a percentage of total shipments
Customer complaints	An analysis of the number and types of customer complaints
Customer acceptance percentage	Number of shipments accepted as a percentage of total shipments; computed for each customer
Warranty claims	An analysis of the number and causes of warranty claims

Illustrative Problem: Measuring Quality

Using many of the examples of the costs of quality identified in Table 3 and the nonfinancial measures of quality listed in Table 4, the following situations demonstrate how a company's progress toward its goal of achieving total quality management is measured and evaluated.

Evaluating the Costs of Quality As shown in Part A of Exhibit 1, three companies, Able, Baker, and Cane, have taken different approaches to achieving product quality. All three companies are the same size, each generating $15 million in sales last year.

Evaluate each company's approach to quality enhancement by analyzing the costs of quality and by answering the following questions.

Which company is more likely to remain competitive in the global marketplace?

Which company has serious problems with its product's quality?

What do you think will happen to the total costs of quality for each company over the next five years? Why?

SOLUTION

The costs of quality have been summarized and analyzed in Exhibit 2. The analysis shows that each company spent between 10.22 and 10.48 percent of its sales dollars on costs of quality. The following statements are based on that analysis.

Which company is more likely to remain competitive in the global marketplace? Able Co. spent the most money on costs of quality. More importantly, however, about 80 percent of the money was spent on costs of conformance. Those dollars spent now will bring benefits in years to come. The company's focus on the costs

Exhibit 1. Measures of Quality—Data for Analysis

A. Costs of Quality	Able Co.	Baker Co.	Cane Co.
Annual Sales	$15,000,000	$15,000,000	$15,000,000
Costs of Conformance to Customer Standards			
Prevention Costs			
Quality training of employees	$ 210,000	$ 73,500	$ 136,500
Quality engineering	262,500	115,500	189,000
Design review	105,000	42,000	84,000
Preventive maintenance	157,500	84,000	115,500
Appraisal Costs			
Setup for testing	$ 126,000	$ 63,000	$ 73,500
Product simulation and development	199,500	31,500	115,500
Quality audits	84,000	21,000	42,000
Vendor audits and sample testing	112,500	52,500	63,000
Costs of Nonconformance to Customer Standards			
Internal Failure Costs			
Scrap and rework	$ 21,000	$ 189,000	$ 126,000
Reinspection of rework	15,750	126,000	73,500
Quality-related downtime	42,000	231,000	178,500
Losses caused by vendor scrap	26,250	84,000	52,500
External Failure Costs			
Warranty claims	$ 47,250	$ 94,500	$ 84,000
Returned goods	15,750	68,250	36,750
Investigation of defects	26,250	78,750	57,750
Customer service	120,750	178,500	126,000

B. Nonfinancial Measures of Quality	Able Co.	Baker Co.	Cane Co.
Vendor Quality Analysis			
20x3	98.20%	94.40%	95.20%
20x4	98.40%	93.20%	95.30%
20x5	98.60%	93.10%	95.20%
Production Quality Level (product defects per million)			
20x3	1,400	4,120	2,710
20x4	1,340	4,236	2,720
20x5	1,210	4,340	2,680
Percentage of On-Time Deliveries			
20x3	94.20%	76.20%	84.10%
20x4	94.60%	75.40%	84.00%
20x5	95.40%	73.10%	83.90%
Order-Return Percentage			
20x3	1.30%	6.90%	4.20%
20x4	1.10%	7.20%	4.10%
20x5	0.80%	7.60%	4.00%
Number of Customer Complaints			
20x3	22	189	52
20x4	18	194	50
20x5	12	206	46

Exhibit 2. Analysis of Costs of Quality

	Able Co.	Baker Co.	Cane Co.
Annual Sales	$15,000,000	$15,000,000	$15,000,000
Costs of Conformance to Customer Standards			
Prevention Costs			
Quality training of employees	$ 210,000	$ 73,500	$ 136,500
Quality engineering	262,500	115,500	189,000
Design review	105,000	42,000	84,000
Preventive maintenance	157,500	84,000	115,500
Subtotal	$ 735,000	$ 315,000	$ 525,000
Appraisal Costs			
Setup for testing	$ 126,000	$ 63,000	$ 73,500
Product simulation and development	199,500	31,500	115,500
Quality audits	84,000	21,000	42,000
Vendor audits and sample testing	112,500	52,500	63,000
Subtotal	$ 522,000	$ 168,000	$ 294,000
Total Conformance Costs	$ 1,257,000	$ 483,000	$ 819,000
Costs of Nonconformance to Customer Standards			
Internal Failure Costs			
Scrap and rework	$ 21,000	$ 189,000	$ 126,000
Reinspection of rework	15,750	126,000	73,500
Quality-related downtime	42,000	231,000	178,500
Losses caused by vendor scrap	26,250	84,000	52,500
Subtotal	$ 105,000	$ 630,000	$ 430,500
External Failure Costs			
Warranty claims	$ 47,250	$ 94,500	$ 84,000
Returned goods	15,750	68,250	36,750
Investigation of defects	26,250	78,750	57,750
Customer service	120,750	178,500	126,000
Subtotal	$ 210,000	$ 420,000	$ 304,500
Total Nonconformance Costs	$ 315,000	$ 1,050,000	$ 735,000
Total Costs of Quality	$ 1,572,000	$ 1,533,000	$ 1,554,000
Total costs of quality as a percentage of actual sales	10.48%	10.22%	10.36%
Ratio of conformance costs to total costs of quality	.80 to 1	.32 to 1	.53 to 1
Ratio of nonconformance costs to total costs of quality	.20 to 1	.68 to 1	.47 to 1
Nonconformance costs as a percentage of sales	2.10%	7.00%	4.90%

of conformance means that only a small amount had to be spent on internal and external failure costs. The resulting high-quality products would lead to high customer satisfaction.

Which company has serious problems with its product's quality? Baker Co. spent the least on costs of quality, but that's not the reason the company is in serious trouble. Over 68 percent of its costs of quality ($1,050,000 of a total of $1,533,000) was spent on internal and external failure costs. Scrap costs, reinspection costs, the cost of downtime, warranty costs, and customer service costs were all high.

Baker's products are very low in quality, which will mean hard times in future years.

What do you think will happen to the total costs of quality for each company over the next five years? Why? When money is spent on costs of conformance early in a product's life cycle, quality is integrated into the development and production processes. Once a high level of quality has been established, total costs of quality should be lower in future years. Able Co. seems to be in that position today.

Baker's costs of conformance will have to increase significantly if the company expects to stay in business. Seven percent of its sales revenue is spent on internal and external failure costs. Because its products are not being accepted by the marketplace, the company is vulnerable to its competitors. It is in a weak position to face competition on a global scale.

Cane Co. is riding the middle road. It is spending a little more than half (53 percent) of its cost-of-quality dollars on conformance, so product quality should be increasing. But the company is still incurring high internal and external failure costs. Cane's managers must learn to prevent such costs if they expect to remain competitive.

Evaluating Nonfinancial Measures of Quality From the information presented in Part B of Exhibit 1, evaluate each company's experience in its pursuit of total quality management.

SOLUTION

The nonfinancial measures presented in Exhibit 1 identify trends for each company for three years—20x3, 20x4, and 20x5. Those data tend to support the findings in the analysis of the costs of quality.

Able Co. For Able Co. in 20x5, 98.6 percent of the raw materials and parts received from suppliers have been high quality, and the quality over the three years has been increasing. The product defect rate, measured in number of defects per million, has been decreasing rapidly, proof that the costs of conformance are having a positive effect. The percentage of on-time deliveries has been increasing, and both the order-return percentage and the number of customer complaints have been decreasing significantly, which means that customer acceptance and satisfaction have been increasing.

Baker Co. Baker Co.'s experience is not encouraging. The number of high-quality shipments of materials and parts from vendors has been decreasing; the product defect rate has been increasing (it seems to be out of control); on-time deliveries were bad to begin with and have been getting worse; more goods have been returned each year; and customer complaints have been on the rise. All those signs reflect the company's high nonconformance costs of quality.

Cane Co. Cane Co. is making progress toward higher quality standards, but that progress is very slow. Most of the nonfinancial measures indicate a very slight positive trend except for percentage of on-time deliveries. More money needs to be spent on the conformance costs of quality.

Measuring Service Quality

Point to Emphasize: Delivery of quality goods and services is not restricted to a specific type or size of organization. Any operation can benefit from providing high-quality goods or services.

The quality of services rendered can be measured and analyzed. Many of the costs of product conformance and nonconformance also apply to the development and delivery of a service. Flaws in service design lead to poor-quality services. Timely service delivery is as important as timely product shipments. Customer satisfaction in a service business can be measured by services accepted or rejected, the number of complaints, and the number of returning customers. Poor service development leads to internal and external failure costs. Many of the costs-of-quality categories and several of the nonfinancial measures of quality can be applied directly to services and can be adopted by any type of service company.

Chapter Review

REVIEW OF LEARNING OBJECTIVES

1. **Define and explain the *just-in-time operating philosophy* and identify the elements of a JIT operating environment.** Just-in-time (JIT) is an overall operating philosophy that requires that all resources, including materials, personnel, and facilities, be used only as needed. Its objectives are to improve productivity and reduce waste. JIT is based on continuous production flow and requires that each part of the production process work in concert with the other components. Direct labor workers in a JIT environment are empowered with expanded responsibilities, which helps to reduce waste in labor cost, space, and production time. The first step in attaining JIT operating efficiencies is to redesign the plant layout, moving machines and processes closer together to reduce throughput time. The elements of a JIT operating environment are (1) maintain minimum inventory levels; (2) develop pull-through production planning and scheduling; (3) purchase materials and produce products as needed, in smaller lot sizes; (4) perform quick, inexpensive machine setups; (5) create flexible manufacturing work cells; (6) develop a multiskilled work force; (7) maintain high levels of product quality; (8) enforce a system of effective preventive maintenance; and (9) encourage continuous improvement of the work environment.
2. **Compare the traditional approach to production with just-in-time operations.** Traditional manufacturing plants are divided into functional departments, with similar machines grouped in each department. Products flow from department to department. Raw materials are ordered well in advance and stored until needed. Work in process and finished goods inventories are usually large. And long production runs are scheduled to reduce setup costs and lower fixed costs per product.

   Just-in-time manufacturing operations are organized in work cells. All machines necessary for the production of a product line are grouped together to reduce the distance between operations and the time it takes to produce a product. Raw materials and parts are ordered as needed. Goods are pulled through the work cell based on actual orders received. Work in process inventories are almost nonexistent, and finished products are shipped when completed. And the size of a production run is based on the size of the order.
3. **Relate JIT to activity-based costing, identify a product's or a service's value chain, and distinguish between value-adding and nonvalue-adding activities.** When converting to a JIT operating environment, managers must try to reduce product throughput time by reducing or eliminating wasted time. They accomplish this in part by reducing or eliminating all nonvalue-adding activities from the production and distribution processes. Such actions also help to reduce costs. To implement ABC, an organization must analyze its entire operation to identify all activities involved in getting its product or service to the customer. Once an activity is identified, it can be analyzed, its value to the organization can be assessed, and it can be improved upon or eliminated. Activities are classified as either value-adding or nonvalue-adding. Value-adding activities add value to a product or service as perceived by the customer. The value chain of a product or service consists of all the activities in its development path that contribute to its marketability. Nonvalue-adding activities add cost to a product or service but do not increase its market value. Nonvalue-adding activities that are necessary for product development are not eliminated, but many nonvalue-adding activities, such as separate inspection, can be eliminated.
4. **Compute product costs for an organization that employs an ABC system in a JIT operating environment.** In a JIT/ABC environment, costs are classified and assigned differently than in a traditional setting. Sophisticated computer monitoring allows many costs to be traced directly to the cells where products are manufactured. Thus, some costs that were traditionally treated as indirect costs are classified as direct costs. These include the costs of materials handling, utilities, operating supplies, and supervision. Costs associated with processing time are grouped as either materials costs or conversion costs. Materials costs include the costs of both direct materials and indirect materials, such as parts and supplies. Conversion costs include the total of direct

labor and manufacturing overhead costs incurred by a work cell. All other costs are considered nonvalue-adding and are targeted for reduction or elimination. Once product costs have been traced to a work cell, the process costing method is used to determine product unit costs.

5. **Define and explain *total quality management,* and identify and compute the costs of quality for products and services.** Total quality management (TQM) is an organizational environment in which all business functions work together to build quality into the firm's products or services. The first stage of a TQM environment identifies and manages the costs of quality. The costs of quality are measures of costs specifically related to the achievement or nonachievement of product or service quality. The costs of quality have two components. One is the cost of conforming to a customer's product or service standards by preventing defects and failures and by appraising quality and performance. The other is the cost of nonconformance—the costs incurred when defects are discovered before a product is shipped and the costs incurred after a defective product or faulty service is delivered. The objective of TQM is to reduce or eliminate the costs of nonconformance, the internal and external failure costs associated with customer dissatisfaction. The high initial costs of conformance can be justified if they minimize the total costs of quality over the life cycle of a product or service.
6. **Use nonfinancial measures of quality to evaluate operating performance.** Nonfinancial measures of quality are related to product design, raw materials input, in-process and delivery control, and customer acceptance. Such measures help a firm meet its goal of continuously improving product or service quality and the production process.

REVIEW OF CONCEPTS AND TERMINOLOGY

The following concepts and terms were introduced in this chapter:

LO 3 **Activity:** An action needed to accomplish the purpose or objective of a function.

LO 5 **Appraisal costs:** The costs of activities that measure, evaluate, or audit products, processes, or services to ensure conformance to quality standards and performance requirements; a cost of conformance.

LO 6 **Computer-aided design (CAD):** A computer-based engineering system with a built-in program to detect product design flaws.

LO 4 **Conversion costs:** The total of direct labor and manufacturing overhead costs incurred by a production department, JIT work cell, or other work center.

LO 5 **Costs of conformance:** The costs incurred to produce a quality product or service; they include prevention costs and appraisal costs.

LO 5 **Costs of nonconformance:** The costs incurred to correct the defects in a product or service; they include internal failure costs and external failure costs.

LO 5 **Costs of quality:** The costs specifically associated with the achievement or nonachievement of product or service quality; they include the costs of conformance and the costs of nonconformance.

LO 5 **External failure costs:** The costs incurred when defects are discovered after a product or service has been delivered to a customer; a cost of nonconformance.

LO 2 **Flexible manufacturing system (FMS):** An integrated set of computerized machines and systems designed to complete a series of operations automatically.

LO 3 **Function:** A group of activities that have a common purpose or objective.

LO 4 **Inspection time:** The time spent either looking for product flaws or reworking defective units.

LO 5 **Internal failure costs:** The costs incurred when defects are discovered before a product or a service is delivered to a customer; a cost of nonconformance.

LO 1 **Just-in-time (JIT) operating philosophy:** An overall operating philosophy that requires that all resources, including materials, personnel, and facilities, be used only as needed, with the objectives of improving productivity and eliminating waste.

LO 4 **Moving time:** The time spent moving a product from one operation or department to another.

LO 3 **Nonvalue-adding activity:** A production- or service-related activity that adds cost to a product or service but does not increase its market value.

LO 5 **Prevention costs:** The costs associated with the prevention of defects and failures in products and services; a cost of conformance.

LO 4 **Processing time:** The actual amount of time spent working on a product.

LO 3 **Process value analysis (PVA):** The process of identifying all activities and relating them to events that cause or drive the need for the activities and the resources consumed.

LO 1 **Pull-through production:** A production system in which a customer's order triggers the purchase of materials and the scheduling of production for the required products.

LO 5 **Quality:** An operating environment in which a company's product or service meets a customer's specifications the first time it is produced or delivered.

LO 4 **Queue time:** The time a product spends waiting to be worked on once it arrives at the next operation or department.

LO 4 **Storage time:** The time a product spends in materials storage, work in process inventory, or finished goods inventory.

LO 3 **Tasks:** The work elements or operating steps needed to perform and complete an activity.

LO 5 **Total quality management (TQM):** An organizational environment in which all functions work together to build quality into the firm's products or services.

LO 3 **Value-adding activity:** A production- or service-related activity that adds value to a product or service as perceived by the customer.

LO 3 **Value chain:** All activities in the development path of a product or service that contribute to its value and marketability.

LO 1 **Work cell:** An autonomous production line that can perform all required operations efficiently and continuously.

REVIEW PROBLEM

Computation of JIT Unit Costs

LO 5 Chaney Food Products Co. installed its first automated just-in-time work cell in December 20x1. The cell began producing large frozen pizzas on January 2, 20x2. Before the JIT cell was installed, the pizzas were processed through four departments: Dough Processing, Meat and Vegetable Preparation, Ingredients Application, and Trimming and Packing. The new JIT cell performs all of these operations in a continuous process and only one skilled operator is needed to run the cell. The company's general manager is interested in how the new cell is affecting the unit costs of the large pizzas and has asked you to prepare a comparative analysis. Data for the calendar quarters before and after installation of the cell are summarized below.

	Large Pizzas	
	Quarter Ended 3/31/x2	Quarter Ended 12/31/x1
Units produced	65,900	43,200
Raw materials		
Pizza dough	$ 36,245	$ 21,600
Meats, cheese, and vegetables	42,835	30,240
Direct labor		
Dough preparation		12,960
Meat and vegetable preparation		10,800
Ingredients application		17,280
Trimming and packaging		21,600
JIT cell	26,360	
Manufacturing overhead		
Indirect labor	19,770	864
Ingredients waste	6,590	25,920
Inspection labor	—	4,320
Lift truck labor	1,977	5,184
Electricity	3,295	1,296
Spoiled units	1,318	6,912
Production scheduling costs	659	8,640
Machine depreciation	9,885	4,752
Building depreciation	2,636	2,592
Supplies	593	432
Storage space costs	659	5,616
Supervisory salaries	7,908	7,776
Machine lubricants	923	648
Repairs and maintenance	3,954	1,728
Total costs incurred	$165,607	$191,160

REQUIRED

1. Compute the unit cost for each cost category (raw materials, direct labor, and manufacturing overhead) for the last quarter of 20x1 and the first quarter of 20x2.
2. Compute and compare total unit costs for the two quarters.
3. Which individual costs were changed the most per unit by the installation of the JIT cell? Should each change have been anticipated? State your reasons.

ANSWER TO REVIEW PROBLEM

1. The unit cost for each cost category and the total unit costs are as shown on the next page.
2. The unit cost of a pizza has decreased by $1.92 ($4.43 – $2.51), or by over 43% of the old cost. The new JIT work cell is profitable.

	Large Pizzas*	
	Quarter Ended 3/31/x2	**Quarter Ended 12/31/x1**
Raw materials		
Pizza dough	$ .55	$ .50
Meats, cheese, and vegetables	.65	.70
Total raw materials unit cost	$1.20	$1.20
Direct labor		
Dough preparation		$ .30
Meat and vegetable preparation		.25
Ingredients application		.40
Trimming and packaging		.50
JIT cell	$ .40	
Total direct labor unit cost	$ .40	$1.45
Manufacturing overhead		
Indirect labor	$ .30	$ .02
Ingredients waste	.10	.60
Inspection labor	—	.10
Lift truck labor	.03	.12
Electricity	.05	.03
Spoiled units	.02	.16
Production scheduling costs	.01	.20
Machine depreciation	.15	.11
Building depreciation	.04	.06
Supplies	.01	.01
Storage space costs	.01	.13
Supervisory salaries	.12	.18
Machine lubricants	.01	.02
Repairs and maintenance	.06	.04
Total manufacturing overhead unit cost	$ .91	$1.78
Product unit cost	$2.51	$4.43

*Unit costs rounded to nearest penny.

3. Nine costs were changed the most by the installation of the JIT cell.
   a. Direct labor decreased by $1.05 per unit. This change could be anticipated because only one operator is now needed to run the cell.
   b. Indirect labor increased by $.28 per unit. This change could be anticipated because more support labor is needed by the JIT cell.
   c. Ingredients waste decreased by $.50 per unit. This change could be anticipated because the JIT cell is more efficient.
   d. Inspection labor cost disappeared. This change could be anticipated because under JIT inspection is performed by cell operators instead of in a separate process.
   e. Lift truck labor decreased by $.09 per unit. This change could be anticipated because in a JIT setting there is very little need to move materials.
   f. Spoiled units decreased by $.14 per unit. This change could be anticipated because there is little spoilage in a JIT cell due to lower inventories on hand.
   g. Production scheduling costs decreased by $.19 per unit. This change could be anticipated because a JIT cell requires less production scheduling than a traditional production operation.
   h. Storage space costs decreased by $.12 per unit. This change could be anticipated because there is very little inventory to store in a JIT setting.
   i. Supervisory salaries decreased by $.06 per unit. This change could be anticipated since fewer employees need direct supervision in a JIT.

Chapter Assignments

BUILDING YOUR KNOWLEDGE FOUNDATION

Questions

1. Briefly describe the just-in-time operating environment.
2. What is pull-through production? In what ways does it differ from push-through production?
3. What is a flexible work cell?
4. What changes occur in the responsibilities of a machine operator in the JIT operating environment?
5. How does the inspection function change in a JIT environment?
6. Why is preventive maintenance of machinery critical to the operation of a JIT work cell?
7. Contrast the traditional manufacturing layout and the JIT production layout.
8. What is process value analysis?
9. What is a nonvalue-adding activity? Why is it important to identify such activities?
10. What is cost management?
11. How has the movement to JIT operations and automated manufacturing facilities affected the role of direct labor in management accounting practices?
12. Name and describe the five time frames included in the traditional manufacturing process.
13. Identify several costs that are accounted for as direct costs in a JIT environment but are treated as indirect costs in a traditional setting.
14. How is quality defined in business? What are the costs of quality?
15. What are two components of the costs of quality? What types of costs make up each component?
16. What are two nonfinancial measures of quality for raw materials? What is each designed to measure?
17. What are two nonfinancial measures of quality for in-process and delivery control? What is each designed to measure?
18. What are four nonfinancial measures of quality for customer acceptance? What is each designed to measure?

Short Exercises

SE 1. **LO 1** *Implementing a JIT Operating Environment*

Match each of the following basic concepts underlying the new methods of manufacturing to the related element of the JIT operating environment.

Basic concepts:

1. Simple is better.
2. The work environment must emphasize continuous improvement.
3. Reduce waste by reducing or eliminating inventories.
4. Any activity or function that does not add value to the product should be eliminated or reduced.

Related elements of the JIT operating environment:

a. Purchase materials and manufacture products as needed, in smaller lot sizes.
b. Perform quick, inexpensive machine setups.
c. Create flexible manufacturing work cells.
d. Enforce a system of effective preventive maintenance.

LO 2 *Traditional Versus Just-in-Time Production*

SE 2. Tell whether each of the following descriptions applies to traditional manufacturing, just-in-time manufacturing, or both.

1. Large departments contain dozens of similar machines.
2. Conveyor belts move the product from one operation to the next.
3. Products can be packaged and shipped in less time, since orders are not moved and queued for each departmental operation.
4. Supporting services, such as repair and maintenance, are close to the manufacturing operations.
5. Travel bins are used to store work in process inventory as it moves between departments.
6. Small operating cells start and complete a product in minimal time, with minimal movement and storage.

LO 3 *Identifying a Product's Value Chain*

SE 3. Which of the following activities would be part of the value chain of a manufacturing company?

Product inspection
Machine drilling
Materials storage
Product engineering
Plating/packing
Cost accounting
Moving work in process
Inventory control

LO 4 *JIT/ABC Product Costing*

SE 4. In a JIT/ABC operating environment, many costs that were traditionally treated as indirect production costs can be traced directly to either a product or a work cell. Which of the following would become direct costs in a JIT/ABC setting?

Building maintenance costs
Machine setup costs
Factory fire insurance costs
Supervision costs
Materials handling costs

LO 5 *Costs of Quality in a Service Business*

SE 5. Modesto-Kropp Insurance Agency incurred the following activity costs related to service quality. Identify each as a cost of conformance (CC) or a cost of nonconformance (CN).

1. Policy processing improvements, $76,400
2. Response to customer complaints, $34,100
3. Training of policy writers, $12,300
4. Losses from policy error, $82,700
5. Policy proofing, $39,500

LO 6 *Nonfinancial Measures of Quality*

SE 6. A fast-food restaurant that specializes in deluxe cheeseburgers has engaged you as a consultant, and you have suggested that management use nonfinancial measures to assess quality. List two factors identifiable by nonfinancial measures that would indicate good quality and two factors that would indicate poor quality.

Exercises

LO 1 *JIT and Global Competition*

E 1. Necula Corporation has been losing money for the past two years. The problem, according to management, is that Necula's foreign competitors are making identical products of higher quality and selling them at lower prices. The competitors have superior production methods and much lower product scrap rates. Necula's management has decided to adopt a just-in-time operating philosophy. How will the JIT operating environment help the company become more profitable? Give specific examples of changes that will increase profits.

E 2. LO 1 LO 2 *JIT Versus Traditional Production Environments*

Tell whether each of the following statements describes a just-in-time (JIT) or a traditional production environment.

1. Minimum inventories are maintained.
2. A push-through method of manufacturing in long production runs is used.
3. All similar machines are grouped together, forming functional departments.
4. Machines are placed in efficient locations, and schedules are developed so that setup times are reduced.
5. Less storage space is needed for inventory.
6. Support functions, such as production scheduling, production quality control, and inventory management, have been reduced.

E 3. LO 2 *Old Versus New Manufacturing Environments*

Downes Industries manufactures casings for computer keyboards. The following machines and operations are involved in the production process.

Mixing machines	The Mixing Department has three machines that mix various chemicals used in the molding operation.
Molding machines	The Molding Department uses six molding machines, each of which can be set up to make any keyboard casing sold by the company.
Trimming machines	In the Trimming Department, casings removed from the molds are trimmed of all excess materials. Six trimming machines are used.
Packing machines	Packing machines wrap and individually box the completed keyboard casings. Each of the two packing machines can keep pace with three trimming machines.

Products are moved from the mixing operation to the molding machines in 200-gallon drums. The drums usually sit for one to three days before their contents are used. Sometimes the chemicals must be remixed before they can be used by the Molding Department. After molding, the casings are stacked on wooden skids and moved to the Trimming Department by small lift trucks. The same procedure is used to move materials from the trimming to the packing operation. Total production time can range from two weeks to three months, depending on the urgency of the order. Christine Downes, the CEO, is not happy with this rate of output. Suggest a plant layout that would change the current operation into a JIT operation without the purchase of new equipment.

E 4. LO 4 *Direct Versus Indirect Costs*

The following cost categories are common in a manufacturing and assembly operation.

Raw materials	Operating supplies
Sheet steel	Small tools
Iron castings	Depreciation, plant
Assembly parts	Depreciation, machinery
Part 24RE6	Supervisory salaries
Part 15RF8	Electrical power
Direct labor	Insurance and taxes, plant
Engineering labor	President's salary
Indirect labor	Employee benefits

Identify each cost as either direct or indirect, assuming it was incurred (1) in a traditional manufacturing setting and (2) in a JIT environment. State the reasons for any changes in classification.

E 5. LO 4 *Product Costing in a Flexible Manufacturing System*

Foster Enterprises, Inc., manufactures wooden serving trays using an FMS work cell. The wood is shaped and the trays are assembled in one continuous operation. September's output totaled 40,300 units. Each unit requires two machine hours of effort. Materials handling cost is allocated to the product based on unit materials cost; engineering design costs are allocated based on units produced; and FMS cell overhead and building occupancy costs are allocated based on machine hours. Operating data for September are as follows.

Materials		
Wood	$96,180	
Hardware	48,900	$145,080
Materials handling		
Labor	$22,649	
Equipment depreciation	7,403	
Electrical power	4,442	
Maintenance	16,284	50,778
Direct labor		
Machinists		46,345
Engineering design		
Labor	$ 8,809	
Electrical power	5,922	
Engineering overhead	3,807	18,538
FMS cell overhead		
Indirect labor	$25,450	
Repairs and maintenance	20,304	
Supervision	16,920	
Equipment depreciation	6,768	
Operating supplies	4,230	
Electrical power	10,152	83,824
Building occupancy overhead		48,360
Total costs		$392,925

Materials handling cost allocation rate per dollar of materials
$50,778 ÷ $145,080 = 35%
Engineering design cost allocation rate per unit
$18,538 ÷ 40,300 = $.46
FMS overhead allocation rate per machine hour
$83,824 ÷ 80,600 = $1.04
Building occupancy allocation rate per machine hour
$48,360 ÷ 80,600 = $.60

Compute the unit cost of one wooden serving tray. Identify the six elements of the computation as part of your answer.

LO 5 *Costs of Quality*

E 6. The Tacinelli Corp. has budgeted quality-related activities for next year. Identify each of the following costs as a cost of conformance or a cost of nonconformance. Further identify each cost of conformance as a prevention or an appraisal cost and each cost of nonconformance as an internal failure or an external failure cost.

1. Returned goods
2. Inspection of finished goods
3. Rework
4. Design review
5. Quality planning activities
6. Processing of customer complaints
7. Maintenance of test equipment
8. On-line statistical process control
9. Reinspection of rework

LO 6 *Nonfinancial Measures of Quality and TQM*

E 7. "A satisfied customer is the most important goal of this company!" was the opening remark of President Brady Rackley at the monthly executive committee meeting of Rackley Company. The company manufactures piping products for customers in sixteen western states. Four divisions, each producing a different type of piping material, make up the company's organizational structure. Rackley, a proponent of total quality management, was reacting to the latest measures of quality data from the four divisions. The data are presented as follows.

	Brass Division	Plastics Division	Aluminum Division	Copper Division	Company Averages
Vendor on-time delivery	95.20%	91.40%	97.10%	89.20%	93.23%*
Production quality rates (defective parts per million)	1,640	2,820	1,270	4,270	2,500
On-time shipments	89.20%	78.40%	91.80%	75.60%	83.75%
Returned orders	1.10%	4.60%	.80%	6.90%	3.35%
Number of customer complaints	24	56	10	62	38
Number of warranty claims	7	12	4	14	9.3*

*Rounded.

Why was Rackley upset? Which division or divisions do not appear to have satisfied customers?

Problems

LO 1 LO 2 *Production Layout*

P 1. Berrios Automotive Products Company manufactures chrome automobile parts. The following manufacturing operations are part of the production of all types of automobile grills.

Assembly	Connecting devices are put on the completed grill.
Stamping	The grill shape is stamped out of a piece of sheet metal.
Plating	A chrome substance is adhered to the heat-treated product.
Receiving	Sheet metal and assembly parts are accepted in the central receiving area.
Welding	Connector pads are attached to the heat-treated product before plating.
Washing	Products are cleaned before being inspected for the first time.
Postassembly inspection	Products are inspected just prior to being packaged.
Raw materials storage	Sheet metal and assembly parts are stored before they are used.
Drilling	Holes are drilled into the products before the connector pads are welded.
Bending	Stamped grills are bent into shape.
Heat treating	All products are heat-treated after passing the preassembly inspection point.
Sheet metal inspection	All sheet metal received is inspected.
Polishing	Plated grills are polished before being assembled.
Skid moving	All grills are moved on large wooden skids from operation to operation.
Shipping	Railroad cars are loaded for shipment to automobile manufacturers.
Packing	Grills are packed in large wooden crates.
Preassembly inspection	All grills are inspected after the washing operation.

REQUIRED

1. Arrange the operations in the order they would occur in a traditional manufacturing system.
2. Assume that just-in-time operations are going to replace the traditional production process. Identify the following:
   a. Operations that would be eliminated
   b. Operations that would be automated
   c. Operations that could be combined into work cells
3. Is this company a good candidate for the JIT environment? Be prepared to defend your answer.

LO 4 *Machine Hours Versus Labor Hours*

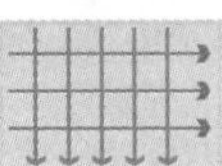

P 2. Kallol Halder has been in the manufacturing business for more than twenty years. Four months ago, Halder Products, Inc., made a major investment in automated machinery. The three new JIT work cells each have seven operating stations and produce chrome automobile bumpers in one operation. Each work cell specializes in one type of bumper; the products are identified as A-Bump, B-Bump, and C-Bump, with A-Bump being the most complex and C-Bump the least complex. After four months of operation, Halder became concerned about the ever-increasing manufacturing overhead rate. Halder had been under the impression that the new automated machinery would reduce production costs. A plantwide overhead rate is still being used, but the machinery installation consultant did suggest switching to individual work cell manufacturing overhead rates, with materials handling costs being treated separately. Those costs are currently included in the total manufacturing overhead cost pool.

The following data are from the past month's records.

	A-Bump	B-Bump	C-Bump
Unit information			
Raw materials cost	$96	$88	$82
Direct labor hours	1.2	1.5	.8
Direct labor cost per hour	$20	$18	$16
Machine hours	4.2	3.1	3
Information totals			
Unit sales during month	50,000	70,000	100,000
Total manufacturing overhead	$2,905,650	$1,186,850	$1,370,000

Halder's policy has been to set selling prices at 160 percent of a product's production cost.

REQUIRED

1. Using total direct labor dollars as a basis, compute the company's plantwide manufacturing overhead rate.
2. Using the application rate computed in **1**, compute the product unit cost and selling price for each type of bumper.
3. Compute a new manufacturing overhead application rate, assuming:
   a. Materials storage and handling overhead equal to 5 percent of the cost of raw materials must be subtracted from the total manufacturing overhead cost.
   b. The manufacturing overhead allocation basis is machine hours.
   c. Product line overhead rates are used rather than a plantwide rate.
4. Using the allocation rates computed in **3**, compute the product unit cost and selling price for each type of bumper.
5. Compare the old and new product selling prices and comment on your findings.

LO 4 *JIT Unit Cost Computations*

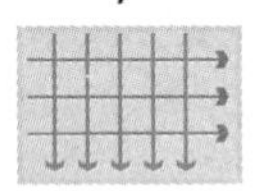

P 3. Albuja Corp. installed an automated just-in-time work cell in its Battery Casings Division at the beginning of the year. Operating data for the first quarter of 20x3 are now available. Prior to the installation of the JIT cell, four operations were performed in functional departments to complete a casing. These departments were Sheet Metal Cutting, Stamping, Shaping, and Finishing. Now all operations are performed in a single cell run by two highly skilled machine operators. The controller is interested in a unit cost comparison and has selected casing FM20 for the analysis. Data for the last two quarters are summarized on the next page.

REQUIRED

1. Compute the unit cost for each cost category for the last quarter of 20x2 and the first quarter of 20x3.
2. Compute and compare product unit costs for the two quarters.
3. Which individual costs were changed the most by the installation of the JIT cell? Should each change have been anticipated? State your reasons.

	Casing FM20	
	Quarter Ended 3/31/x3	Quarter Ended 12/31/x2
Units produced	39,400	21,700
Raw materials		
Sheet metal	$110,320	$ 56,420
Rivets	2,364	1,519
Direct labor		
Sheet metal cutting		26,040
Stamping		20,615
Shaping		16,275
Finishing		19,964
JIT cell	77,224	
Manufacturing overhead		
Indirect labor	86,680	33,852
Inspection labor	—	1,953
Lift truck labor	4,334	2,604
Electricity	21,276	7,378
Materials scrap costs	5,516	7,812
Small tools expense	37,430	25,606
Machine depreciation	22,064	4,774
Production scheduling costs	7,092	7,812
Repairs and maintenance	9,062	4,774
Supervisory salaries	20,488	15,190
Machine lubricants	7,092	2,821
Storage space costs	2,364	11,935
Total costs incurred	$413,306	$267,344

LO 4 **P 4.** *JIT and Activity-Based Costing*

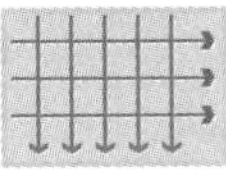

Kalina Products, Inc., produces a line of fax machines for wholesale distributors in the Pacific Northwest. Life Spring Company ordered 150 Model 14 fax machines and Kalina has just completed packaging the order. Before the Life Spring order is shipped, the controller has asked for a unit cost analysis comparing the amounts determined under the company's traditional costing system with amounts computed under the new activity-based costing system.

Raw materials, purchased parts, and production labor costs for the Life Spring order are as follows:

Cost of raw materials	$18,450.00
Cost of purchased parts	$14,800.00
Production direct labor hours	140
Average direct labor pay rate	$15.50

Other operating costs are as follows:

Traditional costing data:

Manufacturing overhead costs were assigned at a rate of 250 percent of direct labor dollars.

Activity-based costing data:

Activities	Cost Drivers	Cost Assignment Rates	Activity Usage for Life Spring Order
Engineering systems design	Engineering hours	$28.00 per engineering hour	18 engineering hours
Work cell setup	Number of setups	$42.00 per setup	8 setups
Parts production work cell	Machine hours	$37.50 per machine hour	84 machine hours
Product assembly cell	Cell hours	$44.00 per cell hour	36 cell hours
Packaging work cell	Cell hours	$28.50 per cell hour	28 cell hours

Building occupancy-related overhead costs are allocated at a rate of $10.00 per parts production work cell machine hour.

REQUIRED

1. Using the traditional costing approach, compute the total cost of the Life Spring order.
2. Using the activity-based costing approach, compute the total cost of the Life Spring order.
3. What difference in the amount of cost assigned to the Life Spring order resulted from the shift to activity-based costing? Does the use of activity-based costing guarantee cost reduction for every product?

P 5.
LO 5 LO 6 *Costs and Nonfinancial Measures of Quality*

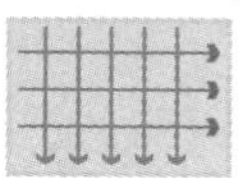

The Abrams Company operates as three autonomous divisions. Each division has a general manager in charge of product development, production, and distribution. Management recently adopted total quality management, and the divisions now track, record, and analyze their costs and nonfinancial measures of quality. All three divisions are operating in a worldwide, highly competitive marketplace. Sales and quality-related data for April are summarized below.

	East Division	Central Division	West Division
Annual sales	$8,500,000	$9,500,000	$13,000,000
Costs of quality			
Setup for testing	$ 51,600	$ 112,800	$ 183,950
Quality audits	17,200	79,100	109,650
Failure analysis	103,100	14,700	92,700
Quality training of employees	60,200	188,000	167,700
Scrap and rework	151,000	18,800	154,800
Quality planning activities	34,400	94,000	108,200
Preventive maintenance	65,800	148,000	141,900
Warranty claims	107,500	42,300	106,050
Customer service	150,500	108,100	154,800
Quality engineering	94,600	235,000	232,200
Product simulation and development	24,700	178,600	141,900
Losses caused by vendor scrap	77,400	23,500	64,500
Returned goods	153,500	16,200	45,150
Product recalls	64,500	32,900	64,500
Total costs of quality	$1,156,000	$1,292,000	$ 1,768,000
Nonfinancial measures of quality			
Defective parts per million	3,410	1,104	1,940
Returned orders	7.40%	1.10%	3.20%
Customer complaints	62	12	30
Number of warranty claims	74	16	52

REQUIRED

1. Prepare an analysis of the costs of quality for the three divisions. Categorize the costs as (a) costs of conformance with subsets of prevention costs and appraisal costs, and (b) costs of nonconformance with subsets of internal failure costs and external failure costs. Compute the total costs for each category for each division.
2. Compute the percentage of sales of each cost-of-quality total for each division (cost ÷ annual sales).
3. Interpret the cost-of-quality data for each division. Is each division's product of high or low quality? Explain your answers. Are the divisions headed in the right direction to be globally competitive?
4. Evaluate the nonfinancial measures of quality in terms of customer satisfaction. Are the results consistent with your analysis in **3**? Explain your answers.

Alternate Problems

LO 4 *JIT and Activity-Based Costing*

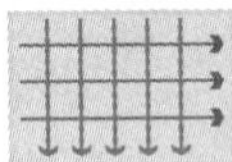

P 6. Morris Computer Company, which has been in operation for ten years, produces a line of personal computers. Kujawa Realtors, Ltd., placed an order for eighty personal computers and the order has just been completed. Morris recently installed a JIT work cell and shifted to an activity-based system of cost assignment. Shawna Lamotte, the controller, is interested in finding out how the ABC system affected the Kujawa order. Raw materials, purchased parts, and production labor costs for the Kujawa order are as follows:

Cost of raw materials	$38,750.00
Cost of purchased parts	21,300.00
Production direct labor hours	220
Average direct labor pay rate	$15.50

Other operating costs are as follows:

Traditional costing data:

Manufacturing overhead costs were assigned at a rate of 280 percent of direct labor dollars.

Activity-based costing data:

Activities	Cost Drivers	Cost Assignment Rates	Activity Usage for Kujawa Order
Electrical engineering design	Engineering hours	$22.00 per engineering hour	32 engineering hours
Work cell setups	Number of setups	$29.40 per setup	11 setups
Parts production work cell	Machine hours	$26.30 per machine hour	134 machine hours
Product testing cell	Cell hours	$32.80 per cell hour	52 cell hours
Packaging work cell	Cell hours	$17.50 per cell hour	22 cell hours

Building occupancy-related overhead costs are allocated at a rate of $9.80 per parts production work cell machine hour.

REQUIRED

1. Using the traditional product costing approach, compute the total cost of the Kujawa order.
2. Using the activity-based costing approach, compute the total cost of the Kujawa order.
3. What difference in the amount of cost assigned to the Kujawa order resulted from the new JIT work cell and the shift to activity-based costing? Does the use of activity-based costing guarantee cost reduction for every product?

LO 5 LO 6 *Costs and Nonfinancial Measures of Quality*

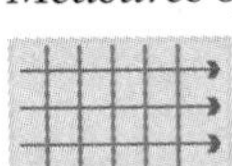

P 7. Rennie Enterprises, Inc., operates as three autonomous companies. Each company has a chief executive officer who oversees its operations. At a recent corporate meeting, the CEOs agreed to adopt total quality management for their operations and to track, record, and analyze their costs and nonfinancial measures of quality. All three companies are operating in a highly competitive worldwide market. Sales and quality-related data for September are summarized on the next page.

	Currence Company	Aspen Company	Prescott Company
Annual sales	$11,600,000	$13,300,000	$10,800,000
Costs of quality			
Sample preparation	$ 69,000	$ 184,800	$ 130,800
Quality audits	58,900	115,550	141,700
Failure analysis	188,500	92,400	16,350
Design review	80,500	176,700	218,000
Scrap and rework	207,000	160,800	21,200
Quality planning activities	49,200	105,600	231,600
Preventive maintenance	92,000	158,400	163,500
Warranty adjustments	149,550	105,600	49,050
Customer service	201,250	198,000	80,050
Quality training of employees	149,500	237,600	272,500
Product simulation and development	34,500	145,200	202,700
Reinspection of rework	126,500	66,000	27,250
Returned goods	212,750	72,600	16,350
Customer complaint processing	109,250	162,450	38,150
Total costs of quality	$ 1,728,400	$ 1,981,700	$ 1,609,200
Nonfinancial measures of quality			
Number of warranty claims	61	36	12
Customer complaints	107	52	18
Defective parts per million	4,610	2,190	1,012
Returned orders	9.20%	4.10%	.90%

REQUIRED

1. Prepare an analysis of the costs of quality for the three companies. Categorize the costs as (a) costs of conformance with subsets of prevention costs and appraisal costs, and (b) costs of nonconformance with subsets of internal failure costs and external failure costs. Compute the total costs for each category for each company.
2. Compute the percentage of sales for each cost-of-quality total for each company.
3. Interpret the cost-of-quality data for each company. Is the company's product of high or low quality? Why? Is each company headed in the right direction to be globally competitive?
4. Evaluate the nonfinancial measures of quality in terms of customer satisfaction. Are the results consistent with your analysis in **3**? Explain your answer.

Skills Development

Conceptual Analysis

SD 1.
LO 1 *JIT in a Service Business*

You are attending the initiation banquet for new members of your business club. The banquet is being held at an excellent restaurant. You are sitting next to two sophomore marketing majors. In discussing their experiences in the accounting course they are taking, they mention that they are having difficulty understanding the just-in-time (JIT) concept. They have read that a company's JIT operating system contains elements that support the concepts of simplicity, continuous improvement, waste reduction, timeliness, and efficiency. They realize that before they can begin to understand JIT in a complex manufacturing environment, they must first understand JIT in a simpler context. They ask you to explain the term and provide an example.

Briefly explain the just-in-time philosophy. Using the elements of a JIT operating system that are presented in this chapter, apply these elements to the restaurant where your banquet is being held. Do you believe the JIT philosophy applies in all restaurant operations? Explain.

Ethical Dilemma

SD 2.
LO 4 *Cost Management and Ethics*

Three months ago, ***Townsend Enterprises*** hired a consultant, Miranda Hong, to assist in the design and installation of a new cost management system for the company. Barry Kaplan, one of Townsend's product/systems design engineers, was assigned to work with Hong on the project. During the three-month period, Hong and Kaplan met six times and developed a tentative design and installation plan for the CMS. Before the plan was to be unveiled to top management, Kaplan asked his supervisor, Gail Carter-Mays to look it over and comment on the design.

Included in the plan is the consolidation of three engineering functions into one. Both of the current supervisors of the other two functions have seniority over Carter-Mays, so she believes that the design would lead to her losing her management position. She communicates this to Kaplan and ends her comments with the following statement, "If you don't redesign the system to accommodate all three of the existing engineering functions, I will see to it that you are given an unsatisfactory performance evaluation for this year!"

How should Kaplan respond to Carter-Mays's assertion? Should he handle the problem alone, keeping it inside the company, or communicate the comment to Hong? Outline Kaplan's options and be prepared to discuss them in class.

Research Activity

SD 3.
LO 2
LO 5 *Just-in-Time Production and Quality*

Many large multinational organizations, as well as organizations in your state, have recently installed automated just-in-time production processes to compete for new domestic and foreign business. Locate an article about an organization that has recently installed a JIT system. Conduct your search using the company annual reports in your campus library, the business section of your local newspaper, or *The Wall Street Journal.*

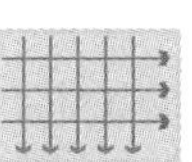

Choose a source that describes the changes the organization made within its plant to increase product quality and to compete as a world-class manufacturer. Prepare a one-page description of those changes. Include in your report the name of the organization, its geographic location, the name of the chief executive officer and/or president, and the dollar amount of the organization's total sales for the most recent year, if stated. Be prepared to present your findings to your classmates.

Decision-Making Practice

SD 4. **LO 2** *Installing JIT Work Cells*

The presidents of three organizations have contracted with your consulting firm for help in improving profitability, and all wish to discuss the possible installation of JIT work cells in their plants. You obtain the following descriptions of their production processes.

Company A: This organization manufactures four models of small private jet airplanes. Capacity for the organization is ten planes per month and they are currently operating at full capacity. Their competition consists of ten organizations in six foreign countries and eight organizations in the United States. The company employs eighteen highly skilled people: three design engineers, thirteen assembly people, and two test pilots. They would like to double their capacity because of the demand for their products.

Company B: This organization manufactures engine blocks exclusively for one automobile maker. They produce 4-, 6-, and 8-cylinder blocks, and each category has at least three different models. The engine block castings arrive directly from the foundry. The organization must mill, bore, drill, tap, finish, and inspect each engine block. All of these operations are currently performed by different departments.

Company C: This organization is a world leader in the manufacture of plastic parts for personal computers. The organization currently produces over five hundred different parts that it classifies into twenty different groupings. Production runs can range from as few as 20 units to as many as 500,000 units. If the plastic parts are allowed to cool for more than six hours during production, they must be reheated before additional processing can be completed.

Identify the organization that you think would benefit most from the installation of JIT work cells. Which organization would probably never need to consider the installation of work cells? Prepare a written analysis that explains your responses.

Managerial Reporting and Analysis

INTERPRETING MANAGEMENT REPORTS

LO 5 LO 6 *Cost of Quality*

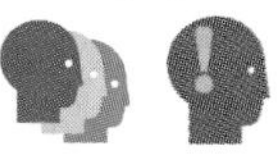

MRA 1. Eric Malarek has been appointed chief accountant for ***Southeast Industries.*** The business has three divisions that manufacture oil-well depth gauges. The industry is very competitive, and Southeast Industries has lost market share in each of the last four years. Three years ago, management announced a companywide restructuring and the adoption of total quality management. Since that time, each of the divisions has been allowed to chart its own path toward TQM. Mr. Malarek is new to the company and has asked to see a summary of the costs of quality for each of the divisions. The following data were presented to him for the past six months.

Southeast Industries
Cost of Quality Report
For the Six Months Ended June 30, 20xx

Sales	Florida Division	Georgia Division	Alabama Division	Company Totals
Sales	$1,850,000	$1,775,000	$1,750,000	$5,375,000
Prevention costs	$ 31,660	$ 47,665	$ 15,270	$ 94,595
Appraisal costs	42,340	32,210	17,980	92,530
Internal failure costs	24,370	22,600	41,940	88,910
External failure costs	32,980	16,450	45,560	94,990
Total costs of quality	$ 131,350	$ 118,925	$ 120,750	$ 371,025

REQUIRED

Evaluate the three divisions' quality control programs by first computing each division's costs of conformance and costs of nonconformance. Also compute quality costs as a percentage of sales for each division. Identify the division that is developing the strongest quality program. What division has been the slowest to react to the management directive? Defend your answers.

FORMULATING MANAGEMENT REPORTS

LO 1 LO 2 LO 3 *Manufacturing Processes and Management Reporting Systems*

MRA 2. ***Classic Clubs, Inc.,*** manufactures professional golf clubs. Demand for the golf clubs is so great that the company built a special plant that makes only custom-crafted clubs. The clubs are shaped by machines but vary according to the customer's sex, height, weight, and arm length. Ten basic sets of clubs are produced, five for females and five for males. Slight variations in machine setup provide the difference in the club weights and lengths.

In the past six months, several problems have developed at the golf club plant. Even though one computer numerically controlled machine is used in the manufacturing process, the company's backlog is growing rapidly. Customers are complaining that delivery is too slow. Quality is declining because clubs are pushed through the production process without proper inspection. Working capital is tied up in excessive amounts of inventory and storage space. Workers are complaining about the pressure to produce the backlogged orders. Machine breakdowns are increasing. Production control reports are not useful because they are not timely and contain irrelevant information. The company's profitability and cash flow are suffering.

Classic Clubs, Inc., has hired you as a consultant to define the problem and suggest a possible solution to the current dilemma. Denise Rodemeyer, the president, asks that you complete your work within a month so that she can prepare and present an action plan to the board of directors at the mid-year board meeting.

REQUIRED

1. In memo form, prepare a response to Rodemeyer. Recommend specific changes in the manufacturing process and the management accounting system. Defend each change that you suggest.
2. To help you prepare this report, answer the following questions.
   a. What kinds of information do you need to prepare this report?
   b. Why is this information relevant?
   c. Where would you go to obtain this information (sources)?
   d. When would you want to obtain this information?

INTERNATIONAL COMPANY

MRA 3. LO 2 LO 3 *Implementing Just-in-Time Principles*

Victor Alfonso recently attended a conference on the implementation of just-in-time principles in manufacturing operations. During lunch, he talked with Arnaldo Pinero, the president of a Mexican corporation that manufactures photographic equipment, and Harold Warioba, the chief executive officer of a Tanzanian textile manufacturer.

Pinero stated that a number of obstacles exist in the implementation of JIT in Mexican plants. He believes that many companies find employees and suppliers unwilling to participate fully in the process of implementing JIT. Also, many managers are integrating only a few components of JIT into traditional manufacturing operations.

Warioba agreed that obstacles also exist for manufacturing operations in Tanzania. He said that his company has encountered difficulty in obtaining loans for new machines, inadequate domestic supplies of materials for mills to operate near capacity, delays in deliveries of materials from international sources, inadequate transportation infrastructure, and unreliable forecasts of product demand.

REQUIRED

1. Which of these obstacles might also exist for U.S. manufacturing organizations that want to implement just-in-time manufacturing principles?
2. What recommendations would you make to help organizations change to a just-in-time operating environment?

EXCEL SPREADSHEET ANALYSIS

MRA 4. LO 3 LO 4 *Excel Analysis*

Quintech Corporation recently installed an automated just-in-time work cell in its Computer Memory Chip Division. Within the new work cell, computer programs communicate how many variations of clusters of electronic circuitry are spot welded to silicon wafers to produce the chips. The company had an activity-based costing system in place before the purchase of the new work cell and has classified costs accordingly. Four divisional activities are accounted for using ABC costing: materials handling, engineering design, machine setup, and building occupancy.

Before the installation of the new JIT work cell, the average cost to produce a single high-quality computer chip was $1.80. The following data were generated by the work cell for the third week in October, when 24,300 high-quality chips were produced.

Costs directly traceable to the work cell	
Raw materials	
Silicon sheets	$12,150
Wire	2,430
Direct labor	
Cell operator	972
JIT cell overhead	
Indirect labor	1,512
Electrical power	620
Operating supplies	236
Supervision	600
Machine maintenance	525
Machine depreciation	2,640
Other traceable overhead	3,830
Total directly traceable costs	$25,515

The following activity-based divisional and work cell data are to be used to assign activity costs for the week:

Divisional activity costs		
Materials handling		
Labor	$ 2,050	
Electrical power	435	
Maintenance	554	
Equipment depreciation	1,060	
Other traceable overhead	440	$ 4,539
Engineering design		
Professional labor	$ 9,450	
Electrical power	916	
Equipment depreciation	1,640	
Other traceable overhead	2,330	14,336
Machine setup		
Labor	$ 3,460	
Electrical power	425	
Tools and equipment depreciation	1,510	
Other traceable overhead	1,955	7,350
Building occupancy		
Building maintenance	$ 5,620	
Heating and electrical power	14,080	
Property fire insurance	1,610	
Other traceable overhead	4,690	26,000
Total divisional activity costs		$52,225

	Automated Work Cell	**Computer Memory Chip Division**
Cost driver data		
Materials handling		
Number of materials moves	23	445
Engineering design		
Number of engineering hours	110	640
Machine setup		
Number of setups	14	196
Building occupancy		
Number of square feet	800	20,000

REQUIRED

Using an Excel spreadsheet:

1. Prepare a detailed analysis showing the computation of the divisional activity cost assignment rates for the week.
2. Compute the costs of the four divisional activities that are assignable to the JIT work cell for the week.
3. Prepare a detailed cost summary for the JIT work cell for the week, including traceable and assigned costs. Assume that there were no beginning or ending work in process inventories for the work cell. The final computation should be the average cost per computer chip for the week.
4. Evaluate the performance of the new work cell in comparison to the traditional approach to computer chip production.

ENDNOTES

1. John Y. Lee and Pauline Nefcy, "The Anatomy of an Effective HMO Cost Management System," *Management Accounting,* Institute of Management Accountants, January 1997, pp. 49–54.
2. James B. Dilworth, *Production and Operations Management,* 5th ed. (New York: McGraw-Hill, Inc., 1993), pp. 347–358.
3. Don Irwin and Victor Rocine, "Self-Directed Work Teams," *CMA Magazine,* September 1994, pp. 10–15. Used by permission of The Society of Management Accountants of Canada.
4. Michael R. Ostrenga, "Activities: The Focal Point of Total Cost Management," *Management Accounting,* Institute of Management Accountants, February 1990, p. 43.
5. Many of the thoughts in this section come from John Hawley Atkinson, Jr., Gregory Hohner, Barry Mundt, Richard B. Troxel, and William Winchell, *Current Trends in Cost of Quality: Linking the Cost of Quality and Continuous Improvement,* a joint study of the Institute of Management Accountants, KPMG Peat Marwick, and William Winchell (Montvale, N.J., 1991).
6. Thomas A. Stewart, "Your Company's Most Valuable Asset: Intellectual Capital," *Fortune,* October 3, 1994, pp. 68–74.
7. Tom Peters, *Thriving on Chaos* (New York: Alfred A. Knopf, 1987), p. 91.

APPENDIX A

The Time Value of Money

Simple Interest and Compound Interest

Interest is the cost associated with the use of money for a specific period of time. Because interest is a cost associated with time, and "time is money," it is also an important consideration in any business decision. *Simple interest* is the interest cost for one or more periods, under the assumption that the amount on which the interest is computed stays the same from period to period. *Compound interest* is the interest cost for two or more periods, under the assumption that after each period the interest of that period is added to the amount on which interest is computed in future periods. In other words, compound interest is interest earned on a principal sum that is increased at the end of each period by the interest for that period.

Example: Simple Interest Joe Sanchez accepts an 8 percent, $30,000 note due in ninety days. How much will he receive in total at that time? Remember that the formula for calculating simple interest is as follows:

$$\begin{aligned} \text{Interest} &= \text{Principal} \times \text{Rate} \times \text{Time} \\ &= \$30{,}000 \times 8/100 \times 90/360 \\ &= \$600 \end{aligned}$$

Therefore, the total that Sanchez will receive is calculated as follows:

$$\begin{aligned} \text{Total} &= \text{Principal} + \text{Interest} \\ &= \$30{,}000 + \$600 \\ &= \$30{,}600 \end{aligned}$$

Example: Compound Interest Ann Clary deposits $5,000 in a savings account that pays 6 percent interest. She expects to leave the principal and accumulated interest in the account for three years. How much will her account total at the end of three years? Assume that the interest is paid at the end of the year and is added to the principal at that time, and that this total in turn earns interest. The amount at the end of three years is computed as follows:

(1) Year	(2) Principal Amount at Beginning of Year	(3) Annual Amount of Interest (Col. 2 × 6%)	(4) Accumulated Amount at End of Year (Col. 2 + Col. 3)
1	$5,000.00	$300.00	$5,300.00
2	5,300.00	318.00	5,618.00
3	5,618.00	337.08	5,955.08

At the end of three years, Clary will have $5,955.08 in her savings account. Note that the annual amount of interest increases each year by the interest rate times the interest of the previous year. For example, between year 1 and year 2, the interest increased by $18 ($318 − $300), which exactly equals 6 percent times $300.

Table 1. Future Value of $1 after a Given Number of Time Periods

Periods	1%	2%	3%	4%	5%	6%	7%	8%	9%	10%	12%	14%	15%
1	1.010	1.020	1.030	1.040	1.050	1.060	1.070	1.080	1.090	1.100	1.120	1.140	1.150
2	1.020	1.040	1.061	1.082	1.103	1.124	1.145	1.166	1.188	1.210	1.254	1.300	1.323
3	1.030	1.061	1.093	1.125	1.158	1.191	1.225	1.260	1.295	1.331	1.405	1.482	1.521
4	1.041	1.082	1.126	1.170	1.216	1.262	1.311	1.360	1.412	1.464	1.574	1.689	1.749
5	1.051	1.104	1.159	1.217	1.276	1.338	1.403	1.469	1.539	1.611	1.762	1.925	2.011
6	1.062	1.126	1.194	1.265	1.340	1.419	1.501	1.587	1.677	1.772	1.974	2.195	2.313
7	1.072	1.149	1.230	1.316	1.407	1.504	1.606	1.714	1.828	1.949	2.211	2.502	2.660
8	1.083	1.172	1.267	1.369	1.477	1.594	1.718	1.851	1.993	2.144	2.476	2.853	3.059
9	1.094	1.195	1.305	1.423	1.551	1.689	1.838	1.999	2.172	2.358	2.773	3.252	3.518
10	1.105	1.219	1.344	1.480	1.629	1.791	1.967	2.159	2.367	2.594	3.106	3.707	4.046

Source: Excerpt from Table 1 in the appendix on future value and present value tables.

Future Value of a Single Invested Sum at Compound Interest

Another way to ask the question in the example of compound interest above is, What is the future value of a single sum ($5,000) at compound interest (6 percent) for three years? *Future value* is the amount that an investment will be worth at a future date if invested at compound interest. A businessperson often wants to know future value, but the method of computing the future value illustrated above is too time-consuming in practice. Imagine how tedious the calculation would be if the example were ten years instead of three. Fortunately, there are tables that simplify solving problems involving compound interest. Table 1, showing the future value of $1 after a given number of time periods, is an example. It is actually part of a larger table, Table 1 in the appendix on future value and present value tables. Suppose that we want to solve the problem of Clary's savings account above. We simply look down the 6 percent column in Table 1 until we reach the line for 3 periods and find the factor 1.191. This factor, when multiplied by $1, gives the future value of that $1 at compound interest of 6 percent for three periods (years in this case). Thus, we solve the problem as follows:

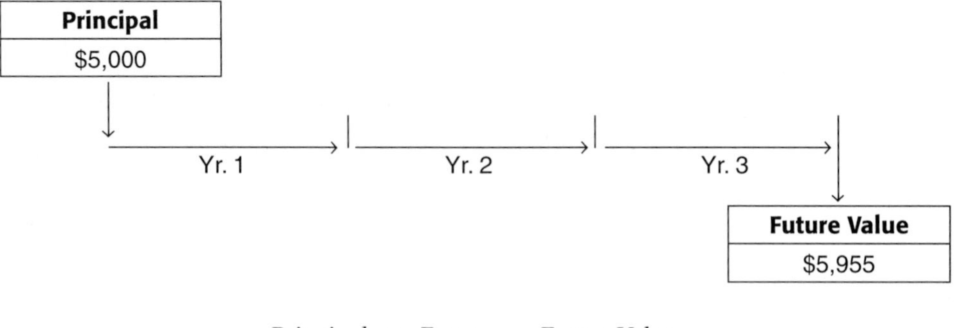

Principal	×	Factor	=	Future Value
$5,000	×	1.191	=	$5,955

Except for a rounding difference of $.08, the answer is exactly the same as that calculated earlier.

Table 2. Future Value of an Ordinary Annuity of $1 Paid in Each Period for a Given Number of Time Periods

Periods	1%	2%	3%	4%	5%	6%	7%	8%	9%	10%	12%	14%	15%
1	1.000	1.000	1.000	1.000	1.000	1.000	1.000	1.000	1.000	1.000	1.000	1.000	1.000
2	2.010	2.020	2.030	2.040	2.050	2.060	2.070	2.080	2.090	2.100	2.120	2.140	2.150
3	3.030	3.060	3.091	3.122	3.153	3.184	3.215	3.246	3.278	3.310	3.374	3.440	3.473
4	4.060	4.122	4.184	4.246	4.310	4.375	4.440	4.506	4.573	4.641	4.779	4.921	4.993
5	5.101	5.204	5.309	5.416	5.526	5.637	5.751	5.867	5.985	6.105	6.353	6.610	6.742
6	6.152	6.308	6.468	6.633	6.802	6.975	7.153	7.336	7.523	7.716	8.115	8.536	8.754
7	7.214	7.434	7.662	7.898	8.142	8.394	8.654	8.923	9.200	9.487	10.09	10.73	11.07
8	8.286	8.583	8.892	9.214	9.549	9.897	10.26	10.64	11.03	11.44	12.30	13.23	13.73
9	9.369	9.755	10.16	10.58	11.03	11.49	11.98	12.49	13.02	13.58	14.78	16.09	16.79
10	10.46	10.95	11.46	12.01	12.58	13.18	13.82	14.49	15.19	15.94	17.55	19.34	20.30

Source: Excerpt from Table 2 in the appendix on future value and present value tables.

Future Value of an Ordinary Annuity

Another common problem involves an *ordinary annuity,* which is a series of equal payments made at the end of equal intervals of time, with compound interest on these payments.

The following example shows how to find the future value of an ordinary annuity. Assume that Ben Katz makes a $200 payment at the end of each of the next three years into a savings account that pays 5 percent interest. How much money will he have in his account at the end of the three years? One way of computing the amount is shown in the following table.

(1) Year	(2) Beginning Balance	(3) Interest Earned (5% × Col. 2)	(4) Periodic Payment	(5) Accumulated at End of Period (Col. 2 + Col. 3 + Col. 4)
1	—	—	$200	$200.00
2	$200.00	$10.00	200	410.00
3	410.00	20.50	200	630.50

Katz would have $630.50 in his account at the end of three years, consisting of $600.00 in periodic payments and $30.50 in interest.

This calculation can also be simplified by using Table 2. We look down the 5 percent column until we reach 3 periods and find the factor 3.153. This factor, when multiplied by $1, gives the future value of a series of three $1 payments at compound interest of 5 percent. Thus, we solve the problem as shown on the next page.

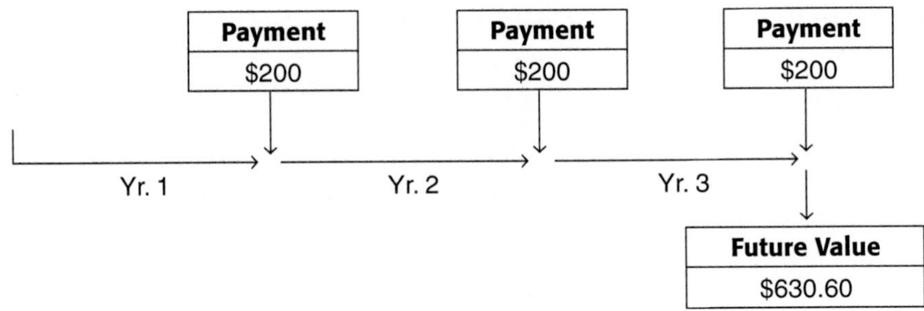

Periodic Payment	×	Factor	=	Future Value
$200.00	×	3.153	=	$630.60

Except for a rounding difference of $.10, this result is the same as the one calculated earlier.

Present Value

Suppose that you had the choice of receiving $100 today or one year from today. Intuitively, you would choose to receive the $100 today. Why? You know that if you have the $100 today, you can put it in a savings account to earn interest, so that you will have more than $100 a year from today. Therefore, we can say that an amount to be received in the future (future value) is not worth as much today as an amount to be received today (present value) because of the cost associated with the passage of time. In fact, present value and future value are closely related. *Present value* is the amount that must be invested now at a given rate of interest to produce a given future value.

For example, assume that Sue Dapper needs $1,000 one year from now. How much should she invest today to achieve that goal if the interest rate is 5 percent? From earlier examples, the following equation may be established.

Present Value ×	(1.0 + Interest Rate)	=	Future Value
Present Value ×	1.05	=	$1,000.00
Present Value		=	$1,000.00 ÷ 1.05
Present Value		=	$952.38

Thus, to achieve a future value of $1,000.00, a present value of $952.38 must be invested. Interest of 5 percent on $952.38 for one year equals $47.62, and these two amounts added together equal $1,000.00.

Present Value of a Single Sum Due in the Future

When more than one time period is involved, the calculation of present value is more complicated. Consider the following example. Don Riley wants to be sure of having $4,000 at the end of three years. How much must he invest today in a 5 percent savings account to achieve this goal? Adapting the above equation, we compute the present value of $4,000 at compound interest of 5 percent for three years in the future.

Year	Amount at End of Year		Divide by		Present Value at Beginning of Year
3	$4,000.00	÷	1.05	=	$3,809.52
2	3,809.52	÷	1.05	=	3,628.11
1	3,628.11	÷	1.05	=	3,455.34

Riley must invest a present value of $3,455.34 to achieve a future value of $4,000.00 in three years.

This calculation is again made much easier by using the appropriate table. In Table 3, we look down the 5 percent column until we reach 3 periods and find the factor .864. This factor, when multiplied by $1, gives the present value of $1 to be received three years from now at 5 percent interest. Thus, we solve the problem as shown below.

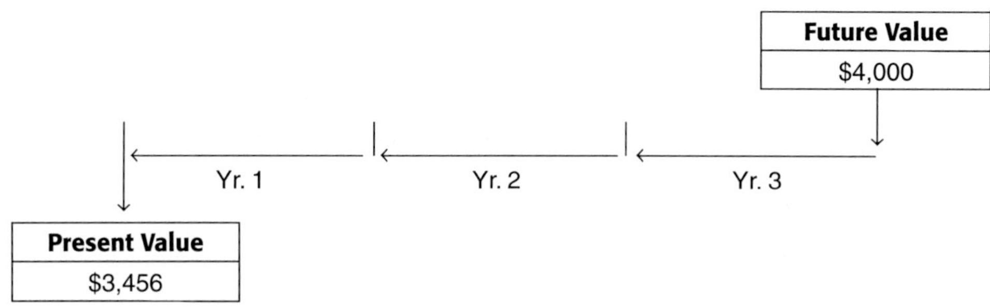

Future Value	×	Factor	=	Present Value
$4,000	×	.864	=	$3,456

Except for a rounding difference of $.66, this result is the same as the one above.

Table 3. Present Value of $1 to Be Received at the End of a Given Number of Time Periods

Periods	1%	2%	3%	4%	5%	6%	7%	8%	9%	10%
1	0.990	0.980	0.971	0.962	0.952	0.943	0.935	0.926	0.917	0.909
2	0.980	0.961	0.943	0.925	0.907	0.890	0.873	0.857	0.842	0.826
3	0.971	0.942	0.915	0.889	0.864	0.840	0.816	0.794	0.772	0.751
4	0.961	0.924	0.888	0.855	0.823	0.792	0.763	0.735	0.708	0.683
5	0.951	0.906	0.863	0.822	0.784	0.747	0.713	0.681	0.650	0.621
6	0.942	0.888	0.837	0.790	0.746	0.705	0.666	0.630	0.596	0.564
7	0.933	0.871	0.813	0.760	0.711	0.665	0.623	0.583	0.547	0.513
8	0.923	0.853	0.789	0.731	0.677	0.627	0.582	0.540	0.502	0.467
9	0.914	0.837	0.766	0.703	0.645	0.592	0.544	0.500	0.460	0.424
10	0.905	0.820	0.744	0.676	0.614	0.558	0.508	0.463	0.422	0.386

Source: Excerpt from Table 3 in the appendix on future value and present value tables.

Present Value of an Ordinary Annuity

It is often necessary to compute the present value of a series of receipts or payments. When we calculate the present value of equal amounts equally spaced over a period of time, we are computing the present value of an ordinary annuity.

For example, assume that Kathy Foster has sold a piece of property and is to receive $15,000 in three equal annual payments of $5,000, beginning one year from today. What is the present value of this sale, assuming a current interest rate of 5 percent? This present value may be computed by calculating a separate present value for each of the three payments (using Table 3) and summing the results, as shown in the table below.

Future Receipts (Annuity)				Present Value Factor at 5 Percent		
Year 1	Year 2	Year 3		(from Table 3)		Present Value
$5,000			×	.952	=	$ 4,760
	$5,000		×	.907	=	4,535
		$5,000	×	.864	=	4,320
Total Present Value						$13,615

The present value of this sale is $13,615. Thus, there is an implied interest cost (given the 5 percent rate) of $1,385 associated with the payment plan that allows the purchaser to pay in three installments.

We can make this calculation more easily by using Table 4. We look down the 5 percent column until we reach 3 periods and find the factor 2.723. This factor, when multiplied by $1, gives the present value of a series of three $1 payments (spaced one year apart) at compound interest of 5 percent. Thus, we solve the problem as shown at the top of the next page.

Table 4. Present Value of an Ordinary Annuity of $1 Received Each Period for a Given Number of Time Periods

Periods	1%	2%	3%	4%	5%	6%	7%	8%	9%	10%
1	0.990	0.980	0.971	0.962	0.952	0.943	0.935	0.926	0.917	0.909
2	1.970	1.942	1.913	1.886	1.859	1.833	1.808	1.783	1.759	1.736
3	2.941	2.884	2.829	2.775	2.723	2.673	2.624	2.577	2.531	2.487
4	3.902	3.808	3.717	3.630	3.546	3.465	3.387	3.312	3.240	3.170
5	4.853	4.713	4.580	4.452	4.329	4.212	4.100	3.993	3.890	3.791
6	5.795	5.601	5.417	5.242	5.076	4.917	4.767	4.623	4.486	4.355
7	6.728	6.472	6.230	6.002	5.786	5.582	5.389	5.206	5.033	4.868
8	7.652	7.325	7.020	6.733	6.463	6.210	5.971	5.747	5.535	5.335
9	8.566	8.162	7.786	7.435	7.108	6.802	6.515	6.247	5.995	5.759
10	9.471	8.983	8.530	8.111	7.722	7.360	7.024	6.710	6.418	6.145

Source: Excerpt from Table 4 in the appendix on future value and present value tables.

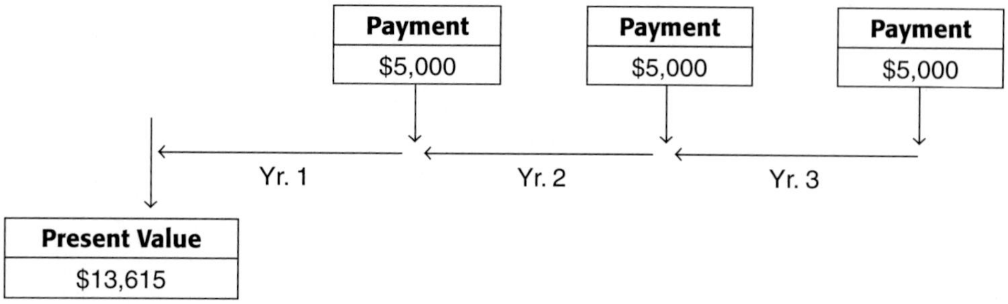

Payment $5,000 | Payment $5,000 | Payment $5,000

Yr. 1 | Yr. 2 | Yr. 3

Present Value $13,615

Periodic Payment	×	Factor	=	Present Value
$5,000	×	2.723	=	$13,615

This result is the same as the one computed earlier.

Time Periods

In all of the previous examples, and in most other cases, the compounding period is one year, and the interest rate is stated on an annual basis. However, in each of the four tables, the left-hand column refers not to years but to periods. This wording is intended to accommodate compounding periods of less than one year. Savings accounts that record interest quarterly and bonds that pay interest semiannually are cases in which the compounding period is less than one year. To use the tables in such cases, it is necessary to (1) divide the annual interest rate by the number of periods in the year, and (2) multiply the number of periods in one year by the number of years.

For example, assume that a $6,000 note is to be paid in two years and carries an annual interest rate of 8 percent. Compute the maturity (future) value of the note, assuming that the compounding period is semiannual. Before using the table, it is necessary to compute the interest rate that applies to each compounding period and the total number of compounding periods. First, the interest rate to use is 4 percent (8% annual rate ÷ 2 periods per year). Second, the total number of compounding periods is 4 (2 periods per year × 2 years). From Table 1, therefore, the maturity value of the note is computed as follows:

Principal	×	Factor	=	Future Value
$6,000	×	1.170	=	$7,020

The note will be worth $7,020 in two years.

This procedure for determining the interest rate and the number of periods when the compounding period is less than one year may be used with all four tables.

Applications of Present Value to Accounting

The concept of present value is widely applicable in the discipline of accounting. Here, the purpose is to demonstrate its usefulness in some simple applications. In-depth study of present value is deferred to more advanced courses.

Imputing Interest on Non-Interest-Bearing Notes

Clearly there is no such thing as an interest-free debt, regardless of whether the interest rate is explicitly stated. The Accounting Principles Board has declared that when a long-term note does not explicitly state an interest rate (or if the interest rate is unreasonably low), a rate based on the normal interest cost of the company in question should be assigned, or imputed.[1]

The following example applies this principle. On January 1, 20x0, Gato purchased merchandise from Haines by issuing an $8,000 non-interest-bearing note due in two years. Gato can borrow money from the bank at 9 percent interest. Gato paid the note in full after two years.

Note that the $8,000 note represents partly a payment for merchandise and partly a payment of interest for two years. In recording the purchase and sale, it is necessary to use Table 3 to determine the present value of the note. The calculation follows.

Future Payment	×	Present Value Factor (9%, 2 years)	=	Present Value
$8,000	×	.842	=	$6,736

The imputed interest cost is $1,264 ($8,000 − $6,736) and is recorded as a discount on notes payable in Gato's records and as a discount on notes receivable in Haines's records. The entries necessary to record the purchase in the Gato records and the sale in the Haines records are as follows:

A = L + OE	Gato Journal			Haines Journal			A = L + OE
− − +	Purchases	6,736		Notes Receivable	8,000		+ + −
	Discount on Notes Payable	1,264		Discount on Notes Receivable		1,264	
	Notes Payable		8,000	Sales		6,736	

On December 31, 20x0, the adjustments to recognize the interest expense and interest income are as follows:

A = L + OE	Gato Journal			Haines Journal			A = L + OE
+ −	Interest Expense	606.24		Discount on Notes Receivable	606.24		+ +
	Discount on Notes Payable		606.24	Interest Income		606.24	

The interest is calculated by multiplying the amount of the original purchase by the interest rate for one year ($6,736.00 × .09 = $606.24). When payment is made on December 31, 20x0, the following entries are made in the respective journals.

A = L + OE	Gato Journal			Haines Journal			A = L + OE
− + − −	Interest Expense	657.76		Discount on Notes Receivable	657.76		+ + + −
	Notes Payable	8,000.00		Cash	8,000.00		
	Discount on Notes Payable		657.76	Interest Income		657.76	
	Cash		8,000.00	Notes Receivable		8,000.00	

The interest entries represent the remaining interest to be expensed or realized ($1,264 − $606.24 = $657.76). This amount approximates (because of rounding differences in the table) the interest for one year on the purchase plus last year's interest [($6,736 + $606.24) × .09 = $660.80].

Valuing an Asset

An asset is recorded because it will provide future benefits to the company that owns it. These future benefits are the basis for the definition of an asset. Usually, the purchase price of the asset represents the present value of these future benefits. It is possible to evaluate a proposed purchase price for an asset by comparing that price with the present value of the asset to the company.

For example, Sam Hurst is thinking of buying a new machine that will reduce his annual labor cost by $700 per year. The machine will last eight years. The interest rate that Hurst assumes for making managerial decisions is 10 percent. What is the maximum amount (present value) that Hurst should pay for the machine?

The present value of the machine to Hurst is equal to the present value of an ordinary annuity of $700 per year for eight years at compound interest of 10 percent. Using the factor from Table 4, we compute the value as follows:

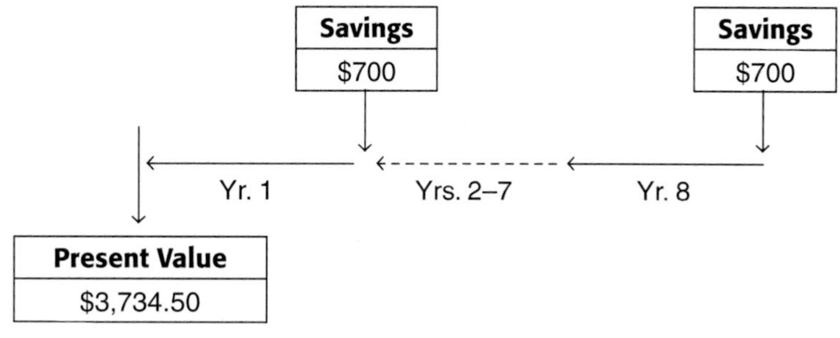

Periodic Savings	×	Factor	=	Present Value
$700.00	×	5.335	=	$3,734.50

Hurst should not pay more than $3,734.50 for the new machine because this amount equals the present value of the benefits that will be received from owning the machine.

Deferred Payment

A seller will sometimes agree to defer payment for a sale in order to encourage the buyer to make the purchase. This practice is common, for example, in the farm implement industry, where the farmer needs the equipment in the spring but cannot pay for it until the fall crop is in. Assume that Plains Implement Corporation sells a tractor to Dana Washington for $50,000 on February 1, agreeing to take payment ten months later, on December 1. When this type of agreement is made, the future payment includes not only the sales price of the tractor but also an implied (imputed) interest cost. If the prevailing annual interest rate for such transactions is 12 percent compounded monthly, the actual sale (purchase) price of the tractor would be the present value of the future payment, computed using the factor from Table 3 (10 periods, 1 percent), as follows:

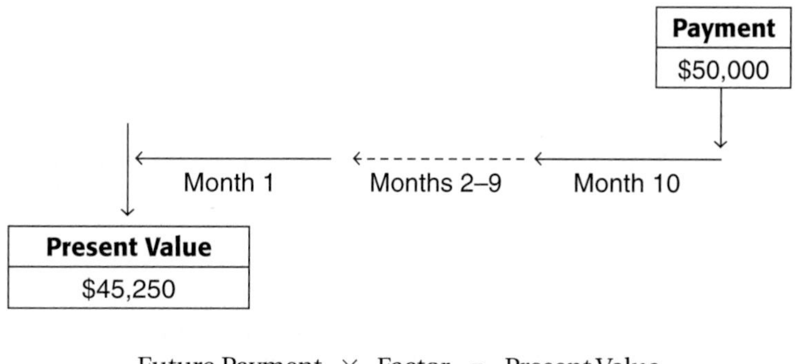

Future Payment	×	Factor	=	Present Value
$50,000	×	.905	=	$45,250

The purchase in Washington's records and the sale in Plains's records are recorded at the present value, \$45,250. The balance consists of interest expense or interest income. The entries necessary to record the purchase in Washington's records and the sale in Plains's records are as follows:

	Washington Journal			Plains Journal			
A = L + OE + +	Feb. 1 Tractor	45,250		Accounts Receivable	45,250		A = L + OE + +
	Accounts Payable		45,250	Sales		45,250	
	Purchase of tractor			Sale of tractor			

When Washington pays for the tractor, the entries are as follows:

	Washington Journal			Plains Journal			
A = L + OE − − −	Dec. 1 Accounts Payable	45,250		Cash	50,000		A = L + OE + + −
	Interest Expense	4,750		Accounts Receivable		45,250	
	Cash		50,000	Interest Income		4,750	
	Payment on account, including imputed interest expense			Receipt on account from Washington, including imputed interest earned			

Investment of Idle Cash

Childware Corporation, a toy manufacturer, has just completed a successful fall selling season and has \$10,000,000 in cash to invest for six months. The company places the cash in a money market account that is expected to pay 12 percent annual interest. Interest is compounded monthly and credited to the company's account each month. How much cash will the company have at the end of six months, and what entries will be made to record the investment and the monthly interest? The future value factor from Table 1 is based on six monthly periods of 1 percent (12 percent divided by 12 months), and the future value is computed as follows:

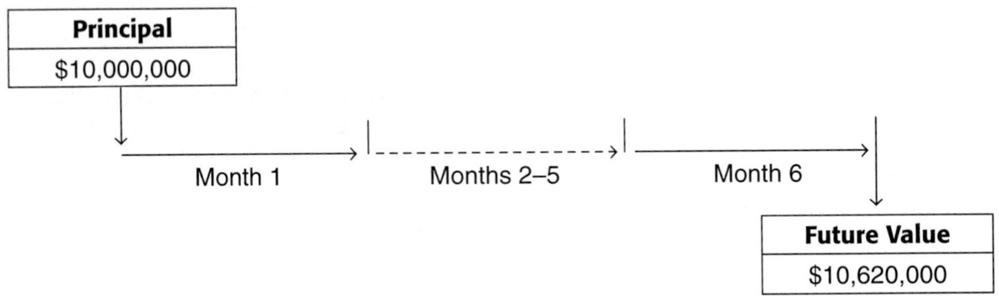

Investment	×	Factor	=	Future Value
\$10,000,000	×	1.062	=	\$10,620,000

When the investment is made, the following entry is made:

A = L + OE + −	Short-Term Investments	10,000,000	
	Cash		10,000,000
	Investment of cash		

After the first month, the interest is recorded by increasing the Short-Term Investments account.

A = L + OE			
+ +	Short-Term Investments	100,000	
	Interest Income		100,000
	One month's interest income $10,000,000 × .01 = $100,000		

After the second month, the interest is earned on the new balance of the Short-Term Investments account.

A = L + OE			
+ +	Short-Term Investments	101,000	
	Interest Income		101,000
	One month's interest income $10,100,000 × .01 = $101,000		

Entries would continue in a similar manner for four more months, at which time the balance of Short-Term Investments would be about $10,620,000. The actual amount accumulated may vary from this total because the interest rate paid on money market accounts can vary over time as a result of changes in market conditions.

Accumulation of a Fund

When a company owes a large fixed amount due in several years, management would be wise to accumulate a fund with which to pay off the debt at maturity. Sometimes creditors, when they agree to provide a loan, require that such a fund be established. In establishing the fund, management must determine how much cash to set aside each period in order to pay the debt. The amount will depend on the estimated rate of interest the investments will earn. Assume that Vason Corporation agrees with a creditor to set aside cash at the end of each year to accumulate enough to pay off a $100,000 note due in five years. Since the first contribution to the fund will be made in one year, five annual contributions will be made by the time the note is due. Assume also that the fund is projected to earn 8 percent, compounded annually. The amount of each annual payment is calculated using Table 2 (5 periods, 8 percent), as follows:

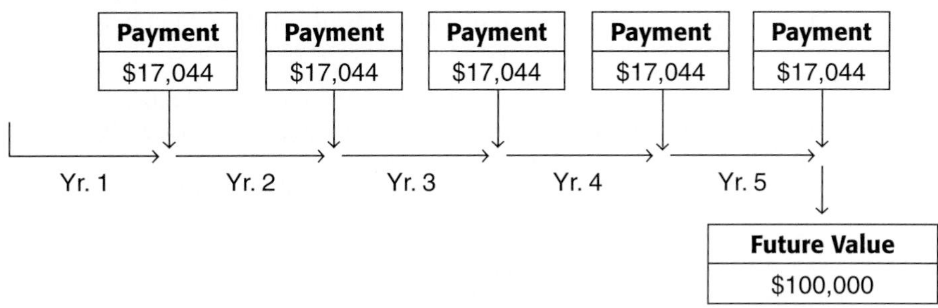

Future Value of Fund	÷	Factor	=	Annual Investment
$100,000	÷	5.867	=	$17,044 (rounded)

Each year's contribution to the fund is $17,044. This contribution is recorded as follows:

A = L + OE			
+	Loan Repayment Fund	17,044	
−	Cash		17,044
	Annual contribution to loan repayment fund		

Other Accounting Applications

There are many other applications of present value in accounting, including accounting for installment notes, valuing a bond, and recording lease obligations. Present value is also applied in such areas as pension obligations; premium and discount on debt; depreciation of property, plant, and equipment; capital expenditure decisions; and generally any problem in which time is a factor.

Exercises

Tables 1 to 4 in the appendix on future value and present value tables may be used where appropriate to solve these exercises.

E 1. *Future Value Calculations*

Wieland receives a one-year note for $3,000 that carries a 12 percent annual interest rate for the sale of a used car.

Compute the maturity value under each of the following assumptions: (1) The interest is simple interest. (2) The interest is compounded semiannually. (3) The interest is compounded quarterly. (4) The interest is compounded monthly.

E 2. *Future Value Calculations*

Find the future value of (1) a single payment of $20,000 at 7 percent for ten years, (2) ten annual payments of $2,000 at 7 percent, (3) a single payment of $6,000 at 9 percent for seven years, and (4) seven annual payments of $6,000 at 9 percent.

E 3. *Future Value Calculations*

Assume that $40,000 is invested today. Compute the amount that would accumulate at the end of seven years when the interest rate is (1) 8 percent compounded annually, (2) 8 percent compounded semiannually, and (3) 8 percent compounded quarterly.

E 4. *Future Value Calculations*

Calculate the accumulation of periodic payments of $1,000 made at the end of each of four years, assuming (1) 10 percent annual interest compounded annually, (2) 10 percent annual interest compounded semiannually, (3) 4 percent annual interest compounded annually, and (4) 16 percent annual interest compounded quarterly.

E 5. *Future Value Applications*

a. Two parents have $20,000 to invest for their child's college tuition, which they estimate will cost $40,000 when the child enters college twelve years from now.

Calculate the approximate rate of annual interest that the investment must earn to reach the $40,000 goal in twelve years. (**Hint:** Make a calculation; then use Table 1 in the appendix on future value and present value tables.)

b. Ted Pruitt is saving to purchase a summer home that will cost about $64,000. He has $40,000 now, on which he can earn 7 percent annual interest.

Calculate the approximate length of time he will have to wait to purchase the summer home. (**Hint:** Make a calculation; then use Table 1 in the appendix on future value and present value tables.)

E 6. *Working Backward from a Future Value*

Gloria Faraquez has a debt of $90,000 due in four years. She wants to save enough money to pay it off by making annual deposits in an investment account that earns 8 percent annual interest.

Calculate the amount she must deposit each year to reach her goal. (**Hint:** Use Table 2 in the appendix on future value and present value tables; then make a calculation.)

E 7. *Determining an Advance Payment*

Ellen Saber is contemplating paying five years' rent in advance. Her annual rent is $9,600. Calculate the single sum that would have to be paid now for the advance rent, if we assume compound interest of 8 percent.

E 8. *Present Value Calculations*

Find the present value of (1) a single payment of $24,000 at 6 percent for twelve years, (2) twelve annual payments of $2,000 at 6 percent, (3) a single payment of $5,000 at 9 percent for five years, and (4) five annual payments of $5,000 at 9 percent.

E 9. *Present Value of a Lump-Sum Contract*

A contract calls for a lump-sum payment of $60,000. Find the present value of the contract, assuming that (1) the payment is due in five years, and the current interest rate is 9 percent; (2) the payment is due in ten years, and the current interest rate is 9 percent; (3) the payment is due in five years, and the current interest rate is 5 percent; and (4) the payment is due in ten years, and the current interest rate is 5 percent.

E 10. *Present Value of an Annuity Contract*

A contract calls for annual payments of $1,200. Find the present value of the contract, assuming that (1) the number of payments is seven, and the current interest rate is 6 percent; (2) the number of payments is fourteen, and the current interest rate is 6 percent; (3) the number of payments is seven, and the current interest rate is 8 percent; and (4) the number of payments is fourteen, and the current interest rate is 8 percent.

E 11. *Non-interest-Bearing Note*

On January 1, 20x0, Pendleton purchased a machine from Leyland by signing a two-year, non-interest-bearing $32,000 note. Pendleton currently pays 12 percent interest to borrow money at the bank.

Prepare entries in Pendleton's and Leyland's journals to (1) record the purchase and the note, (2) adjust the accounts after one year, and (3) record payment of the note after two years (on December 31, 20x2).

E 12. *Valuing an Asset for the Purpose of Making a Purchasing Decision*

Oscaro owns a service station and has the opportunity to purchase a car wash machine for $30,000. After carefully studying projected costs and revenues, Oscaro estimates that the car wash machine will produce a net cash flow of $5,200 annually and will last for eight years. Oscaro feels that an interest rate of 14 percent is adequate for his business.

Calculate the present value of the machine to Oscaro. Does the purchase appear to be a correct business decision?

E 13. *Deferred Payment*

Johnson Equipment Corporation sold a precision tool machine with computer controls to Borst Corporation for $800,000 on January 1, agreeing to take payment nine months later, on October 1. Assuming that the prevailing annual interest rate for such a transaction is 16 percent compounded quarterly, what is the actual sale (purchase) price of the machine tool, and what journal entries will be made at the time of the purchase (sale) and at the time of the payment (receipt) on the records of both Borst and Johnson?

E 14. *Investment of Idle Cash*

Scientific Publishing Company, a publisher of college books, has just completed a successful fall selling season and has $5,000,000 in cash to invest for nine months, beginning on January 1. The company placed the cash in a money market account that is expected to pay 12 percent annual interest compounded monthly. Interest is credited to the company's account each month. How much cash will the company have at the end of nine months, and what entries are made to record the investment and the first two monthly (February 1 and March 1) interest amounts?

E 15. *Accumulation of a Fund*

Laferia Corporation borrowed $3,000,000 from an insurance company on a five-year note. Management agreed to set aside enough cash at the end of each year to accumulate the amount needed to pay off the note at maturity. Since the first contribution to the fund will be made in one year, four annual contributions are needed. Assuming that the fund will earn 10 percent compounded annually, how much will the annual contribution to the fund be (round to nearest dollar), and what will be the journal entry for the first contribution?

E 16. *Negotiating the Sale of a Business*

Horace Raftson is attempting to sell his business to Ernando Ruiz. The company has assets of $900,000, liabilities of $800,000, and owner's equity of $100,000. Both parties agree that the proper rate of return to expect is 12 percent; however, they differ on other assumptions. Raftson believes that the business will generate at least $100,000 per year of cash flows for twenty years. Ruiz thinks that $80,000 in cash flows per year is more reasonable and that only ten years in the future should be considered. Using Table 4 in the appendix on future value and present value tables, determine the range for negotiation by computing the present value of Raftson's offer to sell and of Ruiz's offer to buy.

ENDNOTE

1. Accounting Principles Board, *Opinion No. 21*, "Interest on Receivables and Payables" (New York: American Institute of Certified Public Accountants, 1971), par. 13.

B APPENDIX

Future Value and Present Value Tables

Table 1 provides the multipliers necessary to compute the future value of a *single* cash deposit made at the *beginning* of year 1. Three factors must be known before the future value can be computed: (1) the time period in years, (2) the stated annual rate of interest to be earned, and (3) the dollar amount invested or deposited.

Table 1. Future Value of $1 After a Given Number of Time Periods

Periods	1%	2%	3%	4%	5%	6%	7%	8%	9%	10%	12%	14%	15%
1	1.010	1.020	1.030	1.040	1.050	1.060	1.070	1.080	1.090	1.100	1.120	1.140	1.150
2	1.020	1.040	1.061	1.082	1.103	1.124	1.145	1.166	1.188	1.210	1.254	1.300	1.323
3	1.030	1.061	1.093	1.125	1.158	1.191	1.225	1.260	1.295	1.331	1.405	1.482	1.521
4	1.041	1.082	1.126	1.170	1.216	1.262	1.311	1.360	1.412	1.464	1.574	1.689	1.749
5	1.051	1.104	1.159	1.217	1.276	1.338	1.403	1.469	1.539	1.611	1.762	1.925	2.011
6	1.062	1.126	1.194	1.265	1.340	1.419	1.501	1.587	1.677	1.772	1.974	2.195	2.313
7	1.072	1.149	1.230	1.316	1.407	1.504	1.606	1.714	1.828	1.949	2.211	2.502	2.660
8	1.083	1.172	1.267	1.369	1.477	1.594	1.718	1.851	1.993	2.144	2.476	2.853	3.059
9	1.094	1.195	1.305	1.423	1.551	1.689	1.838	1.999	2.172	2.358	2.773	3.252	3.518
10	1.105	1.219	1.344	1.480	1.629	1.791	1.967	2.159	2.367	2.594	3.106	3.707	4.046
11	1.116	1.243	1.384	1.539	1.710	1.898	2.105	2.332	2.580	2.853	3.479	4.226	4.652
12	1.127	1.268	1.426	1.601	1.796	2.012	2.252	2.518	2.813	3.138	3.896	4.818	5.350
13	1.138	1.294	1.469	1.665	1.886	2.133	2.410	2.720	3.066	3.452	4.363	5.492	6.153
14	1.149	1.319	1.513	1.732	1.980	2.261	2.579	2.937	3.342	3.798	4.887	6.261	7.076
15	1.161	1.346	1.558	1.801	2.079	2.397	2.759	3.172	3.642	4.177	5.474	7.138	8.137
16	1.173	1.373	1.605	1.873	2.183	2.540	2.952	3.426	3.970	4.595	6.130	8.137	9.358
17	1.184	1.400	1.653	1.948	2.292	2.693	3.159	3.700	4.328	5.054	6.866	9.276	10.76
18	1.196	1.428	1.702	2.026	2.407	2.854	3.380	3.996	4.717	5.560	7.690	10.58	12.38
19	1.208	1.457	1.754	2.107	2.527	3.026	3.617	4.316	5.142	6.116	8.613	12.06	14.23
20	1.220	1.486	1.806	2.191	2.653	3.207	3.870	4.661	5.604	6.728	9.646	13.74	16.37
21	1.232	1.516	1.860	2.279	2.786	3.400	4.141	5.034	6.109	7.400	10.80	15.67	18.82
22	1.245	1.546	1.916	2.370	2.925	3.604	4.430	5.437	6.659	8.140	12.10	17.86	21.64
23	1.257	1.577	1.974	2.465	3.072	3.820	4.741	5.871	7.258	8.954	13.55	20.36	24.89
24	1.270	1.608	2.033	2.563	3.225	4.049	5.072	6.341	7.911	9.850	15.18	23.21	28.63
25	1.282	1.641	2.094	2.666	3.386	4.292	5.427	6.848	8.623	10.83	17.00	26.46	32.92
26	1.295	1.673	2.157	2.772	3.556	4.549	5.807	7.396	9.399	11.92	19.04	30.17	37.86
27	1.308	1.707	2.221	2.883	3.733	4.822	6.214	7.988	10.25	13.11	21.32	34.39	43.54
28	1.321	1.741	2.288	2.999	3.920	5.112	6.649	8.627	11.17	14.42	23.88	39.20	50.07
29	1.335	1.776	2.357	3.119	4.116	5.418	7.114	9.317	12.17	15.86	26.75	44.69	57.58
30	1.348	1.811	2.427	3.243	4.322	5.743	7.612	10.06	13.27	17.45	29.96	50.95	66.21
40	1.489	2.208	3.262	4.801	7.040	10.29	14.97	21.72	31.41	45.26	93.05	188.9	267.9
50	1.645	2.692	4.384	7.107	11.47	18.42	29.46	46.90	74.36	117.4	289.0	700.2	1,084

Example—Table 1 Determine the future value of \$5,000 deposited now that will earn 9 percent interest compounded annually for five years. From Table 1, the necessary multiplier for five years at 9 percent is 1.539, and the answer is

$$\$5{,}000 \times 1.539 = \$7{,}695$$

Where r is the interest rate and n is the number of periods, the factor values for Table 1 are

$$\text{FV Factor} = (1 + r)^n$$

Situations requiring the use of Table 2 are similar to those requiring the use of Table 1 except that Table 2 is used to compute the future value of a *series* of *equal* deposits made at the end of each period.

Table 2. Future Value of \$1 Paid in Each Period for a Given Number of Time Periods

Periods	1%	2%	3%	4%	5%	6%	7%	8%	9%	10%	12%	14%	15%
1	1.000	1.000	1.000	1.000	1.000	1.000	1.000	1.000	1.000	1.000	1.000	1.000	1.000
2	2.010	2.020	2.030	2.040	2.050	2.060	2.070	2.080	2.090	2.100	2.120	2.140	2.150
3	3.030	3.060	3.091	3.122	3.153	3.184	3.215	3.246	3.278	3.310	3.374	3.440	3.473
4	4.060	4.122	4.184	4.246	4.310	4.375	4.440	4.506	4.573	4.641	4.779	4.921	4.993
5	5.101	5.204	5.309	5.416	5.526	5.637	5.751	5.867	5.985	6.105	6.353	6.610	6.742
6	6.152	6.308	6.468	6.633	6.802	6.975	7.153	7.336	7.523	7.716	8.115	8.536	8.754
7	7.214	7.434	7.662	7.898	8.142	8.394	8.654	8.923	9.200	9.487	10.09	10.73	11.07
8	8.286	8.583	8.892	9.214	9.549	9.897	10.26	10.64	11.03	11.44	12.30	13.23	13.73
9	9.369	9.755	10.16	10.58	11.03	11.49	11.98	12.49	13.02	13.58	14.78	16.09	16.79
10	10.46	10.95	11.46	12.01	12.58	13.18	13.82	14.49	15.19	15.94	17.55	19.34	20.30
11	11.57	12.17	12.81	13.49	14.21	14.97	15.78	16.65	17.56	18.53	20.65	23.04	24.35
12	12.68	13.41	14.19	15.03	15.92	16.87	17.89	18.98	20.14	21.38	24.13	27.27	29.00
13	13.81	14.68	15.62	16.63	17.71	18.88	20.14	21.50	22.95	24.52	28.03	32.09	34.35
14	14.95	15.97	17.09	18.29	19.60	21.02	22.55	24.21	26.02	27.98	32.39	37.58	40.50
15	16.10	17.29	18.60	20.02	21.58	23.28	25.13	27.15	29.36	31.77	37.28	43.84	47.58
16	17.26	18.64	20.16	21.82	23.66	25.67	27.89	30.32	33.00	35.95	42.75	50.98	55.72
17	18.43	20.01	21.76	23.70	25.84	28.21	30.84	33.75	36.97	40.54	48.88	59.12	65.08
18	19.61	21.41	23.41	25.65	28.13	30.91	34.00	37.45	41.30	45.60	55.75	68.39	75.84
19	20.81	22.84	25.12	27.67	30.54	33.76	37.38	41.45	46.02	51.16	63.44	78.97	88.21
20	22.02	24.30	26.87	29.78	33.07	36.79	41.00	45.76	51.16	57.28	72.05	91.02	102.4
21	23.24	25.78	28.68	31.97	35.72	39.99	44.87	50.42	56.76	64.00	81.70	104.8	118.8
22	24.47	27.30	30.54	34.25	38.51	43.39	49.01	55.46	62.87	71.40	92.50	120.4	137.6
23	25.72	28.85	32.45	36.62	41.43	47.00	53.44	60.89	69.53	79.54	104.6	138.3	159.3
24	26.97	30.42	34.43	39.08	44.50	50.82	58.18	66.76	76.79	88.50	118.2	158.7	184.2
25	28.24	32.03	36.46	41.65	47.73	54.86	63.25	73.11	84.70	98.35	133.3	181.9	212.8
26	29.53	33.67	38.55	44.31	51.11	59.16	68.68	79.95	93.32	109.2	150.3	208.3	245.7
27	30.82	35.34	40.71	47.08	54.67	63.71	74.48	87.35	102.7	121.1	169.4	238.5	283.6
28	32.13	37.05	42.93	49.97	58.40	68.53	80.70	95.34	113.0	134.2	190.7	272.9	327.1
29	33.45	38.79	45.22	52.97	62.32	73.64	87.35	104.0	124.1	148.6	214.6	312.1	377.2
30	34.78	40.57	47.58	56.08	66.44	79.06	94.46	113.3	136.3	164.5	241.3	356.8	434.7
40	48.89	60.40	75.40	95.03	120.8	154.8	199.6	259.1	337.9	442.6	767.1	1,342	1,779
50	64.46	84.58	112.8	152.7	209.3	290.3	406.5	573.8	815.1	1,164	2,400	4,995	7,218

Table 3. Present Value of $1 to Be Received at the End of a Given Number of Time Periods

Periods	1%	2%	3%	4%	5%	6%	7%	8%	9%	10%	12%
1	0.990	0.980	0.971	0.962	0.952	0.943	0.935	0.926	0.917	0.909	0.893
2	0.980	0.961	0.943	0.925	0.907	0.890	0.873	0.857	0.842	0.826	0.797
3	0.971	0.942	0.915	0.889	0.864	0.840	0.816	0.794	0.772	0.751	0.712
4	0.961	0.924	0.888	0.855	0.823	0.792	0.763	0.735	0.708	0.683	0.636
5	0.951	0.906	0.883	0.822	0.784	0.747	0.713	0.681	0.650	0.621	0.567
6	0.942	0.888	0.837	0.790	0.746	0.705	0.666	0.630	0.596	0.564	0.507
7	0.933	0.871	0.813	0.760	0.711	0.665	0.623	0.583	0.547	0.513	0.452
8	0.923	0.853	0.789	0.731	0.677	0.627	0.582	0.540	0.502	0.467	0.404
9	0.914	0.837	0.766	0.703	0.645	0.592	0.544	0.500	0.460	0.424	0.361
10	0.905	0.820	0.744	0.676	0.614	0.558	0.508	0.463	0.422	0.386	0.322
11	0.896	0.804	0.722	0.650	0.585	0.527	0.475	0.429	0.388	0.350	0.287
12	0.887	0.788	0.701	0.625	0.557	0.497	0.444	0.397	0.356	0.319	0.257
13	0.879	0.773	0.681	0.601	0.530	0.469	0.415	0.368	0.326	0.290	0.229
14	0.870	0.758	0.661	0.577	0.505	0.442	0.388	0.340	0.299	0.263	0.205
15	0.861	0.743	0.642	0.555	0.481	0.417	0.362	0.315	0.275	0.239	0.183
16	0.853	0.728	0.623	0.534	0.458	0.394	0.339	0.292	0.252	0.218	0.163
17	0.844	0.714	0.605	0.513	0.436	0.371	0.317	0.270	0.231	0.198	0.146
18	0.836	0.700	0.587	0.494	0.416	0.350	0.296	0.250	0.212	0.180	0.130
19	0.828	0.686	0.570	0.475	0.396	0.331	0.277	0.232	0.194	0.164	0.116
20	0.820	0.673	0.554	0.456	0.377	0.312	0.258	0.215	0.178	0.149	0.104
21	0.811	0.660	0.538	0.439	0.359	0.294	0.242	0.199	0.164	0.135	0.093
22	0.803	0.647	0.522	0.422	0.342	0.278	0.226	0.184	0.150	0.123	0.083
23	0.795	0.634	0.507	0.406	0.326	0.262	0.211	0.170	0.138	0.112	0.074
24	0.788	0.622	0.492	0.390	0.310	0.247	0.197	0.158	0.126	0.102	0.066
25	0.780	0.610	0.478	0.375	0.295	0.233	0.184	0.146	0.116	0.092	0.059
26	0.772	0.598	0.464	0.361	0.281	0.220	0.172	0.135	0.106	0.084	0.053
27	0.764	0.586	0.450	0.347	0.268	0.207	0.161	0.125	0.098	0.076	0.047
28	0.757	0.574	0.437	0.333	0.255	0.196	0.150	0.116	0.090	0.069	0.042
29	0.749	0.563	0.424	0.321	0.243	0.185	0.141	0.107	0.082	0.063	0.037
30	0.742	0.552	0.412	0.308	0.231	0.174	0.131	0.099	0.075	0.057	0.033
40	0.672	0.453	0.307	0.208	0.142	0.097	0.067	0.046	0.032	0.022	0.011
50	0.608	0.372	0.228	0.141	0.087	0.054	0.034	0.021	0.013	0.009	0.003

Example—Table 2 What will be the future value at the end of thirty years if $1,000 is deposited each year on January 1, beginning in one year, assuming 12 percent interest compounded annually? The required multiplier from Table 2 is 241.3, and the answer is

$$\$1,000 \times 241.3 = \$241,300$$

The factor values for Table 2 are

$$\text{FVa Factor} = \frac{(1 + r)^n - 1}{r}$$

Table 3 is used to compute the value today of a *single* amount of cash to be received sometime in the future. To use Table 3, you must first know: (1) the time period in years until funds will be received, (2) the stated annual rate of interest, and (3) the dollar amount to be received at the end of the time period.

Table 3. (*continued*)

14%	15%	16%	18%	20%	25%	30%	35%	40%	45%	50%	Periods
0.877	0.870	0.862	0.847	0.833	0.800	0.769	0.741	0.714	0.690	0.667	1
0.769	0.756	0.743	0.718	0.694	0.640	0.592	0.549	0.510	0.476	0.444	2
0.675	0.658	0.641	0.609	0.579	0.512	0.455	0.406	0.364	0.328	0.296	3
0.592	0.572	0.552	0.516	0.482	0.410	0.350	0.301	0.260	0.226	0.198	4
0.519	0.497	0.476	0.437	0.402	0.328	0.269	0.223	0.186	0.156	0.132	5
0.456	0.432	0.410	0.370	0.335	0.262	0.207	0.165	0.133	0.108	0.088	6
0.400	0.376	0.354	0.314	0.279	0.210	0.159	0.122	0.095	0.074	0.059	7
0.351	0.327	0.305	0.266	0.233	0.168	0.123	0.091	0.068	0.051	0.039	8
0.308	0.284	0.263	0.225	0.194	0.134	0.094	0.067	0.048	0.035	0.026	9
0.270	0.247	0.227	0.191	0.162	0.107	0.073	0.050	0.035	0.024	0.017	10
0.237	0.215	0.195	0.162	0.135	0.086	0.056	0.037	0.025	0.017	0.012	11
0.208	0.187	0.168	0.137	0.112	0.069	0.043	0.027	0.018	0.012	0.008	12
0.182	0.163	0.145	0.116	0.093	0.055	0.033	0.020	0.013	0.008	0.005	13
0.160	0.141	0.125	0.099	0.078	0.044	0.025	0.015	0.009	0.006	0.003	14
0.140	0.123	0.108	0.084	0.065	0.035	0.020	0.011	0.006	0.004	0.002	15
0.123	0.107	0.093	0.071	0.054	0.028	0.015	0.008	0.005	0.003	0.002	16
0.108	0.093	0.080	0.060	0.045	0.023	0.012	0.006	0.003	0.002	0.001	17
0.095	0.081	0.069	0.051	0.038	0.018	0.009	0.005	0.002	0.001	0.001	18
0.083	0.070	0.060	0.043	0.031	0.014	0.007	0.003	0.002	0.001		19
0.073	0.061	0.051	0.037	0.026	0.012	0.005	0.002	0.001	0.001		20
0.064	0.053	0.044	0.031	0.022	0.009	0.004	0.002	0.001			21
0.056	0.046	0.038	0.026	0.018	0.007	0.003	0.001	0.001			22
0.049	0.040	0.033	0.022	0.015	0.006	0.002	0.001				23
0.043	0.035	0.028	0.019	0.013	0.005	0.002	0.001				24
0.038	0.030	0.024	0.016	0.010	0.004	0.001	0.001				25
0.033	0.026	0.021	0.014	0.009	0.003	0.001					26
0.029	0.023	0.018	0.011	0.007	0.002	0.001					27
0.026	0.020	0.016	0.010	0.006	0.002	0.001					28
0.022	0.017	0.014	0.008	0.005	0.002						29
0.020	0.015	0.012	0.007	0.004	0.001						30
0.005	0.004	0.003	0.001	0.001							40
0.001	0.001	0.001									50

Example—Table 3 What is the present value of $30,000 to be received twenty-five years from now, assuming a 14 percent interest rate? From Table 3, the required multiplier is .038, and the answer is

$$\$30,000 \times .038 = \$1,140$$

The factor values for Table 3 are

$$\text{PV Factor} = (1 + r)^{-n}$$

Table 3 is the reciprocal of Table 1.

Table 4 is used to compute the present value of a *series* of *equal* periodic cash flows.

Table 4. Present Value of $1 Received Each Period for a Given Number of Time Periods

Periods	1%	2%	3%	4%	5%	6%	7%	8%	9%	10%	12%
1	0.990	0.980	0.971	0.962	0.952	0.943	0.935	0.926	0.917	0.909	0.893
2	1.970	1.942	1.913	1.886	1.859	1.833	1.808	1.783	1.759	1.736	1.690
3	2.941	2.884	2.829	2.775	2.723	2.673	2.624	2.577	2.531	2.487	2.402
4	3.902	3.808	3.717	3.630	3.546	3.465	3.387	3.312	3.240	3.170	3.037
5	4.853	4.713	4.580	4.452	4.329	4.212	4.100	3.993	3.890	3.791	3.605
6	5.795	5.601	5.417	5.242	5.076	4.917	4.767	4.623	4.486	4.355	4.111
7	6.728	6.472	6.230	6.002	5.786	5.582	5.389	5.206	5.033	4.868	4.564
8	7.652	7.325	7.020	6.733	6.463	6.210	5.971	5.747	5.535	5.335	4.968
9	8.566	8.162	7.786	7.435	7.108	6.802	6.515	6.247	5.995	5.759	5.328
10	9.471	8.983	8.530	8.111	7.722	7.360	7.024	6.710	6.418	6.145	5.650
11	10.368	9.787	9.253	8.760	8.306	7.887	7.499	7.139	6.805	6.495	5.938
12	11.255	10.575	9.954	9.385	8.863	8.384	7.943	7.536	7.161	6.814	6.194
13	12.134	11.348	10.635	9.986	9.394	8.853	8.358	7.904	7.487	7.103	6.424
14	13.004	12.106	11.296	10.563	9.899	9.295	8.745	8.244	7.786	7.367	6.628
15	13.865	12.849	11.938	11.118	10.380	9.712	9.108	8.559	8.061	7.606	6.811
16	14.718	13.578	12.561	11.652	10.838	10.106	9.447	8.851	8.313	7.824	6.974
17	15.562	14.292	13.166	12.166	11.274	10.477	9.763	9.122	8.544	8.022	7.120
18	16.398	14.992	13.754	12.659	11.690	10.828	10.059	9.372	8.756	8.201	7.250
19	17.226	15.678	14.324	13.134	12.085	11.158	10.336	9.604	8.950	8.365	7.366
20	18.046	16.351	14.878	13.590	12.462	11.470	10.594	9.818	9.129	8.514	7.469
21	18.857	17.011	15.415	14.029	12.821	11.764	10.836	10.017	9.292	8.649	7.562
22	19.660	17.658	15.937	14.451	13.163	12.042	11.061	10.201	9.442	8.772	7.645
23	20.456	18.292	16.444	14.857	13.489	12.303	11.272	10.371	9.580	8.883	7.718
24	21.243	18.914	16.936	15.247	13.799	12.550	11.469	10.529	9.707	8.985	7.784
25	22.023	19.523	17.413	15.622	14.094	12.783	11.654	10.675	9.823	9.077	7.843
26	22.795	20.121	17.877	15.983	14.375	13.003	11.826	10.810	9.929	9.161	7.896
27	23.560	20.707	18.327	16.330	14.643	13.211	11.987	10.935	10.027	9.237	7.943
28	24.316	21.281	18.764	16.663	14.898	13.406	12.137	11.051	10.116	9.307	7.984
29	25.066	21.844	19.189	16.984	15.141	13.591	12.278	11.158	10.198	9.370	8.022
30	25.808	22.396	19.600	17.292	15.373	13.765	12.409	11.258	10.274	9.427	8.055
40	32.835	27.355	23.115	19.793	17.159	15.046	13.332	11.925	10.757	9.779	8.244
50	39.196	31.424	25.730	21.482	18.256	15.762	13.801	12.234	10.962	9.915	8.305

Example—Table 4 Arthur Howard won a contest on January 1, 20x8, in which the prize was $30,000, payable in fifteen annual installments of $2,000 every December 31, beginning in 20x8. Assuming a 9 percent interest rate, what is the present value of Mr. Howard's prize on January 1, 20x8? From Table 4, the required multiplier is 8.061, and the answer is

$$\$2{,}000 \times 8.061 = \$16{,}122$$

The factor values for Table 4 are

$$\text{PVa Factor} = \frac{1 - (1 + r)^{-n}}{r}$$

Table 4 is the columnar sum of Table 3.

Table 4. (*continued*)

14%	15%	16%	18%	20%	25%	30%	35%	40%	45%	50%	Periods
0.877	0.870	0.862	0.847	0.833	0.800	0.769	0.741	0.714	0.690	0.667	1
1.647	1.626	1.605	1.566	1.528	1.440	1.361	1.289	1.224	1.165	1.111	2
2.322	2.283	2.246	2.174	2.106	1.952	1.816	1.696	1.589	1.493	1.407	3
2.914	2.855	2.798	2.690	2.589	2.362	2.166	1.997	1.849	1.720	1.605	4
3.433	3.352	3.274	3.127	2.991	2.689	2.436	2.220	2.035	1.876	1.737	5
3.889	3.784	3.685	3.498	3.326	2.951	2.643	2.385	2.168	1.983	1.824	6
4.288	4.160	4.039	3.812	3.605	3.161	2.802	2.508	2.263	2.057	1.883	7
4.639	4.487	4.344	4.078	3.837	3.329	2.925	2.598	2.331	2.109	1.922	8
4.946	4.772	4.607	4.303	4.031	3.463	3.019	2.665	2.379	2.144	1.948	9
5.216	5.019	4.833	4.494	4.192	3.571	3.092	2.715	2.414	2.168	1.965	10
5.453	5.234	5.029	4.656	4.327	3.656	3.147	2.752	2.438	2.185	1.977	11
5.660	5.421	5.197	4.793	4.439	3.725	3.190	2.779	2.456	2.197	1.985	12
5.842	5.583	5.342	4.910	4.533	3.780	3.223	2.799	2.469	2.204	1.990	13
6.002	5.724	5.468	5.008	4.611	3.824	3.249	2.814	2.478	2.210	1.993	14
6.142	5.847	5.575	5.092	4.675	3.859	3.268	2.825	2.484	2.214	1.995	15
6.265	5.954	5.669	5.162	4.730	3.887	3.283	2.834	2.489	2.216	1.997	16
6.373	6.047	5.749	5.222	4.775	3.910	3.295	2.840	2.492	2.218	1.998	17
6.467	6.128	5.818	5.273	4.812	3.928	3.304	2.844	2.494	2.219	1.999	18
6.550	6.198	5.877	5.316	4.844	3.942	3.311	2.848	2.496	2.220	1.999	19
6.623	6.259	5.929	5.353	4.870	3.954	3.316	2.850	2.497	2.221	1.999	20
6.687	6.312	5.973	5.384	4.891	3.963	3.320	2.852	2.498	2.221	2.000	21
6.743	6.359	6.011	5.410	4.909	3.970	3.323	2.853	2.498	2.222	2.000	22
6.792	6.399	6.044	5.432	4.925	3.976	3.325	2.854	2.499	2.222	2.000	23
6.835	6.434	6.073	5.451	4.937	3.981	3.327	2.855	2.499	2.222	2.000	24
6.873	6.464	6.097	5.467	4.948	3.985	3.329	2.856	2.499	2.222	2.000	25
6.906	6.491	6.118	5.480	4.956	3.988	3.330	2.856	2.500	2.222	2.000	26
6.935	6.514	6.136	5.492	4.964	3.990	3.331	2.856	2.500	2.222	2.000	27
6.961	6.534	6.152	5.502	4.970	3.992	3.331	2.857	2.500	2.222	2.000	28
6.983	6.551	6.166	5.510	4.975	3.994	3.332	2.857	2.500	2.222	2.000	29
7.003	6.566	6.177	5.517	4.979	3.995	3.332	2.857	2.500	2.222	2.000	30
7.105	6.642	6.234	5.548	4.997	3.999	3.333	2.857	2.500	2.222	2.000	40
7.133	6.661	6.246	5.554	4.999	4.000	3.333	2.857	2.500	2.222	2.000	50

Table 4 applies to *ordinary annuities,* in which the first cash flow occurs one time period beyond the date for which the present value is to be computed. An *annuity due* is a series of equal cash flows for N time periods with the first payment occurring immediately. The present value of the first payment equals the face value of the cash flow; Table 4 then is used to measure the present value of $N - 1$ remaining cash flows.

Example—Table 4 Determine the present value on January 1, 20x8, of twenty lease payments; each payment of $10,000 is due on January 1, beginning in 20x8. Assume an interest rate of 8 percent.

$$\text{Present Value} = \text{Immediate Payment} + \begin{cases}\text{Present Value of 19 Subsequent}\\ \text{Payments at 8\%}\end{cases}$$

$$= \$10{,}000 + (\$10{,}000 \times 9.604) = \$106{,}040$$

Company Name Index

Note: **Boldface** type denotes real companies.

Subject Index

Note: **Boldface** type indicates key terms.

Career Opportunities in Accounting

	Public Accounting (CPA Firm)	Industry
Contact Organizations	American Institute of Certified Public Accountants (212) 596-6200 www. aicpa.org	Institute of Management Accountants (201) 573-9000 www.imanet.org
Career Choices	Auditor	Controller
	Tax Planner	Financial Executive
	Management Consultant	Internal Auditor
	Financial Advisor	Accounting Manager

	Government or Not-for-Profit Organizations	Graduate Education
Contact Organizations	Federal, State, and Local Government Agencies; Hospitals; Schools; Charitable Organizations	Graduate Schools
Career Choices	Revenue Agent	Law (Tax/Bankruptcy Attorney)
	Budget Analyst	M.B.A. (Business Executive)
	Staff Accountant	M.Acc. (Professional Accountant)
	Treasurer	Ph.D. (College Professor)